DICTIONARY

OF

AMERICAN NAVAL FIGHTING SHIPS

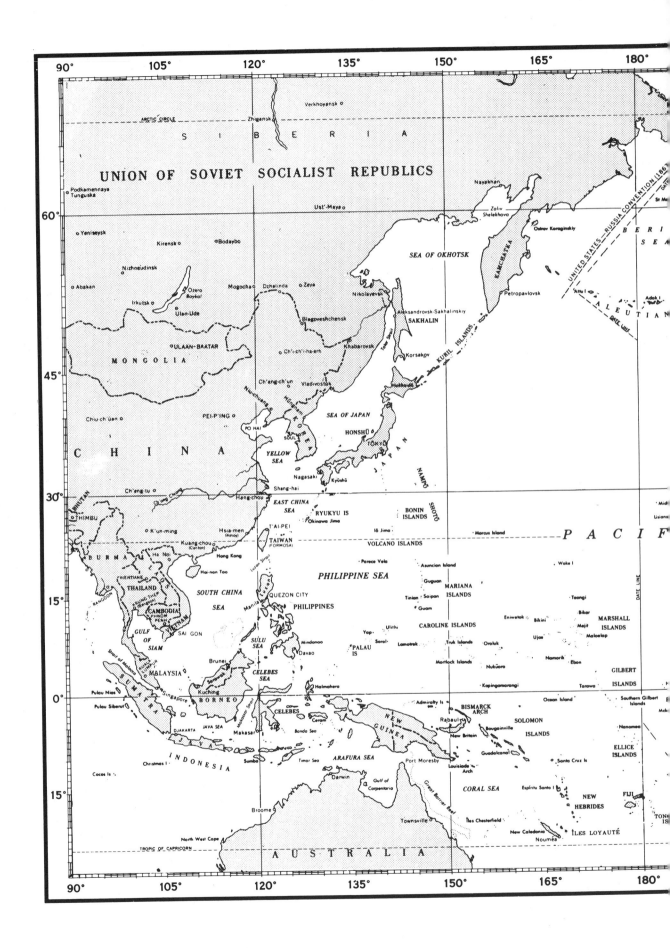

USS *Theodore E. Chandler* (DD–717) at Pearl Harbor in October, 1949, berthed with her *Gearing*-class sister ships *Wiltsie* (DD–716), *Hamner* (DD–718), and *Ozbourn* (DD–846). War-built destroyers of the *Gearing* and the similar *Allen M. Sumner* classes operated in numbers through the Korean and Vietnam conflicts; some *Gearings* still serve as Naval Reserve training ships.

Dictionary of

American Naval

Fighting Ships

VOLUME VII

Historical Sketches—Letters T through V

Appendix—Tank Landing Ships (LST)

JAMES L. MOONEY, Editor

In association with Commander Richard T. Speer, United States Navy, Retired

WITH A FOREWORD BY

ADMIRAL THOMAS B. HAYWARD, United States Navy,
THE CHIEF OF NAVAL OPERATIONS

AND AN INTRODUCTION BY

REAR ADMIRAL JOHN D. H. KANE, JR., United States Navy, Retired,
THE DIRECTOR OF NAVAL HISTORY

NAVAL HISTORICAL CENTER
DEPARTMENT OF THE NAVY
WASHINGTON: 1981

L.C. CARD 60–60198

UNITED STATES

GOVERNMENT PRINTING OFFICE

WASHINGTON, D.C.

FOREWORD

In introducing the first volume of this series over two decades ago, Admiral Arleigh Burke explained that the DANFS project was striving "... to make available in easily accessible form basic information on every naval ship that has served its part in shaping the history and national spirit of the United States." Now, six volumes and some 8,000 ships later, this objective approaches realization. Volume VIII, soon to appear, will complete this monumental task.

Admiral Burke also predicted that the series would be of "... enduring value to the Navy, to students and writers, and to all other Americans in developing a better understanding of the accomplishments of our ships which have ... /made/ our Navy the best in the world." The high praise and wide acceptance expressed by readers over the years signal the fulfillment of this objective. Numerous reprintings of earlier volumes lend additional testimony.

The stories of the famous ships and fighting men contained in this volume are but another chapter in a saga which goes back over 200 years. A reading of these pages can give us insight and inspiration to guide and to motivate us in today's trying times. The careful reader is sure to recognize in the narratives of long-gone ships parallels which can be usefully applied to solving naval problems of tomorrow. The common threads of valor and devotion to duty connect the sailors of the 1980's with their honored predecessors who fought in wooden hulls propelled by the wind. An understanding of this bond will enable the reader to view the Navy of today and that of the future with pride and confidence that a spirit engendered and nourished by a long, honorable, and growing tradition will continue to animate the Navy.

T. B. HAYWARD
Admiral, U. S. Navy

THE DICTIONARY OF AMERICAN NAVAL FIGHTING SHIPS

James L. Mooney, Editor
In association with Richard T. Speer, Commander, United States Navy (Retired)

PRINCIPAL WRITERS

Robert J. Cressman
Christopher N. Kennedy
Roland S. Kennerly
Suzanne MacFarlane
Raymond A. Mann
Luann Parsons
Barbara A. Ponsolle
John C. Reilly, Jr.
Theresa M. Schuster

SECRETARY OF THE NAVY'S ADVISORY COMMITTEE ON NAVAL HISTORY

Richard W. Leopold (Chairman)

Francis L. Berkeley, Jr.
James A. Field
Captain Joy Bright Hancock, USN (Ret.)
Caryl P. Haskins
Jim Dan Hill

John H. Kemble
Augustus P. Loring
Forrest C. Pogue
Gordon B. Turner

INTRODUCTION

With the publication of this volume and Volume VIII—which is soon to follow—a project spanning over a quarter of a century is completed. The eight volumes of this series contain the histories of the almost 10,000 ships which have served in the United States Navy since its inception over 200 years ago. The *Dictionary of American Naval Fighting Ships* is truly unique. Brought to completion, we now have the factual account of the Fleet in useful detail. Volume VII contains the histories of all U.S. Navy ships beginning with the letters "T" through V". Additionally, it includes a comprehensive appendix providing basic data on the 1,095 Tank Landing Ships (LST's) constructed to date. These major ships—which performed service of inestimable value in World War II, Korea, and Vietnam—received insufficient attention in previous volumes, largely due to the fact that so many of them were never named. This appendix accords them some of the recognition which they so richly deserve.

As might be expected in a work containing the history of almost 900 ships, Volume VII contains within its covers the entire spectrum of our Navy. Ships of every size and type, from every era of the Navy's history, are represented in these pages. Biographies of such famous fighting leaders in America's wars as Silas Talbot, Thomas Truxtun and Theodore E. Chandler precede the histories of the ships named to honor them; and the stories of some of our more famous fighting ships are told here. Battleships *Texas* and *Tennessee*, carriers *Tarawa* and *Ticonderoga*, cruisers *Tuscaloosa* and *Vincennes*, destroyers *Tingey* and *Taylor*, and submarines *Tang* and *Trigger* come readily to mind.

However, Volume VII does not consist entirely of glamorous ships. As in the case of earlier volumes in the series, largely due to the letters of the alphabet involved, certain types of ships are represented more extensively than

others. In the case of Volume VII, amphibious ships, minesweepers, and tugs stand in the spot light. Largely unsung in most accounts of our Navy's history, these ships here receive long overdue recognition. The descriptions of their operations in both peace and war help to provide a proper perspective of the Navy as it has served the nation these past 200 years.

Like its predecessors, this volume represents the collective effort of many individuals, a number of whom are not directly affiliated with the Naval Historical Center. However, the work is primarily the product of the Ships' Histories Branch under the supervision of Richard T. Speer. A retired naval officer who served in the same capacity while on active service, Comdr. Speer brought to his position a professional naval expertise which has been of great value in ensuring authenticity of naval terminology and operating practices. In addition, he prepared the LST appendix and took an extensive hand in the review and editing process for the remainder of the volume.

The keel for Volume VII was laid down in 1975, concurrently with the application of finishing touches to Volume VI which was published in 1976. As in the case of Volume VI, the reduced size of the DANFS staff resulted in a longer period of preparation for Volume VII than with the early volumes of the series. Fortunately, the experience and competence of James L. Mooney, the editor of the series since the publication of Volume III, and the skillful diligence of Raymond A. Mann and Ens. Barbara A. Ponsolle helped to overcome this deficiency in numbers. A former staff member, Roland Kennerly, contributed many of the "T" histories before leaving the Ships' Histories Branch. Happily, the Federal Summer Intern program brought us Robert Cressman, Suzanne MacFarlane, and Christopher Kennedy who proved to be adept learners and advanced the publication date significantly. Mr. Cressman deserves special credit. Following his intern apprenticeship, he was retained on a contract basis and made a heavy contribution to the project, both in writing many excellent histories and in helping to locate photographs.

As observant readers will note, Volume VII is richly illustrated. John C. Reilly used his extensive knowledge of naval history in the selection and captioning of pictures. Theresa M. Schuster typed all of the manuscripts. Intimately familiar with the style and format of the project, she was as much assistant editor as typist. This is particularly true in the case of the LST appendix.

Members of other branches of the Naval Historical Center proved to be unfailingly cooperative and helpful. Dr. William J. Morgan of the Research Branch kindly assisted us in untangling knotty problems concerning ships of the American Revolution and of the Early Federal Period. In the Operational Archives Branch, Gerri K. Judkins provided ready access to Action Reports, Submarine War Patrol Reports, and Movement Reports of the World War II era. Barbara A. Gilmore and Judy A. Koontz were equally helpful for the post-World War II period and the field of naval aviation, respectively. Charles Haberlein and Agnes Hoover of the Photographic Section of the Curator Branch provided valuable assistance to Mr. Reilly in the assembly of illustrations. Mr. James E. Smith of the Library Branch saved countless hours of research time in providing project historians with source materials from the Navy Department Library.

Individuals from activities external to the Naval Historical Center were generous in their support. At the Navy and Old Army Branch of the National Archives, Drs. Gibson B. Smith, Timothy Neninger, Robert W. Krauskopf, and Elaine Everly abetted the research efforts of project historians. James Trimble, also of the National Archives, proved to be a prime source of photographic materials. Olga Mager, in the Ships' Deck Logs section of the Office of the Chief of Naval Operations, provided many of the deck logs used. By making the results of his extensive research into the origin of names of U.S. Navy ships wholeheartedly available to the editor, Dennis Green resolved many conflicts and filled innumerable lacunae in that area. Finally, Dr. Martin Gordon, formerly of the U.S. Marine Corps Historical Center, proved to be a most knowledgeable source of information concerning amphibious operations during the Vietnam conflict.

No acknowledgement would be complete without mentioning the members of the Secretary of the Navy's Advisory Committee on Naval History whose wise counsel has been instrumental in the shaping of the entire project. In particular, the passing in 1978 of Dr. Walter Muir Whitehill is noted with extreme regret. Dr. Whitehill served as chairman of the committee for many years, and his loss is keenly felt.

Soon after the publication of this volume, its successor, Volume VIII, will appear and bring the Herculean *DANFS* task to a close. But the Navy's ships will continue to float; to serve, and, when called upon, to fight for their flag. It is our fond hope that the sailors who walk the decks of the ships of our future fleets will stand taller, work harder, and fight longer for having glimpsed through the haze of history the ghostly masts of long gone men-of-war.

JOHN D. H. KANE, Jr.
Rear Admiral, USN (Ret.)
Director of Naval History

1 September 1980

CONTENTS

Page

FOREWORD -- v
INTRODUCTION -- vii
NOTE ON ILLUSTRATIONS -- xi
ABBREVIATIONS AND SYMBOLS -- xii

HISTORICAL SKETCHES:

    LETTER "T" -- 1
    LETTER "U" -- 378
    LETTER "V" -- 433

APPENDIX:

    Tank Landing Ships (LST) --- 569

GUIDE TO THE SERIES --- 732
BIBLIOGRAPHY --- 734

A NOTE ON ILLUSTRATIONS

Negatives for many of the photographs used in this volume are held by the National Archives or the Naval Photographic Center. Negative numbers for those illustrations are included in parentheses at the end of their captions.

Prints of photographs bearing negative numbers with 80–G, 19–N, or 26–G prefixes can be purchased from the Audiovisual Archives Division, National Archives, Washington, D.C. 20408. Those with USN, NH, NR&L, K, or KN prefixes can be purchased from the Command-ing Officer, Naval Photographic Center, Washington, D.C. 20374 (ATTN: Still Pictures).

Unless otherwise specified, all the ships illustrated in this volume are commissioned ships of the U.S. Navy with their names preceded by the identification United States Ship (USS). Ships of the Military Sealift Command are civilian-manned and designated U.S. Naval Ship (USNS). Coast Guard vessels are identified as U.S. Coast Guard Cutter (USCGC).

ABBREVIATIONS AND SYMBOLS

A—alternating current generator.
a.—armament.
AA—antiaircraft.
AB—crane ship.
ABD—advance base dock.
ABDA—American–British–Dutch–Australian Command.
ABSD—advance base section dock.
A/C—Allis–Chalmers Mfg. Co., Milwaukee, Wis.
AC—collier.
ac.—aircraft.
ACM—auxiliary mine layer.
ACR—armored cruiser.
ACV—auxiliary aircraft carrier; or tender.
Act.—acting.
AD—destroyer tender.
ADG—degaussing ship.
AE—ammunition ship.
A.E.F.—American Expeditionary Force (World War I); or Allied Expeditionary Force (World War II).
AEW—airborne early warning (radar picket system).
AF—store ship.
AFD—auxiliary floating dock.
AFDB—large auxiliary floating dry dock (nsp.)
AFDL—small auxiliary floating dry dock (nsp.)
AFDM—medium auxiliary floating dry dock (nsp.)
AFS—combat store ship.
AG—miscellaneous auxiliary.
AGB—icebreaker.
AGC—general communications vessel; or amphibious force flagship (now LCC).
AGD—seagoing dredge.
AGDE—escort research ship.
AGDS—deep submergence support ship.
AGEH—hydrofoil research ship.
AGER—environmental research ship.
AGF—miscellaneous command ship.
AGL—lighthouse tender.
AGM—missile range instrumentation ship.
AGMR—major communications relay ship.
AGOR—oceanographic research ship.
AGP—motor torpedo boat tender.
AGR—radar picket ship.
AGS—surveying ship.
AGSC—coastal survey ship.
AGSL—satellite launching ship.
AGSS—auxiliary submarine.
AGTR—technical research ship.
AH—hospital ship.
AHP—evacuation hospital ship.
AK—cargo ship.
AKA—attack cargo ship (now LKA).
AKD—cargo ship, dock; or deep-hold cargo ship.
AKI—general stores issue ship.
AKL—light cargo ship.
AKN—net cargo ship.
AKS—stores issue ship.
AK(SS)—cargo submarine.
AKV—cargo ship and aircraft ferry.
AKR—vehicle cargo ship.
AL—lightship.
ALCo—American Locomotive Co., Auburn, N.Y.
AM—minesweeper.
AMh—minesweeper, harbor.
AMc—coastal minesweeper

Am–Int—American International Shipbuilding Corp., Hog Island, Pa.
AMS—motor minesweeper.
AMCU—coastal minesweeper (underwater locator); or mine hunter.
AN—net laying ship (now ANL).
ANL—net laying ship (formerly AN).
ANZAC—Australian–New Zealand Force.
AO—oiler; or fuel oil tanker.
AOG—gasoline tanker.
AOE—fast combat support ship.
AOR—replenishment oiler.
AOSS—submarine oiler.
AP—transport.
APA—attack transport (now LPA); or animal transport.
APB—self-propelled barracks ship; or artillery barge.
APb—base repair ship.
APC—cavalry transport; or small coastal transport (formerly APc).
APD—high-speed transport.
APF—administrative flagship.
APG—supporting gunnery ship.
APH—transport fitted for evacuation of wounded.
APL—barracks craft (nsp.).
APM—mechanized artillery transport.
APN—nonmechanized artillery transport.
APP—troop barge, class A.
APR—rescue transport.
APS—mine laying submarine; or transport, submarine.
APSS—transport, submarine.
APT—troop barge, class B.
APV—transport and aircraft ferry.
APY—giant "Y" boat.
AR—repair ship.
ARB—battle damage repair ship.
ARC—cable repairing ship.
ARD—auxiliary repair dock (nsp.).
ARDC—auxiliary repair dock, concrete.
ARDM—medium auxiliary repair dry dock (nsp.).
ARG—internal combustion engine repair ship.
ARH—heavy-hull repair ship.
ARL—landing craft repair ship.
ARM—heavy machinery repair ship.
ARS—salvage ship.
ARSD—salvage lifting ship.
ARST—salvage craft tender.
ARV—aircraft repair ship.
ARVA—aircraft repair ship (aircraft).
ARVE—aircraft repair ship (engine).
ARVH—aircraft repair ship (helicopter).
AS—submarine tender.
ASPB—assault support patrol boat.
ASR—submarine rescue ship.
ASROC—antisubmarine rocket.
ASSA—cargo submarine.
ASSP—transport submarine.
ASW—antisubmarine warfare.
AT—ocean tug.
ATA—auxiliary ocean tug.
ATC—armored troop carrier.
ATF—fleet ocean tug.
ATL—tank landing craft.
Atlas—Atlas Imperial Diesel Engine Co., Mattoon, Ill.
ATO—ocean tug, old.

ATR—rescue tug.
ATS—salvage tug.
aux.—auxiliary.
AV—seaplane tender.
AVB—advance aviation base ship.
AVC—large catapult lighter.
AVD—seaplane tender (destroyer).
AVG—aircraft escort vessel.
avgas—aviation gasoline.
AVM—guided missile ship.
AVP—small seaplane tender.
AVR—aircraft rescue vessel.
AVS—aviation supply ship.
AVT—auxiliary aircraft transport.
AW—distilling ship.
AWK—water tanker.
AZ—airship tender (lighter than air).
B—The letter "B" used as a prefix to a hull number indicates that the ship was built by the United States for a British Comonwealth Navy.
b.—beam.
BAK—British cargo ship.
BB—battleship.
BBG—guided missile capital ship.
bbls.—barrels.
B.C.—British Columbia.
BLM—ballistic intercontinental missile.
BDE—British escort ship.
Beth–Alam—Bethlehem–Alameda Shipyard, Inc., Alameda, Calif.
Beth–Fair—Bethlehem–Fairfield Shipyard, Inc., Baltimore, Md.
Beth–Hing—Bethlehem–Hingham Shipyard, Inc., Hingham, Mass.
BethPac–SanP—Bethlehem Pacific Coast Steel Corp., San Pedro, Calif.
BethPac–SanF—Bethlehem Pacific Coast Steel Corp., San Francisco, Calif.
BethSb–Wilm—Bethlehem Shipbuilding Corp., Wilmington, Del.
Beth–Spar—Bethelem–Sparrows Point Shipyard, Inc., Sparrows Point, Md.
BethSt–Balt—Bethlehem Steel Co., Shipbuilding Div., Baltimore, Md.
Beth–Bklyn—Bethlehem Steel Co., Shipbuilding Div., Brooklyn, N.Y.
BethSt–Quin—Bethlehem Steel Co., Shipbuilding Div., Quincy, Mass.
BethSt–Stat—Bethlehem Steel Co., Shipbuilding Div., Staten Island, N.Y.
Bg—barge.
bhp.—brake horsepower.
blr.—breach-loading rifle.
BM—monitor.
bom—"builders old measurement."
bp.—between perpendiculars (length).
BPDSMS—Basic point defense surface missile system.
Bt.—boat.
btry—battery.
Buda—Buda Diesel Engine Co.
BUEXP—Bureau Express Boiler.
Buff–B—Buffalo Shipbuilding Co., Buffalo, N.Y.
Buff–E—Buffalo Shipbuilding Co., Erie, Pa.
BUMODT—Bureau-modified Thorneycroft boiler.
BUR4DR—Bureau-4-Drum Boiler.
Busch—Busch Sulzer Brothers Diesel Engine Co., St. Louis, Mo.
BUSHIPS—Bureau of Ships (now NSSC).
BW—Babcock & Wilcox Co., Boiler Div., Barberton, Ohio.
BWA—Babcock & Wilcox Co., header-type boiler.
BWA3DR—Babcock & Wilcox 3-drum express-type boiler.
BWHDR—Babcock & Wilcox header-type boiler.
B.W.I.—British West Indies.
BWSHC—Babcock & Wilcox superheat control boiler.
BWSX—Babcock & Wilcox sectional express boiler.

BW2DR—Babcock & Wilcox 2-drum boiler.
BW2DRD—Babcock & Wilcox 2-drum D-type boiler.
BW2DSU—Babcock & Wilcox 2-drum single-uptake boiler.
C—protected cruiser; commanding officer.
CA—heavy cruiser.
CAG—guided missile heavy cruiser.
cal.—caliber.
CAP—combat air patrol.
car.—carronade.
CB—large cruiser.
C/B—Cooper Bessemer.
CBC—large tactical command ship.
CC—battle cruiser; or command ship.
C/C—controlled-circulation boiler.
CCB—command and control boat.
CCS—Combined Chiefs of Staff.
C/E—Combustion Engineering Co., Chattanooga, Tenn.
CED—Combustion Engineering D-type boiler.
CEH—Cummins Engine Co., Inc.
CEHDR—Combusion Engineering header-type boiler.
CENTO—Central Treaty Organization.
CE2DR—Combustion Engineering 2-drum boiler.
CE2DRD—Combustion Engineering 2-drum D-type boiler.
CF—flying-deck cruiser.
CFC—controlled forced circulation.
CG—guided missile cruiser.
CGC—Coast Guard cutter.
CGN—guided missile cruiser (nuclear propulsion).
CH—Cutler-Hammer.
Char—Naval Shipyard, Charleston, S.C. (formerly Navy Yard, Charleston).
Chry—Chrysler Corp.
CIC—Command Information Center.
CinCLant—Commander in Chief, U.S. Atlantic Fleet.
CinCPac—Commander in Chief, U.S. Pacific Fleet.
CIW—Columbian Iron Works, Baltimore, Md.
CL—light cruiser.
cl.—class.
CLAA—Antiaircraft light cruiser.
ClBt—canal boat.
CLC—tactical command ship.
CLG—guided missile light cruiser.
CLK—cruiser hunter-killer ship.
CM—minelayer.
CMc—coastal minelayer.
CMC—Continental Motors Corp.
CNO—Chief of Naval Operations.
C.O.—commanding officer.
compos.—composite drive (2 diesel engines, electric drive; 2 diesel engines, geared drive; hydraulic couple).
const.—construction.
cont.—continued.
Cor.—corvette.
CortRon—escort squadron.
cpl.—complement.
Craig—Craig Shipbuilding Co., Long Beach, Calif.
Cramp—Wm. Cramp & Sons Ship & Engine Building Co., Philadelphia, Pa.
Cres—Crescent Shipyard, Elizabethport, N.J.
CS—scout cruiser.
CSA—Confederate States Army.
CSN—Confederate States Navy.
CSS—Confederate States Ship.
CTB—coastal torpedo boat.
CTF—Commander Task Force.
CTG—Commander Task Group.
Ctr.—cutter.
CTU—Commander Task Unit.
Cur.—Curtis-type turbine.
CV—aircraft carrier.
CVA—attack aircraft carrier.
CVAN—attack aircraft carrier (nuclear propulsion).
CVB—large aircraft carrier.
CVE—escort aircraft carrier.
CVHA—assault helicopter aircraft carrier.

CVL—small aircraft carrier.
CVS—antisubmarine warfare support aircraft carrier; or seaplane carrier.
CVT—training aircraft carrier.
CVU—utility aircraft carrier.
Cwt.—hundred weight.
C.Z.—Canal Zone.
DANFS—Dictionary of American Naval Fighting Ships.
DASH—drone antisubmarine helicopter.
dc.—depth charge.
dcp.—depth charge projector.
dcp. (hh.)—depth charge projector (hedgehog-type).
dct.—depth charge track.
DD—destroyer.
dd.—dry dock.
d/d—diesel direct.
DDC—corvette.
ddd.—diesel direct drive.
DDE—antisubmarine destroyer.
DDG—guided missile destroyer.
DDR—radar picket destroyer.
DE—escort ship.
d/e—diesel electric.
DEC—control escort vessel.
ded.—diesel electric drive.
DEG—guided missile escort ship.
DeL—De Laval Steam Turbine Co., Trenton, N.J.
DeL–FB—De Laval & Farrel-Birmingham.
DeL–Falk—De Laval & Falk.
DeL–GE—De Laval & General Electric.
DeL–Wes—De Laval & Westinghouse.
DER—radar picket escort ship.
de/r—diesel-electric reduction.
derd.—diesel electric reduction drive.
des.—design.
Des—destroyer.
DesDiv—Destroyer Division.
DesRon—Destroyer Squadron.
det.—diesel electric tandem motor drive.
DEW—Distant Early Warning System (a radar network across upper North America).
dgd.—diesel geared drive.
Diehl—Diehl Manufacturing Co., Bridgeport, N.Y.
div.—division.
DL—frigate.
DLG—guided missile frigate.
DLGN—guided missile frigate (nuclear propulsion).
dlt.—double reduction-locked train.
DM—destroyer minelayer; or light minelayer (now MMD).
DMS—high-speed minesweeper; or destroyer minesweeper.
DMZ—Demiltarized Zone.
dp.—displacement; or dual purpose (guns).
dph.—depth of hold.
dr.—draft.
D.r.—Dahlgren rifle.
drd.—diesel reduction drive.
D.sb.—Dahlgren smoothbore.
EAG—experimental miscellaneous auxiliary.
EBCo—Electric Boat Co., Groton, Conn.
ED—Electric Dynamic Co., Bayonne, N.J.
ehp.—estimated horsepower.
EIWHDR—Edgemoor Iron Works header-type boiler.
Ell—Elliot Motor Co., Jeannette, Pa.
EllMach—Ellicott Machine Corp., Baltimore, Md.
ElSpecCo—Electric Specialty Co., Stamford, Conn.
eng.—engine.
enl.—enlisted.
Enter—Enterprise Engine and Foundry Co., San Francisco, Calif.
ew.—extreme width of flight deck.
ex—former.
Exide—Exide Electric Storage Battery Corp., Philadelphia, Pa.
exp.—expansion.
f.—full load (displacement).

Falk–DeL—Falk & De Laval.
Falk–FB—Falk & Farrel-Birmingham.
Falk–GE—Falk & General Electric.
Falk–Wes—Falk & Westinghouse.
FAST—Fast At Sea Transfer equipment.
FB—Farrel-Birmingham Co., N.Y.
FB–Falk—Farrel-Birmingham & Falk.
FB–Wes—Farrel-Birmingham & Westinghouse.
FBM—fleet ballistic missile.
FDL—fast deployment logistics ship.
Fed—Federal Shipbuilding & Drydock Co., Kearny, N.J.
Fiat—Fiat–San Giorgio, Ltd., Turin, Italy.
Flot—flotilla.
FltBtry—floating battery.
FM—Fairbanks Morse diesel, reverse gear drive (manufactured by Fairbanks Morse & Co., Beloit, Wis.).
Fore—Fore River Ship and Engine Co., Quincy, Mass.
Fr.—Frigate.
FRAM—Fleet Rehabilitation And Modernization.
FSch.—F. Schichau Gmbh., Elbing, Germany.
f.t.—fire-tube (Scotch-type boiler).
FW—Foster Wheeler Corp., Mountaintop, Pa.
FWA3DR—Foster Wheeler 3-Drum Express-Type Boiler.
FWH—Foster Wheeler Header-Type Boiler.
FWPFS—Foster Wheeler Pressure-Fixed Supercharged Boiler.
FWSFD—Foster Wheeler Single-Furnace D-Type Boiler.
FWSHC—Foster Wheeler Superheat Control Boiler.
FW2DR—Foster Wheeler 2-Drum Boiler.
FW2DRS—Foster Wheeler 2-Drum Superheat Control Boiler.
gal.—gallon.
Gbt.—gunboat.
gd.—gundeck.
GDEB—Grot—General Dynamics Corp., Electric Boat Div., Groton, Conn.
GDEB—Quin—General Dynamics Corp., Electric Boat Div., Quincy, Mass.
GE—General Electric Co., Schenectady, N.Y.
gen.—generator.
G.g.—Gatling gun.
GM—General Motors Corp., Cleveland Diesel Division, Cleveland, Ohio.
Gond—gondola.
Gould—Gould Storage Battery Co., Trenton, N.J.
gr.—gross (tonnage).
Gulf—Gulf Shipbuilding Corp., Chickasaw, Ala.
Gy—galley.
Hall–S—Hall-Scott.
HBM—His (Her) Britannic Majesty's.
helo.—helicopter.
Herc—Hercules Motor Co., Canton, Ohio.
HH—Harlan and Hollingsworth Corp., Wilmington, Del.
HIJMS—His Imperial Japanese Majesty's Ship.
HL—R. L. Hawthorne, Leslie and Co., Ltd., Newcastle-on-Tyne, England.
HMAS—His (Her) Majesty's Australian Ship.
HMCS—His (Her) Majesty's Canadian Ship.
HMNZS—His (Her) Majesty's New Zealand Ship.
HNMS—Her Netherlands Majesty's Ship.
HORC—Hooven, Owens, Renschler Co., Hamilton, Ohio.
hor3—horizontal triple-expansion.
how.—howitzer.
hp.—horsepower.
HT—Humphreys and Tenant, Ltd., London, England.
HUK—Hunter/Killer; offensive ASW.
Hw—Hunter-wheel.
HwGbt—Hunter-wheel gunboat.
HwStr—Hunter-wheel steamer.
IFS—inshore fire support ship (now LFR).
ihp.—indicated horsepower.
ip.—intermediate pressure.
int.—international.
Irc—ironclad.
IrcFltBtry—ironclad floating battery.

IrcGbt—ironclad gunboat.
IrcRam—ironclad ram.
IrcSlp—ironclad sloop.
IrcStr—ironclad steamer.
IrcStFltBtry—ironclad steam floating battery.
IX—unclassified miscellaneous auxiliary ship.
JCS—Joint Chiefs of Staff.
JHendy—Joshua Hendy.
JTF—Joint Task Force.
k.—knots.
KA—contraction of AKA (attack cargo ship).
Kopp—Koppers Manufacturing Co.
kw.—kilowatts.
l.—length.
LBP—personnel landing boat.
lbp.—length between perpendiculars.
LBS—support landing boat.
LBV—vehicle landing boat.
LCA—assault landing craft.
LCAP—local combat air patrol.
LCB—landing craft, vehicle.
LCC—amphibious comand ship (formerly AGC).
LCC(1)—landing craft, control Mk I.
LCC(2)—landing craft, control Mk II.
LC(FF)—landing craft, infantry (gunboat).
LCI(L)—landing craft, infantry (large).
LCI(M)—landing craft, infantry (mortar).
LCI(R)—landing craft, infantry (rocket).
LCM—landing craft, mechanized.
LCM(2)—landing craft, mechanized, Mk II.
LCM(3)—landing craft, mechanized, Mk III.
LCM(6)—landing craft, mechanized, Mk VI.
LCM(8)—landing craft, mechanized, Mk VIII.
LCPL—landing craft, personnel (large).
LCP(N)—landing craft, personnel (nested).
LCPR—landing craft, personnel, ramped.
LCR(L)—landing craft, inflatable boat (large).
LCR(S)—landing craft, inflatable boat (small).
LCSL—landing craft, infantry (support).
LCSR—landing craft, swimmer reconnaissance.
LCS(S)(1)—landing craft, support (small) Mk I.
LCS(S)(2)—landing craft, support (small) Mk II.
LCT—landing craft, tank.
LCU—landing craft, utility.
LCV—landing craft, vehicle.
LCVP—landing craft, vehicle, personnel.
LFR—inshore fire support ship (formerly IFS, LSMR).
Lht.—lighthouse tender.
LFS—amphibious fire support ship.
LHA—amphibious assault ship (general purpose).
lim.—limiting.
LKA—amphibious cargo ship (formerly AKA).
Loran—long range navigation [system].
lp.—low pressure.
LPA—amphibious transport (formerly APA).
LPD—amphibious transport dock.
LPH—amphibious assault ship.
LPR—amphibious transport, small (formerly APD).
LSD—dock landing ship.
LSFF—flotilla flagship (amphibious).
LSI—landing ship, infantry (giant "Y" boat).
LSI(G)—landing ship, infantry (gunboat).
LSI(L)—landing ship, infantry (large).
LSI(M)—landing ship, infantry (mortar).
LSI(R)—landing ship, infantry (rocket).
LSM—medium landing ship.
LSM(R)—medium landing ship (rocket), (now LFR).
LSS(L)—support landing ship (large) Mk III.
LST—tank landing ship.
LSTH—landing ship, tank (casualty evacuation).
LSTS—landing ship (utility).
LSU—landing ship (utility).
LSV—landing ship, vehicle.
LT—large tug (Army).
lt—light (displacement).
Lufkin—Lufkin Foundry & Machine Co.
LVA—assault landing vehicle.
LVT—landing vehicle, tracked.

LWT—amphibious warping tug.
M—Marine.
M.—mortar.
MAC—Military Airlift Command.
MarAd—Maritime Administration.
MAP—Military Assistance Program.
MB—motor boat.
M.C.—Maritime Commission.
M.C.E.—Maritime Commission Emergency Ship Program ("Liberty" ships).
MSC—mine countermeasures ship.
M.C.V.—Maritime Commission Victory Ship Program ("Victory" ships).
M.D.A.P.—Mutual Defense Assistance Program.
Mfr.—manufacturer.
mg.—machine gun.
MHA—minehunter, auxiliary.
MHC—minehunter, coastal.
MinDiv—mine division.
MinFlot—mine flotilla.
MinLant—Mine Force Atlantic.
MinPac—Mine Force Pacific.
MinRon—mine squadron.
mis.—missile.
mis. ln.—missile launcher.
mk.—mark.
mlr.—muzzle-loading rifle.
MM—minelayer, fleet.
mm.—millimeter.
MMA—minelayer, auxiliary.
MMC—minelayer, coastal.
MMD—minelayer, fast (formerly DM).
MMF—minelayer, fleet.
Mon—monitor.
MON—monitor (new riverine warfare type).
Moran—Moran Brothers Co., Seattle, Wash.
Mssh.—Mosher-type boiler.
mot—motor generator.
mph—miles per hour.
MS—motor ship.
MSA—minesweeper, auxiliary.
MSB—minesweeping boat.
M.S.C.—Military Sealift Command (formerly MSTS).
MSC—minesweeper, coastal (nonmagnetic).
MSCO—minesweeper, coastal (old).
MSD—minesweeper, drone.
MSF—minesweeper, fleet (steel hull).
MSI—minesweeper, inshore.
MSL—minesweeping launch.
MSM—minesweeper, river.
MSO—minesweeper, ocean (nonmagnetic).
MSR—minesweeper, patrol.
MSS—minesweeper, special (device).
MSTS—Military Sea Transportation Service (now Military Sealift Command).
n.—normal (displacement).
NAR—Naval Auxiliary Reserve.
NASA—National Aeronautics and Space Administration.
NaSuCo—National Supply Co.
NATO—North Atlantic Treaty Organization.
NaTran—National Transit Pump & Machine Co., Oil City, Pa.
NATS—Naval Air Transport Service.
NavSea—Naval Sea Systems Command (formerly NSSC and Naval Ordnance Systems Command).
NavSyd—naval shipyard.
NavSyd–Bos—Boston Naval Shipyard, Boston, Mass. (formerly Boston Navy Yard).
NavSyd–Bklyn—New York Naval Shipyard, Brooklyn, N.Y. (formerly New York Navy Yard).
NavSyd–Charl—Charleston Naval Shipyard, Charleston, S.C. (formerly Charleston Navy Yard).
NavSyd–Hunt—Hunters Point Div., San Francisco Bay Naval Shipyard, San Francisco, Calif.
NavSyd–LBeach—Long Beach Naval Shipyard, Long Beach, Calif.

NavSyd–MI—Mare Island Naval Shipyard, Vallejo, Calif.
NavSyd–Norfolk—Norfolk Naval Shipyard, Norfolk, Va. (formerly Norfolk Navy Yard).
NavSyd–Pearl—Pearl Harbor Naval Shipyard, Pearl Harbor, Hawaii (formerly Pearl Harbor Navy Yard).
NavSyd–Phil—Philadelphia Naval Shipyard, Philadelphia, Pa. (formerly Philadelphia Navy Yard).
NavSyd–Ports—Portsmouth Naval Shipyard, Portsmouth, N.H. (formerly Portsmouth Navy Yard).
NavSyd–Puget—Puget Sound Naval Shipyard, Bremerton, Wash. (formerly Puget Sound Navy Yard).
Neafie—Neafie and Levy Ship and Engine Building Co., Philadelphia, Pa.
N.E.I.—Netherlands East Indies.
Nfld.—Newfoundland.
N.G.—New Guinea.
N.I.—Northern Ireland.
NICB—Niclausse-type boiler (built by the Stirling Co., Barberton, Ohio).
Niles—Niles Tool Works Div., General Machinery Corp.
NLSE—New London Ship and Engine Co., Groton, Conn.
NN—Newport News Shipbuilding and Dry Dock Co., Newport News, Va.
NNV—National Naval Volunteers.
NOB—Naval Operating Base.
NOR—Normand-type boiler.
Nordb—Nordberg Manufacturing Co., Milwaukee, Wis.
NOTS—Naval Overseas Transportation Service.
NR—submersible research vehicle (nuclear propulsion).
NROTC—Naval Reserve Officers Training Corps.
N.S.—Nova Scotia.
nsp.—non-self-propelled.
NSSC—Naval Ship Systems Command (formerly BUSHIPS, now part of NavSea).
N.W.I.—Netherlands West Indies.
NYd—Navy yard.
NYd–Pensa—Pensacola Navy Yard, Pensacola, Fla.
NYd–Wash—Washington Navy Yard, Washington, D.C.
NYSb—New York Shipbuilding Corp., Camden, N.J.
off.—officer(s).
OIC—Officer in Charge.
OTC—Officer in Tactical Command.
PA—contraction of APA (attack transport).
PACV—patrol air cushion vehicle.
Palm—N. F. Palmer, Jr., and Co., New York, N.Y.
PARPRO—Peacetime Aerial Reconnaissance Program.
PBM—twin-engine patrol bomber seaplane, known as "Mariner," manufactured by Glenn L. Martin Co.
PBR—river patrol boat.
PBY—twin-engine patrol bomber seaplane, known as "Catalina," manufactured by Consolidated–Vultee Aircraft Corp.
PC—submarine chaser (173').
PCC—control submarine chaser (173').
PCE—patrol escort.
PCEC—control escort (180').
PCER—patrol rescue escort.
PCF—patrol craft, inshore.
PCH—patrol craft (hydrofoil).
PCS—patrol craft, submarine.
PCSC—control submarine chaser (136').
pdr.—pounder.
PE—eagle boat.
PF—patrol escort; or frigate.
PG—patrol gunboat.
PGH—patrol gunboat (hydrofoil).
PGM—motor gunboat.
Phib—amphibious.
PhibRon—amphibious squadron.
P.I.—Philippine Islands.
PIRAZ—positive identification and radar advisory zone.
Pol.—Polaris missile system.

P.Q.—Province of Quebec.
PR—river gunboat.
P.R.—Puerto Rico.
P.r.—Parrott rifle.
PT—motor torpedo boat.
PTC—motor boat subchaser.
PTF—fast patrol craft.
Pusey—Pusey & Jones, Wilmington, Del.
PY—patrol vessel converted yacht.
PYc—patrol vessel converted yacht (coastal).
QIW—Quintard Iron Works, New York, N.Y.
quad.—quadruple.
quint.—quintuple.
R and R—rest and rehabilitation.
r.—rifle.
r. pivt.—rifled pivot gun.
RAF—Royal Air Force.
RAAF—Royal Australian Air Force.
RAN—Royal Australian Navy.
RC—revenue cutter.
RCAF—Royal Canadian Air Force.
RCN—Royal Canadian Navy.
RCS—Revenue Cutter Service.
recip3—reciprocating, triple expansion.
Reg.—Regulus missile system.
rf.—rapid fire.
Rich—Richmond Locomotive Works, Richmond, Va.
Ridg—Ridgeway Dynamo and Electric Co., Ridgeway, Pa.
rkt.—rocket launcher.
RN—Royal Navy.
RNN—Royal Netherlands Navy.
RNZN—Royal New Zealand Navy.
Roach—John Roach and Sons, Chester, Pa.
ROK—Republic of Korea.
RON—squadron.
RU—Reciprocating (Skinner Unaflow).
s.—speed.
sa.—semiautomatic.
SACEUR—Supreme Allied Commander, Europe.
SACLANT—Supreme Allied Commander, Atlantic.
SACMED—Supreme Allied Commander, Mediterranean.
SAR—Search and Rescue, sea air rescue.
sat.—saturated.
sb.—smooth bore.
SC—submarine chaser (110'); or cruiser submarine.
Sc—screw.
SCAJAP—Shipping Control Administrator, Japan.
SCC—control submarine chaser (110').
ScFr—screw frigate.
ScGbt—screw gunboat.
Sch—schooner.
SchBg—schooner barge.
SCOTCH—Scotch fire tube boiler. (All others are water-tube.)
ScSlp—screw sloop-of-war.
ScStr—screw steamer.
ScTug—screw tug.
SEAL—Sea Air and Land (Naval Special Forces).
SEATO—Southeast Asia Treaty Organization.
seabee—construction battalion.
SF—fleet submarine.
Sg.—shell gun.
s-g—single & double reduction gears.
sgl.—single.
SHAEF—Supreme Headquarters Allied Expeditionary Forces.
SHAPE—Supreme Headquarters Allied Powers, Europe.
shp.—shaft horsepower.
SINS—Ships Inertial Navigational System.
SL—ship-of-the-line.
Slp—sloop.
SlpW—sloop-of-war.
SlvBg—salvage barge.
SM—mine laying submarine.
SNAP—anti-snooper air patrol.
SP—motor patrol boat.

sp—self-propelled.
sr—single reduction gears.
S.r.—Sawyer rifle.
SS—submarine; or merchant steamship.
SSA—cargo submarine.
SSB—fleet ballistic missile submarine.
SSBN—fleet ballistic missile submarine (nuclear powered).
SSC—cruiser submarine.
SSG—guided missile submarine.
SSGN—guided missile submarine (nuclear powered).
SSK—antisubmarine submarine.
SSN—submarine (nuclear powered).
SSO—submarine oiler.
SSP—submarine transport.
SSR—radar picket submarine.
SSRN—radar picket submarine (nuclear powered).
SSS—strike support ship.
SST—target and training submarine (sp.).
St—steam.
StBrig—steam brig.
StBt—steamboat.
stbd.—starboard.
StFr.—steam frigate.
Str—steamer.
StRam—steam ram.
StTBt—steam torpedo boat.
StTug—steam tug.
Stw—stern wheel.
StwGbt—stern wheel gunboat.
StwRam—stern wheel ram.
StwStr—stern wheel steamer.
SubDiv—submarine division.
SubFlot—submarine flotilla.
subm.—submerged.
SUBROC—submarine rocket.
SubRon—submarine squadron.
Sun—Sun Shipbuilding and Dry Dock Co., Chester, Pa.
Sup—Superior Marine Manufacturing Co., Milwaukee, Wis.
surf.—surface.
Sw—side wheel.
SwGbt—side wheel gunboat.
SwStr—side wheel steamer.
SwRam—side wheel ram.
SwTug—side wheel tug.
Syd—shipyard.
t.—tonnage.
T.—Maritime Commission standard type.
T—prefix indicating M.S.C. (MSTS) ship.
Tal.—Talos missile system.
Tar.—Tartar missile system.
TB—torpedo boat.
TBS—talk between ships.
td.—turbine direct drive.
ted.—turbine electric drive.
Ter.—Terrier missile system.
terd.—turbine electric reduction drive.
TF—Task Force.
TG—Task Group.
THORN—Thornycroft-type boiler.
Tk.—tanker.
tl.—trial (speed).
TLL—tank lighter.
TLLW—tank lighter (medium tank-well type).
torp.—torpedo(es).
TR—geared turbine drive.
Tr—trawler.
Trans—transport.
TransRon—transport squadron.
Trigg.—Wm. R. Trigg Co., Richmond, Va.
Troy—Troy Engine & Machine Co.
trp.—troop capacity.
tt.—torpedo tubes.
TU—Task Unit.
tur.—turbine.
UDT—underwater demolition team.
UIW—Union Iron Works, San Francisco, Calif.

UIWHDR—Union Iron Works header-type boiler.
U.K.—United Kingdom.
UN—United Nations.
UN–CR—Universal Cruiser.
unrep.—underway replenishment.
USA—United States Army.
USAAC—United States Army Air Corps.
USAAF—United States Army Air Forces.
USAF—United States Air Force.
USAMC—United States Army Medical Corps.
USANF—United States Auxiliary Naval Force.
USAT—United States Army Transport.
USCG—United States Coast Guard.
USCGR—United States Coast Guard Reserve.
USCGS—United States Coast and Geodetic Survey.
USCS—United States Coast Survey.
USMC—United States Marine Corps.
USMCR—United States Marine Corps Reserve.
USMCWR—United States Marine Corps Women's Reserve.
USN—United States Navy.
USNA—United States Naval Academy.
USNR—United States Naval Reserve.
USNRF—United States Naval Reserve Forces.
USNS—United States Naval Ship.
USRCS—United States Revenue Cutter Service.
USRM—United States Revenue Marine.
USS—United States Ship.
USSB—United States Shipping Board.
VB—Navy bombing plane; Navy dive bombing squadron.
VBF—Navy bombing-fighting aircraft; Navy bomber-fighter squadron.
VBT—bombing, torpedo plane.
VC—composite aircraft squadron.
VD—photographic squadron (aircraft).
vert.—vertical.
VF—Navy fighter plane; Navy fighter squadron.
VFB—fighter bombing plane.
VF(M)—fighter plane (two engine).
VF(N)—Navy night fighter squadron.
VG—light transport plane (single engine).
VGF—escort-fighting squadron.
VGS—escort-scouting squadron.
VH—ambulance plane; Navy rescue squadron.
V.I.—Virgin Islands.
VJ—utility plane; Navy utility squadron.
VMB—Marine medium and heavy patrol bomber squadron (land based and seaplane).
VMBF—Marine fighter bomber squadron.
VMD—Marine photographic squadron.
VMF—Marine fighter squadron.
VMF(N)—Marine fighter squadron (night).
VMO—Marine observation squadron.
VMO(AS)—Marine observation squadron (artillery spotting).
VN—training squadron.
VO—observation plane; Navy battleship observation squadron.
VOG—Navy observation plane squadron.
Vog—Henry Vogt Machine Co., Louisville, Ky.
VOGHDR—Vogt header-type boiler.
VP—patrol plane; Navy patrol squadron.
VPB—patrol-bombing plane; Navy medium and heavy patrol bomber squadron (land based and sea based).
VPT—patrol-torpedo plane.
VR—transport plane; Navy transport squadron.
VS—scouting plane; Navy shore based scouting squadron.
VSB—scout-bombing plane.
VSO—scout observation plane.
VT—torpedo plane; Navy torpedo bomber squadron.
VTB—torpedo bombing plane.
VT(N)—Navy night torpedo bomber squadron.
vt2—vertical double-expansion.
vt3—vertical triple-expansion.
VMJ—Marine utility squadron.

vt4—vertical quadruple-expansion.
WAVES—Women Accepted for Voluntary Emergency Service.
Wes—Westinghouse.
Wes-Del—Westinghouse & De Laval.
Wes-Falk—Westinghouse & Falk.
Wes-FB—Westinghouse & Farrel–Birmingham.
WestPac—Western Pacific.
WFB—White–Forster-type boiler (manufactured by Babcock and Wilcox Co.).
Wint—Winton Engine Corp., Cleveland, Ohio.
WIW—Washington Iron Works, Seattle, Wash.
WL—water line.
WM—White and Middleton Co., Springfield, Ohio.
WSA—War Shipping Administration.
wt.—water-tube boiler.
WTDF—water-tube single-furnace boiler.
WWI—World War I.
WWII—World War II.
X—submersible craft (sp.).
XMAP—sweeper device.
YA—ash lighter.
YAG—miscellaneous auxiliary (service craft).
YAGR—ocean radar station ship.
YAR—Yarrow-type boiler.
YC—open lighter (nsp.).
YCD—fueling barge.
YCF—car float (nsp.).
YCK—open cargo lighter.
YCV—aircraft transportation lighter (nsp.).
YD—floating crane (nsp.).
Yd—Yard (Navy).
YDG—district degaussing vessel.
YDT—diving tender (nsp.).
YE—amunition lighter.
YF—covered lighter (sp.); or freight lighter.
YFB—ferryboat or launch (sp.).
YFD—yard floating dry dock (nsp.).
YFN—covered lighter (nsp.).
YFNB—large covered lighter (nsp.).
YFND—dry dock companion craft (nsp.).
YFNG—covered lighter (special purpose) (later YFNX).
YFNX—lighter (special purpose (nsp.) (formerly YFNG).
YFP—floating power barge (nsp.).
YFR—refrigerated covered lighter (sp.).
YFRN—refrigerated covered lighter (nsp.).
YFRT—covered lighter (range tender).
YFT—torpedo transportation lighter.
YFU—harbor utility craft (sp.).
YG—garbage lighter (sp.).

YGN—garbage lighter (nsp.).
Y-gun—Y-type depth charge projector.
YH—ambulance boat.
YHB—house boat.
YHLC—salvage lift craft, heavy (nsp.).
YHT—scow, heating.
YLA—open landing lighter.
YLLC—salvage lift craft, light (sp.).
YM—dredge (sp.).
YMLC—salvage lift craft, medium (nsp.).
YMP—motor mineplanter.
YMS—auxiliary motor minesweeper.
YMT—motor tug.
YN—net tender (boom).
YNG—gate craft (nsp.).
YNT—district net tender.
YO—fuel oil barge (sp.).
YOG—gasoline barge (sp.).
YOGN—gasoline barge (nsp.).
YON—fuel oil barge (nsp.).
YOS—oil storage barge (nsp.).
YP—patrol craft (sp.).
YPD—floating pile driver (nsp.).
YPK—pontoon stowage barge.
YR—floating workshop (nsp.).
YRB—repair and berthing barge (nsp.).
YRBM—repair, berthing, and messing barge (nsp.).
YRBM(L)—submarine repair, berthing, and messing barge (large).
YRC—submarine rescue chamber.
YRDH—floating dry dock workshop (hull) (nsp.).
YRDM—floating dry dock workshop (machine) (nsp.).
YRL—covered lighter (repair).
YRR—radiological repair barge (nsp.).
YRST—salvage craft tender (nsp.).
YS—stevedoring barge.
YSD—seaplane wrecking derrick (sp.).
YSR—sludge removal barge (nsp.).
YSP—stowage pontoon.
YT—harbor tug.
YTB—large harbor tug.
YTL—small harbor tug.
YTM—medium harbor tug.
YTT—torpedo testing barge.
YV—drone aircraft catapult control craft (sp.); or seaplane barge.
YVC—catapult lighter.
YW—water barge (sp.).
YWN—water barge (nsp.).
ZR—rigid airship.
ZRS—rigid airship (scouting).

HISTORICAL SKETCHES

T–1

I

(Submarine No. 52: dp. 1,107 (n.) (surf.), 1,482 (subm.); l. 268′9″; b. 22′10″; dr. 14′2″ (mean); s. 20 k. (surf.), 10.5 k. (subm.); cpl. 38; a. 6 21″ tt., 2 3″; cl. AA–1)

Schley (Submarine No. 52) was laid down on 21 June 1916 at the Fore River Shipbuilding Co. yard in Quincy, Mass., by the Electric Boat Co. of New York; renamed *AA–1* on 23 August 1917 to free the name *Schley* for Destroyer No. 103; launched on 25 July 1918; sponsored by Mrs. Lilian Hovey-King; and commissioned on 30 January 1920 at Boston, Mass., Lt. Comdr. James Parker, Jr., in command.

AA–1 was one of three boats designed and constructed under a project charged with developing fleet submarines; that is, undersea boats possessing the sea-keeping qualities and endurance capability required for long-range operations, as scouts for the surface fleet. On 17 July 1920, while the submarine was being fitted-out, the Navy adopted its modern system of alpha-numeric hull numbers, and the fleet submarine was designated SF–1. On 20 September, she was renamed *T–1*. Thus, by the time she began active service that fall, she was known as *T–1* (SF–1).

T–1's commissioned service lasted less than three years. She operated out of Hampton Roads, Va., training crews and conducting maneuvers along the east coast with other units of the Atlantic Fleet. Throughout the entire period, she remained a unit of Submarine Division 15. However, during her service, flaws in her design and construction—particularly in her propulsion plant—became apparent. On 5 December 1922, *T–1* was placed out of commission and laid up at the Submarine Base, Hampton Roads, Va. Later, she was moved to Philadelphia, Pa. After almost eight years of inactivity, her name was struck from the Navy list on 19 September 1930. Her hulk was broken up, and the materials were sold for scrap on 20 November 1930.

II

(SST–1: dp. 303 (surf.), 347 (subm.); l. 131′3″; b. 13′7″; dr. 12′2″ (mean); s. 10 k. (surf.), 10.5 k. (subm.); cpl. 18; a. 1 21″ tt.; cl. *T–1*)

T–1 (SST–1)—originally projected as AGSS–570—was laid down on 1 April 1952 at Groton, Conn., by the Electric Boat Division of the General Dynamics Corp.;

T–1 (SST–1) on trials, 12 October 1953.   (19–N–144564)

launched on 17 July 1953; sponsored by Mrs. Charles R. Muir; and placed in service on 9 October 1953, Lt. J. M. Snyder, Jr., in command.

After completing trials off the New England coast, *T–1* departed New London in February 1954, bound for the Florida coast. Soon after reaching Key West, she began operations with submarine and antisubmarine warfare (ASW) forces in Florida waters. These duties also took her to Guantanamo Bay, Cuba. On 15 May 1956, *T–1* was named *Mackerel*; but she retained her hull number, SST–1.

Mackerel participated in fleet exercises off the east coast, mainly conducting training and target assignments including some for the Fleet Sonar School at Key West. She made several cruises testing new equipment for submarines. On 2 April 1957, she departed Key West on a special sound-damping project, en route to Annapolis, Md. After more training and target cruises into the late 1950's, she tested acoustical developments for submarine hulls in waters near the British West Indies in the summer of 1963. She again operated in the West Indies in February 1964, performing similar tasks.

She received new equipment at Groton in the spring of 1966 and headed south, arriving at Key West on 26 June. There, *Mackerel* conducted experimental work to acquire data to be used in the development of future Navy submarines. After finishing this assignment in March 1967, the submarine had some of her special equipment removed, and she resumed operations at Key West for the Fleet Sonar School.

Mackerel acted as a target for surface and air ASW forces off the Florida coast and in the Caribbean during the late 1960's and into the 1970's. Sometime in 1971, *Mackerel* was commissioned. She provided target and training services for antisubmarine warfare units of the Atlantic Fleet in the Key West and the Mayport/Jacksonville operating areas in 1971 and 1972. She made her last dive on 21 July 1972. She remained in reduced-complement status from that day until 31 January 1973 but, nevertheless, conducted junior officer and midshipmen training regularly through October 1972. *Mackerel* and her sister *Marlin* (SST–2) were decommissioned on 31 January 1973 in a dual ceremony at the Naval Station, Key West, Fla.; and both were struck from the Navy list on the same day. *Mackerel* was subsequently scrapped.

T–2

I

(Submarine No. 60: dp. 1,107 (n.) (surf.), 1,482 (subm.); l. 268'9"; b. 22'10"; dr. 14'2" (mean); s. 20 k. (surf.), 10.5 k. (subm.); cpl. 38; a. 6 21" tt., 2 3"; cl. *AA–1*)

AA–2 (Submarine No. 60) was laid down on 31 May 1917 at the Fore River Shipbuilding Co. yard in Quincy, Mass., by the Electric Boat Co. of New York; launched on 6 September 1919; sponsored by Miss Madeline Everett; redesignated SF–2 on 17 July 1920; renamed *T–2* on 22 September 1920; and placed in commission at the Boston Navy Yard on 7 January 1922, Lt. Clarke Withers in command.

T–2 was the last of the three T-boats placed in commission and served actively for only 18 months. Her unique mission was long-range scouting and reconnaissance for the surface fleet. Like her sister ships, she operated in Submarine Division 15, training crews and conducting maneuvers with the Atlantic Fleet. By the fall of 1922, design and construction flaws in the three T-boats had become apparent. As a result, *T–2* was decommissioned on 16 July 1923 at the Submarine Base at Hampton Roads, Va., and was placed in reserve there. Later, she was moved to Philadelphia, Pa. Following seven years of inactivity, *T–2* was struck from the Navy list on 19 September 1930. She was broken up, and her metal was sold for scrap on 20 November 1930.

II

(SST–2: dp. 303 (surf.), 347 (subm.); l. 131'3"; b. 13'7"; dr. 12'2" (mean); s. 10 k. (surf.), 10.5 k. (subm.); cpl. 14; a. 1 21" tt.; cl. *T–1*)

T–2 (SST–2) was laid down on 1 May 1952 at Groton, Conn., by the Electric Boat Division of the General Dynamics Corp.; launched on 14 October 1953; sponsored by Mrs. William R. DeLoach; and placed in service on 20 November 1953, Lt. Edward Holt in command.

One of the smallest submarines ever built for the Navy, *T–2* conducted her shakedown and initial trials in the Massachusetts Bay area before getting underway from New London in late January 1954 and proceeding to her home port, Key West, Fla. For nearly two decades, the submarine provided valuable target services for the air and surface units of the Atlantic Fleet and played an important role in the developments in tactics and equipment for both submarine and antisubmarine warfare.

In addition to target and training duty for the Fleet, the submarine participated in various fleet maneuvers. In 1955, from 7 March to 4 April, *T–2* took part in mine warfare exercises, in company with her sister ship *T–1* (SST–1), *Amberjack* (SS–522), *Batfish* (SS–310), and *Chivo* (SS–341), as well as Atlantic Fleet minecraft. Named *Marlin* on 15 May 1956, the submarine was deployed to Guantanamo Bay, Cuba, for services to the Fleet Training Group in July and August 1958, March 1960, and December 1961.

From 1963, *Marlin* operated primarily as a target. On 16 June 1969, *Marlin* departed Key West for overhaul by the Ingalls Shipbuilding Division of Litton Industries, Inc. After calling briefly at St. Petersburg, Fla., en route, she arrived at Pascagoula, Miss., on 23 June and, soon thereafter, commenced her refurbishing. On 17 August, hurricane "Camille" swirled its destructive way in from the Gulf of Mexico. During the tempest, *Marlin* was undocked and towed inland. In the ensuing week, Lt. Comdr. James R. Burnett, in command of *Marlin*, led his crew in assisting the local communities in recovery operations in the wake of the devastating hurricane. Subsequently completing her overhaul on 7 October, *Marlin* sailed for Key West to resume her target operations.

Sometime in 1971, *Marlin* was commissioned. The submarine continued to provide target services to surface and air units of the Atlantic Fleet into 1972, until *Marlin* was decommissioned in a dual ceremony with sister ship *Mackerel* (SST–1) at the naval station at Key West on 31 January 1973. Both submarines were struck from the Navy list on the same day.

In April 1974, *Marlin* was transferred to the Greater Omaha Military Historical Society of Omaha, Nebraska, for use as a memorial. On 25 August 1974, the submarine was dedicated at the opening of "Freedom Park," where she remains on display.

T–3

(Submarine No. 61: dp. 1,107 (n.) (surf.), 1,482 (subm.); l. 268'9"; b. 22'10"; dr. 14'2" (mean); s. 20 k. (surf.), 10.5 k. (subm.); cpl. 38; a. 6 21" tt., 2 3"; cl. *AA–1*)

AA–3 (Submarine No. 61) was laid down on 21 May 1917 at the Fore River Shipbuilding Co. yard in Quincy, Mass., by the Electric Boat Co. of New York; launched on 24 May 1919; sponsored by Mrs. Lilian Terhune Jordan; redesignated SF–3 on 17 July 1920; renamed *T–3* on 22 September 1920; and commissioned on 7 December 1920 at the Boston Navy Yard, Lt. Comdr. Charles Milford Elder in command.

The second of three ships in a program to construct long-rang reconnaissance submarines to operate with the surface fleet, *T–3* joined *T–1* in Submarine Division 15, Atlantic Fleet, soon after commissioning. She operated with that division—later to include *T–2*—conducting maneuvers with the Atlantic Fleet until the fall of 1922. By that time, flaws in the design and construction of the T-boats—particularly in their propulsion plants—caused them to perform poorly. The decision was made to retire all three to the reserve fleet, and *T–3* was the first to go. On Armistice Day 1922, she was decommissioned at Hampton Roads, Va., and berthed at the submarine base located there. Later, she was moved to Philadelphia.

However, *T–3*'s active service did not end there. At the time of the T-boats' decommissioning, the idea of testing German-produced diesel engines in one of them had been bantered about in Navy circles. *T–1* had originally been designated for this purpose, but funds were not then available. In 1925, when money was forthcoming, it was *T–3* that came out of mothballs for the tests. On 1 October 1925, *T–3* was recommissioned at Philadelphia. For the following 21 months, she tested her newly installed 3,000-horsepower M.A.N. diesel engines for the Bureau of Engineering. Early in the summer of 1927, she completed the tests and, on 14 July 1927, was placed out of commission at Philadelphia. After a little over three years of inactivity, her name was struck from the Navy list on 19 September 1930. Her hulk was broken up, and the materials were sold for scrap on 20 November 1930.

T. A. M. Craven

See *Craven* (Vol. II, p. 202) for biography.

(Torpedo Boat No. 10: dp. 146; l. 147'; b. 16'4½''; dr. 4'7''; s. 30 k.; cpl. 30; a. 2 18'' Whitehead tt., 4 1-pdr. r.f.; cl. *Dahlgren*)

T. A. M. Craven (Torpedo Boat No. 10)—a twin-screw torpedo vessel built to a French design (Normand, of Le Havre)—was laid down on 6 December 1897 at Bath, Maine, by the Bath Iron Works; launched on 25 September 1899; sponsored by Miss Amy Craven, granddaughter of Comdr. Craven; and commissioned at the Portsmouth (N.H.) Navy Yard on 9 June 1900, Lt. Comdr. John R. Edie in command.

Ten days later, *T. A. M. Craven* sailed for Newport, R.I., on 19 June 1900. The ship performed training and experimental work there through the summer and into the fall. Returning to Portsmouth in December, the warship was placed out of commission on 5 December 1900.

Recommissioned on 24 October 1902, *T. A. M. Craven* again performed "station work" at Newport, combining research and development activities with training in tactics. She remained at the Naval Torpedo Station, performing these routine but vital duties until she returned to Portsmouth for her second decommissioning which occurred on 22 December 1903.

During 1906 and 1907, *T. A. M. Craven* again operated out of Newport, until assigned to the Reserve Torpedo Flotilla at the Norfolk Navy Yard, Portsmouth, Va., in December 1907. Transferred to Charleston, S.C., in 1908, the torpedo boat operated in the reserve division, working out of Charleston into 1913. During this tour of duty, the ship dropped the initials from her name; and, after 1910, she appears as simply *Craven* on Navy lists.

On 10 September 1913, *Craven* was off the coast of Georgia, en route from Martin's Industry Lightship to Tybee Light. At about 1245, the ship's number one boiler exploded. Ens. W. D. LaMont, the ship's commanding officer, noted a violent explosion which blew a dense cloud of black smoke and gas through the fireroom hatch opening. Once the smoke had cleared, volunteers went below to bring out the wounded men; one, Watertender D. B. Smith, suffered burns on both his hands and feet as he climbed down to rescue Chief Watertender J. W. McCaffrey, who was severely injured by the explosion.

Immediately after the tragedy, *Craven* hoisted distress signals—upside-down ensigns at the signal halyards. The tug *Cynthia*, from Savannah, Ga., saw the flags and altered course to close. She passed a towline to the torpedo boat and began to tow the stricken vessel in—despite the heavy sea running. The tug *Estelle* also arrived on the scene at the same time. Ens. LaMont requested the second tug to put in to Fort Screven to bring doctors out to the torpedo vessel to aid the injured. Eventually, *Craven* tied up to the pier at Fort Screven at 1805, but not before one man of the six injured—Watertender W. O. Milton—had died. Chief McCaffrey later died in the hospital ashore.

Ens. LaMont earned high praise from his division commander, who lauded the young officer for his "excellent judgment shown under such trying conditions." *Craven* herself never returned to active service. On 25 October 1913, the Navy issued orders to place her out of commission. Decommissioned on 14 November, and struck from the Navy list on 15 November 1913, *Craven* was sunk as a target soon thereafter.

T. A. Ward

(Sch.: t. 284; l. 114'6''; b. 28'2''; dph. 9'2''; dr. 10'6''; a. 1 13'' M., 2 32-pdrs.)

Schooner *T. A. Ward* was purchased by the Navy at New York City on 9 October 1861. While the vessel was being fitted out for blockade duty, she was selected for service in the mortar flotilla being established by Comdr. David D. Porter to support Flag Officer David G. Farragut's impending attack on New Orleans. The schooner was armed with a 13-inch seacoast mortar weighing over eight and one-half tons. Two 32-pounders were also installed to give her a low-trajectory punch. The ship was manned by a crew from the receiving ship *North Carolina* and was commissioned at the New York Navy Yard on 17 January 1862, Lt. Walter W. Queen in command.

Late in January, the schooner sailed for Hampton Roads carrying supplies for schooners *George Mangham* and *Adolph Hugel*. From that port, she proceeded to Key West, Fla., where Porter's flotilla was assembling. Early in March, she proceeded thence to Ship Island, Miss., the staging point for Farragut's invasion of the South. In mid-March, the schooners sailed to Pass à l'Outre where they were towed across the bar into the Mississippi on the 18th. Once inside, they waited almost a month while Farragut's steamers labored to get the West Gulf Blockading Squadron's deep-draft ships over the bar and into the river and while other preparations were made for Farragut's attack on the South's greatest city.

On 15 April, revenue cutter *Harriet Lane* towed *T. A. Ward* up the Mississippi to a position just out of range of the Southern guns in Fort St. Phillip and Fort Jackson. There, the crews camouflaged their ships with bushes and tree branches. On the morning of the 18th, Lt. Queen, who also commanded the flotilla's second division, had the schooner towed upstream to a predesignated position on the northeast shore of the river less than 4,000 yards from Fort Jackson. Almost immediately, the guns of the fort opened fire on the schooners which, in turn, began lobbing shells into the Confederate stronghold. Early in the action, a near miss upset several barrels of gunpowder in *T. A. Ward*'s magazine but fortunately did not detonate the explosives. One-half hour later, a shot struck the schooner, damaging her rigging as it smashed through several bulkheads before leaving the vessel through a hole in *T. A. Ward*'s side a few inches above her waterline. Queen then ordered his division to drop downstream a few hundred yards where the schooner's gunners resumed the bombardment as her crew began to repair the damage.

The shelling continued for six days and nights. It reached a crescendo in the wee hours of 25 April to distract the gunners in the Southern forts as Farragut's fleet raced upstream past the Confederate strongholds to take New Orleans.

The following day, New Orleans fell; but Fort St. Philip and Fort Jackson held out until the 28th when they finally surrendered to Porter. On 6 May, *T. A. Ward* retired to Ship Island which the mortar flotilla used as a base for blockade operations to cut off Confederate commerce in the Gulf of Mexico while awaiting Farragut's return from the Mississippi to join in an attack on Mobile, Ala. Early in June, their blockade duty was interrupted by orders which sent the flotilla back up the Mississippi to support Farragut in an attack on Vicksburg which he had been directed to undertake by President Lincoln.

A shortage of steamers in the lower river delayed the flotilla's ascent of the river, but the mortar schooners were on station below Vicksburg on 28 June, in time to bombard the Confederate batteries which guarded the river at that point while Farragut's deep-draft warships dashed past the Southern guns to join Flag Officer Charles H. Davis' Western Flotilla in the upper river.

While Farragut's daring foray past Vicksburg was tactically successful, it was brought to nought strategically by the Union Army's want of sufficient troops to take and hold the river fortress. Thus, after a fortnight's inconclusive operations with Davis, Farragut—supported again by the mortar boats—dashed once more under the Confederate guns and retired downstream to New Orleans.

Meanwhile, events had occurred near Richmond which beckoned *T. A. Ward* back to the east coast. General McClellan's drive up the Peninsula toward the Confederate capital had been halted by General Lee's Army of Northern Virginia in the Seven Days campaign, and the Union's Army of the Potomac was beleaguered in a bridgehead at Harrison's Landing on the northern bank of the James River. As a result, in an effort to save the imperiled Northern troops, Federal Army leaders in Washington asked Gideon Welles for all possible naval support in the James. In compliance, the Union Secretary of the Navy ordered most of Porter's mortar boats back to Hampton Roads, Va., where *T. A. Ward* and her sisters arrived on the last day of July.

By this time, however, the greatest danger to the Union Army had passed; and the mortar vessels were repaired before resuming active operations. When back in top fighting trim, *T. A. Ward* was assigned to the Potomac Flotilla which was then protecting Union communications with Washington by water and attempting to stop Confederate traffic across the Potomac between Maryland and Virginia. Her first contact with the enemy came on the night of 3 and 4 October near Blakistone Island, Md., when she captured a large man-of-war boat which was attempting to slip back to Virginia under cover of darkness. The next night, she took two more boats attempting to run the blockade from Breton and St. Clement's Bays. Later in the month, the ship sailed to the Rappahannock for blockade duty. On 29 October, a party from *T. A. Ward* helped to put out a fire in the American merchant ship *Alleghanian*, which had been set ablaze by a group of Virginians.

By mid-November, the schooner was back on station in the Potomac and captured the sloop *G. W. Green*; a seine boat; and six prisoners near St. Jerome's Creek, Md. She continued to serve in the Potomac Flotilla until transferred to the North Atlantic Blockading Squadron early in the summer of 1863.

T. A. Ward arrived at Hampton Roads on 5 July and soon was stationed off Wilmington where she served on blockade duty into the autumn. On 26 September, orders from Washington directed her to proceed to waters off Charleston, S.C., for duty with the South Atlantic Blockading Squadron.

On 17 October 1863 at Murrell's Inlet, S.C., boat crews from the schooner destroyed Southern merchant schooner *Rover*, before that blockade runner could slip to sea laden with cotton. Three days later, a party from *T. A. Ward* went ashore to reconnoiter and obtain fresh

water; but it was surprised by Confederate cavalry. Ten of the Union seamen were captured. On 12 April 1864, boats from *T. A. Ward* and *South Carolina* seized the blockade-running steamer *Alliance*, which the night before had run aground on Daufuskie Island, S.C., laden with glass, liquor, and soap. On 16 August 1864, a boat expedition from *Saratoga* and *T. A. Ward* captured some 100 prisoners and a large quantity of arms during a daring raid into McIntosh County, Ga. The Union landing party also destroyed a salt works and a bridge across the South Newport River on the main road to Savannah. Between the 23d and the 25th of the same month, men from these two ships engaged Confederate pickets along Georgia's Turtle River.

T. A. Ward spent the autumn and early winter undergoing repairs at Port Royal; but, by New Year's Day 1865, she was on blockade duty off Charleston and she served in nearby waters through the end of the Civil War. In June 1865, she was detached and sailed north. The schooner arrived at Portsmouth, N.H., on 15 July 1865, was decommissioned there on 22 July 1865, and was sold on 25 September 1865.

T. D. Horner

(StwStr.: t. 123; a. 2 12-pdr. r.)

T. D. Horner—a stern-wheel steamer built in 1859 at Brownsville, Pa.—was purchased by the War Department on 18 May 1862 for use on the Mississippi River and its tributaries in the Army's newly established flotilla which was popularly known as the "Ellet Ram Fleet." Commanded and manned by Army personnel, this organization operated in the same waters as the Western Flotilla—later to become the Mississippi Squadron—which had been established the previous summer, also under Army auspices but commanded and manned by Navy personnel. The relationship between these organizations—which often cooperated in carrying out their overlapping missions—was never completely clarified. However, at no time was the Ram Fleet—or were its ships—taken into the Navy. *T. D. Horner* served the Ram Fleet and its successor, the Marine Brigade, as a tug until the latter was dissolved on 24 August 1864.

After the Civil War ended, *T. D. Horner* was sold by the Government on 17 August 1865. She was redocumented for merchant service on 27 November 1865 and plied the Mississippi and its tributaries until New Year's Day 1868 when she hit a bridge at Louisville, Ky., and was damaged beyond economical repair.

Ta-Kiang

Chinese for "Big River."

(Str: t. 510; l. 154'0"; b. 28'0"; dr. 11'0"; dph. 11'6"; cpl. 40)

Ta-Kiang (sometimes spelled *Takiang*)—an oak-hulled, screw steamer built in 1862 at New York City by the shipbuilding firm of Roosevelt and Joyce—was active in the China trade, probably under the British flag to avoid being molested by Confederate raiders and cruisers. In the summer of 1864, the British government chartered the ship to bring troops to Kanagawa, Japan, because of the anti-foreign sentiment then prevalent among certain segments of the Japanese population who were resisting westernization.

As an outgrowth of this hostility to aliens in the summer of 1863, a Prince of Nagato, Mori, of the clan of Choshiu, fortified one side of the Strait of Shimonoseki to close that waterway to western commerce. The following year, the western Treaty powers determined to open those waters once and for all. However, the only American warship then in that part of the

4

world was the sail-powered sloop-of-war *Jamestown*, which could not overcome the strong currents in the strait and thus was unable to participate in any allied expedition to open navigation to foreign shipping.

On 18 August 1864—so that the United States would be represented in the joint Anglo-French-Dutch force—Robert K. Pruyn, the minister resident of the United States in Japan, and Capt. Cicero Price, the commanding officer of *Jamestown*, chartered *Ta-Kiang* from the firm Walsh, Hall, and Co., the agents for the steamer *Ta-Kiang*. Under the terms of the agreement, she was "to carry a landing party, and in every way to assist in the common object, but not to be under fire of the forts."

Before the joint expedition set sail, a mail steamer arrived bringing Japanese diplomats back from France with a treaty that had stipulated, among other provisions, that the Strait of Shimonoseki would be opened within three months. *Ta-Kiang*'s charter was cancelled when word of the treaty first arrived, but the Japanese appeared unwilling to be bound by the agreement. This intransigence left the western powers no alternative to opening hostilities with Choshiu. Accordingly, the United States government rechartered *Ta-Kiang* and took her over on 28 August 1864.

Capt. Price placed Lt. Frederick Pearson, of *Jamestown*, in command of the ship and also transferred 18 men—including a surgeon—and a 30-pounder Parrott rifle to the erstwhile merchantman. Price admonished Pearson to "render any and every other aid in your power to promote the common object, such as towing boats, landing men, and receiving the wounded . . . if required to do so."

On the next day, 29 August, *Ta-Kiang* departed Yokohama in company with the Dutch steam sloop *Djambe* and arrived at the rendezvous point, Hime Shima, on the evening of 1 September. The following day, the remainder of the allied fleet arrived, "making a total of 18 sail." At 1000 on 4 September, the naval force got underway for Shimonoseki, in three columns, with *Ta-Kiang* bringing up the rear of the French column.

The allied ships anchored in sight of the batteries on the shores of Nagato at 1600 that afternoon and, 24 hours later, moved in closer and commenced fire on the forts. By 1730 on the first day of the engagement, all of the batteries within sight had been silenced. During the night, British sailors and marines landed and spiked the guns of one battery. The Japanese commenced the action on 6 September, opening fire on the allied ships at 0600.

During that action, *Ta-Kiang* towed a landing boat from the French steam sloop *Dupleix*, steaming close to the first battery. By noon, a mixed force of British, French, and Dutch troops had taken the batteries. The Westerners repulsed enemy counterattacks with ease; and, before nightfall, "the land forces returned to their vessels."

On 7 and 8 September, *Ta-Kiang* took on board 23 wounded Britons, as well as a surgeon and attendants, and ultimately returned to Yokohama on the evening of 21 September. During the attacks on the Shimonoseki forts, *Ta-Kiang* had fired 18 shells from her Parrott gun "thus identifying herself in this respect with the expedition."

On 22 September 1864, *Ta-Kiang* was returned to her agents for a resumption of mercantile service. Records concerning the ultimate fate of this ship indicate that she was sold to the Japanese government in 1864, becoming *Oye Maru* (or *Ooe Maru*). Some evidence indicates that, in 1869, the ship was returned to the United States flag under Consular documents and was renamed *Peiho*.

Tabberer

Charles Arthur Tabberer—born on 18 December 1915 in Kansas City, Kan.—enlisted in the Naval Reserve on 12 October 1939 and was appointed an aviation cadet on 11 January 1940. Following flight training in Florida at Pensacola and Miami, Cadet Tabberer was designated a naval aviator on 1 November. He was commissioned an ensign in the Naval Reserve on 12 December. After further training at San Diego, Calif., he was ordered to report to Fighting Squadron 5 (VF–5) which was then assigned to *Yorktown* (CV–5).

Ens. Tabberer served with VF–5 throughout his short naval career. Promoted to lieutenant (junior grade) on 29 May 1942, his squadron was assigned to *Saratoga* (CV–3) for the invasion of Guadalcanal in the southern Solomon Islands. Lt. (jg.) Tabberer was one of the 11 "Wildcat" (F4F) pilots lost when elements of the Japanese 25th Air Flotilla opposed the Guadalcanal invasion force on 7 August. Through the efforts of Tabberer and his comrades, the Japanese aerial forces were beaten back. For his sacrifice, Lt. (jg.) Tabberer was awarded the Distinguished Flying Cross, posthumously.

(DE–418: dp. 1,350; l. 306'0"; b. 37'7"; dr. 13'4"; s. 24.3 k. (tl.); cpl. 222; a. 2 5", 10 40mm., 3 21" tt.; cl. *John C. Butler*)

Tabberer (DE–418) was laid down at Houston, Tex., on 12 January 1944 by the Brown Shipbuilding Co.; launched on 18 February 1944; sponsored by Mrs. Mary M. Tabberer; and commissioned on 23 May 1944, Lt. Comdr. Henry Lee Plage, USNR, in command.

On 27 June, *Tabberer* headed toward Bermuda for shakedown training. At the end of a fortnight's post-shakedown availability at the Boston Navy Yard, she got underway on 16 August to escort *Severn* (AO–61) to the Hawaiian Islands. The two ships transited the Panama Canal late that month and reached Pearl Harbor on 7 September. For over a month, the destroyer escort conducted underway training in the waters surrounding the islands. Her exercises included anti-submarine warfare drills and gunfire practice. She also screened carriers *Coral Sea* (CVE–57), *Ranger* (CV–4), and *Saratoga* (CV–3) during night flying qualifications and amphibious support training.

On 16 October, *Tabberer* sortied from Pearl Harbor with Task Group (TG) 12.7, a hunter/killer group built around *Anzio* (CVE–57), formerly *Coral Sea* (CVE–57). Upon arrival at Eniwetok on the 23d, the ships joined Admiral Halsey's 3d Fleet and, on 27 October, stood out of Eniwetok as TG 30.7. After stopping at Ulithi during the first three days of November, the task group headed for the 3d Fleet fueling group's operating area to conduct antisubmarine sweeps. On 18 November, TG 30.7 registered its first kill when *Tabberer*'s sister-ship *Lawrence C. Taylor* (DE–415) sent *I–41* to the bottom after a coordinated depth charge attack with *Melvin R. Nawman* (DE–416). Following a replenishment period at Ulithi, *Tabberer* sortied with TG 30.7 on 9 December to resume antisubmarine sweeps of the Philippine Sea during Task Force 38's Luzon strikes in support of the Mindoro landings.

On 17 December, as *Tabberer* was steaming in company with the 3d Fleet fueling group to the east of the Philippine Islands, rising wind and a choppy sea forced her to break off preparations to take on fuel. The barometer dropped precipitously as the weather grew worse. By evening, the little warship was fighting a full typhoon. During the night, *Tabberer* lost steerageway and could not fight her way out of the deep troughs. She frequently took rolls up to 60 degrees and, on several occasions, approached an angle of 72 degrees from the vertical.

The high winds and seas continued to batter her on the 18th. By 1830, her mast and radio antennae were gone. At 2130, a signalman trying to rig an emergency antenna sounded the "man overboard" alarm. *Tabberer* rushed to the rescue. Once on board, the sailor reported that he was from *Hull* (DD–350) and that his ship had gone down about noon that day. Thus, she was the first ship of the 3d Fleet to learn of the tragedy of 18 December 1944. Though unable to call for help, she immediately embarked upon a search for other survivors. Her rescue efforts continued through the night, all day on the 19th, and into the 20th. In all, she saved 55 officers and men both from *Hull* and *Spence* (DD–512). Later, *Tabberer* was relieved by other units of the fleet, and they rescued an additional 36 men, a few of whom belonged to the crew of the typhoon's third victim *Monaghan* (DD–354). Outstanding rescue efforts during the storm won several members of *Tabberer*'s crew Navy and Marine Corps medals; Lt. Comdr. Plage, the Legion of Merit, and the ship, the Navy Unit Commendation.

On 21 December, the destroyer escort reentered Ulithi lagoon before heading back to Hawaii. She stopped at Eniwetok early in January 1945 and reached Oahu soon thereafter. Following a short availability, she stood out of Pearl Harbor on 29 January. She steamed via Eniwetok and Saipan to screen TF 38 during the air strikes in support of the marines who stormed ashore at Iwo Jima on 19 February. *Tabberer* remained in the Volcano Islands through the first week of March, screening the carriers from enemy submarines and aircraft. Though the task force was subjected to several air attacks and carriers suffered kamikaze and bomb hits, *Tabberer* sustained no damage. On 7 March, she headed for the Philippines and entered San Pedro Bay, Leyte, on the 12th.

From late March to early May, the destroyer escort cruised with various task groups of TF 38 during the invasion of Okinawa. Once again, she protected the American carriers from Japanese submarines and aircraft while their planes struck enemy positions. Although she operated continuously for 52 days and sighted many unidentified planes, the ship never came under attack. Frequently, she rejoined the *Anzio* hunter/killer group for night antisubmarine sweeps.

Tabberer put into Apra Harbor, Guam, on 11 May to replenish and make repairs. On the 23d, she departed again and rejoined *Anzio* for further antisubmarine operations on the sea lanes between Okinawa and the Marianas. On 31 May, *Anzio* planes scored a kill; and *Tabberer* assisted *Oliver Mitchell* (DE–417) in recovering evidence of their success. Following a visit, lasting just over a fortnight, to San Pedro Bay, Leyte, she resumed antisubmarine sweeps with the *Anzio* task group. For the remainder of the war, she hunted Japanese submarines and protected the logistics group during the 3d Fleet's final air assault on the Japanese home islands. During the final month of the war, she destroyed mines and rescued four downed *Anzio* aircrewmen.

After the cessation of hostilities on 15 August 1945, *Tabberer* remained in the Far East to support the occupation forces. She escorted ships between Okinawa; Jinsen, Korea; and Tientsin and Taku, China. She also destroyed mines in the Yellow Sea. On 22 December, the little warship departed Tsingtao, China, to return to the United States. Along the way, she made stops at Okinawa, Eniwetok, and Pearl Harbor before entering San Francisco on 15 January 1946. In April, she shifted to San Diego where she was placed out of commission, in reserve, on 24 April 1946.

Tabberer was recommissioned at San Diego on 7 April 1951, Lt. Comdr. Willard J. McNulty in command. In June, she changed home ports from San Diego to Newport, R.I., and in August reported for duty with the Atlantic Fleet. For the next nine years, she operated along the Atlantic seaboard from Key West, Fla., to Halifax, Nova Scotia. Frequently, she operated in the Caribbean area, often near Guantanamo Bay and Vieques Island. *Tabberer* participated in a variety of exercises and, on several occasions, embarked Naval Academy and NROTC midshipmen for their summer cruises. She left the western Atlantic only once during this period—in the fall of 1957—for a two-month deployment to the Mediterranean. After that, she resumed her operations along the east coast.

On 19 April 1959, the destroyer escort put into port for the last time. At Philadelphia, she began preparations for deactivation. *Tabberer* was placed out of com-

mission, in reserve, in May 1960 and was berthed at Philadelphia for the remainder of her career. On 1 August 1972, her name was struck from the Navy list; and, on 3 October 1973, she was sold for scrapping to Mr. David Hahn of Key West, Fla.

Tabberer earned four battle stars and a Navy Unit Commendation for service in World War II.

Tabora

Minor planet number 721 of the solar system. Discovered in 1911, the new body was named in 1913 during a conference held in Hamburg, Germany, on board the ocean liner *Tabora* of the *Deutsche Ost Afrika Linie*.

(AKA–45: dp. 7,000; l. 426'; b. 58'; dr. 16'; s. 17 k.; cpl. 303; a. 1 5", 8 40 mm.; cl. *Artemis*; T. S4–SE2–BE–1)

Tabora (AKA–45) was laid down under Maritime Commission contract (MC hull 1906) on 4 March 1945 at Providence, R.I., by the Walsh-Kaiser Co., Inc.; launched on 3 May 1945; sponsored by Mrs. Arthur W. Devine; and commissioned on 29 May 1945, Lt. Comdr. Olaf C. Erickson, USNR, in command.

Tabora departed Boston on 9 June and—after nine days of shakedown training out of Hampton Roads, Va.—headed for France. She arrived at Marseilles on 7 July and, the following week, got underway for Panama. She reached Cristobal on the 28th. Two days later, *Tabora* transited the canal and steamed toward the Marshall Islands. She arrived at Eniwetok on 22 August and, the next day, pushed on toward the Philippines. Upon arriving at San Fernando, Leyte, on the last day of August, the ship was assigned to the 5th Fleet.

Tabora loaded troops and vehicles of the 33d Infantry Division and sailed on 20 September for Japan. She arrived at Wakayama, Honshu, on the 25th; unloaded; and, the next day, began the return trip to the Philippines. She transported another load of occupation troops to Matsuyama, Shikoku, in mid-October. On the 24th, *Tabora* was assigned to "Magic-Carpet" duty, returning veterans to the United States. On the last day of October, she got underway for Buckner Bay; loaded 340 marines; and sailed for San Francisco.

Tabora continued shuttling troops from Pacific bases to the United States until early 1946 when she was scheduled for inactivation. *Tabora* was decommissioned on 29 May, returned to the Maritime Commission on 30 June, and struck from the Navy list on 3 July 1946.

Tackle

(ARS–37: dp. 6,500; l. 310'2"; b. 44'6"; dr. 22'6"; s. 10 k.; cpl. 65; a. 1 3")

Tackle (ARS–37), ex SS *W. R. Chamberlain, Jr.*, built in 1912 by the Newport News Shipbuilding and Drydock Co., Newport News, Va., was owned and operated by W. R. Chamberlain and Co.

The ship was acquired through the War Shipping Administration in 1943. She was renamed *Tackle* (ARS–37) on 8 June 1943; taken over by the Navy at Oran, Algeria, on 19 June 1943; and commissioned on 5 August 1943 at Palermo, Sicily. *Tackle* was assigned to the Salvage Force, 8th Fleet, and operated between Algerian ports until early 1944. She took a load of salvage equipment to Bizerte, Tunisia, on 30 March and moved to Palermo, Sicily, on 4 April. The ship shuttled between Sicily, Naples, and North African ports until mid-August.

Tackle sailed with Task Force 84, on 21 August, to participate in the landings on southern France. She arrived at Baie de Cavalaire on the 24th and moved to Port de Bouc on 1 September. On 4 September, *Tackle* was being towed to the fueling and watering berth in the Basin Petrolier by the French tug *Provencal*. At 1425 hours, a mine exploded between the two ships. The

French tug was sunk, and *Tackle* suffered considerable damage to her port side and engine rooms. She was towed to Toulon on the 8th for temporary repairs and, five days later, thence to Palermo. Permanent repairs were completed there on 20 October, and she sailed for Toulon five days later.

Tackle made a voyage from Algeria to Marseilles in November and spent December 1944 shuttling between Algerian ports. On 30 January 1945, she returned to Marseilles. Her designation was changed to ARS(T)–4 on 1 February. The ship steamed to Palermo on the 13th. While she was there, her designation was changed to IX–217. She returned to Algeria on 20 March.

Tackle stood out of Oran on 17 April en route to the United States. She arrived at Norfolk on 18 May; and, on 27 June, it was determined that the ship was unfit for further naval service. *Tackle* was decommissioned on 13 September and struck from the Navy list on 11 October 1945.

Tackle received two battle stars for World War II service.

Tacloban

A city and port on the northeastern coast of Leyte, an island in the Philippines. Tacloban is the capital of Leyte Province.

———

Tulsa (PG–22) (*q.v.*) was renamed *Tacloban* (PG–22) on 18 December 1944 to free the name *Tulsa* for heavy cruiser, CA–129.

Tacoma

A city and port on the coast of Puget Sound in the west central part of the state of Washington. Tacoma is the seat of Pierce County.

I

Harbor tug *Tacoma*, often misspelled *Takoma*, was renamed *Sebago* (*q.v.*) in December 1899 to free the name *Tacoma* for a protected cruiser scheduled to be constructed.

II

(Cruiser No. 18: dp. 3,200 (n.); l. 308'6"; b. 44'0" (wl.); dr. 15'9" (mean); s. 16.58 k. (tl.); cpl. 309; a. 10 5" blr., 3 6-pdr. r., 2 3-pdrs.; cl. *Denver*)

The second *Tacoma* (Cruiser No. 18) was laid down on 27 September 1900 at Mare Island, Calif., by the Union Iron Works; launched on 2 June 1903; sponsored by Miss Julia M. Harris; and commissioned on 30 January 1904, Comdr. R. F. Nicholson in command.

Following a post-commissioning visit to her namesake city, Tacoma, Wash., the protected cruiser voyaged to Hawaii in April and May. She returned to San Francisco on 2 June and, a month later, sailed for Cape Horn. During the voyage, she participated in the search for merchant ship SS *Conemaugh*, which had departed from Valparaiso, Chile, and vanished. After rounding the Horn and steaming up the Atlantic coast of South and North America, *Tacoma* entered New York harbor on 5 November and remained there until joining the North Atlantic Fleet on New Year's Day 1905.

Following the completion of maneuvers off Culebra Island on 25 January, *Tacoma* sailed for Hispaniola where she performed special duty protecting American interests during one of the many periods of turmoil that have troubled that island. Following that assignment, *Tacoma* conducted target practice off the Florida coast between 27 March and 25 April. She returned to New York on 19 May to prepare for a voyage to Europe.

On 18 June, she sailed for France and arrived at Cherbourg on 30 June. She remained there while a bat-talion of sailors went to Paris to participate in ceremonies honoring the remains of John Paul Jones which were being returned to the United States. On 8 July, *Tacoma* departed Cherbourg to escort the remains to their final resting place at Annapolis, Md. After the ceremony at the United States Naval Academy on 24 July, the warship proceeded to Tompkinsville, N.Y. On 5 August, she embarked Japanese diplomats at New York and transported them to Sagamore Hill, President Theodore Roosevelt's summer home at Oyster Bay, N.Y. There, they first met the Russian commissioners for the peace negotiations which were later held at Portsmouth, N.H., and resulted in the termination of the Russo-Japanese War. *Tacoma* returned to Philadelphia on the 8th and conducted training for the Pennsylvania and Massachusetts naval militias before rejoining the North Atlantic Fleet for operations in the Caribbean Sea.

Deployed to the Mediterranean for the first five months of 1906, the ship visited Tangier, Algiers, Ville-franche, Naples, and Genoa. After a trip to Grand Canary Island, she returned to the Mediterranean and visited Alexandria and Port Said before returning to the United States in June.

For the next 10 years, except for an eight-month period in reserve at Philadelphia in 1911 and 1912, *Tacoma* alternated service along the east coast with cruises to the Caribbean and West Indies protecting American citizens and interests there during this turbulent period. In late 1906 and early 1907, Cuba was the major trouble spot; and the cruiser operated along her coasts from late September until mid-November and again from late December until June, visiting Havana, Tunas, Manzanilla, Santiago de Cuba, Cienfuegos, and Guantanamo Bay. She returned to the West Indies again in the spring of 1908 for stops at St. Thomas, St. Christopher, Martinique, Margarita Island, Port Mochima, Cunama, La Guaira, and Curaçao. During the second half of 1908 and the first half of 1909, she observed political conditions in Haiti and Honduras. From July to September of 1909, the cruiser operated off Nicaragua. Later, her itinerary included a visit to Costa Rica and a return to Honduras, all in an effort to bring the steadying influence of American military power to the volatile Latin American republics.

Between January and March of 1910, *Tacoma* cruised off the coast of Nicaragua and visited the Canal Zone and Costa Rica. After a spring voyage to the east coast of the United States, the ship headed back to Central America to protect United States interests there. During the following nine months, she visited Panama, Honduras, Costa Rica, Nicaragua, and Guatemala. In January 1911, pursuant to the orders of the senior naval officer present embarked in *Marietta*, *Tacoma* prevented the converted yacht *Hornet* from participating in the Honduran revolution. Later that month, she landed a force of bluejackets at Puerto Cortez, Honduras, to protect American citizens. In February, her deck was the scene of a peace conference conducted by special commissioner T. C. Dawson. The negotiations brought the revolution to a close and established a new provisional government in Honduras. That summer, *Tacoma* steamed—via Puerto Mexico and Galveston—to New York. She remained at the New York Navy Yard until mid-November when she went into reserve at Philadelphia.

In July 1912, *Tacoma* came out of reserve and was soon on her way back to the troubled waters of the Gulf of Mexico. Late that month, a revolution broke out in Nicaragua and lasted until November. The cruiser patrolled almost incessantly off the Nicaraguan coast at Bluefields and at Great Corn Island from 3 August to 25 October. In November, she headed—via Tampico, Mexico, and Galveston, Tex.—for the navy yard at Boston where she remained through mid-February 1913. By the 22d, she was back patrolling and observing, this time along the coasts of Honduras and Guatemala. The ship returned to New York in July; then operated off the Mexican coast. She cruised off Tampico and Vera

Cruz until January 1914 when she returned to the east coast of the United States for repairs.

Tacoma resumed operations in Mexican waters early in May in the wake of the Tampico Incident and the resultant seizure of the customs house at Vera Cruz. The warship cruised the Mexican coast through September during the latter stages of the Huerta-Carranza struggle and while the new Carranza government consolidated its power against former allies, notably Pancho Villa and Emiliano Zapata.

Late in September 1914, *Tacoma* departed the Mexican coast; steamed, via Jamaica and Cuba, to Haiti, and patrolled off Cape Haitien until early December. After a visit to the Canal Zone, the cruiser returned to Haiti in February; then moved to Santo Domingo in March. On the 21st, she entered the Portsmouth (N.H.) Navy Yard for repairs.

While at Portsmouth, *Tacoma* was placed in reserve. On 19 May 1916, she shifted to Boston, Mass., where she served as receiving ship. On 1 December, she again was placed in full commission. She made another voyage to Mexican waters for patrol duty from January to April of 1917. Upon the entry of the United States into World War I, *Tacoma* returned to the Atlantic seaboard to prepare for convoy duty. During the war, she made five round trips to Europe protecting troop and supply convoys. While returning to the United States from her third voyage to Europe, she stopped at Halifax, Nova Scotia, just when an ammunition explosion in the Belgian relief ship *Mont Blanc* severely damaged the town. *Tacoma* assisted in relief work; and, for three days, the cruiser's officers and men worked diligently to help the devastated port community.

At the end of the war, the cruiser joined the Pacific Squadron and served with it until 1920. Early that year, she returned to her old duty of encouraging stability in the perennially volatile Caribbean. As a unit of the Special Service Squadron, which was ordered to observe events in Latin America and the Caribbean and to protect American interests in those areas, *Tacoma* patrolled the isthmian coast until January 1924. During that time, she was redesignated a light cruiser, CL–20. During a heavy storm on 16 January, the warship ran aground on Blanquilla Reef near Vera Cruz. For almost a week, her crew tried without success to free her, her captain and three crewmen drowning in those attempts. After a board of inquiry, the Navy struck her name from the Navy list on 7 February 1924. She was sold to R. Sebastian of the American Consulate at Vera Cruz on 5 September 1924.

III

(PF–3: dp. 1,430; l. 303′11′′; b. 37′6′′; dr. 13′8′′; s. 20.3 k. (tl.); cpl. 190; a. 3 3′′, 4 40mm., 9 20mm., 2 dct., 8 dcp., 1 dcp. (hh.); cl. *Tacoma*)

The third *Tacoma* was laid down at Richmond, Calif., on 10 March 1943 by Kaiser Cargo, Inc., under a Maritime Commission contract (MC hull 1421) as *PG–111*; redesignated *PF–3* on 15 April 1943; named *Tacoma* on 5 May 1943; launched on 7 July 1943; sponsored by Mrs. A. R. Bergersen; and commissioned on 6 November 1943, Lt. Comdr. Adrian F. Werner, USCG, in command.

After completing shakedown training off the California coast in December, *Tacoma* reported for duty as a training ship in January 1944. She trained prospective frigate crews until 27 June, when she was ordered to proceed to Alaskan waters upon completion of sea trials. However, she was plagued by unsuccessful trials and a boiler room fire and, consequently, did not report for duty at Kodiak, Alaska, until 21 October. For the next four months, *Tacoma* conducted antisubmarine patrols and escorted supply ships and transports along the Alaskan coast and between the various islands of the Aleutians chain, visiting Attu, Adak, Dutch Harbor, and other smaller Alaskan ports.

On 23 February 1945, she departed Dutch Harbor and sailed south for an extensive overhaul—first at San Francisco, then at Bremertown, Wash.—to prepare her for transfer to the Soviet Union. On 10 July, the frigate returned to Alaska, at Cold Bay, and began familiarization training with her prospective Russian crew. She was decommissioned at Cold Bay on 16 August and transferred to the Soviet Navy, in which she served over four years as *EK–12*.

The frigate was returned to the United States on 16 October 1949 at Yokosuka, Japan. She remained there out of commission, in a caretaker status, until the outbreak of hostilities in Korea late in June 1950. She began preparations for activation in August and went back into commission on 1 December at Yokosuka. The next day, she began 15 days of shakedown training out of Yokosuka in Sagami Wan and Tokyo Bay. From the 18th to the 25th, she underwent post-shakedown availability at Yokosuka and put to sea the following day bound for Sasebo, Japan. On the 28th, *Tacoma* headed for the east coast of Korea.

For the next few months, the frigate operated with the UN Blockading and Escort Squadron, Task Force (TF) 95. On 30 January 1951, she joined in the bombardment phase of the amphibious feint at Kansong; and, the following afternoon, she performed the same duty at Kosong. She put in at Pusan on 1 February, then headed for Sasebo two days later. By 5 February, she was back off Korea's eastern coast at Kangnung for a two-day bombardment mission there. On the 7th and 8th, her gunners trained their sights on Yangyang, and then on Hwangpo on the 9th and 10th. When not pounding Hwangpo, *Tacoma* patrolled off Chikute Island. She returned to Sasebo on 13 February and remained there until the 19th, when she headed for Wonsan harbor in North Korea. She arrived off Wonsan on 22 February and, for the next four days, joined in the operations which resulted in the successful landing of 110 Republic of Korea marines on Sin Do on the 24th. The following day, *Tacoma* cleared Wonsan channel to return to Sasebo. She arrived at Sasebo on 27 February and remained there until 10 March, when she got underway for Yokosuka and a restricted availability which lasted until 23 April.

On 3 April 1951, the United States Naval Forces, Far East (NavFE) organization was restructured. As a result, the Service Forces, previously fragmented among separate 7th Fleet and NavFE groups, were consolidated into a new Logistics Group, designated TF 92. When *Tacoma* emerged from the yard at Yokosuka in late April, she was assigned to the new task organization as an escort; and she served in that capacity for the remainder of her United States naval career. From then until September, the frigate escorted supply ships between Japanese and Korean ports and to stations along the Korean coast where she replenished Allied warships. She also conducted antisubmarine patrols and participated in occasional shore bombardments.

On 9 October 1951, *Tacoma* was transferred to the Republic of Korea (ROK). She served in the ROK Navy as *Taedong* (PF–63) until 28 February 1973, when she was decommissioned and returned to the United States Navy. Her name was struck from the Navy list on 2 April 1973, and she was subsequently donated to the ROK Navy as a museum and training ship.

Tacoma earned three battle stars during the Korean War.

IV

(PG–92: dp. 247 (f.); l. 165′; b. 24′; dr. 5′; s. 37.5 k.; cpl. 24; a. 1 3′′, 1 40mm., 4 .50-cal. mg.; cl. *Asheville*)

The fourth *Tacoma* (PG–92) was laid down on 24 July 1967 at Tacoma, Wash., by the Tacoma Boatbuilding Co.; launched on 13 April 1968; sponsored by Mrs. Arne K. Strom; and commissioned on 14 July 1969, Lt. Frank H. Thomas, Jr., in command.

During the fall of 1969, *Tacoma* conducted shakedown training and independent ship exercises along the California coast. While so engaged on 16 October, she joined in a search and rescue mission and recovered a sailor who had fallen overboard from *Neches* (AO–47) the previous night. At the completion of refresher training, she participated in amphibious exercise PHIBELEX/BLT 4–69, off Camp Pendleton, Calif., in early December. In January 1970, she entered Long Beach Naval Shipyard for post-shakedown availability. *Tacoma* returned to San Diego on 20 May and began preparations for deployment to the western Pacific. On 1 August, after two months of operations out of San Diego, she got underway for the Mariana Islands. Following a week-long stopover in Pearl Harbor, the gunboat arrived in her new home port, Apra, Guam, on the 28th.

For almost four years, *Tacoma* alternated between deployments to Vietnam and patrols in the islands of the Trust Territories of Micronesia. Her first tour of duty in Vietnamese waters began on 28 September 1970 when she arrived at Cam Ranh Bay after a week of upkeep at Subic Bay in the Philippines. She was assigned to the Coastal Surveillance Force and participated in search and rescue missions and interdicted communist coastal supply traffic in Operation "Market Time." On 22 November, she and several other units of the Coastal Surveillance Force cooperated in the destruction of a North Vietnamese infiltration trawler. She operated off the coast of Vietnam for two more months and then returned to Subic Bay on 31 January 1971. She remained there two weeks and then headed for Guam, arriving in Apra Harbor on 20 February.

For almost five months, the gunboat underwent overhaul and operated in the vicinity of Guam. On 9 July, she embarked upon her first patrol of the Micronesia Trust Territories. Between then and the 26th, she visited seven islands in the Yap and Palau districts of the Eastern Carolines, conducting surveillance and making goodwill stops. She returned to Guam on the 26th, then departed again on 10 August. While on her second patrol in the Trust Territories, 10 August to 1 September, *Tacoma* visited 19 islands in the Truk and Ponape districts and apprehended a Japanese fishing vessel violating the territorial waters of the Trust Territories at Ngatik Island. She resumed operations in and around Guam on 1 September and was so occupied until early November.

On 5 November, the gunboat departed Guam in company with *Asheville* (PG–84) and headed, via Subic Bay, for Vietnamese waters. On the 29th, she and *Asheville* relieved *Crockett* (PG–88) and *Welch* (PG–93) and resumed "Market Time" operations interdicting communist coastal supply traffic. After almost two months patrolling the Vietnamese coastline, *Tacoma* departed Cam Ranh Bay on 26 January 1972 for a visit to Bangkok, Thailand. There, she welcomed officers of the Royal Thai Navy on board for tours of the ship. On 3 February, she resumed coastal surveillance patrols along the coast of Vietnam. Late in March, trouble in her starboard main engine forced her to Subic Bay for repairs. The gunboat remained there from 29 March to 24 May; then she continued on to Guam, via Yap Island.

Tacoma reached Apra Harbor on 31 May and commenced three months of sea trials, independent exercises, restricted availabilities, and inspections. After a dependents' cruise to Saipan on 3 and 4 September, the gunboat conducted refresher training until 14 October, when she headed back to Vietnam with *Asheville*. Between 20 October and 15 December, she made two patrols along the Vietnamese coast, broken by a visit to Bangkok, Thailand, in mid-November. On 15 December, she cleared Vietnamese waters and set sail for the Philippines. She laid over in Subic Bay from 18 to 21 December awaiting the completion of *Asheville*'s engine repairs. Then, the two gunboats got underway for Guam, where they arrived on the 28th.

During the first three months of 1973, *Tacoma* operated out of Guam, primarily conducting exercises. In February, she made a voyage to Hong Kong, via Subic Bay. The first three weeks in April saw her in port at Apra Harbor preparing for regular overhaul. Yard work on the ship began on 20 April and was completed two months later. In late June and early July, she conducted sea trials and various drills. The gunboat completed type training early in September, then put to sea on 12 September to shadow a Soviet submarine tender and fleet submarine operating in the vicinity of the northern Marianas. She returned to Apra on the 18th and, after a restricted availability, completed sea trials on 27 October. On 5 November, she began another patrol of the eastern Carolines, returning to Guam on the 24th. From 11 to 16 December, *Tacoma* made a Christmas gift tour of the northern Marianas.

Following repairs in December and January and refresher training in late January and early February, the gunboat departed Apra on 13 February 1974 for a three-month cruise. In late February, she participated in exercises with *Midway* (CVA–41), *Oriskany* (CVA–34), and *Marathon* (PG–89), out of Subic Bay. In March, *Tacoma* visited Singapore and cruised the Malaysian coast. Late that month, she visited Bandar Seri Begawan in Brunei on the northern coast of Borneo. After two days at Subic Bay, 4 to 6 May, she headed for Taiwan and visits to Kaohsiung and Keelung. The gunboat returned to Guam on 27 May and commenced preparations to return to the United States.

Tacoma stood out of Apra on 21 June and reached Pearl Harbor on 3 July. Five days later, she continued eastward and arrived in San Diego, Calif., on the 15th. On 1 August, she headed south along the coast of California and Mexico, stopped at Acapulco for two days, and made Rodman, in the Canal Zone, on the 17th. She transited the canal on 22 August and headed, via Guantanamo Bay, Cuba, and Port Everglades, Fla., to her new home port, Little Creek, Va., where she arrived on 2 September.

During the period 14 April–30 June 1975, *Tacoma* was overhauled in the Norfolk area. On 3 September, following underway refresher training, *Tacoma* commenced the mission of serving as a training unit for Royal Saudi Arabian naval personnel. This assignment, calling for operations along the east coast of the United States and in the Caribbean, has continued into 1979.

Tacoma earned two battle stars during the Vietnam War.

Taconic

A ridge in the northern part of the Appalachian Mountains extending along the Massachusetts-New York boundary and into Vermont.

(AGC–17: dp. 13,910 (tl.); l. 459'2"; b. 63'0"; dr. 24'0" (lim.); s. 16.4 k. (tl.); cpl. 633; a. 2 5", 8 40mm.; cl. *Adirondack*; T. C2–S–AJ1)

Taconic was laid down under Maritime Commission contract (MC hull 1710) at Wilmington, N.C., on 19 December 1944 by the North Carolina Shipbuilding Co.; launched on 10 February 1945; sponsored by Mrs. O. W. Turner; acquired by the Navy on 6 March 1945; converted to an amphibious force flagship at the Atlantic Basin Iron Works in Brooklyn, N.Y.; and commissioned there on 16 January 1945, Capt. C. G. Christie in command.

Upon commissioning, *Taconic* began a long tour of duty with the Atlantic Fleet. She served alternately as flagship of the Atlantic Fleet Amphibious Force and of Amphibious Groups 2 and 4. Between June 1946 and June 1949, she participated in CAMID I, II, and III, amphibious warfare exercises conducted in the Chesapeake Bay area and encompassing joint training for Military Academy cadets and Naval Academy midshipmen. Each spring, the amphibious force flagship joined the Atlantic Fleet maneuvers carried out in the Caribbean area.

Taconic (AGC–17) in 1947. Her array of antennas identifies her as an amphibious command ship.   (80–G–704282)

In June 1949, following a yard overhaul at Norfolk, Va., she took part in Operation "Diaper," the transportation of Navy men and their dependents from the Canal Zone to Norfolk.

Taconic remained in active service for 20 more years. During that entire period of time, she retained Norfolk as her home port. She participated in numerous exercises both with the 2d and 6th Fleets, and with units of NATO nations. The amphibious force flagship was deployed to the Mediterranean Sea on eight different occasions in those two decades; and, in the summer of 1958, she served as flagship of the Commander, Middle East Force, during the Lebanon landings. In November 1959, she served as communication and support ship to President Eisenhower during the Pakistan-Afghanistan-India leg of his visit to a number of European and Asian countries. When not deployed with the 6th Fleet, she operated with the 2d Fleet in the western Atlantic and in the Caribbean. The bulk of those operations consisted of exercises; but, on one occasion in March 1957, she carried President Eisenhower's limousines to Bermuda for his meeting with British Prime Minister Harold MacMillan. In January 1963, *Taconic* patrolled the Haitian coast during political unrest in that country. She returned to the Caribbean area for special duty again in May and June of 1965 during similar troubles in the Dominican Republic.

In January 1969, at the beginning of her last year of service, *Taconic* was redesignated LCC–17. After 12 months of operations and preparations for decommissioning, the amphibious force flagship was placed out of commission, in reserve, on 17 December 1969 at Norfolk, Va. She was berthed with the National Defense Reserve Fleet at its James River, Va., berthing area and remained there into October 1979.

Taconnet

A 17th century Abnaki Indian village located at the fork of the Kennebec River near Waterville in what is now Kennebec County, Maine.

(YTB–417: dp. 237; l. 100'0''; b. 25'0''; dr. 9'7''; s. 12 k. (tl.); cpl. 10; cl. *Sassaba*)

Taconnet (YTB–417) was laid down at Curtis Bay, Md., on 23 May 1944 by the Coast Guard Yard; launched on 4 August 1944; sponsored by Mrs. Clyde D. Sterling; completed on 10 February 1945; and delivered to the Navy and placed in service on 13 February 1945.

Taconnet served in the 14th Naval District through the end of World War II. Following the war, she continued to operate in the harbors of the Hawaiian Islands until May 1947 when she was placed out of service, in reserve.

In February 1951, the tug rejoined the active fleet and served at advanced bases in the Pacific area. In February 1962, *Taconnet* was redesignated a medium harbor tug, YTM–417. The tug continued to operate with the Pacific Fleet until sometime in 1969 or 1970 when she was reassigned to the 11th Naval District. As of 1 July 1979, she was still operating in the San Diego area.

Tacony

A section of northeastern Philadelphia on the bank of the Delaware River.

I

(SwStr.: t. 974; l. 205'; b. 35'; dph. 11'6''; dr. 8'10''; s. 15 k.; cpl. 145; a. 2 11'' D. sb., 3 9'' D. sb., 1 24-pdr. how., 2 12-pdrs., 1 brass fieldpiece)

The first *Tacony*—a double-ended, side-wheel steamer built by the Philadelphia Navy Yard—was launched on 7 May 1863; sponsored by Miss Ellie M. Wells, daughter of Lt. Comdr. Clark H. Wells, the captain of the yard at Philadelphia; and commissioned there on 12 February 1864, Lt. Comdr. William T. Truxtun in command.

The double-ender was assigned to the East Gulf Blockading Squadron and sailed south from Philadelphia soon thereafter, bound for Key West. She reached Newport News, Va., on the 15th and entered the Norfolk Navy Yard for repairs to her steering machinery. While the steamer was undergoing this yard work, a despatch arrived reassigning her to the North Atlantic Blockading Squadron. She departed Hampton Roads before dawn on the morning of 27 February, bound for the North Carolina sounds to strengthen Union forces afloat in those dangerous waters against the attacks by the Confederate ironclad ram *Albemarle*, then reportedly nearing completion up the Roanoke River. But for a brief run—via Norfolk—to Washington for repair, she served in the sounds until after the destruction of the *Albemarle* on the night of 27 and 28 October.

In December, *Tacony* left the sounds to join the force Rear Admiral David D. Porter was assembling to destroy the defences of Wilmington; and she participated in the abortive attack against Fort Fisher on Christmas Eve and Christmas Day. She was part of the powerful fleet which Porter led back to Fort Fisher in mid-January 1865, and she supported the effort which finally compelled that valuable Confederate stronghold to surrender on the 15th. She also participated in the attack against Fort Anderson late in the month.

The ship continued blockade duty through the collapse of the Confederacy and then sailed north. She was decommissioned at Boston on 21 June 1865 for repairs. Recommissioned on 16 September 1865, the ship served —but for another period out of commission undergoing repairs from 21 November 1866 to 12 February 1867— until 7 October 1867 when she was decommissioned for the final time at Portsmouth, N.H. *Tacony* remained in ordinary until 26 August 1868 when she was sold. No trace of her subsequent career has been found.

II

(SP–5: dp. 46; l. 82′; b. 13′6″; dph. 7′5″; dr. 4′4″; s. 12.5 k.; cpl. 12; a. 1 1-pdr., 1 mg.)

The second *Tacony* (SP–5)—a wooden screw steam yacht built in 1911 as *Sybilla II* by Mathis Yacht Building Co., Camden, N.J., for John F. Botz, III, Essington, Pa.—was acquired by the Navy on a free lease from Jacob S. Disston, Tacony, Pa., and was commissioned on 24 May 1917.

Tacony was assigned patrol duty in the 4th Naval District through the end of World War I. On 29 November 1918, she was returned to her owner.

Tact

(PG–98: dp. 925; l. 205′0″; b. 33′0″; dr. 14′6″; s. 16 k.; cpl. 87; a. 2 3″; cl. *Temptress*)

Tact (PG–98)—a *Temptress*-class patrol gunboat built for the United States Navy by Collingwood Shipyards, Ltd., Collingwood, Ontario, Canada—was launched on 14 November 1942. However, before seeing any service in the United States Navy, the ship was transferred to the United Kingdom under the Lend-Lease program on 21 June 1943 and served the Royal Navy as HMS *Smilax* until after the end of hostilities in Europe. *Tact* was returned to the United States on 18 October 1946 and sold by the Maritime Commission to the Argentine Republic.

Tadousac

A Montagnais Indian tribe which resided on the Saguenay River, near Quebec, Canada.

(Tug No. 22: dp. 1,000; l. 156′8″; b. 30′0″; dr. 14′7″ (mean); cpl. 62; s. 13 k.; a. 1 mg.; cl. *Bagaduce*)

Tadousac (Tug No. 22)—a steel-hulled, ocean-going fleet tug—was laid down as *Chimo* on 22 July 1918 at Buffalo, N.Y., by the Ferguson Steel and Iron Works; launched on 17 February 1919; renamed *Tadousac* on 24 February; and commissioned on 13 June 1919, Lt. (jg.) Arthur O. Henderson, USNRF, in command.

After fitting out on the Great Lakes, *Tadousac* proceeded via New York to Guantanamo Bay for the annual fleet concentration in Cuban waters. The tug operated out of Guantanamo into the fall of 1920, performing the vital but unglamorous task of towing for the fleet. Subsequently, she was homeported at St. Thomas, Virgin Islands, from late 1920 through the fall of 1922, and at Port-au-Prince, Haiti, from January 1923 through November of that year. After conducting local operations with the 7th and 6th

Naval Districts, respectively, into the summer of 1924, *Tadousac* was decommissioned at Charleston, S.C., on 18 October 1924; was struck from the Navy list on 13 April 1938; and sold to B. J. Maier, of Philadelphia, on 29 December 1938.

Taganak

An island in the Philippines.

(AG–45: dp. 3,000; l. 261′; b. 43′6″; dr. 18′8″; s. 10.2 k.; cpl. 54; a. 1 3″, 1 40mm.)

Taganak (AG–45) was built in 1917 as *War Shell* at Toledo, Ohio, by the Toledo Shipbuilding Co. Acquired by the United States Shipping Board and delivered to the United States Navy for use as a mine carrier, the ship was renamed *Lake Shore*, commissioned at Philadelphia on 11 January 1918, and assigned to the Naval Overseas Transportation Service (NOTS).

Lake Shore was refitted at Philadelphia, armed with one 5-inch gun and one six-pounder, manned with a complement of 64, and got underway for Hampton Roads, Va., on 7 February. The ship loaded a cargo of coal there and sailed for Boston, arriving on the 17th. After discharging her cargo, *Lake Shore* returned to Norfolk on the 27th. She then loaded coal and mines for the North Sea barrage, sailed for Scotland on 7 March, and arrived at Lamlash on the 29th. The steamer returned to Norfolk on 5 May and sailed on the 18th for Boston where she received an extensive overhaul. On 17 June, she proceeded, via New York, to Norfolk where she loaded mines and general cargo. Her convoy sailed on 27 June for Scotland and reached Corpach on 15 July.

Lake Shore returned to Norfolk on 18 August. She made two more trips from Hampton Roads to Europe— one back to the British Isles and one to France—before returning home on 6 February 1919. She was decommissioned on 5 March 1919 and returned to the Shipping Board the next day.

In 1923, *Lake Shore* was sold to the E. K. Wood Lumber Co., Inc., of San Francisco, and renamed *Olympic*. The steamer was operated by the lumber company along the Pacific coast until it was withdrawn from service in 1940.

Early in World War II, to relieve its acute shortage of cargo ships, the Navy reacquired *Olympic* on 23 May 1942. Following repairs, alterations, and refitting at Mare Island, the ship was commissioned as *Taganak* (AG–45) on 23 July 1942, Lt. Comdr. O. H. Pitts, USNR, in command.

Taganak, formally purchased on 28 September 1942, sailed for the South Pacific, via Pearl Harbor, in late October. Upon her arrival at Noumea, New Caledonia, she was sent to New Zealand to return with a load of lumber. The ship then shuttled cargo between New Zealand, New Caledonia, New Hebrides, and the Solomon Islands for the next year. On 19 August 1943, *Taganak* was a few hours out of Noumea en route to Espiritu Santo with a cargo of ammunition when she was attacked by a Japanese submarine. HMNZS *Tui* attacked the enemy with depth charges and forced it to the surface. American dive bombers of Scouting Squadron VS–57 came to the assistance of the New Zealand corvette and aided in the kill of the Japanese submarine *I–17*. Rescue efforts succeeded in saving a few survivors. On 26 October, *Taganak* stood out of Tutuila, Samoa, and headed for the United States laden with copra. The ship arrived at San Pedro, Calif., on 19 November; discharged her cargo, and moved to Oakland for an overhaul.

On 11 February 1944, *Taganak* sailed for the South Pacific to resume shuttling inter-island cargo. She put into Auckland, New Zealand, on 6 February 1945 for repairs and then plied the waters of the South Pacific carrying cargo until after hostilities with Japan ended. The old steamer departed Tutuila on 30 September and headed for the United States. She arrived at San Francisco on 26 October 1945; was decommissioned at Vallejo, Calif., on 25 March 1946; was struck from the Navy list on 12 April; and was sold on 15 November 1946 to the Pillsbury and Martignoni Co., San Francisco, for scrap.

Taghkanic

(ScSlp: dp. 2,400; t. 1,380; a. 12 guns)

In need of fast, powerful warships to strengthen its blockading forces, the Union Navy made plans in 1864 to build eight new sloops-of-war in Federal navy yards. *Taghkanic* was one of these ships, but her construction apparently was not assigned to any specific navy yard before it was obviated by the collapse of the Confederacy. Her name was dropped from the "List of Vessels of the U.S. Navy" sometime in 1866.

Tahchee

A western Cherokee chief who migrated to the Arkansas area early in the 19th century. His raids on the Osage Indians caused the Army to offer a $500 reward for his capture, but a promise of amnesty allowed him to settle down near Fort Gibson. After that, he won renown among Army officers for his skill as a scout and guide.

(YN–43: t. 84; l. 78'; b. 19'3''; dr. 8'6'')

Calatco—a tug built in 1936 by Ira S. Bushey & Sons, Inc., at Brooklyn, N.Y.—was purchased by the Navy on 22 October 1940 from the Canal Lakes Towing Corp., of New York City; renamed *Tahchee* (YN–43); converted for naval service at the New York Navy Yard; and placed in service there on 17 December 1940.

The following day, she departed New York for duty in the 5th Naval District. She reached Norfolk, Va., on the 19th and served there for almost four months. On

2 April 1941, *Tahchee* put to sea and headed north to Philadelphia where she arrived the next day. After a year of inshore patrol duty in the 4th Naval District, she was reclassified a net tender, YNT–11. On 10 April 1943, she reported for duty at Newport, R.I., and completed her Navy career serving in the 1st Naval District based there. During that time, on 7 July 1945, she was redesignated a medium harbor tug, YTM–736. On 1 September 1946, *Tahchee* was placed out of service at Melville, R.I.; and, on 8 November, she was declared surplus to the needs of the Navy. Accordingly, her name was struck from the Navy list on 30 December, and she was turned over to the Maritime Commission for disposal on 4 April 1947.

Tahgayuta

Tahgayuta—a wooden-hulled, screw sloop-of-war to be built in 1863 at Baltimore, Md., by Hazelhurst and Wiegard—was never constructed.

Tahoma

A Salishan Indian word meaning "snow peak." Tahoma is the name of a glacier on the southwestern slope of Mount Ranier in the state of Washington.

I

(ScGbt: t. 507; l. 158'4''; b. 28'; dph. 12'; dr. 10'6''; s. 10 k.; a. 1 10'' D. sb., 2 20-pdr. P. r.; 2 24-pdr. how)

Tahoma—a wooden-hulled, 4th rate screw gunboat constructed during 1861 at Wilmington, Del., by W. and A. Thatcher—was launched on 2 October 1861; and commissioned at the Philadelphia Navy Yard on 20 December 1861, Lt. Comdr. John C. Howell in command.

Assigned to the East Gulf Blockading Squadron, *Tahoma* remained with this force for her entire career through the Civil War. On 26 April 1862, while patrol-

An artist's rendering of the "ninety-day gunboat" *Tahoma*.   (NH 57826)

ling east of Sea Horse Key, Fla., the screw gunboat chased a schooner until the quarry ran aground where she was destroyed. Two months later, *Tahoma* raided St. Mark's, Fla., burned a barracks and destroyed a battery of cannon before heading out to sea, unscathed.

While patrolling off the Yucatan Peninsula on 7 July, *Tahoma* captured the blockade-running schooner *Uncle Mose*, which had sailed unawares up to where the gunboat had anchored. Comdr. Howell later reported that the Confederate captain was astonished "at finding a man-of-war where we were anchored." The prize was laden with 115 bales of badly needed cotton.

After patrol duty in the late summer and early fall, *Tahoma* helped to destroy three important Confederate salt works. On the morning of 6 October, *Tahoma* and *Somerset* lay to off Sea Horse Key and sent ashore a landing party of 111 men in eight boats. A pre-landing bombardment of shell, shrapnel, and cannister fired from the howitzers mounted in two of the boats scattered some 20 to 30 armed Confederate guerrillas.

The sailors quickly landed and deployed to cover the boats. Working parties destroyed 28 boilers and burned all buildings in the vicinity. As Howell subsequently reported, "the expedition was entirely successful . . . no confusion was exhibited on landing . . . no useless expenditure of ammunition, and no one hurt."

While operating along the Florida coast during the first six months of 1863, *Tahoma* captured seven blockade runners: the cotton-laden sloop *Silas Henry* at Tampa Bay on 8 January; British schooner *Margaret* off St. Petersburg on 1 February; the yacht *Stonewall* off Pea Creek on 22 February; schooner *Crazy Jane*, carrying a cargo of cotton and turpentine, near Gadsden's Point on 5 May; cotton-carrying schooner *Statesman* in Tampa Bay on 6 June; the British blockade-running schooner *Harrietton* off Anclote Keys on 18 June; and *Mary Jane*, destroyed on the same day at Clearwater. Also during this period, *Tahoma* engaged a Confederate shore battery at Gadsden's Point on 2 April.

Tahoma and *Adela* landed an expeditionary force at Tampa on 17 October 1863 and burned the steamer *Scottish Chief* as well as the sloop *Kate Dale*. Operating out of Key West from January 1864, *Tahoma* launched two daring raids against Confederate salt works in February of that year.

On the morning of 17 February, a landing force went ashore in two detachments and marched seven miles inland to destroy salt works at St. Marks, Fla. Ten days later, another force went ashore to destroy an even more distant station near Goose Creek. On the latter occasion, the landing party eluded Confederate cavalry and brought off a dozen prisoners, including a captain from an infantry company. Before their destruction, these two salt works had produced some 2,500 bushels of salt—important not only for preserving food but also for making gunpowder.

In the summer, the gunboat steamed north for repairs and was placed out of commission at the New York Navy Yard on 23 July 1864. After the completion of her overhaul, the ship was recommissioned on 13 April 1865 and operated off the east coast until decommissioned at Boston on 27 July of the same year. The ship again served on active duty, this time with the Gulf Squadron, from the fall of 1866 into the summer of 1867. *Tahoma* was decommissioned for the last time on 27 August 1867. The ship was later sold on 7 October that same year at New York.

II

(Coast Guard Cutter No. 60: dp. 1,005; l. 165'; b. 36'; dr. 13'7''; s. 13 k.; cpl. 105; a. 2 3''; cl. *Algonquin*)

The second *Tahoma* (Coast Guard Cutter No. 60) was built at Bay City, Mich., by the Defoe Shipbuilding Co. Completed in 1934, the steel-hulled cutter operated on the Great Lakes between 1934 and 1941, attached to

the 9th Coast Guard district and homeported at Cleveland, Ohio.

As the United States moved closed to full participation in World War II, President Roosevelt issued an executive order on 1 November 1941 transferring the Coast Guard from the Treasury Department to the Navy. Accordingly, *Tahoma* was sometime thereafter reclassified as a gunboat and designated WPG-80.

Although no records have been found delineating *Tahoma*'s service during the first months following Japan's attack on Pearl Harbor, we know that by July 1942, the former cutter had left the Great Lakes to escort Allied convoys in the North Atlantic in the vicinity of Casco Bay, Maine; Ivigtut, Greenland; St. John's and Argentia, Newfoundland; and Sydney, Nova Scotia; into the spring of 1944. The remainder of her naval service was spent in serving on weather and ice patrol duties between Greenland and Iceland and plane guard operations in the same waters. In the latter service, she alternated with the Coast Guard cutters *Frederick Lee* (WPC-139), *Algonquin* (WPG-75), and *Mohawk* (WPG-78) into 1945. At the time of the Japanese surrender in mid-August 1945, *Tahoma* was at sea on a plane guard station.

Released from duty with the Atlantic Fleet on 30 September 1945, *Tahoma* was returned to the Coast Guard for a resumption of peacetime service.

Takana

(Id. No. 3039: dp. 172; l. 69'5''; b. 18'7''; dr. 7'9''; cpl. 8; a. 1 3-pdr.)

Takana (Id. No. 3039)—a steam tug built in 1915 by M. M. Davis and Son, Solomons Island, Md.—was chartered by the Navy on 2 July 1918 from P. Sanford Ross and Co., Jersey City, N.J. Assigned to the 3d Naval District, *Takana* operated in New York harbor until she was returned to her owner on 13 June 1919.

Takanis Bay

A small bay on the southwest coast of Yakobi Island in the Alexander Archipelago off the coast of Alaska.

(CVE-89: dp. 9,570; l. 512'3''; b. 65'2''; ew. 108'1''; dr. 22'6''; s. 19.3 k.; cpl. 860; a. 1 5'', 16 40 mm., 28 ac.; cl. *Casablanca*)

Takanis Bay (CVE-89) was laid down under Maritime Commission contract (MC hull 1126) on 16 December 1943 at Vancouver, Wash., by the Kaiser Shipbuilding Co.; launched on 10 March 1944; sponsored by Mrs. Alden R. Sanborn; and commissioned on 15 April 1944, Capt. A. R. Brady in command.

After shakedown, *Takanis Bay* operated out of San Diego with Fleet Air, West Coast, through the end of hostilities with Japan in mid-August 1945. She tested pilots for carrier operations; and, between 24 May 1944 and 28 August 1945, she qualified 2,509 pilots.

On the latter day, she sailed for Hawaii and was assigned to Carrier Transport Squadron, Pacific. In two trips, she returned 1,300 servicemen to San Diego. Late in September, the carrier was assigned to the "Magic-Carpet" fleet which had been established for the sole purpose of bringing veterans home. At San Diego, bunks for 800 passengers were installed in the carrier, and she made two more round-trip voyages to Hawaii and one to the Tokyo Bay area to repatriate servicemen.

Takanis Bay arrived at San Pedro from her last voyage on 2 January 1946. She moved to Puget Sound in April, where inactivation work was begun, and she was decommissioned on 1 May 1946. *Takanis Bay* was reclassified CVU-89 on 12 June 1955 and was struck from the Navy list on 1 August 1959. She was sold on 29 June 1960 to Hyman-Michaels Co., Chicago, Ill., for scrap.

Takelma

An Indian tribe in Oregon.

(ATF–113: dp. 1,589; l. 205'0''; b. 38'6''; dr. 15'4''; s. 16.5 k.; cpl. 85; a. 1 3'', 2 40mm.; cl. *Abnaki*)

Takelma (ATF–113) was laid down on 7 April 1943 as AT–113 by the United Engineering Co., Alameda, Calif.; launched on 18 September 1943; sponsored by Mrs. George Sutherland; redesignated ATF–113 on 15 May 1944; and commissioned on 3 August 1944.

After her shakedown, the fleet ocean tug operated along the California coast until 16 December when she sailed for Hawaii. She arrived at Pearl Harbor on 5 January 1945 and was routed onward to Eniwetok. The ship towed vessels between various Pacific bases at Ulithi, Leyte, Hollandia, Subic Bay, Manus, Espiritu Santo, and Milne Bay until returning to Pearl Harbor on 15 June 1946. The tug sailed to San Francisco on 28 July; then moved up the coast to Seattle; and remained there until 28 December.

On that day, *Takelma* got underway for Hawaii and arrived at Pearl Harbor on 4 February 1947. She was ordered to begin towing target ships to the Marshall Islands for the atomic bomb tests at Bikini. Her charges on this assignment were berthed at such widely separated ports as Pearl Harbor, San Francisco, and Bremerton. On 6 January 1948, the tug took the power barge *Jacona* (YFP–1) in tow and got underway for Korea. After she delivered the barge to Pusan, *Takelma* made port at Yokosuka, Japan, on 3 February. Five weeks later, she sailed for Pearl Harbor and proceeded thence to the west coast of the United States.

Except for a voyage to the Canal Zone in June, *Takelma* operated in the San Diego-Long Beach area from 22 April to mid-autumn. On 4 November, the tug departed San Diego, bound for the Aleutians, and arrived at Adak 11 days later. On 6 January 1949, she got underway for the Central Pacific and arrived at Midway on the 14th. During the year, she also called at Pearl Harbor, Balboa, Coco Solo, Wake, and Kwajalein.

After communist forces attacked South Korea, the tug headed for the Far East in July 1950 and spent a year operating at Subic Bay and in Japanese waters.

Takelma returned to the United States on 1 July 1951 for a month and was then homeported at Pearl Harbor. She operated out of that port until July 1952.

Takelma stood out of Pearl Harbor on 24 July en route to the Korean war zone via Japan. She arrived at Yokosuka on 7 August; called at Sasebo for four days; and reached Sokcho, Korea, on 19 August. The tug operated in Korean waters, serving at Sokcho, Pusan, and Wonsan, until returning to Sasebo on 18 September. The next day, she got underway for Chinhae, arrived there on the 21st, and returned to Yokosuka. *Takelma* then moved to Sasebo and remained there from 23 October until 29 November when she headed for the Korean ports of Cho Do and Yongyong Do.

Takelma was again at Sasebo from 1 to 16 January 1953 when she returned to the combat zone. She remained there from 18 to 25 January. Her last service during the Korean conflict began when she arrived at Wonsan on 30 January. She returned to Sasebo on 22 February.

She reached Pearl Harbor for repairs on 29 March and then sailed to San Diego. September found the tug back at Pearl Harbor, and she departed there on 26 January 1954 for Sasebo and local operations which lasted until 11 August. From August 1954 to mid-1968, the ship operated from her home port at Pearl Harbor or on deployments to the Far East.

During a time of great American involvement in combat operations in Vietnam, *Takelma* was at "Yankee Station" in the Gulf of Tonkin from 8 July to 15 August 1968 performing special operations for the 7th Fleet, and she returned to that task again on 18 October. She operated in waters off Vietnam until 12 November when she sailed for Pearl Harbor. On 15 November 1969, she got underway for Adak, beginning a four-month tour in the Aleutians which ended on 25 February 1970. On 27 August, she sailed for a six-month deployment to the western Pacific. *Takelma* returned to Pearl Harbor on 23 February 1971 and operated from there until 23 October 1973 when she sailed for the Far East and duty with the 7th Fleet.

The ship returned to Hawaii on 2 May 1974 and rendered services to fleet units there until October 1976 when her home port was shifted to San Diego. On 1

The fleet tug *Takelma* (ATF–113) off Oahu early in 1967.   (KN 14013)

June 1979, *Takelma* commenced service as a naval reserve training ship.

Takelma received two battle stars for Korean service and two for service in Vietnam.

Takoma, see *Tacoma*.

Takos

An Indian word meaning "it is cloudy."

(YTB–546: dp. 260; l. 101'; b. 28'; dr. 11'; s. 12 k.; cpl. 10; cl. *Hisada*)

Takos (YTB–546) was laid down on 10 October 1944 by Ira S. Bushey & Sons, Inc., Brooklyn, N.Y.; launched on 30 July 1945; and commissioned on 11 October 1945.

The large harbor tug was assigned to the New York Navy Yard on 15 November 1945 and operated there until mid-summer of 1946. On 1 August, she got underway for Florida and arrived at Mayport on 13 August. There, *Takos* was placed out of commission, in reserve, on 3 April 1947.

After the start of the Korean War, *Takos* was reactivated in November 1950. On 28 December, the tug headed north for duty in the 1st Naval District. In February 1962, *Takos* was reclassified a medium harbor tug and redesignated YTM–546. She operated in New England waters until 1973 when she was transferred to Norfolk, Va. Here, *Takos* rendered assistance to fleet units of the 5th Naval District into 1975 when she was assigned to the Inactive Fleet at Norfolk, Virginia, where she remained into late 1979.

Talamanca

(AF–15: dp. 6,975; l. 446'10''; b. 60'0''; dr. 25'0'' (mean); s. 16.0 k.; cpl. 238; a. 1 5'', 4 3'')

Talamanca—a combination luxury liner and fruit cargo carrier built in 1931 by Newport News Shipbuilding & Drydock Co., Newport News, Va.—was acquired by the Navy on 16 December 1941 from the United Mail Steamship Co., New York, N.Y.; converted to an auxiliary stores ship at Baltimore, Md., by the Maryland Drydock Co.; designated AF–15 on 27 December 1941; and commissioned on 28 January 1942, Comdr. Nathan W. Bard in command.

Talamanca put to sea for the first time as a naval vessel on 13 February. Six days later, laden with cargo, passengers, and mail, she transited the Panama Canal; proceeded via Talara, Peru, across the southern Pacific; and arrived in Wellington, New Zealand, on 16 March. On 1 April, following a voyage to Melbourne, Australia, and back to Wellington, she headed once more toward the United States. She made a brief stop in Manzanilla, Mexico, on the 16th and reached San Francisco, Calif., on 21 April. Between 9 May and 1 June, *Talamanca* made a round-trip voyage from San Francisco to Pearl Harbor and back again. The stores ship spent the whole month of June in the Mare Island Navy Yard, undergoing further conversion and some repairs.

Talamanca stood out of San Francisco on 8 July with a Hawaii-bound convoy. She reached Pearl Harbor on the 16th and remained there for five days taking on fuel and stores before heading southwest on the 21st. On 1 August, she parted company with the convoy, headed—via the Fiji Islands—for New Zealand, and reached Auckland on the 7th.

For the next three years, Auckland served as *Talamanca*'s home port. Between August 1942 and April 1945, the ship plied the waters of the southwestern Pacific supplying American bases in that area. She visited such places as the Fiji Islands; Espiritu Santo; Efate; Manus; and Napier, New Zealand. The closest she ever came to the combat zone were stops at Guadalcanal, Tulagi, Florida, and the Russell Islands in the Solo-

mons. However, these voyages came in 1944 after the fighting had moved up the Solomons chain past Bougainville and into the Bismarck Archipelago. In all, *Talamanca* made some 36 resupply voyages from Auckland to various bases in the South Pacific and back again, all of them relatively routine affairs.

On 28 April 1945, the stores ship set sail from Auckland for the last time. She headed to Noumea, New Caledonia, thence to Manus, from where she was routed to the Marianas. *Talamanca* reached Saipan on 10 May; discharged cargo; and, on the 15th, shifted to Tinian where she completed discharging her cargo. From Tinian, she sailed, via Eniwetok Atoll, for the west coast. She entered San Pedro, Calif., on 2 June 1945 and loaded cargo. On the 9th, she headed back to the western Pacific. Following fuel-and-water stops at Pearl Harbor and Eniwetok, *Talamanca* entered Apra Harbor, Guam, on 26 June. Her crew unloaded her cargo there; and, four days later, she set sail for Manus. The stores ship arrived at Manus on 3 July and embarked patients from the hospital for transportation to the United States. Two days later, she steamed eastward again. She stopped at Pearl Harbor on 13 July and entered San Francisco Bay on the 19th.

Her passengers disembarked, she moored to a pier at the Moore Dry Dock Co. for overhaul. She completed overhaul and repairs on 31 August and—after degaussing, compass compensation, and trials—began loading cargo on 3 September. On the 9th, she stood out of San Francisco Bay for Pearl Harbor and arrived there on the 14th. Two days later, she continued on to Eniwetok where she stopped on the 23d for fuel and water. From there, she voyaged to Guam, thence to Iwo Jima, where she unloaded cargo. On 8 October, *Talamanca* departed Iwo Jima with Saipan-bound passengers and arrived at her destination that afternoon. She discharged her passengers that same day and her cargo the following day. After stopping at Guam to embark passengers, the stores ship got underway for Hawaii and the United States. She stopped at Pearl Harbor from 27 to 29 October and then continued on to Panama.

The stores ship reverted to her former employment as a fruit carrier on 10 November when she loaded bananas at Puerto Armuelles, Panama, for the War Shipping Administration. She transited the canal on the 13th and set sail for New Orleans, La., the following day. She reached her destination on the 18th and was placed out of commission there on 29 November 1945. She was returned to the War Shipping Administration for eventual return to her owners. Her name was struck from the Navy list on 19 December 1945.

Talbot

John Gunnell Talbot—born on 16 August 1844 at Danbury, Ky.—was appointed a midshipman in 1862 and graduated from the United States Naval Academy on 12 June 1866. Commissioned ensign on 12 March 1868, Talbot attained the rank of master on 26 March 1869 and of lieutenant on 21 March 1870. He was serving as executive officer of *Saginaw* when that steamer grounded on a reef off Ocean Island in the mid-Pacific on 29 October 1870 and broke up. Lt. Talbot and four men volunteered to go to Honolulu, the nearest port, 1,500 miles away, for help.

The men began the voyage in an open boat on 18 November and reached Kauai, Hawaii, on 19 December. However, as the party attempted to get through the heavy surf to shore, their boat capsized. Lt. Talbot and three others drowned while attempting to swim through the rough breakers to shore. The lone survivor reported the wreck of *Saginaw*, and her crew was saved.

Silas Talbot—born on 11 January 1751 in Dighton, Mass.—was commissioned a captain in the Continental Army on 1 July 1775. After participating in the siege of Boston and aiding in the transportation of troops to New York, he obtained command of a fireship and attempted to use it to set fire to the British warship *Asia*.

The attempt failed, but the daring it displayed won him a promotion to major on 10 October 1777.

After suffering a severe wound while fighting to defend Philadelphia, Talbot returned to active service in the summer of 1778 and fought in Rhode Island. As commander of *Pigot* and later of *Argo*, both under the Army, he cruised against Loyalist vessels that were harassing American trade between Long Island and Nantucket and made prisoners of many of them. Because of his success fighting afloat for the Army, Congress made him a captain in the Continental Navy on 17 September 1779. However, since Congress had no suitable warship to entrust to him, Talbot put to sea in command of the privateer *General Washington*. In it he took one prize, but soon thereafter ran into the British fleet off New York. After a chase, he struck his colors to *Culloden*, a 74-gun ship-of-the-line and remained a prisoner until exchanged for a British officer in December 1781.

After the war, Talbot settled in Fulton County, N.Y. He was a member of the New York Assembly in 1792 and 1793 and served in the federal House of Representatives from 1793 to 1795. On 5 June 1794, President Washington chose him third in a list of six captains of the newly established United States Navy. Before the end of his term in Congress, he was ordered to superintend the construction of the frigate *President* at New York. He commanded the Santo Domingo Station in 1799 and 1800 and was commended by the Secretary of the Navy for protecting American commerce and for laying the foundation of a permanent trade with that country.

Captain Talbot resigned from the Navy on 23 September 1801 and died at New York City on 30 June 1813.

The first *Talbot* (Torpedo Boat No. 15) was named for Lt. John Gunnell Talbot; the second and third *Talbot*s (Destroyer No. 114 and DEG–4, respectively) were named for Capt. Silas Talbot.

I

(Torpedo Boat No. 15: t. 46.5; l. 99′6″; b. 12′6″; dr. 3′3″; s. 21.5 k.; cpl. 16; a. 1 1-pdr. R. F., 2 18″ tt. cl. *Talbot*)

The first *Talbot* (Torpedo Boat No. 15) was laid down on 8 April 1897 at Bristol, R.I., by the Herreshoff Manufacturing Co.; launched on 14 November 1897; and commissioned on 4 April 1898, Lt. (jg.) William R. Shoemaker in command.

Talbot cruised down the coast, making calls in Maryland, Virginia, and North Carolina before arriving at Havana, Cuba, on 2 August. She reported to the flagship and received mail for the blockading squadron. At 2100 hours that evening, while en route to Key West for coal, she sighted the dark hull of a ship off the port bow. *Talbot* signalled and stopped her engines, but was still rammed by the tug *Uncas*. The bow of the tug penetrated one foot into the torpedo boat's coal bunker, bending in two frames and crushing the side plating to below the water line. The tug towed *Talbot* to Piedras Cay where temporary repairs were made the next day to enable the damaged ship to proceed to Key West.

Talbot reached Key West on the 5th and got underway 10 days later for New York. She arrived at the New York Navy Yard on 6 September and was ready for sea again in early October. The torpedo boat was then assigned to the Naval Academy for duty supporting midshipmen training, mooring at Annapolis on 10 October. On 11 June 1899, *Talbot* moved to Norfolk to participate in a one-year evaluation of experimental fuel oils. At the completion of this test program, she resumed her duties at the Naval Academy.

Talbot was decommissioned on 20 February 1904 and attached to the Reserve Torpedo Flotilla at Norfolk. She was recommissioned on 31 August 1906 and assigned to special duty between Norfolk and Annapolis. From early 1908 to September 1911, she served at the Torpedo Station, Newport, R.I. On 22 September 1911, *Talbot* was reassigned to Indian Head, Md., for service as a tender. Before assuming the new duty, she proceeded to Norfolk for her annual inspection and was found to be unfit for further naval use.

Talbot was inactivated on 1 May 1912 but retained, "in service," as a ferryboat to be operated between the Washington Navy Yard and the naval facilities at Indian Head. When she arrived at Washington, she was manned by a civilian crew and made an average of three trips a week between the two points. *Talbot* was renamed *Berceau* on 11 April 1918 and reclassified a ferry boat. On 17 July 1920, she was designated YFB–3. She remained on ferry duty until 18 June 1940 when she was placed out of service and towed to Philadelphia.

Berceau was struck from the Navy list on 18 July 1944 and sold for scrap.

II

(Destroyer No. 114: dp. 1,154; l. 314′4″; b. 30′11″; dr. 9′10″; s. 35 k.; cpl. 122; a. 4 4″, 1 3″, 12 21″ tt.; cl. *Wickes*)

The second *Talbot* (Destroyer No. 114) was laid down on 12 July 1917 at Philadelphia, Pa., by William Cramp & Sons; launched on 20 February 1918; sponsored by

The steam torpedo boat *Talbot* (TB–15). Crew members standing on deck give an idea of the size of this predecessor of the destroyer. (NH 63732)

Miss Elizabeth Major; and commissioned on 20 July 1918, Lt. Comdr. Isaac F. Dortch in command.

The destroyer stood out of New York on the 31st and steamed to the British Isles. She made three more round-trip voyages to England and, in December, called at Brest, France. In 1919, she joined the Pacific Fleet and operated with it until 31 March 1923 when she was decommissioned at San Diego. While in reserve, the ship was designated DD–114 on 17 July 1920.

Talbot was recommissioned on 31 May 1930 and joined Destroyer Squadron (DesRon) 10 of the Battle Force at San Diego. She remained with Battle Force until 1937 when she went to Hawaii to support Submarine Force, Pacific Fleet, for a year. In 1939, she served with the Battle Force and the Submarine Force. In 1940 and 1941, the destroyer was based at San Diego.

The day after the Japanese attack on Pearl Harbor, *Talbot* got underway in the screen of *Saratoga* (CV–3) and headed for Hawaii. She arrived at Pearl Harbor exactly a week after the Japanese raid, patrolled off the islands for 10 days, and returned to San Diego. In February 1942, the ship joined the Patrol Force of the 12th Naval District and escorted convoys along the Pacific coast.

Late in May, *Talbot* stood out of Puget Sound to escort *S–18*, *S–23*, and *S–28* to Alaska. They arrived at Dutch Harbor on 2 June and were subjected to a small and unsuccessful air attack the next day. With the exception of three escort trips back to Seattle, the destroyer performed patrol and escort duty in Alaskan waters for the next seven months. On 31 October 1942, the ship was reclassified a high-speed transport and redesignated APD–7. *Talbot* departed Dutch Harbor on 31 January 1943 to be converted by the Mare Island Navy Yard into a small but fast troopship. The work, enabling *Talbot* to transport 147 combat troops, was completed on 15 March.

The next day, the high-speed transport got underway for Hawaii, and she arrived at Pearl Harbor the following week. On 2 April, she headed for Espiritu Santo to join Transport Division (TransDiv) 12. For two months, the APD participated in training exercises with her division and also escorted ships to New Caledonia, New Zealand, Australia, and Guadalcanal.

In mid-June, she joined Task Group (TG) 31.1, the Rendova Attack Group, for the invasion of New Georgia. She and *Zane* (DMS–14) were to capture two small islands that controlled the entrance to Roviana Lagoon from Blanche Channel. The two ships embarked troops of the 169th Infantry Regiment at Guadalcanal; and, on the 30th, they were off their assigned beaches when the assault began. Heavy rains obscured the islands, and *Zane* ran aground at 0230. After landing her troops and supplies without opposition, *Talbot* attempted to pull the minesweeper free but failed. Then *Rail* (ATO–139) arrived and pulled *Zane* free while *Talbot* provided air protection. During the operation, enemy aircraft could be seen attacking the main landing force. On the night of 4 July, the ship and six other high speed transports arrived off Rice Anchorage. During the landing of assault troops the next morning, a Japanese "long-lance" torpedo sank *Strong* (DD–467), one of the destroyers of the bombardment group.

Talbot returned to Guadalcanal to prepare for the occupation of Vella Lavella. On 14 August, she sortied with TG 31.5, the Advance Transport Group of the Northern Landing Force. The assault forces went ashore from the destroyer transports the next morning, unopposed. However, two hours later, the Japanese began air attacks against the ships and kept up the raids throughout the day. Nevertheless, the American fleet suffered no damage and claimed to have shot down 44 of the enemy planes.

The high-speed transport next devoted over a month to escorting smaller ships and carrying supplies to various islands in the Solomons. Late in September, she joined Admiral George H. Fort's Southern Attack Force for the conquest of the Treasury Islands. Eight APD's and 23 smaller landing ships were loaded with troops of the 8th New Zealand Brigade Force. The smaller ships departed Guadalcanal on 23 and 24 October, and the faster destroyer transports left on the 26th. On the 27th, the troops landed on Mono and Stirling islands, and the transports had cleared the area by 2000.

On 3 November, *Talbot* called at Noumea to embark reinforcements for troops who, two days before, had landed on the beaches of Bougainville at Empress Augusta Bay. She arrived on the 6th, disembarked her soldiers, loaded 19 casualties and screened a group of LST's to Guadalcanal. On the 11th, she was back at the beachhead with a resupply echelon. Four days later, she got underway for Guadalcanal. The high-speed transport loaded troops, ammunition, and rations; held a practice landing; and headed for Bougainville. On the 16th, the destroyer transport and her five sister ships rendezvoused with a group of LST's and destroyers. At 0300, a Japanese snooper dropped a flare astern of the convoy. It was followed by enemy bombers which attacked for almost an hour before hitting *McKean* (APD–5) and setting her afire. Although under constant air attack, *Talbot*'s boats rescued 68 crew members and 106 marine passengers from the stricken ship.

Talbot (DD–114), shortly after World War I.   (NR&L(M) 13992)

APD–7 continued to Cape Torokina and arrived there in the midst of another air attack. She landed her troops and headed for Guadalcanal.

After her engines were overhauled at Noumea in December, the ship made a round-trip to Sydney. On 8 January 1944, she departed New Caledonia for Espiritu Santo to pick up a convoy and escort it to Guadalcanal. She arrived off Lunga Point on the 13th and patrolled between there and Koli Point for two weeks. On the 28th, the fast transport embarked elements of the 30th New Zealand Battalion and a group of intelligence and communications specialists of the United States Navy and headed for the Green Islands to participate in a reconnaissance in force.

On the night of 30 January, the destroyer transports landed the raiding party; withdrew from the area; and returned the next night to pick them up. *Talbot* disembarked the New Zealanders at Vella Lavella and the Navy men at Guadalcanal. On 13 February, *Talbot* reembarked New Zealand troops and sortied with TF 31, the Green Islands Attack Group. She was off Barahun Island on the 15th and launched her part of the assault wave. She then shuttled reinforcements and supplies from Guadalcanal to the Green Islands.

On 17 March, the transport loaded elements of the 2d Battalion, 4th Marines, at Guadalcanal and sailed with the amphibious force to the St. Matthias Islands. The marines peacefully occupied Emirau on 20 March, and *Talbot* returned to Purvis Bay. She headed to New Guinea on 4 April to participate in practice landings with the 163d Army Regimental Combat Team (RCT). Two weeks later, she loaded 145 men of that regiment and sortied with TG 77.3, the Fire Support Group, for the assault on Aitape. On the 22d, *Talbot* landed her troops; shelled Tumleo Island; and returned to Cape Cretin. She escorted resupply echelons to the landing area until 10 May when the transports were released by the 7th Fleet.

Talbot joined the 5th Fleet at Guadalcanal on the 13th and began training with underwater demolition teams. On 4 June, she joined a convoy to the Marshalls and arrived at Kwajalein on the 8th. Two days later, the high-speed transport joined TG 53.15 of the Southern Attack Force and got underway for the Marianas. However, she collided with *Pennsylvania* (BB–38) during an emergency turn; and the resulting flooding of several of her compartments forced her to return for repairs. *Talbot* got underway two days later, rejoined the group southeast of Saipan, and was off the beaches there on the 15th, D–Day. During the first days of the operation, she screened the bombardment group. On the 17th, she captured a survivor of a wrecked Japanese boat. The ship developed engine trouble and anchored in the transport area where an enemy plane dropped a stick of bombs off her port bow, but caused no damage. She transferred her underwater demolition team to *Kane* (APD–18) and joined a convoy for Hawaii. She was then routed back to San Francisco for an overhaul that lasted from 11 July to 28 August.

Talbot returned to Pearl Harbor early in September and steamed onward to Eniwetok and Manus. She embarked Underwater Demolition Team No. 3 on 12 October and sortied with TG 77.6, the Bombardment and Fire Support Group, for Leyte. On the 18th, her swimmers made a daylight reconnaissance of the waters between San Jose and Dulag. Although opposed by enemy machine-gun and mortar fire, the team reembarked with no casualties. The transport departed with a convoy and arrived at Seeadler Harbor on the 27th, where she transferred the demolition team to *President Hayes* (AP–39) on the last day of the month.

Talbot headed toward Oro Bay, joined *George Clymer* (AP–57), escorted her to Cape Gloucester, and returned to Seeadler Harbor on the 8th. Two days later, she was anchored there, only some 800 yards from *Mount Hood* (AE–11), when that ammunition ship suddenly exploded and showered her with over 600 pounds of metal and debris. The transport was holed in several places and some crew members were injured.

Talbot's boats searched for survivors but found none.

On 15 December 1944, after the high-speed transport's damage had been repaired at Manus, *Talbot* got underway and proceeded, via Aitape, to Noemfoor Island to participate in amphibious exercises with the 158th RCT. On 4 January 1945, she embarked troops and sortied with Task Unit 77.9.8 for Lingayen Gulf. The ship landed reinforcements at San Fabian the following week and continued on to Leyte. She embarked troops of the 11th Airborne Division on the 26th and headed for Luzon with a convoy. On 31 January, she disembarked the troops as the second wave against Nasugbu and steamed to Mindoro. She loaded mortar and rocket boats and delivered them to Luzon.

On 14 February, the high-speed transport embarked units of the 151st Infantry Regiment and steamed to Bataan. She landed the troops at Mariveles Harbor the next morning and returned to Subic Bay. On the 17th, she took a load of reinforcements to Corregidor. The transport escorted a convoy back to Ulithi and remained there for several weeks before being ordered to Guam. *Talbot* and *LSM–331* proceeded to Parece Vela to conduct a survey of the reef and determine the feasibility of erecting a radio, weather, and observation station there. She returned to Guam on 20 April and reached Ulithi the next day.

On 22 April, *Talbot* joined a convoy bound for Okinawa. Five days later, she began antisubmarine patrols south of Kerama Retto and then, on the 30th, joined a convoy for Saipan. She returned to Kerama Retto and served as a picket ship from 22 May to 6 June when she went back to Saipan. From the Marianas, the high speed transport was routed to Eniwetok, Hawaii, and the United States.

Talbot arrived at San Pedro on 6 July and was to be reconverted into a destroyer. Her classification reverted to DD–114 on 16 July. However, a Board of Inspection and Survey recommended that she be inactivated. *Talbot* was decommissioned on 9 October and struck from the Navy list on 24 October 1945. She was sold to the Boston Metals Co., Baltimore, Md., on 30 January 1946 and scrapped.

Talbot received eight battle stars for World War II service.

III

(DEG–4: dp. 2,643; l. 415′; b. 44′; dr. 24′; s. 27 k.; cpl. 248; a. 1 5″, Tartar, ASROC, DASH; cl. *Brooke*)

The third *Talbot* (DEG–4) was laid down on 4 May 1964 at Bath, Maine, by the Bath Iron Works Corp.; launched on 6 January 1966; sponsored by Miss Frances K. Talbot; and commissioned on 22 April 1967, Comdr. Edwin E. Woods, Jr., in command.

On 8 July, the new guided-missile escort ship departed Hampton Roads, Va., for Puerto Rico for shakedown and missile system trials. *Talbot* next headed north and arrived at her home port, Newport, R.I., on 16 September. The ship conducted special operations off the Virginia Capes from 16 October to 18 November and then spent most of her time until the spring of 1968 undergoing post-shakedown availability. Following firing exercises at the Atlantic Fleet weapons range and antisubmarine operations late in April, the destroyer escort participated in the search for missing nuclear submarine *Scorpion* (SSN–589) in May. She devoted the rest of the year to operations along the Atlantic coast and in the Caribbean.

On 31 January 1969, *Talbot* departed Newport for the Mediterranean and was deployed with the 6th Fleet until she returned on 11 July. After overhaul at the Boston Naval Shipyard was completed on 1 April 1970, *Talbot* conducted local operations before returning to the missile range off Puerto Rico in May for weapons tests, followed by refresher training and four months at Newport. On 28 October 1970, she headed for the Mediterranean and her second tour with the 6th Fleet. The deployment ended at Newport on 2 May 1971, and

The guided-missile escort ship *Talbot* (DEG–4) off Puerto Rico, 1967. (USN 1124862)

she devoted the remainder of the year to east coast operations.

Talbot spent the first part of 1972 conducting tests of the MK–48 torpedo in the Bahamas and off the New England coast. She stood out of Newport on 21 July and proceeded to Roosevelt Roads, Puerto Rico, accompanied by *Farragut* (DLG–6) and *Forrest Sherman* (DD–931). There, *Remora* (SS–487) joined the group on the 26th, and they began combined operations with ships from seven South American navies while circumnavigating South America. *Talbot* made calls in Venezuela, Brazil, Uruguay, Argentina, Chile, Peru, the Canal Zone, and Colombia before returning to Newport on 3 December 1972. She entered the Boston Naval Shipyard on 15 February 1973 for an overhaul that lasted until 14 December.

On 5 January 1974, *Talbot* departed Newport and proceeded to her new home port, Norfolk, Va. From 13 February to 29 April, the ship was deployed on training exercises off Jacksonville, Fla.; Guantanamo Bay, Cuba; and Vieques, Puerto Rico. After a cruise to Newport in May, she entered the Norfolk Naval Shipyard on 17 June for the installation of prototypes of the Oto Melara Mk 75 rapid-fire 76mm gun mount and the Mk 92 fire-control system, intended for use in the new FFG–7 and PHM–1 classes. She stood out of Hampton Roads on 21 October and, from 12 November through 19 December 1974, tested the new systems at the Atlantic Fleet Weapons Range, Culebra, Puerto Rico.

Talbot continued her evaluation work into 1975, alternating three periods of test operations at Culebra with a tender availability alongside *Puget Sound* (AD–38) at Norfolk, local operations in the Virginia capes area, and fleet tactical exercises in the western Atlantic. Her test mission completed, *Talbot* returned to Norfolk on 22 June. After local operations and inspections, she entered the Norfolk Naval Shipyard on 15 September for a three-month overhaul in which her experimental fire-control system and 76mm gun were removed and replaced by her normal 5-inch, 38-caliber gun and fire-control system.

Upon completing overhaul and refresher training in the spring of 1976, *Talbot* departed Norfolk on 22 June for a Mediterranean deployment. The six-month operation included participation in NATO exercises interspersed with port visits and concluded with the ship's return to Norfolk on 10 January 1977. Following post-deployment leave and upkeep, *Talbot* conducted exercises off the east coast until she entered the Philadelphia Naval Shipyard for overhaul on 9 June. Completing overhaul on 7 April 1978, *Talbot* spent the balance of the year in refresher training and participating in Fleet exercises off the east coast and in the Caribbean. On 6 December, she departed the United States for deployment with the Middle East Force in response to the crisis surrounding the deposition of the Shah of Iran. The close of 1978 found *Talbot* en route to the Persian Gulf.

Talbot, Ralph, see *Ralph Talbot*.

Talbot County

Counties in Maryland and Georgia.

(LST–1153: dp. 6,000; l. 382′; b. 54′; dr. 14′5″; s. 14.0 k.; cpl. 190; trp. 197; a. 2 5″; cl. *LST–1153*)

LST–1153 was laid down on 19 July 1945 at Boston, Mass., by the Boston Navy Yard; launched on 24 April 1947; sponsored by Mrs. Lena Mickelson; and commissioned on 3 September 1947.

LST–1153 reported to the Fleet Training Group at Norfolk to begin her shakedown cruise on 21 September. She returned to Boston on 24 October for a post-shakedown yard period and put to sea again on 15 November. Eleven days later, she arrived at her home port, Little Creek, Va. For the next nine years, the tank landing ship operated along the east coast of the United States from New England to Florida and in the Caribbean. On 1 July 1955, *LST–1153* was named *Talbot County*.

Talbot County deployed to the Mediterranean on 31 August 1959, using her bulk fuel tanks to carry more than 240,000 gallons of aviation gasoline to refuel the helicopters of the amphibious squadron attached to the 6th Fleet. After making port calls in France, Italy, Greece, Malta, Gibraltar, Algeria, and Morocco, she returned to the United States on 13 February 1958. The ship was deployed with the 6th Fleet again from April to August 1959 and from October 1960 to May 1961. The remainder of her time, until 1970, was spent in operations along the Atlantic seaboard, ranging from Key West, Fla., to Nova Scotia and various ports in the Caribbean.

Talbot County was decommissioned at Orange, Tex., on 3 April 1970, struck from the Navy list on 1 May 1973, and subsequently scrapped.

Talbot, J. Fred, see *J. Fred Talbott*.

Talita

(AKS–8: dp. 14,350; l. 441′6″; b. 56′11″; dr. 28′4″; s. 12.5 k.; cpl. 214; a. 1 5″, 1 3″; cl. *Acubens*; T. EC2–S–C1)

Talita (AKS–8) was laid down under a Maritime Commission contract (MCE hull 2012) as *Jonathan Jennings* on 23 April 1943 at Portland, Oreg., by the Oregon Shipbuilding Corp.; launched on 12 May 1943; sponsored by Mrs. Paul Ryolfson; acquired by the Navy on a bare boat basis from the War Shipping Administration on 5 November 1943; renamed *Talita* on 13 November 1943; and commissioned on 4 March 1944.

After her conversion into a stores issue ship was completed on 4 March 1944 by the Tampa Shipbuilding Co., Tampa, Fla., she was fitted out and put to sea for a short shakedown cruise. *Talita* got underway from Balboa, Canal Zone, on 1 May bound for the New Hebrides. However, she was diverted to the Solomons and arrived at Guadalcanal on 1 June. After issuing stores there, she proceeded to the New Hebrides.

Talita departed Espiritu Santo on 11 July, reached Eniwetok after a nine-day voyage, and returned to Espiritu Santo on 11 September. She continued resupply runs from there to Majuro, Eniwetok, Ulithi, and Manus until early March 1945 when she headed for the United States.

Talita arrived at San Francisco on 23 March for an overhaul and sailed one month later for the South Pacific. After calling at Pearl Harbor, she shuttled supplies between Eniwetok, Ulithi, Leyte, and Manus until 20 September when she sailed for the Ryukyus. The ship remained at Okinawa from 25 September to 2 October when she got underway for Japan. After offloading supplies at Wakayama, Hiro Wan, and Matsuyama, she returned to Pearl Harbor on 12 November. The next day, she headed for San Francisco.

Talita remained there from 21 November 1945 to 17 February 1946 when she sailed for Hawaii. She arrived at Pearl Harbor on the 25th, was decommissioned on 9 April, and towed back to San Francisco for disposal. *Talita* was transferred to the Maritime Commission on 9 July and struck from the Navy list on 17 July 1947.

Talladega

A county and city in Alabama.

(ScSlp: dp. 2,400; l. 250′6″; b. 38′)

In 1864, the construction of *Talladega*—an *Algoma*-class screw sloop-of-war—was projected by the Navy. Her engines were constructed by the New York Navy Yard, but the Civil War ended before the sloop's keel was laid down. Construction of her hull was postponed

for two years and finally cancelled in 1867. Her engines were later used in another warship. Unfortunately, records identifying the recipient have not been found.

I

(APA–208: dp. 12,450; l. 455′; b. 62′; dr. 24′; s. 17.7 k.; cpl. 692; trp. 1,552; a. 1 5″, 12 40mm.; cl. *Haskell*; T. VC2–S–AP5)

Talladega (APA–208) was laid down under Maritime Commission contract (MCV hull 556) at Richmond, Calif., on 3 June 1944 by the Permanente Metals Corp.; launched on 17 August 1944; sponsored by Miss Marie Tomerlin; and commissioned on 31 October 1944, Capt. Edward H. McMenemy in command.

Following her shakedown cruise, *Talladega* loaded cargo and passengers at San Francisco; got underway for Hawaii on 5 December; and arrived at Pearl Harbor on the 11th. The attack transport conducted amphibious landing exercises with elements of the 28th Regimental Combat Team (RCT), 5th Marine Division, to prepare for the assault on the Volcano Islands. She departed Pearl Harbor on 27 January 1945 and proceeded via Eniwetok to the Mariana Islands.

Talladega sortied from Saipan as a unit of Task Group 56.2, the Assault Group, on 16 February and arrived off Iwo Jima on the morning of the 19th, "D-day." After landing her troops, she remained off the beaches embarking combat casualties for six days before heading back toward Saipan.

Talladega was routed onward through Tulagi and New Caledonia to the New Hebrides. She loaded troops and equipment of the 165th RCT, 27th Infantry Division, at Espiritu Santo on 24 March and departed the next day. Her troops were part of the reserve for the invasion of Okinawa; and, after a stop at Ulithi, she arrived off that island on 9 April. She finished unloading her passengers and cargo by the 14th and returned, via Saipan, to Ulithi.

Talladega was subsequently ordered to the Philippine Islands and arrived at Subic Bay on 31 May. She remained in the Philippines, training elements of the American and 1st Cavalry Divisions for a projected invasion of Japan. However, before the operation began, Japan capitulated.

On 25 August, troops of the 1st Cavalry Division embarked, and the transport headed for Yokohama the next day. She disembarked her passengers there between 2 and 4 September and then returned to the Philippines to pick up soldiers of the 41st Infantry Division for transportation to Japan. The attack transport reached Kure, Honshu, on 5 October.

Talladega returned to Leyte on 16 October for provisions and fuel. The next day, she loaded 1,934 veterans at Samar and sailed for the United States. The ship arrived at San Pedro on 3 November and disembarked her passengers. She made three more round-trips to the Pacific to return troops: to Okinawa in December 1945, to the Philippines in April 1946, and to China in July. When *Talladega* returned to San Francisco in July, she began preparations for inactivation and assignment to the Reserve Fleet. She was placed out of commission, in reserve, on 27 December 1946.

The outbreak of hostilities in Korea on 25 June 1950 increased the Navy's need for active amphibious ships. Consequently, *Talladega* was recommissioned at Hunters Point, Calif., on 8 December 1951. She operated along the west coast until November 1952 when she embarked aviation personnel at San Francisco and steamed westward as a unit of Transport Division 12. The assault transport arrived at Yokosuka, Japan, on 29 November. She loaded men and equipment of the 1st Cavalry Division and headed for the Korean war zone.

Talladega arrived at Pusan on 14 December 1952, unloaded, and returned to Japan on the 18th. During the next nine months, the transport provided amphibious training for the United Nations forces in Japan and redeployed troops from one area in Korea to another. She operated in the war zone during each of the first seven months of 1953, but June. She worked along both coasts, transporting troops and supplies to such ports as Inchon, Koje Do, and Sokcho, before returning to San Diego on 15 August 1953.

During the next 12 years, the transport's operations along the west coast were broken by seven deployments to the western Pacific. In 1965, when United States forces assumed a combat role in South Vietnam, *Talladega* stood out of Long Beach on 27 April for duty with the 7th Fleet. After calling at Pearl Harbor from 2 to 5 May, she proceeded to Guam where she loaded cargo for Vietnam. She delivered the equipment and supplies at Danang on 30 and 31 May. Following upkeep at Subic Bay, the attack transport moved to Okinawa to combat load the 3d Battalion, 7th Marines, for passage to Vietnam. On 1 July, *Talladega* joined Task Group 75.6, composed of *Iwo Jima* (LPH–2) and *Point Defiance* (LSD–31). Marines from the three ships were assault-landed at Qui Nhon and cleared Viet Cong forces from the mountains around Qui Nhon harbor by the 6th. They then reembarked in the ships which remained in the area until 22 July.

From 15 to 25 August, *Talladega* participated in Operation "Starlight," landing marines 10 miles south of Chu Lai. On 12 September, she joined Task Group 76.3 which, in mid-September and early October, conducted the first two raids by a Navy-Marine Corps team in the Vietnamese conflict. On 11 October, the ship returned to Subic Bay and disembarked the marines and then proceeded to Okinawa to unload equipment. After calls at Yokosuka and Pearl Harbor, the transport arrived at Long Beach on 17 November 1965.

Talladega returned to the western Pacific from 14 January to 17 April 1966. During this period, she transported two loads of marines and their equipment from Okinawa to Chu Lai. In 1967, the transport was deployed from 21 July to 1 December. Elements of the 11th Infantry Brigade were transported to Hawaii in July; and, after calling at Guam, *Talladega* proceeded to Subic Bay. She arrived there on 27 August and began loading supplies for Vietnam. However, a change in orders sent her to Japan. The transport arrived at Yokosuka on 7 September, loaded supplies for Operation "Hand Clasp," and headed for Korea the next day. She offloaded supplies at Pusan from 17 to 20 September and returned to Japan. On 12 October, *Talladega* got underway for Vietnam.

Talladega arrived at Vung Tau on 19 October and loaded "Hand Clasp" supplies for delivery to Saigon. She offloaded the supplies between 25 and 31 October. The ship then began the return voyage to the United States. After calling at Hong Kong, Buckner Bay, and Pearl Harbor, she arrived at Long Beach on 1 December 1967.

Talladega was placed in a caretaker status for 18 months before being decommissioned in July 1969. In January 1969, she was redesignated LPA–208. On 20 October 1969, *Talladega* was transferred to the temporary custody of the Maritime Administration and berthed at Olympia, Wash. On 1 September 1971, the ship was transferred to the permanent custody of the Maritime Administration. In July 1972, the transport was moved to Suisun Bay where she remained into October 1979.

Talladega received two battle stars for World War II, two for Korea, and three for Vietnam.

Tallahassee

The capital of Florida.

(Monitor No. 9: dp. 3,255; l. 255'1''; b. 50'; dr. 12'6'' (mean); s. 12.4 k.; cpl. 393; a. 2 12'', 4 4'', 3 6-pdrs.; cl. *Arkansas*)

Florida (Monitor No. 9)—later to become *Tallahassee* (IX–16)—was laid down on 23 January 1899 at the Crescent Shipyard, Elizabethport, N.J., by Lewis Nixon; launched on 30 November 1901; sponsored by Miss Sally Wood; and commissioned on 18 June 1903, Comdr. John C. Fremont in command.

Assigned to the Coast Squadron, *Florida* departed the New York Navy Yard on 6 February 1904, bound via Newport News, Va., for Key West, Fla. She conducted target practice out of Pensacola from late February until late April before heading back up the coast and calling at Charleston, S.C., and Lambert's Point, Va., en route to Annapolis, Md. Arriving at the Naval Academy on 10 May, *Florida* embarked midshipmen early in June for the ship's first training cruise.

During the ensuing voyage, the ship called at Solomons Island, Md., Yorktown, Va., Newport News, and Fort Monroe before visiting the Naval Proving Grounds at Indian Head, Md., and the Washington Navy Yard. She returned to Annapolis on 30 August.

Florida again conducted midshipmen training cruises in the summers of 1905 and 1906. During the latter, the ship was among those reviewed by President Theodore Roosevelt during the Fleet Review at Oyster Bay, Long Island, from 2 to 4 September. Later placed in reserve at the Naval Academy on 11 September, she served as a practice ship for midshipmen until Christmas Day 1906, when she arrived at Norfolk. *South Carolina* and *Michigan* (Battleships Nos. 26 and 27), our first "all-big-gun" capital ships, had been laid down during this month. These ships were to be armed with superfiring turrets, and some apprehension existed as to the possible effect on turret crews when the guns of an upper turret were fired just above the lower one. In two tests carried out in Hampton Roads during March 1907, a 12-inch gun was fired over *Florida*'s turret. Results of these tests demonstrated that gun crews could work inside the gunhouse without injury from muzzle blast.

Placed back in full commission on 4 June 1907 at the Naval Academy, Comdr. Washington I. Chambers in command, *Florida* conducted her fourth midshipmen's training cruise into the late summer of that year. Again placed in reserve at the Naval Academy on 30 August, she conducted practice cruises and training with midshipmen until placed out of commission on 6 January 1908.

Returned to commissioned status on 21 May 1908 at the Norfolk Navy Yard, with Comdr. John G. Quinby in command, the monitor underwent ordnance tests at the yard until again being decommissioned on 19 June 1908. At this time, the ship was renamed *Tallahassee* to clear the name *Florida* for Battleship Number 30.

Subsequently placed in ordinary at Norfolk, she remained there until recommissioned, in reserve, on 1 August 1910, Chief Boatswain Gustav Sabelstrom in command. She operated between the Norfolk and Washington Navy Yards, and in Hampton Roads, Va., into late 1910. She surveyed possible locations for target practices off St. Mary's River, Cobb Point Light, and Liver Pool Point, Md., into late January 1911 before conducting a gunnery practice using the hulk of the erstwhile ram-ship *Katahdin* as a target.

In March 1911, she escorted the former battleship *San Marcos* (ex-*Texas*), to Tangier Sound, Md., in company with survey ship *Leonidas*. *San Marcos* was anchored and grounded to be used for future gunnery practices, and *Tallahassee* served as guard ship into May, returning to Norfolk, Hampton Roads, or Sewall's Point for provisions and to Crisfield, Md., for liberty. From 5 to 9 June, *Tallahassee* pounded the target hulk *San Marcos* in tests of high-explosive shells. Shifting to the Norfolk Navy Yard for repairs, she soon steamed north to the Washington Navy Yard where she received a single 6-inch gun to temporarily augment her battery. She left Washington on 14 July and returned to Tangier Sound to resume firings on *San Marcos*.

Tallahassee returned to the Washington Navy Yard for removal of the 6-inch gun and underwent repairs at Norfolk into the month of November 1912. She subsequently planted range location buoys at Judith Sound, Md., and assisted *Arkansas* (Battleship No. 33) by spotting the latter's fall of shot on *San Marcos*.

She continued ordnance experimentation operations into the late summer of 1914, before entering the navy yard at Norfolk to undergo conversion to a submarine tender, from September to November 1914. She conducted post-repair trials in Hampton Roads before joining the Fleet for maneuvers and exercises into the spring of 1915. *Tallahassee* served Division 1, Submarine Flotilla, Atlantic Fleet, and operated at Chiriqui Lagoon, Almirante Bay, Panama; as well as Cristobal, Canal Zone; and Guantanamo Bay, Cuba. On 9 April 1917, the erstwhile monitor was assigned to the Canal Defense Force.

During World War I, *Tallahassee* operated in the Canal Zone, in the Virgin Islands, and off Bermuda, tending submarines. She continued this duty until she entered the Charleston (S.C.) Navy Yard, where she was decommissioned on 24 March 1919. With the Navy-wide designation of hull-numbers, *Tallahassee* became BM–9 on 17 July 1920, while serving as a training ship at Charleston for the Naval Reserve Force, 6th Naval District. Recommissioned on 3 August 1920, *Tallahassee* was redesignated as IX–16 on 20 July 1921 and decommissioned for the final time on 24 March 1922. She was sold on 25 July 1922 to Ammunition Products Corp., of Washington, D.C.

Tallahassee (CL–61)—laid down as a *Cleveland*-class light cruiser on 2 June 1941 at Camden, N.J., by the New York Shipbuilding Corp.—was subsequently converted to a light aircraft carrier and redesignated CV–23 on 16 February 1942. Before the ship was commissioned, she was renamed *Princeton* (*q.v.*) on 31 March 1942.

Tallahassee (CL–116)—a *Fargo*-class light cruiser—was laid down on 31 January 1944 at Newport News, Va., by the Newport News Shipbuilding and Drydock Co. However, as the collapse of Japan became apparent, the contract for her construction was cancelled on 12 August 1945, and her hull was scrapped on the ways.

Tallahatchie

A river rising in Tippah County, Miss., and flowing some 300 miles southwest to converge with the Yalobusha and form the Yazoo. Tallahatchie is also the name of a county in northwestern Mississippi.

(SwGbt: t. 171; cpl. 51; a. 2 32-pdrs., 4 24-pdr. how.)

Cricket No. 4—a wooden-hulled sidewheel steamer built in 1863 at Cincinnati, Ohio—was purchased there by the Navy from Stephen Morse *et al.* on 23 January 1864. Renamed *Tallahatchie* on 26 January and designated "tinclad gunboat no. 46," the sidewheeler was held at Cincinnati for a fortnight by ice in the Ohio River before she could be moved downstream to Cairo, Ill., to be fitted out and lightly armored.

Acquired by Rear Admiral David D. Porter in response to a request from Commodore Henry H. Bell for light draft gunboats to strengthen United States naval forces in the Gulf of Mexico, *Tallahatchie* headed down the Mississippi on 9 March 1864. The ship's bottom was covered with sheet copper at New Orleans to protect it during salt water operations. When finally ready for action, the ship was commissioned at New Orleans, Acting Master J. W. Saunders in command.

Meanwhile, Porter's Mississippi Squadron had ascended the Red River to support an Army thrust toward Texas. However, the forces had met reverses and were retiring. This left the Union gunboats without land support and in danger of being caught upstream by the falling water level in the river. Now Porter needed help, and *Tallahatchie* ascended the Mississippi and entered the Red River which she patrolled from Fort De Russy to the mouth of the Black River to protect the Mississippi Squadron's waterborne communications.

In the meantime, the crews of Porter's warships and Army engineers dammed the river to allow the ships to ride downstream over the rapids. When the Union gunboats reached safety, *Tallahatchie* returned to New Orleans for duty with the West Gulf Blockading Squadron. She served with this force for the duration of hostilities, operating off the passes of the Mississippi and in Mississippi Sound and Lake Pontchartrain.

On 15 September 1864, while *Tallahatchie* was operating on the lake, her commanding officer, Acting Master J. W. Lennekin, received information warning him that smugglers would attempt to bring out contraband cotton under cover of darkness. Accordingly, he stationed a picket boat off the mouth of the Blind River.

That evening, when the smugglers came out, *Tallahatchie*'s pickets challenged them and ordered them to surrender. Facing imminent capture, the southerners threw overboard a ledger book which contained the details of their illicit activities. Much to the smugglers' chagrin, the book was recovered.

Two days later at the mouth of the Amite River, *Tallahatchie* captured more contraband cotton as well as small quantities of medicines, powder, flour, and other supplies on the banks of Bayou Schinblon. Besides taking the contraband, her landing party went ashore and learned that Conferderate agents had previously purchased ammunition and supplies in the vicinity.

After the coming of peace in the spring of 1865, *Tallahatchie* was decommissioned at Mobile Bay, Ala., on 21 July 1865. Sold at auction to S. W. Roberts on 12 August, the sidewheeler was redocumented as *Coosa* on 25 August. She was subsequently destroyed by fire at Licking River, Ky., on 7 July 1869.

Tallahatchie County

A county in Mississippi.

(LST–1154: dp. 6,000; l. 382'; b. 54'; dr. 14'5''; s. 14 k.; cpl. 190; trp. 197; a. 2 5'', 4 40mm.; cl. *LST–1153*)

LST–1154 was laid down on 4 August 1945 at Boston, Mass., by the Boston Navy Yard; launched on 19 July 1946; sponsored by Mrs. Wilder D. Baker; and commissioned on 24 May 1949, Comdr. Courtland T. Babcock in command.

LST–1154 held her shakedown in the Caribbean and returned to Boston on 8 October. On 12 December, she was assigned duty as flagship for Tractor Flotilla Two. Operating out of Little Creek, Va., her home port, the tank landing ship ranged the eastern seaboard from Labrador to ports in the Caribbean until mid-1958. On 1 July 1955, the LST was named *Tallahatchie County*.

On 12 May 1958, *Tallahatchie County* stood out of Davisville, R. I., and proceeded to the Mediterranean. During the six-month deployment, she visited ports in Spain, Crete, Malta, Greece, Gibraltar, Italy, and Morocco before returning to the United States on 12 December to resume east coast operations. The LST deployed to the 6th Fleet again on 27 July 1959. She returned to Davisville on 11 February 1960 and operated along the east coast until entering the Charleston Naval Shipyard for conversion into an advance aviation base ship.

On 3 February 1962, *Tallahatchie County* was redesignated AVB–2. She now had a complement of 272 and quarters for the 180 men of an aircraft squadron.

Her mission was to be able to beach anywhere that an airfield existed, to unload her 14 mobile support vans, and to be in full operation in four hours. The vans contained spare parts and equipment for weather forecasting, aircraft repairs, electronic repairs, and communications. On 15 May, *Tallahatchie County* got underway for the Mediterranean and arrived at Naples, her new home port, on 8 June 1962.

During the next 17 months, she conducted advance base problems at Souda Bay, Crete, and Cagliari, Sardinia. From 1 November to 15 December 1963, she made a 4,800-mile cruise of the eastern Mediterranean in support of the Naval Oceanographic Office. During the first part of 1964, *Tallahatchie County* was overhauled at an Italian shipyard, *Societa Escercizio Bocini Napoletani*, and then returned to operations in support of the 6th Fleet. During September 1964, she participated in an advance base exercise in conjunction with NATO Operation "Fallex." In February 1965, the advance base ship was called upon to salvage a jet aircraft which had splashed in shallow waters off the coast of Libya. She then returned to Naples to prepare for her longest advance base operation to that time. Patrol Squadron 24 operated from *Tallachatchie's* advance base in Souda Bay from July through September while the runways at the Naval Air Facility, Sigonella, were being repaired.

Tallahatchie County operated out of Naples until 15 January 1970 when she was decommissioned and struck from the Navy list. She was sold for scrap to *Contieri Navali Santa Maria*, Genoa, in July 1970.

Tallahoma

Probably a variant spelling of Tullahoma, a town in central Tennessee, 55 miles northwest of Chattanooga.

Tallahoma—a wooden-hulled, sidewheel, "double-ended" gunboat of the *Sassacus*-class—was constructed at the New York Navy Yard and launched on 28 November 1862. However, since her construction was not completed until 1867—when the Civil War which had prompted her construction had ended—the ship saw no service. After a brief period in ordinary at New York, the ship was sold on 29 August 1868.

Documented as *Mary M. Roberts* on 10 November 1868, the erstwhile gunboat was converted to a barge on 21 December 1870, and she disappeared from the lists of merchant vessels.

Tallapoosa

A navigable river which rises in Paulding County in northwestern Georgia and flows in a generally southwestern direction some 268 miles until it joins the Coosa River in central Alabama in forming the Alabama River.

I

(SwStr.: t. 974; l. 205′; b. 35′; dph. 11′6″; dr. 6′6″; s. 11.5 k.; cpl. 190; a. 2 100-pdr. P.r., 4 9″ D.sb., 2 20-pdr. P.r., 2 24-pdr. how.; cl. *Sassacus*)

The first *Tallapoosa*—a wooden-hulled, double-ended steamer built at the New York Navy Yard by C. W. Booz of Baltimore, Md.—was launched on 17 February 1863 and commissioned on 13 September 1864, Lt. Comdr. Joseph E. DeHaven in command.

As *Tallapoosa* was being fitted out, Confederate cruiser *Tallahassee* was cruising off the Atlantic coast destroying Union shipping from the Virginia Capes to Nova Scotia. Hence, the Union double-ender got underway late in October and spent her first days at sea in seeking the Southern commerce raider. Her futile quest

Tallapoosa, in the gray finish used on ships blockading the southern coast during the Civil War. (NH 270)

took her from New York to Halifax, then south to the Virginia Capes, then back north again to the coast of Nova Scotia. On 4 November, *Tallapoosa* encountered a southeasterly gale, which battered the ship for the next two days, disabled both her rudders, and caused other damage. She finally made port at Boston on the morning of the 7th.

Following repairs at the Boston Navy Yard which lasted over a month and one-half, *Tallapoosa* was assigned to the East Gulf Blockading Squadron. Her most notable duty during this assignment occurred on 11 January 1865 when she assisted in salvaging material and equipment from screw frigate *San Jacinto* which had run aground in the Bahamas on an uncharted reef near Green Turtle Cay off Grand Abaco Island.

After the Civil War ended, *Tallapoosa* served in the Gulf Squadron—cruising in the West Indies and the Gulf of Mexico—until 1867 when she was laid up at the Washington Navy Yard. Reactivated in 1869, the ship became a dispatch vessel, beginning a role which soon brought *Tallapoosa* one of her more interesting missions. In January 1870, she carried Admiral Farragut to Portland, Maine, where he met HMS *Monarch* at the end of that British turreted battleship's voyage across the Atlantic to return to the United States the remains of philanthropist George Peabody who had died in England. Early the following summer, the double-ender carried Farragut from New York City to Portsmouth, N.H., to visit the commandant of the navy yard. It was hoped that the cool sea breezes of New England would improve the aged and ailing admiral's health. As *Tallapoosa* neared Portsmouth on 4 July, she fired an Independence Day salute to her famous passenger, the Navy's highest ranking and most respected officer. Upon hearing the warship's guns, Farragut left his sick-bed, donned his uniform, and walked to the man-of-war's quarterdeck. There he commented, "It would be well if I died now, in harness. . . ." A month and 10 days later, Farragut died at Portsmouth.

In 1872, *Tallapoosa* moved to Annapolis, Md., to serve as a training ship at the Naval Academy. The following year, she became a transport. While she performed this duty, her years of service began to show; and it became apparent that she needed extensive repair work. Hence, the ship was largely rebuilt at Baltimore in 1874 and 1875. There, revitalized and configured as a single-ender, the veteran warship resumed her role as a dispatch vessel and continued performing as such for almost a decade.

Shortly before midnight on 24 August 1884, *Tallapoosa* collided with schooner *J. S. Lowell* and sank about five miles from Vineyard Haven, R.I. After the ship had been raised and repaired by the Merritt Wrecking Company, she was recommissioned at the New York Navy Yard on 11 January 1886. Assigned to the South Atlantic Squadron, *Tallapoosa* departed New York on 7 June 1886, bound for Rio de Janeiro. At the time, South America was plagued by much political and social unrest; and United States warships were needed in the area to protect American interests and commerce. *Tallapoosa* served along the coast of South America until 30 January 1892 when she was condemned as unfit for further service. She was sold at public auction at Montevideo, Uruguay, on 3 March 1892.

II

(CGC: dp. 912; l. 165'10"; b. 32'0"; dr. 11'9" (mean); s. 12.7 k.; cpl. 78; a. 1 4", 2 6-pdrs., 2 mg., 1 Y-gun)

The second *Tallapoosa*—a Coast Guard cutter built in 1915 at Newport News, Va., by the Newport News Shipbuilding and Dry Dock Co.—served the Coast Guard in the Gulf of Mexico from her base at Tampa, Fla., until the United States entered World War I. On 6 April 1917, the cutter was temporarily transferred to the Navy Department. She got underway on the 15th

and headed for the northeast coast of the United States where she served the Navy on antisubmarine patrol during the conflict. After hostilities ended, the Coast Guard cutter was returned to the Treasury Department by an executive order issued on 28 August; and *Tallapoosa* resumed her duty in the Gulf of Mexico, operating out of Mobile. Ala.

Tallulah

A river in Rabun County, Ga., in the far northeastern corner of the state.

(AO–50: dp. 21,650 (tl.); l. 523'6"; b. 68'0"; dr. 30'10" (lim.); s. 14.5 k.; cpl. 338; a. 1 5", 4 3''; cl. *Suamico*; T. T2–SE–A1)

Tallulah (AO–50) was laid down on 1 December 1941 under a Maritime Commission contract (MC hull 321) at Chester, Pa., by the Sun Shipbuilding & Drydock Co.; launched on 25 June 1942; sponsored by Mrs. H. Bowring; acquired by the Navy on 30 July 1942; and commissioned on 5 September 1942, Comdr. Jesse B. Goode in command.

After fitting out at New York, she conducted shakedown training out of Norfolk. *Tallulah* got underway for New York on 17 October 1942 with *Chemung* (AO–30), *Jenkins* (DD–447), and *Chevalier* (DD–451). A week later, she departed New York in company with 32 merchant ships escorted by HMS *Havalock* and four corvettes and proceeded via Guantanamo Bay, Cuba, and Aruba toward Panama. She transited the canal on 9 November and remained at Balboa for three days. On the 12th, she headed westward—via Bora Bora in the Society Islands—to New Caledonia. *Tallulah* remained in Noumea from 12 to 19 December; then made her way to the west coast, arriving at San Francisco on 4 January 1943.

Over the next year, she made five more round-trip voyages to the South Pacific. On three of these, the oiler carried airplanes in addition to her usual oil cargo. On the first of the five, from 4 January until 19 March, the oiler visited the Solomon Islands in addition to New Caledonia and Espiritu Santo. On 15 February, just after she had gotten underway for Guadalcanal, one of her escorts reported and attacked a submarine contact. Late that afternoon, Japanese torpedo bombers dove on the convoy in singles and pairs; but the Allied ships maneuvered radically and put up a hail of anti-aircraft fire. *Tallulah* suffered no hits, and the closest torpedo passed 12 yards astern. For the day's action, her gunners claimed one sure splash and two more possible kills. She arrived off Lunga Point and commenced fueling operations on the 18th. For the next week, she moved between Guadalcanal, Florida Island, and Tulagi, fueling the ships supporting the struggle for Guadalcanal. On 27 February, she reached Espiritu Santo and, three days later, headed back toward the United States.

The middle three voyages were largely uneventful. She sailed from the west coast carrying oil, stores, and planes to various bases in the South Pacific. In addition to Noumea, the oiler visited Samoa, Fiji, and Efate. On 16 October, she departed San Pedro, Calif., on her fifth and last round-trip voyage; arrived in Havannah Harbor, Efate Island, on 5 November; and remained there for eight days, fueling the ships in the harbor. On the 13th, she got underway for fueling-at-sea operations en route to Funafuti in the Ellice Islands, where she anchored four days later. From 19 to 21 November, she was again at sea fueling Task Group (TG) 50.4. Following four more days fueling ships at Funafuti, she stood out of port to replenish the tanks of warships supporting the invasion of the Gilbert Islands during the first week in December. Upon completion of that task, the oiler headed, via Pearl Harbor, back to San Pedro, Calif.

On 13 January 1944, following a brief overhaul, she

once more departed the west cost. This time, however, her destination was the Central Pacific. During the next five months, *Tallulah* shuttled oil and cargo from Pearl Harbor to the forward anchorage established at newly won Majuro Atoll. By early June, anchorages had also been established farther west at Kwajalein and Eniwetok. On 3 June, she departed Majuro and, after a stopover at Kwajalein from 4 to 13 June, arrived in Eniwetok on the 14th. The next day, she put to sea to fuel elements of the 5th Fleet just prior to the Philippine Sea phase of the Marianas campaign. During that battle, the carriers of Task Force 58 broke the back of Japanese sea-borne air power once and for all. Two days after the great air battle, she refueled TG 58.3, built around two of the mighty victors, *Enterprise* (CV-6) and *Lexington* (CV-16). From 1 to 27 July, she conducted fueling operations in and around Eniwetok; then headed for the west coast.

Steaming via Pearl Harbor, *Tallulah* reached Terminal Island, Calif., on 11 August and began overhaul. She stood out again on 26 September and, after fueling-at-sea practice en route, reentered Pearl Harbor on 4 October. She remained overnight and, the following morning, continued on toward the western Pacific. After a stop at Eniwetok on the night of 13 and 14 October, she reached Ulithi on the 19th. On 4 November, she put to sea again to support the Leyte assault. *Tallulah* returned to the lagoon at Ulithi on 17 November and remained until the 23d.

On the 20th, while she was still in Ulithi lagoon, the anchorage was subjected to a *kaiten* attack. At least three of the one-man undersea raiders were sunk. *Mississinewa* (AO-59), anchored off *Tallulah's* starboard bow, took a hit just before 0600 and, by 0900, was at the bottom of the lagoon. *Tallulah* shifted berths to avoid flame and flying debris while members of her crew assisted the survivors of the sunken oiler.

On 23 November, the oiler headed for Hollandia, New Guinea, where she spent a month in exercises and fueling operations. She departed New Guinea on 30 December and steamed—via Mangarin Bay, Mindoro—to Lingayen Gulf, Luzon. She supported the Luzon invasion until late January 1945 when she returned to Ulithi. On 1 February, *Tallulah* was transferred from the 7th to the 5th Fleet for the Iwo Jima invasion. She put to sea on the 16th and conducted fueling-at-sea operations until 3 March, when she returned to Ulithi for upkeep. Ten days later, she exited the lagoon again and resumed fueling the fleet, still operating off Iwo Jima and preparing to soften Okinawa.

For the remainder of World War II, *Tallulah* operated from the base at Ulithi in support of the invasion forces at Okinawa and of the Fast Carrier Task Force during its strikes against Japan and her outposts in China and Southeast Asia. She returned to Ulithi periodically for upkeep and to take on fresh supplies of oil. Then with her tanks full, she carried her precious cargo to the fighting forces. In addition to Ulithi, she visited the base at Leyte Gulf, the forward base at Kerama Retto—located just to the west of Okinawa—and Buckner Bay at the island itself.

The war in the Pacific ended on 15 August, while *Tallulah* was conducting fueling operations at Buckner Bay. She made one more round-trip voyage to Ulithi and back, between 17 August and 1 September; then sailed north on the 20th to fuel ships operating in the vicinity of Jinsen, Korea. During the ensuing three months, she visited China—at Taku Bar, the Gulf of Pohai, and Tsingtao—as well as Nagoya, Kure, Yokohama, and Yokosuka in Japan. On 14 December, *Tallulah* stood out of Yokohama and headed for Pearl Harbor and home.

Soon after her return to the United States, *Tallulah* was decommissioned on 2 April 1946. On 3 October, she was turned over to the War Shipping Administration; and her name was struck from the Navy list. However, on 2 February 1948, she was reacquired by the Navy and, on 1 October 1949, transferred to the Military Sea Transportation Service, now the Military Sealift

Command, to serve as USNS *Tallulah* (TAO-50). Manned by a civilian crew since that time, she plied the oceans of the world, visited most major ports, and kept the Navy supplied with oil and other important liquid cargoes. *Tallulah* was assigned to the Maritime Administration fleet at James River, Va., in May 1975 where she remained into October 1979.

Tallulah earned seven battle stars during World War II.

Talofa

(SP-1016: t. 82; l. 101'0"; b. 15'0"; dr. 5'6" (mean); s. 12 k.; cpl. 19; a. 2 3-pdrs.)

Talofa (SP-1016)—a steam yacht built in 1910 at Neponset, Mass., by George Lawley & Sons—was acquired by the Navy on free lease from Mr. Eben H. Ellison in April 1917 and commissioned on 16 April 1917.

For two years, *Talofa* patrolled in the 1st Naval District, protecting the ports and harbors of New England from the dangers of German marauders. On 24 April 1919, five months after the armistice ending World War I, the yacht was returned to her owner. Her name was subsequently struck from the Navy list.

Taluga

A river in Florida.

(AO-62: dp. 23,235 (tl.); l. 553'0"; b. 75'0"; dr. 32'4" (lim.); s. 18.0 k.; cpl. 313; a. 1 5", 4 3"; cl. *Ashtabula*; T. T3-S2-A1)

Taluga (AO-62) was laid down under a Maritime Commission contract (MC hull 728) on 23 December 1943 at Sparrows Point, Md., by the Bethlehem Steel Co.; launched on 10 July 1944; sponsored by Mrs. Harvey Klemmer; delivered to the Navy at Norfolk on 25 August 1944; and commissioned there on that same day, Comdr. Hans M. Mikkelsen in command.

The oiler left Norfolk on 5 October; stopped at Aruba, Netherlands West Indies, from the 9th to the 11th; and transited the Panama Canal on the night of 13 and 14 October. She reached Pearl Harbor on the 26th and, two days later, continued on to the Marshalls. The oiler entered the Eniwetok lagoon on 26 November and exited on the 28th. On 10 December, she reached Ulithi, which served as her base of operations until the end of World War II.

For the next 11 months, *Taluga* was in and out of Ulithi picking up oil and other supplies there and carrying them to units of the Pacific Fleet. For the most part, her oil and aviation gasoline went to the ships of the Fast Carrier Task Force. During that time, she supported the carrier strikes and landings on Luzon, the Okinawa landings, the strikes on Formosa, and the final 3d Fleet sweep of the Japanese home islands in the summer of 1945. Between April and July of 1945, she spent much of her time in and around the anchorage at Kerama Retto, just west of the southern end of Okinawa. There, on 16 April, she encountered her greatest excitement of the war. Shortly after dawn, 10 kamikazes attacked her formation. One of them dove at the oiler, strafed her deck, and then made for her superstructure. The attacker careened off the ship's bridge and exploded through her forward well deck into a compartment adjacent to her tanks brimming with 300,000 gallons of aviation fuel. However, only 12 men were injured; and the oiler was soon back in action.

Soon after the final 3d Fleet sweep of Hokkaido and Kyushu, Japan capitulated. *Taluga* entered Tokyo Bay on 26 August, 11 days following the cessation of hostilities, and took up duty as station oiler until early October. She then voyaged to Ulithi once more to refill her tanks and returned to Japan for duty as station oiler at Yokosuka. On 18 November, she departed that port to support ships engaged in the occupation of China and Korea. She visited Tsingtao and Jinsen before returning to Yokosuka on 6 December. On 31 January 1946, the oiler put to sea to return to the United States. She arrived in San Pedro, Calif., on 16 February and commenced a four-month yard period.

Following overhaul, she sailed from San Pedro on 15 June for the Far East. For the next year, *Taluga* hauled oil from the Persian Gulf ports of Bahrain and Ras Tanura to American bases in Japan and the Philippines. On 13 June 1947, she got underway from Yokosuka bound for home by the westward route. During that cruise, the oiler visited Singapore and Bahrain before transiting the Suez Canal and stopping at Tangier. On 10 August, she entered port at Norfolk. Three weeks later, the oiler was back at sea and—after an overnight stop at Key West, Fla.—headed for the Mediterranean. She loaded oil at Bahrain from 30 September until 2 October and, following visits to Suez and Tangier, returned to Norfolk on 28 October.

On 4 November, she departed Hampton Roads once more for a cruise to the Middle East. She stopped at Ras Tanura from 30 November to 5 December; then she continued eastward across the Indian Ocean and up through the South China Sea to Yokosuka, Japan, arriving there on the day after Christmas. On the last day of 1947, *Taluga* departed Yokosuka and set a course across the Pacific to Puget Sound, Wash. She reached her destination on 13 January 1948 and began overhaul at the naval shipyard.

Taluga completed overhaul and departed Puget Sound on 19 April. For the next three years, the oiler plied the oceans carrying oil to various American bases the world over. During that period, she made short runs between ports on both coasts as well as long voyages to ports overseas. She served with the 6th Fleet in the Mediterranean on occasion and stopped frequently at the Persian Gulf ports, Ras Tanura and Bahrain. The oiler called most frequently at San Diego, San Pedro, Long Beach, and Seattle on the west coast; Norfolk on the east coast; as well as Galveston, Houston, Cristobal, Guantanamo Bay, and Aruba in the gulf and West Indies areas. On 12 May 1951, *Taluga* departed San Francisco and, during the next month and one-half, made two voyages between California and Alaska. On the first, she made a circuit from Adak to Dutch Harbor to Kodiak before returning to San Francisco on 31 May. The second Alaskan voyage took her to Adak and

Kodiak and was completed on 3 July. During the following months, she shuttled between California ports before departing the west coast for the Far East on 30 July.

While *Taluga* was shuttling oil to bases throughout the world, trouble was brewing in the Far East. On the morning of 25 June 1950, the North Korean People's Army invaded the Republic of Korea. American and other UN troops pushed the North Koreans back as far as the Yalu; and, by winter, the war appeared to be all but over. However, the renewal of the war by the injection of communist Chinese troops required the United States to increase its flow of men and material to strengthen the sagging defenses. By the summer of 1951, *Taluga* was on her way again to join in another Asian war.

She departed Long Beach late in July; stopped at Midway and Kwajalein; and reached Sasebo, Japan, on 23 August. The oiler remained there for a month, then headed for the combat zone on 22 September. Operating from Sasebo at the southwestern tip of Kyushu, *Taluga* supported the blockade and siege of Wonsan and Songjin almost until the end of hostilities. She ranged up and down the eastern coast of Korea supplying oil and aviation fuel to the warships conducting operations along the coast. From March to September of 1952, she returned to the west coast and conducted operations between San Diego and Long Beach. She returned to Korean waters in October and, after almost three months of operations in support of UN naval forces, moved south to Taiwan where she visited Keelung and Kaohsiung and supported the Taiwan Strait Patrol.

In April 1953, *Taluga* sailed from Yokosuka, via Pearl Harbor, and arrived in San Pedro, Calif., early in May. She operated along the west coast, visiting San Diego and Long Beach, until mid-August. On the 17th, she got underway from Long Beach on the first peacetime deployment with the 7th Fleet in a series which lasted until the escalation of the Vietnam War brought the return of a substantial American presence back to the Asian continent.

Interspersed among the routine operations of those deployments were several operations of note—ones which might have presaged the increasing American involvement in Southeast Asia. During the winter of 1954 and 1955, the oiler participated in the evacuation of Chinese Nationalists from the Tachen Islands located just off the mainland. In January 1955, she took station

Taluga (AO–62) off the Philippines in 1957, with the later *Neosho*-class oilers *Kawishiwi* (AO–146) and *Hassayampa* (AO–145).   (80–G–1013403)

off Henriette Passe, near Haiphong, to fuel the transport and relief supply ships evacuating refugees from strife-torn North Vietnam during the latter stages of Operation "Passage to Freedom," instituted in the wake of the Geneva agreements which followed the French defeat at Dien Bien Phu.

Soon thereafter, *Taluga* resumed a series of deployments with the 7th Fleet for another 10 years. In 1965, the United States began expanding its direct participation in the war in Vietnam. *Taluga*'s remaining deployments, therefore, were wartime deployments in or near a combat zone. During the ensuing six years, *Taluga* deployed to the western Pacific six times. On each occasion, she saw service in the war zone along the Vietnamese coast replenishing units of the 7th Fleet operating off the coast. She fueled the larger units as they supported the large carriers conducting strikes inland, and she offered support to the smaller units engaged in Operation "Market Time," the interdiction of North Vietnamese coastal logistics and infiltration. Only once did she depart from her schedule of western Pacific deployments alternated with west coast operations and yard overhauls. That occasion came at the end of her 1970 deployment when she sailed south of the equator to Australia and New Zealand, where she joined in LONGEX–70, the New Zealand annual maritime exercise.

Taluga completed her final deployment as a commissioned Navy ship at Long Beach on 13 November 1971. She conducted operations along the coast for another six months. On 4 May 1972, the oiler was decommissioned and turned over to the Military Sealift Command to participate in a pilot program designed to test the feasibility of reducing the number of Navy men serving in oilers. The operation, named "Charger Log II," was an unqualified success. For the next three and one-half years, her crew—made up of 105 civilians and 16 military men—maneuvered her through 875 underway replenishments in support of the 7th Fleet in the Far East. In late February 1976, she cleared the western Pacific for Oakland, Calif., where she was placed in a ready-reserve status incident to overhaul. USNS *Taluga* completed overhaul in October 1976 and was then reactivated as a fleet support ship assigned to the 3d Fleet in the eastern Pacific. She served in that capacity into October 1979.

Taluga earned four battle stars during World War II, four more during the Korean War, and 12 for the Vietnam War.

Tamaha

A chief of the Mdewakanton Sioux who met and aided Lt. Zebulon Pike during the American explorer's expeditions in 1806 and 1807. Their ensuing strong friendship prompted Tamaha to remain loyal to the United States during the War of 1812 despite the fact that most of the Sioux supported the British. Tamaha not only refused to join the other Sioux in the war against the United States, but served General Clarke as a scout and messenger. On one of his trips, he was imprisoned by a fur trader in the employ of the British and, though threatened with execution, steadfastly refused to divulge any information to the enemy. After the war, in 1816, he visited St. Louis to participate in a council of the 46 chiefs from the upper Missouri. General Clarke took that occasion to present Tamaha a medal of honor for his faithful service to the United States. Tamaha lived to the age of 85, venerated by red man and white man alike. He died in April 1860 at Wabasha, Minn.

(YN–44: dp. 253; l. 105'0"; b. 25'0"; dr. 9'0"; a. 4 .30 cal. mg.)

Rowen Card—a tug built in 1936 at Slidell, La., by the Canulette Shipbuilding Co.—was acquired by the Navy on 25 October 1940 from the Card Towing Line,

Inc., of New York City; renamed *Tamaha* (YN–44); converted to a net tender at the New York Navy Yard; and placed in service there on 17 December 1940.

On 30 December, she departed New York harbor and steamed—via Norfolk, Va.; Charleston, S.C.; Guantanamo Bay, Cuba; the Panama Canal; and San Diego, Calif.—to the Hawaiian Islands. After a long voyage interrupted by port visits, *Tamaha* reached Hawaii on 25 March 1941 and operated for the next five years as a net tender in the 14th Naval District, primarily at Midway Island. On 8 April 1942, she was redesignated YNT–12.

On 1 March 1946, she departed Pearl Harbor in ARD–8 and headed for San Diego, where she was placed out of service on 12 April 1946. On 1 May, *Tamaha* was determined to be surplus to the needs of the Navy, and her name was struck from the Navy list. On 15 January 1947, she was turned over to the Maritime Commission at San Diego, Calif., for disposal.

Tamalpais

A creek and watershed located in Marin County, Calif.; it empties into San Francisco Bay.

(AO–96: dp. 21,650 (tl.); l. 523'6"; b. 68'0"; dr. 30'10" (lim.); s. 15.1 k. (tl.); cpl. 255; a. 1 5", 4 3"; cl. *Escambia*; T. T2–SE–A2)

Tamalpais (AO–96) was laid down at Sausalito, Calif., on 18 September 1944 under Maritime Commission contract (MC hull 1831) by the Marinship Corp.; launched on 29 October 1944; sponsored by Mrs. H. B. Anderson; acquired by the Navy on 20 May 1945; and commissioned that same day, Lt. Cmdr. A. J. Church, USNR, in command.

The fleet oiler departed San Francisco on 7 June for shakedown training out of San Diego. On the 15th, she was ordered to San Pedro to load potable water; and, eight days later, she headed for the Marshall Islands. On 8 July, *Tamalpais* reached Eniwetok and discharged her cargo. The following day, she continued on to Manus, in the Admiralty Islands, where she loaded another cargo of water which she delivered to Ulithi on 22 July. She returned to Manus on the 26th. She put to sea again on 8 August, headed for the Philippines with a fresh water cargo, and arrived at Leyte on 10 August. Four days later, as hostilities in the Pacific were ending, she stood out of Leyte Gulf to rendezvous with Task Group 30.8 off the coast of Japan. The ship entered Sagami Bay on the 28th and anchored in Tokyo Bay on the 30th. There, she issued water to hospital ships and small craft. She remained in Japan—either at Tokyo, Yokosuka, or Sasebo—until March 1946.

On 4 March, *Tamalpais* departed Sasebo for Hong Kong, where she stayed almost two months. On 25 April, she sailed from Hong Kong to return to the United States. She transited the Panama Canal between 22 and 24 May and arrived in Mobile, Ala., on the 28th. On 21 June 1946, she was decommissioned and returned to the War Shipping Administration for layup in the National Defense Reserve Fleet. Her name was struck from the Navy list on 8 July 1946.

On 10 March 1948, *Tamalpais* was reacquired by the Navy, and she was operated by a civilian contractor for the Navy until 1 October 1949, when she was transferred to the Military Sea Transportation Service for duty as a non-commissioned naval vessel manned by civilian personnel. On 28 April 1950, her name was reinstated on the Navy list. For the next eight years, she plied the oceans of the world as USNS *Tamalpais* (TAO–96), visiting major ports the world over and carrying petroleum for the Navy. On 18 December 1957, her name was again struck from the Navy list; and she was transferred to the Maritime Commission's James River Group (Va.), National Defense Reserve Fleet. Sometime between 31 December 1965 and 30 June 1966, *Tamalpais* was turned over to the Department of the Army.

Tamaqua

A borough in Schuylkill County, Pa., founded in 1799 and named for a Delaware Indian chief.

(YTB–797: dp. 356 (f.); l. 109'; b. 31'; dr. 14'; s. 12 k.; cpl. 12; cl. *Natick*)

Tamaqua (YTB–797) was laid down on 16 January 1968 at Marinette, Wis., by the Marinette Marine Corp., and launched on 14 August 1968. Placed in service in November of the same year, *Tamaqua* was assigned to the Pacific Fleet and has served in the western Pacific into October 1979.

Tamaque

A Delaware chief of the Unalachtigo tribe during the mid-18th century. He was initially friendly to the English; but, after the defeat of General Braddock in 1755, he allied himself with the French during the French and Indian War. In 1762, he renewed his friendship with the English through the governor of Pennsylvania and released all his white prisoners. However, his relations with the English soon soured again during Pontiac's conspiracy, and he resumed raids on frontier settlements. Later, just before his death in about 1770, he came under the influence of Moravian missionaries and became a zealous convert to Christianity.

(YN–52: l. 81'0"; b. 21'6"; dr. 10'8")

John E. Matton—a tug built in 1939 at Waterford, N.Y., by John E. Matton & Son, Inc.—was purchased by the Navy on 19 December 1940; converted to a net tender at the New York Navy Yard; renamed *Tamaque* (YN–52) on 9 January 1941; and placed in service on 28 January 1941 at New York City.

On 1 February, *Tamaque* reported to the Commandant, 1st Naval District, for duty at Boston, Mass. She operated in Boston harbor for the next four years, first as a net tender and later as a harbor tug. On 8 April 1942, she was redesignated YNT–20; and, on 4 August 1945, she was reclassified a medium harbor tug, YTM–741. After almost four years of service, *Tamaque* was placed out of service at Marginal Wharf, South Boston, Mass., on 20 December 1945. On 21 January 1946, her name was struck from the Navy list. She was transferred to the Maritime Commission on 6 September 1946 for disposal.

Tamarack

(SP–561: t. 27; l. 80'; b. 13'3"; dr. 4'5" (mean); s. 14 mph.; a. 2 1-pdrs.)

Tamarack—a motor yacht built in 1915 at City Island, N.Y., by Nevins Shipyard—was acquired by the Navy on free lease from E. L. Beard of Flushing, N.Y., on 25 June 1917 and placed in commission on 18 September 1917.

Tamarack was assigned to section patrol duty in the 3d Naval District. She patrolled the coastline and for 17 months protected the ports and harbors of Connecticut, New York, and New Jersey. On 21 February 1919, she was returned to her owner, and her name was struck from the Navy list.

Tamaroa

An American Indian tribe of the Illinois confederacy. In the 17th and 18th centuries, the Tamaroa occupied both sides of the Mississippi River between the mouths of the Illinois and Missouri rivers. They were friendly with the French and deadly enemies of the Chickasaw and Shawnee. They disappeared as a tribe before the advent of the 19th century.

Tamaroa was also the name of the tribe's principal village, located at or near the present site of East St. Louis, Ill.

(AT–62: dp. 705 (n.); l. 151'3½"; b. 27'6"; dr. 10'7"; s. 11 k.)

Tamaroa—a cutter built for the Coast Guard in 1919 at Elizabeth, N.J., by the Bethlehem Shipbuilding Corp.—was transferred to the Navy on 14 May 1936 at San Francisco, Calif.; designated an ocean tug, AT–62; and commissioned at Mare Island Navy Yard on 6 November 1936.

Tamaroa served all of her almost 10-year long Navy career in and around San Francisco, Calif., She was initially assigned to the Commandant, 12th Naval District, and that assignment continued until mid-1942. On 1 January 1938, she was reclassified a harbor tug, YT–136. On 23 July 1942, she was reassigned to the Commander, Western Sea Frontier, continuing to operate in San Francisco harbor. *Tamaroa* was again reclassified on 13 April 1944, when she was designated a large harbor tug, YTB–136. Three months later, she was decommissioned and placed in service. The tug continued to serve in the 12th Naval District until 27 January 1946, when she collided with *Jupiter* (AVS–8) and sank in 42 feet of water in San Francisco harbor. Her name was struck from the Navy list on 25 February 1946.

Tambor

The red rock fish of the Pacific coast.

(SS–198: dp. 1,475 (surf.), 2,370 (subm.); l. 307'3"; b. 27'3"; dr. 15'2"; s. 20 k. (surf.), 8.75 k. (subm.); cpl. 79; a. 10 21" tt., 1 3", 1 40mm.; cl. *Tambor*)

Tambor (SS–198) was laid down on 16 January 1939 by the Electric Boat Co., Groton, Conn.; launched on 20 December 1939; sponsored by Miss Lucia Ellis; and commissioned on 3 June 1940, Lt. Comdr. John M. Murphy, Jr., in command.

After fitting out at New London, *Tambor* got underway on 5 August 1940 for her shakedown cruise which took her to New York City; Washington, D.C.; Morehead City, N.C.; and Houston, Tex. Following further training off Colon, Canal Zone, the submarine returned to New London before holding her acceptance trials and undergoing a post-shakedown overhaul at the Portsmouth (N.H.) Navy Yard. After conducting experiments measuring the effectiveness of depth charges, *Tambor* reported in May 1941 to the Submarine Force, Pacific Fleet.

Tambor began a routine peace-time patrol of Wake Island in late November 1941 and, when war with Japan broke out, she began her first war patrol. However, she was forced to return to Pearl Harbor with one engine out of commission. Routed back to Mare Island where the damage was repaired, the submarine returned to Pearl Harbor in March 1942.

Tambor began her second war patrol on 15 March when she stood out of Pearl Harbor to reconnoiter the areas around Wake, Truk, New Ireland, New Britain, and Rabaul. She made unsuccessful attacks on enemy ships on 30 March and 6 April. On 16 April, she fired two torpedoes at a tanker. One hit, but the submarine's report that the target had been sunk was not verified by postwar examination of Japanese records. *Tambor* returned to Pearl Harbor on 12 May.

After refitting, she was then assigned to Task Group 7.1. The group of six submarines sailed for Midway Island on the 21st to begin patrolling a 150-mile circle in anticipation of the invasion fleet that intelligence had reported was en route there. At 0215 hours on 5 June, *Tambor* sighted four large ships at a range of three miles. Three others soon appeared, but two hours passed before the fleet was identified as two Japanese cruisers escorted by five destroyers. The ships soon outdistanced the submarine; but she promptly radioed their position to Midway. Two days later, *Tambor* sighted a scout plane seven miles away; and she went to 140 feet. Two depth bombs, which exploded close aboard, damaged both her periscopes and cracked all four battery blower motors; so *Tambor* returned to Pearl Harbor on 16 June for repairs.

Her next patrol began on 24 July and ended on 19 September at Fremantle, Australia. *Tambor* searched for enemy shipping in the Marshall Islands. On 7 August near Wotje Island, she sank the converted net tender *Shofuka* with one torpedo which broke her in half. *Tambor* remained in the Marshalls until the 19th when she was ordered to patrol the southern passages to Truk. As there was time to spare before she was to take station there, she prowled through the Caroline Islands. On the 21st near Ponape, the submarine fired a spread of three torpedoes at a freighter and her escort. The first hit the target amidships and the other two aft, blowing off the stern. *Shinsei Maru No. 6* quickly sank. On 1 September, she fired four torpedoes at a tanker off Truk and damaged it with one hit.

Tambor sailed for Hainan Strait on 12 October and laid mines there. On 3 November, she fired three torpedoes at a freighter, but all missed. The submarine eluded detection; and, 30 minutes later, she fired two more. One hit amidships, and *Chikugo Maru* went under by the stern. On the 6th, she fired two torpedoes at a cargo-passenger ship flying the French flag, but both missed. On the 10th, she closed an unarmed sampan, took its crew on board and sank it by gunfire. *Tambor* returned to Fremantle on 21 November for refit during which her deck gun was replaced by a modern 5-inch gun.

From 18 December 1942 to 28 January 1943, *Tambor* patrolled Soenda Strait between Krakatau and Thartway Island. The only target sighted was an enemy destroyer which she attacked on New Year's Day 1943. The submarine's spread of four torpedoes missed, and she went deep to avoid the 18 depth charges that followed.

Tambor sailed from Fremantle on 18 February to carry out a special mission in the Philippine Islands. On 5 March, she landed a small Navy party—with 50,000 rounds of .30-caliber ammunition, 20,000 rounds of .45-caliber ammunition, and $10,000 in currency—on southern Mindanao. On the 22d, she fired three torpedoes at a naval auxiliary southwest of Apo Island and saw one hit. Seven days later, she scored one hit on a freighter out of three torpedoes fired. The submarine returned to Fremantle on 14 April for refit and the installation of a 20-millimeter gun forward of the bridge.

Tambor's seventh patrol took her north of the Malay Barrier from 7 May to 27 June 1943. On 26 May, she fired a spread of three torpedoes at a tanker—all misses. Three days later, three more missed a cargo ship. She tried again several hours later, saw two of the three torpedoes fired score hits, and heard three explosions. As the target was sinking, she fired another spread of three at an accompanying freighter. Some of the crew of *Eiski Maru* escaped in two lifeboats. On 2 and on 6 June, she fired spreads of three torpedoes at cargo ships. The first appeared to break in half, and the second seemed to sink; but there is no record of the sinkings in Japanese official records. On 16 June, *Tambor* fired her last three torpedoes at a tanker off Cam Ranh Bay but all missed.

Tambor stood out of Fremantle for the last time on 20 July en route to Lombok Strait. On 3 August, she sighted five cargomen and a destroyer in Palawan Passage. Three shots at a freighter produced two hits, and one fired at another target missed. However, Japanese records do not indicate any sinking. On 21 August, she sighted an unescorted convoy of three tankers and five freighters. She fired five torpedoes at a pair of freighters, but scored no hits. Two more sped toward a tanker and produced one explosion but no apparent damage. The next day, she sighted another convoy heading in the opposite direction. Making a submerged attack, *Tambor* fired five torpedoes at a large freighter. Three made perfect hits amidships, but all bounced off the side of the ship without exploding. The submarine set sail for Midway Island and arrived there on 7 September. She departed for Pearl Harbor the next day for repairs. Ordered to return to the United States, *Tambor* arrived at San Francisco on 20 November for an overhaul.

Tambor returned to Pearl Harbor on 15 December 1943 and held refresher training during the remainder of the month. She began her ninth war patrol on 5 January 1944. Her assigned area was in the East China Sea. She sighted a *Natori*-class cruiser on the 22d, but lost contact in a rain squall. Six days later, she contacted a convoy of nine ships heading north and tracked it until 0156 hours the next day. She then fired two torpedoes at a cargo ship in a surface attack. Both hit and sent *Shuntai Maru* down by the bow. An escort headed straight for the submarine and ramming seemed inevitable. *Tambor* opened fire with her aft 20-millimeter gun and turned hard to port causing the escort to pass 20 yards astern. After evading the escort, the submarine tried to regain contact with the convoy but failed.

On 2 February, she began tracking two ships. The following morning, she fired two torpedoes at a cargo ship, and both hit amidships. She directed two more at a tanker, and one hit forward of the target's stack. Both *Ariake Maru* and *Goyo Maru* sank. *Tambor* went deep and remained on the bottom under depth charge attack from 0418 to 1315. Ten days later, she encoun-

Tambor (SS–198) off San Francisco, 6 December 1943. Her conning tower is cut down to reduce her silhouette and to accommodate 20-millimeter AA guns.

tered another three-ship convoy. In a night surface attack, the submarine fired a spread of three torpedoes at a cargo ship. As *Tambor* submerged, her crew heard one hit and sink the passenger-cargo ship *Ronsan Maru*.

After repairs at Pearl Harbor, *Tambor* put to sea on 9 April en route to the Marianas. On 18 April, she attacked a 250-ton trawler loaded with food and fresh vegetables. A boarding party from the submarine killed seven members of the Japanese vessel's crew and captured the second officer. The Americans removed the ship's papers and left her afire and sinking. On 10 May, she contacted an eight-ship convoy, escorted by five destroyers and two destroyer escorts. In a submerged attack, *Tambor* fired four torpedoes at a cargo ship and heard two explosions. The submarine went deep and received 50 depth charges from the escorts. *Tambor* surfaced later and attempted to close the convoy once more. However, a destroyer picked her up and subjected her to another depth charge attack. On 26 May, she scored two hits which sank *Chiyo Maru*. *Tambor's* 10th patrol ended at Midway Island on 2 June.

The submarine conducted her next patrol in the waters off southern Hokkaido and near the Kuril Islands from 16 July to 23 August. She fired three torpedoes at a freighter on 28 July and heard three explosions. However, a dense fog prohibited her seeing the results. On 13 August, *Tambor* made a surface attack against a cargo ship and then photographed *Toei Maru* as she lowered two lifeboats and sank in 20 minutes. After returning to Midway, *Tambor* continued to Pearl Harbor for an overhaul and upkeep period.

Tambor returned to Midway on 6 October and sailed the next day for the Tokyo Bay area. On the 15th, she fired four torpedoes at three radar pips and heard one explosion. She was forced to go deep to evade 26 depth charges that were rained down around her. She emerged with no damage and attacked an escort four days later. *Tambor* fired four torpedoes and heard four explosions, but no sinking was verified. The submarine returned to Saipan from 8 to 10 November and then resumed her patrol.

Shortly before midnight on the 15th, *Tambor* fired three torpedoes at a patrol boat, but scored no hits. Forty-five minutes later, three more missed. At 0610, the submarine's commander decided to battle on the surface with his deck guns. Thirty minutes later—as the target began to sink—*Tambor's* crew took two prisoners from the water. She transferred them and a wounded crewman to *Grayson* (DD–435) on the 18th. *Tambor* ended her last war patrol at Pearl Harbor on the 30th.

Routed onward to the United States, *Tambor* arrived at San Francisco on 10 December 1944. After an extended overhaul, the submarine sailed for Puget Sound on 9 March 1945. Upon her arrival there, *Tambor* began training operations with Navy patrol aircraft under Fleet Air Wing 6. On 17 September, she departed the west coast for Portsmouth, N.H. *Tambor* was decommissioned there on 10 December 1945 and placed in reserve. In April 1947, the submarine was assigned to the 9th Naval District to train naval reservists; and she reported to the Naval Reserve Training Center, Detroit, Mich., on 8 December. *Tambor* remained on duty as a reserve training ship until 1959 when a Board of Inspection and Survey found her unfit for further naval service. She was struck from the Navy list on 1 September and subsequently sold for scrap.

Tambor received 11 battle stars for World War II service.

Tampa

A city in Hillsborough County, Fla.

I

(Coast Guard Cutter: dp. 1,181 (n.); lbp. 190'; b. 32'6" (wl.); dr. 14'1" (aft); s. 13 k. (tl.); cpl. 70; a. 3 6-pdrs.; cl. *Unalga*)

Miami—a cutter built for the Revenue Cutter Service

by the Newport News Shipbuilding & Drydock Co.—was launched on 10 February 1912; sponsored by Miss Bernes Richardson; and placed in commission by the Revenue Cutter Service at its depot at Arundel Cove, Md., on 19 August 1912.

During the following five years, *Miami* performed duties typical for cutters. She served several times on the ice patrol off the North American coast between New York and Newfoundland to locate icebergs which might be hazardous to navigation. On other occasions, she operated out of various stations along the eastern seaboard enforcing navigation and fishing laws. Her most frequent bases of operation during that period were Key West and Tampa, Fla.; Arundel Cove, Md.; and New York City. The cutter served overseas once during that half decade, in late June and early July 1914, when she served with the International Derelict Patrol out of Ponta Delgada in the Azores. On 28 January 1915, the Revenue Cutter Service and the Lifesaving Service were merged and named the United States Coast Guard. A year later, on 1 February 1916, *Miami* was renamed *Tampa*.

On 6 April 1917, when the United States entered World War I, *Tampa* was transferred to Navy jurisdiction for the duration of hostilities. During the next four months, she received heavier armament by trading her three six-pounders for four 3-inch guns and a pair of machine guns. After preparations at the Boston Navy Yard, *Tampa* moved to the New York Navy Yard on 16 September and reported for duty to the commanding officer of *Paducah* (Gunboat No. 18). Ordered to duty overseas, the warship departed New York on 29 September in company with *Paducah*, *Sterling*, *B.H.B. Hubbard* (SP–416), and five French-manned, American-made submarine chasers in tow. After stops at Halifax, Nova Scotia, and Ponta Delgada in the Azores, *Tampa* and her sailing mates reached Gibraltar on 27 October 1917.

Tampa's Navy career and war service lasted just 11 months. During that time, she was assigned ocean escort duty protecting convoys from German submarines on the route between Gibraltar and the southern coast of England. On the average, she spent more than half of her time at sea and steamed more than 3,500 nautical miles per month. Between 27 October 1917 and 31 July 1918, she escorted 18 convoys between Gibraltar and Great Britain, losing only two ships out of all those escorted. Though she brought her 4-inch guns into action several times against U-boats, *Tampa's* only verifiable run-in with a German undersea raider proved fatal to the Coast Guard cutter. During the late afternoon of 26 September 1918, *Tampa* parted company with convoy HG–107, which she had just escorted into the Irish Sea from Gibraltar. Ordered to put into Milford Haven, England, she proceeded independently toward her destination. That evening, as she transited the Bristol Channel, the warship crossed the sights of *UB–91*. The U-boat made a submerged attack which sank *Tampa* with a single torpedo.

Little further information on the sinking is available. It appears that the action took place sometime between 2030 and 2100. She disappeared over the horizon at about 1900, and the radio operator on board the convoy flagship reported having felt the shock of an underwater explosion at about 2045. Furthermore, German records of *UB–91's* war cruise specifically identify *Tampa* as the ship she sank "at evening twilight" on 26 September. In all probability, *Tampa* went down rapidly without ever seeing her adversary or bringing her defenses into action. She sank with all hands—115 officers and men as well as 16 passengers. Search and rescue efforts over the succeeding three days turned up only some wreckage, clearly identified as coming from *Tampa*, and a single unidentified body. Her name was struck from the Navy list as of the date of her sinking.

II

(Coast Guard Cutter No. 48: dp. 1,955 (f.); l. 240'; b. 39'1''; dr. 17'9'' (max.); s. 15.5 k.; cpl. 122; a. 2 5'', 1 3'', 2 6-pdrs.; cl. *Tampa*)

Tampa (Coast Guard Cutter No. 48)—a steel-hulled, single-screw cutter—was laid down on 27 September 1920 at Oakland, Calif., by the Union Construction Co.; launched on 19 April 1921; sponsored by Mrs. Joseph P. Conners; and commissioned on 15 September 1921, Lt. Comdr. M. J. Wheeler, USCG, in command.

Tampa got underway for the east coast, transited the Panama Canal on 28 October, and arrived at New York on 7 November. On the 23d, the cutter shifted to Boston, Mass., her home port. In the ensuing years, *Tampa* operated as part of the International Ice Patrol established in the aftermath of the *Titanic* tragedy in 1912. Between March and July—the peak months in which icebergs were regarded as a menace to the northernmost transatlantic sea lanes—*Tampa* conducted regular patrols, alternating with *Modoc* (Coast Guard Cutter No. 39) on 15-day stretches. At the end of each patrol, the cutter would put into Halifax, Nova Scotia, for stores and fuel. Between these cruises in the frigid waters at the northern end of the Atlantic, the cutter operated on exercises and maneuvers, sharpened her skill with target practice and battle drills, and patrolled sailing regattas.

Shifted to the New York division, with headquarters at Stapleton, N.Y., in August of 1932, *Tampa* arrived at her new home port on the 27th of the month. She operated from this base until the late 1930's. During this time, she participated in the drama which accompanied the tragic fire on board the Ward Line steamer SS *Morro Castle*.

At about 0230 on the morning of 8 September 1934, a fire broke out on board the passenger ship as she was returning from a Caribbean cruise. The fires spread rapidly, and incompetent seamanship on the behalf of her captain—who had only taken command after the ship's regular master had died earlier that evening—resulted in the loss of many lives.

Moored at Staten Island when *Morro Castle* caught fire, *Tampa* received word of the disaster at 0436 on the morning of 8 September. She hurriedly recalled her liberty party, got up steam, and put out to sea at 1540. It took two hours to reach the scene of the holocaust; but when she arrived, *Tampa* assumed direction of the rescue operations which, by that time, were already well underway. Surfboats from the Coast Guard's Shark River Station—the first help to arrive—had rescued some 120 people before the New York pilot boat and boats from the Sandy Hook Station appeared and joined in the effort. The cutter *Cahoone* had also been on station for some time.

Tampa passed a towline to the stricken ship, but it soon parted with the sharp crack of a pistol shot and fouled the cutter's screw. *Tampa*, herself, drifted perilously close to shore before the cutter *Sebago* towed her out of danger. When conducted in smooth seas, operations to save lives are difficult enough. The gale raging off the New Jersey shore on the morning of 8 September made matters markedly worse. Nevertheless, the Coast Guardsmen performed feats of great heroism in rescuing the liner's passengers and crew from the storm-tossed waves. During the rescue, *Tampa* had accounted for 140 survivors.

Shifted to Mobile, Ala., in the late 1930's, *Tampa* operated in the Gulf of Mexico into 1941. The cutter came under naval jurisdiction in November 1941, a month before Japan attacked Pearl Harbor. Apparently shifted back to the North Atlantic for coastwise convoy escort runs in the Greenland area, *Tampa* departed Narsarssuak, Greenland, on 3 May 1942 to escort the merchantman *Chatham* to the Cape Cod Canal. The ships stopped briefly at St. John's, Newfoundland, and then pushed on toward the Massachusetts coast. *Tampa* lost track of *Chatham* in dense fog on the 16th but regained contact near the eastern entrance of the canal and safely conducted the merchantman on her way. *Tampa* then searched, unsuccessfully, for a German U-boat reported in the vicinity before she put into Boston on the 17th.

She remained there for repairs and alterations until the 30th when she sailed for Argentia, Newfoundland. While escorting SS *Montrose*, *Tampa* picked up a sound contact and dropped depth charges but could not claim a "kill." On 3 June, *Montrose* ran aground on Moratties Reef. *Tampa*, assisted by two naval vessels, soon floated the merchantman free; and the cutter continued her

USCGC *Tampa* (WPG–48) in the light blue and white camouflage worn by many escort ships in the North Atlantic. Color schemes of this kind were developed in the British and American navies for protection against submarine observation at night and in the overcast weather prevalent in winter on the convoy routes. (26–G–09–20–43(2))

escort mission, routed onward to Greenland. Arriving at Sondrestromfjord on the 10th, *Tampa* conducted harbor entrance patrols before proceeding to Ivigtut. There, she guarded the cryolite mine—which provided ore vitally needed for the production of aluminum—from the 16th to the 26th.

During the last half of 1942, *Tampa*—designated WPG–48 in or around February 1942—conducted 12 more convoy escort missions between Iceland, Greenland, and Nova Scotia. She departed Argentia on 1 January 1943, in company with *Tahoma* (WPG–80), bound for St. John's where she arrived soon thereafter. Moored until the 6th, *Tampa* then got underway to escort a convoy routed to Greenland and then screened two groups of merchantmen—GS–18 and ON–161—to Newfoundland.

On 29 January, she got underway, with *Escanaba* (WPG–77) and *Comanche* (WPG–75), to escort Army transport *Dorchester* and merchantman SS *Biscaya* and SS *Lutz* to Greeland. Bad weather soon hampered the convoy's progress; and the flank escorts, *Comanche* and *Escanaba*, soon experienced difficulties keeping station. Icing had increased their displacement and reduced their speed accordingly. This fact, in turn, slowed the whole convoy. By 2 February, the weather had somewhat improved; but a radio direction finder had discovered the presence of an enemy submarine. *Tampa* accordingly screened ahead, some 3,000 yards from *Dorchester*, while *Escanaba* and *Comanche* were deployed on each flank, 5,400 yards from *Lutz* and *Biscaya*, respectively.

Convoy SG–19, as it was known, soon came into the periscope sights of *U–223*, which maneuvered astern to bring her tubes to bear. The U-boat fired her deadly "fish" which struck *Dorchester* astern at 0355. *Tampa* observed the transport veering hard to port and showing numerous small lights. *Biscaya* quickly fired two green signal rockets and executed an emergency turn to avoid fouling the mortally stricken *Dorchester*.

Three minutes after *Dorchester* had been struck, her master ordered her abandoned. As the ship went down, four Army chaplains gave up their life jackets to soldiers who had none to ensure the survival of others at the expense of themselves. Meanwhile, *Escanaba* and *Comanche* searched for *U–223*, while *Tampa* escorted *Lutz* and *Biscaya* to Skovfjord before returning to assist in the hunt for survivors. *Tampa* subsequently searched for survivors on the 4th, but sighted only numerous bodies; two swamped lifeboats manned only by corpses; and seven life rafts. She found no signs of life before she returned to Narsarssuak on 6 February.

Tampa resumed convoy operations, performing local escort in the Greenland area for the remainder of February 1943. She continued these operations through the spring. On 12 June 1943, she departed Narsarssuak with four other escorts, escorting a three-ship convoy for Argentia. The next day, at 0508, she observed smoke on the horizon, and received a report that *Escanaba* was afire. In fact, *Escanaba* had been blown to bits by an explosion of undetermined origin. Only three survivors were picked up by *Raritan* (WYT–93), and one of these died. The other two could not explain what had destroyed their ship.

Tampa escorted convoys for the remainder of 1943 before returning to Boston on the last day of the year for an overhaul which extended through January 1944. She resumed convoy escort operations in the North Atlantic, between Boston and Greenland—primarily in the Argentia and Narsarssuak vicinities—and continued the task through 1944 and into 1945.

With the cessation of hostilities in Europe in May 1945, *Tampa* resumed ice patrols off the Grand Banks in June through August, alternating with *Modoc* (WPG–46) and *Mojave* (WPG–47). Departing Argentia on 6 September 1945, less than a month after the war against Japan ended, *Tampa* operated between that port and Boston, receiving a 30-day availability at the Coast Guard yard in Boston in November and December.

Tampa subsequently cruised on North Atlantic ice patrol duties into August 1946. She was decommissioned late that year and turned over to the Maritime Commission's War Shipping Administration which sold her to Charles M. Barnett, Jr., on 22 September 1947.

Tampico

A major seaport city in Mexico on the Gulf of Mexico.

(Sch.: t. 80; a. 1 gun)

During the Mexican War, *Pueblano*—a wooden-hulled schooner sometimes listed as *Pueblana*—was seized by the 20-gun sloop-of-war *St. Mary's* while on an expedition against Tampico led by Commodore Connor. A prize crew sailed the schooner to the American Navy's staging-point at Anton Lizardo where she was fitted out and renamed *Tampico*.

Under the command of Lt. William P. Griffin, *Tampico* participated in the attack on Vera Cruz and the fortress castle of San Juan d'Ulloa in March 1847. She served in the inshore covering force and fired on what she determined to be Mexican cavalry massing behind the sand dunes along the shore at Vera Cruz.

Vera Cruz fell on 27 March, and the castle of San Juan d'Ulloa surrendered two days later. With the successful conclusion of the investment of Vera Cruz, *Tampico* subsequently took part in the operations against the town of Alvarado. After the close of hostilities with Mexico, the schooner was sold in 1849 at Norfolk, Va.

Tanager

Any of the numerous American, passerine birds. The brightly colored males are unmusical and inhabit woodlands.

I

(Minesweeper No. 5: dp. 840; l. 187'10''; b. 35'6''; dr. 10'3½''; s. 14 k.; cpl. 85; a. 2 3''; cl. *Lapwing*)

Tanager (Minesweeper No. 5) was laid down on 28 September 1917 at New York City, by the Staten Island Shipbuilding Co.; launched on 2 March 1918; sponsored by Mrs. G. H. Bates; and commissioned on 28 June 1918, Lt. (jg.) Michael Higgins in command.

After operating locally out of Boston through the late summer of 1918, *Tanager*, in company with *Western King*, departed New London, Conn., on 26 September, bound for the Azores. The minesweeper subsequently operated out of Punta Delgada on local escort duties with the Azores detachment through the fall, before pushing on toward Portugal and reaching Lisbon on the day after Christmas 1918. Later in her tour in European waters, she delivered a case of serum to *Georgia* (Battleship No. 15) which apparently was trying to combat an outbreak of influenza.

In the spring, *Tanager* was assigned to the Minesweeping Detachment established to clear the North Sea Mine Barrage from between the shores of Scotland and Norway and arrived at Kirkwall, Scotland, on 7 May 1919. The barrage—which had been laid during World War I to prevent a sortie by the German High Seas Fleet and forays by German U-boats—now prevented the resumption of the commercial shipping which had criss-crossed the North Sea before the war.

While sweeping Group 9, the third operation conducted by the mine force, *Tanager* suffered damage in heavy weather and was forced to put into Kirkwall for a week of repairs. Besides the hazards posed by Neptune in the stormy North Sea, the mines provided their own particular brand of danger. While sweeping Group 10 late in June, *Tanager* fouled a mine in one of her "kites"; and it exploded close aboard, again forcing the ship to limp to Kirkwall for repairs. The severity of her damage required a period in the Admiralty dock at Chatham.

By late summer, the barrage had been swept. In company with other vessels of her squadron, *Tanager* sailed

Tanager (AM-5) in the North Sea, with minesweeping cables streamed. (NR&L(M) 6753)

for the United States on 1 October and—after stops at Brest, France; Lisbon; and Hamilton, Bermuda—arrived at New York on 19 November. For part of the voyage, from Lisbon to Hamilton, she towed *SC-272*.

Upon completion of permanent repairs at Charleston, S.C., *Tanager* was assigned to the Pacific Fleet in December 1919. She was reclassified AM-5 on 17 July 1920. The minesweeper steamed to the Hawaiian Islands and operated out of Pearl Harbor from 1920 to 1941. Her services for the Fleet included target-towing, participation in mine-laying and minesweeping exercises, and transportation of men and mail. In addition, she took part in scientific expeditions to the Necker and Nihoa Islands in the Hawaiian chain and operated briefly at Wake Island in the summer of 1923 during an ornithological survey. In August 1925, she served on a plane guard station for the PN flying boats' unsuccessful flight from the west coast to Hawaii.

Her routine duties at Pearl Harbor were twice interrupted. In early 1928, she was assigned duty as station ship at Pago Pago, Samoa; and, late in March, she unsuccessfully attempted to free SS *Steelmaker*, aground on Mitchell Island. In 1930, *Tanager* operated between Mare Island and San Diego, Calif., for a time, towing and assisting in the preparation of many decommissioned flush-deck, four-pipe destroyers for inactive berthing at the Destroyer Base at the latter place.

In early 1941, *Tanager* received a major overhaul which transformed her silhouette. Her heavy foremast and boom were removed; splinter-shielding was added around her guns and upper bridge; and a depth-charge track was fitted astern. Thus outfitted, she lost excess topside weight and now had better fields of fires for her antiaircraft battery. Assigned to Mine Division 9, Asiatic Fleet, *Tanager* sailed from Pearl Harbor on 11 May 1941, bound for the Asiatic Station. The minecraft proceeded via Guam to the Philippines. En route, she plane-guarded for two PBY's being flown out as rein-

forcements for Admiral Thomas C. Hart's air patrol forces.

Calling at Guam from 29 to 30 May, *Tanager* arrived at Manila on 5 June. She commenced local operations almost immediately and, for the next few months, made patrols off the Corregidor minefields; towed targets for destroyer and submarine exercises; and conducted minesweeping and minelaying duties. From October through December, *Tanager* participated in the laying of an antisubmarine net across Mariveles Bay, Bataan —a difficult operation accomplished in spite of the fact that there were no specialized net-laying craft in the Philippines.

On 8 December 1941 (7 December east of the International Date Line), Japanese planes struck Pearl Harbor and plunged the United States into the Pacific War. On the next day, Japanese planes destroyed General Douglas MacArthur's Far Eastern Air Force on the ground on its Philippine fields and struck the Cavite Navy Yard on the 10th. *Tanager* lay alongside Machina Wharf when the high-level bombers came over dropping their lethal loads. In the ensuing holocaust, the minesweeper managed to leave the area. Others were not so fortunate. *Bittern* (AM-36) was wrecked; *Sealion* (SS-195) was sunk alongside a pier; and *Peary* (DD-226) and *Pillsbury* (DD-227) were damaged. More importantly, Cavite was destroyed as an operating base for the Asiatic Fleet.

With Cavite out of commission and Manila declared an "open city" on Christmas Day 1941, American and Filipino forces withdrew to Bataan and Corregidor. *Tanager* carried the equipment and staff of the Commandant, 16th Naval District, Rear Admiral Francis W. Rockwell, out to the "Rock" during his withdrawal; and she subsequently operated out of Corregidor on inshore patrol duties. In ensuing months, *Tanager* and her dwindling number of sister ships and former China river gunboats lived a furtive, hunted existence. *Tanager* served almost until the bitter end. On 4 May

1942, the day of the commencement of the Battle of the Coral Sea, the minesweeper was hit by shore battery fire from Japanese guns emplaced on Bataan. Mortally hit, she sank off Corregidor that day.

Tanager was struck from the Navy list on 8 May 1942 and received one battle star for her valiant service in the Philippine campaign in 1941 and 1942.

II

(AM–385: dp. 890; l. 221'1''; b. 32'2''; dr. 10'9'' (mean); s. 18.1 k. (tl.); cpl. 117; a. 1 3''; cl. *Auk*)

The second *Tanager* (AM–385) was laid down at Lorain, Ohio, on 29 March 1944 by the American Shipbuilding Co.; launched on 9 December 1944; sponsored by Mrs. Thomas Slingluff; and commissioned on 28 July 1945, Lt. Comdr. Oscar B. Lundgren, USNR, in command.

Tanager steamed via the St. Lawrence River to Boston, Mass., in late July and early August. In October, she moved south to the Naval Amphibious Base at Little Creek, Va., for shakedown training and minesweeping exercises in the Chesapeake Bay area. For almost six years, *Tanager* operated with the 2d Fleet along the eastern seaboard and in the Caribbean area. She conducted minesweeping exercises and supported the training efforts of the Mine Warfare School at Yorktown, Va. On three occasions—once each in 1948, 1950, and 1951—she did tours of duty with the Naval Mine Countermeasures Station, located at Panama City, Fla.

On 2 September 1951, she departed Charleston, S.C., for the Mediterranean Sea. While she was deployed with the 6th Fleet, she conducted more minesweeping exercises and visited many of the famous ports in the area. Among those were Mers-el-Kebir, Gibraltar, Naples, Monaco, Cannes, Venice, Malta, and Genoa. In February 1952, *Tanager* returned to Charleston and resumed operations with the 2d Fleet. After repairs at Charleston and a voyage to Norfolk and back, the minesweeper began her second Mediterranean deployment in April 1953. During that cruise, she added some new ports-of-call to her itinerary, notably Tangier, Palermo, Marseille, Leghorn, Salonika, and Seville. She also participated in a number of minesweeping exercises with other units of the 6th Fleet. *Tanager* re-entered Charleston on 26 October 1953.

Following minesweeping exercises along the southeastern coast of the United States and in the Caribbean, she entered the yard at Savannah Machine & Foundry Co. on 29 June 1954 for repairs. On 23 September, the minesweeper departed Savannah and headed for Beaumont, Tex. She arrived on the 28th and entered the drydock the same day. She was refloated on 8 October and towed to the naval station at Orange, Tex. Two months later, on 10 December 1954, *Tanager* was decommissioned and berthed there with the Atlantic Reserve Fleet. On 7 February 1955, the minesweeper was redesignated MSF–385. On 4 October 1963, *Tanager* was transferred to the Coast Guard for use as a training cutter. Her name was struck from the Navy list on 1 November 1963, and she was commissioned in the Coast Guard as *Tanager* (WTR–885) on 16 July 1964. She was decommissioned once more on 1 February 1972; and, on 15 November, she was sold to Mr. William A. Hardesty of Seattle, Wash.

Tanamo

(Id. No. 2176: dp. 6,000; l. 331'1''; b. 45'2''; dr. 21'1''; s. 12 k.; cpl. 105)

Tanamo (Id. No. 2176)—built in 1914 as *Van Hogendorp* by Swain Hunter and Wigham Richardson, Newcastle-on-Tyne, England—was taken over by the Navy at New York on 9 August 1918 on a bare-boat basis from the Sarnia Steamship Corp., Broadway, N.Y. She was refitted as a refrigerator ship and commissioned on 17 August 1918.

Tanamo, assigned to duty with the Naval Overseas Transportation Service, loaded a cargo of beef and 57 trucks and sailed in a convoy on the 17th for France. Due to boiler trouble, she dropped out of the convoy, entering Halifax on the 30th for temporary repairs and then proceeding on 5 September to New York for additional repairs. On 4 October, *Tanamo* sailed with a convoy for Verdon, arrived there on the 20th and unloaded her cargo.

The ship sailed for home on 3 November and arrived at New York on the 19th. After general repairs and loading 1,479 tons of beef and a deck load of trucks, she returned to St. Nazaire on 14 December 1918. She began her last round-trip voyage from New York to France for the Navy on 15 February 1919.

Upon her return to New York on 2 April, the ship was scheduled for demobilization. *Tanamo* was decommissioned on 24 April 1919 and returned to her owner.

Tananek Bay

A misspelling of Tonowek Bay which is located in Alaskan waters north of the Gulf of Esquibel between Prince of Wales Island and Hecata Island.

Tananek Bay (CVE–88) was renamed *Cape Esperance* (q.v.) on 6 November 1943.

Tancred

Tancred de Hauteville (1078?–1112)—a Norman hero—joined the first Crusade (1096–1099) and distinguished himself as a military leader during the capture of Nicaea and Tarsus, the siege of Antioch, the capture of Jerusalem, and the Battle of Ascalon. Subsequently becoming Prince of Galilee and, later, of Edessa, Tancred's valorous deeds are recounted in Tasso's *Jerusalem Delivered*.

(BAT–13: dp. 763; l. 143'0''; b. 33' 0''; dr. 17'0''; s. 14 k.; cpl. 34; a. 1 3'', 4 20mm; cl. *Oriana*)

Tancred (BAT–13) was laid down on 3 September 1942 at Port Arthur, Tex., by the Gulfport Boiler and Welding Works; launched on 1 January 1943; and delivered to the United Kingdom under lend-lease on 18 February 1943.

Tancred, given the pennant number of W–104 in the Royal Navy, departed Port Arthur, Tex., on 8 March for service in the North Atlantic. After six months under the White Ensign, the tug was transferred to Australia on 2 September 1944, and she served the Royal Australian Navy for one year before she was returned to the custody of the United States Navy on 2 September 1945. Retransferred the same day back to the Australians, *Tancred* served "down under" until 2 August 1948, when she was again returned to the custody of the United States.

Sold—via the Office of the Foreign Liquidation Commission—to Australia on 5 August, *Tancred*'s name was struck from the Navy list on 23 March 1949.

Beginning a career with the Australian Salvage Board in 1949, *Tancred* subsequently served under the aegis of the Department of Marine and Harbours, South Australia. Based at Port Adelaide, Australia, the salvage tug still served in this role, as of 1979, with that department.

Taney

Roger Brooke Taney—born on 17 March 1777 in Calvert County, Md.—graduated from Dickinson College in 1795 and soon began law studies at Annapolis, Md. Admitted to the Maryland bar in 1799, he entered politics as a Federalist in the same year and won a term in the Maryland legislature. During the War of 1812, he was among the dissenting Federalists who supported President Madison's foreign policy; and, after peace returned, he won a dominant position in Federalist circles within Maryland.

In 1823, Taney moved to Baltimore where he established a highly successful law practice and enhanced his reputation as an eminent attorney. After the demise of the Federalist Party, he chaired the committee supporting General Andrew Jackson's presidential candidacy and, during a reorganization of the cabinet in 1831, Taney was appointed United States Attorney General.

In this capacity, Taney became President Jackson's principal advisor in the attack on the United States Bank. In September 1833, Jackson gave Taney a recess appointment as Secretary of the Treasury for the special purpose of establishing depositories in state banks into which Federal funds could be transferred. After Congress reconvened, the Senate refused to approve the nomination; and Taney resumed private practice.

On 28 December 1835, President Jackson picked Taney to succeed John Marshall as Chief Justice of the Supreme Court; and, despite Whig opposition, the appointment was confirmed on 15 March 1836.

During his time on the bench, Taney gave opinions in many cases in which he generally upheld states rights and narrowly construed the Constitution's grant of powers to the Federal Government. In the Dred Scott decision in 1857—his most famous—Taney held that Congress had no power to abolish slavery in the territories acquired after the formation of the Federal Government. He held that slavery was a necessary evil as long as negroes remained in the United States, and he further maintained that negroes did not hold citizenship and therefore could not sue in a Federal court.

Throughout the Civil War, Taney continued to resist any infringement of state's rights and believed the Federal Government had erred in pursuing war to bring seceding states back into the Union. Justice Taney died in Washington, D.C., on 12 October 1864.

I

(RC: t. 112; lbp. 73'4''; b. 20'6''; dph. 9'4''; a. 6 12-pdrs.)

Taney—sometimes referred to as Roger B. Taney—was a wooden-hulled, schooner-rigged revenue cutter completed in late 1833 or early 1834 at New York City by Webb and Allen. In January 1834, she embarked on a special cruise off the east and gulf coasts, from Maine to Texas. Relieving revenue cutter Jefferson on station at Norfolk, Va., in November of 1834, Taney later extended her cruising grounds to Baltimore, Md., in October 1837. She sailed to New York for repairs in the summer of 1843.

Taney maintained this schedule of regular cruises with the Revenue Cutter Service until the onset of hostilities with Mexico when she was placed under Navy orders. Although the latter country possessed meager resources for outfitting privateers, commercial interests in the United States feared that she might issue a few letters-of-marque permitting privately-owned armed ships to prey upon American shipping.

Although the Spanish government cooperated in suppressing the few attempts that had been made to outfit privateers in Spanish ports, the United States dispatched Taney—with sloop-of-war Marion and steamer Princeton—to the Mediterranean station to prevent the appearance of Mexican privateers there. Taney arrived at Gibraltar on 29 August 1847 and remained there until she returned to the United States on 22 August 1849.

The revenue cutter departed New York at the end of October 1849 and conducted soundings in the Atlantic before being transferred to the United States Coast Survey in August of 1850. The following year, turmoil raged on the island of Cuba. The United States sought to steer a neutral course by prohibiting "filibustering" from her shores. Taney sailed southward for Florida waters to seek out a suspected lair of filibusters up the St. Illa River. She found nothing suspicious, however, and her commanding officer, Capt. T. C. Rudolph, subsequently reported that apparently the expedition had been cancelled.

Taney returned to New York harbor in the summer of 1852, where she capsized on 3 August. Eventually righted and repaired at the New York Navy Yard, Taney operated out of Eastport, Maine, from January 1853 until October 1855, when she shifted south to cruise out of Savannah, Ga. After being repaired at Norfolk in August 1857, she returned to her station at Savannah. While operating from that base, she was struck by lightning off Tybee Island, Ga., and severely damaged on 30 August 1857.

Taney was subsequently sold on 5 January 1858.

II

(Coast Guard Cutter No. 68: dp. 2,702 (f.); l. 327'; b. 41'2''; dr. 14' (mean); s. 20.8 k.; cpl. 123; a. 2 5'', 2 6-pdrs., 1 1-pdr., 2 .50-cal. mg.; cl. "Secretary")

Roger B. Taney (Coast Guard Cutter No. 68) was laid down on 1 May 1935 at the Philadelphia Navy Yard; launched on 3 June 1936; sponsored by Miss Corinne F. Taney; and commissioned at Philadelphia on 24 October 1936, Comdr. W. K. Thompson, USCG, in command.

Roger B. Taney departed Philadelphia on 19 December, transited the Panama Canal from the 27th to the 29th, and arrived at her home port, Honolulu, Territory of Hawaii, on 18 January 1937. She conducted local operations out of Honolulu through the summer of 1937.

Roger B. Taney had arrived in the Pacific at a time when the United States was expanding its commercial air travel capabilities. The "Clipper" flights across the Pacific to the Far East made islands like Hawaii, Midway, Guam, and Wake important way-stations. Other islands and islets assumed greater importance when a route across the South Pacific was mapped out to Australia and Samoa. The military benefits which accrued to the United States by its expansion onto some of the more strategic bits of land in the broad Pacific were not lost upon President Franklin D. Roosevelt, who undertook, in the late 1930's, to annex territory in the Pacific.

Two such places were Canton and Enderbury Islands. Roger B. Taney played a role in their colonization by the United States. In early March 1938, the Coast Guard cutter loaded supplies and embarked colonists who would establish the claim of the United States upon the two islands that seemed—at least to the uninitiated —to be mere hunks of coral, rock, and scrub in the Central Pacific. Roger B. Taney disembarked four Hawaiians at Enderbury Island on 6 March 1938 and landed a second contingent—of seven colonists—at Canton Island on the next day. The men, assisted by the Coast Guardsmen, erected buildings and laid the foundations for future signal towers.

The Coast Guard's task over the ensuing years leading up to the outbreak of war in the Pacific was to supply these isolated way-stations along the transpacific air routes and to relieve the colonists at stated intervals. Roger B. Taney performed these supply missions into 1940. Meanwhile, tension continued to rise in the Far East as Japan cast covetous glances at the American, British, Dutch, and French colonial possessions and marched deeper into embattled China.

As the Navy and Coast Guard began gradually increasing and augmenting the armament on its vessels to prepare them for the inexorably advancing war, Roger B. Taney underwent her first major rearmament at the Pearl Harbor Navy Yard in December 1940. She received her last major pre-war refit at the Mare Island Navy Yard, Vallejo, Calif., in the spring of the following year, 1941.

On 25 July 1941, the Coast Guard cutter was trans-

Taney (WPG–37) in the Atlantic in April, 1944. (26–G–06–11–44(08))

ferred to the Navy and reported for duty with the local defense forces of the 14th Naval District, maintaining her base at Honolulu. By this time, the ship's name had apparently been shortened to *Taney*.

Outside of another "line island cruise" in the late summer, *Taney* operated locally out of Honolulu into the critical fall of 1941. She conducted regular harbor entrance and channel patrols, alternating often with one of the four old destroyers of Destroyer Divison 80: *Allen* (DD–66), *Schley* (DD–103), *Chew* (DD–106), and *Ward* (DD–139).

The message: "Air Raid, Pearl Harbor. This is no drill" came at 0755 on 7 December, as Japanese planes swept overhead in an attempt to cripple the Pacific Fleet's retaliatory power. *Taney*, moored alongside Pier 6, Honolulu harbor, stood to her antiaircraft guns swiftly when word of the surprise attack reached her simultaneously. As no Japanese attacks were directed at Honolulu harbor, the Coast Guard cutter was only given the opportunity to fire at stray aircraft which happened to venture into her vicinity. She was firing upon unidentified aircraft as late as noon, indicating that the eager Coast Guardsmen were probably shooting at American planes—not Japanese.

Taney patrolled the waters off Honolulu for the remainder of 1941 and into 1942, conducting many depth charge attacks on suspected submarines in the wake of the Pearl Harbor attack. During this time, the ship received the classification WPG–37. On 22 January 1942, the cutter departed Honolulu in company with SS *Barbara Olson*, and arrived at Canton Island on the 28th. After sending a working party ashore to unload supplies, *Taney* screened *Barbara Olson* offshore until 7 February, when both ships got underway to evacuate the American colony on Enderbury Island. Embarking the four colonists at 1015 that day, *Taney* shelled the island and destroyed the buildings there before sailing for Jarvis Island.

Taney subsequently escorted her merchantman consort to Jarvis Island, where she evacuated the four Interior Department colonists and burned all structures to the ground before departing. Reaching Palmyra on the 12th, the ships remained there until the 15th, before

Taney headed back for the Hawaiian Islands, arriving at Honolulu on 5 March.

Taney operated locally out of Honolulu into 1943 before sailing for Boston late that winter. Prior to heading for the east coast, the ship received a regunning at Mare Island, being fitted with four single-mount, 5-inch guns, making her the only ship in her class with this modification. After making port at Boston on 14 March 1944, *Taney* soon shifted south to Hampton Roads, where she arrived on 31 March. Early in April, she departed Norfolk as a unit of Task Force (TF) 66 as convoy guide for convoy UGS–38.

The passage across the Atlantic proved uneventful, as the convoy made landfall off the Azores on 13 April. Some 35 minutes after sunset on the 20th, the convoy was spotted and tracked by the Germans, who launched a three-pronged attack with Junkers 88's and Heinkel 111's participating. Each flew very low, using the shoreline as a background, thus confusing the search radar of the Allied ships. The first wave struck from dead ahead, torpedoing SS *Paul Hamilton* and SS *Samite*. The former, which had been carrying ammunition, blew up in a shattering explosion—and all 504 men on board her were killed in the blast.

The second wave of German torpedo planes bagged SS *Stephen F. Austin* and SS *Royal Star*; during this melee, two torpedoes churned past *Taney* close aboard. The third wave mortally wounded *Lansdale* (DD–426), which later sank. All of the damaged vessels—save *Paul Hamilton* and *Lansdale*—reached Bizerte, Tunisia, on the 21st. *Taney* later departed Bizerte with homeward-bound convoy GUS–38 and arrived at New York on 21 May.

The Coast Guard cutter conducted two more round-trip convoy escort missions, with convoys UGS/GUS–45 and UGS/GUS–52. Detached as a unit of TF 66 on 9 October 1944, *Taney* sailed for the Boston Navy Yard soon thereafter for extensive yard work to convert her to an amphibious command ship. During this metamorphosis, *Taney*—classified as WAGC–37—was fitted with accommodations for an embarked flag officer and his staff, as well as with increased communications and radar facilities. Her main battery, too, underwent change: she now sported two open-mount 5-inch guns, as well as 40 and 20-millimeter antiaircraft guns. With the work completed in early January 1945, *Taney* departed Boston on 19 January, bound for Norfolk, Va.

She conducted shakedown and training in her new configuration before departing the east coast and sailing, via the Panama Canal and San Diego, to Hawaii. Arriving at Pearl Harbor on 22 February 1945, she soon embarked Rear Admiral Calvin H. Cobb and later underwent various minor repairs. New communications equipment was also installed before the ship departed the Hawaiian Islands for the Marshalls on 10 March.

Taney proceeded independently via Eniwetok and arrived at Ulithi on 23 March, remaining there until 7 April. Joining TG 51.8, the amphibious command ship proceeded to Okinawa and arrived off the Hagushi beaches amidst air raid alerts on the 11th. During one raid, her antiaircraft gunners scored at least three hits on a "Betty" bomber which crossed the ship's bow 1,200 yards away, and later during her first day at Okinawa experienced four more "red alerts." The ship briefly shifted to Kerama Retto from the 13th to the 15th before returning to Hagushi on the latter date.

By the end of May, *Taney* had gone to general quarters 119 times, with the crew remaining at battle stations for up to nine hours at a stretch. During this period off Okinawa in April and May, *Taney* downed four suicide planes and assisted in numerous other "kills." The command ship also conducted combat information center duties, maintaining complete radar and air coverage, receiving and evaluating information on both friendly and enemy activities. On one occasion, *Taney*'s duties took her close inshore—close enough to even receive fire close aboard from a Japanese shore battery.

Suicide air attacks by the Japanese continued throughout June, although most were intercepted by combat air patrol (CAP) fighters and downed before they could reach their targets. Such raids took place on 18 out of 30 days that month. On 25 June, at 0120, a float seaplane passed near *Taney*, provoking return fire from the command ship and batteries ashore which combined to splash the intruder. During this month-long period, at least 288 enemy planes attacked the ships in *Taney*'s vicinity, and at least 96 of these were destroyed.

As if the Japanese menace alone were not enough, in mid-July a typhoon forced the ships at Hagushi to take evasive action. *Taney* led a convoy eastward on the 19th and returned the next day when the storm passed. She performed the same duties again on the first day of the following month when she led a convoy to sea on typhoon-evasion operations. The ship returned to its anchorage on the 3d.

The end of the war found *Taney* still off Okinawa. On 16 August, she got underway to support *Pennsylvania* (BB-38) as three Japanese planes were detected approaching from the northeast. One crashed 30 miles to the north, and two splashed into the sea shortly thereafter. On 25 August, TG 95.5 was dissolved, and Rear Admiral Cobb, who had been embarked during the Okinawa campaign, hauled down his flag and departed.

Taney soon proceeded to Japan, where she took part in the occupation of Wakayama, anchoring off the port city on 11 September and sending a working party ashore the next day. While anchored there, *Taney* weathered a typhoon which swirled by on the 17th. She was, in fact, one of the few ships which stayed at her berth during the storm, her ground tackle holding well in the sticky clay bottom.

Departing Wakayama on 14 October, *Taney* returned to the west coast of the United States, via Midway, and arrived at San Francisco on 29 October. Moving on for the east coast, *Taney* transited the Panama Canal and later arrived at her ultimate destination, Charleston, S.C., on 29 November. During the ensuing period of conversion, the Coast Guard vessel was re-

configured as a patrol cutter. She now sported a main battery of a single-mount, 5-inch gun, a hedgehog, a twin 40-millimeter mount, and two 20-millimeter guns, in addition to depth charge tracks and projectors.

Upon shifting back to the west coast, *Taney* was based at Alameda, Calif., into the 1970's. Although she is listed with the ships receiving engagement stars for Korean service, she has no awards listed, indicating her presence only in a support role outside the geographical vicinity of Korean waters. She served as an ocean station weather ship; a fishery patrol vessel; and a search and rescue ship. Having been reclassified back to gunboat—WPG-37—the ship was now reclassified again, this time as a high-endurance cutter, and received the designation of WHEC-37 in June of 1967.

In the spring of 1969, *Taney* participated in Operation "Market Time" off the coast of Vietnam. She served a 10-month tour of duty, providing gunfire support and preventing enemy infiltration along the coastal routes used by the Viet Cong and North Vietnamese forces.

In 1972, *Taney* was shifted back to the east coast and was assigned duty on the last sea-going weather station: "Hotel" off the coasts of Maryland and Virginia. Fitted with a special storm-tracking antenna housed in a distinctive bulbous dome fitted atop her pilot house, *Taney* deployed seven times yearly, conducting 21 deployments 200 miles off the coast. This last ocean station had been established to track storms threatening the middle states on the east coast which had often struck without warning. Eventually, the use of more sophisticated storm-tracking satellites and radars rendered this station obsolete. Hence, Ocean Station "Hotel" was closed down in 1977.

Now based out of Norfolk, Va., *Taney* stands ready to conduct search and rescue missions at sea to protect American fisheries and to enforce the 200-mile limit. She served into 1979 in keeping with the Coast Guard's motto: "Always Ready"—*Semper Paratus.*

Taney received three battle stars for World War II service.

Tang

Any surgeonfish, especially of the several West Indian species.

I

(SS-306: dp. 1,525 (surf.), 2,424 (subm.); l. 311'6"; b. 27'2"; dr. 15'2"; s. 20.25 k. (surf.), 8.75 k. (subm.); cpl. 66; a. 10 21" tt., 1 5", 1 40mm; cl. *Balao*)

The first *Tang* (SS-306) was laid down on 15 January 1943 at Vallejo, Calif., by the Mare Island Navy Yard; launched on 17 August 1943; sponsored by Mrs. Antonio S. Pitre; and commissioned on 15 October 1943, Lt. Comdr. Richard H. O'Kane in command.

Tang completed fitting out at Mare Island and then moved south to San Diego for 18 days of intensive training before sailing for Hawaii. She arrived at Pearl Harbor on 8 January 1944 and conducted two more weeks of exercises in preparation for combat. *Tang* stood out of Pearl Harbor on 22 January to begin her first war patrol in the Caroline-Mariana Islands area.

On the morning of 17 February, she sighted a convoy of two freighters, their escorts, and five smaller ships. The submarine tracked the convoy, plotted its course, and then prepared to attack. An escort suddenly appeared at a range of 7,000 yards and closing. *Tang* went deep and received five depth charges before the escort departed. Undamaged, she returned to periscope depth and resumed the attack. The range on the nearest freighter closed to 1,500 yards, and *Tang* fired a spread of four torpedoes. Three of them hit, and *Gyoten Maru* sank by the stern. The submarine cleared the area by running deep and then attempted to get ahead of the convoy for a dawn attack, but the remaining freighter passed out of range under air escort.

During the night of 22 February, *Tang* made a surface attack on a convoy of three cargo ships and four escorts. She tracked the Japanese ships for half an hour before attaining a firing position 1,500 yards off the port bow of a freighter. A spread of four torpedoes hit *Fukuyama Maru* from bow to stern, and the enemy ship disintegrated. Early the next morning, *Tang* made another approach on the convoy. The escort of the lead ship *Yamashimo Maru* moved from its covering position on the port bow, and the submarine slipped into it and fired four torpedoes. The first hit the stern of the cargoman; the second struck just aft of the stack; and the third burst just forward of the bridge and produced a terrific secondary explosion. The ship was twisted, lifted from the water, and began belching flames as she slid beneath the waves.

On the morning of the 24th, *Tang* sighted a tanker, a freighter, and a destroyer. Rain squalls hampered her as she attempted to attain a good firing position, so she tracked the ships until night and then made a surface attack. She fired four torpedoes and scored three hits which sank the freighter. The two remaining ships commenced firing in all directions, and *Tang* submerged to begin evasive action. She shadowed the enemy until morning and then closed the tanker for a submerged attack. Additional lookouts had been posted on the target's deck and, when the spread of torpedoes from *Tang* struck her, they were hurled into the air with other debris from the ship. *Echizen Maru* sank in four minutes as *Tang* went deep and rigged for the depth charge attack that followed. The next day, the submarine sank *Choko Maru*, a 1,794-ton cargo ship.

Tang contacted a convoy consisting of a freighter, transport, and four escorts on the evening of the 26th. She maneuvered into position to attack the wildly zigzagging transport and fired her last four torpedoes. All passed astern as the transport speeded up. Having expended all of her torpedoes and scored 16 hits out of 24 attempts, the submarine put into Midway Island for refit.

Tang's second patrol began on 16 March and took her to waters around the Palaus, to Davao Gulf, and to the approaches of Truk. She made only five surface contacts and had no opportunity to launch an attack before she was assigned to lifeguard duty near Truk. *Tang* rescued 22 downed airmen and transported them to Hawaii at the conclusion of the patrol.

Her third war patrol was one of the most devastating carried out against Japanese shipping during the war. *Tang* got underway from Pearl Harbor on 8 June and hunted enemy shipping in the East China Sea and Yellow Sea areas. On the 24th, southwest of Kagoshima, the submarine contacted a convoy of six large ships guarded by 16 escorts. *Tang* closed for a surface attack and fired a spread of three torpedoes at one of the ships and quickly launched a similar spread at a second target. Explosions followed, and *Tang* reported two ships sunk. However, postwar examination of Japanese records revealed by the Japanese government show that two passenger/cargo ships and two freighters were sunk. The ships must have overlapped, and the torpedo spread must have hit and sunk two victims in addition to their intended targets. Those sunk— *Tamahoko Maru*, *Tainan Maru*, *Nasusan Maru*, and the *Kennichi Maru*—added up to 16,292 tons of enemy shipping.

On 30 June, while she patrolled the lane from Kyushu to Dairen, *Tang* sighted another cargo ship steaming without an escort. After making an end-around run on the surface which produced two torpedo misses, *Tang* went deep to avoid depth charges; then surfaced and chased the hapless ship until she closed the range to 750 yards. A single torpedo blew *Nikkin Maru* in half, and the merchantman sank.

The next morning, *Tang* sighted a tanker and a freighter. While she sank freighter *Taiun Maru No. 2*, tanker *Takatori Maru No. 1* fled. The submarine trailed

until dark; then fired two torpedoes which sent the latter down. *Tang* celebrated the Fourth of July at dawn by an end-around, submerged attack on an enemy freighter which was near shore. However, with rapidly shoaling water and her keel about to touch bottom, *Tang* backed off; fired a spread of three with two hits; and then surfaced as survivors of the 6,886-ton cargo ship *Asukazan Maru* were being rescued by fishing boats. That afternoon, *Tang* sighted *Yamaoka Maru*, another cargo ship of approximately the same size, and sank her with two torpedoes. The submarine surfaced and, with the aid of grapnel hooks and Thompson submachine guns, rescued a survivor who had been clinging to an overturned lifeboat. While prowling the waters off Dairen late the next night, the submarine sighted a cargo ship and, during a submerged attack with her last two torpedoes, sank *Dori Maru*. The box score for her third patrol was 10 enemy merchant ships sunk that totaled 39,160 tons.

Her fourth war patrol was conducted from 31 July to 3 September in Japanese home waters off the coast of Honshu. On 10 August, she fired a spread of three torpedoes at a tanker near the beach of Omai Saki with no hits. The next day, after locating two freighters and two escorts, she launched three torpedoes at the larger freighter and two at the other. The larger freighter disintegrated, apparently from a torpedo which exploded in her boilers. As the submarine went deep, her crew heard the fourth and fifth torpedoes hit the second ship. After a jarring depth charge attack which lasted 38 minutes, *Tang* returned to periscope level. Only the two escorts were in sight, and one of them was picking up survivors.

On the 14th, *Tang* attacked a patrol yacht with her deck gun and reduced the Japanese ship's deck house to a shambles with eight hits. Eight days later, she sank a 225-foot patrol boat. On 23 August, the submarine closed a large ship; Japanese in white uniforms could be seen lining its superstructure and the bridge. She fired three torpedoes, and two hits caused the 8,135-ton transport *Tsukushi Maru* to slip under the waves. Two days later, *Tang* sank a tanker and an escort with her last three torpedoes and then returned to Pearl Harbor.

After a refit and overhaul, *Tang* stood out to sea on 24 September for her fifth war patrol. After topping off with fuel at Midway, she sailed for Formosa Strait on the 27th. On the night of 10 and 11 October, she sank the cargo ships *Joshu Go* and *Oita Maru*. The submarine continued on patrol until the 23d when she contacted a large convoy consisting of three tankers, a transport, a freighter, and numerous escorts. Comdr. O'Kane planned a night surface attack. *Tang* broke into the middle of the formation, firing torpedoes as she closed the tankers (later identified as freighters). Two torpedoes struck under the stack and engine room of the nearest; a single burst into the stern of the middle one; and two exploded under the stack and engine space of the farthest. The first torpedoes began exploding before the last was fired, and all hit their targets which were soon either blazing or sinking. As the submarine prepared to fire at the tanker which was crossing her stern, she sighted the transport bearing down on her in an attempt to ram.

Tang had no room to dive so she crossed the transport's bow and with full left rudder saved her stern and got inside the transport's turning circle. The transport was forced to continue her swing to avoid the tanker which had also been coming in to ram. The tanker struck the transport's starboard quarter shortly after the submarine fired four stern torpedoes along their double length at a range of 400 yards. The tanker sank bow first and the transport had a 30° up angle. With escorts approaching on the port bow and beam and a destroyer closing on the port quarter, *Tang* rang up full speed and headed for open water. When the submarine was 6,000 yards from the transport, another explosion was observed aboard that ill-fated ship, and its bow disappeared.

On the morning of 24 October, *Tang* began patrolling at periscope level. She surfaced at dark and headed for Turnabout Island. On approaching the island, the submarine's surface search radar showed so many blips that it was almost useless. *Tang* soon identified a large convoy which contained tankers with planes on their decks and transports with crated planes stacked on their bows and sterns. As the submarine tracked the Japanese ships along the coast, the enemy escorts became suspicious; and the escort commander began signaling with a large searchlight. This illuminated the convoy, and *Tang* chose a large three-deck transport as her first target, a smaller transport as the second, and a large tanker as the third. Their ranges varied from 900 to 1,400 yards. After firing two torpedoes at each target, the submarine paralleled the convoy to choose its next victims. She launched stern torpedoes at another transport and tanker aft. As *Tang* poured on full speed to escape the gunfire directed at her, a destroyer passed around the stern of the transport and headed for the submarine. The tanker blew up, and a hit was seen on the transport. A few seconds later, the destroyer blew up, either from intercepting *Tang*'s third torpedo or from shell fire of two escorts closing on the beam. Only the transport remained afloat, and it was dead in the water. The submarine cleared to 10,000 yards, rechecked the last two torpedoes which had been loaded in the bow tubes; and returned to finish off the transport. The 23d torpedo was fired at 900 yards and was observed running hot and straight. The last torpedo was fired. It broached and curved to the left in a circular run. *Tang* fishtailed under emergency power to clear the turning circle of the torpedo, but it struck her abreast the after torpedo room approximately 20 seconds after it was fired. *Tang* sank by the stern. Those who escaped the submarine were greeted in the morning with the bow of the transport sticking straight out of the water. Nine survivors, including the commanding officer, were picked up the next morning by a Japanese destroyer escort. They spent the remainder of the war in prison camps.

In the last attack, *Tang* had sunk *Kogen Maru* and *Matsumoto Maru*. During her brief career, *Tang* was officially credited with sinking 24 Japanese ships which totaled 93,824 tons. *Tang* was struck from the Navy list on 8 February 1945.

Tang received four battle stars and two Presidential Unit Citations for World War II service. Her commanding officer received the Congressional Medal of Honor for *Tang*'s final action.

II

(SS–563: dp. 1,615 (surf.), 2,100 (subm.); l. 269′; b. 27′; dr. 17′; s. 16.3 k. (surf.), 17.4 k. (subm.); cpl. 87; a. 8 21′′ tt., 40 Mk. 49/57 mines; cl. *Tang*)

The second *Tang* (SS–563) was laid down by the Portsmouth (N.H.) Naval Shipyard on 18 April 1949; launched on 19 June 1951; sponsored by Mrs. Richard H. O'Kane; and commissioned on 25 October 1951, Comdr. E. P. Huey in command.

Following trials and training along the east coast, the fast attack submarine was assigned to Submarine Squadron (SubRon) 1, Submarine Force, Pacific Fleet. From her base at Pearl Harbor, *Tang* operated in the Hawaiian Islands, providing services to surface and air antisubmarine warfare (ASW) forces. She also conducted type training. In October 1953, *Tang* commenced her first overhaul which she completed in July of 1954.

Upon emerging from the yard, the submarine began training for her first western Pacific deployment. That cruise began in September and ended at Pearl Harbor in March 1955. She then operated in the Hawaiian area until June, when she headed back to sea for a training cruise in Alaskan waters. *Tang* returned to Pearl Harbor in August and, soon thereafter, began her second overhaul.

On 20 July 1956, *Tang* put to sea on her second deployment to the western Pacific. That deployment set the pattern for seven more between then and 1972. The submarine came under the command of the Commander, 7th Fleet, and provided training services to units of the Japanese Maritime Self Defense Force, the Nationalist Chinese Navy, SEATO naval forces, and the United States Navy. When not cruising Far Eastern waters, she operated among the Hawaiian Islands and underwent overhauls at the Pearl Harbor Naval Shipyard.

On five occasions during that decade-and-one-half, she cruised to the northwestern coast of North America. In March of 1959, during a cold weather training cruise, *Tang* tested a newly developed snorkel de-icer system. In addition, the submarine provided services to the Naval Torpedo Testing Station, at Keyport, Wash., and to Canadian naval forces at Esquimalt, British Columbia. She returned to the Pacific Northwest in late February 1961, following her fourth overhaul at Pearl Harbor, for shakedown training and participation in a 1st Fleet Exercise, SLAMEX. Two years later, she made her third voyage to the northwestern coast of the United States; this time to join in 1st Fleet ASW exercises. In May and June of 1964, *Tang* made a post-overhaul shakedown cruise to the west coast. Four years and two deployments later, *Tang* made her fifth and last voyage to the west coast while still homeported at Pearl Harbor. Two months later, she resumed local operations in the Hawaiian Islands before embarking upon her eighth deployment to the western Pacific in mid-January 1969. Her ninth deployment came after a period of repairs and intense training around Hawaii and lasted from August 1970 until February 1972. Upon her return to Pearl Harbor, she resumed local operations until August, when she again entered the Pearl Harbor Naval Shipyard for extensive repairs and refurbishments.

In May 1972, she left the yard and began preparation for changing home port to San Diego, Calif. Following 10 days at sea and two at San Francisco, *Tang* arrived at the Naval Submarine Facility at San Diego. There she joined Submarine Division 32 of SubRon 3. The ensuing year brought ASW operations with destroyers and air units followed by a two-month restricted availability at the Mare Island Naval Shipyard and a return to normal operations. On 2 April 1973, the fast attack submarine put to sea for the 10th western Pacific deployment of her career. During it, she again participated in surface and air ASW exercises with units of the 7th Fleet and of various Allied navies. After visiting Yokosuka, Sasebo, Chinhae, Kaohsiung, and Pusan, *Tang* returned to San Diego on 12 October 1973. She resumed local operations after a 30-day standdown period, then made preparations for a deployment to South American waters for Exercise UNITAS XV. On 2 October 1974, she headed south to conduct training exercises with surface units and submarines of the United States, Chilean, and Peruvian navies. At the completion of UNITAS XV, *Tang* visited Acapulco, Mexico, before returning to San Diego on 16 December for Christmas standdown. Throughout 1975, she continued to conduct normal operations out of San Diego.

On 11 January 1976, *Tang* commenced overhaul at Mare Island Naval Shipyard where she remained until completion on 20 January 1977. With the exception of a brief MIDPAC deployment in March, *Tang* operated out of her home port of San Diego for the remainder of 1977 and the first half of 1978. On 1 August, *Tang*'s home port was changed to Groton, Connecticut, in anticipation of her forthcoming inter-fleet transfer.

Tang departed San Diego on 23 August and, following a transit of the Panama Canal, arrived at Groton on 30 September. For the remainder of 1978, she engaged in her new primary mission—training Iranian Navy personnel—as well as providing service to units of the Atlantic Fleet.

Tang earned four battle stars for service in Vietnamese waters.

Tangier

An island and a sound in the lower Chesapeake Bay. Both are located near the Maryland-Virginia border. The island belongs to Virginia and the sound to Maryland.

I

(SP–469: l. 62'0''; b. 13'6''; dr. 2'4'' (mean); s. 14 k.; a. 1 1-pdr.)

The first *Tangier* (SP–469)—a motor yacht built by J. Woodtull at Orvington, Va.—was acquired by the Navy from Mr. J. S. Parsons of Norfolk, Va., and was placed in commission on 24 April 1917.

Records of *Tangier*'s service are extremely sketchy. However, it is known that she was acquired for service with the section patrol to protect the harbors and coastal waters of the United States against intrusion by German U-boats. In all probability, she patrolled the waters near Norfolk and in the lower reaches of the Chesapeake Bay because small craft so acquired usually operated in the immediate area of their acquisition. In any event, *Tangier* served the Navy from 24 April 1917 until 22 October 1918, at which time she was returned to her owner.

II

(AV–8: dp. 11,760 (tl.); l. 492'1''; b. 69'6''; dr. 23'9'' (lim.); s. 18.4 k. (tl.); cpl. 1,075; a. 1 5'', 4 3'', 8 40mm.; cl. *Tangier*; T. C3-Cargo)

The second *Tangier* was laid down under a Maritime Commission contract (MC hull 51) as *Sea Arrow* on 18 March 1939 at Oakland, Calif., by Moore Dry Dock Co.; launched on 15 September 1939; sponsored by Mrs. Joseph R. Sheehan; renamed *Tangier* (AV–8) on 3 June 1940; acquired by the Navy on 8 July 1940; and commissioned in ordinary on that same day, Comdr. Clifton A. F. Sprague in command.

Tangier remained at Oakland for over a year, undergoing conversion to a seaplane tender. Finally, on 25 August 1941, she went into full commission and put to sea on her shakedown cruise. At the completion of shakedown training, she was assigned as tender to Patrol Wing (PatWing) 2, based in Hawaii. She arrived at Pearl Harbor on 3 November and moored abaft the former battleship *Utah* now serving as an antiaircraft training ship, AG–16. There, the seaplane tender spent the last month of peacetime caring for her brood of flying boats.

At 0755 on the morning of 7 December 1941, the first of two waves of Japanese carrier-based planes swooped in on the U.S. Pacific Fleet, moored at Pearl Harbor. *Tangier*, still abaft *Utah*, was in the fight from the beginning. Her klaxon sounded general quarters three minutes later; and, by 0800, her antiaircraft batteries opened up on the swarm of "meatball"-emblazoned planes. During the ensuing melee, *Tangier*'s gunners claimed three enemy planes and hits on a midget submarine which had penetrated the harbor's defenses. She and her sister seaplane tender, *Curtiss* (AV–4), shelled the submarine, but destroyer *Monaghan* (DD–354) finished it off with a two-pronged attack, subjecting it to a ramming and following up with a cascade of depth charges. By 0920, the skies were clear of planes, and only the smoke from the burning ships and shore installations remained. *Tangier* began rescuing survivors from capsized *Utah*.

During the next few days, it became apparent that the Japanese would soon attempt a landing on Wake Island, a desolate speck in the ocean but a strategic American outpost located almost astride the 20th parallel, some two-thirds of the way from Oahu to Guam and almost due north of the Marshall Islands. By mid-December, the seaplane tender was loaded with supplies, ammunition, and equipment for the desperate but thus far victorious defenders of Wake Island. Then, she rode idly at anchor for two days while *Saratoga* (CV–3), the carrier around which the Wake relief force was to be built, steamed to Pearl from San Diego. "Sara" entered Pearl Harbor on 15 December, and *Tangier* departed the same afternoon in company with *Neches* (AO–5) and a destroyer division while the carrier refueled. *Saratoga* caught up to the slow-moving little convoy on the 17th, and the task force advanced on Wake.

At this point, Admiral Kimmel was replaced by Admiral Nimitz as Commander in Chief, Pacific Fleet. It was an unfortunate time to make such a change for, in the space of time it took Nimitz to make it from Washington to Pearl Harbor, confusion and indecision reigned in the Pacific. The immediate result was a failure to press home the relief expedition, and this unfortunate combination of circumstances caused the loss of Wake Island and its gallant garrison. On 23 December, after a three-day struggle against overwhelming odds, the defenders succumbed. The relief expedition was ordered back to Oahu. *Tangier* sailed via Midway Island, where she disembarked the men and equipment of Marine Fighting Squadron 221 to bolster that island's defenses and embarked civilian evacuees. The seaplane tender returned to Pearl Harbor on the last day of 1941.

On 11 February 1942, *Tangier* put to sea again and

Tangier (AV–8) off Mare Island in 1941, in dark gray camouflage.   (19–N–25362)

headed, via Pago Pago and Suva, to New Caledonia. She arrived in Noumea on 3 March and relieved *Curtiss* (AV–4) as tender for six flying boats. For the next three and one-half months, she performed routine tender services for PBY's flying long-range searches to the north of New Caledonia, almost as far as the lower Solomons. Between late April and early May, her brood of seaplanes was increased to 12 in anticipation of a fleet action in the Coral Sea. When the battle came to pass, however, her amphibians had to content themselves with rescuing survivors of *Sims* (DD–409) and *Neosho* (AO–23), sunk on 7 May by the Japanese who mistook them for a cruiser and carrier, respectively, and of the torpedoed Greek freighter SS *Chloe*. The search continued until 13 May, days after the end of the crucial battle. Coral Sea was a tactical victory for the Japanese—the U.S. Navy lost more tonnage—but a strategic victory for the United States. It stopped the southward advance of the "Rising Sun" and set the stage for the American victory in the Battle of Midway by temporarily robbing the Japanese of two of their newest fleet carriers, *Shokaku* and *Zuikaku*. *Shokaku* was incapacitated by battle damage, and *Zuikaku* lost a high percentage of her veteran aviators.

After their rescue operations for survivors of Allied ships lost in the Coral Sea action, *Tangier*'s planes resumed normal search operations. On 30 May, two of her seaplanes were forced down at sea by fuel shortage, and a third crashed near Mare Island in the Loyalty group. Destroyer *Meredith* (DD–434) went out to aid the two planes. One was refueled and returned safely, but the other could not take off and had to be sunk. The crew of the third plane reached safety at Mare Island. On 20 June, *Tangier* was relieved by *Curtiss* and, the following day, got underway for the west coast. She reached Pearl Harbor on Independence Day 1942 and stood out again three days later. On the 15th, she arrived in San Francisco and immediately began overhaul.

Tangier completed overhaul in September and, after loading aviation equipment at the Alameda Naval Air Station, departed San Francisco for Pearl Harbor, Suva, and ultimately Espiritu Santo, where she arrived on 29 February 1943. There, she unloaded her stores and commenced tending seaplanes. She continued routine operations until 12 August, when she got underway for Pearl Harbor. *Tangier* made Oahu on the 28th. During September and October, she made two voyages from Pearl Harbor to American Samoa and one to San Diego, before returning to Espiritu Santo on 6 November with a load of aviation cargo. On the 14th, she headed back to the United States, arriving in San Diego on 3 December for another yard overhaul.

On 21 February 1944, the seaplane tender headed west again. She reached Espiritu Santo on 8 March and, after a four-day layover, continued on to Brisbane, Australia, where she became the flagship of the Commander, Aircraft, 7th Fleet, on 21 March. Two days later, she headed north to support General MacArthur's advance up the back of the New Guinea "bird." After stops at Milne Bay and Langemak Bay, she dropped anchor in Seeadler Harbor, Manus, on 31 March. She remained there for three months, tending her Catalinas as they supported the landings at Wakde, Noemfoor, and Biak and generally supported the 7th Fleet's advance. On 31 July, she moved to Woendi Anchorage located just off Biak, at the head of the New Guinea "bird." *Tangier* conducted seaplane operations from there until 19 September, when she got underway for Morotai. The tender arrived off Morotai on the 21st and supported the invasion, undergoing intermittent air attacks, until 1 December, when she headed back to Manus. She anchored in Seeadler Harbor again on 5 December.

Tangier visited Woendi again on 22 and 23 December; then sailed for the Philippines. She entered Kossol Roads, in the Palaus, on Christmas Day and departed again the following day. On 29 December, she arrived in San Pedro Bay, Leyte Gulf, and began operating

her seaplanes from there. For almost a month, her charges supported various operations in the Philippines. These included the Lingayen invasion and air strikes on the numerous smaller islands of the archipelago. In fact, their primary mission appears to have been air-sea rescue work in support of the air strikes.

On 24 January 1945, *Tangier* departed Leyte and headed for Lingayen Gulf, arriving three days later. Her Catalinas and Mariners conducted night barrier patrols of Luzon Strait and the South China Sea along with night searches and antishipping flights along the China coast in the vicinity of Formosa. On 12 February, the seaplane tender moved to Mangarin Bay, Mindoro, to run day searches over the South China Sea as far north as the coast of French Indochina and Hainan Island. She concluded operations from Mangarin Bay on 7 March and headed for Subic Bay, Luzon. She arrived there on the following day and departed on the 11th. *Tangier* anchored in Cabalitian Bay, off Cabalitian Island, on the 12th and commenced seaplane operations. For the next three months, her planes flew searches and antishipping missions over the South China Sea in the direction of Hong Kong, Swatow, and Formosa.

The seaplane tender exited Cabalitian Bay on 17 June and arrived in Subic Bay the following day. Soon thereafter, she moved to Manila Bay, departing there on 25 June. On the 27th, she stopped at San Pedro Bay; then continued east toward the United States. She reached Pearl Harbor on 10 July and San Francisco on 20 July. She was overhauled at the Moore Dry Dock Co. and then ordered back to the Far East for occupation duty. On 24 September, she exited San Francisco and headed back across the broad Pacific. Sailing via Adak, Alaska, she reached the vicinity of Yokosuka during the second week in October. After two months of occupation duty in Japan, *Tangier* moved to Kowloon Bay, China, in December for air-sea rescue, patrol, and courier duty. In January 1946, she returned to Japan for another brief tour of duty with the occupation forces. Late in February, she moved from Sasebo to Okinawa, where she remained until late March.

On the 22d, *Tangier* set sail for the United States. She made a brief visit to Pearl Harbor in early April and transited the Panama Canal in mid-month. She reached Norfolk, Va., on the 29th and Philadelphia, Pa., on 1 May. Following a short voyage back to Norfolk and to Yorktown, Va., the seaplane tender returned to Philadelphia on 11 May to prepare for inactivation. By January 1947, *Tangier* was out of commission, berthed with the Reserve Fleet at Philadelphia. On 1 June 1961, her name was struck from the Navy list; and, on 17 November 1961, she was sold to the Union Minerals & Alloys Corp. for scrapping.

Tangier earned three battle stars during World War II.

Tanguingui

(SP–126: t. 51; l. 63'6''; b. 15'10''; dr. 3'8'' (aft); s. 12 mph.; cpl. 8; a. 1 1-pdr.)

Tanguingui (Sp–126)—a motor yacht built in 1915 at Morris Heights, N.Y., by the New York Yacht Launch & Engine Co.—was acquired by the United States Navy on 28 June 1917 under free lease from Mr. J. C. McCoy of New York City and was placed in commission on 31 October 1917.

Assigned to the 7th Naval District throughout World War I, *Tanguingui* operated out of Key West patrolling along the extreme southern coast of Florida to prevent incursions by German underseas raiders. Following the armistice, she continued to serve the Navy until her main battery, small arms, and ammunition were removed on 6 February 1919. *Tanguingui*'s name was struck from the Navy list on 7 April 1919, and the yacht was returned to her owner two weeks later.

Taniwha

(SP–129: t. 85; l. 112'; b. 15'6''; dr. 6' (aft); s. 14 k.; cpl. 24; a. 1 6-pdr., 2 mg.)

Taniwha (SP–129)—a motor yacht constructed in 1909 at Neponset, Mass., by George Lawley & Sons—was acquired by the United States Navy in 1917 on free lease from Mr. Henry B. Anderson of New York City. Though commissioned on 18 May 1917, she was not formally acquired by the Navy until 29 September 1917.

Assigned to the 3d Naval District, *Taniwha* operated on section patrol protecting waters near New York City against incursions by enemy forces, particularly submarines. Her service to the Navy continued through the end of hostilities which came on 11 November 1918. She was decommissioned on 4 April 1919, and her name was struck from the Navy list on the same day. She was returned to her owner the following June.

Tanner

Zero Luther Tanner—born on 5 December 1835 in Warsaw, N.Y.—was appointed acting ensign on 18 August 1862. During the Civil War, he served in bark *Midnight* and supply ship *Rhode Island*. On 1 December 1864, when the latter captured British paddle wheel steamer *Vixen*, he was placed in command of her prize crew; and, on 13 January 1865, he led the group of boats from *Rhode Island* which landed at Fort Fisher.

During the ensuing decades, while serving on many ships and shore stations, Tanner became a pioneer in and an authority on hydrography. He invented the Tanner sounding machine and is remembered for his book, *Deep Sea Exploration*, as well as for many articles expanding man's knowledge of the sea. Promoted to captain and retired on 29 June 1906, Tanner died at Washington, D.C., on 16 December 1906.

I

Pamina (AKA–34) (*q.v.*) was renamed *Tanner* and reclassified AGS–15 on 15 May 1946.

Tantalus

A legendary king of Lydia condemned to stand in a pool of water up to his chin and beneath fruit-laden boughs only to have the water or fruit recede at each attempt to drink or eat.

(ARL–27: dp. 2,960; l. 328'; b. 50'; dr. 14'1''; s. 11.6 k.; cpl. 253; a. 8 40mm.; cl. *Achelous*)

Tantalus (ARL–27) was laid down on 10 October 1944 at Seneca, Ill., by the Chicago Bridge and Iron Co.; launched on 2 January 1945; sponsored by Mrs. Angeline Colomone; and commissioned on 13 January 1945, Lt. Frank L. Guberlet in command.

Following her conversion into a landing craft repair ship at Jacksonville, Fla., by the Gibbs Engine Works, she conducted her shakedown cruise in the Hampton Roads area. *Tantalus* departed Davisville, R.I., and headed for the Panama Canal Zone. She arrived at Coco Solo on 29 July; was assigned to Service Forces, Pacific Fleet; and then was ordered to proceed via San Diego to Hawaii.

Tantalus stood out of San Diego on 14 August as whistles and sirens of the city proclaimed the Japanese surrender. She called at Pearl Harbor, Eniwetok, and Guam before reaching San Pedro Bay, Leyte, on 11 October. She served there as tender and repair ship for landing craft until 28 March 1946 when she headed for China. *Tantalus* operated at Shanghai and Hankow until late July when she got underway for Okinawa. She remained in the Ryukyus from 5 August to 31 October when she began a return voyage to China. After calling at Tsingtao, the ship arrived at Shanghai on 22 December 1946.

Tantalus was decommissioned in China on 18 January 1947 and released to the Foreign Liquidation Commission for further transfer to the United Nations Relief and Rehabilitation Administration for disposal. *Tantalus* was struck from the Navy list on 7 February 1947.

Tapacola

A small bird of Chile and Argentina, having short, rounding wings and short tail feathers carried erect.

(AMC–54: dp. 275; l. 98'5''; b. 23'7''; dr. 10'8''; s. 10.0 k.; cpl. 17; cl. *Accentor*)

Tapacola (AMC–54) was laid down on 10 January 1941 by Snow Shipyards, Rockland, Maine; launched on 3 July 1941; sponsored by Mrs. George T. Swiggum; and commissioned on 20 September 1941 at the Boston Navy Yard.

Tapacola departed Boston on 19 October for Yorktown, Va., where she held training at the Mine Warfare School before proceeding to Norfolk. Upon her arrival there, on 30 October, she was directed to continue onward to Florida for duty with the 7th Naval District. The minesweeper arrived at Key West on 7 November 1941 and operated in waters off southern Florida until 30 June 1945 when she sailed to Mayport. Her minesweeping gear was removed, and *Tapacola* began towing targets in connection with aviation training at the air station.

On 10 August, her designation was changed to IX–230. She was transferred to the 8th Naval District and arrived at Pensacola on 13 December 1945. On 28 May 1946, *Tapacola* was placed out of service and, the next month, declared surplus to Navy needs.

Tapacola was struck from the Navy list on 29 October 1946.

Taposa

A small Indian tribe which formerly lived on the Yazoo River in Mississippi. Little is known about them other than the name.

Narragansett (YFB–1163) (*q.v.*) was renamed *Taposa* (YFB–1163) on 18 December 1941.

Tappahannock

The cognate name for Virginia's Rappahannock River in Essex County, Va., and the name of an Indian village founded on its southern bank in about 1680.

(AO–43: dp. 7,004; l. 530'0''; b. 68'0''; dr. 30'0''; cpl. 213; a. 1 4'', 4 3'', 12 20mm.; cl. *Mattaponi*)

Jorkay was laid down under a Maritime Commission contract (MC hull 157) on 24 December 1941 at Chester, Pa., by the Sun Shipbuilding Co.; renamed *Tappahannock* and designated AO–43 on 31 March 1942; launched on 18 April 1942; sponsored by Mrs. George Jessup; acquired by the Navy from the War Shipping Administration on 29 May 1942; and converted for Navy service at the Philadelphia Navy Yard between 1 June and 17 July. Nearly midway through this conversion period, the oiler was commissioned on 22 June 1942, Comdr. A. O. R. Bergensen in command.

Following her shakedown, *Tappahannock* reported for duty with Commander, Service Force, Atlantic, on 13 August, and soon got underway for Panama. In the Canal Zone, the oiler took on board 300 tons of stores for Motor Torpedo Boat Squadron (MTBRon) 3, as well as two PT-boats, and left Balboa on 29 August, bound for the South Pacific.

The minesweeper *Tapacola* (AMc–54).   (NR&L(M) 30701)

Tappahannock unloaded her cargo at Noumea, New Caledonia, on 18 September; and then visited Auckland, New Zealand; Pago Pago, Samoa; and Nandi, Fiji Islands, before becoming station tanker at Noumea. There, she fueled a wide variety of ships until 20 November, when she headed for the west coast.

Tappahannock arrived at San Pedro on 11 December and then moved to San Diego, where she remained through the end of the year. Getting underway again on 2 January 1943, the oiler operated briefly out of Dutch Harbor, Alaska, before returning south to San Pedro and San Francisco en route back to the South Pacific.

By early spring, *Tappahannock* was in the Guadalcanal area, as American forces sought to consolidate their hold on the bitterly contested Solomons. On 1 April, a Grumman J2F "Duck," attached to *Enterprise* (CV–6), crashed into the oiler's mainmast and damaged her radar tower and antenna. The ship then shifted her berth from Espiritu Santo to Tulagi Harbor.

On 6 April, she proceeded to Lunga Point, off Guadalcanal, and then commenced transferring fuel and diesel oil to *Kanawah* (AO–1) and *YO–147*, as well as transferring highly volatile aviation gas to shore tanks. Later in the day, at 1930, Japanese planes succeeded in dropping a few bombs astern of *Tappahannock*'s berth during a nuisance raid but did no damage.

The following day found the oiler still off Lunga, pumping aviation gasoline to tanks ashore. At 1130, the ship received an air raid alert for a Japanese attack expected at 1245. Fifteen minutes later, *Tappahannock* intercepted a dispatch ordering all ships in the vicinity to get underway immediately. The oiler disconnected her fueling hose and quickly got underway, in company with *Woodworth* (DD–460) and *Farenholt* (DD–491). The trio then proceeded through the Lunga Channel at their best sustained smokeless speed of 17 knots. Unbeknownst to the American

sailors, they were steaming directly in the path of a segment of Admiral Isoroku Yamamoto's force as he made his last thrust against the American Navy in the Solomon Islands.

At 1510, as the three-ship convoy steamed through a smooth sea, beneath an overcast sky, a "Condition-Red" warning sounded from Guadalcanal. Four minutes later, lookouts noted tell-tale bursts far astern, and then spotted seven planes milling about, as if engaged in a "dog fight." But suddenly the apparent melee became an orderly formation of "Vals."

For the next five minutes, *Tappahannock*, the key target of the Japanese dive bombers, fought for her life. The first Japanese dive bomber came in from off the port quarter—as the ship was swinging to starboard to evade the attack—and dropped her bomb abaft the bridge. The oiler shuddered as the explosion sent up a geyser of water higher than the mainmast. Three cane fenders and a Franklin lifebuoy were carried away topside while a fountain of water showered the bridge. Below, thermo overload switches went dead in the machinery spaces, and the oiler began to lose way.

In the meantime, *Tappahannock*'s gunners concentrated their fire on the Japanese plane; and it dipped lower and lower until it splashed into the water. At the same time, a quick glance in *Woodworth*'s direction revealed that the destroyer was keeping up her share of antiaircraft fire.

While *Tappahannock*'s "black gang" below valiantly fought to get underway again, a second attacker came in from off the oiler's starboard bow, on a course diagonally across the ship and soon entered the concentrated gunfire of one three-inch and three 20-millimeter guns. However, the "Val" stubbornly remained airborne and escaped the hail of steel; but no sooner had the second plane been driven off when three of the oiler's 20-millimeter guns jammed.

43

Her engineers soon were able to get the ship underway again, and *Tappahannock* began to pick up steam. Putting her helm over hard-a-port, the ship prepared to face a third tormentor which came in from directly astern. Apparently—and fortunately for *Tappahannock* —the momentary power-loss had been a good thing since the Japanese pilot misjudged his target's speed and ended up dropping his bomb clear of the ship— the near miss drenching the forecastle antiaircraft gunners with water from the splash.

A fourth "Val" followed the third one, and, in the disbelieving eyes of the gunners astern, "walked right into" the fire of their guns, coming, in the astonished view of one gun captain—"right down the tracer trajectory." Hit after hit began to tear pieces off the "Val" as it wobbled through the hail of gunfire. Its bomb exploded off the oiler's starboard quarter, and *Tappahannock*'s number six 20-millimeter mount on the bridge "polished off" the enemy dive bomber, sending it spinning into the water where it exploded, leaving only a fleeting pall of smoke to mark its passing.

The fifth and final "Val" crossed the ship from starboard to port, on a path directly across her well-deck aft. His bomb detonated just alongside, causing more severe vibrations than the first near miss and leading to fears that, this time, the ship had suffered serious harm. However, a subsequent check of the damage revealed only some dished hull-plates. As suddenly as it had begun, the attack was over.

The oiler's companions had also emerged unscathed, and *Woodworth* claimed downing one "Val." However, behind them at Tulagi, others had not fared as well. *Kanawah* and *Aaron Ward* (DD–483) had been pummelled and sent to the bottom.

The oiler arrived at Espiritu Santo soon thereafter, and repair crews from *Vestal* (AR–4) remedied her topside damage and patched her hull below the waterline. After her repairs had been completed, *Tappahannock* resumed active service as American forces continued to strengthen their hold on the Solomon Islands. At 0023 on the morning of 24 May, the oiler was again the target of a Japanese air attack, but the nocturnal raider dropped only a single bomb and missed.

The oiler continued supporting Allied operations in the South Pacific until late August when she headed home to the west coast. She then conducted two voyages from San Pedro to Pearl Harbor before heading west to support the American invasion of the Gilbert Islands in November and December.

For the remainder of the war, *Tappahannock* conducted vital fueling duties for the Fleet as it pounded westward and northward against the Japanese empire. She earned the remainder of her Pacific battle stars by supporting operations which ranged from the Gilbert Islands to Okinawa Gunto. She supported the occupations of Kwajalein, Majuro, Guam, Tinian, the Southern Palaus, Luzon, Okinawa and aided the fast carriers in their raids on the Bonins, Philippines, and Formosa.

In the course of these operations, she conducted underway replenishments with the task forces and served as station tanker in newly occupied lagoons and harbors. Her task was unglamourous but dangerous and one of the most vital to be entrusted to a support ship. Without "beans, bullets, and black oil," the fast-moving task forces could not have pounded the Japanese empire into submission.

On 18 October 1944, *Tappahannock* refueled ships of Task Group (TG) 58.3 during their retirement from air strikes on Formosa. The Japanese struck back with torpedo plane attacks on the American forces which damaged cruisers *Canberra* (CA–70) and *Houston* (CL–81). On that day, the oiler took on board 185 enlisted men and 12 officers from the stricken *Houston* and, three days later, disembarked them at Ulithi as she reloaded to resume replenishment duties which she faithfully discharged for the next few weeks.

On 20 November 1944, *Tappahannock* again lay at anchor at Ulithi. Her war diary noted that, at 0540, *Case* (DD–370) reported ramming and sinking a submarine. Six minutes later, *Mississinewa* (AO–59) was torpedoed and immediately enveloped in flames. *Tappahannock* went to general quarters immediately to be ready should another attack be launched. At 0824, the oiler picked up 36 survivors from *Mississinewa* which had capsized and sunk.

Between deployments supporting the fast carrier task forces at sea, *Tappahannock* returned to the west coast of the United States calling at the familiar ports of San Pedro and San Diego, Calif., as well as at Astoria, Oreg., before heading west on 21 February 1945 and arriving at Pearl Harbor five days after. Subsequently operating out of Eniwetok, Kerama Retto, and Ulithi, the oiler supported 3d and 5th Fleet operations against the Japanese homeland—duties which she continued as the war progressed closer and closer to Japan.

After the cessation of hostilities on 14 August, *Tappahannock* continued in her vital support role during the occupation of the erstwhile enemy's homeland. She arrived at Tokyo Bay on 26 August 1945 and remained there until 22 November when she steamed for Yokosuka. She proceeded thence to Tsingtao, China, where she arrived seven days before Christmas. The oiler remained, as station tanker, at the one-time German colonial showplace city until 26 April 1946, when she got underway for the Near East to load a cargo of oil.

Tappahannock returned to the China Coast in the late spring, making port at Hong Kong, British Crown Colony, on 7 June. She remained there for the rest of that month and into the next, before a typhoon swirled up the South China Sea, forcing the oiler to sea on 16 July for typhoon evasion. Departing Hong Kong on 6 August, she sailed again for the Near East, for Ras Tanura and Colombo, to load another cargo of petroleum products for delivery to the fleet serving on occupation duty in Japanese and Chinese coastal waters.

On 17 September, *Tappahannock* put into Sasebo, Japan, before heading for Shanghai, China, two days later. She remained there from 22 to 28 September, before sailing for Yokosuka, from which port she operated until 15 October, when she set sail for the west coast, via Pearl Harbor. *Tappahannock* then conducted local operations out of San Pedro and San Francisco into 1947, before getting underway for Yokosuka in April.

Subsequently moving to North China, she arrived at Tsingtao on 20 May and began operations at that China port. While engaged in these duties, she was assigned to the Naval Transportation Service on 1 July and shifted her base to Yokohama, Japan. She remained on duty there until sailing for Norfolk, Va., on 9 September. She steamed via the Suez Canal to the Mediterranean Sea and made port at Norfolk, Va., on 10 January 1948.

The oiler returned to the Mediterranean soon thereafter, transited that body of water and the Suez Canal, and arrived at the Persian Gulf port of Bahrain on 5 April. After filling her tank with petroleum products, she sailed for the east coast of the United States soon thereafter and returned home via the Mediterranean to unload at Portsmouth, N.H., and Norfolk, via Gibraltar, before returning to the Mediterranean in the summer.

For the remainder of the year 1948, *Tappahannock* operated in the Far East, the Mediterranean, and the Near East, calling at ports ranging from Suez to Yokosuka, before eventually returning to the west coast on 1 August. She remained at San Pedro through the summer, fall, and early winter, before shifting to San Diego on 18 December. Early in 1949, she again headed west for the Far East and thence proceeded across the Mediterranean to operate for a time in northern European waters, calling at Bremerhaven, Germany, and Cherbourg, France, before returning to Norfolk on 4 June.

She next operated for a time in the Caribbean— Aruba, Netherlands West Indies; Roosevelt Roads,

Puerto Rico; and Trinidad, British West Indies, before making two round-trip voyages from Houston and Port Arthur, Tex., with petroleum products for Norfolk. She again called at Bremerhaven and Naples before she moved to the Far East, transiting the Suez Canal, calling at Bahrain, transiting the Malacca Straits, and arriving at Manila on 23 October 1949. While en route to the Philippines, *Tappahannock* was transferred to the Military Sea Transportation Service (MSTS) and designated T–AO–43.

From Manila, the oiler travelled to the west coast and arrived at San Francisco on 15 November 1949. She remained on the west coast through the end of the year, until she was decommissioned at San Diego on 3 February 1950 and placed in reserve.

However, *Tappahannock*'s sojourn in reserve was brief; for, before mid-year, communist aggression in Korea triggered a build-up of the Navy's fleets in both oceans to respond to the threat. *Cahokia* (ATA–168) towed the veteran oiler to San Francisco, and arrived on 14 December 1950. Soon thereafter, *Tappahannock* was recommissioned and rejoined MSTS. She proceeded to the east coast and served from there for four years. During the course of these operations, she ranged from the Canal Zone to the Firth of Forth; from Argentia, Newfoundland to Port Arthur, Tex.; and in the North Atlantic to the Caribbean and the eastern seaboard of the United States. In January 1955, *Tappahannock* was again decommissioned and placed in reserve.

On 27 November 1956, *Tappahannock* was towed to the Todd Shipyard, San Pedro, Calif., where she was prepared for reactivation. She was recommissioned on 12 December 1956, Comdr. O. O. Liebschner in command.

She arrived at Aruba on 14 January 1957, picked up a cargo, got underway on the 16th, and proceeded toward Melville, R.I. En route she was diverted to Norfolk. She then conducted one more round trip to Aruba. During the year, her operations ranged from frigid waters inside the Arctic Circle to the warm Caribbean and took her to the Mediterranean. She visited ports in Scotland, Italy, Trinidad, and Germany. On 18 November 1957, *Tappahannock* was decommissioned at Orange, Tex.

The oiler remained laid-up there for over eight years. In 1966, she was towed to the Naval Support Activity, Algiers, La., and fitted out for active service. *Tappahannock* was commissioned at Algiers on 31 May 1966, Capt. Erman O. Proctor in command. The ship got underway for the west coast on 11 July, and arrived at San Diego, her home port, on 6 August.

After operations on the coast of southern California, *Tappahannock* deployed to the Western Pacific (West-Pac) on 25 November 1966 and reached Subic Bay, Philippine Islands, en route to service off the Vietnamese coast. On the day before Christmas—after first topping-off with liquid cargo, mail, and provisions— she headed for "Yankee Station" off the coast of Vietnam. *Tappahannock* supported the 7th Fleet's "Yankee Team" and "Market Time" operations interdicting communist seaborne supply lanes. As in World War II, *Tappahannock*'s duties were not glamorous, but they were vital. In spite of her advancing age and the arrival of newer oilers and replenishment ships, the veteran oiler remained a vital cog in the operations off Vietnam. During the deployment, she steamed 15,000 miles and delivered nearly 135,000 barrels of oil and gasoline.

Returning to the west coast between cruises to the Far East, *Tappahannock* conducted two more West-Pac cruises, continuing her operations in support of 7th Fleet units in the ongoing task of sweeping the sea lanes off embattled South Vietnam. During her second cruise, from March to September 1968, *Tappahannock* transferred 30,305,196 gallons of fuel oil and steamed 42,627 miles in the course of her operations. She returned to the west coast following the second deployment, underwent much-needed repairs, and served as duty oiler for the Fleet Training Group,

and engaged in Fleet exercise Operation "Behavior Pattern." Underway on 6 March 1969, *Tappahannock* proceeded westward for her third and last WestPac deployment.

Initially based at Sasebo, *Tappahannock* went to sea in the third week of April as part of Task Force 71 which was hastily assembled after North Korean MiG fighters had shot down a Navy EC-121 *Constellation* reconaissance plane over the Sea of Japan, killing its entire Navy crew. Once the tensions had abated in the Far East, the oiler headed southward for operations off Vietnam.

These duties on her WestPac deployments were repetitious and never garnered headlines; yet they were necessary and not without a share of danger. On 13 June 1967, during an underway replenishment in the South China Sea, *Repose* (AH-16) suffered a rudder failure and collided with *Tappahannock*. On another occasion, on 4 October 1967, two fueling booms were carried away during an emergency breakaway from *Ranger* (CVA-61). That day, quick action by one of *Tappahannock*'s men averted possible tragedy and loss of life.

Tappahannock supported TG 73.5 on "Market Time" interdiction operations off the South Vietnamese Coast during most of her third deployment. The oiler, by now one of the oldest active-duty ships on the Navy list, was clearly aging; and replacements for many of her worn-out parts were hard to find or unavailable. She nevertheless was able to deliver some 10,000,000 gallons of oil and 50 tons of mail during 138 underway replenishments. At the end of her eventful and memorable last cruise, she returned to Long Beach, Calif., on 21 September 1969. *Tappahannock* was decommissioned at San Diego on 6 March 1970 and went into reserve at the Maritime Administration's berths at Suisun Bay. Struck from the Navy list on 15 July 1976, the globe-travelling veteran of World War II, the Cold War, and Vietnam, remained at Suisun Bay and was awaiting disposition by MARAD in October 1979.

Tappahannock received nine battle stars for World War II service and nine for Vietnam service.

Tarantula

A name applied to Italy's wolf spider, to some Asiatic spiders, and to various species of large, dark, hairy spiders found in the warmer climes of the Americas.

I

Tarantula (Submarine No. 12)—a *B–1*-class submarine—was renamed *B–3* (*q.v.*) on 17 November 1911.

II

(SP–124: t. 159.97; l. 128' 9''; b. 19'3''; dr. 9'; s. 14 k.; a. 2 6-pdrs., 2 .30-cal. mg.)

The second *Tarantula* (SP–124)—a motor yacht built in 1912 at Neponset, Mass., by George Lawley and Son Corp.—was acquired by the Navy on 25 April 1917 from W. K. Vanderbilt of New York City. Assigned to section patrol in the 3d Naval District during World War I, *Tarantula* operated along the coastal waters of Connecticut, New York, and New Jersey until October 1918. On 28 October, she sank about eight miles southwest of the Fire Island light vessel after colliding with the Royal Holland Lloyd Line steamship SS *Frisia*. Her name was subsequently struck from the Navy list.

Tarawa

An atoll in the north central Gilbert Islands located some 90 miles north of the equator and two-thirds of the way along a diagonal drawn from Hawaii to Australia. It was the scene of a bitter and bloody battle from 20 to 24 November 1943. The marines' assault upon the atoll was one phase of Operation "Galvanic," the first jump in the Navy's leap-frog sweep to victory through the Central Pacific.

I

(CV–40: dp. 27,100; l. 888'0"; b. 93'0"; ew. 147'6"; dr. 28'7"; s. 32.7 k. (tl.); cpl. 3,448; a. 12 5", 72 40mm.; cl. *Essex*)

The first *Tarawa* (CV–40) was laid down on 1 March 1944 at the Norfolk Navy Yard; launched on 12 May 1945; sponsored by Mrs. Julian C. Smith, the wife of Lieutenant General Julian C. Smith, USMC, who commanded the 2d Marine Division at Tarawa; and commissioned on 8 December 1945, Capt. Alvin Ingersoll Malstrom in command.

Tarawa remained in the Norfolk area until 15 February 1946, when she sailed for shakedown training in the vicinity of Guantanamo Bay, Cuba, and returned briefly to Norfolk on 16 April before visiting New York in the latter part of the month. She arrived at Norfolk once again on the 30th. From then until late June, the warship completed her post-shakedown overhaul. On 28 June, she exited Hampton Roads bound for the west coast. *Tarawa* transited the Panama Canal early in July and reached San Diego on the 15th.

Following training and upkeep, she left San Diego for a deployment to the western Pacific. The aircraft carrier reached Pearl Harbor on 7 August and soon thereafter continued on her voyage west. She reached Saipan on 20 August and operated in the vicinity of the Mariana Islands until late September when she headed for Japan. After a stop at Yokosuka between 28 September and 3 October and one at Sasebo from 7 to 11 October, the aircraft carrier got underway for the northern coast of China. She arrived in the vicinity of Tsingtao on the 15th and operated in that area until the 30th when she headed back to the Marianas. On 7 November, the carrier reached Saipan and, for the remainder of her Far Eastern tour, conducted operations in the Marianas. The only exception was a brief voyage to Okinawa and back early in January 1947, after which she departed Guam on the 14th to return to Pearl Harbor. The warship arrived in Pearl Harbor on 24 January and remained in Hawaiian waters until 18 February when she got underway for fleet exercises in the vicinity of Kwajalein. As a unit of Task Force (TF) 57, she participated in battle practice attacks upon the carriers of TF 38 until early March. *Tarawa* returned to Pearl Harbor on 11 March for about a month; then headed for the west coast and arrived in San Francisco on 29 April.

After more than 16 months of air operations out of San Francisco and San Diego, *Tarawa* stood out of San Diego on 28 September 1948 and embarked upon a cruise most of the way around the world. She stopped at Pearl Harbor at the end of the second week in October and then continued her voyage on to her first foreign port of call, Tsingtao, China. The carrier arrived there on 29 October and spent the next five weeks observing events in strife-torn northern China. Early in December, she headed south for liberty calls at Hong Kong and Singapore. The warship departed the latter port on 23 December and headed for the newly independent Republic of Ceylon, and arrived at its capital, Colombo, on 29 December. Departing Ceylon on 2 January 1949, she steamed toward the Persian Gulf to call at Bahrain and Jidda before transiting the Suez Canal on the 20th and the 21st. Leaving Port Said, *Tarawa* continued her voyage to Greece, Turkey, and Crete. From Soudha Bay, Crete, the warship headed across the Mediterranean on 8 February. She stopped overnight at Gibraltar on the 12th and 13th and then started out across the Atlantic. On 21 February, she ended her voyage at Norfolk, Va. From then until early summer, the carrier conducted normal operations along the east coast and in the Caribbean area. After inactivation overhaul, *Tarawa* was placed out of commission on 30 June 1949 and was berthed with the New York Group, Atlantic Reserve Fleet.

Her retirement, however, lasted less than 18 months.

Tarawa in 1958, operating as an antisubmarine carrier (CVS–40) with Grumman S2F *Trackers* on her deck. She still mounts her original battery of 5-inch guns and most of her 40-millimeter AA guns. (USN 1046501)

On 30 November 1950, she was ordered reactivated in response to the Navy's urgent need for warships—particularly for aircraft carriers—to prosecute the war which had erupted in Korea the previous summer. On 3 February 1951, *Tarawa* was recommissioned at Newport, R.I., Capt. J. H. Griffin in command. Though reactivated in response to the Korean war, *Tarawa* never saw service in that conflict. Rather, she served as a replacement in the 6th and 2d Fleets for carriers dispatched to the war zone. On 1 October 1952, she became an attack aircraft carrier, and was redesignated CVA–40. The warship finally made it to the Asiatic war zone in the spring of 1954, but long after the July 1953 armistice had ended hostilities.

The ship returned to the east coast in September 1954 and resumed her normal operations. In December, she entered the Boston Naval Shipyard for overhaul and conversion to an antisubmarine warfare (ASW) aircraft carrier. On 10 January 1955, while still undergoing conversion, she was redesignated CVS–40. Her alterations were completed that summer and, after shakedown, the carrier operated around Quonset Point, R.I., conducting training missions with the ASW air squadrons based there. That fall, she participated in exercises with Hunter-Killer Group 4 before returning to Quonset Point to prepare for the 1956 "Springboard" exercise.

Tarawa served with the Atlantic Fleet for the remainder of her active career. She remained on the east coast, operating out of Quonset Point and Norfolk and occasionally visiting the Caribbean area for exercises. In the main, her duty consisted of barrier patrols against the increasingly large Soviet submarine and surface fleet and assignments training pilots for the Atlantic Fleet. In May 1960, however, *Tarawa*'s active career come to an end. She was decommissioned and placed in reserve at Philadelphia, Pa., where she remained until the late 1960's. During her retirement, she received one more change in designation when she became AVT–12 in May 1961. On 1 June 1967, her name was struck from the Navy list; and, on 3 October 1968, she was sold to the Boston Metals Corp., Baltimore, Md., for scrapping.

II

(LHA–1: dp. 38,900 (f.); l. 820'; b. 106'; dr. 26'; s. 24 k.; cpl. 759; trp. 1,903; a. 2 mis. ln., 3 5", Sea Sparrow, 6 20mm., 2 40mm., ac. 28 (helo.); cl. *Tarawa*)

The second *Tarawa* (LHA–1) was laid down in November 1972 at Pascagoula, Miss., by the Ingalls Shipbuilding Corp.; launched on 1 December 1973; sponsored by Mrs. Audrey B. Cushman, the wife of General Thomas J. Cushman, former Commandant of the Marine Corps.; and commissioned on 29 May 1976, Capt. James H. Morris in command.

Tarawa is the first of five ships in a new class of general-purpose amphibious assault ships and combines in one ship type the functions previously performed by four different types: the amphibious assault ship (LPH), the amphibious transport dock (LPD), the amphibious cargo ship (LKA), and the dock landing ship (LSD). She is capable of landing elements of a Marine Corps battalion landing team and their supporting equipment by landing craft, by helicopters, or by a combination of both.

The ship departed Pascagoula on 7 July 1976 and set a course for the Panama Canal. She transited the canal on 16 July and, after a stop at Acapulco, Mex., arrived at San Diego on 6 August. During the remainder of 1976, the amphibious assault ship conducted trials, tests, and shakedown in the southern California operating area.

During the first half of 1977, *Tarawa* was engaged in training exercises off the California coast. On 13 August, she entered Long Beach Naval Shipyard for post-shakedown availability which was completed on

15 July 1978. Following four and one-half months of intensive individual ship and amphibious refresher training with embarked marines, *Tarawa* ended 1978 in her home port of San Diego on Christmas standdown.

Tarazed

A star in the constellation Aquila.

(AF–13: dp. 6,963; l. 447'10"; b. 60'; dr. 26'; s. 18 k.; cpl. 238; a. 1 5", 3 3")

Tarazed (AF–13) was built in 1932 as *Chiriqui* at Newport News, Va., by the Newport News Shipbuilding and Drydock Co.; was acquired by the Navy on 4 June 1941 from the United Fruit Co. through the Maritime Commission on a bare-boat basis; was converted for Navy use by Brewer's Drydock Co., Staten Island, N.Y.; and was commissioned on 14 June 1941, Comdr. J. M. Connally in command.

Tarazed loaded supplies and headed for the coast of North Carolina to provision ships of the Neutrality Patrol. After returning to New York, she got underway late in August for a voyage to Iceland to resupply American and British naval units. When Japan's attack on Pearl Harbor brought the United States into World War II, the store ship was at Halifax preparing to join another convoy bound for Iceland. Upon completion of the voyage, she proceeded to Baltimore for an extensive overhaul before making resupply runs to Newfoundland, Iceland, and Bermuda.

In July 1942, *Tarazed* arrived at Boston from Nova Scotia and took on a cargo for ports in Puerto Rico, Trinidad, and Panama. On 21 September, she returned to Baltimore laden with sugar which was urgently needed in the United States. The ship continued supply runs from Baltimore or Norfolk to the Caribbean until mid-1943. On 8 June 1943, *Tarazed* joined Task Force 65 at Norfolk; headed for North Africa; and arrived at Mers el Kebir, Algeria, on the 22d. She partially unloaded there; and, on the 30th, she steamed to Oran to help provision that port.

On 4 July, *Tarazed* headed for the United States in convoy GUS–9. She arrived at Norfolk on 23 July, was replenished, and set course for Bermuda. After supplying ports there and at Cuba, she returned to the United States, arriving at Bayonne, N.J., on 13 August.

Eight days later, *Tarazed* weighed anchor for North Africa, arriving at Mers el Kebir on 2 September. After calling at Bizerte and Algiers, she returned to the United States in convoy GUS–15 and arrived at Norfolk on 4 October. Late that month, she joined convoy UGS–22 to take war materiel to Oran, Bizerte, and Palermo. Then, with the exception of a voyage to the Mediterranean in April, she transported provisions to the Caribbean during the first five months of 1944.

In June, *Tarazed* delivered provisions to ships in the ports of Plymouth, Swansea, and Portland, England, and at Belfast, Ireland. She steamed from Norfolk on 24 August and arrived at Oran on 4 September to supply ships supporting the invasion of southern France. She continued making logistics runs to the Mediterranean into April 1945 and turned to supplying bases and ports in the Caribbean until 15 December 1945 when she was ordered to report to the 8th Naval District for subsequent disposal.

Tarazed was decommissioned on 4 January 1946, was returned to her owner through the War Shipping Administration at New Orleans the same day, and was struck from the Navy list on 21 January 1946. She served the United Fruit Co. as *Chiriqui* until 1958. She was then sold to *Union-Partenreederei T/S* of Bremen, Germany, and was renamed *Blexen*.

Tarazed received one battle star for World War II service.

Tarbell

Joseph Tarbell—born at Norfolk, Va., sometime around 1780—was appointed midshipman in the Navy on 5 December 1798. He served in *Constitution* and other ships of the Mediterranean Squadron from 1800 to 1804, at the height of America's war with Tripoli. He was present, under Commodore Preble's command, during the demonstration before Tripoli in 1804 and was among those honored by Congress for services rendered during that action. From 19 to 23 June 1813, during the War of 1812, Tarbell commanded a boat-expedition against the British squadron off Craney Island and in the James River. His flotilla of 15 boats fought the enemy for an hour and one-half and succeeded in forcing him to flee. In those actions, his men sank three British boats, took 43 prisoners, and killed 90 of the enemy. Tarbell was commended by his superior, Commodore Cassin, and by the army officers ashore for his gallantry and assistance in the defense of Craney Island. Just over a month later, on 24 July 1813, he was promoted to the rank of captain. Captain Tarbell died at Norfolk, on 24 November 1815.

(Destroyer No. 142: dp. 1,090; l. 314'4½''; b. 30'11¼'' (wl.); dr. 9'10¼'' (full); s. 35.12 k. (tl.); cpl. 122; a. 4 4'', 2 3'', 12 21'' tt.; cl. *Wickes*)

Tarbell (Destroyer No. 142) was laid down on 31 December 1917 at Philadelphia, Pa., by William Cramp & Sons Ship & Engine Building Co.; launched on 28 May 1918; sponsored by Miss Virgie Tarbell; and commissioned on 27 November 1918, Comdr. Halsey Powell in command.

Tarbell operated along the eastern seaboard until September of 1919, when she was reassigned to the Pacific Fleet. Based at San Francisco, she served with Destroyer Division 15, of Destroyer Flotilla 5 and Destroyer Squadron 4, until late January of 1920 when she joined Division 13 of the same flotilla and squadron. In February, her home yard was changed to Cavite in the Philippines; and, the following month, the destroyer joined the Asiatic Fleet. *Tarbell* served on the Asiatic Station until the summer of 1921, when she returned to the Pacific Fleet with her home yard at Puget Sound. She operated with the Pacific Fleet until she was decommissioned on 8 June 1922 and berthed at San Diego, Calif.

On 29 May 1930, *Tarbell* was recommissioned and assigned to Destroyer Division 11, Destroyer Squadron 10, Destroyer Squadrons, Battle Fleet. Her home port was San Diego until January 1931, when it was changed to Charleston, S.C. However, she remained assigned to the same administrative organization until March, when she was reassigned to Destroyer Division 3 of the Scouting Force. Sometime between July and October of 1934, the destroyer changed home ports back to San Diego, but remained a part of the Scouting Force Destroyers. Late in 1936, *Tarbell* returned to the east

coast to prepare for her second decommissioning, this time at Philadelphia.

She remained there until after war broke out in Europe in September 1939. To keep the war out of the Americas, President Franklin Roosevelt issued two Neutrality Proclamations on the 5th and ordered the Navy to form a Neutrality Patrol. A month later, on 4 October 1939, *Tarbell* was placed back in commission at Philadelphia, Lt. Comdr. Edward W. Rawlins in command. She operated in the Atlantic with the Neutrality Patrol for over two years before the Japanese attack on Pearl Harbor jolted the United States into the war.

Tarbell's duties remained much the same after the United States entered the conflict. The destroyer continued to escort convoys and perform antisubmarine work in the northern Atlantic. She shuttled merchantmen back and forth across the ocean and operated out of the east coast ports on rescue missions to pick up survivors of torpedoed ships.

One such rescue mission occurred on 26 March 1942. A Socony tanker, SS *Dixie Arrow*, was torpedoed off Cape Hatteras, N.C., and *Tarbell*'s lookouts sighted her distress flares a little before 0900. The destroyer instantly rang up full speed; and, one-half hour later, she arrived at the scene of the attack. She dropped a depth-charge barrage to drive off any U-boats lurking in the vicinity and then picked up 22 survivors. After a futile search for the enemy submarine, she disembarked the survivors at Morehead City, N.C.

In May 1942, the destroyer began helping in the surveillance of Vichy French warships in the Caribbean. To assure that those French ships were not turned over to the Germans and that, in accordance with the Panama Declaration, there be no transfer of European possessions in America to any non-American power, she was assigned a patrol area around Pointe-a-Pitre, Grand Terre Island, Guadeloupe, and her specific charge was the old training cruiser *Jeanne D'Arc*.

Her rescue missions continued along with observation missions. On the 16th, she rescued 24 members of the crew of SS *Lammont Dupont*, torpedoed four days out of New York. On the evening of 25 May, when word reached her at San Juan of a U-boat attack on *Blakeley* (DD–150), *Tarbell* got underway so rapidly that two of her officers and 13 crewmen were left behind in Puerto Rico. The following day, she picked up eight wounded *Blakeley* crewmen at Martinique and then participated in the search for the U-boat until the afternoon of the 27th. On 2 June, *Tarbell* rescued 19 survivors of SS *Alegrete*. Two days later, the destroyer sighted survivors of the sinking of SS *M. F. Elliott* and brought them aboard, running her tally up to 31 men rescued on that mission.

Following additional escort duty in the Caribbean

An early view of *Tarbell* (DD–142).   (80–G–456187)

and in the Gulf of Mexico, *Tarbell* began screening transatlantic convoys in mid-May 1943. Her first voyage was in the escort of convoy UGS–9 which was augmented by the latest development in antisubmarine warfare (ASW)—an escort carrier. The convoy reached Casablanca safely on 15 June. *Tarbell* returned to the United States at New York, underwent repairs, and conducted training before joining another Casablanca-bound convoy in August. Upon her return to New York, the destroyer resumed local escort work until 22 October, when she departed New York in company with *Croatan* (CVE–25), *Lea* (DD–118), and *Upshur* (DD–144) to cover the passage of another convoy. The unit steamed via Bermuda, where it was joined by *Albemarle* (AV–5), and arrived at Casablanca on 3 November. Following a short voyage to Gibraltar, *Tarbell* headed back across the Atlantic on 10 November. The return convoy entered New York harbor on the 21st.

The following month brought an availability, refresher training, and time spent in training prospective crews for destroyer-type warships. On 26 December, she departed Norfolk in company with *Mission Bay* (CVE–59) and Destroyer Division 61 to cover convoy UGS–28 to North Africa, thence to operate as a hunter/killer group in the vicinity of the Azores. On 31 December, *Lea* was severely damaged in a collision, and *Tarbell* took her in tow for Bermuda. On 3 January 1944, the destroyer was relieved of her towing duties by *Cherokee* (AT–66) and *Twiggs* (DD–591) and caught up with the convoy at Horta in the Azores on the 7th.

After hunting submarines along the convoy routes, *Tarbell*'s group reached Norfolk, Va., on 7 February, and the destroyer set out for a 10-day availability at Boston. Following that, she was assigned to the Air Force, Atlantic Fleet (AirLant) for air crew training operations off Provincetown, Mass. Relieved of that duty in April, she operated for a time in the screen of *Ranger* (CV–4) and *Kassan Bay* (CVE–69). From then until July 1945, she alternated between carrier escort duty and target ship duty with AirLant. On 20 July 1945, *Tarbell* was placed out of commission at Philadelphia. Her name was struck from the Navy list on 13 August 1945, and she was sold for scrapping on 30 November 1945 to the Boston Metal Salvage Co., Baltimore, Md.

Targeteer

(LSM(R)–508: dp. 1,084 (f.); l. 206'3''; b. 24'6''; dr. 6'8'' (max.); s. 12.6 k.; cpl. 138; a. 1 5'', 4 40mm., 8 20mm., 4 4.2 M.; 10 rkt.; cl. *LSM(R)–501*)

LSM(R)–508 was originally projected as *LSM–508*. The landing craft was reclassified as *LSM(R)–508* on February 1945 and laid down on 31 March 1945 at Houston, Tex., by the Brown Shipbuilding Co., Inc. Launched on 28 April 1945, *LSM(R)–508* was commissioned at Houston on 25 June 1945, Lt. Harry E. Montgomery, USNR, in command.

LSM(R)–508 departed Houston on 30 June and arrived at Galveston, Tex., the same day to begin fitting out. She got underway again on 5 July and arrived at Charleston, S.C., five days later, to receive her rocket launchers and undergo alterations. The landing ship shifted to Little Creek, Va., on 31 July. During her shakedown—conducted from 1 to 15 August 1945—Japan capitulated, ending the war in the Pacific.

LSM(R)–508 operated out of Little Creek, off the Virginia Capes, and in the Caribbean—conducting training there out of San Juan, Puerto Rico, and Guantanamo Bay, Cuba—into 1946. Returning to Little Creek on 24 March, the landing ship participated in further local training operations into the summer. After shifting to Baltimore, Md., in July, for repairs, *LSM(R)–508* sailed for Houston in October, transited the Panama Canal on 30 November, and arrived at San Diego, Calif., soon thereafter, to prepare for inactivation. Decommissioned on 5 February 1947, *LSM(R)–508* was placed in reserve at San Diego. She remained

inactive for the next 22 years. During this time, she was named *Gunnison River* on 1 October 1955.

Apparently slated for disposal in late 1959, *Gunnison River* was reinstated on the Navy list early in 1960 and selected for conversion to a drone aircraft catapult control ship. Accordingly reclassified to YV–3 on 26 May 1960, *Gunnison River* was renamed *Targeteer* on 26 June 1960, with Lt. D. S. Chambers the first officer-in-charge. Placed "in service" in March 1961, *Targeteer* was commissioned on 7 April 1961, Lt. J. L. White in command.

Homeported at San Diego, Calif., from 1961 to 1968, *Targeteer* operated under the operational control of Commander, Fleet Training Group, receiving the necessary upkeep and repairs from Service Group 1. Her primary mission included the launch and recovery of radio-controlled drone aircraft and suface drone unit targets—maintained by Utility Unit 3—furnishing simulated "enemy" aircraft and high-speed surface craft for maneuvers and exercises. Dubbed "the world's smallest aircraft carrier," *Targeteer* provided these support services for the Pacific Fleet into 1968.

Decommissioned on 31 December 1968, *Targeteer* was struck from the Navy list on 1 January 1969. The former drone aircraft catapult control craft was subsequently sold to the American Ship Dismantling Co., of Portland, Oreg., on 10 December 1969 and scrapped soon thereafter.

Tarpon

A large, herring-like fish found abundantly in the Gulf of Mexico and the Caribbean Sea.

I

Tarpon (Submarine No. 14) was renamed *C–3 (q.v.)* on 17 November 1911.

II

(SS–175: dp. 1,500 (surf.), 1,990 (subm.); l. 298'0''; b. 25'1''; dr. 15'3''; s. 19.5 k. (surf.), 8.25 k. (subm.); cpl. 73; a. 6 21'' tt., 1 4''; cl. *Porpoise*)

The second *Tarpon* (SS–175) was laid down on 22 December 1933 at Groton, Conn., by the Electric Boat Co.; launched on 4 September 1935; sponsored by Miss Eleanore Katherine Roosevelt, daughter of Assistant Secretary of the Navy Henry L. Roosevelt; and commissioned on 12 March 1936, Lt. Leo L. Pace in command.

Tarpon operated out of San Diego and Pearl Harbor with Submarine Division (SubDiv) 13 for several years and was then assigned to SubDiv 14. In October 1939, SubDiv 14 was transferred to the Philippines, augmenting the six old S-boats at Manila. All submarines there were then reorganized into Submarine Squadron 5. In October 1941, SubDivs 15 and 16 were transferred from Pearl Harbor to Manila, increasing the Asiatic force to 29 submarines. They were divided into five divisions, and *Tarpon* was assigned to SubDiv 203.

Two days after the Japanese attacked Pearl Harbor, 18 submarines departed the Philippines to begin their first war patrol. *Tarpon* was assigned an area off southeastern Luzon. Since all the ships that she definitely identified as Japanese presented unfavorable firing angles, the submarine ended her patrol on 11 January 1942 at Darwin, Australia, without having fired a torpedo.

Tarpon got underway on 25 January for her second patrol which took her to the Moluccas. On the 30th, she sighted a convoy; but, since the enemy ships were well escorted, the submarine abandoned the chase. On 1 February, *Tarpon* fired a spread of four torpedoes at a freighter. One hit. She then fired two more, and both hit the target. Her victim was apparently sinking when the submarine left the scene of the attack, but postwar analysis of Japanese records did not confirm the kill. On 11 February, while investigating a surface contact, *Tarpon* was illuminated by the enemy ship's searchlight. The submarine submerged and went deep but was severely jolted by four depth charges that knocked out her bow planes, rudder angle indicator, and port annunciator. On the night of 23 and 24 February, *Tarpon* ran aground while attempting to navigate Boling Strait, west of Flores Island. Jettisoning ammunition, fresh water, fuel, and torpedoes failed to lighten the ship enough for her to back off. A native boat then took an officer ashore on the island of Adunara, later returning to the submarine with the only white man on the island—a Dutch missionary, Pastor H. von Den Rulst. He informed the submarine's commanding officer, Lt. Comdr. Lewis Wallace, that the next high tide would occur between 1600 and 1800. His warning that Japanese planes had been over the island during each of the past four days caused the crew a bit of uneasiness until flood tide. Then, with three engines backing, the submarine slid off the bottom. She returned to Fremantle on 5 March.

Tarpon's third patrol began on 28 March and ended at Pearl Harbor on 17 May with no contacts except a hospital ship. Her next mission, which took her north of Oahu, lasted only 10 days, from 30 May to 9 June; but the submarine contacted no enemy shipping. She was then routed back to San Francisco for an overhaul which was completed on 30 September.

On 22 October, *Tarpon* stood out of Pearl Harbor to begin her fifth war patrol which took her to waters north of Bougainville. She sighted many fishing boats which were not worthy of a torpedo and terminated the patrol at Midway on 10 December 1942.

Tarpon then returned to Pearl Harbor for a refit and began her next patrol from there on 10 January 1943. Her assigned area was in Japanese home waters, south of Honshu. At 2130 on 1 February, approximately 27 miles south of Mikurashima, the submarine fired four torpedoes at a ship and scored one hit. A follow-up attack with two torpedoes broke the 10,935-ton passenger-cargo ship *Fushima Maru* in two. Four days later, *Tarpon* began patrolling the sea lanes leading to Truk. On 8 February, she made radar contact on a large, unidentified ship. She fired a spread of four torpedoes, and all hit the target. The submarine was forced to go deep by escorts and could not watch the 16,975-ton transport sink. The victim was the *Tatsuta Maru*, bound for Truk with a load of soldiers. *Tarpon* made no further contacts before returning to Midway on 25 February.

Tarpon's seventh patrol, conducted from 29 March to 15 May, produced no ship contacts; but the submarine did bombard the radio station at Taroa with her deck gun until shelling from Japanese batteries ashore prompted her to withdraw from the area.

On 30 July, *Tarpon* again headed for Japanese home waters. On 16 August, she sighted a Japanese task force which included an aircraft carrier of the *Otaka*-class, but its high speed prohibited an attack. On the 21st, the submarine contacted two large, escorted, cargo ships. She fired a spread of three torpedoes at each and damaged both targets. Seven days later, *Tarpon* damaged another freighter as it was leaving Mikura Shima. On 4 September, she sank a patrol ship with all hands and then returned to Midway on 8 September.

Tarpon conducted her ninth war patrol off the coast of Honshu from 1 October to 3 November. On the night of 16 October, she was patrolling the approaches to Yokohama when she sighted a ship which she tentatively identified as a large auxiliary. The submarine tracked the target until 0156 the next morning when she attacked it with four torpedoes which stopped it dead in the water. However, it soon got underway again and headed straight for *Tarpon*. The submarine submerged, went under the ship, and attacked the target from the other side with three more torpedoes which produced one hit in the stern. The enemy still did not sink, so *Tarpon* fired again with a torpedo which struck the target in the same place as the first. The vessel

exploded and disappeared. Postwar examination of enemy records revealed that the victim was the German raider *Michel* (Shiff-28) which had been preying on Allied shipping in both the Atlantic and the Pacific. *Michel* was the first German raider sunk by a United States submarine in the Pacific.

Four days later, *Tarpon* contacted an aircraft carrier and a destroyer. She made a submerged approach and fired four torpedoes at the carrier. However, both ships speeded up and eluded the deadly missiles. On the morning of 23 October, the submarine made radar contact on two ships and fired five torpedoes at the larger target. All apparently passed under the freighter. The submarine returned to Pearl Harbor on 3 November.

Tarpon's next war patrol, which lasted from 4 December 1943 to 12 January 1944, took her to the Marshall Islands. Besides photographing the various atolls—her primary mission—she fired two torpedoes at an inter-island tanker, but both missed.

From 19 June to 8 August, *Tarpon* performed lifeguard duty in the Truk area, but made no rescues. On 14 July, she fired three torpedoes at what was thought to be an inter-island freighter. All missed, and the ship turned out to be a disguised antisubmarine ship. *Tarpon* went deep to evade the depth charges and cleared the area. On the 25th, she made radar contact on a small convoy and fired three torpedoes at the largest ship. All missed, and the submarine closed to engage with her deck guns. After the second shot, the gun jammed, and only the machine guns continued firing. *Tarpon* withdrew to clear the gun and then returned to the attack. She inflicted considerable damage on the enemy ship before she was outgunned and forced to break off the engagement.

Tarpon's final war patrol, from 31 August to 14 October, consisted of lifeguard duty in the Truk area. When she returned to Pearl Harbor, she was ordered to the east coast of the United States. The submarine departed Pearl Harbor on Christmas Eve, 1944, and arrived at New London, Conn., on 17 January 1945.

After operations on the east coast, *Tarpon* was decommissioned at Boston on 15 November 1945. Early in 1947, the submarine was scheduled for duty as a Naval Reserve training ship. *Tarpon* left Boston under tow on 28 March and arrived at New Orleans on 9 April and was placed in service there on the 17th. She served as a training submarine in the 8th Naval District until placed out of service and struck from the Navy list on 5 September 1956. She was later sunk in deep water, probably as a target, southeast of Cape Hatteras, N.C., on 26 August 1957.

Tarpon received seven battle stars for World War II service.

Tarrant

A county in Texas.

(AK–214: dp. 7,450; l. 338'6''; b. 50'; dr. 21'1''; s. 11.5 k.; cpl. 85; a. 1 3''; cl. *Alamosa*; T. C1–M–AV1)

Tarrant (AK–214), was laid down under Maritime Commission contract (MC hull 2168) on 4 December 1944 by the Leathem D. Smith Shipbuilding Co., Sturgeon Bay, Wisc.; launched on 25 February 1945; sponsored by Miss Agnes Iareon; and commissioned on 18 September 1945, Lt. Comdr. F. A. Simmons, USCGR, in command.

Tarrant and her Coast Guard crew reported to the Commander in Chief, Atlantic Fleet, on 24 September as available for her shakedown cruise. However, since World War II had ended, she was ordered to report to the Commandant, 8th Naval District for disposal.

Tarrant reported on 30 September and was decommissioned and returned to the War Shipping Administration on 21 November. *Tarrant* was struck from the Navy list on 5 December 1945.

Tarrytown

A residential and resort town on the Hudson River in Westchester County, N.Y., located about 24 miles north of New York City.

(PC–1252: dp. 348 (tl.); l. 173'8''; b. 23'0''; dr. 10'10''; s. 20.2 k. (tl.); cpl. 65; a. 1 3'', 1 40mm; cl. PC–461)

PC–1252 was laid down on 8 June 1942 at Houston, Tex., by the Brown Shipbuilding Co.; launched on 30 September 1942; sponsored by Miss Joan Keenan; and commissioned on 27 March 1943; Lt. Harry E. Wilkinson, USNR, in command.

Following shakedown near Miami, Fla., PC–1252 reported to the Commander, Eastern Sea Frontier, for duty escorting ships between New York and the Caribbean. From May 1943 to March 1944, she made round-trip voyages from New York City to either Key West, Fla., or Guantanamo Bay, Cuba.

On 25 March, PC–1252 departed New York bound for Falmouth, England, where she arrived on 19 April. After patrolling between Plymouth and Southhampton for over six weeks, she was assigned, on 3 June, to the forces preparing to invade Europe at Normandy. During Operation "Overlord," she was assigned duty covering the assault at "Utah" beach. After the landing forces had fought their way inland, she resumed patrols, first at "Omaha" beach and then at Cherbourg. Later, PC–1252 patrolled the Channel islands and the area around Le Havre.

Exactly one year after the Normandy invasion, on 6 June 1945, PC–1252 departed Europe in company with 15 other escorts. After stops in the Azores and in Bermuda, she reached Miami on 21 June and began overhaul at the Merrill Stevens drydocks. She completed repairs by the end of September and headed north to Norfolk, Va. From there, she was routed farther north for duty out of Melville, R.I. After operating along the northeastern coast of the United States for one year, PC–1252 was decommissioned on 28 June 1946 and joined the Atlantic Reserve Fleet at Philadelphia, Pa. Almost 10 years later, on 15 February 1956, she was named Tarrytown.

In 1960, Tarrytown was earmarked for disposal through the Military Assistance Program. Her name was struck from the Navy list on 1 July 1960, and she was sold to Venezuela the following October. Acquired along with 11 of her sister ships for use in antismuggling patrols, she never saw duty with the Venezuelan Navy. Tarrytown was later discarded by Venezuela, probably after being cannibalized for spare parts for her 10 sisters who were in service.

Tarrytown (PC–1252) earned one battle star during World War II.

Tartar

The single turret monitor Yazoo (q.v.) was renamed Tartar on 15 June 1869. Less than two months later, on 10 August 1869, she resumed her former name, Yazoo.

Tasco

(SP–502: t. 319; l. 109'; b. 32'4''; dr. 12' (aft); s. 10 k.; cpl. 16; a. 2 1-pdrs.)

Tasco (SP–502)—a salvage tug constructed in 1907 at New London, Conn.—was acquired by the Navy from J. Shewan of Brooklyn, N.Y., on 4 August 1917 and was placed in commission on 29 September 1917.

Acquired for use as a minesweeper, Tasco probably saw little service in that specialty since German mining operations along the coast of America were sporadic and unsuccessful compared to those conducted by both sides in the North Sea. Consequently, Tasco spent all of her brief career patrolling the 3d Naval District coastline around New York. She remained in naval service until the spring of 1919. Her name was struck from the Navy list on 22 May 1919, and she was simultaneously returned to her owner.

Tasker H. Bliss

Tasker H. Bliss—born at Lewisburg, Pa., on 31 December 1853—attended the United States Military Academy at West Point where he graduated in 1875 with a reputation for brilliance. He taught at West Point and at the Naval War College in the 1880's and was an advisor to Secretary of War Elihu Root in his reorganization of the Army. Although promotion in the peacetime Army was slow, his record was such that he became Assistant Chief of Staff in 1915 and Chief of Staff in 1917 shortly after the United States entered World War I. As Chief of Staff, Bliss played a key role in the swift mobilization of American forces for combat. He retired in May 1918 and died in Washington, D.C., on 9 November 1930.

(AP–42: dp. 12,568; l. 535'; b. 72'2''; dr. 27'8''; s. 16.5 k.; cpl. 235; trp. 2,435)

Tasker H. Bliss (AP–42) was built in 1921 as President Cleveland in Newport News, Va., by the Newport News Shipbuilding and Drydock Co., and was owned and operated as a passenger liner by the American President Lines. The steamship was chartered by the Army in July 1941 and renamed Tasker H. Bliss. She was converted for troop use and made five Pacific voyages for the Army before being routed on to Baltimore, Md., where she arrived on 15 August 1942. There, the ship was transferred to the Navy on 19 August 1942; was converted for use as a Navy transport by the Maryland Drydock Co., Baltimore, Md.; and was commissioned on 15 September 1942, Comdr. Gerald L. Schetky in command.

Tasker H. Bliss arrived at Norfolk on 22 September and joined Task Force 34. After loading troops and equipment to participate in Operation "Torch," the invasion of North Africa, the ships of the task force sailed on 24 and 25 October for the coast of Morocco.

Tasker H. Bliss was assigned to Task Group 34.9, Center Attack Group, and arrived off Fedhala, Morocco, on 8 November. On the evening of 12 November, she was riding at anchor in Fedhala Roads when the German submarine U–130 slipped in among the ships and fired five torpedoes at three transports. All torpedoes hit their targets, and they burst into flames. The victims were Edward Rutledge (AP–52), Hugh L. Scott (AP–43), and Tasker H. Bliss. All were abandoned, and the first two sank shortly; but Tasker H. Bliss burned until 0230 the next morning and then sank. She was struck from the Navy list on 7 December 1942.

Tasker H. Bliss received one battle star for World War II service.

Tatarrax

An Indian chief, probably of the Pawnee tribe, said to have visited with the Spanish explorer, Coronado, late in the summer of 1541 while the latter was at Quivira on the Kansas River.

(YTB–372: dp. 206; l. 102'2''; b. 24'0''; dr. 9'7''; s. 12 k.; cpl. 12; cl. Allaquippa)

Tatarrax (YTB–372) was laid down as YT–372 at Port Arthur, Tex., during the winter of 1943 and 1944; launched on 8 April 1944; redesignated YTB–372 and placed in service on 15 May 1944.

Tatarrax departed Galveston on 14 June; transited the Panama Canal on the 27th; and reported for duty with the Commander-in-Chief, Pacific Ocean Area. The large harbor tug cleared Balboa on 11 July and arrived in Pearl Harbor on 16 August. By late September, the tug was operating in the Marshall Islands at Eniwetok Atoll. From there, she moved to the Caroline Islands, ariving at Ulithi on Christmas Eve 1944. In August 1945, Tatarrax moved to the Philippines, reaching Leyte on the 28th. She operated there until the spring of 1946 when she headed for the west coast of the United States.

The tug reached Astoria, Oreg., on 3 June and commenced preinactivation overhaul. On 24 October 1946, she was placed out of service, in reserve, and berthed with the Columbia River Group, Pacific Reserve Fleet.

Tatarrax was placed back in service in 1958. She was assigned to the 14th Naval District, and a record exists of her transfer to the Atomic Energy Commission on 15 May 1958, presumably to assist in conducting experiments. The tug remained active in the 14th Naval District until November 1972 when a survey found her to be unfit for further naval service. During that period, she was redesignated a medium harbor tug, YTM–372. *Tatarrax* was struck from the Navy list on 1 May 1973. She subsequently transferred to the University of Hawaii for use in experiments involving the generation of fuel hydrogen from sea water.

Tate

A county in the northwestern corner of Mississippi.

(AKA–70: dp. 13,910 (tl.); l. 459'0"; b. 63'0"; dr. 26'4" (lim.); s. 16.5 k. (tl.); cpl. 395; a. 1 5", 8 40 mm.; cl. *Tolland*; T. C2S–AJ3)

Tate (AKA–70) was laid down under a Maritime Commission contract (MC hull 1398) on 22 July 1944 at Wilmington, N.C., by the North Carolina Shipbuilding Corp.; launched on 26 September 1944; sponsored by Mrs. C. E. Tate; delivered to the Navy on loan-charter on 3 November 1944; and commissioned at Charleston, S.C., on 25 November 1944, Lt. Comdr. William Jordan, USNR, in command.

The attack transport completed shakedown training in the Chesapeake Bay early in December and steamed to Davisville, R.I., to load Hawaii-bound cargo. She headed south on 30 December, transited the Panama Canal between 4 and 6 January 1945, and reached Pearl Harbor on the 18th. She remained in the Hawaiian Islands until 31 January when she departed Port Allen, Kauai Island, for the Marshall Islands.

Tate reached Eniwetok on 4 February and joined Transport Squadron 17, which soon departed for the Philippines. Proceeding via Ulithi Atoll and Kossol Roads, she reached Leyte Gulf on 21 February and made a shuttle to Samar Island to discharge cargo and disembark passengers before beginning preparations for the upcoming invasion of Okinawa. After training for the assault, she combat-loaded the men and equipment of the Army's 77th Infantry Regiment at Tarranguna, Leyte, and on 21 March departed the Philippines with the Western Islands Attack Group. Her destination was Kerama Retto, a small group of islands located to the south and west of Okinawa, which became the fleet's steppingstone to Okinawa itself. Her soldiers and equipment went into action against the islands of Aka Shima, Kuba Shima, Yakabi Shima, and Zamami Shima. By the afternoon of 28 March, the islands of Kerama Retto were secured, and *Tate* joined the other ships in a waiting area.

The attack transport remained in the vicinity of Okinawa through three weeks of April, also participating in the assault on Ie Shima during her last week in the area. On the 22d, she headed for the Marianas, arriving at Saipan on 27 April. Five days later, she headed for the Solomon Islands. *Tate* loaded marines and cargo at Guadalcanal and Tulagi between 8 and 17 May before heading back, via Eniwetok, to the Marianas. Reaching Guam on 4 June, she disembarked the marines and discharged her cargo. On the 13th, the attack transport got underway for the United States.

On 25 July, *Tate* steamed out of San Francisco Bay to return to the combat zone. Stopping at Eniwetok from 5 to 10 August, she reached Guam on the 14th, the day before the cessation of hostilities. From there,

she headed for Ulithi and thence, via Okinawa, to Jinsen, Korea, for occupation duty. *Tate* returned to the Philippines early in October, visiting Manila and Subic Bay. After stops at Tsingtao, China, and Okinawa in late November, the attack transport steamed back to the United States, arriving at Seattle on 13 December. She remained there until 26 February 1946, when she got underway for San Francisco. The ship loaded cargo between 1 and 16 March and then headed for Eniwetok and Kwajalein.

She discharged her cargo at the two atolls and got underway for Panama on 4 April. *Tate* reached the Canal Zone on 23 April; but, instead of entering the canal, she remained on the Pacific side to help in the final removal of Americans from the air base at Seymour Island in the Galapagos. She returned to Balboa on 20 May, transited the canal, and reached Hampton Roads on 28 May. *Tate* was decommissioned on 10 July 1946 and, three days later, was returned to the War Shipping Administration. Her name was struck from the Navy list on 19 July 1946. Sometime between then and 1948, she was purchased by the Luckenbach Steamship Co. of New York City and served that line as SS *Julia Luckenbach* until 1958.

Tate was awarded one battle star for World War II service.

Tatnuck

An Indian village and a nearby stream located in the vicinity of Worcester, Mass.

I

(Tug No. 27: dp. 1,000 (n.); l. 156'8"; b. 30'0"; dr. 14'7" (mean); s. 13.0 k. (est.); cpl. 44; a. 1 mg.; cl. *Bagaduce*)

The first *Tatnuck* (Tug No. 27) was laid down on 3 December 1918 by the Puget Sound Navy Yard as *Iosco*; launched on 21 February 1919; renamed *Tatnuck* on 24 February 1919; and placed in commission on 26 July 1919, Lt. (jg.) Christian Christensen in command.

Upon commissioning, *Tatnuck* was assigned to the 13th Naval District, which encompassed the Pacific northwest and the Alaskan coast. Designated AT–27 on 17 July 1920, she engaged in towing operations for almost all of her 27-year career. The only break came on 15 April 1944, when the Alaska area was established as a separate naval district—the 17th. She did a short tour of duty under the control of the Commandant, 17th Naval District, before reverting to the 13th in May. On 15 May 1944, she was reclassified ATO–27.

The tug served just over two years under that designation in the 13th Naval District before being placed out of commission on 12 September 1946. Her name was struck from the Navy list on 29 October 1946. *Tatnuck* was delivered to the Maritime Commission for disposal on 26 April 1947 and subsequently was sold to the Puget Sound Tug and Barge Co.

II

(ATA–195: dp. 835 (tl.); l. 143'0"; b. 33'10"; dr. 13'2"; s. 13.0 k. (tl.); cpl. 45; a. 1 3"; cl. *ATA–121*)

The second *Tatnuck* (ATA–195) was laid down on 15 November 1944 at Orange, Tex., by the Levingston Shipbuilding Co.; launched on 14 December 1944; and commissioned on 26 February 1945, Lt. (jg.) John Pakron in command.

Following shakedown training in March, *Tatnuck* was briefly assigned to the Atlantic Fleet before being transferred to the Pacific Fleet with her home yard at Pearl Harbor. During the fall of 1945, the ocean tug saw service with the occupation forces in the Far East. On 26 January 1946, she steamed out of the lagoon at Eniwetok Atoll, reached Pearl Harbor on 19 February, and remained there until 30 April when she headed for Puget Sound. *Tatnuck* arrived in Bremerton, Wash., on 3 January 1947.

The auxiliary tug *Tatnuck*   (ATA–195).

For the remainder of her Navy career, *Tatnuck* operated in the 13th Naval District. Generally, her range of operations extended from the ports of southern California north along the coast of North America and west to the Aleutian Islands. However, during each of four of her last five years of service—1966, 1968, 1969, and 1970—she made a voyage to Balboa, the Pacific terminus of the Panama Canal. In the main, her duties consisted of ocean towing, target towing, and salvage work; but occasionally she was also called upon to assist scientists of the University of Washington's Applied Physics Laboratory in their research work for the Navy.

After more than 26 years of service, she was placed out of commission at Bremerton, Wash., on 1 July 1971 and berthed there with the Pacific Reserve Fleet. She was disposed of by sale in June 1979.

Tatoosh

The name of a Makah Indian summer village and of the island on which it is located, off Cape Flattery, Wash. It is sometimes spelled Tatooche.

(YAG–1: t. 2,224; l. 243'4''; b. 42'0''; dr. 21'0''; cpl. 98; a. 4 .50-cal. mg., 2 .30-cal. mg.)

SS *Catherine D.*—a wooden-hulled steamship built in

1918 at Bellingham, Wash., by Pacific American Fisheries, Inc.—was purchased by the Navy on 27 March 1941; renamed *Tatoosh* (YAG–1) on 10 April 1941; placed in reduced commission on 25 April 1941; was converted to a mobile section base by the Puget Sound Navy Yard; and placed in full commission on 17 June 1941, Lt. Comdr. C. W. Eshom, USNR, in command.

Tatoosh was assigned to the 13th Naval District. Though records of her actual locations do not appear to exist, *Tatoosh* may well have been assigned to Alaskan waters soon after her commissioning. At any rate, she was reassigned to the 17th Naval District on 15 April 1944, the day upon which the Alaskan part of the 13th Naval District was officially reconstituted as the 17th Naval District. The ship served in the new naval district for the remainder of her career. A survey board inspected the vessel in August 1944, and she was decommissioned on 1 December 1944. Her name was struck from the Navy list on 11 December 1944, and her hulk was destroyed on 29 September 1945.

Tattnall

Josiah Tattnall was born on 14 June 1794 at Bonaventura, near Savannah, Ga. He was appointed midshipman on 1 January 1812 and attended the Naval School at Washington, D.C., until 1 August when he was assigned to the frigate, *Constellation*. When his ship tried to slip out to sea, the strong British squadron operating in the Chesapeake Bay forced her to put into Norfolk, Va. *Constellation* remained bottled up in Hampton Roads for the duration of the War of 1812, but Tattnall and his comrades still managed to get into the fray. He was among the 100 or so sailors and marines assigned to the shore battery on Craney Island. On 22 June 1813, the British attempted to carry the island by storm in preparation for an attack on nearby Norfolk. Tattnall's battery and a force of American boats gave the attackers a sound rebuff that deterred the British from further attempts to take the city.

In April 1814, Midshipman Tattnall was detached from *Constellation* and, by 24 August, was in command of a force of employees from the Washington Navy Yard. He led them into battle at Bladensburg in an unsuccessful effort to stop the British advance on the American capital. On 14 October, he was ordered to Savannah for duty in *Epervier*. In May 1815, that sloop sailed for the Mediterranean with Commodore Stephen Decatur's squadron to chastise the Algerine pirates. On 17 June, she participated in the capture of the frigate *Mashuda* and, two days later, of the brig *Estedio*. In July, when *Epervier* was ordered back to the United States with dispatches, Tattnall remained in the Mediterranean in *Constellation*. In January 1817, he transferred to *Ontario* and returned in her to the United States.

Promoted to lieutenant on 1 April 1818, Tattnall was assigned to the frigate *Macedonian* on 30 June, and he sailed in her for the Pacific in November. He was detached from *Macedonian* on 30 August 1820 and returned to the United States. Ordered to Norfolk on 26 December 1822, he joined Commodore David Porter's squadron in schooner *Jackall*. Lt. Tattnall served in the West Indies on an expedition to suppress piracy until he was detached on 4 May 1823. On 23 June 1824, Tattnall was ordered to *Constitution* for Mediterranean service. In March 1826, he transferred to *Brandywine* and returned home in her in May. On the 15th of that month, he was granted six months leave, which was later extended into 1828.

Tattnall served in *Erie* from October 1828 to August 1829 and then went on to survey the Tortugas until March 1830. Lt. Tattnall took command of schooner *Grampus* on 15 April 1831 and cruised the West Indies and the Gulf of Mexico. In August 1832, he captured the Mexican schooner, *Montezuma*, which had boarded and robbed an American ship on the high seas. He was detached from *Grampus* in September 1832 and went on leave awaiting orders for almost four years before being ordered in, July 1836, to recruit men for Capt. Thomas ap Catesby Jones' survey and exploration expedition.

Tattnall was promoted to commander on 25 February 1836 and, in April, reported for a three-year tour of duty at the Boston Navy Yard. Following service with the Mediterranean and African squadrons, Comdr. Tattnall joined the Mosquito Division in the Gulf of Mexico in 1846, commanding the steam gunboat, *Spitfire*. During the Mexican War, he took part in the attacks on Vera Cruz, San Juan d'Ulloa, and Tuxpan, and he suffered an arm wound. For his gallantry before Vera Cruz, the state of Georgia presented him with a sword.

In 1848 and 1849, he returned to shore duty at the Boston Navy Yard. On 5 February 1850, he was commissioned captain and, the following month, was given command of *Saranac*. Next, he commanded the Pensacola Navy Yard from July 1851 to June 1854. From August 1854 to November 1855, Capt. Tattnall was flag captain in *Independence* to Commodore Mervine on the Pacific Station. At Hong Kong on 29 January 1858, he relieved Commodore Armstrong taking command of the East India Squadron, breaking his flag in *San Jacinto*. During his two years in the Far East, Commodore Tattnall came to the assistance of a British squadron under fire from the Barrier Forts at the mouth of the Pei Ho River and, on his return voyage early in 1860, carried the first diplomatic embassy from Japan to the United States.

At the outbreak of the Civil War, Capt. Tattnall held command of the Sackett's Harbor Station. Though he opposed secession, Tattnall resigned his commission on 21 February 1861. A week later, Governor Joseph E. Brown commissioned Tattnall as the senior flag officer of the Navy of Georgia. On 26 March 1861, he received his commission as a captain in the Confederate Navy. Tattnall commanded Southern naval units during the defense of Port Royal until the harbor was captured by Union forces on 7 November 1861. From there, he moved to overall command of the defense of Virginia's waters early in March 1862. Tattnall, by then a flag officer in the Confederate Navy as well as the Navy of Georgia, directed CSS *Jamestown* and other warships in captures of Federal merchantmen off Sewell's Point in April 1862.

On 11 May 1862, in the face of advancing Federal forces, Flag Officer Tattnall ordered the destruction of his flagship, CSS *Virginia* (ex-*Merrimack*). He was later acquitted by a court martial of all charges stemming from that action. He resumed command of the naval defense of Georgia on 29 May 1862 and retained it until 31 March 1863, when he turned over command of forces afloat to Comdr. Richard Page and concentrated upon the shore defenses of Savannah. When Savannah fell to General Sherman's troops, Tattnall became a prisoner of war. He was paroled on 9 May 1865 and, soon thereafter, took up residence once more in Savannah. Capt. Tattnall died there on 14 June 1871 and was buried in Bonaventura Cemetery.

I

(DD–125: dp. 1,090; l. 314'4½''; b. 30'11¼''; dr. 9'4'' (mean); s. 35.11 k. (tl.); cpl. 122; a. 4 4'', 2 3'', 12 21'' tt.; cl. *Wickes*)

The first *Tattnall* (DD–125) was laid down at Camden, N.J., on 1 December 1917 by the New York Shipbuilding Corp.; launched on 5 September 1918; sponsored by Miss Sarah Campbell Kollock; and commissioned on 26 June 1919, Comdr. Gordon Wayne Haines in command.

Following trials off the New England coast, *Tattnall* sailed for the eastern Mediterranean. She arrived at Constantinople on 27 July and, for almost a year, operated in Turkish waters. During that time, she also visited ports in Egypt, Greece, Russia, and Syria transporting passengers and mail. In June 1920, the destroyer began her return voyage to the United States. During the voyage home, she was designated DD–125 on 17 July 1920 when the Navy adopted the alpha-numeric system of hull designations. She stopped at ports in Italy and France before entering New York harbor on 22 July. Following overhaul, *Tattnall* put to sea to join the Pacific Fleet. After port calls along the southern coast of the United States and at ports in Cuba, Nicaragua, Mexico, and the Canal Zone, she reached San Diego on 17 December. The warship operated along the California coast until 15 June 1922, when she was decommissioned and placed in reserve at San Diego.

On 1 May 1930, *Tattnall* was recommissioned, Comdr. A. M. R. Allen in command. The warship served with the Battle Force along the west coast until 1931. By 1 July of that year, she had been transferred to the east coast for duty with the Scouting Force Destroyers as a unit of Destroyer Division 7.

A year later, *Tattnall*'s activity was curtailed by her assignment to the rotating reserve. On 1 January 1934, the destroyer resumed a more active role with the Fleet when she began a year of duty with the Scouting Force Training Squadron. Following another period of relative inactivity in rotating reserve, she rejoined the

Training Squadron late in 1935. During the latter part of 1937, the Training Detachment, United States Fleet, was established; and *Tattnall* and the other units of the Scouting Force Training Squadron joined the new organization. The destroyer continued her training duties until November 1938.

On the 17th, she and *J. Fred Talbot* (DD–156) relieved *Dallas* (DD–199) and *Babbitt* (DD–128) as units of the Special Service Squadron. Based in the Canal Zone, *Tattnall* helped to exert the steadying influence of American seapower in Latin America until the squadron was disbanded on 17 September 1940. The warship, however, continued to operate in the Gulf of Mexico and Caribbean Sea out of her home port at Panama. After the United States entered World War II, *Tattnall* began escorting coastwise convoys in her area of operations, frequently through the Windward Passage between Cuba and Hispaniola, one of the most dangerous areas during the height of the Caribbean U-boat blitz. Though she made many sonar contacts and depth charge attacks, *Tattnall* registered no confirmed kills.

Early in July 1943, the destroyer escorted her last Caribbean convoy north from the Windward Passage to Charleston, S.C. She arrived on the 10th, began conversion to a high-speed transport at the navy yard, and was redesignated APD–19 on 24 July. On 6 September 1943, the day following the 25th anniversary of her launching, *Tattnall* completed conversion. She finished her shakedown cruise in mid-September. Following post-shakedown repairs and alterations in late September, the high-speed transport began amphibious training—first, at Cove Point, Md., and later, at Fort Pierce, Fla.

In April 1944, *Tattnall* was designated flagship of Transport Division (TransDiv) 13, the only high-speed transport division in the Atlantic theater. On 13 April, she departed the east coast for Oran, Algeria, in company with *Roper* (APD–20), *Barry* (APD–29), *Greene* (APD–36), and *Osmond Ingram* (APD–35). TransDiv 13 joined the 8th Fleet at the end of April, and *Tattnall* moved to Corsica to practice for her first assignment, the capture of Elba and Pianosa Islands in the Tyrrhenian Sea. However, before the invasion and during her training period, *Tattnall* was called upon to feign a landing near Civitavecchia, Italy, north of Rome, to draw off German reinforcements headed south to turn back the American forces breaking through at Monte Cassino and heading for Rome. The ruse apparently worked. The reinforcements never reached Monte Cassino; and, on the following day, German radio announced an Allied invasion north of Rome.

On 17 June, the invasion troops went ashore on Elba and Pianosa. *Tattnall*'s boats came under machinegun fire, but suffered no serious damage. After the landings in the Tyrrhenian Sea, the high-speed transport began convoy duty between Italian, Sicilian, and North African ports. Following that duty, she resumed amphibious operations, this time with members of the American-Canadian 1st Special Service Force embarked. Their mission was to capture the heavily fortified Hyeres Islands, located just east of Toulon, and hold them during the main landings in the invasion of southern France. On 15 August, the five ships of TransDiv 13 rapidly put 1,600 troops ashore; and the islands were secured within three days. During the next two weeks, *Tattnall* and her sister transports shuttled reinforcements and supplies into southern France and evacuated Allied wounded and German prisoners of war. For the remainder of the year, the high-speed transport escorted convoys between ports in the Mediterranean Sea.

Tattnall returned to the United States at Norfolk on 21 December and began a month-long availability period before heading for the Pacific. She got underway from Hampton Roads on 31 January 1945. After transiting the Panama Canal early in February and making stops at San Diego, Pearl Harbor, Eniwetok, and

Ulithi, the fast transport reached the Okinawa area on 19 April.

The high-speed transport remained in the Ryukyus through the end of the month. During that time, she stood guard on several of the screen stations which circled Okinawa to protect the units of the fleet from attack by kamikazes, Japan's final suicidal attempt to stem the American tide in the Pacific. *Tattnall* fired at enemy planes several times in the days preceding the night of 29 and 30 April; however, it was not until that night that she drew Japanese blood.

Three red alerts before 0200 failed to materialize into enemy attacks; however, at about 0215, bogies began closing her from the west. A twin-engined plane crossed *Tattnall* astern about 3,000 yards distant, and her 40 millimeter gun crews took him under fire. The attacker retired to the fast transport's starboard quarter with one engine ablaze, but only to renew his attack. Again, he dove at *Tattnall*. This time, her gunners finished the job they had begun on his first pass, and he plummeted into the sea. Soon thereafter, a kamikaze approached the warship from her starboard quarter and dove at her. *Tattnall*, her engines at full speed, turned hard to port to evade the attacker. He splashed into the sea close aboard *Tattnall*'s starboard bow. Debris rained down on the ship and pierced her hull above the waterline. Fortunately, she suffered neither casualties nor serious damage.

The following day, *Tattnall* departed Okinawa and headed for the Mariana Islands and convoy escort duty. She arrived at Saipan on 3 May and returned with a convoy to Okinawa on the 20th. The warship resumed picket duty but experienced no more action like that of the night of 29 and 30 April. To be sure, her crew stood long watches and, on 25 May, was at general quarters for 18 hours straight. On that day, two of her sister ships from TransDiv 13, *Barry* and *Roper*, were hit by kamikazes. *Barry* later sank, and *Roper* was sent to a rear area for repairs.

Early in June, *Tattnall* was ordered to report for duty with the Philippine Sea Frontier. She stopped at Saipan on 13 June and reached Leyte on the 17th. Through the end of the war and for almost a month thereafter, she conducted patrols in the Philippines and escorted convoys to Ulithi and Hollandia. On 13 September, *Tattnall* headed back to the United States. After stops at Eniwetok and Pearl Harbor, the fast transport arrived in San Francisco on 30 October.

From there, she was routed north to the Puget Sound Navy Yard and disposition by the Commandant, 13th Naval District. *Tattnall* was decommissioned at Puget Sound on 17 December 1945. Her name was struck from the Navy list on 8 January 1946. She was sold to the Pacific Metal & Salvage Co., of Seattle, Wash., on 17 October 1946 and subsequently was scrapped.

Tattnall received three battle stars for her World War II service.

II

(DDG–19: dp. 3,370; l. 432'; b. 47'; dr. 21'6''; s. 34 k.; cpl. 354; a. 2 5'', 1 Tartar mis. ln., 1 ASROC ln., 6 15.5'' tt.; cl. *Charles F. Adams*)

The second *Tattnall* (DDG–19) was laid down on 14 November 1960 at New Orleans, La., by Avondale Marine Ways, Inc.; launched on 26 August 1961; sponsored by Mrs. Mary Adams Mason; and commissioned on 13 April 1963 at Charleston, S.C., Comdr. William F. Regan in command.

Following commissioning, *Tattnall* conducted sea trials out of Charleston and tested her Tartar and ASROC missile systems in the Charleston; Jacksonville, Fla.; and San Juan, Puerto Rico, operating areas. Late in August, she returned to Charleston before departing again for shakedown training in the Caribbean. The guided-missile destroyer returned to Charleston once again on 20 October for post-shakedown availability. Training, exercises, and local operations followed from early February until late April 1964. After a visit to New York City late in April, she resumed operations from Charleston.

On 8 September, she got underway for her first overseas cruise during which she participated in NATO Exercise "Teamwork," an operation conducted in the Norwegian Sea and in the Bay of Biscay. The exercise ended early in October, and the warship put into Portsmouth, England, on the 3d. *Tattnall* moved from there to Edinburgh, Scotland, for a one-day visit on 12 October, before heading back to the United States. On the 22d, she reentered Charleston and resumed normal operations.

Following missile firings and bombardment practice in the San Juan operating area, *Tattnall* departed the western Atlantic on 7 December for her first deployment to the Mediterranean Sea. On 14 December, she reached the Straits of Gibraltar and became a unit of the 6th Fleet. While in the Mediterranean, she visited Tunis, Genoa, and Naples in Italy; Marseilles and Theoule in France; and Barcelona in Spain. She also participated in several exercises with other units of the 6th Fleet and with ships of foreign navies. On 4 March 1965, she retransited the Straits of Gibraltar and headed back toward the United States.

The guided-missile destroyer made Charleston on 14 March and began an availability period in preparation for her participation in projects for the Chief of Naval Operations. She completed the availability on 19 April and put to sea to conduct Fleet Research Project Number 69. She finished her work on the research project on 7 May and returned to Charleston. *Tattnall* resumed normal operations until 30 August when she put to sea to conduct the first of two additional tasks for the Chief of Naval Operations. This project, designated

D/S 336, sought to insure her combat readiness prior to the second project, O/S 102. During project D/S 336, *Tattnall*'s crew averaged 10 to 12 hours a day at general quarters as they tracked single and multiple-plane air raids and simulated missile firings. Weather conditions hampered the gathering of data so that project D/S 336 was not concluded until 2 October. She put to sea again on 4 October for project O/S 102, a multi-phase test of the combat effectiveness of the *Charles F. Adams*-class guided-missile destroyer. She completed the project early in December and returned to Charleston for availability, holiday leave, and preparation for another Mediterranean deployment.

On 15 February 1966, *Tattnall* departed Charleston once more to join the 6th Fleet. From 27 February to 3 March, she participated in Exercise "Fairgame IV," a Franco-American exercise conducted in the western Mediterranean. On 17 May, she conducted an intelligence surveillance of Russian warships. In June, she joined in another western Mediterranean exercise, "Deep Six." On this cruise, she added Rhodes; Majorca; Thessalonica and Volas, Greece; and Istanbul, Turkey, to her list of ports visited. On 1 July, the warship put to sea from Palma de Mallorca and headed back toward Charleston, where she arrived on 22 August.

Upon arrival, *Tattnall* immediately began her first major overhaul since commissioning. She remained in Charleston Naval Shipyard from 22 August 1966 until 7 March 1967. After exiting the shipyard, she resumed local operations along the southern Atlantic coast of the United States and in the West Indies until early July. Following a week-long visit to New York City from 12 to 19 July, the guided-missile destroyer returned to Charleston to prepare for her third Mediterranean cruise. That deployment lasted through Janu-

Tattnall (DDG–19) conducting trials, 1963.

ary 1968; and, by early February, *Tattnall* was back in Charleston. She resumed normal operations along the southeastern coast of the United States and in the West Indies until June, when she returned to Europe. After a stop in the Azores and a visit to Germany for the "Kiel Week" celebration, *Tattnall* reentered the Mediterranean for another tour of duty with the 6th Fleet. The warship remained in the Mediterranean until mid-November and then returned to the east coast and local operations.

Tattnall continued to operate from Charleston until late July 1969, when she shifted home ports to Mayport, Fla. She arrived in Mayport on 29 July and conducted normal operations until September. From 2 to 24 September, the guided-missile destroyer participated in NATO Operation "Peacekeeper." On the 24th, she entered Amsterdam in the Netherlands for a week, then put to sea for hunter-killer operations and visits to the European ports of Hamburg, Bergen, Edinburgh, and Le Havre. She reentered Mayport on 10 December 1969.

After four months operating out of Mayport, *Tattnall* steamed north to Chespeake Bay, where she assisted in tests conducted at Randle Cliffs, Md., by scientists of the Naval Research Laboratory. She visited Newport, R.I., in mid-month and returned to Mayport on the 25th. Following five months of operations and exercises in the vicinity of Mayport, *Tattnall* steamed to Charleston for her second regular overhaul. She remained in Charleston Naval Shipyard until 24 March 1971, when she began post-overhaul trials. On 22 April, she headed back to Mayport and operations in the Caribbean Sea and the Gulf of Mexico.

On 16 September 1971, the ship departed Charleston bound for nothern Europe and Exercise "Royal Knight." During that cruise, she visited Rosyth, Scotland, and Rotterdam in the Netherlands before returning to Mayport on 22 October. In March 1972, *Tattnall* deployed to the Mediterranean once again. She conducted exercises with other units of the 6th Fleet and with ships of foreign navies. The guided-missile destroyer visited Valencia, Spain; Genoa and Naples in Italy; Patras and Athens, Greece; Kusadasi and Iskenderun, Turkey; Sousse, Tunisia; Menton, France; and Sicily. On 28 August, she changed operational control to the 2d Fleet and headed for Mayport, where she arrived on 5 September. *Tattnall* resumed operations from Mayport until 29 May 1973, when she got underway to participate in a joint American-French exercise conducted in the vicinity of Charleston. In late May and early June, she visited Norfolk, Va., and the Naval Academy at Annapolis, Md. She returned to Mayport on 18 June.

After a month in the Mayport area, *Tattnall* embarked upon her first UNITAS deployment to South America. She visited ports in Brazil, Colombia, Peru, and Uruguay in between operations and exercises conducted with units of those countries' navies. On 15 December, she returned to Mayport and resumed exercises in the western Atlantic and upkeep in her home port through July 1974. On 22 July, she began a two-month restricted availability at Charleston. *Tattnall* returned to Mayport on 21 September and began preparations for another Mediterranean deployment. The guided-missile destroyer departed Mayport on 25 November and changed operational control to the 6th Fleet at Rota, Spain, on 5 December. That tour of duty in the Mediterranean Sea continued through the first five months of 1975. She returned to the United States at Mayport on 6 June and began western Atlantic operations once more. Late in August, she visited Newport, R.I., and then returned to the Florida area on the 29th. She resumed local operations in that vicinity until early October. On 4 October, *Tattnall* arrived at the Philadelphia Naval Shipyard for regular overhaul.

Completing overhaul on schedule on 6 August 1976, *Tattnall* conducted post-overhaul refresher training off the east coast and in the Caribbean. Completing these operations, she returned to her home port of Mayport on 20 November and commenced an availability period and Christmas standdown.

Following participation in a major fleet exercise, CARIBEX 2–77, from 29 January to 10 February 1977, *Tattnall* departed on a seven-month deployment with the 6th Fleet in the Mediterranean on 30 March. She returned to Mayport on 21 October. Holiday leave period followed.

Tattnall operated off the east coast until 12 June 1978 when she departed for a deployment with the Standing Naval Forces, Atlantic (SNFL) in the North Atlantic. This deployment, which concluded at Mayport on 16 December, included various NATO exercises and port visits to the Netherlands, Great Britain, Norway, Belgium, Germany, and Portugal. *Tattnall* finished the year 1978 in port at Mayport.

Tatum

Lawrence Aldridge Tatum—born on 7 December 1894 in Chambers County, Ala.—enlisted in the Navy at Atlanta, Ga., on 29 June 1917 as a hospital apprentice. Following training at San Francisco, he served at the Naval Hospital in Fort Lyon, Colo., and in the receiving ship at Norfolk, Va. On 15 October 1918, he was transferred to *Alabama* (Battleship No. 8), in which he served until 28 May 1919. Pharmacist's Mate 2d Class Tatum completed his enlistment at the Naval Hospital in Philadelphia and was honorably discharged at Atlanta, Ga., on 18 August 1919.

During the ensuing nine years, he attended Atlanta Southern Dental College, Atlanta, Ga., and received his degree as a doctor of dental surgery. On 9 August 1928, Dr. Tatum was appointed an assistant dental surgeon in the Naval Reserve.

Late in August 1940, Lt. Comdr. Tatum reported to the Naval Air Station, Norfolk, Va., for active duty. He was serving in *Wasp* (CV-7) on 15 September 1942, as that carrier and *Hornet* (CV-8) were covering the movement of reinforcements from Espiritu Santo to Guadalcanal. When *Wasp* was torpedoed by a Japanese submarine, Lt. Comdr. Tatum was among those trapped in the carrier's forecastle, cut off from the rest of the ship by raging flames. Rather than trying to save himself by jumping overboard, Tatum remained in the carrier to aid and comfort the wounded. He apparently went down with the ship when she sank. For his "gallant and intrepid conduct," Lt. Comdr. Tatum was awarded the Silver Star Medal posthumously.

(DE–789: dp. 1,400; l. 306'; b. 36'10''; dr. 9'5'' (mean); s. 24 k.; cpl. 186; a. 3 3'', 4 1.1'', 8 20mm., 3 21'' tt., 2 dct., 8 dcp., 1 dcp. (hh.); cl. *Buckley*)

Tatum (DE–789) was laid down on 22 April 1943 at Orange, Tex., by the Consolidated Steel Corp.; launched on 7 August 1943; sponsored by Mrs. Cecile Cofield Tatum; and commissioned on 22 November 1943, Lt. Comdr. William C. D. Bellinger in command.

After shakedown training in the vicinity of Bermuda, the destroyer escort performed escort duty along the east coast until 25 March when she departed Tompkinsville, N.Y., in the screen of a convoy bound for England. She reached Plymouth on 19 April and returned—via Milford Haven, Wales, and Belfast, Northern Ireland—to New York City on 12 May.

Her second and third transatlantic voyages took the ship to North Africa. She departed the east coast on 28 May in the screen of *Kasaan Bay* (CVE–69), *Tulagi* (CVE–72), and *Mission Bay* (CVE–59) headed for French Morocco. Upon delivering planes at Casablanca, the warships returned to the United States on 17 June 1944, and *Tatum* moored at Bayonne, N.J. She joined *Kasaan Bay* and *Tulagi* once again on 28 June as they weighed anchor for Algeria. The ships made Oran on 10 July; and, the next day, *Tatum* got underway to pick up SS *Cross Keys* at Casablanca and escort her to Bizerte, Tunisia. The destroyer escort returned to Oran on the 16th and, four days later, cleared port once again to protect the British carriers HMS *Hunter* and HMS *Stalker* during their passage to Malta. On the 23d, *Tatum* dropped 130 depth charges on a submarine contact but apparently scored no kill. The force reached Malta on 25 July. Augmented by *Kasaan Bay* and *Tulagi*, the unit steamed to Alexandria, Egypt, and then returned to Malta where they arrived on 3 August.

The next day, *Tatum* reported to Naples where she embarked the commander of a landing craft convoy for the impending invasion of southern France. *Tatum* stood out of Naples on 9 August, joined the landing craft in the Gulf of Pozzouli, and escorted them to the staging area at Ajaccio, Corsica. Before dawn on the 15th, the convoy arrived off St. Tropez where *Tatum* transferred the convoy commander to *LCI–196*. She then patrolled off Cape Camarat until the following afternoon. From 17 July until early autumn, *Tatum* protected convoys shuttling between Corsica, Sardinia, and southern France. On 16 October, she departed Marseilles in the screen of a convoy bound for Bizerte and Oran. During the early part of November, *Tatum* escorted another convoy from Oran to Marseilles; then screened the Army transport *Mariposa* to Naples and returned to Oran on 15 November. *Tatum* got underway again on 24 November to screen a convoy back to the United States, arriving at New York on 11 December. The next day, she began conversion to a high-speed transport at Tompkinsville. On 15 December 1944, she was officially redesignated APD–81.

Tatum (APD–81) cleared Tompkinsville on 6 March 1945, steamed to the Chesapeake Bay for training until the 14th, and stood out of Hampton Roads on the 16th in company with *Prentiss* (AKA–102). Following port calls at Panama and San Diego, *Tatum* entered Pearl Harbor on 12 April 1945. She conducted more training in the Hawaiian Islands before getting underway with a convoy headed, via the Marshalls and Carolines, for the Ryukyus.

Tatum arrived off Okinawa's Hagushi beaches on 19 May and reported for duty with the antiaircraft and antisubmarine pickets stationed around the island. At dusk on 29 May, the warship was proceeding to her radar picket station when she was attacked by four enemy planes. As the first intruder swooped in across her bow, *Tatum*'s guns opened up and scored hits on his wing and fuselage. He banked sharply and headed for the ship's starboard side. About 40 feet from her, the plane's left wing and tail struck the water, jarring loose his bomb. It skipped off the surface, struck and careened off the underside of a gun sponson, and pierced *Tatum*'s hull and two of her longitudinal bulkheads. The dud came to rest with its nose protruding eight inches into the passageway inboard of the executive officer's stateroom. The plane also skimmed over the water into *Tatum*, dented her hull, and knocked out her director fire control and communications with the engine room.

Meanwhile, the second and third planes were setting up for their attack. *Tatum* drove one of them off with gunfire, but the other pilot continued on toward the ship until a hail of gunfire caused him to lose control of his aircraft. He banked sharply to the right, passed by *Tatum*'s port side, and splashed about 100 yards astern. Within seconds, his cautious comrade renewed his attack. He dove on the fast transport, barely missing the port wing of her bridge; and *Tatum*'s antiaircraft fire followed him up as he climbed, did a wing-over, and prepared to come in again. His third and final attack carried him across the ship's fantail and into the water about 50 feet from her starboard quarter.

The fourth plane apparently had been holding back waiting for his colleagues to open a favorable route of attack. He then circled, banked to his left, and dove at *Tatum*. Her barrage ripped off part of his left wing, and he plummeted toward the water, splashing into the sea about 30 feet from her port bow. Then an underwater explosion rocked *Tatum* severely but caused no damage.

Despite considerable damage to the fast transport, her crew had all essential equipment back in operation within 15 minutes. Relieved by *Walter C. Wann* (DE–412) later that evening, she stopped at Hagushi to take on a bomb disposal officer and moved two miles out to sea where the dud was disarmed and dropped overboard. *Tatum* returned to Hagushi the following morning; then moved to Kerama Retto for repairs.

Tatum underwent temporary repairs and departed the Okinawa area on 11 June to escort a convoy to Ulithi. From there, she screened *Briareus* (AR–12) to San Pedro Bay, Leyte, where her permanent repairs were completed; and *Tatum* conducted exercises with *Texas* (BB–35), *Mississippi* (BB–41), *Gainard* (DD–706), and *Barber* (APD–57). On 18 August, she departed San Pedro Bay to escort *Idaho* (BB–42) and *Mississippi* to Okinawa, entering Buckner Bay on the 21st.

Tatum spent eight more months in the Far East, assisting in various phases of the post-war occupation and reconstruction. Between 9 and 11 September, she screened a task unit carrying occupation officials from Buckner Bay to Wakanoura Wan, Honshu, Japan. She remained there until 19 September, assisting in the evacuation of Allied prisoners of war. From there, she shifted to Nagasaki where she supplied boats for the evacuation pool. On 25 September, *Tatum* put to sea for Buckner Bay where she arrived the following day. Three weeks later, the high-speed transport sailed for the Philippines. At Manila, she joined a convoy of troopships bound for French Indochina and arrived at Haiphong on 2 November. After embarking soldiers of the Chinese 52d Army, the convoy got underway on the 4th for Chinwangtao where it arrived on the 12th and disembarked the troops.

Tatum continued to shuttle passengers between Chinese ports until mid-April 1946. On the 12th, she stood out of Hong Kong to return to the United States. After stops at Guam, in the Marshalls, and at Pearl Harbor, the ship reached San Pedro, Calif., on 9 May 1946. On the 18th, she resumed her voyage east and arrived at Philadelphia, Pa., on 3 June. By 5 July, she was in the Charleston (S.C.) Navy Yard undergoing inactivation overhaul. In mid-October, the high-speed transport was towed to Green Cove Springs, Fla., where she was placed out of commission on 15 November 1946. *Tatum* remained out of commission, in reserve, until 1 June 1960 when her name was struck from the Navy list. On 8 May 1961, she was sold for scrap to the Southern Scrap Metal Co., New Orleans, La.

Tatum earned two battle stars during World War II.

Taupata

(YAG–26: dp. 200; l. 117'7''; b. 26'2''; d. 6'8'')

Taupata (YAG–26)—built in 1930 by G. T. Niccol at Auckland, New Zealand—was acquired by the United States Navy on 10 November 1942 from the government of New Zealand and was placed in commission on that same day.

Taupata served as an auxiliary service craft at the Pearl Harbor Navy Yard until early 1944. She was decommissioned on 24 April 1944, returned to New Zealand, and was struck from the Navy list on 16 May 1944.

Taurus

A zodiacal constellation represented pictorially by a bull's forequarters.

(AF–25: dp. 6,600 (f.); l. 325'3''; b. 40'4''; dr. 28'8¾''; s. 13.0 k. (tl.); cpl. 114; a. 1 4'', 1 3'')

I

San Benito—a cargo steamer constructed in 1921 at Belfast, Ireland, by the Workman Clark Co., Ltd.—was renamed *Taurus* and designated AF–25 on 20 August 1942; was acquired by the Navy on 2 October 1942 through the War Shipping Administration from the Balboa Shipping Co., Inc., a subsidiary of the United Fruit Co.; was converted to a provision store ship by the Bethlehem Steel Corp. yard in Alameda, Calif.; and was commissioned on 28 October 1942, Lt. Comdr. Edward T. Collins in command.

After over a month of false starts and material casualties, *Taurus* finally loaded cargo and departed San Francisco on 1 December. Her voyage to the South Pacific took the store ship via Pago Pago, Samoa, to Auckland, New Zealand. In the course of the trip, the former fruit carrier suffered at least 32 more engineering casualties and lost a third of her cargo due to the failure of her ice machine. Upon her arrival at Auckland, *Taurus* went into a five-week availability to correct as many of the deficiencies as possible before beginning her tour of duty with the Service Squadron, South Pacific Force.

She completed repairs during the first week in February 1943 and loaded cargo bound for Espiritu Santo in the New Hebrides Islands. On 9 February, she began the first of four round-trip voyages carrying cargo between Auckland and Espiritu Santo to be staged on to the forward areas.

By August, her sphere of operations was widened to include the Solomons. On each of her next six voyages, *Taurus* carried cargo from Auckland, via Espiritu Santo, to Guadalcanal.

Through 1944 and much of 1945, *Taurus* continued to ply the waters of the South Pacific on relatively uneventful supply missions. Early in 1944, she added Napier, New Zealand, and Noumea, New Caledonia, to her ports of call. By late April, she was operating as far north in the Solomons as New Georgia and Bougainville. In May and June, the store ship visited Efate, Napier, Noumea, and Espiritu Santo. July and September brought resupply runs to the Russell Islands in the Solomons. Through the end of 1944 and during the first three months of 1945, *Taurus* continued carrying provisions to the Solomons, primarily to Guadalcanal, Bougainville, and the Russells.

Following overhaul at Auckland from 6 March to 16 April 1945, the ship got underway for Hollandia, New Guinea. Through the end of August, all her voyages—save one to Manus in the Admiralties—were between Auckland and Hollandia. She returned to Auckland on 30 August and departed again nine days later for New Caledonia and thence to the Philippines. After a stop at Noumea between 12 and 14 September, *Taurus* arrived at Samar on the 25th.

From there, she began her voyage back to the United States. By 23 November, she had transited the Panama Canal and had reported for duty with the Atlantic Fleet. Though originally ordered to Norfolk, Va., she was rerouted to New Orleans. She reported to the Commandant, 8th Naval District, on 29 November 1945. On 11 December 1945, *Taurus* was decommissioned and returned, via the War Shipping Administration, to her owner. Her name was struck from the Navy list on 3 January 1946.

II

(T–AK–273: dp. 9,950 (f.); l. 475'; b. 72'; dr. 19'; s. 16 k. (tl.); cpl. 69)

The second *Taurus* (T–AK–273) was laid down as *Fort Snelling* (LSD–23) on 8 November 1944 at Chickasaw, Ala., by the Gulf Shipbuilding Corp. The end of World War II made her services unnecessary, and the Navy cancelled the contract for her acquisition. The unchristened hull changed hands twice before being completed in 1956 as the roll-on/roll-off ship SS *Carib*

Queen for Trailer Marine Transport, Inc. In 1957, the ship received a Military Sea Transportation Service (MSTS) charter for transatlantic service. However, problems in her propulsion system caused delays and repairs which prevented her actually serving MSTS. In March 1958, after Trailer Marine Transport, Inc., had defaulted on her mortgage, the Maritime Administration took over the vessel. She was assigned to MSTS on 15 January 1959, renamed *Taurus*, and designated T–AK–273.

In May 1959, *Taurus* made her first cargo run, from New York to St. Nazaire. Over the next nine years, she continued to carry cargo for MSTS in both the Atlantic and Pacific oceans. On 1 January 1963, *Taurus* was redesignated LSV–8. During the mid-1960's, she carried cargo to ports in South Vietnam in support of the American effort to aid that Southeast Asian nation's struggle against communist aggression.

Never commissioned, *Taurus* went out of service at Yokosuka, Japan, in September 1968. She was transferred back to the Maritime Administration on 25 June 1969 and was sold on the same day to the Union Minerals and Alloy Corp., of New York City. Her name was struck from the Navy list almost two years later, on 22 June 1971.

Taussig

Edward David Taussig was born on 20 November 1847 in St. Louis, Mo. On 24 July 1863, he was appointed a midshipman at the Naval Academy, then—because of the Civil War—temporarily located at Newport, R.I. Midshipman Taussig graduated from the Academy on 6 June 1867 and began his sea duty in *Minnesota*. He was commissioned ensign on 13 January 1869 to date from 18 December 1868.

Following a tour of duty in *Resaca* and *Narragansett*, Taussig embarked upon a succession of assignments ashore. On 1 July 1874, he returned once more to Newport to begin a course of instruction at the Torpedo Station recently established there. On 29 October, Lt. Taussig was transferred to the Hydrographic Office in Washington, D.C. He was detached from the assignment on 28 December and ordered to the Interoceanic Survey. He returned to Washington in April 1875 for duty with the Bureau of Navigation until October. He rounded out his duty ashore with a tour at the Washington Navy Yard from 2 October 1875 until 25 April 1876.

Over the next four years, he served successively in *Juniata*, *Monongahela*, *Trenton*, and *Constellation*. From 19 June 1880 until 12 May 1881, Taussig served at the Naval Academy and, after three months at sea in *Dale*, he returned there for another 21-month tour. Following three years and four months with the Coast Survey, he returned to sea on 1 September 1886 assigned to *Jamestown*.

Between December 1887 and March 1894, Taussig served successively in the Bureau of Navigation, the Library and War Records Office, and as a member of the board at the Columbian Exposition. On 17 March 1894, Taussig became executive officer of *Atlanta*. By October 1895, he was *Richmond*'s executve officer. He reported to *Independence* for temporary duty on 11 February 1896; however, his assignment was changed on the 20th, when he became executive officer of *Monadnock*. After duty with the Hydrographic Office and as Hydrographic Inspector with the Coast Survey between August 1896 and August 1897, he assumed command of the schooner *Matchless*. In May 1898, he started another period of shore assignments which took him first to the Office of Naval Intelligence and thence to the Norfolk Navy Yard as ordnance officer. On 1 August 1898, Taussig took command of *Bennington*.

Following a year and two months in that gunboat, he returned to shore duty on 31 October 1899 in charge of the 13th Light House District. Taussig commanded

Yorktown from 5 June 1900 until 28 October 1901, at which time he was sent to the Washington Navy Yard for ordnance instruction. Late in December, he was transferred to the Boston Navy Yard as its ordnance officer. He remained there until late May 1902 when he assumed command of *Enterprise*. Promoted to captain on 7 November, Taussig was detached from *Enterprise* on 3 December and ordered for duty as Captain of the Yard at Pensacola, Fla.

Capt. Taussig took a course of instruction at the Naval War College from 1 June to 6 August 1903. Between then and February 1907, he commanded successively—*Independence, Massachusetts,* and *Indiana.* He served next as Captain of the Yard at the New York Navy Yard until 28 May 1907 when he went to Philadelphia for general court martial duty through the latter part of December. On 27 December, Capt. Taussig assumed command of both the Norfolk Navy Yard and the 5th Naval District. On 15 May 1908, he was promoted to rear admiral.

Although Rear Admiral Taussig was transferred to the Retired List on 12 November 1909 to date from the 20th, his service to the Navy did not end. Though relieved of command of the 5th Naval District upon retirement, he returned to the colors nine years later as the Commandant, Naval Unit, Columbia University. He held that command from 27 September until 10 December 1918, whereupon he returned to private life. On 29 January 1921, Rear Admiral Taussig died at the naval hospital in Newport, R.I.

(DD–746: dp. 2,200; l. 376'6''; b. 40'10''; dr. 15'8''; s. 34 k.; cpl. 336; a. 6 5'', 12 40mm., 11 20mm., 10 21'' tt., 2 dct., 6 dcp.; cl. *Allen M. Sumner*)

Taussig (DD–746) was laid down on 30 August 1943 at Staten Island, N.Y., by the Bethlehem Shipbuilding & Drydock Co.; launched on 25 January 1944; sponsored by Miss Ellen M. Taussig; and commissioned at the New York Navy Yard on 20 May 1944, Comdr. Joseph A. Robbins in command.

Taussig fitted out at the New York Navy Yard and conducted a five-week shakedown cruise near Bermuda before returning to New York on 13 July for post-shakedown availability. Repairs complete, she got underway on 18 August for more training—this time at Casco Bay, Maine. On 25 August, *Taussig* headed south from Boston and, on 1 September, transited the Panama Canal. From there, she headed north for a one-day stop at San Diego before continuing west to Pearl Harbor. After six days of training in Hawaiian waters, the warship cleared Pearl Harbor on 28 September in company with Destroyer Squadron (DesRon) 61 bound, via Eniwetok, for Ulithi. She entered the lagoon at Ulithi on 19 October and reported for duty with the 3d Fleet.

Upon joining the 3d Fleet, *Taussig* went to work with Task Force (TF) 38. For the remainder of October, the destroyer searched the area just off the Philippines for pilots downed in sweeps of the archipelago during the Leyte invasion. Early in November, she joined the screen of TF 38 itself while its planes continued to support the Leyte operation with covering strikes up and down the Philippine chain. Along with more of the same duty, December brought an added danger—frightful weather. One fatal typhoon late in 1944 swallowed three American destroyers. The December sweeps, made in preparation for the invasion of Luzon at Lingayen Gulf, continued into the first week of January 1945. On 8 January, the fast carriers began their aerial assault on the shores surrounding the South China Sea. *Taussig* screened the flattops while their planes attacked Japanese bases along the Chinese and Indochinese coasts and on the islands of Formosa and Okinawa as well as providing support for the Allied conquest of Luzon. During the night of 20 January, the destroyer helped shepherd TF 38 through the Balintang Channel, in the northern Philip-

pines between Batan and Babuyan Islands, and into the Philippine Sea.

On 23 January, TF 38 returned to Ulithi for a brief rest and replenishment. At midnight three days later, it became TF 58 once again when Admiral Raymond A Spruance relieved Admiral William F. Halsey as commander of the Central Pacific Force. The fast carrier task force sortied from the lagoon on 10 February, and *Taussig* screened Task Group (TG) 58.1 as it headed north to participate in the first carrier-based aerial attack on the Japanese home islands since the Halsey-Doolittle raid of April 1942. On the morning of the 16th, TF 58 arrived at a point some 125 miles southeast of Tokyo. While *Taussig* and her sister destroyers screened them from enemy submarines, the carriers hurled their planes against Tokyo and other targets on Honshu. After another strike on the morning of the 17th, TF 58 steamed south to support the Iwo Jima invasion. While two of TF 58's task groups moved in to support the Iwo Jima assault on 19 February, *Taussig* stood off to the south to screen a refueling rendezvous between TG 30.8 and the three remaining carrier task groups. That same day, the destroyer subjected a submarine contact to an intensive depth-charge attack. Though she apparently failed to sink the boat, *Taussig* succeeded in her primary mission, protecting the carriers.

Task Force 58 cleared the Volcano Islands on 22 February to resume the air offensive against the heart of the Japanese Empire. Bad weather precluded the carrying out of operations against Tokyo and Nagoya which had been planned for the 25th and 26th, respectively, and *Taussig* steamed southwest to strike Okinawa on 1 March. The following day, *Taussig* joined *Vincennes* (CL–64), *Miami* (CL–89), *San Diego* (CL–53) and Destroyer Squadron 61 in a bombardment of Okino Daito Shima. Two days later, the task force returned to Ulithi.

On 14 March, *Taussig* exited Ulithi lagoon to accompany the fast carriers on another raid against Japan. This time the target was Kyushu, the southernmost of the major islands which constitute Japan proper. With the invasion of Okinawa just over a fortnight away, the carriers sought to pulverize airfields from which kamikaze attacks could be launched against the invasion force. During the raids of 18 and 19 March, American planes also attacked Japanese warships at Kure and succeeded in damaging the carriers *Ryuho* and *Amagi* as well as the superbattleship *Yamato*. *Taussig* helped splash two planes on the 18th and the next day screened TF 58 as it retired from the vicinity of Kyushu after a devastating kamikaze attack. She defended her big sisters during the sporadic air attacks of the 20th and, after the task force reorganization of the 22d, she moved off to screen TG 58.1 during the week-long aerial assault inflicted upon Okinawa at the end of March.

On 1 April, the troops stormed ashore at Okinawa to begin the concluding operation of World War II. TF 58 provided air support through the first three months of the campaign, and *Taussig* moved about off Okinawa screening the carrier from Japanese submarines and planes. The entire campaign was characterized by intense enemy air activity, particularly by kamikazes. On 6 April, an "Oscar" dropped a bomb which barely missed *Taussig*. The destroyer responded with her anti-aircraft battery and scored hits on the intruder, but TF 58's combat air patrol finally claimed the tally. On the night of 15 and 16 April, *Taussig* gunners brought down two bombers and, the following day, claimed credit for downing two suicide planes as well as for assisting in the destruction of a "Frances" finished off by a combat air patrol. On 21 April, she teamed up with *San Juan* (CL–54) and DesRon 61 to subject Minami Daito Shima to the wrath of their guns.

At the end of April, *Taussig* returned to Ulithi with TG 58.1 and remained there through the first week in May. On the 8th, she cleared the lagoon to take up station off Okinawa once more. She screened TG 58.1 carriers while their planes supported the ground forces on Okinawa. *Taussig* continued to guard against the enemy's submarines, but his planes remained the most immediate threat. On 25 May, the destroyer helped to bring down three more Japanese aircraft when her radio controllers vectored combat air patrols in to the kill. Three days later, Admiral Halsey relieved Admiral Spruance, and the 5th Fleet again became the 3d Fleet. *Taussig* remained with the same task group which simply changed designations to TG 38.1. Through the first week in June, she continued to protect those carriers off Okinawa while they sent their planes against the beleaguered island's stubborn defenders and against air bases on Kyushu. She then headed south with TF 38 and arrived at the Leyte Gulf base on 13 June to prepare for the expected invasion of the Japanese home islands.

On 1 July, *Taussig* put to sea with TF 38 for the last series of offensive operations in World War II. For the next month and one-half, she cruised off Japan screening the carriers while their planes softened Japan for the expected invasion. Her guns spoke several times during those operations. On the night of 22 and 23 July, she made an antishipping sweep off Honshu with DesRon 61. The destroyers encountered a four-ship Japanese convoy, engaged it with guns and torpedoes, and claimed to have sunk all four enemy ships. Air operations and antishipping sweeps continued until 15 August 1945 when news of Japan's willingness to capitulate brought an end to hostilities.

Taussig remained in the Far East until shortly after the formal surrender ceremony in Tokyo Bay on 2 September. In October, she returned to the United States and began repairs at Seattle. The destroyer remained there until 1 February 1946, when she sailed for a year of duty off the Chinese coast. In March of 1947, *Taussig* returned to the west coast at San Diego, Calif. Upon her return to the United States, she became a school ship for the General Line School at Monterey. For the next three years, the destroyer conducted cruises along the west coast familiarizing officers assigned to the school with operations at sea. In addition, she was frequently called upon to take naval reservists on board for training cruises.

In 1950, her training duties ended. On 1 May, *Taussig* departed San Diego, bound for the western Pacific. En route, she stopped in Hawaii for a few days training and for liberty in the islands. By 1 June, though, she was again underway for Samar in the Philippines.

Just 24 days later, war erupted in the Far East when North Korean troops streamed south across the 38th parallel into the Republic of Korea. Less than 48 hours later, *Taussig*—assigned to DesDiv 92, 7th Fleet—resumed familiar duty in the Sea of Japan screening TF 77 carriers while their planes joined South Korean ground forces in an attempt to stem the communist tide. That duty continued until the second week in July when *Taussig* made visits to Buckner Bay, Okinawa, and to Keelung, Taiwan, before returning to the war zone on the 11th. Over the following six months, the destroyer operated off both coasts of Korea, usually as a unit of the task group built around *Sicily* (CVE–118) and *Badoeng Strait* (CVE–116). She spent the bulk of that time at sea and participated in the operations at Inchon, Pohang, and Wonsan. In late December, *Taussig* also assisted in the evacuation of Wonsan.

Early in 1951, she returned to the west coast, underwent a three-month overhaul at the San Francisco Naval Shipyard, and conducted extensive underway training out of San Diego in preparation for her return to the war zone. On 27 August, *Taussig* headed toward the western Pacific. After stops at Pearl Harbor, Midway, and Japan, she joined the United Nations Blockading and Escort Force, TF 95, off Korea on 20 September. During ensuing operations with that force until 2 October, the destroyer visited Pusan and conducted shore bombardments near the Han River and near Songjin. From 2 October to 2 November, she screened the carriers of TF 77. Between 3 and 23 No-

vember, *Taussig* participated in hunter-killer operations with units of the ROK Navy before heading south for a month with the Taiwan Strait Patrol. She spent Christmas in Sasebo and then rejoined TF 95 on 26 December for more than a month of operations, primarily shore bombardment and night illumination fire along Korea's western coast. Following rest and relaxation in Yokosuka, *Taussig* began her last tour of combat duty of the deployment on 7 February 1952. For the remainder of this assignment, she screened TF 77 while the carriers conducted air operations. On 24 April, the destroyer completed her second Korean War deployment in the Orient and headed back to the United States.

Taussig returned to San Diego on 11 May and, after a month of leave and upkeep, began training operations which continued until 1 October when she entered the Mare Island Naval Shipyard for repairs. In mid-November, she returned to San Diego and, on the 20th, headed west for her third Korean War deployment. She reached Yokosuka on 22 December and, on the day after Christmas, put to sea to join the screen of TF 77. During the following six months, she alternated screening and plane guard duty for the carriers with bombardment and patrol duty with the Escort and Blockading Force as well as hunter-killer group duty and Taiwan Strait patrols. On Independence Day 1953, she headed home.

By the time of the destroyer's departure from the Far East in the summer of 1953, the Korean conflict had wound down almost to inactivity. Over the next decade, *Taussig* made eight more deployments to the western Pacific. Though she continued to operate with the Korean War task organizations, her duty was increasingly modified to peacetime training and "show-the-flag" duty. Between the seventh and eight deployments, she entered the Long Beach Naval Shipyard on 22 January 1962 to begin a nine-month fleet rehabilitation and modernization (FRAM) overhaul, which she completed on 11 October. Her eighth peacetime deployment to the Far East was from April to December of 1963. Upon her return, the warship conducted operations off the west coast until October 1964.

On 23 October 1964, *Taussig* cleared San Diego harbor for another deployment to the western Pacific. She operated in the Hawaiian Islands until Christmas and then continued on to the western Pacific. On 6 January 1965, the destroyer joined a task unit built around *Constellation* (CVA–64) off the coast of Japan to begin duty with the 7th Fleet. During this deployment, the warship saw her first tour of duty off the coast of Vietnam, where civil strife was growing steadily in intensity. Soon the United States would be deeply committed to bolstering the democratic forces in that Southeast Asian country against communist aggression. For the time being, however, *Taussig*'s one short patrol at "Yankee Station" in March constituted her only Vietnam service during her ninth deployment since the Korean War. For the remainder of that deployment, she conducted normal peacetime training and patrol operations, including a tour in the Taiwan Strait Patrol. The destroyer departed the Orient on 2 May and, after a stop at Pearl Harbor, reached San Diego on 24 May. On 24 July, she entered the Long Beach Naval Shipyard to begin regular overhaul which she completed on 8 November. After a month of independent ship's exercises and holiday standdown, she commenced refresher training on 3 January 1966. On 12 February, the ship entered the Long Beach Naval Shipyard for three weeks of sonar repairs.

Following further exercises and shore bombardment qualifications, the destroyer got underway from San Diego on 20 April to return to the Far East to provide naval support for the burgeoning American presence in the Republic of Vietnam. She stopped at Pearl Harbor from 26 to 28 April and then continued on her way—via Guam and the Philippines—to duty off Vietnam. She departed Subic Bay on 26 May for her first real line period of the Vietnamese conflict. On the 27th, she was ordered to assist in a search and rescue mission for flyers downed by typhoon "Judy." On 1 June, she took up station off the coast of Vietnam to provide naval gunfire support for operations ashore. From then until early October, *Taussig* alternated naval gunfire support with plane guard duty for *Constellation* on the southern SAR station off Vietnam.

After 10 days in Subic Bay as naval gunfire support ready ship, the warship headed south on 9 October to participate in Operation "Swordhilt." She refueled at Manus on 15 October and, on the 16th, joined ships of the Australian, New Zealand, and British navies for the 11-day exercise in which antisubmarine warfare and air defense were emphasized. Following Operation "Swordhilt," she visited Australia. On 4 November, Commander, 7th Fleet, cut short her stay at Melbourne by ordering *Tiru* (SS–416) which had run aground on Frederick Reef some 300 miles northeast of Australia. She escorted the damaged submarine into Brisbane on the 7th and sailed two days later for the United States. She stopped at Suva, Fiji, along the way and entered San Diego on the 25th.

Taussig spent the following year engaged in operations out of San Diego. She conducted ASW training operations during the first two weeks of January and underwent hull repairs at Long Beach for the rest of the month. Early in February, she conducted ASW exercises with *Lofberg* (DD–759), *Chevalier* (DD–805), *Scamp* (SSN–588), and *Pomfret* (SS–391), and then entered San Diego for a tender availability from 11 to 24 February. In March, the destroyer visited Acapulco, Mexico, and returned to San Diego on the 23d. On the last day of the month, she moved to Long Beach, where she began additional hull repairs on 1 April. Those repairs were completed exactly a month later, and she returned to San Diego on 4 May. In June and July, she embarked NROTC midshipmen for their summer cruise, conducted gunnery drills at San Clemente Island, and resumed ASW training with *Lofberg, Chevalier, Frank Knox* (DD–742), and *Raton* (AGSS–270). She disembarked the midshipmen on 3 August and returned to San Clemente for naval gunfire support exercises with Marine Corps spotters. For the remainder of the year, she participated in various drills and exercises—primarily in ASW—along the west coast.

Early in December, she put into San Diego to make final preparations for her next deployment. On 28 December, *Taussig* departed San Diego in company with ASW Group 1 bound, via Hawaii, for the western Pacific. She reached Pearl Harbor on 6 January 1968 and, after a week of ASW exercises and another of rest and relaxation, got underway for Yokosuka, Japan. The destroyer never reached that port. On 23 January, units of the North Korean Navy seized the electronic reconnaissance ship *Pueblo* (AGER–2), and ASW Group 1 was diverted to the Sea of Japan. *Taussig* and her colleagues arrived in their patrol area on 29 January and remained on patrol station for 45 days.

Taussig departed the Sea of Japan on 1 March and put into Subic Bay for upkeep three days later. The destroyer left the Philippines on the 12th to take up naval gunfire support station off Vietnam. On 14 March, she relieved *Cone* (DD–866) off the coast of the III Corps area of South Vietnam. That evening, she fired her first round of the deployment in support of Allied forces ashore. *Pritchett* (DD–651) relieved her on 1 April, and *Taussig* arived in Kaohsiung on the 4th for a tender availability. Eleven days later, the warship put to sea to return to Vietnamese waters. On the 15th, she joined the screen of *Bon Homme Richard* (CVA–31) in the Gulf of Tonkin. After five days serving as plane guard for the carrier, *Taussig* parted company with the task unit and proceeded to the III Corps area of South Vietnam for three days of gunfire support duty. The destroyer rejoined ASW Group 1 on the 23d and, after a five-day visit to Hong Kong, conducted ASW exercises near the Philippines en route to "Yankee Station" in the Gulf of Tonkin, where she spent most of May planeguarding *Yorktown* (CVS–10) and *Kitty Hawk* (CVA–

63). On the 26th, *Taussig* headed for Port Swettenham, Malaysia, where she arrived on the 29th. The destroyer put to sea again on 2 June and, by the 5th, was back on station in the Gulf of Tonkin.

After 12 days of plane guard duty, she pointed her bow toward Sasebo for the first leg of her journey home. On 21 June, *Taussig* stood out of Sasebo, formed up on *Yorktown* along with the rest of ASW Group 1, and headed for the California coast. On 5 July, the warship steamed into San Diego and began a six-week post-deployment standdown. She departed San Diego again on 21 August to enter the San Francisco Bay Naval Shipyard for overhaul. Her refurbishing was completed on 26 November, and *Taussig* departed San Francisco to return to San Diego, whence she operated for the remainder of the year.

Taussig spent the first six weeks of 1969 preparing for refresher training, which she commenced on 14 February. For the ensuing six weeks, the destroyer went through a seemingly unending series of drills, inspections, exercises, and battle problems. Finally, however, *Taussig* passed her final examination on 28 March and settled back into routine operations out of San Diego. She departed San Diego on 4 June, in company with *Halsey* (DLG–23), *Herbert J. Thomas* (DD–833), *Pritchett, John R. Craig* (DD–885), and *Hamner* (DD–718). The six destroyers refueled at Pearl Harbor and continued on to Japan, arriving at Yokosuka on the 21st.

Two days later, *Taussig* stood out for Vietnam, reaching Vung Tau on 28 June. From 29 June to 15 July, she provided gunfire support for the Allied ground forces fighting North Vietnamese and Viet Cong units in the IV Corps area of South Vietnam. From here, she headed for Kaohsiung, Taiwan, for a two-day liberty after which the destroyer steamed on to Japan. After a tender availability alongside *Ajax* (AR–6) at Sasebo, *Taussig* entered the Sea of Japan on 4 August to "ride shotgun" for *Benjamin Stoddert* (DDG–22) and *Halsey*. On 24 August, the warship headed for Hong Kong where she arrived on the 28th.

Five days later, she departed Hong Kong and returned to the gunline, this time near the I Corps area of South Vietnam. On 3 September, *Taussig* supported a combined United States-Korean amphibious landing about 20 miles down the coast from Danang. As the only gunfire support for Operation "Defiant Stand," *Taussig* and her crew kept up a hectic pace until 21 September when her relief arrived, and she headed for the Philippines. She completed repairs and departed Subic Bay on 2 October in company with *Hancock* (CVA–19). She did plane guard duty for the carrier in the Gulf of Tonkin until the 11th when she headed for Yokosuka.

Taussig remained in Japan from 16 to 19 October before resuming her voyage home. Forced to turn back to Yokosuka by Typhoon "Ida," she set out once more on 24 October and, after stops at Midway and Pearl Harbor, reached San Diego on 7 November. Leave and upkeep took up the remainder of 1969, and installation of two new gun mounts occupied the first three months of 1970. In April, she entered the Long Beach Naval Shipyard where she received a new sonar dome. Following that, she embarked upon a vigorous training program in preparation for her deployment to the western Pacific scheduled for July.

However, that deployment was cancelled, and *Taussig* was slated for inactivation. From August to December, her crew worked to prepare the destroyer for decommissioning. On 1 December 1970, *Taussig* was placed out of commission at San Diego and berthed with the San Diego Group, Pacific Reserve Fleet. On 1 September 1973, *Taussig* was struck from the Navy list. On 6 May 1974, she was sold to Taiwan, where she served the Taiwan Navy as *Lo Yang* (DD–14).

Taussig earned six battle stars during World War II, eight battle stars during the Korean War, and six battle stars during the Vietnam War.

Taussig, Felix, see *Felix Taussig.*

Taussig, Joseph K., see *Joseph K. Taussig.*

Tautog

A small edible sport fish, also called blackfish or oysterfish, found on the Atlantic coast of the United States. The adult is black, with greenish-gray blotches.

(SS–199: dp. 1,475 (surf.), 2,370 (subm.); l. 307'2''; b. 27'3''; dr. 13'3''; s. 20 k. (surf.), 8.75 k. (subm.); cpl. 65; a. 10 21'' tt., 1 3''; cl. *Tambor*)

The first *Tautog* (SS–199) was laid down on 1 March 1939 at Groton, Conn., by the Electric Boat Co.; launched on 27 January 1940; sponsored by Mrs. Richard S. Edwards; and commissioned on 3 July 1940, Lt. Joseph H. Willingham in command.

Following brief training in Long Island Sound, *Tautog* got underway for the Caribbean on her shakedown cruise which lasted from 6 September to 11 November. She returned to New London and operated from that base until early February 1941 when she was ordered to the Virgin Islands.

Late in April, she returned to New London, loaded supplies, and sailed with two other submarines for Hawaii on 1 May. After calls at Coco Solo and San Diego, they arrived at Pearl Harbor on 6 June. *Tautog* operated in the Hawaiian area until mid-October. On 21 October, she and *Thresher* (SS–200) stood out to sea, under sealed orders, to begin a 45-day, full-time, simulated war patrol in the area of Midway. For 38 consecutive days, the two submarines operated submerged for 16 to 18 hours each day. *Tautog* returned to Pearl Harbor on 5 December.

Two days later—on Sunday, 7 December—*Tautog* was at the submarine base when the Japanese attacked Pearl Harbor. Within minutes of the first enemy bomb explosions on Ford Island, *Tautog*'s gun crews went into action and, with the help of *Narwhal* (SS–167) and a destroyer, splashed a Japanese torpedo plane as it came over Merry Point.

Tautog's first war patrol began on the day following Christmas and took her to the Marshall Islands for reconnaissance work. After 26 days in the area gathering information, particularly of Kwajalein, the submarine returned to Pearl Harbor on 4 February and was routed to Mare Island for upkeep.

On 9 April, *Tautog* headed westward toward Hawaii and started her next war patrol upon leaving Pearl Harbor 15 days later. Her assigned area was again in the Marshalls. On the 26th near Johnston Island, while en route to her station, *Tautog* sighted the periscope of an enemy submarine which was apparently maneuvering to reach a favorable firing position. *Tautog* made

a sharp turn and fired one torpedo which sank Japanese submarine *RO–30.*

Shortly after her arrival in the Marshalls, *Tautog* was ordered to Truk to intercept ships returning from the Battle of the Coral Sea. In the early morning darkness of 15 May, she tracked a darkened ship, but first light of dawn revealed that it bore the markings of a hospital ship. Two days later, *Tautog* heard the propellers of a submarine, and when it appeared, she fired two torpoedes at it. *Tautog* immediately went to 150 feet and remained there until she heard a loud explosion. Although the Japanese ship was not in sight when *Tautog* surfaced, she was not officially credited with a sinking. Later in the morning, *Tautog* sighted another submarine with the designation *I–28* clearly discernible on its conning tower. She fired two torpedoes. One hit and disabled the enemy submarine, and a third sent *I–28* to the bottom.

Tautog sighted two ships departing Truk on 22 May and made a submerged sound attack on the larger. The American submarine's crew thought that they had sunk the target, but the 5,461-ton cargo ship *Sanko Maru* had been only damaged. Three days later, *Tautog* made an attack from periscope depth against a cargo ship. Her spread of torpedoes sent *Shoka Maru* to the bottom. The patrol ended at Fremantle on 11 June.

Her third war patrol, conducted from 17 July to 10 September, took *Tautog* to waters off the coast of Indochina. Hunting there was very poor, and she contacted only one ship, *Ohio Maru*, which she sank on 6 August.

Tautog was refitted by Holland (AS–3) at Albany, south of Fremantle. Loaded with mines, the submarine stood out to sea on 8 October for a combination offensive and mining patrol. On 20 October, her lookouts spotted the dim outline of a ship through a rain squall. Quickly submerging, the submarine determined that the ship was a 75-ton fishing schooner. *Tautog* prepared for battle, surfaced, closed the range, and fired a shot across the schooner's bow which brought her to. The stranger broke the Japanese colors and hoisted a signal flag. Investigation revealed a Japanese crew and four Filipinos were on board. The Filipinos swam over to the submarine and later enlisted in the United States Navy. The Japanese were ordered to take to their boats but refused to do so. Three shells fired in the schooner's stern disabled her rudder and propeller. The Japanese then launched a boat, were given water, and directed to the nearest land. When *Tautog* opened fire to sink the ship, several more Japanese emerged and scrambled into the boat. Ten more rounds left the schooner a burning hulk.

On 27 October, *Tautog* tracked a passenger-cargo ship until dark and fired two torpedoes into her. A fire started in the target aft, her bow rose into the air, and the unidentified ship sank within a few minutes. The next day, a spread of torpedoes fired at another merchantman turned out to be duds. However, escort ships

Tautog (SS–199) as originally built, painted black with her name and hull number in white. Compare this photograph with the wartime view of *Tambor* in this volume. (80–G–456120)

had seen their tracks, and the submarine received a thorough depth charging which caused no serious damage. During the night of 2 November, *Tautog* planted the mines off Haiphong, Indochina, with several exploding as they were emplaced. On 11 November, she fired a torpedo at another passenger-cargo ship. It missed and alerted an escort which gave *Tautog* a severe depth charge attack. Five explosions close to the submarine caused extensive minor damage. The submarine returned to Fremantle 10 days later for repair and refit.

Her fifth war patrol, from 15 December 1942 to 30 January 1943, took *Tautog* to the Java Sea, near Ambon, Timor, and Celebes Islands. She contacted a freighter in Ombai Strait on Christmas Eve and tracked her until 0306 the next morning when she fired a spread of three torpeodes from her stern tubes. Two hits sent *Banshu Maru No. 2* to a watery grave. *Tautog* went deep and began retiring westward. Enemy patrol boats kept her down for 10 hours before they withdrew. That night, *Tautog* was headed for Alors Strait when she sighted a ship, thought to be a freighter, coming west, accompanied by an escort. They suddenly turned toward *Tautog* and were recognized as an antisubmarine warfare team. The submarine went deep but still received a severe pounding. On 5 January 1943, *Tautog* sighted a sail off her port bow and promptly closed the ship. It turned out to be a native craft with a dozen Mohammedan sailors, four women, several babies, some chickens, and a goat on board. After he had examined the ship's papers, *Tautog*'s commanding officer, Lt. Comdr. William B. Sieglaff, allowed the vessel to resume its voyage. On the 9th at 0838, *Tautog* sighted a *Natori*-class cruiser off Ambon, at a range of about 3,000 yards. Three minutes later, the submarine fired its first torpedo. At 0943, her crew heard a loud explosion, and sound reported the cruiser's screws had stopped. In the next few minutes, as the cruiser got underway at reduced speed, *Tautog* fired two more torpedoes. Meanwhile, the enemy cruiser opened with such a barrage that the submarine could not track her for another attack.

Tautog sighted a freighter on 22 January in the Banda Sea, and three of the submarine's torpedoes sent her to the bottom. The victim was later identified as *Hasshu Maru*, a former Dutch passenger-cargo ship which had been taken over by the Japanese. *Tautog* then headed for Fremantle.

Her next patrol was conducted in Makassar Strait and around Balikpapan from 24 February to 19 April. On St. Patrick's Day, she sighted a grounded tanker with topside damage from an air attack. One torpedo, well placed near the stern, produced a secondary explosion; and the ship settled by the stern. On 9 April in the Celebes off Boston Island, *Tautog* contacted a convoy of five ships. She sank destroyer *Isonami* with three torpedoes and then sent the 5,214-ton freighter *Penang Maru* to the bottom with another spread. During this patrol, *Tautog* also sank a schooner, a sailboat, and a motor sampan with her deck guns.

Tautog stood out of Fremantle on 11 May and headed for a patrol area that included the Flores Sea, the Gulf of Boni, the Molucca Sea, the Celebes Sea, and the Moru Gulf. On 20 May, she sank a sampan with her deck guns. On 6 June, the submarine fired a spread of three torpedoes at a cargo ship off the entrance to Basalin Strait. The first torpedo scored a hit 20 seconds after being fired and a yellowish-green flash went up amidships of *Shinei Maru* as she went down. *Tautog* sank the 4,474-ton cargo ship *Meiten Maru* on the 20th, prior to ending her 53-day patrol at Pearl Harbor. The submarine was then routed back to the United States for an overhaul at the Hunter's Point Navy Yard. She held refresher training when the yard work was completed and got underway for Hawaii.

On 7 October, *Tautog* departed Pearl Harbor to patrol in waters near the Palau Islands. On the 22d, she surfaced near Fais Island to shell a phosphate plant. She sank *Submarine Chaser No. 30* on 4 November and

subsequently damaged a tanker and three cargo ships. With all her torpedoes expended, *Tautog* tracked a convoy for two days while radioing its position back to Pearl Harbor before she returned to Midway on 18 November.

Tautog's ninth war patrol began on 12 December 1943 and took her to Japanese home waters, southeast of Shikoku Island and along the southern coast of Honshu. On 27 December, she fired a spread of three torpedoes at a freighter and made a similar attack on a passenger ship. However, she never learned the results of these attacks since enemy escorts forced her to go deep and kept her down for four hours while they rained 99 depth charges down on her. On 3 January 1944, *Tautog* tracked a cargo ship off the mouth of the Kumano Kawa River, approximately one-half mile from the seawall. She fired a spread of three torpedoes, turned, and headed for deep water. The submarine ran up her periscope, but an explosion filled the air with debris and obscured *Saishu Maru* from view as the freighter sank. The sound of approaching high-speed propellers and a closing patrol plane convinced the submarine that it was time to depart.

The next day, *Tautog* made radar contact with a ship and tracked the target while working toward a good firing position. A spread of six torpedoes produced four hits which broke *Usa Maru* in half. When last seen, the cargoman's bow and stern were both in the air. On 11 January, she intercepted two freighters and fired three torpedoes at the first and larger, and one at the second. Escorts forced *Tautog* deep, but timed explosions indicated a hit on each ship. The submarine was later credited with inflicting medium damage to *Kogyo Maru*. She returned to Pearl Harbor on 30 January for a refit by *Bushnell* (AS–15).

Tautog's assignments for her 10th war patrol took her to the cold waters of the northern Pacific near the Kurils, from Paramushiro south to the main islands of Japan and the northeast coast of Hokkaido. The submarine topped off with fuel at Midway and entered her patrol area on 5 March. The submarine's only casualty of the war occurred that day. While several members of her crew were doing emergency work on deck, a giant wave knocked them all off their feet and swept one man overboard.

On 13 March, *Tautog* tracked a freighter until she reached a good position for an attack and then fired two torpedoes which sent *Ryua Maru* under, stern first. She then sighted another ship coming over the horizon and began a submerged approach. The submarine closed the range and fired a spread of three torpedoes that sank the cargo ship *Shojen Maru*. As she headed homeward on the night of 16 March, *Tautog* made radar contact on a convoy of seven ships off the coast of Hokkaido. She maneuvered into position off the enemy's starboard flank so that two ships were almost overlapping and fired four torpedoes. After watching the first one explode against the nearer ship, *Tautog* was forced deep by an escort, but heard two timed explosions and breaking-up noises accompanied by more explosions. *Tautog* pursued the remaining ships and attacked again from their starboard flank. She fired three torpedoes at a medium-sized freighter and four at another ship. A Japanese destroyer closed the submarine, forced her deep, and subjected her to a depth charge attack for one and one-half hours. *Tautog* was officially credited with sinking destroyer *Shirakumo* and the passenger-cargo ship *Nichiren Maru*. She returned to Midway on 23 March.

During her next patrol, from 17 April to 21 May, *Tautog* returned to the Kurils. On 2 May, she sighted a cargo ship in a small harbor between Banjo To and Matsuwa To. The submarine fired four torpedoes from a range of 2,000 yards. One hit obscured the target. An hour later, she fired two more and scored another hit. The 5,973-ton Army cargo ship *Ryogo Maru* settled into 24 feet of water with her decks awash. The next morning, *Tautog* made radar contact in a heavy fog. She closed the enemy ship and fired four torpedoes with two hitting the target. The submarine circled for a follow-up shot, but this was difficult as the water was covered with gasoline drums, debris, and life rafts. When *Tautog* last saw *Fushima Maru* through the fog, her stern was submerged and her bow in the air. On 8 May, the submarine contacted a convoy headed toward Esan Saki. She fired three torpedoes at the largest ship. One hit slowed the target, and two more torpedoes left *Miyazaki Maru* sinking by the stern. Escorts forced *Tautog* deep and depth charged her for seven hours without doing any damage. Four days later, the submarine fired three torpedoes at *Banei Maru No. 2* and watched her disappear in a cloud of smoke.

On 23 June, *Tautog* departed Pearl Harbor for Japanese waters to patrol the east coasts of Honshu and Hokkaido. On 8 July, she stopped a small freighter dead in the water with one spread of torpedoes and followed with another that sank the ship. A lone survivor, taken on board the submarine, identified the ship as *Matsu Maru* which was transporting a load of lumber from Tokyo to Muroran. The next day, *Tautog* was patrolling on the surface, near Simusu Shima, when she sighted a ship coming over the horizon. She submerged, closed the range, identified the ship as a coastal steamer, and surfaced. She fired 21 5-inch shells into the target, starting a fire and causing an explosion that blew off the target's stern. She then rescued six survivors from a swamped lifeboat who identified their ship as the *Hokoriu Maru*, en route from the Bonin Islands to Tokyo laden with coconut oil.

On 2 August, *Tautog* sighted several ships off Miki Saki. She fired three torpedoes at a freighter from a range of 800 yards. The first hit caused a secondary explosion which obscured the target, and the second raised a column of black smoke. When the air cleared, the cargo ship *Konei Maru* had sunk. The submarine was briefly attacked by escorts but evaded them and set her course for Midway. *Tautog* arrived there on 10 August and was routed to the United States for an overhaul.

Tautog was back in Pearl Harbor in early December and, on the 17th, she began her 13th and last war patrol. She called at Midway and Saipan before taking her patrol position in the East China Sea. On 17 January 1945, *Tautog* sighted a ship heading toward her. She attained a good angle on the bow and fired a spread of three torpedoes at the oncoming target. One hit blew off the enemy's bow. *Tautog* fired another torpedo from a range of 700 yards; and the loaded troopship, *Transport No. 15*, disintegrated. The bright moonlight of 20 January disclosed an enemy ship at a range of 10,000 yeards. *Tautog* attacked from the dark side with two torpedoes and then watched the ship sink. The submarine approached the wreckage and rescued one survivor who identified the ship as the motor torpedo boat tender *Shuri Maru*. The tender was en route from Tsingtao to Sasebo and had a complement of 120. The next day, *Tautog* damaged a tanker but could not evaluate the damage as she had to evade enemy escorts that were approaching. On her way back to Midway, the submarine sank a wooden trawler with her deck guns.

Tautog completed her patrol at Midway on 1 February and was assigned to training duty. On 2 March, the submarine shifted her operations to Pearl Harbor to assist aircraft in autisubmarine warfare for one month before heading for the United States. She reached San Diego on 9 April and operated in conjunction with the University of California's Department of War Research in experimenting with new equipment which it had developed to improve submarine safety. On 7 September, she headed for San Francisco to join the Pacific Reserve Fleet. Her orders were subsequently modified, and she got underway on 31 October for the east coast. *Tautog* arrived at Portsmouth, N.H., on 18 November and was decommissioned on 8 December 1945.

Plans to use *Tautog* as a target during atomic bomb tests at Bikini in 1946 were cancelled, and she was assigned to the 9th Naval District on 9 May 1947 as a reserve training ship. The submarine was towed to Wis-

consin and arrived at Milwaukee on 26 December 1947. She provided immobile service at the Naval Reserve Training Center for the next decade. *Tautog* was placed out of service and struck from the Navy list on 11 September 1959. On 15 November 1959, she was sold to the Bultema Dock & Dredge Co., Manistee, Mich., for scrap.

Tautog received 14 battle stars and the Navy Unit Commendation for World War II service.

II

(SSN–639: dp. 4,290 (f.); l. 301'; b. 32'; dr. 26'; s. 20+ k.; cpl. 110; a. 4 21'' tt., SUBROC; cl. *Sturgeon*)

The second *Tautog* (SSN–639) was laid down on 27 January 1964 at Pascagoula, Miss., by the Ingalls Shipbuilding Division of Litton Systems, Inc.; launched on 15 March 1967; sponsored by Mrs. Albert Gore; and commissioned on 17 August 1968, Comdr. Buele G. Balderston in command.

On 30 August, the nuclear-powered attack submarine departed Pascagoula on her way to join the Pacific Fleet. She transited the Panama Canal on 8 September and arrived in Pearl Harbor on the 23d. There, she joined Submarine Division (SubDiv) 12 as its flagship. During the next 12 months, *Tautog* completed her round of post-commissioning tests and trials as well as her shakedown training. She conducted the majority of these operations in Hawaiian waters although, in January and February 1969, the submarine returned to the mainland for trials and repairs at the Puget Sound Naval Shipyard. She completed her shakedown training in September and, on the 15th, began post-shakedown availability which was protracted by the necessity of replacing her entire diesel generator. *Tautog*'s repairs were finally completed on 19 February 1970, and she began normal operations out of Pearl Harbor—mostly torpedo and sonar tracking exercises.

That routine lasted throuh the summer and into the fall. On 9 October, the ship exited Pearl Harbor for her first Far Eastern deployment. She reached Buckner Bay, Okinawa, on the 23d and joined the 7th Fleet. During her stay in the western Pacific, the nuclear attack submarine spent all of her sea time engaged in antisubmarine warfare (ASW) training—usually with units of the 7th Fleet but, on one occasion, with the British cruiser HMS *Aurora*. When not at sea, she made port calls for liberty and repairs at such places as Subic Bay in the Philippines; Hong Kong; Yokosuka, Japan; and the South Korean port of Pusan. The nuclear-powered attack submarine concluded her first tour of duty in the western Pacific on 28 March 1971 when she sailed out of Yokosuka bound for Hawaii. *Tautog* arrived in Pearl Harbor on 5 April and resumed her routine of upkeep in port alternated with periods at sea engaged in ASW training.

The warship pursued that schedule of activities through the remainder of 1971 and during the first three months of 1972. On 21 March 1972, she put to sea for a special operation. During that mission, she called briefly at Guam and at Subic Bay. At the conclusion of the assignment, *Tautog* made a liberty visit to Hong Kong before returning via Guam to Oahu. The submarine arrived back at Pearl Harbor on 31 August and conducted operations in the Hawaiian Islands for the remainder of the year.

On 15 January 1973, the warship entered the Pearl Harbor Naval Shipyard for her first regular overhaul which was not completed until 15 April 1974. On that day, she resumed local operations out of Pearl Harbor which—except for a voyage to the Pacific Northwest which lasted from late July to early September—occupied her time through the first four months of 1975. On 3 May 1975, she exited Pearl Harbor for another series of special operations in the Central and western Pacific. That voyage included a period in drydock at Guam during the first week in June as well as exercises in the Philippines near Subic Bay. Ports of call once again included Subic Bay and Hong Kong but no Korean or

Japanese ports. *Tautog* returned to Pearl Harbor on 18 October and resumed her schedule of training and upkeep.

Type training, independent ship's exercises, inspections, and evaluations—all conducted in the Hawaiian Islands operating area—consumed the submarine's energies for the next 15 months. She did not deploy overseas until the beginning of 1977 when she got underway for a goodwill visit to Mombasa, Kenya. Departing Oahu on 3 January, she reached her destination on the 24th and remained there for a month while her crew saw the sights and she received visitors on board. *Tautog* returned to sea on 24 February and started east. On the way home, she received orders to join a hastily organized task force built around *Enterprise* (CVN–65) and to return to the East African coast. In Uganda, President Idi Amin had precipitated a crisis by rounding up all Americans resident in his country in response to President Carter's condemnation of the murders of two of Amin's Ugandan opponents. While the United States and the world waited for Amin to make his mind up with regard to the hostages, *Tautog* cruised the Kenyan coast—Kenya stands between landlocked Uganda and the Indian Ocean—with the *Enterprise* group both as a show of American resolve to protect her citizens and as a scratch force to try for a rescue had it become necessary. As he had done many times before, Amin eventually relaxed the pressure and freed the foreign hostages. *Tautog* was released from the special task force and resumed her voyage east, arriving at Guam on 19 March. *Tautog* visited Chinhae, South Korea, in April and, on the 20th, arrived in Subic Bay for a series of special operations in the Philippines.

Early in May, *Tautog* made a liberty call at Hong Kong and then returned to Subic Bay on the 18th. Special operations occupied her time in late May and in June. On 3 July the submarine arrived back at Oahu to resume local operations.

Following completion of post-deployment standdown on 8 August, *Tautog* conducted local operations in the Hawaiian area until she departed Pearl Harbor on 2 December to proceed to the Mare Island Naval Shipyard, Vallejo, California, for overhaul. This overhaul, which included the refueling of her nuclear core, took *Tautog* into 1980.

Tavibo

A Paiute chief in Nevada, famed as a medicine man, who died about 1870.

(YT–276: dp. 240; l. 104'; b. 27'; dr. 11'6''; s. 13 k.; cpl. 10)

The steel-hulled steam tug *Thomas Mesick* was acquired by the Navy at New York City on 22 June 1942 from the Mesick Towing Co.; was renamed *Tavibo* on 4 July 1942; was designated YT–276; and was placed in service in the 3d Naval District on that same day.

On 15 May 1944, *Tavibo* was redesignated YTB–246, large harbor tug. The tug operated in the New York area until 30 August 1946 when she was placed out of service. *Tavibo* was struck from the Navy list on 13 December 1946 and transferred to the Maritime Administration on 9 July 1947 for disposal.

Tawah

Tawah (or Tawa), the Sun Clan of the Hopi Indians.

(SwGbt: t. 108: l. 114'; b. 33'; dph. 3'9''; a. 4 24-pdrs., 2 30-pdr. P.r., 1 12-pdr., 1 heavy 12-pdr. sb.)

Tawah (Gunboat No. 29)—a wooden river steamer, formerly named *Ebenezer*—was purchased by Rear Admiral David D. Porter on 19 June 1863 from Ebenezer Blackstone, St. Louis, Mo.

Tawah was assigned to the Mississippi Squadron under the command of Acting Master Alfred Phelps, Jr. In October 1863, she was assigned to patrol the Tennessee River and remained there until the following year.

In April 1864, *Tawah*, *Paw-Paw*, *Key West*, and *Robb* were employed in convoying Army transports up the Tennessee River, in addition to being on the lookout for Confederate shipping. At this time, *Tawah* was reported to be a miserable ship at best and badly in need of repairs.

On 2 November, *Tawah* and *Key West* encountered *Undine* and *Venus*, which the Confederates had captured three days earlier. After a running battle, *Venus* was recaptured. *Undine*, a "tinclad" of eight 24-pounder brass howitzers, was able to outrun the Union ships and escape to the protection of Confederate shore batteries on Reynoldsburg Island. When *Venus* was recaptured, there were two 20-pounder Parrott rifles and over 200 rounds of ammunition on board.

On 4 November, *Tawah*, *Key West*, and *Elfin* were patrolling the river up to protect the Union headquarters and depot at Johnsonville when Confederate forces under the command of General Nathan B. Forrest attacked the city. *Undine* came up river from the protection of the Confederate batteries, and the three Union ships moved down to attack her. The Confederates burned *Undine* and opened fire on the Union ships with their shore batteries. They were using heavy, rifled guns, and the three Union ships were badly outgunned. The Confederates moved their batteries along the shore and severely shelled the three ships as well as other gunboats, transports, and the wharfs. After fighting fiercely for several hours, *Tawah*'s Parrott guns on the starboard bow were disabled; and all three ships had been damaged, in addition to having expended most of their ammunition. The Union gunboats were abandoned and fired to prevent them from falling into Confederate hands. In June 1865, four 24-pounder howitzers and two rifled, steel 12-pounders were salvaged from the hulk of *Tawah*.

Tawakoni

A Caddoan Indian tribe of the Wichita group that lived in Texas on the banks of the middle Brazos and Trinity Rivers during the 18th and 19th centuries.

(ATF–114: dp. 1,330; l. 205'; b. 38'6''; dr. 14'3''; s. 16.5 k.; cpl. 85; a. 1 3''; 2 40mm.; cl. *Abnaki*)

Tawakoni (ATF–114) was laid down on 19 May 1943 at San Francisco, Calif., by the United Engineering Co.; launched on 28 October 1943; sponsored by Mrs. R. F. Parker; and commissioned on 15 September 1944, Lt. Comdr. Clarence L. Foushee in command.

Tawakoni conducted her shakedown training in the San Pedro Bay area from 1 October to 3 November and returned to San Francisco on the 28th. Two days later, the fleet ocean tug headed for Hawaii and arrived at Pearl Harbor on 12 December 1944. On 4 January 1945, she got underway for the Mariana Islands, towing a barracks ship and a gasoline barge. After calling at Eniwetok and Ulithi, she arrived at Saipan on 7 February and joined the 5th Fleet.

Tawakoni was off the Iwo Jima beaches on 19 February as marines of the V Amphibious Corps began the assault on that island. That day, the tug assisted destroyer minesweeper *Gamble* (DM–15) which, on the 18th, had been hit by two 250-pound bombs. On the 25th, the tug suffered minor damage when a heavy surf pounded her against *LST–785* while assisting that ship to beach. *Tawakoni* remained off Iwo until 10 March, performing retraction, towing, and salvage operations for amphibious craft. She towed *LSM–59* to Tanapag Harbor and then returned to Ulithi on 23 March for repairs.

On 27 March, *Tawakoni* sortied with Task Group 51.1, the Western Islands Attack Group, and arrived off Okinawa on 1 April. During the next few days, she helped to retract landing craft and retrieved barges and buoys. On the 6th, as the tug was preparing to get underway to assist *Bush* (DD–529), approximately 50 miles off Okinawa and badly damaged by suicide planes, a kamikaze attack began. She fired on a suicide plane which crashed alongside a nearby LST and, with the aid of two destroyers, splashed another. A third was downed within an hour. As *Tawakoni* neared *Bush*, two planes came in astern for suicide runs. The tug made a quick turn to avoid the first kamikaze, which crossed the bridge and splashed about 50 feet off the port bow. The ship was showered with debris and gasoline but suffered no damage. The ship's gunners shot down the second plane. Meanwhile, *Bush* had sunk. *Tawakoni* stood by *Calhoun* (DD–801) which had been hit by a kamikaze, as the crew of that ship was transferred to *LCS–82*.

On the 16th, *Tawakoni* participated in the invasion of Ie Shima and splashed one enemy plane before towing *Laffey* (DD–724) to the Hagushi anchorage. She continued operating in Okinawa waters until 1 July when, with units of the 3d Fleet, she headed for San Pedro Bay, Leyte.

While the tug was in the Philippines, Japan capitulated. On 15 September, *Tawakoni* returned to Okinawa which was her base until the following spring. She was frequently called from Buckner Bay for services elsewhere: at Wakayama and Hiro Wan from 21 September to 17 October 1945, at Yokohama and Yokosuka from 9 February to 4 March 1946, and at Guam from 11 to 27 March. She stood out of Buckner Bay on 5 April, bound for the United States, and arrived at San Francisco on 11 May.

Tawakoni operated along the California coast until 15 August when she towed *AFD–26* to the Canal Zone. From Balboa, she steamed to Pearl Harbor to take *Skipjack* (SS–184) in tow for delivery to San Francisco. On 23 December 1946, the tug entered the Puget Sound Naval Shipyard and remained until 24 February 1947.

Tawakoni returned to Pearl Harbor on 4 March conducting local operations until 14 May, when she got underway for China. After calling at Kwajalein, Okinawa, and Guam, she arrived at Tsingtao on 12 July. The tug remained in Chinese waters until 1 December 1947 when she headed for Guam and arrived at Apra Harbor on 1 January 1948. During the next two years, *Tawakoni* performed towing services which took her to the Marshalls, Alaska, Panama, Japan, Hawaii, and the west coast of the United States.

Tawakoni stood out of Sasebo on 12 November 1950 and—three days later at Hungnam, Korea—joined Task Force 90, Amphibious Force, Far East. She planted buoys in the channels at Wonsan, Hungnam, and Inchon and provided towing services to ships of the 7th Fleet. She returned to Sasebo on 14 May 1951 and reached Pearl Harbor on 2 July. She made two round trips to Guam before returning to San Diego on 1 December 1951. On 7 January 1952, *Tawakoni* steamed to Seattle; took two covered lighters in tow; and returned to Pearl Harbor on 2 February. On 22 September 1952, the tug got underway for Adak and operated in Alaskan waters until 2 April 1953.

Tawakoni operated in the central and western Pacific for the next 15 years, calling at ports from Alaska to Australia and from Hawaii to Japan. On 9 October 1968, she stood out of Pearl Harbor with a small drydock in tow that was delivered to Danang, South Vietnam, on 6 November. *Tawakoni* then began trawler surveillance at "Yankee Station" with the 7th Fleet until 17 December 1968 when she headed for Singapore. One month later, she returned to Vietnam and operated between there and the Philippines until early April 1969. The ship received repairs and alterations at Pearl Harbor from 15 April until 13 November. During the next six months, the tug shuttled between ports in the Philippines, Vietnam, Japan, and Guam. With the exception of two deployments to the western Pacific,

Tawakoni operated in the Hawaiian area from May 1971 to May 1978. She was deployed to the western Pacific from 28 February to 19 October 1972 and from 19 February to 8 August 1974. On 1 June 1978, *Tawakoni* was struck from the Navy list and sold to Taiwan.

Tawakoni received two battle stars for service during World War II, three for her labors during the fighting in Korea, and four for duty in Vietnam.

Tawasa

The original name of a Muskhogean Indian tribe of the southeastern United States. They were subsequently named "Apalachicola" by the Spaniards.

(AT–92: dp. 1,330; l. 205'; b. 38'6''; dr. 14'3''; s. 16.5 k.; cpl. 85; a. 1 3'', 2 40mm.; cl. *Bannock*)

Tawasa (AT–92) was laid down on 22 June 1942 at Portland, Oreg., by the Commercial Iron Works; launched on 22 February 1943; sponsored by Mrs. Thomas F. Sullivan; and commissioned on 17 July 1943, Lt. Fred C. Clark in command.

Tawasa held her shakedown cruise off the lower California coast in late August and returned to Portland. The tug steamed to San Pedro, Calif., in October and departed there on the 20th for Hawaii, towing two fuel oil barges. She arrived at Pearl Harbor on 4 November and was assigned to Service Force, Pacific Fleet. The next day, the tug headed for the Ellice Islands and arrived at Funafuti on the 20th.

Tawasa was routed onward to the Gilbert Islands and arrived on 26 November at Abemama—which, only the day before, had been taken by American marines. On 3 December, she moved to Tarawa. The tug made round trips between Tarawa and Funafuti in December 1943 and January 1944. On 21 January, she stood out of Tarawa and rendezvoused with Task Force (TF) 52, the Southern Attack Force, for the invasion of the Marshall Islands. Off Kwajalein Atoll on the 31st, *Tawasa* took soundings enabling *Mississippi* (BB–41) to approach the shore for close bombardment. The tug then performed salvage, towing, and screening duty until 18 February when she moved to Eniwetok to assist in the assault that was to strike that atoll the next morning. She supported operations until the atoll was secured and remained in the area for almost two months, providing services to American ships using this new base. *Tawasa* departed the Marshalls on 12 April for a tender availability at Pearl Harbor and to have a radar installed.

The tug returned to the Marshalls on 25 May. On 11 June, she was in the transport screen of TF 52, the Northern Attack Force, when it sortied for the Mariana Islands. Four days later, she was detached to assist LST's as they landed marines and equipment on Saipan. On 7 July, she got underway for Eniwetok.

Tawasa operated with ServRon 10 from 31 July to 24 August 1944 when she joined ServRon, South Pacific. The ship operated in the South Pacific until 9 May 1946 when she departed Noumea for the United States.

From San Pedro, her home port, she operated along the California coast until returning to Pearl Harbor on 27 December 1946. On 23 February 1947, *Tawasa* headed for Japan and an eight-month tour at Yokosuka before returning home on 30 October 1947.

The tug headed for Alaska on 15 June 1948 and operated out of Adak until October when she steamed to Guam for four months. She then remained on the west coast until 10 August 1950 when she got underway for a five-month tour in Alaska. During the next decade, her operations on the west coast were broken by seven deployments to the Far East for operations with the 7th Fleet. On the first of these, from 4 June 1952 to 1 March 1953, *Tawasa* operated with TF 92, the Logistics Support Force which supplied United Nations forces in Korea. She also performed services at the Korean ports of Cho Do, Sokcho, and Chinhae.

Tawasa (ATF–92) departing Subic Bay to take part in Operation *End Sweep* off Haiphong, February, 1973. (K–98130)

Tawasa deployed to the western Pacific again from 13 February to 3 July 1962. On 29 December, she took *Plaice* (SS–390) in tow at San Francisco and delivered the submarine to Pearl Harbor before returning to San Diego on 1 February 1963. She operated with the 7th Fleet from April to November 1964 and with the Alaskan Sea Frontier from June to September 1965. In December 1965, the tug towed *Bunker Hill* (AVT–9) from San Francisco to San Diego. This was the largest operational tow made by a tug of the Pacific Fleet— 33,946 tons. She returned to Alaska from 8 February to 11 April 1967.

Tawasa's next deployment to the western Pacific placed the ship in a combat zone for the third time in her naval career. On 5 February 1968, she stood out of San Diego for San Francisco to pick up *YFN–1126* and deliver the covered lighter to Hawaii. She left her charge at Pearl Harbor on the 17th and headed for the Philippine Islands the following week to provide target services for ships at Subic Bay until 13 April when she headed for Vietnam.

Tawasa arrived at Danang on the 17th and departed the next day for special operations that lasted for a month. She returned to Subic Bay on 21 May for a week and then steamed to Sattahip, Thailand, to provide drone services for the Royal Thai Navy. The tug called at Danang on 19 June and began special operations that lasted until 10 July. Upon conclusion of the mission, the tug called at Hong Kong and Yokusuka before returning to San Diego on 26 August. She entered the Campbell Machine Yard there the following month for an overhaul which lasted until 21 January 1969.

On 5 March, *Tawasa* got underway for the Philippines and Vietnam. She called at Danang and then proceeded to "Yankee Station" for surveillance duty. The ship was relieved on 22 May and sailed, via Hong Kong, for Singapore. However, on 3 June, the tug went to the assistance of *Evans* (DD–754) which had collided with the Australian aircraft carrier *Melbourne*. *Evans* had been cut in two and only the stern section was afloat. *Tawasa* took the section in tow and returned it to Subic Bay before continuing on her original voyage. She was at Singapore on 16 and 17 June and left for Vung Tau with *YF–866* in tow. She dropped off the lighter on the 19th and picked up a repair barge the next day before proceeding, via Subic Bay, to Guam. After returning

to Subic Bay on 8 July, *Tawasa* made two additional voyages to Vung Tau before returning to San Diego on 24 September 1969.

Tawasa was deployed to the western Pacific again from 16 March to 4 October 1970 and from 8 November 1972 to 15 June 1973. In 1971, the tug deployed to Kodiak from July to November to serve as a search and rescue ship.

After returning to San Diego in 1973, *Tawasa* remained in California waters until 1 April 1975 when she was decommissioned and struck from the Navy list.

Tawasa received three battle stars for World War II service, two for Korea, and seven for Vietnam.

Taylor

William Rogers Taylor—born in Rhode Island on 7 November 1811—was appointed midshipman on 1 April 1828. The following year, he was posted to the sloop *St. Louis* of the Pacific Squadron and served in her until 1832. In 1833 and 1834, he attended the Naval School at New York and, in the latter year, was promoted to passed midshipman. The following year, he was assigned to the receiving ship at New York.

Taylor returned to sea in 1836. Assigned to the sloop *Peacock* cruising with the East India Squadron, Passed Midshipman Taylor was called upon to command a short expedition when his ship ran aground on a reef near the entrance to the Persian Gulf. Assuming command of a cutter, he took a diplomatic agent, Edmund Roberts, to Muscat, on the southern shore of the Gulf of Oman, to exchange ratified treaties. The voyage took five days and included a chase by some Moslem pirates. Midshipman Taylor, however, managed to overcome all obstacles and completed his mission successfully.

On 10 February 1840, Taylor was promoted to lieutenant. In 1842 and 1843, he participated in a survey of Tampa Bay on board the brig *Oregon*. During the Mexican War, Lt. Taylor served in the sloop *St. Mary's* and saw action at Tampico Bar on 8 and 15 June 1846. During the siege of Vera Cruz, he commanded an 8-inch gun in the naval battery.

Between the Mexican War and the Civil War, Taylor saw a succession of tours ashore punctuated by a single sea duty assignment. From 1848 to 1850, he served at the Naval Asylum at Philadelphia. His single sea tour came in 1851 and 1852 when he cruised with the Home Squadron in the sloop *Albany*. From then until the beginning of the Civil War, Taylor did a series of tours of ordnance duty, completing his last one at Washington, D.C., in 1861. While serving in this capacity, he was promoted to commander on 14 September 1855.

On 16 July 1862, Taylor was promoted to captain and, soon thereafter, assumed command of the steam sloop-of-war *Housatonic* which served with the South Atlantic Blockading Squadron through the remainder of 1862 and into 1863. He was the senior Union officer off Charleston on 31 January 1863 when the Confederate ironclad rams *Chicora* and *Palmetto State* made their highly successful raid upon the blockading ships. He served as Dahlgren's Fleet Captain during the operations against Morris Island and Forts Wagner and Sumter between 10 and 19 July 1863. In 1864 and 1865, he commanded the steam sloop *Juniata* of the North Atlantic Blockading Squadron and was present during both attacks on Fort Fisher.

Taylor's naval career continued for eight years after the Civil War. On 25 July 1866, he was commissioned commodore and, until 1867, served another tour of ordnance duty. From 1869 to 1871, he commanded the Northern Squadron of the Pacific Fleet, receiving his promotion to rear admiral on 19 January 1871. Rear Admiral Taylor's last assignment was as president of the Board of Examiners in 1872 and 1873. Rear Admiral Taylor was placed on the retired list on 7 November 1873. On 14 April 1889, he died at Washington, D.C.

Henry Clay Taylor was born in Washington, D.C., on 4 March 1845. He was appointed midshipman at the Naval Academy on 28 September 1860. When the Civil War expansion of the Navy engendered a pressing need for junior officers in the fleet, Midshipman Taylor's class was graduated a year early. He was commissioned ensign on 28 May 1863 and posted to the steam sloop *Shenandoah* operating with the North Atlantic Blockading Squadron. In 1864, he was transferred to the sloop-of-war *Iroquois*, in which he visited the Mediterranean and participated in the hunt for the Confederate raider *Shenandoah*.

After the Civil War, Taylor served in a succession of ships on various stations. In 1866 and 1867, he was in *Rhode Island* with the North Atlantic Squadron, and he was assigned to *Susquehanna* from 1867 to 1868. His next tour of duty, in 1868 and 1869, was with the European Squadron in the storeship *Guard*.

Between 1869 and 1880, Taylor sandwiched two tours at sea in between two periods of shore duty. His first assignment ashore—in 1869, 1870, and 1871—was at the Naval Academy. Following that, he was executive officer of *Saranac*, the flagship of the Pacific Squadron, from 1872 to 1874. Over the next three years, Lt. Comdr. Taylor commanded the Coast Survey steamer *Hassler*. In 1877, he came ashore once more, this time assigned to the Hydrographic Office. From there, he went to the Washington Navy Yard where he was serving at the time of his promotion to commander in December 1879.

In 1880, Comdr. Taylor resumed sea duty as the commanding officer of *Saratoga*. In 1884 and 1885, he was on special duty at New York City. From 1885 to 1887, Comdr. Taylor served as a member of the Board of Inspection and then took a leave of absence in 1888. In 1890, he returned to duty to command *Alliance* on the Asiatic Station until September 1891 when he took another leave of absence until December 1892. After six months special duty in 1893, Comdr. Taylor became President of the Naval War College.

In April 1894, he was promoted to captain. Capt. Taylor assumed command of *Indiana* (Battleship No. 1) in December 1894. His ship was assigned to the North Atlantic Squadron, and he commanded her through the Spanish-American War in 1898. In the fall of 1899, Capt. Taylor was detached from *Indiana* and assigned to shore duty. In March 1900, he became a member of the General Board and, 11 months later on 11 February

1901, he was promoted to rear admiral. On 29 April 1902, he assumed the post of Chief of the Bureau of Navigation, which he held until his death on 26 July 1904.

The first *Taylor* (DD–94) was named for Rear Admiral Henry Clay Taylor, and the second *Taylor* (DD–468) commemorates Rear Admiral William Rogers Taylor.

I

(Destroyer No. 94: dp. 1,090; l. 314'4½''; b. 30'11¼'' (wl.); dr. 9'0'' (mean); s. 35 k. (est.); cpl. 122; a. 4 4'', 1 3'', 12 21'' tt.; cl. *Wickes*)

The first *Taylor* (Destroyer No. 94) was laid down on 15 October 1917 by the Mare Island Navy Yard, Calif.; launched on 14 February 1918; sponsored by Miss Mary Gorgas; and commissioned on 1 June 1918, Comdr. Charles T. Hutchins, Jr., in command.

Upon commissioning, *Taylor* joined Division 12 of the Destroyer Force, Atlantic Fleet. She cruised with that fleet through the end of World War I and into the postwar period. By 1 April 1919, she was assigned to Division 8, Destroyer Force. In 1920, *Taylor* was placed in reduced commission though still operating on the Atlantic coast. That summer, on 17 July, the Navy adopted the alpha-numeric hull designation system, and *Taylor* became DD–94. In October, she was placed back in full commission and, until the summer of 1922, operated with Division 8, Flotilla 8, Squadron 3. On 21 June 1922, the destroyer was placed out of commission at Philadelphia.

Taylor remained inactive there until 1 May 1930, when she was placed back in commission, Comdr. George B. Keester in command. She was assigned to Division 33, Squadron 7, Destroyer Squadrons, Scouting Fleet, and operated from Charleston, S.C., until November when she was placed in reduced commission once again. At the same time, *Taylor* was detached from the Scouting Fleet and transferred to Division 47, Squadron 16, Training Squadorn. She was assigned to the 6th and 7th Naval Districts to train reservists and to carry Reserve Officer Training Corps midshipmen on summer cruises.

By 1 April 1931, her unit designation changed completely. Scouting Fleet became Scouting Force, and the destroyer was an element of Division 28 of the Training Squadron. She operated with that unit until early in 1934 when she joined Squadron 19 of the rotating reserve with which she remained until that fall.

On 1 September, she relieved *J. Fred Talbot* (DD–156) on duty with the Special Service Squadron. She cruised the West Indies and the Gulf of Mexico with that little force for the better part of a year to guard American interests during Latin America's sporadic political spasms. By 1 October 1935, *Taylor* was back with the Training Squadron as a unit of the newly established Division 30. She trained reservists until early in 1937 when she returned to the Special Service Squadron in relief of *Manley* (DD–74). The destroyer again patroled the volatile Caribbean area protecting American lives and property.

Upon her return to the United States in 1938, *Taylor* was moored at Philadelphia to prepare for inactivation. The destroyer was placed out of commission on 23 September 1938. Although her name was struck from the Navy list on 6 December 1938, and she was offered for sale in July 1939, *Taylor*'s service to the Navy was not yet at an end. On 11 July 1940, she was selected for use in training damage control parties and was designated Damage Control Hulk No. 40.

Moreover, at least a part of her saw duty in World War II. In May 1942—while patrolling off Martinique—one of her sister ships, *Blakley* (DD–150), lost 60 feet of her bow to a German torpedo. *Taylor*'s bow was grafted onto *Blakeley* at Philadelphia that summer; and, in September, the latter destroyer returned to convoy escort duty in the Atlantic, Caribbean, and Mediterranean. The former *Taylor* continued to serve as a damage control hulk until almost the end of the war. She was finally sold for scrap in August 1945 and delivered to her purchaser on the 8th.

II

(DD–468: dp. 2,050; l. 376'6''; b. 39'4''; dr. 17.9''; s. 35.5 k.; cpl. 329; a. 5 5'', 4 1.1'', 6 20mm., 10 21'' tt., 6 dcp., 2 dct.; cl. *Fletcher*)

The second *Taylor* (DD–468) was laid down on 28 August 1941 at Bath, Maine, by the Bath Iron Works Corp.; launched on 7 June 1942; sponsored by Mrs. H. A. Baldridge; and commissioned on 28 August 1942 at the Charlestown Navy Yard near Boston, Mass., Lt. Comdr. Benjamin Katz in command.

Taylor began her naval career with the Atlantic Fleet. Assigned to Destroyer Squadron (DesRon) 20, the destroyer trained at Casco Bay, Maine, and made her shakedown cruise in the northern Atlantic before beginning duty as a coastwise convoy escort. The latter duty lasted until mid-November when she escorted a transatlantic convoy to a point just off Casablanca. The transit was uneventful, save for the interception of a Spanish merchantman, SS *Darro*. A boarding party from *Taylor* sent the neutral ship off to Gibraltar to prevent her from transmitting information about the convoy to the enemy. *Taylor* returned to the United States at Norfolk early in December and remained there until mid-month.

On 17 December, the warship cleared Hampton Roads in company with Task Force (TF) 13 on her way to duty in the Pacific. After transiting the Panama Canal and stopping at Tutuila in the Samoan Islands, the destroyer reported at Noumea, New Caledonia, on 20 January 1943 for duty in the Southwest Pacific. From Noumea, *Taylor* continued west to Efate in the New Hebrides group, entering Havannah Harbor on the 26th. There, she became a unit of DesRon 21, one of two four-destroyer divisions screening Rear Admiral Giffen's TF 18, comprised of three heavy cruisers, three light cruisers, and two escort carriers.

On 27 January, *Taylor* cleared Havannah Harbor with the other ships of TF 18, one of several task forces sent out to screen an important reinforcement echelon to Guadalcanal. Admiral Halsey, operating upon intelligence which indicated a major Japanese attempt to reinforce their beleaguered garrison on the island, sent out the large screening force in the hope and expectation of a major naval engagement. That sea battle never materialized because the enemy activities upon which he predicated his actions were actually movements preparatory to a Japanese withdrawal. Instead, the enemy subjected TF 18 to a scathing air attack. On the evening of the 29th, enemy "Betty" bombers attacked TF 18 with torpedoes. The ships brushed off the first attack with antiaircraft fire, suffered negligible damage, and raced on to rendezvous with the other elements of the covering force. After a concerted effort, the Japanese fliers finally scored a crippling torpedo hit on *Chicago* (CA–29). When *Louisville* (CA–28) took the stricken cruiser in tow, *Taylor* helped to screen the retiring ships as they steamed out of range of enemy aircraft. The following day, more enemy planes appeared and attacked. After *Chicago* took four more torpedo hits, her crew and the warships covering her abandoned the heavy cruiser to her watery fate and returned to Efate.

On 4 February, *Taylor* and the other ships of DesRon 21 were transferred to TF 67, Rear Admiral Ainsworth's cruiser-destroyer force. Soon thereafter, TF 67 became TF 18, and the former TF 18 became TF 19. In any event, during February and March, *Taylor* screened Ainsworth's cruisers—*St. Louis* (CL–49), *Honolulu* (CL–48), and *Helena* (CL–50)—during operations between Espiritu Santo and Guadalcanal. During the night of 15 and 16 March, she joined *Nicholas* (DD–

449), *Radford* (DD–446), and *Strong* (DD–467) in the fourth bombardment of the Vila-Stanmore plantation located on Kolombangara Island in the central Solomons. On 26 March, the destroyer cleared Espiritu Santo to escort *Kanawha* (AO–1), *Aloe* (YN–1), and six coastal transports to Guadalcanal. The ships reached Tulagi on the 29th; and, while *Kanawha* discharged cargo, *Taylor* resumed operations at sea with Ainsworth's cruisers.

On the nights of 4, 5, and 6 April, she joined them in sweeps up the "Slot" before being ordered back to Tulagi on the 7th to pick up *Kanawha*. When the destroyer was just about to enter Tulagi, a strong Japanese air raid cancelled her mission by severely bombing *Kanawha* before the old oiler could clear the harbor completely. With *Kanawha* disabled, *Taylor* rang up 30 knots and cleared the area via Sealark Channel. During her transit of the channel, the warship claimed the destruction of three enemy planes and hits on two others.

For much of the month, *Taylor* escorted convoys in the Solomons and between those islands and Espiritu Santo. On 20 April, she rejoined TF 18. After a brief tender overhaul, the destroyer accompanied the cruisers up the "Slot" twice during the 10 days between 4 and 14 May to cover mining operations in Vella Gulf. During the second operation, conducted between the 11th and the 14th, she and the other warships bombarded enemy installations at Vila, Bairoko Harbor, and Enogai Inlet.

Between late May and early July, *Taylor* performed escort duty. On 25 May, she cleared Espiritu Santo with *Munargo* (AP–20), escorted the transport to the 180th meridian, and returned to Espiritu Santo on the 30th. During her next assignment—escorting a convoy of troop transports to Guadalcanal and back—she defended her charges against Japanese planes which jumped the task unit on 10 June south of San Cristobal. After repairs at Espiritu Santo, she served with the antisubmarine screen of escort carrier *Sangamon* (ACV–26) until 6 July when she headed for Tulagi to report for duty with TF 31.

For the next four months, *Taylor* supported the invasions of the central Solomons. In July, she supported the New Georgia landings. On the 11th and 12th, the destroyer covered the landing of troops and supplies at Rice Anchorage on Kula Gulf as well as the evacuation of wounded. On the morning of the 12th, she attacked and damaged a Japanese RO-type submarine, but could claim no definite sinking. That afternoon, *Taylor* was temporarily detached from TF 31 and assigned to TF 18. She headed up the "Slot" with Ainsworth's cruisers —the same ones with which she had previously served except that HMNZS *Leander* replaced *Helena* after the latter cruiser was lost in the Battle of Kula Gulf—to intercept a Japanese surface force. That evening, the two forces collided. *Taylor* and the other van destroyers launched torpedoes and then joined the remainder of TF 18 in engaging the enemy with their guns. It may well have been one of *Taylor*'s "fish" that slammed into *Jintsu*'s hull just abaft her number 2 stack and ripped the Japanese cruiser in half. There is no way of knowing for sure, but the accumulated effect of the destroyer's torpedoes and the entire task force's gunfire cost the enemy his flagship and his commander, Rear Admiral Izaki.

Following the Battle of Kolombangara, *Taylor* reported back to TF 31 and resumed support for the amphibious operations in the central Solomons. On the night of 15 and 16 July, the destroyer took *Helena* survivors off Vella Lavella Island where they had found refuge after their ship went down. Almost a week later, on the night of 23 and 24 July, the destroyer supported the landings at Enogai Inlet and participated in another bombardment of Bairoko Harbor. The following morning, her main battery joined in a bombardment of the Japanese positions around the Munda area of New Georgia.

On 30 July, *Taylor* cleared Guadalcanal in company with a troop transport convoy bound for New Caledonia. She was detached en route to Noumea and ordered to join TF 37 at Efate. On 11 August, *Nicholas*, *O'Bannon* (DD–450), *Chevalier* (DD–451), and *Taylor* were ordered to return to Guadalcanal and rejoin TF 31 for the Vella Lavella phase of the central Solomons operation. First, she covered the landings on 15 August. Two days later, the same four destroyers were ordered out of the anchorage at Purvis Bay to intercept a force of troop-laden barges covered by four destroyers. During the ensuing action off Horaniu, a mad melee of torpedoes and gunfire, neither side lost a destroyer; but the Japanese suffered some damage when American shells set *Hamakaze* ablaze. Later, after the enemy destroyers had made good their escape, the Americans turned their attention to the scattered barges and combat craft, sinking two subchasers, an equal number of torpedo boats, and one barge before retiring. Forty-eight hours later, the four American destroyers returned once again to the area northwest of Vella Lavella to seek out enemy barge traffic. They encountered nothing except enemy aircraft and dodged heavy bombing attacks throughout the evening. Over the next nine days, *Taylor* and her division mates made eight more trips up the "Slot"—one of which was to cover mining operations off the west coast of Kolombangara—but saw little or no action.

Taylor departed Guadalcanal and the Solomons on 28 August to escort *Titania* (AKA–13) to Noumea. Then—after a ten-day repair, rest, and relaxation period in Sydney, Australia—the destroyer escorted a troop transport convoy from Noumea to Guadalcanal. She returned to the Tulagi-Purvis Bay area on 30 September and resumed support of the subjugation of Vella Lavella. By this time, the Japanese had already begun to evacuate bypassed Kolombangara and would soon make the decision to do the same at Vella Lavella. Thus, *Taylor* and other destroyers continued their nocturnal forays up the "Slot" to interdict barge traffic. On the night of 20 October, she, *Terry* (DD–513), and *Ralph Talbot* (DD–390) engaged enemy barges and a surface force in the waters between Choiseul and Kolombangara. Four nights later came the big action of the Vella Lavella and Kolombangara evacuations, the Battle of Vella Lavella. While south of New Georgia escorting a convoy, *Taylor*, *Ralph Talbot*, and *Lavalette* were ordered to join *O'Bannon*, *Chevalier*, and *Selfridge* already embroiled in a slugfest with nine Japanese destroyers covering the Vella Lavella evacuation group. During the ensuing battle, the American and Japanese forces traded torpedo salvoes and gunfire, as well as exchanged destroyer *Chevalier* for destroyer *Yugumo*. During the battle, *Selfridge* and *O'Bannon* also received torpedo hits, but neither was lost. *Taylor* went alongside *Selfridge* in the closing moments of the battle and evacuated most of her crew while a skeleton crew began their successful attempt to save the damaged destroyer. She then screened the two cripples while they limped back down the "Slot" to Purvis Bay.

On 17 October, *Taylor* departed the southern Solomons with the other members of DesDiv 41. She and her consorts escorted a convoy of troop transports to Efate, where they reported for duty with TF 37. Between 23 and 26 October, she made a round-trip voyage between Efate and Noumea, escorting *Lassen* (AE–3) to Noumea and *Aldebaran* to Efate. She and her division were reassigned to the Central Pacific Force on 31 October in preparation for the first step in the Navy's central Pacific thrust, the seizure and occupation of the Gilbert Islands. For that operation, she was assigned to the screen of TG 50.1, built around carriers *Lexington* (CV–16), *Yorktown* (CV–10), and *Cowpens* (CV–25). She screened TG 50.1 during the raids on Jaluit and Mili in the Marshalls conducted during the first half of November in preparation for the Gilberts assault. During the actual landings and occupations, she protected her charges from enemy aircraft and submarines while their planes took off to help those of the

escort carriers maintain air supremacy over the islands. Following the Gilberts operation, she steamed with the carriers during raids on the Marshall Islands. Near the end of those forays, she teamed up with *Lavallette* and *San Francisco* (CA–38) to splash two of four enemy "Kates" which attacked the task group just after noon on 4 December.

Following those raids, *Taylor* was ordered back to the United States for extensive yard work, arriving in San Francisco on 16 December. Repairs completed, she put to sea on 1 February 1944 and headed—via Pearl Harbor—back to the western Pacific. She reached Kwajalein in the Marshalls on the 18th. *Taylor* escorted one convoy to Eniwetok Atoll where she joined the screen of carriers *Coral Sea* (CVB–43) and *Corregidor* (CVE–58) on 29 February. The task unit cleared Eniwetok on 29 February and headed for Pearl Harbor, where it arrived on 3 March. After 12 days of training operations and repairs, the destroyer departed Pearl Harbor in the screen of *Sangamon* (CVE–20), *Suwanee* (CVE–27), *Chenango* (CVE–28), and *Santee* (CVE–29), and arrived in Purvis Bay near Guadalcanal on the 27th. She remained there until 5 April when she left for Milne Bay, New Guinea, for temporary duty with the 7th Fleet.

The warship reached Milne Bay on the 7th and, the following day, headed on to Cape Sudest, where she became a unit of TF 77 for the amphibious assault at Humboldt Bay. During the assault, she screened aircraft carriers and acted as fighter director until 24 April when she departed to escort a convoy back to Cape Sudest. From there she moved to Morobe Bay, where she spent the remainder of the month in availability alongside *Dobbin* (AD–3). During the first week in May, *Taylor* escorted a convoy from Cape Cretin to the Hollandia invasion area and acted as fighter director ship once more. She returned to Cape Cretin on 7 May and departed again two days later to screen a convoy of LST's to the Russell Island subgroup in the Solomons. On 13 May, the destroyer reported back to the 3d Fleet in the Solomons, dropped off the convoy, and departed again to screen another convoy to New Caledonia.

On the 24th, she stood out of Noumea in company with DesDiv 41 to return to the Solomons and arrived at her new base of operations, Blanche Harbor, on 27 May. *Taylor* operated out of that port in the northern Solomons and Bismarcks area until early August. On the night of 28 and 29 May, she patrolled off Medina Plantation on New Ireland while her sister ships bombarded the area to neutralize mobile coastal guns. From 1 to 6 June, she operated with DesDiv 41 conducting antisubmarine operations. During the week from 7 to 14 June, *Taylor* and the other ships of DesDiv 41 joined TG 30.4 for hunter-killer antisubmarine operations. On the 10th, she depth-charged an enemy submarine, forced it to the surface, and damaged it heavily with 5-inch and 40-millimeter fire. The submarine submerged again, and *Taylor* made two more depth-charge runs and netted a probable kill. She returned to Blanche Harbor on the 15th and operated in that vicinity until the first week in August.

On 5 August, she changed operational command from the 3d Fleet to the 7th Fleet. She began her duty with that fleet with a practice bombardment of the Aitape area of New Guinea late in August and a practice landing at Moffin Bay conducted on 6 September. Both operations were in preparation for the landings made on the island of Morotai in the Netherlands East Indies on 15 September. For the remainder of the month, she acted as fighter director ship and as a unit of the invasion force's antisubmarine and antiaircraft screen. The destroyer also escorted convoys to the landing area until mid-October.

Between 18 and 24 October, *Taylor* was a unit of the screen for the second reinforcement echelon for the Leyte invasion. During a Japanese aerial assault on the 24th, the destroyer laid a smoke screen to protect the convoy. That night, as the Battle of Surigao Strait opened, *Taylor* and the other destroyers of her division were anchored near the entrance of San Pedro Bay. Though she did not actually join the surface engagement, *Taylor* joined the support force on the following morning. Following that, she patrolled the vicinity of Dinagat Island with a unit known as the "torpedo attack force." On 27 and 28 October, the warship screened TG 77.4, the escort carrier group. During that duty, she rescued a downed fighter pilot of *Enterprise* (CV–6) and a seaman from *Petrof Bay* (CVE–80). Frequently, she helped fend off Japanese air attacks.

On 29 October, she joined TG 77.2 and departed the area of Leyte Gulf. After visits to Seeadler Harbor, Ulithi Atoll, and Kossol Roads, she returned to Leyte Gulf on 16 November. Between 16 and 29 November, the destroyer continued to screen TG 77.2 and to patrol the eastern entrance to the Surigao Strait. Again, she joined her sister ships in beating off heavy enemy air raids, climaxed by a large attack of suicide planes and dive bombers on the 29th. She claimed one sure kill and two assists during those raids. *Taylor* then cleared Leyte Gulf for almost a month at Seeadler Harbor before returning to Leyte on 28 December to prepare for the invasion of Luzon.

Taylor departed Leyte Gulf on 4 January 1945 in the screen for the cruisers in the covering force. The next day, the destroyer sighted two torpedoes running toward her formation. After giving the submarine alarm, *Taylor* launched a depth charge attack on the enemy submarine—a midget. Following those attacks, she rammed the small submarine and sent it on its last dive. During the Allied approach to Lingayen Gulf and in the days following the landings, the Japanese subjected *Taylor* and her sister ships to a series of heavy air raids. *Taylor*'s antiaircraft gunners assisted in splashing at least two of the attackers. Through the end of January, the warship screened the cruisers and the escort carriers on patrol west of Luzon.

From early February through mid-June 1945, *Taylor* operated out of Subic Bay in the Philippines. Between 13 and 18 February, she participated in an extensive bombardment of Corregidor and of the Mariveles Bay area of Luzon to support minesweeping operations and to pave the way for an assault by airborne troops. Early in March, she supported the recapture of Zamboanga on Mindanao during which the destroyer's guns helped reduce enemy shore installations. She also covered the minesweepers while they cleared the way for the invasion force. On 15 March, *Taylor* returned to Corregidor where she bombarded caves on the island's western cliffs. On 26 March, the ship participated in the amphibious assault on Cebu Island, where she joined *Boise* (CL–47), *Phoenix* (CL–46), *Fletcher* (DD–445), *Nicholas*, *Jenkins* (DD–447), and *Abbot* (DD–629) in laying down a heavy pre-landing bombardment.

After a short two-day sightseeing visit to Manila, *Taylor* cleared the Philippines with *Boise*, *Phoenix*, two Australian warships, and four other American destroyers to support the amphibious landings in northeastern Borneo. En route, she captured five Japanese who were attempting to escape from Tawi Tawi on a raft. On 27 April, *Taylor* and her sister ships reached the vicinity of the invasion—Tarakan, a small island located just off the eastern coast of Borneo and north of Makassar Strait. She operated in that area until 3 May and delivered a preinvasion bombardment and call fire. On 3 May, two days after the actual landings, she departed Tarakan to resume duty in the Philippines, where for the remainder of the month she conducted training operations.

In mid-June, *Taylor* rejoined the 3d Fleet at Leyte Gulf and, for the remainder of the war, screened various units of that fleet. During the latter part of the month, she screened aircraft carriers operating south of Okinawa which conducted air strikes on Sakishima Gunto. On 25 June, she returned to Leyte Gulf and remained there until 8 July, when she departed in the screen of TG 30.8, the logistics group for the fast carriers of TF 38. The destroyer operated with TG 30.8

off Honshu until 3 August when she joined the screen of one of the fast carrier task groups, TG 38.4. On 8 August, she resumed duty with the logistics group for five days. On the 13th, *Taylor* rejoined TG 38.4 just in time to be a part of the last offensive actions directed at Japan.

Following the cessation of hostilities on 15 August, she patrolled off Honshu with the fast carriers. On 23 August, she joined *Nicholas* and *O'Bannon* in the screen of *Missouri* (BB–63) and as such was one of the first American warships to enter Tokyo Bay, arriving on 29 August. The destroyer was present at the surrender ceremony conducted on board *Missouri* on 2 September and carried Allied war correspondents to and from the ceremony. She operated in the Far East until 10 October when she departed Tokyo Bay to return to the United States. *Taylor* arrived in San Francisco on 1 November and began preparations for inactivation. On 31 May 1946, the destroyer was decommissioned and placed in reserve at San Diego.

After four years of inactivity, *Taylor* moved to the San Francisco Naval Shipyard on 9 May 1950 and, three days later, began an extensive conversion to an escort destroyer. While still completing conversion, she was officially redesignated DDE–468 on 2 January 1951. On 3 December 1951, *Taylor* was recommissioned at San Francisco, Comdr. Sheldon H. Kenney in command. On 3 February 1952, she put to sea for a two-month shakedown period off San Diego. On 24 March, the escort destroyer headed west to her new home port, Pearl Harbor, and arrived there on the 30th. Following two months in the Hawaiian Islands, *Taylor* set out to return to the western Pacific for the first time since World War II. She stopped at Midway Island and Yokosuka, Japan, before joining TF 77 on 16 June to screen the carriers during air operations off the Korean coast.

During the five months that she spent in the Far East, *Taylor* drew several different assignments. Initially, she operated with the fast carriers and conducted bombardments of enemy-held positions along the coasts of Korea. During the second week in July, she returned to Yokosuka for upkeep and then went to sea again for exercises which included several weeks of hunter-killer operations. On 1 August, the escort destroyer rejoined TF 77 and, in September, stood blockade watch off Wonsan for three weeks. Her blockade duty at Wonsan was far from passive for, on numerous occasions, she was called upon to shell enemy shore batteries and lines of transportation and to screen minesweepers during daily sweeps of the harbor. Late that month, *Taylor* headed south for a tour of duty on the Taiwan Strait Patrol during which she made a weekend port call at Hong Kong. In late October, the escort destroyer returned north to the western coast of Korea where she patrolled with two British warships, the carrier HMS *Glory* and the cruiser HMS *Birmingham*. On 21 November, *Taylor* returned to Yokosuka, completing the first leg of her voyage home.

After conducting patrols in the western Pacific while en route to Hawaii, *Taylor* entered Pearl Harbor on 8 December. Following a month of leave and upkeep, she entered the Pearl Harbor Naval Shipyard for a month of repairs. For the next three months, she conducted shakedown training in the Hawaiian Islands in order to integrate her replacements with the rest of the crew. On 2 May 1953, the warship exited Pearl Harbor to deploy to the western Pacific again. She reached Yokosuka on the 12th and, after visiting that port and Sasebo, put to sea to join a carrier task group—built around *Bairoko* (CVE–115) and HMS *Ocean* off the western coast of Korea. For the most part, she screened the carriers during air operations; however, on two occasions, she patrolled close to the enemy-held shoreline to discourage the North Koreans from attempting to take offshore islands held by United Nations forces. She returned to Sasebo on 1 June for 11 days of upkeep before heading for Okinawa and two weeks of antisubmarine warfare (ASW) training. On 25 June, *Taylor* returned to Japan at Yokosuka, but she departed again almost immediately for duty with the Taiwan Strait Patrol. During that assignment, she visited Hong Kong once again as well as Kaohsiung where she trained sailors of the Taiwan Navy. The escort destroyer returned to Yokosuka on 20 July and, after two days of voyage repairs, departed the Far East. She arrived in Pearl Harbor on 31 July and, the following day, entered the naval shipyard there for a three-month overhaul.

Taylor's return to Pearl Harbor coincided very closely with the formal end to hostilities in Korea. The armistice came on 27 July 1953 when she had just passed the midpoint of her voyage—five days out of Yokosuka and four days from Pearl Harbor. While she saw some action during her two Korean War deployments, they occurred during the relatively quiet, final two years of the conflict. Her subsequent deployments, while they included both duty off Korea and on the Taiwan Strait Patrol, were entirely peaceful in nature until the expansion of the American role in the Vietnamese civil war in 1965.

In the five years between 1 March 1954 and 1 March 1959, *Taylor* completed five more deployments to the western Pacific. During each, she conducted training exercises and made goodwill visits to Far Eastern ports. When not in the Orient, she conducted normal operations out of Pearl Harbor. During her sixth post-Korean War deployment in 1959 and 1960, she visited Australia for the celebration commemorating the victory at the Battle of the Coral Sea in May 1942. Upon her return to Pearl Harbor on 26 May 1960, the escort destroyer conducted normal operations again until December when she entered the Pearl Harbor Naval Shipyard for a major overhaul before deploying to the western Pacific again in August 1961. In lieu of her annual western Pacific deployment, *Taylor* spent the spring and summer of 1962 in the mid-Pacific as one of the support units for Operation "Dominic," nuclear tests conducted in the upper atmosphere. In October, she returned to Hawaii to begin a repair period which saw her through the end of 1962. During that year, she reverted to the classification of destroyer and was redesignated DD–468 on 7 August 1962.

Local operations in the Hawaiian Islands occupied the remainder of 1962 and the first six months of 1963. On 4 June 1963, the destroyer stood out of Pearl Harbor with a hunter/killer group bound for duty with the 7th Fleet. During this deployment to the Far East, *Taylor* called at Kobe, Japan; Hong Kong; Okinawa; and Kushiro as well as the base ports of Yokosuka, Sasebo, and Subic Bay. The call at Kushiro—a fishing port on Hokkaido, the northernmost of the Japanese home islands—constituted *Taylor*'s contributions to the People to People Program and aided immeasurably in developing greater understanding between the peoples of the United States and Japan. Other than that, the warship engaged in numerous unilateral and bilateral training exercises through the remainder of the cruise which ended at Pearl Harbor on 29 November. *Taylor* operated locally in Hawaii until April 1964 when she entered drydock for a three-month overhaul. In July she resumed operations in Hawaiian waters.

Those operations continued throughout most of the fall of 1964. On 23 November, the destroyer cleared Pearl Harbor in company with *Yorktown* (CVS–10) and *Thomason* (DD–746) to return to the Orient. The task unit steamed via Midway Island and, on 3 December, made port at Yokosuka, Japan. Four days later, she put to sea for two weeks of combined antiaircraft/antisubmarine warfare exercises conducted with *Hancock* (CVA–19) and *Strauss* (DDG–16) near Okinawa. On 19 December, the warship returned to Japan at Sasebo and remained there through the holidays and into the New Year. On 4 January 1965, *Taylor* cleared Sasebo and rejoined *Yorktown* and *Thomason* for a voyage to Hong Kong. The three ships remained in the British Crown Colony for five days before clearing port for a series of special operations conducted in the Philippine Sea. At the conclusion of that duty, she put into Subic Bay on 24 February. After four days in the Philippines, *Taylor* headed back to Sasebo, where she arrived on 3 March. Exactly two weeks later, the destroyer got underway for the western portion of the South China Sea. She arrived off the coast of Vietnam on 21 March and patrolled there for the following five weeks. On 27 April, *Taylor* headed back to Yokosuka for a brief stop—from 3 to 6 May—before returning to Hawaii. The destroyer reentered Pearl Harbor on the 13th and conducted local operations in Hawaiian waters. On 6 December, *Taylor* entered the drydock for another overhaul.

The destroyer left the dock in mid-January 1966 and stood out of Pearl Harbor on 7 February and, with the other ships of DesDiv 111, shaped a course for the western Pacific. The warship reached Yokosuka 10 days later and spent eight days undergoing voyage repairs. On 25 February, she departed Yokosuka to join Task Group 70.4 off the coast of Vietnam the following day. She patrolled Vietnamese waters until the Ides of March, when she headed north to patrol the Taiwan Strait. During her stay in the area around Taiwan, she visited Kaohsiung. Her relief arrived on 12 April, and *Taylor* steamed off to Hong Kong for a five-day port call. On the 21st, she returned to Yankee Station to resume operations in support of American and South Vietnamese forces ashore. Among other tasks, she brought her main battery to bear on the enemy and rendered naval gunfire support between 28 April and 1 May. She conducted upkeep at Sasebo in May and ASW drills from 26 May to 10 June before resuming patrols in the Taiwan Strait on the 11th. She cleared the area again on 5 July, rejoined TG 70.4 on 7 July, and put into Yokosuka the following day. After a week of preparations, the warship departed Yokosuka to return to Pearl Harbor, where she arrived on 22 July.

On 2 August, *Taylor* began a tender availability period alongside *Prairie* (AD–15) which lasted through the end of the month. Following a short cruise for gunnery practice, *Taylor* commenced a restricted availability which lasted until late in November. During the first two weeks in December, the destroyer made a round-trip voyage to Pago Pago, American Samoa. She returned to Pearl Harbor on 16 December for holiday leave and upkeep. During the first three months of 1967, the ship conducted local operations around Hawaii, made repairs, and generally prepared to return to the Far East in late spring.

Following an Operational Readiness Inspection in mid-April, she cleared Pearl Harbor on the 18th to join the 7th Fleet in the Orient. On the 25th, she changed operational control from the 1st to the 7th Fleet and, three days later, steamed into Yokosuka. During the first half of June, the destroyer participated in exercises with units of the Japanese Maritime Self Defense Force and ships of the Republic of Korea Navy. After two days in port at Sasebo, she got underway on 19 June for her first line period on Yankee Station. Between 22 May and 25 June, she plied the waters of the Gulf of Tonkin planeguarding for *Hornet* (CV–12) and providing gunfire support for Allied forces operating ashore. On 27 June, *Taylor* put into Subic Bay. After a tender availability at Subic Bay and a visit to Manila, she put to sea on 10 July to participate in SEATO exercise "Sea Dog." Between the 26th and the 28th, she visited Bang Saen on the Gulf of Thailand. After three more days on Yankee Station—from 28 July to 1 August—the destroyer made for Taiwan. She reached Kaohsiung on the 3d and remained until the 15th, when she headed back to the coast of Vietnam. From 19 August to 11 September, she cruised along the Vietnamese coast providing naval gunfire support as needed by the forces operating ashore. She cleared the coast of Indochina on the 12th, and, after a five-day stop at Hong Kong and another tour of duty in the Gulf of Tonkin, she returned to Yokosuka on 11 October. Five days later, she shaped a course back to Hawaii.

Taylor arrived in Pearl Harbor on 23 October, and

the destroyer commenced her regular overhaul on 11 December. Repairs and modifications occupied her time through the first three months of 1968. The warship completed overhaul on 22 March and conducted sea trials during the first week in April. Later, engineering problems forced the postponement of further operations until the end of the month. At that time, she began preparations for refresher training. The warship conducted refresher training in May and June, then got underway for San Diego, Calif., on 27 June. She conducted operations—primarily gunnery drills at San Clemente Island—from 3 to 15 July. On the latter date, she headed back to Hawaii. En route, *Taylor* conducted bombardment exercises at Kahoolawe Island and then entered Pearl Harbor on the 17th. Three weeks later, the destroyer cleared Pearl Harbor on 5 August and set course for the Gulf of Tonkin.

After fueling stops at Midway, Guam, and Subic Bay, she arived on station off Vietnam on 21 August. *Taylor* did plane guard duty for *Intrepid* (CVS-11) for a day; then steamed off with the carrier and destroyers *Maddox* (DD-731) and *Preston* (DD-795) toward Sasebo. She returned to the Gulf of Tonkin on 5 September and conducted air and surface surveillance as well as antisubmarine warfare exercises in addition to planeguarding for the carriers. On the 19th, the destroyer moved in closer to the coast to provide naval gunfire in support of troops ashore. That duty continued until 6 October when she cleared the combat zone to return to Subic Bay for repairs, supplies, and ammunition. On 20 October, the warship took up where she left off and began a week pounding various targets in Vietnam. That line period was followed by visits to Cebu City and Subic Bay in the Philippines. During late November and early December, she resumed duty on the gunline. On 4 December, she cleared the combat zone and set a course through the Luzon Strait to Yokosuka, where she arrived on the 12th. She spent Christmas in Yokosuka, but returned to Yankee Station by New Year's Day 1969.

In mid-January, she departed Vietnamese waters for the last time. After stops at Subic Bay; Manus Island; Melbourne, Australia; Auckland, New Zealand; and Pago Pago, Samoa, the warship arrived back in Pearl Harbor on 28 February. In May, a board of inspection and survey looked her over and determined that she was unfit for further naval service. Early in June, *Taylor* was moved to San Diego, Calif., and was decommissioned. Her name was struck from the Navy list on 2 July 1969, and she was transferred to Italy at the same time. The former American destroyer served in the Italian Navy as *Lanciere* (D-560) until January 1971. At that time, she was decommissioned and struck from the Italian Navy list. She was subsequently cannibalized to maintain her sister ships still serving in the Italian Navy.

Taylor earned 15 battle stars during World War II, two battle stars for the Korean conflict, and six battle stars for Vietnam service.

Taylor, A. B., see *A. B. Taylor*, to be included in the forthcoming revised edition of Vol. I.

Taylor, David W., see *David W. Taylor*.

Taylor, Harry, see *General Harry Taylor*.

Taylor, Lawrence C., see *Lawrence C. Taylor*.

Taylor, Nathaniel, see *Nathaniel Taylor*.

Tazewell

Counties in Illinois and Virginia.

(APA-209: dp. 7,190; l. 455'; b. 62'; dr. 24'; s. 17.7 k.; cpl. 536; trp. 1,562; a. 1 5", 12 40mm; cl. *Haskell*; T. VC2-S-AP5)

Tazewell (APA-209) was laid down under a Maritime Commission contract (MC hull 557) on 2 June 1944 at Richmond, Calif., by the Permanente Metals Corp.; launched on 22 August 1944; sponsored by Mrs. Samuel I. Rosenman; and commissioned on 25 October 1944, Comdr. H. S. Olsen, USNR, in command.

Following shakedown in the San Pedro-San Diego, Calif., area, *Tazewell* arrived at Seattle, Wash., on Christmas Day 1944 and began loading troops and supplies. On 2 January 1945, the transport got underway for Hawaii where she embarked garrison troops for the Palau Islands and steamed onward. She arrived off Peleliu on the 31st. After offloading all cargo and debarking the troops, she joined a Philippine-bound convoy which sortied for Leyte on 6 February and arrived in San Pedro Bay three days later.

Tazewell was assigned to Transport Squadron 17 which became a unit of Task Group 51.1 for the Okinawa invasion. The transport loaded troops and supplies and participated in amphibious training exercises for the forthcoming operation. On 21 March, the task group sortied for Kerama Retto and arrived off that island on the morning of the 26th. All boats were lowered into the water at 0530, and the assault troops stormed ashore at 0800. They met almost no opposition, but the ships came under air attack shortly after 0630 and were forced to remain at general quarters all day.

The task group was steaming in night retirement on 3 April when it was ordered to proceed to a waiting area approximately 200 miles southeast of Okinawa. It arrived there on the 4th and remained until the 13th. *Tazewell* and six other APA's left the formation that morning and returned to Hagushi Anchorage, Okinawa, the next day. On the morning of 16 April, the transport got underway for Ie Shima and, at 0610, launched her boats for the beaches. She departed at 1600 that afternoon but returned the next day to complete unloading her cargo. At 2200 hours on the 27th, a kamikaze plane crashed a liberty ship some 2,500 yards off *Tazewell's* port bow. *Tazewell* promptly lowered her outboard boats to pick up survivors from the ship which sank in eight minutes. Since many other boats were also in the water, *Tazewell's* boats picked up only seven survivors whom they took to *Hope* (AH-7). The other boats rescued many more survivors, minimizing the loss of life.

On 30 April, *Tazewell* received orders to proceed to the Mariana Islands, and she arrived at Saipan on 5 May. On the 22d, she stood out of Saipan en route to the United States and arrived at San Francisco on 6 June. Two days later, she moved up the coast to Seattle for a three-week yard availability period. She departed Seattle on 27 June, bound for the Marianas, and arrived at Tinian on 14 July. By the next morning, the attack transport had debarked all her troops and had unloaded her cargo. She shifted to Saipan that afternoon. On the 16th, the ship sailed independently for the west coast; and she arrived at San Francisco 14 days later. Hostilities with Japan ended while the transport was in drydock at San Pedro; but, when the ship was ready for sea, she was ordered to the Philippine Islands.

Tazewell arrived at Manila on 18 September and waited four days for orders to unload. On the 22d, she was routed to Lingayen Gulf where she debarked passengers and unloaded cargo. The ship returned to Manila on the 24th; loaded cargo and 8th Army troops; joined Transport Squadron 19 at Legaspi Harbor on 2 October; and sortied for Japan two days later. *Tazewell* remained at Yokohoma for 12 days before moving to Sasebo where she embarked approximately 500 marines of the 5th Marine Division to be returned to the United States. She arrived at San Francisco on 9 November and disembarked her passengers.

Tazewell sailed for the Philippines again on 24 November to pick up a capacity load of veterans eligible for discharge. She loaded troops at Manila and Subic Bay. The transport began her return voyage on 17 December and arrived at San Francisco on 5 January 1946. She subsequently made round-trip voyages to Yokosuka to return servicemen to the United States. Upon her arrival at San Francisco on 9 August from the last of these runs, she was assigned to the Pacific Reserve Fleet there for inactivation.

Tazewell was decommissioned at San Francisco on 27 December 1946 and remained in reserve for the next 12 years. *Tazewell* was transferred to the Maritime Administration on 25 September 1958 and was struck from the Navy list on 1 October 1958. She was sold to Zidell Explorations, Inc., Portland, Oreg., on 11 December 1972 and scrapped.

Tazewell received one battle star for World War II service.

Tazha

A Sioux Indian word which means wave of the sea.

(YT–147: dp. 218; l. 100'0''; b. 25'0''; dr. 9'7'' (f.); s. 12 k. (tl.); cpl. 12; cl. *Woban*)

Tazha (YT–147) was laid at Morris Heights, N.Y., on 8 August 1940 by the Consolidated Shipbuilding Corp.; launched on Lincoln's birthday 1941; and completed and placed in service on 14 June 1941.

Tazha served her entire Navy career at Norfolk, Va., in the 5th Naval District. She operated as a harbor tug there from June 1941 until March 1946. On 15 May 1944, she was reclassified a large harbor tug, YTB–147. In March 1946, she was placed out of service, in reserve. The tug remained inactive at Norfolk until July 1952 when she returned to active service at Norfolk. In February 1962, she changed designations once more and became a medium harbor tug, YTM–147. Following 11 more years of service in the harbor at Norfolk, *Tazha* was decommissioned, and her name was struck from the Navy list on 1 May 1973.

Tchifonta

A river in Louisiana—more commonly spelled Chefuncte and occasionally appearing as Tchefuncta or Tchifonctee—which rises near the Mississippi line and flows south some 40 miles to empty into Lake Pontchartrain near the present town of Houltonville. During the War of 1812, a settlement of the same name existed on the shore of Lake Pontchartrain at the river's mouth on land now occupied by the Chefuncte River State Park. Chefuncte is an Indian word meaning chinquapin, an American dwarf chestnut tree.

(Cor.: l. 152'9''; b. 43'; dr. 8'6''; dph. 8'2''; a. 26 long 32-pdrs., 16 42-pdr. car.)

The construction of *Tchifonta*—a large, shallow draft vessel which Howard I. Chapelle calls "a cross between a frigate and a ship sloop"—was begun either late in 1813 or early in 1814 by M. Pechon at Chefuncte, La. However, work on the ship—designed as a blockship to obstruct the Mississippi below New Orleans—was interrupted in the spring or early summer of 1814 under orders from Secretary of the Navy William Jones. Thus, the corvette was still on the ways during America's gallant defence of New Orleans under General Andrew Jackson in January 1815. The ship remained unfinished on the stocks until she was sold sometime during 1820 or thereafter.

Teaberry

Any of several American evergreen plants which bear white, bell-shaped flowers and spicy red berries. During the American Revolution, its small round leaves were dried and used as a substitute for tea. The plant is also called checkerberry and wintergreen.

(YN–29: dp. 700; l. 163'2''; b. 30'6''; dr. 11'8''; s. 12.5 k.; cpl. 48; a. 1 3''; cl. *Aloe*)

Teaberry (YN–29) was laid down on 25 October 1940 by the John H. Mathias Co., Camden, N.J.; launched on 24 May 1941; sponsored by Miss Mary C. Howard; and placed in service on 16 March 1942.

Teaberry operated in the 1st Naval District out of Boston until February 1943 when she shifted to the 7th Naval District at Miami. Late in March, she was ordered to Trinidad and operated from there until 8 March 1944 when she steamed to Charleston, S.C., to prepare for service in the South Pacific.

In May, *Teaberry* sailed for New Guinea via Miami, Guantanamo Bay, the Panama Canal, Bora Bora, and New Caledonia. Upon arrival at Milne Bay on 22 July, she provided services to units of the 7th Fleet and operated out of that port, Langemak, and Hollandia, until ordered to the Philippine Islands early in 1945. The net layer served there until 4 June 1946 when she headed for Hawaii.

Teaberry arrived at Pearl Harbor on 9 July and, on the 14th, proceeded to the west coast. The ship was at San Francisco from 24 July to 9 October when she was assigned to the 19th Reserve Fleet at Astoria, Oreg. She was placed out of commission, in reserve, on 14 December 1946.

Teaberry was recommissioned at Astoria on 19 April 1952 and assigned to the 12th Naval District with San Francisco designated as her home port. She arrived there on 13 May and served in the 12th Naval District until July 1961, rendering such services to the fleet as: training students in net and boom defense techniques; working with the Research and Development Division of the Naval Net Depot, Tiburon, Calif.; and participating in mine planting and recovery exercises. By August 1953, the ship had been equipped as a "diving-type vessel;" and she assisted the Submarine Force, United States Pacific Fleet, in submarine rescue, surface and aerial torpedo recovery, and submarine communications.

Teaberry was again decommissioned on 7 July 1961 and struck from the Navy list on 1 August 1961. On 12 January 1962, *Teaberry* was sold to the Pacific Towboat and Salvage Co., for scrap.

Teak

A tall East Indian tree whose strong, hard wood is known for durability, as well as for insect and warp resistance. Teakwood is especially suited to shipbuilding.

(YN–30: dp. 805 (lim.); l. 163'2''; b. 30'6''; dr. 11'8''; s. 12.5 k. (tl.); cpl. 48; a. 1 3'', 4 20mm., 4 .50 mg.; cl. *Aloe*)

Teak (YN–30) was laid down on 25 October 1940 at Camden, N.J., by John H. Mathias & Co.; launched on 7 July 1941; sponsored by Mrs. E. L. Patch; placed in service on 7 May 1942; and commissioned on 10 December 1942 at Colon, Canal Zone, Lt. Harl Stanley Day, USNR, in command.

At the time of her commissioning, the net tender was assigned to the nets guarding the west gate of the Panama Canal. *Teak* transited the canal on 15 December 1942; departed Balboa on Christmas Eve; and arrived at San Francisco on 6 January 1943. Based at Tiburon Naval Net Depot on West San Francisco Bay, she began tending the harbor's antisubmarine nets on the 10th.

Throughout 1943 and into 1944, *Teak* patrolled and maintained the nets which protected the anchorages and harbor of San Francisco Bay. She inspected the nets, repaired and replaced worn parts and buoys, and freed mooring anchors and an occasional ship fouled in the nets. These routine but vital duties were varied by repairs at Alameda, with gunnery drills in October, and with a voyage to San Pedro in December.

Reclassified a net laying ship and redesignated AN-35 on 20 January 1944, *Teak* passed under the Golden Gate Bridge shortly before sunset on 2 March and set her course for the South Pacific. Proceeding via Samoa, she reached New Guinea on 4 April and began operating out of Milne Bay and the nearby Trobriand Islands. For the next six months, she provided towing services in nearby waters, carried cargoes, placed sonar buoys, and took up unneeded buoys and moorings.

Reassigned to the Leyte Gulf Service Unit of the 7th Fleet Service Force, she departed Humboldt Bay in convoy on 18 October and entered Leyte Gulf on the 24th. For the next few weeks, despite frequent calls to general quarters, she laid net moorings and marker buoys in Leyte Gulf, aided grounded small craft, and made tows. Late in November, she began sonar buoy station duties between Samar and Homohon Islands. On 17 January 1945, she returned to tending and laying moorings. In mid-March, she proceeded to Luzon and operated in Manila Bay, primarily occupied in raising submerged barges, sampans, diesel boats, and steamboats. During this period—while assigned to the Ship Salvage, Fire Fighting and Rescue Unit, Service Force, Pacific—she won the Navy Unit Commendation.

She remained in the Philippines until late in November, when she headed, via the Marianas and Pearl Harbor, for the California coast and arrived at San Pedro on 4 January 1946. She was towed to Astoria by *Mimosa* (AN-26) in June and was decommissioned and placed in reserve on 30 August 1946. She was placed in custody of the Maritime Administration in June 1961, but remained under Navy ownership. *Teak* was sold to Levin Metals Corp., San Jose, Calif., on 16 March 1976.

Teal

Any of several small, short-necked, river ducks common to Europe and America.

(Minesweeper No. 23: dp. 840; l. 187'10''; b. 35'6''; dr. 10'3½''; s. 14 k.; cpl. 85; a. 2 3''; cl. *Lapwing*)

Teal (Minesweeper No. 23) was laid down on 8 October 1917 at Chester, Pa., by the Sun Shipbuilding Co.; launched on 25 May 1918; sponsored by Miss Agnes M. Haig; and commissioned on 20 August 1918 at the Philadelphia Navy Yard, Lt. (jg.) Frederick Meyer in command.

Through the end of World War I and into the spring of 1919, *Teal* served in the 4th Naval District patrolling off the shores of New Jersey, Delaware, and Pennsylvania. On 20 April 1919, the minesweeper reported for duty with the North Sea Minesweeping Detachment. As a unit of Mine Division 2, she labored to clear the North Sea Mine Barrage and remained in European waters until the task had been completed late in the fall of 1919.

Upon her return to the United States toward the end of November, *Teal* was modified for service as an auxiliary aircraft tender. Although not officially designated a "minesweeper for duty with aircraft" until 30 April 1931, she nevertheless served in this capacity throughout the 1920's and into the 30's. Operating out of Norfolk, Va., from the Caribbean in the south to Narragansett Bay in the north, *Teal* supported operations with the air squadrons of the Scouting Fleet. Frequently in company with *Wright* (AV-1) and *Sandpiper* (AM-51), and later with *Lapwing* (AM-1), she visited the Panama Canal Zone where she serviced the squadrons based at Coco Solo. Her normal schedule alternated winter maneuvers in the Caribbean-Gulf of Mexico area with summer training along the New England coast.

By the mid-1930's, *Teal*'s home port was Coco Solo, whence she operated with Patrol Wing (PatWing) 4. *Teal* was redesignated a small seaplane tender, AVP-5,

effective on 22 January 1936. On 18 October of the following year, she and PatWing 4 were reassigned to Seattle, Wash. For almost five years, *Teal* operated throughout the Aleutians chain in support of PatWing 4 operations.

Soon after the opening of hostilities between the United States and Japan, *Teal* moved south to the California coast. In January 1942, the small seaplane tender was assigned to the Pacific Southern Naval Coastal Frontier, the short-lived forerunner of the Western Sea Frontier, but she remained administratively under the commander of the Scouting Force aircraft. She tended the planes of PatWing 8 until March. In July, *Teal* returned to Seattle and duty with PatWing 4 in the Pacific northwest and Alaska areas. Until the end of the war, the small seaplane tender plowed the icy seas between the Aleutian Islands and along the Alaskan coast. She continued to support flying patrol boats; but the drain of warships from the Alaskan theater to other, more active areas frequently required her to be pressed into service as an escort and sometimes as a resupply transport.

Shortly after the cessation of hostilities on 23 November 1945, *Teal* was decommissioned at Seattle; and her name was struck from the Navy list on 5 December 1945. On 19 January 1948, she was delivered to the Maritime Commission at Port Nordland, Wash., and simultaneously sold to Mr. Murray E. Baker.

Teaser

I

(ScTug: t. 65; l. 80'; b. 18'; dph. 7'; cpl. 25; a. 1 32-pdr. r., 1 12-pdr. r.)

In April 1861, the government of Virginia purchased the Philadelphia-built, wooden-hulled, screw tug *Teaser* of Georgetown, D.C., and commissioned her in the Virginia State Navy, Lt. J. H. Rochelle, VSN, in command. Upon the secession of that state, *Teaser* became a part of the Confederate Navy and continued to operate in Virginia waters. With Lt. W. A. Webb, CSN, in command, she took an active part in the battles of Hampton Roads, Va., on 8 and 9 March 1862, acting as tender to CSS *Virginia*. She received the thanks of the Congress of the Confederate States for this action.

Teaser was a pioneer "aircraft carrier" (balloon ship); she also became a pioneer minelayer when ordered, on 17 June, to assist Lee's Army of Northern Virginia. Under Lt. H. Davidson, CSN, she was used by the Confederate Naval Submarine Battery Service to plant and service "torpedoes" (mines) in the James River. While engaging *Maratanza* at Haxall's on the James on 4 July 1862, a Union shell blew up *Teaser*'s boiler and forced her crew to abandon ship. When seized by *Maratanza*, *Teaser* was carrying on board a balloon for aerial reconnaissance of Union positions at City Point and Harrison's Landing.

Later that summer, *Teaser* was taken into the Federal Navy and was assigned to the Potomac Flotilla. With the exception of three brief deployments elsewhere, she plied the waters of the Potomac from Alexandria, Va., south to Point Lookout, Md., to enforce the blockade by interdicting a thriving trade in contraband between the Maryland and Virginia shores.

On 22 September, she captured schooner *Southerner* in the Coan River. On 19 October, while operating in the vicinity of Piney Point in St. Mary's County, Md., she captured two smugglers and their boat as they were nearing the exit of Herring Creek and preparing to cross the river to Virginia. On 2 November, near the mouth of the Rappahannock, the tug surprised three men attempting to violate the blockade in a canoe. She took them prisoner and turned their contraband over to pro-Union Virginians living on Gwynn's Island. Four days later in Chesapeake Bay, *Teaser* took the cargoless sloop *Grapeshot* and captured her three-man crew.

By December 1862, she had moved to the Rappahannock River with other units of the Potomac Flotilla to support General Ambrose P. Burnside's thrust toward Richmond. On the 10th, she exchanged shots with a Confederate battery located on the southern shore of the river about three miles below Port Royal, Va. After Burnside's bloody rebuff at Fredericksburg on 13 December, *Teaser* and her colleagues returned to their anti-smuggling patrol along the Potomac.

Teaser joined *Primrose* to make March 1863 an active month. On the 24th, the two ships sent a boat expedition to reconnoiter Pope's Creek, Va. The landing party found two boats used for smuggling and collected information from Union sympathizers in the area. Almost a week later, on the night of 30 and 31 March, they dispatched a three-boat party to Monroe's Creek, Va. The previous day, a Federal cavalry detachment had surprised a smuggler in the area; and, though the troops captured his goods, the man himself escaped. *Teaser*'s and *Primrose*'s boats succeeded where the Union horsemen had failed, and they gathered some intelligence on other contrabanders as well.

In April 1863, *Teaser* left the Potomac for duty with Acting Rear Admiral S. P. Lee's North Atlantic Blockading Squadron at Hampton Roads. On the 17th, she joined *Alert* and *Coeur de Lion* in an expedition up the Nansemond River west of Norfolk. However, she ran aground, damaged her machinery, and had to retire from the venture.

By mid-summer, *Teaser* was back in action on the Potomac. On the night of 27 July, she captured two smugglers with a boatload of tobacco in the mouth of the Mattawoman Creek just south of Indian Head, Md. She destroyed the boat and sent the prisoners and contraband north to the Washington Navy Yard. During the night of 7 October, *Teaser* and another flotilla ship—extant records do not identify her companion—noticed signalling between Mathias Point, Va., and the Maryland shore. The two ships shelled the woods at Mathias Point, but took no action against the signallers on the Maryland shore other than to urge upon the Army's district provost marshall the necessity of constant vigilance.

On 5 January 1864, *Teaser* and *Yankee* landed a force of men at Nomini, Va., to investigate a rumor that the Southerners had hidden a large lighter and a skiff capable of boating 80 men there. The force, commanded by *Teaser*'s commanding officer, Acting Ens. Sheridan, found both boats, destroyed the lighter, and captured the skiff. During the landing, Confederate soldiers appeared on the heights above Nomini, but the gunboats dampened their curiosity with some well-placed cannon shots.

In April, *Teaser*, *Anacostia*, *Fuchsia*, *Resolute*, and *Yankee* accompanied an Army expedition to Machodoc Creek, Va. At 0500 on the 13th, the four ships cleared the St. Mary's River in company with the Army's steamer *Long Branch* with a battalion of soldiers under the command of General E. W. Hinks. *Long Branch* landed her troops at about 0800 while the five ships covered the operation. A contingent of Confederate cavalry appeared on the southern bank of the Machodoc but retired when *Teaser* and *Anacostia* sent four armed boat crews ashore. The landing party netted a prisoner, probably a smuggler, and a large quantity of tobacco. By the 14th, General Hinks' troops reembarked in *Long Branch* and headed for Point Lookout. *Anacostia* accompanied the Army steamer while the other four warships investigated Currioman Bay and Nomini. They returned to St. Mary's that afternoon to resume patrols.

During the summer of 1864, *Teaser* was called upon to leave the Potomac once more. On this occasion, the Union forces needed her guns to help defend strategic bridges across the rivers at the head of Chesapeake Bay near Baltimore against Brigadier General Jubal Early's raiders. On 10 July, she departed the lower Potomac, rounded Point Lookout, and headed up the Chesapeake Bay. That night, she had to put into the Patuxent River because of heavy winds and leaks in her hull. Before dawn the following morning, she continued up the bay. During the forenoon, the leaks became progressively worse and, by the time she arrived off Annapolis, she had to remove her exhaust pipe for temporary repairs. Early that evening, *Teaser* reached Baltimore where she put in for additional repairs.

The gunboat did not reach her destination, the bridge over the Gunpowder River, until late on the 12th. She was too late. The bridge had already been burned. She returned to Baltimore immediately to report on the bridge and to pick up arms and provisions for the vessels stationed in the Gunpowder River. When she arrived back at the bridge, she found orders to return to the Potomac awaiting her. *Teaser* departed the northern reaches of the Chesapeake and reported back to the Potomac Flotilla at St. Inigoes on the St. Mary's River in late afternoon on 14 April.

For the remainder of the war, *Teaser* and her flotillamates plied the Potomac and contributed to the gradual economic strangulation which brought the South to its knees by April 1865. Less than two months after General Robert E. Lee's surrender at Appomattox Court House, *Teaser* was decommissioned at the Washington Navy Yard on 2 June. Sold at public auction at Washington to Mr. J. Bigler on 25 June, the tug was redocumented as *York River* on 2 July 1865, and she served commercially until 1878.

II

(SP–933: l. 60'0''; b. 12'0''; dr. 3' (aft.); s. 11.2 k.; cpl. 5; a. 2 1-pdrs.)

The second *Teaser*—a wooden-hulled cabin launch built in 1916 at Norfolk, Va., by W. F. Dunn—was acquired by the Navy in November 1917 from George Roper & Brother and was commissioned on 29 November 1917. For the final year of World War I, she operated in the 5th Naval District on section patrol in the vicinity of Hampton Roads. On 27 December 1918, a month and one-half after the signing of the armistice agreement, *Teaser* caught fire and sank. Her name was struck from the Navy list on 15 February 1919.

Tech III

(SP–1055: l. 50'; b. 9'; dr. 3'6'' (aft.); s. 25–30 mph.; cpl. 5; a. 1 mg.)

Tech III (SP–1055)—a motorboat constructed in 1916 at Atlantic City, N.J., by Adolph Apel—was acquired by the United States Navy from Mr. T. Coleman du Pont of Wilmington, Del., on 6 August 1917 and was placed in commission the following day.

Tech III was assigned to the 4th Naval District, but records of her service are extremely sketchy. She was placed out of commission on 19 October 1917; but—since her name does not disappear from the 4th Naval District list of district vessels until the 1 September 1918 issue of the *Navy Directory*—she seems to have remained in the possession of the Navy until the summer of 1918. Presumably, she was returned to her owner sometime in 1918 and her name struck from the Navy list.

Tech Jr.

(Id. No. 1761: l. 20'; b. 8'; dr. 26'' (aft); s. 30.4 k.)

Tech Jr. (Id. No. 1761)—a motorboat built in 1912 by Adolph Apel at Atlantic City, N.J.—was acquired by the Navy on 30 August 1917 under free lease from L. & T. Prettyman of Cambridge, Md. She served only briefly as a section patrol boat in the 5th Naval District before being returned to her owner on 27 November 1917. Her name was struck from the Navy list simultaneously.

Tecumseh

While still a youth, Tecumseh—a Shawnee Indian chief born near the present site of Springfield, Ohio, sometime in or around 1768—won renown as a brave and skillful warrior. He devoted his life to opposing the advance of white settlers. Reasoning that land in North America—especially in the Ohio valley—belonged to all of the tribes in common, Tecumseh maintained that sales of territory by any single tribe to the United States were null and void. After the Federal Government refused to recognize this principle, Tecumseh attempted to organize a great Indian Confederacy to stem the white tide.

However, while he was in the South working to unite the tribes, Federal troops under Governor William Henry Harrison defeated and scattered Indian forces on 7 November 1811 in the battle of Tippecanoe. This defeat doomed the Indian Confederacy.

After Congress declared war on Great Britain the following year, Tecumseh accepted a commission as a brigadier general in the British army. He cooperated with British troops to win a number of victories in the Great Lakes region, including the capture of Detroit. However, Comdr. Oliver Hazard Perry's victory on Lake Erie, late in the summer of 1813, cut British supply lines and prompted them to withdraw along the Thames Valley. Tecumseh and his braves covered the British retirement until American troops led by Harrison—now a major general—caught up with them at Moravian-town. Tecumseh was killed in the ensuing Battle of the Thames on 5 October 1813.

In June 1930, a bronze replica of the figurehead of ship-of-the-line *Delaware* was presented by the Class of 1891 to the United States Naval Academy. This bust—perhaps the most famous relic on the campus—has been widely identified as Tecumseh. However, when it adorned the American man-of-war, it commemorated not Tecumseh but Tamanend, the revered Delaware chief who welcomed William Penn to America when he arrived in Delaware country on October 2, 1682.

I

(Monitor: t. 1,034; l. 223′; b. 43′8″; dph. 13′6″; s. 7 k.; cpl. 100; a. 2 15″ D. sb.; cl. *Canonicus*)

The first *Tecumseh*—an iron-hulled, single-turret monitor—was launched on 12 September 1863 at Jersey City, N.J., by Secor and Co., of New York City; and was commissioned at the New York Navy Yard on 19 April 1864, Comdr. Tunis A. M. Craven in command.

Although slated to strengthen Rear Admiral Farragut's West Gulf Blockading Squadron for forthcoming operations against Confederate fortifications guarding Mobile Bay, *Tecumseh* was ordered to serve temporarily with the North Atlantic Blockading Squadron, then sorely taxed by General Grant's operations against Richmond—particularly by Maj. Gen. Benjamin F. Butler's planned landing to establish a bridgehead across the James at Bermuda Hundred. Early in May, she was assigned to the James River Flotilla; and she ascended the river to guard Union shipping from Confederate naval forces below Richmond.

In order to prevent Confederate warships from coming down from the upper navigable reaches of the James, The Union Army and Navy cooperated to block the channel. *Tecumseh* participated in this effort from 15 to 18 June by sinking four hulks; stretching a heavy boom across the channel supporting a chain cable; extending a heavy boom across the flats; and sinking a schooner along the right hand bank of the river from which a short boom was extended to the flats.

Three days after the obstructions were completed, *Tecumseh*'s commanding officer, Comdr. Craven, noticed that the enemy was building a line of breastworks at Howlett's Farm. *Tecumseh*'s gunners manned their Dahlgrens, and Craven ordered "commence fire." Five heavy shells landed amidst the enemy encampment and work gang. Craven reported, "I threw into it [the Confederate construction gang's vicinity] five 15-inch shells, two of which exploded in the right place, destroying a platform, throwing the plank and timbers in every direction." The Union shells stirred up a veritable hornet's nest. At 1130, the enemy unmasked a battery of four guns.

Tecumseh resumed fire, and Craven ordered *Canonicus* and *Saugus* to engage as well. The enemy guns replied; and, a half-hour later, Confederate ironclads near Dutch Gap commenced what Craven termed "a wild cross-fire." The enemy vessels, however, were concealed by a line of trees, and thus the Union guns could not reach them.

"Our fire was delivered slowly and with great precision," wrote Craven, "most of our shells exploding within the works of the enemy." *Tecumseh* ceased fire at 1330, as Craven gave his crew a half-hour to rest and eat dinner before delivering a slow and devastating fire from 1400 to 1600. During the engagement, the monitor fired 46 15-inch shells and was not struck by any return fire. She and her sister Union warships had turned back the Confederate threat to Grant's riverine supply line.

On 5 July, the monitor got underway in company with *Augusta* and *Eutaw* and resumed her voyage southward. Proceeding "with all practicable dispatch," *Tecumseh* soon arrived in Florida waters, en route to join Farragut's squadron in the Gulf of Mexico. *Tecumseh* lay at anchor at Pensacola on 3 August as a flurry of messages arrived from the Gulf Squadron: one from the Fleet Captain and the other from Farragut himself. Both dispatches evinced the Admiral's impatience to attack Mobile Bay. "When you do not take fortune at her offer," Farragut wrote, "you must take her as you find her." That evening, Union sailors worked under the guns of Fort Morgan and deactivated and sank Confederate moored mines—"torpedoes"—in the main channel, preparatory to Farragut's forthcoming dash into the bay.

Tecumseh arrived off Mobile Bay on the evening of the 4th, thus enabling Farragut to move. Shortly after 0600 on the 5th, the 18-ship Union squadron crossed the bar at the flood tide and moved into the bay with *Tecumseh* leading the van of monitors, *Manhattan*, *Winnebago*, and *Chickasaw*. The ironclads passed between the fortified headlands, to starboard of the lighter-armored wooden steam frigates, in order to take the fire from the heavy guns at Fort Morgan.

Just after 0700, *Tecumseh* opened fire on the Confederate batteries and joined action in earnest. Meanwhile, Rear Admiral Buchanan's Southern squadron—centered around the heavy ironclad ram *Tennessee*—sortied to meet the attackers. *Tecumseh* veered left to engage the Confederate ram. Suddenly, at 0740, a tremendous explosion shook *Tecumseh* to her keel as she made contact with a dreaded "torpedo."

She began to heel rapidly; and men scrambled to abandon ship. Comdr. Craven arrived at the foot of the ladder leading to the main deck simultaneously with the pilot, John Collins. Craven stepped back, saying "After you, pilot," thus permitting Collins to escape. His gallantry cost Craven his life, for the ship sank in a frightfully fast 25 seconds. The monitor carried him down with her as she capsized. As she rolled over and exposed her hull plates, two accurate shells from Fort Morgan added the *coup de grace* to the doomed ship. Besides their captain, 92 other members of *Tecumseh*'s crew perished in the sinking—"intrepid pioneers of the death-strewed path."

II

(Tug: dp. 214; l. 88′6″; b. 21′6″; dr. 9′3″ (mean); s. 11 k.; cpl. 15; a. 1 1-pdr., 1 Gatling)

Edward Luckenbach—a tug laid down by J. H. Dialogue & Son at Camden, N.J., and completed in 1896—was acquired by the Navy from L. Luckenbach & Co.

in the spring of 1898; renamed *Tecumseh;* and placed in commission at New York City on 6 April 1898, Lt. G. R. Evans in command.

Six days after her commissioning, the tug headed south to join in the war against Spain. After stops at Norfolk, Charleston, and Key West, she joined the North Atlantic Fleet's blockade of Cuba on 26 April. Thereafter, she made frequent shuttles between Key West and the area off Havana. She came close to action only once during her four months of service in Cuban waters. On 5 May, she was nearby when *Vicksburg* captured the Spanish fishing schooner *Oriente* in the Gulf of Campeche. The end of hostilities that summer brought the tug north once more. She reached Hampton Roads on 21 August and, after a period of operations between Norfolk and Hampton Roads, she was placed out of commission on 17 September 1898—presumably at Norfolk.

Tecumseh was placed back in commission in 1899 and, by 30 June, was assigned to the Washington Navy Yard as a district tug. The nation's capital remained her duty station for over four decades. She made frequent trips up and down the Potomac River, most often between the navy yard and the proving grounds at Indian Head, Md. She also visited Norfolk from time to time.

During that period, she was twice out of commission. No decommissioning date for the first period exists, but it must have been brief since the annual reports of the Secretary of the Navy for both 1910 and 1911 indicate that she was active at the Washington Navy Yard. In any case, she was decommissioned on 1 July 1911. Her second decommissioning was probably a result of her sinking which occurred at her wharf in Washington about daybreak on 22 October 1919. In any event, she was decommissioned once again on 1 April 1920. On 17 July 1920, when the Navy adopted its alphanumeric system of hull designations, *Tecumseh* was designated YT–24.

The tug was raised, refitted, and—sometime between July 1921 and January 1922—was placed back in commission at Washington where she served through the 1920's and 1930's. In mid-1940, *Tecumseh* was reassigned to the 5th Naval District. On 5 October 1942, her name was cancelled so that it could be assigned to YT–273. However, she continued to serve, known only by her hull designation, *YT–24.* On 15 May 1944, she was redesignated *YTM–24.* Sometime between 15 April 1945 and 25 January 1946, she was decommissioned and struck from the Navy list. On 22 August 1946, she was transferred to the Maritime Commission for disposal.

III

(YT–273: dp. 260; l. 101'; b. 26'; dr. 11'; s. 11 k.; cpl. 19; cl. *Pessacus*)

The third *Tecumseh* (YT–273) was laid down at Brooklyn, N.Y., on 31 August 1942 by Ira S. Bushey & Sons; launched on 30 December 1942; and completed and placed in service on 27 April 1943.

Tecumseh was assigned to the 3d Naval District and served in the New York-Connecticut area. Reclassified a large harbor tug—YTB–273—on 15 May 1944, she continued her towing duties in that area through the end of World War II and into 1946. In March 1946, she was placed out of service, in reserve, and berthed at New London, Conn. The tug was placed back in service a little more than six years later in July 1952. She operated in the 1st Naval District until 1957 when she was transferred south to Charleston, S.C., and the 6th Naval District.

Tecumseh spent the remainder of her Navy career at Charleston. On 24 November 1961, she was reclassified a medium harbor tug and redesignated YTM–273. Less than five months later, on 5 April 1962, her name was changed to *Olathe (q.v.).* Following more than 13 years of service under her new name and classification,

the tug was placed out of service. Her name was struck from the Navy list in June 1975.

IV

(SSBN–628: dp. 7,300 (surf.), 8,250 (subm.); l. 425'; b. 33'; dr. 31'4''; s. 16 k. (surf.), 21 k. (subm.); cpl. 140; a. 16 Polaris mis., 4 tt.; cl. *James Madison*)

The fourth *Tecumseh* (SSBN–628) was laid down on 1 June 1962 at Groton, Conn., by the Electric Boat Division of the General Dynamics Corp.; launched on 22 June 1963; sponsored by Mrs. Robert L. F. Sikes; and was commissioned on 29 May 1964, Comdr. Arnett B. Taylor (blue crew) and Comdr. Charles S. Carlisle (gold crew) in command.

Tecumseh soon departed the east coast, bound for Hawaii. Based at Pearl Harbor, the nuclear-powered submarine deployed to the Marianas on 17 December 1964, arriving at Guam 12 days later to commence deterrent patrols. Alternately manned by "blue" and "gold" crews, she conducted 21 of these missions into 1969.

The submarine was then transferred to the Atlantic Fleet where she proceeded via Pearl Harbor and the Panama Canal to the east coast and arrived at Newport News, Va., on 8 November 1969. Soon thereafter, she entered the Newport News Shipbuilding and Drydock Company yards for a conversion which replaced her Polaris missiles system with its Poseidon counterpart. Emerging from drydock on 9 May 1970, *Tecumseh* underwent a thorough overhaul through that fall and winter before being assigned a new home port of Charleston, S.C., on 18 February 1971.

She conducted sea trials and shakedown out of Charleston before conducting two deterrent patrols in late 1971. Subsequently deployed to Holy Loch, Scotland, *Tecumseh* arrived in Scottish waters on 9 February 1972. She conducted 18 more deterrent patrols out of Holy Loch through 1976 and operates with the Atlantic Fleet into 1980.

Tekesta

Alternative spelling of Tequesta, a piratical Indian tribe which inhabited the area of the present-day Florida counties of Dade and Monroe during the 16th century.

(AT–93: dp. 1,450; l. 205'0''; b. 38'6''; dr. 15'4''; s. 16.5 k. (tl.); cpl. 86; a. 1 3'', 2 40mm.; cl. *Navajo*)

Tekesta (AT–93) was laid down at Portland, Oreg., on 7 September 1942 by the Commercial Iron Works; launched on 20 March 1943; sponsored by Mrs. P. S. Treiber; and commissioned on 16 August 1943, Lt. John O. Strickland in command.

The ocean tug operated on the west coast until mid-December and departed San Francisco on the 15th, bound for Hawaii. She reached Pearl Harbor on Christmas Eve 1943 and towed targets in Hawaiian waters until 20 January 1944. On that date, she joined Task Force (TF) 52, the Southern Attack Force of the Joint Expeditionary Force then preparing for Operation "Flintlock," the assault on the Marshall Islands. *Tekesta* reached Kwajalein Atoll on 1 February and remained in the Marshalls-Gilberts area for the next two months, retracting beached and broached landing craft, laying marker buoys, assisting fueling operations, and performing other salvage and towing operations necessary in the aftermath of the occupation of the Marshall Islands. During this tour of duty, the tug visited Tarawa in the Gilbert Islands and Nanumea in the Ellice Islands as well as Kwajalein, Eniwetok, and Majuro in the Marshalls.

On 12 April, the tug departed Majuro to return to Hawaii and reached Pearl Harbor a week later. There, she performed miscellaneous towing, rescue, and salvage duties until 10 May, when she got underway for Majuro with three barges in tow. En route, her designation was changed to ATF–93 on the 15th. On the 26th, *Tekesta* reached her destination and delivered her charges. She continued westward on 1 June, arriving in Eniwetok lagoon on the 3d. There, she joined TF 52 to prepare for the invasion of the Marianas. On the 11th, she sortied with that task organization bound for its first objective, Saipan.

The tug arrived off Saipan on D-day, 15 June. The following day, she helped to fight off two enemy bombers which flew over her formation. She remained in the Marianas until late July, towing pontoon bridges to the beaches, retracting landing craft, and assisting in repairs and salvage operations. By the time she departed Saipan, that island had been declared secure, but the struggles for Tinian and Guam continued. On 26 July, *Tekesta* headed for the Marshalls, arriving at Eniwetok on the 29th. Following four days turn-around time there, the tug made a round-trip voyage to Guam, returning to Eniwetok on 14 August. She remained at the atoll until the second week in September doing extensive salvage work with grounded craft and towing barges.

Tekesta headed eastward on 9 September and entered Pearl Harbor once more a week later. After trials and salvage operations there, the tug got underway on 26 October, with *Barite* (IX–161) and *YF–625* in tow, and proceeded via Eniwetok to Ulithi where she delivered her charges on 3 December. The tug then settled into a routine of towing and salvage operations which took her to Guam, Saipan, Ulithi, and the Palaus. Those operations, which lasted until March 1945, were broken only by one short period of operations with the fast carriers in mid-December.

On 1 March 1945, *Tekesta* cleared the Palau Islands for the Philippines and arrived in Leyte Gulf on 4 March to join TF 51, the Ryukyu invasion force. By D-day, 1 April, the tug was operating near Okinawa. For the next month and one-half, she was assigned to the anchorage at Kerama Retto. She towed kamikaze-damaged warships into Kerama Retto and assisted in their repairs. She also labored retracting and repairing beached and damaged landing craft. On 7 April, the tug towed *Newcomb* (DD–586) into the anchorage. On the 15th, her gunners helped to bring down a Japanese plane. She assisted *Harding* (DMS–28) into Kerama on the following day. On 4 May, *Tekesta* towed *Aaron Ward* (DM–34) to repairs at Kerama and, five days later, did the same for *Oberrender* (DE–344).

On 14 May, *Tekesta* took up station at Ie Shima and, for the following month, conducted rescue and salvage missions from that islet. She frequently fought off air attacks. On 25 May, while bringing *Spectacle* (AM–305) into Ie Shima, she fired on kamikazes. Three days later, she fired on a four-plane flight of Japanese aircraft. She hit one, but he managed to crash into SS *Brown Victory*. *Tekesta* immediately came to the aid of the stricken merchantman with fire-fighting crews and medical aid. On 10 June, the tug rushed to the aid of *William D. Porter* (DD–579), but only arrived in time to watch helplessly as the destroyer rolled over and slipped beneath the sea. Three days later, she returned to Kerama Retto and, the following day, departed the anchorage with *Newcomb* in tow for the Marianas.

Tekesta remained in the Marianas four days before continuing on to Leyte. She arrived in Leyte Gulf on 4 August and was operating there with Service Squadron 10 when hostilities ceased on the 15th. On the 30th, she put to sea with the first echelon of the Korean Service Group. After stopping at Okinawa on 2 September, she reached Jinsen, Korea, on the 7th. For the next seven months, *Tekesta* operated with the occupation forces in Korea and northern China. During that time, she visited Hong Kong and Shanghai. On 9 April 1946, the tug exited Hong Kong harbor. She stopped in the Philippine Islands at Samar, from 13 to 20

April; touched at Okinawa on the 23d; and reached Sasebo, Japan, early in May. On the 11th, she returned to Shanghai. Later in the month, she visited Subic Bay before returning to China for three more months of duty.

On 23 August, the tug cleared Tsingtao to return to the United States. After stops at Samar, Guam, Kwajalein, and Pearl Harbor, *Tekesta* entered port at San Francisco, Calif., on 12 November. For the following seven months, she was engaged in normal towing and salvage operations along the west coast, ranging from San Francisco as far south as the Panama Canal. On 16 June 1947, she departed San Francisco and headed north. After stopovers at Bremerton and Seattle, she arrived at Kodiak, Alaska, for a year of duty in the Aleutians area. During that period, she called at Dutch Harbor, Fort Glenn, Attu, Adak, Amchitka, and various other ports of call in Alaska and along the Aleutians chain.

On 28 June 1948, *Tekesta* returned to San Francisco and resumed operations along the California coast until early November. On the 4th, she headed west once more. She called at Pearl Harbor and Midway Island before reaching Yokosuka, Japan, on the 30th. In January, she shifted to Tsingtao, China, and operated there until early in March. *Tekesta* departed China on 10 March, visited Okinawa from the 14th to the 18th, and returned to Tsingtao on the 21st. She reentered Yokosuka on 7 April and operated from that port for two months before beginning her return voyage to the United States. Stopping at Wake Island and Pearl Harbor along the way, the tug put into San Francisco on 24 July 1949.

Operating from her base at Long Beach, *Tekesta* made four voyages to the Panama Canal Zone between July 1949 and April 1950. She also carried passengers to nearby ports. She entered Mare Island Naval Shipyard on 4 April 1950 for inactivation. Six days later, she was towed to San Diego. There, she was placed out of commission on the 14th and berthed with the San Diego Group, Pacific Reserve Fleet.

She remained inactive until 24 January 1958, when she was placed in service, Lt. Fred J. Sleinner in charge. She operated under control of the Commandant, 11th Naval District, until 2 July when she was reassigned to the 12th Naval District and based at San Francisco. In August 1959, *Tekesta* resumed duty at San Diego. She was placed out of service early in 1960 and, in May, was transferred to the government of Chile under lease. As of 1 October 1979, she continued to serve Chile as *Sargento Aldea* (ATF–63).

Tekesta (ATF–93) earned four battle stars during World War II.

Telamon

One of the Argonauts of Greek mythology, King of Salamis and father of Ajax.

(ARB–8: dp. 3,960; l. 328′; b. 50′; dr. 11′2″ (lim.); s. 11.6 k.; cpl. 286; a. 2 40mm., 8 20mm.; cl. *Aristaeus*)

On 28 April 1944, before her construction began, *LST–976* was redesignated ARB–8 and named *Telamon*. She was laid down on 5 December 1944 at Hingham, Mass., by Bethelehem-Hingham Shipyard, Inc.; launched on 10 January 1945; and commissioned on 5 February 1945. After steaming to Baltimore, she was decommissioned, underwent conversion at Maryland Drydock Co., and was recommissioned on 1 June 1945 as ARB–8.

On 14 July, the new battle damage repair ship reported for duty with the Pacific Fleet and on the 23rd was assigned Pearl Harbor as her home port and yard. She joined Service Squadron 10 at Guam in September shortly before being placed in the Pacific Fleet Reserve on 11 September 1945. In the spring of 1946, as part of Service Group 1.8, she took part in preparations for Operation "Crossroads" at Bikini Atoll.

On 21 June 1946, before the nuclear tests took place, she departed the atoll and steamed to Kwajalein.

She was decommissioned on 20 May 1947 and joined the San Diego Group Reserve Fleet that same day. She remained inactive until June 1973 when her name was struck from the Navy list. She was subsequently scrapped.

Telfair

A county in southern central Georgia named for Edward Telfair, the second governor of that state.

(APA–210: dp. 14,837 (tl.); l. 455'0''; b. 62'0''; dr. 24'0'' (lim.); s. 17.7 k. (tl.); cpl. 532; trp. 1,562; a. 1 5'', 10 40mm.; cl. Haskell; T. VC2–S–AP5)

Telfair (APA–210) was laid down under a Maritime Commission contract (MCV hull 558) on 30 May 1944 at Richmond, Calif., by Permanente Metals Corp.; launched on 30 August 1944; sponsored by Mrs. J. L. Cauthorn; and commissioned at San Francisco on 31 October 1944, Comdr. Lyle O. Armel, USNR, in command.

Following fitting out at Oakland, Calif., and shakedown and amphibious training off San Pedro, Calif., the attack transport returned via San Diego to San Francisco to load troops and cargo for her first westward voyage.

On the second day of 1945, she sailed westward and reached Pearl Harbor on the 8th. Nine days later, Telfair resumed her voyage carrying elements of the 111th Infantry to the Palaus for garrison duty. She disembarked troops at Peleliu between 30 January and 6 February and then continued on to the Philippines, arriving at Leyte on 9 February to prepare for the invasion of the Ryukyus. In mid-March, the attack transport embarked elements of the Army's 77th Division and sortied from San Pedro Bay with Task Group (TG) 51.1.

The Western Islands Attack Group, as TG 51.1 was called, was responsible for conducting the prelude to the Okinawa invasion by securing the anchorage at Kerama Retto, a small cluster of islands just to the south and west of Okinawa. Accordingly, it was the first element engaged in combat in the vicinity of Okinawa during the actual invasion operation. Between 25 March and 2 April, Telfair participated in the assault

and occupation of those key islets. On 30 March, she reembarked her troops; and, on the afternoon of 2 April, she cleared the roadstead for a waiting area to the south.

That evening, just after 1830, her task group was jumped by 10 or more kamikazes. Telfair and her sister-ship Goodhue (APA–107) ". . . were attacked by three planes in rapid succession." Her gunners and those of Goodhue combined to explode one in mid-air. A second, after richocheting between her starboard and port kingposts, smacked into Telfair's bulwark, then careened over the side. The third, his glide deflected by gunfire, crashed into Goodhue's cargo boom, smashed her after 20-millimeter gun tubs, and joined his compatriot in the sea.

Telfair remained in the vicinity of Okinawa supporting the invasion until 26 April when she got underway for Ulithi Atoll in the Western Carolines. She entered the lagoon on the 30th, replenished, and repaired battle damage until 22 May. On that day, the attack transport headed east to return to the United States. She reached Seattle, Wash., on 13 June, disembarked passengers, and underwent further repairs.

On 26 June, she steamed out of Puget Sound and again pointed her bow westward. On 13 July, she delivered Army hospital units safely to Saipan. Four days later, Telfair left the Marianas, bound for San Francisco, Calif., where she arrived on the last day of July. Putting to sea once more on 12 August, the attack transport shaped a course for Ulithi, but peace had returned to the Pacific before she reached that atoll on the 28th. Over the next two months, she steamed between Luzon and Leyte in the Philippines, visiting Manila from 1 to 13 October. On the 16th, she departed Lingayen Gulf to land occupation troops in Japan. She made Hiro Wan and Kure, at Honshu, on the 20th and subsequently landed her passengers.

At the end of October, Telfair reported for "Magic-Carpet" duty. On 2 November, she arrived at Samar, in the Philippines, where she embarked her first load of veterans for the return voyage to the United States. On the 4th, the attack transport departed the Philippines and, after almost three weeks at sea, entered port at Portland, Oreg. Telfair remained on the west coast until Christmas Eve when she weighed anchor to return to the western Pacific. She stopped at Saipan at the end of the first week in January 1946; then continued on to Manila where she moored on the 12th. For the next two months, she operated in the

USS Telfair (APA–210). The merchant-like appearance of attack transports and cargo ships is belied by their large complements of landing craft.

Philippine Islands, visiting Subic Bay and Samar. She departed Samar on 5 March and, after calling at Pearl Harbor, reached San Francisco on the 25th. On 8 April, she arrived at Stockton, Calif., to begin inactivation overhaul. On 20 July, she was inactive and berthed with the Stockton Group, Pacific Reserve Fleet.

The North Korean attack upon the Republic of Korea in June 1950 returned *Telfair* to life. She was ordered activated on 7 August and actually rejoined the Pacific Fleet when she was recommissioned on 12 September 1950, Capt. John Andrews, Jr., in command. During the period of fighting in Korea, roughly June 1950 to July 1953, *Telfair* deployed to the western Pacific on three separate occasions. During the first, from October 1950 to July 1951, she visited Yokosuka, Kobe, and Sasebo in Japan and Inchon and Chinnampo in Korea, shuttling troops from the former three ports to the latter two. Her first and second Korean War deployments were separated by six months of operations along the west coast of the United States. Her second tour began with her departure from San Francisco on 26 January 1952 and ended upon her return to the west coast at San Diego on 24 May. In the intervening period, she saw no actual Korean service, but steamed between Okinawa, Kobe, Yokosuka, and Sasebo primarily engaged in training United Nations troops in amphibious operations. Her third and final deployment during the Korean conflict began on 30 October 1952 after four months on the west coast. It took her to the already-familiar Japanese ports and to Manila, Subic Bay, and Hong Kong, as well as the Korean ports of Pusan, Inchon, the island of Koje Do and to the vicinity of Sokcho Ri. *Telfair* returned to San Diego on 20 April 1953 and resumed operations in the eastern Pacific.

Between August 1953 and February 1958, *Telfair* made three more deployments to the western Pacific. For the most part, her duties during those visits to the Far East consisted of lifting United Nations troops from now-peaceful Korea; shuttling troops and supplies between American bases in Korea, Japan, Okinawa, and the Philippines; and participating in 7th Fleet amphibious exercises. In August 1954, however, she did depart from her normal routine to participate in Operation "Passage to Freedom," in which Navy ships evacuated Vietnamese refugees from Haiphong in the communist-controlled northern half of newly-partitioned Indochina to Saigon in the pro-western southern portion. During non-deployment periods, *Telfair* conducted west coast operations and leave and upkeep periods in California ports.

On 29 February 1958, *Telfair* was decommissioned once more and laid up with the National Defense Reserve Fleet. A little over two years later, it appeared that her naval career was at an end once and for all. On 1 July 1960, *Telfair* was transferred to the Maritime Administration, and her name was struck from the Navy list. However, the Navy reacquired her on 24 August 1961, and her name was reinstated on the Navy list on 1 September. She was placed in commission for the third time on 22 November 1961, Capt. E. M. Higgins in command.

Telfair's new seven-year lease on life took her to new oceans and new ports of call for, immediately following training off San Diego, she headed for duty with the Amphibious Force, Atlantic Fleet. She transited the Panama Canal on 1 February 1962 and arrived in her new home port, Norfolk, Va., on the 6th. From then until final decommissioning in 1968, she alternated cruises to the Mediterranean as a unit of the 6th Fleet with operations in the western Atlantic as a unit of the 2d Fleet. On her Mediterranean cruises, she joined other units of the 6th Fleet in bi-national and multi-national amphibious exercises. She was also on hand in Greek waters in April 1967 as part of the back-up force protecting American lives and property during the takeover by the military junta in Athens. When assigned to the 2d Fleet, *Telfair* operated from Norfolk

and cruised the Atlantic seaboard, in the Caribbean and in the Gulf of Mexico. She was normally engaged in amphibious exercises with marines from Camp Lejeune, though she also conducted summer training cruises for midshipmen of the Naval Academy at Annapolis, Md.

On 31 October 1968, *Telfair* was decommissioned for the third and final time at the Naval Amphibious Base located at Little Creek, Va. On the following day, her name was struck from the Navy list. On 26 June 1969, she was transferred to the Maritime Administration once more, this time for simultaneous transfer to her purchaser, the Boston Metals Co., of Baltimore, Md., which subsequently scrapped the ship.

Telfair earned one battle star for World War II and three battle stars during the Korean War.

Tellico

A river in Tennessee.

Tellico—a T1–M–BT1 tanker laid down under a Maritime Commission contract (MC hull 2634) on 15 May 1945 at Jacksonville, Fla., by the St. Johns River Shipbuilding Co. and launched on 23 August under the sponsorship of Mrs. Charles W. Olson—was scheduled to be acquired by the Navy on a loan charter basis from the Maritime Commission as *Tellico* (AOG–74). However, as the tanker neared completion, the Navy's need for this type of ship diminished; and the government contract for her construction was cancelled on 27 August 1945, when the ship was only 74.4% complete.

Eventually finished in 1951 by the Todd Shipyard of Brooklyn, N.Y., the oil tanker served under a succession of owners and national flags into the 1970's. She sailed as *Tellico* under the Panamanian flag; as *Transea* under the Liberian ensign; and finally in succession as *Sea Transporter* and *Sea Transport* under the Canadian flag.

Tempest

(SwStr.: t. 161; a. 2 30-pdr. P.r., 2 24-pdr. how., 2 12-pdrs.)

Tempest—a wooden-hulled, sidewheel steamer built in 1862 at Louisville, Ky.—was acquired by the Navy at Cincinnati, Ohio, on 30 December 1864 from Joseph Brown; was converted there to a gunboat by Mr. Brown; and was commissioned on 26 April, Acting Volunteer Lt. Comdr. William G. Saltonstall in command.

Tempest operated with the naval forces in western waters throughout her brief naval career. She served as flagship for Acting Rear Admiral S. P. Lee, while he directed efforts on the Mississippi and its tributaries to prevent the escape of the former President of the Confederacy, Jefferson Davis. She continued in this role while he oversaw the demobilization of the Mississippi Squadron. Rear Admiral Lee hauled down his flag from her on 14 August. The ship was decommissioned at Mound City, Ill., on 30 November 1865, the day after she was sold at public auction there to Robert Carns. *Tempest* was redocumented on 11 December 1865 and remained in merchant service until 1870.

Yuma (q.v.)—a *Casco*-class, shallow-draft, single-turretted monitor—was renamed *Tempest* on 15 June 1869, but reverted to *Yuma* on 10 August of the same year.

Temptress

(PG–62: dp. 925; l. 205'2''; b. 33'0''; dr. 16'3'' (mean);
s. 16.5 k. (tl.); cpl. 87; a. 1 4'', 1 3''; cl. *Temptress*)

HMS *Veronica* (K 37)—a "Flower"-class corvette—
was laid down early in 1940 at Middlesboro, England,
by Smith's Dock Co., Ltd.; and launched on 17 October
1940. After serving the Royal Navy in the Atlantic,
the ship was transferred to the United States on 16
February 1942, renamed *Temptress* and designated
PG–62 the same day; and commissioned in England
by the United States Navy on 21 March 1942.

Through the end of March and the first week in
April, *Temptress* completed shakedown training in
British waters. Late in April, she put to sea with convoy
ON 85 bound for the United States. Upon arrival in
the United States, the gunboat reported for duty to
the Commander, Eastern Sea Frontier. For the remainder of her career, *Temptress* cruised along the
eastern coast of the United States and in the Caribbean. She escorted convoys between various points
along the Atlantic seaboard from New York to Key
West, Fla., as well as to Guantanamo Bay, Cuba.

After a short tour of duty in the 3d Naval District
training NROTC midshipmen early in the summer of
1945, *Temptress* reported to the Commandant, 1st Naval
District, on 7 July for final disposition. On 1 August,
she cleared Boston and, after stopping at Ponta
Delgada, Azores, overnight on the 8th and 9th, arrived
in Great Britain on 14 August. *Temptress* was placed
out of commission on 20 August 1945 at Chatham,
England, and returned to the Royal Navy six days
later. Her name was struck from the Navy list on 19
September 1945. The ship was sold in 1946 and
entered mercantile service as *Verolock*. Sunk in
January 1947, the ship was subsequently raised and
scrapped at Blyth, England, in 1951.

Tenacity

(PG–71: dp. 925; l. 205'2''; b. 33'0''; dr. 16'3'' (mean);
s. 16.5 k. (tl.); cpl. 87; a. 1 4'', 1 3''; cl. *Temptress*)

HMS *Candytuft* (K.09), a "Flower"-class corvette,
was laid down in 1940 at Grangemouth, Scotland, by
the Grangemouth Dry Dock Co.; launched on 8 July
1940; and commissioned in the Royal Navy soon thereafter. The United States Navy acquired her on 4 March
1942 under reverse lend lease; renamed her *Tenacity*
(PG–71); and placed her in commission at New York
on 11 June 1942.

After serving in the Caribbean under the Com-
mandant, Caribbean Sea Frontier, *Tenacity* was trans-
ferred early in September to Vice Admiral Ingram's
South Atlantic Force, later redesignated the 4th Fleet.
She arrived at Trinidad, British West Indies, on 7
September and, for the next 17 months, plied the waters
along the coast of Brazil escorting convoys to various
Brazilian ports, notably Recife and Bahia.

Late in January 1944, the gunboat was detached
from the 4th Fleet, departed Trinidad, and headed
north to Charleston, S.C. She left that port on 24
March and steamed north for duty in the northwestern
Atlantic. *Tenacity* reported at Boston on 28 March
and joined Task Force 24, a surface force which
patrolled and escorted ships between ports in waters
from Boston in the west and Greenland in the east. For
the remainder of her naval service, *Tenacity* visited
ports such as Argentia and St. Johns in Newfoundland,
Grondal and Narsarssuak in Greenland, and Boston,
Mass. She protected ships and convoys, stood plane
guard station for aircraft flying antisubmarine patrol,
and conducted her own patrols against U-boats.

With the end of the war in Europe on 9 May 1945,
Tenacity was no longer needed to fight submarines in
the Atlantic. Since ships of her type were not the
variety needed in the war still being waged against

Japan, it was determined that *Tenacity* and her sisterships should be returned to Great Britain. She departed
Boston harbor for the last time on 1 August and, after
a brief stop at Ponta Delgada in the Azores, arrived in
England on 14 August. *Tenacity* was placed out of
commission on 22 August and transferred back to
Great Britain four days later. Her name was struck
from the Navy list on 17 September 1945.

Tenadores

(Transport: dp. 7,782; l. 485'; b. 55'3''; dr. 27'4'';
s. 17 k.; a. 4 5'', 2 1-pdrs., 2 mg.)

Tenadores was built in 1913 by Workman, Clark and
Co., Belfast, Ireland; owned and operated by the United
Fruit Co.; taken over by the United States Navy on
12 April 1918; and commisioned on 17 April 1918,
Comdr. James B. Gilmer in command.

Tenadores served as a troop transport during the
remainder of World War I. Shortly after midnight on
28 December 1918, the ship grounded in a heavy fog
off the north coast of the Ile d'Yeu, approximately 10
miles from Brest, France.

During unsuccessful efforts to refloat the ship, some
80 tons of supplies were removed from the stricken
vessel and taken to St. Nazaire. On 30 December 1918,
minesweeper *B.H.B. Hubbard* rescued the last members
of the transport's crew. On 2 January 1919, *Hubbard*
returned to *Tenadores* for one last attempt to salvage
the ship but was thwarted by high seas and the hopeless
state of the transport which was lying on her starboard
side and breaking up. The name *Tenadores* was struck
from the Navy list on 18 February 1919.

Tench

A Eurasian freshwater fish related to the dace and
noted for its ability to survive out of water.

(SS–417: dp. 1,845 (surf.), 2,415 (subm.); l. 311'8'';
b. 27'3''; dr. 16'5'' (mean); s. 20.25 k. (surf.), 8.75
k. (subm.); cpl. 81; a. 10 21'' tt., 1 5'', 1 40mm.,
1 20mm., 2 .50-cal. mg.; cl. *Balao*)

Tench (SS–417) was laid down on 1 April 1944 at
the Portsmouth (N.H.) Navy Yard; launched on
7 July 1944; sponsored by Mrs. Claudia Alta (Lady
Bird) Johnson, the wife of Lyndon Baines Johnson, at
that time the Representative from the 10th Congressional District in Texas and later the 36th President
of the United States; and commissioned on 6 October
1944, Comdr. William B. Sieglaff in command.

After completing trials and shakedown training out
of New London, *Tench* departed that port on 20 December for duty in the Pacific. Following brief pauses for
training at Key West and in the Panama Canal Zone,
the submarine reached Pearl Harbor during the latter
part of January 1945. An additional training period
followed her arrival in Oahu, but only a brief one. On
7 February, she stood out of Pearl Harbor, bound for
her first war patrol. After a stop at Saipan for fuel,
Tench returned to sea in company with *Sea Devil*
(SS–400), *Balao* (SS–285), and *Grouper* (SS–214)—the
other three submarines in the coordinated attack group
to which she was assigned.

They left Saipan on 27 February and headed for their
assigned patrol area which began in the region of the
East China Sea southwest of Kyushu and extended
north into the Yellow Sea. On the night of 6 and 7
March, *Tench* passed through the Colnett Strait—south
of Yoku Shima—and into the East China Sea. The four
submarines rotated patrol, weather-reporting, photo-
graphic-reconnaissance, and lifeguard duties. On 18
March, *Tench* received orders to take up lifeguard station off the western coast of Kyushu during 5th Fleet
carrier air raids on Nagasaki. Just before the noon
watch came on duty, the submarine got word of a dye

marker sighting by search planes. Presumably evidence of a downed American aviator, the marker had been sighted in a bay on the coast of Kyushu near the town of Akune.

Under the protective cover of F6F "Hellcat" fighters, *Tench* threaded her way cautiously into the shallow waters of the bay. Just after she discovered that the "sighting" had been the result of a reflection of a shoal spot, she received a severe fright. Caught in waters too shallow for her to dive, she proceeded almost helplessly on the surface while a large flight of aircraft approached her from astern. Fortunately the planes proved to be additional 5th Fleet bombers returning from Nagasaki. *Tench* stood offshore and watched while they loosed their remaining bombs on installations near Akune: a railroad bridge, a fuel dump, and a factory.

The remainder of March proved relatively unproductive. In the absence of targets worthy of torpedoes, the submarine contented herself with the destruction of floating mines and with the sinking of two tiny trawlers on the 28th.

Early on 3 April, an enemy bomber forced her to dive, and she ran submerged for the remainder of the day. That evening, she surfaced once again and soon made radar contact with a good-sized target. The fact that the enemy ship carried radar—coupled with the appearance of a second target larger than the first—indicted that she was some type of warship escorting a merchantman. Darkness and fog dictated a surface attack. *Tench*'s report claims that the target, the large cargoman, took one torpedo hit and erupted in a splendid pyrotechnic display. Unfortunately, there is no evidence to confirm the kill.

Tench's first war patrol had begun soon after the invasion of Iwo Jima and continued past the landings on Okinawa. American planners had foreseen the possibility of Japan's attempting to strike back at the Allied forces with what remained of the Imperial surface fleet. They therefore stationed a picket line of submarines off Japan to serve as an early warning system. *Tench* received orders to join that group of submarines before concluding her war patrol. She was on station off the western coast of the Japanese home islands when the *Yamato* task force sortied on 6 April to contest the Okinawa landings. *Tench* did not sight the enemy warship because they sortied from the Bungo Suido—the eastern exit to the Inland Sea and the station assigned to *Threadfin* (SS–410). When that submarine sent her warning, the picket line was disbanded, and each submarine turned to its own individual mission. Some tried to gain advantageous setups on the *Yamato* force, but *Tench* cleared the area for an air-sea rescue sweep of the East China Sea before ending her patrol. On 8 April, she picked up the pilot and radioman from an *Essex* (CV–9) dive-bomber and then headed for Guam where she arrived on the 14th.

Refit completed and her crew rested, *Tench* returned to sea early in May for her second war patrol. That patrol took her again to the Japanese homeland, but this time to the Tsugaru Strait between Honshu and Hokkaido which constitutes the northern entrance to the Sea of Japan. Her mission was to interdict Japanese shipping as it attempted to run north and south between the Kurils and Tokyo. Her first contact came on 25 May and proved to be an enemy warship. While patrolling on the surface, she sighted a periscope approaching her out of the fog. She submerged immediately, picked the enemy up on her sound gear, and evaded him successfully. During the waning days of May, she sighted little enemy shipping of consequence, though her gun crews dispatched a number of motor luggers, picket boats, steam trawlers, and other small craft to the depths. On 1 June, however, fortune began to favor the submarine. That evening, she encountered the 861-ton *Mikamisan Maru* hugging the coast of Honshu near Shiriya. *Tench* stalked her quarry until 0700 the next morning when she caught the cargoman about one-half mile off shore. In a surface attack, the

submarine scored two torpedo hits on *Mikamisan Maru* and sent her to the bottom. Two days later, *Tench* scored a single hit amidships on the 517-ton *Ryujin Maru* which proved sufficient to sink her. For five days, the submarine worked her way back and forth across the strait, dodging enemy patrols and picket boats, but without finding suitable targets. Then, on the 9th, she came across the big game of her wartime career, the 2,857-ton freighter *Kamishika Maru*. *Tench* sank the merchantman in a submerged attack and spent the rest of the day evading spirited and persistent enemy retaliation. The following day, she dispatched an enemy tanker, the 834-ton *Shoei Maru No. 6* in another submerged attack. Again, the Japanese spit-kit patrol force went after the submarine with everything it had, but failed even to come close.

In fact, *Tench*'s closest call was self-inflicted. On 11 June, she crossed swords with a Japanese destroyer in a night surface attack. After firing a salvo of torpedoes at the enemy from her bow tubes, *Tench* put her rudder hard over to turn and retired rapidly. Just then, the lookouts reported one of her own torpedoes running in a wide circle and on a collision course with *Tench*. Frantic moments of evasive action ensued, but the torpedo hung tenaciously on to its collision course. Once again fortune smiled. The torpedo ran deeply and passed directly under the submarine's stern. *Tench* continued her retirement unaware of the results of her attack—in all probability unsuccessful—but heartened by her escape from what had seemed certain destruction. After five more days of hunting enemy shipping—during which she encountered and sank a motor trawler with gunfire—*Tench* headed toward Midway Island.

Following a refit there, the submarine put to sea on her third and final war patrol. On 29 July, she once again passed through Colnett Strait and entered the East China Sea. On the 30th, she found another motor lugger and punched holes in her with her 40-millimeter gun. She then proceeded to round up the lugger's nine-man Korean crew, all of whom had taken to the water at the first hint of trouble. Between 2 and 4 August, she rode out an East China Sea typhoon and, on the 6th, released her prisoners in a small boat near the Korean coast. That afternoon, she headed in toward the harbor of Osei To, a small island near the western coast of Korea, to conduct a shore bombardment. During that escapade, her guns destroyed four schooners and severely damaged another five schooners, a sea truck, and a motor trawler as well as some warehouses and other dockside installations. *Tench* then shifted north to the Gulf of Pohai, between the Kwantung Peninsula of Manchuria and the Shantung Promontory of China. Her last encounter of the war occurred on 9 August when she surfaced in fog to torpedo and sink a seagoing tug towing two large barges. While the submarine retired from that attack, two Japanese "Betty" medium bombers dropped a bomb apiece some 500 yards off her port beam and then retired themselves. That ended her hostile actions. On 15 August, the Japanese Empire capitulated, and hostilities ceased.

Tench remained on patrol station until 28 August and then headed for Guam where she arrived on 2 September. After a brief stop at Apra, she headed back toward the United States. Following stops at Pearl Harbor and Balboa in the Panama Canal Zone, *Tench* moored at New London, Conn., on 6 October 1945—a year to the day since she had gone into commission. In March 1946, she was placed out of commission in reserve at New London.

Almost four years of idleness ended for *Tench* in October 1950 when she came out of "mothballs" to be converted to a Guppy 1A submarine. Over the next three months, she underwent extensive modifications to improve her performance characteristics for submerged operations. In January 1950, the submarine was recommissioned at Norfolk, Comdr. Frederick N. Russell in command.

Tench's second period of active service lasted just over two decades. For the most part, she conducted

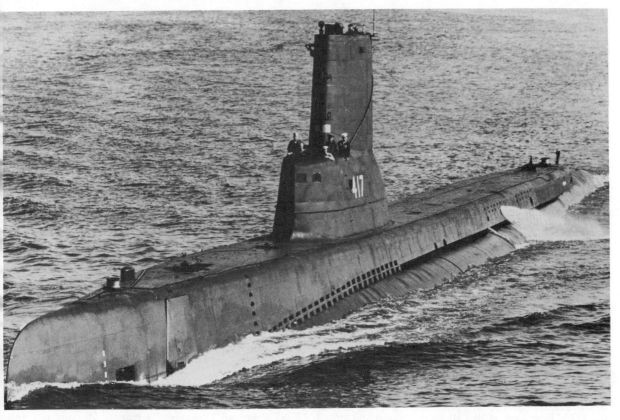

Tench (SS–417) after her Guppy IA conversion, 1965.   (USN 1111882)

routine training operations off the east coast. Initially, she operated out of Norfolk as a unit of Submarine Squadron (SubRon) 6. While so assigned, she made her first deployment to the Mediterranean Sea in January 1952. Upon her return three months later, she resumed her schedule of east coast and Caribbean operations. During the summer of 1955, the submarine changed homeports, leaving SubRon 6 behind for duty with Sub-Ron 2, based at New London, Conn. In addition to periodic fleet exercises, *Tench* served as a school ship for the Submarine School located at New London. That employment continued until October 1961 at which time she stood out of New London on her second deployment to the 6th Fleet in the Mediterranean from which she returned early in 1962. Another extended period of duty with the Submarine School followed. That assignment was augmented by duty with various aviation and surface units in a series of antisubmarine warfare exercises. Early in April 1966, *Tench* broke that routine once again for a four-month cruise with the 6th Fleet. This appears to have been her third and last tour of duty in the Mediterranean. Upon completion of the deployment, she returned once again to her New London-based training operations which occupied the submarine for the remainder of her active career.

During the late summer and early fall of 1968, *Tench* took part in a NATO exercise, Operation "Silvertower," in the eastern Atlantic. During that assignment, she visited ports in the United Kingdom, Germany, and Portugal. The submarine returned to New London on 4 November and began her final 19 months of active service. Near the end of her career, she was reclassified AGSS–417 on 1 October 1969. She was placed in commission, in reserve, at Philadelphia later that month; and, on 8 May 1970, *Tench* was placed out of commission. Berthed at Philadelphia, *Tench* remained in reserve until 1973. On 15 August 1973, her name was struck from the Navy list, and she was subsequently scrapped.

Tench was awarded three battle stars for her World War II service.

Tenedos

An island—now belonging to Turkey and called Bozcaada—in the Aegean Sea about three miles off the coast of Asia Minor and some 12 miles south of the Dardanelles. According to legend, Tenedos was the staging station of the Greek task force under Agamemnon during the Trojan War. It was used by Xerxes as a base during the Persian War and by British Admiral Sir John Thomas Duckworth during operations against Constantinople in 1807.

(Bark: t. 245; dr. 12′)

Tenedos was purchased for the Navy at New London, Conn., on 16 October 1861 by George D. Morgan and R. H. Chappell for use in the "stone fleet." She had been laid up since 12 May 1860 and was among the first contingent of whalers to be purchased for the purpose of being sunk as an obstruction to a Confederate port.

Tenedos, under Master O. Sisson, was loaded with blocks of granite from New England and sailed with other ships of the "stone fleet" for South Carolina on 20 November 1861. Upon their arrival at Port Royal, they were placed at the disposal of Flag Officer Samuel Francis DuPont. Beginning in late afternoon of 19 December and ending the next day, *Tenedos* and 15 other ships were sunk off the bar of Charleston's main channel.

Tenino

A Shahaptian Indian tribe formerly occupying the valley of the Deschutes River in Oregon. It was one of the tribes placed on the Warm Springs Indian Reservation in Jefferson and Wasco Counties, Oreg., by the Wasco Treaty of 1855.

(ATF–115: dp. 1,589; l. 205'; b. 38'6''; dr. 15'4''; s. 16.5 k.; cpl. 85; a. 1 3'', 2 40mm.; cl. *Abnaki*)

Tenino (AT–115) was laid down on 16 June 1943 at Alameda, Calif., by the United Engineering Co.; launched on 10 January 1944; sponsored by Mrs. William Mark; redesignated as ATF–115 on 15 May 1944; and commissioned on 18 November 1944, Lt. Forrest L. Van Camp in command.

Tenino held her shakedown cruise in the San Pedro Bay area until 30 December 1944 when she proceeded to San Diego to load salvage equipment. The next day, the tug got underway for Clipperton Island, off the coast of Mexico, to salvage two Navy ships that were aground there. She arrived on the scene on 4 January 1945 and began salvage operations for *Seize* (ARS–26) which was stranded in the vicinity of *LST–563*. Work continued until the 15th when *Seize* was pulled clear of the beach. *Tenino* started to work on the LST the next day. On 30 January, she lost all of her salvage gear when her No. 3 starboard set of bitts was torn away from her bulwarks. Water poured into the engine room through the openings left by the bitts and the holes around loosened rivets. The tug then proceeded to the lee side of Clipperton Island to effect damage control measures. On 1 February, *Tenino* embarked several patients from the salvage group and headed for Magdalena Bay. The next day, her orders were changed, and she proceeded to Socorro Island where she transferred the patients to a plane on the 3d. The ship arrived at San Diego on the 5th and moved to the Naval Repair Base the next day. On the 9th, she shifted berths to the Concrete Shipbuilding Co., National City, for final repairs.

Tenino departed San Diego on 24 February for San Francisco where she took *Windsor* (ARD–22) in tow for delivery to Hawaii. She delivered the floating drydock to Pearl Harbor on 16 March and began towing *YM–21* toward Guam on 5 April. The tug arrived at Apra Harbor on 6 May and, six days later, headed for Okinawa towing a floating drydock. She reached Buckner Bay on 20 May and served there as an emergency ship until 28 August. In this capacity, *Tenino* engaged in salvage, fire-fighting, and diving operations; performed rescue work; and towed battle casualties.

From 22 July to 7 August, *Tenino* labored to salvage torpedoed attack transport *Marathon* (APA–200). On 12 August, she aided the torpedoed *Pennsylvania* (BB–38). On the 30th, she and *Serrano* (ATF–112) took the battleship in tow and headed for the Marianas. They arrived at Apra Harbor, Guam, on 6 September, and *Tenino* had her engines overhauled there before returning to Okinawa on 25 September. Four days later, the tug stood by to assist endangered ships during a typhoon period. After aiding several ships, *Tenino* found herself fast aground on 9 October. *Bannock* (ATF–81) and *Menominee* (AT–73) pulled her free of the reef on the 11th, and she was repaired in *ARD–17*. *Tenino* continued operating at Okinawa until 19 January 1946 when she got underway for the Philippines with *Flagler* (AKA–181) in tow. Upon delivering that attack cargo ship at Subic Bay, the tug headed back toward the Ryukyus and reached Okinawa on 8 February.

Five days later, she proceeded to the Marshalls. After touching at Saipan and Peleliu, she reached Eniwetok on 27 March but stood out to sea again the next day to retrieve the former Japanese cruiser *Sakawa* which was adrift and out of fuel. The tug returned to Eniwetok on the 31st. A week later, the tug headed for the west coast of the United States.

Tenino reached San Pedro on 24 May and remained there until 11 September when she got underway for the east coast. She arrived at Norfolk on 30 October and was routed via Charleston, S.C., to Orange, Tex. On 18 November 1946, the tug moved to New Orleans for a preinactivation overhaul which lasted until 8 February 1947. *Tenino* returned to Orange on 10 February and was assigned to the Atlantic Reserve Fleet. She was placed out of commission, in reserve, on 17 May 1947 and transferred to the Maritime Administration in September 1961. *Tenino* was struck from the Navy list in September 1962.

Tenino received one battle star for World War II service.

Tennessee

Tennessee, the 16th state, was admitted to the Union on 1 June 1796. The word Tennessee is derived from a Cherokee Indian term which referred to several Cherokee settlements formerly located in territory now within the state.

I

The first *Tennessee*—a former Confederate, side-wheel steamboat—was captured by the West Gulf Blockading Squadron when Rear Admiral David G. Farragut took New Orleans on 25 April 1862. Commissioned in the United States Navy on 2 May 1862, the ship was renamed *Mobile* (*q.v.*) on 1 September 1864.

II

(IrcRam: t. 1,273; l. 209'0''; b. 48'0''; dr. 14'0''; s. 6 k.; a. 2 7⅛'' Brooke rifles, 4 6'' Brooke rifles)

The second *Tennessee*—a casemated, ironclad ram—was laid down at Selma, Ala., sometime in October 1862 by Henry D. Bassett; and she was launched late in February 1863. The ironclad was towed by steamboat *Southern Republic*, whose calliope played "Dixie" as the two steamers tied up at a landing each night during the week-long, 150-mile trip down river. At Mobile, the ironclad's machinery, armament, and armor were installed. The ram was commissioned in the Confederate States Navy on 16 February 1864, Lt. James D. Johnston, CSN, in command.

Tennessee then became flagship for Admiral Franklin Buchanan and proved to be a potent deterrent to any attempts by the Federal Navy to enter Mobile Bay. Though he had wished to force the entrance two years earlier, Rear Admiral Farragut could not seriously entertain such notions until May of 1864. On the 25th he made a run inshore to reconnoiter the defense to the entrance and to get a good look at the South's newest ironclad. *Tennessee* impressed him so much that he concluded that his wooden ships would be no match for her—particularly in the narrow channel dominated by the guns of Fort Morgan. Consequently, he decided to wait for reinforcements in the form of Union iron clads, which did not arrive on the scene until late in July.

On the morning of 5 August 1864, Farragut's fleet—strengthened by the recently arrived single-turret monitors, *Tecumseh* and *Manhattan*, and double-turret monitors, *Chickasaw* and *Winnebago*—began its move toward the entrance to Mobile Bay. As the Union ships steamed past the guns of Fort Morgan, *Tennessee* and the gunboats *Gaines*, *Morgan*, and *Selma* moved forward to engage them. The ironclad ram's underpowered engines gave her insufficient speed to head the invaders off before they steamed into the bay. She exchanged shots with the Federal ships as they moved to a point some three or four miles up the bay, knocking the three Confederate gunboats out of the fight in the process.

At that point, *Tennessee* headed up the bay to take on the Federal fleet single handed. In response, every ship of that fleet tried to grab the glory of sinking the Confederate ram. During the ensuing melee, at least three Union ships succeeded in ramming *Tennessee* but failed to damage her appreciably. Instead, she suffered her most significant damage from Federal gunfire. Both her forward and after gun port covers jammed in the closed position restricting her ability to fire, and her stack was first holed and then shot away making it impossible to keep up sufficient steam to maneuver properly. An 11-inch shell from *Chickasaw* spelled her doom. That shot severed and blew away her rudder chains exposed on the after deck. Robbed of her ability to maneuver and unable to bring a gun to bear, *Tennessee* struck her colors and surrendered at about 1000.

Immediately following her capture, on 5 August, *Tennessee* was commissioned in the United States Navy, Acting Volunteer Lt. Pierre Giraud in charge. The ironclad participated in the Federal assault on Fort Morgan on 23 August which resulted in the fort's capitulation that same day. That autumn, she moved from Mobile to New Orleans for repairs before joining the Mississippi Squadron. She served on the Mississippi through the end of the war in April 1865 and briefly thereafter. On 19 August 1865, *Tennessee* was placed out of commission and was laid up at New Orleans. There, she remained until 27 November 1867 when she was sold at auction to J. F. Armstrong for scrapping.

III

Madawaska (q.v.), a screw frigate, was renamed *Tennessee* on 15 May 1869.

IV

(Armored Cruiser No. 10: dp. 13,712 (f); l. 504'5''; b. 72'10½''; dr. 25'0'' (mean); s. 22.16 k.; cpl. 887; a. 4 10'', 16 6'', 22 3'', 4 3-pdrs., 4 21'' tt.; cl. *Montana*)

The fourth *Tennessee* (Armored Cruiser No. 10) was laid down by the Cramp Shipbuilding Co., Philadel-

phia, Pa., on 20 June 1903; launched on 3 December 1904; sponsored by Miss Annie K. Frazier, daughter of Governor James B. Frazier of Tennessee and subsequently the foundress of the Society of Sponsors of the United States Navy; and commissioned at the Philadelphia Navy Yard on 17 July 1906, Capt. Albert O. Berry in command.

The new armored cruiser departed Hampton Roads, Va., on 8 November 1906 as escort for *Louisiana* (Battleship No. 19) in which President Theodore Roosevelt had embarked for a cruise to Panama to check on the progress of work constructing the Panama Canal. After a brief visit to Puerto Rico on the return voyage, the warships arrived back at Hampton Roads on 26 November. *Tennessee* was present for the Jamestown Exposition held from 7 to 11 June 1907 to commemorate the tricentennial of the founding of the first English settlement in America.

On 14 June, *Tennessee* sailed for Europe and reached Royan, France, on the 23d for duty with the Special Service Squadron. She returned home in August but departed Hampton Roads on 12 October for the Pacific.

Tennessee then patrolled off the California coast until 24 August 1908 when she sailed for Samoa, arriving at Pago Pago on 23 September to resume service with the Pacific Fleet. On 15 May 1910, she arrived at Bahia Blanca to represent the United States at the centenary celebration of the independence of Argentina. On 8 November, the armored cruiser departed Portsmouth, N.H., and proceeded to Charleston, S.C., to embark President William Howard Taft for a round-trip voyage to Panama to inspect progress on the transisthmus canal which was then being constructed. She returned to Hampton Roads on 22 November and then engaged in battle practice off the Virginia coast into February 1911. Following a Mardi Gras visit to New Orleans and a visit to New York early in March, the ship steamed to Cuban waters for two months of operations out of Guantanamo Bay.

The steam frigate *Madawaska*, one of six fast cruisers laid down in 1863, was renamed *Tennessee* in 1869. She is seen here with the spar deck added during that year. (NR&L(O) 14155)

Placed in reserve at the Portsmouth (N.H.) Navy Yard on 15 June 1911, she remained on the east coast for a year and one-half before departing Philadelphia on 12 November 1912 for the Mediterranean. Arriving off Smyrna (now Izmir), Turkey, on 1 December, she remained there protecting American citizens and property during the First Balkan War until 3 May 1913 when she headed home. After reaching Hampton Roads on the 23d, *Tennessee* operated on the east coast until entering the Atlantic Reserve Fleet at Philadelphia on 23 October. On 2 May 1914, she became receiving ship at the New York Navy Yard.

On 6 August, *Tennessee* sailed from New York for duty in Europe through the first half of 1915 supporting the American Relief Expedition. In August, she transported the 1st Regiment, Marine Expeditionary Force, and the Marine Artillery Battalion to Haiti. From 28 January to 24 February 1916, the cruiser served as flagship of a cruiser squadron off Port-au-Prince, Haiti. In March, she embarked a group of dignitaries at Hampton Roads for a two-month, round-trip cruise to Montevideo, Uruguay.

On 25 May, *Tennessee* was renamed *Memphis*, honoring a city of Tennessee, so that the name *Tennessee* could be reassigned to a new warship, Battleship No. 43. In July, the ship got underway for Central America, arriving at San Domingo on 23 July for peace-keeping patrol off the rebellion-torn Dominican Republic. On the afternoon of 29 August, while at anchor in the harbor of San Domingo, *Memphis* was driven ashore by an unexpected tidal wave and totally wrecked. The casualties, including a boatload of *Memphis* sailors returning from shore leave, numbered some 40 men dead or missing and 204 badly injured.

Memphis was struck from the Navy list on 17 December 1917 and sold to A. H. Radetsky Iron and Metal Co., Denver, Colo., on 17 January 1922 for scrapping.

V

(BB–43: dp. 33,190; l. 624'; b. 97'3½''; dr. 31'; s. 21 k.; cpl. 1,401; a. 12 14'', 14 5'', 4 3'' AA, 2 21'' tt.; cl. *Tennessee*)

The fifth *Tennessee* was laid down on 14 May 1917 at the New York Navy Yard; launched on 30 April 1919; sponsored by Miss Helen Lenore Roberts, daughter of the governor of Tennessee; and commissioned on 3 June 1920, Capt. Richard H. Leigh in command.

Tennessee and her sister ship, *California* (BB–44), were the first American battleships built to a "post-Jutland" hull design. As a result of extensive experimentation and testing, her underwater hull protection was much greater than that of previous battleships; and both her main and secondary batteries had fire-control systems. The *Tennessee* class, and the three ships of the *Colorado*-class which followed, were identified by two heavy cage masts supporting large fire-control tops. This feature was to distinguish the "Big Five" from the rest of the battleship force until World War II. Since *Tennessee*'s 14-inch turret guns could be elevated to 30 degrees—rather than to the 15 degrees of earlier battleships—her heavy guns could reach out an additional 10,000 yards. Because battleships were then beginning to carry airplanes to spot long-range gunfire, *Tennessee*'s ability to shoot "over the horizon" had a practical value.

After fitting out, *Tennessee* conducted trials in Long Island Sound from 15 to 23 October 1920. While *Tennessee* was at New York, one of her 300-kilowatt ship's-service generators blew up on 30 October, "completely destroying the turbine end of the machine" and injuring two men. Undaunted, the ship's force, navy yard craftsmen, and manufacturers' representatives labored to eliminate the "teething troubles" in *Tennessee*'s engineering system and enabled the battleship to depart New York on 26 February 1921 for standardization trials at Guantanamo. She next steamed north for the Virgina capes and arrived at Hampton Roads on 19 March. *Tennessee* carried out gunnery calibration firing at Dahlgren, Va., and then drydocked at Boston before full-power trials off Rockland, Maine. After touching at New York, she steamed south; transited the Panama Canal; and, on 17 June, arrived at San Pedro, Calif., her home port for the next 19 years.

Here, she joined the Battleship Force, Pacific Fleet. In 1922, the Pacific Fleet was redesignated the Battle Fleet (renamed the Battle Force in 1931), United States Fleet. For the next two decades, the battleship divisions of the Battle Fleet were to include the preponderance of the Navy's surface warship strength; and *Tennessee* was to serve here until World War II.

Peacetime service with the battleship divisions involved an annual cycle of training, maintenance, and readiness exercises. Her yearly schedule included competitions in gunnery and engineering performance and an annual fleet problem, a large-scale war game in which most or all of the United States Fleet was organized into opposing forces and presented with a variety of strategic and tactical situations to resolve. Beginning with Fleet Problem I in 1923 and continuing through Fleet Problem XXI in April 1940, *Tennessee* had a prominent share in these battle exercises. Yet her individual proficiency was not neglected. During the competitive year 1922 and 1923, she made the highest aggregate score in the list of record practices fired by her guns of various caliber and won the "E" for excellence in gunnery. In 1923 and 1924, she again won the gunnery "E" as well as the prized Battle Efficiency Pennant for the highest combined total score in gunnery and engineering competition. During 1925, she took part in joint Army-Navy maneuvers to test

USS *Tennessee* (BB–43) in the 1930s.   (NR&L(M) 35219)

the defenses of Hawaii before visiting Australia and New Zealand. Subsequent fleet problems and tactical exercises took *Tennessee* from Hawaii to the Caribbean and Atlantic and from Alaskan waters to Panama.

Fleet Problem XXI was conducted in Hawaiian waters during the spring of 1940. At the end of this problem, the battleship force did not return to San Pedro; but, at President Roosevelt's direction, its base of operations was shifted to Pearl Harbor in the hope that this move might deter Japanese expansion in the Far East. Following an overhaul at the Puget Sound Navy Yard after the conclusion of Fleet Problem XXI, *Tennessee* arrived at her new base on 12 August 1940. Due to the increasing deterioration of the world situation, Fleet Problem XXII—scheduled for the spring of 1941—was cancelled; and *Tennessee*'s activities during these final months of peace were confined to smaller scale operations.

On the morning of 7 December 1941, *Tennessee* was moored starboard side to a pair of masonry "mooring quays" on Battleship Row, the name given to a line of these deep water berths located along the southeast side of Ford Island. *West Virginia* (BB–48) was berthed alongside to port. Just ahead of *Tennessee* was *Maryland* (BB–46), with *Oklahoma* (BB–37) outboard. *Arizona* (BB–39), moored directly astern of *Tennessee*, was undergoing a period of upkeep from the repair ship *Vestal* (AR–4), berthed alongside her. The three "nests" were spaced about 75 feet apart.

At about 0755, Japanese carrier planes began their attack. As the first bombs fell on Ford Island, *Tennessee* went to general quarters and closed her watertight doors. In about five minutes, her antiaircraft guns were manned and firing. Sortie orders were received, and the battleship's engineers began to get steam up. However, this quickly became academic as *Oklahoma* and *West Virginia* took crippling torpedo hits. *Oklahoma* capsized to port and sank, bottom up. *West Virginia* began to list heavily, but timely counterflooding righted her. She, nevertheless, also settled on the bottom but did so on an even keel. *Tennessee*, though her guns were firing and her engines operational, could not move. The sinking *West Virgina* had wedged her against the two massive concrete quays to which she was moored, and worse was soon to come.

As the Japanese torpedo bombers launched their weapons against Battleship Row, dive bombers were simultaneously coming in from above. Strafing fighters were attacking the ships' antiaircraft batteries and control positions as high-level horizontal bombers dropped heavy battleship-caliber projectiles modified to serve as armor-piercing bombs. Several bombs struck *Arizona*; and, at about 0820, one of them penetrated her protective deck and exploded in a magazine detonating black-powder saluting charges which, in turn, set off the surrounding smokeless-powder magazines. A shattering explosion demolished *Arizona*'s foreport, and fuel oil from her ruptured tanks was ignited and began to spread. The torpedo hits on *West Virginia* had also released burning oil, and *Tennessee*'s stern and port quarter were soon surrounded by flames and dense black smoke. At about 0830, horizontal bombers scored two hits on *Tennessee*. One bomb carried away the after mainyard before passing through the catapult on top of Turret III, the elevated after turret, breaking up as it partially penetrated the armored turret top. Large fragments of the bomb case did some damage inside the turret and put one of its three 14-inch guns out of operation. Instead of exploding, the bomb filler ignited and burned, setting an intense fire which was quickly extinguished.

The second bomb struck the barrel of the center gun of Turret II, the forward "high" turret, and exploded. The center gun was knocked out of action, and bomb fragments sprayed *Tennessee*'s forward superstructure. Capt. Mervyn S. Bennion, the commanding officer of *West Virginia*, had stepped out on to the starboard wing of his ship's bridge only to be mortally wounded by one of these fragments.

While her physical hurts were relatively minor, *Tennessee* was still seriously threatened by oil fires raging around her stern. When *Arizona*'s magazines erupted, *Tennessee*'s after decks were showered with burning oil and debris which started fires that were encouraged by the heat of the flaming fuel. Numerous blazes had to be fought on the after portion of the main deck and in the officers' quarters on the deck below. Shipboard burning was brought under control by 1030, but oil flowing from the tanks of the adjacent ships continued to flame.

By the evening of 7 December, the worst was over. Oil was still blazing around *Arizona* and *West Virginia* and continued to threaten *Tennessee* for two more days while she was still imprisoned by the obstacles around her. Although her bridge and foremast had been damaged by bomb splinters, her machinery was in full commission; and no serious injury had been done to ship or gunnery controls. Ten of her 12 14-inch guns and all of her secondary and antiaircraft guns were intact. By comparison with most of the battleships around her, *Tennessee* was relatively unscathed.

The first order of business was now to get *Tennessee* out of her berth. Just forward of her, *Maryland*—similarly wedged into her berth when *Oklahoma* rolled over and sank—was released and moved away on 9 December. The forwardmost of *Tennessee*'s two concrete mooring quays was next demolished—a delicate task since the ship's hull was resting against it—and had been cleared away by 16 December. *Tennessee* carefully crept ahead, past *Oklahoma*'s sunken hull, and moored at the Pearl Harbor Navy Yard.

Temporary repairs were quickly made. From Turret III to the stern on both sides of the ship, *Tennessee*'s hull gave mute evidence of the inferno that she had survived. Every piece of hull plating above the waterline was buckled and warped by heat; seams had been opened and rivets loosened. These seams had to be rewelded and rivets reset, and a considerable amount of recaulking was needed to make hull and weather decks watertight. The damaged top of Turret III received a temporary armor patch.

On 20 December, *Tenessee* departed Pearl Harbor with *Pennsylvania* (BB–38) and *Maryland*—both superficially damaged in the Japanese attack—and a screen of four destroyers. From the moment the ships put to sea, nervous lookouts repeatedly sounded submarine alarms, making the voyage something more than uneventful. Nearing the west coast, *Pennsylvania* headed for Mare Island while *Maryland* and *Tennessee* steamed north, arrived at the Puget Sound Navy Yard on 29 December 1941, and commenced permanent repairs.

Working around the clock during the first two months of 1942, shipyard craftsmen repaired *Tennessee*'s after hull plating and replaced electrical wiring ruined by heat. To allow her antiaircraft guns a freer field of fire, her tall cage mainmast was replaced by a tower similar to that later installed in *Colorado* (BB–45) and *Maryland*. An air-search radar was installed; fire-control radars were fitted to *Tennessee*'s main-battery and 5-inch antiaircraft gun directors. Her three-inch and .50-caliber antiaircraft guns were replaced by 1.1-inch and 20-millimeter automatic shell guns, and her 5-inch antiaircraft guns were protected by splinter shields. Fourteen-inch Mark-4 turret guns were replaced by improved Mark-11 models. Other modifications improved the battleship's habitability.

On 25 February 1942, *Tennessee* departed Puget Sound with *Maryland* and *Colorado*. Upon arriving at San Francisco, she began a period of intensive training operations with Rear Admiral William S. Pye's Task Force 1, made up of the Pacific Fleet's available battleships and a screen of destroyers.

However, her role in the war was not to be in the line of battle for which she had trained for two decades. Most of the great battles of the conflict were not conventional surface-ship actions, but long-range duels between fast carrier striking forces. Fleet carriers, with their screening cruisers and destroyers, could maintain relatively high force speeds; and a new generation of fast battleships—beginning with the *North Carolina* (BB–55)-class and continuing into the *South Dakota* (BB–57)- and *Iowa* (BB–61)-classes—were coming into the fleet and were to prove their worth in action with the fast carrier force. But the older battleships—*Tennessee* and her kin—simply could not keep up with the carriers. Thus, while the air groups dueled for the aproaches to Port Moresby and the Japanese naval offensive reached its zenith in the waters west of Midway, the battleship force found itself steaming restlessly on the sidelines.

On 31 May, Admiral Pye sent two of his battleships to search for a Japanese carrier erroneously reported approaching the California coast. Reports of the battle of Midway came in, and Pye sortied from San Francisco on 5 June with the rest of his battleships and destroyers and the escort carrier *Long Island* (AVG–1). The battleship force steamed to an area some 1,200 miles west of San Francisco and about the same distance northeast of Hawaii in the expectation that part of the Japanese fleet might attempt an "end run" raid on our Pacific coast. On 14 June, after it had become clear that Admiral Yamamoto's fleet—reeling from its loss of four carriers 10 days before—had returned to Japanese waters, Pye ordered his force back to San Francisco.

On 1 August, *Tennessee* again sailed from San Francisco with Task Force 1. After a week of exercises the battleships joined *Hornet* (CV–8)—on her way to the South Pacific to support the Guadalcanal operation—and escorted the carrier as far as Hawaii. Arriving at Pearl Harbor on the 14th, *Tennessee* returned to Puget Sound on the 27th for modernization.

California, *Tennessee*'s sister ship, had been sunk in shallow water during the attack on Pearl Harbor. Refloated, and her hull temporarily patched, she returned to Puget Sound in June for permanent repairs which included a thorough modernization. It was decided to include *Tennessee* in this program as well.

By the time *Tennessee* emerged from the navy yard on 7 May 1943, she bore virtually no resemblance to her former self. Deep new blisters increased the depth of her side protection against torpedoes by eight feet-three inches on each side, gradually tapering toward bow and stern. Internal compartmentation was rearranged and improved. The most striking innovation was made in the battleship's superstructure. The heavy armored conning tower, from which *Tennessee* would have been controlled in a surface gunnery action, was removed, as were masts, stacks, and other superstructure. A new, compact, superstructure was designed to provide essential ship and gunnery control facilities while offering as little interference as possible to the fields of fire of the ship's increasingly essential antiaircraft guns. A low tower foremast supported a main-battery director and bridge spaces; boiler uptakes were trunked into a single fat funnel which was faired into the after side of the foremast. Just abaft the stack, a lower structure accommodated the after turret-gun director. *Tennessee*'s old 5-inch battery, and combination of 5″/25 antiaircraft guns and 5″/51 single-purpose "anti-destroyer" guns, was replaced by eight 5″/38 twin mounts. Four new directors, arranged around the superstructure, could control these guns against air or surface targets. All of these directors were equipped with fire-control radars; antennas for surface- and air-search radars were mounted at the mastheads. Close-in antiaircraft defense was the function of 10 quadruple 40-millimeter gun mounts, each with its own optical director, and of 43 20-millimeter guns.

Thus revitalized, and her battleworthiness greatly increased, *Tennessee* ran trials in the Puget Sound area and, on 22 May 1943, sailed for San Pedro. The days of seeming purposelessness were over. Though the slow battleships were still incapable of serving with the carrier striking force, their heavy turret guns could still hit as hard as ever. Naval shore bombardment and gunfire support for troops ashore—then coming to be a specialty in its own right—was well suited for this the earlier generation of battleships which were also still quite usable for patrol duty in areas where fire power was more important than speed. The refurbished *Tennessee*'s first tour of duty combined both of these missions.

Tennessee departed San Pedro with the cruiser *Portland* (CA–33) on 31 May, bound for the North Pacific and arrived at Adak, Alaska, on 9 June to begin patrol operations with Task Force 16, the North Pacific Force. During the Midway operation, the Japanese had occupied the Aleutian islands of Attu and Kiska. Attu was recaptured in May 1943; but Kiska was still in hostile hands; and Japanese air and naval forces still operated in the Aleutians area from bases in the Kuril Islands. *Tennessee* plied back and forth through the legendary fogs and foul weather of the Aleutians with her crew heavily bundled in arctic clothing for protection against intense cold and freezing rain as her radars probed for some sign of the enemy. There was still much to be learned about radar and its pitfalls; on several occasions, convincing images on the radar screens sent patrolling forces to general quarters. During one patrol in July, radio messages reported a force of nine surface ships 150 miles away, steaming rapidly to intercept *Tennessee* and her consorts. Tension grew as the unknown enemy drew closer, and all hands intently prepared for their first action. The radar images were only 45 miles away, and *Tennessee*'s crew were at battle stations when the enemy suddenly disappeared. Where the screens had been displaying what semed to be a hostile squadron, there was nothing. The hostile fleet had been a mere electronic mirage. During this same period, another surface force fought a brief, but energetic, gunnery action with the same kind of electronic "ghost" force south of Kiska. Distant land masses had appeared on ships' early radar sets as ship contacts at much closer ranges.

At about noon on 1 August, *Tennessee* was out on what all thought another routine patrol when the word was passed to prepare to bombard Kiska. At 1310, she began a zigzag approach through the usual murk to the island with *Idaho* (BB–42) and three destroyers. As the water grew more shallow, the ship slowed down and streamed mine-cutting paravanes from her bows. *Tennessee* approached the island from the east, closing to a range from which she could open fire with her 5-inch secondary battery. Her two OS2U *Kingfisher* floatplanes were catapulted to observe fire; and, at 1610, the battleship commenced firing from 7,000 yards. Though the island's shoreline could be seen, the target area—antiaircraft gun sites on high ground—were shrouded in low-hanging clouds and were invisible from the ship. *Tennessee*'s aerial spotters caught an occasional glimpse of the impact area and reported the ship's fire as striking home.

The task group continued along Kiska's southern coast. *Tennessee*'s 14-inch guns chimed in at 1624, hitting the location of a submarine base and other areas with 60 rounds before firing ceased at 1645. Visibility had dropped to zero, and results could not be seen. The battleship recovered her floatplanes, and the force turned back toward Adak.

In the early morning hours of 15 August, *Tennessee* again approached Kiska as troops prepared to assault the island. At 0500, the ship's turret guns began to fire at coastal-battery sites on nearby Little Kiska as the 5-inch guns struck antiaircraft positions on that island. The 14-inch guns then shifted their fire to antiaircraft sites on the southern side of Kiska, while the secondary battery turned its attention to an artillery observation position on Little Kiska and set it on fire. The landing force then went ashore, only to discover that nobody was home.

After the loss of Attu, the Japanese, knowing that Kiska's turn would soon come, decided to save the island's garrison. A small surface force closed the island in dense fog and tight radio silence and, on 27 nd 28 July 1943, succeeded in evacuating 5,183 troops rom Kiska.

Arriving at San Francisco on 31 August, *Tennessee* egan an intensive period of training and carried out attle exercises off the southern California coast before rovisioning and shoving off for Hawaii. After a week's xercises in the Pearl Harbor operating area, the ship leaded for the New Hebrides to rehearse for the invasion of the Gilberts.

The Japanese had occupied Betio on Christmas Day 1941. In nearly two years, with the help of conscripted Korean laborers, they had done a thorough job of digging themselves in. Americans still had a great deal to earn about pre-landing bombardment. Air attacks and laval gunfire damaged, but did not knock out, the beach lefenses; and the landing marines met an intense fire from artillery, mortars, and machine guns. Casualties mounted rapidly, and the landing force asked for all possible fire support. At 1034, *Tennessee*'s 14-inch and 5-inch guns reopened fire. The battleship continued to shoot until 1138, resuming fire at 1224 and firing until a ceasefire order was issued at 1300. The desperately contested struggle went on until dark, with close support being provided by destroyers which closed the beach to fire their 5-inch guns at short range and by waves of carrier planes which bombed and strafed. To reduce the chance of submarine or air attack, *Tennessee* and *Colorado* withdrew for the night to an area southwest of Betio and returned to their fire-support area the next morning to provide antiaircraft protection for the transports and to await a call for gunfire.

The battleships retired to their night area again at dusk. By this time, the battle for the island, its outcome uncertain for the first day and one-half of fighting, had taken a definite turn for the better. By 1600, the Marine commander ashore, Colonel David Shoup, could radio back that "we are winning." *Tennessee* was back in position south of Betio on the morning of the 22d. At 0907, she began to deliver call fire on Japanese defenses at the eastern tip of Betio, dropping 70 rounds of 14-inch and 322 rounds of 5-inch ammunition on gun positions in 17 minutes of shooting.

During the afternoon, the screening destroyers *Frazier* (DD–607) and *Meade* (DD–602) made a sonar contact. Depth charging drove *I–35*, a Japanese long-range submarine, to the surface. Her position was hopeless, but the enemy crew scrambled to man the undersea boat's single 5.5-inch deck gun as *Tennessee*'s secondary guns joined *Frazier* and *Meade* in hurling 5-inch projectiles. *Tennessee* swung clear as *Frazier* rammed the submarine; four minutes later, *I–35* went to the bottom.

Betio was secured by the afternoon of 23 November. *Tennessee* operated in the general area of Tarawa and Abemama atolls, alert for possible counterattacks by air or sea. At dusk on 3 December, *Tennessee* departed the area for Pearl Harbor and, on the 15th, headed for the United States with *Colorado* and *Maryland*. On arrival at San Francisco, four days before Christmas, she was quickly repainted in a "dazzle" camouflage scheme designed to confuse enemy observers. On 29 December, *Tennessee* began intensive bombardment practice, pounding San Clemente Island in rehearsal for the invasion of the Marshall Islands.

In the early morning of 13 January 1944, *Tennessee* set her course for Hawaii with Task Unit 53.5.1 and anchored in Lahaina Roads, off Maui, on the 21st. That day, the ship was inspected by a group headed by Undersecretary of the Navy James Forrestal. On the 29th, *Tennessee*, with Forrestal on board, headed for the Marshalls.

D-Day was set for 31 January 1944. As one attack force landed on the unoccupied Majuro atoll, the major force approached Kwajalein. *Tennessee*, *Pennsylvania*, and two destroyers took up their stations 2,900 yards to the east of the atoll. At 0625, *Tennessee* catapulted off her observation floatplanes; and, at 0701, she began throwing 14-inch salvoes at Japanese pillboxes on Roi Island. Her two forward turrets were busily engaged when fire had to be checked to allow carrier dive bombers to strike the island. Japanese antiaircraft guns opened up on the planes. As soon as the attackers were clear of the area, the ship demolished the enemy guns with two three-gun salvoes. The 5-inch battery then opened up on beach defenses. Main and secondary guns continued to pound Roi and adjacent Namur until noon, the high point of the morning coming when the guns of *Mobile* (CL–63) detonated a Japanese ammunition dump on Namur and sent an enormous mushroom of thick black smoke into the air. At midday, *Tennessee* retired from the firing area to recover and service her spotting planes. Following a welcome midday meal served to the crew at their battle stations, the battleship returned to the fighting and shelled Roi and Namur through the afternoon. At 1700, *Tennessee* turned away to screen supporting escort carriers for the night.

While the fire support ships pounded Roi and Namur on the 31st, marines captured five small nearby islands; and the northern passage into Kwajalein lagoon was cleared for ships to pass in. On 1 February, *Tennessee* and *Colorado*, with *Mobile* and *Louisville*, were back in their assigned area to the eastward and commenced firing at 0708. The ships pounded Namur through the morning; marines began to land on both islands at about noon; and *Tennessee* and her unit continued supporting fire until 1245. Roi fell quickly, but Namur's defenders were well dug in and fought fiercely until the early afternoon on 2 February.

Later that day, the battleship entered Kwajalein lagoon. Vice Admiral Raymond Spruance and Rear Admiral Richard Conolly, commander of the Roi-Namur invasion force, visited Mr. Forrestal on board *Tennessee*; the Undersecretary and his party then went ashore to inspect the newly seized islands and departed the following day by seaplane.

Useful lessons were learned from this operation. Since the Navy had won command of the surface and in the air around the landing area, gunfire support ships could close their objective and fire at what was, for a battleship, virtually point-blank ranges. The heavy, short-range fire of the supporting gunfire ships "met the most sanguine expectations" of the assaulting marines and foretold the shape of operations to come.

By 7 February, the whole Kwajalein atoll was in American hands; and preparations began for the capture of Eniwetok atoll, at the northwest end of the Marshalls group in the direction of the Marianas. Prewar Japanese security had been tight, and little was known about the atoll, but aerial photographs and a Japanese chart found in a beached enemy ship on one of Kwajalein's small islets gave planners enough to work with.

Tennessee arrived at Majuro on 7 February to take on ammunition and supplies before returning to Kwajalein. On the afternoon of the 15th, she sailed for Eniwetok with *Colorado*, *Pennsylvania*, and transports carrying Army troops and marines. Ships of the fast carrier force screened their approach, and cruisers and destroyers opened the action on the morning of 17 February by bombarding Eniwetok island, on the southwest side of the circular atoll, and the smaller islands flanking the selected entry to the lagoon, Deep Passage. Minesweepers cleared Deep Passage and the nearby, though shallower, Wide Passage; and, at 0915, *Tennessee* led the transport convoy into the lagoon and headed for the atoll's northern island of Engebi. The battleship bombarded Engebi while landing forces went ashore on neighboring islets to site artillery pieces. Her 5-inch guns were active during the early evening in support of a marine reconnaissance company which approached Engebi to plant marker buoys for the next day's assault waves and to acquaint themselves with the beaches. During the night, *Tennessee* drew off into the lagoon as light field pieces from the newly captured ground harassed Engebi's defenders. The pre-landing bombardment began at 0700 the next morning, and *Tennessee* joined in at 0733.

Tennessee, her appearance entirely changed by wartime modernization, supports the landing on Iwo Jima. (NR&L(M) 28597)

The first wave went ashore at 0844 and, with the help of supporting ships and planes, had Engebi in their hands by late afternoon.

The atoll was not yet secure. Japanese defenders on Eniwetok and Parry Islands had carefully dug in and camouflaged their positions. Transports and landing vehicles carried a force of soldiers and marines to the southern end of the lagoon and, after a preparatory bombardment, the troops went ashore on Eniwetok. There had not been enough time to give the island a satisfactory softening, and progress was slow.

Tennessee spent the day anchored 5,500 yards north of the island, but her services were not called for until night fell. During the night, Army troops called several times for illumination. Destroyers played their searchlights over Japanese-held areas, while *Tennessee*'s 5-inch guns fired large numbers of star shells. The fight for Eniwetok went on into the afternoon of 21 February, but *Tennessee*'s efforts had, by then, been diverted to Parry Island.

Parry, at the mouth of Deep Channel, was defended by more than 1,300 well-trained, carefully-entrenched Japanese troops. The assault plan called for a careful preliminary working-over with bombs and gunfire, and marine light howitzers began to shell Parry from a nearby islet in the evening of 20 February while carrier planes carried out repeated attacks. *Tennessee* and *Pennsylvania* took up positions 900 yards off Parry during the morning of the 20th and, at 1204, began to blast the island.

The bombardment continued through the 21st, ships and planes taking their turns. Gun crews paused for a "breather" while planes from the escort carriers unloaded their ordnance, then resumed their work. *Colorado*'s 16-inch rifles added to the weight of *Tennessee* and *Pennsylvania*'s 14-inch fire, and *Louisville* and *Indianapolis* joined in with their 8-inch turret guns. *Tennessee* was firing at so short a range that, during the afternoon of the 20th, she was able to take on beach defenses with her 40-millimeter guns.

The final shelling, on the morning of 22 February,

kicked up a dense mixture of smoke and dust as the landing craft went in. *Tennessee*'s heavy guns checked fire at 0852 when the first amphibian tractors were 300 yards from the beach, and her 40-millimeters took up the fire until the vehicles landed. Ships' guns continued to provide support during the first two hours of land fighting but ceased firing as the troops expanded their foothold and advanced across the island. By afternoon, Parry was secured, and Eniwetok atoll was securely in American hands.

On 23 February 1944, *Tennessee* sailed for Majuro. Here, she joined *New Mexico* (BB–40), *Mississippi* (BB–41), and *Idaho* (BB–42). Under the command of Rear Admiral Robert M. Griffin, the battleships sortied from Majuro on 15 March with two escort carriers and a screen of 15 destroyers.

Their objective was the Japanese air and naval base at Kavieng, at the northern end of New Ireland. The Bismarck Archipelago—the two large islands of New Britain and New Ireland—lie just to the east of New Guinea. Rabaul, the by-low legendary Japanese operating base, is at the eastern end of New Britain, just across a narrow channel from New Ireland. About 240 miles northwest of Rabaul, across the Bismarck Sea, is the small Admiralty Island group. Another small island, Emirau, lies northwest of New Ireland and east of the Admiralties. Southeast from Rabaul, the Solomons chain extended for more than five hundred miles. Since the first landing on Guadalcanal in August 1942, the chain had been slowly climbed in a series of strongly contested actions by sea, land, and air. By the end of 1943, American forces held a strong foothold on Bougainville, little more than 200 miles from Rabaul.

The final steps in Rabaul's encirclement and isolation were planned for the spring of 1944. Kavieng was to have been captured early in April, but the success of the land-based air offensive against Rabaul convinced Admiral Nimitz that it would be more profitable to occupy undefended Emirau instead, sending the bombardment ships against Kavieng to convince the Japanese that a landing on New Ireland was planned.

Admiral Griffin, accordingly, headed for Kavieng and, on the morning of 20 March 1944, approached the harbor. Rain squalls and low-hanging clouds shrouded the area as *Tennessee* and the other gunfire ships zig-zagged toward New Ireland. The island appeared through the overcast at 0700. *Tennessee* launched her spotting planes an hour later, and they were soon out of sight in the rain and mist. By 0905, the range to the target was within 15,000 yards, and the battleships opened a deliberate fire. Steaming at 15 knots, *Tennessee* dropped single 14-inch rounds and two- or three-gun salvoes on Kavieng as the bombardment force slowly closed the range. Poor visibility made gunfire spotting difficult, and the pace of firing was held down to avoid wasting ammunition.

Tennessee was about 7,500 yards from the island when her lookouts reported gun flashes from the beach, quickly followed by shell splashes just off the star-board bow and close to one of her screening destroyers. At 0928, *Tennessee*'s port 5-inch guns opened rapid continuous fire at the coastal battery, estimated to consist of four to six 4-inch guns. A 180-degree turn brought the battleship's starboard secondaries to bear, and the duel continued. The Japanese gunners began to get the range, and some projectiles hit close aboard on the starboard beam while others came similarly close to *Idaho*. *Tennessee* was straddled several times and drew away from the shore at 18 knots before checking fire at 0934. Reducing speed to 15 knots and turning back to firing position, *Tennessee* reopened fire at 0936. Her main and secondary batteries pounded the enemy guns for 10 minutes, and nothing more was heard from the Japanese guns. For the next three hours, the ships steamed back and forth off Kavieng, shelling the Japanese airfield and shore facilities. Other coastal gun positions were sighted, but the battleship's 14-inch fire silenced them before they could get off a round. Visibility continued to be a problem; observers in the ships' floatplanes could not get a clear view of the targets. When the 5-inch guns were firing at targets in wooded areas, spotters in the ship's gun directors could not observe hits in the heavy foliage. More than once, rounds had to be dropped in the water to obtain a definite point of reference before "walking" fire onto the desired target.

The bombardment ended at 1235. *Tennessee* turned away and made rendezvous with the covering escort carriers as Admiral Halsey wired his "congratulations on your effective plastering of Kavieng." This diversion had had its effect. While Admiral Griffin's battleships blasted Kavieng, Emirau had been seized without opposition. Pausing at Purvis Bay and Efate, *Tennessee* arrived at Pearl Harbor on 16 April to refurbish and prepare for her next task.

Operation "Forager," the assault on the Marianas, was planned as a two-pronged thrust. Vice Admiral Richmond K. Turner's Task Force 51 was organized into a Northern Attack Force (TF 52), under his command, and a Southern Attack Force (TF 53) under Rear Admiral Richard Conolly. While TF 52 attacked Saipan and nearby Tinian, Conolly's TF 52 was aimed at Guam. The bombardment and fire support force arrayed for this operation included *Tennessee* and seven other older battleships, 11 cruisers, and about 26 destroyers. These ships were divided into two fire support groups. *Tennessee*, with *California*, *Maryland*, and *Colorado*, was assigned to Fire Support Group One (TG 52.17) under Rear Admiral Jesse Oldendorf.

The Northern Attack Force assembled at Hawaii in mid-May 1944. After rehearsals off Maui and Kahoo-lawe, Fire Support Group One sailed for Kwajalein while the transports staged at Eniwetok. On 10 June 1944, *Tennessee* and her task group departed Kwaja-lein, bound for Saipan.

Early on 13 June, as the force approached the Marianas, signs of Japanese activity began to appear. A patrol plane reported sighting a surfaced submarine some 20 miles ahead and attacked it. Another plane shot down a landbased Mitsubishi G4M "Betty" which

had been trailing along 10 miles astern of the ships. Another submarine contact was reported to port of the formation, and screening destroyers dropped depth charges. During the 13th, Vice Admiral Willis A. Lee's Task Group 58.7—seven new fast battleships of the *North Carolina*, *South Dakota*, and *Iowa* classes—temporarily detached from Vice Admiral Marc Mit-scher's Task Force 58—hurled a furious bombardment at Saipan.

Throughout the following night, lookouts reported gun flashes on the horizon, and escorting destroyers attacked suspected submarines. General quarters was sounded at 0400 on 14 June as the old battleships drew near to Saipan. Near the horizon, a Japanese cargo ship, set afire by the guns of *Melvin* (DD–680), burned brightly. Shortly before dawn, Oldendorf's battleships passed to the north of Saipan as the second fire-support group steamed through Saipan Channel at the southern end of the island. The southern group opened fire at 0539. Nine minutes later, *Tennessee* began a methodical bombardment of the selected landing area, the southern portion of Saipan's west coast, in support of mine-sweepers carrying out an assault sweep on the landing zone. Enemy coastal guns had fired a few shots at Oldendorf's ships as they rounded the northern tip of the island, and attacking carrier planes as well as the ships' observation floatplanes encountered heavy anti-aircraft fire. *Maryland* drew fire from a battery con-cealed on a tiny islet off Tanapag harbor. She and *California* turned on this foe and soon silenced it.

Released from this duty, *Tennessee* sailed southward to the area of Agingan Point, at the southwest corner of Saipan and the southern end of the designated land-ing area. Underwater demolition teams (UDT) ap-proached the beach in small craft to reconnoiter the landing beaches and to plant radar beacons which would provide reference points to the next day's land-ing. *Tennessee* closed to 3,000 yards of Agingan Point and, at 0831, opened up with 14-inch, 5-inch, and 40-millimeter batteries. Some smoldering powder grains from the 5-inch guns fell on the port side of the battle-ship's quarterdeck and burst into flame, but were quickly extinguished. Japanese guns dropped shells near the UDT's as mortars and machine guns joined in; at about 0920, projectile splashes began to appear near the supporting ships as batteries on nearby Tinian opened fire. *Cleveland* (CL–55) was straddled, and *California* and *Braine* (DD–630) took hits. *Tennessee* aimed counterbattery fire at the defenders who were opposing the UDT's, and her turret guns fired at Tinian. Shortly before noon, she moved to the north-west to bombard Japanese fortifications on Afetna Point, near the center of the landing zone. At 1331, the ship ceased fire and withdrew from the firing area to recover her seaplanes, later closing *Wadleigh* (DD–689) and *Brooks* (APD–10) to take on board five wounded UDT men for treatment. She joined the rest of her fire support group and took up night stations to the west of Saipan.

D-Day on Saipan was 15 June 1944. Circling to the north of the island, well out of sight from shore during the last hours of darkness, the assault force was off the landing beaches by dawn. Reserve landing forces staged an elaborate feint off Tanapag harbor, hoping to induce the Japanese to reinforce its defenses before the actual landing took place further south. At 0430, the pre-land-ing bombardment began. *Tennessee* joined in at 0540 with a heavy barrage from her main, secondary and 40-millimeter guns from 3,000 yards west of Agingan Point. At 0542, the landing craft and amphibian trac-tors of the landing force began to load and assemble for the movement to shore. Gunfire was lifted at 0630 to allow carrier planes to bombard the island's defenses, resuming at 0700. At 0812, the assault waves headed for the beach. The first went ashore at 0844 and met heavy opposition. The pre-landing bombardment, though prolonged and intense, had left much of the Japanese defenses still able to fight; and, as the 2d and 4th Marine Divisions landed on a 4-mile front south of Garapan, they found that much still remained to be done.

Tennessee's assault station was off the southern end of the landing beach. During the first wave's approach, her guns enfiladed that end of the objective to prepare the way for the right-hand elements of the 4th Division. She checked fire as the troops neared the beach, resuming it a few minutes later as the marines fought to establish themselves ashore. Japanese 4.7-inch field guns, emplaced in a cave on Tinian, opened on *Tennessee.* The battleship commenced counterbattery fire, but the third enemy salvo scored three hits, all of which burst on impact. One projectile knocked out a 5-inch twin gun mount; the second struck the ship's side, while the third tore a hole in the after portion of main deck and sprayed fragments into the wardroom below. An intense fire inside the disabled gun mount was subdued in two minutes by repair parties and men from nearby gun crews; the hit to the hull damaged external blister plating, but was prevented from inflicting further damage by the battleship's heavy belt armor. Eight men were killed by projectile fragments, while 25 more were wounded by fragments and flash burns. *Tennessee's* damages did not prevent her from delivering call fire to help break up a developing Japanese counterattack near Agingan Point before leaving the firing line to make emergency repairs. During the afternoon and night, she took station to screen assembled transports. Four Japanese dive bombers attacked nearby ships at 1845, and *Tennessee's* 5-inch guns briefly engaged them but claimed no hits. That evening, *Tennessee* buried her dead. Tokyo radio claimed victory in the battle for Saipan, stating that they had sunk a battleship which they identified as "probably the *New Jersey.*"

The "sunken" *Tennessee* returned to Saipan Channel early the next day. Several Japanese counterattacks had been stopped during the night, and *Tennessee's* supporting fire assisted the marines in organizing and consolidating their beachhead. During the evening, the first troops of the Army's 27th Infantry Division began to come ashore; another counterattack, this one involving tanks, was turned back during the night of 16 and 17 June.

The original plan had called for landings on Guam on the 18th. However, during the afternoon of the 15th and the early hours of the 16th, Admiral Spruance was advised that Japanese warships were at sea, off the Philippines, heading for the Marianas. The Japanese plan for the defense of these vital islands called for their garrison to hold out while a naval force mounted a counterstroke to destroy the American invasion fleet. By the morning of the 16th, Spruance decided to cancel the attack on Guam while continuing the fight for Saipan and disposing his naval forces for battle. The fast carrier force was sent to counter the Japanese thrust, while the fire-support battleships were to be deployed to the west of Saipan in case the Japanese should evade Task Force 58 and direct a surface thrust at the island. *Tennessee* held station west of Saipan with the other elderly battleships as the two fleets groped toward each other about 150 miles away.

On the 19th, Mitscher's task force clashed with Admiral Jisaburo Ozawa's Mobile Fleet in what was to be called the "Great Marianas Turkey Shoot." By this time, American carrier operations had attained a high level of excellence while the Japanese air arm, its experienced airmen mostly lost during the long campaigns of 1942 and 1943, had to make do with unskilled pilots. The result was striking. In more than eight hours of intense aerial combat, more than 300 Japanese planes were knocked down, most of these by carrier fighters. By the 20th, counterattacking American planes and submarines had sent carriers *Hiyo, Shokaku,* and *Taiho* to the bottom. Thus, Japan's last serious carrier offensive operation ended in disaster.

Ozawa's fleet never got close enough to Saipan for *Tennessee* and her cousins to be called upon. On the 20th, she fueled east of Saipan as the Japanese carrier force headed westward. The next day, she was back on the gun line to blast gun positions on Manigassa Island, off Tanapag harbor. Call fire occupied the afternoon, as she took on several targets near Garapan. *Tennessee's* 14-inch guns commenced firing at 0555 the next day, pounding Garapan from 6,000 yards. Shell hits on the battered town raised clouds of smoke and dust, reminding the battleship's gunners of the Aleutian murk. Fire was shifted onto Mount Tapotchau, east of Garapan, before being returned to Garapan to assist the American troops who were working their way into the southern part of town.

On the night of 22 June, *Tennessee* got underway for Eniwetok where *Hector* (AR–7) repaired her battle damage as the fight for Saipan ground to its end on 9 July. Her next destination was Guam. Departing Eniwetok on 16 July with *California*, she joined Rear Admiral Ainsworth's Southern Fire Support Group (TG 53.5) off Guam in the afternoon of the 19th. The next day, she joined in a systematic bombardment begun on the 8th which was carefully planned to soften up the enemy's defenses while avoiding harm to the island's friendly Chamorro population. *Tennessee* launched her planes; and, at 0742, her turret guns opened fire while the 5-inch battery raked nearby Cabras Island. The ship slowly maneuvered to a position north of Asan Point, several miles north of Apra harbor, where one of two landing beaches was sited. UDT's scouted the beaches while planes laid smoke screens to cover their movements, and the ships' guns kept the Japanese defenders occupied. Firing ceased at midday and resumed late in the afternoon, as *Tennessee* continued to hammer Japanese positions north of Apra.

Shortly after dawn on 21 July, the bombardment ships again took up their work. *Tennessee* renewed her attentions to Cabras Island as the assault waves formed and headed for shore and continued to provide support during the first stage of the landing. At 1003, she ceased firing. Late that day, she put to sea with *California* and *Colorado* and returned to Saipan on 22 July.

Tennessee anchored in Tanapag harbor to replenish ammunition before taking up her night position to the west of Tinian. At 0607 on 23 July, she opened fire on the waterfront area of Tinian Town, as part of a deception scheme intended to convince the strong Japanese garrison that the landing would take place at Sunharon Bay, on the southwest coast of the island. A UDT even made a daylight reconnaissance of the beaches to strengthen the impression, and *Tennessee's* guns supported the frogmen. Fire paused around midday and resumed again in the afternoon before the ship retired to her night position off the island.

Early in the morning of the 24th, *Tennessee* took up her position off Tinian's northwest coast with *California, Louisville* (CA–28), and several destroyers. From 2,500 yards offshore, the ships opened fire at 0532, ceasing fire as the first wave closed the beach at 0747. For the rest of the day, the ship stood by to deliver fire if needed, then retired for the night. In the morning of 25 July, *Tennessee* relieved *California* as the "duty ship" to furnish call fire upon request from the beach. Through the 25th and 26th, *Tennessee* delivered supporting fire by day and star shell by night. After returning briefly to Saipan to replenish on the 27th, the battleship was back on the firing line on the 28th, and her fire supported the advancing marines through the afternoon. Following replenishment at Saipan on the 29th, *Tennessee* began the 30th in support of marines advancing southward through Tinian Town. In the early morning, one of her observation planes collided in midair with a landbased marine OY–1 spotting plane. Both aircraft plummeted to earth behind Japanese lines and burst into flames; the crews of both were killed.

Firing continued through that day and into the 31st, as the marines crowded the last defenders into the southern tip of the island. At 0830 on 31 July, *Tennessee's* guns fell silent, and she returned to Saipan with her task accomplished. On the evening of 2 August, she arrived off Guam to resume fire-support duty. Rejoining Ainsworth's gunfire task group, she delivered call fire and illumination until 8 August when she joined *California* and *Louisville* for the voyage to Eniwetok and thence to Espiritu Santo in the New Hebrides. The ships arrived at Espiritu Santo on 24 August. On 2 September, *Tennessee* arrived at Tulagi for a brief period of amphibious support training.

Meanwhile, decisions had been made which would reshape the Allied offensive in the western Pacific. Meeting at Pearl Harbor in July 1944, President Roosevelt, Admiral Nimitz, and General MacArthur had finally reached an agreement that the Philippines were to be liberated, not merely bypassed. After further discussions, the Joint Chiefs of Staff approved landings beginning at Mindanao, continuing north through Leyte, then taking either Luzon or Formosa and Amoy. During early September, Task Force 38 hit Japanese bases from the Palaus to the Visayas, inflicting considerable damage. Surprisingly little resistance was encountered by the roving carriers, leading to a conclusion that enemy air strength was virtually nonexistent. Nimitz, MacArthur, and Halsey agreed that this eliminated any need for a network of southern air bases to support the capture of the Philippines. Proposed landings on Yap and Mindanao were scrapped, although Morotai was invaded in September and preparations were made for an assault on the Palaus before bypassing the southern Philippines and going into Leyte.

The Palaus were to be *Tennessee's* next objective. This group is not an atoll, but an elongated cluster of islands just north of the Equator and at the western end of the Carolines. The group is about 110 miles long from small islands and reefs to the north through the large island of Babelthuap to the small southern islands of Peleliu and Angaur.

The objectives of the assault force were Kossol Roads, a reef-sheltered anchorage at the northern end of the chain, and the two southern islands; the large Japanese garrison on Babelthuap was to be isolated and left to its own devices. Planes and gunfire ships took turns pounding Peleliu from the morning of 12 September until the assault waves went ashore on the 15th. The battle for that island was to be one of the most bitter of the Pacific war, and organized resistance was not eliminated until November, at a heavy cost in lives.

Tennessee's target was the smaller island of Angaur, a few miles south of Peleliu. On the morning of 12 September, *Tennessee* and *Pennsylvania*, with four light cruisers and five destroyers, began a prolonged bombardment as carrier aircraft did their share.

The flash and roar of bombs and gunfire from ships and planes attacking Peleliu were plain on the horizon as *Tennessee* closed Angaur early on 12 September. The battleship opened fire at 0632, hurling 14-inch shells at targets ashore from 14,000 yards. Through the morning and afternoon, her guns hit coast-defense positions and antiaircraft sites. During the afternoon, minesweepers cleared the approaches to the beaches. By this time, *Tennessee* was only 3,750 yards from shore, and her 40-millimeters had joined in. A prominent masonry lighthouse on the west coast of Angaur was ordered destroyed to keep the Japanese from using it as a gunfire observation point. Twelve 14-inch rounds were aimed at it, scarring the area and scoring three hits, but the tower remained standing. Other targets absorbed *Tennessee's* attention for the next three days. *Tennessee* stood by off Peleliu during the morning of the 15th in case her guns should be needed to assist the assault landing. When this work was completed, she returned on the evening of 16 September to finish off the stubborn tower before the next morning's scheduled landings. As the ship's turret guns trained out on the target, a 6-inch projectile from *Denver* (CL–58) screamed in from the far side of the island and sent the lighthouse crashing down in a cloud of smoke and dust.

Ships and carrier planes pounded the island for five days before Army troops of the 81st Infantry Division went ashore on Angaur on the morning of 17 September. *Tennessee's* guns supported the soldiers through the 19th. By the morning of 20 September, organized resistance was at an end; and the battleship steamed away from the island to Kossol Roads to refuel and to take on ammunition. On 28 September, she arrived at Manus to prepare for her next operation.

Tennessee weighed anchor on 12 October and set her course for Leyte Gulf. Under the supreme command of General MacArthur, Vice Admiral Thomas Kinkaid's 7th Fleet carried two Army corps toward the invasion area. Their objectives were two landing zones on the eastern coast of Leyte. A Northern Attack Force (TF 78) under Rear Admiral Daniel Barbey was aimed at Tacloban, while Vice Admiral Theodore Wilson command TF 79, the Southern Attack Force whose target was Dulag. The old battleships were divided between two fire-support units. *Tennessee*, with *California* and *Pennsylvania*, sailed with the Dulag attack force under Rear Admiral Oldendorf.

During its approach to the Philippines, the invasion force was alert for air and submarine attack; but none came. As the ships steamed under hot, clear skies, their radios brought news of Task Force 38 as the fast carriers ranged an arc from the Ryukyus to Formosa before turning on Japanese air bases in Luzon and the central Philippines. Preliminary minesweeping and bombardment, to clear the way into Leyte Gulf, began on the morning of 17 October 1944. The entrance to the gulf was secured, but the approaches to the objective area were partially swept when Oldendorf, to avoid delaying the operation, decided to order his ships into the gulf. At 0609 on the morning of the 18th, *Tennessee*, with her fire-support unit, entered the channel between Homonhon and Dinagat islands. Paravanes streamed from her bows, and marines were stationed in her upperworks to sink or explode floating mines. The minesweepers continued their work as the heavy ships moved slowly up Leyte Gulf.

Tennessee took up her position off Dulag before dawn on 19 October and, at 0645, began to bombard the landing area north of the town. Her main battery opened up from 8,300 yards, and her secondaries chimed in a few minutes later as she aimed at fortifications and antiaircraft gun emplacements. Catmon Hill, a 1,000-foot elevation just inland, received particular attention from the ships. Japanese planes were reported in the offing, but the only attack came from a horizontal bomber which dropped one bomb into the water near *Honolulu* (CL–48) before being knocked down by gunfire. Heavy shelling continued through the afternoon, and the bombardment ships took up night cruising stations off the mouth of Leyte Gulf.

The landings were scheduled for 20 October; and, at 0600, *Tennessee* opened neutralization fire on the beaches. As the northern force pounded Tacloban and went in to the attack, transports assembled off Dulag and put the landing force into the water. Infantry landing craft armed with heavy mortars (LCI(M)) began dropping shells on reverse slopes at 0915; and, at 0930, the landing waves crossed the line of departure and moved for the beach. At 0945, rocket-firing landing craft (LCI(R)) began to hurl their masses of explosive bombardment rockets at the beach defenses, and the first troops went ashore 15 minutes later. Naval gunfire was shifted inland and to the flanks to assist the landing troops as they began to carve out a beachhead. The landing went well. During the afternoon, *Honolulu* was again attacked, this time by a torpedo bomber which scored a hit and forced the cruiser to withdraw. Night air attacks were feared; a screen of destroyers was placed around the ships in the gulf, smoke was generated, and much nervous firing flared up in the darkness and caused some casualties.

The Japanese Imperial General Headquarters, on noting the scale of the operation being mounted against Leyte, had decided to make that island the focus of a decisive naval counterstroke. The principal surface strength of the Combined Fleet had gone to Lingga Roads, an anchorage in the Lingga Archipelago off Sumatra at the southwest end of the South China Sea, to be near their fuel supply since American submarines had made it increasingly difficult to get oil through to Japan. The surviving carriers had returned to the Inland Sea to train aircrews. Under the Japanese plan, dictated by a combination of geography, logistics, and the lack of adequate carrier aviation, four widely separated forces were to converge on the area of Leyte Gulf in an effort to destroy, at whatever cost, the American invasion force.

While the Japanese fleet set out for Leyte, *Tennessee* continued her work off the beachhead. Fire support was not required from her for the time being, but the increasing tempo of Japanese air activity in the area required her to place herself where her antiaircraft guns could assist in the defense of the assembled transports and cargo ships. In the evening of 21 October, while lying dead in the water in a smoke screen laid to protect the shipping from attacking planes, *Tennessee* was rammed near the stern by the transport *War Hawk* (AP–168). No one was injured, and the battleship's tough hull was little harmed, but her orders for a night fire-support mission were cancelled.

Matters continued to go well ashore, where the town of Tacloban was captured and declared a temporary seat of the Philippine government. Air defense, rather than shore bombardment, was still *Tennessee*'s mission; on the morning of the 24th, enemy planes sank an LCI(L) and damaged a cargo ship before being driven off. A larger raid came in from several directions before noon, hitting American positions on Leyte. The afternoon was mostly quiet. A third attack occurred at 1700. As the enemy aircraft drew away, the battleship's executive officer passed the electrifying word that a Japanese naval task force was expected to try to enter Leyte Gulf that night. The six old battleships of the fire support groups formed columns and moved south to take up positions at the mouth of Surigao Strait, the body of water between Leyte and Dinagat which formed a southern entrance to Leyte Gulf.

The Japanese forces set in motion some days earlier were now approaching their objective. A force of four carriers and two converted hermaphrodite "battleship-carriers" was steaming south from Japan toward the Philippine Sea, while a small surface force under Admiral Shima had sailed from Japanese waters heading for the Sulu Sea. Two striking forces of battleships, cruisers, and destroyers had sailed from Lingga Roads; north of Borneo they separated. The larger force, under Admiral Kurita, passed north of Palawan (losing three cruisers to submarine attack) to transit the Sibuyan Sea and emerge to the north of Samar. A smaller force, commanded by Admiral Nishimura, turned to the south of Palawan and crossed the Sulu Sea to pass between Mindanao and Leyte. Shima's orders directed him to support Nishimura, and his force followed some miles behind Nishimura's.

If the *Sho* plan, as it was called, worked properly, Kurita would approach Leyte Gulf from the north while Nishimura and Shima came up from the south, catching the massed amphibious shipping in the jaws of a vise and destroying it. Ozawa's force was toothless since prolonged heavy casualties and an inadequate pilot training program had left the Imperial Navy with few experienced carrier pilots. The carrier force advancing southward from Japan carried only enough planes to make a convincing decoy; its job was to lure Halsey's 3d Fleet to the north while the converging surface forces did their job.

During the morning of 24 October, carrier planes sighted the three Japanese groups in the Sulu and Sibuyan seas. Recognizing Kurita's as the most powerful, Halsey directed the fast carriers' air groups against him as the Japanese ships steamed across the Sibuyan Sea. With no air cover, Kurita had to endure repeated bomb and torpedo attacks which forced one of his cruisers to turn back with serious damage and, as the day ended, sank the giant battleship *Musashi*. Complaining of the lack of air support, Kurita turned back in midafternoon; and this movement was reported to Halsey by his pilots.

Early on the 24th, a Japanese scout plane from Luzon had spotted Task Force 38 east of that island. All available landbased planes were sent against it, mortally wounding the light carrier *Princeton* (CVL–23). Halsey concluded that the attackers were carrier-based. During the morning, Ozawa's reconnaissance planes sighted Halsey's carriers; and an unproductive air strike was launched against Task Force 38 at 1145. In the afternoon, the Japanese carriers were sighted and, in the evening of 24 October, Halsey ordered the fast carrier force to go after them. Shortly before sunset, Kurita had again reversed course and was heading back in the direction of Leyte Gulf; Halsey had been informed of this, but exaggerated reports of damage inflicted by his planes led him to believe that the Japanese force had been more grievously hurt than was the case. Judging that Kurita was too badly crippled to do any harm to the ships in Leyte Gulf, Halsey continued north through the night. By midnight the Japanese Center Force, as the American commanders referred to it, was pushing, unobserved, toward San Bernardino Strait before turning south toward Leyte Gulf.

Halsey had not sent his planes against the surface forces of Nishimura and Shima, believing that Kinkaid's warships would be able to deal with them. This was to be Oldendorf's job; and, in the evening of the 24th, he deployed his six battleships across the northern end of Surigao Strait. Besides his capital ships, Oldendorf had available eight cruisers and 28 destroyers. These were arranged toward the flanks, the destroyers placed in suitable position to launch torpedo attacks. A great deal of shooting in support of the landing operation had already occurred, and most of the shells remaining in the battleship's magazines were thin-walled, high-capacity bombardment ammunition rather than armor-piercing projectiles. Their handling-room crews carefully arranged the projectile supply so that high-capacity shells would be ready for use against anything smaller than a battleship. The big ships were directed to hold their fire until the enemy was within 20,000 yards to insure as many hits as possible.

The sea was smooth and the moonless night intensely dark as the ships steamed slowly to and fro along their assigned lines of position. *Tennessee* quietly awaited her first action against her own kind.

All available 7th Fleet PT boats had been stationed in Surigao Strait and along its approaches. At 2236, the first PT's made radar contact with Nishimura. Successive torpedo attacks were launched as Nishimura entered Surigao Strait and steamed north, with Shima trailing well behind; Nishimura was annoyed but not injured, though one of Shima's cruisers took a torpedo and had to drop out of the running. Shortly before 0300, Nishimura was well into the strait and taking up battle formation when he was hit by a well-planned torpedo attack by five American destroyers. The battleship *Fuso* was hit and dropped out of formation; other torpedo spreads sank two Japanese destroyers and crippled a third. Another torpedo struck, but did not stop, *Fuso*'s sistership *Yamashiro*. Ten minutes later, another destroyer attack scored a second hit on *Yamashiro*. The disabled *Fuso* had apparently been set afire by the torpedo that had hit her; her magazines exploded at 0338 as *Arizona*'s had on the morning of 7 December; and the two shattered halves of the battleship slowly drifted back down the strait before sinking.

On board *Tennessee*, observers had seen distant flashes of gunfire, star shells, and searchlights as the torpedo boats and destroyers engaged the Japanese. Soon explosions could be heard. At 0302, the battleship's radar picked up Nishimura's approach at nearly 44,000 yards and began to track the lead ship. This was the flagship, *Yamashiro*. With the cruiser *Mogami* and destroyer *Shigure*, she was all that remained of the first Japanese force. At 0351 Oldendorf ordered the flanking cruisers to open fire; and, at 0355, the battleships let fly from 20,500 yards.

Tennessee's forward turret fired a three-gun salvo, and the rest of her 14-inch battery joined in. In this duel, *Tennessee, California,* and the recently arrived *West Virginia* had a considerable advantage over the other battleships. During their wartime modernization, all three had received new Mark 34 main-battery directors provided with Mark 8 fire-control radars and associated modern gunfire computing equipment. The main batteries of the other ships were still controlled by systems developed 20 years or more before and were using earlier Mark 3 radars. This handicap showed in their shooting. Firing in six-gun salvos to make careful use of her limited supply of armor-piercing projectiles, *Tennessee* got off 69 of her big 14-inch bullets before checking fire at 0408. The battle line had increased speed to 15 knots before opening fire, and, as it drew near the eastern end of its line of position, simultaneous turns brought the ships around to a westward heading. *California* miscalculated her turn and came sharply across *Tennessee's* bow, narrowly avoiding a collision and fouling *Tenneesee's* line of fire for about five minutes.

The effect of this intense bombardment was awesome. As one of *Tennessee's* crew described it, "when a ship fired there would be a terific whirling sheet of golden flame bolting across the sea, followed by a massive thunder, and then three red balls would go into the sky; up, arch-over, and then down. When the salvoes found the target there would be a huge shower of sparks, and after a moment a dull orange glow would appear. This glow would increase, brighten, and then slowly dull." Little of the enemy could be seen from *Tennessee.* Occasionally, the vague outline of a ship could be seen against the glare of an explosion; and, at one point, the single stack and high "pagoda" foremast of *Yamashiro* could be seen. Nishimura's three ships found themselves at the focus of a massive crossfire of battleship and cruiser fire. By 0400, both of the larger Japanese ships had been hit repeatedly as they gallantly attempted to return fire; *Mogami,* sorely damaged and her engineering plant crippled, had turned back, and *Yamashiro,* burning intensely, came about to follow. Oldendorf ordered gunfire to cease at 0409, after hearing that flanking destroyers were being endangered by American gunfire. *Yamashiro,* still able to make 15 knots after her frightful beating, was fatally hurt and, at 0419, rolled over and sank with all but a few of her crew. *Mogami* was able to draw out of radar range but had been slowed to a crawl. *Shigure,* more or less overlooked and relatively undamaged, escaped southward.

Shima's force, following along in Nishimura's wake, was unaware of what had befallen. When they were about halfway up Surigao Strait, they sighted what seemed to be two flaming ships; these were the broken halves of *Fuso.* Shima's two cruisers made a radar torpedo attack on what they believed to be American ships but was, in fact, Hibuson Island. "The island," as Samuel E. Morison remarked, "was not damaged." The Japanese admiral decided that Nishimura's force had met with disaster and decided on a retreat. As his ships turned to steam back, cruiser *Nachi* collided with limping, burning *Mogami,* but both vessels were able to continue southward. Collecting *Shigure,* the only other survivor of Nishimura's attack, Shima retired back through the strait. Oldendorf sent some of his cruisers and destroyers after him, and the patrolling PT's joined in. Fire was engaged with the stubborn *Mogami,* but she continued on her way only to be sunk by carrier planes shortly afterward. Destroyer *Asagumo,* her bow blown off by destroyer torpedoes during Nishimura's approach, was sighted and sent to the bottom with her guns still firing. Oldendorf now received reports that Kurita's "crippled" force had emerged from San Bernardino Strait and joined action

east of Samar with some of the supporting escort carrier force stationed there. Plans were hurriedly drawn for another surface battle, and Oldendorf's ships turned toward the northern entrance to Leyte Gulf to defend the landing area.

Their services were, however, not needed. In an epic action off Samar, the escort carriers, destroyers, and destroyer escorts of Rear Admiral C. A. F. Sprague's "Taffy Three" put up so desperate a fight that Kurita judged the odds against him hopeless and turned back. Halsey's carrier planes and surface ships sank all four of Ozawa's decoy carriers, and a submarine finished off a damaged cruiser.

The Battle for Leyte Gulf was over. The last major Japanese naval counterstroke had been defeated, and *Tennessee* had had a share in the last naval action fought by a battle line.

The next several days were quiet ones for *Tennessee,* though the Japanese sent numerous land-based air strikes against Leyte Gulf. On 29 October, the battlewagon's crew was told that their next destination was to be the Puget Sound Navy Yard. Late that day, she got underway for Ulithi with *West Virginia, Maryland,* and four cruisers. From there, she proceeded to Pearl Harbor and thence to Bremerton where she entered the shipyard on 26 November.

Unlike her last yard overhaul, this refit made no remarkable changes in *Tennessee's* appearance. She retained her battery of 10 40-millimeter quadruple anti-aircraft mounts and 43 20-millimeter guns, but her main-battery directors received improved models of the Mark 8 radar, and the Mark 4 radars used with the 5-inch gun directors were replaced by the newer combination of paired Mark 12 and Mark 22 dual-purpose equipments. *Tennessee's* usefulness as an anti-aircraft ship was enhanced by the addition of a model SP height-finding radar. Her pattern camouflage scheme was replaced by a dark gray finish which was calculated to provide a less conspicuous aiming point for kamikaze suicide planes, introduced during the recapture of the Philippines and becoming more and more of a fact of naval life during the winter of 1944 and 1945.

On 2 February 1945, *Tennessee* headed back toward the western Pacific. While she was being refitted, landings had been made in the Central Philippines and on Luzon; and the liberation of the Philippines was nearly accomplished. From its base in the Marianas, the 20th Army Air Force was hitting Japan with B-29s. Their track led past the Bonin Islands, whose garrison could send an early warning to Japanese airfields and gunners in the home islands. To eliminate this danger, provide an advanced base for fighter escorts, and obtain an emergency landing field for damaged bombers, Nimitz had been directed to capture Iwo Jima before going on to the Ryukyus to seize Okinawa as an advanced base for the assault on Japan proper. Japanese resistance on Leyte delayed the landing on Luzon from 20 December 1944 to 9 January 1945, while the landing in the Bonins, scheduled for 20 January 1945, had to be deferred until 19 February. The schedule for landings in the new year was tight; but planners deemed it essential to move as expeditiously as possible since the invasion of southern Japan, scheduled for the fall, depended on the use of Iwo Jima and Okinawa as bases for a long and intensive aerial bombardment.

The Japanese had predicted that a landing would be made on Iwo Jima, and a large garrison of good troops under Lieutenant General Tadanichi Kuribayashi had done a thorough job of digging themselves in. The volcanic island's rugged terrain was heavily fortified with strongly built firing positions supported by a deep and intricate network of tunnels.

B-24 Liberators of the 7th Army Air Force bombed Iwo Jima for 74 consecutive days to soften it up for an assault, and five naval bombardments were delivered. This pounding had no significant effect except to accelerate the work of the defenders.

Steaming by way of Pearl Harbor and Saipan,

Tennessee was just in time to join Rear Admiral W. H. P. Blandy's bombardment force. Blandy, an ordnance specialist, had been Chief of the Bureau of Ordnance earlier in the war. With the expert help of Lt. Col. Donald Weller, USMC, the preinvasion bombardment was thoroughly planned and was modified to meet immediate needs as the shelling progressed. The Japanese defensive tactic called for the landing troops to be stopped on the beaches before they could move inland, and a heavy belt of defenses extended along the shoreline. The mission of the bombarding ships and planes was to break down the Japanese cordon and permit the landing marines to push through before they could be cut to pieces.

Blandy's gunfire force arrived off Iwo Jima early on 16 February 1945. The morning was cool, with occasional rain squalls, and low cloud cover hindered spotting planes. Shortly after daybreak, the warships deployed to their stations, with escort carriers in the near distance providing air cover. Minesweepers began to clear the approaches to the island at 0645, and gunfire opened at 0707. *Tennessee*'s assigned firing course took her along the southeastern shore of Iwo Jima, and her 14-inch guns struck the slopes of Mount Suribachi while the secondaries aimed at the high ground at the north end of the beach. Floatplanes and fighters observing gunfire over the island were followed by dark puffs of antiaircraft fire. Blandy ordered the ships to fire only when air spot could function effectively in the intermittent visibility. Whenever the airplanes could observe the results, the ships kept their fire up through the day. During the afternoon, an OS2U Kingfisher seaplane from the cruiser *Pensacola* (CA–24) found a Japanese "Zeke" on its tail. The observation pilot, determined to put up all the fight he could, went at the fighter though his plane was much slower and less maneuverable, and armed only with one .30-caliber forward-firing machine gun plus a second flexible gun in the observer's cockpit. Against all the odds, the "Zeke" went down in flames.

Visibility was better the next day, and the ships began to approach beaches at 0803. Beginning at 10,000 yards, *Tennessee*, with *Idaho* and *Nevada*, soon closed to 3,000 yards and delivered heavy direct fire to assigned targets while assault minesweeping went on. At 1025, the battleships were ordered to retire to make way for UDT's supported by LCI(G)'s. The defenders concluded that this was the beginning of the actual landing and unmasked guns and mortars in a heavy fire on the gunboats and frogmen. Casualties mounted; one gunboat was sunk, another set afire. The other LCI's returned fire but had to withdraw as the bombardment ships resumed firing against the defenses. Three damaged gunboats came alongside *Tennessee* to transfer their wounded to the battleship's sick bay.

Bombardment continued through the 18th under orders prescribing concentrated hammering of the landing beaches. Once more, *Tennessee*'s big guns pounded Suribachi while her secondaries attacked gun positions overlooking the right flank of the objective area. While the heavier guns fired from ranges varying between 2,200 and 6,000 yards, the 40-millimeter battery raked other targets on cliffs at the north end of the beach and shot up the wrecks of several Japanese ships beached near the shore; these had been used as havens for snipers and machine gunners at Tarawa and in later landings, and were always treated as potential threats. Several fires were started ashore; an ammunition dump exploded spectacularly and burned for several hours. Coastal guns and antiaircraft weapons were still firing when *Tennessee* retired for the night, even though she and *Idaho* had been able to demolish many massive masonry pillboxes with direct hits.

Vice Admiral Richmond K. Turner arrived off Iwo Jima at 0600 on the morning of 19 February with the main body of the invasion force and assumed command. Transports formed up in the darkness and, at daybreak, put their landing craft into the water as troops clambered down the ship's cargo nets. The loaded landing craft circled near the transports as they awaited the signal to land. Tank landing ships moved closer to shore, opened their bow doors, and launched LVT's carrying the first wave of assault troops. Shortly after daylight, a heavy bombardment was opened by the ships of Task Force 54 reinforced by the newer battleships *North Carolina* (BB–55), *Washington* (BB–56), and three cruisers lent for the occasion by Task Force 58. A total of seven battleships, four 8-inch gun heavy cruisers, and three light cruisers armed with 6-inchers laid their fire on the landing areas. At first, the fire was slow and deliberate. It was checked for an air strike, as planes from the fast carrier force delivered bombs, rockets, and napalm before the ships resumed a heavier fire. Beginning at 0850, fire was so adjusted that carrier fighters could strafe the beaches during the last few minutes before H-hour. One minute before H-hour, the turret guns ceased firing, and the secondary guns began to drop a rolling barrage just ahead of the marines as they landed and moved inland. Shore fire control parties (SFCP) accompanied the marines ashore; one SFCP was assigned to work with each of the supporting battleships and cruisers.

The first wave crossed the line of departure at 0830 and landed only a fraction before the scheduled 0900 H-hour. As the troops landed, the Japanese, who had waited out the bombardment in their deep tunnels, manned guns and mortars in protected emplacements and opened an increasingly heavy fire. The ships' guns were kept busy; main batteries took on gun positions as they were located while the lighter guns kept up their barrage ahead of the men on the ground. *Tennessee*'s station was 3,000 yards from Suribachi at the southern end of the landing area, and the water around her was churned by hundreds of vehicles and landing craft as the successive waves moved in. By the end of the day, some 30,000 marines were on Iwo Jima, and some tanks and artillery had been landed.

Ground fighting on Iwo Jima continued until 26 March, as the stubborn Japanese were slowly rooted out of the positions that they continued to defend to the last. Even before the struggle ended, though, Army engineers had patched up the island's battered airstrip; and damaged B–29s were able to seek refuge on dry land instead of ditching. *Tennessee* was a part of this struggle until 7 March, when she sailed for Ulithi. The days after the landing were a steady routine of call fire and counterbattery work as Japanese guns continued to reveal themselves by opening fire on the hovering support ships before being located and taken out. For this purpose, it had been found that single-gun salvoes at close range, using "pointer fire" (in which the gun is directly aimed by telescopic sight), were the most precise and effective. The notion of using a 14-inch naval gun for sniping was rather new, but it seemed to work very well.

Tennessee left the area, having deposited 1,370 rounds of main-battery fire on Iwo Jima along with 6,380 5-inch and 11,481 40-millimeter projectiles. At Ulithi, she began to prepare for the Okinawa operation. Supplies and ammunition were loaded, and the tired sailors stretched their legs and drank beer on tiny Mog Mog Island, whose principal selling point as a vacation resort seemed to be that it did not move underfoot.

Everyone involved knew that this job would be attended by special hazards. Censorship had prevented any mention of the Japanese kamikaze weapon in the American press, but it was much in the mind of the Fleet. Admiral Oldendorf, injured and hospitalized shortly after reaching Ulithi, was replaced by Rear Admiral Morton Deyo, who broke his flag in *Tennessee* on 15 March. On the 21st, Task Force 54, the gunfire force, was underway for the Ryukyus. As Kerama Retto, a small cluster of islands near Okinawa, was taken for use as an advanced base, the battleships arrived off the main island. With *Tennessee* were *Colorado, Maryland, West Virginia, New Mexico,* and *Idaho,* as well as *Nevada, New York, Texas,* and the venerable

Arkansas (BB–33), first commissioned in 1912 and still pulling her weight; she was the only battleship in the fleet still armed with 12-inch guns. With the capital ships came 10 cruisers, 32 destroyer and destroyer escorts, and numerous gun- and rocket-firing LCI's and LSM's.

Shortly after midnight on 26 March 1945, Task Force 54 approached Okinawa with its crews at general quarters in the darkness. At daylight, it deployed; the bombardment began at long range since the nearer waters had not yet been swept for mines. The minesweepers began to work as the ships fired on targets located by previous aerial reconnaissance. No enemy fire answered the American guns though antiaircraft shells pecked at spotting planes. Japanese submarines were in the area, and a number of ships sighted torpedo wakes, but no damage resulted. Planes from the escort carriers and from Task Force 58 mounted strikes on the island, took detailed photographs, and flew air cover for the surface ships. The need for this became quite evident early on the next morning, when a number of kamikazes came in at a time when no combat air patrol (CAP) was overhead. One suicider hit *Nevada*, knocking out one of her turrets; another damaged *Biloxi* (CL–80) at the waterline, while a third went into the water to port of *Tennessee*. The converted "flushdecker" *Dorsey* (DMS–1) was hit by a kamikaze which glanced off the ship, damaging, but not crippling, her.

This was to be the pattern of life off Okinawa during the grueling weeks to come, as the "fleet that came to stay" battled to see the land battle through while keeping itself alive. Long hours at general quarters kept all hands tense and tired as the ships prowled off the island firing at every likely target while reports of suicide attacks piled up.

The day of the landing—1 April 1945, Easter Sunday—was bright and fair, with a gentle breeze. At 0600, Admiral Turner assumed overall command of the operation as Deyo continued to direct the gunfire ships. After a morning bombardment which Morison dscribed as "the most impressive gunfire support that any assault troops had ever had," the landing began. H-Hour was 0830, preceded by the by-now customary intense battering by everything from battleships and carrier planes to sheaves of rockets from flat-bottomed landing craft. As the troops hit the beach, the bombardment was lifted. Early progress was good, meeting surprisingly light opposition. Veterans of earlier landings, and even the intelligence staffs, were puzzled at not having to fight the usual savage struggle to get ashore. Lieutenant General Mitsuru Ushijima, commanding nearly 100,000 defenders—three-quarters of whom were regular Army troops—had decided to make no attempt to stop the landing at the beaches. Instead, he dug his main strength into the hilly southern end of Okinawa, thoroughly fortified as Iwo Jima had been but on a much larger scale. Japanese artillery held its fire during the pre-landing bombardment so that their positions would not be given away; instead of dueling with the ships, they would save their fire for the landing troops. His general idea was to pin down the invasion force and delay it as long as possible, while a massive suicide air offensive wore down the supporting naval forces.

By 18 April, all of northern and central Okinawa was in American hands. The long fight for the Japanese citadel around the old island capital of Naha was to last much longer, and the island was not secured until 21 June. In the meanwhile, the Navy battled by day and night against the unremitting kamikaze offensive. On the afternoon of 12 April, *Tennessee*—instead of taking up a fire-support station—was steaming in air-defense formation. Deyo had been warned that a heavy air attack was on the way and, during the afternoon, it arrived. Some suiciders were knocked down by picket destroyers or splashed by CAP; others, though, got through and aimed themselves at the firing, maneuvering ships. More bandits were shot down by

antiaircraft fire, but *Zellars* (DD–777) was set ablaze by a crashing plane. Five more picked *Tennessee* and came in through puffs of shell bursts and the heavy smoke from *Zellars*. Four were shot down, the last three only hundreds of yards from the battleship. The last diver came down on the bow at a 45-degree angle, was set aflame by 5-inch fire, and plunged into the water. At the same time, an Aichi A6M "Val" dive-bomber, flying low on the starboard bow, headed directly for *Tennessee*'s bridge. Lookouts spotted the "Val" at 2,500 yards, and every automatic weapon that could bear opened up. One of the plane's fixed wheels was torn off, and its engine began to smoke. Heading at first for *Tennessee*'s tower foremast, the Japanese pilot swerved slightly and crashed into the signal bridge. The burning wreck slid aft along the superstructure, crushing antiaircraft guns and their crews, and stopped next to Turret Three. It had carried a 250-pound bomb which, with what was left of the plane, went through the wooden deck and exploded. Twenty-two men were killed or fatally wounded, with another 107 injured.

This was not enough to put *Tennessee* out of action. The dead were buried at sea, and the wounded transferred the following day to the casualty-evacuation transport *Pinkney* (APH–2). The ship's company turned to on emergency repairs; and, by 14 April, the ship was back on the firing line. *Tennessee* remained off Okinawa for two more weeks. On 1 May, Admiral Deyo shifted his flag to a cruiser, and *Tennessee* set her course for Ulithi. Here, the repair ship *Ajax* (AR–6) made repairs, cutting away damaged plating and installing new guns to replace those lost. On 3 June, the ship sailed for Okinawa, arriving on the 9th. By now, the worst was over. Army troops were making a final drive to clear the island, and *Tennessee*'s gunfire again helped to clear the way. With the other old battlewagons, she remained in support until organized resistance was declared at an end on 21 June. By this time, the scene in the air was different. Besides Navy carrier planes, large numbers of Army Air Force fighters were now flying from Okinawa fields; and the days when everything that flew was a cause for alarm had ended—for the time being.

Vice Admiral Oldendorf was subsequently placed in command of naval forces in the Ryukyus, and *Tennessee* flew his flag as she covered minesweeping operations in the East China Sea and patrolled the waters off Shanghai for Japanese shipping as escort carriers sent strikes against the China coast. This was *Tennessee*'s station until V–J Day brought an end to the war in the Pacific. When this glad day came, the big ship was operating out of Okinawa and preparing to take part in the planned invasion of Japan.

The battleship's final assignment of the war was to cover the landing of occupation troops at Wakayama, Japan. She arrived there on 23 September, then went on to Yokosuka. *Tennessee*'s crew had the chance to look over the Imperial Navy's big shipyard and operating base and do some sightseeing before she got underway for Singapore on 15 October. At Singapore, Oldendorf shifted his flag to the cruiser *Springfield* (CL–66), and *Tennessee* continued her long voyage home by way of the Cape of Good Hope.

On the fourth anniversary of Pearl Harbor, the old veteran moored at the Philadelphia Naval Shipyard. During those years, she had hurled 9,347 14-inch rounds at the enemy, with 46,341 shells from her 5-inch guns and more than 100,000 rounds from her antiaircraft battery.

The process of trimming the wartime Navy down to postwar size was already well underway. *Tennessee* was one of the older, yet still useful, ships selected for inclusion in the "mothball fleet;" and, during 1946, she underwent a process of preservation and preparation for inactivation. The work went slowly; there were many ships to lay up and not too many people to do it. Finally, on 14 February 1947, *Tennessee*'s ensign was hauled down for the last time as she was placed out of commission.

Tennessee remained in the inactive fleet for another 12 years. By then, time and technology had passed her by; and, on 1 March 1959, her name was struck from the Naval Vessel Register. On 10 July of that year, she was sold to the Bethlehem Steel Company for scrapping.

Tennessee earned a Navy Unit Commendation and 10 battle stars for World War II service.

Tensas

A river which rises in East Carrol Parish, La., and winds its way south to join the Ouachita at Jonesville.

(SwGbt: t. 41; l. 91'; b. 22'5''; dph. 3'7½''; dr. 4'; a. 2 24-pdr. how.)

Tom Sugg—a wooden-hulled side-wheel steamer built in 1860 at Cincinnati, Ohio—was outfitted as a side-wheel gunboat and served under the name *Tom Sugg*. She operated as a merchant river boat in Arkansas on the White River carrying cotton and general cargo. After the outbreak of the Civil War, she transported arms and horses for Confederate troops near the White River.

On 14 August 1863, USS *Cricket* ascended the Little Red River and captured *Tom Sugg* and *Kaskaskia* at Searcy's Landing. This blow destroyed Confederate river transportation in northern Arkansas and ultimately diminished the flow of supplies to Southern troops east of the Mississippi.

The United States Navy Department purchased the side-wheel gunboat from the Illinois Prize Court on 29 September 1863, and she was commissioned as *Tensas* on 1 January 1864 at Mound City, Ill., Acting Master E. C. Van Pelt in command. She served with the Mississippi River Squadron and was decommissioned on 7 August 1865. She was sold at public auction on 17 August 1865 at Mound City, Ill., to E. B. Trinidad.

Tensaw

A variant form of the name Tensas, a term derived from the Louisiana Indian tribe Taensa.

(YTB–418: dp. 260 (tl.); l. 100'; b. 28'; dr. 11'; s. 12 k.; cpl. 10; a. 2 .50-cal mg.; cl. *Sassaba*)

Tensaw (YTB–418) ex-YT–418, was laid down on 8 August 1944 at the Coast Guard Yard, Curtis Bay, Md.; launched on 11 October 1944; sponsored by Mrs. Albert G. Mariner, Jr.; and placed in service on 8 March 1945.

Late that month, the new large harbor tug reported to the Commandant of the 5th Naval District at Norfolk. In April, she proceeded via the Panama Canal to the Pacific and arrived at Pearl Harbor on 14 May to begin duties in support of the Pacific Fleet. In June 1945, she steamed, via the Marshalls, to the Marianas where she operated through the end of World War II. After Japan capitulated, the tug continued to serve in the Marianas until the Korean War sent her, via the Philippines, to Japan.

Arriving at Yokosuka on 7 February 1951, she supported United Nations forces through the armistice in the summer of 1953. She continued in the western Pacific through the 1950's and into the 1960's. Redesignated a medium harbor tug—YTM—in February 1962, she remained with the Pacific Fleet until July 1967 when she was inactivated, and her name was struck from the Navy list. The tug was subsequently slated for disposal by sale, but no record of her final disposition has been found.

Tercel

The male of various hawks, especially of the peregrine falcon and the goshawk.

(AM–386: dp. 890; l. 221'1''; b. 32'2''; dr. 10'9''; s. 18.1 k. (tl.); cpl. 117; a. 1 3'', 2 40mm.; cl. *Auk*)

Tercel (AM–386) was laid down on 16 May 1944 by the American Shipbuilding Co., Lorain, Ohio; launched on 16 December 1944; sponsored by Mrs. J. H. Thompson; and commissioned on 21 August 1945, Lt. Comdr. M. Dent, Jr., USNR, in command.

Following trials in Lake Erie, *Tercel* headed for the Atlantic via the Great Lakes waterway and the St. Lawrence River. She arrived at Boston on 7 September and was outfitted. Sailing on 2 November, *Tercel* reached Little Creek, Va., the next day for her shakedown cruise.

Tercel was assigned to Mine Forces, Atlantic Fleet, on 1 January 1946, when that organization was activated. She stood out of Norfolk a week later and conducted exercises in the Chesapeake Bay until 21 March. In April, she was assigned to the Mine Warfare School at Yorktown and supported that establishment until 2 July 1946. The minesweeper conducted local operations and participated in exercises along the eastern seaboard from the Caribbean to New London until 20 July 1951 when she arrived at Charleston, S.C.

Tercel stood out of Charleston in early September 1951 for her first deployment to the Mediterranean. While there, she called at Gibraltar and ports in Italy, France, Malta, and Greece. Upon her return to Charleston on 6 February 1952, she resumed her normal east coast routine.

Tercel was again deployed to the Mediterranean from 21 April to 26 October 1953. Then, after approximately eight months of operations in home waters, the minesweeper was transferred to the Atlantic Reserve Fleet for a preinactivation overhaul. The ship was placed out of commission, in reserve, at Orange, Tex., on 10 November 1954. On 7 February 1955, she was redesignated MSF–386 and reclassified a steel-hulled fleet minesweeper. *Tercel* was struck from the Navy list on 1 July 1972 and scrapped.

Terebinth

A small European tree of the Sumac family that yields Chian turpentine.

(AN–59; dp. 1,275; l. 194'6''; b. 37'; dr. 13'6''; s. 12.1 k.; cpl. 56; a. 1 3''; cl. *Ailanthus*)

Terebinth (AN–59) was laid down as *Balm* (YN–78) on 24 March 1943 at New Bern, N.C., by the Barbour Boat Works; launched on 19 August 1943; sponsored by Mrs. J. M. Mitchell; renamed *Terebinth* on 7 December 1943; redesignated AN–59 on 20 January 1944; and commissioned on 5 August 1944, Lt. Sandrup Bernsen, USNR, in command.

Terebinth departed Morehead City, N.C., on 6 August to complete fitting out at the Norfolk Navy Yard. On the 24th, the net laying ship steamed to Melville, R.I., for shakedown training which she completed on 11 September. After operating in the 5th Naval District out of Norfolk for two months, the net layer got underway on 16 November for the west coast. She transited the Panama Canal on the 27th and reached San Francisco on 20 December 1944.

On 26 January 1945, *Terebinth* headed for Hawaii and arrived at Pearl Harbor on 7 February. The following week, the net layer joined a convoy which proceeded, via Johnston Island and Eniwetok, to Ulithi. She was there from 6 to 11 March when she joined units of Mine Squadron 10 bound for the Philippines. The ships arrived at San Pedro Bay 10 days later, prepared for the invasion of the Ryukyu Islands, and sortied on 19 March. They arrived off Kerama Retto on the 26th, and troops of the 77th Infantry Division landed on the beaches there at 0800 that morning. By afternoon, the main islands of the group were under American control, and *Terebinth* began net laying operations in the Aka Shima channel. The northern mooring was completed in the afternoon, and the last of the 1,500-foot net was in place before nightfall. The southern mooring was completed the next morning.

The invasion fleet came under enemy air attack on the first day of the campaign, and raids continued throughout the struggle for the island. A new hazard appeared on the morning of the 28th when lookouts on *Terebinth* sighted an unlighted boat approaching the ship's starboard bow. When challenged, the craft did not reply. Since the unidentified vessel was too close for *Terebinth* to bring her 3-inch gun to bear, the ship's gunners opened fire with small arms. The boat dropped a depth charge near *Terebinth*, veered to starboard, and sped off as a violent explosion shook the net layer. Fortunately, *Terebinth* was not damaged. She then took station at the eastern side of the southern net entrance to Kerama Retto and directed traffic as it entered. The ship remained at this task until 6 April when she joined a salvage group off the Hagushi beaches to aid in retrieving landing craft. On the 29th, she went alongside the damaged *Pinckney* (APH–2) and supplied the transport with electricity for four days while it attended to the needs of wounded men who had been evacuated from the beaches. *Terebinth* remained in the Ryukyus until 6 July when she retired to Leyte.

Terebinth departed San Pedro on 12 August and was approximately 60 miles south of Peleliu on the 15th when she received orders to cease offensive operations against Japan. Two days later, she anchored at Ulithi and began repairing, replacing, and salvaging buoys and nets. She then moved to Kossol Roads in the Palaus to continue the same tasks. On 14 October, the net laying ship set course for Tanapag harbor, Saipan, with a load of nets. She arrived there on the 19th and got underway for the United States on the 26th.

Terebinth arrived at San Diego on 27 November 1945 and, the next day, moved up the coast to San Pedro for inactivation. She was decommissioned on 31 January 1946 and struck from the Navy list on 26 February 1946. The ship was sold to Van Cam Sea Food Co., San Pedro, on 23 April 1946.

Terebinth received one battle star for World War II service.

Teresa

(Id. No. 4478; dp. 6,800; l. 276'9''; b. 49'8''; dr. 24'; s. 10 k.; cpl. 90; a. 2 4'')

Teresa (Id. No. 4478) was built in 1900 as *Austrian* at Port Glasgow, Scotland, by Russel and Co. and owned by Unione Austriaca di Navigazione. The ship was taken over by the United States Shipping Board on 27 September 1917 and chartered to the Army the same day, with a civilian crew. After a dispute between the Army quartermaster and the ship's civilian master, the Army requested that the Navy man the ship. The Navy accepted the ship and commissioned her in the Naval Overseas Transportation Service (NOTS) on 9 January 1918 at Newport News, Va.

Teresa was refitted for naval service and headed for New York on the 29th. She loaded a cargo of Army supplies and returned to Norfolk. On 23 February, the cargo ship got underway with a convoy for France and arrived at St. Nazaire on 4 March. *Teresa* made four additional supply trips to France during the next 16 months. She ended her last voyage at Philadelphia on 28 June 1919 and was decommissioned there on 19 July 1919. The ship was returned to the Shipping Board the same day.

Tern

A sea bird whose body is smaller than the gull which it resembles. It possesses a slender body, a narrow beak, and a deeply-forked tail. The tern inhabits coastal waters on both sides of the Atlantic.

I

(SP–871: t. 18; l. 53'; b. 10'; dr. 2'9''; a. 1 1-pdr., 1 mg.)

The first *Tern* (SP–871)—a motorboat built in 1907 at South Boston, Mass., by Murray and Tregurtha—was acquired by the United States Navy on 28 May 1917 from E. F. Nall of Atlantic City, N.J.; and was commissioned the same day.

Tern operated in the 4th Naval District as a scout patrol boat through the end of World War I. She was returned to her owner on 21 November 1918.

II

(Mine Sweeper No. 31: dp. 950; l. 187'10''; b. 35'6''; dr. 9'9½''; s. 14 k.; a. 1 1-pdr., 2 mg.; cl. *Lapwing*)

The second *Tern* (Mine Sweeper No. 31) was laid down on 7 September 1918 at Morris Heights, N.Y., by the Gas Engine & Power Co. and the C. L. Seabury Co.; launched on 22 March 1919; sponsored by Mrs. Bruce Scrimgeour; and commissioned on 17 May 1919, Lt. Nels Drake in command.

Tern was assigned to the United States Pacific Fleet and steamed to the west coast. On 1 October, the minesweeper joined Train Squadron (TrainRon) 2, Fleet Base Force, at Pearl Harbor. Her squadron operated in support of the Battle Force for the next nine years. *Tern* was designated AM–31 on 17 July 1920 when the Navy first assigned hull numbers to its ships. In July 1927, *Tern* and her squadron moved to San Diego and operated out of that port for six years before their base was shifted to San Pedro, Calif. *Tern* remained with TrainRon 2, Base Force, and accompanied it to Pearl Harbor on 19 June 1941 when the squadron was again assigned to Hawaii.

When the Japanese attacked Pearl Harbor on 7 December 1941, *Tern* was alongside the north end of "Ten Ten" dock undergoing upkeep by *Argonne* (AP–4). All of her machinery was dead, and she was receiving steam and electricity from the dock. She was notified of the attack at 0753 and immediately made preparations to get underway. Twelve minutes later, her gunners opened fire with Lewis machineguns on an incoming enemy plane which was seen to crash near the Officers' Club. At 0943, the minesweeper moved out into the harbor and picked up 47 survivors from various ships. *Tern* then proceeded to *Arizona* (BB–39) to assist in fighting fires but was soon ordered to aid *West Virginia* (BB–48). The fires on *West Virginia* were extinguished at 1430 on 8 December, and the minesweeper moved back alongside *Arizona* until the fires on that battleship were brought under control, shortly after noon on the 9th. *Tern* was not damaged by the Japanese attack.

On 9 January 1942, *Tern* began towing a fuel oil barge to Johnston Island. She delivered it on the 13th and returned to Pearl Harbor. *Tern* got underway for the Society Islands on 9 February, arrived at Borabora on the 18th, and was assigned duty there as station ship. On 1 March, the Base Force was renamed Service Force, Pacific; and, on 1 June, the minesweeper was redesignated AT–142, an ocean tug. She remained at Borabora until 2 January 1943 when she was relieved by *Advent* (AM–83). The tug returned to Pearl Harbor on 27 January and, five weeks later, headed for San Pedro, Calif., and an overhaul.

Tern arrived back at Pearl Harbor on 23 May and joined the Service Squadron, 3d Fleet, operating in the Hawaiian area. Her duties for the next year consisted of recovering training torpedoes, towing targets for bombing and gunnery practice, and assisting other ships. On 15 May 1944, her designation was changed to ATO–142 (Ocean Tug, Old).

On 9 July, *Tern* joined a convoy headed for the Marshall Islands. She arrived at Eniwetok on the 28th and operated from that base for the next five months towing craft to Majuro, Tarawa, Ulithi, and Guam. On 4 January 1945, the tug shifted her base of operations to Ulithi for five months. On 26 May, *Tern* got underway for Leyte, P.I. She arrived at San Pedro on 1 June and was assigned duty as a target towing ship with Submarine Training, Pacific Fleet, at Guam. The tug arrived at Apra Harbor on 20 June and operated with submarines until 1 September when she was relieved by *Cormorant* (ATO–133). The next week, *Tern* began the long voyage, via Eniwetok and Pearl Harbor, to the United States.

Tern arrived at San Francisco in mid-October and began preparing for inactivation. She was decommissioned on 23 November and struck from the Navy list on 5 December 1945.

Tern received one battle star for World War II service.

Ternate

(Id. No. 2697: t. 3,909; l. 393'; b. 51'6''; dr. 20'10''; s. 10 k.; cpl. 62; a. 1 4'')

Ternate (Id. No. 2697) was built in 1907 at Port Glasgow, Scotland, by William Hamilton & Co.; owned and operated by Rotterdamsche Lloyd, Holland; acquired by the United States Shipping Board and delivered to the Naval Overseas Transportation Service (NOTS) on 21 March 1918.

Ternate was commissioned at Newport News, Va., on 6 April 1918, Lt. Cmdr. George W. Jannson in command, and got underway for New York the following week to be refitted for naval use. The cargo ship stood out of New York on the 25th for New Orleans where she loaded Army supplies. *Ternate* returned to New York on 25 May and, that day, joined a convoy for France. She unloaded supplies at Brest, La Pallice, and Verdon from 9 June to 17 July when she began her return voyage to the United States. The ship arrived at Norfolk on 1 August 1918. She then made two more round-trip voyages carrying military cargo to France.

On 2 February 1919, *Ternate* departed Norfolk and proceeded to Savannah and loaded cargo for Italy. En route, she was forced to call at Gibraltar for fuel and finally arrived at Genoa on 17 March. The ship returned to New York on 11 April, was decommissioned, and was returned to the Shipping Board the same day.

Terrebonne Parish

A parish in Louisiana, incorporated in 1822, and located on the gulf coast of the Mississippi delta.

(LST–1156: dp. 5,800 (f.); l. 384'0''; b. 55'0''; dr. 17'; cpl. 160; s. 15 k.; a. 6 3''; cl. *Terrebonne Parish*)

Terrebonne Parish (LST–1156) was laid down as *LST–1156* on 2 January 1952 at Bath, Maine, by the Bath Iron Works; launched on 9 August 1952; sponsored by Miss Anne L. McCrea; and commissioned on 21 November 1952, Lt. Comdr. Henry L. Porter in command.

Following trials and shakedown, *LST–1156* underwent post-shakedown alterations at the Norfolk Navy Yard before commencing operations out of Little Creek with Amphibious Forces, Atlantic Fleet, on 14 September 1953. The ship then conducted training exercises out of Little Creek before entering the Norfolk Navy Yard for conversion to an LST Flotilla flagship, involving the installation of much new communications equipment. *LST–1156* remained on operations out of

Little Creek through June 1955. On 1 July 1955, the ship was named *Terrebonne Parish*, while retaining her designation of LST–1156.

Following operations in the Caribbean and off North Carolina, and overhaul at the Charleston (S.C.) Naval Shipyard, *Terrebonne Parish* conducted a cruise to Lisbon, Portugal, and Port Lyautey, French Morocco, before resuming local operations out of Little Creek. She continued participating in exercises and assault landings in the Caribbean and returned to Norfolk on 14 May 1957 to resume local operations and type training.

On 29 August 1957, *Terrebonne Parish* cleared Norfolk for Morehead City, N.C., and, on the following day, embarked marines, vehicles, and cargo for transport to the Mediterranean. The LST joined units of the 6th Fleet at Taranto, Italy, on 16 September. During the subsequent tour, the ship took part in NATO landing exercises at Saros Gulf, Turkey, and visited ports in Turkey, Greece, Italy, Crete, and Sicily before returning to the United States on 12 February 1958 and resuming local operations out of Little Creek. Following overhaul and refresher training, she again deployed to the Mediterranean with the 6th Fleet in September 1958, serving as part of Service Force, Mediterranean, before returning westward once again to the United States and operations off the east coast and in Caribbean waters.

On 16 June 1959, *Terrebonne Parish* commenced an inland seas cruise, transiting the St. Lawrence Seaway and calling at Iroquois, Cape Vincent, and Port Weller, Ontario; Ashtabula, Ohio; Kenosha, Wisc.; Chicago, Ill.; Milwaukee, Wisc.; Cleveland, Ohio; Erie, Pa.; and Port Colburne and Rochester, N.Y., before returning to her home base of Little Creek on 6 August. Also in 1959, the ship participated in Exercise TRALEX—one of the largest amphibious exercises conducted in that year.

Terrebonne Parish conducted yearly deployments to the Mediterranean, with periodic overhauls and exercises, through 1961. In late October 1962, after the presence of Soviet missiles was detected in Cuba, the United States instituted a "quarantine"—throwing a naval cordon around the island. During these emergency preparations, the LST operated with the Atlantic Fleet Amphibious Force through December, when the crisis finally subsided. Attached to Amphibious Forces, Atlantic Fleet, Amphibious Squadron 6, the ship conducted operations off the Virginia Capes in January and February 1963 and then was overhauled in Jacksonville, Fla., before she again sailed for the Mediterranean.

During her 1963 deployment with the 6th Fleet, *Terrebonne Parish* participated in MEDLANDEX, a joint United States-Spanish exercise wherein 3,000 American and Spanish Marines were landed with support from carrier-based aircraft. The ship remained in the Mediterranean into February 1964 before returning to the United States for amphibious exercises in the spring at Onslow Beach, N.C., and off Camp Pendleton, Va. She proceeded to New York in July to visit the New York World's Fair before taking part in an amphibious exercise with marines and midshipmen off Camp Pendleton.

Early in the autumn, she embarked the men and vehicles of "C" Company, 1st Battalion, 2d Marines, and proceeded for Huelva, Spain, to take part in Exercise "Steel Pike"—where the ship became the first LST to "marry" to an eighteen-section causeway for landing her embarked vehicles. For the remainder of her deployment, the ship took part in landing exercises off Sardinia and Corsica and made visits to ports in Italy, France, and Spain, spending the Christmas holidays in Barcelona, Spain, and New Year's at Valencia.

Returning home to the United States towards the end of March 1965, the ship transported a Marine missile detachment to the Caribbean, and then underwent extensive overhaul for four months by the

Bethlehem Steel shipyard at Baltimore, Md. After refresher training, *Terrebonne Parish* got underway for the Caribbean on 3 March 1966 to begin a four-month deployment to participate in exercises and operations involving beachings and landings. The ship next made two lifts to the Dominican Republic in late August and early September. During this Caribbean tour, a locking device was developed for the sand flaps on the ship's bow doors, to keep them secure while underway. Tests proved that these new devices—installed in January at San Juan, Puerto Rico—were very efficient. As a result, this modification was approved for all LST's.

Terrebonne Parish commenced her 7th Mediterranean deployment on 30 March 1967 when she embarked marines of the 1st Battalion, 6th Marine Regiment, at Morehead City and crossed the Atlantic in company with four minesweepers of Mine Division 83. Upon arriving at Aranci Bay, Sardinia, on 19 April, the ship joined Amphibious Squadron 6, Task Force 61, and soon participated in Exercise "Fairgame Five"—a Franco-American amphibious exercise which brought together elements of the French Army, Navy, Commandos, and Foreign Legion, as well as a joint Navy-Marine team.

The ship headed for the western half of the Mediterranean and proceeded to Italy and Crete for further exercises. While the ship was at Taormina, Sicily, in late July, volunteers from her ship's company and embarked troops went ashore to battle a raging brush fire threatening the town of Giardini.

Leaving Taormina on 7 August and arriving at Porto Scudo, Sardinia, on 12 August, the ship took part in further amphibious exercises before she reembarked her marines after field exercises and proceeded to Malaga, Spain, for further amphibious training operations. The ship subsequently departed Rota, Spain, on 2 September for her return voyage to the United States.

Deploying to the Mediterranean in 1969, the ship moved to the Caibbean early in the following year and also conducted exercises off the east coast before returning to the Mediterranean, in late 1970, for her ninth deployment. The following year, still homeported at Little Creek, Va., and operating under command of Amphibious Forces, Atlantic, *Terrebonne Parish* deployed to the Caribbean for exercises and training activities. These included an operation from 5 to 10 August 1971 in which United States Army and Panamanian National Guard units participated.

Soon after returning from Panama, the ship began preparations for her upcoming transfer to the Spanish government. On 29 October 1971, the ship was decommissioned and turned over to the Spanish Navy at Little Creek, Va. Subsequently renamed *Velasco* and designated L–11, the ship served Spain into 1980.

Terrell County

Counties in Texas and Georgia.

(LST–1157: dp. 5,800 (f.); l. 384′0″; b. 55′0″; dr. 17′; s. 15 k.; cpl. 116; a. 6 3″; cl. *Terrebonne Parish*)

Terrell County (LST–1157) was laid down as *LST–1157* on 3 March 1952 at Bath, Maine, by the Bath Iron Works; launched on 6 December 1952; sponsored by Mrs. John H. Spiller; and commissioned on 14 March 1953, Lt. Comdr. L. I. Reynolds in command.

Following shakedown training and operations out of Little Creek, Va., *LST–1157* departed Morehead City, N.C., on 25 September 1953 with a full load of troops and amphibious vehicles for transfer to the Pacific Fleet and arrived in San Diego on 25 October. Assigned to Amphibious Forces, Pacific Fleet, *LST–1157* operated out of San Diego into February 1954 before getting underway for the Central Pacific. She soon took part in moving natives from northern islands

in the Marshalls to new homes in southern islands in May and June 1954. This lift involved the shipment of lumber for new homes, schools, and churches, as well as of the personal belongings and livestock of the natives.

Returning to a routine of local operations upon arrival at Port Chicago on 2 July, *LST–1157* was named *Terrell County* on 1 July 1955. She departed the west coast on 9 September 1955 for her first Western Pacific (WestPac) deployment, and she operated out of ports in Okinawa and Japan before returning to the west coast and resuming local operations.

Her second WestPac deployment commenced on 13 August 1957. In the succeeding months, *Terrell County* steamed a total of 25,600 miles, conducted three landing exercises and four troop lifts; and transported 500 vehicles and 1,500 men in five beachings and nine "marriages" to landing causeway sections. During this period, she also served as flagship for Landing Ship Squadron ONE. The sudden flare-up of tension halfway around the world in Lebanon temporarily interrupted the LST's routine. The ship sailed for Pearl Harbor and conducted emergency exercises in the Hawaiian area before the Middle Eastern crisis abated.

Departing the west coast on 15 April 1959, the ship headed across the Pacific for her third WestPac deployment. She subsequently returned to San Diego in November and began an extensive overhaul. On 16 June 1960, the ship set sail for her fourth WestPac cruise.

In July 1960, her permanent home port was changed from San Diego to Yokosuka, Japan. In the Far East, *Terrell County* participated in a wide variety of operations with beachings and landings of embarked marines and their equipment. Occasionally, maneuvers with warships of other SEATO powers took place in locales ranging from Thailand to Korea and from Borneo to the Philippine Islands. Liberties at Hong Kong and Tokyo brightened a sometimes uneventful deployment while typhoon evasions, too, were common occurrences.

On 4 August 1964, North Vietnamese torpedo boats reportedly attacked destroyers *Maddox* (DD–641) and *Turner Joy* (DD–951) in the Gulf of Tonkin, off Vietnam. *Terrell County* proceeded to Iwakuni, Japan, where she remained on alert until 20 August, when she headed for Yokosuka and extended upkeep.

Next, local operations in Japanese and Korean waters occupied the ship through the end of 1964. Underway training began the ship's new year and lasted through February and into March 1965. On 12 March, the ship departed the Ryukyus, bound for South Vietnam. She arrived at Danang four days later, unloaded embarked men and cargo, and then returned to Yokosuka for major overhaul.

The ship returned to Vietnamese waters following the refit and transported Marine Air Control Squadron 9 to Chu Lai before returning to Japanese waters. Operational commitments subsequently overrode refresher training out of Yokosuka in July, forcing the ship to embark Naval Beach Group 1. Dispatched to Okinawa on 1 August, *Terrell County* evaded a typhoon en route and made port to load Regimental Landing Team 7 before sailing on the 9th for Chu Lai. Remaining at that American base from 15 to 17 August, the ship evaded two typhoons en route back to Japanese waters before she reached Yokosuka on 25 August.

Following further refresher training and an upkeep period, the LST got underway for South Korea on 21 October and arrived at Pusan two days later. She embarked elements of the Republic of Korea's "Tiger" Division—marking the first time that a Korean expeditionary force had been sent abroad in nearly 1,000 years. Sailing on 25 October, *Terrell County* arrived at Qi Nhon, South Vietnam, on 2 November and debarked her troops.

The ship operated in support of Operation "Blue Marlin" from 4 to 17 November—included in this deployment was a landing near Chu Lai and a trip to

Danang with support equipment on board. Once she completed this assignment, the LST received orders to proceed to Nha Trang and thence to Cam Ranh Bay for further operations. On 21 November, the ship embarked ROK marines and U.S. Army support units for transport to Tuy Hoa.

Soon after reaching Tuy Hoa, the ship, with her troops still embarked, broached in the heavy surf and went aground. On 24 November, *Molala* (ATF–106) and *Mahopac* (ATA–196) succeeded in pulling *Terrell County* "off the beach." Subsequently patched and pumped dry, the LST got underway on 2 December, under tow for Yokosuka, where permanent repairs could be made to her damaged hull.

The restoration work was complete on 22 February 1966, and the ship got underway for Naha, Okinawa. She embarked men and equipment of the Army's 1st Engineering Battalion and transported them to Vietnam. She completed the task on 7 March and then made another transport run from 14 to 26 March, carrying American cavalrymen from Naha to Saigon.

After coastal operations off Vietnam from 27 March to 5 May, *Terrell County* retired to Japan on one shaft, since her starboard shaft had ceased functioning. On 13 May, as the landing ship crept along toward Yokosuka, lookouts sighted the Soviet merchantman *Makhachala* two points abaft the starboard beam and closing. Both ships continued steady on their courses, as *Terrell County* assumed that the heavily-laden Russian would stay clear. Finally, both ships were forced to maneuver radically to avert a collision.

Shaft troubles continued to plague the landing ship but did not interfere with the completion of her transport and cargo missions. She continued these duties into the fall of 1966. In October, *Terrell County* sailed to Subic Bay to serve as the United States' representative at the 22d annual Leyte Gulf celebration which commemorated the American landings of 1944 supported by an earlier breed of LST's.

Subsequently completing a Nuclear Weapons Acceptance Inspection—the first ship in her squadron to do so, *Terrell County* conducted two more transport lifts—both to Chu Lai, Vietnam—before rounding out the year 1966 by joining Task Unit (TU) 76.0.7 as part of the Danang-Chu Lai shuttle. The ship remained with TU 76.0.7 until 18 January 1977, when she sailed for Okinawa. She proceeded thence to her permanent WestPac home port, Yokosuka.

Transport operations to Okinawa, intermingled with type and refresher training exercises, continued through the spring. On 9 July, *Terrell County* relieved *Tom Green County* (LST–1159) as part of Amphibious Ready Group Bravo, TG 76.5, then engaged in the midst of operations "Beaver Track" and "Buffalo." Given the mission of "sea-trailer" or contingency logistics, she carried ammunition, medical supplies, and vehicles assigned to the 2d Battalion, 3d Marine Division, the Marine units bearing the brunt of the fighting ashore. For two months, *Terrell County* supported operations in Quang Tri province, just south of the demilitarized zone (DMZ), and conducted a series of landings in rapid succession: Operations "Bear Chain," "Kangaroo Kick," and "Belt Drive," before heading for Hong Kong on 19 September.

Following visits to Okinawa and Subic Bay, *Terrell County* loaded ammunition and causeway sections and departed Yokosuka on 1 March 1968, bound for Vietnam. However, while steaming in company with *Washoe County* (LST–1165) and *Westchester County* (LST–1167), *Terrell County* lost two causeways which were torn loose by heavy seas. Returning to Yokosuka, the LST obtained replacement sections and embarked Amphibious Construction Battalion (ACB) 1 before getting underway again and rejoining her two sister ships en route to Vietnam. Arriving at Danang on 13 March, the ship delivered her causeways and proceeded to Tien Sha to unload her ammunition and to take on the gear necessary for the ship's forthcoming operations.

Joining the Amphibious Ready Group once again, *Terrell County* operated off My Thuy, Vietnam, from 15 March to 12 April before retiring to Subic Bay. She rendezvoused with *Valley Forge* (LPH–8) off Vietnam on 29 April for operations on station in area "Alice." Subsequently sailing for Hong Kong on 12 May for a five-day visit, *Terrell County* headed for Buckner Bay, Okinawa, to deliver cargo from Danang before moving to Yokosuka for an overhaul which lasted through the summer of 1968. Training and drills occupied the ship well into the fall of that year, before she proceeded back to Vietnam.

From 1 to 7 December, *Terrell County* conducted general drills and gunnery exercises before beaching at Vung Tau to load ammunition. On 10 December, the LST relieved *Washoe County* as support LST for Task Force 115 on Operation "Market Time," the interdiction operation attempting to interrupt North Vietnamese logistics operations in South Vietnamese coastal waters.

On 1 January 1969, *Terrell County* was assigned additional duty as support ship for the fast PCF boats which were aptly nicknamed "swift boats" engaged in riverine operations off the lower Ca Mau peninsula.

Three days after undertaking this duty, the LST launched her LCVP's to participate in an assault north of Song Ong Doc, in conjunction with PCF's and Song Ong Duc regional forces. When Viet Cong gunners opened up on the Allied force, *Terrell County* returned the fire, killing five Viet Cong soldiers and assisting in the successful withdrawal of the assault forces.

Terrell County then participated in other operations against the Viet Cong, firing on positions along the banks of the Song Bo De and Duong Keo rivers, coordinating PCF's, aircraft, and ships' batteries in firing on Viet Cong concentrations and staging areas. As a result of these operations, Viet Cong extortion from local Vietnamese foresters and fishermen in the lower Ca Mau peninsula was substantially, albeit temporarily, curtailed. Relieved as "Market Time" support LST, *Terrell County* got underway on 5 February 1969 for the Philippines and arrived at Subic Bay six days later.

Training and local operations in Japanese, Okinawan, and Philippine waters preceded yet another Vietnam deployment which commenced upon arrival at Vung Tau on 8 May. The next day, the ship relieved *Westchester County* and found that the tempo of operations in the lower Ca Mau peninsula had increased. With 50 men of the Mobile Strike Force embarked, as well as an Army scout helicopter and an Underwater Demolition Team (UDT) detachment, *Terrell County* provided support for multifaceted operations designed to destroy Viet Cong factories, training and supply camps, and extortion stations. She remained on station in the Ca Mau region until 25 June. A visit to Hong Kong from 8 to 24 July preceded the ship's sailing for Yokosuka and upkeep.

The ship subsequently carried causeways to Danang, Vietnam, before resuming duties as support LST for continued interdiction and pacification operations at her old haunt, Ca Mau. From 10 October to 25 November, *Terrell County* supported Operation "Seafloat." With an embarked helicopter detachment, the ship undertook refueling and rearming of helicopters, and provided ammunition and services for PCF's, SEAL teams, and troops.

The ship also undertook small boat and PCF maintenance, as well as providing numerous personal services—laundry and small stores, to name but two. During this period, *Terrell County* established regular mail deliveries to off-shore units by helicopter—the first such services provided in the Ca Mau vicinity. On 15 October, the LST fired a gunfire-support mission against Viet Cong vessels.

On 25 November, *Vernon County* (LST–1161) came

alongside; and *Terrell County* entrusted her "Seafloat" support duties to the newcomer before sailing for Danang. Loading troops and equipment on 30 November, she got underway on 1 December to neutralize a threatened mortar attack before returning and refueling from SS *Hampton Roads.*

Terrell County then returned again to Vung Tau, relieving *Washoe County* as "Seafloat" support vessel, providing fuel, ammunition, and communications support for a brood of smaller craft. She also assisted *Krishna* (ARL–38) by receiving that ship's stores from provision ships and delivering them, and by also serving as a platform upon which *Krishna's* mail and spare parts could be helicoptered in. *Terrell County* also provided repair and maintenance services for PCF's and smaller craft, such as PCR's. She remained at this duty through the spring of 1970.

When American forces invaded Cambodia in the spring of 1970, to deal with troublesome communist "sanctuaries" in the "parrot's beak" area, *Terrell County* operated as "contingency LST" from 17 to 19 May 1970. She then proceeded to Danang to pick up equipment and a "Seabee" causeway section for transport to Yokosuka. Soon after reaching her home port, she commenced an upkeep period which lasted until 1 August.

A trip to Hong Kong and a final deployment to Vietnam rounded out the ship's stay in the Far East. On 1 October, the Panama-registered freighter SS *Tung Yang* lost all power and wallowed in heavy seas. *Terrell County* and *Washoe County* went to the ship's assistance, and *Terrell County* passed a towline to the vessel. By midafternoon on 2 October, *Tung Yang* rode at the end of the towline but, late the next day, the tow parted, and the freighter was once again adrift. *Deliver* (ARS–23), also in the area, soon retrieved the tow, and thus allowed *Terrell County* to proceed for Chu Lai.

After loading retrograde Marine and Navy vehicles, the ship sailed on 6 October for Subic Bay. Arriving on 8 October, the LST took on supplies and got underway on the 9th in company with sister ship *Washoe County* and three MSC's. The two LST's provided support services for these craft during the long voyage to the west coast.

The little convoy arrived at San Diego on Armistice Day, 11 November 1970. After offloading her cargo on the 13th, *Terrell County* proceeded to San Francisco for four days liberty before continuing northward. She reached Bremerton, Wash., on 24 November and was placed in "In Commission in Reserve" status. Her inactivation work lasted into the new year. On 25 March 1971, *Terrell County* was decommissioned at the Puget Sound Naval Shipyard, Bremerton, and placed in the Reserve Fleet there. She was berthed at Pier "D"—Inactive Ship Facility, Bremerton. The LST was sold to Greece in March 1977.

Terrell County received 12 engagement stars for her Vietnam service, as well as the Presidential Unit Citation, the Navy Unit Commendation, and three Meritorious Unit Commendations.

Terrier

I

(Sch.: t. 6; a. 3 guns)

The first *Terrier*, a schooner, was purchased in 1822 at Baltimore, Md., for service in Commodore David Porter's "Mosquito Fleet" in conjunction with the campaign to suppress the West Indian pirates; outfitted at Norfolk, Va., during the latter part of the year; and probably commissioned sometime early in 1823, Lt. Robert M. Rose in command.

Terrier departed Hampton Roads with the other ships of Porter's squadron on 15 February 1823. The ships reached St. Thomas on 3 March and, the follow-

ing day, began patrolling the coast of Puerto Rico. For the next two years, she operated out of the depot Porter established at what is now Key West, Fla. Her area of concentration was the northern coasts of Cuba and Puerto Rico where havens for the pirates abounded and Spanish authority—weakened by the struggle against her former colonies in Central and South America—proved almost non-existent.

Terrier and the seven other shallow-draft schooners acquired at Baltimore were ideally suited to the work of exploring the coastal shallows and shoal waters where the pirates sought refuge and whence they ventured to commit their depredations. That work occupied the ship throughout her brief Navy career. Over the next two years, she remained almost continually on station even during the two outbreaks of yellow fever—in the fall of 1823 and the summer of 1824—which sent the majority of the squadron's ships north to healthier latitudes. Undoubtedly, she participated in many of the small expeditions and skirmishes of the squadron, but there is only one documented instance of the schooner's capturing a prize. That event occurred early in 1824 when she succeeded in retaking a French ship which had been seized by pirates. Unfortunately, the pirate crew escaped ashore to Spanish territory, a refuge into which Americans could not pursue them. The schooner operated in the West Indies until 1825, the year in which a slackening in seaborne piracy enabled the Navy to begin disposing of its special purpose ships on the West Indies station. *Terrier* was one of the ships sold—presumably at auction—during that year.

II

(SP–960: l. 40'; b. 9'; dr. 5'7" (forward); s. 22 mph.; cpl. 9; a. 1 1-pdr., 1 mg.)

The second *Terrier* (SP–960)—a motorboat built by the Great Lakes Boat Building Corp.—was placed in commission on 1 June 1917, although the Navy did not formally acquire her from Mr. Paul Armstrong of Chicago, Ill., until 19 July 1917. Assigned to the 9th Naval District, *Terrier* patrolled the waters of Lake Michigan through the end of World War I. On 10 March 1919, she was returned to her owner; and her name was struck from the Navy list.

Terror

Terror—a screw tug built in 1861 at St. Louis, Mo.—was transferred from the War Department to the Navy on 30 September 1862 and renamed *Ivy* (q.v.).

I

(Mon: dp. 3,295; l. 250'; b. 53'8"; dph. 15'; s. 8.5 k.; cpl. 150; a. 4 15" D.sb.; cl. *Miantonomoh*)

Agamenticus (later renamed *Terror*)—a twin-screw, double-turreted, ironclad monitor—was laid down sometime in 1862 by the Portsmouth (N.H.) Navy Yard; and launched on 19 March 1863. Prior to her commissioning, the ship received an additional deck amidships, extending between the two turrets and over the machinery spaces. This "hurricane deck," added during 1864, provided better ship control and navigational facilities which wartime experience had shown was needed by monitor-type ships. *Agamenticus* was commissioned on 5 May at Portsmouth, Lt. Comdr. C. H. Cushman in command.

Agamenticus operated off the northeast coast of the United States from Maine to Massachusetts until she was decommissioned at the Boston Navy Yard on 30 September 1865. She remained laid-up at Boston for nearly five years. Renamed *Terror* on 15 June 1869, the monitor joined the North Atlantic Fleet on 27 May

1870. She primarily operated between Key West, Fla., and Havana, Cuba, over the next two years. During this time, the monitor and other units of the North Atlantic Squadron stood ready to protect American interests during unrest in Cuba and the West Indies. Early in 1870, the monitor steamed north to join a small, *ad hoc* squadron being formed under the aging Admiral Farragut to take part in funeral services for George Peabody who had died in London. The remains of the well-known merchant and philanthropist were being returned to the United States by HMS *Monarch* escorted by United States corvette *Plymouth*. The American warships met the British turreted battleship off the New England coast late in January and escorted her into the harbor at Portland, Maine. The American ships then proceeded to Boston. Superintending the funeral service was Admiral Farragut's final official duty.

Terror remained with the North Atlantic Fleet until relieved on station at Key West by the single-turreted monitor *Saugus* on 17 May 1872. *Terror*, towed by the tug *Powhatan*, headed north for Philadelphia where she was placed out of commission and laid up on 10 June 1872. The ship then remained in ordinary at League Island into 1874.

During this time, from 1872 to 1874, her deterioration progressively worsened, with dry rot eating away her timbers. She was broken up in 1874 to be nominally rebuilt at Philadelphia by William Cramp and Sons.

II

(Monitor No. 4: dp. 3,990; l. 263'1''; b. 55'6''; dr. 14'8'' (mean); s. 12 k.; cpl. 150; a. 4 10'' blr., 2 4'', 2 6-pdrs., 2 3-pdrs., 2 1-pdrs.; cl. *Amphitrite*)

Terror (Monitor No. 4)—the totally rebuilt version of the earlier monitor of the same name—was an iron-hulled, twin-screw, double-turreted monitor, laid down in 1874 at Philadelphia, Pa., by William Cramp and Sons. Her construction progressed over the next three years until suspended in 1877. Work was resumed six years later, and the monitor was launched on 24 March 1883.

Delivered to the Navy in 1887, the still-unfinished warship was taken to the New York Navy Yard for completion. Over the next seven years, she fitted out at a snail's pace. *Terror* was finally commissioned at New York on 15 April 1896, with Capt. P. F. Harrington in command.

Assigned to the North Atlantic Squadron, *Terror* operated off the east coast of the United States, from Tompkinsville, N.Y., to Hampton Roads and Fort Monroe, Va.; and from Sandy Hook, N.J., to Charleston, S.C., through the winter of 1897 and 1898. The mysterious explosion which wrecked the battleship *Maine* at Havana Harbor on 15 February 1898 materially increased tensions between the United States and Spain. *Terror* sped south from Tompkinsville to join the fleet concentrating in southern waters and arrived at Key West on 2 April 1898.

On 22 April, after receiving orders from President William McKinley, Rear Admiral William T. Sampson, commanding the North Atlantic Squadron from *New York* (Armored Cruiser No. 2), deployed his fleet in preparation for a blockade of the Cuban coast. Three days later, the United States declared war on Spain. *Terror*, which had arrived off Cardenas, Cuba, on the 24th, captured a Cuban vessel—*Almansas*—on the first day of hostilities, but later released her. Over the next two days, the monitor took two Spanish ships, *Ambrosia Bolivar* and *Guido*, and sent the prizes to Florida.

Meanwhile, the whereabouts of the Spanish fleet under Admiral Cervera prompted concern in naval circles in Washington. Intelligence estimates which reached Sampson noted that the Spanish fleet had departed the Cape Verde Islands on the morning of 29 April. Sampson reacted by deciding to meet Cervera's fleet at San Juan, Puerto Rico, the nearest Spanish base in the West Indies. With his flag in *New York*, Rear Admiral Sampson scraped together a makeshift squadron—which included *Terror* and a sistership, *Amphitrite* (Monitor No. 2), as well as battleships *Iowa* (Battleship No. 4) and *Indiana* (Battleship No. 1), *Porter* (Torpedo Boat No. 6), two auxiliaries and a collier—and departed Key West on 3 May.

Terror and *Amphitrite* broke down frequently en route and materially delayed Sampson's passage. At one point, *New York* took both *Terror* and *Porter* in tow. Upon arrival off San Juan on 12 May, the Americans found no Spanish ships in the harbor. In order to "develop their positions and strength," Sampson decided to conduct a brief bombardment of the shore defenses. The squadron stood in for their target at 0400, on 12 May 1898, with the ships cleared for action and the lights of the town clearly visible in the predawn darkness. Sounding general quarters at 0500, the Americans opened fire within 15 minutes, and the Spanish began returning fire at 0523.

Terror stood in, fifth in column, duelling with the Spanish shore batteries in a spirited engagement for the next three hours. As the action wore on, a tremendous volume of white smoke restricted visibility and caused the Admiral to signal "use large guns only" to cut down on the volume of smoke.

Terror expended 31 10-inch shells in three firing passes against the fortifications at San Juan, and scored a direct hit on a battery which the monitor's commanding officer, Capt. Nicholl Ludlow, considered "the most vicious." *Terror*, which had moved close inshore to gain a better firing position, kept up a spirited fire until 0815, when she broke off action and rejoined Sampson's squadron retiring to the northwest.

The monitor subsequently resumed her cruising operations in the West Indies and off Puerto Rico for the duration of hostilities with Spain, into September of 1898. At the conclusion of the "Splendid Little War," *Terror* sailed north for Hampton Roads. Placed in reserve at Norfolk on 18 October 1898, the monitor was decommissioned and placed in ordinary on 25 February 1899.

Taken to Annapolis, Md., late in 1901, *Terror* was recommissioned for service at the Naval Academy and subsequently served as a practice ship for midshipmen. She conducted a summer midshipman cruise in 1905. Later taken up to Philadelphia, Pa., *Terror* was placed in reserve on 11 September 1905 and was decommissioned and laid up at League Island on 8 May 1906.

Struck from the Navy list on 31 December 1915, *Terror* lay at Indianhead, Md., as a test hulk at the Naval Proving Grounds, before being placed on the sale list in June 1920. Although sold for scrap iron on 10 March 1921, *Terror* sank off Shooter's Island, N.Y., sometime in the 1920's. Records indicate that the hulk was raised by the Sorenson Wrecking Company in early 1930, while operating under contract with the Navy. This hulk was presumably scrapped soon thereafter.

III

(CM–5: dp. 5,875; l. 454'10''; b. 60'2''; dr. 19'7''; s. 20.3 k.; cpl. 481; a. 4 5'', 16 1.1'', 14 20mm.; cl. *Terror*)

Terror (CM–5) was laid down on 3 September 1940 by the Philadelphia Navy Yard; launched on 6 June 1941; sponsored by Mrs. Ralph A. Bard; and commissioned on 15 July 1942, Comdr. Howard Wesley Fitch in command.

Following fitting out and shakedown, *Terror*—the Navy's only minelayer built specifically for minelaying—arrived at New York on 30 October 1942 to prepare for her first large-scale operation. With Task Group 38.3, the new minelayer sortied the harbor on 2 November and set her course for North Africa. Rain squalls, strong winds, and heavy seas forced the convoy to alter its course, but its goal remained the same—the support and reinforcement of Operation "Torch."

The large minelayer *Terror* (CM–5), the only ship of her type built by the U.S. Navy during World War II. (80–G–411681)

At dawn on 14 November, *Terror* parted company with the convoy and, escorted by a single destroyer, made her way at 20 knots to the newly taken port of Casablanca. Sunken ships added to the congestion of the harbor as *Terror* fueled *Miantonomah* (CM–10) and supplied that vessel with mines. *Terror* then prepared for her primary mission at Casablanca and the task for which she had been designed, minelaying. Her sortie was delayed on the morning of the 16th due to continued congestion in the harbor. Later, as *Terror*'s crew made ready to get underway, they discovered that a large, "old fashioned" anchor with a heavy chain was fouling the ship's starboard anchor chain. After correcting this problem, *Terror* got underway in company with two minesweepers and, in short order, began laying the minefield which would protect the ships in the harbor. When completed, shortly before dark the same day, the minefield provided Allied shipping a protected channel entrance to Casablanca, stretching seven miles out from El Hank Light, a formidable barrier for any marauding enemy submarine to penetrate. Steaming at 16 knots, *Terror* made her way back to the port just as night fell.

On the following day, despite the obstacles imposed by rudimentary receiving facilities on shore and an extreme shortage of lighters, *Terror* unloaded her cargo of depth charges and ammunition, using a salvaged tank lighter and several wooden barges. Having accomplished her mission, *Terror* departed Casablanca and rendezvoused with a convoy bound for the east coast of the United States. Strong head winds, heavy seas, and the slowness of the convoy made it difficult for *Terror* to keep her station. Off the Virginia Capes, *Terror* was detached from the convoy and made for the Naval Mine Depot, Yorktown. She arrived on 30 November to commence overhaul and training.

In the months that followed, *Terror* operated out of Yorktown, making frequent voyages to the Chesapeake Bay for exercises and occasionally stopping at Norfolk for repairs or overhaul. Often students from the Mine

Warfare Training Facility came on board for instruction tours. Meanwhile, members of *Terror*'s crew, when not attending classes ashore, participated in drills, training, and exercises in gunnery, mine warfare, and damage control. In February, the minelayer assisted *Nuthatch* (AM–60) as that vessel tested the Mark 10 "hedgehog" off Yorktown. After receiving additional antiaircraft guns in May, *Terror* participated in tactical exercises in the Chesapeake Bay through the summer.

Late in September, she began loading mines in preparation for her departure from the Atlantic coast. At Norfolk, she rendezvoused with Task Unit 29.2.5; and, on 2 October, she got underway for the Canal Zone and Pacific ports. On the morning of 19 October, she passed under the Golden Gate Bridge and anchored in San Francisco Bay. The next day, she departed the west coast and steamed via Pearl Harbor to the Ellice Islands.

She arrived at Funafuti on 9 November, unloaded pontoon barges, and took on fresh water. During the nearly three weeks she remained at Funafuti, *Terror* supported the many small craft which surveyed and mined the approaches to the atoll, supplying them with provisions, water, repairs, and medical services. At the same time, she assisted in the conversion of a 1,500-ton covered lighter into a barracks for a construction battalion, sending skilled personnel to speed the work and providing water and mess facilities for the battalion until the task was completed. On the 17th, *Terror*'s gunners fired on the enemy for the first time when Japanese planes bombed the runway on Funafuti. The Japanese raiders dropped 40 bombs near the airstrip, causing a fire which burned for an hour. Another alert followed in the afternoon, but no further action occurred. *Terror* laid mooring buoys in the anchorage before getting underway for Hawaii on 28 November.

Early in December, she loaded mines and gear at Pearl Harbor; then set her course for Tarawa, where she provided heavy equipment and mines for mine details. At night, searchlights from shore combed the dark, spotting enemy planes in an attempt to foil the persistent Japanese raiders.

On Christmas day, *Terror* got underway. She delivered mines and heavy equipment to units at Espiritu Santo and Guadalcanal before arriving at Makin Island on 18 January 1944. The minelayer anchored in the lagoon while her boats surveyed the passes in the reef. She then readied a self-propelled barge to mine the channels. She departed Makin on the 28th and proceeded independently to Tarawa where she embarked Mine Detail 19. On the last day of January, she got underway for Pearl Harbor and took on passengers for transportation to San Francisco. After a three-day stay, she departed the west coast on 21 February with over 500 passengers on board, accommodated on a temporary wooden deck constructed over the tracks on the mine deck. She discharged her passengers at Pearl Harbor on the 26th; then steamed on to Majuro, where she arrived on 10 March.

During the rest of March and into April, she conducted minelaying operations in the Marshalls before getting underway for the Hawaiian Islands on 22 April. There, she underwent repairs, loaded mines, and participated in gunnery exercises before departing on 24 May. In the following months, she carried ammunition, mines, and bombs to the Marshalls and Marianas, returning once to Pearl Harbor to load ammunition. On 17 August, she departed Oahu—this time setting her course for the west coast. *Terror* arrived at San Francisco on the 24th for drydocking and overhaul. On 9 September, she got underway carrying a cargo of ammunition. After loading mines and minesweeping gear at Pearl Harbor, she steamed to Ulithi where she began defensive mining operations.

On 15 October, *Terror* was transferred from ServRon 6 to Minecraft Pacific Fleet. During October and November, she carried cargos to the Marianas, Carolines, and Admiralties. On 25 November, she entered the Navy Yard at Pearl Harbor for repairs and alterations to accommodate the staff of Commander, Minecraft Pacific Fleet. On 6 January 1945, *Terror* assumed duty as the flagship of Rear Admiral Alexander Sharp.

For two weeks, *Terror* conducted exercises out of Pearl Harbor. Then, on 22 January, she got underway and proceeded via Eniwetok to the Carolines. At Ulithi, *Terror* supplied mines and gear to minecraft preparing for the invasion of Iwo Jima. She then steamed on to Tinian to act as tender for minecraft in that second staging area. On 13 February, she departed the Marianas setting her course for the Volcano Islands.

At 0717 on 17 February, *Terror* arrived in the fire support area off the east coast of Iwo Jima. Pre-assault bombardment and minesweeping were well underway when fire from guns on the cliff-lined shore began to interfere with minesweepers operating close inshore, north of the eastern beaches. *Terror* closed the shore to 10,000 yards and, for 20 minutes, added her five-inch gunfire to the bombardment in an attempt to aid the small craft. Nevertheless, the formidable barrage put out by the enemy began to take its toll as first *Pensacola* (CA-24) and then *Leutze* (DD-481) suffered hits. Shortly after noon, damaged landing craft began coming alongside the tender for assistance. *Terror* acted as a casualty evacuation vessel for minesweepers and small craft acting in support of underwater demolition teams. Soon her medical facilities were severely taxed. One after another of these small craft came alongside to transfer their wounded and to receive assistance in repairing their vessels. *Terror* continued her duties off Iwo Jima until 1835 on 19 February when she headed for the Marianas.

On 21 February, she transferred battle casualties to an Army hospital at Saipan; then steamed to Ulithi, where she arrived on the 23d. At that base, she serviced and supplied minecraft staging for the assault on Okinawa. She arrived off Kerama Retto on 24 March to act as flagship and tender for minecraft. *Terror* operated off Kerama Retto until the morning of the 29th when she anchored in that island's harbor. There, despite the constant danger of kamikaze attacks, she performed her dual role as tender and flagship. Her entire complement labored long hours to maintain the supply of water, oil, gear, and ammunition required by minecraft in the area. At the same time, her resources were further strained by the duties imposed by her status as flagship.

On the morning of 2 April 1945, Japanese planes penetrated the harbor. *Terror* took two of the attackers under fire and witnessed the splashing of one plane only 600 yards away. In the following days, *Terror*—responding to warnings to be prepared for attacks by Japanese planes, swimmers, and suicide boats—stationed special night sentries on deck and in a picket boat to intercept any ingenious attackers. Predicted mass air attacks materialized on 6 April when Japanese planes pounded the harbor at Kerama Retto for four hours, coming in on *Terror* from all quarters and keeping her gunners busy. The tender joined other ships in downing two Japanese planes and furnished rescue boats, clothing, and treatment for the survivors of *LST-447* and SS *Logan Victory*.

Throughout April, *Terror* remained at Kerama Retto providing logistic services and receiving casualties from ships hit by kamikazes. Combat air patrols kept raiders outside the harbor most of the time; but, on 28 April, *Pinckney* (APH-2)—anchored nearby—was hit by a suicide plane. *Terror* fired on the enemy aircraft, sent boats to *Pinckney*'s aid, and treated many casualties. During the long and arduous month of April, *Terror*'s crew went to general quarters 93 times, for periods ranging from seven minutes to six and one-half hours.

Minutes before 0400 on 1 May 1945, as *Terror* lay at anchor in Kerama Retto, a kamikaze dove toward the ship. Darting through a hole in the smoke screen and coming in on *Terror*'s port beam, the attacker banked sharply around the stern, then came in from the starboard quarter so rapidly that only one of the minelayer's stern guns opened fire. As the plane crashed into the ship's communication platform, one of its bombs exploded. The other penetrated the main deck before it, too, exploded. The aircraft's engine tore through the ship's bulkheads to land in the wardroom. Fire flared immediately in the superstructure but was soon controlled and, within two hours, was extinguished. Flooding of the magazines prevented possible explosions, and no engineering damage occurred, but the kamikaze had exacted its toll. The attack cost *Terror* 171 casualties: 41 dead, 7 missing, and 123 wounded.

The following day, the battered ship was moored to *Natrona* (APA-214) for emergency repairs. She got underway on the 8th to rendezvous with a convoy bound for Saipan. Since a survey of the vessel revealed that her damage was too great to be repaired in a forward area, *Terror* steamed via Eniwetok and Pearl Harbor to the west coast. She reached San Francisco on 1 June 1945, unloaded ammunition, and then began her overhaul.

Her repairs completed, she departed San Francisco Bay on 15 August and steamed for Korea via the Hawaiian Islands, Saipan, and Okinawa. Moored in Buckner Bay on 16 September, she weathered a furious typhoon. Pounding against *Patoka* (AO-9) put a few holes in *Terror*'s side, but she was soon repaired. On 9 October, while still at Okinawa, she emerged undamaged from another typhoon which beached or wrecked over 100 vessels at Buckner Bay and Unten Ko.

In December, *Panamint* (AGC-13) replaced *Terror* as flagship for Minecraft Pacific Fleet, and the veteran of many Pacific campaigns again crossed the Pacific to arrive at San Francisco in February. She made one voyage to Pearl Harbor in March, then returned to the west coast. *Terror* remained there until February 1947 when she departed San Francisco and steamed through the Panama Canal to embark the Commander, Minecraft Atlantic Fleet, at San Juan late in February. Following exercises in the Caribbean, she operated out of east coast ports until July 1947 when she arrived at the Charleston Navy Yard for inactivation. During the

Korean War, she was placed in service in reserve; and, on 7 February 1955, she was redesignated a fleet mine-layer (MM–5). Her designation symbol was changed to MMF–5 in October 1955, and she was decommissioned on 6 August 1956. In 1971, her hulk was sold to the Union Minerals and Alloys Corporation, of New York City.

Terror received four battle stars for World War II service.

Terry

Edward Terry—born at Hartford, Conn., on 24 January 1839—was appointed midshipman at the Naval Academy on 21 September 1853 and graduated on 10 June 1857. He served in the sloop *Germantown*, attached to the East India Squadron, from 1857 to 1859. By 1861, he was assigned to the steam sloop *Richmond* and served in her with the Western Gulf Blockading Squadron throughout the Civil War. He participated in the engagement with the Confederate ram *Manassas* on 12 October 1861, the artillery duel with Fort McRae and other shore batteries on 22 November, the passage of Forts Jackson and St. Philip, and the capture of New Orleans in late April 1862.

After New Orleans, Farragut's force moved up the Mississippi, and Terry was present when the salt water fleet ran the gauntlet at Vicksburg and joined Flag Officer C. H. Davis' riverine fleet above the Southern stronghold. In January 1863, Terry was promoted to lieutenant commander. On 14 March, his ship joined others of the fleet in bombarding the batteries surrounding Port Hudson so that Farragut could dash past them and establish a blockade cutting the Confederacy's Red River supply line. In his last major engagement, the Battle of Mobile Bay on 5 August 1864, Terry helped to close the last major Conferedrate port on the Gulf of Mexico.

Following the Civil War, Terry alternated between sea duty and a series of shore assignments at the Naval Academy. In 1866 and 1867, he served in the Pacific Squadron in the steam frigate *Powhatan*. His first tour of duty at the Naval Academy followed in 1868 and 1869. He assumed his first command, *Saco*, in 1870 and cruised with the Asiatic Fleet until 1872. During that assignment, on 30 October 1871, he was promoted to commander. He returned to the Naval Academy in 1873 and, by 1875, was appointed Commandant of Cadets,

a post he held until 1878. Comdr. Terry was then ordered to the Pacific Squadron as flag captain in *Pensacola;* first to Rear Admiral C. R. Perry Rodgers and, in 1880 and 1881, to Rear Admiral Thomas H. Stevens. In 1881, he went on leave due to illness. On 1 June 1882, Comdr. Terry died at Manitou Springs, Colo.

I

(Torpedo Boat Destroyer No. 25: dp. 887 (full); l. 293'10''; b. 26'1½'' (wl.); dr. 10'11'' (aft); s. 30.24 k. (tl.); cpl. 89; a. 5 3'', 2 .30-cal. mg., 6 18'' tt.; cl. *Roe*)

The first *Terry* (Torpedo Boat Destroyer No. 25) was laid down on 8 February 1909 at Newport News, Va., by the Newport News Shipbuilding Co.; launched on 21 August 1909; sponsored by Mrs. George Henry Rock; and commissioned on 18 October 1910, Lt. Comdr. Martin E. Trench in command.

Following trials off the east coast, *Terry* joined the Atlantic Fleet Torpedo Flotilla in winter operations in Cuban waters. She conducted both torpedo exercises with the flotilla and general maneuvers with the Fleet as a whole. The routine of winter maneuvers in the Caribbean alternated with spring and summer operations along the New England coast continued until November 1913, when the torpedo boat destroyer arrived at Charleston, S.C., for overhaul.

Soon after entering the navy yard there, *Terry* was placed in reserve. Though still in reserve after her overhaul was completed, *Terry* continued to be active. During 1914, she cruised the coast of Florida; and, by February 1915, she was back in Cuban waters for winter maneuvers. That summer, *Terry* steamed as far north as Newport, R.I., to conduct another round of torpedo exercises. Upon completion of the mission, she returned to her base at Charleston.

By 1 January 1916, the torpedo boat destroyer was operating with a reduced complement destroyer division. On the 31st, she cruised with units of the Atlantic Fleet to Key West, Fla. In May, she steamed from there to Santo Domingo. On 10 June, while maneuvering in the inner harbor at Puerto Plata, she struck a reef and settled until the greater part of the main deck was submerged. On the 13th, under the supervision of the commanding officer of *Sacramento* (Gunboat No. 19), *Terry's* officers and men joined the staff of a wreck-

Terry (DD–25) during builders' trials. Her guns and torpedo tubes have not yet been installed.

ing company in salvage operations. The warship was refloated on 26 July, temporarily repaired by 7 July, and returned to the Charleston Navy Yard on 15 July.

America's entry into World War I saw *Terry* undergoing extensive repairs at Charleston. Upon completion of the yard work, she began duty patrolling along the Atlantic coast and escorting merchantmen bound for Europe. In January 1918, *Terry* put to sea for operations with the destroyer force based at Queenstown, Ireland. There, she escorted convoys through the submarine-infested waters surrounding the British Isles. Her tour of duty at Queenstown was a relatively peaceful, though rigorous, one. While she never sighted a German U-boat nor engaged in combat operations, on one voyage she escorted a convoy which lost one ship to a submarine. On another occasion, on 19 March 1918, she assisted *Manley* (Destroyer No. 74) with casualties after that destroyer was damaged by an accidental depth charge explosion.

In December 1918, *Terry* returned to the United States; and, after 11 months of extremely limited service, she was decommissioned at the Philadelphia Navy Yard on 13 November 1919. She remained there until she was transferred to the Coast Guard on 7 June 1924. She served in the Coast Guard until 18 October 1930, when she was returned to the Navy and restored on the Navy list in a decommissioned status, listed as a "vessel to be disposed of by sale or salvage." On 2 May 1934, *Terry* was sold for scrapping. Her name was struck from the Navy list on 28 June 1934.

II

(DD–513: dp. 2,050; l. 376'6"; b. 39'8"; dr. 17'9"; s. 37 k.; cpl. 273; a. 5 5", 4 1.1", 6 20mm., 10 21" tt., 6 dcp., 2 dct.; cl. *Fletcher*)

The second *Terry* (DD–513) was laid down at Bath, Maine, on 8 June 1942 by the Bath Iron Works; launched on 22 November 1942; sponsored by Mrs. Charles Nagel, Jr., and commissioned at the Boston Navy Yard on 26 January 1943, Comdr. George R. Phelan in command.

After outfitting at Boston in February and shakedown training off Guantanamo Bay, the destroyer returned to Boston for post-shakedown availability. On 2 April, she shifted from Boston to Norfolk. Two days later, she headed north to Argentia, Newfoundland, in the screen of a convoy. *Terry* arrived there on the 8th and departed the following day. She stopped at Portland, Maine, on the 11th to refuel and, the following day, commenced antisubmarine operations off the northeastern coast of the United States.

On 18 April, she had a run-in with a German U-boat. First, *Terry* dropped a pattern of depth charges on a sound contact and waited for results. Then her sonar detected a torpedo running straight for her bow. *Terry* turned to avoid it, and the deadly missile passed astern. Soon thereafter, the destroyer sighted an oil slick and debris and ended the encounter by joining *Brownson* (DD–518) in a futile search for the damaged enemy submarine. On the 20th, the warship put into Narragansett Bay for a few hours to take on fuel and supplies before resuming patrol. She later rescued survivors of a downed Army bomber and put them ashore at New York on 23 April.

Following another brief patrol and a visit to New York City, *Terry* departed the United States on 1 May in the screen of Task Force 67, bound for North Africa. After a stop at Bermuda, the destroyer headed singly for Casablanca, where she arrived on the 12th and commenced a week of repairs and battle practice. On the 19th, she steamed out of Casablanca and headed homeward in company with *Texas* (BB–35). Arriving at the Boston Navy Yard on 31 May, the destroyer entered dry dock. She was refloated on 9 June and got underway the same day. She stopped briefly at Casco Bay, Maine, and at Norfolk, Va., before continuing on to the British West Indies. The destroyer

reached Trinidad on 20 June and spent the ensuing nine days on antisubmarine patrols and in gunnery practice. She departed Trinidad on 29 June, bound for the Philadelphia Navy Yard. Almost at her destination on 3 July, she was ordered to report to Norfolk where she arrived the same day.

Three days later, she put to sea in company with *Yorktown* (CV–10), *Dashiell* (DD–659), and *McKee* (DD–575). The three warships reached the Panama Canal on 10 July. Two days later, *Terry*, *Yorktown*, *McKee*, and *Sigsbee* (DD–502) set out for Hawaii. They arrived in Pearl Harbor on the 24th, and *Terry* conducted exercises in the waters around Hawaii until mid-August. On 19 August, she departed Pearl Harbor for the southwestern Pacific. Steaming with *Fullam* (DD–474) and *Guest* (DD–472), she stopped at Suva, Fiji Islands, before arriving in Havannah harbor, Efate Island, in the New Hebrides on 6 September. After a visit to Noumea, New Caledonia, she returned to Efate briefly before taking up duty in the Solomon Islands late that month.

Terry entered the torturous Solomons campaign late, in mid-September 1943. She saw only the final five months of the campaign and participated in its last two amphibious operations. Her primary missions during her tour of duty in the Solomons consisted of escorting supply convoys and interdicting Japanese barge traffic to keep the enemy from evacuating his bypassed and otherwise useless troops. Infrequently, she also left the Solomons area to visit New Caledonia, either escorting ships there or for availability.

Her first combat in the Solomons came early in October. On the 2d, she was ordered up the "Slot" between Choiseul and Kolombangara along with *Foote* (DD–511), *Converse* (DD–509), and *Jenkins* (DD–447). Their mission was to intercept barges loaded with enemy evacuees from Kolombangara. Before opening the attack, she and her three sister destroyers waited for the enemy to move well out from the island. They sighted their targets at 2114. The four destroyers turned a wide circle to starboard and, five minutes later, opened fire.

Terry fired one salvo, and her fire-direction radar went out. Three minutes later, she ceased fire and commenced repairs. Swiftly, her radarmen restored "sight" to her guns, and *Terry* resumed her barrage almost immediately. The enemy boats returned fire, but *Terry* and the other destroyers pounded them until they disappeared from the radar screen. A bit later, more barges, escorted by a *Wakatake*-class destroyer, hove into sight. *Terry* and her colleagues fired a salvo and launched a spread of torpedoes. The Japanese returned fire, but the torpedoes forced them to cease fire and alter course toward the American warships. Meanwhile, the American destroyers, who had also ceased gunfire in order to launch torpedoes, opened up again with their five-inch batteries. Enemy return fire grew increasingly weaker as they suffered heavily from the American cannonade. *Terry* claimed a straddle on her first salvo, and flashes on the enemy destroyer —thought to be return fire at first—indicated that *Terry*'s salvoes were hitting home. Apparently, Destroyer Division 8's guns had overwhelmed the enemy from the beginning. When the action ended, *Terry* set course for the Gizo Strait.

Terry resumed escort and patrol duties until late in the month. By the beginning of November, she was steaming north again escorting *George Clymer* (APA–27), *Hunter Liggett* (AP–27), and *President Jackson* (AP–37) to Empress Augusta Bay for the Bougainville assault. On 1 November, the day preceding the landings at Cape Torokina, she and *Fullam* fended off an enemy air attack. The gun crews of the little convoy knocked down two of the intruders and scattered the rest. Early the following morning, the troops landed. Terry opened fire at 0545 and continued to support the assault forces throughout the day. The destroyer cleared the area on 3 November and returned south to Florida Island off Guadalcanal.

For the next three months, *Terry* resumed her routine of escorting supply convoys and conducting patrols. She visited Bougainville often and patrolled the Russel and Treasury Islands. The destroyer also made two voyages to Noumea. During the first two weeks in December, she had two scrapes with the enemy. On the 3d, while steaming from Guadalcanal to Bougainville, she came under an almost simultaneous pair of attacks—one from below and one from above. A Japanese submarine fired two torpedoes at her, but she combed their wakes as they passed astern. At almost the same time, enemy fighters swooped in on her. They made several unsuccessful approaches and, after losing one plane to *Terry*'s antiaircraft gunners, abandoned their attack. Eleven days later, she was again making the Bougainville run, and another Japanese plane attempted to attack. *Terry*'s gunfire taught him better manners, and he retired rapidly.

Following more patrols, escort duty, and an availability at Noumea, *Terry* was ordered to cover the last major amphibious operation of the Solomons campaign. She departed Purvis Bay on 13 February 1944, in company with *Braine* (DD–630) and *Warrington* (DD–383). During the landings on 15 February, the three destroyers opened up on an enemy plane, but had to cease fire when he was intercepted by a Marine Corps fighter who "scratched" him. Later, *Terry* and a group of LST's discouraged another Japanese plane, a dive bomber, from pressing home an attack. He remained at extreme range until deciding to clear the area. The destroyer left the Green Islands on 21 February and returned to Tulagi.

Terry's next target was the large Japanese base at Rabaul on New Britain in the Bismark Archipelago. She stood out of Tulagi on 23 February, refueled in the Treasuries, and reached Rabaul just before dawn on the 25th. Her main battery pumped shells into the enemy shore installations in the Vunapore area for 23 minutes. By the time she cleared, at about 0300, several explosions had engulfed the area in a raging fire visible 20 miles out to sea. Her division commander cancelled further bombardment in order to sweep the area of Duke of York Island for a downed pilot. At the conclusion of a futile search, she steamed to New Georgia.

Terry remained in the Southwest Pacific theater for another three months. She screened the task group which carried out the unopposed seizure of Emirau Island on 20 March; then resumed normal patrols and escort duty. On 2 April, she rescued the survivors of a downed B–24. After a liberty call at Sydney, Australia, early in May, she steamed to Efate, where she arrived on the 13th. For the remainder of the month, she conducted exercises with Battleship Division 3, comprised of *Idaho* (BB–42), *New Mexico* (BB–40), and *Pennsylvania* (BB–38).

Terry ended her tour of duty in the Southwest Pacific area early in June 1944 and joined the Central Pacific march. She departed Efate on the 2d with Task Group (TG) 53.14 bound for the Marshall Islands. At Kwajalein Atoll, she joined Admiral Raymond A. Spruance's awesome 5th Fleet. On the 10th, she sortied from the lagoon with elements of that fleet and headed for the Marianas. The first two objectives of the Mariana campaign were Saipan and Tinian. *Terry* was assigned to the Tinian portion of the operation. Her task unit had the dual responsibility of silencing enemy guns on northern Tinian and of rendering Ushi Point airfield useless. She opened fire around 1121 on the morning of 14 June, caused two large explosions, started several fires, and destroyed a radio tower—all at the airfield. That night, she delivered night harassing fire along the west coast of the island.

On the 15th, she returned to bombarding Ushi Point airfield. Later that day, she and *San Francisco* (CA–38) went to the aid of the troops ashore and silenced a Japanese mortar battery that had been responsible for a number of American casualties. Late in the afternoon, after an inconclusive brush with two Japanese

planes, *Terry* retired with her task unit to protect the transports to the south. Before dawn on the 16th, the destroyer joined the screen of battleships *Idaho* and *Pennsylvania* and helped them pound Orote Peninsula on Guam for two hours.

That same day, Admiral Spruance began to concentrate his forces for the imminent Battle of the Philippine Sea. *Terry* was one of the destroyers detached from the screen of Rear Admiral Oldendorf's bombardment group to beef up TF 58's antiaircraft defenses. She joined the screen of TG 58.3 to protect *Enterprise* (CV–6), the veteran of Midway, along with Vice Admiral Mitscher's flagship, *Lexington* (CV–16), *Princeton* (CVL–23), and *San Jacinto* (CV–30).

Steaming just out of range of the American planes, the Japanese played cat and mouse with the 5th Fleet for three days, but Spruance declined to take the bait. Finally, on the 19th, the Japanese launched their attack. The first swarm of enemy raiders never made it to the American ships, and *Terry* did not sight a Japanese plane until 1157 when four of them tried to come in over her quarter. The first, a dive bomber, managed to lay his egg before crashing. The following three torpedo bombers—were not nearly so successful. They made themselves perfect targets approaching low across the destroyer's bow. *Terry*'s gunners teamed up with those of the other ships of the screen to splash each one in succession, before he had an opportunity to release his torpedo. For the remainder of the day, *Terry* saw only unidentified planes at extreme range. The only further excitement occurred just after 1300 when she was rocked by an underwater explosion believed to have been caused by the depth charge of a downed plane.

The Battle of the Philippine Sea, nicknamed the "Great Marianas Turkey Shoot," destroyed the remnants of Japanese carrier-based air power. The occupation of Saipan and Tinian continued unimpaired. *Terry* operated with TG 58.3 until the 22d, when it was apparent that the Japanese were defeated and in full retreat. From that day, 22 June, to 12 July, *Terry* patrolled off Saipan and prowled for submarines. On one occasion, she dropped a pattern of 11 depth charges, but scored no kill. She cleared the Marianas and, on 15 July, entered Eniwetok lagoon. The destroyer patrolled the anchorage against submarines until 17 July when she got underway to return to the Marianas with the Guam invasion force.

The destroyer reached Guam on 22 July, the day after the initial landings, and supported the troops ashore until 10 August. First, she alternated night illumination fire with antisubmarine patrols. Later, she delivered call fire under the direction of spotters stationed ashore. Throughout this period, she delivered night harassing fire and guarded against enemy submarines. On her last day in the Marianas, 10 August, she stood radar picket duty and then sailed for Hawaii.

After a stop at Eniwetok, the warship reached Pearl Harbor on 21 August. There, she made repairs and loaded supplies while her crew enjoyed a bit of shore leave. On 15 September, *Terry* stood out of Pearl Harbor bound for Eniwetok where she arrived on the 30th. Three days later, she departed in the escort of a Ulithi-bound task unit, arriving on 13 October. From there, the destroyer headed back to the United States for overhaul at the Mare Island Navy Yard.

She completed overhaul on 13 December and conducted drills along the coast until the 18th, when she headed west in company with *Missouri* (BB–63). After a brief stop at Pearl Harbor, *Terry* continued her voyage west and rejoined the 5th Fleet at Eniwetok on 5 February. Two days later, she sortied in the screen of the Iwo Jima assault force.

On the morning of 16 February, the destroyer rendezvoused with a group of minesweepers about nine miles south of Iwo Jima. A little after 1000, she opened up on enemy gun emplacements in an effort to protect the minesweepers while they cleared the approaches to the beaches. At about 1432, a Japanese 4-inch gun

The size and appearance of *Terry* (DD–513) are in sharp contrast to those of her predecessor. (80–G–64314)

managed to straddle *Terry*. She rang up speed to 25 knots and lurched ahead while the enemy laid a barrage in her wake. Her 5-inch guns loosed their own salvoes which quickly silenced the offender. Thanks to *Terry*'s gunners, the minesweepers completed their task just after 1600 without losses.

The destroyer cleared the island for the night but returned the following day and resumed counterbattery fire. After the landings on 19 February, she supported the troops ashore with gunfire during the day and screened the ships of Task Force (TF) 54 during the night.

At 0245 on the morning of 1 March, *Terry* was assisting *Capps* (DD–550) in a search for a Japanese submarine, when a low enemy torpedo plane approached her starboard bow. He dropped his torpedo about 1,000 yards from *Terry*. The recognition officer spotted the intruder at precisely that moment and sang out "Torpedo Away." *Terry* leaped ahead at flank speed and came hard right. The torpedo passed harmlessly, 50 yards astern. By 0720, *Terry* was heading for a screening station north of the island. As she passed Kitano Point on the northern coast of Iwo Jima, an enemy battery opened fire and got the destroyer's range immediately. *Terry* responded with her main battery. Her high speed and radical maneuvers did not spoil the enemy's aim and, although eventually silenced, the battery scored a direct hit on the destroyer's starboard main deck. The starboard engine stopped, and *Terry* lost steering control and telephone communications.

Terry opened range with her port engine while *Pensacola* (CA–24), *Nevada* (BB–36), and some destroyers put the shore battery out of action. Ships and boats swarmed to *Terry*'s aid. Medical personnel and repair crews came aboard in surprisingly short order. Her wounded received emergency treatment on board, then were transferrd to hospital ships. *Terry* headed for the southern coast of Iwo Jima where she laid to for two days while undergoing emergency repairs. On 3 March, she cleared the Volcano Islands on the first leg of a long voyage back to the United States.

After interim repairs at Saipan and stops at Eniwetok and Pearl Harbor, she returned to the Mare Island Navy Yard. During the next two months, she received permanent repairs and conducted drills along the California coast. On 13 June, she headed south and briefly conducted exercises in the San Diego area, before escorting *Wasp* (CV–18) to Hawaii. On 11 July, *Terry*, *Wasp*, and *Benner* (DD–807) departed Pearl Harbor to rendezvous with TF 38. For the remaining weeks of the war, she screened the fast carriers during the final raids on the Japanese home islands.

During the months immediately following the end of the war, *Terry* operated in the waters off Japan. She conducted patrols and acted as a courier for the occupation forces. On 1 November, she pointed her bow eastward and headed for home. After a stop at Pearl Harbor, she continued on to San Diego, Calif., where she arrived on 20 November.

For just over a year, *Terry* remained active with the Pacific Fleet, operating out of San Diego. In January 1947, the destroyer was placed out of commission and berthed with the San Diego Group, Pacific Reserve Fleet. *Terry* spent the remainder of her Navy career in reserve, first at San Diego, then at Long Beach, and finally at Bremerton, Wash. Her name was struck from the Navy list on 1 April 1974. She was sold to Peru the following July.

Terry received seven battle stars for her World War II service.

Tesota

A small leguminous tree found in Mexico and the southwestern section of the United States. Also called desert ironwood, the Tesota bears pinnate leaves and purplish white flowers and is known for its extremely hard wood.

(ATA–217: dp. 1,275; l. 194'6''; b. 34'7''; dr. 14'1''; s. 12.1 k.; cpl. 57; a. 2 40mm.; cl. *Palo Blanco*)

ATA–217 was laid down as the net tender *Tesota* (YN–95) on 11 December 1943 at Slidell, La., by the Canulette Shipbuilding Co.; was reclassified a net laying ship and redesignated AN–71 on 20 January 1944; and was launched on 29 July 1944. However, the name *Tesota* was canceled on 10 August 1944, and the ship was reclassified an auxiliary ocean tug and redesignated *ATA–217* on the same day. She was commissioned on 16 January 1945, Lt. H. A. V. Post, USNR, in command.

Following a short shakedown cruise early in February 1945, the tug departed Norfolk for Hawaii and arrived at her home port, Pearl Harbor, on 1 March. After serving there for more than a year, the ship proceeded to the west coast, was decommissioned at Mare Island on 7 May, and was struck from the Navy list on 21 May 1946. *ATA–217* was transferred to the Maritime Commission on 25 March 1947 and was sold the same day to Martinolick Shipbuilding Co., San Francisco.

Teton

A mountain range in the state of Wyoming named for a branch of the Sioux tribe. The word Teton means prairie dweller.

(AGC–14: dp. 13,910; l. 459'2''; b. 63'; dr. 24'; s. 16.4 k.; cpl. 633; a. 2 5'', 8 40mm.; cl. *Mount McKinley*)

Teton (AGC–14) was laid down under Maritime Commission contract (MC hull 1363) as *Water Witch* on 9 November 1943 at Wilmington, N.C., by the North Carolina Shipbuilding Corp.; launched on 5 February 1944; sponsored by Mrs. C. E. Shimp; renamed *Teton* on 7 February 1944; acquired by the Navy on 18 October 1944; and commissioned the same day at Brooklyn, N.Y., Capt. Donald Rex Tallman in command.

Following shakedown in the Chesapeake Bay, the amphibious force flagship, escorted by *Barr* (APD–39), steamed south; transited the Panama Canal; proceeded, via the Mare Island Navy Yard, to Hawaii; and arrived at Pearl Harbor on 19 January 1945. Four days later, Rear Admiral John L. Hall, Commander, Amphibious Group 12, Amphibious Forces, Pacific Fleet, hoisted his flag as his staff came on board.

Teton was attached to a convoy that got underway for the Philippines on 28 January. After stops at Eniwetok, Ulithi, and the Palaus, the force reached Leyte on 21 February. *Teton* next began rehearsals as flagship of Task Force 44 for the forthcoming assault against the Ryukyus. Commodore Clifford Greer Richardson, commanding Transport Squadron 14, and Major General John Hodge, commanding the XXIV Army Corps, embarked with their staffs. On 27 March, *Teton* got underway as flagship of Task Unit 51.13.1 and arrived off Okinawa on 1 April, the day the assault began. She remained there for 72 days controlling the landing operations on the Hagushi beaches and then providing standby control of offensive and defensive air operations. On 11 June, the ship got underway in a convoy bound for the Philippines.

Teton arrived at Subic Bay on the 15th of June and remained there until 17 August. When news of Japan's surrender arrived, Admiral Hall and his staff left the ship to transfer to *Hansford* (APA–106). *Teton* embarked Army forces for the occupation of Japan and proceeded to Honshu, arriving in Tokyo Bay on 29 August.

Teton stood out of Tokyo Bay on 25 September and headed for Guam to embark approximately 750 passengers for transportation to the United States. The ship reached San Francisco on 16 October; disembarked her passengers; and steamed west again three days later.

Teton continued duty with the "Magic-Carpet" Fleet, returning servicemen from Pacific bases to the United States until early 1946. She began inactivation at San Diego in March 1946 and was decommissioned there on 30 August 1946. *Teton* was struck from the Navy list on 1 June 1961 and sold for scrap in March 1962 to Union Minerals and Alloys Corp., New York, N.Y.

Teton received one battle star for World War II service.

Tetonkaha

A river in South Dakota.

(AOG–41: dp. 2,270; l. 220'6''; b. 37'; dr. 13'1''; s. 10 k.; cpl. 62; a. 1 3'', 2 40mm.; cl. *Mettawee*; T. T1–M–A2)

Tetonkaha (AOG–41) was laid down under Maritime Commission contract (MC hull 2067) on 27 September 1944 at Bayonne, N.J., by the East Coast Shipyard, Inc.; launched on 29 October 1944; sponsored by Mrs. J. Scatorwa; and commissioned on 8 December 1944, Lt. Paul J. Hall, USNR, in command.

Tetonkaha departed New York harbor on 30 December 1944 for Hampton Roads; arrived at Norfolk on New Year's Day, 1945; and began her nine-day shakedown the next day. The gasoline tanker stood out to sea on 2 February and headed for the Netherlands West Indies. *Tetonkaha* arrived at Aruba on the 10th; loaded a cargo of aviation gasoline and diesel oil; headed for the California coast; and arrived at San Diego on 1 March. Two days later, the ship proceeded westward to Hawaii and reported to Service Squadron 8 for duty on 14 March.

Tetonkaha supplied aviation gas to outlying islands in the Hawaiian group until August when she began making shuttle runs to Johnston Island. After Service Squadron 8 was dissolved on 1 September, the tanker continued on the Johnston shuttle for the 14th Naval District. *Tetonkaha* was relieved of duty on 6 November and returned to San Francisco in December 1945. She was decommissioned at Mare Island on 22 January 1946; stripped; struck from the Navy list on 12 March; and transferred to the Maritime Commission on 1 July 1946. In 1949, the ship was sold to the Sun Oil Co., Philadelphia, Pa., and renamed *Maumee Sun*.

Texan

(ScStr: dp. 18,000; l. 484'5''; b. 57'; dr. 29'3''; s. 13.5 k.; cpl. 70; a. 1 5'', 1 3'')

Texan (Id. No. 1354)—a passenger liner built in 1902 by the New York Shipbuilding Corp., Camden, N.J., for the American Hawaiian Steamship Co.—was acquired by the United States Shipping Board (USSB) on 18 March 1918; was transferred to the Navy at New York City on the same day; and was commissioned on 23 March 1918.

Assigned to the Naval Overseas Transportation Service after being refitted for naval service, the cargo ship loaded general military supplies and sailed on 9 April with a convoy for France. *Texan* arrived at Brest on the 24th and, after discharging her cargo, began the return voyage to New York on 19 May. Upon her arrival there, she underwent voyage repairs and then loaded supplies, including 405 tons of ammunition and 10 locomotives destined for Marseilles. The ship sailed with a convoy on 18 June and arrived at her destination on 7 July. *Texan* made another round-trip voyage to Marseilles in September and one to Verdon in November and December before returning to New York on 4 January 1919.

On 18 January 1919, *Texan* was transferred to the Cruiser and Transport Force and operated bringing troops of the American Expeditionary Force home from France until 7 August 1919 when she was assigned to the 5th Naval District. *Texan* was decommissioned on 22 August 1919 and returned to the USSB.

Texas

After having been a territory first of Spain and then of Mexico and later an independent republic, Texas was admitted to the Union as the 28th state on 29 December 1845.

(IrcRam: l. 217'; b. 48'6''; dph. 13'; dr. 13'6''; cpl. 50; a. 4 pivots, 2 broadside guns)

CSS *Texas*—a twin-screw, ironclad ram built at Richmond, Va., for the Confederacy—was launched in January 1865. At the time of Lee's evacuation of Richmond on 3 April 1865, she was left unfinished but intact in an outfitting berth at the Richmond Navy Yard—one of only two vessels which escaped destruction by the departing Confederate forces. Captured when the city fell the following day, the ironclad, sister ship of CSS *Columbia*, was taken into the United States Navy, but saw no service. *Texas* was laid up at Norfolk until 15 October 1867 when she was sold at Norfolk to J. N. Leonard.

The first battleship *Texas* returns to New York in triumph after the battle of Santiago, 1898. (NR&L(O)449)

I

(Second Class Battleship: dp. 6,315 (n.); l. 308'10''; b. 64'1''; dr. 22'6'' (mean); s. 17 k.; cpl. 392; a. 2 12'', 6 6'', 12 6-pdrs., 6 1-pdrs., 4 37mm., 4 14'' tt.; cl. *Texas*)

The first *Texas* was laid down on 1 June 1889 at Portsmouth, Va., by the Norfolk Navy Yard; launched on 28 June 1892; sponsored by Miss Madge Houston Williams; and commissioned on 15 August 1895, Capt. Henry Glass in command.

Assigned to the North Atlantic Squadron, the warship cruised the eastern seaboard of the United States. In February 1897, she left the Atlantic for a brief cruise to the Gulf coast ports of Galveston and New Orleans. She resumed Atlantic coast duty in March of 1897 and remained so employed until the beginning of 1898. At that time, she visited Key West and the Dry Tortugas en route to Galveston for a return visit which she made in mid-February. Returning to the Atlantic via the Dry Tortugas in March, the warship arrived in Hampton Roads on the 24th and resumed normal duty with the North Atlantic Squadron.

Early in the spring, war between the United States and Spain erupted over conditions in Cuba and the supposed Spanish destruction of the battleship *Maine* in Havana harbor in February 1898. By 18 May, *Texas* was at Key West, Fla., readying to prosecute that war. On the 21st, she arrived off Cienfuegos, Cuba, with the Flying Squadron to blockade the Cuban coast. After a return to Key West for coal, *Texas* arrived off Santiago de Cuba on the 27th. She patrolled off that port until 11 June on which day she made a reconnaissance mission to Guantanamo Bay. For the next five weeks, she patrolled between Santiago de Cuba and Guantanamo Bay. On 16 June, the warship joined *Marblehead* for a bombardment of the fort on Cayo del Tore in Guantanamo Bay. The two ships opened fire just after 1400 and ceased fire about an hour and 15 minutes later, having reduced the fort to impotency.

On 3 July, she was steaming off Santiago de Cuba when the Spanish Fleet under Admiral Cervera made a desperation attempt to escape past the American Fleet. *Texas* immediately took four of the enemy ships under fire. While the battleship's main battery pounded *Vizcaya* and *Colon*, her secondary battery joined *Iowa* and *Gloucester* in battering two torpedo-boat destroyers. The two Spanish destroyers fell out of the action quickly and beached themselves, heavily damaged. One by one, the larger enemy warships also succumbed to the combined fire of the American Fleet. Each, in turn, sheered off toward shore and beached herself. Thus, *Texas* and the other ships of the Flying Squadron annihilated the Spanish Fleet.

The defeat of Cervera's Fleet helped to seal the doom of Santiago de Cuba. The city fell to the besieging American forces on the 17th, just two weeks after the great American naval victory. The day after the surrender at Santiago, Spain sought peace through the good offices of the French government. Even before the peace protocol was signed in Washington, D.C., on 12 August, American ships began returning home. *Texas* arrived in New York on 31 July and remained in nearby waters until late November.

At that time, she moved south to Hampton Roads where she arrived on 2 December. The warship resumed her peacetime routine patrolling the Atlantic coast of the United States. Though her primary field of operations once again centered on the northeastern coast, she also made periodic visits to such places as San Juan, P.R., and Havana, Cuba, where her crew could view some of the results of their own ship's efforts in the recent war.

Texas went out of commission briefly in 1901 for repairs at the Norfolk Navy Yard but was commissioned again on 3 November 1902. She served as flagship for the Coast Squadron until 1905 and remained in that organization after its commander shifted his flag. By 1908, she had become station ship at Charleston, S.C. On 15 February 1911, her name was changed to *San Marcos* to allow the name *Texas* to be assigned to Battleship No. 35. On 10 October 1911, her name was struck from the Navy list. She was subsequently sunk as a target in Tangier Sound in Chesapeake Bay.

II

(Battleship No. 35: dp. 27,000 (n.); l. 573'0''; b. 95'2½'' (wl.); dr. 29'7'' (f.); s. 21.05 k. (tl.); cpl. 954; a. 10 14'', 21 5'', 4 3-pdrs., 4 21'' tt. (subm.); cl. *New York*)

The second *Texas* (Battleship No. 35) was laid down on 17 April 1911 at Newport News, Va., by the Newport News Shipbuilding Co.; launched on 18 May 1912; sponsored by Miss Claudia Lyon; and commissioned on 12 March 1914, Capt. Albert W. Grant in command.

On 24 March, *Texas* departed the Norfolk Navy Yard and set a course for New York. She made an overnight stop at Tompkinsville, N.Y., on the night of the 26th and 27th and entered the New York Navy Yard on the latter day. She spent the next three weeks there undergoing the installation of the fire control equipment.

During her stay in New York, President Woodrow Wilson ordered a number of ships of the Atlantic Fleet to Mexican waters in response to tension created when an overzealous detail of Mexican Federal troops detained an American boat crew at Tampico. The problem was quickly resolved locally, but fiery Rear Admiral Henry T. Mayo sought further redress by demanding an official disavowal of the act by the Huerta regime and a 21-gun salute to the American flag.

Unfortunately for Mexican-American relations, President Wilson apparently saw in the incident an opportunity to put pressure on a government he felt was undemocratic. On 20 April, Wilson placed the matter before the Congress and sent orders to Rear Admiral Frank Friday Fletcher, commanding the naval force off the Mexican coast, instructing him to land a force at Veracruz and to seize the customs house there in retaliation for the celebrated "Tampico Incident." That action was carried out on the 21st and 22d.

Due to the intensity of the situation, when *Texas* put to sea on 13 May, she headed directly to operational duty without benefit of the usual shakedown cruise and post-shakedown repair period. After a five-day stop at Hampton Roads between 14 and 19 May, she joined Rear Admiral Fletcher's force off Veracruz on the 26th. She remained in Mexican waters for just over two months, supporting the American forces ashore. On 8 August, she left Veracruz and set a course for Nipe Bay, Cuba, and thence steamed to New York where she entered the Navy Yard on 21 August.

The battleship remained there until 5 September when she returned to sea, joined the Atlantic Fleet, and settled into a schedule of normal fleet operations. In October, she returned to the Mexican coast. Later that month, *Texas* became station ship at Tuxpan, a duty that lasted until early November. The ship finally bade Mexico farewell at Tampico on 20 December and set a course for New York. The battleship entered the New York Navy Yard on 28 December and remained there undergoing repairs until 16 February 1915.

Upon her return to active duty with the fleet, *Texas* resumed a schedule of training operations along the New England coast and off the Virginia Capes alternated with winter fleet tactical and gunnery drills in the West Indies. That routine lasted just over two years until the February-to-March crisis over unrestricted submarine warfare catapulted the United States into war with the Central Powers in April 1917.

The 6 April declaration of war found *Texas* riding at anchor in the mouth of the York River with the other Atlantic Fleet battleships. She remained in the Virginia Capes-Hampton Roads vicinity until mid-August conducting exercises and training naval armed-guard gun crews for service on board merchant ships.

In August, she steamed to New York for repairs, arriving at Base 10 on the 19th and entering the New York Navy Yard soon thereafter. She completed repairs on 26 September and got underway for Port Jefferson that same day. During the mid-watch on the 27th, however, she ran hard aground on Block Island. For three days, her crew lightened ship to no avail. On the 30th, tugs came to her assistance, and she finally backed clear. Hull damaged dictated a return to the yard, and the extensive repairs she required precluded her departure with Division 9 for the British Isles in November.

By December, she had completed repairs and moved south to conduct war games out of the York River. Mid-January 1918 found the battleship back at New York preparing for the voyage across the Atlantic. She departed New York on 30 January; arrived at Scapa Flow in the Orkney Islands off the coast of Scotland on 11 February; and rejoined Division 9, by then known as the 6th Battle Squadron of Britain's Grand Fleet.

Texas' service with the Grand Fleet consisted entirely of convoy missions and occasional forays to reinforce the British squadron on blockade duty in the North Sea whenever German heavy units threatened. The fleet alternated between bases at Scapa Flow and at the Firth of Forth in Scotland. *Texas* began her mission only five days after her arrival at Scapa Flow where she sortied with the entire fleet to reinforce the 4th Battle Squadron, then on duty in the North Sea. She returned to Scapa Flow the next day and remained until 8 March when she put to sea on a convoy escort mission from which she returned on the 13th. *Texas* and her division mates entered the Firth of Forth on 12 April but got underway again on the 17th to escort a convoy. The American battleships returned to base on 20 April. Four days later, *Texas* again stood out to sea to support the 2d Battle Squadron the day after the German High Seas Fleet had sortied from Jade Bay toward the Norwegian coast to threaten an Allied convoy. Forward units caught sight of the retiring Germans on the 25th but at such extreme range that no possibility of bringing the enemy to battle existed. The Germans returned to their base that day, and the Grand Fleet, including *Texas*, did likewise on the next.

Texas and her division mates passed a relatively quiescent May in the Firth of Forth. On 9 June, she got underway with the other warships of the 6th Battle Squadron and headed back to the anchorage at Scapa Flow, arriving there the following day. Between 30 June and 2 July, *Texas* and her colleagues acted as escort for American minelayers adding to the North Sea mine barrage. After a two-day return to Scapa Flow, *Texas* put to sea with the Grand Fleet to conduct two days of tactical exercises and war games. At the conclusion of those drills on 8 July, the fleet entered the Firth of Forth. For the remainder of World War I, *Texas* and the other battleships of Division 9 continued to operate with the Grand Fleet as the 6th Battle Squadron. With the German Fleet increasingly more tied to its bases in the estuaries of the Jade and Ems Rivers, the American and British ships settled more and more into a routine schedule of operations with little or no hint of combat operations. That state of affairs lasted until the armistice ended hostilities on 11 November 1918. On the night of 20 and 21 November, she accompanied the Grand Fleet to meet the surrendering German Fleet.

The two fleets rendezvoused about 40 miles east of May Island—located near the mouth of the Firth of Forth—and proceeded together into the anchorage at Scapa Flow. Afterward, the American contingent moved to Portland, England, arriving there on 4 December.

Texas (BB–35) about 1930, as flagship of the United States Fleet. (80–G–1021418)

Eight days later, *Texas* put to sea with Divisions 9 and 6 to meet President Woodrow Wilson embarked in *George Washington* on his way to the Paris Peace Conference. The rendezvous took place at about 0730 the following morning and provided an escort for the President into Brest, France, where the ships arrived at 1230 that afternoon. That evening, *Texas* and the other American battleships departed Brest for Portland where they stopped briefy on the 14th before getting underway to return to the United States. The warships arrived off Ambrose Light on Christmas Day 1918 and entered New York on the 26th.

Following overhaul, *Texas* resumed duty with the Atlantic Fleet early in 1919. On 9 March, she became the first American battleship to carry an airplane when Lt. Comdr. Edward O. McDonnell flew a British-built Sopwith "Camel" off the warship. That summer, she was reassigned to the Pacific Fleet. On 17 July 1920, she was designated BB–35 as a result of the Navy's adoption of the alpha-numeric system of hull designations. *Texas* served in the Pacific until 1924 when she returned to the east coast for overhaul and to participate in a training cruise to European waters with Naval Academy midshipmen embarked. That fall, she conducted maneuvers as a unit of the Scouting Fleet. In 1925, she entered the Norfolk Navy Yard for a major modernization overhaul during which her cage masts were replaced with a single tripod foremast. She also received the very latest in fire control equipment. Following that overhaul, she resumed duty along the eastern seaboard and kent at that task until late in 1927 when she did a brief tour of duty in the Pacific between late September and early December.

Near the end of the year, *Texas* returned to the Atlantic and resumed normal duty with the Scouting Fleet. In January 1928, she transported President Herbert Hoover to Havana for the Pan-American conference and then continued on via the Panama Canal and the west coast to maneuvers with the fleet near Hawaii.

She returned to New York early in 1929 for her annual overhaul and had completed it by March when she began another brief tour of duty in the Pacific. She returned to the Atlantic in June and resumed normal duty with the Scouting Fleet. In April 1930, she took time from her operating schedule to escort SS *Leviathan* into New York when that ship returned from Europe carrying the delegation that had represented the United States at the London Naval Conference. In January 1931, she left the yard at New York as flagship of the United States Fleet and headed via the Panama Canal to San Diego, her home port for the

next six years. During that period, she served first as flagship for the entire Fleet and, later, as flagship for Battleship Division (BatDiv) 1. She left the Pacific once during that time, in the summer of 1936, when she joined in a midshipman training cruise in the Atlantic. Upon completion of that assignment, the battleship immediately rejoined Battle Force in the Pacific.

In the summer of 1937, she once more was reassigned to the east coast, as the flagship of the Training Detachment, United States Fleet. Late in 1938 or early in 1939, the warship became flagship of the newly organized Atlantic Squadron, built around BatDiv 5. Through both organizational assignments, her labors were directed primarily to training missions, midshipman cruises, naval reserve drills, and training members of the Fleet Marine Force.

Soon after war broke out in Europe in September 1939, *Texas* began operating on the "neutrality patrol," established to keep the war out of the western hemisphere. Later, as the United States moved toward more active support of the Allied cause, the warship began convoying ships carrying Lend-Lease material to Great Britain. Sunday, 7 December 1941, found the battleship at Casco Bay, Maine, undergoing a rest and relaxation period following three months of watch duty at Argentia, Newfoundland. After 10 days of Casco Bay, she returned to Argentia and remained there until late January 1942 when she got underway to escort a convoy to England. After delivering her charges, the battleship patrolled waters near Iceland until March when she returned home. For the next six months, she continued convoy-escort missions. Her destinations were various. On one occasion, she escorted Guadalcanal-bound marines as far as Panama. On another, the warship screened service troops to Freetown, Sierra Leone, on the west coast of Africa. More frequently, she made voyages to and from Great Britain escorting both cargo- and troop-carrying ships.

On 23 October, *Texas* embarked upon her first major combat operation when she sortied with Task Group (TG) 34.8, the Northern Attack Group for Operation "Torch," the invasion of North Africa. The objective assigned to this group was Mehedia near Port Lyautey and the port itself. The ships arrived off the assault beaches early in the morning of 8 November and began preparations for the invasion. When the troops went ashore, *Texas* did not come immediately into action to support them. At that point in the war, amphibious warfare doctrine was still embryonic; and many did not recognize the value of a prelanding bombardment. Instead, the Army insisted upon attempting surprise. *Texas* finally entered the fray early in the afternoon when the Army requested her to destroy an ammunition dump near Port Lyautey. For the next week, she contented herself with cruising up and down the Moroccan coast delivering similar, specific, call-fire missions. Thus, unlike in later operations, she expended only 273 rounds of 14-inch and 6 rounds of 5-inch. During her short stay, some of her crew briefly went ashore to assist in salvaging some of the shipping sunk in the harbor. On 15 November, she departed North Africa and headed for home in company with *Savannah* (CL–42), *Sangamon* (ACV–26), *Kennebec* (AO–36), four transports, and seven destroyers.

Throughout 1943, *Texas* carried out the familiar role of convoy escort. With New York as her home port, she made numerous transatlantic voyages to such places as Casablanca and Gibraltar, as well as frequent visits to ports in the British Isles. That routine continued into 1944 but ended in April of that year when, at the European end of one such mission, she remained at the Clyde estuary in Scotland and began training for the invasion of Normandy. That warm-up period lasted about seven weeks at the end of which she departed the Clyde and travelled down the Irish Sea and around the southern coast of England to arrive off the Normandy beaches on the night of 5 and 6 June.

At about 0440 on the morning of the 6th, the battleship closed the Normandy coast to a point some 12,000 yards offshore near Pointe du Hoc. At 0550, *Texas* began churning up the coastal landscape with her 14-inch salvoes. Meanwhile, her secondary battery went to work on another target on the western end of "Omaha" beach, a ravine laced with strong points to defend an exit road. Later, under control of airborne spotters, she moved her major-caliber fire inland to interdict enemy reinforcement activities and to destroy batteries and other strong points farther inland.

By noon, she closed the beach to about a range of 3,000 yards to fire upon snipers and machinegun nests hidden in a defile just off the beach. At the conclusion of that mission, the warship took an enemy antiaircraft battery located west of Vierville under fire.

The following morning, her main battery rained 14-inch shells on the enemy-held towns of Surrain and Trevieres to break up German troop concentrations. That evening, she bombarded a German mortar battery which had been shelling the beach. Not long after midnight, German planes attacked the ships offshore, and one of them swooped in low on *Texas'* starboard quarter. Her antiaircraft batteries opened up immediately but failed to score on the intruder. On the morning of 8 June, her guns fired on Isigny, then on a shore battery, and finally on Trevieres once more.

After that, she retired to Plymouth to rearm, returning to the French coast on the 11th. From then until the 15th, she supported the Army in its advance inland. However, by the latter day, the troops had advanced beyond the range of her guns; and the battleship moved on to another mission.

On the morning of 25 June, *Texas* closed in on the vital port of Cherbourg and, with *Arkansas* (BB–33), opened fire upon various fortifications and batteries surrounding the town. The guns on shore returned fire immediately and, at about 1230, succeeded in straddling *Texas*. The battleship, however, continued her firing runs in spite of shell geysers blossoming about her. The enemy gunners were stubborn and good. At 1316 a 280-millimeter shell slammed into her fire control tower, killed the helmsman, and wounded nearly everyone on the navigation bridge. *Texas'* commanding officer, Capt. Baker, miraculously escaped unhurt and quickly had the bridge cleared. The warship herself continued to deliver her 14-inch shells in spite of damage and casualties. Some time later, another shell struck the battleship. That one, a 240-millimeter armor-piercing shell, crashed through the port bow, entered a compartment located below the wardroom, but failed to explode. Throughout the three-hour duel, the Germans straddled and near-missed *Texas* over 65 times, but she continued

her mission until 1500 when, upon orders to that effect, she retired.

Texas underwent repairs at Plymouth, England, and then drilled in preparation for the invasion of southern France. On 15 July, she departed Belfast Lough and headed for the Mediterranean. After stops at Gibraltar and Oran in Algeria, the battleship rendezvoused with three French destroyers off Bizerte, Tunisia, and set a course for the Riviera coast of France. She arrived off St. Tropez during the night of 14 and 15 July. At 0444, she moved into position for the prelanding bombardment and, at 0651, opened up on her first target, a battery of five 155-millimeter guns. Due to the fact that the troops ashore moved inland rapidly against light resistance, she provided fire support for the assault for only two days. *Texas* departed the southern coast of France on the evening of 16 August. After a stop at Palermo, Sicily, she left the Mediterranean and headed for New York where she arrived on 14 September 1944.

At New York, *Texas* underwent a 35-day repair period during which the barrels on her main battery were replaced. After a brief refresher cruise, she departed New York in November and set a course, via the Panama Canal, for the Pacific. She made a stop at Long Beach, Calif., and then continued on to Oahu. She spent Christmas at Pearl Harbor and then conducted maneuvers in the Hawaiian Islands for about a month at the end of which she steamed to Ulithi Atoll. She departed Ulithi on 10 February 1945, stopped in the Marianas for two days' invasion rehearsals, and then set a course for Iwo Jima. She arrived off the target on 16 February, three days before the scheduled assault. She spent those three days pounding enemy defenses on Iwo Jima in preparation for the landings. After the troops stormed ashore on the 19th, *Texas* switched roles and began delivering support and call fire. She remained off Iwo Jima for almost a fortnight, helping the marines subdue a well dug-in and stubborn Japanese garrison.

Though Iwo Jima was not declared secured until 16 March, *Texas* cleared the area late in February and returned to Ulithi early in March to prepare for the Okinawa operation. She departed Ulithi with TF 54, the gunfire support unit, on 21 March and arrived in the Ryukyus on the 25th. *Texas* did not participate in the occupation of the islands and roadstead at Kerama Retto carried out on the 26th but moved in on the main objective instead, beginning the prelanding bombardment that same day. For the next six days, she delivered 14-inch salvoes to prepare the way for the Army and the Marine Corps. Each evening, she retired from her bombardment position close to the Okinawan shore only to return the next day and resume her poundings. The enemy ashore, preparing for a defense-in-depth strategy as at Iwo Jima, made no answer. Only his air units provided a response, sending several kamikaze raids to harass the bombardment group. *Texas* escaped damage during those small attacks. After six days of aerial and naval bombardment, the ground troops' turn came on 1 April. They stormed ashore against initially light resistance. For almost two months, *Texas* remained in Okinawan waters providing gunfire support for the troops ashore and fending off the enemy aerial assault. In performing the latter mission, she claimed one kamikaze kill on her own and three assists.

Late in May, *Texas* retired to Leyte in the Philippines and remained there until after the Japanese capitulation on 15 August. She returned to Okinawa toward the end of August and stayed in the Ryukyus until 23 September. On that day, she set a course for the United States with troops embarked. The battleship delivered her passengers to San Pedro, Calif., on 15 October. She celebrated Navy Day there on 27 October and then resumed her mission bringing American troops home. She made two round-trip voyages between California and Oahu in November and a third in late December.

On 21 January 1946, the warship departed San Pedro

The missile cruiser *Texas* (CGN–39), July, 1977. (USN 1170359)

and steamed via the Panama Canal to Norfolk where she arrived on 13 February. She soon began preparations for inactivation. In June, she was moved to Baltimore, Md., where she remained until the beginning of 1948. *Texas* was towed to San Jacinto State Park in Texas where she was decommissioned on 21 April 1948 and turned over to the state of Texas to serve as a permanent memorial. Her name was struck from the Navy list on 30 April 1948.

Texas (BB–35) earned five battle stars during World War II.

III

(CGN–39: dp. 11,000 (f.); l. 585'; b. 63'; dr. 31'; s. 30+ k.; cpl. 476; a. 2 5'', 2 Phalanx, ASROC, Harpoon, Standard, 6 Mk.32 tt.; cl. *Virginia*)

The third *Texas* (DLGN–39) was laid down as a guided missile frigate on 18 August 1973, at Newport News, Va., by the Newport News Shipbuilding and Drydock Co.; reclassified as a guided missile cruiser and redesignated CGN–39 on 30 June 1975; launched on 9 August 1975; sponsored by Mrs. Dolph Briscoe, wife of the Governor of Texas; and commissioned on 10 September 1977, Capt. Peter B. Fiedler in command.

Following a nine-week test of the ship's combat systems, *Texas* loaded out weapons at the Yorktown Naval Weapons station in October and underwent refresher training out of Guantanamo Bay, Cuba, in November. *Texas* spent the first three months of 1978 conducting at-sea evaluation of her propulsion and weapons systems off the Virginia capes and in the Caribbean. On 28 March, she transited to her building yard at Newport News to commence a Post Shakedown Availability (PSA) which was completed on 31 July. The remainder of 1978 was spent in individual ship exercises off the east coast and Roosevelt Roads, Puerto Rico, interspersed with periods in *Texas'* home port of Norfolk.

Thaddeus Parker

Thaddeus Parker—born on 13 November 1923 in Cross City, Fla.—enlisted in the United States Navy on 27 June 1941. Upon completion of basic training, Parker was assigned to the U.S. Naval Hospital, Norfolk, Va., as a Hospital Apprentice on 30 August. On 31 October 1941, he was stationed at the Marine Corps Base, Quantico, Va., where he served as a hospital corpsman in the U.S. Naval Hospital, and, after 29 March 1942, in the First Raider Battalion, Fleet Marine Force.

Parker accompanied the Raider Battalion when that unit was ordered to the South Pacific. He was awarded the Navy Cross "for extraordinary heroism while serving as company corpsman during an engagement with enemy Japanese forces on Guadalcanal, Solomon Islands, on the night of September 13–14 1942." The citation further stated: "When his company was almost completely surrounded by the Japanese and under attack from all directions, Parker, with utter disregard for his own personal safety, constantly exposed himself to enemy fire to care for and evacuate the wounded. As a result of his dauntless courage and outstanding devotion to duty, he undoubtedly saved the lives of many of the injured who otherwise might have perished."

Killed in action at New Georgia, Solomon Islands, on July 20, 1943, Parker was posthumously awarded the Purple Heart Medal and the Silver Star Medal with the following citation: "For gallantry in action at New Georgia, Solomon Islands. Disregarding his personal safety, he aggressively moved forward into areas swept by intense, hostile fire to render medical aid to two seriously wounded marines. In courageously attempting to evacuate the second man, Pharmacist's Mate Parker was killed."

(DE–369: dp. 1,350; l. 306'; b. 36'7''; dr. 13'4''; s. 24.3 k.; cpl. 222; a. 2 5'', 4 40mm., 10 20mm., 3 dct., 8 dcp., 3 21'' tt.; cl. *John C. Butler*)

Thaddeus Parker (DE–369) was laid down on 23 May 1944 at Orange, Tex., by Consolidated Steel Corp.; launched on 26 August 1944; sponsored by Miss Ina Lee Parker; and commissioned on 25 October 1944, Lt. Comdr. Duane R. Stoneleigh, USNR, in command.

Following shakedown training off Bermuda from 17 November to 16 December and yard work in Boston, the new destroyer escort got underway on 29 December 1944 for the west coast. She transited the Panama Canal on 7 January 1945 and arrived at San Diego on the 16th.

Four days later, *Thaddeus Parker* headed for Hawaii as the escort for a troopship and reached Pearl Harbor on 26 January. On 5 February, the destroyer escort proceeded to Eniwetok. For the next two months, she escorted ships to Guam and Saipan. On 2 March, *Thaddeus Parker* departed Eniwetok with three other escorts and 12 troop transports that were loaded with marine replacements for battle casualties on Iwo Jima. She lay off that island for several days before being assigned to screening duties. The escort returned to Eniwetok on the 25th and, the following month, was ordered to Ulithi. On 12 May, she rendezvoused with a troop transport, south of the equator, and escorted it to the Palaus.

Thaddeus Parker was assigned to an antisubmarine screen in the vicinity of Peleliu and served as an air-sea rescue ship in Kossol Roads in the Palaus. She rescued a Marine pilot on 19 May and saved another

An early-postwar view of *Thaddeus Parker* (DE–369). (U.S. Naval Institute photo)

on 18 July. On 27 June, she shelled enemy installations at the Koror Naval Base. The escort returned to Ulithi on 20 July and was assigned escort duty. She then made two voyages to Okinawa: the first, escorting a merchant convoy; the second, with the other ships of Escort Division 86.

Thaddeus Parker was at Okinawa when hostilities with Japan ceased; and she waited for almost a month before receiving orders on 11 September to proceed to Honshu, Japan. She was a unit of the southern Japan Occupation Forces from 14 September 1945 to 2 January 1946 when she began her return voyage to the United States. She was assigned to the 19th Fleet at San Diego and was placed out of commission, in reserve, on 31 May 1946.

In March 1951, during the Korean War, *Thaddeus Parker* was removed from the Reserve Fleet and prepared for activation. She was recommissioned at San Diego on 21 September 1951 with Lt. Comdr. John L. Hansen in command. After shakedown training and post-shakedown repairs at the Mare Island Naval Shipyard, the ship returned to San Diego where she operated as a plane guard and participated in antisubmarine operations.

On 14 February, she and other reactivated ships sailed for the east coast to join the Atlantic Fleet. Newport, R.I., was her new homeport. In the spring, she made a cruise to Bermuda and, later, escorted *Block Island* (CVE–106) to the Caribbean for training. She then returned to Newport and remained in the Narragansett Bay area until November when she steamed to Guantanamo Bay for refresher training which she interrupted to return home to Newport for Christmas leave. She returned to Guantanamo in January 1953 to complete the training. In April and May, she provided services to the Training Command at Key West.

In June, the escort made a midshipman cruise to South America, visiting ports in Brazil, Colombia, and the British West Indies. After operations out of Newport, *Thaddeus Parker* made another midshipman cruise the following year. This one took her to Europe from 11 July to 3 September 1954 and included visits to ports in Scotland and France. The ship then operated along the Atlantic seaboard, from Brazil to Nova Scotia until 11 November 1957 when she was assigned duty as a Naval Reserve Training Ship at New York.

Almost a decade later, *Thaddeus Parker* was decommissioned and struck from the Navy list on 1 September 1967. She was sold on 9 July 1968 to Peck Iron and Metals Co., Portsmouth, Va., and scrapped.

Thaddeus Parker received one battle star for World War II service.

Thalia

Thalia (PYc–20) was renamed *Jet* (*q.v.*) on 7 January 1942.

Thane

An Anglo-Saxon nobleman in medieval England who held land of the king in exchange for military support.

119

Escort aircraft carrier *Sunset* (CVE–48) (*q.v.*) was transferred to the United Kingdom under Lend-Lease agreement on 19 November 1943 and served in the Royal Navy as *Thane* (D.48).

Thatcher

Henry K. Thatcher, born in Thomaston, Maine, on 26 May 1806, was appointed a midshipman on 4 March 1823. He was promoted to lieutenant on 28 February 1833; commander on 14 September 1855; captain in 1861; commodore on 3 July 1862; and to rear admiral on 25 July 1866.

Thatcher cruised on the Pacific, Mediterranean, African, and Pacific Stations and held important positions at various shore installations from 1823 to 1862. In 1862 and 1863, he commanded *Constellation* in the Mediterranean. In 1864 and 1865, he commanded *Colorado* and a division of the North Atlantic Blockading Squadron in the attacks on Fort Fisher in December 1864 and January 1865. After the fall of Fort Fisher, he was appointed to command the West Gulf Squadron and immediately began active operations in cooperation with the Army against Mobile, which surrendered on 12 April 1865. On 10 May 1865, the Confederate Naval Forces in the waters of Alabama surrendered to Admiral Thatcher. Sabine Pass and Galveston capitulated in May and June.

Admiral Thatcher was relieved of the command of the West Gulf Squadron and ordered north in early 1866. His last duty was that of port admiral, Portsmouth, N.H., from 1869 to 1870. He was placed on the retired list on 26 May 1868 and died at Boston on 5 April 1880.

I

(Destroyer No. 162: dp. 1,191; l. 314'4½''; b. 30'11¼''; dr. 9'2'' (mean); s. 34.9 k.; cpl. 122; a. 4 4'', 2 3'', 12 21'' tt.; cl. *Wickes*)

The first *Thatcher* (Destroyer No. 162) was laid down on 8 June 1918 at Quincy, Mass., by the Fore River Plant of the Bethelehem Shipbuilding Corp.; launched on 31 August 1918; sponsored by Miss Doris Bentley, the grandniece of Rear Admiral Thatcher; and commissioned on 14 January 1919, Lt. Comdr. Henry M. Kieffer in temporary command. On 25 January, Lt. Comdr. Francis W. Rockwell—who later commanded the 16th Naval District in the Philippines at the outbreak of World War II in the Pacific—assumed command.

Following shakedown, *Thatcher* operated with the Atlantic Fleet into the autumn of 1919. During the transatlantic NC-boat flights in May 1919, the destroyer operated on picket station number 9—one of 21 stations strung out from Newfoundland to the Azores—between her sister ships *Walker* (Destroyer No. 163) and *Crosby* (Destroyer No. 164). Underway at sea, she provided visual and radio bearings for the flying boats as they passed overhead on their way toward Lisbon, Portugal.

Upon completion of this duty, the destroyer—reclassified as DD-162 on 17 July 1920—resumed her routine training operations off the eastern seaboard before heading west in the autumn of 1921 to join the Pacific Fleet. She operated out of San Diego, conducting exercises and training cruises off the west coast until decommissioned at San Diego on 7 June 1922.

Thatcher remained laid-up at San Diego through the summer of 1939. War broke out in Europe on 1 September 1939, when German troops invaded Poland. *Thatcher* was recommissioned at San Diego on 18 December 1939, Lt. Comdr. Henry E. Richter in command, and conducted shakedown and training evolutions off the west coast until transferred to the Atlantic the following spring. Transiting the Panama Canal on 1 April 1940, a month before the situation in Europe

became critical when Germany began her *blitzkrieg* against France and the Low Countries, *Thatcher* subsequently conducted neutrality patrols and training cruises off the east coast and in the Gulf of Mexico through the summer of 1940.

The European situation took a drastic turn with the fall of France in June 1940. British destroyer forces in the wake of the disastrous Norwegian campaign and the evacuation of Dunkirk found themselves thinly spread—especially after Italy entered the war on Germany's side. Prime Minister Winston Churchill appealed to the United States for help.

In response, Roosevelt issued an executive order authorizing the transfer of 50 "over age" destroyers to the British in return for 99-year leases on strategic base sites in the western hemisphere. *Thatcher* was accordingly withdrawn from the Atlantic Squadron and her operations with Destroyer Division 69 for transfer to the Royal Canadian Navy, which had been allocated six of the "50 ships that saved the world," as these vessels came to be known.

As such, *Thatcher* and her five sisters arrived at Halifax, Nova Scotia, on 20 September—the third group of the "flush deckers" transferred. Decommissioned on 24 September 1940, *Thatcher* was struck from the Navy list on 8 January 1941.

Renamed HMCS *Niagara* (I.57), the destroyer departed Halifax on 30 November; proceeded eastward via St. John's, Newfoundland; and arrived in the British Isles on 11 December. Early in 1941, the destroyer was allocated to the 4th Escort Group, Western Approaches Command, and based at Greenock, Scotland. Subsequently transferred to the Newfoundland escort force, *Niagara* operated on convoy escort duties into the summer of 1941. While she was operating with this force, she took part in the capture of a German U-boat, *U-570*.

A Lockheed "Hudson" bomber, flying from Kaldadharnes, 30 miles southeast of Rekyavik, Iceland, located *U-570* running on the surface off the Icelandic coast on 27 August 1941. The "Hudson" attacked the U-boat with depth charges, damaging the enemy craft so severely that she could not submerge. Soon, some of the German crew appeared on deck displaying a large white cloth—possibly a bed sheet—indicating that they had surrendered. Patently unable to capture the submarine herself, the *Hudson* radioed for help.

Niagara sped to the scene and arrived at 0820 on 28 August. Rough weather initially hampered the operation but eventually, by 1800, *Niagara* had placed a prize crew aboard the submarine and had taken *U-570* in tow. During the operation, she also took the 43-man crew of the enemy craft on board. Towed to Thorlakshafn, Iceland, the U-boat eventually served in the Royal Navy as HMS *Graph*.

In January 1942, *Niagara* escorted the tempest-battered Danish merchantman *Triton* into Belfast, Northern Ireland, after the freighter had been severely mauled in a storm at sea. In March the destroyer rescued the survivors from the American merchantman SS *Independence Hall*, which had run aground off Sable Island, Nova Scotia, and had broken in half. The next month, she picked up two boatloads of survivors from the sunken steamer SS *Rio Blanco*, which had been torpedoed by *U-160* on 1 April, 40 miles east of Cape Hatteras, N.C.

The destroyer subsequently underwent boiler repairs at Pictou from May to August 1942 before resuming coastwise convoy operations between Halifax and New York and escort duty in the western Atlantic. Another refit at Pictou came in June and October 1943, before she continued her coastwise convoy escort missions through 1944.

Niagara became a torpedo-firing ship—first at Halifax and later at St. John, New Brunswick—from the spring of 1945 until the end of World War II in mid-August 1945, training torpedomen. Decommissioned on 15 September 1945, *Niagara* was turned over to the

War Assets Corp. on 27 May 1946 and ultimately broken up for scrap soon thereafter.

II

(DD–514: dp. 2,050; l. 376′5″; b. 39′7″; dr. 13′9″; s. 35.2 k.; cpl. 329; a. 5 5″, 10 40mm., 10 21″ tt.; cl. *Fletcher*)

The second *Thatcher* (DD–514) was laid down on 20 June 1942 at Bath, Maine, by the Bath Iron Works Corp.; launched on 6 December 1942; sponsored by Miss Charlotte L. Hyde; and commissioned on 10 February 1943, Lt. Comdr. Leland R. Lampman in command.

The destroyer held her shakedown training in Casco Bay and was then assigned escort duty. She stood out of New York on 29 April with convoy UGF–8 for Casablanca and returned with GUF–8 on 31 May. On 11 June, *Thatcher* departed the east coast for duty in the Pacific. She joined the Pacific Fleet on the 19th and, after calling at Mare Island for armament modifications, arrived at Pearl Harbor on 31 July.

On 22 August, *Thatcher* joined the fast carrier group of Rear Admiral Charles A. Pownall. It steamed toward Marcus Island and launched air attacks against that enemy base on the 31st. The group returned to Pearl Harbor on 7 September.

The following week, the destroyer got underway for the New Hebrides and arrived at Espiritu Santo on the 27th. She performed escort duty between Espiritu Santo and Guadalcanal and then screened a resupply convoy to Vella Lavella in mid-October. In late October, Task Force (TF) 39, composed of Cruiser Division 12 and Destroyer Divisions (DesDiv) 45 and 46, was assembled at Purvis Bay to support the landings on Bougainville. The force—including *Thatcher* in DesDiv 46—sortied on 30 October.

It bombarded the Buka-Bonis airfields on the night of 31 October and 1 November and then made a high-speed run to the southern tip of the island to shell airfields in the Shortlands. After the landings on Cape Torokina on 1 November, TF 39 protected the amphibious forces from enemy interference. That afternoon, TF 39 was ordered to intercept a force of enemy cruisers and destroyers that had left Rabaul to destroy American shipping in Empress Augusta Bay.

At 0227 on 2 November, radar on the American ships showed surface blips at a range of slightly over 35,000 yards. The battle began when the destroyers of DesDiv 45 fired a salvo of 25 torpedoes at the Japanese ships. However, due to a right turn by the enemy to close and to get into battle formation, all of the torpedoes missed.

DesDiv 46—composed of *Thatcher*, *Spence* (DD–512), *Converse* (DD–509), and *Foote* (DD–511)—was protecting the rear of the American formation. These ships held their fire until 0352 when they launched 19 torpedoes against two Japanese destroyers without scoring. However, the American cruisers had been tallying hits on *Sendai* which was soon a blazing wreck. During the ensuing melee, *Foote* was hit by a torpedo that blew off her stern. *Spence* sideswiped *Thatcher*, but the resulting damage did not threaten the survival of either ship. Finally, *Spence* took a hit below the water line that let salt water contaminate her fuel oil. While the Japanese lost the cruiser *Sendai* and the destroyer *Hatsukaze*, the United States suffered no total losses as *Foote* was towed to port and repaired. The next day, the Japanese attacked TF 39 with over 100 aircraft. They lost over 20 planes while scoring two hits on *Montpelier* (CL–57).

A closer inspection of *Thatcher* revealed that her collision with *Spence* had sprung her starboard shaft and had caused extensive dishing of her starboard side amidships. She steamed to Purvis Bay and was routed onward to Noumea where the misaligned screw was repaired. She then returned to Espiritu Santo where she received orders to proceed to the United States for further repairs. On 20 November, *Thatcher* got underway as an escort for *Birmingham* (CL–62), and the ships arrived at San Francisco on 14 December 1943. After her damage had been corrected at the Mare Island Navy Yard, *Thatcher* stood out of San Francisco on 11 February 1944 and steamed to Pearl Harbor for refresher training before rejoining TF 39 on 14 March.

The task force covered the unopposed landings on Emirau Island on the 20th. On 26 March, *Thatcher* was reassigned to TG 58.3 of the Fast Carrier Task Force. She escorted the carriers as their aircraft flew strikes against Palau, Yap, Ulithi, and Woleai in the Caroline Islands from 30 March to 1 April. The task group then retired to the Marshall Islands to prepare for their next assault against Japanese bases.

On 13 April, *Thatcher* escorted the fast carriers to New Guinea as they launched strikes against Hollandia, Wakde, Sawar, and Sarmi on the 21st and 22d to support landings at Aitape and at Tanahmerah and Humboldt Bays. On 29 April, aircraft from the carriers began a two-day attack against Truk, Ponape, and Satawan. On 1 May, *Thatcher* was in the screen of the bombardment group that shelled Ponape.

Thatcher returned to Majuro on 4 May to enter a floating drydock for repairs. She returned to sea late in the month for refresher training and firing exercises. On 26 May, her number 3 5-inch gun accidentally fired into her starboard, midships, 20-millimeter mount killing five men and causing considerable structural damage. Repairs were completed in time for the destroyer to accompany TG 58.4 to the Mariana Islands.

While operating with the group near Saipan on 12 June, *Thatcher* and *Charles Ausburne* (DD–570) were ordered to rescue some aviators in the water near Pagan Island. The two destroyers closed to within five miles of the enemy-held island before reaching the pilots. It was shortly before dark and, as *Charles Ausburne* was picking them up, *Thatcher* investigated a ship which had been sighted about six miles northward. She found a small wooden freighter and took it under fire. The size of the fires which broke out on the target and the subsequent explosions indicated that her cargo was oil and ammunition. Survivors in the water refused the lifelines thrown to them.

Thatcher rejoined her sister destroyer, and they made a sweep of the island seeking further targets. They soon made radar contact, and both ships began firing at 12,000 yards but observed no hits. When they had closed the range to 4,700 yards, *Ausburne* fired star shells which revealed a ship similar to the vessel *Thatcher* had sunk. She then fired another salvo which set the ship afire. The destroyers found no other targets before they rejoined the task group the next morning.

The carriers conducted air strikes against the Bonin Islands on 15 and 16 June and returned to the Saipan area. On 18 June, when TF 58 prepared for a major battle with the Japanese fleet, *Thatcher*'s group took station on the northern flank of the force. During the ensuing action—later referred to as the "Great Marianas Turkey Shoot"—only a few Japanese planes broke through the American fighter cover, and they caused no damage. Meanwhile, the Japanese lost over 300 aircraft.

The next day, *Thatcher* and TG 58.4 were detached from the westward-moving task force to refuel and to continue strikes against Rota and Guam. In the early morning of the 20th, carrier aircraft of the group shot down 18 enemy planes and destroyed 52 more on the ground. On 27 June, *Thatcher* was with the destroyer squadron that was detached to accompany *Miami* (CL–89) and *Houston* (CL–81) on a bombardment mission against Rota and Guam. *Thatcher* and two other destroyers shelled Rota, setting fire to a sugar mill and other buildings, and then joined the other ships off Guam to bombard airfields, shipping, storage tanks, and other worthwhile targets. *Thatcher* shelled the same islands again three days later and continued the operation through 1 July.

She returned to Eniwetok on 6 July with the task group and remained there for a week before heading

Thatcher (DD–514) steaming at high speed with her crew at air-defense stations. (80-G-470546)

back toward the Marianas. The destroyer served with TF 58 until 2 August when she was detached to join the 3d Fleet at Eniwetok. She then joined TG 30.8, the fleet oiler and transport group established to support Admiral Halsey's 3d Fleet. The ship stood out of Eniwetok on 26 August with several oilers and arrived at Seeadler Harbor on the 31st. She spent the next three months with various units of the group as it provided fuel, mail, and planes for TF 38. They first operated in the vicinity of Palau and Yap when the carriers struck west of the Carolines. TG 30.8 then moved to Ulithi as the carriers shifted their strikes westward to the Philippines and Formosa.

Thatcher then joined TG 38.3 for operations in the Philippine Islands. On 14, 15, and 16 December, the carriers launched strikes against Luzon to support the landings on Mindoro. The group retired to refuel, but the rapidly falling barometer indicated a typhoon approaching. *Thatcher* was fueled to 50 percent capacity before the hoses parted due to rough seas. The task force attempted to steam out of the danger area but was near the center of the storm on the 17th and 18th. Three United States destroyers were lost. When the weather cleared and the fleet reassembled, *Thatcher* joined TG 30.8, a supply group, and served with it until 7 January 1945.

On 8 January, *Thatcher* joined a special fueling group composed of six of the fastest oilers, two escort carriers, and eight destroyers to conduct fueling operations in the China Sea for the fast carriers. They accompanied the fast carriers into the South China Sea and took station midway between the Philippines and the coast of Indochina. The destroyer remained on station until the 20th when she headed for Guam with a group of empty oilers. Arriving at Apra Harbor on the 27th, she left for Ulithi and the Philipines the following week.

Thatcher joined the 7th Fleet at Leyte on 10 February and, three days later, escorted a convoy to Subic Bay. From 19 February to 3 March, the destroyer provided fire support for the Army forces ashore. Following two weeks of escort duty, the destroyer joined TG 78.3, the Visayan Attack Group. The group sailed on 15 March and headed directly to the landing beaches on the south coast of Panay.

Thatcher was off the landing beaches on 18 March and fired her only bombardment of the day against two groups of Japanese cut off by guerrillas in villages near the assault area. The 40th Infantry Division landed at 0900 and met very little opposition. As Army troops landed at Negros Occidental on the 29th, the destroyer assisted with call fire and continued the task until 5 April when she was relieved. She refitted at San Pedro to prepare for action in the Ryukyus.

On 13 May, *Thatcher* got underway for Kerama Retto, near Okinawa. The destroyer was assigned to radar picket duty to detect and intercept enemy aircraft before they could enter the transport anchorages. On 20 May, she detected large numbers of Japanese aircraft approaching the anchorage. All ships opened fire, and *Thatcher* maneuvered to bring all batteries to bear on the attacking planes. As a low-flying "Oscar" passed down her port side, she increased her speed to 25 knots and commenced firing with her 20- and 40-millimeter guns. The kamikaze climbed steeply, did a wingover, and dived into the destroyer, striking her aft of the bridge. All power and steering control on the bridge were lost; both radars and the gyro system were out; all external communications were lost; and there was a six- by nine-foot hole between the keel and the bilge. *Boyd* (DD–544) and *Pavlic* (APD–70) came alongside to remove the wounded and help extinguish fires. With 14 killed or missing and 53 wounded, the stricken ship limped into Kerama Retto. *Thatcher* awaited drydock entry until 1 July. On the 13th, she was ready for sea and had to ride out a typhoon in Buckner Bay. On the 19th, a kamikaze slipped into the bay and dived on the destroyer. His aim was not as accurate as his predecessor, and he bounced off the port side, above the water line, to explode and burn alongside. Damage was slight, and only two men were wounded.

Thatcher got underway for the United States on 25 July. After calling at Ulithi, Majuro, Eniwetok, Johnston Island, and Hawaii, she arrived at Bremerton on 20 August. A survey board decided that the ship should be scrapped, and she was decommissioned on 23 November 1945. *Thatcher* was struck from the Navy list on 5 December 1945 and sold on 23 January 1948 to the Lerner Co., Oakland, Calif., for scrap.

Thatcher was awarded 12 battle stars for World War II service.

The Sullivans

The five Sullivan brothers were all born in Waterloo, Iowa, between 1914 and 1920. George and Francis Sullivan, the two oldest, both enlisted in the Navy on 11 May 1937 and served in *Hovey* (DD–208) into June 1941. On 3 January 1942, George and Francis—accompanied by their three younger brothers: Joseph, Madison, and Albert—reenlisted to avenge a friend who had been killed in *Arizona* (BB–39) during the attack on Pearl Harbor on 7 December 1941. All five Sullivans subsequently joined *Juneau* (CL–52) at the New York Navy Yard on 3 February 1942.

Commissioned on 14 February 1942, *Juneau* initially served in the Atlantic but was transferred to the Pacific in August. Late in October, she took part in the Battle of the Santa Cruz Islands and, on 12 November, fought in the fierce night battle off Guadalcanal. In that action, a torpedo severely damaged the ship. The following morning, the crippled cruiser, down by the bow and struggling to make 18 knots, retired from the battle area. Handling sluggishly as she limped through the glassy-calm sea, *Juneau* presented a tempting target for Japanese submarine *I-26* which lurked nearby. One torpedo, or possibly two, hit the damaged cruiser forward and detonated her magazines. The resulting violent explosion tore the ship apart, and she went down in just 42 seconds.

Four of the Sullivans failed to make it topside in time to abandon their doomed ship; but George, wounded the night before, managed to get over the side and pull himself onto a raft. However, he succumbed to his wounds a few hours later. Only 10 of the approximately 140 men thought to have survived the immediate sinking were rescued.

(DD–537: dp. 2,050; l. 376'5''; b. 39'7''; dr. 13'9''; s. 35.2 k.; cpl. 329; a. 5 5'', 10 40mm., 7 20mm., 10 21'' tt., 6 dcp., 2 dct.; cl. *Fletcher*)

The Sullivans (DD–537) was laid down as *Putnam* on 10 October 1942 at San Francisco, Calif., by the Bethlehem Steel Co.; renamed *The Sullivans* on 6 February 1943; launched on 4 April 1943; sponsored by Mrs. Thomas F. Sullivan, the mother of the five Sullivan brothers; and commissioned on 30 September 1943, Comdr. Kenneth M. Gentry in command.

Following shakedown, *The Sullivans* got underway with *Dortch* (DD–670) and *Gatling* (DD–671) on 23 December and arrived at Pearl Harbor five days later. During training operations in Hawaiian waters, the ship was assigned to Destroyer Squadron (DesRon) 52. On 16 January 1944, she steamed out of Pearl Harbor with Task Group (TG) 58.2, bound for the Marshall Islands. En route to Kwajalein Atoll, the group was joined by Battleship Division (BatDiv) 9. Two days later, as the American warships neared their target, picket destroyers were sent ahead to protect the main force from the enemy.

On 24 January, TG 58.2 arrived at the dawn launching point for air strikes against Roi. For two days, *The Sullivans* screened *Essex* (CV–9), *Intrepid* (CV–11), and *Cabot* (CVL–22) as they launched nearly continuous aerial raids. Thereafter, the destroyer continued her operations to the north and northwest of Roi and Namur Islands in the Kwajalein group until 4 February, when TG 58.2 retired to Majuro to refuel and replenish.

Underway at high noon on the 12th, *The Sullivans* screened the sortie of TG 58.2, outward bound for Truk. The same carriers whose planes had blasted Roi and Namur steamed in the van—*Essex*, *Intrepid*, and *Cabot* —now headed for the Japanese fortress-base in the Central Pacific. From the time the group arrived at its launching point on 16 February, the carriers launched what seemed to be nearly continuous air strikes against Truk. "No enemy opposition of any kind was encountered," wrote *The Sullivans'* commander, "indicating that the initial attacks came as a complete surprise."

While the enemy may have been slow to react at the outset, they soon struck back—torpedoing *Intrepid* at 0010 on the 17th. The carrier slowed to 20 knots and lost steering control. *The Sullivans*, *Owen* (DD–536), and *Stembel* (DD–644) stood by the stricken carrier and escorted her to Majuro for repairs. Reaching Majuro on 21 February, the destroyer soon sailed on to Hawaii, arriving at Pearl Harbor on 4 March for drydocking and upkeep.

Underway again on the 22d, *The Sullivans* covered the sortie of TG's 58.2, 58.9, and 50.15 from Majuro, bound for the Palaus, Yap, and Woleai Islands. On the evening of the 29th, while the American warships were approaching the target area, enemy aircraft attacked them but were driven off by the antiaircraft fire from the ships. The next day, *The Sullivans* screened the carriers during air strikes and that evening helped to beat off a Japanese air attack.

After returning to Majuro for replenishment, the warship screened TG 58.2 during air strikes on Hollandia, Tanahmerah, Wakde, and Aitape to support amphibious operations on New Guinea. Late in April, *The Sullivans* participated in support of air strikes on the Japanese base at Truk. On the 29th during one of these raids, the Japanese retaliated with a low-level air attack. American radar picked up four Japanese planes 16 miles away, coming in fast at altitudes varying from 10 to 500 feet. When the planes came within range, *The Sullivans* opened up with one 40-millimeter twin mount and all five 5-inch guns. Two aircraft splashed into the sea due to the firing of the American ships, and one crossing ahead of *The Sullivans* was taken under fire and crashed in flames off her port beam.

The Sullivans arrived off the northwest coast of Ponape on the afternoon of 1 May and provided cover for the battleships led by *Iowa* (BB–61) which bombarded the island. From the disengaged side of the screen, *The Sullivans* fired 18 rounds from extreme range at Tumu Point. She then noted three beached Japanese landing barges and shifted her fire to them. However, she received the general cease-fire order shortly thereafter.

During the task unit's retirement, *The Sullivans* refueled from *Yorktown* (CV–10) and arrived at Majuro on 4 May. Ten days later, TG 58.2 sortied again— bound for Marcus and Wake Islands. Launching the first raid at 0800 on the 19th, the American carriers kept up nearly continuous air strikes with no enemy interruptions for three days. En route back to Majuro, *The Sullivans* and her sister destroyers conducted a thorough but unsuccessful search for a suspected submarine.

On 6 June, *The Sullivans* got underway again, bound for Saipan, Tinian, and Guam to screen carriers in conducting air strikes. On occasion while in the screen, *The Sullivans'* radar picked up enemy "snoopers" around the periphery of the formation—and before dawn at 0315 on the 12th, TG 58.2 shot down one in flames.

The second day's strikes against Saipan took place on the 13th to support the American landings there. Assigned to the duty of communication-linking station between task forces, *The Sullivans* remained within visual sighting distance of both TG's 58.1 and 58.2 during the day. That day, she picked up 31 Japanese merchant seamen after their ship had been sunk offshore and transferred these prisoners to flagship *Indianapolis* (CA–35).

On the 19th, Japanese aircraft attacked the task group. *The Sullivans* picked up a plane visually at a range of less than five miles. "Judies," diving from 23,000 feet, pressed home their attacks. One, taken under fire by *The Sullivans*, took tracer fire from the ship's 20- and 40-millimeter batteries and, moments later, crashed just short of the horizon. American air attacks against Pagan Island, made without enemy retaliation, topped off the Saipan-Tinian-Guam strikes; and *The Sullivans* proceeded with TG 58.2 to Eniwetok for upkeep.

Underway on 30 June, *The Sullivans* resumed work in the screen of carriers launching air strikes to support operations against Saipan and Tinian. During this action, *The Sullivans* served as fighter-direction ship for TU 58.2.4.

On Independence Day, *The Sullivans* joined Bombardment Unit One (TU 58.2.4) to conduct a shore bombardment of airfields, shore batteries, and other installations on the west coast of Iwo Jima. The heavy ships in the group opened fire at 1500, and smoke and dust soon obscured targets along the western shore of the island, making spotting difficult. *The Sullivans*, second ship in a column of destroyers, opened fire at 1548 on planes parked on the southern airstrip. After three ranging salvos, the ship commenced hitting twin-engined "Bettys" parked in revetments along the strip. Five planes blew up, and eight other planes were probably damaged by shrapnel and burning gasoline. Minutes later, an enemy ship resembling an LST came under *The Sullivans* gunfire and caught fire astern. While *Miller* (DD–535) closed to complete the destruction of the enemy vessel, *The Sullivans* and the remainder of the bombardment unit retired and rejoined TG 58.2.

From 7 to 22 July, TG 58.2 operated south and west of the Marianas, conducting daily air strikes on Guam and Rota Islands before returning to Garapan Anchorage, Saipan, to allow the carriers to replenish bombs. Underway at dawn on the 23d, *The Sullivans* accompanied the task group as it sped towards the Palaus for air strikes on the 26th and 27th. She joined TG 58.4 for temporary duty on 30 July and continued air strikes until the 6th of August, when she joined TG 58.7, the heavy bombardment group, and operated with TF 34 until 11 August, when the group returned to Eniwetok for replenishment.

Early in September, as the Navy prepared to take the Palaus, *The Sullivans* supported neutralizing air strikes against Japanese air bases in the Philippines. At dawn on the 7th, she began radar picket duty for TG 38.2 and continued the task through the strikes of the 9th and 10th. From 1800 on 12 September, the ships noted an increase in air activity—observing many bogies which merely orbited the formations as snoopers. The carriers conducted further raids on the central Philippines on the 13th and 14th and then shifted course to the north to subject Manila to air attacks commencing on the 21st. Three days later, American planes again hit the central Philippines.

Returning to Tanapag Harbor, Saipan, at dawn on the 28th, *The Sullivans* went alongside *Massachusetts* (BB–59) for ammunition, provisions, and routine upkeep. However, the cross-swells in the anchorage swept *The Sullivans* hard against the battleship's steel hide, damaging the destroyer's hull and superstructure. Following brief antisubmarine patrol duty, she proceeded to Ulithi on 1 October.

While undergoing tender repairs alongside *Dixie*, *The Sullivans* formed part of a nest of destroyers blown away from the tender during a heavy storm which lashed the anchorage. *The Sullivans* drifted free downwind and got up steam "in a hurry." However, she collided with *Uhlmann* (DD–687). Many small boats were being tossed about, and *The Sullivans* rescued four men from *Stockham*'s gig before it disappeared beneath the waves. As the storm abated on the 4th, the warship returned to Ulithi to complete the abbreviated tender overhaul alongside *Dixie*.

At 1615 on 6 October, *The Sullivans* sortied with the carriers and protected them during raids against targets on Formosa and the Ryukyus. On the evening of the 12th, as the planes returned to the carriers, radar spotted the first of many Japanese aircraft coming down from the north. For the next six hours, approximately 50 to 60 Japanese aircraft subjected the American task force to continuous air attacks. Nearly 45 minutes after sunset, *The Sullivans* sighted a "Betty," coming in low on the starboard side, and took it under fire. During the next 15 minutes, the formation to which *The Sullivans* was attached shot down three planes; between 1856 and 1954, the destroyer herself took five planes under fire. Varying speed between 18 and 29 knots, the formation undertook eight emergency maneuvers. Again and again, timely turns and the great volume of gunfire thrown up by the ships repulsed the enemy air attacks.

The second phase of the attack began at 2105 on the 12th and continued through 0235 on the 13th. The Japanese increased the use of "window" to jam American radar transmissions while their flares lit up the evening with ghostly light. The formation made smoke whenever enemy flare-dropping planes approached, creating an eerie haze effect which helped baffle the enemy pilots. Meanwhile, *The Sullivans* and the other ships in formation executed 38 simultaneous turn movements at speeds between 22 and 25 knots as their guns kept up a steady fire to repel the attackers.

The next day, the carriers again launched successful strikes on Formosa. During the ensuing night retirement, the formation again came under attack by Japanese torpedo-carrying "Betties" which struck home this time and damaged *Canberra* (CA–70). *The Sullivans* then helped to protect the damaged cruiser. On the 14th, "Betty" torpedo bombers scored against *Houston* (CL–81).*The Sullivans* soon joined the screen which guarded the two battle-battered cruisers as they retired toward Ulithi.

Things progressed well until the 16th, when the Japanese mounted a heavy air attack to attempt to finish off the "cripples." *Houston* reeled under the impact of a second hit astern, and *The Sullivans* opened fire on the "Frances" which had made the attack and splashed the Japanese plane. *The Sullivans* and *Stephen Potter* (DD–538) then took a second "Frances" under fire and knocked it down off the bow of *Santa Fe* (CL–60).

The Sullivans rescued 118 *Houston* men and kept them on board until the 18th, when she transferred them to *Boston* (CA–69). While the damaged cruisers were making their way to Ulithi, a Japanese surface force attempted to close the formation before TF 38 intervened to drive them back. *The Sullivans* transferred salvage gear to *Houston* and helped with the ship's many wounded. For his part in directing the destroyer's rescue and salvage attempts, Comdr. Richard J. Baum received his first Silver Star.

On 20 October, *The Sullivans* joined TG 38.2 for scheduled air strikes on the central Philippines in support of the Leyte landings. At dawn of the 24th, reconnaissance located a Japanese surface force south of Mindoro, and the American carriers launched air strikes all day against the enemy warships. That morning, a Japanese air attack developed, and *The Sullivans* downed an "Oscar" fighter plane.

By 25 October, enemy forces were sighted coming down from the north; TF 34, including *The Sullivans*, was formed and headed north, following the carrier groups in TF 38. At dawn on the 25th, the carriers launched air strikes to harass the Japanese surface units, now some 60 miles north. At 1100, TF 34 reversed course, topped-off the destroyers with fuel, and formed fast striking group TG 34.5, with *Iowa* (BB–61), *New Jersey* (BB–62), three light cruisers, *The Sullivans*, and seven other destroyers. The American force missed the Japanese by three hours, but ran across a straggler and reported sinking an *Atago*-class cruiser. Japanese records fail to confirm the claim.

After sweeping south along the coast of Samar hunting for enemy "cripples," *The Sullivans* and other units of TG 34.5 reported back to TG 38.2. The destroyer then remained in the Philippine area, screening the fast carriers and standing by on plane guard duties, through mid-November. At dusk on the 19th, during one of the many air attacks fought off by *The Sullivans*, the destroyer damaged a "Betty" by gunfire and watched it disappear over the horizon, smoking but stubbornly remaining airborne. Six days later, she had better luck when her guns set a Japanese plane afire and splashed it into the sea. Two days later, her task group returned to Ulithi.

The destroyer undertook training exercises from 8 to 11 December before rejoining TG 38.2 to screen its warships during air strikes on Manila and southern Luzon beginning on 14 December. On the 17th, running low on fuel, *The Sullivans* commenced refueling but, with the weather worsening minute by minute, she broke off the operation. A typhoon swept through the Fleet, with the wind clocked at an estimated 115 knots on the morning of 18 December. Three destroyers were sunk and several ships damaged by the winds and waves. *The Sullivans*—aided by the "lucky shamrock" painted on her funnel—emerged from the typhoon undamaged and, on the 20th, commenced searching for men lost overboard from other ships. The lingering bad weather resulted in cancellation of air strikes, and *The Sullivans* retired to Ulithi on Christmas Eve.

After a brief run to Manus and back, escorting *Iowa*, *The Sullivans* sortied from Ulithi on 30 December to screen TG 38.2's air strikes on Formosa in support of the American landings on Luzon. Heavy seas forced a three-day postponement of a high-speed thrust toward the target originally planned for the night of 6 January 1945. During the evening of the 9th, the task force passed through Bashi Channel and entered the South China Sea. Three days later, carrier planes from TG 38.2 swept over Saigon and Camranh Bay, Indochina, hammering at whatever enemy merchantmen they found.

Soon after the conclusion of the air strikes, a bombardment group, TG 34.5, was formed to go after possible "cripples" and dispatch them by surface gunfire. Accordingly, two battleships, two heavy cruisers, three light cruisers, and 15 destroyers raced into Camranh Bay but found it devoid of Japanese shipping. Throughout the day, however, carrier pilots had better luck and enjoyed a veritable "field day" with coastal *marus*. During subsequent air strikes on Hainan Island, Hong Kong, and Formosa, *The Sullivans* served on radar picket duty 10 miles ahead of the task group.

A brief respite for upkeep at Ulithi in late January preceded the ship's deployment with TG 58.2, covering the carriers as they launched devastating air strikes against the Japanese homeland itself, hitting Tokyo and other targets on Honshu on 16 and 17 February. From the 18th through the 21st, American carrier-based air power struck at Japanese positions contesting the landings on Iwo Jima. More strikes were scheduled for Tokyo four days later, but bad weather forced their cancellation. Retiring from the area, TF 58 fueled and commenced a high-speed run at Okinawa at noon on 28 February. Later that day, *The Sullivans* sighted and destroyed a drifting mine. At dawn on 1 March, Hellcats, Avengers, Dauntlesses, and Helldivers pounded Japanese positions on Okinawa. The ships of the task force encountered no enemy opposition from sea or sky and soon retired towards Ulithi.

The Sullivans sortied 12 days later, bound for Kyushu and southern Honshu to support the invasion of Okinawa. Once again screening for TG 58.2, *The Sullivans* stood by as the carriers launched air strikes on 14 March. On 20 March, *The Sullivans* fueled from *Enterprise* (CV-6) at 1152, clearing the carrier's side five minutes later when a kamikaze alert sent the ships scurrying. At 1439, *The Sullivans* commenced maneuvering to go alongside *Enterprise* again—this time to pick up a part for her FD radar antenna. Soon, however, another enemy air attack scattered the ships. As a line had not yet been thrown across to the carrier, *The Sullivans* bent on speed and cleared her as other ships in the task group opened fire on the attackers. A Japanese plane plunged through the antiaircraft fire and crashed into *Halsey Powell* (DD-686) astern as that destroyer was fuelling alongside *Hancock* (CV-19). The stricken destroyer lost steering control and started to veer across the big carrier's bow, and only rapid and radical maneuvering on *Hancock*'s part averted a collision.

The Sullivans soon closed *Halsey Powell* to render emergency assistance. She slowed to a stop 11 minutes later and lowered her motor whaleboat to transfer her medical officer and a pharmacist's mate to *Halsey Powell*, when another kamikaze came out of the skies, apparently bent on crashing into *The Sullivans*. At 1610, the destroyer's radar picked up the "Zeke" on its approach; and, as soon as the motor whaler was clear of the water, *The Sullivans* leapt ahead with all engines thrusting at flank speed.

Bringing right full rudder, *The Sullivans* maneuvered radically while her 20- and 40-millimeter guns sent streams of shells at the "Zeke," which passed 100 feet over the masthead and escaped. Meanwhile, *Halsey Powell* managed to achieve a steady course at five knots; and, with *The Sullivans*, she retired toward Ulithi. However, their troubles were not yet over. At 1046 on

the following day, 21 March, *The Sullivans* picked up a plane, closing from 15 miles. Visually identified as a twin-engined "Frances," the aircraft was taken under fire at 10,000 yards by *The Sullivans*' 5-inch battery. *Halsey Powell* joined in too; and, within a few moments, the "Frances" crashed into the sea about 3,000 yards abeam of *The Sullivans*. At 1250, a combat air patrol (CAP) Hellcat from *Yorktown*, under direction by *Halsey Powell*, splashed another "Frances." At 1320, a CAP Hellcat from *Intrepid*, directed by *The Sullivans*, downed a "Nick" or "Dinah."

On 25 March, *The Sullivans* and *Halsey Powell* arrived at Ulithi, the former for upkeep prior to training exercises and the latter for battle repairs.

The warship next rendezvoused with TF 58 off Okinawa and guarded the carriers supporting the landings on the island. While operating on radar picket duty on the 15th, the ship came under enemy air attack, but downed one plane and emerged unscathed. She continued conducting radar picket patrols for the task group, ranging some 12 to 25 miles out from the main body of the force. On the afternoon of 29 April, she commenced fueling from *Bunker Hill*, but a kamikaze alert interrupted the replenishment, forcing *The Sullivans* to break away from the carrier's side. During the ensuing action, *Hazelwood* (DD-531) and *Haggard* (DD-555) were both struck by Japanese suicide planes, but survived.

Kamikazes continued to plague the ships of TG 58.3 as they supported the troops fighting ashore on Okinawa. Everything from landing craft to battleships was fair game for those Japanese pilots determined to die for their emperor in a blaze of glory. On the morning of 11 May, a kamikaze crashed into *Bunker Hill*. *The Sullivans* promptly closed the carrier to render assistance and picked up 166 survivors. After transferring them to ships in TG 50.8 and replenishing her fuel bunkers, she helped to screen TG 58.3 during air strikes on Kyushu.

In a morning air attack three days later, the gallant old warrior *Enterprise* was hit by a kamikaze. Four enemy planes were shot down in the melee—one by *The Sullivans* in what proved to be her last combat action during World War II.

The Sullivans anchored at San Pedro Bay, Leyte Gulf, on 1 June for recreation and upkeep. She departed Leyte on the 20th, bound, via Eniwetok and Pearl Harbor, for the west coast. The destroyer arrived at Mare Island, Calif., on 9 July and, two days later, commenced her overhaul. She thus missed the final fleet activity which rang down the curtain on the last act of the war. Worn down by a series of blows delivered by American seapower and stunned by the all but unlimited destructive power of two atomic bombs, Japan capitulated on 15 August, ending the war.

Meanwhile, since the return of peace greatly reduced the Navy's need for warships, *The Sullivans* was decommissioned at San Diego on 10 January 1946—soon after her overhaul was completed—and she was placed in the Pacific Reserve Fleet.

The destroyer remained there until May 1951, when she began reactivation work which prepared her for recommissioning on 6 July 1951. The destroyer soon headed south, transited the Panama Canal, and pressed on northward to her home port, Newport, R.I. During the winter of 1951 and 1952, the warship conducted training exercises off the east coast and in the Caribbean.

Late in the summer of 1952, *The Sullivans* departed Newport on 6 September, bound for Japan. Proceeding via the Panama Canal, San Diego, Pearl Harbor, and Midway, she arrived at Sasebo on 10 October but got underway the next day to join Task Force 77 off the eastern shores of Korea. The ship served in the screen of the fast carriers launching repeated air strikes to interdict enemy supply lines and to support United Nations ground forces battling the communists. Remaining on this duty until the 20th, *The Sullivans* steamed to Yokosuka, Japan, for a brief refit.

After a cruise to Buckner Bay, Okinawa, *The Sullivans* rejoined TF 77 on 16 November to resume screening activities and plane guard duty. She supported the carriers as they made the northern-most stab at North Korean supply lines, approaching within 75 miles of the Soviet base at Vladivostok. MiG-15 fighters approached the task force, but combat air patrol Grumman F9F "Panthers" downed two of the attackers and damaged a third in history's first engagement between jet fighters over water.

The destroyer arrived back at Sasebo on 5 December. On 14 December, she joined United Nations forces blockading the Korean coasts—interdicting seaborne traffic and bombarding shore targets both to support United Nations ground troops and to interdict enemy supply operations. Arriving in Area "G" the following day, *The Sullivans* made contact with the enemy on the 16th off Songjin, an important rail terminus and supply center. For the next few days, she bombarded trains and tunnels and frequently opened fire to destroy railroad rolling stock and depots and to prevent repairs to tracks and buildings.

On Christmas Day 1952, as *The Sullivans* scored direct hits on a railroad bridge, she was taken under fire by communist gunners ashore. Fifty rounds from enemy guns failed to touch the ship, although near-misses showered the warship's decks with shrapnel. Counter-battery fire from the ship destroyed at least one of the troublesome shore batteries.

The Sullivans departed Yokosuka on 26 January 1953. On her way home, the warship called at Buckner Bay; at Hong Kong; Subic Bay; Singapore; Colombo, Ceylon; Bombay, India; Bahrein; and Aden, before steaming through the Red Sea, transiting the Suez Canal, and proceeding via Naples to Cannes, France. After a brief fueling stop at Gibraltar, the warship arrived at Newport on 11 April.

The destroyer operated out of her home port well into the summer of 1953, before deploying to the Mediterranean for a tour of duty with the 6th Fleet. She remained on this duty through the end of the year and returned to Newport on 3 February 1954 for operations off the east coast and into the Caribbean through May 1955. She again deployed to European and Mediterranean waters from May to August of that year before returning to Newport late in the summer.

In the years that followed, *The Sullivans* continued alternating east coast operations with Mediterranean deployments. The summer of 1958 saw a communist threat to the security of Lebanon, and President Dwight D. Eisenhower ordered American ships to land troops there to protect Americans and to help stabilize the tense situation. *The Sullivans* supported the landings of marines at Beirut, Lebanon. After their presence had dispelled the crisis, she returned to the United States for a three-month navy yard overhaul and subsequent refresher training in Guantanamo Bay, Cuba.

Back at Newport in March 1959, *The Sullivans* joined a hunter/killer group based around *Lake Champlain* (CV-39). Then, after making a midshipman training cruise in which she conducted antisubmarine warfare operations, the destroyer sailed for another Mediterranean deployment which lasted until she returned home in the autumn.

Operations out of Newport occupied *The Sullivans* until the spring of 1960 when she headed south for ASROC evaluations off Key West, Fla. During this deployment to southern climes, the warship helped to rescue five survivors from a crashed Air Force KC-97 Stratotanker which had splashed off Cape Canaveral.

Following NATO exercises in September, *The Sullivans* visited Lisbon, Portugal, prior to a quick trip through the Mediterranean, Suez Canal, and Red Sea, to Karachi, West Pakistan. In late October and into November, the veteran destroyer participated in Operation "Midlink III," joint operations with Pakistani, Iranian, and British warships. After returning to the Mediterranean, *The Sullivans* conducted exercises with the French Navy and with the 6th Fleet and reached home in time for Christmas.

In January 1961, *The Sullivans* assisted in the sea trials of *Abraham Lincoln* (SSBN-602) off Portsmouth, N.H., before steaming south and taking part in Operation "Springboard." While in the Caribbean, she visited Martinique. Briefly back at Newport early in March, *The Sullivans* soon returned to the West Indies to support marine landing exercises at Vieques, Puerto Rico.

In April, the ship began intensive training in the waters off Florida to prepare to cover a Project Mercury spaceshot. *The Sullivans* joined *Lake Champlain* (CVS-39) at Mayport, Fla., and took station. On 5 May 1961, Comdr. Alan Shepard's space capsule passed overhead and splashed down near *Lake Champlain* and was speedily rescued by helicopters from the carrier. *The Sullivans* then made a midshipmen cruise in June, visiting New York and Halifax, Nova Scotia.

From September 1961 to February 1962, *The Sullivans* underwent a major overhaul in the Boston Naval Shipyard. She proceeded to Guantanamo Bay soon thereafter to train for duty as a school ship. She subsequently served as a model destroyer in which officer students could see and learn the fundamentals of destroyer operation. In May and again in August, *The Sullivans* made training cruises to the Caribbean for the Destroyer School.

In October, after Soviet missiles were discovered in Cuba, *The Sullivans* joined American naval forces blockading the island during negotiations with the Soviet Union over the issue. When the Soviet Government withdrew the strategic weapons, the destroyer returned to Newport.

On 7 January 1963, *The Sullivans* got underway from Newport bound for the Caribbean and another training cruise. Following her return to Newport, she conducted local operations for the Destroyer School. The tragic loss of nuclear submarine *Thresher* (SSN-593) off Boston on 10 April 1963 caused the destroyer to support emergency investigations of the disaster.

For the remainder of 1963 and into the first few months of 1964, *The Sullivans* continued to train officer students. On 1 April 1964, the destroyer was transferred to the naval reserve training force, and her homeport was changed to New York City. Departing Newport on 13 April, the warship proceeded to New York and took on her selected reserve crew. Her cruises with the reserves embarked were devoted mostly to ASW exercises and took the ship to Canadian ports such as Halifax, Nova Scotia; St. John, New Brunswick; and Charlottetown, Prince Edward Island, in the north to Palm Beach, Fla., in the south.

On 7 January 1965, *The Sullivans* was decommissioned at the Philadelphia Naval Shipyard. She remained in reserve into the 1970's. In 1977, she and cruiser *Little Rock* (CG-4) were processed for donation to the city of Buffalo, N.Y., where they now serve as a memorial.

The Sullivans received nine battle stars for World War II service and two for Korean service.

Theenim

A star in the constellation Eridan.

(AKA-63: dp. 13,910; l. 459'; b. 63'; dr. 26'4''; s. 16.5 k.; cpl. 399; a. 1 5", 8 40mm.; cl. *Andromeda*)

Theenim (AKA-63) was laid down under Maritime Commission contract (MC hull 215) on 18 July 1941 at Kearny, N.J., by the Federal Shipbuilding Co.; launched on 31 October 1944; sponsored by Mrs. Joseph Midder; and commissioned on 22 December 1944, Comdr. G. A. Littlefield, USCG, in command.

On 6 January 1945, *Theenim* got underway for Hampton Roads, Va., and a brief shakedown in the Chesapeake Bay-Virginia capes area. After loading at

Norfolk, the attack cargo ship got underway for the South Pacific on the 27th. The ship proceeded via the Panama Canal and Hawaii to the Solomon Islands, arriving at Guadalcanal on 5 March. Assigned to Amphibious Squadron 5, *Theenim* loaded troops and equipment and headed for the Marianas on 15 March. She sortied from the Saipan staging area on 27 March with Task Group 51.2, Demonstration Group "Charlie," for the assault on Okinawa. *Theenim* arrived off the Hagushi Beaches on 1 April, but did not land her troops until the 3d, when she began offloading mobile equipment and debarking marines. Three days later, she helped to splash a "Val" some 1,000 yards off her stern. On the 12th, her gunners shot down a "Zeke" that passed about 60 feet over her bridge. On the 15th, her gunners aided in the destruction of an "Oscar."

The next day, *Theenim* joined a convoy that was retiring to the Marianas, and she arrived at Saipan on 19 April. On 4 June, she stood out of Tanapag Harbor to return to the Solomons to pick up cargo and carry it to Guam where she arrived on 3 July. For the next three months—the last phase of the fighting and the early days of the occupation—the ship shuttled supplies between Saipan, Manus, Guadalcanal, Espiritu Santo, Leyte, Hokkaido, and Honshu. On 5 November, she departed Tokyo Bay for the United States.

Theenim arrived at Portland, Oreg., on 17 November and moved down the coast to San Francisco on 9 December. On 27 December, the ship left the west coast for the Philippines and arrived at Subic Bay on 17 January 1946. She operated in the Philippine Islands until 19 March when she got underway for San Francisco. Upon her arrival on the west coast, the ship was ordered to report to the Atlantic Fleet for disposition. She reached Norfolk on 19 April. *Theenim* was decommissioned and returned to the War Shipping Administration on 10 May and was struck from the Navy list on 12 May 1946.

Theenim received one battle star for World War II service.

Thelma

Acquired by the United States Navy on 11 January 1943, *Thelma* was renamed *Martha's Vineyard* (IX–97) (*q.v.*) on 23 January 1943.

Theodore E. Chandler

Theodore Edson Chandler—born at Annapolis, Md., in 1894 on the day after Christmas—entered the Naval Academy in July 1911. He graduated on 5 June 1915 and received orders to report for duty in *Florida* (Battleship No. 30). Ens. Chandler next served briefly on board *New Hampshire* (Battleship No. 25) beginning training in the use of torpedoes at the end of April 1917. On 2 August, he completed that assignment and, four days later, joined the precommissioning complement of *Conner* (Destroyer No. 72), then being fitted out at the Philadelphia Navy Yard. In May 1918, Lt. (jg.) Chandler sailed in *Conner* to Brest, France, his destroyer's base during the last six months of World War I. After the Armistice, his service in European waters included a brief term as the temporary commanding officer of *Conner*. Chandler returned home in April and, in the following month, reported to the shipyard of the William Cramp & Sons Shipbuilding Co. to help outfit *Chandler* (Destroyer No. 206), named in honor of his late grandfather, former Secretary of the Navy William E. Chandler. After her commissioning in September, he served in that ship until December 1920 when he was detached to return to the United States.

On 2 January 1921, he reported for duty at the Naval Post Graduate School at Annapolis, Md., and began a 29-month series of ordnance-related studies.

On 1 June 1923, he completed training duty and, after a brief leave of absence, reported to Newport News, Va., on 4 July for duty in conjunction with the outfitting of *West Virginia* (BB–48). The battleship went into commission on 1 December, and Chandler served in her until 16 January 1925 when he was transferred to *Colorado* (BB–45). In June 1926, newly-promoted Lt. Comdr. Chandler came ashore once more for a two-year assignment at the Naval Mine Depot, Yorktown, Va. A nine-month tour of duty as gunnery officer in *Trenton* (CL–11) followed. He reported on board *General Alava* (AG–5) on 24 April 1929 but was detached only two days later to assume command of *Pope* (DD–225). In October 1930, he began another series of shore assignments, reporting initially to the Bureau of Ordnance and then to the Army Industrial College before rounding out duty ashore with a brief tour in the office of the Chief of Naval Operations.

On 30 May 1932, Chandler resumed sea duty as gunnery officer on the staff of the Commander, Destroyers, Battle Force. On 2 February 1934, he assumed command of *Buchanan* (DD–131). Between August 1935 and June 1938, he served three successive tours as assistant naval attache: first at Paris, then at Madrid, and finally at Lisbon. He arrived in Camden, N.J., in June 1938 to help fit out *Nashville* (CL–43); and he served as her executive officer until July 1940. Next, he returned to Washington for a 15-month assignment in the office of the Chief of Naval Operations. Near the end of that tour of duty, he was promoted to captain on 18 July 1941.

Chandler relieved Capt. P. P. Powell as commanding officer of *Omaha* (CL–4) on 15 October. Shortly over three weeks later, an event occurred that highlighted Chandler's tour in command of the light cruiser. On the morning of 6 November, *Omaha*, in company with *Somers* (DD–381), came across a darkened ship that acted suspiciously when challenged. That ship—although bearing the name *Willmoto* and purportedly operating out of Philadelphia—proved to be the German blockade runner *Odenwald*, bound for Germany with 3,857 metric tons of raw rubber in her holds. Scuttled by her crew, the German ship began to sink; but Capt. Chandler sent a party on the German vessel that controlled the flooding and salvaged the ship. It proved to be the last time that American sailors received "prize money."

For most of the next 18 months, *Omaha* cruised the waters of the South Atlantic in search of German blockade runners and submarines. That tour of duty ended in April 1943, when Chandler was selected to command United States naval forces in the Aruba-Curaçao area.

On 3 May, he was promoted to rear admiral. In July 1944, Rear Admiral Chandler took command of Cruiser Division (CruDiv) 2, Atlantic Fleet. In that capacity, he participated in Operation "Dragoon," the invasion of southern France executed in mid-August, and commanded the "Sitka-Romeo" force which captured the Iles d'Hyeres just off the coast of Provence. Shortly thereafter, Rear Admiral Chandler was given command of Battleship Division (BatDiv) 2 of the Pacific Fleet. He reported for duty on 2 October in time to command his ships—part of Oldendorf's bombardment group—during the Leyte invasion and helped to repulse the Japanese southern attack group—Nishimura's Force "C" and Shima's 2d Striking Force—in the Surigao Strait phase of the Battle for Leyte Gulf.

On 8 December, Rear Admiral Chandler was shifted to command of CruDiv 4 and flew his flag above *Louisville* (CA–28). During the voyage from Leyte to Lingayen for the invasion of Luzon, Chandler's cruisers came under heavy Japanese air attacks—mostly by kamikazes. Late in the afternoon of 5 January 1945, a group of 16 suicide planes swooped in on the force then about 100 miles from Manila Bay. One of the four successful kamikazes crashed into Rear Admiral Chandler's flagship at her number 2 turret, but she continued in her mission. The next day, however, the cruiser suffered more severely during a repeat performance. At 1730, another suicide plane plunged into the cruiser's starboard side at the bridge. His explosives wreaked havoc with the flag bridge where Rear Admiral Chandler stood. Horribly burned by gasoline flames, the flag officer responded to the occasion like a true sailor. He manhandled fire hoses alongside enlisted men to stop the flames and then waited his turn for first aid with those same ratings. The admiral, his lungs scorched very severely, was beyond help. He died the next day in spite of the Herculean efforts of the medical department.

(DD–717: dp. 2,400; l. 390'6''; b. 40'10''; dr. 19'; s. 35 k.; cpl. 337; a. 6 5'', 12 40mm., 20 20mm., 5 21'' tt., 6 dcp., 2 dct.; cl. *Gearing*)

Theodore E. Chandler (DD–717) was laid down on 23 April 1945 at Kearny, N.J., by the Federal Shipbuilding Co.; launched on 20 October 1945; sponsored by Mrs. Theodore E. Chandler; and commissioned on 22 March 1946, Comdr. Francis O. Fletcher, Jr., in command.

After shakedown near Guantanamo Bay, Cuba, she escorted *Saipan* (CVL–48) and *Leyte* (CV–32) while the two carriers trained new pilots. Then, on 20 September, she stood out of New York bound for the west coast. The destroyer transited the Panama Canal on the 26th and joined Destroyer Squadron (DesRon) 17 at San Diego on 7 October. After amphibious and fleet exercises on the west coast, she departed San Diego on 6 January 1947 bound for Japan.

The warship reached Yokosuka on the 25th and began showing the flag and observing events in China during the struggle between communists and Nationalists. Operating from Japan—where she called at such places as Fukuoka, Kagoshima, and Sasebo—she visited Tsingtao, Hong Kong, Shanghai, and Amoy to keep a wary eye on the events occurring in China until she returned to San Diego on 20 September.

After operating along the west coast for the next year, *Theodore E. Chandler* headed west on 1 October 1948 for her second tour of duty in the western Pacific. That assignment was abbreviated on 24 November when she collided with *Ozbourn* (DD–846) during high-speed, darkened-ship, night maneuvers off Tsingtao. After stops at Tsingtao and at Yokosuka for temporary repairs, she headed back to the west coast on 14 January 1949. The destroyer reached Long Beach on 5 February and, after completing a five-month repair period, resumed operations along the Pacific coast which, save for a run to Pearl Harbor in the fall of 1949, occupied her until events in Korea summoned her back to the Orient.

When the North Korean People's Army invaded South Korea on 25 June 1950, *Theodore E. Chandler* was operating out of San Diego. She spent another nine days at sea; then joined *Helena* (CA–75) and the rest of Destroyer Division (DesDiv) 111 to form the first unit dispatched from the west coast to the new Asian conflict. After brief stops at Pearl Harbor and Yokosuka, she arrived in Sasebo on 25 July.

A brief conference held there organized the various support and escort forces into Task Force (TF) 96. *Theodore E. Chandler* became a unit of Task Group (TG) 96.5, the Japan-Korea Support Group, made up of an escort element, a west Korean supporting element, and two east Korean support elements. DesDiv 111, with *Helena* as flagship, made up one of the rotating, east Korean support elements. On the 26th, the unit departed Sasebo and shaped a course for Korea to conduct shore bombardments in support of United Nations (UN) land forces. En route, however, the task element received orders changing its destination to the Taiwan Strait. *Chandler* and her sister warships completed their mission in the narrow waters separating Taiwan from communist-controlled mainland China and headed for Japan on 2 August. The ships reached Sasebo on the

4th and departed again three days later. Finally, on 7 August, they took up station off the Korean coast.

Initially, they delivered gunfire to relieve the pressure upon the northeastern end of the Pusan perimeter. During her first assignment, *Theodore E. Chandler* steamed to Yongdok to bombard enemy supply lines running south along the coast, bypassing the ROK 3d Division isolated at Chongha, and on toward Pohang where UN lines ended at the Sea of Japan. On 14 August, the destroyer joined *Helena* in a highly successful shoot near Sinchang, during which the two ships destroyed a North Korean supply train and damaged several bridges and tunnels. By the following day, however, North Korean pressure on the Chongha enclave had become so intense that Lt. Gen. Walton H. Walker decided to evacuate the ROK 3d Division by sea. While shipping for the evacuation assembled, the situation at Chongha continued to deteriorate, but the 3d Division relied upon the gunfire delivered by *Chandler* and the other ships of the *Helena* task element to hold back North Korean forces until TF 77 could arrive with the Sunday punch. Even after the carrier planes arrived on the afternoon of the 16th and started close support, the destroyer and her sisters continued to help *Helena* support the ROK forces during the two more days it took to complete the evacuation.

On the 18th, she retired from the Korean coast with the rest of the *Helena* group and set course for Japan. The task element reached Sasebo that same day but on the 23rd returned to Korean waters. The next day, *Chandler* and the other destroyers of DesDiv 111 helped *Helena* subject the railroad cars and warehouses at Tanchon to a severe pounding. On the 26th, the task element arrived off Pohang to relieve the *Toledo* (CA–133) unit in supporting the northeastern end of the UN line. The warships remained in that area with *Helena* until 29 August when they returned to Sasebo for an overnight stopover and, the next day, resumed station off Pohang. After three days off the east coast of Korea, the destroyer reentered Sasebo on 2 September. Ten days later, she headed for the western coast of Korea and the amphibious operation at Inchon.

For almost a month, she cruised the waters of the Yellow Sea. She helped soften the enemy positions until the landings on 15 September and, after that, covered the amphibious forces and conducted bombardments which aided the troops ashore in pushing their advance forward. Early in October, she completed her mission in the Yellow Sea and returned to Sasebo on the 5th. During the next two months, she operated along Korea's eastern coast, interdicting communist supply lines with gunfire. Early in December, she made a very brief stop at Sasebo before beginning a month of duty on station off Hungnam. During the evacuation of UN troops from that North Korean port, *Theodore E. Chandler* once again had the opportunity to aid land forces—hard-pressed since the intervention of communist China in late November—to hold a precarious perimeter during an evacuation operation. The maneuver itself took just less than a fortnight—from 11 December to Christmas Eve—but *Theodore E. Chandler* remained in the general neighborhood for an additional two weeks to dampen somewhat the enemy's victory jubliation by reminding him that strong United States forces remained nearby.

Between 8 and 19 January 1951, she returned to Sasebo and enjoyed her first extended period in port in over three months. When the destroyer put to sea again, she began with an entirely new type of duty, screening the fast carriers of TF 77. For the two months of combat duty before she returned to the United States, the warship alternated between familiar bombardment duty and assignments with the fast carriers. Throughout that period, enemy logistics operations remained the primary target of United States naval might. Finally, on 9 March, she cleared Korean waters to return home; and, after one-day stops at Yokosuka, Pearl Harbor, and San Francisco, the destroyer arrived back in San Diego on 25 March.

During the seven months that the warship spent on the west coast, the conflict in Korea changed from a war of movement and settled down to a war of position, much like that experienced in Europe during World War I—but one in which both sides measured victory by a political, rather than a military, yardstick. The exclusion of total military victory as an objective transformed the struggle into a process of jockeying about for specific geographical advantages which could be translated into diplomatic leverage at the negotiating table. Gains and losses were reported more frequently in yards than in miles. Men died to secure an isolated piece of topography instead of some broader geographic expression. An anonymous hill became more significant than a province.

This change in the nature of the conflict shifted the United Nation's offensive initiative to their naval and air forces. The war of position made enemy lines of communication and supply the targets of interdiction activities by TF 77 and by the blockading forces. Thus, upon *Theodore E. Chandler*'s return to Korea for a second tour of duty during the winter of 1951 and 1952, she settled into more routine assignments. She served with both TF 77, screening the carriers while their aerial arm reached deep into North Korea, and with the UN Blockading and Escort Force (TF 95). The latter duty proved to be more variegated because it involved blockade duty, escort duty, and frequent coastal bombardment missions. Short tours of duty patrolling the Taiwan Strait, visits to Japan, and liberty calls at Hong Kong all served to break up her long stretches of service along the Korean coast.

Her third and final Korean War deployment lasted from January to mid-August 1953 and, with it, came more of the same type of duty she encountered during the preceding assignment. That tour also brought an end to the hostilities when, late in July—after two years of negotiation, see-saw land warfare, and a tight naval blockade—both sides agreed to an armistice. The destroyer remained in the vicinity of Korea for three weeks after hostilities officially ended and then returned to the United States.

In the decade between the end of hostilities in Korea and America's involvement in yet another Asian conflict, *Theodore E. Chandler* participated in peacetime preparations and duties. During that interlude, she deployed to the Far East seven times; and, for the most part, she busied herself in training exercises with 7th Fleet units and with Allied naval units such as those of the Taiwan Navy. She also served periodically with the Taiwan Strait patrol. When not deployed to the Orient, the destroyer trained with 1st Fleet units along the west coast. Most frequently, she conducted antisubmarine warfare (ASW) drills with hunter-killer groups built around aircraft carriers specially modified to stalk submarines. Finally, during that period, she entered the yard twice for rather extensive repairs and modifications. In mid-February 1961, the destroyer began a year-long Fleet Rehabilitation and Modernization (FRAM) overhaul during which the San Francisco Naval Shipyard refurbished her and brought her physical plant up to date. The second extended yard period came in December 1962, when, after her return from the western Pacific, she entered the yard for repairs to her generating plant which she completed in March 1963. At that time, she resumed training operations in the eastern Pacific where, save for a cruise to Hawaii with *Bon Homme Richard* (CVA–31) late in November, she remained until the summer of 1964.

Her next deployment coincided with the beginning of America's extensive buildup in Vietnam. On 19 June, she departed the west coast with ASW Group 1 bound for what appeared to be a normal peacetime deployment to the western Pacific. However, on 2 August, North Vietnamese torpedo boats allegedly made a torpedo attack upon *Maddox* (DD–622) while she cruised international waters in the Gulf of Tonkin. *Theodore E. Chandler* received orders to join the ASW screen of American carriers dispatched to deliver retaliatory air strikes on North Vietnamese torpedo boat bases. After the strikes, the warship resumed her normal duties with ASW Group 1 and the 7th Fleet; but a new Asian conflict cast its shadow upon her and would dominate eight of the 10 years remaining in her career.

Theodore E. Chandler returned to Long Beach on 6 January 1965 for an overhaul at the Long Beach Naval Shipyard. After 10 weeks of refresher training and ASW exercises, she began preparations early in August for another deployment to the western Pacific. She departed Long Beach on 20 August and, following a nonstop voyage in company with DesDiv 92 and oilers *Kennebec* (AO–36) and *Navasota* (AO–106), arrived in Yokosuka on 4 September. Four days later, the warship put to sea again bound for the Philippines. Upon her arrival at Subic Bay, she received orders to the Taiwan Strait, and she patrolled those vital waters from 16 to 20 September. When she returned to the Philippines, *Theodore E. Chandler* began shore bombardment training at the Tabones range.

That duty, however, was interrupted on 30 September by a special assignment. Two days earlier, Indonesian communists—fearful that President Sukarno's failing health might result in their political eclipse—staged a coup. In rapid succession, they captured and executed most Indonesian right-wing military leaders. In response to a potential blood bath, *Theodore E. Chandler* raced through the South China Sea, rendezvoused with the 7th Fleet Amphibious Ready Group, and prepared to evacuate United States citizens from Indonesia should the need arise. Fortunately, that eventuality never came to pass. The Indonesian Defense Minister, General Nasution, managed to elude those sent to liquidate him and led the swift, decisive counterstroke that throttled the revolt before it gained momentum. Consequently, the special task organization was dissolved, and *Theodore E. Chandler* departed the area in company with *Hollister* (DD–788).

During the second portion of the deployment, the warship began regular tours of duty with the naval forces operating off the Vietnamese coastline. On 9 October, she and *Hollister* joined *Bon Homme Richard* to form Task Group (TG) 77.4 which operated on "Dixie Station"—off the central coast of South Vietnam —until the 18th. The next day, she steamed north with the task group to "Yankee Station" whence *Bon Homme Richard* planes struck targets in North Vietnam. After 10 days of air operations, *Theodore E. Chandler* departed the area with the rest of the task group for five days of rest and relaxation at Hong Kong.

The warships left Hong Kong on 11 November to take up station off the coast of North Vietnam again. On the 18th, the destroyer received orders detaching her from the *Bon Homme Richard* group for duty as an antiaircraft warfare (AAW) picket ship. After serving 22 days as an AAW picket, she rejoined the carrier group again on 10 December. The carrier launched air strikes during the following eight days; and then, on the 18th, the entire group shaped a course for Subic Bay and thence proceeded to Hong Kong for another five-day port call.

While in Hong Kong, *Theodore E. Chandler* was detached from TG 77.4 and ordered back to Subic Bay for shore bombardment training. In January 1966, she returned to the coast of South Vietnam and rendered naval gunfire support for the troops operating ashore. On one occasion, the destroyer brought her 5-inch guns to bear on Viet Cong forces staging a major attack on Allied troops and received credit for thwarting the guerrillas. In mid-January, she completed her assignment in the Far East and headed back to the United States.

Following four months of duty in and out of Long Beach, *Theodore E. Chandler* departed that port in June for an extended deployment to the western Pacific. Records of her activities during the 1966 portion of the two years she spent in the Far East are incomplete. However, it can be reasonably assumed that she spent a great deal of time off the coast of Vietnam providing naval gunfire in support of troops ashore, escorting and plane-guarding aircraft carriers during air strikes on targets in both North and South Vietnam, and interdicting enemy coastal logistics operations.

On the other hand, records do tell that she joined *Mansfield* (DD-728) east of Okinawa during the fall of 1966 to patrol the secondary recovery zone for the Gemini 11 space project. When the capsule splashed down successfully in the primary zone located in the Atlantic Ocean, the two destroyers resumed their normal duties. In mid-October, while en route back to the combat zone, she received orders to join *Franklin D. Roosevelt* (CVA-42) and screen that carrier during operations in the Gulf of Tonkin. When the carrier had to return to Yokosuka for repairs in October, *Theodore E. Chandler* went along as escort.

By early November, the warship had returned to Vietnamese waters. Halfway through the forenoon watch on the 13th, she responded to a call for help from SS *Rutgers Victory*, on fire and burning furiously in Nha Trang harbor—about 200 miles northeast of Saigon. Within two hours, the destroyer entered the harbor, the first Navy ship to answer the call. Shortly after her arrival, *Prime* (MSO-446) joined the battle against the flames. *Chandler*'s damage control party led the struggle against the flames burning deep in the stricken ship. Two Army tugs, which also joined the fray, concentrated on cooling the victory ship's hull while *Chandler* and *Prime* crewmen fought the fires themselves. The combined efforts of two Navy ships, two Army tugs, an Air Force firefighting team, and *Rutgers Victory*'s own crew eventually conquered the blaze in a fine display of inter-sevice cooperation, and the warship cleared Nha Trang to resume a heavy schedule of shore bombardment missions.

Records of the subsequent portions of that deployment are much more detailed. The beginning of 1967 found her in Yokosuka and off Tokyo Bay for type training. On the 16th, she headed back to Vietnam to resume gunfire support duty. After bombardments in support of the 1st Air Cavalry's Operation "Thayer II" near Qui Nhon in late January and early February, she departed Vietnamese waters to visit Taiwan and to conduct an ASW exercise in the northern Ryukyus.

The destroyer returned to Japan in mid-February and remained there almost a month before taking up duty on "Yankee Station" in the Gulf of Tonkin with *Bon Homme Richard* on 17 March. Five days later, she shifted her plane-guard service to *Kitty Hawk* (CVA-63) and remained so employed until the 27th when she joined *Bainbridge* (DLGN-25), *Duncan* (DDR-874), and *Henderson* (DD-785) in a fruitless, two-day search for a plane lost at sea. On 29 March, she rejoined *Kitty Hawk* and headed for Subic Bay, whence she operated through 4 April conducting gunnery drills and ASW exercises.

On the 7th, the destroyer returned to Vietnamese waters. After two days of anti-PT-boat training at Danang, she began duty on the south SAR (Search and Rescue) station. Almost a month later, *Arnold J. Isbell* (DD-869) relieved her; and *Theodore E. Chandler* returned to Yokosuka on 11 May. The warship remained in Japan until the end of the month; then steamed south to the Philippines. After two days at Subic Bay, she got underway on 5 June to return to the Gulf of Tonkin. On the 7th, she joined *Constellation* (CVA-64) on "Yankee Station" and served as the carrier's escort and plane guard for five days.

Theodore E. Chandler parted company with the carrier on 12 June and joined *Allen M. Sumner* (DD-692) for an 11-day assignment with Operation "Sea Dragon." The two destroyers moved in close to shore and patrolled the Vietnamese coastline in an effort to interdict enemy waterborne logistics. Working in conjunction with Navy spotter aircraft, they ferreted out enemy cargo barges and sank them with gunfire. On two occasions during the assignment, *Theodore E. Chandler*

came under fire from hostile shore batteries but managed to avoid any hits. The other half of Operation "Sea Dragon" consisted of shore bombardments to destroy depots and marshalling areas as well as to interdict coastal lines of communication. *Theodore E. Chandler* helped to destroy a number of buildings and to silence several North Vietnamese shore batteries that responded to the ships' barrage. On 23 June, her "Sea Dragon" relief arrived and, after two days of operations with *Hancock* (CVA-19), the warship pointed her bow toward Yokosuka where she arrived on the 29th.

Her next line period came during the second week in July. Though it consisted of a mix of assignments similar to previous tours—working with carriers and conducting "Sea Dragon" operations—events occurred to give the duty a slightly different twist in each instance. On 25 July, while the destroyer conducted "Sea Dragon" missions along the coast, the 3d Marine Division called upon her guns to assist them in driving the Viet Cong 806th Battalion west toward waiting South Vietnamese forces. She delivered gunfire along the coast between Quang Tri and Hue and, although the Viet Cong mangaged to evade the marines, the combined effect of naval gunfire and 3d Division amphibious operations still resulted in a major collison between the evacuating enemy and Allied forces. The operation—codenamed "Bear Chain"—ended the next day, and *Theodore E. Chandler* resumed logistics interdiction duty.

Three days later, she was called upon to provide assistance of a different nature. She departed her assigned "Sea Dragon" operating area in company with HMAS *Hobart* to rendezvous with *Forrestal* (CVA-59). A fuel tank dropped off one of the carrier's A-4 aircraft during preparations for take-off, and the flames from it engulfed the ordnance and fuel tanks on nearby planes, causing a series of explosions which bathed her stern area in liquid fire and holed her armored flight deck. *Theodore E. Chandler* joined the group of ships assisting the carrier in removing her wounded and dead and in readying her for a painful retirement to Subic Bay, the first leg of a voyage back to the United States and major repairs.

The destroyer parted company with the carrier shortly after midnight on 30 July in response to orders to return with HMAS *Hobart* to "Sea Dragon" duty off Vietnam. On 8 August, she reentered Yokosuka once more for a brief respite from combat duty. From there, she moved to Subic Bay with a task force built around *Coral Sea* (CVA-43) and, after three days in the Philippines, headed back to Vietnamese waters. During that tour of duty, she provided escort and plane-guard services to *Coral Sea* and, later, to *Intrepid* (CVS-11). Before returning to Yokosuka on 17 October, the warship participated in a series of ASW exercises, visited Hong Kong, and conducted surveillance of Russian trawlers operating in the vicinity.

The destroyer underwent a restricted availability at Yokosuka between mid-October and mid-December. On the 12th, she departed Japan bound for Kaohsiung, Taiwan, where she joined a convoy heading to Vietnam. She departed Kaohsiung on 16 December and relieved *Hamner* (DD-718) in the northern "Sea Dragon" area on 19 December 1967. That duty continued for almost a month until 16 January 1968, when she moved close to the shores of the First and Second Corps Zones of South Vietnam to provide naval gunfire support for the 5th Marines until early February. After another two-week in-port period at Yokosuka, *Theodore E. Chandler* resumed search and rescue duty on the north SAR station in the Gulf of Tonkin followed by five days of shore bombardment in the First Corps Zone once again from 11 to 16 March. After that assignment, she made a leisurely voyage; first to Subic Bay, thence to Taiwan, and finally to Yokosuka where she remained through the third week in April.

On 23 April, the destroyer headed back to Vietnam where, upon arrival, she started logistics interdiction once more. On 6 May, while the destroyer was engaged in a mission to destroy enemy supply traffic, a shore battery opened up on her and scored two 85-millimeter hits before she could silence it with counterbattery fire. One shell penetrated her hull, caused extensive damage in the crew's shower aft, and wounded one man. The other hit glanced off the hull and exploded in the water close aboard. Emergency repairs enabled the ship to return to duty in only three hours and complete her next scheduled mission. Two days later, *Theodore E. Chandler* came under enemy fire again, but she easily evaded the 40 rounds thrown at her and *St. Paul* (CA–73).

On 13 May, she headed back to Subic Bay where her battle damage was quickly repaired enabling the warship to be back in the Gulf of Tonkin by the 20th. PIRAZ duty with *Long Beach* (CLGN–9), a visit to Singapore, and the loss of a gunfire spotting drone to enemy antiaircraft fire near the mouth of the Song Giang River highlighted that combat cruise. *Ozbourn* (DD–846) relieved *Theodore E. Chandler* on 28 June, and she shaped a course for Japan and preparations for the return voyage to the United States. After 11 days in Yokosuka, she and *Hollister* got underway on a voyage that took them to Brisbane, Australia; Wellington, New Zealand; Pago Pago, Samoa; and Pearl Harbor. The two ships pulled into Long Beach on 25 August, and *Theodore E. Chandler* ended a long and arduous deployment for which she later received the Navy Unit Commendation.

On 13 February 1969, *Theodore E. Chandler* completed a four-month overhaul at Long Beach and began 1st Fleet operations along the west coast. After seven months of exercises and training cruises, she departed the west coast on 24 September and headed back to the western Pacific. During that deployment, she spent most of her time at sea off the coast of Vietnam engaged in familiar duty as naval gunfire support ship, SAR picket, and as escort for aircraft carriers. In addition to stops at Sasebo, Yokosuka, and Kaohsiung, she made a port call at Bangkok, Thailand. On 17 March 1970, after six weeks in and out of Sasebo as escort to *Hancock* (CVA–19), the destroyer departed Japan to return to the United States. She reached Long Beach on 1 April and resumed operations with the 1st Fleet. That summer, she participated in an NROTC summer training cruise and then spent all of August and most of September in port at Long Beach. Late the following month, she began preparations to return to the western Pacific; and, on 13 November, the warship departed Long Beach.

During the remainder of her career, *Theodore E. Chandler* made two more deployments to the western Pacific. Though she spent a great deal of time off the coast of Vietnam during both, only the first can be considered a wartime deployment in any real sense. That tour of duty came in the winter of 1970 and 1971 and consisted of duty as plane guard, as SAR picket, and as naval gunfire support ship. The last deployment began in January of 1973, after more than 20 months of normal 1st Fleet operations which included a four-month overhaul at the beginning of 1972. However, soon after she arrived in the Far East, the Vietnam ceasefire ended American involvement in the conflict. During the American withdrawal, she cruised the Gulf of Tonkin as plane guard for the aircraft carriers of TF 77 and then returned to the west coast in July. Upon returning to the United States, she resumed normal operations until the fall. On 1 October 1973, the destroyer was transferred to Naval Reserve training duty at Seattle, Wash. *Theodore E. Chandler* continued that duty until 1 April 1975. On that day, she was decommissioned at Seattle; and her name was struck from the Navy list. On 30 December 1975, she was sold to General Metals, Tacoma, Wash., for scrapping.

Theodore E. Chandler earned nine battle stars during the Korean War and eight battle stars and the Navy Unit Commendation for Vietnam service.

Born on 27 October 1858 in New York City, Theodore Roosevelt spent his childhood in a winning struggle against asthma. He strengthened his body through sheer self will and taught himself to ride, box, and shoot. In 1880, he graduated from Harvard University and turned to the writing of history. Two years later, he published his *Naval War of 1812* which is still regarded as a standard study of the subject.

Also in 1882, he ran as an independent Republican for the state legislature and was elected to represent New York's 21st district. Quickly winning renown as a champion of better government, Roosevelt became minority leader in 1883 and, the following year, headed the Assembly itself.

In 1889, he began six years on the Civil Service Commission in which he opposed corruption in the dispensing of public offices. In 1895, he became president of the New York City Police Board.

In 1897, President McKinley appointed Roosevelt Assistant Secretary of the Navy. He strengthened the Navy and enabled it to begin the war with Spain in a condition of preparedness.

Desiring to participate personally in the fray, Roosevelt resigned his post on 6 May 1898 and helped to organize the 1st Volunteer Cavalry Regiment. In Cuba, he became a hero when he led that regiment—popularly dubbed the "Rough Riders"—in the famous charge up San Juan Hill.

His heroics helped to catapult him into the governorship of New York late in 1898. Two years later, he received the Republican Vice Presidential nomination and was elected with McKinley in November.

On 14 September 1901, McKinley's assassination put Roosevelt in the White House as the 26th President of the United States. He asked Congress for little legislation but used executive power to the hilt to achieve reform.

Early in 1902, he used the long neglected Sherman Antitrust Act to break up the powerful railroad trust, the Northern Securities Company, and won popularity for his achievement as a "trust buster." During the coal strike later that year, by threatening to use troops to work the mines, he forced the miners and owners to accept arbitration which resolved the issue before the crisis became acute.

In 1904, Theodore Roosevelt was reelected overwhelmingly. That popular mandate allowed him to push the reform legislation through Congress.

The Elkins law and the Hepburn Act prevented railroads from charging exorbitant rates and from giving large rebates to preferred customers. The Expedition Act established special three-judge courts to expedite the trial of antitrust suits.

The Pure Food and Drug Act and the Meat Inspection Act protected consumers from the evil practices carried out by the food and meatpacking industries. Roosevelt also dusted off old laws which provided for the establishment of federal parks, national forests, and national preserves of coal, mineral, and petroleum-producing lands to save much of America's natural bounty for succeeding generations.

Roosevelt conducted a vigorous foreign policy. When the Colombian senate refused to ratify the Hay-Herran Treaty—which provided for American construction of and control over an isthmian canal across the Colombian province of Panama—Roosevelt countered by supporting Panamanian insurgents who staged a bloodless coup and immediately agreed to the treaty in their own right. After that, he personally superintended every step of canal construction.

His policy toward other Latin Amercian nations was directed toward protecting them from European intervention. The crowning feat to his diplomacy came in 1905, when Roosevelt played the major role in bringing about the negotiations in Portsmouth harbor which ended the Russo-Japanese War. This contribution to world peace won him the Nobel Peace Prize.

To Roosevelt the aggressive diplomat, a large and efficient navy constituted a primary tool for the conduct of foreign policy. Hence he launched a program to raise the United States Navy up to a high standard of efficiency and strength. He enlarged the fleet, modernized its ships, increased both its officer corps and enlisted complement, and improved efficiency through better training.

Roosevelt reorganized the Navy's operating forces along more rational lines. He called home its ships from stations scattered over the earth and then abolished the stations. He then divided the Navy into three fleets: the Atlantic Fleet (including all battleships), the Pacific Fleet, and the Asiatic Fleet. This change and the increase in personnel allowed the Navy to improve efficiency and to adopt a more realistic training program. The cruise of the Great White Fleet around the world between late 1907 and 1909 might be considered the triumph of his naval policies and the culmination of his efforts to wed military strength to diplomatic endeavor.

Late in February 1909, the battleships of the Atlantic Fleet returned to Hampton Roads and filed past their benefactor in a huge naval review. Early the following month, Theodore Roosevelt passed the reins of government to his hand-picked successor, William Howard Taft, and left the country on a schedule of safaris, hunts, and tours. However, soon after his triumphal return to the United States in 1910, he became disillusioned by Taft's conservatism. In 1912, he tried to win the Republican presidential nomination. When Taft won the Grand Old Party's banner, Roosevelt led his followers out of the party and formed the Progressive Party. The Republican split gave victory to the Democrats, and Woodrow Wilson became president in March 1913.

Roosevelt returned to retirement and resumed writing and travelling. Although neutral at the outbreak of World War I, he quickly became pro-Allied. His outspoken criticism of Wilson's neutrality sought to arouse the country to what he saw as a struggle between benevolent democracy and rapacious, Pan-German imperialism. When the country did enter the war, Roosevelt applied to Wilson for a military command, but the latter ignored him. He hoped to run again for the presidency in 1920, but that last dream was denied him as well for he died peacefully in his sleep on 6 January 1919 at Sagamore Hill, his home at Oyster Bay, N.Y.

I

(ScStr: t. 1,955 (gross); l. 287'0''; b. 40'0'' (wl.); dr. 12'6'' (mean); s. 20.8 k.)

The first *Theodore Roosevelt* (Id. No. 1478)—a steamer built in 1906 at Toledo, Ohio, by the Toledo Shipbuilding Co.—was acquired by the Navy from the Roosevelt Steamship Co. sometime in the spring of 1918 and fitted out as a troop transport during the summer and fall. Though some sources suggest that *Theodore Roosevelt* was never commissioned in the Navy, the fact that the 1919 *Navy Directory* lists Lt. Harry D. Irwin, USNRF, as "comdg U.S.S. Roosevelt" is a strong indication to the contrary. In any event, by 1 November 1918, she was assigned to duty as a cross-channel transport carrying troops back and forth between Great Britain and France. She continued that duty at least until 1 April 1919 and probably returned to the United States sometime in April or May. As of 1 June 1919, the transport was at New York awaiting disposition. On 1 July 1919, she was sold—the purchaser's name is unrecorded—and her name was struck from the Navy list.

II

(SSBN–600: dp. 5,946 (surf.), 6,700 (subm.); l. 382'; b. 33'; dr. 29'; s. 16 k. (surf.), 20+ k. (subm.); cpl. 139; a. 16 Polaris mis., 6 21'' tt.; cl. *George Washington*)

Using components initially assembled for the *Skip-*

jack-class nuclear attack submarine *Scamp* (SSN–588), *SSGN–600* was laid down on 20 May 1958 by the Mare Island Naval Shipyard; named *Theodore Roosevelt* and redesignated SSBN–600 on 6 November 1958; launched on 3 October 1959; sponsored by Mrs. Alice Roosevelt Longworth; and commissioned on 13 February 1961, Comdr. William E. Sims (blue crew) and Comdr. Oliver H. Perry, Jr. (gold crew) in command.

Five days after commissioning, *Theodore Roosevelt* departed Mare Island, bound for the east coast. On 7 March, she became the first fleet ballistic missile submarine (FBM) to transit the Panama Canal. Four days later, she arrived at Cape Canaveral, Fla. After successfully firing her first Polaris A1 missile on 20 March and completing her shakedown training, the submarine arrived in Groton, Conn., on 1 May for post-shakedown availability at the Electric Boat Co. yard. She completed those repairs on 24 June and departed Groton, bound for Charleston, S.C. *Theodore Roosevelt* stopped at Norfolk, Va., along the way and arrived at Charleston on 7 July. Between 7 and 19 July, she loaded Polaris missiles at the Naval Ammunition Depot, Charleston, and made all other preparations for her first deployment. On the 19th, she stood out of Charleston on her first deterrent patrol. She concluded that patrol on 23 September at the FBM base at Holy Loch, Scotland.

Over the next three and one-half years, the submarine made 15 more deterrent patrols, departing from and returning to the Holy Loch base in each instance. Late in the spring of 1965, she departed Holy Loch on her 17th and final patrol of the deployment. She concluded that patrol and the deployment when she arrived in Charleston on 15 June. She unloaded her 16 Polaris missiles and then departed Charleston for New London, Conn., where she arrived on 26 June.

At New London, *Theodore Roosevelt* entered the yard of the Electric Boat Division for an extensive overhaul. Between July 1965 and January 1967, she had her nuclear reactor "refueled" and her Polaris weapon system modified to accept the more advanced Polaris A3 missile. The FBM submarine completed overhaul on 14 January 1967 and launched into sea trials and refresher training, all of which culminated in the successful firing of a Polaris A3 missile at the Cape Kennedy (Cape Canaveral) missile range late in April. At the end of the training period, she returned to Charleston to load missiles and to prepare for another series of deterrent patrols out of Holy Loch. She embarked upon her 18th patrol on 1 June and completed that cruise at the Holy Loch base.

Theodore Roosevelt's second tour of duty operating from the Scotland base proved to be very brief in comparison to her first. Between mid-June of 1967 and February of 1968, she completed her 18th, 19th, 20th, and 21st patrols. On 20 March 1968 while returning to Holy Loch from her 21st patrol, the submarine ran aground off the western coast of Scotland. After drydocking for temporary correction of the damage, she departed Holy Loch on 5 April to return to the United States for permanent repairs. Between 18 and 20 April, she unloaded her missiles at Charleston and then headed north to New London. On the 23d, she arrived in the yard of the Electric Boat Division and commenced an extended repair period. Labor disputes caused delays, and *Theodore Roosevelt* did not complete her repairs until mid-October. She spent the latter part of that month in sea trials and then departed New London on 2 November on her post-repair shakedown cruise. She visited Norfolk, Puerto Rico, and St. Croix before concluding the cruise at Charleston on 27 November. She conducted training operations out of Charleston before deploying to Holy Loch again early in 1969.

That tour of duty lasted until May 1971. During the interim, she conducted nine more deterrent patrols, returning to Holy Loch for refit after each. On 12 May 1971, she stood out of Holy Loch on the 31st patrol of her career. On 20 July, *Theodore Roosevelt* arrived in

The christening ceremony for *Theodore Roosevelt* (SSBN–600) at Mare Island, 3 October 1959.

New London completing both the patrol and the deployment. She remained in New London for three weeks, during which time members of her blue crew and her gold crew were brought together into a single overhaul crew while other members of both crews moved on to other assignments. On 10 August, the FBM submarine headed south to Charleston where she arrived on the 13th. Over the next month, she underwent refit and then departed Charleston on 11 September for special operations. *Theodore Roosevelt* returned to Charleston on the 30th and remained there a week and a day before returning to sea for another three weeks of special operations. The ballistic missile submarine reentered Charleston on 1 November and began a preoverhaul restricted availability. Three weeks later, she officially began her refueling overhaul, which lasted for more than two years.

Theodore Roosevelt completed her overhaul in January 1974. During the following two months, she conducted sea trials out of Charleston. In April and May, shakedown training and nuclear weapons certification preparations occupied her time. In June, she conducted a one-week midshipman familiarization cruise out of New London; then underwent nuclear propulsion safety training before deperming at Norfolk. In mid-June, she received word of her reassignment to the Pacific Fleet with her new home port to be Pearl Harbor, Hawaii. Between July and September, *Theodore Roosevelt* conducted another midshipman training cruise; then settled into predeployment training and preparations. The submarine departed Charleston on 20 September; transited the Panama Canal on 5 October; and, after a nine-day stop for missile loadout at Bangor, Wash., continued on to Pearl Harbor, where she arrived on 4 November. Six days later, she departed Pearl Harbor, bound for the Marianas. She entered port at Guam two weeks later, underwent refit at her new advanced

base there, and began her first deterrent patrol in the Pacific Ocean on 31 December. *Theodore Roosevelt* conducted patrols out of Guam until 16 December 1977 at which time she departed on her 43d deterrent patrol.

Theta

The eighth letter of the Greek alphabet, the symbol for which is θ.

John T. Jenkins, a screw tug, was purchased for the Navy by Rear Admiral David Dixon Porter on 9 December 1864 at Norfolk, Va., and renamed *Theta*. Acquired late in the Civil War, *Theta* probably saw little or no service. There are no records of any deck logs for her, and she is mentioned but once in the *Official Records of the Union and Confederate Navies in the War of the Rebellion*—with reference to her purchase. Her service —if she served at all—was brief and probably consisted of some variety of yard tug duty at Norfolk. She was sold late in 1865—one source indicates that the sale occurred on 17 August 1865—but that transaction remains undocumented. In any event, her name had disappeared from the "List of Vessels of the United States Navy" by 20 January 1866 when the 1866 *Navy Register* was issued.

Thetis

A sea nymph of Greek Mythology. She was the daughter of the sea god Nereus and the mother of the Trojan War hero Achilles.

I

(Aux.Str.: dp. 1,250; l. 188'6''; b. 29'; dr. 17'10''; a. 1 how.)

The first *Thetis*—a three-masted, wooden-hulled

steam whaler built in 1881 at Dundee, Scotland, by Alexander Stephen & Sons—was acquired by the Navy on 2 February 1884 to be employed by the expedition to relieve the polar exploration party under the command of Lt. Adolphus W. Greely, U.S.A. She sailed from Dundee under the command of Lt. L. L. Reamey and arrived in New York on 23 March 1884.

After more than a month of preparations, *Thetis*—now under the command of Comdr. Winfield Scott Schley, who also headed the relief squadron—departed New York on 1 May. Ice flows and heavy weather hampered the search all along the way. *Thetis* did not even reach Upernavik, Greenland, her jumping-off point, until the latter part of the month. She departed that port on the 29th in company with *Bear* and headed north. Along the way, she made stops at the Duck Islands, Cape York, and Littleton Island, arriving at the latter on 21 June. At Littleton Island, her search parties found evidence that Lt. Greely's expedition had stopped there but moved on. They were on the right track. The next day, she moved on to Payer's Harbor and landed search parties on Brevoort Island. More evidence that Greely's party had passed that way also indicated the dire straits in which the expedition found itself. Later that day, the two ships rounded Cape Sabine and, while fighting a howling gale, found Lt. Greely and six companions—alive, but weak from exposure and malnutrition. The other 20 members of the expedition had perished. The following day, the two ships headed south with their precious cargo. After stops at Upernavik, Godhavn, and St. John's, the relief expedition arrived in Portsmouth, N.H., on 1 August. During the five-day stay, rescuers and rescued alike received a tumultuous welcome by the assembled North Atlantic Squadron and enjoyed a warm reception given by the people of Portsmouth. On 5 August, the rescue ships continued south toward New York where they arrived on the 8th. On 26 November 1884, *Thetis* was placed out of commission and was laid up at New York.

After more than two years of inactivity, *Thetis* was recommissioned at New York on 15 January 1887, Lt. William H. Emory, Jr., in command. Between mid-January and mid-March, the ship was fitted out as a gunboat and prepared for a cruise around Cape Horn to the west coast. She departed New York on 24 March and began an eight-month voyage during which she stopped at Rio de Janeiro, Brazil; Montevideo, Uruguay; Valparaiso, Chile; and Callao, Peru. On 13 October, *Thetis* sailed into San Francisco for voyage repairs prior to a brief cruise to Alaskan waters. She departed the Mare Island Navy Yard on 16 November and arrived at Sitka, Alaska, on 4 December. She returned to Mare Island on 9 January 1888 and remained there until 8 April when she embarked upon an extended cruise in Alaskan waters. She returned to Sitka on 18 May and, for the next five months, conducted survey work as far north as Point Barrow visiting Unalaska, St. Michaels, East Cape, and Cape Sabine. On 1 November, she headed south from Sitka and entered San Francisco Bay on the 25th. She spent the following five months at the Mare Island Navy Yard, undergoing repairs and preparing for another Alaska survey assignment. *Thetis* steamed out from the Golden Gate on 20 April and shaped a course north to Sitka, where she arrived on 2 June. Another five months of survey work along the Alaskan coast followed—punctuated again with visits to Unalaska and Point Barrow. She returned to San Francisco on 7 December.

Thetis remained at the Mare Island Navy Yard until July 1890 when she sailed for Central America. A revolution had recently broken out in San Salvador and the insurgents quickly seized power. However, forces of the old government retired to Guatemala which they used as a base for counter-revolutionary

Thetis (center) and *Bear* (left), hampered by ice during their search for the Greely expedition, 1884.

perations. This precipitated war between the two countries. By 27 July, *Thetis* was at San José, Guatemala, beginning a four-month cruise along the coasts of Guatemala and San Salvador to protect American lives and property during the war. During that period, she called several times at La Libertad and Acajulta in San Salvador and at La Union and Ampala, Honduras, in addition to San José, Guatemala. By October, conditions in Central America had quieted sufficiently to allow *Thetis* to return to San Francisco, where she arrived on the 27th. Two days later, she reentered the Mare Island Navy Yard and remained there until the following June.

At mid-month, she departed San Francisco on a four-month assignment in Alaskan waters conducting survey work and patrolling to protect fur seals from poachers. She returned south to San Francisco late in 1891 and remained until the beginning of 1892. In the late spring, she made a brief voyage to the Hawaiian Islands, returning to San Francisco on 18 June. In January 1893, *Thetis* began survey work along the coast of the Baja California peninsula. For the next four years, she conducted those operations in waters between Magdalena Bay and the southern tip of the California peninsula. She returned periodically to San Diego and San Francisco for repairs and supplies. She concluded that duty in the spring of 1897 and arrived back in San Francisco on 24 April. In July 1897, the ship was placed "in ordinary" at Mare Island.

Thetis never again served the Navy. In the spring of 1899, she was transferred temporarily to the Revenue Cutter Service for special duty transporting Siberian reindeer to Alaska. This project was instituted through the cooperation of the Revenue Cutter Service and the Department of the Interior in an attempt to help Alaskan eskimos to learn to herd the animals for food rather than to rely upon their traditional source—the hunt. Between June and October 1899, she transported 31 reindeer from Siberia to Alaska. In the latter month, she was returned to the Navy briefly but was soon retransferred back to the Revenue Cutter Service permanently.

As a commissioned cutter in the Revenue Cutter Service, she spent the next 16 years cruising Alaskan waters bringing justice and carrying supplies to the frontier fringes. During that time, she was based both at Port Townsend, Wash., and San Francisco, Calif. In the spring of 1904, she made a voyage to the Hawaiian Islands to transport illegal Japanese aliens from Lisianski Island to Honolulu. Late in 1909, she returned to Honolulu. From then until the end of her career, she alternated duty in the islands with annual cruises to Alaskan waters.

On 27 April 1916, *Thetis* ended her last voyage for the government at San Francisco. Three days later, she was placed out of commission. On 3 June, she was sold to W. & S. Job & Co. of New York City. Ironically, after years of service on the patrol against seal poachers in the Pacific, she was converted into a sealer herself and operated out of Newfoundland for the next 34 years. In 1950, her hulk was purposely grounded off St. Johns, and she remained there until she broke up.

II

(SP–391: dp. 97.6; l. 127'; b. 16'4''; dr. 7'6'' (aft); s. 12 k.; cpl. 17; a. 2 3-pdrs., 2 mg.)

The second *Thetis* (SP–391)—a steam yacht built in 1901 at Neponset, Mass., by George Lawley & Sons—was purchased by the Navy from Charles H. Fuller of Pawtucket, R.I., on 23 June 1917 and commissioned on 9 July 1917. *Thetis* remained on the Navy's active list for almost two years. During that time, she served as a section patrol boat in the 2d Naval District and patrolled the New England coast between Chatham, Mass., and New London, Conn. Her duty during World War I probably consisted of maintaining a watch along the coast for German U-boats and mines. She

was decommissioned soon after the end of the war, and her name was struck from the Navy list on 31 March 1919. On 19 July 1920, she was sold to Mr. Herman Lee Meader of New York City.

III

(Coast Guard Patrol Boat No. 15: dp. 334; l. 165'; b. 23'9¼''; dr. 7'8½'' (mean); s. 16 k.; cpl. 50; a. 1 3'', 2 1-pdrs.; cl. *Thetis*)

The third *Thetis*—a twin-screw, diesel-powered, steel-hulled Coast Guard patrol boat—was laid down on 9 May 1931 at Bath, Maine, by the Bath Iron Works Corp.; launched on 9 November 1931; and delivered to the Coast Guard on 27 November 1931; and was accepted for service two days later.

Assigned to Division 2, Destroyer Force, on 30 November, *Thetis* departed Bath on 1 December for shakedown training off the eastern seaboard. During this cruise, she visited Washington, D.C. Subsequently transferred to the Special Patrol Force of the New York Division, the ship was stationed initially at Stapleton, N.Y.

By 1934, the vessel had apparently been transferred to Boston, Mass. She remained on duty there through July of 1940. Mid-1941 found *Thetis* shifted south to Key West. As one of the six ships of her class taken over by the Navy, *Thetis* was assigned to the East Coast Sound School, Key West, Fla., on 1 July 1941, concurrently with the establishment of the four Sea Frontiers. By late 1941, the Coast Guard patrol boat was assigned collateral duties in the Gulf Patrol, a unit of Task Force 6. Other ships in this group included Destroyer Division 66, Subchaser Division 31 (less *PC–451*), and three of *Thetis'* sister ships.

Attached to the Sound School at the time of the Japanese attack on Pearl Harbor on 7 December 1941, *Thetis* was classified WPC–115 sometime in or around February of 1942. At about this time, early 1942, German U-boats experienced what they considered a "happy time" off the eastern seaboard, as American vessels were not yet being escorted from place to place. American antisubmarine measures were largely crude and ineffective for nearly the first four or five months of World War II.

On 9 June, while in the course of carrying out her normal training and patrol missions off the east coast of Florida, *Thetis* took part in an unsuccessful search for what was suspected to be a U-boat. However, the torpedoing of the American freighter *Hagan* on the evening of 10 June 1942 gave the American "hunter killer" forces something unquestionably real to hunt for. She was *U–157*, and *Hagan* had been her first victim, being damaged but not sunk by the U-boat.

Accordingly, a "dragnet" was thrown out to find and destroy the submarine before she could attack any other ships. This intensive search effort involved radar-equipped Army B–18 bombers, three destroyers, several PC's, and *Thetis'* sister ship, *Triton* (WPC–116). On 13 June, *Thetis* picked up a definite contact and plunged ahead for the kill. With the unseen target 200 yards two points on the port bow, *Thetis* went to general quarters and continued ahead about 1,000 yards before turning to port and increasing to full power. Regaining contact upon steadying out on her base course—she had temporarily lost it while maneuvering—*Thetis* bore down on the U-boat.

The patrol craft dropped her first depth charges at 1558—five charges set for 200 to 300 feet at five-second intervals. She also launched a further two from the ship's "Y" gun at the time of release of the third charge. After making the run and observing the explosions, *Thetis* turned to starboard to observe the results of her attack, and observed a "water slug" (a disturbance in the water) a short distance to the right of her own wake. As the commanding officer of *Thetis* observed, the "slug" did not resemble the disturbance usually associated with the explosion of depth charges.

Thetis observed pieces of freshly broken wood float to the surface at 1618, as well as articles of clothing. *Thetis* then maneuvered into the flotsam and jetsam and retrieved two pairs of leather submariner's pants of the type usually worn by U-boaters in the northern latitudes.

PE–27 soon made an approach and dropped a marker buoy. *Thetis*, meanwhile, sighted and picked up a tube of lubricant made in Dusseldorf, Germany. While *Thetis* returned to rearm at Key West, *PE–27*, *PC–519*, and *Triton* all carried out attacks—all in actuality unnecessary as *Thetis* had already sunk the U-boat on her first run. *Thetis* came back and conducted one more attack, but *U–157* had already gone to the bottom, entombing her crew in her hull.

Thetis remained with the Navy's East Coast Sound School for the remainder of the war, conducting coastwise convoy escort, sonar training, and antisubmarine patrols for the duration of hostilities. Returned to Coast Guard jurisdiction after World War II and serving into the early 1960's, her name was removed from Coast Guard lists at that time.

Thetis Bay

An inlet at the south end of Tebenkof Bay on the west coast of Kuiu Island in the Alexander Archipelago of Alaska.

(CVE–90: dp. 9,760; l. 512'3''; b. 65'2''; ew. 108'1'' dr. 22'6''; s. 19.3 k.; cpl. 860; a. 1 5'', 16 40mm. ac. 28; cl. *Casablanca*)

Thetis Bay (CVE–90) was laid down under Maritime Commission contract (MC hull 1127) on 22 December 1943 at Vancouver, Wash., by the Kaiser Shipbuilding Co.; launched on 16 March 1944; sponsored by Mrs. Ricco Botta; and commissioned on 21 April 1944, Capt. Donald E. Wilcox in command.

Thetis Bay got underway for San Diego where she conducted brief shakedown training. On 2 June, she moved to San Pedro to load planes and passengers for Pacific bases. The new escort carrier stood out to sea on 5 June; called at Pearl Harbor on the 11th; and continued on, via Makin and Majuro, to Kwajalein. There, she embarked the Army's 50th Engineer Battalion which she offloaded at Pearl Harbor on 5 July. Two days later, the carrier got underway for Alameda with 41 aircraft that needed repairs. She arrived on 13 July and, after offloading the aircraft, proceeded to Terminal Island for a three-week yard period. Between 11 August and 13 September, the escort carrier delivered spare parts, replacement aircraft, and pesonnel to Hawaii and the Marshalls. From September 1944 through mid-April 1945, *Thetis Bay* made five round trip voyages from California ports to bases in the Pacific ranging from Pearl Harbor to Finschhaven, New Guinea.

The former escort carrier *Thetis Bay* as the Navy's first amphibious helicopter carrier (CVHA–1), 1956.

On 12 June 1945, *Thetis Bay* arrived at Pearl Harbor from San Diego with a load of aircraft. There, the aircraft were readied for combat within 72 hours; and the ship got underway for Guam. She arrived at Apra Harbor on 25 June and was assigned to Task Group 30.8 for duty as a replenishment carrier. *Thetis Bay* made her first rendezvous with Task Force 38 on 12 July when she transferred 40 planes to various carriers. She returned to Guam on 22 July and remained there until 24 July to load more aircraft before joining the fast carriers again on the 31st. The ship reloaded at Guam once more and resupplied the task force from 14 August to 8 September when she returned to Apra Harbor en route to the United States.

Thetis Bay arrived at Alameda on 7 September 1945 and was assigned to "Margic-Carpet" duty, returning veterans from overseas bases to the United States. She served in this capacity until January 1946 when she began inactivation. The ship was placed out of commission, in reserve, at Bremerton, Wash., on 7 August 1946.

In May 1955, *Thetis Bay* was towed to the San Francisco Naval Shipyard where she began conversion to the Navy's first assault helicopter aircraft carrier. On 1 July 1955, her designation was changed from CVE-90 to CVHA-1. With that change, she became a complement to the attack transport. Her helicopters supplemented landing craft to give the Navy and Marine Corps the flexibility of a vertical assault capability. She was recommissioned on 20 July 1956, Capt. Thomas W. South, II, in command, and completed conversion six weeks later on 1 September.

The carrier arrived at her new home port, Long Beach, on 20 September. There, helicopter teams from Marine Corps Test Unit No. 1, Camp Pendleton, demonstrated landing and take-off techniques. *Thetis Bay* participated in amphibious training exercises off the California coast before deploying to the Far East on 10 July 1957. She returned to Long Beach on 11 December 1957 and resumed local operations. On 28 May 1959, her designation was changed to LPH-6, amphibious assault ship.

In August 1959, *Thetis Bay* was serving with the 7th Fleet when floods on Taiwan left thousands homeless. On the 12th, she was ordered to proceed from Hong Kong to Taiwan and use her 21 large troop-carrying helicopters to aid the flood victims. By the end of the assistance operation, at noon of the 20th, the ship had delivered a total of 1,600,540 pounds of supplies to the destitute Chinese. In addition, her helicopters had lifted 850 passengers to and from various sites in the flooded area.

In May 1960, *Thetis Bay* participated in a practice night assault landing at Camp Pendleton during which her helicopters carried 1,300 troops and 33 tons of cargo to the objective area. This was the first large-scale night landing of ground forces by carrier-based helicopters.

Thetis Bay deployed to the western Pacific in the spring of 1961. After the assault ship returned to Long Beach, she was transferred to the Atlantic Fleet. She arrived at Norfolk, her new home port, in early December 1961.

During the next three years, the ship operated along the Atlantic coast and in the Caribbean. The highlight of her service with the Atlantic Fleet came during the Cuban missile crisis in October 1962 when she proceeded to the quarantine area with her embarked marine landing team and helicopter squadron ready for action. Fortunately, the resolute response of the United States to the challenge of offensive Soviet missiles in Cuba convinced the Soviet leaders that America would go to war rather than tolerate this threat to the Western Hemisphere. Rather than face a nuclear war, Russia withdrew its missiles, resolving the crisis. Another memorable event in her service occurred in September 1963 when *Thetis Bay* proceeded to hurricane-stricken Haiti. She anchored off Port-au-Prince and launched Marine helicopters carrying medical aid and food supplies to thousands of victims of Hurricane "Flora."

Thetis Bay stood out of Norfolk on 5 January 1964 en route to Philadelphia for inactivation and arrived there the next day. She was decommissioned and struck from the Navy list on 1 March 1964. Her hulk was sold in December 1964 to Peck Iron & Metal Co., Inc., Portsmouth, Va., for scrap.

Thetis Bay received one battle star for World War II service.

Thistle

A plant having spiney, prickly leaves and white, purple, pink, or yellow flowers.

I

(SwGbt: t. 50; a. 1 12-pdr. sb.)

The first *Thistle*—formerly the Army tug *Spiteful*—was transferred by the War Department to the Navy on 1 October 1862.

Thistle deployed with the Mississippi Squadron as a tug and reconnaissance vessel in October 1862 and participated in the capture of Fort Hindman, Arkansas Port, Ark., on 11 January 1863. From 14 to 27 March, she took part in an expedition into Steele's Bayou, Miss., attempting to find an entrance into the Yazoo River, Miss., and a rear approach to the Confederate stronghold at Vicksburg, Miss. After the expedition failed, *Thistle* rejoined the squadron in the Mississippi. There, she performed dispatch and reconnaissance duty for the remainder of the war.

Thistle was decommissioned at Mound City, Ill., on 12 August 1865 and was sold at public auction there on 17 August to J. T. Haight.

II

(SP-1058: dp. 41 (gross); l. 70'; b. 12'; dr. 4'0"
(aft); s. 13 mph.; cpl. 9; a. 1 3-pdr., 1 1-pdr.)

The second *Thistle* (SP-1058)—a wooden-hulled motor boat built in 1907 at Morris Heights, N.Y., by the New York Yacht, Launch & Engine Co.—was acquired by the Navy on free lease from Mr. William Emmerich of New York City on 17 August 1917 and was placed in commission on 26 December 1917. *Thistle* served in the 3d Naval District making patrols of the coast and harbors between New London, Conn., and Barnegat, N.J. However, during her brief service—less than a year—she proved unsuited for the mission required of her, and the Commandant, 3d Naval District, ordered her returned to her owner on 6 July 1918.

Thomas

Clarence Crase Thomas—born on 26 December 1886 in Grass Valley, Calif.—was appointed midshipman on 7 July 1904 and graduated from the United States Naval Academy on 5 June 1908. After service in armored cruiser *Maryland* and gunboat *Yorktown*, he was commissioned ensign on 29 June 1910.

In the next few years, Thomas served in *Denver*, *Cleveland*, and *West Virginia*. Appointed lieutenant (jg.) on 26 June 1913, he was detached from *West Virginia* in the summer of 1914 to attend a post-graduate course in steam engineering at the Naval Academy. He attended Columbia University in late 1915 and, on 24 June 1916, reported on board *Florida* as her electrical officer.

Thomas was commissioned lieutenant on 8 January 1917 and, about a fortnight after the United States entered World War I, was placed in charge of the naval armed guard on the merchant steamship SS *Vacuum* in April. On the 28th, when a lookout reported sighting a German submarine, some 120 miles west of the Hebrides Islands, Lt. Thomas went to the ship's after gun. A few moments later, a torpedo from *U-21* struck *Vacuum* and exploded, throwing Thomas and the gun's crew into the water. The ship sank within two minutes. Picked up by a boat, Thomas soon died of cold and exposure. He was the first United States naval officer to lose his life in the war with Germany and was posthumously awarded the Navy Cross "for distinguished service in the line of his profession as commander of the armed guard crew of the . . . *Vacuum*."

I

(Destroyer No. 182: dp. 1,213; l. 314'4½''; b. 30'11½''; dr. 9'4'' (mean); s. 33.67 k.; cpl. 122; a. 4 4'', 1 3'', 12 21'' tt.; cl. *Wickes*)

The first *Thomas* (Destroyer No. 182) was laid down on 23 March 1918 at Newport News, Va., by the Newport News Shipbuilding and Drydock Co.; launched on 4 July 1918; sponsored by Mrs. Evelyn M. Thomas, widow of Lt Thomas; and commissioned on 25 April 1919, Lt. Comdr. Harry A. McClure in command.

Thomas operated off the east coast on training cruises and exercises until decommissioned at Philadelphia on 30 June 1922. During this service, she was classified DD–182 during the Navy-wide assignment of alphanumeric hull numbers on 17 July 1920. She lay in reserve in the Philadelphia Navy Yard's back channel for the next 18 years.

Recommissioned on 17 June 1940—as the United States Navy expanded to meet the demands imposed by neutrality patrols off American coastlines—*Thomas* was assigned to Destroyer Division 79 of the Atlantic Squadron and operated briefly in training and exercises off the eastern seaboard until transferred to the United Kingdom under the "destroyer-for-bases" agreement. She arrived at Halifax, Nova Scotia, on 18 September 1940 as part of the second increment of the 50 flush-decked, four-piped destroyers exchanged with the British for leases on strategic base sites in the western hemisphere. After a brief familiarization period for the Royal Navy bluejackets assigned to the ship, *Thomas* was officially turned over to her new owners on 23 September 1940. Her name was subsequently struck from the United States Navy list on 8 January 1941.

Simultaneously renamed HMS *St. Albans* (I.15) and commissioned the same day for service in the Royal Navy, the destroyer sailed for the British Isles on 29 September. After calling at St. John's, Newfoundland, en route, she arrived at Belfast, Northern Ireland, on 9 October. *St. Albans* and three sister ships—*St. Mary's* (I.12) (ex-*Bagley*, DD–185); *Bath* (I.17) (ex-*Hopewell*, DD–181); and *Charlestown* (I.21) (ex-*Abbot*, DD–184)—were attached to the 1st Minelaying Squadron as permanent escort force. Operating off the west coast of Scotland, the destroyers participated in some of the earliest minelaying operations in the Denmark Strait which separates Iceland from Greenland.

Between minecraft escort missions, *St. Albans* escorted convoys. On 17 and 18 January 1941, the destroyer searched for survivors from SS *Almeda Star*, torpedoed by *U-96* on the 17th. *St. Albans* underwent repairs at Chatham in February to prepare for her transfer to the Royal Norwegian Navy-in-exile on 14 April. She had no sooner entered service with the Norwegians than she collided with the minesweeper HMS *Alberic*, sinking the minecraft and sustaining enough damage herself to necessitate repairs in the dockyard.

When again ready for action, *St. Albans* joined the 7th Escort Group, operating out of Liverpool. On 12 June, she picked up the survivors from the sunken motor vessel *Empire Dew*—torpedoed that day by *U-48*—and brought them safely to Liverpool.

On 3 August 1941, while bound from Sierra Leone to the United Kingdom in the screen of convoy SL.81, *St. Albans* joined destroyer HMS *Wanderer* (D.74) and the "Flower"-class corvette HMS *Hydrangea* (K.39) in

sinking *U-401*. During subsequent operations screening convoys in shipping lanes between west Africa and the British Isles, *St. Albans* made a score of attacks on U-boats but could not repeat her "kill" performance of 3 August.

During the following autumn, a heavy gale severely damaged *St. Albans* while she was escorting convoy ON 22 on 8 October. The following day brought little respite from the high seas and strong winds, but *St. Albans'* hardy Scandinavian sailors brought her safely into Reykjavik, Iceland. The destroyer's seaworthiness and the seamanship exhibited by her scrappy Norwegian crew elicited a warm commendatory signal from the Commander in Chief, Western Approaches (Cin CWA). In this message of 12 October 1941, he also praised the destroyer's exemplary steaming performance during the previous three months.

St. Albans, meanwhile, continued her escort duties with the 7th Escort Group into 1942. In March, she escorted the damaged carrier HMS *Illustrious* from Liverpool to the Clyde and, in the following month, helped to screen convoy PQ 15 as it carried arms to Russia. During the operation, heavy German air and submarine attacks took a toll of three Allied ships.

In wartime, however, mistakes in identification or errors in navigation sometimes lead to disaster. On one occasion, these factors combined with tragic result when *St. Albans* and the minesweeper HMS *Seagull* sank the Polish submarine *Jastrzab* (ex-British submarine *P-551*) on 2 May. *Jastrzab* had strayed some 100 miles from her correct position in a convoy.

Later that month, the flush-decked destroyer joined the Liverpool Special Escort Division. Among the vessels escorted early in June was the Cunard-White Star liner RMS *Queen Elizabeth*, as the Cunarder steamed from the British Isles toward the Cape of Good Hope with troops bound for the Middle East. Then, after refitting at Falmouth between July and October 1942, *St. Albans* again operated with the Special Escort Division until the end of 1942. In January 1943, she served as a target vessel for training Coastal Command aircraft.

Late in February, she got underway and steamed into the North Sea toward the Scandinavian coast to search for a Norwegian merchantman which was reportedly attempting to escape to sea from Nazi-controlled waters. During this mission, the destroyer was attacked by German aircraft but emerged unharmed.

Shifted to the Western Local Escort Force soon thereafter, *St. Albans* was based at Halifax and operated in convoy escort missions in the western Atlantic for the remainder of 1943. Departing Halifax four days after Christmas of 1943, *St. Albans* arrived in the Tyne on 10 January 1944, where she was soon laid up in reserve. On 16 July, the British transferred the flush decker to the Russian Navy, who renamed her *Dostoiny* ("worthy"). She sailed under the "hammer and sickle" until returned to the British on 28 February 1949 at Rosyth, Scotland.

The veteran of service with the United States, British, Norwegian, and Russian navies was eventually broken up for scrap at Charlestown, England, in April of 1949.

II

(DE–102: dp. 1,240; l. 306'; b. 36'7''; dr. 8'9''; s. 21 k.; cpl. 216; a. 3 3'', 6 40mm., 3 21'' tt., 2 dct., 1 dcp (hh.); cl. *Cannon*)

The second *Thomas* (DE–102) was laid down on 1 January 1943 at Wilmington, Del., by the Dravo Corp.; launched on 31 July 1943; sponsored by Mrs. Herndon B. Kelly; and commissioned on 21 November 1943, Lt. Comdr. David M. Kellogg in command.

On 7 December 1943, *Thomas* got underway for Bermuda to conduct her shakedown cruise which ended on 15 January 1944. During the first part of February, she acted as a school ship at Norfolk and then joined

Task Group (TG) 21.16, a submarine hunter-killer group, centered around escort carrier *Block Island* (CVE–21). *Thomas* remained with the task group until 31 March. During this period, the group sank three German U-boats in the North Atlantic. At 2208 hours on 29 February, *Bronstein* (DE–189) made radar contact with a vessel from a range of 6,500 yards. She, *Thomas*, and *Bostwick* (DE–103) boxed the target; and *Bronstein* fired flares which revealed a surfaced submarine. When *Bronstein* opened fire with her deck guns, the U-boat submerged. The escorts tracked and depth charged the submarine until 0324 when a pattern of depth charges from *Thomas* produced a huge secondary explosion that marked the end of *U–709*. Meanwhile, *Bronstein* had made a second contact and had sunk *U–603* with a pattern of depth charges. The third kill came on St. Patrick's Day when *Bronstein* and *Corry* (DD–463) aided aircraft from *Block Island* in sinking *U–801*.

On 13 April, *Thomas* departed Norfolk, steamed to North Africa with convoy UGS 39, and returned with convoy GUS 39 on the 29th. On 10 June, she was assigned to a hunter-killer group (TG 22.10) whose nucleus was *Card* (CVE–11). The ships hunted German submarines along the southern Great Circle Route. At sunset on 5 July, they were approximately 100 miles south of Sable Island when *Baker* (DE–190) developed a contact. Two depth-charge patterns brought the U-boat to the surface. *Thomas* set a collision course and bore down on the submarine with all guns firing. She sliced through *U–233*'s pressure hull about 20 feet aft of the submarine's conning tower. The U-boat sank stern first in less than a minute. *Thomas* rescued 20 survivors, including the captain. Two days later, she was detached from the task group to return to the Boston Navy Yard for repairs.

Thomas left the yard on 18 July and provided training services for new submarines until the end of August. On 18 September, she rejoined the *Card* group and patrolled in the North Atlantic until 3 November when the ships of the group returned to east coast ports for repairs. On 30 November, the reassembled task group headed back to its asigned area but contacted no enemy submarines during the patrol.

On 29 December, *Thomas* was ordered to return to New York. She sortied again with her hunter-killer group on 16 January 1945. On 14 March, she returned to New York for repairs and rejoined *Card*, off the Florida coast, 10 days later. *Thomas* acted as a plane guard during carrier qualifications for a month and then rendezvoused with convoy KN 32 at Key West to escort it to New York.

On the night of 29 April, the convoy was east of Cape Henry when *Natchez* (PF–2) made sonar contact and sighted the snorkel of a German submarine. The frigate attempted to ram the U-boat, but her quarry went deep. When the ship radioed for help, *Thomas*, *Bostwick*, and *Coffman* (DE–191) went to her assistance. *Coffman* made three attacks; *Thomas* unleashed a creeping barrage; and *Bostwick* moved in, firing a pattern of depth charges. The American sailors heard deep sea explosions about eight minutes later. *Natchez* returned to the attack at 0207, and a pattern of her charges produced a large oil slick. Forty-five minutes later, *Thomas*' sound crew heard a huge underwater explosion. All contact with the submarine was lost, for German submarine *U–548* had been destroyed.

A little more than a week later, Germany surrendered, ending fighting in the Atlantic. *Thomas* conducted exercises in Long Island and Block Island Sounds in May and June. The destroyer escort joined *Mission Bay* (CVE–59) for plane-guard duty in July and August and performed the same duties for *Croatan* (CVE–25) during September and October. On 27 October, the destroyer escort entered New York harbor to participate in the Navy Day celebration. In November, *Thomas* escorted the captured German submarine *U–530* to various ports in Texas.

Thomas was decommissioned at Green Cove Springs, Fla., in March 1946. On 29 October 1948, the destroyer escort was transferred to Taiwan and renamed *T'Ai Ho*. *Thomas* was struck from the Navy list on 22 December 1948.

Thomas received four battle stars for World War II service.

Thomas, Garfield, see *Garfield Thomas*.

Thomas, Harold C., see *Harold C. Thomas*

Thomas, Herbert J., see *Herbert J. Thomas*.

Thomas, Leland E., see *Leland E. Thomas*

Thomas, Lloyd, see *Lloyd Thomas*.

Thomas, Private William H.,
see *Private William H. Thomas*.

Thomas, Solomon, see *Solomon Thomas*.

Thomas A. Edison

Thomas Alva Edison—born on 11 February 1847 in Milan, Ohio—grew up in Michigan. As a child, he was slow in school and very poor in mathematics, but excelled as a reader. Hard work became a characteristic feature of Edison's life at an early age; as a teenager, he had already established a thriving business selling newspapers and candy on trains. In 1863, he became a telegraph operator and, in 1868, went to work for Western Union in Boston, Mass. Throughout that period, however, he also dabbled with chemistry and the application of electricity to telegraphy. He secured

The ballistic-missile submarine *Thomas A. Edison* (SSBN–610).

a patent to his first invention, an electrographic vote recorder, in 1869. That same year, Edison joined the Laws Gold Indicator Co. as general manager and soon established a partnership with two others in the electrical engineering consultation business. He sold his portion of the latter firm in 1870, and the profits therefrom allowed him to establish his own shop with a staff of assistants. In 1874, he made quadruplex telegraphy, the simultaneous transmission of four different messages, practicable and, the following year, developed a resonator for analyzing sound waves. In 1876, the year in which he moved his laboratory to Menlo Park, N.J., he perfected the carbon telephone transmitter. In 1877, Edison invented the phonograph—perhaps his greatest achievement from the standpoint of inventive ingenuity.

If one can regard the phonograph as Edison's greatest invention, the one for which he is best remembered, the incandescent lamp, was not his at all. The principle had been known since Sir Humphry Davy's experiments in 1802, and inventors had toyed with the idea through the first three quarters of the 19th century, hampered at first by the lack of a satisfactory source of electricity and later by the twin problems of short life and poor luminous output. What Edison achieved in 1879, materially aided by better sources of electricity, was a refinement of his predecessors' efforts that produced a lamp with adequate life and luminous output.

Later, in 1883, he made his only truly scientific contribution when he discovered the "Edison effect." He showed that his incandescent lamp could act as a valve admitting negative electricity but rejecting positive. Ironically, he abandoned the discovery because, as an inventor, he saw no practical use for it. Later, his find became the basis for the vacuum tube so important to the development of radio and television transmission and reception.

Edison moved his laboratory to West Orange, N.J., in 1887. In 1891, he invented a "kinetoscope," a device for showing photographs in rapid succession to give the illusion of a moving picture. It was not a motion picture projector in the modern sense, for it utilized neither projector nor screen. It remained for Thomas Armat to devise a machine capable of projecting a picture from film onto a screen in 1895. Edison only acquired the patent to Armat's invention and improved it. He also used the projector in the first commercial showing of motion pictures on 23 April 1896 in New York City. Seventeen years later, he demonstrated a method of synchronizing sound with motion pictures and laid the foundation for sound movies.

When World War I erupted, Edison began devoting a large portion of his talent to defense-oriented inventions. He developed substitutes for drugs, dyes, and other items that the United States had previously imported from blockaded Germany. He also worked on a process to make synthetic carbolic acid and other substances necessary for the manufacture of explosives. He headed the Navy's consultative board and conducted research on such things as torpedo mechanisms, flame throwers, and submarine periscopes. Following the war, he continued his experiments despite his age, looking for improvements in wireless telegraphy, radio, electric power, motion pictures, and even the automobile and airplane. In his eighties, Edison embarked upon the attempt to produce synthetic rubber from domestic American plants. While so engaged, he collapsed in his laboratory on 1 August 1931 and died several weeks later on 18 October.

(SSBN–610: dp. 6,900 (surf.), 8,000 (subm.); l. 410'; b. 33'; dr. 32'; s. 20+ k.; cpl. 110; a. 16 Pol., 4 21'' tt.; cl. *Ethan Allen*)

Thomas A. Edison was laid down on 15 March 1960 at Groton, Conn., by the Electric Boat Division of the General Dynamics Corp.; launched on 15 June 1961; sponsored by Mrs. Madeleine Edison Sloane; and commissioned on 10 March 1962, Capt. Charles M. Young

(Blue crew) and Capt. Walter Dedrick (Gold crew) in command.

Following shakedown training off the eastern coast of the United States, *Thomas A. Edison* loaded Polaris missiles at Charleston, S.C., and embarked upon her first deterrent patrol on 7 November. She concluded that patrol at the base at Holy Loch, Scotland, whence she operated for the next four years and 17 deterrent patrols. In September 1966, her official home port was changed from New London, Conn., to Charleston, S.C., in preparation for her first major overhaul. She ended her 17th patrol at Charleston on 15 October 1966 and began her overhaul on the 28th. She completed repairs on 9 May 1968; and, after post-overhaul sea trials and shakedown, she embarked upon her 18th deterrent patrol on 22 September 1968. Over the next five years she operated out of New London and Rota, Spain, from which ports she conducted another 19 patrols in the Atlantic.

In June of 1973, she was transferred to the Pacific Fleet, arriving in San Diego on 11 July. After a short period of operations with Submarine Group 5, she moved to Vallejo on 6 August to begin another overhaul, this time at the Mare Island Naval Shipyard. On 30 November 1974, the fleet ballistic missile submarine completed repairs and, following shakedown in January and February of 1975, she transited the Panama Canal again in March to fire test missiles near Cape Canaveral, Fla. She concluded that mission in July and retransited the canal on 8 August. *Thomas A. Edison* carried out operations along the west coast until December at which time she headed for her new home port, Guam. As of the beginning of 1980, the fleet ballistic missile submarine continued to conduct deterrent patrols from her base at Guam.

Thomas Blackhorne

(Tr: t. 269; l. 125'5''; dph. 12'7''; s. 10 k.; cl. "Castle")

Thomas Blackhorne (sometimes spelled *Thomas Blackhorn*)—a steel-hulled steam screw trawler built for the British Admiralty in 1917 at Beverley, England, by Cook, Welton, and Gemmell, Ltd.—was leased by the United States Navy in mid-May 1919 for service with the North Sea Minesweeping Detachment and delivered to the Navy at Falmouth, England, where she was commissioned, probably on 16 May 1919.

By July 1919, *Thomas Blackhorne* was no longer involved in active minesweeping operations in the North Sea Mine Barrage fields but was engaged in a support role at the detachment's base at Kirkwall, Scotland. There, she provided sweep wire and stores to the minesweepers based at Kirkwall. She interrupted this duty in early August to steam out to the minefield to recover marker buoys from 4 to 8 August. She then returned to resume her local operations.

Drydocked at Wick to receive a new propeller on 10 September, *Thomas Blackhorne* returned to Kirkwall on the following day to operate between Inverness, Invergordon, and Kirkwall for the remainder of her active career under the stars and stripes. Early in October, she towed the disabled subchaser *SC–38* (which had been damaged in a mine explosion on 25 September) to Harwich, England.

Shifting to Brighton, England, on the 5th, *Thomas Blackhorne* was decommissioned and returned to the Admiralty on the afternoon of 6 October 1919.

Thomas Buckley

(Tr: t. 269; l. 125'4''; b. 22'5''; dph. 12'2''; s. 10 k.; cl. "Castle")

Thomas Buckley—a steel-hulled screw steam trawler built in 1918 at Beverley, England, for the British

Admiralty by Cook, Welton and Gemmell, Ltd.—was chartered by the Navy in May 1919 for service with the North Sea Minesweeping Detachment.

Based at Kirkwall, Scotland, *Thomas Buckley* swept mines in company with *Thomas Laundry* during the detachment's fourth minesweeping operation conducted in early July 1919. She participated in the fifth sweep, in August, serving as buoy marker vessel on 4 and 5 August. The trawler operated locally at Kirkwall through the middle of August, distributing such essentials as kites, slings, and weights—as well as sweep wire—to various minesweepers there, until she returned to the minefields on the 20th.

Receiving an "electronic protective device" from *Avocet* (Minesweeper No. 19), and delivering buoy mooring line to *Turkey* (Minesweeper No. 13), she lay anchored for much of 21 August. The trawler moved out into the minefields on the following day, cruising astern of a squadron of minesweepers. Between 0800 and 1600 that day, *Thomas Buckley*—with riflemen armed with Springfield 1903 rifles—destroyed five mines before making port at Lerwick in the Shetland Islands late that evening. There, she conducted harbor duties before getting underway on the 25th, delivering kites and taking on buoys and gear from other minesweepers. On the 26th, she towed the disabled subchaser *SC–207* to Lerwick before shifting back to Kirkwall to resume local operations.

Thomas Buckley subsequently carried cargoes of sweep and electrode wire, lubricating oil, and gasoline from Invergordon to Kirkwall and conducted transport operations during the early part of October, concluding these duties at Brighton, England, on 6 October. Decommissioned on 7 October 1919, *Thomas Buckley* was returned to the Admiralty the same day.

Thomas C. Hart

Thomas Charles Hart—born on 12 June 1877 in Genessee County, Mich.—graduated from the Naval Academy in 1897 and served his initial tours of sea duty in *Massachusetts* (Battleship No. 2) and in the steam yacht *Vixen*, during the Spanish-American War.

In the years preceding the First World War, Hart filled a variety of sea and shore duty billets: as a junior officer in battleships, torpedo boats, and submarines; as an instructor at the Naval Academy; as aide to an Assistant Secretary of the Navy; and as commander of the Pacific Torpedo Flotilla. By the spring of 1917, Hart was commanding the cruiser *Chicago* and the Submarine Base at New London, Conn., while also acting as Chief of Staff to the Commander, Submarine Force, Atlantic Fleet.

During World War I, Hart served concurrently as commander of Submarine Divisions 2 and 5, with *Bushnell* (Submarine Tender No. 2) as his flagship. One division was based at Bantry Bay, protecting sea approaches to the British Isles; the second was based at Punta Delgada in the Azores, protecting routes to that vital island. In 1918, after temporary duty with the British Admiralty, Hart was appointed Director of Submarines in the Office of the Chief of Naval Operations. Serving in this office as its head until 1922, Hart fought doggedly to improve the lot of the submarine arm of the Navy. His tenacity was responsible for the American Navy's acquisition of surrendered German U-boats after World War I to learn the details of the technical innovations incorporated in the erstwhile enemy craft.

Receiving the Distinguished Service Medal (DSM) for his service as Director of Submarines, Hart spent the ensuing years of the 1920's and 1930's in a succession of sea and shore billets as he advanced up the Navy ladder. He studied at both the Army and Navy War Colleges; commanded the Atlantic Fleet Submarine Divisions, battleship *Mississippi* (BB–42), and Submarine Flotilla 3; served as Assistant Commandant

of the 3d Naval District; Inspector of Ordnance at the Naval Torpedo Station, Newport, R.I.; and Commander of the Control Force. After a tour as Superintendent of the Naval Academy, he went to sea as Commander, Cruiser Division 6, in June 1934. Reporting to the General Board after this tour of sea duty, Hart became its chairman in 1937.

With the temporary rank of admiral, Hart relieved classmate Admiral Harry E. Yarnell as Commander-in-Chief, Asiatic Fleet (CinCAF) on 25 July 1939. For the next two years, as tensions increased in the western Pacific, Hart prepared the small Asiatic Fleet for war with Japan. He reduced the presence of his fleet in Chinese waters and concentrated it in the Philippines to await the onslaught expected momentarily. He also successfully badgered Washington for reinforcements in the way of patrol planes and fleet submarines.

The Japanese attack on Pearl Harbor, coupled with nearly simultaneous assaults on British and Dutch possessions and the Philippines, catapulted the United States into World War II. The Americans, with their Filipino allies, fought a delaying action in the Philippines, while a mixed American, British, Dutch, and Australian (ABDA) military structure was set up to operate from Java in an attempt to hold the Japanese at the Malay Barrier. Given command of ABDA naval forces, Hart directed part of this defense into mid-February 1942. By that point, it had become evident that, despite the brave ABDA sailors, the Japanese were not to be denied. Despite the formidable obstacles, Hart persevered in the face of "discouraging surroundings and complex associations" and earned a gold star in lieu of his second DSM for unfailing judgment, sound decisions, and moral courage.

Transferred to the retired list in July 1942 with the rank of Admiral, Thomas C. Hart nevertheless continued on active duty with the General Board through 1944. From February to April 1944, he was chairman of the committee which conducted the "Hart Inquiry" into the Pearl Harbor attack, a duty which took him to the length and breadth of the Pacific Ocean area.

On 9 February 1945, Hart retired from the Navy to fill an appointment as senator from Connecticut. He served in Congress until 3 January 1947 and did not seek reelection. Admiral Hart then returned to his family home in Sharon, Conn., and died there on 4 July 1971, at the age of 94.

(DE–1092: dp. 3,963 (f.); l. 438'; b. 47'; dr. 25'; s. 25+ k.; cpl. 245; a. 1 5", 1 ASROC ln., 1 Sea Sparrow ln., 4 15.5" ASW tt.; cl. *Knox*)

Thomas C. Hart (DE–1092) was laid down on 8 October 1971 at Westwego, La., by Avondale Shipyards, Inc.; launched on 12 August 1972; sponsored by Mrs. Reginald Bragonier, eldest granddaughter of Admiral Thomas C. Hart; and commissioned on 28 July 1973, Lt. Comdr. Ronald J. Forst in command.

The last combatant ship commissioned at the Boston Naval Shipyard, *Thomas C. Hart* conducted sea trials off the east coast before being homeported in Norfolk, Va. Following shakedown at Guantanamo Bay, Cuba, she returned to the Norfolk Naval Shipyard on 1 February 1974, where she underwent a major structural conversion, altering her after superstructure to accommodate the new Light Airborne Multi-purpose System (LAMPS) facilities. She then steamed out for post-repair trials off the Virginia Capes.

Deploying to the Caribbean, *Thomas C. Hart* conducted weapons systems tests and antisubmarine exercises and, upon completion of these duties, called at Port-au-Prince, Haiti, before returning to Guantanamo Bay for further training. After naval gunfire support qualification at Roosevelt Roads, she cruised to Bermuda for a three-day visit. She left Port Royal Bay on 3 September, having to do a "quick step" to avoid the tropical storm which later became Hurricane Delores, and arrived at Norfolk on 5 September.

In October, following type training in the Narragansett Bay area, the ship qualified for a certificate for unrestricted operations.

With Capt. W. R. Smedburg IV, Commander, Destroyer Squadron 10, and his staff embarked, *Thomas C. Hart* got underway on 18 November for Composite Task Unit Exercise 4–75 and nine days of intensive exercises. The following month, the ship passed her Nuclear Weapons Acceptance Inspection on 11 December and thus became a nuclear-qualified ship.

The early months of 1975 were spent in preparation for *Thomas C. Hart*'s first Mediterranean deployment. This deployment, which lasted from 16 June to 22 December, consisted primarily of operations with *John F. Kennedy* (CV–67) and other escorts while making a number of port visits in company with *Pharris* (FF–1094). On 1 July 1975, the ship was reclassified as FF–1092.

Thomas C. Hart spent the first six months of 1976 engaging in two major fleet exercises in preparation for her four and one-half month, unsupported participation in Unitas XVII later in the year. The first exercise, "Safepass," lasted from 6 to 26 March and involved complex NATO fleet operations out of Halifax, Nova Scotia. The second exercise, "Solid Shield," occurred during the period 13 to 18 May and involved operations off the coast of the Carolinas in support of a full amphibious landing on Onslow Beach. Following an intensive month-long preparation period in June, *Thomas C. Hart* commenced Unitas XVII on 9 July. During the next 18 weeks, the ship circumnavigated the South American continent and operated with host ships from Brazil, Uruguay, Argentina, Chile, Peru, Colombia, and Venezuela. The frigate returned to her home port of Norfolk on 21 November and spent the remainder of the year in post-deployment standdown and holiday leave period.

Early 1977 found *Thomas C. Hart* experiencing a period of maintenance, alteration, and testing. Of most significance was the installation of the Harpoon system, a highly sophisticated surface warfare missile which greatly extended *Thomas C. Hart*'s reach against surface contacts. Most of September was spent in Norfolk preparing for the ship's second Mediterranean deployment. She departed CONUS on 27 September and engaged in seven months of operations with the 6th Fleet before returning to Norfolk again on 26 April 1978. Ports of call included Rota, Spain; Alexandria, Egypt; Istanbul, Turkey; Piraeus, Greece; Venice, Gaeta, and Naples, Italy; and—finally—Majorca; Valencia, and Rota, Spain.

Following post-deployment standdown, *Thomas C. Hart* engaged in CORTRAMID 78, an underway training period for midshipmen, which lasted from mid-June through early July. In late September 1978, *Thomas C. Hart*'s home port was shifted to Philadelphia in anticipation of the commencement of her first regular overhaul since commissioning. *Thomas C. Hart* entered the Philadelphia Naval Shipyard for this purpose on 26 October, and she remained there into 1979.

Thomas Corwin

Thomas Corwin—born on 29 July 1794 in Bourbon County, Ky.—moved to Lebanon, Ohio, in 1798. He was admitted to the bar in 1817 and served in the United States House of Representatives from 1831 to 1840. He was Governor of Ohio from 1840 to 1842 and entered the United States Senate in 1845. He left this post in 1850 to become Secretary of the Treasury under President Fillmore. Corwin returned to private life in 1853 but was reelected to the House in 1858. Lincoln appointed him Minister to Mexico in 1861, and he held this post until 1 September 1864. He died in Washington, D.C., on 18 December 1865.

(Str: l. 213'; cpl. 40; a. 3 guns)

Thomas Corwin was built at Portland, Oreg., in 1876 for the United States Revenue Service. She operated with that organization until 9 April 1898 when she was transferred to the United States Navy during the Spanish-American War. She served in the San Diego, Calif., area until 15 August 1898 when she was returned to the Treasury Department.

Thomas E. Fraser

Thomas Edward Fraser—born on 6 February 1901 in Stafford Springs, Conn.—was appointed to the United States Naval Academy on 3 September 1920. After graduating on 4 June 1924, he served in *Wyoming* (BB–32) for nearly a year and studied torpedo warfare at the Naval Torpedo Station, Newport, R.I., before reporting for duty on board *Worden* (DD–288) on 17 January 1926. He served in that destroyer until 1 May 1930. Following assignments in *Ellis* (DD–154) and at the New York Navy Yard, Fraser reported on 1 March 1934 for duties in connection with the fitting out of *Tuscaloosa* (CA–37). Assignments to the Philadelphia and Portsmouth Navy Yards followed in the late 1930's.

During 1940 and 1941, he briefly commanded, in turn, destroyers *Yarnall* (DD–143), *Claxton* (DD–140), and *Broome* (DD–210). On 10 November 1941, he became commanding officer of *Walke* (DD–416); and, on 20 August 1942, he was appointed to the temporary rank of commander.

On the night of 14 and 15 November 1942, *Walke* was a part of Rear Admiral Willis Augustus Lee's Task Force 64, when it encountered a large Japanese force off Savo Island attempting to bring reinforcements to Guadalcanal. Acting as the senior commander of the four destroyers of the task force, Comdr. Fraser boldly led them into action against the numerically superior Japanese force. The torpedoes and heavy gunfire of the Japanese vessels took a devastating toll of the American destroyers; and, shortly after midnight, Comdr. Fraser gave the order to abandon *Walke*. He was lost in the ensuing action and was posthumously awarded the Navy Cross for his valor and devotion to duty.

(DM–24: dp. 2,200; l. 376'6''; b. 40'10''; dr. 18'10''; s. 34.2 k.; cpl. 363; a. 6 5'', 12 40mm., 8 20mm., 2 .50-cal. mg.; cl. *Robert H. Smith*)

Thomas E. Fraser (DM–24) was laid down as *DD–736* on 31 January 1944 at Bath, Maine, by the Bath Iron Works; named *Thomas E. Fraser* on 1 March 1944; launched on 10 June 1944; sponsored by Mrs. Thomas E. Fraser; reclassified as a destroyer minelayer and redesignated DM–24 on 20 July 1944; and commissioned on 22 August 1944, Comdr. Ronald Joseph Woodaman in command.

Following shakedown training out of Bermuda and mine warfare training out of Yorktown, Va., *Thomas E. Fraser* departed Norfolk on 27 November and proceeded, via the Canal Zone, to the west coast, arriving at San Diego on 12 December. After five days of intensive exercises off San Clemente Island, *Thomas E. Fraser* departed the California coast, steaming in company with *Shannon* (DM–25) and *Harry F. Bauer* (DM–26). On the 21st, the destroyer minelayers rendezvoused with two transports and entered Pearl Harbor on the 26th. *Fraser* devoted the last days of 1944 and most of January 1945 to intensive exercises in the Hawaiian Islands to prepare for her role in the forthcoming assault on Iwo Jima.

On 27 January, *Thomas E. Fraser* got underway to screen Task Group 51.11 as it proceeded via Eniwetok to the Marianas. On the 11th, she reached Saipan, the final staging point for the operation. On the 16th, the force sortied for Iwo Jima. Two hours before dawn on D-day, 19 February, DM–24 left the convoy screen to make an antisubmarine sweep through the transport area off the southern beaches of Iwo Jima. At 0615, she completed the patrol and proceeded to take station in the anchorage screen.

After protecting the transports during the original landings, the minelayer proceeded in mid-afternoon to a fire support sector southeast of Mt. Suribachi. At 1737 —only 1,000 yards from the nearest beach—she began delivering call fire under the direction of a shore fire control party. She poured in five-inch fire on enemy machinegun and mortar nests on the northeast base of the formidable mountain. Shortly before sunset, she shifted her fire to enemy positions in the caves near the base of Mt. Suribachi. Japanese machinegunners on shore fired on the ship but did no damage. That evening, Thomas E. Fraser moved to a position southwest of Mt. Suribachi and delivered call fire and illumination rounds throughout the night. Her star shells made it possible for Marine mortars to foil a Japanese attempt to infiltrate an American position via the sea. In the days that followed, Fraser alternated anchorage screening duties with fire support missions to assist marines fighting ashore. Early on the morning of 21 February, as Fraser was firing on the northeast base of Mt. Suribachi, a near miss by a large shell of undetermined origin caused a hole in her starboard side just below the main deck. Nevertheless, she continued firing on targets of opportunity until late in the afternoon when she returned to anchorage patrol.

During a dusk air raid alert on 23 February, Thomas E. Fraser opened fire on a Japanese airplane as it passed down the port side of the ship, but the raider disappeared, apparently unharmed.

Thomas E. Fraser remained off Iwo Jima through the first week in March, providing screening for the transports and fire support for the marines fighting ashore. She scored hits on enemy supply dumps, machinegun nests, and entrenchments, and knocked out numerous gun emplacements. At night, she often fired star shells or delivered harassment fire.

On 8 March, with the help of a plane spotter, her 5-inch guns scored three direct hits on a Japanese blockhouse. Shortly before sunset that day, she departed that battle-torn island, escorting Lakewood Victory (AK-236).

Arriving at Ulithi on 11 March, the minelayer remained in the lagoon for eight days for upkeep, provisioning, and ammunition replenishment. On the 19th, she got underway in company with Mine Group 2 and steamed for the Ryukyus. Before dawn on the 25th, the minesweepers began sweep operations—part of the large scale American efforts to prepare the waters of the Nansei Shoto for the planned assaults on Kerama Retto and Okinawa. The destroyer minelayer (DM) followed in the wake of the minesweepers, directing their movements and providing fire support. On that day, she fired at shore targets on a number of smaller islands of the Okinawa Gunto, observing direct hits. On the 27th, she fired at targets on the main island of Okinawa. The destroyer minelayer did not retire with the minesweeping group that evening but took up a patrol station off Okinawa and, throughout the night, fired illumination and harassment rounds on the island's southern beaches.

In the early hours of 29 March, Thomas E. Fraser fired on an attacking "Betty," bringing the Japanese plane down in flames. Enemy air attacks became more frequent in the last days of March; and, after midnight on 31 March, the warship drove off an attack by a single Japanese plane. Minutes later, a dive bomber attacked. Hit by 5-inch gunfire from the ship, the enemy aircraft passed overhead and splashed astern. At 0320, a low flying enemy floatplane appeared without warning, dropped a bomb which exploded just off Fraser's port quarter, and disappeared into the night before the ship could fire a single shot. The DM continued her support and direction of the minesweeping group until the completion of its assigned sweeps later that day, then took up her station off Kerama Retto as an anchorage screening vessel.

While screening Mine Division 7 southwest of Kerama Retto on 2 April, the warship took two enemy planes under fire in quick succession, repelling the first

and hitting the second with automatic weapons fire as it passed overhead. The attacker burst into flame and splashed. As dawn approached, the ship fired on other enemy aircraft but scored no more hits. After taking on ammunition at Kerama Retto that afternoon, Thomas E. Fraser got underway to join a transport task unit for night retirement. As the warship approached the convoy, seven "Betties" attacked. Antiaircraft fire from the convoy and its escort downed four enemy planes. However, Henrico (APA-45)—five miles away—took a bomb hit; and a kamikaze found its mark on transport Goodhue's (APA-107) fantail.

Fraser continued screening duties off Kerama Retto until 5 April when she got underway to help escort a convoy of transports to Saipan. En route, orders arrived detaching her from the convoy; and she proceeded with Bache (DD-470) to Guam where they arrived on the 8th.

Following the installation of a new radar antenna, Fraser moved to Saipan on the 18th and, two days later, headed back toward the Ryukyus with a convoy of tank landing ships. After conducting the convoy to a dispersal point off Nakagusuku Wan, the destroyer minelayer took up a screening station off the southern coast of Okinawa. On 28 April, a Japanese plane dove in low from the direction of the island, launched a torpedo which missed the ship, and escaped despite heavy antiaircraft fire. After dark, the ship repelled an enemy air raid and then steamed to assist a hospital ship which had been hit by a Japanese suicide plane. Finding Comfort (AH-6) damaged but proceeding under her own power, Thomas E. Fraser escorted the vessel to Guam where they arrived on 3 May.

The light minelayer was next ordered back to Okinawa to strengthen the thinning ranks of American destroyers on radar picket duty off that island. Steaming on her starboard screw while her port engine was being repaired, the warship left Apra Harbor on 4 May and arrived off Okinawa on the 7th to resume screening and radar picket duties. While operating in the transport screen off Hagushi Beach on the 12th, she helped to fight off a swarm of Japanese suicide planes during the raid in which a kamikaze crashed battleship New Mexico (BB-40).

Throughout the month, she alternated radar picket duty off Okinawa with maintenance and replenishment at Kerama Retto and Hagushi. Late in the day on 24 May, Fraser greeted the first planes of a concerted air attack from the north with gunfire and crashed one of her attackers on Ie Shima. The attack continued into the early hours of the 25th and was at last dispersed after 10 hours and 7 minutes. The ship then spent five days at Kerama Retto for the installation of fighter direction equipment and, on 30 May, resumed her picket duties southwest of Okinawa. As she steamed on station shortly before sunset on 1 June, two low flying torpedo bombers made a surprise torpedo attack. Thomas E. Fraser successfully maneuvered to avoid the torpedoes dropped by the planes and joined the picket group in engaging the intruders.

On 6 June, Thomas E. Fraser relieved J. William Ditter (DM-31), the badly battered target of a mass kamikaze attack, on picket station. Two days later, she returned to Kerama Retto and began preparations for a new assignment—hydrographic survey and sweeping operations between Kerama Retto and Sakishima Gunto. Operating mainly as a buoy planting ship, the destroyer minelayer accompanied sweepers in the southern Nansei Shoto throughout June, returning twice to Kerama Retto to load radar buoys and undergo engineering maintenance. Toward sunset on 21 June, as she lay at anchor in Kerama Retto, Thomas E. Fraser took under fire an enemy plane which had penetrated the screen and had dropped a bomb on the forecastle of nearby Curtiss (AV-4). Joining in the firing, the DM scored an assist when the Japanese plane splashed not far from the seaplane tender.

Into August, Thomas E. Fraser operated out of Buckner Bay, Okinawa, planting buoys to guide minesweeping units clearing the East China Sea. After hostilities ceased, she steamed north to rendezvous with the 3d Fleet. Delays kept the victorious forces hovering off the coast of Honshu for several days. On the 25th, the task force began its approach to Tokyo; and, on the 27th, *Thomas E. Fraser* patrolled Sagami Wan. On the morning of the 28th, she supported *Ellyson* (DMS–19) and *Hambleton* (DMS–20) as they helped to sweep the channel in preparation for the entry of cruiser *San Diego* (CL–53) into Tokyo Bay. She ended August supporting sweepers clearing the Okinoyama minefield and was in Tokyo Bay on 2 September when the peace was signed on board *Missouri* (BB–63).

In September, the minelayer operated with sweep units clearing mines in Kii Suido, in Wakayama anchorage, and off the Pacific coast of the Japanese islands. While anchored in Wakanoura Wan on the 17th and 18th, she weathered a typhoon whose 100-knot gusts forced her to use her engine to ease the strain on her anchor. When the storm abated, she sent out a party to aid survivors and to remove confidential gear and publications from *YMS–478* which had broached and capsized.

She continued off the Japanese coast into October. Following a week at Buckner Bay, she got underway on 25 October for a new sweep area in the East China Sea. Assigned to lay buoys and to assist in navigation, the warship operated in the northern reaches of the East China Sea into November. On 17 November, she put in at Sasebo for fuel and upkeep. On 1 December, she broke out her homeward bound pennant, and the next day departed Japan, steaming via Eniwetok and Pearl Harbor, and arriving in San Diego on 22 December.

On the 26th, she got underway and steamed via the Canal Zone to Norfolk, arriving there on 8 January 1946. Late in March, the destroyer minelayer put in at Charleston for overhaul and remained in that port until late in the year when she participated in a reserve training cruise with *Wisconsin* (BB–64) which continued into January 1947. From February until May, she operated out of various Caribbean ports; then returned to Norfolk. On the last day of June, she departed Hampton Roads; steamed to Recife, Brazil; then proceeded on to the African port of Monrovia for a courtesy and good-will visit during Liberia's centennial celebration. After stopping at Senegal, she returned to the east coast on 16 August.

The destroyer minelayer continued operations off the Atlantic coast ranging as far north as Argentia and as far south as the Caribbean. On 1 December 1947, she was immobilized; but she was again back in service by May 1949. Following local operations out of Guantanamo in July, the ship departed Hampton Roads early in August and called at Cherbourg, France, before returning to the Caribbean where she remained until she returned to Charleston in November.

In September 1950, she broke the routine of training operations off the east coast with a Mediterranean deployment which continued until 22 January 1951 when she departed Oran. In June, she was again underway for European ports, this time on a midshipman cruise which took her to Copenhagen, Plymouth, and Lisbon. In July, she visited Cuba before returning to the east coast. For the next three years, she varied exercises off the Atlantic coast and in the Caribbean with brief voyages to Europe.

In February 1955, she engaged in mine planting off Key West in support of a fleet service mine test program, one of her last assignments. On 10 June 1955, she was placed in reserve; and, on 12 September, she was decommissioned and placed in reserve at Portsmouth (N.H.) Naval Shipyard. Her name was struck from the Navy list on 1 November 1970.

Thomas E. Fraser received three battle stars for World War II service.

Thomas F. Nickel

Thomas F. Nickel—born on 18 July 1921 in Lansing, Mich.—enlisted in the United States Marine Corps Reserve on 3 February 1942 and served at Parris Island, S.C., and Quantico, Va., until ordered overseas on 28 April 1942.

Private Nickel was serving with the 1st Marine Raider Battalion when it landed at Tulagi, Solomon Islands, on 7 August 1942. That day, he ignored hostile machinegun fire as he worked his way forward and knocked out an enemy position with hand grenades, enabling his squad to advance without further casualties. Killed in the attack, Private Nickel was posthumously awarded the Silver Star.

(DE–587: dp. 1,450; l. 306'; b. 37'; dr. 13'9"; s. 23.6 k.; cpl. 221; a. 2 5", 4 40mm., 10 20mm., 2 dct., 8 dcp., 3 21" tt.; cl. *Rudderow*)

Thomas F. Nickel (DE–587) was laid down on 15 December 1943 at Hingham, Mass., by the Bethlehem-Hingham Shipyards; launched on 22 January 1944; sponsored by Mrs. Fred W. Nickel; and commissioned on 9 June 1944, Lt. Comdr. Claude S. Farmer, USNR, in command.

After shakedown training in the Caribbean from 29 June to 26 July, the destroyer escort made one round-trip voyage across the Atlantic escorting convoy UGS–50 to Bizerte, Tunisia, and back before departing Boston with Escort Division 71 on the last day of September, bound for the South Pacific.

She transited the Panama Canal on 15 October and, after calls at the Galapagos and Society Islands, arrived at Espiritu Santo on 1 November. There, after the destroyer escort had taken on 15 aerial torpedoes as deck cargo, she headed for Manus. She delivered her dangerous cargo at Seeadler Harbor on 7 November. Three days later, the ship was anchored there slightly more than a mile from *Mount Hood* (AE–11) when that ammunition ship exploded, but she was not damaged.

Thomas F. Nickel next proceeded to New Guinea and arrived at Humboldt Bay on 21 November. The following week, she again put to sea in the screen of a Philippine-bound convoy. She arrived at San Pedro Bay, Leyte, on 15 December and, two days later, began the return voyage to Hollandia with another convoy. On 28 December, the destroyer escort departed Aitape with Task Group 78.1, the San Fabian Attack Force, which was transporting the 43d Infantry Division to make the initial assault against Luzon. The American ships entered Linagayen Gulf on 9 January 1945, and the DE protected the landings. She was then assigned to the antisubmarine and antiaircraft screen until 18 January. On 10 January, *Dupage* (APA–41) was hit and badly damaged by a suicide plane. A boat from *Nickel* rescued five of that attack transport's crewmen who had been blown overboard and gave them medical attention.

On 18 January, orders sent DE–587 to New Guinea waters to conduct antisubmarine patrols between the islands of Biak and Owi; but, early in February, she found herself heading back to the Philippines in the screen of Task Group 78.6, the third Lingayen reinforcement group. She remained in the Lingayen area of Luzon from 6 February until 7 March. In the following months, the escort performed antisubmarine patrol and escort duty between San Pedro, Subic Bay, and ports in New Guinea and the Carolines. On 6 August, she departed Subic Bay with a convoy to refuel at Buckner Bay and returned to the Philippines escorting *Oak Hill* (LSD–7). In the evening of 12 August, *Oak Hill* reported a periscope on her port quarter and, eight minutes later, a torpedo wake 2,000 yards astern of her. *Thomas F. Nickel* made several depth charge attacks and then lost contact. Both ships arrived safely at Leyte on the 15th, the day hostilities ended.

The destroyer escort made one more round-trip

voyage to Buckner Bay in late August, escorting *Cabildo* (LSD–16) there and returning with *Hocking* (APA–121). She operated in the Philippines until 29 November when she got underway for the United States.

Thomas F. Nickel arrived at San Diego on 18 December 1945 and was decommissioned on 31 May 1946. However, in June, she was assigned to the 12th Naval District as a training ship. On 31 October, she arrived under tow at San Francisco and was subsequently moved to Sacramento for use as a naval reserve armory.

The destroyer escort was reactivated on 8 July 1948 and placed in service as a naval reserve training ship. She made weekend and two-week cruises to Mexico, Canada, Alaska, Pearl Harbor, and Pacific coast ports. After the ship was recommissioned on 22 September 1950, she continued the same duty. She operated out of San Francisco until December 1951 when she moved to San Diego.

On 25 November 1957, *Thomas F. Nickel* was assigned to the Pacific Reserve Fleet. She was decommissioned on 26 February 1958 and berthed at San Diego until she was struck from the Navy list on 1 December 1972. Her hulk was sold for scrap at San Jose, Calif., to the Levin Metals Co. on 9 June 1973.

Thomas F. Nickel received one battle star for World War II service.

Thomas Freeborn

(SwGbt: t. 269; l. 143'4''; b. 25'6''; a. 2 32-pdrs.)

Thomas Freeborn—a sidewheel steamer built in 1861 at Brooklyn, N.Y.—was one of three steam tugs chartered by the Navy in April 1861 for use in the unsuccessful Fort Sumter relief expedition. She was detained at New York, however, and did not sail with the other two ships, *Yankee* and *Uncle Ben*. On 7 May, she was purchased by the Union Navy and, under the command of Comdr. James H. Ward, joined the newly formed "Flying Flotilla" as his flagship. She departed New York on 16 May for duty in the Chesapeake Bay and at Hampton Roads, Va.

In Hampton Roads, *Monticello* and *Thomas Freeborn* engaged Confederate batteries at Sewell's Point, Va., on 19 May. The next day, *Thomas Freeborn* carried Senators Benjamin F. Wade, Zachariah Chandler, and Robert Morrill to Washington, returning to Hampton Roads on 22 May. She again sailed for the Washington Navy Yard on 23 May and took part in the Union occupation of Alexandria, Va., on the 24th. *Thomas Freeborn* deployed on permanent blockade and patrol duty in the Potomac River on 27 May.

There, *Anacostia*, *Resolute*, and *Thomas Freeborn* fired on and silenced Confederate batteries at Aquia Creek, Va., on the last day of May. On 24 June, *Thomas Freeborn* and *Pawnee* shelled Confederate installations at Mathias Point, Va., after having received sporadic shore fire from the batteries earlier. Casualties included Comdr. Ward who was shot and killed while attempting to land on the point during the evening of 27 June. *Thomas Freeborn* returned to the Washington Navy Yard for repairs on 12 July.

Thomas Freeborn soon rejoined the flotilla, capturing sloop *A. B. Leon* off White House Point, Va., on 26 July 1861. On 4 August, she captured schooner *Pocahontas* and sloop *Mary Grey* in Pohick Creek, Va., and, on 10 November, received fire from Confederate batteries on Maryland Point, Va., but sustained no damage. *Thomas Freeborn* captured schooner *Mail* and her cargo of salt in Coan River, Va., on 1 August 1862, and seized and burned schooner *Arctic* in Maryland's Great Wicomico River on 15 September. She captured sloop *Thomas Reilly* on 1 October at the mouth of Quantico Creek, Va.

A landing party from *Thomas Freeborn* cut telegraph lines stretching from Occoquan and Fredericks-burg, Va., to Richmond, Va., on 4 October 1862. On 21 February 1863, *Dragon* and *Thomas Freeborn* engaged a Confederate battery near Fort Lowry, Va.; each vessel received minor damage. *Thomas Freeborn* helped *Yankee*, *Fuchsia*, and *Tulip* destroy a Confederate encampment under construction at Carter's Creek, Va., on 29 April. The vessel spent the remainder of 1863 and all of 1864 on patrol and reconnaissance duty along the Potomac.

Thomas Freeborn was repaired at the Washington Navy Yard in early January 1865. Returning to duty, she captured blockade runner *William Smith* on 3 March in the Piankatank River, Va. On 17 April, she was ordered by the Secretary of War, Edwin M. Stanton, to patrol the Chesapeake Bay from Point Lookout to the mouth of the Patuxent River, Md., in search of the assassins of President Lincoln. Finding nothing, she was ordered to proceed to Cherrystone, Va., on 1 May 1865 and warned of the expected arrival of Confederate ram CSS *Stonewall* from Europe. The steamer returned to the Washington Navy Yard later in the month.

Thomas Freeborn was decommissioned at the Washington Navy Yard on 17 June 1865 and was sold at auction there on 20 July to Anthony Raybold. She was redocumented as *Philip* on 14 September 1865 and finally disposed of in 1887.

Thomas G. Thompson

Thomas Gordon Thompson—born on 28 November 1888 at Rose Bank, Staten Island, N.Y.—received his bachelor's degree from Clark University at Worcester, Mass., in 1914. With the support of a scholarship from the British Iron and Steel Institute, he then began graduate studies at the University of Washington at Seattle. He received his doctorate in chemistry from this institution in 1918. During World War I, Thompson served in the United States Army in the Ordnance and Chemical Warfare Branch, rising to the rank of captain. Returning to the university in 1919, Dr. Thompson was promoted to associate professor in 1923 and to full professor in 1929.

Dr. Thompson—the first American chemist to devote his major efforts to investigating the chemistry of sea water—founded the University of Washington's oceanographic laboratories in 1930. This was an interdepartmental institution which drew its staff from the faculties of the university's departments of physics, chemistry, bacteriology, botany, and zoology. Two years later, as a result of Dr. Thompson's guidance, the university placed a small research vessel, *Catalyst*, in service to perform inshore oceanographic work in the Pacific Northwest.

Over the ensuing years, Dr. Thompson developed methods and techniques for the quantitative determination of elements—such as aluminum, boron, copper, iron, manganese, nickel, strontium, silicon, bromine, iodine, phosphates, and nitrates—which occur, in small quantities, in sea water. In this vein, the professor's main interest lay in determining the relation of the chemical and physical properties of sea water—notably the specific gravity, refractivity, and electrical conductivity.

He participated actively in international geographic and oceanographic ventures, serving or chairing committees and co-authoring studies on specific oceanographic matters. During World War II, Dr. Thompson again served in the United States Army, eventually rising to the rank of colonel.

In 1951, Professor Thompson's efforts in the field of oceanography were rewarded when the university established a department of oceanography. Dr. Thompson was recognized as one of the world's leading oceanographers and one of the pioneers of the chemistry of the sea. Subsequent to his promotion to professor emeritus, the professor's health slowly deteriorated, eventually ending in his death at Seattle, Wash., on 10 August 1961.

(AGOR–9: dp. 1,380 (f.); l. 208'9''; b. 37'4''; dr. 15'3'';
s. 13.5 k.; cpl. 51; cl. *Robert D. Conrad*)

Thomas G. Thompson (AGOR–9) was laid down on
12 September 1963 at Marinette, Wis., by the Marinette
Marine Corp.; launched on 18 July 1964; sponsored by
Mrs. Isabel Thompson, the widow of Professor Thompson; and delivered to the Navy on 4 September 1965.

Specially designed for oceanographic research work,
Thomas G. Thompson was transferred to the University of Washington, for service with that institution's
oceanographic department, in a ceremony at the Boston
Naval Shipyard on 21 September 1965. Manned by a
civilian crew but under the technical control of the
Oceanographer of the Navy, *Thomas G. Thompson*
conducted oceanographic ressearch, performing experiments supporting the national oceanographic programs
of the United States into 1978.

Thomas Graham

(Tr: t. 202; l. 115'6''; b. 22'2''; dph. 12'2''; s. 10 k.;
cl. "Strath")

Thomas Graham—a steel-hulled screw steam trawler
built in 1918 at Bowling, Scotland, by Scott and Sons,
for the British Admiralty—was leased by the Navy for
service with the North Sea Minesweeping Detachment
in May 1919. Based at Kirkwall, Scotland, she served
with the detachment into the summer of 1919. Apparently, the ship's last official duty was to transport the
body of Capt. Roscoe C. Bulmer, the commander of
the North Sea Minesweeping Detachment, from Kirkwall to Inverness, Scotland. Capt. Bulmer had been
severely injured in an automobile accident at Kirkwall
on 4 August 1919 and had died on board *Black Hawk*
(Destroyer Tender No. 9) on the following day.

Thomas Graham was returned to the Admiralty on
7 August.

Thomas H. Barry

(AP–45: dp. 11,250; l. 508'0''; b. 70'9''; dr. 27'3'';
a. 2 5'', 4 3'', 8 .50-cal. mg.)

Thomas H. Barry—a steel-hulled, twin-screw passenger and cargo ship launched on 15 May 1930 as
Oriente by the Newport News Shipbuilding and Drydock Co. for the New York and Cuba Mail and Steamship Company's Ward Line—was acquired by the War
Department in June 1941 for use as an Army transport.

On 29 September 1941, the Acting Chief of Naval
Operations, Rear Admiral Royal E. Ingersoll, sent a
memorandum to the Chief of the Bureau of Navigation,
listing a number of Army transports—including *Thomas
H. Barry*—that were to be "eventually taken over by
the Navy." *Thomas H. Barry* was later designated
AP–45. However, the transport was never taken over
by the Navy and remained under Army control through
the end of World War II.

Thomas Henrix

(Tr: t. 203; l. 115'4''; b. 22'2''; dph. 12'1''; s. 9.5 k.;
cl. "Strath")

Thomas Henrix—a steel-hulled screw steam trawler
built in 1918 at Leith, Scotland, by Hawthorns and
Co., Ltd., for the British Admiralty—was leased by the
United States Navy for service with the North Sea
Minesweeping Detachment. She operated out of Kirkwall, Scotland, supporting the minesweeping operation
in the Barrage between Norway and Scotland. Leased
on 2 June 1919, she was returned to the Admiralty on
6 August 1919.

Thomas J. Gary

Thomas Jones Gary—born on 16 September 1922 in
Texas City, Tex.—enlisted in the Navy on 30 September
1940. When the Japanese attacked Pearl Harbor on 7
December 1941, Seaman 2d Class Gary was on board
California (BB–44). During the raid, the battleship
suffered torpedo and bomb hits which caused extensive
fires and flooding. After he had rescued three or four
wounded men from closed and burning compartments
in the ship, Seaman Gary continued his efforts to save
others until he lost his own life. He was posthumously
commended by the Secretary of the Navy for his courageous action and disregard for personal safety in
assisting his endangered crewmates.

Gary (DE–61) (*q.v.*) and *Gary* (DE–326) were named
for Seaman 2d Class Thomas Jones Gary. The latter
was renamed *Thomas J. Gary* on 1 January 1945.

(DE–326: dp. 1,200 (est.); l. 306'; b. 36'7''; dr. 12'3'';
s. 21.2 k. (tl.); cpl. 216; a. 3 3'', 6 40mm., 10 20mm.,
2 dct., 8 dcp., 1 dcp. (hh.); cl. *Edsall*)

Gary (DE–326) was laid down on 15 June 1943 at
Orange, Tex., by the Consolidated Steel Corporation;
launched on 21 August 1943; sponsored by Mrs. Willie
Mae Gary, mother of Seaman 2d Class Gary; and
commissioned on 27 November 1943, Lt. Comdr. William
H. Harrison, USNR, in command.

Following shakedown exercises out of Bermuda and
post-shakedown overhaul at Charleston, *Gary* reported
to the Commander Caribbean Sea Frontier at Guantanamo for temporary duty on 5 February 1944. She
was detached from that command on 9 March and set
her course for the Straits of Gibraltar, escorting the
first of many transatlantic convoys. Until May of 1945,
Thomas J. Gary operated as an escort vessel in the
Atlantic, safely screening eight convoys from the east
coast to ports in the Mediteranean and the United
Kingdom and back to the United States. While on the
east coast between patrols, *Gary* trained off the coast
of Maine and out of Guantanamo Bay, Cuba, and conducted antisubmarine warfare exercises out of New
London. During June of 1944, she was assigned to the
Navy Fleet Sound School.

In December 1944, she detached from the homebound
convoy she was escorting from British ports to aid
Huron (PF–19) which had collided with a merchantman. On the 9th, she took on board more than 100 Coast
Guardsmen from the badly damaged patrol escort vessel
and then screened her as she was towed to Bermuda.

While the ship was moored at Boston on 1 January
1945, her name was expanded to *Thomas J. Gary*. She
completed her last Atlantic convoy upon her arrival at
New York on 7 May and spent the remainder of the
month preparing for service in the Pacific. Following
refresher training in the Caribbean, she departed waters
off the coast of Haiti on 22 June; steamed, via the
Panama Canal, to the west coast; and departed San
Diego on 12 July with a convoy bound for Hawaii.
She arrived at Pearl Harbor on 20 July to begin repairs
and training.

On 1 August, she departed Oahu with Escort Division
57 and steamed for Saipan. After a brief stop at
Eniwetok, she was rerouted to Guam and arrived at
Apra Harbor on the 13th. The same day, she again
got underway; this time with Carrier Division 27.
As the force steamed toward the Philippines, word of
Japan's surrender reached the ship. Following her
arrival at San Pedro Bay on 17 August, *Thomas J.
Gary* remained in port until the 29th when she departed
Leyte to screen the aircraft carriers of Task Group
(TG) 77.1 during their passage to Korea.

En route, the task group was diverted to Formosa.
With Commander Escort Division 57 embarked, *Thomas
J. Gary* was designated to liberate Allied prisoners of
war who had been held on that island. On 3 September,
she embarked 19 marines from *Block Island* (CVE–106)
charged with arranging the details of the evacuation

of the POW's. Her division commander was also responsible for making the preliminary arrangements for the occupation of Formosa.

Before dawn on 5 September off the coast of Formosa, *Thomas J. Gary* and *Kretchmer* (DE-329) were detached from the escort carrier task group. The destroyer escorts were without navigational guides to indicate the location of mines in waters surrounding the island. Despite the signing of the peace some days before, resistance from die-hard Japanese was a distinct possibility.

At 0718, as the two ships approached the waters most apt to be mined, every precaution was taken to minimize damage and casualties, should the ships strike a mine. The American sailors maintained a state of readiness to repel possible attack, as *Thomas J. Gary*, with her sister ship 500 yards astern, threaded her way at nine knots through the unknown and dangerous waters. Four Combat Air Patrol planes provided cover, and two antimine sweep planes from the carriers relayed word of the sightings of possible mines as the destroyer escorts picked their way through the hazardous approaches to Kiirun, making frequent changes of course to avoid sonar contacts which exhibited a suspicious similarity to those made by mines. One mile north of Kiirun Island, she rendezvoused with a small Japanese tug which led the way into Kiirun Harbor, where a Japanese harbor pilot pointed out the dock to be used.

The ships maintained a condition of modified general quarters and stationed armed guards on shore. A detail headed by *Thomas J. Gary*'s communications officer took over the local Japanese radio station to insure reliable communications between the task group and Japanese authorities in Kiirun for the duration of the evacuation operation. Finally, at 1630, a train arrived bearing Allied prisoners of war who were quickly transferred to the waiting destroyer escorts.

At 1800, provided now with a Japanese pilot and Japanese charts of the minefields in the vicinity of Kiirun, *Thomas J. Gary* got underway. Her commanding officer later dryly reported: "Our outbound route did not coincide with the one used inbound since we discovered that our inbound track crossed several minefields." That night, she rendezvoused with the carriers and transferred the newly freed POW's to the larger ships.

On the 6th, *Thomas J. Gary*, joined by other DE's, returned to Kiirun to transport additional POW's. After transferring most of her passengers to *Block Island* (CVE-106), she got underway for Manila; and, on the 9th, she arrived at Manila to discharge the last 50 of her POW's.

Later in the month, she steamed on to the Ryukyus with the escort carrier group; and she operated out of Okinawa into October, conducting exercises in the East China Sea. On 19 October, while at sea with the escort carrier group, she struck a submerged log which caused considerable damage to her starboard propeller. Slowed to 13 knots, she was forced to leave the formation and put in at Saipan on 23 November for repairs.

She next operated in the Philippines into the new year with calls at Hong Kong and Okinawa. She departed Singapore on 8 April 1946 and set her course via the Suez Canal for the Mediterranean where she spent much of May visiting European ports. On 29 May, she arrived at Charleston to commence drydocking and preservation procedures. On 25 September, tug *Nancy Moran* towed the destroyer escort from Charleston and headed for Green Cove Springs, Fla. She was decommissioned there on 7 March 1947 and placed in reserve.

On 24 July 1956, she was delivered to the Philadelphia Naval Shipyard for conversion to a radar picket escort ship; and, on 1 November 1956, she was redesignated DER-326.

She was recommissioned on 2 August 1957 and spent the remainder of the year in training exercises out of Newport, R.I., and Guantanamo Bay, Cuba. On 30 December, she departed Newport and began duties on the Atlantic Barrier, a part of the North American Defense Command. Operating out of Newport, she completed 12 radar picket assignments in the next year and one-half, breaking the routine duty with a visit to Belgium and the United Kingdom in August 1958.

In July 1959, *Thomas J. Gary* entered the Boston Navy Yard for overhaul. She remained there until 30 October when she got underway for refresher training in waters off the coast of Cuba. On 20 December, she resumed her former duties in the Atlantic alternating North Atlantic Barrier and Contiguous Radar Coverage System assignments.

Early in 1961, she varied radar picket duties with participation in Operation "Springboard;" and, in May, she steamed off Bermuda participating in Operation "Lantbex." In August, she completed a DEW Line assignment in the northeastern Atlantic with a visit to Scotland and finished out the year in overhaul at Boston.

Thomas J. Gary next set her course for Guantanamo for refresher training; then, on 10 July 1962, she steamed from Newport for now familiar North Atlantic picket deployment. Between picket assignments, she put in at Greenock and at Wilhelmshaven for well-earned recreation for all hands. Shortly after her return to Newport on 22 October, she was called upon to conduct patrols in support of the Cuban Quarantine. Relieved of her patrol station off Key West on 29 November, she returned to Newport for availability and a welcome holiday in homeport.

She filled the opening months of 1963 with radar picket duty out of Key West as Southern Tip Picket, and two tours as Sonar School Ship at Key West. In April, a period of tender availability was cut short for *Thomas J. Gary* when she was called upon to take part in the unproductive search for the submarine *Thresher* (SSN-593) lost off the Atlantic coast. She resumed Southern Tip Picket duties in July, and she returned to Newport late in August. On 24 September, she arrived at Boston for overhaul and trials which occupied the remainder of the year.

She opened 1964 with operations in the Caribbean including refresher training and participation in Operation "Springboard." She spent March undergoing availability at Newport and, during April and May, patrolled on picket station off Florida, with time out in May for a good will visit to Fall River, Mass., on Armed Forces Day. She continued picket duties for the rest of the year breaking her routine with gunnery exercises off the Virginia Capes and a visit to the Naval Academy in October.

After participating in the annual exercise Operation "Springboard" again in 1965, she resumed picket duties and, on 30 June, phased out the Southern Tip Picket Station where she had spent so much of her post-World War II career. On 13 September, she departed Newport for a nine-month deployment in the Pacific which took her through the Panama Canal later that month and included support for Operation "Deepfreeze," a scientific expedition to the Antarctic. In March 1966, she departed New Zealand and steamed, via the Suez Canal, to the Mediterranean. Her ports of call in that ancient sea and in the eastern Atlantic included Barcelona, Bremen, Copenhagen, and Edinburgh. She returned to Newport on 21 May 1966.

Thomas J. Gary again got underway from Newport on 24 August and set her course, via the Panama Canal and Pago Pago, to Dunedin, New Zealand, her replenishment port during her participation in Operation "Deepfreeze." Manning her station midway between McMurdo Sound and New Zealand, *Thomas J. Gary* acted as logistics headquarters for Operation "Deepfreeze" and stood ready to provide search and rescue for downed fliers. She remained in southern waters through the end of 1966.

In March, she called at Perth, Australia; then she set her course on the 23d for the Suez Canal. She called at European ports and returned to Newport on 24 May. On 1 July, her home port was officially changed to

Key West. After her arrival there on 9 July, she helped to test experimental equipment during Operation "Combat Keel" late in the year. On 12 December, she returned to Key West for a period of upkeep.

In 1968, she operated out of Key West; conducted refresher training out of Guantanamo; and, in August, participated in support operations for the practice firing of Polaris missiles by nuclear submarine *Daniel Webster* (SSBN–626). Later in the year, she conducted special operations in the Bahamas and acted as school ship for the Fleet Sonar School at Key West.

She continued operations in the Caribbean and off Florida into 1969. In July, she began a special four-month deployment during which she conducted intelligence support activities for antisubmarine forces in the Atlantic and earned a Navy Unit Commendation. She visited the Canary Islands and Malta before returning to Key West late in October.

After participating in Operation "Springboard" off Puerto Rico early in 1970, she got underway on 1 April and steamed across the Atlantic for operations which took her to Spain, Denmark, Germany, and the British Isles. On this deployment, she helped to develop new techniques and tactics in antisubmarine warfare in such an exemplary manner that she was awarded another Navy Unit Commendation. She returned to Key West on 7 September and operated out of that port into 1972 providing surveillance in support of the Atlantic Fleet. Departing Key West on 14 January 1972, she visited Wilhemshaven; then returned via Senegal to the United States. Back in Key West in March, she resumed local operations out of that port which she continued well into 1973.

In September 1973, she began preparations for transfer to the Tunisian government. That month, 33 members of a Tunisian turnover team came on board for training. On 12 October, she got underway from Charleston and crossed the Atlantic, stopping briefly at Ponta Delgada and Palma de Mallorca before arriving at Bizerte on 21 October. The next day, *Thomas J. Gary* was decommissioned in ceremonies at the Quai d'Honneur, Bizerte; and, moments later, the ship was commissioned by the Tunisian Navy as the *President Bourgiba*. Her name was struck from the Navy list that same day.

Thomas Jefferson

For the biography of Thomas Jefferson, see *Jefferson* (III, 512).

I

(AP–60: dp. 11,760; l. 492'; b. 69'6''; dr. 26'9''; s. 18.4 k. (tl.); cpl. 593; trp. 1,265; a. 4 3'', 4 40mm.; cl. *President Jackson*)

The first *Thomas Jefferson* (AP–60) was laid down under Maritime Commission contract (MC hull 56) as *President Garfield* on 5 February 1940 at Newport News, Va., by the Newport News Shipbuilding & Drydock Co. for the American President Lines; launched on 20 November 1940; sponsored by Miss Eugenia Merrill; acquired by the United States Navy on 1 May 1942 from the War Shipping Administration; converted into a troop transport by her builders; and commissioned on 31 August 1942, Comdr. Chauncey R. Crutcher in command.

Following a brief shakedown, the new transport participated in amphibious exercises in the Hampton Roads-Virginia capes area. On 23 October, the transport embarked elements of the 3d Infantry Division and got underway the next day with Task Group (TG) 34.9, the Center Attack Group, for the invasion of North Africa. All units of Task Force (TF) 34, the Western Naval Attack Force, rendezvoused south of Cape Race, Newfoundland, on the 28th and arrived off Morocco on 7 November. *Thomas Jefferson* was one of four transports loaded with the troops that comprised the assault wave against Fedhala. She was in Fedhala Roads at 2353 that night and had her boats in the water before 0200 the next morning. The transport lost 16 of her 33 boats that began the assault, because they landed on a rocky beach approximately three miles from their designated area.

On 11 November, *Jefferson*'s boats rescued survivors of the torpedoed *Joseph Hewes* (AP–50). The next day, they picked up survivors of *Hugh L. Scott* (AP–43), *Edward Rutledge* (AP–52), and *Tasker H. Bliss* (AP–42) which had been torpedoed by the German submarine *U–130*. On the 15th, *Thomas Jefferson* joined a homeward-bound convoy and returned to Norfolk on the 26th.

On 27 December 1942, *Thomas Jefferson* steamed in a convoy bound for the South Pacific. She disembarked troops at New Caledonia and Australia in late January 1943; and, during the passage back to Panama, she was reclassified an attack transport and redesignated APA–30 on 1 February 1943. She departed the Canal Zone on 3 March with a convoy bound, via Norfolk, for New York.

The attack transport returned to Norfolk in mid-April and participated in landing exercises to prepare for the invasion of Sicily. She reached Oran on 22 June with her troops combat loaded. After two more

Thomas Jefferson (APA–30) at New York on 15 April 1943 in a bicolor dark-blue and haze-gray camouflage scheme. (19–N–43939)

weeks of practice landings, she sortied with TG 85.2, Attack Group Two, for the "Bailey's Beach" area of Sicily. The sea was rough on the morning of 10 July as the troops clambered down *Jefferson*'s debarkation nets into landing craft. However, when they did land, there was very little opposition. During the operation, the transport's gunners shot down two enemy planes.

Thomas Jefferson returned to Algeria and was assigned to TG 81.2, the Transport Group of the Southern Attack Force, for the assault on Salerno. She departed Oran on 5 September and arrived off Salerno the night of the 8th. The transport landed her troops on schedule on the beaches in front of Torre di Paestum despite fierce air opposition and steamed to Oran to shuttle reinforcements and supplies to Italy. Then, late in November, she loaded elements of the 82d Airborne Division and headed for the British Isles. After disembarking the paratroopers at Belfast, the transport continued onward to the United States.

Thomas Jefferson arrived at Norfolk on 1 January 1944 and moved up the coast to New York in early February. On the 11th, she stood out to sea with the largest single troop convoy of the war on a return voyage to Belfast. The transport next held weeks of amphibious training before steaming to Weymouth, England, to join the Normandy invasion fleet. On 5 June, *Thomas Jefferson* got underway for France with the mighty Allied armada that was to begin the invasion of "Fortress Europe" and, early the next morning, was at her assigned position off the beaches. Her boats landed their troops at 0630. The ship completed unloading that afternoon and, at sunset, recrossed the channel to Weymouth.

Thomas Jefferson remained in the British Isles for a month before returning to North Africa early in July. From Oran, she was routed to Salerno to practice amphibious operations with the 36th Infantry Division in preparation for the invasion of southern France. She joined TF 87, the "Camel Force," to land assault troops on the east flank of Provence. Departing Palermo, she arrived off the assault area on 14 August. The next morning, her boats landed troops on Red Beach. The transport completed unloading on the 16th and returned to Naples to begin shuttling reinforcements and supplies from Italy, North Africa, and Marseilles to the southern beachhead. On 24 October, she got underway for the United States and arrived at Norfolk on 8 November.

The ship departed Norfolk on 15 December 1944 for the Pacific war zone. She called at San Francisco and arrived at Pearl Harbor on 28 January 1945. Routed on to the South Pacific, the transport trained with marines in the Solomons and then combat loaded them for the assault against the Ryukyus. She was at Ulithi on 17 March and sortied with TG 53.2, Transport Group "Baker," of the Northern Attack Force.

Thomas Jefferson was off the Hagushi Beaches of Okinawa on 1 April when Admiral Richmond K. Turner gave the command to "Land the Landing Force." Her boats left the line of departure at 0800 and landed 30 minutes later. After five days off the bitterly contested island, the transport headed for Saipan and Pearl Harbor. On 8 May, she departed Hawaii carrying troops and cargo for Okinawa. The ship unloaded there and steamed homeward. After calls at Ulithi, Guadalcanal, Espiritu Santo, the Russell Islands, New Caledonia, and Hawaii, she arrived at San Francisco on 15 July. She moved down the coast to San Diego and sailed from there on the 23d to return to the Far East. She called at Pearl Harbor and then headed, via Saipan, to Japan.

Arriving at Sasebo on 22 September, *Thomas Jefferson* got underway for Manila three days later. She returned to Sasebo with occupation troops and supplies on 20 October. The transport was then assigned to "Magic-Carpet" duty, returning servicemen from overseas to the United States. On 4 January 1946, *Thomas Jefferson* was assigned to the Naval Transportation Service to transport servicemen's dependents to Pacific bases. She shuttled passengers and cargo between San Francisco and Pearl Harbor for the next 10 months. On 17 October, the ship departed San Diego for the east coast and arrived at New York on 4 November. She entered the navy yard for alterations and repairs which were not completed until March 1947.

Thomas Jefferson began the return voyage to the west coast on 14 March 1947 and arrived at Oakland on the 30th. Until August 1949, the transport plied between San Francisco and ports in Hawaii, Guam, Midway, Okinawa, Japan, China, and the Philippines. She made another round trip to New York in September and October and returned to San Diego on 10 November. Assigned to the Military Sea Transportation Service for duty on 31 October 1949, she continued her Pacific runs until 1950.

Thomas Jefferson was at San Diego on 25 June 1950 when the North Koreans invaded South Korea. She made a round trip to Yokohama and, on 28 August, headed back to the Far East. The transport called at Yokosuka and Kobe before arriving at Inchon, Korea, on 20 September for eight days. In October, she was again in Korean waters, shuttling troops and cargo from Pusan to Iwon, north of the 40th parallel. The ship returned to Sasebo on 10 November and then got underway for San Francisco.

The attack transport remained at San Francisco from 1 December 1950 to 24 January 1951 when she headed directly to Pusan with troops and cargo. She off-loaded between 8 and 10 February; returned to the United States; and was back at Pusan on 2 April. The next day, the ship got underway for San Francisco, but stayed only to embark troops and supplies before beginning the return voyage, via Amchitka, to Japan. The transport made voyages to Korea again in May and August. She returned to San Francisco on 10 September 1951 and did not sail west of the Hawaiian Islands until 1954.

APA–30 cruised to the Far East in August and December 1954 before returning to San Francisco for inactivation. She was placed in commission, in reserve, on 7 March 1955 and out of commission, in reserve, on 18 July of that year. The transport was struck from the Navy list on 1 October 1958 and transferred to the Maritime Administration for disposal. She was sold to Zidell Explorations, Inc., Portland, Oreg., on 1 March 1973 and scrapped.

Thomas Jefferson received six battle stars for World War II service and four for the Korean conflict.

II

(SSBN–618: dp. 6,900 (surf.), 8,000 (subm.); l. 425'; b. 33'; dr. 32'; s. 20+ k.; cpl. 120; a. 16 Pol., 4 21'' tt.; cl. *Ethan Allen*)

The second *Thomas Jefferson* (SSBN–618) was laid down on 3 February 1961 at Newport News, Va., by the Newport News Shipbuilding & Drydock Co.; sponsored by Mrs. Robert S. McNamara; and commissioned on 4 January 1963, Comdr. Leon H. Rathbun (Blue Crew) and Comdr. Charles Priest, Jr., (Gold Crew) in command.

After shakedown training by both crews and a yard availability period, the fleet ballistic missile submarine was assigned to Submarine Squadron (SubRon) 14 in early October. On 28 October, the Blue Crew took the submarine on her first deterrent patrol which ended at Holy Loch, Scotland, in December 1963. *Thomas Jefferson* continued patrols from Holy Loch for the next four years and also acted as flagship for SubRon 14. In 1966, she returned to New London for two training and rehabilitation periods. She began her 15th deterrent patrol on 12 January 1967 and, upon its completion, returned to Newport News for her first overhaul and refueling. On 17 June 1968, the submarine was ready for sea, and refresher training was held for both crews. Her 16th patrol began on 29 October and terminated at Rota, Spain, on 5 December 1968.

Thomas Jefferson made four deterrent patrols in each of the following years: 1969, 1970, 1971, and 1972. She also conducted special operations in 1970 and 1971. On 20 October 1972, the Gold Crew was awarded a Meritorious Unit Citation for its special operations of the previous year.

Thomas Jefferson completed two patrols in 1973 before returning to the United States to hold midshipman training from 18 June to 31 August. Her last patrol of the year terminated on 12 December 1973. Her 36th, and final, patrol in the Atlantic lasted from 31 January to 22 March 1974. After calling at Norfolk and Charleston, the submarine returned to New London on 22 May. *Thomas Jefferson* was then reassigned to the Pacific Fleet with her new homeport at Vallejo, Calif. She stood out of New London on 7 June en route to the west coast and arrived at Mare Island on the 27th.

On 1 July 1974, *Thomas Jefferson* entered the Mare Island Naval Shipyard for overhaul, refueling, and conversion to the Polaris A–3 missile system. She remained in the yard until 17 November 1975 when she got underway for Bremerton, Wash. The submarine remained in Puget Sound for a month and then moved to San Diego.

During the period January to March 1976, *Thomas Jefferson*'s Blue Crew conducted post-overhaul shakedown operations and then transited the Panama Canal to conduct a Polaris missile firing at Cape Canaveral, Florida. The Gold Crew took over the ship on 4 April and conducted additional post-overhaul shakedown operations which included a missile firing at Cape Canaveral, a transit of the Panama Canal, and a missile loadout at Bangor, Washington, before resuming deterrent patrol operations with the Pacific Fleet on 8 August. *Thomas Jefferson* continued these operations as a unit of Submarine Squadron 15 throughout 1977 and 1978, at the end of which she completed her 44th deterrent patrol.

Thomas Laundry

(Tr: t. 269; l. 125'4''; b. 22'5''; dr. 12'2''; s. 10 k.; cl. "Castle")

Thomas Laundry—a steel-hulled screw steam trawler built in 1918 at Beverley, England, by Cook, Welton, and Gemmell, Ltd., for the British Admiralty—was leased by the United States Navy for service with the North Sea Minesweeping Detachment. Taken over at Falmouth, England, on 16 May 1919, *Thomas Laundry* was commissioned the same day, Lt. (jg.) Franz O. Willenbucher in command.

Arriving at Kirkwall, Scotland, the base for the detachment, on 27 May, via Plymouth, England, *Thomas Laundry* operated locally through June. On 7 July, the trawler departed Kirkwall for the minefields of the North Sea Mine Barrage and joined in the fourth phase of the extensive operations launched to clear the barrage that had once menaced German warships. While sweeping together with *Thomas Buckley*, a sister-ship, *Thomas Laundry* exploded a mine 75 yards astern at 2005 that evening. From the 8th through the 12th, the trawlers swept mines despite rough weather and frequently parting sweep wires.

Later that month, *Thomas Laundry*'s duties assumed a support role as she delivered sweep wire, kites, and weights to minesweepers based at Kirkwall. The trawler also transported men and materiel between the Scottish ports of Inverness and Kirkwall in August before assuming local duties at the latter port again in September, delivering ammunition, guns, sweep wire, and lubricating oil to the ships engaged in the last of the sweeping operations to clear the barrage from the North Sea.

Eventually, *Thomas Laundry* shifted to Brighton, England, where she supported the deactivation of some of her sister ships. She transported the crews of *William Caldwell* and *Thomas Blackhorne* to Harwich on 6 October and that of *Thomas Buckley* to that same port on the 7th. At 1535 on 8 October 1919, *Thomas Laundry* was decommissioned at Brighton and returned to the Admiralty.

Thomas Stone

Thomas Stone—born in 1743 at Poynton Manor in Charles County, Md.—was admitted to the Maryland bar in 1864 and practiced law at Frederick until returning to Charles County about 1771. Stone entered the Continental Congress on 13 May 1775 and, but for a period in 1777, served in that body until October 1778. He won distinction for his work on the committee which drafted the Articles of Confederation. Elected to the Maryland Senate in 1776, Stone represented Charles County in the state legislature until he died at Alexandria, Va., on 5 October 1787.

(AP–59: dp. 14,868; l. 492'; b. 69'6''; dr. 24'8''; s. 16.5 k.; cpl. 379; a. 1 5'', 4 3''; cl. *President Jackson*)

Thomas Stone (AP–59) was laid down under a Maritime Commission contract (MC hull 58) as *President Van Buren* on 12 August 1941 at Newport News, Va., by the Newport News Shipbuilding and Drydock Co.; launched on 1 May 1941; sponsored by Mrs. Alben W. Barkley; and delivered to the American President Line on 11 September 1941. The passenger liner was acquired by the Navy on 14 January 1942; converted for use as a troop transport; and commissioned on 18 May 1942, Capt. O. R. Bennehoff in command.

Thomas Stone loaded troops at Norfolk and, on 26 September, sailed for Ireland with Convoy AT 23. After calling at Halifax en route, she arrived at Belfast on 6 October. She disembarked her troops and then combat loaded men and equipment of the 9th United States Army Division for amphibious exercises off the coast of Scotland before getting underway for the Clyde River on the 26th to participate in Operation "Torch," the Allied invasion of North Africa.

The transport was assigned the task of carrying troops for the British-controlled assault on Algiers. She transited the Straits of Gibraltar on the night of 5 and 6 November. On the morning of the 7th, she was steaming on the left flank of the convoy, second in line astern of *Samuel Chase* (AP–56). At 0535 a torpedo hit the ship's port side, aft, blowing a hole in her bottom; breaking her propeller shaft; and bending her propeller and her rudder to starboard. The convoy continued on, leaving *Thomas Stone* behind, adrift some 150 miles from Algiers, guarded by only British corvette HMS *Spey*. After daylight, an inspection of the damage revealed that the ship was in no immediate danger of sinking but was nevertheless unable to move under her own power.

But Capt. Bennehoff and Major Walter M. Oakes, USA—who commanded the battalion landing team embarked in *Thomas Stone*—were not content to let the transport's troops drift aimlessly in the Mediterranean while others took Algiers. Besides, all on board the damaged ship were in deadly peril from a possible renewal of the submarine attack. To solve both problems, the two officers loaded most of the transport's troops in 24 boats which set out for Algiers Bay under the protection of *Spey*. However, the weather which had been good when the boats left the transport worsened and the frail craft began taking on water. Engine trouble forced the boats to be abandoned one by one and their crews and passengers were transferred to the corvette. When *Spey* finally reached Algiers before dawn on the 8th, she carried all of the crews of the boats and each of their passengers, for every boat had been scuttled. By the time *Spey*'s troops went ashore that morning, they learned that all French resistance had ended.

Meanwhile, two destroyers, HMS *Wishart* and HMS *Velox*, had arrived on the night of the 7th and at tempted to tow *Thomas Stone*. The next morning, HMS *St. Day*, a tug, arrived to assist. Despite bad weather and the twisted remnants of the transport's rudder which made her all but unmanageable, the group of ships finally reached Algiers on the 11th and moored to the Quai de Falaise where she discharged the remaining troops and equipment.

On 19 November, *Thomas Stone* was moved to the outer harbor to make room for two large convoys. An air raid on the night of 24 and 25 November caused additional damage to the ship when a bomb pierced two decks, the hull, and exploded beneath her. On the 25th, a high wind and heavy swells caused the ship to drag both anchors and drove her hard aground, further damaging her hull. While still aground, the transport was reclassified APA–29 on 1 February 1943. Salvage operations continued for over a year, and all equipment and stores were removed. Efforts to refloat the ship continued until the spring of 1944, but the ship was finally placed out of commission on 1 April 1944, and her name was struck from the Navy list on 8 April 1944. Her hulk was sold to Le Materiel Economique, Algiers, for scrap.

Thomas Stone received one battle star for World War II service.

Thomas Washington

Thomas Washington—born on 6 June 1865 at Goldsboro, N.C.—was appointed to the Naval Academy on 17 May 1883. He graduated on 10 June 1887 and, after the required two years of sea duty during which he served on the European Station in *Enterprise* and *Lancaster*, was commissioned ensign in 1889. Over the ensuing three years, he served at sea—first in *Alliance* and then in *Endeavor*—until he was assigned to the office of the Navy's Judge Advocate General in 1892. Subsequently, after duty on several trial boards for general courts martial at the Norfolk and Washington Navy Yards, he was assigned to a succession of ships—*Montgomery*, *Terror*, and *Patterson*—before joining battleship *Indiana* in early 1898. He was in this ship when she helped to defeat the Spanish Fleet under Admiral Cervera on 3 July 1898 in the battle of Santiago.

After a second tour of duty ashore in the office of the Judge Advocate General, Washington served on the General Board. Ordered thence to the Asiatic Station, he joined the staff of Rear Admiral Robley D. "Fighting Bob" Evans, the Commander-in-Chief, Asiatic Fleet, on 29 October 1902. Quartered in battleship *Illinois*, the Asiatic Fleet's flagship, he remained on Evans' staff until detached on 1 June 1904.

Special duty at the Bureau of Navigation followed his return from the Orient and preceded his assuming command of dispatch boat *Dolphin*, the vessel which was then serving as the Secretary of the Navy's yacht. Washington next put in another tour with the Bureau of Navigation for duty before returning to sea in 1912 to command, in turn, gunboat *Yorktown* and cruisers *Charleston* and *Denver* over the next two years.

On 20 April 1914, Washington—by then a captain—assumed the duties of Hydrographer of the Navy. World War I broke out in Europe less than four months after Washington assumed the Hydrographer's duties, depriving the United States of its external sources of oceanographic and hydrographic information. Washington and his small staff responded by independently gathering the necessary data for use by the United States Navy and Merchant Marine.

Relieved as hydrographer on 23 June 1916, Washington was given command of battleship *Florida*. A few months after the United States entered the war in the spring of 1917, *Florida* crossed the Atlantic to operate with the British Grand Fleet. The manner in which he carried out this assignment won Washington the Distinguished Service Medal for "exceptionally meritorious service in a duty of great responsibility." Eleven days after the Armistice—on 22 November 1918—he assumed command of Flagship Division 3, Battleship Force 1, Atlantic Fleet, flying his "flag" alternately in yachts *Aramis* and *Nokomis*. He subsequently commanded Divisions 2 and 4, successively, of the Atlantic Fleet. Detached from this duty on 9 August, he assumed the post of Chief of the Bureau of Navigation on 11 August, with the accompanying rank of rear admiral.

Less than a year later, Washington received orders to duty as Commander in Chief, Asiatic Fleet (CINCAF). He broke his flag in armored cruiser *Huron* on 11 October 1923 and commanded the Fleet until 14 October 1925. During his tour, the Asiatic Fleet provided support for the United States Army's round-the-world flight in the spring of 1924. Operating from the Kurils to Calcutta, the destroyer squadrons of the Fleet sailed on plane-guard stations, transported supplies and spare parts, and provided radio bearings and communications services for the planes, and thus contributed greatly to the success of the flight.

Relieved as CINCAF on 14 October 1925, Washington became Commandant of the Naval Operating Base, San Francisco, Calif., on 19 November 1925, and filled the billet until his retirement on 6 June 1929. Advanced on the retired list to the full rank of admiral on 16 July 1942, Washington died on 15 December 1954 at the Bethesda Naval Hospital, Bethesda, Md.

(AGOR–10: dp. 1,380 (f.); l. 208'9''; b. 37'4'; dr. 15'3''; s. 13.5 k.; cpl. 41; cl. *Robert D. Conrad*)

Thomas Washington (AGOR–10) was laid down on 12 September 1963 at Marinette, Wis., by the Marinette Marine Corp.; launched on 1 August 1964; sponsored jointly by Misses Barbara E. and Ann H. Washington, granddaughters of Admiral Washington; and delivered to the Navy on 17 September 1965.

Transferred to the Scripps Institute of Oceanography, of the University of California, soon thereafter, *Thomas Washington* operates under the control of the Oceanographer of the Navy, with a civilian crew, conducting research experiments in support of the national oceanographic programs of the United States into 1978.

Thomason

Clyde A. Thomason—born on 23 May 1914 at Atlanta, Ga.—enlisted in the United States Marine Corps on 28 December 1934. He served in China and on board *Augusta* (CA–31) before being discharged on 23 December 1940. Sergeant Thomason reenlisted in the Marine Corps Reserve on 8 January 1942 and joined "A" Company, 2d Marine Raider Battalion, the following month.

Sergeant Thomason was killed in action at Makin Island on 17 August 1942 when the battalion raided that island. He was posthumously awarded the Medal of Honor. His citation reads in part: "Leading the advance element of the assault echelon, Sergeant Thomason disposed his men with keen judgment and discrimination and by his exemplary leadership and great personal valor, exhorted them to like fearless efforts. On one occasion, he dauntlessly walked up to a house which concealed an enemy Japanese sniper, forced in the door and shot the man before he could resist. Later in the action, while leading an assault on an enemy position, he gallantly gave up his life in the service of his country. His courage and loyal devotion to duty in the face of grave peril were in keeping with the finest traditions of the United States Naval Service."

(DE–203: dp. 1,400; l. 306'0''; b. 37'0''; dr. 13'6''; s. 23.6 k. (tl.); cpl. 213; a. 3 3''; 8 20mm., 2 dct., 8 dcp., 1 dcp. (hh.), 3 21'' tt.; cl. *Buckley*)

Thomason (DE–203) was laid down on 5 June 1943 at

Charleston, S.C., by the Charleston Navy Yard; launched on 23 August 1943; sponsored by Miss Sara Jeanette Thomason; and commissioned on 10 December 1943, Lt. Comdr. Charles B. Henriques, USNR, in command.

The destroyer escort held shakedown training in the Bermuda area and performed escort duty along the east coast from Newport, R.I., to Panama. She transited the Panama Canal on 21 March 1944 and headed for the New Hebrides. The ship called at Galapagos, the Society Islands, and Samoa before arriving at Espiritu Santo on 18 April. She joined the 3d Fleet and, in addition to performing antisubmarine duty in Indispensable Strait which separates Guadalcanal and Malaita Islands, escorted ships to Guadalcanal.

On 26 May, the DE arrived at Cape Cretin to join the 7th Fleet for operations along the coast of New Guinea. On 3 June, the ship got underway for Wakde and arrived there the following week. On the 13th, her gunners helped Army antiaircraft units repel an enemy air attack. Six days later, she took Army artillery observers along the coast to Sarmi where she shelled enemy emplacements and an air strip. The ship operated from Wakde until 7 August when she shifted her base of operations to Noemfoor, Schouten Islands. In early September, she returned to Espiritu Santo for an overhaul.

On 4 October, *DE-203* stood out to sea to rendezvous with two ammunition ships to escort them to the Palaus. She remained at Kossol Passage for a month, serving as harbor entrance control ship before returning to Hollandia. On 6 November, the destroyer got underway for Maffin Bay. Two days later, *Thomason* and *Neuendorf* (DE-200) bombarded Sarmi and targets along the bay. With the aid of Army spotting planes, the two ships set fire to enemy storehouses and several other buildings.

Thomason headed for the Philippines on 9 November in the screen of a large convoy of landing craft and supply ships. She arrived in Leyte Gulf on the 15th and sailed the same day with a convoy bound for Hollandia. The destroyer escort then conducted intensive antiaircraft and antisubmarine training at Mios Woendi and landing exercises at Aitape with attack transports that were scheduled to participate in the Lingayen operation.

On 28 December 1944, the destroyer escort sortied for Luzon with Task Group 78.1, the San Fabian Attack Force. En route to the Philippines, she was detached to accompany two fuel oil tankers who were scheduled to refuel the escort ships of Task Force 79, which was also en route to Lingayen Gulf.

Thomason began antisubmarine patrols in Mangarin Bay, off Mindoro on 7 January 1945. One month later, she and *Neuendorf* began antisubmarine patrol duty off the west coast of Luzon. At 2222 hours on 7 February, *Thomason*'s surface radar made a contact at a range of 14 miles which was thought to be a small boat. She closed the range and challenged the craft with a flashing light. There was no answer, and surface radar lost contact. However, sonar soon made an underwater contact.

The escort made a hedgehog run but did not fire because she was going too fast. She made another run and fired a pattern of hedgehogs. On both runs, a large submerged mass, outlined by phosphorescence, was seen moving through the water at a depth of between 25 and 50 feet. Four to six of the hedgehogs detonated almost simultaneously, and contact with the target was lost. A heavy oil slick, 250 yards in diameter, rose to the surface. The two ships patrolled until late in the morning, in an expanding search pattern, but never regained contact with the submarine. *RO-55* had been sunk in over 800 fathoms of water.

Thomason returned to Mangarin Bay where she resumed antisubmarine patrols. On the 24th, she rescued

four airmen who had bailed out of their burning Liberator bomber. From March through August, the ship was engaged in antisubmarine patrols and escort duty between various Philippine ports, Palau, and Hollandia. The war was now over. In September, she escorted two convoys from Luzon to Okinawa. On 4 October, *Thomason* stood out of Subic Bay and headed for the United States. She called at San Francisco on the 27th and moved to San Diego for inactivation. *Thomason* was decommissioned on 22 May 1946 and struck from the Navy list on 30 June 1968. In June 1969, she was sold to the National Metal & Steel Corp., Terminal Island, Long Beach, Calif., for scrap.

Thomason received three battle stars for World War II service.

Thomason, John W., see *John W. Thomason.*

Thomaston

A town in Maine. Thomaston was the home of General Henry Knox, the first Secretary of War to serve under the United States Constitution.

(LSD-28: dp. 11,525; l. 510'; b. 84'; dr. 19'; s. 21 k.; cpl. 304; trp. 300; a. 8 3''; cl. *Thomaston*)

Thomaston (LSD-28) was laid down on 3 March 1953 at Pascagoula, Miss., by the Ingalls Shipbuilding Corp.; launched on 9 February 1954; sponsored by Mrs. Mathias B. Gardner; and commissioned on 17 September 1954, Capt. Marion F. Ramirez de Arellano in command.

Following shakedown in the Caribbean, *Thomaston* transited the Panama Canal and joined the Pacific Fleet Amphibious Force. From July through October 1955, *Thomaston* participated in the Arctic Resupply Project, provisioning stations on the Distant Early Warning (DEW) Line before taking part in cold weather landing exercises in the Aleutians in November 1955 and again in January and February 1956.

The landing ship's duties soon took her southward to the warmer climes of the Hawaiian Islands, where she conducted local operations and exercises in March and April. On hand in Santa Barbara, Calif., from 2 to 9 July, for the Semana Nautica Celebration, *Thomaston* returned to the Hawaiian Islands and participated in three landing exercises in the autumn before returning to the west coast to conduct exercises off the Marine Corps base at Camp Pendleton, Calif., during the spring of 1957.

She subsequently deployed to the Western Pacific (WestPac) in 1959 and participated in exercises off Borneo and Korea in June and August of that year. Alternating between the west coast and WestPac, *Thomaston* participated in a busy schedule of operations and cruises into the 1960's. During the international tensions brought on by the United States' discovery of Russian missile sites in Cuba, *Thomaston* sailed via the Panama Canal to the Caribbean and operated with the Atlantic Fleet until tensions abated with the withdrawal of the missiles. She then returned to San Diego on 15 December 1962.

She commenced the year 1963 at her home port, San Diego, and conducted training exercises into February before serving as primary control ship off "Green" Beach, Del Mar, Calif., during Operation "Steel Gate" from 28 February to 8 March 1963. *Thomaston* departed the west coast on 26 March, bound for the Far East, and arrived via Pearl Harbor at Subic Bay on 20 April. Serving with the Amphibious Force of the 7th Fleet, she participated in special operations in the South China Sea from 22 April to 5 May. A second special operation in the South China Sea—again with the Amphibious Ready Group, 7th Fleet—took place in late August and early September.

After operating in Okinawan waters, *Thomaston* departed Yokosuka, Japan, on 4 November, bound for the west coast of the United States. While en route three days later, the LSD received word of a merchantman in distress. Changing course, *Thomaston* found SS *Barbara Fritchie* in heavy seas, dead in the water, having lost a propeller and suffering rudder damage. *Thomaston* took her in tow and headed for Pearl Harbor, transferring the tow to Cree (ATF–84) on the 12th. The LSD's stop at Pearl Harbor was a brief one, though, as she arrived and departed for home on the same day, 15 November.

Making port at San Diego on 21 November, *Thomaston* operated locally and trained through the early fall of 1964, when she sailed for the Philippines on 26 October to commence another WestPac deployment. Arriving at Subic Bay on 16 November, the LSD conducted special operations in the South China Sea, including a dredge lift from Saigon to Danang, South Vietnam, between 21 November and 16 December. Christmas of that year found *Thomaston* again at sea, on "special operations" in the South China Sea. She was present at the initial Marine landings at Danang and Chu Lai, South Vietnam. She remained deployed to WestPac until June of 1965, when she returned to San Diego to conduct routine local operations off the west coast.

Departing San Diego on 10 January 1966 for West-Pac, *Thomaston* arrived in Vietnamese coastal waters on 5 February and immediately commenced operations at Chu Lai and Danang, serving as boat haven at the latter port. She returned to the United States in the spring and remained at San Diego from 9 April to 9 July 1966. The ship then headed back to the western Pacific and operated out of Subic Bay from 28 July through the end of the deployment. She participated in Operations "Deckhouse III" (phases one and two) and "Deckhouse IV" in August and September. In the former, *Thomaston* landed marines north of Vung Tau and served as primary control ship and boat haven during the subsequent operations. She then landed marines at a point just south of the demilitarized zone (DMZ) between North and South Vietnam. She thus continued in her familiar role as primary control ship and boat haven during "Deckhouse IV" and staged boat convoys carrying supplies nine miles up the Cua Vet River to Dong Ha.

Returning to Subic Bay, *Thomaston* later participated in Exercise "Mudpuppy II" which was designed to provide training in river operations for marines. Held on Mindoro in the Philippines, "Mudpuppy II" ended three days before Christmas; and *Thomaston* sailed for Vietnam.

She thus began the year 1967 as she had begun the previous year, in active combat operations against Viet Cong and North Vietnamese Army units along the coastline. Participating in "Deckhouse V" and "Deckhouse VI" into March, *Thomaston*'s participation in the former operation began on 5 January 1967 when she dropped anchor off the mouth of the Song Co Chien River. She helped to launch the thrust of "Deckhouse V," aimed at the delta lowlands of Kien Hoa province, South Vietnam. The combined American and Vietnamese Marine Corps landings successfully challenged Viet Cong forces in this area. Relieved at Vung Tau by *Point Defiance* (LSD–31) on 6 March, *Thomaston* sailed for repairs at Subic Bay, en route home via Hong Kong, Okinawa, Yokosuka, and Pearl Harbor.

Following an extensive overhaul at San Diego from 28 June to 18 December 1967, *Thomaston* departed her home port on 21 February 1968 for her regular deployment to WestPac. After joining the Amphibious Ready Group off Vietnam in the I Corps zone, *Thomaston* commenced operations in support of marines of the Special Landing Forces (SLF) engaged ashore in the defense of Quang Tri province. She spent the month of March steaming in coastwise logistics runs between Danang, Camranh Bay, and the burgeoning Army supply base at Thon My Thuy, known colloquially as "Murder Beach."

During her operations at the latter port, *Thomaston* demonstrated to the Army the versatility of the Landing Ship Dock by serving as an effective repair ship with a built-in drydock. Many small craft and pontoon piers serving the supply base received hull and machinery work by the crew in the ship's capacious well-deck. During this deployment, *Thomaston* proved that the amphibious ship was a natural vehicle for interservice cooperation.

While operating off the coast of South Vietnam with the Amphibious Ready Group, *Thomaston* conducted two search and rescue operations. On the evening of 25 May, a CH–46 helicopter, loaded with mail, passengers, and baggage, lost power in the vicinity of *Valley Forge* (LPH–8) and crashed. The helicopter remained afloat while those on board jettisoned all excess weight. It gradually sank, but fortunately not before all men had safely left the craft. Within a mile of the accident, *Thomaston* dispatched two boats to the scene and recovered not only four of the passengers and crew of the CH–46 (the remainder were picked up by helicopter) but the crew from one of *Valley Forge*'s boats which had capsized upon launching. Later, on 2 June and again while in the vicinity of *Valley Forge*, *Thomaston* picked up men from the carrier who had jumped overboard to escape flames from a flight deck fire.

Thomaston next participated in "Badger Catch III," the withdrawal of the Special Landing Force from the Cua Vet River area bordering on the extreme southern edge of the DMZ. Subsequently, *Thomaston* and her embarked SLF participated in a swift succession of operations against Communist ground forces. Operation "Swift Sabre" plunged into Viet Cong-contested areas of the western shore of Danang harbor on 8 June 1968. Following Exercise "Hilltop XX" in Subic Bay, *Thomaston* participated in "Eager Yankee" which landed elements of the SLF in Quang Tri province near Cua Tu Hien on 9 July before engaging, 13 days later, in "Swift Play" in the coastal area south of Danang. These operations resulted in the capture of significant numbers of weapons and stores and the destruction of operating bases and installations from which the enemy had launched attacks against other "friendly forces." During "Swift Play," *Thomaston* came under shore battery fire for a brief time.

For the next five years, *Thomaston* actively supported the war effort in Vietnam, conducted troop and cargo lifts, and participated in amphibious operations. The tide of war, however, was running against the South Vietnamese; and, by the spring of 1975, concentrated efforts on the part of North Vietnamese and Viet Cong troops put pressure on the crumbling South Vietnamese government.

The end for South Vietnam came during *Thomaston*'s 15th WestPac deployment. The beginning of the year 1975 found the landing ship at Subic Bay, undergoing a needed availability. She departed Subic Bay on 2 February, bound for Singapore where she stayed until the 13th. As a member of Task Group (TG) 76.4, *Thomaston* later returned to port at Subic Bay on the 25th. Her anticipated upkeep period, however, was cut short when the ship was directed to return to sea with TG 76.4. On 2 March, *Thomaston* departed Subic Bay to execute Operation "Eagle Pull," which evacuated Americans and designated Cambodian citizens from the Cambodian capital city of Pnomh Penh. The civilians were to be picked up by helicopters and ferried to the ships offshore.

She remained in readiness until the evening of 5 April, when *Thomaston* was ordered to Phu Quoc Island to assist Vietnamese nationals evacuated from Danang. She transferred food and medical supplies via her LCU's and LCM–8 assault craft to Vietnamese refugees quartered on Military Sealift Command (MSC) vessels.

TG 76.4 executed "Eagle Pull" on 11 April, and *Thomaston* took part as a plane guard on station to the south. Upon the successful completion of the operation, designated units of the group proceeded to

Sattahip, Thailand, to debark civilians airlifted from Cambodia. Meanwhile, *Thomaston* sailed for the Philippines, arriving at Subic Bay on the morning of 17 April, but her much deserved in-port period was again abbreviated by operational necessity. Underway once more at 2330 on the 18th, *Thomaston* sailed for Vietnamese waters to take part in the *Gotterdammerung* of South Vietnam—the evacuation of the besieged capital, Saigon.

On 29 April, Operation "Frequent Wind" commenced at 1500. During the next nine hours, *Thomaston* received 811 Vietnamese, American, and other refugees. During this operation—for which the ship received the Meritorious Unit Commendation—*Thomaston* received evacuees via helicopter, landing "choppers" as large as CH–46's on her flight deck aft. All Vietnamese citizens were to be processed and placed aboard MSC ships; American citizens would be retained on board for transportation to the Philippines. Although limited by space, all individuals were provided with food, clothing, and medical attention. Makeshift shelters, "tents" made from marines' blankets, were set up on board.

Returning to Subic Bay on 3 May, *Thomaston* immediately commenced preparations for her homeward voyage. Civilians embarked during "Frequent Wind" were debarked at Subic Bay. The ship then headed on for the west coast of the United States, via Buckner Bay, Okinawa; and Pearl Harbor; and arrived at San Diego on 6 June 1975.

Thomaston subsequently operated with the Pacific Fleet in 1976, conducting training and local operations in waters off Okinawa, Japan, Korea, and Hawaii, before returning to San Diego at the close of the year.

Following a material inspection by the Navy Board of Inspection and Survey in January 1977, *Thomaston* commenced preparations for her forthcoming overhaul. On 1 June, she entered Todd Shipyard, Seattle, Wash., for the most extensive overhaul conducted on an amphibious ship to that time. Lasting 18 months and costing nearly $30 million, the overhaul was completed on 7 December 1978. *Thomaston* returned to her home port of San Diego on 14 December and remained there into 1979.

Thomaston received 11 battle stars, one Navy Unit Commendation, and two Meritorious Unit Commendations for Vietnam service.

Thompson

Richard Wigginton Thompson—born on 9 June 1809 in Culpepper County, Va.—left Virginia in 1831; lived briefly in Louisville, Kentucky; and, later that year, settled in Lawrence County, Ind. There, he taught school, kept a store, and studied law at night. Admitted to the Bar in 1834, he practiced law in Bedford, Ind., and served for four terms in the Indiana Legislature from 1834 to 1838. He served as President Pro Tempore of the Indiana Senate for a short time and briefly held the office of Acting Lieutenant Governor. In the Presidential Election of 1840, he zealously advocated the election of William Henry Harrison. Thompson then represented Indiana in the United States Congress, serving in the House of Representatives from 1841 to 1843 and again from 1847 to 1849.

Following the Civil War, Thompson served as judge of the 18th Circuit Court of the state of Indiana from 1867 to 1869. In 1877, President Rutherford B. Hayes appointed him Secretary of the Navy; and he held that office until 1881.

Retiring to Indiana, Richard W. Thompson lived out the remainder of his days in his adopted state. He died on 9 February 1900 at Terre Haute, Ind.

Robert Means Thompson—born on 2 March 1849 in Corsica, Pa.—was appointed to the United States Naval Academy on 30 July 1864. Graduating tenth in the class of 1868, Thompson first went to sea in *Contocook* in the West Indian Squadron. He later served in

Franklin, Richmond, and *Guard* of the Mediterranean Squadron; as well as in *Wachusett* and at the Naval Torpedo Station, Newport, R.I.

Commissioned ensign on 19 April 1869 and promoted to master on 12 July 1870, he resigned from the Navy on 18 November 1871 to study law in his brother's office. After he was admitted to the Pennsylvania Bar in 1872, he was still not satisfied with his legal training so he studied law at Harvard and graduated from that school in 1874. Thompson subsequently practiced law in Boston and was a member of the Boston Common Council from 1876 to 1878. He later became interested in mining and smelting enterprises.

He was an organizer of the Navy Athletic Association and the donor of the Thompson Cup which is awarded to the midshipman who contributes most to the advancement of athletics at the Naval Academy. He also helped to organize the New York Chapter of the United States Naval Academy Alumni Association and served as its first president and as a trustee of the Naval Academy Alumni Association at Annapolis, Md.

Thompson was president of the Society of Naval Architects and Marine Engineers and president of the Navy League. He also visited Japan at the invitation of the Japanese government and was awarded the Order of the Rising Sun, Second Class, by the Emperor. He also received the Order of Gustavus Vasa by the government of Sweden, and the Cross of Commander, Legion of Honor, by the French government.

Robert Means Thompson died on 5 September 1930 at Fort Ticonderoga, N.Y.

The first destroyer named *Thompson*, DD–305, was named for Richard Wigginton Thompson; the second, DD–627, for Robert Means Thompson.

I

(DD–305: dp. 1,308; l. 314'4½''; b. 30'11½''; dr. 9'10''; s. 35.0 k.; cpl. 122; a. 4 4'', 1 3'', 12 21'' tt.; cl. *Clemson*)

The first *Thompson* (DD–305) was laid down on 25 September 1918 at San Francisco, Calif., by the Bethlehem Steel Corp.; launched on 15 January 1919; sponsored by Mrs. Herbert H. Harris; and commissioned at the Mare Island Navy Yard, Vallejo, Calif., on 16 August 1920, Lt. Comdr. H. L. Best in command.

On 4 September, *Thompson* departed San Francisco for a shakedown training cruise which took her as far southward as Magdalena Bay, Mexico. She returned to San Diego, Calif., on 29 September, to operate with the Battle Fleet as part of Destroyer Division (DesDiv) 32, Destroyer Squadron (DesRon) 11. After initial fleet operations off the west coast, *Thompson* departed from San Diego on 7 January 1921 to take part in fleet maneuvers off Panama and later off the Chilean coast, south of Valparaiso.

Departing from Valparaiso on 4 February, she steamed with DesDiv 32 to Balboa, Canal Zone, and thence to La Union, El Salvador. Departing that port on 27 February, she proceeded north and soon resumed operations out of San Diego. Her cruises ranged as far north as Seattle, Wash.

Following her return from exercises to the northward on 21 June, she operated off the California coast. On 10 December, she departed San Diego and steamed to the Puget Sound Navy Yard, Bremerton, Wash., for regular overhaul.

Upon completion of the refit, *Thompson* headed for San Diego on 8 February 1922 for resumption of operations with the Battle Fleet. In the following years, she worked out of San Diego and took part in winter and spring maneuvers off Panama, on occasion transiting the Panama Canal for fleet exercises in the Caribbean Sea.

On 15 April 1925, *Thompson* steamed with the Fleet from San Francisco for fleet problems in Hawaiian waters. Upon completion of this training on 1 July, she departed Pearl Harbor with the Fleet, bound for a goodwill cruise to Australia and New Zealand. **After** calling at Pago Pago, Samoa, on 10 and 11 **July,** she arrived at Melbourne, Australia, on the 23d and received a rousing welcome. In company with sisterships *Kennedy* (DD–306), *Decatur* (DD–341), and *Farquhar* (DD–304), *Thompson* left Melbourne on 6 August and made port at Dunedin, New Zealand, four days later.

Putting out to sea after a 10-day visit there, *Thompson* visited Wellington from 22 to 24 August. She then proceeded home across the Pacific, via Pago Pago and Pearl Harbor, and reached San Diego on 26 September.

For the remainder of her career, *Thompson* continued her operations with DesDiv 32, DesRon 11. Early the next year, she made a brief visit to the east coast, calling at Norfolk, Va., Newport, R.I., and New York, N.Y., before returning to San Diego and serving out the rest of her days in operations along the west coast.

Under the terms of the 1930 London Naval Treaty limiting naval tonnage and armaments, *Thompson* was decommissioned on 4 April 1930; struck from the Navy list on 22 June 1930; and sold for scrap on 10 June 1931.

Following her sale, she served as a floating restaurant in lower San Francisco Bay during the depression years of the 1930's. In February 1944, the Navy repurchased the ship and partly sank her in the mud flats of San Francisco Bay, where Army and Navy aircraft carried out bombing runs with dummy bombs.

II

(DD–627: dp. 2,500; l. 348'3''; b. 36'1''; s. 37.4 k.; cpl. 276; a. 4 5'', 4 40mm., 5 21'' tt.; cl. *Gleaves*)

The second *Thompson* (DD–627) was laid down on 22 September 1941 at Seattle, Wash., by the Seattle-Tacoma Shipbuilding Corp.; launched on 15 July 1942; sponsored by Miss Sara Thompson Ross; and commissioned on 10 July 1943, Lt. Comdr. Lee A. Ellis in command.

Following operations along the west coast, Thompson departed San Diego on 19 August, bound for the east coast. She arrived at Norfolk on 1 September, prior to departing the next day for the coast of Maine and arriving at Casco Bay on 3 September. The destroyer then headed south to the Boston Navy Yard where she underwent repairs. She next engaged in exercises off the Massachusetts coast before returning to Casco Bay on 23 September for training.

On 5 October, she escorted *Arkansas* (BB–33) into New York and joined the screen for *Texas* (BB–35) for nine days of exercises in shore bombardment and

The destroyer *Thompson* (DD–627) refuels from the battleship *Arkansas* (BB–33) in April, 1944, while rehearsing for the invasion of Normandy. (80–G–244198)

other drills before joining Convoy UGS–21 which sailed from Norfolk, bound for North Africa. *Thompson* served as an escort, keeping ships in the channel as they plodded out to sea and prodding them to close up and keep in formation, while her echo-ranging gear was alert for prowling submarines off Chesapeake Bay. One day out, 16 October, the wind and sea rose, presaging a heavy storm which served to scatter parts of the convoy and cause *Thompson* to note in her log numerous times, "telling stragglers to close up." After the transatlantic voyage, *Thompson* was released from escort duty on 31 October to proceed to Casablaca, French Morocco.

One week later, the destroyer, attached to DesDiv 36, was homeward-bound with Convoy GUS–20. On 24 November, *Thompson* entered New York harbor with the convoy and then proceeded independently to the New York Navy Yard for voyage repairs. She sailed for Casco Bay on 5 December and conducted refresher training en route.

On 7 December, *Thompson* and *Baldwin* (DD–624) screened *New Jersey* (BB–62) as the battleship conducted high-speed runs and turning trials. Later that day, the three ships engaged in night illumination and spotting practice before carrying out the same program on 8 December.

After returning to Casco Bay, *Thompson* again put to sea, bound for Norfolk. During the night of 10 December, the winds increased to 70 knots with high seas and a low barometer. By 0735, it became necessary to rig in her already battered whaleboats and reduce speed to 12 knots. *Thompson* put into Norfolk on 12 December. Two days later, she joined Convoy UGS–27, bound for North Africa. On 27 December, she made a depth charge run on what her log termed "a questionable target."

Entering Casablanca harbor on 3 January 1944, *Thompson* and her fellow escorts were soon assigned to Convoy GUS–27, bound for Norfolk, where they arrived on the 24th. After alternating between New York, Boston, and Casco Bay, she departed Norfolk on 18 March, bound for Trinidad.

Returning to Norfolk six days later, *Thompson* operated along the east coast until mid-April when she joined the build-up of forces for the invasion of western Europe. On 18 April, she rendezvoused with *Baldwin*, *Arkansas*, *Tuscaloosa* (CA–37), *Nevada* (BB–36), and the rest of DesRon 18—to which *Thompson* was attached—and sailed for England. This force arrived at Plymouth on 28 April and prepared for duties during the forthcoming invasion.

On 4 May 1944, *Thompson* participated in landing exercise "Fabius," one of the many preliminaries to the landing on Normandy. On the 9th, she conducted shore bombardment practice at Slapton Sands, England; on the 13th, she fired antiaircraft practice off Ailsa Craig, Scotland; and, on 16 May, she engaged in division tactics and further bombardment exercises off the Irish coast.

On 15 April, she anchored at Belfast Lough, Ireland. The following day, 16 April, *Nevada*, *Texas*, and DesDiv 36 departed for exercises off the Irish coast before returning to Belfast Lough. Three days later, on 19 April, General Dwight D. Eisenhower inspected the ship.

Underway on the 20th, she conducted anti-"E" Boat exercises through the 22d. In these operations, she fired starshells and practiced illumination tactics for dealing with the foreseen danger of the *Schnellboote*. After more shore bombardment practice, in which her 5-inch and 40-millimeter gunners exercised at their battle stations and sharpened up their gunnery, she put out of Belfast Lough for Plymouth and thence proceeded to Portland, where she arrived on 27 April.

The next day, German Heinkel-111's bombed and mined the harbor, causing no small amount of work for harried minesweeper crews. But, with this danger soon swept away, the Allied forces could resume the nearly complete preparations for the upcoming Normandy invasion.

On 5 June, she joined Task Group (TG) 124.7, Convoy 0–1, bound for Omaha beach. She and her charges arrived off the Normandy beaches after an uneventful, but storm-tossed, evening.

Thompson then received her fire support orders to take station off Point de la Percee as a unit of TG 124.9. En route, she stood to action stations, her guns trained out and ready for any eventuality as the drama of history's greatest landing operation unfolded around her.

She arrived off Point du Hoc as Army rangers were struggling to gain a foothold on the rocky promontory. *Thompson*'s spotters could not momentarily see much, as Army aerial bombardments had obscured the area with smoke and dust. But when the haze cleared away, the destroyer's main battery opened fire with a vengeance, tongues of flame flashing from her gun muzzles as her salvos screamed shoreward. One by one, her targets of opportunity disappeared as her salvos struck "on target." She then lay-to, like a cat with a cornered mouse, awaiting remaining enemy guns to reveal themselves with tell-tale flashes.

Later in the day, she cruised closer inshore and located three giant German "Wurzburg" radar antennae. Once again, her spotting was deadly accurate, and one of the radar "dishes" toppled over, shattered by *Thompson*'s shells. Soon after, the wreckage of the two other antennae joined the first one in the dust.

Thompson's smaller guns also got into the fray. Her 40-millimeter batteries shredded concealments of shore batteries and sniper nests, working in close conjunction with shore-spotting teams who ferreted out the hidden enemy. Among her other targets was a fortified house. Solidly constructed, it had withstood numerous coastal storms. But on 6 June 1944, its solid Norman masonry could not hold up to a few rounds of five-inch high explosives; and down it tumbled, into a pile of rubble.

The following day, 7 June, *Thompson*'s straight-shooting gunners were at it again—this time, in support of the Rangers at Point du Hoc. Once more, her 40-millimeter and 5-inch batteries shot the enemy out of his sniper nests and gun positions before setting course for Portland, to anchor in Weymouth Bay to replenish her depleted fuel and ammunition stocks.

On 8 June, *Thompson* and her old companion, *Satterlee*, steamed back to Omaha beach. On the evening of 9 June, the Germans struck back in a stealthy E-boat attack. *Thompson*, screening as part of the Allied naval craft gathered there, joined in commencing fire on the intruders who were successfully driven off, retiring to the northward at high speed. On 10 June, her 20- and 40-millimeter gunners splashed a low-flying German "snooper" airplane.

At 0100 on 11 June, another E-boat attack developed from the northward. Here, as before, the long hours spent in night illumination and spotting practice exercises paid off handsome dividends. *Thompson* fired starshells, which blossomed in the darkness to turn night into day, and revealed the shadowy E-boats. British steam gunboats *Grey Goose* and *Grey Wolf* then darted in to ward off the intruders under the watchful eye of the destroyermen.

On 12 June, *Thompson* embarked a party which included Admiral Ernest J. King, General Dwight D. Eisenhower, General George C. Marshall, and General Henry H. Arnold and transported them across the channel to the invasion beaches at Omaha and then returned to Plymouth with Admiral King and his party embarked.

She continued to operate off Normandy beaches throughout the remainder of June 1944, steaming often between Seine Bay, France, and Plymouth, England. On one occasion, she served as flagship of Rear Admiral Alan G. Kirk, Naval Commander, Western Task Forces, for a quick visit to Cherbourg; on another, she once more served as a transport for General Eisenhower.

On 24 July 1944, *Thompson* steamed for North Africa, transiting the Straits of Gibraltar and arriving at Bizerte four days later. Underway in company with the rest of DesDiv 36 on the 29th, she left Bizerte bound for Oran, Algeria, arriving on the 30th. *Thompson* reached Naples on the 6th of August and joined the Allied expeditionary forces amassing for Operation "Anvil Dragoon," the invasion of southern France. Underway with Convoy SF-1, bound for the assault area, *Thompson* served in the screen and patrolled offshore throughout the operation from 15 to 21 August.

After a brief tender availability from 28 August to 1 September, she returned to the southern France beachheads to continue patrols through 18 September before steaming to Mers-El-Kebir, Morocco, where she arrived four days later, on 22 September. On the 23d, she departed Mers-El-Kebir and headed for the United States.

Arriving at Bermuda on 1 October, she commenced Navy Yard availability on 3 October, which lasted through the 27th of that month. For the remainder of 1944, *Thompson* operated off the east coast of the United States.

On 3 January 1945, the destroyer joined Convoy UGS-66, bound for North African ports. Entering Mers-El-Kebir on the 20th of January, she remained in North African waters until 1 February, when she joined the screen of Convoy GUS-68, en route to the United States. Arriving off New York on 13 February, the New York section of the convoy was detached. *Thompson* remained with the Boston section and continued on to that Massachusetts port, where she commenced a 10-day navy yard availability on 15 February.

Following these repairs, she steamed to Norfolk, Va., conducting gunnery exercises en route. On 1 March, she sortied with Convoy UGF-21, bound for North Africa, and arrived in North African waters on 12 March. The following month, after returning to the United States, she again escorted a North African convoy, this time UGS-85, commencing on 7 April.

On 30 May, *Thompson* was reclassified as a fast minesweeper and redesignated DMS-38. She spent the month of June undergoing conversion for her new mission, commencing on the 5th. She completed her yard work on the 29th.

During a post-conversion period, she conducted her first minesweeping exercises, with magnetic sweep equipment, in Chesapeake Bay. She also calibrated her radar, conducted antiaircraft exercises, and practiced laying mines. On 1 August, she departed the Virginia capes and steamed toward the Canal Zone, where she arrived on 7 August.

While underway on 14 August, she received the news that Japan had surrendered. On 18 August, she arrived at San Diego.

During September, *Thompson* moved westward, stopping at Pearl Harbor on 8 September and Eniwetok on the 21st. Arriving at Buckner Bay on 28 September, she put in just in time to take on fuel and head out to sea as a typhoon swirled its stormy way north. Shortly after the ship returned to Buckner Bay, yet another typhoon warning scrambled the Fleet and set it seaward into the East China Sea once more. On 9 October, the storm center smashed through Okinawa, but *Thompson* was well-clear and suffered no damage. She and her sistership in Mine Division (MineDiv) 61, formed a scouting line 4 miles apart on 10 October, keeping careful lookout while returning to Buckner Bay, searching for life rafts, derelicts, or men in the water.

On 16 October, *Thompson*, in company with MineDiv 61, headed to sea from Buckner Bay to commence sweeping operations in area "Rickshaw" in the Yellow Sea. En route the following day, *Thompson* sighted several floating mines and destroyed them by gunfire.

On 19 October, the force arrived at "Rickshaw," joined by *PGM-29*, *PGM-30*, and *PGM-31*. *Thompson* began her initial actual minesweeping at the north-east end of known mine lanes. The following day, *Thompson* swept her first mine—the first one swept by the task group. By 17 November, "Rickshaw" had been swept clean of Japanese mines, with *Thompson* scoring high with 64 mines located and destroyed.

After a short tender availability at Sasebo, Japan, the base of operations for MineDiv 61, *Thompson* steamed to Nagoya, Japan, to become flagship of the task group sweeping nearby waters. Completing this operation by mid-December, the minesweeper steamed back via Wakayama to Sasebo. During the last week in 1945, she assisted in the unsuccessful search for survivors of *Minevet* (AM-371), sunk by a mine explosion off Tsushima, northwest of Kyushu, Japan.

The ship spent January and February 1946 in Japanese home waters, and then steamed for Bikini Atoll to assist in sweeping operations to prepare the area for Operation "Crossroads" tests of atomic bombs to be conducted there in July. Before the tests took place, *Thompson* headed back to the United States. She remained at San Francisco, Calif., through July and then spent two months in overhaul at the Mare Island Navy Yard, Vallejo, Calif. From Mare Island, she returned to San Francisco to operate out of that port until late in the year. After six months of operation at San Francisco, she sailed for China on 10 February 1947 and proceeded via Pearl Harbor, Guam, and Kwajalein to Tsingtao.

Following six months duty with American occupation forces in Chinese waters, *Thompson* returned to the United States in early September 1947 and arrived at San Diego, Calif., on 2 October. Transferred to the operational command of Destroyers, Pacific Fleet, with the abolition of the Pacific Fleet Minecraft command, *Thompson* operated out of San Diego as a destroyer until 29 April 1948, when she returned again to Mare Island for a two-month overhaul. In July, she returned to San Diego and underwent training operations off the west coast, activities in which she was engaged for the remainder of 1948.

In January 1949, *Thompson* again set course for China in company with Destroyer Division 52. En route, however, the ships received orders to put about for the west coast after spending a few days in Hawaii, arriving at San Diego on 4 February 1949.

Thompson and three of her sister fast-minesweepers then became Mine Squadron (MineRon) One and were assigned to the General Line School at Monterey, Calif. They alternated in these operations between Monterey and San Diego for the remainder of 1949. After spending the first three months of 1950 in routine exercises and cruises out of San Diego, *Thompson* steamed for Pearl Harbor on 6 April 1950 for a three-month overhaul.

While in the yard, she received news that North Korean armed forces had invaded South Korea, crossing the 38th parallel. Completing her overhaul ahead of schedule, *Thompson* returned to San Diego on 20 July and began an accelerated and rigorous underway training period which lasted through August and part of September 1950.

On 4 October 1950, *Thompson* and sistership *Carmick* (DMS-33) departed San Diego, Calif., and arrived at Pearl Harbor five days later. The next day, they got underway for Midway. Twenty-four hours from their destination, orders directed them to patrol off Wake Island during the meeting of General Douglas MacArthur and President Harry Truman. *Thompson* remained there overnight, refueling at sea from *Guadalupe* (AO-32) before proceeding to Japan, arriving at Sasebo on the 21st.

While *Thompson* and *Carmick* had steamed across the Pacific, United Nations forces had been rallying after the initial heavy losses and retreats at the hands of the communist armies. Accordingly, the American Eighth Army put heavy pressure on North Korean troops, pushing them towards Pyongyang, on the west coast of Korea. This thrust was stretching the Army's supply lanes. To remedy this problem, an operation was mounted to open up the mined port of Chinnampo.

Yet to do this deed required ingenuity and resourcefulness; not the least of which involved a lack of minesweeping craft at the start of operations. *Thompson* and *Carmick*, newly arrived in the Land of the Morning Calm, were detailed to join the makeshift minesweeping organization recently established under Comdr. M. N. Archer. Consisting of *Forrest Royal* (DD–872), *Catamount* (LSD–17), *Horace A. Bass* (APD–124), *Pelican* (AMS–32), *Swallow* (AMS–36), and *Gull* (AMS–16), LST Q–007, four Republic of Korea minesweepers, and a helicopter from *Rochester* (CA–124), this task group performed a nearly impossible feat in slightly over two weeks. Before too long, American ships were bringing in supplies to the advancing Eighth Army. After a week of patrol duties off the newly swept port escorting logistics ships now able to utilize the channel, *Thompson* left the bitterly-cold region behind for a week of repairs and resupply at Sasebo.

In early November, however, the entry of Chinese communist forces into the war vastly altered the strategic picture. In the face of heavy onslaughts, United Nations troops retreated. One port which served as an evacuation point was Chinnampo, familiar to *Thompson*'s men as a result of the sweeping operation conducted a scant month before.

While United Nations warships conducted bombardments of advancing communist troops, *Thompson* escorted troopships out of the harbor in dense fog and through treacherous tidal currents to assist in the evacuation. For her part in this action, *Thompson* received the Navy Unit Commendation.

After replenishment, she served as harbor control vessel at Inchon, Korea. Two days after Christmas, she suddenly received orders to head for Sasebo, where MineRon 1 was to be regrouped. Arriving at the Japanese port on 27 December, she departed on 30 December 1950 in company with *Doyle* (DMS–34) and *Endicott* (DMS–35) for minesweeping assignments on the east coast of Korea. There, she spent close to three weeks engaged in clearance sweeps so that support ships could take fire-support stations to assist ground forces ashore.

In late January 1951, after a month in the arduous and cold conditions of that region, *Thompson* returned to Sasebo for repairs. These included drydocking for work on the hull; and, as a result of the docking period, the availability was extended another three weeks, before she departed for minesweeping operations again in mid-February.

Now using Wonsan, Korea, as a base, she operated to the northward, eventually sweeping Kyoto Wan deep, 50 miles south of the Manchurian border. While sweeping off the key railway nexus of Songjin, *Thompson* ran across a new minefield and cut seven mines as she passed through on her sweep. Later, she operated in the screen for *Missouri* (BB–63) and *Manchester* (CL–83), while they operated in that area on shore bombardment duties.

At Chuuron Jang, she herself destroyed two railroad bridges with her pinpoint gunnery. Also during this period, she took part in "junk-busting" operations up and down the coast, being on the lookout for suspicious junks used by communist forces for infiltration and minelaying operations. On one occasion, while underway north of Songjin, she sighted six North Korean junks in a cove. Once again, as at the Normandy "D-day" landings, *Thompson*'s gunners opened fire with a vengeance and sank all six communist boats.

After a month of such operations, she returned to Sasebo for upkeep. From 1 April to 3 November, *Thompson* returned to shell communist defense positions, supply lines, and troop concentrations. On 14 June 1951, however, it was the enemy's turn to hit back.

Thompson's gunners had just completed the destructions of a railroad bridge near Songjin when communist shore batteries opened fire, soon straddling the ship. One shell struck the bridge and knocked out the ship's fire control gear. In retaliation, *Thompson*'s gunners destroyed one enemy battery and damaged another. With three dead and three wounded, *Thompson* retired.

On 3 November, *Thompson* departed from Korean waters, homeward bound. She steamed into San Diego bay on 20 November and thence proceeded to the Mare Island Navy Yard for overhaul. After post-repair trials, she conducted operations on the west coast and underwent a restricted availability at Long Beach, Calif. *Thompson* spent the remainder of 1951 and the first part of 1952 in continental United States waters before departing San Diego on 23 June 1952.

Arriving at Pearl Harbor six days later, she continued on to Yokosuka, where she arrived on 18 July. After a short availability alongside *Frontier* (AD–25), *Thompson* proceeded to Songjin, Korea, arriving off that port on 11 August 1952.

In contrast to her earlier Korean tours, when her minesweeping duties were intermingled with destroyer-type operations, *Thompson* was now free to operate as a destroyer for coast patrol and gunfire support duties. Sweeping was now done by AM's and AMS's; and was all done at night.

The communists, too, had changed tactics. More guns were brought in to defend the coasts, while enemy accuracy had improved as well. On 20 August 1952, once more off Songjin, *Thompson* was taken under fire by a Chinese battery. A shell hit the flying bridge, killing four and wounding nine. *Thompson* attempted to return the fire, but the excellently concealed shore guns made the return shelling's accuracy difficult and ineffective. Retiring from the scene, the stricken *Thompson* transferred her casualties to *Iowa* (BB–64), then operating 15 miles south of Songjin.

Five days later, the minesweeper arrived at Sasebo on 25 August for tender availability repairing her engines and battle damage, before she headed north to Songjin. She remained off this unlucky port from 13 September to 12 October 1952, occasionally patrolling to the northernmost extremity of the United Nations blockade before again returning to Sasebo.

From 3 November to 1 December 1952, *Thompson* operated in Wonsan harbor, as part of the United Nations blockade forces there. As such, she was in range of communist guns on many occasions. The object of enemy fire at least four times, *Thompson* received damage for the third time when straddled on 20 November 1952, while acting as gunfire support ship for *Kite* (AMS–22) which was conducting a sweep of the inner harbor. From three widely spaced points, enemy guns took the minesweepers under fire, catching *Thompson* amidships on the starboard side as she was laying clouds of oily black smoke between *Kite* and the shoreline.

Returning to Yokosuka for repairs to the battle damage, *Thompson* spent Christmas in that Japanese naval port. New Year's, however, once again found the fast minesweeper at Songjin. After two more tours there, into February of 1953, *Thompson* headed back to the United States in company with *Carmick*. With refueling stops at Midway and Pearl Harbor, she finally arrived at San Diego on 14 March 1953.

Operating with MineDiv 11, she based on the west coast for the remainder of the year. Commencing on 8 June 1953, *Thompson* served as a Columbia Movie Studio "prop" during the filming of the Herman Wouk novel, *The Caine Mutiny*. Operating out of San Francisco for one week, *Thompson* became *Caine*, while at the same time serving as the model for many of the Columbia sets used in the filming of the on board scenes.

After taking part in two exercises in late September 1953, she operated out of San Diego until 1 December 1953, when she reported to the Pacific Reserve Fleet to prepare for inactivation. On 18 May 1954, *Thompson's* commission pennant was hauled down and the ship placed in reserve. On 15 July 1955, she was reclassified as a destroyer and redesignated DD–627. She was struck from the Navy list on 1 July 1971 and sold to the American Ship Dismantlers, Inc., of Portland, Oreg., on 7 August 1972 for scrapping.

Thompson received two battle stars for Wold War II service and seven battle stars and the Navy Unit Commendation for her Korean War service.

Thompson, James, see *James Thompson.*

Thompson, Robert M., see *Robert M. Thompson.*

Thompson, Sara, see *Sara Thompson.*

Thompson, Smith, see *Smith Thompson.*

Thor

The Norse god of thunder.

(AKA–49: dp. 7,000 (tl.); l. 426'0''; b. 58'0''; dr. 16'0'' (lim.); s. 16.9 k. (tl.); cpl. 303; a. 1 5'', 8 40mm.; cl. *Artemis;* T. S4–SE2–BE1)

Vanadis (AKA–49) was laid down on 18 April 1945 under a Maritime Commission contract (MC hull 1910) at Providence, R.I., by the Walsh-Kaiser Co., Inc.; launched on 8 June 1945; sponsored by Mrs. J. Henry Gill; acquired by the Navy on 9 July 1945; and commissioned the same day, Lt. Comdr. E. B. Williams in command.

Following shakedown out of Hampton Roads, *Vanadis* arrived at Newport, R.I., on 4 August and began shuttling back and forth between that port and Hampton Roads. In mid-December, the attack cargo ship headed for the Gulf of Mexico. After visiting Mobile, Ala.; Gulfport, Miss.; and Jacksonville, Fla., she arrived at Boston. On 6 February, she reported to the Commandant, 1st Naval District, for inactivation. *Vanadis* was placed out of commission on 27 March 1946. Her name was struck from the Navy list on 5 June 1946; and, on 2 July, she was transferred to the Maritime Commission.

After almost nine years of inactivity—berthed with the National Defense Reserve Fleet at James River, Va.—*Vanadis* was reacquired by the Navy on 14 April 1955 and reinstated on the Navy list as *AKA–49.* On 30 June, she entered the Bethlehem Steel Co.'s yard at Baltimore, Md., for conversion to a cable repair ship. She was redesignated ARC–4; and, on 14 November 1955, she was renamed *Thor.* On 3 January 1956, *Thor* completed her conversion and was recommissioned, Comdr. R. H. Thomas in command.

The cable repair ship operated in the Atlantic through

The cable laying and repairing ship *Thor* (ARC–4).

1956. In February 1957, she reported to the Pacific Fleet and, until the fall of 1958, operated out of San Francisco repairing and laying cables. She returned to the Atlantic in September 1958 and served there until the summer of 1961, when she was temporarily assigned to the Pacific again. The cable repair ship returned to operations in the Atlantic in December. Following an overhaul at Boston in the spring of 1962, *Thor* deployed to the Pacific once more for cable repair operations in the northern reaches of that ocean. In October, she returned to the eastern side of the Isthmus of Panama and busied herself with cable repair duties and oceanographic projects in the Caribbean Sea. For the next five and one-half years, *Thor* continued to repair and lay cables in the western Atlantic and in the West Indies. Occasionally, she also participated in more oceanographic projects. During that half decade, she ranged as far north as Nova Scotia and as far south as the Caribbean. Periodically, she also conducted operations in the Gulf of Mexico.

On 20 April 1968, the ship departed Norfolk and steamed, via the Panama Canal and San Diego, for the Central Pacific. She conducted special operations in the vicinity of Midway Island and returned to Hawaii on 16 June for several days before departing Pearl Harbor on the 24th for the Marianas. She reached Guam on 5 July and spent the next month repairing cable around that island. She returned to Pearl Harbor on 13 August and operated in the Hawaiian Islands until she headed back toward the mainland on 7 November. Following a brief stop at Long Beach, Calif., *Thor* returned to Norfolk on 6 December.

Over the next four years, *Thor* deployed to the Pacific three times. In August 1969, after seven months of operations along the east coast, she headed, via the Panama Canal and San Diego, to Pearl Harbor. Through November, she conducted operations near Midway Island and then returned to the Atlantic via Pearl Harbor, Long Beach, and the Panama Canal. In February 1970, she entered the Bethlehem Steel Shipyard in Boston to begin a year-long overhaul and repair period. In mid-February 1971, the cable repair ship resumed normal operations until late June when she deployed to the Pacific once more. She reached Hawaii on 29 July and departed again on 9 August for cable operations in the northernmost reaches of the Pacific, near the Aleutians chain. She completed those repairs late in the month and, after visits to Esquimalt, British Columbia, and San Diego, retransited the canal on 20 September and arrived in Portsmouth, N.H., eight days later. During the first seven months of 1972, the cable repair ship operated along the eastern seaboard again. On 24 July, *Thor* departed Norfolk for her last assignment in the Pacific Ocean. She arrived at Alameda, Calif., on 11 August and conducted cable laying operations from there into late November. On the 24th, the ship cleared Alameda. She passed through the Panama Canal on 4 December and arrived back at Portsmouth on the 12th.

On 17 January 1973, *Thor* embarked upon her last overseas cruise as a commissioned ship in the Navy. She arrived in Swansea, England, 10 days later and, after two days in port, put to sea for cable operations. From 14 to 18 February, she visited the Submarine Base at Holy Loch, Scotland, before resuming cable operations near the Arctic Circle. She completed her assignment at the end of the month and, after another visit to Holy Loch during the first week in March, headed back to the United States. On 17 March, she returned to the Portsmouth Naval Shipyard to begin preparations for decommissioning incident to her transfer to the Military Sealift Command.

Thor (ARC–4) was decommissioned at Portsmouth on 2 July 1973 and simultaneously transferred to the custody of the Military Sealift Command. USNS *Thor* (T–ARC–4) operated with the Military Sealift Command, primarily in the Pacific, until April 1974 when she was returned to the Maritime Administration to

be placed in reserve. Since then, she has been berthed with the National Defense Reserve Fleet at Suisun Bay, Calif.

Thorn

Jonathan Thorn—born on 8 January 1779 at Schenectady, N.Y.—was appointed a midshipman on 28 April 1800. Subsequently serving with the Navy during the Tripolitan War, Thorn volunteered to take part in the hazardous expedition to destroy the captured frigate *Philadelphia*, which lay beneath the guns of the shore batteries in heavily defended Tripoli harbor. On 16 February 1804, Lt. Stephen Decatur, Jr., led a party of these volunteers in the ketch *Intrepid* into Tripoli and burned the erstwhile American frigate.

Attached to the schooner *Enterprise*, Thorn was then assigned to *Gunboat No. 4*, under Decatur's command. In this vessel, he participated in the attack on Tripoli, with Commodore Edward Preble's squadron on 3 August 1804. Specially commended by Decatur for his conduct in this battle, Thorn received command of one of the Tripolitan gunboats captured and commanded this vessel in the engagement with the Tripolitan pirates on 7 August.

Commissioned a lieutenant on 16 February 1807, Thorn became the first commandant of the New York Navy Yard at age 27. In 1810, he was granted a two-year furlough to command John Jacob Astor's sailing bark *Tonquin* in a voyage slated to take the ship to the Pacific Northwest to establish a fur trading post. Anchoring off Nootka on 5 June 1811, after a voyage which had taken the ship around Cape Horn to the Hawaiian Islands and to the mouth of the Columbia River, Thorn soon began trading with the local Indians. Angered by what they considered a bad business deal, the Indians came on board *Tonquin* and, in a brief, bloody action, massacred Thorn and his crew.

———

The name *Thorn* was assigned on 22 January 1941 to DD–505, an experimental 1,150-ton destroyer ordered on 9 September 1940 from the Federal Shipbuilding and Drydock Co., Kearny, N.J. However, the contract was cancelled on 10 February 1941 and replaced by a contract for the *Gleaves*-class destroyer, *Thorn* (DD–647).

I

(DD–647: dp. 1,630 (f.) ; l. 348′4″; b. 36′1″; dr. 17′5″; s. 37 k.; a. 4 5″, 4 40mm., 7 20mm., 5 21″ tt., 6 dcp., 2 dct.; cl. *Gleaves*)

The first *Thorn* (DD–647) was laid down on 15 November 1942 at Kearny, N.J., by the Federal Shipbuilding and Drydock Co.; launched on 28 February 1943; sponsored by Mrs. Beatrice Fox Palmer; and commissioned on 1 April 1943, Lt. Comdr. Edward Brumby in command.

Following shakedown and trials out of Casco Bay, Maine, *Thorn* joined Destroyer Squadron (DesRon) 19. Between 28 May 1943 and 2 January 1944, the destroyer conducted four round-trip convoy escort missions on the New York-Norfolk-Casablanca route—the first trip as part of Task Force (TF) 69 and the other three as part of TF 64. On her last convoy run, she escorted two oilers to Punta Delgada, in the Azores, in company with *Stockton* (DD–646)—the first ships to enter the port under the terms of the new agreement between the Allies and the government of Portugal.

On 3 January 1944, the day after *Thorn* arrived back in New York harbor, *Turner* (DD–648) blew up and sank in Ambrose Channel, 5,000 yards astern of *Thorn*. Calling away the ship's motor whaleboat, *Thorn* sent a rescue party to try to recover survivors. Lt. James P. Drake, USNR, and Boatswain's Mate, First Class E. Wells were awarded Navy and Marine Corps Medal for their bravery in the rescue of three *Turner* survivors; and three other men received commendation bars for their part in the operation.

Late in January, *Thorn* sailed for the Pacific and transited the Panama Canal on the 29th. Ordered to report to relieve DesRon 1 in New Guinea waters, the destroyer and her sisters of DesDiv 37 headed for the southwest Pacific. *Thorn* was detoured to Guadalcanal and Rendova to escort a detached oiler group. She finally arrived at Milne Bay, New Guinea, on 29 February.

Thorn moved directly from there to Cape Sudest where, on 4 March, the destroyer embarked troops and supplies of the Army's 7th Cavalry Division and immediately proceeded to Los Negros Island for the invasion of the Admiralties. In addition to making three additional escort trips between Cape Sudest and Seeadler Harbor, *Thorn* participated in two shore bombardments of Pityili Island, conducted antisubmarine patrols north of the Admiralties, and acted as a fighter director vessel.

On 10 April—while making a practice torpedo run during preparations for forthcoming Allied landings at Hollandia—*Thorn* struck an uncharted reef. Damage to her screws and shafts forced the ship back to the west coast for an overhaul. En route home, she escorted *Massachusetts* (BB–59) to Bremerton, Wash. She subsequently escorted *Thetis Bay* (CVE–90) from the Puget Sound Navy Yard to San Francisco, Calif., where she eventually arrived on 22 May.

After completing her overhaul at the Hunter's Point Navy Yard, *Thorn* conducted refresher training and then escorted *Mississippi* (BB–41) to Hawaii. She arrived at Pearl Harbor on 11 August. She then escorted *Maryland* (BB–46) to Purvis Bay, Solomon Islands, where she joined escort carrier Task Unit (TU) 32.7.1 and proceeded to the Palaus for the landings on 15 September. During this deployment as screen and plane guard, *Thorn* rescued the crews of three Grumman TBM "Avenger" torpedo planes which had "ditched."

Detached from escort duty at the end of September, *Thorn* joined the 7th Fleet at Manus, in the Admiralties, on 3 October. As American forces massed for the initial assaults on the Japanese-occupied Philippine Islands, *Thorn* joined the fire support screen for TF 77. She entered Leyte Gulf on the night of the 18th and screened battleships and cruisers during their early shore bombardments.

As Allied troops swarmed ashore two days later, the destroyer provided interdiction fire at Abuyog, south of the Leyte beaches, and patrolled the southern end of Leyte Gulf for the following week. At dawn on the 21st, *Thorn*'s gunners opened fire on a Japanese Aichi "Val" and sent the enemy dive bomber splashing into the sea near the transport area. On the 22d, the destroyer and *Portland* (CA–33) splashed another enemy aircraft.

During the fierce night action at Surigao Strait, *Thorn* screened the American battleships as they mauled the Japanese force coming through the strait. Originally ordered to conduct a torpedo attack on the Japanese battle line, *Thorn* and her mates were recalled as the Japanese fled posthaste from the direction whence they had come. *Thorn* then formed up with the lefthand flank of cruisers and destroyers and headed south to polish off the "cripples" from the Japanese force. The American ships came across one Japanese destroyer and smothered it with fire which summarily dispatched it to the depths. During her 17 salvoes, *Thorn* observed 12 hits.

That evening, *Thorn*'s division received orders to lie-to off Homonhon Island, to conduct a torpedo attack on a Japanese force expected from the eastward. The enemy, however, retired into the San Bernardino Strait that afternoon, and the American destroyer unit was recalled on the 26th.

Ordered to Ulithi, *Thorn* departed Philippine waters to rejoin the 3d Fleet in the Carolines, for duty with the Fast Carrier Task Force. From 5 to 24 November, *Thorn* participated in TF 38's strikes against Japanese targets in the Philippines, screening and planeguarding for the fast carriers. She returned to Ulithi with TG 30.8 for duty with a logistics support group. She subsequently resumed planeguarding, this time standing by escort carriers. She assisted *Cape Esperance* (CVE–88) during the 18 December typhoon. Following this heavy storm—which sank three destroyers—*Thorn* searched for survivors in the storm area.

During the carrier strikes on Lingayen in early January 1945 and the subsequent carrier raids on Japanese shipping in the South China Sea, *Thorn* escorted a fast oiler group for replenishment evolutions with the aircraft carriers. While returning to the Carolines, via Leyte Gulf and the Mindoro Strait, *Thorn* rescued the crew of a downed TBM and the pilot of a crashed fighter before arriving at Ulithi on the 27th. The destroyer again screened oilers during the operations against Iwo Jima and also entered waters near the strategic island to screen heavy fire support units. On 21 February, *Thorn* and *Ute* (ATF–76) learned that *Bismarck Sea* (CVE–95) had been struck by two Japanese suicide planes, and they rushed to aid the stricken ship. However, when they searched the scene, the escort carrier had already gone to the bottom, the victim of Japanese kamikazes.

Two days in Ulithi followed the ship's return; and, on 13 March, *Thorn* reformed with the 5th Fleet support group built around *Detroit* (CL–8) for the Ryukyu operations. On 25 March, *Thorn* and *Aylwin* (DD–355) made depth charge attacks on a sonar contact and observed an oil slick after the last drop. They conducted a retirement search before rejoining the formation on the 26th, but could not verify that the contact had actually been a submarine.

Thorn susbequently conducted four escort missions with the replenishment group, escorting oilers into Kerama Retto to fuel the fire support ships off Okinawa and making her first run on 1 April. On the second run, *Thorn* observed two enemy planes splashing into the sea, victims of combat air patrol (CAP) fighters and ship gunfire. On the third, a kamikaze crashed *Taluga* (AO–62), two miles astern, while another enemy suicide plane splashed alongside a nearby small patrol craft.

The destroyer then spent two weeks at Ulithi, replenishing for further operations with the logistics support group. She rejoined the oilers and supply ships at sea on 28 May. On 5 June, *Thorn* rode out her second major typhoon, steaming through the eye of the storm at 0530. Two days later, she joined a group of four damaged escort aircraft carriers which were retiring to Guam.

On 4 July, soon after screening the CVE's out of the "front lines" for repairs, *Thorn* resumed work with the replenishment and support group and continued screening and supporting it through the surrender of Japan. During this period, she sank seven drifting mines.

Following Japan's surrender, *Thorn* steamed off Tokyo Bay until 9 September, when the entire group entered Sagami Wan. The next day, the support group's base was established at the Yokosuka Naval Base, where *Thorn* remained through the end of September.

Streaming her homeward-bound pennant, *Thorn*, in company with DesRon 19, steamed out of Tokyo Bay on 8 October and joined *Tennessee* (BB–43) and *California* (BB–44) off Wakayama the following day. On 15 October, the group sailed on the first leg of their homeward-bound voyage, subsequently stopping at Singapore, Colombo, and Cape Town. The destroyer eventually arrived in New York on 7 December 1945, via St. Helena and Ascension Islands in the Atlantic. After a month's overhaul, she proceeded to Charleston, S.C., where she was decommissioned and placed in reserve on 6 May 1946.

Thorn lay in reserve through the 1950's and 60's. Struck from the Navy list on 1 July 1971, the ship's hulk was authorized for use as a target and was sunk by aircraft from *America* (CVA–66) in November 1973.

Thorn received seven battle stars for her World War II service.

II

(DD–988: dp. 7,600 (f.); l. 563'; b. 55'; dr. 19'; s. 30 k.; cpl. 250; a. 2 5'', ASROC, Sea Sparrow, 2 Mk. 32 tt.; cl. *Spruance*)

The second *Thorn* (DD–988) was laid down on 29 August 1977 at Pascagoula, Miss., by the Ingalls Shipbuilding Division of Litton Systems, Inc., and launched on 3 February 1979 with Mrs. Patricia Palmer Ansley serving as sponsor. *Thorn* was scheduled to be commissioned in early 1980.

Thornback

A slender member of the shark family native to northern Atlantic waters ranging from the temperate to the arctic. The thornback has a long pointed snout and a sharp spine at the end of each dorsal fin.

(SS–418: dp. 1,570 (surf.), 2,415 (subm.); l. 311'8''; b. 27'3''; dr. 15'5''; s. 20.25 k (surf.), 8.75 k. (subm.), cpl. 81; a. 10 21'' tt., 1 5'', 1 40mm., 1 20mm.; cl. *Balao*)

Thornback (SS–418) was laid down on 5 April 1944 by the Portsmouth (N.H.) Navy Yard; launched on 7 July 1944; sponsored by Mrs. Peter K. Fischler; and commissioned on 13 October 1944, Comdr. Ernest P. Abrahamson in command.

Thornback stood out of New London, Conn., on 20 March 1945 bound, via the Panama Canal, for the Hawaiian Islands. She arrived at Pearl Harbor on 25 May and conducted training in Hawaiian waters prior to getting underway on 11 June for the western Pacific. As she stood down the Pearl Harbor channel, a formation of LCI's, running down the wrong side of the channel, forced *Thornback* to crowd dangerously near the extreme edge of the channel. In the process, the submarine damaged her sound dome, necessitating repairs and a two-day delay in departing.

She set sail for Saipan on the 13th, but she was rerouted to Guam. En route to the Marianas, *Thornback* conducted an average of four training dives daily, in conjunction with battle problems, drills, and emergency surfacing exercises, before she arrived at Guam on 25 June.

As lead ship of a wolf pack nicknamed "Abe's Abolishers," *Thornback* stood out to sea on 30 June, bound for the Japanese home islands. By this point in the war, American and British task forces steamed within easy gun range of Japanese coastal targets with near impunity. Japan's merchant marine and Navy had dwindled in size. Allied submarines and aircraft had taken an ever increasing toll. In the air, Japan's once vaunted air forces had been struck from the skies. Sweeping ahead of 3d Fleet Task Forces, the "Abolishers" made antipicket boat sweeps in the Tokyo-Yokohama area before proceeding to hunting grounds off the east coast of Honshu and south of Hokkaido.

Rough seas, strong winds, and generally poor visibility prevailed during *Thornback*'s patrol. She sighted a hospital ship on 5 July and let it pass. Six days later, a minor fire in the pump room caused a temporary shutdown in the number one air conditioning plant before swift repairs enabled the ship to continue as before.

On the 15th, *Thornback* sighted *Sea Poacher* (SS–406), and the two boats exchanged information on their hunting areas. They also swapped movies, precious commodities for boosting morale on board the crowded

submersibles. Six days later, *Thornback* proceeded north to patrol off Erimo Seki, an area which had recently seen a series of devastating carrier raids by Admiral William F. Halsey's Fast Carrier Task Force 38. The submarine's commanding officer noted somewhat humorously, "This area should be about as heavily travelled as the Sahara Desert after the working over it just had. . . ."

His assessment was correct—only straggling merchantmen and small patrol craft hugged the barren coasts. On 26 July, at 0320, *Thornback* submerged 8,000 yards off Hei Saki. At 0400, the submarine's sound gear picked up the "pinging" projected by a snooping Japanese escort ship, and she came to periscope depth to have a look.

Carefully maneuvering into position, *Thornback* fired one shot from her stern tubes at 0429 and soon heard a small explosion which stopped the enemy's screws. Almost immediately the submariners picked up new sounds—two more escorts, "pinging" and coming aggressively closer. After sizing up the new attackers, *Thornback* felt that they were too small to use a torpedo on—besides, a Japanese floatplane had begun circling the area. A rowboat with a few Japanese sailors amidst a pile of flotsam testified to the fact that the first ship was no longer there. Satisfied that their quarry had been sunk, the submarine cleared the area. One of the other escorts gave up the chase and picked up survivors of her sunken sister. "All antisubmarine vessels have closed the beach," *Thornback*'s commander later recorded, "and seem to be pinging away at the rocks."

Three days later, by periscope, the submarine spotted a 950-ton "sea truck," similar to *Sanko Maru*, at 2,000 yards, close inshore. Unescorted, the Japanese presented a tempting target for a gun attack; but, no sooner had *Thornback*'s periscope shears and bow broken the surface, than the target slipped into the misty weather. Not to be daunted, *Thornback* followed, playing a cat and mouse game, and fired five torpedoes. All missed. She later sighted the enemy again, missed with three more torpedoes, and took the "sea truck" under fire. Despite poor visibility, *Thornback* closed to 300 yards and scored numerous hits with the 40-millimeter guns. The target, however, was able to move closer inshore and escaped in the fog which closed around her like a shroud.

The submarine lurked on the surface off Hokkaido on 31 July and again tangled with some of the numerous Japanese patrol craft. She sighted a 100-foot patrol boat at 500 yards and closing. *Thornback*'s five-inch deck gun was trained out, but her crew could not keep their sights on the attacker through the telescopes and switched to open sights. Meanwhile, the 40-millimeter gun opened a devastating barrage at the enemy craft as it came steadily on a collision course. These shells continually hit the escort ship along the waterline and in the pilot house, probably killing the occupants on the bridge.

Thornback had passed her target once at 300 yards and came about for a second pass when the forward torpedo room reported sharp noises forward. Further amplification showed that the noise was caused by enemy machine gun bullets striking the submarine's hull. Resuming the attack, *Thornback* swung back into action, with visibility only 300 yards and lessening. Her 40-millimeter fire continued to maul the Japanese vessel, shooting away one of her masts and leaving her limping shoreward at only 3 knots. After securing from battle stations, *Thornback* passed through an oil slick and noted a mast from the heavily hit patrol craft.

Later on the 31st, *Thornback* rendezvoused with *Sea Poacher* off Kessennuma and proceeded north to pick up *Angler* (SS–240) en route to a projected shore bombardment mission against Hokkaido. The sight of the three submarines cruising on the surface moved *Thornback*'s commander to write: "On this clear and sunny day, the three ships in perfect column on a flat

USS *Thornback* (SS–418), 1963.   (USN 1086056)

sea made a beautiful picture tearing along at 18.5 knots."

At 1402 on 1 August, this part of "Abe's Abolishers" —*Thornback*, *Angler*, and *Sea Poacher*—made landfall off their target of Urakawa, Hokkaido. They swung parallel to the beach with guns manned and ready. Twelve minutes later, slowing to 10 knots, *Thornback* and her consorts opened fire with 5-inch and 40-millimeter batteries at a range of 4,200 yards. The first few rounds from *Thornback*'s five-incher went wild, but the crew soon locked onto the range. Firing by hand after the foot firing plunger broke off, *Thornback*'s gunners eventually sent 100 rounds of 5-inch shells shoreward, heavily damaging a factory and a power plant. "The firing took 22 minutes and was of inestimable value to the entire crew," wrote the submarine's commanding officer. "The training was excellent and the boost to morale tremendous."

Thornback set sail for Midway after the shelling of Urakawa, and arrived at the atoll on 8 August. Seven days later, Japan—hemmed in by veritable armadas of Allied ships and planes which were able to roam almost at will and unchalleneged off her coast and in her skies —surrendered.

Thornback soon returned to the United States, where she was decommissioned at New London on 6 April 1946 and was placed in the Atlantic Reserve Fleet. Subsequently brought to the Portsmouth Naval Shipyard, she was converted and reactivated as a Guppy II–A. On 2 October 1953, the submarine was recommissioned, Lt. Comdr. Thomas C. Jones, Jr., in command, and assigned to Submarine Squadron (SubRon) 4.

Shaking down in her new configuration, the submarine performed a "first" for submarines on 6 November 1954, when she snorkled in the Mississippi River at New Orleans from the Industrial Canal to the foot of Canal Street. With SubRon 4, the ship was based at Key West, Fla., and visited Caribbean ports before entering the Charleston (S.C.) Naval Shipyard in February 1956 for overhaul. Upon completion of this work, the submarine was deployed to the Mediterranean for a tour with the 6th Fleet before returning to Key West in March 1957. While with SubRon 4, *Thornback* participated in operations supporting the Operational Development Force, the Fleet Sonar School, and the Fleet Training Unit at Guantanamo Bay, Cuba.

On 2 June 1958, *Thornback* departed the Caribbean, bound for Londonderry, Northern Ireland, and operations with the joint Royal Navy-Royal Air Force antisubmarine school. While thus engaged, the submarine damaged her port propeller at Derry and became the first American submarine to be docked at Faslane by the Royal Navy. *Thornback* returned to the 6th Fleet and her second Mediterranean deployment which lasted from 2 July to 24 September 1958.

For the remainder of the ship's active career, she was based out of Charleston, conducting deployments to the North Atlantic, the Mediterranean, and to the Caribbean and operating in a support capacity as newer submarine types joined the Fleet. Placed in a reduced-manning status on 14 April 1971, the ship was turned over to the Turkish Navy on 1 July 1971 and renamed *Uluc Ali Reis* (S–338). Decommissioned from the United States Navy on that same date, she was later struck from the Navy list on 1 August 1973.

Thornback received one battle star for her World War II service.

Thornborough

An alternate spelling of Thornbrough. At the age of 7, Edward Thornbrough—born on 27 July 1754 at Plymouth Dock, England—went to sea in the 74-gun line of battleship *Arrogant* and spent most of the next six decades serving in the Royal Navy. Perhaps the first highlight of his career occurred during his service in the sloop *Falcon* off the coast of Massachusetts at the outset of the American Revolution. During a boat expedition to take possession of an American schooner which had run aground in Cape Ann harbor while attempting to escape from *Falcon*, Thornbrough was seriously wounded by fire from the shore.

Thornbrough later won renown during the wars with France caused by the French Revolution. After Waterloo, he served for three years at Portsmouth as Commanded in Chief before retiring in 1818. Admiral Sir Edward Thornbrough died on 3 April 1834.

———

On 10 June 1943, before her construction began, *Thornborough* (DE–565) was assigned to the Royal Navy. The *Buckley*-class destroyer escort was laid down on 22 September 1943 at Hingham, Mass., by the Bethlehem Steel Co.; launched on 13 November 1943; and completed and transferred to the United Kingdom under Lend-Lease agreement and commissioned in the Royal Navy on 31 December 1943.

Thornborough (K.574) served in the English Channel and off Normandy in 1944. In the summer and fall of that year, the "Captain"-class frigate operated as a radar ship with prowling motor torpedo boat groups off the coast of Flanders, protecting Allied support shipping and preventing German ships from supplying hard-pressed units ashore, or from mining waters used by the Allies. In July and August off Cape D'Antifer, she engaged enemy E-boats and attacked a German convoy. In November, she again took part in an attack on enemy E-boats in the Scheldt Estuary.

For the remainder of the war, *Thornborough* operated in the North Sea and in the Atlantic. She was nominally returned to the United States on 30 January 1947, and her name was struck from the Navy list on 7 February. On 24 April 1947, she was sold to Athens Piraeus Electricity Co., Ltd., Athens, Greece, to be broken up.

Thornhill

Leonard W. Thornhill—born on 17 August 1915 in Lamison, Ala.—was appointed to the Naval Academy on 19 June 1934, graduated on 2 June 1938, and was commissioned an ensign. After serving at sea in *Pennsylvania* (BB–38) until September 1939 and in *J. Fred Talbot* (DD–156) until July 1940, he was transferred to Pensacola for flight training. Thornhill received his naval aviator's wings on 23 January 1941 and soon thereafter reported for duty at the Naval Air Station at Opa-Locka, Fla.

Following another assignment ashore at San Diego, Calif., Thornhill joined carrier-based Torpedo Squadron (VT) 2 on 13 August 1941. After the Japanese attack on Pearl Harbor, Thornhill served with his ship, *Lexington* (CV–2), during the first month of the war, patrolling the Johnston-Palmyra-Oahu triangle against possible enemy incursions. In February and March, he participated in the carrier's offensive patrols in the Coral Sea and in the attacks on Japanese installations at Salamaua and Lae located on the northern coast of New Guinea.

Early May found *Lexington* patrolling the Coral Sea after two weeks of upkeep in Pearl Harbor. Thornhill piloted one of the 12 TBD–1 torpedo bombers launched during mid-morning on 7 May to seek out and destroy Japanese forces converging on the Australian base at Port Moresby. At 1135, VT–2 encountered the light carrier *Shoho* and immediately launched a well coordinated attack in conjunction with Bombing Squadron (VB) 2. While VB–2 took some of the fighter pressure off the torpedo bombers, Thornhill and his comrades split formation and attacked the carrier from both directions astern. All 12 planes made their runs and drops successfully and without loss to themselves. The "Devastators" claimed nine hits from 12 drops, one of which was credited to Lt. (jg.) Thornhill. The coordinated attacks of VT–2 and VB–2 sent *Shoho* to the bottom—the first enemy carrier sunk by American forces in World War II.

The following day, during the second phase of the Battle of the Coral Sea, Thornhill went aloft with VT–2 at 0910 in search of the two remaining Japanese carriers, *Shokaku* and *Zuikaku*. After failing to encounter the enemy ships at their supposed location, Thornhill and his squadron mates initiated a "box search" to find their quarry. Sometime after 1100, they found their target, fleet carrier *Shokaku*. At 1142, VT–2 commenced its attack; and the carrier began a long, slow turn to the right which allowed each TBD–1 to make its "run without splitting across the stern." The attack ended just eight minutes later, and VT–2 began the flight home claiming five hits on *Shokaku*—all of which proved later to be wishful thinking. Only the dive bombers succeeded in damaging the enemy carrier.

During the return flight, VT–2 planes began to run low on fuel as a result of their drawn-out search earlier that morning. All planes cut back power in order to make the flight most economically. Even so, Lt. (jg.) Thornhill could not make it. His "Devastator" ran out of fuel some 20 miles short of home, and he had to ditch in the ocean. Though a destroyer went to their rescue, Thornhill and his crew perished at sea. For his contribution to the destruction of *Shoho* carried out with ". . . complete disregard for his own personal safe-

ty . . .," Lt. (jg.) Thornhill was awarded the Navy Cross posthumously.

(DE–195: dp. 1,240; l. 306'0''; b. 36'7''; dr. 11'8''; s. 20.9 k. (tl.); cpl. 216; a. 3 3'', 6 40mm., 10 20mm., 2 dct., 8 dcp., 1 dcp. (hh.); cl. *Cannon*)

Thornhill (DE–195) was laid down on 7 October 1943 at Newark, N.J., by the Federal Shipbuilding & Drydock Co.; launched on 30 December 1943; sponsored by Mrs. J. E. Thornhill, the mother of Lt. (jg.) Thornhill; and commissioned on 1 February 1944, Lt. John B. Shumway, USNR, in command.

The destroyer escort got underway on 18 February, held shakedown training out of Bermuda, and returned to New York exactly one month later. *Thornhill* served as a training ship at Norfolk during April. In May, she returned to New York to escort a part of Convoy UGS–42 to Norfolk. The 108-ship convoy sortied from Hampton Roads on 13 May, bound for North Africa. *Thornhill* arrived at Bizerte on 1 June and returned to New York on the 29th with a westbound convoy. Late in July, the destroyer escort screened another convoy to North Africa and returned to New York on 7 September 1944.

During the next eight months, *Thornhill* made four more escort voyages to England and France. On 9 June 1945, she and the other ships of Escort Division (CortDiv) 55 got underway for Guantanamo Bay and proceeded thence through the Panama Canal to the west coast of the United States. The division arrived at San Diego on 9 July. CortDiv 55 stood out to sea five days later and arrived at Pearl Harbor on the 19th to join the Destroyer Force, Pacific Fleet.

Thornhill and her division departed with SS *Empress of Australia* on 8 August, bound for the Marshalls, and reached Eniwetok the day after hostilities with Japan ceased. She remained in the Marshalls until 7 December when she and *Wingfield* (DE–194) headed back toward Hawaii. The two ships arrived at Pearl Harbor on 13 December 1945, and *Thornhill* served as a weather patrol ship there during January 1946. The destroyer escort sailed for home on 2 February and, after calling at San Diego, arrived at the Boston Navy Yard on 7 March. The next week she got underway for Green Cove Springs, Fla., to be inactivated. She was decommissioned on 17 June 1946 and assigned to the Atlantic Reserve Fleet.

Thornhill was transferred to Italy under the Military Assistance Program on 10 January 1951 and was struck from the Navy list on 26 March that same year. She serves the Italian Navy as *Aldebaran* (F–590).

Thornton

James Shepard Thornton—born on 25 February 1826 at Merrimack, N.H.—was appointed midshipman in the United States Navy on 15 January 1841 and served in the sloop-of-war *John Adams* during the Mexican War. The outbreak of the Civil War found him serving on the Atlantic coast in brig *Brainbridge*. He later became executive officer in Farragut's flagship *Hartford* and was serving in her when she and other ships of the West Gulf Blockading Squadron dashed past Forts St. Philip and Jackson on 24 April 1862 to capture New Orleans. He continued to serve in *Hartford*, with great credit, during the engagement with the Confederate ram *Arkansas*, during duels with the Vicksburg batteries, and in other operations on the Mississippi River.

In August 1862, he assumed command of gunboat *Winona* which was stationed with the Union blockading force off Mobile Bay, Ala. On 13 September, the gunboat shelled and destroyed a Confederate steamer lying under the protection of the guns of Fort Gaines. He subsequently became executive officer of *Kearsarge* and received a vote of thanks from Congress for gallantry during the successful engagement with the Confederate raider *Alabama* off Cherbourg, France, on 20 June 1864.

After the Civil War, he commanded *Kearsarge* on the South Pacific Station. Thornton was commissioned captain on 24 May 1872. Captain Thornton died at Germantown, Pa., almost three years later on 14 May 1875.

I

(Torpedo Boat No. 33: dp. 269 (f.); l. 175'0'' (wl.); b. 17'6''; dr. 5'2''; s. 27.57 k. (tl.); cpl. 28; a. 3 1-pdrs. rf., 3 18'' tt.; cl. *Blakeley*)

The first *Thornton* (Torpedo Boat No. 33) was laid down on 16 March 1899 at Richmond, Va., by the William R. Trigg Co.; lanched on 15 May 1900; sponsored by Miss Mary Thornton Davis; and commissioned on 9 June 1902, Ens. Samuel Brown Thomas in command.

Thornton participated in the summer maneuvers of the North Atlantic Fleet off the eastern coast of the United States. In November and December, the torpedo boat moved south to the West Indies for combined winter maneuvers. On 28 January 1903, she returned to Norfolk, and she was assigned to the Reserve Torpedo Flotilla on 16 February.

On 19 June 1905, *Thornton* was placed back in full commission; and, the following month, she made a brief visit to Annapolis, Md. On 21 July, she was again decommissioned and entered the Norfolk Navy Yard. Three months later, the torpedo boat rejoined the Reserve Torpedo Flotilla at Norfolk. Recommissioned on 19 June 1907, she was assigned to the 3d Torpedo Flotilla; and, over the next several years, she operated along the eastern seaboard and cruised the Gulf of Mexico. In the fall of 1909, she joined several other torpedo boats in ascending the Mississippi River as far as St. Louis. The following December, she entered Charleston, S.C., and, on the 22d, was decommissioned and assigned to the Reserve Torpedo Flotilla at Charleston.

Though the Reserve Torpedo Flotilla was abolished in 1914, *Thornton* remained inactive at Charleston until 1917. She was in reserve until 14 March 1914 when the Reserve Torpedo Flotilla was disbanded. After that, she was placed in commission, in ordinary, at the Charleston Navy Yard until 1917.

With America's entry into World War I, *Thornton* was placed back in full commission on 7 April 1917. She was converted to a minesweeper and, on 22 May, departed Charleston for Norfolk. Attached to the 5th Naval District, she performed minesweeping operations in Hampton Roads and off Cape Henry. On 8 April 1918, she collided with *Joseph F. Bellows* (SP–323) in Hampton Roads. Because of exsensive damage, *Thornton* was towed to the Norfolk Navy Yard where she was decommissioned on 11 May 1918. On 1 August 1918, she was redesignated *Coastal Torpedo Vessel* No. 16. A board of inspection and survey examined her in March 1919 and recommended that she be sold. On 12 May 1919, her name was struck from the Navy list. Fifteen months later, near the end of August 1920, she was sold to the Southern Oil & Transport Corp., of New York City.

II

DD–270: dp. 1,215 (n.); l. 314'4½''; b. 30'11½''; dr. 9'9¾'' (aft); s. 34.72 k. (tl.); cpl. 122; a. 4 4'', 1 3'', 12 21'' tt.; cl. *Clemson*)

The second *Thornton* (DD–270) was laid down on June 1918 at Squantum, Mass., by the Bethlehem Shipbuilding Corp.; launched on 2 March 1919; sponsored by Miss Marcia Thornton Davis; and placed in commission at Boston on 15 July 1919, Comdr. A. G. Stirling in command.

On 26 August, *Thornton* sailed for Europe. Following a port call in the Azores, the destroyer reached the Strait of Gibraltar on 15 September. For the remainder of 1919, she visited a number of ports, both in the Mediterranean and along the Atlantic coast of Europe.

The ship returned to Boston on 12 February 1920 and remained there until 27 March, when she weighed anchor for the Pacific. After calls at several ports on the Gulf of Mexico, the destroyer transited the Panama Canal on 30 April. She then steamed slowly up the western coast of Mexico, stopping along the way at Salina Cruz, Manzanillo and Guaymas to show the flag. On 27 May, *Thornton* reached San Diego and, for the next two years, conducted operations along the California coast. On 24 May 1922, *Thornton* was placed out of commission and laid up at the Destroyer Base, San Diego.

Thornton remained in reserve throughout the 1920's and 1930's. On 25 May 1940, she was ordered recommissioned for conversion to a seaplane tender. Accordingly, she was recommissioned, in ordinary, on 24 June 1940 and moved to the San Francisco yard of the Bethlehem Steel Co. for conversion. On 2 August 1940, *Thornton* was officially redesignated a seaplane tender (destroyer), AVD–11. Her alterations were completed early in 1941, and she was placed in full commission on 5 March 1941, Lt. Comdr. Wendell F. Kline in command. On 8 April, she reported for duty to Commander-in-Chief, Pacific Fleet, at San Pedro. Ten days later, the seaplane tender arrived in Pearl Harbor, and she operated in the Hawaiian Islands until August 1942. During her 16 months in the islands, she made frequent voyages to Midway, Wake, Palmyra and other outlying islands of the 14th Naval District.

On the morning of 7 December 1941, she was moored at the Submarine Base at Pearl Harbor. Her action report for that day states that the Japanese opened their attack on Pearl Harbor at 0756 and that *Thornton*'s crew, led by four reserve ensigns, was at action stations two minutes later. They fought back with every available weapon—four .50-cal. machineguns, three Lewis guns, three Browning automatic rifles, and twelve .30-cal., bolt-action Springfields. The combined fire of *Thornton* and *Hulbert* (AVP–6) accounted for at least one Japanese torpedo bomber and discouraged two more from making a run on *Neosho* (AO–23) as the oiler changed berths during the second dive-bombing attack between 0910 and 0917. *Thornton* fought hard and bravely during the attack on Pearl Harbor and was fortunate enough to suffer no casualties.

Following the Pearl Harbor attack, she was stationed at French Frigate Shoals with *Ballard* (AVD–10) as aircraft rescue ships for the planes engaged in the expanded air searches. After the victory at Midway, she resumed her runs between the outlying islands of the 14th Naval District—though the Japanese occupation had removed Wake Island from her itinerary—until August 1942. On the 25th, *Thornton* steamed out of Pearl Harbor, headed north, and arrived at Kodiak, Alaska, on the 30th. For the next two months, the seaplane tender cruised the icy Alaskan seas as a part of Task Force 8. She visited Kodiak, Attu, and Chernofski before departing Kodiak for Pearl Harbor on 21 October.

Thornton stopped at Pearl Harbor from 30 October to 10 November, then headed for duty in the South Pacific. After short periods of duty at Suva in the Fiji Islands, Funafuti in the Ellice Islands, and at Vanikoro in the Santa Cruz Islands, she moved to Espiritu Santo in the New Hebrides, arriving on 18 July 1943. The seaplane tender remained at Espiritu Santo until 11 November, when she put to sea for Guadalcanal in the Solomons. Between 13 and 15 November, she made a round-trip run between Guadalcanal and Espiritu Santo to escort *Chandeleur* (AV–10) from the latter to the former.

Following duty in the Solomons and a stop at Pearl Harbor from 5 to 8 February, *Thornton* returned to the west coast at Mare Island on 17 February 1944. She remained on the west coast for the next 10 months conducting normal operations and undergoing extensive repairs. On 3 December 1944, the warship departed San Pedro to return to the western Pacific.

From mid-December 1944 until late February 1945, *Thornton* was at Pearl Harbor. On the 22d, she got underway for operations to prepare for the assault on Okinawa. She stopped at Eniwetok early in March, then moved on to Ulithi, the staging area for Okinawa.

On 5 April 1945, while operating in the Ryukyus as part of the Search and Reconnaissance Group of the Southern Attack Force, *Thornton* collided with *Ashtabula* (AO–51) and *Escalante* (AO–71). Her starboard side was severely damaged and open to the sea. On 14 April, she was towed into Kerama Retto. On the 29th, a board of inspection and survey recommended that *Thornton* be decommissioned, beached, stripped of all useful materiel as needed, and then abandoned. She was beached and decommissioned on 2 May 1945. Her name was struck from the Navy list on 13 August 1945. In July 1957, *Thornton*'s abandoned hulk was donated to the government of the Ryukyu Islands.

Thornton earned three battle stars for World War II service.

Thorson, Private John F., see *Private John F. Thorson.*

Thrasher

Any of a number of thrushlike birds which are known as singers and mimics.

Prior to being launched, *Thrasher* (Submarine No. 26) was renamed *G–4* (*q.v.*) on 17 November 1911.

I

(MB: l. 45'; b. 9'5''; dr. 4'6'' (forward); s. 9½ mph.; cpl. 7; a. 1 Lewis mg.)

Petrel (SP–546)—a motorboat built by Murray & Tregurtha at South Boston, Mass.—was acquired from Mr. Edgar Pierce on 14 May 1917; and placed in commission at Boston on 22 May 1917.

Petrel served on section patrol in the 1st Naval District through her entire naval career, operating from the Boston section base. On 2 August 1918, she was renamed *Thrasher*, to avoid confusion with Navy gunboat *PG–2* which also carried the name *Petrel*. Eventually, however, she lost that name also and went only by her number, *SP–546*. Unfortunately, no date for that change is available in the records, though the *Ships Data U.S. Naval Vessels*, issued on 1 November 1918, lists her simply as *SP–546* and shows both former names, *Thrasher* and *Petrel*. She served the Navy until 11 June 1919 when her name was struck from the Navy list. On 2 September 1919, she was sold to Mr. Henry X. Kelley of Boston, Mass.

II

(MSC–203: dp. 320 (lt.); l. 144'; b. 28'; dr. 9'; s. 13 k. cpl. 39; a. 2 20mm.; cl. *Redwing*)

The second *Thrasher* (MSC–203) was laid down as AMS–203 on 1 April 1954 at Tampa, Fla., by the Tampa Marine Co.; launched on 6 October 1954; sponsored by Mrs. Fred T. Henke; redesignated MSC–203 on February 1955; and commissioned on 16 August 1955, Lt. (jg.) Frank Mabbett McCraw, Jr., in command.

Two weeks later, *Thrasher* steamed for Charleston, her home port, to join Mine Force, Atlantic Fleet. But for a visit to Havana, Cuba, the wooden-hulled nonmagnetic coastal minesweeper spent the remainder of 1955 operating in South Carolina and Florida waters. She assumed duties as an active element of Mine Force, Atlantic, on the last day of the year; and, on New Year's Day 1956, her home port was changed to Yorktown, Va. The minesweeper's duties there included search and rescue missions for aircraft downed off the Virginia coast.

Assigned to the Experimental Mine Warfare School at Key West in 1957, the coastal minesweeper operated off the east coast and in the Caribbean until 7 February 1958 when she departed Key West and steamed via the Panama Canal and Manzanillo, Mexico, to the California coast, arriving at San Diego on the 28th. As

The coastal minesweeper *Thrasher* (MSC–203), with equipment on her main deck for sweeping moored, magnetic, and acoustic mines. Built of wood and nonmagnetic alloys, *Thrasher* and her contemporaries were improved versions of the wooden minecraft of World War II.

signed for a time to Scripps Institute of Oceanography, *Thrasher* surveyed ocean currents off Monterey, Calif., in March. That summer, she cooperated with Warner Brothers during the shooting of the film "Up Periscope," and then returned to her primary duty plying California's coastal waters as a minesweeper with the San Diego Harbor Defense Command. In the fall, she trained sailors of the Turkish Navy and later, when the Turkish Navy received a minesweeper from the United States under the Mutual Aid for Defense Program, continued to lend assistance during shakedown.

Early in 1959, *Thrasher* joined Fleet Training Group, San Diego, for underway exercises. In April, she moved north to Seattle to conduct tests on the new "MM–1" automatic degaussing system; then returned to southern California for annual minesweeping exercises conducted out of Long Beach. On 8 May 1959, *Thrasher* departed San Diego and steamed independently to Hawaii for additional tests of the new degaussing system which had been designed to compensate for changes in latitude and longitude. After successfully completing the tests, she returned to San Diego on 6 June and, later in the summer, provided assistance in channel conditioning to the harbor defense unit at San Francisco. In the fall, she acted as an observation ship for aerial minelaying operations conducted by Fleet Air Wing 14 off San Diego and conducted additional tests of the new degaussing system. In December 1959, *Thrasher* was transferred to the 12th Naval District and assigned a new home port of San Francisco for duty with that port's harbor defense unit.

She took up her new duties in January and, in February, acted as target ship for *Mero* (SS–378) despite heavy seas which rolled the minesweeper up to 50 degrees. After work on her degaussing system and installation of "Shoran" at the Hunter's Point Naval Shipyard, *Thrasher* participated in minesweeping exercises out of Long Beach, earning a letter of commendation from Commander Mine Force, Pacific Fleet, for her performance. Late in the fall, she helped to salvage and refloat *YW–91* which had run aground at Santa Rosa Island. In this operation, *Thrasher* earned another letter of commendation.

The minesweeper continued assignments off the west coast until she was decommissioned on 1 August 1961. Placed in service as a reserve training ship for the 12th Naval District, she operated in that capacity for the next 14 years, conducting weekend training cruises and occasional fortnight refresher training cruises for her selected reserve crew. During that time, she visited various California and Mexican ports. In the summers of 1966 and 1967, she joined *Ruff* (YMS–327) and *Cormorant* (MSC–122) to form naval reserve Mine Division 13 for exercises, including a month of operations in 1967 off the coasts of Washington and Canada. That same year, *Thrasher* increased her number of reserve crews from one to two and stepped up her training activities correspondingly. In 1973, she made another summer cruise to northern ports, calling at ports in Oregon, Washington, and British Columbia.

In March 1975, she made her last reserve training cruise, coducting minesweeping exercises in Monterey Bay before returning to San Francisco. Towed to the inactive ship facility at Mare Island on 1 May 1975, she was inactivated and her name struck from the Navy list on 1 July. Late in 1975, she was transferred to the Republic of Singapore; and, into 1976, she served in the Republic of Singapore's Navy as RSS *Mercury.*

Threadfin

Any of a family of fishes related to the mullets and distinguished by filamentous rays on the lower part of the pectoral fin.

(SS–410: dp. 1,525 (surf.), 2,415 (subm.); l. 311'8"; b. 27'3"; dr. 15'3" (mean); s. 20.25 k. (surf.), 8.75 k. (subm.); cpl. 81; a. 10 21" tt., 1 5", 1 40mm., 1 20mm., 2 .50-cal. mg.; cl. *Balao*)

Threadfin (SS–410) was laid down on 18 March 1944 at the Portsmouth (N.H.) Navy Yard; launched on 26 June 1944; sponsored by Mrs. Frank G. Fox; and commissioned on 30 August 1944, Comdr. John J. Foote in command.

Training and trials out of Portsmouth followed her final completion late in September. After transiting the Panama Canal in mid-November, the submarine reached Pearl Harbor early in December and conducted intensive training in preparation for her first war patrol. She stood out of Pearl Harbor on Christmas Day. Early in January 1945, she reached her assigned patrol area in the waters just south of Kyushu. There, she spent 30 of her 54 days at sea. She encountered numerous enemy aircraft, patrol craft, and fishing vessels, but only six targets worthy of a torpedo.

On 30 January, *Threadfin* sighted a large enemy patrol craft, but prudently allowed her to pass unmolested in the hope of drawing a bead on any merchant vessels for which she might be running interference. Presently, a 2,000-ton coastal freighter—escorted by two patrol vessels and a plane—crossed her path. *Threadfin* fired a spread of six torpedoes from a range of about 2,900 yards. At least one of them struck home, obscuring the target in smoke and steam. The cargoman probably sank; but *Threadfin* could not verify that result visually because the escorts drove her deep with a persistent, though ineffective, depth charge attack.

Two days later, the submarine encountered a Japanese *RO–60*-class submarine. However, the enemy's course changes kept *Threadfin* from gaining an advantageous attack setup; and the Japanese "pig-boat" disappeared in the distance. *Threadfin* next happened upon two freighters escorted by three patrol craft. This time, the small convoy's position close inshore defied the American submarine's efforts to attack.

The following day, she mistook another patrol vessel for a cargo ship and discovered her mistake in just enough time to make a deep dive to safety. That escapade also robbed her of a chance at a small convoy consisting of two small cargomen and two escorts. She sighted the convoy later when she returned to periscope depth; but, by then, the ships had passed out of range. A week later, she launched six torpedoes at a minesweeper 2,500 yards distant. In spite of an excellent fire-control solution, all six missed. They apparently ran too deeply. Three days later, she concluded a somewhat discouraging, but still successful, first war patrol at Midway Island.

Following a month there for refit and training, *Threadfin* embarked upon her second war patrol on 14 March. She initially joined a coordinated attack group composed of herself, *Sea Dog* (SS–401), and *Trigger* (SS–237). During her five-day tour with that wolf pack, *Threadfin* made two attacks on enemy shipping. On the afternoon of 28 March, she came across two Japanese destroyer escort-type warships and apparently dispatched one with a single hit from a spread of six torpedoes. The stricken warship's screws stopped while her colleague's depth charge attack deprived *Threadfin* of definite knowledge of the ultimate result. That evening, the submarine tangled with a convoy composed of two small trawlers and four luggers. During the ensuing surface gun engagement, the submarine inflicted serious damage on two of the luggers, moderate damage on the trawlers, and minor damage on the remaining pair of luggers. Though disconcerting, the Japanese return fire proved ineffectual.

On 31 March, that group was dissolved, and *Threadfin* received orders to join *Hackleback* (SS–295) and *Silversides* (SS–236) near Bungo Suido, the primary entrance to the Japanese Inland Sea which separates Honshu from Kyushu and Shikoku. The new attack group's primary assignment was to guard against an undetected sortie of the remainder of Japan's fleet during the Allied assault on Okinawa. On the evening of 6 April, *Threadfin* made radar contact with what later proved to be an enemy task force built around Japan's super battleship, *Yamato*. Passing up a tempting opportunity in order to carry out her prime directive, *Threadfin* flashed the warning to 5th Fleet headquarters afloat off Okinawa.

Completing that phase of her mission, the submarine tried desperately to regain attack position on the force, but its speed denied her a second chance. On the whole, however, her radio was probably more valuable than her torpedoes would have been. Her timely warning enabled the planes of Task Force 58 to ambush and sink *Yamato* and to destroy most of her consorts as well.

A second mission of the submarine consisted of lifeguard duty to rescue downed American airmen. Her first war patrol afforded her no opportunity to pursue such a humane mission; but, near the end of the second, she rescued a half-drowned P–51 pilot. Though he had swallowed large quantities of water, artificial respiration soon brought him around. That proved to be the last noteworthy event of the patrol; and, after a refueling stop at Midway on 30 April, *Threadfin* concluded her second war patrol at Pearl Harbor on 4 May.

At Pearl Harbor, she underwent refit followed by a brief four-day training period before departing on her third and final war patrol. She stopped briefly at Guam for voyage repairs; then continued on to her assigned area in the Yellow and East China Seas. She closed her first victim, a three-masted schooner, to inspect her and determine her nationality. Finding her to be enemy-operated and worthy of attack, the submarine opened up with her 5-inch deck gun. Fifteen hits later, the schooner vanished beneath the waves. *Threadfin* rescued nine crewmen from the schooner and learned that her victim had been bound for Dairen, laden with coal. The next day, the submarine encountered a freighter sunk in shallow water and surrounded by small boats, apparently conducting some variety of salvage operations. She fired a single torpedo which caused the wreck to settle a further 10 feet and which she hoped would suspend the suspected salvage operations. Closer inspection, however, indicated that the boats were fishing, not conducting salvage operations.

Soon thereafter, *Threadfin* sighted a four-masted cargo schooner and sank her in a gun attack. The following afternoon, her deck gun accounted for another cargo schooner. On the 19th, she stopped a group of five two-masted cargo junks for inspection but allowed them to continue their voyage after identifying them as friendly Chinese. The next night, she made a surface radar torpedo attack on an enemy ship shrouded by heavy fog. She loosed a spread of five torpedoes, of which two found their mark. The target sank within five minutes without ever being visually sighted from *Threadfin*. The submarine concluded her offensive operations near the Strait of Tsushima. After a day of submerged patrolling without sighting a worthwhile target, she received word that night that *Sea Robin* (SS–407) had come upon a patrol craft heading north and four small cargomen heading south. While *Sea Robin* took on the patrol craft, *Threadfin* hit the small convoy. During the ensuing night gun action, she sank two of the four tiny merchantmen and forced the other two into *Sea Robin*'s path. The two American submarines dispatched all four to "Davy Jones Locker." On the return trip from her final war patrol, *Threadfin* rescued three survivors from a downed American flying boat and took them to Guam where she arrived on 27 July.

From 27 July to 12 August, the submarine refitted at Guam in preparation for her fourth war patrol, but that patrol never occurred. While she conducted post-refit training, the Japanese capitulation ended hostilities. On 18 August, she got underway from Guam to return to the United States. She transited the Panama

Canal on 16 September and reported for duty with the Atlantic Fleet. Six days later, she tied up at the naval base at Staten Island, N.Y.

The balance of *Threadfin*'s 28-year career proved to be routine in nature. Initially, she operated out of New London, Conn., serving as a training platform for the officers and men learning the ropes at the Submarine School. That duty apparently lasted until December 1952, at which time the submarine was decommissioned to enter the Portsmouth (N.H.) Naval Shipyard for an extended conversion overhaul.

Over the next eight months, *Threadfin* received extensive modifications in an effort to make her more effective in underwater operations—more truly a submarine than simply a submersible. When she emerged from the shipyard the following summer, her hull had been streamlined and her sail modified. In addition, she lost one of her four diesel engines to make room for auxiliary equipment displaced by an expanded sonar facility. Finally, her underwater performance was boosted by the installation of two "greater capacity" batteries—they actually produced the same power as the old style batteries but in a smaller, lighter physical plant—and a snorkel permitted extended submerged cruising. At the completion of her Guppy IA conversion, *Threadfin* was recommissioned at Portsmouth on 7 August 1953, Lt. Comdr. Daniel G. Bailey in command. In October, she conducted her post-conversion shakedown cruise and, early the following month, reported for duty as a unit of Submarine Squadron 4 at Key West, Fla.

Over the remaining 19 years of her career, *Threadfin* operated off the east coast. She participated in several exercises each year and frequently conducted summer training cruises for Naval Academy and NROTC midshipmen. Though based in Key West, she made visits to Gulf ports such as New Orleans and often ventured north to New London, Conn. In October 1962, she participated in President Kennedy's quarantine of Cuba during the missile crisis. The following summer, the submarine made what, on the basis of sparse records, appears to be her only post-war overseas deployment with the 6th Fleet in the Mediterranean Sea.

After successive years of routine operations in the Caribbean and Atlantic, *Threadfin* was placed out of commission on 18 August 1972 and transferred to Turkey that same day. She served in the Turkish Navy on loan, as *Birinci İnönü* (S–346) until the following summer. On 1 August 1973, her name was struck from the Navy list. Two weeks later, she was returned to the United States Navy and concurrently sold to Turkey. As of November 1977, she continued to serve actively in the Turkish Navy as *Birinci İnönü*.

Threadfin was awarded three battle stars for World War II service.

Threat

(AM–124: dp. 890; l. 221'2''; b. 32'2''; dr. 10'9''; s. 18. k.; cpl. 105; a. 2 3'', 4 20mm., 2 .30-cal. mg., 2 dct. 4 dcp.; cl. *Auk*)

Threat (AM–124) was laid down on 15 December 1941 at Savannah, Ga., by the Savannah Machine and Foundry Co.; launched on 15 August 1942; sponsored by Mrs. Allan M. Robinson; and commissioned on 1 March 1943, Comdr. Allan M. Robinson, USNR, in command.

In March and April of 1943 *Threat* completed shakedown and exercises off the east coast as she prepared for duty as a convoy escort on the Eastern Sea Frontier. During April, the minesweeper escorted convoys along the Atlantic coast; and, on 11 May, she got underway for her first transatlantic voyage. The convoy arrived at Casablanca on 1 June 1943; and, on 9 June, *Threat* departed North Africa with a convoy bound for New York. Throughout 1943, she continued escort duties in the Atlantic, completing three voyages to North Africa and numerous convoy shuttles along the Eastern Sea Frontier and into the Caribbean.

Early in 1944, *Threat* helped to protect a convoy as it steamed via the Azores to the British Isles. After this mission, *Threat* remained in the Falmouth area for repair. In April and May, she operated out of Batten Bay and conducted exercises with ships of the British Royal Navy in preparation for Operation "Overlord," the invasion of Europe.

On 2 June 1944, the ship was sealed and briefing commenced. On 5 June 1944, *Threat* departed Tor Bay with a minesweeper unit to take part in Operation "Neptune," the assault phase of "Overlord." *Threat* helped clear the channels to be used by fire support vessels in the Baie de la Seine. In the days which followed, *Threat* witnessed the sinking by mines of *Glennon* (DD–620), *Tide* (AM–124), and *Rich* (DE–695). On 8 June, while aiding the disabled *Rich*, *Threat* narrowly missed becoming the victim of a mine which sank the destroyer escort off Cardonet Bank.

A shore battery fired on *Threat* as she was running acoustic and magnetic sweeps off Cherbourg on 9 June. The doughty sweeper returned the fire with her 3-inch gun, silencing two shore gun employments and blowing up a small ammunition dump. Commander, Mine Squadron 7, commended *Threat* for her performance that day and gave special praise to the smart ship-handling operations entailed. Throughout June, *Threat* continued to sweep waters off the French coast, occasionally drawing fire from German shore batteries but escaping unscathed. While she swept channels for fire support ships in preparation for the bombardment of Cherbourg, she was subjected to heavy fire from enemy shore emplacements. In July, *Threat* conducted daily sweeps of the Baie de la Seine, necessitated by the delayed action and time release settings of mines left by the German forces.

After replenishment at Plymouth late in July, *Threat* returned to the Mediterranean. In August, she escorted convoys between Gibraltar and North Africa before proceeding to Corsica where she cleared shipping channels despite the activity of enemy aircraft. On 19 August, she got underway for assault areas on the southern coast of France. Operating out of St. Tropez and the Golfe de Fos, *Threat* conducted support activities for Operation "Anvil."

In September, *Threat* continued sweeps, patrols, and minewatching missions off the southern coast of France. Following a quick run to Naples for provisions and fuel, she returned to the French coast to supply YMS's and to continue minesweeping. Early in October, *Threat* escorted a convoy to Bizerte before engaging in visual sweeps for mines off the German-held Italian coast. While pursuing her minesweeping duties, *Threat* exchanged gunfire with enemy shore batteries on more than one occasion before returning to French waters late in October.

Throughout November, *Threat* operated off France's southern coast. She cleared fire support channels and patrolled for floating mines in the area between Cannes and San Remo, before departing Cannes on 27 November 1944 for provisioning and ammunition replenishment at Bizerte.

The sweeper continued operations in the western Mediterranean in December. Early in the month, she swept mines off Cagliari, Sardinia; and, on 28 December, she departed Oran, escorting TG 81.14 bound for American ports. On 17 January 1945, she arrived at Norfolk after nearly a year of action in European waters.

Threat remained on the east coast for major overhaul and the installation of SA-2 radar until 26 April when she departed Miami and steamed, via the Canal Zone and San Diego, for Hawaii. She arrived at Pearl Harbor on 26 May 1945 and commenced gunnery and minesweeping exercises in preparation for her new assignment in the Pacific. On 11 June, she got underway for Ulithi where she rendezvoused with a convoy en route to Okinawa.

After her arrival at Buckner Bay on 6 July, *Threat*

soon joined sweeping operations in the China Sea. She continued these duties after peace came in August and, in September, took part in the clearing of heavily mined Tsugaru Strait in preparation for the naval occupation of Ominato Bay. Through October and November, *Threat* continued sweeps in the East China Sea operating out of Honshu and Sasebo. In December, she plied the waters off Shanghai before setting course for San Diego and inactivation.

Threat was decommissioned on 31 May 1946, reclassified as a steel-hulled fleet minesweeper (MSF–124) on 7 February 1955, and struck from the Navy list on 1 July 1972.

Threat received three battle stars for World War II service.

Thresher

A class of shark which is harmless to man and easily recognizable because its tail is longer than the combined length of body and head.

I

(SS–200: dp. 1,475 (surf), 2,370 (subm.); l. 207'2''; b. 27'3'; s. 20 k. (surf.), 8.75 k. (subm.); cpl. 59; a. 10 21'' tt., 1 3'', 1 .30-cal. mg., 1 .50-cal. mg.; cl. *Tambor*)

The first *Thresher* (SS–200) was laid down on 27 April 1939 at Groton, Conn., by the Electric Boat Co.; launched on 27 March 1940; sponsored by Mrs. Claud Jones; and commissioned on 21 August 1940, Lt. Comdr. William L. Anderson in command.

Following training and sea trials, *Thresher* got underway from New London, Conn., on 25 October for engineering trials in Gravesend Bay, N.Y., and shakedown off the Dry Tortugas.

She operated along the east coast through the end of 1940 and into 1941. During a call at Annapolis, Md., *Thresher* hosted Rear Admiral Russell Willson as a guest on 31 April before she got underway the following day for the Caribbean. After emerging on the Pacific side of the Panama Canal on 9 May and stopping at San Diego from the 17th through the 21st, *Thresher* arrived at Pearl Harbor on 31 May. She operated out of the Hawaiian Islands into the fall of 1941, as tensions rose in the Far East and the United States prepared for war in both oceans.

Thresher and sister-ship *Tautog* (SS–198) departed the submarine base at Pearl Harbor on 31 October bound for a simulated war patrol north of Midway atoll. They both carried fully-armed torpedo warheads. *Tautog* returned first; and, on 7 December, *Thresher* neared the Hawaiian Islands to end her part of the cruise. Escorted by *Litchfield* (DD–336) through Hawaiian waters lest she be mistaken for a Japanese submarine, *Thresher* received word at 0810 that Pearl Harbor was under attack by Japanese aircraft.

Litchfield promptly set off to join American light forces departing from the harbor, leaving *Thresher* alone to conduct her first real war patrol. However, the destroyer was ordered back to escort the submarine; radio contact between the two ships was established; and a rendezvous arranged.

At the pre-appointed time, *Thesher* poked up her periscope to have a look, and noticed a destroyer— similar to *Litchfield*—approaching, bows-on. The submarine's commander and a signalman felt certain that the oncoming ship was *Litchfield*. Nevertheless, instead of a warm reception from friends, she got a hot reception from the destroyer's forward gunners, who opened fire on the submarine as soon as her black conning tower broke the surface.

Quickly reappraising the situation, *Thresher* immediately went deep to avoid the attentions of "friendly forces." She again tried to enter the harbor on the 8th, but was driven off by depth-bombs from a patrol plane, before *Thornton* (AVD–11) finally arrived to provide safe-conduct for the submarine at midday on the 8th.

Departing Pearl Harbor on 30 December, *Thresher* headed for the Marshalls and Marianas. Reconnoitering Majuro, Arno, and Mili atolls from 9 to 13 January 1942, the submarine shifted to waters off Japanese-held Guam in the early morning darkness of 4 February. A little before daybreak, she sighted a small freighter seven miles north of Agana Harbor and closed for the attack. She loosed a three-torpedo spread, holing the ship and sending her down by the bow and dead in the water. *Thresher* then fired another spread of torpedoes, but all mised due to the target angle. When the submarine returned to the scene one-half hour later, the once-wallowing freighter was no longer in sight; and *Thresher* felt that she had scored a "kill." Her claim, however, was not substantiated in postwar accounting.

For the next six days, *Thresher* reconnoitered the seas between Tinian and Rota in the Marianas, having departed the Guam area to evade possible Japanese antisubmarine measures. She found nothing there and set a course for home. While en route, an overzealous Navy plane attacked the ship on 24 February but, fortunately, did not damage the submarine which returned safely to Pearl Harbor on the 26th.

The newly refitted fleet boat then departed Pearl Harbor on 23 March for waters near the Japanese home islands. As a subsidiary mission on this patrol, *Thresher* was to gather meteorological data in the waters off Honshu and report it to Pearl Harbor. This information was needed by Vice Admiral Halsey's task force—centered around aircraft carriers *Enterprise* (CV–6) and *Hornet* (CV–8)—then approaching the Japanese home islands. Embarked in *Hornet* were 16 Army B–25 medium bombers, under the command of Lt. Col. James H. Doolittle, which would take off at sea and fly to Japan for strikes on Tokyo on 18 April. Conducting routine exercises and drills while en route, *Thresher* sighted a large Japanese freighter on the morning of 10 April. She closed for the attack and launched a three-torpedo spread. All three missed, and the freighter escaped in the mist. When the target emerged from the murk, her course precluded a further attack; and the frustrated submarine proceeded on her way.

She sighted a second target later that day, and her hunting was better this time around. One torpedo broke the back of the 3,000-ton freighter *Sado Maru* off Yokohama harbor, sending her beneath the waves in three minutes. Enemy antisubmarine craft picked up *Thresher* within 30 minutes of the sinking, and the submarine began a game of hide-and-seek. During one depth-charge attack, the boat lost depth control and began plunging towards unexplored depths before her bow was trimmed, and she regained control.

On the 13th, while running on the surface to recharge her batteries, *Thresher* took a high wave over her conning tower. Water cascaded down the open conning tower hatch and rushed into the ship, grounding many electrical circuits. For a short time, there was a decided danger that chlorine gas would be released to endanger the crew, but quick thinking and damage control action prevented that development. Eventually, all short circuits were repaired; and the boat pumped out.

The next day, *Thresher* departed her assigned patrol area and turned her attention to gathering meteorological data. *Thresher* conducted periscope patrols in the advance screen of Halsey's task force, searching for any enemy craft that could warn the Japanese homeland. She was detached from this duty on the 16th and, after evading two Japanese patrol planes, returned home to Pearl Harbor on the 29th.

Commencing her fourth war patrol on 26 June, *Thresher* headed for waters between the Palaus and the Marshalls. She approached a tanker off Enijun Pass on 6 July and commenced an attack. One torpedo struck home near the stern, and *Thresher* felt a muffled explosion. Large amounts of smoke boiled into the sky from the stricken tanker's stern. Soon, Japanese aircraft arrived on the scene and assisted the two surface escorts during an ensuing three-hour depth bomb counterattack. The submarine then resumed her search for "targets of opportunity."

Midway between Kwajelein and Wotje atolls, *Thresher* sighted the 4,836-ton motor torpedo boat tender *Shinsho Maru*. Two torpedo hits caused tremendous explosions to shake the area, and *Shinsho Maru* sank beneath the waves. The submarine then withdrew to await expected Japanese countermeasures. Within the hour, two depth charges shook the ship, and 10 minutes later, a banging and clanking alerted *Thresher* to the fact that the Japanese were apparently bringing a large grapnel into play in an attempt to capture the submarine.

Thresher fought for her life. After applying full right rudder, she made a 10 minute, high-speed run which shook her free from the giant hook. Then, as a depth charge exploded near her conning tower, the boat went into deeper water. With a bending and twisting turn, the submarine left the enemy behind, with some 30-odd depth charges exploding in her wake. Shaken but not seriously damaged, *Thresher* made minor repairs as she headed for Truk to reconnoiter the passes leading into this enemy naval bastion.

Missing a freighter with torpedoes on the night of 20 July, *Thresher* surfaced in a rain squall before daybreak on the 21st. The boat's sonar picked up the sound of screws, close and closing. Soon an enemy patrol craft came into view, approaching on a collision course. Surprisingly, the Japanese chose not to ram, but instead put over his helm hard right, and came to a parallel course some 50 yards away. With the two antagonists perhaps mutually astonished to find each other in the area, *Thresher* "pulled the plug" to dive deep, while the enemy's guns fired close but ineffective salvoes into the water ahead of the disappearing submarine.

After escaping by silent-running to the Palaus, *Thresher* tangled with an enemy "Q"-ship off Ambon in the former Netherlands East Indies. The two torpedoes that she fired at the enemy failed to detonate, and the "Q"-ship subjected *Thresher* to an eight-charge barrage before giving up the attack. Since she had been reassigned to the Southwest Pacific Submarine Forces, *Thresher* sailed for Australian waters and terminated her fourth war patrol at Fremantle on 15 August.

Following refitting, *Thresher* loaded mines and departed Fremantle on 15 September, bound for the Gulf of Siam. She fired torpedoes at two freighters north of Lombok Strait on 19 September but was unable to determine the results of her attacks. On the night of the 25th, luck again failed to smile on the submarine as a single torpedo streaked beneath a large, high-speed target in the Sulu Sea.

Thresher later surfaced at 2300 and proceeded on a course which took her north to Pearl Bank. There, in the northernmost reaches of the Gulf of Siam, she made one of the first mine plants by a submarine in the Pacific war. These strategic "plants" by *Thresher* and her sisters, in subsequent patrols, covered Japanese shipping lanes in areas in the southwest Pacific command previously unpatrolled by submarines. Later these minefields filled the gap between patrol zones along the coastal waters of Malaya, Siam, and Indochina, when many submarines were diverted to participate in the Solomons campaign.

While reconnoitering off Balikpapan, Borneo, and the Celebes coast, *Thresher* sighted a tanker aground on a reef off Kapoposang Island in the Java Sea. *Thresher* soon surfaced for a deck-gun attack and left the enemy ship with decks awash. The submarine then returned to her base at Fremantle on 12 November for refit.

Underway from Fremantle on 16 December, she arrived off Soerabaya, Java, on Christmas Day. She intercepted a convoy of freighters, escorted by two destroyers, several subchasers, and two aircraft. Slipping past the escorts, *Thresher* sent five torpedoes towards the leading three ships. Two successive explosions followed. Rising to periscope depth, the submarine observed the second ship in the column down by the bow, with her stern up in the air and her screws, still revolving, out of the water. A second ship lay dead in the water, enveloped in smoke. Escaping unscathed from this tangle with a coastal convoy, *Thresher* sighted an enemy aircraft carrier the next night, but was picked up by escorts and held at bay for more than an hour while the tempting task force faded into the night.

On the night of 29 December, *Thresher* made contact with the 3,000-ton freighter *Haichan Maru*. Just before midnight, she fired a spread of torpedoes at the cargoman; but all missed or ran too deep. Undaunted, *Thresher* waited for the moonrise and then surfaced to utilize her deck gun. Outmaneuvering the enemy, who tried to ram her, *Thresher* scored eight hits in succession amidships with her 5-inch main battery, stopping *Haichen Maru* dead in the water. A single torpedo finished the deck gun's work, and the enemy vessel slipped beneath the waves stern first in the predawn darkness of 30 December 1942.

Returning to Fremantle on 10 January 1943, the submarine got underway 15 days later for her seventh war patrol. At 1100 on 14 February, *Thresher* made contact with a Japanese *I-65*-class submarine to the east of Thwartway Island. She launched two torpedoes; but one turned out to be a dud, and the other exploded harmlessly on the ocean bottom. Turning north and firing deck guns, *Thresher*'s adversary soon disappeared from sight over the horizon.

Three days later, *Thresher* reconnoitered Flying Fish Cove, off Christmas Island, and photographed docks, houses, phosphate loading areas, and gun emplacements. Then, after proceeding to the Flores Sea, she intercepted a three-ship convoy escorted by two antisubmarine vessels on 21 February. Loosing a two-torpedo salvo, *Thresher* scored a hit with one on the stern of transport *Kuwayama Maru*. *Thresher* then evaded 13 depth charges before returning to periscope depth a little more than an hour later. She observed her target lying dead in the water while barges carried troops from the first transport to an undamaged sister. As escorts searched the waters nearby, *Thresher* closed and torpedoed the second transport as it was lying-to during the transfer of survivors from the first. Two loud explosions reverberated in the background as the submarine lived to avoid possible countermeasures.

The following day, *Thresher* returned to celebrate Washington's Birthday by finishing off *Kuwayama Maru*. The enemy ship, by then abandoned, jack-knifed into a "V" shape and sank within three minutes.

Thresher prowled for more game and came upon a tanker and a freighter on 2 March. A single torpedo hit on the 5,232-ton tanker *Toen Maru* sank the ship. The freighter, sighting the torpedo wakes, took evasive action to avoid being hit. Then, a nearby escort arrived on the scene and kept *Thresher* at bay while the second target escaped. The submarine subsequently concluded this patrol with her arrival at Fremantle on 10 March.

Her eighth war patrol (from 4 April to 23 May) was uneventful, but her ninth saw the submarine score another "kill." Off Balikpapan, Borneo, she sighted a three-ship convoy, escorted by a sole destroyer on the night of 30 June. After an unrewarding try with a trio of torpedoes, *Thresher* dodged the escort's depth charging attack and returned with the scent of a kill. Tracking with radar, *Thresher* set a tanker ablaze from stem to stern and scored hits on the 5,274-ton passenger-freighter *Yoneyama Maru*, which sent the hapless merchantman to the bottom of Makassar Strait.

Later, while heading for Tambu Bay on the morning of 5 July, *Thresher* tracked a tanker. Chasing her quarry along the Celebes coast, the submarine lurked nearby until the escort left the tanker. *Thresher* then closed, loosed three torpedoes, and scored one hit on the bow of the enemy vessel. However, this blow failed to stop the tanker, which fired her guns to keep *Thresher* at bay as she escaped at high speed.

Four days later, *Thesher* arrived off Catmon Point, Negros Island. Under cover of darkness, the submarine surfaced and delivered 500 pounds of stores and 40,000 rounds of ammunition to Filipino commandoes. In addition, the crew of the submarine contributed their personal rations of cigarettes, matches, soap, candy, and other personal gear to those brave men who were resisting Japanese occupation. Receiving intelligence documents in return, *Thresher* got underway for a resumption of her war patrol shortly before midnight on 9 July. *Thresher* soon departed the Philippines and sailed via Pearl Harbor and Midway to the west coast for a major overhaul at the Mare Island Navy Yard, Vallejo, Calif.

Newly refitted, *Thresher* departed the west coast on 8 October and arrived at Pearl Harbor one week later. She commenced her tenth war patrol as she departed the Hawaiian Islands on 1 November, bound for the waters north of the Carolines. Prowling north of Truk, *Thresher* commenced tracking a five-ship convoy on the morning of 12 November and slipped past two escorts shortly before midnight.

She fired a spread of three "fish" into *Muko Maru*, a 4,862-ton transport. Then, an attack on another *Maru* failed, as a second trio of torpedoes missed their mark. Escorting antisubmarine craft hunted in vain for the American attacker, dropping 20 depth charges in a harassing barrage.

Thresher's 11th war patrol took her to the South China Sea below Formosa. While cruising on the surface on 10 January 1944, *Thresher* sighted a pair of masts, low on the horizon, and quickly dove to avoid possible detection. Coming to periscope depth soon thereafter, she approached cautiously, keeping in mind that the ship may have been the advance screen of a convoy. The contact proved to be a 150-ton trawler. *Thresher* battle-surfaced, and her gun crews tumbled out on deck to man the guns. Opening the action from 6,000 yards, the submarine expended 45 5-inch shells; 1,000 rounds of .50-caliber machinegun fire; and 770 20-millimeter shells. Finally, the trawler went down. The submarine's war patrol report noted the tonic effect on the submersible's crew: "Not much damage was done to the Imperial war effort," the commanding officer, Comdr. Duncan C. MacMillan, commented, "but the action had a good psychological effect on the crew."

Thresher next set course for the Luzon Strait, between Batan Island and Luzon, in the Philippines. At 1143 on the 15th, *Thresher* came to the surface, only to spot a Japanese aircraft carrier and an escorting destroyer soon thereafter. The submarine "pulled the plug" and submerged but soon came up to periscope depth to observe the enemy destroyer rapidly approaching. With insufficient time to maneuver for a "down the throat" shot, *Thresher* went deep and rigged for silent running. The destroyer churned overhead and dropped four depth charges—none of which fell very close to the submarine. After remaining above the submarine for two hours, the escort finally turned away, leaving *Thresher* unscathed.

Again coming to periscope depth at 1700, *Thresher* soon sighted a four-ship convoy escorted by a sole subchaser at a range of 12,000 yards. Surfacing at 1911, *Thresher* began the chase, tracking the convoy by radar. The three leading targets steamed in column formation, roughly 500 to 800 yards apart, with the fourth some 6,000 yards astern. The escort was between the third and fourth merchantmen. Approaching from the westward, to take advantage of the moonrise, the submarine stalked her prey, whose behavior had been, to a point, predictable.

Previously zigzagging every 10 minutes, the convoy changed course at 2155—giving *Thresher* an excellent setup for her stern tubes. At 2207, the submarine let fly with four torpedoes from 1,800 yards at the lead ship, the 6,960-ton freighter *Tatsuno Maru*. *Thresher* observed two hits; and the vessel, with her bow in the air, was observed in a sinking condition.

Thresher next fired three bow tubes at the second target—later identified as 4,092-ton freighter *Toho Maru*. Three torpedoes struck the ship—evidently a tanker—and literally blew her to pieces. The cargo of oil burst into flames and illuminated the night as brightly as day.

The third ship commenced fire with deck guns on *Thresher*, passing down the port side at 800 yards away. With the submarine now illuminated by the burning oil, and with her after tubes spent, *Thresher's* historian noted later "that our usefulness for the moment was over." Accordingly, *Thresher* dove as bullets from the approaching escort splashed nearby.

Thresher counted some 20 explosions from depth charges before the patrol craft left an hour later. When she surfaced, *Thresher* observed that she was again all alone and then commenced patrolling along the Singapore-to-Japanese Empire trade route.

On 26 January, however, *Thresher* made radar contact with a small convoy. Closing her sighting, the submarine soon spotted two ships steaming along beneath the overcast night skies. At 0011, *Thresher* fired three torpedoes from her bow tubes at the 1,266-ton freighter *Kikuzuki Maru*, before the submarine bent on full-speed ahead and hard right rudder to clear the area. Her "fish" scored a bullseye, and the quarry disappeared within a minute.

A second spread of torpedoes, fired 35 seconds after the first, plowed into 2,205-ton *Kosei Maru*, which sank soon thereafter. A fourth target made off to the south at high speed, "spraying the ocean with 5-inch ammunition." Resuming the approach at 0020, *Thresher* doggedly tailed the Japanese freighter for four hours before reaching a favorable attack position. Firing her last torpedoes at 0446, *Thresher* began to build up speed and had just commenced a turn when one torpedo struck the enemy ship, causing a tremendous explosion.

The blast slowed the freighter, but its tremendous concussion stopped the submarine dead in the water. All four main engines overspeed trips were actuated; cork insulation flew; lights broke; clocks stopped; and water poured down the antenna trunk. By the time *Thresher* regained battle readiness, the enemy was too far away to encourage further pursuit.

Well within the range of shore-based aircraft, *Thresher* quit the chase. Escorts, alerted to the fact that an American submarine was prowling in the vicinity, arrived on the scene and conducted a three-hour long, but futile, depth-charging. On the 28th and 29th, *Thresher* patrolled the Formosa-to-Palau shipping route, in the area of the Luzon Strait, before returning via Midway to Pearl Harbor where she arrived on 18 February. There, Lt. Comdr. MacMillan was awarded the Navy Cross for his aggressive action during the patrol.

Thresher went to sea on 18 March, departing Pearl Harbor for the central Carolines. She remained on air-sea rescue station during American carrier strikes on Truk, bombarded Oroluk Atoll on 11 April, and photographed islands in that group. The submarine played "hide and seek" with numerous enemy aircraft and witnessed several American bombing raids on Truk. She sighted only two enemy ships and was unable to attack either, before she returned to Pearl Harbor on 8 May.

On 14 June, the submarine headed out for her 13th war patrol. She joined a wolf pack—consisting of *Apogon* (SS–308), *Guardfish* (SS–217), and *Piranha* (SS–389)—on the 25th. Nicknamed the "Mickey Finns" and under the overall command of Capt. William V. O'Regan, the group picked up "ditching signals" from a downed aircraft that afternoon and changed course to investigate. Arriving in the vicinity on the 27th, they found only a drop tank and no trace of plane or pilot.

Over the succeeding days, the submarines observed several planes but contacted only a few fishing vessels and small patrol craft. This drought of targets continued until 11 July, when *Thresher* made radar contact

with a group of six ships steaming on the Formosa-Luzon route. As she changed course to intercept, the submarine dispatched contact reports to the other ships. *Guardfish* and *Apogon* picked up the contact, but *Piranha* could not. *Thresher* deployed to a position 15,000 yards astern of the convoy, to trail the enemy group and be ready to pick off stragglers. *Guardfish* took the enemy's port flank. *Apogon* maneuvered to the convoy's starboard quarter.

A Japanese escort latched on to *Thresher*, however, and trailed the submarine, depriving her of a chance to attack the convoy. Meanwhile, *Piranha* managed to sink a 6,504-ton passenger cargo ship, while *Apogon* was rammed and forced to return to her base for repairs.

Rendezvousing on the 13th, the remaining submarines resumed their hunting. At 1600 on the 16th, *Thresher* sighted smoke on the horizon. She surfaced and dispatched a contact report. After a cat-and-mouse period of some two hours, *Thresher* noted that the convoy consisted of six ships: a large tanker, three freighters, and two escorts.

Thresher closed her prey beneath a clear and dark night sky. At 2329, with the range to the near escort at 2,000 yards, she opened fire. Three torpedoes sped from the forward tubes at the lead escort; three at the first freighter. Comdr. MacMillan then turned *Thresher* 150 degrees to port and launched four torpedoes at the second freighter. The submarine sighted four explosions and heard six soon thereafter, as she departed at high speed.

Commencing her reload at midnight, *Thresher* returned to the area and continued the attack on the convoy which had been pared down to three ships: a freighter, the oiler, and an escort. At 0118, the submarine fired two bow tubes at the escort and three at the leading freighter. She then swung 165 degrees to starboard to fire stern shots at the oiler. Soon thereafter, she heard at least six explosions. The escort promptly began a depth charge barrage. When *Thresher* returned to periscope depth, she found that the convoy had remained stubbornly afloat. Commencing another reload at 0122, the submarine continued to stalk her crippled prey.

Although still reloading tube number six, *Thresher* fired two bow tubes at the freighter; two at the oiler and one at the escort. Then, *Thresher* swung about and fired one stern tube at the latter. Two torpedoes exploded at 0246, and the cargo ship sank immediately. One minute later, two "fish" struck the oiler. A tremendous explosion lighted the entire sky, and the ship sank within 15 seconds.

While it could not be ascertained whether or not the last escort actually went down, the effect of two torpedo hits made it likely that she had been heavily damaged. All torpedoes expended, *Thresher* headed for Midway. The submarine claimed to have destroyed the entire convoy, but a post-war assessment only credited her with two cargo vessels: the 4,916-ton *Sainei Maru* and the 2,838-ton *Shozan Maru*.

Thresher did, however, receive the Navy Unit Commendation and the citation noted the "outstanding heroism . . . persistent and daring coverage of Japanese-controlled waters . . . striking fiercely at the enemy in a brilliantly-executed attack on the night of 16 and 17 July 1944."

Upon completion of voyage repairs, *Thresher* stood out of Midway on 23 August, bound for her 14th war patrol which would take her to the Yellow and East China Seas. Six days later, while cruising on the surface, *Thresher* was battered by heavy seas which caused the ship to roll some 53 degrees from the vertical and produced waves up to 50 feet high.

Thresher arrived off the Japanese home islands on September and made intermittent sweeps with her radar. Rounding the southern tip of Kyushu, the submarine sighted several small craft before making contact with a minelayer and two subchasers on the 10th

Clearing the vicinity at high speed, *Thresher* headed for new patrol grounds.

The submarine was twice frustrated on the 13th, when a large oiler passed far out of reach and a freighter—attacked with four torpedoes—remained stubbornly afloat. An escorting aircraft harried the submarine and prevented her from attempting further attacks.

At 1531 on 18 September, *Thresher* sighted the masts, funnel, and bridge of a ship on the horizon. After determining the enemy's base course and zigzag plan, *Thresher* surfaced and locked the freighter onto radar contact at 1923. Another pip, an escort vessel, soon appeared on the radar screen.

By 2100, *Thresher* had maneuvered into position off the enemy's port bow and waited for the Japanese ships to make a zig which would place the submarine at a desirable point for the attack. *Thresher* closed in for the kill and loosed four torpedoes as the group turned to the right. The quarry, however, elected to move contrary to the hunter's expectations; and the first spread ran wide of its targets. *Thresher*, still undetected, quickly came about and fired four stern "fish" from 1,200 yards.

The second spread ran true and struck the 6,854-ton freighter *Gyoku Maru*. The explosions broke the cargoman's back, and she quickly slipped from sight. *Thresher* retired at high speed when she detected the presence of three additional ships—including light cruiser *Yubari*—rapidly closing.

Reloading, *Thresher* turned upon her pursuers, loosing a spread of torpedoes which barely missed. Subsequently evading her hunters and shifting to waters off Manchuria, the submarine sighted only fishing craft until the 26th, when a large cargo vessel hove into sight at 0944. *Thresher* surfaced at 1315 and headed for the nearest point on the enemy's zigzag course. One hour later, the submarine spotted a floatplane on patrol, and hurriedly "pulled the plug" to submerge. As she went deep, one depth charge exploded nearby.

Staying under until 1600, *Thresher* came to the surface and picked up her target at 1815. The submarine then tracked her quarry until after sunset. *Thresher*'s commander postulated that the enemy vessel was bound for Daisei Gunto and accordingly plotted course to intercept the enemy vessel before she could reach that destination, some three hours later.

Attacking from the bright moon side, *Thresher* fired two bow tubes—aiming one torpedo at the hull near the mainmast and one at the fore. Both struck home, and the 1,468-ton freighter *Nissei Maru* broke up and sank within one minute.

The following day—26 September—*Thresher* came upon a 5,000-ton oiler and cut loose with four tubes from a range of 4,000 yards. On *Thresher*'s bridge, observers saw the enemy vessel, *Koetsu Maru*, disappear within a minute. Having now expended all of her torpedoes, *Thresher* headed for Midway. En route, on 3 October, the submarine sighted, tracked, and approached a small trawler. After sunset, *Thresher* surfaced and manned her deck guns. After firing 27 rounds of 5-inch ammunition, the submarine soon received an answer in the form of shells which fell around the submarine and forced her to back off. When it became too dark to see the target, *Thresher* left the trawler alone and resumed her passage to Midway.

After fueling at Midway on 8 October, *Thresher* sailed for the Hawaiian Islands and arrived at Pearl Harbor on the 12th. Following a lengthy refit, *Thresher* got underway on 31 January 1945 and proceeded to the Marianas in company with *Tilefish* (SS-307), *Shad* (SS-235), and *Peto* (SS-265). Remaining at Saipan overnight, 12 and 13 February, the "wolf pack" pushed on toward its assigned patrol areas north of Luzon in the Philippines. However, *Thresher*'s 15th war patrol proved to be largely unproductive. Only two of her contacts developed into torpedo attacks. One failed due to the target's shallow draft; and, in the second, the

quarry shook off the hunter with evasive maneuvers. *Thresher* did, however, conduct air-sea guard patrols, standing ready to rescue ditched airmen; and conducted a shore bombardment of Basco Harbor, Batan Island, on 28 March. The latter part of this patrol was conducted in company with *Piranha* and *Puffer* (SS-268).

Clearing her patrol station soon thereafter, *Thresher* nested alongside *Fulton* (AS-11) for voyage repairs before pushing on for Oahu on 4 April. Arriving at Pearl Harbor 20 days later, *Thresher* thus ended her active combat service upon conclusion of her 15th war patrol. Undergoing a routine refit and voyage repairs, *Thresher* subsequently rendered target training services out of Pearl Harbor and Eniwetok. She was operating out of the latter base on 15 August 1945 when news of Japan's surrender reached her.

Thresher cleared Eniwetok on 15 September, arrived at Pearl Harbor seven days later, and stood out of Hawaiian waters on the 26th. Making port at San Francisco, Calif., on 4 October, the submarine subsequently left the west coast on the 31st. She transited the Panama Canal on 10 November and arrived at Portsmouth, N.H., eight days later. She was placed out of commission there on 13 December 1945.

The veteran submarine was recommissioned on 6 February 1946. She remained at her berth while her reduced complement prepared the ship for a voyage to the Pacific where she was slated for use as a target in Operation "Crossroads," the atomic bomb tests at Bikini Atoll in the Marshall Islands. However, during the refurbishing, it was decided that the ship had deteriorated beyond economical repair, and work was stopped. *Thresher* was decommissioned for the final time on 12 July 1946. Her name was struck from the Navy list on 23 December 1947, and she was sold for scrapping on 18 March 1948 to Max Siegel of Everett, Mass.

Thresher received 15 battle stars and a Navy Unit Commendation for World War II service.

II

(SSN–593: dp. 3,700 (surf.), 4,300 (subm.); l. 278'6''; b. 31'8''; s. 20+ k.; cpl. 100; a. 4 tt.; cl. *Thresher*)

The second *Thresher* (SSN–593) was laid down on 28 May 1958 by the Portsmouth (N.H.) Naval Shipyard; launched on 9 July 1960; sponsored by Mrs. Frederick B. Warder; and commissioned on 3 August 1961, Comdr. Dean W. Axene in command.

Following trials, the nuclear attack submarine took part in Nuclear Submarine Exercise (NUSUBEX) 3–61 off the northeastern coast of the United States from 18 to 24 September.

On 18 October, the submarine headed south along the east coast. After calling at San Juan, Puerto Rico, she conducted further trials and test-fired her torpedo system before returning to Portsmouth on 29 November. The ship remained in port through the end of the year and spent the first two months of 1962 evaluating her sonar system and her Submarine Rocket (SUBROC) system. In March, the submarine participated in NUSUBEX 2–62, an exercise designed to improve the tactical capabilities of nuclear submarines, and in antisubmarine warfare training with Task Group ALPHA.

Off Charleston, the ship undertook operations observed by the Naval Antisubmarine Warfare Council, before she returned briefly to New England waters from whence she proceeded to Florida for SUBROC tests. However, while mooring at Port Canaveral, the submarine was accidentally struck by a tug which damaged one of her ballast tanks. After repairs at Groton, Conn., by the Electric Boat Company, the ship returned south for more tests and trials off Key West. *Thresher* then returned northward and remained in dockyard hands through the early spring of 1963.

In company with *Skylark* (ASR–20), *Thresher* put to sea on 10 April 1963 for deep-diving exercises. In addition to her 16 officers and 96 enlisted men, the

A bow view of the nuclear submarine *Thresher* (SSN–593), 24 July 1961.   (USN 1057645)

submarine carried 17 civilian technicians to observe her performance during the deep-diving tests.

Fifteen minutes after reaching her assigned test depth, the submarine communicated with *Skylark* by underwater telephone, apprising the submarine rescue ship of difficulties. Garbled transmissions indicated that —far below the surface—things were going wrong. Suddenly, listeners in *Skylark* heard a noise "like air rushing into an air tank"—then, silence.

Efforts to reestablish contact with *Thresher* failed, and a search group was formed in an attempt to locate the submarine. Rescue ship *Recovery* (ASR–43) subsequently recovered bits of debris, including gloves and bits of internal insulation. Photographs taken by bathyscaph *Trieste* proved that the submarine had broken up, taking all hands on board to their deaths in 1,400 fathoms of water, some 220 miles east of Boston.

Thresher was officially declared lost in April 1963.

Thrush

A bird of a family of approximately 700 species and sub-species. The thrush is found world-wide and is known for its beautiful songs.

I

(Minesweeper No. 18: dp. 840; l. 187'10''; b. 35'5''; dr. 8'10''; s. 14 k.; cpl. 85; a. 2 3''; cl. *Lapwing*)

The first *Thrush* (Minesweeper No. 18) was laid down on 27 May 1918 at Wilmington, Del., by Pusey and Jones Co.; launched on 15 September 1918; sponsored by Mrs. J. E. Taylor; and commissioned on 25 April 1919, Lt. (jg.) F. T. Mayes in command.

Following shakedown, *Thrush* arrived in Kirkwall, Scotland, on 5 June and served with Squadron 3 of the Minesweeping Detachment which was busy clearing the North Sea Mine Barrage which had effectively contained the German Navy during World War I. Detached on 25 November, the minesweeper called at Brest, France, before returning to the United States.

Subsequently assigned to Mine Division 3, Mine Squadron 4, the ship was designated AM–18 on 17 July 1920. *Thrush* joined the Pacific Fleet and was based at San Pedro, Calif., before her base of operations was shifted to Pearl Harbor. Engaging in peacetime exercises and maneuvers in the Hawaiian Islands into the early spring of 1922, the minesweeper was decommissioned at Pearl Harbor on 3 April and placed on the inactive list.

After over 13 years in reserve, the minesweeper was recommissioned at Pearl Harbor on 31 October 1935 and refitted at the Mare Island Navy Yard, Vallejo, Calif. There she was converted to a small seaplane tender and redesignated AVP–3 on 22 January 1936. The tender operated out of Seattle, Wash., with Aircraft Base Force through April 1937. She then proceeded to Coco Solo, Canal Zone, in October, to tend planes attached to Patrol Wing (PatWing) 3.

Operating with Aircraft Scouting Force through 1939, the seaplane tender was attached to PatWing 5 tending a brood of planes at San Juan, Puerto Rico, when World War II began in Europe. In January 1940, she moved to the Virgin Islands and worked out of St. Thomas until March. She then returned to San Juan and remained there through December, continuing her operations in support of the Neutrality Patrol.

Anchoring off the mouth of the St. John's River, near Jacksonville, Fla., *Thrush* stood plane-guard duty while tending a covey of Martin PBM Mariners through January and February of 1941. Switched to Tucker's Island, near Hamilton, Bermuda, *Thrush* continued her plane-tending duties through March, on occasion serving as a small cargo vessel to transport supplies from ships to docks and depots on shore.

The seaplane tender then performed similar duties at San Juan, Puerto Rico, and in the British West Indies until she departed Trinidad on 28 November, bound for Brazil. She arrived at Para on 7 December 1941, the day Japanese planes swept down on the American base at Pearl Harbor in a devastating raid which plunged the United States into World War II.

Thrush conducted wartime patrols out of Para before moving her base of operations to Natal, Brazil, on 20 December. Refuelling planes, carrying supplies, and serving as a seagoing "jack-of-all-trades"—even as a floating radio station upon occasion—*Thrush* continued operations off the Brazilian coast through the early spring of 1942.

On 18 May, Brazilian Lloyd steamer SS *Commandante Lyra* fell victim to a German U-boat's torpedoes

USS *Thrush* (AM–31). Many of these sturdy steel-hulled minesweepers served through World War II in a variety of roles.

off Cape San Roque, Brazil. *Thrush* responded to the merchantman's signal requesting assistance. When she reached the burning ship, she sent over a salvage party to fight both the flames which blazed in two holds and the flooding which had already entered several compartments. The seaplane tender passed a towline to the stricken merchantman and towed her 200 miles to Fortaleza Bay.

The ship continued operations out of Natal and Recife, Brazil, through October 1942. She departed Fortaleza Bay on 14 October, bound, via Trinidad and San Juan, for Norfolk. Arriving at Hampton Roads on 1 November, the ship underwent an overhaul and upkeep period at the Norfolk Navy Yard before 12 days of gunnery training and other exercises in Chesapeake Bay through 26 December. The ship then called at Mayport and Jacksonville, Fla., before arriving at San Juan on 8 January 1943. Pressing on to Trinidad, *Thrush* spent one week at the British West Indian port before heading for Brazil and arriving at Belem on the 25th. She then operated off the coast of Brazil escorting coastal convoys until 4 April, when she departed Belem and proceeded homeward—via Trinidad, San Juan, Guantanamo, and the Windward passage—and reached Norfolk on 22 April.

On 2 May, *Thrush* arrived at Quonset Point, R.I., to begin training operations which lasted through the summer. Engaged in antisubmarine drills, the seaplane tender towed targets for dive-bomber practices; retrieved practice torpedoes; and acted as an escort for "R"-type submarines engaged in training exercises with aircraft. Upon completion of this duty, the ship moved south and made port at Norfolk on 9 August for availability which lasted through 11 September.

Heading further south, *Thrush* took part in the dismantling of naval air bases at Almirante Bay, Panama, and at Moneypenny Anchorage, Nicaragua. She then deployed to Baltra Island in the Galapagos group during November and returned to Panamanian waters in December.

Operating in the Canal Zone through January 1944, *Thrush* subsequently carried an Army surveying party to the Cocos Islands and to the Honduran coast in March before towing a Navy oil barge back to Panama. From April through September, the ship participated in submarine training exercises off Key West and towed targets for submarines and aircraft before putting into the Norfolk Navy Yard for availability.

Following repairs, she headed south, via Trinidad, to Dutch Guiana and arrived at Paramaribo on 19 November. She anchored off the mouth of the Surinam River and commenced tending Martin PBM's—a duty which lasted through March of 1945, punctuated briefly by an inspection at Trinidad. Subsequently, *Thrush* returned to the routine operations of beaching and repairing aircraft, fueling them, and feeding their crews. Acting also as a floating radio station, the seaplane tender continued these duties from her return from Trinidad on 24 March to 4 June.

After making port at San Juan on 12 June, *Thrush* commenced a month-long repair period before getting underway for the Hawaiian Islands. She transited the Panama Canal and called at Manzanillo, Mexico, and San Diego en route, and reached Pearl Harbor on 26 August. The tender remained in Hawaiian waters through 20 September and then returned to the west coast at San Pedro, Calif., on 30 September. She next returned to the Atlantic—via Manzanillo, Mexico, and the Panama Canal—and arrived at Norfolk on 1 November.

The following day, she set out for Massachusetts waters, via New York City and the Cape Cod Canal, and arrived in Boston on 4 November 1945. There, the Navy decided that the venerable seaplane tender was beyond economical repair. *Thrush* was decommissioned on 13 December 1945 and struck from the Navy list on 8 January 1946. Transferred to the Maritime Commission on 19 August, she was sold to John A. Pohl, of Haworth, N.J., on 21 August.

(MSC–204: dp. 320 (lt.); l. 144'; b. 28'; dr. 9'; s. 13 k.; cpl. 39; a. 2 20mm.; cl. *Redwing*)

The second *Thrush* (MSC–204) was laid down as AMS–204 on 7 May 1954 at Tampa, Fla., by the Tampa Marine Co.; launched on 5 January 1955; sponsored by Mrs. Edgar S. Russell; redesignated MSC–204 on 7 February 1955; and commissioned on 8 November 1955, Lt. (jg.) Richard Anthony Dallamura in command.

Late in November 1955, the new coastal minesweeper reported at Charleston for duty with Mine Division 42 and then conducted shakedown in Chesapeake Bay. In 1956, she moved to Yorktown, her new homeport; carried out assignments for the Mine Warfare School; and in August proceeded to Norfolk, her base for Operation "Hideaway." Early in 1957, she was assigned to the 6th Naval District and homeported at Key West. There she tested and evaluated new mine warfare equipment for the Mine Warfare Evaluation Detachment.

In 1958 and 1959, she participated in mine warfare exercises out of Charleston and Norfolk, including NATO exercises. In August 1959, she again shifted home ports, this time to Coco Solo at the Atlantic entrance of the Panama Canal. She operated from that base until 1962 when she was ordered to Miami. There, she trained naval reserve crews for nine years. In 1971, she moved to Port Everglades, whence she continued her assignment with the Naval Reserve Force. At times, she served as a training ship for three reserve crews: two underway crews and an in-port maintenance unit—all elements of the Selected Reserve System. Conducting reserve cruises, visiting east coast ports, and ranging as far as the Bahamas for minesweeping exercises, she continued training Florida Reserves for the Mine Warfare Service, Atlantic Fleet, into 1975. In 1976, she was transferred to the Naval Oceanographic Office.

Thuban

A star of 3.6 magnitude, the brightest body in the constellation Draco. Thuban was at one time the pole star and was important in ancient Egyptian religion.

(AKA–19: dp. 13,910; l. 459'3''; b. 63'; dr. 26'4'' (lim.); s. 16.5 (tl.); cpl. 456; a. 1 5'', 4 3'', 18 20mm.; cl. *Andromeda*; T. C2–S–B1)

Thuban (AKA–19) was laid down under a Maritime Commission contract (MC hull 203) on 2 February 1943 at Kearny, N.J., by the Federal Shipbuilding and Drydock Co.; launched on 26 April 1943; sponsored by Miss Madeleine Carroll; acquired by the Navy on 9 June 1943; and commissioned on 10 June 1943 at the Brooklyn Navy Yard, Comdr. James C. Campbell, USNR, in command.

On 23 June 1943, *Thuban* got underway from Gravesend Bay and anchored the next day in Hampton Roads. Following a week of tests and exercises, the new attack cargo ship, escorted by *Griswold* (DE–7), departed Norfolk and steamed southward conducting intensive drills and exercises en route to the Canal Zone. After transiting the Panama Canal on 5 and 6 July, *Thuban* continued on independently to the California coast and arrived at San Diego on the 13th.

In the days that followed, she conducted landing craft exercises; and, on the 22d, she arrived at Oakland to load cargo for the assault on Japanese-occupied islands in the Aleutian chain. On 5 August, she commenced exercises at Adak and on the 15th anchored off Quisling Cove, Kiska, to take part in what was expected to be an assault on a Japanese stronghold. However, the landing turned out to be unopposed. *Thuban* remained in the Aleutians until late in the month while American forces reoccupied the islands. She then steamed south, touched at San Francisco, and arrived at San Diego on 6 September.

On the 16th, the ship set her course for the Hawaiian Islands and arrived at Pearl Harbor on the 22d. After loading cargo, she departed on 2 October, escorted by *Gamble* (DM-15) and bound for the Ellice Islands. On the 8th, the attack cargo ship arrived at Funafuti to discharge her cargo; then continued on to anchor at Wellington Bay, New Zealand, on the 19th. There, she embarked elements of the 2d Marine Division and participated in exercises in preparation for the coming assault on Tarawa. On 1 November, she got underway and on the 8th arrived at Efate, where, for two days, she conducted landing craft exercises in Meli Bay. On the 13th, she departed the New Hebrides to take part in Operation "Galvanic," the conquest of the Gilbert Islands.

Before dawn on "D-day," 20 November 1943, *Thuban* arrived at her assigned position in the transport area off Betio Island and began lowering boats and "amphtracs" for the initial assault on Tarawa. All of her boats were in the water by 0435, and *Thuban* prepared to unload cargo. At 0551, as she maneuvered to maintain her station in the transport area, enemy shore batteries found the range of the transports, and a shell landed between *Thuban* and *Doyen* (APA-1). The transports quickly headed out to sea, beyond range of the shore batteries, but not before additional shells landed among them, providing many anxious moments.

Nightly air raids on the island, a reported periscope sighting, and bomb explosions on Betio marked the tense days that followed. *Thuban* continued unloading cargo and supplied fuel and repairs for her own boats and those of other ships. *Thuban* lost three men to enemy action during this operation, and four of her landing craft were sunk as they moved toward the beach. Shore parties sent her a number of casualties which taxed her limited medical facilities. Discharging cargo on call, *Thuban* remained off Betio until 27 November, when she departed the Gilberts in company with Task Group (TG) 53.8 and headed for the Hawaiian Islands.

After disembarking troops and equipment of the 2d Marine Division at Hilo and Honolulu, *Thuban* embarked Army units. Then, operating out of Pearl Harbor, she conducted training exercises in Maalaea Bay, Maui, into the new year to prepare for the conquest of the Marshall Islands. Attached to the 5th Amphibious Force, she departed Pearl Harbor on 21 January 1944 and arrived off Kwajalein on 31 January. At 0410 on 1 February, she began lowering and dispatching her landing craft, 18 of which took part in the initial landings on the islands of the atoll that day. For four days, she unloaded powder, projectiles, tanks, and other items as her boats supported landings on the islands of the atoll. Then, on the 6th, she began reloading troops and cargo.

During Operation "Flintlock," *Thuban's* boats were constantly busy; and, because of the nature of the seas and the beaches, the landing craft took a beating, often requiring repairs after only two trips. On the 7th, while receiving fuel from *Thuban*, *Sigsbee* (DD-502) tore a two-foot long hole in the cargo ship's starboard plating. *Thuban* effected repairs, put to sea the next day, and headed for Hawaii with *Colohan* (DD-658) in tow.

Off Oahu on the 19th, she transferred the destroyer to a tug and entered Pearl Harbor to discharge equipment, cargo, and troops. The next day, she delivered landing craft to the amphibious training base at Kauai and departed the Hawaiian Islands. She moored at San Diego on the morning of the 29th and, during March and April, participated in extensive training operations off the coast of southern California. On 1 May, she departed San Francisco to rejoin the 5th Amphibious Force, encountered foul weather and mountainous seas during the passage to Hawaii, and arrived at Pearl Harbor on the 6th. Through the remainder of May, she conducted rehearsals for coming amphibious operations.

On the 18th, she loaded cargo and troops of the 4th Marine Division and, on the 29th, got underway with TG 52.15 bound via Eniwetok for the assault on the Marianas. Late on the 14th, she approached Saipan. In the dark predawn on the 15th, exploding star shells lighted the sky on *Thuban's* port beam. Ships of the screen reported the sinking of a submarine as *Thuban* steamed around the northern tip of the island and headed south, sighting Saipan for the first time at 0445. Before sunrise, she lay to in the transport area and began lowering her boats. As the first assault waves hit the beach in the faint light of early dawn, *Thuban's* crew enjoyed a grandstand view of "D-day" on Saipan, especially of the shoreline south of Charankanoa where her own landing craft were operating.

Late that day, as the transports commenced night retirement, a group of seven Japanese dive bombers attacked. One plane dropped a bomb near a destroyer some 3,000 yards off *Thuban's* starboard bow, but an eruption of antiaircraft fire from *Thuban* and her sister ships of the transport group drove the attackers away. Numerous alarms sounded during the night, and *Thuban* helped to repel two additional raids.

In the days that followed, *Thuban* continued to unload her vital cargo to supply the forces on shore, furnished ammunition for light cruiser *Montpelier* (CL-57), and took on casualties from Marine and Army units on the beach, occasionally approaching within less than a mile of the shore. Despite frequent air alerts, the attack cargo ship was soon remaining in the transport area unloading through the night. Toward midnight on the night of 22 and 23 June, a shell from an enemy battery on Tinian passed low over the number three hatch and burst nearby on the port beam, but *Thuban* escaped damage. All hands remained at battle stations during the night as *Thuban* took on casualties, made smoke, and continued unloading.

On the 26th, *Thuban* completed discharging her cargo. During air attacks that night, an enemy plane dropped a stick of bombs 2,000 yards from *Thuban*, and a low-flying Japanese aircraft crashed the superstructure of *Mercury* (AK-42) off *Thuban's* port beam before plunging into the water. That same night, a surprise Japanese counterattack on shore left large numbers of wounded near Garapan requiring evacuation. Anchored off Susupe Point on the morning of the 27th, *Thuban* embarked 91 injured men filling sick bay, the main deck, and many quarters areas to overflowing with stretcher cases. The attack cargo ship's crew assisted in bathing, bandaging, and feeding the wounded while the ship's one doctor and his assistants aided the most severely injured. On this hectic day, *Thuban* also fueled, watered, and provisioned various ships. That evening, as the ship made smoke during a prolonged period of air raids, phosphorescent bombs hit the beach near Susupe Point, and a bomb narrowly missed one of her landing craft in the process of transporting a load of wounded. Action continued after midnight as five bombs hit the beach 2,000 yards from the ship's position.

Departing Saipan on the 28th, *Thuban* arrived at Eniwetok on 1 July and transferred her patients to ships better equipped to care for them. After fueling and loading ammunition urgently needed by American warships supporting the assault on the Marianas, *Thuban* departed the Marshalls on the 15th.

Returning to Saipan on the 19th, she provided fuel, water, and ammunition to ships of the Marianas invasion force, took on empty brass, and repaired landing craft. Early on the morning of the 24th, seven of her tank lighters took part in the initial landings on Tinian. On the 28th, *Thuban* got underway and steamed in convoy via Eniwetok to the Hawaiian Islands, arriving at Pearl Harbor on 10 August. There, following amphibious exercises off Maui, she embarked Army troops; rendezvoused with TG 33.3; and headed via the Marshalls for the Admiralty Islands, arriving at Manus on 3 October.

Assigned to Task Group 79.3 for the impending amphibious assault on Leyte, she departed Seeadler Harbor on 14 October in company with Transport Division

177

7 and rendezvoused with Attack Group Able. In the early hours of "A-day," 20 October, the formation fought the strong currents of the Surigao Strait and drove off a Japanese dive bomber before arriving in the outer transport area. While the battleships delivered a pre-assault bombardment, *Thuban* began lowering her boats. Throughout the morning, she unloaded cargo; and her landing craft joined the assault waves which raced to the beach. Although interrupted by calls to general quarters and the necessity to make smoke when an air attack was imminent, for three days she discharged a steady stream of vital ammunition, engineering equipment, trucks, trailers, and rations for the troops on shore. On the morning of the 21st, two enemy planes came in low, evading detection, and dropped bombs near *Custer* (APA–40), 1,000 yards astern of *Thuban*. On the 23d, she unloaded the last of her cargo; departed the Philippines; and steamed via Manus to arrive at Oro Bay, New Guinea, on 4 November.

After loading personnel and equipment of the 11th Airborne Division, she departed New Guinea on the 11th and returned to Leyte Gulf a week later. Through the 22d, she unloaded her cargo despite 37 calls to general quarters. During this period, a number of aerial dogfights occurred in her area and, although *Thuban* was not attacked directly, she helped to repel enemy raiders on four occasions. Her mission completed, she departed the Philippines on the 24th and anchored in Humboldt Bay on the 29th.

On 13 December, she continued on to Aitape Roads, Tamara Island. During the next two weeks, hampered by rolling treacherous surf and 10- to 15-foot swells, she loaded cargo and equipment of the Army's 43d Division Artillery. *Thuban* then joined Transport Division 7 during rehearsals for the impending Lingayen Gulf landings, embarked troops of the 43d Artillery, and on 29 December 1944 departed New Guinea with Task Group 78.1, bound for the Philippines.

The passage was marked by the sighting of an enemy aerial snooper and the sinking of a Japanese midget submarine by *Taylor* (DD–468) south of Apo Island. Early on 9 January 1945, the attack cargo ship entered Lingayen Gulf. No enemy opposed her approach; and, by 0900, her landing craft were in the water, and *Thuban* had begun to discharge her cargo. During a twilight air alert that day, enemy attackers dropped bombs nearby, and *Thuban* fired on a Japanese fighter plane. During the predawn darkness on 10 January, enemy torpedo boat attacks in the area prompted *Thuban* to establish a boat patrol to defend the ship against surprise attack. As *Thuban* made smoke during the ensuing morning twilight, a lowflying Japanese plane made a strafing run on the ship. Despite its advantage of surprise, the raider made no hits but escaped before *Thuban* could open fire. As the ship unloaded the last of her cargo on the night of 11 and 12 January, a Japanese plane splashed 500 yards away off her starboard beam; and, as dawn approached, she narrowly avoided damage when two bombs fell only 200 yards off her port quarter. Later in the day, she got underway and set a course southward.

As *Thuban* steamed toward Leyte Gulf on the morning of the 13th, a Japanese suicide plane attempted to glide-dive into the attack cargo ship. Despite heavy fire from *Thuban*, the kamikaze pressed the attack until the last possible moment, then banked to port and dove, crashing the bridge of *Zeilin* (APA–3), 1,300 yards away from *Thuban*.

Thuban anchored in Leyte Gulf on the 15th but got underway three days later, bound for the Schoutens, and arrived at Biak Island on the 22d. After loading elements of the Army's 41st Division, she departed New Guinea on 2 February, paused briefly in Leyte Gulf, and arrived off Mindoro Island on the morning of the 9th. There she lowered her boats and began unloading which continued through the night as Allied mop-up operations on Mindoro reached completion. Underway on the 10th, she proceeded via Leyte and Ulithi to the Volcanos. Arriving at a point 70 miles southeast of Iwo Jima in company with TG 12.6 on 9 March, she remained there until the morning of the 17th when she proceeded to the hard-won island and embarked tired, battered, but victorious Marine units. She weighed anchor on the 27th and reached Saipan on the 29th, where she loaded cargo of the 5th Marine Division Air Transport Group. She departed the Marianas on 14 April and steamed to the Hawaiian Islands where she discharged her cargo before continuing on to moor in San Francisco Bay on the 27th.

Following repairs, she loaded fleet issue stores at the Oakland Naval Supply depot and departed San Francisco Bay on 19 July 1945. She stopped at Ulithi on 4 August, rendezvoused with elements of Service Squadron 6 on the 8th, and throughout that month provisioned ships of the 3d Fleet off the coast of Honshu as they awaited the occupation of Japan. After the formal surrender ceremony in Tokyo Bay, she continued to supply American ships, visiting anchorages on the Korean and China coasts into the new year.

Transferred to the Naval Transportation Service early in 1946, she operated between the west coast of the United States and various Pacific island groups, including the Marianas and Japan, participating in occupation duties until the outbreak of the Korean War in the summer of 1950.

After taking on Army cargo at Oakland, she departed the west coast early in August 1950 and arrived at Yokohama on the 29th to discharge her cargo and complete outfitting for her return to the role of attack cargo ship. After combat loading and embarking Army and Navy personnel, *Thuban* proceeded to Kobe and, on 11 September 1950, got underway with TG 90.2 bound for Operation "Chromite"—the assault on Inchon. En route to its destination, the task group encountered heavy seas as it skirted a typhoon; and *Thuban* was forced to fall behind to repair a hydraulic line carried away by rough seas. Repairs completed, *Thuban* rejoined the task group and, on the 15th, approached the outer transport area at Inchon. That day, her boats joined in the first assault waves; and, in the days that followed, the veteran attack cargo ship discharged personnel, cargo, and equipment in support of the invasion.

On the 20th, she departed Inchon to return to Yokohama. There, she loaded units of the 7th Division and on 29 September returned to Inchon. Early in October, she took on stores and troops at Yokosuka; then proceeded to Pusan for final staging for the scheduled Iwon landings. Underway on the 28th, she arrived at Iwon Ko on the following day. On the completion of her mission in this landing, she departed Iwon Ko on 6 November. Later that month, she carried elements of the Army's 3d Division from Japan to Wonsan; then returned to Yokohama on the 21st. On the 23d, she sailed for home and arrived at San Francisco on 7 December.

Early in 1952, she returned to the east coast and took up her duties supplying the American Fleet in Atlantic and Caribbean waters. Throughout the 1950's, she continued the familiar round of east coast and Caribbean ports, varied by a voyage to Japan in 1953 and by participation in various fleet exercises in the Atlantic. While deployed in the Mediterranean in the fall of 1956, *Thuban* took part in extensive exercises. Increasing tension in the Middle East exploded into war on 30 October, and *Thuban* was called upon to evacuate American nationals from Egypt early in November. She embarked 1,500 evacuees at Alexandria and, on 5 November, departed that troubled port. After transferring her passengers at Suda Bay, she returned to exercises with the 6th Fleet.

She participated in NATO exercises in the Mediterranean in 1957 and in November returned to the east coast and routine peacetime operations. During the Cuban crisis in October 1962, she operated for two months in Caribbean waters supporting the American naval quarantine.

Decommissioned in October 1967, *Thuban* was placed in the Atlantic Reserve Fleet and was berthed at Norfolk. On 1 January 1969, she was reclassified an amphibious cargo ship and redesignated LKA–19. She remained in the National Defense Reserve Fleet into October 1979.

Thuban received seven battle stars for World War II service and three for Korean War action.

Thunder

(Slp.)

Blockade runner, *Annie Dees*, was captured by Union screw gunboat *Seneca* off Charleston, S.C., on 20 November 1862 and was purchased by the Navy from the New York Prize Court on 9 December 1863.

Renamed *Thunder*, the sloop joined the South Atlantic Blockading Squadron for use as a tender. During October 1864, she operated off Wassaw Sound, Ga., and returned to Port Royal, S.C., in November for repairs. *Thunder* serviced blockade vessels off the Savanah River, Ga., in January and February 1865 and spent most of the remaining months of the war on duty off Tybee Island, S.C.

Thunder was sold at Port Royal on 8 August 1865 to John Smith.

Thunderer

The monitor *Passaconaway* (q.v.) was renamed *Thunderer* on 15 June 1869 and again renamed *Massachusetts* on 10 August 1869.

Thurlow, L. K., see *L. K. Thurlow*.

Thurston

Counties in Nebraska and Washington.

The county in Nebraska was named for John Mellen Thurston. Born on 21 August 1847 in Montpelier, Vt., J. M. Thurston was admitted to the Wisconsin bar in 1869 and subsequently achieved prominence in Nebraska as an attorney, a railroad executive, and a political leader. After serving in the United States Senate from 1895 to 1901, Thurston practiced law in Washington, D.C., and in Omaha, Nebraska, until he died on 9 August 1916.

The county in the state of Washington was named for Samuel Royal Thurston. Born in Monmouth, Maine, on 15 April 1816, S. R. Thurston moved to Burlington, Iowa, in 1845; practiced law there; and edited the *Iowa Gazette*. Early in 1849, he settled in Oregon and, when that territory was organized later that year, he was elected as its first delegate to the United States Congress. He took his seat on 3 December 1849 and served until 3 March 1851. While returning home from the national capital to the Northwest Pacific coast, Thurston died at sea on 9 April 1851.

(AP–77: dp. 13,910; l. 459'3''; b. 63'0''; dr. 23'0''; s. 16.5 k. (tl.); cpl. 456; trp. 1,306; a. 4 3'', 4 40mm.; cl. *Thurston*; T. C2–F)

Thurston (AP–77) was laid down under Maritime Commission contract (MC hull 134) as SS *Del Santos* on 9 December 1941 at Kearney, N.J., by the Federal Shipbuilding & Drydock Co. for the Mississippi Shipping Co.; launched on 4 April 1942; sponsored by Mrs. Dorothy W. Necht; and delivered on 11 July 1942.

The ship was acquired by the Navy from the War Shipping Administration under a bare boat charter on 13 September 1942 and was renamed *Dauphin* and designated AP–77 on 16 September. However, to avoid confusion with a Canadian ship named *Dauphin*, the ship was again renamed on 18 September, this time as *Thurston*. Commissioned on 19 September 1942, with Capt. Jack E. Hurff in command, *Thurston* was converted into an auxiliary transport by the Atlantic Basin Iron Works, Brooklyn, N.Y., and was ready for sea on the 24th.

Following shakedown training out of Little Creek, Va., and landing exercises with Army units at Solomons Island, Md., the transport sortied on 24 October with Task Group (TG) 34.9, the Center Attack Force, for the invasion of North Africa. Her holds and decks were combat-loaded with men and equipment of the 15th Infantry Regiment. On the morning of 8 November, she arrived in the transport area off Fedhala, French Morocco. Since her troops were assigned to the reserve force, she did not begin disembarking them until late that evening. On the 13th, *Thurston* entered Casablanca harbor to finish unloading supplies and equipment. She began her return voyage on the 15th and arrived at Hampton Roads 11 days later.

Two round-trip voyages across the Atlantic carrying reinforcements to North Africa were next on her agenda. She then spent March and April undergoing repairs and alterations. On 10 May, the ship sailed with convoy UGF–8A for Oran with troops to be used in the invasion of Sicily. In early June, *Thurston* embarked units of the 16th Infantry Regiment and headed to Algiers for landing rehearsals. On 6 July, she sortied with Task Force (TF) 81 and, on the 9th, arrived in the assault area off Gela. The ship landed the troops early the next morning, completed unloading on the 12th, and returned via Algiers to Oran. On 22 July, she headed to New York for more troops and supplies and was back at Oran on 2 September. Five days later, she embarked 600 German prisoners of war and disembarked them at New York on the 22d.

On 8 October, the transport—loaded with American troops—joined Convoy UT–3 and debarked them at Gourock, Scotland, on the 17th. She then proceeded to Glasgow to pick up Canadian troops, returned to Gourock, and joined a convoy for North Africa. The convoy arrived off Algiers on 6 November and, that evening, was subjected to an air attack in which *Beatty* (DD–640), SS *Santa Elena*, and the Dutch ship SS *Mornix Van St. Aldegonde* were torpedoed and sunk while Allied ships splashed six German planes. The remainder of the convoy arrived at Naples two days later, and *Thurston* disembarked the Canadians. She then moved to Palermo to pick up elements of the American 1st Armored Division for passage to Scotland. After a week at Gourock, the transport got underway for the United States on the last day of November and reached New York on 9 December 1943.

Thurston carried troops from New York to Liverpool in January 1944; to Gourock in February; and to Cardiff, Wales, in April. When the ship finished unloading at Cardiff on 4 April, she proceeded to Loch Long for three weeks of landing exercises to prepare for the invasion of Hitler's "Fortress Europe." She anchored at Portland, England, on the 29th and sustained minor damage there on 28 May when a German bomb exploded 30 yards off her port side.

In the evening of 5 June, *Thurston* began the channel crossing to Normandy with Assault Group O–3. At 0333 the next morning, she was anchored about 10 miles off the "Omaha" beaches and landed her troops on schedule at H-hour. She lost three of her boats in the initial assault wave and two in the 2d wave. That evening, the transport left the area and returned to Portland the next morning to remain "on-call" until the 19th.

On 4 July, *Thurston* got underway and proceeded, via Oran, to Naples with a load of lorries and M–4 tanks. After unloading on the 17th, she remained at Naples until 13 August, when—loaded with assault troops—she sortied with the Assault Group of TF 84 (Alpha Force) for the invasion of southern France. She was off Baie de Pampelonne, France, on the morning of the 15th and launched the assault wave which went ashore with little opposition. The next morning, she got underway for Oran. Late in September, the transport loaded French troops and landed them at Lardier on the 30th. She then operated in resupply convoys from North Africa and Italy to the beaches until 25 October when she joined a covoy headed to the United States.

The ship arrived at New York on 6 November and began an overhaul that lasted until 19 December. She called at Norfolk the next day and got underway for the Pacific on the 21st. She transited the Panama Canal on 27 December 1944 and arrived at San Francisco on 5 January 1945. There, the transport loaded passengers and cargo and headed for Hawaii. She reached Pearl Harbor on the 22d; debarked the passengers; embarked garrison troops; and proceeded via Eniwetok to the Marianas.

The transport was at Saipan from 11 to 16 February, whence she sortied with Transport Group Able of the Attack Force for the assault against Iwo Jima. *Thurston* remained off the Iwo beaches from 19 to 26 February before she was finally ordered to land her troops. She finished unloading cargo the next day and headed back toward the Marianas. She arrived at Saipan on 2 March, called at Guam the next day to off-load 33 battle casualties, and then proceeded to the Solomons. *Thurston* called at Tulagi on the 12th and continued to Espiritu Santo to load elements of the Army's 27th Infantry Division. From there, her itinerary took her, via Ulithi, to Okinawa. The ship debarked her troops at the Hagushi Beaches on 9 April and, five days later, headed for the Marianas, whence she was routed, via Ulithi and Manus, to New Caledonia. She embarked 917 homeward-bound passengers and battle casualties at Noumea on 11 May and debarked them at San Francisco on 26 May.

Thurston took on Army troops on 9 June and proceeded, via Eniwetok and Ulithi, to the Philippines. She arrived at Manila on 8 July, discharged her troops and cargo there, moved to Tacloban, and embarked homeward-bound naval personnel. The transport called at Ulithi to pick up more sailors and, as the war ended, anchored at San Francisco on 14 August. On the 25th, the ship began a voyage to the Philippines with more Army troops and arrived at Manila on 15 September. There, the ship was assigned to "Magic-Carpet" duty, returning servicemen home from overseas.

Thurston was next ordered to the Solomons. On 4 October, while en route to Guadalcanal, she sighted a 28-foot dory which showed no sign of life. However, a blanket in the forward cockpit aroused suspicion of the deck officer, who sent a landing craft to see if anyone was on board. The LCVP circled the dory at very close range before moving alongside. As the boat officer stepped aboard the dory, three Japanese armed with grenades in both hands emerged from under the blanket and hurled them at the officer and the boat. The boat officer tumbled overboard and the boat crew abandoned the LCVP over the "off-side" before the grenades exploded. A second LCVP with a fully-armed crew was launched to rescue the crew of the first boat. As soon as they were picked up, *Thurston* opened fire with her machine guns and finally sank the dory with a 3-inch shell. The boat crew suffered no casualties, and the LCVP was recovered. The ship then called at Guadalcanal, Espiritu Santo, New Caledonia, and arrived at Seattle on the 30th.

The transport made three more "Magic-Carpet" voyages: to the Philippines in December 1945 and in March 1946, and to Okinawa and Japan in May. When she arrived at San Francisco on 20 June, she began preparations for inactivation. *Thurston* was decommissioned and returned to the War Shipping Administration on 1 August 1946 and resumed the name *Del Santos*. She was struck from the Navy list on 28 August 1946.

Del Santos was sold to the Waterman Steamship Co. in 1948. The following year, she was renamed *Chickasaw*. She remained in merchant service as *Chickasaw*

until 7 February 1962 when she ran aground on Santa Rosa Island off the coast of California.

Thurston received seven battle stars for World War II service.

Tiburon

A large voracious shark found in the Caribbean and along both the Atlantic and Pacific coasts of Central America.

Tiburon (SS–529), a *Balao*-class submarine, was authorized on 19 July 1940. Her construction was to be undertaken by the Boston Navy Yard but was cancelled on 29 July 1944.

Tickler

(Sloop: dp. 50)

Tickler—a 50-ton sloop—was acquired by the Navy at New Orleans, La., in August 1812. Little is known of this vessel other than the fact that she apparently served as a dispatch boat at New Orleans during the War of 1812. She was sold in 1818.

Ticonderoga

A village in Essex County, N.Y., on La Chute River, 100 miles north of Albany. The name is an Iroquois Indian term which means "between two lakes" and refers to Lake George and Lake Champlain. Here, the French built a fort called Carillon in 1755, but it was captured four years later by British troops under General Amherst. Early in the American Revolution, on 10 May 1775, Ethan Allen and his "Green Mountain Boys" captured the fort from the British. General Sir John Burgoyne recaptured the fort in May 1777, holding it until his surrender at Saratoga, N.Y., on 17 October 1777.

I

(Sch: t. 350; l. 120'; a. 8 long 12-pdrs., 4 long 18-pdrs., 3 32-pdr. car.)

The first *Ticonderoga*—a merchant steamer built in 1814 at Vergennes, Vt.—was purchased by the Navy at Lake Champlain and converted to schooner rigging; and relaunched on 12 May 1814.

Ticonderoga rendered gallant service with Captain Thomas Macdonough's squadron during the Battle of Lake Champlain on 11 September 1814. Commanded by Lt. Stephen Cassin, *Ticonderoga* compelled sloop HMS *Finch* (formerly USS *Growler*) to surrender after riddling her with shot and forcing her aground. She also assisted in the capture of sloop HMS *Chubb* (formerly USS *Eagle*), and repelled several boarding attempts by British gunboats. Midshipman Hiram Paulding was on board *Ticonderoga* during the battle and used his pistol to discharge a cannon when firing matches proved defective. During the two-and-one-half hour engagement, six members of *Ticonderoga*'s crew were killed, and six others were wounded.

After the war, *Ticonderoga* was laid up at Whitehall, N.Y. A decade later, she was pronounced unworthy of repair and sold at public sale on 19 July 1825.

II

(ScSlp: dp. 2,526; l. 237'0''; b. 38'2''; dr. 17'6''; s. 11 k.; a. 1 150-pdr. P.r., 1 50-pdr. D.r., 6 9'' D.sb., 2 24-pdr. how., 2 12-pdr. r., 2 heavy 12-pdr. sb.)

The second *Ticonderoga* was laid down by the New York Navy Yard in 1861; launched on 16 October 1862;

Ticonderoga anchored at Venice, with St. Mark's in the background. Rolled hammocks are stowed along the gunwales, and the crew is at quarters for inspection. Bulwark sections forward and aft of the stack can be lowered, as they are here, to permit the use of pivot guns.

sponsored by Miss Katherine Heaton Offley; and commissioned at New York on 12 May 1863, Commodore J. L. Lardner is command.

Ticonderoga went south on 5 June 1863 for duty as flagship of the West Indies Squadron and, after stopping at Philadelphia, arrived at Cape Haitien on 12 June. She patrolled waters off the Virgin Islands, Barbados, Tobago, Trinidad, and Curaçao protecting Union commerce. *Ticonderoga* returned to Philadelphia for repairs in September. She was relieved as flagship of the squadron in October and sent to the Boston Navy Yard.

Operating out of Boston, *Ticonderoga* searched unsuccessfully off Nova Scotia for the captured steamer *Chesapeake* from 11 to 16 December. In June 1864, she hunted Confederate commerce raiders off the New England coast, putting into Portland harbor, Maine, on 26 June. There, *Ticonderoga* received a telegram on 10 July ordering her to track down and destroy the marauding Confederate raider CSS *Florida*. Her search lasted until October and carried *Ticonderoga* as far south as Cape San Roque but was stopped because of mechanical troubles and insufficient fuel. She returned to Philadelphia late in October.

Ticonderoga left Philadelphia bound for Hampton Roads, Va., on 31 October. She was assigned to the North Atlantic Blockading Squadron on 4 November and deployed off Wilmington, N.C. *Ticonderoga* participated in the first, unsuccessful attempt to take Fort Fisher, N.C., on 24 and 25 December, losing eight men killed and 20 wounded on the first day of the assault when a 100-pounder Parrott rifle exploded. A landing party from *Ticonderoga* assisted in the capture of the fort on 15 January 1865.

Ticonderoga joined the South Atlantic Blockading Squadron on 19 January. After a brief tour of duty, she left for Philadelphia in March and was decommissioned there on 5 May.

Ticonderoga was recommissioned for service with the European Squadron in 1866. She remained with the Squadron through 1869, visiting ports in the Mediterranean, on the continent, and along the English and African coasts. The vessel was extensively repaired in 1870 and reported for duty with the South Atlantic Squadron at Rio de Janeiro on 23 August 1871. After over two years of service on the coast of South America, she was reassigned to the North Atlantic Squadron in January 1874. The ship was decommissioned at Portsmouth, N.H., on 24 October and remained laid up there until 1877.

Ticonderoga was recommissioned on 5 November 1878 and ordered to embark upon a cruise around the world, Commodore Robert W. Shufeldt commanding. The expedition was of a commercial nature, intended to expand existing trade relations and establish new ones. *Ticonderoga* sailed eastward from Hampton Roads on 7 December and stopped at ports including Madeira, Monrovia, Cape Town, Aden, Bombay, Penang, Singapore, Manila, Hong Kong, Nagasaki, Fusan, Honolulu, and San Francisco. *Ticonderoga* arrived at Mare Island, Calif., for extensive repairs on 9 November 1880. During the two-year mission, she had visited over 40 ports and steamed in excess of 36,000 miles without a mishap.

She left Mare Island in March 1881 and returned to New York on 23 August. She was decommissioned there a final time on 10 September 1882 and declared unfit for further service. *Ticonderoga* was sold at Boston on 5 August 1887 to Thomas Butler & Co.

III

(Id. No. 1958: t. 5,130 (gross); l. 401.1'; b. 53.2'; dph. 27.5; dr. 25'6'' (mean); s. 11 k.; a. 1 6'', 1 3'')

Camilla Rickmers (spelled *Kamilla Rickmers* in German)—a steamer built in 1914 by *Rickmers Aktien Gesellschaft*, at Bremerhaven, Germany, and operated by *Rickmers Reismühlen Reederei & Schiffbau Aktien Gesellschaft*—was seized by United States Customs officials in 1917; turned over to the Navy; fitted out as an animal transport; renamed *Ticonderoga*; and commissioned at Boston in the Naval Overseas Transportation Service (NOTS) on 5 January 1918, Lt. Comdr. James J. Madison, USNRF, in command.

Ticonderoga departed Boston on 16 January and reached Newport News, Va., three days later. There, she loaded a cargo of automobiles, trucks, animals, and sundry other Army supplies before moving north to New York City to join a convoy which sailed for France on 20 February. *Ticonderoga* entered port at Brest on 7 March and began discharging her cargo. She completed unloading operations and departed France on the 23d to return to the United States. She arrived at New York on 8 April and the following day headed for Norfolk, Va., to undergo repairs and take on cargo before returning to New York on the 30th.

On 3 May, *Ticonderoga* steamed out of New York harbor once more, bound for Europe. She reached Brest on 18 May and proceeded southeast along the coast of France to the Gironde estuary where she unloaded her cargo and took on ballast for the return voyage. The transport put to sea on 10 June and entered Hampton Roads 15 days later. *Ticonderoga* took on another Army shipment at Newport News and joined an east-bound convoy at New York on 12 July. She delivered her cargo at the Gironde estuary once more, laying over there from 28 July to 21 August before heading home.

Ticonderoga loaded another Army cargo at Norfolk between 5 and 19 September. She then steamed to New York where she joined a convoy bound for Europe. On 22 September, *Ticonderoga* cleared New York for the last time. During the night of the 29th and 30th, the transport developed engine trouble and dropped behind the convoy. At 0520 the following morning, she sighted the German submarine *U–152* running on the surface; and she cleared for action. For the next two hours, her gun crews fought the enemy in a losing battle. The U-boat's gunners put her forward gun out of commission after six shots, but the 6-inch gun aft continued the uneven battle. Almost every man on board *Ticonderoga*—including her captain—suffered wounds. Eventually, the submarine's two 5.9-inch guns succeeded in silencing *Ticonderoga*'s remaining gun. At 0745, *Ticonderoga* slipped beneath the sea. Of the 237 sailors and soldiers embarked, only 24 survived. Twenty-two of those survivors were in one life boat and were picked up by the British steamer SS *Moorish Prince* four days later. The other two, the executive officer and the first assistant engineer, were taken prisoner on board the U-boat and eventually landed at Kiel, Germany, when *U–152* completed her cruise. *Ticonderoga*'s name was subsequently struck from the Navy list.

Ticonderoga (CV–19) was renamed *Hancock* (q.v.) on 1 May 1943 when the names of CV–14 and CV–19 were switched.

IV

(CV–14: dp. 27,100; l. 888'; b. 93'0'' (wl.); ew. 147'6''; dr. 28'7''; s. 33 k.; cpl. 3,448; a. 12 5'', 72 40mm., ac. 80+; cl. *Essex*)

The fourth *Ticonderoga* (CV–14) was laid down as *Hancock* on 1 February 1943 at Newport News, Va., by the Newport News Shipbuilding & Dry Dock Co.; renamed *Ticonderoga* on 1 May 1943; launched on 7 February 1944; sponsored by Miss Stephanie Sarah Pell; and commissioned at the Norfolk Navy Yard on 8 May 1944, Capt. Dixie Kiefer in command.

Ticonderoga remained at Norfolk for almost two months outfitting and embarking Air Group 80. On 26 June, the carrier shaped a course for the British West Indies. She conducted air operations and drills en route and reached Port of Spain, Trinidad, on the 30th. For the next 15 days, *Ticonderoga* trained intensively to weld her air group and crew into an efficient wartime team. She departed the West Indies on 16 July and headed back to Norfolk where she arrived on the 22d. Eight days later, the carrier headed for

Panama. She transited the canal on 4 September and steamed up the coast to San Diego the following day. On the 13th, the carrier moored at San Diego where she loaded provisions, fuel, aviation gas, and an additional 77 planes, as well as the Marine Corps aviation and defense units that went with them. On the 19th, she sailed for Hawaii where she arrived five days later.

Ticonderoga remained at Pearl Harbor for almost a month. She and *Carina* (AK–74) conducted experiments in the underway transfer of aviation bombs from cargo ship to aircraft carrier. Following those tests, she conducted air operations—day and night landing and antiaircraft defense drills—until 18 October when she exited Pearl Harbor and headed for the western Pacific. After a brief stop at Eniwetok, *Ticonderoga* arrived at Ulithi Atoll in the Western Carolines on the 29th. There she embarked Rear Admiral A. W. Radford, Commander, Carrier Division 6, and joined Task Force (TF) 38 as a unit of Rear Admiral Frederick C. Sherman's Task Group (TG) 38.3.

The carrier sortied from Ulithi with TF 38 on 2 November. She joined the other carriers as they resumed their extended air cover for the ground forces capturing Leyte. She launched her first air strike on the morning of the 5th. The planes of her air group spent the next two days pummeling enemy shipping near Luzon and air installations on that island. Her planes bombed and strafed the airfields at Zablan, Mandaluyong, and Pasig. They also joined those of other carriers in sending the heavy cruiser *Nachi* to a watery resting place. In addition, *Ticonderoga* pilots claimed six Japanese aircraft shot down and one destroyed on the ground, as well as 23 others damaged.

Around 1600 on the 5th, the enemy retaliated by sending up a flock of planes piloted by members of the suicide corps dubbed kamikaze, or "Divine Wind," in honor of the typhoon that had destroyed a Chinese invasion fleet four centuries previously. Two of the suicide planes succeeded in slipping through the American combat air patrol and antiaircraft fire to crash *Lexington* (CV–16). *Ticonderoga* emerged from that airborne *banzai* charge unscathed and claimed a tally of two splashes. On 6 November, the warship launched two fighter sweeps and two bombing strikes against the Luzon airfields and enemy shipping in the vicinity. Her airmen returned later that day claiming the destruction of 35 Japanese aircraft and attacks on six enemy ships in Manila Bay. After recovering her planes, the carrier retired to the east for a fueling rendezvous.

She refueled and received replacement planes on the 7th and then headed back to continue pounding enemy forces in the Philippines. Early on the morning of 11 November, her planes combined with others of TF 38 to attack a Japanese reinforcement convoy, just as it was preparing to enter Ormoc Bay from the Camotes Sea. Together, the planes accounted for all the enemy transports and four of the seven escorting destroyers. On the 12th and 13th, *Ticonderoga* and her sisters launched strikes at Luzon airfields and docks and shipping around Manila. This raid tallied an impressive score: light cruiser *Kiso*, four destroyers, and seven merchant ships. At the conclusion of the raid, TF 38 retired eastward for a refueling breather. *Ticonderoga* and the rest of TG 38.3, however, continued east to Ulithi where they arrived on the 17th to replenish, refuel, and rearm.

On 22 November, the aircraft carrier departed Ulithi once more and steamed back toward the Philippines. Three days later, she launched air strikes on central Luzon and adjacent waters. Her pilots finished off the heavy cruiser *Kumano*, damaged in the Battle off Samar. Later, they attacked an enemy convoy about 15 miles southwest of *Kumano*'s not-so-safe haven in Dasol Bay. Of this convoy, cruiser *Yasoshima*, a merchantman, and three landing ships went to the bottom. *Ticonderoga*'s air group rounded out their day of

TICONDEROGA
(THE BIG "T")

DEDICATED TO CAPTAIN DIXIE KIEFER, U. S. N.

WORDS AND MUSIC BY

EDDIE FRITZ, Jr., Mus. 2c U.S.N.R.

Design by H.B.McGee

HILLIARD-CURRIE
MUSIC PUBLISHERS
54 W. RANDOLPH ST., CHICAGO, ILL.

Ticonderoga (CV–14) is one of the relatively few Navy ships to have had a piece of music written in her honor. This song was published in 1944.

destruction with an aerial rampage which cost the Japanese 15 planes shot down and 11 destroyed on the ground.

While her air group busily pounded the Japanese, *Ticonderoga*'s ship's company also made their presence felt. Just after noon, a torpedo launched by an enemy plane broached in *Langley*'s (CVL–27) wake to announce the approach of an air raid. *Ticonderoga*'s gunners raced to their battle stations as the raiders made both conventional and suicide attacks on the task group. Her sister ship *Essex* (CV–9) erupted in flames when one of the kamikazes crashed into her. When a second suicide plane tried to finish off the stricken carrier, *Ticonderoga*'s gunners joined those firing from other ships in cutting his approach abruptly short. That afternoon, while damage control parties dressed *Essex*'s wounds, *Ticonderoga* extended her hospitality to that damaged carrier's homeless airmen as well as to *Intrepid* (CV–11) pilots in similar straits. The following day, TF 38 retired to the east.

TF 38 stood out of Ulithi again on 11 December and headed for the Philippines. *Ticonderoga* arrived at the launch point early in the afternoon of the 13th and sent her planes aloft to blanket Japanese airbases on Luzon while Army planes took care of those in the central Philippines. For three days, *Ticonderoga* airmen and their comrades wreaked havoc with a storm of destruction on enemy airfields. She withdrew on the 16th with the rest of TF 38 in search of a fueling rendezvous. While attempting to find calmer waters in which to refuel, TF 38 steamed directly through a violent, but unheralded, typhoon. Though the storm cost Admiral Halsey's force three destroyers and over 800 lives, *Ticonderoga* and the other carriers managed to ride it out with a minimum of damage. Having survived the tempest's fury, *Ticonderoga* returned to Ulithi on Christmas Eve.

Repairs occasioned by the typhoon kept TF 38 in the anchorage almost until the end of the month. The carriers did not return to sea until 30 December 1944 when they steamed north to hit Formosa and Luzon in preparation for the landings on the latter island at Lingayen Gulf. Severe weather limited the Formosa strikes on 3 and 4 January 1945 and, in all likelihood, obviated the need for them. The warships fueled at sea on the 5th. Despite rough weather on the 6th, the strikes on Luzon airfields were carried out. That day, *Ticonderoga*'s airmen and their colleagues of the other air groups increased their score by another 32 enemy planes. The 7th brought more strikes on Luzon installations. After a fueling rendezvous on the 8th, *Ticonderoga* sped north at night to get into position to blanket Japanese airfields in the Ryukyus during the Lingayen assault the following morning. However, foul weather, the bugaboo of TF 38 during the winter of 1944 and 1945, forced TG 38.3 to abandon the strikes on the Ryukyu airfields and join TG 38.2 in pounding Formosa.

During the night of 9 and 10 January, TF 38 steamed boldly through the Luzon Strait and then headed generally southwest, diagonally across the South China Sea. *Ticonderoga* provided combat air patrol coverage on the 11th and helped to bring down four enemy planes which attempted to snoop the formation. Otherwise, the carriers and their consorts proceeded unmolested to a point some 150 to 200 miles off the coast of Indochina. There, on the 12th, they launched their approximately 850 planes and made a series of antishipping sweeps during which they sank a whopping 44 ships, totalling over 130,000 tons. After recovering planes in the late afternoon, the carriers moved off to the northeast. Heavy weather hindered fueling operations on the 13th and 14th, and air searches failed to turn up any tempting targets. On the 15th, fighters swept Japanese airfields on the Chinese coast while the flattops headed for a position from which to strike Hong Kong. The following morning, they launched antishipping bombing raids and fighter sweeps of air installations. Weather prevented air operations on the 17th and again made fueling difficult. It worsened the next day and stopped replenishment operations altogether, so that they were not finally concluded until the 19th. The force then shaped a course generally northward to retransit Luzon Strait via Balintang Channel.

The three task groups of TF 38 completed their transit during the night of 20 and 21 January. The next morning, their planes hit airfields on Formosa, in the Pescadores, and at Sakishima Gunto. The good flying weather brought mixed blessings. While it allowed American flight operations to continue through

Hit by two *kamikazes* off Formosa on 21 February 1945, *Ticonderoga* was saved by the heroic efforts of her crew. (80-G-273437)

the day, it also brought new gusts of the "Divine Wind." Just after noon, a single-engined Japanese plane scored a hit on *Langley* with a glide-bombing attack. Seconds later, a kamikaze swooped out of the clouds and plunged toward *Ticonderoga*. He crashed through her flight deck abreast of the No. 2 5-inch mount, and his bomb exploded just above her hangar deck. Several planes stowed nearby erupted into flames. Death and destruction abounded, but the ship's company fought valiantly to save the threatened carrier. Capt. Kiefer conned his ship smartly. First, he changed course to keep the wind from fanning the blaze. Then, he ordered magazines and other compartments flooded to prevent further explosions and to correct a 10-degree starboard list. Finally, he instructed the damage control party to continue flooding compartments on *Ticonderoga*'s port side. That operation induced a 10-degree port list which neatly dumped the fire overboard! Firefighters and plane handlers completed the job by dousing the flames and jettisoning burning aircraft.

Wounded denizens of the deep often attract predators. *Ticonderoga* was no exception. The other kamikazes pounced on her like a school of sharks in a feeding frenzy. Her antiaircraft gunners struck back with desperate, but methodical, ferocity and quickly swatted three of her tormentors into the sea. A fourth plane slipped through her barrage and smashed into the carrier's starboard side near the island. His bomb set more planes on fire, riddled her flight deck, and injured or killed another 100 sailors—including Capt. Kiefer. Yet, *Ticonderoga*'s crew refused to submit. Spared further attacks, they brought her fires completely under control not long after 1400; and *Ticonderoga* retired painfully.

The stricken carrier arrived at Ulithi on 24 January but remained there only long enough to move her wounded to hospital ship *Samaritan* (AH–10), to transfer her air group to *Hancock* (CV–19), and to embark passengers bound for home. *Ticonderoga* cleared the lagoon on 28 January and headed for the United States. The warship stopped briefly at Pearl Harbor en route to the Puget Sound Navy Yard where she arrived on 15 February.

Her repairs were completed on 20 April, and she cleared Puget Sound the following day for the Alameda Naval Air Station. After embarking passengers and aircraft bound for Hawaii, the carrier headed for Pearl Harbor where she arrived on 1 May. The next day, Air Group 87 came on board and, for the next week, trained in preparation for the carrier's return to combat. *Ticonderoga* stood out of Pearl Harbor and shaped a course for the western Pacific. En route to Ulithi, she launched her planes for what amounted to training strikes on Japanese-held Taroa in the Marshalls. On 22 May, the warship arrived in Ulithi and rejoined the Fast Carrier Task Force as an element of Rear Admiral Radford's TG 58.4.

Two days after her arrival, *Ticonderoga* sortied from Ulithi with TF 58 and headed north to spend the last weeks of the war in Japanese home waters. Three days out, Admiral Halsey relieved Admiral Spruance, the 5th Fleet reverted back to 3d Fleet, and TF 58 became TF 38 again for the duration. On 2 and 3 June, *Ticonderoga* fighters struck at airfields on Kyushu in an effort to neutralize the remnants of Japanese air power—particularly the Kamikaze Corps—and to relieve the pressure on American forces at Okinawa. During the following two days, *Ticonderoga* rode out her second typhoon in less than six months and emerged relatively unscathed. She provided combat air patrol cover for the 6 June refueling rendezvous, and four of her fighters intercepted and destroyed three Okinawa-bound kamikazes. That evening, she steamed off at high speed with TG 38.4 to conduct a fighter sweep of airfields on southern Kyushu on the 8th. *Ticonderoga*'s planes then joined in the aerial bombardment of Minami Daito Shima and Kita Daito Shima before the carrier headed for Leyte where she arrived on the 13th.

During the two-week rest and replenishment period she enjoyed at Leyte, *Ticonderoga* changed task organizations from TG 38.4 to Rear Admiral Gerald F. Bogan's TG 38.3. On 1 July, she departed Leyte with TF 38 and headed north to resume raids on Japan. Two days later, a damaged reduction gear forced her into Apra Harbor, Guam, for repairs. She remained there until the 19th when she steamed off to rejoin TF 38 and resume her role in the war against Japan. On the 24th, her planes joined those of other fast carriers in striking ships in the Inland Sea and airfields at Nagoya, Osaka, and Miko. During those raids, TF 38 planes found the sad remnants of the once-mighty Japanese Fleet and bagged battleships *Ise*, *Hyuga*, and *Haruna* as well as an escort carrier, *Kaiyo*, and two heavy cruisers. On 28 July, her aircraft directed their efforts toward the Kure Naval Base, where they pounded an aircraft carrier, three cruisers, a destroyer, and a submarine. She shifted her attention to the industrial area of central Honshu on the 30th, then to northern Honshu and Hokkaido on 9 and 10 August. The latter attacks thoroughly destroyed the marshalling area for a planned airborne suicide raid on the B–29 bases in the Marianas. On the 13th and 14th, her planes returned to the Tokyo area and helped to subject the Japanese capital to another severe drubbing.

The two atomic bombs dropped on Hiroshima and Nagasaki on the 6th and 9th, respectively, convinced the Japanese of the futility of continued resistance. On the morning of 15 August, *Ticonderoga* launched another strike against Tokyo. During or just after that attack, word reached TF 38 to the effect that Japan had capitulated.

The shock of peace, though not so abrupt as that of war almost four years previously, took some getting used to. *Ticonderoga* and her sister ships remained on a full war footing. She continued patrols over Japanese territory and sent reconnaissance flights in search of camps containing Allied prisoners of war so that air-dropped supplies could be rushed to them. On 6 September—four days after the formal surrender ceremony on board *Missouri* (BB–63)—*Ticonderoga* entered Tokyo Bay.

Her arrival at Tokyo ended one phase of her career and began another. She embarked homeward-bound passengers and put to sea again on the 20th. After a stop in Pearl Harbor, the carrier reached Alameda, Calif., on 5 October. She disembarked her passengers and unloaded cargo before heading out on the 9th to pick up another group of veterans. *Ticonderoga* delivered over a thousand soldiers and sailors to Tacoma, Wash., and remained there through the 28th for the Navy Day celebration. On 29 October, the carrier departed Tacoma and headed back to Alameda. En route, all of the planes of Air Group 87 were transferred ashore so that the carrier could be altered to accommodate additional passengers in the "Magic-Carpet" voyages to follow. Following the completion of those modifications at the Pearl Harbor Naval Shipyard in November, the warship headed for the Philippines and arrived at Samar on 20 November. She returned to Alameda on 6 December and debarked almost 4,000 returning servicemen. The carrier made one more "Magic-Carpet" run in December 1945 and January 1946 before entering the Puget Sound Naval Shipyard to prepare for inactivation. Almost a year later, on 9 January 1947, *Ticonderoga* was placed out of commission and berthed with the Bremerton Group of the Pacific Reserve Fleet.

On 31 January 1952, *Ticonderoga* came out of reserve and went into reduced commission for the transit from Bremerton to New York. She departed Puget Sound on 27 February and reached New York on 1 April. Three days later, she was decommissioned at the New York Naval Shipyard to begin an extensive conversion. During the ensuing 29 months, the carrier received the numerous modifications—steam catapults to launch jets, a new nylon barricade, a new deck-edge elevator and the latest electronic and fire control equipment—necessary for her to become an integral unit of the fleet. On 11 September 1954, *Ticonderoga* was recommissioned at New York, Capt. William A. Schoech in command.

In January 1955, the carrier shifted to her new home port—Norfolk, Va.—where she arrived on the 6th. Over the next month, she conducted carrier qualifications with Air Group 6 in the Virginia Capes operating area. On 3 February, she stood out of Hampton Roads for shakedown near Cuba, after which she returned via Norfolk to New York for additional alterations. During the late summer, the warship resumed carrier qualifications in the Virginia capes area. After a visit to Philadelphia early in September, she participated in tests of three new planes—the A4D–1 "Skyhawk," the F4D–1 "Skyray," and the F3H–2N "Demon." *Ticonderoga* then returned to normal operations along the east coast until 4 November when she departed Mayport, Fla., and headed for Europe. She relieved *Intrepid* at Gibraltar 10 days later and cruised the length of the Mediterranean during the following eight months. On 2 August 1956, *Ticonderoga* returned to Norfolk and entered the shipyard to receive an angled flight deck and an enclosed hurricane bow.

Those modifications were completed by early 1957; and, in April, she got underway for her new home port—Alameda, Calif. She reached her destination on 30 May, underwent repairs, and finished out the summer with operations off the California coast. On 16 September, she stood out of San Francisco Bay and shaped a course for the Far East. En route, she stopped at Pearl Harbor before continuing west to Yokosuka, Japan, where she arrived on 15 October. For six months, *Ticonderoga* cruised Oriental waters from Japan in the north to the Philippines in the south. Upon arriving at Alameda on 25 April 1958, she completed her first deployment to the western Pacific since recommissioning.

Between 1958 and 1963, *Ticonderoga* made four more peacetime deployments to the western Pacific. During each, she conducted training operations with other units of the 7th Fleet and made goodwill and liberty port calls throughout the Far East. Early in 1964, she began preparations for her sixth cruise to the western Pacific and, following exercises off the west coast and in the Hawaiian Islands, the carrier cleared Pearl Harbor on 4 May for what began as another peaceful tour of duty in the Far East. The first three months of that deployment brought normal operations—training and port calls. However, on 2 August, while operating in international waters in the Gulf of Tonkin, *Maddox* (DD–731) reported being attacked by units of the North Vietnamese Navy. Within minutes of her receipt of the message, *Ticonderoga* dispatched four, rocket-armed F8E "Crusaders" to the destroyer's assistance. Upon arrival, the "Crusaders" launched Zuni rockets and strafed the North Vietnamese craft with their 20-millimeter cannons. The *Ticonderoga* airmen teamed up with *Maddox* gunners to thwart the North Vietnamese attack, leaving one boat dead in the water and damaging the other two.

Two days later, late in the evening of the 4th, *Ticonderoga* received urgent requests from *Turner Joy* (DD–951)—by then on patrol with *Maddox*—for air support in resisting what the destroyer alleged to be another torpedo boat foray. The carrier again launched planes to aid the American surface ships, and *Turner Joy* directed them. The Navy surface and air team believed it had sunk two boats and damaged another pair. President Johnson responded with a reprisal to what he felt at the time to be two unprovoked attacks on American seapower and ordered retaliatory air strikes on selected North Vietnamese motor torpedo boat bases. On 5 August, *Ticonderoga* and *Constellation* (CV–46) launched 60 sorties against four bases and their supporting oil storage facilities. Those attacks reportedly resulted in the destruction of 25 PT-type

boats, severe damage to the bases, and almost complete razing of the oil storage depot. For her quick reaction and successful combat actions on those three occasions, *Ticonderoga* received the Navy Unit Commendation.

After a return visit to Japan in September, the aircraft carrier resumed normal operations in the South China Sea until winding up the deployment late in the year. She returned to the Naval Air Station, North Island, Calif., on 15 December 1964. Following post-deployment and holiday standdown, *Ticonderoga* moved to the Hunter's Point Naval Shipyard on 27 January 1965 to begin a five-month overhaul. She completed repairs in June and spent the summer operating along the coast of southern California. On 28 September, the aircraft carrier put to sea for another deployment to the Orient. She spent some time in the Hawaiian Islands for an operational readiness exercise then continued on to the Far East. She reached "Dixie Station" on 5 November and immediately began combat air operations.

Ticonderoga's winter deployment of 1965 and 1966 was her first total combat tour of duty during American involvement in the Vietnam War. During her six months in the Far East, the carrier spent a total of 115 days in air operations off the coast of Vietnam, dividing her time almost evenly between "Dixie" and "Yankee Stations," the carrier operating areas off South and North Vietnam, respectively. Her air group delivered over 8,000 tons of ordnance in more than 10,000 combat sorties, with a loss of 16 planes, but only 5 pilots. For the most part, her aircraft hit enemy installations in North Vietnam and interdicted supply routes into South Vietnam, including river-borne and coastwise junk and sampan traffic as well as roads, bridges, and trucks on land. Specifically, they claimed the destruction of 35 bridges as well as numerous warehouses, barracks, trucks, boats, and railroad cars and severe damage to a major North Vietnamese thermal power plant located at Uong Bi north of Haiphong. After a stop at Sasebo, Japan, from 25 April to 3 May 1966, the warship put to sea to return to the United States. On 13 May, she pulled into port at San Diego to end the deployment.

Following repairs she stood out of San Diego on 9 July to begin a normal round of west coast training operations. Those and similar evolutions continued until 15 October, when *Ticonderoga* departed San Diego, bound via Hawaii for the western Pacific. The carrier reached Yokosuka, Japan, on 30 October and remained there until 5 November when she headed south for an overnight stop at Subic Bay in the Philippines on the 10th and 11th. On the 13th, *Ticonderoga* arrived in the Gulf of Tonkin and began the first of three combat tours during her 1966–67 deployment. She launched 11,650 combat sorties, all against enemy targets located in North Vietnam. Again, her primary targets were logistics and communications lines and transportation facilities. For their overall efforts in the conduct of day and night strikes on enemy targets, *Ticonderoga* and her air group earned their second Navy Unit Commendation. She completed her final line period on 27 April 1967 and returned to Yokosuka, from which she departed again on 19 May to return to the United States. Ten days later, the carrier entered San Diego and began a month-long, post-deployment standdown. At the beginning of July, the warship shifted to Bremerton, Wash., where she entered the Puget Sound Naval Shipyard for two months of repairs. Upon the completion of yard work, she departed Bremerton on 6 September and steamed south to training operations off the coast of southern California.

On 28 December, *Ticonderoga* sailed for her fourth combat deployment to the waters off the Indochinese coast. She made Yokosuka on 17 January 1968 and, after two days of upkeep, continued on to the Gulf of Tonkin where she arrived on station on the 26th and began combat operations. Between January and July, *Ticonderoga* was on the line off the coast of Vietnam for five separate periods totalling 120 days of combat duty. During that time, her air wing flew just over 13,000 combat sorties against North Vietnamese and Viet Cong forces, most frequently in the continuing attempts to interdict the enemy lines of supply. In mid-April, following her second line period, she made a port visit to Singapore and then, after upkeep at Subic Bay, returned to duty off Vietnam. On 9 July, during her fifth and final line period, Lt. Comdr. J. B. Nichols claimed *Ticonderoga*'s first MiG kill. The carrier completed that line period and entered Subic Bay for upkeep on 25 July.

On the 27th, she headed north to Yokosuka where she spent a week for upkeep and briefings before heading back to the United States on 7 August. *Ticonderoga* reached San Diego on the 17th and disembarked her air group. On the 22d, she entered the Long Beach Naval Shipyard for post-deployment repairs. She completed those repairs on 21 October, conducted sea trials on the 28th and 29th, and began normal operations out of San Diego early in November. For the remainder of the year, she conducted refresher training and carrier qualifications along the coast of southern California.

During the first month of 1969, *Ticonderoga* made preparations for her fifth consecutive combat deployment to the southeast Asia area. On 1 February, she cleared San Diego and headed west. After a brief stop at Pearl Harbor a week later, she continued her voyage to Yokosuka where she arrived on the 20th. The carrier departed Yokosuka on the 28th for the coast of Vietnam where she arrived on 4 March. Over the next four months, *Ticonderoga* served four periods on the line off Vietnam, interdicting communist supply lines and making strikes against their positions.

During her second line period, however, her tour of duty off Vietnam came to an abrupt end on 16 April when she was shifted north to the Sea of Japan. North Korean aircraft had shot down a Navy reconnaissance plane in the area, and *Ticonderoga* was called upon to beef up the forces assigned to the vicinity. However, the crisis abated; and *Ticonderoga* entered Subic Bay on 27 April for upkeep. On 8 May, she departed the Philippines to return to "Yankee Station" and resumed interdiction operations. Between her third and fourth line periods, the carrier visited Sasebo and Hong Kong.

The aircraft carrier took station off Vietnam for her last line period of the deployment on 26 June and there followed 37 more days of highly successful air sorties against enemy targets. Following that tour, she joined TF 71 in the Sea of Japan for the remainder of the deployment. *Ticonderoga* concluded the deployment—a highly successful one for she received her third Navy Unit Commendation for her operations during that tour of duty—when she left Subic Bay on 4 September.

Ticonderoga arrived in San Diego on 18 September. After almost a month of post-deployment standdown, she moved to the Long Beach Naval Shipyard in mid-October to begin conversion to an antisubmarine warfare (ASW) aircraft carrier. Overhaul and conversion work began on 20 October, and *Ticonderoga* was redesignated CVS-14 on the 21st. She completed overhaul and conversion on 28 May 1970 and conducted exercises out of Long Beach for most of June. On the 26th, the new ASW support carrier entered her new home port, San Diego. During July and August, she conducted refresher training, refresher air operations, and carrier landing qualifications. The warship operated off the California coast for the remainder of the year and participated in two exercises—HUKASWEX 4–70 late in October and COMPUTEX 23–70 between 30 November and 3 December.

During the remainder of her active career, *Ticonderoga* made two more deployments to the Far East. Because of her change in mission, neither tour of duty included combat operations off Vietnam. Both, however, included training exercises in the Sea of Japan with ships of the Japanese Maritime Self Defense Force. The first of these two cruises also brought operations in the Indian Ocean with units of the Thai Navy and a transit of Sunda Strait during which a ceremony was held to commemorate the loss of *Houston* (CA–30) and HMAS *Perth* in 1942.

In between these two last deployments, she operated in the eastern Pacific and participated in the recovery of the Apollo 16 moon mission capsule and astronauts near American Samoa during April of 1972. The second deployment came in the summer of 1972; and, in addition to the training exercises in the Sea of Japan, *Ticonderoga* also joined ASW training operations in the South China Sea. That fall, she returned to the eastern Pacific and, in November, practiced for the recovery of Apollo 17. The next month, *Ticonderoga* recovered her second set of space voyagers near American Samoa. The carrier then headed back to San Diego where she arrived on 28 December.

Ticonderoga remained active for nine more months, first operating out of San Diego and then making preparations for inactivation. On 1 September 1973, the aircraft carrier was decommissioned after a board of inspection and survey found her to be unfit for further naval service. Her name was struck from the Navy list on 16 November 1973, and arrangements were begun to sell her for scrap.

Ticonderoga received five battle stars during World War II and three Navy Unit Commendations, one Meritorious Unit Commendation, and 12 battle stars during the Vietnam War.

V

(CG–47: dp. 8,910; l. 563'; b. 55'; dr. 29'; s. 30+ k.; a. 1 mis. ln., 2 5", 2 Phalanx, Standard missile, Harpoon, ASROC, 6 15.5" tt.; cl. *Ticonderoga*)

The fifth *Ticonderoga* (CG–47) was laid down on 21 January 1980 at Pascagoula, Miss., by the Ingalls Shipbuilding Division of Litton Industries and was scheduled to be launched in March 1981. Her projected delivery date was January 1983.

Tide

(SP–953: l. 143'; b. 22'9"; dr. 12.5' (aft); s. 11 mph.; a. 2 1-pdrs.)

Tide (SP–953)—a tug built in 1916 at Manitowoc, Wis., by the Manitowoc Shipbuilding Co.—was acquired by the Navy on 14 June 1918 from the Bay State Fishing Co., of Boston, Mass., to serve as a minesweeper in the 1st Naval District. Though never commissioned by the Navy, she may have been armed and manned by naval reservists to patrol the waters of the 1st Naval District during the closing months of World War I. In any event, her name was struck from the Navy list sometime between November 1918 and October 1919.

I

(AM–125: dp. 890; l. 221'2"; b. 32'2"; dr. 10'9"; s. 18.1 k.; cpl. 105; a. 2 3", 4 20mm., 2 dct., 4 dcp., 1 dcp. (hh.); cl. *Auk*)

Tide (AM–125) was laid down on 16 March 1942 at Savannah, Ga., by the Savannah Machinery and Foundry Company; launched on 7 September 1942; sponsored by Mrs. Ruth Hangs; and commissioned on 9 May 1943, Lt. Comdr. Alvin Robinson, USNR, in command.

Following shakedown training out of Key West and Norfolk, *Tide* got underway from Hampton Roads for her first transatlantic voyage. On 17 July, as she steamed in convoy for North Africa, the minesweeper collided with an infantry landing craft, *LCI–267*, which she had just provisioned. Damage to the sweeper included sprung plates and two minor hull punctures which were repaired at sea. *Tide* arrived at Casablanca on 18 July and was soon on her way again escorting a convoy bound for American ports.

During the homeward voyage on 29 July, a sonar contact prompted *Tide* to drop depth charges on what she thought was an enemy submarine. Although a later search revealed an oil slick, no submarine sinking was confirmed.

Following her arrival at New York on 9 August, *Tide* operated on the Eastern Sea Frontier until 30 September. In October and November, she made another successful Atlantic crossing, returning to New York on 25 November 1943.

During December, *Tide* participated in exercises off the Maine coast and conducted mine warfare training off Yorktown. Convoy duties in the waters of the Eastern Sea Frontier and the Caribbean occupied her during January 1944. On the 25th, *Tide* got underway again for what was to be her longest convoy escort assignment. Departing Charleston, she steamed, via Bermuda and the Azores, for the United Kingdom.

Tide completed this voyage at Milford Haven harbor, England, on 10 March and spent the remainder of the month operating out of Falmouth. In April and May, she escorted convoys in British coastal waters and engaged in exercises with minesweepers of the Royal Navy in preparation for the invasion of Europe. In the last week of May, *Tide* made sweeps out of Babbacombe Bay.

On 5 June, *Tide* got underway from Tor Bay with Minesweeper Squadron "A," a unit assigned to the "Utah" area. Later that day, German mines began to take their toll as *Osprey* (AM–56), a squadron member, went down. As the day wore on, *Tide* swept channels off the Normandy beaches for fire-support ships and continued sweeps the next day, D-day. During the night of 6 and 7 June, she joined other vessels in guarding Carentan Estuary to prevent the sally of enemy E-boats.

On the morning of 7 June, *Tide* swept the area inshore and between St. Marcauf and Barfleur to clear lanes for fire-support ships. At 0940, while recovering her gear, *Tide* drifted over the Cardonet Banks and struck a mine which exploded with such force that she was lifted out of the water. The explosion broke her back, blasted a tremendous hole in her bottom, and tore away all bulkheads below the waterline causing immediate and irreversible flooding.

Tide's commanding officer, Lt. Comdr. Allard B. Heywood, USNR, died soon after the initial explosion, and Lt. Comdr. George Crane, the ship's executive officer, directed efforts to assist the stricken vessel and to rescue survivors. *Threat* (AM–124) and *Pheasant* (AM–61) tried to aid *Tide*, but the ship was beyond saving. When *Swift* (AM–122) attempted to tow the damaged ship to the beach, the strain broke her in two. She sank only minutes after the last survivors had been taken off.

Her name was struck from the Navy list on 29 July 1944.

Tide received one battle star for World War II service.

Tidewater

That region of the Commonwealth of Virginia on the coastal plain and along the shores of the Chesapeake Bay as well as along the James, York, Rappahannock, and Nansemond Rivers. It was the region of the United States first settled permanently by English colonists at the beginning of the 17th century.

(AD–31: dp. 16,800 (f.); l. 492'0''; b. 70'0''; dr. 27'6''; s. 18.0 k. (tl.); cpl. 1,017; a. 1 5'', 8 40mm., 12 20mm.; cl. *Shenandoah*)

Tidewater (AD–31) was laid down on 27 November 1944 at the Charleston Navy Yard; launched on 30 June 1945; sponsored by Mrs. Robert N. S. Baker; and commissioned at Charleston, S.C., on 19 February 1946, Capt. Frank H. Ball in command.

Since World War II ended some five months before the destroyer tender was placed in commission, she remained active only long enough to complete sea trials. She did not report for duty with the active fleet but was decommissioned and ordered to the reserve group berthed at Charleston. There, she became accommodation ship for members of the staff of the Commander, Submarine Group 3. That duty continued through the outbreak and first 15 months of hostilities in Korea. By that time, the increased need for ships to support United Nations land forces fighting in that Asian country brought the destroyer tender into her first real active service. On 2 October 1951, *Tidewater* was recommissioned at Charleston, S.C., Capt. Harold S. Harnly in command.

Tidewater, however, did not participate directly in the hostilities that brought her back to active duty. Instead, between late 1951 and early 1954, she operated exclusively along the eastern seaboard of the United States. After shakedown training in the Chesapeake Bay area, she reported for duty with Destroyer Flotilla (DesFlot) 4 in February 1952. At her home port, Norfolk, Va., she supported the destroyers of DesFlot 4 with her repair facilities. Over the next two years, the ship departed that port on a number of occasions to participate in various exercises. During the fall of 1952, *Tidewater* joined ships of other NATO powers in Exercise "Mainbrace" for six weeks of train-

Tide (AM–125) off Normandy on 7 June 1944, her back broken by a mine. (80–G–651676)

ing. The following February, she joined other Navy ships in the Caribbean for her first of many annual "Springboard" exercises, after which she resumed duty at Norfolk tending the destroyers of DesFlot 4. In July 1953, the destroyer tender moved south to Charleston to render her services to the ships of the Mine Force. She returned to Norfolk in mid-August and entered the naval shipyard for overhaul on the 12th. At the completion of overhaul, she put to sea for the Carribean and refresher training on 2 November. *Tidewater* returned to Norfolk on 1 December and resumed tending destroyers until February 1954 when she headed south to participate in her second "Springboard" exercise. Upon completion of that duty, the destroyer tender headed across the Atlantic for her first deployment with the 6th Fleet in the Mediterranean.

With that assignment, *Tidewater* set a pattern which endured for the remainder of her Navy career. Over the next 13 years, she made 10 deployments to the Mediterranean, alternating that service with 2d Fleet duty along the Atlantic coast of the United States. During each tour of duty with the 6th Fleet, she made port calls at various harbors along the length of the "middle-sea" littoral. While serving on her fourth deployment in the summer of 1960, the destroyer tender had the honor to play host to Queen Fredricka of Greece. Her eighth deployment to the Mediterranean came in the spring of 1967, just before the outbreak of the Six-Day War between the Arabs and Israel. During that brief conflict, *Tidewater* hurried to Suda Bay, Crete, where she served as an advanced base ship for 6th Fleet units standing watch in the eastern Mediterranean for the duration of hostilities.

When not in the Mediterranean, she busied herself in support of the warships of the Atlantic Fleet from her base at Norfolk, Va., and at other ports along the eastern seaboard. When in the area, she joined in various exercises, most frequently in Operation "Springboard," the annual Carribean-based exercise conducted by the ships of the Atlantic Fleet. She also underwent periodic overhauls to refurbish herself and modernize her equipment. The most significant of those occurred in June 1962 when, at the conclusion of her fifth Mediterranean tour, she entered Norfolk Naval Shipyard for an extensive overhaul which included the installation of a helicopter pad and concomitant equipment to expand her logistics support capabilities.

Tidewater completed her 10th Mediterranean deployment on 2 May 1969. She resumed tender duty with the warships of the Atlantic Fleet out of Norfolk and remained so occupied through the end of the year and into 1970. In August 1970, she received word that she would be decommissioned the following spring. She served as flagship for the Commander, Cruiser-Destroyer Group 4, from 10 September until 13 November, at which time she began preparations for inactivation. On 4 January, the United States Navy agreed to lease *Tidewater* to the Indonesian Navy upon decommissioning. Accordingly, when she was placed out of commission at Norfolk on 20 February 1971, she was turned over to the Indonesian Navy and recommissioned as *Dumai*, Col. Mardianus Aruf in command. Since then, *Dumai* has remained active with the Indonesian Navy.

Tiger

I

(ScStr: t. 9,950; l. 410'; b. 56'; dph. 29'6''; dr. 27'6½''; s. 10.5 k.; cpl. 114; a. 1 5'', 1 3'')

The first *Tiger* (Id. No. 1640)—a single-screw, steam freighter built at San Francisco, Calif., by the Union Iron Works—was completed in June 1917 and operated as a merchant ship by the Standard Transportation Co., of Delaware, until chartered by the War Department on 12 November 1917. The ship was fitted out at New York for the Army Transportation Service, received a Navy armed guard on 30 November, and carried supplies to France for the American Expeditionary Force through the autumn of 1918. On 23 December at Norfolk, Va., the ship was transferred to the Navy Department and commissioned the same day.

Assigned to the Naval Overseas Transportation Service and refitted for naval service, *Tiger* took on a cargo of food and general Army supplies and departed Hampton Roads on 9 January 1919, bound for France. The ship reached Le Havre on the 24th and discharged her cargo. After voyage repairs, she got underway on 7 February and proceeded, via Norfolk, to New York where she arrived on 3 March. There, she was inspected and found suitable for conversion to a troop transport. On 7 March 1919, the ship was transferred to the United States Cruiser and Transport Force to assist in the formidable task of returning some two million American troops from Europe. By mid-summer, most of the doughboys had been returned; and *Tiger* was transferred to the 3d Naval District on 29 July. The ship was decommissioned on 23 August and returned to her owner the same day.

II

(WPC: dp. 220; l. 125'; b. 24'; dr. 6'9" (mean); s. 11 k.; cpl. 38; a. 1 3''; cl. *Active*)

The second *Tiger*—later classified during World War II as WPC–152—was a steel-hulled, twin-screw, Coast-Guard cutter built in 1927 at Camden, N.J., by the American Brown Boveri Electric Corp. She was commissioned at Camden on 3 May 1927.

Tiger operated out of the Coast Guard base at Stapleton, N.Y., until shifting to Norfolk, Va., and arriving there on 6 June 1933. Subsequently, the 125-foot cutter was transferred to Hawaii and operated out of Honolulu. In the summer of 1941, she came under Navy jurisdiction and was assigned to the local defense forces of the 14th Naval District. Equipped with depth charges and listening gear, *Tiger* operated out of Honolulu—in company with her sister ship *Reliance* and the 327-foot cutter *Taney*—into the critical fall of 1941. On 7 December, the Japanese Navy launched a surprise attack on the Pacific Fleet at its Pearl Harbor base. *Tiger*—patrolling off Barber's Point that morning—won her sole "battle star" on this date.

Little is known of the ship after this point other than that she operated out of Honolulu for the duration of the war on local patrol and antisubmarine duties. In 1948, *Tiger* was decommissioned and sold.

Tiger received one battle star for her World War II service.

Tigress

(Sch.: t. 52; lbp. 50'; b. 17'; dph. 5'; cpl. 27; a. 1 32-pdr.)

Amelia—a schooner built at Erie, Pa., by the firm of Adam and Noah Brown—was launched in the spring of 1813, probably in April. Acquired by the Navy for service with Captain Oliver Hazard Perry's forces on Lake Erie, *Amelia* was renamed *Tigress* and placed under the command of Lt. Augustus H. M. Conkling.

Tigress took part in the spirited engagement at Put-in-Bay on 10 September 1813, the Battle of Lake Erie. Perry's resounding victory over Commodore Robert H. Barclay's squadron in this battle forced the British to abandon their plans for transfrontier raids with their Indian allies into American territory. Instead, since their position in the area around Detroit had been rendered untenable by American control of Lake Erie, the British withdrew.

Perry consequently convoyed American troops into the territory formerly held by the British, investing Malden on 23 September and Detroit on the 27th. On 2 October, a small naval flotilla—*Tigress, Scorpion,* and *Porcupine*—under the command of Lt. Jesse D. Elliott—ascended the Thames River to support an overland expedition under General William Henry Harrison. In the ensuing Battle of the Thames, Harrison's army routed the mixed British and Indian force. The Indian leader Tecumseh was klled in the battle which forced the British to withdraw from the vicinity, never more to threaten the American northwest territories.

Tigress subsequently sailed for Lake Huron, where she took part in blockading operations into the summer of 1814. She and *Scorpion* drew the task of standing watch on the entrance to the Nautawasaga River, the sole outlet to the lake for the town of Machilimackinaw. By early September, the situation in this town was desperate. If the blockade were not lifted within a fortnight, dwindling food supplies would force the British to surrender.

To avert such a development, four boatloads of British and Indians set out from Machilimackinaw on the night of 3 September 1814. They slipped alongside *Tigress*—which was anchored close inshore—and boarded the schooner. A brief and bloody battle followed; and—although "warmly received" by the vessel's crew—the British captured the ship in five minutes. "The defense of this vessel," wrote Lt. Bulger, in command of the attackers, "did credit to her officers, who were all severely wounded."

While the surviving officers and men were sent ashore as prisoners of war, Bulger retained the greater part of the boarding party on board and kept the ship's American flag flying. *Scorpion* soon arrived on 5 September and anchored some two miles distant. Bulger, in a daring stroke, ran the captured *Tigress* alongside *Scorpion* and captured her, too. Both American vessels and their captured crews were later taken to Machilimackinaw.

The British renamed their prizes soon thereafter. *Tigress* became HMS *Surprise*—an appropriate name in view of the nature of her capture—and *Scorpion* became HMS *Confiance*. Both subsequently served the Royal Navy until laid up at the Colborne Basin, Ontario, Canada, and dismantled.

In the spring of 1933, *Tigress'* remains were raised and placed on the town dock at Penetanguishene, Ontario.

II

(ScTug: a. 1 how.)

The second *Tigress*—a screw tug—was chartered by the Navy at Baltimore, Md., from A. C. Hall sometime in the summer of 1861 prior to 20 August. At some now unknown date, she was purchased by the Navy. She departed Baltimore on 20 August, bound for the Washington Navy Yard.

Tigress joined Capt Thomas T. Craven's Potomac River flotilla on 26 August and operated largely in patrol activities. On two occasions in early September, she carried captured runaway slaves to Capt. Craven's flagship, *Resolute*.

On the evening of 10 September, while *Tigress* was on patrol off Indian Head, Md., steamer *State of Maine* ran down the tug and sank her. The ship's wreck was subsequently raised; but, on 22 November 1862, she was deemed not worth the expense of repair. She was subsequently sold at public auction, with half of the proceeds going to her former owner, A. C. Hall, who had raised the wreck.

III

(ScStr: t. 360; l. 139'; b. 27'; dr. 15'; dph. 16.2')

The third *Tigress*—a screw steamer constructed in 1871 at Quebec, Canada, by Harvey and Co.—rescued 19 members of an Arctic expedition from an ice flow in Baffin Bay in May of 1873 and brought them into her home port, St. John's, Newfoundland, with the first

reports of the loss of the expedition's ship, *Polaris*. She was so well-suited structurally for cruising icy Arctic waters that she was chartered by the United States Navy for service during the search for *Polaris* and the remainder of that ship's company. She was then manned by a Navy crew under the command of Comdr. James A. Greer.

Tigress' orders were to make her way as near to *Polaris'* last reported position and there to begin the main portion of the search. She cleared New York on 14 July, visited St. John's, and put in at Godhaven, Greenland, on 6 August for coal. Between the 8th and the 10th, she moved from Godhavn to Upernavik where she took on coal and provisions from *Juniata*. The next day, the steamer headed north, following the Greenland shore as closely as she dared. On her way, she searched North Star Bay, Northumberland Island, and Harstene Bay without success. On 14 August, she discovered the camp on Littleton Island at which the people from *Polaris* had passed the previous winter. From the natives then in possession of the camp, the searchers learned that the *Polaris* crew had departed the previous June in boats constructed of materials salvaged from the ship and that *Polaris* herself sank soon thereafter. *Tigress'* crew gathered what papers and instruments they found in the camp and reembarked.

On the 15th, the steamer shaped a course to the south and, following a stop at Melville Bay to communicate with the authorities at Tessuisak, reentered Godhavn on 25 August. After coaling from *Juniata* again, *Tigress* resumed the search by crossing Baffin Bay and heading southward along the coast of Baffin Island to Cumberland Sound and back to the coast of Greenland. There, she searched the area between Ivigtut and Liskenaes. She searched the Davis Strait until 16 October when she had to put into St. Johns for coal. There, she learned that the rest of *Polaris'* crew had been rescued and had arrived in Scotland. After a fortnight in port, *Tigress* cleared St. John's on 30 October and, on 9 November, returned to New York where she was returned to her civilian crew.

IV

(Motorized Yawl: t. 24 (gross); l. 56'; b. 15'3"; dr. 4'3"; s. 7 mph; cpl. 8; a. 1 1-pdr., 1 mg.)

The fourth *Tigress*—a yawl built in 1905 at Bridgeport, Conn., by W. A. Robinson—was inspected by the Navy on 26 June 1917 as a potential section patrol craft in the 7th Naval District. Though never purchased by the Navy, she was chartered temporarily, armed, and manned by naval reservists. The yawl was placed in commission on 18 August 1917 and operated in the vicinity of Tampa, Fla., through the end of World War I. After hostilities ended, she was returned to her owner.

Tigrone

A tiger shark found mainly in tropical waters.

(SS–419: dp. 1,579 (surf.), 2,416 (subm.); l. 311'8"; b. 27'3"; dr. 15'5"; s. 20.25 k. (surf.), 8.75 k. (subm.); cpl. 81; a. 10 21" tt., 1 5", 1 40mm., 1 20mm., 2 .50-cal. mg.; cl. *Balao*)

Tigrone (SS–419) was laid down on 8 May 1944 by the Portsmouth (N.H.) Navy Yard; launched on 20 July 1944; sponsored by Mrs. Charles F. Grisham; and commissioned on 25 October 1944, Comdr. Hiram Cassedy in command.

Tigrone completed fitting out in mid-November and conducted training out of Portsmouth and New London before departing the Submarine Base at New London on the last day of 1944. After 10 days of training at the Fleet Sound School, the new submarine got underway on 16 January. Steaming via the Canal Zone, she paused for a week of training off Panama; then set her course for Hawaii, conducting extensive practice approach exercises with *Riverside* (APA–102) en route. On 16 February, she arrived at Pearl Harbor to prepare for her first war patrol.

On 9 March, she departed Oahu and steamed westward, arriving at Guam on the 19th. After a three-day pause to repair a main engine, she got underway on the 21st in company with *Bullhead* (SS–332) and *Blackfish* (SS–221), members of a combined attack group, led by her own commanding officer, Comdr. Hiram Cassedy. Joined by *Seahorse* (SS–304), the submarines set their course for the South China Sea where they formed a scouting line in hopes of intercepting Japanese shipping.

Seahorse was mistakenly strafed and bombed by a "friendly" but overanxious B–24 on the 24th. *Tigrone's* first brush with the enemy came on the 29th in the South China Sea when she dove to avoid an enemy "Oscar" and, at 50 feet, felt the jolt of a small explosion over the forward battery compartment, apparently the concussion of a small bomb dropped by the enemy plane. The new submarine emerged from this encounter without damage and continued her patrol of the sea lanes off the China coast.

In the days that followed, she made an unsuccessful attempt to intercept a convoy spotted by American planes. Then, on 3 April, she began lifeguard duties off the eastern shore of Hainan. On the 5th, *Tigrone* again managed to evade a bomb dropped by a high flying Japanese plane. On the 8th, she assumed a lifeguard station off Kuannan and began steering five mile legs to maintain her station, when the ship's commanding officer noted a wake which he took to be one of the ship's own. Two minutes later, the appearance of a torpedo 500 yards away on the port bow gave startling proof that the wake was that of an enemy submarine. As *Tigrone* swung left, the torpedo passed her abeam, less than 60 yards away. She then submerged and rigged for silent running, remaining below for over two hours.

On the 9th, she took up a lifeguard station off Mofu Point and continued patrols off Hainan until the 15th when she departed the area late in the day. She bombarded Pratas Reef with 5-inch gunfire on the 16th and joined *Rock* (SS–274) three days later to fire on targets including towns and docks on Batan Island. She ended her first war patrol at Guam on 24 April 1945.

After refitting by *Apollo* (AS–25), *Tigrone* departed Apra Harbor on 19 May, took on torpedoes at Saipan the same day, and on the 20th got underway for her assigned area. On the 25th, she sighted Sofu Gan Island and Tori Shima before taking up her lifeguard station south of Honshu and west of the Nanpo Shoto. That same day, she rescued a downed flier from the 19th Fighter Command, Iwo Jima.

Early on the morning of the 27th, *Tigrone* engaged a Japanese lugger which countered the submarine's 5-inch and 40-millimeter fire with machinegun fire. As *Tigrone* turned away from the raking fire of the lugger, heavy seas washed over her main deck, knocking three of the submarine's crewmen against the gun and injuring them. Despite intermittent heavy rain, *Tigrone* finished off the lugger with 5-inch fire. The final and telling round caught the lugger dead center, set it afire, and stopped it dead in the water. High seas made boarding a hazardous proposition, so the battered enemy vessel was left to burn, and *Tigrone* returned to her lifeguard station.

Early on the afternoon of 28 May, the submarine rendezvoused with a Navy bomber which had signalled its distress. The plane ditched 500 yards from *Tigrone*, and the submarine's crew quickly rescued five survivors from the water. In the next two days, *Tigrone* proved her skill as a lifeguard ship as she responded to frequent calls for aid and rescued 23 men from the Philippine Sea. On the afternoon of the 24th, *Tigrone* answered a call for assistance from a severely damaged "Catalina" seaplane which had nosed into a wave on takeoff from a rescue operation. Quickly arriving on the scene, the submarine took on board 16 survivors, the crew and twice-rescued passengers of the disabled seaplane.

Soon the submarine was searching again—this time for survivors of other downed aircraft who had been reported by circling planes to be floating on rafts in *Tigrone's* lifeguard area. Night fell before the submarine located the rafts; but, early on the 30th, she surfaced and, despite 30-foot waves, resumed the search. Friendly aircraft aided her efforts, and *Tigrone's* persistence was rewarded when she at last located seven Army aviators afloat on a raft. These tenacious survivors had been washed overboard several times during the night but had climbed back each time. The heavy seas made rescue difficult and time-consuming, but finally the exhausted aviators were brought safely on board the submarine. *Tigrone* jauntily sent out the message, "*Tigrone* has saved the air force and is now returning to Iwo Jima with 28 rescued zoomies," and noted that she had set a new record for lifeguard proficiency.

On 1 June, *Tigrone* put in at Iwo Jima to disembark her passengers and on the next day, despite continuing radar problems, again got underway, returning to her patrol area on the 3d. Plagued by fog and radar malfunctions, *Tigrone* at last was forced to request lifeguard duty when a persistent loud scraping noise in the vicinity of her starboard shaft rendered normal submarine patrol and attack functions hazardous, if not impossible.

Operating south of Honshu, *Tigrone* joined the "Lifeguard League" and on the 26th recovered an aviator who had parachuted from his disabled fighter, rescuing him from the water only six minutes from the time his parachute blossomed. During the two days that followed, she took on rescued aviators from other submarines and set her course for Guam on the 28th. She ended her second war patrol on 3 July at Apra Harbor, having rescued a total of 30 aviators on this war patrol.

Following refitting by *Proteus* (AS–19), *Tigrone* departed Guam on 31 July and, after the usual stop at Saipan for torpedoes, arrived on lifeguard station. As the submarine approached within 100 miles of Honshu, the news arrived that Russia had declared war on Japan. Patrolling nearer and nearer Honshu as American planes made strikes on Tokyo and other cities of the Japanese homeland, *Tigrone* encountered increasing numbers of Japanese search planes.

On the 11th, the first reports of Japanese surrender were received; but, for two more days, *Tigrone* continued her patrols, approaching within 50 miles of the shore of Sagami Wan as she pursued lifeguard duties. On the 13th, with Navy pilots helping to spot targets, she bombarded Mikomoto Island, scoring 11 hits on a radio station and lighthouse tower. The submarine claimed this action as the final bombardment of the war. On the 14th, *Tigrone* rescued another aviator who had been forced to parachute from his plane and, later in the day, spent an anxious half hour attempting to evade persistent sonar contacts which turned out to be birds.

On the 15th, she received orders to cease all attacks; and, the next day, the official statement of Japan's surrender was published. She patrolled off the east coast of Japan as far north as Sendai and Todo Saki. Then, on the 30th, she rendezvoused with "Benny's Peacemakers" and, on the last day of August, moored in Tokyo Bay. She departed Tokyo on 2 September and made her way via Hawaii and the Canal Zone to New London, arriving there early in October 1945.

Later that month, she visited Washington, D.C., for Navy Day activities and, late in December, reported to the 16th Fleet at Philadelphia for preservation procedures preparatory to inactivation. She was towed to New London and placed out of commission, in reserve, on 30 March 1946.

Tigrone (AGSS–419) during her last year of active service, with an experimental sonar equipment prominently installed in her bow.

On 12 April 1948, her designation was changed to SSR, radar picket submarine. In June, she was towed from New London to Portsmouth for conversion. She was recommissioned on 1 November 1948 and, early in 1949, conducted shakedown out of Portsmouth in preparation for her new duties as an Arctic radar picket. That summer, she joined Submarine Division 62 operating out of Norfolk to begin activities evaluating new radar equipment and techniques for long range air defense. She continued in this role until 1957, operating in the Atlantic and Caribbean and completing five Mediterranean deployments with both American and NATO forces. On 1 August 1957, her status was changed to in commission, in reserve; and, on 1 November, she was decommissioned. She was assigned to the Atlantic Reserve Fleet and berthed at Philadelphia.

Redesignated SS–419 on 3 February 1961, she was recommissioned on 10 March 1962 and underwent overhaul and conversion at the Philadelphia Naval Shipyard before reporting to New London for refresher training on 22 September. On 15 November, she departed New London for four weeks of shakedown out of Puerto Rico; and, on 14 December, she returned to New London to remain there into the new year. From April through August 1963, she operated in the Mediterranean on deployment with the 6th Fleet. She then returned to New London for local operations and to provide services for the Submarine School. On 1 December 1963, she was redesignated an auxiliary submarine AGSS–419. Early in 1964, she was fitted out with an experimental sonar unit. Through the end of 1964, she operated in conjunction with the Naval Underwater Sound Laboratory and the Submarine School, testing and evaluating the new equipment.

In 1965, she underwent a major eight-month overhaul and modification at the Philadelphia Naval Shipyard. Her torpedo tubes were removed, two forward compartments thoroughly sound isolated, and a new experimental sonar system, the Brass III, was installed. Operating as a research and development vessel in cooperation with the United States Underwater Sound Laboratory, she began duties which would fill the remaining years of her long career. Assigned primarily to data collection and sonar and acoustic tests in connection with the Brass program, she operated out of New London, conducting underwater systems tests as well as research in sound propagation.

In 1968, she visited British and Norwegian Sea ports; spent September through December in antisubmarine warfare exercises; and trained reserves. She continued

her research assignments, joining with HMS *Grampus* in the early months of 1972 for a joint American-British oceanographic operation in the eastern Atlantic. She operated occasionally in Caribbean waters, taking part in Operation "Springboard" in 1973 and 1974. While moored at the Submarine Base in New London, on 25 October 1974, *Tigrone* observed the 30th anniversary of her commissioning. Into 1975, she continued research activities off the east coast, which included a visit to Bermuda in March and operations with air units off Jacksonville and Atlantic City.

On 5 May, she began pre-inactivation procedures and, on 27 June 1975, was decommissioned at the Naval Submarine Base, Groton, Conn. At the time of her decommissioning, *Tigrone* was the oldest submarine in commission in the United States Navy, as well as the last unit of the submarine force still in operation to have taken part in combat action in World War II. Her name was struck from the Navy list on that same day, and she was sunk as a target on 25 October 1976.

Tigrone received two battle stars for World War II service.

Tilefish

A large, yellow-spotted deepwater food fish.

(SS–307: dp. 1,526; l. 311'10"; b. 27'4"; dr. 15'2"; s. 20.25 k. (surf.), 8.75 k. (subm.); cpl. 66; a. 10 21" tt., 1 5", 1 40mm., 2 .50-cal. mg.; cl. *Balao*)

Tilefish (SS–307) was laid down on 10 March 1943 at Vallejo, Calif., by the Mare Island Navy Yard; launched on 25 October 1943; sponsored by Mrs. Wilson D. Leggett; and commissioned on 28 December 1943. Lt. Comdr. Roger Myers Keithly in command.

During February and March 1944, *Tilefish* underwent trials and shakedown off the California coast before getting underway for Hawaii. On 3 April, the submarine departed Pearl Harbor for her first war patrol setting course for the Japanese home islands. While patrolling in the "Hit Parade" area east of Honshu *Tilefish* sighted many enemy aircraft but found few targets for her torpedoes. Early in the patrol, she was hampered by the failure of her fathometer; and throughout the mission, she was plagued by periscope fogging and overcast weather which ruled out celestial navigation. Finally, on the morning of 11 May, the novice submarine and her crew encountered their first opportunity for action. *Tilefish* sighted a small convoy and launched a determined attack. Choosing a pas senger liner as her target, the submarine unleashed a spread of torpedoes, scoring a hit under the ship's bridge. As *Tilefish* dove amid the sounds of explosions, she experienced problems which caused her inadvertently to take on a large amount of water. Before the situation was brought under control, *Tilefish* had made a hair-raising dive to 580 feet, well below test depth. Too deep to be reached by the depth charges of her pursuers, she evaded their attack and continued her patrol. Finding contact with the enemy to be very light, *Tilefish* requested another patrol area and was assigned to the northern Marianas where she searched for targets on 19 and 20 May. She completed this patrol at Majuro on 29 May 1944.

After a refitting by *Bushnell* (AS–15), *Tilefish* departed Majuro on 22 June 1944 and headed with an attack group for the Luzon Strait area. In company with *Sawfish* (SS–276) and *Rock* (SS–274), *Tilefish* set course, via Batan Island and Bashi Channel, for her assigned position. On the morning of 18 July, *Tilefish* launched a torpedo attack on a large convoy and had the satisfaction of seeing a freighter sustain two hits. Meanwhile, *Rock* had joined in the attack and was being held down by a destroyer of the convoy's screen. At 1050, *Tilefish* made a torpedo attack on the destroyer. Seeing their menacing wakes, the enemy ship attempted to evade the torpedoes, but the first hit under its forward mount and wrapped her bow around the bridge. A second hit added to the destroyer's damage. Before *Tilefish* was forced down by enemy aircraft, she caught one last glimpse of the destroyer, listing and dead in the water. Nine minutes later, the submarine made a periscope sweep and found no sign of the enemy ship.

In the days that followed, the submarine patrolled the waters east of Formosa attempting to intercept the convoy which she had damaged on the 18th. On 26 July, *Tilefish* surfaced just at the moment when *Sawfish* launched a three-torpedo attack on a Japanese *I–52*-class submarine. *I–29* exploded, leaving behind only smoke and flames. On 31 July, after *Sawfish* had reported a convoy contact off Luzon, *Tilefish* set course to intercept the enemy ships but never found the quarry. *Tilefish* fueled at Midway before completing her second patrol at Pearl Harbor on 15 August.

Tilefish departed Oahu on 10 September 1944. This patrol, conducted in the Sea of Okhotsk and off the Kuril

Islands, was made difficult by rough seas which produced swells reaching heights of 30 to 40 feet. Despite the problems imposed by high seas, *Tilefish* sank a small trawler with her four-inch gun on the 23d. Early in October, she destroyed two small cargo vessels as they were leaving Hitokappu Wan, Yetorofu Jima. During the mid-watch on 13 October, an adventurous owl came on board. The feathered seafarer was promptly dubbed Boris Hootski and made official ship's mascot. In the following days, *Tilefish* claimed two more kills—a cargo ship and a wooden-hulled antisubmarine vessel. On the 17th, to prevent its being salvaged, she blew out the stern of a vessel grounded west of Shimushiru Island. *Tilefish* ended her third patrol at Midway on 24 October 1944.

On 15 November, *Tilefish* got underway for the Kuril Islands. During the first half of this patrol, she operated in northern waters but was hampered by bitterly cold weather, poor visibility, and hurricane-force winds. The mountainous waves forced the submarine to submerge to ride out the storm. On the 25th, *Tilefish* entered the Sea of Okhotsk to patrol the coast of Shimushiru. Snow frosted the periscope and prevented accurate identification of possible targets. By 16 December, *Tilefish* had moved up to take up a lifeguard station off Najima Saki. On the morning of 22 December, she sank *Chidori*, a torpedo boat, and evaded a Japanese counterattack of depth charges and aerial bombs without damage. She departed the patrol area on 24 December and arrived at Pearl Harbor on 2 January 1945.

After refitting by *Orion* (AS–18), *Tilefish* set course for the Marianas in company with *Thresher* (SS–200) and *Peto* (SS–265) on 31 January 1945. En route, she participated in exercises and searched for the survivors of a downed American plane. Underway from Saipan on 13 February, *Tilefish* proceeded independently to her patrol area in the Nansei Shoto where she prowled the traffic lanes in search of targets. She reported sinking a 90-ton cargo ship in a morning gun attack on 28 February before taking up a lifeguard station in support of planned strikes on Amami Shima. On 1 March, she rescued a flier from *Hancock* (CV–19) whose plane had splashed and sank only 500 yards off the starboard bow of the submarine. She sent a fishing trawler to the bottom on 4 March. On the following

Tilefish (SS–307) after World War II, in a gray-and-black camouflage scheme used on submarines toward the end of the war.

day, in the course of a daylong attack on a freighter, she sank a Japanese minesweeper which was escorting the cargo ship. From 10 to 19 March, she performed lifeguard duties in support of strikes on Nagoya and other Japanese targets. After patrolling the approaches to Tokyo Bay on 22 March, *Tilefish* set course, via Midway and Pearl Harbor, for San Francisco. After undergoing overhaul, she returned to Pearl Harbor on 11 July and was soon underway for Midway and Saipan. When the war in the Pacific ended, *Tilefish* was on lifeguard station off the Ryukyus. She continued lifeguard duties and patrols in the western Pacific until 7 September when she returned to Pearl Harbor.

Early in 1946, *Tilefish* returned to San Francisco and operated off the west coast throughout most of the year. In May, she participated in wolf pack exercises, and in September took part in live load training, using the hulk of the former SS *Schuyler Colfax* as a target. In October, she made a brief trip to the Hawaiian Islands and then returned to the west coast. From January 1947 to September 1950, *Tilefish* continued to operate out of California ports with occasional voyages to Pearl Harbor. During this period, she conducted underway training and took part in fleet exercises off the west coast.

On 5 September 1950, *Tilefish* departed Pearl Harbor for Japan. From 28 September 1950 through 24 March 1951, the submarine operated out of Japanese ports conducting patrols in Korean waters in support of the United Nations campaign in Korea. She made reconnaissance patrols of La Perouse Strait to keep the Commander, Naval Forces Far East, informed of Soviet seaborne activity in that area. After this tour, the submarine resumed her routine of operations out of Hawaiian and west coast ports until 1957. Highlights of this period were convoy attack exercises in Hawaiian waters and a goodwill visit to Acapulco, Mexico, early in June 1956.

Following a period of reduced status and overhaul, *Tilefish* again got underway in April 1957 for Far Eastern waters. During this deployment, she visited ports in Japan and the Ryukyus before completing the cruise at San Diego on 27 September 1957.

On 16 September 1958, the veteran submarine made way via Pearl Harbor for Midway and the Marshalls. With four civilian geophysicists on board from the Hydrographic Office, the submarine completed a submerged survey of Eniwetok, Wake, and Midway, operating at sea for nearly three months. She returned to San Diego on 5 December 1958 for inactivation.

Tilefish was decommissioned on 12 October 1959, underwent overhaul at the San Francisco Naval Shipyard, and was recommissioned on 30 January 1960. Her final decommissioning was in May of 1960. She was sold to the Venezuelan government to be known as ARV *Carite*. *Tilefish* was struck from the Navy list on 1 December 1960.

Carite served in the Venezuelan Navy into the 1970's. While in the service of Venezuela, during the filming of the movie "Murphy's War" in 1969 and 1970, the submarine played the part of a German U-boat hiding in the Amazon River. For the role, she was modified by the addition of a "cigarette deck" aft of her sail and was painted in a "dazzle" camouflage pattern.

Carite was decommissioned by the Venezuelan Navy on 28 January 1977 and scheduled to be cannibalized for spare parts.

Tilefish received five battle stars for World War II service. She received one battle star for Korean service.

Tillamook

A large and prominent Salish Indian tribe which occupied the shores of Tillamook Bay and its tributary rivers in northwestern Oregon.

I

(Tug No. 16: dp. 415; l. 122'6''; b. 24'0''; dr. 12'10'' (mean); s. 10.55 k.; cpl. 20; a. 2 3-pdrs.)

The first *Tillamook* (Tug No. 16) was laid down on 6 January 1914 at Seattle, Wash., by the Seattle Construction & Dry Dock Co.; launched on 15 August 1914 and placed in service soon thereafter.

The tug steamed south to San Francisco and reported to the Commandant, 12th Naval District, for duty at the Mare Island Navy Yard. *Tillamook* served her entire 33-year Navy career towing and assisting ships at Mare Island. During her service, the tug changed designations three times. On 17 July 1920, when the Navy adopted the system of alpha-numeric hull designations, she became AT–16. Almost 16 years later, on 31 January 1936, a number of old tugs previously classified as ocean tugs were reclassified as yard craft, and *Tillamook* became YT–122. She received her final classification—as a medium harbor tug, YTM–122—on 13 April 1944. Following that, she served three more years at Mare Island before she was placed out of service and turned over to the Maritime Commission for disposal on 28 April 1947.

II

(SP–269: t. 24 (gross); l. 59'0''; b. 12'6''; dr. 4'9''; s. 9.5 k.; cpl. 9; a. 1 3-pdr., 2 mg.)

The second *Tillamook*—a motor yacht built in 1911 at Port Clinton, Ohio, by the Matthews Boat Co.—was acquired by the Navy from Mr. D. C. Whitney of Detroit, Mich., on 14 May 1917 and was placed in commission on 1 June 1917 as *SP–269*.

Assigned to the 9th Naval District, *SP–269* patrolled the waters of Lake Michigan without the benefit of her name to avoid confusion with Tug No. 16 which was also named *Tillamook*. She remained active in the 9th Naval District until the fall of 1919. Often official papers referred to her as *Tillamook* (SP–269), particularly those regarding her disposal. *SP–269* was sold to Mr. George Jerome of Detroit, Mich., on 20 November 1919.

III

(ATA–192: dp. 835 (tl.); l. 143'0''; b. 33'10''; dr. 13'2''; s. 13.0 k. (tl.); cpl. 45; a. 1 3''; cl. *ATA–121*)

The third *Tillamook* (ATA–192) was laid down as *ATA–192* on 19 October 1944 at Orange, Tex., by the Levingston Shipbuilding Corp.; launched on 15 November 1944; and commissioned on 23 January 1945, Lt. (jg.) W. C. Heck in command.

After shakedown training in the Gulf of Mexico, *ATA–192* departed Galveston, Tex., on 21 February transited the Panama Canal a week later and headed north. After visits to Acapulco, Mexico; San Diego Calif.; and Portland, Oreg., the tug arrived in Pearl Harbor on 28 April. On 10 May, *ATA–192* sailed for duty in the western Pacific. During the waning days of World War II, she towed ships between various anchorages in the western Pacific. She visited Guam late in June and Okinawa in mid-July. From there, the tug moved south to Leyte in the Philippines, where she remained from 20 to 30 July. Early in August, she headed eastward and proceeded via Ulithi and Pearl Harbor to the west coast. The tug arrived in San Francisco on 1 September at the time of Japan's formal surrender ceremony in Tokyo Bay, across the Pacific and the international date line.

After almost a month in port at San Francisco, *ATA 192* got underway for Pearl Harbor bound for the atomic bomb tests at Bikini Atoll in the Marshalls. *ATA–192* spent four months in the Marshalls during Operation "Crossroads." She ferried personnel, helped fight fires caused by the tests and, on one occasion towed the former Japanese battleship *Nagato*, once

Admiral Isoroku Yamamoto's flagship as Commander in Chief, Combined Fleet. During her stay in the Marshalls, the tug also was a frequent visitor to Kwajalein and Eniwetok Atolls. On 8 September 1946, she left Kwajalein lagoon to return to the United States. After a five-day stopover at Pearl Harbor, she reached San Francisco on 12 October and began the procedure for her post-test radiological clearance.

On 15 November, she departed San Francisco and headed north. After stops at Bremerton and Seattle in Washington, *ATA-192* arrived at Kodiak, Alaska, on New Year's Day 1947 to begin an extended tour of duty in the 17th Naval District. In February, she underwent repairs at Puget Sound Naval Shipyard; and, early in March, she returned to Alaskan waters. Over the next 10 years, she steamed between various ports in Alaska and along the Aleutians chain. On 31 May 1948, she was named *Tillamook*. For the first half of her decade in Alaskan waters, *Tillamook* operated out of Kodiak and, after 25 April 1952, out of Adak. In addition to the usual towing operations, the ship also conducted search and rescue missions. On 27 May 1957, *Tillamook* was ordered out of commission, in reserve. However, that order was rescinded on the following day, and she was reassigned to the Pacific Fleet for duty with the Service Force, Pacific Fleet. From then until well into the fall of 1960, the tug was homeported at Pearl Harbor and conducted towing operations for the Pacific Fleet Service Force.

In November 1960, she was reassigned again, this time to Far Eastern waters guarded by the 7th Fleet. On 17 November, *Tillamook* reached Japan at her new home port, Yokosuka. During her first four years in the western Pacific, she performed towing operations between such bases as Sasebo, Yokosuka, and Subic Bay. The highlight of this period of duty was a visit to Sihanoukville, Cambodia, in April of 1962. Late in 1964, when the American presence in Vietnam began to increase, *Tillamook* also began to visit the ports of that nation. However, her missions in Vietnamese waters up to 1965 were brief port visits to deliver tows at such places as Danang.

During 1965, however, the tug began to participate in combat operations in the expanding conflict in Southeast Asia. In February, she assisted the disabled Coast Guard cutter *Chautauqua* (WPG-41) into Yokosuka for repairs and then returned to combat operations along the Vietnamese coast. In April, *Tillamook* joined the surveillance forces attempting to interdict enemy infiltration and coastwise logistics operations. She assisted a South Vietnamese Navy patrol boat, *PC-04*, in destroying enemy junks beached near Vung Ro. In August, she resumed operations towing district and landing craft between various Far Eastern bases and did not return to Vietnamese waters until December when she towed *YFNB-2* and *YR-71* from Subic Bay to Danang. *Tillamook* visited Vietnam again in January of 1966 when she brought a barge into Camranh Bay.

After another period of towing operations outside of the combat zone, the tug rejoined the American naval forces in Vietnam in August of 1966. She provided gunfire support for forces operating on the Long Tau branch of the Saigon River. In December, while attempting to retrieve a drifting barge, four of her crew became separated from the ship. In the night, the barge drifted ashore, and *Tillamook* provided covering fire through the night to protect the four sailors from nearby enemy troops. The following morning, a small landing craft rescued the men. *Tillamook* returned to Subic Bay soon thereafter. While in Subic, the tug answered a call for a rescue mission with only the duty section embarked. The call came in around 2200 one evening, and the tug got underway immediately to rendezvous with SS *Enid Victory* which was unable to return to port because of a damaged engine. *Tillamook* brought the merchantman safely back to Subic Bay. During 1967, *Tillamook* made three short visits to Vietnam—one to Vung Tau in mid-March, another to Danang in late June, and the third to Vung Tau again early in December. However, she spent most of the year occupied with routine operations in Japanese and Philippine waters. The year 1968 was much the same—though highlighted by a visit to Singapore in June and three short visits to Danang, one each in the months of January, June, and September. In 1969 and 1970, *Tillamook* made only four brief stops in Vietnam—at either Vung Tau or Danang. Her routine of tows between Japan and the Philippines was broken only by an escort mission to Keelung, Taiwan, in mid-September of 1970.

The year 1971 was *Tillamook*'s last as a commissioned Navy ship. In January and February, she operated in Japanese waters out of Yokosuka. Early in March, she made another round-trip voyage to Keelung and returned to Japan at Sasebo on the 19th. The following day, she began a voyage that took her to Pusan, Korea, and Buckner Bay, Okinawa, before she returned to Yokosuka on the 28th. The tug remained in port in Yokosuka for the brief duration of her Navy career. On 1 July 1971, *Tillamook* was decommissioned at Yokosuka and was leased to the Republic of Korea (ROK) under the provisions of the Military Assistance Program. She served the ROK Coast and Geodetic Survey until 1976 when she was scheduled to be returned to the United States Navy for final disposition. Her name was struck from the Navy list on 15 April 1976.

Tillamook earned two battle stars during the Vietnam War.

Tillman

Benjamin Ryan Tillman was born on 11 August 1847 in Edgefield County, S.C. In July 1864, Tillman left school to enter the Confederate Army, but his service to the South during the Civil War was prevented by serious illness. He served as governor of South Carolina from 1890 to 1894; and, during his administration, he founded Clemson Agricultural and Mechanical College. He entered the United States Senate on 4 March 1895, and he held the position of senator for the remainder of his life. During World War I, Tillman was chairman of the Senate Committee on Naval Affairs until his death on 3 July 1918.

I

(DD–135: dp. 1,090; l. 314'4½''; b. 31'8''; dr. 9'8¼'' (aft); s. 35 k.; cpl. 122; a. 4 4'', 1 3'', 12 21'' tt., 2 dct.; cl. *Wickes*)

The first *Tillman* (Destroyer No. 135) was laid down on 29 July 1918 by the Charleston (S.C.) Navy Yard; launched on 7 July 1918; sponsored by Miss Mary Y. Tillman, the granddaughter of Senator Tillman; reclassified DD–135 on 17 July 1920, during the Navy-wide assignment of alphanumeric hull numbers; and commissioned on 10 April 1921, Lt. Louis R. Vail in command.

Following shakedown, *Tillman* operated out of Charleston with Division 20, Squadron 9, Destroyer Flotilla 1, Atlantic Fleet, until the summer of 1921. Operating with half of her normal complement by the following winter, the destroyer trained and cruised with Division 33, Squadron 8, Atlantic Fleet Destroyer Squadrons into the spring of 1922. Soon thereafter, *Tillman* was decommissioned on 3 July 1922 and laid up at the Philadelphia Navy Yard.

After almost eight years of inactivity, *Tillman* was placed back in commission at Philadelphia on 1 May 1930, Lt. Comdr. Alfred Y. Lanphier in command. Returning to Charleston, the destroyer operated with Division 23, Squadron 7, of the Scouting Fleet Destroyer Squadrons. Transferred to Division 48 by 1 January 1931, *Tillman* conducted training cruises for

USS *Tillman* (DD–135) at Charleston, S.C., 14 June 1921.   (19–N–10556)

naval reserve trainees and NROTC midshipmen until late in the spring of 1933, when she shifted to Boston to train reservists and NROTC midshipmen of the 1st Naval District.

As part of the Scouting Fleet Training Squadron, *Tillman* eventually returned to Charleston and alternated tours of active training duty with periods moored in "rotating reserve." On 1 January 1934, she returned to full-time active duty with the Training Squadron and resumed training cruises. The destroyer continued to alternate periods in the rotating reserve with assignments to training duty into the late 1930's. Later assigned to Destroyer Division (DesDiv) 29 of Destroyer Squadron (DesRon) 10, she worked out of Charleston and Boston, training reservists and NROTC midshipmen, participating in Fleet landing exercises in the Caribbean; conducting battle practices and drills; and showing the flag at ports along the eastern seaboard and in the Caribbean. She continued this schedule until she was again decommissioned on 15 June 1939.

Two and one-half months later, German forces attacked Poland, triggering World War II in Europe. Early in the spring of 1940, the tide turned against the Allies, as Germany launched a devastatingly successful blitzkrieg. In addition, German U-boats terrorized transatlantic convoys and took heavy tolls of merchantmen and escorts alike. By summer, Britain stood alone against Hitler, with only the English Channel between her and the hitherto victorious German legions.

The Royal Navy's destroyer forces had taken a bad beating in the Atlantic, as well as in the Norwegian debacle and the evacuation of Dunkirk. At this point, the newly installed prime minister, Winston Churchill, appealed to President Franklin Roosevelt for help. Accordingly, on 23 July 1940, the two leaders agreed on a "destroyers for bases" exchange, whereby the United States would transfer 50 overaged flush-decked destroyers to the British in return for 99-year leases on sites for strategic bases in the Western Hemisphere.

As one of the 50 ships, *Tillman* recommissioned at Philadelphia on 24 August 1940. About three months later, she moved up the coast to Halifax, Nova Scotia, the transfer point for the "50 ships that saved the world." On 21 November 1940, she arrived at that port with the remainder of her division, DesDiv 72, the last group of ships to be turned over to the Royal and Royal Canadian Navies.

Decommissioned on 26 November 1940, *Tillman*'s name was struck from the Navy list on 8 January 1941. Commissioned in the Royal Navy as HMS *Wells* (I.95) on 5 December 1940, the destroyer suffered damage on the 9th in a collision with sister ship HMS *Newmarket* (G.47), the former USS *Robinson* (DD–88). She was thus unable to sail for the British Isles until 4 February 1941. Getting underway on that date in company with HMS *Newark* (G.08), the former USS *Ringgold* (DD–89), *Wells* encountered a heavy gale in which she lost her topmast. *Newark* soon suffered engine failure and had to be towed back to Halifax.

Wells eventually arrived in the United Kingdom and was soon assigned to the 17th Destroyer Division, which provided escorts for the 1st Minelaying Squadron. During this time, she carried out a number of mining operations off the western coast of Scotland.

Between these operations, *Wells* escorted convoys to and from Iceland. On 10 June 1941, while operating south of this strategic isle, she attacked a U-boat but without success. Two days later, she encountered another U-boat and went to the attack, but the explosion of her own depth charges damaged her and forced her to give up the search.

Following refitting at Hull, England, in the autumn of 1941, *Wells* returned to convoy escort duty. On 16 January 1942, she intercepted an SOS from SS *R. J. Cullen*—an American merchantman which had run aground on the southeast side of Barra Island, in the outer Hebrides, west of Scotland. Heavy seas initially made launching a boat a virtual impossibility, but *Wells* stood by until lifeboats and tugs arrived and transported the steamer's crew safely ashore.

While escorting two transports later that spring, *Wells* and *Brighton* (I.08) (ex-USS *Cowell* (DD–167) were bombed by German aircraft west of the Faroes but escaped damage. During November, *Wells* conducted convoy escort operations with Convoy KX-6 supporting Operation "Torch," the invasion of North Africa, and returned to the United Kingdom in December with Convoy MKF–3 to soon resume escort duties with Iceland-bound convoys.

After serving another tour of convoy escort and minelaying escort duties, *Wells* was transferred to Rosyth in August 1943 and operated with the Rosyth Escort Force, screening coastwise convoys between the Firth of Forth and the Thames estuary. Early in 1945, after refitting at the Clyde in late 1944, she became a target ship for aircraft training with the Western Approaches Command, a role in which she erved until reduced to reserve status at Greenock after World War II, in mid-1945. Decommissioned in July 945, *Wells* was subsequently scrapped at Troon, Scotland, on 24 July 1945.

II

DD–641: dp. 1,630; l. 348′3′′; b. 36′1′′; dr. 17′5′′; s. 37.4 k.; cpl. 276; a. 4 5′′, 4 1.1′′, 5 20mm., 5 tt., 2 dct., 6 dcp.; cl. *Gleaves*)

The second *Tillman* (DD–641) was laid down on 1 May 1941 at Charleston, S.C., by the Charleston Navy Yard; launched on 20 December 1941; sponsored by Mrs. Charles Sumner Moore; and commissioned on 4 June 1942, Lt. Comdr. Francis Douglas McCorkle in command.

From June until September 1942, *Tillman* underwent sea trials and shakedown off the east coast. In September and October, the new destroyer escorted convoys and participated in exercises on the Eastern Sea Frontier before getting underway on 23 October from Chesapeake Bay with a convoy bound for Operation "Torch"—the invasion of North Africa.

Shortly before midnight on 7 November, *Tillman* reached a point some six miles off the coast of Africa and began screening the unloading transports of the Center Attack Group during the successful assault on Fedhala. While screening off the transport area, *Tillman* engaged an enemy patrol vessel, *W–43*, which had attempted to slip six merchant ships into the transport area despite the destroyer's warnings. After coming under fire from *Tillman*'s five-inch guns, the patrol vessel exploded and beached. *Tillman* later captured three French merchantmen. On 10 November, American troops advancing on Casablanca from the east came under fire from enemy destroyers. *Tillman, Augusta* (CA–31), and *Edison* (DD–439) attacked the enemy ships, at the same time drawing fire from the shore batteries including that at El Hank. Maneuvering at speeds up to 34 knots, *Tillman* fired on the enemy ships, leaving one vessel steaming in circles, before she returned to her station off the transport area. On 12 November, *Tillman* departed the area escorting a convoy which weathered 50- to 60-foot seas before arriving safely at New York on 1 December.

Tillman continued convoy duty in the wintry Atlantic and then participated in exercises off Casco Bay, Maine. Departing New York harbor in the early hours of 8 February 1943, a dark night with unusually strong tides, *Tillman* sideswiped the paravane boom of an improperly illuminated merchant vessel anchored directly in the channel. After repairs at New York, *Tillman* operated on the Eastern Sea Frontier in February and March, performing escort duties and participating in exercises. In the spring, the destroyer protected convoys in the Atlantic and Mediterranean.

On 5 July, she screened the sortie from Oran of a convoy bound for Operation "Husky," the invasion of Sicily. In the days that followed, the destroyer provided neutralizing fire on beach defenses and picked off artillery which menaced troops landing near Scoglitti. Before dawn on 10 July, *Tillman* fired her first salvo into Yellow Beach at 0331, as the assault got underway. At 0430, a stick of six bombs dropped by enemy aircraft exploded 300 yards off *Tillman*'s starboard bow, temporarily knocking out her radar. An hour later, *Tillman* silenced a shore battery which had been firing on Yellow Beach. Enemy air attackers, flying in low over the land where they were indiscernible by radar, harrassed landing troops and supporting ships. Fear of hitting troops on the beaches forced the Allied ships to withhold their fire when aiming at the low-flying planes. During the night of 10 and 11 July, *Tillman* patrolled off the invasion beaches. On the 11th, she repelled enemy air bombing attacks and supplied fire missions called in by shore observers. On 15 July, *Tillman* returned to Oran to guard returning transports.

During the remainder of 1943, *Tillman* escorted convoys in Mediterranean and Atlantic waters, experiencing many dangerous moments as she protected vulnerable merchant vessels from enemy submarines and airplanes. While en route from New York to Bizerte on 2 September 1943, one day after passing through the Strait of Gibraltar, *Tillman* was attacked by a German torpedo plane. Patchy haze limited visibility to 2,000 yards when the plane, incorrectly identified as friendly, dropped torpedoes. Quick maneuvering saved *Tillman* from destruction by the torpedo which crossed about 30 yards ahead and passed down her port side trailing a sinister wake. During the same attack, *Kendrick* (DD–612) was damaged by a German torpedo. Two days later, the convoy arrived at Bizerte, but the illusion of safety in port was dispelled on 6 September by a 30-minute air attack on the harbor. *Tillman* engaged the attackers with her main battery and machine guns. Thirteen members of her crew were injured when a spent shell exploded on the deck of the ship.

On 6 November 1943, as she steamed off the coast of Algeria, *Tillman* helped repel a German air attack on the port quarter of a convoy carrying troops and supplies for the Italian campaign. An estimated 25 German aircraft, many equipped with glider-bombs, took part in the raid, and sank two merchantmen and the destroyer *Beatty* (DD–640). In the first wave of the attack, a Dornier 217 singled out *Tillman* as the target of her glider-bomb. The radio-controlled missile came in at a terrific speed, but *Tillman*'s machine guns splashed it in a violent explosion only 150 yards off the destroyer's port bow. Soon after, a second glider intended for *Tillman*'s destruction splashed and exploded, again only 150 yards away, as *Tillman* shot down its launching plane. A third glider splashed off the ship's starboard beam as its parent craft turned back in the face of *Tillman*'s concerted fire. During this first stage of the attack, *Tillman* maneuvered constantly and rapidly to evade the gliders. Her own safety temporarily secured, *Tillman* then turned her guns on planes attacking the convoy and splashed another attacker. Soon, the final and fiercest phase of the attack began as five German planes attacked *Tillman*. As her main battery engaged the raiders, *Tillman* turned left full rudder to evade torpedoes, two of which passed nearly parallel to the ship at distances of 60 and 100 feet. Moments later, as the destroyer swung to port to regain her station, a heavy explosion shook the ship. This detonation, thought to have been caused by a torpedo exploding in the destroyer's wake, caused her no serious damage; and she turned to the task of rescuing survivors from the sinking merchant freighter SS *Santa Elena*. She then proceeded to Philippeville to disembark the survivors.

During December 1943 and throughout 1944, *Tillman* escorted convoys between ports in the United States, the Mediterranean, and the United Kingdom. Occasionally, she varied this duty with overhaul at New York or exercises off New England. In the first three months of 1945, *Tillman* participated in exercises in the Caribbean and off the east coast before departing on 28 March from Delaware Bay and steaming via the Canal Zone and San Diego for Hawaii.

Following her arrival at Pearl Harbor on 21 April, she took part in exercises in Hawaiian waters, then departed the area on 1 May. Until September, *Tillman* performed life guard and antisubmarine picket duties out of Guam and Ulithi. On 5 September at Tamil Harbor, the commanding officer of the Japanese garrison on Yap Island formally surrendered to the American Atoll Commander from Ulithi on board *Tillman*.

The destroyer continued to operate in the Carolines and southern Marianas until 3 November 1945 when she proceeded to Pearl Harbor. Then, continuing on, she steamed via the Panama Canal to the east coast, arriving at Charleston on 11 December 1945 for inactivation.

Tillman was decommissioned on 6 February 1947 and was struck from the Navy list in March 1972.

Tillman received three battle stars for World War II service.

Tills

Born in Manitowoc, Wis., on 9 March 1918, Robert George Tills enlisted in the Naval Reserve as a seaman second class on 24 May 1937 and reported for active duty on 14 June. After serving until 14 July 1938, Tills was appointed an aviation cadet on 3 August and reported to the Naval Air Station, Pensacola, Fla., for flight training on 26 August 1938.

On 18 September 1939, 17 days after Hitler's German legions marched into Poland and commenced hostilities in Europe, Tills was commissioned an ensign in the Naval Reserve, and reported to Patrol Wing 2, Patrol Squadron 21, on 5 December. On 14 April 1941, Tills was augmented to regular Navy status and commissioned as ensign.

By this time, Ensign Tills was flying neutrality patrols with Patrol Wing 10, based on the tender *Langley* (AV–3) in the Philippines at Cavite. With war imminent, Commander in Chief, Asiatic Fleet, Admiral Thomas C. Hart, deployed his surface units to the southward, away from the vulnerable Manila Bay anchorages so tantalizingly in reach of Japanese land-based bombers on Formosa. As part of this southern movement, *William B. Preston* (AVD–7) received orders dispatching her to Malalag Bay, near Davao Gulf, on the southeastern coast of Mindanao. Dropping anchor on 1 December, she served as an advance base for three PBY's assigned the duty of patrolling the eastern reaches of the Celebes Sea.

Ensign Tills flew one of the Catalinas, and the planes alternated on aerial reconnaissance flights. Early on 8 December 1941, a radio dispatch crackled over the airwaves into the destroyer-seaplane tender's radio room: "Japan started hostilities; govern yourselves accordingly." The terse message alerted all hands, and *William B. Preston* and her planes prepared for war.

One plane took off immediately to search the seas for signs of the Japanese; while the other two, including the one to which Tills was attached, remained in the serene waters of Malalag Bay, their crews ready to take off at once. *William B. Preston* shifted her anchorage from the two Catalinas to lessen the chances that one bomb, aimed at the ship, would also damage the aircraft. Anxious eyes peered intently into the lightening skies for signs of Nipponese aircraft.

Shortly before 0800, nine Mitsubishi A5M4 "Claudes" from Japanese carrier *Ryujo*, escorting 13 Nakajima D3A–1 "Vals," swept around the narrow point of land screening Malalag Bay from Davao Gulf. Leaving the destroyer seaplane tender alone for the time being, the "Claudes" strafed the helpless PBY's, turning them into collanders of metal and fabric and setting them afire. Ensign Robert Tills died in the fusillade of bullets from the Japanese strafers, the first American naval officer killed in the defense of the Philippines.

(DE–748: dp. 1,450; l. 306'; b. 36'10''; dr. 13'9''; s. 24 k.; cpl. 221; a. 3 3'', 2 40mm., 10 20mm., 2 dct., 8 dcp., 1 dcp. (hh.), 3 21'' tt.; cl. *Cannon*)

Tills (DE–748) was laid down on 23 June 1943 at San Pedro, Calif., by the Western Steel and Pipe Co.; launched on 3 October 1943; sponsored by Miss Helen Irene Tills, the sister of the late Ensign Tills; and commissioned on 8 August 1944, Lt. Comdr. James L. Brooks, USNR, in command.

Tills was assigned to Escort Division (CortDiv) 53 and conducted trials and shakedown off San Diego before post-shakedown availability at Terminal Island. On 16 October, the ship departed the west coast in the screen for Task Group (TG) 19.5, which included escort carriers *Makin Island* (CVE–93), *Lunga Point* (CVE–

94), *Salamaua* (CVE–96), and *Bismarck Sea* (CVE–95). She reached Pearl Harbor on the 23d and took part in antisubmarine operations in Hawaiian waters for the remainder of 1944.

On 2 January 1945, *Tills* departed Pearl Harbor for exercises with TG 12.3, before the hunter-killer group headed for the Marshalls. Arriving at Eniwetok on 15 January, the destroyer escort remained there a fortnight before beginning exercises on the 29th.

Tills weighed anchor on 5 February for a hunter-killer mission. In this, like the other operations staged from the Marshalls, the ship sailed easterly by day and westerly by night to a distance some 400 miles east of Eniwetok. Her patrolling of this stretch of the Pacific between the Hawaiian Islands and the Marshalls continued for 10 days before *Tills* returned to Pearl Harbor for availability alongside tender *Algor* (AD–34).

The ship conducted post-availability exercises off Oahu before screening for *Sangamon* (CVE–26) in late February, while the escort carrier's planes carried out night flight training operations. Returning to Pearl Harbor on 2 March, the ship two days later joined TG 19.3, formed around *Kasaan Bay* (CVE–69). Two five day training cruises followed, before *Tills* was briefly reassigned to TG 19.2, whose nucleus was *Tripoli* (CVE–64).

After routine training and availability at Pearl Harbor, the destroyer escort embarked 2 Navy officers and 23 Navy and Marine enlisted men for transportation to the Marshalls. On 29 March, she rendezvoused with *Gilligan* (DE–508) and *Whitman* (DE–24) which helped her to screen a 17-ship convoy, PD–355T, to Eniwetok. After making port on 6 April, *Tills* rejoined TG 12.3, which conducted hunter-killer operations between the Hawaiian Islands and the Marshalls.

Following her 14 April return to Eniwetok, the escort ship remained with TG 12.3, steaming on antisubmarine patrols east of the Marshalls. On 20 April, a typhoon upset the group's routine by grounding *Corregidor*'s aircraft and pitching the small destroyer escorts in the heavy seas and 70-knot winds. The storm finally abated three days later, and the battered task group returned to Eniwetok.

Designated Task Unit (TU) 96.6.7, *Tills* departed the Marshalls on 30 April and arrived at Ulithi on 3 May. Two days later, the destroyer escort rendezvoused with UOK–9 and screened that convoy to the Ryukyus. En route to Okinawa, *Tills* sighted an abandoned Japanese patrol boat and sank the vessel with gunfire and depth charges.

Dropping anchor off Hagushi Beach on 10 May, the destroyer escort got underway soon thereafter and relieved *Starling* (AM–64) on screening duty in the transport area. On the 12th, *Tills* went to general quarters upon learning that enemy aircraft had been sighted. Spotting two planes emerging from a smoke screen, her gunners opened fire with the 40-millimeter battery before a sharp-eyed lookout noted that the planes were "friendly." The Bofors guns ceased firing immediately, and the aircraft flew away undamaged.

Following her duties with the transport screen off Okinawa, *Tills* was assigned to the screen of Carrier Division 22 which contained escort carriers *Santee* (CVE–29), *Chenango* (CVE–28), and *Block Island* (CVE–106). As these small carriers steamed toward Sakishima, their planes loaded bombs and prepared to launch. Their target, Sakishima, had been serving as a refueling base for Japanese aircraft shuttling between Kyushu and Formosa and was thus an important link in the chain of airbases which supplied Japan's dreaded kamikaze offensive with its deadly aircraft. *Tills* served as antisubmarine screen and plane guard for these strikes which commenced on 1 June. The group returned to Kerama Retto to rearm and refuel before proceeding northward on 20 June for further strikes.

Four days later, the destroyer escort returned to hunter-killer operations and maintained antisubmarine

198

atrols on a continuous basis until making port at Jlithi for availability alongside *Oahu* (ARG–5). For he remainder of July and into August, *Tills* continued ntisubmarine operations on the sea lanes converging in he Western Caroline basin.

As the war progressed to its conclusion in the Pacific, *Tills* commenced a needed availability at Guam. While in Apra Harbor, the destroyer escort received ord that an atomic bomb had been dropped on Hiroshima, Japan, on 6 August. As *Tills* entered dry-ock *ABSD–6* three days later for repairs to her sonar ome, a second atomic blast hit Nagasaki. While the estroyer escort was docked, in company with *Torrance* AKA–76), *Roberts* (DE–749), and SS *A. McKensie*, irwaves brought the welcome news that Japan had urrendered on 15 August. The long Pacific war was ow over.

After remaining at Apra Harbor until 29 August, he destroyer escort headed for Saipan which she eached later that day. She remained there for almost month. On 24 September, she was assigned to duty vith Transport Squadron 12 at Buckner Bay, Okinawa. Following her arrival at Nagasaki with transports ringing American occupation forces, *Tills* made two ound trips between Nagasaki and Manila before mak-ag port at Saipan on 21 October, ending the initial eg of her homeward-bound voyage. Two days later, a company with three sister ships, the remainder of ortDiv 53. *Tills* weighed anchor, headed for Hawaii, nd reached Pearl Harbor on 31 October.

Tills departed Hawaiian waters on 2 November, ound for the west coast. En route, the ship received ord that a large transport plane had crashed into he sea off Oahu, and she was ordered to aid in the earch for possible survivors. Of the eight people escued, *Tills* picked up two and soon transferred them *Casablanca* (CVE–55) where more complete medical reatment was available.

Arriving at San Diego on 9 November, *Tills* under-vent six days of availability before sailing for Panama n the 17th. Eight days later, on 25 November, she ransited the Panama Canal for the first time.

Departing Coco Solo on 27 November, the destroyer scort proceeded to Hampton Roads for further avail-bility in the Norfolk Navy Yard and initial prepara-ions for decommissioning. On 16 January 1946, *Tills* eported to the St. John's River berthing area to ommence initial preservation work for her eventual ecommissioning in June 1946.

Reactivated early in 1947 to an "in-service status," he ship was towed to Miami, Fla., where she was artially fitted out. In July, she made a two-week train-ag cruise to San Juan, Puerto Rico, with naval re-ervists on board. The following month, she entered the harleston (S.C.) Naval Shipyard for overhaul. Re-urbished by November, *Tills* was homeported at Miami nd operated along the east coast from Boston to anama and in the Caribbean, primarily training eservists.

Tills was placed back in full commission at Charles-n, S.C., on 21 November 1950, with Lt. Comdr. Elmo . Zumwalt in command. The destroyer escort sub-equently operated off the east coast as a training ship, ndertaking refresher and reserve training cruises. Iomeported at Charleston, S.C., the ship took part in xercise "Convex III" from 27 February to 20 March 952 and in Operation "Emigrant" from 6 to 12 Octo-er 1952. In between these tasks, she made her first ruise to European waters in the summer of 1952, call-ag at Lisbon, Portugal, and Archachon, France, in une.

Continuing her reserve training cruises off the east ast through the summer of 1955, *Tills* cruised to urope again and, after calling once more at Lisbon, dded Cadiz, Spain, to her itinerary. In 1956, the de-royer escort undertook a total of 13 naval reserve ruises.

On 1 May 1958, *Tills'* home port was moved to Boston, Mass., shifting the locus of her operations northward to the northeastern coast of the United States and to the Canadian provinces of Nova Scotia and Newfoundland.

On 1 September 1959, after the ship had conducted reserve training and refresher training cruises for over a year, her home port was moved still farther north to Portland, Maine. On 18 October 1959, *Tills* was de-commissioned and placed in service as a unit of the Selected Reserve Training Program. Administrative control was accordingly shifted from Commander, Destroyer Force, Atlantic Fleet, to Commandant, 1st Naval District.

After making weekend reserve cruises through the summer of 1961, *Tills* was recommissioned on 1 October 1961 in response to the Berlin Crisis, with Lt. Comdr. W. L. Rich, USNR, in command. Following a six-week repair period at Newport, R.I., and refresher training in Guantanamo Bay, Cuba, the ship operated out of her home port of Norfolk, Va.

After the crisis situation eased, *Tills* returned to her erstwhile home port of Portland, Maine, on 12 July 1962 and was decommissioned there on 1 August 1962. Attached to Reserve Destroyer Squadron 30 and Re-serve Destroyer Escort Squadron, 1st Naval District, *Tills* operated out of South Portland, Maine, in an in-service basis and resumed making weekend reserve training cruises. On these brief voyages, she conducted antisubmarine exercises and steamed up and down the St. Lawrence Seaway. Moving to Newport on 20 Octo-ber 1963, the ship underwent a one-month tender availability during which she received new torpedo tubes which replaced her old ones and her K-guns. She returned to Portland on 17 November and remained there for the remainder of the year.

During 1964, *Tills* participated in a number of diverse and interesting events. After a tender avail-ability alongside *Grand Canyon* (AD–28) from 22 March to 18 April, *Tills* returned to the Naval Re-serve Training Center at South Portland before getting underway for Boston on 13 June. A highlight of her reserve cruise was a four-day visit to the New York World's Fair.

After returning to her Maine base, the ship held an open house on 4 July and then visited Rockland, Maine, for the annual Rockland Seafood Festival on 3 August. On 28 August, *Tills* served as patrol ship for the annual Starboat Yacht Races off Winthrop, Mass.

After subsequently participating in joint United States-Canadian antisubmarine exercises, the ship re-turned to the Naval Training Center at Portland for repairs before resuming her training cruises, a mission she faithfully carried out for the remainder of her career.

Found unfit for further service, *Tills* was struck from the Navy list on 23 September 1968. On 3 April 1969, the ship was sunk as a target off the east coast.

Timbalier

A bay on the coast of Louisiana near New Orleans.

(AVP–54: dp. 2,592; l. 310'0''; b. 41'2''; dr. 13'6''; s. 18.2 k.; cpl. 367; a. 1 5'', 8 40mm.; cl. *Barnegat*)

Timbalier (AVP–54) was laid down on 9 November 1942 at Houghton, Wash., by the Lake Washington Shipyard; launched on 18 April 1943; sponsored by Mrs. S. B. Dunlap; and commissioned on 24 May 1946, Capt. James E. Johnson in command.

Timbalier departed the Seattle area on 20 June and reached San Francisco two days later. Shifting to Alameda, the seaplane tender loaded stores and air-plane spare parts before heading for San Diego on 26 June. She conducted trials and shakedown off the west coast through 27 July, when the ship steamed south for Panama. She transited the canal on 3 Au-gust and proceeded up the coast to New York.

Timbalier (AVP-54) about 1946, in the overall haze-gray color scheme first applied to many naval ships nea the end of World War II. Small bow numbers were retained for some time after the war ended.

Timbalier remained at the New York Naval Shipyard into the autumn. She got underway on 8 November, put into Norfolk the next day, and remained in the vicinity of Hampton Roads into December.

On the 3d, *Timbalier* got underway from Hampton Roads and proceeded to San Juan, Puerto Rico, where she arrived on 7 December and reported for duty to the Commander, Fleet Air Wing (FAW) 11. Based at Trinidad, the seaplane tender operated in the Caribbean and off the east coast of the United States, tending the Martin P5M Mariners of FAW 11 until late 1954.

Timbalier was decommissioned on 15 November 1954 and placed in the Atlantic Reserve Fleet. Her name was struck from the Navy list on 1 May 1960, and the seaplane tender was subsequently sold on 20 December 1960 to Panagiotis Kokkinos, of Piraeus, Greece.

Timmerman

Grant F. Timmerman—born on 14 February 1919 in Americus, Kansas—enlisted in the United States Marine Corps on 28 October 1937. He served at various Marine Corps posts and stations on the west coast and in China before the outbreak of World War II.

Sergeant Timmerman participated in the invasion and capture of Tarawa in November 1943 as a member of the 2d Marine Division. In June and July 1944, he served as a tank commander with the 2d Battalion, 6th Marines, in action against enemy Japanese forces on Saipan. Sergeant Timmerman was awarded the Bronze Star Medal for his conduct on 15 and 16 June 1944. His citation reads: "Continuously exposed to shattering blasts from Japanese mortars during hazardous night and day landing operations, Sergeant Timmerman steadfastly manned his gun and delivered vigorous, accurate fire against bitter enemy counterattacks, thereby assisting vitally in the maintenance of our position."

Serbeant Timmerman was posthumously awarded the Medal of Honor for conspicuous gallantry and intrepidity at the risk of his life during action against Japanese forces on 8 July 1944. "Advancing with his

tank a few yards ahead of the infantry in support a vigorous attack on hostile positions, Sergeant Timme man maintained steady fire from his antiaircraft s mount machinegun until progress was impeded by series of enemy trenches and pillboxes. Observing target of opportunity, he immediately ordered the ta stopped and, mindful of the danger from the muzz blast as he prepared to open fire with the 75-mm. [gun fearlessly stood up in the turret and ordered the i fantry to hit the deck. Quick to act as a grenade, hurl by the Japanese, was about to drop into the open turr hatch, Sergeant Timmerman unhesitatingly blocked t opening with his body, holding the grenade against h chest and taking the brunt of the explosion. His exce tional valor and loyalty in saving his men at the cost his own life reflect the highest credit upon Sergea Timmerman and the United States Naval Service. gallantly gave his life in the service of his country."

(DD–828: dp. 2,420; l. 391'0''; b. 41'0''; dr. 19'0 s. 40 k. (tl.); cpl. 367; a. 6 5'', 12 40mm., 10 20mm cl. *Gearing*)

Timmerman (DD–828) was laid down on 1 Octob 1954 at Bath, Maine, by the Bath Iron Works; assign to the Atlantic Reserve Fleet on 19 November 194 launched on 19 May 1951; sponsored by Mrs. Fr Timmerman; and commissioned on 26 September 195 Comdr. Edward E. Hoffman in command.

Timmerman was constructed as an experiment light weight, advanced design destroyer to test a evaluate, under operating conditions, advanced desi experimental engineering equipment. As a unit of t Operational Development Force, 1st Naval Distri Boston, she tested her new propulsion system for t next four years. On 11 January 1954, her designati was changed to AG–152, a miscellaneous auxiliary sh

The ship was decommissioned at Boston on 27 Ju 1956. She was moved to Philadelphia in Septemb and assigned to the Reserve Fleet. In early 19 *Timmerman* was declared unfit for further service a struck from the Navy list on 4 April 1958. On 21 Ap

1959, she was sold to the Boston Metals Co., Baltimore, Md., and scrapped.

Timor

(Ship: t. 289)

Timor was one of a number of ships acquired early in the Civil War by the Union Navy Department for the purpose of sinking as an obstruction in channels and harbors important to the Confederacy. Purchased on 30 October 1861 at Sag Harbor, N.Y., she sailed with the first contingent of "stone whalers" (see Volume V, Appendix I, pages 427–437), which departed New England ports on 20 November 1861, bound for Savannah. En route, Atlantic gales severely tried the fleet and damaged *Timor*'s canvas and hull so severely that she was forced to put in at Gloucester on 4 December. After being towed to Boston for repairs, she again set her course southward on 20 December.

No longer required at Savannah, *Timor* sailed instead to Charleston where, for a short time, she was turned over to the Army Quartermaster. However, when preparations began for blocking Maffitt's Channel, a secondary entrance to Charleston Harbor, *Timor* was returned to the stone fleet. She was sunk as an obstruction in Maffitt's Channel at the mouth of Charleston harbor on 25 or 26 January 1862, along with some 12 other ships.

Tingey

Thomas Tingey was born in London on 11 September 1750. As a youth, he served in the British Navy commanding a blockhouse at Chateaux Bay on the Labrador coast. He later commanded merchant vessels in the West Indies before coming to the colonies and investing in the East India trade. According to unverified tradition, Tingey served in the Continental Navy during the War for Independence.

In September 1798, Tingey was commissioned a captain in the United States Navy and distinguished himself in the undeclared war with France as commander of the man-of-war *Ganges*. During that time, Tingey commanded a squadron which cruised the waters of the Windward Passage between Hispaniola and Cuba to protect American shipping from French privateers. Tingey commanded *Ganges* as she took four prizes and known for his bloodless encounter with the British frigate *Surprise*.

In January 1800, Tingey was appointed to supervise construction of the new navy yard at Washington, D.C., and became its first commandant on 23 November 1804. In the summer of 1814, as the British advanced on Washington, the Secretary of the Navy ordered Tingey to set fire to the yard. Tingey returned after the withdrawal of the British forces and commanded the yard until his death on 23 February 1829. Commodore Tingey was buried with military honors in what is now known as Congressional Cemetery, Washington, D.C.

I

(Torpedo Boat No. 34: dp. 165 (n.); l. 175'0'' (wl.); b. 17'6''; dr. 4'8'' (mean); s. 24.94 k. (tl.); cpl. 28; a. 3 1-pdr. rf., 3 18'' tt.; cl. *Blakely*)

The first *Tingey* (Torpedo Boat No. 34) was laid down on 29 March 1899 at Baltimore, Md., by the Columbian Iron Works; launched on 25 March 1901; sponsored by Miss Anna T. Craven, the great-great-granddaughter of Commodore Thomas Tingey; and commissioned at Norfolk, Va., on 7 January 1904, Lt. John F. Marshall in command.

Tingey then joined the Reserve Torpedo Flotilla at its base at the Norfolk Navy Yard and remained there for the first third of her Navy career. For the most part, she lay tied up at pierside; but, periodically she got underway to insure her material readiness should a need for her services ever arise. By 1908, she was reassigned to the 3d Torpedo Flotilla, but she remained relatively inactive at Norfolk. In 1909, she was listed as a unit of the Atlantic Torpedo Fleet. However, all three organizations to which she was assigned appear simply to have been different names for the same duty —lying at pierside in reserve.

Sometime late in 1909, *Tingey* moved south from Norfolk to Charleston, S.C., where she was promptly placed in reserve again on 22 December 1909. The torpedo boat remained at Charleston, in various conditions of reserve, but apparently always still in commission. Infrequently, she got underway to test her machinery. In 1917, *Tingey* moved north to the Philadelphia Navy Yard where she was placed out of commission on 8 March 1917. A month later on 7 April 1917, she was recommissioned and moved further north to patrol the coastal waters of the 1st Naval District during the period the United States participated in World War I. In September 1918, the torpedo boat's name was cancelled so that it could be given to Destroyer No. 272, one of the new *Clemson*-class destroyers. The older vessel then became *Coast Torpedo Boat No. 17*. Two months later, Germany sued for the armistice which ended hostilities. *Coast Torpedo Boat No. 17* was placed out of commission at Philadelphia on 30 January 1919, and she was struck from the Navy list on 28 October 1919. On 10 March 1920, she was sold to the Independent Pier Co., of Philadelphia, Pa.

II

(Destroyer No. 272: dp. 1,215 (n.); l. 314'4½''; b. 30'11½''; dr. 9'9¾'' (aft); s. 34.53 k. (tl.); cpl. 122; a. 4 4'', 1 3'', 12 21'' tt., 2 dct.; cl. *Clemson*)

The second *Tingey* (Destroyer No. 272) was laid down on 8 August 1918 at Quincy, Mass., by the Bethlehem Shipbuilding Corp.; launched on 24 April 1919; sponsored by Miss Mary Velora Arringdale; and commissioned at the Boston Navy Yard on 25 July 1919, Comdr. Alfred W. Brown in command.

After fitting out, the destroyer proceeded to the west coast and joined Division 31, Squadron 2, Flotilla 10, at San Diego late in December. For the next two and one-half years, the destroyer operated out of San Diego with the Pacific Fleet. During most of that period, however, she had only 50 percent of her normal complement. Consequently, though she did conduct operations and patrols along the western coast of Mexico, she remained in a quasi-reserve status throughout her brief period of commissioned service. She made but one organizational change during her active career and that came in the latter part of 1921 when she was reassigned to Division 29, Squadron 10.

In 1922, the antimilitarist feeling prevalent following World War I combined with the government's policy of financial retrenchment to cause the deactivation of a substantial portion of the Navy's recently expanded destroyer fleet. *Tingey*, therefore, was placed out of commission on 24 May 1922, berthed at San Diego, and remained there for the remainder of her career. After 14 years of inactivity, *Tingey*'s name was struck from the Navy list on 19 May 1936. She was sold to the Schiavone-Bonomo Corp., of New York City, on 29 September 1936 and was scrapped in December.

III

(DD–539: dp. 2,050; l. 376'1''; b. 39'7''; dr. 17'9''; s. 37 k.; cpl. 273; a. 5 5'', 4 40mm., 4 20 mm., 10 21'' tt., 2 dct., 6 dcp.; cl. *Fletcher*)

The third *Tingey* (DD–539) was laid down on 22 October 1942 by the Bethlehem Steel Co., San Francisco, Calif.; launched on 28 May 1943; sponsored by Mrs.

Garry Owen; and commissioned on 25 November 1943, Comdr. John Odgers Miner in command.

Following shakedown off the west coast, *Tingey* departed San Francisco for the Pacific theater on 2 February 1944. The destroyer participated in exercises out of Pearl Harbor in February and March before screening a convoy en route to the Marshalls early in April. On 13 April, she sortied Majuro to join Rear Admiral Marc A. Mitscher's fast carrier attack force. Later that month, while supporting carrier strikes on Eton and Dublon in the Truk Islands, *Tingey* suffered casualties during an engagement with Japanese aircraft.

Tingey continued on her mission acting as a member of the destroyer screen for Battleship Division 7. On 1 May, *Tingey* participated in the bombardment of Tumu Point to eliminate the site as a Japanese submarine and air base. On 29 April, *Tingey* continued screening duties for the task force while one of its cruiser units bombarded Satawan Island.

On 15 May, *Tingey* sortied Majuro in company with Rear Admiral Alfred E. Montgomery's carrier task group and set course for Marcus and Wake Islands. Early in June, she steamed as a member of Task Force (TF) 58 for the Philippine Sea. During the following week, she operated in the vicinity of Saipan and Tinian participating in the Battle of the Philippine Sea. The carriers of the group launched strike after strike against Guam and Rota and decimated the massed attacks of enemy aircraft flung at them by Japanese Admiral Ozawa in the 19 June battle, later known as "the Great Marianas Turkey Shoot." Also in June, *Tingey* accompanied the group as it conducted air strikes on Pagan Island.

On the last day of June, *Tingey* sortied from Eniwetok with Rear Admiral Ralph E. Davison's carrier task group for air strikes in the Bonins. She then rejoined the 5th Fleet off Saipan to support invasion forces in the Marianas. On 21 July, the carriers launched 10 strikes in support of the assault on Guam. After replenishment at Saipan, *Tingey* set course for the northern Palaus where she supported carrier air sweeps and strikes. She then assumed screening duties for Rear Admiral Gerald F. Bogan's carrier task group as it conducted strikes on enemy concentrations on Guam.

After mooring at Eniwetok for upkeep and inspection, *Tingey* resumed her duties late in August. During the first two weeks of September, she supported carrier strikes on Leyte, Bulan, and Samar, before proceeding to Luzon. There, the destroyer encountered night enemy attacks while supporting carrier strikes on the Philippines. After replenishment at Tanapag Harbor, *Tingey* got underway for Ulithi where she conducted antisubmarine patrols.

In October, *Tingey* continued operations with Mitscher's fast carrier force. On 17 and 18 October, she supported strikes on Visayan Island; and, on the 24th, the carriers launched strikes in the Battle of the Sibuyan Sea. Steaming off San Bernardino Strait on the night of 25 and 26 October, *Tingey* joined with the battleships and cruisers of the task group to sink the *Nowaki*. This ill-fated Japanese destroyer was a straggler from Admiral Kurita's Center Force retiring from the Battle off Samar. Following this engagement, *Tingey* steamed northward for strikes on Manila Bay; then returned in the first week of November for additional strikes on Luzon and Bicol.

Departing Ulithi on 14 November, *Tingey* steamed for the Philippines. En route, she weathered a typhoon which swallowed up three destroyers on 18 December. After a fruitless search for survivors, the carrier group aborted planned strikes on Luzon because of bad weather and rough seas and returned to Ulithi.

On 30 December 1944, the task group conducted strikes on Formosa and Luzon. In January 1945, *Tingey* proceeded to the South China Sea for strikes on French Indochina and Hong Kong before returning to Ulithi. In February, she participated in Operation "Jamboree" strikes on Tokyo Bay and experienced enemy air attacks as she performed screening duties in support of the Iwo Jima landings. She accompanied carriers making strikes on Kyushu and Okinawa in March. When enemy aircraft bombed carrier *Franklin* (CV-13) on the 19th, causing fire and extensive damage, *Tingey* rescued survivors and escorted the battered vessel to Ulithi.

During April and May, enemy air activity was frequent as *Tingey* screened carriers providing direct air support for ground troops on Okinawa. *Tingey* made three assists, splashed a Japanese raider, and rescued downed fliers from *Essex* (CV-9) and *Bunker Hill* (CV-17). Under constant enemy air attacks, *Tingey* continued her duties off Okinawa in May, making one quick run north to Kyushu on 13 May for air strikes. *Tingey* spent most of June undergoing upkeep in the Philippines before getting underway for San Francisco. On 9 July, she arrived at Mare Island where she remained until the end of the war. *Tingey* was decommissioned in March 1946.

The outbreak of the Korean War led to *Tingey's* recommissioning on 27 January 1951. After two months of operations out of San Diego, she was soon taking part in American efforts in the Korean conflict. Following a brief period at Pearl Harbor in May, *Tingey* steamed via Sasebo and Yokosuka for Korea. From August to December 1951, she operated off Wonsan on the east coast of Korea supplying gunfire support for United Nations ground troops, conducting antimining and shore bombardment patrols off Hungnam, and destroying many enemy targets. In December, *Tingey* provided support for Republic of Korea (ROK) commando raids before getting underway for Yokosuka on 4 December.

Tingey spent the first six months of 1952 in San Diego; then steamed on 11 July, via Midway and Pearl Harbor, toward Korea. On 13 August, *Tingey* was again off the east coast of Korea providing gunfire support for ROK forces ashore. She also engaged in antisubmarine searches and conducted night patrols between Nan Do Island and the Korean peninsula. During this six-month tour off Korea, *Tingey* completed successful fire missions on enemy troops, railroads, and gun and mortar positions. She departed Korea on 26 January 1953 and arrived at San Diego on 16 February.

In mid-August, she got underway again for WestPac arriving off Korea on 10 November 1953. During this tour, *Tingey* operated out of Sasebo, Japan conducted missions off the east and west coasts of Korea; and visited Taiwan and the Philippines before she returned to San Diego in April 1954.

Tingey again departed San Diego on 16 November 1954 for operations in the East China Sea and the Sea of Japan. During this tour, she plied the waters of Taiwan Strait to protect Taiwan against invasion and also conducted surveillance of shipping. *Tingey* trained Chinese Nationalist personnel and visited Bangkok and Manila before setting course for Hong Kong on 27 January. Between January and April, she operated off Taiwan, Korea, and Okinawa; then steamed in May for San Diego. In the following three years *Tingey* served additional tours in the Far East. Returning from WestPac in 1957, she operated out of San Diego as a naval reserve training ship until 1962 when SEATO exercises sent *Tingey* to the Far East once more. After completing these exercises, she returned to San Diego to resume reserve training cruises.

On 1 August 1963, *Tingey* was involved in a collision with *Vammen* (DE-644) off southern California. *Tingey* sustained no casualties and was able to return to San Diego under her own power despite severe flooding and damage. She was decommissioned on 3 November 1963, and her name was struck from the Navy list.

Tingey received eight battle stars for World War II service and five battle stars for the Korean War.

Tingles

An island off the Atlantic coast of Maryland, more frequently listed as Tingle and Tingee.

(AG–144: dp. 705; l. 176'; b. 32'; dr. 14')

Tingles (AG–144)—a former Army freight supply ship built in 1944—was acquired by the Navy late in 1947, probably in September; named *Tingles* (AG–144) on 21 November 1947; and placed in service at Subic Bay in the Philippines on 2 December 1947.

Tingles was assigned to the ferry run between Subic and Sangley Point. While operating in the Philippines, she was redesignated a light cargo ship, AKL–13, on 31 March 1949. In May 1949, she was reassigned to the Service Force, Pacific Fleet and departed Subic Bay on 27 May 1949 under tow by *Mataco* (ATF–86). After stops at Guam and at Kwajalein, she reached Pearl Harbor on 25 June and reported to the Commandant, 14th Naval District, for outfitting and commissioning.

On 11 August, it was decided that she should not be outfitted or commissioned. Consequently, early in September, *Tingles* departed Pearl Harbor in company with *LSIL–1092* and *Genesee* (AOG–8) and proceeded to San Francisco, Calif., where she arrived on the 12th. On 10 November 1949, the ship was placed out of service, in reserve, and was berthed with the San Francisco Group, Pacific Reserve Fleet. *Tingles* remained there until 16 December 1953 when she was moved to Stockton, Calif., her berthing area until her name was struck from the Navy list on 1 April 1959. She was subsequently sold to be converted for private use.

Tinian

A 20-square mile island of the southern Marianas assigned by the League of Nations to Japan as a mandate after World War I. It was captured by United States marines after fierce fighting from 24 July to August 1944.

CVE–123: dp. 11,373; l. 557'1''; b. 75'; ew. 105'2''; dr. 32'; s. 19 k.; cpl. 1,066; a. 2 5'', 36 40mm., ac. 34; cl. *Commencement Bay*)

Tinian (CVE–123) was laid down on 20 March 1945 at Tacoma, Wash., by the Todd-Pacific Shipyards, Inc.; launched on 5 September 1945; sponsored by Miss Grace L. Woods; and accepted by the Navy on 30 July 1946.

Never commissioned, the escort aircraft carrier was assigned to the Pacific Reserve Fleet, 19th Fleet, at Tacoma, Wash. On 12 June 1955, the ship was reclassified as an escort helicopter aircraft carrier and redesignated CVHE–123. On 9 June 1958, *Tinian* arrived at San Diego, under tow, and was berthed at South Tee Pier. In May 1959, she was again reclassified, this time as a cargo ship and aircraft ferry, AKV–23.

Tinian remained with the San Diego Group of the Reserve Fleet until 1 June 1970 when she was struck from the Navy list. Her hulk was sold to Levin Metals Co., San Jose, Calif., on 15 December 1971 for scrap.

Tinosa

A poisonous, black, tropical fish.

SS–283: dp. 1,526; l. 311'10''; b. 27'4''; dr. 16'10''; s. 20.25 k. (surf.), 8.75 k. (subm.); cpl. 60; a. 10 21'' tt., 1 3'', 2 .50-cal. mg., 2 .30-cal. mg.; cl. *Gato*)

The first *Tinosa* (SS–283) was laid down on 21 February 1942 at Vallejo, Calif., by the Mare Island Navy Yard; launched on 7 October 1942; sponsored by Mrs. William E. Molloy; and commissioned on 15 January 1943, Lt. Comdr. Lawrence Randall Daspit in command.

After preliminary operations, the submarine proceeded to Hawaii, arriving at Pearl Harbor on 16 April 1943. Over the next two years, she completed twelve war patrols in the Pacific and was credited with sinking 16 enemy ships, totaling 64,655 tons.

On her first war patrol, conducted from 3 May to 19 June 1943, *Tinosa* damaged three enemy ships in the waters east of Kyushu, Japan, while sustaining some depth-charge damage herself. After refitting at Midway, she got underway on 7 July to patrol the sea routes between Borneo and Truk. Handicapped by the faulty firing mechanism of her Mark 14 torpedoes, she damaged only a single tanker on her second patrol before returning to Hawaii on 4 August.

Tinosa next departed Pearl Harbor on 23 September. While prowling waters near the Carolines on the morning of 6 October, *Tinosa* sighted a lone tanker. In a midday torpedo attack, she damaged the enemy ship; then quickly dove to 150 feet. Four depth charges exploded nearby, springing open lockers and knocking men off their feet in the after torpedo room. Moments later, a fire broke out in the motor room but was quickly brought under control. Throughout the afternoon, *Tinosa* and *Steelhead* (SS–280) continued to harass the tanker until evening, when they had the satisfaction of seeing their target go down, sinking by the stern.

At sunset on 6 October, *Tinosa* bombarded a radio station on Alet Island, near Truk. She ended the patrol at Midway on 16 October. Departing Midway on 27 October, *Tinosa* headed for the Palau-Truk sea lanes. On the morning of 22 November, she sighted two cargo ships and two small escort craft steaming in convoy. The submarine fired six torpedoes, scoring hits on both cargo ships. The entire action took only five minutes and left her between two mortally stricken ships, her position clearly marked by torpedo wakes leading out ahead and astern—a perfect fix for the enemy escorts. Amid the sounds of the cargo vessels breaking up, *Tinosa* dove deep to avoid the certain counter attack of the escort vessels. A short time later, four depth charges exploded close by the submarine, knocking out her planes, gyro, steering, internal communications, and other equipment. She made a wild climb to 250 feet, then dove to 380 feet, before her crew regained control. *Tinosa* then resumed evasive tactics which enabled her to elude the remnants of the convoy late in the afternoon.

During an attack on a convoy on 26 November, *Tinosa* sank Japanese cargo ship *Shini Maru* and then dodged 34 depth charges, none of which caused her any damage. She emerged from this encounter with a torpedo stuck in her number 5 tube but managed to remedy the problem and headed for the Molucca Passage-Palau traffic lanes. On 3 December, she sighted a large passenger-cargo vessel, the *Azuma Maru*, protected by a single escort. At 1820, *Tinosa* launched a torpedo attack from periscope depth, damaging the Japanese ship. At 2101 while maneuvering on the surface as she sought to finish off the *Azuma Maru*, *Tinosa* came under fire from the now blazing cargo vessel; and, minutes later, she narrowly avoided being rammed by the crippled enemy ship which circled out of control because of a damaged rudder. At 2120, *Tinosa* fired three more torpedoes, and the *Azuma Maru* disappeared, leaving behind a fiercely burning spot of oil and debris. The submarine then eluded the enemy escort and returned to her patrol area. She concluded this patrol at Fremantle, Australia, on 16 December 1943.

After sailing on 10 January 1944 for the South China Sea, *Tinosa* landed an intelligence team and its supplies at Labian Point, North Borneo, under cover of darkness on the 20th, before proceeding to the Flores Sea. Two days later, she sank *Koshin Maru* and *Seinan Maru* and damaged a third ship in a running attack on a convoy off Viper Shoal. In another action on the night of 15 and 16 February, *Tinosa* drew gunfire from the ships of a convoy as she torpedoed and sank *Odatsuki Maru* and *Chojo Maru*. She ended her fifth patrol at Pearl Harbor on 4 March 1944.

In company with *Parche* (SS–384) and *Bang* (SS–385), *Tinosa* got underway for the East China Sea and her sixth patrol on 29 March. Operating off Japan and the Ryukyus, this wolf pack preyed successfully on passing convoys by stationing units along well-traveled routes. The submarines made six major attacks on this patrol. *Tinosa* herself sank two Japanese cargo ships, *Taibu Maru* and *Toyohi Maru*, in a night attack on 4 May. On this patrol, she also sank a trawler with her 4-inch gun on 9 May and claimed to have damaged three other vessels. The submarine arrived at Majuro on 15 May.

After refitting, *Tinosa* departed the Marshalls on 7 June, bound for the East China Sea. On 18 June, she resorted to unusual tactics in attacking a three-masted 400-ton fishing sampan which had withstood her gunfire. *Tinosa* closed the enemy vessel, doused her with fuel oil, and set her ablaze by tossing flaming, oilsoaked rags on her deck. Shortly after dawn on 2 July, Japanese planes and patrol vessels forced *Tinosa* to go deep near Nagasaki and kept her down until dusk. The following day, the submarine sank two passenger-cargo ships in an attack on a convoy, adding *Konsan Maru* and *Kamo Maru* to her list of kills. Following this patrol, *Tinosa* reported to Hunters Point, Calif., on 7 August, for a much needed overhaul.

Tinosa departed San Diego on 7 November 1944 and proceeded, via Pearl Harbor, to Nansei Shoto to reconnoiter its waters and to test new FM sonar equipment in locating Japanese mines. After 58 days at sea, *Tinosa* returned to Pearl Harbor.

On 17 March 1945, *Tinosa* got underway from Tanapag Harbor in the Marshalls. Despite unexplained damage in her bow plane rigging gear, *Tinosa* proceeded to the Nansei Shoto area and resumed testing the mine-detecting capabilities of her temperamental FM sonar. She also observed Japanese shipping and took reconnaissance photographs before ending the patrol at Apra Harbor, Guam, on 7 April.

On 28 April, *Tinosa* headed for Truk. Her FM sonar equipment—which she had received while at Guam—remarkably improved her sonar range, and she gathered data on sonar performance throughout the voyage. On 3 May, she narrowly escaped damage from bombs dropped by an enemy airplane off Moen Island. Although there was no opportunity to attack enemy shipping during this patrol, *Tinosa* bombarded a Japanese installation on Ulul Island on the night of 14 May. She also made numerous photographs which she turned over to intelligence officers upon her arrival at Guam on 16 May.

Tinosa got underway for the Sea of Japan on 29 May. En route, she rescued 10 survivors of a ditched B–29. Acting on this special mission as a member of a wolf pack selected to initiate Operation "Barney," an incursion into the Sea of Japan, *Tinosa* accomplished the dangerous task of plotting mines in Tsushima Strait on 6 June. Following the completion of this special mission, *Tinosa* made six aggressive torpedo attacks, sank three cargo ships, and—during the daylight hours of 12 June—launched a brilliant surface battle against the *Keito Maru*, a Japanese sea truck. Having sunk four Japanese vessels and damaged a fifth, she completed her 11th patrol arriving at Pearl Harbor on 4 July.

After refitting, *Tinosa* set course for her 12th patrol on 11 August. Before she reached her assigned area, this patrol was terminated by Japan's capitulation. On 26 August 1945, she departed Midway for an overhaul at San Francisco. After operating off the west coast from January to June 1946, she was placed in reserve. In January 1947, *Tinosa* was placed out of commission.

The Korean War precipitated her recommissioning in January 1952. However, she was decommissioned on 9 December 1953, and her name was struck from the Navy list on 1 September 1958. The use of her hull for experimental and training purposes was authorized on 2 March 1959.

Tinosa received nine battle stars for World War II service. She received the Presidential Unit Citation for her fourth, fifth, and sixth war patrols.

II

(SSN–606: dp. 3,700 (surf.), 4,300 (subm.); l. 278'; b. 31'7''; dr. 28'5''; s. 15+ k. (surf.), 25+ k. (subm.); cpl. 96; a. 4 tt., SUBROC; cl. *Permit*)

The second *Tinosa* (SSN–606) was laid down on 24 November 1959 by the Portsmouth (N.H.) Naval Shipyard; launched on 9 December 1961; sponsored by Mrs. Samuel B. Stratton, the wife of Congressman Samuel B. Stratton of New York; and commissioned on 17 October 1964, Comdr. Robert B. Brumsted in command.

Following shakedown out of New London, the submarine underwent availability at her builder's yard from April to June 1966 before making a cruise to Faslane, Scotland, and the Caribbean. After an overhaul which lasted from March through June 1967, the ship provided services for the Naval Underwater Sound Laboratory at New London through the first three months of 1968. During this tour, *Tinosa* was based briefly at Port Everglades, Fla., as well as at New London and visited Bermuda in the course of her operations. At the end of this experimental and test duty, *Tinosa* began local operations out of New London.

Tinosa continued to work off the eastern seaboard and in the Caribbean into 1969. During her major overhaul in the spring of that year, she received submarine safety improvements designed in the wake of the tragic loss of *Thresher* (SSN–593) in April 1963.

USS *Tinosa* (SSN–606).

Following the completion of this yard period, *Tinosa* resumed active operations off the eastern seaboard and into the familiar waters of the Caribbean Sea and continued the routine into the middle of 1971. In July, she crossed the Atlantic for visits to ports in northern Europe and for deployment in the Mediterranean with the 6th Fleet. After operating out of Sardinia and Holy Loch during this period, she returned home in December to conduct tests in conjunction with a project sponsored by the Massachusetts Institute of Technology.

Tinosa worked out of New London from 1 February 1973 until the end of March, operating with submarines and surface craft on exercises and maneuvers. After a three-day visit to the Naval Academy in late April, where she served in a familiarization program for midshipmen, *Tinosa* underwent a tender availability alongside *Fulton* (AS–11) at New London. In ensuing months, the submarine was twice deployed to Bermuda and operated off Andros Island before participating in joint United States-Canadian antisubmarine warfare exercises in December off the Florida coast.

After being drydocked in *ARD–5* at New London from January to March of 1974, *Tinosa* departed her home port on 19 May, bound for the Mediterranean, and conducted her second deployment with the 6th Fleet through the summer months. She visited Bizerte from 24 June to 1 July and was the first nuclear-powered submarine to visit Tunisia.

Returning to New London on 16 November, the ship operated locally out of her homeport into late February 1975. Subsequently operating in the Narragansett Bay area into the spring of that year, *Tinosa* departed New London on 23 July, bound for Charleston, S.C. She later shifted south to operate off the Florida coast. The ship underwent a major overhaul at the Ingalls Shipbuilding yard at Pascagoula, Miss., from late 1975 to 12 December 1977. She then resumed operations with the Atlantic Fleet commencing with two months of weapons system testing in the Caribbean from 13 February to 20 May 1978. This was followed by a combined exercise with units of the Canadian Navy off Florida in mid-April. Most of the summer was spent in preparing for *Tinosa*'s forthcoming deployment to the Mediterranean. On 13 September, she departed New London for five months of operations with the Sixth Fleet. At the end of 1978, the nuclear attack submarine was in upkeep in La Maddalena, Sardina, following operations with a NATO task force composed of United States, British, Italian, and Turkish naval units.

Tinsman

Carl Welby Tinsman—born on 29 March 1924 in Anne Arundel County, Md.—enlisted in the United States Naval Reserve on 19 August 1942 and served in the destroyer *Eberle* (DD–430) as a seaman second class. While patrolling some 650 miles off the coast of Brazil on 10 March 1943, *Eberle*, *Santee* (CVE–29), *Savannah* (CL–42), and *Livermore* (DD–429) intercepted the German blockrade runner *Karin*, flying a Dutch flag. Not fooled by the false colors, *Eberle* and *Savannah* closed the enemy ship at flank speed and fired warning shots across her bow. *Karin*'s crew promptly set her afire and began to abandon ship.

Tinsman was a member of the 14-man party from *Eberle* which boarded the blazing ship and attempted to save the prize. Displaying exceptional courage, Tinsman continued his efforts to put out the fire until a sudden explosion of a demolition charge ended his life. He was posthumously awarded the Silver Star for his heroic action.

(DE–589: dp. 1,450; l. 306'; b. 37'; dr. 13'9"; s. 23.5 k.; cpl. 221; a. 2 5", 4 40mm., 10 20mm., 2 dct., 8 dcp., 1 dcp. (hh.); cl. *Rudderow*)

Tinsman (DE–589) was laid down by the Bethlehem-Hingham Shipyard, Hingham, Mass., on 21 December 1943; launched on 26 June 1944; sponsored by Mrs. James Corley, sister of Seaman Tinsman; and commissioned on 26 June 1944, Lt. William G. Grote, USNR, in command.

Following fitting out and trials, the destroyer got underway on 21 July 1944, proceeded to Bermuda on shakedown, and returned to Boston on 19 August. On 11 October, she departed Boston harbor and, the next day, joined a convoy bound, via the Panama Canal, for the South Pacific. She arrived at Seeadler harbor in the Admiralty Islands late in November and, after training exercises, headed for New Guinea. On 2 December, she reached Hollandia, but was soon at sea again escorting a convoy to Leyte.

On 14 December, while *Tinsman* was in San Pedro Bay, a Japanese suicide plane grazed the bridge of a nearby tanker. A week later, the destroyer escort was back in New Guinea waters, anchoring in Humboldt Bay. The day after Christmas, she was on the move again, this time for waters off the Vogelkop Peninsula of New Guinea for antisubmarine patrol.

In the first days of the new year, she escorted a convoy to San Pedro Bay; then, on 6 January 1945, she departed Leyte to screen a convoy bound for Lingayen Gulf, Luzon. Japan, attempting to stop the mighty American naval force steaming northward, unleashed swarms of kamikaze planes. On 12 January—as *Tinsman* escorted a slow-moving group consisting of an oiler, tugs, and tows—enemy suicide planes attacked her convoy. During the day, the American ships fought off four Japanese attackers, splashing two enemy planes. On the 13th, *Tinsman*'s guns opened up on yet another Japanese aircraft which soon went out of control and splashed. On the 14th, *Tinsman* anchored in Lingayen Gulf and retired the next day toward Leyte, arriving in San Pedro Bay on the 18th to prepare for the landings at Nasugbu, Luzon.

Tinsman departed Leyte Gulf on 27 January 1945 with Amphibious Group 8 and, on the 31st, arrived at Nasugbu Bay where troops of the 11th Airborne Division landed without serious opposition. The real threat came that night as a large number of Japanese "Q-boats" attacked the American ships. Armed with impact bombs, these small, sinister craft swarmed out of the darkness and attempted to ambush *Lough* (DE–586) as she patrolled not far from *Tinsman*. *Tinsman* provided illumination enabling *Lough* to foil the attack, sinking at least six of the enemy vessels. *Tinsman* departed Luzon on 2 February in a convoy bound for Mindoro. Throughout February, she shuttled between Mangarin Bay and Nasugbu Bay on escort duty.

Early in March, she left Leyte Gulf, bound for New Guinea. After taking on stores at Hollandia, *Tinsman* returned to the Philippines and resumed escort duty. In mid-April, she made a voyage to the Palaus; and, in July, she varied her routine of convoy duty with visits to Ulithi and Hollandia before returning to the Philippines.

Although the war ended in August, *Tinsman* remained in the Far East, operating mainly in the Philippines. She also made voyages to Hollandia and Tientsin before setting course for home on 29 November. Steaming via Eniwetok and Pearl Harbor, she arrived at San Pedro, Calif., on 18 December 1945.

She was later berthed at San Diego, where she was placed out of commission on 11 May 1946. On 15 May 1972, her name was struck from the Navy list; and, on 14 September 1973, her hulk was sold to Levin Metals Corporation, San Jose, Calif., for scrapping.

Tinsman received two battle stars for World War II service.

Tioga

A village of Iroquoian Indians that lived near the present site of Athens, Pa., until it was burned by Colonel Hartley in 1778. The name of the village—an Indian term variously translated as "at the forks," "swift current," and "gate"—has been given to a river that rises in Bradford County, Pa., and flows westward and then loops northward and flows to Corning, N.Y., where it joins the Cohocton. Counties in New York and Pennsylvania are also called Tioga.

I

(SwGbt.: t. 819; l. 209'; b. 34'11''; dph. 12'3''; dr. 10'2''; s. 11.5 k.; cpl. 105; a. 1 10'' D.sb., 1 100-pdr., 6 24-pdr. how.; cl. *Genessee*)

The first *Tioga*—one of 12 double-ended steam gunboats laid down in the summer and fall of 1861—was launched by the Boston Navy Yard on 18 April 1862; sponsored by Mrs. H. P. Grace; and commissioned on 30 June 1862, Lt. George W. Rodgers in command.

The double-ender sailed for Hampton Roads late that day, joined the North Atlantic Blockading Squadron upon her arrival there on 5 July, and promptly ascended the James to support Union troops beleaguered in a small pocket on the north bank of the river. Lee's Army of Northern Virginia had recently defeated McClellan's Army of the Potomac in the Seven Days Campaign and penned the Northern forces in a bridgehead at Harrison's Landing where they were protected by the guns of

Union warships and fed by Federal supply ships. The Union gunboats, charged with maintaining control of the James for the North to assure the continuation of McClellan's waterborne support, constituted an independent division of the North Atlantic Blockading Squadron called the James River Flotilla.

While in the James River Flotilla, *Tioga* escorted supply ships and frequently exchanged fire with Southern batteries and sharpshooters ashore. One of her more unusual duties during this assignment was the chore of protecting the barge which carried and launched an observation balloon to reconnoiter Confederate positions and troop deployments. Thus, it has been claimed jocularly that she was one of the first warships to screen an aircraft carrier.

During much of August, *Tioga* helped to cover the movement of Union troops as McClellan evacuated the peninsula between the James and the York Rivers and transferred his troops north by water to protect Washington. After the withdrawal had been largely completed, the James River Flotilla was broken up on 29 August, with a dozen of its ships being transferred to the Potomac Flotilla and the remainder reverting to the direct control of Rear Admiral Louis M. Goldsborough who commanded the North Atlantic Blockading Squadron.

The crew of the USS *Tioga* muster for gunnery drill as the ship lies at anchor off Bangor, Maine, during the Civil War. Men like these were the backbone of the Federal naval effort. (NH 85666)

Tioga was one of the Union warships sent north to strengthen Federal control of the Potomac and, by doing so, to beef up the Union forces afloat ready to defend Washington. At this time, Lee was defeating Pope's Army of Virginia in the Second Battle of Bull Run, greatly endangering the Federal capital.

However, before *Tioga* could become an effective part of the Potomac Flotilla, a change of orders reassigned her to the newly established West India Squadron, formed—under the command of Commodore Charles Wilkes—to counter the threat posed by the recent commissioning of the Confederate commerce raider *Florida* and the expected activation of the steam warship then being built for the South in England under the designation 290 which would prey on Northern shipping as *Alabama*. While *Tioga* never encountered either of these adversaries which would win renown under Confederate colors, she did compile an impressive score against blockade runners.

She took her first prize on St. Valentine's Day 1863, when she overhauled *Avon* and sent that English schooner to Key West, Fla., for adjudication. On 13 March, she captured another British schooner, *Florence Nightingale*, laden with cotton and without papers. Nine days later, she made a prize of the English side-wheel steamer *Granite City*. The British sloop *Justina* struck her colors to the gunboat on 23 June. On 20 June, while cruising in company with *Santiago de Cuba* and *Octorara*, *Tioga* sighted a strange steamer; and the three Union ships gave chase. When they noticed a large quantity of cotton floating in the water, *Tioga* and *Octorara* hove to and picked up the jettisoned cargo, while *Santiago de Cuba* kept up the pursuit and overtook the English steamer *Victory* which she sent to Boston under a prize crew. A week later, *Tioga* captured *Julia* as that English schooner attempted to slip through the Union blockade laden with cotton and rosin. On 25 September, she took Confederate steamer *Herold* which had escaped from the South with a cargo of cotton and naval stores.

Three days before the gunboat made this capture, orders had left Washington to transfer *Tioga* to the East Gulf Blockading Squadron. After beginning her new assignment, the double-ender participated in the capture of sloop *Last Trial* near Key West; but thereafter she spent much of the autumn undergoing repairs at Key West. Early the following year, she resumed her success as a bane to blockade runners. She took an unidentified schooner—laden with salt, liquors, coffee, arms, and other items badly needed by the South—off Grand Bahama Island on 4 January 1864. On 20 March, she overhauled the sloop *Swallows*—laden with cotton, rosin, and tobacco—and sent her to Boston. About the same time, she chased and overtook the sloop *Oriental*.

Late in the spring of 1864, yellow fever broke out on board *Tioga*; and, on 19 June, she was ordered north. She arrived at Portsmouth, N.H., on the 27th and was decommissioned two days later but remained in quarantine in the lower harbor until October.

After an overhaul had been completed and the Civil War had ended, *Tioga* was recommissioned at Portsmouth on 6 June 1865 and cruised off the New England coast through the summer. In October, the ship was transferred to the Gulf Squadron; and she arrived at Pensacola on 30 November. The double-ender cruised in the gulf, principally off the coast of Texas, through the winter and into the spring of 1866. Ordered north, *Tioga* arrived at New York on 8 May and was laid up in the navy yard there until she was sold on 15 October 1867.

II

(Launch: dp. 131; l. 81′10′′; b. 20′; dr. 8′8′′ (mean); s. 9.8 k.; cpl. 11; a. none)

One of the two *Tioga*s to operate under naval control during World War I was the harbor cutter *Tioga*, built at Solomons Island, Md., for the United States Coast Guard. Launched on 4 May 1916, the ship was commissioned on 17 October 1916, Master's Mate Albert M. Totzke, USCG, in command.

When the United States entered World War I, the Treasury Department transferred all Coast Guard ships and craft to the Navy, effective 6 April 1917. *Tioga* operated on local patrol duties in the 5th Naval District through the end of hostilities in November 1918 and into the following summer.

Transferred back to the Coast Guard on 28 August 1919, *Tioga* was apparently placed out of commission soon thereafter, as Coast Guard records indicate that the ship was "recommissioned" at the Coast Guard Depot, South Baltimore, Md., on 5 December 1921. The harbor cutter operated briefly at Baltimore, her pre-war home port, before being assigned to the Norfolk, Va., station on 1 January 1923.

Operating out of Norfolk for the next six years, *Tioga* returned to Baltimore for repairs in the spring of 1929. Upon completion of that yard period which commenced on 3 May, *Tioga* stood out of Baltimore on 13 June to return to Norfolk. Subsequently placed out of commission there on 15 March 1930, the launch was sold to M. J. Gross of New York City on 26 April 1930.

(Tug: t. 73 (gross); l. 74′8′′; b. 18′8′′; dph. 8′5′′)

The second *Tioga* to see naval service during World War I was the wooden-hulled tug built in 1916 at Solomons, Md. She was carried in the 1 November 1918 edition of *Ship's Data, U.S. Naval Vessels* and listed as serving in the 5th Naval District. Apparently, she was never commissioned and probably performed local towing operations within the district. One of her typical missions was her towing of the wooden-hulled motor launch *Vaud J.* from Baltimore to Indian Head, Md., in the autumn of 1918. *Tioga* disappears from Navy and mercantile lists in 1919, and her subsequent fate remains a mystery.

Tioga County

Counties in southern New York and northern Pennsylvania. The former was established in 1791; the latter, in 1804.

(LST–1158: dp. 6,225; l. 384′; b. 56′; dr. 16′1′′; s. 14 k.; cpl. 151; a. 6 3′′; cl. *LST–1156*)

LST–1158 was laid down on 16 June 1952 at Bath, Maine, by the Bath Iron Works; launched on 11 April 1953; sponsored by Mrs. Joseph A. Callaghan; and commissioned on 20 June 1953, Lt. Comdr. Charles R. Patton in command.

Following shakedown out of Little Creek, Va., *LST–1158* shifted to the west coast in January 1954 and operated out of San Diego, Calif. For the next few years, the tank landing ship worked along the west coast and in the Hawaiian Islands. On 2 July 1955, the ship was named *Tioga County*.

The ship conducted two western Pacific (WestPac) deployments between January 1957 and mid-1960, interspersed with local operations and cruises to the Hawaiian Islands. While en route from the Philippines to Yokosuka, Japan, *Tioga County* went to the aid of a stricken Taiwanese fishing craft on 2 February 1960. Bucking gale-force winds and 17-foot seas, the LST passed lines to the foundering craft and drew her alongside. The ship's crew passed lifejackets down to the fishermen and brought them up via a Jacob's ladder, including one of the nine who had injured his leg.

Following her return to the west coast from the second WestPac deployment, the ship resumed local operations out of San Diego. In August 1961, the ship sailed north for Alaskan waters and operated in the Aleutians for three months. On one occasion off Attu, the ship battled high seas and gales up to 80 knots. She returned to San Diego on 1 December 1961.

Sailing for Hawaii following leave and upkeep, *Tioga County* participated in joint Army-Navy exercises in the islands before returning to the California coast. She conducted local operations and training out of San Diego, on occasion between the west coast and the Hawaiian Islands, into 1965. On 31 May of that year, the ship was selected as the test bed for the "Sea Sparrow" missile; and she participated in these tests until June, when she was commended by the Raytheon Corporation for her part in the development of the missile system.

In July 1965, *Tioga County* departed San Diego, bound for Hawaii. During her five-month deployment, she operated out of Pearl Harbor and worked with the Army 25th Infantry Division on exercises. Although the ship was scheduled to spend Christmas in San Diego, a change of plans sent her to the Far East for her third WestPac deployment.

Arriving at Subic Bay en route to Vietnamese waters, she loaded barbed wire and aviation fuel tanks and got underway for Danang in mid-January 1966. After delivering her cargo there, she embarked troops and served as a "combat taxi" for the Army 101st Airborne Division, making troop and vehicle lifts between Phan Rang and Tuy Hoa and carrying up to 1,000 troops each time.

After shifting briefly to Subic Bay for a drydocking for repair of her screws, *Tioga County* soon returned to Vietnamese waters to take part in Operation "Double Eagle," off Quang Ngai province. She made numerous beachings to load troops and cargo and earned her first engagement star for this action.

Following this logistics support evolution, the LST returned to the west coast—via Hong Kong; Yokosuka, Japan; and Pearl Harbor—and reached San Diego on 14 May 1966.

Tioga County conducted local operations along the west coast until 2 March 1967, when she got underway for her fourth WestPac deployment. Proceeding via Pearl Harbor, Guam, and Subic Bay, the LST arrived at Danang on 28 April with 43 vehicles and other cargo.

Following a run to Okinawa, *Tioga County* returned to Vietnam and became the first LST of her class to participate in duty with the Mobile Riverine Assault Force.

Arriving at Vung Tau on 6 June, the ship loaded 30,000 cases of "C" rations; 700 tons of Army ammunition, and 350 tons of miscellaneous cargo. She transited the Song Cua Thieu to the 9th Infantry's advanced base at Dong Tam and took on board 369 men of "B" and "C" companies of the 3d Battalion, 9th Infantry.

Under the aegis of Commander, River Flotilla 1, *Tioga County* served in the Rung Sat special zone of the Mekong Delta region, supporting "search-and-destroy" missions against Viet Cong (VC) troops. She acted as a "Mekong Hilton" to the men who were based on board and served as a mobile ammunition and supply depot. In addition, she accompanied the rest of the riverine force up the Song Soirap to Nha Be for close support of both artillery and infantry combat operations.

Difficulty with the ship's generators forced her back to Subic Bay for repairs before she returned to Vietnamese waters in late July. She then joined Amphibious Ready Group Alfa off the coast of Viet Nam near the Demilitarized Zone (DMZ). Here she participated in Operations "Beacon Gate," "Beacon Guide," and "Beacon Point." During this period, in addition to logistics support operations, *Tioga County* conducted her first combat landing as her LCVP's put a Marine landing team ashore on the coastal region of Quang Ngai province—a known VC stronghold near the DMZ—with the initial landing wave.

Detached from this duty on 6 September, *Tioga County* sailed for the United States, steamed via Yokosuka and Pearl Harbor, and arrived back at her homeport on Navy Day, 27 October. The LST conducted local operations and training out of San Diego into

1970, before she conducted her fifth and final WestPac deployment from 5 January to 7 July.

Decommissioned on 23 December 1970, *Tioga County* was placed in reserve at San Diego with the inactive fleet. Activated in mid-1972 for service with the Military Sealift Command, *Tioga County* was designated T–LST–1158 and operated as such until she was transferred to the Maritime Administration in 1973 to be laid up in the National Defense Reserve Fleet. Struck from the Navy list on 1 November 1973, the former tank landing ship is in the Maritime Administration custody at Suisun Bay into 1978.

Tioga County received three battle stars for Vietnam service.

Tippecanoe

A river which runs west and south across Indiana from Lake Tippecanoe, in Kosciusko county, to converge with the Wabash River near the site of a battle of the same name. On 7 November 1811, troops under the command of General William Henry Harrison, then governor of Indiana Territory and, later, President of the United States, met and defeated warriors of Tecumseh's Indian confederation.

(Monitor: dp. 2,100; l. 224'0''; b. 43'8''; dr. 13'6''; a. 2 15'' D.sb.; cl. *Canonicus*)

Tippecanoe—a single-turreted monitor constructed in 1862 by Miles Greenwood in Cincinnati, Ohio—was renamed *Vesuvius* on 15 June 1869 and then *Wyandotte* (*q.v.*) on 10 August 1869.

(Id. No. 2141: t. 5,644; l. 415'3''; b. 56'; dr. 25'6'' (aft); s. 11 k.; a. 1 5'', 1 3'')

SS *Holsatia*—a steamer built in 1914 at Dumbarton, Scotland by A. McMillan & Son, Ltd.—served the German flag Hamburg-America Line until seized by the United States government early in 1917. She was renamed *Tippecanoe* and was turned over to the United States Shipping Board (USSB) to serve as an Army cargo transport.

Evidence suggests that the Navy intended to take over the ship, but *Tippecanoe* never appeared on the Navy list. That may have been due to the brevity of her service. Her name did appear in the *Navy Directory* over a three-month period in the summer of 1918. Perhaps she was transferred to the Navy but was sunk before her name was published on the Navy list. Perhaps she was sunk before the Navy's plans to acquire her came to fruition. The fact that she carried a Navy armed-guard gun crew during her single voyage under the American flag strongly suggests that the ship was never officially a Navy unit. However, she was inspected by a representative of the Commandant, 12th Naval District, in December 1917 and was fitted out for service by the Navy at San Francisco. In any event, the USSB assigned her to a convoy during the summer of 1918; and, on 25 July 1918, some 500 miles west of Brest, a torpedo from *U–91* abruptly ended her brief career.

I

(AO–21: dp. 16,800 (f.); l. 477'10''; b. 60'3''; dr. 27'8'' (lim.); s. 11.0 k. (tl.); cpl. 208; a. 2 5'', 2 3''; cl. *Patoka*)

Tippecanoe (AO–21) was laid down on 1 October 1919 at Newport News, Va., by the Newport News Shipbuilding & Drydock Co.; launched on 5 June 1920; delivered to the United States Shipping Board late that year; and acquired by the Navy at the Mare Island Navy Yard on 6 March 1922.

The oiler *Tippecanoe* (AO–21) off Mare Island, 14 November 1942. Her wide expanse of black boot topping shows that her oil tanks are empty of cargo. (19–N–36906)

Tippecanoe remained inactive at Mare Island for almost two decades before she was finally placed in commission on 6 March 1940, Comdr. Hugh W. Olds in command. The oiler was assigned to Squadron 8, Base Force Train, and operated between the west coast and the Hawaiian Islands for the next two years. Her most frequent ports of call were Pearl Harbor, San Pedro, San Francisco, San Diego, and Seattle.

When the Japanese attacked Pearl Harbor on 7 December 1941, fortune ordained that *Tippecanoe* be safe in San Francisco. During the first three months of the war, the oiler steamed up and down the west coast between San Diego, San Pedro, San Francisco, and Seattle. She did not leave the west coast until 3 February when she headed back to Hawaii. She entered Pearl Harbor on the 17th and lay over there until 3 March when she headed for the South Pacific. After a brief stop at Pago Pago, Samoa, the ship put to sea on 15 March and headed to an area north of New Caledonia to fuel Rear Admiral Frank Jack Fletcher's Task Force (TF) 17. She returned to the vicinity of Samoa on 26 March, visited Tongatabu on 6 April, and put into Noumea, New Caledonia, on the 26th.

On 1 May, the oiler put to sea to rendezvous with TF 17 once more. She made contact with Rear Admiral Aubrey W. Fitch's task unit—built around *Lexington* (CV–2)—and, on the 2d and 3d, fueled the venerable carrier and her supporting ships. Drained bone dry, *Tippecanoe* then headed for Efate where she arrived on 4 May, the day Rear Admiral Fletcher's *Yorktown* (CV–5) airmen struck the Japanese seaplane base at Tulagi to open the preliminaries of the historic action that stopped Japan's southward advance. During the Battle of the Coral Sea itself, *Tippecanoe* remained in the haven at Efate. On 8 May, she got underway and, for a time, joined Vice Admiral William F. Halsey's recently arrived TF 16—built around carriers *Enterprise* (CV–6) and *Hornet* (CV–8). She stopped at Noumea on 11 May and then continued on to Samoa, reaching Tutuila on 24 May. Four days later, she put to sea to return to Hawaii and entered Pearl Harbor on the 30th. On 1 July, she left Oahu to conduct nearly a month of operations with TF 18 before returning on the 26th.

Tippecanoe departed Pearl Harbor on 9 August 1942 and reached Alaskan waters on the 15th to begin three years in the frigid northern latitudes of the Pacific. For the remainder of the war, she steamed the resupply circuit between such ports as Kodiak, Dutch Harbor, Adak, Akutan, Cold Bay, and Attu and made periodic voyages south to Seattle and San Francisco to replenish. In May 1943, she supported the invasion of Attu, but from a safe distance in port at Adak. By the latter part of the summer, the Aleutians had been secured, and her travels among the American bases in the area became routine.

On 15 August 1945, when hostilities in the Pacific ceased, *Tippecanoe* was en route from Seattle to Dutch Harbor. After visits to Adak and Attu during the latter half of the month, the oiler headed for Japan for several months of duty supporting the occupation forces. She arrived at Ominato on 8 September and, after a month there, moved on to Tokyo. During her two remaining months in Japan, she visited Aomori, Yokohama, and Yokosuka. She departed Yokosuka on 28 November to return to the United States and entered San Francisco on 18 December. On 6 March 1946, *Tippecanoe* was decommissioned at Mare Island Naval Shipyard. Her disposal was authorized on 19 March, and her name was struck from the Navy list on 12 April. She was transferred to the Maritime Commission on 7 October and was sold to the National Metal & Steel Co. on 20 November 1946.

Tipton

Counties in Indiana and Tennessee.

The Tennessee county is named for Capt. Jacob Tipton, a native of North Carolina who was killed on 4 November 1791 during a battle on a branch of the Wabash River near Ft. Wayne, Ind., between United States troops led by Major General Arthur St. Clair and a confederated Indian army composed primarily of Miami Indians.

The Indiana county was named for Senator John Tipton, a veteran of the Indian Wars and the War of 1812, who represented Indiana in the United States Senate from 1832 until shortly before his death on 5 April 1839.

(AKA–215: dp. 7,125; l. 338'6''; b. 50'0''; dr. 21'1''; s. 11.5 k. (tl.); cpl. 85; a. 1 3''; cl. *Alamosa*; T. C1–M–AV1)

Tipton (AKA–215) was laid down under Maritime Commission Contract (MC hull 2169) on 28 December 1944 at Sturgeon Bay, Wis., by the Leathem D. Smith Shipbuilding Co.; launched on 13 March 1945; sponsored by Mrs. W. F. Maister; transferred to the Navy Department on 7 September 1945; and commissioned on

9 October 1945, Lt. Comdr. H. E. Gray, USCGR, in command.

Upon commissioning, the cargo ship was transferred to the custody of the Coast Guard for maintenance and operation and was manned by a Coast Guard crew. *Tipton* was decommissioned and permanently transferred to the Coast Guard on 4 March 1946. She was struck from the Navy list on 20 March 1946.

Tirante

A silvery, enlongated "cutlass fish" found in waters off Cuba.

(SS–420: dp. 1,570 (surf.), 2,416 (subm.); l. 311'8''; b. 27'2''; dr. 15'3'' (mean); s. 20.25 k. (surf.), 8.75 k. (subm.); cpl. 66; a. 10 21'' tt., 1 5'', 1 40mm., 1 20mm., 2 .50-cal. mg.; cl. *Balao*)

Tirante (SS–420) was laid down on 28 April 1944 by the Portsmouth (N.H.) Navy Yard; launched on 9 August 1944; sponsored by Mrs. William B. Sieglaff, wife of Comdr. Sieglaff; and commissioned on 6 November 1944, Lt. Comdr. George L. Street III in command.

Following shakedown training in Long Island Sound and training in waters off Panama and off Oahu, Hawaii, *Tirante* departed Pearl Harbor on 3 March 1945, bound for Japanese home waters. Prowling to the westward of Kyushu, the submarine patrolled the approaches to Nagasaki. She had good hunting. She sank the 703-ton tanker *Fuji Maru* on 25 March and followed this success with the sinking of the 1,218-ton freighter *Nase Maru* three days later. After the latter attack, Japanese escorts kept *Tirante* down for seven hours, before she slipped away from her hunters, unscathed.

On 31 March, *Tirante* shelled and sank a 70-ton lugger with 5-inch and 40-millimeter gunfire and, on 1 April, missed an LST-type vessel with a spread of three torpedoes. The submarine soon shifted to waters off the south coast of Korea, near the Strait of Tsushima. At twilight on 6 April, she battle-surfaced and captured a small Japanese fishing vessel and took its three crewmen prisoner before sinking the prize.

The following day, *Tirante* torpedoed a 2,800-ton cargo freighter loaded with a deck cargo of oil drums. The submarine surfaced, looked over the debris, and directed nearby Korean fishing craft to pick up two survivors who were clinging to pieces of wreckage. Nevertheless, although observers on the submarine reported witnessing the *Maru's* sinking, post-war examination of Japanese records failed to confirm the "kill."

Having broken the Japanese codes, American naval intelligence men were able to anticipate Japanese movements. One intercepted enemy message told of an important convoy steaming toward *Tirante's* area. In response to this information, the submarine laid an ambush on 9 April. Picking out two targets, she fired three torpedoes at each. One spread missed, but the other struck the 5,500-ton transport *Nikko Maru*—carrying homeward-bound Japanese soldiers and sailors from Shanghai. As the important auxiliary slipped beneath the waves, enemy escorts leapt to the offensive. To ward off the counterattack, *Tirante* fired a "cutie" (homing torpedo) at one of the escorts and heard subsequent "breaking-up noises." But again, post-war accounting failed to confirm the sinking.

Tirante resumed her relentless prowling of the Yellow Sea between Quelpart Island (Cheju Do) and the mouth of the Yangtze. She soon received an intelligence report which informed her that an important Japanese transport was at Cheju, the main port on Quelpart Island. Under cover of darkness, *Tirante* boldly began her approach on the surface. In defiance of possible enemy radar or patrolling planes or ships, she closed the coast and penetrated the mine- and shoal-obstructed waters within the 10-fathom curve line. Prepared to fight her way out, *Tirante* then entered the harbor where she found three targets: two escort vessels and the 4,000-ton *Juzan Maru.*

The submarine launched three torpedoes at the *maru,* which blew up in an awesome explosion. The conflagration clearly illuminated *Tirante* and alerted the *Mikura-*class escort vessel *Nomi* and *Kaibokan No. 31* which immediately got underway toward the invading submersible. While she headed back out to sea at flank speed, *Tirante* launched a spread of torpedoes which hit and destroyed both pursuers. En route to Midway, the submarine captured two Japanese airmen (bringing her prisoner total to five) and concluded her first war patrol on 25 April.

Tirante's stellar performance earned Comdr. Street the Medal of Honor. Lt. Edward L. Beach, the executive officer—and later commander of *Triton* (SSRN–586) during the submarine's submerged circumnavigation of the globe—received the Navy Cross. The ship, herself, was awarded the Presidential Unit Citation.

Tirante departed from Midway on 20 May as command ship of the nine-boat "wolfpack" dubbed "Street's Sweepers." They patrolled the Yellow and East China Seas on the lookout for enemy targets—by then dwindling in number. *Tirante* located a four-ship convoy on 11 June, in the familiar hunting grounds off Nagasaki. She evaded the three escorts long enough to get a shot at the lone merchantman, an 800-ton cargo freighter, and pressed home a successful attack. Post-war Japanese records, though, do not confirm a "kill."

The next day, *Tirante* pulled off nearly a repeat performance of her hit-and-run raid at Cheju. She crept into Ha Shima harbor, some seven miles from Nagasaki and picked out the 2,200-ton *Hakuju Maru* moored alongside a colliery. From a range of 1,000 yards, the submarine fired a "down the throat" shot at the cargoman which exploded with a roar. The second "fish" failed to detonate, but the third completed the destruction begun by the first. As shells from shore guns fell around her, *Tirante* bent on speed and cleared the area.

Resuming her roving patrols, *Tirante* and her sisters played havoc with shipping between Korea and Japan, destroying junks carrying supplies from Korea to the Japanese home islands. Boarding parties from the submarine would take off the skippers for questioning, put the crew in life boats, and set the craft afire. *Tirante* bagged a dozen in this manner and also destroyed two heavily armed picket boats with surface gunfire before returning to Guam on 19 July.

Tirante departed Guam on 12 August on what would have been her third war patrol. The end of the war, however, cut this operation short and the submarine put into Midway on the 23d. Eventually sailing for the east coast of the United States, *Tirante* moored at the Washington Navy Yard in October—at which time Comdr. Street received his Medal of Honor in a White House ceremony. Shifting to Staten Island, N.Y., on 31 October, the submarine remained there until moving to New London, Conn., on 8 January 1946. After conducting training operations out of New London, *Tirante* was decommissioned and placed in reserve on 6 July 1946 at her Connecticut home port.

Subsequently converted to greater underwater propulsive power (GUPPY) configuration, *Tirante* was recommissioned on 26 November 1952, at the Portsmouth Naval Shipyard. After conducting her shakedown to Bermuda and operating in the Atlantic as far north as Iceland, the submarine returned to the east coast of the United States to prepare for her first deployment with the 6th Fleet.

In the ensuing two decades, *Tirante* conducted six more Mediterranean deployments, interspersed with a regular schedule of exercises and maneuvers with Fleet units in the North Atlantic, off the east coast and in the Caribbean and the Gulf of Mexico. The ship participated in joint exercises with NATO forces; sometimes served as a target for antisubmarine warfare exercises; and, on occasion, assisted the Fleet Sonar

Tirante (SS–420) as a streamlined Guppy IIA submarine, July 1962. A sonar dome is prominent on her forecastle.

School at Key West, Fla., in the development of ASW tactics and weapons.

Decommissioned at Key West, Fla., on 1 October 1973, and struck from the Navy list the same day, *Tirante* was sold on 11 April 1974 to Union Minerals and Alloys of New York, for scrapping.

Tirante received two battle stars and a Presidential Unit Citation for her World War II service.

Tiru

A member of the lizardfish family. Voracious and carnivorous, this fish is found in the Mediterranean and the Atlantic—especially in the Bermuda area and Caribbean.

(SS–416: dp. 1,525 (surf.), 2,415 (subm.); l. 311'8''; b. 27'3''; dr. 15'3''; s. 20.25 k. (surf.), 8.75 k. (subm.); cpl. 81; a. 10 21'' tt., 1 5'', 1 40mm.; cl. *Balao*)

Tiru (SS–416)—laid down on 17 April 1944 at Vallejo, Calif., by the Mare Island Navy Yard—remained in an uncompleted state for three years as a result of the curtailment of the submarine building program at the end of World War II. In the fall of 1947, the Navy decided to complete *Tiru* as a "Guppy" (greater underwater propulsive power) snorkel boat. Its altered design incorporated improvements resulting from the Navy's recent combat experience and German technical development. *Tiru* was launched on 16 September 1947; sponsored by Mrs. John P. Cromwell, the widow of Capt. John P. Cromwell, who rode *Sculpin* to his death rather than risk divulging important war

plans under torture; and commissioned on 1 September 1948, Comdr. Charles N. G. Hendricks in command.

Tiru conducted training and trials off the west coast before heading for Hawaii on 10 February 1949. Homeported at Pearl Harbor and attached to Submarine Squadron (SubRon) 12, the "Guppy" submarine operated in Hawaiian waters for a year and one-half before conducting a 12-day snorkel voyage from Pearl Harbor to the west coast which ended upon her arrival at San Diego on 27 June 1950.

On 9 June 1951, *Tiru* sailed for the Far East and her first Western Pacific (WestPac) deployment. While in Asiatic waters, she operated in support of United Nations forces engaged in combatting communist aggression in Korea. Then, after departing Yokosuka, Japan, on 26 November, the warship arrived at Pearl Harbor on 6 December. Her operations in the Hawaiian area continued until 24 February 1952, when *Tiru* got underway for her second WestPac deployment.

Between 1952 and 1959, *Tiru* conducted four more WestPac deployments, interspersed with local operations—providing services for antisubmarine warfare (ASW) exercises and conducting type-training. Operating with the 7th Fleet from 1 January to 17 April 1959, on her seventh WestPac tour, *Tiru* returned to Pearl Harbor for a major overhaul, entering the shipyard on 4 May 1959 for a fleet rehabilitation and modernization (FRAM) conversion to a "Guppy" III. In the course of the work, the ship took on a new and different external appearance. Her hull was lengthened by 12 feet; she acquired a new conning tower, five feet longer than its predecessor; and a fiberglass sail was added. Internally, increased sonar and ordnance equipment greatly enhanced the ship's capabilities in those key areas. On the last day of the year 1959, *Tiru* emerged from the overhaul a virtually "new" ship.

From 1 January to 10 November 1960, *Tiru* conducted local operations out of Pearl Harbor to prove the worth of the FRAM/Guppy III conversion. After testing and honing her capabilities, the submarine departed Pearl Harbor on 10 November for another 7th Fleet deployment. She later returned to Pearl Harbor on 10 May 1961 upon completion of her eighth WestPac cruise.

Local operations out of her home port occupied the rest of 1961 and the first few months of 1962. She again was deployed to WestPac in March and April before returning to Hawaiian waters on 3 May. The next month, the ship operated with a carrier task force on ASW "hunter-killer" exercises. While the submarine was engaged in a firing exercise, a torpedo malfunction in her after torpedo room seriously damaged the compartment, and 18 men were overcome by toxic gases. Quick reaction averted a more serious tragedy and earned four men—one officer and three enlisted men—Navy and Marine Corps medals.

The ship conducted three more WestPac deployments through 1965 before she returned to a schedule of local operations. *Tiru* entered another major overhaul on 6 December 1965—one which saw the installation of a masking system to cover the ship's own noise while snorkeling. Further internal alterations improved both her fighting capacity and her habitability. She conducted sea trials until 14 June 1966 when she departed Hawaii for the Naval Torpedo Station at Keyport, Wash., for an alignment and testing of her weapon system. The submarine departed the west coast on 9 July, bound for Hawaiian waters, and made port at Pearl Harbor nine days later to commence pre-deployment operations.

After a 16-day passage from Hawaii, *Tiru* arrived at Brisbane, Australia, on 12 October. Three days later, she sailed to commence ASW exercises in the Coral Sea with warships of the Australian, British, New Zealand, and United States Navies. The nine-day exercise provided for submarine patrol, reconnaissance, and attack operations against both carrier and destroyer task forces before the submarine returned to Brisbane on 26 October.

On 2 November, *Tiru* got underway for Subic Bay, Philippine Islands. One day out, the submarine ran aground on Frederick Reef. For two anxious days and nights, *Tiru* attempted to extricate herself from the predicament by backing off under her own power, but to no avail. On 6 November, civilian tug *Carlock* and Australian destroyer HMAS *Vendetta* came to the rescue, arriving on the scene and commencing salvage operations under the direction of a 7th Fleet salvage officer. Returning to Brisbane, *Tiru* was drydocked at South Brisbane Dockyard for emergency repairs and damage estimates.

Following temporary repairs to her sonar dome, outer hull, and keel, the submarine gingerly made her way from Australia to the United States Naval Ship Repair Facility, Yokosuka, Japan. En route, *Tiru* called at Guam to provision alongside *Proteus* (AS-19) and pick up new crew members. Arriving at Yokosuka on 29 November, the submarine entered drydock for restricted availability.

Once repaired, *Tiru* left Yokosuka on 9 January 1967 for Chin Hae, Korea, and while in transit provided services for an Iwakuni-based patrol plane squadron. Operating with Republic of Korea (ROK) ASW forces from 15 to 17 January, *Tiru* arrived back at Yokosuka on the 22d for upkeep. From 7 February to 20 March, the submarine conducted special operations before returning for further upkeep prior to a "Yankee Station" deployment off Vietnam. She later operated with Nationalist Chinese forces on ASW exercises; conducted additional special operations; and again provided services for patrol plane squadrons based at Iwakuni, before returning to Hawaii on 15 May.

Spending the remainder of the year 1967 on local operations out of Pearl Harbor, *Tiru* commenced the year 1968 as a unit of Submarine Division (SubDiv) 72, SubRon 7, and Submarine Flotilla (SubFlot) 5. On 16 May, the submarine was shifted to operational control of Commander, 7th Fleet, with her home port changed to Yokosuka, Japan. Departing the western Pacific on 4 October after a tour which had included a transit through the Vietnam war zone, *Tiru* returned to the west coast; and her home port was changed to San Francisco, Calif., while she became a unit of SubDiv 52, SubRon 5, SubFlot 1.

Overhauls and local operations occupied the ship until 12 November 1969, when *Tiru* sailed west for another WestPac deployment. Transferred to the command of the Commander, 7th Fleet, on 6 December, the submarine arrived at Yokosuka on 10 December. Five days later, she got underway for special operations which took her into 1970.

Tiru participated in Exercise "Sea Rover," with United States and Australian naval units, before heading home for the United States at the conclusion of her WestPac deployment. While approaching Guam for voyage repairs, she routinely copied the evening weather broadcast which was accompanied by an urgent alert notifying the ship of a search and rescue (SAR) operation underway to look for and rescue survivors of a small craft which had been adrift for two days in a heavy sea. An extensive search by Guam-based SAR forces had thus far turned up nothing, but *Tiru* located the five people—two of them Japanese nationals—and rescued them, despite darkness and high seas. Soon after *Tiru*'s arrival at Guam on 14 April 1970, the Japanese consul visited the submarine to express his government's appreciation for the ship's rescue mission.

Subsequently arriving at San Diego on 8 May after a brief period at Pearl Harbor, *Tiru* conducted local operations and underwent an overhaul prior to being transferred to the Atlantic Fleet on 1 August 1970. Underway on the 6th of August for Charleston, S.C., her new home port, *Tiru* called at Acapulco, Mexico; Rodman, Canal Zone; transited the Panama Canal; and visited Kingston, Jamaica, before reaching Charleston harbor on 2 September. For the remainder of the year, the ship conducted local operations, provided services, and underwent type training—activities which continued into 1972. Later transferred to SubFlot 6, SubRon 4, SubDiv 41, during 1972, *Tiru* operated in the Caribbean and off the lower east coast of the United States, with two deployments to European waters, into 1975.

On 1 July 1975, *Tiru* was decommissioned and struck from the Navy list to be sold to the Turkish government. An American arms embargo imposed on Turkey as a result of the Cyprus tensions between Greece and Turkey delayed the sale, however, even though negotiations and arrangements had been well into the planning stages. As of the end of 1979, the submarine's status was uncertain.

Tisdale

Ryland Dillard Tisdale was born on 15 November 1894 at the Naval Ordnance Proving Ground (now the Naval Ordnance Station) located in Charles County, Md., about 25 miles south of Washington, D.C. He was appointed a midshipman at the Naval Academy on 7 July 1911 and graduated on 5 June 1915. Between his commissioning and the entry of the United States into World War I, Ens. Tisdale served in *Virginia* (Battleship No. 13) and *Nevada* (Battleship No. 36).

On 5 June 1917, less than two months after the declaration of war, Tisdale reported on board SS *Antilles*, apparently for duty with an armed-guard gun crew assigned to that chartered Army transport. He served in that ship until she was torpedoed off Brest, France, on 17 October.

Lt. Tisdale subsequently received a special letter of commendation from the Secretary of the Navy for displaying ". . . coolness and courage in command of the forward guns, . . ." and for not leaving his post ". . . until he was forced to dive from the bridge of the sinking vessel." Tisdale also assisted other *Antilles* survivors onto life rafts. He was picked up by either *Alcedo* (SP–166) or *Corsair* (SP–159) and taken into Brest. On 23 October, he took passage in *Bridge* (Supply Ship No. 1) for Britain, where he reported for duty to the senior United States Navy officer present. After temporary duty in *Seattle* (Armored Cruiser No. 11), he returned to the United States on 12 December.

In late January 1918, Tisdale took a three-week course of instruction at the Fuel Oil Testing Plant in Philadelphia. From there, he went to Bath, Maine, for duty in connection with the outfitting and commissioning of *Wickes* (Destroyer No. 75). When she was placed in commission on 31 July, Lt. Tisdale became her engineering officer. From *Wickes*, he went to *Lamberton* (Destroyer No. 119) as executive officer and in December 1919 moved to *Hogan* (Destroyer No. 178) where he held the same post.

Tisdale's tour of duty in *Hogan* ended on 11 June 1920 when he reported to the Naval Academy for postgraduate studies in engineering. A year later, he checked in at the New York Navy Yard for practical instruction during the summer, before entering Columbia University on 28 September for further course work which lasted until the early summer of 1922, when he moved to the General Electric Co. in Schenectady, N.Y., until the end of July. Tisdale rounded out his scholastic efforts late that summer with six weeks of study at the Westinghouse Electric and Manufacturing Co., at Pittsburgh, Pa.

Tisdale returned to sea duty in the fall of 1922. On 16 October, he reported to *Argonne* (AP–4) in Philadelphia and, on 8 November, transferred to *California* (BB–44). He served in that battleship until April 1925, when he went ashore once more, this time to a billet in the Bureau of Engineering. In 1927, he completed his tour in Washington and returned to sea as executive officer of *Bridge* (AF–1). On 25 September 1928, he reported for duty at Shanghai, China. Five days later, he assumed his first command, the Asiatic Fleet destroyer *Stewart* (DD–224). That command lasted 13 months. He was detached on 31 October 1929 and, after a month with the 16th Naval District, Lt. Comdr. Tisdale took over his second command, *Palos* (PG–16), and began patrolling the upper reaches of the Yangtze in that gunboat. During this tour of duty, Lt. Comdr. Tisdale earned the Navy Cross. Late in July 1930, he and his ship were in the vicinity of Changsha when that city was attacked, taken, looted, and lost by Chinese communists. Tisdale and his crew assisted in the evacuation of Americans and other foreigners. He also led his crew and ship past the city for two firing passes as a show of force to discourage looting of the foreign concessions. The citation states, in part, that, ". . . the loss of American and other foreign property was limited by his timely action."

Lt. Comdr. Tisdale's next assignment took him to the Georgia School of Technology for a two-year tour of duty with the Naval Reserve Officers Training Corps detachment located there. From there, he went back to the Asiatic Fleet to join the staff of the Commander, Destroyer Squadron 5. He served in that capacity from 19 January to 11 November 1935 when he became Captain of the Yard at Olongapo in the Philippines. Tisdale was placed on the retired list on 30 June 1936, with the rank of commander.

In 1940, the United States began preparing for the contingency of war. Comdr. Tisdale returned to the colors in July and served for a brief period in the Bureau of Ships at Washington, D.C. In October, he was relieved of duty; however, within another month, he was back on active duty. On 14 January 1941, Comdr. Tisdale reported for duty at the Cavite Navy Yard near Manila in the Philippines. Tisdale spent the remainder of his life in the Philippines. He served in the defense of those islands after the Japanese invasion on 8 December 1941. After the surrender at Corregidor in May 1942, Comdr. Tisdale continued to resist the enemy on Mindanao. On 23 May 1942, he was killed at Tamparan in Lanao Province during action with Moros—who had collaborated with the Japanese.

(DE–33: dp. 1,140; l. 289′5″; b. 35′0″; dr. 8′3″ (mean); s. 21 k.; cpl. 156; a. 3 3″, 4 1.1″, 9 20mm., 2 dct., 8 dcp., 1 dcp. (hh.); cl. *Evarts*)

BDE–33 was laid down at Mare Island Navy Yard on 23 January 1943 as one of the warships to be transferred to the United Kingdom under the terms of the lend-lease agreement. However, her allocation to the Royal Navy was canceled; and she was named *Tisdale* and redesignated DE–33 on 23 June 1943 when a destroyer escort recently laid down at Boston, DE–228, was assigned to the Royal Navy in her stead. *Tisdale* was launched on 28 June 1943; sponsored by Mrs. Elizabeth M. Tisdale, Jr.; and commissioned on 11 October 1943, Lt. Comdr. Theodore Wolcott in command.

Following shakedown, *Tisdale* cleared Treasure Island, Calif., on 5 December 1943. Six days later, she moored at Pearl Harbor in the Hawaiian Islands. The destroyer escort conducted training in the vicinity of Oahu until the 23d, when she got underway for the Central Pacific. After stops at Canton Island and Abemama, she reached Tarawa Atoll—in the Gilbert Islands—on 9 January 1944. Between 16 and 20 January, she made two voyages between Tarawa and Funafuti in the Ellice Islands, ending up at Funafuti on the 20th. On the 23d, *Tisdale* stood out of Funafuti to participate in Operation "Flintlock," the seizure and occupation of Kwajalein and Majuro Atolls in the Marshall Islands. However, the destroyer escort saw no action in the operation and only put into Majuro after it had been secured.

The destroyer escort moored at the dock in Pearl Harbor at mid-morning on 13 February. She underwent repairs until the first week in March. On 3 March, she cleared the harbor to return to the Marshalls. After a stop at Johnston Island, she moored at Majuro just after noon on the 12th. Three days later, *Tisdale* exited the lagoon in the screen of a convoy bound for the Gilberts. She arrived at Tarawa on St. Patrick's Day and remained there for almost two months screening ships into and out of the atoll. On 12 May, she exited the lagoon in company with *Fleming* (DE–32) and *Eisele* (DE–34) and set course for Pearl Harbor, where she arrived on the 19th.

Following a 10-day availability at the DE docks, she got underway on 29 May in the screen of Rear Admiral Blandy's floating reserve for the Marianas invasion. *Tisdale* and her charges staged through Kwajalein, stopping there from 9 to 11 June before continuing on to the Marianas. Soldiers and marines stormed ashore at Saipan on the 15th. The destroyer escort, however, remained some distance from the island, continuing to screen the reserve force. On 16 June, Admiral Spruance decided to commit the floating reserve, and the Army's 27th Infantry Division landed at dusk. *Tisdale* escorted the ships into position off Saipan for the landings and began duty screening the transport area.

During the Battle of the Philippine Sea, the warship covered the transports against the possibility of an enemy end run and the contingency of Japanese planes penetrating Task Force 58's reinforced antiaircraft screen. Neither eventuality materialized, and *Tisdale* saw no action until 24 June when she accompanied *Colorado* (BB–45) on a bombardment of Saipan. Later that day, she joined *Stringham* (APD–6) in the channel between Tinian and Saipan where they fired shells to illuminate that stretch of water to interdict Japanese attempts to reinforce the Saipan garrison. The following morning, she returned to the transport area and resumed her duties in the antisubmarine screen. On 2

July, she began screening ships on their nightly retirements from Saipan. Six days later, *Tisdale* went into action against the next objective in the Marianas, Tinian, by delivering night harassing fire and illuminating fire in the area around Tinian Town and Sunharon Harbor.

On the 12th, she cleared the Marianas and escorted a convoy to Eniwetok until the 21st, when she headed back to the Marianas. The destroyer escort arrived off Saipan on 25 July and resumed her familiar duty screening transports during the campaign on Tinian. On 16 August, just before the assault on Guam, she departed the Marianas once more. Steaming via Eniwetok, she reached Pearl Harbor on 27 August and began a 20-day availability. She conducted trials and training exercises in the Hawaiian Islands until October.

Tisdale departed Oahu in the screen of a convoy on 2 October and arrived in Eniwetok lagoon on the 13th. From then until late February 1945, she escorted convoys. This duty took her back and forth between Eniwetok and Ulithi. The single exception was a round-trip voyage to Manus in late January and early February. During the return voyage, she attacked a sonar contact on 3 February and, although she received no official credit for it, she probably sank a Japanese submarine.

On 25 February, *Tisdale* exited the lagoon at Eniwetok in company with *Thetis Bay* (CVE–90). The task unit reached Apra on the 28th, and she conducted operations with the escort carrier well into the first week in March. On 5 March, the two warships headed back to Eniwetok, entering the lagoon on the 8th. Three days later, she headed out of the Eniwetok anchorage with a Ulithi-bound convoy. She made her destination on 16 March and, five days later, headed for the Ryukyu Islands with the escort carriers of Support Carrier Unit 2.

On 25 March, the warships arrived in their area of operations to the south of Okinawa, the objective in Operation "Iceberg." The carriers launched their planes to support the invasion of Okinawa, and *Tisdale* helped protect them from enemy submarine and air attacks. Though enemy planes occasionally approached the task unit, *Tisdale* saw no real air action because the combat air patrol either splashed them or chased them away. On the 31st, she was transferred to the screen of Support Carrier Group 1; but her duties remained as before.

On 17 April, the warship closed the Hagushi beaches at Okinawa for the first time; then retired to screen refueling operations. On 20 April, she did her first duty as a radar picket ship. That same day, *Tisdale* departed the Ryukyus to screen *West Virginia* (BB–48), *Portland* (CA–33), and *Biloxi* (CL–80) to Ulithi. After five days at Ulithi, she departed the atoll on 29 April. She escorted a convoy to Okinawa and arrived off the Hagushi beaches once more on 3 May. For the next month, she stood radar picket duty at various stations around the island, occasionally putting into the anchorage at Kerama Retto for mail, provisions, and other supplies.

On 14 June, *Tisdale* departed Okinawa and headed for Leyte in the Philippines. After some repairs, she cleared Leyte on 30 June and steamed—via Eniwetok and Pearl Harbor—back to the United States. She arrived in San Francisco on 1 August and, four days later, moved north to Portland, Oreg. The Japanese agreed to capitulate on 15 August, and *Tisdale* began decommissioning procedures soon thereafter. She was decommissioned on 17 November 1945, and her name was struck from the Navy list on 28 November 1945. She was sold to A. G. Schoonmaker Co., Inc., of New York City on 2 February 1948 and scrapped the following month.

Tisdale earned four battle stars during World War II.

———

Tisdale (DE–278)—an *Evarts*-class destroyer escort—was laid down at the Boston Navy Yard on 5 June 1943.

Later that month, she was assigned to the United Kingdom under the provisions of the lend-lease agreement. Accordingly, her name was cancelled on 23 June and reassigned to DE–33. On 19 October, she was officially transferred to the Royal Navy and placed in commission as HMS *Keats* (K 482). She was returned to the United States Navy on 27 February 1946. *DE–278* was struck from the Navy list on 20 March 1946 and sold to George H. Nutman, Brooklyn, N.Y., on 19 November 1946.

Titania

A satellite of the planet Uranus.

(AK–55: dp. 13,910 (tl.); l. 459'2"; b. 63'; dr. 26.5 (lim.); s. 16.5 k.; cpl. 266; a. 1 5", 4 3", 8 .50-cal. mg., 2 dcp.; cl. *Arcturus*; T. C2–F)

Titania was laid down as *Harry Culbreath* under Maritime Commission contract (MC hull 132) on 25 October 1941 at Kearney, N.J., by the Federal Shipbuilding and Drydock Co.; renamed *Titania* and designated AK–55 on 16 February 1942; launched on 28 February 1942; sponsored by Mrs. Bennett Champ Clark; acquired by the United States Navy on 27 March 1942 and commissioned on 27 May 1942, Lt. Comdr. Dale E. Collins in command.

Titania began her career plying coastal waters between New York and Norfolk during the summer of 1942. On 19 September, the new cargo vessel got under way from Hampton Roads for training in Chesapeake Bay; then, in October, she conducted landing exercises to prepare for the Allied invasion of North Africa.

Late in November, she departed Norfolk and steamed eastward to play her part in Operation "Torch." As a member of the Southern Attack Group, she arrived in the transport area eight miles from Safi around midnight on 7 November 1942. Early in the morning a landing craft from the ship rescued the crew of a tank landing craft which had been destroyed by a gasoline explosion. In the afternoon, she entered Safi Harbor; began discharging vital equipment and stores and, 78 hours later, had unloaded her entire combat cargo. On the afternoon of 12 November, as *Titania*, escorted by *Cole* (DD–155), steamed toward Fedhala, German U-boat *U–130* unsuccessfully attacked them. A few days later, after delivering landing craft at Fedhala, *Titania* steamed home.

During the first two weeks in December, *Titania* underwent repairs and was combat loaded at Norfolk to prepare for service in the Pacific. On 17 December, she got underway from Hampton Roads in convoy, steamed through the Panama Canal on Christmas Day and arrived at New Caledonia on 18 January. During January and February, she operated out of Noumea, making runs to Espiritu Santo and Guadalcanal with troops and equipment.

Titania's reclassification as an attack cargo ship on 1 February 1943 changed her destination to AKA–13. In the following months, she continued to carry men and materiel to the Solomons. Unloading at Guadalcanal was a hazardous business for, at any time, Japanese airplanes might appear to harrass the transport or attack nearby targets ashore. Whenever this occurred, *Titania* got underway as her men raced to their general quarters stations. When the last raider disappeared, the ship pulled back into port and resumed unloading. On 5 March, while the transport was steaming from Guadalcanal to New Caledonia with a load of disabled aircraft, an unidentified plane dropped three bombs unnervingly close to her—only 10 to 20 yards astern.

On 7 April, she again got underway for the Solomons. After discharging much of her cargo at Tulagi and Gavutu, the transport moved to Lunga Point to finish unloading. In May, *Titania* operated between

Noumea and Guadalcanal and made one voyage to Efate. On the 13th, *Titania* witnessed an air engagement taking place over Cape Esperance as American planes intercepted Japanese raiders attempting to approach Henderson Field.

Late in May, she arrived at Wellington, New Zealand, for repairs in drydock. She returned to Noumea on 1 July and spent almost four months transporting military equipment, stores, and troops in the waters east of Australia.

In the last week of October, *Titania* departed Guadalcanal to rehearse the coming assault on Bougainville, the northernmost of the Solomons. On 1 November, she took part in Operation "Cherryblossom," the initial landing at Cape Torokina, Bougainville. Anchored off the beach, while unloading marines and their equipment that day, *Titania* twice came under air attack. During one of these raids, her guns opened up on a "Kate" which had dropped its bombs near a destroyer and then passed over the transport group. Hit by machine gun fire from the attack transport, the Japanese plane began to smoke; then splashed several miles away. By 1739 that evening, *Titania* had finished unloading, freeing her to depart Bougainville that night and head for Guadalcanal.

On 8 November 1943, *Titania* was back at Empress Augusta Bay, Bougainville, unloading needed troops and equipment when the Japanese struck with a full-scale air raid. Shortly after noon, five different waves of three to four "Vals" each attacked the unloading transports. *Fuller* (AP–14) was damaged during this attack, but *Titania* escaped unscathed, despite three bombs which exploded nearby and one dud which barely missed the ship. Meanwhile, *Titania* splashed five attackers and damaged at least two more.

Throughout the remainder of 1943 and into the new year, *Titania* continued to operate in the Solomons. On 12 January 1944, she disembarked elements of the 12th Marines, as well as supplies and equipment for units of the American Division, then operating near Cape Torokina. After finishing the month with division tactical exercises off Tambunuman Beach, Guadalcanal, she visited New Zealand in February before ending the month with tactical and amphibious exercises out of New Caledonia. Throughout the following months, she continued ferrying men and materiel in the Solomons and Bismarcks. She stopped at Kwajalein early in June and, later that month, set her course for the Marshalls.

With elements of the 3d Marine Division embarked, *Titania* got underway from Eniwetok on 17 July, bound for the assault on Guam. At 0606 on the 21st, *Titania* was lying to in the transport area six miles off Asan Point. Minutes later, she hoisted out her landing craft; and, at 0830, the first wave of the 3d Marine Division landed on the northwest shore of Guam between Asan and Adelup Points. The ship began unloading cargo shortly before 1000 and, for the next four days, discharged vital materiel, including ammunition, to support American fighting men in the bitter struggle taking place on shore. On 26 July, she departed Guam and set her course for the Marshalls, arriving at Eniwetok on 30 July.

In September, she operated out of New Guinea where the 7th Fleet was preparing for the coming assault on the Philippines. Early in October, she participated in exercises with Transport Division 6; then, on Friday, 13 October, headed for Humboldt Bay, the staging area for the impending invasion of Leyte. Assigned to the Palo Attack Group, *Titania* entered Leyte Gulf on the morning of 20 October. At 0845, *Titania* began releasing her boats which carried supplies and equipment for the American Army's 24th Division. At 1400, she approached within two miles of the beach to facilitate unloading. Later in the afternoon, as the Army's *Light Tanker No. 425* came alongside *Titania* to help her unload, one of the tanker's machine guns accidentally discharged, making 100 holes in *Titania*'s side and severing her degaussing cable in two places. Yet no serious damage resulted; and the next day, after discharging over 1,000 tons of cargo, the cargo ship departed Leyte Gulf, returning to New Guinea on the 27th.

After loading cargo at Humboldt Bay for the 32d Army Division, she got underway on 9 November in company with a 25-transport convoy steaming for Leyte. On 13 November, the Japanese launched four air raids at the convoy. During one of these attacks, a "Jill" torpedo bomber dove out of a cloud and levelled off at 100 feet for an approach. *Titania* joined in the firing which soon splashed the raider. On the morning of 14 November, the ship arrived in San Pedro Bay. During the day, she unloaded supplies and equipment of the 32d Army Division and also splashed a Japanese plane which sank only 1,500 yards off her starboard bow. On 15 November, she finished discharging her cargo and departed. Early in December 1944, the transport took part in exercises in Huon Gulf, New Guinea, then anchored in Seeadler Harbor. On the last day of the year, she got underway from Manus and steamed for the Philippines in company with the Luzon Attack Force.

In the days which followed, Japan launched mass kamikaze attacks to deter this formidable invasion force. On 6 January 1945, combat air patrol (CAP) planes shot down a Japanese plane just 1,000 yards from *Titania*'s port bow. Air activity picked up two days later as the convoy's CAP downed four planes. A "Val" approached from *Titania*'s port quarter, crossed her stern, and dropped one bomb 100 yards from the ship's port quarter and another only 50 yards off her starboard bow. *Titania* and other members of the convoy had taken the plane under continuous fire and finally splashed it only 100 yards off her starboard bow.

On 9 January, as *Titania* anchored off Crimson Beach, the Lingayen Gulf landings began. Despite a heavy cross swell which made unloading difficult, *Titania* serviced small craft and discharged her cargo of vehicles, ammunition, and gasoline, as well as personnel. On the 18th, she got underway for the Netherlands East Indies where she loaded supplies and equipment of the 33d Infantry Division. Throughout February and March, she continued to support ground forces in the Philippines.

On 17 April, *Titania* began loading supplies and equipment for Australia's 26th Infantry Brigade (Reinforced). She got underway on 27 April for the assault on Tarakan Island and arived off Yellow Beach on P–day, 1 May. *Titania*'s first shore parties discovered soft, sticky, mud beaches and a 10-foot tidal range, both of which slowed and hampered unloading efforts. Finding the pier badly burned but its supporting structure intact, *Titania* sent a work party ashore to obtain logs to restore the pier to usable condition. Seventy tons of bridge planking from the transport's hold completed the repair job and made it possible for trucks to load from the pier at four hatches. Under these improved conditions, *Titania* discharged the materials, engineering equipment, and supplies needed to construct and operate an airfield at Tarakan by the 9th. She retired toward Morotai that day and remained at anchor there throughout the rest of the month.

In early June, the veteran attack transport was again underway, this time with elements of the 9th Australian Division of the Australian I Corps on board, bound for Brunei Bay. On 10 June, Z–day, the transport arrived off the "Oboe Six" assault area and unloaded her cargo despite a surprise air attack by a Japanese "Nick" which dove out of low clouds and dropped a bomb which exploded some 300 yards off her port beam. *Titania* departed Brunei Bay on the following afternoon.

After loading an Australian division at Morotai, *Titania* engaged in rehearsals for the coming reoccupation of Balikpapan. She arrived off the coast of Borneo on 1 July to unload units of the Australian I Corps and members of Company "A," United States Engineering Boat and Shore Regiment. Anchored in the transport area, the ship did not come under fire, although her landing boats were fired on by mortars and machine guns as they landed their cargoes on Red Beach. *Titania* unloaded 575 tons of cargo, including high explosives, and departed Balikpapan at 1930 the same day.

Throughout the remainder of July, *Titania* was at anchor at Morotai. On 30 July, she got underway and visited San Pedro Bay, Leyte, and Ulithi, before steaming for the Hawaiian Islands. At Pearl Harbor, she loaded LVT's (track landing vehicles) for shipment to the United States, embarked personnel, and departed on 22 August.

After more than two and one-half years in foreign waters, the veteran arrived at Bremerton, Wash., on 30 August for overhaul which lasted through the end of October.

In the early months of 1946, *Titania* operated out of California ports, then steamed to Samar, arriving on 1 March. She remained in the Philippines until May when she returned to the west coast for repairs. Throughout the next two years, she continued to shuttle between the west coast of the United States and the islands of the Pacific, carrying cargoes to occupation forces. In September 1948, she departed Pearl Harbor and proceeded via the Panama Canal to the east coast, arriving at Yorktown, Va., on 6 November. She again passed through the Panama Canal in December en route to Eniwetok, Guam, and Saipan. On 16 March 1949, she arrived at San Francisco and remained through the spring and summer, operating in coastal and Alaskan waters.

In October 1949, she was assigned to the Military Sea Transportation Service but retained her commissioned status and Navy crew.

When fighting broke out in Korea on 25 June 1950, *Titania* was at Yokohama. Early in July, she carried troops and cargo from Naha to Pusan; then returned to Japan to embark marines and troops of the 1st Cavalry Division for the assault on Pohang. Underway on 16 July, the darkened ship crossed the Japanese Inland Sea and passed between Kyushu and Honshu through the Shimonoseki Strait, arriving off the assault area at 0415 on 18 July. Debarkation was uneventful; and, by 2225, her landing craft had returned to the ship, their mission completed. *Titania* remained anchored at Geitjetsu Wan until 23 July when she got underway for Yokosuka.

Following the Pohang operation, the transport returned to the United States, arriving at San Diego on 7 August. There, she began taking on ammunition and marine cargo; but, in the early hours of 15 August, before the loading had been completed, a fire broke out in her number 1 boiler. Within three hours, the fire was brought under control, but the damage incurred required two weeks of repairs. It was 3 September before *Titania* got underway for Japan. As she crossed the Pacific, she skirted Typhoon Missantha, encountering 53-knot winds before she arrived at Kobe on 21 September.

On 25 September, only 10 days after the initial landings at Inchon, *Titania* arrived off that port to unload marines, equipment, and ammunition, and to embark members of the 1st Naval Beach Group. Although *Titania* did not come under fire, frequent alerts and the sights and sounds of night shore bombardment made this a tense operation. Her mission completed, *Titania* departed Inchon on 1 October. She made additional voyages to Inchon and Wonsan carrying combat cargo before getting underway from Yokohama on 17 November 1950 for San Francisco.

Until the signing of the armistice on 27 July 1953, *Titania* continued to carry men and materiel between American ports and the Far East. Much of her time was spent rearming and provisioning ships at sea in the waters off Korea. Rough seas, rain, and snow hampered the ship's operations during the winter months, taxing the resilience and resourcefulness of her crew on many occasions. Following the cessation of hostilities in th summer of 1953, *Titania* remained in the Far Eas operating out of Japanese ports and in Korean water until February 1954 when she returned to San Fran cisco.

On 15 July 1954, she departed San Francisco steam ing, via the Hawaiian Islands and Japan, for the Philip pines. She operated out of Subic Bay until Octobe when she visited Hong Kong and Sasebo before gettin underway from Japan on 6 November. After spendin the early months of 1955 in California ports, *Titani* was decommissioned on 19 July 1955. Her name wa struck from the Navy list on 1 July 1961.

She received seven battle stars for World War I service and was awarded the Navy Unit Commendatio seven times. She also received seven battle stars fo Korean service.

Tivives

A name probably coined by the United Fruit Co. fron the Spanish words "*ti*" and "*viveres*" and roughly translated as "your food."

(ScStr.: t. 5,017; lbp. 378′9″; b. 50′4″ (wl.); dr 22′6½″ (mean); dph. 29′1″; s. 12.5 k.; cpl. 91; a 1 5″, 1 3″)

Tivives—a United Fruit Co. refrigerated ship built in 1911 at Belfast, Ireland—was chartered at New York City by the Navy on 5 July 1918 from the United Fruit Co. and commissioned the same day.

Assigned to the Naval Overseas Transportation Service, *Tivives* loaded 1,603 tons of beef and eight motor trucks and, on 13 July, sailed in convoy for France. The Allied ships reached Gironde on the 28th and, the next day, moved to St. Nazaire where she discharged her cargo. The ship next proceeded to Verdon whence she sailed in convoy on 15 August for home. After reaching New York City on the 26th, she underwent minor repairs, took on 1,704 tons of beef, and got underway on 2 September, bound once more in convoy for Europe. After unloading at Rochefort, the refrigerated ship departed Verdon on the 30th and returned to New York on 13 October. Only six days later, *Tivives* steamed ou of New York harbor and headed eastward across the Atlantic with more beef for General Pershing's "dough boys." She reached Verdon on 6 November.

Five days later, as the ship was discharging her cargo, Germany signed the armistice ending hostilities One week thereafter, *Tivives* headed home; and she reached New York on 3 December.

There, she took on 1,857 tons of beef and butter and got underway on Christmas Day. The ship reached Verdon on 4 January 1919, unloaded her cargo, picked up a cargo of American military equipment, and sailed for the United States on the 22d. The ship reached New York on 5 February but, 10 days later, began her last naval crossing, laden with beef for Europe. She moored at Verdon on the last day of February and, after delivering her beef, set her course homeward on 15 March.

After reaching New York on the 27th, the ship began preparations for demobilization. She was decommissioned on 25 April and returned to her owner.

Tjikembang

The Dutch spelling of Cikembang, a river in west Java, east of Bandung.

(ScStr.: t. 5,028; l. 510′6″; b. 58′4″ (wl.); dr. 27′5′ (mean); dph. 31′2″; s. 12.5 k.; cpl. 70)

Tjikembang—a freighter completed in early 1914 a Flushing, Holland, by *Koninklijke Maatschappij d Schelde* and owned and operated under the Dutch flag by the Java-China-Japan Line—was laid up in the Philippine Islands early in World War I. Seized by

American customs officials soon after the United States entered the conflict, the ship was taken over by the Navy from the United States Shipping Board on 22 March 1918 and commissioned on 12 April.

Assigned to the Naval Overseas Transportation Service, *Tjikembang* took on a cargo of hemp and sugar and then got underway on 11 May, bound for the east coast of the United States. After proceeding via the Hawaiian Islands and the Panama Canal, she arrived at New York City on 28 July. There, she unloaded her cargo, picked up 7,410 tons of Army supplies, and sailed on 9 August in a convoy bound for France. She reached St. Nazaire on the 28th, discharged her cargo, and departed the European continent in a homeward-bound convoy on 14 September.

After returning to New York on the 28th, she underwent extensive repairs and modifications which converted her to an animal transport. Upon completion of the yard work at the Robbins Drydock Co., the ship loaded 3,296 tons of general cargo, and a number of horses and mules. She got underway with a convoy for France on 27 October and reached La Pallice on 15 November, four days after the armistice ended hostilities.

After discharging her cargo, the ship set her course for the Virginia capes on the 28th and reached Norfolk, Va., on 15 December. She underwent repairs there which lasted until 19 January 1919. On that day, she sailed for New York where she arrived on the 23d and was decommissioned on 22 February. After eight months of being laid up in reserve there, the ship was returned to the Shipping Board on 22 October 1919.

Tjisondari

The Dutch spelling of Cisondari, a river in west Java, near Bagor.

(ScStr.: dp. 17,350 (n.); l. 434'0"; b. 58'4" (wl.); dr. 26'10" (mean); s. 12.0 k.; cpl. 70; a. 1 6", 1 3")

Tjisondari—a freighter built in 1915 at Flushing, Holland, by *Koninklijke Maatschappij de Schelde* and owned and operated under the Dutch flag by the Java-China-Japan Line—was seized by American customs officials in the Philippine Islands at Manila after the United States entered World War I. The ship was taken over by the Navy from the United States Shipping Board on 22 March 1918 and commissioned on 3 April.

Assigned to the Naval Overseas Transportation Service, the ship sailed five days later for the west coast of the United States and reached San Francisco on 5 May. There, she was refitted for naval service, loaded with Army supplies, and got underway on the 29th for the east coast. After steaming south to Panama, she transited the canal, proceeded north along the Atlantic coast, and arrived at New York on 20 June. Following minor repairs and bunkering with coal, *Tjisondari* sailed in convoy on Independence Day for France. The Allied ships reached Brest on the 19th; and, the next day, she began discharging her cargo at St. Nazaire. She headed homeward in convoy on 15 August and returned to New York on the 26th.

After taking on another cargo of Army supplies, the vessel got underway again in convoy for Europe on 6 September. Her convoy made port at St. Nazaire on the 25th and proceeded thence to Brest where she unloaded. Sailing for the United States on 17 October, she entered New York harbor on the 28th. While there, stalls were built in the ship enabling her to carry 721 horses. The ship then took on cargo, filled her stalls with horses, and sailed once more for France on 27 November. The ship entered Quiberon Bay on 9 December, discharged her cargo, and headed home. However, after she passed between Cape May and Cape Henlopen, the ship ran aground and damaged her hull while ascending the Delaware River. Hence, when she finally

reached Philadelphia on 5 January 1919, the vessel badly needed yard work.

Repairs and reloading delayed the ship at Philadelphia until she got underway on 19 February, bound for Denmark laden with flour. She discharged her cargo at Copenhagen and headed homeward on 29 March.

Tjisondari made port at New York on 10 April and, following voyage repairs, headed for Hampton Roads on the 23d. She took on board a cargo of oil at Norfolk and carried it—via the Panama Canal, San Francisco, and Hong Kong—to the Philippines. She reached Manila on 23 May. Three months later, on 23 August, the ship was decommissioned and returned to her owner.

Tlingit

A name for those Indian peoples who make up the Koluschan linguistic family. They inhabit the islands and the coast of Canada and Alaska.

(YTB–497: dp. 345 (f.); l. 100'0"; b. 25'0"; dr. 10'0"; s. 12 k. (tl.); cpl. 8; cl. *Sassaba*)

Tlingit (YTB–497)—a large harbor tug—was laid down on 15 December 1944 at Brooklyn, N.Y., by Ira S. Bushey & Sons; launched sometime early in 1945; and placed in service at the New York Navy Yard on 21 August 1945.

Few records of *Tlingit*'s operations have survived; but, in September, she was at Coco Solo in the Canal Zone, en route to Hawaii. At Pearl Harbor, she replaced *Nahasho* (YTB–535), when—or shortly before—that tug was placed out of service in November. By the summer of 1946, *Tlingit* had moved to the Far East and qualified for the China service medal between 11 July 1946 and 20 June 1947. Following that tour of duty, she returned to the west coast; and, on 31 March 1948, she was placed out of service, in reserve.

The tug remained at the Puget Sound Naval Shipyard until she was reactivated on 17 November 1950 for service in the 17th Naval District. She arrived in Kodiak, Alaska, in February 1951 and served there until May 1957 when she returned south to San Francisco. She served in the 12th Naval District for the remainder of her career. In February 1962, she was reclassified a medium harbor tug and became YTM–497. In June 1963, *Tlingit* was placed out of service and her name was struck from the Navy list.

Toad

(MB: l. 26'0"; b. 5'6"; s. 16.5 k.; cpl. 5)

Toad—a wooden motor boat built in 1914 by D. R. Shackford—was acquired under free lease from D. R. Shackford by the Navy on 4 August 1918. *Toad* was commissioned on 4 September 1918 and used on section patrol in the 5th Naval District. She was returned to her owner on 27 January 1919.

Tocobaga

A tribe of Timucaan Indians who once resided on the west coast of Florida.

Tocobaga (YTB–709)—a *Hisada*-class harbor tug—was slated to be built at San Pedro, Calif., by the Bethlehem Steel Co., but the contract for her construction was cancelled on 1 October 1945.

Tocsam

(MB: t. 13; l. 41'; b. 10'1"; dr. 3'0" (mean); cpl. 6; a. none)

Tocsam—a motorboat built in 1910 at Oxford, Md.,

by the Landing Yacht Building Company—was acquired by the Navy from G. H. Lohr on 2 July 1918; and commissioned at Charleston, S.C., on 21 August 1918, Ens. B. A. Hagood, USNRF, in command.

Tocsam served on section patrol in the Charleston area until the Armistice which ended hostilities on 11 November. Then, her services no longer required, *Tocsam* was decommissioned on 15 December 1918 and returned to her owner the following day.

Todd

Counties in Kentucky, Minnesota, and South Dakota.

The Kentucky county was named for John Todd who —during the American Revolution—took part in the capture of Kaskaskia and Vincennes under General George Rogers Clark. He was killed in the Battle of Blue Licks on 19 August 1782. Todd was the great-uncle of Mary Todd Lincoln.

The Minnesota and South Dakota counties were named for John Blair Smith Todd, an 1837 graduate of West Point who followed a distinguished career in the Army—from the Seminole War to the Civil War—with service as a political leader in the Dakota territory. He was governor of the territory from 1869 to 1871. He died at Yankton, S.D., on 5 January 1872.

(AKA–71: dp. 13,910; l. 459'2"; b. 63'0"; dr. 26'4"; s. 16.5 k. (tl.); a. 1 5", 8 40mm.; cl. *Tolland*; T. C2–S–AJ3)

Todd (AKA–71) was laid down under Maritime Commission contract (MC hull 1400) on 10 August 1944 at Wilmington, N.C., by the North Carolina Shipbuilding Corp.; launched on 10 October 1944; sponsored by Mrs. R. Gregg Cherry; acquired by the Navy from the War Shipping Administration on 14 November; and commissioned on 30 November 1944, Lt. Comdr. Charles A. Johnson, USNR, in command.

The attack cargo ship held shakedown training in the Chesapeake Bay and then moved up the coast to Davisville, R.I., to load cargo. On 4 January 1945, *Todd* began an independent voyage to Hawaii. She transited the Panama Canal on 11 January and arrived at Pearl Harbor on the 26th. She unloaded her cargo, participated in training exercises for two weeks, and got underway for New Caledonia on 12 February.

On 22 February, *Todd* arrived at Noumea to await further orders. During the next 10 weeks, the ship moved only once and that was to carry tracked landing vehicles 50 miles up the coast to Uarai Bay for the Army. She left Noumea on 3 May and proceeded, via Manus, to the Philippines. The cargo ship arrived at Leyte on 16 May and headed for Hollandia 12 days later. She loaded troops and supplies and returned to Manila on 17 June. *Todd* then made two more round-trips from the Philippines to New Guinea. The ship was unloading cargo at Subic Bay when hostilities with Japan ceased. She embarked occupation troops, with their equipment, at Manila and got underway for Japan on 27 August. The troops disembarked at Yokohama on 2 September. A voyage from the Philippines to Okinawa and another from the Philippines to Japan followed. In October and early November, she made calls at Hong Kong and Tsingtao before proceeding to Sasebo. *Todd* embarked elements of the 5th Marine Division and departed Japan for the United States on 7 December.

The ship arrived at San Diego on 22 December 1945 and disembarked her passengers. She moved to San Pedro the next day and off-loaded ammunition. *Todd* proceeded to San Francisco on 9 January 1946 and entered the Hunters Point Naval Shipyard for voyage repairs. Between 15 February and 15 March, the attack cargo ship made one last voyage to Hawaii. On 5 April, *Todd* stood out of San Francisco bound for Norfolk and inactivation. She arrived on 1 May and was decommissioned on 25 June 1946. *Todd* was returned to the War Shipping Administration the next day and was struck from the Navy list on 19 July 1946.

Toiler

(ARS–47: dp. 1,190; l. 213'6"; b. 43'0"; dr. 13'9"; s. 16 k. (tl.); cpl. 120; a. 1 3", 4 40mm.; cl. *Diver*)

On 3 May 1944, the name *Toiler* was assigned to ARS–47—a *Diver*-class salvage ship to be built at Napa, Calif., by the Basalt Rock Co.—but the contract for construction of that ship was cancelled on 12 August 1945.

Toka

A word in the Sioux language meaning sea mist.

(YT–149: dp. 325; l. 100'0"; b. 25'0"; dr. 9'7" (f.); s. 12 k.; cl. *Woban*)

Toka (YT–149) was laid down on 3 October 1940 at Bay City, Mich., by the Defoe Bridge & Metal Works; launched on 15 April 1941; completed and delivered to the Navy on 24 May 1941; and placed in service on 3 June 1941.

Not long thereafter, *Toka* reported for duty with the 4th Naval District at Philadelphia, Pa., where she served as a district tug throughout World War II and for almost 24 years thereafter. During her service there, she changed designations twice. On 15 May 1944, she became a large harbor tug and received the hull designation YTB–149. Some 18 years later, she was still assigned to Philadelphia when she was redesignated a medium harbor tug, YTM–149, in February 1962. However, in 1968, *Toka* changed assignments from the 4th Naval District to the 13th Naval District. She was placed out of service, in reserve, at Bremerton, Wash., in November 1978.

Token

(AM–126: dp. 890; l. 221'2"; b. 32'2"; dr. 10'9"; s. 18.1 k.; cpl. 102; a. 2 3", 4 20mm., 2 dct., 4 dcp.; cl. *Auk*)

Token (AM–126) was laid down on 21 July 1941 at Chickasaw, Ala., by the Gulf Shipbuilding Corp.; launched on 28 March 1942; sponsored by Mrs. Charles Hunt Ross; and commissioned on 31 December 1942, Lt. Comdr. William H. Harrison, USNR, in command.

After shakedown cruises off the Florida coast and in the Gulf of Mexico, the new minesweeper steamed from Miami on 2 April 1943; transited the Panama Canal; and arrived at San Francisco on 1 May. Following training and escort duty in western coastal waters, she departed San Francisco on 28 August for the New Hebrides. From October until the following June, *Token* escorted convoys between Espiritu Santo and Guadalcanal. Late in June, she proceeded via Florida Island to Sydney, Australia. A severe vibration developed en route, and *Token*'s stay in Sydney was prolonged for the replacement of bent and damaged propeller blades. She departed Sydney on 30 July 1944 and proceeded to the Solomons, where she spent the month of August conducting exercises and undergoing additional repairs.

In September, *Token* engaged in minesweeping in the Palau and Ulithi groups before proceeding to Manus where the 7th Fleet was concentrating for the invasion of Leyte. On 17 October, while conducting minesweeping operations en route to Leyte, *Token* was caught in a typhoon which caused her some minor damage. Following two days of minesweeping in Leyte Gulf, *Token* anchored in the south transport area off Leyte on 24 October. The next day, *Token* scored several hits on an enemy aircraft and rescued a downed flier from *Sangamon* (CVE–26). Heavy air activity continued until *Token* got underway for the Admiralties arriving at Manus on 5 November.

Token steamed from Manus on 14 November and proceeded via Pearl Harbor and San Francisco to Portland, Oreg., where she underwent major overhaul. On 13 April, *Token* departed the west coast for Pearl Harbor where she resumed escort duty.

Arriving off Okinawa on 20 May 1945, at a time of mass kamikaze attacks, *Token* experienced her first of many days of enemy air activity. While performing screening activities on the 28th, *Token* rescued and captured two survivors from a splashed Japanese plane. After repairs at Kerama Retto in June, she swept waters off Okinawa, in the East China Sea, and in Tokyo Bay. In the following months, *Token* continued sweeps of formerly contested waters off the Pescadores and China before steaming—via Sasebo, Kyushu, and Pearl Harbor—to Charleston, S.C. She then operated off the east coast until finally berthing in June 1947 at Orange, Tex., where she was assigned to the Atlantic Reserve Fleet, Texas Group, and placed out of commission on 6 January 1948.

Recommissioned on 12 April 1951, *Token* participated in training exercises off Charleston in company with Mine Squadron 8, Mine Force, Atlantic Fleet. Departing from Charleston in August, *Token* headed for the Mediterranean and touched at Gibraltar, Istanbul, Naples, and Seville before returning to Charleston on 7 February 1953.

She operated off the Atlantic and gulf coasts before being inactivated and decommissioned again on 16 April 1954. *Token* was reclassified a steel-hulled fleet minesweeper on 7 February 1955 and redesignated MSF–126. Her name was struck from the Navy list on 1 December 1966.

Token received four battle stars for World War II service.

Toledo

Cities in Ohio, Illinois, Iowa, and Oregon.

Toledo (PF–33) was renamed *Dearborn* (q.v.) on 18 August 1943.

I

(CA–133: dp. 13,600; l. 674'11''; b. 70'10''; dr. 20'6''; s. 33 k.; cpl. 1,142; a. 9 8'', 12 5'', 40 40mm., 28 20mm.; cl. *Baltimore*)

Toledo (CA–133) was laid down on 13 September 1943 at Camden, N.J., by the New York Shipbuilding Corp.; launched on 6 May 1945; sponsored by Mrs.

Edward J. Moan; and commissioned at the Philadelphia Naval Shipyard on 27 October 1946, Capt. August J. Detzer, Jr., in command.

On 6 January 1947, the heavy cruiser got underway for a two-month training cruise in the balmy waters of the West Indies. After completing shakedown training out of Guantanamo Bay, she visited St. Thomas in the Virgin Islands; Kingston, Jamaica; and Port-au-Prince, Haiti, before returning north to Philadelphia and a three-week post-shakedown availability. On 14 April, she departed Philadelphia and shaped a course across the Atlantic. *Toledo* steamed through the Mediterranean, transited the Suez Canal, crossed the Indian Ocean, and arrived at Yokosuka, Japan, on 15 June. *Toledo* remained in the Far East visiting Japanese and Korean ports in support of occupation forces until October. On the 21st, she stood out of Yokosuka for her first transpacific voyage and steamed via Pearl Harbor to Long Beach, Calif., where she arrived on 5 November.

Toledo made two more peacetime deployments to the western Pacific before the outbreak of the Korean War in 1950. On 3 April 1948, she departed Long Beach in company with *Helena* (CA–75) and shaped a course for Japan. She arrived in Yokosuka on the 24th and began her second tour of occupation duty patrolling for contraband smugglers. Later that spring, the cruiser made a goodwill cruise to the Indian Ocean during which she stopped at Karachi, Pakistan; Singapore, Malaya; Trincomalee, Ceylon; and Bombay, India. After her return to the northwestern Pacific in early summer, *Toledo* operated out of Tsingtao, China, during the evacuation of Chiang Kaishek's Nationalist Chinese forces to Taiwan. On 16 September, the warship departed the China coast and headed for Bremerton, Wash. She entered the Puget Sound Naval Shipyard on 5 October for her first major overhaul. The cruiser's refurbishing was completed on 18 February 1949; and she headed back to Long Beach for six months of training along the coasts of California, Mexico, and the Isthmus of Panama. Among other exercises, she participated in Operation "Miki," a simulated air-sea assault on Pearl Harbor. On 14 October, *Toledo* stood out of Long Beach to resume duty in the Far East. For eight months, she cruised the waters between Japan, China, the Philippines, and the Marianas.

Toledo returned to Long Beach on 12 June 1950. Less than two weeks later, at 0400 in the morning of 25 June, forces of North Korea's communist regime burst across the 38th parallel and streamed south to engulf the Republic of Korea (ROK). Ten days later, *Toledo* pointed her bow west once more and embarked upon her fourth cruise to the Orient and her first tour of combat duty.

She made a brief stop at Pearl Harbor en route and continued on to Sasebo, where Rear Admiral J. M. Higgins, Commander, Cruiser Division 5, broke his

USS *Toledo* (CA–133) presents the characteristic silhouette of the war-built *Baltimore* class of heavy cruisers. (19–N–119403)

flag in her on 18 July. Eight days later, the cruiser took up station off the eastern coast of Korea a few miles north of Pohang, near Yongdok. She teamed up with Destroyer Division 91 to form one of the two alternating East Coast Support Elements of Task Group (TG) 95.5. From 27 to 30 July, *Toledo*, *Mansfield* (DD–728), and *Collett* (DD–730) bombarded North Korean communication arteries which started at Yongdok and ran north between the mountains and the sea to the 38th parallel. On 4 August, the task element joined Air Force fighters in a combined air-sea strike on an enemy-held village near Yongdok. The following day, her 8-inch guns, directed by airborne controllers, rendered call-fire for the front-line troops. *Toledo* then moved some 70 miles north to the area around Samchok where she cruised along a 25-mile stretch of coastline and shelled a number of targets. During that interdiction run, she demolished a bridge, chewed up highway intersections, and generally wreaked havoc on communist supply lines. On the 6th, *Helena* relieved *Toledo*, enabling her to return to Sasebo for upkeep.

The warship resumed station off the Korean coast on 15 August and operated with *Rochester* (CA–124), *Mansfield*, *Collett*, and *Lyman K. Swenson* (DD–729) along a 40-mile length of coast from Songjin south to Iwon. After a number of bombardment missions, she returned to Sasebo again on the 26th and remained there until 31 August when she headed for a week of duty off Pohang Dong.

Toledo's next important mission was the landing at Inchon in mid-September. The heavily armed and fortified island of Wolmi Do—located in the harbor—threatened the success of the operation. Therefore, *Toledo* and her previous consorts—augmented by *Gurke* (DD–783), *De Haven* (DD–727), and Royal Navy warships, HMS *Jamaica* and HMS *Kenya*—entered the harbor to silence the island's guns on 13 September. The destroyers led the way through the mine-infested channel and moved in close to draw enemy fire while the cruisers stood off waiting for the North Koreans to betray their positions. By early afternoon, the artillery duel had begun; and the enemy suffered most. That evening, the cruisers and destroyers retired for the night. They returned the next day to finish the job. Then, after two days of preparatory bombardment, marines of the 3d Battalion Landing Team, 5th Marines, stormed Wolmi Do's defenses. Meanwhile, *Toledo* redirected her fire to support the 1st Marines who were about to land on Blue Beach just south of Inchon proper. After reportedly destroying three gun emplacements and a number of machine gun nests, closing two tunnels, hitting trenches and mortar positions, *Toledo* retired for the night at 1525.

Toledo continued fire-support missions until early October. However, after the 18th, the marines had advanced beyond the range of her 8-inch guns; and *Toledo* shifted to support troops mopping up bypassed pockets of enemy resistance. On 5 October, she departed the area and steamed for Sasebo.

The cruiser returned to the Korean coast at Chaho Han on 13 October, conducted shore bombardments in preparation for the amphibious operation at Wonsan, and reentered Sasebo the following day. The warship got underway again a little before midnight on the 18th and arrived off Wonsan early the next morning. For the next three days, she supported the marines during their advance inland from Wonsan.

On 22 October, *Toledo* departed Korea and, after stops at Sasebo and Yokosuka, headed for the United States on the 27th. Steaming via Pearl Harbor, she arrived in Long Beach on 8 November and remained there until the 13th when she headed for San Francisco. The following day, she entered the Hunter's Point Naval Shipyard and began a three-month overhaul. Refurbishment completed, *Toledo* left the yard on 24 February 1951 and returned to Long Beach the next evening. Following a round-trip voyage to San Diego,

the warship weighed anchor on 2 April to return to the western Pacific. She stopped over at Pearl Harbor from the 7th to the 9th and then continued on to Sasebo where she arrived on the 18th.

Toledo began her second tour of duty in the Korean combat zone on 26 April. For the next month, she cruised off the coast near Inchon where she provided gunfire support for the front-line troops of the I Corps guarding the Han River line during the communist spring offensive of 1951. Throughout that month, however, the enemy generally remained well beyond the river, out of range of the cruiser's 8-inch battery.

On 26 May, she steamed north to Kansong and joined Task Element 95.28 to conduct an interdiction bombardment of the area. Then, between 28 and 30 May, the enemy did venture close enough to the Han to allow *Toledo* to bring her main battery to bear, but only at extreme range. The cruiser spent the first 10 days of June at Yokosuka; then returned to the Korean coast on the 12th. On 18 June, she teamed up with *Duncan* (DD–874) and *Everett* (PF–8) to pummel the important enemy logistics junction located at Songjin.

The warship made a brief visit to Sasebo before heading back to Wonsan where, on the 27th, she joined *Bradford* (DD–545) in shelling the enemy ashore. The following evening, she endured her first hostile fire when shore batteries opened up on the cruiser and came dangerously close on several occasions.

Toledo's tour of duty along the eastern coast of Korea lasted until late November. She bombarded Wonsan, Songjin, and Chongjin and rescued several downed pilots—one, from *Boxer* (CV–21), twice. Late in October, her guns supported the 1st Marine Division in operations near Kansong. While conducting a shore bombardment on 11 November, she again came under fire from an enemy shore battery which scored some close near misses.

On 24 November, *Toledo* completed her deployment to the western Pacific and stood out of Yokosuka to return to the United States. After a pause at Pearl Harbor from 1 to 3 December, she continued on to Long Beach, where she arrived on the 8th. After a month of leave and upkeep, *Toledo* began seven months of duty operating out of Long Beach, conducting drills and training exercises along the west coast of the United States until mid-August. On 16 August 1952, the cruiser stood out of Long Beach to return to the western Pacific. After the customary stop at Pearl Harbor, she arrived in Yokosuka on 8 September.

Toledo embarked upon her third combat tour along the coast of Korea on 12 September when she stood out of Yokosuka. During the latter part of the month, her 8-inch guns aided the American X and the ROK I Corps. She supported the United Nations forces' limited offensives and holding actions while armistice talks dragged on. Periodically, she cleared that area to participate in gun strikes near Wonsan and in coastal patrols. On 24 September, she was called upon to provide continuous illumination fire and to silence an enemy 120-millimeter howitzer while United Nations forces recaptured positions recently lost to the communists.

She made an overnight port call at Sasebo on the 29th and 30th, visited the Bonin Islands from 2 through 4 October, and stopped at Yokosuka on the 5th and 6th, before taking up station on the bombline once more on the 8th. On 11 October, she joined the carriers of TF 77 and, for the next three months, alternated frequently between that duty and shore bombardment assignments. On 12 October, an enemy 75-millimeter gun managed to straddle her with eight rounds before 48 rounds from her 5-inch battery silenced it. Just before 0200 on the 14th, a gun opened fire from the same spot, scoring three near misses but no hits.

Other than those instances and some long-range snooping by MiG 15's, little action came *Toledo*'s way during her third and final Korean War deployment. In mid-January, she visited Hong Kong for rest and relaxation before resuming patrols off Wonsan and Song-jin and fire support duties for the American X and ROK I Corps. On 28 February 1953, *Toledo* departed Yokosuka and shaped a course for the United States. Following an overnight stop at Oahu on the night of 10 and 11 March, the cruiser moored at Long Beach on St. Patrick's Day, 1953. She departed Long Beach on 13 April and, after a two-day call at San Diego, arrived in San Francisco on the 16th. There, she entered the Hunter's Point Naval Shipyard for a five-month overhaul.

Toledo was still undergoing repairs when hostilities in Korea ended with the armistice of 27 July 1953. She departed San Francisco on 10 September and, after operations along the coast, headed for Pearl Harbor on 20 October. The cruiser reached Yokosuka on 7 November and began her seventh deployment to the Far East. Though the Korean conflict had ended the previous summer, American forces continued to patrol the waters along the Korean peninsula; and *Toledo* joined them in the endeavor. In fact, she spent the next six months operating out of Sasebo and Yokosuka in the waters between Japan and Korea and in the East China Sea. She visited Pusan, Inchon, and Pohang as well as Okinawa and Hong Kong. In addition to patrolling the neutral waters off the Korean coast, she periodically conducted exercises with the carriers of TF 77.

On 13 April 1954, the warship entered Yokosuka for upkeep following exercises in the Sea of Japan and preparatory to her return home. Three days later, she began her transpacific passage. She made the usual call at Pearl Harbor and tied up at Long Beach on May Day.

With one notable exception, *Toledo*'s eighth deployment to the Far East set the pattern for all those to follow. After almost five months of normal operations along the western coast of the United States, the cruiser cleared Long Beach on 14 September. She stopped at Pearl Harbor on the 21st for five days of rest and relaxation and then continued her voyage to Yokosuka where she arrived on 7 November. For the most part, her deployment consisted of training operations, goodwill calls at a number of ports, and general patrol and show-the-flag duties. During this tour of duty, she visited Hong Kong, Kobe, Nagasaki, Beppu, Subic Bay, and Manila.

The single exception to this peaceful routine came in January 1955. *Toledo* joined TF 77 in the waters between Taiwan and the communist Chinese mainland to support another evacuation of Nationalist Chinese forces—this time from the Tachen Islands. She took station about 1,500 yards off the islands as flagship of the naval gunfire support group. Throughout the operation, she and the other units of the group provided close-in support for the amphibious craft engaged in the actual evacuation. At the completion of that operation, the cruiser resumed the duties which became her normal Far Eastern routine.

On 5 March 1955, she departed Japan in company with *Pittsburgh* (CA–72) to return to the United States and arived in Long Beach 17 days later. She conducted operations along the west coast until 16 June when she began a four-month overhaul at the Puget Sound Naval Shipyard in Bremerton, Wash. The cruiser resumed duty late in October and cruised the west coast until early in 1956.

Toledo's active Navy career lasted four more years. During that period, she made four more deployments to the western Pacific. All save one consisted of routine operations, conducted out of bases in Japan and in the Philippines. The one exception came early in 1958. The cruiser cleared the west coast on 19 February and reached Japan early in March. However, after visiting Sasebo and Yokosuka, she headed south to Australia rather than to normal 7th Fleet operations. She reached Sydney on 30 April and remained there for five days as a guest of the Australian government during the 25th anniversary celebration of the Battle of the Coral Sea. After Sydney, *Toledo* also visited Melbourne before returning north to Japan via Okinawa to resume 7th Fleet operations. The deployment ended on 26 August 1958 when *Toledo* steamed back into Long Beach.

The warship made one more deployment to the western Pacific between 9 June and 25 November 1959. On 5 January 1960, she entered Long Beach Naval Shipyard to begin inactivation overhaul. *Toledo* completed preparations and was placed out of commission at Long Beach on 21 May 1960. She was moved to San Diego soon thereafter and remained there, in reserve, for the next 14 years. On 1 January 1974, her name was struck from the Navy list, and she was sold to the National Metal & Scrap Corp. on 30 October 1974.

Toledo earned five battle stars for service during the Korean War.

Tolland

A Connecticut county which was in turn named for a town in Somerset, England.

(AKA–64: dp. 13,910 (tl.); l. 459'2''; b. 63'; dr. 26'4'' (lim.); s. 16.5 k. (tl.); cpl. 375; a. 1 5'', 8 40mm.; cl. *Tolland*; T. C2–S–AJ3)

Tolland (AKA–64) was laid down under a Maritime Commission contract (MC hull 1385) on 22 April 1944 at Wilmington, N.C., by the North Carolina Shipbuilding Corp.; launched on 26 June 1944; sponsored by Miss Beverley Peebles; delivered to the Navy under loan-charter on 13 August 1944; and commissioned at Charleston, S.C., on 4 September 1944, Comdr. Edward J. Kingsland, USNR, in command.

Assigned to Task Group 29.7, *Tolland* departed Hampton Roads on 14 October bound for Hawaii, transited the Panama Canal on 21 October, and arrived at Pearl Harbor on 5 November.

The ship devoted the next month to amphibious maneuvers and exercises off Maui before heading back to the west coast on 6 December and making port six days later. Returning to Pearl Harbor on 23 December, the ship spent Christmas and New Year's in Hawaiian waters before embarking on further training in preparation for combat operations across the Pacific.

The day and night exercises continued through the third week of January 1945 as the ship's crew honed its skills in cargo loading and unloading, boat-handling, and antiaircraft gunnery. *Tolland* got underway with Task Force 53 on 27 January, bound for Eniwetok with marines of the 5th Marine Division and a construction battalion or "seabee" unit embarked.

Following brief stops at Eniwetok and Saipan, *Tolland* anchored off Iwo Jima on 19 February to commence 10 days of unloading. After the initial landings had been blessed with good weather, rough tides hampered subsequent support operations. In spite of these natural impediments, the operations proceeded. In the vicious tidal conditions on the steep beaches, three of the ship's LCVP's and one LCM sank, but the men on board were saved. One unmanned amphibious craft struck the port propeller, and a Japanese shell clipped a radio antenna for the ship's only damage. Twenty-five marines, wounded on shore in heavy fighting with the fanatical Japanese defenders, were evacuated to the ship for medical treatment while the ship lay to off the beachhead.

The stars and stripes flew proudly over Mt. Suribachi as Marine forces secured the island after bitter fighting. *Tolland* and her companion AKA's in the squadron left the Bonins for a period of waiting, training, provisioning, and repairs, while American forces marshalled for the asault on an island one step closer to the Japanese homeland itself—Okinawa. Drydocked at Espiritu Santo late in February, *Tolland* then combat-loaded elements of the Army 27th Division and cleared the New Hebrides on 1 April 1945, bound for the Ryukyus.

With Kerama Retto secured earlier in the Okinawa campaign, *Tolland* put in on 9 April and anchored as a floating reserve with Task Force 53. American forces endured terrific air attacks from the Japanese defenders, now nearly reduced to this last island defense post on their very doorstep. The attack cargo ship's crew stood to general quarters for hours at a time—night and day—some sleeping and eating at their stations during lulls in the action, to be so many steps closer to their guns at the sound of the alarm. In one of the 22 air attacks encountered during her eight-day deployment off Okinawa, *Tolland*'s guns downed a Japanese "Betty" bomber on 12 April. On 15 April, an "Oscar" flew low over the transport area, attracting fire and spinning into the sea in flames as *Tolland* and other ships shared the kill.

Departing from the Ryukyus on 16 April, *Tolland* proceeded via Saipan to Ulithi and engaged in nearly continuous exercises and drills through 14 May, when she was ordered to Angaur in the Palau Islands. Loading heavy guns soon after her arrival, she set out for the Philippines, to off-load her cargo at Cebu on 24 May, before moving to Subic Bay and anchoring there for three weeks of upkeep and training.

Subsequent to her rest period at Subic Bay, the ship proceeded to Manila where she remained from 22 to 28 June. She then steamed to Leyte where she embarked troops, vehicles, and equipment of the Army 323d Division for amphibious training.

By this time, preparations for the invasion of Japan were proceeding apace. Estimates of fanatical and suicidal Japanese resistance projected astronomical casualties for both defender and invader alike, with untold devastation forecast. Accordingly, heavy air attacks by American B–29's pounded key Japanese targets while units of the American and British Navies steamed often close inshore, bombarding coastline targets.

The entire month of July found *Tolland* and her sisters engaged in training for the projected invasion of Japan, conducting exercises in Subic Bay and Lingayen Gulf. While the attack transport was at Lingayen, word came that American B–29's had dropped atomic bombs on Hiroshima and Nagasaki. Now hardpressed on all sides and hemmed in by armadas of sea and air forces, Japan capitulated on 15 August 1945. After a brief stop at Subic Bay from 17 to 19 August, *Tolland* proceeded to Batangas Bay, Luzon, on the 20th and then moved on to Tokyo where she was present when Japanese representatives signed the formal articles of surrender on the deck of battleship *Missouri* (BB–63).

Returning to the Philippines, the ship arrived at Zamboanga on 2 September, where she embarked units of the Army 41st Cavalry Division for transportation to Kure, Japan, for duty with the Allied occupation forces. Provisioning at Manila after delivering the Army troops, she embarked elements of the Chinese 52d Army at Tonkin Gulf, French Indochina, and transported them to Chinwangtao, China, at the base of the Great Wall.

On 14 November, *Tolland* departed Taku, China, and pointed her bow toward home, arriving at Seattle on 20 November 1945 as Task Unit 78.19.6, and remaining in the Pacific northwest until 28 February 1946, when the ship departed for Port Hueneme.

On 11 March 1946, with cargo loaded on board earmarked for Guam, *Tolland* departed the west coast. She arrived at Apra Harbor on 27 March and remained there until 20 April when she departed for Panama. Making port at Balboa on 13 May, she transited the Panama Canal and reported to Commander in Chief, Atlantic Fleet, for duty on 14 May. Departing Panamanian waters on the 16th, she proceeded for Hampton Roads and arrived at Norfolk on 21 May.

Tolland was decommissioned on 1 July 1946 and returned to the War Shipping Administration on 2 July. Seventeen days later, on 19 July 1946, her name was struck from the Navy list.

Purchased by the Luckenbach Steamship Co., Inc., she was renamed SS *Edgar F. Luckenbach* and served under this company's flag through 1959.

Tolland received two battle stars for her World War II service at Iwo Jima and Okinawa.

Tollberg

Maynard W. Tollberg—born on 17 February 1904 in North Branch, Minn.—enlisted in the United States Naval Reserve on 24 September 1923 and was honorably discharged on 15 September 1927. He reenlisted on 23 June 1942 with the same rating and was assigned duty on board *La Vallette* (DD–448).

On the afternoon of 30 January 1943, during the second day of the Battle of Rennell Island, *La Vallette* was screening the damaged cruiser *Chicago* (CA–29) when 11 enemy torpedo planes attacked. *La Vallette* received a torpedo hit in her forward engine room which killed 22 members of the crew. Watertender Second Class Tollberg, although fatally scalded by high temperature steam, painfully climbed up the fireroom ladder and emerged on the main deck through a hatch which had been blown open by the detonation. Despite severe pain and partial blindness, he expended his dying strength trying to close the control valve through which oil was pouring into the fireroom below, where a number of his helpless shipmates were trapped. Tollberg then collapsed and soon died of his wounds. He was posthumously awarded the Navy Cross.

(APD–103: dp. 1,650; l. 306′0″; b. 37′0″; dr. 12′7″; s. 23.6 k. (tl.); cpl. 204; trp. 162; a. 1 5″, 6 40mm.; cl. *Crosley*)

Tollberg (APD–103) was laid down as DE–593 on 30 December 1943 at Hingham, Mass., by the Bethlehem Shipbuilding Co.; launched on 12 February 1944; sponsored by Mrs. Maynard W. Tollberg; converted to a high speed transport; and redesignated APD–103 on 17 July 1944; and commissioned on 31 January 1945, Lt. Comdr. Edward F. Butler, USNR, in command.

The new ship stood out of Boston on 18 February for shakedown training off Bermuda. She left Bermuda on 9 March and arrived at Hampton Roads, Va., on the 11th. Two weeks later, she got underway to escort *Rankin* (AKA–103) to the Canal Zone. *Tollberg* transited the Panama Canal on the 31st and, the next day, proceeded independently to California. She reached San Diego on 9 April and, six days later, sailed for Hawaii.

The transport arrived at Pearl Harbor on the 22d, but left again on 4 May and proceeded, via Eniwetok, to Ulithi. The ship got underway on 31 May with *Cross* (DE–448) to escort *Poseidon* (ARL–12), *Minotaur* (ARL–15), and *Moose* (IX–114) to Okinawa. She arrived at the Hagushi beach area on 4 June and was assigned to picket duty in the antiaircraft and antisubmarine screen. The high-speed transport had only one opportunity to fire at a distant Japanese aircraft. On 8 August, she and *Abercrombie* (DE–343) joined *California* (BB–44) and *Nevada* (BB–36) to screen the battleships to the Philippines. The next day, *Tollberg* rescued a pilot from *California* whose plane had swamped while taxiing in to be picked up. The warships arrived at Leyte on the 11th, and the transport remained there for nine days.

Tollberg departed the Philippines on the 20th to escort a convoy to Okinawa and returned on the 29th. Between 20 September and 3 October, she escorted Transport Squadron 14 to Wakayama Wan, Japan, and back to Leyte. On 2 November, she left Manila to carry passengers for Okinawa and, after escorting *Estes* (AGC–12) to Shanghai, disembarked them at Buckner Bay on the 7th. Five days later, she was back at Manila. Between 24 and 26 November, the transport embarked 156 passengers at Samar for passage to the east coast of the United States.

Sailing the next day, *Tollberg* called at Eniwetok, Pearl Harbor, San Diego, and the Canal Zone before arriving at Norfolk, Va., on 30 December 1945. She remained at Norfolk until 26 March 1946 when she headed for the West Indies. After two months in the Caribbean, the ship was at the New York Naval Shipyard from 20 May to 24 July; and she then entered the Charleston Naval Shipyard for preservation work which continued from 26 July to 12 November.

Tollberg arrived at Green Cove Springs, Fla., on 13 November; was decommissioned there on 20 December 1946; and entered the Atlantic Reserve Fleet. In September 1959, she was towed from Mayport, Fla., to Sabine Pass, Tex., and laid up with the Texas Reserve Group. *Tollberg* was struck from the Navy list in November 1964 and transferred to the Government of Colombia under the Military Assistance Program on 14 August 1965. She serves the Colombian Navy as *Almirante Padilla* (DT–03).

Tollberg received one battle star for World War II service.

Tolman

Charles E. Tolman—born on 25 June 1903 in Concord, Mass.—entered the United States Naval Academy in the summer of 1921 and graduated on 4 June 1925. After serving in battleship *Utah* (BB–31), he was transferred to *Worden* (DD–288) in 1926. Tolman then completed training courses at the Naval Torpedo Station, Newport, R.I., and at the Submarine Base, New London, Conn. He served in submarines *O–4* in 1928 and *S–22* from 1929 to 1932 when he returned to the Naval Academy for two years. Tolman served in submarine *S–46* in 1934 and commanded *S–30* from April 1935 to May 1937. He was attached to the Office of the Chief of Naval Operations for 17 months before assuming command of *Spearfish* (SS–190) on 7 October 1939. In January 1941, Tolman joined the staff of Commander, Submarines, Atlantic Fleet.

Comdr. Tolman became the commanding officer of *De Haven* (DD–469) upon her commissioning on 21 September 1942. The destroyer steamed to the South Pacific in November 1942 and supported operations in the Solomons. On the afternoon of 1 February 1943, while escorting landing craft, *De Haven* was attacked by six Japanese dive bombers. Fighting off the attackers, the destroyer splashed three enemy planes before a bomb struck her navigating bridge, stopped her, and killed Comdr. Tolman. Two more hits and a near miss doomed *De Haven*, which sank within two minutes. Comdr. Tolman was posthumously awarded the Navy Cross for his valiant leadership.

(DM–28: dp. 2,200; l. 376'6"; b. 40'10"; dr. 18'10"; s. 34.2 k. (tl.); cpl. 363; a. 6 5", 12 40mm.; cl. *Robert H. Smith*)

Tolman (DM–28) was laid down as DD–740 on 10 April 1944 at Bath, Maine, by the Bath Iron Works; reclassified a destroyer minelayer and redesignated DM–28 on 19 July; launched on 13 August; sponsored by Mrs. Helen Tolman; and commissioned on 27 October 1944, Comdr. Clifford A. Johnson in command.

The minelayer held her shakedown training off Bermuda during November and December and returned, via Norfolk, to Boston. On 13 January 1945, *Tolman* departed Boston to escort *Pittsburgh* (CA–72) to the west coast. She called at San Diego on the 27th and then escorted *Birmingham* (CL–62) to Hawaii. She participated in exercises at Pearl Harbor until 23 February before heading for Eniwetok and Ulithi. On 19 March, *Tolman* sortied from Ulithi with Task Group 52.4 to provide fire support and antisubmarine screening for the minesweepers clearing channels prior to the amphibious assault on the Ryukyus. On 22 March, she began clearing the approaches to the beaches of Okinawa.

Shortly after midnight on 28 March, she encountered eight Japanese motor torpedo boats. The enemy closed to 4,000 yards when *Tolman* opened fire with her 5-inch and 40-millimeter batteries. The DM increased her speed to 34 knots and maneuvered radically to avoid torpedoes. Two of the enemy boats exploded and sank as the remainder laid a smoke screen. The minelayer briefly lost contact, but used radar-controlled fire against the remaining boats and fired star shells to ferret them out. The last boat was seen to slow, apparently in trouble, just before it was blown up. The ship evidently made a clean sweep of the torpedo boats as a search revealed nothing, and no boats had been seen leaving the area.

Later that morning, *Tolman* was approximately 500 yards from *Skylark* (AM–63) when *Skylark* struck and detonated a mine against her hull. As *Tolman* moved in to pass a tow line to the stricken ship, *Skylark* hit a second mine and began settling rapidly. *Tolman* backed full to clear the mined area, but her boats, together with *PC–1228* and *PC–1179*, rescued 105 survivors.

On 29 March, during several enemy air attacks, *Tolman* reported splashing one plane of three in the first raid; one of two in the second attack; and, with the aid of *Barton* (DD–722) and *Wiley* (AM–29), two of three in the third. Later, she shot down a kamikaze that was approaching her in a suicide dive. The minelayer then proceeded to Kerama Retto to transfer *Skylark*'s survivors to other ships.

On the morning of 30 March, *Tolman* contacted three enemy torpedo boats at a range of 3,000 yards. She went ahead at flank speed and made a hard turn to port. One torpedo passed astern and another was reported off her starboard bow. A third exploded astern, causing considerable vibration. On 3 April, she screened Transport Division 17 to a waiting area approximately 150 miles southeast of Okinawa and remained there for 10 days before returning to the Hagushi beaches.

Tolman grounded off Nagunna Reef on the morning of 19 April and remained aground. Two tugs then pulled her free on the 25th, and *Clamp* (ARS–33) towed her to Kerama Retto for repairs. She entered drydock on 15 May and was not ready for sea until late in June. On 28 June, the ship got underway for the United States. After arriving at San Pedro on 21 July, she began permanent repairs that were completed on 8 November.

The minelayer stood out for the Far East early in December and arrived at Sasebo on the day after Christmas. She operated out of Sasebo until February 1946 and then shifted her base of operations to Pusan, Korea, for three months. The ship began the return voyage to California on 4 May and arrived at San Francisco on 27 May 1946. Proceeding down the coast to San Diego in January 1947, she was decommissioned on the 29th. *Tolman* was reclassified a fast minelayer, MMD–28, in January 1969. She was struck from the Navy list on 1 December 1970.

Tolman received one battle star for World War II service.

Tolovana

A small river in central Alaska. It rises in the mountains just to the west of Fairbanks and flows into the Tanana River, one of the primary tributaries of the Yukon River.

(AO–64: dp. 25,440 (lim.); l. 553'0"; b. 75'0"; dr. 32'4" (lim.); s. 18.3 k. (tl.); cpl. 313; a. 1 5", 4 3", 8 40mm.; cl. *Cimmarron*; T. T3–S2–1)

Tolovana (AO–64) was laid down on 5 June 1944 under a Maritime Commission contract (MC hull 730) at Sparrows Point, Md., by the Bethlehem Steel Co.; launched on 6 January 1945; sponsored by Mrs. Richard M. Bissell, Jr.; acquired by the Navy on 24 February 1945; and commissioned that same day, Lt. Comdr. Carleton G. Long, USNR, in command.

Following shakedown training in Chesapeake Bay and repairs at the Norfolk Navy Yard, *Tolovana* put to sea on 25 March bound ultimately for the western Pacific. En route, she stopped at Houston, Tex., from 30 March to 2 April; loaded diesel oil; and continued on her way. The oiler transited the Panama Canal on 6 April and, after further repairs at Balboa, resumed her voyage west. On 23 April, she reached Pearl Harbor and reported for duty with the Service Force, Pacific Fleet. After completing voyage repairs and loading aviation gasoline, *Tolovana* stood out of Pearl Harbor on 28 April. On 9 May, she entered the lagoon at Ulithi Atoll in the Western Carolines and reported for duty with Service Squadron 10. Three days later, she returned to sea bound via Kossol Roads in the Palaus to Leyte Gulf. *Tolovana* discharged the aviation gasoline portion of her cargo at Kossol Roads on 14 and 15 May and transferred her diesel oil to gasoline oilers at San Pedro Bay, Leyte, between 17 and 31 May.

Since her tanks had not been contaminated with fuel oil and gasoline constituted the commodity in greatest need at Okinawa, *Tolovana* was earmarked for duty shuttling it between Ulithi and the combat area which was considered too dangerous for merchant tankers. She returned to Ulithi from Leyte on 2 June and loaded her first full cargo of gasoline. For the remainder of the war, the oiler steamed back and forth between Ulithi and the Ryukyus delivering aviation and automobile gasoline to the tank farm on Okinawa. She experienced frequent air attacks but suffered no combat damage.

When the war ended in mid-August, *Tolovana* was at Okinawa. During the immediate postwar period, she continued to make the Okinawa-Ulithi gasoline shuttle in support of occupation forces. Later that fall, she widened her sphere of operations to include such ports as Jinsen, Korea; and Yokosuka, Japan. In May 1946, she moved to the Marshall Islands to support Operation "Crossroads," the atomic bomb tests conducted at Bikini Atoll. She remained in that area until 17 June when she headed back to the United States. *Tolovana* reached Long Beach, Calif., on 5 July and entered the naval shipyard for her first overhaul since commissioning.

On 22 September, the ship emerged from the naval shipyard revitalized and began two years of duty along the western coast of North America. During the greater part of that period, *Tolovana* provided logistics support for bases in Alaska and in the Aleutians chain. She made frequent calls at Adak, Attu, Kodiak, and Anchorage while operating from Seattle, Wash., and periodically returned to California ports for visits and overhauls. She also made a voyage apiece to Guam and to Pearl Harbor during the period. In August 1948, *Tolovana* bade farewell to the cold waters of Alaska and headed via the Panama Canal to Bremerhaven, Germany, where she stopped over for five days in mid-September. The oiler returned to the west coast late in October, reaching Long Beach on the 19th, and resumed logistics support missions along the western seaboard and in the Aleutian Islands.

During the ensuing years, she continued such duty. However, her sphere of operations widened to include ports in the western Pacific, in the Indian Ocean, and the Mediterranean Sea. Frequently, she called at such ports as Ras Tanura in Saudi Arabia to take on petroleum products directly from the producers and then carry them to American bases in Japan and the Philippines. In August 1949, the Naval Transport Service—with which she had been serving since December 1949—was reconstituted as the Military Sea Transportation Service (MSTS). When transferred to the new organization, ships like *Tolovana* ceased to be commissioned ships in the Navy, though they continued to perform their familiar logistics support function for the Navy as well as for the other services.

The outbreak of war in Korea during the summer of 1950 increased Navy requirements for oilers engaged in direct support of the combat fleet. Thus, they were recalled from MSTS' general logistics operations and converted to perform such missions. *Tolovana* entered Mare Island Naval Shipyard on 15 February 1951; emerged ready for duty just over three months later; and, on 24 May, was recommissioned, Capt. E. C. Madsen in command. However, the oiler did not deploy immediately to the combat zone. Instead, she resumed operations off the west coast until early July when she made a voyage to Guam. On 24 July, *Tolovana* departed Guam and shaped a course for Pearl Harbor where she arrived on 8 August. She spent the remainder of the month there, preparing to deploy to the Far East and the Korean combat zone.

On 1 September, the oiler stood out of Pearl Harbor and headed west. Just under two weeks later, she arrived in Sasebo, Japan, and reported for duty with Task Force (TF) 77. Between 20 September and 18 December, *Tolovana* provided logistic support for the carriers of TF 77 and their supporting forces as well as for United Nations units operating ashore at Chosen, Songjin, and Wonsan. On 18 December, the ship returned briefly to Sasebo and departed the same day on a voyage to Okinawa, Taiwan, and Hong Kong, during which she provided support for American forces at Okinawa and for those engaged in the Taiwan Strait patrols. *Tolovana* returned to Sasebo on 31 January 1952 and resumed her support role refueling and replenishing units of TF 77 operating off the Korean coast.

On 18 March, the oiler returned to Japan at Yokosuka and, after two days of preparations, sailed for the west coast of the United States. She arrived in San Pedro, Calif., on 1 April and began two months of training operations. On 7 June, *Tolovana* put to sea bound for the Trust Territories in the central Pacific where, for the next six months, she delivered fuel and supplies from Pearl Harbor to the mid-Pacific islands: Midway, Eniwetok, and Kwajalein. She stopped at Hawaii on 12 December for the last time before returning to the west coast. The next day, the ship shaped a course for Long Beach and entered the port on the 19th.

Over the next six years, *Tolovana* deployed annually to the western Pacific. In each case, she departed the west coast during the summer months and returned in December or January. Her duties normally consisted of logistics missions in support of TF 77 and of the Taiwan Strait patrol. However, during the first of these six tours, she was called upon to join in Operation "Passage to Freedom"—the evacuation of French and loyal Vietnamese from Haiphong in communist North Vietnam to South Vietnam following the collapse of French rule in Indochina. The remaining five deployments to the Far East involved routine logistic support for units assigned to TF 77 and to the Taiwan Strait patrol. When not cruising Asiatic waters, *Tolovan* punctuated training operations off the California coast with upkeep and periodic overhauls.

In January 1960, *Tolovana* returned to the west coast completing the last in her series of six, regular summer-fall deployments to the Far East. This, however, did not signal an end to such duty but rather to its regularity. In fact, over the next four years, she completed five tours of duty in Asian waters. During the second of this series, she was called upon to support those units of the fleet sent to Southeast Asia late in March 1961 to bolster the resolve of pro-western forces in Laos crumbling in the face of a major push on the part of Pathet Lao guerillas supported by North Vietnamese regulars. Though American resolve lessened the probability of a complete collapse of the anticommunist faction in Laos, the crisis did not die away until after *Tolovana* left the Far East in May to return home. She began her next tour of duty in the western Pacific in October 1961 and returned to the United States in February 1962. The following summer, the oiler participated in Operation "Dominic," a nuclear test conducted at Christmas Island during June and early July 1962.

After another relatively routine assignment with the 7th Fleet between October 1962 and April 1963, *Tolovana* entered a decade in which her service mirrored the increasingly more direct involvement of United States forces in the conflict in Vietnam. During that period, she made eight deployments to the western Pacific; and, on each, her crew members qualified for combat campaign ribbons. During the first of this series of tours, American presence remained small, and *Tolovana* spent comparatively little time in support of the operations there. However, by the time of her next cruise to the western Pacific—July to November 1965—America's buildup had begun in earnest. From that point on, she concentrated upon replenishing ships in the combat zone, returning briefly to Subic Bay in the Philippines or to Yokosuka or Sasebo in Japan to refill her tanks. The fact that *Tolovana* never came under enemy fire did not diminish her effectiveness. She contributed to the success of underway replenishment operations—pioneered by the Navy during World War II—which, in turn, enabled American warships to remain in action for extended periods of time and bring the full weight of their naval might to bear on the struggle.

On the other hand, there were breaks in the routine. She called at various liberty ports in the Far East such as Hong Kong; Bangkok, Thailand; Yokosuka and Sasebo in Japan; and Kaohsiung, Taiwan. During the 1967 and 1968 deployment, she was ordered north to provide logistics support for ships which answered the call of *Pueblo* (AGER–2), captured on the high seas in violation of international law by forces of the North Korean Navy. However, the major change in routine came between the deployments when she returned to the west coast for upkeep, training, repairs, and periodic overhauls.

Her eighth and last wartime deployment came in September 1972, and she was still in the western Pacific in January 1973 when American involvement drew to a close. The oiler remained in the Far East until the following May and then departed Subic Bay to return to Long Beach where she arrived on the 24th. After three months in port at Long Beach, *Tolovana* resumed local operations in the southern California operating area until July 1974 when she stood out of San Diego for the last western Pacific cruise of her career. That assignment continued until January 1975 at which time she returned to San Diego. Between 31 March and 1 April, the veteran oiler made the transit from San Diego to Mare Island Naval Shipyard. On 15 April 1975, *Tolovana* was decommissioned, and her name was struck from the Navy list that same day.

Tolovana (AO–64) earned one battle star during World War II, two battle stars for the Korean conflict, and 12 battle stars and the Navy Unit Commendation for service off Vietnam.

Tolowa

An Athapascan Indian tribe of northwestern California that formerly occupied the coast from the Klamath River to the Oregon line.

(ATF–116: dp. 1,589; l. 205'0''; b. 38'6''; dr. 15'4''; s. 16.5 k. (tl.); cpl. 85; a. 1 3'', 2 40mm.; cl. *Abnaki*)

Tolowa was laid down as AT–116 on 28 July 1943 at Alameda, Calif., by the United Engineering Co.; redesignated as ATF–116 on 15 May 1944; launched on 17 May 1944; sponsored by Mrs. B. D. Bales; and commissioned on 26 December 1944, Lt. Eugene G. Sheasby, USNR, in command.

The tug held shakedown training in the San Diego-San Pedro area in January and February 1945. On 27 February, she got underway for Hawaii with a barge in tow and arrived at Pearl Harbor on 12 March. Eleven days later, she proceeded via Eniwetok to

Ulithi. *Tolowa* left Ulithi on 7 May bound for the Philippines with *Ginnabar* (IX–163) and *YC–755* in tow. She delivered her charges at Leyte on 13 May and returned to Ulithi to deliver a concrete ship and a barge to Leyte.

On 8 June, *Tolowa* joined a convoy of 12 tugs, 20 tows, and two escorts en route to Okinawa. She arrived at Kerama Retto on 12 June and embarked a fire-fighting team. The ship then took station off Ie Shima as an emergency salvage and fire-fighting tug. The tug operated in the Okinawa area until the end of hostilities in August.

On 11 September, she headed for the Philippines and operated there until late in October, when she took two tows from Subic Bay to Hong Kong. She returned to Subic Bay on 2 November and, six days later, headed again for Chinese waters. After operating out of Shanghai and Tsingtao from 16 November 1945 to 1 April 1946, she called at Sasebo en route back to the Philippines. On 16 April, *Tolowa* began the long return voyage to the United States. She called at Eniwetok, Kwajalein, Johnston, and Oahu before arriving at San Diego on 9 July. The ship proceeded to San Pedro the next day, remaining there until 6 August when she got underway for the east coast to be inactivated.

After a stay at New Orleans from 12 September to 9 November, *Tolowa* shifted to Orange, Tex. The tug was decommissioned on 27 January 1947 and struck from the Navy list on 11 November 1970.

Tolowa received one battle star for World War II service.

Tom Bowline

(Sch.: t. 260; cpl. 90; a. 12 guns)

Tom Bowline—a schooner—was purchased by the United States Navy in late 1814 at Portsmouth, N.H., for use as a storeship, Lt. B. V. Hoffman in command. Subsequently proceeding to New York, she joined *President*, *Hornet*, and *Peacock* in preparations for a raiding foray into the East Indies.

President's sortie on 14 January 1815, however, ended in disaster—grounding and suffering severe damage, the frigate fell victim and captive to a superior British squadron on the following day—15 January. On the 22d, a strong northeasterly gale blew up and provided the three other American ships at New York an opportunity to escape the vigilant eyes of the British blockaders. *Tom Bowline* bent on storm canvas to accompany *Hornet* and *Peacock* in their bid for freedom of the open sea.

Unaware of *President*'s fate, the three ships made for Tristan de Cunha for the prearranged rendezvous. *Hornet* became separated en route, leaving her two consorts to press on without her. *Tom Bowline* and *Peacock* reached the volcanic island on 18 March—only to be driven off by a gale.

Hornet arrived five days later, but her landfall coincided with the appearance in the area of British brig-sloop *Penguin*. The two ships closed for action, and *Hornet* damaged *Penguin* seriously enough to warrant destruction of the Briton. The sighting of strange sail on the horizon hastened *Hornet*'s burning of the prize, but apprehension turned to relief as the sails proved to be *Peacock* and *Tom Bowline* returning to Tristan de Cunha for the planned rendezvous. *Tom Bowline* embarked the *Penguin*'s captive crew and took the prisoners to Rio de Janeiro, Brazil.

Records giving details of *Tom Bowline*'s subsequent service have not been found, but the vessel was apparently sold in 1818.

Tom Green County

A county in western Texas, established in 1874 and named in honor of Brigadier General Tom Green of the Confederate Army.

Green—born in Amelia County, Va., on 8 June 1814—graduated from the University of Tennessee and Princeton College and was admitted to the Tennessee bar in 1835. Coming to Texas in December 1835, Green enlisted in the Volunteer Auxiliary Corps of the Texas Army at Nacogdoches on 14 January 1836 and took part in the Battle of San Jacinto the following spring. After that victory, he was promoted to assistant adjutant general. With Texas independence achieved, he briefly returned to Tennessee before returning to the "Lone Star State" in 1837.

Subsequently becoming clerk of the Texas Supreme Court in 1841, he participated in an expedition against the Indians on the upper Colorado River in 1841. He served as a captain in the Travis County Volunteers at the time of the Rafael Vasquez invasion in March 1842. During the Mexican War, Green raised a company of volunteers and served as a captain under John Coffee Hays.

Resigning his clerkship upon the commencement of hostilities in the Civil War, he entered the Confederate Army as a colonel in Sibley's Brigade and participated in the invasion of New Mexico in 1862. On 1 January 1863, Green commanded the expedition mounted in "cotton-clad" steamers *Neptune* and *Bayou City* which recaptured Galveston.

Green was next transferred to Louisiana, where he won renown as a cavalry leader. Some officers said that he was second only to J.E.B. Stuart. At the battles of Mansfield and Pleasant Hill, Green's Brigade conducted forays and guerrilla warfare, harassing Union supply lines and rear areas.

In the spring of 1864, during a Federal drive to cut off Texas as a storehouse of supplies for the Rebel cause, Green led his men in an ill-fated attack on Union gunboats at Blair's Landing, La. On 12 April 1864, while leading a cavalry charge to the very bank of the river, Green was decapitated by shellfire.

Admiral David Dixon Porter paid tribute to the fallen Confederate cavalryman in saying that Green was "one in whom the rebels place more confidence than anyone else. He led his men to the very edge of the bank, they shouting and yelling like madmen—losing General Green has paralyzed them; he was worth 5,000 men to them."

(LST–1159: dp. 2,590; l. 384'; b. 55'; dr. 17'; cpl. 116; s. 15 k.; a. 6 3''; cl. *LST–1156*)

Tom Green County (LST–1159) was laid down as *LST–1159* on 2 September 1952 at Bath, Maine, by the Bath Iron Works; launched on 2 July 1953; sponsored by Mrs. R. T. Cowdrey; and commissioned on 12 September 1953, Lt. Comdr. Stephen J. Nemeth in command.

Initially attached to Amphibious Forces, Atlantic Fleet, LST–1159 conducted shakedown in Guantanamo Bay and the Caribbean before commencing local opera-

Tom Green County (LST–1159) in 1959. Her prominent stack distinguishes her from earlier classes of tank landing ships. (USN 1045200)

tions out of Norfolk and Little Creek, Va. She departed Norfolk on 24 February 1954 for duty with Amphibious Forces, Pacific Fleet, and, after a transit of the Panama Canal, reached the west coast on 20 March. The tank landing ship operated out of her new home port, San Diego, until 20 September, including calls at San Francisco and San Pedro, Calif., and Esquimalt, British Columbia, in her itinerary.

En route to the Far East, LST–1159 stopped briefly at Pearl Harbor before proceeding on toward Japan. While on the voyage across the Pacific, the ship was diverted to join Task Force (TF) 98 in Southeast Asian waters and arrived at Henriette Pass, near the port of Haiphong, French Indochina, on 29 October. Taking part in Operation "Passage to Freedom," LST–1159 transported refugees from the northern part of what became a divided Vietnam, to the southern ports of Tourane (Danang) and Saigon. On 29 November 1954, her job in the massive humanitarian effort completed, the tank landing ship proceeded toward her original destination.

LST–1159 proceeded via Subic Bay, Philippine Islands, and Hong Kong, British Crown Colony, and arrived at Yokosuka, Japan, on 22 December. The tank landing ship paid calls on the Japanese ports of Moji, Sasebo, and Kobe before a deteriorating international situation resulted in the ship's call to duty with TF 76 at Buckner Bay, Okinawa, on 3 February 1955. She sortied from Okinawa soon thereafter and took part in the evacuation of the Tachen Islands from 8 to 13 February, moving 2,144 civilians, 1,100 troops, 600 tons of ammunition, and 37 vehicles to Formosa in two round trips. Soon after completing these operations, LST–1159 was named Tom Green County.

Returning via Sasebo, Japan, and Inchon, Korea, to the United States, Tom Green County made port at San Diego on 2 April to begin a period of local operations out of that port. On 14 October, the tank landing ship entered the Mare Island Naval Shipyard at Vallejo, Calif., for a four-month yard period which lasted until February of 1956.

Moving back to San Diego following the overhaul, Tom Green County departed the west coast for her second Far East deployment on 24 April and arrived at Pearl Harbor on 4 May. Underway on 7 May, the ship made port at Yokosuka on the 24th and operated in the Far East for the remainder of 1956, touching at her normal ports of call, such as Sasebo, Iwakuni, Nagasaki, and Yokosuka, Japan; Buckner Bay and Naha, Okinawa; as well as Hong Kong and Iwo Jima, before returning to Yokosuka on 22 November.

On 23 January 1957, the tank landing ship departed Japanese waters for Hawaii and reached Pearl Harbor on 9 February. Tom Green County conducted local operations between the Hawaiian Islands and the west coast for the remainder of the year, with calls at San Diego, Monterey, Oakland, San Francisco, and Camp Pendleton, before she headed for Pearl Harbor.

Deployed again to the Far East, Tom Green County made port at Yokosuka on 4 July 1958 to commence amphibious support exercises and training cruises to familiar places: Buckner Bay, Naha, Subic Bay, and a new port on the itinerary, the Nationalist Chinese base at Kaohsiung, Taiwan. She remained engaged in these activities through the fall of 1958, before returning, via Pearl Harbor, to San Diego to round out the year. Local operations between the west coast and Pearl Harbor occupied the ship through 1959.

In July 1960, new orders dictated the tank landing ship's change of home port from San Diego to Yokosuka and assigned Tom Green County as flagship of Landing Ship Division 92. She continued her operations much as before, but maintenance work was now conducted in Japanese yards, obviating returns to United States for overhauls. Local operations, interspersed yard periods, and training exercises kept the tank landing ship engaged through 1962.

Following the ship's participation in Operations "Tulungan" (9 March to 9 April 1962) and "Lone Eagle" (14 to 23 October), at Subic Bay and Okinawa, respectively, Tom Green County went on alert as events half-way around the world threatened peace. The presence of Russian IRBM's in Cuba brought on a head-to-head confrontation between the Soviet Union and the United States. Ready for any eventuality, the Navy prepared itself, world-wide. Tom Green County sailed for Naha on the 24th of October, moored at the LST ramp, and took on board marines and their equipment. After the crisis passed, the ship returned to her normal operating schedule, making for Iwakuni on the 27th to off-load, before proceeding to Yokosuka.

Upkeep from 2 to 25 November at Yokosuka preceded the ship's type-training exercises through 29 November. Tom Green County paid a port visit at Beppu, Japan, from 1 to 3 December before returning to her home port on the 7th. Underway three days later, the ship made for Numazu, Japan, to load marines and materiel for transport to Okinawa and arrived on the 15th. The tank landing ship off-loaded, headed for Japanese waters, and arrived at Yokosuka on 19 December before getting underway again on Christmas Eve for Tokyo. Tom Green County departed the Japanese capital city on the 28th and returned to Yokosuka, where she spent the remainder of the year in upkeep status.

The following year saw more of the same activities in store for the tank landing ship. Port visits to Tsoying, Taiwan (12 to 14 March 1963); Hong Kong (16 to 22 March); Osaka, Japan (8 to 15 April); and Taipei, were interspersed with local operations out of Yokosuka. Tom Green County participated in Operations "Flagpole" (16 to 28 June) and "Bayonet Beach" (31 August to 9 September) along the eastern coast of South Korea, transporting embarked marines and vehicles to landing beaches and putting them ashore. Following her return to Japanese home waters with a visit to Kagoshima from 9 to 15 November, the ship proceeded to Sasebo for three weeks of upkeep. Conducting type training in Buckner Bay, she on-loaded marines for transport to Numazu and subsequently arrived home at Yokosuka on 20 December.

As the situation in Southeast Asia worsened, the United States began to take a more active part in the Vietnam conflict. Operation "Jungle Drum," towards the end of 1965, landed marines in southern Thailand. With increasing American commitments in Vietnam, Tom Green County participated in Operations "Piranha" and "Double Eagle" in January and February of 1966. The latter was the first large-scale amphibious landing under combat conditions since Inchon. In June 1966, the tank landing ship came under the operational and administrative command of Landing Ship Squadron 9; and, in November, the ship commenced support commitments for the Vietnam Coastal Surveillance Force, engaged in monitoring and interdicting offshore small craft traffic, TF 115.

The year 1967 found the ship participating in further combat operations: "Beacon Torch," "Beaver Track," "Bear Chain," and "Kangaroo Kick." As an element of Amphibious Ready Group Bravo (TG 76.5), Tom Green County received the Meritorious Unit Commendation for these operations conducted between 18 June and 4 August 1967. During this deployment in Southeast Asia, the ship also underwent a yard overhaul at Yokosuka from 16 August to 17 November before she returned to Vietnamese waters.

On 22 March 1968, Tom Green County arrived in the Mekong Delta region to commence a deployment as support LST for the Riverine Assault Force. On 15 April, Viet Cong insurgents attacked the ship with recoilless-rifle and automatic-weapons fire. Tom Green County shuddered under the impact of nine hits taken in quick succession. Following repairs of her battle damage, the tank landing ship resumed operations with Amphibious Ready Group Alpha (TG 76.4) and participated in Operation "Swift Pursuit," before returning to the Mekong in December to commence resupply duties for

TG 117.2—Mobile Riverine Group Bravo. While en route on 28 December, *Tom Green County* came under rocket fire from Viet Cong gunners and took seven hits on her port side.

Repairing the damage and continuing her assigned missions, she conducted her operations in the Bassac River near Can Tho. On 21 January 1969, while beached at Vung Tau and loading supplies for a routine convoy run, the ship again came under fire as Viet Cong launched a rocket barrage directed at the loading ramp and the adjacent airstrip. One rocket (122 millimeter) impacted on the fantail and exploded in the mess decks of *Tom Green County*, inflicting heavy materiel damage and wounding several men in the after part of the ship.

Retracting and anchoring at Vung Tau Bay, *Tom Green County* effected temporary repairs before being relieved by *Whitfield County* (LST-1169) to sail for Yokosuka and permanent repairs. En route to Japanese waters, the ship's company arrived at a novel method of preparing and consuming their meals, as the regular galley and messing facilities had been rendered useless by the battle damage. Besides subsisting on makeshift rations, the crew "char-broiled" steaks on jury-rigged "grills" fashioned from empty 55-gallon oil drums. Steak-grilling continued unabated through even inclement weather—in which case the whole "steak-grilling" operation was moved to the tank deck.

On 2 February, the ship made port at Yokosuka, to commence a long repair period, after which she conducted support operations for an assault boat school at Numazu while undertaking independent steaming exercises. Sudden troop deployments in Vietnam resulted in a recall to Southeast Asian waters, and *Tom Green County* accordingly sailed for Vung Tau on 23 June. En route, the ship trained in riverine warfare tactics.

Tom Green County relieved *Whitfield County* on 4 July 1969 at My Tho, near Dong Tam, and spent the next six weeks supporting the operations of TF 117, as it prepared to "wrap up" its operations in the Mekong Delta region. While at My Tho and in the "Delta," the tank landing ship served as a floating supply base and a transient barracks ship for members of the Army 9th Division who were being processed for stateside duty. *Tom Green County* also gave the Viet Cong a dose of their own medicine—firing over 3,000 rounds of 3-inch/50-caliber counter-battery harassment and interdiction fire, while maintaining a vigilant watch for swimmer-sappers who might attempt to mine the ship while she lay at anchor.

On 18 August, the day before the disestablishment of the Mobile Riverine Force, *Tom Green County* departed Vietnamese waters and steamed for Subic Bay, arriving in the Philippines on the 23d of the month. Taking on provisions after arriving, the tank landing ship proceeded for Keelung, Taiwan, on the 23d, making port four days later. Underway for the Marianas on 2 September, the ship stopped briefly at Guam before pressing on with a Micronesian cruise, calling at Koror, Babelthuap, and Yap, before returning to Guam and subsequent operations transporting men and materiel to Yokosuka.

On 25 October, with the ship's dependents on board, *Tom Green County* cruised from Yokosuka to Tokyo, unloading the dependents upon arrival and on-loading a 5-ton, 135-foot totem pole from Alaska, to transport it to the World's Fair—Expo '70—at Osaka. Operation "Totem Pole" proceeded to completion on 27 October when the ship docked at Kobe and unloaded her unusual cargo.

After a one-night liberty, *Tom Green County* joined *Vernon County* (LST-1161), *Washoe County* (LST-1165), and *Westchester County* (LST-1167) in support of Operation "Keystone Lift" from Danang, where they made port on 5 November. Four and one-half hours later, the tank landing ship got underway for Kin Red, Okinawa, with elements of the 3d Battalion, 12th Marines, embarked; and arrived at her destination on the 11th, unloaded and disembarked the troops; and headed

back toward Yokosuka. En route, however, the ship was redirected to Danang for another lift, and she took on board a full cargo of railroad rolling stock. Her ship's historian nicknamed *Tom Green County* the "Ghost Ship of Danang" because of her nocturnal loading operation in which she arrived after dark and was gone before the dawn. On the night of the 25th, *Tom Green County* made port at Okinawa; unloaded in just one and one-half hours; and steamed for Yokosuka, her job completed. Four days later, on the afternoon of 29 November, the ship arrived at her home port in time to spend Thankgiving of 1969 at "home."

Returning to the business of transporting marines soon thereafter, *Tom Green County* completed one round-trip haul from Okinawa to Numazu before making port at Yokosuka on 13 December for a year-end leave and upkeep period.

For the next two years, *Tom Green County* remained in the Far East serving as she had done since she was first homeported at Yokosuka. Late in 1971, she was ordered home to the United States and her home port changed to San Diego. The tank landing ship departed Japanese waters on 27 October and made port at Pearl Harbor on 12 November for a seven-day stay before beginning the last leg of her voyage to the west coast. Upon her arrival at San Diego on 28 November, she soon commenced preinactivation preparations; and, on 23 December, she cruised in San Diego harbor, commencing the training of the new Spanish crew slated to take over the ship. On 5 January 1972, *Tom Green County* was decommissioned and transferred to Spain. Renamed *Conde de Venadito* and designated L–13, she serves the Spanish Navy through 1979.

Tom Green County was awarded 12 engagement stars, two Navy Unit Commendations, and one Meritorious Unit Commendation for her Vietnam service.

Tomahawk

A river in Wisconsin.

Waterway (LSD–15)—formerly *Tomahawk*—was renamed *Shadwell* (*q.v.*) on 6 April 1944.

I

(AO–88: dp. 21,650 (tl.) ; l. 523'6''; b. 68'; dr. 30'10'' (lim.) ; s. 15.1 k.; cpl. 267; a. 1 5'', 4 3''; cl. *Escambia*; T. T2–SE–A2)

The first *Tomahawk* (AO–88) was laid down under Maritime Commission contract (MC hull 1267) on 1 June 1943 by Marinship Corporation of Sausalito, Calif.; launched on 10 October 1943; sponsored by Mrs. W. L. Kidneigh; and commissioned at Portland, Oreg., on 16 April 1944, Comdr. Benjamin Watkins Cloud in command.

Early in July 1944, *Tomahawk* completed her shakedown off the west coast and steamed via Pearl Harbor for the Marshalls. The oiler arrived at Eniwetok on the 24th, reported for duty with Service Squadron 10, and was soon underway for fueling operations in the Marianas. During August, she contributed logistic support for the final stages of the fight for the Marianas.

On 26 August, *Tomahawk* departed Eniwetok for Manus with a logistics task unit for the 3d Fleet. Steaming from Seeadler Harbor on the 31st, she relieved oilers *Schuylkill* (AO–76) and *Millicoma* (AO–73) which had collided. Through September and October, *Tomahawk* continued fueling duties for the 3d Fleet, operating out of Seeadler Harbor. On 18 October, she rendezvoused with the damaged cruisers *Houston* (CL–81) and *Canberra* (CA–70) as they returned from a successful Fast Carrier Task Force strike on Formosa. After refueling the battle-scarred ships and their escort, *Tomahawk* continued on to her assigned area where she provided support for units active in the battle for Leyte Gulf.

On 20 November 1944, *Tomahawk* was anchored at Ulithi when a Japanese midget submarine penetrated the lagoon. The undersea raider sent fleet oiler *Mississinewa* (AO–59) down in flames before being rammed and sunk by destroyer *Case* (DD–370) just a mile and one-half from *Tomahawk*.

As the year ended, *Tomahawk* continued fueling missions and, in January, ranged as far as Leyte Gulf in support of the 5th Fleet. In the early months of 1945, *Tomahawk* continued to operate out of Ulithi providing direct logistic support to the fleet in and near the combat zone. During the first two weeks of February, she fueled units of Admiral Raymond A. Spruance's 5th Fleet preparatory to operations off Nanpo Shoto and, later in the month, supported Task Force 58 which was striking targets in the Tokyo area. In March, *Tomahawk* fueled units in preparation for strikes on Nansei Shoto and Japan. While at Kerama Retto early in April, *Tomahawk* fought off enemy air raiders and later suffered some minor damage to her plating and degaussing cable while fueling *Arkansas* (BB–33). Returning to Ulithi in April, *Tomahawk* continued underway replenishment operations in support of the Fast Carrier Task Force before steaming from Ulithi in May, bound for overhaul at Portland, Oreg.

Repairs completed, she got underway again on 20 July 1945 and proceeded via San Francisco to Pearl Harbor. The successes of American naval forces in the Pacific made it possible for her to make the entire voyage to the Carolines without an escort. She arrived at Ulithi just in time for the unconditional surrender of Japan. She subsequently performed fueling tasks and exercises with units of Admiral William F. Halsey's 3d Fleet, operating out of Tokyo and Ulithi before departing Tokyo late in October. *Tomahawk* steamed via San Francisco and the Panama Canal for the east coast and arrived at Norfolk on 11 December 1945.

Tomahawk was decommissioned on 5 January 1946 and was struck from the Navy list on 21 January 1946. Following reconversion at Norfolk, she was turned over to the Military Sea Transportation Service. Through the remaining 1940's and throughout the 1950's, she served in decommissioned status, carrying fuel for the American fleet around the world. In September 1961, the tanker was transferred to the Maritime Administration, assigned to the National Defense Reserve Fleet, and berthed in Suisun Bay, Calif. In 1966, she was converted to a container ship, renamed *Maine*, and sold to the Hudson Waterways Corp.

Tomahawk received six battle stars for World War II service.

II

YTB–789: dp. 356 (f.); l. 109'; b. 31'; dr. 14'; s. 12 k.; cpl. 12; cl. *Natick*)

The second *Tomahawk* (YTB–789) was laid down in January 1966 at Marinette, Wis., by the Marinette Marine Corp.; launched on 5 May 1966; and delivered to the Navy on 7 June 1966. Her fitting-out period ended on 8 July 1966, and the large harbor tug reported to the 10th Naval District, San Juan, Puerto Rico, and provided tug and tow services out of Roosevelt Roads until reassigned to the 6th Naval District in the spring of 1971 and stationed at Mayport, Fla., where she has served into 1980.

Tomatate

An erroneous spelling of Tomtate, a food fish of warm American waters having a compressed body, a toothless palate, and conical jaw teeth.

Tomatate (SS–421) was renamed *Trutta* (*q.v.*) on 24 September 1942.

Tombigbee

A river in Alabama which connects Birmingham with the Gulf of Mexico at Mobile. It rises in northeastern Mississippi and flows south by southeast into western Alabama, and joins the Alabama River to form the Mobile. The name itself is derived from Choctaw Indian words for "coffin makers."

(AOG–11: dp. 4,142 (f.); l. 310'9''; b. 48'6''; dr. 15'8''; s. 14 k.; cpl. 120; a. 4 3''; cl. *Patapsco*)

Tombigbee (AOG–11) was laid down on 23 October 1942 at Savage, Minn., by Cargill, Inc.; launched on 18 November 1943; sponsored by Mrs. F. R. Stoltz; and commissioned on 13 July 1944 at New Orleans, Lt. Comdr. A. O. Askland, USNR, in command.

Following shakedown, *Tombigbee* departed Galveston on 13 August, bound for the west coast; transited the Panama Canal en route; and reached San Diego on the 28th. Pushing on for the western Pacific, the tanker arrived at Pearl Harbor on 4 September, where she paused briefly before proceeding on to Eniwetok, in the Marshalls, where she joined Service Squadron 10.

Her tanks filled with fresh water instead of the oil for which she was designed, *Tombigbee* began replenishing the tanks of the ships of the Fleet and worked out of Guam and Ulithi as she continued this duty for the remainder of the year. The ship's first taste of combat came while she lay anchored at Ulithi on 20 November 1944. A Japanese midget submarine slipped into the anchorage area and torpedoed the oiler *Mississinewa* (AO–59) which was anchored less than 1,500 yards from *Tombigbee*.

The tanker remained on the Guam-Ulithi "express" water supply run through January 1945. On 7 February, while she was steaming toward Guam, orders rerouted *Tombigbee* to Saipan. Subsequently removed to Tinian, with a full load of water, she supplied water until 19 February, when she joined Task Group (TG) 50.9 and got underway for the Volcano Islands. At 0924 six days later, *Tombigbee* was detached from the task group and entered the harbor at Iwo Jima. There, the water carrier lay-to and kept out of the line of fire of the supporting battleships, cruisers, and destroyers. Rough seas hampered her water-discharging operations, but the need for fresh water overrode considerations such as the desire to avoid minor hull damages caused by the ships bumping and scraping each other in the tossing waves.

After remaining in the Iwo Jima area until 9 March, the ship proceeded to Guam where she reloaded her holds with more of her precious liquid cargo. Later in the month, *Tombigbee* joined the invasion force heading for the Ryukyus.

On 1 April, Easter Sunday, the day broke cool and slightly overcast—with a calm sea—a perfect day for an amphibious operation. *Tombigbee* arrived off the beaches of Okinawa at 0545 and steamed to a position on the eastern side of the island and close to the transport group. As she neared the anchorage, a Japanese suicide plane—intent on bigger game than the water carrier—flew past the tanker's starboard side and crashed into *Hinsdale* (APA–120) before that ship could unload her troops.

The next day, *Tombigbee* shifted her anchorage to Hagushi on the western side of the island. During succeeding weeks, *Tombigbee*'s men saw numerous suicide planes crash into combat ships and auxiliaries. Meanwhile, they often remained at general quarters up to 20 hours a day while supplying water to landing craft and amphibious warfare ships. The ship made trips to Kerama Retto and reloads from fleet tankers that brought water from the Philippines. *Tombigbee* remained at Okinawa through the end of the war, and her historian noted that "the entire harbor went wild" when news arrived that Japan had accepted unconditional surrender terms.

The tanker departed the Ryukyus on 21 September, bound for Japanese waters, and, two days later, arrived at Sasebo to participate in occupation operations. She twice returned to Okinawa for reloading. By November, Army and Navy doctors judged the water supply around Nagasaki as fit, and the tanker began replenishing her depleted tanks with local water to supply the ships still on duty in Japanese ports.

Following this tour of duty, for which she received the Navy Occupation Service Medal, *Tombigbee* supported the ships participating in the atomic bomb testing in the Marshalls at Bikini Atoll, from 1 April to 5 September 1946. During the assignment, she made periodic trips to Eniwetok for replenishment of water. Four days after her arrival at Pearl Harbor on 14 September, the ship headed for the west coast for an overhaul which lasted into 1947. Upon her return to the western Pacific, she began conducting local operations in the Marshalls—at Eniwetok and Kwajalein—which continued from 13 January to 14 March. Then, following brief repairs at Pearl, *Tombigbee* was again deployed to the Far East. She operated out of Guam; Yokosuka, Japan; Pusan and Jinsen (Inchon), Korea; Tsingtao, China; and Buckner Bay and Naha, Okinawa; as well as at Manila in the Philippine Islands. The tanker remained in the Far East until 1 August, when she departed Tsingtao, bound for Long Beach. After overhaul, the ship returned to the Orient and touched at familiar ports before heading for the west coast late in the summer of 1949 for inactivation. On 12 December 1949, *Tombigbee* was placed out of commission, in reserve, at the Mare Island Naval Shipyard, Vallejo, Calif.

The North Korean invasion of South Korea, commencing on 25 June 1950, triggered the reactivation of many Navy ships, including *Tombigbee*. The gasoline tanker was recommissioned at Mare Island on 28 July 1950 and was deployed to the Middle Pacific (MidPac) operating area where she served until near the end of hostilities in Korea. On 13 May 1953, she sailed for the northern Pacific and operated in that area until 22 December when she was transferred back to MidPac.

The tanker conducted logistic support operations in the Pacific through 1964, taking part in various fleet operations. During the period from 1953 to 1964, the ship participated in Operations "Rocky Shoals" (22 October to 22 December 1958), "Twin Peaks" (13 May to 31 May 1959), "Blue Star" (26 February to 6 April 1960), "Long Haul" and "Pack Mule" (8 September to 20 October 1960), "Green Light" (10 May to 28 June 1961), and "Silver Sword" (27 October to 6 November 1961), and her areas of operation ranged from Maui, Hawaii, to Yokosuka, Japan.

She deployed to the Far East in the spring of 1962, conducting logistic support operations out of Subic Bay, Philippines, from 16 May to 8 June befor proceeding to Yokosuka and technical availability. For the remainder of the year, the ship conducted local operations out of Pearl Harbor before departing the Hawaiian area on 18 December for Port Lyttelton, New Zealand, and participation in Operation "Deep Freeze 1963." Following a port visit to Lyttelton from 5 to 9 January 1963, *Tombigbee* pressed on for the colder climes of McMurdo Sound and conducted operations in support of "Deep Freeze" from 18 to 22 January before returning—via Wellington, New Zealand and Sydney, Australia—to Pearl Harbor. After local operations out of Pearl, the tanker was deployed to the Marshalls for local petroleum-carrying operations through the late summer before returning once again to the Hawaiian Islands for local operations and technical availability at Pearl Harbor.

Tombigbee continued her unglamorous but vital support duties in the Pacific. She was again deployed to the Marshalls—Kwajalein and Eniwetok—and also conducted local operations out of Pearl. Returning to the west coast in the spring, the tanker participated in Exercise "Pinetree" from 21 to 28 May 1964 before returning to Pearl Harbor. Two shuttle runs between

Pearl Harbor and Kaneohe Bay, Hawaii; classified operations, and technical and restricted availability at the Navy Yard, Pearl Harbor, occupied the ship through late October, before she was again deployed to the Philippines. While in the Far East, *Tombigbee* operated out of Subic Bay; Kaohsiung, Taiwan; Hong Kong; and Yokosuka—before departing Japan on 7 June and arriving at Pearl Harbor on the 18th. She remained in Hawaiian waters for the rest of 1965.

Upon completion of her regular overhaul at Pearl Harbor, *Tombigbee* conducted regular refresher training before departing Pearl on 21 February 1966 for passage to Subic Bay, where she made port on 12 March. Deploying to coastal waters off Vietnam, the tanker conducted two logistic support deployments, from 18 March to 6 June, and from 11 July to 28 August, before returning to Pearl Harbor for restricted availability, independent ship exercises, and operations as a submarine target reference vessel.

Homeported at Pearl Harbor in 1967, *Tombigbee* began the new year with operations with Submarine Flotilla 5 and Destroyer Flotilla 5 on antisubmarine warfare exercises off Maui before she conducted exercises in anticipation of her second WestPac deployment. On 6 September, she departed Pearl Harbor, bound, via Guam and Subic Bay, for Vietnam, and arrived at Danang on 4 October. She conducted logistics support operations in the I Corps tactical zone from 4 October to 2 December, from 29 December 1967 to 26 January 1968, and from 25 February to 19 March. Availability at Subic Bay punctuated her tours in the combat zone.

Following a return to Pearl Harbor for overhaul and independent ship exercises, *Tombigbee* was redeployed to WestPac. She arrived at Danang on 23 November for further operations in I Corps tactical zone, supporting the Vietnamese counteroffensive operation. On 22 December, while engaged in these activities, she assisted *LCU–1500* which encountered difficulties and was in danger of being swept ashore and foundering in heavy surf. Continuing under the operational command of Naval Support Activity, Danang, *Tombigbee* carried her support mission of supplying petroleum products for air and ground forces engaged in combatting Communist forces in the I Corps zone through the middle of the year 1969.

Following a routine return to Pearl Harbor for upkeep and availability, the tanker was again deployed off Vietnam with Service Squadron 5 through 1971, supporting Operation "Market Time" in the Vietnamese coastal waters, with periodic visits to such ports as Singapore; Kaohsiung, Taiwan; Hong Kong; Brisbane, Australia; and Subic Bay. She also conducted surveillance operations of Soviet warships operating in the vicinity of American forces in the South China Sea.

After returning to Pearl Harbor at the end of the year 1971, *Tombigbee* was placed in reduced operating status from 1 February 1972. From 31 May to 7 July, the ship underwent inactivation preparations; and, on the latter date, 7 July, the ship was decommissioned at Pearl Harbor and transferred to the Greek Navy. Renamed *Ariadni* (A–414)—after the mythical daughter of King Minas who helped Theseus to escape from the labyrinth—the ship has served with the Hellenic Navy as a support tanker through 1979.

Tombigbee was awarded two battle stars for World War II service and 11 engagement stars for her service in the Vietnam War.

Tomich

Peter Tomich—born on 3 June 1893 in the village of Prolog in what is now Yugoslavia—enlisted in the United States Navy on 23 January 1919 and initially served in *Litchfield* (DD–336).

On the morning of 7 December 1941, Chief Water tender Tomich was on duty in the boiler room of *Utah* (AG–16) while the ship lay in Pearl Harbor, moored off Ford Island. Shortly before 0800, Japanese planes from a powerful carrier task force swept down on the unsuspecting American fleet. Within the first few moments of the attack, *Utah* took two torpedoes and began flooding rapidly.

As the ship began to roll over on her beam ends and "abandon ship" was ordered, Tomich lingered below, securing the boilers and making certain that all men were out of the engineering spaces. In so doing, Tomich was unable to escape before *Utah* capsized and trapped him below. For his "extraordinary courage and disregard of his own safety" during the attack, Tomich was posthumously awarded the Medal of Honor.

(DE–242: dp. 1,200; l. 306'0"; b. 36'10"; dr. 12'3"; s. 19.5 k.; cpl. 216; a. 3 3", 2 40mm., 8 20mm., 2 dct., 8 dcp., 1 dcp. (hh.); cl. *Edsall*)

Tomich (DE–242) was laid down on 15 September 1942 at Houston, Tex., by the Brown Shipbuilding Co.; launched on 28 December 1942; sponsored by Mrs. O. L. Hammonds; and commissioned on 27 July 1943, Lt. Comdr. H. A. Hull in command.

Following commissioning, *Tomich* got underway from Galveston on 12 August and reached New Orleans on the following day. The destroyer escort departed Louisiana waters on the 19th, bound for Bermuda and four weeks of shakedown training. On 23 September, *Tomich*, in company with *Farquhar* (DE–139), departed Bermuda and escorted *Merrimack* (AO–37) to Norfolk before sailing for Charleston, S.C., and availability.

Tomich sailed for Cuba on 9 October and further training in Caribbean waters, reaching Guantanamo Bay on the 12th. Five days later, the escort vessel rendezvoused with Army transport *George Washington* and escorted her to Kingston, Jamaica. *Tomich* immediately returned to Cuba. Upon her arrival back at Guantanamo Bay later the same day, 17 October, she received orders to search for *Dorado* (SS–248) which had sailed from New London on 6 October and had been expected to arrive at the Canal Zone on the 14th. *Tomich* hunted for the missing submarine until the 22d but failed to locate any trace of it.

Six days later, the destroyer escort set course for Hampton Roads to screen *Pike* (SS–173) to Norfolk. Released from this duty on the 30th, she returned to Guantanamo Bay before heading north again and making port at Norfolk on 5 November.

Nine days later, *Tomich* joined the screen of Convoy UGS–24, bound for French Morocco. On 2 December, after her charges had all made port, she dropped anchor off Casablanca. Arriving in New York on Christmas morning, 1943, after escorting Convoy GUS–24, *Tomich* secured alongside pier "K" of the New York Navy Yard for availability which lasted into 1944.

On 5 January 1944, *Tomich* departed the yard and proceeded to Block Island Sound for gunnery and antisubmarine warfare training off Montauk Point, Long Island. Five days later, the ship steamed for Norfolk, Va., in company with other units of Escort Division (CortDiv) 7, to join other ships of Task Force 63 in escorting Convoy UGS–30 to Casablanca. After a brief independent run to Gibraltar, where she moored alongside famed British battleship HMS *Warspite*, *Tomich* departed the British base on 4 February and rendezvoused with Convoy GUS–29 the next day.

Detached from the convoy screen on the 8th, she proceeded to the Azores, where she met SS *Phoenis Banning* and SS *Abraham Baldwin*. Rejoining GUS–29 with her two charges, *Tomich* continued ocean escort duties through the 17th. On the following day, the destroyer escort again received orders for independent duty and escorted *Mattaponi* (AO–41) and SS *Sangara* to Bermuda before returning north to the New York Navy Yard for availability commencing on 22 February.

Tomich got underway on 5 March 1944 for Bayonne, N.J., where she underwent deperming before proceeding to Montauk Point for refresher training. The destroyer escort sailed for Hampton Roads and arrived at Norfolk on the 11th. Two days later, she sailed for Tunisia as an escort for Convoy UGS–36.

On 30 March, the convoy passed through the Straits of Gibraltar, bound for Bizerte. During the evening watch of the 31st, *Tomich* homed in on a sonar contact and went to general quarters, proceeding to track down the echo. Dropping two 13-charge patterns, *Tomich* remained at general quarters throughout the night and instituted an antisubmarine patrol in company with HMS *Black Swan*. About 0401, as *Tomich* rejoined the screen, her lookouts spotted enemy aircraft off her port bow. Zig-zagging independently on the port bow of the convoy, the destroyer escort opened fire with her entire antiaircraft battery at 0410. During the 20-minute attack, the enemy aircraft, twin-motored Ju. 88's, came in low and fast; but the heavy antiaircraft fire of the escorts drove off their attackers with no loss to themselves.

After all of her charges had reached port safely, *Tomich* was assigned to homeward-bound Convoy GUS–36 but detached on 13 April to proceed to Oran, Algeria, for inspection of her starboard shaft. After investigation revealed that all was in order, the ship rejoined her convoy on the 14th. She subsequently arrived at New York on 2 May and underwent availability at the navy yard before she proceeded to Casco Bay for refresher training.

Returning to Norfolk on the 20th, *Tomich* sailed as part of TF 64, escorting Convoy UGS–43 bound for Bizerte. After reaching North Africa, *Tomich* was detached from convoying long enough to escort *Carib* (AT–82), which was towing *Menges* (DE–320) to the Azores. When she arrived at Horta, *Tomich* rejoined homeward-bound Convoy GUS–43.

Availability at the New York Navy Yard in early July preceded further training exercises in Casco Bay, Maine, before the ship returned to Norfolk on 1 August to begin another round-trip escort mission with UGS–50 and GUS–50. Following another yard availability, she made a coastal convoy run from New York to Boston. Then, training in Casco Bay occupied the ship into October. On the 10th, *Tomich* arrived at Quonset Point, R.I., for special radar and antisubmarine warfare tests and exercises with *Barracuda* (SS–163) and shore-based planes from Quonset Point Naval Air Station. On the 13th, *Tomich* departed the area and returned to Casco Bay on the 14th for further training exercises before arriving at Norfolk on 4 November.

On 7 November, in company with the rest of CortDiv 7 and *Core* (CVE–13), *Tomich* got underway from the Naval Operating Base at Hampton Roads for Bermuda and antisubmarine "hunter-killer" group training. Arriving on 10 November, the group engaged in intensive exercises for the remainder of the month before returning to New York on 6 December. *Tomich* operated along the east coast of the United States on antisubmarine operations in the western Atlantic for the remainder of the year 1944 and into the spring of 1945.

Following an overhaul at the Boston Navy Yard in May and June, the ship steamed to the Caribbean. Departing Guantanamo Bay on 16 July 1945, she transited the Panama Canal on the 18th and arrived at San Diego on the 26th. Standing out of that port on the 31st, she conducted exercises while en route to Hawaii and reached Pearl Harbor on 7 August as the war in the Pacific drew to its climax. The inexorable advance of American air and naval forces—topped by the dropping of atomic bombs on Hiroshima and Nagasaki—compelled Japan to surrender unconditionally. Meanwhile, *Tomich* continued training exercises in Hawaiian waters, prior to departing Pearl Harbor on 20 August, bound for the western Pacific.

Tomich made port at Saipan on the 29th of August before proceeding independently to the Bonins on 1 September. The destroyer escort relieved *Helm* (DD–388) on air-sea rescue station on 5 September for a five-day stint before heading for Iwo Jima and replenishment. She operated in waters between Iwo Jima, Okinawa, and Saipan for the remainder of the year 1945 and into 1946 before heading for China. She made port at Tsingtao on 13 January 1946. She remained on duty in Chinese waters until 10 April when she departed Shanghai for Hawaii. Arriving at Pearl Harbor on 21 April, she proceeded via the west coast to the Panama Canal.

Following her arrival on the east coast, the ship underwent inactivation preparations at Charleston, S.C., from May through late August. *Tomich* then proceeded to Mayport, Fla., and arrived on 4 September. Following further inactivation procedures there, *Tomich* was placed out of commission, in reserve, at Green Cove Springs, Fla., on 20 September 1946. She remained there until her name was struck from the Navy list on 1 November 1972, and she was scrapped.

Tomich received one battle star for World War II service.

Tommy Traddles

(MB: l. 46'; b. 14'; dr. 1'10" (mean); s. 8 k.; cpl. 7; a. 1 1-pdr., 1 mg.)

Tommy Traddles was a wooden-hulled cabin motor launch built in 1906 at Morris Heights, N.Y., by Ralph E. Monroe, and originally owned by V. B. Hubbell; later acquired and used by D. R. Hoornbeeck. Purchased in 1915 by Dr. J. B. Leffingwell of Bradenton, Fla., the pleasure craft was under private ownership until World War I.

After the United States entered the war in the spring of 1917, the Navy conducted a widespread search for suitable patrol craft to guard the nation's shorelines against possible infiltrators. Accordingly, *Tommy Traddles* was purchased by the Navy on 25 June 1917 for use as a section patrol boat. After being delivered to the Navy on 4 August, the motor launch was deemed unsuitable for this duty and returned to her owner on 4 September 1917.

Tonawanda

From the creek which rises in Wyoming County, N.Y., and flows northwest through Niagara County to empty into the Niagara River. Tonawanda is a Seneca Indian word meaning "swift water," referring to river rapids.

I

(Mon: t. 1,564; dp. 3,400 (approx.); l. 258'6"; b. 52'9"; dph. 14'; dr. 12'8"; s. 10.5 k.; cpl. 150 (approx.); a. 4 15" D.sb.; cl. *Miantonomah*)

The first *Tonawanda*—a double-turreted coastal monitor built by the Philadelphia Navy Yard—was launched on 6 May 1864; and commissioned on 12 October 1865, Comdr. William Ronckendorff in command. Completed too late for service in the Civil War, *Tonawanda* was decommissioned at the Washington Navy Yard on 22 December 1865. Reactivated on 23 October 1866 for duty as a training ship at the United States Naval Academy, she was serving in that capacity when she was renamed *Amphitrite* (q.v.) on 15 June 1869. Her assignment at Annapolis ended in 1872, and she was taken to the Delaware River and broken up in 1873 and 1874 by the Harlan and Hollingsworth Co., Wilmington, Del.

II

(AN–89: dp. 775 (tl.); l. 168'6"; b. 33'10"; dr. 10'10" (f.); s. 12.3 k. (tl.); cpl. 46; a. 1 3"; cl. *Cohoes*)

The second *Tonawanda* (AN–89) was laid down on 12 September 1944 at Sturgeon Bay, Wis., by the Leathem D. Smith Shipbuilding Co.; launched on 14 November 1944; sponsored by Mrs. Charles N. Barnum; and commissioned on 9 May 1945, Lt. Edward F. McLaughlin in command.

The net laying ship departed Sturgeon Bay on 19 May and, after a voyage across the Great Lakes and down the St. Lawrence River, arrived in Boston, Mass., on 4 June. After a short availability, she moved to Melville, R.I., on the 19th for shakedown training and daily net laying drills in Narragansett Bay. *Tonawanda* stood out of Boston harbor again on 18 July and shaped a course south to Key West and thence to the Panama Canal. She transited the canal on 2 and 3 August and continued her voyage to San Pedro, Calif., where she arrived on 15 August, the day after hostilities in the

Though not placed in service by the Navy, *Tommy Traddles* is typical of the many small craft used for patrol duty during World War I.   (NH 84932)

Pacific ceased. She reported for duty in the 11th Naval District and, for the next 10 weeks, *Tonawanda* operated in the 11th Naval District at San Pedro, Seal Beach, Long Beach, and Port Hueneme, disposing of nets and salvaging net buoys. On 27 November, the ship stood out of San Pedro Bay and headed back to the Panama Canal which she transited on the 8th. Continuing north, *Tonawanda* arrived in Norfolk, Va., on 19 November and reported for duty with the Service Force, Atlantic Fleet.

On 3 January 1946, she received orders to duty in the 7th Naval District and, on the 4th, stood out of the Chesapeake Bay and turned south. She reached Miami, Fla., on 7 January and began assisting in hydrographic triangulation surveys in the Florida-Cuba-Bahamas area. That duty lasted until 7 April when the net laying ship departed Miami in company with *Marietta* (AN–82) for New Orleans. *Tonwanda* remained in New Orleans from 25 April to 11 May, when she shifted to Orange, Tex., to prepare for inactivation. *Tonwanda* was decommissioned on 9 August 1946 and berthed at Orange.

On 18 March 1952, after almost six years in reserve, *Tonawanda* was recommissioned at Orange, Lt. Clarence A. Tennehill in command. After trials off Sabine Pass, Tex., she departed the Texas coast on 21 March bound for New England duty in the 1st Naval District. The ship arrived in Boston on 1 April and entered the Bethlehem Simpson Shipyard to complete outfitting. On 10 June, she moved to the Net Depot at Melville, R.I., where she began seven years of experimental net installation duties in the vicinity of Melville and Boston. Periodically, she departed the New England coast to conduct underway training and mine warfare tactics exercises in the Chesapeake Bay and off the Virginia capes. On two occasions, from 28 August to 21 October 1955 and from 2 May to 30 June 1956, temporary duty with the Mine Warfare Evaluation Detachment, Key West, interrupted her routine along the New England coast. During those two periods, she assisted other ships assigned to the detachment in experiments in mine planting, testing, recovery, and in overall mine warfare tactics development. After each of these tours, she resumed normal operations out of Melville and Boston.

On 16 November 1959, *Tonawanda* departed Boston and headed for Bayonne, N.J., to prepare once more for inactivation. On 18 December 1959, *Tonawanda* was decommissioned at Bayonne and assigned to the New York Group, Atlantic Reserve Fleet. She remained there until 25 May 1960 when she was leased to the government of Haiti under the terms of the Military Assistance Program. As of late 1979, she was still serving the Haitian government as *Jean Jacques Dessalines* (MH–10) when she was disposed of by sale by the United States.

Tonkawa

An Indian tribe which lived in central Texas during most of the 18th and 19th centuries. The Tonkawa were war wanderers who lived chiefly on game—mostly buffalo. In 1859, they were placed on a reservation at the Washita River. In 1862, nearly half of the 300 remaining members were massacred by the Delaware, Shawnee, and Caddo warriors for allegedly aiding the Confederacy. Refugees fled to Fort Griffin, Tex. In 1884, the survivors were moved to a small reservation near Ponca City, Okla.

I

(ATA–176: dp. 835; l. 143'0''; b. 33'10''; dr. 13'2''; s. 13 k.; cpl. 45; a. 1 3''; cl. *ATA–121*)

The first *Tonkawa* (ATA–176) was laid down as *ATR–103* on 30 January 1944 at Orange, Tex., by the Levingston Shipbuilding Co.; launched on 1 March 1944; sponsored by Mrs. R. F. Parker; redesignated *ATA–176* on 15 May 1944; and commissioned on 19 August 1944, Lt. (jg.) Ralph T. Crane, USNR, in command.

After a brief shakedown cruise in the Gulf of Mexico, the auxiliary ocean tug stood out of Galveston on 22 September bound, via Miami, for the Canal Zone. She arrived at Colon on 4 October and departed Balboa on the 20th for the South Pacific. *ATA–176* called at Borabora and Manus before anchoring in Milne Bay, New Guinea, on 20 December. Assigned to the Service Force, Pacific Fleet, the tug got underway on 30 December 1944 for Hollandia and arrived on 5 January 1945. She took *Etamin* (IX–173) in tow and sortied with a convoy for the Philippines on the 10th. She arrived at San Pedro Bay on the 22d and returned to Humboldt Bay on 12 February. During the next eight months, *ATA–176* operated between ports in New Guinea, Emirau, Morotai, Borneo, and various Philippine islands.

On 20 October 1945, the auxiliary tug stood out of Manila to search for an Army barge that had been reported adrift to the northwest. She found the barge on the 26th and towed it to Okinawa. *ATA–176* then returned to Manila Bay on 5 November 1945. After operations in the Philippines, she called at Guam in April 1946 and left Apra Harbor on 2 May towing

The district tug *Tonkawa* (YTB–796), her mast hinged back to permit her to operate in cramped spaces.

AFD–3 to Midway. She delivered her charge there on the 15th and headed for the United States. The tug arrived at San Francisco on 1 June and remained at the Naval Supply Depot, Oakland, with a crew supplied by the 12th Naval District until 30 June 1947. On that day, *ATA–176* was decommissioned and placed "in service," manned by a civilian crew. On 16 July 1948, the ship was named *Tonkawa.*

Towkawa served in the 12th Naval District until 8 May 1956 when she was placed out of service, in reserve. *Tonkawa* was struck from the Navy list on 1 August 1961.

Tonkawa (YTB–710)—a *Hisada*-class harbor tug— was slated to be built at San Pedro, Calif., by the Bethlehem Steel Co., but the contract for her construction was cancelled on 1 October 1945.

II

(YTB–786: dp. 356 (f.); l. 109'; b. 31'; dr. 14'; s. 12 k.; cpl. 12; cl. *Natick*)

The second *Tonkawa* (YTB–786) was laid down on 22 December 1965 at Marinette, Wis., by the Marinette Marine Corp.; launched on 15 March 1966; and placed in service in June 1966. *Tonkawa* was then assigned to duty at Advanced Bases, Atlantic Area, and provided tug and tow services for the Atlantic Fleet into October 1979.

Tonopah

An alternative spelling of the word tunanpin which means "black bear" and refers variously to sub-clans of the Iowa, Missouri, and Oto Indian tribes of North America.

Nevada (*q.v.*), a double-turreted monitor, was renamed *Tonopah* on 2 March 1909 so that the name *Nevada* could be assigned to Battleship No. 36.

Tonowek Bay

A bay in the western part of the Prince of Wales archipelago of Alaska.

Tonowek Bay (CVE–104) was renamed *Munda* (*q.v.*) on 6 November 1943.

Tonti

Chevalier Henry de Tonti—often spelled Tonty— was born in Gaeta, Italy, about 1650. In 1678, he sailed for Canada as LaSalle's lieutenant and devoted the remaining quarter century of his life to exploring and settling the Mississippi basin. He died at Mobile, Louisiana (now Alabama), in September 1704.

(AOG–76: dp. 2,022 (lt.); l. 325'; b. 48'; dr. 19'; s. 10 k. (tl.); cpl. 38; cl. *Tonti*; T1–M–BT2)

Tonti (AOG–76)—originally slated for use by the British under the terms of the Lend-Lease Program— was laid down under a Maritime Commission contract (MC hull 2648) as *Tavern* on 16 May 1945 at Houston, Tex., by the Todd-Houston Shipbuilding Corp.; launched on 23 August 1945; and sponsored by Mrs. E. Bornkman. Work on completing the ship was suspended on 26 August 1945.

Work was subsequently resumed, and the vessel was completed in December 1945. Apparently named *Tonti* by the Maritime Commission at this time, she was leased on 24 June 1948 at Orange, Tex., to the Marine Transport Lines, Inc. Operating at first under the supervision of the Naval Transportation Service and,

after September 1949, under the auspices of the Military Sea Transportation Service, the gasoline tanker carried liquid cargoes for the Navy. She plied the waters of the Atlantic, the Caribbean, and the Gulf of Mexico, ranging as far north as the Labrador Sea. *Tonti* continued operations through the 1950's. In July 1960, she was returned to the custody of the Maritime Administration and placed in the National Defense Reserve Fleet. On 13 January 1965, she was transferred to the Colombian Navy under the "grant aid" program and served as *Mamonal* (BT–62) until 1975 when she was scrapped.

Tontogany

A town in Wood County in northwestern Ohio named for a local Indian chief.

(YTB–821: dp. 356 (f.); l. 109'; b. 31'; dr. 14'; s. 12 k.; cpl. 12; cl. *Natick*)

Tontogany (YTB–821) was laid down on 4 December 1972 at Marinette, Wis., by the Marinette Marine Corp.; launched on 16 May 1973; and delivered to the Navy on 28 July 1973. Placed in service in July 1973, *Tontogany* was attached to the 5th Naval District and operated at Norfolk, Va., where she provided tug and towing services, waterfront fire protection, and pilot assistance. Late in 1977, she was shifted to the 6th Naval District, Charleston, S.C., where she served into October 1979.

Tooele

A mining town 25 miles southwest of Salt Lake City, Utah.

(PC–572: dp. 270; l. 169'7''; b. 20'9''; dr. 8'7''; s. 20.2 k. (tl.); a. 2 3''; cl. *PC–451*)

PC–572 was laid down on 27 September 1941 at Portland, Oreg., by the Albina Engine & Machinery Works, Inc.; launched on 28 February 1942; sponsored by Mrs. Ernest Haycox; and commissioned on 19 June 1942, Lt. Comdr. Arthur H. Middleton, USNR, in command.

The submarine chaser joined the Northwest Sea Frontier on 4 July and, after completing shakedown training on the 31st, began antisubmarine patrols in Puget Sound. On 31 August, she stood out for Kodiak, Alaska, and arrived there on 4 September. For the next five months, *PC–572* served as an escort and on local antisubmarine patrols around Kodiak and Seward. In February 1943, she moved her base of operations to the Aleutian Islands and—in addition to antisubmarine patrols at Dutch Harbor, Adak, and Attu—escorted merchant ships through Akutan Pass into the Bering Sea.

The ship returned to Puget Sound in November and entered the navy yard there for an overhaul that lasted from 23 November 1943 to 25 February 1944. She escorted a convoy to San Diego and returned to Puget Sound to resume antisubmarine patrols. On 15 April, *PC–572* joined Western Sea Frontier at San Francisco for antisubmarine and harbor entrance patrol duty.

On 3 September, operational control of *PC–572* was shifted to Commander in Chief, Pacific Fleet, and she got underway for Hawaii on the 23d. The ship called at Pearl Harbor on 30 September and was routed onward to the Marshall Islands. She arrived at Eniwetok on 15 October and began escorting convoys under Commander, Task Force 96. The submarine chaser screened Allied shipping from Eniwetok to Saipan in October; to Peleliu and Ulithi in November; to Peleliu again in December 1944; and to Ulithi in January and February 1945. In March, she rendezvoused at the equator with merchant ships coming from the South Pacific and protected them as they steamed to Eniwetok

In late April, *PC-572* got underway for the Gilbert Islands and arrived at Tarawa on 13 May to assume duties as an air-sea rescue ship. On 19 October, she began the return voyage to the United States and, after stops at Makin, Majuro, and Hawaii, arrived at San Francisco on 6 December. On 31 December 1945, *PC-572* got underway for the east coast and arrived at Charleston on 29 January 1946. She entered the navy yard for an overhaul and was ready for sea on 8 April.

The submarine chaser arrived at San Juan on 31 May 1946 and operated in the Caribbean until November 1949 when her home port was changed to Norfolk. During the next 10 years, the ship operated out of that base along the east coast, as well as from Washington, D.C., and Newport, R.I. On 15 February 1956, the ship was named *Tooele*. *Tooele* was decommissioned on 9 February 1959 at Green Cove Springs, Fla., and assigned to the Atlantic Reserve Fleet. She was struck from the Navy list on 1 July 1960.

Tooele received one battle star for World War II service.

Topa Topa

An alternate form of Topatopa, a Chumash Indian village in California.

Topa Topa (AF-29) was renamed *Graffias* (q.v.) on 12 October 1943.

Topawa

A Papago Indian ceremony or game roughly translated as "It is a bean." Topawa is also an Indian village in Arizona.

(YTB-419: dp. 345 (f.); l. 100'0''; b. 25'0''; dr. 9'7''; s. 12 k.; cpl. 8; cl. *Sassaba*)

Topawa (YTB-419) was laid down at the Coast Guard Yard at Curtis Bay, Md., sometime in the first half of 1944; launched on 14 October 1944; sponsored by Mrs. Frank J. Kuska; completed on 13 March 1945; and delivered to the Navy on 24 March 1945.

Topawa was placed in service with the 1st Fleet in the 12th Naval District. By March 1946, she had moved to the Central Pacific at Eniwetok Atoll in the Marshall Islands. Late in May, she moved to Kwajalein in the Marshalls and served there until 23 November when she headed back toward Eniwetok. *Topawa* reentered Eniwetok on 25 November but remained there only nine days before continuing on to Guam. Officially reassigned to the Marianas command in early 1947, the tug spent the next 19 years performing various towing assignments in and around Apra Harbor. In February 1962, she was reclassified a medium harbor tug and received the new hull designation, YTM-419. In 1966, she was reassigned to the Pacific Fleet. The tug operated with that fleet for the remaining nine years of her career. In September 1975, her name was struck from the Navy list, and she was put up for sale in June 1977.

Topaz

A red, yellow, or pink transparent mineral used as a semi-precious gem. The name is also used in conjunction with yellow sapphires and yellow quartz.

PYc-10: dp. 160; l. 111'8''; b. 18'11''; dr. 7½'' (mean); s. 13 k.; a. 1 3'', 2 30-cal. mg., 3 dct.)

Doromar—a yacht built in 1931 by the Luders Marine Construction Co., Stamford, Conn.—was acquired by the Navy on 14 February 1941 from Mr. W. McCullough; renamed *Topaz* and designated PYc-10 on 3

March 1941; converted to a coastal patrol yacht by Robert Jacob, Inc.; and placed in commission at New York on 14 July 1941.

Topaz cleared New York on 21 July and headed south. She stopped at Norfolk, Va., from 25 July to 5 August and then continued on to Charleston, S.C., where she arrived on the 7th. Three days later, she steamed on to Miami, whence she departed the 15th. After a two-day visit to Guantanamo Bay, Cuba, the coastal patrol yacht headed for Cristobal in the Canal Zone. She arrived in the Canal Zone on 22 July 1941 and reported for duty to the Commandant, 15th Naval District.

For the next three years, *Topaz* patrolled the close approaches to the Panama Canal and the coastlines of the Canal Zone. On 12 August 1944, she departed the 15th Naval District and the Canal Zone. After stopping at Guantanamo Bay and Charleston, she reached Philadelphia, Pa., on 31 August 1944. She was placed out of commission there on 27 September and was turned over to the War Shipping Administration for disposal. Her name was struck from the Navy list on 14 October 1944.

Topeka

The capital of Kansas and the seat of Shawnee County. Topeka is located in the northeastern section of the state.

I

(Gbt.: dp. 2,255 (n.); l. 259'4''; b. 35'0'' (wl.); dr. 19'5'' (aft); s. 16 k.; cpl. 167; a. 6 4'', 6 3-pdrs., 2 1-pdrs., 1 Colt mg.)

Diogenes—a steamer built in 1881 by Georg Howaldt at Kiel, Germany—was acquired by the Navy from the Thames Iron Works, London, England, on 2 April 1898; renamed *Topeka*; and placed in commission the same day, Lt. John J. Knapp in command.

Topeka cleared Falmouth, England, on 19 April and arrived at Tompkinsville, N.Y., on 1 May. The following day, she moved to the New York Navy Yard to begin a two-month overhaul during which she received her armament and generally prepared for duty on the Cuban blockade. The gunboat departed New York on 30 June and, after a five-day stop at Key West, Fla., joined the blockading forces off Havana on 11 July. That same day, she was assigned station off Bahia de Nipe, located on the northeastern shore of Cuba almost directly opposite Santiago de Cuba on the island's southeastern coast. On 17 July, she and *Maple* captured the Spanish sloop *Domingo Aurelio* off Bahia de Nipe. Four days later, *Topeka* joined *Annapolis*, *Wasp*, and *Leyden* in a foray into Bahia de Nipe. The four warships encountered no real resistance from the Spanish and, therefore, easily captured the port and sank the Spanish cruiser *Jorge Juan*, abandoned by her crew.

Following the capture of the Bahia de Nipe littoral, *Topeka* steamed to Key West with dispatches. She returned to Cuban waters on 28 July and remained until 5 August, when she again steamed to Key West. She made one more voyage to Cuba in mid-August, visiting Port Francis on the 14th before heading north on the 15th. After stops at Key West and Hampton Roads, she visited Provincetown and Boston, Mass., and then arrived at the New York Navy Yard on 13 September. *Topeka* exited New York harbor on 22 October and reached Philadelphia the following day. She remained there until 19 November when she sailed for the Caribbean. During that cruise, she visited Cuba, Haiti, San Domingo, and Puerto Rico before returning—via Norfolk and Newport, R.I.—to Boston, Mass., early in February 1899. On 15 February 1899, *Topeka* was placed out of commission at the Boston Navy Yard.

USS *Topeka* prepares to sail from New York Navy Yard after her conversion to a gunboat. The receiving ship *Vermont*, originally a ship-of-the-line, appears in the background.

After 18 months of inactivity, the gunboat was re-commissioned at Boston on 15 August 1900, Comdr. Francis H. Delano in command. She departed Boston on 19 September and, after a five-day stop at Tompkinsville, N.Y., embarked upon a training cruise to the Mediterranean Sea on 27 September. Steaming via the Azores and Lisbon, Portugal, and Gibraltar, she entered the Mediterranean on 7 November. During the cruise, she visited Villefranche, Genoa, Leghorn, Naples, Algiers, and Tangier. *Topeka* transited the Straits of Gibraltar on 5 January 1901 and, after visits to the Azores and to St. Vincent and Barbados in the West Indies, returned to the United States at Hampton Roads, Va., on 4 March 1901.

For more than a year, *Topeka* operated along the southeastern coast of the United States and in the West Indies, working out of Norfolk and the South Carolina ports of Charleston and Port Royal. On 16 May 1902, the gunboat cleared Port Royal and headed—via Port-au-Prince, Haiti, and San Juan, Puerto Rico—to the Caribbean for a summer training cruise in the waters off Venezuela. Over the next three months, when not conducting gunnery drills, she was a frequent caller at the Venezuelan ports of Puerto Cabello and La Guaira as well as at nearby Curaçao in the Danish West Indies. She departed Puerto Cabello on 23 August 1902 and reached Hampton Roads on 5 September. That same day, she entered the Norfolk Navy Yard for three months of repairs.

On 10 December, *Topeka* completed repairs and departed Norfolk to join the fleet in the West Indies. She reached Culebra on the 16th and, for the following two months, conducted exercises in the West Indies and the Caribbean. On 21 February 1903, the ship got underway from Kingston, Jamaica, to return to the United States. She arrived in Charleston, S.C., on 1 March, and began operations along the length of the eastern seaboard. Those operations occupied her until late in the year.

On 10 December, she steamed out of Hampton Roads to return south to the Caribbean Sea—Gulf of Mexico area. After a visit to New Orleans, La., between 16 and 22 December, she began duty with the Caribbean Squadron. In January and early February of 1904, she cruised along the coast of Panama in the wake of the revolution which separated that republic from Colombia and paved the way for the construction of the Panama Canal. During the latter part of February, *Topeka* visited Kingston, Jamaica; Guantanamo Bay, Cuba; and San Juan, Puerto Rico, before joining other units of the fleet off the coast of San Domingo late in the month. She plied the waters around Hispañola through the end of March protecting American lives and interests while civil strife tore the island asunder.

Topeka left the West Indies on 30 March and returned to the United States upon her arrival at Charleston on the 5th. On 15 May, the warship reported for duty at Newport, R.I., and, for the next four months, participated in wireless telegraphy experiments conducted off the New England coast. During October and November, *Topeka* participated in the trials of three new warships—*Colorado* (Armored Cruiser No. 7), *West Virginia* (Armored Cruiser No. 5), and *Pennsylvania* (Armored Cruiser No. 4). Late in November, she resumed duty along the east coast.

On 5 January 1905, *Topeka* stood out of Newport News, Va., to return to the West Indies. She stopped at Key West for 11 days, from 11 to 22 January and then continued on to Cuba. Between 23 and 25 January, the warship gathered hydrographic and commercial information at Havana. She coaled at Bahia de Nipe on the 27th and headed for Puerto Rico, where she trained with the North Atlantic Fleet until 17 February. She operated out of Guantanamo Bay from 1 February to 22 March and then headed back to the United States. After visits in Florida at Key West and Pensacola, *Topeka* arrived in Hampton Roads on 11 April. On the 23d, the gunboat again headed south to the troubled waters of the West Indies. She arrived off the Dominican Republic on the 28th and patrolled the coastline of that strife-torn country into August. On 13 August, the gunboat weighed anchor at Guantanamo Bay and shaped a course for Portsmouth, N.H., where she arrived on the 21st. *Topeka* was placed out of commission on 7 September 1905 and assigned duty as station ship at Portsmouth.

She remained at Portsmouth—serving as station ship, auxiliary to *Southery*, and as a prison ship—until the summer of 1916. On 14 June 1916, she was recommissioned and moved to New York where she served as receiving ship until decommissioned again on 14 September. Two weeks later, she departed New York, under tow by *Uncas*, and returned to Portsmouth. There, she served as a training ship for 1st Naval District recruits throughout the United States' participation in World War I.

On 24 March 1919, *Topeka* was recommissioned at Boston, Comdr. Earl P. Finney in command. After fitting out, she cleared Boston on 28 May and headed south. She arrived in Charleston, S.C., on 9 June and reported for duty with the American Patrol Detachment. From then until late October, she cruised the Gulf of Mexico along the coast of Mexico. The gunboat returned to Charleston on 23 October. *Topeka* was placed out of commission on 21 November 1919 and was turned over to the Commandant of the Charleston Navy Yard. On 17 July 1920, the Navy adopted the alpha-numeric system of hull designations, and the gunboat became PG–35. Almost a year later, on 1 July 1921, she was redesignated IX–35. On 1 July 1922, *Topeka* was put up for sale. However, no satisfactory bids were forthcoming; and the vessel was withdrawn from the market on 29 September.

Topeka was recommissioned again on 2 July 1923 and was turned over to the 4th Naval District as a training ship for Philadelphia units of the Naval Reserve Forces. She served in that capacity until 2 December 1929, when she was decommissioned for the last time. On 2 January 1930, her name was struck from the Navy list. In accordance with the terms of the London Treaty for the Limitation and Reduction of Naval Armaments, she was sold to the Union Shipbuilding Co., of Baltimore, Md., on 13 May 1930, for scrapping.

II

(CL–67: dp. 10,000; l. 608'4"; b. 66'3"; dr. 25'0"; s. 31.6 k. (tl.); cpl. 1,410; a. 12 6", 12 5", 28 40mm., 10 20mm.; cl. *Cleveland*)

The second *Topeka* (CL–67) was laid down on 21 April 1943 by the Bethlehem Steel Co. yard located at Quincy, Mass.; launched on 19 August 1944; sponsored by Mrs. Frank J. Warren; and commissioned at the Boston Navy Yard on 23 December 1944, Capt. Thomas L. Wattles in command.

After shakedown in the West Indies and post-shakedown repairs, *Topeka* departed Boston on 10 April 1945 for duty with the Pacific Fleet. The following day, she joined *Oklahoma City* (CL–91); and the two ships steamed via Culebra Island and Guantanamo Bay to the Panama Canal. They transited the canal on 19 April and reported for duty with the Pacific Fleet on the 20th. The next day, *Topeka* and her steaming mate headed for Pearl Harbor, where they arrived on 2 May. Following almost three weeks of gunnery exercises in the Hawaiian Islands, the cruiser sailed west from Pearl Harbor as the flagship of Cruiser Division (CruDiv) 18. She entered Ulithi Atoll in the Western Carolines on 1 June and, after three days in the anchorage, put to sea with *Bon Homme Richard* (CV–31), *Oklahoma City*, *Moale* (DD–693), and *Ringgold* (DD–500) to rendezvous with Task Force (TF) 38.

On her first cruise with the fast carriers, she screened them against enemy air attack while their planes made three raids against targets in the enemy's home islands and the Ryukyus. On 8 June, TF 38 aircraft hit Kanoya on Kyushu—the home of Japanese naval aviation. The

next day, they struck the Ryukyu Islands—specifically Okino Daito, located a little over 200 miles west of Okinawa. The third and final strike of her first combat cruise came on 10 June and provided the cruiser with her initial opportunity to join the fray. While TG 38.1 aircraft bombed and strafed the airfield on Minami Daito, the ships in the screen—*Topeka* among them— moved in and took the other installations under fire. At the conclusion of that action, *Topeka* moved off with the rest of TG 38.1 bound for San Pedro Bay, Leyte.

After spending the latter half of June at Leyte for relaxation and replenishment, the light cruiser returned to sea on 1 July with TF 38 for the final six-week carrier sweep of the Japanese home islands. The task force made a fueling rendezvous on the 8th and then began a run-in toward Tokyo which the American planes bombed on 10 July. Next, the ships moved north to Honshu and Hokkaido for a two-day antishipping sweep of the area around Hokadate and Muroran. They retired from the area for another fueling rendezvous on the 16th, but returned to the vicinity of southern Honshu and resumed the aerial blitz of Tokyo on the 17th and 18th. On the night of the latter date, *Topeka* had another opportunity to strike the enemy directly when she joined *Atlanta* (CL–104), *Duluth* (CL–87), *Oklahoma City*, and the destroyers of DesRon 62 in an antishipping sweep of the entrance to Sagami Nada near the sea approaches to Tokyo. During that sweep, she fired her guns at Japanese installations located on Nojima Zaki, the point of land which marks the eastern terminus of the entrance into Sagami Nada. Completing another replenishment retirement between 19 and 23 July, the task force resumed its air raids on central Japan with two extensive forays against shipping in the Inland Sea on the 24th and the 28th, respectively.

A typhoon at the end of July forced the task force to take evasive action and postpone further air operations until the second week in August. At that time, *Topeka* steamed north with TF 38 while the carriers moved into position to send sortie after sortie against heavy concentrations of enemy aircraft on northern Honshu. Those raids—launched on 9 and 10 August— proved eminently successful, wiping out what was later learned to be the transportation for 2,000 shock troops being assembled for a one-way, suicide mission to destroy the B-29 bases on Tinian. The carrier planes paid return visits to Tokyo on the 12th and 13th and were taking off to repeat those attacks when a message arrived on the 15th, telling of Japan's capitulation.

Topeka patrolled Japanese waters until mid-September, at which time she entered Tokyo Bay. She remained there until 1 October, the day she began her homeward voyage to the United States. The cruiser stopped briefly at Okinawa on the 4th to embark 529 veterans and resumed her eastern progress on the 5th. On 19 October, she arrived in Portland, Oreg., and disembarked her passengers. Ten days later, she steamed south to San Pedro, Calif., for overhaul. On 3 January 1946, the warship put to sea to return to the Far East. She reached Yokosuka, Japan, on the 24th and began duty supporting American occupation forces in Japan, China, and in the Central Pacific islands. During that tour of duty, which lasted until the following fall, she called at Sasebo, Japan; Tsingtao and Shanghai in China; Manila in the Philippines; and Guam in the Marianas. The cruiser returned to San Pedro, Calif., on 20 November.

Following an overhaul and operations along the west coast, she headed back to the Orient on 22 September 1947. Upon her arrival at Yokosuka, Japan, on 10 October, she became a unit of TF 71. Operating from bases at Shanghai and Tsingtao, the warship patrolled the north China coast while civil war raged on shore between Nationalist and communist factions. She concluded that duty early in March and entered Nagasaki, Japan, on the 8th. Following visits to Sasebo and Kure, *Topeka* sailed for the United States on 25 April and arrived in Long Beach on 7 May. Later that month, she moved to Pearl Harbor for a four-month overhaul at the completion of which she returned to the west coast. Late in October, the warship resumed local operations out of Long Beach and out of San Diego. She remained so occupied until February 1949. On 25 February, she arrived in San Francisco to prepare for inactivation. *Topeka* was decommissioned there on 18 June 1949 and berthed with the local group of the Pacific Reserve Fleet.

Early in 1957, *Topeka* was towed from San Francisco to the New York Naval Shipyard which she entered on 15 April to begin conversion to a guided missile cruiser. On 23 May, she was officially redesignated CLG–8. During the almost three years it took to convert her, the cruiser was extensively modified. She retained only half her original gun battery, losing her two after 6-inch triple turrets and her three after 5-inch double mounts. The removal of those guns made room for the installation of her twin Terrier surface-to-air missile launcher and related ancillary equipment.

On 26 March 1960, *Topeka* was recommissioned, Capt. Frank L. Pinny, Jr., in command. In July, she made the passage from New York to the west coast. From August to October, the refurbished cruiser conducted shakedown training in the southern California operating area and then reported for duty at her home port, Long Beach. During the ensuing three years, *Topeka* alternated two peacetime deployments to the western Pacific with repair periods and local operations on the west coast. Her two tours in the Orient were characterized by visits to such places as Hong Kong, the Philippines, Okinawa, and a number of ports in Japan as well as exercises with other ships of the 7th Fleet and of Allied navies. When not deployed to the Far East, she conducted training operations, upkeep, and repairs.

In March 1964, she embarked upon her third deployment to the western Pacific since being recommissioned. That deployment began routinely enough with fleet exercises in May and calls at Japanese, Taiwanese, Malaysian, and Philippine ports. However, in August, North Vietnamese torpedo-boats attacked *Maddox* (DD–731) on the 2d and then returned to attack *Maddox* and *Turner Joy* (DD–951). This action—known as the Gulf of Tonkin incident—gave the remaining part of *Topeka*'s deployment a more wartime character. *Topeka* cruised the waters of the Gulf of Tonkin while American involvement in the Vietnam conflict began to gather momentum. It was more than a year, though, before she steamed into war in earnest. Late in October, she started for home and reentered Long Beach near the end of the second week of November. For the next 12 months, she viewed the developing war from afar—operating out of west coast ports, undergoing repairs and modifications, and conducting exercises with the 1st Fleet.

On 29 November 1965, however, she headed back to the western Pacific for the first deployment during which her primary mission was to support the American and South Vietnamese forces fighting the communists. On that tour of duty, she served as the flagship for the Commander, Cruiser-Destroyer Group, 7th Fleet. In that capacity, the ship operated in the South China Sea and in the Gulf of Tonkin providing naval gunfire support for the troops ashore and supporting carrier air operations by conducting search and rescue missions for downed aircrews. She punctuated tours of duty in the combat zone with port visits to Yokosuka, Japan; Hong Kong; and the Philippine ports of Manila and Subic Bay. Her six-month deployment ended on 28 May 1966 when *Topeka* reentered Long Beach.

Five months of normal west coast operations—upkeep, training exercises, and the like—followed. On 31 October, the guided missile cruiser entered the naval shipyard for an overhaul during which her weapons systems were updated; and her engineering plant was overhauled. On 13 March 1967, she completed the yard

overhaul and began sea trials and, later, refresher training. She finished those evolutions early in June and resumed local operations. On 1 August, the warship put to sea from Long Beach for her first deployment to the Mediterranean Sea. She stopped at Norfolk on 12 and 13 August to embark the Commander, Cruiser-Destroyer Flotilla 12, and his staff and then sailed for Palma de Majorca on the 14th. On the 20th, *Topeka* joined the 6th Fleet and, on the 22d, relieved *Galveston* (CLG–3) as flagship for TG 60.2. During her five months with the 6th Fleet, she ranged the length of the "middle sea." In late September and early October, the warship participated in NATO exercise "Eager Beaver," conducted in the eastern end of the Mediterranean. In mid-October, she conducted operations in the Ionian and Tyrrhenian Seas on her way back to the western end.

In January 1968, she concluded her first tour of duty in the Mediterranean with another NATO exercise—this one an amphibious operation. On the 12th, she was relieved by *Columbus* (CG–12) at Rota, Spain. The cruiser then headed back to the United States. After stops at Puerto Rico and in the Canal Zone, *Topeka* reentered Long Beach on 29 January.

On 2 February, the warship began a five-week availability at the Long Beach Naval Shipyard. The guided-missile cruiser departed Long Beach again on 15 March, bound for her new home port, Mayport, Fla. After arriving at her destination on 21 March, *Topeka* remained in port for upkeep until 6 May when she returned to sea for refresher training at Guantanamo Bay, Cuba. Returning to Mayport on the 26th, the ship began preparations for another deployment to the Mediterranean—the last deployment of her career.

Topeka departed Mayport on 29 June and, after gunnery exercises at Culebra Island near Puerto Rico, she headed across the Atlantic. On 9 July, she relieved *Columbus* at Malaga, Spain, and began 6th Fleet operations. The warship's final deployment proved to be routine in nature. She visited ports all along the Mediterranean littoral and conducted operations in all portions of the middle sea from the Aegean and Ionian Seas in the east to the Riviera ports in the west. Spain, Italy, Greece, Turkey, and France—as well as the islands of Malta, Crete, and Majorca—provided her with interesting ports of call. *Topeka* concluded her assignment with the 6th Fleet on 9 December at Rota when she was relieved once again by *Columbus*. That same day, she headed for Mayport, arriving 10 days later.

On 30 January 1969, *Topeka* steamed out of Mayport and proceeded north for inactivation. After a stop at Yorktown, Va., to off-load her ordnance, she arrived in Boston on 5 February. There, she completed inactivation preparations; and, on 5 June, *Topeka* was placed out of commission. The warship was towed to Philadelphia and was berthed with the reserve fleet group there. On 1 December 1973, her name was struck from the Navy list; and, on 20 March 1975, she was sold to the Southern Scrap Material Co., Ltd., for scrapping.

Topeka was awarded two battle stars for her World War II service and three battle stars for her Vietnam service.

Topenebee

A noted American Indian chief of the Potawatomie tribe of southern Michigan during the late 18th and early 19th centuries. Topenebee became an adherent of Tecumseh during the latter's uprising in the second decade of the 19th century. He was present at the Dearborn Massacre of 15 August 1812 and was instrumental in saving the lives of a number of settlers.

(YTB–373: dp. 206; l. 102′2′′; b. 24′0′′; dr. 9′7′′; s 12 k.; cpl. 12; cl. *Allaquippa*)

Topenebee (YTB–373), a large harbor tug, was constructed early in 1944 by the Gulfport Boiler & Welding Works, Inc., at Port Arthur, Tex., and was placed in service on 25 May 1944.

Topenebee left Galveston, Tex., on 13 June and arrived in the Canal Zone on the 26th. After almost three weeks in Panama, during which she transited the canal, the tug departed Rodman on 15 July for duty in the 14th Naval District. She arrived in Pearl Harbor on 20 August. For the next 23 years, *Topenebee* served in the Hawaiian Islands, primarily operating at and steaming between Midway Island and Pearl Harbor. On 1 May 1947, she was placed out of service, in reserve, at Pearl Harbor.

However, she was active again by 21 October 1948 and on her way to Midway to replace *YTB–129*, while the latter was undergoing overhaul. In January 1949, her temporary duty at Midway was formalized as a reassignment. In June of 1950, *Topenebee* received orders to head for Pearl Harbor for inactivation. However, later that month, communist forces invaded South Korea; the tug's tour of duty at Midway was extended; and orders for her decommissioning were cancelled. She remained active in the 14th Naval District until November of 1953 at which time she was placed out of commission, in reserve, at Pearl Harbor. In December of 1956, *Topenebee* came out of reserve and rejoined the active fleet.

For the next decade, she plied the waters of the 14th Naval District. In February 1962, she was reclassified as medium harbor tug and was redesignated YTM–373. In 1967, a Board of Inspection and Survey found *Topenebee* to be unsuitable for further naval service. Accordingly, she was decommissioned, and her name was struck from the Navy list on 1 June 1967. Records delineating her final disposition are not extant; but, in all probability, she was sold—possibly for private use. More probably, however, she was scrapped.

Topila

The feminine form of the Mexican term for constable.

(ScStr: dp. 11,484; l. 394'0''; b. 59'0''; dr. 23'2''; s. 11 k.; a. 2 5'')

Topila—a steel-hulled, oil tanker launched on 12 June 1913 at Newport News, Va., by the Newport News Shipbuilding and Dry Dock Co. and delivered to the East Coast Oil Co. on 22 July 1913—was acquired by the Navy at Philadelphia late in the summer of 1917 and was commissioned on 8 September 1918.

Assigned to the Train, Atlantic Fleet, the tanker carried fuel oil from petroleum centers on the coast of the Gulf of Mexico to ports along the Atlantic seaboard and in Europe. When the Naval Overseas Transportation Service (NOTS) was established on 9 January 1918, *Topila* was one of the original ships assigned to that organization. At that time, she had been at sea for five days laden with oil destined for England. Upon her arrival at Devonport on 19 January, she discharged her cargo, got underway for home four days later, and reached New York on 13 February.

The ship subsequently made two more round-trip voyages to European waters under NOTS orders: one to Portsmouth, England, and the other to Verdon, France. She returned to New York from the latter on the final day of March and resumed voyages carrying fuel from Port Arthur, Tex., to ports on the east coast. Decommissioned on 24 June 1918, she was simultaneously transferred, via the United States Shipping Board, to the Southern Pacific Co.

Torch

(Sch.: t. 260; lbp. 106'; b. 26'0''; dph. 11'9''; a. 2 long 18-pdrs., 8 18-pdr. car.)

Torch—a privateer schooner purchased at Baltimore,

Md., in 1814 and initially commanded by Lt. Wolcott Chauncey—formed part of the "flying squadron" slated to cruise the West Indies to wage war on British commerce towards the end of the War of 1812. However, the ratification of the Treaty of Ghent on 18 February 1815 terminated hostilities before the squadron, then forming at New York, could get to sea to undertake wartime operations.

The kidnapping and piratical activities of the Algerians soon dispelled the hard-won peace which had so recently come to the United States. Only five days after hostilities with Great Britain ceased, the United States declared war on Algeria. Subsequently, a squadron under the command of Capt. Stephen Decatur, in *Guerriere*, set sail from New York on 20 May, bound for the Mediterranean.

On 19 June, the Americans made landfall off Cape Gata, Spain, and soon sighted *Mashouda*, the frigate flying the flag of Algerian Admiral Rais Hammida. Giving chase, the yankee squadron heavily damaged the enemy ship—decapitating Hammida with a 32-pounder shot in the process—and forced her to surrender.

The remainder of the squadron set out in search of other Algerian vessels while *Mashouda* was sent to Cartagena under guard of *Macedonian*. Off Cape Palos, Spain, this remainder spotted 22-gun brig *Estido* and bent on sail to make contact. The wily enemy, however, ran into shoal waters where the heavier American frigates feared to go for danger of running aground.

Torch, whose shallower draft permitted her to give chase, joined *Epervier*, *Spitfire*, and *Spark* in forcing *Estido* aground. The Americans took possession of the enemy brig and 83 prisoners.

The successful conclusion of the campaign to force the Algerians to abandon their piratical ways followed thereafter. *Torch* subsequently returned home to the United States and was sold on 3 April 1816.

Torchwood

Any of a family of tropical American trees and shrubs with hard, heavy, fragrant, resinous, streaky, yellowish-brown wood.

(AN–55: dp. 1,275 (tl.); l. 194'6''; b. 37'0''; dr. 13'6'' (lim.); s. 12.1 k. (tl.); cpl. 56; a. 1 3''; cl. *Ailanthus*)

Torchwood (YN–74) was laid down on 22 June 1943 at Stockton, Calif., by the Pollock-Stockton Shipbuilding Co., redesignated AN–55 on 20 January 1944; launched on 19 February 1944; sponsored by Mrs. Henry F. Bruns; and commissioned at San Francisco on 12 May 1944.

After fitting-out, *Torchwood* cleared San Francisco on 3 June 1944 and arrived in San Pedro, Calif., two days later to begin a month of training. On 3 July, she put to sea, bound for Hawaii, and arrived at Pearl Harbor on the 11th. After almost a fortnight in the Hawaiian Islands, she got underway on 23 July and shaped a course for the southwestern Pacific. She made a brief stop at Funafuti in the Ellice Islands on 7 August and, 10 days later, reached Milne Bay, New Guinea, where she reported for duty with the 7th Fleet. *Torchwood* served in the anchorage at Milne Bay through mid-September and then moved forward to support the landings in the Netherlands East Indies at Morotai. By early December, she was at Manus in the Admiralty Islands, but she got underway again on the 4th and returned to Milne Bay on the 6th. Three days later, she moved on to Hollandia, where she operated for a month from 14 December 1944 to 15 January 1945. After a short tour of duty at Woendi—between 18 and 25 January—she returned to Hollandia, where she served until late June.

On 2 July 1945, *Torchwood* took station in Leyte Gulf with the underwater defense forces and remained there through the end of the war. On 17 November 1945, she headed back to the United States and, after stops at

Eniwetok and Pearl Harbor, reached San Francisco on 22 December. On 7 January 1946, she headed south and, two days later, arrived in San Pedro, her base until 7 July when she sailed for Hawaii. The ship entered Pearl Harbor on the 16th, and remained there until 24 August when she got underway for the western Pacific.

After two very brief stops—one at Eniwetok and the other at Guam—*Torchwood* arrived in Subic Bay in the Philippines on 14 September. There, she reported to the Commander, Philippine Sea Frontier, to await decommissioning for her transfer to the government of China by the Foreign Liquidation Commission. On 2 October, she departed Subic Bay and headed for China. She arrived in Shanghai on the 7th and, on the 26th, was decommissioned. That same day, she was turned over to the Foreign Liquidation Commission which, in turn, transferred her to the Chinese Maritime Customs Service. *Torchwood*'s name was struck from the Navy list on 23 April 1947.

Tornado

Winnebago (q.v.) was renamed *Tornado* on 15 June 1869 but resumed the name *Winnebago* on August of the same year.

Toro

A name applied to various fish including the cowfish, the catalufa, and the cavallo.

(SS–422: dp. 1,570 (surf.), 2,415 (subm.); l. 311'8''; b. 27'3''; dr. 15'5'' (mean); s. 20.25 k. (surf.), 8.75 k. (subm.); cpl. 81; a. 10 21'' tt., 1 5'', 1 40mm., 1 20mm., 2 .50-cal. mg.; cl. *Balao*)

Toro (SS–422) was laid down on 27 May 1944 at the Portsmouth (N.H.) Navy Yard; launched on 23 August 1944; sponsored by Mrs. Alan G. Kirk; and commissioned on 8 December 1944, Comdr. James D. Grant in command.

Following her completion on 26 December 1944, *Toro* participated in training exercises out of Portsmouth, Newport, and New London before arriving at Key West on 11 February 1945. She provided services to the Fleet Sonar School; then, on the 28th, departed Key West in company with *Bumper* (SS–333), bound for the Canal Zone were she underwent a week of intensive training. The two submarines set a westward course for Hawaii on 15 March and arrived at Pearl Harbor on 1 April. *Toro* conducted training exercises out of that port with Submarine Division 101 until 24 April when she departed Oahu in company with *Billfish* (SS–286). She arrived at Saipan on 6 May and, after one false start, got underway for her first war patrol on the 10th.

After arriving in her patrol and lifeguard area south of Shikoku and east of Kyushu on the 16th, she occasionally encountered Japanese planes as she pursued her duties. On the 18th, following a probable periscope sighting, *Toro* detected a transmission on Japanese submarine radar frequency and attempted to close the contact but was unsuccessful.

As she patrolled Bungo Suido, she was often assigned as lifeguard for air strikes against the Japanese islands. While off Omino Shima before sunrise on the 25th, she received word that a B–29 was in trouble. She began the search in state four seas with only fair visibility and, two hours after dawn, homed in by friendly air cover, she rescued two Army aviators who had been floating in their lifejackets for three and one-half hours. Twenty minutes later, she rescued another aviator and then continued her search for additional survivors until late in the day. While patrolling on the surface the following morning, she made radar contact with a possible target at 2,000 yards. The submarine turned toward the contact and shortly there-

after a torpedo wake crossed her bow, indicating that an enemy vessel had first located her. *Toro* dove and had no further contact with the unseen attacker. *Toro* continued patrols and lifeguard duty in Bungo Suido until 14 June when she set her course for the Marianas. She moored at Apra Harbor five days later.

Following refit by *Fulton* (AS–11), she got underway from Guam on 14 July; paused briefly at Saipan for fuel, water, and the replacement of her torpedoes with Mark 18's; and arrived in her patrol area on the 24th. Late in the day, she was drawn far out of her assigned area in a fruitless search for a downed flier. The departure of *Toro*'s air cover at 1800 left her in a most dangerous situation due to the expected passage of an American task force on an antishipping sweep. Unable to clear the area in time, *Toro* made radar contact with the task force at 2055. Despite attempts to establish her identity, *Toro* was soon the target of two obviously unfriendly American ships which bore down on the submarine at a speed of 22 knots and bracketed her with gunfire at a distance of 7,400 yards. *Toro* attempted to establish her identity using a flare, smoke bombs, and sonar; but the ships were still firing when she passed 150 feet. The beleaguered submarine continued down to 400 feet and rigged for depth charges. The surface vessels, thinking that they had sunk a Japanese picket boat, remained in the area for half an hour searching for survivors without discovering that their target had been a friendly submarine. An hour after midnight, *Toro* surfaced and set her course back to her patrol area.

That morning, she returned to her lifeguard station and, in the afternoon, rescued three British aviators afloat on a raft. She maintained her station for carrier strikes against Japan on the 28th and, shortly after noon on the 30th, received a distress message from an Army Mustang plane. After circling his plane over the submarine the pilot parachuted from the crippled aircraft at an altitude of only 800 feet. Within seven minutes, *Toro*'s crew brought the aviator on board.

She transferred the rescued British fliers to *Gabilan* (SS–252) on 1 August. On the 5th, while patrolling her lifeguard area for planes returning from bomber raids on the Japanese islands, *Toro* sighted dense dense black smoke on the horizon and, receiving reports of a downed pilot in the area, put on all possible speed to investigate the source of the smoke. Less than 20 minutes later, she picked up an Army aviator afloat in his lifeboat impressively marked by a smoke display. Minutes later, a second Army aviator jumped from his plane nearby, and again *Toro* had a flier on board within seven minutes of the time his parachute opened.

At mid-month, Japan capitulated. After destroying a number of mines south of Honshu, the submarine departed the area on the 17th and proceeded via Guam to Midway where she arrived on 27 August.

On 4 September, she departed Midway and proceeded via Pearl Harbor and the Panama Canal to east coast ports. She arrived at Philadelphia on 31 October to prepare for inactivation. In January 1946, *ATR–67* towed the submarine to New London, where, on 7 February 1946, *Toro* was decommissioned and placed in reserve.

Toro was recommissioned on 13 May 1947, and she reported for duty to Submarine Squadron 2, Atlantic Fleet, on the 28th. She conducted hunter/killer exercises, made a simulated war patrol in the Arctic Sea and joined fleet tactical exercises in the Mediterranean. On 28 January 1950, she joined Submarine Development Group 2; and her operations helped to refine submarine tactics, weapons, and equipment. She worked in the Atlantic and Caribbean until July 1952, when she reported to Submarine Squadron 2 at New London and assumed new duties training submariners. During the next 10 years, she combined these activities with type training and services to ships and aircraft engaged in antisubmarine warfare exercises. She also participated in Operation "Springboard" and made one

Mediterranean cruise. She was redesignated auxiliary submarine (AGSS) in July 1962 and, on 22 November 1962, as her Navy career drew to its close, she made her 11,000th dive while operating in Long Island Sound.

In February 1963, she was ordered to berth with the Philadelphia Group, Atlantic Reserve Fleet, for demilitarization and non-industrial stripping; on 11 March 1963 she was decommissioned; and on 1 April 1963 her name was struck from the Navy list. She was slated to be sunk in an attempt to locate *Thresher* (SSN–593) (*q.v.*), but the plan was abandoned, and *Toro* was later sold and scrapped.

Toro received two battle stars for World War II.

Torpedo

Torpedo was designed and partially constructed in New York City by inventor Robert Fulton for the purpose of towing "torpedoes" against British ships engaged in blockading New York harbor during the War of 1812.

Work commenced on the ship in 1814, but Fulton died before she was completed. His workmen proved incapable of proceeding without him, so the work was suspended. Although never launched or formally christened, she was carried on the Navy register from 1814 to 1818. Her unfinished hulk remained in a corner of the New York Navy Yard nearly totally submerged, at least until 1820.

Torrance

A county in the state of New Mexico.

(AKA–76: dp. 14,160; l. 459'2''; b. 63'; dr. 26'4''; s. 16.5 k.; cpl. 395; a. 1 5'', 8 40mm., 16 20mm.; cl. *Tolland*)

Torrance (AKA–76) was laid down under a Maritime Commission contract (MC hull 1382) on 1 April 1944 at Wilmington, N.C., by the North Carolina Shipbuilding Corp.; launched on 6 June 1944; sponsored by Miss Marlene DeKay; acquired by the Navy on 20 June and towed to the Bethlehem Steel Company plant at Hoboken, N.J., for conversion to an attack cargo ship; and commissioned on 18 November 1944, Lt. Comdr. George A. Euerle, USNR, in command.

Following commissioning, *Torrance* underwent 10 days of trials in Long Island Sound before setting course for Hampton Roads on 28 November. Soon after arriving in Norfolk the next day, the cargo ship conducted shakedown training in Hampton Roads. Leaving Norfolk after shaking down, *Torrance* headed for the west coast.

Upon arrival in Caribbean waters on 17 December, she received orders to proceed to San Francisco, Calif. She entered the Pacific from the Panama Canal on Christmas Eve and arrived in San Francisco on 2 January 1945.

There she took on board supplies earmarked for South Pacific bases and set out for South Sea isles on the 13th.

She made port at Milne Bay, New Guinea, on 31 January, then proceeded to Manus, in the Admiralties, where she arrived on 3 February. *Torrance* next returned to the New Guinea coast, this time to Hollandia, where she arrived on Saint Valentine's Day. Receiving orders directing her to the Philippines, the ship joined Transport Division 49, Transport Squadron 17, bound for Leyte.

Torrance and other ships in her division engaged in intensive exercises off Cabuagan Island, near Leyte, in mid-March. On 21 March, the attack cargo ship embarked the men and materiel of the Army Engineers 305th Regimental Combat Team and joined a convoy bound for the Ryukyus.

Torrance arrived in waters off Okinawa early in the campaign but remained in reserve off the Hagushi beaches until her division launched a feint attack and landing on the southeast coast of Okinawa on 19 April 1945.

She completed the diversionary operation and returned briefly to Hagushi before delivering combat supplies to Ie Shima. Then, back at Hagushi, she unloaded the remainder of the cargo carried in her capacious holds. During these operations, both nature and the Japanese joined forces to attempt to thwart the American onslaught, but to no avail. Fragile landing craft carried their loads to the beaches, braving heavy seas and stiff breezes while death-dealing *kamikazes* swept down from the Japanese home islands. *Torrance*'s antiaircraft gunners stood to their weapons and fired out streams of tracer which clawed at the attacking planes and sent two of them spinning into the sea.

The Nipponese assault came not only from the skies —in the form of kamikazes—and from the sea—in the small, fast suicide motor boats which endangered both warship and auxiliary alike—but from strategically emplaced and cleverly concealed shore batteries as well. These guns made their presence felt with salvoes which landed uncomfortably close among the coveys of transports and their escorts. Like frightened quail, the transports—including *Torrance*—shifted anchorage to safer waters, as destroyers and cruiser gunfire and carrier-based planes dealt with the troublesome shore guns.

Despite the difficulties engendered by wind and wave, suicide plane or shore battery, the conquest of Okinawa moved steadily forward. *Torrance* cleared the battle area and dropped anchor at Saipan on 5 May to await further orders. On 22 May, she departed the Marshall Islands, bound for the west coast of the United States.

The attack cargo ship reached San Francisco on 6 June and commenced voyage repairs which lasted until the 24th, when she set out for Seattle, Wash. *Torrance* remained in the northwest coastal waters until she once more headed westward into the Pacific.

Arriving at Eniwetok on 17 July for an 11-day layover, she unloaded her cargo from the United States. For the remainder of the war, the attack cargo ship operated in support of the Fleet and its bases in waters of the Philippines and off Korea and provided supplies for the American occupation forces in the Japanese home islands. She first reached Japan when she made port at Sasebo on 23 November 1945.

From there, she steamed back to Seattle, where she arrived on 10 December and remained into the New Year. Late in January, she shifted south and moored at San Francisco on 27 January 1946. She made one more cargo-carrying voyage to Pearl Harbor before returning to the west coast en route to the Canal Zone.

Transiting the Panama Canal on 29 April, *Torrance* pointed her bow towards Jacksonville, Fla., where she received orders to report to the Commandant of the 5th Naval District, Norfolk, Va., for disposition. Arriving in Hampton Roads on 9 May 1946, she was decommissioned at Norfolk on 20 June 1946. Delivered to the War Shipping Administration two days later, *Torrance* was struck from the Navy list on 3 July 1946 and laid up with many of her sisters in the James River.

Purchased by the Alcoa Steamship Company of New York in 1948, the erstwhile attack cargo ship was renamed SS *Alcoa Roamer* and engaged in the freight-carrying trade through 1968. Given the name SS *Eldorado* when taken over by the Clairship Navigation Corp. of New York, she continued in cargo activities through 1971.

Torrance received one battle star for her World War II service.

Torrington

A British name. Three earlier *Torringtons* served in the Royal Navy. The first *Torrington* was acquired in

1654 and named for a town in Devonshire, the scene—during England's First Civil War—of a victory of the Parliamentarian force commanded by Sir Thomas Fairfax.

The second and third *Torrington* were named for Admiral George Byng, Viscount Torrington, who entered the Royal Navy in 1678 and rose steadily until he was appointed First Lord of the Admiralty in 1727. His greatest triumph at sea was probably his victory over the Spanish Fleet off Cape Passaro, Sicily. He died on 17 January 1733.

Torrington (BDE–568)—a *Buckley*-class destroyer escort—was laid down under the lend-lease program on 22 September 1943, at Hingham, Mass., by the Bethlehem Steel Co.; launched on 27 November 1943; and commissioned by the Royal Navy on 18 January 1944.

Following commissioning, *Torrington* shook down in Casco Bay, Maine, and off Bermuda, before proceeding to England, via St. John's and Argentia, Newfoundland.

After arriving in British home waters on 20 April 1944, the new DE operated in the English Channel area and first tasted combat on 21 July 1944 off Cape D'Antifer. In company with HMS *Melbreak* that day, *Torrington* engaged a German destroyer and four motor-torpedo boats ("E" boats) and drove them away from vital supply lines supporting the Allied invasion of western France.

Besides patrolling in the Channel, *Torrington* also served in the Atlantic and the North Sea. On 11 March 1945, she sank a German midget submarine, or *Seehund*, off Ramsgate, England. Two days later, she destroyed a second *Seehund* off Dunkirk, France, sinking the enemy submersible during a determined depth charge attack.

After Germany surrendered, the DE was returned to the United States on 11 June 1946. *Torrington* (BDE–568) was struck from the Navy list on 15 October 1946 and sold on 26 September 1947 for scrap.

Torry

An island near the southeastern shore of Lake Okeechobee, Fla.

(AG–140: dp. 500; l. 177'; b. 33'; dr. 10'; s. 13 k. (tl.); cpl. 37; a. none; cl. *Camano*)

Torry—a cargo ship built for the Army in 1944 by Ingalls Shipbuilding Corp., Decatur, Ala., as freight supply ship *FS–394*—was acquired by the Navy on 22 February 1947 at Subic Bay, Luzon, Philippines; named *Torry* and designated AG–140 on 3 April 1947; and commissioned at Guam on 5 July 1947.

In August 1947, she began operating in the Marianas and Carolines, performing logistic and routine patrol functions. She was reclassified AKL–11 on 31 March 1949 and continued her activities among the Pacific islands. While at Guam on 24 July 1951, she was loaned to the Department of the Interior and was permanently transferred to that department and struck from the Navy list on 29 January 1952. She served with the Department of the Interior providing sea transportation among the islands of the Pacific Trust Territory until 1961 when she was sold to Socony Mobil Oil Co., Inc. Two years later, she was transferred to American M.A.R.C., Inc., of Inglewood, Calif., and, in 1965, was transferred to the Western Offshore Drilling and Exploration Co., Sante Fe Springs, Calif.

Torsk

A food fish of the North Atlantic, also known as the cusk or tusk. The torsk, a member of the cod family, can reach a length of three feet and weigh as much as 30 pounds.

(SS–423: dp. 1,570; l. 311'8''; b. 27'3''; dr. 15'5'' (mean); s. 20.25 k. (surf.), 8.75 k. (subm.); cpl. 81; a. 1 5'', 1 40mm., 1 20mm., 2 .50-cal. mg., 10 21'' tt.; cl. *Balao*)

Torsk (SS–423) was laid down on 7 June 1944 at the Portsmouth (N.H.) Navy Yard; launched on 6 September 1944; sponsored by Mrs. Allen B. Reed; and commissioned on 16 December 1944, Comdr. Bafford E. Lewellen in command.

Completed on the last day of 1944, *Torsk* trained out of Portsmouth, Newport, and New London until 11 February, when she headed for Florida. On the 16th, the submarine arrived at Port Everglades where she provided services for antisubmarine research. She departed that Florida port on 20 February, transited the Panama Canal, and reached Hawaii on 23 March.

After a repair and training period, she got underway from Pearl Harbor for her first war patrol. *Torsk* paused briefly at Guam en route to an area off Kii Suido which she reached on 11 May and began lifeguard duty. Air contacts were few in this period, and the submarine found no opportunity to conduct rescue operations. Toward midnight on 11 May, she set course for her patrol area off the northeastern coast of Honshu. She arrived there on the 13th and, for two days, attempted to contact other members of the wolf pack, "Lewellen's Looters." On the 16th, she made rendezvous with *Sandlance* (SS–381) and *Cero* (SS–225). For more than a fortnight, their careful coverage of the east coast of Honshu turned up nothing more interesting than mines.

On 2 June, while patrolling between Honshu and Hokkaido, *Torsk* came upon a small coastal minelayer. The submarine fired six torpedoes—which the small vessel avoided by maneuvering—and then dove and rigged for depth charges which did not materialize. *Torsk* had another disappointing encounter on the 4th when, while patrolling off Kobe Saki, she fired four torpedoes at a 700-ton freighter without scoring. The following day, she set her course homeward, stopped at Midway on the 11th, and returned to Pearl Harbor on the 16th.

After refitting and the installation of new equipment, the submarine got underway for her second war patrol on 17 July. She spent the first two days of August at Guam and set her course for the Sea of Japan.

She passed through the minefields of Tsushima Strait on 10 August and, on the morning of the 11th, rescued seven Japanese merchant seamen who had survived the sinking of the *Koue Maru* some four days before. Early that afternoon, the submarine entered her patrol area and, on the following morning off Dogo Island, *Torsk* made a submerged periscope attack which sank a small coastal freighter.

On the 13th, she patrolled off Ando Saki and, after sighting a number of fishing boats during the morning, sighted another small freighter which she promptly sank. Later the same day, she made an unsuccessful attack on a cargo ship as it entered Wakasa Wan; then dodged through a 75-boat fishing fleet; and outdistanced the *maru*'s escort.

Off Amarubi Saki on the morning of the 14th, *Torsk* sighted a medium cargo ship and took up the chase. A 745-ton "Kaibokan"-class patrol escort vessel accompanied the freighter to seaward, presenting the submarine with a tempting target. At 1035, as the freighter and her escort approached Kasumi Ko, *Torsk* launched one of the new experimental Mark 28 torpedoes at the escorting ship. Minutes later, the "fish" found its mark; an explosion bent the stern of the frigate up to a 30-degree angle, and shortly thereafter the target sank. As the freighter entered the harbor half an hour later, *Torsk* attempted to sink her but was unsuccessful, possibly because the torpedoes struck undetected reefs near the mouth of the harbor.

Around noon, another frigate appeared, apparently a reinforcement which had been called in. Continuing her aggressive action, *Torsk* fired a Mark 28 torpedo at the frigate which had already detected the submarine's presence. Comdr. Lewellen then initiated deep submergence procedures and ordered the crew to rig for silent running. After a tense five minutes, she reached 400 feet and there she launched another torpedo, this time the new acoustic Mark 27. Almost immediately, a loud explosion announced that the first torpedo had found its mark, and a minute later a second explosion sounded, followed by strong breaking up noises. The secret new torpedoes had proven their worth in battle, and *Torsk* was credited, not only with two enemy warships, but also with sinking the last Japanese warship sunk in World War II. Held down by enemy planes and patrol vessels, the submarine remained submerged more than seven hours. Then, she surfaced and headed for the Noto peninsula.

On the 15th, following four highly successful days of aggressive patrolling, *Torsk* received word of the cessation of hostilities. She continued her patrol in the Sea of Japan, conducting visual and photo surveillance and destroying floating mines. On the 31st, what was thought to be a torpedo wake was sighted, an indicator that not everyone had heard the news of the war's ending.

The submarine set her course for the Marianas on 1 September, passed through Tsushima Straits on the 3d, and arrived at Guam on the 9th, successfully completing her second war patrol.

She departed the Marianas on the next day, proceeded via Pearl Harbor and the Canal Zone, and arrived at New London in mid-October. For the next seven years, she operated out of that port serving as a training ship, participating in exercises and tests, and occasionally making naval reserve training cruises. In June 1949, she was assigned to Submarine Squadron 2; and, in the summer of 1950, she was deployed to the Mediterranean. The ship returned to New London in the fall for fleet exercises and, the following year, extended her operations into the Caribbean.

Early in 1952, she completed her conversion to a fleet-snorkel submarine and was deployed again to the Mediterranean that summer. Returning on 27 November, she continued operations out of New London ranging from Halifax to Havana as she trained prospective submarine personnel and laid exercise mine fields. In 1955, she was reassigned to Submarine Squadron 6 at Norfolk. There, her duties included services to aircraft and surface ships to help them hone their skills in antisubmarine warfare. She made frequent Caribbean voyages and participated in Operation "Springboard." In June 1959, she proceeded via the Saint Lawrence Seaway to the Great Lakes, visited various ports on Lake Ontario and Lake Michigan, then returned to the Norfolk operating area in mid-August.

In the early 1960's, she made Mediterranean deployments; joined Commonwealth countries in Exercise "New Broom X"; and continued her duties in training antisubmarine forces in the Atlantic. During the Cuban Crisis in the fall of 1962, she patrolled in support of the blockade of that Caribbean island.

On 4 March 1964, the veteran submarine was decommissioned and, following modifications at the Boston Navy Yard, was assigned to the Washington Navy Yard for use in training reserves. *Torsk* operated out of Washington until 1971 and, on 15 December of that year, was struck from the Navy list. On 26 September 1972, she was turned over to the state of Maryland to be used as a museum in the Inner Harbor at Baltimore.

Torsk received two battle stars for World War II service.

Tortola

The main island of the British Virgin Islands. Located between St. John and Virgin Gorda, this rugged island was first settled in 1648 by Dutch buccaneers.

(PF–91: dp. 1,246; l. 301'6''; b. 36'6''; dr. 13'8''; s. 20 k.; cpl. 194; a. 3 3'', 4 40mm.; cl. *Tacoma*)

Originally classified as a gunboat and designated PG–199, *Tortola* was reclassified as a frigate and redesignated PF–91 on 15 April 1943; her keel was laid down on 16 October 1943 at Providence, R.I., by the Walsh Kaiser Co., Inc.; launched on 16 November 1943; completed on 15 May 1944; and transferred under lend-lease agreement to the United Kingdom on the same day. She served the British Navy as *Tortola* (K.595).

The ship operated in the Arctic in 1944 with the 20th Escort Group on the Russian convoy route into December. She augmented this with service in the Atlantic in both 1944 and 1945. With the end of the war, she proceeded to the United States, arriving at Boston on 9 May 1946, and was returned to the United States Navy on 22 May 1946. On 17 June, she was authorized for transfer to the Maritime Commission for disposal; and, on 3 July 1946, her name was struck from the Navy list. Sold to John J. Duane Co. of Quincy, Mass., on 17 January 1947, she was resold to Washburn Wire Co. of Philippsdale, R.I., on 10 September 1947 and scrapped.

Tortuga

A group of desert coral islets—60 miles west of Key West, Fla.—which were discovered in 1513 by Spanish explorer Ponce de Leon. In 1861, the United States government completed Fort Jefferson on Garden Key, and this bastion remained in Union hands throughout the Civil War. It later was used as a prison until abandoned in 1874. During the 1880's, the Navy established a base at Tortuga; and it subsequently set up a coaling and a wireless station there as well. During World War I, a seaplane base was established on the islet; but it was abandoned soon thereafter.

(LSD–26: dp. 4,490; b. 72'2''; dr. 18'0''; s. 15.4 k.; cpl. 326; a. 1 5'', 12 40mm.; cl. *Casa Grande*)

Tortuga (LSD–26) was laid down on 16 October 1944 by the Boston Navy Yard; launched on 21 January 1945; sponsored by Mrs. George D. Payne; and commissioned on 8 June 1945, Lt. Comdr. Raymond G. Brown, USNR, in command.

Commissioned during the final phase of World War 11, *Tortuga* conducted shakedown in the Virginia capes area and was at Colon, Canal Zone, en route to the Pacific combat area on 15 August 1945 when she received news of Japan's surrender. The dock landing ship soon proceeded to Buckner Bay, Okinawa, and subsequently operated in Korean and Chinese waters, repairing small craft and serving in the mobile support unit attached to Amphibious Forces, Pacific Fleet. Operating initially out of Jinsen (now Inchon), Korea, *Tortuga* subsequently conducted her support missions out of Tsingtao, Taku, and Shanghai, China; Hong Kong; and Yokosuka, Japan. In the spring of 1947, the ship returned to the west coast of the United States, via Guam and Pearl Harbor, and was decommissioned and placed in reserve at San Diego on 18 August 1947.

Following the communist invasion of South Korea in the summer of 1950, *Tortuga* was recommissioned on 15 September 1950, Comdr. Elof W. Hermanson in command. Reactivated in response to the Navy's need for amphibious ships created by the war in Korea, the landing ship dock underwent an abbreviated refitting and shakedown before she sailed for Japan on 29 December. Proceeding via Pearl Harbor and Eniwetok, she arrived at Sasebo on 3 February 1951. *Tortuga* participated in a feint landing which preceded the operation mounted to recapture the strategic port of Inchon.

About this time, intelligence reports indicated that the Chinese communists might take advantage of American preoccupation with the war in Korea by mounting an invasion, across the Taiwan Strait, of Nationalist-held Formosa. American strategists felt

The dock landing ship *Tortuga* (LSD–26).   (U.S. Naval Institute photo)

that, in such an endeavor, the Chinese would utilize many seagoing junks since, in operations off Korea, vessels of this type had proven to be almost unsinkable. Accordingly, *Tortuga* raised eight 60-foot junks from the depths of Inchon harbor and transported them to Yokosuka to be studied to determine what ordnance would be most effective against them.

Tortuga remained in the Far East through 1952 for two more Korean deployments. During the first, the landing ship provided support services at Inchon; and, in the second, she took part in the massive amphibious feint at Kojo, North Korea, from 13 to 16 October 1952, and in operations off Wonsan, supporting minecraft in November and December. During 1953, *Tortuga* participated in the Korean prisoner-of-war exchange after the Panmunjom Armistice and also conducted landing exercises and maneuvers in the Far East and off the west coast of the United States.

Tortuga was deployed to the Western Pacific (West-Pac) again in 1954. The signing of the Geneva accords which ended the fighting between the French and Viet Minh resulted in the creation of two Vietnams—north and south. The former was to be in communist hands; the latter was to be governed by non-communist leaders. Diverted to Haiphong from Yokosuka, *Tortuga* arrived at her destination on 21 August 1954 to take part in the massive evacuation of French nationals, in Operation "Passage to Freedom," as well as the moving of Vietnamese refugees who chose not to live in the north under communist domination. The landing ship conducted four round trips from Haiphong in the north to Tourane (now Danang), Saigon, and Nha Trang in the south, before she returned to Yokosuka on 4 October. For the remainder of the year, she conducted minesweeper support operations in Korean waters.

During the 14 years from 1955 to 1969, *Tortuga* would remain employed in a regular schedule of deployments to WestPac. She was based at San Diego until 30 June 1966, when her home port was changed to Long Beach. In between deployments—which included exercises and equipment lifts and labors to help maintain the 7th Fleet's readiness—*Tortuga* conducted local operations out of west coast ports and underwent progressive modifications during regular availabilities.

As American involvement in Southeast Asia deepened during the latter half of the 1960's, *Tortuga*'s deployment schedule accordingly reflected her role in the buildup of Allied strength to attempt to check com-

munist domination of Southeast Asia. On 4 August 1964, North Vietnamese torpedo boats attacked *Maddox* (DD–731) and *Turner Joy* (DD–951) in the Gulf of Tonkin. As a direct result, the United States took ever-increasing steps to aid the South Vietnamese government in its attempt to combat Viet Cong insurgent activity within its borders. Within a few years, American involvement had been broadened from one of advising Vietnamese troops to the actual commitment of massive land, sea, and air forces. Soon after receiving word of the Tonkin Gulf incident, *Tortuga*—combat-loaded—got underway from Buckner Bay. She remained underway in the South China Sea from 6 August to 19 September before returning to Subic Bay.

For the remainder of the year 1964, *Tortuga* operated out of Yokosuka and conducted troop and equipment lifts between Japan and Okinawa until she headed home and arrived back at San Diego on 18 December. In February 1965, the landing ship proceeded to Camp Pendleton, Calif., to participate in Exercise "Silver Lance," the largest peacetime landing exercise ever held. In June, she commenced a WestPac deployment. She proceeded to Buckner Bay and Danang and, after operating in the Orient through the early summer, returned to Long Beach in late August 1965. She subsequently conducted a lift to Okinawa before she returned to San Diego for refresher training.

Tortuga sailed for Vietnamese waters on 1 March 1966, arrived at Vung Tau on 18 April, and relieved *Belle Grove* (LSD–2) as support ship for "Game Warden"—the Navy's operation designed to interdict the flow of communist supplies along the coastlines of South Vietnam. Initially, *Tortuga* operated in the Rung Sat special zone between Saigon and Vung Tau, helping to guard the entrance to the shipping channels snaking through Viet Cong territory to the capital city.

Tortuga shifted to the Mekong Delta region on 12 June to serve as a floating base for the Navy's fast PBR's of TF 116 and for a detachment of Army Bell UH–1B Huey helicopter gunships. The PBR's, attached to River Patrol Squadron 512, were small yet relatively heavily armed craft. Each mounted a .50-caliber machine gun forward and an "over-and-under" combination mount of one .50-caliber machine gun mounted over an 81-millimeter mortar aft. The helicopters, too, were relatively heavily armed, packing a "punch" of rockets of varying sizes and up to six machine guns. Initially, the helicopters were Army

244

"choppers" from the 145th Aviation Detachment. However, by the end of *Tortuga*'s tour, they were Navy aircraft from Task Force "Sea Wolf." Together, the PBR's and Hueys conducted their patrols and forays into the verdant jungle waterways; the PBR's knifing through the muddy sandy-colored waterways while the helicopters flew close cover above.

Occasionally, the hard-hitting teams would strike "pay-dirt," by capturing enemy munitions. On one occasion, on 12 June at the mouth of the Co Chien River, *Tortuga*'s PBR's participated in the capture of a large stock of guns and munitions captured from a damaged communist trawler which had been forced aground and set afire.

During her support operations with the riverine assault groups, *Tortuga* received a number of distinguished visitors ranging from General William C. Westmoreland, Commander, Military Assistance Group; Rear Admiral N. G. Ward, Commanding Naval Forces, Vietnam; as well as United States Ambassador to South Vietnam Henry Cabot Lodge; and news commentator Chet Huntley, who brought with him an NBC camera team to record a news story on *Tortuga*'s river patrol base activities.

Her deployment completed in the summer of 1966, *Tortuga* got underway on 30 August and steamed via Japan to the west coast. She arrived at San Diego on 7 November for leave, upkeep, and overhaul. The refit lasted through April of 1967, modernizing the ship and preparing her for another WestPac deployment. Following a period of refresher training and amphibious exercises, *Tortuga* sailed on 21 July 1967 from San Diego and arrived, via Hawaii, Guam, and the Philippines, at Danang on 5 September.

Upon arrival, *Tortuga* relieved *Monticello* (LSD–34) with Amphibious Ready Group (ARG) "Bravo" and operated with that unit into the fall of 1967. She took part in Operations "Fortress Sentry" and "Formation Leader," before her detachment from ARG "B" on 9 November. Subsequently, *Tortuga* loaded a cargo of disabled or damaged CH–46 helicopters for transport from Danang to Okinawa, where the "choppers" were repaired for further service. For the remainder of the year, from 3 to 31 December, *Tortuga* conducted cargo lifts from Japanese ports to Vietnam and vice-versa.

Tortuga then returned to the west coast—via Yokosuka, Buckner Bay, Subic Bay, Hong Kong, and Pearl Harbor—and arrived at Long Beach on 9 March 1968. For the remainder of the year, the landing ship conducted exercises and local operations out of Long Beach, until again deploying to WestPac in February 1969. On 17 February, while en route to Yokosuka, *Tortuga* conducted her first underway refueling—with *Cook* (LPR–130)—receiving 31,000 gallons of Navy Special Fuel Oil (NSFO). Upon arrival at Yokosuka, *Tortuga*'s in-port time was extended to allow the on-loading of a complete destroyer radar system for transport to Subic Bay. Underway on 11 March with her special cargo, the landing ship soon reached Subic Bay, unloaded, and proceeded for Kaohsiung, Taiwan, en route to South Vietnam.

On the last leg of her Vietnam-bound voyage, *Tortuga* instituted a stepped-up shipboard defense program consisting of daily general quarters drills, exercising especially with the ship's guns and in damage control problems—for the ship had received intelligence reports that a Viet Cong rocket attack was expected to coincide with her arrival at Danang. When paraflares were sighted on the horizon at 0200 on 14 March, *Tortuga* knew that she had arrived at her destination and went to general quarters. The expected attack failed to materialize, though, and *Tortuga* unloaded her cargo unmolested but at piers which, only the day before, had been rocketed by the Viet Cong. When the off-loading was completed, *Tortuga* shifted her berth far away from most of the shipping in the harbor. There, boat crews bent to the task of loading old ammunition on the ship. Meanwhile, one boat crew, composed of one officer and five enlisted men, armed with rifles and

Thompson submachine guns, kept a constant vigil in an LCVP which circled the ship at a distance of 60–70 yards. Periodically, at odd intervals, the boat's crew would drop percussion grenades in the water in an effort calculated to discourage enemy frogmen. When the task was completed, the ship got underway for the Philippines.

Reaching Subic Bay after an uneventful passage, the ship unloaded the explosives and soon received orders to transport a much-needed suction dredge up the Saigon River to Nha Be, through territory largely controlled by the Viet Cong. At Tan My, *Tortuga* embarked the dredge and a warping tug and got underway. During the transit of the Saigon River, the landing ship stood to general quarters, keeping a sharp eye for enemy attempts to impede the progress of the ship. The enemy failed to appear, however, and *Tortuga*, her dredge, and her tug arrived at Nha Be soon thereafter.

From 5 to 20 May, *Tortuga* participated in "Daring Rebel," an operation mounted to seek out and destroy Viet Cong rest camps on Barrier Island, 15 miles south of Danang. Joining *Duluth* (LSD–6), *Winston* (LKA–97), and *Okinawa* (LPH–3), *Tortuga* closed the beachhead, while *White River* (LSMR–536) stood offshore to provide initial bombardment. When *White River* launched a heavy rocket barrage shoreward, "Daring Rebel" got underway. Landing craft splashed ashore while troop-carrying helicopters quickly airlifted troops ashore in the vertical-envelopment phase of the operation. For the next two weeks, *Tortuga* served as primary control ship for the operation which located and destroyed caches of food and ammunition and Viet Cong rest camps.

The landing ship again served as primary control ship (PCS) in Danang harbor during "Gallant Leader," a follow-up to "Daring Rebel." Relieved by *Duluth* on 23 May, *Tortuga* set sail soon thereafter for Buckner Bay and simulated combat landings during exercises with Assault Craft Unit 1 in late June. In July, *Tortuga* transported the first increment of marines and their equipment for "Keystone Eagle," from Cua Vet, South Vietnam, to White Beach, Okinawa, before returning up the Saigon River to Nha Be with a load of palletized cargo.

Subsequently supporting Operation "Sea Float," delivering two pontoons and 32 pallets of ammunition from Nah Be to Tan My, *Tortuga* onloaded men and equipment from "Charlie" Battery, 1st Light Antiaircraft Missile Battalion (LAAM), First Marine Air Wing, at Danang harbor for transport to the west coast of the United States. In this last operation, the second increment of "Keystone Eagle," *Tortuga* headed "stateside" for the last time, and arrived at Seal Beach, Calif., on 12 September 1969, unloading the 58 Hawk missiles of the 1st LAAM Battalion, USMC, and then proceeding to the Long Beach Naval Shipyard.

Tortuga disembarked her marines and proceeded to pier 7 where she was moored outboard of *Carter Hall* (LSD–3). On 3 January 1970, *Tortuga* got underway for the Inactivation Facility at Mare Island, where she was decommissioned on 26 January 1970. Transferred to the temporary custody of the Maritime Administration (MARAD) on 6 October 1970, the ship was berthed at Suisun Bay, Calif., where she was later placed in permanent custody of MARAD on 1 September 1971. She was carried on the Navy list into 1977. Her name then disappeared from the list.

Tortuga was awarded five engagement stars for her Korean War service and eight for service off Vietnam.

Totem Bay

A bay on the southern shore of Kupreanof Island in the Alexander Archipelago in the southern panhandle of Alaska.

Totem Bay (CVE–111) was renamed *Vella Gulf* (CVE–111) (*q.v.*) on 6 April 1944.

245

Toucan

A brightly colored and easily tamed bird of the American tropics. It is characterized by its large but thin beak.

(AM–387: dp. 890; l. 221'1''; b. 32'2''; s. 18.1 k.; cpl. 117; a. 1 3'', 2 40mm., 2 dct.; cl. *Auk*)

Toucan (AM–387) was laid down on 16 February 1944 at Cleveland, Ohio, by the American Shipbuilding Co.; launched on 15 September 1944; sponsored by Miss Rose B. Jackiewicz; and commissioned on 25 November 1944, Lt. Comdr. S. H. Squibb, USNR, in command.

The minesweeper departed Cleveland on 28 November and proceeded via the Great Lakes and the St. Lawrence River to Boston where she arrived on 15 December. *Toucan* spent the next four months preparing for duty in the western Pacific.

Toucan departed Charleston on 20 April, transited the Panama Canal, and arrived at San Diego on 6 May. Three days later, the minesweeper sailed for Hawaii and arrived at Pearl Harbor on the 15th.

Getting underway again on the 27th, the ship served in the screens of various convoys as she proceeded to the Ryukyus via Eniwetok, Guam, and Ulithi.

Reaching Okinawa as American forces pushed ever closer to Japan's home islands, *Toucan* swept the waters surrounding the Ryukyus and then performed escort duty and sweeping operations with the 3d Fleet as it hammered away at Japanese ports, cities, and airfields through the end of July.

With the collapse of Japan under the massed weight of an Allied naval armada and the unexpected destructive capacity of two atomic bombs, the task of clearing the offensive and defensive minefields in Pacific seas began in earnest. From 14 to 24 August, *Toucan* took part in the "Skagway" sweep in the East China Sea and Ryukyus area. A call at Shanghai, China, punctuated two further sweeping operations—from 7 September to 2 October and from 25 to 30 October. The latter was conducted in the Kyushu-Korea area. All told, she steamed over 40,000 miles and swept 134 mines in the East China Sea, the lower Yangtze River, and in the Chusan Archipelago. On 6 February 1946, *Toucan* left Japanese waters and headed for the west coast, arriving at San Francisco on 23 March 1946. Moving to San Diego on 24 April, she began preparations for inactivation and was placed out of commission, in reserve, there on 1 July 1946.

The outbreak of hostilities in Korea in June 1950 increased the Navy's need for minecraft. Accordingly, *Toucan* was recommissioned on 27 October and operated on the west coast for more than a year.

On 4 January 1952, *Toucan* sailed for Sasebo and called at Pearl Harbor and Midway before reaching Sasebo on 2 February. She commenced Korean War operations in the Hungnam and Wonsan areas on 21 February, streaming her sweeping gear and hunting for the dangerous North Korean mines. With periodic repairs at Sasebo, *Toucan* operated primarily off Wonsan. From February through August 1952, the ship fired more than 8,000 rounds of ammunition at communist shore targets—trading fire with the enemy on many occasions and dodging everything from 76 millimeter shells to small arms fire.

Her duties included the disruption of the North Korean fishing trade. The ship took 13 prisoners while destroying three sampans and damaging 22 more. The plucky minesweeper also scored hits on enemy bunkers, box cars, and railroad trestles before departing Korean waters on 1 August to head for Long Beach, Calif.

The minesweeper returned to the Korean fighting zone the following year and continued her sweeping and interdiction operations in the vicinity of the Cho-Do, Paengyoung-Do, and Cheju-Do island areas from June to September 1953. The ship sailed for California and operated along the west coast from the time of her arrival at Long Beach on 3 December 1953 through 17 July 1954.

Toucan returned to the Far East in the summer of 1954 and reached Inchon, Korea, on 14 August. Two days later, she got underway for the west coast of Korea and operated primarily in the Taeyongyong-Do and Tojang Po vicinity. She departed Sasebo on 11 January 1955 and proceeded to Hong Kong only to

The newly completed *Toucan* (AM–387) at Cleveland, 24 November 1944. She is in "dazzle" camouflage with numerous 40-millimeter and 20-millimeter AA guns and a single 3-inch 50-caliber gun forward. The prominent loop antenna amidships is part of a radio direction finder installation. (NH 68592)

return to Japanese waters a fortnight later. Her stay at Sasebo was brief. Four days later, she weighed anchor for Keelung, Formosa, and thence moved to the Tachen Islands. On 7 February, the minesweeper took part in the evacuation of Chinese Nationalists from the Tachen group and disembarked the evacuees at Sasebo a week later.

During this mission, *Toucan* was redesignated MSF-387 on 7 February 1955.

Departing Sasebo only two days after her arrival from the Tachens, *Toucan* headed home and arrived at Long Beach on 11 March. She operated on the west coast as a unit of Mine Division 71 until August 1956 when she began another deployment to the Far East. She called at Yokosuka, Kobe, Sasebo, Fukuoka, Beppu, and Kagoshima, Japan, as well as Keelung, Formosa, before returning to Long Beach on 21 December.

On 1 May 1957, *Toucan* was inactivated and assigned to the Pacific Reserve Fleet, berthing at the Columbia River, Oreg., Group. Upon disestablishment of this group, the minesweeper was transferred to Bremerton, Wash., where she remained until 27 May 1964. On that day, she was withdrawn from the reserve fleet for conversion and transfer to the Republic of China, effective on 22 December 1964.

Toucan received three battle stars for World War II and two battle stars for the Korean War.

Toucey

Issac Toucey—born on 5 November 1796 in Newtown, Conn.—was admitted to the bar in 1818 and began two full terms in the United States House of Representatives on 4 March 1835. He served as Governor of Connecticut in 1846 and 1847 and as Attorney General under President Polk from 21 June 1848 to 3 March 1849. After a stint in the state legislature in 1850 and 1851, Toucey represented Connecticut in the United States Senate from 12 March 1852 to 3 March 1857. He was Secretary of the Navy under President Buchanan from 6 March 1857 to 3 March 1861.

After retiring from public office upon Lincoln's inauguration, Toucey resumed the practice of law. He died in Hartford, Conn., on 30 July 1869.

The first ship built by the Mare Island Navy Yard was launched as *Toucey* on 3 March 1859 but, at the request of her namesake, the Secretary of the Navy, was renamed *Saginaw* (*q.v.*) before being commissioned on 5 January 1860.

I

(Destroyer No. 282: dp. 1,215 (n.); l. 314'4½''; b. 30'11½'' (wl.); dr. 9'9¾''; s. 34.95 k.; cpl. 122; a. 4 4'', 1 3'', 12 21'' tt.; cl. *Clemson*)

Toucey (Destroyer No. 282) was laid down on 26 April 1919 at Squantum, Mass., by the Bethlehem Shipbuilding Corp.; launched on 5 September 1919; sponsored by Miss Elizabeth Alden Robinson; and commissioned at Boston on 9 December 1919, Comdr. Reuben B. Coffey in command.

Soon after commissioning, *Toucey* began duty with the Atlantic Fleet as a unit of Division 42, Flotilla 7, Squadron 1. Based at Newport, R.I., for the next seven years, she operated along the eastern seaboard and in the West Indies. During the summer, the destroyer cruised the northern latitudes off the New England coast, training in destroyer operations. Each winter, she headed south for the annual fleet concentration held in waters near the Panama Canal and for gunnery training at the range near Puerto Rico. Sometime between 1 July 1921 and 1 January 1922, she was reassigned to Division 25 of Squadron 9 and began operating with only 50 percent of her normal complement. However, by 1 January 1923, her full comple-

ment had been restored and, still assigned to the same squadron and division, she began operating with the newly organized Scouting Force.

Late in 1926, she appears to have been temporarily assigned to the American naval forces operating in Europe. By 1 January 1927, her base of operations had been moved from Newport, R.I., to Norfolk, Va. From the sketchy records which exist, she appears to have served the remainder of her career with the Scouting Force destroyers operating out of Norfolk.

In the spring of 1930, she moved to Philadelphia to prepare for inactivation. On 1 May 1930, *Toucey* was decommissioned at Philadelphia. Her name was struck from the Navy list on 22 October. The former destroyer was sold on 17 January 1931 and scrapped sometime in 1934.

Tourist

(PYc–32: dp. 185; l. 150'0''; b. 26'1''; dr. 10'2''; cpl. 32)

Tourist—a steel-hulled steam yacht built as *Calumet* in 1903 by George Lawley & Son at South Boston, Mass., and later renamed *Kehtoh*—was acquired by the Navy on 23 March 1942 from Edward Baletti of Weehawken, N.J. Retaining her civilian name, *Tourist* was classified a patrol craft and designated PYc–32. Assigned to the 3d Naval District for patrol service, the vessel was found unsuitable for this duty and was returned to her owner on 18 May 1942.

However, on 7 August 1942, the Navy reacquired the ship, classified her as a miscellaneous district auxiliary and designated her as *YAG–14*. Conversion work began at the Frank McWilliams shipyard, Staten Island, N.Y., and progressed until she was 98 percent complete, when the remainder of the work was undertaken at the Bethlehem Steel Co. yard in Brooklyn, N.Y.

YAG–14 was placed in service by the Commandant, 3d Naval District, on 12 December 1942. On 3 January 1943, she got underway for Miami, via the inland waterway system.

Attached to Service Squadron 9, she was readied at Charleston, S.C., for service with the Fleet Sound School, Key West, Fla. She arrived there on 2 April 1943 and was placed in commission the following day. For the remainder of 1943 and into 1944, the ship served the Fleet Sound School as a training vessel for sonar operators. On 11 August 1944, *YAG–14* was decommissioned. Struck from the Navy list on 22 August 1944, she was transferred to the War Shipping Administration, Maritime Commission, and sold on 20 February 1945.

Tourmaline

A mineral of variable color, consisting of a complex silicate which makes a striking gem when transparent and cut.

(PY–20: dp. 750; l. 154'; b. 26'6''; dr. 10'6''; s. 13 k.; cpl. 161; a. 2 3'', 4 .50-cal. mg., 2 dct.)

Tourmaline (PY–20)—a yacht built in 1930 at Bath, Maine, by the Bath Iron Works as *Sylvia*—was purchased by the Navy on 16 May 1941 from Logan G. Thomson. She entered the Marine Basin Co., Brooklyn, N.Y., on 23 June, for conversion before proceeding to the New York Navy Yard where she was commissioned as *Tourmaline* (PY–20) on 19 September 1941, Lt. Comdr. Charles E. Judge, USNR, in command.

The converted yacht departed New York harbor on 2 October and arrived at Norfolk, Va., two days later. She operated out of Hampton Roads during the two remaining months that the United States remained technically at peace. After Japan's attack on Pearl Harbor, she conducted her initial war patrols off the east coast based at Norfolk and at Charleston, S.C.

USS *Tourmaline* (PY–20) at Brooklyn in August 1941, in dark early-wartime camouflage. (19–N–25372)

The early part of the year 1942 found *Tourmaline* operating between Norfolk and Key West, Fla. On 29 June, she departed Key West to escort a convoy of merchant vessels to Norfolk. En route back toward Charleston, she assisted *Landsdowne* (DD–486) to pursue an underwater contact; but neither ship managed to locate the suspected U-boat. The yacht arrived at Charleston on 5 July. Her next mission called for her to escort a convoy to the British West Indies. She reached Guantanamo Bay, Cuba, on the 19th, establishing a pattern which lasted through much of her subsequent patrolled in that vicinity through early August before sailing for Key West on the 12th of that month.

After cruises on patrols in Florida waters, she departed Key West on 27 October—in company with *SC–499*, *SC–641*, and *SC–675*—to escort five merchantmen to Havana, Cuba. *Tourmaline* next headed for New York, where she arrived on 7 November. She returned to Guantanamo Bay, Cuba, on the 19th, establishing a pattern which lasted through much of her subsequent service in which she escorted convoys between New York and ports in the Caribbean. On 13 December 1942, five days out of New York, *Tourmaline*'s underwater sound gear picked up a strong metallic echo. She speeded to attack and dropped three depth charges before her steering gear was damaged. Forced to steer with her engines, the escort broke off the chase, and her quarry escaped.

After the damage was repaired, *Tourmaline* resumed escort duty and continued convoy work until 25 January 1944. On that day, the yacht received orders to report to the 1st Naval District, where she joined the Naval Local Defense Force based at Boston, Mass. For the remainder of 1944 and into June 1945, *Tourmaline* patrolled the waters off the Massachusetts coast through the end of the war in the Atlantic.

Decommissioned on 18 July 1945, *Tourmaline* was temporarily laid-up at the Mystic Shipbuilding Company and Repair Yard, East Boston, Mass. Struck from the Navy list on 13 August 1945, she was transferred to the War Shipping Board, Maritime Commission, on 3 January 1946. On 23 January 1946, Andrew

M. Embiricos and Manuel E. Kulukundis, of the Greek War Relief Association, Inc., purchased the yacht under its original name, *Sylvia*.

Usage (AM–130) (*q.v.*) was transferred to the United Kingdom on 7 June 1943 and served with the Royal Navy as *Tourmaline* (J.339).

Towaliga

A river in Georgia which rises in Spalding County and flows southeast to empty into the Ocmulgee River. The word, Towaliga, is a Creek Indian term meaning "scalp place." Creek war parties apparently stopped on the bank of this stream to dry scalps.

(AOG–42: dp. 2,270; l. 220'6''; b. 37'0''; dr. 13'1''; s. 10 k. (tl.); cpl. 62; a. 1 3'', 2 40mm.; cl. *Mettawee*; T. T1–M–A2)

Towaliga (AOG–42) was laid down under Maritime Commission contract (MC hull 2068) on 29 September 1944 at Bayonne, N.J., by the East Coast Shipyard Inc.; launched on 29 October 1944; sponsored by Mrs. Michael Canose; acquired by the Navy on 6 December 1944; and commissioned on 14 December 1944, Lt. Robert H. Smith in command.

The gasoline tanker called at Norfolk on 9 January 1945 and began shakedown training in the Chesapeake Bay the next day. On 11 February, she joined a convoy bound for the West Indies and arrived at Aruba, Netherlands Antilles, 10 days later. After filling her cargo tanks, the ship proceeded through the Panama Canal to the west coast; spent 14 and 15 March at San Diego; and sailed for Hawaii on the 16th. She reached Pearl Harbor on 28 March and, for the next four months, shuttled diesel oil and aviation gasoline from Hawaii to Johnston Island. In mid-August, while the ship was undergoing an overhaul in dry dock at Pearl Harbor, hostilities ended.

Upon completion of the yard work, *Towaliga* got underway for Japan and, after stops at Eniwetok and Saipan, arrived at Osaka on 9 October 1945. The ship operated from Osaka until 16 August 1946 when she was ordered to China. She arrived at Tsingtao on the 19th and was placed in a standby status with a reduced crew, preparatory to being decommissioned. On 6 December, the ship's complement was filled, and she began training Chinese crews. *Towaliga* was decommissioned on 10 May 1947 and transferred to the Republic of China under the lend-lease program. The ship was nominally returned to the United States on 17 February 1948 but simultaneously transferred permanently to China.

Towaliga was struck from the Navy list on 12 March 1948.

Towers

John Henry Towers—born on 30 January 1885 at Rome, Ga.—graduated with the Naval Academy class of 1906 and was commissioned ensign in 1908, while serving in battleship *Kentucky*. He was later assigned to battleship *Michigan* before being sent to Hammondsport, N.Y., in 1911 for aviation duty.

Under the tutelage of Glenn Curtiss, Towers qualified as a pilot in August of that year and went on to supervise the establishment of the Navy's first aviation unit at Annapolis, Md., in the fall. He travelled to California where, in conjunction with the Curtiss Flying School at North Island in San Diego, he took part in developing and improving naval aircraft types.

After returning east thereafter, Towers was nearly killed in the summer of 1912. While he was flying as a passenger on 20 June, his plane was caught in a sudden downdraft and plummeted earthward. The pilot, Ens. W. D. Billingsley, was thrown from the aircraft and killed. Towers, too, was wrenched from his seat but managed to catch a wing strut and stayed with the plane until it crashed into the Chesapeake Bay. Interviewed by Glenn Curtiss soon thereafter, Towers recounted the circumstances of the tragedy; and the report and resultant recommendations eventually led to the design and adoption of safety belts and harnesses for pilots and their passengers.

On 5 March 1913, the Navy designated Towers Naval Aviator No. 3; and, in January 1914, he became the executive officer of the Naval Air Station at Pensacola, Fla. When Vera Cruz was occupied by the Navy and marines that spring, Towers commanded the aviation unit carried to that port in battleship *Mississippi* and cruiser *Birmingham*. In August 1914, one month into World War I, Towers was ordered to London as assistant naval attaché—a billet he filled until he returned to the United States in the autumn of 1916. Once back home, he supervised the establishment of the Naval Flying Corps—then in its infancy—and went on to become Assistant Director of Naval Aviation with the establishment of the Division of Aviation within the Navy Department.

In February 1919, Towers was placed in charge of the proposed transatlantic flight of the NC-flying boats and, while commanding *NC–3*, led the division from Trepassy Bay, Newfoundland. Though their ultimate destination was Lisbon, Portugal, *NC–1* and *NC–3* encountered dense fog off the Azores and had to land to take bearings. Due to the heavy seas, neither could take off again; and the latter soon began shipping water. Towers and his crew managed to keep the flying boat afloat for 52 hours and eventually made Punta Delgada on Sao Miguel Island. *NC–4* went on to complete the transatlantic crossing, arriving at Lisbon on 27 May. For his part in the operation, Towers received the Navy Cross.

Between the autumn of 1919 and the late winter of 1922 and 1923, Towers served at sea—as the executive officer of *Aroostook* and as the commanding officer of

old destroyer *Mugford*, which had been redesignated an aircraft tender. Then, after a tour as executive officer at Pensacola Naval Air Station, he spent two and one-half years—from March of 1923 to September of 1925—as an assistant naval attaché, serving at the American embassies at London, Paris, Rome, the Hague, and Berlin. Returning to the United States in the autumn of 1925, he was assigned to the Bureau of Aeronautics and served as a member of the court of inquiry which investigated the loss of dirigible *Shenandoah*.

Towers next commanded *Langley* (CV–1) from January 1927 to August 1928. He received a commendation for "coolness and courage in the face of danger" when a gasoline line caught fire and burned on board the carrier in December 1927. Towers personally led the vigorous and successful attempt to suppress the flames kindled by the explosion and thus averted a catastrophe.

After shore duty in the Bureau of Aeronautics—successively serving as head of the plans division and later, as assistant bureau chief—Towers joined the staff of the Commander, Aircraft, Battle Force, Rear Admiral Harry E. Yarnell, in June 1931. He was among the staff which planned a successful "attack" on Pearl Harbor during the Joint Army-Navy Exercise No. 4 in the Hawaiian Islands in February 1932—an operation which was to be duplicated on a larger scale by the Japanese in December 1941.

Between June of 1933 and June of 1939, Towers filled a variety of billets ashore and afloat: he completed the senior course at the Naval War College in 1934; commanded the Naval Air Station at San Diego; again served on the staff of ComAirBatFor; commanded *Saratoga* (CV–3); and became Assistant Chief of the Bureau of Aeronautics. On 1 June 1939, he was named Chief of the Bureau of Aeronautics with the accompanying rank of rear admiral.

As bureau chief, Towers organized the Navy's aircraft procurement plans while war clouds gathered over the Far East and in the Atlantic. Under his leadership, the air arm of the Navy grew from 2,000 planes in 1939 to 39,000 in 1942. He also instituted a rigorous pilot-training program and established a trained group of reserve officers for ground support duties. During Towers' tenure, the number of men assigned to naval aviation activities reached a high point of some three quarters of a million.

Promoted to vice admiral on 6 October 1942, Towers became Commander, Air Force, Pacific Fleet. From this billet, he wisely and effectively supervised the development, organization, training, and supply of the Fleet's growing aviation capability. For his sound judgment and keen resourcefulness, Towers received, successively, the Legion of Merit Medal and the Distinguished Service Medal.

In August 1945, Towers was given command of the 2d Carrier Task Force and Task Force 38, Pacific Fleet. On 7 November 1945, he broke his flag in *New Jersey* (BB–6) as Commander, 5th Fleet. On 1 February 1946, he hoisted his flag in *Bennington* (CV–20) as Commander in Chief, Pacific Fleet, a post he held until March of 1947.

After chairing the Navy's General Board from March to December 1947, Towers retired on 1 December 1947. After retirement, Towers served as President of the Pacific War Memorial, a New York-based scientific foundation; as assistant to the President of Pan American World Airways; and as President of the Flight Safety Council. Admiral Towers died in St. Albans' hospital, Jamaica, N.Y., on 30 April 1955.

(DDG–9: dp. 3,370; l. 437'; b. 47'; dr. 27'3''; s. 30 k.; cpl. 354; a. 2 5'', Tar., ASROC, 6 21'' tt.; cl. *Charles F. Adams*)

Towers (DDG–9) was laid down on 1 April 1958 at Seattle, Wash., by the Todd Shipyard Corp.; launched on 23 April 1959; sponsored by Mrs. Nathaniel

Rotoreau, Jr.; and commissioned on 6 June 1961 at the Puget Sound Naval Shipyard, Bremerton, Wash., Comdr. L. D. Cummins in command.

Homeported at San Diego, Calif., *Towers* carried out trials and local operations off the southern California coast into September 1961. She then conducted her shakedown cruise to Callao and Lima, Peru; Balboa, Panama Canal Zone; and Acapulco, Mex., before she deployed to the Western Pacific (WestPac) for the first time in the early spring of 1962.

She arrived at Sydney, Australia, on 30 April to represent the United States during the 20th observance of the anniversary of the Battle of the Coral Sea and shifted to Melbourne a week later. She then continued her WestPac deployment with visits to Yokosuka and Sasebo, Japan; Buckner Bay, Okinawa; Subic Bay, Philippines; Keelung, Taiwan; and Bangkok, Thailand. She then returned home via Guam and Hawaii.

Following a routine schedule of local operations out of San Diego from 1 January to 17 May 1963, *Towers* departed her home port on 18 May, bound for the Far East. En route, she stopped at Pearl Harbor and Midway and later took part in exercises and operations off Japan and in the Philippines. She returned to San Diego on 28 November 1963 and operated along the southern California coast through the end of 1964.

Towers departed San Diego on 5 January 1965, bound for her third WestPac tour. As American forces became increasingly involved in the Vietnam War—escalating from an advisory capacity to active combat—the Navy's role in Vietnamese coastal waters expanded. *Towers* participated in three main facets of the 7th Fleet's operations in the Gulf of Tonkin and the South China Sea. She performed screening and plane-guard duties for fast carrier task forces on "Yankee Station," providing protection with her missiles and her rapid-fire 5-inch battery. In addition, she conducted search and rescue (SAR) patrols on the northern station; and made interdiction patrols in conjunction with Operation "Market Time."

Upon the conclusion of this tour, the guided missile destroyer sailed for home on 10 May. En route to the Hawaiian Islands, she participated in Operation "Sailor Hat," a special blast test to determine deficiencies in modern ship construction, and arrived home at San Diego on 26 June.

From 31 January to 6 February 1966, *Towers* participated in Operation "Buttonhook," a joint United States and Canadian exercise off the west coast of Canada and the United States which emphasized anti-submarine warfare (ASW) techniques. Following availability at the Long Beach Naval Shipyard during March, *Towers* took part in Operation "Gray Ghost" from 12 to 22 April. This exercise dealt with air control intercept tactics and antiaircraft warfare (AAW) measures to prepare the ship for her upcoming deployment to the Gulf of Tonkin, off Vietnam. In addition, the ship trained to become proficient in tactics to utilize against possible motor torpedo (PT) boat attacks.

Departing San Diego on 4 June, *Towers* steamed west, via Pearl Harbor, Guam, and Subic Bay, to Vietnam. She expended some 3,266 rounds of 5-inch ammunition between 2 and 17 July, off target areas which included the "Rung Sat Special Zone." Her target assessment included the destruction of 17 enemy buildings and damage to 118 more, the sinking of three sampans, the killing of 11 Viet Cong soldiers, and the destruction of a bridge.

The guided missile destroyer returned to Subic Bay for upkeep and further training in PT-boat countermeasures before she returned to the Gulf of Tonkin to take up her position on the northern SAR station on 1 August. For the next month, she deployed with *Wiltsie* (DD–716), keeping on the alert to spot downed pilots and to direct friendly helicopters to the rescue.

On 6 August, *Towers* directed an HU–16 helicopter to the site of a downed aviator some 69 miles from the ship. The next day, *Towers* directed another HU–16 to a spot behind the enemy-held island of Cac Ba, where two Air Force men had bailed out. The "chopper" successfully rescued them from behind communist lines. In the next two weeks, the ship participated in two more rescues—picking up two more Air Force pilots in one and a Navy flyer in the other.

Towers' most daring rescue came on the last day of her tour on the SAR station. On 31 August, a Navy plane was hit by antiaircraft fire over Haiphong, and the pilot bailed out of his doomed aircraft directly over the enemy harbor. As he floated down under his parachute to face what seemed certain capture, *Towers* and *King* (DLG–10) closed to within visual range of Haiphong harbor. Then *King's* helicopter sped in under the guidance of *Towers'* experienced controllers and picked up the pilot, whisking him out of danger from beneath the enemy's very nose.

After a brief rest and recreation period, *Towers* returned to the SAR station again on 1 October. However, flying weather turned out to be poorer at this time of year, and air operations were sharply curtailed. Hence, *Towers* spent much of her time on this tour patrolling the Tonkin Gulf.

Sailing for home on 21 November, *Towers* departed Yokosuka and ran into heavy seas while en route to the west coast, suffering minor storm damage before she arrived at her home port on 3 December. After operations at sea from January to mid-March, *Towers* underwent a major overhaul at Hunters' Point Naval Shipyard from 14 April to 19 October. The guided missile destroyer then operated out of San Diego through the spring of 1968.

Towers then readied herself for her next WestPac deployment. Her preparation included screening and shore bombardment exercises with *New Jersey* (BB–62), the world's only active battleship. Departing San Diego on 5 September, *Towers* made stops at Pearl Harbor and Subic Bay before arriving off the I Corps tactical zone to commence "Sea Dragon" operations.

While escorting and screening *New Jersey*, *Towers* knocked out two artillery and three antiaircraft gun sites; destroyed 55 meters of trenches; sank two logistics craft; set off 19 secondary explosions; and killed an estimated 10 enemy soldiers. On 1 October, the ship rescued two downed airmen just south of the demilitarized zone (DMZ). The flyers, Capt. James Spaith, USMC, and his observer, 1st Lt. U. S. Grant, USMC, had been shot down when their Douglas A4F "Skyhawk" had been hit while spotting gunfire for *New Jersey*.

Towers furnished gunfire support for South Vietnamese Army units in January 1969 and shelled shore targets for the American 3d Marine Division and the 101st Airborne Division, both north and south of Danang. From her anchorage inside Danang harbor, the guided missile destroyer fired frequent night-harassment and counter-rocket site fire against communist positions in the surrounding countryside. Her damage assessments for this duty included destruction of targets such as troop concentrations, bunkers, footbridges, and supply-carrying sampans.

Following upkeep at Subic Bay, she planeguarded on "Yankee Station" for *Constellation* (CVA–64) and returned to the I Corps operating zone for urgent gunfire support duties. She provided support for Operation "Daring Endeavor," launched to destroy enemy troop concentrations south of Danang. Commended for her part in this action, *Towers* remained on the scene from 17 to 30 November. She again provided anti-rocket support out of Danang from the 21st through the 25th. In addition, she provided gunfire for Korean marines and the Army's 101st Airborne.

Towers then sailed north to the Philippines for upkeep at Subic Bay before proceeding to Singapore for rest and recreation. She arrived back on "Yankee Station" three days before Christmas, to assume the role of escort commander for *Intrepid* (CVS–11). After two days of this duty, however, the guided missile destroyer was back in the IV Corps operating area on night-harassment fire duties against the communist ground forces.

New Year's Day 1970 found the ship still engaging the enemy in the IV Corps' zone, supporting Vietnamese ranger battalions. During this period, *Towers'* 5-inch rifles wreaked havoc upon Viet Cong and North Vietnamese troop concentrations, bunkers, sampans, and footbridges. The ship then spent a few days at Hong Kong before she returned to the "gunline," once more at Danang. She supported the 3d Marine Division, operating north and south of Danang, blasting enemy troops and structures, again in support of Korean marines and the 101st Airborne. During the latter period, she again stood duty at Danang, her guns ready to reply to communist rocket sites.

Shifting again to "Yankee Station," *Towers* joined the screen of *Hancock* (CVA–19) on station with TG 77.5 until 7 February. She then sailed for Subic Bay for three days of upkeep before proceeding on to Yokosuka. Departing Japanese waters on 21 February, *Towers* soon headed east and brought this WestPac deployment to a close when she sailed into San Diego harbor on 4 March.

Towers spent much of the year 1970 on routine local operations in the vicinity of her home port in preparation for future WestPac deployments. On 4 September, while conducting refresher training out of San Diego, the ship directed a helicopter to rescue the pilot from an F–8 "Crusader" that had crashed nearby. The embarked evaluation team from the Fleet Training Group gave the ship a grade of "outstanding" during this "unscheduled evolution."

Deploying again to WestPac on 7 January 1971, *Towers* proceeded to Vietnamese waters, via Pearl Harbor and Midway. While she proceeded west on the 20th, one of the other ships in her convoy, *Roark* (DE–1053), suffered a major engine room fire which stopped her dead in the water. *Towers* turned-to and lent a hand. After the fire was extinguished, the guided missile destroyer took *Roark* in tow until *Quapaw* (ATF–110) arrived and took over the towing.

Towers arrived back on the gunline on 8 February and provided gunfire support until the 21st, when she moved to "Yankee Station" to provide plane-guard service for *Ranger* (CVA–61). On 6 March, a member of the carrier's flight deck force was blown over the side during launching operations. *Towers* quickly sped to the scene, rescued the sailor, and returned him to his ship.

A short visit to Subic Bay followed, as did another tour on the gunline and the northern SAR station. The ship then returned to Subic Bay for upkeep and then made still another tour as plane guard and screen for *Kitty Hawk* (CVA–63). She departed WestPac on 1 July. Arriving at San Diego on the 15th, *Towers* operated out of her home base into the early spring of 1972. Gunnery exercises, underway training evolutions (with emphasis on ASW and AAW tactics); plane-guarding for *Midway* (CVA–41); and an upkeep and inport period all followed as the ship prepared for her upcoming WestPac deployment.

Events in Vietnam, however, forced a change in plan for *Towers* and rapidly accelerated her return to the war zone. Although not scheduled for deployment until September, she departed the west coast on 20 June, bound once more for the gunline. A massive Viet Cong and North Vietnamese assault had battered South Vietnamese forces in key Quang Tri province and resulted in emergency measures for the supporting naval forces offshore. During the voyage from the west coast to the South China Sea, the ship assisted in the rescue of six crewmen from a downed B–52 "Stratofortress" near Guam and received a commendation from the Secretary of the Navy.

A curtailed two-day upkeep period at Subic Bay preceded the ship's sailing on 13 July for the gunline.

Heavy commitments and long hours of gunfire support duty in support of ARVN troops followed from 17 to 28 July as *Towers* participated in Operation "Lamson–72." From 29 July to 5 August, the ship operated on "Linebacker" strikes against targets to the northward of the DMZ, in North Vietnam, as part of Task Unit 77.1.2. On several occasions during this time, she came under fire from communist shore batteries.

The intense gunfire support duties assigned to the ship soon wore out the linings of her two 5-inch guns, so the ship sailed for Sasebo, where she spent the week from 9 to 15 August undergoing a re-gunning. She soon returned to the "gunline" and supported ARVN troops off Hue. The destroyer also fired night "Linebacker" strikes on 24 and 25 September, rounding out the month with gunfire support missions fired for the 1st ARVN division.

A visit to Hong Kong for needed rest and recreation for her crew soon followed, and an upkeep period at Subic Bay preceded the ship's return to Vietnamese waters on 21 October. She supported the ARVN 22d Division near Qui Nhon and around Quang Tri. She then again visited Subic Bay and Kaohsiung, Taiwan, before returning to the gunline again from 3 to 8 December. For the rest of the month, *Towers* fired gunfire support missions against North Vietnamese troop concentrations near Quang Tri. Spirited exchanges of gunfire with enemy shore batteries took place on numerous occasions during this period.

She finished the year 1972 again serving as plane guard for *Constellation* on "Yankee Station" and closed out her gruelling seven-month deployment on the last day of the year, when she sailed for Yokosuka. From there, she returned home via Midway and Pearl Harbor.

This deployment turned out to be the destroyer's last in support of the Vietnam War. The "Vietnamization" plan placed the burden of self-defense on the shoulders of the South Vietnamese, as American land, sea, and air forces were withdrawn from combat in January and February of 1973. *Towers* operated out of San Diego from 1973 through 1976, pursuing a regular schedule of local operations, routine upkeep and overhaul periods, and underway training evolutions.

She departed San Diego on 30 July 1976 for her first extended overseas deployment in three years. She conducted exercises and local operations in the Far East, participating in Exercise "Sharkhunt XVII" with the Taiwanese Navy before shifting to the Indian Ocean for an extended cruise. She then took part in "Midlink 76" with units of the Iranian, Pakistani, British, and American Navies in mid-November before participating in "Multiplex/Missilex-76" with United States 7th Fleet units in the South China Sea.

Following port visits to Hong Kong from 6 to 12 January and Bangkok from 29 January to 4 February 1977, *Towers* engaged in a coordinated ASW exercise, "Sharkhunt XX," with the Taiwanese Navy from 22 to 25 February. She returned to San Diego on 21 March to complete a seven-month, three-week deployment. Post-deployment operations off the west coast were highlighted by a port visit to Vancouver, British Columbia, from 9 to 17 July for the annual Sea Festival. *Towers'* last significant operations at sea for the year occurred during the period 12 to 16 September when she conducted naval gunfire support exercises on the range at San Clemente Island. On 23 September, the guided missile destroyer commenced a four-month availability at San Diego which took her into the new year.

Post-availability trials commenced on 26 January 1978, and *Towers* spent the next nine months evaluating her radar detection and tracking system during numerous at-sea operations for that purpose. On 14 November, the ship got underway for Long Beach where she entered the Naval Shipyard on the 15th for commencement of a regular overhaul which took her into 1979.

Towers received one Navy Unit Commendation, one Meritorious Unit Commendation, and four battle stars for her service in Vietnam.

Towhee

A North American bird of the finch family.

(AM–388: dp. 890; l. 221'1''; b. 32'2''; s. 18.1 k.; cpl. 117; a. 1 3'', 2 40mm.; cl. *Auk*)

Towhee (AM–388) was laid down on 21 March 1944 at Cleveland, Ohio, by the American Shipbuilding Co.; launched on 6 January 1945; sponsored by Mrs. C. E. Conners; and commissioned on 18 May 1945, Lt. T. N. Humble, USNR, in command.

Towhee departed Cleveland on 26 May, bound for the Massachusetts coast, via the Canadian ports of Montreal and Halifax, Nova Scotia, and arrived at Boston on 10 June. The minesweeper remained at this port through 23 July, undergoing a major overhaul, before proceeding to Little Creek, Va., for a continuation of overhaul and shakedown.

Leaving the Norfolk area on 21 September, *Towhee* headed south for Panama, transited the Panama Canal, and joined the Pacific Fleet on 30 September. A short availability at Craig Shipyard, San Pedro, Calif., in October prepared the ship for her departure from the west coast; and she got underway for Pearl Harbor on 3 November and arrived eight days later. On the 21st, the minesweeper departed the Hawaiian Islands, but an engineering casualty on the following day forced her return to Pearl Harbor.

After spending a month under repair, *Towhee* again sailed for Japan on 28 December and proceeded via Eniwetok, Saipan, Guam, and Samar in the Philippines. Escorting YMS's, the minesweeper reached Sasebo on 1 February 1946 and commenced a short availability alongside *Nereus* (AS–17) for voyage repairs.

Departing Sasebo for Saishu To, she spent one week in those waters and then shifted her operations to Tsushima before returning to Sasebo. Assigned as flagship, Task Unit 96.6.2, she participated in part of the gigantic minesweeping operations designed to clear the waters around the Japanese home islands of mines sown during the war and commenced her sweeps in Tsushima Strait on 17 March.

After a month of operations, *Towhee* departed Sasebo on 22 April, bound for the west coast, via Eniwetok and Pearl Harbor. *Towhee* stood into San Diego on 20 May before proceeding on to transit the Panama Canal on 9 June and rejoin the Atlantic Fleet. After a two-day layover at Coco Solo, Canal Zone, the minesweeper got underway north and arrived at Charleston, S.C., on 17 June.

Towhee remained on active duty with the Atlantic Fleet through 1953 and was decommissioned and laid up at Orange, Tex., in March 1954. On 7 February 1955, a fleet-wide redesignation of minecraft resulted in *Towhee* being redesignated as MSF–388. The minesweeper remained inactive through November of 1963. In December of that year, the ship proceeded to Philadelphia for activation and conversion to an oceanographic survey ship to replace *Requisite* (AGS–18). She was recommissioned on 1 April 1964 and redesignated AGS–28. Assigned to Service Force, Atlantic Fleet, and homeported in Norfolk, Va., the ship completed underway training by July at Guantanamo Bay, Cuba. *Towhee* then commenced a series of five oceanographic survey operations through the summer of 1965 before assisting in builder's trials for a nuclear submarine in the late summer.

Navigational difficulties caused a premature return from the ship's sixth survey operation in late October, necessitating a tender availability alongside *Cadmus* (AR–14) before the survey ship departed Norfolk on 6 December and deployed once more for survey operations in the western Atlantic.

The ship remained with the Atlantic Fleet through May 1966, when she underwent a tender availability alongside *Amphion* (AR–13) to prepare for shifting her operations back to the Pacific. Upon completion of the tender availability, *Towhee* entered the Norfolk Naval Shipyard for installation of new communications equipment and air conditioning. She departed the shipyard on 1 July and the Norfolk area six days later, bound for Pearl Harbor. After stopovers at the Canal Zone and at Mazatlan, Mex., *Towhee* made port at Pearl Harbor on 12 August.

Assigned to ServRon 5, the oceanographic survey vessel underwent voyage repairs soon after arriving in Hawaiian waters and continued availability through September. From 18 October to 5 November, the ship conducted underway training operations and refresher training. On 9 November, the ship got underway for her first Far Eastern deployment.

After layovers at Guam in the Marianas and at Subic Bay in the Philippines, *Towhee* dropped anchor in Touraine Bay, off Danang, South Vietnam, on 9 December. Survey operations conducted between the time of her arrival and her departure on 12 January 1967 were frequently hampered by gale winds and high seas. The ship subsequently returned, via Subic Bay and Guam, to Hawaiian waters and reached Pearl Harbor on 6 February.

Following a survey in the vicinity of Midway Island, the ship entered the naval shipyard at Pearl Harbor for 10 days of upkeep. *Towhee* then conducted underway training prior to entering *ARD–30* for routine predeployment underwater hull inspection. On 18 September, *Towhee* departed Pearl Harbor, bound for the ship's second WestPac deployment, and stopped briefly at Guam en route to the Gulf of Thailand. Arriving off the western coast of Vietnam for survey operations during the latter part of October, *Towhee*'s operations continued into December, when she made a visit to Bangkok, Thailand, over Christmas 1967. *Towhee* headed for Hawaii in April and conducted local operations in the Hawaiian area until 25 November 1968, when the survey ship headed for the west coast.

Towhee underwent a material inspection on 19 and 20 March 1969 at the conclusion of her west coast deployment, and the surveying board found the ship unfit for further service. *Towhee* was decommissioned on 30 April 1969, and custody was transferred to the Inactive Ship Facility at Vallejo, Calif. On 1 May 1969, *Towhee* was struck from the Navy list and sold to the Learner Co. of Oakland, Calif., on 6 March 1970, for scrapping.

Towle, Private John R., see *Private John R. Towle.*

Towner

A county in North Dakota named for Oscar M. Towner, a prominent farmer, land owner, and political leader of the Dakota Territory. Towner—born in 1842—served in the territorial legislature. He died in 1897.

(AKA–77: dp. 13,910; l. 459'2''; b. 63'0''; dr. 26'4''; s. 16.5 k. (tl.); cpl. 395; a. 1 5'', 8 40mm.; cl. *Tolland*; T. C2–S–AJ3)

Towner (AKA–77) was laid down under Maritime Commission contract (MC hull 1383) on 8 April 1944 at Wilmington, N.C., by the North Carolina Shipbuilding Corp.; launched on 13 June 1944; sponsored by Mrs. Harold Broudy; acquired by the Navy from the War Shipping Administration on 27 June 1944; and commissioned on 3 December 1944, Comdr. Robert P. Erdman in command.

Following shakedown training in the Chesapeake Bay area from 14 to 23 December, the attack cargo ship loaded cargo at Bayonne, N.J., and, with *Sheliak* (AKA–62), got underway on 4 January 1945 for the Pacific. The two ships transited the Panama Canal on 10 January and headed for Hawaii the next day, arriving at Pearl Harbor on the 25th.

Towner stood out to sea again on 9 February bound for New Caledonia and arrived at Noumea 10 days later. For the next two and one-half months, she made shuttle runs to Uarai Bay and participated in amphibious training exercises. In late April, *Towner* loaded elements of the 710th Tank Battalion and, with Transport Division 33, sortied on 3 May for the Philippines. She unloaded at Dulag on the 16th and reported to the 7th Fleet the following week. On 27 May, she sailed independently, via Hollandia, to Milne Bay to load a deck cargo of boats which she delivered to Manus. In early June, she loaded base hospital units at Lae for transportation to the Philippines and unloaded them at Manila on the 16th. From mid-June to mid-October, she shuttled troops and cargo from New Guinea to the Philippines.

On 26 August, *Towner* joined the Transport Division of the 3d Amphibious Force at Cebu to assist in carrying troops and equipment of the Americal Division to Japan. The convoy sortied on 1 September and arrived at Yokohama a week later. *Towner* discharged her troops and cargo and was back in the Philippines on the 17th. In early October, she made another round-trip to Tokyo Bay. The cargo ship departed Leyte on 24 October and, after calling at Okinawa and Taku, arrived at Tsingtao on 17 November. On 2 December 1945, *Towner* proceeded—via Guam, Guadalcanal, the Russells, and Hawaii—to the United States.

Towner arrived at Seattle on 25 January 1946 and entered the Bremerton Naval Shipyard for voyage repairs. She got underway for the east coast on 19 March and arrived at Norfolk on 10 April. *Towner* was decommissioned on 10 June 1946, returned to the War Shipping Administration on 13 June, and was struck from the Navy list on 19 June 1946.

Townsend

A sound off the coast of New Jersey.

———

Construction of *Townsend* (AV–18)—a *Kenneth Whiting*-class seaplane tender—was originally assigned to the Philadelphia Navy Yard but was cancelled on 14 November 1944. A contract for building the ship was awarded to the Todd Pacific Shipyard, Tacoma, Wash., on 1 December 1944; and her keel was laid down on 30 June 1945. However, the contract was terminated on 11 August 1945.

Toxaway

(MB: t. 9; l. 52'; b. 11'3''; dr. 2'6'' (mean); s. 13.8 k.; cpl. 9; a. 1-1pdr., 1 mg.)

Toxaway—a wooden-hull motorboat built in 1917 at Morris Heights, N.Y., by the Gas Engine and Power Co. and the Charles L. Seabury Co.—was acquired by the Navy on 9 June 1917 from J. H. Nunnally. Designated SP–743, the boat was commissioned on 12 June 1917, attached to the 2d Naval District, and operated out of Newport, R.I., on section patrol through the Armistice. On 2 December 1918, *Toxaway* was returned to her owner.

Trabajador

(Tug: dp. 148; l. 111'; b. 26'1''; dr. 10'6'')

Trabajador—a tug completed in 1931 at Hong Kong, British Crown Colony, by the Hong Kong and Whampoa Dock Co., Ltd.—was taken over by the Navy from the Visayan Stevedore-Transportation Co., and was assigned to the 16th Naval District on 13 December 1941, Lt. (jg.) Trose E. Donaldson, USNR, in command.

Trabajador—misspelled as *Trobagador* in the correspondence establishing the Inshore Patrol—operated in Manila Bay with the Base Section of the Inshore Patrol from the day of her "commissioning" until her loss the following spring. In his book, *They Were Expendable*, William L. White credits *Trabajador* with serving for a time at Sisiman Cove, Bataan, as the tender to Motor Torpedo Boat Squadron 3, prior to the withdrawal by American and Filipino forces from that beleaguered peninsula.

Trabajador was ultimately sunk off Corregidor, probably by Japanese artillery fire coming from Bataan, and remained on the bottom of Manila Bay until well after World War II ended. She was subsequently raised, repaired, and renamed *Resolute*. She apparently remained in operation as a tug, in the Philippines, into the late 1970's.

Trabajador received one battle star for her World War II service.

Tracer

(AGR–15: dp. 10,710 (f.); l. 441'6''; b. 57'¼''; dr. 22' (mean); s. 11 k.; cpl. 151; a. 2 3''; cl. *Guardian*; T. Z–EC2–S–C5)

William J. Riddle—a "Liberty ship"—was laid down under a Maritime Commission contract (MC hull E–2340) on 24 December 1944 at Panama City, Fla., by the J. A. Jones Construction Co., Inc.; launched on 31 January 1945; sponsored by Mrs. Marion Harders; and, upon completion in early 1945, was delivered to the War Shipping Administration, Maritime Commission.

William J. Riddle operated with Moore-McCormack Lines and the Waterman Steamship Corp. from 1945

A prewar view of *Toxaway* (SP–743). (NH 84930)

to 1947. When hostilities ended in the Far East in mid-August 1945, the "Liberty ship" was steaming from Hawaii to the Philippines. Converted to a cattle carrier the following year, she operated as such through the end of 1946. Changed back to a dry cargo carrier by March of 1947, she voyaged to European and Mediterranean ports until the summer of 1947 when she was laid up in the Maritime Commission's National Defense Reserve Fleet and berthed in the James River, Va. She remained there for 10 years.

The Navy selected *William J. Riddle* for conversion to a radar picket ship in May of 1957. Towed to the Charleston (S.C.) Naval Shipyard soon thereafter, conversion work began on 24 May 1957. Renamed *Interrupter*, and classified as AGR–15, the erstwhile "Liberty" was commissioned at Charleston 16 October 1958, Lt. Comdr. George S. Harrison in command.

Following shakedown in Guantanamo Bay, Cuba, and post-shakedown availability at her conversion yard, *Interrupter* sailed for the Pacific. She transited the Panama Canal on 26 January 1959 and arrived at her home port, San Francisco, Calif., on 12 February, the sixth AGR to join newly formed Radar Picket Squadron 1.

Fitted out with the latest radar detection equipment, *Interrupter* and her seven *Guardian*-class sister ships were designed to serve as the seaborne eyes of the North American Air Defense Command—the naval link in the chain of early-warning stations covering the Pacific approaches to the United States. Her mission was to "detect, report, and track enemy airborne threats approaching by overseas routes and to control the intercepts used to destroy such threats."

Before putting to sea for her first patrol, she conducted training evolutions with Air Force officers embarked on board for familiarization with the ship's mission. In addition, *Interrupter*'s officers and men familiarized themselves with the Air Force's part in this vital mission. On 6 March 1959, *Interrupter* sailed from San Francisco on her first barrier patrol.

On 4 September 1959, *Interrupter* was renamed *Tracer* to eliminate confusion with some of her sister ships with similarly sounding names.

Between 1959 and 1965, *Tracer* conducted patrols at sea, at various picket stations in the Western Contiguous Radar Line. The ship proved to be an efficient vessel and received awards for administrative and operational efficiency on several occasions. As more sophisticated early-warning systems came into operational use, the need for the AGR's diminished accordingly. Deactivated in 1965, *Tracer*'s name was struck from the Navy list on 1 September 1965. She was then transferred to the Maritime Commission and laid up at Suisun Bay, Calif., where she remained through the late 1960's.

Tracker

Tracker (BAVG–6) was laid down on 3 November 1941 at Seattle-Tacoma, Wash., by the Seattle-Tacoma Shipbuilding Corp.; launched on 7 March 1942; and transferred to the United Kingdom on 31 January 1943 under the provisions of the lend-lease agreement.

Designated by the British as a "Ruler"-class aircraft escort vessel, she served in the North Atlantic, operating mostly east of Newfoundland protecting merchant convoys from predatory German submarine wolfpacks. Early in 1944, she moved to the Arctic to escort Allied convoys on the dangerous run to the Soviet Union. As part of an augmented escort group designed to discourage aggressive German submarines, she helped to protect convoy JW 58 which sailed for Russia late in March. On the eastward voyage, planes from *Tracker* assisted in the sinking of German submarines *U–355* and *U–288*, bringing to four the number of submarines sunk by the convoy's escort. The fine performance of *Tracker*'s aircraft helped to prove the soundness of a new air organization and tactics introduced on this convoy.

Participating in the invasion of Normandy in June 1944, *Tracker* served the Royal Navy through the end of World War II and was returned to the United States on 29 November 1945. She was later sold to Rio de la Plata S.A. de Navigacion de Ultramar, Buenos Aires; and, from 1950 until 1964, operated as an oiler under Argentine registry. She was scrapped in August 1964.

Tracy

Born on 5 April 1830, near Oswego, N.Y., Benjamin Franklin Tracy was reared on a farm and educated at Oswego Academy. Admitted to the New York Bar in 1851, Tracy served as district attorney of Tioga County, N.Y., from 1853 to 1859. Elected to the State Assembly in 1861, he urged full support of the national government in the Civil War.

In the summer of 1862, Tracy raised the 109th and 137th New York Volunteer regiments and took the field as a colonel with the former. During the bloody Wilderness Campaign in the spring of 1864, he led his troops with conspicuous gallantry. Tracy's bravery and steadfastness in the arduous and difficult campaign won him the brevet rank of Brigadier-General and the Medal of Honor.

For the remainder of the war, Tracy served as a colonel in the 127th Regiment and commanded the military prison and the recruiting camp at Elmira, N.Y.

In 1866, after the end of the Civil War, President Andrew Johnson appointed Tracy district attorney for the eastern district of New York. In 1873, he resumed his private practice in Brooklyn, N.Y. From 1881 to 1882, he assumed duties as judge of the New York Court of Appeals.

In 1889, President Benjamin Harrison appointed the lawyer to the post of Secretary of the Navy. He entered at once into the program of building up the Navy with new, modern ships and of enacting much-needed reforms. During his administration, battleships *Iowa*, *Indiana*, *Massachusetts*, and *Oregon* and cruiser *Brooklyn* were completed or authorized. He also organized the naval militia and established the Board of Construction and Repair to correlate the work of various bureaus.

Following an active career in public service and leaving the Navy in better shape than he had found it upon taking office as Secretary, Tracy retired to his Tioga County farm where he raised horses until his death on 6 August 1915.

(DD–214: dp. 1,308; l. 314'4½"; b. 30'11"; dr. 9'9"; s. 35.0 k.; cpl. 132; a. 4 4", 1 3", 12 21" tt.; cl. *Clemson*)

Tracy (DD–214) was laid down on 3 April 1919 at Philadelphia, Pa., by the William Cramp and Sons' Shipyard; launched on 13 August 1919; sponsored by Mrs. Frank B. Tracy; and commissioned on 9 March 1920, Comdr. Lawrence P. Treadwell in command.

Following commissioning, Tracy cruised on shakedown to the Dry Tortugas before returning to Philadelphia. She steamed with Destroyer Division (DesDiv) 39 for duty in the Near East, arriving at Constantinople, Turkey, in early June 1920.

With the troubled international situation in the Near East, American naval forces "showed the flag" and stood ready to protect American lives and property. *Tracy* touched at principal Black Sea ports and also visited cities along the coasts of Palestine and Egypt, as well as Mediterranean Turkey.

As the bloody civil war cast its dark shadow over Russia and the Bolsheviks swept all before them, the White Russians were forced to evacuate. *Tracy* was one of the ships which embarked hundreds of refugees at Sevastopol and carried them to Constantinople.

In June 1921, she sailed with her division for the Far East, transiting the Suez Canal and touching at ports in India, Ceylon, French Indochina, and Java before finally reaching Manila late in August 1921.

Tracy initially operated independently with the South China Patrol and "showed the flag" at the ports upon which she called. Detached from this duty in the spring of 1923, she steamed to Japan for a goodwill cruise before proceeding to Chefoo for summer maneuvers.

Anchored at Dairen, Manchuria, in early September 1923, *Tracy* received orders to get underway immediately for Yokohama, Japan, which had been rocked by a severe earthquake. Upon arrival, she participated in the initial relief work there and carried refugees from Yokohama to Tokyo. She sent repair parties ashore to assist in laying fresh water lines and remained in the Yokohama area for two weeks before heading for Shanghai.

There, her landing party went ashore to guard the American-owned Shanghai Light and Power Company until relieved on 12 October 1923 by a force from armored cruiser *Huron*. Proceeding to Manila, she spent some time in that port before commencing a cruise to southern Philippine ports on 26 November. For the remainder of her tour in the Asiatic Fleet, she carried out flag-showing cruises and exercises before departing for the United States on 8 May 1925. At Midway, her division was relieved by DesDiv 39.

Arriving in San Diego, Calif., on 17 June, *Tracy* was refitted and received new fire-control instruments. She departed the west coast on 24 June and proceeded, via the Panama Canal, to New York City. Spending the next two years with the Scouting Fleet, *Tracy* wound up her tour by taking part in the reinforcement operations for the Special Service Squadron in Nicaraguan waters during the revolution and civil strife which had broken out in that country in November and December 1926.

Following overhaul by the Norfolk Navy Yard, *Tracy* returned briefly to Nicaraguan waters in March 1927 and then proceeded north. Steaming from Newport, R.I., on 1 June with DesDiv 38, she visited Queenstown, Northern Ireland, before touching at ports in Scotland, England, Belgium, France, Portugal, Spain, Algeria, Tunisia, and Italy. Departing Gibraltar on 28 January 1928, she operated in the Atlantic for one month before orders transferred DesDiv 38 to the Battle Fleet. Based at San Diego from 1 April 1928 until the spring of 1929, *Tracy* served on occasion as plane guard destroyer with *Lexington* (CV-2) and *Saratoga* (CV-3) before preparing at Mare Island Navy Yard, in June and July 1929, for duty in the Far East.

DesDiv 38 relieved DesDiv 45 at Pearl Harbor, Hawaii, and then proceeded to Japan for a goodwill visit, arriving at Yokohama on 26 August 1929.

In accordance with the Asiatic Fleet's routine, *Tracy* alternated duty in China ports in the summer with operations in the Philippines during the winter. The months in between were spent in cruises along the Chinese coast, engaged in "showing the flag" and exercises. During the fall of 1930, after a cruise to the Netherlands East Indies, she was fitted out for extended independent duties as station ship, Chefoo, China.

Japan's seizure of Manchuria in September 1931 and the fighting between Japanese and Chinese forces around Shanghai in February 1932 enlivened the Asiatic Fleet's duty at this juncture; but *Tracy's* activities were limited to keeping a watchful eye on American interests. Later in the year, the destroyer received orders assigning her once again to the Battle Force, and she left the Asiatic Fleet for the last time.

Tracy took part in maneuvers and exercises in the Pacific and off the west coast before being reclassified as a destroyer-minelayer and redesignated DM-19 on 30 June 1937. *Tracy* was then assigned to Mine Division 1 and operated out of Pearl Harbor with the Battle Force.

In late 1941, her division entered the navy yard at Pearl Harbor for overhaul. On 7 December 1941, *Tracy* lay at berth 15 of the yard with her machinery, boilers, and guns dismantled. Most of her complement were living in the receiving barracks ashore, and only a skeleton crew was on board. As Japanese planes swept overhead, *Tracy's* crew boarded their ship and sought to find ways to fight back.

Some sailors went to *Cummings* (DD-376) and helped to man her guns; others boarded *Pennsylvania* (BB-38) and assisted in fighting the battleship's antiaircraft batteries. Meanwhile, back on board *Tracy*, the remaining destroyermen, after assembling three .30-caliber Lewis guns and two .50-caliber Brownings, did their best to drive off the attackers. When the raid ended, a party of 10 men from the destroyer minesweeper assisted in fighting fires raging on board stricken *California* (BB-44).

Following the interrupted overhaul at the navy yard, *Tracy* went to sea to commence wartime operations. On 31 March 1942, she assisted in laying a minefield near French Frigate Shoals before returning to Pearl Harbor and conducting local operations. She then headed for Suva, in the Fiji Islands, on 23 July. Seven days later, in company with *Breese* (DM-18) and *Gamble* (DM-15), *Tracy* arrived at Suva before proceeding from there to Espiritu Santo.

At bases in the Southwest Pacific, American forces prepared for their first amphibious thrust of the war, aimed at the Solomon Islands. *Tracy*, in Task Force (TF) 62, arrived off the beaches of Guadalcanal on 7 August, as the guns of American cruisers and destroyers awoke the Japanese to a thundering reveille. She took part in the bitterly fought campaign for the islands in the Solomons, engaged in the unglamorous but vital tasks of escort duty and antisubmarine patrol. She operated between Espiritu Santo and the battle zones through the summer and fall of 1942 before returning to Pearl Harbor in December for a brief refit. On 18 December. she set out for New Caledonia, escorting a west-bound convoy, and arrived with her charges at Noumea on 2 January 1943.

Designated a unit in TF 66, she operated out of Noumea and Nandi, on occasion engaged in laying minefields around the American and Allied bases. She also delivered much-needed gasoline to Henderson Field, on Guadalcanal, for the aircraft of the "Cactus Air Force," whose planes carried the battle to the enemy from the air.

By late January 1943, the Japanese had decided to abandon Guadalcanal and had begun to evacuate as many men as could be plucked from the steamy island and ferried through the gauntlet of American sea and air power. Increased enemy surface activity with corresponding air cover tipped off the Americans that major Japanese troop movements were afoot; and orders went out to try to derail the "Tokyo Express" by any means possible—mines, PT-boats, and air strikes.

On 1 February 1943, a large force of Japanese destroyers was sighted heading for "Ironbottom Sound." *Tracy*, as task group leader, led *Montgomery* (DM-17) and *Preble* (DM-20) in laying a field of 300 mines between Doma Reef and Cape Esperance. That night, Japanese destroyer *Makigumo* struck one of these mines and was damaged so badly that she was scuttled. Nevertheless, the Japanese managed to extricate the remnants of their garrison from Guadalcanal.

Following this action, *Tracy* rejoined TF 62 for escort duty and touched at Noumea, Tulagi, and Efate before heading for Hawaii on 19 April. She reached Pearl Harbor on 1 May and, 11 days later, headed toward San Francisco for a much-needed overhaul at Mare Island.

After refitting, *Tracy* departed San Francisco on 22 May and spent the next few months engaged in "milk runs"—convoys between the Hawaiian islands and the west coast. On 10 August, she departed Pearl

Harbor and steamed to Samoa and thence set her course toward Espiritu Santo and the South Pacific.

At the end of November 1943, *Tracy* led a division of minelayers in placing an offensive minefield near Bougainville in preparations for the landings there.

Next, operating out of Noumea for the remainder of 1943, *Tracy* called at Funafuti, Espiritu Santo, and Guadalcanal through December. On 1 January 1944, she steamed in convoy with *President Jackson* (AP–37), *President Hayes* (AP–39), *President Adams* (AP–38), *Titania* (AK–55), and *Alhena* (AK–26) to the Fiji Islands, arriving at Nandi on 5 January.

Underway again the following day, *Tracy* escorted another convoy to Guadalcanal, conducting gunnery exercises en route, and arrived on the 10th. Later in the month, she departed Efate, New Hebrides, bound for New Caledonia in company with *President Hayes*. During the passage, they fought through a storm before arriving at Noumea on the 19th. Upon the completion of refueling there, she proceeded to Wellington, New Zealand. For the remainder of January and continuing into May, she threaded her way among the Pacific isles, escorting convoys and carrying out exercises en route.

On 3 June, she arrived in San Francisco to commence overhaul at Hunters Point. Upon conclusion of the yard work, *Tracy* underwent refresher training off the west coast, ranging as far north as Seattle and Bremerton, Wash. On 31 August, she departed Seattle in company with SS *Cushman K. Davis*, bound for Oahu, and arrived at Pearl Harbor on 9 September.

After a navy yard availability from 12 to 24 September, she got underway on the 29th, bound for the Marshalls in company with Convoy BD–110T. Arriving at Eniwetok on 8 October, she commenced further convoy runs between Eniwetok and Pearl Harbor; and Pearl Harbor and San Francisco; arriving back on the west coast on 6 November 1944. Following a brief layover in San Diego, *Tracy*'s bow headed west toward Honolulu, before escorting another eastbound convoy back to San Francisco.

With Iwo Jima secured, the Navy then turned its attention to Okinawa, with *Tracy* taking part in this action as well, serving as buoy-laying and mine disposal vessel, arriving off that island on 1 April 1945. While in support of the Okinawa invasion, she engaged in antisubmarine and antismall boat patrols off the Fleet anchorages. While operating in this vital screening duty, she rescued survivors from *LCI(G)–82* which had been hit by a Japanese suicide motorboat. In a period of heavy air activities, when many a ship writhed in agony after being struck by the *kamikaze*, *Tracy* bore a charmed life, emerging from the arduous Okinawa campaign unscathed. She departed for Ulithi on 16 April and arrived on 22 April at the sprawling atoll to commence a period of upkeep and availability which lasted until 2 May. Continuing operations in the western Pacific, she took part in convoy escort duties through July, when she escorted an LST convoy from Okinawa to Leyte, anchoring in San Pedro Bay, Leyte, P.I., on 3 July. From 5 to 17 July, she underwent tender availability before entering floating drydock *ARD–2* for hull repairs.

Under the operational control of Minecraft, Pacific Fleet, she anchored at San Pedro Bay through the middle of August. On 10 August, her radio picked up an unofficial Japanese broadcast which announced that Japan had agreed to accept unconditional surrender terms. *Tracy*'s log noted: "Much blowing of whistles and searchlight displays by Fleet units present."

On 15 August, she got underway as part of the screen for TU 72.5.38; and, while en route to Okinawa, she received word to cease all offensive activities. Entering Buckner Bay, Okinawa, on 20 August, she lay at anchor for five days before transferring Mark VI buoys from *Weehawken* (CM–12) to various other fast minesweepers gathering to commence the job of sweeping up the mines sown during the war.

The end of the war in the Pacific in August marked only the beginning of *Tracy*'s participation in the gigantic minesweeping efforts in Japanese home waters. From Buckner Bay, the ship proceeded to Japan, and she arrived in Nagasaki Wan on 11 September, one of the first Allied ships to enter that expanse of water. She served as buoy-laying and mine-disposal vessel during the minesweeping operations which cleared the sea lanes outside of that key seaport and continued these duties until late in October, when she sailed for home.

Her career as a fighting ship in the United States Navy all but over, *Tracy* pointed her bow towards home on 25 October and called briefly at Buckner Bay en route to Pearl Harbor. Arriving at the Hawaiian base in mid-November, she departed there on the 18th, bound —via San Diego, Calif., and Salina Cruz, Mexico—for the Panama Canal. She arrived at New York in December 1945 and was decommissioned on 19 January 1946. Struck from the Navy list on 7 February 1946, she was sold to the Northern Metals Company of Philadelphia, Pa., and scrapped later in the year.

Tracy received seven battle stars for her World War II service.

Traffic

(dp. 280; lbp. 106'0''; b. 29'4''; dr. 9'0'' (mean); s. 10 k.)

Traffic—a wooden-hulled, derrick-rigged, freight steamer constructed in 1891 by D. McCarty at South Brooklyn, N.Y.—was apparently placed in commission at New York sometime in 1894. She spent her entire 30-year Navy career at the New York Navy Yard transporting passengers and freight between ships and shore. On occasion, she also doubled as a tug.

On 9 May 1922, *Traffic* was placed out of commission. However, it would appear that she continued to serve at the New York Navy Yard until 1924, because her replacement, *Transfer*, was not activated until then. *Traffic*'s name was struck from the Navy list on 29 January 1924. On 15 April 1924, she was sold to Joseph F. O'Boyle of New York City.

Tramp

(SP–646: l. 82'; b. 10'6''; dr. 2'8'' (mean); s. 20 k.; cpl. 10; a. none)

Tramp—a wooden-hulled steam yacht built in 1901 at Bristol, R.I., by the Herreshoff Manufacturing Co. —was acquired by the Navy on 13 July 1917 from Raymond B. Price of New York City. Designated SP–646, *Tramp* was assigned to the 2d Naval District and served on section patrol through the end of World War I. On 28 March 1919, *Tramp* was sold to Thomas Butler and Company, Boston, Mass.

Tranquillity

(AH–14: dp. 15,400; l. 520'0''; b. 71'6''; dr. 24'0''; s. 17.5 k. (tl.); cpl. 568; cl. *Haven*; T. C4–S–B2)

Tranquillity (AH–14) was laid down under Maritime Commission contract (MC hull 745) as *Marine Dolphin* on 20 August 1943 at Chester, Pa., by the Sun Shipbuilding & Drydock Co.; renamed *Tranquillity* on 22 June 1944; launched on 25 July 1944; sponsored by Miss Carol P. Meekins; acquired by the Navy from the Maritime Commission on 14 August 1944; converted into a hospital ship at New York City by the Atlantic Basin Iron Works; and commissioned on 24 April 1945, Capt. Merrittt D. Mullen, USNR, in command.

The hospital ship got underway for Hampton Roads on 5 May and arrived at Norfolk the next morning.

Tramp (SP–646) before her acquisition by the Navy.   (NH 84931)

Following shakedown training from 8 to 18 May and a short yard period for alterations, she stood out to sea on 6 June, bound for Hawaii; transited the Panama Canal on 14 June; and arrived at Pearl Harbor on the 27th to join the Service Force, Pacific Fleet.

On 11 July, *Tranquillity* proceeded to Ulithi and served as the base hospital ship from 22 July to 3 August. On the latter date, she was sent to the Palaus to take on board the survivors from cruiser *Indianapolis* (CA–35) which had been sunk by a Japanese submarine several days earlier. She arrived at Peleliu the next morning; embarked 166 survivors; and headed for Guam where the patients were disembarked on the 8th.

Tranquillity returned to Ulithi on 10 August but was ordered to sea the next day to rendezvous with the 3d Fleet some 350 miles off the coast of Japan. Following a fortnight with the 3d Fleet, the hospital ship headed for Guam. On the 27th, she took on 766 patients at Apra Harbor and stood out for the United States. She disembarked the patients at San Francisco on 11 September and then returned to Hawaii, arriving at Pearl Harbor on the 26th. She was attached to the "Magic-Carpet" Fleet, returning armed forces personnel from overseas bases to the United States. The ship arrived at Guam on 18 October, picked up 788 patients, and disembarked them at San Francisco on 3 November. On 9 November, the ship was reclassified as a hospital transport and redesignated APH–114. The ship made two more voyages with the "Magic-Carpet" Fleet and returned to San Francisco on 30 January 1946.

Tranquility got underway for the east coast on 18 February and arrived at Philadelphia on 22 March. Three days later, she was redesignated AH–14. *Tranquillity* was placed out of commission, in reserve, on 26 July 1946 and struck from the Navy list on 1 September 1961.

Tranquillity received one battle star for World War II service.

Transfer

(Self Propelled Lighter: dp. 700; l. 110'0''; b. 30'0''; dr. 10'0''; s. 8 k.)

Transfer—a steam-propelled, derrick-rigged, freight lighter—was laid down on 18 August 1904 at the New York Navy Yard; launched on 24 May 1905; and placed in sevice at New York on 19 July 1910.

Transfer spent her entire Navy career in the 3d Naval District assigned to the New York Navy Yard. Though initially carried on the Navy list as a tug, she performed all varied duties of a freight lighter, primarily transporting people, cargo, stores, and other items between ships and shore.

Records documenting the milestones of the ship's career are sparse; but we can assume that she was commissioned sometime during her first dozen years of service since documents indicate that she was decommissioned on 6 October 1922. She remained in that status until 6 February 1924 when she was recommissioned to replace *Traffic*. Ten years later, *YF–211* took over her duties; and *Transfer* was decommissioned once again on 8 February 1934.

Transfer apparently remained out of commission for the remainder of her career, though in all probability, she continued to serve the Navy. Little is known of her service, but her boiler plant provided heat to cruisers *Honolulu* (CL–48) and *Helena* (CL–50) during the winter of 1938 and 1939 while the former underwent post-shakedown availability and the latter completed construction. On 8 March 1941, *Transfer* received the alpha-numeric designation, IX–46. *Transfer's* name was struck from the Navy list on 16 September 1945 as a result of an inspection and survey. In January 1945, the Commandant, 3d Naval District, was authorized to dispose of her and sold her for scrapping on 8 April 1945.

Trapper

(ACM–9: dp. 1,320; l. 188'2''; b. 37'0''; dr. 12'6''; s. 12.5 k (tl.); cpl. 69; a. 1 40mm.; cl. *Chimo*)

Trapper (ACM–9) was built for the United States Army as *Maj. Gen. Arthur Murray* at Point Pleasant, W. Va., by the Marietta Manufacturing Co.; acquired by the Navy on 2 January 1945; converted into an auxiliary minelayer by the Navy Yard, Charleston, S.C.; and commissioned on 15 March 1945, Lt. Richard E. Lewis, USNR, in command.

After shakedown training in the Chesapeake Bay area during April, *Trapper* got underway on 11 June and proceeded—via Manzanillo, the Panama Canal, and San Diego—to the Pacific war zone. In mid-August, while the minelayer was en route to Hawaii, Japan capitulated. The ship arrived at Pearl Harbor on 21 August and was routed westward, via Eniwetok, Saipan, and Okinawa, to Japan.

Trapper arrived at Kobe on 25 November 1945 and operated out of that port repairing minesweeping gear until 1 February 1946 when she shifted her base of operations to Wakayama for a month. On 11 March, the minelayer got underway for the United States. En route, she called at Saipan, Eniwetok, Kwajalein, Johnston, and Hawaii before arriving at San Francisco on 2 May. *Trapper* was decommissioned and transferred to the United States Coast Guard on 20 June 1946 and struck from the Navy list on 19 July 1946.

The former auxiliary minelayer served with the Coast Guard until early 1959 as *Yamacraw* (WARC–333). She was reacquired by the United States Navy on 17 April 1959 and commissioned at New York on 30 April as ARC–5, a cable repair ship.

Yamacraw was assigned to the 3d Naval District for the next six years. She operated from Portsmouth, N.H., to Bermuda and spent much of her at-sea time conducting research projects for the Office of Naval Research and for the Bell Telephone Laboratories.

On 2 July 1965, *Yamacraw* was decommissioned, transferred to the permanent custody of the Maritime Administration, and struck from the Navy list.

Trathen

James Trathen—born at sea off the coast of Maine on 28 August 1811—entered the Navy as an Acting Volunteer Lieutenant on 26 August 1861. Assigned to command bark *Midnight*, he took his ship south in November 1861 for duty with the Gulf Blockading Squadron. Patrolling off the coast of Texas—independently for a large part of the time—*Midnight* from time to time bombarded Confederate positions ashore. With only a two-week rest period at Key West in June 1862, Trathen's bark remained on blockade duty through August, when she was ordered north.

Subsequently assuming command of the steamer *Mount Vernon*, Trathen joined the North Atlantic Blockading Squadron in October 1862. Patrolling off Wilmington, N.C., his ship apprehended eight merchantmen of various registries trying to run the cordon of Union ships off the Confederacy's shores. On 31 July 1863, under the heavy guns of Fort Fisher, Trathen daringly captured the steamer *Kate*. On 16 May 1865, he was promoted to lieutenant commander.

After returning to civilian life on 26 May 1866, Trathen died in Washington, D.C., on 19 June 1903.

(DD–530: dp. 2,050; l. 376′2″; b. 39′7″; dr. 17′9″; s. 35.5 k.; cpl. 273; a. 5 5″, 10 40mm., 7 20mm., 10 21″ tt., 6 dcp., 2 dct.; cl. *Fletcher*)

Trathen (DD–530) was laid down on 17 March 1942 at San Francisco, Calif., by the Bethlehem Steel Co.; launched on 22 October 1942; sponsored by Mrs. Cassin Young, wife of Capt. Cassin Young who was awarded the Medal of Honor for his valor as commanding officer of *Vestal* (AR–4) during the Japanese attack on Pearl Harbor; and commissioned on 28 May 1943, Comdr. Alvoord J. Greenacre in command.

Following training operations in the Hawaiian area, *Trathen* joined Rear Admiral Willis A. "Ching" Lee's Task Force (TF) 11 to take part in the reoccupation of Baker Island. The target isle, a tiny elliptical speck of land, lay nearer to the Japanese-held northern Gilberts than Funafuti in the Ellice group and presented a valuable staging area for projected aerial search and photo reconnaissance missions against the Japanese mandates. Lee, in *Hercules* (AK–41), led TF 11's sortie from Pearl Harbor on 25 August 1943, and his ships arrived off Baker on 1 September. While the transports and *Ashland* (LSD–1) disembarked their troops and disgorged their cargoes shoreward, *Trathen* stood by and provided fighter-direction services to the Grumman F6F Hellcats from *Belleau Wood* (CVL–24) and *Princeton* (CVL–23). During the action, the destroyer directed the F6F's to a radar contact 32 miles away. They soon came upon the snooping Kawanishi "Emily" flying boat and dispatched her so fast that no radio report from the Japanese got out over the airwaves. Two days later, *Trathen* again vectored the Hellcats to another "Emily" which they also splashed into the sea.

With Baker secure and the priceless airfield constructed and ready for use by 11 September, *Trathen* headed for Hawaii. On 29 September, the ship commenced screening operations for Task Group (TG)

14.5, as it sortied from Pearl Harbor, bound for Wake Island. Under the command of Rear Admiral Alfred E. Montgomery, this fast carrier task force—the largest yet assembled—consisted of *Essex* (CV–9), *Yorktown* (CV–10), *Lexington* (CV–16), *Cowpens* (CVL–25), *Independence* (CVL–22), and *Belleau Wood*. On 5 and 6 October, Montgomery's planes made six strikes, flying 738 combat sorties while battleships and cruisers provided their heavy gunfire for further harassment of the Japanese-held island. Despite a cracked high pressure turbine casing, *Trathen* retired with the task force back toward the Hawaiian Islands and arrived at Pearl Harbor on the 11th.

Temporary patching at Pearl Harbor permitted the destroyer to proceed to Bremerton, Wash., and permanent repairs at the Puget Sound Navy Yard. The ship sailed for the Hawaiian Islands on 21 November and reached Pearl Harbor six days later. Following training exercises with land-based aircraft off Oahu, *Trathen*'s commanding officer was designated Commander, Task Unit (TU) 16.15.2, and his ship joined *Martin* (DE–30) and SS *Mormacport*. The ships sailed via Canton Island, Funafuti, and Tarawa to Makin Island where they arrived on 18 December. The next day, the destroyer sped 125 miles to the scene of a downed PBY Catalina, rescued the patrol bomber's crew, and returned to Makin on the 20th. On the return leg of the mission, the ship's radar picked up a formation of Japanese medium bombers bound for the Gilberts. Evidently attracted to bigger game, the bombers sped on. However, one which passed over the ship was taken under fire but apparently suffered no damage.

After pressing on to Abemama Island, *Trathen* and *Le Hardy* (DE–20) got underway on Christmas Day 1943 to escort SS *Mormacport* back to Hawaii. One day out, an "Emily" spotted the three-ship convoy but stayed tantalizingly out of reach of the Allied ships' guns. Detaching *Le Hardy* that evening, *Trathen* and *Mormacport* proceeded on to Hawaii and arrived at Pearl Harbor on New Year's Day 1944.

Trathen conducted gunnery exercises in the Hawaiian area before departing Pearl Harbor on 23 January, bound for the Marshalls.

Entering Kwajalein lagoon on 2 February, *Trathen* relieved *Schroeder* (DD–500) off Kwajalein Island as a fire-support ship and shelled Japanese positions ashore until the fire control party could locate no further targets. On the 5th, *Trathen* joined *McCord* (DD–534) and cruisers *Minneapolis* (CA–36) and *San Francisco* (CA–38) off Gugegwe delivering support fire for the three battalions of marines, embarked in six LST's, as they swarmed ashore in LVT(A)'s and 17 amphtracs, with 16 Sherman tanks. At 0720, *Trathen* commenced fire with her main battery, sending 5-inch shells whistling shoreward. The destroyer and her consorts then stood by as the landing craft reached the beach.

Trathen continued to provide gunfire support until the Kwajalein operations ended on 7 February. The destroyer headed for Majuro on the 8th and arrived there the next day. On the 10th, *Trathen* returned to Kwajalein to conduct antisubmarine patrols.

Trathen next formed up with *Indianapolis* (CA–35) off Eniwetok. Based on an intelligence report that the island was unoccupied, the American warships carried out relatively light bombardment. In the meantime, analysis of papers captured at Kwajalein revealed that Eniwetok was, in fact, defended by tough, crack Japanese troops.

Too late for a radical change of plans, *Indianapolis* and near-sister *Portland* (CA–33), accompanied by *Trathen* and *Hoel* (DD–553), stationed themselves on the flanks of the LCI(G)'s, with waves of LVT's in the middle. *Trathen* screened the former cruiser while *Hoel* drew the latter, and the ships joined the gunboats (LCI(G)) in firing on the island.

Eniwetok soon fell to the mailed fist of American land and sea power. *Trathen* furnished fire support intermittently until the 29th of the month and thereafter remained at Eniwetok until 4 March when she headed for Majuro for a tender availability. Then, following exercises at Purvis Bay in the Solomons and patrol duty between the Emirau and New Hanover Islands, *Trathen* subsequently joined the 7th Fleet on 3 May.

The destroyer departed Manus, in the Admiralties, on 15 May in company with TF 74 and 75, bound for New Guinea waters. The target island, Wakde—occupied in 1942 by the Japanese—possessed an excellent airstrip and vital facilities which would be immensely useful to the Allies as they "island-hopped" closer to the Philippines and Japan. Arriving on the 17th, *Trathen* provided gunfire support for the force which landed on Wakde and later operated off the coast supporting the operation until the 25th, when the ship sailed for Biak.

The next target on the Navy's timetable, this island—the largest of the Schoeten Islands group—lay fringed with coral reefs. The attack force scheduled to bombard the island arrived off the landing beaches 15 minutes ahead of schedule; and, at 0629 on the morning of 27 May, the 6-inch guns of cruisers *Phoenix* (CL–45), *Boise* (CL–47), and *Nashville* (CL–43) began lobbing the first of 1,000 rounds of shells shoreward, while the destroyers looked for "game" along the landing beaches —such as small Japanese patrol craft.

At 1100, four Japanese fighters made half-hearted passes over the airstrips on Biak. Two fighter-bombers came over late in the afternoon shortly thereafter followed by four twin-engined planes—three of which were destroyed by antiaircraft fire. The fourth was damaged. *Trathen* remained on patrol station off the Schoetens until 31 May, when she retired to Humboldt Bay to rejoin TF 75.

The Japanese' first reinforcement attempt towards Biak had been detected, and the Nipponese had turned back. On 3 June, as the enemy was retreating, TF 74 and 75 received orders to go after the fleeing Japanese. At 2318 on 3 June, *Trathen* got underway with the other units of Destroyer Division (DesDiv) 48 and gave chase. The next day, 10 Japanese "Val" dive bombers tried to pounce on the American force but were driven off. On the 5th, Japanese torpedo bombers attacked American forces, and one of them fell to *Trathen's* heavy antiaircraft fire.

Subsequently, the enemy launched a second effort aimed at reinforcing their beleaguered outpost on Biak. Six Japanese destroyers—three with troops embarked and three towing landing barges—joined cruisers *Aoba* and *Kinu* north of Misool Island, west of the "parrot beak" of New Guinea. The enemy force was under Rear Admiral Sakonju in destroyer *Shikinami*. Proceeding towards Biak, the Japanese reinforcement group remained undetected until 10 B–25 Mitchells, escorted by P–38 Lightnings, spotted them and launched a devastating attack which sank *Harusame* and damaged three of her sister destroyers. Resuming the run to Biak once the planes had departed, the Japanese continued on an unknowing collision course with Vice Admiral V.A.C. Crutchley's cruisers and destroyers prowling between Biak and Hollandia.

Unaware of Sakonju's position, Crutchley decided to commence a sweep parallel to the coast of Biak. About 2200 on the night of 8 June, a PB4Y bomber on night patrol, detected the Nipponese force and reported five unidentified ships making 12 knots in the direction of Crutchley's cruisers and destroyers. Deploying for battle on a northerly course, the British Admiral ordered his ships to general quarters. The Japanese simultaneously detected the American's presence and turned to fire torpedo spreads before retiring.

Trathen, in DesDiv 48, followed astern of DesDivs 42 and 47, under orders from Crutchley to pursue the fleeing enemy. Then, while the two divisions charged ahead on the heels of the retreating Nipponese, *Trathen* and her division mates fell back on orders to screen Crutchley's cruisers.

The American force never caught up with the enemy and returned to Humboldt Bay on the following day. *Trathen* subsequently participated in the invasion of Noemfoor Island. Assigned to TG 77.2, the covering force, she conducted shore bombardment missions there on 2 July before retiring to Humboldt Bay. She later served in the covering forces during the landings at Cape Sansapor, New Guinea, on 30 July, laying smoke screens and patrolling 25 miles off shoreline to cover the invasion.

Recreation and availability at Sydney, Australia, from 13 to 20 August, provided *Trathen's* officers and men with a welcome respite from the toils of war. Heading back north after a week of Australian hospitality, the destroyer conducted exercises and drills in the vicinity of Purvis Bay in preparation for the Western Carolines Operation. On 6 September, she departed from Purvis Bay as part of TG 32.5. After screening the carriers as they launched devastating air strikes in support of the Palau invasion, the destroyer retired on 26 September to refuel and replenish depleted ammunition stocks in Kossol passage.

With the dissolution of her task, the destroyer headed for Manus and arrived there on 2 October. Next assigned to TG 77.4, *Trathen* set her course towards Leyte Gulf in the Philippine Islands. Landings on Dinagat and Suluan Islands in the entrance to Leyte Gulf commenced on the 17th; and the destroyer stood by to provide antiaircraft and gunfire support. Three days later, three Japanese fighters roared low over the area which *Trathen* was guarding. Within minutes, the ship's gunners splashed their second plane of the war; and the destroyer even managed to capture the aircraft's pilot whom they transferred to carrier *Sangamon* (CVE–26).

Again on the 24th, Japanese aircraft harassed the ships of the invasion force, and the alert combat air patrol (CAP) downed two more of the enemy. *Trathen* retired to Manus early in November but returned to Leyte Gulf on the 16th for patrols in Surigao Strait. Relieving *Sigourney* (DD–643) on the 19th, *Trathen* remained in the Philippines until the 23d when she headed to the Western Carolines. After sinking a medium barge with 5-inch and 40-millimeter fire en route, she reached Ulithi on 25 November.

Exercises off Ulithi occupied the ship from 30 November to 29 December before *Trathen* joined TG 38.2 on 5 January 1945. She served as plane guard and screening vessel for this group and TG 38.5 through the end of the month. The former group participated in preinvasion strikes on the island of Luzon before turning to the South China Sea for a series of strikes on Japanese-held Formosa from 9 to 11 January. The French Indochina coast next received its share of attention, with Japanese shipping and coastal installations feeling the might of the American naval air arm. Then, moving northward against virtually no opposition from Japanese planes or ships, the task group aircraft bombed Hong Kong and Hainan Island. Monsoon and typhoon-type winds and seas buffeted the group on the 17th and 18th, with *Trathen's* inclinometer registering a staggering 67 degrees from the vertical at the height of the storm.

After leaving the South China Sea through the Balintang Channel, *Trathen* and her mates participated in more strikes against Formosa and in raids on Sakishima Gunto which served Japan as a staging area for the kamikazes. In the course of her plane-guarding duties, *Trathen* steamed astern of *Hancock* (CV–19) on 21 January and witnessed the detonation of an Avenger as it landed hard on the flight deck. One man was blown overboard by the explosion, but *Trathen* soon fished him from the water.

Following the strikes on Okinawa, *Trathen* got underway from Ulithi on 10 February to support carrier operations between Iwo Jima and the Japanese home islands. Six days later, TF 58 commenced the first strikes against Tokyo launched from 150 miles southeast of the Imperial city. After a night retirement, the group conducted further strikes the next day. With the landings at Iwo Jima, *Trathen* arrived in the vicinity on the 20th and screened the carriers as they conducted air strikes for the next four days supporting the American marines fighting for that fanatically defended island.

The force swept north with *Trathen* in its screen and arrived at a point off Tokyo at dawn on the 25th to launch strikes to hit the Japanese capital again. That night, the carriers steamed in the direction of Nagoya, but heavy weather cancelled the strikes scheduled to be launched against that industrial city on the 26th. While in Japanese waters, *Trathen* and her division mates sighted a number of floating mines. The destroyer herself sank one with gun fire on 27 February.

Following availability at Ulithi, *Trathen* returned to the "front lines" on 14 March, rendezvousing with TG 58.4 in preparations for air strikes on the Japanese home islands and on Okinawa. Temporarily detached to pick up a downed pilot, the destroyer rejoined the group as it plowed on towards Japan. She later sank several more floating mines while screening the carriers against air attacks. Slashing through CAP and antiaircraft fire, some kamikazes managed to crash into their targets and give their lives for the Emperor. Antiaircraft fire from *Trathen*'s group accounted for five of the winged marauders, but one hit *Intrepid* (CV–11) on 18 March.

Nine days later, *Trathen*, in company with battle cruisers *Guam* (CB–1) and *Alaska* (CB–2), cruisers *Flint* (CL–97) and *San Diego* (CL–53) and four other destroyers left the carriers to bombard Minami Daito Shima. All ships shelled the target area with impunity. The battlecruisers, light cruisers, and destroyers rejoined the carriers on 28 March and resumed their screening duties.

In the months that followed, American forces—aided by the small British Far East Fleet—continued hammering at the Japanese homeland with air strikes and bombardments by surface ships. On 11 April, still attached to TF 58, *Trathen* hammered away at attacking Japanese planes with her antiaircraft batteries. During the third raid that day, a 5-inch shell from a "friendly" ship hit the destroyer near her number five 5-inch mount handling room. It killed three men, wounded 21, and rendered the after mount inoperative.

Tender availability soon made good the damage, and *Trathen* returned to the Fleet. Departing Ulithi on 3 May, she rejoined TF 58 on the 5th near Okinawa. Six days later, *Bunker Hill* (CV–17), flagship of TF 58, was hit by a kamikaze. Another Japanese pilot, with similar intentions for *Trathen*, dived toward the destroyer. While the ship's guns hammered at the suicide plane, help came from the air. A "friendly" fighter, braving the antiaircraft fire from his own ships, also attacked the kamikaze which crashed into the sea off *Trathen*'s port bow.

Anchoring in Ulithi lagoon for a needed rest, *Trathen* got underway again 10 days later and sortied with TG 58.4 to screen the carrier.

On 4 June, air operations were cancelled as the barometer began to plummet. The storm center of a typhoon passed some 70 miles to the southeast, and the ships in company with *Trathen* emerged unscathed from the fringes of the storm. On 6 June, while carrying out plane-guard duties, the destroyer rescued the two-man crew of a downed SB2C Helldiver. She recovered both men, but the pilot was dead when he was brought on board.

These operations proved to be *Trathen*'s last of World War II, for she soon departed Leyte to begin the long voyage back to the United States. After a stop at Pearl Harbor, *Trathen* arrived at Seattle, Wash., on 9 July 1945, for an overhaul at the Todd Shipbuilding Co. While the destroyer was in the shipyard, the war in the Pacific ended. Upon completion of the refit, the ship sailed for San Diego on 29 September and arrived there on 2 October. On 18 January 1946, *Trathen* was decommissioned and berthed with the San Diego Group, Pacific Reserve Fleet.

When North Korean forces swept southward across the 38th parallel on 25 June 1950, the United States soon came to the aid of the embattled South Koreans. Called out of reserve service on 14 June 1951, *Trathen* was recommissioned on 1 August. As flagship of Destroyer Squadron (DesRon) 28, the ship was transferred to the Atlantic Fleet on 5 October, based at Norfolk, Va., and operated off the east coast and in the Caribbean through the end of 1952.

Subsequently ordered to the Far East, *Trathen* arrived at Sasebo, Japan, on 12 February 1953. During her Korean deployment, *Trathen*'s main and secondary batteries pounded railroad lines, trains, bunkers, and transformer stations. On 11 March, the destroyer joined the "Train Buster Club" when she destroyed a railroad train. Two days later, after the ship completed her patrols between Wonsan and Hungnam, she was relieved on station to return to Sasebo for repairs. Later becoming a part of TF 77, *Trathen* continued on duty until 7 June. She departed Sasebo on the following day, bound for Hong Kong.

Returning to the United States via Southeast Asia and the Mediterranean, *Trathen* operated with the Atlantic Fleet until January 1955, when she was transferred back to the Pacific Fleet and subsequently deployed to the Western Pacific (WestPac). On 21 April, *Trathen* departed Long Beach to begin successive West-Pac deployments which would last through 1964, interspersed with tours of duty on the west coast. When in the Orient, she followed a varied itinerary visiting such ports as Kaohsiung, Taiwan; Hong Kong; Sasebo and Yokosuka, Japan; as well as Pearl Harbor, Guam, Midway, and Subic Bay. During this period, she took part in antisubmarine, antiaircraft, and other exercises; served as plane guard when operating with fast carrier forces, and patrolled the Taiwan Strait as part of American forces protecting that island.

While *Trathen* was at Kaohsiung during her last deployment to WestPac, word arrived early in August of the "Tonkin Gulf Incident." Getting underway shortly thereafter, *Trathen* operated at sea throughout the remainder of the month but for brief replenishments at Kaohsiung. Relieved on station, *Trathen* sailed for Hong Kong to serve as station ship before traveling to the South China Sea to support naval operations off the coast of the Republic of South Vietnam. On 8 October 1965, the destroyer departed for eastern waters and proceeded via Guam and Midway to the west coast.

After arriving at Long Beach on 28 October, the destroyer conducted routine carrier operations off the west coast. On 12 February 1965, *Trathen* reported to the Commander, San Diego Group, Pacific Reserve Fleet, to begin her second inactivation period at the Todd Shipyard, San Pedro, Calif. On 15 March, she made her final voyage at the end of a towline. Brought to San Diego, she completed the process of deactivation and was decommissioned on 11 May 1965 and placed in reserve. A survey of the ship conducted in June 1972 reported that the costs of modernization to *Trathen* would be disproportionate to the value of the ship. Accordingly, *Trathen* was struck from the Navy list on 1 November 1972.

Trathen received eight battle stars for World War II service and one for Korean service.

Traveler

(SP–122: t. 18; l. 50'3''; b. 10'8''; dr. 4'6'' (aft); s. 10 mph; cpl. 6; a. 1 1-pdr., 1 mg.)

Traveler (SP–122)—a motorboat built in November 1914 at Port Clinton, Ohio, by the Mathews Boat Co.—was acquired from Mr. John D. Meyers of Miami, Fla., on 5 May 1917 and was placed in commission on 14 July 1917. *Traveler* was assigned to the 7th Naval District and was based at Key West, Fla., whence she conducted patrols to protect American coastal trade routes from submarine and mining incursions. Following the armistice in November 1918, the motorboat continued to serve at Key West. On 9 September 1919, she and seven other section patrol boats anchored in the North Beach Basin at Key West were completely destroyed by a hurricane. The wreckage of the eight boats was hauled out immediately following the storm and burned. Her name was struck from the Navy list on 4 October 1919.

Traveller

(Smack: t. 36)

Commodore Edward Preble acquired the fishing smack, *Traveller*, in June of 1805 to carry supplies to the American ships operating in the Mediterranean. Little is known of the craft other than she was apparently commanded by Sailing Master Benjamin C. Prince, and that she was sold to a Sir Alexander Ball in December of 1805.

Traverse County

A county in western Minnesota.

(LST–1160: dp. 5,777 (f.); l. 384'; b. 56'6''; dr. 17'; s. 14.5 k.; cpl. 600; a. 6 4''; cl. *LST–1156*)

LST–1160 was laid down on 18 December 1952 at Bath, Maine, by the Bath Iron Works Corp.; launched on 3 October 1953; sponsored by Mrs. Omar R. King; and commissioned on 19 December 1953, Lt. Comdr. James W. Perkins in command.

Late in January 1954, the tank landing ship moved, from Boston—where she had completed outfitting—to the Naval Amphibious Base at Little Creek, Va. On 26 March, after seven weeks of shakedown training in the Virginia capes operating area and three weeks of post-shakedown availability, *LST–1160* became an active unit of the Atlantic Fleet Amphibious Force. Between the spring of 1954 and the summer of 1955, the ship completed seven training exercises to sharpen her skill as an amphibious warfare ship. Those drills frequently took her south to the West Indies, most often to Vieques Island near Puerto Rico where embarked marines practiced amphibious landings. On 1 July 1955, *LST–1160* was named *Traverse County*. Not long thereafter, she was awarded the Battle Efficiency "E" as the outstanding ship of LST Flotilla 4. Late in 1955, *Traverse County* entered the Philadelphia Naval Shipyard for a four-month overhaul. The tank landing ship exited the shipyard in April 1956 and, following a month of refresher training, resumed operations out of Little Creek. The remainder of 1956 saw her periodically embarking marines at Morehead City, N.C., and putting them ashore at Little Creek and at nearby Camp Pendleton.

At the beginning of 1957, *Traverse County* completed preparations for her first deployment with the 6th Fleet. During the next 11 years, *Traverse County* performed eight tours of duty in the Mediterranean. Most often, her operations with the 6th Fleet included visits to ports in Spain, France, Italy, Greece, Turkey, and along the North African coast. She often conducted training exercises with units of friendly foreign navies. However, during her 1958 deployment, a crisis erupted in Lebanon at the far eastern end of the Mediterranean; and, in July, the LST joined other 6th Fleet units and Amphibious Squadron 6 LST's in landing marines at Beirut to help stabilize the situation. The remainder of her Mediterranean assignments proved to be more routine in nature.

When not attached to the 6th Fleet, *Traverse County* operated out of Little Creek, Va. Her western Atlantic duties frequently took her to the West Indies and the Caribbean where, in addition to the usual amphibious exercises, she performed supply missions to various American bases in the area under the auspices of the

Commander, Service Force, Atlantic Fleet. Such was her assignment in the fall of 1962 when United States surveillance of Cuba uncovered the siting of offensive missiles on that island by the Russians. When the crisis occurred, President John F. Kennedy invoked a successful quarantine of Cuba to secure the removal of those weapons. During that operation, *Traverse County* provided support as a combat ready unit. However, the Soviet Union withdrew the missiles; and the tension abated enabling the LST to resume her normal routine early in 1963. She returned to supplying Caribbean bases and conducting amphibious exercises at Little Creek, Onslow Beach, N.C., and at Vieques Island near Puerto Rico.

The Cuban Missile Crisis proved to be her last internationally significant operation. After 1962, she resumed her routine, alternating Mediterranean deployments with east coast operations. She completed her eighth and last 6th Fleet assignment in December 1968. During 1969, she conducted another series of amphibious exercises at her old haunts—Little Creek, Onslow Beach, and Vieques. Similar operations carried her into 1970; but, on 7 March, she headed for the Panama Canal and a tour of special duty. After transporting the 8th Marine Engineering Battalion from Morehead City, N.C., to Vieques Island, she arrived at Colon, Canal Zone, on the 12th. She transited the canal and embarked scientists and equipment of the Smithsonian Institution for research operations in the vicinity of the Secas Islands of Panama. That duty lasted until 3 April when she returned to Rodman in the Canal Zone. Between the 3d and the 24th, the tank landing ship transported Army Reserve troops and their equipment between Rio Hato and Rodman and carried Operation "Handclasp" supplies to Guayaquil, Ecuador. On 27 April, she reembarked the Smithsonian scientists for another week of research operations. Upon her return to Rodman early in May, the ship entered the Panama Canal Company's Mt. Hope Shipyard for repairs. She exited the shipyard on 11 June, retransited the canal, and joined the Caribbean Amphibious Ready Group for a day before returning to Rodman for further orders. Late in June, she transported more Army reservists between Rio Hato and Rodman.

On 7 July, she headed back to the United States for inactivation. *Traverse County* reached Little Creek on the 15th. Later that fall, *Traverse County* was placed out of commission. Sometime thereafter, she was moved to the Atlantic Reserve Fleet berthing area at Orange, Tex. There she remained until 7 June 1972, at which time she was transferred to the Military Sealift Command. She served with that organization until 1 November 1973 when her name was struck from the Navy list. The ship was then transferred to the Maritime Administration and berthed with the National Defense Reserve Fleet group at Suisun Bay, Calif.

Travis

On the night of 12 June 1813 in the mouth of the York River, Captain Samuel Travis, USRCS—commanding officer of revenuer cutter *Surveyor*—prepared his ship to fight off an expected attack by British forces. When the enemy party boarded their ship, Travis and crew ignored the overwhelming numerical superiority of their attackers and defended *Surveyor* with fierce and fearless valor until overwhelmed. The commander of the British boarding party so admired Travis' intrepid effort that he returned his sword.

(WPC–153: dp. 220; l. 125'; b. 23'6''; dr. 9'; s. 11 k.; cpl. 38; a. 1 3''; cl. *Active*)

Travis—a steel-hulled, twin-screw, diesel-powered Coast Guard cutter built in 1927 at Camden, N.J., by the American Brown Boveri Corp.—was commissioned in mid- or late 1927, with Boatswain's Mate J. S. Turner in charge. Built to combat the rum-running trade, *Travis* operated out of Stapleton, N.Y., Morehead City,

N.C., and Rockland, Maine, successively, through the 1930's. The latter port served as her home base from 1937 to the summer of 1941, when the Coast Guard was placed under naval control for the duration of the national emergency brought on by the war in Europe.

Apparently shifted to Argentia, Newfoundland, in either late 1941 or early 1942 to support the Atlantic Fleet in the Battle of the Atlantic, *Travis*—designated WPC–153—picked up a sound contact at 1100 on 8 February 1942 while patrolling off Placentia Bay. She dropped a depth charge which temporarily disabled her sound gear. Once the cutter regained the contact, she dropped another pair of charges. While the Coast Guardsmen noted an oil slick, there was no definite confirmation of a "kill."

Travis apparently remained in these northern climes into the winter of 1942. On 20 December, she came across the disabled freighter *Maltran* which was in danger of running aground on a poorly charted rocky shore. The cutter attempted to tow off the ship, but the hawser parted. Meanwhile, *Mohawk* (WPG–78) happened by and, at the request of *Travis*, rendered assistance. The second cutter relieved the first in the towing operation and succeeded in taking *Maltran* in tow at 0315 on 21 December, while *Travis* operated as an antisubmarine screen. Eventually, the little group successfully navigated the dangerous uncharted waters and emerged to make passage to the swept channel at Argentia.

Subsequent records are sparse, but the ship undoubtedly remained in active service through the end of the war and into the 1950's. Eventually, her home port became Port Everglades, Fla., by 1960, and she remained in service there until decommissioned in 1963. She was sold soon thereafter.

Traw

London Lewis Traw—born on 1 April 1903 at Pocahontas, Ark.—enlisted in the United States Marine Corps on 15 December 1924 and, in the course of a career which spanned 18 years, achieved the rank of platoon sergeant. He served with the marine detachment on board *Oklahoma* (BB–37) for two years during the 1920's and in China from August 1936 until February 1938.

In October 1942, he was serving with the 1st Marine Division as it fought to seize and hold Guadalcanal. In the course of that bitter battle, Sgt. Traw displayed intrepidity and courage as he directed the fire of the machine guns in his section despite tremendous enemy fire and repeated assaults by Japanese forces far outnumbering his own. Under his inspiring leadership, the platoon made a major contribution to the rout and destruction of a Japanese regiment. On 27 October 1942, Sergeant Traw was killed in action near Lunga on Guadalcanal.

He was posthumously awarded the Silver Star for his role in this action.

(DE–350: dp. 1,350; l. 306'; b. 36'7''; dr. 9'5'' (mean); s. 24.3 k.; cpl. 222; a. 2 5'', 4 40mm., 10 20mm., 2 dct., 8 dcp., 1 dcp. (hh.), 3 21'' tt.; cl. *John C. Butler*)

Traw (DE–350) was laid down on 19 December 1943 at Orange, Tex., by the Consolidated Steel Corp.; launched on 12 February 1944; sponsored by Mrs. Jennie Traw, mother of Sgt. Traw; and commissioned on 20 June 1944, Lt. Comdr. James T. Kilbreth, Jr., USNR, in command.

For a week after her commissioning, *Traw* conducted preliminary tests and exercises. Then, on 28 June 1944, she departed Orange, Tex., and arrived at Galveston for drydocking. On 7 July, the new destroyer escort got underway in company with *Leland E. Thomas* (DE–420) and *Jesse Rutherford* (DE–347) for her shakedown cruise to Bermuda. Exercises out of Great Sound occupied the remainder of the month as *Traw*'s

crew drilled and brought the new ship to battle-readiness.

Following repairs and trials at the Boston Navy Yard, she steamed independently to Norfolk, arriving on 28 August 1944. On 30 August, the destroyer escort began a period of activity as a training ship. Daylong cruises to the Chesapeake Bay, with a balance crew on board for training, occupied *Traw* until late in September. On the 24th, she departed Norfolk escorting *Solomons* (CVE–67) and entered the swept channel at New York early the next day.

Operating as a unit of Escort Division 78, *Traw* got underway on 6 October 1944 in Convoy UGF–15 bound for the Mediterranean. The destroyer escort entered the swept channel at Gibraltar on 17 October and, on the 20th, anchored in the harbor at Marseilles. After escorting a small convoy to North Africa, *Traw* departed Oran on the 26th with a convoy steaming westward for the United States. Late in the day on 16 November, she left the convoy protecting *Solomons*. As the severe weather of the crossing moderated, *Traw* delivered her charge safely to Narragansett Bay. She then continued southward, discharged ammunition at the Ammunition Depot, Earle, N.J., and reported to the New York Navy Yard for overhaul. Her repairs completed, *Traw* rendezvoused with *Cowie* (DD–632) and *Barracuda* (SF–4) on 19 November in Block Island Sound for antisubmarine exercises. In company with other destroyer escorts, she continued exercises until halted by severe weather on the 21st.

She returned to New York and, on 25 November, was again underway escorting Convoy UGF–17 B. On 5 December, *Traw* left her picket station to pick up official mail at Rosia Bay. Three days later, she acted as navigational guide when the convoy entered the channel at Marseilles. After escorting a seven-ship convoy to Oran, she departed Mers el-Kebir on 13 December as a convoy escort. The voyage was uneventful, and she arrived at New York on 23 December.

Traw completed overhaul at New York; then set her course for Norfolk, arriving on 10 January to prepare for the long voyage to the Pacific. On 19 January, she got underway for the Canal Zone. She entered the Pacific on the 25th; and, three days later, she moored at Seymour Island in the Galapagos for fueling. Assigned to Escort Division 78, Pacific Fleet, she steamed independently on 1 February, via Bora Bora, for the Admiralties. On 22 February, she passed through the antisubmarine nets and anchored in Seeadler Harbor.

After fueling and upkeep, she joined other DE's in exercises. Then, on the 27th, she began the escort duties which she would continue until the end of the war. Throughout March and April, *Traw* protected convoys moving between New Guinea and the Philippines. In May, she made a single voyage to the Palaus; then returned to Leyte where she conducted patrols. She remained in Philippine waters into June, varying convoy and patrol duties with antisubmarine warfare exercises. In July and August, she escorted convoys to Ulithi and Okinawa and returned to the Philippines where she continued her escort duties into September.

Late in November she steamed, via Samar and the Marshalls, to Hawaii, arriving there on 19 December. She departed Pearl Harbor in April 1946 and returned to the west coast, remaining in California ports until her decommissioning at San Diego on 7 June 1946.

Her name was struck from the Navy list on 1 August 1967. Her hulk was sunk as a target off Baja California, Mexico, on 17 August 1968.

Treasure

An island just off the western coast of Florida near St. Petersburg.

(YFB–24: l. 65'; b. 13'; dr. 4'; cl. *YFB–19*)

Treasure (YFB–24) was laid down on 16 June 1942 at Seattle, Wash., by the Shain Manufacturing Co.;

launched on 1 August 1942; and delivered to the Navy at Puget Sound Navy Yard on 9 November 1942. The ferryboat was assigned to duty in the 14th Naval District and was placed in service at Johnston Island on 22 January 1943.

Treasure carried passengers in the vicinity of Johnston Island through the end of World War II and for almost a year thereafter. In May 1946, the ferryboat was transferred to Pearl Harbor where she served until ordered deleted from the 14th Naval District's list of service craft on 2 July 1946. She was placed out of service at Pearl Harbor on 30 August 1946, and her name was struck from the Navy list on 10 June 1947. In July 1947, she was sold to Mr. William H. Pinney of Honolulu, Hawaii.

Trefoil

I

(ScStr: t. 370; l. 145'7''; b. 23'9''; dr. 11'2''; cpl. 44; a. 1 30-pdr. P.r., 1 12-pdr. how.)

Trefoil—a wooden-hulled screw steamer built in 1864 by clipper ship designer Donald McKay—was purchased by the Navy on 4 February 1865 and commissioned at the Boston Navy Yard, Boston, Mass., on 1 March 1865, Acting Master Charles C. Wells in command.

Trefoil proceeded south to the Gulf of Mexico and arrived at Mobile Bay on 24 March. She served in the West Gulf Blockading Squadron under Rear Admiral Henry Knox Thatcher through the end of the Civil War, operating mainly as a dispatch boat between Pensacola and Mobile.

In July 1865, she returned north to the Boston Navy Yard where she was decommissioned on 30 August 1865. Placed in ordinary in 1866, the steamer was sold at auction on 28 May 1867 to a Mr. L. Litchfield.

II

(IX–149: dp. 10,960 (f.); l. 366'4''; b. 54'; cpl. 54; a. 1 40mm.; cl. T. B7–D1)

The second *Trefoil* (IX–149)—a non-self-propelled, concrete-hulled cargo barge constructed in 1944 under a Maritime Commission contract (MC hull 1329) by the Barrett, Hilp & Belair Shipyard in San Francisco—was acquired by the Navy on 5 March 1944 as *Midnight*; designated IX–149; and placed in service on 9 March 1944, Lt. Neal King, USNR, in charge.

Midnight completed conversion for Navy use on 28 March and was assigned to the Service Force, Pacific Fleet. That same day, she was towed out of San Francisco on her way to the Central Pacific. After a stop at Pearl Harbor, she continued her voyage and arrived in Majuro Lagoon on 4 May. For the next five months, she served at Majuro and Eniwetok. During that time, she was renamed *Trefoil* on 10 June 1944. On 5 October, *Current* (ARS–22) towed her out of Eniwetok and on to Ulithi where she arrived on the 16th. She remained there for 10 months on duty with Service Squadron 8. In August 1945, she was towed from Ulithi to Leyte in the Philippines where she arrived on the 28th. *Trefoil* remained there until 9 November, when she was towed out for Guam in the Marianas. The barge reached Apra Harbor on the 16th.

Trefoil served at Guam for the remainder of her Navy career. Early in 1946, she was chosen as one of the support ships for Operation "Crossroads," the atomic bomb tests conducted at Bikini Atoll that summer. However, soon thereafter, that decision was rescinded and another made to dispose of her. Action on that decision was also deferred, and she was used to house Stockton-Pollack employees building a drydock in Apra Harbor. Her reprieve ended in September 1947

when she was determined to be in excess of the needs of the Navy. On 28 May 1948, the barge was turned over to the Foreign Liquidations Commission of the State Department for disposal; and she was sold to the Asia Development Corp. of Shanghai, China. Her name was struck from the Navy list on 22 December 1948. The barge, however, remained at Apra Harbor because she was impounded due to a dispute over ownership of the vessel between the Asia Development Corp. and Moellers Ltd., of Hong Kong. Though the resolution of the dispute and final disposition of the barge is unknown, all available Navy records name the Asia Development Corp. as her rightful owner.

Trego

A county in Kansas named for Capt. Edward P. Trego of the 8th Kansas Regiment who was killed during the Battle of Chicamauga on 19 September 1863.

(AKA–78: dp. 13,910; l. 459'2''; b. 63'0''; dr. 26'4''; s. 16.5 k. (tl.); cpl. 247; a. 1 5'', 8 40mm.; cl. *Tolland*; T. C2–S–AJ3)

Trego (AKA–78) was laid down under Maritime Commission contract (MC hull 1384) on 14 April 1944 at Wilmington, N.C., by the North Carolina Shipbuilding Corp.; launched on 20 June 1944; sponsored by Mrs. M. W. Nettles; acquired by the Navy on 4 July 1944; and commissioned on 21 December 1944, Lt. Comdr. James F. Hunnewell, USNR, in command.

The attack cargo ship held shakedown training in the Chesapeake Bay area in early February 1945 and then loaded cargo at Norfolk. She stood out of Norfolk on 16 February bound for Hawaii, transited the Panama Canal on Washington's Birthday, and arrived at Pearl Harbor on 8 March. The ship unloaded; participated in training exercises for a week; discharged her landing boats; and on 31 March got underway for San Francisco to replace them and to load equipment for the 5th Marine Division which had just returned from Iwo Jima.

Trego discharged her cargo at Pearl Harbor on 19 April; loaded men and equipment of the 7th Air Force; and sailed on 2 May with a convoy bound, via Eniwetok and Ulithi, for Okinawa. After unloading her troops and supplies at the Hagushi beaches between 3 and 11 June, the ship returned to Pearl Harbor. On 19 July, she headed for Guam laden with maintenance equipment and arrived at Apra Harbor on 30 July. The following week, she got underway for the South Pacific; picked up equipment at Guadalcanal and at the Russells; and delivered it back at Guam on the 29th. On 8 September, she headed for the Philippines to join Transport Squadron 20 of the 5th Amphibious Force. She and the other ships of the squadron embarked the entire 25th Infantry Division and sortied for Japan on 1 October. However, due to several typhoons, the convoy did not reach Nagoya until the 28th. The ships began unloading immediately and finished on 1 November. After disembarking their troops, the squadron disbanded; and *Trego* got underway on 2 November for the South Pacific. She called at Milne Bay on the 11th; at Manus in early December; at Batavia on 18 December 1945; and at Guam on 11 January 1946.

On 18 January, the cargo ship headed for the United States and reached San Diego on 5 February. She stood out to sea on 29 March, bound for the east coast and inactivation. She arrived at Norfolk on 17 April. Decommissioned there on 21 May, *Trego* was returned to the War Shipping Administration the next day and was struck from the Navy list on 5 June 1946.

Trego received one battle star for World War II service.

Trembler

A torpedinoid fish of the West Indies and Brazil.

Trembler (SS–424) was renamed *Quillback* (*q.v.*) on 7 December 1943.

Trenton

The capital city of New Jersey and of Mercer County. It is located at the head of navigation on the Delaware River about 28 miles northeast of Philadelphia.

During the American Revolution, Trenton was the site of a decisive American victory. On Christmas night 1776, Washington led the remnants of the Continental Army across the Delaware River in a blinding snow storm. At dawn on 26 December, he caught the Hessian garrison at Trenton by surprise. This total victory netted the Americans 1,000 prisoners and huge quantities of small arms, cannon, and munitions. More importantly, it revived the cause of independence which had suffered greatly during the retreat from New York after the Battle of Long Island the previous August.

I

(ScStr: dp. 3,800; l. 253'; b. 48'; dr. 20'6'' (mean); s. 14½ k.; cpl. 477; a. 11 8'' mlr., 2 20-pdr. blr.)

The first *Trenton*—a wooden-hulled screw steamer—was laid down by the New York Navy Yard in 1875; launched on New Year's Day, 1876; sponsored by Miss Katherine M. Parker; and commissioned on 14 February 1877, Capt. John Lee Davis in command.

Trenton departed New York on 8 March 1877 and reached Villefranche, France, on 18 April. The follow-ing day, Rear Admiral John L. Worden broke his flag in her, and she became flagship of the European Station. A week after the American warship reached the Mediterranean, Russia declared war on Turkey. Consequently, *Trenton* and the other ships of the squadron alternated tours of duty in the eastern Mediterranean protecting United States citizens and other foreign nationals resident in or visiting Turkish possessions. On 9 May, she departed Villefranche for Smyrna, Turkey, and—but for a run to Salonika from 9 to 13 June with *Marion*—remained there until 25 August when the flagship left the eastern Mediterranean behind to return to Villefranche. Next, *Trenton* visited Marseilles for two weeks in mid-September then steamed back to Villefranche on the 18th and remained there until Christmas Day when she put to sea to return to the eastern Mediterranean. Reentering Smyrna on the second day of 1878, she showed the flag there until 16 March when she sailed for Piraeus, the port-city for Athens, Greece. On 2 April, she got underway again for Villefranche, touching at La Spezia and Leghorn in Italy en route.

On 17 July, she headed for Gibraltar and, on the 24th, exited the Mediterranean. She cruised north, visited Lisbon, Portugal; Cherbourg, France; and Yarmouth, England; and then returned to the Mediterranean, reaching Villefranche in mid-October. *Trenton* resumed her cruises between Mediterranean ports, adding Genoa, Naples, and Tangiers to her itinerary in the spring of 1879. In June, she again headed out through the Straits of Gibraltar to visit Portsmouth, England; Terneuzen, Holland; Antwerp, Belgium; and Copenhagen, Denmark. She was back at Villefranche late in September. In mid-November, she sailed to Gibraltar and waited there until 7 December for *Constellation* to arrive with *Trenton*'s replacement crew. The warship remained in the western Mediterranean until early April 1880.

USS *Trenton* on the Asiatic Station.

On the 3d, she headed east once more. After stops at Naples and at Alexandria, Egypt, the warship began cruising the Aegean again. She visited Smyrna, Tenedos, and Chamak Kelessi in Turkey as well as Piraeus before returning to Villefranche on 25 May. After a visit to Marseilles on 7 June, the flagship left the Mediterranean for the third time during this deployment and made another cruise to English, Belgian, and Dutch ports.

Trenton returned to the western Mediterranean in August and operated there until 7 September 1881 when she sailed for the United States. She arrived in Hampton Roads on 12 October and, three days later, moved up the York River for the Yorktown centennial celebration. On 22 October, the warship departed Yorktown and the following day arrived in the New York Navy Yard. There, she was decommissioned on 9 November.

Reactivated on 18 September 1883, *Trenton* departed New York in November for duty on the Asiatic Station. Steaming via the Mediterranean, the Suez Canal, Ceylon, and Singapore, she arrived at Hong Kong on 1 May 1884 to begin two years of cruising in the Far East. She visited ports in China, Korea, and Japan, carrying out various diplomatic missions. On occasion, *Trenton* sent landing parties ashore in China and Korea to protect American nationals and other foreigners during periods of internal unrest. The warship completed this tour of duty in the spring of 1886; departed Yokohama, Japan, on 9 May; retraced her voyage back across the Indian Ocean, through the Suez Canal and the Mediterranean Sea, and across the Atlantic to reach Hampton Roads on 2 September. She entered the Norfolk Navy Yard on 9 September and was decommissioned for repairs on the 17th.

On 16 May 1887, she was placed in commission once again. On 25 July, she exited Hampton Roads and headed south for Brazil. En route, *Trenton* stopped at St. Vincent in the Windward Islands and entered Rio de Janeiro on 10 September for a fortnight visit. After touching at St. Thomas on the return voyage, she dropped anchor in New York harbor on 3 November.

Almost three months later, on 30 January 1888, *Trenton* sailed for the Pacific. The voyage took her more than a year to complete, for she had to steam around Cape Horn at the southern end of South America. After stops at Panama and Tahiti, the warship reached Apia, Samoa, on 10 March 1889 and joined other units of the Pacific Squadron. Six days later, while still at anchor in Apia harbor, *Trenton* was wrecked by a hurricane. Before abandoning ship, however, her crew assisted in the rescue of *Vandalia's* ship's company. *Trenton* was declared a total loss, and her name was struck from the Navy list on 13 April 1891.

Trenton's eagle figurehead. The national eagle was a popular motif in the decoration of American warships.

(CL–11: dp. 7,500 (n.); l. 555'6''; b. 55'0'' (wl.); dr. 14'3'' (mean); s. 33.91 k. (tl.); cpl. 458; a. 12 6'', 4 3'', 2 3-pdrs., 10 21'' tt.; cl. *Omaha*)

The second *Trenton* (CL–11) was laid down on 18 August 1920 at Philadelphia, Pa., by William Cramp & Sons; launched on 16 April 1923; sponsored by Miss Katherine E. Donnelly; and commissioned on 19 April 1924, Capt. Edward C. Kalbfus in command.

On 24 May, the light cruiser stood out of New York harbor for her shakedown cruise in the Mediterranean Sea. On 14 August, while in transit from Port Said, Egypt; to Aden, Arabia; *Trenton* was ordered to Bushire, Persia. She arrived on the 25th and took on board the remains of Vice Consul Robert Imbrie. She received and returned the gun salute to the late vice consul and departed the same day. Following stops at Suez and Port Said, Egypt; and at Villefranche, France; *Trenton* arrived at the Washington Navy Yard on 29 September.

In mid-October, while *Trenton* was conducting gunnery drills in the Norfolk area, powder bags in her forward turret exploded, killing or injuring every member of the gun crew. During the ensuing fire, Ens. Henry Clay Drexler and Boatswain's Mate, First Class, George Cholister attempted to dump powder charges into the immersion tank before they detonated but failed. Ens. Drexler was killed when the charge exploded, and Boatswain's Mate Cholister was overcome by fire and fumes before he could reach his objective. He died the following day. Both men were awarded the Medal of Honor, posthumously.

Later that month, *Trenton* steamed north to join in the futile search for a lost Norwegian ship. Following that mission, the light cruiser operated along the east coast until 3 February 1925, when she departed Philadelphia to join the rest of the Scouting Fleet of Guantanamo Bay, Cuba. After gunnery exercises, the fleet headed for the Panama Canal and transited it in mid-month. On the 23d, the combined forces of the Battle Fleet and Scouting Fleet departed Balboa and steamed north to San Diego. En route, the ships participated in a fleet problem, then assembled in the San Diego-San Francisco area. On 15 April, the United States Fleet put to sea for the Central Pacific and conducted another battle problem en route—this one designed to test fully the defenses of the Hawaiian Islands. After reaching Hawaiian waters, the Fleet as a whole conducted tactical exercises there until 7 June when most of the Scouting Fleet headed back toward the Atlantic.

Trenton—in Light Cruiser Division 2—sortied with the Battle Fleet on 1 July for a cruise to the South Pacific and visits to Australia and New Zealand. After stopping at Samoa, the ships visited the ports of Melbourne, Wellington, Sydney, Auckland, Dunedin, and Lyttleton. Late in August, Light Cruiser Division 2 turned homeward and steamed via the Marquesas and Galapagos Islands and the Panama Canal to rejoin the Scouting Fleet near Guantanamo Bay on 4 October. After gunnery practice, *Trenton* returned to Philadelphia on 9 November.

In January 1926, *Trenton* joined the other units of the Scouting Fleet and returned to Guantanamo for gunnery drills and tactical exercises. On 1 February, she departed Cuba with them, bound for Panama. During the next six weeks, she participated in combined maneuvers with units of both Battle Fleet and Scouting Fleet. In mid-March, the units of the Scouting Fleet returned to their home yards for repairs before leaving for summer training cruises with naval reservists and tactical exercises in the area around Narragansett Bay. In mid-September, she returned to Guantanamo Bay for winter maneuvers.

Trenton participated in maneuvers until just before Christmas when the units of the Scouting Fleet dispersed to their home ports for the holidays. Early in 1927, she joined the Scouting Fleet in combined maneuvers with the Battle Fleet near Guantanamo Bay. In May, *Trenton* was called upon to transport Col. Henry L. Stimson, a special observer in Nicaragua during a period of internal disorder. She embarked Col. and Mrs. Stimson at Corinto and carried them back to Hampton Roads. Following a review by President Coolidge in June, the various units of the two fleets departed Hampton Roads for their normal summer routines. Light Cruiser Division 2, of which *Trenton* was flagship, operated off Narragansett Bay; then, in the fall, rejoined the Scouting Fleet for gunnery and tactical exercises along the east coast between Chesapeake Bay and Charleston, S.C.

In January 1928, *Trenton* and her division embarked marines at Charleston and returned to Nicaragua, where they landed to assist in supervising the elections which resulted from Col. Stimson's visit. She and her sister-ships rejoined the Scouting Fleet at Guantanamo and resumed maneuvers. On 9 March, Light Cruiser Division 2 parted company with the Scouting Fleet. The four light cruisers rendezvoused with the Battle Fleet off the California coast and headed for Hawaii, conducting drills en route. After exercises in the Hawaiian Islands, *Trenton* and *Memphis* (CL–13) cleared Honolulu to relieve Light Cruiser Division 3 on the Asiatic Station. During that tour of duty, she entertained Col. Henry L. Stimson, this time as Governor General of the Philippines. She participated in joint Army-Navy maneuvers in the Philippines and patrolled the northern Chinese coast, on one occasion putting a landing force ashore at Chefoo.

In May 1929, *Trenton*'s division was detached from the Asiatic Fleet, and she steamed back to the United States along with *Memphis* and *Milwaukee* (CL–5). The light cruiser was overhauled at Philadelphia in the latter part of 1929 and then rejoined the Scouting Fleet. During the next four years, *Trenton* resumed the Scouting Fleet schedule of winter maneuvers in the Caribbean followed by summer exercises off the New England coast. Periodically, however, she was ordered to the Isthmian coast to bolster the Special Service Squadron during periods of extreme political unrest in one or more of the republics of Central America.

In the spring of 1933, *Trenton* moved to the Pacific and became flagship of the Battle Force cruisers. She operated in the eastern Pacific until September 1934. At that time, the ship returned to the Atlantic side of the Panama Canal to cruise with the Special Service Squadron. Over the next 15 months, *Trenton* visited ports in the Caribbean, in Central America, and South America as the squadron conducted a good-will cruise to Latin America. In January 1936, she retransited the canal and, after an overhaul at the Mare Island Navy Yard, rejoined the Battle Force until late in the spring of 1939. During that period, she made her second cruise to Australia in the winter of 1937 and 1938 for the sesquicentennial of the first colonization of that continent.

In May 1939, she returned to the Atlantic and, after a stop at Hampton Roads, got underway on 3 June for Europe. There she joined Squadron 40–T, a small American naval force which had been organized in 1936 to evacuate United States citizens from Spain and to protect American interests during the Spanish Civil War. *Trenton* patrolled the western Mediterranean and waters off the coast of the Iberian peninsula until mid-July 1940 when she returned to the United States. During her homeward voyage, the light cruiser carried Luxembourg's royal family then in flight from Nazi aggression.

In November, *Trenton* reentered the Pacific and rejoined the Battle Force, becoming an element of Cruiser Division 3. From 1941 to mid-1944, the ship served with the Southeast Pacific Force. At the time of America's entry into the war early in December of 1941, she was moored at Balboa in the Canal Zone. During the early part of 1942, *Trenton* escorted convoys to Bora Bora in

Trenton (CL–11) at Madeira during her service with Squadron 40–T, a Curtiss SOC *Seagull* floatplane on her catapult. The flag at the bow of her boat, in the foreground, shows that the U.S. Consul is on board.

he Society Islands where the Navy was constructing a 'uel depot. From mid-1942 to mid-1944, she patrolled he western coast of South America between the Canal Zone and the Strait of Magellan.

On 18 July 1944, *Trenton* headed north for duty in waters surrounding the Aleutians. After stopping for a time at San Francisco, she arrived at Adak, Alaska, on 2 September. A month later, she shifted bases to Attu. In October, *Trenton* joined *Richmond* (CL–9) and nine destroyers in two sweeps of the northern Kuril Islands—one between the 16th and the 19th and the second between the 22d and the 29th—as a diversion during the invasion of Leyte. She returned to the Kurils again on 3 January 1945 to bombard enemy installations on Paramushiru Island, then resumed Alaskan patrols.

For the remainder of the war, *Trenton* patrolled the waters of Alaska and the Aleutian Islands and made periodic sweeps of the Kuril Islands. On 18 February, she returned to Paramushiru to pound shore installations. A month later, she bombarded Matsuwa. On 10 June, the light cruiser shelled Matsuwa once more and made an antishipping sweep before conducting another bombardment during the evening hours of the 11th. Between 23 and 25 June, *Trenton* conducted her last offensive operation of the war, an antishipping sweep of the central Kurils. Task Force 94 split into two units. *Trenton* encountered no enemy shipping, but the other unit sank five ships of a small convoy.

Not long after that operation, the light cruiser steamed south for yard work. She reached San Francisco on 1 August, and the end of the war found her at Mare Island Navy Yard awaiting inactivation overhaul. Early in November, she headed south to Panama. *Trenton* transited the canal on the 18th, arrived at Philadelphia a week later, and was placed out of commission there on 20 December 1945. Her name was struck from the Navy list on 21 January 1946. On 29 December 1946, she was delivered to her purchaser, the Patapsco Scrap Co. of Bethlehem, Pa., for scrapping.

Trenton earned one battle star for World War II service.

III

(LPD–14: dp. 16,913 (f.); l. 569'; b. 105'; dr. 22'; s. 31 k.; cpl. 454; trp. 1,436; a. 4 3''; cl. *Austin*)

The third *Trenton* (LPD–14) was laid down at Seattle, Wash., on 8 August 1966 by the Lockheed Shipbuilding & Construction Co.; launched on 3 August 1968;

sponsored by Mrs. Richard J. Hughes; and commissioned on 6 March 1971, Capt. Karl R. Thiele in command.

Trenton got underway on 9 April for the east coast and reached her home port, Norfolk, Va., on 12 May. The amphibious transport dock remained in port until 1 June when she departed Hampton Roads for shakedown training out of Guantanamo Bay, Cuba. However, on 28 June, her shakedown cruise was interrupted when a steam valve in her number two engine room ruptured, killing four sailors instantly and severely injuring six others. The injured men were "medevaced" first to Guantanamo Bay and thence to the burn ward of the Army Hospital at Fort Sam Houston, Tex. There, two of the six subsequently died as a result of their injuries.

Trenton returned to Guantanamo Bay for interim repairs and then made her way back to Norfolk on one engine, arriving on 6 July. After repairs at the Norfolk Naval Shipyard, she completed shakedown training off the Virginia Capes and in the Guantanamo Bay operating area. On 9 November, the ship returned to Norfolk and remained there through the end of 1971.

On 17 January 1972, *Trenton* rounded Cape Charles and headed north to participate in Exercise "Snowy Beach." She arrived off Reid State Park, Maine, three days later and participated in the cold weather amphibious exercise until the 23d when she headed home. On 4 February, she stood out of Hampton Roads bound for the Gulf of Mexico in company with *Ponce* (LPD–15). The two ships reached New Orleans on 9 February and, for the next six days, served as "hotel" ships for ROTC and military participants in the Mardi Gras Festival.

Trenton returned to Norfolk on 20 February and resumed her east coast-West Indies routine. Following amphibious training at Onslow Beach, N.C., and sea trials near Norfolk, she visited the Caribbean in April with other units of Amphibious Squadron (PhibRon) 4. She then devoted the rest of the early summer to exercises and training at Onslow Beach and at Norfolk before preparing for her first Mediterranean deployment.

The ship departed Norfolk on 28 July, embarked marines at Morehead City, N.C., on the 29th, and headed across the Atlantic on the 30th. She reached Rota, Spain, on 10 August and, with the other units of PhibRon 4, was incorporated into the 6th Fleet as Task Force (TF) 61. She spent the remainder of the year and most of the first month of 1973 in the Mediterranean. During that six-month period, *Trenton* participated in six amphibious landing exercises (Phiblex's), most of which were conducted in cooperation with the military services of foreign nations. In September, she conducted a landing exercise at Timbakion, Crete, with units of the Italian Navy. Greek and Italian ships joined her later that month for Phiblex 3–73 conducted at Alexandroupolis, Greece. In mid-October, troops of the French Foreign Legion provided the opposition for a landing exercise at Corsica. *Trenton* visited Izmir, Turkey, in mid-September and, in mid-December, concluded her exercise schedule at Porto Scuda, Sardinia, with Phiblex 6–73. On 16 January 1973, she headed home; and, 10 days later, she entered the Naval Amphibious Base at Little Creek, Va.

On 1 March, *Trenton* shifted to the administrative command of PhibRon 10. On the 27th, she embarked marines at Morehead City and headed for Onslow Beach, where she participated in Exercise "Exotic Dancer VI." On 7 April, the warship headed south to Vieques Island, near Puerto Rico. From 10 to 14 April, *Trenton* joined other Navy ships in Exercise "Escort Tiger XIV," which consisted of training for disaster assistance to the island countries of the Caribbean. During this Caribbean cruise, she visited Maracaibo, Venezuela; San Juan, Puerto Rico; and St. Thomas in the Virgin Islands before embarking the marines at Vieques on 3 May. After a port visit at Ponce, Puerto Rico, *Trenton* carried her marines to Guantanamo Bay for a four-day exercise. On 14 May, she departed the Caribbean and, after disembarking the marines on 17 May, reached Norfolk on the 18th.

On 11 June, *Trenton* steamed out of Hampton Roads for northern Europe. She reached Kiel, Germany, on the 22d, and, for the next week, participated in the annual "Kiel Week" naval celebration. Early in July, she visited Portsmouth, England, and, at mid-month, put into Rotterdam in the Netherlands. The amphibious transport dock bade farewell to Europe at Rotterdam on 21 July and headed back to the United States.

Trenton spent the remainder of the summer conducting drills in the Virginia capes operating area and in preparation for her second Caribbean deployment of the year. On 1 October, she shifted from PhibRon 10 to PhibRon 8. On the last day of that month, she embarked marines at Morehead City and headed south. For the remainder of the year, she cruised the Caribbean, visiting ports in Puerto Rico, the Virgin Islands, and in the Netherlands Antilles as well as conducting amphibious exercises at Vieques Island. The amphibious transport dock returned to Norfolk on 14 December.

During the first four months of 1974, *Trenton* conducted operations out of Little Creek and Norfolk and prepared for duty in the Mediterranean. On 10 May, she embarked marines at Morehead City and put to sea. Ten days later, she reached Rota, Spain, and joined the 6th Fleet. For the next six months, she cruised the Mediterranean, visiting ports and conducting exercises. In July, *Trenton* participated in the evacuation of 286 refugees from strife-torn Cyprus to Beirut, Lebanon. While with the 6th Fleet, she participated in four amphibious exercises. One—Operation "Good Friendship/Double Effect"—included ships of the Turkish Navy. On 20 October, she steamed out of Rota to return to the United States. She arrived in Norfolk on 31 October and operated in the western Atlantic through the end of 1974.

On 7 March 1975, she embarked marines at Morehead City and headed south. After an amphibious assault exercise at Onslow Beach from 8 to 10 March, she continued south to the Caribbean. During the two-month cruise, *Trenton* participated in four exercises, two of which—"LantReadEx 2–75" and "Rum Punch"—were held in cooperation with units of the British and Dutch navies. She returned to Norfolk on 28 April. In May, she hosted a class from the Naval War College, conducted a midshipman training cruise for the Naval Academy, and returned to Onslow Beach for joint service Exercise "Solid Shield." During the early summer,

Trenton prepared for overhaul. On 14 August, she headed north to New York, moored at the Coastal Dry dock & Repair Co. on the following day, and commenced a nine-month overhaul.

On 12 May 1976, *Trenton* completed her overhaul and following loadout at Little Creek, Va., she deployed to Guantanamo Bay, Cuba, on 6 July for refresher training. Returning to Norfolk on 17 August, the ship's next three months was spent in preparation for a forthcoming Mediterranean deployment. On 15 November, *Trenton*, with embarked elements of Marine Battalion Landing Team 1/6, formed Mediterranean Amphibious Ready Group 3–76 and operated with the Sixth Fleet until she returned to Norfolk on 12 May 1977.

Following post-deployment standdown which ended on 30 June, *Trenton* spent the remainder of 1977 conducting midshipman training cruises, engaging in amphibious exercises, and participating in COMPTUEX 3–77, which involved units of the Standing Naval Force Atlantic.

The year 1978 found *Trenton* embarking elements of Battalion Landing Team 1/2 and deploying to the Caribbean from 30 January to 7 March to participate in Atlantic Fleet Readiness Exercise 1–78. The succeeding four months were spent in preparations for a return to the Mediterranean. The ship, with embarked elements of Marine Battalion Landing Team 2/8, departed Morehead City on 27 July, as part of Mediterranean Amphibious Ready Group 2–78. The remainder of 1978 was spent with the Sixth Fleet in that sea.

Trepang

A marine animal sometimes called a sea slug or a sea cucumber—having a long, tough, muscular body—found in the coral reefs of the East Indies.

I

(SS–412: dp. 1,562 (surf.), 2,424 (subm.); l. 311'10"; b. 27'4"; dr. 15'2"; s. 20.25 k. (surf.), 8.75 k. (subm.); cpl. 66; a. 10 21" tt., 1 5", 1 40mm., 1 20mm., 2 .50-cal. mg.; cl. *Balao*)

SS–412 was originally projected as *Senorita* but was renamed *Trepang* on 24 September 1942. The submarine was laid down on 25 June 1943 at Vallejo, Calif., by the Mare Island Navy Yard; launched on 23 March 1944; sponsored by Mrs. R. M. Davenport, the wife of the submarine's prospective commanding officer; and commissioned on 22 May 1944, Comdr. Roy Milton Davenport—already a three-time Navy Cross winner—in command.

Following shakedown out of San Diego, *Trepang* departed the west coast on 15 August 1944 and proceeded to Hawaii where her crew trained and prepared the ship for combat. Setting out from Pearl Harbor on 13 September for her first war patrol, the submarine prowled the waters south of Honshu, the largest and most important of Japan's home islands. She remained below during daylight hours and came up after dark to get a better view as she recharged her batteries and filled up with fresh air. On the night of 30 September *Trepang* spotted a fast convoy departing Tokyo Bay. The submarine gave chase and closed in on a group of ships which included two large tankers, a small freighter, and an escort. The submarine fired an overlapping spread of torpedoes which struck the freighter 750-ton *Takunan Maru*, and sent her to the bottom.

On 10 October, *Trepang* attacked her second convoy which consisted of a pair of tankers and a single escort. Although the submarine claimed a "kill," a postwar assessment of the action did not credit her with a sinking. The following day, the error was reversed. The submarine fired four torpedoes at another Japanese ship, and her commanding officer recorded that all of the "fish" had missed. This time, however, postwar accounting credited *Trepang* with the destruction of the 1,000-ton *Transport No. 105*.

On 12 October, the submarine cruised some 12 miles southwest of the entrance to Tokyo Bay. Soon after she came to the surface, and her radar swept the surrounding seas. Four pips showed themselves on the phosphorescent screen—two large and two small—which were identified as two battleships and two destroyers.

Despite the fact that the phosphorescent waters would make his submarine stand out starkly in the night, Davenport closed at flank speed and fired a full spread of six torpedoes. The "fish" sped through the water toward their targets. He claimed success when explosions rumbled across the water, and flames lit up the night. Davenport turned the submarine to present her stern tubes to the enemy and loosed four more torpedoes. These all missed.

Davenport's gallant and skillfully pressed attacks won him his fourth Navy Cross. He felt that he had damaged a *Yamashiro*-class battleship and had sunk a destroyer; but, unfortunately, a study of Japanese records after the war did not verify either claim.

Her supply of torpedoes exhausted, *Trepang* cleared the area and headed for the Marshalls. She reached Majuro on 23 October for voyage repairs alongside *Bushnell* (AS-15) and brief training which lasted until 16 November. On that day, *Trepang* got underway for the Philippines leading a wolfpack which also included *Segundo* (SS-398) and *Razorback* (SS-394).

The weather was dark, windy, and rough on 6 December, as *Trepang*'s conning tower broke the surface after a day's submerged inshore patrol off Luzon. While shifting course toward deeper water, she detected a group of ships approaching from the northward. Upon closing to investigate, *Trepang* counted seven large ships and three escorts in the convoy which slowly approached the Philippines.

Trepang radioed news of her "find" to her packmaster and then submerged. The submarine shot straight and true—sending freighter *Banshu Maru No. 31* and *Jinyo Maru* to the bottom in quick succession and damaging a third vessel—*Fukuyo Maru*. However, as *Trepang* came about to administer the *coup de grace* to *Fukuyo Maru*, the third cargo ship "obligingly blew up and sank." Meanwhile, as *Segundo* and *Razorback* arrived on the scene, *Trepang* fired all of her remaining torpedoes at a fourth ship which, she reported, blew up and sank soon thereafter. However, this fourth sinking was not confirmed by Japanese records. In the meantime, the other two American submarines were trying to finish off the fleeing remnants of the shattered convoy and managed to sink two ships—one with the aid of American naval aircraft. *Trepang*, now out of torpedoes, sped back to Pearl Harbor, arriving before Christmas.

Following this war patrol, Davenport, one of the most highly decorated submariners of the war, left *Trepang* for shore duty as an instructor at the Naval Academy.

Again sailing for Honshu, *Trepang*—now under Comdr. Allen Russell Faust—teamed up with *Piper* (SS-409), *Pomfret* (SS-391), *Bowfin* (SS-287), and *Sterlet* (SS-392) on an anti-picket boat sweep past Nanpo Shoto, the eastern island chain south of Tokyo, to clear the sea lanes for the carriers of Task Force 58 which in turn was about to strike the Japanese home islands to neutralize them during the assault on the strategic island of Iwo Jima. *Trepang* encountered no worthwhile targets during the patrol and had to settle for performing lifeguard duty for carrier assaults on Tokyo. On 24 February 1945, the submarine sank the 875-ton freighter *Usuki Maru* and blew the bow off another small coastal vessel. While maneuvering to finish off the crippled ship, several antisubmarine vessels appeared on the scene from behind a nearby headland and converged on the fleet boat. *Trepang* dove deep as the Japanese subjected her to a seven-hour depth charge barrage.

Following her return to Guam in March, *Trepang* headed for the Yellow Sea, a "hazardous duty" area due to its vast stretches of shallow water. Despite the danger, the submarine performed well, bagging the 1,000-ton

landing craft, *Transport No. 146*, on 28 April; the 4,667-ton, heavily laden freighter, *Miho Maru*, two days later; and *Minesweeper No. 20* which blew sky-high with a hit on her magazine on 4 May. In addition, the submarine surfaced to shell a junk with a load of lumber. The sole member of this victim's crew, a Korean, understood little sign language, and looked to be of little value for intelligence purposes, so he was put back on board his barely seaworthy craft, with tools and food, and sent on his way. Leaving the Yellow Sea, *Trepang* did a short tour of lifeguarding for B-25 strikes on Shanghai, China, and for the continuing series of B-29 raids on Tokyo, before she returned to Guam.

Trepang's fifth war patrol was divided into two parts —the first saw the ship operating in a lifeguard capacity while the second gave her a more offensive role off northeastern Honshu and eastern Hokkaido. In the former role, she arrived on station to the southeast of Tokyo Bay. Having experienced two previous tours of lifeguarding, *Trepang*'s men expected a series of long, dull days, spent moving in circles, squares, or triangles to break the monotony.

However, shortly before noon on her first day, lookouts spotted a blossoming parachute overhead and soon saw the splash of a crashed P-51 Mustang fighter damaged while escorting B-29's to Tokyo. *Trepang* bent on full power and soon picked up the downed aviator, 2d Lt. Lamar Christian, USAAF, safe and sound. During the maneuver, another Mustang, piloted by 1st Lt. Frank Ayres, USAAF, radioed that it, too, was in trouble; and the pilot requested permission to bail out. *Trepang* replied telling Ayres to "be patient" until the first rescue was complete. Ayres circled the submarine until Christian was safely on board the submarine. Ayres then executed a perfect jump and landed some 400 yards away from *Trepang* and was soon hauled on board.

Three days after rescuing the two airmen, *Trepang* turned them over to *Tigrone* (SS-419) which was on her way home with 30 other aviators already on board. In the middle of the transfer, the submarines picked up a radio message from a "Boxkite" (rescue search plane) that a B-29 Superfortress crew, downed the previous day, was floating a mere seven miles from the Japanese seaport of Nagoya. Accompanied by *Springer* (SS-414), which had also been discharging passengers to *Tigrone*, *Trepang* surged ahead.

The two submarines raced to save the Superfortress's crew. *Trepang* put on full speed and arrived on the scene first. She found eight survivors in four groups of rafts, spread over about four miles of ocean. By the time *Springer* arrived on the scene, *Trepang* had picked up seven of the fliers. *Springer* picked up the last man.

En route to a rendezvous with *Devilfish* (SS-292), *Trepang* sighted a small, troop-laden freighter and sank the ship with her deck guns. A dozen or so Japanese soldiers from the flaming vessel refused to be picked up and taken prisoner and so were left to drown.

Subsequently patrolling off the eastern coast of Honshu, *Trepang* went scoreless until July, when she spotted a coastal convoy of three ships. She torpedoed and sank the lead ship—*Koun Maru No. 2*—but the other vessels conducted evasive action and sped away from the scene at full speed.

Satisfied that she had done her best, *Trepang*, heading to seaward, suddenly shuddered under the impact of two depth bomb explosions. A solitary Japanese plane had spotted *Trepang*'s shadow in the shallow waters and had attacked with depth bombs. Fortunately, all missed their mark.

Given another lifeguarding assignment, *Trepang* stood on the alert to pick up possible downed airmen from British and American carrier strikes on the Japanese home islands. During this tour in July 1945, she rescued one pilot—Lt. (jg.) Bill Kingston, USNR. In addition, on 14 July, she witnessed a shore bombardment conducted by three battleships and a heavy cruiser against Kamaishi.

By now, the war was moving fast, and *Trepang* returned to Pearl Harbor for a refit. There, she watched the tumbling succession of staggering headlines—first the atomic bombs on Hiroshima and Nagasaki; the Russian entry into the Far Eastern War; Japan's tentative acceptance of surrender terms, and finally—on 15 August—peace at last.

After completion of her refit, *Trepang* departed Pearl Harbor and arrived at San Diego on 3 September 1945. Decommissioned on 27 June 1946 and placed in reserve at Vallejo, Calif., at the Mare Island Navy Yard, *Trepang* remained in reserve into the 1960's. She was redesignated as an auxiliary submarine and classified AGSS–412 on 11 June 1962. Struck from the Navy list on 30 June 1967, the submarine was authorized for disposal on 22 December 1967. She was subsequently sunk as a target during Exercise "Strike Ex 4–69" on 16 September 1969 by the combined gunfire of *Henderson* (DD–785) and *Fechteler* (DD–870).

Trepang received five battle stars for World War II service and a Navy Unit Commendation.

II

(SSN–674: dp. 2,860 (surf.), 4,630 (subm.); l. 292′0″; b. 32′0″; dr. 29′0″; s. 20+ k.; cpl. 107; a. 4 21″ tt., SUBROC; cl. *Sturgeon*)

The second *Trepang* (SSN–674) was laid down on 28 October 1967 at Groton, Conn., by the General Dynamics Electric Boat Division; launched on 27 September 1969; sponsored by Mrs. Melvin R. Laird, wife of the Secretary of Defense; and commissioned on 14 August 1970, Comdr. Dean Sackett, Jr., in command.

Following local operations out of New London, Conn. *Trepang* proceeded to the Arctic early in 1971. From 22 February to 22 March, the nuclear attack submarine operated beneath the northern ice cap, conducting extensive tests to provide data for her weapons systems, as well as carrying out scientific experiments concerning the movement, composition, and geological history of the cap itself.

After returning to New London via Faslane, Scotland, *Trepang* was soon deployed to the warmer climes of the Caribbean, departing from her home port on 22 April and subsequently making port at Frederiksted, St. Croix, Virgin Islands, for weapons systems acceptance and evaluation trials. Back in New England waters for local operations, *Trepang* again headed south for further tests. Later in the year, in November, the submarine conducted independent operations in the North Atlantic.

Following her return to her homeport on 5 February 1972, she subsequently underwent standdown and upkeep, as well as type training and equipment grooming in local operating areas. During this period, *Trepang* again conducted a second extended deployment into the northern Atlantic from 24 July to 25 September 1972, returning to New London via Halifax, Nova Scotia. For the remainder of the year, *Trepang* operated off the east coast between New London and Ft. Lauderdale, Fla.

An interim four-week drydocking period at the Portsmouth (N.H.) Naval Shipyard preceded the ship's 1973

The launch of *Trepang* (SSN–674) at Groton, Connecticut.   (USN 1141366)

operations, before the attack submarine headed south for weapons tests off the Florida coast. Completing a four-week upkeep period on 22 April, the ship completed a Nuclear Technical Proficiency Inspection before returning to New London, where she completed an Operational Reactor Safeguards examination on 4 May.

On 8 June, *Trepang* departed New London for a six-month deployment with the 6th Fleet in the Mediterranean. She participated in several special operations with this Fleet during the increased tension brought on by the Yom Kippur War in the Middle East in October 1973. The attack submarine returned to her home port at the end of November 1973 for upkeep and standdown leave period.

Trepang got underway on 15 February 1974 for a special operation which lasted through 9 April. The ship then spent three days at Holy Loch, Scotland, before sailing for New London. She continued local operations and training off the east coast through her change of home port on 1 October 1974, when the submarine was assigned to Portsmouth, N.H. She spent the remainder of the year 1974 in drydock in annual overhaul.

Trepang was assigned to Submarine Squadron 10 during March 1975. She spent the period from April to August completing the overhaul and carrying out crew training and recertification. Following sea trials in late October, *Trepang* returned to New London on 7 November for an intensive post-overhaul upkeep alongside *Fulton* (AS-11).

Departing New London on 1 December, *Trepang* conducted post-overhaul weapons systems acceptance testing at Roosevelt Roads, Puerto Rico, and five days of acoustic trials off Frederiksted, St. Croix, Virgin Islands, before departing St. Croix on 17 December and returning to New London on 22 December.

Trepang spent the early part of the year 1976 preparing for an extended cruise. She deployed to the Mediterranean from June to November, operating with the 6th Fleet. She returned to New London upon conclusion of the deployment and observed post-deployment standdown into 1977.

In mid-January 1977, *Trepang* participated in Exercise "CARIBEX 77." The spring was devoted to individual ship exercises which included a Nuclear Technical Proficiency Inspection (NTPI), a Mk–48 Torpedo Proficiency Inspection, and an Operational Readiness Inspection, all of which were completed successfully. An extensive refit period, which included drydocking, took place in May and early June. Midshipman orientation cruises followed; and, in September, *Trepang* conducted pre-deployment work-up and certification. The nuclear attack submarine then engaged in an Atlantic training mission from mid-October to mid-December with the ship returning to Groton in time for Christmas.

January 1978 found *Trepang* finishing a post-deployment standdown. The remainder of January, February, and March were devoted to type training and participation in NATO Exercise "Safepass." *Trepang* spent the summer working up for a scheduled Mediterranean deployment. The deployment was subsequently cancelled to permit the ship's participation in a special CNO project. The remaining months of 1978 were spent in the evaluation of project-associated equipment, with alternate periods at sea followed by periods in port devoted to equipment maintenance. *Trepang* departed Groton on 27 November to conclude the year at sea while continuing to participate in the special project.

Trever

Born in Waupan, Wis., on 11 June 1885, George Arthur Trever was appointed to the Naval Academy in May 1905 and graduated on 4 June 1909. He spent the years prior to his commissioning in cruises in *Pennsylvania* (Armored Cruiser No. 4); *Princeton*

(Gunboat No. 13); and *Annapolis* (Gunboat No. 10). Receiving the single gold stripe of an ensign while serving in *Rowan* (Torpedo Boat No. 8) on 5 June 1911, Trever assumed command of that vessel later that month. In September 1912, he was transferred to *Farragut* (Torpedo Boat No. 11); and he commanded her until early 1914, when detached to report on board *Cheyenne* (Monitor No. 10).

Following his tour in *Cheyenne*, newly promoted Lt. (j.g.) Trever was ordered to *H–1* (Submarine No. 28), then attached to the Pacific Fleet. After a two-year tour of duty commanding *H–1*, he reported for duty at the Mare Island Navy Yard. In the spring of 1917, Trever reported to the Puget Sound Navy Yard, Bremerton, Wash., to supervise the building of *N–1* (Submarine No. 53), then on the ways at the Seattle Construction and Drydock Company, Seattle, Wash. *N–1* was commissioned on 26 September 1917 and operated out of Puget Sound until transferred to New York late in the year for patrol duties in the Atlantic. In May 1918, Trever was ordered to the Fore River Shipbuilding Company, Quincy, Mass., to assist in fitting out *O–5* (Submarine No. 66). He assumed command of the new O-boat on 9 June 1918 and received the temporary rank of lieutenant commander on 1 July 1918.

On 5 October 1918, during post-commissioning trials, an explosion occurred on board *O–5*, in which Trever and a crewman were injured. Nine days later, at the naval hospital, Brooklyn, N.Y., on 14 October 1918, Lt. Comdr. George A. Trever died as a result of the severe and multiple injuries suffered in the shipboard tragedy.

(DD–339: dp. 1,308; l. 314'4½''; b. 30'11½''; dr. 9'10''; s. 35.0 k.; cpl. 122; a. 4 4'', 1 3'', 12 21'' tt.; cl. *Clemson*)

Trever (DD–339) was laid down on 12 August 1919 at Vallejo, Calif., by the Mare Island Navy Yard; launched on 15 September 1920; sponsored by Mrs. Bess McMillan Trever, widow of Lt. Comdr. George A. Trever; and commissioned on 3 August 1922, Lt. H. E. Snow in command.

After shakedown, *Trever* was placed in out-of-commission status, with Destroyer Division 44, at San Diego, Calif., on 17 January 1923. She reposed in "red lead row" until called to active duty on 2 June 1930. As part of Destroyer Division (DesDiv) 15 and later, DesDiv 10, she operated out of San Diego with the Battle Force until reclassified as a high-speed minesweeper and redesignated DMS–16 on 19 November 1940. Then, she worked out of Pearl Harbor through 1941, assigned to Mine Division (MineDiv) 4, Mine Squadron 2, as part of the Base Force, United States Fleet.

On 7 December 1941, *Trever* lay moored in West Loch, Pearl Harbor, with sister ships *Zane* (DMS–14), *Wasmuth* (DMS–15), and *Perry* (DMS–17)—the entire complement of MineDiv 4, nested together off the Pearl City Yacht Club. Shortly before 0800 that Sunday morning, Japanese aircraft swept over the Pacific Fleet's base in a daring stroke calculated to immobilize the Fleet at a single blow.

MineDiv 4's ships commenced firing almost immediately. *Trever*'s .50-caliber Browning machine guns concentrated on one attacker strafing the Pearl City Yacht Club and caused the enemy plane to plunge into a hillside and explode. A second, bolder raider peeled off to strafe the nested minecraft, soon lost its wings in a hail of bullets, and tumbled across the flak-torn sky until it crashed and burned near Beckoning Point.

The forthcoming signal to sortie resulted in a frenzied scramble to reach the open ocean. Many ships, including *Trever*, left behind commanding officers who were unable to reach their departing ships. During the hasty exit, *Trever* embarked the captain and executive officer of *Henley* (DD–391). Later in the morning, these two officers returned to their own ship by an ingenious,

The "flushdeck" destroyers *Long* (DD–209) and *Trever* (DD–339) in tactical exercises off the California coast during the 1930's.

if unorthodox, method. With the threat of a submarine attack, a direct-alongside high-line transfer was out of the question. *Henley* assumed a position ahead of *Trever* and reeled out a long manila line with a life raft attached. *Henley*'s two officers climbed down into the raft, and, after a wet and bumpy ride in choppy seas, reached their own ship and were taken on board.

Trever's own commanding officer, Lt. Comdr. D. A. Agnew, who had gone to sea in *Wasmuth*, boarded his own ship in mid-afternoon as it swept the Pearl Harbor channel. For the next few months, *Trever* conducted more minesweeping operations, as well as local escort missions and antisubmarine patrols.

On 15 April, *Trever* and *Hopkins* (DMS–13), as Task Group (TG) 15.2, got underway to escort a six-ship convoy from Honolulu to the California coast, arriving at San Pedro on 25 April. Soon afterwards, *Trever* entered the Mare Island Navy Yard for an extensive overhaul, including the removal of her 4-inch mounts and the installation of 3-inch antiaircraft guns and 20-millimeter Oerlikon cannons.

Newly refitted, *Trever* joined TG 15.6 and escorted a west-bound convoy to Oahu, arriving at Pearl Harbor on 2 July. She remained in Hawaiian waters until the 12th, when—in company with *Zane*, *Hopkins*, *Navajo* (AT–64), and *Aldebaran* (AF–40)—she steamed for Tutuila, Samoa; and Tongatabu in the Tonga Islands. Upon arrival, these ships joined Task Force (TF) 62 which was preparing for the first American amphibious assault of the war in the Pacific, the thrust into the Solomon Islands.

Arriving off Guadalcanal on 7 August, *Trever* helped to screen the transports until she was detached with *Hovey* (DMS–11) and *Hopkins* to bombard targets ashore.

While the American ships steamed in column some 3,000 yards away, Japanese shore batteries on Gavutu Island opened fire at 0807. One minute later, as the enemy's shells straddled the American formation, *Trever*'s 3-inch guns, accompanied by the stentorian chatter of her 20-millimeter guns, barked out a telling reply. At 0830, her shells silenced the troublesome gun with a direct hit; and, five minutes later, the destroyer minesweepers ceased fire and withdrew.

Later, while she was conducting sweeping operations with MineRon 2, her antiaircraft fire helped to drive off enemy bombers which had attacked the transport areas. The following day, twin-engined "Betty" bombers swept over the American ships. *Trever* commenced firing at 1203. In the brief, four-minute, running fight, she helped to splash four bombers.

That evening, a Japanese cruiser force threaded its way down "the Slot" between Guadalcanal and Savo Island and surprised five Allied cruisers (four American and one Australian) and their attendant destroyers. In the brief, bitter night battle known as the Battle of Savo Island, *Vincennes* (CA-44), *Quincy* (CA-39), *Astoria* (CA-34), and Australian *Canberra* were sunk. Providentially for the Americans, the Japanese commander inexplicably decided not to press further on down the strait, where he might have caught the anchored American transports, some still heavily laden with supplies for the marines ashore. On 9 August, *Trever* helped to screen the transports as they retired to Noumea, New Caledonia.

After various escort assignments, *Trever* joined TF 65 on 14 September and departed Espiritu Santo for a run to Guadalcanal with reinforcements and supplies for the hard-pressed marines. TF 65 arrived off the island on the 17th and hastily unloaded before retiring toward Noumea, where it arrived on the 22d.

On 10 October, *Trever*, as part of Mine Squadron 2, escorted *McCawley* (AP-10) and *Zeilin* (AP-9) from Espiritu Santo to the Solomons. Upon their arrival on 13 October, *Trever* and *Hovey* received orders to search for survivors of the Battle of Cape Esperance, fought on the night of 12 October.

During the day's search, *Trever* took on board 34 enemy survivors, including three officers. One raft of eight refused to surrender but put up a fight, giving *Trever* no recourse but to destroy it and its occupants. Returning to the transport area, *Trever* transferred her prisoners to *McCawley* and headed back to Espiritu Santo with the returning transports.

Trever next headed back to the Solomons with *Zane* and arrived at Tulagi on 25 October 1942 with torpedoes, ammunition, and aviation fuel for Motor Torpedo Boat Squadron 3. After unloading, they remained there, expecting orders to bombard Japanese positions along Guadalcanal's coast. The directive did not come, but something else did—a message intercepted at 1000, telling that three Japanese destroyers were standing down the strait, apparently to bombard the airstrip at Henderson Field.

Two choices were open to Lt. Comdr. Agnew of *Trever*, who was in command of the task unit. One was to head for the Maliala River to join *Jamestown* (PG-55) and the damaged *McFarland* (AVD-14) which were both well camouflaged. By following this plan, *Zane* and *Trever*, both uncamouflaged, might attract the Japanese into the area, thus assuring the destruction of all four highly vulnerable American ships. Not wishing to be thus caught like "rats in a trap," Agnew decided on the second alternative, a dash for safety.

Shaping course for Sealark Channel, the two old minecraft got underway and bent on speed to clear the area. At 1014, three distinctive silhouettes came over the horizon into view, hull-down and "bones-in-teeth."

The "black gangs" on the American ships were able to pound and cajole 29 knots from the old machinery. However, the Japanese, making 35 knots, gained rapidly and opened fire with their 5.5-inch guns while still out of range of the Americans' 3-inchers. The first enemy shells whistled overhead and sent up fountains of water several hundred yards beyond the minecraft, and the next salvo fell some 300 yards astern.

Trever and *Zane* dodged nimbly and kept up a steady fire from their 3-inch guns as exploding shells drenched their decks with spray. The Japanese then drew blood by hitting *Zane* amidships and killing three men.

Agnew now decided that his ships could not make Sealark Channel and chose instead to attempt a high speed transit of shoal-studded Niella Channel. Just as the Americans were changing course, the Japanese broke off the action, perhaps remembering their primary mission.

Three days later, *Trever* and *Zane* once again conducted a resupply run to Tulagi, each carrying 175 drums of gasoline lashed to her deck. Continuing such runs through January 1943, *Trever* then steamed to Australia for overhaul, arriving at Sydney on 27 January. She returned to Espiritu Santo on 28 February before calling at Wellington, New Zealand, on 31 May.

Returning to escort duties, she accompanied LST-343 from Lunga Roads to the Russell Islands on 20 June 1943. After nightfall, a twin-float Japanese biplane—a "washing machine Charlie"—came over and dropped bombs on the two ships, sending them to general quarters and provoking an angry return fire from *Trever*'s 20-millimeter guns.

The old destroyer minesweeper next took part in operations in the New Georgia campaign. On the 29th, Rear Admiral George H. Fort hoisted his flag to *Trever*'s main as Commander, TG 31.3. That night, in company with *Schley* (APD-14), *McKean* (APD-5), and seven infantry landing craft (LCI's), *Trever* departed Wernham Cove, Russell Islands. At daybreak the next morning, the APD's launched their landing boats. The troops stormed ashore at Oliana Bay, taking the Japanese defenders by surprise. Later that day, with the objective secured, Rear Admiral Fort disembarked at Renard Sound.

On 5 July, American forces struck hard at Kula Gulf to occupy Rice Anchorage and thus to prevent Japanese reinforcements from reaching Munda from Vila. *Trever* embarked 216 men of the Army's 3d Battalion, 148th Infantry Regiment, and joined bombardment and transport groups in the assault.

On 5 August, *Trever* joined *Honolulu* (CL-48)— which had lost her bow to a "long-lance" torpedo during the Battle of Kolombangara—and escorted the damaged cruiser from Espiritu Santo to Pearl Harbor. On 19 August, *Trever* got underway to escort an eastbound convoy to San Francisco.

After a month's overhaul at Mare Island, *Trever* steamed for Pearl Harbor on 8 October and touched there briefly before heading for Guadalcanal. On Armistice Day, she joined the screen for *American Legion* (AP-35) and escorted her to Empress Augusta Bay. Later that month, *Trever* took part in the landings at Cape Torokina, Bougainville.

Trever devoted the next year to escort missions and target towing duty in the South and Central Pacific. Perhaps the highlight of this service came in October 1944 when she joined the screen for torpedoed cruisers *Houston* (CL-81) and *Canberra* (CA-70) and escorted them safely to Ulithi.

On 18 December, as *Trever* was escorting a convoy toward the Western Carolines, the wind velocity began to increase steadily, with the seas rising and the barometer falling. By 1440, typhoon conditions prevailed. Visibility dropped to zero, and torrential rains deluged the ship while mountainous waves and 90-knot winds threatened to tear her apart. Heavy seas carried away the two motor whaleboats and bent and twisted their davits. At 1630, a man making emergency repairs topside was washed overboard; and *Trever* immediately began a search for the missing sailor. Two hours later, she picked up her man: bruised, battered, and in shock —but alive.

The following day, *Trever* put into Guam and transferred her injured seaman to the naval hospital on shore. On 22 December, she reached Eniwetok. On 24 December, she and Army transport *Santa Isabel* got underway for Hawaii, arriving at Pearl Harbor on the last day of 1944. Continuing her homeward journey, *Trever* moored alongside the Mole Pier at the Naval Repair Base, San Diego, and began overhaul on 9 January 1945.

Upon completion of her repairs, she headed for Oahu on 25 March 1945. For the remainder of the war, *Trever* operated out of Pearl Harbor, where she had entered the hostilities with Japan four years before. On 4 June 1945, she was reclassified as a miscellaneous auxiliary and designated as AG-110.

On 22 September 1945, she departed Pearl Harbor for the last time and steamed to San Diego. After repairs, she proceeded via the Canal Zone to Norfolk, Va., where she arrived on 21 October 1945. She was decommissioned on 23 November 1945, struck from the Navy list on 5 December 1945, and sold for scrapping on 12 November 1946.

Trever received five battle stars for her World War II service.

Triana

Rodrigo de Triana was the lookout in *Pinta* who first sighted land on 12 October 1492 during Columbus' first voyage to the New World. Although no documentary evidence has been found linking the ship and the man, *Triana* was probably named for the discoverer of America.

I

(Tug: dp. 450; lbp. 137'; b. 26'; dr. 9'6'' (mean); s. 10 k.)

The first *Triana*—an iron-hulled screw tug built at New York, N.Y., by William Perrine—was launched on 29 April 1865 and was apparently completed sometime after January 1866. Initially laid up at Washington, D.C., *Triana* had entered service at the Washington Navy Yard by or before the summer of 1867.

Triana was subsequently shifted to the New York Navy Yard, Brooklyn, N.Y., where she operated from 1880 to 1887. Subsequently assigned "special service" duty at the Naval Torpedo Station, Newport, R.I., *Triana* performed services supporting experimental torpedo work being carried on there. In addition, she served as an accommodation vessel for men under instruction at that station.

The tug remained in service at Newport until she was struck from the Navy list on 13 April 1891. *Triana* was sold on 2 May 1891.

II

(IX-223: dp. 14,230; l. 441'6''; b. 56'11''; dr. 27'9''; s. 12.0 k. (tl.); cpl. 98; a. 2 3''; cl. *Triana*; T. EC2-S-C1)

The second *Triana* (IX-223) was laid down on 27 December 1943 under Maritime Commission contract (MCE hull 2559) as *Elinor Wylie* at Los Angeles, Calif., by the California Shipbuilding Corp. for the McCormick Steamship Lines; launched on 24 January 1944; sponsored by Mrs. William O'Brien; renamed *Triana* on 21 May 1945; acquired by the Navy from the War Shipping Administration on a "bare-boat" basis on 24 May 1945; and commissioned at Pearl Harbor the same day, Lt. Wyman W. Hodgkins, USNR, in command.

The ship had been severely damaged by an underwater explosion in 1944 and was not considered seaworthy when fully loaded. Nevertheless, during the period 24 May to 29 July, she was patched up, strengthened, and converted into a floating storage ship by the Pearl Harbor Navy Yard.

On 30 July, *Triana* got underway for the Marshall Islands and arrived at Eniwetok on 11 August. One of her holds was consigned to fleet freight, and the remaining cargo space was utilized for drum storage. On 24 September, after the vessel had taken on some 4,500 tons of cargo, her number 2 hold began leaking, and further loading operations were cancelled. The leaks were temporarily stopped, and the ship continued to receive and discharge fleet freight and drum lubricating oil until 30 November.

On 1 December, *Triana* got underway for Guam to unload 8,896 drums of lubricating oil. She arrived at Apra Harbor on the 5th and departed for the United States on 24 December 1945. The cargo ship arrived at San Francisco on 15 January 1946 to prepare for inactivation. *Triana* was decommissioned and returned to the War Shipping Administration on 21 February 1946 and struck from the Navy list on 12 March 1946.

Triangulum

A constellation in the northern triangle of the Zodiac.

(AK-102: dp. 14,550; l. 441'6''; b. 56'11''; dr. 28'4''; s. 12.5 k. (tl.); cpl. 206; a. 1 5'', 4 40mm.; cl. *Crater*; T. EC2-S-C1)

Triangulum (AK-102) was laid down under Maritime Commission contract (MCE hull 1669) on 14 May 1943 as *Eugene B. Daskam* at Wilmington, Calif., by the California Shipbuilding Corp.; renamed *Triangulum* on 27 May 1943; launched on 6 June 1943; sponsored by Mrs. D. H. Mann; acquired by the Navy on 19 June 1943 from the War Shipping Administration on a "bareboat" basis; converted to Navy use at the Destroyer Base, San Diego; and commissioned on 30 July 1943, Comdr. Eugene J. Kingsland, USNR, in command.

Assigned to the Naval Transportation Service, the auxiliary cargo ship moved up the coast to load cargo at San Francisco and stood out to sea with a convoy on 28 August, bound for the New Hebrides. She arrived at Espiritu Santo on 2 October and, for the next five months, shuttled troops and cargo between ports in Australia and New Guinea.

Triangulum embarked part of a battalion of Army combat engineers at Lae and sortied on 14 April 1944 with Task Group (TG) 77.1, the Western Attack Group, for the invasion of Hollandia. On the morning of 22 April, she began landing her 700 troops on the beaches of Humboldt Bay. The ship completed discharging cargo by 1800 the next day and departed in a convoy bound, via Buna, for Milne Bay. She then resumed her supply runs between Australia and New Guinea.

The ship loaded combat cargo at Manus and got underway for Hollandia on 7 November to rendezvous with a convoy proceeding to the Philippines. She arrived at Leyte Gulf on the 19th and began discharging supplies. During her visit there, Japanese planes frequently attacked Allied shipping; and, during a raid on Thanksgiving Day, four of her men were wounded by friendly antiaircraft fire. On 4 December, she departed the area for Australia and, after calling at Hollandia, arrived at Brisbane on 17 December 1944. *Triangulum* shuttled supplies from Australia to South Pacific bases, mostly in New Guinea, for the next year. The supply runs were broken by three voyages to the Philippines: in January, May, and August 1945. On 8 November, she stood out of Leyte to load cargo at Hollandia, Biak, Milne Bay, and Manus to be transported to the United States.

On the last day of 1945, the ship arrived at San Francisco where she was stripped for inactivation and ordered to join the Reserve Fleet in Hawaii. *Triangulum* arrived at Pearl Harbor on 23 February 1946 and was decommissioned there on 15 April. In May 1947, she was towed back to San Francisco and returned to the Maritime Commission on 2 July. *Triangulum* was struck from the Navy list on 17 July 1947.

Triangulum received two battle stars for World War II service.

Trident

A three-pronged spear, symbolic of authority, carried by Poseidon, sea god of the ancient Greeks.

(AMc–107: dp. 195 (est.); l. 98'5''; b. 23'6''; dr. 10'8'';
s. 10 k.; cpl. 17; a. 2 .50-cal. mg.; cl. *Accentor*)

Trident (AMc–107) was laid down on 25 April 1941
at Rockland, Maine, by Snow Shipyards; launched on
8 October 1941; and placed in service at Boston on 18
February 1942, Ens. Edmond J. Massello, USNR, Officer in Charge.

Following a training period at the Mine Warfare
School, Yorktown, *Trident* reported to Section Base,
Boston, for duty with the 1st Naval District. During
the first week in March 1942, the wooden-hulled coastal
minesweeper plied the waters of Boston harbor and its
approaches, performing tasks which would soon become
familiar. At night, she functioned as a guard and escort
vessel; then, as sunrise came, she began daily exploratory sweeps, searching for moored, magnetic, and sonic
mines in the harbor and its approaches. At times, severe
weather or low visibility forced *Trident* to secure from
sweep operations; and, in foggy weather, she helped to
regulate harbor traffic.

Continuing instruction, drills, and periods of repair
broke the minesweeper's routine. After *Trident* was
assigned to the harbor entrance control post, she had
occasion to locate and investigate suspicious small
craft—a welcome diversion from the usual inner harbor
activities.

In June 1942, the 1st Naval District command was
incorporated into the Northern Group of the Eastern
Sea Frontier, and *Trident* continued her duties in
coastal waters for over three years until 8 August
1945, when she arrived at Charleston and reported to
the Commandant, 6th Naval District, for disposition.
She was placed out of service on 16 November 1945,
and her name was struck from the Navy list on the
28th. On 22 October 1946, *Trident* was transferred to
the Maritime Commission; and she was subsequently
sold to Benjamin Feldman of New York City.

Trieste

A seaport in northeastern Italy at the head of the
Adriatic Sea. The bathyscaph was named for the town
in appreciation for the support which its people rendered during the novel submersible's development.

(Bathyscaph: t. 50; l. 59'6''; b. 11'6''; dr. 18' (f.);
cpl. 2)

Trieste—a research bathyscaph—was the development of a concept first studied in 1937 by the Swiss
physicist and balloonist, Auguste Piccard. World War
II abruptly terminated Piccard's work in Belgium on
his deep-sea research submarine—a bathyscaph—and he
did not resume it until 1945. Piccard later worked with
the French government on the development of such a
craft, until invited to come to Trieste, Italy, in 1952,
to commence the construction of a new bathyscaph.
Scientific and navigational instruments to equip the
craft came from Switzerland, Germany, and Italy.
There, on the southern shore of the Gulf of Naples, at
the Navalmeccanica, a civilian shipyard near Naples,
Trieste took shape. In August 1953, the bathyscaph
was placed in the water for the first time. On 11 August
1953, Professor Piccard and his son Jacques made the
trial dive—to a depth of five fathoms.

Between 1953 and 1956, *Trieste* conducted many dives
in the Mediterranean. In 1955, Dr. Robert Dietz, of the
United States Navy's Office of Naval Research (ONR),
met Professor Piccard in London and discussed the
project. During their talks, Piccard invited Dietz to
Italy to see the bathyscaph. During his visit the following year, Dietz invited Piccard to the United States to
discuss the bathyscaph's future as an American submersible.

A group of American oceanographers and underwater
sound specialists visited Castellamare, Italy, the following summer, 1957, and tested and examined *Trieste*.

They eventually recommended that the craft be acquired
by the United States government. They thought that
the submersible was the ideal craft to participate in
Project "Nekton"—an inspection of the deepest point
in the world's oceans, the Challenger Deep, off the
Marianas.

Thus, in the fall of 1958, *Trieste* was transported to
San Diego, Calif., her new home port. Starting in
December of that year, *Trieste* made several dives off
San Diego. Fitted with a stronger sphere, fabricated
by the Krupp Iron Works of Germany, *Trieste* was
taken to Guam for Project "Nekton." With *Wandank*
(ATR–109) as support vessel, *Trieste* climaxed her
participation in Project "Nekton" on 23 January 1960
when Lt. Don Walsh, USN, and Jacques Piccard—the
professor's son who had accompanied the bathyscaph to
the United States to instruct the Navy in its operation
and maintenance—descended seven miles to the bottom of the Challenger Deep. The world's record descent
had taken nine hours.

Between 1960 and 1962, after *Trieste* was overhauled
at San Diego upon her return from Guam and Project
"Nekton," the bathyscaph conducted many dives in the
San Diego area. In November 1962, another period of
repairs commenced. At this time, a new bathyscaph
float was on the drawing board, and construction began
early in 1963. *Trieste*'s modifications were proceeding
apace when the submarine *Thresher* (SSN–593) sank
off the Massachusetts coast. *Trieste* was brought across
country to Boston, where she soon entered the search
to locate the lost submarine. She made five dives before
returning to the Boston Naval Shipyard for repairs.
Trieste later conducted five more dives. In August, during this series, she discovered the debris from *Thresher*,
including the submarine's sail which still clearly carried
the number "593." About this time, the bathyscaph—
then 10 years old—began to show signs of age.

Hence *Trieste*—her search mission accomplished—
was returned to San Diego, where she was taken out
of service. For her part in the search, however, the
bathyscaph and her commander, Comdr. Donald A.
Keach, received the Navy Unit Commendation. Subsequently, *Trieste* was transported to the Washington
Navy Yard where she was placed on exhibit in the Navy
Memorial Museum in early 1980.

Trieste II

See *Trieste* for an explanation of the name.

(Bathyscaph: t. 46 (long); l. 67'; b. 15'; dr. 12'5'';
cpl. 2)

Trieste II was designed by the Naval Electronic
Laboratory, San Diego, Calif., as a successor to *Trieste*
—the Navy's pioneer bathyscaph. Built at the Mare
Island Naval Shipyard, *Trieste II* incorporated the
Terni, Italian-built sphere used in *Trieste* with an entirely new bathyscaph float—one more seaworthy and
streamlined. Completed in early 1964, *Trieste II* was
placed on board USNS *Francis X. McGraw* (T-AK–
241) and shipped, via the Panama Canal, to Boston.

Commanded by Lt. Comdr. John B. Mooney, Jr.,
Trieste II conducted dives in the vicinity of the loss
site of *Thresher*—operations commenced by the first
Trieste the year before. She recovered bits of wreckage,
positively fixing the remains as that of the lost
Thresher, in September 1964.

Subsequently shipped back to San Diego, *Trieste II*
underwent a series of modifications until April 1965,
when she was launched on 19 April to undertake the
first of many dives as test and training vehicle for the
Navy's new deep submergence program. After a series
of dives off San Diego, *Trieste II* underwent further
modifications at Mare Island to improve the craft's
undersea navigation, control, and small object recovery.

As the bathyscaph continued her operations as test
vehicle for the deep submergence program, she quali-

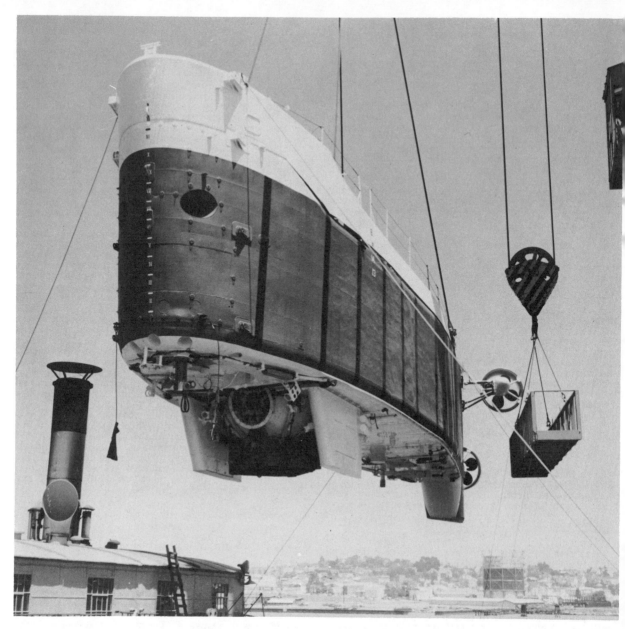

The research bathyscaph *Trieste II*. Controlled from the pressure-resistant sphere seen on the underside, *Trieste II* is equipped with cameras, sonars, and sensors for scientific observation at great depths. Her instrumentation can be varied to suit the mission in hand.

fied four officers as "hydronauts"—the beginning of a burgeoning oceanographic operation. *Trieste II*'s valuable experience in deep submergence operations has helped in the design and construction of other deep-diving submersibles which could be used in rescuing crews and recovering objects from submarines in distress below levels reachable by conventional methods.

This unique craft was listed only as "equipment" in the Navy inventory until the autumn of 1969. On 1 September 1969, *Trieste II* was placed in service, with the hull number X–1. Reclassified as a deep submergence vehicle (DSV) on 1 June 1971, *Trieste II* (DSV–1) continued her active service in the Pacific Fleet into 1980.

Trigger

The triggerfish is any of numerous deep-bodied fishes of warm seas having an anterior dorsal fin with two or three stout erectile spines.

I

(SS–237: dp. 1,552 (surf.), 2,415 (subm.); l. 311'8''; b. 27'3''; dr. 15'3''; s. 20.25 k. (surf.), 8.75 k. (subm.); cpl. 80; a. 10 21'' tt., 1 3'', 2 .50 cal. mg.; cl. *Gato*)

The first *Trigger* (SS–237) was laid down on 1 February 1941 at Mare Island, Calif., by the Mare Island

Navy Yard; launched on 22 October 1941; sponsored by Mrs. Walter N. Vernou; and commissioned on 30 January 1942, Lt. Comdr. Jack H. Lewis in command.

The submarine sailed for Hawaii on 22 May and reached Pearl Harbor the following week. She sortied for Midway with Task Group 7.2 on the 29th in anticipation of a Japanese attack on that island. Her station was northeast of Midway, and she remained there without contacting any enemy shipping until she was ordered back to Pearl Harbor on 9 June.

On 26 June, *Trigger* got underway for the Aleutians to patrol an area west of Cape Wrangell, Attu Island. She encountered no enemy shipping before calling at Dutch Harbor on 8 August en route back to Hawaii.

Trigger's second war patrol, conducted from 23 September to 8 November, took her to Japanese home waters. In the early morning hours of 5 October, the submarine sighted smoke on the horizon and headed for it. A vessel soon appeared, coming toward the submarine. As the target approached, the submarine identified it as a small ship. *Trigger* then surfaced and manned her machine guns. However, when the submarine neared the target, she learned that the Japanese ship was larger than she had at first appeared to be. Enemy shells soon began exploding close to *Trigger*, and the 4,000-ton ship turned and came on fast in an attempt to ram. The submarine barely avoided a collision as she submerged for an attack. *Trigger* fired two torpedoes and heard one hit. She then surfaced and gave chase, only to have the target again open fire. The submarine missed with three more torpedoes and then discontinued the pursuit.

Before dawn on the morning of 17 October, *Trigger* made a surface attack on a freighter off the Bungo Strait. She fired two spreads of torpedoes which sank *Holland Maru* with her guns still firing. That night, a destroyer came out of Bungo Strait and dropped a string of depth charges near the submarine. *Trigger* fired three torpedoes "down the throat" at the onrushing Japanese destroyer and, one minute later, observed an explosion so powerful that it threw enough flame and water into the air to obscure the target. When the air cleared, the enemy ship was still intact, suggesting that *Trigger's* first torpedo may have exploded prematurely, detonating the next two by its turbulence. The submarine fired one more torpedo as the enemy disappeared, but failed to score a hit.

Near midnight of the 20th, *Trigger* fired a spread of four torpedoes from a range of 900 yards in a surface attack upon a 10,000-ton tanker. Two torpedoes hit the enemy ship as it turned in an attempt to ram. The submarine went to 100 feet to evade a Japanese counterattack and heard a heavy explosion as either gasoline, magazines, or the boilers blew up. She then came up to periscope level but found nothing in sight. Four days later, *Trigger* attacked a large enemy tanker, riding high in the water. A spread of three torpedoes produced three observed hits, one near the target's stern. The screws of the enemy ship stopped, and she began emitting heavy white smoke aft. But she soon got underway again. *Trigger* fired her last torpedo at the ship as it was moving off and missed. That night, she surfaced and began her homeward voyage.

From 3 December 1942 to 22 January 1943, the submarine conducted a combined minelaying and offensive patrol in waters surrounding the Japanese home islands. On 20 December, she began planting a minefield off Inubo Saki, Honshu. *Trigger* planted the northern half of the field and was working on the southern part when a cargo ship passed her, heading into the newly-laid mines. Five minutes later, a violent explosion rocked the freighter which sank as an escort circled her. The submarine later heard another explosion from the direction of the minefield and, when she surfaced the next day, found the field was covered by smoke.

On 22 December, *Trigger* sighted a ship approaching from Uraga and made a surface attack. A spread of three torpedoes produced one hit forward of the bridge, and the target started to settle by the bow. The submarine fired one more torpedo into the ship and, when last seen, *Teifuku Maru* was awash forward with her screws nearly out of the water. On 31 December 1942, she attacked a cargo ship loaded with planes. *Trigger* fired three torpedoes from 700 yards and watched two hit. The target began to list to starboard and was down by the bow. Sound reported a heavy secondary explosion. The submarine came up to periscope level and saw the freighter with her stern high out of the water and a destroyer approaching. She went deep and when she next came up for a look, there was nothing to be seen.

On 10 January 1943, a Japanese destroyer approached *Trigger*, and the submarine fired three torpedoes from 1,500 yards. One hit under the well deck and folded the destroyer's forecastle up at a 45-degree angle; and another hit the target's stern. Soon *Okikaze* sank on an even keel.

Trigger stood out of Midway on 13 February to patrol off the Palaus. Two weeks later, she fired four torpedoes at a freighter, but the target managed to steer between them. Heavy air cover prevented a second attack. On 4 March, the submarine attacked a freighter in a rain squall, but all three of her torpedoes missed. On the 15th, *Trigger* sighted a convoy steaming in two columns. There were two freighters in the right hand column and three in the left with an escort on the outboard bow of each. She worked her way between the two columns and fired three torpedoes at each of the leading ships. She hit the lead freighter in the left hand column twice but missed her target on the right because it unexpectedly changed course. *Trigger* than fired three more torpedoes at the right lead ship at a range of 700 yards and observed two hits before the escorts forced her to go deep. When she surfaced again, there was nothing to be seen. *Trigger* was later officially credited with having sunk *Momoha Maru*, a 3,103-ton cargo ship.

That night, the submarine fired six torpedoes at a ship that was being towed by a smaller freighter. Five of the torpedoes missed, and the sixth made a circular run and passed over the submarine's engine room. A shaken crew broke off the attack.

On 20 March, the submarine fired three torpedoes at the lead ship in a convoy of four cargomen. One hit caused the target to list 10 degrees to port and stop, but it soon got underway and rejoined the convoy. *Trigger* terminated the patrol at the Submarine Base, Pearl Harbor, on 6 April.

Between 30 April and 22 June, the submarine made a patrol which returned her to Japanese home waters. On 28 May, *Trigger* contacted two freighters off Iro Saki and launched three torpedoes at the larger. One hit its target aft. When last seen, the ship was down by the stern. The next day, the submarine fired a spread of three torpedoes at a small cargo ship. Two missed and the third exploded prematurely. She then launched a fourth which apparently hit but failed to explode. On 1 June, the submarine was searching for Japanese shipping off Sagami Nada when she sighted two columns of smoke. She closed the range toward a firing position, made out two cargo ships, and fired a spread of three torpedoes at each target. Hit in her stern, the lead ship, *Noborikawa Maru*, sank immediately. The second ship saw the torpedo wakes, turned, and passed between them. *Trigger* then fired a torpedo at the oncoming ship; but, if the torpedo reached the target, it failed to explode. On the 10th, *Trigger* sighted an aircraft carrier protected by two destroyers. She closed and sent six torpedoes streaking toward the Japanese flattop. The submarine heard four hits before she went deep to avoid the escorts which kept her down for several hours. The damaged carrier *Hiyo* limped into Tokyo Bay and was out of action for almost a year. The next day, the submarine began her return voyage to Pearl Harbor.

On 1 September, after a yard overhaul, *Trigger* was ready to begin her sixth war patrol. It took her into the East China Sea, off the China coast, north of Formosa. On the 17th, she made two hits on a Japanese freighter, one aft and one on the bow, but both torpedoes proved to be duds. The next day, she again contacted the same ship and fired four torpedoes at her. One struck *Yowa Maru*, and the 6,435-ton cargo ship slid beneath the waves.

The 21st of September was *Trigger's* best day. She was patrolling some 30 miles north of the Hoka Sho light when she sighted a convoy of three tankers and three freighters protected by Japanese planes. The submarine attacked the tankers first, firing three torpedoes at the leader and three at the second. One hit aft was seen on the lead tanker, and flames shot over 500 feet into the air. Her crew, dressed in whites, could be seen running forward to escape the fire. One torpedo hit the second tanker amidships, and it broke in half beneath the stack and sank immediately. *Trigger* turned and fired three stern tubes at the third tanker. This target swung toward the submarine, and all three torpedoes missed. *Trigger* then fired another torpedo which hit the ship's starboard side. When the submarine went deep her commanding officer slipped and fell into the periscope well as the quartermaster was lowering it. He supported himself on his elbows, and the quartermaster heard his shouts in time to prevent a serious accident. Sonar reported two more explosions before the submarine came up to periscope depth to resume the at-

tack. *Trigger* fired two bow torpedoes at the third freighter in the column and scored two hits on the target which went down by the bow. The submarine then made two more attacks on the freighter, but all of her torpedoes either missed or were duds. During the three and one-half hours of action, *Trigger* sank two tankers, *Shiriya* and *Shoyo Maru*, and a freighter, *Argun Maru*, for a total of 20,660 tons of enemy shipping. The submarine returned to Midway on 30 September to be refitted and rearmed.

The East China and Yellow Seas were *Trigger's* objective for her seventh patrol. She stood out of Midway on 22 October and proceeded to her patrol area. At 2200 hours on 1 November, she sighted a convoy that was steaming in two columns. When a ship in the nearer column overlapped one in the more distant group, she fired a spread of three torpedoes at them. One torpedo struck the nearer freighter in her bow and one hit the farther ship amidships. The submarine saw the nearer ship go down by the bow, before she herself was forced to go deep where she was severely depth-charged by two escorts. In the early morning of the 2d, *Trigger* fired three torpedoes at a freighter and scored one hit. At 0050 hours, she attacked the ship again with a spread of another three. Two of them hit forward, and *Yawata Maru* went down, bow first, in a vertical plunge. Two hours and 25 minutes later, *Trigger* fired three torpedoes at a 7,148-ton transport. All torpedoes hit the

The crew of *Trigger* (SS–237) celebrate the four torpedo hits which damaged the Japanese carrier *Hiyo*.

ship, and *Delagoa Maru* disintegrated. On 5 November, the submarine attacked a convoy of three cargo ships protected by one destroyer and two planes. *Trigger* fired three bow tubes at the second ship in the convoy and one bow tube at the third before she went deep to avoid the escort which dropped 20 depth charges. Thinking she was clear, the submarine came to periscope depth and was greeted by five near bomb misses.

On 13 November, *Trigger* made a submerged approach on a convoy of nine merchantmen and four escorts. After the Japanese ships zigged, the submarine found herself between two columns of ships. But her bow tubes were empty! She attacked the last and biggest ship, believed to be a transport, from a range of 800 yards with a spread of four torpedoes. The target, which carried a large deck cargo, took one hit aft and one under her stack. The submarine went deep, received a short depth charge attack, and came up to periscope depth to learn that her target had gone down. On the 21st, *Trigger* sighted a cargoman and closed the range to 2,000 yards before firing four torpedoes. Two hits started the victim down by the bow as the submarine's crew took turns at the periscope to watch *Eizan Maru* sink. More than a fortnight later, the submarine arrived at Pearl Harbor on 8 December 1943.

Trigger stood out to sea on New Year's Day 1944 to begin her eighth war patrol, this time in the Truk-Guam shipping lanes. On 27 January, she sighted the conning tower of an *RO*-class submarine dead ahead. *Trigger* set up to fire a bow shot from a range of 800 yards. She came to periscope depth and saw that the Japanese submarine, then less than 100 yards away, was preparing to attack. *Trigger* went to 150 feet, expecting a torpedo at any minute, but sound heard no torpedo screws. She came up to periscope depth and saw the Japanese periscope so she decided to make an end around. When *Trigger* returned to periscope depth, the enemy had disappeared.

Four days later, she contacted a convoy of three ships accompanied by two *Fubuki*-class destroyers. The submarine scored two hits on the coastal minelayer *Nasami* which disappeared in a cloud of smoke and debris. The nearer destroyer began closing the range, and *Trigger* missed it with four aft tubes. She caught up with the convoy again and fired five torpedoes at the last ship. Two hits produced flames that reached mast head height and several secondary explosions that marked the end of the 11,933-ton converted submarine tender *Yasukuni Maru*. Over three weeks later, the submarine terminated the patrol when she arrived at Pearl Harbor on 23 February.

On 23 March, *Trigger* headed for the Palaus on her ninth war patrol. In the early morning of 8 April, she contacted a convoy of approximately 20 large ships with an estimated 25 escorts and closed to attack. When she raised her periscope, she saw a destroyer 150 feet away firing at the scope and attempting to ram. The submarine loosed four torpedoes at the convoy and went deep as several more escorts joined the attack. On her way down, she heard four explosions. *Trigger* ran at 300 feet or more for 17 hours as six escorts dogged her trail and rained down numerous depth charges. Six exploded extremely close. When the submarine surfaced, her forward torpedo room was flooded to her deck plates; the hull air induction and most compartments were in about the same condition. The bow planes, trim pump, sound gear, and both radars were all dead. Her radio antenna was grounded, and the submarine could not transmit. The crew spent the next four days making repairs "by use of spares, baling wire, and considerable ingenuity."

Trigger met *Tang* (SS–306) on the 14th and exchanged information by line gun. The next day, *Trigger*'s executive officer went on board *Tang* by a rubber boat, to borrow an air compressor part and to make plans for a coordinated search and attack. On the 18th, *Tang*'s executive officer delivered spare parts for the air compressor to *Trigger*, and she continued on patrol.

Shortly before midnight on the 26th, the submarine contacted a convoy of six ships off the eastern Palaus. She fired six torpedoes, from 2,400 yards, at four ships that were closely bunched and overlapping. Four hits were seen and heard from a big explosion on each ship. Suddenly, a terrific explosion blew up one of the closer ships. One of the more distant ships stood straight up on her bow and then sank immediately. At six minutes after midnight, *Trigger* fired three torpedoes at a group of ships and heard one timed explosion. At 0157, she fired four torpedoes at a damaged cargo ship and two at an escort. The cargo ship received two more hits. Five minutes later, the submarine fired three stern tubes at a group of three escorts, and the middle one disappeared in a cloud of smoke. During the attack, *Trigger* sank the 11,739-ton passenger-cargo ship *Miike Maru* and heavily damaged the destroyer escort *Kasado*, the 9,467-ton cargo ship *Hawaii Maru*, and the 8,811-ton cargo ship *Asosan Maru*. *Trigger* returned to Pearl Harbor on 20 May and, four days later, headed for the United States for a major overhaul. She arrived at San Francisco on 31 May and, after overhaul, returned to Hawaii on 11 September.

On 24 September, *Trigger* got underway to take station off the east coast of Formosa and perform life guard patrol for bomber strikes due on 12 October. The morning of the strikes, she rescued a pilot from *Bunker Hill* (CV–17) whose burning plane had crash-landed nearby. On the 19th, as the invasion of the Philippines was about to begin, she contacted a convoy of two *Atago*-class cruisers, one *Natori*-class, two other light cruisers, and several destroyers with air cover. *Trigger* had no chance to fire but reported the contact. On 30 October, she fired four torpedoes at a tanker but missed. She then fired another four from her stern tubes and heard one hit the target before running up the periscope to watch the other three blow off part of the stern, but the ship did not sink. *Trigger* went deep as 78 depth charges were rained down on her within the next hour but caused no damaged. The damaged 10,021-ton tanker *Takane Maru* was later sunk by *Salmon* (SS–182) and *Sterlet* (SS–392). The next morning, *Trigger* received word from *Salmon* that she had been heavily damaged by depth charges and was unable to submerge. *Trigger* rendezvoused with *Salmon* that night and was joined by *Silversides* (SS–236) and *Sterlet* to escort the damaged submarine to Saipan. They were provided with air cover from the Marianas and arrived at Tanapag Harbor on 3 November. A week later, *Trigger* departed with six other submarines but was ordered to discontinue her patrol on the 17th and returned to Guam.

On 28 December 1944, *Trigger* headed for the Bungo Strait-Kii Strait area to begin her 11th war patrol. At 2105 on 3 January 1945, she sighted a light; and radar made a doubtful contact. Thirty minutes later, a torpedo passed by her starboard side. She reversed course and cleared the area but returned two days later. That day, she sighted a periscope at 2,000 yards; and—realizing that instead of hunting, she was being hunted—she slipped away.

On the 29th, she made radar contact from 23,000 yards on a large convoy with six escorts and well-covered by aircraft. As she closed, the moon came out bright and clear. An enemy bomber turned and started in as radar picked up another plane coming in astern at 5,000 yards. The submarine went deep, and the convoy slowly pulled away. The next day, the ship was ordered to terminate her patrol, and she returned to Guam on 3 February.

Trigger stood out to sea on 11 March to begin her 12th war patrol and headed for the Nansei Shoto area. On the 18th, she attacked a convoy west of the islands, sinking the cargo ship *Tsukushi Maru No. 3* and damaging another. The attack was reported on the 20th, and the submarine was subsequently ordered to radio as many movements of the convoy as possible to help find a safe passage through a known mined area of the East China Sea. On the 24th, *Trigger* was ordered to begin patrolling west of the islands the next day, outside the 100 fathom curve, and to steer clear of restricted areas. On the 26th, she was ordered to join a wolf pack called "Earl's Eliminators" and to acknowledge receipt of the message. A weather report came from the submarine that day but no confirmation of her having received the message. The weather report was *Trigger*'s last transmission. On 4 April, she was ordered to proceed to Midway, but she had not arrived by 1 May and was reported as presumed lost.

Post-war records indicate that she torpedoed and sank the repair ship *Odate* on 27 March. The next day, Japanese planes and ships joined in a two-hour attack on a submarine at a position 32°16′ N. and 132°05′ E. The attack was heard by *Silversides* (SS–236), *Seadog* (SS–401), *Hackleback* (SS–295), and *Threadfin* (SS–410) in adjacent areas. *Threadfin* was the only one of these submarines that had been attacked that day, and she reported that she heard many depth charges and several heavy explosions east of her position after the attack on her ceased. *Trigger* was struck from the Navy list on 11 July 1945.

Trigger received 11 battle stars for World War II service and the Presidential Unit Citation for her fifth, sixth, and seventh war patrols.

II

(SS–564: dp. 1,615 (surf.), 1,990 (subm.); l. 269′; b. 27′; dr. 17′; s. 15.5 k. (surf.), 18.3 k. (subm.); cpl. 88; a. 8 21″ tt.; cl. *Tang*)

The second *Trigger* (SS–564) was laid down on 24 February 1949 at Groton, Conn., by the Electric Boat Co.; launched on 14 June 1951; sponsored by Mrs. Roy S. Benson; and commissioned on 31 March 1952, Comdr. Edward L. Beach in command.

Following shakedown training off Rio de Janeiro, Brazil, the attack submarine returned to her home port, New London, and participated in local operations for the remainder of the year. She was back in the Caribbean in February, returned to New London on 28 March, and continued east coast operations until 16 August 1957. She then joined *Nautilus* (SSN–571) and proceeded to the Arctic. The submarine spent 10 days at the ice pack in the north Greeland Sea and made several short trips under the ice pack. From 16 September to 1 October, she participated in the North Atlantic Treaty Organization (NATO) Operation "Strikeback." She then called at Portland, England, and Le Havre, France, en route back to New London to resume normal operations.

On 14 January 1958, *Trigger* entered the Portsmouth (N.H.) Naval Shipyard for major alterations. Her four high-speed diesel engines were replaced by three medium-speed engines. The submarine was cut in two and lengthened by nine feet. On 15 August, she got underway for New London and refresher training. She stood out of New London on 2 February 1959 for extended operations in the North Atlantic. She called at Faslane, Scotland, and returned to her home port in late April.

On 1 August, *Trigger* joined Submarine Squadron (SubRon) 4 at Charleston, S.C., her new home port, and, in late September and early October, participated in NATO Exercise "Fishplay." The submarine conducted operations out of Charleston for the next decade. She was deployed to the 6th Fleet in the Mediterranean during the periods: 10 April to 6 August 1962; 7 July to 29 October 1966; and 7 October 1969 to 2 February 1970. From 6 January to 6 August 1964, she underwent modifications in connection with the SUBSAFE program; and, from 3 January 1968 to 6 June 1969, her hull was again lengthened to accommodate more sonar equipment.

On 10 August 1970, *Trigger* departed Charleston for the west coast and assignment to the Pacific Fleet. She called at Montego Bay, Rodman, and Acapulco en route, and arrived at San Diego, her new home port, on 5 September to join SubRon 3. On 18 November, the submarine got underway for Bangor, Wash., to spend a month testing the Mk 48 torpedo. From 3 March to 7 June 1971, *Trigger* returned to Bangor to participate in Mk 48 Torpedo Selection Test Plan operations. Following yard work at the Hunter's Point Naval Shipyard from July 1971 to April 1972, she made a voyage to the Nanoose Bay Acoustic Test Range and returned to San Diego on 25 May.

On 17 October, *Trigger* stood out to sea on her first WestPac deployment. She called at Christmas Island on the 31st and arrived at Auckland, New Zealand, on 10 November. The operational control of *Trigger* was shifted to the Commander, 7th Fleet; and she participated in Exercise "Longex 7," a combined fleet problem utilizing ships from the navies of the United States, New Zealand, Canada, and Australia. The submarine departed Auckland on 1 December and arrived at Subic Bay on the 18th. From 29 December 1972 until 25 January 1973, *Trigger* was underway conducting special submarine operations. She left the Philippines on 3 February and, after calling at Hong Kong, participated in a joint United States-Canadian exercise off Taiwan. The ship sailed for Yokosuka on the 20th and remained in Japan undergoing repairs until getting underway for the United States on 16 March.

The submarine arrived at San Diego on 5 April. On 25 June, she started training a crew of the Italian Navy to operate the ship. *Trigger* was decommissioned and transferred to the Government of Italy on 10 July 1973. She was struck from the Navy list on 2 July 1973 and served the Italian Navy as INS *Livio Piomarta* (S–515).

Trilby

The heroine in a novel of the same name by George du Maurier. An attractive young Parisian laundress, Trilby—under the guidance of Svengali—wins renown as an artist's model and later as a singer.

(MB: l. 37′0″; b. 7′8″; dr. 3′0″ (forward); s. 12 mph.; cpl. 4; a. 1 mg.)

Trilby—a wooden-hulled motorboat—was acquired by the Navy from the Governor of Maine, Carl E. Milliken, on 29 June 1917. Designated SP–673 on 13 July, *Trilby* was assigned to the 1st Naval District as a section patrol vessel. By 11 August 1917, she had begun patrolling the harbor at Bath, Maine, and she continued to operate in the vicinity of that port at least until 11 November of that year. No records documenting her service—if any—beyond that date have been found. In any case, she was subsequently deemed unsuitable and was returned to her owner on 5 July 1918.

Trimount

Following her purchase by the Navy, *Trimount* was renamed *Chaffinch* (q.v.) and designated AM–18 on 17 December 1940.

Tringa

A bird of the sandpiper family.

(ASR–16: dp. 2,150 (f.); l. 251′4″; b. 42′0″; dr. 14′11″ (lim.); s. 16.0 k.; cpl. 102; a. 2 3″, 2 40mm.; cl. *Chanticleer*)

Tringa (ASR–16) was laid down on 12 July 1945 at Savannah, Ga., by the Savannah Machine & Foundry Co.; launched on 25 June 1946; sponsored by Mrs. Nola Dora Vassar, the mother of Curtis L. Vassar, Jr., missing in action; and commissioned on 28 January 1947, Lt. Comdr. Paul C. Cottrell in command.

Upon commissioning, *Tringa* was assigned to Submarine Squadron (SubRon) 8 and operated out of the submarine base at New London, Conn. During her first six years of active service, she remained close to the eastern seaboard. Fortunately, her services as a submarine rescue vessel were not required. On the other hand, *Tringa* remained busy practicing simulated submarine rescues and serving as target ship and recovery ship for submarines in torpedo-firing drills. In addition, she participated in a number of rescue experiments for the Bureau of Ships, testing diving bells, submarine buoys, ground tackle, mooring gear, and related equipment.

Her most significant contribution during those six years came in January 1950 when *Missouri* (BB–63) ran aground in the vicinity of Thimble Shoals Light and Old Point Comfort, Hampton Roads, Va. *Tringa* and her sister rescue vessels joined tugs in refloating the battleship on 1 February.

In August of 1953, *Tringa* was called upon to cross the Atlantic Ocean to aid *Harder* (SS–568), which had broken down off the coast of Ireland. The ship returned to New London with the submarine and then resumed operations along the east coast of the United States. During the early months of 1955, *Tringa* escorted *Nautilus* (SSN–571), the world's first atomic-powered ship, during her sea trials.

That fall, she joined *Albacore* (AGSS–569) for experiments at Portsmouth, N.H. The submarine rescue vessel conducted deep submergence tests on a new submarine rescue chamber, RC–21. In the midst of that operation, RC–21 parted its tow and sank in 230 feet of water. *Tringa* spent the next 25 days struggling against foul weather, treacherous currents, and fouled wreckage, but successfully salvaged RC–21 in the end. For their part in the operation, three officers and 10 divers assigned to *Tringa* received commendations.

Early in 1957, she began serving as school ship for the submarine Prospective Commanding Officers' School. That duty took her to the warm waters of the British West Indies in April and again in July. After her return to normal duty at New London, *Tringa* was called upon to assist the newly-constructed Peruvian submarine *Iquiqui*, which on 27 August had run aground on Long Sand Shoal in Long Island Sound. The rescuer arriver on the scene, passed a tow wire to the stranded boat, and pulled her off at the next high tide.

Late in the summer, a voyage to Europe broke *Tringa*'s routine. On 3 September, she stood out of New London in company with *Fulton* (AS–11) and a submarine group to participate in a NATO fleet exercise. En route to Scotland, *Tringa* made a brief side trip to Newfoundland to deliver a critically-ill *Fulton* crewman to the naval hospital at Argentia. She reached Rothesay on 13 September but soon moved on to Portland, England. During the two-day trip, hurricane "Carrie" struck and enlivened *Tringa*'s passage through the Irish Sea. On 28 September, the ship departed England and headed for France. At Le Havre, she provided tender services for the submarines returning from the exercises until 11 October when she headed home toward the United States.

Tringa reentered Newport on 23 October and, after three weeks of upkeep, sailed for Bermuda and another tour of duty with the submarine Prospective Commanding Officers' School. In January 1958, she served as target ship for the submarine school at New London and recovered practice torpedoes fired at her. She underwent her biennial overhaul at Boston that spring and, after refresher training in June, made a two-week goodwill cruise to Canadian ports in July.

Tringa returned to New London on 22 July and, through the first month and one-half of 1959, trained divers, served as target and torpedo recovery ship for New London-based submarines, and conducted drills. On 25 February, she got underway for Norfolk, Va., where she served as *Kittiwake*'s (ASR–13) stand-in during that ship's overhaul. She operated as a temporary unit of SubRon 6 until 1 April at which time she departed Norfolk and moved north. After a brief rendezvous with *Torsk* (SS–423) during the latter's post-overhaul dives and a three-day stopover at Philadelphia, *Tringa* returned with the submarine to New London on the 9th.

After demonstrating her rescue capabilities during an operational readiness inspection, she resumed training divers, conducting underway training, and providing services to submarines. She also escorted submarines during their post-construction trials. In this regard, *Tringa* assisted *Barbel* (SS–580) in May and *Seadragon* (SSN–584) in October. In December, the ship escorted the fleet ballistic missile (FBM) submarine *George Washington* (SSBN–598) on her trials. In January 1960, she conducted diving operations in Narragansett Bay with a group of four Norfolk-based minesweepers in a search for debris from an exploded aircraft. Following the annual "Springboard" exercise in mid-February, *Tringa* visited Puerto Rico, the Virgin Islands, and the Dominican Republic before resuming duty out of New London late in March. Toward the end of the following month, the ship sailed to Ft. Lauderdale, Fla., where she spent a month as recovery ship for the Naval Ordnance Test Facility's missile program. In May, she returned north and, after a visit to Kingston, N.Y., and a brief rendezvous with *Dogfish* (SS–350) for that submarine's sea trials and deep dives, *Tringa* returned to New London to prepare for overhaul.

Following post-overhaul refresher training, *Tringa* resumed her normal duty out of New London. In December, she began assisting in the fleet ballistic missile submarine ordnance evaluation program by recovering test missiles fired in practice. The following spring, she returned to Norfolk to serve as "ready duty ASR" for most of the Atlantic coast during a period when the other Atlantic Fleet submarine rescue vessels were either in overhaul or deployed overseas. By July 1961, however, she was able to return to New London and resume her usual routine. In the fall, she steamed south to Florida but remained in southern waters only briefly —assisting the Bureau of Weapons in tests—before the requirements of the FBM program called her back to New London.

Over the next two years, the ship alternated two deployments to the Mediterranean with 2d Fleet operations along the eastern seaboard. After returning from submarine operations near Bermuda, *Tringa* operated from New London until early in April 1962. At that time, she put to sea for a three-month deployment during which she provided support services to 6th Fleet submarines. After visiting a number of Mediterranean ports, she left the "middle sea" in July 1962 and visited Lisbon, Portugal, and then headed for Scotland. At Holy Loch, she picked up an APL and a YRDM for tandem tow to the United States and departed the British Isles on 12 August. *Tringa* delivered her charges to Norfolk on 3 September and continued on to New London where she arrived on the 5th. After four weeks of leave and upkeep, she resumed duty escorting and towing targets for units of Submarine Flotilla (SubFlot) 2.

Tringa underwent another overhaul from March to July 1963 and, after refresher training, resumed duty with Atlantic Fleet submarines. In August, she visited the site of *Thresher*'s (SSN–593) sinking to support units operating with the deep submergence vehicle *Trieste*. In mid-September, she escorted *Thomas Jefferson* (SSBN–618) during trials. Later that month, she was called upon to assist *Grouse* (MSCO–15) aground on the Massachusetts coast at Cape Ann. Her divers attached cables to *Grouse*, but three attempts to pull the stranded ship off the rocks failed. *Grouse* was destroyed by fire, and *Tringa* returned to New London on 30 September. Normal operations and escort duty for two newly constructed FBM submarines—*Nathan Hale* (SSBN–623) and *Lafayette* (SSBN–616)—occupied the ship for the remainder of the year.

Tringa deployed to the Mediterranean for the second time on 3 April 1964 and returned to the United States on 1 September. After a three-week upkeep period, she resumed local operations by escorting *Haddo* (SSN–604) and *Tecumseh* (SSBN–628) during their sea trials. That employment occupied her to the end of 1964 and through 1965.

She cleared New London on 31 January 1966 to participate in Operation "Springboard." Three days out of port, the ship was ordered to the Mediterranean to join in the search for the nuclear weapon missing after the mid-air collision of a B–52 bomber with a C–135 cargo plane. Upon her arrival off Palomares, Spain, *Tringa* was fitted out with underwater television equipment with which she conducted visual inspections of sonar contacts while her divers assisted in the recovery. The submarine rescue ship completed her part of the operation on 25 March and headed back to New London, where she arrived on 9 April. Local operations out of New London occupied her time until the end of September when she entered the James S. Munro Shipyard at Chelsea, Mass., for overhaul.

Tringa completed overhaul on 10 January 1967 and then returned to New London. She remained there until 30 January when she sailed for the West Indies. During February and the first week in March, the ship underwent inspection and survey at San Juan, conducted refresher training near Guantanamo Bay, and assisted in test-firings of SUBROC missiles at the Grand Turk missile range. On 15 March, *Tringa* reentered New London and began preparations for a deployment to European waters. The ship cleared New London on 3 April and reported for duty at Rota, Spain, later in the month. She operated along the Spanish and Portuguese coasts for two months, escorting submarines, towing targets, and recovering practice torpedoes. On 14 June, *Tringa* headed for the submarine base at Holy Loch, Scotland. During the following month, she provided services to the submarines based there and visited Dublin and Londonderry. On 26 July, she returned to New London from her European deployment and took up duties with SubFlot 2 once again.

The submarine rescue vessel served in coastal waters of the United States for the remainder of 1967 and throughout 1968. During that period, she departed northeastern coastal waters only once, in mid-November 1968, when she made a short cruise to Bermuda with units of SubRon 8. On 6 January 1969—in company with *Sea Robin* (SS–407), *Becuna* (AGSS–319), *Halfbeak* (SS–352), and *Thornback* (SS–418)—she departed New London and headed for duty with the 6th Fleet. She reached Rota, Spain, on 20 January and joined United States naval forces assigned to the Mediterranean area. The deployment with the 6th Fleet lasted until 15 April when she left Rota and headed back across the Atlantic. *Tringa* entered New London on the 25th and began post-deployment leave and upkeep. A little over two months later, the ship resumed operations from New London and remained so occupied until the end of November when she entered the Boston Naval Shipyard.

Tringa completed overhaul early in March 1970. During refresher training, she received orders reassigning her to Submarine Division 121 based at Key West, Fla. She reported to her new home port on 29 April; and, for the rest of the year, she operated in the Gulf of Mexico and along the southeastern coast of the United States. Early in June, the ship accompanied *Darter* (SS–576) during her sea trials. Later that month, she picked up a Cuban refugee family adrift on the ocean some 35 miles from Key West and brought them into that port. Through the fall of 1970, *Tringa* continued normal operations from Key West.

Over the next five years, *Tringa* alternated tours of duty in the Mediterranean with service along the east coast of the United States. Within that time period, she made two deployments with the 6th Fleet: the first during the spring of 1971 and the second in the summer of 1972. Upon her return to the United States on each

occasion, she resumed her duties at Key West conducting torpedo exercises with Atlantic Fleet submarines.

In June of 1973, *Tringa* rushed to the rescue when disaster struck a civilian deep-submergence vehicle test project. On the 17th, she received orders to go to the aid of Dr. Edmund Link, whose submersible, the "Sea-Link," was reported "in distress, bottomed in approximately 360 feet of water with four men on board." *Tringa* made a four-point moor above the stricken craft and for two days provided a platform for divers engaged in the rescue operation. Finally, on 18 June, a civilian salvage vessel, *A. B. Wood*, arrived on the scene and joined in the salvage/rescue operation. Utilizing a television camera and a crane, *A. B. Wood* succeeded in hauling "Sea-Link" to the surface that night. Though *Tringa* divers tried to revive the two men in the after chamber of the submersible by warming it with HeO_2 and hot water, the two men were pronounced dead at 0800 on 20 June. The two men in the forward chamber survived.

The following month, *Tringa* was reassigned to New London, Conn., and spent August and September engaged in the familiar role of standby rescue and target recovery ship for New London-based submarines. Following an overhaul which lasted from November 1973 until mid-February 1974, the ship returned to duty at New London. The next three years brought *Tringa* more routine duty supporting Atlantic Fleet submarines, testing diving equipment, training divers, and escorting newly built submarines on their trial cruises. The ship departed the western Atlantic only once during that period, in July 1975, to participate in a series of oceanographic surveys conducted from the submarine base at Holy Loch, Scotland. She returned to New London early the following November and operated along the eastern seaboard until 30 September 1977 when she was decommissioned at the Submarine Base, New London, Conn. Her name was struck from the Navy list concurrently with decommissioning.

As of the beginning of 1978, she awaited final disposal.

Trinity

A river in California.

(AO–13: dp. 16,800; l. 477'10''; b. 60'; dr. 26'2'' (mean); cpl. 107; a. 2 5''; cl. *Patoka*)

Trinity (AO–13) was laid down on 10 November 1919 at Newport News, Va., by the Newport News Shipbuilding and Drydock Co.; launched on 3 July 1920; and commissioned on 4 September 1920, Comdr. Harry M. Bostwick, USNRF, in command.

Following shakedown, *Trinity* got underway from Chesapeake Bay on 11 February 1921, bound for the Mediterranean. She arrived at Malta and delivered general stores for *Pittsburgh* (CA–4) before proceeding for Spalato, Dalmatia, with fuel oil for American ships operating in the Adriatic. After a three-day layover at Spalato, she got underway on 8 March for Venice, where she arrived on the 12th. She eventually called at Pola, Italy, before making port at Brindizi to take on fuel oil and general supplies for the naval base at Constantinople, Turkey, and American naval forces operating in Turkish waters. Following the delivery of this cargo, *Trinity* sailed from Gibraltar on 4 April and arrived at Tompkinsville, Staten Island, N.Y., on the 17th. Subsequently based at Norfolk and assigned to the Naval Transportation Service, the oiler operated along the east coast and in the Caribbean until she was decommissioned on 22 December 1923 and laid up at the Philadelphia Navy Yard.

She remained there, inactive, until growing tension in both Europe and the Far East prompted the Navy to enlarge its building programs, and to recondition and recommission old ships. Accordingly, *Trinity* was recommissioned at Philadelphia on 21 June 1938. She transported cargoes of oil from ports on the Gulf of Mexico to Guantanamo Bay, Cuba, and the Panama Canal Zone.

Transferred to the Pacific Fleet early in 1939, *Trinity* carried oil to Dutch Harbor, Alaska, for use by the Coast and Geodetic Survey. In the summer, she turned her attention to the Far East and conducted voyages from ports on the west coast of the United States and in the Netherlands East Indies to the Philippine Islands, delivering fuel oil to storage facilities such as those on Sangley Point, near Cavite. Late in 1940, the oiler was assigned to the Asiatic Fleet.

She departed Manila Bay on 28 February 1941 to commence the first of eight round-trip voyages from Manila, in that year, to ports in oil-rich Borneo and the Netherlands East Indies. As war clouds gathered on the horizon in the summer of 1941, an organization plan was drawn up which designated *Trinity* as part of the Manila-based Task Force 2.

At the end of the eighth voyage, *Trinity* arrived at Manila on 3 December. On 8 December, she lay alongside the fuel docks at Sangley Point, discharging oil to the storage tanks ashore, when she received word from Admiral Thomas C. Hart that "Japan has commenced hostilities—govern yourselves accordingly."

With Japanese air attacks expected momentarily, Hart decided to send the two Navy oilers, *Trinity* and *Pecos* (AO–6), and seaplane tender *Langley* (AV–3) south from Manila Bay. Later that day, these three valuable auxiliaries, shepherded by *Pope* (DD–225) and *John D. Ford* (DD–228), departed in a hastily assembled convoy. Two days later, while the American ships sailed for Borneo, 80 Japanese bombers and 52 fighter planes attacked the American navy yard at Cavite, destroying it as a base for the Asiatic Fleet. *Trinity* had departed the area just in time.

The convoy reached Balikpapan, Borneo, on 14 December; and *Trinity* now commenced her wartime operations with the hard-pressed Asiatic Fleet. After a one-month stay there fueling Allied warships, she steamed first to Koepang Bay, Timor, and then to Kebola Bay, at Amor Island, in the Netherlands East Indies. Standing out of Kebola Bay on 17 January 1942, *Trinity* set course for Australia, escorted by *Alden* (DD–211) and *Edsall* (DD–219). Shortly after 0630, a Japanese submarine fired three torpedoes at the oiler. All missed their target. *Alden* then searched for the enemy, made contact, and dropped a pattern of depth charges. In the resulting confusion, however, the American destroyer lost contact with the enemy and abandoned the search.

Upon her arrival at Darwin, *Trinity* filled the depleted fuel bunkers of *Holland* (AS–3) and *Otus* (AS–20), the tenders to the Asiatic Fleet submarine forces operating in the Malay Barrier. (*Canopus* (AS–9) had been left at Manila Bay to provide for the Manila-based submarines.) When she had delivered this "liquid gold," orders came for *Trinity*, *Otus*, and *Holland* to accompany *Black Hawk* (AD–9) and four destroyers on a voyage to the south coast of Java to establish a base there.

Dropping anchor at the congested port of Tjilatjap, she remained there a week before Vice Admiral William A. Glassford, Commander, United States Naval Forces, Southwest Pacific (COMSOWESPAC), dispatched her to Iran to obtain refined fuel oil to relieve the critical fuel shortage in the war zone. Departing Tjilatjap on 17 February in company with *Edsall*, she proceeded independently after her escort was ordered back to port and arrived at Abadan, Iran, on 9 March.

The first United States warship in local memory to have visited this part of the world, *Trinity* gathered valuable intelligence material on local conditions in Iraq and Iran, including observations of the port-of-entry (Abadan) for war materials slated for use by the Soviet Union. She also collected oceanographic data on the Persian Gulf. After loading her vital cargo, she headed for Fremantle on 17 March.

Unfortunately, Java fell even before *Trinity* arrived at her destination. Although Allied forces had been driven out of the Malay Barrier, they gathered in Australia to begin building for the long road back. COMSOWESPAC retained *Trinity* for the Persian Gulf-Fremantle run, calling at such varied ports as Basra, Iraq; Bahrein, Arabia; Diego Garcia, Chagos Archipelago; Bombay, India; and Geraldton and Albany, Australia; as well as the now-familiar ports of Abadan and Fremantle. On one occasion, in November 1942, the ship encountered a typhoon in which heavy seas, whipped by 70-knot winds, enveloped the ship and destroyed two motor whaleboats.

In 1943, with Papuan New Guinea secured and the Buna-Gona campaign successfully resolved, *Trinity* moved her base to Milne Bay, New Guinea, where she arrived on 13 August 1943 and came under the control of Commander, Base Force, 7th Fleet. Attached to this command for the remainder of the year, *Trinity* plied the Milne Bay-Brisbane route, while also touching at Cairns and Townsville, Australia. When anchored at Milne Bay, she provided oil for miscellaneous Allied ships. She subsequently moved north to commence operations in the Buna-Cape Cretin vicinity, an area in which she remained until early March.

During the next few months, she proceeded back to Milne Bay and thence to Port Moresby before heading for Cairns and completing the round trip to Milne Bay on 24 July 1944. Operating out of the New Guinea area, she worked as shuttle tanker and harbor feeder, anchoring at such places as Manus in the Admiralties, Humboldt Bay and Hollandia on the north coast of New Guinea, and at Biak in the Schouten Islands.

By January 1945, as the war progressed steadily towards the Japanese homeland, *Trinity* continued her unglamourous but vital job of plying the triangular New Guinea-Shouten Islands-Admiralty Islands route, shuttling cargoes of oil needed to keep the warships of the Fleet in operation. Arriving at Leyte, Philippines, in May 1945, she returned to waters from which she had been driven so unceremoniously in those dark days of December 1941. For the remainder of her active service, she operated in the western Pacific through the end of the war and the early months of the occupation.

Trinity departed Samar on 12 January 1946, bound for home. After stops at Eniwetok and Pearl Harbor, she arrived at the Mare Island Naval Shipyard on 22 February and reported to Commandant, 12th Naval District. The oiler remained there until decommissioned on 28 May. Struck from the Navy list on 3 July, she was delivered to the Maritime Commission's War Shipping Administration on 5 September 1946. Sold to the Colonial Steamship Corp. in 1951, the veteran tanker was renamed *Seabeaver*.

Trinity received one battle star for her World War II service.

Tripoli

A joint land-sea operation against Derna during the war between the United States and the Barbary state of Tripoli which resulted in the capture of that fortress city on 27 April 1805. After a long and grueling march across the desert from Alexandria, William H. Eaton—the American naval agent in the Barbary states—led a polyglot force of Arabs, Greek mercenaries, and a small detachment of marines in storming the Tripolitan defensive positions. Gunfire from United States warships *Hornet*, *Nautilus*, and *Argus*, and the valor of the marines—commanded by Lt. Presley Neville O'Bannon, USMC—were instrumental in achieving the American victory which has been immortalized by the phrase from the Marine Corps hymn, ". . . to the shores of Tripoli. . . ."

I

(CVE–64: dp. 7,800; l. 512'3''; b. 65'; ew. 108'1''; dr. 22'6''; s. 19 k.; cpl. 860; a. 1 5'', 16 40mm., 20 20mm.; cl. *Casablanca*; T. S4–S2–BB3).

The first *Tripoli* (CVE–64)—an escort aircraft carrier built under a Maritime Commission contract (MC hull 1101) at Vancouver, Wash.—was laid down by the Kaiser Shipbuilding Co. on 1 February 1943 as *Didrickson Bay* (ACV–64); renamed *Tripoli* on 3 April 1943; launched on 13 July 1943; sponsored by Mrs. Leland D. Webb; and commissioned on 31 October 1943, at Astoria, Oreg., Capt. Wendell G. Switzer in command.

Following shakedown training off the California coast, the escort carrier entered the repair base at San Diego, Calif. There, on 4 January 1944, gasoline was inadvertently and unknowingly dumped into the water around the forward part of the ship, on the starboard side. Acetylene torch sparks set the volatile mixture ablaze, and flames quickly spread from the bow to frame 82, engulfing the forward galley walkway and the island superstructure. Yardcraft and the ship's force battled the flames and soon had the blaze under control, but not before one man had died.

Subsequently repaired, *Tripoli* departed San Diego on 31 January, bound for the Panama Canal and duty with the Atlantic Fleet. She arrived at her new home port, Norfolk, Va., on 16 February. Embarking Composite Squadron 13—Wildcat fighters and Avenger bombers—the escort carrier put to sea on 15 March as the center ship in Escort Carrier Task Group (TG) 21.15. Supported by five destroyer escorts of Escort Division (CortDiv) 7, *Tripoli* patrolled west of the Cape Verde Islands to break up German U-boat refuelling activities in that area.

After providing air cover for a convoy routed to the British West Indies, *Tripoli*'s covey of Wildcats and Avengers searched the sea lanes northwest, southwest, and west of the Cape Verdes before putting into Recife, Brazil, on 5 April to refuel and provision. Back at sea again two days later, *Tripoli* continued the routine of daily launchings and recoveries of her planes, guarding the Allied sea lanes against the incursions of enemy U-boats.

About one hour before sunrise on 19 April, one of *Tripoli*'s Avengers made radar contact with a German U-boat as the submarine cruised on the surface awaiting the arrival of her "Milch Cow" or refuelling partner. The enemy, *U–543*, put up a spirited antiaircraft barrage while the Avenger made three attacks. A pattern of rockets bracketed the dodging, twisting submarine on the first pass as the Germans prepared to "pull the plug" and dive for comparative safety. On the second run, the plane's depth charges failed to release, giving the enemy submersible all of the time she needed to dive. Leaving only swirling water, the U-boat evaded the plane's last attack—a mine dropped in the tell-tale swirl but, in so doing, also missed her fuelling rendezvous with "Milch Cow" *U–408*.

Returning to Norfolk on 29 April, *Tripoli* underwent voyage repairs before embarking Composite Squadron 6—12 Avengers and 9 FM–2 Wildcats. She then formed up with CortDiv 7 and departed Hampton Roads on 24 May for further searches in the vicinity of the Cape Verdes. Four days out, she changed course to intercept a German submarine estimated to be proceeding southwest from a position west of the Madeira Islands. When no contact was made by 30 May, *Tripoli* and her consorts steamed north to rendezvous with a convoy bound for Nova Scotia.

Following her return to Norfolk on 18 June, *Tripoli* spent two months in carrier qualification training off Quonset Point, R.I., before making port again at Norfolk on 15 July. Embarking Composite Squadron 6, she conducted two weeks of pilot qualifications in the Chesapeake Bay area before departing Hampton Roads on 1 August, bound for her new base of operations, Recife.

Screened by *O'Toole* (DE–527) and *Edgar G. Chase* (DE–16), the escort carrier proceeded south until 1 August, when *O'Toole* developed a sonar contact and gave chase. *Tripoli*'s planes laid patterns of sonobuoys at the initial point and dropped smoke floats and float lights on an oil slick. Picking up the "scent," *O'Toole* straddled the floats with her hedgehog projectiles and

depth charges and soon radioed victoriously "We hit the rodent!" A brief visual examination of the evidence—debris and a large quantity of diesel oil—satisfied the hunter-killer group that they had indeed sunk an enemy submarine. However, a post-war examination of German records did not confirm the kill. As night fell, *Tripoli* vectored two planes to another sonar contact by *O'Toole*, and four depth bombs thundered—thrashing the sea, keeping another U-boat down and running.

Tripoli and her group then returned to Recife on 13 August and reported for duty with Admiral Jonas H. Ingram's 4th Fleet. Designated as the center of TG 47.7, the escort carrier put to sea on 22 August with the four destroyer escorts of CortDiv 24 to operate against a homeward-bound German submarine estimated to pass at 25° south latitude and 5° west longitude.

After a fruitless search pursuing two fading sonar contacts in the mid-South Atlantic narrows, *Tripoli* and her group returned to Recife on 11 September for provisioning and fuelling. Underway again two days later, TG 47.7 headed out to conduct another search—this time along the estimated track of two U-boats slated to rendezvous for refuelling. One of the target U-boats was *U–1062*, a "Milch Cow" bound from Penang, Malaya, with a cargo of valuable petroleum products for the German war effort. Ordered to fuel *U–219*, outward-bound for the Far East, *U–1062* prepared to rendezvous with her smaller sister boat in the South Atlantic narrows—directly in the path of the *Tripoli* escort group.

Passing to the westward of the Cape Verdes, TG 47.7 made rendezvous with the *Mission Bay* (CVE–59) escort group to conduct a joint hunter-killer operation against the two enemy boats. Round-the-clock searches by prowling, radar-equipped Avengers continued with unrelaxed vigilance until 40 minutes after sunset on 28 September, when a TBF piloted by Lt. William R. Gillespie, USNR, reported a definite contact with the surfaced *U–219* only 11 miles from the enemy's estimated track.

Gillespie went in to conduct a low-level rocket attack, but heavy flak slapped the intrepid airman's plane and crew into the sea. Another Avenger, drawn to the battle, braved the maelstrom of flak to conduct another rocket run and also dropped depth bombs, while a Wildcat strafed the twisting and turning U-boat which struggled desperately to dodge the harassing attacks by the American planes.

Indeed, *U–219* emerged from the fracas unscathed; but *U–1062* did not enjoy similar good fortune. *Fessenden* (DE–242), one of *Mission Bay*'s screen, homed in on sonobuoy indications on 30 September and killed the "Milch Cow" with a four-charge pattern. In the meantime, *U–219* was not yet out of the proverbial woods—one of *Tripoli*'s Avengers dropped depth bombs on the fleeing boat on 2 October. Keen-eared American sonarmen felt that they had definitely "killed" the submersible, but postwar accounting showed that *U–219* had escaped to Batavia, Java.

When fuel supplies ran low, *Tripoli* came about and made port at Recife on 12 October. She conducted one further search of the narrows from 26 October to 12 November before heading for a much-needed overhaul at Norfolk. Subsequently, the escort carrier sailed for the Pacific and, after transiting the Panama Canal and touching at San Diego, arrived at Pearl Harbor 10 days into the new year, 1945.

Tripoli transferred Composite Squadron 8 ashore to conduct operations from Hilo, Hawaii, before she loaded a miscellaneous cargo of fighters and bombers to be offloaded at Roi, in the Marshall Islands, where she made port on 20 February 1945. Returning to Pearl Harbor after this ferry run, the escort carrier commenced training operations which would continue through the end of the war and into the late fall of 1945. With Japan's surrender and the welcome end to hostilities in the Pacific, *Tripoli* was assigned to the gigantic "Magic-Carpet" operation.

Arriving at San Diego on 29 August with 500 Navy veterans, *Tripoli* returned to Pearl Harbor on 8 September before resuming local operations—including night carrier qualifications—through November. She subsequently made one trip with Army passengers to San Pedro, Calif., and a further "Magic-Carpet" run to San Diego. The carrier departed the west coast on 15 January 1946 for deactivation overhaul at Norfolk. On 22 May 1946, the need for her services no longer pressing, *Tripoli* was decommissioned and laid up, in reserve.

Communist aggression in Korea in the summer of 1950 resulted in the return of many of the Navy's reserve ships to active service to support American operations in the Far East. Acordingly, *Tripoli* was recommissioned at New York on 5 January 1952, Capt. Raymond N. Sharp in command. Assigned to the Military Sea Transportation Service (MSTS), Atlantic Area, the erstwhile "hunter-killer" began her new career as an aircraft transport and ferry.

Over the next six years, *Tripoli* conducted 44 transport voyages, mostly to European and Mediterranean ports but with one visit to Hawaii and two to the Far East. Following the ship's third voyage to Europe, *Tripoli* was berthed at the Port Newark Terminal on 5 August 1952 where she loaded 45 Republic F–84 Thunderjet aircraft, 90 wingtip fuel tanks, and related gear for transport to the Far East. After going to sea on 7 August, bound for Japan, *Tripoli* steamed via the Panama Canal and San Diego and made port at Yokosuka with her vital cargo on 5 September,

where cranes lifted the reinforcements ashore—soon to be in action in their ground-attack role in Korea.

After onloading battle-damaged aircraft for repairs in the United States, the carrier embarked 245 Navy and Marine Corps personnel for rotation back to Alameda Naval Air Station, Calif. Making port on the west coast on 22 September, she then put to sea for the Far East a second time, once again carrying jet aircraft to Yokosuka, as well as transporting men of the Sea Echelon of Boat Unit 1. Loading a cargo of helicopters and military passengers, *Tripoli* returned to the west coast and arrived at Alameda on Armistice Day 1952. Subsequently making her sole Hawaiian voyage under MSTS, *Tripoli* then headed east to finish out her career with transport voyages to European and Mediterranean ports.

Receiving "smart ship" awards from MSTS in the intervening years, *Tripoli* was reclassified a utility carrier and redesignated CVU–64 on 12 June 1955. Again redesignated T–CVU–64 on 1 July 1958, *Tripoli* was decommissioned at New Orleans, La., on 25 November 1958 and subsequently struck from the Navy list on 1 February 1959. Her hulk was then scrapped by a Japanese firm in January 1960.

II

(LPH–10: dp. 18,000 (f.); l. 602'; b. 84'; ew. 105'; dr. 29'; s. 24+ k.; cpl. 556; tr. 2,677; a. 8 3'', 20 helo.; cl. *Iwo Jima*)

The second *Tripoli* (LPH–10) was laid down on 15 June 1964 at Pascagoula, Miss., by the Ingalls Ship-

Tripoli (LPH–10) off Vietnam in February 1969, with Marine CH–46A troop-carrying helicopters on deck.

building Corp.; launched on 31 July 1965; sponsored by Mrs. Jane Cates, the wife of General Clifton B. Cates, former Commandant of the Marine Corps; and commissioned on 6 August 1966 at the Philadelphia Naval Shipyard, Capt. Henry Suerstedt, Jr., in command.

Following three months fitting out at Philadelphia, the amphibious assault ship put to sea on 6 November, bound for the west coast. She transited the Panama Canal at mid-month and arrived at her home port, San Diego, on the 22d. Final acceptance trials, shakedown training, and post-shakedown availability at Long Beach occupied the warship until she embarked Marine Heavy Helicopter Squadron (HMH) 463, elements of Marine Observation Squadron (VMO) 6, and some members of the staff of the Commander, Amphibious Squadron (ComPhibRon) 5 on 1 May 1967 and departed San Diego, bound for the western Pacific.

On 22 May, she arrived in the combat zone off the coast of Vietnam and disembarked HMH 463 and VMO 6 at Danang on the 23d and 24th before joining TG 76.5, just then finishing up amphibious landing Operation "Belt Tight" in the I Corps zone just south of the demilitarized zone (DMZ) between North and South Vietnam. She headed for the Philippines on 25 May, arrived in Subic Bay on the 27th, and relieved *Princeton* (LPH–5) as flagship of Amphibious Ready Group (ARG) "Bravo"/TG 76.5. In that capacity, she embarked not only the task group commander's staff but also the staff of the Commander, Special Landing Force (SLF) "Bravo" CTG 79.5, the 3d Battalion, 3d Marine Regiment (Battalion Landing Team (BLT) 2/3), the men and aircraft of Marine Medium Helicopter Squadron (HMM) 164, Surgical Evacuation Team "Bravo," and Detachment "Bravo" of Tactical Squadron (TacRon) 11. On 8 June, she departed Subic Bay for an extended tour of duty in Vietnamese waters.

During her 1967 deployment, *Tripoli* participated in eight amphibious operations, all conducted along the coast of the I Corps tactical zone located in the northernmost part of South Vietnam. Her first operation, codenamed "Beacon Torch," began on 18 June when marines of SLF "Bravo" were flown into the vicinity of Hoi An, located on the coast midway between the DMZ and the southern limit of I Corps tactical zone. Between 18 June and 2 July, the marines operated ashore, initially engaging an enemy force of about 100 men. After an air strike broke the enemy resistance, they concluded their mission with a search and destroy sweep to wipe out the remnants of that force. All the while, *Tripoli* remained offshore providing logistic support, medical evacuation services for casualties, and a platform from which to launch air support missions by the embarked Marine attack squadron. On 2 July, she received the special landing force back on board and immediately headed north to the coast of Quang Tri province to answer a call for assistance from Marine Corps units near Con Thien which had suffered heavily from bombardments by North Vietnamese regulars. The ensuing Operation "Beaver Track" pitted SLF "Bravo" against the North Vietnamese troops to relieve the pressure on Marine Corps units based ashore with the III Marine Amphibious Force (MAF). Simultaneously with Operation "Beaver Track," SLF "Alfa"—embarked in *Okinawa* (LPH–3)—went ashore to engage the same enemy forces in Operation "Bear Claw." The two battalion landing teams joined III MAF marines based ashore in a week-long struggle followed by an eight-battalion search and destroy sweep. Throughout the 12 days of "Beaver Track/Bear Claw," *Tripoli* steamed offshore within easy helicopter range to provide logistical, medical, and ground support. The two landing forces were later credited with a third of the 1,100 enemy casualties and with no small part in breaking up the enemy attack.

"Beaver Track/Bear Claw" ended on 14 July, and both battalion landing teams returned to their ships on the 17th. The respite from combat, however, proved brief. At dawn three days later, *Tripoli*'s marines stormed ashore in a combined waterborne-airborne amphibious assault on the exposed seaward flank of the Viet Cong 806th Battalion near Quang Tri City. The enemy forces avoided contact with the marines by retiring hastily to the west where they were badly mauled by South Vietnamese troops. BLT 2/3 reembarked in *Tripoli* on the 27th for another brief rest before the equally brief amphibious Operation "Kangaroo Kick" which commenced on 1 August. *Tripoli*'s marines landed in Quang Tri province, north of Hue. Though the operation ended only three days later, the marines did not reembark for the voyage to Subic Bay. Instead, they changed operational control to III MAF while *Tripoli* and the rest of TG 76.5 spent two weeks at the Philippine naval base for upkeep.

Tripoli returned to the Vietnamese coast near Hue on the 20th and backloaded SLF "Bravo" in time for the marines to participate in Operation "Belt Drive." On 27 August, the battalion landing team once more went ashore—via both helicopter and landing craft—in Quang Tri province. Viet Cong and North Vietnamese resistance proved slight; and, after a three-day sweep of the Hai Lang forest, the troops reembarked in *Tripoli* on 5 September. That same day, *Dupont* (DD–941) suffered a hit from enemy guns on Cape Lay, North Vietnam. *Tripoli*—located not far away—went to her assistance and evacuated 12 casualties by helicopter for treatment on board the amphibious assault ship. On the 17th, because her entire complement of CH–46A helicopters had been grounded, *Tripoli* launched the first all-boat landing from an LPH. In spite of swells eight to twelve feet high, a rain squall, 30- to 40-knot winds, and visibility frequently less than one-half mile, the boat landings for Operation "Fortress Sentry" came off almost without a hitch. Ashore near the Cua Viet river some seven miles south of the DMZ, the marines moved inland but encountered no enemy resistence until the 23d. Then, artillery and air support quickly extinguished the enemy's will to fight, and the operation was terminated on the 25th. The troops reembarked between 25 and 27 September, and the task group headed back to Subic Bay for six days in port.

Tripoli returned to Vietnam at Danang early in October and loaded 39 defective CH–46A helicopters for transportation to Okinawa where their tail pylons were to be replaced. Shortly after she departed Danang on 7 October, her lookout spied an Air Force F–105 which crashed into the sea about two miles ahead. One of her helicopters flew to the scene, rescued the pilot, and returned him to the ship for medical treatment. Not long thereafter, her lookouts caught sight of a second survivor of the crash. By the time her helicopter arrived on the scene, an Air Force chopper had already picked up the man. *Tripoli*'s helo assisted in the operation by taking on board the Air Force crewman who had jumped in to assist the survivor into the lift harness.

The amphibious assault ship returned from the Ryukyus to Vietnamese waters at mid-month. On the 17th, CH–53 helicopters carried the battalion landing team to a point 10 miles south of Phu Bai in Thua Thien province. The following day, the marines changed operational control to III MAF ashore for a search and destroy sweep along Route 1. Meanwhile, *Tripoli* supplied logistic support until she cleared Vietnamese waters on 1 November, bound for Okinawa with another 18 defective CH–46A helicopters. After brief stops at Okinawa and Subic Bay, the amphibious assault ship returned to Danang on 10 November. After reembarking SLF "Bravo," she prepared for her last amphibious operation of the deployment, Operation "Badger Hunt." On the 14th, the landing force was lifted some 25 miles inland to the area near An Hoa in Quang Nam province. After silencing sporadic enemy resistance near the landing site, *Tripoli*'s marines joined elements of the shore-based 7th Marines in a successful search-and-destroy operation. *Tripoli* supported the landing force through the end of the operation on the 27th, when the marines returned to the ship. She entered Danang on the 29th and began transferring the troops of the battalion landing team and their supporting elements to *Valley Forge* (LPH–8). The next day, 30 November, *Valley Forge* relieved *Tripoli* as flagship, TG 76.5; and *Tripoli* got underway to return to the United States via Okinawa and Yokosuka. She arrived in San Diego on 23 December 1967 and began post-deployment standdown.

Tripoli completed a restricted availability at Long Beach between late January and the end of March 1968. During the first three weeks of April, she conducted a series of individual ship exercises and then rounded out the month with amphibious training. From 6 to 17 May, the ship conducted refresher training and then returned to San Diego to prepare for her second WestPac deployment. On 12 June, the amphibious assault ship stood out of San Diego on her way to the Far East. She stopped briefly at Pearl Harbor and at Okinawa before arriving at Subic Bay on 1 July. Between the 2nd and the 5th, she embarked the 2d Battalion, 7th Marines, HMM 265, Detachment "Bravo" of TacRon 13 and other supporting units of the ARG "Bravo." On the 6th, she departed Subic Bay and arrived the following day in the Vietnam combat zone.

Tripoli's second tour of duty in the Orient closely followed the pattern of her first. During the next seven months, she patrolled the coast of Vietnam near the I Corps tactical zone just below the DMZ in a position to launch her landing contingent quickly whenever they were needed by Marine Corps, Army, and South Vietnamese forces operating ashore. The first of her eight amphibious operations came the day after she arrived in the combat zone. Following preliminary naval bombardment, Operation "Eager Yankee" opened with a combined airborne and waterborne assault. The marines of SLF "Bravo" charged ashore about 10 miles east of Phu Bai on the coast of the Thua Thien province. They then wheeled right and pressed north toward a known Viet Cong haven. The enemy avoided contact; and, on the 16th, the marines joined shore-based forces in Operation "Houston IV." That operation ended on 22 July, and the battalion landing team returned to the ship the same day.

However, the marines enjoyed precious little respite. While *Tripoli* proceeded to the scene of a new operation, feverish preparations allowed her to send SLF "Bravo" ashore again just 17 hours after the completion of reembarkation. For Operation "Swift Play," the troops rode helicopters ashore to an area about 10 miles southwest of An Hoa, deep inland in Quang Nam province. The assault forces spotted several enemy formations, but no engagements resulted. The following day, BLT 2/7 transferred to the control of III MAF to conclude an operation designed to parry a major enemy thrust toward Danang. The landing force remained ashore operating under the commanding general, 1st Marine Division, in defense of Danang through the months of August, September, and November. Meanwhile, *Tripoli* steamed on station offshore providing logistics and medical support, departing Vietnamese waters twice between 22 July and 5 November. In mid-August, she steamed to Subic Bay for repairs; and, in early October, she voyaged via Subic Bay to Kaohsiung, Taiwan, for a liberty call. During all other periods, she remained off the Vietnamese coast providing support services to the marines of BLT 2/7 operating ashore.

On 5 November, the special landing force ended more than three months of combat duty ashore and reembarked in *Tripoli*. Five days later, HMM 165's helicopters and *Tripoli*'s landing craft carried the troops ashore once again. In Operation "Daring Endeavor," the marines sought out and destroyed enemy fortifications and captured large quantities of rice. They con-

cluded the action on the 17th and returned to the ship that same day. Three days later, the amphibious assault ship launched her fourth landing, another combined waterborne and airborne operation directed at an area in Quang Nam province, just south of Danang. During Operation "Swift Move," initial opposition proved very light; and the landing force quickly transferred to the control of the 1st Marine Division for further action ashore in the continued defense of Danang against Viet Cong and North Vietnamese units. *Tripoli* continued support activities for the battalion landing team until 3 December when she offloaded what remained aboard of the marines' equipment at Danang preparatory to departing Vietnam for a liberty call at Hong Kong. After a five-day visit to the British Crown Colony, she continued on to Subic Bay for a two-week availability. On 27 December 1968, she headed back to Danang. On 1 January 1969, she embarked BLT 3/26 and HMM–164 to reconstitute SLF "Bravo."

During the remainder of her second tour of duty in the Far East, *Tripoli* participated in two more amphibious operations. The first of these, Operation "Bold Mariner," was hailed as the largest such maneuver since the Allied landings during World War II. Aimed at the Batangan Peninsula of Quang Ngai province, where the entire population was considered hostile, the operation sought to cordon off the peninsula and trap the 300 or so guerillas operating there. Both special landing forces, "Alfa" and "Bravo," joined South Vietnamese troops and soldiers of the Americal Division in forming the cordon. Following a feint near Mo Duc, the amphibious force headed for the real landing area. Navy guns softened the objective beaches, and the troops went ashore on 13 January—all by helicopter. While the operation continued, *Tripoli* remained offshore providing her marines with the ever-needed logistical support and medical facilities. By 6 February, the troops ashore had thoroughly combed the peninsula for Viet Cong troops so BLT 3/26 turned the mop-up operation over to the American and South Vietnamese soldiers and returned to the ship.

The reembarkation of the marines was completed by 9 February, just in time for *Tripoli* to launch her last amphibious operation of the deployment. The expected enemy Tet offensive required South Vietnamese troops to be withdrawn from Operation "Taylor Common," then in progress near An Hoa in Quang Nam province. SLF "Bravo" was to replace those troops in Operation "Defiant Measure." The landings began at 0800 on the morning of 10 February, and the offloading of men and equipment continued for several days. *Tripoli* remained in the area until the 16th. Operation "Defiant Measure" was concluded on that day—though the marines remained ashore to continue Operation "Taylor Common." HMM–164 was disembarked before *Tripoli* began her voyage home. She departed Vietnam that same day and arrived in Subic Bay on the 18th. There, she turned over her duties to *Valley Forge*. On the 22d, she got underway for Yokosuka, Japan, and badly needed repairs before continuing on to the United States. She finally arrived back in San Diego on 19 March and began post-deployment standdown.

Tripoli remained on the west coast until November. After leave and upkeep, she began an availability period at the San Diego yard of the National Steel Company which continued until 11 August. Following refresher training in September and amphibious training in October, she stood out of San Diego on 1 November to return to the Far East. After a brief stop at Guam on the 15th for fuel, she continued on to Danang, South Vietnam, where she arrived five days later.

During *Tripoli*'s third deployment to the western Pacific, the combat operations along the Vietnamese coast which had characterized her first two deployments were totally absent. Instead, she busied herself with a series of amphibious training exercises and a series of "Keystone" operations redeploying Marine Corps units. Her first mission, Operation "Keystone Cardinal," began on 20 November when she loaded the marines and equipment of BLT 3/4 for transportation to Okinawa. At Okinawa between 24 November and 2 December, she disembarked BLT 3/4 and embarked BLT 2/9, HMM–165, and supporting units to constitute SLF "Alfa." On 2 December, she departed Okinawa bound for the Philippines. She conducted upkeep at Subic Bay between 5 and 12 December and two amphibious exercises at Zambales on the 13th and 14th.

She returned to Vietnamese waters on the 17th and cruised the area without incident until the 25th when she headed back to Subic Bay. In the Philippines, minor repairs and more amphibious exercises occupied her until 6 January 1970. She made a six-day cruise to Vietnam and then returned to the Philippines on the 12th for more training. On the 25th, she disembarked SLF "Alfa" at Subic Bay in preparation for a voyage to Vietnam to pick up homeward-bound marines. She entered Danang on 31 January and began embarking personnel from HQ, III MAF, 1st Marine Air Wing, 1st Marine Division, and III MAF Logistics Command.

Later that evening, she got underway for home. After a non-stop voyage of 17 days, she arrived in San Diego on 16 February. She moved to Long Beach on the 23d to replace a cracked screw and departed that port on the 27th to return to the western Pacific. She reached Subic Bay on 15 March.

Tripoli operated in the Philipines and at Okinawa conducting amphibious exercises in preparation for an exercise with units of South Korean forces. She arrived in Korean waters on 18 April and, two days later, began Operation "Golden Dragon." The combined American-South Korean amphibious exercise lasted until the 25th. *Tripoli* returned to Okinawa on the 27th. She briefly operated off Danang at the end of the first week in May and then visited Hong Kong for a week in mid-month. Late in May, she returned via Subic Bay to Okinawa to disembark SLF "Alfa" and then moved to Danang where she disembarked ComPhibRon 9 and his staff and took on cargo for the voyage home. *Tripoli* got underway on 7 June and reached San Diego on the 24th.

Tripoli spent the next 15 months on the west coast. Following post-deployment upkeep and local operations, she conducted carrier qualifications in the southern California operation area in August and an amphibious exercise off Camp Pendleton. For the remainder of 1970, the ship occupied herself with individual ship's exercises and upkeep in preparation for an overhaul which began on 1 February 1971. She left Hunter's Point on 1 June, fully revitalized, and returned to San Diego on the 3d to prepare for refresher training which took place in late June and early July. Amphibious refresher training filled the latter half of July. She made two brief training cruises during the first week in August: one with NROTC midshipmen embarked and the other with Marine Corps reservists on board. Local operations and preparations for her fourth WestPac deployment occupied the rest of August and the entire month of September. On 1 October, *Tripoli* stood out of San Diego bound for the Far East. After stops at Pearl Harbor and Okinawa, she arrived in Subic Bay on the 28th.

The ship conducted amphibious training operations in the Philippines and made port visits to such places as Keelung and Kaohsiung in Taiwan and Sasebo, Japan. During her return from Sasebo to Subic Bay, she received orders to deploy to the Indian Ocean with TF–74, a special contingency task force built around *Enterprise* (CVAN–65) in response to the Indo-Pakistani War which erupted on 3 December. The amphibious assault ship remained in the Indian Ocean for the duration of the brief war. The fighting ended on 15 December; and, two days later, Pakistan officially accepted the loss of its eastern provinces which became the independent nation, Bangladesh. *Tripoli* remained

with TF–74 in the Indian Ocean and the Bay of Bengal until early 1972.

She returned to Subic Bay on 14 January and resumed training operations punctuated by visits to Singapore, Hong Kong, and Kobe, Japan. She began operations in Vietnamese waters at the beginning of April, operating on Yankee Station to provide search-and-rescue and medical evacuation services. She departed the combat zone twice, once for upkeep at Subic Bay and later to exchange battalion landing teams at Okinawa. At the end of June, she resumed flight operations in connection with troop movements. However, instead of carrying embarked marines inland for amphibious landings, her helicopters moved Vietnamese troops from point to point ashore. On 29 June, *Tripoli*-assigned helicopters helped to transport 1,400 Vietnamese marines from Tam My to the vicinity of Quang Tri City during the allied counteroffensive to recapture areas of the I Corps tactical zone which had been overrun by North Vietnamese troops. As this operation—codenamed "Lam Son 72"—progressed, *Tripoli* remained off shore, evacuating casualties and waiting should the reserves be required. That necessity came shortly before noon on 11 July, when her helicopters helped to insert the reserve Vietnamese marine battalion—picking them up near Route 553 and landing them behind enemy lines, about a mile and one-half north-northwest of Quang Tri City. On the 20th, *Tripoli* departed Vietnamese waters bound for the Philippines where heavy monsoons had caused extensive flooding. She reached Subic Bay on 23 July and conducted relief operations until 4 August, at which time she set course for the United States.

Tripoli arrived at San Diego on 20 August and remained there until 10 October. After a six-day amphibious exercise near Hunter Liggett Point, the amphibious assault ship returned to home port where she stayed through the end of the year. During the first two months of 1973, she operated out of San Diego and prepared to deploy to the Far East once more. She stood out of San Diego on 6 March for her fifth deployment to the western Pacific. Steaming via Pearl Harbor—where she made a three-week stop for repairs to her high pressure turbine—she arrived in Subic Bay on 17 April. There she remained and, when not plagued by material casualties to her main propulsion plant, conducted training preparatory to Operation "Endsweep," the removal of American mines from North Vietnamese waters. Though scheduled to sail for Haiphong on 16 June, she was delayed by more problems in her propulsion plant. Nevertheless, early the next morning, *Tripoli* headed for North Vietnam and arrived at Haiphong on the 19th. That morning, the Commander, TF 78, embarked in the amphibious assault ship and began negotiations with North Vietnamese representatives over the conduct of Operation "Endsweep." Meanwhile, *Tripoli*'s embarked air group began providing logistics support and inter-ship transportation services.

Major issues in the negotiations were resolved by the 28th, and minesweeping operations began early that morning. Throughout the operation, the ship provided a platform for helicopters engaged both in minesweeping operations and for those providing logistics and transport services. Periodically, she retired from the area to replenish and to evade typhoons. Otherwise, she remained in the minesweeping area until 18 July when she departed North Vietnamese waters in company with *Inchon* (LPH–12) and *Ogden* (LPD–5), bound for Luzon. Four days after her arrival back in Subic Bay, the last American operation in Vietnamese territory ended, and the "Endsweep" task force was dissolved. Operations reverted to CTG 76.5/ARG "Bravo." That organization lasted only two days for—on the 27th—the Commander, PhibRon 1, broke his flag in *Tripoli*, and she became flagship for TG 76.4/ARG "Alfa."

But for a round-trip voyage to Okinawa early in

September, the ship operated out of Subic Bay for the remainder of her deployment. Main propulsion plant problems, however, continued to plague her for, on the return trip, she went dead in the water not far to the northwest of Subic Bay. *Beaufort* (ATS–2) went out and towed her into port. After repairs, *Tripoli* occupied her remaining time in the Far East with amphibious exercises in the Philippines. On 11 October, *Okinawa* relieved her as flagship of TG 76.4, and *Tripoli* headed for home. She arrived in San Diego on 27 October and remained there through the end of the year.

Between January 1974 and the end of 1976, *Tripoli* made two relatively routine deployments to the western Pacific. The first lasted from late July 1974 until late January 1975. During that time period, she operated out of Subic Bay and engaged primarily in amphibious training exercises in the Philippines. The second deployment—from mid-February to late October 1976—saw a repetition of this routine but also included a voyage to Guam for disaster relief duty as a result of typhoon "Pamela." She also participated in two joint American-Korean amphibious exercises conducted near Pohang, Korea, in March and June, respectively. The second deployment ended on 25 October when she arrived in San Diego, remaining there into 1977.

The first six months of 1977 were spent in a Planned Restricted Availability (PRAV) at the Naval Station, San Diego, for the purpose of increasing propulsion reliability during the next deployment. While the PRAV concluded on 28 June, it was necessary to tow *Tripoli* to the Long Beach Naval Shipyard to use the yard's extensive facilities for the reinstallation of *Tripoli's* low pressure turbine. The work was completed on 26 July; and, following successful sea trials, *Tripoli* returned to San Diego on 28 July. Succeeding months were spent in refresher training and workup for the ship's forthcoming deployment to the western Pacific. On 3 November, *Tripoli* departed San Diego. Chopping to control by the Commander, 7th Fleet, on 25 November, she spent the next seven months in WestPac, returning to San Diego on 22 July 1978. Following post-deployment standdown, *Tripoli* received an inspection by the Naval Board of Inspection and Survey in September. On 16 October, the ship commenced a three-month PRAV in preparation for a scheduled deployment to the western Pacific in 1979.

Tripoli earned nine battle stars for service in the Vietnam conflict.

Trippe

John Trippe—born in 1785 in Dorchester County, Md.—was appointed a midshipman in the Navy on 5 April 1799. During the Quasi-War with France, he made his first cruise in the frigate *Constitution* and later served in the schooner *Experiment*. On 21 May, he was assigned to Commodore Richard Dale's flagship *President*, and he served in her until early 1802 in operations against the Tripolitan corsairs in the Mediterranean.

He returned to the United States in April 1802 and received a furlough to make a mercantile voyage. On 24 May 1803, the Navy Department ordered Trippe to *Vixen* as an acting lieutenant. The schooner sailed for the Mediterranean on 3 August and joined Commodore Preble's squadron off Tripoli on 14 September 1803.

Lt. Trippe served with distinction in the Mediterranean until the fall of 1805. On 3 August 1804, he led his crew of *Gunboat No. 6*, manned by another midshipman and nine sailors, to victory over the 36-man crew of a large Tripolitan boat. Trippe and his men boarded the enemy, and Trippe himself grappled with the leader of the pirates. Though his adversary towered over him, Lt. Trippe used his own agility and tenacity to emerge victorious in a desperate hand-to-hand struggle. Seriously wounded, he was unable to

participate in the next three of Preble's five attacks on Tripoli. However, by the beginning of September, he had recovered sufficiently to resume command of *Gunboat No. 6* for the fifth and final assault carried out on the 3d. For his gallentry in action against the Barbary pirates, Lt. Trippe received a sword and a commendation from Congress.

Trippe returned to the United States in November 1805, but 1806 found him back on duty in the Mediterranean. In 1808, Trippe served at Charleston, S.C., enforcing the embargo legislation. He took command of *Enterprise* on 23 January 1809, departed New York on 24 June, and headed for Holland. On 31 July, he reached Amsterdam, where he delivered official dispatches and conducted negotiations which helped cement commercial relations between The Netherlands and the United States. Having helped open Dutch ports to American shipping, he weighed anchor on 10 October and reentered New York harbor on 2 December.

On 26 April, Trippe transferred to the command of *Vixen* and, a month later, departed New Castle, Del., bound for New Orleans. Off Stirrup Key on 24 June, *Vixen* came under the fire of a British ship, HMS *Moselle*. When summoned on board the Britisher, Trippe refused, cleared *Vixen* for action, and demanded an explanation of *Moselle's* untoward action. Her captain responded with an apology, stating that he had mistaken the American man-of-war for a Frenchman. *Vixen* then continued peacefully on her way and put into Havana, Cuba, six days later. On 9 July 1810, while en route from Havana to New Orleans, Lt. Trippe died.

I

(Sloop: t. 60; cpl. 35; a. 1 long 32-pdr.)

Contractor—a merchant sloop purchased by the Navy on the Niagara River in New York in 1812—was converted to a warship by Henry Eckford of New York; renamed *Trippe;* and placed in commission soon thereafter, Lt. Thomas Holdup in command.

For awhile, *Trippe* and her sister ships, fitted out on the Niagara River, were bottled up by British shore batteries at Fort George. However, Commodore Chauncey's squadron joined the troops under Col. Winfield Scott in a combined attack upon the fort, and it fell on 27 May 1813. The fall of Fort George forced the British to evacuate Fort Erie as well. With the river open, Chauncey's ships began passage of the Niagara rapids on 6 June 1813 and, on the 19th joined Oliver Hazard Perry's fleet at Erie, Pa.

Trippe and the rest of Perry's squadron remained at Erie for another month. At first, the need for additional men to complete its crews kept the fleet in port. Later, a British blockade restricted its movement. However, the British were not exceedingly vigilant; and, on 4 August, *Trippe* and the other ships crossed the bar to leave Erie harbor. They remained near Erie until the 12th when they set sail for the western end of Lake Erie.

Perry established his operating base in Put In Bay at South Bass Island. That location afforded him excellent lines of communications with American forces to the south and put him within easy striking distance of Commodore Robert Barclay's British fleet, based just inside the mouth of the Detroit River at Amherstburg.

For over a month, the British ships remained at their base under the protection of heavy shore batteries. However, Barclay had to order his ships out of the river in order that supplies might be delivered to British troops operating near the Detroit River. They weighed anchor on 9 September and departed Amherstburg. At sunrise the following morning, American lookouts sang out, "Sail ho." Perry's ships, including *Trippe*, cleared for action and headed out in the line of battle with flagship *Lawrence* in the lead. Though they outnumbered the British nine ships to six, the Americans were outgunned

54 to 63. Undaunted, Perry, hampered by light winds, edged his men-of-war closer to the enemy.

By midday, the two forces opened fire. The British concentrated on the lead American ships, *Lawrence*, *Caledonia*, and *Niagara*. Meanwhile, *Trippe*—stationed near the rear of the American force—fought a long range duel with *Lady Prevost* and *Little Belt*, battering *Lady Prevost* severely. The Britisher's captain and her first lieutenant received serious wounds, and she herself, reduced to an unmanageable wreck, fell off to leeward. Perry's flagship suffered similar damage, but he moved his flag to *Niagara* and ordered his ships forward, through the enemy line. *Trippe* charged ahead, firing furiously. The British resisted the American onslaught heroically, but—one by one—they struck their colors. When *Chippeway* and *Little Belt* attempted to flee, *Trippe* and *Scorpion* overhauled them and herded them back to their defeated fleet.

The Battle of Lake Erie, *Trippe*'s only action in the War of 1812, assured American control of Lake Erie and enabled American troops led by General William Henry Harrison to win a decisive victory in the Battle of the Thames. Throughout the remainder of her career, *Trippe* carried supplies to support General Harrison's land operations. In October, the British attacked Buffalo at the east end of the lake and forced the Americans to evacuate the city. They found *Trippe* aground near Buffalo Creek and set fire to her. She and her cargo of supplies burned completely.

II

(Torpedo Boat Destroyer No. 33: dp. 742 (n.); l. 293'10''; b. 26'1½'' (wl.); dr. 9'5'' (aft); s. 30.89 (tl.); cpl. 83; a. 5 3'', 2 .30-cal. mg., 6 18'' tt.; cl. *Roe*)

The second *Trippe* (Torpedo Boat Destroyer No. 33) was laid down on 12 April 1910 at Bath, Maine, by the Bath Iron Works; launched on 20 December 1910; sponsored by Mrs. John S. Hyde; and commissioned at the Boston Navy Yard on 23 March 1911, Lt. Frank D. Berrien in command.

Upon commissioning, *Trippe* joined the torpedo boat destroyers and submarines assigned to the east coast as a unit of the Atlantic Torpedo Fleet. For the next

three years, she conducted routine operations along the east coast. In 1911, she completed trials and participated in exercises off Newport, Boston, and the Virginia capes. She made her first cruise to southern waters in 1912. She cleared Newport on 3 January and dropped anchor in Guantanamo Bay 11 days later. Following three months of training at Guantanamo Bay and in the Gulf of Mexico, the torpedo boat destroyer returned north in April and entered Boston harbor on the 21st. After repairs, *Trippe* resumed training operations off the northeastern coast. On 2 January 1913, the warship headed south once more for three months of tactical exercises and gunnery drills out of Guantanamo Bay and in the Gulf of Guacanayabo. She returned to Boston on 14 April and spent the remainder of 1913 in operations off the coast between Boston and Norfolk, Va.

Trippe began 1914 as she had the previous two years —by heading south and conducting battle practice in the Caribbean through the end of March. However, in April, the Tampico incident brought her to the shores of Mexico, when American sailors and marines went ashore at Vera Cruz and seized the customs house on the 21st. *Trippe* arrived off *Tampico* on the 22d and patrolled the area for a week to prevent arms from being landed. On 1 May, she steamed south to Vera Cruz where she conducted more patrols and supported the battleships and cruisers operating in the vicinity. Near the end of the month, *Trippe* cleared Mexican waters; and, on the 31st, entered Boston harbor.

At the completion of an extensive overhaul, the warship conducted trials and drills in the Boston area from mid-August to late September. On 30 September, *Trippe* arrived at Newport for a week of operation before heading south. She shifted to Hampton Roads in mid-October and participated in exercises there and at Lynnhaven Bay for a month before returning to Boston.

The warship spent December and the first three weeks of 1915 in the Boston area and, on 26 January, arrived in Guantanamo Bay to resume her schedule of winter drills in the Caribbean. Late in March, *Trippe* pointed her bow northward once more and reached Boston on 6 April. After her normal round of maneuvers off the northeastern coast, the torpedo boat destroyer returned to Boston on 23 October. A little less than two months

Trippe (DD–33) moored at Queenstown during World War I. Her camouflage pattern was calculated to make it difficult for a submarine commander to make an accurate estimate of her heading, necessary for accurate torpedo firing. (NR&L(M) 5369)

later—on 13 December 1915—*Trippe* became a unit of the newly-organized 2d Reserve Flotilla. On 5 January 1916, she was designated a "Destroyer operating with reduced complement;" and, on the 27th, she was placed in ordinary at the Boston Navy Yard.

The threat of war, however, made her retirement a brief one. *Trippe* was placed in full commission once again at Boston on 25 July 1916, Lt. (jg.) Roy P. Emrich in command. During the following eight months, *Trippe* trained along the coast in preparation for the increasingly probable entry of the United States into World War I. The United States declared war on the German Empire on 6 April 1917. *Trippe* continued to operate off the coast until early May, when she entered Boston and commenced preparations for duty overseas.

On 21 May 1917, the destroyer cleared Boston for Great Britain. After a call at St. John's, Newfoundland, she arrived in Queenstown on the southern coast of Ireland, the location of a major wartime American destroyer base. She paused only long enough to refuel and make voyage repairs before clearing the harbor on 5 June for her first patrol. From Queenstown, she escorted Allied convoys on the last leg of their voyage from America to France and England. Her field of operations, situated as it was in the war zone which had been established around the British Isles by Germany on 5 February 1915, was the prime hunting ground of High Seas Fleet U-boats. When not engaged in escorting convoys, *Trippe* patrolled the waters around Queenstown in an effort to detect and destroy as many enemy submarines as possible.

The warship had only one verified scrape with German U-boats. On 18 September 1917, she and *Jacob Jones* (Destroyer No. 61) were steaming in company some 350 miles west of Brest, France, when—shortly after 0200—she sighted the distinctive wake of the periscope of a submarine running on a parallel course, but in the opposite direction. *Trippe* dropped depth charges, but without "visible results," and continued on to rendezvous with an eastbound convoy. That night, she dueled with another adversary—the sea. In a raging storm, waves carried her starboard waist gun platform overboard. *Trippe*, however, successfully shepherded her convoy into Quiberon Bay, France, made repairs quickly, and resumed her grueling routine.

Through the final year of the war, *Trippe* and her sister ships slowly bested the enemy. Convoys of merchant ships carried troops and supplies to France, where the armies of the Allies grew steadily. By the fall of 1918, they reached a point of overwhelming superiority over those of the Central Powers. On 11 November, the day of the signing of the armistice, *Trippe* was in port at Queenstown. Just over a month later, she cleared that Irish port, refueled at the Azores and Bermuda, and returned to Boston on 3 January 1919. After six months of operations along the eastern seaboard, the destroyer entered the Philadelphia Navy Yard on 23 July for preinactivation overhaul. On 6 November 1919, *Trippe* was decommissioned and placed in reserve at Philadelphia.

Trippe's inactivity lasted five years. By 1924, Prohibition had spawned a thriving traffic in smuggling alcoholic beverages. The Coast Guard's small fleet, charged with stopping the illegal importation of alcohol, was unequal to the task. Consequently, President Coolidge proposed to increase that fleet by 20 of the Navy's inactive destroyers, and Congress authorized the necessary funds on 2 April 1924. Coast Guardsmen and Navy yard workers overhauled *Trippe*'s hull, stripped her of depth charge gear and torpedo tubes, and removed one of her four guns. On 7 June 1924, *Trippe* was transferred to the Treasury Department; and, on 24 June, she was placed in commission as *Trippe* (CG–20), Lt. Comdr. John H. Cornell, USCG, in command. For the next four years, the former Navy destroyer operated along the northeastern coast out of New London, Conn., as a cutter of the Coast Guard's "rum patrol."

Trippe was placed in reduced commission at New London on 5 January 1929. That October, she was moved to Stapleton, N.Y. From January to March 1930, she was overhauled at the New York Navy Yard. After a month of gunnery exercises off St. Petersburg, Fla., she returned to Stapleton on 23 April to resume operations along the coast. On 18 December, *Trippe* cleared Stapleton for the Philadelphia Navy Yard. The Coast Guard decommissioned *Trippe* at Philadelphia on 15 April 1931 and returned her to the Navy on 2 May. She remained in reserve at Philadelphia until 1934 when she was scrapped. Her name was struck from the Navy list on 5 July 1934. She was sold to Michael Flynn, Inc., of Brooklyn, N.Y., on 22 August 1934.

III

(DD–403: dp. 1,850; l. 341'0"; b. 35'5"; dr. 9'10" (mean); s. 38.5 k.; cpl. 230; a. 4 5", 4 .50 cal. mg., 16 21" tt., 3 dct.; cl. *Benham*)

The third *Trippe* (DD–403) was laid down on 15 April 1937 by the Boston Navy Yard; launched on 14 May 1938; sponsored by Miss Betty S. Trippe; and placed in commission on 1 November 1939, Lt. Comdr. Robert L. Campbell in command.

Trippe spent the remainder of 1939 outfitting at Boston. In January 1940, she visited Newport, R.I., to take on torpedoes and Yorktown, Va., to load depth charges before heading for the Gulf of Mexico. Following shakedown training in the Gulf of Mexico and the Caribbean, she returned to Boston on 20 March 1940. After completing her post-shakedown overhaul, *Trippe* departed Boston on 24 June ultimately to join the Caribbean portion of the Neutrality Patrol. She voyaged via Hampton Roads to San Juan, Puerto Rico, where she arrived early in July only to return north at mid-month for a two-day visit to Washington, D.C. On 26 July, *Trippe* entered San Juan once more to begin Neutrality Patrol duty in earnest.

For eight months, the destroyer roamed the warm waters of the West Indies to prevent the European belligerents from waging war in the western hemisphere. During that period, she escorted *Tuscaloosa* (CA–37), with President Roosevelt embarked, upon a tour of bases in the Caribbean. She saw the President safely into Charleston, S.C., on 14 December and then headed for Philadelphia and quick repairs. After a two-day visit to Norfolk at the end of the first week in January 1941, *Trippe* steamed south to Guantanamo Bay, Cuba, where she conducted neutrality patrols until spring.

On 21 March, the warship began a two-month overhaul at Boston. On 24 April, while *Trippe* continued repairs, President Roosevelt extended the Neutrality Patrol to the very edge of the German war zone. When *Trippe* emerged from her refit in May, she visited Norfolk and then trained out of Newport until early June. On 11 June, she joined the screen of *Texas* (BB–35) for her first extended patrol in the North Atlantic. On 29 June, *Texas* and her escorts passed through the periscope sights of a U-boat. The puzzled German captain almost perpetrated an incident by attacking; but, unable to match Task Force 1's speed, he gave up the chase late that afternoon. Blissfully unaware of the danger, the battleship steamed on with *Trippe* and her sister destroyers. The following day, they ended their patrol at Newport.

Trippe continued patrolling out of Newport, first with *Texas* and then with *New York* (BB–34), through July and the first fortnight in August. On 15 August, the warship shifted her base to Boston and Provincetown. On the 25th, she cleared Boston to escort *Mississippi* (BB–41) to Argentia. After more than a month of training and antisubmarine operations off Newfoundland, *Trippe* departed Argentia on 11 October in company with *Yorktown* (CV–5), *New Mexico* (BB–40), *Quincy* (CA–39), *Savannah* (CL–42), and seven other destroyers. After anchoring briefly at Casco Bay, Maine, and patrolling the area between that port and Boston, the warships headed for a mid-ocean rendezvous to relieve the Royal Navy escort of a westbound convoy. On her return voyage, *Trippe* parted company with the escort off Portland, Maine, and put into Casco Bay. On 9 November, she departed the Maine coast in the screen of *Ranger* (CV–4), *Vincennes* (CA–44), and *Quincy* to meet another westbound convoy and escort it to the United States.

In mid-November, *Trippe* escorted *Ranger* south to the West Indies and screened flight operations conducted from that carrier in the vicinity of Trinidad until early December. She was returning north with the carrier on 7 December when the Japanese attack on Pearl Harbor jolted the United States into World War II. America's entry into the war, however, did not change *Trippe*'s assignment. She continued to escort transatlantic convoys and to hunt U-boats. She stopped at Norfolk for a week and then headed for Newport on 15 December. Just before dawn on the 16th, an Army bomber approached her from the north and after making several passes dropped a stick of bombs and reported sinking a German destroyer in Block Island Sound. *Trippe* emerged unscathed—the bombs exploded some 200 yards off her bow—and continued on to Newport where she arrived that same day.

Over the next 10 months, *Trippe* was all over the northwestern Atlantic. She escorted coastwise traffic between ports along the eastern seaboard. She relieved British warships in mid-ocean and escorted their convoys into American ports as well as screening eastbound convoys as far as mid-ocean where British warships took over. The destroyer patrolled off such diverse places as Argentia, Newfoundland, and the North Carolina capes. Her escort duties took her as far south as the Panama Canal and the West Indies, as far north as Newfoundland, and, on one occasion, as far east as Londonderry in northern Ireland. Twice, *Trippe* searched for survivors of torpedoed merchantmen—once off Hampton Roads early in February and again near Bermuda in June. She also made two fruitless attacks on what she believed to be submerged U-boats. Now and then, she even found time to conduct drills and gunnery training.

In October 1942, *Trippe* cleared the Chasapeake Bay area and steamed north to Newport where she arrived on the 7th. For the next two weeks, she operated with *Massachusetts* (BB–59) while the new battleship practiced shore bombardment for the upcoming invasion of French North Africa. During the pre-dawn hours of 19 October, she was steaming for Casco Bay when *Benson* (DD–421) struck *Trippe* on her starboard quarter, killing four *Trippe* crewmen and injuring three others. On 13 November, *Trippe* completed repairs at New York and got underway for antisubmarine warfare training at New London, Conn.

Following almost a month of training and escorting coastal convoys, *Trippe* departed New York in the screen of her first convoy bound for Casablanca. She returned to New York on 7 February 1943 and conducted more training. In April, the destroyer made another round-trip voyage to Morocco and escorted a coastal convoy to Norfolk before heading for the Mediterranean. On 10 May, the warship arrived at Oran, Algeria. She then screened convoys between that port and Bizerte, conducted patrols, and practiced shore bombardment in preparation to support the Allied landings on Sicily.

On 9 July, the destroyer left Oran in the screen of a Sicily-bound convoy and was still at sea when Allied troops clambered ashore the following day. She arrived off Gela on the 14th, the day following the landings at that port, and patrolled that area until the 20th when she returned to Oran. However, the destroyer arrived back at Sicily the same day—this time at Palermo. Three days later, the *Luftwaffe* attacked the anchorage. To elude radar, the German medium bombers ap-

proached from the south, low over the Sicilian mountains, and circled the targets. As *Trippe* zigzagged to evade bombing and strafing planes, her 5-inch battery barked defiantly. When the raid was over, she claimed credit for one of the German eagles.

Up north, while Lieutenant General Patton's armored columns moved across the northern coast of Sicily and side-stepped heavy enemy formations with amphibious landings, the Navy supported his advance. *Trippe* left Palermo on 4 August in company with *Savannah* (CL–42) to support the advance with naval gunfire. On the 5th, she bombarded bridges at Terranova. During the next two days, the destroyer joined *Philadelphia* (CL–41) before supporting the landings at Sant'Agate di Militello. *Trippe*'s guns paved the way for the troops landing at Brolo on the 11th; and, on the 16th, her main battery supported the amphibious end-run at Spadafora. The following day, Sicily was declared secured; and *Trippe* headed north with three PT boats to accept the surrender of the Aeolian Islands of Lipari and Stromboli.

The Italian mainland was the destroyer's next target. In the early hours of 20 August, *Trippe* and *Wainwright* (DD–419) shelled a railroad bridge at Fiume Petrace; then turned south to Bizerte and escorted a convoy to Palermo. *Trippe* next returned to Bizerte and on 31 August, proceeded to Oran.

British troops landed at Reggio, Italy, on 3 September to begin the long, bitter drive up the Italian peninsula. Two days later, *Trippe* put to sea to escort a convoy to the assault beaches at Salerno, just south of Naples. This attack, aimed at turning German defenses in the south of Italy, was launched on the morning of 9 September 1943. The troops ran into heavy enemy resistance. The *Luftwaffe* and heavy coastal batteries took a heavy toll of the landing force, but *Trippe* and other fire support ships brought their batteries to bear and helped the troops ashore consolidate their beachhead.

After several round-trip voyages between Salerno and Oran, she returned to the Bay of Naples on 16 October. Early on the morning of the 13th, while *Trippe* was escorting a convoy from Naples to Oran, the German submarine *U–371* attacked the convoy and quickly sank *Bristol* (DD–453). *Trippe* searched briefly for the attacker, but concentrated upon rescuing *Bristol*'s survivors, so the U-boat escaped.

Trippe occupied the next month with convoy operations in the western Mediterranean and patrol work of Oran. On 18 November, she sailed from Gibraltar with *Brooklyn* (CL–40) and a screen of British and United States destroyers. Off Casablanca, they rendezvoused with battleship *Iowa* (BB–61), which had just borne President Roosevelt on the first leg of his journey to the Allied conferences at Cairo and Teheran. *Trippe* escorted *Iowa* through the Straits of Gibraltar to Oran then screened the battleship as she steamed westward again through the Straits into the Atlantic and proceeded to Casablanca to await President Roosevelt's return. After shepherding her charge to that port, *Trippe* turned back to Algiers and resumed her patrol operations.

On the afternoon of 16 December, the destroyer put to sea in company with *Edison* (DD–439) and *Woolsey* (DD–437) to hunt for the survivors of a torpedoed merchantman. While searching for castaways, the three warships also sought the U-boat itself. Early that evening, they made radar contact on *U–73* steaming on the surface. *Woolsey* switched on her searchlights, and *Trippe*'s fire control radar locked onto the target. The two destroyers immediately opened up with their main batteries and pumped salvo after salvo of 5-inch shells into the German submarine. Six minutes after visual contact, *U–73* went down for the last time—all the way to the bottom. While *Woolsey* picked up the German submariners, *Trippe* made sure that *U–73* had no colleague lurking in the area. The destroyers then returned to Oran.

At the beginning of 1944, the destroyer was at Palermo, Sicily. On 21 January, she got underway to support the Allied landings at Anzio, located farther up the Italian peninsula near Rome. The next day, she took station with *Brooklyn* and *Edison*, and her guns supported the troops going ashore. Two days later, she fought off a *Luftwaffe* air attack. She returned to gunfire support on the 25th and bombarded enemy troops and vehicles. On 31 January, she pounded troop concentrations and vehicles and demolished an observation post. *Trippe* hit two German strong points on 5 February. She was relieved of duty on the gunline on 10 February and returned to Oran, rescuing two downed British flyers along the way.

On 23 February, *Trippe* steamed to Casablanca where she joined a hunter-killer group built around *Card* (CVE–11) and got underway for the United States. During the voyage, the escort carrier and the five destroyers in her screen conducted air, sound, and radar searches for German submarines. *Trippe* parted company with the task unit on 4 March and, after a stop at Bermuda, put into New York for a month of upkeep. Following refresher training, she conducted hunter-killer operations out of Casco Bay. Late in May, she escorted *Hancock* (CV–19) on the first leg of the new carrier's shakedown cruise before joining *Cooper* (DD–695) for electronics countermeasure experiments in Chesapeake Bay. She put into Norfolk on 3 June, but departed the next day with *Ticonderoga* (CV–14) for air operations off the Virginia capes. From 19 June until Independence Day 1944, *Trippe* conducted exercises in the Gulf of Paria near Trinidad. On 9 July, she returned to Boston with *Hancock* and began a 19-day availability. Between 28 July and 23 October, the destroyer made two round-trip voyages between the United States and southern Italy escorting convoys to and from that bitterly contested campaign. For the remainder of the year, she conducted training near Casco Bay and screened *Shangri La* (CV–38) during air operations near Trinidad. Late in February 1945, *Trippe* escorted another convoy to the Mediterranean, this time to Oran. She returned to New York during the first week in April and began a brief yard period.

Repairs complete, *Trippe* headed south with a convoy bound for the Canal Zone. She transited the canal, stopped at San Diego, and arrived in Pearl Harbor on 16 May. She spent several weeks in the Hawaiian Islands conducting shore bombardment drills in preparation for duty with the 5th Fleet in the Central Pacific. However, the landings for which she prepared never came to fruition. Instead, the ship headed west in mid-June and escorted convoys between various islands in the Central Pacific, including Iwo Jima, Saipan, Ulithi, and Okinawa. The brevity of her stopovers protected her from the wrath of the kamikazes. She was en route to Okinawa with a convoy on 15 August, when she received word of the cessation of hostilities. *Trippe* remained in the Far East participating in the surrender negotiations with Japanese garrisons remaining in the Marianas and Bonin Islands. On 5 November, she returned to Saipan and began a month of patrols, training, and air-sea rescue operations north of that island. On 15 December, she cleared Guam to return to the United States.

Her homecoming was brief, however, for on 15 January 1946, she steamed back to Pearl Harbor to prepare for Operation "Crossroads," the atomic bomb tests conducted at Bikini Atoll. Four months later, the tests were ready to go forward. *Trippe* entered Bikini lagoon on 1 June. The destroyer missed the first explosion, an air-burst on 1 July; but the second test, an underwater detonation on the 25th, made her so radioactive that it was unsafe to approach her. *Trippe*'s radioactive contamination forced the Navy to keep her at Bikini where she was subjected to an intensive study. *Trippe* was decommissioned there on 28 August 1946. Over the next 18 months, her hull deteriorated to the point of making it almost impossible to keep her afloat. On

3 February 1948, she was towed to deep water off Kwajalein and sunk by gunfire. Her name was struck from the Navy list on 19 February 1948.

Trippe earned six battle stars for World War II service.

IV

(DE–1075: dp. 3,963 (f.); l. 438'; b. 47'; dr. 25'; s. 25+ k.; cpl. 245; a. 1 5", 1 ASROC/Standard missile 1n., 1 Sea Sparrow 1n., 4 15.5" ASW tt.; cl. *Knox*)

The fourth *Trippe* (DE–1075) was laid down on 29 July 1968 at Westwego, La., by Avondale Shipyards, Inc.; launched on 1 November 1969; sponsored by Mrs. John S. Foster; and commissioned at Charleston, S.C., on 19 September 1970, Comdr. Allen B. Higgenbotham in command.

Trippe completed outfitting during the first week in February 1971, loaded ammunition at the weapons station on the 7th and 8th, and cleared Charleston on the 9th. Following a five-week stay at Newport, R.I., the escort ship got underway on 23 March to conduct shakedown training in the Caribbean. During that cruise, she visited Guantanamo Bay, Cuba; Frederiksted, St. Croix, in the American Virgin Islands; Puerto Rico; and Andros Island in the Bahamas. She interrupted her shakedown cruise from 22 to 28 April to conduct a surveillance mission off the coast of Haiti just after the death of the President of Haiti, François Duvalier. She resumed training on 29 April and continued it until 23 May when she headed for home. *Trippe* entered Newport again on 25 May and remained there until 6 July, conducting final trials between 14 and 16 June. The ship entered the Boston Naval Shipyard on 7 July and began post-shakedown availability, which included the installation of one sonar and two missile systems. She completed sea trials on 9 December and returned to Newport 10 days later.

On 10 January 1972, she departed Newport for operations in the Caribbean. On the 26th, just before reaching the Virgin Islands, *Trippe* encountered a burning merchantman, SS *Fiona C*. A boarding party from *Trippe* succeeded in dropping *Fiona C*.'s anchor to keep her from drifting ashore on Culebra Island. After notifying Coast Guard authorities of the burning ship's exact position, *Trippe* continued on into the harbor at St. Thomas. From 28 January to 18 February, she conducted a series of Standard and Sparrow III missile test firings for the Operational Test and Evaluation Force and then returned north, arriving at Newport on 22 February. From then until 28 April, she remained in the Newport area, putting to sea only once—from 13 to 17 March—to participate in COMPTUEX 8–72. Between 28 April and 11 May, *Trippe* joined in LANTREADEX 4–72. She returned to Newport on 11 May and remained for almost a month.

On 5 June, she departed Newport bound for the Pacific. She transited the Panama Canal on 10 June and, after stops at Oahu and Guam, joined the 7th Fleet at Subic Bay in the Philippines on Independence Day. Five days later, *Trippe*, in company with *America* (CVA–66), headed for the combat zone off the coast of Vietnam. For the next month, she conducted combat operations in the Gulf of Tonkin. She served as a planeguard for *America* and conducted naval gunfire support missions for troops ashore in the vicinity of Quang Tri City and of the old imperial capital, Hue. The warship returned to Subic Bay on 13 August.

Soon after her arrival, *Trippe* was ordered to the Middle East to fulfill missions originally assigned to damaged *Warrington* (DD–843). On 16 August, she departed the Philippines and, after visits to Singapore and Ceylon, arrived in Manama, Bahrain. For almost three months, she conducted goodwill visits to Middle Eastern ports—stopping at Bandar Shapur, Iran; Sitrah, Bahrain; Karachi, Pakistan; Djibouti in the French territory of Afars and Issas; Victoria in the

Trippe (DE–1075) early in 1972. An ASROC launcher is on her forecastle; the similar launcher at her stern fires point-defense surface-to-air missiles. (K–93346)

Seychelles Islands; Tamatave, Malagasy Republic; and Mombasa, Kenya.

At Mombasa, she turned her duties over to *Sellars* (DDG–11) on 2 November and headed back to the United States. En route home, *Trippe* stopped at Lourenco Marques, Mozambique; Luanda, Angola; Dakar, Senegal; and Bermuda. On 2 December, she moored at Newport and began post-deployment standdown.

Trippe opened 1973 in port at Newport preparing for a restricted availability at the Boston Naval Shipyard. Between 9 and 12 January, she made a brief run to Earle, N.J., to offload ammunition and, on 6 February, entered the shipyard. During her almost five months in the yard, *Trippe*'s DASH flight deck and hangar were enlarged to accommodate a light airborne multipurpose system (LAMPS) manned helicopter for antisubmarine warfare, antiship missile defense, search and rescue, and general utility missions. She also received the interim surface-to-surface missile (ISSM) system. The escort ship completed her availability on 27 June, loaded ammunition at Charleston on the 29th, and headed for Guantanamo Bay, Cuba. After refresher training and missile and gunfire qualifications at Vieques Island, she operated with Carrier Division 6 late in July. *Trippe* returned to Newport on 29 July to prepare for her upcoming deployment.

On 30 August, she departed Newport in company with *Dewey* (DLG–14) and *Harry E. Yarnell* (DLG–17). On 7 September, she reported for duty with the 6th Fleet at Lisbon, Portugal. Three days later, she joined units of other NATO navies in Operation "Quickshave," which ended on the 20th. After a visit to Falmouth, England, she headed for the eastern Mediterranean, where she operated with Task Force (TF) 60. For the remainder of the deployment, *Trippe* screened TF 60 carriers, located submarines of the Soviet Mediterranean Squadron, and participated in gunfire exercises. On 14 January 1974, *Trippe* turned her duties over to her relief at Rota, Spain, and headed home. She returned to Newport on the 24th and began a month-long, post-deployment standdown. On 28 February, she departed Newport and, on 1 March, entered her new home port, Charleston, S.C. For the remainder

of the year, *Trippe* operated along the east coast conducting training and exercises.

On 9 January 1975, the warship left Charleston and headed for a tour of duty in the Indian Ocean. Steaming via the Cape of Good Hope, she reported on 13 February for duty with the Middle East Force at Mombasa, Kenya. Four days later, *Trippe* headed north to Bandar Abbas, Iran, where she arrived on the 27th. There, she entertained the Shah's nephew, Prince Shafique, a captain in the Imperial Iranian Navy and commander of its Destroyer Squadron 1.

From there, she voyaged on a tour of visits to ports on the Indian Ocean littoral, among which were Karachi, Pakistan; Djibouti, French territory of Afars and Issas; and Hodeidah, Yemen. Her series of port visits was interrupted late in March when she was called upon to observe political conditions in Saudi Arabia after the assassination of King Faisal. On 1 April, she resumed her itinerary by calling at Jidda, Saudi Arabia, to embark Saudi naval personnel for training. From there, she headed for Bahrain. During that voyage, she encountered units of the Soviet Indian Ocean Squadron off Socotra Island. After five days in Manama, Bahrain, she put to sea on 16 April to observe those same Soviet ships during their Exercise "Okean 75." Upon release from that duty, *Trippe* visited Bandar Abbas again on the 30th. The warship completed her middle eastern tour at Mombasa on 28 May and headed —via the Suez Canal and the Mediterranean Sea—to the United States. After stopping at Rota, Spain, and crossing the Atlantic, she entered Charleston on 29 June. The next day, *Trippe* was redesignated a frigate FF–1075. Following a summer of training and a midshipman cruise, the frigate began overhaul at Charleston on 6 October.

Trippe completed overhaul on 23 June 1976. The succeeding three months were spent in the Caribbean where the fleet frigate conducted refresher training. Proceeding to her home port, Charleston, on 8 October, *Trippe* spent the remainder of 1976 conducting a rigorous schedule of inspections in preparation for a forthcoming deployment to the Middle East.

Following a technical restricted availability from 27 December 1976 to 29 January 1977, *Trippe* departed from Charleston on 31 January. The ship made a series of visits to West African ports while en route to the Mediterranean for a transit of the Suez Canal. From 8 March to 14 July, *Trippe* was under the operational control of Commander Middle Eastern Force. Concluding her deployment, *Trippe* returned to Charleston on 15 September. On the conclusion of post-deployment standdown, the ship conducted a host of inspections, both underway and in port.

December 1977 and January 1978 were spent preparing for an April deployment as well as an intervening fleet exercise, "READEX 1–78," conducted in the Caribbean during February. On 4 April, *Trippe* deployed to the Mediterranean, returning on 26 October. The customary post-deployment standdown followed which concluded the year 1978.

Trippe earned one battle star for service off the coast of Vietnam.

Tristram Shandy

The hero—and the shortened title—of the novel, *The Life and Opinions of Tristram Shandy, Gentleman*, which was written by Laurence Sterne between the years 1759 and 1767.

(SwGbt.: t. 444; l. 222'; b. 23'6''; dr. 6'4''; s. 12 k.; a. 3 12-pdrs., 1 20-pdr. P.r.)

Tristram Shandy—a schooner-rigged, iron-hulled sidewheel steamer completed in 1864 at Greenock, Scotland—was originally owned by Matthew Isaac Wilson, a Liverpool, England, merchant. The ship subsequently sailed for the Bahamas, whence she took part in British efforts to continue trade with Southern states during the American Civil War.

On her first attempt to run the Federal blockade, *Tristram Shandy* outdistanced a Union pursuer by dumping cargo overboard to gain a few more knots of speed. After reaching Wilmington, N.C., she returned to Nassau to pick up another cargo earmarked for the Confederacy.

Successfully slipping through the blockade, she unloaded at Wilmington and took on board a valuable cargo of cotton, turpentine, and tobacco. In addition, $50,000 in Confederate specie reposed in the ship's safe. On 15 May 1864, the steamer attempted to slip to sea under the protective covering of a rain squall. The ship was darkened to avoid detection by roving Union patrols, but her funnels suddenly commenced throwing highly visible flames. Union gunboat *Kansas* spotted the telltale light and gave chase. For two hours, *Kansas* pursued and slowly gained on the fleeing blockade runner. Meanwhile, *Tristram Shandy*'s master frantically called down for more steam. The fugitive steamer's engineer zealously carried out the orders from the bridge until a valve failure stopped her engine. Slowly, the blockade runner lost way and lay dead in the water, an easy prey for Union sailors. A boarding party from *Kansas* rigged a towline to the prize, and the blockader towed her to Beaufort, N.C. The erstwhile blockade runner was then taken to Massachusetts where the Navy purchased her from the Boston Prize Court.

Repaired and converted to a gunboat at the Boston Navy Yard, the ship proceeded to Hampton Roads, Va., where she was commissioned on 12 August 1864, Acting Vol. Lt. Edward F. Devens in command. Eleven days later, the ship arrived off Wilmington on 23 August and began duty as a blockader. On 7 September, her lookout sighted a strange ship. However, the distance between the two ships was too great, and the quarry slipped away. Her next chance came on 31 October when she joined *Santiago de Cuba* and *Mount Vernon* in pursuing a blockade runner which escaped after a three-hour chase.

On 3 December 1864, a blockade runner, whose name could not be determined, ran aground off the western bar at Wilmington, at Marshall Shoals. Although within range of Fort Fisher's guns, *Tristram Shandy* closed the disabled blockade runner to destroy her before she could be salvaged by Southern forces. Commencing fire with her Parrott rifle and her 3-pounders, the Union gunboat soon reduced the grounded runner to a blazing wreck, down by the bow and sinking from numerous hits. Meanwhile, Confederate batteries opened fire on the gunboat, and several Southern shells splashed close alongside. Through skillful maneuvering by her commanding officer, *Tristram Shandy* emerged unscathed, as she kept behind the clouds of smoke from her own guns and thus confused the Confederate lookouts spotting for the fort's heavy rifles.

On Christmas Eve, in an attempt to take Fort Fisher and thus close the Confederacy's last major seaport, Rear Admiral David D. Porter deployed a large fleet of gunboats, ironclads, and transports off the fort and commenced laying down a heavy shore bombardment. Army forces slated to take part in the operation, under General Ben Butler, arrived from northward too late to commence operations on the first day. Ill feeling resulted between Butler and Porter, with the former officer returning to Washington and the operation temporarily shelved.

After participating in the initial December bombardments of Fort Fisher, *Tristram Shandy* took part in the second assault which commenced on Friday, 13 January 1865. A frontal assault by sailors and marines drawn from landing forces in the Fleet suffered disastrously as fusilades of gunfire from Confederate sharpshooters and cannoneers swept them down as wheat before a scythe. Meanwhile, Army forces attacked from the landward side, storming the fort's relatively undefended rear. By 15 January, Fisher was secured in Union hands, and the last barrier to Wilmington was removed, enabling the Union to stop the flow of supplies through the Confederacy's last seaport.

Tristram Shandy resumed patrol operations off Wilmington; and, on 25 January 1865, she captured blockade runner *Blenheim*. The runner's captain and crew had not received the news of the fall of Fort Fisher and anchored off Mound Battery. He thus fell prey to Union sailors from the gunboat, who boarded *Blenheim* and captured her easily.

On 31 January, *Tristram Shandy* joined the East Gulf Blockading Squadron and remained with that group into the spring. Returning north, she served as a dispatch vessel with Union forces operating in Hampton Roads. Admiral Porter embarked in *Tristram Shandy* on 14 April, after the admiral had previously escorted President Lincoln on a tour of the devastated fallen Confederate capital of Richmond, Va. Two days later, the ship moored at Baltimore, where the admiral was greeted with the sad news that the President had been assassinated the previous night in Washington.

On 26 April, the ship returned to Hampton Roads to continue her duties as a dispatch vessel, operating off the Virginia capes, concurrently serving as a lookout and keeping watch for the Confederate ram *Stonewall*, believed to be still at sea and unaware that hostilities had ceased.

Tristram Shandy then conveyed Confederate prisoners to Fort Pulaski, Georgia, in late May and returned to Hampton Roads on 2 June. Upon arrival, she was assigned to duty as a roving vessel operating under the direct orders of the Commander of the North Atlantic Squadron, for his use in inspecting the various ships and stations under his command.

On 21 June 1865, her name was changed to *Boxer* (q.v.). Her service as a warship finished, *Tristram Shandy* was laid up at Philadelphia in the late summer of 1865. She remained in reserve until sold on 1 September 1868 to J. N. Middleton, of Philadelphia, who renamed her *Firefly*.

The erstwhile blockade runner and gunboat operated subsequently in mercantile service under a succession of owners until she ran aground off Havana, Cuba, and was declared a total loss in 1874.

Triton

A Greek demigod of the sea who was the son of Poseidon and Amphitrite. Triton, who possessed a man's body above the waist and that of a fish below, used his conch-shell trumpet alternately to summon storms and to still the sea.

I

(Tug: dp. 212; lbp. 96'9''; b. 20'9''; dr. 9' (mean); s. 13 k.)

The first *Triton*—a steam-powered, steel-hulled tug constructed in 1889 at Camden, N.J., by J. H. Dialogue —was purchased by the Navy in September of 1889; and placed in commission soon thereafter.

The tug spent her entire career operating from the navy yard at Washington, D.C. She frequently steamed down the Potomac to the naval reservation at Indian Head, Md., which was home first to the Naval Proving Grounds in the 1890's and then to the Naval Powder Factory during the first half of the 20th century. In all probability, *Triton* conveyed barges laden with materials to be utilized in the testing of naval guns and in the production of gunpowder and explosives. During the year 1900 alone, she recorded 198 round-trips between Washington and Indian Head. She continued to serve the Navy at Washington through World War I and into the 1920's. On 17 July 1921, the Navy designated her YT–10 in accordance with the new system of alphanumeric hull designations. She remained in service until early in 1930. Her name was struck from the Navy list on 19 May, and she was sold on 15 September.

II

(StTug: t. 98; l. 81'; b. 19'; dr. 10' (aft); s. 10 k.; cpl. 10)

The second *Triton* (Id. No. 3312)—a tug built in 1889 at Philadelphia, Pa., by Neafie & Levy—was acquired by the United States Navy on 17 October 1918 from the Independent Pier Co., of Philadelphia, Pa.; and was placed in commission at Philadelphia on 25 October 1918.

Acquired less than a month before the Armistice which ended World War I, *Triton* served only briefly. The Navy had planned to use *Triton* as a minesweeper and patrol craft in the 4th Naval District, but the end of hostilities in Europe on 11 November 1918 obviated the need for her. In all probability, she spent her entire four-month naval career at Philadelphia, either moored at pierside or, at most, serving as a tug. In any event, *Triton* was returned to her owner on 8 March 1919, and her name was struck from the Navy list that same day.

III

(SS–201: dp. 1,475 (surf.), 2,370 (subm.); l. 307'2''; b. 27'3''; dr. 13'3''; s. 20 k. (surf.), 8.75 k. (subm.); cpl. 59; a. 10 21'' tt., 1 3'', 2 .50-cal. mg.; cl. *Tambor*)

The third *Triton* (SS–201) was laid down on 5 July 1939 by the Portsmouth (N.H.) Navy Yard; launched on 25 March 1940; sponsored by Mrs. Ernest J. King, wife of Rear Admiral (later Fleet Admiral) Ernest J. King; and commissioned on 15 August 1940, Lt. Comdr. Willis A. Lent in command.

The new submarine held her shakedown training in the Caribbean from 14 January 1941 to 26 March and then conducted training and minelaying exercises in the Portsmouth-New London area. *Triton* departed Portsmouth on 1 July, transited the Panama Canal on the 12th, and arrived at San Diego on the 20th. Nine days later, she and *Trout* (SS–202) headed for Hawaii and arrived at Pearl Harbor on 4 August.

Assigned to Submarine Division 62, *Triton* made a training cruise to Midway from 30 August to 15 September and then participated in local and fleet operations in the Hawaiian area. On 19 November, the submarine headed west to conduct a practice war patrol and arrived off Wake Island on the 26th. On 8 December, she saw columns of smoke rising over the island but assumed that it was caused by construction work being done ashore. That night, when she surfaced to charge her batteries, she was informed by radio that Wake and Pearl Harbor had been bombed and was ordered to stay out of range of Wake's guns. The next morning, *Triton* observed the Japanese bombing the island. On the night of the 10th, she was surfaced, charging her batteries, when flashes of light from Wake revealed a destroyer or light cruiser on a parallel course. The submarine was silhoutted against the moon, and the enemy ship turned towards her. *Triton* went deep and began evasive action. When the Japanese ship slowed astern, the submarine came to 120 feet and fired four stern torpedoes. Her crew heard a dull explosion 58 seconds later and believed that one of her torpedoes had hit the target. The submarine then went to 175 feet and cleared the area. On 21 December, the submarine was ordered to return to Hawaii, and she arrived back at Pearl Harbor on the last day of the year.

On 25 January 1942, *Triton* got underway for the East China Sea and her second war patrol. She was off Kyushu on 17 February when she contacted a freighter. The submarine fired four torpedoes and scored one hit in the target's stern. The ship stopped for a few minutes and then slowly got underway. That evening *Triton* attacked another freighter with two torpedoes at a range of 1,200 yards. One hit the Japanese cargo ship aft of her well deck, and the maru went dead in the water and began settling. Soon, several heavy explosions marked the end of *Shinyo Maru No. 5.* Four days later, the submarine intercepted two cargo ships. She sank *Shokyu Maru* with two torpedoes but could not attack the second ship because of its speed and the appearance of a four-engine patrol plane. On the night of the 27th, the submarine was on the surface for a battery charge when she sighted a ship approximately three miles away. She closed to attack and fired two torpedoes. One torpedo hit, but haze over the water and smoke from the damaged ship prohibited a second attack. *Triton* made no further contacts and returned to Pearl Harbor on 17 March.

Triton got underway on 13 April to return to the East China Sea. Ten days later, the submarine contacted a 1,000-ton trawler near Marcus. After missing with two torpedoes, she surfaced to battle with her deck guns and left the trawler a sinking wreck. On May Day, the submarine sighted six freighters, in two columns, escorted by two torpedo boat escorts. She fired two torpedoes, and both hit the leading ship. *Triton* then fired two torpedoes at the next freighter but both missed. The submarine passed under the convoy and fired two more torpedoes at the damaged cargo ship. One missed, but the other broke the back of *Calcutta Maru*, which promptly sank. The submarine contacted an escorted convoy on 6 May and fired two torpedoes which missed the last ship. *Triton* next spotted a destroyer coming to the rear of the convoy, fired twice more, and went deep to elude it. Her sonar heard two violent explosions. At that point, the submarine maneuvered around and ahead of the convoy to position for another attack. When she attained the desired angle, she fired four torpedoes—two at the third ship and two at the fourth. *Triton* heard two explosions from the first spread but none from the second as she was forced to take evasive action. The submarine later returned to periscope depth, but no ships were in sight. The convoy had cleared the area after the freighter *Taiei Maru* and the transport *Taigen Maru* had sunk. On 15 May, she sank two deep-sea fishing boats with her deck guns. The next day, she spotted an aircraft carrier and a destroyer at a range of six miles but could not close the range. She then radioed a report of the contact, but it was not acknowledged. *Triton* sighted a Japanese submarine on 17 May and fired a torpedo from 6,200 yards into *I–164*. Parts of the target were blown 100 feet into the air, and *I–164* went down by the stern. Four days later, she fired four torpedoes at another enemy submarine, but all missed. The patrol terminated at Pearl Harbor on 4 June, as the Battle of Midway began.

Triton's fourth war patrol took her to Alaskan waters and lasted from 25 June to 24 August. On Independence Day, she was patrolling in a heavy fog, in the vicinity of Cape Sabok, when the fog lifted enough to reveal a Japanese destroyer. The submarine trailed the enemy all day, in and out of patches of fog, until she had closed the range to 3,000 yards. *Triton* then fired two torpedoes, and one hit the target amidships. The destroyer *Nenohi* capsized to port and slid under the waves. *Triton* sighted a freighter on the 28th but lost it in a fog bank. The same thing happened the next day. On 9 August, *Triton* saw an enemy submarine's periscope and prepared to attack. However, the Japanese sub struck first, forcing *Triton* to go deep as enemy torpedoes passed overhead. On the 15th, *Triton* fired four torpedoes at a darkened ship from a range of 1,500 yards. There were two consecutive explosions, and flames shot over two hundred feet into the air. To *Triton*, the enemy ship appeared to be larger than a destroyer. However, there is no official record of a sinking on that date. The submarine made no further contacts before returning to Pearl Harbor on 7 September. She then entered the navy yard for an overhaul that lasted until 6 December.

On 16 December, *Triton* got underway for a position 20 miles east of Wake on the Midway-Wake route. She was one of three submarines stationed between the two islands to mark the way for Army Liberator bombers in strikes on Wake and to rescue the crews of any planes forced down at sea. She made no rescues; but, on the night of 23 December, she aided in guiding the Liberators in a night bombing attack on the island. On Christmas Eve, the submarine sighted the mast of a ship on the horizon that was headed for Wake anchorage. *Triton* closed to 1,000 yards and fired two torpedoes. One hit under the stack and the other hit under the foremast. *Amakasu Maru No. 1* was obliterated in a cloud of smoke and steam as she went under. The submarine then set a course for Brisbane. On 28 December, she sighted an enemy ship, closed to 7,000 yards, and fired three torpedoes into the transport *Omi Maru*. The ship sank almost immediately and, although there was much wreckage, no survivors were seen. *Triton* was then ordered to patrol the Truk-Rabaul-New Guinea shipping lanes, north and northwest of New Ireland, and arrived on station on 30 December 1942.

On 10 January 1943, *Triton* stalked an unidentified vessel but withheld her attack upon observing that the target was marked as a hospital ship. Three days later, she fired four torpedoes at a tanker and scored one hit. When the enemy ship began firing at her periscope, the submarine went deep to begin an end around. About 20 minutes later, the submarine returned to periscope depth and launched a spread of four torpedoes. Two geysers of water rose amidship as high as the target's bridge, but no explosions followed. The next day, *Triton* attempted to attack a freighter, but an escort forced her down where she was subjected to a two-hour depth charge attack. On the 16th, she attacked two cargo ships, scoring two hits on the first and one on the second; but her victims forced her to submerge before she could evaluate the damage. Later that day, *Triton* fired her last three torpedoes at a large freighter but heard no explosions. She then headed for Australia and reached Brisbane on 26 January.

On 16 February, *Triton* began her sixth and final war patrol, hoping to destroy enemy shipping between the Shortland Basin and Rabaul. Ten days later, she reported that she had seen smoke on the 22d and that the Japanese had installed radar at Buka. On 6 March, the submarine attacked a convoy of five destroyer-escorted ships, sinking the cargo ship *Kiriha Maru* and damaging another freighter. One of her torpedoes made a circular run, and *Triton* crash-dived to evade it. She attacked another convoy on the night of 8 March and claimed that five of the eight torpedoes she had fired scored hits. She could not observe the results or make a follow-up attack because gunfire from the escorts forced her down. On 11 March, *Triton* reported that she was chasing two convoys, each made up of five or more ships. She was informed that *Trigger* (SS–237) was operating in an adjoining area and ordered to stay south of the equator. On the 13th, *Triton* was warned that three enemy destroyers in her area were either looking for a convoy or were hunting American submarines.

On 15 March, *Trigger* reported that she had attacked a convoy and had been depth charged. Even though attacks on her ceased, she could still hear distant depth charging for about an hour. No further messages from *Triton* were ever received. Post-war examination of Japanese records revealed that on 15 March 1943 three Japanese destroyers attacked a submarine a little northwest of *Triton*'s assigned area and subsequently observed an oil slick, debris, and items with American markings. On 10 April 1943, *Triton* was reported overdue from patrol and presumed lost.

Triton received five battle stars for World War II service.

IV

(Coast Guard Patrol Boat No. 16: dp. 337; l. 165'; b. 25'3''; dr. 8'6''; s. 16 k.; cpl. 50; a. 1 3'', 2 1-pdrs.; cl. *Thetis*)

The fourth *Triton*—a steel-hulled, diesel-powered Coast Guard patrol boat—served almost simultaneously with the submarine of the same name. The contract for her construction was let on 17 November 1933 to the Marietta Manufacturing Co., Point Pleasant, W. Va.; and, a little over a year later, on 20 November 1934, the ship was placed in commission, Lt. Comdr. George C. Carlstedt, USCG, in command.

Assigned to the homeport of Gulfport, Miss., *Triton* operated in the Gulf of Mexico from at least 1 January 1935. On 1 July 1941, four months in advance of the directive whereby the United States Coast Guard was transferred from the Treasury Department to the Navy, *Triton* and five of her sister ships were turned over to the Navy. This action occurred simultaneously with the establishment of the four Sea Frontiers.

Four *Thetis*-class patrol boats, including *Triton*, were assigned to the East Coast Sound School, Key West, Fla., for duty as patrol and training vessels. Their collateral duties included operating under the aegis of Commander, Task Force 6, on gulf patrol duties. At the time of the Japanese attack on Pearl Harbor, 7 December 1941, *Triton* was operating out of Key West. In or around February of 1942, *Triton* was classified as a patrol craft and given the alphanumeric hull number WPC–116.

Although American warships had been actively engaged in patrol and escort missions in the Battle of the Atlantic even before Pearl Harbor, their techniques for combatting the dangerous German submarines were, in January and February 1942, still far from adequate. U-boats operating off the eastern seaboard experienced what they called "the happy time," before American convoys could be organized. In some cases, Allied ships would be sunk because they were silhouetted by lights in non-blacked out cities along the shoreline.

Triton's antisubmarine warfare (ASW) training missions were conducted along with local patrol and escort duties out of Key West from 1941 into 1945. She had her first brush with what she presumed to be an enemy submarine on 21 February 1942. On that day, she made one attack but without success. Over the next few days, upon occasion joined by *PC–445* and *Hamilton* (DD–141), *Triton* conducted more attacks but did not draw blood.

On 9 June 1942, when SS *Lake Ormoc* reported an enemy submarine on the surface in her vicinity, *Triton* directed *Thetis* (WPC–115) to make the search. *Triton*, meanwhile, contacted the submarine *R–10* (SS–87) which had been conducting exercises with the patrol vessels in that same area. When *PC–518* took over the job of escorting *R–10* back to Key West, *Triton* joined *Thetis* in search of the submarine. Eventually, *PC–518* and *Noa* (DD–343) joined the hunt. *Triton* attacked with depth charges but, after a further search, concluded that the target was a "non-submarine," probably a tidal rip in the Gulf Stream.

Triton's next recorded ASW operation came soon thereafter, during the concentrated search and destroy mission mounted to find the U-boat which torpedoed the American steamer SS *Hagan* on the night of 10 June. The hunt, which involved radar-equipped Army B-18 bombers, three destroyers, several PC's, and *Triton* and *Thetis*, took three days. On the 12th, in an area well known for "false contacts," *Triton* attacked what she thought to be a submarine but later evaluated to be otherwise. Later that day, although not picking up propeller noises, the contact seemed strong to *Triton*'s sonar operator; and the ship attacked. Again, the result was the same—negative.

The next day, however, was different. *Thetis* picked up *U–157* trying to escape the "dragnet" and destroyed her in a single depth charge attack. That patrol craft recovered two pairs of leather submariner's pants and a tube of lubricant marked "made in Dusseldorf." There were no survivors. *Triton* took part in further attacks, along with the other ships of the hunter-killer group based on Key West; but, by that point, the enemy submersible had already been killed.

Triton remained with the Sound School, apparently, into 1945. On 10 February, while *PC–1546* was engaged in "Robot Bomb Patrol," she picked up what she evaluated as a submarine contact. She and *Triton*, also in the vicinity, then conducted attacks but found no evidence that a kill had been made.

Triton apparently remained in the Gulf of Mexico region for the remainder of her active service in the Coast Guard. Reverting to Treasury Department control after the end of World War II, *Triton* was reclassified from WPC–116 to WMEC (Medium Endurance Cutter)–116 sometime in 1966. Her post-war duty station was at Corpus Christi, Tex., until 1967. She was subsequently scrapped.

V

(SSR(N)–586; dp. 5,800 (surf.), 7,900 (subm.); l. 447'; b. 37'; s. 20½ k. (surf.), 20½ k. (subm.); cpl. 159; a. 6 tt.; cl. *Triton*)

The fifth *Triton* (SSR(N)–586) was laid down on 29 May 1956 at Groton, Conn., by the Electric Boat Division of the General Dynamics Corp.; launched on 19 August 1958; sponsored by Mrs. John Will; and commissioned on 10 November 1959, Capt. Edward L. Beach in command.

Triton put to sea on her shakedown cruise on 15 February 1960, bound for the South Atlantic. She arrived in the middle Atlantic off St. Peter and St. Paul Rocks on 24 February to commence a history-making voyage. Having remained submerged since her departure from the east coast, *Triton* continued on south towards Cape Horn, rounded the tip of South America, and headed west across the Pacific. After transiting the Philippine and Indonesian archipelagoes and crossing the Indian Ocean, she rounded the Cape of Good Hope and arrived off the St. Peter and Paul Rocks on 10 April—60 days and 21 hours after departing the mid-ocean landmark. Only once did her sail break the surface of the sea, when she transferred a sick sailor

to *Macon* (CA–132) off Montevideo, Uruguay, on March. She arrived back at Groton on 10 May, having completed the first submerged circumnavigation of th earth.

Triton's globe-girdling cruise proved invaluable t the United States. Politically, it enhanced the nation' prestige. From an operational viewpoint, the cruis demonstrated the great submerged endurance an sustained high-speed transit capabilities of the firs generation of nuclear-powered submarines. Moreove during the voyage, the submarine collected reams o oceanographic data. At the cruise's conclusion, *Trito* received the Presidential Unit Citation and Captai Beach received the Legion of Merit from Presiden Dwight D. Eisenhower.

Following her post-shakedown availability, *Trito* assumed her duties as a radar picket submarine i August 1960. She was then deployed to Europea waters with the 2d Fleet to participate in NAT(exercises. She climaxed the deployment with a port vis to Bremerhaven, West Germany.

For the first half of 1961, *Triton* conducted opera tional patrols and training exercises with the Atlanti Fleet. During this period, the rising threat posed b Russian submarine forces increased the Navy's de mands for nuclear-powered attack submarines wit antisubmarine warfare (ASW) capability. Accordingl upon the demise of the Navy's radar picket submarin program, *Triton* was redesignated SSN–586 on 1 Marc 1961 and entered the Portsmouth (N.H.) Naval Ship yard in June 1962 for conversion to an attack sut marine.

In March 1964, upon completion of this overhau *Triton*'s home port was changed from New Londor Conn., to Norfolk, Va. On 13 April 1964, *Triton* becam the flagship for the Submarine Force, Atlantic Flee and served in that role until relieved by *Ray* (SSN 653) on 1 June 1967. Eleven days later, *Triton* wa shifted to her original home port of New London.

Because of cutbacks in defense spending, *Triton* scheduled 1967 overhaul was cancelled indefinitely, an the submarine—along with 50 other vessels—was sched uled for inactivation. From October 1968 through Ma of 1969, the submarine underwent preservation an inactivation processes and was decommissioned o May 1969. On the 6th, *Triton* departed New Londo under tow and proceeded to Norfolk where she wa placed in the inactive fleet. She remained berthed a Norfolk into 1980.

Triton received both a Presidential Unit Citation an a Navy Unit Commendation during her service wit the fleet.

Tritonia

A plant cultivated for its long, sharply-pointe leaves and yellow, red, and orange flowers.

(SwGbt: dp. 202; l. 178'; b. 22'4''; a. 1 heavy 12-pdr 1 light 12-pdr.)

Tritonia—a side-wheel steamer built as *Sarah S. N Cary* in 1863 at East Haddam, Conn.—was purchase by the Navy at Hartford, Conn., on 1 December 186: and commissioned at the New York Navy Yard o 23 April 1864, Lt. Roswell H. Lamson in command.

With *Stepping Stones* and *Delaware*, *Tritonia* serve in a special torpedo and picket division established i the James River, Va., on 12 May 1864. The divisio patrolled the river to keep it clear of Confedera vessels, torpedoes, and fire rafts.

On 26 July, *Tritonia* left the division for duty wit the West Gulf Blockading Squadron. She arrived i Mississippi Sound on 5 August, the day of Admir Farragut's victory in Mobile Bay, and spent the r mainder of the month operating as a dispatch vess between New Orleans and that historic body of wate On 8 and 9 September, boat crews from *Tritoni*

Rodolph, *Stockdale*, and Army transport *Planter* destroyed several large Confederate salt works at Salt House Point in Bon Secours Bay, Ala. As they returned to Mobile Bay on 11 September, the vessels were fired upon but suffered no casualties.

Tritonia resumed blockade duty, towing the captured schooner *Medora* to New Orleans on 15 December for adjudication. She then operated in Mobile Bay until the end of the war and later at Pensacola and New Orleans. On 29 January 1866, *Tritonia* carried a company of Army troops up the Tombigbee River and recaptured the steamer *Belfast* which had been seized by guerrillas and taken up that stream. The joint expedition also recovered the steamer's cargo of cotton and captured five guerrillas as well.

Tritonia was sold at public auction at New York on 5 October 1866; redocumented as *Belle Brown* on 19 November; and lost at sea in 1880.

Triumph

(AM–323: dp. 890; l. 221'2''; b. 32'2''; dr. 10'9'' (mean); s. 18.1 k. (tl.); cpl. 105; a. 1 3'', 4 40mm.; cl. *Auk*)

BAM-323 was laid down for the Royal Navy on 27 October 1942 at Seattle, Wash., by the Associated Shipbuilding Corp.; taken over by the United States Navy in late 1942 or early 1943; named *Triumph* and designated AM–323 on 23 January 1943; launched on 25 February 1943; and commissioned on 3 February 1944, Lt. Comdr. Carl R. Cunningham, Jr., USNR, in command.

Following outfitting at Seattle, Wash., and shakedown training along the California coast, *Triumph* stood out of San Francisco on 1 May as a unit in the escort of an Oahu-bound convoy. She arrived in Pearl Harbor on the 10th and, after a five-day layover, joined the screen of a convoy bound for the Marshall Islands. She entered the lagoon at Majuro on 25 May; two days later, headed back to Hawaii with 24 passengers embarked; and reached Pearl Harbor on 2 June. She got underway again late in the month to escort another convoy to the Marshalls. She reentered Pearl Harbor on 16 July and prepared for her first deployment in the combat zone.

On 12 August, *Triumph* stood out of Pearl Harbor with a convoy bound initially for the Solomon Islands. The minesweeper arrived at Florida Island near Guadalcanal on 24 August and conducted minesweeping rehearsals in the Russell Islands to prepare for the invasion of the Palaus. On 8 September, she departed Guadalcanal with Task Group (TG) 32.4, the transport screen for the Palau Islands invasion force. *Triumph* reached Kossol Passage at dawn on 15 September and began sweeping mines from the prospective anchorage there. The first day passed without mishap, and the minesweepers retired from Kossol Passage for the night. However, at about 1430 the next day, *Wadleigh* (DD–689) struck a mine while supporting the sweeping of Kossol Passage as destruction vessel. At 1540, *Triumph* sent a fire and rescue party to assist the destroyer—by then completely without power—and took over her duties as destruction vessel. Over the next half hour, the minesweeper destroyed five floating mines by gunfire. Following that, she stood by *Wadleigh* until dark, providing what assistance she could. She then took up screening station for the night. Minesweeping operations continued on a daily basis until midday on the 18th when *Triumph* began devoting herself entirely to screening and harbor control duties. The little warship remained in the Palaus until mid-October—though at Peleliu after 30 September—and then got underway to screen a convoy to the Solomons.

After stops in the Russell Islands and at Tulagi, *Triumph* returned to the Palaus on 21 October. She remained there until late November, performing antisubmarine screening duty at Peleliu in the south and

at Kossol Passage in the north, as well as escorting ships between the two.

On 11 November, *Triumph* left the Palaus in company with a New Guinea-bound convoy. She reached Humboldt Bay on the 15th and sailed for Ulithi on the 20th. Ordered back to Humboldt Bay on the 22d, the minesweeper returned two days later. After taking on fuel and provisions, she stood out of Humboldt Bay for San Pedro Bay, Leyte, on the 26th in company with *General M. L. Hersey* (AP–148), *Hopewell* (DD–681), and Coast Guard cutter *Spencer*. *Triumph* reached recently invaded Leyte on the morning of 30 November and began preparations for the flanking landings at Ormoc Bay on the western shore of the island. After five days patrolling the San Pedro Bay anchorage against enemy submarine incursions, the ship got underway as a unit of TU 78.3.6. En route, *Triumph* and her traveling companions suffered a kamikaze attack when three "Zekes" dove on the unit. The first tried to crash *Requisite* (AM–109) but missed and splashed down between that ship and *Triumph*. The second fighter tried a bombing run but was brought down by the combined antiaircraft fire of the task unit. The pilot of the third plane prudently declined to attack. Later that day, a group of medium bombers overflew the unit but made no attack.

Just before noon, the minesweeper and her mates reached Ormoc Bay and streamed their sweep gear to complete their mission. Unmolested, the group of minesweepers completed their sweeping by 2125 that night and took up station in the screen of the Ormoc Bay attack force. The following morning, the Army 77th Division landed unopposed just south of Ormoc town and in the enemy's rear area. The only Japanese attempt to oppose the operation consisted of aerial attacks—both conventional and kamikaze. Though the attacks cost the American naval forces two warships sunk, *Mahan* (DD–364) and *Ward* (APD–16), two more severely damaged, *Liddle* (APD–60) and *Lamson* (DD–367), and an LSM abandoned; they failed to impede the landings and the progress of the troops ashore. *Triumph* departed Ormoc Bay late on the morning of the 7th and headed back to San Pedro Bay. Though her task unit occasionally engaged enemy aircraft during the intermittent air attacks, she concentrated on her role as a part of the antisubmarine screen while the destroyers of the outer screen bore the brunt of the attack. The raids ceased at dark; and, early the next morning, TU 78.3.6 reentered San Pedro Bay.

Triumph remained at San Pedro Bay until the afternoon of 12 December when she got underway to participate in the occupation of Mindoro. On the second day out, the task organization came under aerial attack. Just after midday, a kamikaze crashed the flagship *Nashville* (CL–43), and the light cruiser was forced to drop out of formation and return to San Pedro Bay with *Stanly* (DD–478).

Additional raids occurred that afternoon, but they caused no damage. By the morning of 14 December, the unit was passing Negros Island; and *Triumph*, along with the rest of the minesweepers, received orders to sweep the waters ahead of the force. During that sweep, the unit was attacked by a formation of three "Oscars." The enemy planes dropped three bombs off *Triumph*'s port quarter but caused no damage. An American combat air patrol drove the raiders off, and the minesweepers completed their mission by late afternoon. Just after midnight on 15 December, *Triumph* and her mates reached the beaches on the southwestern coast of Mindoro.

At 0225, they began sweeping the invasion approaches. They completed their task less than three hours later and moved out while the invasion force moved in. Later, she joined in sweeps of Pandarochan Bay; then returned to Mindoro Strait to form up for the return to Leyte. At 1830, she departed Mindoro and, after a brief but intense aerial attack at dusk, voyaged peacefully back to the anchorage at San Pedro

Bay, anchoring there a little after 0800 on the 18th. For the remainder of the month, she remained at San Pedro Bay and conducted antisubmarine patrols in Leyte Gulf.

On 2 January 1945, the minesweeper once again departed San Pedro Bay—this time to participate in the initial invasion of Luzon. The four-day voyage to the beaches at Lingayen Gulf was punctuated by a number of Japanese air assaults. An inconclusive air-to-surface battle on the night of 2 January was followed by the first attack in earnest on the 3d. Shortly after dawn, a formation of "Zekes" pounced on the convoy. One near-miss of the oiler Cowanesque (AO–79) caused a fire amidships. All ships joined in a withering fire that discouraged suicide runs; and, consequently, no ship suffered a direct hit.

The next morning, enemy planes approached the formation, but combat air patrol downed some and chased others away. On the 5th, general quarters sounded five times before noon, but Triumph observed no planes. Later, three warships peeled off to chase two Japanese destroyers sighted off the convoy's quarter. The enemy ships, however, managed to escape. At 1700, a formation of "Vals" hit the task force. Six of them attempted suicide crashes, but only one came close to its target—an LCI—which lost its mast in the encounter. Early the next morning, the force reached its destination off the beaches at Lingayen Gulf.

Between 6 and 9 January, Triumph conducted pre-invasion sweeps of the assault areas in Lingayen Gulf. Though the main task force was subjected to incessant enemy air attacks, the minesweeper continued her minesweeping almost unmolested. Each night, she retired from Lingayen Gulf and took up screening station for the transports and cargo ships. On the 9th, the ground troops stormed ashore at Lingayen, and Triumph kept a close watch for enemy submarines and suicide boats. She remained in Lingayen Gulf until the 14th—riding at anchor during the last three days of that period—and then got underway with a Leyte-bound convoy of LST's and LCI's. After transiting the Sulu Sea, the Mindanao Sea, Surigao Strait, and Leyte Gulf, the Allied ships arrived in San Pedro Bay on the 19th.

She remained there until 25 January when she headed out to resume action off Luzon. She reached Subic Bay and swept its coastal waters. On 4 February, she departed and headed back to Leyte, stopped at San Pedro Bay from 8 to 13 February, then put to sea once again on her way to the Marianas.

Triumph entered Apra Harbor, Guam, and reported for duty with the 5th Fleet. Two days later, she set a course for Ulithi, the staging area for Operation "Iceberg," the invasion and occupation of the Ryukyus. She arrived at Ulithi the following day and began a period of rest, repairs, and rehearsals.

Early in the afternoon of 19 March, Triumph sailed out of the lagoon at Ulithi with the Ryukyu Islands invasion force. When she arrived at her destination early on the morning of the 24th, Triumph and her division mates joined Shea (DM–30) and a patrol craft in minesweeping operations. On the 26th, destroyer Halligan (DD–584) struck a mine, and it caused explosions in her forward magazine which ripped off most of her forward section. Two ships of Triumph's unit proceeded to assist the stricken warship but managed to rescue only 172 members of Halligan's 325-man complement.

The following day, the division swept 15 mines of which total Triumph claimed three. On the 28th, her formation endured its first air raid of the campaign when three enemy planes dived in to attack. The formation responded with a lively fusillade which splashed all three. The minesweeper continued sweeping operations through the end of the month. She and her colleagues concluded their mission on the eve of the landings, 31 March, and began duty with the task force's antisubmarine screen.

At 0600 the following morning—April Fool's Day and Easter Sunday rolled into one—landing craft started their move shoreward; and, soon thereafter, the first wave of marines and soldiers hit the beaches on Okinawa.

During the ensuing four months, Triumph alternated screening duties with minesweeping operations. On several occasions during that time, she became directly involved in the incessant air attacks launched by the Japanese against the invasion force. On 16 April when Taluga (AO–62) received a kamikaze hit, Triumph was soon at hand to rescue three men blown overboard in the action. The minesweeper herself almost required such assistance on the 18th when a "Kate" torpedo bomber apparently tried to crash into her. Near sunset he came in from astern up the port side, passed under her port yardarm, and splashed down not far from Triumph.

The air raids continued, but their primary targets remained the radar picket destroyers. Consequently, Triumph experienced few actual surface-to-air engagements. On 11 May, while she patrolled off Ie Shima, she brought two enemy planes under fire but could not definitely claim credit for the one splashed by anti-aircraft fire. Combat air patrol accounted for the other one. Between mid-May and mid-June, she executed her patrols and sweeps under relatively calm circumstances.

On 15 June, however, she experienced another potentially fatal adventure. At dusk, Triumph was patrolling north of Kerama Retto when an enemy torpedo bomber executed a near-perfect run on her. Initially, the plane was thought to be friendly, though the radarman continued to track the unidentified aircraft just in case. The pilot lined his plane up with the moon, made a well-executed approach, and launched his torpedo. Two sharp-eyed sailors on board Triumph spied the torpedo splash, raised the alarm, and the warship immediately went hard to starboard to evade the torpedo. It passed in her wake, a scant 30 yards astern. Darkness precluded any real antiaircraft response, so Triumph resumed her patrols. Three days after that attack, the minesweeper put into Kerama Retto for supplies and upkeep.

Triumph remained in Kerama Retto through the end of June. On the 30th, she got underway to rehearse for sweeps into the East China Sea. Those preparations continued until Independence Day when she sortied with TU 39.11.6. She arrived in the assigned area with the rest of her unit on the 5th and conducted a highly productive, eight-day sweep unimpaired by Japanese air activity. She returned to Buckner Bay, located on the western coast of Okinawa, on Bastille Day. There she replenished and refueled over a three-day period before returning to the East China Sea to resume mine sweeping operations.

However, just before beginning that mission, she was detached from the East China Sea minesweeping force and was ordered to report to TF 39 for further orders. On 17 July, she was forced to leave the anchorage at Buckner Bay to evade a typhoon. After serving in the antisubmarine screen of the ships forced out of the anchorage, the warship returned to Buckner Bay on 21 July and remained there, awaiting orders, until 5 August. On that day, she stood out of the bay as a unit in the screen of a convoy of tank landing ships.

Two days later, she took PGM–11 in tow after the latter ship suffered an engine casualty. On the 11th, Triumph parted company with the convoy to tow PGM–11 into Apra Harbor, Guam. With Pledge (AM–277) and YMS–341 in escort, the minesweeper entered Apra Harbor on the morning of 12 August. Three days later, she received word of the Japanese capitulation.

Triumph remained at Guam for a month undergoing repairs. She departed on 12 September to participate in the occupation of Japan and former Japanese possessions. She served her entire tour of occupation duty at Okinawa, arriving there on 18 September and departing again on 19 October. After stops at Guam and

Hawaii, she returned to the United States at San Francisco on 15 December. She underwent an extensive overhaul at the Kaiser shipyard at Richmond, Calif., from 19 January to 12 June 1946 and then began operations along the west coast. That duty continued until *Triumph* was placed out of commission at San Diego on 30 January 1947.

Triumph remained in reserve at San Diego until early 1952. After extensive preparations during the late fall of 1951 and the winter of 1952, she was recommissioned at San Diego on 28 February 1952. The warship reported for duty with the Pacific Fleet early in April and ultimately to the Atlantic Fleet on 19 May. Operating out of Charleston, S.C., the minesweeper served along the southern portion of the eastern seaboard and in the Caribbean until mid-September when she deployed to the Mediterranean for service with the 6th Fleet. Following another tour of duty in the western Atlantic early in 1954 and a second deployment to the Mediterranean during the winter of 1954 and 1955, *Triumph* began preparations for deactivation in the spring of 1955. On 7 February 1955 she was redesignated MSF–323. On 29 August 1955, *Triumph* was decommissioned and placed in reserve at Green Cove Springs, Fla.

There, she remained until late in 1959. During that period, she changed designations again on 4 December 1959 when she became MMC–3. Late in 1959, the decision was made to transfer her to Norway under the Military Assistance Program. On 27 January 1961, she was transferred to the Norwegian Navy. Her name was struck from the Navy list on 1 March 1961.

Triumph was awarded six battle stars for World War II service.

Trocadero Bay

A strait in the eastern part of Bucareli Bay in the Prince of Wales archipelago of Alaska.

Trocadero Bay (CVE–119) was renamed *Point Cruz* (*q.v.*) on 5 June 1944.

Troilus

One of about 40 asteroids known as the Trojan planets and named for heroes of Greece and Troy mentioned in the Iliad. Troilus, planet No. 1208, is named for the son of Priam, king of Troy.

(AKA–46: dp. 7,000 (tl.); l. 426′; b. 58′; dr. 16′ (lim.); s. 16.9 k.; cpl. 303; a. 1 5″, 8 40mm.; cl. *Artemis*; T. S4–SE2–BE–1)

Troilus (AKA–46) was laid down under a Maritime Commission contract (MC hull 1907) on 18 March 1945 at Providence, R.I., by the Walsh-Kaiser Co., Inc.; launched on 11 May 1945; sponsored by Mrs. Arthur G. B. Metcalf; acquired by the Navy and commissioned on 8 June 1945, Lt. Comdr. Nathan McKenzie, USNR, in command.

Following shakedown training in the Chesapeake Bay, *Troilus* departed Norfolk on 11 July and steamed independently via the Canal Zone to Hawaii. She arrived at Pearl Harbor on 1 August, disembarked passengers, fueled, and again got underway. Until 15 August, when the surrender of Japan was announced, she conducted intensive amphibious exercises in Maalaea Bay, Maui, operating with units of Transport Squadron 22.

With news of the war's end, she returned to Pearl Harbor and began loading ammunition, equipment, gasoline, trucks, trailers, and even airplanes for the occupation of Japan. On 7 September, *Troilus* departed the Hawaiian Islands and proceeded via the Marianas to Japan. She anchored in Wakayama harbor on the morning of 27 September and had all her boats in the water in less than 40 minutes. Despite continuous heavy rainfall and a rough eight-to-ten-foot surf which tossed two LCV's high on the beach beyond retraction, *Troilus* unloaded cargo throughout the day. On the 29th, she disembarked over 200 troops from the 98th Division's 368th Field Artillery. After the successful completion of her mission, *Troilus* departed Wakayama on 1 October, bound for the Philippines.

Early in October, she stopped at Subic Bay and at Manila Bay before anchoring in Lingayen Gulf on the 12th to take on additional passengers and cargo for the occupation of Japan. She discharged troops at Wakayama harbor on the 25th, then continued on to anchor at Nagoya on the 27th. Early in November, she began "Magic-Carpet" duties transporting American troops back to the United States. She embarked 485 passengers at Buckner Bay on 11 November; then set her course for California the following day. *Troilus* arrived at San Francisco on the morning of 29 November and lost no time in disembarking her homeward-bound passengers.

Following repairs at Graham Shipyard, Oakland, the attack cargo ship got underway for Japan on 24 December 1945, but en route received orders diverting her to Hawaii. *Troilus* put in at Pearl Harbor on 16 January and, on the 23d, set her course for California. She discharged passengers and mail at San Pedro on 30 January and then returned to San Francisco to take on a capacity load of landing craft for transportation to the east coast. She departed that port on the 12th and steamed via the Panama Canal and Norfolk to New York. During March, crews removed equipment and gear from the vessel in preparation for her disposition. On 11 April, *Troilus* made her last voyage under her own power, steaming up the Hudson River to moor at the Eureka Shipyard, Newburgh, to remove remaining materials and to undergo preservation procedures. Her decommissioning took place minutes before noon on 14 June 1946. Her name was struck from the Navy list on 8 July 1946, and she was delivered to the Wartime Shipping Administration on 28 August 1946. She was laid up by that agency until 17 April 1967 when she was sold to the Union Metals and Alloy Corporation, of New York City, and scrapped.

Trollope

Henry Trollope—born on 20 April 1756 in Bucklebury, Berkshire, England—entered the Royal Navy in April 1771 and served on the coast of North America in *Captain* and *Asia*. He helped cover the retreat of British troops from Concord and participated in the Battle of Bunker Hill. During the War of American Independence, he served with distinction on the American coast and in the English Channel.

Following the return of peace, Trollope lived in Wales for eight years before returning to sea in 1790 as commanding officer of *Prudente*. Rising steadily in rank during the war with France, he displayed outstanding leadership, wisdom and courage during the mutiny which broke out in the fleet in May 1797, first persuading his own ship's rebellious crew to return to duty and then inducing the mutineers of two other men-of-war to obey orders. The following October, Trollope reached the high point of his combat service as his ship *Russell* fought with great valor in the Battle of Camperdown. Admiral Trollope spent most of the years after Waterloo in retirement and died on 2 November 1839.

Trollope (DE–566)—a *Buckley*-class destroyer escort built for the United Kingdom under lend-lease—was laid down on 29 September 1943 at Hingham, Mass., by the Bethlehem Steel Co.; launched on 20 November 1943; and delivered to the Royal Navy on 10 January 1944 and commissioned the same day.

The "Captain"-class frigate served the Royal Navy in the English Channel and off Normandy during 1944. After less than six months of service, her career was cut short when she ran aground near Arromanches-les-Bains, France, on 6 July 1944. Assessed as a total constructive loss, she was officially returned to the United States Navy on 10 October 1944.

Her name was struck from the Navy list on 13 November 1944. She was sold to John Lee of Belfast on 9 January 1947, and she was scrapped in 1951.

Trouncer

Perdido (CVE–47) (*q.v.*) was transferred to the United Kingdom under lend-lease agreement on 31 January 1944 and served the Royal Navy as *Trouncer*.

Troup

(Brig: a. 16 guns)

Troup—a 16-gun brig whose builder is unknown—was acquired by the Navy in 1812 at Savannah, Ga., and was used as a guard and receiving ship there for the duration of the War of 1812. She was sold at Savannah in 1815.

Trousdale

A county in northern Tennessee named for William Trousdale.

Born on 23 September 1790, Trousdale fought in the Creek War, the War of 1812, the Seminole War, and the Mexican War. Wounded twice at the Battle of Chapultepec, he was made a brevet brigadier-general in the United States Army on 13 September 1847. After serving as Governor of Tennessee from 1849 to 1851, he became Minister to Brazil in 1852 and held that post until he retired from public life in 1857. General Trousdale died at Nashville, Tenn., on 27 March 1872.

(AKA–79: dp. 13,910 (tl.); l. 459'2"; b. 63'0"; dr. 26'4" (lim.); cpl. 362; a. 1 5", 8 40mm.; cl. *Tolland*; T. C2-S-AJ-3)

Trousdale (AKA–79) was laid down under a Maritime Commission contract (MC hull 1386) on 22 April 1944 at Wilmington, N.C., by the North Carolina Shipbuilding Corp.; launched on 3 July 1944; sponsored by Mrs. J. R. Craig; delivered to the Navy under loan-charter on 24 July 1944; and commissioned at Hoboken, N.J., on 21 December 1944, Lt. Comdr. William J. Lane, USNR, in command.

The attack cargo ship conducted shakedown training off Long Island, N.Y., and in the Virginia capes area and proceeded to Bayonne, N.J., to load cargo earmarked for the Pacific theater of operations. On 27 January, *Trousdale* headed for the open sea in company with *Charles E. Brannon* (DE–446), bound for Panama. She transited the Panama Canal on 2 February and sailed for Hawaii on 3 February.

Reaching Pearl Harbor on 17 February, *Trousdale* spent the next 25 days unloading cargo; making minor repairs; and waiting for orders. In mid-March 1945, she on-loaded her first combat cargo-miscellaneous units of the 10th Army, including signal battalions, military police, a weather squadron, communications companies, bomb disposal units, and occupational government personnel, together with 200 vehicles and 900 tons of equipment. On 14 March 1945, *Trousdale* set out for the Marshall Islands.

After anchoring at Eniwetok on 22 March, the ship headed for the Carolines, arriving at Ulithi on 29 March. She got underway for the Ryukyus on 13 April and arrived off Okinawa on the 17th.

Trousdale anchored off Hagushi beach while the amassed battleships, cruisers, and destroyers shelled Japanese defenses further inland. After commencing unloading that evening, she temporarily suspended operations as Japanese "kamikazes" flew in from the north to attempt to crash American ships engaged in the landings.

Hampered by kamikazes and bad weather conditions with heavy seas and high winds, the ship lay off the beach for the next six days, engaged in nearly continuous unloading operations. On 22 April, she joined a south-bound convoy and, on 27 April, made port at Saipan, where she transferred all of her landing craft, save two, to other ships.

Crossing the equator on 7 May, *Trousdale* anchored off Guadalcanal on the 9th and soon commenced loading equipment belonging to rear-echelon units of the 6th Marine Division. On 18 May, the ship weighed anchor and steamed for Tulagi, where she loaded landing craft and set out, via Eniwetok and Saipan, for Guam, arriving there on 7 June.

On 13 June, the attack cargo ship sailed for the west coast, making port at San Francisco. The ship then underwent minor repairs and loaded a cargo of oil and a new set of landing craft before setting a westerly course on 10 July, bound for Tinian, the American B–29 bomber base in the Marianas.

Meanwhile, the war in the Pacific was drawing to a close as American forces swept close to the Japanese home islands themselves. Carrier planes and ships offshore bombarded coastal targets; planes and ships made the sea lanes untenable for Japanese sea power; and the Japanese air force rapidly dwindled in numbers.

Arriving at Tinian on 27 July, the ship commenced offloading immediately and was working hard at the task on 5 August when an American B–29 bomber exploded an atomic bomb over Hiroshima. *Trousdale* completed discharging her cargo on the 8th and shifted her anchorage to Saipan the same day. While she was anchored there on 15 August, word came through that Japan had accepted the terms of the Potsdam Declaration and capitulated to the Allies. The long and bloody war in the Pacific was over.

Yet for *Trousdale*, and ships like her, the occupation operations were just commencing. Accordingly, the ship departed Saipan on 29 August, arriving at Okinawa on 4 September. The attack cargo ship spent a week loading Army equipment for occupation forces and, in company with three other AKA's, sailed on 11 September for Korea.

En route, lookouts sighted mines drifting in the murky waters of the East China and Yellow Seas. Gunfire from the ships destroyed these menaces to navigation. The ships made port at Jinsen on 13 September and commenced offloading soon after arrival. The AKA's encountered difficulties posed by the 20- to 30-foot tidal range which permitted larger landing craft to discharge cargo only at specific times. After completing the unloading operations, the ships headed back to Okinawa, arriving there on 18 September.

Trousdale then embarked marines for passage to Taku, China. Anchoring off Taku Bar, the ship sent her landing boats up the Wei River for special duties, while unloading the marines for occupation duty. Orders soon came, sending *Trousdale* to the Philippines. She departed the China coast on 6 October, and—after steaming through a typhoon so intense that the ship's inclinometer recorded 55-degree rolls—reached Manila on 13 October 1945. There, the ship took on fuel and provisions and was soon underway for Hong Kong. Upon her arrival in the vicinity of the British Crown Colony of Hong Kong, the ship prepared to embark Chinese soldiers for passage to North China.

Chiang Kai-shek, as he had done during the war with Japan, sought American assistance in his as yet undeclared war against the communists. This included the air lift and sea lift of Nationalist troops to cities in northern China, population centers rapidly coming under the influence of the communist forces who had taken pains to encourage popular support while fighting the Japanese.

Accordingly, *Trousdale* took on board large contingents of Chinese troops, many of whom had never before been on a ship. Commencing the loading on 24 October, the operation was completed the next day, and the ship sailed with her human cargo for Chinwangtao at the base of the Great Wall of China. Making port on 30 October, she offloaded her troops and returned southward for another load—the Chinese First Division—making port at Hong Kong on 7 November and departing two days later for Tsingtao where she arrived on 14 November.

While remaining at Tsingtao, the ship received urgent boiler repairs. The attack cargo ship got underway again on 14 November for Japan and arrived at Sasebo on the 20th. The ship sailed on New Year's Day, 1946, bound, via Midway Island, for the west coast.

Trousdale moored at San Diego, Calif., on 18 January 1946, but soon headed for Panama and steamed through the Canal on 2 February, exactly one year to the day since her first transit. She arrived at Norfolk, Va., on 11 February and, six days later, headed for the New York Navy Yard to prepare for decommissioning.

On 6 March, the attack cargo ship departed New York on her last voyage as a United States Navy man-of-war and arrived at Norfolk on the following day. *Trousdale* was decommissioned on 29 April 1946, returned to the War Shipping Board of the Maritime Commission on the 30th, assigned to the National Defense Reserve Fleet, and berthed in the James River. Her name was struck from the Navy list on 8 May 1946.

The ship was sold in 1947 to the Waterman Steamship Company, of Mobile, Ala., and served as a merchant ship under the name *Lafayette* until purchased in 1954 by the Ocean Transportation Co., Inc., New York, N.Y., and renamed *Ocean Deborah*. In 1962, she was purchased by the Central Gulf Steamship Corp., New Orleans, La., and renamed *Green Dale*. She served under that name until 1970 when she was sold to a purchaser in Taiwan; and, presumably, she was soon scrapped.

Trousdale received one battle star for her World War II service at Okinawa.

Trout

Any of certain small, fresh-water fishes, highly esteemed by anglers for their gameness, their rich and finely flavored flesh, and their handsome (usually mottled or speckled) coloration.

I

(SS–202: dp. 1,475 (surf.), 2,370 (subm.); l. 307′2″;
  b. 27′3″; dr. 13′3″; s. 20 k. (surf.), 8.75 k. (subm.);
  cpl. 59; a. 10 21″ tt., 1 3″, 2 50-cal. mg.; cl. *Tambor*)

The first *Trout* (SS–202) was laid down on 28 August 1939 by the Portsmouth (N.H.) Navy Yard; launched on 21 May 1940; sponsored by Mrs. Walter B. Woodson; and commissioned on 15 November 1940, Lt. Comdr. Frank W. Fenno, Jr., in command.

On 2 July 1941, following preliminary operations along the east coast, *Trout* and *Triton* (SS–201) departed New York, bound for the Pacific. After transiting the Panama Canal and stopping at San Diego, the submarines arrived at Pearl Harbor on 4 August 1941.

Trout conducted training operations with Submarine Division 62 until 29 November when she stood out of Pearl Harbor to conduct a simulated war patrol off northern Midway. During the patrol, the submarine ran submerged from 0500 to 1800 each day. On the morning of 7 December, she received word of the Japanese attack on Pearl Harbor. That night, the submarine observed two ships shell Midway. She was about 10 miles distant and proceeded toward the enemy ships at full speed, but they retired before she arrived. Frustrated in being unable to fire a shot, she continued her patrol until 20 December 1941 when she returned to Pearl Harbor.

On 12 January 1942, *Trout* stood out of Pearl Harbor with 3,500 rounds of ammunition to be delivered to the besieged American forces on Corregidor. She topped off with fuel at Midway on the 16th and continued westward. On the 27th, near the Bonin Islands, she sighted a light off her port bow, closed to 1,500 yards of the vessel, and fired a stern torpedo which missed. She

Trout (SS–202) returns to Pearl Harbor on 14 June 1942.

closed to 600 yards; discovered that her target was a submarine chaser; and, as she had been warned to avoid small ships, resumed her course for the Philippines. On 3 February, *Trout* rendezvoused with a torpedo boat off Corregidor and was escorted to South Dock. She unloaded the ammunition; refueled; loaded two torpedoes; and requested additional ballast. Since neither sandbags nor sacks of concrete were available, she was given 20 tons of gold bars and silver pesos to be evacuated from the Philippines. She also loaded securities, mail, and State Department dispatches before submerging shortly before daybreak to wait at the bottom in Manila Bay until the return of darkness. That evening, the submarine loaded more mail and securities before she was escorted through the mine fields out to open water. *Trout* set a course for the East China Sea which she entered on the 10th.

That afternoon, *Trout* fired a torpedo at a freighter from a range of 2,000 yards but missed. The submarine then closed the target before firing two more which both hit the freighter. Approximately 25 minutes later, her sonar heard four explosions that were the boilers of *Chuwa Maru* blowing up as she sank. That evening, *Trout* was returning through the Bonins when she sighted a light. She changed course, closed the range to 3,000 yards, and fired two torpedoes at the ship. Both missed. In the time that lapsed between firing the first and the second torpedo, an enemy torpedo passed down *Trout*'s port side. As the submarine went to 120 feet, another torpedo passed overhead. *Trout* came up to periscope depth and fired a third torpedo at the target and blew it up. Sound picked up another ship running at full speed, but there was no opportunity to attack it. *Trout* was credited with sinking a small patrol ship of approximately 200 tons. When she reached Pearl Harbor on 3 March, the submarine transferred her valuable ballast to a cruiser.

The submarine's third war patrol, conducted from 24 March to 17 May, took her to Japanese home waters. On 9 April, *Trout* was patrolling between Ichie Saki and Shioni Misaki when she sighted two small cargo ships. She fired two torpedoes at each target, but all missed. The next day, she fired one torpedo at a small steamer and missed again. On 11 April, she attacked a large freighter with two torpedoes. One hit the target but did not sink it. Finally, on the 24th, the submarine hit a 10,000-ton tanker with two torpedoes off the coast of Shiono, and it headed for the beach. A sweep of the periscope showed a cargo ship going to the aid of the tanker. *Trout* fired one torpedo and missed. She then closed to 500 yards and fired another torpedo that hit with a tremendous explosion. When last seen, the cargo ship, too, was heading for shallow water. Four days later, the submarine attacked a 1,000-ton patrol vessel or minesweeper with a torpedo which sank it in two minutes. On 30 April, *Trout* attacked two ships off Shimo Misaki but missed both. On 2 May, the submarine sank the 5,014-ton cargo ship *Uzan Maru*. Two days later, she fired a spread of two torpedoes at what was thought to be a freighter. The first torpedo missed, but the second hit forward of the bridge, sinking the converted gunboat *Kongosan Maru*. The submarine was then subjected to a six-hour depth charge attack before she could clear the area.

Trout stood out of Pearl Harbor on 21 May as a unit of Task Group 7.1, the Midway Patrol Group, which consisted of 12 submarines. Her station was south of the island as nine of the submarines were positioned fan-like to the west of Midway in preparation for the Japanese attack. At 0812 on 4 June, *Trout* sighted a Japanese fighter plane preparing to attack from astern. She went deep and heard a series of light explosions. On 9 June, *Trout* passed through a large oil slick and some debris before rescuing two Japanese from a large wooden hatch cover. She returned to Pearl Harbor on 14 June without firing a torpedo.

On 27 August, the submarine proceeded via the Marshalls to the Caroline Islands and began patrolling off

Truk. She was detected by patrol craft on 10 September and was forced to go deep for one and one-half hours while they rained down 45 depth charges. The next day, she sighted a large transport, but escorts forced her to go deep and clear the area. On the 21st, the submarine fired three stern torpedoes at a naval auxiliary. The first torpedo broke the ship in half, and the next two hit the aft section. The victim was subsequently identified as *Koei Maru*, a converted net tender. A week later, *Trout* picked up a carrier group consisting of a light aircraft carrier, two cruisers, and two destroyers. The submarine closed to 1,500 yards and fired a spread of five torpedoes. She heard two timed explosions and saw the carrier *Taiyo* (*Otaka*) slow, with smoke pouring out of her starboard side near the water line. *Trout* heard high-speed screws approaching and went to 200 feet as a pattern of 10 depth charges shook her severely.

On 3 October, *Trout* was going to reconnoiter Otta Pass. Six miles west of South Islands, she came to periscope depth to obtain a navigational fix. Just as the periscope was lowered, there was a violent explosion, close aboard, that shook the ship violently. The entire crew was stunned by the shock. One man was thrown from his bunk, and another was knocked off his feet. *Trout* crash-dived to 150 feet. As she passed 80 feet on the way down, another bomb exploded without effect. Since both periscopes were out of commission, the submarine headed for Australia and arrived at Brisbane on the 13th.

Trout's sixth war patrol began on 26 October and took her to waters around the New Georgia Islands. On 13 November, she was patrolling 80 miles north of Indispensable Strait when she saw a *Kongo*-class battleship accompanied by destroyers and six aircraft. The submarine fired a spread of five torpedoes with a depth setting of 25 feet; all missed; and she cleared the area. The patrol ended when the submarine returned to Brisbane 10 days later.

On 29 December 1942, *Trout* stood out to sea to patrol off North Borneo. The submarine contacted a large tanker off Miri on 11 January 1943 and fired three torpedoes from a range of 2,000 yards. The first two hit the target amidships, but the third exploded prematurely. Four minutes later, there was a heavy explosion from the direction of the target. Since postwar examination of Japanese records shows no sinking, the damaged ship must have managed to limp back to port.

Ten days later, off Indochina, *Trout* fired two torpedoes at a cargo ship from 700 yards and watched as the unidentified ship sank immediately. On 29 January, the submarine fired three torpedoes at a destroyer and watched each run true to the target. However, all proved to be duds. On 7 February, she sighted tanker *Misshin Maru* moored off Lutong. She made a submerged approach, fired two torpedoes at the target, heard one explosion, and observed smoke rise from the stern of the tanker. However, no sinking upon this occasion was confirmed.

One week later, *Trout* fired two torpedoes at what she thought to be a tanker as it emerged from a rain squall. The first torpedo blew off the target's bow, but the second one was a dud. As the enemy ship was still steaming at eight knots, the submarine surfaced for battle with her deck guns. *Trout* opened fire, but soon seven of her men were wounded by enemy machine gun fire. She then swung around and fired a stern torpedo and watched *Hirotama Maru* turn her stern straight up with her screws still turning and slip under the waves. The patrol ended when the submarine arrived at Fremantle on 25 February.

Trout was next ordered to plant mines in Api Passage. She got underway on 22 March and, on 4 April while en route from Balaboc Strait to Miri, fired a spread of three torpedoes at a naval auxiliary. One hit the target amidships, raising a 20-foot plume of water into the air; but the warhead did not explode.

Trout fired a fourth torpedo; but the ship saw its wake, turned, and dodged it. The next day, she fired three torpedoes at another ship with no results. *Trout* planted 23 mines in Api Passage on 7 and 8 April and then began patrolling the Singapore trade route. On the 19th, she fired four torpedoes at a freighter but scored no hits. Later in the day, she fired a spread of three torpedoes at a tanker and missed. *Trout* sighted two trawlers on the 23d and battle surfaced. Her deck guns soon stopped the first ship dead in the water and set it on fire; they then turned the second one into a burning wreck. Since there was only one torpedo remaining, the submarine headed for Fremantle, where she arrived on 3 May.

From 27 May to 20 July, *Trout* performed a special mission during an offensive war patrol. On 9 June, she missed a transport with three torpedoes. She then landed a five-man Army team at Labangan, Mindanao. On the 15th, the submarine fired a three-torpedo spread which destroyed the tanker, *Sanraku Maru*. She contacted three small coastal steamers on 26 June and sank two of them with her deck guns. On 1 July, she sank *Isuzu Maru* with four torpedoes. Eight days later, *Trout* picked up a party of five American officers off the south coast of Mindanao and headed for Fremantle.

Trout stood out to sea on 12 August to patrol the Surigao and San Bernardino straits. On 25 August, she battled a cargo-fisherman with her deck guns and then sent a boarding party on board the Japanese vessel. After they had returned to the submarine with the prize's crew, papers, charts, and other material for study by intelligence officers, the submarine sank the vessel. Three of the five prisoners were later embarked in a dinghy off Tifore Island.

On 9 September, she fired three bow tubes at an *I–62*-class submarine off Surigao Strait. Thirty-five seconds later, there was a loud explosion which apparently stopped the target's screws. *Trout's* sound crew reported a torpedo approaching her port beam, and she went to 100 feet. After she heard a second explosion, *Trout* came to periscope level, but found no sign of *I–182* which she had sunk. On the 22d, one of the remaining Japanese prisoners died of self-imposed starvation and was buried at sea.

The next day, the submarine sighted two ships with an escort. One was a freighter with a deck load of planes, and the other was a passenger-cargo. *Trout* fired a spread of three torpedoes at each of the targets. She saw and heard two hits on each. The freighter *Ryotoku Maru* sank stern first. The transport was being abandoned. The submarine proceeded close aboard and passed 12 to 15 life boats. There was a good fire on the transport which was low in the water with her bow nearly awash. Sound heard a heavy explosion from *Yamashiro Maru* and, seven minutes later, *Trout* could see no trace of her. That night, the submarine set a course for Hawaii and arrived at Pearl Harbor on 4 October 1943.

The submarine was then routed back to the United States for a prolonged overhaul at the Mare Island Navy Yard. She was ready for sea in January 1944 and returned to Pearl Harbor late that month.

On 8 February, the submarine began her 11th and final war patrol. *Trout* topped off with fuel at Midway and, on the 16th, headed via a great circle route toward the East China Sea. She was never heard from again.

Japanese records indicate that one of their convoys was attacked by a submarine on 29 February 1944 in the patrol area assigned to *Trout*. The submarine badly damaged one large passenger-cargo ship and sank the 7,126-ton transport *Sakito Maru*. Possibly one of the convoy's escorts sank the submarine. On 17 April 1944, *Trout* was declared presumed lost.

Trout received 11 battle stars for World War II service and the Presidential Unit Citation for her second, third, and fifth patrols.

II

(SS–566: dp. 2,108 (surf.), 2,700 (subm.); l. 278'; b. 27'1''; dr. 20'; s. 16.3 k. (surf.), 17.4 k. (subm.); cpl. 89; a. 8 tt.; cl. *Tang*)

The second *Trout* (SS–566) was laid down on 1 December 1949 at Groton, Conn., by the Electric Boat Co.; launched on 21 August 1951; sponsored by Mrs. Albert H. Clark, the widow of Lt. Comdr. Albert H. Clark, the last commanding officer of *Trout* (SS–202); and commissioned at the submarine base at New London, Conn., on 27 June 1952, Comdr. George W. Kittredge in command.

Trout operated out of New London as a unit of Submarine Squadron (SubRon) 10 from 1952 to 1959. During this period, she conducted training and readiness operations with ships of the fleet and NATO nations, operating from the North Atlantic to the Caribbean Sea. She engaged in sonar evaluation tests, practice ASW exercises, and submerged simulated attack exercises. During submerged exercises in polar waters in company with *Harder* (SS–568), *Trout* sailed 268 miles beneath Newfoundland ice floes, setting a distance record for conventionally powered submarines.

In August 1959, *Trout* shifted her home port to Charleston, S.C., where she was assigned to SubRon 4. She was deployed to the 6th Fleet in September 1959 for her first Mediterranean cruise. Four months later, while returning home, she represented the United States at Bergen, Norway, during the 50th anniversary celebrations commemorating the birth of the Norwegian Navy's submarine arm.

In February 1960, *Trout* performed as a test bed for Bureau of Ships shock tests. She won her first Battle Efficiency "E" award in 1961. In early 1963, the submarine rendered services for the Operational Test and Evaluation Force before commencing a six-month overhaul at Charleston in July of that year.

During the remaining years of the 1960's, *Trout* made three more Mediterranean deployments as a unit of the 6th Fleet. Between deployments, she participated in training and developmental exercises off the east coast and in the Caribbean. In July 1970, she was assigned to the Pacific Fleet.

Homeported at San Diego, Calif., *Trout* conducted two Western Pacific (WestPac) deployments—in 1972 and 1975—primarily providing submarine services during ASW exercises conducted by warships of the United States, South Korean, or Nationalist Chinese navies. Between these deployments, the submarine participated in antisubmarine warfare exercises and conducted local operations off the southern California operating areas, punctuating this service with weapons tests in the Pacific Northwest, out of Puget Sound.

After returning from her second WestPac deployment to San Diego on 29 January 1976, *Trout* operated off the west coast until receiving orders on 1 December changing her home port to Philadelphia. She was decommissioned and struck from the Navy list on 19 December 1978.

Truant

(PYc–14: dp. 395; l. 138'; b. 17'4''; dr. 6'7''; s. 10 k.; a. 2 3'')

In the years following the outbreak of World War II in Europe, during which international tension also worsened in the Far East, the United States Navy augmented the Fleet to meet the growing threat. It also sought yachts, trawlers, and other suitable ships in which to train the officers and men needed by newly constructed warships.

On 3 July 1941, as a part of the latter program, the Navy chartered, on a bare-boat basis, *Truant*, a steel-hulled steam yacht built in 1892 at Bristol, R.I., by the Herreshoff Manufacturing Co. Henry Ford had purchased the ship in 1938 and had her extensively refitted. When he offered the yacht for the duration of the emergency, the Navy agreed to his request that she be allowed to retain her name during her Navy service. The ship was classified a coastal yacht and designated PYc–14, assigned to the 9th Naval District on 11 July, and commissioned on 16 July 1941 at the Great Lakes Naval Training Station, Ill., Lt. Charles G. Campbell, USNR, in command.

Truant plied the waters of Lake Michigan on training cruises until mid-September; then headed for Dearborn, Mich., where she arrived on 20 September 1941. She remained there in winter quarters near the Ford Motor Company plant until the early spring of 1942, when she resumed her training cruises. On board this slim, graceful craft, officers and men of the growing and expanding Navy received schooling in basic gunnery and seamanship, which prepared them to serve on fighting ships in the war zones of the Pacific, the Atlantic, and the Mediterranean. With the onset of winter in 1942, she again tied up at her "winter quarters" at the Ford Motor Company plant at South Chicago, Ill., for the cold months and remained there into the spring of 1943.

The yacht then engaged in training exercises and maneuvers in Lake Michigan into November. On 17 November 1943, *Truant* was decommissioned at the Ford Motor Company plant at Dearborn and returned to her owner. On 6 December 1943, her name was struck from the Navy list.

Truckee

A river of eastern California and western Nevada which rises in Lake Tahoe. The river was named after an Indian guide who showed the river to the Stevens Party in 1844.

Designed as a coastal tanker (Type T1–M–BT1) and originally named *Eola*, *Truckee* (AOG–75) was laid down under Maritime Commission contract (MC hull 2635) on 28 May 1945 at Jacksonville, Fla., by St. John's River Shipbuilding Corp. She was scheduled for acquisition by the United States Navy on loan from the Maritime Commission and to be manned by the Coast Guard, but her acquisition was cancelled on 29 August 1945. Sponsored by Mrs. Michael J. Ryan, she was launched on the following day but remained in an unfinished state for three years pending disposal by the Maritime Commission.

From 1948 until 1950, International Tankers, Panama, owned *Truckee*, but it was not until July 1951 that Maryland Drydocking Company completed the ship. From that time until 1971, she served as an oil carrier

for Standard Oil of California under the name *California Standard*. She acquired the name LSCO *Transpacific* in 1971 and operated for Luzon Stevedoring Corp., Manila.

I

(AO–147: dp. 11,600 (lt.); l. 655'; b. 86'; dr. 35'; s. 20 k.; cpl. 265; a. 8 3''; cl. *Neosho*)

Truckee (AO–147) was laid down in December 1953 at Camden, N.J., by the New York Shipbuilding Corp.; launched on 19 March 1955; sponsored by Mrs. Murrey L. Royar; and commissioned on 18 November 1955, Capt. Joseph W. Leverton in command.

Assigned to the Atlantic Fleet, the new oiler reported for duty with Service Squadron 4 off Norfolk in January 1956 and spent February in the Caribbean. In May, she carried fresh water, her first cargo, to Bermuda and the following month got underway for her first transatlantic voyage. With a group of midshipmen embarked for training, she steamed to Copenhagen and through the North Sea; then stopped at Sheerness, England, before turning to the United States.

On 19 September, she departed Norfolk; set her course southward and, throughout October, acted as flagship and supplied fuel and repairs for a hydrographic survey group operating in the vicinity of two South Atlantic island groups—Ascencion Island and Fernando de Noronha. In November, she returned to the Virginia capes and, before the year was out, had ranged as far as Portugal serving the fleet.

In 1957, she continued to ply the waters of the North Atlantic and Caribbean until August when she again headed south to operate with the Atlantic Survey and Cable Group in the mid-South Atlantic. In addition to her regular duties, *Truckee* served as flagship on this operation. She returned to Norfolk in April 1958 and, in June, sailed for European waters. She stopped at Portuguese, Norwegian, and British ports before returning to the United States in August. *Truckee* operated out of Norfolk throughout the remainder of 1958 and during the early months of 1959.

In June 1959, she took part in refresher training out of Guantanamo; then, in August, moved north to fuel ships providing support for President Eisenhower's air trip to Europe. Late in the month, she stopped at Greenock; and she returned to the Norfolk area in September. The oiler remained with the 2d Fleet into the new year, conducting a midshipman cruise in the summer of 1960 and steaming northward in the fall to take part in NATO exercises inside the Arctic Circle. *Truckee* then headed southward to warmer climates and welcome Mediterranean ports. The oiler spent Christmas and New Year's at Cannes and continued her de-

USS *Truckee* (AO–147)

ployment with the 6th Fleet into 1961, making over 160 fuelings at sea between November 1960 and February 1961.

Into the 1960's, *Truckee* alternated 6th Fleet Mediterranean cruises with 2d Fleet duty in the Atlantic. On her Mediterranean deployment which began in February 1962, the oiler served as flagship, Commander, Service Force, 6th Fleet. During the Cuban Quarantine operations in the fall of 1962, *Truckee* fueled 152 ships in 50 days, while serving as flagship for Commander, Service Squadron 4.

In 1963, while continuing her regular round of duties with the 2d Fleet, she was awarded the Golden "E" since she had won the Battle Efficiency Award for five consecutive years. In 1964, she participated in NATO Exercises "Teamwork" and "Masterstroke" in the North Atlantic; and, late in the year, she underwent 10 weeks of yardwork at Baltimore to provide adequate accommodations for the extra staff she would carry when used as a flagship.

On 1 March 1965, *Truckee* departed Norfolk for an eight-month deployment in the Mediterranean. During this cruise, she served as flagship for Commander, Service Force, 6th Fleet, participated in several major exercises, fueled over 400 ships and visited ports in five countries. On 6 November, she returned to Norfolk and rejoined the 2d Fleet.

In 1966, she received her eighth consecutive combat efficiency "E" award, but her activities were curtailed in mid-summer when she began an extensive overhaul at Norfolk, which was not completed until the new year.

In January 1967, the oiler conducted refresher training out of Guantanamo Bay, Cuba; and, late in March, set her course for the Mediterranean, supporting the 6th Fleet and serving as Service Force flagship. In May, tension mounted in the Mideast as Arab-Israeli relations grew increasingly abrasive. On the morning of 5 June, *Truckee* was fueling carrier *America* (CVA–66) when word came that war had broken out between these two mideast neighbors. *Truckee* provided fuel and coordinated the support which enabled the carriers and their escorts to remain on station during this explosive situation. Although the technical research vessel *Liberty* (AGTR–5) was mistakenly bombed and torpedoed by the Israelis some days later, American military involvement was limited to maintaining readiness during the tense situation. After the crisis subsided, *Truckee* returned to Norfolk in September and participated in NATO exercises during November.

In the first half of 1968, *Truckee* alternated upkeep and Caribbean cruises. The oiler was damaged by a collision with *Wasp* (CVS–18) which occurred in June while she was removing fuel from the carrier. In July and August, *Truckee* underwent repairs at Norfolk and, in September, got underway for the Mediterranean. During this deployment, she fueled 158 ships, visited seven countries, and pumped 35 million gallons of fuel before returning to the United States in April 1969 for fleet operations on the Atlantic coast and in the Caribbean. Later in the year, she underwent overhaul and took part in refresher training out of Cuba.

She began another Mediterranean deployment in April 1970 and embarked 6th Fleet's Service Force Commander at Rota. Again, as in 1967, *Truckee* was on the scene when new violence threatened in the Mideast. From 9 September 1970 until 8 October, the tanker supplied the naval forces standing off the coast of Israel during the Jordanian Crisis. Pumping day and night during 27 of her 30 days at sea, she earned the Meritorious Unit Commendation for her fine performance. On 18 November, *Truckee* returned to Norfolk and began the conversion of her plant to burn Navy Distillate Fuel.

The oiler plied the Atlantic from Nova Scotia to the Virgin Islands in 1971, supporting NATO and Atlantic Fleet operations. She participated in Exercise "Rough Ride" in June. After that 10-day NATO exercise involving ships from five countries, she supported a

NATO sea power demonstration off Norfolk in September.

February 1972 found *Truckee* again underway, via the Caribbean, for the Mediterranean. At the end of this deployment with the 6th Fleet, she returned to the east coast in November and, at year's end, had pumped a total of 50 million gallons of fuel.

On deployment with the 6th Fleet again in 1973, *Truckee* provided support during yet another Middle East crisis, the October War. After an emergency sortie from Palma on 7 October occasioned by the heaviest Arab-Israeli fighting since 1967, *Truckee* remained in the eastern Mediterranean until ordered to standdown from alert posture on 18 November 1973. During this cruise, the tanker pumped 25 million gallons of fuel to NATO and United States ships and steamed 25,000 miles.

In 1974, *Truckee* remained on the east coast operating out of Norfolk. She also underwent an extended overhaul which took seven and one-half months and was not completed until January 1975. In the summer of 1975, she participated in Exercises "National Week" and "Dawn Patrol" in the eastern Mediterranean. Later in August, she shifted operations to the western Mediterranean before departing Rota in October at the end of her 10th Mediterranean deployment.

On 3 November, she returned to Norfolk for overhaul. In February 1976, she returned to duty with the 2d Fleet operating out of Norfolk with occasional visits to other east coast ports. Second Fleet operations took *Truckee* to Guantanamo in May and to Puerto Rico in July, and she continued local operations out of Norfolk for the remainder of the year.

The early months of 1977 were spent in preparations for *Truckee*'s forthcoming deployment to the Mediterranean. She departed Norfolk for operations with the 6th Fleet on 31 March. Following six months of providing fuel to units of that fleet, *Truckee* returned to CONUS, arriving in Norfolk on 21 October. A two-week, post-deployment standdown was followed by an availability devoted primarily to overhaul of the ship's entire Mk 56 gun fire control system. The close of the year found the fleet oiler in her home port.

During the period 6 January to 11 July 1978, *Truckee* conducted operations in the Caribbean on four separate occasions. An upkeep followed; and then, on 25 August, *Truckee* departed Norfolk for a two and one-half month deployment to the North Atlantic. Port visits during the deployment included Rotterdam, Netherlands; Kiel, Germany; and Lisbon, Portugal. The ship returned to Norfolk on 30 October, and she continued local operations out of that port into 1979.

Truett

Quincy H. Truett was born in Quitman, Ga., on 3 April 1932. He enlisted in the Navy on 14 September 1951 at Jacksonville, Fla., and, during the later stages of the Korean War, saw duty in destroyers *John W. Thomason* (DD–760) and *Floyd B. Parks* (DD–884). Subsequently, he served successfully in *Tulare* (AKA–112), *Chilton* (APA–38), and *Tawasa* (ATF–92). From 1 August 1965 to September 1966, Truett served with the Naval Support Activity, Danang, in South Vietnam. Following a tour of duty with the Key West Test and Evaluation Detachment, he trained at the Naval Amphibious Base at Coronado, Calif., in preparation for his return to Vietnam. On 13 September 1968, Chief Boatswain's Mate Truett transferred to River Patrol Flotilla 5 and joined River Division 551.

On the night of 20 January 1969, his division was operating on the Kinh Dong Tien Canal. Truett was patrol officer for two of four river patrol boats escorting an armored troop carrier. The entire unit came under intense enemy fire, and the boat ahead of Truett's erupted in flames. When the blaze forced the patrol boat's crew into the water, Chief Truett ordered his own craft to the rescue. Seemingly oblivious to the enemy gunfire streaming at him, Chief Truett maintained a constant covering fire throughout the rescue of the crew of PBR 8137. Though mortally wounded, Chief Truett continued to fight until the successful completion of the rescue. Chief Truett died of his wounds that same day. For his ". . . extraordinary heroism . . ." Chief Boatswain's Mate Truett was posthumously awarded the Navy Cross.

(DE–1095: dp. 3,963 (f.); l. 438'; b. 47'; dr. 25'; s. 27 k.; cpl. 245; a. 1 5'', ASROC, LAMPS, 4 15.5'' tt.; cl. *Knox*)

Truett (DE–1095) was laid down on 27 April 1972 at Westwego, La., by Avondale Shipyards, Inc.; launched on 3 February 1973; sponsored by Mrs. Geraldine Truett Walter; delivered to the Navy on 24 May 1974 at the Norfolk Naval Shipyard, Portsmouth, Va.; and commissioned there on 1 June 1974, Comdr. James W. Egerton in command.

On 20 August, *Truett* departed Hampton Roads and headed for the West Indies. After arriving at Guantanamo Bay, Cuba, on 3 September, the ocean escort devoted the next six weeks to a feverish series of drills and exercises to prepare for duty in the Atlantic Fleet. On 8 October, *Truett* completed shakedown training and sailed for home. After a brief stop at St. Thomas in the Virgin Islands, *Truett* returned to Norfolk on 18 October.

Following local operations in the Hampton Roads area and repairs at the Norfolk Naval Shipyard, *Truett* got underway in April 1975 to conduct further tests and to train some 40 officers attending the Surface Warfare School. In May, she embarked her LAMPS helicopter and its detachment of officers and men. On 24 May, the ocean escort cleared Norfolk to participate in Exercise "Solid Shield." After nine days of hard work, she returned to Norfolk to prepare for a "Unitas" deployment. During her stay at Norfolk, the Navy reclassified the ship as a frigate on 1 July 1975 and redesignated her FF–1095.

Twenty days later, the frigate left Norfolk and set a course for the Panama Canal. En route, she conducted exercises with units of the Colombian Navy. *Truett* transited the canal on 8 August and headed down the western coast of South America. For the duration of "Unitas XVI," she trained with units of various South American navies, among which were those of Peru, Chile, Argentina, Uruguay, Brazil, and Venezuela. In the course of the deployment, she visited many ports and rounded Cape Horn at the southern tip of South America. After conducting exercises with the navies of the east coast nations of South America, she made a brief stop at Trinidad before returning home to Norfolk on 8 December. During the first two months of 1976, she resumed normal operations out of Norfolk.

Between 3 and 21 March, *Truett* participated in an ASW-and-convoy-operations exercise, "Safepass 76," with units of NATO's Standing Naval Force, Atlantic. Succeeding months were spent in preparation for the ship's forthcoming NATO deployment in the North Atlantic. Departing Norfolk on 14 June, *Truett* spent the next six months engaging in two major fleet exercises and visiting 20 ports from Norway to Portugal. The fleet frigate returned to Norfolk on 17 December and spent the remainder of the year enjoying a period of leave and a tender availability.

The greater part of 1977 was spent in priming the ship for deployment to the Mediterranean late in the year. During this workup period, *Truett* engaged in two major Atlantic Fleet exercises and underwent six inspections or qualifications. On 27 September, she departed for the Mediterranean and operations with the 6th Fleet which took her into the new year.

On 2 February 1978, *Truett* transited the Suez Canal and operated with the Middle East Force in the Red Sea and Gulf of Aden during the Ethiopian/Somalian crisis. Her operations there included a 56-day, continuous at-sea period. Returning to the Mediterranean in April, *Truett* arrived back in Norfolk on 25 April. The summer was spent conducting operations off the east coast, and the fleet frigate then proceeded to Braswell Shipyard, Boston, for a regular overhaul which commenced on 27 September. The ship remained there into 1979.

Trumbull

Jonathan Trumbull—born on 12 October 1710, at Lebanon, Conn.—graduated from Harvard College in 1727 and returned to Lebanon to prepare for the ministry. After the death of his brother Joseph, who had been their father's business associate, he joined his father in business in 1731. Trumbull soon made a name for himself in commerce, establishing direct trade relationships with Great Britain instead of dealing through intermediaries in Boston or New York, as most Connecticut merchants had done. His business acumen enabled his enterprises to flourish, until an unexplained reversal in 1766 threw his firm into virtual bankruptcy.

While engaged in commercial ventures, he was active in politics and eventually rose to be speaker of the Connecticut General Assembly. He advanced to the Deputy Governorship in 1766 and served in that capacity for three and one-half years. With the death of Governor William Pitkin in October 1769, Trumbull became the governor of the colony. During the decade between the Stamp Act and the Battle of Lexington, while tensions increased between the 13 colonies and Great Britain and war clouds thickened over English settlements in North America, Trumbull staunchly supported colonial rights.

Trumbull's major contribution to the Continental cause, though, lay in harnessing his business skill to the pressing task of providing war material for the Continental Army. He made Connecticut a primary source for supplies for General Washington's troops, assuring them a somewhat steady—if sparse—flow of food, clothing, and munitions.

Late in the war, a whispering campaign, later determined to probably have been started by the British in order to discredit him, weakened his political position in his home state. While completely vindicated by a legislative investigation of his administration in January 1782, Trumbull continued to lose popularity in Connecticut because of his controversial, unpopular plan for half-pay for disbanded officers from the Continental Army.

Wearied by political life, Trumbull retired from public life in May 1784 and devoted the remainder of his life to the study of theology. Trumbull died on 17 August 1785. Bolstered by his unshakable faith that "the Lord reigneth," he had substantially aided the Continental cause during the War for Independence.

I

(Gy.: t. 123; lbp. 72'4''; b. 19'7''; dph. 6'2''; cpl. 80; a. 1 18-pdr., 1 12-pdr., 2 9-pdrs., 6 6-pdrs.)

The first *Trumbull*—a shoal-draft galley built on Lake Champlain at Skenesboro, N.Y., under the direction of Brigadier General Benedict Arnold—was launched on 10 September 1776 and began active service soon thereafter, Capt. Seth Warner in command.

Trumbull transported a draft of reinforcements to Crown Point, N.Y., as General Arnold's forces sought to hurry to completion a squadron of small vessels—mostly galleys and cannon-carrying gondolas, or "gundalows"—to oppose the expected British push down the lake toward Fort Ticonderoga. The Americans sought to retain possession of the lake—which they had controlled since early in the war—and thus engaged in a shipbuilding race with the British, who were also constructing a fleet of specially designed lake craft. Since there were no roads parallel to the lake, the British were forced to launch their invasion southward by water instead of by land. Control of Lake Champlain was thus vital to the success of British plans.

Trumbull was among Arnold's vessels that anchored in the lee of Valcour Island, south of Plattsburgh, N.Y., by early October, to await the British onslaught. With 25 ships, the British outnumbered the Americans by 10; and, in view of this numerical inferiority, Arnold's second-in-command urged a withdrawal. Nevertheless, despite his squadron's inferiority, Arnold bravely stood and fought.

Initially, the Americans' position favored them, as on the morning of 11 October 1776, Capt. Thomas Pringle's 25-vessel "fleet" sailed past Valcour Island and failed to discover Arnold's ships until he was south of them. Then, forced to attack from the leeward, Pringle's ships sailed up to meet Arnold's which were deployed in a crescent-shaped formation, anchored across Valcour Bay. In the resultant action, the Americans suffered heavy damage to *Washington, Congress,* and *New York;* and the loss of *Royal Savage* and *Philadelphia.* The action ended at nightfall when the British withdrew and anchored, thinking that the Americans could not escape.

Under cover of darkness and fog, the surviving ships in Arnold's squadron muffled their oars to slip past the unsuspecting British. However, before they could reach safety, a contrary wind sprang up and slowed their progress southward. The British weighed anchor, gave chase, and soon overhauled the Americans. In the ensuing battle, Arnold lost his own flagship, the galley *Congress,* and five other ships.

Trumbull escaped the holocaust, only to be captured by the British the following year, 1777, and was eventually destroyed.

Thus, the Battle of Valcour Island ended in a crushing tactical defeat for the Americans since it all but annihilated Arnold's flotilla and left the British in full control of Lake Champlain. However, the dominance of Arnold's little warships on the lake during the first year and one-half of the Revolutionary War had prevented British troops from invading the newly independent colonies from Canada through the Lake Champlain, Lake George, Hudson River corridor. Then, when the Royal Navy finally did manage to best Arnold's flotilla at Valcour Island in the autumn of 1776, winter was too close to permit English land forces to take advantage of British victory by a thrust down the corridor to attack Washington's army from the rear. This gave the colonies additional time to recruit, train, and arm the forces which the following year stopped a British invasion in a decisive victory at Saratoga, N.Y., which has been called the turning point of the American Revolution. Thus, while losing on a tactical level at Valcour, the Americans won a strategic victory which ultimately enabled them to achieve independence.

II

(Fr.: t. 700; cpl. 199; a. 24 12-pdrs., 6 6-pdrs.)

The second *Trumbull*—one of the 13 frigates authorized by the Continental Congress on 13 December 1775 —was probably laid down in March or April 1776 at Chatham, Conn., by John Cotton and was launched on 5 September 1776.

However, after the frigate had been launched, her builders discovered that her deep draft would make it extremely difficult to get the ship across the bar at the mouth of the Connecticut River into Long Island Sound. The following spring, as *Trumbull* lay in the river at Saybrook awaiting assistance in getting out to deep water, her safety became a matter of great concern to Continental naval authorities. In April, General Tryon—the Royal Governor of New York—to lead a raid into neighboring Connecticut. Tryon's forces landed at Fairfield, marched inland, and

burned Continental public stores at Danbury. A small force of Americans harassed the British troops as they marched back to their ships. Fortunately, Tryon did not attack the berth on the Connecticut River where *Trumbull*—protected by neither guns nor warships—lay virtually defenseless.

After three years of inactivity, *Trumbull* was finally freed in 1779. Capt. Elisha Hinman suggested that casks of water be lashed alongside, port and starboard, with stout ropes running beneath the keel. When the casks were pumped out, they rose and lifted the ship just enough in the water so as to permit passage over the bar. *Trumbull* then was fitted out for sea at New London, Conn., under the direction of Nathaniel Shaw. On 20 September 1779, Capt. James Nicholson received command of the frigate.

Nicholson did not receive his cruising orders, though, until the following spring. Late in May 1780, *Trumbull* sailed for her first foray into the Atlantic. Action was not long in coming. At 1030 on 1 June 1780, *Trumbull*'s masthead lookout sighted a sail to windward. In order to remain undetected for as long as possible, the frigate furled her sails until 1130. Then, upon ascertaining the strange ship's size, *Trumbull* then made sail and tacked towards what soon proved to be the British 32-guns letter-of-marque, *Watt.*

Nicholson delivered a short exhortation to his men, who "most chearfully [sic] decided to fight." By noon, Nicholson noted that his ship seemed to "greatly outsail" the enemy and determined to utilize this advantage by moving to windward of the enemy.

Watt challenged *Trumbull,* running up the Cross of St. George and firing a gun. *Trumbull,* in order to keep her true identity cloaked until the last possible moment, also ran up the British colors. *Watt*'s commanding officer, Capt. Coulthard, initially mistook *Trumbull* "for one of his Majesty's cruizing [sic] frigates" but soon became suspicious of the frigate's movements and closed to windward. His suspicions were confirmed when *Trumbull* failed to respond to a "private signal."

Watt gave "three cheers and a broadside" to commence what historian Gardner W. Allen considered "one of the hardest-fought naval engagements of the war." *Trumbull* soon ran up Continental colors and returned the first broadside at a range of 80 yards. For two and one-half hours, the two ships traded shot in a fierce action. The range—never wider than 80 yards—most of the time was under 50 yards; and once the ships' yards nearly became locked together. *Watt* twice set the frigate afire; *Trumbull*'s shot caused fires on board the letter of marque that proved impossible to extinguish until the Briton had cut away much of her rigging. Most of the men in *Watt*'s tops were either killed, wounded, or driven below.

The British ship's hull, rigging, and sails were shot to pieces. Holed below the waterline, the letter of marque took on water at an alarming rate, and her danger was compounded by the fact that the American guns had left her with only one operable pump. *Trumbull* fared little better. Captain of Marines Gilbert Saltonstall subsequently noted: "We were literally cut all to pieces; not a shroud, stay, brace, bowling, or other rigging standing. Our main top mast shot away, our fore, main mizzen, and jigger masts gone by the board . . ."

Trumbull lost eight killed and 31 wounded; *Watt* suffered 13 killed and 79 wounded. Both badly battered, the frigate and letter of marque broke off action and retired from the scene of battle. Nicholson eagerly wanted to continue to pursue his adversary until he had been convinced that—even if he managed to repair his only surviving mast—the condition of his crew would not permit another engagement.

Trumbull weathered a gale while struggling back to Connecticut and reached Nantasket on 14 June, three days after *Watt* had limped into New York. Nicholson subsequently reported that "was [sic] I to have my choice . . . I would sooner fight any two-and-thirty gun frigate . . . on the coast of America, than to fight that ship over again. . . ."

In the meantime, the Continental Board of Admiralty, after congratulating Nicholson on the "gallantry displayed in the defense" against *Watt*, urged him to speed the outfitting of his ship for further service. Lack of money and scarcity of men combined to keep the frigate inactive at Philadelphia for the first part of the year 1781.

On 8 August 1781, *Trumbull*—the last remaining frigate of the original 13 authorized by Congress in 1775—eventually departed from the Delaware capes in company with a 24-gunned privateer and a 14-gun letter-of-marque. Under their protection was a 28-ship merchant convoy. On 28 August 1781, lookouts on the American ships spotted three sails to the eastward; two tacking to give chase to the convoy.

At nightfall, a rainsquall struck with terrific force and carried away *Trumbull*'s fore-topmast and her main topgallantmast. Forced to run before the wind, the frigate separated from the convoy and their escorts, and soon found herself engaged with the frigate HMS *Iris*, the former Continental frigate *Hancock*, and the 18-gun ship *General Monk*, the former Continental privateer *General Washington*. Even with the "utmost exertion," the wrecked masts and sails could not be cleared away. Knowing he could not run, Nicholson decided to fight.

Trapped, *Trumbull* "beat to quarters," but three-quarters of the crew failed to respond, and instead fled below. Undaunted, Nicholson bravely gathered the remainder. For one hour and 35 minutes, *Trumbull* and *Iris* remained engaged; *General Monk* soon closed and entered the contest as well. "Seeing no prospect of escaping in this unequal contest," Nicholson later wrote, "I struck. . . ." Eleven Americans were wounded and five killed during the engagement before *Trumbull* struck her colors.

Trumbull, by this point almost a wreck, was taken under tow by the victorious *Iris* to New York. However, because of her severe damage, the British did not take the frigate into the Royal Navy; and the details of her subsequent career are lost in the mists of unrecorded history.

III

(SlpW.: t. 400; a. 18 12-pdrs.; cpl. 220)

The third *Trumbull*—an 18-gun sloop-of-war whose construction was financed by public subscription of the citizens of Norwich, Conn.—was apparently begun in mid-1799, under the direction of Naval Agent Joseph Howland. Commanded by Master Commandant David Jewett, *Trumbull* was apparently completed early the following year and, after fitting out, departed New London, Conn., in late March 1800. She joined *Charlotte* at New York and escorted the heavily-laden provision ship to the West Indies where she replenished the American squadron operating against the French in that vicinity.

Soon after her arrival in April, *Trumbull* began patrolling on station, ever alert for French merchantmen and warships as she protected American merchantmen in the area. She captured the armed French schooner *Peggie* in early May. On 3 August, *Trumbull* took the 10-gun French schooner *Vengeance*. Among the 130 people on board the prize were women and children and several officers of one of the rival factions in the civil war then raging on the island, Hispanola. The following day, the sloop captured another Fench vessel; one which is variously recorded as *Tulipe*, *Tullie*, or *Cullie*.

Ordered home with *Vengeance* as a prize, *Trumbull* arrived at New London late in the summer. After quick repairs there, *Trumbull* returned to her patrol station off Santo Domingo in October 1800, transporting Navy Agent Thomas T. Gantt to St. Kitts to relieve Thomas Clarkson.

Trumbull subsequently cruised off Puerto Rico for a time before she returned north in the spring of 1801. Arriving at New York, *Trumbull* was sold later that year; and her crew was discharged.

Trumpeter

George Nelson Trumpeter—born on 2 September 1919 in Monaco, Pa.—enrolled in 1938 at the Carnegie Institute of Technology College of Engineering and, during his three years there, participated in the Reserve Officer Training Program. On 5 March 1941, he enlisted in the Naval Reserve as a seaman second class and within two weeks began elimination flight training at Naval Reserve Aviation Base, Philadelphia. In April, he was transferred to the Naval Air Station, Jacksonville, Fla.; and, in May, he received an appointment as an Aviation Cadet. In October, he became a naval aviator and, on 5 December 1941, was commissioned an ensign and assigned to Advanced Carrier Training Group, Atlantic Fleet, Norfolk. On 1 October 1942, he was promoted to the rank of Lt. (jg.).

Assigned for duty with the Southern Attack Force of Operation "Torch," Lt. Trumpeter flew his F4F fighter from the deck of escort carrier *Santee* (CVE-29) on the morning of D-day, 8 November 1942. Taking off in light winds at 0545 in *Santee*'s first launch of the day, he joined a flight of six Wildcats for combat air patrol over the transport and carrier areas of Safi. Lt. Trumpeter was lost while returning from this mission and was listed as killed in air combat action.

Originally, *Trumpeter* (CVE-37) was to be built under a Maritime Commission contract (MC hull 248), but the supervision of the contract for her construction was reassigned to the Navy on 30 April 1942. First classified as an aircraft escort vessel, AVG-37, the ship was redesignated an auxiliary aircraft carrier, ACV-37, only five days before her keel was laid down on 25 August 1942 at Tacoma, Wash., by the Seattle-Tacoma Shipbuilding Corp. Launched on 15 December 1942, the ship was again redesignated on 15 July 1943, this time as CVE-37.

Turned over to the United Kingdom at Portland, Oreg., on 4 August 1943, the *Bogue*-class carrier served with the Royal Navy in the North Atlantic in 1943 and 1944. In the latter year, she was assigned to convoy duty in the icy and treacherous Arctic. In March 1945, she escorted JW65 on the danger-fraught Russian convoy route. That convoy lost two merchant ships and the British sloop *Lapwing* to German U-boats at the mouth of Kola Inlet. She completed her wartime service in Norwegian waters in 1945.

Trumpeter arrived at Norfolk on 20 March 1946, was decommissioned by the Royal Navy on 6 April, and was returned to the custody of the United States the same day. She was struck from the Navy list on 21 May 1946 and, on 2 May 1947, was sold to the Waterman Steamship Co., Mobile, Ala.

DE-279—originally named *Trumpeter*—was renamed *Kempthorne* in June 1943 when the Bureau of Ships decided that, upon completion, the *Evarts*-class destroyer escort would be turned over to the United Kingdom. Laid down on 5 June 1943 by the Boston Navy Yard, the warship was launched on 17 July 1943 and was formally transferred to the United Kingdom on 23 October 1943 under terms of the Lend-Lease agreement.

Kempthorne (K.483) served the Royal Navy in the North Atlantic as a "Captain"-class frigate through the end of World War II. In May 1945, she was one of two British warships which presided over the surrender of the German U-boats at Trondheim, Norway. While still in England, *Kempthorne* was returned to the custody of the United States on 20 August 1945 and was commissioned in the United States Navy the same day for the voyage home. The destroyer escort arrived at Philadelphia on 8 September 1945 and was decommissioned at the navy yard there on 17 October. Struck from the Navy list on 1 November 1945, *Kempthorne* was scrapped by 28 May 1946.

I

(DE–180: dp. 1,240; l. 306'; b. 36'8''; dr. 11'8''; s. 20.9 k. (tr.) ; cpl. 216; a. 3 3'', 2 40mm., 10 20mm., 2 dct., 8 dcp., 1 dcp. (hh.), 3 21'' tt.; cl. *Cannon*)

Trumpeter (DE–180) was laid down on 7 June 1943 at Newark, N.J., by the Federal Shipbuilding and Drydock Co.; launched on 19 September 1943; sponsored by Mrs. Hazel Vivian Trumpeter, mother of Lt. Trumpeter; and commissioned on 16 October 1943, Comdr. John R. Litchfield in command.

While *Trumpeter* was completing outfitting at New York Navy Yard only three days after her commissioning, sparks from a workman's burner set off a small fire on a line between the dock and the port side of the ship. An alert fire watch at the scene quickly extinguished the fire, and damage to the new destroyer escort was averted. On the 28th, she underwent dock trials and deperming and finished the month with underway trials in New York harbor.

Early in November, *Trumpeter* departed New York, setting her course for Bermuda. She moored in Port Royal Bay on the 6th and in the following weeks participated in extensive shakedown and indoctrination exercises. Antisubmarine tactics, convoy escort technique, gunnery, night illumination, cruising and screening exercises occupied her days. Each evening, she returned to Bermuda to anchor in Great Sound. Antisubmarine runs, practice fueling at sea, towing, mailpassing and emergency steering drills readied the new destroyer escort and her crew for the rigors of wartime Atlantic operations.

At last, on 2 December, *Trumpeter* got underway for New York where she underwent alterations and voyage repairs. On 16 December, she departed New York and set her course northeast. The same day, she moored at Quonset Point Naval Air Station and reported for temporary duty with the Antisubmarine Development Detachment, Atlantic Fleet (ASDEVLANT). There she took part in testing newly developed antisubmarine gear until 17 January when she departed Narragansett Bay for New York. After repairs to one of her main propulsion generators, she resumed her duties at Quonset Point, remaining there until 13 February when she detached from ASDEVLANT and made way for New York. Following routine upkeep, she got underway with Task Group (TG) 27.2 on the 20th, steaming southward with two escort carriers and two DE's, bound for Brazil.

Late in the morning on the first day of March, she arrived at Recife, reported for duty with the 4th Fleet; then continued on to arrive at Rio de Janeiro on the 7th. She moored at Bahia on the 17th for 10 days availability and routine upkeep. On the 28th, she got underway with *Straub* (DE–181) and *Gustafson* (DE–182) ; then, on the 31st, she rendezvoused with *Solomons* (CVE–67) and reported to CTG 41.6 for her first antisubmarine patrol.

For the next five months, *Trumpeter* conducted patrols out of Brazilian ports with antisubmarine task groups. The escort carrier hunter-killer group was an innovation in antisubmarine warfare which effectively blunted the efficiency of German submarines in the Atlantic shipping lanes. Each group, composed of one escort carrier and its screen of destroyer escorts or old destroyers, aggressively sought out and destroyed enemy submarines in Atlantic waters with notable success. When *Trumpeter* began patrols in March 1944, however, German submarine activity was not so extensive as it had been earlier in the war; and many of her patrols were uneventful.

In June, while *Trumpeter* was patrolling in mid-Atlantic with *Solomons*, a plane from the carrier detected the presence of a German submarine. Planes dispatched from *Solomons* eventually sank the submarine. While *Trumpeter* remained behind to screen the carrier, *Straub* and *Herzog* (DE–178) set out for the area of the sinking, some 40 miles away, to rescue survivors. The two DE's picked 23 Germans from the waters, but the flier, whose bold low altitude bombing run had finished off the U-boat, was still missing when the search was ended.

Trumpeter's routine of patrol interspersed with periods of repair and upkeep was varied in August with four days of antisubmarine exercises and night battle practice out of Recife. She departed on 1 September and, on the 3d, joined *Memphis* and *Cannon* (DE–99) en route to Rio de Janeiro. During two weeks in that port, she underwent availability and prepared for her first Atlantic crossing. Finally, on 22 September 1944, she departed Brazilian waters escorting transports *General M. C. Meigs* (AP–16) and *General W. A. Mann* (AP–112) carrying troops of the Brazilian Expeditionary Force bound for the European theater of war.

On 4 October, she anchored in Gibraltar Bay but, less than six hours later, was again underway for the east coast. Arriving at New York on 13 October, she commenced 30 days of availability and drydocking; then, on 14 November, she set her course for South America, conducting firing practice as she steamed southward. At 1700 on the 23d, she saw the welcome sight of the Fortaleza harbor blimp, proceeded to that Brazilian port, paused briefly, and then steamed on to arrive at Recife on 25 November. In December, she engaged in gunnery practice and, later in the month, made routine patrols out of Recife with *Marblehead* (CL–12) and *Micka* (DE–176). On the 24th, she moored at Bahia and remained there undergoing availability until 2 January when she got underway again for patrol. In the next three months, she continued Atlantic patrols; then, early in March, she escorted *Omaha* (CL–4) from Recife to Montevideo.

Trumpeter departed Uruguay on 22 March 1945, steamed northward, and arrived at New York on 8 April. Following availability and dry-docking, she took part in antisubmarine exercises in Casco Bay. On 24 April, while patrolling off the New England coast, she struck an underwater object which damaged her sonar gear, making it necessary for her to detach from the task group (TG 22.6) and put in to Norfolk for repairs. She rejoined the task group on the 26th and into May continued antisubmarine patrols. On 8 May, she arrived at New London to begin antisubmarine warfare exercises. Later in the month, she proceeded to New York where she joined the screen of UGS 94 when it departed the United States on the 22d. Stopping briefly in the Azores, *Trumpeter* steamed for Mediterranean ports. The convoy members dispersed to their various destinations on 7 and 8 June, and the destroyer escort continued on to Oran for a short stay before departing the Mediterranean. After refueling at Horta, she steamed on, arrived at Boston on 19 June, and began a prolonged period of availability.

Underway again on 23 July, she set her course for the Caribbean and, on the 27th, arrived at Guantanamo Bay for refresher training in gunnery, antisubmarine warfare, damage control, and shore bombardment. On 10 August, she departed Cuba and steamed, via the Canal Zone, to San Diego. Following a period of availability, *Trumpeter* departed the west coast on the 27th on orders from the 11th Naval District. She arrived at Pearl Harbor on 2 September and alternated exercises with carrier rescue duties until late in October when she began weather station patrols in the North Pacific.

She returned to the Hawaiian Islands in December and, on the 18th, got underway for the Canal Zone. She arrived at Boston early in January 1946 and remained in east coast ports until February when she reported to the 16th Fleet at Green Cove Springs, Fla., to await inactivation.

She was decommissioned on 14 June 1946. Her disposal was deferred pending a possible transfer to a foreign government, but the transaction failed to materialize, and *Trumpeter*'s inactivation was completed in December 1947. Her name was struck from the Navy list on 1 August 1973, and her hulk was authorized for sinking as a target in Atlantic Fleet tests.

Trumpetfish

Any of several fishes so-called for their deep, compressed body and long, tubular snout.

(SS–425: dp. 1,570 (surf.), 2,415 (subm.); l. 311′8″; b. 27′3″; dr. 15′5″; s. 20.25 k. (surf.), 8.5 k. (subm.); cpl. 81; a. 10 21″ tt., 1 5″, 1 40 mm., 1 20mm.; cl. *Balao*)

Trumpetfish (SS–425) was laid down on 23 August 1943 at Philadelphia, Pa., by William Cramp Shipbuilding Co.; launched on 13 May 1945; sponsored by Mrs. Oswald S. Colclough; and commissioned on 29 January 1946, Lt. Comdr. Raphael C. Benitez in command.

A combined shakedown and goodwill cruise to Caribbean ports in the early spring of 1946 preceded the submarine's westward cruise to Pearl Harbor. Highlighting the ship's training operations in Hawaiian waters was her intentional torpedoing of the large Japanese submarine *I–400* which had been captured at the end of World War II.

Trumpetfish returned to the east coast for local operations out of New London, Conn., and, late in 1946, was briefly based at Annapolis to conduct training cruises for Naval Academy midshipmen. In the summer of 1947, as the ship underwent a Guppy II conversion, her hull was streamlined, a snorkel system was added, and higher capacity batteries were installed. The net result of the conversion enhanced the ship's offensive capabilities and increased her maximum submerged speed.

Attached to Submarine Squadron 4, based at Key West, Fla., *Trumpetfish* conducted local operations and training exercises off the east coast. In September 1953, she participated in NATO Exercise "Mariner" and then was deployed to the Mediterranean with the 6th Fleet.

After returning home, the ship operated along the east coast and in the Caribbean through 1955. Following duties out of Key West in January and February 1956, *Trumpetfish* proceeded to Guantanamo Bay for service with the Fleet Training Group. In July, the ship took part in midshipmen training cruises from Annapolis to Guantanamo Bay and back.

In the fall of 1956, the ship joined a hunter-killer group for a deployment to Europe and the Middle East.

Departing Norfolk on 1 October 1956, *Trumpetfish* sailed for European waters and participated in training exercises as she crossed the Atlantic. After calling at Brest, France, *Trumpetfish* suddenly received word of a crisis in the Levant.

President Nasser of Egypt had nationalized the previously British-owned Suez Canal, and prevailing Arab-Israeli tensions had erupted into warfare while British and French troops attacked Egyptian positions. *Trumpetfish* made her best speed for Suda Bay and joined the 6th Fleet in peace-keeping missions in the eastern Mediterranean. With the cessation of hostilities, *Trumpetfish* resumed her Mediterranean cruise, operating briefly with the Italian fleet before returning to Key West on 28 January 1957.

The submarine conducted local operations out of her home port until 29 August, when she got underway for European waters and fall NATO exercises. Air, surface, and submarine forces of NATO nations engaged in tests and exercises to hone their capabilities to defend the NATO nations against possible aggression. After returning to Key West on 25 October, *Trumpetfish* operated out of that base conducting training and exercises into 1959.

During her next Mediterranean deployment, she snorkeled through the Strait of Bonifacio between Corsica and Sardinia. In August 1959, as part of Atlantic Fleet dispersal plans, *Trumpetfish*'s home port was changed to Charleston, S.C. During January and February of 1960, the submarine took part in operations in the North Atlantic before briefly visiting Scotland. She subsequently participated in exercises in the western Atlantic Ocean, before a major refit at Charleston during 1961 modernized the ship to a Guppy III configuration. The alterations increased her capabilities by adding 15 feet to her length, by giving her better weapons and electronics, and by extending her range.

Trumpetfish resumed a schedule of local antisubmarine warfare operations out of Charleston, alternating deployments to the Mediterranean and duty with the 6th Fleet. She participated in emergency operations during the tension precipitated by the Cuban Missile Crisis in October 1962. The submarine later participated in several inter-type fleet exercises in home waters and in the Caribbean. *Trumpetfish* underwent a routine yard period at Charleston before taking part in Exercises "Plumb Bob I" and "Minibex" in 1965. After a Mediterranean deployment in early 1966, the ship took part in "Plumb Bob II" and provided services for the David Taylor Model Basin.

Subsequently assigned the primary mission of providing services for antisubmarine warfare forces, *Trumpetfish* stood ready to conduct mining and reconnaissance missions as well. On 12 January 1970, the

Trumpetfish (SS–425), streamlined during her *Guppy* overhaul for better submerged performance.

submarine departed Charleston for Cape Kennedy, provided services en route to *Remora* (SS–487), and conducted type training exercises. A port visit to Cape Kennedy occupied 16 to 18 January, before the submarine got underway for Fort Lauderdale, Fla., to provide services for the Naval Ordnance Laboratory Test Facility (NOLTF) there. Ten days of local operations at the NOLTF preceded the ship's providing services for *Henry Clay* (SSBN–625) during the nuclear submarine's sea trials off the Florida coast from 5 to 8 February. Subsequently taking part in Operations "Springboard" and "Exotic Dancer III," *Trumpetfish* headed for Philadelphia and a yard overhaul which would last through the summer and fall and into December 1970.

After the long overhaul, the submarine participated in type and refresher training off the east coast before she headed for the Caribbean in the spring. Among her activities were those which provided services for the German Republic's destroyer *Lütjens* between 7 and 14 May. The exchange of several crew members with the German ship during this time provided a valuable and enlightening experience.

On 5 June, after participating in a fleet mine test, *Trumpetfish* commenced six weeks of pre-deployment upkeep, with sea trials from 12 to 16 July. On the 23d, the submarine departed for South American waters and Operation "Unitas XII." Joining Task Force (TF) 86, *Trumpetfish* arrived at Cartagena, Colombia, on 6 August, prior to transiting the Panama Canal to proceed down the Pacific coast of South America. She crossed the equator on 20 August and made port at Callao, Peru, on the 30th. The ship operated with TF 86 for two weeks after the four-day port visit at Callao, before arriving at Valparaiso, Chile, on 17 September.

The submarine traversed the inland waterway and the Strait of Magellan and arrived at Punta Arenas, Chile, on 4 October. She conducted operations during "Unitas XII" off the Atlantic coast of South America, with visits to Mar Del Plata, Argentina, and Rio de Janeiro, Brazil, before rejoining TF 86 at La Guaira, Venezuela, on 2 December. Bidding farewell to the task force four days later, the ship sailed for Charleston and arrived at her home port eight days before Christmas 1971.

Trumpetfish remained with SubRon 4, operating out of Charleston through 1972. She deployed to the Caribbean again on 25 January 1973. Later conducting torpedo tests off Newport, R.I., the submarine operated with British aircraft carrier HMS *Ark Royal* off San Juan, Puerto Rico, in May, before returning to Charleston on the 30th of that month. Upkeep, type training, and services for Patrol Wing 11 in the Jacksonville, Fla., area preceded the ship's arrival at Charleston on 15 August to prepare for decommissioning.

On 15 October 1973, at Charleston, *Trumpetfish* was decommissioned and struck from the Navy list. She was next turned over to the Brazilian government and renamed *Goiaz* (S–15), with Commander Edouardo Russo her first commanding officer. As *Goiaz*, the submarine operated with the Brazilian Navy into 1980.

Trutta

A variety of trout, distinguished from the typical trout by its small, black spots and its smaller and fewer scales.

(SS–421: dp. 1,570 (surf.), 2,416 (subm.); l. 311'8"; b. 27'3"; dr. 15'5"; s. 20.25 k. (surf.), 8.75 k. (subm.); cpl. 81; a. 10 21" tt., 1 5", 1 40mm., 2 20mm., 2 .50-cal. mg.; cl. *Balao*)

Originally assigned the name *Tomtate*, SS–421 was renamed *Trutta* on 24 September 1942; laid down on 22 May 1944 by the Portsmouth (N.H.) Navy Yard; launched on 18 August 1944; sponsored by Mrs. Edward C. Magdeburger; and commissioned on 16 November 1944, Comdr. Arthur C. Smith in command.

Following outfitting and shakedown, *Trutta* underwent 30 days of intensive training in the Portsmouth-New London area and then set a course southward and steamed via the Canal Zone to arrive at Pearl Harbor on 25 February 1945. After a period of advanced training, *Trutta* got underway from Oahu with *Parche* (SS–384) and *Lionfish* (SS–298)—members of a coordinated attack group under *Trutta*'s direction—and arrived at Saipan on 30 March. The following day, as she was leaving Tanapag Harbor on her first war patrol, the submarine struck a cable connected to an oil drum adrift in the charted channel and was forced to return to Saipan to repair her damaged propeller blades. The submarine finally got underway on 3 April and proceeded as rapidly as possible toward her patrol area.

On 7 April, she changed course in an attempt to intercept a Japanese naval force which had sortied from Bungo Suido late the day before. It was feared that this task force—headed by *Yamato*, the world's largest battleship—would interrupt the assault on Okinawa to the south. Despite her full-power running, *Trutta* did not intercept the Japanese ships because they changed their course. Nevertheless, the Japanese force did not reach Okinawa because on that day fliers from the carriers of Vice Admiral Mitscher's Task Force 58 sank *Yamato*, light cruiser *Agano*, and destroyer *Hamakaze*, and inflicted irremediable damage to three other destroyers which the Japanese scuttled. After receiving news of this successful battle, *Trutta* headed southward on the 9th. Proceeding via the Nansei Shoto, she avoided the hostile notice of enemy aircraft and weathered gale force winds and force-five seas before entering her patrol area in the East China Sea on the afternoon of the 11th. There, she patrolled along the Shanghai-Quelpart Island traffic routes. On the 13th, while pursuing an antisubmarine force of three Japanese destroyers, she passed through an uncharted minefield before the ships changed course and outdistanced her.

While patrolling near the entrance to Daito Wan on the western coast of Korea on 18 April, she sank one small freighter with gunfire and damaged another. Off the China coast on the 22d, *Trutta* narrowly escaped damage when an enemy float plane dropped two bombs which exploded over the diving submarine. Shortly after midnight three days later, as *Trutta* patrolled west of Quelpart Island, lookouts on the submarine's bridge were startled to see a torpedo pass astern. As *Trutta* put on speed and turned parallel to the torpedo's wake, another torpedo passed by her port side moving from stern to bow, a sinister reminder that she was not alone in the Yellow Sea. Fortunately, *Trutta* observed no further sign of the Japanese submarine, and she continued her patrols until the 26th when she headed for Guam.

Late in the day, on the 27th, as she passed between Akuseki Shima and Takara Shima in the northern Ryukyus, she made contact with a Japanese plane—the harbinger of a prolonged coordinated holddown attempt. The next morning, finding her adversary of the night before replaced by two "Betties," the submarine, low on air and battery power, sent a message indicating that she would have to surface and fight it out if the situation did not improve before noon. A little more than an hour later, 10 American fighters from Okinawa appeared and routed the Japanese planes. Friendly air cover remained with the submarine until she recharged her batteries and filled her air flasks. She then proceeded independently to the Marianas, arriving at Guam on 4 May.

Following refitting and exercises with battleship *South Dakota* (BB–57), *Trutta* got underway on 2 June in company with *Queenfish* (SS–393). She weathered a typhoon before arriving on lifeguard station on the 7th. That day, while standing lifeguard duty for air strikes on Kobe, the submarine rescued a downed Army aviator who had been adrift in a small rubber boat for nearly a week and, the day before, had also weathered the typhoon.

As air raids against the cities of the Japanese homeland intensified, *Trutta* manned a lifeguard station south of Kyushu, made patrols just off Bungo Suido, and conducted visual and photo reconnaissance of Tori Shima, approaching to within about one mile of the island. On 21 June, she departed Bungo Suido to join sister "Street's Sweepers" patrolling the Yellow and East China Seas. She conducted patrols west of Tsushima Strait and then fired a few diversionary rounds of 5-inch fire on Hirado Shima before moving west to take up patrol along the southwest coast of Korea. On 1 July, her persistence paid off when, after pursuing a sailing vessel, she discovered a fleet of schooners. Working quickly to take advantage of surprise and to prevent the ships from fleeing to nearby shallow water, *Trutta* sank seven of the three- and four-masted schooners in a four-hour action. Crew members boarded and searched two of the vessels and put the schooner crews in lifeboats before destroying the ships.

On the 6th, while patrolling the southern approaches to Daito Wan, she came upon a tug towing three schooners, quickly dispatched the tug and two of its tows with 5-inch fire, and left the third in flames. She continued patrolling along the Korean coast until the afternoon of 12 July when she departed the area and set her course for the Marianas.

She arrived at Guam on the 18th, underwent refitting by *Fulton* (AS–11), and then got underway on the 12th for her third patrol. Before *Trutta* arrived in her assigned area, she received official word that peace negotiations had obviated continuing her patrol; and the submarine set a northeast course. She arrived at Midway on 24 August; and, two days later, she headed home via Pearl Harbor and the Panama Canal. After calls at New Orleans and other gulf and east-coast ports, she arrived at New London early in January 1946 and reported to the 16th Fleet for inactivation. By March 1946, she had been placed out of commission. She remained in the Reserve Fleet until 1951 when she was reactivated at New London. Recommissioned on 1 March 1951, she operated out of that port until 4 May 1952 when she was again decommissioned, this time at Charleston. Following conversion to a "Guppy II A" submarine, she was recommissioned on 2 January 1953 and joined Submarine Squadron 4 at Key West.

For the next 19 years, she operated out of Key West, plying the Atlantic, the Caribbean, and the Gulf of Mexico. During this period, she also made six deployments to the Mediterranean. She assisted in the evaluation of new weapon systems, including electronic counter-measure equipment; served as an antisubmarine warfare training target; trained naval reserves; and participated in fleet exercises. Shortly after her transfer to Squadron 12 on 1 August 1959, she rescued five Cuban refugees who had been adrift in a rubber boat for two days. Still homeported at Key West, she continued her duties through the 1960's, breaking routine with goodwill visits to American and Mediterranean ports, and earning a number of Battle Efficiency "E's." Moored at Key West in November 1969, she celebrated the 25th anniversary of her first commissioning.

Her long career with the United States Navy drew to its close in 1972. In June of that year, she trained a turnover crew of the Turkish Navy, and the veteran submarine was decommissioned on 1 July and turned over to the Navy of the Republic of Turkey. Her name was struck from the Navy list on that same day.

Trutta received two battle stars for World War II service.

Truxtun

Thomas Truxtun was born on 17 February 1755 near Hempstead, Long Island, New York. When his father died in 1765, young Truxtun came under the guardianship of John Troup of Jamaica, Long Island. Two years later, at the age of 12, he embarked upon a seafaring career, sailing with Captains Joseph Holmes and James Chambers in the London trade. At 16, he was pressed into service in the Royal Navy on board HMS *Prudent*. Truxtun's British commanding officer observed the lad's natural abilities and offered him aid in securing a midshipman's warrant. However, Truxtum declined, obtained his release through the good offices of influential friends, and returned to mercantile service. By the age of 20, he had risen to command of *Andrew Caldwell* in which he brought large quantities of gunpowder into Philadelphia in 1775. Later that year, his ship was seized by HMS *Argo* off St. Kitts in the West Indies.

By the time Truxtun made his way back to Philadelphia, the colonies had reached the point of open rupture with the mother country. He signed on as a lieutenant in *Congress*, the first privateer to be fitted out for service against Great Britain. During the remainder of 1776, Truxtun participated in the capture of several prizes off the coast of Cuba. In 1777, he fitted out Continental Navy sloop *Independence* and sailed her to the Azores where he took three prizes. Upon his return, Truxtun fitted out *Mars* and made a highly successful cruise in the English Channel. Successively, he commanded *Independence* once more and then, in turn, *Commerce* and *St. James*.

In addition to privateering, Truxtun's ships also carried precious cargoes of military stores to the colonies. On one voyage in *St. James*, he landed the most valuable cargo brought into Philadelphia during the Revolution. At a dinner in Truxtun's honor, George Washington declared his services had been worth those of a regiment. On another occasion, *St. James*—still under his command—carried Thomas Barclay, the American consul, to France. En route, he also managed to disable a 32-gun British ship.

Following the Revolution, Truxtun resumed his career in mercantile service and commanded *Canton*, the first Philadelphia ship to enter the China trade. When the United States Navy was organized, he was selected as one of its first six captains on 4 June 1798. He was assigned command of one of the new frigates then under construction. His ship, *Constellation*, was completed late in June; and he put to sea immediately to prosecute the undeclared naval war with revolutionary France.

The frigate, accompanied by a squadron of smaller ships, operated in the West Indies between St. Christopher and Puerto Rico. On 9 February 1799, Truxtun scored the first of his two most famous victories. After an hour's fight, *Constellation* battered *Insurgente* into submission, killing 29 and wounding 44 of the French frigate's crew. Truxtun brought *Insurgente* into St. Christopher where she was refitted and commissioned in the United States Navy.

Almost a year later, on 1 February 1800, he sighted the 50-gun French frigate *La Vengeance*, chased her all day, and finally overhauled her that evening. For the next five hours, Truxtun used superior American gunnery and the prevailing heavy seas to his advantage and, by 0100, completely overcame *La Vengeance*'s initial broadside superiority. During the action, the French warship had struck her colors several times, but darkness had prevented Truxtun from seeing the signal. Accordingly, the engagement continued until every gun on board the Frenchman went silent. The French frigate then sheered off to flee, and *Constellation*'s battle-damaged rigging made it impossible for the American frigate to pursue her escaping victim. After refitting *Constellation* at Jamaica, Truxtun returned with her to Norfolk late in March.

After commanding frigate *President* in the West Indies from mid-1800 to May 1801, Truxtun was appointed to command the squadron then fitting out for the Tripolitan expedition. Through a misunderstanding engendered by his request to have a captain appointed to command his flagship *Chesapeake*, Truxtun's unintended resignation from the Navy was accepted in Washington.

Commodore Truxtun retired first to Perth Amboy, N.J., and thence to Philadelphia, where he was active in local politics for the rest of his life. In 1809, he led the agitation in Philadelphia against the Embargo. The following year, he was unsuccessful in his bid for a seat in Congress under the Federalist banner. From 1816 to 1819, Truxtun served as the sheriff of Philadelphia. Commodore Truxtun died at Philadelphia on 5 May 1822 and was interred there at Christ Church.

I

(Brig: t. 329; lbp. 102'6''; b. 28'2''; dr. 12'3'' (mean); dph. 13'0''; a. 10 32-pdr. car., 2 long guns)

The first *Truxtun*—a brig laid down in late December 1841 at Portsmouth, Va., by the Norfolk Navy Yard— was launched on 16 April 1842; and commissioned on 18 February 1843, Lt. George P. Upshur in command.

On 16 June, *Truxtun* stood out of Hampton Roads for her first cruise. The brig reached Gibraltar on 9 July, received a visit from the American consul on the 16th, and sailed on the 18th to continue her cruise. On 26 July, she hove into sight of Majorca and, the following day, dropped anchor in Port Mahon. She remained there until 28 August when she resumed her cruise. During the ensuing month, the brig proceeded to the eastern Mediterranean and visited several Aegean ports before putting into Constantinople on 29 September. There, she conducted several missions for the American charge d'affaires before departing the Levant late in October. Sailing via Port Mahon again, *Truxtun* left the Mediterranean in mid-November and headed for Norfolk where she arrived on 28 December. In mid-January 1844, she moved to Philadelphia where she was placed out of commission on 6 February.

On 13 June 1844, *Truxtun* was placed back in commission, Comdr. Henry Bruce in command. Two weeks later, she sailed down the Delaware River and passed between the capes into the Atlantic. After visiting Funchal, Madeira, the warship joined the African patrol. She took up station off Tenerife in the Canary Islands to begin duty suppressing the slave trade. For 16 months, *Truxtun* patrolled off the Atlantic bulge of the African continent. During that time, she visited Monrovia, Liberia; and Sierra Leone as well as the islands of Mayo, St. Jago, and St. Vincent. She also took at least one prize, a schooner which was outfitted and taken into the United States Navy as *Spitfire*. On 30 October 1845, the brig weighed anchor at Monrovia, and she headed west toward the United States. On 23 November, she arrived at the Gosport Navy Yard where she was placed out of commission once more on 28 November 1845.

In mid-May 1846, war broke out between the United States and Mexico. *Truxtun* was recommissioned at Norfolk on 8 June under the command of Lt. Edward W. Carpender. On the 15th, she passed El Morro castle and anchored in Havana harbor, Cuba. For the next six weeks, the brig operated off the coast of Cuba. On 2 August, the warship cleared Havana and, on the 9th, joined the blockading American fleet just off the Mexican coast at Sacrificios Island. On the 12th, Lt. Carpender received orders instructing him to relieve sloop of war *John Adams* on station off Tampico. Early in the evening on 14 August, the brig was heading north in a gale about 100 miles from her destination. She turned in towards land in order to be able to provision ashore the following morning. That maneuver brought her dangerously close to Tuxpan Reef, and she soon ran hard aground. The gale continued to blow and drove her harder upon the reef. Still, her officers and crew tried to free her and declined a Mexican offer to surrender. On the morning of the 15th, she dispatched one of her cutters to the anchorage at Anton Lizardo to seek help.

Though stuck fast on the reef, the little warship refused to strike her colors and prosecuted the blockade to the best of her ability. On the 16th, she sighted a sail on the horizon. With the gale still churning the sea, *Truxtun* dispatched a cutter to investigate the stranger. The boarding party discovered that she was Mexican and promptly seized her. They sailed the prize toward *Truxtun* in an effort to help the stricken warship but could not get close enough to assist her. Lt. Carpender finally determined that further effort to save his ship would be fruitless. He sent some supplies to the men on board the captured Mexican and ordered them to Anton Lizardo with the prize and with a message indicating his intention to surrender to the Mexicans.

After putting the Mexican crew ashore at Tuxpan, the prize headed for Anton Lizardo. En route, she encountered a schooner. A long sea chase ensued; but, late in the evening of the 18th, *Truxtun*'s prize claimed one of her own. With a prize crew of four on board the new captive, the two small ships set off for the American anchorage. Though they became separated in the night, both prizes reached their destination—the first, on the 22d; and the second, a day later.

Meanwhile, *St. Mary's* had entered Anton Lizardo after having previously picked up the cutter and crew *Truxtun* had dispatched for help on the 15th. In response to the information given him by *St. Mary's*, Commodore Conner, the commander of the Home Squadron, ordered *Princeton* and *Falmouth* to *Truxtun*'s aid. *Princeton* hove into sight of the grounded brig early in the afternoon of the 20th and sent a landing party ashore under a flag of truce. The landing party learned that Lt. Carpender and the remainder of his crew had surrendered three days earlier. The following day, *Princeton* sent a boarding party to *Truxtun*; but they did not succeed in getting on board until the 22d. Finding that the Mexicans had already taken most of what was salvageable, they took the rest and set fire to the ship. She burned to the waterline and was subsequently struck from the Navy list.

II

(Torpedo Boat Destroyer No. 14; dp. 605 (f.); l. 248'0'' (wl.); b. 23'1¼''; dr. 10'11'' (max.); s. 30 k. (tl.); cpl. 72; a. 2 3'' rf., 6 6-pdr. rf., 2 18'' tt.; cl. *Truxtun*)

The second *Truxtun* (Torpedo Boat Destroyer No. 14) was laid down on 13 November 1899 at Sparrows Point, Md., by the Maryland Steel Co.; launched on 15 August 1901; sponsored by Miss Isabelle Truxtun; and commissioned on 11 September 1902, Lt. Archibald H. Davis in command.

Upon commissioning, *Truxtun* was assigned to the 2d Torpedo Flotilla, and her commanding officer was appointed commander of the flotilla. She conducted trials out of Norfolk until 14 January 1903 and received her final acceptance on 24 April. In August, she participated in maneuvers off Frenchman's Bay, Maine, in the Presidential review by Theodore Roosevelt at Oyster Bay, and in a joint Army-Navy exercise off Portland, Maine.

On 26 September, the 2d Torpedo Flotilla became a unit of the Coast Squadron, North Atlantic Fleet. *Truxtun* joined that squadron in target practice off the Massachusetts coast before returning to Norfolk later that fall for repairs.

For the next four years, *Truxtun* operated along the Atlantic coast and in the Caribbean. In December 1907, she and five other destroyers assembled in Hampton Roads with the battleships of the Atlantic Fleet. President Theodore Roosevelt reviewed the fleet once more and then, this "Great White Fleet" passed between Capes Charles and Henry to embark upon its famous round-the-world voyage. *Truxtun* escorted the fleet on the first leg of its voyage, going as far as the west coast. Along the way, she visited ports in Brazil, Chile, Peru, Panama, and Mexico. The fleet reached

Truxtun (Torpedo-Boat Destroyer No. 14), one of the first 16 American destroyers authorized in 1898. (NR&L(O) 898)

San Francisco in May 1908, and the destroyers were detached and reassigned to the Pacific Torpedo Fleet, an organization not administratively assigned to the Pacific Fleet. After repairs at Mare Island Navy Yard that summer, *Truxtun* joined her sister destroyers in a training voyage to Hawaii and Samoa. She returned to the west coast at San Diego, her new base of operations, early in December. She began her duty along the Pacific coast of North America with a voyage to Alaskan waters, visiting Seattle, Sitka, Seward, Skagway, and Juneau.

Truxtun remained in the Pacific until the summer of 1917. During the intervening period, she continued to be active with the Pacific Torpedo Fleet making cruises out of San Diego. On 25 March 1912, the Pacific Reserve Fleet was established under the command of Rear Admiral Alfred Reynolds. This organization was established in response to severe manpower shortages and was not similar in any respect to the contemporary reserve or "mothball" fleet. By 1 June 1912, *Truxtun* joined the Pacific Reserve Fleet; however, she remained somewhat active, periodically putting to sea to check her machinery and to maintain herself ". . . in constant readiness for sea."

Her reserve status was short-lived. She was placed back in full commission on 12 October 1912 and resumed normal activity along the coast. On two occasions, in the summer of 1914 and again in the summer of 1916, the torpedo boat destroyer steamed to Mexican waters to protect American interests during the series of political convulsions that plagued that nation during the second decade of the twentieth century. By July 1916, she had returned to semi-inactivity as a unit of the reserve division of the Coast Torpedo Force—later redesignated Division 2 (Reserve), Coast Torpedo Force. As before, however, she conducted sporadic cruises along the California coast to maintain herself in a state of readiness.

On 18 February 1917, *Truxtun* was returned to full commission for the third and final time, Lt. James G. Ware in command. Initially, she was assigned to patrol duty in the area of the Panama Canal. On 6 April 1917, the day the United States entered World War I, she departed Colon harbor and headed south to Puerto Colombia, Colombia, where she watched the German ship SS *Prinz August Wilhelm* which was anchored in the harbor. She was relieved by *Stewart* (Destroyer No. 13) on 14 April and returned to Colon the following day. For almost three months, she patrolled the Pacific coastal waters of Panama and Colombia, periodically doubling as a submarine tender. On Independence Day 1917, she transited the Panama Canal and, the following day, departed Balboa in company with *Stewart*, *Preble* (Destroyer No. 12), and *Whipple* (Destroyer No. 15). The four destroyers reached Hampton Roads on 13 July. Through the end of August, *Truxtun* patrolled Chesapeake Bay and conducted maneuvers off the coast. She made port calls at New York and Philadelphia, on one occasion acting as escort for *Texas* (BB–35).

On 31 August, *Truxtun* departed Philadelphia for duty in the Azores. After a short stop-over in Bermuda, she arrived at Ponta Delgada on 16 September. The destroyer operated from Ponta Delgada until early December. She and *Whipple* met SS *Caproni* on 30 September and escorted her into Ponta Delgada on 3 October. In mid-October, she made a short voyage to Funchal, Madeira Island, and back. Later that month, she participated in a search for the survivors of a torpedoed ship. *Truxtun* cleared Ponta Delgada on 6 December and headed—via Gibraltar—for France. She reached Brest on 15 December. Operating from that port, the destroyer convoyed merchant ships and conducted patrols against German U-boats for the remainder of World War I.

During the ensuing 12 months, she experienced two adventures. The first came on the night of 17 April 1918 when the explosives-laden steamship SS *Florence H.* exploded into flame in Quiberon Bay. For steering his destroyer into the flaming seas surrounding the stricken munitions carrier and helping to rescue many of her crewmen, *Truxtun*'s commanding officer, Lt. Ware, was awarded the Distinguished Service Medal. Her second scrape involved the enemy. At about 0900 on 18 May, while escorting a convoy, she sighted an underwater disturbance and immediately charged to the attack. The warship dropped several patterns of depth charges and fired several rounds from her guns. However, many of the depth charges failed to function properly. The U-boat, believed to have been *UC–56*, made good her escape; and *Truxtun* returned to the convoy at about 0930.

Just over a month after the armistice ended World War I, *Truxtun* bade farewell to Europe. Departing Brest on 18 December in company with *Flusser* (Destroyer No. 20), *Stewart*, *Whipple*, and *Worden* (Destroyer No. 16), she steamed, via Ponta Delgada and Bermuda, back to the United States. She entered the Delaware River on 3 January 1919 and was decommisioned at Philadelphia on 18 July. Her name was struck from the Navy list on 15 September 1919. She was sold to Joseph G. Hitner, of Philadelphia, on 3 January 1920 for conversion to mercantile service as a motor fruit carrier.

III

(DD–229: dp. 1,215 (n.); l. 314'4½''; b. 30'11½'' (wl.); dr. 9'9¾''; s. 35.18 k. (tl.); cpl. 122; a. 4 4'', 1 3'', 12 21'' tt.; cl. *Clemson*)

The third *Truxtun* (DD–229) was laid down on 3 December 1919 at Philadelphia, Pa., by William Cramp & Sons; launched on 28 September 1920; sponsored by Miss Isabelle Truxtun Brumby; and commissioned at the Philadelphia Navy Yard on 16 February 1921, Lt. Comdr. Melville S. Brown in command.

Upon commissioning, *Truxtun* completed shakedown and began duty along the east coast with the Atlantic Fleet as a unit of Division 39, Destroyer Squadron 3. She operated with that unit along the Atlantic seaboard until the fall when she was reassigned to Division 43, Squadron 15. During the winter of 1921 and 1922, the destroyer joined the fleet in maneuvers and exercises near Guantanamo Bay, Cuba.

In March 1922, Division 43 returned north to Newport, R.I., to prepare for service in the Asiatic Fleet. On 22 June 1922, *Truxtun* departed Newport and proceeded, via the Mediterranean, the Suez Canal, and the Indian Ocean, to the Far East which she reached in mid-August. By early September, she and several sister destroyers of Division 43 joined the main elements of the Asiatic Fleet off Chefoo on the northern coast of China. Late in October, the fleet headed south to its winter base at Manila in the Philippines, from whence it conducted exercises until the following spring.

Truxtun served with the Asiatic Fleet for the next 10 years. During that decade, she alternated summer cruises in Chinese waters with winter maneuvers in the Philippines. This routine was punctuated by special unusual assignments. For instance, in June 1924, she and the other five destroyers of Division 43 helped to form a chain of picket ships across the Yellow Sea for the Army's global flight. More often, however, internecine warfare in China brought *Truxtun* to the coast of that troubled nation to protect American lives and property. She spent a total of eight out of the 13 months between September 1926 and October 1927 patrolling the Yangtze River while a myriad of factions in China clawed at another—and anyone else who happened to cross their paths. The destroyer returned to the Yangtze Patrol twice more—from 1 March to 14 April 1930 and from January through March 1932—when internal political convulsions in China threatened foreign lives and property.

On 18 April 1932, *Truxtun* departed Manila and the Asiatic Fleet to join the destroyers attached to the Battle Force. After stops at Guam, Midway, and Hawaii, she reached Mare Island Navy Yard on 13 May. For the next seven years, she cruised the Pacific, as far north as Alaska and as far south as the Panama Canal, participating in maneuvers with her big sisters of the Battle Force. Only once, in 1934, did she leave the Pacific. On 9 April, she cleared San Diego and transited the Panama Canal. After calling at Port-au-Prince, Haiti, *Truxtun* steamed north to New York City, arriving on 31 May. Following that visit, she cruised the eastern seaboard. On 15 September, the destroyer stood out of Hampton Roads, retransited the canal, and returned to San Diego on 9 November to resume operations with the Battle Force.

On 27 April 1939, *Truxtun* steamed out of San Diego and headed for the canal once more. She reached Norfolk on 15 May and joined Destroyer Division 27, Atlantic Squadron. The destroyer cruised the east coast of the United States while war clouds gathered in Europe. Soon after the outbreak of war in September, *Truxtun* began enforcing the provisions of President Franklin Roosevelt's proclamation of American neutrality by patrols and escort duty off the Atlantic coast, in the Gulf of Mexico, and in the Caribbean. In late May and early June 1940, the warship made a voyage to Casablanca in French North Africa and then resumed neutrality patrols off Florida and in the Caribbean.

Following repairs at Norfolk in December 1940 and January 1941, *Truxtun* cleared Hampton Roads on 6 February. The next day, she reached Newport, R.I., where she joined Destroyer Division 63, Squadron 31. Between late February and mid-March, she made two voyages to Halifax, Nova Scotia, returning to the United States at the Washington Navy Yard on both occasions. On 15 March, the destroyer returned to Newport and resumed patrols and exercises. For the remainder of her career, *Truxtun* patrolled the North Atlantic sea lanes and escorted convoys from New England and Canadian ports—via Argentia, Newfoundland—to Reykjavik, Iceland.

On Christmas Day 1941, *Truxtun* departed Boston in the screen of Convoy HX–168. She arrived at Reykjavik on 13 January 1942 and, six days later, headed back to Argentia with Convoy ON–57. At 0415 on 18 February while acting as escort to *Pollux* (AKS–2) in Placentia Bay, Newfoundland, *Truxtun* ran aground on Ferryland Point. She broke up almost immediately after grounding and, in spite of the heroic efforts of the local populace, lost 110 members of her crew to the elements. Her name was struck from the Navy list on 25 March 1942.

IV

(APD–98: dp. 1,650 (tl.); l. 306'0''; b. 37'0''; dr. 12'7'' (lim.); s. 23.6 k. (tl.); cpl. 204; trp. 162; a. 1 5'', 6 40mm.; cl. *Crosley*)

The fourth *Truxtun* (DE–282) was laid down on 13 December 1943 at the Charleston Navy Yard as a *Rudderow*-class destroyer escort; launched on 9 March 1944; sponsored by Miss Norton Truxtun; redesignated a high-speed transport, APD–98, on 15 July 1944; and commissioned on 9 July 1945, Lt. Comdr. Paul A. Bane, USNR, in command.

Truxtun departed Charleston on 24 July for shakedown training in the vicinity of Guantanamo Bay, Cuba, until 25 August, 10 days after the cessation of hostilities with Japan. Three days later, the high-speed transport entered Norfolk, Va., for post-shakedown availability. On 10 September, she cleared Hampton Roads for a two-week, round-trip voyage to Miami, Fla. Returning to Norfolk late in September, she prepared for inactivation. On 9 November, *Truxtun* again headed for Florida—this time bound for the Atlantic Reserve Fleet berthing area at Green Cove Springs. Arriving there on 16 November, she completed preparations for inactivation and was decommissioned on 15 March 1946.

Truxtun spent the remainder of her Navy career in reserve, at Green Cove Springs until 1961, then at Orange, Tex. On 24 June 1963, *Truxtun*'s name was cancelled in order that it might be assigned to DLGN–35. For the 18 months remaining in her Navy career, she was identified simply as *APD–98*. On 22 November 1965, she was sold to Taiwan under the provisions of the Military Assistance Program and served with the Taiwanese Navy as *Fu Shan* (PF–35). Two months after the sale, on 15 January 1966, *APD–98* was struck from the Navy list.

V

(DLGN–35: dp. 8,659 (f.); l. 564'; b. 58'; dr. 30.5'; s. 31 k.; cpl. 492; a. 1 5'', 2 3'', 1 mis. ln., Terrier, ASROC, 6 15.5'' ASW tt.; cl. *Truxtun*)

The fifth *Truxtun* (DLGN–35) was laid down on 17 June 1963 at Camden, N.J., by the New York Shipbuilding Corp.; launched on 19 December 1964; co-sponsored by Mrs. Kirby H. Tappan and Mrs. Scott Umstead; and commissioned on 27 May 1967, Capt. David D. Work in command.

Truxtun cleared Camden on 3 June and headed for the west coast. En route, she visited Yorktown and Norfolk, Va.; Guantanamo Bay, Cuba; Rio de Janeiro, Brazil; and Mar del Plata, Argentina. The guided missile frigate rounded Cape Horn on 10 July and entered the Pacific Ocean. After port calls at Valparaiso, Chile, and Mazatlan, Mexico, *Truxtun* reached Long Beach, her home port, on 29 July. After conducting trials there in late summer and early fall, she commenced shakedown training in November. She interrupted shakedown twice: on 10 and 11 November for Operation "Bell Anchor" and again from 27 November to 3 December for Exercise "Blue Lotus."

The nuclear-powered warship completed her shakedown training and, on 2 January 1968, got underway for the western Pacific. She made an overnight stop at

Pearl Harbor on the 7th and 8th and arrived in Sasebo, Japan, on the 19th. Five days later, *Truxtun* and *Enterprise* (CVAN–65) departed Sasebo and headed for the Sea of Japan in response to North Korea's seizure of American environmental research ship *Pueblo* (AGER–2). She operated in the Sea of Japan until 16 February when she headed south for her first line period off the coast of Vietnam. After a brief overnight stop in Subic Bay on the 19th and 20th, the guided missile frigate set a course for "Yankee Station" in the Gulf of Tonkin. *Truxtun* spent the majority of the remainder of her deployment in the Far East operating off the coast of Vietnam. While in the combat zone, she conducted search and rescue (SAR) missions, stood guard against North Vietnamese air attacks as a positive identification radar zone (PIRAZ) picket ship, and served as plane-guard ship for carriers *Enterprise*, *Bon Homme Richard* (CVA–31), and *Ticonderoga* (CVS–14). *Truxtun* punctuated her line periods with calls at Singapore, Hong Kong, Danang, and Subic Bay. She departed Subic Bay on 6 July, steamed east toward the United States, and reentered Long Beach on the 19th.

For the next four months, the warship operated along the west coast. She acted as plane guard for *Ranger* (CVA–61), *Kitty Hawk* (CVA–63), *Enterprise*, and *Yorktown* (CVS–10) while those carriers conducted landing qualifications for pilots. In mid-November, *Truxtun* became an antisubmarine warfare school ship and trained student sailors in the techniques of hunting submarines. Early in December, the guided missile frigate returned to Long Beach to prepare for overhaul. In January 1969, she shifted to Bremerton, Wash., where she entered the Puget Sound Naval Shipyard for refurbishing which lasted until April. The ship then resumed operations along the west coast which continued until 23 September when she got underway for her second deployment with the 7th Fleet.

After a stop at Pearl Harbor, the guided missile frigate arrived at Subic Bay on 20 October. Again, she spent much of her deployment cruising along the coast of embattled Vietnam, taking time periodically to make port calls at Hong Kong, Singapore, and Subic Bay. However, in addition to acting as plane guard for carriers and standing duty as PIRAZ and SAR ship, she also served as a peacetime aerial reconnaissance protective (PAPRO) picket in the Sea of Japan and participated in the Taiwan Strait patrol. Just before departing the Far East, she conducted exercises in the vicinity of Okinawa and then made her final port visit at Sasebo, Japan, from 6 to 11 March 1970.

Truxtun returned to Long Beach on 23 March and launched into a round of inspections and training cruises. In June, the warship embarked 40 NROTC midshipmen for their summer training cruise. During the first part of the cruise, she fired missiles on the Pacific missile range and visited San Francisco and Seattle. On 13 July, she departed Seattle for Pearl Harbor to conduct the second part of the training cruise. On 29 July, *Truxtun* returned to Long Beach from Hawaii, disembarked the midshipmen, and resumed normal operations. For the remainder of the summer, she conducted exercises and underwent various inspections. From 16 to 25 October, she moored alongside *Gompers* (AD–37) for a tender availability. Following one more period of exercises at sea late in October, she entered the Long Beach Naval Shipyard in preparation for a three-month restricted availability which began on 2 November 1970.

Truxtun's yard work was completed in mid-January, and the frigate then conducted type training and ASW exercises before preparing to deploy to the western Pacific once more. She returned to Long Beach on 22 January 1971 and remained there until 2 February when she got underway for Pearl Harbor. After a two-day layover in Hawaii, she resumed her voyage to the Far East on 9 February and reached Subic Bay on the 20th. During that deployment, *Truxtun* returned to her familiar routine along the coast of Vietnam, standing

PIRAZ picket duty and conducting exercises and tests. She visited Yokosuka, Japan, several times and made single stops at Hong Kong and Sattahip, Thailand. In late April, she also patrolled the Taiwan Strait for two days.

On 6 July, she completed her final line period of the deployment and left the Gulf of Tonkin. After a visit to Subic Bay, she set a course, on the 10th, for Fremantle, Australia, where she spent a week at the end of July. Following port calls at Pago Pago, Samoa, and Pearl Harbor, she moored at Long Beach on 17 August and began post-deployment standdown. Through the end of September, *Truxtun* received visitors on board and conducted drills to improve and to test her missile and gunnery marksmanship. During the first week in October, a Board of Inspection and Survey inspected *Truxtun*; and, on the 8th, she began a restricted availability during which she was modified to utilize the Light Airborne Multi-purpose System (LAMPS). From 18 November to 9 December, she conducted post-availability dock trials and type training as well as testing the newly installed LAMPS system. On 14 December 1971, a team from Naval Air Systems Command inspected and certified *Truxtun*'s LAMPS installation.

During the first six months of 1972, *Truxtun* operated out of her home port in North American coastal waters. She conducted exercises, entertained visitors, and underwent several inspections. Following another restricted availability in June, she spent July preparing for her fourth tour of duty with the 7th Fleet.

On 13 July, she departed Long Beach with HMNZS *Canterbury*, bound for the western Pacific and for her most eventful series of line periods off Vietnam. She parted company from *Canterbury* on 18 July and put into Pearl Harbor the following day. On the 23d, *Truxtun* resumed her voyage to the Orient and moored at Subic Bay on 4 August. Four days later, she loaded ammunition and got underway for her first line period in the Gulf of Tonkin. Over the next five months, the guided missile frigate stood both SAR and PIRAZ picket duty. During these assignments, she evaded at least three typhoons. Her busiest week came between 8 and 15 October, when her radarmen vectored the combat air patrol to six MiG kills, three of which occurred on the 15th alone. By the end of her deployment, she had teamed up with the combat air patrol to down five more, bringing her victory tally to 11 MiG's. In October, November, and January, *Truxtun* briefly joined the Taiwan Strait patrol. She also made port calls at Sasebo, Singapore, Hong Kong, and Yokosuka. On 21 January 1973, *Reeves* (DLG–24) relieved her on the north SAR station, and *Truxtun* headed, via the Taiwan Strait, for Japan. She stopped at Yokosuka from 26 to 30 January before continuing on, via Pearl Harbor, to Long Beach, where she arrived on Lincoln's Birthday.

Post-deployment standdown took up the ensuing month. On 19 March, she moored alongside *Piedmont* (AD–15) and commenced a tender availability which lasted until late April. *Truxtun* then resumed operations in and out of Long Beach. In May, she conducted type training off the California coast and naval gunfire support qualifications at San Clemente Island. On 7 June, the warship began embarking Naval Academy and NROTC midshipmen for their summer cruise. For the next two months, she trained the midshipmen, carrying them to ports along the west coast as well as to Hawaii.

She debarked the midshipmen on 27 July and began preparations for her fifth deployment to the Far East. On 17 August, *Truxtun* got underway from Long Beach, bound for the western Pacific. En route, she stopped at Pearl Harbor and reached Subic Bay on 5 September. She punctuated relatively uneventful tours of duty on PIRAZ station in the Gulf of Tonkin with port visits to Sattahip, Singapore, Manila, and Yokosuka. *Truxtun* also conducted missile exercises and ASW drills. On 9 December, she stood out of Subic Bay, sifted through the San Bernardino Strait, and headed for home. On Christmas Eve 1973, the guided missile frigate moored at Long Beach and began preparations for her first complex overhaul.

On 25 January 1974, *Truxtun* cleared Long Beach for Bremerton, Wash. Four days later, she entered the Puget Sound Naval Shipyard. There, the warship began a major 18-month overhaul during which her nuclear reactors were "refueled." On 30 June 1975, near the end of that repair period, *Truxtun* was reclassified a nuclear-powered guided missile cruiser and was redesignated CGN-35. On 31 July, she completed the overhaul and all attendant tests and trials and sailed for San Diego. She arrived in her new home port on 4 August and resumed normal operations in the southern California area. That schedule occupied her for the following 12 months.

On 30 July 1976, the guided missile cruiser headed out of San Diego, bound for the western Pacific. After two weeks of training in the Hawaiian Islands, she continued her voyage west on 16 August; and, after a somewhat circuitous cruise that took her to Wellington in New Zealand and Melbourne in Australia, *Truxtun* arrived in Subic Bay on 25 September. She conducted operations in the Philippines for about a month and then departed Subic Bay on 28 October, bound for the Indian Ocean and participation in Operation "Midlink 76." She arrived in Karachi, Pakistan, on 9 November for three days of briefings in preparation for the exercise. From 13 to 21 November, the warship joined in the multinational exercise in the waters off the coast of Pakistan. She returned to Karachi at the conclusion of "Midlink" on the 21st and remained there until the 24th at which time she headed back to Subic Bay. Local operations in the Philippines occupied the remainder of the year. From 4 to 13 January 1977, *Truxtun* made a round-trip voyage to Hong Kong and back. She completed READEX 1-77 between 15 and 21 January and then again headed for the Indian Ocean in company with *Enterprise* (CVN-65) and *Long Beach* (CGN-9). En route, she and her travelling companions conducted exercise "Merlion III" with units of the Singapore Armed Forces on the 25th. *Truxtun* participated in Operation "Houdini" in mid-February and visited Port Victoria in the Seychelle Islands. She returned to Subic Bay on 13 March and, four days later, got underway for the United States.

After an 11-day non-stop voyage, she reentered San Diego on 28 March. The guided missile cruiser conducted a four-week restricted availability and then resumed operations along the California coast. For six months, the warship conducted routine independent ship's exercises, gunnery drills, and antisubmarine warfare training. She spent the month of November at the Puget Sound Naval Shipyard undergoing repairs to her nuclear power plant and returned to San Diego on 4 December. For the remaining three weeks of 1977, *Truxtun* operated out of her home port.

The first three months of 1978 were spent in operations off the west coast in preparation for *Truxtun*'s forthcoming deployment to the western Pacific. The ship departed San Diego on 4 April and spent the next six months in operations with the 7th Fleet which took her as far west as the Arabian Sea and as far south as Perth, Australia. *Truxtun* returned to San Diego on 27 October. Local operations out of San Diego, following post-deployment standdown, concluded the year.

Truxtun was awarded seven battle stars and the Navy Unit Commendation for service in the Vietnam conflict.

Tryon

James R. Tryon—born on 24 September 1837 at Coxsackie, N.Y.—was appointed an Acting Assistant Surgeon (Volunteer) on 17 March 1863. After serving briefly at the United States Naval Hospital in New York City, Tryon spent the last two years of the Civil War at Pensacola, Fla., caring for sick and wounded officers and men of the West Gulf Blockading Squadron.

After duty ashore in Boston and Washington, Tryon served in *Idaho* on the Asiatic Station from 4 February 1870 to 9 December 1872. Next came an assignment in New York City from 1873 to 1876. Following two years in *Swatara* on the North Atlantic Station, he was transferred to *Vandalia*. Next came duty in New York City for two and one-half years and service in *Alaska* on the Pacific Station until 1883. He served on board *Quinnebaug* on the European Station and off Africa until 1887 when he was assigned to the Medical Examining Board in New York.

Tryon was promoted to medical inspector on 22 September 1891 and served in *Chicago* on the North Atlantic Station until 1893 when he was promoted to Surgeon General of the United States Navy with the rank of commodore. The culmination of his career came on 7 September 1893 when Commodore Tryon became Chief of the Bureau of Medicine and Surgery and Surgeon General. He retired on 24 September 1899. In 1911, Tryon was promoted to the rank of read admiral, retroactive to his date of retirement. Admiral Tryon died on 20 March 1912 at the Naval Hospital in New York City where he had begun his naval career almost half a century before.

(APH–1: dp. 9,920; l. 450'0"; b. 62'0"; dr. 23'6"; s. 18 k. (tl.); cpl. 455; trp. 1,274; a. 1 5", 12 40mm.; cl. *Tryon*; T. C2–S1–A1 (c))

Tryon (APH–1) was laid down under Maritime Commission contract (MC hull 175) on 26 March 1941 at Oakland, Calif., by the Moore Drydock Co., as *Alcoa Courier*; launched on 21 October 1941; sponsored by Mrs. Roy G. Hunt; renamed *Comfort* in June 1942; renamed *Tryon* on 13 August 1942; acquired by the Navy from the Maritime Commission on 29 September 1942; and commissioned on 30 September 1942, Comdr. Alfred J. Byrholdt in command.

The transport evacuation ship got underway for San Diego on 9 October and departed from there on the 21st, bound for New Caledonia. On 7 November, she arrived at Noumea; joined the Service Squadron, South Pacific; and remained with that organization for the next 15 months, evacuating combat casualties from the Solomons to Suva, Noumea, Wellington, Auckland, and Brisbane. On her return trips to the forward areas, she carried priority cargo and troops for forces fighting the Japanese.

Tryon's first combat duty came in the Marianas during the summer of 1944. On 16 July, she joined Task Force 51 at Lunga Point and sortied for the invasion of Tinian. The hospital transport arrived off the beaches on the 24th, combat loaded with troops and equipment. After unloading, she embarked casualties for a week and then got underway for the Marshalls. The ship called at Eniwetok, New Caledonia, Espiritu Santo, and the Russell Islands before anchoring off Guadalcanal on 27 August.

Tryon embarked 1,323 marines of the 1st Marine Division and sortied on 8 September, with Transport Division 6 of Task Force 32, for the assault on the Palaus. She was off the beaches of Peleliu on the morning of the 15th and disembarked elements of the assault wave. Then, serving as a hospital evacuation ship, she embarked 812 combat casualties and, on the 20th, stood out for Manus. She disembarked the patients at Seeadler Harbor four days later and headed back to Peleliu the next morning. The ship remained off the beaches from 28 September to 4 October and then joined a convoy bound for the Solomons.

When *Tryon* arrived at Tulagi on 11 October, she was assigned to the 7th Fleet to participate in the Leyte campaign. She called at Hollandia and Humboldt Bay en route and reached Leyte on the 30th. The ship completed unloading the next day and began the return voyage to the South Pacific. The transport loaded troops and cargo at Langemak Bay from 13 through 27 December and headed for Manus on 28 December 1944. On 2 January 1945, *Tryon* stood out of Manus with

Task Group 77.9, the reinforcement group, for the invasion of Luzon on the beaches of the Lingayen Gulf. She arrived off San Fabian on the morning of the 11th and began unloading troops and supplies. From 13 to 27 January, she received casualties on board and headed to Leyte Gulf where they were transferred to *Hope* (AH–9) and *Bountiful* (AH–7). On 2 February, she joined a convoy and departed for the Solomons.

On 22 February, the evacuation hospital ship got underway and proceeded via Pearl Harbor to the United States for an overhaul. She arrived at San Francisco on 11 March and remained in the navy yard until 20 May. After refresher training in San Diego, she sailed for Hawaii on 3 June and arrived at Pearl Harbor the following week. The transport then called at Eniwetok, Guam, and San Francisco before returning to Hawaii on 2 August. The next day, she headed for Guam and arrived there on the 15th to hear that hostilities with Japan had ceased. *Tryon* was routed to the Philippines, embarked occupation troops at Leyte, and joined a convoy for Japan on 1 September. The transport disembarked the troops at Yokohama and received liberated Allied prisoners of war cn board for transportation to the Philippines. She disembarked them at Manila on the 18th.

On 1 October, *Tryon* was assigned to the "Magic-Carpet" fleet which was established at the end of the war to return troops to the United States. She served with it through the end of the year. In mid-January 1946, the ship was slated for inactivation. She was decommissioned at Seattle on 20 March 1946, returned to the War Shipping Administration in April, and struck from the Navy list on 17 April 1946.

Tryon was turned over to the United States Army on 17 July 1946 and converted into a troop transport by the Todd Shipyard, Seattle, Wash. She emerged from the yard on 25 August 1947 and was placed in service as *Sgt. Charles E. Mower*. The Secretary of Defense, by a directive dated 2 August 1949, established a unified sea transportation service; and, on 1 March 1950, the ship was transferred back to the Navy Department, assigned to the Military Sea Transportation Service, and designated T–AP–186.

Sgt. Charles E. Mower operated as a dependent transport shuttling between San Francisco and Pearl Harbor until she was inactivated in 1954. *Sgt Charles E. Mower* was placed out of service, in reserve, on 16 June 1954; transferred to the reserve fleet at Suisun Bay; and struck from the Navy list on 1 July 1960.

Tryon (APH–1) received six battle stars for World War II service.

Tucana

A constellation of the Southern Hemisphere not far from the pole and on the opposite side from the Southern Cross.

AK–88, an *Enceladus*-class cargo ship, was originally authorized under Maritime Commission contract (MC hull 651) and assigned the name *Symmes Potter*. The name *Tucana* was assigned to her by the Navy on 30 October 1942; and, on 1 January 1943, her contract was transferred from the Maritime Commission to the supervision of the Navy. AK–88 was laid down on 24 April 1944 at Camden, N.J., by the Penn-Jersey Shipbuilding Corp.; launched on 13 September 1944; and sponsored by Mrs. Patrick J. Cushing. On that same day, she was reassigned and delivered to the Army, and her name was struck from the Navy list.

Tucker

Born on 1 November 1747 in Marblehead, Mass., Samuel Tucker began his naval career in the spring of 1760 as a cabin boy in the Massachusetts Bay Colony

warship, *King George*. He subsequently sought his fortune in the merchant service, rising to command of a ship in July 1774. Tucker was in England at the outbreak of the American War for Independence, but returned to Massachusetts in the autumn of 1775.

Upon his return to the colonies, Tucker was selected by General George Washington to command a small flotilla of armed schooners which he had purchased and fitted out to prey on the shipping which was bringing supplies from England to America to support British troops in the colonies. Tucker also served as commanding officer of the schooner *Franklin*.

In that schooner and later in schooner *Hancock*, Tucker swept the seas around Boston and off the Massachusetts coast, taking many prizes in the year 1776. His first, taken jointly with the schooner *Lee*, came on 29 February, when the two Continental ships cornered the 300-ton *Henry and Esther*, bound for Boston laden with wood from Halifax, Nova Scotia.

In April 1776, in *Hancock*, Tucker sighted two supply brigs making for Boston. Standing in to the harbor very near to the protecting cannon of British warships anchored in the roadstead, he soon captured brigs *Jane* and *William*, out of Ireland. Tucker brazenly sailed up and took both from beneath the very noses of the British Navy, escaping with the two ships and their valuable cargoes of foodstuffs and other items needed by the Continental Army.

Because of his distinguished record, Tucker was given command of the new Continental Navy frigate *Boston* in March 1777. On 21 May, *Boston* and sister frigate *Hancock* set sail from Boston to raid the King's commerce on the high seas. Cruising in the North Atlantic, eight days out of their home port, the raiders captured a small brig laden with cordage and duck.

On 30 May, they sighted a convoy of troopships escorted by the 64-gun HMS *Somerset*, which soon set course to engage Manley's *Hancock*. Sizing up the situation in his experienced mariner's eye, Tucker bent on sail to go after the transports to wreak havoc among them. At that point, *Somerset's* commanding officer decided not to engage *Hancock*, since his primary mission was to protect the transports. Thus, *Hancock* escaped nearly certain devastation at the hands of the 64-gun Britisher. Tucker's timely action and good shiphandling were undoubtedly major factors in the Briton's decision.

On 7 June, *Boston* and *Hancock* engaged HMS *Fox* and made her a prize after a heated battle. One month later, on 7 and 8 July 1777, HMS *Flora*, HMS *Rainbow*, and HMS *Victor* attacked the three Continental ships and took *Hancock* and *Fox*. Only *Boston* escaped.

For the remainder of 1777, Tucker, in *Boston*, carried out commerce-raiding forays in the North Atlantic and off the northeast coasts before being selected for a special mission. On 13 February 1778, Capt. Samuel Tucker was rowed ashore to Braintree, Mass., where he soon sat down for a hasty and early meal with the family of John Adams. Soon, Adams, the newly appointed minister to France, and his son, John Quincy, were taken out to *Boston* and lodged on board as preparations for heading out to sea were completed.

Encountering heavy seas and wind halfway across the Atlantic, *Boston* nearly dismasted in a gale. On another occasion, three British warships gave chase to the solitary Continental frigate and its distinguished passenger. The unpleasant surroundings of a dank and dismal English prison were not relished by anyone, least of all Adams, who would have been considered a traitor to the crown. Avoiding contact with British ships as much as possible, Tucker was finally forced to fight.

Encountering a British privateer, Tucker maneuvered *Boston* to cross the enemy's "T." With devastating effect, *Boston's* guns thundered and sent shot down the length of the Britisher, and soon, the Briton struck her colors. Arriving safely at Bordeaux on 1 April, Adams would have stories to tell in future days about his eventful cruise with Samuel Tucker in *Boston*.

Cruising in European waters from the spring of 1778 until the fall of that year, Tucker took four more prizes before returning to Portsmouth, N.H., on 15 October. In 1779, two cruises in the North Atlantic netted nine prizes for Tucker and his mariners before orders sent *Boston* to Charleston, S.C., to help defend that port against the British onslaught.

On 11 May 1780, Charleston surrendered, after a siege, and the warships in harbor were captured, along with most of their officers and men. Tucker was among the prisoners but would not remain so for long, as he received parole on 20 May and was exchanged for British Capt. Wardlaw, whom Tucker had captured when *Boston* took HMS *Thorn* in September 1779.

On 11 January 1781, Tucker assumed command of *Thorn*, now a privateer. After taking seven prizes, he was again captured in an engagement with HMS *Hind* off the mouth of the St. Lawrence River.

He and his crew were treated kindly and taken to Prince Edward Island. One day, having had permission to go to Halifax, Tucker escaped and made his way to Boston. In an era where chivalry in war was still very much alive, Tucker wrote a letter of apology to the British garrison commander for his escape. At his own request, Tucker was paroled.

When the war had ended and independence had been secured for the fledgling United States, Tucker received hearty thanks from Congress. During the years following the establishment of peace, the old mariner from Marblehead sailed packets from America to Bremen, Germany, until he retired to farming, in Maine, in 1792.

Yet, when the young United States once again went to war with Britain in the War of 1812, Samuel Tucker returned to active service, commanding a schooner which protected the coast of Maine from British privateers. In 1813, he captured the British privateer *Crown* in a short, sharp engagement, putting an end to the harassment of Maine coastal trade which had been posed by the Briton.

Changing his residence to Massachusetts, Tucker settled down once again to a life of farming. In 1823, he was awarded a small pension, retroactive to 1818.

After holding positions of public trust in his home state of Massachusetts and having lived a life of adventure on the high seas, Samuel Tucker died at the age of 86 in Bremen, Maine, on 10 March 1833.

I

(Destroyer No. 57: dp. 1,205; l. 310′; b. 29′10′′; dr. 10′4½′′; s. 29.50 k.; cpl. 89; a. 4 4′′, 4 21′′ tt.; cl. *Tucker*)

The first *Tucker* (Destroyer No. 57) was laid down on 9 November 1914 at the Fore River Shipbuilding Company, Quincy, Mass.; launched on 4 May 1915; sponsored by Mrs. William Garty, the great, great, granddaughter of Capt. Samuel Tucker; and commissioned on 11 April 1916, Lt. (jg.) Frank Slingluff, Jr., in temporary command until Lt. Comdr. Benyaurd B. Wygant assumed command 13 days later.

Following commissioning, *Tucker* commenced trials off the east coast before reporting to Division 8, Destroyer Force, United States Atlantic Fleet. While World War I raged in Europe, *Tucker* and units of the Fleet conducted exercises and maneuvers in southern and Cuban waters into the spring of 1917.

Steaming independently in the West Indies, she received word of the United States' declaration of war on the Central Powers on 6 April 1917. Upon this notification of the commencement of hostilities, *Tucker* soon joined the Fleet at its anchorage in the York River before being ordered to proceed to the Boston Navy Yard, Mass., for fitting-out for war.

The immediate and pressing need for escort ships led to the deployment of American destroyers to Queenstown, Northern Ireland, commencing with the departure of six ships on 24 April under Comdr. J. K. Taussig. Later, *Tucker*, in company with *Rowan* (Destroyer No. 64), *Cassin* (Destroyer No. 43), *Ericsson* (Destroyer No. 56), *Winslow* (Destroyer No. 53), and *Jacob Jones* (Destroyer No. 61) set out from Boston on 7 May as the second contingent of United States ships designated to operate in conjunction with British surface forces patrolling off the Irish coast.

Arriving on 17 May, *Tucker* and her sister ships soon commenced wartime operations. On 12 June, she rescued 47 survivors from the stricken merchantman SS *Poluxena*; on 1 August, she saved 39 men from the torpedoed SS *Karina*. For the remainder of 1917 and into the late spring of 1918, *Tucker* operated out of Queenstown, hunting German submarines, escorting and convoying ships through the submarine-infested war zones, and providing assistance to ships in distress.

By the early summer of 1918, as American forces poured into the war on the Western Front and swelled in numbers on the continent of Europe, the need for escorts to convoy the ships that bore the men and materiel grew apace. Thus, American destroyers were progressively transferred to the eastern Atlantic to augment the escort forces already operating in that war zone.

In June 1918, *Tucker* joined the escorts working out of Brest, France. On 1 August, while steaming out to meet an inbound convoy, she received word that the group's escort, the French cruiser *Dupetit-Thouars*, had been torpedoed and sunk by a German submarine. The American destroyer soon arrived on the scene and helped to save the survivors of the stricken French warship from the waters of the Bay of Biscay. *Tucker*'s efforts, and those of the five other American destroyers who were also present, were rewarded by a commendation from the *Prefet Maritime*, on behalf of the French Ministry of Marine.

While taking part in the campaign to eradicate the German submarine menace preying upon Allied shipping, *Tucker* obtained her share of the submarine hunting the day after assisting in the rescue of *Dupetit-Thouars*' crew, on 8 August. Sighting a U-boat, *Tucker* sped to the attack, dropping depth bombs on the undersea enemy. The British Admiralty gave credit to *Tucker* for a "possibly sunk" as a result of the attack. As antisubmarine warfare was in its infancy, however, attempts to verify the "kill" proved to be inconclusive.

On 11 November 1918, the armistice was signed, and hostilities ceased along the war-torn Western Front. As American forces withdrew from Europe and headed home to the United States, *Tucker* carried passengers and mail between French and British ports. Departing from Brest for the last time on 16 December 1918, she headed for Boston, Mass., and a period of repairs in the navy yard.

In July 1919, she departed Boston and cruised along the coastlines of Massachusetts and Maine, engaged in recruiting duty. In October 1919, she was placed in reserve in Philadelphia, Pa., where she remained until placed out of commission on 16 May 1921. On 17 July 1920, *Tucker* was designated DD–57.

The prohibition of liquor, instituted by law on 17 January 1920, soon resulted in widespread and blatant smuggling of alcoholic beverages along the coastlines of the United States. The Treasury Department discovered that the Coast Guard simply did not have the ships to constitute a successful patrol. To cope with the problem, President Calvin Coolidge authorized the transfer, in 1924, of 20 old destroyers, then in reserve and out of commission, from the Navy to the Coast Guard.

On 25 March 1926, *Tucker* was activated and acquired by the Coast Guard, part of a second group of five to augment the original 20. Designated CG–23, she joined the "rum patrol" and chased rum runners, aiding in the attempt to enforce prohibition laws.

On 4 April 1933, the greatest disaster which aeronautics had experienced up to that time occurred off the New Jersey coast. The airship *Akron* (ZRS–4) crashed in a storm and carried 73 men to their deaths, including Rear Admiral William A. Moffett, Chief of the Bureau of Aeronautics. *Tucker* received word of the crash and sped to the scene. Upon arrival, she found that German motorship *Phoebus* had pulled four men from the sea—one of whom died shortly after being rescued. The survivors were transferred to *Tucker* and were disembarked at the New York Navy Yard.

After Congress had passed the 21st Amendment to the Constitution to end prohibition, *Tucker* was returned to the Navy on 30 June 1933. Her name was cancelled on 1 November 1933 to free the name *Tucker* for DD–374; and, thereafter, the old destroyer was known by her hull designation *DD–57*. For a time, *DD–57* served as a Sea Scout training ship, docked at Sandy Hook, N.J. Struck from the Navy list on 24 October 1936, *DD–57* was sold on 10 December 1936 and reduced to a hulk two days before Christmas 1936.

II

(DD–374: dp. 1,500; l. 341'4''; b. 34'8''; dr. 17'; s. 36.5 k.; cpl. 158; a. 5 5'', 12 21'' tt.; cl. *Mahan*)

The second *Tucker* (DD–374) was laid down at Portsmouth, Va., on 15 August 1934 by the Norfolk Navy Yard; launched on 26 February 1936; sponsored by Mrs. Leonard Thorner; and commissioned on 23 July 1936, Lt. Comdr. George T. Howard in command.

Following shakedown training, *Tucker* joined the destroyer forces attached to the United States Battle Fleet and was based at San Diego, Calif. As part of Destroyer Squadron 3, Destroyer Division 6, she operated with the Battle Force along the west coast and in the Hawaiian Islands. In February 1939, she took part in Fleet Problem XX, the naval exercise in the Caribbean personally observed by President Franklin D. Roosevelt from *Houston* (CA–30).

As the international situation in the Pacific worsened, President Roosevelt ordered the Fleet to remain in Hawaiian waters after the conclusion of exercises in the spring of 1940. *Tucker* then operated between the west coast and Hawaii through the end of the year. On 14 February 1941, she arrived at Pearl Harbor, from San Diego, and then proceeded to New Zealand, arriving at Auckland on 17 March to "show the flag" in that area of the world.

Returning to Pearl Harbor from the South Pacific, she took part in routine exercises at sea before returning to her home port of San Diego, Calif., on 19 September. Getting underway again after a short stay, *Tucker* steamed to Hawaii as part of Task Force 19 and began operations anew in the Hawaiian Islands in

November. After one month of maneuvers in the Hawaiian operating area, she returned to Pearl Harbor for a tender overhaul.

On 7 December 1941, *Tucker* lay peacefully moored at berth X–8, East Loch, Pearl Harbor, in the center of a nest of five destroyers and tender *Whitney* (AD–4); to port of *Tucker* lay *Selfridge* (DD–375) and *Case* (DD–370); to her starboard were *Reid* (DD–365) and *Conyngham* (DD–371), with *Whitney* outboard of *Conyngham*. Suddenly the drone of airplane engines and the roar of exploding bombs and torpedoes shattered the Sunday morning calm; Japanese planes swept over the harbor and wheeled above like hawks.

On board *Tucker*, GM2c W. E. Bowe observed the unfolding attack and promptly manned a machine gun on the ship's after superstructure, commencing fire even before the general quarters alarm sounded. Within two minutes, the after 5-inch guns came into action, joining the concentrated gunfire emanating from the nest of ships in which *Tucker* lay. This veritable storm of shells and bullets produced hits on two enemy aircraft, both of which spun into the lush green hills and exploded.

As the damaged fleet licked its wounds and rolled up its sleeves to begin the war, *Tucker* patrolled off Pearl Harbor before spending the succeeding five months escorting convoys between the west coast and Hawaii. *Tucker* then received new orders sending her to the South Pacific.

With the reinforcement of United States island bases in the Pacific, *Tucker* escorted *Wright* (AV–1) to Tutuila, American Samoa, as part of the drive to fortify these outposts. The destroyer then escorted her charge to Suva, in the Fiji Islands, and thence to Noumea, New Caledonia. Steaming then for Austrialia, she arrived at Sydney on 27 April. After taking on fuel the following day, she visited Melbourne, Perth, and Fremantle before heading back to Sydney.

In company with *Wright*, *Tucker* returned to Suva arriving there on 3 June 1942, the day before the commencement of the climactic Battle of Midway. For the remainder of June and into the first week of July *Tucker* operated out of Suva; then relieved *Boise* (CL–47) on 10 July on convoy escort duties. On 30 July, the destroyer arrived at Auckland and, the following day steamed for the Fiji Islands.

At Suva, she received orders to escort the SS *Nira Luckenbach* to Espiritu Santo; and, on 1 August, the two ships departed by way of a route north of Efate Island and west of the Malekula Islands. Threading their way through the Bruat channel, both ships then set courses to enter the Segond Channel for the final leg of their voyage to Espiritu Santo. At 2145, *Tucker*

USS *Tucker* (DD–374) at Mare Island, 11 March 1942. Like other destroyers of her age, she has had some of her tophamper cut down and antiaircraft guns installed.

struck a mine which exploded and broke the destroyer's back. She slowed to a halt, mortally stricken, and began folding up like a jacknife.

The explosion instantly killed three men. *Nira Luckenbach* quickly sent boats to aid in rescuing the destroyermen as they abandoned their sinking ship.

By the next morning, *YP-346* had arrived on the scene and attempted to tow the stricken destroyer into shallower water to facilitate salvage operations. *Breese* (DMS-18) also arrived and stood by as *YP-346* valiantly struggled to beach the foundering *Tucker*. However, the efforts soon came to naught; and *Tucker* jacknifed and sank in 10 fathoms at 0445 on 4 August 1942.

The minefield into which she had steamed had been laid by United States forces only the day before, on 2 August, and its existence had not yet been radioed to *Tucker* and *Nira Luckenbach*. Thus, *Tucker*'s commanding officer and her crew had no idea of the dangerous waters into which they had steamed so unknowingly. The destroyer's only casualties were three men killed in the initial explosion and three more listed as "missing."

Her name was struck from the Navy list on 2 December 1944.

Tucker received one battle star for her World War II service.

Tucker, Henry W., see *Henry W. Tucker*.

Tucson

A city in, and the seat of, Pima County, Ariz.

(CL–98: dp. 6,000; l. 541'6''; b. 53'2''; dr. 20'0''; s. 33 k.; cpl. 623; a. 12 5'', 16 40mm., 16 20mm., 8 21'' tt.; cl. *Oakland*)

Tucson (CL-98) was laid down on 23 December 1942 at San Francisco, Calif., by the Bethlehem Steel Co.; launched on 3 September 1944; sponsored by Mrs. Emmett S. Claunch, Sr.; and commissioned on 3 February 1945, Capt. Arthur D. Ayrault in command.

Following outfitting at San Francisco and shakedown out of San Diego, *Tucson* sailed for the western Pacific on 8 May. She stopped at Pearl Harbor on 13 May for three weeks of additional training before resuming her voyage west on 2 June. She stopped overnight at Ulithi on 13 and 14 June, then continued on to the Philippines, and reached Leyte on the 16th. The cruiser was assigned to the screen of the Fast Carrier Task Force, TF 38, specifically to that of Rear Admiral Gerald F. Bogan's Task Group (TG) 38.3 built around carriers *Essex* (CV-9), *Ticonderoga* (CV-14), *Randolph* (CV-15), *Monterey* (CV-26), and *Bataan* (CVL-29).

Tucson joined the fast carriers just in time to participate in their final rampage against the Japanese Empire and its inner defenses. On 1 July, she sortied from Leyte Gulf with TF 38 and headed north to the Japanese home islands. On the 10th, the flattops launched planes against Tokyo. On the 14th and 15th, TF 38's air groups struck Hokkaido and northern Honshu. They returned to southern Honshu on the 17th and 18th to blast Tokyo again and then left the area for almost a week. On 24 and 28 July, she appeared with the carriers south of Shikoku while their planes hit shipping in the Inland Sea. On the 30th, they zeroed in on Kobe and Nagoya. After that, they retired south to fuel and replenish before striking out northward. By the second week of August, *Tucson* was off northern Honshu screening the carriers while their planes pounded the island once more. She then accompanied them south to pummel Tokyo again on the 13th. Two days later, Japan capitulated.

Though hostilities had ceased in mid-August and the Japanese had surrendered formally on 2 September, *Tucson* remained in the Far East, steaming with TF 38 to the east of Honshu, covering the occupation forces moving into Japan. On 20 September, she cleared the

The antiaircraft cruiser *Tucson* (CL–98) in weathered dark camouflage finish during the latter part of the Pacific war. Ships of this class were considerably smaller than other light cruisers of their time.

area and, two days later, stopped at Okinawa before shaping a course back to the United States. En route, she called at Pearl Harbor and then arrived in San Francisco on 5 October. On the 23d, the warship headed down the coast to San Pedro, where she participated in the Navy Day celebration on the 27th and 28th. On the 29th, she shifted to San Diego where she reported for duty with Pacific Fleet Training Command as an antiaircraft gunnery training ship. Between November 1945 and August 1946, the antiaircraft cruiser trained about 5,000 officers and men in the use of 5-inch and 40- and 20-millimeter antiaircraft guns. She interrupted her training duties periodically to represent the Navy at special events held in various ports on the Pacific coast.

On 6 September, she entered the Puget Sound Naval Shipyard for a three-month overhaul to get ready for duty under the Commander, Destroyers, Pacific Fleet. For the next two months, *Tucson* trained out of San Diego in preparation for a fleet exercise to be conducted near Hawaii. On 24 February 1947, the cruiser stood out of San Diego and cruised Hawaiian waters as an element of the force charged with the defense of the islands against an aggressor force moving in from the western Pacific. At the completion of the exercise, the warship put into Pearl Harbor on 11 March. However, she got underway again on the 18th to participate in the fruitless search to the northwest of Hawaii for survivors of the wrecked SS *Fort Dearborn*.

On 27 March, *Tucson* returned to San Diego and resumed normal west coast operations until late summer. She again departed the west coast on 28 July and proceeded, via Pearl Harbor, to the Far East, arriving at Yokosuka, Japan, on the 15th. For the next two months, the warship cruised the waters of the Yellow Sea and the East China Sea making observations during the Communist-Nationalist struggle for supremacy in Manchuria and northern China. During that period, she visited Shanghai twice and Tsingtao once. *Tucson* returned to Yokosuka on 19 October, stayed overnight, and sailed the next day for the United States, arriving at San Diego on 6 November. The cruiser resumed west coast operations and, for the brief remainder of her active career, remained so engaged.

On 9 February 1949, *Tucson* reported to Mare Island Naval Shipyard to begin preparations for inactivation. On 11 June 1949, she was decommissioned and berthed with the San Francisco Group of the Pacific Reserve Fleet. She remained in reserve at Mare Island until 1 June 1966 when her name was struck from the Navy list. The former warship served as a test hulk until 1970. On 24 February 1971, the hulk was sold to the National Metal & Steel Corp., of Terminal Island, Calif., for scrapping.

Tucson earned one battle star during World War II.

Tucumcari

A city in and the seat of Quay County, New Mexico. The name is derived from the Comanche Indian word "tukamukaru," which means to lie in wait.

(PGH–2: dp. 57; l. 80′; b. 22′; dr. 14′; s. 50 k.; cpl. 13; a. 1 40mm., 4 .50-cal. mg., 1 81mm. M.; cl. *Tucumcari*)

Tucumcari (PGH–2) was laid down on 1 September 1966 at Seattle, Wash., by the Marine Branch of the Boeing Company's Aerospace Group; launched on 15 July 1967; and delivered to the Navy on 7 March 1968. Placed "in service" on that day, the ship's first officer-in-charge was Lt. Marvin H. Mandles, USNR.

Tucumcari—an extremely fast, highly maneuverable, experimental hydrofoil gunboat designed to perform well even in heavy weather—represented the culmination of 10 years of hydrofoil development. The new gunboat arrived in San Diego, her home port, in July 1968. She conducted operational evaluation tests with Amphibious Forces, Pacific Fleet, and participated in exercises. In addition, the craft conducted day and night operations with the Fleet with ships ranging from cruisers to patrol craft. During her tour of duty in San Diego, she performed a mission of mercy, rendezvousing with a Navy tug beyond helicopter range and receiving on board one of the tug's crewmen for transportation to San Diego for emergency leave.

After a year of operations out of San Diego, *Tucumcari* was deployed to Vietnamese waters. She spent most of her six months in the combat zone assigned to Operation "Market Time," the inshore patrol established to stop the flow from the north of communist arms and infiltrators. While performing this duty, she logged 200 hours of foilborne operations including day and night, all-weather, and high sea-state missions. She also conducted underway replenishments with larger fleet units and vertical replenishment from helicopters. The latter even included medical evacuation operations and the transfer of cargo loads.

Tucumcari returned to San Diego in March 1970 and operated off the west coast until transferred to the Atlantic Fleet in August. After operating off the east coast into 1971, *Tucumcari* was slated to deploy to northern Europe and to the Mediterranean to demonstrate the capability of hydrofoil propulsion for other NATO nations. It was hoped that the demonstration would stimulate the development and production of a NATO guided missile hydrofoil.

Tucumcari was loaded on board *Wood County* (LST-1178) on 22 March 1971 and secured in a specially constructed cradle on the main deck. Three days later, *Wood County* got underway for Copenhagen, Denmark, and the first of demonstration "flights" for the hydrofoil gunboat. Arriving in Copenhagen on 8 April, *Tucumcari* was offloaded on the 13th and readied for her first tests. While in Danish waters, the patrol craft participated in Exercise "Evil Edge," a joint West German, Danish, and American patrol boat exercise. During "Evil Edge," the gunboat made simulated attacks against West German destroyers. *Tucumcari* was subsequently put through her paces at Olpenitz, Germany; Rosyth, Scotland; Portsmouth, England; and Brest, France, before the northern and western European phase of the tests were concluded and *Wood County* with the hydrofoil gunboat stowed on deck, sailed for Toulon, France, on 6 July to commence the Mediterranean phase of the deployment.

After demonstrating at Toulon, *Tucumcari* conducted further operations at Athens, Greece; Golchuk, Turkey; Brindisi and Augusta, Italy; and in the Tyrrhenian Sea, concluding the last of these tests on 25 September. Then, on 1 October, with *Tucumcari* safely nestled on board, *Wood County* sailed for Little Creek, Va.

Homeported at Little Creek, Va., *Tucumcari* operated with the Atlantic Fleet Amphibious Force into the autumn of 1972. On 16 November of that year, she ran aground seven miles west of Puerto Rico during night operations with amphibious forces. Fortunately, she suffered no personnel casualties. While she was being pulled off the coral reef, the craft incurred more damage, so severe that she could not be economically repaired. Accordingly, she was struck from the Navy list on 7 November 1973 and transferred to the Naval Ship and Research Development Center at Annapolis, Md. She was subsequently used as a test hulk for structural evaluation and fire containment tests into the mid-1970's.

Tudno

(SwStr: t. 754; l. 265′4″; b. 32′6″; dr. 11′4″; cpl. 74)

The steel-hulled paddle steamer *H. T. Jackson* was built in 1891 at Glasgow, Scotland, by Fairfield Co.

Tucumcari (PGH–2), foilborne at high speed.

Ltd., and renamed *Saint Tudno* around 1913. While the exact terms of the transfer are not known, the English Channel excursion steamer was apparently loaned to the United States Navy sometime near the end of World War I.

Known only as *Tudno,* the ship served under the Stars and Stripes from about the time of the armistice to 21 August 1919. Her log reports that one officer reported on board the ship as early as 21 October 1918. As of 1 December 1918, her commanding officer was Lt. (jg.) William J. Brown, USNRF. There is no record of any commissioning, nor is the ship carried on any contemporary listings of United States naval vessels.

In any event, the little-documented *Tudno* performed valuable service at Brest, France, in the gigantic effort to return the doughboys home from "over there." She ferried troops from the docks of Brest to the waiting transports—transports that ranged from the giant *Leviathan* (Id. No. 1326) to *New Jersey* (Battleship No. 16); from the Cunarder *Aquitania* to the armored cruisers *Frederick* (Armored Cruiser No. 8) and *Huntington* (Armored Cruiser No. 5).

During the course of *Tudno*'s service at Brest, some important people trod her decks—even if only for a brief time. President Woodrow Wilson and his party came ashore from *George Washington* (Id. No. 3018) on 13 December 1918 as the President prepared to take part in the Paris Peace Conference. *Tudno* later transported the Chief Executive and his party back to *George Washington* on 15 February 1919 and again carried him from that ship to shore on 13 March. Later in that month, *Tudno* conveyed Secretary of the Navy Josephus Daniels and his party from *Leviathan* to the docks at Brest; and, on 14 April, the paddle steamer transported Secretary of War Newton D. Baker and Army General John J. Pershing to Brest's Pier 5.

Tudno continued her troop-ferrying duties into the spring and summer months and, on 23 June, "received word of German(y)'s Signature of [the] Peace Treaty; great rejoicing thruout [sic] harbor." Six days later, *Tudno* dressed ship and moved out into the harbor, mooring alongside *George Washington;* soon the French yacht *Dolmer* drew alongside, and President Wilson crossed *Tudno*'s deck to the waiting transport, having achieved what he fervently hoped would be a lasting peace.

Subsequently, *Tudno* took Secretary of State Robert Lansing to the liner SS *Rotterdam* on 13 July. Six days later, the paddle steamer took a party of 200 West Point cadets and 300 sailors from *Leviathan* to shore for a visit to Paris.

Her last troop-ferrying duty came on 12 August 1919, when she took 1,400 men out to the transport *Powhatan* (Id. No. 3013). Two days later, *Tudno* took on board a case of Pyrene fire extinguishers and eight tires for delivery to United States Naval Headquarters, London, England; and, on the 16th, embarked 12 passengers. Underway at 1755 that day, *Tudno* arrived at Southampton, England, on the 17th. On the morning of 21 August, *Tudno* was handed over to the British; and her crew was transferred to *Laub* (Destroyer No. 263), moored alongside.

The sidewheeler resumed mercantile service as *Saint Tudno* and retained that name even though she changed flags—to Dutch ownership in about 1922. She disappears from *Lloyd*'s lists in 1923–1924.

Tulagi

An island of the south central Solomons in the southwestern Pacific. Located south of Florida Island and north of Guadalcanal, Tulagi was the scene of the beginning of the struggle for the Solomons when Japanese forces occupied the island on 3 May 1942. It was captured by United States Marines later that year when they landed there on 7 August and wrested control of the island from the Japanese.

(CVE–72: dp. 7,800; l. 512'3"; b. 65'; ew. 108'1"; d 22'6"; s. 19 k.; cpl. 860; a. 1 5", 16 40mm., 2 20mm.; cl. *Casablanca*; T. SA–S2–BB3)

Tulagi (CVE–72) was laid down on 7 June 1943 a Vancouver, Wash., by the Kaiser Co., Inc., as *Fortaze Bay* (ACV–72); and redesignated CVE–72 on 15 Jul 1943. However, her name was corrected to rea *Fortaleza Bay* on 19 October 1943, and the ship wa renamed *Tulagi* on 6 November 1943; launched on 1 November 1943; sponsored by Mrs. James Duke Barner and commissioned on 21 December 1943, Capt. Josep Campbell Cronin in command.

The new escort carrier got underway from Seatt on 17 January 1944 bound for San Francisco whe she was immediately pressed into service ferryin stores, airplanes, and military personnel to Hawai She departed Pearl Harbor for the homeward voyage o 29 January and arrived at San Diego with her loa of passengers on 4 February. Throughout most o February, she participated in training exercises out o San Diego before steaming, via the Canal Zone, fo Hampton Roads, Va. Following her arrival at Norfol on 17 March, *Tulagi* underwent overhaul and carrie qualification tests.

Tulagi embarked a load of Army Air Forces plane late in May and departed New York on the 28th i convoy with two other carriers and their screen. O 6 June, *Tulagi* entered her first foreign port as sh steamed the swept channel approach to Casablanc After disembarking her cargo, the carrier took o passengers including a group of 35 prisoners of wa and then headed home.

After arriving at Norfolk on 17 June 1944, *Tula* got underway late in June for Quonset Point, R.I where she embarked personnel, planes, and equipmen On the last day of the month, she departed Narragar sett Bay with Rear Admiral Calvin T. Durgin on boar as Commander, Task Group 27.7, and steamed eastwar conducting squadron and battery training in route t Oran, Algeria. *Tulagi* visited Malta on 26 July an then spent the following weeks conducting exercise which included a dress rehearsal out of African an Italian ports for the coming Operation "Dragoon," th invasion of southern France.

On D-day, *Tulagi* steamed in formation 45 miles o the invasion beach; and, at 0546, she launched her firs flight of Hellcats. In the next week, aircraft from *Tulagi* flew a total of 68 missions and 276 sorties, i flicting considerable damage on the enemy. Weathe was generally good as carrier-based planes conducte spotting missions and made strikes at various target ashore, including gun emplacements and railway facil ties. On 21 August, *Tulagi*'s last day in support o Operation "Dragoon," German forces were in retrea before the Allied thrust. *Tulagi*'s fliers conducted devastating attack along the line of march of a Germa convoy which snarled the roads for miles aroun Remouline and crowned her achievements of the day b downing three German Ju 52's.

After taking on supplies and fuel at Oran, she g underway for home on 6 September. Following a quic overhaul at Norfolk, the escort carrier set her cours for Panama; transited the Canal; and arrived at Sa Diego on 26 October. There, she embarked two ai squadrons for transportation to Hawaii and departe the west coast on 29 October 1944.

Following her arrival at Pearl Harbor on 5 Novembe the carrier participated in antisubmarine warfare an gunnery exercises. On the 24th, she got underway i company with a special antisubmarine task grou which conducted sweeps as it steamed via the Mar shalls and Ulithi for Saipan. Throughout Decembe *Tulagi* continued antisubmarine activities in the Palau and the southern Marianas.

On the first day of the new year, 1945, *Tulagi* g underway for Lingayen Gulf and the impending inva sion of Luzon. Meanwhile, the Japanese in the Philip pines had assigned more than 100 suicide planes fo

concerted attack on *Tulagi*'s task force. The convoy
passed through Surigao Strait into the Mindanao Sea
3 January. In the following three days, the kamikazes
took their toll. On the 4th, reports of enemy aircraft in
the area became more frequent; and, late in the afternoon, a suicide plane splashed while trying to dive into
Lunga Point (CVE–19). Moments later, observers on
Tulagi saw the conflagration which marked the death
throes of *Ommaney Bay* (CVE–79), the victim of another kamikaze. On the morning of 5 January, enemy
air attackers continued to menace the convoy as it
steamed through Mindoro Strait and into the South
China Sea. Although fighters from the carrier splashed
two "Zekes," three enemy aircraft succeeded in penetrating the defenses of the convoy. Two were splashed,
but one managed to crash into cruiser *Louisville* (CA–
28), a member of the convoy's screen.

When landing began at Lingayen Gulf on 9 January
1945, *Tulagi* launched her planes for air strikes on land
targets, anti-snooper patrols, and air cover for American vessels. On 12 January, *Tulagi* supplied air support
for the Lingayen Gulf beachhead; and, the next day,
her port battery shot down a suicide plane which had
singled out the carrier for destruction. Before it
splashed, the attacker, deflected from *Tulagi* by withering antiaircraft fire, crossed astern and to starboard
of the escort carrier and vainly attempted to dive into
a alternate target. On 17 January, the Army Air
Forces assumed responsibility for direct air support of
American operations in Lingayen Gulf; and *Tulagi*'s
fliers turned their attention toward the Zambales coast
where they provided cover for support and protection
forces near San Narciso. On 5 February, *Tulagi*
arrived at Ulithi after a grueling period of sustained
flight operations during which her planes had been in
the air for all but two of 32 days.

Tulagi departed Guam on 21 February to conduct
hunter-killer exercises in support of the assault on
Iwo Jima before joining a task unit in area Varnish
west of Iwo Jima on 1 March. She supplied air support
and antisubmarine patrols until departing the area on
4 March, bound for Ulithi. Arriving there on 14
March, she prepared for the invasion of the Ryukyus.
Assigned alternately to antisubmarine and direct
support activities, *Tulagi* operated continuously off the
coast of Okinawa from the end of March until early
June. On 3 April, four "Zekes" attacked her formation,
and all were splashed. On the 6th, while *Tulagi* was
anchored at Kerama Retto for rearming, a Japanese
air attack penetrated air space over the harbor. The
carrier took one of her attackers under fire at 4,000
yards, but the Japanese plane came harrowingly close
before turning aside to dive into a nearby LST which
burst into flames 200 feet high. Minutes later, *Tulagi*
splashed another attacker and chased off a third with
her accurate fire. The next day, *Tulagi* resumed her
station off Okinawa, providing planes for air strikes
called in by ground observers and for running photo-
reconnaissance and patrol missions. On the 13th, after
she launched a special strike against the airfields of
Miyako Jima, she began antisubmarine operations
along the shipping lanes approaching Okinawa.

Following this long and arduous tour, *Tulagi* arrived
at Guam on 6 June 1945. The carrier departed the
Marianas on the 8th, bound for San Diego. She remained on the west coast throughout the summer undergoing overhaul, trials, and training. Peace came while
she was at San Diego, but she departed the west coast
again on 4 September and steamed via Hawaii for the
Philippines. At Samar, she embarked planes for transportation back to the United States and reached Pearl
Harbor in October. After returning to San Diego in
January 1946, the veteran escort carrier reported to the
19th Fleet at Port Angeles, Wash., on 2 February 1946
for inactivation. She was decommissioned on 30 April
1946 and struck from the Navy list on 8 May 1946.

Tulagi received four battle stars for World War II
service.

Tulare

A county in the south central part of California which
contains the Sequoia National Park and the Tule River
Indian Reservation. The name Tulare is derived from
the word tule, a large bullrush. Because of the abun-
dance of tules which grew in its marshy ground, the
name Tulare was given, in the 16th century, to the
entire San Joaquin Valley.

The contract for the acquisition of *Tulari* (AK–217)
was canceled early in 1945, before the ship was completed.

I

(AKA–112: dp. 9,190; l. 564'0''; b. 76'0''; dr. 26'0'';
cpl. 435; a. 12' 3''; cl. *Tulare*; T. C4–S–1a)

Tulare (AKA–112) was laid down under a Maritime
Administration contract as *Evergreen Mariner* (MA
hull 32) on 16 February 1953, at San Francisco, Calif.,
by the Bethlehem Pacific Coast Steel Corp.; launched
on 22 December 1953; sponsored by Miss Carolyn
Knight, daughter of the governor of California, Goodwin J. Knight; renamed *Tulare* and designated as
AKA–112 on 10 June 1954. The ship was then converted to an attack cargo ship by her building yard;
turned over to the Navy on 10 January 1956; and
commissioned on 12 January 1956, Capt. Donald W.
Todd in command.

After a year's operations off the west coast, punctuated by one round trip to Pearl Harbor, *Tulare* departed San Diego on 11 February 1957 for her first
deployment to the western Pacific. In the course of her
operations in the Far East, she participated in amphibious exercises at Buckner Bay, Okinawa; called at four
Japanese ports: Yokohama, Yokosuka, Sasebo, and
Shimoda; visited Sydney, Australia; Singapore; and
Pusan, Korea, before returning via Pearl Harbor to
San Diego on 26 September. She then took part in
amphibious exercises off the west coast until November
1957 when she entered the Long Beach Naval Shipyard
for repairs.

The ship's second deployment to the Far East took
her to Yokosuka and Sasebo, Japan; Okinawa; Hong
Kong; Guam; the Philippine Islands; and Pearl Harbor, before she returned to San Diego on 16 March
1959. In the spring and summer of that year, *Tulare*
operated in the San Diego area and took part in Operation "Twin Peaks." Standing out of San Diego on 13
October, she headed west for extended operations in
oriental waters, highlighted by a goodwill tour of eight
Japanese cities.

The first few months of 1960 saw the ship participating in Operation "Blue Star," the largest amphibious
operation in the western Pacific since the landings at
Inchon, Korea, in September 1950. After returning to
San Diego on 29 April 1960, *Tulare* operated locally in
exercises off the west coast, with troop and cargo lifts,
until sailing for her fourth deployment to the western
Pacific on 19 June 1961. Her special duty on the outbound voyage was to carry cargo to Wake Island. After
unloading there, *Tulare* continued on to Japan. Following two weeks at Yokosuka, the ship visited Beppu,
Japan, and headed for Inchon and Pohang, Korea, to
take part in Operation "Sharp Edge," in which she
embarked 300 Army troops with their equipment. *Tulare*
then visited Hong Kong and several Japanese ports
during the summer and early fall of 1961. En route to
the Ryukyus in October, *Tulare* was designated command ship for search and rescue operations for merchantmen *Pioneer Muse* and *Shiek*, both aground off
Kito Daito Shima. While *Tulare* directed the operation,
Princeton (CVS–37) arrived on the scene and contributed her Marine helicopters which plucked the survivors from the stranded ships.

Soon after reaching Okinawa, *Tulare* participated in
Operation "Warm Up," with other units of Amphibious
Squadron 3. On 16 November 1961, the ship departed

Tulare (LKA–112) in the Pacific early in 1969.   (K–67590)

the Far East for the west coast and arrived at San Diego on 12 December 1961.

On 6 October 1962, *Tulare* sailed for her fifth tour in the Orient. Five days out, she assumed new duties as an acting amphibious assault ship for Amphibious Squadron 3, after *Iwo Jima* (LPH–2) had received a summons to the Atlantic Fleet during the Cuban Missile Crisis. Operating in this capacity for two weeks, the attack cargo ship steamed for Subic Bay where she loaded all supplies and ammunition originally earmarked for *Iwo Jima*. Primed for action, *Tulare* remained on alert for the first two months of the deployment. The easing of tensions, however, allowed the ship to return to a routine operating schedule. She later took part in SEATO Operation "Jungle Drum II" off Thailand, before visiting Nagasaki, Sasebo, and Yokosuka in March and April of 1963.

She returned to the west coast in the middle of April for overhaul and local operations in the San Diego area, including various phases of amphibious, underway, and operational readiness training. Operations "Pine Tree" and "Cherry Tree" occupied her during the spring of 1964, before she departed the west coast on 18 June for her sixth deployment to the western Pacific.

After initial routine cruising, *Tulare* evaded typhoons in late July and early August before tensions flared suddenly in Southeast Asia. North Vietnamese torpedo boats attacked *Maddox* (DD–731) and *Turner Joy* (DD–951) on 2 and 4 August. *Tulare* quickly loaded marines and equipment, headed south, and joined Task Force (TF) 76 in maintaining a posture of readiness in the South China Sea. After returning to Okinawa and making a brief yard stop at Subic Bay in the Philippines, the attack cargo ship was ordered in November 1964 to the coast of Vietnam. However, before she could join American naval forces operating off Vietnam, her orders were changed to allow for local operations between Okinawa and Japan. About a fortnight later, the ship headed home and arrived off San Diego on 18 December.

Early in 1965, the ship participated in Exercise "Silver Lance," at Camp Pendleton, Calif., involving over 50 ships and 10,000 marines—the amphibious force gearing itself to conditions expected in a landing in Vietnam. After spending March and April 1965 in port at San Diego, the ship conducted underway and re-

fresher training in May. Then the stepped-up temp of operations in Southeast Asia resulted in the ship making two special voyages to Japan and Okinaw carrying troops and equipment.

Tulare returned to the west coast late in the yea but soon was deployed again to WestPac, departing th west coast on 12 February 1966 and steaming vi Hawaii to Chu Lai, Republic of Vietnam. She off-loade her cargo between 6 and 9 March and then proceede via Sasebo to Okinawa. The ship later returned to Ch Lai with 47 vehicles and 1,211 tons of other cargo. Fo the remainder of the year, she operated in the Orien visiting Buckner Bay, Okinawa; Subic Bay, Phili pines; Hong Kong; Bangkok, Thailand; Camranh Ba Phan Rang, and Tuy Hoa, Vietnam; and Yokosuka an Sasebo, Japan. During the year 1966, the ship steame a total of 43,397 miles; transported 2,076 men, 8,89 tons of cargo, and 483 vehicles; spent 50 days off Viet nam in combat-related operations; and conducted 1 underway replenishments to ships of the Fleet on dut in the South China Sea.

After being drydocked at Richmond, Calif., upon he return to the west coast, *Tulare* conducted trainin through late September before she got underway fo the Hawaiian Islands on 18 October. She deployed t WestPac with cruises to Subic Bay and Okinawa befor getting underway for Vietnam on 4 December. Sh relieved *Washtenaw County* (LST–1166) in providin logistic support for Amphibious Ready Group (ARG Alfa, at Danang on 6 December. Underway on the 8t she operated for the next 11 days with ARG Alfa befor being relieved by *Wexford County* (LST–1168) on 1 December. From Christmas of 1967, *Tulare* conducte lifts in support of marines battling North Vietnames and Viet Cong forces in the vicinity of Hue and Cu Vet. She returned to Subic Bay for overhaul on 2 January 1968.

As war continued to rage over devastated and trou bled Vietnam, the United States' involvement becam progressively deeper, and *Tulare* continued her su port operations until returning to the west coast lat in the summer of 1968. On 1 January 1969, the shi was redesignated LKA–112. She commenced her 10t WestPac deployment on 30 January 1969, departin San Diego in company with *Paul Revere* (LPA–248 *Belle Grove* (LSD–2), *Alamo* (LSD–33), *Cook* (APD 130), *Tortuga* (LSD–26), and *Valley Forge* (LPH–8) ound, via Pearl Harbor and Okinawa, for Southeast Asia. She arrived in her operating area off Vietnam n 7 March and delivered her cargo on the following ay before returning to sea to be replenished while nderway by *Caliente* (AO–53), *Niagara Falls* (AFS–), and *Mattaponi* (AO–41). She conducted local operaions between the Philippines and Okinawa before rriving in her operating area on 8 July to take part n three and one-half weeks of operations supporting peration "Brave Armada" while serving with the mphibious ready group.

After a run from Danang to San Diego, Calif., in hich she transported marines, she subsequently renezvoused with gunboats *Defiance* (PG–95) and *Welch* PG–93) on 27 October off the coast of Mexico before teaming to Acapulco, Mexico, early in November. She onducted local operations out of San Diego for the emainder of the year 1969 and ended the year prearing for an upcoming voyage to the Far East.

Getting underway from San Diego for Vietnam on 3 January 1970, *Tulare* steamed independently and rrived at Danang on 10 February. She embarked narines and loaded cargo soon after her arrival and eturned home on 2 March. The ship got underway rom San Diego for the Mare Island Naval Shipyard, allejo, Calif., on 23 March, and arrived there two ays later to commence overhaul. Drydocked from 22 April to 21 May, *Tulare* emerged from the shipyard n 30 June and got underway for the San Diego operting area and refresher training which lasted until 1 September. On 21 September, the ship commenced reparations for another WestPac deployment; and she ot underway on 2 November for Okinawa.

From 1971 to 1973, the ship conducted regular deploynents in support of American operations in Vietnam, p to the time of the American withdrawal from that rea in February 1973. Thereafter, she conducted troop nd cargo lifts to American bases on Okinawa, Japan, nd the Philippine Islands supporting the American nilitary presence in the Far East. In between these VestPac deployments, *Tulare* operated off the southern California coast, participating in local operations and mphibious exercises.

Removed from the active amphibious force on 1 July 975 and assigned to the Naval Reserve Force, *Tulare* perated from San Francisco, actively involved in the Naval Reserve Training Program, into 1979.

Tulare received 11 battle stars, one Navy Unit Comnendation, and one Meritorious Unit Commendation for ietnam service.

Tularosa

A river in western New Mexico which rises in Catron County, drains a portion of the Apache National Forest, nd flows into the San Francisco River. The name, ularosa—which is derived from the Spanish and means eddish reeds or willows—has also been given to a illage in Otero County, New Mexico.

AOG–43: dp. 2,270 (lim.); l. 220′6″; b. 37′; dr. 13′1″ (lim.); s. 10 k.; cpl. 62; a. 1 3″, 2 40mm., 3 20mm.; cl. *Sequatchie*; T. T1–M–A2)

Tularosa (AOG–43) was laid down under a Maritime Commission contract (MC hull 2069) on 31 Octoer 1944 at Bayonne, N.J., by the East Coast Shipards, Inc.; launched on 17 December 1944; sponsored y Miss Patricia Hefferman; acquired by the Navy on January 1945; and commissioned at the New York Navy Yard on 10 January 1945, Lt. (jg.) Rex Montomery Stagner in command.

On 4 February 1945, the new gasoline tanker teamed southward for shakedown training in the hesapeake Bay. On 9 March, she and *Dour* (AM–223) ot underway for Bermuda. On the 12th, she moored t St. George's Island to discharge barrels of kerosene which she had taken on at Norfolk. A few days later,

she called at Aruba to take on gasoline and diesel oil; then set her course, via the Panama Canal, for the west coast; and arrived at San Diego on 8 April. She departed the west coast on the 12th and reached Pearl Harbor on the 23d.

In May, she made a voyage to Canton Harbor, in the Phoenix Islands; and then returned to Pearl Harbor on the 21st. Throughout her time in the Pacific, *Tularosa* operated out of Oahu, carrying aviation fuel and gasoline to Johnston Island and Midway. She continued her duties into 1946, departed Pearl Harbor on 30 January, and returned to the west coast on 12 February.

Assigned to the 12th Naval District for disposition, *Tularosa* was stripped and was decommissioned on 23 April 1946. Her name was struck from the Navy list on 21 May 1946, and she was transferred to the Maritime Commission on 28 August.

Tulip

I

(ScGbt.: t. 183; l. 97′3″; b. 21′9″; dph. 9′6″; dr. 8′; cpl. 57; a. 2 24-pdrs., 1 20-pdr. P.r.)

Tulip—a wooden-hulled, steam lighthouse tender built at New York City in 1862 and 1863 as *Chih Kiang* by Jowett & Company for the Chinese Navy—was purchased by the Navy on 22 June 1863 at New York.

Renamed *Tulip* and refitted for service as a tug and gunboat, the screw steamer joined the Potomac River Flotilla in August 1863. That force patrolled the river protecting Union waterborne communications between the nation's capital and the port cities of the divided nation during the Civil War. She initially performed towing duties at the Washington Navy Yard, and then served with the flotilla in operations against Confederate forces in the Rappahannock. In the latter duties, the ship carried Federal troops and supported naval landing parties which from time to time went ashore for operations against Confederate traffic across the river.

As she continued this wartime riverine service into 1864, *Tulip* developed a defective starboard boiler. Comdr. Foxhall A. Parker, commanding the Potomac Flotilla, ordered the ship home to the Washington Navy Yard so that repairs could be made to correct her defective propulsion plant. *Tulip* got underway on 11 November with orders restricting her steaming on the port boiler only. Not long after departing from St. Inigoes Creek, St. Mary's County, Md., her engineers, against all orders, began supplying steam to the starboard boiler. When abreast Ragged Point, the boiler exploded and tore the fragile ship apart—killing 47 men instantly—of the 57-man complement. Of the 10 survivors, two died later as a result of the injuries received in the violent explosion which claimed the ship.

II

(Lht.: dp. 774; l. 190′0″; b. 30′0″; dr. 10′7″ (mean); dph. 16′0″; cpl. 32)

The second *Tulip*—a lighthouse tender completed in 1908 at Camden, N.J.—operated off the east coast for the Lighthouse Service. At the entry of the United States into World War I, the entire Lighthouse Service was incorporated into the Navy for the duration of hostilities. *Tulip* continued her east coast service under Navy control through the end of the war. *Tulip* was returned—with the entire Lighthouse Service—to the custody of the Department of Commerce on 1 July 1919.

Tullibee

Any of several whitefishes of central and northern North America.

I

(SS–284: dp. 1,525 (surf.), 2,424 (subm.); l. 311'6"; b. 27'2"; dr. 15'3"; s. 20.25 k. (surf.), 8.75 k. (subm.); cpl. 80; a. 10 21" tt., 1 4"; cl. *Gato*)

The first *Tullibee* (SS–284) was laid down on 1 April 1942 at Mare Island, Calif., by the Mare Island Navy Yard; launched on 11 November 1942; sponsored by Mrs. Kenneth C. Hurd; and commissioned on 15 February 1943, Comdr. Charles F. Brindupke in command.

Tullibee held shakedown training from 8 to 30 April and departed for Hawaii on 8 May. She arrived at Pearl Harbor on 15 May and held further training exercises in Hawaiian waters. Numerous air fitting leaks developed, and she was docked for repairs twice. When this proved ineffective, the submarine entered the navy yard until 11 July.

On 19 July, *Tullibee* got underway for the Western Caroline Islands and her first war patrol. On the 28th, she sighted a passenger-cargo ship, accompanied by an escort and an aircraft that prevented an American attack. On 5 August, the submarine began patrolling the Saipan-Truk traffic lanes. Five days later, she sighted smoke on the horizon which proved to be three freighters with an escort. *Tullibee* closed the range to 2,700 yards; fired one torpedo at the ship on the right and three at the vessel on the left. As the submarine fired the first torpedo, a ship rammed her and bent her number one periscope. She went deep and was depth charged by the escort as the ships sped away. As they had been set to run at a depth of 15 feet—too deep for the draft of the largest target—none of the torpedoes exploded.

On 14 August, *Tullibee* sighted a convoy of three freighters with an escort and began an end-around run to get into good attack position. She fired a torpedo from a range of 3,000 yards and went deep. It missed, and she returned to periscope depth to fire three torpedoes at the last ship. It apparently saw their wakes as it turned and combed them. The submarine again went deep. When she surfaced, the targets had escaped. On the 22d, *Tullibee* sighted a convoy of five ships escorted by two destroyers; closed to 2,000 yards; and fired three torpedoes at the nearest freighter. Two minutes later, she fired three more at another ship. As she went deep to avoid a destroyer heading her way, she heard one explosion. She soon heard the bursts of two more torpedo explosions, followed by breaking-up noises. When she surfaced, she sighted over 1,000 empty 50-gallon oil drums, but no ships. Postwar examination of Japanese records indicated that *Tullibee* had damaged one freighter and had sunk the passenger-cargo ship *Kaisho Maru*. The patrol terminated when the submarine reached Midway Island on 6 September.

On 28 September, *Tullibee* began her second war patrol. Her assigned area was in the East China Sea between the Ryukyus and the China coast. On 4 October, she sighted a convoy of nine passenger-cargo ships with three destroyer escorts. The submarine pulled well ahead of the convoy and tracked them until the next morning. At 0058, she fired a spread of three torpedoes at a large freighter with one hitting the target a minute later. Another spread of three from the bow tubes produced two bits on a heavily laden cargo ship. Minor explosions and breaking-up noises began immediately as *Chicago Maru* sank. Twelve days later, *Tullibee* contacted a convoy of seven ships with three escorts which later separated into two groups; one hugging the China coast and the other heading for Pescadores Channel. She attacked the largest ship in the last group with six torpedoes. One hit the target. The submarine began an end-around run and fired four torpedoes at another ship. Two torpedoes soon broached, and *Tullibee* broke off the attack. She went deep and rigged for silent running to evade the escorts. On 5 November, the submarine was running submerged near Okinoyerabu Shima when she sighted a large, three-story building on the island. She surfaced and fired 55 shells into the barracks before retiring at full spee[d]. She began the voyage back to Hawaii the next day a[nd] reached Pearl Harbor, via Midway, on the 16th. H[er] official score for this patrol was one passenger-carg[o] ship sunk, a tanker damaged, and a passenger-carg[o] ship damaged.

Tullibee's third patrol was in a wolf pack wit[h] *Halibut* (SS–232) and *Haddock* (SS–231). The tr[io] sortied from Pearl Harbor on 14 December 1943 f[or] the Marianas to intercept enemy shipping plying b[e-] tween Truk and Japan. On 2 January 1944, *Tullib[ee]* sighted a Japanese I-class submarine on the surfa[ce] and fired four torpedoes at a range of 3,000 yard[s.] The enemy saw the wakes and combed the four [of] them as *Tullibee* was forced deep by an enemy floa[t] plane which dropped six bombs.

On 19 January, *Haddock* reported that she had dam[-] aged the Japanese aircraft carrier *Unyo* which limpe[d] to Saipan. *Tullibee* sighted the carrier there on th[e] 25th, close ashore and well protected by escorts an[d] aircraft. The submarine remained on station for sever[al] days awaiting an opportunity to sink the carrie[r.] However, when she surfaced on the 28th, she learne[d] that the carrier had slipped away. Three days late[r,] the submarine made radar contact with two target[s.] She fired three torpedoes at what appeared to be [a] freighter and swung left to fire one at the escort. Th[e] first target, net tender *Hiro Maru*, took two hits, di[s-] integrated, and disappeared in about one minute. Th[e] torpedo fired at the escort missed, and the submarin[e] went deep to evade. *Tullibee* cleared the area the fo[l-] lowing day and returned to Pearl Harbor on [1] February.

On 5 March, *Tullibee* stood out of Pearl Harbor t[o] begin her fourth war patrol. Nine days later, she calle[d] at Midway to top off her fuel and then proceeded t[o] her patrol area in the Palaus. She was scheduled t[o] support carrier strikes against those islands on 30 an[d] 31 March. On 25 March, *Tullibee* arrived on statio[n] and began patrolling. The next day, she made rada[r] contact on a convoy consisting of a large passenge[r-] cargo ship, two medium-sized freighters, a destroye[r,] and two other escorts. The submarine made sever[al] surface runs on the transport but kept losing her [in] rain squalls. *Tullibee* finally closed to 3,000 yards an[d] fired two torpedoes from her bow tubes at the targe[t.] About two minutes later, the submarine was rocke[d] by a violent explosion. Gunner's Mate C. W. Kukye[n-] dall—on the bridge at the time—was knocked unco[n-] scious and thrown into the water. When Kukyendall[—] the sole survivor—regained consciousness, the su[b-] marine was gone. Apparently, one of her own torpedo[es] ran a circular course and sank the submarine whic[h] had launched it. *Tullibee* was struck from the Navy li[st] on 29 July 1944.

Tullibee received three battle stars for World War [II] service.

II

(SSN–597: dp. 2,317 (surf.), 2,640 (subm.); l. 273['] b. 23'7"; dr. 21'; s. 12.9 k. (surf.), 16 k. (subm.[)] cpl. 58; a. 4 tt.; cl. *Tullibee*)

The second *Tullibee* (SSN–597) was laid down o[n] 26 May 1958 at Groton, Conn., by the Electric Bo[at] Div. of the General Dynamics Corp.; launched on 2[7] April 1960; sponsored by Mrs. John F. Davidson, th[e] widow of Comdr. Charles F. Brindupke; and commi[s-] sioned on 9 November 1960, Comdr. Richard S. Jortber[g] in command.

Following her shakedown in January 1961, *Tullib[ee]* engaged in sonar evaluations and nuclear submarin[e] tactical exercises with Submarine Developmental Grou[p] 2, operating out of New London, Conn., into 196[2.] During this period, the ship visited Bermuda on sever[al] occasions, as well as San Juan, Puerto Rico.

In July 1964, *Tullibee* participated in fleet exercise[s] in antisubmarine warfare (ASW) tactics with NAT[O]

Tullibee (SSN–597), the only ship of her class.   (USN 1051125)

nits. The submarine resumed developmental work in
965 and operated in this capacity into the fall of that
ear. On 28 October, her home port was temporarily
hanged to Portsmouth, N.H., when the ship entered
he Portsmouth Naval Shipyard, Kittery, Maine, for
n extensive overhaul. She remained in drydock for 754
ays—emerging on 2 January 1968.

Shifted back to New London, *Tullibee* deployed to the
aribbean Sea in January 1969 following refresher
raining and continued developmental work during
969 and 1970. On 1 August 1970, *Tullibee* departed
ew London, bound for the Mediterranean and the
hip's first service with the 6th Fleet. During this
eriod, she took part in NATO and 6th Fleet exercises
nd made port visits to Athens, Greece; Naples, Italy;
nd Rota, Spain, before returning to New London on
4 December, having travelled some 20,000 miles in
35 days.

In early 1971, the submarine returned to develop-
ental exercises once more to work on SSN tactics
nd also made a port visit to Cape Canaveral, Fla.
articipating in a major NATO exercise in the western

Atlantic, *Tullibee* visited Halifax, Nova Scotia, before
she received the Meritorious Unit Commendation for
her contingency operations in the Mediterranean during
the previous year (from 9 September to 31 October
1970). For the remainder of the year 1971, *Tullibee*
operated in the western Atlantic on NATO and ASW
exercises. During this period, too, *Tullibee* received
the Arleigh Burke Fleet Trophy for significant improvement in the ship's battle efficiency and readiness for
that fiscal year.

The submarine conducted regular operations with the
Atlantic Fleet Submarine Force into 1974, operating
off the east coast and in the Caribbean. Following one
Caribbean cruise in the fall of 1974, *Tullibee* departed
New London on 28 April 1975 for her second deployment to the 6th Fleet. After operating in the Mediterranean into the fall of that year, the submarine returned to New London in October for an extended
period of upkeep.

Tullibee subsequently participated in sonar evaluation tests with HMS *Matapan* (D 43) in the Caribbean,
in two separate deployments between April and June

1976, before undergoing another extended upkeep period. The SSN conducted ASW operations and local operations into the fall of 1976, before she departed New London on 12 November for her third Mediterranean deployment. After serving in the 6th Fleet into the spring of 1977, she returned to her home port on 24 April. During the remainder of the year, *Tullibee* underwent three upkeep periods interspersed with ASW exercises off the east coast of the United States. The early months of 1978 were spent in preparation for her fourth Mediterranean deployment. Departing New London in March, the submarine conducted operations with various units of the 6th Fleet. The deployment was marred somewhat by a propulsion casualty which necessitated a two-month repair period spent at Rota, Spain. *Tullibee* returned to New London on 30 August. Operations out of that port took *Tullibee* into 1979.

Tullibee received a Meritorious Unit Commendation for her service with the 6th Fleet.

Tulsa

A city in Oklahoma.

(PG–22: dp. 1,760 (f.); l. 241'2''; b. 41'2½''; dr. 12'8''; s. 12.0 k.; cpl. 159; a. 3 4'', 2 3-pdrs.; cl. *Asheville*)

Tulsa (PG–22) was laid down on 9 December 1919 at Charleston, S.C., by the Charleston Navy Yard; launched on 25 August 1922; sponsored by Miss Dorothy V. McBirney; and commissioned there on 3 December 1923, Lt. Comdr. Robert M. Doyle, Jr., in temporary command. Lt. Comdr. Doyle assumed his regular duties as executive officer on 14 December 1923 when Comdr. MacGillivray Milne assumed command.

The patrol gunboat cleared Charleston on 19 January 1924, bound for the Caribbean to join the Special Service Squadron. She called at Key West, Fla., on 22 January, before proceeding to Baytown, Tex., where she took on fuel four days later.

The ship spent the next five years on station in Central American waters, "showing the flag" and calling at such places as Tuxpan and Vera Cruz, Mexico; Guantanamo Bay, Cuba; and at ports in Puerto Rico and the Canal Zone. In between cruises with the Special Service Squadron, she returned to Boston, Mass., for yard repair work.

When civil strife broke out in Nicaragua in the late 1920's, details of marines and bluejackets from *Tulsa* landed to protect lives and preserve property. When not engaged in these duties, the patrol gunboat conducted routine training exercises in waters near the Panama Canal Zone and visited ports in Honduras.

En route for the west coast late in 1928, *Tulsa* transited the Panama Canal as she prepared for duty in the Far East. She departed San Francisco, Calif., on 24 January 1929, called at Honolulu and Guam, and proceeded to Manila.

Designated flagship of the South China Patrol on 1 April 1929, *Tulsa* operated out of Hong Kong, British Crown Colony; and Canton, China, for cruises up the Pearl River and along the south China coast. At Canton in May 1929, she witnessed the bombing of Chinese naval vessels by airplanes of the opposing faction in a Chinese civil war flaring at the time.

Relieved in June by *Mindanao* (PR–8) as flagship of the South China Patrol, she steamed up the coast to Shanghai, beginning a two-week deployment with the Yangtze Patrol in which she cruised as far upriver as Hankow. Assigned new duties as station ship at Tientsin in north China, *Tulsa* headed north in July 1929 to serve as a mobile source of information for the Commander in Chief, Asiatic Fleet (CINCAF).

She continued under the direct operational control of CINCAF into the 1930's, being later reassigned to the South China Patrol and observing conditions along the south China coast during the period following the outbreak of the undeclared Sino-Japanese war in Ju 1937. As tensions increased in the Orient in 1940 and 1941, Admiral Thomas C. Hart, CINCAF, incrementally reduced the Asiatic Fleet's presence in Chinese water. Withdrawn to the Philippines in May 1941, *Tul* joined the Inshore Patrol, guarding the sea approach to Manila Bay.

On 10 December 1941, two days after the outbreak war in the Philippines, a heavy Japanese air attack devastated Cavite, the base of the Asiatic Fleet, near Manila. Standing in from the Corregidor minefield *Tulsa* anchored off the burning base as the last Japanese planes departed. She called away all of her boat and sent fire and rescue parties ashore to bring what wounded could be rescued from the holocaust. A 1900, she recalled all hands that were ashore; an within hours, *Tulsa*, *Asheville* (PG–21), *Lark* (AM 21), and *Whippoorwill* (AM–35) retired toward Bali papan, Borneo.

After a brief stay at that port, she called at Maka sar before receiving orders to proceed to Surabay Java, in the Netherlands East Indies, where she spe Christmas. Then, steaming independently, she cruise to Tjilatjap, on the south coast of Java, where he landing force began to receive training in jungle wa fare. The plan to use *Tulsa*'s bluejackets as infantry a last-ditch defense of Java never progressed beyon the initial training stage, and her erstwhile grou troops returned to the ship as she was being outfitte to become a convoy escort vessel.

Equipped with a home-made depth charge rack co structed by the ship's crew, *Tulsa* now boasted an ant submarine capacity and began escorting merchantme along the south coast of Java to Tjilatjap, the only po on the island still out of reach of Japanese bomber While engaged on convoy duty in late February, *Tuls* received orders to proceed to a point 300 miles to th south of Java. En route, she learned that her missio included searching for survivors of *Langley* (AV–3 sunk on 26 February 1942. When she arrived at th scene, however, she found only traces of wreckage, b no survivors. Unbeknownst to *Tulsa*, *Langley*'s sur vivors had already been rescued by *Whipple* (DD–217 and *Edsall* (DD–219).

After this apparently fruitless rescue attempt, *Tuls* came upon the scene of the sinking of British merchan ship *City of Manchester*. *Whippoorwill* already had be gun rescue operations, yet needed medical facilitie which *Tulsa* had on board. The gunboat hove to an assisted the minesweeper in the lifesaving, then re turned to Tjilatjap where she awaited instruction ready for sea at a moment's notice.

With Java being rapidly encircled by the onrushin Japanese, orders to retire were not long in coming. O 1 March 1942. *Tulsa*, *Asheville*, *Lark*, and *Isabel* (PY 10) crept out of Tjilatjap, bound for Australia. Whil the other three ships steamed resolutely onward, *Ash ville* soon developed engine difficulties and fell behin only to be trapped and sunk by superior Japanese sur face forces.

Tulsa and her two companions arrived in Australia waters shortly thereafter. They were the last surfac ships of the Asiatic Fleet to survive the Japanese on slaught in the East Indies; and they escaped, by hairsbreadth, the fate which befell *Asheville*.

For the seven months following her arrival in Fre mantle, she engaged in routine patrols off the Austra lian coast before being refitted at Sydney in Octobe 1942. Here, she received British ASDIC, degaussin equipment, Y-guns, and 20 millimeter Oerlikons. Thu outfitted, she served once again as a convoy escort, occa sionally towing targets as well.

In the latter half of 1942, she was attached to Sub marine Forces, Southwest Pacific, and operated inde pendently out of Brisbane as a target for the sub marines out of Fremantle. She then gave submariner practice in making approaches and battle surfacing.

Tulsa (PG–22) at Hong Kong, April 1941.

With the beginning of the Buna-Gona offensives in New Guinea, *Tulsa* escorted PT boats to take part in that campaign and operated between Milne Bay, New Guinea, and Cairns, Australia. When the PT boat base at Kona Kope, on the southeastern shores of Milne Bay, was established in November 1942, *Tulsa* brought in much-needed equipment to aid in the operations being conducted from that base. But five days before Christmas 1942, *Tulsa* grounded on an uncharted pinnacle and damaged her ASDIC gear, necessitating a return to yard facilities for repairs.

Soon returning to the war zone, she resumed patrols off Milne Bay. On the night of 20 January 1943, six Japanese bombers attacked the ship. In the short, sharp action which followed, *Tulsa* put up a spirited defense with her 3-inch and 20-millimeter antiaircraft battery, driving off the attackers with no damage to herself, while dodging 12 bombs.

For the remainder of 1943, she continued operating in the New Guinea-Australian area, tending PT boats, escorting supply ships, and serving as flagship of the 7th Fleet. On one occasion while serving as a PT boat tender, *Tulsa* towed *PT–109*, later commanded by Lt. (jg.) John F. Kennedy, USNR, future President of the United States.

After a major overhaul in December 1943, she resumed operations in the Milne Bay-Cape Cretin area. She departed the bay on 8 January 1944, with a fuel barge in tow, en route to Cape Cretin. There, she joined HMAS *Arunta*, USS *LST–453*, and SS *Mulcra*, to serve as headquarters ship for Capt. Bern C. Anderson, Commander, Task Unit 76.5.3.

Under the control of Commander, Escorts and Minecraft Squadrons, 7th Fleet, she served in the Finschhafen-Buna area and participated in the Hollandia strike on 26 April 1944 and the Wakde landing on 17 May. She then continued in her role of escort vessel and patrol craft in the New Guinea-Australia area before proceeding to the Philippines in November 1944.

Returning to the scene of her hurried departure nearly four years before, *Tulsa* continued operations with the 7th Fleet in the Philippines. On 18 December 1944, she was renamed *Tacloban*, after a town on the island of Leyte, where American forces had landed a scant two months earlier.

As the United States Navy swept northward towards the Japanese home islands, and fierce fighting ensued on Okinawa and Iwo Jima, *Tacloban* performed the necessary tasks of convoy escort and local patrol vessel at fleet anchorages. On 26 August 1945, she was detached from duty with the Local Defense Force, Macajalar Bay, on the northwestern coast of Mindanao, and sent to Leyte. Arriving a week later, she received orders to accompany *Ingham* (WPG–35) and *LCI–230* to Buckner Bay, Okinawa.

On 7 September, en route to her destination, *Tacloban* was slowed by an overheated bearing, and her speed dropped to 3.1 knots. Left to proceed in company with *LCI–230*, *Tacloban* limped into Buckner Bay on 13 September. Task Force 74, to which she had been attached, sailed for Shanghai, China, two days later; but *Tacloban*, an "Old China Hand," could not make the trip and remained at Buckner Bay.

Following voyage repairs, she continued across the Pacific and arrived at Pearl Harbor on 18 December 1945. Thirteen days later, she headed for the California coast and arrived at San Francisco, Calif., on 10 January 1946.

Aged and worn, she was decommissioned on 6 March 1946; struck from the Navy list on 17 April; and turned over to the War Shipping Administration, Maritime Commission, on 12 October 1946, for disposal.

Tulsa received two battle stars for her World War II service.

On 27 November 1944, the name *Tulsa* was assigned to CA–129, an *Oregon City*-class heavy cruiser to be built at Quincy, Mass., by the Bethlehem Steel Company's Fore River Plant. However, on 12 August 1945 —before the ship's keel had been laid—the contract for her construction was cancelled.

Tuluran

A small island located just off the northwestern shore of Palawan Island in the Philippine Archipelago.

(AG–46: dp. 4,500 (lim.); l. 261'0''; b. 43'6''; dr. 18'8'' (lim.); s. 9.0 k.; cpl. 45; a. 1 3'', 3 20mm.)

Anna Shafer—a cargo ship built in 1917 at Toledo, Ohio, by the Toledo Shipbuilding Co. and renamed *Tuluran* on 6 May 1942—was acquired by the Navy through the War Shipping Administration and designated AG–46 on 16 October 1942; completed conversion at the General Engineering & Drydock Co., Alameda, Calif., on 8 December 1942; and commissioned at San Francisco on 11 December 1942, Lt. F. G. Isbell, USNR, in command.

Three days later, *Tuluran* joined the Pacific Fleet Service Force. On Christmas Eve, the ship stood out of San Francisco, bound for the South Pacific. After stopping at Pearl Harbor from 6 January to 22 February 1943, *Tuluran* continued on to Samoa, arriving in Tutuila on the 28th. She operated at Samoa for the next nine months before departing Tutuila on 26 November bound for the United States. After a one-day stop at Pearl Harbor on 11 December, she continued on to San Diego, Calif., where she arrived on 23 December. For the next four months, *Tuluran* underwent an extensive overhaul.

On 19 April 1944, *Tuluran* departed the west coast to return to the South Pacific and duty shuttling cargo between bases in the rear areas of the war zone. She stopped at Pearl Harbor from 29 April to 2 May and returned to Tutuila on 13 May. This time, however, she only remained overnight and, the following day, resumed her voyage. The cargo ship reached the New Hebrides Islands on the 21st. Eight days later, *Tuluran* departed Espiritu Santo to deliver cargo to the southern Solomons. She reached Guadalcanal on 5 June and remained there until the 20th when she headed back to the New Hebrides, arriving at Espiritu Santo on 3 July. She remained until early August when she moved to the New Guinea area where she operated from 17 August until the beginning of October, when she steamed via Espiritu Santo to the Solomons. After serving at Guadalcanal until mid-November, the ship made her first voyage to the Central Pacific.

Following visits to Saipan in the Mariana Islands and to Peleliu in the Palaus, she returned to the southwestern Pacific in mid-December. She visited the Russell Island subgroup in the Solomons from 17 to 19 December and spent a month at Noumea, New Caledonia, from 24 December 1944 to 24 January 1945, before returning to Espiritu Santo on the 27th. She departed the New Hebrides once more on 19 February and headed back to the Solomon Islands, where she operated for the next two months. During that tour of duty, she returned to Guadalcanal first and then visited the Treasury subgroup, Bougainville, the Green Islands, and the Russells again as well as making a side trip to Emirau Island.

On 3 April, the cargo ship departed the Russell subgroup and headed back to the Central Pacific. For the remainder of the war, *Tuluran* carried cargo between the American bases and anchorages established at various atolls in the Marshalls, Carolines, and Marianas. Her itinerary over the last five months of the war included Eniwetok, Ulithi, Peleliu, Guam, and Saipan. On 8 August, a week before the cessation of hostilities, *Tuluran* stood out of Eniwetok bound for Hawaii. Japan capitulated a week before the ship arrived in Pearl Harbor. *Tuluran* spent three days at Oahu and then continued her voyage east on 24 August.

On 3 September, she entered San Francisco; and, on 20 December 1945, *Tuluran* was decommissioned. She was stripped of usable materiél at Mare Island Naval Shipyard. Her name was struck from the Navy list on 8 January 1946, and the Commandant, 12th Naval District, turned her over to the Maritime Commission for final disposition on 1 July 1946. On 26 December, she was sold to the American Iron & Metal Co. and subsequently scrapped.

Tumult

(AM–127: dp. 890; l. 221'2"; dr. 10'9"; s. 18.1 k.; cpl. 102; a. 2 3", 6 20mm., 2 .30-cal. mg., 2 dct., 4 dcp.; cl. *Auk*)

Tumult was laid down on 21 July 1941 at Chickasaw, Ala.. by the Gulf Shipbuilding Corp.; launched on 19 April 1942; sponsored by Mrs. D. M. Pierce; and commissioned on 27 February 1943, Comdr. Charles E. Judge, USNR, in command.

Following tests and fitting out, *Tumult* began escort duties on the Eastern Sea Frontier late in March 1943. In April, the new minesweeper participated in antisubmarine warfare training out of Key West. On the 21st, she began minesweeping, fueling, and antiaircraft drills in company with other minesweepers on Virginia's York River. Then, on the 24th, she got underway for Bermuda and searched en route for survivors from the freighter *Santa Catalina* which had been sunk. *Tumult* discovered debris and a life ring on the 26th but failed to find any survivors.

Following repairs at Norfolk, the minesweeper escorted a group of small coastal transports which departed from Charleston on 15 May. The short voyage to Key West afforded her practice in escort procedures. *Tumult* got underway again on the 20th and set her course for the Panama Canal and the Pacific. Early in June, she paused briefly at Manzanillo, Mexico, to obtain emergency medical aid for a member of her crew and then continued on to San Diego. Provisioning, exercises, and repairs there occupied the remainder of June and most of July. On 21 July, the minesweeper got underway for San Franciscisco where she remained throughout most of August. On the 28th, she finally set course for the Pacific war zone, escorting a convoy of vulnerable, slow-moving, cargo vessels which pulled a section of portable dock *ABSD–1*. *Tumult* spent the entire month of September shepherding these awkward charges across the Pacific. On 2 October, having safely delivered the convoy, *Tumult* anchored at Espiritu Santo.

Throughout the remainder of 1943 and into 1944, *Tumult* escorted convoys among the Solomon Islands and between the Solomons and New Caledonia. Short periods of availability at Espiritu Santo and minesweeping exercises off Savo Island varied the sweeper's duties until late in June when she departed Port Purvis for a week of recreation and rehabilitation in Sydney, Australia. In July, she returned to the Solomons to resume the familiar routine of convoy protection.

Late in August, she participated in tactical maneuvers and minesweeping exercises in the Russells preparing for the impending assault on the Palaus. Underway from Guadalcanal on 8 September, *Tumult* screened her task group on station until her arrival off Peleliu on D-day, 15 September 1944. Early that morning, she began sweeps off Angaur Island and, during the days which followed, alternated minesweeping duties with patrolling and screening of the transport area.

Tumult got underway from Peleliu on 19 September and set her course for yet another island strike—the assault on Ulithi. She arrived off the atoll on 21 September and, through the following days, swept for mines to prepare this prize anchorage for use by American vessels. On 23 September, the day of the unopposed landings, she swept 21 mines before a contact mine fouled her sweep gear and forced her to retire to the disposal area to rid herself of both her port sweeping gear and the otherwise inextricable, offending mine. *Tumult* departed Ulithi on 25 September with a convoy of transports bound for Dutch New Guinea.

After repairs, she departed Manus on 10 October 1944 with a sweeping unit of TG 77.5 bound for the Philippines. On the 17th, *Tumult* began sweeping Surigao Strait in gale force winds; and on the 19th—the day before General MacArthur's landing on Leyte—she swept 26 contact mines which attested to the thoroughness of the Japanese defenses. On the 23d, she anchored in the tranport area of Leyte Gulf. In the days that followed, Japanese air raiders kept antiaircraft crews busy; and, on the 25th, *Tumult*'s gunners scored a hit on a "Val" which went down in flames two miles off the port quarter. The next day, *Tumult* fired on 11 Japanese planes and had reason to thank her luck as a bomb dropped 300 yards away off her starboard bow. Later that day, she splashed a "Sally" which went down one mile off her port bow. On the 28th, *Tumult* got underway for Manus.

After repairs at Seeadler Harbor, she set her course eastward and steamed via Pearl Harbor and San Francisco to Portland, Oreg., and arrived there on 7 December. *Tumult* underwent overhaul and shakedown on the west coast; then departed Long Beach on 23 April 1945. She arrived at Pearl Harbor on 1 May for a week of exercises before rendezvousing with a convoy bound for the Marianas. On 22 May, she arrived at Guam but soon was underway again with a slow-moving convoy steaming for Okinawa. On 4 June, typhoon winds forced the convoy, whose tows and tugs were experiencing extreme difficulty in holding course, to disperse. Two days elapsed before rendezvous with the last of the stragglers had been achieved. On the 9th, *Tumult* screened the convoy as it entered Buckner Bay, and then she proceeded on to Kerama Retto.

On the 11th, the minesweeper began patrolling off Okinawa. As she steamed on station on the evening of the 16th, explosions rent the night, and fire illuminated the horizon some eight miles away as destroyer *Twiggs* (DD–591) went down, the victim of a kamikaze. *Tumult* continued on picket off Okinawa until 30 June, with only brief respites at Kerama Retto for availability and provisioning. She then participated in four days of exercises before setting course for sweeps in area "Juneau" of the East China Sea. On 17 July, *Tumult* was provisioning at Buckner Bay when a typhoon warning prompted her to depart on short notice, leaving behind her navigator and engineering officer as she headed out to sea. For three days, she steamed northward outdistancing the typhoon; then returned to Okinawa to complete her interrupted logistic tasks.

As the war ended, *Tumult* was sweeping in area "Skagway" off the coast of Kyushu, Japan. A few days later, she rendezvoused with the 3d Fleet as it steamed northward. On 28 August, *Tumult* and three other minesweepers swept past the headlands of Tokyo Bay and into the harbor. The once busy Japanese port presented a bleak and unnervingly quiet appearance. Only a single battleship, *Nagato*, and a few smaller vessels remained; and a lone beached destroyer added to the desolation of the scene, as the victorious American ships entered the harbor.

Tumult immediately began sweeping the anchorage and, in the following days, helped to remove minefields at the harbor entrance. During most of September, she swept off the eastern coast of Honshu, clearing Sagami Wan and Ishinomaki Wan. While the minesweeper was anchored in Tokyo harbor on the 27th, a motor whaleboat capsized nearby in heavy seas. *Tumult* launched her own whaleboat and rescued 20 survivors from the stormy waters of the bay. Early in October, the minesweeper sat out a typhoon in Tokyo Bay; then got underway for Sasebo where she stopped before departing Japan for sweeps in area "Klondike" in the Yellow Sea.

On 30 October, accidental engine room flooding left one of *Tumult*'s main propulsion motors inoperable, stopping her port shaft. On the first day of November, she headed for Japan and underwent repairs at Sasebo until the end of the year. In January 1946, she steamed via Eniwetok and Pearl Harbor to San Pedro, Calif., arriving there on 15 February. She departed the west coast on 3 March and proceeded via the Panama Canal to Charleston, S.C.

In June, she made a training cruise out of Jacksonville, Fla., and spent the rest of 1946 and most of 1947 operating along the east coast. In November of the latter year, she varied her peacetime duties with minesweeping off Argentia, Newfoundland.

From January 1948 until July 1952, *Tumult* continued to operate out of Atlantic ports and made three Caribbean cruises. On 25 August 1952, *Tumult* departed Charleston with Minesweeper Division 82, setting her course for the British Isles. In ensuing months, the veteran minesweeper participated in NATO exercises and visited many Mediterranean ports. She returned to Charleston on 7 February 1953 and resumed her duties out of east coast ports, which she continued until 21 July 1954 when she arrived at Orange, Tex., for inactivation.

Two months later, on 21 September 1954, *Tumult* was placed out of commission. On 7 February 1955, she was redesignated a steel-hulled fleet minesweeper (MSF–127). Her name was struck from the Navy list on 1 May 1967. Her hulk was later purchased by the Southern Scrap Metal Co., Ltd., New Orleans, La.

Tumult received five battle stars for World War II service.

Tuna

Any of numerous large, vigorous, spiny-finned fishes including some highly esteemed for sport and food.

Submarine No. 27 was laid down as *Tuna* on 20 October 1909; however, on 17 November 1911, she was renamed *G–2* (*q.v.*) and served in the Navy under that name.

I

(SP–664: t. 81 (gross); l. 94'0''; b. 16'0''; dr. 4'0'' (mean); s. 12 k.; cpl. 19; a. 1 1-pdr., 1 mg.)

The first *Tuna* (SP–664)—a motor yacht built in 1911 at Baltimore, Md., by the Neilson Yacht Building Co.—was acquired under free lease from Mr. Edward L. Welch of Philadelphia, Pa., on 11 June 1917 and was commissioned on 12 June 1917. During World War I, *Tuna* was assigned to the Block Island section base in the 2d Naval District and patrolled the coastline between Long Island and Martha's Vineyard. On 11 January 1919, she was returned to her owner, and her name was struck from the Navy list.

II

(SS–203: dp. 1,475 (surf.), 2,370 (subm.); l. 307'2''; b. 27'3''; dr. 13'3'' (mean); s. 20 k. (surf.), 8.75 k. (subm.); cpl. 59; a. 10 21'' tt., 1 3'', 2 .50-cal. mg., 2 .30-cal. mg.; cl. *Tambor*)

The second *Tuna* (SS–203) was laid down on 19 July 1939 at Vallejo, Calif., by the Mare Island Navy Yard; launched on 2 October 1940; sponsored by Mrs. Wilhelm L. Friedell; and commissioned on 2 January 1941, Lt. Comdr. J. J. Crane in command.

Tuna departed San Diego, Calif., on 19 May 1941 for Pearl Harbor and shakedown training. Operations in Hawaiian waters revealed that the submarine's torpedo tubes were misaligned. This problem necessitated her returning to Mare Island for repairs. When the Japanese attacked Pearl Harbor on 7 December 1941, *Tuna* lay in drydock at Mare Island. She set out for Pearl Harbor on 7 January 1942.

The first of *Tuna*'s 13 war patrols lasted from 25 January to 21 March 1942, as she roved the waters of the East China Sea. On 4 March off Kyushu, a 4,000-ton cargo ship steamed into the crosshairs of *Tuna*'s periscope. Soon after, the *maru* disappeared beneath the waves as *Tuna*'s first kill. For the rest of the cruise, however, hunting was poor, and the unidentified *maru* remained the submarine's only victim during her initial war patrol.

Standing out of Pearl Harbor on 14 April, *Tuna* once again set her course towards the Japanese home islands and the hunting off Honshu. She added another score to her tally by sinking the 805-ton cargo ship,

Toyohara Maru, on 15 May before returning to Pearl Harbor on 16 June.

Following refit, *Tuna* became Task Unit 8.5.12, with orders to proceed to the Aleutian Islands. This third war patrol commenced on 13 July, but her only contact with the Japanese came on 9 August when *Tuna* sighted a Japanese I-boat on the surface. She lost it shortly thereafter in heavy weather. Later in the month, she supported the Army occupation of Adak Island by transporting a colonel and six enlisted men from Dutch Harbor to Kuluk Bay between 25 and 27 August. She returned to Pearl Harbor on 5 September.

After routine overhaul, *Tuna* set out from Pearl Harbor on 9 November. She made only one contact during her fourth war patrol, firing two torpedoes at a Japanese destroyer operating off New Georgia Island on 12 December. Both missed their mark. Three days after Christmas 1942, *Tuna* arrived at her new base, Brisbane, Australia.

Setting out again on 18 January 1943 to begin patrol number five, she arrived in waters off the east coast of Vella LaVella six days later. Expending 16 torpedoes in five futile daylight attacks, *Tuna* pressed home determined forays only to be driven deep by intense enemy antisubmarine countermeasures. Kept on station between New Ireland and Buka after 11 February, *Tuna* launched further attacks—but from excessive ranges—which only resulted in still more frustration for *Tuna*'s submariners. Dispatched next to interdict traffic from reinforcing Vila Plantation and Munda, *Tuna* remained luckless and was forced deep and endured depth-charge attacks before ending the patrol on 7 February.

After refitting at Brisbane, *Tuna* set out on her sixth war patrol on 4 March to take up a position in the Bismarck Archipelago, off Lyra Reef, on the northeast side of New Ireland. En route, she patrolled west of Bougainville. On 16 March, she received orders to shift her position to a point southeast of a line between Mussau and Manus Islands in the Admiralties. Late in the afternoon of 29 March, she sighted a convoy of four merchantmen, with two escort ships and two aircraft. After stalking the convoy all night, *Tuna* attacked the following morning, firing three torpedoes at the largest vessel. Two hits, and the 4,697-ton *Kurohime Maru* plunged to the bottom.

On 4 April, *Tuna* changed patrol zones, prowling now to the northwest of the Manus-Mussau line in the East Caroline Basin on the traffic lanes to Rabaul. After no further attack opportunities developed, *Tuna* returned to Brisbane on 20 April.

On 19 May, en route to her war patrol station for the seventh patrol, *Tuna* came under attack by a Japanese submarine which fired one torpedo at the American ship before breaking off the attack. After that brush with destruction, *Tuna* prepared to bombard Wakde Island with her deck guns; but the presence of Japanese subchasers forced a change in plans.

On 29 July 1943, as *Tuna* set out from Brisbane on her eighth patrol, a Royal Australian Air Force patrol bomber attacked her, dropping three bombs close aboard. The resultant damage necessitated 17 days of major repairs at Brisbane, delaying her departure for the eighth patrol until 21 August. Once on station, two attack opportunities presented themselves, but neither one bore fruit.

Arriving back at Fremantle on 14 October, *Tuna* refitted alongside *Pelias* (AS–14) before proceeding on her ninth patrol which commenced on 7 November. After transiting the Molucca Strait, *Tuna* prowled in the Java and Flores Seas. Attacking a freighter in a rain squall on 21 November, *Tuna* launched four torpedoes; but only one hit the enemy merchantman. On 12 December, the submarine had better luck. The 5,484-ton cargo ship *Tosei Maru* fell victim to her torpedoes, becoming the largest kill in *Tuna*'s war career to that date.

Following her ninth patrol, *Tuna* proceeded across the Pacific to Hunters Point, Calif., where she arrived on 6 April for a major overhaul. After refitting, she headed for Pearl Harbor, her base of operations for war patrol number 10. Departing Pearl Harbor on 24 April, she soon commenced roving the Palaus. On 4 May, *Tuna* sighted a 100-ton trawler. Bound for Wake Island with classified documents on board, *Takima Maru* put up a fight when taken under fire by the submarine's two 20-millimeter guns. In the face of the returned fire, *Tuna* opened up with her 3-inch deck gun and scored a hit on the first salvo, holing *Takima Maru* near the stern. Ten minutes later, the trawler settled beneath the waves, stern first, leaving the waters littered with secret papers and the surviving Japanese.

Meanwhile, *Haddock* (SS–231) arrived on the scene and assisted in the pickup of confidential documents and prisoners. Each submarine picked up 30 documents; *Tuna* fished out three prisoners—one of whom died later. The two remaining prisoners were transferred to *Haddock*.

Ten days later, *Tuna* bombarded the phosphate works on Fais Island with 24 rounds from her deck gun. After the remainder of her patrol proved fruitless, the submarine returned to the Marshall Islands arriving at Majuro Atoll on 21 June.

After commencing her 11th patrol upon departing Majuro on 15 July, *Tuna* roamed the sea lanes of the Japanese home islands, off Shikoku and Kyushu. Her radar picked up tempting targets, but bad luck continued to dog the ship's efforts to make contact and launch attacks. On occasion, the superior surface speed of the hunted enabled it to easily outrun the hunter, and good antisubmarine measures by the Japanese escort ships forced *Tuna* to proceed cautiously. On 5 September, she arrived at Pearl Harbor empty-handed.

Following refit, *Tuna* departed Pearl Harbor on 8 October, bound for the western Pacific. In conjunction with Operation "King Two," the invasion and liberation of the Philippine Islands, *Tuna* operated in a wolf pack, "Roach's Raiders," in company with *Haddock* and *Halibut* (SS–232). During this 12th patrol, *Tuna* contacted seven ships; but made only one attack, "unsuccessful," before arriving at Saipan on 2 December.

Tuna's final war patrol began on 6 January as she left Saipan to take position off the west coast of Borneo. From 28 to 30 January 1945, *Tuna* conducted a special mission, reconnoitering the northeast coast of Borneo. She did not attempt a landing due to enemy activity. From 2 to 4 March, *Tuna* accomplished her second special mission of the patrol, landing personnel and 4,400 pounds of stores near Labuk Bay. During the patrol, she sighted no contacts deemed worthy of torpedo fire, and *Tuna* returned to Fremantle on 13 March 1945.

Thereafter, based at Fremantle, *Tuna* operated on training duty until she sailed for Leyte on 13 April. The submarine touched at Subic Bay and Saipan before returning to Pearl Harbor on 5 September. From there, she proceeded to San Francisco, arriving on 14 September.

After moving through the Panama Canal to the east coast, *Tuna* remained in commission, in the inactive fleet, to assist in the maintenance and security of other submarines sent to Portsmouth, N.H., for tests. In this capacity, she served with Submarine Division 162, Submarine Squadron 16, Inactive Fleet, New London Group, until she was selected as a target vessel for the upcoming atomic bomb tests at Bikini Atoll in the Marshall Islands.

After once again transiting the Panama Canal, *Tuna* arrived at Pearl Harbor on 2 March 1946 and reported for duty with Commander, Joint Task Force 1. In company with *Skipjack* (SS–184), *Skate* (SS–305), and *Searaven* (SS–196), *Tuna* departed Pearl Harbor on 21 May 1946.

Upon her arrival at Bikini Atoll, nine days later, *Tuna* was assigned a place among the target vessels anchored in the atoll. The first bomb was detonated on

1 July 1946, and the second followed 24 days later. Receiving only superficial damage, *Tuna* departed for Kwajalein on 22 August 1946 en route to Pearl Harbor and the west coast. On 5 September, she arrived in Hawaiian waters, mooring at the submarine base.

Underway for the west coast on 7 October, she arrived at the Mare Island Naval Shipyard a week later, where she moored with the 19th Fleet. Scheduled for decommissioning on 11 December 1946, she was retained as a radiological laboratory unit and subjected to numerous radiological and structural studies while remaining at Mare Island. No preservation work was undertaken on the ship, and she was decommissioned on 11 December 1946. On 20 September 1948, *Tekesta* (ATF–93) towed *Tuna* from Mare Island for the submarine's "last patrol." On 24 September 1948, *Tuna* was sunk in 1,160 fathoms of water off the west coast and struck from the Navy list on 21 October 1948.

Tuna received seven battle stars for her World War II service.

Tunica

A small Indian tribe which lived on the lower Mississippi until the beginning of the 18th century. Pressure from the Chickasaws forced them to migrate to the northwestern portion of what is today the state of Mississippi. By the late 19th century, the Tunicas had all vanished from that area.

(ATA–178: dp. 835 (tl.); l. 143'0''; b. 33'10''; dr. 13'2''; s. 13.0 k. (tl.); cpl. 45; a. 1 3''; cl. *ATA–121*)

ATA–178 was laid down on 10 May 1944 at Orange, Tex., by the Levingston Shipbuilding Co.; launched on 15 June 1944; and commissioned on 15 September 1944, Lt. J. L. Robinson in command.

Late in September, *ATA–178* picked up two barges at New Orleans for towing to Hawaii. The tug transited the Panama Canal, stopped at San Diego, and reached Pearl Harbor on 10 December 1944. After a brief layover in Hawaii, she departed Pearl Harbor to tow one of the 10 sections of a drydock to Guam, where she arrived on 14 January 1945.

Not long after her arrival in the Marianas, *ATA–178* was assigned to the Samoan Defense Command. Between 10 February and 28 May, she towed supply barges between various bases in the South Pacific. Late in May, *ATA–178* joined other tugs in towing bargeloads of equipment from the South Pacific to bases nearer to the active theaters of operations. During the final three months of the war, she called frequently at Guam, Leyte, Manus, Eniwetok, and Kwajalein to deliver equipment-laden barges.

Following the cessation of hostilities, she reported to Noumea, New Caledonia, where she underwent her first major overhaul. When that was completed, she resumed her duties in support of the disestablishment of South Pacific bases until April 1946. On the 24th, she departed Tutuila, Samoa, and headed via Pearl Harbor to San Diego, where she arrived on 31 May. On 18 June, the tug stood out of San Diego for the east coast. She transited the canal during the second week in July and arrived in New York on 24 July. A week later, she headed south and reported for duty at Mayport, Fla., on 22 August. For the next 16 months, she towed inactivated ships between Mayport, Charleston, and Savannah. On 23 December 1947, *ATA–178* was placed out of commission and berthed with the Texas Group, Atlantic Reserve Fleet.

ATA–178 spent the remainder of her Navy career in reserve. On 16 July 1948, she was named *Tunica*. After almost 14 years of inactivity, *Tunica* was transferred to the Maritime Administration in October 1961 for lay-up with the National Defense Reserve Fleet at Beaumont, Tex. Eleven months later, on 1 September 1962, her name was struck from the Navy list. She was finally disposed of by the Maritime Administration sometime during fiscal year 1971.

Tunis

A seaport, the capital city of Tunisia, on the Mediterranean coast of North Africa.

Tunis was renamed *Aquila* (AK–47) (*q.v.*) on 3 September 1941.

Tunisien

Crosley (DE–108)—a *Cannon*-class destroyer escort laid down on 6 June 1943 at Wilmington, Del., by the Dravo Corp.—was slated for transfer to France on 11 February 1944; renamed *Tunisien*; and launched on 17 February 1944. Operating with the French Navy, she escorted a convoy carrying French troops for the assault on Toulon as a part of Operation "Dragoon," the invasion of southern France in August 1944. Later that year, she was with Convoy UGS–40 when it was attacked by more than 20 German bombers 50 miles east of Algiers on the evening of 11 May. *Tunisien* was permanently transferred to France under the Mutual Defense Assistance Program on 21 April 1952.

Tunny

Any of several oceanic fishes resembling the mackerel. The tunny, which is found in all warm seas, can reach a length of 10 feet and weigh in excess of 1,000 pounds.

I

(SS–282: dp. 1,525 (surf.), 2,424 (subm.); l. 311'8''; b. 27'3''; dr. 16'10'' (mean); s. 20.25 k. (surf.), 8.75 k. (subm.); cpl. 80; a. 10 21'' tt., 1 5'', 1 40mm., 1 20mm., 2 .50-cal. mg; cl. *Gato*)

The first *Tunny* (SS–282) was laid down on 10 November 1941 at Vallejo, Calif., by the Mare Island Navy Yard; launched on 30 June 1942; sponsored by Mrs. Frederick G. Crisp; and commissioned on 1 September 1942, Lt. Comdr. Elton Watters Grenfell in command.

Following shakedown training out of California ports, *Tunny* arrived in the Hawaiian Islands on 12 December 1942. After an additional week of training and two weeks of availability, she got underway from Submarine Base, Pearl Harbor, on 12 January 1943 for her first war patrol. For nearly a week, rough seas hampered the progress of the submarine. Then, as she approached the Ryukyus, sea traffic increased. Sightings of sampans became frequent, and *Tunny* often dove to avoid detection by suspicious looking trawlers.

At 0530 on the 26th, *Tunny* sighted masts and a stack over the horizon indicating a possible target. During the day, she lessened the distance between herself and her quarry; and, near dusk, she closed a 400-ton trawler. Finding the prey not worth a torpedo, the submarine surfaced and opened fire with her deck gun. Soon darkness forced her to discontinue the attack, and she continued on her way.

On the 29th, she began patrolling off Formosa. An hour and one-half before midnight on 31 January, her periscope at last disclosed a worthwhile target. A freighter approaching Takao Ko. *Tunny* fired two "fish" from her bow tubes, but the freighter made a radical change of course which enabled her to evade the lethal torpedoes. When her target counterattacked and dropped two depth charges, *Tunny* broke off the attack and submerged.

On the first day of February, *Tunny* set her course for the China coast, running on the surface. As darkness fell on the 2d, she was only hours from Hong Kong, expecting to make landfall on Tamkan Island by daybreak. At 2130, she made radar contact; and, through the night, drew closer to her as yet unseen quarry.

A light rain was falling and visibility was poor when, half an hour before morning twilight, *Tunny* began a radar approach. Rapidly shoaling water less than 20 fathoms deep and land masses on two sides of the submarine limited her maneuverability. At 2,200 yards, the extreme phosphorescence of the water illuminated her wake and betrayed her presence to the enemy ship, which began signalling the unidentified intruder with a blinker light. Despite her detection, *Tunny* continued the approach until she was only 1,000 yards from the target and then fired three torpedoes. The Japanese ship, now discernible as a loaded tanker, began to maneuver radically and opened fire on the submarine. Undeterred, *Tunny* submerged and continued the attack, firing a second volley from her stern tubes. One of these torpedoes hit the side of the tanker with a thud, but without explosion, and a small column of water erupted just forward of the tanker's bridge. Duds and prematures were a problem for American submarines early in 1943, and verification that this torpedo had indeed hit the tanker, but failed to detonate, was forthcoming when members of the tanker's crew dashed to the spot in question and began examining the impact area with flashlights. Despite continuous fire from the ship and the proximity of land, *Tunny* managed to stay within firing range of her target by travelling at full speed. After the tanker successfully evaded *Tunny*'s third salvo, the submarine fired a last torpedo from 1,600 yards as the intended victim reached the passage into Hong Kong. Following this disappointing conclusion to her attack, *Tunny* dove in anticipation of search planes which appeared within two hours and continued their surveillance throughout the day.

After dark on 3 February, while patrolling Lema Channel, *Tunny* made radar contact with a sizeable target. On this very dark night, visual identification was impossible; but, at 2005, the submarine approached to 900 yards and made a three-torpedo attack. The sound of the target's screws ceased immediately, and *Tunny* claimed to have sunk this unidentified ship which had been seen only on radar. When the submarine surfaced at daybreak the following day, the submariners discovered an unexpected visitor on deck—a six-foot black and yellow striped snake.

On the 4th, *Tunny* set her course for Swatow, keeping to the shoreline in hopes of intercepting shipping. En route, she passed a large hospital ship well marked and brilliantly lighted. On the 6th and 7th, *Tunny* patrolled off Swatow. Numerous junks plying the Formosa and Swatow banks at all hours added to the hazards imposed by shallow water and an inoperable fathometer and made it impossible for *Tunny* to approach the shore closer than six miles.

Early on the morning of 8 February, she went deep to avoid a plane revealed by radar. When she surfaced, she discovered a freighter 10,000 yards off her beam. She shadowed the target during the day and, after sunset, made her approach and launched two torpedoes from a distance of 830 yards. Due to bad runs, neither of these took effect, but they did alert the freighter, which opend fire on *Tunny*. The submarine fired two shots from her bow tubes, but one torpedo missed, and the other circled around to the right. *Tunny* then drew ahead for a surface approach and fired three more torpedoes. Two of these found the mark; but one put on an amazing show, veering sharply first to the left and then to the right, before hitting the target. The *Kusayama Maru*, a heavily-laden, 5,000-ton cargo ship, sank by the stern in 20 minutes; and *Tunny* had scored her first confirmed kill. As she proceeded on toward Takao, a searchlight suddenly pierced the dark not far ahead, and *Tunny* dove to avoid detection.

The next day, *Tunny* sighted a large transport. Undetected by two nearby patrol vessels and a plane, she made her approach and scored two hits on the transport with her remaining torpedoes. However, the ship did not sink and later left the area.

On 11 February, *Tunny* set her course for Midway. En route, she used a combination of 20-millimeter and 5-inch gunfire to sink a 100-ton fishing trawler. On the 20th, she made contact with the harbor escort and proceeded to moor at Midway, completing her first aggressive and successful patrol. She later continued on to Hawaii, arriving at Pearl Harbor on 24 February 1943.

After refitting by tender *Sperry* (AS–12) and three days of training, *Tunny* departed the Hawaiian Islands on 18 March, paused at Midway for replacement of her periscope, and got underway for Wake on the 24th. Later, Commander, Submarine Force, Pacific Fleet, would describe *Tunny*'s second war patrol as belonging "in that exceptional category of one of the outstandingly aggressive patrols of the war."

On 27 March 1943, *Tunny* arrived off Wake Island and operated within a 200-mile circle all day, flooding down the decks awash when within 30 miles of the island. Before dawn the next morning, she closed to within 10 miles of the Japanese-held island and watched as its awakening occupants turned on their lights. A motor torpedo boat and two patrol boats passed by less than 600 yards from the submarine without detecting her presence. Trailing these vessels, *Tunny* came upon a cargo ship; and all hands scrambled to battle stations. Shortly after sunrise, the submarine launched her attack, firing two torpedoes from a range of 700 yards. The first found its mark and blew the stern off the enemy ship, but the buoyancy of the lightly loaded vessel kept it afloat. *Tunny* was maneuvering at periscope depth to avoid depth charges dropped across her bow at a range of 300 yards when the first of several aerial bombs fell close aboard. The submarine dove to 280 feet. When she attempted to surface an hour later, *Tunny* was again driven down by an aerial adversary. Later in the morning, travelling submerged at 150 feet, she set her course for her assigned patrol area.

On 31 March, she entered he patrol area in the Carolines; and, on 1 April 1943, she conducted submerged patrols off North Pass, Truk, and later in the day on the Japanese naval base's western approaches. Failing to find any action in these areas, she surfaced late in the afternoon on 2 April and set her course for the channel between Puluwat and Pulap Islands. Later that day, as she patrolled off Alet Island, *Tunny* made radar contact with a ship dead ahead. Heading in for a flank attack, she sighted a *Momo*-class destroyer 1,000 yards astern of her chosen target. *Tunny* fired three torpedoes from 960 yards and noted a hit in the forward hold of the Japanese cargo ship before diving to 300 feet to avoid the attention of the destroyer. Minutes later, a series of nine depth charges tumbled down in search of the submarine, but exploded at too shallow a depth to achieve their purpose. Some 15 minutes later, as *Tunny* started up to take a look, she was jolted by a deep-set depth charge which caught her at 260 feet, but caused only minor damage—a small price to pay for the sinking of *Toyo Maru No. 2*. Before midnight, the destroyer gave up the search, and the submarine surfaced and set her course for the Namonuito group to the north.

Late on the 4th, *Tunny* headed west to intercept traffic reported north of McLaughlin Bank. On 7 April, while patrolling in that area, the submarine took advantage of a rain squall to approach within 1,000 yards of a radar-tracked target. She then fired two torpedoes at the *Kosei Maru*, an 8,000-ton passenger-cargo ship, scoring a hit amidships and one aft, and dove immediately to escape the inevitable wrath of the escorting *Hibiki*-class destroyer which had been patrolling just ahead of the now-stricken transport. The ensuing depth charge counterattack continued until the descroyer lost contact with the submarine in a heavy rain squall. Having added a third cargo ship to her list of kills, *Tunny* retired from the scene of the attack.

On the 8th, the submarine surfaced in a downpour to continue patrols north of West Fayu Island. Later that day, she set her course to intercept a convoy reported to be southwest of Truk. At 2228 on 9 April, she made radar contact with a formation less than three miles distant and went to four engines to maneuver into position for an attack. In a few minutes, the formation changed course, putting *Tunny* in position to slow down to two-thirds speed and head in, flooded down to decks awash to avoid detection. As the convoy became visible, *Tunny*'s commanding officer, Comdr. James A. Scott, could hardly believe his luck. On the starboard bow was a large aircraft carrier; to port, two auxiliary carriers; and on each bow of the formation, a destroyer. Given this perfect setup, *Tunny* maneuvered to swing the bow on twin targets, but her plans were disrupted when three small boats similar to motor torpedo boats appeared only 300 yards off her port bow. *Tunny* quickly dove to 40 feet, turned right, ninety degrees, and fired four torpedoes from her stern tubes at one of the auxiliary carriers from a distance of 880 yards. As she turned her attention to other targets, four torpedo explosions sounded through the night.

Signalling from her new target gave executive officer Lt. Comdr. Roger Keithly at the conn a final check on the target's bearing, and *Tunny* released a salvo of six torpedoes from her bow tubes at the large carrier. Her surprise attack completed, *Tunny* immediately dove amidst the cacophony of depth charges and churning screws. The depth charges rocked the submarine but did no damage; and the crackling and grinding noises heard throughout the ship, as well as on sonar, led those on board the submarine to believe that their lethal "fish" had found their mark. In all this noise and confusion, *Tunny* unobtrusively slipped away to the north. Later, examination of Japanese records showed that this attack was ruined by prematures and duds, and that damage to the enemy had been minor. However, the skill and daring with which the raid was conducted remained an example of excellence and prompted the Commander, Submarine Force, Pacific Fleet, to commend *Tunny*'s commander for his actions on this patrol as "an illustrious example of professional competence and military aggressiveness."

An hour and one-half after midnight on 10 April, the submarine surfaced and set her course to return to her patrol area. While approaching North Pass about 25 miles out of Truk on 11 April, *Tunny* dove when a searchlight suddenly broke the night, 500 yards ahead on the starboard bow. No depth charges followed, and the source of the light—not sizeable enough to be detected on radar—was presumed to be a small boat.

Early on the afternoon of the 11th, a contact, at first thought to be a patrol boat, turned out to be a Japanese submarine. The designation symbol of the enemy submarine was emblazoned on her conning tower, spelling out *I-9* in large white characters. Boldly taking the offensive, *Tunny* fired her three remaining forward "fish" at the submarine, only to see the vessel turn away and parallel the course of the death-dealing torpedoes. *Tunny* then began her own evasive procedures, going deep and away from the Japanese submersible—and none too soon. Minutes later, she tracked two torpedoes which passed harmlessly astern. An enemy plane added bombs to *Tunny*'s immediate concerns, but she rigged for silent running and weathered the attack by remaining submerged until after nightfall.

That same evening, as *Tunny* lay on the surface in the bright moonlight, charging her batteries, she made radar contact with a ship moving at 18 knots. Within minutes, the contact materialized into an enemy destroyer steaming on the starboard bow. *Tunny* dove to 44 feet and began to swing for a stern shot when the belligerent destroyer increased speed to a thundering 30 knots and headed in from a distance of less than 1,400 yards. As the submarine dove for 400 feet, the explosions of nine depth charges fairly close by pursued her. Silent running and a quick reversal of course eventually shook off the menacing destroyer, and *Tunny* returned to the surface after the moon set, noting only minor damage from the attack.

In the days that followed, *Tunny* patrolled off East Fayu Island and north of Mogami Bank before setting her course for Saipan on the 15th. Her surveillance of Magicienne Harbor disclosed that it was not in use. Seeking targets, the submarine passed through Saipan Channel and later discovered two cargo ships in Garapan Harbor. Prevented from attacking by the presence of intervening reefs, *Tunny* departed the area and moored in the lagoon at Midway on 23 April for a welcome rest. So aggressive had been her handling on this eventful patrol that not one of her firing ranges exceeded 1,000 yards. She was awarded the Presidential Unit Citation for this outstanding patrol.

After refitting at Midway, *Tunny* continue on to Hawaii for additional repairs. She departed Pearl Harbor on 25 May 1943 and, after fueling at Johnston Island, got underway on the 27th for Eniwetok. Her first contact with the enemy on this third war patrol came early in the afternoon on 31 May when she dove to avoid a radar contact whose speed identified it as a plane. As *Tunny* passed 300 feet, a bomb exploded over her after torpedo room breaking lights and thermometers, flooding the after torpedo tubes, and causing miscellaneous other damage. An unsatisfactory makeshift repair of the broken bridge speaker prompted a note in the war patrol report that "the only dependable communication system was the open hatch and a powerful set of lungs." Other repairs were completed before nightfall, and *Tunny* continued on her way. She patrolled off Eniwetok for two days; then moved on to her assigned area, arriving at Truk on 6 June.

As this patrol progressed, *Tunny* discovered that antisubmarine action by the Japanese at Truk had shifted to aerial detection. On 7 June, her first day of patrol, she was harassed by a single float biplane and an ineffectual Japanese destroyer. *Tunny* found the enemy biplanes a great nuisance, since her radar detected them late or not at all. Soon she came to regard the aircraft as an arch-enemy which thwarted attacks

Tunny (SSG–282) after her conversion to a missile submarine. The watertight hangar abaft her sail holds a *Regulus* cruise missile.

on convoys by hovering overhead and guiding possible targets around the submarine, out of firing range.

On 14 June, as *Tunny* cruised on the surface following a submerged patrol east of Murilo Island in the Hall group, one of her lookouts sighted a convoy bearing 090 degrees. Made up of two small freighters and a large transport and accompanied by two destroyers, the convoy was a tempting target. As *Tunny* made her approach, an unoberved escort vessel suddenly challenged her with a searchlight and several rounds of 4-inch fire which fell astern. The submarine dove to 300 feet but continued her approach. She then surfaced and fired four torpedoes at the transport from a range of 3,400 yards. Three explosions and a tremendous cloud of smoke and water over the target indicated that *Tunny* had damaged the enemy vessel. The submarine dove to avoid the escorts, but no depth charging ensued. Shortly after midnight, as she ran on the surface attempting to intercept the convoy, an undetected vessel fired shots which splashed astern; and *Tunny* dove again.

As June wore on, *Tunny* continued patrols as far as Saipan without success. On the 26th, she conducted routine and photographic reconnaissance of Saipan Harbor and Tinian Channel and, later that day, surfaced to patrol the Truk-Empire shipping lanes east of Rota Island. Patrolling off Harnum Point and Rota harbor on 28 June, *Tunny* sighted a converted gunboat zigzagging madly, went to battle stations, and dispatched the enemy vessel with a salvo of three torpedoes from 1,500 yards. Sighting an armed trawler bearing down on her, the submarine dove. Those on board felt the concussion of three sharp explosions close aboard, perhaps from aerial bombs, as *Tunny* went deep and rigged for silent running, maneuvering to avoid the trawler. Seconds later, two heavy explosions marked the death throes of *Tunny*'s most recent victim. *Tunny* was chased down again by the trawler when she attempted to surface an hour later. Returning to periscope depth some three hours after the attack, her commanding officer at the periscope was relieved to find no sign of the trawler, but his relief quickly turned to alarm when the periscope revealed a close-up of the bomb bay of a Mitsubishi 97 at 300 feet, directly overhead. This time *Tunny* waited four hours before surfacing again 13 miles from Guam.

She patrolled off Guam until 4 July when she received orders to leave the area. Early the next day, she set\ her course for Johnston Island. Japanese aircraft continued to badger the submarine for two days as she proceeded toward Hawaii. After taking on fuel and provisions at Johnston Island on the 11th, she completed her third patrol at Pearl Harbor on the 14th.

After refitting and three days of training, *Tunny* departed Hawaii on 5 August for Midway. She arrived at Midway on the 9th and was again underway on the 10th. On the 18th, she sighted Pagan and Alamagan Islands; and, on 22 August, she entered her assigned area in the Palaus and began patrols. Early in the morning of the 24th, she sighted a six-ship convoy as it emerged from Toagel Mlungui Pass. *Tunny* trailed the convoy until she could obtain a good firing position; and, at moonrise on the 25th, she submerged to 40 feet and began her approach. At 0140, she fired three torpedoes and then another two in rapid succession. She then ducked her periscope and dove to avoid being rammed by the first target. The convoy passed overhead as *Tunny* dove deep in expectation of depth charges. She heard her torpedoes explode at the end of their run, but the absence of depth charges was both welcome and unexpected. Near dawn, *Tunny* made another attack, launching six torpedoes at ships of the convoy without success. Meanwhile, a destroyer escort had joined the convoy. Alerted to *Tunny*'s presence, she now bore down on the submarine. *Tunny* dove; and, for the next two hours, the enemy ship remained overhead pinging and tracking. The destroyer escort dropped two patterns of six depth charges close by the submarine but finally gave up the search. At noon,

Tunny came to periscope depth and, finding no sign of the convoy, set her course for Toagel Mlungui, securing from battle stations after an exhausting 15 hours.

At midmorning on the 26th, she spotted two vessels with a submarine chaser escort approaching Toagel Mlungui Pass and launched a five-torpedo attack. As *Tunny* dove, the screws of the first ship were heard to stop; and, shortly thereafter, two depth charges exploded overhead. Two minutes later, another pattern of depth charges exploded all around the submarine. A small fire broke out in the maneuvering room, causing main power to be lost momentarily. In order to check the fire, the main motors were stopped for one minute; then started again. Although the fire was small, dense smoke from burning insulating varnish made it difficult at first to assess the damage. Meanwhile, *Tunny*'s bow planes jammed and the submarine climbed to 200 feet, then went into a steep glide which took her down to 380 feet before control was regained. Within five minutes, cooly efficient damage control parties had restored operating conditions to nearly normal; and the submarine began her retirement to the southwest. Once again the sound of screws caused tense moments for those on board *Tunny*, but this time no depth charges fell.

Early that evening, *Tunny* surfaced and headed away from the heavily-travelled lanes she had been patrolling in order to assess her damages and effect repairs. Inspection disclosed considerable damage to the bow, ripped-up plating aft of the torpedo room, and sheared-off rivets and bolts. The torpedo room pressure hull was badly dished in between frames; and this damage in turn immobolized the bow plane tilting gears. The explosions had jammed the gyro spindles in the stern torpedo tubes, impaired the usefulness of sound and radar gear, and caused other damage visible throughout the ship. Sailors inspecting topside found fragments of the destructive depth charges scattered over the deck.

For two days, her crew labored to restore her to order and make the necessary repairs. Having done everything within his means to restore *Tunny* to normal operating condition, her commanding officer found her still short of combat readiness. Her bow planes, despite all efforts, were still inoperative; her bow bouyancy tank unuseable; and various other problems, which could not be remedied at sea, remained. Thus, on 29 August 1943, she departed her patrol area leaving these hunting grounds to other submarines in better condition. The war-scarred submarine moored at Pearl Harbor on 8 September.

After a preliminary assessment of battle damage, *Tunny* departed Pearl Harbor on 11 September 1943. She arrived at Hunters Point on 17 September for overhaul and repairs and remained there until 2 February 1944. Then, repairs and tests completed, she departed the west coast. *Tunny* returned to Hawaii a week later, underwent voyage repairs and training, and departed Pearl Harbor for her fifth war patrol on 27 February.

She stopped at Midway on 2 March, got underway the next day for the Palaus, and entered her patrol area on the 15th. On the 20th, a persistent observation plane kept *Tunny* down for three hours off the entrance to Toagel Mlungui and dropped eight light bombs without damaging the submarine. In the following days, the submarine patrolled the northern and western approaches to the islands.

On 22 March, *Tunny*'s radar picked up what proved to be a large convoy. Day was breaking, and *Tunny* was maneuvering for a position ahead when an escorting destroyer appeared on the radar at 14,000 yards. The enemy soon sighted the submarine and challenged her with a blinker. *Tunny* took advantage of a nearby rain squall for concealment and continued to close the convoy, keeping a watchful eye on the destroyer. Despite bad visibility and the pinging of the escort, *Tunny* continued her approach and soon found herself in the midst of a group of tankers and cargo ships. Choosing two heavily loaded cargo ships for her targets, she launched a six-torpedo attack and heard or observed hits on both. Immediately, attention on board *Tunny* was diverted when a small tanker nearly collided with the submarine. *Tunny* now obtained a setup on a destroyer moving at high speed across her stern, fired four Mark 18 torpedoes, then dove quickly even as depth charges from a nearby trawler exploded on the port quarter. During the next four hours, the Japanese ships dropped 87 depth charges in an effort to finish off the submarine but without effect. Late in the day, *Tunny* surfaced and began a futile search for stragglers and cripples from the morning's attack. She found only debris and an oil slick.

At 2119 on the 23d, while patrolling off Angaur Island, *Tunny* picked up a radar contact which she identified by sight as a large I-class submarine. For nearly an hour and one-half, *Tunny* and the enemy submarine maneuvered for position, each attempting to prevent the other from obtaining a shot. Then, at 2324, *Tunny* fired four torpedoes from a range of 1,900 yards, swung hard to starboard to prevent a collision, and dove to avoid a possible return attack. Before the hatch was closed, two hits were heard and felt and a flash was seen inside *Tunny*'s conning tower. For one terrible moment, observers on board *Tunny* feared that their own submarine had been hit. As *Tunny* dove to 150 feet and began circling the area, the screws of the enemy submarine stopped, and a crackling racket began and continued for an hour. When the noise ceased, *Tunny* surfaced and cleared the area, but Japanese submarine *I-42* had met her end.

Tunny returned to waters off Toagel Mlungui and resumed patrols. On the morning of 29 March, she observed a large number of small vessels leaving Malakal Harbor, none worth an attack. Apparently the enemy had somehow received word of the 5th Fleet's impending bombing attack on Japanese installations in the Carolines and made a desperate attempt to clear the area. Late in the afternoon, a larger formation appeared: the 63,000-ton Japanese battleship *Musashi*, one light cruiser, and three destroyers, also fleeing the expected aerial bombardment. After a daring approach, *Tunny* fired six torpedoes at the battleship from her bow tubes. The torpedoes passed directly under an alert detroyer of the screen which immediately hoisted flags to warn the battleship, swung parallel to the torpedo tracks, and made a run on the submarine. *Tunny* went deep and ran for the southwest while the destroyer dropped 38 depth charges in a short, but concentrated counterattack. Toward sunset, the submarine lost contact with the formation. Later that night, she encountered what she thought to be the same force and was held down for two hours by one of the escorting ships. Hits by two of *Tunny*'s torpedoes had damaged but failed to slow the powerful battleship.

At 0200 on 30 March, *Tunny* arrived on station to begin lifeguard duties for the 5th Fleet's air attack on the Palaus. At 0700, a series of explosions followed by the appearance of heavy smoke from the vicinity of the harbor indicated that American planes were finding their mark. During the morning, more than 100 planes passed over the submarine on their return from the strike. Then, as *Tunny* circled on station shortly after noon, two American torpedo bombers approached. One sheared off for a strafing attack which was not completed; the other went into a steep glide and released a bomb from an altitude of 300 feet. Incredulous watchers on the submarine saw the bomb cross over the deck gun on the bow, pass the bridge at what appeared to be no more than arm's length, and strike the water with a tremendous impact, only 10 yards to starboard of the forward engine room. The entire ship lifted with a snap as if it had collided with an underwater object, and an explosion followed some seconds later, throwing personnel and gear in all directions in the maneuvering and after torpedo rooms. Damage to the main control cubicle and to *Tunny*'s remaining torpedoes resulted. *Tunny* completed repairs during the night, and the next morning manned her lifeguard

station as before, only a little more wary of "friendly" aircraft.

Tunny departed the Palaus on 2 April, stopped at Milne Bay on the 7th, and arrived in Australia on 11 April. She received the Presidential Unit Citation for this patrol.

Following refit, the submarine departed Brisbane on 29 April and set her course for New Guinea. She underwent voyage repairs at Milne Bay; then proceeded via Langemak Bay to her patrol area in the Marianas. She arrived in the patrol area on 11 May and, in the days that followed, encountered many enemy planes as she patrolled off Saipan and Guam.

On 17 May, she received a report from *Sand Lance* (SS–381) of a convoy in the area and set out to intercept it. Late in the afternoon, she sighted the smoke of her quarry; and, just after sunset, the masts came into view. The convoy consisted of three cargo ships escorted by a like number of destroyers. Racing against fading twilight, *Tunny* made her approach; launched a spread of three torpedoes at the second ship of the column; then rapidly fired three more at the last cargo ship. Before the converging escorts forced her down, *Tunny* observed that a hit had left the last ship of the column down by the stern, emitting clouds of dense black smoke. Although the escorting vessels dropped 81 depth charges, none fell close; and *Tunny* withdrew to the southeast, having scored her sixth kill of the war, a 4,900-ton cargo ship, the *Nichiwa Maru*. Shortly after midnight, *Tunny* surfaced and saw an ill-fated cargo ship, the victim of *Sand Lance*, ablaze from stem to stern. Frequent minor explosions punctuated the night as the ship went down in the darkness.

As *Tunny* continued patrols in the Marianas, she sighted numerous aircraft and noted explosions and burning ships—apparently the work of *Silversides* (SS–236). At this time, however, planes attached to enemy convoys seemed effective in detecting *Tunny* and routing convoys around her, out of range of her torpedoes.

On 8 June, she rendezvoused with *Pilotfish* (SS–386) and *Pintado* (SS–387) to form a coordinated attack group, the "Blair Blasters." The three submarines formed a scouting line for a patrol across the western Pacific to the South China Sea. *Tunny* passed through Balintang Channel on 14 June and sighted Luzon the next morning. While returning through Balintang Channel on 16 June, she made a surface approach on a small sampan and sank it with gunfire. She conducted patrols in the Philippine Sea until 22 June when she parted company with the attack group. On the 29th, she fueled at Midway; then proceeded to Oahu, having travelled over 14,500 miles on her sixth war patrol.

After refitting, she departed Pearl Harbor on 4 August 1944 as a member of a coordinated attack group called "Ed's Eradicators." With wolf pack members *Barb* (SS–220) and *Queenfish* (SS–393), she set her course, via Midway, for the South China Sea. She arrived in her patrol area on 25 August. Her first action came hours after midnight on the 31st when the wolf pack attacked a convoy. *Queenfish* was the first to score a hit, and *Tunny* witnessed the explosion of a tanker, the victim of her sister submarine. As *Tunny* maneuvered in the bright moonlight, she was suddenly startled by gunfire, which seemed to those on board to come from all directions. She dove and avoided damage from the depth charges which soon followed. Later on the same day, a hit by *Barb* alerted the convoy's air escort to *Tunny*'s presence; and she was forced down again without opportunity to launch her torpedoes. Time after time, the submarine surfaced only to be forced down by escorting planes as the attack on the convoy continued into the evening.

A second disappointing day came on the heels of the first. *Tunny* patrolled submerged for most of 1 September in order to avoid enemy aircraft. Late in the afternoon, she was advancing westward on a scouting line formed by the wolf pack, when she sighted a plane dead ahead and about six miles distant. She immediately began to dive, but 90 seconds later, as she passed 110 feet, two bombs hit close aboard aft, sending the ship upward at an eight degree angle and causing extensive damage. As the third and fourth bomb exploded, *Tunny* was already heading for 300 feet to assess her damages.

Inspection disclosed that the bombs had dished in the hull plating in the vicinity of the after torpedo room and the maneuvering room, causing a leak in a vent riser. Less than 10 minutes after the Japanese plane had been sighted, the commanding officer decided to discontinue the patrol. Throughout the ship, sheared off valves and bolts, damaged meters, clocks, and gauges attested to the force of the bomb's explosion. In addition, all three radio antennae were down, a leak in her pressure hull had been aggravated, and *Tunny*'s rudder action indicated possible damage. She set her course for Balintang Channel and surfaced late in the day on 2 September. *Tunny* continued to sight Japanese airplanes as she made her way to Hawaii. She completed this patrol on 17 September at Pearl Harbor.

Tunny departed Oahu for California on 20 September; and, on the 26th, she arrived at Hunter's Point for battle damage repairs and an overhaul. She returned to Hawaii in January 1945 and, after a training period, departed Pearl Harbor on 3 February for her 8th war patrol.

On St. Valentine's Day, she entered Tanapag harbor and moored to *Fulton* (AS-11) for repairs to her main engine. Later in the month, she conducted sonar tests out of that port. On 5 March, she departed Saipan and, in the days that followed, was slowed by heavy seas as she proceeded to her patrol area in the Ryukyus.

On 13 and 14 March, she conducted a special reconnaissance mission off the Nansei Shoto in preparation for landings planned for Okinawa on 1 April. On the 14th, *Tunny* plotted over 230 mines which she detected on sonar as she travelled through the hazardous waters at 150 feet. On the 15th, all hands breathed a sigh of relief as *Tunny* got underway for her patrol area, her special mission safely and successfully completed.

Her pursuit of a distant convoy ended in disappointment on the 18th, when a change of course allowed the cargo ships and their escort to slip away from *Tunny* around sunset. For two days, the submarine patrolled off Amami O Shima; then, on the 23d, she took up a lifeguard station. Days later, as *Tunny* searched for a downed flier, a twin-float enemy plane took her by surprise and dropped two bombs. One fell quite close but caused only minor damage to the submarine. As the month drew to its close, *Tunny* rescued two fliers from *Intrepid* (CV-11) and one from *Bennington* (CV-20) as those ships took part in the assault on Okinawa.

On 1 April, *Tunny* completed her lifeguard duties and set her course for Midway. En route, she sank a 200-ton lugger with her deck gun. After stopping at Midway, she arrived at Oahu on 14 April.

Following refitting and a week of sonar and approach training, *Tunny* departed Pearl Harbor on 14 April for her ninth war patrol. She stopped at Guam for repairs and additional sonar exercises; then got underway on 28 May. *Tunney*, *Skate* (SS-305), and *Bonefish* (SS-223) formed the second group of "Hydeman's Hellcats" known as "Pierce's Polecats." On 2 June, *Tunny* passed through the Nansei Shoto and, as she approached Kyushu two days later, encountered increasing small boat traffic. On 5 June, *Tunny* passed through Korea Strait, repeating the hair-raising task of mine detection by sonar, this time in Nishi Suido. She plotted over 80 mines; then continued on to conduct patrols on the western shore of Honshu.

Operating in the supposedly inviolable waters of the Sea of Japan, the wolf pack attacked shipping and made exploratory attempts to enter Japanese harbors. Late on 9 June, *Tunny* attacked a cargo vessel. One torpedo hit the enemy vessel with a thud but failed to explode; and *Tunny* discontinued the attack. In the harbor-entering phase of the patrol, *Tunny* closed the breakwater of Etomo Ko to 8,000 yards shortly before midnight on 12 June. Town and waterfront lights provided illumination, but no suitable target could be found, and the submarine cleared the harbor before midnight. A few minutes later, *Tunny* approached within 5,000 yards of the harbor mouth at Uppuri Wan but discreetly withdrew when searchlights located and then brilliantly illuminated the intruder.

On 16 June, *Tunny* sighted numerous rafts filled with the Japanese survivors of a successful action by *Bonefish* and later took prisoner a Japanese chief petty officer who had escaped from the sinking ship. On the following day, as *Tunny* and *Bonefish* closed a radar-located target, *Tunny* suddenly found herself the object of gunfire, with the closest shot falling only 200 yards off her port beam. She quickly changed course and eluded both the gunfire and the depth charges which followed. On 19 June, shallow coastal water foiled *Tunny*'s attack on a 4,000-ton cargo ship.

Tunny rendezvoused with *Skate* on the 23d to depart the Sea of Japan. She remained off Hokkaido for two days on the chance that she might be able to aid *Bonefish*, missing since her request to make a daylight submerged patrol of Toyama Wan some days earlier. On the 27th, *Tunny* discontinued her vigil; proceeded via the Kuril Islands and Midway; and arrived at Pearl Harbor on 6 July.

The submarine then made her way back to the west coast. *Tunny* was decommissioned on 13 December 1945 and placed in the Mare Island Group, 19th Fleet.

Communist aggression in Korea placed new demands on the resources of the Navy and led to *Tunny*'s being placed in commission, in reserve, on 28 February 1952. She saw no service at this time, however, and was decommissioned in April 1952. On 6 March 1953, she was placed in commission for the third time. Converted to carry guided missiles, she was reclassified SSG-282 and served as a Regulus-missile submarine for nearly 12 years.

For the first four of those years, she operated out of Point Mugu, contributing to the development of the Regulus missile system. Except for a short period of type training, *Tunny* engaged entirely in the launching and guidance of Regulus missiles for purposes of missile evaluation in the development of the system. In 1957, she shifted her base of operations to Hawaii where she conducted deterrent patrols and fired exercise missiles.

In May 1965, the Regulus missile system was phased out, and *Tunny* was redesignated SS-282. She remained in the Hawaiian operating area until the end of the year, conducting training exercises and providing various other services. In 1966, she was converted to a troop-carrying submarine and redesignated APSS-282. In February 1967, *Tunny* began missions in unconventional warfare, operating off the coast of Vietnam. She conducted reconnaissance in preparation for amphibious assault operations and gathered navigational and oceanographic information. Ideally suited for transporting small teams for specialized operations as well as for gathering information, she participated in Operation "Deckhouse VI."

On 1 January 1968, the veteran submarine was reclassified LPSS-282. She was decommissioned on 28 June 1969; and, on 30 June 1969, her name was struck from the Navy list. She was designated for disposal as a mobile target.

Tunny received nine battle stars and two Presidential Unit Citations for her World War II service. She received five battle stars for her operations during the Vietnam War.

II

(SSN-682: dp. 4,290 (f.); l. 301'; b. 32'; dr. 26'; s. 20+ k.; cpl. 110; a. 4 21'' tt., SUBROC; cl. *Sturgeon*)

The second *Tunny* (SSN-682) was laid down on 22 May 1970 at Pascagoula, Miss., by the Ingalls Shipbuilding Division of Litton Systems Inc.; launched on 10 June 1972; sponsored by Mrs. Lola Aiken; and commissioned on 26 January 1974 at Charleston, S.C., Comdr. Dennis Y. Sloan in command.

Tunny remained at Charleston, her home port, until March when she moved to Groton, Conn., for two weeks of in-port training at the submarine base. Between March and June, she conducted shakedown training in the West Indies and along the east coast. From June to August, the nuclear-powered submarine conducted normal operations out of Charleston before heading north to the Portsmouth (N.H.) Naval Shipyard where she began post-shakedown overhaul on 12 August. The warship completed repairs on 5 October and headed back to Charleston where she resumed normal training operations.

In February 1975, *Tunny* began preparations for her first deployment to the Mediterranean. She stood out of Charleston and headed across the Atlantic on 6 March and changed operational control to the 6th Fleet 10 days later. During the first part of her tour in the Mediterranean, the submarine operated with Task Force (TF) 60 conducting antisubmarine (ASW) exercises with the other ships of the unit. Following refit and tender upkeep in June and early July at Santo Stefano, Sardinia, *Tunny* rejoined the 6th Fleet as a unit of TF 69 and resumed ASW training. After participating in a major 6th Fleet exercise late in July and early in August, the warship departed the Mediterranean for home. She changed operational control from 6th Fleet to the Atlantic Fleet Submarine Force on 17 August and arrived in Charleston 12 days later. After post-deployment standdown in September and a shipyard availability at Charleston in October and November, she resumed operations—mostly type training—out of Charleston on 20 November.

Type training along the South Carolina and Florida coasts occupied her time during the first month of 1976. February brought inspections and examinations; and, in March, she participated in two special operations designed to help develop and evaluate submarine tactics. In May, *Tunny* began preparations for her second tour of duty with the 6th Fleet but did not embark upon that assignment for over two months. In the meantime, she conducted one exercise—in mine warfare—in June. Finally, on 26 July, she sailed out of Charleston on her way to the Mediterranean. Following a visit to Lisbon, Portugal, the attack submarine joined the 6th Fleet on 11 August. After a month of ASW training, highlighted by Exercise "National Week XXI," the warship put into Santo Stefano for a month of upkeep alongside *Howard W. Gilmore* (AS-16). In October, she returned to sea for ASW training operations punctuated periodically with a visit to Naples or upkeep at Santo Stefano. That routine continued until 11 December, when she departed Santo Stefano to return to the United States. Arriving in Charleston on 22 December, she commenced a combination of holiday leave and upkeep and post-deployment standdown.

January 1977 found *Tunny* undergoing an extensive upkeep following her Mediterranean deployment. She then resumed operations off the east coast which extended through the spring and summer months. In mid-September, the attack submarine commenced a two-month Selected Restricted Availability (SRA) at the Norfolk Naval Shipyard which was concluded in late November, followed by a short sea trial period. Following refresher training at the Naval Submarine School, New London, *Tunny* returned to Charleston for the Christmas holidays.

Tunny spent January and part of February 1978 preparing for a North Atlantic deployment which commenced in late February and concluded in late April. In July, *Tunny*'s home port was changed to Pearl Harbor, Hawaii, and the ship transited to that port on 19 August. The remainder of the year was devoted to local operations in preparation for a forthcoming deployment to the western Pacific in 1979.

Tunxis

An American Indian tribe which derived its name from *Wuttunkshau*, or "the point where the river bends." This term referred to the bend of the Farmington River, near Farmington and Southington, Conn., in what is now Hartford County. The tribe resided there until they sold most of their territory to the English in 1640 and disappeared soon thereafter.

I

(Mon: t. 614; l. 225'; b. 45'; dr. 6'6''; cpl. 69; a. 2 guns; cl. *Casco*)

The first *Tunxis* was launched on 4 June 1864 at Chester, Pa., by Reaney, Son, and Archbold; and commissioned at the Philadelphia Navy Yard on 12 July 1864.

On 21 September 1864, the light-draft monitor departed the sheltered waters of the navy yard on her maiden voyage. However, she soon began taking on water at such an alarming rate that she came about and returned to Philadelphia, where she was decommissioned later in the month.

On 19 October 1864, *Tunxis* entered William Cramp and Sons' Shipyard, Philadelphia, for extensive refit and rebuilding. On 12 July 1866, two years to the day since her first commissioning, the monitor emerged from the complete overhaul far more seaworthy than before. Nevertheless, since her class design had proven disappointing, she was immediately laid up at League Island Navy Yard.

On 15 June 1869, her name was changed to *Hydra*; and, on 10 August, this ship was renamed *Ostego*. In 1874, *Ostego* was broken up for scrap, having never seen active service.

II

(AN–90: dp. 785; l. 146'; b. 33'10''; d. 10'10''; s. 12.3 k.; cpl. 46; a. 1 3''; cl. *Cohoes*)

The second *Tunxis*—originally projected as YN–119 —was redesignated AN–90 on 17 January 1944; laid down on 2 May 1944, at Duluth, Minn., by the Zenith Dredge Co.; launched on 18 August 1944; sponsored by Mrs. Edward J. Thye, wife of the Governor of Minnesota; and commissioned on 28 March 1945.

Decommissioned on 30 June 1945, the net tender remained in reserve until activated on 20 February 1953. Originally operating out of the 5th Naval District, she was transferred to the 6th District on 4 January 1954 and based at Charleston, S.C.; Savannah, Ga.; and at Key West, Fla. *Tunxis* participated in Atlantic Fleet exercises off the east coast from 13 to 22 November 1954 before returning to Charleston.

On 15 April 1955, the ship was placed "in commission in reserve" before being decommissioned on 20 July of that year. In August 1963, *Tunxis* was transferred under the Military Assistance Program to the government of Venezuela. She serves the Venezuelan Navy as *Puerto Nutrias* (H–02).

Tupelo

A city in, and the seat of, Lee County, Miss.

Tupelo (YN–75) was renamed *Winterberry* (q.v.) on 3 April 1943.

Turaco

A large, brilliantly colored African bird having a long tail and prominent crest.

(AMc–55: dp. 275; l. 98'5''; b. 23'7''; dr. 10'9''; s. 10 k.; cpl. 17; a. 2 .50-cal. mg., 4 .30-cal. mg.; cl. *Accentor*)

Turaco (AMc–55) was laid down on 17 January 1941

at Rockland, Maine, by the Snow Shipyards; launched on 28 July 1941; sponsored by Mrs. F. C. Gatcombe; placed in service on 9 October 1941, Lt. (jg.) Allard B. Heyward, USNR, Officer in Charge.

The new coastal minesweeper completed fitting out at Boston Naval Shipyard; then got underway on 19 October 1941. She arrived at Yorktown on the 21st for a period of training in mine warfare. On 30 October, the wooden-hulled coastal minesweeper arrived at Norfolk and, soon thereafter, headed southward. Early in November, she reported for duty to the Commandant, 7th Naval District.

On 19 February 1942, a German submarine torpedoed and sank SS *Pan Massachusetts*, the first American ship lost to enemy action in the waters of the Gulf Sea Frontier. In the summer of 1942, as German submarines took their grim toll of merchant shipping, *Turaco* pursued her duties. German submarines laid minefields which were discovered by patrolling American vessels—often enough, only after American ships had been damaged or lost. The small coastal minesweepers joined the larger sweepers (AM's) in clearing these fields on the Eastern and Gulf Sea Frontiers.

As the war wore on, *Turaco* continued her duties with the 6th and 7th Naval Districts. Increased availability of ships and airplanes, improved understanding of antisubmarine warfare, and greater organizational efficiency all contributed to decreasing merchant ship losses on the Gulf Sea Frontier.

As World War II drew to its close in June 1945, *Turaco* served with Naval Air Operational Training Commands at Mayport and Fort Lauderdale, Fla. Following a brief assignment in July with the Bureau of Ordnance, 7th Naval District, the minesweeper proceeded to Miami for alterations. Early in August, as it became clear that the fighting would soon end, she reported to the Commandant, 6th Naval District, at Charleston for disposition.

Turaco was placed out of service on 30 November 1945 and was struck from the Navy list on 19 December of the same year. In September 1947, she was transferred to the Maritime Commission and was sold to Henry H. Berman, Newark, N.J.

Turandot

A "minor planet" or asteroid of our solar system discovered by Max Wolf in 1904 and named by him after the title character in the Pucini opera of the same name.

(AKA–47: dp. 4,087; l. 426′; b. 58′; dr. 16′ (lim.); s. 16.9 k.; cpl. 303; a. 1 5′′, 8 40mm., 10 20mm.; cl. *Artemis*; S4–SE2–BE–1)

Turandot (AKA–47) was laid down under Maritime Commission contract (MC hull 1908) on 29 March 1945 by the Walsh-Kaiser Co., Inc., Providence, R.I.; launched on 20 May 1945; sponsored by Mrs. Charles H. MacLeod; and commissioned on 18 June 1945, Lt. Comdr. Francklyn W. C. Zwicker, USNR, in command.

Following fitting out and conversion at the Boston Navy Yard, *Turandot* made her shakedown cruise in the Chesapeake Bay in July 1945. After undergoing availability at Norfolk, the new attack cargo ship took on passengers and cargo; then departed Hampton Roads on 24 July, bound for the Canal Zone. She transited the Panama Canal on 30 July and, early the next day, rendezvoused with *Barbero* (SS–317) for exercises en route to the Hawaiian Islands. On 10 August, she parted company with the submarine and made her way independently to Oahu, arriving at Pearl Harbor on 14 August 1945.

After discharging her cargo, she embarked 172 Army troops and departed the Hawaiian Islands on 7 September, setting her course for the New Hebrides. She arrived at Espiritu Santo on the 17th, discharged her

passengers, loaded cargo, and embarked elements of the 85th Construction Battalion.

On 22 September, she got underway for the Marshalls. After fueling at Eniwetok, she continued on and arrived at Wake Island on 6 October. The following day, she discharged her cargo and passengers and returned to Eniwetok to begin "Magic-Carpet" duties, carrying troops back to the United States. She embarked more than 600 veterans, then got underway on 13 October and steamed via a great circle route to California. On Friday, 26 October, she entered San Pedro Harbor and disembarked her happy passengers. After voyage repairs at Terminal Island, she again got underway on 3 November, steaming for the Marianas. On the 19th, *Turandot* arrived at Saipan. This time, she was to serve as a magic carpet for more than a thousand returning troops. She departed Saipan on the 27th and completed the crossing at San Pedro on 12 December.

Voyage repairs occupied most of the remainder of the month. *Turandot* opened the new year with a voyage to San Diego; then, on the 24th, continued southward and steamed, via the Panama Canal, to the Atlantic. On 5 February, she arrived at Hampton Roads and was delivered on 25 June 1946 to the Maritime Commission for custody pending disposal. She decommissioned on 21 March 1946 and was struck from the Navy list on 17 April 1947.

On 4 November 1954, the former attack cargo ship was reacquired by the Navy; reclassified a cable repair ship, redesignated ARC–3, and renamed *Aeolus* (q.v.). Her conversion was completed on 15 May 1955 at Baltimore by the Key Highway Plant of the Bethlehem Steel Co. The ship was accepted for limited service and recommissioned later that month.

Turbot

A large, brown and white flatfish, valued as a food.

Turbot (Submarine No. 21) was renamed *G–3* (q.v.) on 11 November 1911.

Turbot (SS–427)—a *Balao*-class submarine—was laid down on 13 November 1943 at Philadelphia, Pa., by the Cramp Shipbuilding Co., but the contract for her construction was cancelled on 12 August 1945. Her partially completed hulk was later launched and, in 1950, was assigned to the Naval Ship Research and Development Center, Annapolis, Md. There, it is used for research and development in connection with the control and reduction of machinery noise in submarines.

Turkey

A large game and poultry bird, allied to the pheasant and native to North America. Benjamin Franklin suggested that the abundant wild turkey, which had provided food for the early settlers in the New World, should be chosen as the national bird.

I

(Minesweeper No. 13: dp. 840; l. 187′10′′; b. 35′5′′; dr. 8′10′′; s. 14 k.; cpl. 85; a. 2 3′′; cl. *Lapwing*)

The first *Turkey* (Minesweeper No. 13) was laid down on 19 August 1917 at Chester, Pa., by the Chester Shipbuilding Co.; launched on 30 April 1918; sponsored by Mrs. W. T. Smith; and commissioned on 13 December 1918, Lt. John H. McDonald in command.

Although completed too late to see service during World War I, *Turkey* took part in the gigantic operation to clear the mine barrage which had been laid in the North Sea during this conflict. This system of minefields constituted a formidable obstacle to the resumption of trade in the aftermath of the war. After steaming across the Atlantic, the new minesweeper arrived at Kirkwall, Scotland, on 20 April 1919 and joined the American forces massing there to begin clearing the shipping lanes between Scotland and Norway.

Soon thereafter, *Turkey* got underway for mine-sweeping operations in the North Sea. During her second operation (which ran from 8 to 29 May), a mine exploded directly beneath *Turkey* on 16 May. The disabled minesweeper crept to Lyeness, at Scapa Flow, where she was drydocked for repairs.

Her damage was corrected in time for *Turkey* to take part in the project's fifth operation, commencing on 22 July. Eight days later, the minesweeper suffered a condenser failure. After receiving a cannibalized unit from the disabled *Pelican* (Minesweeper No. 27), she resumed operations in mid-August.

Fair weather conditions, unusual for the North Sea, enabled the ships to make excellent progress. While thus engaged, *Turkey* fouled a mine in her sweep gear; and it exploded close aboard, causing minor damage. However, the ship effected quick repairs at sea and continued operations without missing the proverbial step. By the 16th, *Turkey*'s group had swept a record 1,373 mines.

Deteriorating weather conditions, however, hampered the clearing of group 13, in an operation begun on 5 September. After delaying putting to sea due to heavy fog, the ships got underway to carry out their assignment but seemed dogged with misfortune and bad luck from the beginning. *Oriole* (Minesweeper No. 7) snared a mine which exploded in one of her "kites," damaging both kite and ship and forcing her to limp home. *Swan* (Minesweeper No. 34) closed *Turkey* to obtain more sweep wire to replace her depleted stock, but the capricious sea slammed the two ships together, forcing *Swan* out of action and back to port for repairs.

By November of 1919, the colossal job of sweeping the barrage had been completed. On 25 November, *Turkey* and her 34 sister ships received orders detaching them from duty in the North Sea. Taking on fuel at Brest, France, *Turkey* departed European waters but soon ran into bad weather off the Azores. Bucking heavy seas and high winds, the ship used a large amount of her fuel and exhausted it completely, long before she reached Bermuda. Destroyer tender *Panther* (AD-6) passed a towline to the minesweeper and eventually brought her to Bermuda.

Following her return to the United States, *Turkey* began operating out of New York in the waters of the 3d Naval District. On 17 July 1920, the minesweeper was designated AM-17 when the Navy adopted its modern alphanumeric system of hull numbers. In 1921, the ship shifted to the Pacific to join the Pacific Fleet Train. Based at Pearl Harbor, she operated as part of Mine Division 4 and Mine Division 6 until decommissioned there on 12 April 1922.

After a decade and one-half in reserve, *Turkey* returned to the west coast in September 1937 and was fitted out at the Mare Island Navy Yard, Vallejo, Calif. Recommissioned there on 15 August 1938, *Turkey* subsequently operated out of San Pedro, Calif., through 1939.

As the Fleet shifted to Pearl Harbor in late 1939 and early 1940, *Turkey* followed and operated out of Pearl Harbor into 1941. On 7 December of that year, she lay moored in a nest of her sister ships at the Coal Docks at Pearl Harbor, when Japanese planes launched a surprise attack on the unsuspecting Pacific Fleet.

A Naval Reserve ensign, who had experienced only six months of sea duty, led the ship's defense until her commanding officer could return to the ship. The crew tumbled to battle stations at the sound of the general quarters alarm and quickly manned the main battery of two 3-inch guns. In addition, two Lewis guns atop the tall pilot house went into action. A number of riflemen armed with Springfield 1903 bolt-action rifles roamed the decks looking for good vantage points from which to fire at the attacking planes. Twenty minutes after the raid began, *Turkey* backed clear of the next ship to improve her field of fire and continued the fight.

When all Japanese planes had departed the area, *Turkey* and her sister ships labored to salvage the critically damaged battleships which were partially sunk in the mud and oily waters off Ford Island. *Turkey* remained engaged in these operations until 1 April 1942, when she departed Pearl Harbor for Samoan waters.

Relieving *Kingfisher* (AM-25) as station ship at Samoa, *Turkey* operated in Samoan waters through the end of the year and into 1943. She conducted mine-sweeping patrols, provided local escort services, and towed targets for the Marine shore batteries on Samoa. On 1 June 1942, she was reclassified as an ocean-going tug and given the designation AT-143. She also supported Marine raider landing exercises.

On 14 April 1943, *Turkey* visited Bowditch Island on an inspection and discovered two castaways who had been there for nearly a month. The two had been treated well by the local populace and were in good shape.

After receiving repairs from 21 to 30 April, the minesweeper became station ship at Tutuila. She returned to Pearl Harbor in June and thence proceeded to the west coast and a major overhaul at Mare Island. Following trials off the west coast, she headed for Hawaii and arrived at Pearl Harbor on 20 October.

Operating out of the Fleet's Hawaiian base, *Turkey* towed targets for naval aircraft and recovered practice torpedoes through January 1944. Operating as a unit of Service Squadron 6, she conducted these activities through late February, after which she underwent more repair work at Pearl Harbor from 1 March to 24 April.

Following post-repair trials and practice torpedo-recovery operations in Hawaiian waters, she headed for the Marshalls on 10 May 1944—in company with *Preserver* (ARS-8) and towing barges *YOGL-7* and *YW-68*—and arrived at Majuro on 25 May. Five days later, *Turkey* headed for Kwajalein with *YF-412* and *YF-383* in tow and in company with *ATR-46*, making port there on 1 June. Upon delivering her tows, she proceeded back to Majuro. Meanwhile, on 15 May 1944, she had been reclassified as an old ocean tug and redesignated ATO-143.

On 4 June, she commenced ammunition replenishment operations at that base for cruisers *Santa Fe* (CL-60), *Biloxi* (CL-80), and *Mobile* (CL-63). For the remainder of the summer, *Turkey* operated in the Marshalls, towing small barges between Majuro, Kwajalein, and Eniwetok, undergoing a brief overhaul alongside *Ajax* (AR-6) at Majuro from 29 August to 2 September and conducting harbor operations. Then, on 5 October, she headed for Ulithi.

After harbor duty there, she sailed for Ngulu Atoll on 17 October to assist in salvage operations for *Montgomery* (DD-121), which had been damaged by a mine explosion earlier that day. She returned to Ulithi on the 23d and, four days later, assisted the torpedo-damaged *Houston* (CL-81) into the harbor after the cruiser had been struck off Formosa by a Japanese aircraft-launched torpedo.

While *Turkey* was towing *YOG-21* alongside *Essex* (CV-9), the minesweeper's foremast caught in one of the carrier's flight deck radio antenna braces and was broken in three places. On 21 November, *Turkey* went to the assistance of the tanker *Mississinewa* (AO-59) which had been struck by a Japanese manned torpedo. The minesweeper closed to help put out the fires. Despite valiant firefighting efforts, the oiler rolled over and sank some three hours later, the war's first victim of Japan's *Kaiten*.

Following a short overhaul period at Ulithi in December 1944, *Turkey* commenced assisting in fueling operations of Fleet carriers there early in January 1945; and, but for a brief drydock period from 9 to 13 January, she continued the task through the end of the month.

In early February, she assisted in preparations for the Iwo Jima landings before proceeding, via Kossol Roads in the Palaus, to San Pedro Bay, off Leyte. *Turkey* then continued operations as part of the Service Squadron, South Pacific Forces, in harbor activities at Ulithi in March through May 1945. After getting underway again for Leyte on 7 May, she served as a retriever for a tow convoy, keeping a lookout for barges and other craft which might slip their tows en route. Arriving in San Pedro Bay on 13 May, she commenced harbor operations and continued them until 7 June, when she began 10 days of upkeep alongside *Prometheus* (AR–3).

She operated between Leyte and Ulithi through the end of hostilities in mid-August before stopping at Kwajalein on the 24th. On 30 August, she got underway for Hawaii and reached Pearl Harbor on 11 September. From there, she proceeded to San Francisco.

Turkey was decommissioned on 6 November 1945; struck from the Navy list on 28 November 1945; and sold and delivered to the Hawley Forge and Manufacturing Co., of San Francisco on 30 December 1946.

The coastal minesweeper *Turkey* (MSCO–56), October 1966. Except for removal of most of her guns and addition of newer radar, she is little changed from her original configuration.

Turkey received one battle star for her World War II service.

II

(YMS–444: dp. 320; l. 136'; b. 24'6''; dr. 8' (mean); s. 14 k.; cpl. 33; a. 1 3'', 2 20mm., 2 .50-cal. mg., 2 dct., 2 dcp.; cl. *YMS–1*)

The second *Turkey* was laid down as *YMS–444* on 16 November 1943 at Kingston, N.Y., by C. Hiltebrant Dry Dock Co., Inc.; launched on 20 July 1944; and commissioned on 26 December 1944, Lt. George H. H. Huey, USNR, in command.

YMS–444 completed fitting out at New York and, in January 1945, made a shakedown voyage to Little Creek. On 6 February, she arrived at Norfolk and remained there while members of her crew attended Fire Fighting School. Then, late in February, she returned to New York. In March, the auxiliary motor minesweeper began operating out of Tompkinsville, N.Y.

On 20 July, she departed New York and, after a stop at Miami, steamed through the Panama Canal to the California coast, arriving at Los Angeles on 8 September. On the 17th, she set her course westward for Pearl Harbor and the Marshalls. Although the war was over when *YMS–444* arrived in the Pacific, there were still enormous tasks left for the minesweepers. *YMS–444* pursued her duties operating out of Saipan and Eniwetok in October 1945. In November, she moved on to the Ryukyus and Japan, sweeping mines in the Kyushu-Korea and Honshu areas, and remained in Japanese waters into the new year.

On 24 February 1946, she departed Kure and set her course, via the Marianas and Marshalls, for Pearl Harbor and California. After pausing at San Pedro in April, she got underway for the Canal Zone on the 27th. It was 6 June before she departed the Canal Zone and set her course, via Charleston, for New York. She was decommissioned on 30 August 1946 and remained in the 3d Naval District as a Naval Reserve training ship.

For the next six years, *YMS–444* operated out of New York ports and on the Great Lakes. On 1 September 1947, she was named *Turkey* and redesignated a motor minesweeper (AMS–56). She was placed in commission, in reserve, in April 1950, and she returned to active status on 21 November.

Turkey returned to the Atlantic in March 1952 and was assigned to serve with the Mine Forces, Atlantic Fleet, in August. During the following four years, she operated out of east coast ports with occasional voyages to the Caribbean. On 7 February 1955, she was reclassified an old coastal minesweeper MSC(O)–56. She arrived at Charleston on 9 November 1956 and was decommissioned there on 23 November 1956. Then, on 1 May 1957, she departed Charleston, steamed via New York, Halifax, and Montreal, and reported to the Commander, 4th Naval District, Toledo, Ohio, on 27 May 1957.

In 1960, *Turkey* was transferred to the 1st Naval District to continue as a Reserve training ship. As such, she operated out of Fall River, Mass., until September 1968 when she was replaced as a training ship by *Jacana* (MSC–193). Her name was struck from the Navy list as of October 1968, and she was sold in August 1969.

Turner

Daniel Turner—probably born at Richmond on Staten Island in 1794—was appointed a midshipman in the Navy on 1 January 1808. Following brief duty at the New York Naval Station, he served in *Constitution* on the North Atlantic Station. On 8 June 1812, he received orders to Norwich, Conn., where he took command of the gunboats located there.

On 14 March 1813, two days after receiving his commission as a lieutenant, Turner was sent to Sackett's Harbor, N.Y., located on the shores of Lake Erie. There, he took command of *Niagra*, a brig in Oliver Hazard Perry's squadron. However, just before the Battle of Lake Erie, he relinquished command to Capt. Jesse D. Elliott and assumed command of *Caledonia*. The little brig played an important role in the Battle of Lake Erie on 10 September 1813 because, at one point in the action, her two 24-pounder long guns were the only ones in Perry's flotilla capable of returning the distant fire of the three heaviest British ships then in the process of pounding Perry's flagship *Lawrence*. For his part in the American victory at Lake Erie, Lt. Turner received the praise of Perry, a vote of thanks and a medal from Congress, and a sword from the state of New York.

In the summer of 1814, Turner succeeded to the command of schooner *Scorpion*, and he cruised Lakes Erie and Huron in her supporting army operations around Detroit and blockading British forces at the Nottawasaga River and Lake Simcoe. On 6 September 1814, Turner and his command were captured by the British when he brought *Scorpion* alongside the former American schooner *Tigress* which, unbeknownst to him, had been captured a few days earlier. After a period of imprisonment at Mackinac, Lt. Turner returned to the United States in exchange for a British prisoner of war.

Between 1815 and 1817, Turner cruised the Mediterranean in the frigate *Java* commanded by his old superior on the Great Lakes, Oliver Hazard Perry. During that deployment, *Java* visited Algiers and Tripoli in a show of American naval strength calculated to impress the Barbary pirates and intimidate them into honoring their treaties with the United States. In 1817, *Java* returned to Newport, R.I., to be laid up.

Between 1819 and 1824, Turner returned to sea in the schooner *Nonsuch* attached to a squadron commanded again by Oliver Hazard Perry. In addition to hunting West Indian pirates, his ship sailed up the Orinoco River to carry Perry on a diplomatic mission to the Venezuelan government under Simon Bolivar. During the return downriver, Perry and many of the crew contracted yellow fever. Turner was close at hand when his mentor died at Trinidad on 23 August 1819. During the remaining years of Turner's assignment to *Nonsuch*, his ship worked along the east coast of the United States, patrolled in the West Indies to suppress piracy, and made a brief cruise to the Mediterranean in 1824.

Following shore duty at Boston, Turner returned to sea in 1827 for a three-year assignment with the West India Squadron, as the commanding officer of *Erie*. In 1830, he came ashore again for three years at the Portsmouth (N.H.) Navy Yard.

Promoted to captain on 3 March 1835, Turner spent a long period waiting orders before returning to sea in 1839 in command of *Constitution*. He sailed the Pacific Station in "Old Ironsides," until he was relieved in 1841. From 1843 to 1846, he commanded the American squadron which operated along the Brazilian coast. From that duty, he reported ashore again as Commandant, Portsmouth (N.H.) Navy Yard. Capt. Turner died suddenly on 4 February 1850 at Philadelphia, and he was buried in Greenmount Cemetery in Baltimore, Md.

I

In November 1936, *Turner* (DD–259) was converted to a water barge and redesignated YW–56. Dropping her name, she served as *YW–56* until 10 February 1943 at which time she was named *Moosehead* (*q.v.*) and redesignated IX–98.

On 22 January 1941, the name *Turner* was assigned to DD–506, an experimental 1,150-ton destroyer ordered on 9 September 1940 from the Federal Shipbuilding and Drydock Co., Kearny, N.J. However, the contract was cancelled on 10 February 1941 and was replaced by a contract for a 1,630-ton destroyer of the *Gleaves*-class, *Turner* (DD–648).

II

(DD–648: dp. 1,630; l. 348'4''; b. 36'1''; dr. 17'5''; s. 37 k.; cpl. 261; a. 4 5'', 4 1.1'', 5 20mm., 5 21'' tt., 3 dcp. (mousetrap), 2 dct.; cl. *Gleaves*)

The second *Turner* (DD–648) was laid down on 15 November 1942 at Kearny, N.J., by the Federal Shipbuilding & Drydock Co.; launched on 28 February 1943; sponsored by Mrs. Louis E. Denfeld; and commissioned on 15 April 1943 at the New York Navy Yard, Lt. Comdr. Henry S. Wygant in command.

Turner completed outfitting at the New York Navy Yard and then conducted shakedown and antisubmarine warfare training out of Casco Bay, Maine, until early June. On the 9th, she returned to New York to prepare for her first assignment, a three-day training cruise with the newly commissioned carrier, *Bunker Hill* (CV–17). Returning to New York on 22 June, she departed again the next day on her first real wartime assignment, service in the screen of a transatlantic convoy. First, she sailed with a portion of that convoy to Norfolk, Va., arriving that same day. On the 24th, the convoy departed Hampton Roads and shaped a course eastward across the Atlantic. After an uneventful voyage, she escorted her convoy into port at Casablanca, French Morocco, on 18 July. She departed with a return convoy on the 23d and arrived back in New York on 9 August. Later that month, she was in the screen of a convoy to Guantanamo Bay, Cuba, making a brief stop at Hampton Roads along the way. On the return trip, she rendezvoused with HMS *Victorious* and accompanied the British carrier to Norfolk.

During the first two weeks of September, *Turner* conducted ASW training at Casco Bay, Maine, and then returned to New York to prepare for her second transatlantic voyage. On 21 September, the destroyer headed south to Norfolk. She arrived there on the 23d and, the following day, headed out across the Atlantic with her convoy. After an 18-day passage, during which she made one depth-charge attack on a sound contact, *Turner* arrived at Casablanca on 12 October. Four days later, she departed again and headed for Gibraltar to join another convoy. The warship reached the strategic base on the 17th and, after two days in port, stood out to join the screen of Convoy GUS–18.

On the night of 23 October, *Turner* was acting as an advance ASW escort for the convoy when she picked up an unidentified surface contact on her SG radar. At 1943, about 11 minutes after the initial radar contact, *Turner*'s lookouts made visual contact with what proved to be a German submarine running on the surface, decks awash, at about 500 yards distance. Almost simultaneously, *Turner* came hard left and opened fire with her 5-inch, 40-millimeter, and 20-millimeter guns. During the next few seconds, the destroyer scored one 5-inch hit on the U-boat's conning tower as well as several 40-millimeter and 20-millimeter hits there and elsewhere. The submarine began to dive immediately and deprived *Turner* of any opportunity to ram her. However, while the U-boat made her dive, *Turner* began a depth-charge attack. She fired two charges from her port K-gun battery, and both appeared to hit the water just above the submerged U-boat. Then, as the destroyer swung around above the U-boat, *Turner* rolled a single depth charge off her stern. Soon after the three depth charges exploded, *Turner* crewmen heard a fourth explosion, the shock from which caused the destroyer to lose power to her SG and FD radars, to the main battery, and to her sound gear. It took her at least 15 minutes to restore power entirely.

Meanwhile, she began a search for evidence to corroborate a sinking or regain contact with the target. At about 2017, she picked up another contact on the

SG radar—located about 1,500 yards off the port beam. *Turner* came left and headed toward the contact. Not long thereafter, her bridge watch sighted an object lying low in the water. Those witnesses definitely identified the object as a submarine which appeared to be sinking by the stern. Unfortunately, *Turner* had to break contact with the object in order to avoid a collision with another of the convoy's escorts. By the time she was able to resume her search, the object had disappeared. *Turner* and *Sturtevant* (DE–239) remained in the area and conducted further searches for the submarine or for proof of her sinking but failed in both instances. All that can be said is that probably the destroyer heavily damaged an enemy submarine and may have sunk her. No conclusive evidence exists to support the latter conclusion.

On the 24th, the two escorts rejoined the convoy, and the crossing continued peacefully. When the convoy divided itself into two segments according to destination on 4 November, *Turner* took station as one of the escorts for the Norfolk-bound portion. Two days later, she saw her charges safely into port and then departed to return to New York where she arrived on 7 November.

Following 10 days in port, the warship conducted ASW exercises briefly at Casco Bay before returning to Norfolk to join another transatlantic convoy. She departed Norfolk with her third and final convoy on 23 November and saw the convoy safely across the Atlantic. On 1 January 1944, near the end of the return voyage, that convoy split into two parts according to destination as *Turner*'s previous one had done. *Turner* joined the New York-bound contingent and shaped a course for that port. She arrived off Ambrose Light late on 2 January and anchored.

Early the following morning, the destroyer suffered a series of shattering internal explosions. By 0650, she took on a 15-degree starboard list; and explosions—mostly in the ammunition stowage areas—continued to stagger the stricken destroyer. Then, at about 0750, a singularly violent explosion caused her to capsize and sink. The tip of her bow remained above water until about 0827 when she disappeared completely taking with her 15 officers and 123 crewmen. After nearby ships picked up the survivors of the sunken destroyer, the injured were taken to the hospital at Sandy Hook. A Coast Guard Sikorsky HNS–1 flown by Lt. Comdr. F. A. Erickson, USCG—in the first use of a helicopter in a life saving role—flew two cases of blood plasma, lashed to the helicopter's floats, from New York to Sandy Hook. The plasma saved the lives of many of *Turner*'s injured crewmen. *Turner*'s name was struck from the Navy list on 8 April 1944.

III

(DD–834: dp. 2,425; l. 390'6''; b. 40'10''; dr. 18'6''; s. 34.6 k. (tl.); cpl. 345; a. 6 5'', 12 40mm., 10 21'' tt.; cl. *Gearing*)

The third *Turner* (DD–834) was laid down on 13 November 1944 at Bath, Maine, by the Bath Iron Works Corp.; launched on 8 April 1945; sponsored by Miss Louise Leahy, granddaughter of Fleet Admiral William D. Leahy; and commissioned on 12 June 1945 at the Boston Navy Yard, Comdr. Ellis B. Rittenhouse in command.

Immediately following her commissioning, *Turner* began undergoing conversion to destroyer picket ship at Boston while her crew attended intensive specialized schools in preparation for picket duty. In mid-July, she arrived at Guantanamo Bay and, while she was undergoing shakedown in Cuban waters, Japan capitulated, ending World War II.

Late in August, the ship returned to Boston for post-shakedown availability. In the second week of September, she resumed training exercises in the Caribbean and in Atlantic coastal waters. On 8 October, she departed Norfolk and steamed—via Pensacola, the

Panama Canal, and San Diego—to Hawaii, arriving at Pearl Harbor on 28 November. There, she prepared for duty in the Tokyo area and, on 10 December, departed the Hawaiian Islands and proceeded to Japan.

She operated out of Japanese ports with Task Group 55.4, Task Force 54, and other elements of the 5th Fleet until 24 March 1946 when she departed Yokosuka and proceeded via Midway to Pearl Harbor. She remained at Oahu until 29 May when she got underway and proceeded to Roi Island. In June and July, she participated in Operation "Crossroads"—the atomic bomb tests at Bikini Atoll—during which she was flagship of Destroyer Squadron 5 and supported air operations for Section Baker of the tests. She returned to Pearl Harbor on 30 July, got underway again on 7 August, and steamed into San Diego harbor on the 13th. The ship operated along the west coast until August 1947, mainly participating in hunter-killer and fleet exercises.

After loading ammunition at San Pedro, the destroyer, in company with Destroyer Division 132, departed that port on 26 August 1947; steamed via the Hawaiian Islands and Japan; and arrived at Tsingtao on 20 September. She visited various China coast ports before her return to San Diego on 5 May 1948. For nearly a year, she operated out of California ports, conducting reserve training cruises and inter-type exercises.

Turner was reclassified a radar picket destroyer on 18 March 1949. She departed San Diego on 4 April, steamed via the Panama Canal, and arrived at Newport, R.I., on 21 April 1949. There, she received additional electronic equipment enabling her to carry out her new duties. Throughout the 1950's, she conducted reserve training cruises, participated in fleet exercises, and frequently made 6th Fleet deployments. On her eighth Mediterranean cruise in 1958, she acted as a picket ship for Task Force 61 during the Lebanon crisis.

In 1959, she shifted homeport to Mayport, Fla., and continued to pursue the same duties. At the New York Naval Shipyard in 1960, she underwent a Fleet Rehabilitation and Modernization (FRAM) overhaul which improved her radar and sonar capabilities in antiaircraft and antisubmarine warfare. In 1961, the Charleston Naval Shipyard installed a new variable depth sonar, adding to *Turner*'s submarine detection equipment. Into the 1960's, she alternated frequent Mediterranean cruises with routine Atlantic training exercises, Atlantic picket duty, and special assignments. In 1962, she joined Task Force 140, the Project Mercury Recovery Force; and, in 1964, she added a Red Sea and Persian Gulf deployment to a Mediterranean voyage. In November and December of that year, she remained on station in the Caribbean in support of the Gemini II space shot.

Armed conflict flared in the Caribbean in April 1965; and, from 8 through 25 May, *Turner* operated with Task Force 128 in support of the American presence in the Dominican Republic. She again provided assistance to the American space program in February 1966 when she patrolled an alternate recovery station—at a point midway between South America and Africa, not far from the equator—as a backup site for a project Apollo landing.

While in the Caribbean on routine training in August 1967, *Turner* conducted a search for a disabled motor boat which had been adrift in the Windward Passage with 11 passengers on board. After a four-hour hunt, she located and assisted the boat and its occupants. During her 14th Mediterranean deployment late in January 1968, she directed the fruitless search for the missing Israeli submarine *Dakar;* and, while operating with *Independence* (CVA–62) in the Mediterranean in October of that year, *Turner* rescued two survivors of a downed plane.

Early in 1969, she completed her 15th Mediterranean deployment and returned to the United States. In April, she arrived at Mayport and was decommissioned

there on 26 September. Her name was struck from the Navy list that same day, and, on 13 October 1970, she was sold to Southern Scrap Material, Ltd., New Orleans, for scrapping.

Turner Joy

Charles Turner Joy—born on 17 February 1895 in St. Louis, Mo.—entered the Naval Academy in 1912 and graduated from there on 3 June 1916. He reported for duty in newly commissioned *Pennsylvania* (Battleship No. 38). That fall, his ship became flagship of the Atlantic Fleet when Admiral Henry T. Mayo shifted his flag from *Wyoming* (Battleship No. 32) to *Pennsylvania*. Ens. Joy remained with the flagship throughout America's participation in World War I and was still on board in December 1918 when she helped to escort *George Washington* when that transport carried President Woodrow Wilson to France for the peace conference in Paris.

He was detached from *Pennsylvania* in January 1921 to study ordnance engineering. After study at several places, he received a master's degree from the University of Michigan late in 1923. On 15 November 1923, he reported for duty as Aide and Flag Lieutenant to the Commander, Yangtze Patrol. Two years later, Joy became executive officer of destroyer *Pope* (DD–225). Following six months of service with that Asiatic Fleet destroyer, Joy went to Washington to join the Aviation Ordnance section of the Bureau of Ordnance. He returned to sea in January 1928 as asistant gunnery officer in *California* (BB–44) and served in that capacity until ordered to the Naval Mine Depot at Yorktown, Va., in May 1931 for duty as ordnance officer.

Two years later, Lt. Comdr. Joy took over his first command, *Litchfield* (DD–336). Following that assignment, he was posted to the staff of the Commander, Battle Force Destroyers, as gunnery and operations officer. In mid-year 1937, Comdr. Joy reported for duty at the Naval Academy where he eventually became the head of the Ordnance and Gunnery department. That duty lasted until May 1940 when he returned to sea as executive officer of *Indianapolis* (CA–35), then serving in the Atlantic with the Scouting Force. His last prewar assignment began in February 1941 when he became operations officer on the staff of the Commander, Scouting Force, Pacific Fleet, embarked first in *Indianapolis* and, later, in *Lexington* (CV–2). Joy's duty from February 1941 to September 1941 involved a number of organizational changes which do not lend themselves to a succinct, clear description. Suffice it to say that he remained an operations officer and worked with both the staff of the Commander, Pacific Fleet Scouting Force, and with that of the Commander, Task Force (TF) 11, during the early weeks of the war in the Pacific.

In September 1942, Capt. Joy assumed command of *Louisville* (CA–28), then assigned to TF 8 in the Aleutian Islands. There, he directed his ship during convoy-escort missions between the various bases in the island chain and in an occasional bombardment of Japanese-held Kiska. In November, Capt. Joy's ship was reassigned to the southwestern Pacific. After a stop at New Caledonia, he reported for duty with TF 67, then engaged in the naval phase of the struggle for Guadalcanal. On 29 January 1943, Capt. Joy and his ship managed to get into the last of the major naval actions of the Guadalcanal campaign, the Battle of Rennel Island. For the most part, however, his Southwest Pacific duty consisted of protective patrols east of Guadalcanal while American land forces completed their subjugation of the island. The third phase of his command of *Louisville* brought a second tour of duty in the Aleutian Islands. In April, he took his ship north via Pearl Harbor to join TF 16 for the occupation of Attu and Kiska. Between 11 and 30 May, he directed her activities during the assault and occupation of Attu. In July, he conducted a preinvasion bombardment of Kiska.

After eight months in Washington as head of the Pacific Plans Division in the headquarters of the Commander in Chief, United States Fleet, newly frocked Rear Admiral Joy assumed command of Cruiser Division (CruDiv) 6 in April 1944. He led CruDiv 6 during the Mariana Islands assaults, the Battle of the Philippine Sea, and in the carrier strikes on Formosa, Okinawa, and the Philippines in preparation for the invasion of the Philippines. Later, during operations to liberate the archipelago, Rear Admiral Joy's cruisers participated in the Leyte assault, the Battle for Leyte Gulf, and the invasion of Luzon at Lingayen Gulf. In February 1945, he directed his division in support of the assault and occupation of Iwo Jima. Rear Admiral Joy also participated in the final amphibious operation of the war, the invasion of Okinawa, serving as Senior Officer Present Afloat at Buckner Bay. In that capacity, he "directed the unloading operations, arranged salvage and rescue operations, and carried out fire support duties in the face of intense enemy air and kamikaze attacks."

Rear Admiral Joy ended his tour of duty as Commander, CruDiv 6, on 8 June 1945 and took over Amphibious Group 2 soon thereafter. The end of the war in August found him in Coronado, Calif., preparing his command for the expected landing on the Japanese home islands. When the Japanese capitulation obviated that invasion, the Navy quickly shifted Rear Admiral Joy to duty in conjunction with the occupation of Japan and that empire's former possessions. He served initially in China as Commander, Yangtze Patrol Force, and then at Hong Kong as Commander, TF 74. Upon his return to the United States, the admiral served a three-year tour of duty, from June 1946 to August 1949, as commanding officer of the Naval Proving Ground, Dahlgren, located on the banks of the southern Potomac River in King George County, Va.

Joy put on his third star on 1 August 1949 and, that fall, became Commander, Naval Forces, Far East (NavFE). Vice Admiral Joy was serving in that capacity during the summer of 1950 when communist troops from North Korea invaded South Korea. He commanded all United Nations naval forces between June 1950 and May 1952, coordinating logistics, reconnaissance, minesweeping, bombardment, antisubmarine, and air operations. In no small measure, the success of the Inchon landing was due to his talents as overall commander of the naval forces involved. The last year of his tour of duty in the Far East coincided with the beginning of the peace negotiations with the North Korean government. Vice Admiral Joy served as senior United Nations delegate at the conference from its beginning in July 1951 until his relief on 23 May 1952. On 4 June 1952, he was also relieved of command of United States Naval Forces, Far East, and returned home shortly thereafter. Vice Admiral Joy rounded out a full career of service as Superintendent of the Naval Academy/Commandant, Severn River Naval Command, from 4 August 1952 until relieved of duty pending retirement on 1 July 1954. Upon retirement, he was raised to the rank of full admiral. Admiral Joy spent a brief two-year retirement at La Jolla, Calif., before his death at San Diego on 13 June 1956.

(DD–951: dp. 4,200 (f.); l. 418'6''; b. 45'; dr. 22'6''; s. 33 k.; cpl. 360; a. 3 5'', 2 3'', 6 15.5'' tt., 1 dct., 2 dcp. (hh.); cl. *Forrest Sherman*)

Turner Joy (DD–951) was laid down on 30 September 1957 at Seattle, Wash., by the Puget Sound Bridge & Dredging Co.; launched on 5 May 1958; sponsored by Mrs. C. Turner Joy; and commissioned on 3 August 1959, Comdr. Ralph S. Wentworth, Jr., in command.

Following a pre-shakedown goodwill cruise to Central and South American ports and shakedown out of San Diego, *Turney Joy* began, early in 1960, duty as flagship both of Destroyer Squadron (DesRon) 13 and

Destroyer Division (DesDiv) 131. Based at Long Beach, Calif., she formed part of an antisubmarine warfare (ASW) task group built around *Hornet* (CVS–12). She conducted exercises along the California coast until 17 May when she sailed with the task group for the western Pacific.

After stops at Pearl Harbor and Apra, Guam, she stood air-sea rescue duty near the Marianas for President Dwight D. Eisenhower's flight to visit several Asian nations. After returning to Apra briefly, the destroyer moved via the Philippines to Bangkok, Thailand. *Turner Joy* crossed the President's path once more in July when the Red Chinese used the latter's visit to Nationalist Chinese Taiwan as a pretext for shelling the tiny islands, Quemoy and Matsu. A tense month of duty with the Taiwan Strait patrol followed as the United States Navy demonstrated America's support for one of her allies. In mid-August, the warship moved north for exercises with 7th Fleet carriers along the coast of Japan. That duty rounded out her first western Pacific deployment, and the destroyer got underway for Yokosuka, Japan, and headed home.

Turner Joy returned to Long Beach on 16 November. Over the next 18 months, she completed an extensive overhaul and participated in numerous 1st Fleet exercises along the California coast. In October 1961, the destroyer was transferred to DesDiv 191 of DesRon 19 and assumed duty as flagship for both. On 2 June 1962, she stood out of Long Beach with an ASW task group built around *Hornet* (CVS–12). On her way to the Far East, the warship participated in exercises with Amphibious Squadron 5 in the Hawaiian Islands. Later, she joined the screen of *Hancock* (CVA–19) operating off the southern coast of Honshu, Japan. Her second deployment to the Orient was characterized by a series of exercises with ships of the 7th Fleet and of Allied navies. Areas of operations included the Sea of Japan, the Pacific east of Japan, and the South China Sea. After a final series of drills conducted with *Bonhomme Richard* (CVA–31), the destroyer completed that tour of duty at Yokosuka, Japan, early in December. On the 7th, she headed back to the United States where she arrived on the 21st. The ensuing 14 months brought another overhaul as well as further 1st Fleet exercises in the waters along the west coast. Those evolutions continued into 1964; and, in March, the destroyer began preparations for overseas movement.

On 13 March 1964, *Turner Joy* departed Long Beach to embark upon her most celebrated tour of duty in the Far East. The third western Pacific deployment of her career began routinely enough. After calling at Pearl Harbor on her way west, the destroyer joined the task group built around *Kitty Hawk* (CVA–63) for operations in the Philippine Sea, followed by a cruise through the South China Sea to Japan. Further training operations and port visits ensued, as the deployment continued peacefully. During late July, *Turner Joy*, while attached to a carrier task group built around *Ticonderoga* (CVA–14), began making "watch dog" patrols off the coast of Vietnam where a vicious civil war had been raging at varying levels of intensity since the end of World War II. In the afternoon of 2 August *Maddox* (DD–731), engaged in a similar patrol, called for assistance when three North Vietnamese motor torpedo boats attacked her. As *Maddox* evaded the torpedo boats, aircraft from *Ticonderoga* joined her in knocking out two of the hostile craft. Meanwhile *Turner Joy* raced to *Maddox* to provide additional surface strength. By the time she reached *Maddox*, the remaining boat had fled; but *Turner Joy* remained with *Maddox*, and the two destroyers continued their patrols of the gulf.

Less than 48 hours later, *Turner Joy*'s radar screens picked up a number of what appeared to be small high-speed surface craft approaching, but at extreme range. As a precaution, the two destroyers called upon *Ticonderoga* to furnish air support. By nightfall, the unidentified radar echoes suggested that North Vietnamese small craft were converging upon the two American warships from the west and south. *Turner Joy* reported that she sighted one—maybe two—torpedo wakes, then rang up full speed, maneuvered radically to evade expected torpedoes, and began firing in the direction of the unidentified blips. Over the next two and one-half hours, *Turner Joy* and planes from *Ticonderoga* fired at the supposed hostile craft. Reports claimed that at least two of those were sunk by direct hits and another pair severely damaged, and that the remaining assailants retired rapidly to the north. Whether or not the North Vietnamese attacked the two ships on the 4th remains a mystery. Only they know for sure. It could well have been that bad weather and the freakish radar conditions—for which the Gulf of Tonkin is famous—caused radar echoes to appear on *Turner Joy*'s screen and prompted her captain and crew to take defensive action in consideration of the events two days earlier.

In any event, the "Tonkin Gulf Incident" prompted American retaliation. *Constellation* (CVA–64) joined *Ticonderoga* off North Vietnam the following day; and, together, they launched 64 sorties against the bases from which the attacks had been launched and against an oil storage depot known to have been used to support those bases. Planes from *Constellation* hit the communist motor torpedo boat bases at Hongay and Loc Chao in the north while *Ticonderoga* aircraft went after three targets in the south: the motor torpedo boat bases at

Quang Khe and Phuc Loi as well as the Vinh oil storage depot. At the last-named target, American planes set fire to 12 of the 14 oil storage tanks sending almost 10 percent of North Vietnam's oil reserves up in smoke. Of more lasting significance both to the warship and the country, however, the incident prompted Congress to pass the Tonkin Gulf resolution, the legal foundation for the direct involvement of the United States in a bloody and costly war in Indochina for the ensuing eight and one-half years. Throughout that period, *Turner Joy* served repeatedly in the conflict.

Following the excitement of the first week in August, the destroyer resumed more routine operations in the South China Sea. She concluded her deployment when she reached Long Beach on 2 October—two months to the day since she had rushed to the aid of *Maddox*. The destroyer conducted normal operations out of Long Beach until 18 December when she entered the naval shipyard for a three-month overhaul. Late in March, she began refresher training out of San Diego. West coast operations occupied her until 10 July, when she departed Long Beach with DesRon 19, bound once again for duty in the Orient. At the end of a 21-day transit, *Turner Joy* joined *Coral Sea* (CVA–43) near the end of the month. During August and the first three weeks of September, the destroyer served both as an escort for the carrier and as a detached radar picket ship.

On 23 September, she moved into the Gulf of Thailand near the west coast of South Vietnam to participate in

USS *Turner Joy* (DD–951)

one of the earliest naval gunfire support missions conducted along that section of the coastline. After a brief respite in Subic Bay for upkeep, the warship returned to shore bombardment duty in October, this time along South Vietnam's southeastern coast between Cape St. Jacques and Chu Lai. On the 25th, she provided callfire for American and South Vietnamese forces operating ashore in the vicinity of Chu Lai itself. During the mission, her guns destroyed a number of enemy positions and figured prominently in the repulse of a Viet Cong attack. Near the conclusion of that 24-hour action, a 5-inch round misfired; and, during the ensuing efforts to clear the chamber, the shell detonated. The explosion damaged the gun mount, killed three sailors, and wounded three more. That event forced her departure from the combat zone. After landing the three casualties at Danang, *Turner Joy* set course for Subic Bay in the Philippines. After a week of repairs, the destroyer departed Subic Bay in company with *Ticonderoga* (CVA–14) for screening duty in the South China Sea, followed by port calls at Hong Kong and at Yokosuka, Japan. At the end of the year, she returned to naval gunfire support duty off the coast of South Vietnam.

On 3 January 1966, the destroyer resumed plane guard duty with *Ticonderoga* in the South China Sea. The destroyer patrolled with the carrier on "Yankee Station" until the 14th when she headed, via Subic Bay, for Long Beach. *Turner Joy* arrived home on 1 February and, two weeks later, began a month-long restricted availability. From the completion of her overhaul in March through the end of May, the destroyer remained in Long Beach engaged in upkeep, repairs, and in training the numerous replacements who had reported on board. On 11 June, she put to sea once again to conduct a midshipman training cruise, during which she visited Pearl Harbor, Seattle, and San Francisco. *Turner Joy* concluded that operation on 29 July when she disembarked the midshipmen at Long Beach. Later that summer, she again visited Seattle in conjunction with that city's annual Seafair celebration. Additional training and upkeep at Long Beach followed and occupied her until the second week in October. At that time, she returned to sea to participate in fleet exercise "Baseline II," after which she proceeded to Long Beach for a series of repairs in preparation for another tour of duty in the western Pacific. *Turner Joy* stood out of Long Beach on 18 November and—after visits to Pearl Harbor, Midway, and Guam—entered port at Kaohsiung, Taiwan, on 11 December.

Turner Joy's fourth deployment to the western Pacific brought her three tours of duty off the coast of Vietnam and concluded with a visit to Australia. On 15 December, she departed Kaohsiung and headed for the coastline of the II Corps area of South Vietnam. The destroyer reached her zone of operations on the 18th and, for the next month, conducted shore bombardments in support of American and South Vietnamese troops operating ashore. She concluded that assignment on 17 January 1967 and headed for the Philippines. After two weeks of availability at Subic Bay and a five-day liberty visit to Hong Kong, *Turner Joy* returned to the Vietnamese coast on 10 February. For almost a month, she delivered gunfire support for troops ashore, this time in the I Corps zone of South Vietnam. That duty ended on 3 March, and a nine-day tender availability alongside *Jason* (AR–8) in Sasebo, Japan, followed.

On 21 March, the destroyer resumed station off Vietnam. This time, however, off the coast of North Vietnam. Instead of supporting American and South Vietnamese troops directly through shore bombardments, she did so by interdicting enemy logistical efforts in Operation "Sea Dragon." Though primarily directed at the enemy's water-borne logistics, "Sea Dragon" also struck wherever possible at the enemy's overland supply lines. During her 26 days on station engaged in "Sea Dragon" operations, *Turner Joy* fired on a

number of shore targets in addition to an even larger number of enemy waterborne logistics craft. On 7 April, while firing on some enemy craft beached near Cap Mui Ron, the destroyer came under the fire of a North Vietnamese shore battery. During that exchange, she suffered a direct hit on the fantail and a near-miss air burst above the forward mast. The hit astern penetrated the deck to the supply office, damaging records therein as well as pipes and cables in the overhead. Several rounds of 5-inch VT fragmentation projectiles in mount 53 ammunition stowage area also suffered damage and had to be discarded. Shrapnel from near misses wounded a member of *Turner Joy*'s repair party and peppered her bow while the air burst above the forward mast put her air-search radar out of service except for its IFF aspect. The damage, however, was not severe enough to curtail her tour of duty; and she remained on station until relieved by HMAS *Hobart* on 16 April.

Two days later, the destroyer arrived in Subic Bay, and she entered drydock, soon thereafter, for repairs to her strut bearing, the bow, the peak tank, and her air search radar antenna. Concurrently with this yard work, she conducted a tender availability with *Piedmont* (AD–17) to prepare her for visits to Australia and New Zealand during the forthcoming celebration of the 25th anniversary of the Battle of the Coral Sea. Repairs and availability completed, she stood out of Subic Bay on 24 April in company with *McKean* (DD–784). En route to Melbourne, the two ships stopped at Manus in the Admiralty Islands and at Brisbane, Australia. The ship reached Melbourne on 8 May; and, while she remained there until the 13th, her crew enjoyed Australian hospitality in the city and replied in kind on board. Between 13 and 17 May, she made a rough transit of the Tasman Sea and arrived in Auckland, New Zealand, on the latter date for the second phase of her Coral Sea celebration. She remained in Auckland until 22 May at which time she and *McKean* put to sea to return to the United States. After a stop at Pago Pago, American Samoa, the two ships rejoined *Gridley* (DLG–21) and *Maddox* on 26 May to reconstitute DesRon 19 for the voyage home. After a brief fueling stop at Pearl Harbor on 2 June, the warships arrived in Long Beach on the 8th. Between June and September, *Turner Joy* went through a month of post-deployment standdown followed by training operations in the waters off southern California. On 18 September, she arrived at Bremerton, Wash., for a two-month shipyard availability at the Puget Sound Naval Shipyard. In mid-November, she returned to Long Beach and resumed operations along the California coast.

That duty continued until late February 1968 when she entered the Long Beach Naval Shipyard for a restricted availability in preparation for her fifth deployment to the Far East. *Turner Joy* stood out of Long Beach on 12 March and—after stops at Oahu, Midway, and Guam—arrived in Subic Bay on 4 April. Over the following five months, the destroyer conducted operations along the coast of Vietnam similar to those performed during previous deployments. She delivered naval gunfire support for American and South Vietnamese troops in South Vietnam and conducted "Sea Dragon" patrols along the coast of North Vietnam to interdict enemy waterborne logistics traffic. Her tours of duty on the gunline took her to the I, II, and IV Corps areas of South Vietnam. As during previous deployments, she punctuated assignments in the combat zone with visits to Subic Bay and to Buckner Bay, Okinawa, for fuel, supplies, and repairs, as well as to Kaohsiung, Taiwan; and Hong Kong for rest and relaxation. She completed her last tour of duty of the deployment off the Vietnamese coast on 4 September and, after a brief tender availability at Subic Bay, headed homeward on 8 September. Retracing her outward-bound voyage with stops at Guam, Midway, and

Pearl Harbor, *Turner Joy* entered Long Beach on the 26th.

Upon her return to the United States, the warship began preparations for her regular overhaul. She entered the Long Beach Naval Shipyard on 28 November and remained there until late February 1969. When post-overhaul trials ended on 15 March, the ship resumed normal operations out of Long Beach. During April and May, she participated in a 1st Fleet combined ASW/AAW exercise as a part of her refresher training. She completed those operations during the latter half of May; and, after a brief availability alongside *Bryce Canyon* (AD-36), she embarked NROTC midshipmen on 5 June for the two-month 1969 summer training cruise. At the end of the cruise, *Turner Joy* debarked the midshipmen on 1 August and resumed training in the southern California operating area.

On 18 November, she got underway from Long Beach to return to the Orient. Following a four-day layover at Pearl Harbor and brief fuel stops at Midway and Guam, she arrived in Subic Bay on 11 December. After a five-day availability alongside *Prairie* (AD-15), the destroyer stood out of Subic Bay bound for Danang, South Vietnam, and gunfire support duty off the coast of the I Corps zone. By New Year's Day 1970, she was on her way to "Yankee Station" to act as plane guard for Task Force (TF) 77 aircraft carriers. On 4 January, she headed back to Subic Bay where she remained until the 18th. She completed another three-week tour on the gunline on 10 February and then shaped a course for Sasebo, Japan, whence she operated until early in March. After a liberty call in Hong Kong, *Turner Joy* returned to the Vietnamese coast and resumed gunfire support missions until early April. On 3 April, she rendezvoused with *Shangri La* (CVA-38) and then made port calls at Subic Bay and Bangkok, Thailand, before embarking upon her final gunline assignment on 19 April. She returned to Subic Bay on 10 May for a final visit before heading back to the United States on the 17th.

The destroyer arrived back in Long Beach on 1 June and began a three-month restricted availability in the naval shipyard. She completed the availability early in October and began sea trials and training in the southern California operating area. Early in December, *Turner Joy* reentered the Long Beach Naval Shipyard to be readied for her redeployment to the western Pacific. On 26 January 1971, she stood out of Long Beach on her way to rejoin the 7th Fleet. She entered Subic Bay on 16 February and went into drydock for several days while both her propellers were replaced. On 5 March, she exited Subic Bay for a tour of naval gunfire support duty along the Vietnamese coast. That assignment—carried out along the I Corps zone coastline near Danang—ended on 2 April; and she headed for "Yankee Station" and two weeks of plane guard duty with the TF 77 aircraft carriers. Following a five-day port call at Subic Bay, *Turner Joy* took up position at "Yankee Station" again on 27 April—this time as escort for the PIRAZ (positive identification and radar advisory zone) ship. She performed that duty until 30 April; then, after three days evading a typhoon, she moved in close to the I Corps shoreline to resume gunfire support duties.

On 14 May, the destroyer shaped a course for Subic Bay. Following a five-day gunfire exercise at the Tabones range, she departed the Philippines to make liberty visits to Bangkok, Thailand, and Hong Kong. In late June, she did another tour of duty on PIRAZ station and provided plane guard services to *Kitty Hawk* (CVA-63). A brief liberty call at Subic Bay followed; and then, on 30 June, she embarked upon a voyage to Australia and New Zealand. During July, she made visits to the Australian towns of Brisbane and Sydney as well as the New Zealand port, Auckland. On the 26th, *Turner Joy* got underway for home. She arrived back in Long Beach on 10 August and con-

ducted normal post-deployment evolutions through the remainder of 1971.

In February 1972, the destroyer began an extensive overhaul. Over the ensuing six months, she received entirely new 5-inch 54-caliber gun mounts; and her propulsion plant underwent conversion to enable it to burn Navy distillate fuel. Extensive other modifications, installations, and renovations also took place between February and August. From August to December, she busied herself with various trials and tests at sea, conducted refresher training, and prepared for her next assignment to the Far East. Her voyage west began on 6 December and ended with her arrival at Subic Bay on the 29th. Two days later, she put to sea for her first tour on the gunline. It also proved to be her last. She delivered gunfire support intermittently for 28 days. Then, on 28 January 1973, American participation in the Vietnam conflict ended with a negotiated ceasefire.

For the remainder of that deployment, *Turner Joy* participated in a variety of operations—including Operation "Endsweep," the removal of American mines from the waters around Haiphong harbor, as well as antisubmarine warfare exercises and carrier operations in the South China Sea. She punctuated those assignments with port visits to Subic Bay; Hong Kong; Kaohsiung, Taiwan; and Sasebo, Japan. On 13 June, she headed home via Yokosuka and arrived in Long Beach on the 22d. She spent the period from then until mid-October engaged in upkeep and a restricted availability. On 17 October, she departed Long Beach and set course for her new home port, San Diego. Upon arrival there, she began normal operations—engineering and gunnery exercises at sea alternated with upkeep in port.

That routine continued until April 1974, at which time she began preparations for her first peacetime deployment to the western Pacific in a decade. She stood out of San Diego on 6 May, reached Pearl Harbor on the 12th, and completed a brief assignment with *Ranger* (CVA-61) in the Hawaiian operating area on the 24th. On that day, she departed Oahu and continued her voyage west. *Turner Joy* arrived in Subic Bay on 4 June and, for the next two months, conducted local operations in company with *Ranger*. On 1 August, the destroyer departed the Philippines for a goodwill visit to Surabaja, Java, and a liberty call at Hong Hong. She returned to the Philippines on 31 August and conducted local operations out of Subic Bay for two months before heading homeward on 3 October. The warship arrived in San Diego on 22 October and, after a month of post-deployment leave and upkeep, began a normal schedule of operations in the southern California operating area.

Turner Joy ended 1974 and began 1975 engaged in a rather extensive availability which was completed in mid-April. At the conclusion of that repair period, she resumed operations along the coast of southern California. Refresher training, FleetEx 2-75, and a midshipman training cruise occupied her from April through August. On 2 September, she departed San Diego for the 11th deployment of her career to the western Pacific. However, after a two-week stop at Subic Bay, her western Pacific assignment was transformed into a tour of duty in the Indian Ocean.

On 13 October, she departed Subic Bay in company with *Midway* (CV-41), *Fanning* (DE-1076), and *Sacramento* (AOE-1) bound ultimately for Bandar Abbas, Iran. Along the way, she visited Singapore and Sri Lanka and participated in exercises with the Singapore Navy. The destroyer arrived in Bandar Abbas on 13 November whence she and her sailing companions participated in the CENTO exercise, "Midlink." During that operation, she joined units of the British, Iranian, and Pakistani navies in practicing a broad spectrum of naval tactics—ASW, AAW, surface engagements, gunnery drills, and missile shoots.

"Midlink" ended on 25 November, and *Turner Joy*

briefly stopped again at Bandar Abbas before heading for the Philippines on the 29th. She arrived back in Subic Bay on 12 December and remained there until 9 January 1976. Routine operations in the Philippines, exercises in the South China Sea and the Sea of Japan —as well as visits to ports in Taiwan and Japan— characterized the remainder of that deployment. On 17 March, she stood out of Yokosuka to return to the United States. After stops at Midway and Pearl Harbor, she reentered San Diego harbor on 4 April. Following post-deployment standdown, the destroyer reverted once more to training operations out of San Diego.

As a result of long years of service in Vietnam and two delays in a scheduled overhaul, however, *Turner Joy* was unable to successfully complete her Operational Propulsion Plant Examination. This deficiency made it necessary for the ship to spend the remainder of 1976 in port correcting propulsion deficiencies.

The year 1977 was spent largely in port due to recurring material problems. In September, however, *Turner Joy* was underway briefly for local operations. Pre-overhaul standdown began in mid-October; and, on 7 November, the ship was towed to the Long Beach Naval Shipyard for a regular overhaul designed to completely renovate her entire engineering plant. The entire year of 1978 was spent in overhaul.

Turner Joy received nine battle stars for her Vietnam service.

Turner, Richmond K., see Richmond K. Turner.

Turquoise

A gem, composed of hydrous phosphate of aluminum and copper, whose color ranges from a greenish-grey to sky blue.

(PC–459: dp. 565; l. 172'; b. 26'; dr. 11'; cpl. 60; a. 1 3'', 2 dct.)

Ohio—a diesel yacht built in 1922 at Newport News, Va., by the Newport News Shipbuilding and Dry Dock Co.—was laid down on 1 August 1922; launched on 16 September 1922; and delivered exactly two months later to Edward Willys Scripps, the publisher of the Scripps Howard newspapers. After Scripps died on board the yacht on 12 March 1926, as she lay anchored in Monrovia Bay, Liberia, the yacht served a succession of owners under the names *Maramichi*, *Walucia III*, *Kallisto*, and *Entropy*.

On 21 August 1940, as America girded for World War II, the United States Navy purchased *Entropy* from Robert V. G. Furman of Schenectady, N.Y., classified her a submarine chaser, and designated her PC–459. Since American submarine chasers were unnamed during World War II, the ship was known simply by her hull number, *PC–459*. The luxury craft entered the Gibbs-Jacksonville Yard at Jacksonville, Fla., on 25 September 1940 for conversion for naval use. On 5 December 1940, *PC–459* was placed in commission at Jacksonville, Lt. Comdr. Cecil G. McKinney, USNR, in command.

Following commissioning, *PC–459* put into Charleston (S.C.) Navy Yard on 9 December for fitting out. After spending the remainder of December 1940 and the better part of January 1941 in training exercises and shakedown, she got underway for Cuban waters in company with *Seminole* (AT–65) on 21 January. After a brief stay at Guantanamo Bay, *PC–459* set out on 30 January for Puerto Rico.

Upon arrival at San Juan on 1 February 1941, *PC–459* was reclassified a patrol yacht, designated PY–18, and named *Turquoise*. Operating under the Commandant of the 10th Naval District, *Turquoise* patrolled Caribbean waters through July as the Battle of the Atlantic moved ever closer to neutral waters on the American coast. On 1 August, when the Navy commissioned the Naval Operating Base at Trinidad, British West Indies, the patrol yacht received orders to report there for duty as temporary station ship.

She remained in the vicinity of Trinidad until early December, when she returned to Charleston for refit. On 7 December, the day after she entered the navy yard, the Japanese attacked Pearl Harbor. Four days later, on 11 December, Italy and Germany declared war on the United States.

Her refit shortened, *Turquoise* steamed back to Puerto Rico and arrived on 20 December. She operated in the Caribbean on local patrols into the early spring, when she returned to Charleston for availability. Upon the conclusion of the overhaul, she set out for San Juan on 9 April 1942. Upon arrival, she received orders to escort a YP and a dredge to Trinidad and then to report to the Commandant of the Naval Operating Base there for orders.

Besides inshore patrol duties out of Trinidad, she also escorted local convoys in the Caribbean area, called at such ports as Gonaives and Port-au-Prince, Haiti, besides the already-frequented San Juan, Trinidad, Key West, and Guantanamo Bay. But for occasional refits at Charleston, she continued such operations through most of 1943. In December 1943, she received orders to proceed to the Canal Zone.

Arriving on 24 December 1943, she was transferred under lend-lease to the Ecuadorian Navy on 29 January 1944. The yacht operated under the Ecuadorian flag as *Nueve de Octobre* (the 9th of October) through 1949. She was sold to the Ecuadorian government on 13 May 1949 and was struck from the Navy list on 7 June 1949.

Renamed *Esmeraldas*, after a port city in Ecuador, she served with the Ecuadorian Navy into 1953. *Esmeraldas* ran aground in the Guayas River, near Guayaquil, and was declared a total loss on 9 September 1953.

Turquoise did not receive any battle stars for her World War II service.

Turtle

The first *Turtle* was named for the marine reptile; the second for Turtle Town, a small unincorporated town in Polk County, Tenn.

I

(Submarine: t. 1 (approx.); l. 7'6''; dhp. 6'; s. 2 to 3 k.; cpl. 1; a. 1 "torpedo")

The first *Turtle* was designed in 1771 by David Bushnell, a Yale student, and built with the help of his brother, Ezra Bushnell, in 1775 at Saybrook, Conn. The submersible was named *Turtle* because Bushnell thought that this unique craft bore some resemblance to "two upper tortoise shells of equal size, joined together."

Conceived as a means of breaking the British blockade of Boston harbor, the submersible embodied four basic requirements for a successful military submarine: the ability to (1) submerge, (2) to maneuver under water, (3) to maintain an adequate air supply to support the operator of the craft, and (4) to carry out effective offensive action against an enemy surface ship.

Turtle could be made to submerge by simply flooding her bilges with sea water. To surface, the man operating the submarine would pump out the bilges. A crude conning tower, fitted with round, glass ports projected some six or seven inches above the surface of the water. This arrangement allowed the operator to see where he was going and permitted light to illuminate the equipment necessary to operate the submarine. When submerged, *Turtle* was illuminated by instruments made of a phosphorescent wood known as "fox fire."

Maneuverability in the horizontal plane was achieved by a hand- or foot-cranked propeller fitted at the bow. Ascent or descent was made possible by a second propeller fitted just ahead of the low conning tower arrangement. It was possible for *Turtle*'s operator to propel the craft forward by utilizing the foot-treadle to operate the bow propeller while simultaneously using the hand-operated second propeller to move the craft up or down. Steering was accomplished by a tiller. The combination of the craft's shape and the ballast load—700 pounds (500 fixed and 200 detachable)—gave *Turtle* a low center of gravity and made her quite stable.

Air was supplied by a pair of tubes fitted through the conning tower hatch. Valves in these pipes would automatically shut them while the vessel was submerged. The tubes themselves actually resembled a crude snorkel arrangement.

As to the craft's offensive capability, Bushnell invented a "torpedo" which would be carried into action and then jettisoned to be secured against an enemy ship's hull. The "torpedo" was an egg-shaped casing filled with 150 pounds of gunpowder and fitted with a rudimentary clock-work detonator. Fitted piggy-back style abaft the conning tower, the "torpedo" was to be fastened to a bolt screwed into the enemy's hull. The clock-work mechanism—set for about an hour's time —would then set off the charge, hopefully after the submarine had cleared the area. Apparently, during *Turtle*'s trials, Bushnell tested this aparatus against a hulk in the Conecticut River.

Bushnell attempted to keep his strange work a secret and completed *Turtle* in late October or early November of 1775. However, word leaked out, due probably to the Tory sympathies of a local postmaster who would periodically read letters written by one of Bushnell's friends, who knew of the invention. To the British, the craft seemed potentially dangerous.

Encouraged in his endeavors by men like George Washington, Thomas Jefferson, and Benjamin Franklin, among others, Bushnell continued to perfect his device —almost entirely with his own dwindling funds. Although Bushnell planned to deploy *Turtle* to Boston, that operation was obviated when General Howe evacuated the city on 17 March 1776 despite his successes at Breed's and Bunker hills and withdrew north to Nova Scotia.

After reinforcements arrived, Howe set sail from Halifax on 10 June and began landing his troops at Staten Island, N.Y., on 5 July. Bushnell accordingly offered the services of his submarine to General Washington who provided the young inventor with funds and "other aids to carry his plan to execution."

Bushnell had planned to use his brother Ezra as the operator of the submarine when she went into action against the British. However, Ezra fell ill shortly before Bushnell had planned to launch his invention's combat career. With Ezra's illness, there was no one who knew enough to operate the craft outside of Bushnell himself. Bushnell accordingly approached General Parsons of the Connecticut militia to call for three volunteers to undergo an accelerated training program. The one volunteer who apparently distinguished himself by his abilities was Sergeant Ezra Lee.

Meanwhile, as *Turtle* underwent minor alterations over a 10-day period, the military situation in the New York area changed dramatically. Late in August, Washington's army retreated from Long Island, as Howe occupied Governor's Island. The time to prove the submarine's effectiveness had come.

Bushnell picked out the imposing 64-gun HMS *Eagle*—the flagship of Admiral "Black Dick" Howe (General Howe's brother)—as his choice for a target. This vessel, under the command of Capt. Henry Duncan, lay moored with the rest of the large British squadron to the north of Staten Island.

Sergeant Lee clambered down the narrow conning tower hatch late in the evening of 6 September 1776 and, at 2230, set out on his mission. Towed downstream "as nigh the fleet they dared," *Turtle* was cast off, undetected. Lee hove about and rowed for nearly two and one-half hours before the tide slackened. He rowed under the stern of his target and, as he neared *Eagle*'s imposing bulk, he could see men on deck. The sound of their voices wafted down to his ears in the muggy pre-dawn darkness. Once this close, Lee shut all doors and prepared to descend beneath the royal man-of-war's hull.

Turtle sank deeper and came up under the hull. However, his efforts to attach the "torpedo" to the ship's hull were frustrated by copper-sheathing, or marine growth, or perhaps merely a hard spot in the hull which prevented the drill from boring into the ship bottom. Lee tried again after failing in the first attempt but apparently lost control of the craft. *Turtle* "immediately rose with great velocity" and broached two or three feet from *Eagle*'s side. Fortunately, the sergeant's craft "sunk like a porpoise" and submerged before a chance glance from British sailors on deck revealed his presence.

Lee initially thought to try again but decided against it. Daybreak might bring the chance of his being discovered. Deeming it "the best generalship" to clear the area, he retreated as fast as he could, traveling mostly submerged but surfacing every few minutes to get his bearings. The tide, however, made the passage difficult. Soon, some 300 or 400 British soldiers clambered atop the parapet on the fort on the English-held Governor's Island and saw the little craft steering a "crooked and zig-zag" course past the island. Presently, curiosity spawned the desire to take action, and a 12-oared cutter put out from shore with six men in it.

Lee eyed them cautiously and waited until they closed to within 50 and 60 yards. He then "let loose the magazine (torpedo) in hopes that if they should take me they would likewise pick up the magazine, and then we would all be blown up together." As Lee later recorded, however, "But as kind Providence would have it, they (the British) took fright," and returned to the island, to the sergeant's "infinite delight."

Turtle and her intrepid operator were eventually towed to safety by American boats which spotted the submarine. The "torpedo" soon drifted with the tide past Governor's Island, directly toward the anchored mass of British ships—both warships and transports. Suddenly, the "torpedo" blew up "with a tremendous explosion, throwing up bodies of water to a great height." This succeeded in alarming the British enough to cut their cables and slip downstream to the southward of Staten Island.

Two subsequent attempts to blow up British ships followed. Each, conducted from Fort Lee (Manhattan having fallen later that summer), was unsuccessful. On 9 October 1776, two British frigates, HMS *Phoenix* and HMS *Roebuck*, accompanied by the 20-gun HMS *Tartar* and three tenders, stood up the lower Hudson. They ignored the futile cannonade from Forts Washington and Constitution and quickly disposed of a small Continental squadron. Among the American ships lost was the small sloop carrying *Turtle*. Lee and Bushnell both escaped injury and reached shore. The first American submarine, however, sank to the bottom of the Hudson.

Although soon recovered, *Turtle* saw no further service. Her eventual fate remains a mystery.

II

(Research submersible: t. 21; l. 26′; b. 8′; s. 2.5 k.; cpl. 2)

AUTEC II (an acronym for the Atlantic Underwater Test and Evaluation Center's second submersible)—a research submersible capable of operating at depths in excess of one mile—was built at Groton, Conn., by the Electric Boat Division of the General Dynamics Corporation. Renamed *Turtle* on 3 December 1968, the research craft was launched eight days later—on 11 December—and sponsored by Mrs. Edward J. Fahy, the wife of Rear Admiral Fahy, the Commander of the Naval Ships' Systems Command. Completed in 1969, the submersible—in company with a sister craft, *Sea Cliff*—underwent sea trials in the Bahamas, basing on the support ship *Maxine D.*

Placed in service in June 1970, *Turtle* was assigned to the Pacific Fleet. Given the hull number DSV–3 on 1 June 1971, the submersible operated in "active, in service," status until January of 1973, when she was commissioned. Since that time, *Turtle* has performed research work for the Navy into 1980.

Tuscaloosa

A city in the state of Alabama.

I

(CA–37: dp. 9,950; l. 588'2''; b. 61'9''; dr. 19'5''; s. 32.7 k.; cpl. 708; a. 9 8'', 8 5'', 8 .50-cal. mg.; cl. *New Orleans*)

Tuscaloosa (CA–37) was laid down on 3 September 1931 at Camden, N.J., by the New York Shipbuilding Co.; launched on 15 November 1933; sponsored by Mrs. Thomas Lee McCann, wife of Lt. Thomas L. McCann and the niece of the Hon. William B. Oliver, Representative of the 6th District of Alabama; and commissioned on 17 August 1934, Capt. John N. Ferguson in command.

Tuscaloosa devoted the autumn to a shakedown cruise which took her to Rio de Janeiro, Buenos Aires, and Montevideo, before she returned to the New York Navy Yard shortly before Christmas. She then underwent post-shakedown repairs which kept her in the yard into March 1935.

The heavy cruiser soon shaped a course for the west coast. After a stop at Guantanamo Bay, Cuba, she transited the Panama Canal on 7 and 8 April and then steamed north to San Diego, where she joined Cruiser Division (CruDiv) 6 in time to participate in Fleet Problem XVI staged in May in the northern Pacific off the coast of Alaska and in waters surrounding the Hawaiian Islands. This operation was divided into five distinct phases which might be aspects of some real naval campaign of the future in which the United States would take the strategic offensive.

Tuscaloosa subsequently was based at San Pedro, Calif., whence she conducted routine exercises and local operations with CruDiv 6. In the spring of 1936, the heavy cruiser participated in Fleet Problem XVII, taking place off the west coast of the United States, Central America, and the Panama Canal Zone. The five-phase exercise was devoted to preparing the fleet for antisubmarine operations, testing communications systems, and training of aircraft patrol squadrons for extended fleet operations.

In May 1937, the Fleet again exercised in Alaskan waters and in the vicinity of the Hawaiian Islands and Midway, practicing the tactics of seizing advanced base sites—a technique later to be polished to a high degree into close support and amphibious warfare doctrines. *Tuscaloosa*, as part of the "augmented" Scouting Force, "battled" the Battle Force that spring.

In April and May 1938, the heavy cruiser participated in Fleet Problem XIX, which was conducted in the vicinity of Hawaii. This operation gave the Navy added experience in search tactics; in the use of submarines, destroyers, and aircraft in scouting and attack; in the dispositions of the Fleet and the conduct of a major fleet battle.

In addition, the exercise again dealt with the matter of seizing advanced fleet bases and defending them against minor opposition. Fleet Problem XIX also tested the capabilities of the Hawaiian Defense Force, aug-

menting it with fleet units to help to defend the islands against the United States Fleet as a whole. The last phase of the exercise exercised the Fleet in operations against a defended coastline.

Tuscaloosa departed San Diego on 3 January 1939 and proceeded, via the Panama Canal, to the Caribbean. She took part in Fleet Problem XX, in the Atlantic to the east of the Lesser Antilles, before undergoing a brief refit at the Norfolk Navy Yard. She than joined *San Francisco* (CA–38) and *Quincy* (CA–39) for a goodwill tour of South American ports. Between 8 April and 10 May, the division—under the command of Rear Admiral Husband E. Kimmel—visited Caracas, Rio de Janeiro, Montevideo, and Buenos Aires before transiting the storm-tossed Strait of Magellan. The three cruisers drove their bows deep into heavy seas and battled gale-force winds as they made the difficult passage on 14 and 15 May. The division then sailed up the west coast of South America, visiting Valparaiso, Chile, and Callao, Peru, before transiting the Panama Canal and returning to Norfolk, where she arrived on 6 June.

Tuscaloosa remained off the east coast into the summer of 1939. In August, she carried President Franklin D. Roosevelt to Campobello Island, New Brunswick. En route, off Portsmouth, N.H., the Commander in Chief witnessed salvage operations in progress on the sunken *Squalus* (SS–192) which had stayed down after a test dive on 24 May 1939. On 24 August, following visits to Campobello and several ports in Newfoundland, President Roosevelt disembarked at Sandy Hook, N.J.

A week later, the German Army invaded Poland, plunging Europe into war. The outbreak of World War II on 1 September 1939 found *Tuscaloosa* at NOB Norfolk. On the 5th, President Roosevelt established the Neutrality Patrol; and, the next day, the cruiser departed for her first patrol which kept her at sea until she returned to her home port on the 11th. Three days later, the heavy cruiser departed Norfolk and spent the remainder of September and most of October engaged in gunnery training and conducting exercises out of Guantanamo Bay and San Juan, Puerto Rico. She departed the Caribbean on 27 October, bound for Hampton Roads, and arrived at Norfolk on 5 November and, but for gunnery exercises off the Virginia capes from the 13th to the 15th, remained in the Hampton Roads areas until mid-December.

Meanwhile, the Neutrality Patrol found itself keeping track of German merchantmen in waters of the western hemisphere. At the outbreak of hostilities, there had been some 85 German ships near the Americas. One of those, the North German (Norddeutcher) Lloyd (NDL) liner *Columbus*—the 13th largest steamship in the world—had been on a tourist cruise when war caught her in the West Indies. She put into Vera Cruz, Mex., where she fueled and prepared to make a break for home.

The liner departed Vera Cruz on 14 December 1939 but soon thereafter was picked up and shadowed by the destroyer *Benham* (DD–397). In ensuing days, a succession of United States warships—totaling seven in all—trailed the liner. Capt. Wilhelm Daehne, *Columbus*' master, was careful to keep his ship within the 300-mile neutrality zone until she was abreast of the Delaware capes. He then headed east.

Tuscaloosa, meanwhile, had been ordered out to participate in the chase. On 16 December, two days after *Columbus* departed Vera Cruz, *Tuscaloosa* stood out of Norfolk, bound for her patrol station. She soon relieved *Cole* (DD–155) and *Ellis* (DD–154)—two flushdeckers —and at 1450 on 19 December, spotted the British destroyer HMS *Hyperion*, guns trained out and battle ensigns streaming, standing toward *Columbus*. *Hyperion* radioed *Tuscaloosa*: "What ship are you escorting?" *Tuscaloosa* remained silent, but *Hyperion* was soon radioing *Columbus* to heave to and not use her radio. Two shots whistled across the German liner's bow.

For Capt. Daehne, there remained only one alternative. After having carefully planned for that eventuality, he scuttled his ship. All but two of his crew—a complement that included nine women stewardesses—succeeded in going over the side and manning the lifeboats. Since *Hyperion* clearly had no room for the 577 Germans who had abandoned the liner, she radioed *Tuscaloosa*, asking politely if the cruiser could handle the survivors.

From his motor launch, Capt. Daehne kept the lifeboats together while *Tuscaloosa* embarked the 567 men and nine women. He then followed them to safety on board the cruiser which provided hospitality for the shipwrecked mariners who were glad to be on board an American cruiser as rescued seamen and not in a British warship as prisoners-of-war. The bulk of the survivors were put up in the cruiser's seaplane hangar that had been cleared out to facilitate its use as a large berthing area; and the women were berthed in sick bay.

Tuscaloosa took the survivors to New York—the only port equipped to handle such a large and sudden influx of aliens—and disembarked them at Ellis Island between 1610 and 1730 on 20 December for officials to process. Ultimately, most of *Columbus'* officers and men returned, via the Pacific, to their native land. Meanwhile, *Tuscaloosa* departed New York on the 21st and arrived at Norfolk the following day.

The heavy cruiser remained at Norfolk into the New Year, 1940, and departed her home port on 11 January, bound for the West Indies. On the voyage to the Caribbean, she was accompanied by her sister ship, *San Francisco*; Battleship Division 5—less *Wyoming* (BB-43); and *Manley* (APD-1), the prototype, high-speed transport. *Tuscaloosa* and her consorts arrived at Culebra on the 16th and, two days later, shifted to Guantanamo Bay. There, she participated in fleet exercises from the 18th to the 27th. Departing Guantanamo on the latter day, *Tuscaloosa* returned to Norfolk on 29 January and entered the navy yard there for special alterations to fit her out for service as a residential flagship.

Tuscaloosa departed the Norfolk Navy Yard on 2 February and moored at NOB Norfolk. Two days later, she got underway for Cuba, arriving at Guantanamo on the 7th, only to sail three days later for Pensacola, Fla., in company with *Lang* (DD-399). The two ships exercised en route and arrived at Pensacola on the 14th.

The next day, *Tuscaloosa* embarked President Roosevelt and his guests and departed in company with *Jouett* (DD-396) and *Lang* for a cruise to Panama and the west coast of Central America. The voyage gave the President an opportunity to discuss Pan-American defense with leaders of Latin American nations. Steaming to the Pacific coast of Central America, Roosevelt inspected the Pacific defenses of the Panama Canal. In addition, he fished regularly at a variety of locations but, as he later recounted, caught "damned few fish." On the return passage through the canal, on 27 February, Roosevelt conferred with United States Navy, Army, and Air Corps officers to discuss the defense of the vital passage.

After disembarking the President at Pensacola, *Tuscaloosa* proceeded north to Norfolk and from thence to the New York Navy Yard for a three-month overhaul. During her sojourn at Brooklyn, Hitler's legions conquered France in June 1940 and won mastery of continental Europe. Soon thereafter, *Tuscaloosa* returned to the neutrality patrol and conducted monotonous but intensive patrols in the Caribbean and Bermuda areas through the summer and fall months of 1940.

On 3 December 1940 at Miami, President Roosevelt embarked in *Tuscaloosa* for the third time for a cruise to inspect the base sites obtained from Great Britain in the recently negotiated "destroyers for bases" deal. In that transaction, the United States had traded 50 old flush-decked destroyers for 99-year leases on bases in the western hemisphere. Ports of call included Kingston, Jamaica; Santa Lucia, Antigua; and the Bahamas. Roosevelt fished and entertained British colonial officials—including the Duke and Duchess of Windsor—on board the cruiser.

While the President cruised in *Tuscaloosa*, American officials in Washington wrestled with the problem of extending aid to Britain. Having barely weathered the disastrous campaign in France in the spring and the Battle of Britain in the summer, the United Kingdom desperately needed war materiel. American production could meet England's need, but American neutrality law limiting the purchase of arms by belligerents to "cash-and-carry" transactions was about to become a major obstacle, for British coffers were almost empty. While pondering England's plight as he luxuriated in *Tuscaloosa*, the President hit upon the idea of the "lend-lease" program to aid the embattled British.

On 16 December, Roosevelt left the ship at Charleston, S.C., to head for Washington to implement his "lend-lease" idea—one more step in United States' progress towards full involvement in the war. Soon thereafter, *Tuscaloosa* sailed for Norfolk and, on 22 December, embarked Admiral William D. Leahy, the newly designated Ambassador to Vichy France, and his wife, for passage to Portugal. With the "stars and stripes" painted large on the roofs of Turrets II and III, and her largest colors flying, *Tuscaloosa* sailed for the European war zone, initially escorted by *Upshur* (DD-144) and *Madison* (DD-425).

After disembarking the Ambassador to Vichy France at Lisbon and returning to Norfolk on 11 January 1941, the cruiser went to sea on maneuvers that kept her at sea until 2 March. She subsequently arrived at the newly opened American naval facility at Bermuda, on 8 April, the day after the base's commissioning. Her consorts included *Ranger* (CV-4), *Wichita* (CA-45), and destroyers *Kearny* (DD-432) and *Livermore* (DD-429). Based at Bermuda, *Tuscaloosa* continued patroling shipping lanes in the North Atlantic, enforcing the neutrality of the United States.

Elsewhere in the Atlantic, the war between the British and the Germans took an anxious turn late in May when German battleship *Bismarck* and heavy cruiser *Prinz Eugen* broke out into the Atlantic. On 24 May, *Bismarck* had sunk the vaunted HMS *Hood* in the Denmark Strait and had temporarily eluded pursuit.

Bismarck's escape into the swirling mists of the Atlantic prompted orders which sent *Tuscaloosa* to sea immediately. Most of the crew on liberty at the time could not be rounded up in time, so the ship set out for the hunt with personnel "shanghaied" from *Vincennes* (CA-44) and *Quincy* and a group of reserve ensigns who happened to be on board for a reserve cruise. However, before the cruiser reached waters where she hoped to find the *Bismarck*, British warships—directed by an American naval reserve ensign piloting a British PBY—succeeded in pounding *Bismarck* to junk on 27 May, avenging the loss of *Hood*."

Tuscaloosa soon returned to the tedium of neutrality patrolling. As the United States continued in a slow but deliberate fashion to become involved, however, the tenor of events soon changed for the heavy cruiser. On 8 August, she departed Bermuda for Newfoundland and soon embarked General Henry H. "Hap" Arnold, head of the Army Air Corps; Rear Admiral Richmond K. Turner, Director of the War Plans Division of the Navy; and Capt. Forrest Sherman. She joined *Augusta* (CA-31) off New York; and, together, the two ships, escorted by a screen of three destroyers, proceeded to Argentia, Newfoundland.

Augusta, bearing President Roosevelt, and her consorts soon arrived in the barren anchorage where the British battleship HMS *Prince of Wales*—with Prime Minister Churchill embarked—awaited her. The ensuing discussions between the two heads of state hammered out the "Atlantic Charter."

Tuscaloosa (CA–37) at Scapa Flow, April 1942. Her "dapple" finish was widely used during her first year of war time operation. (80–G–12018)

Returning from Argentia upon the conclusion of the Anglo-American talks, *Tuscaloosa* conveyed Under Secretary of State Sumner Welles to Portland, Maine. Three weeks later, in September, the cruiser overtook the first American troop convoy to Iceland, as American marines relieved British troops guarding that strategic island which lay like a pistol pointed at England.

Tuscaloosa soon received new orders which assigned her to a task group built around battleships *Idaho* (BB–40), *Mississippi* (BB–41), and *New Mexico* (BB–42). *Wichita* and two divisions of destroyers joined *Tuscaloosa* in the screen of the men-of-war. Under the two-starred flag of Rear Admiral Robert C. "Ike" Giffen, the Denmark Strait patrol worked out of wind-swept, cold Hvalfjordur, Iceland—known to Americans as "Valley Forge."

The similarities between the Continental Army's historic winter campground and the Icelandic region were not just confined to a homonymous relation of their names. The bitter cold, wind, and snow and the wartime operations seemed similar—the latter in the form of daily patrols, unceasingly vigilant for any signs of the "enemy." *Tuscaloosa* and *Wichita* "stripped ship" for war, removing accumulated coats of paint and other inflammable and nonessential items before they set out for sea on 5 November. As the task force steamed toward Iceland, its warships were constantly alert to the possibility of an imminent sortie by the German battleship *Tirpitz*, the sistership of the late *Bismarck*.

While *Tirpitz* failed to show herself, the American ships continued to conduct "short of war" operations which became increasingly warlike as time went on. The attempted torpedoing of *Greer* (DD–145); the damaging of *Kearny* in October; the sinking of *Reuben James* (DD–245) by a German U-boat; and the torpedoing of *Salinas* (AO–9) all pointed to the fact that American ships were becoming involved in the fighting.

Meanwhile, tensions heightened in the Pacific, as Japan continued her undeclared war against China; took over French Indochina; and proceeded apace with plans to move southward against British and Dutch colonial possessions. The Japanese strike at Pearl Harbor on 7 December plunged the United States into "real" war at last, in both oceans, for Germany and Italy declared war on the United States on 11 December.

On 6 January 1942, *Tuscaloosa* stood out of Hvalf-

jordur in company with *Wichita* and two destroyers—*Grayson* (DD–435) and *Meredith* (DD–434)—for training cruise to the Denmark Strait. After returning to port three days later, the heavy cruiser moved on to Boston for a navy yard overhaul from 8 to 20 February. She conducted refresher training out of Casco Bay and then underwent another brief refit at New York before joining Task Group (TG) 39.1, under the command of Rear Admiral John W. Wilcox, Jr., whose flag flew in *Washington* (BB–56).

The task group sortied from Casco Bay and struggled through gale-whipped seas, bound for Scapa Flow in the Orkney Islands—the British Home Fleet's base. On 27 March, Rear Admiral Wilcox apparently suffered a heart attack and was washed overboard from *Washington*. The heavy seas ruled out rescue attempts; and the task group's commanding officer soon disappeared in the stormy Atlantic. With Wilcox' death, Rear Admiral Giffen, whose flag flew in *Wichita*, assumed command of TG 39.1.

Tuscaloosa arrived at Scapa Flow on 4 April and immediately took on board a British signals and liaison team. She was initially employed with the British Home Fleet on training duties and later took part in covering runs for convoys to North Russia.

At that period, Anglo-American naval operations frequently were mounted in an attempt to lure *Tirpitz* out of her snowy Norwegian lair. One such attempt, Convoy PQ–17, resulted in disaster in June 1942. The following two months found *Tuscaloosa* still active in convoy protection and covering assignments.

In mid-August, *Tuscaloosa* received orders to carry supplies—including aircraft torpedoes, ammunition, and medical equipment—to North Russia. Soon after she and two destroyers set out on the mission, a member of the cruiser's crew developed symptoms of spinal meningitis. The sick man was quickly put ashore at Seidis fjord, Iceland; and the group got underway again on 19 August, bound for Kola Inlet.

The next day, *Tuscaloosa* and her screen—which by that time consisted of three destroyers (two American and one British)—were spotted by a snooping German reconnaissance plane. The task force changed course and, assisted by the worsening visibility in the northern latitudes, managed to shake the intruder. On the evening of 22 August, two more British destroyers joined *Tuscaloosa*'s screen; and, the following day, a Russian escort guided them to Kola Inlet.

All hands turned-to and unloaded the valuable cargo

The cruiser then took on fuel; prepared to get underway; and, just before departure, embarked 243 passengers, most of whom were survivors of ships which had been sunk while serving in earlier convoys to Russia. Many of them had endured the special tribulation and agony of PQ–17. With her human cargo thus on board, *Tuscaloosa* cleared Kola Inlet on 24 August and reached Seidisfjord on the 28th.

She remained there but briefly before steaming to the mouth of the River Clyde, where she disembarked her passengers. Detached from the Home Fleet shortly thereafter, *Tuscaloosa* headed for Hvalfjord and proceeded thence to the United States for an overhaul.

On 8 November 1942, Operation "Torch"—the code name of the Anglo-American effort to wrest North Africa from the hands of the Vichy French—got underway. Off Casablanca, French Morocco, steamed *Tuscaloosa* and her old companion, *Wichita*, joined by new *Massachusetts* (BB–59) as part of the covering force. As American troops splashed ashore, *Tuscaloosa*'s guns, aided by accurate spotting from the cruiser's scout planes, thundered and sent shells whistling shoreward into the French positions. In the harbor, French ships scurried about like tadpoles as they prepared to sortie against the attackers.

French battleship *Jean Bart*, incomplete and immobile, nevertheless packed a powerful punch in her 15-inch guns and loosed heavy and accurate salvoes, straddling the American ships several times with giant shell splashes. French shore batteries at Table d'Aukasha and El Hank also proved troublesome; but the combined might of Allied sea and air power silenced both the shore batteries and *Jean Bart* as well.

After being narrowly missed by torpedoes from a Vichy submarine and shells from *Jean Bart*'s heavy rifles, *Tuscaloosa* retired from the battle zone to refuel and to replenish her ammunition. After this, she remained offshore in support of the invasion and then headed back to the United States for refit.

Following repairs, she rejoined in covering convoys bound for the North African front, as American forces and their British and Free French allies sought to push the Germans and Italians out of Tunisia. Next, from March through May 1943, *Tuscaloosa* operated in a task force on training exercises off the east coast of the United States.

Besides honing its fighting edge, this group formed a fast, mobile, and ready striking force, should German surface ships slip through the Allied blockade to terrorize Allied shipping in the Atlantic. In late May, she escorted RMS *Queen Mary*, which bore British Prime Minister Churchill to New York City. After rejoining the task force for a brief time, *Tuscaloosa* joined *Augusta* at the Boston Navy Yard for a 10-day work period.

After leaving Boston, she escorted RMS *Queen Elizabeth* to Halifax, Nova Scotia, before rendezvousing with *Ranger* and proceeding to Scapa Flow to resume operations with the British Home Fleet. *Tuscaloosa* conducted sorties into the North Sea, in company with British and American units, in attempts to once again entice German heavy units to sea. However, the hope of drawing the Germans into a decisive sea fight diminished each passing day as the enemy apparently sought to stay in his protected waters.

On 2 October, *Tuscaloosa* formed part of the covering force for *Ranger* while the carrier launched air strikes against port installations and German shipping at Bodo, Norway, in Operation "Leader." These first American carrier strikes against European targets lasted from 2 to 6 October and devastated the area. German shore-based aircraft attacked the striking force only to be summarily shot down by covering American fighters.

Shortly afterward, the Germans did elect to come out to sea, conducting a foray against the important Allied weather station on Spitzbergen Island. *Tirpitz* and other heavy units subjected the installation and its garrison to a severe shelling before retiring—unscathed—to their Norwegian lair.

Tuscaloosa took part in the relief expedition to reestablish the station before the onset of winter. Assigned to Force One, the cruiser loaded two LCV(P) and cargo and departed Seidisfjord in company with four destroyers—three British and one American—on 17 October. Force Two, covering Force One, consisted of HMS *Anson*, HMS *Norfolk*, *Ranger*, and six destroyers.

On the morning of the 19th, *Tuscaloosa*'s group arrived at devastated Spitzbergen and immediately commenced unloading operations. While ice "growlers" and pinnacles hampered antisubmarine screening by the destroyers' sound gear, *Tuscaloosa* fielded a party of 150 men on shore to unload supplies and equipment to reestablish the weather station. By nightfall, the cargo had been safely unloaded, and the force left the area. After fueling at Seidisfjord, the cruiser proceeded to the Clyde to disembark the survivors of the original Spitzbergen garrison.

Tuscaloosa conducted one more sweep of the Norwegian coast in an attempt to draw German fleet units to sea, but the enemy chose not to give battle. Upon the cruiser's return to Iceland, she was detached from the Home Fleet and proceeded to New York, where she began major overhaul on 3 December 1943.

Upon completion of the refit in February 1944, *Tuscaloosa* engaged in Fleet exercises and shore bombardment practice out of Casco Bay until April and then entered the Boston Navy Yard for installation of radio intelligence and electronic countermeasures gear. Later that month, she embarked Rear Admiral Morton L. Deyo, Commander, CruDiv 7, and task force commander, and set out for the Clyde to join the Allied Forces massing for the assault on the European continent.

During the interim period prior to D-day, *Tuscaloosa* conducted further short bombardment practice and engaged in further exercises. Her aviation unit exchanged their venerable Curtiss SOC "Seagulls" for British Supermarine Spitfires and checked out in them for spotting purposes. Yet, they remained shore-based for the remainder of their time operating in support of the invasion.

On 3 June, *Tuscaloosa* steamed in company with the task force bound for the Normandy beaches. At 0550, 6 June 1944, she opened fire with her 8-inch battery; and, three minutes later, her 5-inch guns engaged Fort Ile de Tatihou, Baye de la Seine. For the remainder of D-day, coast defense batteries, artillery positions, troop concentrations, and motor transport all came under the fire of *Tuscaloosa*'s guns which were aided by her air spotters and by fire control parties attached to Army units on shore. Initial enemy return fire was inaccurate, but it improved enough by the middle of the day to force the cruiser to take evasive action.

On the afternoon of 9 June, *Tuscaloosa* returned to Plymouth to replenish her depleted ammunition. Back in the vicinity of Ile St. Marcouf on the evening of the 11th, she remained on station in the fire-support area until the 21st, providing gunfire support on call from her shore fire control party operating with Army units. She then returned to England.

Five days later, on 26 June, the Army's 7th Corps mounted a landward assault against Cherbourg, supported by ships of the covering force from the seaward side. For four hours, *Tuscaloosa* and her consorts dueled with the accurate German shore batteries. During the action, the enemy frequently straddled the British and American ships and forced them to take evasive action. Great clouds of smoke and dust, kicked up by the intense bombardment conducted from sea and land, initially hampered Allied fire. By noontime, however, visibility improved and greatly aided the accuracy of the bombardment.

In July, with the beachhead secured in Normandy and Allied forces pushing into occupied France,

Tuscaloosa steamed from Belfast to the Mediterranean to join British, French, and American forces assembling for Operation "Anvil/Dragoon," the invasion of southern France.

Following preliminary bombardment exercises off Oran, French North Africa, *Tuscaloosa* was based at Palermo, Italy, and got underway on 13 August. Two days later, *Tuscaloosa* commenced fire at 0635 and continued to pound targets ashore until the combined Allied forces stormed onto the beaches at H-Hour, 0800. Then, moving off the 100-fathom curve, *Tuscaloosa* leisurely cruised the shoreline, visually inspecting it for targets of opportunity. A troublesome pillbox at the St. Raphel breakwater provoked *Tuscaloosa*'s attention, and the cruiser's 8-inch shells soon destroyed it. Air spotters located a field battery, and *Tuscaloosa*'s gunners promptly knocked it out of action with three direct hits.

For the next 11 days, the cruiser delivered fire support for the right flank of the Army's advance to the Italian frontier. She engaged German shore batteries and fought off air attacks. The raids—conducted by Junkers 88's and Dornier 217's singly, or in small groups—usually occurred during the covering force's nightly retirement from the beachheads. Of the high altitude variety, these aerial assaults included the use of radar-controlled glider bombs. However, radar counter-measures and jamming devices, as well as effective evasive action and gunfire, thwarted these twilight and nocturnal attacks.

In September, when Allied forces had secured footholds in both western and southern France, *Tuscaloosa* returned to the United States for refitting at the Philadelphia Navy Yard. After a short exercise period in Chesapeake Bay, she steamed via the Panama Canal to the west coast and reported to the Commander in Chief, Pacific Fleet. After stopping briefly at San Diego, she proceeded on westward to Pearl Harbor, where she conducted various exercises before steaming to Ulithi to join Commander, 3d Fleet in January 1945.

Following her sortie from Ulithi, she joined the bombardment group off Iwo Jima at dawn on 16 February. Three days later, as waves of landing craft bore marines shoreward to invade the island, *Tuscaloosa*'s guns pounded Japanese positions inland. Then, after the Americans had reached land, her batteries supported their advances with incessant fire and illumination. This continued from 19 February to 14 March, throughout all phases of the bitterly fought campaign to wrest the island from the Japanese.

Returning to Ulithi after the Iwo Jima operation, she spent four hectic days replenishing stores, ammunition, and fuel in preparation for the next operation—Okinawa, at the end of the chain of Japanese home islands. On Palm Sunday, 25 March, *Tuscaloosa*'s main and secondary batteries opened fire on shore targets pinpointed by aerial reconnaissance. Only allowed a six-day respite in the middle of the arduous campaign for replenishment purposes, *Tuscaloosa* stood on duty for the entire operation.

Tuscaloosa's charmed life in the face of everything the Axis could throw at her still held through the maelstrom of the kamikazes which came at the invasion ships and their escorts from all quarters. The "Divine Wind" came down from the Japanese home islands, in the form of planes piloted by pilots so loyal to their Emperor that they unhesitatingly gave their lives to defend their home soil.

Tuscaloosa's gunners splashed two of the intruders. One, headed for the fantail of *Texas* (BB–35), flew apart as the cruiser's shells splashed her in the old battleship's wake. The other headed for an escorting destroyer in the screen only to be splashed after hitting a curtain of fire from the cruiser's guns.

Only the mop-up of determined resistance ashore remained when *Tuscaloosa* departed from Okinawa on 28 June. Two days later, she arrived in Leyte Gulf, Philippine Islands; there reporting to Commander, 7th Fleet, for duty. Six weeks later, with Allied warship bombarding her shores with near impunity and Allie planes sweeping her skies clear of rapidly dwindling numbers of her defending aircraft, Japan surrendered The explosion of two atomic bombs—one over Hiroshima and the other above Nagasaki—had sealed Japan's fate in August 1945.

On 27 August, *Tuscaloosa*, in company with other units of the 7th Fleet, departed Subic Bay in the Philippines, bound for Korean and Manchurian waters She touched at Tsingtao, China, en route, and proceeded to cruise off the newly liberated ports of Dairen and Port Arthur, Manchuria; Chefoo, Taku, Weihaiwe and Chinwangtao, China, before finally anchoring of Jinsen (now Inchon), Korea, on 8 September to support the landings of marines nearby.

After a stay of 22 days, *Tuscaloosa* put to sea once more on 30 September, bound for Taku, China, to support marines landing there. She next sailed for Chefoo on 6 October but, en route, received orders changing her destination to Jinsen to take on provisions

As Chinese Nationalist and communist forces jockeyed for position to control formerly Japanese-held territory, American forces stood by in the uneasy role of observers. *Tuscaloosa* arrived off Chefoo, then held by the communists, on 13 October. Remaining until 3 November, she lay at anchor off the port, keeping well informed on the situation ashore through daily conferences with officials of the communist Eighth Route Army. During this period, puppet troops, who had been loyal to the Japanese during the war, clashed with communist forces near Chefoo.

On 3 November, she put to sea, bound for Tsingtao where the cruiser spent one evening before proceeding down the China coast to call at Shanghai. There, she took on board 214 Army and 118 Navy passengers for "Magic-Carpet" transportation home for demobilization

She arrived in Hawaii on 26 November, where additional passenger facilities were installed, and took on board 206 more men before departing Hawaiian waters on the 28th and arriving at San Francisco on 4 December. After voyage repairs, the ship sailed for the South Pacific on 14 December, via the Solomon Islands and proceeded to Noumea, New Caledonia.

Tuscaloosa embarked troops at Guadalcanal, moved to the Russell Islands where she took on more passengers, and arrived at Noumea on New Year's Day 1946. By that afternoon, the ship got underway for the west coast with more than 500 passengers.

She arrived at Pearl Harbor nine days into the new year; fueled; and picked up additional demobilized servicemen to transport home. She sailed for San Francisco on 10 January and arrived five days later. On 29 January, the men delivered, *Tuscaloosa* stood out of San Francisco bound for the east coast on her last cruise as an active member of the Fleet.

Placed out of commission at Philadelphia on 13 February 1946, *Tuscaloosa* remained in reserve there until she was struck from the Navy list on 1 March 1959. Her hulk was sold on 25 June 1959 to the Boston Metals Co., of Baltimore, Md., for scrapping.

Tuscaloosa received seven battle stars for her World War II service.

II

(LST–1187: dp. 8,342; l. 522'3''; b. 69'5''; dr. 15'; s 20 k.; cpl. 231; a. 4 3''; cl. *Newport*)

Tuscaloosa (LST–1187) was laid down on 23 November 1968 at San Diego, Calif., by the National Steel and Shipbuilding Co.; launched on 6 September 1969; sponsored by Mrs. Thomas F. Connolly; and commissioned on 24 October 1970, Comdr. Harry W. Kinsley, Jr., in command.

Tuscaloosa spent the remainder of the year alternating in underway and upkeep periods. On 4 January 1971, she began duty off the coast of California as a est ship evaluating *John C. Calhoun*'s (SSBN–630) sensors.

She continued a rigorous training schedule out of San Diego, her home port, into the spring when she prepared for a deployment to the western Pacific. The tank landing ship loaded a cargo of Quonset hut components and a tank-deck load of LVT's, tanks, and heavy construction vehicles and departed the west coast on 18 May 1971.

Arriving at Okinawa on 1 June, *Tuscaloosa* unloaded and proceeded—via Subic Bay, Philippines—to Danang, South Vietnam. After taking on a cargo of Marine Corps equipment, she returned home to San Diego on 5 July and began an extensive post-shakedown availability which lasted into the fall. On 1 October, *Tuscaloosa* got underway for a seven-month WestPac deployment, in company with Amphibious Squadron 5— *Tripoli* (LPH–10); *Duluth* (LPD–9); *Anchorage* (LSD–36); *Mobile* (LKA–115); and *Schenectady* (LST–1185).

For the remainder of the year, the landing ship conducted exercises and operations in the Philippines and off Okinawa. She operated with marines, took part in amphibious exercises, and ended the year at Sasebo, Japan.

The ship got underway for the Ryukyus on 4 January 1972 but was delayed by a collision with a Japanese patrol craft. The next day, after an informal investigation ascertained that she had not suffered any damage, she resumed her voyage to Okinawa where she embarked marines and transported them to Yokosuka. Following repairs to her bow doors, the ship sailed for the Philippines and arrived at Subic Bay on 15 February. There, the ship loaded a cargo of generators and delivered them to Vungtau, South Vietnam.

The ship returned to Japan soon thereafter, transporting marines and equipment, before she headed back to the Philippines for amphibious exercises. Then, upon completion of these exercises, *Tuscaloosa* got underway, in company with *Mobile* and *Denver*, and proceeded via Okinawa to Vietnamese waters, arriving on "Yankee Station" in the Tonkin Gulf on 6 April. She remained on station until 3 May, when she proceeded via Danang to Subic Bay. *Tuscaloosa* subsequently returned to Vietnam and operated both at Danang and on "Yankee Station" until late May.

The LST next supported Thailand contingency operations by transporting Marine Corps equipment and Navy construction battalion tools. She then returned to Subic Bay and pressed on to the United States at the end of her grueling 10-month deployment.

She engaged in local operations and amphibious exercises off the California coast into mid-1973, before she again deployed to WestPac on 29 August, her holds filled with Project "Handclasp" material for delivery to communities in the Philippines. *Tuscaloosa* later participated in Operation "Pagasa II" in conjunction with units of the Philippine Navy and operated out of Subic Bay for the remainder of the year, with calls at Hong Kong and Kaohsiung, Taiwan, on her itinerary.

Commencing 1974 with exercises with Korean naval units in Operation "Fly Away," *Tuscaloosa* visited Keelung, Taiwan, in late January, before departing Okinawa on 11 February 1974 and returning via Pearl Harbor to the west coast of the United States. The next major item on *Tuscaloosa*'s agenda was a major overhaul by the Todd Shipyards at Seattle, Wash., which began on 9 July.

On 3 August, an 11-man rescue and assistance party from the ship assisted *Moctobi* (ATF–105) in rescuing USNS *Lipan* which had collided with another vessel in the Strait of Juan de Fuca and lay dead in the water in danger of sinking. Prompt salvage efforts over a three-day period enabled *Lipan* to return to port for repairs.

After *Tuscaloosa*'s own repairs and overhaul had been completed, she rejoined the fleet on 12 December and operated along the California coast into the spring of 1975. She again deployed to WestPac on 1 April, getting underway from San Diego in company with two Korean minecraft and *Barbour County* (LST–1195) for Pearl Harbor and Okinawa.

While *Tuscaloosa* and her three consorts sailed westward, the situation in Southeast Asia deteriorated rapidly. Both the South Vietnamese and Cambodian governments were tottering and their forces falling back under the onslaught of communist troops. *Tuscaloosa* arrived at Pearl Harbor on 6 April and proceeded on toward the Ryukyus on the same day. Arriving at Okinawa on the 18th, the LST's crew urgently offloaded her cargo and pressed on the next day for Subic Bay. After a full-power run, she arrived there on the 21st and embarked 280 stragglers who had been unable to return to their ships—*Enterprise* (CVAN–65), *Midway* (CVA–41), and *Hancock* (CVA–19)—when the carriers pulled out hurriedly to participate in "Frequent Wind," the evacuation of Saigon.

Tuscaloosa now turned-to to support Operation "New Life"— escorting 26 former South Vietnamese Navy ships to the Philippines. During the seven-day passage, she provided over 200 pallets of food and medical supplies per day and earned the Meritorious Unit Commendation while thus engaged. In addition, she sent salvage and repair parties to various ships to effect any repairs necessary to keep the less seaworthy Vietnamese ships afloat. Two craft were evacuated and sunk by gunfire from *Tuscaloosa* to eliminate possible hazards to navigation. In addition, four Vietnamese craft were temporarily taken over by the United States Navy and placed under the command of four officers from *Tuscaloosa*.

From Subic Bay, *Tuscaloosa* proceeded to Okinawa and, upon arrival there, was ordered to make best possible speed for the Gulf of Thailand. Four days later, when nearly at her destination, she was ordered to turn back. The evacuation of the area had been completed, and her services were no longer needed. Thereafter, the LST continued routine operations during this WestPac deployment before returning to the west coast of the United States on 17 November 1975. She conducted another deployment to the western Pacific during the period 29 March to 17 November 1977 and spent the period 3 February to 10 December 1978 in regular overhaul at San Diego. *Tuscaloosa* continued to operate with the Pacific Fleet into 1979.

Tuscaloosa earned four battle stars and a Meritorious Unit Commendation during her Vietnam service.

Tuscana

Probably a variant spelling of Tucana, the name of a constellation of the southern hemisphere.

(AKN–3: dp. 14,350 (tl.); l. 441'6''; b. 56'11''; dr. 28'4'' (lim.); s. 12.5 k.; cpl. 228; a. 1 5'', 1 3'', 12 20mm.; cl. *Indus*; T. EC2–S–C1)

AKN–3 was laid down as *William R. Cox* under Maritime Commission contract (MC hull 2406) on 5 December 1943 at Baltimore, Md., by the Bethlehem-Fairfield Shipyard, Inc.; launched on 29 December 1943; sponsored by Miss Cheshire Cox; acquired by the Navy under bareboat charter and renamed *Tuscana* on 8 January 1944; converted to a net cargo ship at Baltimore by the Maryland Drydock Co.; and commissioned on 28 March 1944, Comdr. Thomas J. Butler, USNR, in command.

Tuscana arrived at Hampton Roads on 6 April 1944 and operated out of that port, conducting drills and shakedown in Chesapeake Bay. On 26 April, she set her course via the Canal Zone for Hawaii. She entered Pearl Harbor on 23 May, provisioned, took on passengers, and got underway for the Marshalls on the 26th.

She arrived at Kwajalein on 5 June; got underway on the 27th, steaming with barge *YC–1008* in tow; and arrived at Eniwetok on 29 June. On 20 July, while attempting to transfer a passenger to *Vega* (AK–17) during a rain squall, *Tuscana*'s Buoy Boat No. 1 became stranded on a reef. When pounding seas forced the boat's crew to abandon her, a boat from destroyer *Downes* (DD–375) came to the rescue and saved all hands. On the 27th, *Tuscana* departed Eniwetok, with other net cargo ships and an escort, and set her course for the Marianas.

Tuscana anchored at Garapan on 1 August, detached men and cargo for the operation of harbor and waterfront facilities, and on the 7th began net operations. Throughout the remainder of the month, *Tuscana*'s crew labored to assemble and launch anti-torpedo nets which were towed into place and installed by the smaller net laying ships (AN's). On this, her first net laying assignment, *Tuscana* provided nets to protect Mutcho Point and Garapan harbor from submarine attack. After completing this vital task, *Tuscana* arrived at Pearl Harbor on 11 September and began loading stores, buoys, and net materials.

On the 19th, she got underway with a slow convoy of eight ships and three escorts bound for the Marshalls. After a few days at Eniwetok, she continued on toward the Carolines and arrived at Ulithi on 9 October. Here, conferences on net laying took place on board the ship. Then, on 15 October, *Tuscana*'s crew began net assembly. On the 26th, she began delivering nets to smaller net laying ships which towed them into place and installed them to protect the lagoon anchorage. On the 28th, *Tuscana* assembled the last net of this operation. The same day, *Viburnam* (AN–57), a member of the task unit working with *Tuscana*, struck a Japanese mine which caused severe damage to the net layer and underscored the ever-present hazards of warfare in the Pacific.

Tuscana embarked passengers on 11 November and, on the following day, got underway and steamed via Eniwetok to the Hawaiian Islands. Throughout most of December, she remained at Pearl Harbor undergoing repairs. Then, on the 27th, she set her course again for the Marshalls and spent a week at Eniwetok before proceeding on to the western Carolines. Shortly after midday on 20 January 1945, she passed through Mugai Channel and anchored at Ulithi. Although hampered at first by rough seas. *Tuscana* supplied moorings and assembled 1,260 yards of anti-torpedo net for Towachi Channel and an additional 6,390 yards for use elsewhere in the approaches to Ulithi. On 12 February 1945, her assignment completed, she departed Ulithi.

In March, she underwent drydocking at Pearl Harbor; then took on cargo and passengers. She returned to Ulithi on 4 April 1945, and, on the 12th, departed that port steaming in convoy for Okinawa. She anchored off the Hagushi landing beaches on the 18th. Near dusk each evening, the general alarm sounded, a regular reminder of the danger of Japanese air raiders. On 2 May, sailors on board *Tuscana* saw the flash of firing off the ship's starboard quarter and later observed the glow of an explosion which they thought marked the fiery end of a Japanese suicide boat. On 6 May, *Tuscana* began to assemble nets and moorings to screen the anchorage.

Early in the day on the 28th, as *Tuscana* lay anchored in Buckner Bay, a swarm of kamikazes attacked. For *Tuscana*, the action began at 0725, when a Japanese airplane crashed into a merchant ship only 800 yards off her starboard bow. For over 30 minutes, *Tuscana* fought off the airborne raiders. At 0735, a suicide plane crashed into *Sandoval* (APA–194). Soon thereafter, *Tuscana* opened fire on her first enemy plane; and, moments later, another came in toward her port bow. *Tuscana*'s guns opened on the attacker and kept it under fire until it disappeared in the low overcast. At 0744, she engaged a third aircraft and splashed it 600 yards off the port bow. She then turned her attention to the rescue of two survivors from *Sandoval*. At 0755, yet another Japanese plane came in range, and *Tuscana* splashed this raider some three

miles away. During the fight, *Tuscana* lost her starboard mainmast boom, which was toppled and damaged beyond operational use, and her topping lift was carried away by friendly fire. At 0758, *Tuscana*'s guns opened on the last of the attackers and ceased fire five minutes later, just as a kamikaze crashed merchant ship *Josia Snelling*. At 0900, the all clear was sounded, and *Tuscana* emerged from her encounter with the enemy without personnel loss and with the knowledge of having assisted in the splashing of two enemy planes.

During an early afternoon alert on 3 June 1945 *Tuscana*'s gunners splashed a Japanese aircraft only 500 yards off her starboard quarter. On the 6th, she got underway and proceeded via Saipan and the Hawaiian Islands to the California coast. On 6 July, she anchored in San Francisco Bay to begin a prolonged period of overhaul. While the ship underwent extensive repairs, members of her crew attended school in damage control, fire fighting, and radar. During this interlude, hostilities ended in the Pacific.

Late in August, *Tuscana* completed dock trials and tests; then provisioned and got underway on 7 September. Steaming via Pearl Harbor, she arrived at Okinawa on 14 October and began discharging her cargo. Late in the month, as she was proceeding to Japan, she sighted and destroyed a floating mine. The ship anchored at Sasebo on the 25th. She returned to Okinawa in November; then continued on to Hawaii and reached Pearl Harbor on 10 December. She discharged passengers and cargo there; and, on 1 December, she set her course for Balboa. Steaming via the Panama Canal, she arrived at Norfolk on 1 January 1946.

The net cargo ship was decommissioned on 28 January 1946 and returned to the War Shipping Administration the next day. Her name was struck from the Navy list on 25 February 1946. Laid up under the name *William R. Cox*, the ship remained in custody of the Maritime Administration until she was sold in the late 1960's to Horton Industries, Inc., and scrapped.

Tuscana received two battle stars for World War II service.

Tuscarora

A mountain range in south-central Pennsylvania. The name is Iroquois Indian and means "hemp gatherers."

I

(ScSlp.: dp. 1,457; l. 198'6''; b. 33'2''; dr. 14'10''; s. 11 k.; a. 2 11'' D.sb., 2 32-pdrs. 33 Cwt., 4 32-pdrs. 57 Cwt., 1 30-pdr. P.r.)

The first *Tuscarora* was laid down on 27 June 1861 at Philadelphia, Pa., by Merrick & Sons; launched on 24 August 1861; sponsored by Miss Margaret Lardner and commissioned on 5 December 1861, Comdr. Tunis A. M. Craven in command.

Later that month, *Tuscarora* sailed for Southampton, England, under orders to capture or sink the cruiser CSS *Nashville*. *Nashville* had run the blockade on 26 October and docked at Southampton after crossing the Atlantic, becoming the first vessel to show the Confederate flag in English waters. She finally weighed anchor and departed on 3 February 1862, but *Tuscarora* was unable to pursue her as English law required that two belligerent vessels leave port separated by not less than 24 hours. Disgusted, Comdr. Craven sailed for Gibraltar where, upon his arrival on 12 February, he found the raider CSS *Sumter*—Comdr. Raphael Semmes in command—anchored.

For almost two months, Craven and Semmes exchanged verbal broadsides both with each other and with the British authorities. Semmes then cleverly feigned preparations for departure, only to abandon *Sumter* in port on 11 April. *Tuscarora* remained at Gibraltar until relieved by her sister ship, *Kearsarge*,

12 June. She put in at Cadiz, Spain, on 15 June, for repairs.

On the 23d, she received orders to sail immediately for England and to deploy off the coast in search of the recently launched Confederate raider CSS *Alabama*. *Tuscarora* reconnoitered the southern coasts of England and Ireland and scoured the Irish channel without finding any trace of the vessel. She returned to Spanish waters in September and cruised off the Azores during October, but again found nothing. On 1 December 1862, *Tuscarora* was ordered to remain off the European coast and to protect American shipping. On 15 March 1863, she reported that she had no intelligence that Confederate vessels were operating in her area. She returned to the Philadelphia Navy Yard later that month.

Tuscarora left Philadelphia on 6 June 1863, bound for the New York Navy Yard. She got underway again on 14 June to search for the bark CSS *Tacony* and patrolled off Bermuda before putting into Hampton Roads, Va., for supplies on 22 June. Two days later, she headed north and cruised between Cape Henry and the coast of Nova Scotia before arriving at Boston 12 days later. During her time at sea, she failed to locate *Tacony*. During August, *Tuscarora* searched for Confederate raiders off the Grand Banks, Newfoundland, but encountered none before she returned to Boston on 5 September.

Early in October, *Tuscarora* left Boston for duty with the North Atlantic Blockading Squadron. She arrived off Wilmington, N.C., on the 7th and was ordered to Beaufort, N.C., where she served as a storeship. The vessel subsequently returned to Boston and was decommissioned there on 4 June 1864.

Tuscarora was recommissioned at Boston on 3 October 1864 and reassigned to the North Atlantic Blockading Squadron. She put in at Hampton Roads on 8 October and took up blockade station off Wilmington. *Tuscarora* participated in the unsuccessful attempt to take Fort Fisher, N.C., on 24 and 25 December. In mid-January 1865, she returned to waters off Wilmington, and a landing party from the vessel helped to capture the fort on the 15th. She suffered three men killed and 12 wounded during the assault.

The next day, *Tuscarora* was reassigned to the South Atlantic Blockading Squadron. Towing monitor *Canonicus*, she sailed for Port Royal, S.C., on 17 January, and arrived on the 20th to deploy off Georgetown, S.C. She was transferred to the blockade off Ossabaw Sound, Ga., on 5 March 1865, and escorted President Jefferson Davis, his family, and other captured Confederate officials aboard the steamer *William P. Clyde* from Port Royal to Hampton Roads on 16 to 19 May. After disembarking her famous passengers at Fort Monroe, *Tuscarora* continued north to the Boston Navy Yard where she was decommissioned on 30 May.

Tuscarora was recommissioned later in the year and sailed on 2 November 1865 for the Pacific Ocean via Cape Horn. She served with the South Pacific Squadron from 1866 until May 1869. She stood off Valparaiso, Chile, during the Spanish bombardment on 31 March 1866 and was also present at Callao, Peru, when the Spanish shelled it on 2 May. In 1867, *Tuscarora* stopped at Tahiti and other islands of the Society group. She also touched at Fiji, where she received payment of awards made to United States citizens in 1855 and 1858 for injuries and losses sustained as a result of acts of the natives.

Tuscarora returned to South America in 1868 and was placed at the disposal of the Chilean government to assist victims of the great earthquake which had

The wooden steamer *Tuscarora* after the Civil War with ensigns at her mastheads to celebrate a holiday. (NR&L(O) 2806)

occurred on 18 November 1867. In February 1869, she investigated the imprisonment of the United States consul at Buenaventura, Colombia, and moved to Valparaiso at the end of the month. She departed Valparaiso on 12 May bound for the North Atlantic and arrived at Key West, Fla., on 28 July. *Tuscarora* ended the year stationed at Aspinwall, Colombia, now Colon, Panama.

Tuscarora remained at Aspinwall until April 1870; then returned to Key West. She cruised off the coast of Cuba in June and escorted the ironclads *Wyandotte*, *Ajax*, and *Manhattan* from New Orleans to Key West. After again cruising the Caribbean, she arrived at Portsmouth, N.H., on 31 January 1871 and was decommissioned there on 10 February. She was recommissioned on 16 May 1872 and assigned to the South Pacific Station. *Tuscarora* left Portsmouth on 22 June and arrived at Valparaiso on 9 September. She remained in South American waters through June 1873, sailing for San Francisco via Acapulco on 17 May. After her arrival on 25 June, *Tuscarora* departed San Francisco and surveyed the sea floor off the northwest coast to determine a suitable route for a submarine cable. The vessel returned to San Francisco on 6 November.

In January 1874, *Tuscarora* took soundings for a submarine cable route between the United States, Japan, and China. The ship arrived at Honolulu, Oahu, in February where a force of 150 officers, bluejackets, and marines from her and from *Portsmouth* quelled a large riot that followed the election of King David Kalakaua. Order was restored by the 20th. After performing additional survey work, *Tuscarora* returned to San Francisco for refitting in October.

Tuscarora was transferred to the North Pacific Station on 11 October 1874 and left for Honolulu on 1 November with orders to take soundings of the ocean bottom every 30 nautical miles. She remained at Honolulu through January 1875. The vessel touched at Samoa in March and returned to Honolulu in June and to San Francisco in July. She left in September and performed survey work in the South Pacific, visiting the Fiji Islands, Australia, and Samoa. She returned to San Francisco and was decommissioned at the Mare Island Navy Yard on 14 September 1876. *Tuscarora* was laid up for repairs during 1877.

Tuscarora was recommissioned at Mare Island on 10 January 1878, and was assigned special oceanic survey work off the western coasts of both Central and South America. She returned to Mare Island for repairs on 30 June 1879 but headed south again on 25 September to resume her duties. *Tuscarora* again returned to Mare Island on 21 April 1880 and was decommissioned there on 31 May for repairs. The repairs and modifications were never completed, and the vessel was struck from the Navy list in 1883.

Tuscarosa was sold at Mare Island to W. E. Mighell on 20 November 1883.

II

(AT–77: dp. 530 (lt.); l. 135'0''; b. 30'0''; dr. 14'2'')

The second *Tuscarora* (AT–77) was laid down late in 1940 at Orange, Tex., by the Levingston Shipbuilding Co. on the company's own initiative. She was acquired by the Navy in January 1941; launched on 17 July 1941; named *Tuscarora* (AT–77) on 23 July 1941; and commissioned on 13 December 1941.

On the day of her commissioning, *Tuscarora* got underway from Orange for her shakedown cruise which she completed at Charleston, S.C., on 21 December. On 8 January 1942, the tug cleared Charleston and headed north to her first duty station, Norfolk, Va. She arrived in Hampton Roads on the 14th and began duty as a harbor tug. For the duration of World War II, *Tuscarora* served as a harbor tug at Norfolk. Her duties varied from guarding submarine nets to towing targets and ammunition barges as well as assisting ships into and out of port. During her stay at Norfolk, the tug changed designations twice. On 5 November 1942, she was officially designated a harbor tug and her hull number was changed to YT–341. Later, on 15 May 1944, when many older tugs received new designations, *Tuscarora* became a large harbor tug, YTB–341.

After World War II, she left Hampton Roads on 9 October, rounded Cape Henry, and shaped a course south. Following a brief stop at Fort Lauderdale, Fla., she arrived in Key West and reported for duty at the Antisubmarine Development Detachment Section Base located there. For almost two years, the tug operated in the Gulf of Mexico and the West Indies supporting the forces engaged in developmental work for antisubmarine warfare equipment, tactics, and doctrine.

On 1 July 1947, *Tuscarora* was reassigned to the 7th Naval District but remained stationed at Key West until November of 1953 when she was decommissioned and placed in reserve with the Green Cove Springs (Fla.) group of the Atlantic Reserve Fleet. *Tuscarora* remained with the reserve fleet for eight years. In November of 1958, the tug changed classifications for the third time when she was redesignated an auxiliary ocean tug, ATA–245. On 1 September 1961, her name was struck from the Navy list, and she was transferred to the Maritime Administration for lay-up with the National Defense Reserve Fleet at James River, Va. She remained there until sometime between 30 June 1970 and 30 June 1971, during which period she disappeared from the inventory of the Maritime Administration.

Tuscola

(YT–280: dp. 400 (f.); l. 110'0''; b. 27'0''; dr. 11'4''; s. 12 k.; cpl. 12; cl. *YT–215*)

YT–280 was constructed during the winter of 1943 and 1944 at Stamford, Conn., by the Luders Marine Construction Co. Soon after she was placed in service, the tug was named *Tuscola* on 28 April 1944. Less than a month later, on 15 May 1944, she was reclassified a large harbor tug and received the designation YTB–280.

Tuscola was assigned initially to the 12th Naval District and probably performed general towing duty in and around San Francisco. She served there until the spring of 1946 when she moved to the east coast for duty in the 1st Naval District. For almost two decades, *Tuscola* plied the waters off the New England coast, towing ships and other craft around and between such ports as Portsmouth, N.H.; Portland, Maine; Boston, Mass.; and New London, Conn. She also visited the Canadian cities of Quebec and Montreal. Sometime in 1963, the harbor tug was decommissioned, and her name was struck from the Navy list.

Tuscumbia

A city in and county seat of Colbert County in northwest Alabama. Tuscumbia is located on the Tennessee River approximately 108 miles northwest of Birmingham. Tuscumbia was named in 1822 for a Cherokee Indian chief.

I

(SwScGbt: dp. 915; dr. 7'; a. 3 11'' D. sb., 2 9'' D. sb.)

The first *Tuscumbia* was built in 1862 at Cincinnati, Ohio, by Joseph Brown; launched on 2 December; and commissioned at Cairo, Ill.; on 12 March 1963, Lt. Comdr. James W. Shirk in command.

Tuscumbia assisted in the recapture of Fort Heiman on the Tennessee River from 12 to 14 March 1863. The vessel destroyed Confederate watercraft used to ferry troops across the river and enfiladed Southern entrenchments situated behind the fort. At the end of the month, she entered the Mississippi.

In the spring and early summer of 1863, *Tuscumbia* perfomed valuable service during amphibious operations against Vicksburg, Miss. On 1 April, she carried Admiral David D. Porter and Generals Grant and Sherman on a reconnaissance expedition up the Yazoo River to determine the practicality of landing a force above Vicksburg at Hayne's Bluff. *Tuscumbia* withdrew under heavy fire from shore batteries, prompting the decision to shift operations below Vicksburg to Grand Gulf. *Tuscumbia* participated in the run past the Vicksburg batteries to New Carthage on the night of 16 and 17 April 1863, towing the damaged transport *Forest Queen* to safety. On 20 April, *General Sterling Price* and *Tuscumbia* reconnoitered the Mississippi from New Carthage to Grand Gulf and took part in the attack on the Confederate works at Grand Gulf on 29 April. During the attack, *Tuscumbia* suffered five casualties and was put out of action after taking 81 hits.

Tuscumbia was quickly repaired and fired upon the Vicksburg batteries on 19 and 22 May. During the attack on the 22d, *Benton, Mound City, Carondelet,* and *Tuscumbia* silenced three water batteries and destroyed four guns. *Tuscumbia* returned to the naval station at Memphis, Tenn., for repairs in August but was laid up in November. She was repaired at Memphis in May 1864 and was assigned patrol duty between Cairo and the head of the Tennessee River. After further repairs at Mound City, Ill., in October, she was inactivated in February 1865.

Tuscumbia was sold at auction at Mound City to W. K. Adams on 29 November 1865.

II

(YTB–762: dp. 356 (f.); l. 109'; b. 31'; dr. 14'; s. 12 k.; cpl. 12; cl. *Natick*)

The second *Tuscumbia* (YTB–762) was laid down in September 1945, at Portland, Oreg., by the Commercial Iron Works; launched in November 1945, and completed in January 1946. Records of her subsequent career are scarce but the ship apparently lay in reserve for a decade and one-half and was not placed in service until December 1961. She then served at San Diego, attached to the 11th Naval District, until shifted to Pearl Harbor, Hawaii, to operate in the 14th Naval District providing the necessary tug and tow services to support the Pacific Fleet from 1963 to and into 1978.

Tusk

An alternate name for the cusk, a large edible saltwater fish related to the cod.

(SS–426: dp. 1,570 (surf.), 2,415 (subm.); l. 311'8''; b. 27'3''; dr. 16'5'' (mean); s. 20.25 k. (surf.), 8.75 k. (subm.); cpl. 81; a. 10 21'' tt., 1 5'', 1 40mm., 1 20mm., 2 .50-cal. mg.; cl. *Balao*)

Tusk (SS–426) was laid down on 23 August 1943 at Philadelphia, Pa., by the Cramp Shipbuilding Co.; launched on 8 July 1945; sponsored by Mrs. Carolyn Park Mills; and commissioned on 11 April 1946, Comdr. Raymond A. Moore in command.

Tusk completed her shakedown cruise in the southern Atlantic with a round of goodwill visits to Latin American ports. She called at Rio de Janeiro and Bahia in Brazil, Curaçao in the Netherlands West Indies, and at Colon in the Canal Zone before returning to New London in June. For the next year, she conducted operations along the east coast between New London and Wilmington, N.C. During the first month of 1947, *Tusk* participated in a fleet tactical exercise in the Central Atlantic. A three-month overhaul at Philadelphia followed by oceanographic work along the Atlantic shelf in conjunction with Columbia University and the Woods Hole Oceanographic Institute occupied

her until October 1947 when she entered the Portsmouth Naval Shipyard for a "Guppy II" conversion.

Over the next seven months, *Tusk* received extensive modifications to improve her submerged performance characteristics. Four "greater capacity" batteries replaced her old larger ones. Her hull became more streamlined—the anchors were recessed into the hull and the propeller guards were removed—to improve her overall hydrodynamic design for underwater operations. Her sail was streamlined and enlarged to house the snorkel, a device added to allow her to operate on diesel power at periscope depth and to recharge her batteries while running submerged. All of these changes helped to convert *Tusk* from simply a submersible surface ship into a truer submarine. They increased her submerged range; and, though she lost about two knots in surface speed, her submerged speed increased from just under 10 knots to about 15.

The newly converted submarine returned to active duty early in the summer of 1948. She conducted her shakedown training and made a simulated war patrol to the Canal Zone in June and July. She returned to the United States in August and visited the Naval Academy at Annapolis where her presence allowed about 1,000 fourth classmen to see at first hand the latest development in submarine design. That fall and winter, *Tusk* resumed normal operations, participating in exercises with other United States and NATO forces. She ranged from the Caribbean Sea in the south to above the Arctic Circle in the north. The beginning of 1949 brought a more restricted radius of operations. During the first six months of that year, she served with Submarine Development Group 2 based at Newport, R.I. In July, *Tusk* rejoined the multinational forces of NATO for another round of exercises in the North Atlantic. During these exercises, she visited Londonderry, Northern Ireland; and Portsmouth, England.

During the final phase of those exercises, *Tusk* was operating in a unit which also included the submarine *Cochino* (SS–345). On 25 August, while steaming through a gale off the coast of Norway, *Cochino* suffered an explosion in one of her batteries. *Tusk* rushed to the aid of the stricken submarine, providing medical supplies for *Cochino*'s injured by way of life rafts. One such raft capsized in heavy seas sending a *Cochino* officer and a civilian employee of the Bureau of Ships into the icy Arctic waters. Both were recovered, but during the administration of artificial respiration on board *Tusk*, another wave broke over her deck washing away the civilian and 11 *Tusk* crewmen. Only four sailors were subsequently rescued. After those tragic events, *Tusk* and the limping *Cochino* headed for Hammerfest, Norway. Along the way, another explosion erupted in *Cochino*'s after battery. The second detonation sealed *Cochino*'s doom. Water literally poured through her battered hull. *Tusk* came alongside in heavy seas and lashed herself to the sinking submarine. Under the worst possible conditions, *Tusk* took all of *Cochino*'s crew off safely. Minutes later *Cochino* took her final plunge; and *Tusk* headed for Hammerfest.

That fall, the submarine returned to the United States to resume east coast operations out of New London in support of the Submarine School. She made cruises north to Halifax, Nova Scotia, and south to Bermuda. Her duty with the Submarine School continued until the middle of 1951 when she was assigned once more to Submarine Development Group 2. That assignment, punctuated by regular exercises with the fleet, continued until the summer of 1952 when she returned to an operational unit, Submarine Squadron (SubRon) 10. Normal east coast duty out of New London lasted until late in the year at which time *Tusk* was deployed to the Mediterranean for a six-month tour with the 6th Fleet. Her return to the United States early in the summer of 1953 brought more local operations out of New London. During the first

USS *Tusk* (SS–426), 1967. (USN 1122574)

part of 1954, the submarine operated in the Caribbean. Then, after four months of local operations out of New London, she sailed for northern European waters. That tour brought port visits to Belfast, Ireland; and Glasgow, Scotland; as well as training exercises with NATO forces in the northern Atlantic.

The first four years of the 1950's established the pattern for the remainder of *Tusk's* Navy career. She saw four additional Mediterranean deployments between 1954 and 1973. Initially, however, a long stretch of east coast operations intervened between overseas deployments. Six years elapsed between her 1954 northern Europe assignment and her second Mediterranean cruise late in 1960. The fall of 1961 brought another round of NATO exercises followed by joint American-Canadian training operations in the western Atlantic. Another three-year period of New London-based local operations occurred before she was deployed again to Europe in the fall of 1964 for more NATO training. During the spring and summer of 1966, *Tusk* returned to the Mediterranean for her third tour of duty with the 6th Fleet. Late 1966 brought a resumption of duty in American coastal waters which lasted until early 1967. During the summer of 1967, the submarine returned to northern European waters, visiting several ports and participating in yet another series of multinational NATO exercises. That November, she joined in binational American-Canadian exercises in the western Atlantic before resuming her east coast routine. Throughout 1968 and during the first half of 1969, the ship continued New London-based operations, including services to nuclear-powered submarines *Jack* (SSN–605) and *Lafayette* (SSBN–616). In July, she made her fourth deployment to the Mediterranean, returning to east coast operations in October.

After almost three years of that New London-based routine, *Tusk* set out for her fifth and final tour of duty with the 6th Fleet. She concluded that cruise the following October. The submarine rounded out the final year of her career with normal operations along the eastern seaboard, primarily in the New England vicinity. On 18 October 1973, *Tusk* was decommissioned at New London, Conn., and was simultaneously transferred, by sale, to the Taiwan Navy. Her name was struck from the Navy list on the same day.

Tuskegee

A city in Alabama and the seat of Macon County. It is probably best known as the location of the Tuskegee Institute, a coeducational college for Negroes founded by Booker T. Washington in 1881.

(YTB–806: dp. 356 (f.); l. 109'; b. 31'; dr. 14'; s. 12 k.; cpl. 12; cl. *Natick*)

Tuskegee (YTB–806) was laid down on 25 September

1969 at Sturgeon Bay, Wis., by Peterson Builders, Inc.; launched on 15 April 1970; and delivered to the Navy on 2 October 1970. Placed in service during October, the large harbor tug was attached to the 11th Naval District and was soon in operation out of San Diego, Calif. She provided tug and tow assistance for Fleet units at this port into 1976 when she was shifted to Hawaiian waters for operations out of Pearl Harbor which she has continued into 1978.

Tutahaco

An Indian name said to have been applied by members of Coronado's expedition (1540–1541) to a group of villages on the Rio Grande in New Mexico near the present-day town of Bernalillo.

(YTB–524: dp. 218 (tl.); l. 101'; b. 28'; dr. 11'; s. 12 k. (tl.); cpl. 10; cl. *Hisada*)

Tutahaco (YTB–524) was laid down on 1 May 1945 at Jacksonville, Fla., by Gibbs Corporation Marine Repair Yard; launched in August 1945; and completed and delivered to the Navy on 6 November 1945.

Placed in service, the large harbor tug began duties with the 10th Naval District, San Juan, Puerto Rico, early in 1946. Redesignated a medium harbor tug—YTM—on 2 February 1962, she was still in service, assigned to the 10th Naval District, in 1980, after almost 30 years in the Caribbean.

Tutuila

An island in American Samoa.

I

(PG–44: dp. 395; l. 159'5''; b. 27'1''; dr. 5'5'' (mean); s. 14.37 k.; cpl. 61; a. 2 3'', 10 30-cal. mg.)

Tutuila (PG–44) was laid down on 17 October 1926 at Shanghai, China, by the Kiangnan Dock and Engineering Works; launched on 14 June 1927; sponsored by Miss Beverly Pollard; and commissioned on 2 March 1928, Lt. Comdr. Frederick Baltzly in command.

Assigned to the Yangtze Patrol (YangPat) and redesignated a river gunboat (PR–4) on 15 June 1928, *Tutuila* cruised on shakedown up the Yangtze River from Shanghai to I'Chang, where she joined sister ship *Guam* (PR–3) in mid-July. Convoying river steamers through the upper reaches of the Yangtze on her first passage through the scenic gorges, she flew the flag of Rear Admiral Yates Stirling, Jr., Commander, Yangtze Patrol (ComYangPat). *Tutuila's* shallow draft enabled her to traverse the treacherous rapids of the gorges with ease, so that the fluctuating water levels did not hinder her year-round access to the upper stretch of the Yangtze. Her duty with Yang-Pat offered excitement and variety: conducting roving armed patrols; convoying merchantmen; providing armed guards for American flag steamers; and "showing the flag" to protect American lives and property in a land where civil strife and warfare had been a way of life for centuries.

Dealing with sniping by bandits or warlord troops in the 1920's and 1930's required both tact and—upon occasion—a few well-placed rounds of 3-inch or .30 caliber gunfire. One incident which called for a mixture of diplomacy and force came in 1929, when Lt. Comdr. S. E. Truesdell was in command of the gunboat.

He called on the Chinese warlord from whose territory some rifle shots had come. During a discussion of the incident, the general explained that his men were merely "country boys, who meant no harm." Truesdell replied that he, too, had some "country boys" among his own crew. He noted that he had found them tinkering with the after 3-inch gun, pointing it at the general's conspicuous white *yamen* (headquarters), as they practiced their range-finding. Truesdell's rejoinder bore immediate fruit—the sniping ceased forthwith!

In 1937, the complexion of life for the Yangtze gunboats changed. The undeclared Sino-Japanese War began in July and spread to the Yangtze valley in August and September. Japanese river operations effectively bottled up the river for neutral gunboats, and their proximity to war zones produced incidents such as the sinking of the *Panay* (PR–5) by Japanese aircraft on 12 December 1937. On 3 August 1938, *Tutuila* followed *Luzon* (PR–7) up the river to Chungking, as the YangPat flagship carried the American Ambassador, Nelson T. Johnson, to that river port.

Tutuila remained at Chungking as station ship with little hope of relief. Further Japanese operations resulted in the capture of Hankow in October 1938, making river travel below the former Chinese capital city subject to harassment and obstruction by the Japanese Navy. Such conditions resulted in the virtual stranding of *Tutuila* at Chungking, where she remained through 1941.

After the fall of Hankow, the Chinese moved their capital up river to *Tutuila*'s station—Chungking. Japanese forces thus stepped up the intensity of their attacks on that city, and air raids were common occurrences during the spring, summer, and fall. Only winter bad weather prevented the Japanese from year-round heavy raids. Moored at Lungmenhao lagoon, *Tutuila* bore a charmed life until 31 July 1941, when Japanese bombs landed close aboard, holing the ship at her waterline and destroying the ship's motor skimmer with its outboard motor.

By late 1941, as the situation in the Far East worsened, four gunboats remained with YangPat. Admiral Hart's reduction of naval forces in Chinese waters cut this number to two. *Luzon*—with Rear Admiral William A. Glassford, ComYangPat, embarked—departed from Shaighai for Manila on 28 November 1941 in company with *Oahu* (PR–6). *Wake* remained at Shanghai as station ship; *Tutuila*, beyond hope of escape, remained marooned at Chungking.

Shortly after his arrival in Manila, Rear Admiral Glassford deactivated the Yangtze Patrol on 5 December 1941. Within a few days, Japanese air attacks had devastated Pearl Harbor; and hostilities were underway with a rapidity which caught *Wake* unawares at Shanghai, where she was captured. For *Tutuila*, however, this news only heightened the anxiety.

Her complement of two officers and 22 enlisted men was ordered to depart from Chungking without their ship. She was then taken under the jurisdiction of the Naval Attaché attached to the American Embassy. She was decommissioned on 18 January 1942, the same day *Tutuila*'s crew flew out of the city. The attaché delivered the ship to an authorized representative of the Republic of China on 16 February 1942. Then, under terms of lend-lease, the United States leased the gunboat to China on 19 March 1942, her name becoming *Mei Yuan* which can be translated as "of American origin." The name *Tutuila* was struck from the United States Navy list on 25 March 1942.

The ship was permanently transferred to the Chinese government on 17 February 1948. She served the Nationalist Navy until near the end of the Civil War which ravaged China after World War II. As Communist forces advanced upon Shanghai, the Nationalists abandoned and scuttled *Mei Yuan* to prevent her capture. Her subsequent fate is unknown.

II

(ARG–4: dp. 14,350; l. 441'6''; b. 56'11''; dr. 23'; s. 12.5 k.; cpl. 528; a. 1 5'', 3 3'', 4 40mm.; cl. *Luzon*; T. EC2–S–C1)

Arthur P. Gorman was laid down under a Maritime Commission contract (MC hull 1179) on 11 August 1943 at Baltimore, Md., by the Bethlehem Steel Co.; renamed *Tutuila* on 8 September and designated ARG–4; launched on 12 September; transferred to the Navy when 80 percent complete for conversion to an internal combustion engine repair ship on 18 September; converted by the Maryland Drydock Co.; and commissioned there on 8 April 1944, Comdr. George T. Boldizsar in command.

Tutuila underwent shakedown in Hampton Roads from 20 April to 24 May before sailing for the Panama Canal and proceeding via San Diego, Pearl Harbor, and Eniwetok to the South Pacific.

Early in August, the repair ship joined Service Squadron (ServRon) 10, based at Purvis Bay, in the once hotly contested Solomon Islands. *Tutuila* served the Fleet as a floating advance base as it swept its way across the Pacific toward Japan. For the final year of the war, the repair ship engaged in round-the-clock work schedules which seldom slackened.

Tutuila aided in the build up for the operations which led to the liberation of the Philippines from the Japanese yoke. Upon completion of this campaign, American task forces set their sights on islands closer to the Japanese homeland. Iwo Jima and Okinawa fell to the telling power of American shells, bombs, and troops which stormed ashore supported by a great Allied armada. Soon, the Allied navies were within shelling distance of the Japanese home islands themselves.

During this time, the repair ship operated first out of Manus, in the Admiralties, before moving to Ulithi in the Carolines. In the wake of the liberation of the Philippines, *Tutuila* arrived at Leyte on 24 May 1945 and provided repair services there to a wide variety of ships and smaller craft from the date of her arrival until the end of hostilities.

Yet, *Tutuila*'s work was far from over. As American and Allied forces prepared for occupation of the Japanese homeland, the ship joined those forces headed north for duty off Nippon's shores. On 30 August, *Tutuila*—in company with *Jason* (ARH–1), *Whitney* (AD–4), and 11 smaller ships—set out on the first leg of the voyage northward. One day out, a typhoon lashed at the convoy, forcing the slower repair ship to remain with the "small boys" while *Jason* and *Whitney* received orders to run for Japan. On 2 September, having weathered the storm and shepherded her charges to safe harbor, *Tutuila* dropped anchor in Buckner Bay, Okinawa.

From there, *Tutuila* proceeded with a 33-ship convoy, bound for Korea, making port at Jinsen (now called Inchon) on 24 September 1945. She operated there as a maintenance vessel for ships engaged in the repatriation of Japanese prisoners of war. She continued this work after moving to Taku, China, where she arrived on 26 January 1946.

Departing Taku on 30 March, the ship steamed to Shanghai, China, where she dropped anchor on 2 April.

Six days later, she sailed for the United States. The ship transited the Panama Canal and arrived at New Orleans on 20 May. Following repairs, she moved to Galveston, Tex., on 9 June 1946 for deactivation and was decommissioned there six months later, on 7 December 1946.

She lay basking in the Texas sun until the summer of 1950, when North Korean troops crossed the 38th parallel and invaded South Korea. As the United States armed forces mobilized to support the United Nations effort, *Tutuila* received the call to return to active service. Towed to Orange, Tex., she was reconditioned with new shop machinery which replaced her 5-inch and 40-millimeter guns and their magazines. On 7 May 1951, the ship was recommissioned and assigned to the Service Force, Atlantic Fleet.

Tutuila arrived at Norfolk on 30 May 1951 and served there until 13 October, when she proceeded to Baltimore for one week before returning to Hampton Roads where she remained from 23 October 1951 to 16 June 1952.

Calling briefly at Guantanamo Bay, Cuba, from 20 to 23 June, she operated out of Norfolk again from 28 June to 15 August and from 22 August to 30 October, with a stint at New York in between. She continued this routine of east coast operations from 1952 through 1957, with occasional calls at Port-au-Prince, Haiti; Havana, Cuba; and Guantanamo Bay.

In 1957, the ship paid good will calls to Bermuda in June and Nova Scotia in August, with groups of Explorer Scouts embarked for each cruise. In October 1958, *Tutuila* again visited Havana and then proceeded to Philadelphia, where she took part in a special project for reclaiming materiel from ships in reserve before returning to Norfolk. She underwent a major overhaul at the Norfolk Navy Yard from 31 October 1958 to 21 January 1959 before proceeding to Guantanamo Bay late in March. But for a round-trip cruise to Port-au-Prince from 10 to 12 April, the ship served there until summer when she returned to the Virginia capes for antisubmarine exercises. The ship continued her operations out of Norfolk until the autumn of 1962.

On one occasion, the repair ship encountered merchantman SS *William Johnson* in distress while en route to Norfolk and, within a short time, *Tutuila* sent over a repair crew to correct the engineering casualty.

American reconnaissance planes flying over Cuba in the fall of 1962 noticed unusual activities there; and, when photographic prints were developed, the unusual items and activities were found to be Russian-built missiles and missile sites. In reaction to this threat, President John F. Kennedy ordered the Navy to throw a cordon around Cuba—instituting a "quarantine" of the island. In this tense climate, Navy destroyers and patrol planes formed a picket line, turning back Russian ships carrying missiles.

Tutuila proceeded to Morehead City, N.C., where she rendered services to Amphibious Squadron 6 before stopping at Norfolk to load cargo and proceed south to support the quarantine line. Basing out of Roosevelt Roads and Vieques, Puerto Rico, the ship provided supplies and services for the ships engaged in blockading Cuban sea lanes.

After the Soviet Government complied with President Kennedy's demand for the withdrawal of the missiles and all of their associated technicians, sites, and the like, tensions eased. *Tutuila* proceeded north toward Norfolk but encountered a storm—much like the one weathered in 1945, with 80-knot winds and heavy seas—which caused a three-day delay in her returning to home port.

Operating out of Norfolk and Charleston, S.C., through 1964, the ship provided repair services during Operation "Springboard" in January of 1965. Visits to San Juan and Roosevelt Roads, Puerto Rico; Frederiksted and St. Croix, in the American Virgin Islands; and Fort Lauderdale, Fla.; provided the crew with sightseeing and recreational activities in between her

regular duties out of the east coast ports of Norfolk and Charleston. In March 1965, *Tutuila* participated in a program to reclaim materiel and special equipment installed on radar picket destroyers which were currently being decommissioned at Bayonne, N.J.

As flagship of ServRon 4, *Tutuila* returned to Norfolk before heading south to the strife-torn Dominican Republic. While performing repair and support duties during the months of April and May, the ship conducted a special series of operations geared toward supplying needed petroleum products to light and power facilities in Santo Domingo after rebel gunfire had prevented normal tanker deliveries.

For the remainder of the year 1965, she continued operations out of Norfolk following the Dominican intervention, calling at San Juan and Guantanamo Bay for refresher training after her annual Portsmouth overhaul. During March and April 1966, *Tutuila* underwent extensive preparation for overseas deployment, as repair shops, berthing and messing spaces were air-conditioned, and new communications equipment was procured and installed.

The repair ship sailed from Norfolk on 9 May and transited the Panama Canal on 18 May. After brief stops at Pearl Harbor and at Subic Bay in the Philippines, the repair ship arrived at An Thoi, Phu Quoc Island, in the Gulf of Siam, to support Operation "Market Time" off the coast of South Vietnam.

Relieving *Krishna* (ARL–28) on 19 July, *Tutuila* commenced servicing the nimble and hard-hitting PCF's, or "Swift" boats, attached to Division 11. WPB's of the Coast Guard's Division 11 were based on *Tutuila* as well. The following month found *Tutuila*'s LCM's and their crews participating in Operation "Seamount," an Army-directed landing operation to clear the southern Phu Quoc Island of enemy forces. Landing South Vietnamese troops at four locations, *Tutuila*'s boats also carried supplies and ammunition to the Allied ground forces while helicopters evacuated casualties to the repair ship for medical attention.

Krishna returned to An Thoi on 8 October to relieve *Tutuila*, which then steamed to Bangkok, Thailand, for rest and relaxation for her crew. The repair ship then arrived back off the Vietnamese coast, reaching Vung Tau, off Cape St. Jacques, on 18 October. Here she supported Operations "Market Time," "Game Warden," and "Stable Door" through the end of 1966.

The opening days of the new year, 1967, saw the repair ship taking up support duties for the Mobile Riverine Force established at Vung Tau for operations in the Mekong Delta. Here, she assisted in the preparation of ASPB's and other small patrol craft until *Askari* (ARL–30) arrived and took over the major repair and maintenance work.

Tutuila conducted in-country availability for the first time on *Hisser* (DER–100) on 9 January. Her repair crews finished another difficult job in just five days—the overhauling and repairing of the troublesome diesel generators of *Benewah* (APB–35).

Turned over to the operational control of Commander, Naval Support Activity, Saigon, in April 1967, the ship commenced services to LST's engaged in operations off the mouth of the Mekong River. During this period, the repair ship continued to provide support and maintenance facilities for craft of the Mobile Riverine Assault Force and supported Coastal Division 13 as well. Further, *Tutuila*'s 3-inch guns spoke in anger for the first time in the Vietnam conflict, as the ship undertook a shore bombardment in the Rung Sat Special Zone, providing harassment and interdiction fire into an area of suspected Viet Cong activity north of Vung Tau.

Returning to An Thoi in October 1967, *Tutuila* relieved *Krishna* and provided support for coastal divisions of Navy and Coast Guard before proceeding to Kaohsiung, Taiwan, for five days of upkeep in late November. She returned to Vung Tau on 7 December to continue supporting coastal interdiction operations.

The repair ship remained at Vung Tau until taking over duties at An Thoi in April 1968 from *Krishna*. While remaining on station through the summer, *Tutuila* also trained South Vietnamese sailors in the operation of PCF's, four of which had been transferred to the Republic of Vietnam in August. *Tutuila's* hard work earned the Navy Unit Commendation as a result of the labors conducted at both Vung Tau and An Thoi.

Extensive improvements in habitability highlighted the yard work conducted at Yokosuka in January 1969, while the main engine, auxiliary pumps, and the three main generators were all subjected to thorough overhauling. On 21 March, the ship departed from Yokosuka for sea trials and refresher training—a virtually new ship both inside and out. The final week of training completed by 22 April, *Tutuila* cleared the Japanese isles on the 27th; bound, once more, for Vietnam.

After a five-day visit to Hong Kong en route, the ship dropped anchor at Vung Tau on 14 May. She commenced work almost immediately, conducting a temporary availability on *Brule* (AKL–28) before 1 June and filling 36 work requests from *Mark* (ARL–12) as well as repair work and availability requirements for local YFR craft and the Republic of Korea *LSM–610*.

On 12 June, *Tutuila* got underway for An Thoi, where she supported the continuation of "Market Time," as well as "Seafloat" and "Sealord," while maintaining PCF's, YFU's, *APL–21*, and several LST's.

For the months of June and July, the ship also undertook further training operations—repairing 17 Vietnamese Navy PCF's and training 39 Vietnamese bluejackets in diesel engine overhaul. *Saint Francis River* (LSMR–525) underwent two weeks of restricted availability, adding to the repair ship's already busy and round-the-clock schedule. Fulfilling these and other requests for South Vietnamese, Korean, Thai, and United States Navy units, *Tutuila* remained busy for the remainder of her active career off Vietnam—receiving three Navy Unit Commendations in the process. Late in 1971, she was selected for transfer to the Republic of China Navy.

On New Year's Day 1972, *Tutuila* departed Vung Tau after six years of combat support duties. Many times she had hoisted PCF's or other patrol craft onto pontoons alongside for complete overhauls; her crew had taught their Vietnamese counterparts the intricacies of diesel power plants and generators. Her guns had even conducted one offensive shore bombardment. Vietnam lay behind her as she headed for Hong Kong on 1 January 1972. Six days of bad weather jostled her before she finally made port at the British Crown Colony on 7 January.

Her stay at Hong Kong was not all rest and relaxation, however, as much lay ahead to be done in preparation for the transfer to the Chinese Navy. *Tutuila's* crew gave her a "face lift" which included painting; overhauling engines; and getting her records and accounts in order. She departed Hong Kong on 13 January and arrived at Subic Bay two days later, where, upon arrival, the work of off-loading supplies and ammunition began.

Departing Subic Bay on 29 January, *Tutuila* made port at Kaohsiung on 2 February to the accompaniment of a Chinese military band which played tunes from the dockside. For the next three weeks, final checks were undertaken to put the finishing touches on the transfer. Finally, by 21 February 1972, all was in readiness. On that day, *Tutuila* was decommissioned and struck from the Navy list. Transferred to the Nationalist Chinese Navy, she was renamed *Pien Tai* and serves as a supply ship into 1979.

Tutuila received seven battle stars, three Navy Unit Commendations, and two Meritorious Unit Commendations for her Vietnam service.

Tweedy

Albert William Tweedy, Jr., was born on 22 March 1920 and attended public schools in Winnetka, Ill., and Hingham, Mass., before he enrolled at Williams College, Williamstown, Mass., in the fall of 1938. In the summer of 1939, he completed Marine Corps' Platoon Commander School at Quantico, Va., and, at the end of his sophomore year, left college to become a Marine Aviation Cadet. Following flight training at Squantum, Mass., and Pensacola, Fla., he was commissioned a Second Lieutenant in the United States Marine Corps Reserve on 14 October 1941.

Assigned to the 2d Marine Aircraft Wing, Fleet Marine Force, he was stationed at San Diego and Hawaii before reporting for duty with Marine Scouter-Bomber Squadron (VMSB)–241 at Midway early in 1942. He served as Assistant Flight Officer and Assistant Communications Officer for the squadron before becoming its Communications Officer late in May.

Early on the morning of 4 June 1942, Lt. Tweedy took off from Midway in his "Dauntless" Navy dive-bomber (SBD–2). Minutes later, the Battle of Midway commenced as planes from the Japanese carriers pounded the Marine installations on Midway, and outdated American fighter planes based at Midway were bloodily dispatched by the newer and nimbler Japanese Zeros in the opening stages of the battle.

On that morning, Lt. Tweedy flew with Major Lofton Henderson's division of VMSB–241. Although stripped of its fighter protection, this division nonetheless attempted a glide-bombing attack on Japanese carrier *Hiryu*. Despite a fearsome antiaircraft barrage and repeated attacks by the numerically superior enemy fighter planes, Lt. Tweedy dove his aircraft to a perilously low altitude before releasing a bomb over the enemy carrier. Japanese fighters then attacked and splashed his slow-moving bomber, killing Lt. Tweedy. He was posthumously awarded the Navy Cross for his extraordinary heroism, cool courage, and conscientious devotion to duty.

(DE–532: dp. 1,350; l. 306'; b. 36'10''; dr. 13'; s. 24 k.; a. 2 5'', 4 40mm., 10 20mm., 2 dct., 8 dcp.; cl. *John C. Butler*)

Tweedy (DE–532) was laid down on 31 August 1943 by the Boston Navy Yard; launched on 7 October 1943; sponsored by Mrs. Albert William Tweedy, mother of Lt. Tweedy; and commissioned on 12 February 1944, Lt. Comdr. Thomas Donald Cunningham in command.

On completion of her fitting out, *Tweedy* departed Boston on 1 March and steamed for Bermuda where she conducted shakedown exercises through the end of the month. En route from Bermuda to Boston on 30 and 31 March, the destroyer escort conducted an unproductive 13-hour search for a German submarine known to be lurking in the coastal shipping lanes.

She began April moored in Boston, then moved south for firing tests in the Chesapeake Bay before arriving at Miami on the 18th. There, she began the duties which were to occupy her throughout most of World War II. Assigned to the Naval Training Center, Miami, she operated off the Florida Keys, conducting indoctrination cruises for student officers and nucleus crews. Occasionally putting in at Charleston for repairs or alterations, she continued in this essential but inconspicuous role, supplying the fleets with trained personnel, into the early months of 1945. In April 1945, she rescued six downed aviators from a Navy flying boat and conducted a submarine search north of San Salvador.

In June 1945, she put in at Charleston to undergo availability in preparation for assignment to Destroyer Escort Division 63. From mid-June until late October, she participated in exercises in Casco Bay with that division. On 21 October, she moored at Boston for Navy Day activities. The ship got underway on 8 November, bound for Florida, and arrived at Green Cove Springs on the 11th. There, she prepared for inactivation. On 10 May 1946, she was decommissioned and placed in reserve.

Towed from her Florida berth late in March 1949, she underwent conversion and repairs at Charleston and Bath, Maine, which continued into the autumn of 1950. She arrived at Boston in November 1950 and remained there until she was recommissioned on 2 April 1952. Following exercises out of Guantanamo Bay, Cuba, she finished out the year as a training ship for the Fleet Sonar School at Key West.

For the next three years, *Tweedy* conducted reserve training and midshipman cruises in addition to assignments at the Fleet Sonar School at Key West and participated in the annual Operation "Springboard" in the Caribbean. In 1956, she added submarine hunter-killer exercises in the North Atlantic—during which she tested new antisubmarine warfare equipment—to her activities. Late in the summer of 1957, she was deployed on her first Mediterranean cruise and, before returning to Key West in November, participated in Operation "Deepwater."

In June 1958, the ship became a Naval Reserve training ship. Following refresher training in Cuban waters, she assumed duties as flagship for Reserve Escort Squadron 4, training reservists from the 6th Naval District. The ship was placed out of commission, in reserve, on 20 June 1959, but she conducted weekend training cruises out of Pensacola for over two years.

In response to the Berlin Crisis of August 1961, *Tweedy* was recommissioned on 2 October of that year. Following refresher training, she was assigned the home port of Newport and commenced antisubmarine barrier duties in the Caribbean early in 1962. Throughout the year, she engaged in fleet and type exercises, made goodwill visits, and served as flagship for Escort Squadron 12. On 12 June, as *Tweedy* steamed from Pensacola to Norfolk, she came upon nine Cuban nationals in distress after two days at sea in an open, 14-foot boat. *Tweedy* aided the refugees and, later in the day, transferred them to Coast Guard representatives for assistance on their way to Miami.

On 1 August 1962, the destroyer escort was again decommissioned and returned to reserve training ship status. Operating out of Florida ports, she continued in that capacity until late in May 1969 when she departed St. Petersburg for the last time. On 29 May, she arrived at Orange, Tex., for inactivation; and, in June, her name was struck from the Navy list. In March 1970, she was assigned to Naval Air Atlantic for destruction as a target.

Twiggs

Levi Twiggs was born in Richmond County, Ga., on 23 May 1793 and was commissioned a second lieutenant in the United States Marine Corps on 10 November 1813. During the War of 1812, he saw action on board *President* and was captured when that frigate was taken, after a gallant defense, by a squadron of four British warships. After being imprisoned at Bermuda, he was freed when word of the Treaty of Ghent reached that island. Over two decades later, he took part in the Indian Wars in Florida and Georgia in 1836 and 1837. When the war with Mexico opened, Major Twiggs requested an active part in the fighting and was attached to the Marine Battalion which left New York in June 1847. He was felled by enemy fire as he led a storming party in the assault on Chapultepec before Mexico City on 13 September 1847.

I

(Destroyer No. 127: dp. 1,306 (f.); l. 314'4½''; b. 30'11½'' (wl.); dr. 9'9½'' (aft); s. 35.04 k.; cpl. 122; a. 4 4', 2 3'', 12 21'' tt., 2 dct.; cl. *Wickes*)

The first *Twiggs* (Destroyer No. 127) was laid down

on 23 January 1918 at Camden, N.J., by the New York Shipbuilding Corp.; launched on 28 September 1918; sponsored by Miss Lillie S. Getchell, the granddaughter of Major Twiggs; and commissioned at the Philadelphia Navy Yard on 28 July 1919, Comdr. Isaac C. Johnson, Jr., in command.

Following shakedown, the destroyer joined Division 16, Squadron 4, Pacific Fleet, late in October 1919 and operated out of San Diego, Calif., on training cruises through the spring of 1922. While performing this duty, *Twiggs* was classified DD–127 on 17 July 1920 during the Navy-wide assignment of alphanumeric hull numbers. A combination of factors—increased operating costs, manpower shortages, and the general antimilitary climate which followed World War I—resulted in a reduction of the Navy's active Fleet. Accordingly, *Twiggs* was decommissioned at San Diego on 24 June 1922.

After almost eight years of inactivity, *Twiggs* was placed in commission again on 20 February 1930 at San Diego, Lt. Comdr. Thomas S. King II in command. She became flagship of Destroyer Division (DesDiv) 14 and conducted operations out of San Diego with the Battle Fleet until late in the year. Early in February 1931, she headed south from San Francisco with the Battle Fleet to participate in the annual Fleet concentration with the Scouting Fleet. At the end of the exercises on 25 March 1931, *Twiggs* was reassigned to the Scouting Fleet, soon to be redesignated the Scouting Force as a result of the Fleet Reorganization of 1 April 1931. *Twiggs'* new home port was Charleston, S.C., whence she operated as flagship of DesDiv 7 until late in the spring of 1933. Sometime between 1 April and 1 July 1933, she rejoined the Battle Force destroyers on the west coast as a unit of DesDiv 6, Destroyer Squadron (DesRon) 2. The destroyer was completely active until 1 November 1933 when she joined Rotating Reserve DesRon 20 at San Diego. She remained there in a caretaker status, with a minimum crew on board, until 1 July 1934 when she returned to fully active duty with DesDiv 4, DesRon 2. She operated out of San Diego with the Battle Force destroyers until late in 1936 when she began preparations for decommissioning. On 6 April 1937, *Twiggs* was placed out of commission and berthed at San Diego once again.

Towards the end of the destroyer's sojourn in San Diego's "red lead row," Germany invaded Poland on 1 September 1939. To augment the "neutrality patrol" which President Roosevelt had placed around the eastern seaboard and Gulf ports, the Navy quickly set the wheels in motion to recommission 77 destroyers and light minelayers which had lain in reserve at either Philadelphia or San Diego. As part of this operation, *Twiggs* was recommissioned at San Diego on 30 September 1939, Comdr. Lyman K. Swenson—who was later killed in *Juneau* (CL–52) at Guadalcanal in November 1942—in command.

As flagship for DesDiv 64, DesRon 32, *Twiggs* initially operated out of San Diego on shakedown and training cruises through November. In company with eight of her sister ships, she transited the Panama Canal early in December. Soon after reaching her new base at Key West, Fla., *Twiggs* got underway to shadow the British destroyer HMS *Hereward*. Later in the month, she joined sister ship *Evans* (DD–78) and *Vincennes* (CA–44) in keeping a close watch on the Australian light cruiser HMAS *Perth* as the British man-of-war prowled the Gulf of Yucatan on the alert to intercept the German liner *Columbus* which was attempting to slip through the Royal Navy to safety in Germany. The Americans maintained such a close surveillance of the Australian ship that her exasperated commander, Capt. F. B. "Fearless Freddie" Farncomb, was heard to remark: "Queer idea of 'neutrality' these Americans have! "

During her subsequent operations with DesDiv 64, *Twiggs* conducted neutrality patrols, training cruises for Naval Reserve contingents, battle practices, and exercises through the summer of 1940.

Meanwhile, by the spring of 1940, the Allied cause had taken a decided turn for the worse, as Norway fell after a disastrous British-Norwegian defense, and France and the Low Countries crumbled under the German blitzkrieg. In addition, German submarines, preying upon the convoys which served as England's lifeline, began taking heavy tolls on merchantman and escort alike. After the fall of France, Britain found herself very much alone in her struggle to prevent German hegemony in Europe.

With British destroyer forces in bad shape—the beatings taken in Norway, in the Atlantic convoy lanes, and in the Dunkirk evacuation had cut deeply into the Royal Navy list of escort ships—Prime Minister Winston Churchill appealed to the United States for aid. By the summer of 1940, President Franklin D. Roosevelt hit upon a solution to the problems respectively facing the United States and Great Britain. Accordingly, he and the Prime Minister reached the "destroyers for bases" agreement, whereby the United States transferred 50 overage, flush-decked, four-piped destroyers to the British in return for 99-year leases on strategic base sites in the Western Hemisphere.

As the summer of 1940 gave way to fall, *Twiggs* began preparation for her transfer to the United Kingdom. She arrived at Halifax, Nova Scotia, the turnover point for the "50 ships that saved the world," on 16 October 1940. The destroyer was decommissioned on the 23d, and her name was struck from the Navy list on 8 January 1941.

Turned over to the Royal Navy on 23 October 1940, the flush-decker became HMS *Leamington* (G.19), with Comdr. W. E. Banks—a holder of the Distinguished Service Order—in command. She shifted to St. John's, Newfoundland, whence she departed on 4 November as part of the 4th "Town" Flotilla, bound for the British Isles. En route to Belfast, Northern Ireland, she and her sister ships passed through the scene of the action fought on the 5th by the armed merchant cruiser HMS *Jervis Bay*, in defense of the homeward-bound Convoy HX-84, against the German "pocket battleship" *Admiral Scheer*. *Jervis Bay*'s gallant delaying action enabled 32 of the 37 ships in the convoy to escape, although she herself was sunk in the action. *Leamington* searched for survivors but could find no signs of life.

Proceeding via Belfast, Northern Ireland, *Leamington* arrived at Plymouth, England, on 15 November. There, the destroyer was allocated to the 2d Escort Group, Western Approaches Command, based at Londonderry. She conducted convoy escort missions across the Atlantic into 1941. While in the screen of Convoy SC-48—as it was being attacked by German U-boats for more than a week—*Leamington* teamed with the destroyer HMS *Veteran* in sinking *U-207* off the east coast of Greenland on 11 September.

On 27 March 1942, *Leamington* added another "kill" to her record when she and three other destroyers sent *U-587* to the bottom as the U-boat threatened Middle East-bound troop convoy WS-27. That summer, as the flush decker steamed toward North Russia in the screen of the ill-fated convoy, PQ-17, the powerful German battleship *Tirpitz* (sister to the famed *Bismarck* which had been sunk on 28 May 1941) was reported on the prowl. Since the massed convoy would present too easy pickings for such a powerful adversary, the ships were scattered. However, such tactics exposed the Allied ships to the attacks of German U-boats and aircraft. As a result, 23 of the 34 ships in PQ-17 were sunk. No other Russian convoy during the entire war suffered so severely.

Leamington was refitted at Hartlepool, England, between August and November 1942 and then resumed convoy escort missions in the Atlantic. On 12 November, the Panamian registry merchantman SS *Buchanan* was torpedoed by *U-224*. Thirteen days later, *Leamington*, assisted by aircraft, located the last of the freighter's four lifeboats and took aboard its 17 uninjured sailors.

In October 1942, the Royal Navy transferred *Leamington* to the Royal Canadian Navy, who employed her in the defense of shipping in the western Atlantic over the next 14 months. She experienced extremely bad weather, with extensive icing conditions, while operating in the North Atlantic in late 1942 and early 1943. At one point, the ship reached Halifax after a severe gale on 22 January 1943, coated from bridge to foc'sle deck with ice varying from 2 to 10 feet thick.

On 14 May 1943, *Leamington* collided with *Albatross* (AM-71) and was docked at Halifax for repairs but managed to be seaworthy again by the end of the month. She then sailed south to Norfolk, which she reached on 27 June, and underwent permanent repairs there until September.

Departing Halifax on 22 December, *Leamington* returned to the British Isles and reverted to Royal Navy control. After a period of service based at Rosyth, Scotland, the flush-deck destroyer was placed in reserve at the Tyne. However, on 16 June 1944, the British loaned the ship to the Russians, who renamed her *Jgoochyi* or *Zhguchi* (meaning "scorcher"). She served under the Russian flag through 1949 and was returned to Great Britain in 1950. She was subsequently broken up for scrap at Newport, England, on 26 July 1951.

II

(DD-591: dp. 2,050; l. 376'6''; b. 39'4''; dr. 17'; s. 35.5 k.; cpl. 273; a. 5 5'', 7 20mm., 10 40mm., 10 21'' tt., 6 dcp., 2 dct.; cl. *Fletcher*)

The second *Twiggs* (DD-591) was laid down on 20 January 1943 at Charleston, S.C., by the Charleston Navy Yard; launched on 7 April 1943; sponsored by Mrs. Roland S. Morris; and commissioned on 4 November 1943, Comdr. John B. Fellows, Jr., in command.

Following a shakedown cruise to Bermuda in December 1943, *Twiggs* operated out of Norfolk as a training ship until 12 May 1944, when she departed Hampton Roads in company with *Franklin* (CV-13), *Cushing* (DD-797), and *Richard P. Leary* (DD-664) and proceeded, via the Panama Canal and San Diego, to Hawaii.

After arriving in Pearl Harbor on 6 June 1944, *Twiggs* took part in exercises and drills in Hawaiian waters and escorted convoys operating between Oahu and Eniwetok. Throughout most of July, *Twiggs* worked out of Eniwetok alternating exercises with escort and radar picket duties. On 19 August, she returned to Pearl Harbor to begin rehearsals for the long-awaited return to the Philippines.

On 15 September, in preparation for the assault on Leyte, *Twiggs* departed Pearl Harbor as a member of Destroyer Squadron 49, screening Task Group 79.2, Transport Attack Group "Baker," which steamed via Eniwetok for Manus in the Admiralty Islands. After final preparations for the impending invasion, she departed Seeadler Harbor on 14 October. Arriving off Leyte on 20 October, *Twiggs* helped to provide antiaircraft protection for the transports during the landings. In the following days of heavy enemy air activity, she continued to support the invasion and, on one occasion, rescued a downed flier from *Petrof Bay* (CVE-80). *Twiggs* departed Leyte on 25 October, steamed via Mios Woendi Island to Manus, and arrived at Seeadler Harbor on 1 November.

Twiggs next rendezvoused with *Haraden* (DD-585) and *Halligan* (DD-584) for escort duty among the Palau Islands. Stationed east of Mindanao, she protected convoys on the approaches to Leyte.

On 10 December, *Twiggs* left Kossol Roads, between Peleliu and Angaur, with a task force bound for the occupation of Mindoro Island. Luzon was the key to the liberation of the Philippines, and Mindoro was the first step in the assault on Luzon. From December 13 through the 17th, *Twiggs* provided antiaircraft cover for the force as it steamed through Surigao Strait and the Mindoro Sea.

Late in 1944, Japan began organized and concerted use of kamikazes. On 13 December, a Japanese suicide plane crashed into *Haraden* (DD–585). *Twiggs* aided the severely damaged destroyer, fighting fires and treating casualties. She was then detached from the convoy to guide *Haraden*, which had lost communications and radar in the engagement, until the battered vessel made visual contact with a tow convoy off Silino Island. *Twiggs* then returned to the Mindanao Sea and resumed her duties with the task unit. Army Air Force flights out of Leyte augmented escort protection of the convoy. *Twiggs* retired to the Palaus on 20 December.

Twiggs sortied from Kossol Roads on 1 January 1945 protecting a large task force intended for the invasion of Luzon. In the Sulu and South China Seas, several ships of the convoy were hit by Japanese plane attacks; and, on 4 January 1945, *Twiggs* rescued 211 survivors of *Ommaney Bay* (CVE–79), destroyed by fire and explosion following an attack by a suicide plane. Raids by both torpedo and kamikaze planes continued as *Twiggs* operated northwest of Cape Bolinao in support of the Lingayen assault. After taking on food and ammunition at Mindoro, *Twiggs* briefly ran antisubmarine patrol off the entrance of Manganin Bay. Underway on the 21st, she arrived in Ulithi on 25 January for minor repairs and maintenance in preparation for the conquest of the Volcanos.

Twiggs joined Task Force 54 which sortied from Ulithi on 10 February for rehearsals at Loesip Island. On 16 February, the force arrived off Iwo Jima where *Twiggs* quickly began fire support for pre-assault underwater demolition operations off the eastern beaches. She also conducted screening and harassing activities, firing on Japanese shore units and providing illumination. On the 17th, a suicide plane attack on *Twiggs* resulted in a close call when the plane, in an obvious attempt to crash into the destroyer, crossed her fantail before hitting the water off her port beam and sinking without exploding. The destroyer continued activities to support American ground forces during the grueling battle for Iwo Jima. On 10 March, she retired toward the Carolines, arriving at Ulithi two days later for rest and replenishment.

On 25 March 1945, *Twiggs* arrived off Okinawa to take part in the preinvasion bombardment. In addition to antisubmarine and antiaircraft patrols, she supported ground forces with night harassing fire. Suicide planes were very active at this time, as the Japanese desperately defended the island. On 28 April, a day of heavy air activity, a kamikaze splashed close aboard *Twiggs* while she was on radar picket duty with Task Group 51. Bomb blast and fragmentation from the splashed airplane and bomb blew in the hull plating between the main and first platform deck causing structural damage. The underwater body was dished in, and the starboard propeller was bent. *Nestor* (ARB–6) repaired the damage; and, on 17 May, *Twiggs* returned to duty with the gunfire and covering forces off Okinawa.

In June, the battle for Okinawa was drawing to its close. *Twiggs* continued radar picket duties in the western fire support area and supported strikes on Iheya Shima and Iheya-Aguni with pre-landing bombardment and gunfire support. On 16 June, *Twiggs* was on radar picket duty off Senaga Shima in the western fire support area. At 2030, a single, low-flying plane dropped a torpedo which hit *Twiggs* on her port side, exploding her number 2 magazine. The plane then circled and completed its kamikaze mission in a suicide crash. The explosion enveloped the destroyer in flame; and, within an hour, she sank. Despite the hazard of exploding ammunition from the blazing *Twiggs*, 188 survivors were rescued from the oily waters. Among the 152 dead and missing was her commanding officer, Comdr. George Phillip.

Twiggs was struck from the Navy list on 11 July 1945; and, in 1957, her hulk was donated to the government of the Ryukyu Islands.

Twiggs received four battle stars for World War II service.

Twilight

Twilight was renamed *Ormsby* (q.v.) and designated APA–49 on 10 March 1943.

Twin Falls

A county in southern Idaho and the city which serves as its seat of government.

(T–AGM–11: dp. 8,010 (f.); l. 455'; b. 62'; dr. 20'; s. 19 k. (tl.); cpl. 56; cl. *Twin Falls*; T. VC2–S–AP3)

Twin Falls Victory was laid down under a Maritime Commission contract (MCV hull 167) on 27 December 1944 at Portland, Oreg., by the Oregon Shipbuilding Corp.; launched on 6 February 1945; sponsored by Mrs. J. B. Pfietor; and delivered to Pope & Talbot, Inc., of Portland, Oreg., the first of several companies to operate her under contract with the War Shipping Administration. By April 1958, she was out of service and laid up with the National Defense Reserve Fleet at its berthing area on the James River in Virginia.

On 1 July 1964, she was acquired by the Military Sea Transportation Service to become a range instrumentation ship assigned to missile tracking duty on the Air Force's Eastern Test Range in the Atlantic Ocean. Renamed *Twin Falls*, designated AGM–11, and operated by a civil service crew, she served as a mobile tracking platform for recording data on missiles and satellites that were out of range of land-based tracking stations.

In October 1969, the Air Force determined that *Twin Falls* was no longer necessary to its mission. Placed out of service early in 1970, she was slated for disposal. Her name was struck from the Navy list on 1 September 1972, and she was transferred, via the Department of Commerce, to New York City on 2 November to serve as a training facility for that city's Food and Maritime Trade High School.

Twining

Nathan Crook Twining was born on 17 January 1869 at Boscobel, Wis. He was appointed a naval cadet in 1885 and graduated from the United States Naval Academy on 7 June 1889. During the Spanish-American War, he served in *Iowa* (Battleship No. 4) in Cuban waters and later was executive officer of *Kearsarge* (Battleship No. 5) when that ship circumnavigated the globe with the "Great White Fleet." He commanded *Tacoma* (Cruiser No. 18) during the bombardment of Vera Cruz in 1914. During World War I, he served as Chief of Staff for Admiral Sims, Commander of Naval Forces in European waters, and was also a member of the Allied War Council. Rear Admiral Twining retired early in 1923 and died on 4 July 1924 at Nantucket, Mass.

(DD–540: dp. 2,050; l. 376'5''; b. 39'7''; dr. 17'9''; s. 35.2 k.; cpl. 329; a. 5 5'', 7 20mm., 10 40mm., 10 21'' tt., 6 dcp., 2 dct.; cl. *Fletcher*)

Twining (DD–540) was laid down on 20 November 1942 at San Francisco, Calif., by the Bethlehem Steel Co.; launched on 11 July 1943; sponsored by Mrs. S. B. C. Wood; and commissioned on 1 December 1943, Comdr. Ellis Kerr Wakefield in command.

Twining departed San Francisco on 21 December for shakedown training and completed the cruise at San Diego on Christmas Day. Following exercises out of that port, she returned to San Francisco; loaded passengers and cargo; and got underway on 11 February 1944.

Twining arrived at Pearl Harbor on the 17th to begin three months of training exercises, maneuvers, and drills, as her crew honed its skills in bombardment, fire support, and amphibious landing operations in preparation for Operation "Forager."

On 31 May, the destroyer departed the Hawaiian Islands in company with Fire Support Group 1 of the Saipan invasion forces. She arrived at Kwajalein on 8 June, fueled, and commenced antisubmarine patrols off the harbor entrance. On the 10th, *Twining* screened the sortie of the task group from the lagoon; headed for the Marianas; and arrived off Saipan at dawn on the 14th. Steaming along the island's eastern shore, she screened cruiser *Montpelier* (CL–57); joined briefly in the pre-assault bombardment and, late in the afternoon, engaged in a running battle with a coastal battery. Leading *Stockham* (DD–683) and *Montpelier*, *Twining* closed the shore to 3,000 yards and joined in the fire which silenced the enemy guns. As darkness fell, she took up her station to screen vessels supplying night harassment fire at Garapan on Saipan's west coast.

The next day, D-day, she continued screening duties and fired on selected shore targets while marines landed on the western side of the island. Japanese planes appeared at dusk, but none came within range of *Twining*'s guns. She spent most of the 16th in the unproductive pursuit of a sound contact and, at dusk, joined in the bombardment of Magicienne Bay. During the night, her guns scored hits on a Japanese ammunition dump near Aslito airfield.

Early on the morning of 17 June, *Twining* joined Destroyer Division 106 and steamed to rendezvous with Vice Admiral W. A. Lee's battleships in anticipation of fleet action. The American assault on the Marianas had drawn the Japanese Combined Fleet northward for an attempt to repulse the thrust.

The 18th passed uneventfully except for sightings of a few snoopers. Then, at dawn the next day, a lone, unidentified plane closed the formation; took fire from *Twining* and others; circled; and disappeared. The ensuing lull lasted until 1008 when *Alabama* (BB–60) reported a large number of aircraft approaching from the west. Steaming on picket station 10 miles west of the formation, *Twining* caught sight of the first wave of attackers at 1049. Throughout the battle, combat air patrol (CAP) planes disrupted the enemy onslaught, shooting down many Japanese aircraft and thwarting the approach of the rest. In her first antiaircraft action, *Twining* splashed two of the planes which got through and also was credited with an assist. During the attacks, the destroyer was the target of two bomb drops but suffered no damages. For *Twining*, the Battle of the Philippine Sea was over in 26 minutes. No further Japanese planes attacked nearby during the day, although pilots from the American carriers continued to pick off intruders.

On the 20th, *Twining* steamed west in search of the enemy fleet. Late in the day, the carriers launched an air strike; and, when darkness came, many planes had not returned. *Twining* turned on her searchlight as a marker for the aircraft and rescued survivors of planes which had gone down in the darkness. At dark on the 21st, the task force abandoned the pursuit of the elusive Japanese fleet and reversed course, steaming eastward to look again for survivors of the air strike force caught by darkness of the day before. On the 23d, *Twining* fueled at sea; then set course for the Marianas, screening oiler *Cahaba* (AO–82).

At Saipan again on the 25th, *Twining* conducted shore bombardment off Mutcho Point. Throughout the remainder of June, she continued to operate off Saipan, providing shore bombardment, night harassment and illumination fire, as well as screening transports and engaging enemy aircraft. In Magicienne Bay early on the evening of the 28th, *Twining* witnessed an impressive exchange of fire between marine units on the south side of the bay and Japanese on the north. Later in the evening, Japanese planes attacked, peppering seaward waters with bombs. Observers on board the destroyer watched as shore fire scored a hit on an enemy plane overhead; then saw the plane fall in flames some four miles away. Just before midnight on 30 June, as *Twining* patrolled off Nafutan Point, two enemy planes

attempted to make runs on Aslito airfield but were turned back by heavy fire from the destroyer.

Into July, *Twining* continued her duties off Saipan, supplying screening, fighter direction, and fire support. She also made occasional voyages to Tinian for bombardment missions. Off the northern tip of Saipan on the night of 6 and 7 July, *Twining*'s crew was kept busy firing on numerous Japanese airplanes which had apparently chosen the ship both as a reference point for their approach to the runway on Marpi Point and as a target for their bombs. Nine planes made approaches during this raid, although only one dropped a bomb. Flares from the planes often illuminated the scene as the destroyer's gunfire drove off all nine, none of which managed to land on the Japanese-held airstrip. In the days that followed, *Twining* remained on picket station, occasionally firing on enemy troop concentrations on the island.

On 24 July, she screened *Montpelier* and *New Orleans* (CA–32) as they shelled Japanese positions on Tinian. The following day, the destroyer fired support missions to screen American troops advancing up the western shore of the island. *Twining* continued her support of the invasion of Tinian through the end of the month, steaming on station between Tinian and Saipan and occasionally firing at Japanese targets on the island.

On 1 August, *Twining* moved to a new fire support assignment off the southeast coast of Tinian. She made the first of three bombardment runs at 0130 and later stood in to 1,500 yards from shore to pound enemy-held slopes and caves with gunfire.

On the 7th, *Twining* departed Saipan, escorting slow-moving *LST–130* to Eniwetok. A week later, she entered the atoll where her worn strut bearings were replaced.

Twining departed Eniwetok on 15 September to rendezvous with Rear Admiral Gerald F. Bogan's Fast Carrier Task Group and thereafter devoted most of her effort for the rest of the war to protecting aircraft carriers. Arriving off Luzon on the 21st, *Twining* guarded the carriers as they launched strikes despite cloudy weather, squalls, and low visibility. Following the launching of further strikes from an attack position off San Bernardino Strait on the 24th, the task group headed eastward and arrived off Saipan on the 28th. From there, the destroyer conducted antisubmarine patrols until the 30th when the task group got underway for the western Carolines and entered Ulithi lagoon on 6 October.

At dusk on the 11th, the task force sortied to get into a position for a strike on Formosa, the first in a series of raids intended to destroy the usefulness of that highly fortified island as an air base and a staging area for Japanese forces during the impending landings on Leyte.

For three days, planes from the carriers hit targets on Formosa; and, each evening, Japanese raiders attacked the American ships. On the 12th, *Twining* rescued several downed fliers. That evening, enemy planes attacked her formation in an action which continued until midnight. A Japanese plane threatened the destroyer from an altitude of 300 feet. After *Twining* opened fire, the raider attempted to crash into her but rapidly lost altitude and splashed 300 yards off her port bow, spreading flaming gasoline over water near the ship.

In the days that followed, enemy air activity continued to be heavy. On the 14th, an enemy bomber dropped two bombs which narrowly missed the destroyer.

On the 18th and 21st, the carriers of TG 38.2 launched strikes against targets in the Philippines to support American landings on Leyte. Before dawn on the 24th, reports of American plane sightings of the Japanese Fleet began to reach the destroyer. That day, as *Twining* continued her routine screening duties, planes from the carriers struck telling blows against Admiral Kurita's "Center Force" in the Sibuyan Sea.

That night, her task force turned north to attack a Japanese carrier force which had been sighted north of Luzon. Daylong strikes launched from the American flattops sank four enemy carriers of Admiral Ozawa's Northern Force in an action known as the Battle off Cape Engãno. On the 26th, planes from TG 38.2 attacked crippled Japanese ships in the Visayan Sea. On the 29th, *Twining* rescued a downed flier from *Hancock* (CV–19).

But for occasional runs to Ulithi for ammunition, *Twining* remained with the carriers throughout November as they hammered Japanese fortifications in the Philippines. On 10 December, the destroyer got underway with Rear Admiral Montgomery's Fast Carrier Task Group to act as picket during strikes on Luzon in support of the landings on Mindoro. On the 14th, she rescued a pilot from *Hornet* (CV–12) and had him on board four and one-half minutes after his plane hit the water.

On the 17th, in rapidly worsening weather conditions, the formation rendezvoused with fueling units; and *Twining* filled her oil tanks. During a typhoon which battered the task force the next day, the weight of her full load of fuel gave *Twining* the added stability she needed to weather 65-foot seas and 50-degree rolls. Ordered to stand by the disabled *Monterey* (CVL–26) as the light carrier burned, dead in the water, *Twining* maintained a position near the stricken vessel throughout the storm. *Twining* came through the tempest with no major damage but lost one man overboard.

As dawn broke in moderating weather on 19 December, the destroyer accompanied the task force as it steamed on for a strike on Luzon; but, when bad weather aborted the strike, she returned to the scene of the typhoon to search for survivors from the three destroyers which had sunk during the storm, before returning to Ulithi on Christmas Eve to repair storm damage.

Admiral Halsey's 3d Fleet departed on 30 December and set course for strikes on Formosa, the Ryukyus, and the China coast to prevent Japanese interference with the coming landings on Luzon at Lingaygen Gulf. *Twining* screened the carriers as they launched strikes against the enemy in the Philippines, on Formosa, and in French Indochina.

Twining returned to Ulithi on 26 January for drydocking, provisioning, and training exercises. She got underway again on 10 February with Rear Admiral Davison's Carrier Task Group bound for waters near the Japanese home islands. After naval aircraft raided military targets in the Tokyo area on the 16th and 17th, the task group headed south toward the Volcano Islands.

Twining was on picket station off Iwo Jima on 19 February, D-day, as the carrier force launched strikes and fighter cover for the landings. Four days later, the destroyer again headed north protecting carriers steaming toward the Japanese homeland, but bad weather foiled the carriers. On 1 March, the task group launched strikes on the Ryukyus before steaming to the Carolines.

In mid-March, Task Force 58 departed Ulithi to conduct strikes on the airfields near Kyushu on the 18th. The next day, as the group was en route to Kobe, carrier *Franklin* (CV–13) suffered extensive damage when hit by two bombs. *Twining* helped to protect the damaged vessel as she withdrew. On the 20th, a Japanese plane attempted to finish off the battered carrier only to be chased off by a hail of fire from the escorting ships. On the 22d, having safely conducted *Franklin* out of danger, *Twining* set her course for Nansei Shoto. On 27 March, *Twining* screened destroyer *Murray* (DD–576)—which had taken an aerial torpedo through her bow above the water—until that ship had completed temporary repairs. The next day, *Twining* headed north in search of the Japanese fleet, then returned to Okinawan waters on the 31st, and resumed duty as a picket for carrier operations.

On the first day in April, the carriers resumed strikes on Okinawa in support of landings there. On the 6th, the group came under attack from massed kamikazes as Japan vainly tried to repulse the Allied assault. During a two-hour period, *Twining*'s group splashed five kamikazes; but the destroyer was on the opposite side of the formation and had no opportunity for a clear shot.

The following day, she screened the carriers as they steamed north to intercept Japanese warships approaching Okinawa. A 380-plane strike located the Japanese ships in the East China Sea, near Amami Oshima, and sank superbattleship *Yamato*, light cruiser *Yahagi*, and four destroyers. Enemy air activity was frequent; and, on 13 April, *Twining* chased off an aerial intruder which had approached her picket post.

A few days later, she retired to Ulithi for repairs. On 4 May, she again got underway from Ulithi, this time with Task Group 58.1, bound for strikes on Kyushu in support of operations on Okinawa. As the formation approached the Japanese islands, enemy pilots became bolder; and *Twining* fired on a number of planes. Throughout the remainder of May and into June, she continued to protect the carrier force as it operated off Okinawa.

On 4 June, the barometer reading began to drop; and winds picked up. Winds reached 70 knots by 0600, and *Twining* again faced the might of a typhoon but emerged undamaged and resumed her picket duties late in the day. Following strikes on Kyushu, she detached from the group on 10 June to escort *Dashiell* (DD–659) to Leyte.

After upkeep and availability in San Pedro Bay, she screened *Yorktown* (CV–10) in Leyte Gulf as the carrier exercised a newly-assigned air group. Early in July, *Twining* joined Task Force 38, with Admiral W. F. Halsey embarked in *Missouri* (BB–63), for seven days of intensive training exercises in preparation for the long-awaited assault on the Japanese homeland. On 10 July, the task force arrived off Tokyo and, four days later, began launching strikes. On the 24th, *Twining* joined in antishipping sweeps off the Kure-Kobe area and, on the night of 24 and 25 July, took part in the bombardment of Shiono-Misaki airfield. Frequent enemy air activity occurred as *Twining* screened the carriers. Air strikes against Kure and Kobe late in July were followed early in August by additional strikes against northern Honshu. On 9 August, a kamikaze attempted to crash into *Twining* but, under intense fire from the ship, overshot the destroyer. At 0605 on 15 August, *Twining* heard the carriers recall strikes bound for Tokyo targets; and, two hours later, Radio San Francisco announced the welcome news of Japan's unconditional capitulation.

Late in August, *Twining* stood by in Sagami Wan to provide fire support for the occupation of Yokosuka Naval Base; but the landings took place without incident. The same procedure was repeated at Tateyama Wan on 3 September with the same peaceful result. On the 9th, the destroyer began support of minesweeping activities off Sendai, Choshi; then returned to Tokyo Bay on the 16th for repairs and replenishment.

Twining next participated in training exercises before getting underway for the United States on 31 October. She steamed, via Pearl Harbor, with Destroyer Squadron 53 and, on 20 November, entered Puget Sound for overhaul at Bremerton. On 14 June 1946, she was decommissioned at San Diego. Assigned to the Naval Reserve Training Program in August, *Twining* operated out of west coast ports and made voyages to Hawaii and Mexico as part of her training activities.

Twining was recommissioned on 10 June 1950. After operations on the west coast, she departed San Diego on 20 August 1951 and steamed, via Hawaii and Japan, to waters off Korea.

With Commander, Destroyer Division 172, embarked on *Twining*, the destroyer joined the screen of Fast Carrier Task Force 77 late in September and also supplied counterbattery fire in support of minesweepers in the vicinity of Hungnam. In October, *Twining* operated in the waters of Tongjoson Bay, participating in the interdiction of Wonsan harbor where she engaged shore batteries and fired on buildings, road intersections, and railroads. She occasionally supplied fire called for by aircraft or shore fire control centers. On 9 October, the destroyer scored a hit on an ammunition storage area setting off a violent explosion and numerous fires.

Two days later, *Twining* proceeded to Hungnam harbor to thwart communist efforts to remine swept waters there. That night, as she steamed near the channel entrance, an unidentified jet made a quick surprise attack, dropped two bombs, strafed the destroyer, and escaped into the overcast. The bombs dropped nearby, but the destroyer suffered no damage. After sinking a sampan and engaging a shore battery, *Twining* set her course for Yokosuka.

Twining spent November in upkeep and training exercises and devoted December to antisubmarine hunter-killer exercises off Okinawa. On the 11th, she headed for the east coast of Korea for interdiction and close support missions. The destroyer ended the month screening Task Force 77 and began the new year with upkeep at Sasebo. On 22 January 1952, *Twining* departed Japan to return to Wonsan. There, she fired on vehicles, warehouses, and enemy troop concentrations and, on the 30th, rescued a downed American pilot. She operated in Wonsan harbor until 19 February, when she got underway for Japan. Following voyage repairs, she departed Yokosuka, steamed via Midway and Pearl Harbor for the west coast, and arrived at San Diego on 10 March.

She remained in California ports until 1 November 1952 when she sailed for the Far East and her second tour of duty in Korean waters. In the months that followed, she operated off the east coast of Korea, carrying out patrol and reconnaissance missions, firing on shore targets, supplying night illumination for island garrisons in Wonsan harbor and fire support for minesweepers.

In March, she anchored in Buckner Bay before moving to Formosa to train personnel of the Chinese Nationalist Navy in gunnery and damage control. On 8 April, she rendezvoused with *Oriskany* (CVA–34) to provide antisubmarine screening for the carrier and conducted patrols of the North Formosa Strait before returning to Japan in mid-April. In May, the destroyer departed Yokosuka, setting her course for Pearl Harbor and Long Beach. She operated out of California ports throughout the remainder of 1953.

Although the Korean War was at an end, *Twining* continued to alternate cruises in the Far East with operations on the west coast until June 1963 when she returned to San Diego from exercises with the British, New Zealand, and Australian navies. In May 1964, the destroyer was transferred from Destroyer Squadron 5 to Reserve Destroyer Squardon 27 and began conducting training cruises for reserves. She was decommissioned and stricken from the Navy list on 1 July 1971 and was sold on 16 August 1971 to Taiwan for use by the Chinese Nationalist Navy under the name of *Kwei Yang* (DD–8).

Twining received eight battle stars for World War II service and five for Korean service.

Two Sisters

(Sch.: t. 54; a. 1 12-pdr.)

Two Sisters—a schooner built in 1856 at Baltimore—was captured on 21 September 1862 by Union steamer *Albatross* off the mouth of the Rio Grande River while attempting to slip through the Federal blockade to Brownsville, Tex., with a cargo of 87 bales of gunny cloth needed by the Confederacy for baling cotton. Subsequently purchased by the Navy from the Prize Court at Key West, Fla., *Two Sisters* was commissioned on 30 January 1863 at Key West, Acting Master William A. Arthur in command.

Assigned to the East Gulf Blockading Squadron, *Two Sisters* took her first prize on 1 February—seizing sloop *Richards* off Boca Grande, Mexico. On 30 April, the Union schooner captured cotton-carrying blockade runner *Agnes* off the Tortugas, before taking schooner *Oliver S. Breese* off Anclote Keys, Fla.

Two Sisters continued her patrols on the blockade through the spring, summer, and early fall, keeping a wary eye on the route between Bayport, Fla., and Havana, Cuba. On 15 October, she, *Sea Bird*, and *Fox* assisted *Honduras* in the capture of the Havana-bound British steamer *Mail*, which had attempted to run the blockade laden with cotton and turpentine. Bayport proved to be a good hunting ground. *Two Sisters* also captured schooner *Maria Alberta* there on 27 November.

On 13 January 1864, while *Two Sisters* was stationed off the mouth of the Suwanee River, a boat crew debarked from her and captured schooner *William* with its cargo of salt, bagging, and rope. The Union schooner's patrol duty was broken in May by service as tender to steam frigate *San Jacinto*. She then resumed independent blockade service through the onset of winter.

On 3 December 1864, *Two Sisters* participated in an early amphibious-type operation. Her boats and crews joined others from *Nita*, *Stars and Stripes*, and *Hendrick Hudson*, all under the command of Acting Lt. Robert B. Smith, in a raid on Tampa Bay, Fla., in which they destroyed the large Confederate salt work at Rocky Point.

Two Sisters subsequently remained on duty blockading the Florida coast for the duration of the Civil War. *Two Sisters* was sold in a public auction to J. Jones on 28 June 1865.

Tybee

An island off the coast of Georgia.

(Str.: t. 28; l. 63'; b. 11'8''; dph. 7'; dr. 5'; cpl. 5; a. none)

Tybee—a steam launch built for the United States Revenue Cutter Service by J. H. Dialogue and Son, of Camden, N.J., and completed late in 1895—was delivered to the Revenue Cutter Service on 19 November 1895. Three days later, she sailed for Savannah, Ga., where, after a voyage which touched at Baltimore, Md.; Norfolk, Va.; Beaufort, N.C.; and Charleston, S.C., she arrived on 21 January 1896.

She conducted local operations at Savannah through the turn of the century and, on occasion, patrolled regattas staged in the Savannah area. After the United States entered World War I on 6 April 1917, *Tybee* was taken over by the Navy and served on local patrol duties out of Savannah for the duration of hostilities. She was returned to the Treasury Department on 28 August 1919.

Assigned to the gulf division on 11 October 1920, *Tybee* was subsequently assigned a permanent station at Savannah on 1 January 1923. She lost the name *Tybee* on 6 November of the same year and was classified and named *AB–15*. She alternated bases between Norfolk and Savannah for the remainder of her career. She was condemned on 23 June 1930 and sold to D. E. Little of Jacksonville, Fla., on 25 September 1930.

Tyee

Early in 1917, *Tyee*—a 316-ton screw steam tug completed in 1884 at Port Ludlow, Wash., and operated by the Puget Sound Tugboat Co.—was inspected in the 13th Naval District for possible use as a naval patrol craft in the Puget Sound area. Although she was given the Navy designation SP–1366, she was apparently never taken over by the Navy.

Tyler

Charles Tyler—born in 1760—entered the Royal Navy in 1771 and rose in rank during service in a number of British men-of-war. Despite an injury to his left leg in 1777 which left him permanently lame, he continued to serve the Navy—for the most part afloat—through much of the War for American Independence and the Napoleonic wars. He commanded the 80-gun ship of the line *Tonnant* during the battle of Trafalgar. Tyler was knighted in 1815 and was promoted to admiral in 1825. He died at Gloucester on 28 September 1835.

During her naval service, the Civil-War, sidewheel gunboat *Tyler* retained a part of her merchant name, *A. O. Tyler*. DE–567 was named by the Royal Navy for Sir Charles Tyler.

(SwGbt.: t. 575; l. 180′0″; b. 45′4″; dr. 6′0″; dph. 7′8½″; s. 8 k.; a. 1 32-pdr., 6 8″)

A. O. Tyler—a side-wheel steamer built in 1857 at Cincinnati, Ohio—was acquired by the War Department on 5 June 1861; converted to a river gunboat; and renamed *Tyler*.

From June 1861 to 1 October 1862, *Tyler* served in the Western Flotilla, an Army organization—led by naval officers—created to gain and maintain for the Union control of the Mississippi River and its tributaries. Commissioned in September 1861, she participated in an attack on the Confederate batteries located near Hickman and Columbus, two railroad towns located on the Mississippi River in western Kentucky. During the action, she also traded shots with the Confederate gunboat *Jackson*. On 7 October, she returned to Columbus to duel with the Southern batteries once again. A month later, when the Confederates tried to cut off two columns of Federal troops invading pro-Southern, south-

eastern Missouri, Brigadier General Grant mounted an expedition to clean out the Confederate camp at Belmont, Mo. *Tyler* and *Lexington* escorted the transports from Cairo to Belmont and then moved downriver and bombarded the Confederate batteries across the river at Columbus, Ky. Confederate reinforcements crossed the river and counterattacked, but *Tyler* and *Lexington* abandoned their attack on the works at Columbus, broke up the Southern counterattack, and covered the withdrawal of the outnumbered Federal contingent.

The gunboat remained relatively quiet until February 1862, making only one reconnaissance trip down the river at the end of the first week in January. However, when General Grant decided to advance up the Cumberland and Tennessee Rivers, he called upon the gunboats to support his move. The campaign resulted in the fall of Forts Henry and Donelson—on 6 February and 16 February, respectively. These victories opened the whole of the Tennessee-Cumberland water system to Federal forces, made Confederate positions in western Kentucky untenable, and threatened Nashville, Tenn.

Though she was present as a participant at the captures of both forts, *Tyler*'s most significant contribution came in the brief interlude between the two capitulations. During the period 6 to 10 February, the gunboat joined *Conestoga* and *Lexington* in a raiding expedition farther up the Tennessee River to Florence, Ala. Along the way, they destroyed a railroad bridge located about 25 miles above Fort Henry and then continued upriver in pursuit of some Confederate gunboats. At Florence, Mussel Shoals stopped any additional advance; but, during the run between the railroad bridge and Florence, the Union force succeeded in capturing three of the fleeing gunboats, and its advance forced the Southerners to destroy six others.

One of the captured ships, *Eastport*, proved to be one of the best contemporary river steamers and had been earmarked for conversion to an ironclad. Her capture robbed the South of what would have been a formidable addition to her riverine forces and gave the Northerners a valuable addition to theirs. On the return downriver

An artist's depiction of the gunboat *Tyler* on the Mississippi with a siege "mortar boat" in the foreground. (NR&L(O) 1535)

to join in the campaign against Fort Donelson, *Tyler* and her consorts took with them a large amount of captured naval stores—notably a quantity of timber and iron the Southerners had collected for *Eastport*'s conversion to an ironclad and which the Union forces used in their own conversion of the captured vessel.

After participating in the two-day action which culminated in the surrender of Fort Donelson—the Cumberland River fort, *Tyler* resumed operations on the Tennessee River in support of Grant's advance southward along the river's banks through western Tennessee. On 6 and 7 April, when Confederate forces under General Albert Sydney Johnston surprised Grant's troops in southwestern Tennessee near Pittsburg Landing and began pushing them back into the river, *Tyler* and *Lexington*—moored nearby—brought their guns to bear when the Confederates attempted to protect their right flank by anchoring it on the river bank. *Tyler* and *Lexington* delivered a devastating enfilading fire that forced the Southern right flank to fall back. Grant's troops took advantage of the withdrawal to mount a general advance supported by naval ordnance. Thus, victory ensued when debacle seemed imminent. In Grant's own words, "in this repulse much is due to the presence of the gunboats."

Later, on 19 April, *Tyler* moved farther south, back to Florence, Ala., where she captured the Confederate transport *Albert Robb* and burned another Southern ship, *Dunbar*. But, after Shiloh and the capture of Island No. 10 on the Mississippi, the North shifted the emphasis of its war in the west to conquering that mighty river in an effort to divide the Confederacy in two. Fort Pillow fell on 4 June and Memphis, Tenn., on the 6th. Vicksburg, Miss., was the next obstacle, and it took more than a year to remove it. Those efforts occupied *Tyler* intermittently for the ensuing 13 months. Her first action of the Vicksburg campaign came in mid-July when she joined the ironclad *Carondolet* and the *Queen of the West* in probing the Yazoo River above Vicksburg in search of the incomplete, Confederate, ironclad ram *Arkansas* which had eluded capture at Memphis and sought refuge far up the Yazoo. The falling waters of the Yazoo forced *Arkansas* downriver; but, by then, she was virtually complete and ready for battle.

On 15 July, the Union probe and the falling river brought *Tyler* and her colleagues into a collision with *Arkansas*. After a brisk exchange of cannonades, *Carondolet* was disabled. Only *Tyler*, abandoned by *Queen of the West*, remained to suffer the full onslaught of the powerful Southern warship. Recognizing the futility in attacking her adversary unsupported, *Tyler* reluctantly retreated with *Arkansas* in pursuit. After a running fight all the way down the Yazoo, the two warships reached the Union fleet lying near the confluence of the two rivers. *Tyler* sought refuge among the fleet while *Arkansas* ran through it, delivering salvo after salvo into the aggregate of ships, and moored safely under the protection of the Vicksburg shore batteries.

During the first phase of the siege of Vicksburg, *Tyler* participated in the joint Army-Navy expedition up the Yazoo River to establish a landward advance on the Confederate stronghold. That expedition lasted from 7 December 1862 until 3 January 1863. Though the expedition showed no immediate fruits, the land campaign, in conjunction with the waterborne attacks, eventually brought Vicksburg to her knees. In the meantime, *Tyler* saw action in two other operations—the first was to open Arkansas to invasion and the second was in support of the slow strangulation of Vicksburg. In mid-January, she joined other units of the squadron in escorting Army transports to Fort Hindman which guarded Arkansas Post, Ark., on the invasion route to Little Rock. Federal forces carried that fort finally on 9 January 1863 after a combined sea and land campaign. Following that expedition, the

gunboat resumed a patrol routine on the Mississippi until late April.

On the 29th, she joined another expedition up the Yazoo, and it resulted in the fall of the important fortifications on Haynes Bluffs on 1 May. That operation was the gunboat's last major role in the reduction of Vicksburg which surrendered to Union forces on Independence Day 1863. *Tyler* resumed her support for Army troops upriver invading Arkansas. On the day that Vicksburg surrendered, the gunboat brought her guns to bear on an attacking Confederate force near Helena, Ark., and, once again, saved the day for Federal rams.

For the remainder of the war, she participated in the invasion of Arkansas, operating principally on the White River. Her last major scrape with the Confederates came on 24 June 1864 far up the White River near Clarendon, Ark., when she engaged the Southern shore batteries which damaged and captured the gunboat *Queen of the West*. The beginning of 1865 found her still on the White River; but, by May, she was at Memphis, Tenn. In June, *Tyler* moved to Mound City, Ill., where she remained until sold at auction there on 17 August 1865 to Mr. David White, of St. Louis, Mo.

Tyler—a projected *Buckley*-class destroyer escort designated DE–567—was assigned to the United Kingdom on 10 June 1943; and her keel was laid down on 6 October 1943 at Hingham, Mass., by the Bethelehem Steel Co. The ship was launched on 20 November 1943 and delivered to the Royal Navy under lend-lease on 14 January 1944.

In 1944, *Tyler*—a "Captain-class" frigate—served the Royal Navy in the English Channel and participated in the invasion of Normandy. In 1945, she alternated escort duty in the Atlantic with Channel operations. One of her more exciting moments came on the evening of 27 January 1945, when she joined *Keats* and *Bligh* in sinking the German U-boat *U–1051* between St. George's Channel and the Irish Sea.

After the war ended, *Tyler* steamed back to the United States and arrived at Philadelphia on 31 October 1945. She was formally returned to the United States Navy in November of that year and, on 8 January 1946, was struck from the Navy list. On 23 May 1946, she was sold to Hugo Neu of New York City and later resold to the Northern Metal Co., Philadelphia. She was scrapped in the summer of 1946.

Typhon

A character in Greek mythology. Typhon, the son of Tartarus and Gaea, was a giant who dared to make war on heaven. For this offense, the angry Jupiter hurled him to earth and buried him beneath Mt. Etna.

(ARL–28: dp. 4,100; l. 328'; b. 50'; dr. 11'2''; s. 11.6 k.; cpl. 253; a. 1 3'', 8 40mm.; cl. *Achelous*)

On 14 August 1944—before her construction began—LST–1118 was reclassified a landing craft repair ship (ARL–28). The ship was named *Typhon* 19 September 1944, and her keel was laid down on 17 October 1944 at Seneca, Ill., by the Chicago Bridge and Iron Co.; sponsored by Mrs. F. E. Kitteredge, the ship was launched on 5 January 1945 and commissioned on 18 January 1945, Lt. Bernard M. Jacobsen, USNR, in command.

Typhon proceeded down the Illinois Waterway and the Mississippi River and reached New Orleans on 20 January. She then moved to Mobile, Ala., to repair her propeller blades which she had damaged soon after leaving Seneca. When again ready for sea, *Typhon* proceeded, via Panama City, Fla., to Baltimore, Md., where she arrived on 13 February. Three days later, she was decommissioned there for completion as a landing craft repair ship. While the conversion was in progress, the ship's officers and men underwent special training at Camp Bradford, Va., with additional instruction in amphibious warfare at Little Creek, Va.

On 18 June 1945, *Typhon* was recommissioned, Lt. Thomas S. Moulton, USNR, in command. Ten days later, she got underway for Hampton Roads to conduct her shakedown training in the Norfolk area. After post-shakedown inspections, the ship departed Norfolk on 22 July; picked up a load of pontoons at Davisville, R.I.; and headed, via the Panama Canal, for the west coast. En route, the repair ship received word that Japan had surrendered, ending the war in the Pacific. Putting into San Diego on 18 August, she unloaded her pontoons and, 10 days later, got underway for the Hawaiian Islands, arriving at Pearl Harbor on 7 September.

After two months there, she headed westward and proceeded, via the Marianas, to Japan. Anchoring off Yokosuka on 16 November, she remained in Japanese waters until early 1946 when she made a brief run back to the Marianas. Returning to Japan with supplies, the repair ship reached Nagasaki on 13 February and remained there until late March, when *Typhon* headed for China, arriving at Shanghai on 30 March. For almost a year, the ship operated out of Hong Kong and Shanghai, working to support American occupation forces in China.

Late in February 1947, she prepared to return home and arrived at San Diego on 29 March. Decommissioned, *Typhon* was laid up in reserve in 1947 at San Diego. On 1 July 1960, her name was struck from the Navy list, and the ship was sold on 23 February 1961 to Al Epstein of New Orleans, La.

Typhoon

The Navy acquired tanker *Typhoon* on 19 October 1943. Although Navy records indicate that the ship was renamed *Villalobos* and designated IX–145 on 3 November 1943, she served as *Typhoon* until sometime late in 1944, when she began using her new name, *Villalobos* (*q.v.*).

Tyrrell

A county in North Carolina named for Sir John Tyrrell, a lord proprietor of Carolina.

(AKA–80: dp. 14,160; l. 459'2''; b. 63'; dr. 26'4''; s. 16.5 k.; cpl. 395; a. 1 5'', 8 40mm., 16 20mm.; cl. *Tolland*; T. C2–S–AJ3)

Tyrrell (AKA–80) was laid down on 6 May 1944 under Maritime Commission contract (MC hull 1387) at Wilmington, N.C., by the North Carolina Shipbuilding Corp.; transferred to the Navy on 30 July and towed to Baltimore on 8 August for conversion to an attack cargo ship by the Key Highway plant of the Bethlehem Steel Co.; and commissioned on 4 December 1944, Lt. Comdr. John L. McLean, USNR, in command.

After shakedown training in the Virginia capes area, the attack cargo ship departed Hampton Roads on 5 January 1945 and steamed through the Panama Canal to Hawaii. After spending the last week of the month in Pearl Harbor, the ship embarked 33 Navy passengers and proceeded, via Eniwetok, to the Carolines and discharged her passengers at Ulithi on 13 February. Two days later, she proceeded via the Palaus to the Philippines. After her arrival in Leyte Gulf on 21 February, the ship commenced preparations for the assault on the Ryukyus.

At dawn on 1 April 1945, the Southern Attack Force, to which *Tyrrell* was attached, arrived off Hagushi, Okinawa. At 0550, as battleships, cruisers, and destroyers commenced bombardment of Japanese defenses— *Tyrrell* began lowering her boats. By 0644, the last of her landing craft was in the water and headed for the beach.

For the next nine days, *Tyrrell* remained off Okinawa, supporting the conquest of that island stronghold. On 2 April, a twin-engined Japanese bomber attempted to crash the ship, diving through a storm of antiaircraft fire. In an attempt to ram the bridge, the plane sheared off the ship's main radio antenna, hit the lower yardarm support on the starboard side of the mainmast, and continued on to sideswipe the starboard 5-ton cargo boom at the number 5 hatch. As the plane splashed alongside, it blew up and showered the cargo ship's decks with pieces of wreckage.

On 4 April, *Minneapolis* (CA–36) came alongside to receive 600 rounds of eight-inch projectiles and 1,200 cans of powder. In turn, *Tyrrell* received all of the cruiser's empty shell casings. The following day, while at anchor in the transport area, *Tyrrell*'s gunners joined in damaging an attacking Japanese bomber.

Upon completion of unloading on 9 April, *Tyrrell* retired, via Guam and Pearl Harbor, to the west coast, arriving at San Francisco on 11 May. She then made two runs to Pearl Harbor carrying cargo. On 27 July, the cargo ship got underway for the Marshalls.

While en route to Majuro, she received orders on 4 August diverting her to Roi, where she arrived on 9 August. Four days later, while she unloaded cargo at Majuro, word was received that Japan had surrendered.

Tyrrell next steamed, vai Kwajalein, to Saipan where she embarked men and material of the 2d Marine Division destined for the occupation of Japan. On the morning of 23 September 1945, *Tyrrell* arrived off the devastated Japanese port city of Nagasaki and began disembarking her troops and equipment. The attack cargo ship next proceeded to the Philippines, arriving at Manila on 27 September. She then shuttled between the Philippines and Japan, supporting occupation activities by transporting supplies to such ports as Wakayama and Nagoya. On 13 November 1945, *Tyrrell* departed Nagoya, bound for Seattle, Wash.

After voyage repairs at the Puget Sound Naval Shipyard, she returned to Japan, this time to deliver supplies for the American occupation forces at Kure, arriving there on 10 January 1946. Departing Japanese waters on 2 February, she proceeded through the Panama Canal to the east coast.

Upon her arrival at Norfolk on 4 March 1946, *Tyrrell* reported to the Commandant, 5th Naval District, for disposition. She was decommissioned at Norfolk on 19 April, returned to the War Shipping Administration on 22 April, and struck from the Navy list on 1 May 1946.

Purchased in 1948 by the Pacific Far East Line, Inc., of Delaware, and homeported in San Francisco, the ship was renamed SS *California Bear* and served as a freight carrier through 1961, when she was again renamed—this time SS *America Bear*. She was sold in 1963 to the Central Gulf Steamship Corp.; homeported in New Orleans, La.; and renamed SS *Green Lake*. After plying the waters of the Caribbean under this name from 1963 to 1968, she was taken over by the United States Department of Commerce and named SS *Oceanic Cloud*, a capacity in which she served through 1971.

Tyrrell received one battle star for her World War II service.

U

U–111

Former German Submarine: dp. 798 (surf.), 996 (subm.); l. 235½'; b. 20¾'; dr. 11¾'; s. 16.4 k. (surf.), 8.4 k. (subm.); cpl. 36; a. 6 20'' tt., 1 4.1'', 1 3.4''; cl. U–111)

U–111 was laid down early in 1917 at Vegesack, Germany, by Bremer Vulcan under subcontract to the

Germaniawerft in Kiel; launched on 5 September 1917; completed by *Germaniawerft* in Kiel; and commissioned in the Imperial German Navy on 30 December 1917, *Kapitänleutnant* Beyersdorff in command.

After completing her shakedown cruise on 17 March 1918, she was posted to the *IV U-Flottille, Hochseeflotte* (Fourth Submarine Flotilla, High Seas Fleet). She departed Heligoland, a fortified island and naval base located well inside the German Bight, on 25 March. After the outward voyage, which took her around the Orkney Islands, west of the Hebrides Islands, and south along the western coast of Ireland, she arrived in her patrol area near St. George's Channel during the first week in April. On the 7th, she sighted her first target, the 2,346-ton British steamer SS *Boscastle*. The submarine made a surface torpedo attack and sank the ship with a single torpedo. *Boscastle*, however, proved to be her only victim during this first cruise. She operated in the vicinity of St. George's Channel for another five days without encountering further shipping and then began the voyage home to Germany. After backtracking along the route she had taken on the outward voyage, *U-111* returned to Germany at Emden on 24 April.

A month and three days later, the U-boat exited the Ems estuary to begin her second cruise to raid Allied merchantmen. From the Ems, she headed through the North Sea. On 28 May, her second day out, she came upon a small Danish steamer, the 393-ton SS *Dronning Margrethe*. Declining to waste a valuable torpedo on such small game, *U-111* brought her deck guns to bear and sank the Dane with gunfire. From the North Sea, she followed substantially the same route as on her initial voyage, reaching St. George's Channel early in June. After an unsuccessful patrol off the entrances to St. George's and the English Channels, the U-boat retired from the area and again retraced her outward route. On 22 June just outside the Skaggerak, during the last leg of her homeward voyage, the submarine encountered a Norwegian sailing vessel laden with timber for English mines. Once again, she scorned the use of a torpedo in favor of her 4.1-inch and 3.4-inch deck guns and riddled the 272-ton SS *Rana* with gunfire. Leaving that ship sinking, *U-111* headed south through the North Sea for Wilhelmshaven, where she arrived on 26 June.

U-111's third and final combat cruise proved to be the least successful of all. She departed Wilhelmshaven on 25 August, transited the Kiel Canal, and headed north through the Baltic Sea around Denmark to debouch into the North Sea by way of the Skaggerak. Thence, she rounded the Orkneys and the Hebrides and headed south along the west coast of Ireland. The U-boat then transited St. George's Channel and entered the Irish Sea. Stormy weather and heavy seas plagued her throughout the cruise, and she appears to have encountered no Allied shipping. She followed the same route back to Germany and concluded her last patrol at Emden on 30 September.

Apparently, *U-111* remained in port at Emden through the cessation of hostilities on 11 November. Nine days after the armistice, she was surrendered to the Allies and interned at Harwich, England. When the United States Navy expressed an interest in acquiring several of the latest types of U-boats, the Allies allocated six boats—*U-117, U-140, UB-148, UB-88, UC-97,* and *U-164*—to the United States on condition that they be destroyed within a year of the transfer. In March 1919, 12 officers and 120 enlisted men arrived in England to ferry the six submarines back to the United States. The crew assigned to *U-164* found the submarine in such atrocious condition that it was impossible to ready her for the Victory Bond drive—the ostensible reason for which she had been acquired. For that reason, American authorities in England arranged to secure the substitution of *U-111* for the cannibalized and dilapidated *U-164*. Soon thereafter, she was placed in commission in the United States Navy, Lt. Comdr. Freeland A. Daubin in command.

Since she had been substituted for *U-164* at the very last minute, *U-111* did not put to sea on 3 April with the rest of the Ex-German Submarine Expeditionary Force. She remained in Harwich for an additional four days while her crew conducted a crash familiarization course and completed last-minute repairs. Finally, on 7 April, she steamed out of Harwich and stood down the English Channel. Rather than follow the route taken by the other U-boats via the Azores and Bermuda, *U-111*'s commanding officer sought to make up the time he had lost by heading directly across the Atlantic via a great circle route. Fog, gales, and heavy seas harassed the U-boat all the way across the ocean. On one occasion, she came near sinking when she began filling with water because of an open sea-cock. However, one of her crewmen crawled under her engines and into the slimy dark water to find and close the offending apparatus. In spite of adversity, *U-111* made her passage successfully and moored in New York on 19 April, in plenty of time to carry out her tasks in the Victory Bond campaign.

At New York, swarms of tourists, reporters, and photographers roamed throughout the submarine. Navy technicians and civilian shipbuilders also came to try to learn everything they could about German submarine construction in the brief time before *U-111* departed New York for visits to various ports on the Victory bond circuit. For the bond drive, the coasts of the United States and the country's major waterways were divided into five different regions, one for each of the captured U-boats except *U-140*. *U-111* visited ports along the New England coast and received visitors in conjunction with the sales campaign. The submarine completed her assigned itinerary late in the summer of 1919. Following that, she and *UB-148* were subjected to an extensive series of performance tests before being laid up at the Philadelphia Navy Yard. During the summer of 1921, she returned to sea for another series of tests, this time as a target for gunnery and aerial bombardment tests. As a result of those experiments, her battered hulk went to the bottom of the ocean sometime in July 1921.

U-117

(Former German Submarine: dp. 1,164 (surf.), 1,512 (subm.); l. 267½'; b. 24½'; dr. 13¾'; s. 14.7 k. (surf.), 7 k. (subm.); cpl. 40; a. 1 5.9'', 1 3.4'', 2 mine tubes, 42 mines, 4 20'' tt.; cl. *U-117*)

U-117—a UE-II series long-range minelayer submarine—was laid down in 1917 at Hamburg, Germany, by *Aktiengesellschaft Vulcan;* launched on 10 December 1917; and commissioned in the Imperial German Navy on 28 March 1918, *Kapitänleutnant* Otto Dröscher in command.

After shakedown, *U-117* was posted to the *U-Kreuzer Verband* (Submarine Cruiser Unit) on 1 June 1918. Over the next five weeks, she completed fitting out at Kiel and prepared for her single patrol during the war.

On 11 July, *U-117* departed Kiel and took the eastern route through the Baltic around Denmark and out into the North Sea by way of the Skaggerak. After rounding the Shetland Islands, she set a course for the coast of North America to lay minefields off the coast of the United States and to conduct cruiser warfare. During the voyage across the Atlantic, heavy weather foiled her attempts to attack two lone steamers, two convoys, and a small cruiser.

However, once she reached the American coastal zone on 8 August, her luck improved. Two days later, *U-117* encountered a fleet of fishing craft and went on a spree, sinking nine of the vessels with explosives and gunfire. On the 12th, she sighted the ballast-laden SS *Sommerstadt* and, after observing that the Norwegian

The former German minelaying submarine U–117 at Philadelphia Navy Yard, 8 July 1919. Radio antenna masts were erected while cruising on the surface and taken down before submerging.

steamer was armed, made a submerged attack that sank her with a single torpedo. The following day, the U-boat made another submerged torpedo attack and hit the 7,127-ton American tanker *Frederick R. Kellogg* bound from Tampico, Mex., for Boston with 7,500 barrels of crude oil. The action occurred only 12 miles north of the Barnegat Light, in shallow water which enabled the ship to be salvaged.

Later that same day, the minelayer submarine began the other half of her duty by laying mines near Barnegat Light. That field later claimed a victim when SS *San Saba* struck a mine and sank on 4 October. On 14 August, *U–117* took a break from mining operations to resume cruiser warfare when she encountered an American schooner. The U-boat brought her deck guns to bear on the sailing vessel and sent her to the bottom with gunfire. However, shortly thereafter, the hunter became the hunted when an American seaplane forced the submarine to seek refuge beneath the ocean. The plane and *SC–71* subjected *U–117* to a brief barrage of bombs, and *SC–71* attacked the submarine with depth charges before losing track of her.

The next day, *U–117* resumed her mine laying operations off Fenwick Island Lightship. That field later claimed two victims, one damaged and the other sunk. On 29 September, *Minnesota* (Battleship No. 22) struck one of those mines and suffered extensive damage. The Naval Overseas Transportation Service cargo ship *Saetia* (Id. No. 2317) entered the same field on 9 November, struck a mine, and sank. Later that day— still 14 August—the submarine moved farther south and, after laying a third minefield near Winter Quarters Shoal Lightship, halted an American sailing vessel, the 1,613-ton *Madrugada*, and sank her with gunfire. A patrolling American seaplane foiled a subsequent attempt by the U-boat that day to stop another sailing ship.

On 16 August, *U–117* resumed her mining operations, this time off Cape Hatteras, N.C. The approach of the 6,978-ton British steamer SS *Mirlo* interrupted her mine laying labors. Approaching the target submerged, *U–117* fired a single torpedo which sent the merchantman to the bottom. Following that attack, the submarine resumed her mining duties and laid her fourth and final minefield. At that point, a severe shortage of fuel forced the U-boat to head for Germany.

The return voyage proved to be both more eventful and more successful than the outward-bound cruise. On 17 August, she stopped a Norwegian sailing ship, the 2,846-ton *Nordhav*, out of Buenos Aires, bound for New York laden with linseed. *U–117* crewmen placed bombs on board the cargo carrier which sank the prize. Three days later, the U-boat engaged in an unsuccessful surface gun duel with an unidentified, strongly armed steamer. On the 26th, she stopped the 162-ton *Rush* and sank that American trawler with bombs placed on board. The next day, *U–117* caught sight of another Norwegian freighter, SS *Bergsdalen*, steaming in ballast from La Pallice to Baltimore. Justifying her action with the observation that this modern Viking Norwegian mounted a gun, the submarine attacked unheralded and submerged, sinking her quarry with a single torpedo. Three days later, on 30 August, she encountered her final two victims. The submarine stopped two 136-ton British fishing trawlers, *Elsie Porter* and *Potentate*, and sank both by placing explosive charges on board.

After an unsuccessful attempt at a torpedo attack on a lone British steamer, SS *War Rance*, on 5 September, *U–117* concentrated on making the final run-in toward the Skagerrak and safety. Her critical fuel shortage forced the submarine to make wireless contact with *U–140* on 8 September to set up a fuel replenishment rendezvous. The two U-boats met on the 12th and 13th near the Faroe Islands, and *U–117* took on about 5,000 gallons of diesel oil before continuing on toward Kiel. The submarine pulled into Kiel rather ignominiously on 22 September, having had to call upon a patrolling torpedo boat to tow her the last few miles into port.

For the rest of the war, *U–117* remained inactive. On 23 October 1918, she was reassigned to the *I U-Flotille, Hochseeflotte* (1st Submarine Flotilla, High Seas Fleet); however, she remained in a shipyard— probably at Kiel—for the duration.

The armistice of 11 November 1918 ended hostilities, and its terms required Germany to turn her submarines over to the Allies. *U–117* surrendered at Harwich, England, 10 days later.

During the succeeding weeks, the United States Navy expressed an interest in acquiring several former German submarines to serve as exhibits during a Victory Bond campaign. *U–117* became one of the six U-boats set aside for that purpose. In March 1919, her American crew took over the submarine and placed her in special commission, Lt. Comdr. Aquilla G. Dibrell in command.

After a hectic time preparing for sea, *U–117* stood down the English Channel from Harwich on 3 April in company with *Bushnell* (Submarine Tender No. 2),

UB–88, *UB–148*, and *UC–97*. This unlikely American task organization—dubbed the Ex-German Submarine Expeditionary Force—called at the Azores and at Bermuda before reaching New York City on 27 April where the submarines were soon opened to the public. Tourists, photographers, reporters, Navy Department technicians, and civilian submarine manufacturers all flocked in to see the six war trophies. Then orders came for her to begin a series of port visits to sell Victory Bonds. *U–117* drew one of the east coast itineraries and, although exact information regarding her ports of call is not available, she did stop at Washington, D.C., and spent a significant period of time at the navy yard located there. At the conclusion of the bond drive late that summer, the U-boat was laid up at the Philadelphia Navy Yard along with *U–140* and *UB–148*. There, she remained—partially dismantled—until taken out to sea in June 1921 to act as a target for aerial bombing tests conducted by the Navy and Army. On 22 June 1921, *U–117* was sunk by bombing off the coast of Virginia, near Cape Charles.

U–140

(Former German Submarine: dp. 1,930 (surf.), 2,483 (subm.); l. 311'; b. 29¾'; dr. 17¼'; s. 15.8 k. (surf.), 7.6 k. (subm.); cpl. 62; a. 2 5.9", 2 3.4", 6 20" tt.; cl. *U–139*)

U–140—a large, heavily armed submarine cruiser—was laid down early in 1917 at Kiel, Germany, by *Germaniawerft;* launched on 4 November 1917; and commissioned in the Imperial German Navy on 28 March 1918, *Korvettenkapitän* Waldemar Kophamel in command.

Though one of the very few German submarines to receive a name, *Kapitänleutnant Weddigen*—after the commander of *U–9* who had startled the world at the outbreak of the war by sinking in quick succession the British cruisers *Aboukir, Cressy,* and *Hogue*—the U-boat was known more generally as *U–140*. She completed her shakedown cruise early in June and was posted on the 5th to the *U-Kreuzer Verband* (Submarine Cruiser Unit) to conduct long-range cruiser warfare off the coast of the United States.

On 2 July, she stood out of Warnemunde on Germany's Baltic coast, passed around Denmark through the Skaggerak into the North Sea, thence moved north around the Shetlands, and set a course for North America. On 11 July, she sighted an eight-ship convoy and attempted a submerged attack. However, heavy seas made depth control impossible, and the attempt failed. Four days later, she spied four large, fast passenger liners similar in construction to SS *Mauritania* and SS *Lusitania*. However, their speed, course, and distance precluded an attack; and *U–140* continued her voyage.

On the 19th, she encountered and stopped a Danish ship, SS *Olaf Maersk*. After inspecting the ship's cargo and satisfying herself as to the propriety of the Dane's papers, which indicated that she was carrying petroleum and gasoline for the Swiss government, *U–140* allowed the neutral merchantman to proceed on toward her destination.

The submarine reached the coastal waters off North America, just south of Newfoundland, on 26 July and opened her campaign with a running gun battle with the 13,967-ton British steamer SS *Melitia*. The merchantman was too fast for the submarine and gradually made good her escape. That evening, *U–140* engaged another British ship, the 4,147-ton SS *British Major* in another surface gun battle. The U-boat's slight superiority in speed allowed her to close range with her quarry only very gradually, and gathering darkness forced her to break off the action before she was able to get the enemy's range. The next day, however, the submarine scored her first victory. Just south of Halifax, Nova Scotia, she stopped the Portuguese

sailing ship *Porto*, carrying a cargo of lumber. In order to save ammunition and torpedoes for more valuable and dangerous game, *U–140*'s boarding party placed explosive charges at strategic points in the ship and exploded them to sink her. The next day, bad luck struck once more when difficulties controlling depth spoiled an attempted submerged attack on SS *Kermanshah*, a 4,948-ton American cargo ship. The heavy seas which contributed to her inability to follow through on the attack also precluded any attempt at pursuit.

The first week in August, however, brought the heretofore all but hapless commerce raider a series of victories. On the 1st, she made a submerged attack on the 7,029-ton Japanese ship SS *Tokuyama Maru* and scored a torpedo hit. When the explosion proved to be less than fatal, *U–140* surfaced to deliver the coup de grace with her deck guns.

Three days later, the U-boat attempted a submerged torpedo shot at a steamer armed with a 4.7-inch gun. That try was unsuccessful, and the submarine had to surface to bring her 5.9-inch guns to bear. The American tanker SS *O. B. Jennings* fought back gamely for 22 minutes, but a 5.9-inch shell hit her magazine and put her gun out of action. At that point, *O. B. Jennings'* crew abandoned ship; and the submarine closed range and sank her. After finishing off the ship, *U–140* turned her attention to the crew adrift in boats. Her commanding officer interrogated the crew members, took *O. B. Jennings'* second officer prisoner, and then cleared the area.

On 5 August, she stopped the American sailing ship *Stanley M. Seaman*, bound from Newport News to Santo Domingo with a cargo of coal, and sank her with explosive charges. The next day, she stopped a 3,024-ton American merchantman—also carrying coal—and sank her with explosives.

During the latter encounter, the submarine had been in full view of the Diamond Shoals Lightship which began sending wireless reports on *U–140*. The submarine responded by taking the lightship under fire; and, as soon as her crew abandoned the lightship, the U-boat sank it with gunfire.

Four days passed before the U-boat encountered another target. On 10 August, she tried to stop a 6,062-ton Brazilian steamer, SS *Aberaba*, but an American destroyer happened upon the scene and foiled the attempt. *U–140* made an emergency dive while the destroyer dropped a barrage of 16 depth charges. The submarine suffered a number of leaks in her pressure hull as a result of the attack and began leaking fuel as well. That damage limited her operations along the United States coast to another week. During those seven days, she encountered only one ship, the 7,781-ton American ship SS *Pastores* with which she traded a few shots before the steamer escaped. Finally, on the 17th, the loss of about 9,000 gallons of fuel forced *U–140* to begin the long voyage home.

The cruise back to Germany did not, however, end her combat activities. On 22 August, she engaged the 7,523-ton armed British merchantman SS *Diomed* in a gun battle and scored her last victory of the war when *Diomed* succumbed to the submarine's 5.9-inch gunfire and slid beneath the sea. The next afternoon, *U–140* traded salvoes with an armed American ship; but gathering darkness covered SS *Pleiades'* escape. *U–140* had to break off the action and resume her homeward voyage. On 12 and 13 September, she stopped near the Faroe Islands to transfer about 5,000 gallons of fuel to *U–117*. A week later, *U–140* re-entered Kiel to end an 81-day cruise during which she claimed to have sunk over 30,000 tons of Allied shipping.

The submarine apparently spent the remaining weeks of World War I in port at Kiel. The terms of the armistice which ended hostilities on 11 November 1918 required Germany to dismantle or to surrender her submarines. Accordingly, *U–140* was turned over to the British on 23 February 1919 and interned at Harwich, England.

In the meantime, the United States Navy had expressed a desire to acquire several former German U-boats for use in a Victory Bond campaign during the summer of 1919. *U–140* was set aside for those purposes, and her American crew took control during the latter half of March. The submarine was placed in special commission soon thereafter, Lt. Comdr. G. A. Hulings in command.

Accounts vary as to how *U–140* actually made the voyage to the United States. One source indicates that she made the voyage under her own power with *Bushnell* (Submarine Tender No. 2) and four of the other five U-boats of the Ex-German Submarine Expeditionary Force. On the other hand, in his account, Vice Admiral Charles A. Lockwood, Jr.—who served in and later commanded *UC–97*—stated that *U–140* preceded *Bushnell* and the four U-boats which sailed with her by several days. He also maintained that she was towed to New York by a collier, but he failed to identify the ship. Be that as it may, *U–140* arrived in New York sometime during May 1919.

The submarine was opened for a time to public viewing at New York. No records have been found delineating *U–140*'s subsequent service. At the end of the summer, she was laid up at the Philadelphia Navy Yard and remained there, partially dismantled, until the summer of 1921. At that time, she was taken out to sea to serve as a target in aerial bombardment tests. Following those tests on 22 July 1921, *Dickerson* (DD–157) sank *U–140*'s battered hulk with gunfire.

U–2513

(Former German Submarine: dp 1,621 (surf.), 1,819 (subm.); l. 251'9''; b. 21'9''; dr. 20'3''; s. 15½ to 16 k.; cpl. 57; a. 6 21'' tt., 4 20 mm.; cl. *U–2501*)

U–2513—a former German Type XXI submarine constructed in late 1944 and early 1945 by Blohm & Voss at Hamburg, Germany—was surrendered to the Allies at Horten, Norway, after the collapse of Nazi Germany in May 1945. No records have been found to indicate whether or not she was ever commissioned in the *Kriegsmarine*, but the location of her surrender suggests that she may well have been at least placed in service—though perhaps hastily in the spring of 1945 to escape advancing Allied forces. In any event, it is certain that she made no war cruises. Documents covering her activities between May 1945 and mid-1946—at which time the United States Navy took possession of her—are likewise unavailable. In all probability, however, she lay at dockside in some port in occupied Germany or perhaps in an Allied harbor.

The first real record of her activities begins in August 1946 with her arrival in Charleston, S.C. Presumably, that arrival coincided with the end of her voyage from Europe to the United States. At Charleston, the submarine underwent an extensive overhaul which was completed late in September. On the 24th, she departed Charleston and headed for Key West, Fla. The following day, she began six months of duty which included both evaluation tests of the U-boat's design and duty in conjunction with the development of submarine and antisubmarine tactics.

On 15 March 1947, she headed north from Key West, bound for the New England coast, and arrived at Portsmouth, N.H., on the 22d. She remained there until 8 September when she began six weeks of operations out of Portsmouth and New London, Conn., under the auspices of the Commander, Submarines, Atlantic Fleet. She concluded that duty on 15 October and departed New London to return to Key West. *U–2513* resumed her old duties at Key West five days later and continued them until the summer of 1949. In mid-June 1949, the submarine moved from Key West north—via Norfolk, Va.,—to Portsmouth, N.H., where she was placed out of service in July 1949. She remained at Portsmouth until August 1951 at which time she was

moved to Key West. On 2 September 1951, the Chief of Naval Operations ordered that *U–2513* be sunk by gunfire. Presumably, that decision was carried out soon thereafter—though the exact date of the action is not recorded.

U–3008

(Former German Submarine: dp. 1,621 (surf.), 1,819 (subm.); l. 251'9''; b. 21'9''; dr. 20'3''; s. 15½ to 16 k.; cpl. 57; a. 6 21'' tt., 4 20mm.; cl. *U–2501*)

U–3008—a former German Type XXI submarine built in late 1944 and early 1945 by *Aktiengesellschaft Weser* at Bremen, Germany—was surrendered to the Allies at Kiel, Germany, in May 1945 immediately following the collapse of Nazi Germany. Probably never commissioned in the *Kriegsmarine* before the end of the war, the U-boat was turned over to the United States Navy in the summer of 1945. She departed Europe early in August and reached New London, Conn., on the 22d. On 13 September, she moved to Portsmouth, N.H., where she began an extensive overhaul the following day. Work proceeded on an intermittent basis due to the lack of final and total approval of the vessel's allocation to the United States by the Allied powers concerned. However, by the spring of 1946, the naval shipyard received orders to proceed with the overhaul as expeditiously as possible and to place the submarine in service immediately upon its completion. *U–3008*'s overhaul was completed by mid-summer, and she went into service on 24 July 1946, Comdr. Everett H. Steinmetz in charge.

U–3008 was assigned initially to Submarine Squadron (SubRon) 2 and operated along the New England coast out of New London, Conn., and Portsmouth, N.H. That duty continued until the end of March 1947. On the 31st, she departed New London bound ultimately for Key West, Fla., and duty with the Operational Development Force. En route, the U-boat stopped off at Norfolk for three weeks of underway operations with Task Force 67. She continued south on 19 April and arrived at Key West on the 23d. There, she reported for duty with SubRon 4 and began working with the Operational Development Force. That duty involved the development of submarine and antisubmarine tactics and lasted until October 1947 when she returned to New London. The U-boat conducted operations out of New London and Portsmouth between October 1947 and February 1948. On 28 February, she stood out of New London to return to Florida. She reached Key West on 5 March and resumed duty with the Operational Development Force. She remained so engaged until the end of the first week in June. On the 7th, she headed north once more and arrived in Portsmouth on the 11th. On 18 June 1948, *U–3008* was placed out of service at the Naval Base, Portsmouth, N.H. Though out of service, *U–3008* apparently remained a Navy test hulk for several years because she was in the Navy drydock at Roosevelt Roads at the time she was offered for sale in 1955. She was sold to Loudes Iron & Metal Co. on 15 September 1955, and the purchaser took possession of her on 17 January 1956. She was subsequently scrapped.

UB–88

(Former German Submarine: dp. 510 (surf.), 640 (subm.); l. 182'; b. 19'; dr. 12'; s. 13.6 k. (surf.), 8 k. (subm.); cpl. 34; a. 5 20'' tt., 1 4.1''; cl. *UB–88*)

UB–88 was laid down in February 1917 at Hamburg, Germany, by the *Aktiengesellschaft Vulcan;* launched on 11 December 1917; and placed in commission in the Imperial German Navy on 26 January 1918, *Oberleutnant zur See* Johannes Ries in command.

After shakedown in the North and Baltic Seas, *UB–88* was assigned to the *I U-Flotille Flandern* (1st Subarine Flotilla, Flanders) at Zeebrugge on the Belgian ast. She departed Kiel, Germany, on 4 June and eaded via the eastern route, around Denmark and rough the Skaggerak, south to Zeebrugge. During e voyage to her first duty station, the submarine ored her first victory. Passing down the east coast of ngland on the 10th, she encountered a convoy of five reighters and six trawlers escorted by two destroyers nd a pair of aircraft. In a submerged attack, she red a single torpedo which struck and sank the 1,555-n Swedish steamer SS *Dora*. The convoy's escorts nducted a brief depth charge attack, but *UB–88* scaped with negligible damage. Two days later, she rrived safely in Zeebrugge and reported for duty with *U–Flotille Flandern*.

Between June and October, *UB–88* conducted three ar cruises out of Zeebrugge. The first—along the east oast of England—began when she put to sea on 20 une. On the third day out, she encountered a south-ound convoy between Flamborough Head and Sunder-nd. She made a submerged torpedo attack and suc-eeded in sinking another Swedish steamer, the 1,624-n SS *Avance*. The following day, the U-boat ran into nother south-bound convoy, numbering about 30 ships. ne of those ships rammed her main periscope, but the ubmarine managed a successful submerged attack sing her secondary periscope and sank the 1,706-ton ritish ship SS *London*. The convoy's escorts answered ith nine depth charges, but the submarine managed to vade their attacks. During the pre-dawn hours of 25 une, she encountered and sank another British teamer, the 4,482-ton SS *African Transport*. The 25th as *UB–88*'s lucky day for, that evening, she ran onto 20-ship convoy heading south. The U-boat sank SS *oorlands* and then survived a 16-charge depth bomb-ng by the convoy escorts.

Four days later, *UB–88* scored another double in one ay. Just before sunrise, she made a surface torpedo ttack and sank the small British steamer SS *Sixth Six*. Iear dusk that evening, she singled SS *Florentia* out f a north-bound convoy and sank her in another sur-ace torpedo attack. Two days later, she concluded the ruise at Zeebrugge.

On 29 July, the submarine put to sea again to hunt llied merchant shipping in the English Channel. While perating between Le Havre and the Isle of Wight, he encountered two steamers escorted by a French estroyer and launched two torpedoes. One hit the ,045-ton British steamer SS *Bayronto* while the other hissed completely. Though damaged, *Bayronto* made it hto port because the French destroyer prevented *UB–8* from finishing off her victim by barraging her with 5 depth charges. Two days later, off Brest, the sub-harine met a large American convoy bound for France. *JB–88* attempted to maneuver into position for a sub-herged torpedo attack, but the convoy changed course hd foiled her efforts. Shortly before the convoy entered ort at Brest, the four escorting cruisers parted com-any with it and made for the open sea. In so doing, hey presented a target that the U-boat's commander ould not pass up. She fired a torpedo at one of the varships, but it missed its mark. For her impertinence, *JB–88* suffered a staggering depth-charge barrage of 5 to 20 minutes in duration. She sustained severe con-ussion damage to her electrical system, but prompt and fficient damage control enabled her to remain in action hd to continue the patrol.

The following day, she scored her third daily double.)perating to the south of Brest, she came upon a outh-bound convoy escorted by armed trawlers and porting observation balloons. The U-boat drew a bead n SS *Lake Portage* and fired a torpedo at the 1,998-on American ship, which sank soon thereafter. Later, he singled SS *Berwind*, another American ship, out of north-bound convoy and sank her with a single tor-edo. The following day, another north-bound convoy rossed her path. In a submerged attack, *UB–88* tor-edoed and sank a 1,901-ton Norwegian steamer, SS

Hundvaago. She rounded out that cruise with one last attack on 9 August during the return voyage to Zee-brugge. The submarine scored a torpedo hit on the 4,090-ton British ship SS *Anselma de Larringa* near the mouth of the Seine River. Although damaged, her victim succeeded in reaching a friendly port. *UB–88* continued her homeward voyage and reentered Zee-brugge on 11 August.

After almost a month of preparations, the U-boat returned to sea on 7 September for her final cruise as a unit of *I U-Flotille Flandern*. Following a long voyage through the North Sea, around the Orkney Islands, and down the west coast of Ireland, she reached her opera-tions area off the northern part of France's west coast on 14 September. Two days later, she claimed her first victim of the patrol when she fired the torpedo which sank SS *Philomel*, a 3,050-ton British steamer travel-ling south in convoy with about 19 other ships. Three days later, she fired two torpedoes at a 30-ship convoy. Apparently both missiles hit the same ship, SS *Fanny*, a 1,484-ton Swedish steamer bound from England to Bordeaux with a cargo of 1,930 tons of coal. The fol-lowing day, she began her long return voyage to Zee-brugge via the same route—around the British Isles and through the North Sea. En route home, shortly after midnight on 22 September, she encountered her last target, SS *Polesley*. In a surfaced attack, *UB–88* scored a torpedo hit which sent the 4,221-ton British steamer to the bottom just off the coast of Cornwall. The submarine then resumed her course and entered Zeebrugge on 29 September. She remained there only overnight. The next day, she got underway to return to Germany. On 3 October, she arrived in Heligoland and joined her new unit *II U-Flotille, Hochseeflotte* (2d Submarine Flotilla, High Seas Fleet). She remained inactive—first at Heligoland and, then, at Wilhelms-haven—through the end of World War I.

Soon after the 11 November armistice ended hostili-ties, *UB–88* surrendered along with the other warships of the High Seas Fleet. They were interned—probably at Harwich, England—on 26 November 1918. When the United States Navy expressed an interest in acquiring several German submarines to be used in conjunction with the current Victory Bond drive and to enable American crews to learn their supposed secrets, *UB–88* and five other boats were allocated to the United States with the agreement that they would be destroyed upon the conclusion of the bond campaign. Naval personnel were dispatched from the United States early in 1919, and they took over the warship on 23 March 1919. Soon thereafter, *UB–88* was placed in special commission for the voyage across the Atlantic, Lt. Cmdr. Joseph L. Nielson in command.

After a brief period allotted to the crew to make repairs and familiarize themselves with the foreign submarine's machinery, *UB–88* stood out of Harwich on 3 April in company with *Bushnell* (Submarine Tender No. 2) and three other former German U-boats—*U–117*, *UC–97*, and *UB–148*. That task unit, dubbed the Ex-German Submarine Expeditionary Force, steamed via the Azores and Bermuda to New York, where it arrived on 27 April. Not long after reaching New York, *UB–88* and the other four boats became the center-stage attraction for a horde of tourists, reporters, and photographers, as well as for technicians from the Navy Department, submarine builders, and equipment suppliers. During her stay in New York, *UB–88* re-ceived additional refurbishment in preparation for her participation in the bond drive.

Finally, orders arrived dispersing five of the six U-boats to different sections of the American coasts and waterways for visits to various ports along the way. *UB–88* drew the longest itinerary of the five U-boats. She was assigned to the ports on the east coast south of Savannah, Ga.; ports on the Gulf coast; the Missis-sippi River as far north as Memphis, Tenn.; and the west coast. She departed New York on 5 May in company with her tender, the Coast Guard ship *Tus-*

carora. On the first part of the cruise, she visited Savannah, Jacksonville, Miami, and Key West. At the time she departed Key West, the submarine had to bid farewell to *Tuscarora*, because boiler trouble forced the cutter to remain there for repairs. *Bittern* (Minesweeper No. 36) became her tender and escorted the U-boat through the remainder of her voyage.

From Key West, *UB–88* headed for Tampa, thence to Pensacola; and on to Mobile and New Orleans. At the latter port, she entered the Mississippi River. For the next month, she made calls at ports large and small along the great river. Though her schedule originally called for her to travel as far north as St. Louis, Mo., she made it only as far as Memphis before the rapidly-falling water level forced her to cut short her voyage on the Mississippi and head downriver. *UB–88* returned to New Orleans on 1 July and entered drydock for repairs to her port tail shaft. The submarine completed repairs on 22 July and departed New Orleans to begin a cruise to ports along the Texas coast and thence to the Canal Zone. A breakdown between Houston, Tex., and Colon, Canal Zone, meant that *Bittern* had to tow the submarine the final 200 miles into Colon. After receiving repairs, provisions, and visitors, *UB–88* transited the canal on 12 August. Following a two-day visit to Balboa, she headed north along the Mexican coast to San Diego and, after stops at Acapulco and Manzanillo in Mexico, reached her destination on 29 August.

The last leg of her voyage took the submarine north to San Pedro, Santa Barbara, Monterey, and San Francisco in California; Astoria and Portland in Oregon; and Seattle, Tacoma, and Bremerton in Washington. On the return voyage, she stopped at San Francisco only, departing that port on 6 November for the submarine base at San Pedro, where she arrived the next day. After being laid up at San Pedro for four months, *UB–88* began the dismantling process on 1 April 1920. That operation was completed by 31 August, and *UB–88* was placed out of commission on 1 November 1920. The following spring, the U-boat returned to sea for the last time; and, on 1 March 1921, she took her final plunge when *Wickes* (DD–75) sank her with gunfire.

UB–148

(Former German Submarine: dp. 523 (surf.), 653 (subm.); l. 182′; b. 19′; dr. 12′; s. 13.6 k. (surf.), 8 k. (subm.); cpl. 34; a. 5 20″ tt., 1 3.4″; cl. *UB–142*)

UB–148—a UB.III series, small, coastal submarine—was laid down during the winter of 1917 and 1918 at Bremen, Germany, by *Aktiengesellschaft Weser;* launched on 7 August 1918; but never commissioned in the Imperial German Navy. She was completing preparations for commissioning when the armistice of 11 November ended hostilities. Two days later, she was interned at the Swedish naval base located at Karlskrona, Sweden, to await her fate.

By the terms of the armistice, Germany was required to destroy her aircraft and submarines or surrender them to the Allies. On 26 November, *UB–148* was surrendered to the British at Harwich, England. Later, when the United States Navy expressed an interest in acquiring several former U-boats, to use in conjunction with a Victory Bond drive, *UB–148* was one of the six boats allocated for that purpose. Her American crew, sent to England early in March 1919, took her over later that month, began preparing her for the voyage to America, and placed her in commission, Lt. Comdr. Harold T. Smith in command.

The U-boat departed England on 3 April 1919 in company with *Bushnell* (Submarine Tender No. 2) and three other submarines—*U–117*, *UB–88*, and *UC–97*. That task organization, the Ex-German Submarine Expeditionary Force, steamed via the Azores and Bermuda to New York, where it arrived on 27 April. After a period of repairs, the submarines were opened for visits by the public. Tourists, reporters and photographers joined Navy technicians and civilian ship builders in swarming over *UB–148* and the other submarines. Following that, *UB–148* received instruction to call at ports along the east coast of the United States in the immediate vicinity of New York City in conjunction with the bond drive. At the conclusion of the drive that summer, she and *U–111* were subjected to extensive tests and trials to evaluate their performance capability. When that experimentation ended, she joined *U–117* and *U–140* at the Philadelphia Navy Yard, where they were laid up pending final disposition. She was dismantled at Philadelphia; and, during the summer of 1921, her hulk was used in gunnery and aerial bombing tests conducted off the east coast. Following those tests, *UB–148* was sunk by gunfire from *Sicard* (DD–346).

UC–97

(Former German Submarine: dp. 491 (surf.), 57 (subm.); l. 184¼′; b. 18¾′; dr. 12½′; s. 11.5 k. (surf.), 6.6 k. (subm.); cpl. 32; a. 3 20″ tt., 1 3.4″, 6 mine tubes, 14 mines; cl. *UC–90*)

UC–97, a minelaying submarine, was laid down late in 1917 at Hamburg, Germany, by Blohm & Voss an launched on 17 March 1918. She was never commissioned in the Imperial German Navy because the armistice of 11 November ended hostilities before the submarine was ready for sea. She was surrendered according to the terms of the armistice and was probably interned at Harwich, England.

In any event, the United States Navy expressed an interest in acquiring several of the surrendered German submarines for display purposes in conjunction with a Victory Bond drive. Early in 1919, *UC–97* and five other U-boats were allotted to the United States. Officers and sailors went to England in March and took possession of the boats on the 23d. Soon thereafter, *UC–97* was placed in special commission for the voyage to the United States, Lt. Comdr. Holbrook Gibson in command.

The American crew worked feverishly to prepare the submarine for the voyage across the Atlantic. However, faulty machinery kept *UC–97*'s crew from completing its mission until she was well out to sea. Thus, when she put to sea with *UB–88*, *U–117*, and *UB–148* on 3 April, *Bushnell* (Submarine Tender No. 2) had to tow her. However, by late afternoon of her first day at sea, the U-boat's American crew succeeded in getting her diesel engines running; and for the remainder of the voyage, she moved under her own power.

Her unit, which received the interesting name, Ex German Submarine Expeditionary Force, steamed first to Ponta Delgada in the Azores and thence to Bermuda. From Bermuda, the four U-boats and *Bushnell* set course for New York City, where they arrived on 27 April after a rough voyage. At New York, the boats became the objects of interest to a horde of visitors. Reporters, photographers, and tourists joined Navy Department technicians and civilian submarine builders in swarming over and through *UC–97* and the other boats. Soon, however, the U-boat received her itinerary for the Victory Bond campaign. Of the six regions into which the coastal areas and major waterways of the United States were divided, *UC–97* drew the Great Lakes region. That assignment required her to negotiate the locks of the Canadian-controlled St. Lawrence canal system. *UC–97*'s refusal to break with traditional practice on board a man-of-war and fly the Union Jack at the fore caused trouble at each Canadian port of call along the way. However, her commanding officer, Lt. Comdr. Charles A. Lockwood, Jr.—who later rose to fame in World War II as Commander, Submarines, Pacific Fleet—stuck to his guns and was later vindicated by Canadian naval officers who applauded his pertinacious observance of time-honored naval tradition.

Once she cleared the last locks and entered the Great Lakes, *UC–97* began a whirlwind series of visits to American ports, large and small, along the littoral of Lakes Ontario, Erie, Huron, and Michigan. Though scheduled to visit Lake Superior ports as well, the U-boat had to cut short its voyage because of wear on the engines. Thus, in August, she started back down the coast of Lake Michigan toward Chicago, where she arrived at the beginning of the last week of the month. At Chicago, her crew turned *UC–97* over to the Commandant, 9th Naval District. She was laid up at the Great Lakes Naval Station until 7 June 1921 when she was taken out into Lake Michigan and sunk as a target during naval reserve gunnery drills.

U. S. Grant

Two ships have borne the name *U. S. Grant* while serving in the United States Navy. For the biography of Ulysses S. Grant, see *Ulysses S. Grant* on page 394.

I

(RC: t. 263; l. 163'; b. 25'; s. 10 k.; cpl. 39; a. 4 guns)

U. S. Grant—frequently identified simply as *Grant*—was a wooden-hulled, screw, steam, revenue cutter built in 1870 and 1871 at Wilmington, Del., by the Pusey and Jones Corp. The cutter was assigned to the New York station on 19 January 1872 with Capt. George R. Slicer, USRCS, in command.

For the next two decades, *U. S. Grant* operated off the east coast from Block Island Sound to the mouth of the Delaware River. She was withdrawn from this duty on 29 September 1893 to be refitted for duty in the Pacific. She departed New York on 6 December, bound for Port Townsend, Wash. En route, the revenue cutter called at Barbados; Bahia, Brazil; Montevideo, Uruguay; Valparaiso, Chile; Callao, Peru; San Diego and San Fracisco, Calif., and arrived at Port Townsend on 23 April 1894, ending a voyage of 73 days and 20 hours.

In the ensuing years, *U. S. Grant* operated out of Port Townsend, protecting the salmon fisheries and, when necessary, extending assistance to ships of the Bering Sea whaling fleet.

She continued her peacetime routine in the Pacific northwest into the late 1890's. Arriving at San Francisco on 7 April 1898, *U. S. Grant* was placed under Navy control four days later, on 11 April, as the United States girded for war with Spain. Retaining her coast guard crew, the revenue cutter operated under Navy aegis as a unit of the Naval Auxiliary Service through July. Returned to the Treasury Department on 16 August 1898, *U. S. Grant* resumed her peacetime activities, patrolling the same northwest Pacific coastlines of Washington and Alaska which she had covered during her brief wartime naval service.

On 23 January 1906, the Pacific Mail Line steamer *Valencia* became stranded off Cape Beale Light, near Vancouver Island, British Columbia. Of the 164 people on board, 126 perished in the tragedy. *U. S. Grant* assisted in operations to recover the bodies of the victims and later transported them to Seattle.

U. S. Grant conducted her last cruise in the summer of 1906, patrolling the salmon fisheries off the Washington coast in the vicinity of Point Wallace, Wash. Subsequently taken out of service, the revenue cutter was sold on 28 November 1906 to A. A. Cragin, of Seattle, Wash.

II

(ScStr: dp. 15,010; l. 508'2''; b. 55'3''; dr. 27'6''; dph. 31'8''; s. 15 k.; cpl. 211; trp. 1,244; a. 4 6'', 2 1-pdrs., 2 mg.)

Konig Wilhelm II—renamed *Madawaska* in 1917 and *U. S. Grant* in 1922—was a steel-hulled screw steamer launched on 20 July 1907 at Stettin, Germany, by Vulcan *Aktiengesellschaft*. Built for the transatlantic passenger trade, *Konig Wilhelm II* operated between Hamburg, Germany, and Buenos Aires, Argentina, under the house flag of the Hamburg-Amerika Line, until the outset of World War I in 1914. Voluntarily interned at Hokoben, N.J., to avoid being captured by the Royal Navy, the passenger liner was seized after the United States entered the war on 6 April 1917, as were all other German vessels in American ports. Before agents of the Federal Government took possession of the ship, her German crew unsuccessfully attempted to render her unusable by cracking her main steam cylinders with hydraulic jacks.

Following repairs to the damaged machinery, *Konig Wilhelm II* was assigned the identification number 3011 and commissioned on 27 August 1917, Lt. Charles McCauley in temporary command pending the arrival of Comdr. Edward H. Watson. Renamed *Madawaska* on 1 September—the ship was assigned to the Cruiser and Transport Force of the Atlantic Fleet. During World War I, she conducted 10 transatlantic voyages in which she carried nearly 12,000 men to Europe.

After the armistice of 11 November 1918, *Madawaska* made seven more voyages, bringing 17,000 men home from the European theater. She completed the last of these runs upon her arrival at New York on 23 August 1919. She was decommissioned on 2 September and simultaneously transferred to the War Department.

Sailing for the Pacific soon thereafter, *Madawaska* embarked elements of the Czech Legion at Vladivostok, Russia, early in 1920, as part of the evacuation of that force in the wake of the Russian Civil War in Siberia. The ship sailed to Fiume, Yugoslavia, and disembarked her Czech passengers to return to their homeland. Subsequently sailing for New York, *Madawaska* was inactivated and turned over to the Shipping Board for lay-up.

The following year, however, the War Department reacquired the vessel and authorized a major refit for her before she could resume active service. During this overhaul, which would last through the spring of 1922, the ship was fitted with modern marine water-tube boilers for greater safety in operation and to enable the ship to make increased speed. On 3 June 1922, at Brooklyn, N.Y., the transport was renamed *U. S. Grant*; Princess Cantacuzene, wife of Major General Prince Cantacuzene, Count Speransky of Russia, and a granddaughter of General Ulysses S. Grant, christened the ship.

For almost two decades, *U. S. Grant* soldiered on in the Army Transport Service, maintaining a regular schedule of voyages carrying troops, passengers, and supplies along a route which included calls at San Francisco, Calif.; Honolulu, Territory of Hawaii; Guam; Manila, Philippine Islands; Chinwangtao and Shanghai, China; the Panama Canal Zone, and New York. For many of these years of service in the Pacific, *U. S. Grant* served as the sole source of refrigerated stores from the United States. Her periodic arrivals at Apra Harbor invariably produced a temporary improvement in the diet of Americans living in Guam.

On one voyage to Guam, the transport was nearly lost. On the late afternoon of 19 May 1939, *U. S. Grant* ran aground on the dangerous inner reef in the as-yet unfinished harbor. Fortunately, the accident did not occur during typhoon season. The combined efforts of *Penguin* (AM–33) and *Robert L. Barnes* (AG–27) failed to budge the ship off the coral, leading the Acting Governor of Guam, Comdr. George W. Johnson, to hit upon a plan of action in collaboration (by radio) with Capt. Richmond K. Turner, in *Astoria* (CA–34), which was then en route to the island.

For 21 hours, members of the U.S. Naval Insular Force and local stevedores unloaded 300 tons of cargo from the grounded *U. S. Grant*, while much of her fuel was transferred to *Robert L. Barnes* and *Admiral Halstead*. *Astoria*—en route for the United States after carrying Japanese Ambassador Hiroshi Saito's ashes back to his homeland—arrived at 0630 on 21 May. She took up her assigned position, as did *Penguin*, *Robert L. Barnes*, and *Admiral Halstead;* at 0809, *U. S. Grant* lurched free of the coral reef, to the accompaniment of cheers from the transport's crew. The island's newspaper, *The Guam Recorder*, subsequently reported in its June 1939 edition: "The short time in which the difficult operation was carried out was due to the efficient cooperation of all . . . involved, the Army, Navy, and Merchant Marine." All cargo was soon reloaded, and *U. S. Grant* resumed her voyage.

She continued under the aegis of the Army Transportation Service through 1940. Then, as war clouds gathered in the Pacific and Atlantic, *U. S. Grant* was subsequently reacquired by the Navy. Armed with seven 3-inch guns (she had been unarmed while serving as an Army transport), the vessel was refitted at the Mare Island Navy Yard, Vallejo, Calif., and was commissioned on 16 June 1941, Capt. Herbert R. Hein in command. Continuing her service as a transport, the ship received the classification of AP–29.

U. S. Grant operated between ports on the west coast and into the Aleutian Islands through the outbreak of war in the Pacific on 7 December 1941. She carried passengers and cargo to Alaskan ports as the United States built up its defenses in that area against possible thrusts by Japan. In February and March 1942, *U. S. Grant* conducted voyages to the Hawaiian Islands. During the former month, she returned some 1,000 enemy aliens (mostly Japanese with a sprinkling of Germans) for placement in internment camps in the southwestern United States. Among these passengers was prisoner of war number one, Lt. Kazuo Sakamaki, whose midget submarine had run aground off Barber's Point, Oahu, on 7 December 1941. In April, *U. S. Grant* resumed trips to Alaskan ports, carrying troops from Seattle to American bases on the Alaskan mainland and in the Aleutians, and continued this vital routine until the spring of 1942.

The Battle of the Coral Sea during May 1942 convinced the Japanese that a thrust at Midway Island was imperative, in an attempt to draw out the American fleet—particularly the dwindling number of vital carriers. Consequently, a powerful Japanese fleet sailed for Midway, while a smaller task force headed northward for the Aleutians to launch a diversionary raid. Carrier-based planes from the carrier *Ryujo* struck Dutch Harbor, Alaska, on 3 June; and Japanese troops occupied Attu and Kiska islands on the 7th.

During this time, *U. S. Grant* carried troops to Kodiak, Alaska, and Cold Bay into the summer. She narrowly escaped being torpedoed while proceeding from Seattle to Dutch Harbor in convoy on 20 July. Alert lookouts picked out the tracks of two torpedoes, and evasive action enabled the ship to avoid the deadly "fish" which passed close aboard, from starboard to port.

The venerable transport disembarked Army troops at Massacre Bay on 14 June, three days after the initial landings. The following month, as American and Canadian troops prepared to assault Kiska, Rear Admiral Francis W. Rockwell broke his flag in *U. S. Grant* as Commander, Task Force 51.

During this operation, *U. S. Grant* served as combination transport and communications vessel. The Americans eventually discovered that the Japanese had stolen away like nomads, leaving only a few dogs to "contest" the landings, and had completed their evacuation, undetected by the Allies, by 28 July. During the Kiska landings, the transport not only carried Army troops, but also a Mexican liaison group; a detachment of Canadian troops, and a group of civilian correspondents.

After a period of repairs in late 1943, which laste into 1944, *U. S. Grant* resumed coastwise voyages Alaska. From April to December, she shifted to th eastern Pacific to operate between Hawaii and the we coast. She often embarked medical patients to retur them to the west coast from Hawaiian area hospital Arriving at San Francisco after one such voyage o 23 January 1945, *U. S. Grant* disembarked passenge and got underway the same afternoon without pa sengers or escort, bound for the Caribbean. Transitin the Panama Canal, after embarking passengers a Balboa, the ship operated in the Caribbean for th next six months, between the West Indies and Ne Orleans, La., until the end of the war.

U. S. Grant returned to Pacific duty in Septembe departing San Francisco on the 18th for Okinawa, vi Eniwetok. She arrived at Okinawa on 12 October, i the wake of a destructive typhoon, and took on boar 1,273 passengers for transportation to the Unite States, getting underway from the island on 21 O tober.

Arriving at San Francisco on 7 November, *U. . Grant* disembarked her passengers soon thereafte One week later, on 14 November, the transport wa decommissioned and returned to the War Departmen Her name was struck from the Navy list on 28 N vember.

Turned over to the Maritime Commission, the ers while transport and veteran of two world wars wa sold to the Boston Metals Co. on 24 February 1948 fo scrapping.

U. S. Grant received one battle star for her Worl War II service.

Uhlmann

Robert William Uhlmann—born on 16 August 191 at Pittsburgh, Pa.—attended the College of Engineer ing, University of Michigan, from 1937 until 1940. O 27 September 1940, he enlisted in the Naval Reserve a an apprentice seaman and, during November an December, trained in *Arkansas* (BB–33). Followin his appointment as a midshipman in the Naval Reserv on 17 March 1941, he trained at the Midshipma School, Northwestern University, Chicago, Ill., and o 12 June 1941 was commissioned ensign. After add tional training, he reported to Patrol Squadron 2 on 1 August 1941. This squadron, a part of Patr Wing 2 stationed at Naval Air Station, Kaneohe Ba was redesignated Patrol Squadron 12 (VP–12) o 28 October 1941.

On the morning of 7 December 1941, as the incredu lous Commander of Patrol Wing 1 investigated repor that a plane of the dawn patrol had depth-charged Japanese submarine only a mile from the entrance t Pearl Harbor, nine Japanese fighters circled low ove the airfield at Kaneohe and then attacked, machin gunning the control tower and leaving planes in flame in the bay and on the ramp. The men of VP–12 spran into action without regard for personal safety, exposin themselves to the deadly fire of the enemy planes a they sought to save planes not yet destroyed and fight off the raiders. The Japanese fighters strafe automobiles trying to reach the field and concentrate attention on men attempting to man guns in th grounded planes. Everyone on station joined the dut sections in combatting the surprise attackers.

While across the island in Pearl Harbor the Pacifi Fleet fought for survival, Fleet Air Detachment, Nav Air Station, Kaneohe, waged its own battle against th Japanese attackers with only rifles and machine gun A short time later, a second wave of enemy planes fle over, bombing vulnerable hangars and planes, and de stroying the hangar where many members of Patr Squadron 12 were obtaining replenishment ammunitio for machine guns. Additional strafing attacks followe and, before the morning was over, eight patrol bombe seaplanes were destroyed, and all 35 planes which ha been on the ground when the attack began were out of commission. Air station personnel shot down two Japanese planes and scored hits on the fuel tanks of seven others, but the material and human costs were high. Among the dead at the end of the battle was Ensign Uhlmann who had joined with VP–12 in the courageous attempt to repulse the enemy.

(DD–687: dp. 2,050; l. 376'5"; b. 39'7"; dr. 17'9"; s. 35.2 k. (tl.); cpl. 329; a. 5 5", 10 40mm., 7 20mm., 2 dct., 6 dcp., 10 21" tt.; cl. *Fletcher*)

Uhlmann (DD–687) was laid down on 6 March 1943 at Staten Island, N.Y., by the Bethlehem Steel Co.; launched on 30 July 1943; sponsored by Mrs. C. F. Uhlmann, mother of Ens. Uhlmann; and commissioned on 22 November 1943 at the Brooklyn Navy Yard, Comdr. Selden G. Hooper in command.

After shakedown out of Bermuda and post-shakedown availability, the destroyer joined Destroyer Squadron 56 on 24 January 1944. Two days later, she got underway to escort *Wasp* (CV–18) to Trinidad. She then transited the Panama Canal, touched at San Diego, and arrived at San Francisco on 16 February. There, she embarked passengers for transportation to Hawaii and departed the west coast on the 17th in company with *Birmingham* (CL–62) and *Newcomb* (DD–586).

She arrived at Pearl Harbor on the 23d. During March, *Uhlmann* underwent availability, conducted training, and rendered occasional convoy screening services in Hawaiian waters. In April, she conducted carrier escort training exercises and honed her skills in shore bombardment and radar tracking in preparation for assignment to carrier screening duties. Two hours after sunset on the 24th, while *Uhlmann* was participating in training exercises in Hawaiian waters as an antisubmarine screening ship for the carriers of Task Group 19.2, she was struck amidships by destroyer *Benham* (DD–796). The collision tore an eight-by-ten-foot hole in *Uhlmann*'s hull below the water line, flooding her firerooms and the forward engine room. The following day, she was taken in tow by *Tekesta* (AT–

93) and returned to Pearl Harbor on the 26th. After temporary hull and engine repairs, she set her course for San Francisco on 17 May, steaming on her port engine with her forward fire and engine rooms out of commission. On the 24th, she moored at Hunter's Point and, for the next two months, underwent extensive repairs.

In August, she returned to Pearl Harbor and resumed training exercises including torpedo firing and antisubmarine warfare drills. After one false start, she departed Oahu on 18 September with *South Dakota* (BB–57) and *Woodworth* (DD–460) and set her course for the Admiralties. En route to Manus, she was diverted to the western Carolines and reported to 3d Fleet at Ulithi on 30 September. During a typhoon on 3 October, a nest of three destroyers drifted down on *Uhlmann* and pierced three holes in her starboard side. A few hours later, the destroyer made an emergency sortie from the lagoon with Task Group 38.2; but, by nightfall, high seas had carried away her emergency damage control measures and flooded the anchor windlass room. She returned to Ulithi on the 4th for repairs by *Dixie* (AD–14) and, on the 6th, was underway for an at-sea rendezvous with Task Force 38—the 3d Fleet's Fast Carrier Force—the following day.

At noon on the 9th, the carriers began a high-speed approach to a launch position for strikes on the Ryukyus. On the 10th, planes launched by the carriers struck Okinawa, destroying enemy aircraft, shipping, and shore installations in preparation for the projected landings on Leyte, Cebu, and Negros.

After fueling at sea on the 11th, TF 38 began a high-speed approach on Formosa for two days of strikes on that island, again in support of the impending American assault on the Philippines. On 12 and 13 October, as the carriers steamed 85 miles east of Formosa and launched strike after strike against that island, *Uhlmann* operated in their antiaircraft screen. Planes from the carriers attempted to destroy Japanese air strength on Formosa to eliminate that island as a staging base for the enemy.

Shortly after dusk on the 12th, low flying Japanese bombers and torpedo planes approached Task Group

Uhlmann (DD–687) as a "four-gun *Fletcher*." Her fifth 5-inch gun has been replaced by 3-inch 50-caliber antiaircraft guns with directors. (USN 1064865)

38.2 from the west and northwest. Although most of the Japanese planes were intercepted by the task force's combat air patrol, more than a dozen broke through and attacked the formation. *Uhlmann* opened fire on a Japanese medium torpedo bomber at 7,000 yards. But, undeterred, the plane continued to approach the zigzagging destroyer from port until it was hit at close range by *Uhlmann*'s 40-millimeter fire, crossed over the ship, and splashed 100 yards off the destroyer's starboard bow. The plane sank at once leaving a large quantity of gas and oil floating on the sea.

A second wave of attackers followed two minutes after the first, and *Uhlmann*, maneuvering with the formation, joined in the fire which downed some seven Japanese raiders during the night. At 2200, she hit an enemy plane which burst into flame and illuminated the moonless overcast night before splashing off the stern of the ship. Minutes before midnight, *Uhlmann* picked up another aerial intruder on radar and opened up with 5-inch fire. The plane countered by dropping flares as a diversionary tactic and pulled away, but *Uhlmann*'s deadly fire found its mark as the raider burst into flame and splashed into the sea. The destroyers began laying smoke around midnight, and the raids tapered off. For the remainder of the night, Japanese planes merely approached within 6 to 7 miles, dropped flares, and retired without attacking the formation.

Japanese planes again ventured near the formation late on the 14th only to be routed by night fliers of the combat air patrol. The next day, TF 38 began a high-speed run in for strikes on Luzon, with *Uhlmann* providing antisubmarine protection for the fast carriers of TG 38.2. On the 16th and 17th, the carriers launched heavy strikes on Luzon concentrating on ships and installations in the Manila Bay area. Late on the 17th, the formation set a southerly course to get into position for strikes farther south, with the fighter planes of the task force dispersing light Japanese air opposition en route. Steaming east and northeast of Samar, the task force made strikes on Negros on the 20th in strategic support of the landings on Leyte and also provided direct air support for those landings.

Meanwhile, upon first sighting American minesweepers in the approaches to Leyte Gulf, Japan had sent her naval forces into Philippine waters. On the 24th, *Uhlmann* protected the carriers of Rear Admiral Gerald F. Bogan's TG 38.2 as they launched strikes against the Japanese Center Force which was approaching San Bernardino Strait. In an action known as the Battle of the Sibuyan Sea, American naval aircraft sank Japanese super battleship *Musashi* and damaged several other enemy warships. At 2022 that evening, Task Force 38 turned north to seek out and destroy the Japanese Northern Force whose carriers had been spotted north of Luzon where they had been stationed in the hope of luring the 3d Fleet away from the beaches of Leyte.

However, a gallant little group of American destroyers, destroyer escorts, and escort carriers had fought off the overwhelmingly superior Japanese Center Force and induced it to abandon its plan of attacking the amphibious ships which were supporting the Allied beachheads on Leyte. Thus, when TG 34.5 returned within aircraft range of San Bernardino Strait, the chastened Japanese Center Force had already retreated back through that strategic passage to safety.

In the days that followed the historic battle for Leyte Gulf, *Uhlmann* continued to screen TG 38.2 while its carriers conducted strikes on land targets, including raids on Luzon on the 29th and 30th. Shortly before noon on the 29th, as the carriers recovered aircraft from a strike against Japanese targets in the Manila area, *Uhlmann* left the formation to investigate what appeared to be the splash of a downed plane but was later determined to be a bomb splash. As the destroyer attempted to discover the cause of the splash, a Navy torpedo bomber from *Hancock* (CV–19) made a water landing nearby, and *Uhlmann* quickly rescued the pilot

and two crewmen. Meanwhile, an enemy attack had materialized, and the destroyer went to general quarters, increased her speed to 25 knots, and executed evasive maneuvers as she attempted to rejoin the formation. As she steamed to her assigned position, she joined in the general fire against the attackers—10 to 12 Japanese planes which made notably inaccurate high altitude bombing runs and retired after one or two of their members had been splashed by the American ships' accurate fire.

On 4 November, TF 38.2 began a high-speed approach for strikes on Luzon. For two days, carrier-based aircraft pounded Luzon and Bicol. Then, on the 7th, *Uhlmann* set her course for Ulithi. En route, heavy seas caused flooding in the boatswain's stores and chain locker; and *Uhlmann*, accompanied by *Yarnall* (DD–541), left the formation and ran with the wind while damage-control measures were being effected. She arrived at Ulithi on the 9th, underwent repairs, and got underway again on the 16th. She rendezvoused with TG 38.2 the following day and took up an antisubmarine screening station. Following carrier strikes on Luzon on the 19th, *Uhlmann* returned to Ulithi on the 22d.

The destroyer conducted exercises out of Ulithi until 10 December when she got underway and rendezvoused with Task Force 38 on the 12th. On the 14th, 15th, and 16th, the carriers made strikes against air installations on Luzon and against shipping in water off that island to support landings on Mindoro. Toward dusk on the 16th, the task force began its retirement. As the American warships fueled northeast of Samar on the 17th, weather conditions worsened. At 1330, *Uhlmann* abandoned fueling from *Massachusetts* (BB–59) due to rough seas and 26-knot winds stirred up by an approaching typhoon. On the 18th, *Uhlmann* recorded 69-knot winds, and rolls up to 58 degrees as the typhoon's center passed within 30 miles of the formation. During the afternoon, winds decreased; and, by 2000, they had subsided to 25 knots. On the 19th and 20th, the ships of the battered task force resumed fueling which continued into the next day while its escorts searched for survivors of the three destroyers which had failed to survive the tropical storm. Late on the 20th, due to heavy seas, the carriers aborted a high-speed run in for strikes on Luzon; and *Uhlmann* returned to the storm area and searched for survivors. She made port at Ulithi on Christmas Eve.

Underway again with TG 38.1 on the 30th, she screened the carriers during strikes on Formosa and Luzon early in the new year and, an hour before midnight on 9 January 1945, transited Bashi Channel into the South China Sea. The carriers launched strikes on French Indochina, Formosa, and Hong Kong before retiring from the South China Sea on the 19th. Steaming 75 miles north of Luzon at dusk the next day, the formation came under attack by enemy aircraft, and *Uhlmann* joined other ships of the formation in repelling raiders. Following strikes on Formosa and Okinawa, TF 38 returned to Ulithi on the 26th. That day, the 3d Fleet was redesignated 5th Fleet and placed under the command of Admiral Raymond A. Spruance.

Following antisubmarine training, *Uhlmann* got underway from Ulithi with TG 58.2 on 10 February. During a Japanese air raid on the 16th, the first of two days of strikes on the Tokyo area, *Uhlmann* took under fire an enemy fighter which made a low-glide, diving attack on the ship's port beam and dropped a bomb 100 yards in the wake of destroyer *Halsey Powell* (DD–686). Neither destroyer suffered any damage in this exchange. On the 19th, *Uhlmann* screened TF 58 as it steamed north of Iwo Jima launching strikes on that island in support of the initial landings there. On the 20th, mechanical difficulties in her steering mechanism forced *Uhlmann* to part company with the task force, and she put in at Ulithi on 23 February for repairs.

Underway on 14 March, she rendezvoused with TG 58.2 on the 16th. On the 17th, the carriers began a high speed run in for strikes on Kyushu. While the planes of TF 58 pounded that Japanese homeland, *Uhlmann* protected the carriers from air and submarine attack. Air activity began early on the 18th; and *Uhlmann*, acting as linking vessel between TF 58 and its picket line, began firing on aerial snoopers before dawn. Shortly before 0700, she joined the picket line and, at 0956, rescued three Navy aviators from a torpedo bomber which had splashed nearby.

Throughout the day and into the night, alerts prompted by Japanese surveillance planes brought the ship's crew to general quarters. Four minutes before midnight, *Uhlmann* opened fire on an enemy aircraft at 10,000 yards. The plane burst into flame and splashed 7,000 yards off the destroyer's starboard quarter and burned brightly for several minutes. Air activity continued into the early hours of the 19th. Before dawn that day, *Uhlmann* joined *Cushing* (DD–797) in firing on a high-altitude Japanese raider which burst into flames and splashed. Fifty miles off the eastern shore of Shikoku on the morning of the 19th, a Japanese plane dove toward the destroyer and, despite fire from the ship, dropped a small bomb which hit 50 feet off the ship's starboard quarter. No further action occurred that day as *Uhlmann*, screening TG 58.2, proceeded southward to rejoin the rest of TF 58 southeast of Kyushu.

Ships of the task force began refueling on the 20th but were forced to discontinue when an air attack developed in mid-afternoon. *Uhlmann* was transferring aviation personnel to *San Jacinto* (CVL–30) at 1453 when a kamikaze dove at carrier *Hancock* (CV–19), missed, and crashed into *Halsey Powell* (DD–686). *Uhlmann* fired on enemy dive bombers throughout the remainder of the afternoon, was hit by some shrapnel, but suffered no casualties. Air activity continued to be heavy as strikes on Japan continued on the 21st. During a surprise attack early in the afternoon, a bomb fell only 200 yards from *Cushing* (DD–797), and another bomb narrowly missed a carrier of the force. Ten minutes before midnight on the 22d, while *Uhlmann* steamed on picket station, she made a surface radar contact which was later identified as a Japanese submarine. In company with *Haggard* (DD–555), she proceeded at high speed toward the submerging target and stood by while *Haggard* forced the unlucky enemy ship to the surface with depth charges. *Haggard* then rammed the submarine which exploded and sank. *Uhlmann* escorted the slightly damaged destroyer back to Ulithi where they arrived on the 25th.

She departed Ulithi on the 30th and set a north-westerly course. After weathering a typhoon on 2 April, she rendezvoused with TG 58.4 on the 5th and, toward dusk, began an approach for strikes on Okinawa. Following rendezvous with TF 58, she alternated radar picket and screening duties as the carrier-based planes pounded Okinawa.

In April, Japan began concentrated massed kamikaze attacks against American ships in the waters of the Ryukyus; and the carrier forces, despite their discreet distance from Okinawa, were not exempt from the attentions of the suicide planes. On the 12th, combat air patrol from the formation splashed three "Zekes" within sight of *Uhlmann* as she stood her picket station 25 miles north of TF 58. Two days later, snoopers and nuisance raiders kept the air patrol occupied in the afternoon and early evening.

On radar picket with TG 58.4 on the 17th, *Uhlmann* joined in fire that downed two enemy aircraft, one of which splashed near *Benham* (DD–796) causing minor damage to that ship. That night, *Uhlmann* added her depth charges to a combined attack which sent Japanese submarine *I–56* to the bottom. Late on the afternoon of the 29th, as enemy planes began closing from the northward, destroyer *Haggard* (DD–585) joined *Uhlman* to strengthen the picket station in the face of attack. Minutes before 1700, a Japanese fighter plane, taken under fire by *Uhlmann*, nosed over and dove toward *Haggard*. The crash and explosion of the suicide plane and its bomb tore a hole in *Haggard*'s starboard side, flooding her firerooms and number one engine room, and leaving her dead in the water. Meanwhile a second "Zeke" began a run in. *Uhlmann* splashed the attacker close aboard *Haggard* and rescued two of the damaged destroyer's crew from the water. *Uhlmann* then requested assistance from the task group which responded with a combat air patrol of two divisions. An hour later, light cruiser *San Diego* (CL–53) and Destroyer Division 104 came to the aid of the stricken destroyer. *Uhlmann* escorted *Haggard* a short distance toward Kerama Retto and returned to her picket duty the next day. She screened the carrier strike force until 11 May when she headed for the Carolines. The ship arrived at Ulithi on the 14th.

Underway with TG 58.4 on the 24th, the destroyer returned to a strike launch area off Okinawa and resumed her picket duties. On the 28th, operational control of the task force was returned to the 3d Fleet and TG 58.4 became TG 38.4. *Uhlmann* continued patrolling picket station and screening the fast carriers until 13 June when she arrived at San Pedro Bay, Leyte, for replenishment and maintenance. On 1 July, she set a northerly course; and, throughout July, the carriers conducted strikes on targets in the Japanese islands to soften up this last stronghold of Japanese power for the projected invasion. On the 25th, *Uhlmann* joined specially formed TG 35.3 for an antishipping sweep across Kii Suido between Honshu and Shikoku. Two hours after midnight on this completely overcast night, *Uhlmann* bombarded a radio tower on the southern tip of Uwano Hanto while other ships of the group shelled nearby airfields.

Until the cessation of hostilities on 15 August, *Uhlmann* continued to operate with the carrier force as it launched strikes against Japan. On 23 August, she rendezvoused with TF 47—a combined British-American force—for temporary escort duty in connection with the occupation of Japan. She arrived in Sagami Wan on the 27th, and immediately manned a picket station. On the 30th, while acting as plane guard for *Cowpens* (CV–25), she rescued that carrier's landing signal officer who had jumped over the side in an attempt to rescue the pilot of a downed plane. That same day, the destroyer anchored in Sagami Wan, ending 61 days of continuous operation and, on the 31st, shifted anchorages to Tokyo Bay.

Her occupation duties included mail, freight, and passenger runs between Iwo Jima and Japanese ports. Late in October, she participated in training exercises; then, on the 31st, departed Yokosuka, steamed via Pearl Harbor, and arrived at Bremerton late in November. Following alterations, she got underway on 20 April 1946 and arrived at San Diego on the 24th. There, on 14 June 1946, she was decommissioned and placed in reserve. On 12 August, she was assigned to the Naval Reserve Training Program and underwent an overhaul at Terminal Island before reporting to the Commandant, 11th Naval District, in November 1946.

Operating out of San Diego, she trained reserve crews until the end of the decade. On 23 May 1950, she was recommissioned, but remained in reserve and, that summer, made a southward voyage, visiting Central and South American ports. She returned to San Diego in July and, on 18 November, was assigned active status.

On 27 January 1951, she reported to the Commander in Chief, Pacific Fleet, for duty and, on 16 June, departed San Diego with units of Destroyer Division 152, setting her course for Korean waters. Assigned to TF 77—the fast carrier force operating in the Sea of Japan—*Uhlmann* resumed the screening and plane guard duties which had occupied much of her time in World War II. She later joined TF 95, a blockade and escort force, and carried out day and night bombardment of the Korean coast. While conducting a routine observation patrol off Wonsan Harbor's Hodo Peninsula on the morning of 20 August, the destroyer came under fire from seven enemy shore batteries. Gun flashes on the beach provided a warning only moments before shells began to fall 1,000 yards from the destroyer. All hands went quickly to battle stations as *Uhlmann* commenced evasive maneuvers, increased to flank speed, and opened fire on the shore installations. In short order, she reduced the enemy on shore to two guns, while she steamed among near misses, some of which came as close as 15 yards. Fragments from the shell explosions carried away a radio antenna during the half hour engagement. Ordered by TG 95.2 to break off the action, *Uhlmann* withdrew out of range of the shore batteries.

In the fall, she patrolled Formosan waters and participated in hunter-killer antisubmarine training off Okinawa. In November, she rejoined TF 77 and, operating in the Sea of Japan, rescued several pilots before leaving Yokosuka on 22 January 1952.

She returned to San Diego on 6 February and, in the months that followed, underwent drydocking and alterations which included the installation of new armament. She conducted exercises; then departed San Diego on 11 August 1952 in company with Destroyer Division 152, escorting *Kearsarge* (CV–12) and *Toledo* (CA–133) to the Far East.

During this seven-month Korean deployment, *Uhlmann* operated with fast carrier forces, conducted hunter-killer activities, and patrolled off Formosa. She also conducted shore bombardment which destroyed enemy gun emplacements, a factory, and storage facilities, while damaging buildings, bunkers, and railways. On the morning of 3 November, as she was firing interdiction rounds on a railroad and tunnel on the east coast of North Korea near Hangwon, the destroyer was taken under fire by shore guns, mortars, and machine guns. Brought to alert by shell splashes only 100 yards off her port bow, *Uhlmann* accelerated to 25 knots, began evasive maneuvers, and opened fire with her 3-inch and 5-inch guns. She scored a direct hit on an enemy gun emplacement and suffered only minor damages in the exchange. However, she emerged from the encounter with 13 wounded. After putting in at Hong Kong over Christmas, she departed Yokosuka on 3 March 1953, steamed via Midway and Pearl Harbor, and arrived at San Diego on 19 March 1953.

Following exercises off the west coast, *Uhlmann* was again deployed to the western Pacific. She proceeded via the Hawaiian Islands, and she arrived at Yokosuka on 20 November 1953. During this seven-month tour, the destroyer plied waters off Japan and Korea and engaged in training and operations out of Yokosuka and Sasebo with TF 77. In February 1954, *Uhlmann* joined with elements of the French and British Far Eastern Fleets for Exercise "Sonata" which included extensive antisubmarine warfare training and visits to Philippine and Indochina ports. During March, she embarked personnel of the Nationalist Chinese Navy for training.

While patrolling Formosa Strait in the first week of March, she assisted the grounded Chinese Nationalist merchant ship, *Kiang Shan* which was stranded on an island in the Pescadores. In the course of a daring rescue of crewmen from the Chinese steamer, *Uhlmann* lost her whaleboat and bent her propellers, shafts, and rudder on reefs in the shallow water. After the successful completion of her mission, she put in at Kaohsiung on the 5th. To prevent vibration damage to her reduction gears, she was towed from that port on the 11th and, on 14 March, arrived at Subic Bay for repairs. On her return to San Diego, she resumed the stateside routine of upkeep and training.

Over the net 15 years, *Uhlmann* made 11 more deployments to the western Pacific (WestPac). On deployment to the Far East in 1954 with Destroyer Division 152, she took part in the evacuation of the Tachen Islands—located off Hangchou Wan—in the American attempt to defuse the explosive situation which had developed between Nationalist China and the People's

Republic of China. In 1958, during a period of heightened tension over the Chinese offshore islands, the destroyer again supported American interests in the Far East. Between deployments, *Uhlmann* operated out of San Diego, participating in fleet exercises, receiving upkeep, and performing goodwill assignments.

In the 1960's, trouble flared in the area formerly known as French Indochina; and *Uhlmann* served three more wartime tours in Pacific waters, this time off the coast of Vietnam. Her duties included gunfire support of land action, often coordinated by an airborne spotter, illumination missions, and routine bombardment assignments. Off Vietnam in 1965, she searched junks for contraband; supplied shore bombardment; and served as a plane guard for carrier *Bonhomme Richard* (CV–31). In 1968, a year of heavy fighting in the Republic of Vietnam, *Uhlmann* acted as a plane guard in the Gulf of Tonkin and fired 50 naval gunfire support missions off Hue.

In 1969, she participated in fleet exercises in Hawaiian waters; then, on 1 October, she returned to the west coast and assumed new duties as a Group I Naval Reserve Training Ship operating out of Tacoma. For the next three years, she conducted reserve training cruises out of that port and participated in fleet exercises. During Exercise "Head Beagle" in August 1970, she conducted intensive training in the Strait of Juan de Fuca and off the coast of Washington in conjunction with Canadian naval forces.

The oldest commissioned destroyer in the Navy, she was found unfit for service on 24 November 1971; and, on 15 July 1972, *Uhlmann*, the Navy's last *Fletcher*-class destroyer, was decommissioned at the Naval Reserve Center Pier, Tacoma. Her name was struck from the Navy list the same day, and she was transferred to the custody of the Inactive Ship Facility, Bremerton, for disposal. She was later scrapped.

Uhlmann received seven battle stars for World War II service, two for Korean War service, and five for Vietnam War service.

Ukiah

A city located in western California about 54 miles north-northwest of Santa Rosa. It is the seat of government for Mendocino County.

(PC–1251: dp. 280; l. 173'8''; b. 23'0''; dr. 10'10''; s. 20.2 k. (tl.); cpl. 65; a. 1 3'', 1 40mm.; cl. PC–461)

PC–1251 was laid down on 8 June 1942 by the Brown Shipbuilding Co. at Houston, Tex.; launched on 12 September 1942; sponsored by Miss Betty Ann Woolsey; and commissioned on 27 February 1943, Lt. L. C. Mably, USNR, in command.

PC–1251 conducted shakedown training briefly under the auspices of the Commander, Submarine Chaser Training Center, Miami, Fla., and then began antisubmarine patrols and convoy-escort duty in the Caribbean on the Guantanamo Bay-Aruba-Trinidad circuit. Sometime after mid-year, the submarine chaser switched from the Guantanamo to Trinidad convoys to the New York to Key West run. That duty lasted until late November, at which time she began a yard overhaul at Miami, Fla. Another six months of escorting convoys in the Gulf of Mexico and along the east coast followed her yard period at Miami.

By late spring of 1944, the U-boat menace in the western Atlantic had abated sufficiently to allow for the reassignment of a significant portion of the Navy's escort fleet to the Pacific theater. On 31 May, she departed Miami and headed for Pearl Harbor. She transited the Panama Canal on 12 June, made a stop at San Diego from 22 June to 8 July, and arrived in Pearl Harbor on 15 July. She conducted maneuvers out of Pearl Harbor until 12 August at which time she got underway for the Solomon Islands. The warship arrived at Florida Island, near Guadalcanal in the Solomons, n 24 August. She remained in the Solomons until 4 September at which time she got underway with Task Force (TF) 32 for the invasion of the Palau Islands. En route, she served as a unit of the antisubmarine screen for the Angaur Tractor Group carrying the Army's 81st Division which served both as a floating reserve and, if not needed to reinforce the marines on Peleliu, as the Angaur invasion force. On the day following the Peleliu invasion, PC–1251 supported the 81st Division's assault on Angaur—first by acting as control vessel for Red Beach on the island's northwestern coast and then by screening the transport area against possible Japanese submarine attack. After the beachhead was established, PC–1251 shifted entirely to antisubmarine patrols and convoy-escort duty. From October 1944 until February 1945, the submarine chaser acted as a unit of the antisubmarine screen which patrolled Angaur and Peleliu as well as the eastern entrance to the anchorage at Kossol Roads. In addition, she also escorted convoys between Saipan, Manus, Eniwetok, Ulithi, and the Palaus.

At the end of January, she shifted her sphere of operations from the Palau Islands to islands farther east—escorting convoys between Guam, Ulithi, and Eniwetok. After a month on that circuit, PC–1251 cleared the western Pacific altogether, departing Eniwetok on 1 March 1945. Ten days later, she escorted her convoy into Pearl Harbor and, the following day, commenced a two-month overhaul. On 7 May, she emerged from that yard period and began three weeks of training and escort duty in the Hawaiian Islands. Her service at Hawaii ended on 25 May when PC–1251 stood out of Pearl Harbor to return to the western Pacific. She arrived back at Eniwetok on 5 June and, for the remainder of the war, escorted convoys between various advanced bases in the Central Pacific as well as to and from Okinawa in the Ryukyus. Though she had missed the opening phase of the final operation of the war, PC–1251, nevertheless, spent most of her remaining wartime service in direct support of that campaign. By the time the Japanese finally capitulated in mid-August, she had moved south to the Philippine Islands and had begun patrols and escort missions between ports in that archipelago—most frequently between the Manila area of Luzon to San Pedro Bay at Leyte. On 20 August, she was redesignated PCC–1251.

On 21 September, she stood out of Leyte Gulf in the screen of a convoy bound for Hiroshima, Japan. En route, she and her charges, six LST's, stopped off at Okinawa for several days, from 26 September to 2 October. PCC–1251 escorted the LST's into Hiro Wan on the 6th. She stayed at Hiroshima until the 12th, at which time she put to sea, bound for Guam. The submarine chaser arrived at Apra Harbor on 18 October. She remained moored to pierside at Guam from mid-October 1945 to late April 1946. On 24 April, she departed Guam and headed back to the United States via Eniwetok and Pearl Harbor. She reached Astoria, Oreg., on 24 May and, three days later, shifted to Portland. Following inactivation overhaul at Kaiser Shipyards in Portland, PCC–1251 was towed back to Astoria on 12 July. On 3 August, she was decommissioned and berthed with the Columbia River Group, Pacific Reserve Fleet. There, she remained for the next 15 years. On 15 February 1956, PCC–1251 received the name Ukiah. On 1 July 1960, her name was struck from the Navy list, presumably in preparation for the submarine chaser's disposal. While information on her final disposal is not available, Ukiah was probably scrapped.

Ukiah was awarded one battle star for World War II service.

Ulitka Bay

A bay on the northwestern corner of Noyes Island which is located off the southernmost coast of Alaska, a few miles east of Prince of Wales Island.

Prior to the laying of her keel, Ulitka Bay (CVE–91) was renamed Makassar Strait (q.v.) on 6 November 1943.

Ulua

An important foodfish of the tropical Pacific.

Ulua (SS–428)—a Tench-class submarine—was laid down on 13 November 1943 at Philadelphia, Pa., by the Cramp Shipbuilding Co., but the curtailment of naval construction programs, in the closing days of the war against Japan, resulted in the suspension of further construction on 12 August 1945. The partly completed submarine was launched in January 1946 and towed to the Portsmouth (N.H.) Naval Shipyard for maintenance, prior to beginning her career as a test hull. Towed to Norfolk, Va., in 1951, she participated in tests to gather research data on new weapon and submarine design. Ulua's usefulness to the Navy ended, and her name was struck from the Navy list on 12 June 1958. Her hulk was sold for scrap on 30 September 1958 to the Portsmouth Salvage Co., Inc.

Ulvert M. Moore

Ulvert Mathew Moore—born on 26 August 1917 at Williamson, W.Va.—enlisted in the Naval Reserve on 15 October 1940 at Washington, D.C., and served as a seaman 2d class until appointed an aviation cadet on 14 January 1941. After flight training at Jacksonville and Miami, Fla., into the summer of 1941, Moore then received advanced carrier training at Norfolk, Va.

Assigned to Torpedo Squadron (VT) 8—embarked in Hornet (CV-8)—soon thereafter, Moore was killed in action on 4 June 1942, during the Battle of Midway. Flying a Douglas TBD-1 Devastator, Ens. Moore perished in VT-8's gallant torpedo attack—led by Lt. Comdr. John C. Waldron—against the Japanese carrier Akagi of the Midway-bound task force under Vice Admiral Chuichi Nagumo. Moore was awarded a posthumous Navy Cross for pressing home his attack despite being grimly aware that VT-8 had neither fighter cover nor enough fuel to return to Hornet. However, the sacrifice of "Torpedo 8" was not in vain. The attack drew down the Japanese combat air patrol and left the skies above open for the attack of the dive bombers which soon crippled three Japanese carriers on the first day of the battle and thus paved the way to an American victory.

(DE-442: dp. 1,350; l. 306'; b. 36'8''; dr. 9'5'' (mean); s. 24 k.; cpl. 186; a. 2 5'', 4 40mm., 10 20mm., 3 21'' tt., 2 dct., 8 dcp., 1 dcp. (hh.); cl. John C. Butler)

Ulvert M. Moore (DE-442) was laid down on 2 December 1943 at Houston, Tex., by the Brown Shipbuilding Co.; launched on 7 March 1944; sponsored by Mrs. L. E. Moore, mother of Ens. Moore; and commissioned on 18 July 1944, Lt. Comdr. Franklin D. Roosevelt, Jr., USNR—the son of the President—in command.

Following shakedown off Bermuda, the destroyer escort screened Shamrock Bay (CVE-84) from New York to Norfolk on 18 September before departing the latter port on 5 October in company with Kendall C. Campbell (DE-443). The two DE's escorted Taluga (AO-62) and Aucilla (AO-56) to Aruba, Dutch West Indies, and thence conveyed them to the Canal Zone before continuing on by themselves to the west coast of the United States, arriving at San Diego on 22 October. Ulvert M. Moore and her sister ship subsequently sailed for the Hawaiian Islands, escorting Colorado (BB-46) from San Pedro to Pearl Harbor between 24 and 30 October.

When *Ulvert M. Moore* had refueled there, urgent orders sent her to sea to join a hunter-killer group based around *Corregidor* (CVE–58) which was searching for *I-12*. That Japanese submarine had torpedoed and sunk the American merchantman SS *John A. Johnson* on 30 October. *Corregidor's* unit, designated Task Group (TG) 12.3, operated between Hawaii and the west coast until 19 November, when it returned to Pearl Harbor.

After repairs alongside *Yosemite* (AD–19) from 20 to 23 November, *Ulvert M. Moore* put to sea on the 24th with TG 12.4, centered around *Tulagi* (CVE–72), bound for the Carolines, via Eniwetok in the Marshalls. TG 12.4 conducted antisubmarine patrols en route and reached Eniwetok on 2 December and Ulithi on the 7th. Upon its arrival at the latter, the group was reclassified TG 30.6. The destroyer escort and her mates then operated on antisubmarine patrols in an area from the Marianas in the north to the Palaus in the south.

Following this duty, *Ulvert M. Moore* replenished her stores at Kossol Roads, Palaus, and got underway on New Year's Day 1945 as part of the screen for TG 77.4—the 14 escort aircraft carriers which would furnish close air support for the landing operations on Luzon and provide air cover for the fire support group, TG 77.2—bound for Luzon. Snooping Japanese planes showed up on the 3d, approached the formation, but kept just out of range.

Ulvert M. Moore went to general quarters twice in the predawn hours of 4 January, fueled from *Suamico* (AO–49), and spent the afternoon delivering mail via highline transfer to other ships in the task force. While she was casting off from alongside *Minneapolis* (CA–36), her lookouts noted a Japanese plane slipping into the return flight pattern of the carriers. This kamikaze soon crashed into *Ommaney Bay* (CVE–79) shortly after 1714, 1,000 yards away from *Ulvert M. Moore's* starboard bow.

A heavy explosion rocked the "jeep carrier" from stem to stern, and large fires soon broke out along her starboard side. The destroyer escort headed for the scene at full speed and picked up four men—one of whom died before he could be brought aboard ship. All three suffered from flash burns and shock. *Ommaney Bay* continued to burn fiercely and eventually had to be sunk by a torpedo from *Burns* (DD–588) at 1845 that day.

With bogies in the vicinity at 0039 on 5 January, *Ulvert M. Moore* went to general quarters and remained there until 0205. The destroyer escort went to general quarters three more times that day, twice for enemy aircraft and once for a contact which turned out to be friendly. At 1655, the destroyer escort received reports of approaching Japanese aircraft. Soon Japanese torpedo planes attacked the starboard side of the formation, giving *Ulvert M. Moore* a few moments before three "Oscar" fighters approached from port. Opening fire from 5,000 yards with her 5-inch battery and from 3,000 yards with her 40-millimeter Bofors guns, *Ulvert M. Moore* downed one "Oscar" which burst into flames and disintegrated.

Elsewhere in the immediate vicinity, Japanese planes crashed into the Australian heavy cruiser HMAS *Australia* and *Stafford* (DE–411). The latter, holed on her starboard side aft, between the after engine room and fire room, initially seemed lost as fire broke out on board. *Ulvert M. Moore* closed to port and took off 54 men and 3 officers while *Halligan* (DE–584) nudged alongside to starboard and took off additional crewmen.

Ulvert M. Moore received orders to stand by *Stafford*, along with *Halligan* and the fleet tug *Quapaw* (AT–12) which arrived to take the stricken destroyer escort in tow. Gunfire from *Halligan* and *Ulvert M. Moore* splashed a "Val" dive-bomber early on the 6th, before *Ralph Talbot* (DD–390) relieved *Halligan* at 1849 on that day. Another Japanese plane ventured too close to the little formation on the 7th, and *Ulvert M. Moore's* gunners splashed it.

After transferring the crewmen of *Stafford*—who had been embarked in *Ulvert M. Moore*—to *Ralph Talbot*, the destroyer escort resumed antisubmarine patrols in the vicinity of Mindoro Island as part of Task Unit (TU) 77.4.1. While thus engaged, she received orders to assist *La Vallette* (DD–448) in searching for a Japanese submarine reported by a plane to be running on the surface in the vicinity. Accordingly, *Goss* (DE–444) accompanied *Ulvert M. Moore* and joined *La Vallette* and *Jenkins* (DD–447). At 1557 on 30 January, *La Vallette* made contact and dropped a depth charge barrage but observed no results and soon lost the contact. The group continued to search throughout the night with negative results.

On 31 January, *Ulvert M. Moore* secured from the search at 1607 and steamed to join up with TG 77.4. En route, the destroyer escort received a radio message from *Boise* (CL–47) telling of a surfaced submarine on a southeast bearing 8 miles away. *Bell* (DD–587) and *O'Bannon* (DD–450) left *Boise's* screen to investigate. *Bell* closed to four miles before the enemy submarine—identified by postwar accounting as RO–115—submerged. At 2037, *Ulvert M. Moore* received orders to assist in the search and arrived at the scene to complete the hunter-killer group. The destroyer escort detected the submarine at 2152 but briefly lost the contact. Regaining the contact at 2210, she fired her first "hedgehog" pattern four minutes later. At 2227, she fired another "hedgehog" pattern; and three explosions rumbled up from below—muffled noises intermingling with "crunching noises." Twice more, the destroyer escort attacked like a persistent terrier. Another pattern of 7.2-millimeter projectiles left the "hedgehog" mount at 2302, hit the water and plunged downward; 12 seconds later a sharp "crack" followed, as did "distinct and definite bubbling and hissing noises." Men on the destroyer escort's fantail reported seeing a large bubble burst on the surface.

Ulvert M. Moore closed the vicinity of the strong contact at 2336 and again at midnight. The eighth attack proved to be the killer; for, 15 seconds after the "hedgehog" depth charges hit the water, three violent explosions sent out concussions felt by topside personnel in *Ulvert M. Moore* and the three other ships. A last explosion rumbled up from below—the death agony of the RO-boat and a "definite bluish light similar to burning gas" was noted. For two hours, the ships searched the vicinity to confirm the "kill." Men topside in *Ulvert M. Moore* noted the strong odor of diesel oil, an object which resembled a life jacket, small boxes and pieces of deck planking, and a considerable amount of paper.

Ulvert M. Moore retired to Ulithi and remained there from 6 to 18 February before departing with other ships of CortRon 70 and *Tulagi*, as part of TU 50.7.3 to provide antisubmarine protection for the carriers which would furnish close air support for the forces attacking Iwo Jima. The ship thus began her most grueling period, as she steamed continuously for 78 days to support this operation and the subsequent one against Okinawa. The destroyer escort operated with *Tulagi* and, later, *Anzio* (CVE–57), southeast of Okinawa. During the Okinawa operation, President Roosevelt died on 12 April, a loss felt not only by the nation and the Fleet, but by Comdr. Roosevelt, *Ulvert M. Moore's* commanding officer.

Returning to Guam on 6 June, *Ulvert M. Moore* soon shifted to Ulithi for major repairs. On 19 June, the destroyer escort put to sea with TG 30.8, the group providing logistics support for Admiral William F. Halsey's air strikes against the Japanese home islands. She operated with this unit until returning to Guam on 24 July. Three days later, the ship joined the hunter-killer group based around *Salamaua* (CVE–96), in operating on antisubmarine patrol northeast of Luzon.

Two atomic bombs—dropped on Hiroshima and Nagasaki on 6 and 9 August, respectively—hastened the collapse of Japanese resistance. At this time, *Ulvert M. Moore* was operating with *Salamaua* on antisubmarine patrol east of Formosa, a duty in which she remained engaged until putting into Leyte on 25 August.

Ulvert M. Moore screened TG 32.1, the supporting escorts for TF 32, then en route to Tokyo Bay for the Japanese surrender. On 2 September, the escort vessel entered Tokyo Bay, in the words of her ship's historian, as "a fitting culmination to approximately 14 months of strenuous operation."

After conducting antisubmarine and mine patrol duties in Japanese home waters, escorting Japan-bound transports with occupation forces embarked, and destroying floating mines with light-caliber gunfire, *Ulvert M. Moore* operated in the Philippines into the winter before she returned via Pearl Harbor to the United States. Arriving at San Diego on 22 November, the destroyer escort was decommissioned there on 24 May 1946 and placed in reserve.

Ulvert M. Moore remained inactive until the onset of the Korean War in the summer of 1950. The destroyer escort was accordingly recommissioned at San Diego on 27 January 1951 and assigned to CortRon 9. After shakedown, she departed San Diego on 19 April, bound for the Far East.

Arriving at Sasebo, Japan, on 17 May 1951, *Ulvert M. Moore* joined Task Force 72 for Formosa patrol duty, standing guard off Taiwan, to deter against possible communist Chinese incursions against the Nationalist Chinese. The destroyer escort was detached from this duty on 10 June and arrived at Buckner Bay two days later. She then conducted hunter-killer exercises as she steamed north to Japan.

Arriving at Yokosuka on 16 June, she departed there nine days later and headed for the west coast of Korea to join the British carrier HMS *Glory* for screen and patrol duty. In August, *Ulvert M. Moore* participated in bombardment and covering operations at Wonsan, Korea, during minesweeping operations there and came under fire for the first time from communist shore batteries. Her guns covered the retirement of the more lightly constructed minecraft and earned the ship a "well done." After conducting frequent patrols north to Songjin and Chongjin, Korea, for shore bombardment and anti-junk patrol, the destroyer escort put into Sasebo on 25 August for refit.

The following month, *Ulvert M. Moore* continued her operations off the coast of Korea undertaking bombardment and call-fire missions in support of United Nations ground troops at Wonsan, Songjin, and Chongjin on the east coast of Korea. Near the end of the month, the ship proceeded towards Okinawa, conducting hunter-killer exercises en route.

However, Typhoon "Ruth" prevented successful completion of their evolution and forced *Ulvert M. Moore* and the other ships of CortRon 9 back towards Korea. Arriving off Hungnam on 14 October, the destroyer escort proceeded to her interdiction patrol station and watched for enemy junk traffic off the coast. Early on the morning of 17 October, communist shore batteries shelled the ship, lobbing a salvo close aboard the escort vessel. One shell hit the after steering engine room, and fragments killed one man almost instantly. In addition, the splinters wounded an officer and an enlisted man. Efficient and rapid damage control work soon repaired the damage, allowing the ship to return to action. *Ulvert M. Moore* remained on the station—conducting shore bombardment, serving on antisubmarine patrol, and patrolling to locate and destroy enemy junks or mines—until she departed Korean waters on 6 November, arriving at San Diego, via Japan, on 26 November.

After an overhaul at the San Francisco Naval Shipyard and antisubmarine and air defense training off the coast of California, *Ulvert M. Moore* got underway for the Far East and her second tour off Korea, departing San Diego on 18 October 1952.

Ulvert M. Moore subsequently took part in operations interdicting communist coastal rail traffic and harassing enemy logistics movements. She remained thus engaged until 19 December before conducting a period of hunter-killer exercises off Okinawa between 27 December 1952 and 9 January 1953.

On 31 March, *Ulvert M. Moore*'s commanding officer assumed duties as Commander Task Group (CTG) 95.3, to enforce Japanese and South Korean fishing rights off Korean coastlines, before she sailed for the west coast of the United States, making port at San Diego on 6 June 1953. After conducting local operations, including antisubmarine, air defense, and type training evolutions, *Ulvert M. Moore* again sailed for the Far East, departing the west coast for Yokosuka on 20 May 1954.

During this tour, the ship's duties consisted primarily of escorting fleet tankers and ammunition ships. In addition, she also participated in a marine landing exercise, a hunter-killer training operation, and conducted antisubmarine exercises with Colombian, British, and Dutch naval units. She weathered three major typhoons during the deployment: "Grace," while moored at Sasebo; "June," during a sortie with a typhoon-evasion task force from Tokyo Bay; and "Lorna," while at sea off the southeast coast of Japan. Upon completion of her tour, *Ulvert M. Moore* departed Yokosuka, bound for San Diego via Midway and Pearl Harbor. While en route home, she encountered a storm which battered her for 10 days and produced many heavy rolls in the storm-tossed seas.

Ulvert M. Moore subsequently conducted three more WestPac deployments into 1958. During one of these, in early 1958, she participated in Operation "Skyhook." Placed out of commission, in reserve, on 10 October 1958 at Astoria, Oreg., the destroyer escort remained inactive until struck from the Navy list on 1 December 1965. She was authorized for destruction as a target vessel on 18 April 1966 and subsequently sunk off San Nicholas Isle on 13 July 1966 by aircraft from *Coral Sea* (CVA–43) and by surface gunfire.

Ulvert M. Moore (DE–442) was awarded five battle stars for her World War II service and three for Korea.

Ulysses

A character in Greek mythology and the protagonist of Homer's epic poem, the *Odyssey*, which tells of his arduous voyage back to Ithaca, his home, after the Trojan War.

(Panama Collier No. 1: dp. 19,585; l. 536'; b. 65'; dr. 28'1''; dph. 39'6''; cl. *Ulysses*)

Ulysses (Panama Collier No. 1)—a steel-hulled screw steamer designed by the Navy and constructed at Sparrows Point, Md., by the Maryland Steel Co. under naval supervision—was launched on 12 December 1914 and, on 17 April 1915, was delivered at the Norfolk Navy Yard to the Panama Canal Co.

Ulysses shuttled between Hampton Roads and the Canal Zone, carrying coal to Cristobal, into 1917. During World War I, the ship received a main battery of one 5-inch gun and a 3-incher and a Navy armed guard crew to man them while the ship continued to discharge her longstanding duties. The guns were apparently removed shortly after the armistice ended hostilities. Throughout the war, *Ulysses* belonged to the Panama Canal Co. and operated under the control of the Panama Canal Railroad Co. She continued in this status after peace returned until 1929, the last year in which her name appeared on shipping registers.

I

(ARB–9: dp. 4,100 (lim.); l. 328'0''; b. 50'; dr. 11'2''; s. 11.6 k. (tl.); cpl. 286; a. 8 20mm.; cl. *Aristaeus*)

Originally slated for construction as *LST–967* but redesignated ARB–9 on 14 April 1944 and named

Ulysses on 28 April 1944, *Ulysses* was laid down on 2 November 1944 at Hingham, Mass., by the Bethlehem-Hingham Shipyard; launched on 2 December 1944; and commissioned on 27 December 1944. After proceeding to Baltimore, she was decommissioned on 9 January 1945; converted to a battle damage repair ship by the Maryland Drydock Co.; and recommissioned on 20 April 1945, Lt. James L. Johnstone, USNR, in command.

In May, the new battle damage repair ship conducted shakedown exercises in Chesapeake Bay; then, on the 22d, she departed Norfolk in company with *Patroclus* (ARL–19). She steamed via the Panama Canal and San Pedro and arrived at San Francisco on the morning of 1 June. There, she loaded stores and pontoons before getting underway from San Francisco Bay on the 28th.

After *Ulysses* had been at sea for only six hours, the bolts, plates, and turnbuckles holding the pontoons in place began to show signs of bending under the stress of the ocean voyage; and the ship was ordered back to San Francisco for additional work on the pontoon mounts. At noon on 6 July, she again got underway and set her course, via Pearl Harbor and Eniwetok, for the Marianas. She arrived at Saipan on 6 August—just over a week before Japan capitulated—and reported to Commander, Service Division 103.

During the remainder of 1945, she carried out repair assignments while based in turn at Saipan and at Okinawa. At Buckner Bay on 9 and 10 October 1945, she weathered a devastating typhoon during which she collided three times with *LST–717*. The repair ship lost three anchors in attempting to hold her position in the anchorage during the height of the storm and emerged from the ordeal with a six-foot hole in one side.

In January 1946, *Ulysses* shifted operations to Shanghai; then, in March, she set her course for the United States. After transiting the Panama Canal and unloading ammunition at Charleston in mid-May, she pro-

ceeded to Jacksonville for preservation work. On September, she reported to the 16th Fleet; and, on February 1947, she was decommissioned and joi the Atlantic Reserve Fleet at Green Cove Springs, F She remained there until 1961 when her name v struck from the Navy list.

Ulysses S. Grant

Ulysses Simpson Grant—born on 27 April 1822 Point Pleasant, Ohio—graduated from the United Sta Military Academy on 1 July 1843. He served with tinction in the war with Mexico—under Gener Zachary Taylor and Winfield Scott, taking part in battles of Resaca de la Palma, Palo Alto, Monter and Vera Cruz. He was twice brevetted for bravery: Molino del Rey and Chapultepec. After growing rest during frontier duty in the peacetime Army, he resign his commission in 1854 and attempted to pursue care in business and farming.

Shortly after the outbreak of the Civil War, Gr was commissioned a colonel in the 21st Illinois Vol teer Infantry. He later became brigadier general volunteers on 7 August 1861. Following the captu of Fort Henry and Fort Donelson in February 18 President Abraham Lincoln promoted Grant to ma general of volunteers. These victories opened Tenne to federal forces, and earned Grant the nickname "unconditional surrender."

He doggedly pursued the Confederate Army and w impressive—but costly—victories at Shiloh, Vicksbu and Chattanooga. His willingness to fight and ability win impressed President Lincoln who appointed Gr lieutenant general and gave him overall command the Army.

Grant left Major General William T. Sherman immediate charge of all troops in the west and mov

Ulysses S. Grant (SSBN–631) alongside the submarine tender *Proteus* (AS–19), 1965. (USN 1113229 C)

headquarters to Virginia where he turned his attention to the long frustrated Union effort to take Richmond. Despite heavy losses and difficult terrain, the army of the Potomac kept up a relentless pursuit of General Robert E. Lee's troops and won bloody contests in the Wilderness, at Spotsylvania, at Cold Harbor, and at Petersburg. His relentless pressure finally forced Lee to evacuate Richmond early in April 1865 and forced him to surrender at Appomattox Courthouse on 9 April 1865. Within a few weeks, the War between the States was over.

Grant became *ad interim* Secretary of War on 12 August 1867—when Johnson suspended Secretary Stanton—and held the office until early the next year. He ran for the presidency on the Republican ticket in 1868 and won the election. His two terms were marred by economic, social, and political turmoil; but Grant himself was not involved in the scandals, and his personal reputation emerged untarnished.

He devoted his twilight years to writing and completing his two volumes of *Personal Memoirs* which were published the year of his death. Grant died on 23 July 1885, at Mt. McGregor, N.Y.

(SSBN–631: dp. 7,300 (surf.), 8,250 (subm.); l. 425'; b. 33'; dr. 31'4''; s. 20+ k.; cpl. 140; a. 16 Poseidon mis., 4 21'' tt.; cl. *James Madison*)

Ulysses S. Grant (SSBN–631) was laid down on 18 August 1962 at Groton, Conn., by the Electric Boat Div. of the General Dynamics Corp.; launched on 2 November 1963; sponsored by Mrs. David W. Griffiths, the great-granddaughter of General Grant; and was commissioned at Groton on 17 July 1964, Capt. J. L. From, Jr., in command.

Following shakedown, the fleet ballistic missile (FBM) submarine got underway from Groton in early December 1964, bound for the Pacific. Transiting the Panama Canal on New Year's Eve, she arrived at Pearl Harbor in January 1965. The FBM submarine was deployed to Guam, in the Marianas, and operated from there into 1970. She conducted 18 deterrent patrols before returning to the east coast of the United States, departing the western Pacific in December 1970. After an overhaul at Charleston, S.C., *Ulysses S. Grant* was deployed to Holy Loch, Scotland, and operated in the European area until September 1975.

Returning home at that time, the submarine continued to operate with the Atlantic Fleet on deterrent patrols into 1980.

Umpqua

A river in Oregon rising near Roseburg and meandering northwest before emptying into Winchester Bay and the Pacific Ocean. The river in turn was named for the Umpqua Indians, a small tribe of Athabascan linguistic stock.

(Mon: dp. 1,175; l. 225'; b. 45'; dr. 6'; s. 9 k.; a. 2 11'' D. sb.; cl. *Casco*)

Umpqua—a single-turreted, twin-screw monitor—was laid down in March 1863 at Brownsville, Pa., by Snowden & Mason; launched on 21 December 1865; and completed on 7 May 1866.

Umpqua was a *Casco*-class monitor intended for service in the shallow bays, rivers, and inlets of the Confederacy. These warships sacrificed armor plate for a shallow draft and were fitted with a ballast compartment designed to lower them in the water during battle to reduce the target they provided enemy guns.

However, when the first of the light-draft monitors were launched in the spring of 1864, the Navy discovered that serious errors had been made in calculating their displacements. They proved to have a scant three inches of freeboard—even without turret, guns, and stores. As a result, the Navy Department ordered

on 24 June 1864 that *Umpqua*'s deck be raised 22 inches to provide sufficient freeboard. Upon delivery, the monitor was laid up at Mound City, Ill.; and she saw no commissioned service. In August 1868, she was moved to New Orleans, La. Her name was changed to *Fury* on 15 June 1869, but she resumed the name *Umpqua* on 10 August 1869.

Umpqua was sold at New Orleans on 12 September 1874 to Nathaniel McKay.

I

(Tug No. 25: dp. 1,000; l. 156'8''; b. 30'; dr. 14'7'' (mean); s. 13.0 k.; cpl. 42; a. 1 mg.; cl. *Bagaduce*)

The first *Umpqua* (Tug No. 25) was laid down on 19 February 1919 at Buffalo, N.Y., by the Ferguson Steel and Iron Works; launched on 18 September 1919; and commissioned at Buffalo on 6 December 1919, Lt. (jg.) W. F. Verleger in command.

Umpqua—as one of a class of ships regarded as "exceptionally powerful seagoing tugs"—spent nearly all of her active service operating out of Charleston, S.C., in the 6th Naval District. During that lengthy period—more than two and one-half decades—the single-screw, steel-hulled steam tug performed heavy duty towing and tug operations for the Atlantic Fleet into the 1940's.

In World War II, the seagoing tug performed coastal towing operations out of Charleston and ranged into the Gulf of Mexico. Among the ships she towed were patrol craft (PC's), amphibious vessels (LCI's and LST's), pontoon barges, and the incomplete hull of DE–774 (named *Russell M. Cox* but cancelled before she was to be completed). She also towed merchantmen and assisted vessels in distress.

Reclassified as an old ocean-going tug, ATO–25, on 15 May 1944, *Umpqua* was decommisioned at Charleston on 24 May 1946; her name was struck from the list of naval vessels on 3 July of the same year. She was transferred to the Maritime Commission for disposition on 4 December 1946.

II

(ATA–209: dp. 835 (tl.); l. 143'0''; b. 33'0''; dr. 13'2'' (lim.); s. 13 k. (tl.); cpl. 45; a. 1 3''; cl. *ATA–174*)

Although orginally designated *ATR–136*, *Umpqua* was laid down as *ATA–209* on 15 December 1944 at Port Arthur, Tex., by Gulfport Boiler and Welding Works; launched on 2 February 1945; and commissioned on 2 April 1945, Lt. Paul L. Cortney, USNR, in command.

Following shakedown in the Gulf of Mexico, *ATA–209* reported on the last day of April to Service Force, Atlantic. On 19 May, the auxiliary ocean tug departed New Orleans towing *YF–756*. She steamed via the Panama Canal and San Diego to Hawaii, arriving at Pearl Harbor early in July.

She operated on towing assignments between the Hawaiian Islands and the Marshalls until October when she set her course via San Francisco and the Panama Canal for Charleston. Arriving on 27 November, she reported to the Commandant, 6th Naval District, for duty; and, in April 1946, she was permanently assigned to that command. On 16 July 1948, she was named *Umpqua*.

Her primary job was that of towing ships, barges, and gunnery targets. She also participated in rescue and recovery operations. Her routine duties were performed mostly along the Atlantic and Gulf coasts and in the Caribbean, and they occasionally took the tug as far north as Nova Scotia. In the 1950's, she took part in calibration of radio navigation systems; and, in the 1960's, she assisted in oceanographic operations towing MONOB I, the Bureau of Ships' mobile sound lab, to study sites in the Caribbean. In 1965, she varied her duties with the retrieval of a Titan III rocket booster in support of NASA tests. On two occasions, she towed old Liberty ship hulls loaded with unserviceable ammunition to a disposal area in the Atlantic where the ammunition was detonated, and the hulls were sunk.

In July 1967, *Umpqua* was transferred to the Service Force, Atlantic Fleet, and was assigned to Service Squadron 8. *Umpqua* continued her towing duties, assisting disabled and damaged naval vessels. Occasionally, she participated in torpedo recovery and mineplanting in conjunction with exercises of various Atlantic Fleet units. In May and June of 1970, she towed *Darby* and *Tweedy*—formerly DE–218 and DE–532, respectively—to sea for use as targets for destruction.

In 1971, as her career with the United States Navy drew to a close, *Umpqua* took part in Operation "Springboard" one last time and made one of her longest tows when she pulled ammunition ship *Great Sitkin* (AE–17) 120 miles to Puerto Rico after the ship had gone dead in the water at sea. In June 1971, *Umpqua* began training a Colombian Navy crew in preparation for the transfer of the tug. On 1 July, she was decommissioned; her name was struck from the Navy list; and she was turned over to the government of Colombia under the Military Assistance Program.

Unadilla

A river which rises in Columbia County, N.Y., and meanders southwesterly before emptying into the Susquehanna River. Unadilla is an Iroquoian Indian noun meaning "place-of-meeting."

I

(Gbt.: t. 507; l. 158'; b. 28'; dph. 12'; dr. 9'6''; s. 8 k.; a. 1 20-pdr. P.r., 1 11'' D. sb., 2 24-pdr. how.)

The first *Unadilla*, a screw gunboat, was laid down at New York City by John Englis and the Novelty Iron Works in the late spring of 1861; launched on 17 August; and commissioned at the New York Navy Yard on 30 September, Lt. Napoleon Collins in command.

The vessel was one of 23 "90 Day" gunboats hurriedly constructed in less than three months shortly after the outbreak of the Civil War in April 1861. In October 1861, *Unadilla* joined the South Atlantic Blockading Squadron under Rear Admiral Samuel F. Du Pont and participated in the capture of Forts Walker and Beauregard in Port Royal Sound, S.C., on 7 November. During the bombardment, the gunboat was struck six times but suffered no casualties and sustained minor damage to her hull and rigging. Control of Port Royal Sound enabled the Union Navy to coordinate the blockade of the southern Atlantic seacoast more effectively for the duration of the war.

On 10 November, Lt. Collins in *Unadilla* assumed command of Union naval forces off Beaufort, S.C., for the purpose of restoring order to the town following its capture two days before. *Unadilla* and *Pembina* next proceeded to St. Helena Sound, S.C., on 24 November to reconnoiter Confederate positions at Hunting Island, Otter Island, and at the mouths of the Morgan and Coosaw rivers. The two gunboats conducted a survey up the Ashepoo River on 27 November. *Unadilla* returned to the Ashepoo on 6 December, but her engines failed, forcing the vessel back to Port Royal under tow on 9 December.

In January 1862, *Unadilla* joined *Pembina* on patrol in Wright's River, S.C. On 28 January, the gunboats fired upon and drove back two Confederate steamers attempting to reach Ft. Pulaski, Ga., and damaged three others. *Unadilla* remained in Wright's River through April, making several reconaissance expeditions up both the Wright's and New rivers in March and investigating rumors that the Confederates were

building a large ironclad warship at Savannah, Ga. She was temporarily deployed in the Savannah River, Ga., in mid-April and, on 24 April, received orders to return to Port Royal.

Unadilla left Port Royal for blockade duty off Charleston, S.C., on 28 April. On 10 May, she caught the English schooner *Mary Teresa* attempting to run into Charleston with a cargo of salt and assorted merchandise. *Unadilla* delivered the schooner's two passengers to the authorities and sent the vessel north to the New York prize court; then on 20 and 21 May, she joined *Pembina*, *Ottawa*, and the surveying steamer *Bibb* in Stono Inlet, S.C., where the Union flotilla captured six armed Confederates. On a second inspection of Stono Inlet and Stono River on 29 May, the vessel found the river free from Confederate obstructions and floating batteries, making it possible for Federal troops to cross in safety. *Unadilla* remained on duty in the Stono River until 4 July, when she returned to Port Royal to help repulse a Confederate attack upon Port Royal Island.

Unadilla left Port Royal on 12 July for reconnaissance duty in Ossabow Sound, Ga., and its tributaries. There, during an exploratory expedition up the Ogeechee River on 29 July, *Unadilla*, *Huron*, and *Madgie* exchanged heavy gunfire with Confederate Fort McAllister for over an hour before retiring down the stream. On 4 August, while patrolling between the Ogeechee and Vernon rivers in Ossabow Sound, *Unadilla* captured the British blockade-running steamer *Lodona* and her cargo of foodstuffs, dry goods, and building materials. The gunboat returned to New York for repairs on 19 August.

When she was again ready for action, *Unadilla* resumed reconnaissance duty in the rivers and inlets of the South Carolina and Georgia coasts. She sailed to Port Royal from the North Edisto River, S.C., in late December for repairs and supplies, and then joined the blockading force off Charleston on 2? December 1862. There, *Unadilla* captured the screw steamer *Princess Royal* on 29 January 1863 after chasing the blockade runner aground. *Princess Royal* proved to be a rich catch, as she was laden with rifled guns, small arms, ammunition, and two powerful steam engines intended for ironclads. She was a valuable vessel herself and was later taken into the Union Navy. *Unadilla* ended the month by helping the Fleet to beat back an attempt to raise the blockade made during the foggy early morning hours of 31 January by the newly completed Confederate rams CSS *Chicora* and *Palmetto State*. Before they were repulsed, the two ironclads largely destroyed both *Mercidita* and *Keystone State*, killing one quarter of the crew of the *Keystone State*. The near success of the attack prompted Confederate General P.G.T. Beauregard to exuberantly, and erroneously, proclaim the blockade of Charleston lifted.

Unadilla left the blockade off Charleston on 6 February to join with *Commodore McDonough* for reconnaissance activity in Stono Inlet and Stono River. In addition to routine patrol duties, *Commodore McDonough*, *Unadilla*, and *Pawnee* entered the Kiawah River, S.C., on 28 February to ascertain if it were possible for the Confederates to install batteries on John's Island, but found that it was not. On 14 March, *Unadilla* received orders to return to the Charleston blockade to counter increased blockade running activity. There, the gunboat served with the reserve force during Rear Admiral Du Pont's monitor attack upon the strong Confederate forts in Charleston harbor on ? April. However, the Southern defenders put up such a vigorous defense that the Union fleet was compelled to disengage. Reporting on the action, Rear Admiral Du Pont commented that to continue the attack "would have converted a failure into a disaster."

Shortly after the attack, *Unadilla* returned to her previous duty station in the Stono Inlet where she engaged a Confederate floating battery on 25 May. She remained there a month before being ordered to pro-

FORT ANDREWS.   PEMBINA.   TATNALL'S FLEET.   UNADILLA.

GUN-BOATS ENTERING SAVANNAH RIVER ABOVE FORT PULASKI.

Unadilla, seen here with her sister ship *Pembina*, formed part of the Federal squadron which entered the Savannah River through a channel above Fort Pulaski on 22 February 1862. Cut off from support, the Confederate garrison at Fort Pulaski surrendered on 11 April. (NR&L(O) 20001)

eed to the command of the blockade off Wassaw Sound, Ga., on 24 June. She put into Port Royal for repairs in August and returned to Wassaw Sound in September. From her post off Tybee Island, Ga., the gunboat conducted frequent reconnaissance surveys and reported upon both suspected Confederate troop movements in the area and the construction and movements of the ram CSS *Savannah*. In January 1864, she underwent repairs at Port Royal and, in March, was dispatched to St. John's River, Fla., for reconnaissance and convoy duties. After striking a sand bar, *Unadilla* returned to Port Royal in May where carpenters discovered that the battle-weary vessel needed an extensive overhaul. *Unadilla* was detained briefly in Ossabow Sound but, on 19 June, finally received orders north to the Philadelphia Navy Yard.

Repairs completed, *Unadilla* departed Philadelphia on 22 October, bound for Hampton Roads, Va., and duty with Rear Admiral David Dixon Porter's North Atlantic Blockading Squadron. On 22 November, she was dispatched to the blockade off New Inlet, N.C. She next served with the blockade off Wilmington and Beaufort, N.C., in early December and participated in the unsuccessful first amphibious assault upon Confederate Fort Fisher in the Cape Fear River, N.C., on 24 and 25 December. The fleet returned two weeks later and took the fort during a second amphibious assault between 13 and 15 January 1865. The Union vessels continued up the Cape Fear River toward Wilmington, and *Unadilla* assisted in the attack and capture of Fort Anderson on 18 February. On 23 February, she was ordered to proceed to Hampton Roads and served in the James River, Va., squadron doing routine reconnaissance work until the end of the war.

Unadilla was decommissioned at the New York Navy Yard on 4 May 1865 but was recommissioned on 20 December 1866 for duty with Rear Admiral Henry H. Bell's Asiatic Squadron in 1867, primarily for use in the suppression of Chinese pirates. *Unadilla*, together with *Aroostook*, *Maumee*, and assorted small gunboats of other nations, was credited with stopping most of the pirate depredations by 1868. The gunboat also visited Bangkok in June of 1868 to deliver arms and exchange diplomatic pleasantries with the King of Siam and his ministers. Soon thereafter, *Unadilla* was condemned as being too unseaworthy to be sent safely back to the United States and was sold on station on 9 November 1869.

II

(Harbor Tug No. 4: dp. 355; l. 110'; b. 25'; dr. 9'11" (mean) ; s. 12 k.; a. none)

The second *Unadilla* (Harbor Tug No. 4) was laid down on 29 April 1895 at Vallejo, Calif., by the Mare Island Navy Yard; and launched on 21 September 1895. Assigned to the Mare Island Navy Yard, *Unadilla* operated there through two world wars, performing local tug and tow services and providing waterfront fire protection. During this four-decade tour, the tug was given the hull number classification YT–4 on 17 July 1920 and reclassified YTM–4 on 15 May 1944. Declared surplus to the needs of the United States in September 1945 and slated for disposal, *Unadilla* was subsequently struck from the Navy list and delivered to the War Shipping Administration in May 1947.

III

(ATA–182: dp. 860; l. 143'; b. 33'; dr. 14' (mean); s. 14 k.; cpl. 46; a. 1 3''; cl. *ATA–121*)

Although originally projected as steel-hulled, seagoing, rescue tug *ATR–109*, the third *Unadilla* was reclassified an auxiliary ocean tug and redesignated ATA–182 on 15 May 1944; laid down on 30 June 1944 at Orange, Tex., by the Levingston Shipbuilding Co.; launched on 5 August 1944; and commissioned on 16 October 1944.

Following shakedown training out of Norfolk, Va., *ATA–182* transited the Panama Canal and then supported fleet operations in the Pacific through the cessation of hostilities with Japan and into 1946. During this period, she operated at Ulithi, Eniwetok, and Leyte, primarily towing floating drydocks. Returning to the west coast late in 1946, *ATA–182* was decommissioned on 26 November 1946 at Portland, Oreg., and placed in reserve there.

After being named *Unadilla* on 16 June 1948, she retained her hull number designation ATA–182. The ship was recommissioned at Astoria, Oreg., on 3 May 1951. She moved south and conducted refresher training out of San Diego, Calif., into the winter. Proceeding to Seattle, Wash., on 3 January 1952, she arrived there on the 8th and picked up three YFN's for towing to the Hawaiian Islands. Departing on 11 January, *Unadilla* and her three unwieldy charges labored through heavy seas in a 17-day passage to Pearl Harbor. During the voyage, one YFN broke loose but was soon recovered.

Deploying to the Western Pacific (WestPac), *Unadilla* proceeded via Guam to Japan and arrived at Sasebo on 17 March. The tug towed targets until late August for fleet units conducting underway training exercises off the southern coast of Honshu. During this deployment, the ocean-going tug was twice employed in Korean waters: on the first occasion, she put into Cheju Do to escort a damaged LST back to Sasebo; and, on the second, *Unadilla* carried a medical unit to Ullong Do to combat a typhus epidemic. The medical mission resulted in the ship's receiving the Korean Presidential Unit Citation.

Departing WestPac on 21 August, *Unadilla* arrived at San Diego on 6 September, via Parl Harbor. The ship towed targets off the coast of southern California through February 1953; towed *YFR–888* from Panama to Long Beach from 3 to 16 March; and deployed to WestPac again in the late summer of that year. She arrived at Sasebo on 5 September, via Pearl Harbor and Midway.

Unadilla spent her second WestPac deployment much like the first, towing targets for exercising units of the 7th Fleet off the southern coast of Japan from September 1953 to March 1954. Escorting *Gypsy* (ARSD–from Kwajalein to Pearl Harbor while en route the west coast, the tug arrived at San Diego on April. She conducted local operations from May August, towing targets for the Fleet Training Gro at San Diego. Following a regular yard overhaul a an inspection period, *Unadilla* resumed these operatio in January 1955.

Unadilla subsequently sailed for the Pacific Nort west and arrived at Astoria, Oreg., on 29 April 195 Placed in reserve on that date, the ocean-going t prepared for deactivation. Decommissioned and plac in reserve on 22 July, she lay in reserve at Portla until struck from the Navy list on 1 September 196 Shifted to the Maritime Administration (MARA lay-up facility at Olympia, Wash., the erstwhi ocean-going tug was towed to the MARAD facility Suisun Bay, Calif., in 1971. She was disposed of som time between 1972 and 1975.

Unadilla received two battle stars for her Kore War service.

Unalga

(RC: dp. 1,181 (n.); lbp. 190'; b. 32'6''; dr. 14'1 (aft); s. 13 k.; cpl. 70; a. 3 6-pdrs.; cl. *Unalga*)

Unalga—a Coast Guard cutter built by the Newpo News Shipbuilding & Drydock Co.—was launched 10 February 1912; sponsored by Miss Elizabeth Hille and commissioned by the Revenue Cutter Service (RC at its depot at Arundel Cove, Md., on 23 May 1912.

Unalga spent the summer of 1912 fitting out. June, she received her guns at Washington, D.C., a

The Coast Guard cutter *Unalga*. (26–G–10–23–40(01))

mpleted installing them at Baltimore in July and ugust. On 6 September, she received orders to report the Commander, Northern Division, Pacific Coast, CS, at Port Townsend, Wash.

She departed Baltimore that day and, after stops at ewport News and Norfolk, she headed out into the tlantic. She reached the Straits of Gibraltar on 11 ctober and, three days later, continued on toward aples, Italy, where she arrived on the 19th. She got nderway again on the 25th; stopped at Malta from 5 to 29 October; and arrived at Port Said, Egypt, e northern terminus of the Suez Canal, on 1 November.

While *Unalga* made her way from port to port eastard across the Mediterranean, Bulgaria, Serbia, reece, and Montenegro took advantage of the Italourkish War in Libya to form the Balkan League and escend upon the embattled Ottoman Empire. Greek nd Serbian armies invaded European Turkey in an ffort to liberate Ottoman possessions populated by neir kinspeople. While the Greeks and Serbs moved to Macedonia, three Bulgarian armies drove heading into Thrace, invested Adrianople, and defeated urkish armies at the battles of Kirk Kilissa and ule Burgas. The success of that drive alarmed the reign community in Constantinople lest the capital all to the invader with all the murder and mayhem ttendant upon a Balkan war.

To protect Americans and other foreigners in Turkey n the event that Constantinople should fall, the United tates Ambassador, Mr. Rockhill, asked that warships e sent to the Levant. In response to this request, the Javy Department dispatched *Brutus* and planned to end two other warships. The Treasury Department rdered *Unalga* to remain at Port Said and place herelf under the orders of Ambassador Rockhill should eed for her services arise. During the six weeks she tayed at Port Said, the tempo of hostilities decreased n Thrace because the Bulgars failed to breach the Chatalja Line held by the Turks athwart the road to Constantinople. On 3 December, the Turks and Bulgars oncluded a preliminary armistice preparatory to the eace conference which began in London in late December. On 17 December, the same day the conference egan, *Unalga* departed Port Said to transit the Suez Canal and continue her interrupted voyage to the west oast of North America.

After stops at Aden, Ceylon, Singapore, Manila, okohama, Japan, and Honolulu, the cutter arrived at 'ort Townsend on 22 March 1913. Five days after eporting to the Commander, Northern Division, vas reassigned to the Bering Sea Fleet. On 3 May, he departed Port Townsend for her first cruise to Alaskan waters. During that assignment, she visited Kodiak and Unalaska before returning to Port Townsnd on 11 August. On 3 October, *Unalga* was reasigned to the Southern Division and, on the 21st, got underway for San Francisco, where she arrived four days later. The cutter served with the Southern Division until detached on 25 March 1914. After spending he first 20 days of April at Oakland, Calif., undergoing epairs, she headed back to Alaska and duty in the Bering Sea.

For the next three years, the cutter alternated between assignments with the Northern Division and the Bering Sea Fleet. After World War I broke out in Europe on 1 August 1914, she took on the added esponsibility of enforcing America's neutrality laws. In February 1915, she also started patrols to enforce he provisions of the 1911 convention between the United States, Great Britain, Japan, and Russia for he protection of fur seals. Those two responsibilities, as well as her normal duties, took her to a number of Alaskan ports such as Seward, Juneau, and Skagway in addition to Unalaska and to such places as Cook's Inlet, Slime Banks, the Pribilofs, and St. Matthew's Island.

When the United States entered World War I on 6 April 1917, President Woodrow Wilson issued an Executive Order which placed the Coast Guard under the jurisdiction of the Navy Department for the duration of hostilities; and *Unalga* joined the Navy. Though assigned to the seagoing fighting service, she continued to discharge her former duties. She made a cruise a year to the Alaska-Bering Sea area during the summer months of 1917, 1918, and 1919. On each cruise, she transported mail and supplies to fishermen and natives in inaccessible areas, provided medical assistance where needed, and aided vessels in distress. During the 1918 cruise, she also participated in the settlement of a labor dispute that arose in several canneries. In addition to the routine described above, she continued patrols in support of the fur seal protection convention. Since the nation was at war, *Unalga* also kept a vigilant watch for enemy ships, but the slight probability of the appearance of a German, Austro-Hungarian, or Turkish ship in the northern Pacific allowed her to concentrate on her peacetime mission. In all probability, *Unalga* never fired her guns in anger during her first hitch with the Navy.

The hostilities ended with the armistice of 11 November 1918, but the Coast Guard continued under Navy jurisdiction for another nine months. On 28 August 1919, the Treasury Department resumed control. On that day, the names of all Coast Guard ships which had served the Navy were struck from the Navy list. *Unalga* hardly noticed the change, however, because she continued her Bering Sea cruises and Northern Division assignments just as before. The cutter cruised the Alaskan and northern Pacific coasts, making calls at familiar ports through the 1920's. At the conclusion of her summer cruise to the Bering Sea in 1930, she departed Port Townsend to return to the east coast for the first time in 18 years. On 5 September, she arrived at an unspecified depot (probably the one at Arundel Cove, Md.). In any case, she was placed out of commission there on 16 February 1931 and, two days later, moved to Philadelphia for extensive repairs. She departed the navy yard on 27 June 1931 to return to the depot, probably for additional work since she was not placed back in commission until 23 April 1932.

On 14 May, she headed south for duty at Port Everglades, Fla., where she arrived on the 24th. She served at that port and at Fort Lauderdale until sometime in 1934. In September of 1933, the cutter served briefly with the Navy again when she was called upon to patrol the waters of the Florida Strait during the series of revolts in Cuba which finally resulted in the beginning of Fulgencio Batista's 25-year dictatorship. On 1 November, she was released from that duty and, the next day, was ordered to report to the Commander, Southern Area (USCG) for further orders. She resumed normal operations from the Coast Guard station at Port Everglades until sometime in 1935 when she was transferred to San Juan, Puerto Rico.

Unalga served at San Juan for most of her remaining active career. On 1 November 1941, President Franklin D. Roosevelt transferred the Coast Guard to the jurisdiction of the Navy Department; and *Unalga* rejoined the Navy. Classified as WPG–53 sometime in 1942, she spent the entire war operating out of San Juan, conducting antisubmarine patrols under the auspices of the Commandant, 10th Naval District. The paucity of information on her World War II service suggests that she never encountered the enemy. Sometime in 1945, the cutter was reassigned to the 5th Naval District, operating in and around Norfolk. Subsequently decommissioned and turned over to the War Shipping Administration, *Unalga* was sold in July 1946.

Uncas

A Mohican chief—the son of Owenoco—was born in or near 1588. In 1626, he married the daughter of Sassacus, chief of the Pequots, and thus became a chief of the Pequot tribe. When a rebellion against Sassacus lead to his banishment, Uncas fled to the Narragansett tribe; but he subsequently made peace with the Pequots and returned. In 1637, he joined the English in a war against the Pequots, receiving a portion of captured Pequot land. This conduct earned him the enmity of the Pequots, Narragansetts, and other Indian tribes. In 1643, Uncas defeated the powerful Narragansett chief Miantonomo and executed him at the behest of the English colonists. In 1648 the Mohawks, Pocomtocks, and other Indian tribes made war on Uncas but failed to defeat him. Besieged by the Narragansett chief Pessacus, he was saved by Ensign Thomas Leffingwell. In gratitude, it is said that Uncas gave the Englishman all the land on the site of present-day Norwich, Conn. During his life, he allied with the English in all the wars waged against the Indians, ending with King Philip's War in 1675. Uncas died in 1682 or 1683.

I

(ScStr.: t. 192; l. 118'6''; b. 23'4''; dph. 7'6''; s. 11.5 k.; a. 1 20-pdr. P.r., 2 32-pdrs.)

Uncas—a screw steamer built at New York City in 1843—was purchased by the Navy there on 20 September 1861 from Dudley Buck for use with the Coast Survey. She was refitted at the New York Navy Yard from September 1861 to February 1862 and placed in service early in March, Acting Master Lemuel G. Crane commanding.

However, before *Uncas* could begin her duties for the Coast Survey, the Confederate ironclad ram *Virginia* attacked the Union warships blockading Hampton Roads, sinking frigates *Cumberland* and *Congress* and endangering their consorts. As a result of the havoc created by the resurrected *Merrimack*, *Uncas* was sent to Hampton Roads to strengthen the Union naval forces still afloat there. She had arrived in that strategic roadstead by 14 March and, three days later, was officially transferred to the Navy and assigned to the North Atlantic Blockading Squadron. Unfortunately, by that time, *Uncas'* brief service had revealed serious deficiencies in the ship; and she was ordered to Baltimore for repairs. While she was being readied for action, the Navy again changed its plans for the vessel and sent her to the western part of the Gulf of Mexico where Flag Officer Farragut was preparing

for his daring attack on New Orleans. On 10 Apr the steamer entered the Mississippi where she w needed to help locate positions for Commander David Porter's mortar boats during his impending bombar ment of Forts St. Philip and Jackson. Farragut planne to use her as a gunboat in the Mississippi Sound. How ever, her machinery broke down again almost immed ately, and the ship returned north for further repai before beginning either task.

The deficiencies were quickly corrected; and, on th 26th, the ship was steaming to Port Royal, S.C., join Flag Officer Samuel F. Du Pont's South Atlant Blockading Squadron—when she captured the schoone *Belle* 30 miles northwest of Charleston, S.C. The *Bel* was operating out of Nassau, New Providence, an purportedly bound for Philadelphia with a cargo of salt, pepper, and soap. *Uncas* remained only briefly a Port Royal, being assigned on 29 April 1862 to th blockade of St. Simon's Sound, Ga., and all inlan waters extending from St. Catherine's to St. Andrew Sounds.

Uncas next received orders to Florida, arriving i the St. John's River on 11 June 1862. *Uncas* first sa action on 1 September 1862 when she and *Patroo* engaged a company of Confederates at St. John's an Yellow Bluffs. Scattered incidents following this initi clash led to a major encounter with Southern batterie at St. John's Bluff on 11 September 1862. The engage ment lasted four hours and 20 minutes. During th action, *Uncas* fired 143 shells and 13 solid shot whil *Patroon* expended 60 shells. *Uncas* suffered consider able damage to her upperworks but weathered the fir and forced the defending Confederates to abandor temporarily, the fort. The ship and officers drew prais from Flag Officer Du Pont for their conduct. *Uncas* an *Patroon* fought a second, minor battle at the bluffs o 2 October 1862. *Uncas* continued patrol and reconnais sance work on the river through the winter and int the spring of 1863. On 10 March 1863, in company wit *Norwich*, *Uncas* escorted Army transports up the St John's River with troops who landed and occupie Jacksonville, Fla.

On 10 June 1863, Flag Officer Du Pont ordered *Unca* to Port Royal for repairs. The vessel's deteriorate condition upon arrival prompted further orders o 4 July 1863 directing *Uncas* to proceed to the New Yor Navy Yard. *Uncas* was stricken and sold at publi auction at the New York Navy Yard on 21 Augus

GENL. BURNSIDE'S EXPEDITION.

The steamer *Uncas*, with steam sloop *Tuscarora* and gunboat *Winona*, escort Army transports on their way to cap ture Roanoke Island and cut Albemarle Sound off from the sea early in 1862. (NR&L(O) 20062)

1863. She was redocumented as *Claymont* on 20 November 1863 and remained in merchant service until abandoned in 1886.

II

(ScTug: dp. 441; l. 119'8''; b. 25'; dr. 12' (mean); s. 12 k.; cpl. 15; a. 1 1-pdr., G.g.)

The second *Uncas*—built as *Walter A. Luckenbach* in 1893 by John H. Dialogue and Sons, of Camden, N.J., for the Luckenbach and Co. shipping firm, of New York, N.Y.—was acquired by the Navy on 2 April 1898 for Spanish-American War service as an ocean-going tug; was renamed *Uncas* and commissioned on 6 April 1898, Lt. Frederick R. Brainard in command.

Assigned to the North Atlantic Fleet, *Uncas* operated on blockade duty off Matanzas on the north coast of Cuba. On 3 May 1898, *Uncas*, in company with *Hudson*, captured the Havana-bound Spanish sailing vessel *Antonio Suarez*. On 13 July, again in company with *Hudson*, the tug overtook two sloops. Together, *Hudson* and *Uncas* captured one sloop—*Bella Yuiz*, a Spanish vessel bound for Havana—and sank the other, taking two prisoners.

After the conclusion of hostilities, *Uncas* underwent repairs at the Philadelphia Navy Yard before she sailed south for the Caribbean, via Port Royal, S.C. In the fall of 1899, *Uncas* inspected lighthouse facilities in the Danish West Indies and at Puerto Rico before she served a brief tour towing Army Quartermaster Corps barges. She then resumed lighthouse inspection and harbor survey duties in the Puerto Rican area and, during this tour, carried a selection board to Culebra Island to seek out a site for a target range.

While engaged in local operations in Puerto Rican waters into the late winter of 1901, *Uncas* assisted *Mayflower* off a shoal near San Juan on 15 March 1901. She subsequently carried Army passengers and towed targets for Army Coast Artillery units at San Juan into mid-1901. Sandwiched in between her routine operations, *Uncas* towed the disabled merchantman SS *Longfellow* from Arecibo, Puerto Rico, to San Juan, for repairs, on 14 November 1901.

Operating as a tender for the North Atlantic Fleet, *Uncas* continued her Caribbean-based operations, carrying dispatches, mail, and provisions and serving again on lighthouse inspection duties into 1902. She carried an inspection and survey team to look over land on Culebra for a possible coaling station site from 26 to 28 June 1903 before she headed north for temporary duty at the Norfolk Navy Yard.

Returning to the Caribbean soon thereafter, *Uncas* operated out of San Juan for the first half of the year 1904 before she returned to the Norfolk Navy Yard for repairs. The tug subsequently received assignment to Guantanamo Bay and operated out of that port on "special" and "general" service with the Fleet until she was assigned to the Norfolk Navy Yard in late 1915.

On 7 June 1916, while operating at the Washington Navy Yard, *Uncas*—by then designated Ocean Tug No. 51—was inspected and adjudged to be no longer satisfactory for service off the Atlantic coast.

As a result, she conducted only local operations out of Washington through the end of World War I. *Uncas* was redesignated as a yard tug—YT–110—on 10 June 1921. Decommissioned at Washington on 6 March 1922, she was struck from the Navy list on 14 March and put up for sale. Purchased by the Wood Towing Corp., of Norfolk, Va., on 25 July 1922, the tug then entered mercantile service and operated out of the Norfolk area.

III

(MB: t. 13; l. 60'; b. 10'; dr. 2' (mean); s. 20 k.; cpl. 8; a. 1 .30-cal. mg.)

The third *Uncas*—a wooden-hulled motorboat built in 1917 by the Greenport Basin and Construction Co., of Greenport, Long Island, N.Y.—was acquired by the Navy from Charles L. Poor, of New York City, on 28 June 1917, for use during World War I as a section patrol boat. Assigned to the 3d Naval District and given the designation SP–689, the motorboat—operating without a name since a tug named *Uncas* was already on the Navy list—conducted local patrol operations out of Section Base No. 6 at Bath Beach, N.Y., for the duration of the war. She was returned to her owner on 31 December 1918.

IV

(YT–242: l. 100'; b. 25'; dr. 10'; s. 12 k.)

The fourth *Uncas* (YT–242)—formerly *Susan Moran* and *Southwind*—was built at Orange, Tex., by the Levingston Shipbuilding Co. and acquired by the Navy on 21 March 1942. She operated actively as part of the Service Force, Atlantic Fleet, for the duration of World War II. Her most memorable service came in early November 1942 when she helped to defend Convoy SC–107 as it steamed through the U-boat-infested North Atlantic from Halifax, Nova Scotia, to the United Kingdom. *Uncas* was placed in inactive status at Boston in March 1946. She was struck from the Navy list in January 1947 and sold to private ownership on 16 May 1947.

Uncas received one battle star for her World War II service.

Undaunted

I

(Tug: dp. 450 (est.); l. 143'0''; b. 28'0''; dr. 17'0'' (aft); s. 11.5 k. (tl.); cpl. 29; a. 1 3'', 2 mg.)

The first *Undaunted* (SP–1950)—a tug built in 1917 at San Francisco, Calif., by the Union Iron Works—was acquired by the Navy from the Rolph Navigation & Coal Co. on 14 November 1917 at San Francisco; fitted out as a tug at the Mare Island Navy Yard; and commissioned on 5 February 1918.

Soon after commissioning, *Undaunted* departed San Francisco bound for the coast of France. She operated as a tug in support of United States naval forces in Europe through the end of World War I in November 1918.

Sometime in the first half of 1919, she returned to San Francisco as a unit of the Pacific Fleet Train, the name then applied to what the Navy now calls the Service Force. While serving the Pacific Fleet, she received the designation AT–58 in July 1920 when the Navy adopted its alphanumeric system of hull designations. Later, on 27 February 1936, she became a harbor tug and was designated YT–125. At that time, her commissioned status was probably downgraded to "in service." By 1938, she was assigned to the 12th Naval District; and she remained based at San Francisco.

On 1 May 1939, *Undaunted* was placed back in full commission. However, that change endured only briefly; for, on 30 June, she reverted to her former "in service" status. In all likelihood, it was sometime during the two-month period she spent in full commission that *Undaunted* made the voyage from San Francisco to her new duty station on the east coast. By 28 May 1939, her home yard had been changed to Norfolk, Va.; and it is reasonable to assume that she arrived in the Hampton Roads area about that time. On 16 July 1940, the vessel once again became an ocean tug and resumed her former designation, AT–58. On 1 August, she was placed back in full commission at Norfolk; and records indicate that, by early October, she was assigned to the 5th Naval District on special duty but with her home port at Washington, D.C.

The tug *Undaunted* (AT–58).

For the next five years, she plied the waters of the Potomac River and the Chesapeake Bay, towing ships and other craft between Norfolk, Baltimore, and Washington as well as to and from ports between the three places. On 15 May 1944, a mass redesignation of tugs occurred, and *Undaunted* was reclassified an old ocean tug with the designation ATO–58. The tug was decommissioned for the last time on 1 July 1946 at the Norfolk Naval Shipyard. Her name was struck from the Navy list on 25 September 1946, and she was delivered to the Maritime Commission for disposal on 19 March 1947.

II

(ATR–126: dp. 835 (tl.); l. 143'0''; b. 33'10''; dr. 13'2''; s. 13 k.; cpl. 45; a. 1 3'', 2 20mm.; cl. *ATA–170*)

The second *Undaunted* was laid down as rescue tug *ATR–126* on 27 November 1943 at Port Arthur, Tex., by the Gulfport Boiler and Welding Works; reclassified auxiliary ocean tug *ATA–199* on 15 May 1944; launched on 22 August 1944; and commissioned on 20 October 1944, Lt. Guy S. Flanagan, Jr., USNR, in command.

Following shakedown out of Galveston, *ATA–199* paused briefly at New Orleans on 18 November, then put to sea the same day to rendezvous with a convoy bound for the Panama Canal with sections of an advance base dock *ABSD–5* in tow. *ATA–199* acted as retriever tug for the convoy and, on the 22d, took over a tow from a tug which had broken down. Arriving at the Canal Zone on the 29th, she spent over two weeks as a member of Service Squadron 2, pulling various units through the locks. On the 21st, she departed the Canal Zone again acting as the retriever tug for a Philippine-bound convoy, steamed via the Marshalls and Carolines, and arrived at Leyte on 24 February 1945.

She operated in Leyte Gulf until 23 March when she departed San Pedro Bay towing fleet ocean tug *Serrano* (ATF–112). She arrived at Ulithi four days later and joined Service Squadron 10. In the months that followed she operated in the Philippines, Marianas, Carolines, Solomons, and Admiralties towing vessels that varied from lighters to wrecking derricks. In June and July, she towed pontoon barges from the Russell Islands to Okinawa; then on the morning of 29 July, she departed Buckner Bay and headed for the west coast, with the battered destroyer, *Hugh W. Hadley* (DD–774), in tow. During her homeward voyage—as she proceeded via Saipan, Eniwetok, and Pearl Harbor—Japan capitulated. The tug weathered a typhoon before reaching San Francisco on 26 September, at the end of a tow of nearly 7,000 miles.

Exactly one month later, she got underway again and returned to Pearl Harbor early in November. *ATA–199* operated out of Oahu until 11 April 1946, when she departed Pearl Harbor, with a section of *ABSD–7* in tow, and proceeded—via west coast ports and the

Panama Canal—to Norfolk where she delivered her tow on 21 July. She remained there until 24 August when she set her course via Panama City, Fla., and, on 7 September, arrived at New Orleans. Operating from that base, she conducted tows between various gulf ports until 24 June 1947 when she arrived at Beaumont, Tex., for inactivation overhaul.

On 25 August 1947, she proceeded to Orange, Tex., where she was decommissioned the same day and assigned to the Texas Group, Atlantic Reserve Fleet. The tug was named *Undaunted* on 16 July 1948 and transferred to the custody of the Maritime Administration—although still owned by the Navy—in September 1961. By January 1963, her name was struck from the Navy list. She was later transferred to the Bureau of Commercial Fisheries.

Underhill

Samuel Jackson Underhill—born on 25 August 1917 at Jericho, N.Y.—received a bachelor of science from Yale University and attended Harvard Law School before enlisting in the Naval Reserve as a seaman 2d class on 8 November 1940. After serving briefly at Floyd Bennett Field, Brooklyn, N.Y., Underhill was appointed an aviation cadet and was transferred on 6 February 1941 to the Naval Air Station, Jacksonville, Fla., for flight training. He subsequently underwent further training at Miami; was designated a naval aviator on 15 July; and was commissioned an ensign in the Naval Reserve on 6 August. Following advanced flight training at Norfolk, he reported to Scouting Squadron 5 (VS-5).

In May 1942, when Rear Admiral Frank Jack Fletcher's Task Force 17 steamed in the Coral Sea seeking to foil Japan's attempt to extend her influence southward, Underhill was with VS-5 on board carrier *Yorktown* (CV-5). He flew his Dauntless dive-bomber when VS-5 raided Tulagi on the morning of 4 May. On the morning of the 7th, a coordinated attack group of 17 SBD's from VS-5 took off from *Yorktown* and, in clear skies with unlimited visibility, launched a dive bombing attack on Japanese light carrier *Shoho*. The American planes scored nine direct hits and two near misses that sent the hapless enemy flattop to the bottom.

On the 8th, the two naval forces at last found one another and the stage was set for the first great naval action between aircraft carriers, the Battle of the Coral Sea. On the morning of 8 May, *Yorktown* launched the SBD's of VS-5, dividing the group to accomplish separate missions. One division joined in the attack on Japanese carrier *Shokaku* and, diving from 17,000 feet through broken cloud cover, dropped bombs which bent the enemy carrier's deck sufficiently to prevent the launching of her aircraft. As the bombers pulled out, Japanese fighter planes swarmed out to repel them but were fought off by the Americans.

Later that morning, dive bombers of VS-5 conducted anti-torpedo plane patrol around *Yorktown*'s formation. Pressed into service due to the lack of fighters, the slower Dauntless dive-bombers were at a disadvantage with the Japanese attackers. At 1110, eight of the American bombers intercepted and engaged a group of about 17 Japanese fighter planes, shot down six of the enemy and damaged seven more. When the fierce action was over, Ensign Underhill was numbered among those lost in the fight to protect the carrier. He was posthumously awarded the Navy Cross for his extraordinary heroism.

(DE–682: dp. 1,400; l. 306'0"; b. 37'; dr. 13'6"; s. 24 k.; cpl. 213; a. 3 3", 10 20mm., 4 40mm., 4 1.1", 2 dct., 8 dcp., 1 dcp. (hh.); cl. *Buckley*)

Underhill (DE–682) was laid down on 16 September 1943 at Quincy, Mass., by the Bethlehem Steel Company's Fore River Shipyard; launched on 15 October 1943; sponsored by Mrs. Bertha Underhill, aunt of Ensign Underhill; and commissioned on 15 November 1943, Lt. Comdr. Sidney R. Jackson, USNR, in command.

Following shakedown out of Bermuda, the new destroyer escort got underway from Boston on 17 January 1944; arrived at Guantanamo on the 22d; and reported to Commander, Caribbean Sea Frontier, for duty. She operated out of Trinidad and Guantanamo escorting convoys until late in May when she escorted SS *George Washington* from Kingston, Jamaica, to Miami.

Following repairs and alterations at Boston and training exercises in Casco Bay, Maine, *Underhill* got underway before dawn on Independence Day and steamed from Hampton Roads to screen UGS 47, a large, slow convoy bound for Mediterranean ports. *Underhill* conducted battle drills and investigated sonar contacts during the long, uneventful Atlantic voyage. In the Mediterranean on the 21st and 22d, she responded to several air raid warnings, but no enemy action materialized, although the last three convoys to pass along this route had been attacked by German planes. As she entered the inner harbor at Bizerte on the 24th, the destroyer escort struck a submerged object, which badly damaged her port propeller and shaft, and prompted her to head for Oran the following day. After arriving at that port on 27 July, she underwent temporary repairs; then, on 5 August, departed North Africa. Early on the 6th, she joined the escort of Convoy GUS 47, with which she arrived safely at New York on 18 August. Six days later, Lt. Comdr. Robert M. Newcomb relieved Lt. Comdr. Jackson as commanding officer of the destroyer escort.

During the remainder of 1944, *Underhill* continued Atlantic convoy escort duties. In September, she conducted UGS 54 to Plymouth, England, and, late in October, returned with a group of tank landing ships. She escorted Convoy UGS 60 from Boston to Mers el-Kebir in November; then engaged in antisubmarine warfare exercises out of Oran with French submarine *Doris*. She departed that Algerian port on 3 December escorting GUS 60 and reached New York on the 21st.

She left New York on 9 January 1945 for a temporary assignment with Submarine Forces, Atlantic. Operating out of New London, she served as a training and escort ship for submarines; took part in exercises in Block Island Sound and Long Island Sound; and trained intensively in antisubmarine warfare.

On 8 February, she departed from New London and rendezvoused with HMS *Patroller* to escort the British escort carrier to the Canal Zone. *Underhill* then steamed—via the Panama Canal, the Galapagos, and Bora Bora—to the Admiralties and arrived at Seeadler Harbor on 15 March 1945.

During the next three months, she escorted convoys among the Philippines, the Admiralties, and ports on the coast of New Guinea. In mid-July, she arrived at Okinawa for eight days of antisubmarine patrol duty in nearby waters. On the 22d, she departed the Ryukyus as the largest and lead ship in the screen for a convoy of seven tank landing ships and a merchant ship carrying the battle-weary soldiers of the 96th Division to Leyte.

On the morning of 24 July, the discovery of a distant Japanese plane alerted the convoy. However, the snooper never approached closer than 10 miles and, within half an hour, disappeared from view. Subsequent events suggested that this plane had been gathering information on the convoy and reporting the data to nearby submarines.

Early that afternoon, *Underhill* made sound contact with an unidentified object whose lack of movement seemed to indicate that it was not a submarine. Moments later, her lookouts sighted a mine directly in the path of the convoy only 25 yards away, and Lt. Comdr. Newcomb quickly warned his charges to change course to avoid it. As the convoy steamed clear of the lethal object, the destroyer escort attempted to sink the mine by gunfire; but, despite direct hits, the mine neither exploded nor sank.

Meanwhile, the sonar contact had begun to look more promising, and Newcomb ordered submarine chaser *PC–804* to investigate. The PC dropped depth charges which brought a submarine to periscope depth. On board *Underhill*, the word went out to "stand by to ram," but, when the submarine went deep, the order was changed to "prepare for depth charge attack." The concussion of the exploding depth charges shook the ship; and dark, oily, debris-filled water bubbled to the surface where the submarine had been.

Almost immediately, lookouts sighted the periscopes of two more submarines on collision courses with the ship. Again the word was passed to stand by to ram. Throughout the ship, men braced themselves for the expected collision. Then, two jolts shook the ship. Almost immediately, they were followed by two violent explosions, caused by one, or perhaps two, *kaiten*— Japanese midget suicide submarines. The explosions, which severed the ship in two at the forward fire room, flung a tremendous quantity of oily water over the still floating aft section of the unlucky *Underhill*, knocking down men and washing some overboard, but also dousing possible fires in that portion of the ship. Guns mounted forward were blown aft, and it soon became apparent that the bridge and mast had been blown off. Soon, survivors on the floating after section of the ship began to realize the extent of the damage.

Although hampered in their rescue efforts by the necessity to pursue sound contacts and by alarms over real and imagined periscope sightings, *PC–803* and *PC–804* quickly came to the aid of survivors in the water and on the slowly sinking aft section. On board *Underhill*, the wounded were brought to the boat and main decks. The survivors displayed fine training and discipline as they calmly and efficiently went about their individual tasks—aiding the injured and attempting to control the damage. Of the 238 men on board *Underhill* when she struck the midget submarines, only 125 survived. Among the dead was her commanding officer, Lt. Comdr. Robert M. Newcomb, who had been with the ship since her commissioning.

Shortly after 1800, the last of the survivors was removed from the floating section which had been listing to port and slowly sinking. The hulk was then sunk by 3-inch and 40-millimeter fire from the patrol craft.

Underhill's name was struck from the Navy list on 1 September 1945.

Underwriter

I

(SwGbt: t. 341; l. 170'; b. 23'7''; dr. 8'1''; a. 1 80-pdr. r., 1 8'' sb.)

The first *Underwriter*—a side-wheel steamer built in 1852 at Brooklyn, N.Y.—was purchased by the Navy at New York on 23 August 1861; and commissioned there on 22 August, Lt. James M. Prichett in command.

Assigned to the Potomac Flotilla, *Underwriter* arrived in the Potomac River off Aquia Creek, Va., ill-prepared for active duty, and proceeded to the Washington Navy Yard on 28 August for extensive repairs and alterations. While laid up, she was transferred to the North Atlantic Blockading Squadron. The vessel sailed for Hampton Roads, Va., on 3 October and joined the blockade off Hatteras Inlet, N.C., on 9 October.

Underwriter, *General Putnam*, and *Ceres* left Hatteras Inlet on 14 November and proceeded southwest to Ocracoke Inlet. There, they scuttled three stone-filled hulks, effectively closing the inlet to Confederate shipping. The three vessels also participated in the capture of Confederate works on Roanoke Island, N.C., on 7 and 8 February 1862, and saw action during the capture of Elizabeth City on 10 February.

On 13 February, *Underwriter*, *Lockwood*, *Shawsheen*, and *Whitehead* proceeded up the North River, N.C., and placed obstructions at the mouth of the Albemarle and Chesapeake Canal. *Underwriter* also assisted in the capture of New Berne, N.C., on 13 and 14 March, knocking out a Confederate battery along the Neuse River during the attack. After additional support duties in both Pamlico and Albemarle Sounds, the vessel returned to Baltimore on 1 June for repairs.

Underwriter left Baltimore in late July 1862 and returned to New Berne. She remained in the Neuse River off New Berne performing various reconnaissance and dispatch assignments—occasionally moving to different points in the North Carolina sounds. *Underwriter* sailed to Plymouth, N.C., in August and towed the prize schooner *Young Rover* to New Berne on 13 August. She was ordered to report to Plymouth for reconnaissance duty on 4 December and sailed from there to Hatteras Inlet on 17 December. On 4 January 1863, she sailed down the Chowan River 15 miles beyond Winfield, N.C., and destroyed Confederate supplies.

Underwriter evacuated Union forces from Winfield during the siege and threatened capture of Plymouth in April. She was stationed in Albemarle Sound later that month and returned to Plymouth in May. *Underwriter* stood down the Neuse River in June and was ordered to report to the blockade off Hatteras Inlet on 16 December. She returned to New Berne on 10 January 1864.

While lying at anchor off New Berne, *Underwriter* was captured by a Confederate boat crew early on the morning of 2 February. The Southerners were led by Commander John Taylor Wood, grandson of President Zachary Taylor and nephew of President Jefferson Davis. Wood and his ment caught *Underwriter* by surprise and took her in hand-to-hand combat, killing Acting Master Jacob Westervelt and capturing most of the vessel's officers and crew. The gunboat did not have steam up, forcing the Confederates to burn her as they were under heavy fire from surrounding Union batteries. *Underwriter* burned to the waters' edge. However, her boilers and engines survived relatively unscathed and were later salvaged.

II

(ScTug: t. 170; l. 121'; b. 22'; dr. 9'3'' (mean); s. 13 k.; cpl. 22)

The second *Underwriter*—an iron-hulled screw tug built in 1880 and 1881 at Camden, N.J., by John H. Dialogue and rebuilt in 1903—was taken over by the Navy at New Orleans, La., from the Pilot's Association of New Orleans on 1 July 1918 and assigned the identification SP–1390. Commissioned on 9 August, with Boatswain Joseph W. Elfert, USNRF, in command, *Underwriter* was formally purchased by the Navy on 1 September.

The ship operated on minesweeping duties off the mouth of the Mississippi River for the duration of World War I. Retained for service after the armistice, *Underwriter* was used on salvage duties and in training Naval Reserve seamen in minesweeping through 1919.

Underwriter was classified YT–44 on 17 July 1920 and was renamed *Adirondack* on 15 October 1920. The ship remained in the 8th Naval District on local harbor tug operations and towed vessels between New Orleans and Pensacola, Fla., through 1921. *Adirondack* was decommissioned on 1 March 1922 and was sold to B. Mitchell of New Orleans on 6 June of the same year.

Undine

A mythical female water nymph capable of acquiring a soul through marriage with a mortal.

I

(StwGbt: dp. 179)

The first *Undine*—a steamer built in 1863 at Cincinnati, Ohio, as *Ben Gaylord*—was purchased by the

Navy at Cincinnati on 7 March 1864 and commissioned there in April.

Undine joined the Mississippi Squadron and, in May 1864, was deployed in the Mississippi River between Fort Adams and Natchez, Miss. She soon left the Mississippi and operated during early July in the Tennessee River in support of Union forces ashore. While standing off Clifton, Tenn., *Undine*, Acting Master John L. Bryant in command, struck a snag and partially sank on 25 July. Her crew was able to transfer the ship's guns ashore to defend Clifton from Confederate attack before taking measures to raise the vessel. *Undine* was successfully refloated on 1 August after the arrival of the pump steamer *Little Champion* on 31 July.

Undine, *Key West*, and transports *City of Pekin*, *Kenton*, and *Aurora* left Clifton on 9 October on an expedition to capture Eastport, Miss. This operation was launched to prevent cavalry forces under Confederate General Nathan Bedford Forrest from crossing the Tennessee River at Eastport and to provide an outpost against an expected advance of General Hood. However, the Union force was ambushed by shore batteries on 10 October as it landed troops near Eastport. After a heated, 30-minute exchange with the batteries, *Undine* and *Key West* evacuated troops caught ashore in the withering crossfire and escorted the disabled transports back downstream. The battered expedition returned to Paducah, Ky., at sundown on 12 October.

After repairs were completed, *Undine* resumed patrol and reconnaissance duty along the Tennessee River. On 30 October, she convoyed the transport *Anna* from Johnsonville, Tenn., to Sandy Island. While returning to Johnsonville, Acting Master Bryant heard artillery reports coming from the river below Sandy Island and ordered *Undine* turned about to investigate. Near Paris Landing, *Undine* was again ambushed. Transports *Venus* and *Cheeseman* soon joined her and engaged the Confederates. Three hours later, both transports were disabled, and *Undine* was out of ammunition and crippled by a broken engine. Bryant hauled down his flag and surrendered *Undine*, *Venus*, and *Cheeseman*. He was later exonerated by a board of inquiry.

The Confederates wasted little time putting the captured Union vessels to use. While patrolling the Tennessee River on 2 November, *Key West* and *Tarwah* engaged *Undine* and *Venus*. *Venus* was retaken, but *Undine* escaped, badly damaged, to the protection of Confederate batteries at Reynoldsburg Island. There, she was burned by the Confederates on 4 November to prevent her recapture by Union gunboats attacking the island. Her destruction came in the wake of General Nathan Bedford Forrest's unsuccessful attempt to cross the Tennessee River at Johnsonville. If the Confederate plan had succeeded, General William Tecumseh Sherman's supply line would have been exposed, and the Union Army's march through Georgia and South Carolina would have been endangered.

After the Civil War, the hulk of *Undine* was one of several in the Tennessee River ordered raised or wrecked on 20 June 1865. Two 24-pounder howitzers were recovered from the vessel later that month.

II

(Launch: l. 61'5''; b. 11'0'')

The second *Undine* was a wooden-hulled launch built in 1893 at Brooklyn, N.Y., by the New York Navy Yard. She was utilized there as the Commandant's barge from 1893 to 1910, after which time she disappears from lists of United States Navy miscellaneous craft.

Unicoi

A county and a mountain range in Tennessee. The word unicoi is derived from the Cherokee term "unaka" which means white.

(IX–216: dp. 13,150 (lim.) ; l. 416'; b. 54'0''; dr. 27'1''; cpl. 70; a. 1 4'', 1 3'', 8 20mm.)

Unicoi (IX–216) was built in 1920 at Tampa, Fla., by Oscar Daniels Co. She was owned first by the United States Shipping Board and later by the Maritime Commission. In the late thirties or early forties, she was renamed *Excelsior*; but, by 1942, she was again called *Unicoi*.

Late in the afternoon of 15 July 1942, as *Unicoi* steamed southward off Cape Lookout, N.C., with convoy King Sail 520, a German submarine struck without warning and torpedoed three merchant vessels of the formation. Moments later, the submarine surfaced in the middle of the convoy only 350 yards from *Unicoi*. The ship's alert armed guard quickly took advantage of this unusual opportunity and fired a shell, scoring a hit on the submarine. Meanwhile, the two planes which supplied the convoy's air cover approached the submarine and dropped their depth charges. One charge actually hit the submarine and slid off before detonating. In all, four depth charges at close range finished off German submarine *U–576* which left behind black oil, debris, and bubbles as she went to the bottom.

Unicoi continued on with the convoy to Key West where, on the 28th, she joined Convoy WAT–10 bound for Caribbean ports. The ship parted company with the convoy on 1 August off Guantanamo Bay and set her course via the Panama Canal to New Zealand.

Around this time, she came under the control of the War Shipping Administration and was operated by American Export Lines, Inc. She continued operations in the Pacific until 20 April 1945 when she was transferred to the United States Navy outside Tacloban in Leyte Gulf. Accepted from the War Shipping Administration on bareboat charter, *Unicoi* was commissioned on 23 April 1945.

Designated an unclassified miscellaneous auxiliary ship (IX), she reported for duty with Service Squadron 8, Service Forces, Pacific; but, due to her age and disrepair, underwent extensive overhaul at Seeadler Harbor before taking up her duties as a mobile dry storage ship early in August, shortly before Japan capitulated. On the 7th, as she entered the channel at Green Island with a cargo of provisions for the island's Construction Battalion Maintenance Unit, she went aground. After unloading her cargo, shifting ballast and discharging 65 tons of fresh water over the side, she was refloated with the assistance of two landing craft late in the afternoon. Undamaged, she proceeded via Bougainville to the Treasury Islands where she loaded nets, buoys, and other equipment for transportation to the Philippines.

She arrived at Samar on 4 September and remained in the Philippines until 6 December when she set her course via Pearl Harbor for the west coast. *Unicoi* arrived at San Francisco on 2 February 1946, was decommissioned on 16 April, and returned on the same day to the War Shipping Administration at Suisun Bay, Calif. Her name was struck from the Navy list on 1 May 1946, and she was later sold to the Walter W. Johnson Co. for scrapping.

Unicorn

The narwhal—a marine mammal which inhabits Arctic seas and is related to the whale and the porpoise—has a single tusk which often grows to nine feet in length suggesting the horn of a unicorn. Indeed, the narwhal is frequently called the sea unicorn.

The contract for the construction of *Unicorn* (SS–429)—a *Tench*-class submarine authorized on 9 July 1942 and scheduled to be built at Philadelphia, Pa., by the Cramp Shipbuilding Co.—was cancelled on 29 July 1944.

The contract for the construction of *Unicorn* (SS–436)—a *Tench*-class submarine laid down on 25 April 1945, at Groton, Conn., by the Electric Boat Co.—was terminated on 7 January 1946. However, it was reinstated on 26 February 1946 for "completion of specific items." The submarine was launched on 1 August 1946; sponsored by Mrs. William A. Rowan; and accepted by the Navy on 3 September.

Towed to the Portsmouth (N.H.) Naval Shipyard on 15 September, the boat was moved to New London two months later and assigned to the Atlantic Reserve Fleet. She remained out of commission, in reserve, until 29 July 1958, when her name was struck from the Navy list.

Unimak

A bay on the southern side of Unimak Island, Alaska, in the Aleutians.

(AVP–31: dp. 2,592; l. 310'9"; b. 41'2"; dr. 13'6"; s. 18.2 k.; cpl. 367; a. 1 5", 4 40mm., 8 20mm., 2 dcp. (mousetrap); cl. *Barnegat*)

Unimak (AVP–31) was laid down on 15 February 1942 at Harbor Island, near Seattle, Wash., by the Associated Shipbuilders, Inc.; launched on 27 May 1942; sponsored by Mrs. H. B. Berry, the wife of Capt. H. B. Berry, the personnel officer of the 13th Naval District; and commissioned on 31 December 1943, Comdr. Hilfort C. Owen in command.

Following shakedown and fitting-out into late January 1944, the small seaplane tender departed San Diego, Calif., on 20 March, bound for the Canal Zone. Arriving at Balboa eight days later, the seaplane tender operated on the Pacific coast of Central America into April, providing logistics support to advanced seaplane bases at Santa Elena Bay, Ecuador, and at Aeolian Bay, Battra Island, in the Galapagos group. She soon shifted to Coco Solo on the Caribbean side of the Canal and transported men and materiel to Barranquillas, Colombia, arriving there on 25 April.

After escorting SS *Genevieve Lykes* back to Coco Solo on 23 and 24 June, *Unimak* conducted routine exercises with patrol planes into July. On 4 July, she received reports that a tanker near her position had been torpedoed and headed for the damaged ship. When she arrived on the scene late that day, she found the tanker still underway, making for the Panama coast. She immediately commenced screening the disabled ship and, aided by an escort of Army and Navy planes, shepherded the tanker safely to Colon late on the following afternoon.

Soon thereafter, *Unimak* shaped her course towards the last reported position of Navy blimp *K–53*. At 1532 on 9 July, the seaplane tender sighted two yellow rubber rafts and the wreckage of the crashed blimp floating on the water. At 1558, *Unimak* took on board nine survivors and sank the unsalvagable blimp by collapsing the bag with 40-millimeter gunfire; the ship then landed the survivors at Portland Bight, Jamaica.

A few days later, on 12 July, *Unimak* joined with *John D. Edwards* (DD–216) in hunting for a submarine reported to be lurking nearby. Within a few days, word of a crashed plane sent the two ships speeding for the last reported position of an aircraft. *Unimak* located only wreckage and one body and buried it at sea on 16 July.

Unimak remained in the Caribbean through the autumn, tending patrol planes, conducting logistics support missions for advanced seaplane bases, and occasionally towing targets for the patrol planes training in the area. On 15 December, *Rockaway* (AVP–29) relieved *Unimak*, releasing her to steam north via Norfolk to Boston, Mass.

Arriving there at the end of December 1944, *Unimak* underwent availability at the Boston Navy Yard for the entire month of January 1945. She got underway for England on 14 February, but an engineering casualty forced the ship to return to Boston for a major propeller shaft alignment which lasted into March.

On 7 April, *Unimak* got underway for the British Isles and proceeded, via Bahia Praia in the Azores, to Bristol, on the first of two voyages to England to bring back supplies and men from decommissioned Navy patrol plane squadrons in the British Isles. On the second voyage, from 5 to 15 June, *Unimak* transported the men and materiel of Patrol Bomber Squadrons 103 and 105 from Bristol to Norfolk.

Departing Hampton Roads on 20 July, bound for the west coast, the ship transited the Panama Canal on the

The former seaplane tender *Unimak* (AVP–31), seen here in San Francisco Bay as the Coast Guard cutter *Unimak* (WAVP–379).

26th and arrived at San Diego on 3 August. She got underway for Pearl Harbor on the 12th. The seaplane tender subsequently operated in the Hawaiian chain until 7 September when she headed for the Aleutians.

She operated in northern climes—calling at Adak, Kodiak, and Attu, Alaska; and once at Petropavlovsk, Siberia—into November of 1945 before heading southward to prepare for inactivation. Subsequently reporting to Commander, 19th Fleet, in December, *Unimak* was decommissioned on 26 July 1946. She remained in reserve until transferred to the Coast Guard on 14 September 1948. She served the Coast Guard as *Unimak* (WAVP–379).

Union

I

(SwStr: t. 956; l. 184'6''; b. 33'6''; dr. 11'3''; s. 7 k.; a. 4 68-pdrs.)

The first *Union* was laid down at the Norfolk Navy Yard, Portsmouth, Va., in 1841; launched in late 1842; and commissioned at Norfolk in early 1843, Lt. W. W. Hunter in command.

The Navy tested various designs of propulsion machinery during the transition to steam power in the early 19th century. Among these first experiments were *Union* and *Water Witch*—each fitted with an innovation named the Hunter Wheel.

The Hunter Wheel was named after Lt. W. W. Hunter and consisted of a conventional paddle wheel drum placed horizontally within the vessel below the waterline. The paddles were so arranged as to project from a suitable opening in the side of the ship when at right angles to the keel. Water was kept from entering by a cofferdam placed around the paddle wheel drum and against the side of the ship.

Union left Norfolk on a trial cruise in February 1843. She stopped at Washington, Boston, New York, and Philadelphia before returning to Norfolk in June. Although both Lt. Hunter and Secretary of the Navy Abel P. Upshur highly praised the vessel, it was later discovered that her engines wasted too much energy uselessly driving the paddle wheels through the water-filled cofferdam inside the ship. Later that year, *Union* put into the Washington Navy Yard for repairs.

Union joined the Home Squadron in 1844 and conducted a second series of test runs ending in early 1845. She was placed in ordinary at the Washington Navy Yard on 30 February. While she was laid up, it was decided to replace her original engines with ones of greater power. The alterations were completed at Washington in 1846 but failed to increase the efficiency of the paddle wheels. The ship was placed in ordinary at Norfolk as of November 1847.

In 1848, *Union* was sent to the Philadelphia Navy Yard and converted into a receiving ship. Her machinery and paddle wheels were removed at this time and sold. *Union* remained at Philadelphia as a receiving ship until sold there in 1858.

II

The second *Union* was a Mexican schooner captured by *Prineton* off Tampico, Mexico, on 14 November 1846. She joined the Navy later that month, Lt. J. A. Winslow in command, but was wrecked on a reef off Vera Cruz on 16 December.

III

(ScGbt: t. 1,114; l. 220'; b. 34'; dr. 16'; s. 13.5 k.; a. 1 12-pdr. r.)

The third *Union*—a screw steamer built at Mystic, Conn.—was chartered by the Navy on 24 April 1861 at Philadelphia, Pa.; and was commissioned there on 16 May 1861, Comdr. John R. Goldsborough in command.

The next day, *Union* was assigned to the Atlantic Blockading Squadron, and she steamed south to cruise off Charleston, S.C., and Savannah, Ga., on 28 May. However, she soon headed back north and captured schooner *F. W. Johnson* at sea off the mouth of the Chesapeake Bay on 1 June. The following morning, she arrived at Hampton Roads with the prize.

After coaling, *Union* returned to the blockade off Savannah and captured the brig *Hallie Jackson* there on the 10th. She arrived off Charleston, S.C., on the morning of the 18th and, later that day, captured the blockade runner *Amelia*. *Union* sent *Amelia* north to Philadelphia in the charge of a prize master and delivered the prize's crew to Fort Monroe, Va., on the 23d.

Union left Hampton Roads on 27 June to rejoin the blockade off Charleston. She sustained considerable damage to her superstructure and rigging in a collision with the Spanish ship *Plus Ultra* on 2 July. She was

The steamer *Union*, completed in 1843. (NR&L(O) 18705)

temporarily repaired at sea and sailed for Hampton Roads to refuel on 15 July. En route north, *Union* stopped at Georgetown, S.C.; Wilmington, N.C.; Ocracoke Inlet, Hatteras Inlet, and Hatteras Cove in search of blockade running activity and reached her destination on 18 July.

Union was next deployed on blockade duty off Cape Hatteras. On 28 July, she found the Northern merchant brig *B. T. Martin*—which had been captured by Confederate privateer *York*—hard aground north of the cape and destroyed the prize. She briefly put into Hampton Roads for coal on 5 August, then immediately returned to blockade duty off Hatteras, where she forced the Confederate privateer *York* aground on the 9th. *Union* returned to Hampton Roads on 14 August for emergency repairs and put into Baltimore the next day for alterations.

While undergoing repairs, *Union* was transferred to the Potomac Flotilla on the 16th. She left Baltimore the next day and arrived in the Potomac River off Aquia Creek, Va., on 19 August. The vessel performed routine reconnaissance and dispatch duties in the Potomac and, despite heavy fire from shore, burned a large Confederate schooner in Dumfries Creek on 11 October. *Union* suffered no casualties during the action and received special commendation for her daring exploit from the Secretary of the Navy, Gideon Welles. The vessel remained in the Potomac until ordered north on 5 December. She was decommissioned at the Philadelphia Navy Yard on 10 December.

Union was recommissioned on 20 January 1863 and detailed to the Gulf of Mexico for use as a supply and dispatch vessel. She spent the remainder of the war operating between New York; Hampton Roads; Port Royal, S.C., and points scattered along the Florida coast and the shore of the Gulf of Mexico.

Union also compiled an impressive list of captures during this time. These included the blockade-running British schooner *Linnet*, captured on 21 May 1863 west of Charlotte Harbor, Fla., and the English steamer, *Spaulding*, taken off St. Andrew's Sound, Ga., on 11 October. On 14 January 1864, *Union* seized steamer *Mayflower* and her cargo of cotton near Tampa Bay, Fla.; and, on 26 April, she captured schooner *O.K.* south of the bay. The supply vessel's final prize was sloop *Caroline*, captured at Jupiter Inlet, Fla., on 10 June 1864.

Union completed several dispatch and supply missions after the war ended and was decommissioned at New York on 29 September 1865. She was sold at auction there to W. H. Starbuck on 25 October and was redocumented as *Missouri* on 8 December. The steamer remained in merchant service until she caught fire and sank in the Bahamas on 22 October 1872, some 25 miles northeast of Abaco. This disaster cost the lives of some 69 persons.

IV

(AKA–106: dp. 6,433; l. 459'0''; b. 63'0''; dr. 26'0''; s. 17 k.; cpl. 387; a. 1 5'', 8 40mm., 16 20mm.; cl. *Tolland*; T. C2–S–AJ3)

The fourth *Union* (AKA–106) was laid down as *North Carolina* (MC–1697) on 27 September 1944 by the North Carolina Shipbuilding Co., Wilmington, N.C.; launched on 23 November 1944 and renamed *Union* at the time of launching; sponsored by Mrs. William Olive Burgin; moved to the Bethlehem Shipbuilding Co. at Hoboken, N.J., to undergo conversion into an attack transport for use by the United States Navy; and commissioned on 25 April 1945, Comdr. Hartwell T. Doughty in command.

After provisioning and receiving ammunition on 6 May, *Union* proceeded to Norfolk, Va., for shakedown training. She returned to the Norfolk Navy Yard on 15 May for availability and loading before departing for Pearl Harbor. On 27 May, the ship left Norfolk for the Canal Zone and arrived at Hawaii on 18 June

1945. After unloading her cargo and undergoing availability for repairs, *Union* left Honolulu on 16 July en route to Eniwetok and Guam. Stopping briefly at Eniwetok on 24 July, *Union* proceeded to Guam where she arrived on 2 August 1945.

The ship received orders to transport cargo to Leyte in the Philippines and got underway on 20 August. Upon arrival, she was directed to unload and proceed at once to Cebu where she loaded and transported units of the Americal Division to Japan as part of Transport Squadron (TransRon) 13, consisting of some 22 ships. The group steamed into Yokohama harbor on 8 September, and she unloaded her cargo and the Army personnel. Two days later, *Union* got underway for a turnaround trip to the Philippines. She was diverted to Okinawa to pick up repatriated prisoners of war for Guam where she arrived on 16 September. *Union* remained at Guam through 2 October when she set course for Tsingtao, China, to transport marines for occupation duty.

On 24 October 1945, *Union* anchored at Manila, then made a round trip to Subic Bay with *Leo* (AKA–60) to pick up landing craft replacements for the entire squadron. The ship departed Manila Bay on 30 October for Haiphong, French Indochina, to embark elements of the 52d Chinese Nationalist Army for transportation to Chinwangtao, North China. Having disembarked the troops and equipment on 12 November, *Union* proceeded to Taku, China, and remained there until she received orders on 1 December. The following day, she set course for Manila Bay, Philippines, thence to San Pedro, Calif., via Pearl Harbor. She arrived in California on 29 December.

Union operated out of San Diego conducting local operations between periods of upkeep. Caught in the tremendous postwar personnel turnover, *Union* sometimes operated with less than 50 men on board. In early September 1946, she was called upon to transport typhoon relief supplies to Guam. Some ports visited were Pearl Harbor; Guam; Saipan; Samar Island, Philippines; Tsingtao, and Taku, China. Her amphibious expertise contributed to her success during Operation "Shaft Alley" in Samar and also in resupplying marines at Guam and Peking. Christmas morning of 1946 found *Union* anchored off Taku Bar where she celebrated the New Year.

Throughout January and February 1947, *Union* conducted operations at Samar Island, Philippines; Tsingtao, China; and Guam. On 23 February, she departed Samar for San Diego via Pearl Harbor. The ship arrived at San Diego on 22 March, then sailed to the Puget Sound Naval Shipyard for a scheduled overhaul. On 14 May, the ship departed Puget Sound for San Diego via San Francisco and began preparing for "Barex–47," the 1947 Point Barrow supply expedition. After loading at Port Hueneme, *Union* and *Muliphen* (AKA–61) departed for Seattle on 7 July. On 30 July, the expedition left Seattle for the purpose of delivering supplies to agencies north of the Arctic Circle. After unloading at Point Barrow and Wainwright, Alaska, she loaded empty oil drums and old ammunition at Kodiak, Alaska, and delivered her cargo to Seattle on 24 August.

Personnel shortages throughout the Navy necessitated *Union*'s restricted mobility status for about eight months after she returned to San Diego on 6 September 1947. During the summer of 1948, *Union* repeated the Point Barrow resupply trip. On 26 July 1948, "Barex–48" got underway from Seattle. *Union* returned to San Diego on 24 August and finished out the year conducting local operations, which included Operations "Satanic" and "Demon."

On 10 January 1949, *Union* departed San Diego for "Microex–49," a cold weather amphibious operation off Kodiak and Whittier, Alaska. The ship returned to San Diego on 25 February and conducted a month of local operations before undergoing overhaul at the Puget Sound Naval Shipyard, Bremerton, Wash., from

31 March to 10 May 1949. Returning to San Diego, *Union* prepared for a third Point Barrow trip. The off-loading at Point Barrow, Alaska, was accomplished from 3 to 6 August. On 16 August, *Union* arrived back at Port Hueneme, Calif., and then proceeded to San Diego. She spent the remainder of 1949 in San Diego conducting local operations with the exception of Operation "Miki," a major amphibious exercise in the Hawaiian area held during the month of October.

Union departed Pearl Harbor on 7 November and arrived at Seattle, Wash., for a one-day stay. She returned to her home port on 21 November and operated in the San Diego area until 22 May 1950 when she set course for Yokosuka, Japan, arriving on 6 June.

The Korean War began on 25 June 1950. On that day, *Union* was underway conducting landing exercises at Sagami Wan, Honshu, Japan. She stopped briefly at Yokosuka before arriving at Sasebo on 3 July for repairs. Repairs and training continued at Yokosuka until *Union* sailed to Yokohama on 11 July to embark Army troops and equipment for transportation to Pohang, Korea, on 18 July. Having delivered her cargo, the ship returned to Yokosuka on 25 July and conducted various exercises until 4 September when she arrived at Kobe, Japan, to reload. On 11 September, *Union* got underway for Jinsen, Korea, where boat landings took place four days later amidst mortar, machine gun, and rifle fire. On 21 September, *Union* departed for Sasebo, Japan, with seven casualties on board. After delivering the casualties, *Union* travelled to Kobe, Japan, arriving on the 4th of October. She set course for Inchon, Korea, that day and arrived four days later to unload marines and equipment. She stopped at Yonghung Man Kosen, Korea, for five days before arriving at Yokosuka on 2 November. *Union* then got underway for San Diego, Calif., returning to her home port on 22 November 1950.

Union then proceeded to the San Francisco Naval Shipyard for a regular overhaul which lasted from 1 December 1950 to 14 February 1951. She returned to San Diego on 24 February and operated in her home port area until 5 July. At that time, she set sail for the Puget Sound Naval Shipyard, Bremerton, Wash., for a month of repairs.

The next assignment for *Union* was the first of two resupply trips to the Pribilof Islands of St. Paul and St. George in the Bering Sea, the homeland of the largest fur-seal herd in the world. *Union*'s primary mission was to deliver tons of supplies to personnel of the Bureau of Commercial Fisheries who worked on the two small islands. The ship arrived back at San Diego on 4 September.

Later in September, *Union* sailed to Subic Bay, Philippines, carrying heavy earth-moving equipment. She then began forward area amphibious training with the 45th Army Division off the island of Hokkaido, Japan. During December, the ship sailed to Hong Kong and lifted Allied troop replacements to Inchon, Korea. *Union* returned to Sasebo, Japan, on 22 December and remained in port through 15 January 1952.

On 19 January 1952, the ship returned to Yokosuka, Japan, and conducted operations between Yokosuka, Chigasaki, and Sasebo until March of that year.

On 19 March 1952, *Union* helped to shift a battalion of marines from Sokcho Ri, a harbor on the east coast of Korea, to the west coast. After the lift was accomplished, the ship returned to Yokosuka, Japan, on 5 April. After a trip to Buckner Bay on 19 April and several round trips between Yokosuka and Sasebo, she embarked troops and landed them on the island of Koje-do on 21 May. *Union* departed Yokosuka on 14 June for San Diego via Pearl Harbor. She arrived at San Diego on 2 July 1952 and spent the remainder of the summer in local operations and upkeep. In September, she sailed north to San Francisco for a regular shipyard overhaul by Mechanix, Inc., which lasted from 25 September to 24 November 1952. *Union* spent the remainder of the year in the San Diego area.

The first half of 1953 was spent in refresher training and local operations in the San Diego area. On 14 July, *Union* sailed for her fifth cruise to the Orient. The war in Korea was concluded by a truce on 27 July, and *Union* arrived at Yokosuka, Japan, on 9 August. She received orders to Korea and transported North Korean prisoners of war from Koje-do to Inchon in two trips which fully occupied the month of August. From September through November, *Union* divided her time between Japan, Korea, and Hong Kong. The ship got underway for the United States on 1 December 1953 and returned to San Diego on 19 December 1953, in time for a leave and upkeep period over the holidays.

January through April 1954 found *Union* engaged in local operations and upkeep in the San Diego area. On 26 April, she sailed for San Francisco via Port Hueneme, Calif. From 3 May to 2 July, *Union* underwent a regular overhaul at the Todd Shipyards Corp., Alameda, Calif. The ship returned to San Diego on 11 July and spent the summer in refresher training.

On 1 October, *Union* joined Amphibious Squadron 1; and, on the 23d, she departed for a sixth Western Pacific (WestPac) deployment. *Union* arrived at Yokosuka, Japan, on 10 November and underwent voyage repairs. She visited the Japanese ports of Osaka and Sasebo and celebrated Christmas at sea en route to Korea. While training Korean Marine Corps and Navy units, *Union* ushered in the New Year at Chin Hae.

In January 1955, *Union* proceeded to Subic Bay, Philippines, via Sasebo, Japan. After a restricted availability at Subic and a visit to Hong Kong, *Union* departed in February for the Tachen Islands where she and other ships assisted in the evacuation of Chinese Nationalist troops and refugee civilians. Having landed the evacuees at Keelung on 13 February, *Union* visited Hong Kong, Yokosuka, and Beppu, Japan.

After loading men and equipment of the First Marine Division at Inchon, *Union* departed on 3 April for a quick turn-around trip to San Diego. She returned to Pusan, Korea, on 20 May and arrived back at San Pedro, Calif., on 12 June with Marine air group personnel and equipment.

Union spent the month of January 1956 participating in Operation "Cowealex" which called for a landing on Umnak Island in the Aleutians. Rough weather necessitated changing the landing site to Unalaska Island in Makuskin Bay. The ship returned to San Diego on 9 February and conducted local operations. *Union* then left California en route to Pearl Harbor to participate in a landing exercise, "Hawrltlex 1–56" which concluded on 11 April. She arrived at San Diego on 23 April and spent the months until November taking part in local operations and undergoing upkeep. Late in August, *Union* made a brief trip to Vancouver, British Columbia, to represent the United States Navy in the Pacific National Exhibit. On 13 November 1956, the ship sailed for San Francisco and an overhaul at the San Francisco Naval Shipyard at Hunters Point.

Having completed her regular overhaul, *Union* returned to San Diego on 27 January 1957 and conducted refresher training. She then took part in a number of amphibious exercises off Coronado Roads. In early June, *Union* turned in her 5-inch stern gun and her 20-millimeter mounts to the Naval Repair Facility, San Diego. In July, she participated in Operation "Workhorse," a local landing exercise.

On 23 August 1957, *Union* got underway for WestPac via Pearl Harbor. She arrived at Yokosuka, Japan, on 12 September and underwent restricted availability. *Union* then visited Kure, Nagoya, and Chigasaki Beach before returning to Yokosuka to pick up Marine Corps cargo for Naha, Okinawa. On 4 November, she sailed for Subic Bay, Philippines. *Union* spent the remainder of the year in cargo-carrying tasks which took her to Taiwan, the Philippines, Hong Kong, and Okinawa. Christmas and New Year's Day were spent in Subic Bay, Philippines.

USS *Union* (AKA–106) at Brooklyn, 29 April 1945. (80–G–320976)

The year 1958 began with a week-long visit to Hong Kong, after which she proceeded to Yokosuka. On 5 February, *Union* departed Yokosuka for Okinawa to prepare for Operation "Strongback," a major 7th Fleet amphibious assault exercise at Dingalen Bay, Luzon, Philippines, in which destroyers, cruisers, and carriers took part in screening, gunfire, and air support tasks. D-day was 1 March, and *Union* returned to San Diego, via Pearl Harbor, on 2 April.

April, May, and June 1958 were occupied with leave, upkeep, and local operations in the San Diego area. *Union* underwent a material inspection during July, and a resupply expedition to the Pribilof Islands scheduled for August was cancelled due to the Lebanon crisis which broke in early July. During September, the ship took part in "Phiblex 2–59," a full-scale land-

ing exercise for the First Marine Division at Camp Pendleton.

After spending October in the San Diego area, *Union* sailed on 10 November for San Francisco and another regular yard overhaul. After off-loading cargo and ammunition, she arrived at the Mare Island Naval Shipyard for overhaul which lasted from 17 November 1958 to 16 January 1959.

Union returned to San Diego in 25 January. Shortly thereafter, she underwent refresher training, followed by amphibious training commencing on 17 March which completed her "working up." On 16 April, *Union* sailed for WestPac. On 22 April, she was detached and proceeded independently to Guam, thence to Subic Bay, Philippines. Throughout June, *Union* remained in the vicinity of Okinawa. She participated in Exercise

"Reconnex 1–60" off Irimote Jima, Japan, from 20 to 28 June.

On 10 July 1959, *Union* and *Comstock* (LSD–19) embarked the 3d Anti-Tank Battalion and sailed for Numazu, Japan, to commence the first phase of Operation "Tankex." Other ports which *Union* visited in connection with the operation were Kobe and Joji. In September, *Union* performed three weeks of duty as station ship in Hong Kong.

On 1 November 1959, *Union* set sail for San Diego via Pearl Harbor. She arrived at San Diego on 24 November and ended the year with a leave and upkeep period for the holiday season.

During the first six months of 1960, *Union* conducted local operations and necessary upkeep and repair periods in her home port area of San Diego. In February, she participated in Operation "Swan Dive," a Marine landing at Camp Pendleton. In May, she took part in Operation "Big Top," in which Marine air and naval surface units combined to land marines on Camp Pendleton beaches with an airlift of helicopter-borne troops among the initial assault waves.

On 21 June, *Union* deployed to WestPac via Pearl Harbor. During the first part oif the deployment, the ship made stops at Guam; Okinawa; Subic Bay, Philippines; Hong Kong; and Yokosuka, Japan, conducting various cargo-personnel lifts. In September, *Union* embarked the Army's 1st Battle Group of the 2d Infantry at Inchon, Korea, for a practice exercise on the beaches of Pohang Dong, Korea, and returned to Inchon.

In October, *Union* visited the Japanese ports of Kure, Numazu, and Kobe. She carried out a people-to-people program which included an orphans' party, exchange of wardroom visits with Japanese officers, a tour of the ship by Japanese officers and petty officers, two visits for an evening meal by Japanese students from universities and colleges, a presentation of several utility items to a Numazu orphanage, and several softball games.

During a second visit to Hong Kong in November, *Union* acted as station ship. In December, she completed her WestPac deployment and returned to San Diego. A Christmas leave period commenced on 22 December.

The early weeks of 1961 were spent in leave and upkeep in anticipation of the regular overhaul commencing 15 February. Completed under four separate commercial repair contracts, the extended completion date was 26 April 1961. May, June, and July were spent in the San Diego area, where *Union* underwent two intensive training periods followed by leave and upkeep.

Departing San Diego on 4 August, *Union* was chartered by the Department of Commerce to make her second and the Navy's last resupply trip to the Pribilof Islands. Cargo off-loading operations commenced at St. George Island early on the 21st. Strong winds, high seas, and thick fog made this entire operation a challenge to seamanship and perseverance. The ship arrived at Seattle, Wash., on 3 September and disembarked passengers and cargo. The following year, the Department of Commerce would carry on this work with its own vessel, thus ending a Navy mission initiated in the 1920's by executive order of President Coolidge.

After five weeks in San Diego preparing for deployment, *Union* sailed for her home port on 16 October. Upon her arrival at Pearl Harbor, the ship took part in Operation "Silver Sword," a landing exercise of 5,000 marines on the beaches of Maui. The landing commenced one minute after midnight on the 30th of October. On 15 November. Amphibious Squadron 1 sailed from Pearl Harbor. *Union* and *Washburn* (AKA–108) broke off from the squadron and arrived at Sasebo on 28 November 1961. After voyage repairs at Sasebo, *Union* steamed to Hong Kong where she served as station ship for the remainder of the year, 16 December 1961 through 14 January 1962.

Union was relieved as station ship on 15 January, and she sailed for Subic Bay, Philippines. After 10 days of upkeep, *Union* returned to her work of amphibious operations and participated in the "Away All Boats" exercise.

The ship then sailed for Buckner Bay, Okinawa, to load a cargo of Marine Corps equipment. In February, *Union* learned that her deployment had been extended two weeks so she could participate in Operation "Tulungan," a SEATO exercise in which the United States Navy and Marine Corps, the Royal Australian Air Force, and Philippine units took part. An unusually long operation, "Tulungan" lasted from mid-February to mid-April. *Union* left Yokosuka for San Diego on 17 April.

After arriving in San Diego on 5 May 1962, *Union* spent May and June in leave, upkeep, and training exercises in the San Diego area. On 26 July, she steamed for an interim overhaul lasting from 1 August to 7 September at Seattle, Wash. Refresher training commenced off San Diego on 5 October. On 27 October, *Union* got underway for the Panama Canal with Task Group (TG) 53.2. Having transited the Panama Canal on 5 November, *Union* moored at Cristobal, Canal Zone, and later anchored at Limon Bay, Colon. *Union* arrived at Guantanamo Bay, Cuba, on 30 November to take part in the Cuban quarantine. She conducted cargo operations at Roosevelt Roads and Vieques, Puerto Rico, and enjoyed liberty at Kingston, Jamaica. On 2 December, *Union* got underway for California via the Panama Canal. She arrived back at San Diego on 16 December and spent the remainder of 1962 in leave and upkeep.

January 1963 was spent in preparing for and participating in amphibious operational training off Coronado, Calif. In February, *Union* got underway for the naval ammunition depot at Seal Beach, Calif., where the ammunition which had been on board for possible use during the Cuban crisis was off-loaded. The remainder of the month was spent preparing for Exercise "Steel Gate." At the completion of "Steel Gate," *Union* commenced preparation for her deployment to WestPac.

Union departed San Diego on 26 March for the transit to Okinawa via Pearl Harbor. While underway, she participated in Exercise "Windmill," which simulated a merchant convoy. After off-loading at Pearl Harbor and Okinawa, *Union* arrived at Sasebo, Japan, for routine voyage repairs. It was May when *Union* arrived at Yokosuka, Japan, to off-load material and accomplish routine upkeep.

Union's next mission was to participate in the 24th annual Black Ship Festival at Shimoda, Japan. This festival commemorates the arrival in Shimoda of Commodore Perry and his squadron of "Black Ships" in 1854. Having brought good will to Shimoda, *Union* next steamed to Sasebo for upkeep, then on to Pusan, Korea, where she provided facilities for Korean units to stage a ship-to-shore movement. June arrived with *Union* underway for Naha, Okinawa, to embark marines for the upcoming Operation "Flagpole" at Kuryongpo, Korea. Typhoon Shirley greatly hampered the landing phase of the operation, but it was finally completed despite torrential rains, floods, washed out roads, and dense fog.

After a port visit to Kure, Japan, *Union* off-loaded "Flagpole" gear at Buckner Bay, then underwent a period of upkeep at Yokosuka. It was there that she embarked midshipmen for a cruise which took her to the ports of Keelung, Taiwan; Hong Kong; and Subic Bay, Philippines, where the midshipmen debarked.

The ship travelled to Inchon, Korea, to prepare for Exercise "Bayonet Beach," which provided for ship-to-shore movements in the area of Pohang, Korea. After the exercise, *Union* sailed from Iwakuni, Japan, to Subic Bay, Philippines, with Marine aviation ordnance equipment. After a period of upkeep at Yokosuka, she visited Kobe, Japan, and met with an anti-American demonstration staged by the Japanese Peace Committee, a communist organization.

On 20 October 1963, *Union* proceeded south to Okinawa to rendezvous with her squadron and begin the transit to San Diego via Pearl Harbor. She arrived on 13 November and enjoyed a period of liberty. As the year came to an end, *Union* was preparing for an upcoming yard overhaul.

January 1964 found *Union* in San Diego concluding a leave and upkeep period. On 18 January, she sailed for San Francisco and, four days later, proceeded to Richmond, Calif., for drydocking at the Willamette Iron and Steel Co. Drydocking was completed on 6 February and the remainder of the overhaul on 26 March. *Union* returned to San Diego on 4 April and, on the 27th, reported for four weeks of intensive refresher training. Training reached a successful culmination on 22 May, and a two-week upkeep period followed.

From 8 to 19 June, *Union* participated in amphibious refresher training at Coronado, Calif. A period of availability alongside *Klondike* (AR–22) followed; and, from 3 to 12 July, *Union* was assigned an upkeep period. *Union* enjoyed an extended period of upkeep from 17 July to 24 August when Operation "Cascade Columbia II," scheduled to commence on 13 August, was cancelled as a result of the tense military situation in Vietnam.

After conducting a midshipmen cruise and on-loading supplies and marines, *Union* got underway from San Diego on 25 August to participate in Exercise "Sea Bar" at Solo Point, Wash. Two days later, *Union* proceeded independently to Astoria, Oreg., to take part in the 44th annual Astoria Regatta and Fish Festival. On 1 September, Exercise "Sea Bar" got underway for nine days of amphibious landings. On 14 September, *Union* returned to her home port and underwent a material inspection.

The ship next began to prepare for Exercise "Hard Nose," a major amphibious landing exercise involving 39 ships and some 11,000 marines. The 12-day exercise began on 6 October and concluded on the beach of Camp Pendleton on the morning of 17 October. Upon returning to San Diego, *Union* began an extended period of upkeep in preparation for an upcoming WestPac deployment.

On 16 November, *Union* departed San Diego for a 5,900-mile transit of the Pacific Ocean. On 7 December, she arrived at Buckner Bay, Okinawa. After off-loading and readying the boat group, *Union* got underway for local operations. On 20 December, *Union* set course for Subic Bay, Philippines. Three days later, she moored at Rivera Point, Subic Bay. The crew received an unexpected treat when comedian Bob Hope and his troupe presented their annual Christmas show at Subic Bay on 28 December 1964.

Union began the New Year 1965 with a round-trip from Subic Bay to Buckner Bay, Okinawa, and Hong Kong. She returned to Subic Bay on 23 January and conducted task group operations throughout the month of February. On 8 March, *Union* anchored at Danang, South Vietnam. On 12 March, she departed for Yokosuka, Japan, where she went into drydock until 29 March. After spending several days moored pierside, *Union* departed on 6 April for special operations at Buckner Bay, Okinawa. On 14 April, the ship anchored at Danang, South Vietnam, along with *Cook* (APD–130), *Henrico* (APA–45), and amphibious assault ship *Vancouver* (APD–2). They transported marines to Danang, bringing the total to nearly 8,000.

Upon leaving Danang, South Vietnam, *Union* sailed to an anchorage at the mouth of the Hue River and remained there until 19 April. She anchored briefly at Buckner Bay, Okinawa, before conducting four days of special operations culminating in a landing at Baie De Dung, Vietnam. On 16 May, *Union* again returned to Buckner Bay, only to sail again four days later for Chu Lai harbor, Vietnam, conducting special operations en route. On 27 May, she arrived at Danang harbor, South Vietnam, and proceeded to Yokosuka, Japan, arriving there on 4 June 1965.

Union departed the Far East and arrived at San Diego, Calif., on 23 June. The month of July was spent undergoing tender availability with *Klondike* (AR–22). After loading ammunition at Seal Beach, Calif., *Union* again departed for Buckner Bay, Okinawa, arriving on 28 August. The ship set course for Yokosuka, Japan, on 31 August; and, after a nine-day visit, *Union* sailed for Pearl Harbor, Hawaii, arriving there on 21 September. Two days later, she got underway for San Diego, Calif., where she arrived on 30 September.

October and November were spent in port at San Diego. In mid-December, she got underway for local operations, and *Union* finished the year 1965 moored at her home port.

The first six months of 1966 were spent in amphibious refresher training and restricted availability at San Diego. During July, *Union* prepared for deployment by loading ammunition and Marine cargo. On 27 July, the ship departed for another WestPac cruise. She arrived at Okinawa on 22 August, then continued to Danang, South Vietnam, where she back-loaded BLT 3/3 (Battalion Landing Team, 3d Battalion, 3d Marine Regiment) and transported the marines to Okinawa for a recreation and retraining cycle. *Union* then proceeded to Camranh Bay, South Vietnam, where, on 15 September, elements of the Republic of Korea Marines were loaded for transportation to Chu Lai. When this offload had been completed, boiler troubles forced *Union* into an availability at Subic Bay from 27 September through 7 October.

With all repairs completed, *Union* commenced a lengthy period of support operations for Commander, Military Assistance Command, Vietnam, which extended to 21 November. The ship arrived at Okinawa on 26 November and, after a few days for liberty and replenishment, loaded elements of BLT 1/9. She sailed for Subic Bay, Philippines, on 3 December. After her detachment from this duty, *Union* set course for Sasebo on 13 December, looking forward to a holiday upkeep period which lasted through the 27th. As the year closed, *Union* was once again at Okinawa loading BLT 4/4. On the final day of 1966, a practice turnaway landing was conducted at Chin Wan in preparation for actual movement across the beach that would follow on New Year's Day.

The first day of 1967 found *Union* in the last phase of her WestPac tour. After landing craft training operations in the Okinawa area, *Union* departed Okinawa en route to Danang, Vietnam. After off-loading and back-loading Marine vehicles, the ship returned to Okinawa on 14 January. An upkeep period at Sasebo, Japan, began on 17 January and was followed by rest and recreation at Keelung, Taiwan, and Kobe, Japan. On 15 February, *Union* set course for Yokosuka, Japan, spending 10 days in port there and then departing for San Diego. *Union* entered San Diego Bay on 15 March 1967, completing her 15th WestPac cruise.

After a month-long leave period, preparations began for Operation "Alligator Hide," an amphibious assault at Coronado Roads, Calif. Following the operation, *Union* spent 13 days in port and, on 15 May, conducted individual ship exercises. On 29 May 1967, *Union* suddenly received orders to perform duties as a reconnaissance ship, trailing the Russian trawler *Peleng*, which had been operating off the coast of southern California near Catalina and San Clemente Islands. *Union* stayed within close range of the trawler for 10 days. On 5 June, she was relieved on station by *Taussig* (DD–746) and returned to San Diego.

After an administrative inspection, the ship made preparations for overhaul which commenced on 8 July at Pacific Ship Repair, Inc., San Francisco, Calif. She returned to her home port on 1 October to prepare for refresher training. A month-long refresher training period ended on 1 December and was followed by an amphibious inspection which was completed on 22 December. *Union* spent the 1967 holiday season moored at her home port.

The new year, 1968, began with *Union* enjoying a leave period which lasted until 26 January. On 1 February, *Union* departed San Diego for another WestPac deployment. *Union* arrived at Buckner Bay, Okinawa, on 26 February. She operated off the coast of Vietnam transporting much-needed equipment and ammunition. From 20 to 27 March, the ship participated in Operation "Former Champ" with Nationalist Chinese ships and marines in Taiwan. On 7 April, *Union* escorted *Asheville* (PGM–84) to Subic Bay, Philippines, for engineering repairs. After a brief stop at Yokosuka, Japan, the ship set course for San Diego via Pearl Harbor. *Union* arrived at her home port on 16 September 1968 after completing a seven-month deployment.

Upon returning to San Diego, *Union* enjoyed a month-long period of leave. On 16 October, she commenced an upkeep period followed by a period of restricted availability which lasted through 30 November. The ship conducted independent ship's exercises before commencing a holiday leave period on 14 December.

From 1 January to 1 August 1969, *Union*'s schedule was filled with all types of operational training, inspections, and upkeep evolutions in the San Diego–San Francisco area. *Union* conducted training exercises at Acapulco, Mexico, from 14 to 27 April; and, from 17 to 21 June, the ship took part in Exercise "Bell Call," an amphibious operation which included embarkation, withdrawal, movement, demonstration, simultaneous surface and helicopter assault, and subsequent troop exercise ashore.

On 1 August 1969, *Union* departed San Diego en route to Pearl Harbor, thence to Yokosuka, Japan, arriving on 23 August. After a brief upkeep period, she departed on 29 August for Okinawa where she spent three days conducting amphibious exercises. On 5 September, *Union* got underway for Danang, Vietnam. She transported cargo from Danang to Okinawa until 19 November when she departed Danang for Subic Bay, Philippines.

Having off-loaded three-fourths of the ship's ammunition in preparation for a homeward transit, *Union* proceeded to Okinawa on 26 November to complete her off-loading. She departed Okinawa three days later for the long voyage to San Diego where she arrived on 18 December. *Union* deviated from her course twice; on 6 December to transport an injured marine to a hospital on Midway Island as soon as possible; the next day, to assist in the restoration of the French Frigate Shoals Loran station at Tern Island, Hawaii. The remainder of 1969, from 18 to 31 December, was devoted to a leave period for *Union*'s crew.

Union was placed out of commission, in reserve, on 5 June 1970 and transferred to the Maritime Administration at Suisun Bay, Calif. On 1 September 1976, she was stricken from the Navy list. *Union* was sold in September 1977 to National Metal and Steel Corp. of Terminal Island, Calif., for scrapping.

Union was awarded two battle stars for Korean service and nine battle stars for her Vietnam service.

Uniontown

A city in Fayette County in southwestern Pennsylvania which was settled about 1767, incorporated as a borough in 1796, and as a city in 1916. Fort Necessity, the site of George Washington's first "command decision" during the French and Indian War, is situated near Uniontown; General Braddock's grave is also nearby. The city is also the birthplace of Generals George C. Marshall and Henry H. "Hap" Arnold.

(PF–65: dp. 2,415; l. 303'11''; b. 37'6''; dr. 13'8''; s. 19 k.; cpl. 214; a. 3 3'', 8 40mm., 2 dct., 8 dcp., 1 dcp. (hh.); cl. *Tacoma*; T. S2–S2–AQ1)

Uniontown (PF–65) was laid down under a Maritime Commission contract (MC hull 1489) as *Chatta-*

nooga on 21 April 1943 at Sturgeon Bay, Wis., by the Leathem D. Smith Shipbuilding Co.; launched on 7 August 1943; sponsored by Mrs. Cecilia Daniel; brought to New Orleans, La., for completion on 4 April 1944; renamed *Uniontown* on 16 August 1944 to free the name *Chattanooga* for CL–118; and commissioned on 6 October 1944, Comdr. Richard E. Morell, USCG, in command.

Following shakedown in the Caribbean and a brief visit to Charleston, S.C., *Uniontown* joined Task Force 61 at Hampton Roads, Va., on 27 December 1944 for duty as a convoy escort. Two days later, the Coast Guard-manned escort vessel got underway for the first of three round-trip voyages across the Atlantic, escorting convoys to Oran, Algeria, and back. Her first round trip lasted from 29 December 1944 to 11 February 1945; the second round trip commenced on 15 March and ended with the ship's return to New York on 9 April. On 28 April, *Uniontown* got underway for North Africa and her last wartime convoy escort run.

While en route to Algeria, *Uniontown* received word that German forces had surrendered at Rheims on 7 May, ending the long European war. Arriving at Oran on the 13th, *Uniontown* soon got underway for the United States and reached Philadelphia on 8 June for conversion to a weather ship. On 3 July, outfitted for weather patrol duties, she set out for Newfoundland and arrived at Argentia two days later.

On 13 July, *Uniontown* commenced operations at Weather Station No. 3 and remained on station until 2 August. The ship returned to Grondal, Greenland, from 3 to 20 August in between deployments on weather patrol. The frigate served on Weather Station No. 1 from 22 August to 11 September and subsequently at Weather Station No. 3 from 2 to 20 October before she returned to the Boston Navy Yard. A month later, *Uniontown* headed for Hampton Roads and arrived at Norfolk on 30 November 1945.

On 20 December 1945, the warship was decommissioned at the Portsmouth Naval Shipyard, Norfolk, Va., and was struck from the Navy list on 8 January 1946. She was then sold to the Argentine government in July 1947, in whose service she was renamed *Sarandi*.

Union Victory

Union Victory was renamed *Perseus* (q.v.) and designated AF–64 on 4 December 1961.

Unit

(ScTug: t. 57; dr. 8'; s. 7.5 k.)

Unit—steamer *Union* built at Philadelphia, Pa., in 1862—was purchased at Boston, Mass., on 2 June 1864. *Unit* was assigned to the North Atlantic Blockading Squadron and served as a tug and repair vessel in Hampton Roads, Va., for the duration of the Civil War. In June 1865, the tug was sent to New York City.

Unit was sold at auction there on 12 July 1865 to C. and E. T. Peters. Redocumented as a merchant steamer on 6 September 1865, *Unit* remained in mercantile service until 1902.

United States

(Fr: t. 1,576; lbp. 175'; b. 43'6''; dr. 23'6''; s. 11 k.; cpl. 364; a. 32 long 24-pdrs., 24 42-pdrs. car.)

The first *United States*—one of six frigates authorized by Congress on 27 March 1794—was designed by naval architect Joshua Humphreys and Capt. Thomas Truxtun; was built at Philadelphia; was launched there on 10 May 1797; and was commissioned on 11 July, Revolutionary War naval hero, Capt. John Barry, in command.

413

The frigate *United States* engages HMS *Macedonian*. (KN 2880)

United States—the first American warship to be launched under the naval provisions of the Constitution—entered the water four months before the launching of sister ship *Constellation* at Baltimore and five and one-half months before that of *Constitution* at Boston. She was fitted out at Philadelphia during the spring of 1798 and, on 3 July, was ordered to proceed to sea.

Ten days later, the new frigate—in company with *Delaware*, a former merchantship which had been acquired by the Government and fitted out for naval service—rounded Cape Henlopen and stood out to sea. The two ships quickly set a course for Boston where they were to add the newly purchased 20-gun ship *Herald* and the revenue cutter *Pickering* to their little fleet. During her voyage north, *United States* performed admirably, constantly pulling ahead of *Delaware* and exceeding Barry's most sanguine expectations. However, when he reached Boston, Barry learned that *Herald* and *Pickering* would not be ready to sail for several weeks. The commodore decided that the need for American naval power in the Caribbean was too great to permit him to wait for them, so *United States* and *Delaware* departed Nantasket Roads on 26 July and headed for Barbados.

The voyage south was enlivened by encounters with several ships, but none proved to be French. The two warships reached Bridgetown on 21 August but stood back out to sea only some three hours later. At dawn

the next day, a lookout spotted a strange sail; and the Americans gave chase. During the pursuit, *United States* quickly outstripped *Delaware* and, by early afternoon, was within range of the fleeing ship. Two rounds from the frigate brought the quarry to, and she proved to be the French, 10-gun privateer *Sans Pareil* of Guadaloupe.

The frigate continued to hunt for French vessels in ensuing weeks but did not take her next prize until 4 September when a day-long chase was rewarded by eight-gun privateer *Jalouse*'s surrender. At noon on the 7th, the *United States*, escorting the latter prize, and *Delaware*, shepherding *Sans Pareil*, got underway for home. Three days later, *Delaware* and her prize set off in pursuit of a strange sail; and, on the 13th during a gale at night, *United States* became separated from *Jalouse*. Thus, she was alone when she entered the Delaware on 18 September.

After almost a month in home waters, the frigate put to sea again on 17 October with orders to cruise between Cape May, N.J., and the New England coast. However, a fierce storm arose the following day and battered *United States* as it forced her south to a point some 250 miles off Cape Hatteras, N.C. When the tempest abated, the frigate painfully began working her way back north; but she did not anchor in the Delaware until the evening of the 30th.

More than a month and one-half ensued as the ship

underwent repairs. On 18 December, she put to sea again and headed back to the West Indies where Barry was to command the American squadron. She reached the Caribbean a fortnight later and began cruising among the islands of the West Indies. On the morning of 3 February 1799, the *United States* sighted a strange sail near Martinique and set out in pursuit. Over five hours later, she pulled within range of the fleeing vessel and opened fire. Her third round struck the schooner and went through the unfortunate vessel from stern to stem, leaving her in a sinking condition. The frigate then attempted to close the foundering ship, but her victim sank before *United States* could reach her. The men on the frigate rescued the schooner's survivors and learned that the sunken vessel had been *L'Amour de la Patrie*, a six-gun privateer.

On the 16th, the frigate arrived in waters off Guadaloupe and attempted to negotiate an exchange of prisoners under a flag of truce. However, shore batteries opened fire on the boat carrying Barry's envoy, forcing it to return to the frigate. Six days later, a similar effort met with better luck, and Barry arranged to exchange his 58 prisoners from *L'Amour de la Patrie* for an equal number of American sailors.

On the 26th, Barry sighted two unknown sails east of Marie Galente and overtook one, the 430-ton *Cicero* which had been taken by the French privateer *Democrat*. He put a prize crew on her and resumed his pursuit of *Democrat*. However, by dark, the privateer escaped into shoal water off Maria Galente.

Meanwhile, more commissioned ships of the United States Navy had been arriving in the Caribbean so that by mid-March Barry's squadron contained two frigates, three ships, and four revenue cutters. The venerable commodore displayed great skill in deploying these warships throughout the West Indies so that he could afford maximum protection to American merchant shipping while discouraging French aggression. On 26 March, the *United States* took the French privateer schooner *La Tartueffe* and its prize American sloop *Vermont* southeast of Antigua.

On 19 April off St. Christopher, Barry turned over command of the squadron to Commodore Truxtun; and the *United States* sailed for home escorting a convoy of some 30 merchantmen. Barry wanted to be back in waters near Philadelphia so that he could discharge the members of her crew whose enlistments were expiring and so that he could protect shipping from Europe expected to be approaching the American coast during the late spring and summer. The frigate reached New Castle, Del., on 10 May.

At the end of some two months in home waters, the *United States* got underway from New Castle unexpectedly during a storm on 6 July when her cable parted. Since Barry had already received sailing orders, he let the ship move right on downriver. She emerged from the Delaware capes that night and sailed down the coast to Hampton Roads where she anchored on 22 July.

After receiving a new bowsprit, the frigate got underway on 13 August in company with *Insurgent*. Sometime after she got out to sea, the ships parted, and the *United States* sailed south along the Atlantic coast to the mouth of the St. Mary's River. She then turned north and moved back up the seaboard and anchored off Newport, R.I., on 12 September. There, Barry received orders to wait for further instructions. When they arrived, they sent Barry and his ship across the Atlantic to Europe.

On 3 November 1799, *United States* sailed for France with American commissioners appointed by President John Adams to negotiate a settlement of the issues dividing the two erstwhile allies. She returned to New York in April 1800 and was laid up for repair of the damage she had suffered during a severe storm in the Bay of Biscay. In the fall, the frigate received orders to resume duty as flagship of the West Indies Squadron but—because a treaty of peace with France had been signed—she was recalled soon after she reached the Caribbean and returned to Chester, Pa., on 28 April.

On the last day of his administration, President Adams signed a bill authorizing his successor, Thomas Jefferson, to dispose of all naval vessels except the frigates. Accordingly, *United States* departed Chester on 17 May and proceeded to the eastern branch of the Potomac River, where the Federal government was establishing the Washington Navy Yard. *United States* was decommissioned there on 6 June 1801 and was laid up with four other frigates built under the legislation of 27 March 1794: *President, Constellation, Congress,* and *Chesapeake*.

United States remained in the Potomac until 1809 when orders were given to ready her for active service. On 10 June 1810, the frigate—now under the command of Capt. Steven Decatur, Jr., one of the midshipmen on her first cruise—sailed to Norfolk, Va., for refitting. While she was at Norfolk, Capt. John S. Carden, R.N., of the new British frigate HMS *Macedonian*, wagered Capt. Decatur a beaver hat that his vessel would take *United States* if the two should ever meet in battle.

The opportunity to settle the bet came sooner than either officer expected, as the United States declared war on Great Britain on 19 June 1812. *United States*, the frigate *Congress*, and the brig *Argus* joined Commodore John Rodgers' squadron at New York and put to sea immediately, cruising off the east coast until the end of August. The squadron again sailed on 8 October 1812, this time from Boston. Three days later, after capturing *Mandarin, United States* parted company and continued to cruise eastward. At dawn on 25 October, five hundred miles south of the Azores, lookouts on board *United States* reported seeing a sail 12 miles to windward. As the ship rose over the horizon, Capt. Decatur made out the fine, familiar lines of *Macedonian*.

Both ships were immediately cleared for action and commenced maneuvers at 0900. Capt. Carden elected not to risk crossing the bows of *United States* to rake her, but chose instead to haul closer to the wind on a parallel course with the American vessel. For his part, Decatur intended to engage *Macedonian* from fairly long range, where his 24-pounders would have the advantage over the 18-pounders of the British, and then move in for the kill.

The actual battle developed according to Decatur's plan. *United States* began the action at 0920 by firing an inaccurate broadside at *Macedonian*. This was answered immediately by the British vessel, bringing down a small spar of *United States*. Decatur's next broadside had better luck, as it destroyed *Macedonian*'s mizzen top mast, letting her driver gaff fall and so giving the advantage in maneuver to the American's frigate. *United States* next took up position off *Macedonian*'s quarter and proceeded to riddle the hapless frigate methodically with shot. By noon, *Macedonian* was a dismasted hulk and was forced to surrender. She had suffered 104 casualties as against 12 in *United States*, which emerged from the battle relatively unscathed.

The two ships lay alongside each other for over two weeks while *Macedonian* was repaired sufficiently to sail. *United States* and her prize entered New York Harbor on 4 December amid tumultuous national jubilation over the spectacular victory. Wherever they went, Capt. Decatur and his crew were lionized and received special praise from both Congress and President James Madison. *Macedonian* was subsequently purchased by the Navy, repaired, and had a long and honorable career under the American flag.

After repairs, *United States*—accompanied by *Macedonian* and the sloop *Hornet*—sailed from New York on 24 May 1813. On 1 June, the three vessels were driven into New London, Conn., by a powerful British squadron, and *United States* and *Macedonian* were kept blocked there until the end of the war. However, Decatur was transferred to the frigate *President* in the spring of 1814, and he took the officers and crew of

United States with him to his new command. *Hornet* managed to slip through the blockade on 14 November 1814 and escaped to sea.

After the end of the War of 1812, the American government turned its attention back to the Mediterranean where Algiers had resumed preying upon American shipping while the United States was preoccupied by its recently concluded war with Great Britain. On 23 February 1815, President Madison requested that Congress declare war on Algiers; and it voted favorably on his recommendation on 2 March.

Work fitting out two American squadrons promptly began—one at Boston under Commodore William Bainbridge and one at New York under Commodore Steven Decatur, Jr.

The *United States* was assigned to the former but required, after being bottled up in port for the latter part of the War of 1812, some repairs and refitting. Thus, she was not ready for sea when Bainbridge departed Boston on 3 July. Exactly two months later, the frigate—under the command of Capt. John Shaw—departed that port and headed for the Mediterranean. When the frigate reached Gibraltar, Shaw learned that a treaty of peace with Algiers had been signed; but, since the Barbary states had made a habit of changing their minds when no longer under duress, it seemed prudent to keep an American squadron in the Mediterranean. Thus, after both Decatur and Bainbridge had sailed for home, the *United States* remained behind, within easy reach of the North African coast and ready to remind Barbary rulers of their treaty commitments. The senior American naval officer in the region, Capt. Shaw became commodore and commanded the squadron until Commodore Isaac Chauncy arrived on 1 July 1816 and took overall command. Nevertheless, the *United States*—despite losing her position as flagship, continued to serve in the Mediterranean until she sailed for home in the spring of 1819 and reached Hampton Roads on 18 May of that year. The frigate was decommissioned on 9 June 1819 and laid up at Norfolk.

United States did not sail again until 1824. From 1824 to 1827, she was deployed with the Pacific Squadron under Commodore Isaac Hull and protected American shipping and commercial interests. She put into the Philadelphia Navy Yard in 1828 for extensive repairs and remained there until 1830 when she was placed in ordinary at the New York Navy Yard. The frigate remained at New York through 1832 and was thoroughly modernized. She served in the Mediterranean Squadron from 1833 to 1838 and was deployed with the Home Squadron during 1839 and 1840.

United States was repaired at Norfolk in 1841 and was designated the new flagship of the Pacific Squadron in January 1842. She left Hampton Roads on 9 January, bound for the Pacific via Cape Horn. Herman Melville, the future author of *Moby Dick*, enlisted as an ordinary seaman on board *United States* at Honolulu, Hawaii, on 17 August 1843.

The vessel returned to the United States in 1844 and was placed out of commission at Boston on 14 October. She was recommissioned there on 18 May 1846 and was detailed to the African Squadron for duty helping to suppress the illicit slave trade. *United States* joined the Mediterranean Squadron in 1847 and served in European waters until ordered home late in 1848. She was decommissioned on 24 February 1849 and placed in ordinary at Norfolk.

United States rotted away at Norfolk until 20 April 1861 when the navy yard was captured by Confederate troops. Before leaving the yard, Union fire crews failed to burn the vessel along with other abandoned ships, thinking it unnecessary to destroy the decayed relic. The Confederates, pressed for vessels in any kind of condition, thought otherwise and, after pumping her out, commissioned the frigate CSS *United States*, often called *Confederate States*, on 29 April. On 15 June, she was ordered to be fitted out as a receiving ship

A 1948 artist's conception of the projected aircraft carrier *United States* (CVB–58). She is shown here operating McDonnell FH–1 *Phantom* fighters and Lockheed P2V–3C *Neptune* twin-engine bombers, a version of the P2V designed for carrier operation. (80–G–706108)

and was provided with a deck battery of 19 guns for harbor defense.

In this role, she served her new owners well but was ordered sunk in the Elizageth River, Va., to form an obstruction to Union vessels when the Confederates abandoned the navy yard in May 1862. Surprisingly, the ancient timbers of the frigate were found to be so strong and well-preserved as to ruin one whole box of axes when attempts were made to scuttle her, and it was necessary to bore through the hull from inside before she settled to the muddy bottom of the river.

Shortly after the destruction of ironclad ram *Virginia* on 11 May 1862 and the surrender of the Norfolk Navy Yard to Union troops, *United States* was raised and towed to the yard by federal authorities. She remained there until March 1864, when the Bureau of Construction and Repair decided to break her up and sell the wood. This work was delayed until late 1865, when the Bureau ordered on 18 December that the gallant old frigate be docked at Norfolk and immediately broken up.

United States (CC–6)—a *Lexington*-class battle cruiser—was laid down on 25 September 1920 by the Philadelphia Navy Yard. However, her construction was halted on 8 February 1922 when the vessel was only 12.1 percent complete. Under the terms of the Washington Treaty for the Limitation of Naval Armaments of 1922, the unfinished hulk of *United States* was sold on 25 October 1923 for scrap.

United States (CVA–58) was laid down on 18 April 1949 at Newport News, Va., by the Newport News Shipbuilding and Dry Dock Corp., but her construction was terminated only five days later on the 23d. The 'super-carrier' had been designed to launch atomic bomb-carrying, long-range aircraft and had been an object of controversy between the military services. Designed without a fixed-superstructure, the 1,090-foot, 33-knot carrier would have been, at the time of her scheduled completion, the world's largest aircraft carrier.

Upham

Frank Brooks Upham—born on 7 September 1872 at Ft. Apache, Ariz.—was appointed to the Naval Academy on 6 September 1889 and graduated on 2 June 1893. Following the completion of the two required years of postgraduate sea duty—which he served on the Pacific Station in protected cruiser *Philadelphia*—Upham was commissioned an ensign on 1 July 1895 and joined *Olympia* (Cruiser No. 6) on 18 July before she sailed for the Far East to become the flagship of the Asiatic Squadron. At the time of the Spanish-American War, Upham was on the staff of the Commander in Chief, Asiastic Squadron, Commodore George Dewey; and the young officer received his baptism of fire during the Battle of Manila Bay.

He advanced up the officer ranks of the Navy, eventually attaining flag rank in 1927. During the years before World War I, Upham's sea duty embraced tours in *Oregon* (Battleship No. 3), *New Jersey* (Battleship No. 16), and *South Dakota* (Armored Cruiser No. 9); he also commanded *Olympia* and the yacht *Scorpion*. He served tours of duty ashore at Newport, R.I., at the Naval War College and in Washington at the Bureau of Ordnance. His overseas shore duty began in the summer of 1911 when he took up the duties of Assistant Naval Attache at Tokyo and Peking, shortly before the outbreak of the Chinese Revolution in October of that year.

During World War I, Upham commanded *Columbia* (Cruiser No. 12) and *Pueblo* (Armored Cruiser No. 7) and won the Navy Cross for leading the latter during the "difficult, exacting, and hazardous" convoy escort missions across the Atlantic.

In the years following the armistice, Capt. Upham was Chief of Staff to the Commander, Battleship Force, Atlantic Fleet—Rear Admiral Hilary P. Jones—before serving successive tours of shore duty: in Paris as naval attache and in Washington assigned to the Office of Naval Intelligence. He commanded *Tennessee* (BB–43) from September 1924 to March 1926 and subsequently filled the billet of commandant of the naval air station at Pensacola, Fla. He capitalized on this assignment to earn his naval aviation observer's wings. Reaching flag rank in June 1927, *Upham* successively commanded Battleship Division 3 and Submarine Divisions, Control Force, and served as Chief of the Bureau of Navigation.

Given the temporary rank of admiral on 18 August 1933, Upham returned to the Far East as Commander in Chief, Asiatic Fleet, and broke his flag in cruiser *Augusta* (CA–31) commanded by Capt. (later Fleet Admiral) Chester W. Nimitz. Relieved by Admiral Orin G. Murfin in October 1935, Upham returned to the United States to serve as chairman of the General Board from 20 December 1935 to 30 September 1936. Placed on the retired list on 1 October 1936, Rear Admiral Upham died in San Francisco, Calif., on 15 September 1939.

(APD–99: dp. 1,390; l. 306'; b. 37'; dr. 12'7''; s. 24 k.; cpl. 204; a. 1 5'', 6 40mm.; cl. *Crosley*)

Upham (DE–283) was laid down on 13 December 1943 at Charleston, S.C., by the Charleston Navy Yard; launched on 9 March 1944; and sponsored by Mrs. Mabel Upham, the widow of Admiral Upham. The ship was redesignated APD–99 on 17 July 1944 and was converted to a high-speed transport by the Charleston Navy Yard. She was commissioned on 23 July 1945, Lt. Richard E. Farwell, USNR, in command.

Upham conducted her shakedown training in Guantanamo Bay, Cuba, from 8 August to 10 September; during the cruise, the war in the Pacific came to an end with Japan's capitulation in mid-August. Thus, too late to participate in combat, the fast transport exercised with an operational training unit in Chesapeake Bay until 5 October. She then served a brief tour of training duty out of Miami, Fla., from 8 to 22 October.

Then, shifting north to Hampton Roads, *Upham* reached Norfolk in time for Navy Day festivities before sailing for Jacksonville, Fla., to prepare for inactivation. Decommissioned on 25 April 1946, *Upham* was placed in the Reserve Fleet group on the St. John's River at Green Cove Springs, Fla. The ship remained inactive until struck from the Navy list on 1 June 1960.

Sold to the government of Colombia in January 1962, the erstwhile fast transport was converted for service as a floating power station and, while not carried on the Colombian Navy list, presumably served in that capacity into the 1970's.

Upshur

John Henry Upshur—born on 5 December 1823 in Northampton County, Va.—was appointed a midshipman on 4 November 1841 and initially served at sea with the Mediterranean Squadron. During the war with Mexico, Upshur was assigned to *St. Mary's* as that brig participated in operations against Tampico. He also served ashore with the naval battery during the attacks against Vera Cruz in March 1847. In the years preceding the Civil War, Upshur carried out assignments in the Mediterranean, the West Indian, and the African Squadrons. He also performed brief tours of duty at the Naval Academy and at the Washington Navy Yard as an ordnance officer. From 1853 to 1856, Upshur served in *Supply* during Commodore Matthew Calbraith Perry's expeditions to Japan which opened that nation to the west.

During the Civil War, Upshur participated in the capture of the Southern forts at Hatteras Inlet which opened the Carolina sounds to Union forces. He was executive officer of *Wabash* during the expedition which wrested Port Royal, S.C., from Confederate hands. Later on, he served in the South Atlantic Blockading Squadron during operations against Charleston. He returned to the North Atlantic Blockading Squadron in time for the abortive joint expedition against Fort Fisher late in December 1864. He was also in the expedition which finally carried the Southern works guarding Wilmington in mid-January 1865.

After the Civil War, Upshur served in a succession of sea and shore billets, culminating in his service as commander of the Pacific Squadron from 1882 to 1884. Rear Admiral Upshur retired in 1885 and died in Washington, D.C., on 30 May 1917.

William Peterkin Upshur—born on 28 October 1881 in Richmond, Va.—graduated from the Virginia Military Institute and received a commission as second lieutenant in the United States Marine Corps on 1 February 1904. Over the ensuing three and one-half decades, Upshur rose in rank and eventually became a major general on 1 October 1939.

After tours of sea duty in the Marine detachments of *Maine* (Battleship No. 10) and *Kearsarge* (Battleship No. 5), Upshur successively served ashore at Panama; the Marine Barracks at Norfolk, Va.; Port Royal, S.C.; and Mare Island, Calif., before being ordered to the transport *Buffalo*. Assignments with Marine detachments in the Philippine Islands and in China preceded his return home for duty at the Marine Barracks in Philadelphia, Pa.

During his next tour of duty—in Haiti—Upshur won the Medal of Honor. While his detachment of mounted marines forded a river in a deep ravine, they came under the fire of some 400 Haitian Caco bandits from an ambush. Leading his men forward through the heavy fusillade, Upshur succeeded in establishing a defensive position which protected his command for the night. At daybreak on the folowing day, 24 October 1915, Upshur led a fierce counterattack which caught the Cacos unawares and routed them. This action materially aided the marines in their eventual capture of the Haitian stronghold, Fort Dipitie.

Following his return to the continental United States, Upshur performed shore duty at Philadelphia; Annapolis, Md.; and Quantico, Va., before sailing for France in World War I. Following the war, he served in shore billets in repeat tours at Philadelphia, Quantico, and Haiti, before attending the Army Staff School at Ft. Leavenworth, Kansas, in 1924 and 1925.

Serving in *California* (BB-44) on the staff of the Commander, Battle Force, United States Fleet, in 1929. Upshur attended the Naval War College in 1931; and served briefly at Headquarters, Marine Corps, in Washington, D.C., before attending the Army War College. In the late 1930's Upshur again served ashore at Headquarters, Marine Corps; and later commanded the Marine Corps Base at San Diego.

Upshur's last post was that of Commander, Headquarters of the Department of the Pacific, at San Diego—a billet which he filled on 9 December 1941. Major General Upshur subsequently died as a result of injuries suffered in a plane crash near Sitka, Alaska, on 21 July 1943.

The first *Upshur* (Destroyer No. 144) was named for Rear Admiral John Henry Upshur; and the second *Upshur* (T–AP–198) was named for Major General William Peterkin Upshur, USMC.

I

(Destroyer No. 144: dp. 1,247; l. 314'4½''; b. 30'11¼''; dr. 9'½'' (mean); s. 34.61 k.; cpl. 113; a. 4 4'', 2 .30-cal. mg., 12 21'' tt.; cl. *Wickes*)

Upshur (Destroyer No. 144) was laid down on 19

February 1918 at Philadelphia, Pa., by William Cram and Sons' shipyards; launched on 4 July 1918; spo sored by Mrs. Alexander Gustavus Brown, the gran daughter of Rear Admiral Upshur; and commission at the Philadelphia Navy Yard on 23 December 191 Comdr. William V. Tomb in command.

Following shakedown and fitting out, *Upshur* d parted Newport, R.I., on 20 May 1919, bound via t Azores for north European waters. She arrived Devonport, England, on 16 June and shifted to Harwi two days later before subsequently calling at Helig land, Germany; Copenhagen, Denmark; and the fr city of Danzig. She eventually returned, via Harwi and Ponta Delgada, to the United States, arriving New York City on 22 July.

Assigned to the Pacific Fleet soon thereafter, *Upsh* transited the Panama Canal, bound for San Dieg her base of operations until the spring of the followi year. During her time at San Diego, the ship conduct gunnery and torpedo training and local coastal oper tions. In April 1920, *Upshur* got underway and pr ceeded via Honolulu, Pearl Harbor, Midway, and Gua to the Far East, arriving at Cavite, in the Philippin on 20 May. She soon sailed for duty on the low Yangtze River.

At Yochow on 16 June, troops of warlord Chan Ching-yao murdered American missionary, William Reimert. At Hankow when the incident occurred, *U shur*, acting under urgent orders, got underway for t trouble spot on the 22d—departing with such gre haste that four of her complement (one officer an three enlisted men) were left behind. Arriving Yochow on the 23d, *Upshur* sent ashore a landing par of one officer and 40 men at 1805 on 25 June to prote the American mission. Two days later—when loc tensions had eased—they were reembarked.

The Standard Oil Company's steamer *Mei F* arrived at Yochow on the 28th and delivered 100 bags rice for refugees in the vicinity. Over the ensuing day *Upshur* delivered that food staple to the Americ mission. In the meantime, the Commander in Chi Asiatic Fleet, Admiral Albert Gleaves, arrived Yochow in *Elliott* (Destroyer No. 146) to observe t local situation. Eventually, the offending Chinese offic in charge, Chang Ching-yao, was removed, and t Chinese foreign office, while investigating the incide expressed its profound regrets.

Upshur remained on the Yangtze until 9 July, wh she resumed routine operations—target practices a torpedo drills. For her tour on the river, the destroy received commendation in the Secretary of the Nav annual report, noted as being "especially serviceable establishing radio communication along the river."

Upshur conducted exercises in the Philippine Islan in the winter and in Chinese waters, off Chefoo, the summer, with more training and "showing the fla cruises in between. During her tour in the Asia Fleet, *Upshur* was reclassified DD–144 on 17 Ju 1920. After completing her assignment in the Far Ea early in 1922, the destroyer arrived back on the we coast in the spring and was decommissioned at S Diego on 15 May 1922 and placed in reserve.

Recommissioned on 2 June 1930, Lt. Comdr. Mort L. Deyo in command, *Upshur* operated with the Batt Fleet and Scouting Force, first on the west coast a later on the east, until decommissioned on 22 Decemb 1936 at Philadelphia. She was berthed in the Philad phia Navy Yard until the autumn of 1939.

Soon after the outbreak of war in Poland in Se tember 1939, President Roosevelt declared the neutrali of the United States and ordered the establishment a Neutrality Patrol off the eastern seaboard and g coast on 5 September. To augment the ships first a signed to this duty, the Navy began reactivation of light minelayers and destroyers. Accordingly, *Upsh* went back into commission at Philadelphia on 4 Octob a little over a month after Germany invaded Pola Attached to the Atlantic Squadron of the United Sta fleet, *Upshur* interspersed her routine training evolutions—battle practices, torpedo exercises, and tactical maneuvers—with patrols safeguarding America's neutral shores along the Atlantic and gulf coasts.

Upshur's routine was broken briefly in December 1939. On the 13th, the North German Lloyd Line steamship *Columbus* slipped out of Vera Cruz, Mexico, in an attempt to reach Germany and slip through the British blockade. She had not reckoned with the Neutrality Patrol, however, that persistently shadowed the liner from the moment she stood out of the Mexican port. *Upshur* participated in the tracking and reporting of the steamer, the 13th largest merchant steamship in the world. *Columbus* ultimately met her doom on 19 December; she scuttled when confronted by the British destroyer HMS *Hyperion*. American cruiser *Tuscaloosa* (CA-37), standing nearby, rescued *Columbus*' crew.

The rapid fall of France in the spring of 1940 caused alarm in the western hemisphere that French possessions in the West Indies might fall into German hands. American planners quickly drew up contingency plans to take these isles by force if necessary. In the event of such an invasion, *Upshur* and her sisters in Destroyer Squadron 30 were slated to screen the counterbattery and gunfire support group built around *Texas* (BB-35), *Vincennes* (CA-44), and *Chester* (CA-27). Fortunately for France and the United States, skillful diplomacy obviated such flexing of America's naval muscles; and the crisis abated by the autumn of 1940.

In between the routine neutrality patrol assignments and training, *Upshur* was called upon to perform a special escort mission. On 23 December 1940, the heavy cruiser *Tuscaloosa* departed Norfolk with William D. Leahy, Ambassador to Vichy France, and his wife, embarked, bound for Lisbon, Portugal. *Upshur* and the new destroyer *Madison* (DD-425) escorted the heavy cruiser, until they were detached on Christmas Day to return to Norfolk while the cruiser proceeded on, unescorted, on her diplomatic mission.

In March 1941, the Support Force was established for the United States Fleet, under the command of Rear Admiral Arthur LeRoy Bristol. Based at Narragansett Bay, this group prepared for assignment to "distant seas" and was formed around the nucleus of *Denebola* (AD-12), *Albemarle* (AV-5), *Belknap* (AVD-8), and *George E. Badger* (AVD-3). Four patrol plane squadrons and three destroyer squadrons—the last including *Upshur*—rounded out the Support Force.

Over the ensuing months, *Upshur* operated alternately out of Argentia; Newport, R.I.; Philadelphia; Narragansett Bay; Boston; and Reykjavik, Iceland, after its occupation by the United States that summer. On 11 September, the destroyer departed Argentia, bound for a rendezvous with an outward-bound convoy headed for the British Isles.

Five days later, a convoy of 50 merchantmen of British and Allied nationalities—classified as HX-150 —put to sea from Halifax, Nova Scotia, escorted locally by Canadian units. On 17 September, about 150 miles out of Argentia, the American escort group under Capt. Morton L. Deyo, which included *Upshur*, met up with the British convoy. The ensuing days witnessed the five American destroyers shepherding the convoy towards the "Mid-Ocean Meeting Point" (MOMP). *Upshur* steamed on the port side of the convoy, 500 to 1,000 yards out, searching with her sound equipment in a 30-degree sector during the day, and patrolling 500 to 1,000 yards out at night. The Americans brought the convoy safely to the MOMP, where British ships— two destroyers and four corvettes—picked up the England-bound ships. The five American destroyers then convoyed the Iceland-bound section of the convoy to Reykjavik. This convoy was the first one assisted by the United States Navy in the Battle of the Atlantic.

This mission proved to be only the beginning of American escort operations prior to the formal entry of the United States into World War II, as ships of the

Support Force escorted 14 convoys between 16 September and 30 October. As the months wore on, clashes of American warships with German submarines grew in frequency and intensity. *Kearny* (DD-432) was damaged by a German torpedo on 17 October, and *Salinas* (AO-19) suffered a similar fate on the 30th. The next day, *Reuben James* (DD-145) was sunk by *U-552*. Over the ensuing period from 1 November to 7 December 1941, Support Force destroyers conducted seven round-trip convoy missions in shepherding 14 convoys consisting of some 550 ships across the North Atlantic.

Besides the ever-present danger from lurking U-boats during these missions, there always existed the difficulties posed by the weather of the North Atlantic. Biting cold winds and raging seas combined to make life miserable on board the older destroyers like *Upshur*. Storm damage often forced ships back into port for repairs, and heavy concentrations of ice formed by the heavy spray and cold temperatures often dangerously increased a ship's top-hamper. Damages inflicted by Neptune often changed the schedules for the escorting destroyers, giving some very little time to rest and refit in port before having to go out on another arduous convoy mission.

On the other hand, the weather could also be an effective ally in that convoys were sometimes given the advantage of fogs which blotted out their presence from the prying eyes of U-boat periscopes. While sometimes giving the friendly forces more than a few anxious moments, the weather also gave the enemy just as difficult a time. In the period following full-scale American entry into the war with the Japanese attack on Pearl Harbor on 7 December 1941 and until the middle of February 1942, Support Force destroyers escorted a dozen convoys in each direction across the Atlantic—750 ships—in comparative safety.

On the night of 4 February 1942, *Upshur* departed Londonderry, Northern Ireland, in company with *Gleaves* (DD-423), *Dallas* (DD-199), *Roper* (DD-147), and the "Secretary"-class Coast Guard cutter *Ingham*. Throughout the day on the 5th, the ships hunted a U-boat whose intentions seemed to be to follow the Americans to their outbound convoy assignment. Seven times the destroyers and the Coast Guard cutter attacked the submarine, dropping 30 depth charges, but could not "kill" the elusive submersible.

After rendezvousing with Convoy ON-63 on the morning of 7 February, the escorts shaped a course southwest with the 30 merchant vessels, shepherding them along in the wintry seas. *Upshur*'s lookouts spotted a U-boat running on the surface two miles away and gave chase, but the German lookouts were alert, and the submarine submerged before *Upshur* could attack.

For two hours, *Upshur* and *Ingham* scoured the area, dropping 15 depth charges before they returned to their stations. *Upshur* had no sooner returned to station when she again spotted the U-boat—8,000 yards away. Accelerating to flank speed, the flush-decker headed towards the enemy, only to have the U-boat submerge out of sight once more. *Upshur* fired two rounds from her forward 3-inch gun—both shells splashing around the enemy's disappearing conning tower. *Gleaves* soon arrived on the scene and assisted *Upshur* in searching for the U-boat. Neither ship was able to make contact with the enemy that day nor the next, but they succeeded in preventing the German submersible from making contact with the convoy and managed to bring all of their charges safely into port.

Over the ensuing two years, *Upshur* operated on convoy escort missions with the Atlantic Fleet. Her duties took her from the eastern seaboard of the United States to the mouth of the Mediterranean Sea, from the inhospitable climes of the North Atlantic to the tropical Caribbean. As the Allies slowly gained the upper hand in the Battle of the Atlantic, newer and more modern destroyers replaced the aging flush-deckers as front-line convoy escorts. Throughout 1944, *Upshur* operated between Norfolk, Va., and Quonset Point, R.I., serving as plane guard and target vessel during qualification trials for aircraft carriers. During this period, she worked successively with *Kasaan Bay* (CVE–69), *Ranger* (CV–4), *Mission Bay* (CVE–59), *Tulagi* (CVE–72), *Tripoli* (CVE–64), *Wake Island* (CVE–65), *Prince William* (CVE–31), and *Solomons* (CVE–67). Reclassified as a miscellaneous auxiliary, AG–103, on 3 June 1945, *Upshur* was plane-guarding for the new *Essex*-class carrier *Lake Champlain* (CV–39) when Japan capitulated on 15 August, ending the war in the Pacific.

Decommissioned at Norfolk, Va., on 2 November 1945, *Upshur* was struck from the Navy list on 11 November; was sold to the Northern Metals Co. of Philadelphia on 26 September 1947; and was scrapped by April 1948.

II

(T–AP–198: dp. 11,203 (f.); l. 533'9''; b. 73'3''; dr. 27'1''; s. 19 k.; cpl. 216; tr. 2,500; cl. *Barrett*; T. P2–S1–DN3)

Passenger cargo liner *President Hayes* was laid down in 1949 under a Maritime Commission contract (MC hull 2916) at Camden, N.J., by the New York Shipbuilding Corp., for the American President Lines. However, late in June 1950, before the ship could be completed in her civilian configuration, war broke out in Korea. The Navy acquired *President Hayes* on 15 September 1950, renamed the liner *Upshur*, and designated her T–AP–198 on 2 January 1951. Launched on 9 January 1951 and sponsored by Mrs. Charles Sawyer, the wife of President Truman's Secretary of Commerce, *Upshur* was converted by her builder to a troop and dependent transport and, on 20 December 1952 at Camden, was placed in service with the Military Sea Transportation Service (MSTS).

For the next two decades, *Upshur* operated out of New York providing service for troops and dependents on numerous transatlantic cruises to Bremerhaven, Germany; Mediterranean ports in North Africa, Turkey, Greece, and Italy; and Caribbean ports. She operated under the aegis of MSTS, Atlantic, until transferred to the Maritime Administration on 2 April 1973. Simultaneously retransferred on that day to the Maine Maritime Academy, the ship was renamed *State of Maine* and based at Castine.

Soon after beginning this service, the erstwhile troop transport got underway for a two-month training cruise to the Caribbean and to South America with cadets from the Maritime Academy embarked. In 1974 *State of Maine* cruised to northern Europe and visited Leningrad, Helsinki, Antwerp, and Glasgow. The cruise marked the first time in many years that an American training vessel had called at a Russian port.

Upshur, Abel P., see *Abel P. Upshur*.

Upshur, George P., see *George P. Upshur*.

Uranus

One of the more remote of the known major planets discovered in 1781 by Sir William Herschel. The planet itself was named for the personification of heaven, Uranus was the husband (or son) of Gaea (Earth) and the father of Titans, Furies, the Cyclops, and giants. Hating his offspring, Uranus confined them to Tartarus but was attacked and dethroned by his son Chronus.

(AF–14: dp. 3,348 (f.); l. 269'6''; b. 39'6''; dr. 16'; s. 12 k.; cpl. 93; a. 1 4''; cl. *Uranus*)

Uranus (AF–14)—built in 1933 as *Helga* at Elsinore near Copenhagen, Denmark, by Helsingoors Shipbuilding Works, for J. Lauritzen—had previously operated as *Caravelle* (1938 to 1940) and *Marie* (1940 to 1941). She served in the fruit trade between her home country—Denmark—and Central American republics and became a ship without a country upon the fall of her homeland to the invading Germans in the spring of 1940.

Acquired by the Navy from the United States Maritime Commission on 11 August 1941, *Marie* soon entered the Robbins Drydock Co. yard at Brooklyn, N.Y., for conversion to a naval stores ship. Renamed *Uranus* and classified AF–14, the ship was placed in commission at Brooklyn on 27 October 1941, Comdr. Orrin J. Hewitt in command. During the ship's subsequent shakedown period, the Japanese attacked Pearl Harbor and the United States entered World War II in both oceans. *Uranus* departed Norfolk, Va., on 20 December and arrived at Halifax, Nova Scotia, on Christmas Eve. Five days later, she pushed on for Iceland.

Uranus served as a floating refrigerated storage vessel and provided stores and provisions to American forces in Iceland into the summer of 1943. During this

The refrigerated store ship *Uranus* (AF–14) at Norfolk, 11 December 1943. (19–N–60186)

time, her ports of call included Hvalfjordur, Seydisfjordur, Reykjavik, and Akureyi. In these in-hospitable and unpredictable northern waters, the ship ran aground off Akureyi while on a coastwise passage at 0129 on 10 April 1943, coming to a stop on a sloping gravel beach which was reputedly once the fairway between two holes of a coastal golf course. After repeated attempts, with the assistance of *Symbol* (AM–123) and *Kewaydin* (AT–24), the storeship was finally refloated on the 13th.

Following repairs, she departed Icelandic waters on 21 August, with men and equipment from a Navy construction battalion on board but, due to contrary winds and currents, did not make port at her Davisville, R.I., destination until 3 September. After discharging passengers, the storeship proceeded on for New York, arriving three days later. She then pressed south for Norfolk, where she soon commenced a lengthy overhaul.

Uranus—now outfitted with a new refrigeration system—departed the east coast on 20 December and, five days later, reached a rendezvous with a convoy bound for the Pacific. Clearing the Panama Canal on the first day of 1944, the storeship headed on for Pearl Harbor on 3 January, proceeding independently, and reached Oahu on the 23d.

She conducted two round-trip Pacific passages between San Francisco, Calif., and Pearl Harbor and Midway, before she sailed for Majuro in the Marshalls. For the remainder of the year 1944, *Uranus* conducted routine cargo and stores-carrying runs between Midway and Pearl Harbor to the west and San Pedro, Calif., to the east. Overhauled at San Francisco in April 1945, the ship was based at this port for the remainder of the war in the Pacific. She subsequently participated in "Magic-Carpet" operations to bring veterans back to the United States from the erstwhile Pacific battle zones.

Decommissioned on 8 May 1946 at Norfolk, *Uranus* was delivered to the War Shipping Administration of the Maritime Commission on 9 May and was struck from the Navy list on 21 May.

Returned by the Maritime Commission to her original owner, J. Lauritzen, the former naval stores ship was renamed *Maria Dan* in 1946 or 1947 and operated in the mercantile trade until 1960.

Urdaneta

Andres de Urdaneta—a subordinate of Miguel Lopez de Legaspi—helped to establish the first Spanish colony in the Philippine Islands in 1565. He also founded the city of Manila and discovered the eastward-flowing currents and winds which enabled Spanish ships to sail from the Philippines via Guam to Mexico.

(Gbt: dp. 42; lbp. 70'5''; b. 12'3''; dr. 4'9'' (mean); s. 8 k.; cpl. 15; a. 1 1-pdr., 1 37mm., 1 Colt mg.)

Urdaneta—occasionally misspelled *Undaneta*—was an iron-hulled gunboat built for the Spanish government at the Cavite Arsenal near Manila, Philippines, in 1882 and 1883 and was apparently captured by the Army during the Spanish-American War in 1898. Acquired from the War Department by the Navy on 17 January 1899, *Urdaneta* went into commission on 2 June 1899.

The gunboat conducted local patrols into the summer months to interdict the flow of munitions and arms to insurrectionists in the Philippines resisting American attempts to establish sovereignty. On 17 September 1899, *Urdaneta* ran aground in the Orani River, near Manila, on a soft mud shoal. Insurrectionists along the river soon opened a withering enfilading fire, killing the gunboat's commanding officer, Naval Cadet Welborn C. Wood, and some of his crew. The Filipinos quickly rushed the stranded vessel and captured the remainder of the crew not slain by the murderous fire from the jungle-lined banks.

Apparently recovered by the Navy, *Urdaneta* resumed her service in the spring of the following year, being commissioned at Cavite on 12 May 1900. She departed Cavite on the 14th and served for a time as guard ship at Olongapo before shifting to Subic, and eventually, to Cavite, where she spent the remainder of May undergoing repairs and alterations.

Urdaneta subsequently operated as guard vessel at Subic Bay and conducted surveys in connection with the impending visits of the commission investigating naval base sites in the Philippines. She remained engaged in these vital but unglamourous duties until she was decommissioned on 12 December 1902 at Cavite. Struck from the Navy list on 15 December 1904, *Urdaneta* was apparently reinstated on the Navy list as a tug, although there is no extant record of this event. The ship is listed in *Ship's Data, United States Naval Vessels* editions for 1912 through 1916 as a yard tug operating at Cavite. Her subsequent fate is unknown.

Urgent

Urgent (ARS–38)—a *Bolster*-class salvage ship—was scheduled to be built at Napa, Calif., by the Basalt Rock Co., Inc.; but the end of the war in the Pacific obviated her construction. Accordingly, the contract for building the vessel was terminated on 12 August 1945.

Usage

Usage (AM–130) was laid down on 1 January 1942 at Chickasaw, Ala., by the Gulf Shipbuilding Corp.; launched on 4 October 1942; and transferred to the United Kingdom under lend-lease on 7 June 1943.

Usage, an *Auk*-class minesweeper, served with the Royal Navy as *Tourmaline* (J 339) in the Atlantic in World War II. She was returned to United States custody in January 1947, struck from the Navy list, and transferred to the Foreign Liquidation Commission for disposition. Sold to Turkey, she served with the Turkish Navy under the name *Cardak* until 1974.

Utah

Utah was admitted to the Union on 4 January 1896 as the 45th state. It takes its name from a tribe of Indians who dwelt in that area—know as Utes. The hunting grounds for that tribe embraced three-quarters of the territory enclosed by the present boundaries of that state.

(Battleship No. 31: dp. 21,825 (n.); l. 521'6''; b. 88'3''; dr. 28'4'' (mean); s. 20.75 k.; cpl. 1,041; a. 10 12'', 16 5'', 2 21'' tt.; cl. *Florida*)

Utah (Battleship No. 31) was laid down on 9 March 1909 at Camden, N.J., by the New York Shipbuilding Co.; launched on 23 December 1909; sponsored by Miss Mary Alice Spry, daughter of Governor William Spry of Utah; and commissioned at the Philadelphia Navy Yard on 31 August 1911, Capt. William S. Benson in command.

After her shakedown cruise—a voyage that took her to Hampton Roads, Va.; Santa Rosa Island and Pensacola, Fla.; Galveston, Tex.; Kingston and Portland Bight, Jamaica; and Guantanamo Bay, Cuba—*Utah* was assigned to the Atlantic Fleet in March 1912. She operated with the Fleet early that spring, conducting exercises in gunnery and torpedo defense, before she entered the New York Navy Yard on 16 April for an overhaul.

Departing New York on 1 June, *Utah* briefly visited Hampton Roads and then steamed to Annapolis, Md., where she arrived on the 5th. There, she embarked

Naval Academy midshipmen and got underway on the 10th for the Virginia capes and the open Atlantic. She conducted a midshipmen training cruise off the New England seaboard well into the summer before disembarking her contingent of officers-to-be back at Annapolis on 24 and 25 August. Soon thereafter, the battleship headed for the Southern Drill Grounds to conduct gunnery exercises.

For a little over two years, the dreadnought maintained that schedule of operations off the eastern seaboard, ranging from the New England coast to Cuban waters. During that time, she made one cruise to European waters, visiting Villefranche, France, from 8 to 30 November 1913.

Utah began the year 1914 at the New York Navy Yard and sailed south on 5 January. After stopping at Hampton Roads, she reached Cuban waters later in the month for torpedo and small arms exercises. However, due to tension in Mexico, *Utah* sailed for Mexican waters in early February and reached Vera Cruz on the 16th. She operated off that port until getting underway for Tampico on 9 April with several hundred refugees embarked.

Soon thereafter, it was learned that a German steamship, SS *Ypiranga*, was bound for Vera Cruz with a shipment of arms and munitions earmarked for the dictator Victoriano Huerta. *Utah* received orders to search for the ship and put to sea and reached Vera Cruz on the 16th. When it appeared that the shipment might be landed, the Navy took steps to take the customs house at Vera Cruz and stop the delivery. Accordingly, plans were drawn up for a landing at Vera Cruz, to commence on 21 April 1914.

Utah consequently landed her "battalion"—17 officers and 367 sailors under the command of Lt. Guy W. S. Castle—as well as her Marine detachment, which formed part of the improvised "First Marine Brigade," made up of detachments of marines from the other ships that had arrived to show American determination. In the ensuing fighting, in which the men of *Utah*'s bluejacket battalion distinguished themselves, seven won medals of honor. Those seven included Lt. Castle, the battalion commander; company commanders Ens. Oscar C. Badger and Ens. Paul F. Foster; section leaders, Chief Turret Captains Niels Drustrup and Abraham Desomer; Chief Gunner George Bradley; and Boatswain's Mate Henry N. Nickerson.

Utah remained at Vera Cruz for almost two months

before returning north to the New York Navy Yard in late June for an overhaul. Over the next three years, the battleship operated on a regular routine of battle practices and exercises from off the eastern seaboard into the Caribbean, as the United States readied its forces for the possible entry of the United States into the worldwide war that broke out in July 1914.

After the United States finally declared war on 6 April 1917, *Utah* operated in the waters of the Chesapeake Bay as an engineering and gunnery training ship and continued that duty until 30 August 1918, when she sailed for the British Isles with Vice Admiral Henry T. Mayo, Commander in Chief, United States Atlantic Fleet, embarked.

Fears of possible attacks by German heavy units upon the large convoys crossing the Atlantic with troops and munitions for the western front prompted the dispatch, to European waters, of a powerful force of American dreadnoughts to Irish waters. *Utah*—as part of that movement—reached Brerehaven, Bantry Bay, Ireland, on 10 September. There, she became the flagship of Rear Admiral Thomas S. Rodgers, Commander, Battleship Division 6. Until the signing of the armistice on 11 November 1918, *Utah*, along with the sisterships *Oklahoma* (Battleship No. 37) and *Nevada* (Battleship No. 36), operated from Bantry Bay, covering the Allied convoys approaching the British Isles, ready to deal with any surface threat that the German Navy could hurl at the valuable transports and supply ships.

After the cessation of hostilities, *Utah* visited Portland, England, and later served as part of the honor escort for the transport *George Washington* (Id. No. 3018), as that ship bore President Woodrow Wilson into the harbor of Brest, France, on 13 December 1918. The following day, *Utah* turned homeward and reached New York on Christmas Day 1918.

Utah remained at anchor in the North River, off New York City, until 30 January 1919. During that time, she half-masted her colors at 1440 on 7 January due to the death of former President Theodore Roosevelt and, on the 8th, fired salutes at half-hour intervals throughout the day in memory of the great American statesman.

Utah carried out a regular routine of battle practices and maneuvers, ranging from the New England coast to the Caribbean, into mid-1921. During that time, she was classified as BB-31 on 17 July 1920, during the Navy-wide assignment of hull numbers.

USS *Utah* (BB–31), after a partial modernization had given her a pole mainmast in place of an original cage mast. Boiler uptakes have been trunked into a single stack. (19–N–11021)

Ultimately departing Boston on 9 July 1921, *Utah* proceeded via Lisbon, Portugal, and reached Cherbourg, France, soon thereafter. There, *Utah* became the flagship for the United States naval forces in European waters. She "showed the flag" at the principal Atlantic coast ports of Europe and in the Mediterranean until relieved by *Pittsburgh* (CA–4) in October 1922.

Returning to the United States on 21 October 1922, *Utah* then became the flagship of Battleship Division (BatDiv) 5, United States Scouting Fleet and operated with the Scouting Fleet over the next three and one-half years.

Late in 1924, *Utah* was chosen to carry the United States diplomatic mission to the centennial celebration of the Battle of Ayacucho (9 December 1824), the decisive action in the Peruvian struggle for independence. Designated as flagship for the special squadron assigned to represent the United States at the festivities, *Utah* departed New York City on 22 November 1924 with General of the Armies John J. Pershing, USA, and former congressman, the Honorable F. C. Hicks, embarked, and arrived at Callao on 9 December.

Utah disembarked General Pershing and the other members of the mission on Christmas 1924, so that the general and his mission could visit other South American cities inland on their goodwill tour. Meanwhile, *Utah*, in the weeks that followed, called at the Chilean ports of Punta Arenas and Valparaiso before she rounded Cape Horn and met General Pershing at Montevideo, Uruguay. Reembarking the general and his party there, the battleship then visited in succession: Rio de Janeiro, Brazil; La Guaira, Venezuela; and Havana, Cuba, before ending her diplomatic voyage at New York City on 13 March 1925.

Utah spent subsequent summers of 1925 and 1926 with the Midshipman Practice Squadron and, after disembarking her midshipmen at the conclusion of the 1925 cruise, entered the Boston Navy Yard and was decommissioned on 31 October 1925 for modernization. During that period of alterations and repairs, the ship's 'cage' mainmast was replaced by a lighter pole mast; she was fitted to burn oil instead of coal as fuel; and her armament was modified to reflect the increased concern over antiaircraft defense. Interestingly, *Utah* and her sistership *Florida* (BB–30) never received the more modern "tripod" masts fitted to other classes.

Utah was placed back in commission on 1 December 1925 and, after local operations with the Scouting Fleet, departed Hampton Roads on 21 November 1928, bound for South America. Reaching Montevideo on 18 December, she there embarked President-elect and Mrs. Herbert C. Hoover; the Honorable Henry T. Fletcher, Ambassador to Italy; and members of the press. *Utah* transported the President-elect's party to Rio de Janeiro, Brazil, between 21 and 23 December, and then continued her homeward voyage with Mr. Hoover embarked. En route, the President-elect inspected the battleship's crew while at sea, before the ship reached Hampton Roads on 6 January 1929.

However, *Utah*'s days as a battleship were numbered. Under the terms of the 1922 Washington Naval Treaty, *Utah* was selected for conversion to a mobile target, in place of the former battleship *North Dakota*; and, on 1 July 1931, *Utah*'s classification was changed to AG–16. Her conversion—carried out at the Norfolk Navy Yard—included the installation of a radio-control apparatus. After having been decommissioned for the duration of the conversion, *Utah* was recommissioned at Norfolk on 1 April 1932, Comdr. Randall Jacobs in command.

Utah departed Norfolk on 7 April to train her engineers in using the new installations and for trials of her radio gear by which the ship could be controlled at varying rates of speed and changes of course—maneuvers that a ship would conduct in battle. Her electric motors, operated by signals from the controlling ship, opened and closed throttle valves, moved her steering gear, and regulated the supply of oil to her boilers. In addition, a Sperry gyro pilot kept the ship on course.

Returning to port on 21 April, *Utah* passed her radio control trials off the Virginia capes on 5 May. On 1 June, *Utah* ran three hours under radio control, with all engineering stations manned; over the next two days, she made two successful runs, each of four hours duration, during which no machinery was touched by human hands. Observers, however—two in each fire room and two in each boiler room—kept telephone information and recorded data.

Her trials completed, *Utah* departed Norfolk on 9 June. After transiting the Panama Canal, she reached San Pedro, Calif., on 30 June, reporting for duty with Training Squadron 1, Base Force, United States Fleet. She conducted her first target duty, for cruisers of the Fleet, on 25 July, and later, on 2 August, conducted rehearsal runs for *Nevada* (BB–36), *Utah* being controlled from *Hovey* (DD–208) and *Talbot* (DD–114).

Over the next nine years, the erstwhile battleship performed a vital service to the fleet as a mobile target, contributing realism to the training of naval aviators in dive, torpedo, and high level bombing. Thus, she greatly aided the development of tactics in those areas. On one occasion, she even served as a troop transport, embarking 223 officers and men of the Fleet Marine Force at Sand Island, Midway, for amphibious operations at Hilo Bay, Hawaii, as part of Fleet Problem XVI in the early summer of 1935. She then transported the marines from Hawaii to San Diego, Calif., disembarking them on 12 June 1935.

That same month, June 1935, saw the establishment of a fleet machine gun school on board *Utah* while she continued her mission as a mobile target. The former dreadnought received her first instructors on board in August 1935, and the first students—drawn from the ships' companies of *Raleigh* (CL–7), *Concord* (CL–10), *Omaha* (CL–4), *Memphis* (CL–13), *Milwaukee* (CL–5), and *Ranger* (CV–4)—reported aboard for training on 20 September. Subsequently, during the 1936 and 1937 gunnery year, *Utah* was fitted with a new quadruple 1.1-inch machine gun mount for experimental test and development by the machine gun school. Some of the first tests of that type of weapon were conducted on board.

Utah—besides serving as a realistic target for exercises involving carrier-based planes—also towed targets during battle practices conducted by the Fleet's battleships and took part in the yearly "fleet problems." She transited the Panama Canal on 9 January 1939 to participate in Fleet Problem XX—part of the maneuvers observed personally by President Franklin D. Roosevelt from the heavy cruiser *Houston* (CA–30).

After providing mobile target services for the submarines of Submarine Squadron 6 in the late autumn and early winter of 1939, *Utah* devoted the eight months that followed to special machine gun practices. The following summer, *Utah* sailed for the Hawaiian Islands, reaching Pearl Harbor on 1 August 1940, and fired advanced antiaircraft gunnery practice in the Hawaiian operating area until 14 December 1940, when she sailed for the west coast, returning to Long Beach four days before Christmas.

For the next two months, *Utah* operated as a mobile bombing target off San Clemente Island, Calif., for planes from Patrol Wing 1, and from the carriers *Lexington* (CV–2), *Saratoga* (CV–3), and *Enterprise* (CV–6). *Utah* returned to Hawaiian waters on 1 April 1941, embarking gunners for the Advanced Antiaircraft Gun School, men drawn from *West Virginia* (BB–48), *Oklahoma* (BB–37), *Colorado* (BB–45), *Phoenix* (CL–46), *Nashville* (CL–43), *Philadelphia* (CL–41), and *New Orleans* (CA–32).

Over the weeks that followed, she trained her embarked gunnery students in control and loading drills for the 5-inch batteries, firing runs on radio-controlled drone targets as well as .50-caliber and 1.1-inch firing on drones and balloons. *Utah* put into Los Angeles harbor on 20 May and there embarked Fleet Marine Force passengers for transportation to Bremerton, Wash. Putting the marines ashore a week later, the ship entered the Puget Sound Navy Yard on 31 May 1941.

During the ensuing overhaul, *Utah* received repairs and alterations designed to make her a more effective gunnery training ship. The alterations included the addition of 5-inch/38-caliber guns in single mounts with gunshields—similar to those fitted on the more modern types of destroyers then in service. She also lost her prewar colors, being repainted in overall measure one camouflage—dark gray with pale gray tops. With war paint thus donned, *Utah* sailed for Hawaiian waters on 14 September, after visits to Port Townsend, Wash., and San Francisco and San Pedro, Calif. She arrived at Pearl Harbor soon thereafter and carried out antiaircraft training and target duties through the late autumn.

Utah completed an advanced antiaircraft gunnery cruise in Hawaiian waters shortly before she returned to Pearl Harbor in early December 1941, mooring off Ford Island in berth F–11. On the morning of 7 December 1941, the senior officer on board—the captain and executive officer were ashore on leave—was Lt. Comdr. Solomon S. Isquith, the engineer officer.

Shortly before 0800, men topside noted three planes—taken for American planes on maneuvers—heading in a northerly direction from the harbor entrance. They made a low dive at the southern end of Ford Island—where the seaplane hangers were situated—and began dropping bombs.

The attack on the fleet at Pearl Harbor lasted a little under two hours, but for *Utah*, it was over in a few minutes. At 0801, soon after sailors had begun raising the colors at the ship's fantail, the erstwhile battleship took a torpedo hit forward, and immediately started to list to port.

As the ship began to roll ponderously over on her beam ends, 6-by-12-inch timbers—placed on the decks to cushion them against the impact of the bombs used during the ship's latest stint as a mobile target—began to shift, hampering the efforts of the crew to abandon ship. Below, men headed topside while they could. One, however, Chief Watertender Peter Tomich, remained below, making sure that the boilers were secured and that all men had gotten out of the engineering spaces. Another man, Fireman John B. Vaessen, USNR, remained at his post in the dynamo room, making sure that the ship had enough power to keep her lights going as long as possible.

Comdr. Isquith made an inspection to make sure men were out and nearly became trapped himself. As the ship began to turn over, he found an escape hatch blocked. While he was attempting to escape through a porthole, a table upon which he was standing—impelled by the ever-increasing list of the ship—slipped out from beneath him. Fortunately, a man outside grabbed Isquith's arm and pulled him through at the last instant.

At 0812, the mooring lines snapped, and *Utah* rolled over on her beam ends; her survivors struck out for shore, some taking shelter on the mooring quays since Japanese strafers were active.

Shortly after most of the men had reached shore, Comdr. Isquith, and others, heard a knocking from within the overturned ship's hull. Although Japanese planes were still strafing the area, Isquith called for volunteers to return to the hull and investigate the tapping. Obtaining a cutting torch from the nearby *Raleigh* (CL–7)—herself fighting for survival after taking early torpedo hits—the men went to work.

As a result of the persistence shown by Machinist S. A. Szymanski; Chief Machinist's Mate Terrance MacSelwiney, USNR; and two others whose names were unrecorded, 10 men clambered from a would-be tomb. The last man out was Fireman Vaessen, who had made his way to the bottom of the ship when she capsized, bearing a flashlight and wrench.

Utah was declared "in ordinary" on 29 December 1941 and was placed under the control of the Pearl Harbor Base Force. Partially righted to clear an adjacent berth, she was then declared "out of commission not in service," on 5 September 1944. *Utah*'s name was struck from the Navy list on 13 November 1944. Her partially submerged hulk still remains, rusting, at Pearl Harbor with an unknown number of men trapped inside.

Of *Utah*'s complement, 30 officers and 431 enlisted men survived the ship's loss; 6 officers and 58 men died—four of the latter being recovered and interred ashore. Chief Watertender Tomich received the Medal of Honor posthumously for his selfless act in ensuring the safety of others.

Utah (AG–16) received one battle star for her World War II service.

Ute

A tribe of Shoshonean Indians formerly living in Colorado, Utah, and New Mexico. The Utes went on the warpath in 1879 and massacred white settlers at the White River Agency in Colorado. On 29 September 1879, the braves of the tribe met Army troops under Major Thornburgh and, in the ensuing battle, gained the upper hand, forcing the soldiers to retreat and erect a barricade of wagons and dead horses. Thereafter, the Indians besieged the Army until 5 October, when troops under General Merritt arrived and put the Indians to flight. Once subdued, the Utes were placed on reservations in Utah, Colorado, and New Mexico.

(AT–76: dp. 1,589 (tl.) ; l. 205'0'' ; b. 38'6'' ; dr. 14'3'' s. 16.25 k.; cpl. 85; a. 1 3'', 2 40mm.; cl. *Navajo*)

Ute (AT–76) was laid down on 27 February 1942 at Alameda, Calif., by the United Engineering Co.; launched on 24 June 1942; sponsored by Mrs. Robert Tate; and commissioned on 13 December 1942, Lt. William F. Lewis in command.

After shakedown training in the San Francisco Bay region, *Ute* got underway on 10 February 1943, bound for Alaskan waters, and reached Dutch Harbor a week later. *Ute* immediately sailed for Amchitka, Alaska, where she participated in the salvage operations on the attack transport *Arthur Middleton* (APA–25) which had been thrown aground in one of the vicious "williwaws" common to that area of the world.

Throughout March, *Ute*, assisted by the fleet tug *Tatnuck* (AT–27), continued in her efforts to haul the stranded attack transport off the beach. *Ute* utilized two sets of beach gear in the attempt to free the vessel. *Ute* interrupted that work only once during the month —to assist the merchantman SS *Wallace* to clear the harbor after the merchantman's mooring had parted.

After suspending her operations on the *Arthur Middleton* for the first week of April because of bad weather, the plucky auxiliary resumed her work when the weather cleared on the 8th. Success crowned her efforts the following day, when the attack transport shuddered free of the beach. Within a few days, *Ute* and *Tatnuck* got underway and towed *Arthur Middleton* to Dutch Harbor where they arrived on the 13th.

Ute fueled and left immediately for aptly named Cold Bay where she assisted the stranded Russian merchantman *Krasnyl Oktyabr*. Passing a tow line to the Soviet vessel, *Ute* pulled her free the next day. That mission completed, the fleet tug cleared Cold Bay for Women's Bay where she took two tank landing craft (LCT's) in tow and proceeded via Dutch Harbor to Sweeper's Cove.

During the first week of May, *Ute* assisted in laying an antisubmarine net at Sweeper's Cove. On the 6th she joined TF 51 as the carriers were steaming toward the Kuril Islands for strikes against Paramushiro to support the invasion of Attu. While the task force was returning from the raid—which *Ute* had participated in as a salvage unit—reduced visibility caused the tug to be separated from the rest of the force. After failing to regain her position, *Ute* received orders to proceed to Attu.

Reaching that island on 12 May, *Ute* immediately found employment during the initial landings there. The merchantman SS *Perida*—transporting an Army combat team—had struck a pinnacle rock, rupturing two holds, and was in danger of foundering. The tug passed a line to the stricken vessel and pulled her out of danger to a position near the beach where she could unload her vital cargo.

Transferring pumps and other salvage gear to *Perida*, *Ute* continued salvage operations from the 12th to the 28th. During that period, enemy air raids enlivened the proceedings and caused several ships to stand out to sea. *Ute*, like a faithful companion, stayed near the stranded *Perida* to lend a hand should the occasion arise. On the 29th, *Ute* passed a towline to *Perida* and took her to Adak. The valuable tug then rounded out the month towing targets.

Ute remained at Adak until 8 June, when she headed for Shemya Island. En route there, she assisted the subchaser/patrol craft, *PC–487*, which had only a short time before rammed and sunk a Japanese submarine, *I–24*. Taking the submarine chaser's men and equipment on board, the tug stood by the scene of the action until relieved on station by *Lamberton* (DMS–2).

Upon reaching Shemya, *Ute* went to work dynamiting shoal spots until the 16th. On that day, she was ordered to Nizki Island to assist SS *MacVeigh* after that merchantman had been stranded on a reef. *Ute* easily pulled the vessel free and assisted *Tatnuck* in towing her to Massacre Bay.

Ute carried out a small repair job on an Army tug and then commenced salvage operations on SS *MacVeigh*. That task kept her busy until the 28th when she left to tow an antisubmarine net to Shemya. Two days later, the tug returned at flank speed to Attu and soon thereafter proceeded to Alexai Point to assist the grounded *Hulbert* (AVD–6).

Throughout the first three weeks of July 1943, *Ute* attempted to pull *Hulbert* off the beach and still continued her efforts to salvage SS *MacVeigh*. She interrupted those efforts on the 19th to assist the grounded merchantman *Delwood*. However, an LCT passed between the two ships, cutting the towline. Again passing a line, *Ute* persisted in her attempt to free the ship and finally succeeded in getting the ship off the rocks. Unfortunately, the damage to *Delwood* proved to be greater than at first thought; and, soon after she had been refloated, she was in a dangerously "sinking condition." Thirty minutes later, *Delwood* listed heavily to port and began to go down by the stern.

Ute cut herself free from the foundering merchantman with an acetylene torch. Happily, no men were lost in the operation. *Ute* later took the damaged LCT in tow and delivered her to Massacre Bay.

Ute operated at Massacre Bay, Attu, until 7 August when she towed two LCT's to Constantine Harbor, Amchitka. After leaving her tow there, the tug picked up another LCT and proceeded to Adak which she reached on the 10th. Two days later, she sailed with the Kiska-bound attack force. However, that operation proved to be unnecessary, since the Japanese had evacuated the island a short time before, leaving only a few stray dogs to contest the invasion.

Weather and mines still endangered the ships. The latter damaged the destroyer *Abner Read* (DD–526); and, on 18 August, *Ute* towed that destroyer to Adak.

A few days later, *Ute* returned to Kiska with a barge in tow. On the 26th, she got underway to investigate the report that a sunken Japanese submarine lay in the vicinity of Twin Rocks. Divers sent down from *Ute* confirmed the report, locating a submarine lying on her port side in 10 fathoms of water.

On 13 September, *Ute* proceeded to the location of the disabled *LST–461*; but upon reaching the scene soon thereafter, found that *LST–461* was already underway, travelling at the end of a towline astern of the tug

Robert Preston. *Ute* returned to Kiska Harbor and, the next day, took a barge in tow. The towline parted, however, and heavy weather forced the tug to abandon her attempt to regain the barge.

Two days later, *Ute* proceeded to Buldir Island to assist *LCT–356*. Arriving there on the 19th, the tug took the landing craft in tow and subsequently delivered her safely to Kiska.

For the remainder of September, the fleet tug tackled a number of odd jobs, such as clearing fouled anchors and recovering tackle from sunken Japanese vessels. On the 29th, she recovered a Navy plane which had capsized in the harbor.

Ute continued salvage evolutions on sunken and damaged enemy ships in the harbor before she moved to Adak in early October. There, the tug underwent a needed availability alongside a tender until the 22d when she returned to Kiska and sailed thence to Attu. There, *Ute* pulled the merchantman, SS *Ole E. Rolvaag* off the beach, with little trouble, and spent the remainder of the month searching for Army barges reported adrift at sea.

After failing to locate the derelicts, *Ute* returned to Massacre Bay on 1 November. A week later, she salvaged a PT-boat and towed it to a mooring buoy. The next day, the tug once more headed for Kiska and spent the days salvaging sunken Japanese ships. The fickle Alaskan weather added to her workload, and *Ute* again found herself engaged in pulling ships free of the beach. The destroyer *King* (DD–242), an old "flush-decker," ran aground at Kuluk Bay, Adak; and *Ute* pulled her free on the 27th before proceeding to Lash Bay, Tanaga Island, for salvage operations on *LST–451*.

Neptune's capricious antics in wintry Alaskan waters continually interrupted *Ute*'s work on the LST, and heavy seas finally forced the tug from the anchorage. She cruised at sea until the weather moderated and then returned to pull the landing ship free a few days later. With the LST in tow, *Ute* started out for Adak, but weather and sea conditions worsened and forced the ships to take shelter in the lee of Tanaga Island for two days before continuing.

After finally delivering the LST, *Ute* fueled and rushed to aid the Russian merchantman *Valery Chkalov*, a ship that had split in half in the heavy seas. Arriving a few hours later, *Ute* stood by while *Cree* (ATF–84) took the after section of the halved ship in tow and then herself went to work recovering the forward half. *Ute* rescued a Soviet seaman from one of the hulks after the man jumped overboard into the freezing waves.

The next morning, *Ute* secured a grapnel to the wreck and towing commenced. The following day, the wire parted. After several unsuccessful attempts to secure another towline to the hulk, the resourceful American sailors welded a 400-pound anchor to a depth charge arbor and fired it off in the direction of the wreck. A second try at this ingenious method succeeded when one of the flukes of the anchor caught on the Russian ships' deck. After taking up the slack, *Ute* towed the hulk once more.

Two hours later, though, the towing wire chafed and parted. With the derelict drifting aimlessly in the stormy seas, no move could be made to resume the tow until the tempest abated. Then, five volunteers clambered on board the drifting bow section and took the line passed from *Ute* and once more secured the anchor chain to the wreck. Finally, on 22 December, *Ute* transferred her charge to an Army tug at Sand Bay, Great Sitkin Island. Soon after returning to Adak, Rear Admiral F. E. M. Whiting presented Lt. William F. Lewis, *Ute*'s commanding officer, with the Legion of Merit for his performance of duty in the tug.

Subsequently, the day after Christmas 1943, *Ute* got underway for Shemya Island to assist grounded SS *Scotia*. On the way, a heavy storm forced *Ute* to seek protection in the lee of Tanaga Island. Thence, under new orders, the fleet tug pushed on via Attu to Kiska where she obtained additional salvage and diving equipment necessary for the *Scotia* salvage project.

Just before the salvage operations on the grounded *Scotia* could commence, the ship's master gyro compass failed, holding up the salvage work for nearly two weeks before repairs could be effected. No sooner had work begun, than *Ute* was forced to shift to Tanaga Island to aid the grounded *YMS–127*. Three days later, the fleet tug pulled the motor minesweeper off the rocks and towed her to Adak before returning to Attu at the end of the month.

Early in February 1944, *Ute* was assigned to standby salvage duty during another bombardment of Japanese installations on Paramushiro. Led by the light cruisers *Richmond* (CL–9) and *Raleigh* (CL–7), the American ships conducted a successful shelling; and *Ute* returned to Adak.

One week later, the busy fleet tug proceeded to Constantine Harbor, at Amchitka, to save a gasoline barge. After cruising off the harbor entrance for a day waiting for the weather to improve, *Ute* entered the harbor and commenced operations. Upon completion of her mission four days later, she proceeded to Kiska—to shift a cruiser's moorings—and thence moved on to Adak to tow targets. However, bad weather prevented the scheduled gunnery exercises, and the fleet tug returned to Attu.

Ute operated on standby during another bombardment of Japanese installations on Paramushiro early in March. After returning to Attu, she shifted to Adak, delaying long enough to tow targets there in mid-month before shifting to Great Sitkin Island. During the last week of March, *Ute* towed the bow section of the Russian merchantman *Valery Chkalov* to Dutch Harbor. She later returned to Great Sitkin in April to prepare the after section of that ship for towing. Departing Great Sitkin on 1 May, *Ute* delivered the bow section of *Valery Chkalov* to Vancouver, British Columbia, on the 21st and then pushed on to Seattle for an availability. During that stint in Aleutian waters, the ship was reclassified as a fleet tug, ATF–76.

After repairs and alterations at the Puget Sound Navy Yard during June and most of July, the fleet tug left Puget Sound on 28 July and pointed her bow once more toward Alaskan waters.

Stopping long enough at Kodiak to pick up a tow, *Ute* proceeded to Dutch Harbor, where she was drydocked for repairs to her bilge keel. Underway with her tow again a few days later, the fleet tug ultimately reached Adak on 21 August.

For the first half of September, *Ute* remained at Adak, doing odd jobs and towing sleds for gunnery exercises before she proceeded to Dutch Harbor on 14 September. Except for a salvage job to perform on *YP–87*, the remainder of the month proved uneventful.

In October, *Ute* put to sea to assist the Russian merchantman SS *Altgelt* which was reportedly breaking up at sea. However, the Soviet ship reached Kodiak safely; and *Ute* returned to Dutch Harbor for the remainder of the month. The ship then sailed south for another availability, this time at the Pacific Repair and Drydock Co. in Oakland, Calif.

With repairs and trials behind her, *Ute* cleared San Francisco Bay on 16 December 1944, in a convoy bound for the Hawaiian Islands. She reached Pearl Harbor two days into the new year, 1945. A week later, she pushed on for the Marshalls.

Towing *Limestone*, a concrete supply barge, *Ute* touched first at Majuro, then at Eniwetok where she arrived on 1 February 1945. There, the fleet tug was assigned to the logistics support group of TG 50.8 to service the main striking force of the 5th Fleet with oil and provisions while underway and thus enable the Fleet to stay at sea nearly continuously to support the Iwo Jima campaign.

On 9 February, *Ute* sortied in company with TG 50.8 for an area east of Iwo Jima and remained at sea for the rest of the month. On the 16th, Vice Admiral Marc

A. Mitscher's carrier planes bombed airfields, aircra factories, and shipping in the Tokyo area and repeat those strikes on the 17th as well.

On the 21st, *Ute* attempted to assist escort carri *Bismarck Sea* (CVE–95), damaged by a Japanese kam kaze. However, before *Ute* could arrive on the scer *Bismarck Sea* sank. After searching for survivors, t fleet tug returned to her station in the task group.

Task Goup 50.8 returned to Ulithi for a rest, puttii into that lagoon on 6 March, but sortied again a for night later to support the Fleet in the operation agair Okinawa Gunto. As before, *Ute* steamed in compar ready to perform her vital but unglamorous salva mission. However, except for sighting numerous min in the vicinity, the tug found this assignment u eventful.

Ute cruised with TG 50.8 until 16 April, when s was detached to head for Okinawa. Once again, she w ordered to assist one of the kamikaze-damaged flatto —this time the fleet carrier *Franklin* (CV–13). Ho ever, *Franklin* recovered her power of self-propulsi before *Ute* arrived.

On the night of 24 May, *Ute* fired at—but missed— Japanese plane that roared by, close aboard. The ne morning, however, her gunners splashed a "Val" th had attempted to bomb the helpless SS *William B. Al son*. A few hours later, *Ute* got underway and churn to the assistance of the high-speed minesweeper *Butl* (DMS–29), kamikazied off the anchorage.

At dusk on that day, after assisting the damag *Butler*, *Ute* proceeded to Chimu Wan to extinguish fire on *PC–1603* and to assist that patrol craft whi had been hit by two kamikazes. During the night, t efforts of the firefighters succeeded, and *Ute* prepar to take the craft in tow.

However, before *Ute* could get a line to the submari chaser, new orders sent the tug to the assistance the destroyer *Braine* (DD–630), also the victim of kamikaze, 40 miles east of Okinawa. *Ute* got underwa but as she did so, a "Val"—pursued by a trio Corsair fighters (Vought F4U's)—attacked her.

Undeterred by *Ute*'s gunfire and that of the thr fighters, the "Val" made a suicide dive in the directi of the fleet tug. Fortunately, the airmen and *Ute* gunners gained the upper hand and splashed the "Va into the sea about 50 yards on *Ute*'s port quarter.

Ute's usefulness was proved before the month w out as she assisted ships on the picket lines (freque targets of kamikazes) and in the harbors. On the 17t she towed an LSM from the Hagushi beach anchora to Kerama Retto and, the following day, salvaged t damaged tank landing craft, *LCT–1335*. After *Da* (DD–519) took a kamikaze on 28 April, *Ute* set out her aid; but, since *Daly* could make it to Kerama Ret under her own power, *Ute* returned to Hagushi. Th night, the fleet tug opened fire on a Japanese pla which attacked ships in the anchorage nearby, and t suicider crashed about 500 yards from the ship.

The next day, *Haggard* (DD–555), damaged by kamikaze, required assistance. *Ute* brought the strick "tin can" to Kerama Retto before being sent to Buckn Bay for duty. Shortly after arriving there, the tu salvaged an LCI (landing craft, infantry) that ha hit a reef and later relieved another tug in towing a ammunition barge. Then, for nearly two weeks, *U* performed repairs on the damaged merchantman, S *William B. Allison*.

Ute located the damaged kamikazied destroyer *Brai* on the afternoon of 27 May and delivered her, at t end of a towline, to Kerama Retto the following mor ing. *Ute* next returned to the crippled *William Allison*—then leaking badly and threatening to sink but interrupted that work the next day to condu salvage operations on *LST–844*.

After pulling the LST off a reef on 2 June, *U* returned to *William B. Allison* and commenced pumpi operations. Three days later, she went to the assistan of *J. William Ditter* (DM–31), after that light min yer had mixed it up with Japanese suiciders, and towed the damaged ship to Kerama Retto, the refuge for battered and sinking ships.

Ute managed to pitch in with some antiaircraft action of her own on the 11th and shot down a Japanese plane that passed over her during a suicide run.

By this time, one of *Ute's* engines was out of operation, so the fleet tug sailed for Saipan on the 16th, exactly two months after she had first made landfall at Okinawa. During that period, the ship had been at general quarters between 20 and 30 percent of the time, saw antiaircraft fire nearly every night, and observed Japanese aircraft numerous times. After reaching Saipan, she proceeded on to Leyte Gulf for availability.

Moored alongside *Jason* (ARH–1), *Ute* underwent repairs and alterations through mid-August 1945 when Japan capitulated. She remained in San Pedro Bay until the 28th, when she proceeded in convoy back to Okinawa.

With the war now over, *Ute* was sent to occupy lower Korea. Early in September, she proceeded to Jinsen (now Inchon), Korea, where she remained through mid-month. She headed for Shanghai, China, on the 18th, and reached the mouth of the Yangtze a few days later. After taking on a pilot, the fleet tug proceeded up the Whangpoo River to Shanghai, where she remained for the remainder of the month.

On 1 October, *Ute* towed the Yangtze River lightship into position at the mouth of that river and returned to Shanghai soon thereafter. Early in the second week of October, the fleet tug received orders to proceed up the Yangtze, taking in tow with her four lighters laden with aviation gasoline.

Reaching Hankow on the 16th, she discharged her cargo there and returned to Shanghai within a few days. Six miles above Keichow, two mines detonated close aboard, dislocated the tug's shaft bearings, ruptured her fuel tanks, and caused considerable damage throughout the ship. *Seize* (ARS–26) assisted the crippled fleet tug; and *Tekesta* (ATF–93) took over *Ute's* barges. The little convoy reached Shanghai on 1 November. On that day, *Ute* went alongside the heavy-hull repair ship *Dixie* (ARH–14) and remained there undergoing temporary repairs through the end of the month.

On 15 December, *Ute* got underway for the Marianas —in company with and towed by *ATR–72*—and reached Guam on the day after Christmas. From that island, she continued on via Eniwetok and Kwajalein to the United States and arrived at San Francisco on 27 February 1946. After a drydocking at the San Francisco Naval Shipyard from 5 to 19 April, the tug proceeded north to Astoria, Oregon, where she was placed in out-of-commission, in-reserve, status on 13 July 1946.

Called back to service in the Korean War mobilization, *Ute* was recommissioned at Tongue Point, Oreg., on 14 September 1951. Upon completion of an overhaul at Oakland on 23 November 1951, she sailed for San Pedro and four weeks of intensive underway training. On 4 January 1952, *Ute* departed San Diego and headed for the Far East, stopping at Pearl Harbor for two weeks en route. After touching at Sasebo, Japan, *Ute* proceeded on to the Korean war zone.

From 23 February to 21 March 1952, *Ute* operated in Wonsan harbor, primarily laying buoys to mark swept channels and at Nan Do laying mooring buoys for boats in rough weather. She made one trip to Hungnam to replace a vital navigation buoy. During that period, *Ute* also participated in shore bombardments at Wonsan, Hungnam, and Songjin, engaging targets of opportunity.

On 27 February in Songjin harbor, *Ute* cleared the fouled screw of the minesweeper *AMS–34*. On 14 March, she assisted the Republic of Korea (ROK) minesweeper, *AMS–518*, with emergency repairs after that vessel had broken her starboard propeller shaft and suffered a flooded engine room. Following the emergency repairs, *Ute* took the minesweeper to Chinhae, Korea.

Not only did *Ute* perform salvage duties and shore bombardments at Wonsan, but she also was assigned picket stations inside the harbor and performed other duties that included the detail of taking mail and supplies to islands held by friendly forces. She also supplied American and ROK small craft with fuel, provisions, and some 20,000 gallons of fresh water.

Upon completion of her first tour in Korean waters, *Ute* returned to Sasebo for a short period of replenishment. Her second trip to the combat zone took her to Cho Do, on the western coast of Korea, where she operated from 31 March to 27 April. Her numerous duties included: furnishing local escort and fire support for LST's en route to Cho Do or Sok To, carrying mail and stores for friendly ships in the immediate vicinity, and repairing friendly LCM's and minesweepers. Each night, *Ute* conducted picket patrols.

On 6 April, *Ute* commenced salvage of an ROK salvage ship that had run aground and needed help to pull free and out of danger. During the operation, *Ute* drew heavy fire from communist shore batteries; 21 rounds landed between 20 to 100 feet from the ship. However, the valiant fleet tug bore a charmed life, for she was able to maneuver safely out of gun range on every occasion, and her crew suffered no casualties.

On 24 April, *Ute* fired a shore bombardment mission and earned the nickname "Good Shoot *Ute*" from the American and British forces blockading the Korean west coast. Fires started by the ship's shells burned all night. The crew also noted several explosions indicating damage done to the enemy. That engagement proved to be the last before she retired from Korean waters.

During her replenishment at Sasebo, *Ute* received emergency orders to assist a SCAJAP LST that had broached at Cheju Do island. This task kept the tug busy from 29 April to 11 May, when, with her task completed, she returned to Sasebo.

Ute's fourth trip to the combat zone took her back to Cho Do, on the west coast of Korea. Her duties were similar to those of her earlier stays on the line but placed more emphasis on the ship's repair capabilities. She furnished 10,000 gallons of fresh water to small craft during that particular tour and conducted a successful salvage operation on a damaged LCM that had been beached during a storm. After refloating the craft, she delivered it to an LSD for repairs.

On the night of 15 June 1952, *Ute* was ordered to take a wooden barge—laden with a cargo of gasoline, oil, food, and water—to an island deep in enemy waters which was held by friendly troops. Since it was imperative that the delivery be made under cover of darkness, *Ute* threaded her way to the island which was located only 35 miles from the mouth of the Yalu River and in an area reportedly patrolled heavily by communist aircraft. Innumerable navigational hazards and poorly charted waters made the passage an anxious one; but, by navigating with her radar, the tug made the trip successfully and delivered the barge and its eagerly-awaited cargo in record time. Returning to Cho Do before daybreak, *Ute's* combat air patrol—provided lest she be discovered by enemy planes—was not needed.

Ute's other duties during this time included the evacuation of wounded and the transportation of prisoners of war (POW's) to the British light cruiser, HMS *Ceylon*. Other routine tasks included the stopping and searching of alien sampans coming down the Yellow Sea from the north. Relieved on station, *Ute* proceeded to Yokosuka, Japan, for a well-earned rest.

That autumn, *Ute* labored in Korean waters for a fifth time, from 20 August to 30 September 1952. During that time, she operated in company with the destroyer *Bradford* (DD–545) and, on one occasion, witnessed that "tin can's" firing on MiG jets that passed close by. The tug performed salvage work and fired eight more shore bombardment missions.

Having logged 155 days in the combat zone, *Ute* headed for Pearl Harbor on 7 October. After a yard availability there, the tug picked up the disabled *PC-1141* at Johnston Island, returning her to Pearl Harbor on 26 January 1953.

Ute plied the Pacific, performing routine towing duties, to Midway and Wake Islands, before she began her second Western Pacific (WestPac) deployment early in September. She then operated in Far Eastern waters until the following March, when she returned via the Marshalls to Pearl Harbor.

Over the ensuing decade, *Ute* conducted numerous WestPac deployments and operated in the northern Pacific as well. Her missions included tows, salvage work, and search and rescue missions. During those years, *Ute* was homeported at Pearl Harbor and ranged from Japan to Indochina; from Johnston Island to Bikini Atoll; and from Adak—her old "stomping grounds"—to the Marianas.

Early in 1966, American involvement in Vietnam began to show in the ship's routine. The tug departed Sasebo on 27 March, bound for South Vietnam, with *APL-55* in tow. Shifting to Danang soon after her arrival at Camranh Bay, she towed *YD-127* to Subic Bay, Philippines, between 6 and 10 April. Ten days later, the veteran tug relieved *Bausell* (DD-845) in shadowing a Soviet trawler to keep the Russian ship from interfering with the operations of American carriers in Tonkin Gulf.

After continuing that "skunk patrol" for five days, *Ute* salvaged the merchantman, SS *Excellency*, a ship that had run aground while carrying munitions to Vietnam. She arrived at the scene—at Triton Island, 180 miles southeast of Danang—on 26 April and, after surveying the bottom offshore, began laying beaching gear. After tearing *Excellency* from the bulldog grip of the reef at 1602 on 30 April, *Ute* returned to the Tonkin Gulf on 1 May to resume "skunk patrol."

Relieved by *Abnaki* (ATF-96) at Danang in mid-May, *Ute* put into Hong Kong on the 22d for rest and recreation. She operated in southeast Asian waters into the summer, touching at Kaohsiung, Taiwan; Subic Bay; Singapore; and Sattahip and Bangkok, Thailand, before returning to Subic Bay for upkeep.

After a brief visit to Japanese waters, *Ute* returned to Pearl Harbor in early October. She did not return to WestPac operating areas again until the following summer. She performed services for the Royal Thai Navy between 28 and 30 August and then towed *APL-55* from An Thoi, Vietnam, to Sasebo, Japan. For a month that autumn, from 15 October to 15 November, *Ute* carried out surveillance of a Soviet "trawler" in the Tonkin Gulf with TF-77, before conducing salvage operations on *Clarke County* (LST-601) at Doc Pho, Vietnam.

Ute spent much of 1970 in the southeast Asian area —numbering Camranh Bay, Vung Tau, Danang, Sattahip, and Singapore among her ports of call. After participating in salvage operations with SS *Laredo Victory* near Midway, *Ute* returned to the west coast of the United States, towing two old *Fletcher*-class hulks, ex-*O'Bannon* (DD-450) and ex-*Nicholas* (DD-449) from Pearl Harbor to the Mare Island Naval Shipyard between 31 January and 14 February 1971.

Subsequently deploying to the northern Pacific operating area and then to Pearl Harbor in mid-year, *Ute* spent much of that autumn undergoing salvage and refresher training in Hawaiian waters. Deploying to WestPac again in early November, *Ute* "chopped" to the 7th Fleet on 13 November.

Ute did not return to continental American waters until 1972; her home port was officially changed from Pearl Harbor to San Diego on 15 October. One of her first tasks upon arrival "stateside" was the tow of the erstwhile fleet carrier *Bunker Hill* (CV-17) to San Clemente Island in November for shock tests. After the tests were completed, *Ute* returned *Bunker Hill* to San Diego. Commander, Destroyer Squadron 33 re-

ported that the overall success of the tests ". . . ca be largely attributable to the expertise and versatilit of USS *Ute* in performing a variety of assignments.

Ute performed coastwise tow and tug services fo the Fleet, off the southern California coast, into 197 Her WestPac service was not over, however, for sh commenced yet another deployment on 7 January 197 Over the seven months that ensued, *Ute* visited suc ports as Pearl Harbor; Subic Bay and Poro Point i the Philippines; Singapore; Hong Kong; Yokosuk Kure, and Sasebo in Japan; Keelung, Taiwan; an Pusan, South Korea. The Fleet utilized her services i such diverse activities as torpedo recovery, targe tows, diver requalification, and ocean towing. Sh capped off the deployment by towing *YMS-789* fro Poro Point to Tacoma, Wash. One month of hecti activity followed her return from WestPac, and the the ship was decommissioned and simultaneously turne over to the Military Sealift Command (MSC) on 3 August 1974.

Manned by a civilian crew, the valuable vetera served actively with MSC into the late 1970's an remained on the Navy list as of October 1979.

Ute received three battle stars for her World War I service, two for her Korean War service, and nine fo her service in Vietnam.

Utina

Olata Quae Utina (ca. 1565) was a leading chief o the now-extinct Timucua Indians who occupied th territory along the middle reaches of the St. John River in Florida near the present-day site of S Augustine.

(AFT-163: dp. 1,589 (tl.); l. 205'0''; b. 38'6''; d 15'4'' (lim.); s. 16.5 k. (tl.); cpl. 85; a. 1 3'', 40mm., 4 20mm.; cl. *Abnaki*

Utina (ATF-163) was laid down on 6 June 1945 a Charleston, S.C., by the Charleston Shipbuilding Drydock Co.; launched on 31 August 1945; sponsore by Mrs. Jonathan Yerkes; and commissioned at th Naval Base, Charleston, on 30 January 1946, Lt. A. Vetro in command.

Since commissioning, the major portion of *Utina* long Navy career was spent in the western Atlanti and in the West Indies. She carried out a variety towing missions, helping damaged ships into por towing decommissioned ships to berthing areas, towin targets for gunnery exercises, and the like. Throughou her active career, *Utina* was closely associated with th American naval base at Guantanamo Bay, Cuba. Righ after commissioning, she conducted her shakedow training out of that port, and when she completed i Guantanamo Bay became her home port for over fiv years. In 1951, she was reassigned to Norfolk bu continued to deploy each year to the base in Cuba fo several weeks of operations—frequently in conjunctio with the annual "Springboard" fleet exercises held i the West Indies. She was at Guantanamo Bay i February of 1964 when Cuban Premier Castro cut o the base's water supply. When the United States go ernment decided to respond by permanently servin the water link to illustrate the base's self sufficienc *Utina* played an important role by bringing in Gua tanamo Bay's first potable water before two larg tankers could be activated for the purpose.

Throughout her quarter of a century of service wit the Navy, *Utina* altered her routine of operations alon the eastern seaboard and in the West Indies only twic In May of 1965, she embarked upon her only deplo ment to the 6th Fleet in the Mediterranean. He missions, however, remained the same though the em phasis shifted to target towing for 6th Fleet surfac gunnery exercises. She returned to Norfolk in earl

The fleet tug *Utina* (ATF–163).

October 1965 and resumed 2d Fleet services once more. Her second departure from her primary zone of operations came in June of 1967 when she steamed to Iceland to assist *Aeolus* (ARC–3) in a special project. The tug returned to Norfolk on 13 July 1967 and resumed east coast-West Indies operations for the remaining four years of her career. On 3 September 1971, *Utina* was decommissioned at Norfolk, and she was transferred, on a loan basis, to the Venezuelan Navy. She was commissioned as *Felipe Larrazabal* (R 21) and served in the Venezuelan Navy until December of 1977. At that time, she was returned to the United States Navy, retransferred to Venezuela on a sale basis, and her name was struck from the Navy list—all simultaneously. As of the beginning of 1980, she was still active with the Venezuelan Navy.

Utowana

TR.: t. 414 (gross); l. 168'9''; b. 27'9''; dr. 15'9'' (aft.); s. 12 mph.; cpl. 32)

Utowana (SP–951)—a yacht built in 1891 at Philadelphia, Pa., by Neafie & Levy and rebuilt as a trawler at Staten Island, N.Y., in 1917 for the Commonwealth Fisheries Co., Boston, Mass.—was acquired by the Navy during the summer of 1917 for service as a minesweeper in the 1st Naval District and placed in commission on 30 October 1917, Lt. Comdr. Reuben K. Dyer, USNV, in command.

Though some records indicate that the ship was later renamed *Victorine*, they give no date for the renaming. Moreover, the trawler was consistently referred to hereafter as *Utowana* both in official and unofficial publications. In any event, the trawler was assigned to Division 13, Squadron 5, Patrol Force. That organization, made up various types of ships and craft, was responsible for patrol and escort duties overseas. In addition to the European bases such as Brest in France and Queenstown in Ireland, ships of the Patrol Force operated in such diverse areas as the Caribbean and the Azores. While no records have been found indicating where *Utowana* served before arriving on the French coast early in 1918, she operated briefly at Bermuda and perhaps for a short period at Ponta Delgada in the Azores. It is known that she departed Newport, R.I., on 4 November 1917 in company with *Hannibal*, *Helenita* (SP–210), *Margaret* (SP–527), *May* (SP–164), *Rambler* (SP–211), and *Wenonah* (SP–165). Each yacht towed a submarine chaser. After five days at sea and in spite of a breakdown apiece for *Margaret, May, Helenita* and *Utowana*, the little task group arrived in Hamilton, Bermuda. Apparently, *Helenita* and *Utowana* remained behind in Bermuda when the other four yachts—augmented by *Cythera* (SP–575), *Artemis* (SP–593), and *Lydonia* (SP–700) departed Hamilton on 18 November bound for Ponta Delgada. Presumably, *Utowana*—like *Helenita*—stayed in Bermuda to conduct patrols in surrounding waters, though it is also possible that she remained behind for repairs. Records giving details simply do not exist.

In any event, the former yacht reached the French coast in February 1918. Thereafter, in all probability, she provided escort services to coastal convoys and conducted antisubmarine patrols of French coastal waters. About the time of the armistice, the armed trawler began to assist *Favorite* (SP–1385) in salvage and repair work. Following the armistice, she probably continued her salvage work. *Utowana* returned to the United States in August 1919 and was assigned to the 3d Naval District. She was placed out of commission on 11 September 1919. Just over a year later, on 13 September 1920, she was sold to the Denton Shore Lumber Co., Tampa, Fla.

The trawler *Utowana* shortly before her acquisition by the Navy; the "C" on her funnel refers to her owner, the Commonwealth Fisheries Company of Boston.

Uvalde

A county in southwestern Texas, the home of former Vice President John Nance "Cactus Jack" Garner.

(AKA–88: dp. 13,910 (tl.); l. 459'3"; b. 63'0"; dr. 26'4" (lim.); s. 16.5 k.; cpl. 366; a. 1 5", 8 40mm., 18 20 mm.; cl. *Andromeda*; T. C2–S–B1)

Uvalde (AKA–88) (formerly projected as the merchant freighter *Wild Pigeon*) was laid down under a Maritime Commission contract (MC hull 1188) on 27 March 1944 at Oakland, Calif., by the Moore Drydock Co.; launched on 20 May 1944; sponsored by Mrs. George J. Kean; and commissioned on 18 August 1944, Lt. Comdr. William M. McCloy, USNR, in command.

After fitting out at Oakland, *Uvalde* ran her trials before departing San Francisco Bay on 29 August, bound for San Pedro, Calif. She conducted extensive shakedown training out of that port before she shifted to San Diego, Calif., there to train in amphibious warfare from 15 through 30 September in company with the attack transport *Appling* (APA–58).

In yard hands at Terminal Island, Calif., for postshakedown availability until 10 October, *Uvalde* got underway and churned out of Los Angeles harbor, bound for San Francisco. *Uvalde* consequently loaded cargo at that port from 11 through 19 October.

Departing "Frisco" on 20 October, *Uvalde* reached Manus, in the Admiralty Islands, on 6 November. Over the next few days, the ship lay at anchor in Seeadler Harbor, Manus, awaiting orders for onward routing. While there, she witnessed the volcanic explosion of the ammunition ship *Mount Hood* (AE–11) at 0820 on 11 November. Fortunately at a distance far enough away to be unaffected by the blast, *Uvalde* responded to the emergency by sending medical assistance and supplies to some of the other ships closer to where the ill-fated ammunition ship had been anchored—ships that had taken heavy casualties when shrapnel from the atomized *Mount Hood* had ripped into them.

Subsequently, three days after the *Mount Hood* tragedy, *Uvalde* got underway to unload cargo at East Murzim Dock. Completing that evolution a little over a week later, on the 21st, *Uvalde* got underway for New Guinea on the 29th, reaching Milne Bay, her destination, on 3 December.

The attack cargo ship then took on board 100 tons of miscellaneous cargo earmarked for the 489th Port Battalion, Transportation Corps, 6th Army. She shifted to Oro Bay, New Guinea, within a few days, then loading additional cargo—1,025 tons of vehicles, gasoline, and organizational equipment for the 6th Army. On 21 December, *Uvalde* and her escort, *J. Douglas Blackwood* (DE–219) got underway for the Admiralties, reaching their destination the following day.

Uvalde spent Christmas at Manus before she got underway on her first "mission of war" as part of Task Group (TG) 77.9 on 2 January 1945, shaping course for the island of Luzon. The attack cargo ship subsequently entered Lingayen Gulf on the morning of 1 January and, at 0925, sent her first wave of landing craft onto the beaches. During her ensuing stay at Lingayen Gulf, *Uvalde*'s sailors witnessed their first attacks by the Japanese kamikazes on ships in the vicinity.

On the 13th, *Uvalde* weighed anchor, shifting to Leyte and reaching there on the 16th. Two days later, the attack cargo ship got underway again, this time headed for the Schouten Islands. Bound for Biak, *Uvalde* reached her destination on the 23d and commenced loading cargo at dock number 2 soon thereafter.

Completing loading on 2 February, *Uvalde* returned to Leyte, joining formation with TG 78.5 on the following day. Subsequently anchoring in Leyte Gulf on the 6th, the attack cargo ship pushed on for Mindoro the following day, arriving on the 9th. Twenty-seven hours later, the ship completed the unloading evolution, receiving a "well done" from Capt. R. W. Abbott, the officer in tactical command of the task group.

Uvalde returned to Leyte and, over the days that ensued, prepared for her next operation. For six weeks the attack cargo ship participated in the practice evolutions that ultimately led up to the final big assault landing of the war in the Pacific—the invasion of Okinawa in the Ryukyus.

The amphibious cargo ship *Uvalde* (AKA–88), 1959. (USN 1044340)

Underway on 27 March, *Uvalde* reached the assault areas on 1 April, the day of the initial landings. By noon of that day—Easter Sunday—the loading operations were proceeding apace. At 0559 on 3 April, *Uvalde*'s gunners drew their first blood, downing a suicider making a run on the nearby attack transport *Latimer* (APA–152). *Uvalde* received official credit for the kill—she soon sported a miniature Japanese flag on her bridge.

Off Okinawa from 1 to 9 April, *Uvalde* spent much of her time at general quarters due to the heavy Japanese aerial resistance. The attack cargo ship subsequently weighed anchor on the 9th and headed for Saipan in the Marianas, en route to her ultimate destination, Pearl Harbor.

After provisioning ship at Pearl, *Uvalde* returned to the western Pacific, departing the Hawaiian Islands on 0 May. Reaching Eniwetok in the Marshalls 10 days later, the attack cargo ship got underway for Guam in the Marianas after exchanging cargo and embarking passengers. *Uvalde* then discharged and unloaded at Guam before she proceeded for the west coast of the United States, her course shaped for San Francisco.

Departing Guam on 27 June, *Uvalde* arrived at the Golden Gate on 12 July, en route to Everett, Wash., for drydocking and repairs. Reaching Everett on the 6th, the ship underwent nearly two weeks of repair work there, completing her assigned availability on 28 July.

Departing the Pacific Northwest on 1 August, *Uvalde* proceeded to San Francisco to load cargo in preparation for her return to the western Pacific theater of operations. Completing the loading process on 11 August, the attack cargo ship got underway for the Hawaiian Islands on the 12th. She was at sea when, at 1400 on 14 August 1945, President Harry S. Truman announced in a radio broadcast address that a state of war no longer existed between the United States and Japan. World War II was over at last.

For *Uvalde*, the war had been a short one, but there still remained the duty of returning the many soldiers, sailors, marines, and airmen home from the fighting fronts. The attack cargo ship took part in those operations well into 1946, also earning the Navy's Occupation Service Medal for operations in China waters in ensuing months.

Up until mid-1950, *Uvalde* transported troops and cargo to American outposts in Asia, supporting the United States presence in that area of the world. *Uvalde* participated in the United Nations' efforts to stem North Korean aggression after that nation invaded neighboring South Korea in June 1950, deploying to Korean waters with troops and cargo on numerous occasions.

New Year's Day 1951 found *Uvalde* at Sasebo, Japan; nine days later she got underway, bound for the west coast of the United States, and she reached her destination two weeks later on the 24th. Shifting to the Mare Island Naval Shipyard for repairs and alterations on the 30th, the attack cargo ship remained in yard hands until early April, when she shifted to San Diego to conduct underway training evolutions.

After three weeks of post-repair training, *Uvalde* shifted to the naval supply center at Oakland, Calif., when she loaded cargo earmarked for the Far East. The attack cargo ship subsequently made three round-trip voyages, touching at Sasebo and Yokosuka in the west and Oakland in the east over the remainder of 1951.

Uvalde spent much of 1952 engaged in the same shuttle operations that had kept her occupied since the onset of the Korean War. She visited Korean waters in the latter half of the month of March 1952, touching at Sokcho Ri and Paengyong Do before resuming her west coast-to-Japan shuttle voyages with her termini at Oakland, Sasebo, and Yokosuka. During August, 1952, the ship made a short recreational stop at Pearl Harbor.

During the late autumn of 1952, *Uvalde* remained in Japanese waters, undergoing a drydocking at Yokosuka in late November before she sailed for Oakland on the 23d of that month. Reaching Treasure Island, San Francisco, on 8 December, the attack cargo ship went into the naval shipyard at Mare Island three days later.

Uvalde overhauled at Mare Island into mid-February, 1953, after which time she conducted the usual underway training evolutions before resuming west coast-to-Japan shuttle voyages. She called at Korean ports once, visiting Pohang in May 1953, spending most of her time in Japanese waters. Ports included during that cruise included Sasebo, Yokosuka, and Nagasaki.

February through July of the following year, 1954, was spent in shuttle service between the Naval Supply Center, Oakland, and the Far East, with a recreational visit to Nagasaki in April. During July, the ship arrived at Yokosuka and, after a trip to Sasebo and return, loaded a cargo of rice and medical supplies, setting sail for French Indochina to assist in Operation "Passage to Freedom."

Uvalde reached Tourane Bay, French Indochina, on 28 August and remained there, supporting "Passage to Freedom" operations until 10 September, when she got underway to return to Oakland. Over the next few years, *Uvalde*'s routine would remain much the same, sailing back and forth across the Pacific on the supply line from the west coast of the United States to American military bases in the Far East.

"Mothballed" in 1957 and becoming a part of the Reserve Fleet, *Uvalde* was struck from the Navy list on 1 July 1960 but was reinstated on 1 September 1961, because of the Berlin Crisis. *Uvalde* was recommissioned on 18 November 1961, Capt. C. A. Baldwin in command.

Ordered to duty with the Atlantic Fleet, the attack cargo ship—with a new lease on life—got underway for Guantanamo Bay, Cuba, and five weeks of training in December. After a voyage that had taken her via Mazatlan, Mexico; the Panama Canal; and Guantanamo (where she engaged in refresher training operations as scheduled), *Uvalde* reached her new assigned home port, Norfolk, Va., in February 1962. She thus became a part of the Amphibious Force of the Atlantic Fleet.

After a post-shakedown overhaul, *Uvalde* took part in amphibious exercises at Vieques, Puerto Rico (Lant-PhibLex 1–62) in April—her first major exercise since recommissioning. By the end of the year 1962, the veteran attack cargo vessel had deployed on various 2d Fleet exercises and maneuvers in the western Atlantic and Caribbean areas. Attached to Amphibious Squadron (PhibRon) 10 from 22 October to 5 December, *Uvalde* supported the Fleet during the Cuban Missile Crisis, when President John F. Kennedy "quarantined" Cuba over the presence of offensive Soviet missiles on that strategic isle.

Subsequently, *Uvalde* spent all of January, 1963, engaged in pre-deployment upkeep. She sailed on 4 February, shaping course for the Mediterranean, and operated with the 6th Fleet through mid-May, touching at Naples, Italy; Athens, Greece; Izmir, Turkey; Rhodes, Greece; Golfe Juan, France; and Barcelona, Spain; during the course of her operations.

After returning to Norfolk for upkeep and independent ship exercises, *Uvalde* deployed to the Caribbean as part of the Amphibious Ready Squadron, calling at San Juan, Puerto Rico, during that cruise that carried over into late February 1964 as part of Phib Ron 8. She deployed again to the Caribbean from late June to late September, 1965, before she later participated in Exercise "Steel Pike I;" during the latter cruise, she visited Gran Canaria, Tenerife, in the Canary Islands.

Returning to her home port, Norfolk, in late November, *Uvalde* shifted to the New York Naval Shipyard, Brooklyn, N.Y., on 7 January. She remained there undergoing repairs and alterations, until 28 April, after which time she headed south, ultimately conducting refresher training in Guantanamo Bay.

In late June, *Uvalde* supported the American intervention in the Dominican Republic, serving as "bulk fuel control ship" between 18 and 28 June. The ship then conducted independent exercises and underwent some needed upkeep through mid-July.

Uvalde subsequently trained out of Little Creek, Va., for 10 days in July before resuming scheduled independent ship exercises and upkeep periods out of and at, Norfolk. That autumn, she deployed to the Mediterranean for the second time as a unit of Phib Ron 10. During that cruise—lasting into mid-March 1966—*Uvalde* operated with Task Force 61, visiting Marseilles and Toulon, France; Malta; Naples, Genoa, and Livorno, Italy; Barcelona and Mazarron, Spain and Porto Scudo and Santa Manza, Corsica.

Reaching the end of the deployment, *Uvalde* left Palma, Majorca, in her wake on 17 March, bound for Rota, Spain, the turnover point, where she would be relieved of her duties with the 6th Fleet. She then began her homeward-bound voyage on 20 March, setting course for Morehead City, N.C.

Midway across the Atlantic, *Uvalde* picked up distress signals from a Danish merchantman, the refrigerator ship SS *Chilean Reefer*. One of the freighter's crewmen was desperately ill and needed prompt medical attention—care that the ship was apparently unable to supply. *Uvalde* immediately reversed course and sped to her assistance. The attack cargo ship took on board the patient, transferring him from *Chilean Reefer* in an LCM, where treatment commenced as soon as he came on board. The sailor remained on board to return to a hospital in the United States for treatment.

Uvalde ultimately reached Morehead City and there disembarked her detachment of marines and off-loaded their equipment. *Uvalde*'s crew, eager to continue on the homeward-bound leg of their voyage after the six month Mediterranean cruise, worked all night to unload the ship so that the ship could sail the next morning, as soon as possible. *Uvalde* reached her home port, Norfolk, on 3 April 1966. As her commanding officer wrote in retrospect: "It was a good deployment, but it was even better to be back home again."

The attack cargo ship subsequently deployed to the Mediterranean one more time in her career, from April to August of 1967, returning to Morehead City, N.C. on 14 September and Norfolk the following day. She remained on active operations with the Atlantic Fleet into 1968, but she was ultimately declared "unfit for further service." Replaced by a *Charleston*-class attack cargo ship, with significant increases in combat vehicle and cargo stowage and better combat characteristics, *Uvalde* was decommissioned and struck from the Navy list on 1 December 1968.

Transferred to the Maritime Administration on 2 June 1969 for disposal, *Uvalde*'s hulk was simultaneously sold to Levin Metals Corp., of San Jose, Calif., and scrapped.

Uvalde earned one battle star for her World War II service and three for the Korean War.

V

V–1

V–1 (SF–4) was renamed *Barracuda* (*q.v.*) on 19 February 1931 and redesignated SS–163 on 1 July 1931.

V–2

V–2 (SF–5) was renamed *Bass* (*q.v.*) on 19 February 1931 and redesignated SS–164 on 1 July 1931.

V–3

V–3 (SF–6) was renamed *Bonita* (*q.v.*) on 19 February 1931 and redesignated SS–165 on 1 July 1931.

V–4

V–4 (SF–7) was renamed *Argonaut* (*q.v.*) on 19 February 1931 and reclassified as a minelaying submarine and redesignated SM–1 on 1 July 1931. She was subsequently further redesignated APS–1 on 22 September 1942.

V–5

V–5 (SC–1) was renamed *Narwhal* (*q.v.*) on 19 February 1931 and redesignated SS–167 on 1 July 1931.

V–6

V–6 (SC–2) was renamed *Nautilus* (*q.v.*) on 19 February 1931 and redesignated SS–168 on 1 July 1931.

V–7

V–7 (SC–3) was renamed *Dolphin* (*q.v.*) on 19 February 1931 and redesignated SS–169 on 1 July 1931.

V–8

V–8 (SC–4) was renamed *Cachalot* (*q.v.*) on 19 February 1931 and redesignated SS–170 on 1 July 1931, prior to the laying of her keel on 21 October 1931.

V–9

V–9 (SC–5) was renamed *Cuttlefish* (*q.v.*) on 19 February 1931 and redesignated SS–171 on 1 July 1931, prior to the laying of her keel on 7 October 1931.

V–43

(Former German Torpedo-boat Destroyer: dp. 1,106; l. 261'3"; b. 27'3"; dr. 13'1"; s. 34.5 k.; cpl. 87; a. 3 88mm., 6 20" tt., 24 mines; cl. *V–43*)

V–43—a large, German torpedo boat destroyer—was laid down in the latter part of 1914 at Stettin, Germany, by the *Aktiengesellschaft Vulcan*; launched on 27 January 1915; and placed in service in the Imperial German Navy on 28 May 1915, probably under the command of *Kapitänleutnant* Carl.

V–43 was assigned to VI Torpedo Flotilla, High Seas Fleet, operating out of Wilhelmshaven. For the most part, she and her sisters in VI Torpedo Flotilla screened German minesweeping operations in the eastern portion of the North Sea and patrolled against British incursions into the German Bight. On 24 April 1916, she accompanied Vice Admiral Hipper's battle cruisers on a shore bombardment of the English coast near Lowestoft. During the mission, she did not have an opportunity to launch any torpedoes. She returned to Jade Bay the following day.

Sometime during the following month, *V–43* entered the yard for repairs—probably at Wilhelmshaven—because the official German account of the war, *Der Krieg zur See 1914–1918*, lists her in the Jutland task organization chart with the note "*Auf Werften: nahm an der Schlacht nicht teil*"—"in the yard: took no part in the battle." In any event, *V–43* subsequently returned to active duty with VI Torpedo Flotilla. For the remainder of 1916, she operated with 12 Torpedo Half Flotilla out of the Ems estuary and Jade Bay patrolling the North Sea. By December 1916, she became the flagship of the half flotilla.

Late in January 1917, *V–43* and the other torpedo boat destroyers of VI Torpedo Flotilla were reassigned to the Commander, Torpedo Flotillas, Flanders. On the 22d, the two half flotillas departed Wilhelmshaven, exited the German Bight into the North Sea, and rounded the northwestern corner of the Netherlands. That evening as the warships passed down along the coast of the Netherlands, they encountered two British forces—the first, a three-ship group of light cruisers and the second, a full flotilla of destroyers. The Germans fired torpedoes and guns and, as the British cruisers turned to evade the torpedoes, dashed past them down the Channel toward Zeebrugge. However, VI Torpedo Flotilla did not escape unscathed. Its flagship, *V–69*, received heavy damage from the cruisers' guns and, after engaging the destroyers, was forced to retire to the Dutch coast for repairs at Yimuiden. The remaining German warships then engaged the British destroyers and managed to sink one of them before arriving safely in Zeebrugge early the following morning. *V–43* carried out *V–69*'s duties as flagship of the entire flotilla until 20 February when she was relieved of that responsibility by *S–49* and resumed her role as flagship of 12 Torpedo Half Flotilla.

For the next two months, VI Torpedo Flotilla operated out of Zeebrugge. *V–43*, however, was undergoing repairs at Ostend during the flotilla's only other action of its short tour of duty along the Belgian coast. On 29 March, *V–43* departed Zeebrugge in company with the other ships of her flotilla to conduct a short commerce raid on their way back to Wilhelmshaven and resumption of duty guarding the German Bight. On the way, they encountered only one small British steamer, SS *Mascot*, which *V–67* and *G–95* sank with gunfire. That afternoon, the ships of the flotilla dropped anchor in Wilhelmshaven.

For the remainder of the war, *V–43* conducted patrols in the German Bight and protected German minesweeping operations in that area. Early on the morning of 17 November 1917, while covering the minesweepers, she and the other ships of 12 Half Flotilla joined the cruisers *Frankfurt*, *Pillau*, *Königsberg*, and *Nürnberg* in a running battle with British cruisers and battlecruisers. During that fight, the torpedo-boat destroyer managed to launch two torpedoes, but neither scored a hit. One passed close to HMS *Royalist* and the other 30 yards ahead of HMS *Cardiff*. The German destroyers and cruisers covered the minesweepers' retirement toward Heligoland, and the British broke off action at about 0950 when the German battleship *Kaiser* and *Kaiserin* moved up to support the light forces.

Over the next year, *V–43* operated in the German Bight. During the fall of 1918, the blockade and four years of war undermined Germany's ability and will to fight. In November, the German High Command sued for an armistice which was formalized on 11 November 1918. Under the conditions of that armistice, the High Seas Fleet was to be interned by the Allies. The greater portion of the fleet, including *V–43*, went to the British base at Scapa Flow in the Orkney Islands. The erstwhile German warships lay at anchor there, tended by German nucleus crews while surrender negotiations at Versailles dragged on. Finally, on 21 June 1919, the crew of *V–43* joined a large number of their comrades in a last defiant act against the victors. Rather than surrender their ships, they tried to scuttle them. *V–43* sank, but she was later raised and repaired. Almost a year later, she was turned over to the United States Navy at Rosyth, Scotland, and commissioned on 4 June 1920 for the Atlantic passage. She was placed out of commission at Norfolk, Va., on 30 August 1920. After spending almost a year there, she was sunk off Cape Henry, Va., on 15 July 1921 by gunfire from *Florida* (BB–30).

Vaga

A Spanish feminine adjective meaning "wandering" or "roving."

(YT–116: dp. 529; l. 148'6"; b. 26'; dr. 12'10" (mean); cpl. 28)

General Weeks—a single-screw, steel-hulled harbor tug—built at Shanghai, China, for the United States Army Quartermaster Corps—was completed in 1910 and operated out of Manila Bay, performing tug and towing services in the Philippines until transferred to the Navy on 7 April 1930. Classified YT–116, the tug was inactivated at the Cavite Navy Yard on 22 May—presumably to fit out for naval service—and was renamed *Vaga* on 29 July 1931.

Commissioned at Cavite on 1 August, with Boatswain Glen B. Swortwood in command, *Vaga* commenced local operations out of the navy yard which would occupy her throughout the ensuing decade, as war clouds gathered over the Far East. She provided tug and tow services at Cavite, Sangley Point, and Manila and, on occasion, performed ferry duty between Cavite and Manila. She also assisted warships of the Asiatic Fleet to moor and unmoor at the wharves of Cavite before and after overhauls. Only six days before the outbreak of war in the Far East, *Vaga* assisted *Houston* (CA–30)—the heavy cruiser which would later win fame in the Java campaigns—in mooring at her anchorage after the warship completed her accelerated overhaul at Cavite on 2 December 1941.

On 8 December (7 December east of the international date line), the Japanese initiated a series of strikes at American, Dutch, and British possessions in the Far East. At 0350 on that day, the radio operator at Olongapo picked up Admiral Thomas C. Hart's warning message: "Japan started hostilities, govern yourselves accordingly." Soon the alarms were sounding in the Philippines as the United States cleared for action. That morning, the 1st Battalion, 4th Marines, under Lt. Col. Curtis T. Beecher, USMC, embarked in *Vaga* for Mariveles, on the Bataan peninsula.

Two days later, on 10 December, the Japanese—after having neutralized American air power the day before—nearly obliterated the Cavite Navy Yard, rendering it unusable by the Asiatic Fleet as an advanced base. On 31 December, *Vaga* was assigned to the Inshore Patrol, to safeguard Corregidor's shorelines and to oppose the movement by water of Japanese men and materiel along the shores of Manila Bay. Operating out of Corregidor, *Vaga* performed yeoman service until almost the bitter end. On 5 May 1942—just two days before the enemy forced Corregidor's surrender—*Vaga* was scuttled off the island to prevent her from being captured. *Vaga* was struck from the Navy list on 24 July 1942.

Vaga received one battle star for her World War II service.

II

(YTB–374: dp. 320 (f.); l. 102'0"; b. 25'0"; dr. 10'0"; cpl. 12; s. 12 k.; cl. *Allaquippa*)

The second *Vaga* (YT–374) was laid down on 21 March 1944 at Port Arthur, Tex., by the Gulfport Boiler and Iron Works, under a contract from the General Motors Corp.; launched on 6 May 1944; reclassified YTB–374 on 15 May 1944; and completed and delivered to the Navy on 31 May 1944.

Placed in service soon thereafter, *Vaga* was initially allocated to the 14th Naval District and proceeded to the Hawaiian Islands to perform tug and tow services and to provide waterfront fire protection at the important Pacific Fleet base at Pearl Harbor. Subsequently placed out of service, in reserve, at San Diego, with the Pacific Reserve Fleet, in March 1946, *Vaga* remained inactive through the late 1950's.

Reactivated in January 1961 and reclassified YTM–374 in February 1962, *Vaga* resumed her harbor tug duties at San Diego, Calif., with the service force of the Pacific Fleet. For the next decade, she operated out of that port until taken out of service and struck from the Navy list on 1 October 1972. She was sold in August 1973.

Vagrant

(PYc–30: dp. 120 (lt.); l. 117'7"; b. 25'2"; dr. 10'0"; cpl. 14; s. 12.0 k.; a. 2 .50-cal. mg.)

Vagrant—a steel-hulled, single-screw yacht—was laid down on 9 January 1941 at Bath, Maine, by the Bath Iron Works; launched on 24 May 1941; and was delivered to her purchaser, Harold S. Vanderbilt, on 13 September 1941. The Navy acquired *Vagrant* on 23 March 1942 for use as a district patrol craft. Although initially designated and classified as the unnamed *YP–258*, the yacht was reclassified a coastal patrol vessel and received the hull number PYc–30 on 2 April 1942; a subsequent order, dated 8 April 1942, authorized the retention of the name *Vagrant*. Fitted out at City Island, N.Y., by the Robert Jacob, Inc., yard, *Vagrant* was commissioned on 9 May 1942, Lt. (jg.) George T. Elliman, USNR, in command.

After shakedown out of New London, Conn., and Boston, Mass., *Vagrant* arrived at Newport, R.I., on 11 August 1942 for special duty under the orders of the Commander, Eastern Sea Frontier. Successively transferred to the 1st and 3d Naval Districts for local operations in a patrol and training capacity, *Vagrant* was decommissioned and placed "in service" on 29 December 1943. She performed training duties with the 3d Naval District for the duration of the war with Germany.

On 30 May 1945, the Commandant, 3d Naval District, authorized *Vagrant* to be inactivated, preparatory to her turnover to the War Shipping Administration (WSA). Placed "out of service" and laid up on 6 August, *Vagrant* was struck from the Navy list on 1 September and transferred to the WSA on 14 December.

After return to her pre-war owner, H. S. Vanderbilt, *Vagrant* changed hands in about 1949 when she was acquired by Ralph C. Allen of Oyster Bay, N.Y. Subsequently picked up by the Orion Shipping and Trading Co., *Vagrant* remained on the *Lloyd's Register of Yachts* until 1956 or 1957, when her named disappeared from the lists.

Valcour

An island in Lake Champlain, southeast of Plattsburgh, N.Y. A crucial naval engagement took place off that island on 11 October 1776, when a Continental force under General Benedict Arnold met a superior British fleet. Although the British bested Arnold's makeshift flotilla, the delay forced upon the enemy by the long time it took them to construct vessels for service on the lake resulted in a year's postponement of their attempt to invade the colonies—a year in which the Americans prepared to meet the British Army. When they finally started their thrust down the Lake

Champlain, Lake George, and Hudson River corridor in the fall of 1777, the English Army was defeated and captured in the Battle of Saratoga.

(AVP–55: dp. 1,776; l. 310'9''; b. 41'2''; dr. 11'11'' (mean); s. 18.5 k.; cpl. 367; a. 1 5'', 8 40mm., 8 20mm., 2 rkt.; cl. *Barnegat*)

Valcour (AVP–55) was laid down on 21 December 1942 at Houghton, Wash., by the Lake Washington Shipyard; launched on 5 June 1943; and sponsored by Mrs. H. C. Davis, the wife of Capt. H. C. Davis, the intelligence officer for the 13th Naval District. *Valcour* was taken to the Puget Sound Navy Yard for completion, but the heavy load of war-damage repairs conducted by that yard meant that her construction assumed a lower priority than the repair of combatant vessels. As a result, *Valcour* was not completed until well after World War II ended. She was commissioned at the Puget Sound Naval Shipyard (the former Puget Sound Navy Yard) on 5 July 1946, Comdr. Barnet T. Talbott in command.

Ordered to the Atlantic Fleet upon completion of her shakedown—conducted between 9 August and 9 September off San Diego—*Valcour* transited the Panama Canal between 17 and 21 September and reached the New York Naval Shipyard on 26 September for post-shakedown availability. *Valcour* subsequently operated out of Norfolk, Va.; Quonset Point, R.I.; Cristobal, Canal Zone; and Guantanamo Bay, Cuba; tending seaplanes of the Fleet Air Wings, Atlantic, through mid-1949.

Having received orders designating her as flagship for the Commander, Middle Eastern Force (ComMid-EastFor), *Valcour* departed Norfolk on 29 August 1949; steamed across the Atlantic and the Mediterranean; stopped at Gilbraltar and at Golfe Juan, France; transited the Suez Canal; and arrived at Aden, a British protectorate, on 24 September. Over the months that ensued, *Valcour* touched at ports on the Indian Ocean and Persian Gulf—Bahrein, Kuwait; Ras Al Mishab, Basra; Ras Tanura, Muscat; Bombay, India; Colombo, Ceylon; and Karachi, Pakistan. She returned to Norfolk on 6 March 1950—via Aden, Suez; Pireaus, Greece; Sfax, Tunisia; and Gibraltar. Late in the summer—after a period of leave, upkeep, and training—the seaplane tender returned to the Middle East for her second tour as ComMidEastFor

flagship which lasted from 5 September 1950 to 15 March 1951.

On the morning of 14 May 1951, two months after she returned to Norfolk, *Valcour* headed out to sea for independent ship exercises. While passing the collier SS *Thomas Tracy* off Cape Henry, Va., she suffered a steering casualty and power failure. As *Valcour* veered sharply across the path of the oncoming collier, she sounded warning signals. *Thomas Tracy* attempted to make an emergency turn to starboard but her bow soon plowed into the seaplane tender's starboard side, rupturing an aviation gas fuel tank.

An intense fire soon broke out and, fed by the high-test aviation gas, spread rapidly. To make matters worse, water began flooding into the ship's ruptured hull. Although fire and rescue parties on board went to work immediately, the gasoline-fed inferno forced many of the tender's crew to leap overboard into the swirling currents of Hampton Roads to escape the flames that soon enveloped *Valcour*'s starboard side. The situation at that point looked so severe that Capt. Eugene Tatom, the tender's commanding officer, gave the order to abandon ship.

Thomas Tracy, meanwhile, fared better. Fires in that ship were largely confined to the forward hold and she suffered no injuries to her crew; she managed to return to Newport News with her cargo—10,000 tons of coal—intact. *Valcour*, on the other hand, became the object of exhaustive salvage operations. Rescue ships, including the submarine rescue ship *Sunbird* (ASR–15) and the Coast Guard tug *Cherokee* (WAT–165) sped to the scene of the tragedy. Fire and rescue parties—in some cases forced to utilize gas masks—succeeded in bringing the blaze under control but not before 11 men had died, and 16 more had been injured. Another 25 were listed as "missing."

Towed back to Norfolk—reaching port at 0200 on the 15th—*Valcour* underwent an extensive overhaul over the ensuing months. During those repairs, improvements were made in shipboard habitability—air-conditioning was installed—and the removal of her single-mount 5-inch gun forward gave the ship a silhouette unique for ships in her class. The reconstruction task was finally completed on 4 December 1951.

Valcour rotated yearly between the United States and the Middle East over the next 15 years, conducting yearly deployments as one of the trio of ships in her class that served alternately as flagship for Com-

USS *Valcour* as the administrative flagship of the Middle East Force (AGF–1). Her white color scheme is intended to help her air conditioning system cope with the area's heat.

MidEastFor. There were several highlights to the ship's lengthy Middle East deployments. In July of 1953, during the ship's fourth cruise, *Valcour* aided a damaged cargo vessel in the Indian Ocean and then escorted her through a violent typhoon to Bombay, India. In May 1955, men from *Valcour* boarded the blazing and abandoned Italian tanker *Argea Prima* at the entrance to the Persian Gulf, even though the ship at the time was laden with a cargo of 72,000 barrels of crude oil, and proceeded to control the fires. Once the seaplane tender's fire and rescue party had performed their salvage operation, *Argea Prima*'s crew reboarded the ship; and she continued her voyage. Later, *Valcour* received a plaque from the owners of the tanker in appreciation of the assistance rendered to their ship.

Valcour performed her duties so efficiently that the Chief of Naval Operations congratulated ComMidEast-For for her outstanding contribution to good foreign relations and for her enhancement of the prestige of the United States. The ship was also adjudged the outstanding seaplane tender in the Atlantic Fleet in 1957 and was awarded the Battle Readiness and Excellence Plaque and the Navy "E" in recognition of the accomplishment. During *Valcour*'s 1960 cruise, she became the first American ship in 48 years to visit the Seychelles Islands, an archipelago in the Indian Ocean. In 1963, *Valcour* earned her second Navy "E".

In between her deployments to the Middle East, *Valcour* conducted local operations out of Little Creek, Va.; Guantanamo Bay; and Kingston, Jamaica. In 1965, the ship qualified as a "blue nose" by crossing the Arctic Circle during operations in the Norwegian Sea.

She completed her 15th cruise on 13 March 1965 and soon thereafter was selected to continue those duties on a permanent basis. She was reclassified as a miscellaneous command flagship, AGF-1, on 15 December 1965 and departed the United States for the Middle East on 18 April 1966 for her 16th MidEastFor cruise.

Valcour's mission was that of command post, living facility, and communications center for ComMidEast-For and his staff of 15 officers. Demonstrating American interest and good will in that area of the globe, *Valcour* distributed textbooks, medicine, clothing, and domestic machinery (such as sewing machines, etc.) to the needy, under the auspices of Project "Handclasp." Men from *Valcour* helped to promote good relations in the countries visited by assisting in the construction of orphanages and schools; by participating in public functions; and by entertaining dignitaries, military representatives, and civilians. In addition, while watching merchant shipping lanes, *Valcour* stood ready to rescue stricken ships and to evacuate Americans during internal crises.

Homeported at Bahrain—an independent sheikdom in the Persian Gulf—since 1965, *Valcour* became the permanent flagship for ComMidEastFor in 1971. Relieved as flagship by *La Salle* (LPD–3) in the spring of 1972, *Valcour* returned to Norfolk, Va., via Colombo; Singapore; Brisbane, Australia; Wellington, N.Z.; Tahiti; Panama; and Fort Lauderdale, Fla. After four days at the last-named port, she arrived at Norfolk on 11 November, completing the 18,132-mile voyage from the Middle East.

After being stripped of all usable gear over the ensuing months, *Valcour* was decommissioned on 15 January 1973 and shifted to the Inactive Ship Facility at Portsmouth, Va., so that she could be prepared for service as a test-bed for electromagnetic tests held under the auspices of the Naval Ordnance Laboratory (NOL), White Oak, Md. Her name was struck from the Navy list simultaneously with her decommissioning. Towed from Norfolk to Solomons Island, Md., branch of NOL the following March, she soon thereafter began her service as a test ship for the EMPRESS (Electromagnetic Pulse Radiation Environment Simulation for Ships) facility. The erstwhile seaplane tender and command ship was sold by the Navy in May 1977.

Valdez

Phil Isadore Valdez—born on 13 April 1946 in Dixon, N.M.—graduated from Espanola (N.M.) High School in May 1965 and enlisted in the Navy on 1 November 1965. After completing basic training, he was trained at the Naval Hospital Corps School at San Diego, Calif. Advanced to the rating of hospitalman in May 1966, Valdez served at the Naval Hospital, Key West, Fla., until 19 December 1966 at which time he was transferred to the 1st Battalion, 1st Marines, Fleet Marine Force, serving ashore in Vietnam near Danang.

On the morning of 29 January 1967, Valdez was assigned as corpsman with the 3d Platoon when that unit was flown in by helicopter to provide support for the embattled Company "H," 2d Battalion. Upon landing, Valdez' unit came under heavy sniper fire, and several marines went down as a result. The hospitalman sprang into action instantly. First, he ran about 70 meters across open land being raked by enemy fire to aid a fallen marine. He helped that man to a safer place and quickly dressed his wounds. After completing that task, he dashed back out into the hail of fire to assist another wounded marine some 50 meters away. Upon reaching his new charge, he positioned himself so as to protect the wounded man from the enemy fire and began to dress his wound. At that point, the enemy got his range; and Valdez fell to their fire, mortally wounded. His ". . . heroic action and selfless devotion to duty . . ." saved the lives of two wounded marines and, in recognition of his ". . . conspicuous gallantry and intrepidity in action," HN Valdez was advanced to the rate of hospitalman, third class, and awarded the Navy Cross, both posthumously.

(DE–1096: dp. 3,963 (f.); l. 438'; b. 47'; dr. 25'; s. 27+ k.; cpl. 245; a. 1 5", 1 ASROC/Standard missile ln., 1 Sea Sparrow ln., 4 15.5" ASW tt.; cl. *Knox*)

Valdez (DE–1096) was laid down on 30 June 1972 at Oswego, La., by the Avondale Shipyard; launched on 24 March 1973; sponsored by Mrs. Manuelita Valdez, the mother of Hospitalman Third Class Valdez; and commissioned on 27 July 1974 at Charleston, S.C., Comdr. Joe D. Peden in command.

Valdez spent the following three months in Charleston fitting out and completing final trials. She departed Charleston on 27 October, bound for Guantanamo Bay, Cuba, whence she operated for the next seven weeks. Upon completion of her shakedown cruise, she returned to Charleston for a month of leave and upkeep followed by inspections and preparations for post-shakedown availability. That availability began on 25 February 1975 and ended on 11 April. At that juncture, she began normal operations out of Charleston and, later, participated in Exercise "Solid Shield," an amphibious landing and convoy protection exercise conducted during the last week in May and the first week in June near Morehead City, N.C. On 6 June, the ocean escort returned to Charleston and resumed the normal routine until 18 August. During that period, she was reclassified a frigate and redesignated FF–1096 on 30 June 1975.

On 18 August, the frigate steamed out of Charleston for her first overseas deployment. She changed operational control to the 6th Fleet upon arrival at Rota, Spain, on the 29th. From there, the frigate moved into and across the Mediterranean Sea to Egypt. She transited the Suez Canal on 5 September and the next day reported for duty with the Middle East Force at Djibouti in the French Territory of the Afars and Issas. During her tour of duty with the Middle East Force, *Valdez* participated in bilateral exercises with units of the naval forces of France, Iran, Abu Dhabi, and Pakistan as well as of the Air Force of Kuwait. She also embarked officers of the Saudi Arabian Navy for training and participated in the multinational CENTO exercise codenamed MidLink–75. Ports of call included Bandar Abbas, Iran; Bahrain; Kuwait; Sharjah and Abu Dhabi in the United Arab Emirates; Karachi, Pakistan; Assab, Ethiopia; Victoria in the Seychelles; and Jidda, Saudi Arabia.

On 31 January 1976, *Valdez* retransited the Suez Canal on her way home. She recrossed the Mediterranean Sea and arrived back in Rota on 5 February where she remained until the 8th. Between 11 and 14 February, she visited Brest, France, where she participated in a gun salute symbolic of the first salute ever fired to the flag of the independent United States. From there, she set course—via the Azores and Bermuda—to return to Charleston. *Valdez* reentered her home port on 25 February.

After leave and upkeep, she resumed normal 2d Fleet operations out of Charleston. That duty lasted until September when she began preparations for another 6th Fleet deployment.

On 4 October, she stood out of Charleston and arrived in Rota 10 days later. On the 16th, *Valdez* reentered the Mediterranean. The ship spent the remainder of the year and the initial months of 1977 engaged in operations with the 6th Fleet. *Valdez* returned to Charleston on 21 April and commenced 30 days of leave and upkeep.

Following a summer devoted to operations off the east coast, the fleet frigate began preparations for another overseas period, this time a deployment to the North Atlantic. She departed Charleston on 27 September to join a NATO task group for Exercise "Combined Effort." During the next two months, *Valdez* engaged in other NATO exercises at sea interspersed with port visits. Her ports of call included Lisbon, Portugal; Portsmouth, England; Amsterdam, the Netherlands; Bremerhaven, Germany; and Cherbourg, France. *Valdez* returned to Charleston on 2 December and remained there into the new year.

The ship got underway on 16 January 1978 for a three-month good will cruise to West Africa and South America. Countries on her agenda consisted of Morocco, Guinea-Bissau, Liberia, Togo, Ivory Coast, Nigeria, Senegal, and Brazil. *Valdez* returned to Charleston on 18 April. A month of repairs and leave followed. The summer was spent conducting operations out of her home port. On 12 September, *Valdez* departed Charleston for Boston where she commenced a regular overhaul on 15 September at the Bethlehem Steel shipyard. The ship remained there into 1979.

Valdez, Private Jose F., see *Private Jose F. Valdez.*

Valeda

(MB: t. 19 (gross); l. 59'5''; b. 12'6''; dr. 4'2'' (mean); s. 10.5 k.; cpl. 10; a. 1 1-pdr., 1 .30-cal. mg.)

Valeda (SP–592)—a wooden-hulled cabin motor launch completed in 1908 at Stamford, Conn., by the Stamford Motor Co.—was acquired by the Navy from F. B. Richards of Cleveland, Ohio, on 9 July 1917; and was commissioned on 12 July 1917 at Rockland, Maine, Chief Quartermaster Cecil C. Wescott in command.

Attached to the 1st Naval District, Rockland Section, *Valeda* operated on harbor and harbor entrance patrols for the duration of World War I. After the armistice, she was decommissioned on 4 Febuary 1919 at Baker's Yacht Basin, Quincy, Mass., and struck from the Navy list on 1 October 1919. *Valeda* was subsequently sold to J. R. C. McBeath, of Atlantic, Mass., on 2 January 1920.

Valencia

A county in western New Mexico.

(AKA–81: dp. 13,910; l. 459'2''; b. 63'; dr. 26'4''; s. 16.5 k.; cpl. 415; a. 1 5'', 8 40mm., 16 20mm.; cl. *Tolland*; T. C2–S–AJ3)

Valencia (AKA–81) was laid down under a Maritime Commission contract (MC hull 1389) on 20 May 1944 at Wilmington, N.C., by the North Carolina Shipbuilding Corp.; launched on 22 July 1944; sponsored by Mrs. C. L. Merritt; acquired by the Navy on 18 August 1944; converted for Navy use by the Bethlehem Steel shipyard, Key Highway plant, Baltimore, Md.; and commissioned there on 9 January 1945, Lt. Comdr. Rodney A. Blake, USNR, in command.

Following fitting out, shakedown, and initial exercises in the Hampton Roads area, *Valencia* got underway from the Naval Operating Base, Norfolk, Va., at 0938 on 10 February, in company with *Medea* (AKA–31), bound for the Canal Zone. The ships transited the Panama Canal on the 17th and proceeded on to the Hawaiian Islands, making port at Pearl Harbor on 2 March.

Shifting to Honolulu on the 8th, *Valencia* moored at the Army Transport Dock and loaded a total of 145 officers and enlisted men before getting underway on the 14th for the Marshalls. Escorted by *PC–1139* up to a point 30 miles from Pearl Harbor, the attack cargo ship proceeded independently for the remainder of her passage and arrived at Eniwetok on 22 March. Again traveling singly, *Valencia* got underway for the southern Carolines three days later and arrived off Ulithi after a week's voyage. However, a typhoon prevented her from entering the harbor; and she steamed away from the storm center at slow speeds until early on the following day, when quieter seas and improved visibility permitted her to reach her destination.

The auxiliary remained at Ulithi from 1 to 13 April, preparing for participation in her first operation. *Valencia* got underway for Okinawa at 1617 on the 13th, in Division "Able" of Task Group 55.8, in company with *Okanogan* (APA–220), *Jerauld* (APA–174), *Lenoir* (AKA–74), *Lumen* (AKA–30), SS *Kelso Victory*, and SS *Typhoon*. The four-day passage was highlighted by a suspected submarine contact which sent all ships to general quarters and by the sighting of a stray mine which escort vessels destroyed.

Valencia anchored off Hagushi beach, Okinawa, at 0921 on 17 April, commenced discharging cargo at 1815, and ceased at 1945. All ships began making smoke at 2024, upon receipt of an air raid alert, completely covering the anchorage area within a few moments. *Valencia* later observed antiaircraft fire from the forces ashore and noted reports of enemy aircraft being in the vicinity two or three times, before securing from general quarters at 2239. Due to pevailing heavy surf conditions, the beaches were closed to landings on the 19th, as high winds kicked up heavy seas which greatly hampered unloading. Heavy swells continued to hinder operations into subsequent days, as rough seas made it difficult to hold boats alongside, sweeping them against the steel hide of the ship. Despite this handicap and two "red alerts" on the evening of 20 and 21 April, the crew, aided by a force of 83 marines (two officers and 81 enlisted men) managed to unload the ship's cargo by evening on the 21st.

Valencia engaged in hoisting in her boats and making ready for sea throughout the night of the 21st and commenced disembarking her marine stevedoring party at 0620 on the 22d. Another "red alert" interrupted the boat-hoisting process at 0710, but the resumption of the task at 0900, when the "all clear" was sounded, enabled the ship to soon be ready for sea. Accordingly, the ship got underway at 1317 on 22 April for the Marianas in Task Unit 51.29.20.

Arriving at Saipan on 1 May, *Valencia* transferred most of her landing craft (LCVP's, LCPL's, and LCM's) to the boat pool and got underway for Noumea, New Caledonia, on the 3d. She loaded Army equipment; Navy construction battalion vehicles and equipment; and embarked passengers for destinations on the cargo ship's itinerary. *Valencia* got underway at 1508 on 20 May and, between that time and her arrival at Eniwetok on the 30th, called at Guadalcanal and Tulagi, embarking and debarking passengers and picking up new boats. She remained at Eniwetok from 1 to 26 June, awaiting orders, before getting underway for the Marianas. She reached Guam at 1900 on 29 June to unload LCVP's, vehicles, and general cargo at Apra Harbor.

The attack cargo ship then shifted to Tanapag Harbor, Guam, to finish unloading before proceeding on to the west coast of the United States, dropping anchor in San Francisco Bay on 31 July. *Valencia* remained at anchor until the 9th, when she shifted to Pier 90–B, San Francisco, to begin loading general cargo earmarked for the Philippines. During this time, the war in the Pacific came to an end after Japan, reeling from the steady Allied pounding and two atomic bombs, capitulated on 15 August 1945.

Sailing for the Philippines on 18 August, *Valencia* arrived off Samar on 6 September, unloaded all holds by the 19th, and subsequently moved on to Manila Bay, Subic Bay, and Lingayen Gulf in succession. Subsequently, the attack cargo ship embarked men and equipment of the 25th Division of the 6th Army for occupation duty in Japan. On 1 October, she got underway for Wakayama as part of TU 54.8.1. Detached from the convoy for a brief period on 6 October to destroy a floating unidentified object, she expended 292 rounds of 20-millimeter ammunition before resuming her passage with the group—her mission completed.

Arriving off Honshu on the 7th, *Valencia* remained in the Wakayama area until the 25th. During this period, a typhoon passed just west of the anchorage area of Wakanoura Wan on 10 and 11 October. Winds up to 90 knots swept across the bay, forcing *Valencia* to ride out the typhoon by using her anchors and main engines. Her mission at Wakayama completed by the 25th, the attack cargo vessel got underway on that date for Nagoya, Japan. After transiting the swept channel to the ship's destination, she anchored first off Yokkaichi Ko—the transport anchorage—and then shifted to alongside a pier where she discharged cargo, troops, and eight Army LCM's, and remained until the 14th. Having embarked 268 men for transportation to the United States on the 13th, the ship got underway on the 14th for San Francisco.

While en route, the destination of the ship was changed to Portland, Oreg., and she made port there on 28 November. Remaining at Portland until 17 December, the ship shifted to San Francisco and then conducted one round-trip voyage to Pearl Harbor and back before departing the west coast on 14 February 1946 for the east coast. Transiting the Panama Canal on the 24th, *Valencia* arrived at New York, N.Y., on 3 March, via Little Creek, Va., before proceeding back to the Hampton Roads vicinity and arriving at the Norfolk Navy Yard on the 7th.

Decommissioned on 8 May 1946, the ship was delivered to the War Shipping Administration, Maritime Commission, five days later. Her name was struck from the Navy list on 21 May 1946.

Acquired by the Lykes Lines, the vessel was renamed SS *Genevieve Lykes* and entered mercantile service soon thereafter. Acquired by T. J. Stevenson and Co., Inc., of New York City, in 1947, the vessel was renamed *Garden City*. She remained in service with this firm until her name disappeared from the merchant registers in 1971.

Valencia received one battle star for her World War II service.

Valentine

An asteroid, number 447, discovered by the astronomers Wolf and Schwassmann in October 1899.

(AF–47: dp. 7,125; l. 338'6''; b. 50'0''; dr. 21'1''; s. 11.5 k.; cpl. 83; a. 1 3'', 6 20mm.; cl. *Adria*; T. R1–M–AV3)

Valentine (AF–47) was laid down under a Maritime Commission contract (MC hull 2339) at Beaumont, Tex., by the Pennsylvania Shipyards, Inc. Launched on 3 February 1945 and sponsored by Mrs. P. Blaschke, the ship was placed "in service" on 19 June 1945 for ferrying and departed Beaumont on 25 June, bound for Galveston, Tex. There, at the Todd-Galveston Shipyard, Inc., *Valentine* underwent conversion to a refrigeration ship. She was commisioned at Galveston on 19 July 1945, Lt. John W. Perdue in command.

After shakedown and post-shakedown availability, *Valentine* departed Galveston on 2 August, bound for Mobile, Ala. She loaded her first cargo of fleet supplies there and got underway on 10 August for the Pacific. While en route, the ship received word that Japan had surrendered on 14 August 1945. *Valentine* transited the Panama Canal on the 16th and departed Balboa shortly after noon on the 17th for the Hawaiian Islands.

Valentine arrived at Pearl Harbor late in the morning of 5 September, discharged her first cargo, reloaded with fleet issue supplies over the ensuing days, and sailed for Okinawa on 21 September for onward routing. Two days out of Buckner Bay, on 7 October, the barometer began to plummet; and, as *Valentine*'s historian recorded, "all indications pointed to some pretty rough weather." Aerological reports indicated that a typhoon was passing ahead of the ship, and it was expected, initially, to go up the China coast. However, late on the 8th, the storm's course changed. In view of that development, *Valentine* reversed course to stay out of its center. The ship rode out the typhoon; 60-knot winds drove waves and spray as high as the bridge. By the morning of the 9th, the wind and waves had calmed sufficiently to enable the ship to continue on toward Okinawa. Although buffeted about in the heavy seas, *Valentine* had fared much better than other ships of the fleet that had been trapped at Okinawa as the center of the typhoon swirled destructively across Buckner Bay.

The refrigeration ship lingered at Buckner Bay from 1345 on the 11th to 1735 on the 12th before she got underway for the China coast. Arriving at Shanghai on the 16th, *Valentine* unloaded her cargo—part of which consisted of Thanksgiving dinners for American servicemen stationed at that port—before she eventually weighed anchor for Hong Kong shortly after noon on the 25th. While leaving Shanghai via a swept channel, *Valentine* encountered a mine that she sank with gunfire in the middle of that waterway. Later on in her voyage to the British Crown Colony, as she passed the southern tip of Formosa, her lookouts sighted another stray mine 50 yards ahead; a quick course change enabled the vessel to slip by within a narrow margin before she destroyed that mine, too, with gunfire to end its threat to shipping.

Valentine arrived at Hong Kong at 0916 on 31 October, unloaded her cargo over the ensuing days, and sailed for home on 10 November. She arrived at San Francisco on 8 December to take on another load of fleet issue supplies. All hands had hoped for a "stateside" Christmas, but this was not to be, as *Valentine* weighed anchor for the Far East on 22 December—three days before Christmas.

After the ship tarried at Okinawa, she was routed on to Japan, her holds laden with supplies for the American occupation forces. She touched at the Japanese ports of Sasebo, Kure, and Kobe, in succession, into late February 1946. She departed Kobe shortly before noon on 26 February and arrived back at San Francisco on 21 March. Loading cargo on a fleet issue basis, *Valentine* departed the west coast, one month later, on 21 April, bound again for the western Pacific.

She remained at Pearl Harbor from 30 April to 5 May before she proceeded on toward the Marshalls and arrived at Majuro on the 13th. She provided fresh and frozen provisions to ships of the fleet at Kwajalein, Roi, Bikini Atoll, Eniwetok, and Wake Island before she returned via Pearl Harbor to the west coast, arriving at San Francisco on 16 July. During her brief service career, *Valentine* sailed 47,770 miles and delivered 6,400 tons of cargo.

Decommissioned at San Francisco on 6 August 1946, *Valentine* was transferred to the War Shipping Administration soon thereafter. She was struck from the Navy list on 8 October 1946.

Valeria

Minor planet number 611, discovered on 24 September 1906 at Taunton, Mass., by Joel Metcalf, a Unitarian minister and amateur astronomer, who made the initial identification of 41 minor planets.

(AKA–48: dp. 7,000 (tl.); l. 426'0''; b. 58'0''; dr. 16'0''; s. 16.9 k.; cpl. 303; a. 1 5'', 8 40mm., 10 20mm.; cl. *Artemis*; T. S4–SE2–BE1)

Valeria (AKA–48) was laid down under a Maritime Commission contract (MC hull 1909) on 8 April 1945 at Providence, R.I., by the Walsh-Kaiser Co.; launched on 29 May 1945; sponsored by Mrs. A. D. Hunter; and transferred to the Navy on 28 June 1945 and commissioned the same day, Lt. Comdr. Robert Smith Trower III in command.

The new attack cargo ship departed Boston on 9 July; conducted shakedown training in the Chesapeake Bay; and got underway on 29 July, bound for the Canal Zone. She transited the Panama Canal on 5 August and steamed westward, conducting gunnery exercises en route. During her passage to Oahu, hostilities ended in the Pacific. On the 18th, *Valeria* moored at Pearl Harbor.

On 7 September, she got underway for Noumea. Ten days later, the ship reached Espiritu Santo where she took on troops from *Achenar* (AKA–53) and *Turandot* (AKA–47). On the 19th, *Valeria* proceeded to Noumea where she disembarked her passengers. Underway again the next day, she returned to Espiritu Santo on on the 22d. There, on the 25th, the attack cargo ship loaded elements of the 85th Construction Battalion and departed the New Hebrides the following day. She steamed via Eniwetok and delivered her cargo and passengers at Wake Island early in October.

She completed discharging her cargo there on the 12th and reported for "Magic Carpet" duties—transporting returning servicemen from the Pacific islands to the United States mainland. Before the end of the year, she made two round trips carrying returning Army veterans from Eniwetok and Saipan to west coast ports.

Assigned to the 5th Naval District on 5 January 1946, *Valeria* departed Los Angeles, Calif., on the 11th, steamed via the Panama Canal to the Atlantic coast, and arrived at Norfolk on 1 February. She was decommissioned on 18 March, and her name was struck from the Navy list on 17 April. *Valeria* was delivered to the War Shipping Administration at Lee Hall, Va., on 26 June 1946.

Valiant

I

(Cutter: t. 13; l. 60'; b. 12'6''; dr. 8'; s. 8 k.; cpl. 9; a. 1 1-pdr., 1 .30-cal. mg.)

The first *Valiant* (SP–535)—a wooden-hulled sailing cutter completed in 1896 by Charles S. Drowne—was rebuilt in 1907 and was fitted with an auxiliary engine to augment her sails in 1917. The vessel was acquired by the Navy under free lease from Henry M. Warren; and commissioned at Philadelphia on 29 May 1917, Ens. R. F. Watson, USNRF, in command.

Valiant operated on 4th Naval District patrol duties, locally, in the Cape May, N.J., area for the duration of World War I. She was subsequently decommissioned

at the Corinthian Yacht Club, near Philadelphia, Pa., on 11 January 1919, and returned to her owner soon thereafter.

II

(PC–509: dp. 190; l. 150'0''; b. 24'0''; dr. 8'6'' (mean) (f.); s. 15 k.; a. 1 3'')

Vara—a yacht constructed in 1929 by the Herreshoff Manufacturing Co. at Bristol, R.I.—was acquired from Mr. Harold S. Vanderbilt on 7 October 1940; converted for naval service at the New York Navy Yard; designated *PC–509*; and commissioned at New York City on 27 December 1941.

Assigned to the Panama Canal Zone, *PC–509* operated from that point escorting convoys in the Gulf of Mexico and the Caribbean Sea for the duration of her brief Navy career. She reached the Canal Zone on 2 February and pursued a varied itinerary during the first 14 months of her career as a convoy escort. She visited Guantanamo Bay and Havana in Cuba; Jacksonville, Miami, and Key West in Fla.; as well as Charleston, S.C. In May 1943, however, she began to concentrate upon the Canal Zone-Guantanamo Bay circuit exclusively. On 15 July 1943, *PC–509* was named *Valiant* and redesignated PYc–51. Over the last 15 months of her service, she escorted seven convoys from Panama to Guantanamo Bay and returned in the screen of a Panama-bound convoy after the first six. Between convoys, she conducted routine patrols and participated in submarine searches, though it appears that she never saw combat.

After escorting her seventh convoy safely into Guantanamo Bay on 25 August 1944, *Valiant* headed north for inactivation. She stopped briefly at Charleston on 28 August and arrived in Philadelphia on the 31st. There, she was placed out of commission sometime in September and was turned over to the Commandant, 4th Naval District, for disposal. Her name was struck from the Navy list on 14 October 1944, and she was sold by the War Shipping Administration on 15 June 1945.

Vallejo

A city on San Pablo Bay in western California which in turn was named for General Mariano G. Vallejo. Fleet ballistic missile submarine SSBN–658 also bears the name of this distinguished Californian. See *Mariano G. Vallejo* for his biography.

Vallejo (PF–97) was projected as a *Tacoma*-class frigate, but her construction was cancelled in December 1943.

Vallejo (CL–112) was projected as a *Fargo*-class light cruiser to be built at Camden, N.J., by the New York Shipbuilding Corp. under a 9 July 1942 authorization; but her construction was cancelled on 5 October 1944.

Vallejo (CL–146) was laid down as a *Worcester*-class light cruiser on 16 July 1945 at Camden, N.J., by the New York Shipbuilding Corp. However, her construction was cancelled on 8 December 1945; and her hulk was subsequently scrapped.

Vallejo, Mariano G., see *Mariano G. Vallejo*.

Valley City

(ScStr.: t. 190; l. 127'6''; b. 21'10''; dph. 7'6''; dr. 8'4''; s. 10 k.; a. 4 32-pdr. 42 Cwt.)

Valley City—a wooden-hulled screw-steamer built at Philadelphia in 1859—was purchased by the Navy at

New York City on 26 July 1861; and commissioned at the New York Navy Yard on 13 September 1861, Lt. James C. Chaplin in command.

The next day, *Valley City* left New York to join the Potomac Flotilla commanded by Capt. Thomas T. Craven. She arrived in the Potomac River off Occoquan Creek, Va., on the 17th and began patrol and reconnaissance duties. She exchanged gunfire with a Confederate battery at Freestone Point, Va., on 25 September. *Valley City* was reassigned to the North Atlantic Blockading Squadron under Flag Officer Louis M. Goldsborough in October but first put into the Baltimore Navy Yard, Md., for emergency repairs to her funnel. After a brief stop in Hampton Roads late in December, the repaired steamer was deployed with the blockade off Hatteras Inlet, N.C., on 4 January 1862.

Valley City remained off Hatteras Inlet for one month and then participated in the successful amphibious assault upon Roanoke Island, N.C., on 7 and 8 February. The victory closed supply lines to the Confederate-held Norfolk Navy Yard and was largely responsible for the evacuation of that vital naval facility three months later. Following the capture of Roanoke Island, *Valley City* assisted in the capture of Elizabeth City, N.C., on the 10th. During the attack, a shot passed through the steamer's magazine and exploded in a locker containing fireworks. When Lt. Chaplin and others went below to extinguish the fire, they found Quarter Gunner John Davis seated calmly above an open barrel of powder to keep the fire out, while passing powder to the upper deck. For his incredible valor on this occasion, Davis received the Medal of Honor. *Valley City* remained in the North Carolina sounds and participated in the capture of New Berne on 13 and 14 March and the subsequent clearing of the Neuse River. She returned to Baltimore for repairs on 2 June.

In September, *Valley City* was assigned patrol and reconnaissance duty in Virginia's York River. She was reassigned to Plymouth, N.C., on 25 October to protect Union troops stationed there. On the evening of 2 November, she led a reconnaissance expedition up the Roanoke River to Hamilton which she left a week later and returned to New Berne. In January 1863, the vessel returned to the Norfolk Navy Yard for a new propeller and underwent further repairs and alterations at Baltimore before deploying off Washington, N.C., in April. *Valley City* fired upon Confederate positions near Blount's Creek, N.C., on 15 April, then left to join Lt. Charles W. Flusser's command at Plymouth on 19 April.

Valley City performed routine patrol and reconnaissance duties off Plymouth through July. On the 26th, the steamer helped to protect Union forces ashore during a joint expedition up the Chowan River, N.C. Later, while serving as a mail steamer, the vessel collided with the U.S. transport *Vidette* on 21 September and suffered one fatality. *Valley City* sailed for Hampton Roads on 27 November and proceeded on to Baltimore for repairs and did not return to New Berne until 19 February 1864, when she resumed her now familiar patrol and reconnaissance activities.

Valley City was pesent at the evacuation of Washington, N.C., in May and captured the schooner *M. O'Neill* there on 5 May. During the summer months of May through September 1864, the steamer played an important role in support of Union forces ashore and afloat in scattered operations in the Roanoke, Chowan, Pamlico, Pungo, and Scuppernong rivers of North Carolina. On 28 October, *Valley City* plucked Lt. William Barker Cushing from the Roanoke River after his daring, successful torpedo attack upon the Confederate ram CSS *Albemarle* at Plymouth and, from 29 October to 1 November, assisted in the recapture of Plymouth itself. While on an expedition up the Roanoke River on 20 December, the vessel suffered two casualties in a surprise attack by hidden Confederate shore batteries at Poplar Point, N.C.

Valley City remained active during the last few months of the war, rendering assistance to an Army expedition to Colerain, N.C., in January 1865, and participating in a reconnaissance patrol up the Chowan River to Winton, N.C., in early April. In May, *Iosco*, *Valley City*, and a picket boat captured a motley collection of small Confederate watercraft during a sweep of the Roanoke River and also dragged the bottom for sunken guns and unexploded torpedoes.

Early in the summer, the steamer returned north and was sold at public auction at New York City on 15 August 1865. She was redocumented for merchant service on 28 December and was lost at sea off Cape San Blas, Fla., on 30 January 1882.

Valley Forge

A locality in Chester County, Pa., where the Continental Army suffered bitter cold and privation during the winter of 1777 and 1778 while British troops basked in warmth and plenty in nearby Philadelphia. Yet, because of the inspiring example of leaders like Washington and skillful training by drill instructors like von Steuben, the American Army emerged from its winter encampment with renewed self confidence, courage, and fighting ability. The name Valley Forge has since become a symbol of the triumph of American patriotism and self-sacrifice.

Valley Forge (CV–37)—an *Essex*-class aircraft carrier—was renamed *Princeton* (q.v) on 21 November 1944.

I

(CV–45: dp. 36,380; l. 888'0''; b. 93'0''; dr. 28'7''; s. 32.7 k.; cpl. 3,448; a. 12 5'', 72 40mm.; ac. 80; cl. *Ticonderoga*)

Valley Forge (CV–45)—built with money raised by the citizens of Philadelphia in a special war bond drive—was laid down on 7 September 1944 by the Philadelphia Navy Yard; launched on 18 November 1944; sponsored by Mrs. A. A. Vandegrift, wife of the Commandant of the Marine Corps; and commissioned on 3 November 1946, Capt. John W. Harris in command.

Following fitting out, the new carrier got underway on 24 January 1947 for shakedown training which took her via Norfolk to Guantanamo Bay, Cuba, and the Canal Zone. She completed the cruise on 18 March and returned to Philadelphia for post-shakedown overhaul. The ship left Philadelphia on 14 July, headed south, and transited the Panama Canal on 5 August. She arrived at her home port, San Diego, on the 14th and joined the Pacific Fleet. Following the embarkation of Air Group 11 and intensive air and gunnery training in coastal waters, the aircraft carrier—flying the flag of Rear Admiral Harold L. Martin, Commander of Task Force 38—got underway for Hawaii on 9 October. The task force devoted almost three months to training operations out of Pearl Harbor before sailing for Australia on 16 January 1948. After a visit to Sydney, the American warships conducted exercises with units of the Royal Australian Navy and then steamed to Hong Kong.

During a voyage from the British crown colony to Tsingtao, China, orders arrived directing the task force to return home via the Atlantic. With her escorting destroyers, the ship continued the round-the-world trip with calls at Hong Kong; Manila; Singapore; Trincomalee, Ceylon; and Ras Tanura, Saudi Arabia. After operating for a time in the Persian Gulf, she became the largest aircraft carrier to transit the Suez Canal. The ship finally arrived at San Diego, via the Mediterranean Sea, the Atlantic Ocean, and the Panama Canal.

Valley Forge deployed to the Far East, departing the west coast on 1 May 1950. While anchored in Hong Kong harbor on 25 June, the warship received electrifying news that North Korean forces had begun stream-

A 1946 view of *Valley Forge* (CV–45), with a single Curtiss SB2C–4 *Helldiver* and two Vought F4U *Corsairs* on her flight deck. (80–G–703585)

ing across the 38th parallel into South Korea. Departing Hong Kong the next day, the carrier steamed north to Subic Bay, where she provisioned, fueled, and set her course for Korea.

The first carrier air strike of the Korean conflict was launched from *Valley Forge*'s flight deck on 3 July 1950. Outnumbered and outgunned, the South Korean troops battled desperately against veritable tides of communist invaders. Waves of Douglas AD Skyraiders and Vought F4U Corsairs struck the North Korean airfield at Pyongyang while Grumman F9F–2 Panthers flew top cover. Tons of bombs from the attacking American planes pounded hangars, fuel storages, parked Russian-built aircraft, and railroad marshalling yards. Meanwhile, the escorting Panthers downed two Yak–9's and damaged another.

In spite of attempts by United Nations forces to interdict the steady flow of communist infantry and armor, the North Koreans steadily pushed the defending South Koreans back into a tenuous defense perimeter around Pusan. On 18 September 1950, the American landing at Inchon outflanked the communist forces while United Nations forces broke out of the perimeter to the south. During this period of bitter struggle, *Valley Forge*'s Air Group 5 made numerous daily strikes against North Korean targets. Troop concentrations, defensive positions, and supply and communications lines were repeatedly "fair game" for the bombs of the Skyraiders and the rocket and cannon fire from the Panthers and Corsairs. Over 5,000 combat sorties delivered 2,000 tons of bombs and rockets between 3 July and 19 November 1950.

Returning to San Diego for overhaul, *Valley Forge* arrived on the west coast on 1 December, only to have sailing orders urgently direct her back to Korea. In the interim, between the carrier's leaving station and her projected west coast overhaul, the communist Chinese had entered the fray, launching a powerful offensive which sent United Nations' troops reeling back to the southward. Accordingly, *Valley Forge* hurriedly embarked a new air group, replenished, and sailed on 6 December for the Far East. Rendezvousing

441

with TF 77 three days before Christmas of 1950, *Valley Forge* recommenced air strikes on the 23d—the first of three months of concentrated air operations against the advancing communist juggernaut. During her second deployment, the ship launched some 2,580 sorties in which her planes delivered some 1,500 tons of bombs.

The communist blitzkrieg wavered to a halt by the end of January 1951, and United Nations forces once again pushed the invaders northward past the strategic 38th parallel. After nearly 10 months continuous duty in frequently chilly and always inhospitable Korean coastal waters, *Valley Forge* sailed for the United States on 29 March 1951. Following a major overhaul that lasted into autumn, the ship emerged to become the first American carrier to return to Korea for a third deployment.

On 11 December 1951, *Valley Forge* launched her first air strikes in railway interdiction. Rockets, cannon fire, and bombs from the ship's embarked air group, and those of her sister ships also on station, hammered at North Korean railway targets—lines, junctions, marshalling yards, and rolling stock. Anything that could possibly permit the enemy to move his forces rapidly by rail came under attack. By June, *Valley Forge*'s train-busting Skyraiders, Corsairs, and Panthers had severed communist rail lines in at least 5,346 places.

Valley Forge returned to the United States in the summer of 1952 but was again deployed to the Far East late in the year. In October 1952, she was reclassified an attack carrier and redesignated CVA–45. On 2 January 1953, she began the new year with strikes against communist supply dumps and troop-billeting areas behind the stalemated front lines. While the propeller-driven Skyraiders and Corsairs delivered tons of bombs on their targets, the jet Panthers conducted flak-suppression missions using a combination of cannon fire and rockets to knock out troublesome enemy gun sites. This close teamwork between old- and new-style planes made possible regular strikes against Korea's eastern coastlines and close-support missions to aid embattled Marine Corps or Army forces on the often bitterly contested battle lines. *Valley Forge* air groups dropped some 3,700 tons of bombs on the enemy before the ship left the Korean coast and returned to San Diego on 25 June 1953.

After a west-coast overhaul, *Valley Forge* was transferred to the Atlantic Fleet and reclassified—this time to an antisubmarine warfare support carrier—and redesignated CVS–45. She was refitted for her new duties at the Norfolk Naval Shipyard and then rejoined the Fleet in January 1954. The face-lifted carrier soon got underway to conduct exercises to develop and perfect the techniques and capabilities needed to carry out her new duties.

Conducting local operations and antisubmarine warfare exercises, *Valley Forge* operated off the east coast through late 1956, varied by a visit to England and the eastern Atlantic for exercises late in 1954. Her operations during this period also included midshipman and reservists' training cruises and occasional visits to the Caribbean.

Carrying out training operations out of Guantanamo Bay in 1957, *Valley Forge* accomplished a naval "first" in October, when she embarked a Marine detachment and twin-engined HR2S–1 Mojave helicopters. Experimenting with the new concept of "vertical envelopment," *Valley Forge*'s helicopters air-lifted the marines to the beachhead and then returned them to the ship in history's first ship-based air assault exercise. On 1 April 1958, Rear Admiral John S. Thach—the pilot who, early in World War II, devised the famous "Thach Weave" fighter tactic which was used so successfully by American Navy pilots against the Japanese Zero fighter planes—hoisted his two-star flag to the carrier's main as the ship became flagship of Task Group (TG) Alpha. This group, built around *Valley Forge*, included

eight destroyers, two submarines, and one squadron each of antisubmarine helicopters, planes, and a land-based Lockheed P2V Neptune. A significant development in naval tactics, TG Alpha concentrated solely on developing and perfecting new devices and techniques for countering the potential menace of enemy submarines in an age of nuclear propulsion and deep-diving submersibles.

Valley Forge remained engaged in operations with TG Alpha through the early fall of 1959, when she then entered the New York Naval Shipyard for repairs. The ship returned to sea on 21 January 1960, bound for maneuvers in the Caribbean. During her ensuing operations, the carrier served as the launching platform for Operation "Skyhook." This widely publicized scientific experiment involved the launching of three of the largest balloons ever fabricated, carrying devices to measure and record primary cosmic ray emissions at an altitude of between 18 and 22 miles above the earth's surface.

Following a deployment in the eastern Mediterranean —during which she called at ports in Spain, Italy, and France—*Valley Forge* returned to Norfolk to resume local operations on 30 August, continuing antisubmarine exercises as flagship of TG Alpha through the fall of 1961. The carrier participated in a Project "Mercury" operation, and her helicopters retrieved the space capsule launched by a rocket from Cape Canaveral on 19 December. Two days later off Cape Hatteras, in response to an SOS, *Valley Forge* sped to tanker SS *Pine Ridge*, which had broken in two during a storm. While the survivors of the stricken ship clung tenaciously to the after half of the tanker, the carrier's helicopters shuttled back and forth to pick up the men in distress. Soon, all 28 survivors were safe on board *Valley Forge*.

Entering the Norfolk Naval Shipyard on 6 March 1961 for overhaul and modification to an amphibious assault ship, *Valley Forge* was reclassified as LPH–8 on 1 July 1961 and, soon thereafter, began refresher training in the Caribbean. She returned to Hampton Roads in September and trained in the Virginia capes area with newly embarked, troop-carrying helicopters. In October, the ship—as a part of the Atlantic Fleet's ready amphibious force—proceeded south to waters of Hispaniola and stood by from 21 to 25 October and from 18 to 29 November to be ready to evacuate any American nationals from the Dominican Republic, should that measure become necessary during the struggle for power which afflicted that nation in the months following the assassination of the long-established dictator, Generalissimo Rafael Trujillo.

After returning home late in the year, *Valley Forge* sailed from Norfolk on 6 January 1962, bound for San Diego and duty with the Pacific Fleet. At the end of three months of training off the west coast, the amphibious assault ship steamed westward for duty in the Far East with the 7th Fleet. With the flag of the Commander, Ready Amphibious Task Group, 7th Fleet, at her main, *Valley Forge* closed the coast of Indochina under orders to put ashore her embarked marines. In Laos, communist Pathet Lao forces had renewed their assault on the Royal Laotian Government; and the latter requested President Kennedy to land troops to avert a feared, full-scale communist invasion of the country. The amphibious assault ship airlifted her marines into the country on 17 May; and, when the crisis had abated a few weeks later, carried them out again in July.

For the remainder of 1962, the ship operated in the Far East before returning to the west coast of the United States to spend the first half of 1963 in amphibious exercises off the coast of California and in the Hawaiian Islands.

Valley Forge entered the Long Beach Naval Shipyard on 1 July 1963 for a Fleet Rehabilitation and Modernization overhaul, including the installation of improved electronics and facilities for transporting and andling troops and troop helicopters. Putting to sea again on 27 January 1964, the newly modernized assault ship rejoined the fleet and, following local operations and training, departed Long Beach once more for another WestPac deployment.

She stopped at Pearl Harbor and Okinawa, en route to Hong Kong, and then steamed to Taiwan. In June, she joined ships of other SEATO navies in amphibious exercises and then visited the Philippines where in July she was awarded the Battle Efficiency "E."

On 2 August 1964, North Vietnamese torpedo boats attacked destroyer *Maddox* (DD-731) in the Gulf of Tonkin. *Valley Forge* then spent 57 days at sea off the Vietnamese coast in readiness to land her marines should the occasion demand.

Returning—via Subic Bay, Okinawa, and Midway—to Long Beach on 5 November, *Valley Forge* made two round-trip voyages to Okinawa carrying marines and aircraft before commencing a WestPac deployment in the South China Sea in the fall of 1965. With a Marine landing force embarked and flying the flag of Commander, Amphibious Squadron 3, *Valley Forge* conducted intensive training exercises in the Philippines while preparing for service in Vietnam.

In mid-November, the amphibious assault ship stood by in reserve during Operation "Blue Marlin" and then airlifted her marines ashore for Operations "Dagger Thrust" and "Harvest Moon" before spending the Christmas season "in the crisp freshness of an Okinawan winter." After embarking a fresh Marine battalion landing force and a medium transport helicopter squadron, she sailed for Vietnam on 3 January 1966. Following pauses at Subic Bay and Chu Lai, *Valley Forge* arrived off the Vietnamese coast on the 27th and, two days later, launched her landing forces to take part in Operation "Double Eagle."

Remaining on station off the coast, the ship provided logistic and medical support with inbound helicopters supplying the men ashore and outbound "choppers" evacuating casualties for medical treatment back on the ship. Reembarking her landing team on 17 February, *Valley Forge* proceeded northward, while her marines took a breather. The second phase of "Double Eagle" commenced two days later, and the ship's marines again went ashore via helicopter to attack enemy concentrations.

By February 26th, the operation had drawn to a close; and *Valley Forge* reembarked her marines and sailed for Subic Bay. Following a round trip to Danang, the carrier steamed back to the west coast for an overhaul and local training along the California coast before again deploying to WestPac. Upon her return to Vietnamese waters, the ship took part in operations off Danang before she again returned to the United States at the end of the year 1966.

After undergoing a major overhaul and conducting training off the west coast, *Valley Forge* returned to the Far East again in November 1967 and took part in Operation "Fortress Ridge," launched on 21 December. Air-landing her troops at a point just south of the demilitarized zone (DMZ), the ship provided continual supply and medical evacuation (MedEvac) services for this "search and destroy" operation aimed at eliminating North Vietnamese and Viet Cong units which threatened American and South Vietnamese troops. The completion of this operation on the day before Christmas 1967 did not mark the end of *Valley Forge*'s operations for this year, however, as she was again in action during Operation "Beaver Tooth," near Quang Tri in northern South Vietnam.

Upkeep at Danang preceded her deployment to her new station off Dong Hoi, where she provided her necessary resupply and MedEvac support for Allied troops operating against communist forces. Operation "Badger Catch," commencing on 23 January 1968 and extending through 18 February, took off for the Cua Viet River, south of the DMZ, before the ship set her course for Subic Bay and much-needed maintenance.

Subsequently returning to the fray in Vietnam, *Valley Forge* operated as "Helo Haven" for Marine helicopter units whose shore bases had come under attack by communist ground and artillery fire. During Operation "Badger Catch II," from 6 March to 14 April, Marine "choppers" landed on board the carrier while their land bases were being cleared of Viet Cong and North Vietnamese troops. Following a routine refit at Subic Bay, the ship took part in Operation "Badger Catch III" from 28 April to 3 June. She then moved to Danang and prepared for Operation "Swift Saber" which took place from 7 to 14 June. Landing Exercise "Hilltop XX" occupied the ship early in July. Then, *Valley Forge* transferred her marines and helicopters to *Tripoli* (LPH-10) and headed home via Hong Kong, Okinawa, and Pearl Harbor. She reached Long Beach on 3 August.

Following five months on the west coast which included local operations and an overhaul, the amphibious assault ship returned to the Far East for the last time, departing Long Beach on 30 January 1969.

At San Diego, she embarked a cargo of Marine CH-53 Sea Stallion helicopters for delivery to transport squadrons in Vietnam. The ship stopped at Pearl Harbor and paused near Guam while one of her helicopters carried a stricken crewman ashore for urgent surgery. She loaded special landing-force equipment at Subic Bay and embarked the Commander, Special Landing Forces Bravo and a squadron of Marine CH-46 transport helicopters. On 10 March, the carrier began operating in support of Operation "Defiant Measure," steaming off Danang as her helicopters flew missions "on the beach." This was completed by the 18th, and *Valley Forge* debarked her helicopters before steaming to Subic Bay for upkeep.

After her return to Danang on 3 May, the amphibious assault ship reembarked her helicopters as well as part of a battalion landing team of marines who had been taking part in fighting ashore. The carrier continued to operate in the Danang area during the weeks that followed, her helicopters flying frequent support missions, and her marines preparing for further combat landings.

During late May and early June, *Valley Forge* received visits from Secretary of the Navy John Chafee and Vice Admiral William F. Bringle, Commander, 7th Fleet. She offloaded her marines at Danang on 10 June and embarked a battalion landing team for transportation to Okinawa, where she arrived on the 16th. The landing team conducted amphibious exercises with *Valley Forge* for 11 days and boarded the ship for a voyage to Subic Bay where they continued the training process. *Valley Forge* returned to the Danang area on 8 July and resumed flying helicopter support for Marine ground forces in the northern I Corps area. The ship took evasive action to avoid an approaching typhoon and then began preparations for an amphibious operation.

Operation "Brave Armada" began on 24 July with a helicopter-borne assault on suspected Viet Cong and North Vietnamese positions in Quang Ngai Province. *Valley Forge* remained in the Quang Ngai-Chu Lai area to support this attack until its completion on 7 August. She then steamed to Danang to debark her marines. General Leonard F. Chapman, the Commandant of the Marine Corps, visited *Valley Forge* that same day. The ship sailed for Okinawa on the 13th, arriving four days later and debarking her helicopter squadron before getting underway again to evade another typhoon. She proceeded to Hong Kong, dropping anchor there on 22 August, the day on which she received a message announcing her forthcoming inactivation. She returned to Danang on 3 September to load material for shipment to the United States and sailed that evening for Yokosuka for three days of upkeep before leaving the Far East.

Valley Forge got underway from Yokosuka on 11 September and anchored at Long Beach on the 22d. After leave and upkeep, she offloaded ammunition and equipment at Seal Beach and San Diego. The ship returned to Long Beach on 31 October to prepare for decommissioning. This process continued through the new year; and, on 15 January 1970, *Valley Forge* was placed out of commission. She was turned over to the Inactive Ship Maintenance Facility at San Diego. Her name was struck from the Navy list on the same day. After the failure of attempts to raise funds for using the ship as a museum, she was sold on 29 October 1971 to the Nicolai Joffre Corp., of Beverly Hills, Calif., for scrap.

Valley Forge was awarded eight battle stars for Korean War service and nine for Vietnam service, as well as three Navy Unit Commendations.

Valor

I

(AMc–108: dp. 195 (est.); l. 98′5″; b. 23′6″; dr. 10′6″ (mean); s. 10 k.; cpl. 17; a. 4 .50-cal. mg.; cl. *Accentor*)

Valor (AMc–108) was laid down on 27 May 1941 at Rockland, Maine, by the Snow Shipyards, Inc.; launched on 8 November 1941; co-sponsored by Misses Jane and Noreen Brannan; and placed in service on 24 March 1942 at the Boston Navy Yard.

Although records are sketchy and inconclusive, the coastal minesweeper appears to have operated in the waters of the 1st Naval District, primarily out of Boston, throughout her brief career. She also served for some time out of the Woods Hole Section Base. She was attached to the Northern Group, Eastern Sea Frontier, at the time of her loss on 29 June 1944.

Late that day, she was patrolling the southern approaches to the Cape Cod Canal, alert to the possible presence of enemy intruders on this highly traveled coastal route. Minutes before 2200, as she patrolled north of Cuttyhunk Island in Buzzard's Bay, *Valor* was struck by *Richard W. Suessens* (DE–342). Within three minutes, the small ship sank in the shallow waters off Mishaum Point at the western entrance of Buzzard's Bay. The destroyer escort rescued seven survivors; but, although five other vessels joined in the search which continued until sunrise, the seven remaining men on board were never found. The following day, the survivors were transferred to facilities at the Naval Operating Base, Newport, R.I.

Salvage operations began the day after the collision. On 14 October, her name was struck from the Navy list. In January 1945, her hull was sold to the Newport Shipyard, Inc.

II

(AM–472: dp. 775; l. 172′; b. 35′; dr. 10′; s. 14 k.; cpl. 70; a. 1 40mm., 2 .50-cal. mg.; cl. *Aggressive*)

The second *Valor* (AM–472) was laid down on 28 April 1952 at Manitowoc, Wis., by the Burger Boat Co.; launched on 13 May 1953; sponsored by Mrs. Walter J. Kohler; towed through the Great Lakes and down the St. Lawrence River to Boston, Mass.; and commissioned at Boston on 29 July 1954, Lt. Charles R. Davis in command.

Following preliminary trials, *Valor* joined Mine Division (MinDiv) 82, Mine Squadron (MinRon) 8, Mine Force, Atlantic Fleet, on 14 September. Immediately thereafter, she steamed to Key West, Fla., where she conducted shakedown training through the end of the year. In February 1955, she entered the Charleston Naval Shipyard for an extensive overhaul. On the 7th of that month, she was redesignated MSO–472.

Valor completed repairs and modifications in October and rejoined the Mine Force, though on a detached assignment at the Engineering Experimental Station

at Annapolis, Md., as an engineering prototype. That phase of testing ended on 23 November; and *Valor* returned to Charleston but continued experimental duty until December. After that, the minesweeper began normal duty with the Atlantic Fleet Mine Force based at Charleston. That service—broken only by a voyage to Halifax, Nova Scotia, in April and May of 1956 and by a six-month deployment to the Mediterranean Sea from 29 August 1957 to 12 February 1958—lasted until March of 1958.

On 1 March 1958, she began a 10-year association with the Navy Mine Defense Laboratory located at Panama City, Fla. On 16 March, she departed Charleston and, on the 29th, arrived in her new home port. In July of 1959, after 15 months of duty at Panama City—punctuated by an overhaul at Charleston during the winter of 1958 and 1959—*Valor* took her first break from mine countermeasures development work when she was deployed to northern European waters. Departing Charleston on 24 July, the minesweeper arrived in Ostend, Belgium, on 11 August. There, she changed operational control from the United States Navy to the Belgian *Force Navale* and joined the Belgian Minesweeper Division 191. On 17 August, she and the other elements of the division departed Ostend for a voyage to the waters surrounding the Belgian Congo.

The warships arrived in Congolese waters on 9 September and commenced a series of multinational minesweeping exercises involving American, Belgian, and Portuguese units. The exercises ended on 21 September, and *Valor* and her division mates headed back to Ostend where they arrived on 17 October. *Valor* continued to operate locally out of Ostend, with the Belgian minesweeper division, until 15 January 1960 when she returned to United States Navy control and headed—via Rota, Spain—back to the United States. The minesweeper arrived back in Panama City, Fla., on 14 February 1960.

Over the next eight years, *Valor* continued to operate out of Panama City in support of the mine countermeasures development program of the Navy Mine Defense Laboratory. However, that routine was broken frequently—on three occasions by six-month deployments to the 6th Fleet in the Mediterranean Sea, but more often by overhauls, refresher training, and exercises in the West Indies. Her association with the Mine Defense Laboratory ended on 1 March 1968 when she received orders transferring her to MinDiv 44 and reassigning her to Charleston as her home base.

The ship operated from that port for the remaining two years of her Navy career. During that period, *Valor* made one more deployment to the Mediterranean between April and August of 1968. Early in October 1969, the minesweeper began a pre-rehabilitation overhaul at Charleston in preparation for extensive modifications to update her equipment. She never finished those modifications for, early in 1970, a board of inspection and survey found her to be beyond economical repair and recommended that she be disposed of. She was decommissioned sometime in July 1970, and her name was struck from the Navy list on 1 February 1971. On 30 August 1971, she was sold to Mr. Charles Gural, of Rahway, N.J., for scrapping.

Valparaiso

The second largest city in Chile and the most important seaport on the Pacific coast of South America. Valparaiso (which means "Vale of Paradise")—located 75 miles northwest of Santiago—was founded in 1536 by the conquistador Juan de Saavedra and now occupies a semicircular area containing 19 hills.

(t. 402; l. 117′6″; b. 27′6″; cpl. 36; a. none)

Valparaiso—a brig built at Baltimore, Md., in 1836—was one of a class of vessels popularly called "Baltimore clippers" because of their reputation for speed and outstanding performance. *Valparaiso* was purchased by the Navy at New Bedford, Mass., on 22 November 1861.

The sailing vessel was originally intended to be sunk on 20 January 1862 at the entrance to Charleston harbor, S.C., as part of the second "Stone Fleet." These stone fleets—the first of which was sunk at Charleston on 20 December 1861—consisted of older vessels, mostly derelicts, filled with large boulders. They were intended to aid Northern efforts to blockade the Southern coastline in the early days of the Civil War when the Union Navy was still relatively small.

However, instead of deploying with her sisters at the bottom of Charleston harbor as originally planned, *Valparaiso* joined the South Atlantic Blockading Squadron of Flag Officer Samuel F. Du Pont and served as a storeship at Port Royal, S.C. She remained at Port Royal for the duration of the war.

After the collapse of the Confederacy, the old brig was sold at public auction at Bay Point, S.C., on 2 September 1865.

Valve

(ARS–28: dp. 1,897; l. 183'3"; b. 37'; dr. 14'8"; s. 12.0 k.; cpl. 65; a. 1 3"; cl. *Diver*)

Valve (ARS–28) was laid down on 17 November 1942 at Bellingham, Wash., by the Bellingham Marine Railway Co.; launched on 20 May 1943; sponsored by Mrs. Henry Foss; and commissioned on 24 February 1944, Lt. W. D. Mooney, USNR, in command.

Following shakedown, the salvage ship departed the west coast at San Francisco on 18 April 1944, bound for Hawaii with a trio of sled targets in tow, and arrived at Pearl Harbor 12 days later. She remained at the Pacific Fleet's base, operating locally, into the fall. Early in this tour, she assisted in fire-fighting operations on burning LST's in West Loch, Pearl Harbor, in the wake of the destructive explosions which eventually sank five of these ships on 21 and 22 May. She spent four hours fighting the blazes before she was ordered to clear the area due to the danger of exploding ammunition carried in the LST's. On 23 May, she returned to West Loch and extinguished the blaze in the hulk of *LST–480*.

Valve commenced salvage operations on the sunken *LST–535* on 31 May, her divers making 225 dives in 41 days. She worked on the wreck, removing such items as 15 tons of live ammunition, 10 LVT's, and a great deal of wreckage, from 31 May to 30 August. At noon on the latter day, she got underway to aid *LCI(G)–566*, aground off Wahie Point, Lanai. After pulling the landing craft free, she resumed salvage operations on *LST–535* on 5 September. *Valve* prepared the ship's hulk for blasting by 8 October and, with this task completed, sailed for Eniwetok 10 days later.

Valve served as flagship for the commander of a Guam-bound convoy—containing *Bond* (AM–152) and *SC–1036* and three merchantmen—from 10 to 14 November, before the ship conducted salvage and clearance operations in Tanapag Harbor, Guam, into December 1944. During this period, she salvaged *Sparks* (IX–196) and prepared the hulk of Japanese freighter *Keiyo Maru* for sinking at sea.

After shifting to Saipan soon thereafter to relieve *Anchor* (ARS–13), *Valve* operated out of Saipan on local salvage operations and harbor clearance duties through the end of the year and into the spring of 1945. She departed Saipan for Iwo Jima on 28 May 1945, towing the hulk of Japanese merchantman *Toyoto Maru*.

Next serving on local convoy escort duties between Iwo Jima and Guam, *Valve* shifted to Okinawan waters in July. Between 18 and 31 July, the salvage vessel went to general quarters during 15 "flash-red" alerts. On 28 July, *Valve* and *Jicarilla* (ATF–104) put out fires which had broken out in number three hold of

SS *John A. Rawlins*. Before Japan surrendered on 15 August, the salvage ship endured 14 more "flash-red" alerts while in Okinawan waters.

She conducted salvage operations in inner Naha harbor at Okinawa into the winter of 1945. When *Colbert* (APA–145) struck a drifting mine while on typhoon evasion on 17 September, *Valve* towed the stricken ship to a safe anchorage in Okinawa. *Valve* rode out another severe typhoon which swirled its way into the fleet anchorage on 9 October. During the storm, SS *Richard S. Oglesby* twice fouled *Valve*, and *LST–826* collided with the salvage ship as well. Fortunately, *Valve* suffered only minor damage.

Valve subsequently conducted salvage operations on other typhoon-damaged ships—including *Wateree* (ATF–117), *Sacandaga* (AOG–40), *LST–823*, *LST–534*, and *Vandalia* (IX–191)—through December 1945. The salvage vessel then conducted local salvage and harbor clearance operations at Okinawa into the spring of 1946. In May, she assisted in the preparations at Bikini Atoll for Operation "Crossroads" before sailing via Pearl Harbor for the west coast.

Decommissioned on 26 August 1946, *Valve* was struck from the Navy list on 12 March 1948 and sold to Walter H. Wilms on 26 July 1948.

Vamarie

(Yacht: t. 45 (gross); l. 70'2"; b. 15'3"; dr. 10'4"; cpl. 14)

Vamarie—a ketch-rigged ocean racing yacht designed by Jasper Morgan of Cox and Stevens, Inc.—was built in 1933 at Bremen, Germany, by Abeking and Rasmussen, for S. Vadim Makaroff of Oyster Bay, Long Island. With Makaroff at the helm, the slim racing yacht participated in nine ocean races between 1934 and 1936, sailing over 30,000 miles. Donated to the Regiment of Midshipmen at the United States Naval Academy, Annapolis, Md., on 11 November 1936, *Vamarie* served as the Navy's racing yacht in local races in Chesapeake Bay during the racing season in 1937. The following summer, on 22 June 1938, *Vamarie* was entered in the race from Newport, R.I., to Bermuda marking the first time that the yacht returned to "blue water" in two years. Four days later, the yacht, commanded by Capt. John F. Shafroth, came in 18th out of 22 vessels in her class and 29th out of the 44 total entries.

Vamarie participated in further local races into 1939. On 8 March 1940 she was classified IX–47. The yacht was officially assigned to the Naval Academy on 22 October 1940 and was placed in service on 10 November 1944. She operated under the aegis of the Severn River Naval Command until authorized for disposal on 24 February 1955. Struck from the Navy list on 22 June 1955, *Vamarie* was broken up in December of the same year.

Vammen

Clarence Earl Vammen, Jr.—born in Aberdeen, Wash., on 17 October 1919—attended Pomona (Calif.) Junior College before he enlisted in the Naval Reserve on 17 February 1941 at Long Beach, Calif. After his initial duty at the Naval Reserve Aviation Base, Long Beach, Seaman 2d Class Vammen was transferred to the naval air station at Pensacola, Fla., on 27 March. On 3 April, he was discharged at his own request to accept an appointment as an aviation cadet.

Vammen reported to the Naval Air Station (NAS), Pensacola, on 4 April for flight training. Detached on 19 August and transferred to NAS, Miami, for further training, Vammen was appointed a naval aviator (heavier-than-air) on 23 September. Completing his instruction on 20 October, he accepted the rank of ensign that day.

Assigned to Advanced Carrier Training Group, Pacific Fleet, soon thereafter, Vammen continued his training until joining Torpedo Squadron (VT) 6, based on the carrier *Enterprise* (CV–6), on 28 April 1942. He joined the ship within two weeks of the completion of the famous Halsey-Doolittle Raid on Tokyo, 18 April 1942, and just before his carrier and *Hornet* (CV–8) proceeded south toward the Coral Sea to meet an expected Japanese thrust. Unfortunately, the two flattops were too late to assist *Lexington* (CV–2) and *Yorktown* (CV–5) in the critical Battle of the Coral Sea which took place from 4 to 8 May.

Although she missed the Coral Sea action, *Enterprise* —"The Big E"—did participate in the pivotal Battle of Midway one month later. Ensign Vammen, by that point assigned to Scouting Squadron (VS) 6, did not take part in the strikes of 4 June against the Japanese carrier fleet. He received his baptism of fire, however, soon enough.

On Friday evening, 5 June, Vammen—flying a Douglas SBD–3 Dauntless, with Aviation Machinists' Mate 2d Class M. W. Clark in the rear seat—took off with eight other planes of VS–6, as part of the strike launched to locate and sink what had been erroneously reported as two enemy carriers. Subsequently, the SBD's from *Enterprise* and *Hornet* found and attacked what they reported to be a "Japanese CL" (light cruiser)— a ship that turned out to be the destroyer *Tanikaze*. The Dauntlesses that made the dusk attack failed to score any hits with their 500-pound bombs on the twisting, turning destroyer. Vammen, who had never received instruction in night carrier recoveries, made his first night landing—not on *Enterprise*, but on *Hornet*.

The next morning, on 6 June, Vammen joined *Hornet*'s planes in attacking the fleeing Japanese heavy cruisers *Mogami* and *Mikuma*, a strike that inflicted such severe damage on the latter that she sank later that day. Unfortunately, Vammen and his gunner failed to return from that mission.

For his part in the Battle of Midway, however, Ensign Vammen—cited for "courage and unflinching devotion to duty"—was awarded the Distinguished Flying Cross, posthumously.

(DE–644: dp. 1,400; l. 306'0''; b. 37'0''; dr. 9'5'' (mean); s. 23.5 k.; cpl. 186; a. 3 3'', 4 1.1'', 10 20mm., 3 21'' tt., 2 dct., 8 dcp., 1 dcp. (hh.); cl. *Buckley*)

Vammen (DE–644) was laid down on 1 August 1943 at San Francisco, Calif., by the Bethlehem Steel Co.; launched on 21 May 1944; sponsored by Mrs. Earle Morgan, aunt of the late Ens. Vammen; and commissioned on 27 July 1944, Lt. Comdr. L. M. King, Jr., USNR, in command.

Following commissioning, *Vammen* fitted out through mid-August 1944 and later conducted her shakedown out of San Diego, Calif., into late September before undergoing a post-shakedown availability at her builder's yard. Underway for Pearl Harbor, Territory of Hawaii, on 13 October, the new destroyer escort convoyed SS *Phillipa* to the Hawaiian Islands before reporting for duty to Commander, Service Force, Pacific, on 21 October.

For the remainder of October and all of November, the destroyer escort trained out of Pearl Harbor, operating in company with vaious submarines and aircraft carriers, perfecting techniques of antisubmarine warfare and escort duty. She then escorted SS *Cushman Davis* via Funafuti in the Ellice Islands to Espiritu Santo, before she steamed independently to Pearl Harbor, arriving at the Pacific Fleet's main base three days after Christmas 1944.

Vammen plane-guarded for *Bataan* (CVL–29) early in January 1945 before escorting the merchantman, SS *Exira*, to Eniwetok in the Marshalls from 9 to 16 January. While returning to Pearl Harbor, *Vammen* responded to a radio request for assistance from *LST–598* which had an ill crewman. The destroyer escort rendezvoused with the landing ship at sea on 20 January and took the sick man on board. The following day, off Johnston Island, *Vammen* transferred the man to a hospital boat, sent from that outpost, for medical treatment ashore. The destroyer escort arrived back at Pearl Harbor on the 23d.

At the end of the month, *Vammen* sailed for the Marshalls, escorting Convoy PD–278–T, consisting of the attack transports *Montrose* (APA–212) and *Mountrail* (APA–213). Departing Pearl Harbor on 30 January, PD–278–T arrived at Eniwetok on 7 February. *Vammen* then headed for Hawaii the next day and, on the 10th, relieved *Witter* (DE–667) as escort for the escort carriers *Kitkun Bay* (CVE–71) and *Salamaua* (CVE–96) en route. They subsequently reached Pearl Harbor on the 17th.

The destroyer escort conducted one more convoy escort run to the Marshalls before she participated in her first major action. She shepherded PD–310–T— the attack transports *Meriwether* (APA–203), *Menard* (APA–201), and *Allendale* (APA–127)—from 22 February to 2 March, the day of their arrival at Eniwetok.

Three days later, she (as one of nine escorts) sortied with a 10-ship convoy bound for Ulithi and Kossol Roads. Detached on 9 March, she escorted the merchantman SS *Westward Ho* to Kossol Roads and, two days later, departed the Palaus and proceeded to the Philippines in company with the landing ship *Ozark* (LSV–2) and *Westward Ho*, reaching Rizal, Leyte, on the 13th.

After patrolling the entrance to Leyte Gulf from 14 to 18 March, *Vammen* underwent an availability at San Pedro Bay alongside tender *Markab* (AD–21). With those repairs completed within a week's time, the destroyer escort sortied on 25 March, bound for Okinawa and her baptism of fire.

Steaming as part of the screen for Tractor Group "Easy," *Vammen* reached the Ryukyus on 1 April, the day of the initial landings on Okinawa. Detached from duty with Task Unit (TU) 51.14.2—for which the ship's commanding officer had been screen commander —*Vammen* was assigned to the western half of screening station A–39. Later that day, she received orders to screen LST Group "Dog" during its night retirement. While maneuvering at 15 knots through the congested transport area under poor visibility conditions, the destroyer escort struck a heavy floating object with her bow at 2100. A few seconds later, an explosion occurred beneath her stern, as though a depth charge had exploded under the ship.

After noticing marked vibrations, *Vammen* reduced speed to 10 knots. Repair parties reported no evident damage, but the vibrations indicated damage to shafts or propellers. As it turned out, the ship's starboard propeller had been damaged and required replacement. Nevertheless, she completed hr assigned mission proceeding to rendezvous with the LST group on its night retirement.

At 0645 the next day, she resumed her screening station, A–39, but because of her reduced speed capacity, was ordered to take station A–50. Fortunately for *Vammen*, she was never attacked by enemy aircraft.

Vammen remained on station off Okinawa until 8 April. Due to the frequent enemy air raids, her crew spent an average of 10 to 12 hours a day at their general quarters stations, but, as Comdr. King noted in his report of the ship's operations, "no undue fatigue or effect on morale or efficiency" resulted. Offered no opportunity to fire at enemy aircraft during her time off Okinawa, *Vammen* conducted two "hedgehog" attacks on suspected submarine contacts, neither with observable results.

With the additional problem of a burnt-out drive motor in her surface-search (SL) radar, *Vammen* departed Okinawa on 8 April, screening LST Group 17 to Leyte. Arriving at San Pedro Bay on the 14th, she underwent repairs alongside *Markab* before she was drydocked in *ARD–16* to have the damaged starboard propeller replaced. Undocking on the 17th, *Vammen* returned to Okinawa at the end of April, screening LST Group 41.

Detached from that escort duty on 2 May, *Vammen* received orders to head for the scene of a submarine sighting at 1514 on the 5th. She arrived on the scene at 1723 and commenced a search plan in company with *Halloran* (DE–305), but found nothing. The ships abandoned the search at 1100 the following day, and *Vammen* soon resumed her screening role off Okinawa.

The destroyer escort remained off Okinawa, screening incoming ships and off transport areas, for the rest of May. On 28 May, while anchored at the northern end of the transport area in Hagushi Bay, *Vammen* picked up TBS reports of incoming aircraft—"bogies"—commencing beyond 50 miles. A short while later, the destroyer escort's radar picked up one enemy plane, a "Tony," first at 10 miles and then one mile away as it circled across the ship's bow.

The "Tony" suddenly emerged from the low clouds on the escort's starboard quarter, and all of *Vammen*'s 20-millimeter Oerlikons that could bear opened up, joining the other ships nearby in putting up a fierce barrage of fire. The "Tony" strafed a tug nearby but —hit in the tail and right wing—burst into flame, lost altitude, and crashed into the water without exploding, clear of any ships.

Underway on 3 June, *Vammen*—awarded an "assist" in the downing of the plane on 28 May—escorted an Okinawa-to-Leyte convoy between 3 and 8 June, sinking a Japanese mine with gunfire en route. After repairs alongside *Markab* and a docking in *ARD–18* for repairs to her sound gear—which had been inoperative since 22 May—the destroyer escort sailed for Lingayen in company with sistership *Cole* (DE–641), on her way back to Okinawa.

For the remainder of June, *Vammen* performed the unglamorous but vital duty of screening transports and of providing local escort services to incoming convoys. She ultimately departed the Ryukyus in early July and steamed to Ulithi before returning once more to Okinawa on the 15th, commencing patrol at station D–1, off Buckner Bay, on the 22d.

Subsequently returning to Ulithi in early August, the destroyer escort returned to Okinawa on the 12th and, after fueling, got underway on the 13th, as part of the screen for an Okinawa-to-Ulithi convoy. It was while underway with that convoy two days later that the ship received the welcome news of Japan's capitulation. *Vammen*'s commanding officer recorded the event: "1745, On basis of communique No. 467, all offensive action against Japanese ceased."

Vammen reached Ulithi on the 18th and, after escorting Convoy UOK (Ulithi to Okinawa) 52 to Okinawa from 27 to 31 August, returned to Ulithi at the beginning of September. Subsequently visiting Guam and Saipan, *Vammen* reached Pearl Harbor on 9 November on her way back to the west coast of the United States.

The ship underwent a lengthy availability at the Puget Sound Naval Shipyard, Bremerton, Wash., that lasted into 1946. She shifted southward to San Diego and departed that port on 20 February, bound for the Hawaiian Islands, reaching Pearl Harbor on 27 February. She sailed from Oahu on 4 March and proceeded via Guam to China.

Vammen supported the American occupation forces in their operations from the spring of 1946 into the autumn, touching at ports such as Tsingtao and Shanghai, China; and Kowloon. Departing Shanghai on 1 July 1946, the destroyer escort reached Pearl Harbor on 16 July via Guam and Eniwetok. She then set out for the west coast, reaching San Diego on 28 July.

The destroyer escort next underwent an availability at Terminal Island, Calif., and San Pedro in early September and shifted to San Diego in mid-month. *Vammen* was subsequently decommissioned at San Diego on 3 February 1947 and placed in reserve. She was inactivated on 2 April 1947.

The Korean War meant a new lease on life for *Vammen*; she was reactivated and heavily modified to enable her to perform a specialized antisubmarine warfare (ASW) role. With a redesigned bridge, trainable forward-firing ASW projectors ("hedgehogs") and improved sonar capabilities, *Vammen* thus became one of the most modern ASW vessels in the Fleet.

Recommissioned at Mare Island, Calif., on 15 February 1952, *Vammen* operated off the west coast, out of San Diego and in the southern California area, into the summer of the following year, training. On 19 July 1953, she left San Diego behind, bound for her first deployment to the Western Pacific (WestPac) since her recommissioning.

After proceeding via Pearl Harbor, Midway, and Yokosuka, *Vammen* arrived at Sasebo, Japan, on 23 August but got underway the next morning for the key port of Wonsan on the eastern coast of North Korea. She operated off Wonsan, performing patrol and gunfire support duties, from 25 August to 17 September before she returned to Sasebo.

Vammen returned to Wonsan at the end of October and, after performing a second tour of gunfire support and patrol there, returned to the west coast of the United States. Departing Wonsan on 11 November, the destroyer escort reached San Diego on 2 December via the Shimonoseki Straits, Yokosuka, Midway, and Pearl Harbor.

Over the next six years, *Vammen* alternated in training operations off the coast of California—operating primarily out of San Diego—and conducting regular WestPac deployments.

The latter provided her with excellent training opportunities. In 1955 and again in 1958, she made cruises through the Western and Central Carolines, the Bonins, the northern Marianas, and the Volcano Islands, parts of the Trust Territories of the Pacific Islands administered by the Navy. She kept a figurative "eye" on local conditions on the various atolls and islands, keeping a lookout for illegal activities in trading and shipping. Her surveillance missions varied in format. On some occasions, she would send a landing party ashore via motor whaleboat or outboard motor-powered rubber raft; and, on other occasions, *Vammen* would remain offshore while her men scanned the island with binoculars. During the former, a pharmacist's mate (the ship's doctor) would accompany the landing party to provide medical care and advice for the sick.

On another occasion, while enroute to WestPac in company with *LeRay Wilson* (DE–414), *Vammen* visited Port Lyttleton, New Zealand, the seaport for Christchurch. From 3 to 8 February 1958, the two destroyer escorts remained there, while *Vammen* transferred 51 sacks of mail destined for Operation "Deepfreeze" personnel in Antarctica.

In April 1960, *Vammen* was selected as a Group I Naval Reserve Training (NRT) ship; on 21 May, she was redesignated a Group II NRT ship. On 18 June 1960, the destroyer escort was decommissioned and placed "in service."

After becoming an NRT ship, *Vammen* soon began to provide training for reserve surface divisions of the 11th Naval District. Those men came on board for both dockside and underway training. On the third weekend of each month and for two weeks each summer, *Vammen* embarked her selected reserve crew. She then conducted ASW, gunnery, and other shipboard training drills off the coast of California between Long Beach and San Diego. In August 1960, *Vammen* conducted her first annual two-week training cruise with her selected reserve crew embarked. For her performance during those evolutions, the destroyer escort received the highest grade assigned to an NRT ship of her type.

She subsequently conducted her second two-week cruise the following summer, 1961, ready for instant mobilization that came sooner than anyone in her crew probably realized. That autumn, the Cold War tensions that escalated over Berlin and in the Far East resulted in the reactivation of 40 NRT ships for active duty. Accordingly, on 2 October 1961, *Vammen* was recommissioned at Long Beach, Comdr. Charlie S. Nelson, USNR, in command.

Following her recommissioning, *Vammen* underwent her regularly scheduled overhaul at the Todd Shipyard. Transferred to Pearl Harbor as her new home on 15 December 1961, *Vammen* sailed for another WestPac deployment on 6 January 1962. She deployed with a hunter-killer group and arrived at Pearl on the 12th. She began refresher training soon thereafter.

Assigned to Escort Division (CortDiv) 72, *Vammen* sailed for the Philippines on 24 February. After logistics stops at Midway and Guam for fuel and minor voyage repairs, the destroyer escort reached Subic Bay on 11 March. After a brief period of upkeep, *Vammen* visited Manila in company with *Marsh* (DE–699) and *Charles E. Brannon* (DE–446) from 16 to 18 March. On the 19th, the three ships got underway for the Gulf of Siam.

Arriving off the southern tip of South Vietnam on 21 March, *Vammen* and *Charles E. Brannon* relieved *Wiseman* (DE–667) and *Edmonds* (DE–406) on the following day and assumed the duties of training units of the small South Vietnamese Navy in that area. From that day until 9 April, *Vammen* remained on station in the Gulf of Siam, off the coast of South Vietnam, maintaining American presence in that area. Heavy pressure from communist Viet Cong forces inside South Vietnam had brought about a commitment of force there as the United States sought to bolster the American-backed regime. After visiting Subic Bay for a week of upkeep and conducting a port visit to Hong Kong, *Vammen* returned to her station in the Gulf of Siam. Originally, the ship's schedule had called for the ship to visit Japan and return to Pearl Harbor after visiting Hong Kong, but—as *Vammen*'s commanding officer reported ". . . the efforts of *Vammen* and the other ex-NRT ships on the South Vietnam training mission were apparently of such value that it was decided to retain Escort Division 72 on the mission through mid-May."

There were further changes of plan afoot for *Vammen*, as was evidenced during the second deployment in the Gulf of Siam. On 13 May, *Vammen* and *Charles E. Brannon* were diverted from their training duties under Task Force 72 and were ordered to report for duty to commander, TG 76.5. Complying, the two destroyer escorts subsequently screened *Valley Forge* (LPH–8), *Navarro* (APA–215), and *Point Defiance* (LSD–31) while that group took a Marine Corps expeditionary force to Bangkok, Thailand. The 3d Battalion, 9th Marines, embarked in the amphibious group were sent to Thailand in an effort to provide the friendly regime with troops to deter any communist moves across the Mekong River. Following that operation, *Vammen* and her sistership escorted TG 76.5 back to Subic Bay, arriving there on the 23d.

Vammen subsequently visited Yokosuka, Japan, and participated in Exercise "Powerdive"—with 7th Fleet units in the Japan area—before she returned via Midway Island to her home port, Pearl Harbor, on 18 June. At Pearl from 18 June to 11 July, *Vammen* enjoyed the longest consecutive in-port period since February of that year, undergoing much-needed repairs and maintenance. On 11 July, *Vammen*, in company with *Colahan* (DD–658), *Marsh*, and *Wiseman*, sailed for the west coast of the United States.

After her arrival at Long Beach on 17 July, *Vammen* was decommissioned on 1 August, resuming her role as an NRT ship. For the next seven years, *Vammen* continued her duties as an 11th Naval District NRT ship, based at Long Beach, and operating primarily in the Long Beach-Los Angeles-San Pedro area. During that time, she ranged as far north as British Columbia and as far south as Ensenada, Mexico. Age ultimately caught up with the veteran destroyer escort; and, in the summer of 1969, she was adjudged unfit for further service.

Placed out of service on 12 July 1969, *Vammen*'s NRT crew was transferred to *Maddox* (DD–731); and the ship herself was turned over to the Naval Inactive Ship Maintenance Facility, San Diego. Struck from the Navy list on 12 July 1969, *Vammen*'s stripped hull was utilized in a "Condor" missile test on 4 February 1971 and, as a result of the damage suffered on that date, sank on 18 February.

Vammen (DE–644) earned one battle star for her World War II service and one engagement star for her Korean War service.

Vanadis

An alternative name for Freya, the Norse goddess of love and beauty.

Vanadis (AKA–49) was converted to a cable repair ship in 1955 and renamed *Thor* (ARC–4) (q.v.) on 14 November 1955.

Van Buren

Martin Van Buren—born in Kinderhook, N.Y., on 5 December 1782—began the study of law at age 14 and was admitted to the bar seven years later, beginning a law practice at Kinderhook. During his tour as a state senator from 1812 to 1820, Van Buren became a regent of the University of the State of New York in 1815 and, the following year, became attorney general of the state. In 1820, Van Buren had a part in organizing one of the first American political "machines," the Albany Regency.

Elected to the United States Senate in 1821, he was reelected to another term six years later. In 1828, however, he was elected Governor of New York, and took office in 1829, only to resign in March of that year to become President Andrew Jackson's Secretary of State. His most important achievement in that post was an agreement with Great Britian allowing a resumption of trade between the United States and the British West Indies, commerce banned at the close of the War of Independence.

Resigning his post in 1831, he was chosen as Minister to Great Britain but did not receive confirmation. He did, however, receive the nod as Andrew Jackson's running mate in the 1832 election and became Vice President. At the end of Jackson's second term, Van Buren, his hand-picked successor, was elected President in 1835 and took office on 4 March of the following year.

During Van Buren's presidency, the nation suffered a financial panic and depression. In addition, the Seminole War—a long and costly period of hostilities—brought condemnation from some quarters who decried the cost of the conflict in money and lives. In international affairs, the Canadian seizure and burning of the American ship *Caroline* in late 1837 caused great tension between the United States and Great Britain until the incident was settled by the Webster-Ashburton treaty.

Although the unanimous choice of his own party for the 1840 elections, Van Buren lost the election to the war hero, General William Henry Harrison. Although he was the leading contender for his party's nomination in 1844, Van Buren lost the bid to James K. Polk, who went on to win the Presidency.

In 1848, Van Buren's political career ended. Nominated by the Free-Soil party—which opposed the extension of slavery—the former President's candidacy split the Democratic Party in his home state. Ultimately, Zachary Taylor benefitted from that split. After the 1848 election, Van Buren spent two years in Europe, before he returned to the United States to live in retirement at Kinderhook. He died there on 24 July 1862.

The first *Van Buren*, a revenue cutter, was named [f]or President Van Buren; the second *Van Buren* (PF-[4]2), honors the small city of Van Buren, Ark.

I

Sch: t. 112; lbp. 73'4¼''; b. 20'2''; dph. 7'4''; a. 4
12-pdrs.)

The building of the first *Van Buren*, a schooner-[r]igged revenue cutter, was authorized on 26 June [1]839. That same day, the Secretary of the Treasury [o]rdered Lt. J. C. Jones, USRM, to superintend her [c]onstruction at Baltimore. Reported ready for use on [1]9 November 1839, the ship entered service with the [R]evenue Marine on 2 December 1839, Capt. Henry [P]rince, USRM, in command.

Few records apparently exist to indicate the nature [o]r extent of *Van Buren*'s service in late 1839 and 1840. [I]t can be assumed that she performed the usual duties [a]ssigned to the ships of the Revenue Marine (a fore-[r]unner of the United States Coast Guard), keeping [w]atch off the coast of the United States for smugglers [o]r shipwrecks, ready to enforce the laws of the land [o]r rescue survivors from disasters at sea.

With the outbreak of the Seminole War in Florida [i]n the late 1830's, the Revenue Marine came under the [c]ontrol of the Navy for cooperation with Army forces [i]n their campaign to put down the Seminoles. On 30 [J]uly 1841, the Secretary of the Navy wrote to the [S]ecretary of the Treasury, Thomas Ewing, transmit-[t]ing the "authority of the President" to transfer the [r]evenue cutters *Jefferson*, *Madison*, and *Van Buren* [t]o the Navy's jurisdiction. Ewing, on 2 August, con-[s]equently relieved 1st Lieutenant John McGowan, [U]SRM—*Van Buren*'s commanding officer—"from the [u]sual duties arising under the Revenue laws," and [d]irected him to place himself, and his ship, under the [d]irection of the Navy.

As part of the "Mosquito Fleet" under Lt, John T. [M]cLaughlin, *Van Buren* operated as a unit of the [N]avy's "riverine" force, in conjunction with Army [t]roops, in battling the wily and elusive Seminole foe. [S]uch duty proved exacting, the officers and men under-[g]oing "every species of privation and toil." The Semi-[n]ole Wars had produced a riverine conflict similar to [t]hat waged in the Mekong Delta over a century and a [q]uarter later.

At the end of nearly a year of such service, *Van [B]uren*, *Madison*, and *Jefferson* put into Norfolk by 23 [J]uly 1842. Six days later, the Secretary of the Treasury [i]ssued instructions to the Collector of Revenue to re-[c]eive the vessels and put them back into the service of [t]he Revenue Marine. She was accordingly transferred [f]rom Navy control on 18 August 1842.

Ordered to Charleston, S.C., on 22 August, *Van Buren* [o]perated out of that port over the next three years. [D]uring that time, she underwent repairs at Baltimore [i]n May and June 1844.

When the United States went to war with Mexico in [1]846, *Van Buren*—under the command of Capt. Thomas [F]. Rudolph, USRM—received orders on 20 May from [R]obert J. Walker, Secretary of the Treasury, to take [o]n board a "full supply of ammunition and stores for [t]hree months" and sail for the Gulf of Mexico. Eight [d]ays later, with instructions to report to the Collector [o]f Customs at New Orleans, *Van Buren* stood out of [C]harleston.

However, as the schooner put to sea, a bolt of [l]ightning struck the fore-royal mast and so damaged it [t]hat Capt. Rudolph was compelled to bring the ship [b]ack into harbor the same day. After repairs to the [d]amaged mast, *Van Buren* cleared Charleston again on [4] June and headed for the gulf.

The cutter reached Belize. Honduras, simultaneously [w]ith the revenue cutter *Walter Forward* on 30 July [a]nd later sailed as part of the squadron commanded by [C]apt. John A. Webster, USRM, for blockade duty off

the coast of Mexico. *Van Buren* took station off Vera Cruz.

Reported unfit for sea on 4 October, *Van Buren* lay at Southwest Pass, near New Orleans, preparing for a voyage to Soto la Marina, a town on the northeastern coast of Mexico. Three days later, the ship's officers remonstrated against that proposed cruise because of the ship's unseaworthiness. Ordered to proceed without delay to New York, *Van Buren* accordingly sailed for that port on 11 November 1846. She saw no further active service and was sold on 1 June 1847.

II

(PF-42: dp. 2,100; l. 303'11''; b. 37'6''; dr. 13'8'';
s. 20 k.; cpl. 190; a. 2 3'', 4 40mm., 9 20mm., 2 dct.,
8 dcp., 1 dcp. (hh.); cl. *Tacoma*)

The second *Van Buren* (PF-42) was laid down under a Maritime Commission contract (MC hull 1453) on 24 June 1943 at Los Angeles, Calif., by the Consolidated Steel Corp.; launched on 27 July 1943; sponsored by Mrs. Edward J. O'Hara; and commissioned at Terminal Island, Calif., on 17 December 1943, Lt. Comdr. Charles B. Arrington, USCG, in command.

Van Buren conducted shakedown off the west coast before departing San Pedro, Calif., on 9 March 1944, bound for the western Pacific. She sailed in company with sister ship *Ogden* (PF-39) and escorted the merchant tanker SS *Fort Erie* to Espiritu Santo from 23 to 29 March. Departing that port on the 30th, the frigate arrived at Milne Bay, New Guinea, on 2 April.

On 21 April, Vice Admiral Marc Mitscher's task force of carriers, battleships, cruisers, and destroyers began pounding Japanese airfields and defensive positions on Hollandia, Wakde, Sawar, and Sarmi, New Guinea, to neutralize them during an impending amphibious operation under the command of Rear Admiral Daniel E. Barbey. The next day, Army troops began splashing ashore at Aitape and Humboldt Bay. *Van Buren* escorted convoys supporting this operation into May and June.

As Army forces encountered stiff enemy resistance ashore, naval units were often called upon to render gunfire support. *Van Buren* received such a request on the afternoon of 9 June. At 1740, the patrol frigate opened with her main battery, firing salvoes at Japanese troop concentrations near a road in the Sarmi-Sawar sector. Ten days later, the warship again conducted a gunfire-support mission for the Army, this time near Maffin Village. The following day, *Van Buren* lobbed 150 rounds of 3-inch and 180 of 40-millimeter into the troublesome Maffin Village sector. Directions from an Army spotting plane provided information on enemy positions. Lying to off the beach, *Van Buren* soon demolished her targets and started many fires. An Army plane again provided call-fire guidance on the 23d, when *Van Buren* once more supported Army troops struggling against the Japanese defenders ashore, breaking up troop concentrations and destroying communications and supplies.

Van Buren subsequently screened the ships supporting the Cape Sansapor operations in August and continued escort operations into the autumn. On 10 November, *Van Buren* departed Humboldt Bay, bound for Cape Sansapor with a convoy of four LST's (LST-454. LST-465, LST-471, and LST-697). En route on 16 November, the frigate saw an Army plane crash four miles away and altered course to close. The ship's motor whaleboat soon rescued the aircraft's crew unhurt.

One week later, while participating in operations in the Philippines, *Van Buren* went to general quarters when *El Paso* (PF-41) radioed a contact report of an unidentified plane closing their vicinity. *Van Buren's* SA radar picked up the enemy at 18 miles; her SL receivers picked up the contact at 6 miles. Although ready for action, the frigate did not get a chance to engage, as the plane veered away and passed along the opposite side of the convoy, well beyond the American warship's gun-range.

Van Buren continued her convoy escort and screening duties with the 7th Amphibious Force, in the Philippines, into late 1944. After escorting a convoy to Leyte in mid-December, *Van Buren* sailed via Manus, in the Admiralties, to Hawaii. Arriving at Pearl Harbor on 2 January 1945, *Van Buren* operated as a training ship attached to the Pacific Fleet's destroyer forces through the spring of 1945. Shifting to the west coast of the United States soon thereafter, the patrol vessel arrived at San Francisco on 2 July. Assigned to Commander, Western Sea Frontier, the warship was fitted out as a weather ship and operated as such through the end of hostilities with Japan and into the year 1946.

Departing San Francisco on 13 March 1946, *Van Buren* transited the Panama Canal and arrived at Charleston, S.C., on 3 April. Decommissioned on 6 May 1946, *Van Buren* was struck from the Navy list on 19 June 1946 and sold soon thereafter to the Sun Ship-building and Drydock Co., of Chester, Pa., for scrapping.

Van Buren received three battle stars for World War II service.

Van Buren, John J., see *John J. Van Buren.*

Van Nassau, Jan, see *Jan Van Nassau.*

Van Valkenburgh

Franklin Van Valkenburgh—born on 5 April 1888 at Minneapolis, Minn., and appointed a midshipman on 15 September 1905—graduated from the Naval Academy on 4 June 1909. After service in *Vermont* (Battleship No. 20) and in *South Carolina* (Battleship No. 26), Van Valkenburgh was commissioned ensign on 5 June 1911. Traveling to the Asiatic Station soon thereafter, he joined *Rainbow* (Submarine Tender No. 7) at Olongapo, Philippine Islands, on 11 September. He reported to *Pampanga* (Gunboat No. 39) as executive officer on 23 June 1914 for a short tour in the southern Philippines before his detachment on 4 August.

After returning to the United States, Lt. (jg.) Van Valkenburgh joined *Connecticut* (Battleship No. 18) on 11 November. Following postgraduate work in steam engineering at the Naval Academy in September 1915, he took further instruction in that field at Columbia University before reporting to *Rhode Island* (Battleship No. 17) on 2 March 1917. The entry of the United States into World War I found Van Valkenburgh serving as the battleship's engineering officer. Subsequent temporary duty in the receiving ship at New York preceded his first tour as an instructor at the Naval Academy. On 1 June 1920, Van Valkenburgh reported on board *Minnesota* (Battleship No. 22) for duty as engineer officer, and he held that post until the battleship was decommissioned in November 1921.

He again served as an instructor at the Naval Academy—until 15 May 1925—before he joined *Maryland* (BB-46) on 26 June. Commissioned commander on 2 June 1927 while in *Maryland*, he soon reported for duty in the Office of the Chief of Naval Operations on 21 May 1928 and served there during the administrations of Admirals Charles F. Hughes and William V. Pratt. Detached on 28 June 1931, Van Valkenburgh received command of *Talbot* (DD-114) on 10 July and commanded Destroyer Squadron 5 from 31 March 1932.

After attending the Naval War College, Newport, R.I., and completing the senior course in May 1934, Comdr. Van Valkenburgh next served as inspector of naval materiel at the New York Navy Yard before

going to sea again as commanding officer of *Melvi* (AD-2) from 8 June 1936 to 11 June 1938. Promot to captain while commanding *Melville*—on 23 Decemb 1937—he served as inspector of materiel for the Naval District from 6 August 1938 to 22 January 19.

On 5 February 1941, Van Valkenburgh relieved Ca Harold C. Train as commanding officer of *Arizo* (BB-39). Newly refitted at Puget Sound, *Arizo* served as flagship of Battleship Division 1 for the mainder of the year, based primarily at Pearl Harb with two trips to the west coast. On 4 December, t battleship went to sea in company with *Nevada* (B 36) and *Oklahoma* (BB-37) for night surface pract and, after conducting these gunnery exercises, return to Pearl Harbor independently on the 5th to moor berth F-7 alongside Ford Island.

Both Capt. Van Valkenburgh and the embark division commander, Rear Admiral Isaac C. Kie spent the next Saturday evening, 6 December, board. Suddenly, shortly before 0800 on 7 Decemb Japanese planes roared overhead, shattering the Su day peace and punctuating it with the explosion bombs and the staccato hammering of machine gu Capt. Van Valkenburgh sped forward from his cal and arrived on the navigation bridge where he imme ately began to direct his ship's defense. A quarte master in the pilot house asked if the captain want to go to the conning tower—a less-exposed position view of the Japanese strafing—but Van Valkenbur refused to do so and continued to man a telepho fighting his ship.

A violent explosion suddenly shook the ship, throwi the three occupants of the bridge—Van Valkenburg an ensign, and the quartermaster, to the deck, a shattering the bridge windows. Dazed and shaken, t ensign stumbled through the flames and smoke a escaped, but the others were never seen again. A co tinuing fire, fed by ammunition and oil, blazed f two days until finally put out on 9 December. A su sequent search recovered only Capt. Van Valkenburg class ring.

The captain was posthumously awarded the Med of Honor—the citation reading in part: "for devoti to duty . . . extraordinary courage, and the comple disregard of his own life." In gallantly fighting his sh he directed its defense in the tragically short ti allotted him.

(DD-656: dp. 2,050; l. 376'6''; b. 39'8''; dr. 13' (mean); s. 37 k.; cpl. 319; a. 5 5'', 6 40mm., ?0mm., 10 21'' tt., 2 dct., 6 dcp.; cl. *Fletcher*)

Van Valkenburgh (DD-656) was laid down on 15 N vember 1942 at Chickasaw, Ala., by the Gulf Shipbui ing Corp.; launched on 19 December 1943; sponsor by Mrs. Marguerite Van Valkenburgh, widow of Ca Van Valkenburgh; and commissioned at the Alaba State Docks, Mobile, on 2 August 1944, Comdr. Ale ander B. Coxe, Jr., in command. The ensign hoist upon commissioning that afternoon was the same th had flown above *Arizona's* fantail at Pearl Harbor the morning of 7 December 1941.

Van Valkenburgh conducted trials and structu firing tests after her initial fitting-out period a while returning from her gunnery tests on 7 Augu received a request for help from the Army tug *LT-* The destroyer altered course and soon came across t disabled tug, with three barges laden with explosives tow. *Van Valkenburgh* patrolled on various cours around *LT-18*, standing by to render assistance if nec sary, until help arrived early on the 8th. Returning Mobile, the destroyer continued the fitting-out proce before getting underway for Bermuda on 20 Augu

Van Valkenburgh conducted her shakedown traini out of Great Sound, Bermuda, into late September a on the 26th, headed for Charleston, S.C., and po shakedown availability. Shifting to Hampton Roa soon thereafter, the destroyer conducted training evo ions before rendezvousing with *Wilkes Barre* (CL–03) on 22 October.

Van Valkenburgh escorted that new light cruiser to the Canal Zone and transited the Panama Canal on 7 October. At Balboa, *Mannert L. Abele* (DD–733) joined the two warships, and the three continued on together, bound for San Diego, Calif. Between 10 and 16 November, they escorted a convoy of troop transports to the Hawaiian Islands, conducting training operations off Lanai, Maui, before arriving at Pearl Harbor on the 17th.

Van Valkenburgh subsequently operated out of Pearl Harbor, engaging in an intensive slate of training activities. She made practice torpedo runs, antiaircraft firings, and shore bombardments—exercises occurring in such an endless parade that it moved a *Van Valkenburgh* sailor to write that "the real thing could be no more of a strain."

Van Valkenburgh trained in Hawaiian waters through the end of December 1944 and, after a tender availability alongside *Yosemite* (AD–19), headed for the western Pacific and her first combat operation, departing Pearl Harbor on 27 January 1945. After touching at Eniwetok en route, the destroyer reached Saipan in the Marianas, where dress rehearsals were held for the landings slated to take place on Imo Jima in the Volcano Islands. After two days of exercises at Saipan, the fleet sortied for Iwo Jima.

The morning of 19 February dawned gray and wet as the force reached their objective. *Van Valkenburgh* soon commenced her patrols as part of the three-deep screen around the unloading transports and took her turn at firing gunfire support for the marines ashore. For a week off Iwo, the destroyer alternately screened, escorted, and bombarded.

As transports and freighters unloaded their holds and disembarked their mottle-garbed marines, *Van Valkenburgh* received orders to escort a group of empty ships back to the Marianas. After shepherding a group to Saipan, *Van Valkenburgh* returned to Iwo Jima at noon on 3 March. Five days later, she made another trip to Saipan, returning on 18 March to resume screening duties as escort for an amphibious group.

After joining that unit, *Van Valkenburgh* participated in landing rehearsals and exercises on neighboring Tinian and learned that the destination for that group was Okinawa, in the Ryukyu chain, only 350 miles from the enemy's homeland. On 27 March, as part of TG 51.2, *Van Valkenburgh* sailed for her second combat operation.

Van Valkenburgh's group was ordered to feint a landing on the southwest coast of the island to draw off the Japanese defenders, while the main force approached from the westward. On the morning of 1 April, while the "Demonstration Group" gathered off the southern beaches, the 6th Army and several marine units splashed ashore on the western side of the island.

"While opposition on land was slow in gathering," wrote *Van Valkenburgh*'s ship's historian, "air opposition was immediate." As the destroyer made her sweep close inshore, a suicider crashed *LST–884*, a ship loaded with ammunition and an embarked detachment of marines. Fortunately, the plane carried no bomb, but holed the ship near the waterline forward, starting fires in the double bottom.

Van Valkenburgh stood by *LST–884* for eight hours, sending the stricken ship a fire and rescue party and fire-fighting equipment under the command of Lt. Comdr. W. Brown (attached to the staff of Capt. V. D. Chandler, screen commander embarked in *Van Valkenburgh*) to aid in fighting the blazes. Due in large part to the work of Brown's party, the fires were extinguished; and, in spite of an initially dangerous starboard list, *LST–884* reached Kerama Retto under tow. Three officers and 15 enlisted men from the destroyer received decorations, the highest being Silver

Stars to Lt. Comdr. Brown and Lt. J. D. McCormich, USNR.

On 4 April, *Van Valkenburgh* retired almost 100 miles to the east of Okinawa with the feint group whose maneuvers had accomplished their purpose. That group remained as a floating reserve, occasionally detaching transports to disembark their needed troops and marines on Okinawa, until they sailed back to the Marianas, reaching Saipan on 15 April.

Four days later, *Van Valkenburg* returned to Okinawa, and spent the initial part of that tour in the inner screen, patrolling the transport area just off the beach. "The first night . . .," the destroyer's commanding officer recounted, ". . . we had eighteen raids and not one of them turned out to be friendly."

As *Van Valkenburgh* subsequently entered the anchorage at Kerama Retto, a group of small, rocky islands 15 miles off the southwestern coast of Okinawa, her men saw the after-effects of other ships' encounters with the "Special Attack Corps," or, the kamikaze. After seeing the devastation wrought by the suicide planes, *Van Valkenburgh* headed out to report and relieve *J. William Ditter* (DM–31) on radar picket station (RP) 14, as support ship to *Wickes* (DD–578).

Seventy-two miles to the northwest of Okinawa, RP–14, was, in the words of *Van Valkenburgh*'s commanding officer, "more nearly in the direction of Japan than anywhere else." The proximity to Japanese air bases soon became evident. Within six hours of her assuming station, the local combat air patrol (CAP), controlled by *Wickes*, had shot down 21 planes. *Van Valkenburgh* herself accounted for another and assisted in destroying a second.

Van Valkenburgh also went to the aid of a second kamikaze victim, *LCS–15*, which was hit by a flaming suicider and sank immediately. The destroyer picked up the ship's survivors; and her doctor, assisted by his pharmacist's mates, worked into the wee hours of the morning on the wounded, some of them badly burned.

Over half of the following 63 days which the destroyer spent in Okinawan waters were spent on one of the 15 stations surrounding the island itself. The radar picket ships not only provided an early warning of the approach of enemy aircraft or surface units but also drew fire. The Japanese concentrated their kamikazes on the picket line of destroyers and smaller units like LCI's and LCS's.

During those weeks, no one rested. Few, if any, of the crew even bothered to undress when attempting sleep. Most slept fully-clothed, awaiting the general quarters alarm. *Van Valkenburgh* experienced at least two general quarters alarms per night; often four or five times between 2100 and dawn. As soon as it was light, Corsairs of the Marine air wing based ashore reported for duty on each station, joining with carrier-based aircraft to form the CAP.

On 28 April, within a week of her rescue of the survivors of *LCS–15*, *Van Valkenburgh* made her third "Good Samaritan" trip. *Twiggs* (DD–591) and *Daly* (DD–519), on RP–1, drew the ire of a determined group of suiciders. *Daly* suffered heavy casualties when a kamikaze, plummeting downward, exploded just before it was about to crash the bridge on the port side. Among those killed by the shrapnel and flying debris was the ship's doctor.

Van Valkenburgh went alongside *Daly* and transferred her doctor, Lt. M. E. Smale, to her stricken sistership, along with Pharmacist's Mate 3d Class Charles B. Reed, to attend the wounded. Since neither *Daly* nor the other kamikazied ship required any further assistance, *Van Valkenburgh* returned to her station and later embarked Doctor Smale and Pharmacist's Mate Reed at Kerama Retto.

Between her tours on the radar picket stations, *Van Valkenburgh* received upkeep back at Kerama Retto and conducted one shore bombardment mission. It was a one-night assignment at Buckner Bay, where she blasted pockets of Japanese resistance on the southern tip of Okinawa. The next day, however, she steamed back to the picket line.

The busiest time for *Van Valkenburgh* came on the evening of 17 May, when, in company with *Douglas H. Fox* (DD–779) and a group of four LCI's, she was on patrol on RP–9. The CAP had just returned to base, and the group wondered when they could secure from the evening alert when suddenly the word came: "Several planes approaching from the west—very low —on the deck."

Over the next 30 minutes, a "melee" took place. "Apparently," *Van Valkenburgh*'s commanding officer recalled, "we were marked for 'liquidation' that night as RP–10 had been on the night of the sinking of the *Little*." With "everybody for himself," *Van Valkenburgh* twisted and turned, maneuvering while firing with every gun that could be brought to bear. At one point, five blips appeared on the radar screen within a four-mile radius.

Two Japanese planes splashed—victims of *Van Valkenburgh*'s direct fire—one only 50 yards off the fantail. *Douglas H. Fox* splashed two more, and the pair of destroyers teamed up for a fifth kill. Unfortunately for *Douglas H. Fox*, one kamikaze found its mark, crashing that destroyer's forward gun mount.

Van Valkenburgh closed her stricken sister and rendered what aid she could. While thus engaged, she diverted her attention long enough to lay down a barrage to discourage a seventh Japanese plane "who appeared to be calculating his chances in on the attractive target of the two slow-moving destroyers." At a range of 12 miles, the plane suddenly disappeared from the radar screen, and *Van Valkenburgh* claimed that her antiaircraft fire had scored again.

After assisting *Douglas H. Fox*, *Van Valkenburgh* patrolled the area to search for possible missing men. The night prowl proved fruitless, but the ship was later relieved to hear that only one man of the stricken destroyer's complement remained unaccounted for.

Subsequently, *Van Valkenburgh* was deployed to RP–16, in company with *Robert H. Smith* (DM–23), and spent a relatively quiet patrol until her radar picked up the approach of *Shubrick* (DD–639), en route to relieve *Robert H. Smith*. While *Shubrick* was still some 10 miles away and as *Van Valkenburgh* was about to secure from general quarters, the latter's radar picked up two low-flying bogies, 10 miles to the north and closing.

Van Valkenburgh and *Robert H. Smith* cleared for action, but the pair of planes turned and headed for the newcomer, *Shubrick*. *Van Valkenburgh* passed a warning to her sistership, but too late. At 0010 on 29 May, one of the two enemy aircraft crashed *Shubrick* astern. *Van Valkenburgh*'s lookouts saw the splash of fire in the pre-dawn darkness and heard the "crump" of the explosion.

Communicating her intentions to *Robert H. Smith*, *Van Valkenburgh* veered off and headed for her damaged sister. She arrived to find that the kamikaze had blown a 30-foot hole in the starboard side, and one of the stricken destroyer's own depth charges had exploded, causing further damage. With the situation looking grim, *Van Valkenburgh* came alongside at 0113, taking on board survivors—some of whom had been badly wounded.

"Gear of all types was carried, dumped, and hurled across from the sinking destroyer," as she transferred classified material and all unnecessary personnel. Again *Van Valkenburgh*'s Doctor Smale transformed the wardroom into a dressing station to minister to the casualties. "Once more our decks and passageways bore the stretchers of the dead and dying," wrote *Van Valkenburgh*'s commanding officer. In the wardroom, "plasma flowed in life-giving torrents."

With flooding controlled and fires extinguished, *Shubrick* remained doggedly afloat. *ATR–9* soon arrived on the scene and towed the crippled destroyer to Kerama

Retto. *Van Valkenburgh* had performed "Good Samaritan" duty for the fourth time.

The attacks, however, did not cease. On the evening of 5 June, while on RP–11 in company with *Cassin Young* (DD–793) and *Smalley* (DD–565), *Van Valkenburgh* came under a concentrated torpedo attack. About dusk on that day, four or five planes closed, low from the west and heavy with bombs and torpedoes. *Van Valkenburgh*'s 40-millimeter Bofors batteries hurled out shell after shell, peppering the skies with flak. One bomber launched its torpedo—the "fish" passing 10 yards ahead of the ship—but did not emerge from the attack. The destroyer's 40-millimeter barrage slapped it into the sea. The second tordepo dropped, which was aimed in *Van Valkenburgh*'s direction, passed astern.

Following that last incident, *Van Valkenburgh*'s sailors noted a definite slackening in the Japanese attacks. The massive B–29 raids on the home islands together with the attrition caused by steady pounding by American carrier-based air power, had slowed the Japanese down considerably.

Late on 24 June, *Van Valkenburgh* finally left the forward areas, bound for the Philippines. For the ensuing fortnight, the ship rested at San Pedro Bay, Leyte, enjoying a breather from the hectic pace of operations that had lasted for over two months.

Early in July, she put to sea as part of a surface force comprised of the new large cruisers *Alaska* (CB–1) and *Guam* (CB–2), four light cruisers, and seven destroyers. Assigned to operate along the China coast between Formosa and Shanghai, the force searched for any signs of Japanese surface ship activity in that area but found no opposition of any kind. Ready for anything when they put to sea, *Van Valkenburgh*'s sailors found the situation almost anticlimactic. As one member of the crew wrote: "Our tension relaxed considerably and our sweep took on the aspect of tactical maneuvers in Chesapeake Bay."

Neither ships nor planes inquired or resisted the task force's progress, as the ships set a course back to Okinawa after a five-day patrol, 200 miles off Shanghai. The task force commander offered consoling thoughts: "If the lack of action is a disappointment at least we have the satisfaction of knowing that the East China Sea was under 'our control.'"

Subsequently returning to Buckner Bay, *Van Valkenburgh* lay at anchor there when, at 2100 on 10 August 1945, "all Hell broke loose." Something akin to a 4th of July celebration occurred, as some 150 warships threw everything they had—searchlights; tracers; red, white, and green flares; and star shell—into a 15 minute celebration that commemorated the word that the Japanese were entertaining thoughts of surrender. The demonstration subsided as quickly as it had formed and darkness again descended upon Buckner Bay. Two days later, however, the torpedoing of *Pennsylvania* (BB–38) brought home the fact that war was still very much "on." It was not until after 15 August that the signal "cease present operations" could be hoisted, indicating that the war was over at last.

On 7 September, *Van Valkenburgh* stood out of Buckner Bay in company with *Anthony* (DD–515), *Wadsworth* (DD–516), *Beale* (DD–471), and *Ammen* (DD–527), as screen for the carriers *Suwannee* (CVE–80), *Chenango* (CVE–28), *Cape Gloucester* (CVE–109), and *Birmingham* (CL–62), bound for Japan and occupation duty in the erstwhile enemy's waters. For the week that followed, the group operated off the coast of Kyushu, southwest of Nagasaki, Japan, while aircraft from the carriers patrolled the island and coast and assisted in locating mines in the clearance operation paving the way for entry into the harbor at Nagasaki.

On 15 September, as *Van Valkenburgh* steamed into Nagasaki harbor, every available vantage point topside was occupied by men silently taking in the incredible devastation wrought by the atomic bomb dropped on the city over a month before. During her week there, *Van Valkenburgh* stood by as Allied prisoner war were taken on board the hospital ship *Haven* (AH–12) which lay moored at the port's principal dock. For the next six weeks, *Van Valkenburgh* remained in Japanese waters, carrying out two courier trips to Takayama, Honshu, Japan, on the Inland Sea.

Finally, her tour of duty in the Far East completed, *Van Valkenburgh* sailed for the United States on 17 November, departing Sasebo on that day, bound for the west coast. Reaching San Diego on 6 December—via Midway and Pearl Harbor—the destroyer soon pushed on for the east coast, transiting the Panama Canal on 18 and 19 December. Making port at Charleston, S.C., two days before Christmas of 1945, *Van Valkenburgh* was decommissioned and placed in reserve on 12 April 1946.

On 31 August 1950, some two months after North Korean troops swarmed into South Korea, the Navy ordered *Van Valkenburgh*'s activation in light of the recently erupting Far Eastern crisis. Accordingly, *Van Valkenburgh* was recommissioned at Charleston on 7 March 1951, Comdr. C. A. Marinke in command. She trained off the Virginia capes and up the coast to Nova Scotian waters, as well as into the Caribbean, from Guantanamo Bay to Culebra, Puerto Rico.

Van Valkenburgh subsequently departed Norfolk on 8 May; transited the Panama Canal between 20 and 22 May; and reached Yokosuka, Japan, on 17 June, via San Diego, Pearl Harbor, and Midway.

Leaving Yokosuka in her wake on 22 June, *Van Valkenburgh* spent the next 36 days at sea with Task Force 77, screening the fast carriers as they launched their strikes against communist forces ashore. Putting into Sasebo at the end of July, the destroyer spent a brief period in-port before she got underway on 1 August for the "bomb line."

Van Valkenburgh relieved *Brown* (DD–546) as Task Element (TE) 95.28 shortly after noon on 3 August. Operating under the control of Commander, Task Group (TG) 95.2 Commander, East Coast Blockading and Patrol Group, the destroyer commenced a period of operations in support of the I Corps, Republic of Korea (ROK) Army. No sooner had she actually commenced those activities, than she received a call for a direct fire. She expended 20 rounds of 5-inch shells against enemy positions before conducting night inshore patrol from Kojo, south to the "bomb line."

Over the ensuing days, *Van Valkenburgh* expended over 2,400 rounds of ammunition against a variety of targets—ranging from houses to bunkers, artillery positions to sampans, trenches to tents and supply dumps, frequently using air spotters. She conducted her patrol operations in company with ROK *YMS–514.* On one occasion—9 August 1952—*Van Valkenburgh* dueled with a communist shore battery. Taking 10 rounds of 76-millimeter projectiles from Suwan Dan, the destroyer returned immediate counterbattery and slow destructive fire, using airspot, expending 51 rounds of 5-inch projectiles.

After being relieved by *Tingey* (DD–539), *Van Valkenburgh* operated in the Far East into the autumn. She visited the Japanese ports of Yokosuka, Hakodate, and Ominato and touched at Keelung, Formosa, before she patrolled the Formosa Strait. She then visited Kaohsiung, Formosa, and Hong Kong, but returned to the Formosa Strait for a second stint of patrol duty. Then, after a week's upkeep at Subic Bay, from 10 to 17 October, *Van Valkenburgh* headed for the United States. She completed a circumnavigation of the globe, sailing via Singapore, Federated Malay States; Colombo, Ceylon and Ras Tanura, Aden; the Suez Canal—transiting that waterway on 14 November; Naples and Genoa, Italy; Cannes, France; and Gilbraltar; reaching Norfolk, Va., on 12 December.

After remaining at Norfolk through the Christmas and New Year's holidays, *Van Valkenburgh* operated in the Vieques, Puerto Rico, area in March 1953. She then returned to Norfolk, where she was placed in reserve, but still in commission, in August 1953. Taken to Philadelphia later that same month, *Van Valkenburgh* remained in reserve at that port until she was decommissioned on 26 February 1954.

Transferred on loan to the Government of Turkey on 28 February 1967, *Van Valkenburgh* became *Izmir* (D–340) and operated with the Turkish Navy into the early 1970's. Struck from the Navy list on 1 February 1973, the destroyer was returned to the United States on 15 February but was simultaneously sold to Turkey. She remained with the Turkish Navy into 1980.

Van Valkenburgh won the Navy Unit Commendation for her service off Okinawa, was awarded three battle stars for her World War II duty and received one for Korean War operations.

Van Voorhis

Bruce Avery Van Voorhis—born on 29 January 1908 in Aberdeen, Wash.—grew up in Nevada and was appointed to the Naval Academy in June 1925. Following graduation from the Academy on 6 June 1929, Ens. Van Voorhis reported for duty in *Mississippi* (BB–41). That assignment lasted until November 1930 when he transferred to the naval air station at Pensacola, Fla., for aviation training. He received his wings on 3 September 1931 and was assigned to *Maryland* (BB–46) as a member of Observation Squadron 4B (VO–4B). In June 1934, he transferred to Bombing Squadron (VB) 5B on board *Ranger* (CV–4) and, soon thereafter, to VB–2B attached to *Saratoga* (CV–2). From July 1935 until May 1937, he served in the Panama Canal Zone and flew patrols from Coco Solo with Patrol Squadron (VP) 2F. The following June, 1938, Van Voorhis returned to carried-based aviation and served first in *Enterprise* (CV–6), then in *Yorktown* (CV–5), and finally back to *Enterprise.* In June 1940, Van Voorhis joined the aviation unit assigned to *Honolulu* (CL–48) where he served for a year. In July 1941, he reported for duty at the Naval Air Station, Anacostia, where he served until November 1942.

In December, Van Voorhis, a lieutenant commander since July, assumed command of VP–14, but soon thereafter took command of VB–102. While serving in that capacity, Lt. Comdr. Van Voorhis gave his life for his country near Hare Island of Kapingamarangi Atoll, the southernmost of the Eastern Caroline Islands. After a 700-mile flight alone, Lt. Comdr. Van Voorhis launched successive bombing and strafing attacks on the enemy ground installations. During his onslaught, he succeeded in destroying a radio station, antiaircraft emplacements, and at least one airborne fighter as well as three others on the water. However, the strength of Japanese aerial opposition eventually forced Van Voorhis lower and lower until either the intense antiaircraft barrage, the fighters, or—perhaps—his own bomb blasts knocked him out of the sky near the island. For the ". . . conspicuous gallantry and intrepidity . . ." he displayed in his ". . . lone but relentless battle against overwhelming opposition . . ." Lt. Comdr. Van Voorhis was awarded the Medal of Honor, posthumously.

(DE–1028: dp. 1,892 (f.); l. 314'6"; b. 36'9"; dr. 17'3¼"; s. 27 k.; cpl. 198; a. 2 3", Weapon ALFA, 6 15.5" tt.; cl. *Courtney*)

Van Voorhis (DE–1028) was laid down on 29 August 1955 at Camden, N.J., by the New York Shipbuilding Co.; launched on 28 July 1956, sponsored by Mrs. Kathryn Van Voorhis, the widow of Lt. Comdr. Van Voorhis; and commissioned at Philadelphia, Pa., on 22 April 1957, Lt. Comdr. Joseph J. Doak, Jr., in command.

Following shakedown training near Guantanamo Bay, Cuba, during the summer, *Van Voorhis* reported at Newport. R.I., for duty with Escort Squadron (CortRon) 14. The destroyer escort conducted operations along the east coast of North America until May 1958 when she sailed across the Atlantic for a cruise with the 6th Fleet. While operating with other ships of the 6th Fleet near Crete, she was ordered to the eastern end of the Mediterranean in mid-July to patrol off the Levantine coast. She supported the marines who landed in Lebanon in response to President Chamoun's request for help during a crisis precipitated by Arab nationalist factions in reaction to his administration's pro-Western policies and its adherence to the "Eisenhower Doctrine." President Eisenhower's personal representative, Robert Murphy, helped the factions to negotiate a settlement which resulted in the election of General Chahib to the presidency on 31 July. President Chamoun's refusal to yield office before the expiration of his term kept the country in turmoil until late September. However, political conditions in Lebanon remained highly volatile, so American forces remained there until after General Chahib took office in September. During this period, *Van Voorhis* alternated normal 6th Fleet operations with patrols off Lebanon. Late in September, the warship departed the Mediterranean and returned to Newport early in October.

Upon her return, the warship operated along the east coast until February of 1959 when she joined the other ships of her squadron in a three-month cruise to South America. She reentered Newport late in April and resumed local operations once more. She continued that employment through June 1960. The following month, she departed the United States for duty in the eastern Atlantic. During that six-week cruise, *Van Voorhis* joined other Navy ships and units of Allied navies in a NATO exercise. She also visited Greenwich, England, and Greenock, Scotland, before returning to Newport where, after upkeep, she resumed antisubmarine warfare operations. She remained so occupied through the remainder of 1960. Over the following two years, the destroyer escort continued the routine of summer operations out of Newport and winter training in the West Indies. In the autumn of 1962, when the United States subjected Cuba to a quarantine in order to keep offensive missiles from the strategically situated island, *Van Voorhis* moved to Mayport, Fla., to support the blockade-type operation. After spending the last week of the quarantine in Mayport, she returned north without having actually participated in the operation.

In December, the warship began preparations for another overseas deployment. On 15 February 1963, she cleared port for a three-month goodwill cruise to Africa—"Solant Amity IV." During the first half of the cruise, she moved south, along the eastern coast of Africa, and called at Monrovia, Liberia; Lagos, Nigeria; Pointe Noiro in the Congo; and Capteown, South Africa. After rounding the Cape of Good Hope, she moved north, up the eastern coast of Africa, and visited Lourenco Marques, Mozambique; Diego Suarez in the Malagasy Republic; and Mombasa, Kenya. She continued north to Aden, transited the Red Sea and the Suez Canal and entered the Mediterranean on 1 May. During the first two weeks of May, *Van Voorhis* crossed the Mediterranean making liberty calls at Athens, Naples, and Barcelona along the way. She rounded out the voyage with one-day stops at Gibraltar and the Azores and reentered Newport on 24 May.

Following upkeep, she conducted ASW exercises in July and made a midshipman cruise to Bermuda. Additional ASW training off the Florida coast ensued before the ship returned to Newport in October. For the remainder of 1963 and throughout 1964, the destroyer escort operated along the eastern seaboard. On 8 August 1964, she was reassigned to CortRon 8 as the squadron flagship. She continued ASW training exercises through 1964 and during the first part of January 1965.

During the latter part of the month, the ship entered the Boston Naval Shipyard for a six-week availability during which she received control equipment associated with the Drone Antisubmarine Helicopter (DASH) system. The installation was completed early in March, and *Van Voorhis* departed Boston on the 9th to par-

ticipate in the annual "Springboard" exercises conducted in the Caribbean. Upon completion of that assignment, *Van Voorhis* returned north to receive her DASH helicopters. She arrived in Norfolk on 29 March and began three weeks of tests and qualifications with the DASH system. The first destroyer escort to receive DASH, *Van Voorhis* completed her qualification trials in April and returned to her home port on the 21st.

The ship continued to work out of Newport through the following four and one-half years, primarily conducting operations in the western Atlantic. She sharpened her antisubmarine warfare skills constantly as she participated in numerous exercises along the entire North American coastline and in the Caribbean. In 1966 and 1967, she made cruises around South America in which she visited a number of South American ports and participated in bilateral and multilateral exercises with warships of various South American countries. During the first five months of 1969, her sphere of operations was centered around Florida and the West Indies. In June, she returned to Newport for a short time before resuming operations in the Caribbean in July. Through the fall and winter of 1969, she alternated between Newport and the Fleet Sonar School at Key West, Fla.

In January 1970, *Van Voorhis* began preparations for conversion to a research and development platform to test the Interim Towed Array Surveillance System (ITASS). Late that month, her DASH equipment was removed to make room for the ITASS submarine detection gear. On 9 February, she entered the Bethlehem Steel Shipyards in East Boston to begin the actual conversion. Over the next month, her new equipment was installed, and her DASH hangar was modified to provide a berthing area for the additional crew members necessitated by the ITASS. *Van Voorhis* completed the conversion early in March and, for the next four months, she conducted a series of tests on the experimental equipment in the vicinity of Bermuda.

From late June to late August, she prepared to deploy to the Mediterranean. She departed Newport on 26 August 1970, passed thorugh the Straits of Gibraltar on 6 September, and arrived at Naples on the 9th. The destroyer escort operated with the 6th Fleet, conducting surveillance patrols with her new ITASS gear until near the end of November. During the intervening two months, she also called at such places as Barcelona, Mallorca, Crete, and Naples. On 17 November, she turned the 6th Fleet ITASS responsibility over to her relief, *Lester* (DE–1022). After a liberty call at Palma de Mallorca and change of operational control at Rota, Spain, *Van Voorhis* set out to recross the Atlantic on 26 November and arrived in Newport on 6 December.

Van Voorhis began 1971 in port at Newport and operated from that base during the first eight months of the year. In September, the warship underwent an inspection and survey which found her to be unfit for further naval service. She remained moored at Newport until the following summer. *Van Voorhis* was decommissioned on 1 July 1972, and her name was struck from the Navy list simultaneously. On 15 June 1973, she was sold to the Union Minerals and Alloys Corp., of New York City, and was subsequently scrapped.

Vance

Joseph Williams Vance, Jr.—born on 4 December 1918 in Memphis, Tenn.—attended Southwestern University (The College of the Mississippi Valley) in Memphis from 1936 to 1938 and later the University of Florida at Gainesville before he enlisted in the Naval Reserve on 26 July 1940 as an apprentice seaman. After serving at sea in *Arkansas* (BB–33) during the late summer and early fall, he was appointed midshipman on 22 November and reported to *Prairie State* (IX–15) for further training.

Commissioned ensign on 28 February 1941, Vance drew Asiatic Fleet duty and joined *Parrott* (DD–218) in the Philippine Islands on 16 April. His ship conducted maneuvers and exercises in the Philippine Archipelago through the summer of the critical year, 1941; and, as the international situation continued to be "tense and unpredictable," was dispatched on 24 November with her division—Destroyer Division (DesDiv) 58—to Tarakan, Borneo.

Soon after the Japanese attacked Pearl Harbor on 7 December 1941 (8 December west of the date line), Parrott and her sister ships joined the American-British-Dutch-Australian (ABDA) effort to stem the Japanese tide sweeping down from the north. Parrott operated in the Netherlands East Indies archipelago until the fall of Java, participating in two major engagements—the Battle of Makassar Strait (24 January 1942) and the Battle of Badoeng Strait (20 February 1942).

For his gallantry during the first action, Ens. Vance was awarded the Bronze Star. As the ship's torpedo officer, Vance had charge of the destroyer's 12-tube battery of 21-inch torpedo tubes—in effect the ship's "main battery." On 23 January, DesDiv 58 began a final approach to the town of Balikpapan, Borneo, captured only that day by the Japanese. Dutch "scorched earth" policies and a Dutch air raid had set fire to most of the vital petroleum storage areas, starting blazes which clearly silhouetted the Japanese transports lying to offshore.

On 24 January, in the initial phase of the Battle of Makassar Strait, Vance and his torpedo crews had bad luck. All eight torpedoes missed on the first run. The division turned and tried again—this time with success. Three "fish" ran straight and true from Parrott's tubes on the port battery, sinking 3,500-ton transport Sumanoura Maru. Within minutes, Parrott teamed up with Pope (DD–225) and Paul Jones (DD–230) in delivering a torpedo attack on Tatsukami Maru, holing her and sending her to the bottom shortly thereafter. Soon the American force retired in the confusion of the melee while the Japanese area commander sent his escorts on a wild goose chase after American submarines!

Vance's bronze star citation took note that he had skillfully fired four salvoes in a battle at close range, in which a wide variety of target speeds and approaches had been used and had directed the fire by means of an old-fashioned open sight. By his "ability, resourcefulness, and devotion to duty," Vance contributed substantially to Parrott's performance in the United States Navy's first surface action victory—a tactical one at best—in the war against Japan.

Parrott then continued her operations in defense of the Malay barrier, taking part in the Battle of Badoeng Strait on 20 February—an action in which the ship was damaged. The destroyer ended up in Fremantle with the remnants of the Asiatic Fleet scattered by the Battle of the Java Sea from 27 February to 1 March. Vance remained in Parrott through the spring, when he received promotion to lieutenant (junior grade) on 15 June 1942.

As Allied forces gathered for the assault on Japanese-held Guadalcanal, Vance received orders to HMAS Canberra, as liaison officer with the Australian Navy. Canberra, once the prewar flagship of the Australian squadron, departed Wellington, New Zealand, on 22 July, bound for Guadalcanal and what was to be her final action. On 8 August, the Australian cruiser helped to screen American transports off the landing beaches and then in the evening retired, in company with Chicago (CA–29), to a night screening position south of Savo Island.

Unbeknownst to the Allied force, a Japanese cruiser formation steamed undetected down "the Slot" between Guadalcanal and Savo Islands. They soon opened fire with guns (8- and 5.5-inch) and the dreaded "long lance" torpedoes. Chicago took a torpedo forward, but Canberra took the worst punishment in the form of a veritable hail of shells which soon reduced her to a blazing wreck. During the engagement, Lt. (jg.) Vance was killed in action.

(DE–387: dp. 1,200; l. 306'0''; b. 36'7''; dr. 8'7'' (mean); s. 21 k.; cpl. 186; a. 3 3'', 2 40mm., 8 20mm., 3 21'' tt., 2 dct., 8 dcp., 1 dcp. (hh.); cl. Edsall)

Vance (DE–387) was laid down on 30 April 1943 at Houston, Tex., by the Brown Shipbuilding Co.; launched on 16 July 1943; sponsored by Mrs. John W. Vance, mother of the late Lt. (jg.) Vance; and commissioned on 1 November 1943, Lt. Comdr. E. A. Anderson, USCG, in command.

Following shakedown off Bermuda, Vance became the flagship for Escort Division (CortDiv) 45—a Coast Guard-manned unit—and convoyed a group of oil tankers from Norfolk, Va., to Port Arthur, Tex., and back. Upon her return to Norfolk, she served as a training ship for destroyer escort crews while awaiting the arrival of the rest of her division.

In February 1944, the ship conducted local escort operations before joining the New York section of Convoy UGS–33, bound for Gibraltar. Her section rendezvoused off Norfolk with the remainder of the convoy and its flagship, Bibb (WPG–31), and set out across the Atlantic. On 7 March, Vance departed Casablanca with GUS–33 for the return voyage and put into the New York Navy Yard on the 23d for availability.

Vance next got underway on 12 April, with the other ships of CortDiv 45 and a Navy-manned destroyer escort division, to screen the 102 merchantmen of convoy UGS–39 to Tunisia. Arriving at Bizerte on 3 May, the warship left Tunisian waters eight days later, bound for New York with GUS–39. Off Oran on the 14th, a German U-boat slipped through the screen of escorts and torpedoed two merchantmen. Vance, holding the "whip" position of the screen (where she had the duty of shepherding stragglers) came up through the convoy, sighted the periscope, and attempted to ram. The U-boat "pulled the plug" and dove deeper, evading the onrushing escort's sharp bow.

Vance remained on the scene for 10 hours, subjecting the U-boat to depth-charge and hedgehog attacks, until relieved by a squadron of Navy destroyers. Three days later, after an extensive hunt, the relief ships sank U–616.

Altogether, Vance made eight round-trip voyages to the western Mediterranean and followed each with availability at either Boston or New York. Four times the ship engaged in training exercises out of Casco Bay—sharpening up her antisubmarine and gunnery skills. On 14 July 1944, Vance helped to fight off a German air attack against an Allied convoy off Oran. During most of the voyages, the destroyer escort held the "whip" position in the convoy—a grueling and sometimes frustrating detail since merchantmen frequently displayed a lack of discipline and straggled behind the convoy. Carrying the division doctor on board, Vance on occasion would take on board men from other ships for medical treatment.

On 2 May 1945, Vance departed New York with her last Mediterranean-bound convoy. On the morning of 11 May—four days after Germany had surrendered—Vance sighted a light up ahead in the convoy and rang down full speed to investigate. Upon closing the light, the destroyer escort discovered a surfaced U-boat, U–873, which had been at sea for 50 days. While the submarine began to run, Vance hailed the erstwhile enemy in German by bullhorn, ordering the submariners to heave to. Vance placed a prize crew on board the captured U-boat who delivered the prize at Portsmouth, N.H., on the 16th.

Vance then underwent alterations to her antiaircraft armament and soon got underway for the Pacific. However, she arrived too late to participate in anything but training operations and returned to the east coast for decommissioning. In mid-October 1945, she underwent a pre-deactivation availability before proceeding south to Green Cove Springs, Fla. On 27 February 1946, *Vance* was decommissioned and placed in reserve.

The ship remained in "mothballs" for the next nine years, before she was towed to the Mare Island Naval Shipyard in November 1955 for conversion to a radar picket destroyer escort. The extensive alterations involved the addition of: improved air-search radar, extensive communications equipment, and complete facilities for fighter-direction operations. It also entailed the enclosing of the entire main deck areas amidships to provide accommodations for officers and men. Designated DER–387, *Vance* was recommissioned on 5 October 1956 at Mare Island, Lt. Comdr. Albert M. Brouner in command.

Between March of 1957 and the end of the year, *Vance* was homeported at Seattle, Wash., as a unit of CortDiv 5 and completed eight patrols on various stations of the Radar Early Warning System in the northern Pacific. Each tour lasted approximately 17 days, and the ship maintained a round-the-clock vigil with air-search radars, tracking and reporting every aircraft entering or approaching the air space of the northwestern United States. On Labor Day 1957, *Vance* drew emergency duty—an engineering casualty prevented the assigned ship from going out—and got underway in a fast 75 minutes. Although she was only manned at 60 percent of her complement (because many of her officers and men were ashore on leave or liberty and could not be notified in time to return to the ship before she weighed anchor) *Vance* was deployed for 12 days and completed a successful mission.

On 1 June 1958, the radar picket escort ship's home port was changed to Pearl Harbor; and she began operating with CortRon 7. One month later, she departed Hawaiian waters for a 29-day patrol on the mid-ocean picket lines which provided radar coverage from Alaska to Midway Atoll. *Vance* thus became the first ship on the Distant Early Warning (DEW) line in the Pacific and the first to sail under the newly organized Pacific barrier patrol. In mid-January 1959, following routine overhaul and refresher training at Pearl Harbor, *Vance* again took station on the mid-Pacific stretch of ocean on her second DEW-line deployment.

Vance continued to conduct regular DEW-line patrols until May of 1960, when CortRon 7 was dissolved. At that time, she rejoined CortDiv 5 and served with her old unit into 1961. On occasion, the picket ship took Russian trawlers under surveillance—undoubtedly while the communist vessel was returning the compliment.

Early in 1961, *Vance*'s communications capabilities were extensively augmented during an overhaul at Pearl Harbor. After resuming DEW-line patrols late in the spring, the ship received orders in August 1961 designating her an ocean station vessel with TF–43, Operation "Deepfreeze 62." Temporarily based at Dunedin, New Zealand, *Vance* served as a communication relay ship for aircraft bringing in vital supplies to the Antarctic stations from New Zealand. She remained on station in the cold, bleak, southern waters into March 1962, when she headed home via Melbourne, Australia, and Papeete, Tahiti, to Pearl Harbor. She soon resumed duties on the DEW-line and—but for periodic interruptions for maintenance, replenishment, and training—devoted herself to the task of operating mainly off the Aleutian Islands through February 1965.

In the mid-1960's, with the advent of improved radar and early-warning capabilities, the radar picket escort ship was rapidly approaching obsolescence. However, as the United States stepped up its efforts to aid the South Vietnamese government in countering internal and external communist aggression, the ship received a new lease on life. In Vietnam, a ship of this nature could be invaluable for coastal patrol work. Accordingly, in February 1965, *Vance* was ordered to the Western Pacific (WestPac). On 25 March 1965, sh[e] sailed from Pearl Harbor, in company with *Briste[r]* (DER–327) and *Forster* (DER–334), as Task Grou[p] (TG) 52.8, bound for the Philippines.

En route from Subic Bay to waters off the coast o[f] Vietnam, *Vance* rescued Capt. Leland D. Holcom[b] USAF, who had ejected from a burning F-100 Supe[r] Sabre fighter plane. *Vance* took station in Operatio[n] "Market Time" on 11 April 1965. From that day unt[il] the 24th, she operated near the 17th parallel as part of Task Unit (TU) 71.1.1. During the assign[-] ment, she maintained communications between airborn[e] Convair EC–121K Constellations and Commander, T[U] 71.1.1, in *John W. Thomason* (DD–760). Subsequentl[y] from 15 May to 4 June, *Vance* returned to "Marke[t] Time" surface surveillance—this time in the Gulf o[f] Thailand near the border dividing South Vietnam fro[m] Cambodia. She operated in company with small min[e] sweepers (MSO's) and embarked a Vietnamese Nav[y] liaison officer to aid in the ship's "visit and searc[h]" activities. She continued these activities until sailin[g] for Hawaii early in September and arrived at Pea[rl] Harbor on the 18th.

Vance returned to "Market Time" station in mid[-] January 1966, and then participated in Operatio[n] "Masher," the amphibious operation designed to clea[r] northern Binh Dinh province of Viet Cong insurgent[s.] Next moving to the Gulf of Thailand once more, th[e] destroyer escort conducted close-support and logistic[] operations with Navy PCF's (swift boats) and Coas[t] Guard WPB's in interdicting communist coastal suppl[y] traffic, often boarding 30 vessels per day.

Underway on 11 April to patrol off Cap de Ca Ma[u,] the southernmost tip of South Vietnam, *Vance* moni[-] tored coastal junk traffic and seagoing vessels, survey[-] ing traffic patterns in the South China Sea. Later, o[ff] Binh Dinh, she closed to investigate a trawler an[d] came under fire from Viet Cong ashore. Although th[e] ship's skin was pocked by bullets, *Vance* briskly re[-] turned the fire with her 3-inch battery, driving awa[y] or killing the unseen but pestiferous snipers.

In a more humanitarian vein, *Vance* and a "Swift[""] rescued 56 men, women, and children from a swampe[d] boat near Qui Nhon. For several hours, *Vance*'s me[n] cleaned and fed babies; made old women as comfort[-] able as possible; and gave away blankets, towels, an[d] food. Relieved by *Haverfield* (DER–393) late in Jul[y,] *Vance* headed for Hawaii and got as far as the Sa[n] Bernadino Strait before she was ordered to retur[n] to Vietnam for further "Market Time" duty. On [] August, *Surfbird* (ADG–383) relieved the destroye[r] escort on station and allowed *Vance* to sail again vi[a] the Philippines for Pearl Harbor.

On 15 January 1967, *Vance* returned to the Far Ea[st] for another 7th Fleet deployment and relieved *Koine[r]* (DER–331) off the mouth of the Saigon River. Onc[e] again, *Vance*'s duties involved hunting for contraban[d] carrying craft attempting to infiltrate from the nort[h] to deliver their cargoes to the Viet Cong. *Vance* tracke[d] all ocean-sized vessels and stopped and searched jun[ks] and sampans—tedious and frustrating but vital wor[k.]

The ship conducted two more "Market Time" patrol[s] during her third WestPac deployment and, betwee[n] missions, underwent a tender availability at Kaohsiun[g,] Taiwan; rest and recreation at Hong Kong; and upkee[p] at Subic Bay. At the end of her last "Market Time[""] assignment, she patrolled the Taiwan Strait betwee[n] communist China and Taiwan before returning t[o] Pearl Harbor for routine overhaul. In late 1967, th[e] ship began her final WestPac deployment in which he[r] duties were similar to those of her third deploymen[t.] She subsequently returned to the west coast of th[e] United States late in 1968 for inactivation.

Placed in reserve, at the Inactive Ship Facilit[y,] Vallejo, *Vance* was decommissioned on 10 October 196[9,] struck from the Navy list on 1 June 1975, and schedule[d] to be used as a target.

Vance received seven battle stars for service i[n] Vietnam.

Vancouver

A city in the state of Washington.

LPD–2: dp. 13,600 (f.); l. 522'; b. 100'; dr. 20'; s. 21 k. (tl.); cpl. 436; a. 4 3''; cl. *Raleigh*)

Vancouver (LPD–2) was laid down on 19 November 1960 at Brooklyn, N.Y., by the New York Naval Shipyard; launched on 15 September 1962; sponsored by Mrs. Stuart Symington; and commissioned on 11 May 1963, Capt. Thomas C. Harbert, Jr., in command.

After completing builders trials at New York and shakedown training out of Norfolk, Va., the amphibious transport dock ship departed the latter port on 14 August and laid a course for the west coast. She transited the Panama Canal on 20 August and—after making a side trip to Acapulco, Mex., in the process of assisting a disabled fishing vessel—arrived in San Diego, her permanent home port, on the 31st.

Late in September and early in October, *Vancouver* made the traditional visit to her namesake city—Vancouver, Wash.—and then returned to San Diego for seven weeks of training. Underway training occupied the first four weeks while amphibious training took up the last three. In mid-December, she welcomed on board the newly appointed Secretary of the Navy, Paul H. Nitze, and the Commander in Chief, Pacific Fleet, Admiral U.S. Grant Sharp, as well as several other high ranking Navy and Marine Corps officers, and treated them to a display of her multifaceted amphibious capabilities.

USS *Vancouver* (LPD–2) disembarks mechanized landing craft (LCM) from her flooded well deck; a Sikorsky CH–37C *Mojave* transport helicopter is on the flight deck. The LPD can land troops and equipment simultaneously by water and by air. (USN 1103218)

In mid-February 1964, the ship moved from San Diego to Long Beach where she entered the naval shipyard for post-shakedown availability. She finished repairs on 21 May, completed final acceptance trials early in June, and then returned to San Diego. Late in June, the amphibious transport dock ship made another voyage north to Canada for a visit to another namesake city, British Columbia, in time to participate in that city's annual maritime festival. On the way back home, she stopped in San Francisco for the Independence Day weekend and then reentered San Diego on 7 July. At that point, she began her operational schedule. She participated in three amphibious warfare exercises between July and October and then began preparations for her first deployment to the Far East.

Her first tour of duty with the 7th Fleet coincided with the beginning of the rapid acceleration of American involvement in South Vietnam heralded by the Gulf of Tonkin incident in August 1964. She departed San Diego on 16 November, loaded marines at Port Hueneme, and set out across the Pacific on the 17th. Vancouver arrived in Buckner Bay, Okinawa, on 6 December, and unloaded her passengers. Embarking another Marine battalion at Okinawa on 21 December, she moved to Subic Bay in the Philippines, where she traded her second load of marines for a third which she transported to Okinawa in January 1965.

Sometime in February, the ship embarked elements of the 9th Marine Expeditionary Brigade and, on 8 March in company with Henrico (APA–45) and Union (AKA–106), landed the marines at Danang, South Vietnam, to protect the perimeter of the airbase there and free South Vietnamese troops for other combat duties. During the remaining three months of her first deployment to the Orient, Vancouver twice revisited Vietnam—on both occasions on resupply missions. In June, she concluded her deployment and headed home. However, less than two months after her return, she embarked marines for a special troop lift to the widening conflict in Vietnam. She departed the west coast on 5 August and did not return until 5 October. At that point, she began the normal schedule of upkeep and training exercises at San Diego and other points along the California coast.

During the first week in July, Vancouver embarked LVT's and Battalion Landing Team (BLT) 1/26 (1st Battalion, 26th Marines) in preparation for her second 7th Fleet assignment. On the 9th, she put to sea and, after a two-day stop at Pearl Harbor from 14 to 16 July, arrived at Subic Bay on 28 July. There, she became a unit of the newly constituted 7th Fleet Amphibious Ready Group (ARG), Task Group (TG) 76.5—a self-contained mobile amphibious assault team made up of a Special Landing Force (SLF), marines and support units, and the ships which served as their transportation and mobile bases. In a series of training exercises held in the Philippines, the Navy-Marine Corps teammates honed their skills for an almost instant response to any need for amphibious support or reinforcement in the 7th Fleet's zone of operations.

Quite naturally, Vietnam constituted the area most in need of such a capability at that time. Accordingly, the ARG concluded its amphibious training on 12 August, reembarked the landing force, and sailed for the waters off Vietnam. Between 16 and 29 August, Vancouver participated in her first combat action during Operation "Deckhouse III" which consisted of two landings at a point some 60 miles east of Saigon. The first phase, from 16 to 20 August, saw BLT 1/26 move ashore in both modes—waterborne and airborne—against minor opposition and later destroy a fortified, Viet-Cong-held village. During the second set of landings, 22 to 29 August, the marines sent ashore changed operational control from the ARG to the authorities ashore to assist in Operation "Toledo," a search-and-destroy mission to deprive the enemy of valuable caches of arms and supplies. At the conclusion of "Deckhouse III," Vancouver returned to Subic Bay for 10 days of upkeep.

Departing the Philippines on 12 September, the sh[ip] began her second amphibious assault, Operation "Dec[k]house IV," on 15 September in the vicinity of the C[ua] Viet River in Quang Tri Province just south of t[he] demilitarized zone (DMZ). The landings constituted [the] seaward arm of the larger Operation "Prairie" bei[ng] conducted by American and South Vietnamese forc[es] ashore to destroy North Vietnamese Army fortific[a]tions, bunkers, and supply caches in the area and [to] stem intensified infiltration across the DMZ. Durin[g] their 10 days ashore, the marines of the SLF e[n]countered heavy resistance and accounted for 254 [of] the enemy killed before they reembarked on 25 Septe[m]ber. At the conclusion of the operation, Vancouver di[s]embarked her portion of BLT 1/26 troops at Dana[ng] and headed for Okinawa.

After she embarked BLT 3/3 there, she returned [to] Vietnamese waters on 6 October and steamed with t[he] contingency force in the area off the DMZ for t[he] next 22 days. On 28 October, she disembarked BL[T] 3/3 and, two days later, embarked BLT 3/26 f[or] transportation to the Philippines. She departed Dana[ng] on 1 November and arrived in Subic Bay on the 12t[h]. During December, she participated in an amphibiou[s] exercise, "Mudpuppy II," at Mindoro and conducte[d] upkeep at Subic Bay. On the 30th, the amphibiou[s] transport dock ship got underway for Vietnames[e] waters and arrived near Vung Tau the following da[y].

There, near the entrance to the Saigon River, sh[e] began another amphibious operation in the "Deckhouse" series—"Deckhouse V," on 4 January 1967. It laste[d] until the 15th and was a joint United States-Sout[h] Vietnamese effort utilizing marines of both nation[s]. Vancouver embarked more than 500 South Vietnames[e] marines at Vung Tau on the 4th and, after a two-da[y] delay caused by bad weather, sent her binational forc[e] ashore on the 6th by both assault craft and helicopte[r]. In spite of continued bad weather and her first exper[i]ence with riverine operations, the ship and her boa[ts] remained in the area for 10 days, providing the nece[s]sary logistics support for the SLF operating ashor[e]. After reembarking the SLF and South Vietnames[e] marines on 15 January and then disembarking th[e] latter again at Vung Tau the following day, she de[]parted Vietnam to return to the Philippines.

The ship arrived at Subic Bay on the 19th b[ut] remained only two days before continuing on to Ok[i]nawa where she exchanged BLT 1/9 for BLT 1/4 la[te] in January. Following a visit to Keelung, Taiwan, sh[e] returned to the Philippines early in February and co[n]ducted an amphibious exercise, "Mudpuppy III," wit[h] the marines of BLT 1/4. Another brief rest and relax[a]tion period at Subic Bay at the end of the first week i[n] February preceded her departure from the Philippine[s] on the 12th. Vancouver resumed duty with the ARG o[n] 14 February and, two days later, began her part i[n] Operation "Deckhouse VI," another two-phase amphib[i]ous assault in support of operations of wider scop[e] being conducted ashore.

At the conclusion of Operation "Deckhouse VI," th[e] amphibious transport dock ship visited Subic Bay[;] Hong Kong; Okinawa; and Yokosuka, Japan, befor[e] departing the latter port on 24 March to return hom[e] to San Diego. After a three-day stop at Pearl Harbo[r] at the end of the month, she arrived in San Diego on [] April.

Following an unusually long period in port at Sa[n] Diego, Vancouver resumed operations along the we[st] coast in July. In addition to single-ship underwa[y] training, she revisited Vancouver, British Columbi[a], in July to participate in a Fleet Assembly as part o[f] the Canadian Centennial Celebration. Late that mont[h] the ship resumed local operations which included unde[r]way training and amphibious refresher training. Th[at] employment occupied her for the remainder of th[e] year and the first month of 1968.

On 1 February 1968, the ship departed San Dieg[o] bound for Okinawa to begin another tour of duty wit[h] the 7th Fleet. She stopped at Pearl Harbor from 8 [to]

0 February and, after being diverted from Okinawa on the 12th, arrived in Danang on the 23d to disembark her marines, urgently needed to stem the 1968 Tet offensive. The following day, *Vancouver* got underway for Subic Bay where she arrived on the 26th. On the 27th, she changed operational control to TG 76.5 and became part of the 7th Fleet ARG once more. On 29 February, the ship steamed out of Subic Bay for the Cua Viet River area of Vietnam where she began supporting the SLF, operating ashore since late January. While continuing that mission, she put into Danang on 10 March and spent the next two weeks repairing boats as well. In April, she steamed around off the DMZ providing support for BLT 3/1 until 10 April when she headed back to the Philippines.

Vancouver arrived in Subic Bay on the 15th and remained there until the 26th at which time she got underway to return to Vietnamese waters. The amphibious transport dock ship arrived on station near the mouth of the Cua Viet River and began providing logistics support to elements of BLT 3/1 committed to defensive positions in the vicinity of Dong Ha. That duty lasted until 3 June when she reembarked the SLF.

On 6 June, *Vancouver* began a combat operation, code named "Swift Sabre." The SLF moved ashore in two groups. One group assaulted beaches in landing craft while the other group flew well inland in helicopters. Both groups then began moving toward one another in a sweep of Elephant Valley in Thua Thien province to eliminate a frequent source of hostile mortar fire on the Danang air base. After supporting the marines for a week, *Vancouver* received a replacement SLF, BLT 2/7, when BLT 3/1 changed operational control to military authorities ashore. The new battalion landing team came on board on 14 and 15 June, and *Vancouver* set a course for the Philippines on the 15th. She entered Subic Bay on the 18th and began a 10-day upkeep period. Between 30 June and 3 July, the ship participated in the amphibious exercise "Hilltop XX" and then departed Subic Bay on 5 July for her last tour of duty in Vietnamese waters during the 1968 deployment.

Immediately upon her arrival off Vietnam, she began preparations for the amphibious operation, "Eager Yankee." In the predawn of 9 July, destroyers *Benner* (DD–807) and *O'Brien* (DD–725) shattered the silence and sporadically lighted the darkness with gunfire. At the conclusion of the prelanding bombardment, *Vancouver*, as primary control ship for the boat phase of the assault, began shuttling marines ashore some 10 miles east of Phu Bai. The first elements of BLT 2/7 went ashore in LVT's and began establishing defensive positions and clearing landing zones for the airborne phase of the operation. The ship remained in the area providing logistics support for the marines as they drove northwest toward a known Viet Cong haven. After a week without contacting the enemy, *Vancouver*'s landing force joined shore-based units in Operation "Houston IV" while the ship continued in her support role. The second operation ended on 22 July, and the marines reembarked that same day.

However, they did not remain on board for long because, on the following day, Operation "Swift Play" began. In that operation, an all-helicopter affair, the marines landed well inland about 10 miles southwest of Hoi An in east central Quang Nam province. They failed to contact the enemy during the helicopter assault and, the following day, changed operational control to authorities ashore while *Vancouver* played her usual support role. She remained in the vicinity until 19 August at which time she headed back to Subic Bay without her Marine Corps contingent.

The warship arrived in Subic Bay on 21 August and spent the next six days engaged in turnover operations with her relief, *Ogden* (LPD–5). On 27 August, she put to sea bound for Hong Kong where she arrived on the 29th. After a five-day rest and relaxation period, she departed Hong Kong for Okinawa. Diverted to

Subic Bay by a typhoon, she continued her voyage via the San Bernardino Strait and finally arrived at Okinawa on 9 September. The following day, she set sail for Yokosuka, Japan, where she arrived on the 12th for five days of upkeep.

On the 17th, *Vancouver* began her voyage home. She reentered San Diego on 28 September and, after a month of post-deployment standdown, resumed local operations along the California coast.

That employment lasted until early in February 1969 when she began the first portion of her regular overhaul at San Francisco. That phase of the task was completed in mid-April and, after a brief return to San Diego, the ship entered the Long Beach Naval Shipyard for drydocking. The refurbishing was finished near the end of May, and *Vancouver* returned to San Diego on the 28th. Following two months of inspections and refresher training, the ship loaded vehicles and cargo at San Diego and got underway for the western Pacific on 1 August. She made a three-day stop at Pearl Harbor from the 8th to the 11th; then resumed her voyage and arrived at Okinawa on 21 August. After unloading cargo at Buckner Bay, she got underway for Vietnam on the 24th. Upon arriving at Tau My, South Vietnam, on 27 August, *Vancouver* unloaded cargo there and at Danang before departing Vietnam that same day.

On the 29th, she arrived in Subic Bay and began turnover operations to relieve *Paul Revere* (LPA–248) of duty with ARG "Bravo" (TG 76.5). A week later, on 6 September, she put to sea with TG 76.5 for her first line tour with the amphibious ready group. She arrived off Danang two days later and entered the harbor on the 10th to unload more cargo. On 12 September, she and her group participated in Operation "Defiant Stand" by staging an amphibious feint about 10 miles south of the actual landing beaches to draw off defenders while ARG "Alfa" stormed ashore. The task group completed its deception early that morning and headed back out to sea to steam around until needed again. That routine, punctuated by brief visits to Danang and a series of amphibious and other exercises, occupied her until late October.

On 20 October, *Vancouver* began a new phase in her participation in the Vietnam War. Operation "Defiant Stand" had been the last amphibious operation of the war. On the heels of President Richard M. Nixon's announcement of the staged withdrawal of large numbers of American troops from the conflict, the amphibious ready group began carrying out the withdrawal. On 20 October, *Vancouver* moved from Danang to Cua Viet and began loading elements of BLT 1/4. She completed Operation "Keystone Cardinal" on 22 October and set course for Okinawa the following day. She disembarked the marines at Okinawa on 25 and 26 October but remained at the island for liberty until 2 November. After embarking BLT 1/9, she headed for Subic Bay where she disembarked the marines on the 4th.

Following a week of repairs at Subic Bay, she reembarked BLT 1/9 on the 12th, conducted an amphibious assault exercise on the 13th, and got underway for Vietnam on the 14th. The new line period, unlike those before, consisted entirely of steaming well off the coast outside the territorial waters of Vietnam in order that the amphibious ready group's presence not be construed as a violation of President Nixon's troop reduction in Vietnam. She continued steaming in the new operating area until 23 November at which time she retired toward the Philippines. She entered Subic Bay on the 27th. Another practice landing in the Philippines followed on 1 December, and *Vancouver* repaired storm damage sustained during the transit from Vietnam to the Philippines.

On 6 December, the ship once more got underway for the coast of Vietnam. She arrived off Danang on the 9th; but, four days later, she left the combat zone for visits to Hong Kong, Taiwan, and Okinawa. *Vancouver* returned to the Vietnamese coast on the last day of 1969. New Year's Day 1970, however, brought her departure from the area on her way back to the Philippines. She entered Subic Bay on the 11th and remained in the Philippines until the 20th when she started a round-trip voyage to Okinawa. The ship returned to Subic Bay on the 27th and remained in the area until 4 February when she headed for Taiwan. After a patrol of the Taiwan Strait, she entered port at Kaohsiung, Taiwan, for a four-day visit. She returned to Subic Bay on 21 February and began turnover operations with her relief ship *Denver* (LPD-9). On 4 March, she departed Subic Bay for Okinawa where she delivered cargo on 6 March. Continuing her voyage on the 7th, she stopped at Danang on 11 March, unloaded cargo, and headed back to Okinawa where she refueled on the 14th before continuing on toward the United States.

Vancouver arrived in Del Mar, Calif., on 27 March and, the following day, moved to the San Diego Naval Station for drydocking and repairs. Repairs were completed early in June, and the ship departed San Diego on 10 June with Naval Academy midshipmen embarked for their summer cruise. She arrived in Yokosuka on 24 June and departed again on the 29th. The ship visited Hong Kong between 4 and 8 July and stopped at Danang on 9 and 10 July to load cargo bound for the United States. On the way back home, she stopped at Pearl Harbor from 24 to 27 July and then reentered San Diego on 1 August. Local operations out of San Diego, including LVT training and amphibious refresher training, occupied the ship's time through the end of the year and for the first three months of 1971.

On 30 March, *Vancouver* put to sea to return to the western Pacific. She made a two-day stop at Pearl Harbor at the end of the first week in April and arrived in Subic Bay on the 19th. The ensuing six weeks brought amphibious training and port visits to Singapore and Kaohsiung. In June, the ship carried cargo from Vung Tau and Danang in the Vietnam to Subic Bay and Okinawa. Early in July, *Vancouver* participated in an amphibious exercise at Zambales and then departed the Philippines on the 19th for a week at Hong Kong. On 28 July, the ship returned to the Philippines at Mindoro for more amphibious exercises. August brought voyages to Sasebo, Japan, and Kaohsiung, Taiwan; and, early in September, she returned to the Philippines for another round of practice landings at Zambales.

On 9 September, *Vancouver* left Subic Bay to pick up cargo in Vietnam. She stopped at Danang, Qui Nhon, and Camranh Bay before returning to Subic Bay on the 17th. On 25 September, she embarked upon a round-trip voyage to Okinawa and returned to Subic Bay on 9 October. On 14 October, *Vancouver* set out on her voyage back to the United States, stopping en route at Okinawa and Pearl Harbor before arriving back in San Diego, Calif., on 5 November.

The amphibious transport dock ship remained in San Diego through the end of 1971 for post-deployment standdown and for the usual holiday leave and upkeep period. On 11 January 1972, *Vancouver* began local operations along the California coast. That duty lasted until 10 June, when she embarked midshipmen for the annual training cruise and got underway for the Far East. During the midshipman cruise, the ship made a visit to Yokosuka, Japan, and two each to Hong Kong and Subic Bay in the Philippines. Late in July, she headed back to the west coast, arriving at San Diego on 4 August. There, on the 21st, *Vancouver* began her regularly scheduled overhaul.

The ship completed post-overhaul sea trials early in February 1973 and conducted type and refresher training until mid-March. On 17 March, *Vancouver* again deployed to the western Pacific. She arrived in Sasebo, Japan, on 4 April then continued her voyage on the 5th. She briefly stopped at Okinawa on 6 April and arrived in Subic Bay on the 8th.

On the 9th, she relieved *Cleveland* (LPD-7) as one of the support ships for Operation "End Sweep," the clearing of American mines in the harbors of North Vietnam as a result of the withdrawal of American forces from the Vietnamese civil war. During April, May, and June, the amphibious transport dock ship alternated tours of duty in Vietnamese waters in support of the minesweeping forces with liberty and upkeep periods in Philippine ports. She also made periodic liberty calls at Hong Kong and at various Japanese ports.

The ship completed her last tour of duty in Vietnamese waters on 18 July and headed back to the Philippines, arriving in Subic Bay on the 20th. For her remaining two months in the Far East, *Vancouver* visited Hong Kong; the Japanese ports Numazu, Kagoshima, and Iwakuni. She returned to the Philippines early in September, whence she put to sea on the 19th to return home. After stopping overnight at Pearl Harbor on 2 and 3 October, the ship continued on to San Diego where she arrived on the 9th and began a year of operations along the California coast. Her tasks included: helicopter qualifications, landing craft training, and full scale amphibious warfare exercises.

On 18 October 1974, she concluded her west coast schedule and got underway for the western Pacific. She stopped at Pearl Harbor on 25 and 26 October and continuing her voyage on the 26th, arrived in Buckner Bay, Okinawa, on 9 November. Though assigned to ARG "Alfa" as relief for *Ogden* (LPD-5), *Vancouver* began her first real peacetime deployment to the Far East in more than a decade. For the next six months, she spent most of her time alternating between Okinawa and the Philippines conducting a series of amphibious exercises and transporting marines and cargo.

She did, however, return to the Indochina peninsula that spring to participate in Operation "Eagle Pull," the evacuation of Vietnamese and Cambodian refugees in the wake of the collapse of the non-communist governments in those nations. At the end of the deployment, she departed Okinawa on 20 May and arrived back in San Diego on 6 June.

She resumed west coast operations almost immediately with type training and a weapons inspection. Similar duty occupied her through the end of the year and during the first nine months of 1976. On 25 September 1976, she headed back to the western Pacific once more. She made a three-day stop at Pearl Harbor at the beginning of October and put in at Kwajalein Atoll on the 10th for ARG commanding officers to conduct turnover briefings. From Kwajalein, she continued her voyage to Broad Sound, Australia, where she arrived on 21 October. There, she conducted a rehearsal landing in preparation for the Operation "Kangaroo II" landing exercises conducted between 24 and 29 October in conjunction with Austrilian military and naval forces. At the conclusion of Operation "Kangaroo II," *Vancouver* made a five-day visit to Sydney, Australia, and then got underway for Okinawa. She reached her destination on 20 November, disembarked one group of marines, and took on another. The following day, she headed for Subic Bay, arriving there on the 24th to begin a three-week availability. Late in December, *Vancouver* embarked upon a voyage to Taiwan and Hong Kong observing New Year's Eve at the latter port.

After a return to Okinawa and Subic Bay early in January 1977, the ship visited Singapore during the latter half of the month. She returned to the Philippines on 11 February and conducted exercises in the vicinity of Subic Bay until mid-March. On 16 March, the amphibious transport dock ship put to sea, bound for Inchon, Korea. During the latter part of March and early part of April, she participated in amphibious training with units of the South Korean military. On 12 April, she stopped at Okinawa and the next day headed back to the Philippines. *Vancouver* arrived in Subic Bay on 16 April but departed again on the 28th for a round-about voyage home. She made stops at Okinawa, Eniwetok, and Pearl Harbor before arriving back in San Diego on 21 May. After a month of post-

eployment standdown, the ship entered the Bethlehem
teel Co. shipyard at San Pedro, Calif., for her regualr
verhaul. She remained there into 1978.

Vancouver completed her overhaul satisfactorily on
8 April 1978. A rigorous period of refresher training
ut of San Diego followed in preparation for the ship's
orthcoming deployment to the western Pacific. *Van-
ouver* departed from San Diego on 31 August and
pent the remainder of the year in operations with
he 7th Fleet. Her schedule took her to Eniwetok Atoll,
Iarshall Islands; Subic Bay, Philippines; Pusan,
Lorea; and Hong Kong, B.C.C.

Vancouver (LPD-2) earned 11 battle stars for service
n the Vietnam conflict.

Vandalia

A city in Illinois on the Kaskaskia River. Vandalia
vas the state capital from 1820 to 1839 and today is
he seat of Fayette County. The origin of the name
s uncertain, but the name probably is derived from
he Germanic Vandal tribe. Other explanations of
he name hold that it is a latinization of a Dutch
amily name or that it refers to a small Indian tribe
f the early 19th century.

I

(Slp: t. 614; l. 127'4''; b. 34'6''; dr. 16'6''; cpl. 150;
a. 4 8'' Sg., 16 32-pdrs.; cl. *Boston*)

The first *Vandalia*—an 18-gun sloop-of-war—was laid
own at the Philadelphia Navy Yard in 1825; launched
n 1828; and commissioned on 6 November of that year,
Comdr. John Gallagher in command.

Vandalia left Philadelphia on 16 December 1828,
ound for duty with the Brazil Squadron off the eastern
eaboard of South America. She remained off the
oasts of Brazil and Argentina for the next three years,
elping to protect American citizens and mercantile
nterests during a period of continuing political unrest
n the continent of South America. She returned to
Vorfolk, Va., on 18 December 1831; was decom-
nissioned the next day; and remained inactive until 4
October 1832 when she was recommissioned for serv-
ce with the West Indies Squadron. *Vandalia* again put
nto Norfolk in August 1834 and was decommissioned
here on the 24th for major repairs. Recommissioned
n the last day of the year, she joined the West Indies
Squadron in January 1835 and served with that or-
anization into the summer of 1838 protecting Amer-
can citizens and property in the West Indies; cooper-
ting with land forces in Florida during the second
Seminole Indian War; and helping to suppress the
lave trade. After almost three months laid up under-
oing repairs from 30 August to 24 November, the
hip was reactivated and returned to duty for a year
n the Caribbean, ending when her commissioning pen-
ant was again hauled down at Norfolk on 23 Novem-
er 1839.

Following more than two years on the stocks, the
hip was returned to commission on 3 February 1842,
oined the newly created Home Squadron in 1842,
nd performed routine patrol and reconnaissance duties
t scattered points as far north as Newfoundland and
as far south as the mouth of the Amazon River. During
a visit to Haiti in the early spring of 1845, an epidemic
f yellow fever broke out in the ship. She returned
mmediately to Norfolk, was decommissioned on 30
April, and was laid up. During the sloop's period in
rdinary which lasted until 1849, she was lengthened
oy 13 feet in 1848. The renovated *Vandalia* was recommissioned on 9 August 1849 and joined the Pacific
Squadron on 5 September 1849 as that organization
was expanding to service the territory which the United
States had recently acquired on the Pacific coast. She
made several visits to the Hawaiian Islands in 1851
before returning to the New York Navy Yard on 6
October 1852 and going out of commission again on
the 14th.

Vandalia's rest ended on Valentine's Day 1853, and
the ship soon joined Commodore Matthew C. Perry's
East Indies Squadron. She was present at Commodore
Perry's historic entrance into Tokyo Bay on 13 February 1854 and in 1855 helped to protect American
interests in China during the Taiping Rebellion. *Vandalia* was decommissioned at the Portsmouth (N.H.)
Navy Yard on 30 September 1856 but was recommissioned on 11 November 1857 for duty with the Pacific
Squadron. In 1859, the warship rescued survivors of
the American clipper ship *Wild Wave*, wrecked off
Oeno and Pitcairn Islands, and conducted an expedition against natives at Waya, Fiji Islands, following
the murder of two American citizens. *Vandalia* returned to the New York Navy Yard early in 1860
and was decommissioned on 6 January of that year but
was recommissioned there on 8 November and assigned
to duty with the East Indies Squadron.

With the outbreak of the Civil War in April 1861,
Vandalia was called back home and assigned to the
South Atlantic Blockading Squadron on 31 May for
blockade duty off Charleston and Bull's Bay, S.C. There,
she captured the schooner *Henry Middleton* on 21
August and assisted in the capture of the sailing ship
Thomas Watson in 15 October. The vessel also participated in the successful amphibious assault upon
Roanoke Island, N.C., on 7 and 8 November. This
victory closed the supply lines to Confederate-held
Norfolk Navy Yard and was largely responsible for
the evacuation of that vital naval facility six months
later. *Vandalia* put into New York on 24 November to
deliver the officers and crew of the wrecked steamer
Governor.

Vandalia soon returned to duty with the South
Atlantic Blockading Squadron and was deployed off
Tybee Roads, Ga., in December. She remained at Tybee
until April 1862, at which time she was ordered to
proceed to the blockade at Wassaw Sound, Ga. The
sloop returned to Port Royal, S.C., in June and took up
blockade duty off Charleston in July. She served at
Port Royal as a guardship in September and was repaired and resupplied there in November. Later that
month and in December, she cruised along the outside
line of the blockade off Charleston and Port Royal
Bay, performing reconnaissance duties as well as
giving practical sailing experience to recent Naval
Academy graduates. On 12 December, the vessel was
ordered north for major structural repairs at New York.

Vandalia was decommissioned at the New York Navy
Yard on 4 February 1863 and then sailed for Portsmouth, N.H., on 17 October for use as a receiving and
guard ship. She remained at Portsmouth until broken
up there sometime between 1870 and 1872.

II

(ScSlp: dp. 2,033; lbp. 216'; b. 39'; dph. 20'; a. 8 guns;
cl. *Swatara*)

The second *Vandalia*—a screw sloop—was laid down
at the Boston Navy Yard, Mass., in 1872 and commissioned there on 10 January 1876.

Vandalia was soon deployed with the European
Squadron and spent most of the next three years cruising in the Mediterranean along the coasts of Africa,
the Middle East, and Turkey. She put into Villefranche,
France, in October 1877, and left on 13 December with
the former President, General Ulysses S. Grant, as a
passenger. During the next three months, the screw
sloop of war touched at ports in Italy, Egypt, Turkey,
and Greece before President Grant disembarked at
Naples on 18 March 1878. After making several more
Mediterranean cruises, *Vandalia* received orders to return to the United States later that year. She put into
Boston on 13 January 1879 and departed on 7 April,
bound for Norfolk, Va., and duty with the North Atlantic Squadron.

USS *Vandalia* as flagship of the Pacific Squadron.

Vandalia remained with the North Atlantic Squadron for five years. During this time, she performed patrol, reconnaissance, and convoy escort duty off the eastern seaboard of the United States. The vessel was also active off the Grand Banks and in the Gulf of Mexico and the Caribbean. *Vandalia* was detached from the squadron in 1884 and put out of commission at the Portsmouth (N.H.) Navy Yard on 14 October for a thorough overhaul.

Repairs continued for over a year before *Vandalia* was ready for recommissioning on 15 February 1886. The sloop left New York on 14 August, heading westward for duty with the Pacific Squadron as the flapship of Rear Admiral Louis A. Kimberly. *Vandalia* remained with the squadron into 1889, seeing duty in the Hawaiian Islands and Samoa, as well as along the Pacific coasts of North, Central, and South America. The sloop put into the Mare Island Navy Yard, San Francisco, for repairs on 11 October 1888.

While *Vandalia* lay at Mare Island, relations between American and German officials at Apia, Samoa, became increasingly strained. Late in the winter of 1889, at the behest of the American consul in Samoa. *Vandalia*, *Trenton*, and *Nipsic* sailed for Samoa and reached Apia Harbor early in March to balance the presence of the German vessels SMS *Adler*, *Olga*, and *Eber*. The British were ably represented by HMS *Calliope*. On 15 and 16 March 1889, each of these vessels suddenly became trapped in the harbor when violent, hurricane-force winds roared out of the northeast, driving mountainous waves before them. *Adler*, *Olga*, and *Eber* were all either sunk or hopelessly grounded and torn apart on the sharp reef, and together lost a total of 150 officers and crew killed. The powerful engines of *Calliope* barely enabled the vessel to get to sea in a dramatic performance that drew cheers from the crews of the American vessels. However, despite heroic efforts by the officers and crews of *Vandalia* and *Trenton*, the two vessels tore their bottoms out upon the reef on 16 March. *Vandalia* struck at about noon and sank until her docks were completely awash, forcing her crew to

scramble into the rigging. *Trenton* grounded alongside *Vandalia* at 2200 that evening, but enough of her main deck remained above water to allow *Vandalia*'s crew to climb on board. After the hurricane began *Nipsic* was driven ashore on a sandy beach and was later salvaged.

American casualties totalled 49 killed, 43 from *Vandalia* alone. The survivors from *Vanadalia*, *Trenton*, and *Nipsic* soon sailed for Mare Island on board a chartered steamer, but *Vandalia* and *Trenton* themselves were so battered that they were soon dismantled and their scrap donated to the Samoans.

III

(IX–191: dp. 22,491; l. 516'6''; b. 68'1''; dr. 28'8''; s. 10 k.; cpl. 105; a. 1 4'', 1 3'')

Walter Jennings—a twin-screw, steel-hulled tanker completed in 1921 by the Federal Shipbuilding Co. of Newark, N.J., for the Standard Oil (New Jersey) Co.—served under the aegis of Standard Oil through the 1920's and 1930's. Allocated to the Navy by the Maritime Commission's War Shipping Administration in late 1944, the ship was renamed *Vandalia* on 18 October 1944, being designated as an "unspecified auxiliary" (IX), and given the classification IX–191. She was accordingly taken over from the War Shipping Administration on 23 December 1944 and was commissioned on the same day, Lt. R. P. Morrison, USNR, in command, at Pearl Harbor, Hawaii.

She departed Pearl Harbor on 27 February 1945 for Eniwetok in the Marshalls and made port on 11 March Routed to Saipan with a Marianas-bound convoy, *Vandalia* developed an engine casualty and was forced to reverse course and turn back to Eniwetok for repairs The vessel got underway on 18 March but was rerouted on the 23d to Ulithi in the Carolines. Entering the harbor at her destination two days later, she proceeded to her assigned berth—remaining there into the summer as station tanker at Ulithi.

She subsequently shifted to Buckner Bay, Okinawa, to serve as storage tanker there in September. On 9 October, a particularly heavy and violent typhoon swept over Okinawa. *Vandalia* ran aground at 1518, coming to rest about 200 yards from Miyegusuku lighthouse on Naha Island and sinking rapidly. The 40-knot winds lashed the ship, and heavy seas pounded the old tanker unmercifully. One engine failed, and the ship went out of control, carried along with the fury of the typhoon, as the ship's force determinedly tried to pump out the engine room, fire room, and after compartments. She came to rest listing to starboard, and the danger immediately confronting the commanding officer, Lt. John F. Auge, USNR, was that of the ship capsizing. Accordingly, Auge gave the order to abandon ship—which was done by 0740 on the 10th. There were no casualties.

Auge observed that the ship appeared to be damaged beyond economical repair but nonetheless stationed a guard on board to prevent pilferage. A guard was retained on board until 20 November when, after stripping her of whatever remained of value, *Vandalia* was decommissioned and abandoned.

Struck from the Navy list on 5 December 1945, the tanker was eventually purchased by the China Merchants and Engineers, Inc., for scrap, on 31 December 1948.

IV

(PC-1175: dp. 280; l. 173'8''; b. 23'0''; dr. 10'10''; s. 20.2 k. (tl.); cpl. 65; a. 1 3'', 1 40mm., 1 dcp. (Mousetrap), 2 dct.; cl. *PC-461*)

PC-1175 was laid down on 8 June 1943 at Sturgeon Bay, Wis., by the Leathem D. Smith Shipbuilding Co.; launched on 7 August 1943; sponsored by Miss Joan Burgess; and commissioned on 1 December 1943 at New Orleans, Lt. Peter J. Brennan, USNR, in command.

The submarine chaser soon moved to Miami, Fla., for operational training and then to Kest West for shakedown. On 23 January 1944, she embarked upon her first mission, escorting a convoy on the Key West-to-Galveston leg of its voyage. For the next four months, she served under the operational control of the Commander, Gulf Sea Frontier. Her duties consisted of escort missions for coastwise convoys in the Gulf of Mexico and frequently involved runs from gulf coast ports to the Canal Zone.

On 28 May, the submarine chaser departed Key West to escort the French submarine *Le Centaure* to New York. After arriving there on 1 June, she changed operational control from the Gulf Sea Frontier to the Eastern Sea Frontier. Though her theater of operations changed, *PC-1175*'s duties remained the same—escorting coastal convoys and conducting antisubmarine patrols. When not engaged in her usual round-trip escort missions between New York and Guantanamo Bay, Cuba, *PC-1175* conducted antisubmarine warfare (ASW) training—most frequently in Long Island Sound but occasionally out of Guantanamo Bay—or made offensive ASW patrols in PC units built around a gunboat or a frigate.

Late in the spring of 1945, the ship received orders to duty with the Pacific Fleet Service Force. Departing New York on 8 June, the submarine chaser transited the Panama Canal at mid-month and arrived in San Diego on the 27th. Four days later, on 1 July, she departed San Diego for duty in the Central Pacific. After a 10-day stop at Pearl Harbor from 9 to 19 July, she resumed her voyage and arrived in Eniwetok lagoon on the 29th. After a week at Eniwetok, *PC-1175* got underway for the Marianas on 5 August. Three days later, she arrived at Saipan where she remained for another three days before returning to sea, bound for the Volcano Islands. She made Iwo Jima on 16 August, the day after the cessation of hostilities in the Pacific. She patrolled the waters around Iwo Jima for four days and then headed back toward the Marianas on the 20th. The subchaser reached Saipan on 23 August and took up patrol duty once again, this time in the waters around that island and Tinian. On 6 September, four days after the formal Japanese surrender ceremony in Toyko Bay, *PC-1175* departed Saipan, bound for Okinawa. She made a brief stop at Iwo Jima on 8 September and arrived off Hagushi beach on 12 September.

The submarine chaser spent most of the first year of peace patrolling the Central Pacific. She visited the Volcano and Bonin Islands, the Marianas, and the Carolines. On 25 May 1946, the submarine chaser stood out of Guam on the first leg of her voyage home. However, engine failure interrupted that voyage on 28 May; and *PC-1175* had to lay to until the next day when *Sylvania* (AKA-44) took her in tow. The two ships entered the lagoon at Eniwetok on the last day of May, and *PC-1175* began repairs to her engines immediately. Those repairs were completed by 4 June, and she resumed her homeward-bound voyage on that same day. The warship made a five-day stopover at Pearl Harbor between 11 and 16 June and then continued on to the west coast. She arrived at Astoria, Oreg., on 23 June and, four days later, moved to Portland for additional yard work at the Commercial Iron Works. She completed those repairs on 10 August and moved, under tow, back to Astoria. On 16 August 1946, *PC-1175* was placed out of commission at Astoria and was berthed with the Columbia River Group, Pacific Reserve Fleet. She remained there for the next 11 years. On 15 February 1956, she was named *Vandalia*; and, in July 1957, she was transferred, on a loan basis, to the Taiwan Navy. She served Taiwan as *Han Kiang* (PC-124). During that service, probably sometime late in 1968 or early in 1969, she ran aground and was severely damaged. Her name was struck from the Navy list on 15 June 1969, and her wreck was sold to the Taiwan Government for scrapping.

Vandenberg, Hoyt S., see *General Hoyt S. Vandenberg*.

Vanderbilt

Cornelius Vanderbilt—born on 27 May 1794 on Staten Island, N.Y.—began his career ferrying freight from Staten Island to New York City. About a decade later, he and Thomas Gibbons challenged Robert Fulton's monopoly of commercial navigation of New York State waters. Fulton's monopoly was eventually overturned by the Supreme Court in *Gibbons* v. *Ogden* (1824) in a landmark case defining federal power over interstate commerce. Soon after this decision, Vanderbilt embarked upon an ambitious, worldwide, steamboat enterprise of his own in which he acquired the nickname "Commodore" along with a reputation for toughness and determination.

In the 1860's, Commodore Vanderbilt diversified into railroads. He bought up small, unprofitable lines and joined them to form the New York Central Railroad System. During the financial panic of 1873, he sponsored building projects that alleviated the effects of the panic in New York City. He subsequently donated one million dollars to Central University—which thereafter was called Vanderbilt University—in Nashville, Tenn. He died in New York City on 4 January 1877.

(SwStr.: dp. 3,360; l. 331'; b. 47'6''; dr. 19'; s. 14 k.; a. 2 100-pdr. P.r., 12 9'' D.sb., 1 12-pdr.)

Vanderbilt—originally a transatlantic passenger and mail steamer—was built by Jeremiah Simonson of Greenpoint, Long Island, N.Y., in 1856 and 1857; chartered by the Army shortly after the start of the Civil War in April 1861; offered to the Army by her owner, Commodore Cornelius Vanderbilt, in early 1862; and transferred to the Navy on 24 March.

A wartime view of USS *Vanderbilt*.

Popularly known as "Vanderbilt's Yacht," the former flagship of Commodore Cornelius Vanderbilt's North Atlantic Mail Steamship Line began her military career in Hampton Roads, Va., intended for use as a ram against the Confederate ironclad CSS *Virginia*. Commodore Vanderbilt, himself, suggested filling the bow of the vessel with concrete and reenforcing it with iron plating. This was not done, however, and *Vanderbilt* was turned over to the Navy on 24 March and fitted with a heavy battery of 15 guns at the New York Navy Yard during the summer of 1862. She left New York on 10 November and—after conducting a brief search for CSS *Alabama*, the most destructive Confederate commerce raider of the entire war—put into Hampton Roads on 17 January 1863.

Ten days later, *Vanderbilt* received orders to conduct a much longer and more thorough search for *Alabama*. This year-long cruise took the vessel to the West Indies, eastern coast of South America, Cape of Good Hope, St. Helena, Cape Verde, the Canary Islands, Spain and Portugal. During the West Indies portion of her deployment, *Vanderbilt* served as flagship of Commodore Charles Wilkes' Flying Squadron. During the search, *Vanderbilt* captured the blockade-running British steamer *Peterhoff* on 25 February, off St. Thomas, Virgin Islands, causing a dispute between the British and Americans as to the disposition of mail carried aboard the steamer. President Lincoln eventually ordered the mail returned to the British. *Vanderbilt*'s captures also included the British blockade runner *Gertrude*, taken off Eleuthera Island in the Bahamas on 16 April, and the British bark *Saxon*, seized at Angra Peguena, Africa, on 30 October. *Saxon* was suspected of having rendezvoused with and taken cargo off CSS *Tuscaloosa* earlier. However, pursuing leads as to the whereabouts of *Alabama*, herself, became increasingly frustrating as *Vanderbilt* would often arrive at a port only to discover that her quarry had departed only a few hours earlier. She eventually returned to New York in January 1864 for repairs without ever having sighted the Confederate vessel.

Vanderbilt left New York in September and cruised off Halifax, Nova Scotia, searching for blockade runners. The Halifax-Wilmington, N.C., route for blockade runners was used heavily at this time owing to outbreaks of yellow fever at Bermuda and Nassau. Nevertheless, the Union cruiser failed to take any prizes and put into Boston, Mass., on 13 October. She was deployed with the blockade off Wilmington in November and participated in the unsuccessful first amphibious assault upon Confederate Fort Fisher in the Cape Fear River, N.C., on 24 and 25 December. The Fleet took the fort during a second amphibious assault on 13 and 15 January 1865. *Vanderbilt* returned to New York in late January, remaining until 24 March when she left for the Gulf of Mexico ferrying new recruits. From there, she proceeded to Charleston, S.C., towing the uncompleted Confederate ram *Columbia* from Charleston to Norfolk in May, and towed the *Onondaga* from Norfolk to New York in June. *Vanderbilt* served as a receiving ship at the Portsmouth (N.H.) Navy Yard during the summer of 1865.

The Civil War now over, *Vanderbilt* sailed from Portsmouth on 14 August and put into the Philadelphia Navy Yard on 27 August to be fitted out for a cruise around Cape Horn. She left Philadelphia on 25 October and arrived in Hampton Roads three days later. There, she was designated flagship of a special squadron consisting of herself, *Tuscarora*, *Powhatan*, and *Monadnock*. The squadron was commanded by Commodore John Rodgers and intended to increase the Pacific Squadron to a 14-ship force. The vessels left Hampton Roads on 2 November and arrived at San Francisco, Calif., on 21 June 1866 after stopping at most major South American ports while circumnavigating the South American continent.

Vanderbilt was decommissioned at Mare Island, Calif., on 30 June, but was soon recommissioned and, on 13 October, sailed from San Francisco to Honolulu, Hawaii, with the Hawaiian monarch, Queen Emma, on board. The cruiser returned to San Francisco on 3 December and remained there at anchor until placed in ordinary at Mare Island on 24 May 1867. She lay there, in ordinary, until sold on 1 April 1873 to Howe & Company of San Francisco. Her new owners removed her machinery, gave her a graceful clipper bow, and full rigging. Renamed *Three Brothers*, she spent most of her time in the grain trade between San Francisco, Le Havre, Liverpool, and New York where she acquired an enviable reputation for speed and handling. "Vanderbilt's Yacht" served successive owners until 1899, at which time the vessel, now a coal hulk, was sold for scrap at Gilbraltar.

Vanderburgh

A county in the far southwestern corner of Indiana bounded on the south by the Ohio River. The city of Evansville is situated in Vanderburgh County and takes up much of its area.

(APB–48: dp. 4,080 (lim.); l. 328'0''; b. 50'0''; dr. 11'2'' (lim.); s. 10 k. (tl.); cpl. 137; trp. 302; a. 8 40mm.; cl. *Benewah*)

Vanderburgh (APB–48)—a tank landing ship converted during construction to a self-propelled barracks ship—was laid down on 12 January 1945 at Evansville, Ind., by the Missouri Valley Bridge & Iron Co.; launched on 20 April 1945; sponsored by Mrs. C. A. Bailey; and commissioned at New Orleans on 3 July 1945.

The ship conducted brief shakedown training late in July and, in mid-August, headed via the Panama Canal Zone for Hawaii. *Vanderburgh* arrived at Pearl Harbor on 2 September where she stopped for six days before continuing on to the Far East for duty supporting American occupation forces there. After stops at Eniwetok and Guam, she arrived in Sasebo, Japan, on 2 October. *Vanderburgh* remained briefly at Sasebo before moving to Hiro Wan, a bay on Japan's Inland Sea near Hiroshima and Kure. She remained there, providing living quarters for occupation personnel until early 1946. At that time, the ship headed eastward, stopped at Pearl Harbor, and arrived at San Francisco on 8 April 1946.

There, she began temporary duty as accommodation ship and simultaneously began preparations for inactivation. On 30 January 1947, she was placed out of commission and was berthed in Stockton, Calif., in the Pacific Reserve Fleet. She remained in reserve until 1 April 1972 when her name was struck from the Navy list. On 15 November 1972, the former *Vanderburgh* was sold to Mr. Ronald M. Fraser, of Portland, Oreg., for scrapping.

Vandivier

Norman Francis Vandivier—born on 10 March 1916 in Edwards, Miss.—entered the Indiana National Guard in 1935 and was promoted to corporal before he completed his enlistment on 1 July 1938. He enlisted in the Navy on 6 July 1939 at Grosse Ile, Mich., for aviation training and was enrolled as a seaman second class. On 20 October, Vandivier took the oath of office as an aviation cadet in the Naval Reserve and soon began pilot training at the Naval Air Station, Pensacola, Fla. He received his wings on 21 May 1940 when he was designated a naval aviator. At the completion of additional training, he was commissioned an ensign in the Naval Reserve on 28 June 1940. That same day, he was assigned to Bombing Squadron 6 on board the carrier *Enterprise* (CV–6) to which he reported on 1 August.

Ens. Vandivier served in *Enterprise* throughout his brief naval career. Between August 1940 and December 1941, he flew training missions from her flight deck and cruised between the islands of the Pacific. However, during those relatively idyllic months, relations between the United States and Japan steadily deteriorated. On the morning of 7 December 1941, events came to a head when the Japanese launched a surprise air attack on Pearl Harbor.

At that time, Ens. Vandivier was on board *Enterprise* which was some 200 miles from the battle and on her way back to Hawaii after ferrying Marine Corps Fighter Squadron 211 to Wake Island. Rather than return to port, *Enterprise* conducted a fruitless search for the attacking enemy force. She finally put into Pearl Harbor on the afternoon of 8 December to refuel and replenish before again getting underway the next morning to resume patrols which continued through the end of the year.

On 11 January 1942, the carrier departed Pearl Harbor to assist *Yorktown*'s task force in protecting a reinforcement convoy which safely disembarked its marines at Samoa on the 23d.

Two days later, the *Enterprise* task force was ordered to head for the Marshall Islands and begin America's first offensive action against the Japanese Empire. Bombing Squadron 6 flew off *Enterprise* just before dawn on 1 February, and its three divisions winged toward Kwajalein. Ens. Vandivier and his comrades reached that atoll just before 0730, divided themselves into two flights, and immediately began their attack. Vandivier flew the second plane in the 2d division, and so his was probably the 7th or 8th plane to dive on the ships and installations located near and on Kwajalein islet at the extreme southeastern end of the atoll. Because of the fires and smoke caused by his predecessors' bombs and the dangerously low altitude to which he dove before dropping his bombs, the results of Ens. Vandivier's drop were not readily discernible. However, the fact that he continued his dive until almost the last possible moment makes it highly probable that his attack was successful. Later, he was credited with a near miss on a cargo ship. Subsequently, he destroyed a barracks and received the Air Medal for ". . . meritorious conduct . . ." during the raid.

Ens. Vandivier landed on *Enterprise* around 0900. Within 45 minutes, his plane was rearmed, refueled, and back in the air making for Maloelap Atoll. At 1030, he followed his division leader into a steep dive on Taroa islet and delivered another successful attack on enemy installations. After that raid, Vandivier returned to his ship which rapidly moved out of the area.

The young Navy pilot's next action came on 25 February when Bombing Squadron 6 and Scouting Squadron 6 flew off *Enterprise* to bomb Wake Island, by then in Japanese possession. A week later, he rose from *Enterprise*'s flight deck to strike Marcus Island. While this attack, like the one on Wake, was of limited strategic value, the entire series of raids offered Ens. Vandivier and his comrades invaluable flying experience.

In April, *Enterprise* provided air cover for *Hornet* (CV–8) which was carrying 16 Army, twin-engine B-25's under the command of Lt. Col. James Doolittle. Ens. Vandivier made his closest approach to Japan on 18 April when the bombers rose from *Hornet* to make their daring one-way raid on Tokyo. Immediately after the launch, the two carriers and their escorts reversed course and cleared the area. Vandivier reentered Pearl on 25 April. Five days later, *Enterprise* took the flyer to sea once more and raced to reinforce carriers *Lexington* (CV–2) and *Yorktown* (CV–5) in the South Pacific. However, time and distance conspired to prevent Ens. Vandivier from participating in the Battle of the Coral Sea—which ended before his ship could reach the area—and she was ordered back to Hawaii to ready herself for an even more important mission.

Enterprise returned to Pearl Harbor on 26 May. Ens. Vandivier and his shipmates began feverish preparations to meet an expected Japanese thrust at Midway Island. Two days later, his ship headed back to sea to take station off Midway. On the 30th, *Yorktown* put to sea to join *Hornet* and *Enterprise* some 235 miles northeast of Midway. Planes from the three carriers searched diligently for the enemy force during the next three days; but it was a Midway-based PBY Catalina flying boat that made first contact with the Japanese invasion force on the morning of 3 June, about 700 miles from the island.

While Midway-based bombers attacked the enemy transport force that afternoon, Ens. Vandivier waited with the other pilots for news of their own special targets—the Japanese carriers. At 0545 the following morning, another Catalina from Midway found the enemy flattops. *Enterprise* and *Hornet* raced to close the Japanese while *Yorktown* recovered search planes.

At about 0705, *Enterprise* planes began rumbling down her flight deck and wobbling into the air. By 0730, the whole attack group was aloft. As they made off to attack the enemy, Ens. Vandivier formed his SBD Dauntless dive bomber up with the other planes of Bombing 6's 3d Division. Led by the carrier's group commander, Lt. Comdr. Clarence "Wade" McClusky, the formation winged its way toward the enemy carrier striking force, composed of four of the six carriers which had attacked Pearl Harbor.

At 0920 when the planes reached the point where they expected to find the enemy carriers, the airmen gazed down upon empty ocean. At this point, the air group commander made a hard decision. His planes were low on fuel; and, if they initiated a search, some aircraft might not make it back to the carriers. On the other hand, if the strike returned to *Enterprise* and missed the enemy carriers, Midway might fall. Worse yet, Japanese bombers might knock out *Enterprise*, *Hornet*, and *Yorktown*, leaving little or nothing between America and the forces of the Japanese Empire. Therefore, the American pilots ignored their fuel problem and began searching for the enemy. At 1005, they spied, on the horizon to the northwest, the silhouettes of three large carriers and a number of escorts. At first, several pilots thought that their leader had brought them back to their own ships; but closer inspection revealed pagoda masts and yellow flight decks. These ships could only be Japanese.

As the attack commenced, the Dauntless dive bombers of Bombing 6 jockeyed for position with those of Scouting 6. Vandivier's division followed the 2d division whose commander saw that many of Scouting 6's bombs were only near missing the "left hand" aircraft carrier —now known to have been Nagumo's flagship *Akagi*. Rather than follow the 1st division in its attack on *Kaga*, which seemed well taken care of with critical hits, the 2d and 3d divisions bore down on *Akagi*. In due course, it was Ens. Vandivier's turn. Over he went and then down, toward the flagship of the Pearl Harbor attack force. He released his bomb—whether or not it was a hit or a near miss will never be known—and pulled out of the dive. He banked his plane and headed home. He later reported by radio that he was making a water landing, but he and his gunner were never seen nor heard of again.

In spite of a critical fuel shortage, Vandivier had pressed home his attack against the flagship of Japan's main carrier strength. His bravery is indicative of the spirit and determination which, perhaps above all else, won the crucial Battle of Midway for America and paved the way for ultimate victory. For his selfless contributions to that victory, Ens. Vandivier—promoted to lieutenant (junior grade) on 30 June 1942 retroactively to 15 April 1942—was awarded the Navy Cross Medal, posthumously, for ". . . extraordinary heroism and distinguished service. . . ."

(DER–540: dp. 1,350; l. 306'0''; b. 36'7''; dr. 13'4''; s. 24.3 k. (tl.); cpl. 222; a. 2 5'', 1 dct., 1 dcp. (hh.); cl. *Wagner*)

Vandivier (DER–540) was laid down at the Boston Navy Yard on 8 November 1943 as a *John C. Butler*-class destroyer escort DE–540; launched on 27 December 1943; and was sponsored by Mrs. Mary Hardin Vandivier. Since World War II came to an end before she was completed, work on her gradually tapered off and was finally suspended on 17 February 1947. Seven years later, on 1 July 1954, work was resumed to complete her and to convert her to a destroyer escort radar picket ship. She was redesignated DER–540 on 2 September 1954 and was placed in commission on 11 October 1955, Lt. Comdr. Frank B. Correia in command.

During the remainder of 1955, *Vandivier* completed outfitting at Boston, moved to Newport, R.I., and prepared for her shakedown cruise. On 14 January 1956, she cleared Newport to conduct her shakedown training in the West Indies. Over the next two months, she operated in the vicinity of Roosevelt Roads, P.R., and near Guantanamo Bay, Cuba. She also made port visits to Ponce and San Juan in Puerto Rico as well as to Guantanamo Bay and Havana in Cuba.

On 15 March, *Vandivier* departed Havana to return to New England. She arrived at Boston on the 20th and underwent post-shakedown availability there until the second week in April, when she returned to Newport to begin duty as a radar picket ship with the Atlantic Fleet.

Throughout her brief Navy career as an active unit of the fleet, *Vandivier* served along the Atlantic seaboard and operated out of Newport. Her duties consisted solely of patrols off the coast as a sea-going extension of the distant early warning system during the height of the Cold War. She cruised on station for periods of approximately two weeks in duration while her radar equipment scanned the horizon for any airborne intruders—missiles or planes. When not on station, she conducted upkeep in port at Newport and made special event cruises. In 1956, she conducted cruises for the American Society of Planners and for women officer candidates as well as for her crewmen's families.

She began 1957 with duty on the picket station between 2 and 16 January and again from 28 January to 7 February. Following upkeep and a three-month overhaul, she headed south to Guantanamo Bay, Cuba, on 10 June. Arriving there four days later, *Vandivier* conducted refresher training until mid-July. On the 12th, she departed Cuban waters to return north. After a brief stopover at Norfolk, she continued north to Fall River, Mass. Upon completion of the availability, the ship got underway on 1 August and steamed toward Rockland, Maine, to participate in the Maine Seafood Festival. On 4 August, she put to sea to resume radar picket duty. For the remainder of the year, *Vandivier* alternated between two-week tours of duty on the picket line with one-week in-port periods at Newport.

The year 1958 began much the same way as the previous year ended. Until May, the warship stood 14-day watches on the radar picket station followed by a week of upkeep in Newport. On 8 May, she stood out of Newport for a visit to Bermuda in the British West Indies. After a three-day visit, she resumed her routine on the so-called Atlantic Barrier Patrol until September. On 20 September, she had the honor of escorting President Dwight D. Eisenhower during the America's Cup Races held off Narragansett Bay. On the following day, *Vandivier* resumed duty guarding the country from the threat of aerial sneak attack.

That duty occupied her for the remainder of 1958 and all of 1959. Throughout 1959, only two events varied her routine of radar picket operation out of Newport. In April, she made a two-day visit to Bermuda; and, on 5 September, she made another dependents' cruise for the families of her officers and men. Otherwise, it was business as usual—two weeks on station followed by a week in Newport—with periodic availabilities thrown in for good measure. The year 1960 brought more of the same duty but only for part of the year. On 30 June 1960, after all preparations,

Vandivier was decommissioned and placed in reserve with the Philidelphia Group, Atlantic Reserve Fleet. *Vandivier* remained in reserve until late 1974 when she was sunk as a target. Her name was struck from the Navy list on 1 November 1974.

Vanguard

A satellite launching system developed by the Naval Research Laboratory for the International Geophysical Year of 1957 and 1958.

Mission San Fernando (T–AO–122) (*q.v.*) was converted to a missile range instrumentation ship in 1964 and 1965 and was renamed *Vanguard* (T–AGM–19) on 1 September 1965.

Vara

Vara—a yacht constructed in 1929 at Bristol, R.I., by the Herreshoff Manufacturing Co.—was acquired by the Navy from Harold S. Vanderbilt on 7 October 1940. Converted for naval service by the New York Navy Yard, the ship was reclassified as a patrol craft and commissioned as *PC–509* on 27 December 1941. She was subsequently renamed *Valiant* (*q.v.*) on 15 July 1943 and simultaneously reclassified as PYc–51.

Varian

Bertram Stetson Varian, Jr.—born on 26 November 1920 at Weiser, Idaho—enlisted in the Navy as a seaman 2d class on 3 December 1940 at Boise, Idaho, and received an appointment as aviation cadet on 15 February of the following year. Following flight training at Pensacola, Fla., he was designated a naval aviator on 8 September 1941 and was commissioned an ensign in the Naval Reserve on 4 October.

Varian received further instruction with the Advanced Carrier Training Group and reported to *Enterprise* (CV–6) on 3 April 1942, joining Bombing Squadron (VB) 6. Flying from *Enterprise* during the pivotal Battle of Midway on 5 June 1942, he flew with the third division of "Bombing Six" in their attack against the Japanese carrier *Akagi*. VB–6 pressed home their attack—often diving to very low altitudes to ensure their bomb's delivery—and severely crippled Vice Admiral Chuichi Nagumo's flagship.

The victory had not been attained without cost, however, as only a third of the 15 Douglas SBD Dauntlesses that *Enterprise* launched earlier that day returned to their carrier. Among those lost were Ensign Varian and his gunner, ARM3c C. R. Young, who were forced to take to their rubber boat when their plane ditched 50 miles northeast of the Japanese task force. They were never seen again.

For his "extraordinary heroism" and "distinguished service" in pressing home his attack against heavy odds and knowing that very little fuel remained with which to return to friendly forces, Ensign Varian received a posthumous Navy Cross.

(DE–798: dp. 1,400; l. 306'; b. 36'10''; dr. 9'5'' (mean); s. 24 k.; cpl. 186; a. 3 3'', 4 1.1'', 8 20mm., 2 dct., 8 dcp., 1 dcp. (hh.); cl. *Buckley*)

Varian (DE–798) was laid down on 27 August 1943 at Orange, Tex., by the Consolidated Steel Corp.; launched on 6 November 1943; sponsored by Mrs. Arnold F. Brunkow, sister of the late Ens. Varian; and commissioned on 29 February 1944, Lt. Comdr. C. W. Petrie, USNR, in command.

After fitting out, *Varian* conducted shakedown out of Bermuda for the last half of the month of March 1944. She then joined the homeward-bound ships of Convoy GUS–33 on 30 March and helped to escort them to Hampton Roads, Va. Following repairs at Boston and further training out of Casco Bay, *Varian* shifted south and rendezvoused with Mediterranean-bound Convoy UGS–44 on 2 June. After subsequently shepherding GUS–44 from Bizerte to Hampton Roads, the destroyer escort arrived at New York on 18 July. She then conducted two more round-trip convoy missions, with UGS/GUS–51 from mid-August to mid-September and with UGS/GUS–58 until mid-November, before she was assigned to the first "hunter-killer" group—formed on 30 November 1944 to track down and destroy enemy submarines.

Varian and her sisters accordingly underwent intensive training for 26 days. They received special instruction, principally in high-frequency direction finding and gunnery; and spent 60 hours perfecting unit tactics for coordinated attacks on maneuvering submarines. Before they put to sea, the ships—grouped as Task Unit (TU) 27.1.1—practiced every type of known antisubmarine warfare attack, rehearsing them in simulated operating conditions.

In less than a month after TU 27.1.1's departure from Casco Bay on the day after Christmas of 1944, the new, crack unit proved the "hunter-killer" concept valid. On the morning of 16 January 1945, *Varian*, *Hayter* (DE–212), *Otter* (DE–210), and *Harry E. Hubbard* (DE–748) hunted down *U–248* and sank her after a dogged two-hour hunt, 500 miles north of the Azores. A little over three months later, on 24 April, *Varian* and nine other DE's tracked down the U-boat that had recently torpedoed *Frederick C. Davis* (DE–136). The 10 American DE's avenged their sister's loss with a punishing depth charge barrage that forced *U–546* to the surface, where the DE's then destroyed her with gunfire. *Varian* picked up nine survivors.

The end of the war in Europe on 7 May 1945 saw many of Germany's U-boat fleet still at sea. On 12 May, *Varian* rendezvoused with one of these *unterseebooten*, *U–805*, and a party from the destroyer escort, led by Lt. (jg.) Earl D. Stevenson, USNR, boarded the submarine and brought her to the east coast.

Following upkeep at the Boston Navy Yard, *Varian* got underway on 23 May and proceeded via New York to Hampton Roads. Shifting to Miami, Fla., soon thereafter, the destroyer escort operated in a training role, providing practical experience for newly commissioned officers until 16 July. The next day, earmarked for conversion to a radar picket ship, *Varian* arrived at Charleston for availability. However, her conversion was cancelled; and the ship soon resumed training operations in the Caribbean.

On 2 September, the ship departed Culebra, Puerto Rico, and she steamed north to New London, Conn., for training duty with Atlantic Fleet submarines. At New Haven, Conn., for Navy Day festivities, *Varian* subsequently sailed south for inactivation at Green Cove Springs near Jacksonville, Fla. Arriving there, via Boston, on 27 November, *Varian* was decommissioned on 15 March 1946 and placed in reserve. She was later shifted to the Texas group of the Reserve Fleet at Orange. There, she remained through the 1960's. Struck from the Navy list on 1 December 1972, *Varian* was sold on 12 January 1974 to the Southern Scrap Metal Co., Ltd., of New Orleans, for scrapping. Towed by three tugs, the erstwhile U-boat killer began her final voyage on 31 January.

Varian received two battle stars for her World War II service.

Varuna

A Vedic god—originally of the sky but later of the god of waters—who guarded immortality, truth, and right and punished evildoers.

I

(ScGbt.: t. 1,300; l. 218'; b. 34'8''; dph. 18'3''; a. 8 8'', 2 30-pdr. P.r.)

The first *Varuna*—originally intended for merchant

Artist's impression of the steam gunboat *Varuna* during her brief service with the West Gulf Blockading Squadron.

service between New York and New Orleans—was laid down in late January or early February 1861 at the Mallory Yard, Mystic, Conn.; launched there in the following September; and purchased by the Navy at New York City on 31 December of that same year.

On 10 February 1862, she was ordered to remain in New York until *Monitor* was ready for action so that she might escort the new ironclad from New York to Hampton Roads, Va., to protect the wooden-hulled Union blockaders there from the Southern armored ram, CSS *Virginia*. However, these orders were revoked later that same day; and *Varuna* was assigned to the newly established West Gulf Blockading Squadron. En route south late in February, *Varuna* put into Port Royal, S.C., for repairs, where ship's commanding officer, Commander Charles S. Boggs, assumed temporary command of the harbor on 24 February during Flag Officer Samuel F. Du Pont's absence. The gunboat finally joined Rear Admiral David G. Farragut's West Gulf Blockading Squadon on 6 March.

On 24 April, *Varuna* was with the squadron during Farragut's daring nighttime dash past Confederate works guarding the Mississippi below New Orleans— Fort Jackson and Fort St. Philip. At the height of the melee, *Varuna* was rammed twice by the steamer CSS *Governor Moore* and struck twice again immediately thereafter by the cottonclad ram CSS *Stonewall Jackson*. After striking *Varuna*, Lt. Beverly Kennon, CSN in command of one of the Confederate warships, *Governor Moore*—found himself unable to depress his guns far enough to fire upon the Union vessel; and so he shot through the bow of his own ship and used the resulting hole as a gun port. Although fatally damaged, *Varuna* backed off from the Confederate vessels and continued to subject them to a withering fire until rising water silenced her guns. Her determined fight contributed greatly to Farragut's complete victory on the lower Mississippi.

Rear Admiral Farragut's stunning victory and subsequent capture of New Orleans, itself, electrified the North. *Varuna*'s part in the Union triumph was soon commemorated in George H. Bowker's poem, *The Varuna*, which appeared in the *Philadelphia Press* on 12 May.

II

(AGP–5: dp. 3,960; l. 328'; b. 50'; dr. 13'6''; s. 12 k.; cpl. 283; a. 1 3'', 8 40mm., 8 20mm.; cl. *Portunus*)

LST–14 was laid down on 23 August 1942 at Neville Island, Pa., by the Dravo Shipbuilding Yard; launched on 9 December 1942; sponsored by Mrs. R. J. Mitchell; renamed *Varuna* and designated AGP–5 on 13 January 1943; completed as an LST by Dravo on 26 March 1943 and placed in reduced commission on that date; towed to Tampa, Fla., where she was converted to a motor torpedo boat tender (AGP); and commissioned on 31 August 1943, Lt. Comdr. L. W. Borst, USNR, in command.

Following her shakedown in the Gulf of Mexico, *Varuna* sailed for the Pacific on 4 October and proceeded via Guantanamo Bay, Cuba, to the Panama Canal which she transited on the 22d. When two days out of Balboa, the ship left the convoy to receive an emergency appendectomy patient from *LST–219*. Following a successful transfer, and while steaming to rejoin the convoy, *Varuna* and *LST–219* collided on 27 October. There were no casualties in either ship, but the damage sustained forced both vessels to return to Panama for repairs.

Drydocked at Balboa from 9 to 20 November, *Varuna* got underway on 3 December for the Society Islands and arrived at Bora Bora on Christmas Eve. She remained there until the 28th, when she got underway on the second leg of her passage, and arrived at Pago Pago, Samoa, on 2 January 1944.

However, *Varuna* did not linger long in Samoan waters, for she pushed toward Suva, Fiji Islands, on 5 January and then proceeded via Noumea, New Caledonia, and Espiritu Santo, New Hebrides, to the Solomon Islands. She reached Lunga Point, Guadalcanal, on the 11th and then moved to Tulagi where she unloaded her cargo of motor torpedo boat (MTB) base equipment. Calling at Rendova harbor, Rendova Island, and later at Blanche harbor, Treasury Islands, *Varuna* conducted her first repair job on 17 February, when she repaired *PT–105*. She remained at the Blanche harbor base through the remainder of the month of

February—repairing an average of four PT-boats per day—before she shifted her operations to Nissan Harbor, Green Island.

Establishing the PT-boat base at Green Island, *Varuna* was now situated at the base perhaps nearest to Japanese territory. Located half-way between New Ireland and Bougainville—both occupied by the Japanese and both well north of the nearest Allied bases—Green Island served as a staging area for the five MTB squadrons attached to *Varuna*. These PT's were earmarked to harass the Japanese seaborne supply lane from New Britain, New Ireland, and the Shortlands, and to assist in the blockade of Rabaul.

The ship's historian later recorded that it was while at Green Island that "Tokyo Rose" first mentioned *Varuna*. The vessel had been cut off from vital supplies while at Green Island and had been unable to get any more—or so said "Rose." Several days later, as the historian recounted, a PC came alongside to offer *Varuna* a share of her own meager stores. "The *Varuna* declined with thanks," the historian wrote, saying that "she had plenty of everything."

Varuna operated out of Green Island until 31 July, when she returned to the Treasury Islands for a 20-day stay. Returning to Green, she loaded men and equipment of Motor Torpedo Boat Squadron (MTBRon) 27, and departed her estwhile base on the 24th, reaching Manus in the Admiralties two days later. Although initially slated to stage from there, a change of plan routed *Varuna* and her PT boats to Mios Woendi on the northern tip of New Guinea. Departing Manus on 7 September, the MTB tender and her brood—MTB-Rons 27 and 28—arrived at Mios Woendi on the 13th, via Humboldt Bay, New Guinea.

For the next 17 days, *Varuna* took on stores, fuel, water, and gasoline in preparation for her next operations and, in company with MTBRon 27, departed for the Palaus. Arriving in Kossol Roads on 1 October, the MTB tender set up shop providing support services for the PT's which had been assigned the task of patrolling the large fleet anchorage there. In addition, the "Peter Tares" (PT's) were to patrol and blockade the Japanese-held island of Babelthuap and other small islands of the group.

Varuna received a "flash red" alert on the 30th at 0855; and, while other ships got underway, she received orders to remain at anchor to act as communication link for screening vessels and the PT's and to render assistance as necessary. At 1220, the ship picked up a single twin-engined "Sally" coming in low and fast. It dropped one bomb near a floating drydock and roared on towards the anchored MTB tender. *Varuna* opened fire with 3-inch, 40-millimeter, and 20-millimeter guns, repelling the attack by enveloping the plane in tracer fire and causing the attacker to veer off in the direction of Babelthuap.

Varuna remained at Kossol Roads until the day after Christmas 1944, when she sailed for San Pedro Bay, Leyte, arriving on 29 December. She remained in the bay until 25 January 1945, tending the boats from MTBRon 27 and repairing boats from other squadrons engaged in the local operations against the Japanese. In addition, towards the end of this period, *Varuna* staged for the invasion of Olongapo and Subic Bay on the island of Luzon.

She served in this support role in the capture of the Olongapo region, tending and repairing "Peter Tares." As American forces began their march to recapture Manila and the Bataan Peninsula, *Varuna*'s boats blockaded the Bataan shoreline, serving a dual purpose in keeping reinforcements from coming in and those trapped Japanese from getting out; blockading Corregidor and Fort Drum in Manila Bay; and patrolling the bay. This action continued until late in April, with *Varuna* remaining in Subic Bay until 5 May.

Following a period of repairs which included a dry-docking, the MTB tender anchored off Samar to prepare for the impending strike against the Japanese-held

island of Borneo. Departing Samar on 23 June, *Varuna* steamed singly for Tawi Tawi in the Sulu Archipelago, arriving on 26 June. She spent the following day fueling and making repairs to boats from MTBRons 10 and 27 before getting underway on the 28th.

Arriving off Balikpapan on 1 July, *Varuna* found that rough seas in Makassar Strait made docking of the PT's to be almost impossible. Allied forces meanwhile rapidly secured a beachhead, forcing the Japanese defenders into the hinterlands, and minesweeping operations cleared a channel to the inner harbor of Balikpapan. There, *Varuna* again set up shop to tend her group of torpedo boats. Up to this point, the Japanese had made little resistance from the air; but, late in July, the enemy began nearly continual air attacks for five days running. On one such attack, bombs splashed astern of *Varuna* but far enough away so as to not cause any damage.

Her boats, during this period, conducted regular patrols off the Borneo coast and across Makassar Strait to the Celebes. *Varuna* tended her brood, supporting their harassing activities to the enemy until 0237 on 15 August 1945, when word came to cease offensive action. Two atomic bombs and increased Allied pressures had forced Japan to accept the unconditional surrender terms of the Potsdam Declaration.

Varuna subsequently proceeded for Bobon Point, Samar, to assist in the decommissioning of PT boats. Arriving on 10 September, the MTB tender spent the next two months in the Philippines supporting this activity. On 20 November, she sailed for the United States and proceeded—via Guam, Pearl Harbor, and the Panama Canal—to New York City. Decommissioned on 4 January 1946, *Varuna* was struck from the Navy list on 1 May 1946 and sold to Stavenger Tankrederi for scrap soon thereafter.

Varuna received four battle stars for her World War II services.

Vashon

An island lying in Puget Sound, Wash., between the cities of Seattle and Tacoma. In 1792, the British sea captain, Capt. George Vancouver, named the island for his friend, Capt. James Vashon.

(YFB–19: dp. 20 (lt.); l. 65'; b. 17'; dr. 5'; cl. *Vashon*)

Vashon (YFB–19) was a wooden-hulled ferryboat completed at the Puget Sound Navy Yard, Bremerton, Wash., in April 1941. Placed in service in the spring of 1941, *Vashon* operated as a ferry craft attached to the 13th Naval District through World War II. Placed out of service, in reserve, in March 1948, *Vashon* was subsequently sold in July 1958. No details of her subsequent fate have been found.

Vassar, Matthew, see Matthew Vassar.

Vaud J.

(MB: t. 63 (gross); l. 101'0''; b. 19'8''; dr. 4'6'' (mean); s. 8.6 k.; cpl. 8; a. none)

Prior to World War I, *Vaud J.*—a wooden-hulled cabin motor launch built in 1907 at Wildwood, N.J., by Thomas Johnson—was owned by A. L. Dunn, of Govans, Md. The Navy inspected the motor boat on 8 April 1917 and deemed her "not suitable for either Army or Navy use." Apparently, the Navy later revised its appraisal since it again inspected the craft on 23 September 1918 at Bear Creek, near Baltimore, Md.

Acquired by the Navy soon thereafter, *Vaud J.* was taken over by the Navy on 27 September but not commissioned. Designated SP–3361, *Vaud J.* was assigned to the Bureau of Ordnance and towed to the Naval Proving Ground at Indian Head, Md., by the tug *Tioga* and operated there in connection with range construction work into the spring of 1919.

Sold on 30 June 1919 and simultaneously struck from the Navy list, *Vaud J.* became the property of the Chesapeake Water Supply Co. She was carried on lists of American merchant vessels into the early 1920's, but her owner was not listed. From 1924 to 1929, the craft was owned by Hurley Booye of Cape May, N.J., until either late 1929 or early 1930 when she was purchased by Harry Mogok of Cape May. *Vaud J.* operated until 1932, when her name disappears from the mercantile listings.

Vaux, Richard, see *Richard Vaux.*

Vedette

I

(ScStr.: t. 441; l. 199'6''; b. 26'0''; dr. 12'0''; cpl. 61; a. 3 3'', 2 Colt mg.; 10 mines)

Virginia—a steel-hulled, single-screw steam yacht designed by G. L. Watson and built at Bath, Maine, by Bath Iron Works for New York merchant Isaac Stern —was delivered on 23 December 1899. In 1916, the yacht was acquired by the financier and philanthropist Frederick W. Vanderbilt of New York City and renamed *Vedette.* The Navy acquired the ship from him on a free-lease basis on 4 May 1917. Earmarked for convoy escort and patrol duty overseas, *Vedette* was classified SP–163 and was commissioned at the New York Navy Yard on 28 May 1917, Lt. Comdr. Chester L. Hand in command.

Vedette and five other former yachts got underway from Tompkinsville, N.Y., bound for Bermuda on 9 June on the first leg of their voyage to France. *Sultana* (SP–134) and *Christabel* (SP–162) were the first to weigh anchor; *Harvard* (SP–209), *Kanawha* (SP–130), *Noma* (SP–131), and *Vedette* followed. The ships formed up into divisions, with *Vedette* leading the second group.

On the evening of the 12th, they anchored in St. George harbor and remained in Bermuda for a little over three days, coaling ship and taking on water. The vessels got underway again on the morning of the 16th and reached the Azores on the 25th.

After coaling and taking on water and provisions, *Vedette* and her consorts began their passage to Brest. En route, they soon encountered abundant evidence that they were entering a war zone. *Vedette* spotted "considerable floating wreckage and a cork life belt" upon which no name was visible on the evening of the 2d. The next morning, she spotted more of the same: boxes, barrels, a broken life-belt, and pieces of planking from an anonymous ship—or ships—mute evidence of a sinking. The squadron sighted the French coast at 0440 on 4 July; but, before they could make it into port, *Christabel* broke down; and *Vedette* stood by until her damaged consort could get underway again. Later, as the ships made their way toward Brest, a French torpedo boat came out and greeted the American force that was among the first ships of the United States Navy to reach French waters in World War I.

Over the next 10 days, *Vedette* prepared for the operations that lay ahead. She finally put to sea, in company with *Harvard,* on the morning of 16 July.

Her first patrol pretty much set the standard theme for the many that followed. The two ships initially headed for the middle of the patrol line 10 miles off the coast, extending from the northward and westward of Ushant to the southward of Belle Isle. *Vedette* patrolled the southern half of the line while *Harvard* prowled the northern. *Vedette* returned to Brest on the 19th, without having met the enemy, but she did encounter more wreckage, including life rings from an unidentified ship. She twice more patrolled the area

between Brest and Ushant, near Belle Isle, before the end of July.

Vedette remained in port the first few days of August, and she suffered slight damage on the morning of 3 August when *Christabel*—while shifting moorings— raked her stern, carrying away the flagstaff and damaging the after rail. Nevertheless, *Vedette* stood out to sea at 1700 that afternoon in the screen of an outward-bound convoy of 10 merchantmen which were also protected by *Harvard,* three French patrol vessels, and two British ships. *Vedette* left that convoy at 0050 on the 4th and patrolled the vicinity until 0650, when she picked up a Brest-bound convoy of 19 merchantmen escorted by three patrol boats. *Vedette* anchored at Brest at 1025 the same day, but her respite was short. Less than six hours later, she stood out with a convoy of 16 merchantmen, three French patrol boats, and *Harvard.*

Vedette left that convoy when it passed out of the coastal danger zone and waited to pick up a Brest-bound convoy at 1655 on the 5th. While en route in, *Harvard* broke down; and *Vedette* stood by until her longstanding partner was ready to proceed.

Still en route to Brest during the pre-dawn hours of 6 August, *Vedette* sighted a "suspicious vessel" at 0320 and opened fire with her number two 3-inch gun. The shot fell well forward of the stranger, who soon signalled that she was a French patrol boat. *Vedette*'s first shot of the war had been aimed at a "friendly" ship.

The yacht was docked at Brest shortly after noon that day for alterations. After the work was completed during the forenoon watch on the 7th, the ship was towed back to her former berth, where she provisioned and made ready to return to the Ushant-Brest patrol line.

Vedette escorted an outward-bound convoy late on the 9th, and an inward-bound one on the 10th, before she and *Harvard* were assigned to another outward-bound group of 10 merchantmen and two French patrol vessels. At 2010, *Vedette*'s watch heard an explosion astern, accompanied by several blasts of a ship's whistle. A British merchantman, last in line of the convoy, had struck a mine; nearby, a French vessel rescued 14 men before the rapidly sinking Briton disappeared. Twelve men had died in the explosion.

After delivering the convoy to Quiberon Bay, *Vedette* anchored at 0645, but that evening again got underway —with a convoy of eight merchantmen, two French patrol vessels, and *Harvard*—and arrived back at Brest with that group at noon on the following day. On the morning of the 15th, *Vedette* was underway again and conducted convoy escort operations through the next day.

At 0650 on 17 August, the Greek steamship *Pontoporos*—bound from Tyne Dock to Spezia with a cargo of 4,600 tons of coal and 2,000 tons of coke—was hit by a torpedo on the starboard beam. The missile exploded eight feet below the waterline, abreast the engine room, and tore up the decking topside.

Vedette rang up full speed ahead and stood about, hunting for the submarine. Unable to make contact with the enemy, the yacht picked up 27 men from a lifeboat, including the master of *Pontoporos,* a Captain Panas, at 0715. Two more men were transferred from a French fishing boat five minutes later. *Vedette* soon cast the lifeboat adrift at 0725 and circled the sinking ship; at 0740, *Pontoporos* sank from sight. After *Vedette* reached Port Heliguen later that morning, she turned the 29 survivors over to French authorities.

Vedette continued the same routine of operations— interspersed with periods of upkeep, maintenance, and provisioning—through the remainder of that summer and autumn and into 1918. On 20 January 1918, Lt. Comdr. Hand was relieved as commanding officer by Lt. Charles A. Pownall who would command carrier task forces during World War II. By January 1918, the ship's armament reflected the multi-national character of the escort work performed out of Brest, for not only did she carry her original allotment of 10 Sperry Mk. I "Mines" (American), but also was equipped with eight French Guirand charges and three British Type "D" ones! By the next summer, that had again changed, and the ship carried, by that point, 21 American Mark 2 depth charges.

Vedette's routine changed little in 1918. Her only encounter with the enemy, however, came on 5 August 1918.

Underway from Quiberon Bay at 0435 that day, she was steaming at the head of a convoy of 11 ships; other escorts were *Harvard*, *Remlik* (SP-157), and *Stewart* (Coast Torpedo Vessel No. 13). At 0802, the convoy passed Point de Chats abeam to port, distance three miles; at 0812, the ships changed course so that by 0835, they were off Pen Men, abeam to port at a distance of two and one-half miles. At 0924, *Vedette*'s watch felt a slight jar; within a minute, they saw that SS *Hundvaago* had taken a torpedo and was sinking rapidly.

Vedette went to full speed ahead and sprang to general quarters. At 0927, Signalman 3d Class Nye, Chief Quartermaster Teiper, and the officer of the deck saw a submarine off the starboard quarter of the convoy. *Vedette* heeled as the helm was put over at hard right rudder and she raced toward the enemy. She sounded five short blasts on the whistle, but a merchant ship obstructed the yacht's view of the submarine, and the periscope disappeared. *Vedette* immediately commenced a search, circling and trying to locate the enemy submersible.

At 0935, *Vedette* received orders from *Harvard* and, in company with *Stewart*, quickly proceeded to reform the panic-stricken convoy. Within 20 minutes, *Hundvaago* had disappeared, another U-boat victim. An hour before noon, *Vedette* resumed her position at the head of the convoy and, 45 minutes later, took station on the port flank of the convoy.

Things were not quiet for long, however. At one minute past noon, a French seaplane, attracted to the scene of the torpedoing, dropped a smoke bomb, indicating the presence of what looked like a submarine. *Vedette* again went to general quarters and put over hard right rudder as she sped off to the hunt. She soon picked up a small oil wake about 200 yards east of the smoke bomb and dropped a barrage of eight depth charges at 1215. Ten minutes later, having seen "no further evidence of a submarine," *Vedette* rejoined the convoy, taking station on the port bow.

Stewart later dropped four depth charges over a 15-minute period but failed to learn whether or not she had tangled with a submarine. She nevertheless continued the hunt, in company with *Vedette*, *Harvard*, and *Remlik*, while the newly arrived *Tucker* (Destroyer No. 57) joined the convoy's screen.

However, *Vedette*'s work for that day was not complete until she had assisted a downed French seaplane from the French Naval Air Service. At 1718, another French plane had dropped a message requesting aid in Bay de Douarnez. A bit under an hour later, *Vedette* lowered her motor boat that took the pilots aboard and took the disabled plane in tow. When the ship reached her destination, she lowered a whaleboat which took up the tow and safely delivered the French plane.

Vedette would never again have that much excitement in a single day. Thereafter, her duties for the remainder of the war were placid as she continued to escort convoys to and from Brest and patrolled offshore in between convoy runs. Less than a month after the armistice stilled the guns of World War I, she departed Brest for the last time when she weighed anchor on 6 December for the long voyage home.

Steaming in company with *Emeline* (SP-175), *Corona* (SP-813), *Nokomis* (SP-609), and *Sultana*, *Vedette* arrived at Ponta Delgada at 1025 on 11 December. She coaled ship there, took on provisions, and brought aboard 133 bags of coal to store on deck for the transatlantic voyage. Underway at 0702 on the 15th, the squadron anchored in St. George's harbor, Bermuda, on the morning of 24 December but got underway again on Christmas Day on the last leg of their voyage.

Shortly after leaving Bermuda, *Emeline*, *Nokomis*, and *Corona* steamed off "on duty assigned," leaving *Vedette* along with *Sultana*—one of her companions on her voyage to Europe in the summer of 1917. The two yachts entered New York harbor on the afternoon of 28 December, home at last.

At 0900 on the 30th, *Vedette* moved up the East River to the New York Navy Yard. By noon, her trio of 3-inch guns, her machine guns, and small arms had been removed.

On 4 February, at Tebo's Yacht Basin, *Vedette* was returned to her owner. She was struck from the Navy list the same day.

II

(MB: l. 32'0'')

Vedette—a wooden-hulled, launch-type motor boat built in 1914 at Bayonne, N.J., by the Elco Co.—was acquired by the Navy during World War I from the Panama Canal Co. for use as a section patrol boat. The vessel served in the Canal Zone for the duration of hostilities and was returned to her owner on 31 December 1918.

Veendijk

(Id. No. 2515: dp. 16,000; l. 434'; b. 54'; dr. 28.7' (mean); dph. 34.9'; s. 12 k.; cpl. 70; a. 1 5'', 1 3'')

Veendijk (Id. No. 2515), a steamer constructed in 1914 by the Sunderland Shipbuilding Co. at Sunderland, England, for the Holland-America Steamship Line, was seized by United States customs officials at New York in March of 1918; turned over to the Navy on 28 March 1918; and commissioned at New York on 5 April 1918, Lt. Comdr. William S. P. Keyes, USNRF, in command.

Assigned to the Naval Overseas Transportation Service, she was refitted for naval service at New York before embarking upon her first mission late in April. On the 17th, she departed New York with an Army cargo, bound for France. She arrived in Brest on 13 May but moved to La Pallice the following day. After unloading her cargo, the freighter departed La Pallice on 17 June in convoy for New York. She reached her destination on 2 July and began a repair period. She loaded more cargo and stood out of New York on 13 July, bound for St. Nazaire, France, where she arrived on 30 July. The cargo ship departed France on 21 August and arrived back in New York on 4 September. During the remaining two months of the war, *Veendijk* made one more round-trip voyage to France and back. Following the armistice in November, she continued to serve the Navy. Between late November 1918 and late June 1919, the ship made another voyage to France and back as well as a round-trip voyage to Montevideo, Uruguay. Upon her return to New York on 25 June 1919, *Veendijk* began preparations for going out of service. On 2 August 1919, she was placed out of commission at New York. On 21 August, her name was struck from the Navy list, and she was returned to the Holland-America Steamship Line. She resumed mercantile service with the Holland-America line until sometime in 1933, at which point her name disappeared from merchant ship registers.

Vega

A star of the first magnitude in constellation Lyra used frequently by navigators.

I

(SP–734: t. 276 (gross); l. 175'0''; b. 20'4''; dr. 7'9''
(mean); s. 15 k.; cpl. 69; a. 1 3'', 1 6-pdr., 2 mg.)

Lyndonia—a steel-hulled, steam yacht designed by
Charles L. Seabury and built in 1907 at Morris Heights,
N.J., by the Gas Engine and Power Co. and the Charles
Seabury Co.—was acquired by the Navy from the noted
Philadelphia publisher Cyrus H. K. Curtis on 5 Sep-
tember 1917. Designated SP–734 and converted for
Navy use at the Philadelphia Navy Yard, the former
yacht was placed in commission on 4 December 1917,
Lt. Comdr. John J. McCracken in command.

Lyndonia departed Philadelphia on 22 December
bound for Bermuda in company with *Venetia* (SP–431)
and tugs *Gypsum Queen* (SP–430) and *Montauk* (SP–
1213). At 1020 the following day, *Lyndonia* blew two
tubes in her forward boiler; at 1800, all tubes in the
after boiler blew as well. As the ship slowly lost steam,
she signalled *Venetia* of her plight. Accordingly, at
1820, *Montauk* passed a hawser to *Lyndonia* and took
her in tow. On Christmas Day, while en route to the
Virginia capes, the remaining boiler tubes blew, leaving the ship without any steam whatever.

As if losing steam were not enough, 10 minutes
later, the hawser parted, leaving *Lyndonia* adrift for
nearly 20 minutes before she was again taken in tow.
Subsequently, *Joseph F. Bellows* (SP–323) pulled
Lyndonia to the Norfolk Navy Yard where the yacht
then underwent repairs in drydock.

Lyndonia got underway on 4 February for New
London, Conn., and arrived off the Delaware capes
the following day, only to encounter heavy ice floes
which blocked further passage. She accordingly returned to Norfolk and remained there into the spring,
serving as dispatch and mail boat in the Chesapeake
Bay. During this tour of duty, on 20 February, the
ship was renamed *Vega*.

On 22 April, *Vega* sailed for Philadelphia. Arriving
there the following day, she was attached to the 4th
Naval District and based at Cold Spring Inlet, near
Cape May, N.J., for patrols off the New Jersey coast.

On 25 June, *Vega* sighted a ship resembling a surfaced submarine at long range. Going to general quarters, *Vega* altered course to close the unidentified craft
and flashed recognition signals and challenges in Morse
code. The ship would not respond, however, and *Vega*
opened fire with her 6-pounder forward—firing six
quick shots before the target hove to. Upon closer investigation, the unidentified ship turned out to be SS
Skandeborg, a Danish merchantman bound from Cuba
to New York with a general cargo—mostly sugar. No
member of the Danish vessel's crew knew Morse code—
hence her seeming reluctance to reply to *Vega*'s
challenges!

The warship continued her operations out of Cold
Spring Inlet into the fall of 1918. During this period,
she also undertook local escort duties.

On 28 October, following repairs at the New York
Navy Yard, *Vega* sailed south to Annapolis, where she
arrived three days later to commence duties as a training ship for midshipmen at the Naval Academy. She
remained in the Annapolis vicinity from 1 November
to 4 December before she got underway for Pensacola,
Fla., on 5 December.

Reaching Pensacola three days before Christmas,
1918, *Vega* conducted local operations out of Pensacola
until 22 March 1919, when she got underway for
Philadelphia. The yacht remained at the Philadelphia
Navy Yard through the spring and summer months,
and was decommissioned on Friday, 13 September
1919. She was subsequently sold to Charles H. Crocker,
of San Francisco, Calif., on 20 December 1921.

II

(AK–17: dp. 11,320; l. 401'1''; b. 54'0''; dr. 20'0''; s.
11.5 k.; cpl. 227; a. 2 5''; cl. *Sirius*)

Lebanon—a single-screw, steel-hulled freighter built
in 1919 under a United States Shipping Board contract at Hog Island, Pa., by the American International
Shipbuilding Co.—was acquired by the Navy on 2 December 1921. Renamed *Vega* and given the classification of AK–17, she fitted out for Navy service and commissioned at the Boston Navy Yard on 21 December
1921, Lt. William H. Newman, USNRF, in command.

Assigned to the Naval Transportation Service, *Vega*
served the pre-World War II Navy from Atlantic to
Pacific on cargo runs which included calls at both
east and west coast ports, as well as visits to the Far
East and the Caribbean. During the first three years
of her naval service, *Vega* completed six round-trip
voyages from San Francisco to Asiatic waters before
returning home in October 1924. In successive summers
from 1925 to 1928, the cargo vessel operated between
Seattle, Wash., and Alaskan ports, carrying supplies
and stores to naval radio stations at St. Paul and
Dutch Harbor. In addition, *Vega* and sistership *Sirius*
(AK–15) carried general freight, heavy guns, and
ordnance parts in support of Marine peace-keeping
activities in Nicaragua. Among *Vega*'s cruises were
voyages in 1928 carrying supplies for the Bureau of
Fisheries, Commerce Department, to seal rookeries on
Pribilof and other Alaskan islands. She returned with
seal skins garnered during supervised killings.

Vega operated in unglamorous but vital logistical
duties into the 1930's as the tide of war crept closer
toward the United States. On 6 December 1941, *Vega*
arrived at Honolulu, Hawaii—her holds laden with
ammunition for the Naval Ammunition Depot, Pearl
Harbor, and an Army derrick barge in tow—moored
to Pier 31 and commenced unloading her cargo at 0100
on 7 December. When Japanese planes swept over
Oahu, *Vega* went to general quarters as civilian stevedores continued the arduous job of unloading her
dangerous cargo. Since the Japanese were after bigger
game, the Hog Islander and her vital cargo emerged
from the attack unscathed.

Vega remained in the Hawaiian Islands until 3
January 1942, when she got underway with a cargo
of civilian automobiles and pineapples. She arrived at
San Francisco 10 days later and soon entered Mare
Island Navy Yard for refit. She returned to Hawaiian
waters on 10 March. After detaching her tow, *Progress*
(AMc–98), and unloading construction gear, the cargo
vessel loaded another cargo of pineapples and civilian
dependents' gear and got underway for the west coast
on 20 March.

Transferred to the operational control of Commandant, 13th Naval District, *Vega* departed San
Francisco for Tacoma, Wash., on 9 April. From then
until 9 January 1944, the cargo vessel operated out of
Tacoma and Seattle, carrying vital construction materials and supporting American operations against
the Japanese invaders in the Aleutian Islands. On
one run, *Vega* delivered a cargo of naval stores and
ammunition, as well as some 20-millimeter antiaircraft
guns for the garrison at Dutch Harbor—only a few
days before the devastating bombardment of that base
by a Japanese cruiser task force in early June 1942.

The ship returned to San Francisco early in 1944 and
was soon assigned to Service Squadron (ServRon) 8.
During the next year, the cargo vessel supported three
major amphibious operations—in the Marianas, the
Western Carolines, and at Okinawa—carrying vital
supplies and construction materials to assist the famed
"Seabees" in establishing the advance bases so necessary to the smooth operation of the Fleet. She picked
up her first load of pontoon barges at Pearl Harbor and
got underway for the Gilbert Islands on 31 January.
However, her orders were changed en route, sending
her to the Marshalls. She arrived at Kwajalein atoll on
6 March, unloaded the barges, and returned to San
Francisco for another load. Departing San Francisco
on 18 May, she unloaded at Guam before steaming back

Vega (AK–17) moors at New York Navy Yard during the 1920s with the help of a commercial tug.

to the Russells to pick up another load at Banika Island.

On 23 October 1944, *Vega* commenced loading empty brass powder cans at Ulithi in the Carolines, while her embarked "Seabee" battalion—the 1044th—assembled self-propelled barges brought out in SS *Claremont*. Subsequently, the cargo vessel sailed for Eniwetok where she took on board another load of brass casings, heading for Pearl Harbor on 30 December, en route to the west coast. She made port at San Francisco, a familiar terminus for the ship, on 18 January 1945. *Vega* departed the west coast with another load of barges on 9 March bound, via Eniwetok and Ulithi, for the Ryukyus. Dropping anchor off Okinawa on 13 June, *Vega* began assembling pontoon barges; and, three days later, during a Japanese air raid on her anchorage, the cargo vessel downed a twin-engined bomber before its pilot could drop his bombs.

Departing Okinawa on 6 July, the cargo vessel sailed, via Pearl Harbor, for the west coast and arrived at San Pedro soon thereafter. Offloading empty brass picked up at Pearl Harbor, *Vega* transported a cargo of dry stores to San Francisco before proceeding on to Oakland, Calif., where she was decommissioned on 15 January 1946. Struck from the Navy list on 12 March, she was turned over to the Maritime Commission on 1 July. The veteran cargo vessel was sold on 6 August to the National Metals and Steel Corp. for scrapping.

Vega received four battle stars for her World War II service.

III

(AF–59: dp. 15,150 (f.); l. 502'0''; b. 72'0''; dr. 29'0''; s. 21 k.; cpl. 350; a. 8 3''; cl. *Rigel*; T. R3–S–4A)

The third *Vega* (AF–59) was laid down on 7 June 1954 at Pascagoula, Miss., by the Ingalls Shipbuilding Corp.; launched on 28 April 1955; sponsored by Mrs. Theodore C. Lonnquest; and commissioned on 10 November 1955, Capt. Floyd T. Thompson in command.

Following shakedown, *Vega* sailed for the west coast and duty with the Pacific Fleet. Between January 1956 and mid-1964, *Vega* made 13 deployments to the Far East, usually about four months in length. During this time, the versatile storeship sailed an average of over 30,000 miles per year and routinely visited Yokosuka and Sasebo, Japan; Hong Kong; Subic Bay, Philippines; and Kaohsiung, Formosa, with an occasional run to Kobe and Iwakuni, Japan. In 1956, *Vega* set a record for ships of her type when she provisioned *Shangri-La* (CVA–38) at a rate of 218 tons per hour. In 1963, the *Vega* again proved herself to be the Navy's fastest working storeship as she delivered 117 tons of provisions to *Ranger* (CVA–61) in just 27 minutes, giving her a transfer rate of 245 tons per hour.

From October 1964 to January 1965, *Vega* participated in Fleet operations off the coast of Vietnam before she returned to the United States in February 1965. Returning to Vietnamese waters in the late spring, she once more supported 7th Fleet units. While underway in the South China Sea on 8 September 1965, *Vega* was the scene of an unusual change of command, when Capt. T. A. Melusky relieved Capt. R. E. Hill as commanding officer. The ceremony took place at 0128, on the port wing of the bridge, by the light of red-filtered flashlights, with the ship darkened during an underway replenishment of *Constellation* (CVA–62). The storeship returned to the United States in October 1965.

Vega was again deployed to the 7th Fleet from February to May of 1966. During this time, the ship replenished her first two nuclear-powered ships, *Bainbridge* (DLGN–25) and *Enterprise* (CVAN–65).

473

Later, during her next WestPac tour, *Vega* conducted 125 underway and 26 in-port replenishments—more than during any other deployment. Besides her normal Japanese ports of call, she also visited Danang and An Thoi, Vietnam, while calling for the first time at Singapore.

As American involvement in Vietnam deepened, *Vega*'s deployment schedule reflected this increase in operations. While deployed in the summer of 1966, *Vega* steamed in company with *Hector* (AR–7), *Ashtabula* (AO–51), *Parricutin* (AE–18), and *Currituck* (AV–7). From 22 August to 21 November, she supported "Yankee-Station" and "Market-Time" operations.

She remained thus employed, with regular deployments to WestPac through 1969. In between her deployments to the "Yankee-Station" or to "Market-Time" zones, *Vega* maintained a regular schedule of local operations, overhauls, and refresher training upon return to the west coast. Homeported at San Francisco, Calif., *Vega* continued her unglamorous but vital duty of providing the necessary supplies to keep the Fleet and its men in top operating condition.

After loading at Oakland, Calif., from 24 March to 4 April 1969, *Vega* sailed on 5 April for Yokosuka, Japan.

Her normal routine of operations was interrupted later that month, when North Korean MiG fighters shot down an American EC–121 surveillance aircraft over the Sea of Japan. As tensions rose between Pyongyang and Washington, the 7th Fleet responded to the crisis by dispatching a task force which included the nuclear attack carrier *Enterprise* to the vicinity. *Vega* joined Task Group (TG) 73.7 on 24 April in support of Task Force (TF) 71 in the Sea of Japan and performed 17 underway replenishments between the 24th and the 29th.

With the relaxation of tensions, *Vega* was detached on the latter date and resumed her regular WestPac replenishment operations to the 7th Fleet. *Vega* began her first line period for 1969 on 9 May and replenished 22 ships before returning to Subic Bay on the 16th. On 31 May, the refrigerator ship commenced a 37-hour replenishment operation with *Niagara Falls* (AFS–3) in Subic Bay, delivering some 1,057.5 tons of provisions.

On 9 June, *Vega* got underway to support "Market Time" operations. She replenished in port at An Thoi on 13 June, at Vung Tau on the 15th, Camranh Bay on the 16th, and at Danang on the 17th, before carrying out nine underway replenishments on "Yankee Station," over the next six days.

Returning to Subic Bay on 27 June, the ship remained there until 6 July, when she sailed for Yankee Station—as bad weather had grounded all COD (carrier onboard delivery) aircraft, and supplies needed to be delivered to the Fleet. She arrived on station on 8 July and, alongside *Oriskany* (CVA–34) four days later, conducted her longest underway replenishment, from 1737 on 12 July to 0105 on the 13th—a period of seven hours and 28 minutes.

Soon thereafter, *Vega* shifted to Hong Kong, where her commanding officer became the administrative Senior Officer Present Afloat (SOPA) on 23 July. She and *Rowan* (DD–702) got underway on the 27th to avoid typhoon "Viola" which was then swirling its way up the China coast. Returning two days later, *Vega* resumed her SOPA duties and continued to carry them out until she departed that port on 8 August, bound for Sasebo. There, the supply ship loaded Fleet freight and soon sailed for the west coast of the United States, arriving at San Francisco, Calif., on 5 September, where she remained for the rest of 1969.

After entering the Hunters Point Naval Shipyard on 2 January 1970 for her regular overhaul, *Vega* spent three months in dockyard hands before she emerged on 2 April to commence refresher training out of San Diego. She trained in the southern California operating area into the summer, before shifting on 21 August to the Army Refrigerator (Reefer) Piers at Oakland, Calif. There, she conducted a predeployment loadout of goods for shipment to the western Pacific.

Vega again got underway on 11 September, bound for Subic Bay, and crossed the 160th meridian on 26 September to commence officially her WestPac tour. After evading typhoon "Hope" en route, *Vega* stopped briefly at Subic Bay before she pressed on 8 October for her first line tour of the deployment on Yankee Station off the coast of Vietnam. She returned to Subic on 22 October. During this tour, she transferred over 226 tons of foodstuffs during underway replenishments.

Her second line period saw the ship transfer 290 tons of provisions to ships with TF 77 on Yankee Station. Bangkok, Thailand, provided welcome relief for liberty parties before the ship returned to the line a third time on 29 November. Operating in support of "Market Time," *Vega* transferred some 392 tons of food—Christmas supplies—to ships engaged in the daily interdiction patrols of the sea lanes. Further, the ship delivered some 67 tons of supplies to Danang, Camranh Bay, Con Son, An Thoi, and Hon Choi—all in South Vietnam.

After visiting Hong Kong from 13 to 21 December, *Vega* spent Christmas at Kaohsiung, Taiwan, and then returned to Subic Bay to load supplies. Before the year was out, the supply ship was underway again—for her fourth line period off Vietnam. During this swing, the ship transferred 300 tons of food to ships on "Yankee Station" and "Market Time" patrols. Many sailors on the ships she supplied probably enjoyed the fresh fruit acquired on Taiwan during the ship's visit there prior to deploying off the Vietnam coastline.

The supply vessel conducted two more swings on the patrol line in the sea lanes off Vietnam into early 1971. Extremely difficult weather conditions hampered such operations on 29 and 30 January 1971, but the men on the ships involved rose to the occasion and accomplished the successful transfer of 100 tons of food without incident. Offloading 342 tons of supplies at the Naval Supply Depot, Subic Bay, from 8 to 10 March, the ship departed the Philippines to visit Japan. While en route, however, *Vega* was dispatched to search for a Japanese fishing vessel in distress off Yonakuni Jima. Conducting the search in heavy seas and beneath leaden grey overcast skies, *Vega*'s efforts were uncrowned with success, as she found no trace of the distressed ship.

Vega eventually visited Sasebo, from 17 to 20 March, before she got underway for Pearl Harbor, en route to her ultimate destination of Alameda, Calif.

Making port at the Naval Air Station, Alameda, on 6 April, *Vega* later served from 13 to 17 May as host ship at San Francisco for HMCS *Terra Nova*. *Vega* then entered Triple "A" Shipyard, San Francisco, on 27 May for a restricted availability which increased the ship's transfer capabilities. Completing these modifications on 23 July, the ship conducted a program of type training off the California coast from the 26th through the 30th, before she sailed north to call at the annual Sea Fair at Seattle, Wash.

During a subsequent refit, again carried out at San Francisco's Triple "A" Shipyard in the summer and again in the fall of 1971, *Vega* received modifications that further improved her cargo-handling capacities. Specifically, number 3 hold was modified to handle pre-palletized cargo; and existing helicopter facilities were upgraded. In addition, a 4,000-pound pallet conveyor belt was added, as well as battery-charging facilities and a new forklift garage. In between yard periods, the cargo vessel participated in local operations and type training exercises.

From 1972 through 1974, *Vega* continued fulfilling her primary mission of supplying units afloat and ashore with necessary food and cargo. She regularly deployed to the far reaches of the western Pacific operating area and conducted replenishments to ships at sea on "Yankee Station" and "Market Time" patrols and carried out support operations with the Mobile Logistics Support Force. The tempo of the Vietnam war, however, began to change. By the spring of 1973,

American involvement on the southeast Asian mainland was drawing to a close.

After deploying to the line three times in early 1975, *Vega* sailed from Subic Bay on 22 March 1975, to provide logistics services for TG 76.4, standing by in the Gulf of Thailand to execute Operation "Eagle Pull," the evacuation of Cambodian refugees fleeing the communist takeover of that country. She conducted replenishment operations with a wide variety of ships. Returning to Subic Bay to reload on 31 March, she set sail for the second increment of "Eagle Pull," rejoining the forces in the Gulf of Thailand on 5 April. After conducting replenishments with *Frederick* (LST–1184), *Durham* (LKA–114), *Long Beach* (CLGN–9), *Reasoner* (DE–1063), *Blue Ridge* (LCC–19), *Okinawa* (LPH–3), and *Thomaston* (LSD–28), she arrived at Phu Quoc Island to provide supply support for Cambodian refugees, and transferred some 12.4 tons of refugee subsistence items to *Dubuque* (LPD–8) and *Peoria* (LST–1183). Rendezvousing with TG 76.4 on the 9th, the busy supply vessel again returned to Phu Quoc on the 10th and to Subic Bay on the 13th.

Underway from Subic Bay on 23 April, *Vega* sailed for the coast of South Vietnam. By this juncture, the government of South Vietnam was collapsing, leaving tons of American-supplied equipment intact for the communist forces. Operation "Frequent Wind" was launched to evacuate Vietnamese fleeing the onslaught, lest they be left behind and fall into communist hands. For the next few days, *Vega* replenished United States and South Vietnamese Navy ships, delivered passengers and mail, and transferred refugee supplies to vessels loaded with fleeing South Vietnamese. Underway at sea from 25 to 30 April, the supply ship arrived off Vung Tau on 1 May and replenished South Vietnamese naval units *YFU–69*, *HQ–3*, *HQ–800*, and *HQ–801* as well as conducted a vertical fleet supply replenishment with *Mars* (AFS–1) and fleet supplies and mail for five other Navy ships.

Heading for Subic Bay, *Vega* served as escort for the "New Life" flotilla, heavily laden with Vietnamese refugees and their belongings. Arriving at Subic Bay on the 6th, she stood in with the first contingent of refugee vessels—some 70 craft in all, of all shapes and sizes. Underway for a resumption of escort duties later that day, *Vega* stood out to sea; she subsequently refueled from *Taluga* (T–AO–62) on the 7th before conducting underway replenishments over the next two days with *Midway* (CVA–41), *Badger* (DE–1071), and *Ashtabula* (AO–51). Arriving at Subic Bay on 10 May to load supplies, she got underway soon thereafter, in company with *Harold E. Holt* (DE–1074), for refugee vessel escort duties.

On 13 May, communist Cambodian forces seized the American-owned containership, SS *Mayaguez*, off Koh Tang Island, Cambodia. Both *Vega* and *Harold E. Holt* made full speed ahead for the area, while American forces soon mobilized for quick and decisive strikes to gain the release of the ship and its crew from the hands of the Cambodians. Arriving on the 15th, *Vega* stood by to provide services while *Harold E. Holt* moved in and delivered a detachment of marines, who boarded the containership. While the incident was brought to a conclusion by the swift recapture of the ship and her crew, the routine task of conducting underway replenishments to ships of the 7th Fleet in southeast Asian waters continued unabated in the wake of the fall of Vietnam and Cambodia.

Vega returned to San Francisco, Calif., on 4 August, following a circuitous route via Cebu and Subic Bay, Philippines; Hong Kong, British Crown Colony; Buckner Bay, Okinawa; and Pearl Harbor. A tally of the ships' activities on her most eventful WestPac cruise showed the ship to have completed some 105 underway, 15 boat, and 38 vertical replenishments— the last utilizing the capabilities of helicopters for rapid and increased transport of supplies from ship to ship. A total of some 2,848.9 tons of provisions, including 136.8 tons of refugee supplies, were transferred. The ship then underwent restricted availability from 18 to 19 August.

For the remainder of the ship's active service career with the United States Navy, *Vega* operated off the west coast, conducting local operations, and later deployed to the Philippines, Hong Kong, Taiwan, Japan, and Okinawa for her final WestPac deployment. She arrived at San Francisco on 21 December 1976 and immediately commenced leave and upkeep.

On 21 January 1977, *Vega* shifted to berth 23 south, Mare Island Naval Shipyard, to commence standdown prior to inactivation. She was decommissioned on 29 April 1977 and struck from the Navy list the same day.

Vega earned 10 battle stars for her service to units of the 7th Fleet during the Vietnam war.

Vela

One of four subdivisions of Argo, a large constellation of the Southern Hemisphere, named for the sails of *Argo*, the ship used by Jason on his voyage in quest of the golden fleece.

(AK–89: dp. 5,202 (est.); l. 269'10''; b. 42'6''; dr. 20'9''; (est. mean); s. 10.25 k.; cpl. 83; a. 1 3''; cl. *Enceladus*; N3–M–A1)

Vela (AK–89) was originally scheduled for construction under a Maritime Commission contract (MC hull 652) and was assigned the name *Charles A. Ranlett*. However, her construction was transferred to the supervision of the Navy on 1 January 1943. She was laid down as *Vela* (AK–89) on 5 June 1944 at Camden, N.J., by the Penn-Jersey Shipbuilding Corp.; launched on 15 January 1945; sponsored by Mrs. Elbert Bradford Ferguson; and transferred to the Army on 17 January 1945. Her name was struck from the Navy list on 8 February 1945.

On 11 June 1952, *Vela* was returned to the Navy and transferred to the Military Sea Transportation Service. She was placed in service at Baltimore the following day and was reinstated on the Navy list on 22 August. She operated out of New York through 1958, ranging from Canadian coastal waters to the Caribbean on supply missions. Later transferred to the Maritime Administration and placed in the National Defense Reserve Fleet, she was berthed in the Hudson River until she was sold on 23 November 1970 to Hierros Ardes, S.A., Spain, and scrapped.

Vella Gulf

A naval engagement in the Solomons campaign of World War II, fought in Vella Gulf between the islands Vella Lavella and Kolombangara on the night of 6 and 7 August 1943. In the battle of Vella Gulf, six American destroyers—*Dunlap* (DD–384), *Craven* (DD–382), *Maury* (DD–401), *Lang* (DD–399), *Sterett* (DD–407), and *Stack* (DD–406)—engaged a group of four enemy destroyers attempting to reinforce Japanese troops on Kolombangara. The American warships closed, undetected, and fired torpedoes which sank *Hagikaze*, *Arashi*, and *Kawakaze*.

(CVE–111: dp. 11,373; l. 557'1''; b. 75'; ew. 104'; dr. 32'; s. 19 k.; cpl. 1,066; a. 2 5'', 36 40mm., 24 20mm., ac. 34; cl. *Commencement Bay*)

Vella Gulf (CVE–111) was laid down as *Totem Bay* on 7 February 1944 at Tacoma, Wash., by the Todd-Pacific Shipyards, Inc.; renamed *Vella Gulf* on 26 April 1944; launched on 19 October 1944; sponsored by Mrs. Donald F. Smith; and commissioned on 9 April 1945, Capt. Robert W. Morse in command.

Following initial local operations in Puget Sound, *Vella Gulf* sailed for San Diego and arrived there on 4 May to pick up the initial increment of her assigned Marine air group. After embarking them at the naval

The recently commissioned *Vella Gulf* (CVE–111) in Puget Sound 21 April 1945. *Commencement Bay*-class escort carriers could operate more planes than their predecessors and embodied design improvements to increase endurance and resistance to damage. (19–N–81247)

air station, the escort aircraft carrier conducted shakedown off the southern California coast and embarked the remainder of her group during this period. At the completion of a post-shakedown availability, she departed the west coast on 17 June, bound for Hawaii. She arrived at Pearl Harbor on 25 June and conducted 11 days of intensive training operations.

Vella Gulf departed Pearl Harbor on 9 July; stopped at Eniwetok in the Marshalls on the 16th to refuel; and proceeded on to Guam, where she arrived four days later. On the 23d, she sailed for the Marianas to conduct air strikes against Rota and Pagan Islands. The next day, she launched 24 sorties against Pagan Island with her FG-1D Corsairs, Hellcat photographic aircraft, and TBM-3E Avenger bombers. Three days later, the escort carrier launched 21 sorties against Rota, with a dozen Corsairs, eight Avengers and one Hellcat taking part. Light antiaircraft fire from Japanese guns peppered the skies but failed to reach the American planes. Two planes returned from the mission having conducted their attacks from such a low altitude that shrapnel from their own bomb explosions slightly damaged their tail surfaces.

The day after the Rota strike, the ship flew off her planes to Saipan and then returned to Apra Harbor, Guam, on 2 August, for a three-day breather before heading for Okinawa on the 5th. She arrived at Buckner Bay four days later. Her one night spent in the anchorage there was a memorable one since, during the evening, word arrived that surrender negotiations with the Japanese were in progress and prompted many ships and shore-based units to set off pyrotechnics.

Vella Gulf arrived back at Guam on 15 August in time to receive the welcome news that Japan had capitulated. *Vella Gulf* participated in the initial occupation operations of the Japanese home islands. She provided food and fuel to other Fleet units off the coast and, in late August, alternated with *Gilbert Islands* (CVE–107) in furnishing air cover for a replenishment group. The escort carrier then sailed for Tokyo Bay and arrived there on 10 September.

Departing Japanese waters on 21 September, *Vella Gulf* embarked 650 men at Okinawa for passage back to the west coast of the United States. After a brief stop at Pearl Harbor, she arrived at San Francisco, Calif., on 14 October. She subsequently operated in the Puget Sound area as training ship for escort carrier personnel until late March 1946, when she sailed for the coast of southern California and arrived at San Diego on 27 March. However, her stay there was brief,

for she soon got underway again, touched at Port Angeles, and pushed on to Tacoma, Wash., where she began inactivation on the last day of the month. Moved to Seattle on 7 April, the ship was placed in inactive status, out of commission, on 9 August 1946.

Placed in reserve at Tacoma, the vessel remained there into the 1960's. Reclassified as a helicopter carrier (CVHE) on 12 June 1955, *Vella Gulf* was later transferred to the Military Sea Transportation Service; and she was again reclassified—this time to T–AKV–11. However, she never returned to active service. Struck from the Navy list on 1 June 1960, she was reinstated on 1 November of the same year. Struck for the second time on 1 December 1970, the erstwhile escort carrier was sold to the American Ship Dismantlers, Inc., of Portland, Oreg., on 22 October 1971 and scrapped.

Vella Gulf received one battle star for her World War II service.

Velocipede

(MB: t. 25; l. 60′0″; b. 11′8″; dr. 2′11′ (mean); cpl. 8; a. 1 1-pdr., 1 mg.)

Velocipede (SP-1258)—a motor boat constructed at Morris Heights, N.J., by the Charles L. Seabury Co.—was acquired by the Navy on 27 October 1917 under free lease from Mr. K. C. Atwood, Jr., of New York City, N.Y., for use as an aeronautical patrol boat; and commissioned on 14 November 1917.

Assigned to the 7th Naval District, *Velocipede* served on patrol duties at the Naval Air Station, Miami, Fla., until after the armistice had ended hostilities on 11 November 1918. She remained in Navy hands until 6 February 1919 when she was returned to her owner.

Velocity

I

(Sch.: t. 87; a. 2 12-pdr. how.)

The first *Velocity* was a British blockade-running schooner captured by *Kensington* and *Rachel Seaman* at Sabine, Tex., on 25 September 1862; and was purchased by the Navy from the Key West prize court, Key West, Fla., on 30 September.

Velocity joined the West Gulf Blockading Squadron shortly after her acquisition, deploying with the blockade off Sabine Pass. There, on 25 November, she assisted *Kensington*, *Rachel Seaman*, and another prize vessel, *Dan*, in the capture of the British schooner *Maria* and the Confederate schooner *Course*. *Velocity* was, herself, recaptured together with *Morning Light* on 21 January 1863 at Sabine Pass, resulting in a temporary lifting of the Union blockade on the Texas coast. She is believed to have continued to serve as a Confederate gunboat, but her final disposition is unknown.

(MB: l. 85′6′′; b. 17′6′′; dr. 4′9′′ (mean); cpl. 5; a. 1 3-pdr., 2 mg.)

Velocity—advertised as an "unsinkable" fishing craft —was constructed at Morris Heights, N.Y., by the noted boat-builder, Charles L. Seabury, and owned by W. W. Stephens prior to World War I when she was inspected for naval service. Assigned the classification SP–446, *Velocity* was apparently earmarked for section patrol duties. However, no logs exist, nor has other evidence been found to confirm or to disprove her naval service.

II

(AM–128: dp. 890; l. 221′2′′; b. 32′2′′; dr. 10′9′′; s. 18.1 k.; cpl. 105; a. 1 3′′, 2 40mm.; cl. *Auk*)

The second *Velocity* (AM–128) was laid down on 21 July 1941 at Chickasaw, Ala., by the Gulf Shipbuilding Co.; launched on 15 April 1942; sponsored by Mrs. K. B. Hover, the wife of the shipbuilder's destroyer hull foreman; and commissioned on 4 April 1943, Lt. Comdr. Joseph L. Bull, Jr., USNR, in command.

After fitting out and conducting sea trials, *Velocity* took on further supplies, underwent yard work at New Orleans, conducted minesweeping training out of Burwood, La., and practiced antisubmarine tactics out of Key West, Fla. Departing the Florida Keys on 3 May, the minecraft arrived at Norfolk, Va., on the 6th and escorted a coastal convoy to Charleston, S.C., before undergoing further yard work at the Norfolk Navy Yard.

Departing Norfolk on 6 June, *Velocity* arrived at Key West three days later, en route to the Panama Canal Zone. She then escorted eight LST's across the Gulf of Mexico to Balboa, before she transited the canal on 18 June. She departed the Panama Canal Zone on the 24th, but her onward routing was cancelled; and she put back into port soon thereafter. She conducted local operations out of Balboa into July, after which time she transported a cargo of diesel fuel oil to Baltra Island, in the Galapagos group, to alleviate a critical fuel shortage there. When she returned to Balboa, she conducted further local operations, including towing targets for the planes from a carrier task group training in the vicinity—carriers including *Princeton* (CVL–23), *Lexington* (CV–16), and *Belleau Wood* (CVL–24).

Velocity subsequently escorted floating drydocks *ABD–1* and *ABD–2* and their tows, *Sombrero Key* and *Stratford Point*, to the New Hebrides Islands, arriving at Espiritu Santo on 24 September. The minesweeper soon shifted to Noumea, New Caledonia. She operated out of this port on convoy escort and local patrol duties into mid-1944, escorting ships to the New Hebrides, the Solomons, the Ellice Islands, and the Bismarck Archipelago.

In mid-August, *Velocity* joined the 3d Fleet. On 8 September, she departed Guadalcanal in company with Task Group (TG) 32.17, in the screen, escorting a convoy bound for the invasion of the western Carolines. Soon thereafter, *Velocity*, in company with *Triumph* (AM–323) and *Competent* (AM–316), arrived off Kossol Roads early on 15 September. Together, the three ships swept 13 mines. The next day, *Wadleigh* (DD–689) struck a mine which very nearly broke the ship's back and sank her. However, prompt damage control saved the destroyer, and *Velocity* was among the ships which sent a fire and rescue party to lend assistance to the stricken *Wadleigh*.

Upon completion of the operation at Kossol Roads, *Velocity* shifted to Ulithi, arriving on the last day of September. Here, the minesweeper conducted sweeping operations in the harbor before serving as a convoy escort, screening ships to Humboldt Bay, New Guinea. Soon thereafter, she then shifted to Seeadler Harbor, at Manus in the Admiralties.

Velocity departed Manus on 10 October with the remainder of her division, Mine Division (MinDiv) 14. Arriving off Leyte Gulf on the 17th, the minecraft and her sisters commenced sweeping the area in the path of the invasion slated to begin on the 20th. On the 19th, a Japanese "Val" dive bomber dropped a bomb near the ship and attempted to strafe her but was driven off by brisk antiaircraft fire. That evening, *Velocity* and MinDiv 14 swept ahead of the battleships of Rear Admiral Oldendorf—the same ships which a few nights hence would win the Battle of Surigao Strait. *Velocity* operated as mine-disposal vessel for the division and ended up with a tally of 24 mines sunk and 15 destroyed.

She conducted sweeping operations on the day of the landings, 20 October, at Leyte and continued this duty until the 23d, at which time she and her sister sweepers were ordered to join the antiaircraft screen for the transports. On the 26th, when a formation of twin-engined "Betty" bombers attacked the anchorage area, *Velocity* splashed one of the attackers. During the confused melee, an American Grumman F6F Hellcat fighter went down due to a fuel shortage. *Velocity* quickly sent her motor whaleboat to pick up the aviator, but a boat from *Token* (AM–126) arrived on the scene first. On the 27th, however, *Velocity* took her turn at bat and rescued a pilot from a crashed American plane.

Following the Leyte operation, *Velocity* departed the Philippines on 28 October and proceeded via Manus to Portland, Oreg., where she arrived on 4 December. After a major availability at the Albina Engine and Machine Works Dock there, the minesweeper departed Portland on 3 March, bound for San Pedro, Calif. Subsequently shifting to San Francisco, *Velocity* departed the west coast on 4 April and arrived at Pearl Harbor on the 14th.

Departing Hawaiian waters two days later, *Velocity* escorted *Sangay* (AE–10) to Guam, via Eniwetok, in the Marshalls. She then moved to Saipan, where she joined the 5th Fleet. Shifting to Kerama Retto, Okinawa, on 11 May, the minesweeper operated in the Ryukyus as minesweeper, antiaircraft vessel, and antisubmarine ship. When *Halloran* (DE–305) was kamikazed on the night of 21 June, *Velocity* went to her aid.

On 4 July, *Velocity* departed Kerama Retto for minesweeping operations in the East China Sea. With her base of operations now at Buckner Bay, Okinawa, the ship proceeded to sweep 13 mines between 4 and 30 July and continued operations into the East China Sea into August and past the end of the war with Japan. In the operation concluded on 25 August, *Velocity* tallied a score of 35 mines located and destroyed. The minesweeper operated in Japanese waters into October 1945, between Honshu and Hokkaido, to clear shipping lanes for the ships of the occupation forces. During this time, she was based at Ominato, Japan.

After a brief period at Shanghai, China, at the end of December 1945, *Velocity* shifted to Japanese waters. Departing Sasebo, Japan, on 21 January 1946, *Velocity* arrived at San Francisco on 1 March, via Saipan, Eniwetok, and Pearl Harbor. Decommissioned and placed in inactive status on 7 October 1946, the minesweeper remained in reserve through the 1960's. During this time, her classification was changed to fleet minesweeper, and she was designated MSF–128 on 7 February 1955. Struck from the Navy list on 1 July 1972, *Velocity* was simultaneously sold to the Mexican government. She serves as *Ignacio L. Vallarta* (G.14) into 1980.

Velocity received five battle stars for her World War II service.

Venango

A county in northwestern Pennsylvania which contains the site of the first successful oil well, drilled in 1859.

(AKA–82: dp. 13,910 (tl.); l. 459'2''; b. 63'0''; dr. 26'4''; s. 16.5 k.; cpl. 247; a. 1 5'', 8 40mm., 16 20mm.; cl. *Tolland*; T. C2–S–AJ3)

Venango (AKA–82) was laid down under a Maritime Commission contract (MC hull 1391) on 6 June 1944 at Wilmington, N.C., by the North Carolina Shipbuilding Co.; launched on 9 August 1944; sponsored by Miss Alana Jane Matthes; placed briefly in service from 25 to 30 August 1944 while being towed to New York harbor for conversion by the Bethlehem Steel Co., Hoboken, N.J.; and commissioned on 2 January 1945, Lt. Comdr. Thurman A. Whitaker, USNR, in command.

Following trials in Long Island Sound and shake-down training in Chesapeake Bay, the new attack cargo ship got underway from Norfolk on 2 February; transited the Panama Canal on the 8th; and reached Pearl Harbor on Washington's Birthday. There, she reported to Amphibious Forces, Pacific, for duty as a unit of Transport Division (TransDiv) 63. She commenced discharging cargo on the 27th and, the following day, was reassigned to TransDiv 56.

After unloading the cargo she had taken on at Norfolk, *Venango* proceeded on 4 March to Army Transport Pier 26 at Honolulu and began taking on cargo for the impending assault on Okinawa. On the 14th, she embarked troops, vehicles, and gear of the Army's 82d Signal Construction Battalion. The next day, she got underway for a staging point in the Marshalls. On the 23d, she anchored at Eniwetok; then, on the 25th, again got underway and steamed for the Western Carolines. Off Ulithi on the 29th, she rode out a typhoon—high winds and heavy squalls—and then entered the lagoon the next day and anchored. With elements of Task Group 55.8 steaming in a four-column formation, she departed Ulithi on the afternoon of the 13th and headed for the Ryukyus.

About dawn on 17 April, lookouts on the attack cargo ship sighted Okinawa off the ship's starboard beam, some 16 miles away. Later that morning, she anchored off Okinawa and began unloading her boats at 1830. In the days that followed, *Venango* continued discharging the troops, cargo, and equipment of the 82d Signal Battalion. Often at dawn and dusk, the call to general quarters alerted all hands that enemy air raiders were nearby. Although *Venango* sighted no Japanese planes, enemy raiders hit numerous nearby land targets as the cargo ship lay at anchor off Okinawa. On 22 April, she departed the Ryukyus and reached Saipan on the 27th.

On 1 May, she shifted from the anchorage to a dock in Tanapag harbor to load equipment and cargo of the 21st Naval Construction Battalion for transportation to Okinawa. Two days later, she departed Saipan in convoy and, on the 27th, stood into Nakagusuku Wan. Numerous air raids alerts marked the days that followed. An hour after midnight on 31 May, *Venango* began discharging her cargo. Frequent alerts continued as she emptied her holds. On 3 June, a Japanese bomber splashed in the transport area; and, the next day, *Venango* made an emergency sortie with a six-ship merchant convoy to ride out an approaching typhoon. However, the typhoon did not strike Okinawa; and *Venango* returned to Nakagusuku Wan on the 5th and resumed unloading. On the 6th, action picked up; and observers on the cargo ship witnessed the air attack in which destroyer minelayers *Harry F. Bauer* (DM–26) and *J. William Ditter* (DM–31) downed six Japanese aircraft, despite serious damage to both ships by kamikazes.

Venango departed Okinawa in convoy on the 19th and steamed via Saipan to Pearl Harbor where she arrived on 29 June. She shifted berths to Honolulu harbor on

7 July. There, she loaded miscellaneous cargo, including beer, lumber, cement, and tar, before getting underway on the 13th and steaming independently for the Western Carolines. The same day, main engine damage forced her to reverse her course; and, on the 14th, she found herself back at Pearl Harbor for repairs.

The attack cargo ship again departed Oahu on the 23d, proceeded independently via Ulithi, and arrived at Hydrographer Bank in the Palaus on 6 August. Anchored between Peliliu and Angaur, she loaded cargo and got underway late the following afternoon. She entered Leyte Gulf on the morning of 9 August, unloaded cargo, and was anchored in Guiuan Roadstead off Samar on the 15th, when Japan capitulated. After discharging the remainder of her cargo, she began taking on 8th Army troops and equipment on 1 September. Underway on the 3d, she anchored in Manila Bay on the 5th; then, two days later, joined the sortie of Transport Squadron (TransRon) 24, bound for Yokohama.

Early on the morning of the 13th, the ships formed a single column and steamed into Tokyo Bay. *Venango* docked at Yokohama to unload her cargo and, on the 18th, weathered a typhoon. The following day, she departed Tokyo Bay in company with TransRon 24 and set her course for Guam. She arrived at Apra Harbor on the 23d, loaded cargo of the 3d Marines, 6th Marine Division and, on the 30th, set her course for China. On 12 October, she moored at Tsingtao and began discharging cargo. Still in company with Trans-Ron 24, she departed the Chinese coast on 17 October and anchored in Manila Bay on the 23d. In November, she carried elements of the 52d Chinese Army from Haiphong to Chinwangtao, China; then, on the 20th, she departed the Gulf of Pohai off Taku and set her course for the west coast of the United States. Early on the morning of 6 December, she entered the Strait of Juan de Fuca and, in mid-afternoon, moored at the Naval Station, Seattle, and discharged her passengers.

Following repairs, she got underway on 1 February 1946 and steamed via San Francisco and the Panama Canal to Norfolk where she arrived on the 25th. She was decommissioned there on 18 April; and, on 22 April, she was returned to the War Shipping Administration. Her name was struck from the Navy list on 1 May 1946.

Sold to the Waterman Steamship Corp., she operated out of Mobile, Ala., beginning in 1948. In 1953, she was transferred to Isbrandtsen Co., Inc., and for more than 10 years operated out of New York under the name *Flying Eagle*. In the early 1970's, she operated out of New Orleans as *Del Alba* and was owned by Delta Steamship Lines. By 1975, she was no longer listed in the *Record* of the American Bureau of Shipping.

Venango received one battle star for World War II service.

Vencedor

(MB: t. 90 (gross); l. 90'; b. 17'; dr. 3'11'' (mean); s. 10.5 k.; cpl. 15; a. 1 6-pdr., 1 1-pdr.)

Vencedor (SP–699)—a wooden-hulled motorboat completed in 1909 at Neponset, Mass., by George Lawley and Sons, and originally named *Tekla*—was acquired by the Navy on a free lease basis from H. H. Luedinghams on 19 June 1917; and commissioned at the New York Navy Yard on 30 August 1917, Ens. David Crow, USNRF, in command.

Operating out of Section Base No. 6, 3d Naval District, *Vencedor* performed harbor patrol duties into the summer of 1918 when she began carrying dispatches and towing targets. After continuing this duty through the armistice, *Vencedor* was decommissioned at City Island, N.Y., on 26 February 1919 and returned to her owner.

Vendace

A whitefish native to certain lakes in Scotland and England.

The name *Vendace* was assigned to SS–430—a *Tench*-class submarine to be built at Philadelphia, Pa., by the Cramp Shipbuilding Co.—but the contract for her construction was cancelled on 29 July 1944.

Venetia

(PY: t. 589 (gross); l. 226'0''; b. 27'0''; dr. 15'0''; s. 13 k.; cpl. 69; a. 4 3'', 2 mg.)

Venetia—a single-screw, steel-hulled steam yacht built in 1904 at Leith, Scotland, by Hawthorne and Co. to plans drawn up by the designers Cox and King—was acquired by the Navy on 4 August 1917 from industrialist John Diedrich Spreckles for use as a patrol craft. Designated SP–431 and fitted out at the Mare Island Navy Yard, Vallejo, Calif., *Venetia* was commissioned at Mare Island on 15 October 1917, Comdr. Lewis B. Porterfield in command.

The converted yacht departed Mare Island on 23 October, transited the Panama Canal on 6 November, and reached Philadelphia on 15 November. The ship underwent alterations at the Philadelphia Navy Yard—including the installation of new radio equipment—before she sailed for New York on 3 December. Following minor repairs at the New York Navy Yard from 4 to 15 December, *Venetia* returned to Philadelphia.

Four days before Christmas, *Venetia* sailed for European waters with *SC–67* (allocated to the French Navy) in tow and in company with the converted yacht *Lydonia* (SP–700) which, in turn, had the French *SC–173* in tow. The next day, they rendezvoused with *Montauk* (SP–392), *Gypsum Queen* (SP–430), and *Barnegat* (SP–1232) off the Delaware Breakwater and headed for Bermuda where they arrived on the 26th and remained into the new year, 1918. The group got underway on the next leg of the transatlantic passage on 7 January and reached the Azores on the 23d. *Venetia* subsequently spent five days at sea, searching for a French subchaser (*SC–319*) which had been separated from the convoy. The yacht eventually departed Ponta Delgada on 8 February in company with *Nahant* (SP–1250) and *Penobscot* (SP–982)—each ship towing a French subchaser. Arriving at Port Leixos, Portugal, on the 13th, *Venetia* got underway again five days later, with the French *SC–172* in tow, and arrived at Gibraltar on the 18th.

While undergoing voyage repairs, *Venetia* received a new depth charge rack and releasing gear. Thus outfitted, *Venetia* sailed on 2 March 1918 in the screen for a 28-ship convoy, bound for Bizerte, Tunisia. Other escorts sharing the mission included *Cythera* (SP–575), *Artemis* (SP–593), and the French trawler *Isole*. Six days later, *Venetia* got underway back toward Gibraltar, escorting eight vessels, and returned to her home port on 12 March. Based at Gibraltar, the ship performed similar convoy escort missions in the Mediterranean for the duration of hostilities.

Her first contact with the enemy came that spring. On 11 May 1918, *Venetia* was steaming off the port quarter of a 7-knot convoy bound for Gibraltar, when a torpedo steaked past her bow, some 150 to 200 yards ahead. Lookouts on the armed yacht then sighted "a large amount of water" spouting into the air over the bow of SS *Susette Fraisinette*, a French steamship about 100 yards away. The merchantman had been torpedoed by *UB–52* and later sank at 0412. While the French trawler *Isole* picked up 34 survivors from *Susette Fraisinette*, *Venetia* cruised in widening circles until 0520, carrying out a sector search for the offending U-boat. At 0527, the yacht's maintop lookout sighted *UB–52* eight or nine miles away, standing well off the convoy's track and on a course between west and southwest.

Venetia, at general quarters, headed for *UB–52* at full speed, keeping the submarine bearing one point to starboard, at intervals, as the submarine continued standing off to westward. Soon, the yacht gained perceptibility, and the U-boat came into better view. Her periscopes were down, and lookouts in the yacht noted that the enemy submersible mounted a single gun (a 3.4-inch weapon) forward of the small conning tower. The fact that the German's bow seemed "unusually high" out of the water—coupled with the fact that there was "no perceptible bow-wave"—led Comdr. Porterfield to hope that either the enemy's diving apparatus was disabled ". . . or that he decided to shoot it out."

As *Venetia* bore down on *UB–52*, Porterfield laid out his battle plan: keep the U-boat one point on the starboard bow, open up with 3-inch gunfire at about 6,500 yards, machine guns at 2,000, "and finish by ramming him at full speed." Unfortunately, the U-boat's commander, *Oberleutnant zur See* Launburg, saw *Venetia*'s approach and ordered his ship to dive. Porterfield took *Venetia* over where the U-boat had just "pulled the plug" and initiated a search. *Venetia* steamed in the vicinity, within a five-mile circle, probing until 0738. During that time, she dropped 13 depth bombs and subsequently set a course to keep the enemy from making further attacks on the convoy.

Twelve days later, *UB–52* met her doom in the Adriatic at the hands of the British submarine HMS *H–4*. Survivors from the U-boat reported that *Venetia*'s efforts had not only prevented further attacks on the convoy but had driven *UB–52* off. Since Porterfield's action in doggedly pursuing the U-boat had aided substantially in saving the convoy, he received commendations from the British Senior Naval Officer, Gibraltar; from Commander in Chief, Mediterranean; and from the American Patrol Force commander, Rear Admiral Wilson.

Back at sea with a convoy outward bound from Gibraltar soon thereafter, *Venetia*'s next encounter with the enemy came within a week of her brush with *UB–52*. Just before nightfall on 17 May, the armed yacht was steaming on an irregular zig-zag pattern when the British steamship SS *Sculptor* took a torpedo from *U–39*. *Venetia*, two and one-half to three points abaft the beam of the stricken merchantman and 1,300 yards away, simultaneously sounded general quarters and rang down emergency full speed ahead.

As the yacht passed astern of *Sculptor*, Porterfield assumed that, after making her attack, the submarine had turned aft on the starboard side of the convoy. *Venetia* consequently dropped 300-pound depth charges set at 150-foot depth, between 1901 and 1902. At that point, the yacht's foretop lookout reported that he could see the wake of a submarine moving through the water. Ensign Willis L. DeCamp took station in the foretop and confirmed the lookout's report.

Venetia altered course and dropped depth charges ahead of the wake at 1906, 1908, 1909, 1911, and 1913. Meanwhile *Surveyor* stood by the damaged merchantman, and *Venetia* radioed Oran to send a tug. *Wheeling* (Gunboat No. 14) assisted in the attack, dropping seven depth charges; *Venetia* subsequently stood by *Sculptor* with orders to get her underway, if possible, in tow, and circled the crippled ship at 12 knots. By this time, British trawler *Corvi*, French trawler *Isole*, and French subchasers *SC–171* and *SC–350* picked up survivors and were standing by. *Venetia* then ordered *Isole* to rejoin the convoy.

However, the escorts were not nearly as successful driving away the attacker this time. Twice more, *U–39* closed the convoy, sinking British steamer SS *Mavisbrook* at 2028 and then damaging SS *Elswick Grange* at 2320. The latter eventually reached port under tow.

Venetia's next encounter with the enemy came less than two months later. On 20 July, the warship departed Gibraltar, bound for Genoa, Italy, as part of the screen for a convoy of 17 ships. Her fellow escorts were British trawler *Kodama*, British sloop *Narcissus*,

Italian trawler *Porto Torres*, and American converted yacht *Wenonah* (SP–165).

Three days into the voyage, an enemy submarine, lurking nearby, torpedoed the British merchantman SS *Messidor* at 1924. At that time, *Venetia* was steaming at 11 knots some 800 yards astern and was zigzagging to starboard of the convoy. Hearing the explosion, *Venetia* went to full speed and headed toward the front of the convoy. Between 1926 and 2000, she searched for the U-boat and dropped two British and 11 American depth charges. During that time, the ship once sighted a suspicious wake on the starboard bow. *Venetia* came hard right but, upon investigation, decided that the wake had not been made by either a submarine or a torpedo.

While the yacht continued searching for the submarine, she kept within sight of the sinking *Messidor* which her crewmen could see plainly in the moonlight. At 2025, the patrol craft passed within hailing distance of *Kodama* which was busy picking up survivors, asking for a count on the survivors and the missing. *Kodama* replied that she had not finished counting; after telling the trawler to steam in a circle and continue counting until totals had been reached, *Venetia* continued the search for the U-boat.

Venetia neared *Kodama* again shortly under an hour later, and ascertained the count of survivors to be 33, with one man missing. Porterfield—not at all certain that *Messidor* would sink—wondered if he should not retain *Messidor*'s officers to accompany the steamer to port in case she could be towed in. He prepared a wireless message to Algiers asking for a tug and escort to either Algiers or Bougie, and stating that he would stand by *Messidor* until 0500 the next morning. However, all of his speculations were soon rendered academic, as *Messidor* began listing rapidly to starboard at 2230. Ten minutes later, the freighter rolled over and sank. *Venetia* then headed northward to catch up with the convoy and joined at 0746 on 24 July; two days later, the convoy arrived at Genoa without further incident.

Venetia returned to Gibraltar with a 20-ship convoy on 1 August after an uneventful passage. The next day, Comdr. Porterfield was relieved by Capt. C. F. Howell, USCG, as commanding officer. On the 16th of that month, the armed yacht began a refit and overhaul at Gibraltar, entering drydock on the 26th for hull repairs. *Venetia* put to sea on 14 September with an 11-ship convoy and arrived at Genoa six days later. She returned to her home base on 26 September, convoying 19 ships safely to port.

Venetia subsequently conducted two more round-trip convoy escort voyages—one to Genoa and one to Bizerte—before she departed Gibraltar on 6 November, bound for Madeira, in company with *Surveyor*. The ships arrived at Funchal, Madeira, on the 9th, and *Venetia* departed on the 11th, the day that the armistice was signed at Compiegne, France, ending World War I. The armed yacht made arrival at Ponta Delgada, in the Azores, on the 13th, en route to Gibraltar, which she reached on the 19th.

During her last month in European waters, *Venetia* made a round-trip voyage to Portugal before sailing for the United States on 21 December, towing *SC–223*, as part of a homeward-bound subchaser detachment built around the tender *Hannibal*. Later towing *SC–330*, the yacht reached Ponta Delgada on the day after Christmas. Subsequently touching at St. Thomas, Virgin Islands; Santo Domingo, Dominican Republic; and Port-au-Prince, Haiti, *Venetia* arrived at Guantanamo Bay on 31 January 1919. She transited the Panama Canal on 3 February and reached San Francisco on the 20th. One week later, on 27 February 1919, *Venetia* shifted to the Mare Island Navy Yard where she was decommissioned, and all of her military fittings were removed. She was returned to her owner on 4 April 1919.

Venetia remained under the ownership of the entrepreneur John D. Spreckles until his death in June of 1926. The graceful yacht was then sold to James Play-

fair, who owned the ship from 1928 to 1939. The ownership of the erstwhile convoy escort and patrol craft changed hands again in 1940, when R. S. Misener acquired the ship. After some 65 years in operation—the latter years on the Great Lakes—she disappeared from the *Lloyd's Register of Yachts* in 1968.

Venetian Maid

(MB: t. 13 (net); l. 60'0''; b. 10'0''; dr. 2'4'' (mean); a. 1 1-pdr., 1 mg.)

Early in World War I, *Venetian Maid*—a wooden-hulled motor boat designed by Carlton Wilby and completed in 1916 at Detroit, Mich., by the American Boat Co.—was slated to be acquired by the Navy from Thomas Hunter for use as a section patrol boat. She was assigned the designation SP–188 and scheduled to be delivered to the Navy on 14 June 1917. However, records indicate that the boat was never actually taken over by Federal authorities.

Vengeance

I

(Brig: a. 12 guns)

The first *Vengeance*—a former merchant ship and dockyard tender—was one of four vessels procured and fitted out by the French government in February 1779 to form a special squadron under command of Capt. John Paul Jones. The other three vessels were the frigate *Bonhomme Richard*, the frigate *Pallas*, and the cutter *Cerf*.

On 19 June 1779 the squadron sailed from L'Orient, France, accompanied by the frigate *Alliance* to escort French merchantmen and troop transports to Bordeaux, and also to cruise against the British in the Bay of Biscay. On the second day out, *Alliance* fouled *Bonhomme Richard*, causing sufficient damage to force the squadron to return to port for repairs on 1 July. *Vengeance*, *Pallas*, and *Cerf* soon put out to sea, and cruised briefly off Belle-Ile to protect American and French commerce from British privateers before returning to port.

The entire squadron sailed again on 14 August 1779, this time embarking on an extended cruise northwest around the west coast of Ireland into the North Sea and then down the east coast of Scotland and England. Four days out, the *Monsieur*, a French privateer accompanying the squadron, captured a ship and left with her prize the next day. A large vessel outran the Americans during a chase on 19 and 20 August, but the squadron overtook *Mayflower* on 21 August and sent that British brig to L'Orient as a prize. The vessels separated during a storm on the night of 26 August but reassembled on the night of 1 and 2 September. The following day, they took an Irish brigantine returning from Norway; and, on 15 September, they captured two colliers. Unfavorable winds frustrated an attempt to attack the port of Leith, Scotland, on 17 September.

While off Spurn Head, England, on 22 September, Jones received a report from *Vengeance* that the English Baltic Fleet was approaching from the northeast. Capt. Jones immediately ordered *Vengeance* to stand out to sea, find *Alliance*, and tell her to rendezvous with the squadron off Flamborough Head, England. The Americans encountered the fleet of 41 ships under convoy of the frigate HMS *Serapis* and the sloop-of-war *Countess of Scarborough* the next day. During the ensuing battle, Capt. Jones in *Bonhomme Richard* captured *Serapis* against tremendous odds, losing his own ship but gaining an international reputation for gallantry and daring both for himself and the fledgling Continental Navy. *Pallas* took *Countess of Scarborough* to complete the victory.

All told, the American squadron took 16 merchant vessels as prizes during the voyage; *Vengeance*, herself claiming three. Jones' exploits also left the English coastline in considerable uproar for the duration of the war. *Vengeance* remained with the Navy until American independence was secured in 1783 and was then returned to France.

II

(Brig: a. 3 guns)

The second *Vengeance*—a brig—was purchased by the Navy at Boston, Mass., in 1805 for use as a bomb ketch against the Barbary pirates. Commanded by Lieutenant William Lewis, she left Boston for the Mediterranean on 19 June and was with Capt. John Rodgers' squadron of 13 warships when it appeared off Tunis on 1 August. Impressed by the American show of force, the Bey of Tunis elected to accept American peace terms, and *Vengeance* did not see action. Her subsequent movements are unknown, but she was broken up at New York City in 1818.

Vent

(ARS–29: dp. 1,897; l. 183'3''; b. 37'; dr. 14'8''; s. 12.0 k.; cpl. 65; a. 1 3''; cl. *Diver*)

Vent (ARS–29) was laid down on 29 January 1943 at Bellingham, Wash., by the Bellingham Marine Railway Co.; launched on 30 June 1943; and commissioned on 7 April 1944, Lt. Howard H. Bothell, USNR, in command.

Following shakedown, *Vent* departed Long Beach, Calif., with *YC–1043* in tow, on 16 June 1944. She arrived in Hawaiian waters 11 days later and delivered her tow. She participated in salvage operations on five LST's which had been set afire by an accidental explosion and had sunk in West Loch, Pearl Harbor, on 21 May. On 23 July, she sailed for the South Pacific and arrived at Funafuti, Ellice Islands, on 7 August. From there, she pushed on for Milne Bay and Manus.

Subsequently operating out of Espiritu Santo in the New Hebrides, *Vent* touched at Efate, Noumea, and Guadalcanal. She arrived off Utupua Island on 30 November and, from 1 to 3 December, conducted salvage operations, in company with *Apache* (ATF–67) and *Tawasa* (ATF–92), for SS *Dominican Victory*, grounded off Basilisk Reef.

The salvage ship returned to Pearl Harbor in March 1945 for an overhaul and, while in the Hawaiian Islands, salvaged Fleet Marine Force equipment sunk off Hilo from 3 to 5 May. On 2 June, she sailed west once more and proceeded via Eniwetok in the Marshalls to the Marianas. The ship conducted harbor clearance and salvage operations in Tanapag Harbor, Saipan, into the summer of 1945. The end of the war in August, however, meant little to the ship's deployment—for there was much salvage work to be done in the wake of the war.

The destructive typhoon which swirled into the fleet anchorage at Buckner Bay, Okinawa, in October 1945, swept many small craft ashore. *Vent* participated in salvaging a number of AFD's grounded on the beaches of Buckner Bay. The salvage ship later operated in the Marianas before she sailed, via Pearl Harbor, for the west coast of the United States and arrived at San Pedro, Calif., on 21 June 1946.

Subsequently decommisioned on 30 August 1946, *Vent* was struck from the Navy list on 12 March 1948 and sold to Henry J. Barbey on 30 June 1948.

Venture

I

(MB: t. 48 (gross); l. 80'0''; b. 13'0''; dr. 4'0''; cpl. 14; a. 1 3-pdr., 1 1-pdr.)

The first *Venture* (SP–616)—a wooden-hulled, screw steam yacht designed by F. D. Lawley and completed as *Shadow* in 1916 at South Boston, Mass., by George Lawley and Sons Corp.—was acquired by the Navy under free lease from Mrs. Sarah L. Silsbee of Isleboro, Maine, on 28 April 1917 and commissioned the same day, Chief Boatswain's Mate Zidon C. Long, USNRF, in command.

Attached to the 5th Section, 1st Naval District, Portsmouth, New Hampshire, *Venture* operated out of the Portsmouth Navy Yard through the end of World War I, conducting security patrols and performing dispatch duties. Following the armistice, she was decommissioned on 5 February 1919 and returned to her owner.

II

(PC–826: dp. 138 (f.); l. 110'0''; b. 17'6''; dr. 6'0'' (mean) (f.); s. 17 k. (tl.); cpl. 24; a. 2 .50-cal. mg., 4 dc.)

Vixen—a wooden-hulled yacht built in 1931 by the Consolidated Shipbuilding Corp. at New York City—was acquired on 27 December 1941; designated *PC–826*; and commissioned on 10 March 1942.

PC–826 was assigned to the 3d Naval District and, for the duration of World War II, escorted coastwise convoys along the seaboard encompassed within the 3d Naval District and participated in searches for reported German U-boats. However, her entire career appears to have passed without any combat action. On 15 July 1943, *PC–826* became *Venture* and received the designation PYc–51. On 25 September 1944, she was reduced from "in commission" status to "in service" status and continued so for the remaining 13 months of her Navy career. After the war ended, the yacht was placed out of service at New York on 10 October 1945; and her name was struck from the Navy list on 24 October. On 12 April 1946, she was delivered to the War Shipping Administration berthing facility located on Long Island, N.Y., to be sold.

III

(MSO–496: dp. 775; l. 172'; b. 35'; dr. 10'; s. 14 k.; cpl. 70; a. 1 40mm., 2 .50-cal. mg.; cl. *Aggressive*)

The third *Venture* (MSO–496) was laid down on 11 January 1955 at Ft. Lauderdale, Fla., by Broward Marine Inc. as AM–496; redesignated MSO–496 on 7 February 1955; launched on 27 November 1956; sponsored by Mrs. Leroy Williams, wife of the Governor of Florida; and commissioned on 3 February 1958, Lt. Comdr. James H. Agles in command.

Following shakedown training at Guantanamo Bay, Cuba, during March and April, *Venture* conducted local minesweeping operations out of Charleston, S.C., until late June at which time she entered the Charleston Naval Shipyard for post-shakedown availability. That repair period lasted until 1 December when she began preparations to deploy to the Mediterranean Sea. Although her home port was changed from Charleston, S.C., to Panama City, Fla., on New Year's Day 1959, the minesweeper embarked upon her first Mediterranean cruise from the former port on 9 January as the flagship of Mine Division (MinDiv) 81. After a routine tour of duty with the 6th Fleet, *Venture* returned to Charleston on 30 May for a tender availability at the naval shipyard and normal operations out of Charleston until late summer.

On 3 August 1959, the minesweeper departed Charleston, bound finally for Panama City, Fla., her new home port. For the next dozen years, she served the Navy's Mine Defense Laboratory located there. For the remainder of her career, the minesweeper and her division mates helped that institution to develop mine warfare countermeasures. When not operating under the auspices of the laboratory, she performed mine warfare training exercises under the direction of the Commander, Mine Squadron 8. In addition, she periodically

Venture (SP–616) and five other commandeered patrol craft moored at Portsmouth Navy Yard, 16 May 1917. From left to right an unidentified craft; *Gypsy* (SP–55); *Doris B. IV* (SP–625); *Venture*; an unidentified schooner; and *Comber* (SP–344) illustrate the variety of types and sizes of small craft taken over for local patrol duty during World War I.

provided services in support of the research and developmental work carried on by the Operational Test and Evaluation Force—frequently in conjunction with the Naval Mine Defense Laboratory mentioned above—and by the Naval Ships Research and Development Center (popularly dubbed the David Taylor Model Basin) located at Carderock, Md.

During that time period, *Venture* departed the immediate area of the eastern Gulf of Mexico infrequently. On occasion, she made visits to Norfolk, Charleston, and Mobile, but those calls either were very brief or were made strictly for the purpose of repairs and availabilities. Early in 1969, however, she did clear the Panama City area for a tour of duty overseas. Between 10 January and 16 June 1969, she made her second and last deployment to the 6th Fleet—almost a decade to the day after she had begun her first Mediterranean mission.

Back in Panama City by mid-June, the minesweeper resumed duty assisting in the development of mine countermeasures. That task carried the warship through the last two years of her naval career. Just before she began inactivation preparations, she became flagship of MinDiv 21 when the Atlantic Fleet Mine Force was reorganized; and MinDiv 81 was transformed into MinDiv 21. *Venture* began preparations for her inactivation on 3 May 1971 at Charleston. She was decommissioned there on 2 August 1971 and, on 10 November, was berthed with the Norfolk Group, Atlantic Reserve Fleet. In September 1977, *Venture*'s name was struck from the Navy list; and she was slated to be sold for scrap. As of 21 April 1978, no final disposition had been consummated.

Venus

One of the major planets of the solar system, Venus moves in an orbit between Earth and Mercury and, at its brightest, is far more brilliant than any fixed star, often being visible in full daylight.

(AK–135: dp. 14,550; l. 441'6''; b. 56'11''; dr. 28'4''; s. 12.5 k.; cpl. 206; a. 1 5'', 4 40mm.; cl. *Crater*; T. EC2–S–C1)

William Williams was laid down under a Maritime Commission contract (MCE hull 263) on 5 July 1942 at Richmond, Calif., by the Permanente Metals Corp., Yard No. 2; launched on 21 August; sponsored by Mrs. Paul S. Marrin; was delivered to her owners, the Isthmian Steamship Lines, on 8 September; and operated in the Pacific for the remainder of 1942 and into 1943. On 2 May 1943, while near Suva, Fiji Islands, *William Williams* was torpedoed by Japanese submarine *I–19*, commanded by Lt. Takaichi Kinashi who, while commanding this I-boat, had torpedoed *Wasp* (CV–7), *North Carolina* (BB–55), and *O'Brien* (DD–415) with the same spread of torpedoes off Guadalcanal on 15 September 1942. Kinashi chose not to finish off the crippled "Liberty ship," however, and cleared the area. *William Williams*, meanwhile, abandoned by her crew, remained afloat though heavily damaged.

Reboarded, *William Williams* was towed to Fiji and thence to Auckland, New Zealand, where the Navy acquired the ship on 6 November 1943 from the War Shipping Administration under a bareboat charter. Enough repairs to make the ship seaworthy were effected, and she was commissioned as *Venus* on 10 November, Lt. Comdr. George H. L. Peet in command.

Towed from Auckland, *Venus* arrived at Sydney, Australia, where she was decommissioned and placed "in service" on 4 December. Docking and conversion work at the port were delayed due to higher priorities being assigned to other ships and labor troubles at the dockyards themselves. Once these obstacles were overcome, work proceeded apace—a difficult task due to the fact that the conversion was accomplished in a foreign yard with non-standard materials. Designated AK–135, the ship was placed back in commission on 26 September 1944. On 4 October, she commenced her shakedown and soon loaded general cargo and dry provisions before she sailed for the Admiralties on 26 October.

She reached Manus four days later and discharged some of her cargo. There, she also received her main battery, a single 5-inch, dual-purpose gun. The ship witnessed an air raid on 9 November, but the attack was directed at another vicinity, and the cargo vessel did not participate in the action. The following day, *Mount Hood* (AE–11) blew up in a cataclysmic explosion while handling ammunition at Seeadler Harbor. All but a few of her crew (those who were ashore at the time) were killed in the blast which not only atomized the ammunition ship but severely damaged other ships nearby. *Venus* responded to this emergency by sending a boat to assist in medical operations with 30 units of blood plasma.

During the ship's stay at Manus, several cases of diphtheria developed on board, and all hands were restricted to the ship. On 28 November, *Venus* sailed for Dutch New Guinea, arrived at Hollandia the following day, and stayed until Christmas Eve, when she headed for Aitape—arriving there on Christmas Day. On 27 December 1944, the cargo vessel got underway for Cape Sansapor, where she supplied LST's attached to Task Group (TG) 77.5, which later took part in the landings at Lingayen Gulf. Proceeding to Morotai upon completion of these revictualling operations, she unloaded the remainder of her cargo and fueled various small craft of the Royal Australian Navy.

On 4 January 1945, during *Venus'* stay at Morotai, Japanese aircraft conducted a bombing raid on the nearby land base, but the planes were driven off by antiaircraft fire and night fighters. Six days later, *Venus*, her holds empty, sailed with five other ships to Hollandia, where she took on board passengers. While proceeding thence to Australia, she encountered heavy gales but arrived safely at Brisbane on 23 January.

The ship underwent repairs soon after she arrived while concurrently loading equipment of the 109th Fleet Hospital unit and of the 544th Construction Battalion (CB or "Seabees") for transport to the Philippine Islands. She departed Brisbane on 4 February, proceeded via Manus and Hollandia, and joined a convoy off the Dutch New Guinea coast. The Allied ships arrived at Guiuan Roadstead off Samar on 27 February. Part of the Seabee unit soon went ashore to begin building the hospital, while the remainder stayed on board to unload equipment and stores. Eventually, as more Seabees could be accommodated ashore, the job of unloading passed on to *Venus'* crew. Despite the lack of barges and experienced stevedores, *Venus* succeeded in unloading all equipment and supplies earmarked for the hospital unit before she joined a southbound convoy on 8 April, got underway for the Admiralities, and arrived at Manus one week later.

Proceeding thence to Emirau, *Venus* loaded the remnants of the 77th CB Battalion and their equipment, accomplishing this on 25 April before getting underway for Brisbane to load more of the 77th Battalion's equipment. Besides the full load of cargo, *Venus* also accommodated 600 passengers, and additional galley and bunking facilities were set up on deck beneath makeshift shelters to take care of these men. The cargo vessel then headed north for the Philippines, via Milne Bay, and arrived at Manila on 13 June to commence

offloading and to disembark her passengers. Five days later, the ship shifted to a berth alongside a sunken Japanese cargo ship.

With the erstwhile enemy freighter serving as a dock, *Venus* offloaded the remainder of her cargo—experiencing two air raid alerts during her stay at Manila—and completed these operations by 30 June. She then pressed southward for the Admiralties and loaded 1,500 tons of bombs for transport to Bougainville in the Solomons. The installation of a gyro compass delayed her sailing until 25 July, but the ship arrived at Empress Augusta Bay on the 29th.

Eleven days later, *Venus* departed Torokina, Bougainville, bound for the New Hebrides and arrived at Espiritu Santo on 11 August. She loaded material for drydock *ABSD–1*, loading from lighters in Pallikulo Bay. Due to poor loading conditions, the job was not completed until 7 September, when she was ready to sail for the Philippine Islands. During her stay at Espiritu Santo, word arrived that Japan had surrendered; and, for the first time since commissioning, the ship could sail at night without having to "darken ship."

Venus arrived at Samar on 20 September and discharged her cargo before moving on to Subic Bay. She sailed from Cebu on 15 December, bound for the Hawaiian Islands, and arrived at Pearl Harbor on 16 March. Decommissioned on 18 April 1946, the ship was subsequently towed by *Hitchiti* (ATF–103) to the west coast, departing Pearl Harbor on 5 December 1947 and arriving at San Francisco on the 13th.

Declared surplus to Navy needs, the ship was struck from the Navy list on 19 February 1948. Stripped for disposal, she was returned to the Maritime Commission on the 27th and was placed in the National Defense Reserve Fleet at Suisun Bay, Calif. The ship was scrapped at Oakland, Calif., in August 1961.

Venus received one battle star for her service during World War II as *William Williams*.

Verbena

A large genus of herbs or subshrubs mostly native to the Americas.

(ScGbt.: t. 104; l. 74'; b. 17'6''; dr. 8'; s. 12 mph; a. 1 20-pdr. P.r., 1 12-pdr. sb.)

Verbena—originally the wooden steamer *Ino* built at Brooklyn, N.Y., in 1864—was purchased by the Navy at New York City on 7 June 1864 and commissioned at the New York Navy Yard on 11 July 1864.

On 19 July, the vessel was attached to the Potomac Flotilla for duty as a tug. Two days later, she deployed in the Potomac River off Point Lookout, Md.; and she served for most of the duration of the Civil War as a tender to the ironclad *Roanoke*. After the collapse of the Confederacy, *Verbena* received orders on 5 May 1865 to proceed to the Washington Navy Yard, where she was decommissioned on 13 June.

Verbena was sold at public auction there to W. E. Gladwick on 20 July; redocumented as *Game Cock* on 9 September; renamed *Edward G. Burgess* on 7 July 1885; and dropped from the registry in 1900.

Verdi

(MB: l. 75'0''; b. 11'5''; dr. 3'6''; s. 15 k.; a. 1 1-pdr., 1 mg.)

Verdi (SP–979)—a wooden motorboat built in 1909 at Morris Heights, N.Y., by the Charles L. Seabury Co. and the Gas Engine and Power Co.—was acquired by the Navy from Walter J. Green, of Utica, N.Y., on 30 June 1917. Homeported during her civilian service at Clayton, N.Y., on the St. Lawrence River, *Verdi* was assigned section patrol duties with the 9th Naval District. She served in the Great Lakes through the armistice of 11 November 1918, which ended World War I, and was returned to her owner on 4 December 1918.

Verdin

A tiny, yellow-headed titmouse found in the south-western United States.

Verdin (ASR–17)—projected as a *Chanticleer*-class submarine rescue vessel—was to be built at Savannah, Ga., by the Savannah Machine Foundry; but, because of Japan's collapse, the contract for her construction was cancelled on 12 August 1945.

I

(YMS–471: dp. 320 (f.); l. 136'0''; b. 24'6''; dr. 6'1''; s. 12 k.; cpl. 33; a. 1 3'', 2 20mm.; cl. *YMS–1*)

PCS–1439 was laid down on 5 September 1943 at Jacksonville, Fla., by the Gibbs Gas Engine Co.; redesignated *YMS–471* on 27 September 1943; launched on 23 May 1944; and commissioned on 27 October 1944.

Following brief shakedown training, *YMS–471* proceeded to Charleston, S.C., and began escorting coastwise convoys and conducting minesweeping operations. That duty ended in April 1945 when she was transferred to the Pacific Fleet. After a long voyage which took her by way of the Panama Canal, San Diego, Pearl Harbor, Eniwetok, Guam, and Saipan, the minesweeper finally joined the 3d Fleet off Okinawa in June. During the last week of the month, she and the other ships of Mine Squadron (MinRon) 105 swept mines from the Buckner Bay, Kerama Retto, and Unten Ko areas of the Ryukyus. In July, *YMS–471* ventured into the East China Sea for mine disposal operations.

At the time Japan capitulated, the minesweeper was undergoing repairs at San Pedro Bay, Leyte. Soon thereafter, she headed north to begin the monumental job of clearing mines from waters around Japan for transports bringing American occupation forces and supporting shipping. She concentrated on sweeping the approaches to the island of Honshu and remained at the task from 8 September 1945 until 20 February 1946, when she began preparations for the voyage back to the United States. The minesweeper reached the west coast in April 1946 and returned home to Charleston in June to begin demobilization.

Though never actually decommissioned, she remained inactive at Charleston until early in 1947, when she embarked upon a refresher training cruise in the West Indies. She also participated in a fleet exercise held off Cuba. On 18 March 1947, near the conclusion of the exercise, *YMS–471* was named *Verdin* and was redesignated AMS–38. After a tour of duty at Yorktown, Va., serving as a training platform for the students of the Mine Warfare School, *Verdin* returned to Charleston in November where she remained until the following spring. In April 1948, she entered the Charleston Naval Shipyard for repairs and then put to sea once again for refresher training out of Norfolk. In November, the minesweeper participated in cold weather fleet exercises off Newfoundland before returning to warmer waters.

This time, she reported to Panama City, Fla., for duty at the Navy's mine countermeasures research facility. For the next six years, *Verdin* alternated between mine warfare research duty at Panama City and mine warfare school ship operations at Yorktown. Periodic overhauls, mine and convoy exercises, and refresher training punctuated these two primary assignments. In November 1954, *Verdin* transferred back to Charleston where she became flagship for Mine Division 43. She spent her last eight active months there as an operational unit of the Mine Force. On 7 February 1955, she was redesignated MSC(O)–38. On 1 July 1955, she reported to Green Cove Springs, Fla., for

inactivation. There, she went into reserve on 30 August 1955. A little over four years later, on 1 November 1959, her name was struck from the Navy list. No documents have been found giving details of her final disposition.

Verdin (MSC(O)–38) earned three battle stars for World War II service as *YMS–471*.

Vergana

Possibly a euphonious contraction of the Spanish phrase *vergas en alto*, meaning "all ready to sail."

(ScStr: t. 128; l. 145'; b. 17'10''; dr. 8'6''; dph. 9'4''; s. 12 k.; cpl. 19; a. 2 1-pdrs.)

Vergana—a steel-hulled, single-screw, schooner-rigged steam yacht—was built in 1897 by T. S. Marvel of Newburgh, N.Y. Owned first by F. S. Flower of New York City and later by Wilbert Melville of Los Angeles, Calif., the ship was acquired by stationer and printer Charles H. Crocker in either late 1916 or early 1917. She was registered at San Francisco, Calif. and homeported at Belvedere Cove, Calif., at the time of America's entry into World War I, when the Navy evinced an interest in the ship for local patrol duties.

Although some records indicate that *Vergana* was delivered to the Navy on 4 May 1917, her deck log records that her first commanding officer, Ens. E. Dahlgren, USNRF, reported on board the ship on 16 April 1917. The ship was commissioned on 10 July 1917.

Vergana—classified as SP–519—performed harbor entrance patrol duty at San Francisco for the duration of World War I. She alternated with *Sentinel* (SP–180), *SP–647* (formerly *California*), and the Coast Guard vessel *Golden Gate* underway at the mouth of San Francisco Bay or stationary at guard duty beside a pier. She performed those duties almost continuously, with periods of upkeep and liberty breaking that routine.

Decommissioned at the Mare Island Navy Yard, Vallejo, Calif., on 16 January 1919, *Vergana* apparently remained in reserve thereafter. Reclassified an old district patrol craft, OYP–519, on 17 July 1920, the ship was ordered sold on 30 September 1921. An initial sale, of that date, was never consummated; but, on 25 February 1922, *Vergana* was sold to Louis A. Fracchia of Oakland, Calif.

Veritas

Minor planet No. 490, discovered on 3 September 1902 by astronomer Max Wolf of Heidelberg, Germany. The planet is named for a mythological goddess, the daughter of Time and Saturn.

(AKA–50: dp. 7,080; l. 426'0''; b. 58'0''; dr. 16'0''; s. 16.9 k.; cpl. 303; a. 1 5'', 8 40mm.; cl. *Sidonia*; T. S4–SE2–BE1)

Veritas (AKA–50) was laid down under a Maritime Commission contract (MC hull 1911) on 26 April 1945 at Providence, R.I., by the Walsh-Kaiser Co., Inc.; launched on 16 June 1945; sponsored by Mrs. Fred B. Smith; and commissioned on 19 July 1945, Lt. Comdr. A. S. Brooks, USNR, in command.

Into the fall of 1945, *Veritas* operated along the Atlantic coast, making cargo runs which took her as far north as Boston and ranged south to Hampton Roads, Va. After loading cargo at Norfolk from 22 to 26 October, *Veritas* got underway on the 26th for Bermuda and the only duty which took her away from the eastern seaboard of the United States.

The cargo vessel returned to Norfolk and transported cargo to Baltimore in December and made stops at Bayonne, N.J., and New York City before heading for Hampton Roads early in 1946. She arrived at Norfolk on 17 January 1946 and was decommissioned on 21 February 1946. Struck from the Navy list on 12 April 1946, the cargo vessel was delivered to the Maritime Commission on 29 June 1946, in whose custody she remained until disappearing from registers of American merchant shipping in 1949.

Vermilion

A parish in far southern Louisiana bordering on the Gulf of Mexico and a county in eastern Illinois bordering on Indiana.

(AKA–107: dp. 13,910 (tl.); l. 459'2''; b. 63'0''; dr. 26'4'' (lim.); s. 16.5 k. (tl.); cpl. 425; a. 1 5'', 8 40mm., 16 20mm.; cl. *Tolland*; T. C2–S–AJ3)

Vermilion (AKA–107) was laid down under a Maritime Commission contract (MC hull 1700) on 17 October 1944 at Wilmington, N.C., by the North Carolina Shipbuilding & Drydock Co.; launched on 12 December 1944; sponsored by Mrs. Rex Freeman; delivered to the Navy incomplete on 23 December 1944; moved to the Todd Shipyard at Brooklyn, New York; completed as a Navy attack cargo ship and placed in commission at Brooklyn on 23 June 1945, Capt. F. B. Eggers in command.

Assigned to the Atlantic Fleet and based at Norfolk, Va., *Vermilion* spent more than a year after commissioning engaged in shakedown and refresher training. That routine occupied her time until late in 1946. In November of that year, she made a cruise to South American waters and resumed duty out of Norfolk upon her return. Normal Atlantic Fleet operations—including midshipman summer training cruises, amphibious exercises, type training and reserve training cruises—took up *Vermilion*'s time for almost three years. On 26 August 1949, she was decommissioned and berthed with the Reserve Fleet Group located at Orange, Tex. The outbreak of the Korean War in the summer of 1950 interrupted her inactivity. She was recommissioned at Orange on 16 October 1950, Capt. A. Jackson in command.

Though the Korean War occasioned *Vermilion*'s return to active duty, she never saw service in that conflict. Instead, she replaced more combat-ready ships in the Atlantic Fleet and released them for duty in the Far East. After shakedown training, the attack cargo ship began normal operations with the Atlantic Fleet. That employment continued until the summer of 1951 when she participated in Operation "Bluejay," the first large scale seaborne lift of supplies to the new air base under construction at Thule, Greenland. She returned from that mission to Norfolk on 29 August 1951 and resumed operations with the Atlantic Fleet. During

the summer of 1952, the ship returned to Thule on another supply mission. She completed that operation on 25 August when she returned to Norfolk and to duty with the Atlantic Fleet. The end of the year and the beginning of 1953 saw her operating in the West Indies out of the base at Guantanamo Bay, Cuba. She returned to Norfolk on 2 February and once again started normal duty out of that port.

For the next five years, *Vermilion* participated in Atlantic Fleet amphibious exercises at Onslow Beach, N.C., and in the Caribbean. She also conducted independent ship's exercises and made cruises the length of the Atlantic seaboard. In June of 1958, the attack cargo ship left the east coast of the United States for a six-month deployment to the Mediterranean Sea. She returned home in December and resumed her normal schedule of operations.

Her routine of amphibious exercises, independent ship's exercises, and the like continued until the fall of 1962 when she was deployed to the West Indies to support the American quarantine of Cuba during the Cuban missile crisis. Following that mission, the ship returned once again to her familiar routine of operations out of Norfolk. In May 1963, she once more departed the east coast for a deployment with the 6th Fleet in the Mediterranean.

Vermilion returned to Norfolk on 17 October and began another four-year stint of operations along the Atlantic seaboard and in the Caribbean. In January 1968, she departed Morehead City, N.C., with Marine Air Control Squadron 6, bound—via the Panama Canal and Pearl Harbor—for the Ryukyus. She arrived in Buckner Bay, Okinawa, on 22 February and departed those islands on the 25th with Marine Air Control Squadron 8 embarked. She disembarked the air squadron at Morehead City on 30 March and returned to Norfolk on the 31st. Following a six-month overhaul at the Norfolk Naval Shipyard, during which she was redesignated LKA–107 on 14 August, *Vermilion* resumed Atlantic Fleet operations in November. She continued to operate out of Norfolk for over two years. On 13 April 1971, the ship was decommissioned at Norfolk. She was transferred to the Maritime Administration on 27 July 1971 for layup in the National Defense Reserve Fleet at James River, Va. Her name was struck from the Navy list on 1 January 1977.

Vermillion

A bay—frequently spelled Vermilion with only one "L"—located in the Gulf of Mexico off the coast of Louisiana, southeast of Vermilion Parish and southwest of Iberia Parish.

Vermillion (AKA–107) at Vieques on maneuvers, 1949. (80–G–445319)

Vermillion (ACV–52) was laid down on 10 May 1943 by the Seattle-Tacoma Shipbuilding Co. as a *Prince William*-class auxiliary aircraft carrier; redesignated an escort aircraft carrier, CVE–52, on 10 June 1943; assigned to Great Britain on 23 June 1943; launched on 27 September 1943; and accepted by Great Britain on 20 January 1944. Commissioned in the Royal Navy as HMS *Smiter* (D.55), a "Ruler-class" escort carrier, she served the British throughout the remainder of World War II. She returned to the United States at Norfolk on 20 March 1946 and was officially transferred back to the United States Navy on 6 April 1946. She was immediately determined to be surplus to the needs of the Navy and was designated for sale. Her name was struck from the Navy list on 6 May 1946. On 28 January 1947, she was sold to the Newport News Shipbuilding and Drydock Co., Norfolk, Va., for conversion to mercantile service. She was subsequently resold to *Compania Argentina de Navigacion Dodero, S.A.*, and entered mercantile service in 1948 at Buenos Aires as SS *Artillero*.

Vermillion Bay

See *Vermillion* above for name source.

Vermillion Bay (CVE–108)—a *Commencement Bay*-class escort carrier—was renamed *Kula Gulf* (*q.v.*) on 6 November 1943, prior to the laying of her keel.

Vermont

Vermont, the 14th state, was admitted to the Union on 4 March 1791. She was the first to enter after the ratification of the Constitution by all 13 of the original states. The name Vermont is a French term, meaning "green mountains" and was first used by the French explorer Samuel de Champlain in 1612 to describe the area east of Lake Champlain.

I

(SL: t. 2,633; lbp. 197'1½''; b. 53'6''; dph. 21'6''; cpl. 820; a. 20 8'' Sg., 64 32-pdrs.; cl. *North Carolina*)

The first *Vermont* was one of nine, 74-gun warships authorized by Congress on 29 April 1816. She was laid down at the Boston Navy Yard in September 1818; finished about 1825; and kept on the stocks until finally launched at Boston on 15 September 1848 in the interest of both space and fire safety considerations. However, *Vermont* was not commissioned at this time. Instead, the already aged ship of the line remained in ordinary at Boston until the outbreak of the Civil War in April 1861. At this time, the cavernous hull of the vessel was badly needed as a store and receiving ship at Port Royal, S.C., and she was commissioned at Boston on 30 January 1862, Comdr. Augustus S. Baldwin in command. She received orders to sail for Port Royal for duty with Rear Admiral Samuel F. Du Pont's South Atlantic Blockading Squadron on 17 February and left Boston on 24 February under tow by the steamer *Kensington*.

That evening, a violent northwest gale accompanied by snow struck the vessels while off Cape Cod Light, Mass. *Kensington* let go the tow lines, but *Vermont* refused to obey her helm, broached, and had all her sails and most of her boats blown and torn away. The gale raged for 50 hours; and, by the morning of the 26th, *Vermont* was drifting eastward with no rudder, her berth deck flooded, and much of the interior of the vessel destroyed. Later, on the 26th, *Vermont* sighted the schooner *Flying Mist*, hailed her, put a man on board and persuaded her captain to return to the east coast and report the helpless condition of the ship to naval authorities. Rescue vessels began to reach the

stricken warship on 7 March and enabled *Vermont* to sail into Port Royal under her own power on 12 April

Vermont remained anchored at Port Royal, where she served the South Atlantic Blockading Squadron as an ordnance, hospital, receiving, and store ship and drew praise from Rear Admiral Du Pont. Secretary of the Navy Gideon Welles ordered the vessel to return to New York for "public service" on 25 July 1864. She left Port Royal on 2 August and was replaced there by her sister ship-of-the-line *New Hampshire*. *Vermont* remained at New York for the next 37 years, serving both as a store and receiving ship. She was condemned and struck from the Navy list on 19 December 1901 and was sold at New York on 17 April 1902.

II

(Battleship No. 20: dp. 16,000 (n.); l. 456'4''; b. 76'10''; dr. 24'6'' (mean); s. 18 k.; cpl. 880; a. 4 12'', 8 8'' 12 7'', 20 3'', 12 3-pdrs., 4 1-pdrs, 4 .30-cal. mg. 2 .30-cal. Colt mg.; cl. *Connecticut*)

The second *Vermont* (Battleship No. 20) was laid down on 21 May 1904 at Quincy, Mass., by the Fore River Shipbuilding Co.; launched on 31 August 1905; sponsored by Miss Jennie Bell, the daughter of Governor Charles J. Bell of Vermont; and commissioned at the Boston Navy Yard on 4 March 1907, Capt. William P. Potter in command.

After her "shaking down" cruise off the eastern seaboard between Boston and Hampton Roads, Va., *Vermont* participated in maneuvers with the 1st Division of the Atlantic Fleet and, later, with the 1st and 2d Squadrons. Making a final trial trip between Hampton Roads and Provincetown, Mass., between 30 August and 5 September, *Vermont* arrived at the Boston Navy Yard on 7 September and underwent repairs until late in November 1907.

Departing Boston on 30 November, she coaled at Bradford, R.I.; received "mine outfits and stores" at Newport, R.I.; and picked up ammunition at Tompkinsville, Staten Island, N.Y.; and arrived at Hampton Roads on 8 December.

There, she made final preparations for the globe-girdling cruise of the United States Atlantic Fleet. Nicknamed the "Great White Fleet" because of the white and spar color of their paint schemes, the 16 pre-dreadnought battleships sailed from Hampton Roads on 16 December, standing out to sea under the gaze of President Theodore Roosevelt who had dispatched the ships around the globe as a dramatic gesture toward Japan, a growing power on the world stage.

Vermont sailed as a unit of the 1st Division, under the overall command of Rear Admiral Robley D. "Fighting Bob" Evans, who was concurrently the Commander in Chief of the Fleet. Over the ensuing months, the battleship visited ports in Chile, Peru, Mexico, California, Hawaii, New Zealand, Australia, the Philippines, Japan, China, and in the Mediterranean, before she returned to Hampton Roads—again passing in review before President Roosevelt—on Washington's Birthday, 22 February 1909. During the voyage, *Vermont*'s commanding officer, Capt. Potter, was advanced to flag rank and took command of the division; his place was taken by Capt. (later Admiral) Frank Friday Fletcher.

Following her return to the United States, *Vermont* underwent repairs at the Boston Navy Yard from 9 March to 23 June and then rejoined the fleet off Provincetown. She subsequently spent the 4th of July at Boston as part of the 1st Division of the Fleet before spending nearly a month, from 7 July to 4 August, in exercises with the Atlantic Fleet. Subsequently coaling at Hampton Roads, the battleship conducted target practice off the Virginia capes in the operating area known as the Southern Drill Grounds.

For the remainder of 1909, *Vermont* continued maneuvers and exercises, broken by visits to Stamford,

Conn., for Columbus Day festivities and to New York City for the observances of the Hudson-Fulton Celebration from 22 September to 9 October. She spent the Christmas holidays at New York City, anchored in the North River.

The battleship then moved south for the winter, reaching Guantanamo Bay on 12 January 1910. For the next two months, she exercised in those Caribbean climes, returning to Hampton Roads and the Virginia capes for elementary target practice that spring. Ultimately reaching Boston on 29 April, the battleship underwent repairs at that yard through mid-July, before embarking members of the Naval Militia at Boston for operations between that port and Provincetown from 22 to 31 July.

Vermont subsequently visited Newport and then sailed for Hampton Roads on 22 August, where she then prepared for target practices between 25 and 27 September, before visiting New York City with other ships of the Atlantic Fleet.

After minor repairs at the Philadelphia Navy Yard, the battleship sailed for European waters on 1 November. Reaching the British Isles a little over two weeks later, Vermont—with other units of the 3d Division, Atlantic Fleet—visited Gravesend, England, from 16 November to 7 December and then called at Brest, France, where she remained until heading for the West Indies on 30 December.

Vermont engaged in winter maneuvers and drills out of Guantanamo Bay, Cuba, from 13 January 1911 to 13 March, before sailing for Hampton Roads. In the ensuing weeks, the battleship operated in the Southern Drill Grounds and off Tangier Island in the Chesapeake Bay, where she conducted target practice. After dropping off target materials at Hampton Roads on 8 April, Vermont sailed later that day for Philadelphia where she arrived on 10 April and entered drydock.

Later in the spring, Vermont resumed her operations with the other pre-dreadnought battleships of the 3d Division. She operated off Pensacola, Fla., and ranged into the Gulf of Mexico, calling at Galveston, Tex., from 7 to 12 June before returning to Pensacola on 13 June for provisions.

Shifting northward to Bar Harbor, Maine, Vermont spent the 4th of July there before she drilled and exercised with the Fleet in Cape Cod Bay and off Provincetown. The battleship then operated off the New England seaboard through mid-August, breaking her periods at sea with a port visit to Salem and alterations at the Boston Navy Yard. She then shifted south to conduct experimental gunnery firings and autumn target practice in the regions from Tangier Sound to the Southern Drill Grounds.

After repairs at the Norfolk Navy Yard from 12 September to 9 October, Vermont rejoined the Fleet at Hampton Roads before participating in the naval review in the North River, at New York City, between 24 October and 2 November. She then maneuvered and exercised with the 1st Squadron of the Fleet before returning to Hampton Roads.

Touching briefly at Tompkinsville on 7 and 8 December, Vermont reached the New York Navy Yard on the latter day for year-end leave and upkeep and remained there until 2 January 1912, when she sailed for the Caribbean and the annual winter maneuvers. She operated in Cuban waters, out of Guantanamo Bay and off Cape Cruz, until 9 March, when she sailed for the Norfolk Navy Yard and an overhaul that lasted into the autumn.

She departed Norfolk on 8 October and reached New York City on the 10th. She participated in the naval review at that port from 10 to 15 October before embarking Commander, 2d Division, Atlantic Fleet, at Hampton Roads between 16 and 18 October.

Vermont subsequently worked out of Hampton Roads, in the Virginia capes-Southern Drill Grounds area, into December. During that time, she conducted target practices and twice participated in humanitarian deeds, searching for the stranded steamship SS Noruega on

2 November and assisting the submarine B-2 (Submarine No. 11) between 13 and 15 December.

The battleship spent Christmas 1912 at the Norfolk Navy Yard before steaming for Cuba and winter maneuvers. En route, she visited Colon, Panama, a terminus of the nearly completed Panama Canal, and reached Guantanamo Bay on 19 January 1913. She subsequently operated out of Guantanamo and Guayancanabo Bay until sailing for Mexican waters on 12 February.

Vermont arrived at Vera Cruz on the 17th and remained at that port into the spring, protecting American interests until 29 April, when she sailed north to rejoin the fleet in Hampton Roads. The battleship conducted one midshipman's training cruise that summer, embarking the midshipmen at Annapolis on 6 June. After rejoining the fleet, Vermont cruised in Block Island Sound and visited Newport.

The battleship then received her regular overhaul at Norfolk from July into October before she conducted target practice off the Southern Drill Grounds. Vermont then made her second European cruise, departing Hampton Roads for French waters on 25 October, reaching Marseilles on 8 November. Ultimately departing that Mediterranean port—on 1 December—Vermont reached the Norfolk Navy Yard five days before Christmas, making port on the end of a towline because of storm damage to a propeller.

Soon after she had completed her post-repair trials and had begun preparations for the spring target practice with the Fleet in the Southern Drill Grounds, tension in Mexico beckoned the battleship. Departing Hampton Roads on 15 April, Vermont reached Vera Cruz very early in the morning of 22 April in company with Arkansas (Battleship No. 33), New Hampshire (Battleship No. 25), South Carolina (Battleship No. 26), and New Jersey (Battleship No. 16). Her landing force—a "battalion" of 12 officers and 308 men—went ashore after daybreak that same day as United States forces occupied the port to block an arms shipment to the dictator Victoriano Huerta. In the fighting that ensued, two officers from the staff were awarded Medals of Honor: Lt. Julius C. Townsend, the battalion commander, and Surgeon Cary DeV. Langhornes, the regimental surgeon of the 2d Seaman Regiment. During the fighting, Vermont's force suffered one fatality, a private from her Marine detachment, killed on the 23d. But for a visit to Tampico, Mex., from 21 September to 10 October, Vermont remained in that Mexican port into later October.

Over the next two and one-half years, Vermont maintained her schedule of operations off the eastern seaboard of the United States, ranging from Newport to Guantanamo Bay, before she lay in reserve at Philadelphia from 1 October to 21 November 1916. Vermont subsequently supported the Marine Corps Expeditionary Force in Haiti from 29 November 1916 to 5 February 1917 and then conducted battle practices out of Guantanamo Bay. She ultimately returned to Norfolk on 29 March 1917.

On 4 April 1917, Vermont entered the Philadelphia Navy Yard for repairs. Two days later, the United States declared war on Germany. The battleship emerged from the yard on 26 August 1917 and sailed for Hampton Roads for duty as an engineering training ship in the Chesapeake Bay region. She performed that vital function for almost the entire duration of hostilities, completing the assignment on 4 November 1918, a week before the armistice stilled the guns of World War I.

Her service as a training ship during the conflict had been broken once in the spring of 1918 when she received the body of the late Chilean ambassador to the United States on 28 May 1918; embarked the American Ambassador to Chile, the Honorable J. H. Shea, on 3 June; and got underway from Norfolk later that day. The battleship transited the Panama Canal on the 10th; touched at Port Tongoi, Chile, on the 24th; and arrived at Valparaiso on the morning of 27 June.

There, the late ambassador's remains were accompanied ashore by Admiral William B. Caperton and Ambassador Shea. Departing that port on 2 July, *Vermont* visited Callao, Peru, on the 7th, before retransiting the Panama Canal and returning to her base in the York River.

Vermont entered the Philadelphia Navy Yard on 5 November and was there converted to a troop transport. She subsequently sailed from Norfolk on 9 January 1919 on the first of four round-trip voyages, returning "Doughboys" from "over there." During her time as a transport, the battleship carried some 5,000 troops back to the United States, completing her last voyage on 20 June 1919.

Prepared at the Philadelphia Navy Yard for inactivation, *Vermont* departed the east coast on 18 July, sailing from Hampton Roads on that day, bound for the west coast. After transiting the Panama Canal, the battleship visited San Diego, San Pedro, Monterey, and Long Beach, Calif.; Astoria, Oreg.; and San Francisco, Calif., before reaching the Mare Island Navy Yard, Vallejo, Calif., on 18 September. There, the battleship was decommissioned on 30 June 1920. She was subsequently reclassified as BB–20 on 17 July of that same year.

Vermont remained inactive at Mare Island until her name was struck from the Navy list on 10 November 1923. She was then sold for scrapping on 30 November of the same year in accordance with the Washington Treaty limiting naval armaments.

Verna & Esther

(MB: t. 12; l. 48'0''; b. 10'2''; dph. 4'8''; dr. 3'6'' (mean); s. 7 k.; cpl. 4; a. 1 1-pdr.)

Verna & Esther—a single-screw, wooden-hulled motor boat built in 1912 at Kennebunk, Maine—was acquired by the Navy from Ens. F. K. Williams of Princetown, Mass., on 6 August 1917; and commissioned on 10 September. Designated SP–1187, *Verna & Esther* served in the 1st Naval District as a target range boat during World War I. Soon after hostilities ceased, she was returned to her owner on 30 November 1918.

Vernon County

Counties in Missouri and Wisconsin and a parish in Louisiana.

(LST–1161: dp. 5,777; l. 384'; b. 56'6''; dr. 17'; s. 14.5 k.; cpl. 600; a. 6 3''; cl. *LST–1156*)

LST–1161 was laid down on 14 April 1952 at Pascagoula, Miss., by Ingalls Shipbuilding Corp.; launched on 25 November 1952; sponsored by Mrs. Hugh White, the wife of the then-governor of Mississippi; and commissioned on 18 May 1953, Lt. Comdr. D. E. Sutherlin in command.

After conducting her shakedown cruise, *LST–1161* operated off the eastern seaboard, out of Little Creek, Va., and Morehead City, N.C., through mid-February 1954. She subsequently deployed twice to the Caribbean operating areas during the year 1954. During an exercise at Vieques, Puerto Rico, between 11 April and 7 May 1954, the ship participated in the filming of the movie "Away All Boats." The LST entered the naval shipyard at Philadelphia, Pa., for extensive modifications on 28 July. Once those alterations and repairs were completed, the tank landing ship headed for Little Creek, reaching the amphibious base there on 19 December. The ship received the name *Vernon County* on 1 July 1955.

Vernon County operated with the Amphibious Forces of the Atlantic Fleet, alternating between Norfolk and Little Creek as her "home ports." During her years of operations from those places, she deployed regularly to the North Atlantic, Mediterranean, and Caribbean areas. In 1958, she was transferred to the Pacific Fleet, sailing via the Panama Canal to her new assigned home port—San Diego, Calif.

After operating from San Diego for over a year and one-half, conducting regular periods of underway training and local operations off the southern California coast, *Vernon County* changed home ports for the last time. On 16 June 1960, the tank landing ship departed the west coast, bound for Yokosuka, Japan. Together with seven additional LST's, *Vernon County* would comprise Amphibious Squadron (PhibRon) 9. They reached Yokosuka on 6 August.

Vernon County subsequently formed an integral part of the amphibious forces supporting the Southeast Asia Treaty Organization (SEATO), participating in SEATO's Operation "Tulungan" in May 1962. In so doing, she became one of the first American amphibious vessels to transport marines to Thailand.

Her first years in Yokosuka saw the ship participating in many major amphibious exercises, including those named "Pony Express" and "Sharp Edge." After an upkeep period in June 1962, *Vernon County* transported marines from Subic Bay, Philippines, to Iwakuni, Japan; she paid a port call at Karatsu, Japan, reportedly the first American man-of-war to visit that port since the Korean War.

February of the following year saw *Vernon County* at Kobe, Japan; in March, she visited Tsoying and Kaohsiung, Taiwan, and spent much of April at Subic Bay. That June, she participated in Operation "Flagpole," a joint 7th Fleet-Republic of Korea (ROK) naval exercise. Before returning to her home port, Yokosuka, the LST called at Shimonoseki, Japan; Naha, Okinawa; and Keelung, Taiwan.

After her return to Yokosuka and subsequent refresher training at Numazu, Japan, *Vernon County* took part in Operation "Litgas" in company with other SEATO naval units. Subsequently returning to Hong Kong, via Yokosuka, the tank landing ship visited Kobe in mid-July 1964.

For a few days, *Vernon County* trained in nearby Sagami Wan when an international incident occurred in the waters of the Gulf of Tonkin. With the 7th Fleet alerted during the "Tonkin Gulf" crisis that flared up immediately, *Vernon County* embarked marines and steamed for Vietnam. For the next 60 days, as part of the force thrown into Southeast Asian waters ready for any contingency, *Vernon County* veritably hugged the coast of that war-torn country.

Vernon County was then relieved on station and proceeded back to Yokosuka, but the respite offered was, in retrospect, only a short one. In January 1965, trouble again flared in Vietnam, and the tank landing ship again headed for Vietnamese waters to provide amphibious support. Departing her home port on 8 February, *Vernon County* proceeded to Iwakuni, Japan, and Naha, Okinawa, before pushing on to Danang and arriving on the 18th. Upon arrival, she disembarked Company "C," 7th Engineer Battalion, to provide construction support for the light antiaircraft ("Hawk") missile battery then being emplaced there, thus completing the "Hawk" deployment—yet another step in American commitment to aid the South Vietnamese.

Over the ensuing months, *Vernon County* conducted her operations: loading, offloading, stand-by alerts, and the landing of marines and equipment on South Vietnamese shores under conditions that varied from flower girls to light machinegun fire. In April, *Vernon County* landed marines at Danang, South Vietnam, and brought turn-around loads from Okinawa. Once this landing was completed, *Vernon County* sailed north and took part in one of the largest amphibious undertakings since Inchon (in Korea), when she participated in the landings at Chu Lai, South Vietnam. In that operation, three battalion landing teams and a Navy mobile construction battalion went ashore with a twofold mission: (1) extend American influence, and (2) initiate construction of an airfield.

More turn-around loads followed to insure the steady flow of supplies and equipment to support the ever-expanding beachhead and the development of a landing strip to support the operations of a Marine Air Wing. As marine reinforcements arrived in the Western Pacific (WestPac) area, *Vernon County* continued to load and land supplies at Chu Lai.

While the ship was carrying out her duties in that capacity, American intelligence picked up evidence that a Viet Cong (VC) force was massing for an attack on the recently arrived marines at Chu Lai. Accordingly, a joint Marine-ARVN (Army of the Republic of Vietnam) operation was planned and launched on 6 August 1965 to search for the VC. In that evolution, code-named "Thunderbolt," the marines and ARVN soldiers did not find the VC in strength, but only met scattered resistance. Nevertheless, the operation proved to be, in retrospect, a "Successful experiment in command and control."

Subsequently, however, the interrogation of a VC deserter revealed the location of the 1st VC Regiment. It was, as thought, moving toward Chu Lai. Accordingly, another operation, code-named "Starlite," was expeditiously planned.

Vernon County embarked elements of the 3d Battalion, 3d Marines (Battalion Landing Team) (BLT) 3, under Lieutenant Colonel Joseph E. Muir, USMC, at Chu Lai, and sailed south along the coast to An Thuong, where she put the troops ashore in one phase of "Starlite." The operation, involving amphibious, heli-borne, and ground forces, started out as a search and destroy operation but soon escalated into a battalion-sized offensive against the VC. "Starlite" thwarted the incipient VC move toward Chu Lai, some nine miles to the north, the main battle taking place in the Van Truong village complex.

The marines discovered communication equipment, numerous documents, munitions, rice, and propaganda —all leading intelligence men to estimate that the hamlet of Van Thuong had served as a VC command post. During the operation, marines of the 3d Marine Amphibious Force (MAF) clearly bested the enemy forces, annihilating the 60th VC Battalion and severely crippling the 40th Battalion. It was the first big battle for the marines, who came away from "Starlite" confident in their ability to meet the enemy on the field of battle and defeat him.

Late in October, *Vernon County* sailed for Korean waters and, with other units of the 7th Fleet, participated in the movement of the ROK "Tiger" Division to Vietnam. Subsequently, *Vernon County* took part in direct lifts of equipment and troops to Vietnam before returning to Yokosuka on Christmas Day 1965.

After operating locally out of her home port and in Vietnamese waters, primarily at Chu Lai, *Vernon County* replenished and underwent a period of upkeep at Subic Bay in the Philippines. She then returned to intracoastal shipping operations off the coast of South Vietnam and even penetrated the Mekong Delta to pay a port call at Saigon. The tank landing ship returned to Yokosuka in early June.

Vernon County trained briefly in Japanese waters—at Numazu—before going to Okinawa, and from there to Hong Kong. Returning to Vietnamese waters upon conclusion of that liberty-port visit, the tank landing ship headed for Subic Bay, via Danang and Camranh Bay, soon thereafter, for 13 days of upkeep in the Philippine Islands. Returning to Yokosuka after conducting lifts of men and materiel to Okinawa and Sasebo, *Vernon County* remained in her home port until 21 September 1966.

Ordered back to Vietnam, *Vernon County* operated in support of Operation "Market Time," the coastal interdiction of communist supply traffic off the coast of South Vietnam, serving as "mother ship" for the fast patrol craft used for those evolutions. *Vernon County* remained on station with "Market Time" until 29 November. From there, she went on to Yokosuka, commencing a regularly scheduled yard overhaul on 8 December 1966.

Completing those repairs and alterations on 15 March 1967, *Vernon County* ran sea trials and conducted refresher training before visiting Kobe in April. Subsequently, the tank landing ship returned to Yokosuka, where she conducted more training during May.

Leaving Yokosuka in her wake on 6 June, *Vernon County* was heading for Sasebo when she received orders directing her to sail for Vietnam. Upon arrival, *Vernon County* became a part of the Mobile Riverine Force (MRF), a joint Navy-Army assault unit conducting search and destroy missions in the Mekong Delta region. While assigned to the MRF, *Vernon County* was a veritable picture of versatility: she carried ammunition for Army troops, fire support bases, and the Navy's river patrol boats; she carried boats, clothing, batteries, and "C" rations for troops in the field; purified and supplied fuel to various riverine craft; housed, fed, and entertained over 340 additional Army and Navy combat personnel; and logged over 780 helicopter landings on her "flight deck."

Relieved from MRF support duties on 20 August 1967, *Vernon County* headed for Chu Lai, and from there to Keelung, Taiwan. Reaching the latter port on 30 August, the tank landing ship spent five days there before moving on, ultimately returning to her home port, Yokosuka, on 8 September.

Vernon County remained in port until 5 October 1967, when she headed south for Ora Wan, Okinawa, to conduct two days of training with marine amphibious forces. Upon completion of training, the tank landing ship shifted to Subic Bay, where she loaded various items for churches, schools, and hospitals at Tacloban on the island of Leyte. She departed Subic Bay on 18 October and was to represent the United States at ceremonies commemorating General Douglas MacArthur's famous "return" to the Philippines on the 20th. A typhoon brewing in the vicinity, however, forced a cancellation of the evolution. *Vernon County* subsequently returned to Subic Bay, whence she sortied on 23 October for Yokosuka.

Arriving at her destination on 1 November, *Vernon County* remained in port until the 20th, at which time she got underway for Naha, Okinawa, and from there for Subic Bay. Upon reaching the Philippines, the ship was assigned to Amphibious Ready Group (ARG) "Bravo."

Underway for Vietnam on 18 December, *Vernon County* arrived off the mouth of the Cua Viet river two days later. Over the days that ensued, prior to Christmas 1967, the tank landing ship took part in Operation "Fortress Ridge" in company with the other units of ARG "Bravo." In that operation, marines from the group landed, unopposed, and swept through the sandy, marshy regions north of the Cua Viet, encountering several pockets of enemy resistance. Helicopter gunships, air strikes, naval gunfire, and artillery all assisted in subduing the enemy in what proved to be the last pre-Christmas truce operation.

After Christmas, *Vernon County* took part in her second amphibious operation within a month, when she participated in Operation "Badger Tooth," between 26 December 1967 and 2 January 1968. Heliborne and landing craft-borne marines met no opposition in the initial landing, 13 miles east of Quang Tri city but, on the 27th, encountered a stubborn and well-disciplined North Vietnamese unit in the fortified town of Thon Tham Khe. Several hours of intense fighting ensued, with the enemy eventually withdrawing from the fight.

Vernon County operated with ARG "Bravo," Task Group (TG) 76.5, until 3 February, operating off the coast between Danang and the demilitarized zone (DMZ). After completing her part in Operations "Fortress Ridge" and "Badger Tooth," she remained offshore, devoting a good deal of her time to training because of the slow tempo of operations after missions against the VC.

Vernon County, when relieved of duty with TG 76.5, headed for Japan and returned to her home port of Yokosuka for a scheduled two-month overhaul, after which time she sailed for Korean waters. She conducted joint training with ROK naval units, including a United States detachment from Amphibious Construction Battalion 1 embarked with four pontoon causeways and associated equipment. After a complete slate of exercises, the tank landing ship returned to Japan for upkeep. She then sailed for Okinawa, there loading cargo before proceeding back to Vietnam.

Offloading her cargo at Wunder Beach, Danang, *Vernon County* shifted operations to the Mekong River Delta region, where she assumed duties of support LST for mobile riverine forces. From 25 May to 21 June, *Vernon County* operated as support ship for Task Force (TF) 115, Mobile Riverine Force (MRF) "Alfa." During that period, the group operated at Ben Tre, Dong Tam, Vinh Long, Sa Dec, My Tho, Can Tho; all in the Mekong, or IV Corps, area of Vietnam. In the little over three-week period, *Vernon County* traveled some 556.5 miles through Vietnamese rivers.

The MRF, a joint Army-Navy operation, relied upon the support services rendered by the duty LST. *Vernon County* served as a floating warehouse wherein 600 tons of ammunition, plus non-ordnance support material, could be stowed in the capacious tank deck area. From those supplies, the LST supported Navy river craft, Army operations in the field, and Army fire support bases. She, in turn, was replenished by another LST that came up river from the port of Vung Tau.

A good deal of activity took place during that period of both base and ship defense; 15 to 20 rounds of 3-inch gunfire were fired nightly for harassment and interdiction; all gunmounts were manned continuously throughout the nocturnal hours, to be fired while the crew was proceeding to their general quarters stations. In addition, six sentries patrolled the pontoons moored alongside, and on the main deck; boats patrolled 150 to 200 yards away, remaining alert for possible swimmers, mines, or traffic of a suspicious nature. Periodically, percussion grenades were tossed into the water as antiswimmer measures.

The ship also served as a landing pad for helicopters making resupply runs both to and from the ship to units in the field; whenever the ship made a transit of the waterways of the Mekong Delta, she stood at general quarters with .50-caliber and .30-caliber machine guns mounted to provide the ship with close-range firepower when needed.

Upon relief by *Washtenaw County* (LST–1166) on 21 June at Can Tho, *Vernon County* proceeded down the Bassac River to the South China Sea, before she headed to Subic Bay for generator repairs. En route and three days out of Vietnamese waters, the ship's commanding officer, Lt. Comdr. L. D. Mott, was stricken with acute appendicitis, necessitating an emergency medevac (medical evacuation) by air. Subsequently, the ship reached Subic Bay on 24 June.

Upon arrival, however, it was found that the ship's generators could not be repaired there, so she sailed for Naha, Okinawa, with retrograde cargo on board, en route back to Japan. She offloaded her cargo at Naha and proceeded on, reaching Yokosuka on 13 July. There, the repairs were effected. While at her home port, the ship received the Navy Unit Commendation for her service with the Mobile Riverine Force.

Vernon County subsequently returned to Vietnamese waters, lifting cargo to Vung Tau and offloading it while at anchor on 14 August. The following day, she proceeded to Nha Be, where she relieved *Windham County* (LST–1170) as support LST for Mobile Riverine Assault Force "Bravo." For the next two months, *Vernon County* operated primarily in the Nha Be region but also at the junction of the Soirap and Vamn Co rivers. Midway through that period, the base was shifted to Dong Tam, where the LST remained until relieved by *Caroline County* (LST–525) on 16 October.

Sailing to Kaohsiung, Taiwan, with a cargo of retro-

grade jeeps, and encountering typhoon "Hester" en route, *Vernon County* visited Hong Kong for rest and recreation before returning to her home port in late October; she remained there for the rest of the year.

Underway again for Vietnam on 6 January 1969, *Vernon County* encountered engineering difficulties en route to her initial destination, Naha. Reaching Okinawa on the 10th, she offloaded her cargo—54 tons of cargo and 303 tons of vehicles—before setting sail for Subic Bay for four days of upkeep and repair work on her engineering spaces. By 17 January, the problem was corrected, thus permitting the tank landing ship to get underway and proceed for her ultimate destination, Vietnam.

Lifting cargo that proved to be about the "smallest in the history of the vessel"—one man and two tons of LCPL equipment—*Vernon County* disembarked her passenger and unloaded the equipment upon arrival at Vung Tau. Shifting to the Mekong Delta region soon thereafter, *Vernon County* embarked 360 troops and support units and relieved *Whitfield County* (LST–1169) as support ship for TF 117.

From 17 January to 24 March, *Vernon County* deployed with TF 117, a mobile riverine force. Once again, the ship served as a floating warehouse for ammunition, fuel, and other support materiel; a mooring point for river patrol craft; and a helipad for the detachment of four "choppers."

The most noteworthy events of the deployment occurred in the ship's direct contact with the enemy. During the post-Tet offensive period in the latter part of February and early days of March, *Vernon County* took two near-misses from North Vietnamese Army (NVA) mortar batteries located on the south bank of the Song My Tho river at about 0230 on 22 February. One landed approximately 25 meters off the starboard side near an ammunition pontoon; the other landed some 25 meters off the port quarter. A large rocket missed the ship, landing harmlessly 200 yards away. *Vernon County* manned her battle stations and returned the fire with 46 rounds of 3-inch gunfire.

The next day, NVA/VC automatic weapons fire came in the direction of the LST, most rounds concentrated on one of the pontoons alongside or at the bridge. On the 25th, lookouts spotted a swimmer 50 yards from the stern; grenades from M–79 launchers were soon directed at him, thoroughly saturating the area. A body was sighted soon thereafter, the grenades apparently having done their work.

The following day, the ship came in for further attention from VC sappers. A deck sentry sighted a dark object floating in the water near the fantail and fired two M–16 rounds, quickly resulting in a violent thrashing about in the water below. Shortly thereafter, the target—probably a sapper—sank.

Closely related to the ship's activities was a recoilless rifle attack on the Philippine tug, *Kangaroo*, 500 yards downriver from *Vernon County*. The tug sustained serious damage, and fires broke out on board; the LST's rescue and assistance team boarded the crippled ship and promptly extinguished the fires, performing temporary repairs on the tug's damaged superstructure as well. The "quick and professional" action on the part of *Vernon County* resulted in 27 letters of commendation and a bronze star for the ship's sailors who participated in the salvage operation.

Relieved on station by *Windham County* (LST–1170) on 24 March, *Vernon County* sailed for Yokosuka, via Penang, Malaysia; Danang; Subic Bay; and Okinawa. She reached Yokosuka on 22 April and subsequently remained in port for slightly more than a month.

After conducting refresher trials in company with *Tom Green County* (LST–1159), *Vernon County* sailed to Korean waters, where she loaded a World War II-vintage PT-boat hull on 5 June for eventual transfer to a stateside museum. She began her return voyage to Yokosuka on the following day.

Vernon County began her next line tour on 5 July, sailing once more for Vietnamese waters, this time in company with *Westchester County* (LST–1167). Arriving on the 13th, *Vernon County* loaded "A" Company, 3d Motor Transport Battalion, 3d Marine Division— 264 marines, five naval enlisted men, 10 officers, 49 vehicles, and 44 tons of miscellaneous equipment—and departed Danang on the evening of the 13th. Five days later, *Vernon County* and *Westchester County* arrived at Kin Red, Okinawa, and discharged their cargoes and disembarked their passengers.

Although the ship was slated to return to Vietnamese waters, enginering casualties diverted her to Subic Bay for repairs. From Subic, she was ordered, upon completion of repairs, to join ARG "Bravo," operating off the I Corps zone in the northern part of South Vietnam.

Vernon County carried out training activities in the days that ensued, lifting 185 field troops from "E" Company, 2d Battalion, 26th Marines, from Chu Lai to Danang. Debarking the marines on 10 August, *Vernon County* loaded cargo that day for shipment to Okinawa. Although initially slated to depart on 10 August, the loss of the ship's stern anchor forced a delay of one full day. The ship ultimately accomplished the cargo lift, however, reaching White Beach, Okinawa, on 16 August. She participated in exercises over the succeeding days before proceeding to sea at 2300 on 19 August to evade typhoon "Cora." Subsequently, the ship proceeded to Taiwan for rest and recreation at the port of Keelung.

With the end of the Taiwan stay, however, the ship put to sea again to return to Yokosuka. En route, she rescued three Taiwanese fishermen early on the evening of 29 August, the event taking place northeast of Taiwan. The fishermen, who had been adrift for a week, were returned later that evening to a naval vessel of the Nationalist Chinese Navy.

Vernon County operated between Okinawa and Japan through mid-October, after which time she returned to Vietnamese waters, sailing to Danang in company with *Washoe County* (LST–1165), *Westchester County*, and *Tom Green County*. Reaching Danang on 4 November, *Vernon County* embarked 147 marines of the Headquarters and Service Company, 9th Motor Transport Battalion, 53 vehicles, and 58 tons of equipment. The lift, designated "Keystone Cardinal," was scheduled to terminate at Kin Red, Okinawa. En route, however, heavy seas held progress to a virtual standstill while three days out of Danang. *Vernon County* suffered storm damage—two perpendicular cracks began to develop on opposite sides of her mast, directly below the radar platform. Diverted to Subic Bay, the tank landing ship effected repairs there before proceeding on and ultimately unloading her cargo at Kin Red on 17 November.

Vernon County returned to Vietnam soon thereafter, initially to Vung Tau, where she took on a load of amunition to be delivered to the LST supporting TF 115's riverine operations. From Vung Tau, *Vernon County* proceeded to the vicinity of the Ca Mau Peninsula and there relieved *Terrell County* (LST–1157) on station. The operation, known as "Market Time," kept the ship on station for eight weeks. Operating slightly to the north of Square Bay and Point de Damau, the LST remained at anchor 90 percent of the time, about 5,000 yards from shore. During that time, she acted as a floating landing pad for support helicopters; provided goods and services to small craft operating on the coastal interdiction and patrol functions of the "Market Time" operation; assumed the role of naval gunfire support ship; and established the central communications point for TG 115.7.

Vernon County performed all of her duties well, servicing and rearming helicopter gunships, providing supplies to her frequent customers—PCF's ("Swift boats") and PGM's (motor gunboats)—and hurling call fire ashore.

Relieved by *Washoe County* on 21 January 1970, *Vernon County* sailed first to Hong Kong, and from there to the Philippines, the latter in connection with the first leg of the lift known as "Keystone Bluejay."

Provisioning at Subic Bay, *Vernon County* returned to Vietnamese waters on 19 February, embarking men and equipment of Marine Air Group (MAG) 12, Marine Air Base Support Squadron (MABS) 12, and Marine Air Tactical Control Unit (MAC TU) 62 shortly after her arrival.

Departing Chu Lai in company with *Westchester County*, the LST sailed to Iwakuni, Japan, reaching that destination ahead of schedule on 27 February. The two ships then sailed for Yokosuka, arriving soon thereafer. *Vernon Couny* subsequently sailed to Korean waters, participating in Operation "Golden Dragon"— a joint ROK-United States Navy operation—before returning to Japanese waters and the port of Sasebo.

The LST operated between Japan and Okinawa into the summer. During one of her in-port periods, the ship received a visit from Admiral Elmo Zumwalt, Jr., the Chief of Naval Operations, on 16 May.

Following an availability and refresher training, *Vernon County* departed Yokosuka in company with gunboat *Crockett* (PG–88). She was diverted to Subic Bay to meet an additional two gunboats to escort to Vietnamese waters. Necessary upkeep items, however, could only be completed by *Vernon County* and *Welch* (PG–93), who then proceeded to sea as scheduled to resume the transit to Camranh Bay. Once within Vietnamese waters on 29 September, *Welch* proceeded independently, leaving *Vernon County* to proceed to Vung Tau to relieve *Westchester County* as "Market Time" support LST.

Her responsibilities and activities generally similar to previous deployments on "Market Time," *Vernon County* remained on station supporting TF 115 until 5 November. Then, after a period of time at Hong Kong, the LST returned to Japan, reaching Yokosuka four days before Christmas of 1970.

She began the new year 1971 in drydock number one at Yokosuka, Japan, at the naval ship repair facility. During the first few weeks of the year, the ship took on a decidedly different appearance, because, instead of the standard Navy "haze gray," *Vernon County* had been painted white overall in preparation for the ship's next—and perhaps most interesting—deployment. During the week of 7 February, the final preparations were made for *Vernon County* to become, by necessity, totally self-sufficient, far from the Navy's logistic, maintenance, and support areas. After taking on part of the necessary stores and equipment, she sailed for Okinawa to pick up the rest before proceeding on her way, bound for remote Diego Garcia, in the Chagos Archipelago, with an interim stop at Singapore.

Vernon County ultimately reached Diego Garcia shortly after 1700 on 9 March and, the next day, began underwater reconnaissance and beach surveys. On the 11th, the first formal construction of a United States Navy communication station began which was to forge another link in the globe-gridling system of transmitting and receiving stations. The following day, the 12th, *Vernon County* became the first LST in history to beach at the largely unexplored isle, offloading much of her heavy equipment to prepare a staging site for the reception of the many tons of supplies and equipment needed to build the station.

As the days passed, the atoll began to change; the ship rode higher in the water as equipment was unloaded. Temperatures on deck averaged 122 degrees between 1000 and 1500 each day; "tropical" hours soon commenced: 0400 to 1400. The men of Underwater Demolition Team 12 and a platoon of seabees removed underwater obstacles, installed buoys, marked anchorages, cleared land and set up a tent city, and began laying down an airfield. By the time *Monticello* (LSD–35) and *Charleston* (LKA–113) arrived, the base camp was fully ready, as was a harbor. Later, having established a self-sustaining shore party, *Vernon County* made two additional voyages to and from Diego Garcia, picking up more men and supplies at Singapore, Cocos Island, and Mauritius.

During the last few days of her deployment to Diego Garcia, the ship was repainted back to her standard "haze gray"—a sure sign that the time had come for the ship to sail away from the isle upon which she had established a base camp and the beginnings of a communication station.

Vernon County returned to the Philippines via Australia and transferred military vehicles from the Sangley Point Naval Air Station (which was being turned over to the Philippine government) to Okinawa in early June. She ultimately returned to her home port, Yokosuka, on the afternoon of 19 June.

The tank landing ship conducted another tour of duty in Vietnamese waters that summer, again performing the duties of "Market Time" support ship, a job that entailed her staying close to shore and serving as a landing platform for helicopters, a haven for patrol boats, and a supplier of food, fuel, water, lodging, and ammunition for both helos and patrol craft. Turning over those duties to *Windham County* on 6 September, *Vernon County* remained on patrol off the coast of South Vietnam on another phase of "Market Time" support, turning over those duties to *Washtenaw County* on 19 October before proceeding to Bangkok, Thailand, for rest and recreation.

Departing that Thai city on 27 October for Hong Kong, *Vernon County* spotted a Thai fishing boat in distress one day out. Several of the ship's engineers boarded the small craft and diagnosed the problem as an electrical failure in the engine. After completing repairs to the fishing craft's engine, *Vernon County*'s men received a present of four boxes of fresh crabs and squid in grateful appreciation of services rendered by the Navy men. Happy possessors of a picture of *Vernon County* and cigarettes given in return by the LST, the fishing craft sailed off. "We might have been forgiven for being proud of our role as Good Samaritans," the ship's cruise book recorded. "In any case, the crabs were delicious."

Vernon County ultimately spent the remainder of her active naval career in the Far East, returning twice more to Vietnamese waters and serving once more as "Market Time" support LST. The ship visited the familiar ports of Subic Bay, Hong Kong, Vung Tau, Kuching, Malaysia, and Singapore, among others. She also served another tour with the Amphibious Ready Force in the Gulf of Tonkin in early October 1972.

Decommissioned on 14 June 1973 at Yokosuka, Japan, *Vernon County* was transferred to the Venezuelan Navy on 29 June 1973 on loan. Assigned the name *Amazonas* (T–21), the tank landing ship was permanently transferred, via cash sale, in December, 1977. She was simultaneously struck from the Navy list.

Vernon County earned a Presidential Unit Citation (28 February to 25 March 1969), three Meritorious Unit Commendations, three Navy Unit Commendations, and 13 battle stars for her Vietnam War service.

Vesole

Kay Kopl Vesole was born on 11 September 1913 in Pzedboz, Russia (now in Poland). Sometime thereafter, his family immigrated to the United States and settled in Iowa where he later attended the State University of Iowa. On 19 October 1942, he accepted an appointment as an ensign in the naval reserve. Ens. Vesole studied at a series of naval training schools during the remainder of 1942 and the first part of 1943. Beginning at the Naval Training School, Tucson, Ariz., he transferred to the Naval Training Station (Local Defense) at Boston, Mass., in January 1943. The following month, he moved from Boston to Gulfport, Miss., to enter the Armed Guard School. In April, he moved to the Armed Guard Center located at New Orleans, whence he was routed to Panama City, Fla., to take command of the armed guard gun crew on board a merchant ship.

By December 1943, Ens. Vesole commanded the armed guard crew assigned to the Liberty ship SS *John Bascom*. On the night of 2 December, his ship was riding at anchor in Bari, Italy, when a massive air raid of 105 Ju. 88 medium bombers attacked the port. During that raid, Vesole's ship was bombed and sunk. However, before she went down, Ens. Vesole heroically directed the defense of the ship despite severe multiple wounds. When it became apparent that the ship would sink, he led a party below and supervised the evacuation of the wounded. Once in the lifeboat, he manned an oar and helped to row the boat ashore even though he had only one functional arm. When he reached land, Ens. Vesole still disregarded his wounds in order to help pull survivors out of the oil-covered and flaming waters and to get them safely into a nearby bomb shelter. Finally, an ammunition explosion inflicted still further wounds on the officer—wounds that soon proved fatal. For ". . . his exceptional fortitude and self-sacrificing concern for others . . .," Ens. Vesole was awarded the Navy Cross, posthumously.

(DD–878: dp. 2,425; l. 390'6''; b. 40'10''; dr. 18'6''; s. 34.5 k.; cpl. 345; a. 6 5'', 16 40mm., 5 21'' tt., 1 dcp. (hh.), 6 dcp., 2 dct.; cl. *Gearing*)

Vesole (DD–878) was laid down on 3 July 1944 at Orange, Tex., by the Consolidated Steel Corp.; launched on 29 December 1944; sponsored by Mrs. Kay K. Vesole; and commissioned on 23 April 1945, Comdr. H. E. Townsend in command.

Following a short visit to Galveston, Tex., *Vesole* got underway on 11 May for Guantanamo Bay, Cuba. She completed shakedown training on 10 June and left the West Indies, bound for Norfolk, Va. The ship arrived at Norfolk on the 12th and began conversion to a radar picket destroyer. The alterations were completed on 29 July, and the ship stood out of Chesapeake Bay for additional training along the east coast and in the West Indies.

She concluded training on 13 August and set a course for the Panama Canal. While en route, she received word of the Japanese capitulation but continued on toward the Pacific Ocean. She transited the canal on 16 August, reported for duty with the Pacific Fleet, and continued on to San Diego, where she arrived on 24 August. On the 28th, the destroyer put to sea once again and steamed to Pearl Harbor where she joined aircraft carrier *Boxer* (CV–21) for the voyage to Japan.

During her more than a year in the Far East, *Vesole* conducted numerous training evolutions, usually in company with a carrier task group—most frequently with *Boxer*, *Lexington* (CV–16), or *Intrepid* (CV–11). She ranged the China coast, making visits frequently at Tsingtao and Shanghai, and also calling at the Japanese ports of Tokyo, Kure, and Yokosuka. On two occasions during the winter of 1945 and 1946, the warship made round-trip voyages from Japan to the Marianas and back. Later in 1946, she added Okinawa and Hong Kong to her itinerary while continuing to stop at Japanese, Chinese, and Philippine ports of call. In November of 1946, she departed Tsingtao for the last time and headed home. After a stop at Guam on the 29th and a similarly brief visit to Pearl Harbor, she arrived in San Diego on 16 December.

On 6 January 1947, the destroyer stood out of San Diego in company with the other units of Destroyer Division (DesDiv) 141 and headed, via the Panama Canal, back to the east coast. She made a six-day layover at Norfolk from 23 to 29 January and arrived at the New York Naval Shipyard where she began a three-month overhaul. She completed repairs on 30 April and put to sea for sea trials. In June, she conducted refresher training. Various exercises out of Newport, R.I., occupied her time until 2 September at which time she put to sea, bound for European waters. She arrived in Plymouth, England, on 11 September and spent the next five months visiting such ports as Antwerp, Belgium, and Lisbon, Portugal, as well as a number of British ports. She departed Plymouth on 4 February 1948 and headed back to the United States. On St. Valentine's Day 1948, *Vesole* arrived back in Newport.

A short, four-month period of normal operations along the east coast ensued. On 5 June, the ship once again embarked upon a voyage to western Europe, this time with Naval Academy midshipmen embarked and in company with a carrier task force built around *Coral Sea* (CV–43). Conducting all manner of training evolutions along the way, *Vesole* steamed to Lisbon, Portugal, and thence into the Mediterranean. The task group operated in the Mediterranean until 12 July at which time it headed for Guantanamo Bay, Cuba. Following another month of training in the West Indies, *Vesole* disembarked the midshipmen at Annapolis on 24 August and then entered the Boston Naval Shipyard for a two-month overhaul. In November, the warship began post-overhaul refresher training first in Narragansett Bay and later in the West Indies.

Following five months of normal 2d Fleet operations, *Vesole* departed Newport on 18 April 1949 for another deployment to the Mediterranean Sea. That assignment, which consisted primarily of training duty, lasted until 17 September, when the warship pointed her bow homeward. She reentered Newport on the 25th and resumed operations along the east coast. That employment, which included both cold weather and Caribbean duty, lasted until 3 May 1950 when she got underway from Norfolk with TG 88.1 to return to the Mediterranean.

Over the next five months, the destroyer visited a host of ports along the Mediterranean littoral and conducted a number of exercises in cooperation with the fast carriers as well as amphibious training and independent ship's drills. She concluded that tour of duty in the "middle sea" late in September and returned to the United States at Norfolk on 4 October.

The ship began a yard overhaul almost immediately, and it lasted until 15 February 1951 at which time she began a six-week period of refresher training in the West Indies. The warship returned to Norfolk on 3 April and began preparations for another cruise to the Mediterranean. On 15 May, *Vesole* departed Norfolk to join the 6th Fleet. Once again, she conducted a variety of training exercises—including a multinational one, Operation "Beehive," with units of the British, French, and Italian navies—punctuated by frequent calls at ports throughout the Mediterranean. The destroyer took leave of the Mediterranean at Gibraltar on 23 September and returned to Norfolk on 6 October.

Vesole resumed normal 2d Fleet operations once more. These included a major Atlantic Fleet exercise, amphibious exercises, and a convoy exercise. After a short visit to the New York Naval Shipyard for the installation of new electronic gear, she steamed back to Norfolk to prepare for another deployment to the Mediterranean Sea. She departed Norfolk on 21 April 1952 and, for the next six months, executed the normal 6th Fleet schedule of exercises and port visits. The warship left Lisbon, Portugal, on 11 October and arrived back in Norfolk on the 20th.

For the next five months, *Vesole* underwent extensive alternations at the Norfolk Naval Shipyard. She traded her 40-millimeter antiaircraft battery for six 3-inch 50-caliber rapid fire guns in dual mounts. Her aftermast was removed, and a taller mast was installed forward. In addition, she received much highly sophisticated radar, electronic, and communications equipment. She completed the alterations at the end of March 1953 and, late in April, put to sea for refresher training in the Guantanamo Bay operating area. At the conclusion of refresher training, the destroyer returned to Norfolk, arriving there on 14 June. She resumed operations out of Norfolk until sailing once again for the Mediterranean on 16 September 1953.

Over the next decade, *Vesole* continued to alternate deployments to the 6th Fleet in the Mediterranean with periods of normal operations along the east coast and in the West Indies. During her 1958 tour of duty, *Vesole* earned the Armed Forces Expeditionary Medal as a unit of the contingency force established in the eastern Mediterranean during the internal crisis in Lebanon.

In 1962, she earned that same award as a result of the quarantine placed on Cuba due to the siting of Russian missiles on that island. The destroyer participated actively in that operation, patrolling the area between Key West, Fla.. and Havana, Cuba. She inspected two of the Russian merchant ships charged with removing the missiles from Cuba and visually accounted for 12 of the 42 missiles. Other than for her participation in those two crises, the decade between 1953 and 1963 passed routinely with training duty along the east coast, Mediterranean deployments, overhauls, and the like.

January of 1964 found her in the Philadelphia Naval Shipyard undergoing a fleet rehabilitation and modernization (FRAM) overhaul to improve her antisubmarine warfare capabilities. The alterations included significant superstructure modifications and internal changes. Living compartments and messes were improved, but more importantly, she received a drone antisubmarine helicopter (DASH) hangar—for later augmentation with the helicopter itself—as well as new radar, electronic warfare equipment, and an antisubmarine rocket (ASROC) launcher.

The warship completed her FRAM modifications late in September of 1964 and, on 7 October, departed Philadelphia for her new home port, Newport, R.I., her base for operations with the Atlantic Fleet as a unit of the Hunter/Killer Antisubmarine Warfare Group. That duty continued until late in 1965 when she embarked upon her only deployment to the Vietnam war zone. She spent late 1965 and early 1966 engaged in "Market Time" operations off the Vietnamese coast—the interdiction of enemy coastwise logistics operations—and in gunfire duties supporting the troops fighting ashore. She also served intermittently in the antisubmarine screen of the carriers operating off Vietnam in the Gulf of Tonkin.

After upkeep at Subic Bay, she got underway with DesRon 24 to return to Newport. Steaming via the Indian Ocean, the Suez Canal, the Mediterranean Sea, and the Atlantic Ocean, *Vesole* arrived back in Newport on 8 April 1966.

During the next six years, the warship made four deployments overseas: three with the Middle East Force in the Indian Ocean and one with NATO's Standing Naval Force in the eastern Atlantic and in European waters. After seven months of normal east coast duty, *Vesole* departed Newport and headed via the Mediterranean and the Suez Canal to her first tour of duty with the Middle East Force stationed in the Indian Ocean. On 29 December, she transited the Suez Canal and relieved *Johnston* (DD–821) at Port Sudan. That assignment consisted entirely of training evolutions and goodwill visits to East African and Persian Gulf ports. She concluded that tour of duty on 28 February 1967 when she retransited the Suez Canal and reentered the Mediterranean. She crossed the "middle sea" and the Atlantic Ocean and arrived back in Newport on 21 March.

Normal operations, as far south as Jacksonville, Fla., occupied her time for the remainder of the year. During the first two months of 1968, she conducted exercises in the West Indies before returning north for a yard overhaul. The warship entered the Boston Naval Shipyard on 12 April 1968 and remained there until 19 August. Following refresher training in the West Indies in September and October, *Vesole* returned to Newport on 7 November to prepare for her next deployment.

On 6 January 1969, the destroyer stood out of Newport bound for the Netherlands and duty with NATO's

Standing Naval Force in the Atlantic. She reached Den Helder on 18 January and began her five-month tour of duty. That assignment was made up of a series of multinational fleet exercises and goodwill visits to western European ports. On 17 May, following a NATO review in which Queen Elizabeth II of Great Britain participated, she concluded her assignment in European waters and headed back to the United States. *Vesole* returned to the United States at Norfolk on 2 June and reentered her home port, Newport, almost a month later on 1 July. The warship remained there over six weeks, before getting underway on 19 August to proceed to her new home port, Charleston, S.C.

Vesole operated out of Charleston for the remainder of the year and during the first two months of 1970. On 3 March, she left Charleston to deploy for a second time to the Indian Ocean. On this occasion, she took the long route, around the Cape of Good Hope, calling at various African ports along the way. She reported for duty with the Middle East Force at Diego Suarez in the Malagasy Republic during the second week in April. For the next six months, the destroyer plied the Indian Ocean conducting exercises—alone, with other ships of the Middle East Force, and with units of foreign navies—making port calls along the Indian Ocean littoral. She was finally relieved of that duty at Mombasa, Kenya, during the second week in August. The destroyer departed Mombasa on 14 August and, again taking the Cape of Good Hope route, headed back to Charleston, where she arrived on 18 September.

Vesole operated along the east coast of the United States for just over a year. During that time, she participated in tests of the Harpoon missile system and of the Poseidon missile. She planeguarded for aircraft carriers conducting pilot carrier qualifications and participated in a number of exercises. On 23 September 1971, she got underway from Charleston, bound ultimately for her last tour of duty with the Middle East Force. After stops at Recife, Brazil, and several African ports, the warship arrived in Majunga in the Malagasy Republic on 29 October to report for duty. Once again, goodwill port visits and exercises highlighted her deployment. After only four months in the Indian Ocean, she was relieved by *Charles P. Cecil* (DD–835) at Mombasa during the second week in February 1972. On Lincoln's Birthday 1972, the destroyer began the long voyage home. Again rounding the Cape of Good Hope and crossing the Atlantic, she arrived back in Charleston on 11 March 1972. She conducted local operations out of Charleston until 5 July when she entered the Charleston Naval Shipyard for a four-month overhaul.

When *Vesole* emerged from the shipyard in November 1972, she began her last four years as an active ship in the Navy. Those four years brought three more overseas cruises—two with the 6th Fleet in the Mediterranean and one to South America for a series of UNITAS exercises with South American navies. Immediately following overhaul, the warship conducted sea trials and refresher training which continued until March of 1973. On 19 March, she returned to Charleston to begin converting her main propulsion plant to the use of Navy distillate fuel. That conversion was completed on 24 May at which time she returned to sea for trials and then for normal 2d Fleet operations. On 27 July, she departed Charleston for UNITAS XIV, a series of binational exercises conducted in cooperation with various South American navies. During that deployment, she transited the Panama Canal to operate in the Pacific with units of the Peruvian and Chilean navies. The deployment also brought exercises with the navies of Colombia, Brazil, Uruguay, and Argentina. *Vesole* ended her long UNITAS voyage back at Charleston on 15 December.

After the holidays, she began 11 months of duty out of Charleston. Gunnery, ASROC, and tropedo exercises predominated during that time, but she also trained with aircraft carriers. On 15 November 1974, she departed Charleston to return to the 6th Fleet in the Mediterranean after a four-year hiatus. That deployment lasted until 5 May 1975 at which time she departed Rota, Spain, to return to the United States. The ship arrived back in Charleston on 15 May; and, after an availability alongside tender *Sierra* (AD–18), she resumed operations at sea out of Charleston. The warship remained so employed until the beginning of 1976, her last year of active service to the Navy.

On 6 January 1976, *Vesole* departed Charleston for her final overseas deployment, fittingly enough with the 6th Fleet. She arrived in Rota, Spain, on 17 January and entered the "middle sea" on the 19th. During that deployment, she participated in Exercise "Silver Fox," conducted in the Black Sea, and constituted a unit of the contingency force dispatched to the eastern Mediterranean from 3 April to 15 May as a result of internal strife in Lebanon. *Vesole* concluded that deployment at Charleston on 28 July 1976. The destroyer was placed out of commission there on 1 December 1976. Her name was struck from the Navy list on that same day; and, as of January 1980, her transfer to a foreign government was still pending.

Vesole earned two battle stars for her service in the Vietnam conflict.

Vesta

(ScStr.: dp. 4,400 (n.); lbp. 270'4"; b. 38'1" (wl.); dr. 19'; s. 9 k.; cpl. 48)

Vesta (Id. No. 2506)—a cargo steamer built in 1907 at Rotterdam in the Netherlands by *Rotterdam Droogdoek Maatschappij* for the *Koninklijke Nederlandsche Stoomboot Maatschappij*—was seized by United States customs officials at New York on 21 March 1918. Though listed in the 1 November 1918 edition of *Ship's Data, U.S. Naval Vessels* as commissioned the same day in the Naval Overseas Transportation Service, *Vesta* was never actually taken over nor was she ever commissioned by the Navy. Instead, she was held by the United States Shipping Board as part of the Emergency Fleet Corporation's real assets. She was returned to her owners sometime late in 1919 or early in 1920 and resumed mercantile service which lasted until the mid-1940's. She disappeared from the mercantile lists in 1946.

Vestal

A virgin—dedicated to Vesta, the Roman goddess of hearth and fire—who tended the sacred fire kept perpetually burning on her altar.

(Collier No. 1: dp. 12,585; l. 465'9"; b. 60'1"; dr. 26'0" (mean); dph. 36'6"; s. 16.0 k.; cpl. 90; a. none; cl. *Vestal*)

The construction of *Erie* (Fleet Collier No. 1) was authorized on 17 April 1904; but the ship was renamed *Vestal* in October 1905, well before her keel was laid down on 25 March 1907 at the New York Navy Yard, Brooklyn, N.Y. Launched on 19 May 1908, *Vestal* was placed in service, with a civilian crew, at her builders' yard on 4 October 1909.

Vestal served the fleet as a collier, operating along the Atlantic coast and in the West Indies, from the autumn of 1909 to the summer of the following year. Then, after a voyage to Europe to coal ships of the Atlantic Fleet in those waters, the ship returned to the United States, reaching the Philadelphia Navy Yard. She was taken out of service at the Boston Navy Yard on 25 October 1912.

Converted to a fleet repair ship at the Boston Navy Yard, *Vestal* was commissioned there on 3 September 1913, Comdr. Edward L. Beach in command. After fitting out, *Vestal* departed her conversion yard on 26 October for Hampton Roads, Va., where she conducted

USS *Vestal* during her service as a collier (1909–12), her grimy hull giving evidence of hard work.

her shakedown between 29 October to 10 November. After touching at Key West, Fla., for coal on 14 November, *Vestal* moved on to Pensacola, Fla., her base for operations as a repair ship for the Atlantic Fleet.

Vestal alternated between duty off the eastern seaboard with service in the West Indies until the spring of 1914, when she joined the fleet at Vera Cruz, Mexico, in the wake of the occupation of that port in April. The auxiliary vessel provided repair services at Vera Cruz from 2 May to 20 September before she sailed for Boston, escorting the cruiser *Salem* to the navy yard there for overhaul.

Vestal then operated off the Virginia capes and in Guantanamo Bay, Cuba, before she returned to the Boston Navy Yard on 10 June 1915, after calls at New York City and Newport, R.I. She took on stores and provisions at Boston and underwent repairs there before she rejoined the fleet at Narragansett Bay on 19 May 1916.

After the United States entered World War I the following spring, *Vestal* sailed overseas to support the ships of the Fleet in the waters of the United Kingdom. The auxiliary provided repair and overhaul services to the 1st Destroyer Flotilla, based at Queenstown, Northern Ireland, for the duration of hostilities and into 1919. Returning to the United States in that year, *Vestal* served the Scouting Force and the Battle Fleet until 1925, when she underwent a major overhaul and a conversion of her propulsion system from the use of coal to the burning of oil as fuel. During the Navy-wide assignment of alphanumeric hull numbers on 17 July 1920, *Vestal* was classified as a repair ship, AR–4. Highlighting that service was her role in salvage work conducted on *S–51* (SS–162), the submarine rammed and sunk by the merchant ship SS *City of Rome* on 25 September 1925. *Vestal* conducted her salvage operations from October to early December 1925 and again from 27 April to 5 July 1926. During the latter period, the submarine was raised from her watery grave.

Vestal subsequently joined the Pacific Fleet in 1927 and participated in the yearly Fleet problems and maneuvers as part of the training. When the Fleet was shifted permanently to Hawaiian waters upon the conclusion of Fleet Problem XXI in the spring of 1940, *Vestal* followed and was based at Pearl Harbor.

After returning to the west coast for an overhaul at the Mare Island Navy Yard, Vallejo, Calif., *Vestal*

steamed back to Pearl Harbor, resuming her vital, but unsung, duties. On 6 December 1941, she was moored alongside *Arizona* (BB–39), at berth F 7, off Ford Island, to provide services to the battleship during her scheduled period of tender upkeep between 6 and 12 December.

The next day, however, the ordered routine of a peacetime Sunday in port was rudely shattered shortly before 0800. Explosions from bombs and torpedoes began to reverberate across the waters of the harbor as Japanese carrier-based aircraft swept down upon the ships of the Fleet anchored or moored in their berths. At 0755, *Vestal* went to general quarters, manning every gun from the 5-inch broadside battery to the .30-caliber Lewis machine guns on the bridge wings. At about 0805, her 3-inch gun commenced firing.

At about the same time, two bombs—probably intended for the more valuable battleship inboard—hit the repair ship. One struck the port side, penetrated three decks, passing through a crew's space, and exploded in a stores hold, starting fires that necessitated flooding the forward magazines. The second hit the starboard side, passed through the carpenter shop, the shipfitter shop, and left an irregular hole, about five feet in diameter, in the bottom of the ship.

The problem of maintaining antiaircraft fire soon became a secondary one to the ship's fight for survival that ensued. The 3-inch gun jammed after three rounds, and the crew was working to clear the jam when a cataclysmic explosion blew *Vestal*'s valiant gunners overboard.

At about 0820, *Arizona*, moored inboard, had taken a torpedo that had passed beneath the repair ship's stern; almost simultaneously, a bomb penetrated *Arizona*'s deck after glancing off the faceplate of number 2 turret and exploded in the black powder magazine below. The resultant explosion touched off adjacent main battery magazines. Almost as if in a volcanic eruption, the forward part of the battleship exploded, and the concussion from the explosion literally cleared *Vestal*'s deck.

Among the men blown off *Vestal* was her commanding officer, Comdr. Cassin Young. The captain swam back to the ship, however, countermanded an abandon ship order that someone had given, and ordered the ship underway. Fortunately, the engineer officer had anticipated just such an order, and already had the "black gang" hard at work getting up steam.

Topside, things looked bleak. The fiery explosion touched off oil from the ruptured tanks of the stricken battleship and, in turn, caused fires to start on board *Vestal*, aft and amidships. At 0845, men forward cut *Vestal*'s mooring lines, freeing her from the dying battleship, and she got underway, steering by engines alone. A tug pulled *Vestal*'s bow away from the inferno engulfing *Arizona* and the repair ship, and the latter began to creep out of danger, although she was slowly assuming a list to starboard and taking water aft. At 0910, *Vestal* anchored in 35 feet of water off McGrew's Point.

Upon further reflection, however, with the draft aft increasing to 27 feet and the list to six and one-half degrees, Comdr. Young decided upon another course of action. "Because of the unstable condition of the ship," Young explained in his after-action report, "(the) ship being on fire in several places and the possibility of further attacks, it was decided to ground the ship." Underway at 0950, less than an hour after the Japanese attack ended, *Vestal* grounded on Aiea Shoal soon thereafter.

Young—who was awarded the Medal of Honor for his actions on 7 December—subsequently commended his officers and men. "The conduct of all officers and enlisted men was exemplary and of such high order that I would especially desire to have them with me in the future engagements."

Although damaged herself, *Vestal* participated in some of the post-attack salvage operations, sending repair parties to the overturned hull of the battleship *Oklahoma* (BB–37) so that welders could cut into the ship and rescue men trapped there when she turned turtle after being ripped by Japanese torpedoes.

Over the ensuing days, *Vestal*'s men turned to the task of repairing their own ship because yard facilities in the aftermath of the Japanese surprise attack were at a premium. Within a week of the raid, *Vestal*'s crew had pumped out the oil and water that had flooded the compartments below the waterline and cleared out the damaged and gutted holds—all work that had to be completed before the rebuilding process could begin.

After repairs and alterations and operations at Pearl Harbor, *Vestal* received orders on 12 August 1942 to proceed to the South Pacific. She set sail for Tongatabu in the Tonga Islands. She arrived there two weeks later, on the 29th, at a key time—less than a month after the launching of Operation "Watchtower," the invasion of the Solomon Islands. Over the months that followed, the Japanese would contest the Americans and their Australian and New Zealand allies with skill and tenacity.

During *Vestal*'s 60 days at Tongatabu, she completed 963 repair jobs for some 58 ships and four shore activities. Included were repairs to such men-of-war as *Saratoga* (CV–3) (torpedoed by *I–26* on 31 August); *South Dakota* (BB–60) (damaged from grounding at Lahai Passage, Tonga Islands, on 6 September); and *North Carolina* (BB–55) (torpedo damage suffered on 15 September).

One of the more difficult jobs was the one performed on *South Dakota*. The battleship had run aground on an uncharted reef and put into Tongatabu for emergency repairs. *Vestal*'s divers commenced their work at 1600 on 6 September and began checking the ship's seams. With only six divers working, *Vestal*'s party operated until 0200 on the 7th and reported the damage as a series of splits extending along some 150 feet of the ship's bottom. By the next morning, 8 September, *Vestal*'s skilled repairmen, together with men of the battleship's crew, managed to mend the damage sufficiently to allow the ship to return to the United States for permanent repairs.

When *Saratoga* put into Tongatabu after being torpedoed by *I–26* on 31 August, *Vestal*'s divers combined forces with *Navajo* (AT–64) to inspect the damage and later trim and brace the hole. Pumps managed to clear the water out of the flooded fireroom and tons of cement were poured in the hole to patch

the damaged area. Within 12 days of her arrival at Tongatabu, "Sister Sara" was able to return to the United States.

Vestal subsequently sailed for the New Hebrides on 26 October, but a change of orders brought her to New Caledonian waters instead, and she reached Noumea on 31 October. Her arrival could not have been more timely because the Battle of the Santa Cruz Islands had occurred just a few days before. *South Dakota* and *Enterprise* (CV–6), two of the most heavily damaged ships, were at Noumea.

A bomb hit on the latter had buckled a 30- by 60-foot section of the flight deck, aft, bulging it about four feet above deck level. In addition, the hit flooded the after elevator machinery room and blew out bulkheads and damaged furniture in "officer's country." Ordered to sea before the damage was completely repaired, the carrier took with her two *Vestal* officers and a large repair party, who continued work up until two hours before the ship went into action again. Those *Vestal* men were included in the Presidential Unit Citation awarded the "Big E."

South Dakota, like *Enterprise*, had suffered major damage. She had taken a bomb hit on one of her 16-inch gun turrets; had been torn by shrapnel; and had collided with *Mahan* (DD–364) during the battle. The destroyer had not only holed the battleship's starboard side, but had left an anchor in the wardroom. Even though *Vestal* repair parties were busy with *Enterprise*'s urgent repairs, they also went to work on the damaged *South Dakota*, listing her over to patch the hole on the battleship's starboard side at the waterline. Her craftsmen repaired the wardroom (removing *Mahan*'s anchor in the process), patched shrapnel holes, and put sprung hatches and damaged fire mains in order. She was back in action in a scant five days.

During her time at Noumea, *Vestal* completed 158 jobs on 21 ships; she departed that port on 13 November; reached Espiritu Santo three days later; and began a year's schedule of repair service. During the next 12 months, *Vestal* tackled some 5,603 jobs on 279 ships and 24 shore facilities. Some of the outstanding repair jobs were on combatants, ships damaged during the bitter naval engagements in the Solomons in late 1942 and early 1943. There were: *San Francisco* (CA–38), ripped by heavy caliber hits during the night battle off Savo Island on 13 November 1942; *New Orleans* (CA–32) and *Pensacola* (CA–24), the latter with a torpedo hole measuring 24 by 40 feet, a flooded after engine room, and two propeller shafts broken; the Australian light cruiser HMAS *Achilles*, which, besides shrapnel and collision damage, had taken a direct hit on her after turret; and the torpedoed and fire-damaged cargo ship *Alchiba* (AK–23).

In addition, she performed repairs on the torpedoed light cruiser *St. Louis* (CL–49), the torpedoed Australian light cruiser HMAS *Hobart*; the bomb-damaged transport *Zeilin* (AP–9); and others, including *Tappahannock* (AO–43) and HMNZS *Leander*. She also corrected battle damage to and performed alterations on 12 LST's and a large number of miscellaneous lesser ships. Only once during that time, from 27 May to 2 June 1943, did the ship herself undergo repairs.

One of the most outstanding pieces of salvage work performed by the *Vestal* was for *Pensacola*, heavily damaged at the Battle of Tassafaronga. A torpedo had caused such extensive damage aft that the heavy cruiser's stern was barely attached to the rest of the ship and swayed gently with the current. A few frames, some hull plating, and one propeller shaft were practically all that still held the aftermost section to the rest of the ship. As *Vestal*'s commanding officer later recounted, "Never had an AR (repair ship) been presented with such a task; no records on how it should best be done were available."

By trial and error, and some known facts from previous experience, however, *Vestal*'s workers turned-to. The hole was plugged and braced for stability, compartments that could be were sealed and pumped out;

three propellers of about seven tons each were pulled off to reduce drag. "One has to be something of an artificer," her commanding officer recounted, ". . . to realize the problems that came up to do with this job, such as underwater welding and cutting, which was still a fairly new thing." *Vestal*'s force used a dynamite charge to jar one propeller loose and had to burn through the shaft of another to get it off.

After *Pensacola* came *Minneapolis* (CA–36), torpedoed amidships and with 75 feet of her bow missing. *Vestal* put her in shape, too, for a trip to a "stateside" yard where permanent repairs could be made. "So it went," continued the commanding officer, ". . . one broken, twisted, torpedoed, burned ship after another was repaired well enough to make a navy yard or put back on the firing line."

On 18 November 1943, *Vestal* departed Espiritu Santo, bound for the Ellice Islands, and reached her destination, Funafuti, on the 22d. During her brief stay there, the repair ship completed some 604 major repair tasks for 77 ships and for eight shore activities. Her outstanding job during that tour was her work on the light carrier *Independence* (CVL–22).

Underway for Makin on 30 January 1944, *Vestal*'s orders were changed en route, the ship proceeding instead for the Marshalls. She reached Majuro atoll on 3 February. The big repair job awaiting her there was that for the battleship *Washington* (BB–56), which had suffered heavy collision damage forward. Although estimates called for it to be a 30-day job, *Vestal*, often working 24-hour shifts, completed the task in only 10 days. After that, *Washington* sailed for Pearl Harbor to receive permanent repairs.

In need of repairs herself—especially new evaporators—*Vestal* departed Majuro and sailed, via Pearl Harbor, for the Mare Island Navy Yard. Upon conclusion of those repairs, the addition of new equipment, alterations, and a general overhaul—and a vari-colored paint job—*Vestal* departed Mare Island on 8 September, bound for the Carolines. Her voyage took her via Pearl Harbor and Eniwetok. At the latter place, she picked up tows for the remainder of her voyage, a cement barge, *Chromite*, and the Navy ammunition barge YF–254. She reached Ulithi on 15 October 1944.

During the ship's sojourn at Ulithi, *Vestal* completed 2,195 jobs for 149 ships—including 14 battleships, nine carriers, five cruisers, five destroyers, 35 tankers, and other miscellaneous naval and merchant ships. Her biggest repair job of that time was the light cruiser *Reno* (CL–96), torpedoed off San Bernardino Strait by Japanese submarine *I–41* on the night of 3 November. Once again, *Vestal*'s workers performed their tasks quickly and efficiently, having *Reno* on her way in a short time for permanent repairs in a "stateside" yard.

Underway for the Marianas on 25 February 1945, *Vestal* arrived at Saipan two days later, to commence what would be over two months of service there, principally repairing amphibious craft used for the Iwo Jima invasion. While *Vestal* lay at anchor at Saipan, the Okinawa invasion commenced on 1 April 1945. Less than a month later, *Vestal* sailed for Kerama Retto, a chain of islands off the southwestern tip of Okinawa, and arrived there on 1 May.

During May, *Vestal* went to general quarters 59 times as Japanese planes made suicide attacks on the ships engaged in the bitter Okinawa campaign. Experience proved that the best defense against the suiciders was a smoke or fog screen produced by all ships that blended into one gigantic mass of low-hanging clouds. For that purpose, *Vestal* had two boats equipped with fog generators and several barrels of oil. Besides the fog generators, smoke pots would be thrown over the bow of the ship to emit a dense, white, sickly-smelling smoke for about 15 minutes apiece. Besides the danger posed by suiciders, deck sentries kept a sharp lookout for any enemy who might attempt to swim out to the ships with mines or explosive charges.

At Kerama Retto, *Vestal*'s big job was repairing destroyers, and her jobs included the kamikaze-damaged *Newcomb* (DD–586) and *Evans* (DD–552).

Vestal remained at Kerama Retto through mid-June before she got underway on the 23d for Nakagusuku Wan, later renamed Buckner Bay. She arrived there later that day. The repair ship remained in that body of water for the remainder of the war. At 2055 on 10 August 1945, a pyrotechnic display burst forth as word arrived telling that Japan was entertaining thoughts of surrender. "So great was the display of fireworks and so immense the feeling of victory that once the tension had been broken, the true peace announcement received at 0805, August 15, 1945, caused hardly a ripple of enthusiasm: nevertheless the spirit of victory was uppermost in the hearts and conversations of all hands."

The main danger to the fleet after Japan surrendered was typhoons. *Vestal* had sortied twice from Buckner Bay before "V-J Day"—once on 19 July and once on 1 August. On 16 September, *Vestal* sortied for the third time on typhoon evasion, returning to the harbor the next day after having ridden out 68-knot winds and heavy seas.

Vestal carried out storm-damage repairs over the ensuing days before another typhoon—the fourth for the Ryukyus that year—swirled in from the sea on the 28th. Upon receipt of orders from Commander, Service Division 104, *Vestal* weighed anchor and headed out to sea at 1500, her stem sluicing seaward from Buckner Bay. "The glassy sea, humid atmosphere, and falling barometer portended the approaching engagement between ship and her relentlessly violent foes, sea and wind."

The merchantmen *Fleetwood* and *Kenyon Victory* took positions 800 yards astern and in single file with *Vestal* leading the way, steaming westward and away from the threatening blackness massing to the east of Okinawa. Overhauling a four-ship convoy, Capt. H. J. Pohl, *Vestal*'s commanding officer, assumed command of the now seven-ship group. The ships met the fierce winds head-on to lessen the roll and steered to take the surging seas on the quarter, maneuvering skillfully to prevent damage or, worse, loss. By late in the afternoon of the third day, Pohl, the convoy's commodore, had his ships back in Buckner Bay, safe and sound.

That particular storm-evasion sortie proved only to be a realistic exercise compared to what came next. On 6 October, *Vestal* received typhoon warnings of a tropical storm 400 miles in diameter with winds of 100 knots near the center, moving west-northwest at 17 knots.

At 0015 on the 7th, *Vestal* and all ships present in Buckner Bay received word to prepare to execute typhoon plan "X-ray" upon on hour's notice. By mid-afternoon, those orders arrived; and the fleet began stirring itself to action for its survival. Among the first vessels to get underway was *Vestal*, the venerable repair ship clearing the harbor entrance at 1600, steaming due east. Ultimately, *Beaver* (ARG–19) and the merchantmen *Hope Victory*, *Grey's Harbor*, and *Esso Rochester* joined her.

Rising seas, increasing winds, and a plummeting barometer ushered in Monday, 8 October, but *Vestal* and her brood maintained their eastward course through the next day, 9 October—the day when the typhoon struck Okinawa with unparalleled force. At that time, *Vestal* was steering a "crazy-patch course," eluding the storm that included seas up to 40 feet high and winds registering between 50 and 65 knots. Hoping for a possible entry into Buckner Bay on Wednesday, 10 October, *Vestal* headed westerly, bucking strong head winds.

At 1405 on 10 October, while *Vestal* headed back to Buckner Bay, a signalman on the flying bridge called out: "Life raft on port bow." "Second life raft on port beam," came another cry only a few moments later. Barely perceptible several thousand yards to port were tiny specks, rising with the waves—specks which turned out to be the survivors of the sunken *LSM–15* that had gone down in the fury of the typhoon during the previous night.

Ordering the other ships to proceed independently, *Vestal* put about to port and shortly thereafter swung to windward of the nearest life raft. In the lee thus formed, the repair ship lowered a motor whaleboat; that craft picked up 17 men from the first raft. Ultimately, 15 more survivors clambered up the boarding nets to safety—a total of two officers and 30 men recovered from the sea.

Entering Buckner Bay at dusk, *Vestal* witnessed the savage typhoon's aftermath with the dawn of the 11th. Once again, *Vestal* immediately turned to the task of repairing the battered ships of the fleet.

Subsequently, *Vestal* performed her vital service functions supporting the occupation of China and Japan, before she sailed back to the United States. Her disposal delayed in order to allow the ship to perform decommissioning work on other ships referred to the 13th Naval District for disposal, *Vestal* was ultimately decommissioned at the Puget Sound Naval Shipyard on 14 August 1946. Struck from the Navy list on 25 September of the same year, she lay inactive for the next two and one-half years before stripping began on 20 May 1949. Her hulk was sold on 28 July 1950 to the Boston Metals Co., Baltimore, Md., and subsequently scrapped.

Vestal (AR–4) received two battle stars for her World War II service.

Vester

(MSA: t. 117 (gross); l. 96′4″; b. 18′4″; dr. 5′9″ (mean); s. 7.6 k.; cpl. 24; a. 2 1-pdrs.)

Vester—a wooden-hulled freight boat completed in 1876 at Boothbay, Maine—was acquired by the Navy from the Delaware Fish Oil Co. on 24 May 1917; designated SP–686; and commissioned on 2 June 1917, Ens. J. T. H. Anderson, USNRF, in command.

Assigned to the 4th Naval District, *Vester* operated on patrol duties until 21 October, when she was transferred to the district minesweeping squadron. Based then at the Section Base at Lewes, Del., the ship appears to have spent most of her active duty alongside a pier with her engines out of commission. After 11 September 1918, she was shifted to routine patrol duties when her antiquated single-expansion power plant would permit.

She remained thus engaged until decommissioned at Cape May, N.J., on 15 May 1919. *Vester* was sold on 15 January 1920 to Hayes and Anderton, of New York City.

Vesuvius

An Italian volcano located on the eastern side of the Bay of Naples. Its most famous eruption, on 24 August 79 A.D., completely destroyed the city of Pompeii and the town of Herculaneum.

I

(Bomb Ketch: t. 145; lbp. 82′5″; b. 25′5″; dr. 8′4″; cpl. 30; a. 1 13″ mortar, 8 9-pdrs., 2 24-pdrs.)

The first *Vesuvius*—a bomb ketch built by Jacob Coffin at Newburyport, Mass.—was launched on 31 May 1806; and commissioned in or before September 1806, Lt. James T. Leonard in command.

Vesuvius departed Boston for the Gulf of Mexico but, while en route on 19 October, ran aground in the Gulf of Abaco. The ship lost her rudder and floated free only after her crew had jettisoned all of her guns and their carriages; her shot and shell; and even part of the kentledge. She finally reached New Orleans on 27 November.

Repaired and rearmed with 10 6-pounders, the ship subsequently sailed for Natchez and operated out of that port from February 1807 until returning to New Orleans on 30 May. *Vesuvius* was then ordered north for further repairs and arrived at New York on 1 August.

The ship apparently remained in the New York area until the spring of 1809, when she again sailed for New Orleans. Embarking upon duties to suppress slave traders and pirates operating out of the trackless bayous, *Vesuvius* cruised off the mouth of the muddy Mississippi and into the Gulf of Mexico, alert for any sign of illegal activity.

The crew's vigilance was rewarded in February 1810 when, under the command of Lt. Benjamin F. Read, *Vesuvius* gave chase to a pirate vessel off the mouth of the Mississippi and captured *Duc de Montebello*—a schooner named by Frenchmen who had been expelled from Cuba by the Spanish government. Dispatched to New Orleans, the buccaneer ship was condemned. In the same month, boats from *Vesuvius*, under the command of Midshipman F. H. Gregory, captured pirate schooner *Diomede* and slaver *Alexandria*—the latter with a full cargo of slaves on board and flying British colors.

Four months later, Comdr. David Porter, commander of the New Orleans station, embarked in *Vesuvius* before the bomb ketch departed New Orleans on 10 June 1810, bound via Havana, Cuba, for Washington. Also making the passage were Porter's wife and the Porters' ward, eight-year-old James Glasgow Farragut. The lad —who would later change his name to David Glasgow Farragut and ultimately become the Navy's first admiral—was experiencing his first sea voyage.

After repairs at the Washington Navy Yard, the ketch pressed on for New York and arrived on 6 September 1810. *Vesuvius* was placed in ordinary, and her crew was transferred to *Enterprise*.

In 1816, *Vesuvius* served as a receiving ship at New York. A survey conducted in April 1818 revealed that the cost to repair and refit the ship would be, in the survey's words, "exhorbitant." Still carried on the Navy list as a receiving ship through 1821, *Vesuvius* was broken up in June 1829 after being damaged beyond repair on 4 June when the old steamship *Fulton* exploded alongside.

II

(Bomb Brig: t. 239; l. 97′0″; b. 26′0″; dph. 10′0″; dr. 9′8″ (forward), 11′4″ (aft); a. 1 10″ mortar)

The second *Vesuvius*—a coastal cargoman built in 1845 at Williamsburg, N.Y., as *Saint Mary*—was acquired by the Navy at New York in 1846 for use with the blockading squadrons in the Gulf of Mexico. Records of the ship's service are sketchy at best, especially for her early service in the Navy. However, reports indicate that she apparently operated as *Vesuvius*, off Vera Cruz, although one source dates her renaming as occurring on 5 January 1847. In August of 1846, after many members of her crew contracted yellow fever while on duty off Vera Cruz, *Vesuvius* put into Bermuda en route north for recuperation.

She was probably refitted at New York, as records indicate that, under the command of Comdr. George A. Magruder, she departed from that port towards the end of the winter of 1846 and 1847, arriving at Laguna del Carmen, Mexico, on 7 March 1847, for blockade duty. *Vesuvius* was assigned to the port of Laguna. At this juncture, Commodore Matthew Galbraith Perry—commanding the Gulf Squadron—appointed Magruder the military governor of the town, and the commander was of great value to Perry as an administrator. The majority of time spent by *Vesuvius* on the Gulf station was spent at Laguna, where she logged the shipping movements of vessels both inside and outside of the harbor.

In the spring of 1847, when Commodore Perry launched his expedition against Tuxpan, *Vesuvius* was withdrawn temporarily from Laguna to support the operation. The Mexicans defending the town with 650 men led by General Cos were ideally situated to command its approaches. The assault on the Mexican defensive works was launched by a 1500-man landing force drawn from the ships' crews. Twenty-five officers and men from *Vesuvius*, led by Commander Magruder, took part in this action and were present when the stars and stripes were raised over the captured city.

Twelve days later, Perry launched an all-out assault against Tabasco, the last remaining large port commanded by the Mexicans on the Gulf coast. Although captured earlier by American forces, Tabasco had fallen again to Mexican hands. After leaving guardships at Coazacoalcos and Tuxpan, Perry arrived off Frontera on 14 June 1847, at the mouth of the river which led to Tabasco. Shifting his flag again to *Scorpion*, Perry and his squadron commenced the passage up the tortuous channels. At "Devil's Bend," concealed Mexican sharpshooters opened fire from the dense chaparral along the riverbank. *Scorpion*, *Washington*, *Vesuvius*, and the flat-bottomed "surfboats" returned the fire; *Vesuvius*' 10-inch mortar shells dispersed the snipers; thus allowing the squadron to continue its way upriver.

At six in the evening, the squadron anchored for the night and arranged barricades about the decks to protect the American sailors against sniper fire. During the night, Mexican forces placed obstructions in the only navigable channel.

Meanwhile, landing parties from Perry's ships stealthily scaled the steep cliffs which rose from the river. They then rushed the works in a sudden assault which surprised the Mexican troops and put them to flight. During the attack, the gunboats forced their way up the river under the command of Lt. David D. Porter, who would later win fame during the Civil War.

Fort Iturbide, mounting six guns, soon fell to a landing force commanded by Lt. Porter, thus clearing the final obstacle from the road to Tabasco. Accordingly, detachments from *Scorpion* and *Spitfire* took possession of this objective on the 16th.

Vesuvius remained in the Gulf of Mexico, at Laguna, through the end of the year 1847. Under the command of Lt. S. W. Godon, the brig captured American schooner *Wasp* on 10 October 1847, which was engaged in illicit trading, and later captured four bungos. *Vesuvius* moved to Campeache on 8 March 1848 and then back to Laguna late in April. She operated there until sailing north in mid-summer. The brig arrived at Norfolk on 1 August and was sold there the following October.

Tippecanoe—a *Canonicus*-class monitor—was renamed *Vesuvius* on 15 June 1869 and subsequently renamed *Wyandotte* (*q.v.*) on 10 August 1869.

III

(Dynamite Gun Cruiser: dp. 930; l. 252′4″; b. 26′5″; dr. 9′0″; s. 21 k.; cpl. 70; a. 3 15″, 3 3-pdrs.)

The third *Vesuvius*—a unique vessel in the Navy inventory which marked a departure from more conventional forms of main battery armament—was laid down in September 1887 at Philadelphia, Pa., by William Cramp and Sons Ships and Engine Building Co., subcontracted from the Pneumatic Dynamite Gun Co. of New York, N.Y.; launched on 28 April 1888; sponsored by Miss Eleanor Breckinridge; and commissioned on 2 June 1890 at the Philadelphia Navy Yard, Lt. Seaton Schroeder in command.

Vesuvius carried three 15-inch pneumatic guns, mounted forward side-by-side. In order to train these weapons, the ship had to be aimed, like a gun, at its target. Compressed air projected the shells from the "dynamite guns." The explosive used in the shells themselves was actually a "desensitized blasting gelatin" composed of nitrocellulose and nitroglycerine. It was less sensitive to shock than regular dynamite but still sensitive enough that compressed air, rather than powder, had to be utilized as the propellant. Ten shells per gun were carried on board, and the range of flight —varying from 200 yards to one and one-half miles— depended on the amount of air entering the firing chamber.

Vesuvius sailed for New York shortly after commissioning and then joined the Fleet at Gardiner's Bay, N.Y., on 1 October 1890. She operated off the east coast with the North Atlantic Squadron into 1895. Highlights of this tour of duty included numerous port visits and participation in local observances of holidays and festivals, as well as gunnery practice and exercises. Experience showed that the ship's unique main battery had two major drawbacks: first, the range was too short; second, the method of aiming was crude and inaccurate.

Decommissioned on 25 April 1895 for major repairs, *Vesuvius* re-entered service on 12 January 1897, Lt. Comdr. John E. Pillsbury in command. The ship got underway from the Philadelphia Navy Yard, bound for Florida, and operated off the east coast through the spring of the following year, 1898. By this time, American relations with Spain were worsening. The American Fleet gathered in Florida waters, and *Vesuvius* hurried south from Newport, R.I., and arrived at Key West on

The "dynamite cruiser" *Vesuvius*, her yacht-like appearance broken by the muzzles of three dynamite guns near her bow.

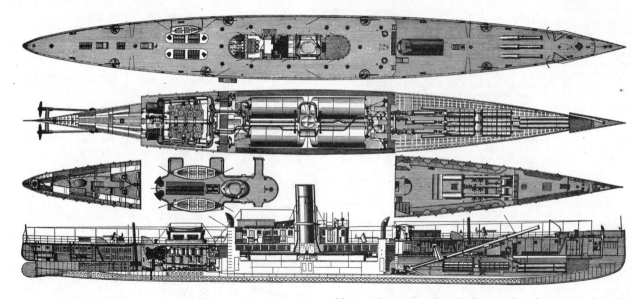

These drawings illustrate *Vesuvius'* internal arrangement. Most of her forepart is taken up by three 15-inch compressed-air guns and banks of air tanks. Like submarine torpedo tubes, these guns were fixed. They were traversed by turning the ship; elevation was adjusted by by varying the compressed-air propulsion charge.

13 May. She remained there until the 28th, when she headed for blockade duty in Cuban coastal waters. *Vesuvius* performed special duties at the discretion of the Fleet Commander in Chief and served as a dispatch vessel between Cuba and Florida into July of 1898.

On 13 June, *Vesuvius* conducted the first of eight shore bombardment missions against Santiago, Cuba. The cruiser stealthily closed the shore under cover of darkness, loosed a few rounds of her 15-inch dynamite charges, and then retired to sea. Psychologically, *Vesuvius'* bombardment caused great anxiety among the Spanish forces ashore, for her devastating shells came in without warning, unaccompanied by the roar of gunfire usually associated with a bombardment. Admiral Sampson wrote accordingly, that *Vesuvius'* bombardments had "great effect."

After hostilities with Spain ended later that summer, *Vesuvius* sailed north and called at Charleston, S.C.; New York, and Newport, before reaching Boston. Taken out of active service on 16 September 1898, *Vesuvius* remained at the Boston Navy Yard until 1904, when she began conversion to a torpedo-testing vessel. *Vesuvius* lost her unique main battery and acquired four torpedo tubes—three 18-inch and one 21-inch. Recommissioned on 21 June 1905, *Vesuvius* soon sailed for the Naval Torpedo Station at Newport to begin her new career.

She conducted torpedo experiments at the station for two years until decommissioned on 27 November 1907 for repairs. Recommissioned again on 14 February 1910, *Vesuvius* remained at Newport for the next 11 years, on occasion serving as station ship, into 1921. Decommissioned and ordered appraised for sale on 21 October 1921, *Vesuvius* was sold for scrap on 21 April 1922 to J. Lipsitz and Co., Chelsea, Mass.

IV

(AE–15: dp. 5,504; l. 459'; b. 63'; dr. 29'; s. 16 k.; cpl. 255; a. 1 5'', 4 3'', 2 40mm.; cl. *Wrangell*)

The fourth *Vesuvius* (AE–15) was laid down under a Maritime Commission contract (MC hull 1381) by the North Carolina Shipbuilding Company, Wilmington, N.C.; launched on 26 May 1944; acquired by the United States Navy on 4 July 1944; and commissioned on 16 January 1945, Comdr. Flavius J. George in command.

The ship underwent builder's trials out of Brooklyn, N.Y., and then began shakedown out of Hampton Roads, Va., in the Chesapeake Bay. On 17 February, she sailed to Earle, N.J., to onload ammunition. She then headed for the island of Ulithi, via the Panama Canal, on 5 March. She reached her destination on 5 April and promptly unloaded and took on more cargo. *Vesuvius* departed for Okinawa on 10 April where she became part of Service Squadron 6. In this role, she replenished ammunition to the Fleet in the waters around Okinawa. In July 1945, Vesuvius joined a rearming group off Honshu, Japan, to support raids on Japan by the 3d Fleet. She detached on 2 August and set sail for Leyte Gulf, Philippines. While there, word of the Japanese capitulation was received on 15 August 1945. The ship remained in the Philippines until 28 October, when she left for the United States. After transiting the Panama Canal, *Vesuvius* joined the Service Force, Atlantic Fleet. The ship arrived at Yorktown, Va., on 14 December 1945.

Vesuvius departed Yorktown on 10 January 1946, bound for Leonardo, N.J., to discharge her cargo and ship's ammunition to the Naval Ammunition Depot. On 7 February, she headed for Orange, Tex., arriving there on 13 February to commence her pre-inactivation overhaul. *Vesuvius* was placed out of commission, in reserve, at Orange on 20 August 1946.

In response to the needs imposed by the Korean conflict, *Vesuvius* was recommissioned on 15 November 1951. She remained at Orange and Beaumont, Tex., for outfitting and readying for sea until 7 January 1952, when she departed for San Diego. Having arrived on 14 February, the ship conducted exercises and loaded ammunition at Port Chicago, Calif., before sailing on 22 March for Sasebo, Japan.

She arrived at Sasebo on 3 May 1952 and, after voyage repairs, began supplying ammunition to the ships of Task Force (TF) 77 on patrol off the east coast of Korea. On 1 December, *Vesuvius* headed for the United States, arriving at San Francisco on 18 December for overhaul.

Over the next decade, *Vesuvius* was to make 11 more extended deployments to the western Pacific where she serviced units of the 7th Fleet. These operations were interspersed with port visits to Japan, Okinawa, Taiwan, the Philippines, and Hong Kong. Periods on the west coast of the United States were spent in overhaul and in the conduct of underway training.

On 24 June 1963, *Vesuvius* commenced her 13th post-World War II deployment to the western Pacific, making stops at Pearl Harbor and at Guam for repairs and arriving at Yokosuka on 4 August. She serviced the 7th Fleet throughout August. In October, she visited Sasebo and Kagoshima, Japan; Subic Bay, Philippines; and Buckner Bay, Okinawa. In November, she visited Hong Kong and spent the entire month of December 1963 in and out of Yokosuka, Japan.

Vesuvius began the year 1964 in Yokosuka making final preparations for her homeward passage. On 7 January, she got underway for San Francisco via the great circle route. She arrived on 31 January and spent February and March moored to the pier at Port Chicago. A brief trip to San Diego and participation in an exercise with other units of the 1st Fleet occupied April, and *Vesuvius* spent May in an upkeep status at Concord. On 6 July, she was underway for coastal operations. August and September saw the ship in and out of port, training and providing services to the Fleet Training Group. In October, she participated in operations with members of the 1st Fleet. On 20 November 1964, *Vesuvius* returned to Concord for upkeep and a holiday leave period. She got underway on 18 December for the Mare Island Annex, where she spent the holiday season.

The ship made a brief trip to San Diego beginning on 4 January 1965 before returning to Concord on 15 January. She began reloading cargo in preparation for deployment and got underway for the Far East on 1 February. *Vesuvius* reached Subic Bay, via Pearl Harbor and Guam, on 28 February. She then began operations in the South China Sea interrupted by brief returns for the onload of cargo in Subic Bay. In July 1965, she received a well-earned respite from her duties in Hong Kong. After a week there, she resumed operations. Having made 182 underway replenishments during the deployment, *Vesuvius* returned to Concord, Calif., on 28 November.

Vesuvius began the year 1966 by steaming on 3 January to the Puget Sound Naval Shipyard at Bremerton, Wash., to undergo repairs for six weeks. After leaving Bremerton, the ship headed south to Concord to onload ammunition. On 5 March, she sailed for San Diego for refresher training. Shortly after arrival, a 26-inch crack in one of her hull plates was discovered. She promptly began transferring her load of ammunition to other ships. By 26 March, the ammunition had been successfully offloaded; and, on 28 April 1966, *Vesuvius* proceeded to the Bethlehem Steel Shipyard in San Francisco. On 14 May, *Vesuvius* deployed for the western Pacific. From 13 June through 27 November 1966, *Vesuvius* conducted replenishment operations between the Philippines and the South China Sea. In December, she stopped at Pearl Harbor on her way home, where an unusual cargo was embarked—$9,700,000 was brought on board for a special currency lift back to the United States. Shortly before Christmas, *Vesuvius* reached Concord.

The year 1967 found the ship berthed at Mare Island preparing to undergo her first major overhaul since 1962. Following completion of overhaul at the Mare Island Naval Shipyard and underway training, *Vesuvius* departed for the western Pacific on 15 July 1967, bound for Subic Bay. Except for brief periods in Hong Kong, *Vesuvius* came off the line in the South China Sea only long enough to fill her hold with more ammunition.

Near the end of January 1968, *Vesuvius* sailed to Yokosuka on her return trip to the United States, only to be recalled to the seas off Vietnam following the *Pueblo* incident. *Vesuvius* finally returned to the San Francisco Bay area on 17 March 1968, offloaded, proceeded to the Naval Shipyard at Mare Island and, on 4 April, entered the Triple A Shipyard in San Francisco for extensive repairs and upkeep. Repairs were completed on 10 May, and the ship began refresher training in June. Following inspections and loadout, *Vesuvius* deployed again on 31 July 1968. She reached Subic Bay on 20 August for receipt of ammunition, then began operations in the Vietnam area. She remained on line through 3 December, when she left for a period of rest and recreation in Hong Kong. She departed there on 10 December to return to Vietnam.

Vesuvius remained on line through January and February 1969. In late February, she sailed into Bangkok, Thailand. From Bangkok, the ship went to Subic Bay to commence her final loadout before heading home. After a brief stop in Hawaii, *Vesuvius* arrived in Concord on 1 April 1969. In late April, the ship underwent six weeks of restricted availability at a commercial yard in San Francisco. Late in June, she steamed for San Diego and refresher training and exercises. By 23 July, she had returned to San Francisco and began three weeks of loadout for yet another deployment. *Vesuvius* departed for the western Pacific on 17 September 1969. After stopovers in Pearl Harbor and Yokosuka, she touched at Subic Bay for a few days before starting her line period off Vietnam.

During this deployment, *Vesuvius* conducted seven line runs in the South China Sea and the Tonkin Gulf in support of 7th Fleet operations. On 25 April, she left

The ammunition ship *Vesuvius* (AE–15).

for home with stops at Kobe, Japan, and Pearl Harbor. She arrived at Concord on 23 May 1970. The ship entered a three-month upkeep in San Francisco from July to October followed by a predeployment inspection. On 9 November, *Vesuvius* departed the San Francisco area for intensive training in San Diego and, on 6 December, steamed back to Port Chicago for a holiday leave period.

Vesuvius again departed for the western Pacific on 4 January 1971. She arrived at Subic Bay on 25 January, and, one week later, was underway for her first line run of the deployment. On 20 February, she pulled into Singapore and then proceeded shortly thereafter to the Philippines for a 15-day upkeep period. *Vesuvius* then resumed her assignment of providing ammunition logistics support to the 7th Fleet and Royal Australian Navy units off the coast of Vietnam. On 2 August 1971, *Vesuvius* left Subic Bay for San Francisco, arriving on 1 September. After offloading ammunition at Concord Naval Weapons Station, the ship moved to the Mare Island Naval Shipyard for a month of standdown. On 4 October, she entered a six-week upkeep. Upon completion, she returned to Concord on 19 November. *Vesuvius* departed Concord on 29 November for refresher training off San Diego, returning to Mare Island on 4 December.

Vesuvius got underway on 3 January 1972 and, on 5 January, commenced refresher training in San Diego. She returned to Concord on 29 January. Preparations for deployment began immediately, and the ship left California on 14 February. Upon arrival at Subic Bay, *Vesuvius* again supported combat operations for the 7th Fleet. On 29 June, she began upkeep and returned to action on 18 July. Her duties were interrupted for short trips to Hong Kong and Bangkok in August and October. In December, she entered drydock at Subic Bay to replace her propeller, but she promptly returned to Vietnam and ended the year in the combat zone.

The ship returned to Concord on 3 March 1973. After offloading ammunition, the ship moved to Mare Island. The ship was scheduled for upkeep from April to July. However, a message was received from the Chief of Naval Operations in July to prepare the ship for decommissioning. On 14 August 1973, *Vesuvius* was decommissioned and transferred to the Inactive Ship Maintenance Facility at Mare Island for further disposition. She was struck from the Navy list on 14 August 1973.

Vesuvius received two battle stars for World War II, two battle stars for the Korean War, and 10 battle stars for her service in Vietnam.

Viburnum

A large genus of shrubs or trees related to the honeysuckle family. Some species in the United States include the blackhaw, sheepberry, withe rod, and dockmackie.

(AN–57: dp. 1,275; l. 194'6"; b. 37'0"; dr. 13'6"; s. 12.1 k.; cpl. 56; a. 1 3", 3 20mm.; cl. *Ailanthus*)

Viburnum (AN–57)—a wooden-hulled, net-laying ship—was originally classified as YN–76 when the ship's keel was laid on 9 December 1943 at Stockton, Calif., by the Pollock-Stockton Shipbuilding Co. Reclassified to AN–57 on 1 January 1944, the ship was launched on 26 April 1944; sponsored by Mrs. R. F. Chavin, the wife of Brigadier General R. F. Chavin, USA, the commanding officer of the United States Army's Stockton Ordnance Depot. *Viburnum* was commissioned at the Pollock-Stockton yard on 2 June 1944, Lt. Benjamin A. Smith, USNR, in command.

After shakedown out of the Naval Net Depot, Tiburon Bay, Calif., and post-shakedown repairs and alterations at Long Beach, *Viburnum* departed Treasure Island, San Francisco, Calif., on 15 August, bound for Pearl Harbor with two high-speed sled targets in tow. The net-layer reached Pearl Harbor on 27 August,

delivered her tows, and subsequently pushed on for Majuro, in the Marshall Islands, where she arrived on 15 September. Assigned to Service Squadron 10, *Viburnum* shifted to Ulithi, in the Carolines, soon thereafter.

On 28 October 1944, *Viburnum* was tending the net installation at Doa Channel, Ulithi. Late that morning she picked up a net section from the depot ship *Tuscana* (AKN–3) and proceeded to stretch a double net section early in the afternoon. At 1457, a sudden violent explosion blew the port side of the forecastle deck upward, and the ship's commanding officer, Lt. Smith, ordered all hands to stand by to abandon ship. The blast had killed two men and blown a dozen others over the side. The latter were swiftly rescued by a boat from *Volans* (AKS–9). *Arapahoe* (ATF–68) came alongside *Viburnum* at 1550, joined shortly thereafter by *Zuni* (ATF–95); the latter consequently moored the stricken net-layer alongside the destroyer tender *Dixie* (AD–14) for a thorough check of the damage.

The ensuing investigation revealed that a Japanese submarine mine had blown a hole in the starboard side of the ship extending 10 frames' length (from frame 10 to frame 20) and to a point within five feet of the main deck. The explosion had broken the keel, and the hole extended about eight feet up from the keel on the port side. In ensuing days, a work crew from *ARB–6* cleared away the wreckage, and the ship's force recovered the bodies of the two men killed. From November 1944 to January 1945, *Viburnum* received repairs from *Jason* (ARH–1) and *Vestal* (AR–4) before she was docked in *AFDL–32* and repaired enough to resume active operations about 9 February 1945.

Viburnum remained at Ulithi, performing limited harbor work in a protected harbor, into the spring of 1945. She sailed for the west coast of the United States on 9 May, stopped briefly at Pearl Harbor en route and arrived at San Francisco on 5 June. Due to the heavy workload on west coast yards for repairs to damaged combatant vessels, the Navy did not desire full restoration of *Viburnum*. Accordingly, the net-laying ship was decommissioned and placed in an "in-service" status on 12 July 1945. *Viburnum* was placed out of service on 3 January 1946, and her disposal was authorized on 17 January. Her name was struck from the Navy list on 21 January, and the former net-layer was transferred to the United States Maritime Commission on 12 August 1947. The vessel was simultaneously delivered to Walter K. Wilms and Co., at Suisun Bay, and was probably scrapped soon thereafter.

Vicksburg

A city in Mississippi located on a bluff at the mouth of the Yazoo River; founded in 1812; and named for Newitt Vick (1766–1819), the owner of a plantation on the present site of the city. During the American Civil War (1861–1865), General Ulysses S. Grant besieged the city from 19 May to 4 July 1863, when it surrendered, giving the North control of the Mississippi River and its tributaries and contributing greatly to the eventual overall Union victory.

I

(ScGbt.: t. 886; l. 185'; b. 33'; dr. 13'8"; s. 9 k.; a. 1 100-pdr. P.r., 4 30-pdr. P.r., 1 20-pdr. P.r., 1 20-pdr. sb.)

The first *Vicksburg*—a wooden steamer built in 1863 at Mystic, Conn.—was purchased by the Navy at New York City on 20 October 1863; and commissioned at the New York Navy Yard on 2 December, Lt. Comdr. L. Braine in command.

On 7 December, a group of 17 Confederate sympathizers masquerading as passengers seized the steamer *Chesapeake* off Cape Cod, Mass. The panic caused by that daring Confederate exploit prompted the Navy to order *Vicksburg* on 21 December to take up station off Sandy Hook, N.J., and detain for inspection all commercial ships outbound from New York. She performed similar duty off Staten Island, N.Y., through January 1864 until she was finally relieved on 8 February and ordered to sail for Hampton Roads, Va., for duty with the North Atlantic Blockading Squadron.

Vicksburg put into Hampton Roads two days later and was deployed with the blockade off Wilmington, N.C., on the 18th. In the spring, while on temporary duty off the coast of South Carolina, the gunboat seized the blockade-running British schooner *Indian* east of Charleston on 30 April. Returning to North Carolina, *Vicksburg* towed the stricken mortar schooner *Oliver H. Lee* to Beaufort, N.C., on 17 and 18 May and chased a blockade runner on the 31st, recovering 79 bales of cotton thrown overboard by the vessel's crew. The gunboat put into Hampton Roads for repairs in June.

On 11 July, *Vicksburg* received orders north to Annapolis, Md., to help protect Union emplacements there from Confederate raiders. She arrived off Annapolis in the Severn River on the 13th. Lt. Comdr. Braine found that the town was apprehensive over the proximity of Confederate forces and was mainly defended by 300 patients from the local hospital. Together with the gunboat *Daylight*, Lt. Comdr. Braine organized the town defenses and predicted that he would "give the rebels a warm reception." That day, he also sent a boat party up the South River under the command of Acting Ensign Francis G. Osborn. The two-day expedition destroyed all means of crossing the South River and thereby protected the rear of the Union forces at Annapolis. *Vicksburg* received orders to return to Hampton Roads on the 15th, arrived there on the 17th, and left for the blockade off Wilmington later in July in a convoy consisting of the side wheel steamer *Nansemond* and four tugs.

While deployed on patrol and reconnaissance duty off Wilmington, *Vicksburg* unsuccessfully chased a blockade-running side-wheel steamer on the night of 6 August and another on the night of the 23d which she

found aground at daylight the next morning. The gunboat underwent repairs soon thereafter and spent September making an extensive survey of Confederate Fort Fisher and of other Southern land defenses in the Cape Fear River. After completing this mission on 10 October, she assisted in the capture of the new, steel-hulled, blockade-running British steamer *Bat* off the Cape Fear River and, on the 20th and the 24th, participated in two unsuccessful nighttime chases of blockade-running steamers in the same area. *Vicksburg* remained off the Cape Fear River for the duration of the year and, on 26 December, assisted in covering the evacuation of troops after the unsuccessful first attack upon Fort Fisher on 24 and 25 December.

Vicksburg began the final year of the war assisting Union forces in mop-up operations following the fall of Fort Fisher during a second amphibious assault which took place between 13 and 15 January 1865. She also participated in the bombardment of Half Moon Battery, situated on the coastal flank of the Confederate defense line which crossed Cape Fear Peninsula six miles above Fort Fisher, on 11 February. On the 22d, she was ordered north to Hampton Roads. In March, *Vicksburg* was one of several vessels sent to White House, Va., to support General Grant's siege of Richmond by keeping open navigation between White House and the mouth of the York River.

With the end of the Civil War in April 1865, *Vicksburg* was decommissioned at the New York Navy Yard on 29 April and sold at auction to C. C. & H. Cable on 12 July. She was documented for merchant service on 7 August 1865. Her name last appeared on lists of merchant vessels in the autumn of 1868.

II

(Gunboat No. 11: dp. 1,010; l. 204'5"; b. 36'0"; dr. 12'9" (aft); s. 12.71 k. (tl.); cpl. 143; a. 6 4", 4 6-pdr. R.F., 2 1-pdr. R.F., 1 Colt mg.; cl. *Annapolis*)

The second *Vicksburg* (Gunboat No. 11) was laid down in March 1896 at Bath, Maine, by the Bath Iron

An early-1900s view of the gunboat *Vicksburg* in white hull and buff upperworks, the standard finish for steel ships at that time.

Works; launched on 5 December 1896; sponsored by Miss Trowbridge; and placed in commission at the Portsmouth (N.H.) Navy Yard on 23 October 1897, Comdr. A. B. H. Lillie in command.

Vicksburg stood out of Newport, R.I., on 16 January 1898 and, after two months in the Caribbean, returned north as far as Norfolk, Va., late in March. On 26 April—the day after the United States Congress declared that a state of war with Spain had existed since the 21st—*Vicksburg* stood out of Chesapeake Bay and headed south to join Rear Admiral William T. Sampson's North Atlantic Fleet in blockading the northern coast of Cuba. She reached Key West, Fla., on May Day and, after three days there, got underway to join the blockade.

For the next three months, *Vicksburg* patrolled the Cuban coast near Havana, returning to Key West periodically for fuel and provisions. During her tour of duty in Cuban waters, she captured three blockade runners. In May, she took *Oriente* and *Fernandito* on the 5th and 7th, respectively. Both were small unarmed sailing ships bound from the Gulf of Campeche to Havana with cargoes of fish. The gunboat took each to Key West where they were condemned by a prize court. Her third and final capture came more than a month later on 24 June when she encountered *Ampala*, a 150-ton sailing vessel, bound from Havana to Truxillo. Though *Ampala* carried no cargo save provisions for her passengers, *Vicksburg* took her to Key West where she, too, was duly condemned. On one occasion, *Vicksburg* came under the fire of a shore battery near Havana. By August, hostilities in Cuba were ending, and the need for blockading ships diminished. *Vicksburg* departed Cuban waters on the 14th and, after a three-day stop at Key West, continued north to Newport where she arrived on 23 August. During the remaining months of 1898 and the first five months of 1899, she operated along the east coast and in the Caribbean. On 24 May 1899, *Vicksburg* was placed out of commission at Boston, Mass.

Almost a year later, on 15 May 1900, the gunboat was recommissioned at Newport, R.I., Comdr. E. B. Barry in command. After six months of operations in the Atlantic, *Vicksburg* stood out of Boston on 9 November for duty on the Asiatic Station. She sailed via the Mediterranean Sea and the Suez Canal and arrived at Cavite—on the island of Luzon in the Philippines—on 2 February 1901. During the first of her three years in the Far East, *Vicksburg* joined other Navy units in supporting the Army's campaign against the insurrection in the Philippines which followed Spain's ceding the islands to the United States. *Vicksburg* herself contributed significantly to the success of those operations when she assisted Army forces in capturing the leader of the revolt, Emilio Aguinaldo, at Palawan Island in March 1901. She also cooperated with the Army again in June during the occupation of Puerta Princessa and Cuyo, the two major cities on the island.

In 1902, the warship moved north and, for the remaining two years of her tour, cruised the waters off the coasts of China, Japan, and Korea. She spent the entire first quarter of 1904 at Chemulpo, Korea, protecting American interests during the initial stages of the Russo-Japanese War. On 9 June 1904, *Vicksburg* took leave of Asia when she stood out of Yokohama, Japan, and shaped a course for home. She reached Bremerton, Wash., on 29 June but later moved south to the Mare Island Navy Yard near San Francisco, Calif. There, she was placed out of commission, in reserve, on 15 July 1904.

After almost five years of inactivity, *Vicksburg* was placed back in commission at Mare Island on 17 May 1909, Comdr. Alexander S. Halstead in command. The gunboat departed San Francisco on 16 June and headed south to the coast of Mexico and the Isthmus of Panama. During the next four years, she cruised the western coast of Central America in an effort to support American diplomatic moves to maintain peace in the revolution-prone nations in the area. For that pur-

pose, she made calls at ports in Mexico, Honduras, El Salvador, Guatemala, and Panama. Conditions in Nicaragua were especially volatile during those years, and *Vicksburg* returned to Corinto and other Nicaraguan ports time and time again.

During the early summer of 1912, she began operating primarily along the California coast. In late August, she cruised south for an extended courtesy visit to Guayamas, Mexico. The gunboat returned to the United States at San Diego on 3 November. Following repairs at the Mare Island and the Puget Sound navy yards, she began duty with the Washington Naval Militia on 18 June. That service occupied her almost completely until the United States entered World War I in the spring of 1917. The only exception came in May and June of 1914 when she was placed back in full commission for a brief cruise to Mexico. Upon her return to Puget Sound, she reverted to reserve status and resumed training duty with the Washington Naval Militia.

On 6 April 1917, the United States associated herself with the Allied Powers in World War I by declaring war on the German Empire. A week later, on 13 April, *Vicksburg* was placed back in full commission at Puget Sound. The gunboat patrolled the western coasts of the United States and Mexico through the end of the war. That German influence was particularly strong in Mexico during the war is evidenced by the fact that Germany started reasonably serious negotiations to persuade Mexico to enter the war on the side of the Central Powers. The famous Zimmermann telegram—which offered Mexico the opportunity to recoup her losses in the American Southwest—contributed greatly to the United States' decision to go to war against Germany. Thus, the Navy had to flex its muscles convincingly to dissuade Mexico from assisting the Central Powers. *Vicksburg* and the other ships which patrolled the Mexican coasts helped provide the influence necessary to keep that nation out of the enemy camp.

As a result of her mildly pro-German attitude, Mexico became a center for German activity in the western hemisphere, particularly after the United States entered World War I. Incidents involving German nationals occurred frequently. One such incident provided *Vicksburg* with the single concrete reward for her vigilance. On 17 March 1918, she anchored off the harbor at Viejo Bay, Mexico, in response to information that a ship carrying German nationals would attempt to leave the port. At 1225, she sighted the schooner *Alexander Agassiz* standing out to sea under the American flag and immediately got underway to intercept her. The schooner tried to make a dash for it, but a shot across her bow forced *Alexander Agassiz* to heave to and submit to a search.

Vicksburg's boarding party made some interesting discoveries. The schooner carried 14 people, of whom five were German and six were Mexican. Two others were women, one of whom was purportedly the vessel's owner. The remaining passenger was an American, probably the informant upon whose advice the capture was made since he is listed in *Vicksburg*'s war diary as ". . . one American spy. . . ." The motorized sailing vessel also carried some small arms and a quantity of ammunition as well as a "German flag." The people were taken on board *Vicksburg*, and the five Germans were put in irons.

Vicksburg justified the capture on the fact that the schooner carried enemy nationals and that she possessed no proper ship's papers. In a three-hour discussion held that afternoon with the Captain of the Port, the British vice consul, and commanding officers of other American ships in the area, *Vicksburg*'s commanding officer supported his action further with the fact that the passengers were seen to throw articles overboard just before the boarding party arrived and with the suggestion that *Alexander Agassiz* had been fitted out as a raider. That shaky proposition was later repudiated by an American prize court which ordered that restitution be made to the owner of the schooner. It now seems

Three members of *Vicksburg*'s crew—Machinist 2/cl. A. E. Flesher, Shipfitter 2/cl. F. R. Shuster, and Carpenter's Mate 2/cl. C. A. Kilwinski—pose in front of a painted backdrop for a souvenir photo of the kind so popular during the second half of the last century. (Courtesy Navy/Marine Corps Museum, Treasure Island, California)

likely that the five Germans were simply making a desperate attempt to return home.

Later that month, *Vicksburg* delivered her prize to San Diego and the prisoners to Los Angeles. She then resumed her patrols off California and remained so occupied through the remaining months of the war. The gunboat continued her active service for almost a year after hostilities stopped in November 1918. On 16 October 1919, she was finally decommissioned for the last time at Puget Sound; and, four days later, she was transferred to the Washington State Nautical School. *Vicksburg* served as a training ship with the school until 1921. During this period, she received the designation PG–11 on 17 July 1920, when the Navy adopted the alphanumeric system of hull designations.

On 2 May 1921, *Vicksburg* was transferred once more —this time to the Coast Guard—and her name was struck from the Navy list. She was renamed *Alexander Hamilton* on 18 August 1922 and served as a training ship at the Coast Guard Academy until 1930. The Coast Guard decommissioned her on 7 June 1930, stripped her, and towed her to the depot at Curtis Bay, Md., where she was permanently assigned as station ship. Sometime between 1 July 1935 and 1 July 1936, she was renamed *Beta* and, by 1 July 1940, she had been reassigned to New London, Conn., as a station ship.

In 1942, she was towed back to Curtis Bay where she served as a training platform for machinist's mates and water tenders. That duty lasted until 30 December 1944 when she was finally placed out of service completely. On 28 March 1946, the hulk was turned over to the War Shipping Administration for final disposition. Presumably, she was scrapped.

Laid down as *Vicksburg*, late in 1941, CL–81 was renamed *Houston* (q.v.) on 12 October 1942, prior to launching.

III

(CL–86: dp. 10,000; l. 610'1"; b. 66'4"; dr. 25'0" (max.); s. 33 k.; cpl. 992; a. 12 6", 12 5", 28 40mm., 10 20mm.; cl. *Cleveland*)

Cheyenne (CL–86) was laid down on 26 October 1942 at Newport News, Va., by the Newport News Shipbuilding and Drydock Co., but, exactly one month later, was renamed *Vicksburg*. The light cruiser was launched on 14 December 1943; sponsored by Miss Muriel Hamilton, the daughter of Mayor J. C. Hamilton, of Vicksburg, Miss.; and commissioned at the Norfolk Navy Yard on 12 June 1944, Capt. William C. Vose in command.

The ship was fitted out for sea at Norfolk into July and conducted the preliminary phases of her shakedown in Chesapeake Bay prior to sailing for the British West Indies on 7 August. The light cruiser, then operating out of Trinidad, completed her shakedown training in the Gulf of Paria between 12 and 30 August; conducted shore bombardment exercises off Culebra, Puerto Rico, on 1 September and, on the following day, sailed for Hampton Roads in company with the old flushdecked destroyers *Broome* (DD–216) and *Simpson* (DD–221).

Returning to Hampton Roads soon thereafter, *Vicksburg* then conducted radar spotting practice at *YAG–13* and at a battle raft on the 9th, and fired a drone practice off Cape May on the 10th. She underwent a postshakedown overhaul at the Boston Navy Yard from 11 to 24 September; ran standardization trials off Rockland, Maine; and then took part in naval radiation laboratory tests in the vicinity of Deer Island in Boston harbor. After availability at Boston, *Vicksburg* operated in Narragansett Bay, Block Island Sound, and Long Island Sound, serving as a precommissioning training vessel for crews of large combatant warships between 5 October and 15 December.

Vicksburg returned to the Norfolk Navy Yard on 17 December and remained there until she ran her post repair trials in the Chesapeake Bay on the last two days of 1944. The warship departed Hampton Road on New Year's Day 1945 and rendezvoused with the destroyers *Rodman* (DD–456) and *Emmons* (DD–457) at the entrance to the Chesapeake Bay to form Task Group (TG) 21.12. *Vicksburg* and her escorts arrived at Cristobal, Canal Zone, four days later; transited the Panama Canal that afternoon; and moored at NOB Balboa where TG 21.12 was dissolved.

Vicksburg got underway for the Hawaiian Islands on 6 January 1945 and arrived at Pearl Harbor on the 17th. The light cruiser then conducted exercises of Oahu—aircraft tracking, firing at drones, fighter direction, radar calibration, and long and short range battle practices—through the end of January.

Vicksburg departed Pearl Harbor at 0800 on 5 February, and arrived at Saipan, in the Marianas, on the 13th. There, she was fueled from the fleet oiler *Enoree* (AO–69) and prepared for the ship's upcoming operation—and her baptism of fire—the bombardment of Iwo Jima.

The following day, *Vicksburg* left Saipan and joined other units of TG 52.19 at sea. On the 15th, the light cruiser became part of Task Unit (TU) 54.9.2, movement group "Baker"—consisting of herself; the battleships *Nevada* (BB–36) and *Idaho* (BB–42); the heavy cruisiers *Chester* (CA–27) and *Pensacola* (CA–24); and screening destroyers. That force soon split into two fire support units. *Vicksburg* joined *Chester* and *Pensacola* and took station at 0651 to commence bombarding the shore. At 0709, *Vicksburg* catapult-launched the first of her plane sorties and commenced fire. Directed by the ship's spotter in a Vought OS2U Kingfisher, the light cruiser's 6-inch guns opened up from a range of 12,000 yards, shelling enemy installations on the northern end of the island of Iwo Jima.

Squalls cut down the visibility for the spotting aircraft; but, occasionally, the aircrew managed to glimpse the target area. At 0808, *Vicksburg* completed the first phase of her bombardment mission and recovered her plane to refuel it. At 0947, the light cruiser commenced the second phase of her assigned mission. Still hampered by bad weather over the target, the spotters doggedly remained airborne and directed gunfire as well as they could through the spotty cloud cover. By afternoon, however, visibility had increased markedly, allowing the ship to assess her gunfire as landing "on target," in the third phase.

Vicksburg had launched her Kingfisher at 1249 piloted by Lt. J. B. Nabors, Jr. At 1414, listeners on the radio circuit heard Nabors report that his aircraft was being fired upon by Japanese antiaircraft guns. Shortly thereafter, a Japanese A6M5 "Zeke" fighter attacked the slower, more vulnerable Kingfisher. The ensuing air battle did not last long, however, and ended happily for the American side, when another Kingfisher—from *Pensacola*—bagged the "Zeke," enabling *Vicksburg's* plane to resume her air spotting activities unhindered by enemy interference in the air.

One-half hour later, *Vicksburg* completed Phase III of her gunfire assignment and recovered the Kingfisher. Shortly before 1600, the light cruiser again launched one of her brood of floatplanes and, at 1618, commenced Phase IV from a range of 10,000 yards. After completing the firing at 1727 and subsequently recovering her aircraft, *Vicksburg* and her consorts were joined by the other fire support ships in retiring for the night at 14 knots.

Vicksburg remained off Iwo Jima, providing gunfire support for the landings, into March and headed for Ulithi on the 5th to replenish and provision before putting to sea again on the 14th in TG 58.1, part of the 5th Fleet's fast carrier striking arm, which was then undertaking air strikes to neutralize Japanese air power as the Allies prepared to invade Okinawa.

Vicksburg's first brush with the Japanese while engaged in that screening duty came on 18 March, 100 iles east of the Japanese home island of Kyushu. A "Betty" made a torpedo attack on the cruiser, dropping er "fish" while the ship was in the middle of a tight mergency turn. The torpedo churned by the bow, some 5 yards ahead of the ship, and proceeded parallel to he cruiser's port side. Within 20 minutes, another nemy plane closed, dropped flares, and departed— urried along on its way by antiaircraft fire from the hips of TG 58.1.

Soon thereafter, *Vicksburg*—already at general quar- ers—opened fire with her 40-millimeter battery. The lane came in through the formation, and *Vicksburg*'s Bofors guns began blasting the plane after it had lready been set ablaze by fire from other ships. Moments later, it splashed.

At 0600, a "Frances" closed the formation and ap- roached one of the carriers in the group from astern. t soon executed a wingover and dived on the carrier hrough a curtain of flak. The enemy never reached his estination, however, for the heavy wall of gunfire— robably from the carrier herself—knocked the "Fran- es" into the water.

Slightly less than two hours later, a "Judy" bored in or a surprise attack and passed over *Vicksburg*. The ight cruiser's battery blasted away at the intruder and cored three definite hits before 5-inch gunfire (probably rom either the destroyer *Harrison* (DD–573) or light ruiser *Miami* (CL–89)) blasted the enemy from the ky.

Meanwhile, the carriers' planes battered Japanese argets ashore on the Japanese home islands. The ruisers and destroyers in the screen had no rest, for he Japanese came back again on the next day. At 0715, a Japanese plane dived toward *Wasp* (CV–18) and cored one bomb hit. *Vicksburg* soon opened fire on the nemy plane. As it turned, either to make another at- ack or to escape the American fighters from the com- at air patrol, the Japanese plane was rocked by a roximity burst from one of *Vicksburg*'s shells. The last knocked off a wing and set the plane afire. It then pun into the sea—a confirmed "kill."

While she was supporting strikes against Japanese argets to weaken the enemy's ability to defend against he impending invasion of the Ryukyus, *Vicksburg* estroyed eight Japanese planes. In addition, one of the hip's Kingfishers rescued a Marine aviator from the waters off the Japanese home islands.

Later detached from service with TG 58.1, *Vicksburg* hifted to a position off Okinawa for shore bombard- ment and close support duties. Highlighting the opera- ion for the light cruiser was firing nearly 2,300 rounds f 6-inch and 5-inch projectiles in a six-hour time pan, supporting an Army advance up the southern art of the island. Some of her targets were only a ew hundred yards ahead of the advancing troops—a ituation that required accurate shooting. *Vicksburg*'s uns blasted Japanese gun positions, caves, and strong- oints during the ship's long hours of firing and load- ng ammunition on the veritable "front lines."

After leaving the Ryukyus late in the Okinawa cam- aign, *Vicksburg* supported a minesweeping operation n the China Sea until 24 June, when she sailed for he Philippine Islands.

Vicksburg remained in Philippine waters through the apanese capitulation on 15 August 1945. Five days ater, on the 20th, the light cruiser departed San Pedro Bay, Leyte, as part of TU 30.3.7, in company with the estroyers *Moale* (DD–693), *Rowe* (DD–564), and *Lowry* (DD–770). While the ships proceeded toward a point off the Japanese home islands—where they would rendezvous with a fast carrier striking force—*Lowry* ighted and exploded a drifting mine.

Vicksburg joined TG 38.2 on 24 August—part of Vice Admiral John S. McCain's task force—and was replen- shed and provisioned at sea. TG 38.2 covered the approaches to Tokyo Bay prior to, and during, the formal Japanese surrender on 2 September 1945. Three lays later, *Vicksburg* entered Tokyo Bay.

There, Rear Admiral I. J. Wiltse, Commander, Cruis- er Division 10, shifted his flag to *Vicksburg;* and, on 20 September, the light cruiser departed Tokyo Bay as part of a 3d Fleet task group under the command of Rear Admiral John F. Shafroth and proceeded to Oki- nawa, where she anchored at Buckner Bay, on the 23d. There, 2,200 passengers came on board for transporta- tion back to the United States.

Five days after arrival in Pearl Harbor on 4 October, *Vicksburg* led the sortie of the 3d Fleet for the United States. On the 15th, the Fleet passed in review in San Francisco Bay, Calif. *Vicksburg* remained in that port until 26 October when she got underway to shift to Monterey Bay, Calif., to take part in Navy Day observ- ances there on the 27th. The ship reached Long Beach on 31 October but shifted to Portland, Oreg., on 6 November to participate in Armistice Day services be- fore returning to Long Beach on the 16th.

Placed in the Terminal Island Naval Shipyard in San Francisco Bay on 17 January 1946 for availability, *Vicksburg* emerged from the overhaul and moderniza- tion as perhaps the most modern ship of her class. On 20 May 1946, *Vicksburg* became the flagship for Vice Admiral Frederick C. Sherman, Commander, 3d Fleet, who shifted his flag from *Iowa* (BB–61) on that date. Two days later, the ship moved to San Diego, where she moored at the Naval Air Station (NAS). She remained there into September, when she became the temporary flagship of Vice Admiral A. E. Montgomery.

Vicksburg was ultimately decommissioned on 30 June 1947 at San Francisco, Calif. She remained "moth- balled" until struck from the Navy list on 1 October 1962. Sold to the National Metal and Steep Corp., Terminal Island, Calif., on 25 August 1964, she was then scrapped.

Vicksburg received two battle stars for her World War II service.

Victor

I

(MB: t. 50; l. 71'6''; b. 15'; dr. 3'3'' (mean); s. 12 k.; cpl. 10; a. 1 3'', 2 mg.)

The first *Victor* (SP–1995)—a wooden-hulled motor- boat constructed at Camden, N.J., by Clement A. Troth and completed in 1917—was leased by the Navy on 27 November 1917 from George H. Earle, Jr., of Haver- ford, Pa.; and commissioned on 26 December 1917, Ens. George H. Earle, III, in command.

Operating out of Cape May, N.J., *Victor* patrolled the entrance to Delaware Bay for the duration of the war. During her naval service, two incidents stood out to enliven her otherwise uneventful routine; and both occurred in February 1918.

While the boat was on patrol on the 10th of the month, an explosion in the vessel's engine room started a fire at 1530. The crew fought the flames with fire extinguishers and formed a bucket brigade back to the stern. Not having a wireless, *Victor* hoisted dis- tress signals—including an upside down national ensign —fired a gun to attract attention to her plight, and sounded her klaxon horn. Meanwhile, her small boat was manned, lowered, and sent out to obtain assistance as the fire made enough headway to convince some on board that their chance of putting it out was slim.

Members of the crew not fighting the fire began to construct a makeshift raft out of doors, tops of berths, hatchways, and tables, while still others moved ammu- nition astern to prevent its catching fire and exploding. All life preservers were moved on deck, ready for use. However, the dogged efforts of the firefighters brought the blaze under control by 1605; and it was completely extinguished by 1610. Soon thereafter, *Emerald* (SP– 177) arrived on the scene and towed *Victor* back to port for repairs.

On 25 February, while *Victor* lay at anchor at the section base, a seaplane, piloted by Ens. Walker Weed,

USNRF, tried to make a landing at Cold Spring Inlet, but instead fell on the opposite side of the base, on the beach. An explosion followed the crash, and the plane burst into flames with its occupants still on board. Sounding "man overboard," *Victor* and *Emerald* sent boats shoreward with rescue parties.

The pilot, Ensign Weed, his clothes afire, stumbled from the blazing aircraft and plunged headlong into the water to extinguish the flames. Meanwhile, his passenger, named Bennett, staggered out of the fire but passed out before he could reach the water's edge. *Victor*'s men ran to his aid, extinguished the fire, and saw to it that the injured flyer's wounds were dressed and treated.

Victor remained on harbor entrance patrol duties at Cape May until four days before the armistice which ended the war in Europe. Shifted then to Delaware River patrol duties in the area of the antisubmarine nets, *Victor* sailed for Camden, N.J. She was decommissioned there on 21 November 1918 and returned to her owner.

II

(AMc–109: dp. 190; l. 98'5''; b. 23'6''; dr. 10'6'' (mean); s. 10 k.; cpl. 17; a. 2 .50-cal. mg., 2 .30-cal. mg.; cl. *Accentor*)

The second *Victor* (AMc–109)—a wooden-hulled, coastal minesweeper—was laid down on 14 July 1941 at Rockland, Maine, by the Snow Shipyard, Inc.; launched on 6 December 1941; sponsored by Miss Virginia Hanson; and placed in service at the Boston Navy Yard on 17 April 1942.

Following training at the Mine Warefare School, Yorktown, Va., *Victor* operated locally in the Tidewater region for nearly one year before shifting to the 3d Naval District in March 1943 for local operations. After the end of the war with Germany, she moved to Charleston, S.C., in June of 1945 for mine clearance operations. *Victor* worked locally in the 6th Naval District until placed out of service there on 31 October 1945. Simultaneously laid up in reserve in the Wando River, the minesweeper was declared surplus and authorized for delivery to the War Shipping Administration (WSA) on 5 November for disposal. Struck from the Navy list on 16 November 1945, the erstwhile minecraft was delivered at Charleston by the WSA to her purchaser, Eugene Marino of Gloucester, Mass., on 28 October 1946.

Victoria

In Roman mythology, Victoria was the goddess of victory; she was called Nike in Greek lore. The Civil War steamer of that name was named for her.

The second *Victoria* (AO–46) was named for the river in the western part of the Northern Territory of Australia.

The third *Victoria* (T–AK–281) was named for the city in Victoria County, Texas, established in 1824 and incorporated in 1839. The college of the same name was established in 1926.

I

(ScGbt.: t. 254; l. 113'; b. 22'; dph. 10'6''; s. 12 k.; a. 1 30-pdr. P.r., 2 8'' sb.)

The first *Victoria*—a wooden steamer built at Kensington, Pa., in 1855—was purchased by the Navy at New York City on 26 December 1861 for blockade duty during the Civil War; and was commissioned at the New York Navy Yard on 13 March 1862, Lt. Comdr. George A. Stevens in command.

Upon her commissioning, *Victoria* was assigned to Rear Admiral Louis M. Goldsborough's North Atlantic Blockading Squadron and left New York, bound for Hampton Roads, Va., on 17 March 1862. She arrived there on the 20th, reconnoitered the mouth of the Rap-

pahannock River, Va., from the 25th to the 31st, and towed the gunboat *Chocura* to the Baltimore Navy Yard, Md., on 2 April. She returned to Hampton Roads on the 4th but, on the 17th, was ordered to join the blockade off Wilmington, N.C.

Victoria operated exclusively in the coastal waters sounds, rivers, and inlets of North Carolina during the remainder of her active naval career. In company with other Union blockaders, she compiled an impressive list of prizes but often failed to capture sighted blockade runners because of her greatly inferior speed and generally poor condition. The first successful capture was the steamer *Nassau* and her cargo of Enfield rifles and ammunition, seized by *Victoria* and *State of Georgia* off Confederate Fort Caswell, N.C., on 28 May. Also off Fort Caswell, *Victoria*, *Mount Vernon*, and *Mystic* chased aground and destroyed the blockade runner *Emily* standing in for Wilmington on 26 June. *Victoria* sailed for Beaufort, N.C., for repairs on 30 August returned to the blockade off New Inlet, N.C., on 4 September, and put into the Norfolk Navy Yard, Va., for more extensive repairs on the 21st.

Repairs completed, *Victoria* left Norfolk on 8 December, arriving at her old duty station off Wilmington on the 9th. She immediately resumed her routine patrol and reconnaissance activities and, on 25 December, prevented an unidentified blockade-running steamer from landing ashore below the Cape Fear River, N.C. On 28 December, she chased a large steamer near Little River, N.C., and landed a small reconnaissance party near the mouth of the river on the 31st. *Victoria* captured the brig *Minna* and her cargo of salt and drugs near Shallote Inlet, N.C., on 18 February 1863. After another unsuccessful pursuit of a blockade runner on the night of the 24th, *William Bacon* and *Victoria* seized the blockade-running British steamer *Nicolai I* off Cape Fear, N.C., on 21 March.

During the remainder of the year, *Victoria*'s already fragile structural condition steadily deteriorated, prompting her disgruntled captain to complain in August that the vessel was unfit to remain with the blockade off Wilmington. Nevertheless, she continued on station and, after several more unsuccessful pursuits of blockade running steamers, finally put into the Norfolk Navy Yard for temporary repairs in early October. After a brief return to duty later in the month, at which time she captured a small sloop off Little River on the 15th, *Victoria* entered the Norfolk Navy Yard for a major overhaul in November.

These latest repairs took almost six months to complete, and *Victoria* did not leave the navy yard for the Wilmington blockade until late April 1864. Once there, she fired upon, chased aground, and destroyed the blockade-running steamer *Georgiana McCaw* near Wilmington on 2 June 1864. However, the gunboat again began to deteriorate soon thereafter and spent most of the remainder of the year in hopeless, frustrating pursuits of blockade runners. *Victoria* was damaged further in a collision with the steamer *Cherokee* that summer and eventually returned to the Norfolk Navy Yard for a new round of repairs in December.

Victoria remained at Norfolk for the duration of the war, where she was decommissioned on 4 May 1865. She was sold at auction at New York City to L. A. Edwards on 30 November; redocumented on 13 June 1866; and dropped from documentation in 1871.

II

(AO–46: dp. 13,179 (n.); l. 435'0''; b. 56'0''; dr. 26'6''; s. 11 k.; cpl. 59; a. 1 5'', 1 3'')

The second *Victoria* was originally built in 1917 as the steel-hulled, single-screw tanker *George G. Henry*. Constructed at San Francisco, Calif., by Union Iron Works, the ship was chartered by the United States Navy from her original owners, the Los Angeles Petroleum Co., on 23 August 1918; and commissioned at New York City the same day, Lt. Comdr. George F. Weeden, USNRF, in command.

Designated Id. No. 1560, *George G. Henry* departed New York on 29 August 1918, bound for European waters carrying aviation gasoline and Army medical stores. After discharging that cargo at Le Havre, France, the tanker touched at Spithead and Plymouth, England, before setting out across the Atlantic on her way back to the east coast of the United States.

At 0850 on 29 September, *George G. Henry* sighted the German submarine *U–152* on the surface, 5,000 yards off her port beam, went to general quarters, and opened fire at once with her forward gun. Attempting to keep the submarine directly astern, the tanker steered a northerly course and brought her after gun to bear on the enemy.

George G. Henry's gunners at the after mount managed to hurl 21 rounds at the enemy, landing several shells close aboard and forcing the surfaced submarine to maneuver radically. At 0905, *U–152* managed to score a hit on the tanker. The German shell pierced the American ship's after deck, damaging the steering gear and destroying the after magazine.

While flames enveloped the fantail, *George G. Henry* steered to bring her forward gun to bear while damage control parties fought the fires aft. Well-placed salvoes managed to keep the enemy away, while six smoke floats dropped over the side produced a dense, impenetrable smoke screen that shielded the tanker for some 20 minutes.

U–152, however, passed the weather side of that bank of smoke and renewed the action, landing shells close aboard. Shrapnel flailed the superstructure of the tanker, wounding 14 men. The after gun, though, still had some fight left. Its crew managed to get off two remaining rounds at 1015. Ten minutes later, the submarine gave up the chase and broke off the action.

In subsequent reports, Comdr. Weeden credited his ship's survival to Ens. George R. Thompson, USNRF, the head of the engine room force. Working amidst flames and acrid smoke, Thompson and his men remained below, working the vital machinery, allowing *George G. Henry* to maintain speed throughout the running battle. Three men under Thompson's command —members of the "black gang"—received honors: Chief Water Tender Hal Neargardt, USN, and Fireman First Class W. W. Reese received Navy Crosses and Fireman First Class W. T. Vail was awarded the Distinguished Service Medal.

Having escaped one danger, *George G. Henry* encountered another before she reached New York. Shortly after midnight on 3 October 1918, about 110 miles east of Cape Sable, she made an emergency turn to avoid an oncoming convoy, but to no avail. Her bow cut deeply into the collier *Herman Frasch* (Id. No. 1617) forward of that ship's poop deck. The latter's bow rose perpendicularly, slipped back and crushed *George G. Henry*'s port rail, hung suspended in the air for a few fleeting moments, and then slid off into the sea. *George G. Henry* immediately put over life rafts and boats, and with her searchlight beams sweeping the waves, searched for survivors. She picked up 65 men during the hunt which lasted until daybreak.

George G. Henry returned to New York on 6 October. After repairs at Shewen's Dry Dock, Brooklyn, N.Y., *George G. Henry* shifted to Bayonne, N.J., where she loaded a cargo of ammunition, gasoline, and military stores between 7 and 11 November. On the latter day— the day that the armistice ending World War I was signed—the ship touched briefly at Staten Island, N.Y., before sailing for France.

George G. Henry made three peacetime voyages to French ports—Le Havre, Rouen, Paulliac, Furt, and Blaye—carrying cargoes of oil from New York and Louisiana. After completing her last NOTS voyage upon arrival at New York on 5 May 1919, *George G. Henry* entered Shewen's Dry Dock for voyage repairs three days later. There, she was decommissioned and returned to her owner on 21 May 1919, and her name was simultaneously struck from the Navy list.

Over the next two decades, *George G. Henry* plied the trade routes of the Atlantic and Pacific, first under the colors of the Pan-American Petroleum and Transport Co. and then for the Standard Oil Co. In July 1940— due to the restrictions of the Neutrality Act—the ship was sold to the Panama Transport Co., a subsidiary of Standard Oil of New Jersey, and continued operating under Panamanian registry.

Laid-up for two months at Solomons Island, Md., for repairs, she was placed in service between South American (Caribbean) oil ports, the east coast of the United States, and the Canary Islands. She made six voyages in 1939; 17 in 1940; and 19 in 1941.

Her Far Eastern voyage in 1941 proved eventful. On 28 April 1941, *George G. Henry* sailed from New York; she subsequently loaded a cargo of petroleum products at Aruba, in the Netherlands West Indies, early in May and—after discharging that cargo at Balboa, Canal Zone, and at the ports of Golfito and Quepos Point, Costa Rica—proceeded to San Pedro, Calif. There, she loaded a cargo earmarked for Far Eastern ports. She touched at Honolulu, Territory of Hawaii, to top off her own fuel bunkers and then pushed on to the Philippines, reaching Manila on 29 June, a little over two months out of New York.

Over the next six months, time-chartered to the Standard-Vacuum Oil Co., *George G. Henry* carried oil from Balikpapan and Palembang, Dutch East Indies; Tarakan, Borneo; and Miri, Sarawak, to ports in the Philippines, to Shanghai, and to Hong Kong. Meanwhile, war clouds were thickening in the skies over that area of the world, as the Rising Sun of Japan began to cast a lengthening shadow over American, British, and Dutch colonial possessions. In fact, as the tanker steamed toward Manila during the first few days of December 1941, Japanese invasion forces were already headed toward their jump-off points—their arrival timed to coincide with a diversionary strike to be launched against the ships of the United States Pacific Fleet at Pearl Harbor, Territory of Hawaii.

However, oblivious to those events, *George G. Henry* arrived at Manila on 4 December 1941 with a cargo of 69,550 barrels of oil that had been taken on board at Palembang, Java, and at Tanjong Oeban, on Bintang Island, near Singapore. By 8 December 1941 (7 December east of the International Date Line), the tanker had already discharged the part of her cargo consigned for delivery at Manila and was preparing to leave that port for Cebu, in the southern Philippines, to discharge the remainder. That, however, was not to be.

As she stood out of the harbor area, *George G. Henry* received a signal from the Army signal station on the island of Corregidor, the fortress standing like a sentinel at the entrance of Manila Bay: "No ships are allowed to leave port." It was not long before the merchant seamen on board found out the reason for that order: Pearl Harbor had been attacked. The United States and Japan were at war.

Although in civilian colors at the outset of hostilities, *George G. Henry* had acquired a coat of "war gray" by 10 December. On that day, she lay anchored in Manila Bay when Japanese planes came over just after noon and leisurely pounded the Cavite Navy Yard, almost erasing it from the face of the map. During the raid, bombs splashed near the tanker, between *George G. Henry* and the Filipino freighter *Sagoland*. "The nearest explosion," wrote a member of the tanker's crew later, "caused our ship to roll and vibrate as if she were breaking up on the rocks." Fortunately, the tanker emerged unscathed.

After that raid, it was obvious that Cavite and Manila Bay were not safe for surface ships. Hastily assembled convoys began heading southward, but *George G. Henry* remained behind where her vital cargo was needed. On 12 December—the day on which Japanese troops splashed ashore at Aparri and Vigan in northern Luzon and at Legaspi on the southeast coast of that island—*George G. Henry* was moored at Pier 7, the largest commercial pier in Manila's port area and an easily distinguishable landmark, to discharge her remaining cargo. By that evening, the tanker had pumped ashore 69,500 barrels of oil to storage tanks ashore. That task completed, *George G. Henry* returned to her anchorage to await further orders.

Two days later, her master, Capt. Jens G. Olsen, received the authorization to take *George G. Henry* south—provided that the escape be made at night. Thus, at sunset on the 15th of December, *George G. Henry* headed for the channel through the minefield that had been sown between Corregidor and the Bataan peninsula. She soon discovered, however, that the channel—supposedly lighted with three buoys—was dark. As she slowed, a strong current carried the tanker inexorably toward the deadly minefield. *George G. Henry* went full speed astern and got out of immediate danger but still found herself in a very perilous situation.

Fortunately for *George G. Henry*, *Bulmer* (DD–222) came along and, when her commanding officer learned of the tanker's plight, led *George G. Henry* through the swept channel to safer waters. The tanker then proceeded unmolested across the Sulu Sea, steamed southward past the island of Tawi Tawi, and reached Balikpapan, Borneo, on 20 December, having made the passage from Manila in four days, eight hours, and three minutes—a record run according to her engineer's log.

There, *George G. Henry* filled her bunkers with 75,000 barrels of fuel oil and sailed on Christmas Eve for the Netherlands East Indies. She reached Soerabaya on the 26th and anchored offshore the next day to await further instructions. When she finally received those orders, the tanker proceeded to the south entrance of Soerabaya harbor, directly through unswept areas of minefields laid by the Dutch Navy.

Underway again on the last day of 1941, *George G. Henry* departed Soerabaya, bound for Australian waters. Convoyed by *Boise* (CL–47), *Pope* (DD–225), and *John D. Ford* (DD–228)—as well as by two submarines and the destroyer tender *Black Hawk* (AD–9)—the tanker reached Port Darwin, Australia, on 6 January 1942. Her first job was to pump 13,900 barrels of fuel oil into the depleted bunkers of *Pecos* (AO–6).

George G. Henry remained at Port Darwin into early February, fueling ships of the Asiatic Fleet and, upon occasion, Australian naval vessels. Among her American customers were *Langley* (AV–3), *Tulsa* (PG–22), *Lark* (AM–21), *Heron* (AVP–4), *Alden* (DD–211), *Barker* (DD–213), *Bulmer* (DD–222), *John D. Ford*, *Parrott* (DD–218), *Parry* (DD–226), *Pope*, and *William B. Preston* (AVD–7).

By the second week of February, *George G. Henry's* Balikpapan cargo was largely depleted; she thus departed Port Darwin on 11 February, bound for Fremantle. Barnacles and seaweed hampered the old tanker's progress, and she crept along at 7 knots, ultimately reaching her destination on 22 February.

George G. Henry, *Trinity* (AO–13), and *Pecos* provided the hard-pressed units of the Asiatic Fleet with the vital fuel oil with which the men-of-war of that fleet battled against heavy odds, as did the dwindling numbers of Dutch, British, and Australian ships pushed before the Japanese tide of conquest. Ultimately, Japanese force proved too much. The Battle of the Java Sea on the last two days of February and the fall of Java less than a week later meant that the Japanese had managed to destroy the pre-war Dutch colonial empire and also conquered many British possessions as well. Within two months, the Philippines, too, would be in Japanese hands.

George G. Henry fueled the four surviving American ships that took part in the Battle of the Java Sea, the destroyers *John D. Ford*, *Alden*, *Paul Jones* (DD–230), and *John D. Edwards* (DD–216), soon after they arrived in Australian waters. By the end of March, there was less of a need to fuel surface ships of the Asiatic Fleet, so the tanker was dispatched to Melbourne, Australia, turning over hoses and fittings to the government-chartered tanker *Erling Brovig*, before she set sail for Melbourne on 29 March.

Reaching her destination on 8 April, *George G. Henry*

began fueling Army transports for their return voyage to the United States. Her first customer at Melbourne was the former luxury liner *President Coolidge* which would embark former Philippine President Manuel Quezon for transportation to the United States. From her moorings, the men of the *George G. Henry* saw General Douglas MacArthur escort his friend Quezon on board *President Coolidge* before she sailed.

On 15 April 1942, while at Yarraville, a suburb of Melbourne, *George G. Henry* was taken over by the Navy under a bareboat charter. The ship's master, Capt. Jens G. Olsen (who, incidentally, had sailed in *George G. Henry* as a boatswain and had been the last civilian crewman to leave the ship when she was taken over by the Navy in World War I)—a member of the Naval Reserve—was called to active duty as a lieutenant commander and given command of the ship.

Taken to Sydney for extensive conversion, overhaul, and fitting-out for naval service, *George G. Henry* was first renamed—erroneously—*Victor* on 20 April, before the correct name, *Victoria*, was received upon the ship's arrival at Sydney on 25 April. Classified as AO–46, *Victoria* was fitted out for service at Mort's Dock and Engineering Co. (Chapman's Branch) under the supervision of Royal Australian Naval authorities at Garden Island. Survivors from *Langley*, *Peary*, and *Pecos* made up the ship's new crew.

Following the completion of the conversion—during which she received a battery of two 3-inch guns and machine guns—*Victoria* awaited further orders in Sydney harbor. Underway on 18 November 1942 with a cargo of Navy special fuel, she joined a convoy of merchantmen, SS *Paul Revere*, SS *Benjamin Franklin* and SS *William Williams*—the future USS *Venus* (AK–135)—escorted by two Australian corvettes HMAS *Whyalla* and HMAS *Townsville*. En route, they were joined by another Australian corvette that served as an antisubmarine screen. After touching briefly at Brisbane on the 21st for further orders, the convoy now consisting of *Victoria* (guide) and *Benjamin Franklin* got underway for Townsville the following day. Reaching Cleveland Bay, Brisbane, via Townsville *Victoria* commenced fueling Allied warships in those waters and continued those duties at Challenger Bay, Palm Islands, on 3 December. She subsequently alternated serving at Challenger Bay and at Dunk Island Harbor before returning to Brisbane on Christmas Eve.

Victoria there became a unit of Task Force (TF) 50. The other ships in that group were *Gold Star* (AK–12) and *Mizar* (AF–12). As ordered, the tanker fueled the warships of TF 44—HMAS *Australia* (heavy cruiser), HMAS *Hobart* (light cruiser), *Phoenix* (CL–46), and various destroyers. *Victoria* remained at Brisbane through New Year's Day 1943.

Shifting to Townsville in company with the Australian minesweeper HMAS *Geelong* and the merchantman SS *Jason Lee* between 4 and 8 January, *Victoria* reached her destination on the 8th, where she remained for three days before shifting her operations back to Challenger Bay. For the next eight months, *Victoria* operated off the coasts and harbors of the Australian continent, ranging from Townsville to Cairns; from Brisbane to Dunk Island Harbor; from Sydney to Stoke's Bay, Flinders Island; and to the Queensland ports of Mackay and Gladstone. During that time, the ship picked up the nickname "The Galloping Ghost of the Aussie Coast."

After that stint of operations, *Victoria* departed Townsville on 28 August 1943, in company with six merchantmen. On the 29th, four Australian naval vessels joined as escorts, as did *LST–470* and *APc–2* *Victoria* and the rest of the convoy reached Milne Bay, New Guinea, on the last day of August.

Subsequently, *Victoria*, the Australian ammunition ship RFA (Royal Fleet Auxiliary) *Yunnan*, and *APc–22* departed Milne Bay on 2 September, bound for Porlock Harbor, New Guinea. *Victoria* and her escorts reached that port on the 3d, concurrently with the first assault echelon slated to land on the Huon Peninsula.

near Lae, New Guinea. The next day, Australian troops of the 9th Division went ashore in conjunction with a parachute landing in the Markham Valley.

Victoria—no stranger to danger—remained at Porlock continuously for over two months, in an undefended harbor, in company with *Yunnan*, providing advance logistics base services. She furnished support for Destroyer Squadron 5 and other ships and was the only source of fuel oil north of Milne Bay during the Lae-Salamaua campaign. Early in October, the ship's fuel supply was replenished from the bunkers of the British tanker, SS *Luxor*.

Although the enemy resistance on shore at Lae, and later at Salamaua, was initially light, enemy air attacks, in strength, commenced about noon on the first day and continued at night from that point on. The attacks usually were conducted by small groups of enemy aircraft. Ships either arriving or departing the landing areas—and resupply echelons—usually came under persistent and determined aerial raids. The first damage occurred to the destroyer *Conyngham* (DD-371) on 4 September.

Those air attacks conducted by the enemy never came in *Victoria*'s direction, although the venerable old oiler was well within range of Japanese air bases on New Britain and New Guinea. Although radarless, the valuable auxiliary kept her radio tuned on the frequencies of the destroyers in the area. In that fashion, on the radio warning net, she kept abreast of the latest inbound raids.

On at least two occasions, *Victoria* interrupted fueling operations upon receipt of the warning and sounded general quarters. Lookouts picked out the "bogies" visually as Japanese, but the planes did not attack and remained out of gun range. At other times, men in *Victoria* could see the antiaircraft fire blossoming in the skies over Oro Bay, 40 miles away, and could hear the explosion of ordnance. "On such occasions," wrote Lt. Comdr. F. E. Clark, then the ship's executive officer, "we were agreeably surprised that the enemy did not attack the tempting target offered by a lightly-armed oiler and ammunition ship lying in an undefended harbor."

Relieved by another old Asiatic Fleet companion—the oiler *Trinity*—on 8 November 1943, *Victoria* hoisted anchor and headed for Milne Bay. Even her last day at Porlock Harbor was lively. An Army Air Corps P-38 Lightning from the 471st Fighter Squadron went down nearby, and her pilot, 2d Lt. Fred Durkin, USAAF, parachuted into the water near the ship. *Victoria*'s crew immediately hauled him on board, thus accomplishing the ship's first rescue.

Reaching Milne Bay on 9 November after proceeding independently from Porlock Harbor, *Victoria* then pressed on, without escort, for Australian waters, reaching Brisbane on the 15th for a period of well-deserved recreation for the crew and engine repairs for the ship herself.

Five days before Christmas, with a full cargo of fuel, *Victoria* got underway for Townsville in company with 11 merchantmen, three LCI's, and three escort vessels. The convoy dispersed on the 21st, and *Victoria* proceeded independently to her destination on the 22d, anchoring in Cleveland Bay to await further orders. On Christmas Eve, Convoy TN-197 was formed and sent on its way—*Victoria* included—to New Guinea. The ships reached Milne Bay on the 28th, where the convoy was dissolved. The following day, *Victoria* got underway for Buna, New Guinea. Soon after her arrival there later that day, she commenced fueling operations.

Transferring the remainder of her cargo of fuel oil to *Trinity* on the last day of 1943, *Victoria* headed for Milne Bay on New Year's Day 1944. After loading fuel oil from SS *Corinth*, the oiler then proceeded to an anchorage near Milne Bay and commenced fueling Allied warships. On the 25th, *Victoria* rendezvoused at sea with Australian heavy cruiser, HMAS *Shropshire*, and fueled her. Two days later, she headed for Buna in company with the motor minesweeper *YMS-73* and

the subchasers *SC-741* and *SC-650* to discharge a cargo of fuel oil to *Trinity*. That mission completed, *Victoria* proceeded independently to Milne Bay, reaching there on 30 January.

Departing Milne Bay on 27 February, *Victoria* headed for Langemark Bay, Finschhafen, with Convoy BG-46, reaching her destination two days later. The ship subsequently fueled Allied warships in that port until 3 April, when she sailed for Seeadler Harbor, at Manus, in the Admiralty Islands.

Reaching that port on 5 April, *Victoria* immediately commenced fueling vessels in need. Because the harbor shore establishments were still not yet in full operating status, the valuable auxiliary ship acted as signal station for the harbor and cooperated with every activity requiring her assistance. For the work performed by the officers and men, *Victoria* was highly commended by the Commander, Subordinate Command, New Guinea Area.

Escorted by HMAS *Kiana*, *Victoria* departed Manus on 14 May, bound once again for New Guinea. She reached Humboldt Bay on the 16th and began the busiest fueling period of the ship's career. The ship frequently conducted her operations at night as well as during the day. From her anchorage, she could see enemy planes bombing Allied airdromes nearby. At times like that, only her pumps were stopped while all hands remained ready to resume fueling when the "all clear" sounded.

During her time at Humboldt Bay, she fueled such ships as *Nashville* (CL-43), *Phoenix* (CL-46), *Boise* (CL-47), as well as the Australian heavy cruisers HMAS *Australia* and HMAS *Shropshire* and numerous destroyers attached to those task forces.

After remaining at Humboldt Bay less than a month, *Victoria* got underway on 5 June, bound for Seeadler Harbor. Escorted by the fast transport *Kilty* (APD-137) and the frigate *Ogden* (PF-39), the tanker reached her destination on the 7th and commenced fueling operations immediately. She subsequently sailed to Hollandia, arriving there on the 28th.

For the remainder of the summer, *Victoria* continued her vital support operations for the 7th Fleet as they conducted the "island-hopping" in the Southwest Pacific theater of war. She fueled Allied warships at Mios Woendi, at Humboldt Bay, and Hollandia. Operating out of Mios Woendi, *Victoria* fueled ships taking part in the assaults against the Philippines and Borneo that commenced that autumn. While at Mios Woendi, she fueled the badly damaged "jeep carriers" from the Battle of Leyte Gulf: *Kalinin Bay* (CVE-68), *Fanshaw Bay* (CVE-70), *White Plains* (CVE-66), and *Kitkun Bay* (CVE-71), on 29 October, four days after that epic battle.

After refueling Task Group (TG) 78.6 off Biak, New Guinea, on 28 January 1945, *Victoria* resumed her routine fueling operations at Mios Woendi, duties she discharged through mid-April 1945. Proceeding independently for Hollandia on 19 April, *Victoria* reached her destination the next day, turning over cargo to *Arayat* (IX-134) and taking on stores that had accumulated for the ship at that port. She then pushed on for Seeadler Harbor, which she reached on 23 April.

After fueling Allied warships at Seeadler Harbor, *Victoria* was drydocked in *ABSD-4* on 10 June for an overhaul. On the 16th, she was refloated and shifted to the Repair Base at Lombrum Point, Los Negros Island, for engine and hull work. That overhaul was completed on 21 August, a little less than a week after Japan capitulated.

The ship then loaded a full cargo and—under orders from Commander, Service Force, 7th Fleet—departed Seeadler Harbor on 22 August, bound for the Philippines. "If this 'Galloping Ghost' could speak," the ship's commanding officer wrote, "she would surely have said the same words as General MacArthur, 'I shall return.;'" During the time that *Victoria*, ex-*George G. Henry*, had been away from the Philippine Archipelago, she had issued 2,136,228 barrels of Navy special fuel oil.

Reaching Manila Bay on 2 September 1945—the day that Japan signed the formal articles of surrender in Tokyo Bay—*Victoria* commenced fueling operations immediately. Less than a month later, her tour of duty in the Pacific theater at a close, *Victoria* departed the Philippines on orders from Commander, Service Squadron 7. The ship departed on that date with an "exceptionally well done" message from ComServRon 7 and Commander, Service Division 73. With 76 sailors embarked as passengers, *Victoria* headed for the United States.

Taking the "Great Circle Route" north of Mindanao, Kure, and Rivella Gigardo Islands, *Victoria* participated in an air-sea rescue operation a week after leaving Manila. On 18 October, she served as station ship for rescue planes and as radio ship for smaller ships involved in the operation that led to the rescue of crews from a ditched Boeing B–29 Superfortress and a Consolidated PBY Catalina. Three days later, the ship sank a large floating mine with gunfire.

Making port at Balboa, Canal Zone, on 15 November, the ship transited the Panama Canal on the next day and reached Cristobal. She then sailed across the Gulf of Mexico to Mobile, Ala., where she arrived on the 22d. Decommissioned on 14 December 1945 and delivered to the War Shipping Administration (WSA) of the Maritime Commission simultaneously, *Victoria* was struck from the Naval Vessel Register on 8 January 1946.

Victoria earned four battle stars during her World War II service.

III

(T–AK–281: dp. 15,199; l. 455'3''; b. 62'0''; dr. 22'0'' (max.); s. 19.7 k.; cpl. 87; a. none; cl. *Norwalk;* T. VC2–S–AP3)

The third *Victoria* (T–AK–281) was one of four "Victory Ships" transferred from the Maritime Administration to the Navy in the mid-1960's for conversion to fleet ballistic missile (FBM) resupply cargo ships. She had been laid down under a Maritime Commission contract (MC hull V–526) as *Ethiopia Victory* on 20 January 1944 at Richmond, Calif., by the Permanente Metals Corp., Shipbuilding Division, for the Agwilines shipping firm; launched on 20 April 1944; and sponsored by Mrs. Michael F. Novak. Eventually placed in reserve in the years following World War II, *Ethiopia Victory* was transferred to the Navy on 13 August 1964 and taken to the Philadelphia Navy Yard for conversion.

In her designed role, the ship was to provide complete logistics services to a deployed FBM tender. One of her holds was modified to carry missiles in an upright position; in addition, she could carry refrigerated provisions, submarine torpedoes, spare parts, and fuel. On 22 May 1965, the ship was renamed *Victoria* and classified as T–AK–281.

Entering service with the Military Sea Transportation Service (MSTS) in October 1965, *Victoria* operated with MSTS until that agency became the Military Sealift Command (MSC) on 1 August 1970. She presently serves under the auspices of MSC, Atlantic, into 1980.

Victorine

Though one record indicates that *Utowana* (SP–951) (*q.v.*) was renamed *Victorine,* all other sources—both official and unofficial—consistently refer to her as *Utowana* throughout her Navy career. Furthermore, the one file that addresses her as *Victorine* makes no indication as to when the name change occurred.

Victorious

(Freighter: dp. 16,400; l. 440'1½''; b. 56'0''; dr. 29'9'' dph. 38'0''; s. 10.5 k.; cpl. 97)

Victorious—a steel-hulled, single-screw cargo vessel built under a United States Shipping Board contract by the Bethlehem Shipbuilding Corp., Union Iron Works plant, San Francisco, Calif.—was inspected by the Navy at San Francisco on 5 October 1918 and was earmarked for operation by the Naval Overseas Transportation Service (NOTS). She was commissioned at San Francisco on 19 October 1918.

Victorious—designated Id. No. 3514—proceeded to Port Costa on the 25th, arriving on 18 November seven days after the armistice ended World War I. The cargo vessel took on a full load of flour and, on the 22d, sailed, via the Panama Canal, for New York. Arriving there on 13 December, *Victorious* got underway for England four days after Christmas 1918.

Victorious reached London on 14 January 1919, discharged her cargo of flour, and loaded 2,300 tons of steel billets and 200 steel rails before sailing for the United States on 30 January. Arriving back at New York on 13 February, the cargo vessel was placed out of commission on 25 February 1919. She was simultaneously struck from the Navy list and returned to the USSB.

Victory

(StwGbt.: t. 160; l. 157'; b. 30'3''; dr. 5'; s. 5 mph.; a. 24–pdr. how.)

Victory—a wooden merchant steamer built at Cincinnati, Ohio, in 1863 and originally named *Banker*—was acquired by the Navy at Cincinnati in May 1863; was commissioned at Cincinnati on 8 July; but was not formally purchased by the Navy until 15 July.

Victory was one of the lightly armor-plated gunboats of the Mississippi Squadron called "tinclads" which were used during the Civil War for shallow water patrol and reconnaissance duty on the Tennessee, Ohio, and Cumberland rivers. On the day of *Victory's* commissioning, 8 July, Confederate General John Hunt Morgan crossed the Ohio River into Indiana at the head of a 6,000-man raiding party. From the 10th to the 19th, *Victory, Moose, Reindeer, Springfield, Naumkeag,* and *Allegheny Belle* chased Morgan as he proceeded eastward along the river. Union cavalry ashore prevented him from recrossing the Ohio to safety in the South. While *Victory* and three of the gunboats remained scattered downstream on the 19th to prevent the raiding party from doubling back, the Federals finally trapped Morgan at Buffington Island and forced him to attempt a crossing. The try failed miserably, and most of the Confederates surrendered. Morgan, himself, escaped with a few followers only to be caught near New Lisbon, Ohio, one week later.

Victory remained with the Mississippi Squadron for the duration of the war, performing patrol, reconnaissance, convoy, and dispatch duty. On 14 April 1864, she helped to repulse a raid on Paducah, Ky.; and—on 4 November, as part of a squadron of six gunboats—aided the successful defense from a carefully staged Confederate attack on Johnsonville, Tenn., led by the famed Confederate cavalryman, Lt. Gen. Nathan B. Forrest.

After the Confederacy collapsed, *Victory* was decommissioned at Mound City, Ill., on 30 June 1865 and sold at public auction there to W. Thorwegen on 17 August. She was documented as *Lizzie Tate* on 7 October 1865 and was reduced to a barge on 22 November 1867. At this time, her wake vanished into the mists of history.

Vidette

A variant spelling of *Vedette*, a French term meaning a small guard or patrol vessel.

(MB: l. 56'; b. 9'4'')

Vidette—a wooden-hulled, sheathed launch built at Cowes, England, on the Isle of Wight—was apparently acquired by the Navy sometime in either late 1907 or early 1908. From then until either late 1910 or early 1911, she was utilized at Brooklyn, N.Y., at the New York Navy Yard as the commandant's barge. She then moved to Portsmouth, Va., to perform similar duty at the Norfolk Navy Yard through the end of World War I. Although one source lists the craft as being transferred to the Coast Guard on 3 May 1919, no record of her subsequent service has been found.

Vidofner

(ScStr.: t. 27; l. 58'9''; b. 11'; dr. 3'6'' (mean); s. 14 k.; cpl. 10; a. 1 1-pdr., 1 mg.)

Vidofner (SP-402)—a small, wooden-hulled, screw steamer completed in 1906 at South Boston, Mass., by Murray and Tregurtha—was acquired by the Navy on 19 May 1917 from S. H. Freihefer, H. M. Pfiel, and E. G. Schmidneiser and was commissioned at the Philadelphia Navy Yard on 7 June 1917, Lt. (jg.) Edgar S. Husband, USNRF, in command.

Following an overhaul and a short trial run down the Delaware River to test her engines, *Vidofner* was assigned to local navy yard patrol duties at Philadelphia and commenced her initial patrol on 31 July. During this first night out, she arrested two men in a row boat and eight men in a cutter as they tried to enter the reserve basin area—a forbidden zone. When these men were returned to their respective ships, they were identified and released. In this same vein, the patrol craft picked up a man in a skiff, on 2 August, "who was acting suspiciously." When the man was identified by the yard quartermaster, he, too, was released.

At 1115 on 5 August, an aide from the district commandant's office arrived at the dock and requested that *Vidofner* make ready to get underway at once. Accordingly, an inspection party boarded the vessel; and she headed downstream toward *Henderson* (Transport No. 1), which had grounded earlier that day. Early the following day, after the inspection party had been transferred to the stranded troopship, *Vidofner* headed back to the navy yard and relieved *Little Aie* on patrol at 0800. Two hours later, *Vidofner* stopped tug *Sam Weller* near a restricted area and ordered her out. When the tug failed to comply quickly enough, the patrol boat fired two shots in the air—sufficient prodding to hurry the tug on her way.

Vidofner remained on patrol duty at the Philadelphia yard until assigned to northern net patrol at the mouth of the Delaware Bay on 31 August. Her first month on patrol in that area was uneventful. On 8 October, however, the relative calm of her existence was blown to the winds as a heavy storm swept across Delaware Bay, threatening to scatter the flotilla on patrol duty there. *Vidofner* dragged anchor at 0730 and fouled *Seagull* (SP-544) before getting underway and clearing the other SP-boat. After taking "a bad pounding" in the rough seas, *Vidofner* dropped both anchors and moored off Brown Shoal Buoy in hopes of riding out the storm.

The tempest did not let up, though, and continued instead with unabated fury. *Seagull*, unable to get underway, drifted off into the pre-dawn darkness on the 9th, dragging her anchors and sending out SOS signals. Ordered to make for the breakwater at Lewes, Del., where some measure of shelter was afforded, *Vidofner* got underway and made haven—*Seagull* eventually arrived by 0815 at the end of a towline.

After shifting her base of operations to Cape May, N.J., on 13 October, *Vidofner* performed net patrol duties in the Delaware capes area until she was decommissioned at Essington, Pa., near Philadelphia, on 7 December 1917 and returned to her owners.

View, A.J. See *A. J. View*, to be included in the forthcoming revised edition of Vol. I.

Vigil

(YAGR-12: dp. 10,760 (f.); l. 441'6''; b. 57'; dr. 24'; s. 12.5 k.; cpl. 154; cl. *Guardian*; T. ZEC2-S-C5)

SS *Raymond Van Brogan* was laid down under a Maritime Commission contract (MCE hull 2339) on 14 December 1944 at the Wainwright yard of the J. A. Jones Construction Co. in Panama City, Fla.; launched on 27 January 1945; sponsored by Mrs. Mary Anne Durham; and delivered to the War Shipping Administration on 10 February 1945.

Following a shakedown cruise in the Gulf of Mexico, the ship transited the Panama Canal on 19 February and headed for Terminal Island, Calif., where she was turned over to A. J. Bull & Co. for operation under contract to the War Shipping Administration. She performed several resupply missions in the Pacific theater, carrying aircraft as well as other war materiel and some troops. Following the end of World War II, the War Shipping Administration transferred her contract to the Waterman Steamship Corp., which firm

The yacht *Vidofner*, her polished woodwork and wicker furniture giving her an air of quiet luxury, before acquisition by the Navy.

The radar picket ship *Vigil* (YAGR–12) on 2 April 1957, newly converted from a *Liberty*-type merchant cargo ship. Masts and kingposts support search and height-finding radars and a club-like *Tacan* aircraft navigation beacon.

operated her from Mobile, Ala. In the summer of 1947, SS *Raymond Van Brogan* was taken out of service and berthed with the National Defense Reserve Fleet at Mobile, Ala. Nine years later, in June 1956, she was brought out of the Maritime Commission's reserve fleet for conversion to a radar picket ship and active service with the Navy. She was moved to Philadelphia where she completed her conversion at the naval shipyard. On 7 August 1956, she received a new name and her Navy hull designation to become *Vigil* (YAGR–12). She completed conversion early in 1957 and was placed in service on 5 March 1957, Lt. Comdr. Stanley Abstetar, USNR, in command.

During *Vigil*'s eight-year naval career, she was assigned to the Continental Air Defense Command and served as one of that organization's radar picket ships operating as seaward extensions of its radar coverage system. The ship operated out of Davisville, R.I., during her entire period of service and spent on the average of 200 days per year actually engaged in picket patrols in waters off the coast of New England. On 28 September 1958, she was redesignated AGR–12, thereby dropping her yard craft designation and becoming a commissioned auxiliary. On 3 March 1965, *Vigil* was placed out of commission. Her name was struck from the Navy list on 1 April 1965, and she was returned to the Maritime Commission for lay up with the Hudson River Group of the National Defense Reserve Fleet. On 23 November 1970, she was sold to the Spanish firm, Revalorizacion de Materiales, for scrapping.

Vigilance

(AM–324: dp. 890; l. 221'2''; b. 32'2''; dr. 10'9'' (max.); s. 18.1 k.; cpl. 105; a. 1 3'', 2 40mm., 6 20mm., 2 dct., 1 dcp. (hh.); cl. *Auk*)

Vigilance (AM–324) was originally laid down for the Royal Navy under the lend-lease program as HMS *Exploit* (BAM–24) on 28 November 1942 at Seattle, Wash., by the Associated Shipbuilding Corp. However, the United States Navy decided to keep the ship and renamed her *Vigilance* (AM–324) on 23 January 1943. Launched on 5 April 1943, the minesweeper was commissioned at her builder's yard on 28 February 1944, Lt. Comdr. William C. Hayes, USNR, in command.

After fitting-out, radio direction finder calibration, sea trials, and minesweeping indoctrination, *Vigilance* departed Seattle on 21 March, bound for southern California for type training, shakedown, and training in antisubmarine warfare (ASW) tactics.

Escorting *PCS–1396* and *PCS–1404*, the new *Auk*-class minecraft departed San Diego on 4 May, bound for Hawaii. Upon her arrival at Pearl Harbor on 11 May, *Vigilance* delivered 111 bags of mail to the Fleet Post Office and, three days later, got underway with *Triumph* (AM–323) for the Marshall Islands. The two minesweepers screened *William Ward Burrows* (AP–6), *Fortune* (IX–146), and *Boreas* (AF–8) to Majuro which they reached on 25 May.

Vigilance departed Majuro at 0800 on the 26th to return to Hawaii, intercepted *Megrez* (AK–126) en route, and relieved *PC–548* of escorting that cargo ship for the remainder of the voyage to Oahu. After arriving at Pearl Harbor on 2 June, *Vigilance* underwent upkeep and maintenance before moving to Brown's Camp, Oahu, for experimental minesweeping evolutions which she conducted into mid-June.

On 14 June, *Vigilance* weighed anchor as part of the screen for Convoy 4313–A, a group of three Navy cargo ships, three civilian merchantmen, and refrigerator ship *Arctic* (AF–7). *Crouter* (DE–11) and *Pursuit* (AM–108) joined *Vigilance* in escorting the convoy to Eniwetok where they arrived on 25 June.

During the second of two more round-trip runs from Pearl Harbor to the Marshalls, *Vigilance* suffered an engine casualty—a damaged exhaust manifold—that was beyond the capacity of the ship's force to handle. Accordingly, she went alongside *Zeus* (ARB–4) at Eniwetok on 24 September for repairs.

Making port back at Pearl Harbor on 5 October, the ship underwent more repairs and maintenance work and tested minesweeping gear off Brown's Camp. After getting underway for the Marshalls again on 23 October, escorting *Ocelot* (IX–110), *Vigilance* twice picked up "doubtful" submarine contacts—on 24 and 28 October—and fired hedgehog patterns on both occasions. She made port at Eniwetok on 3 November but got underway for Guam two days later, escorting a convoy consisting of SS *Fred Lykes*, SS *Cape Bon*, SS *Cape Kildare*, SS *Rockland Victory*, and USAT *General M. M. Patrick*.

The minesweeper subsequently performed local escort duty between Guam, Peleliu, and Ulithi, arriving at the latter on 14 November. She patrolled the approaches to Mugai channel, Ulithi, from the 17th through the 19th. Five minutes before sunrise on 20 November, while on patrol station number 4, *Vigilance* sighted a small wake 700 yards broad on the starboard quarter. Southbound on her patrol, the minesweeper had swung wide to avoid fouling the screen of an outward-bound task group of three destroyers, a cruiser, and other vessels when she made the sighting. She then put over ull right rudder and accelerated to full speed as her rew went to battle stations. With depth charges set on shallow" the minecraft bent on speed to make an attack ut, much to her chagrin, found that the wake had ompletely disappeared. In the midst of all the hulls nd wakes created by the Saipan-bound task group, icking up the contact proved impossible.

Vigilance signalled the location of the wake to *ummings* (DD–365). Moments later, the cruiser in he convoy signalled that she sighted a periscope on er starboard quarter. *Case* (DD–370) arrived on the cene first and disposed of what proved to be a midget ubmarine by ramming and depth charges.

After that incident, *Vigilance*—aided by a pair of rumman TBF's from VMTB–232—remained on patrol ff the channel entrance. At 0031 on 21 November, a BF bore in low from astern, as if to challenge the ninecraft. Men in *Vigilance* thought that the plane night have been a new arrival, unfamiliar with their hip. The plane suddenly made a sharp bank. A wing-ip caught in the water and the plane plunged into he sea about one-half mile from *Vigilance*. The plane vas immediately enveloped in flame; and, shortly there-fter, the aircraft's depth charges exploded.

To compound the confusion, a second TBF came in nd, thinking the wreckage on the water was a sur-aced submarine, strafed the floating plane. *Vigilance* aunched her motor whaleboat at 0051 and picked up urvivor—Corporal Robert M. DeHart, USMC—who ad almost miraculously remained alive despite the rash, the explosion, and the machine gun fire. *Vigilance* ontinued the search in the hope of picking up other urvivors but found none. At 0524, the minecraft was rdered to transfer the wounded man to hospital facili-ies ashore.

Without let-up except for an occasional day or so of naintenance and upkeep, *Vigilance* patrolled off Ulithi's Mugai channel for the remainder of the year.

Following an escort mission to the Palaus from 5 to 11 January 1945, *Vigilance* returned to Ulithi on the 12th, only to find a full-scale antisubmarine alert in progress. She commenced patrolling station number 7 n company with *PC–1179* before receiving orders to patrol off the Zowariyau and Piiriperiperi channels. hifting to a retiring search in company with *Impec-able* (AM–320) soon thereafter, *Vigilance* was relieved of this duty by *Spangler* (DE–696) and returned to Ulithi.

After local patrol operations off the Mugal channel, Vigilance performed local escort missions between Ulithi and Kossol Roads and from Kossol Roads to Seeadler Harbor, at Manus, in the Admiralties. For the latter part of February, the minesweeper served as sub-marine listening watch and harbor entrance patrol ves-sel at Kossol before she returned to Ulithi.

From 6 to 8 March, *Vigilance* lay alongside *Terror* (CM–5) undergoing availability in preparation for the upcoming operation against the Ryukyus. *Vigilance* got underway for Nansei Shoto on 19 March and steamed in cruising formation with Mine Division (MinDiv) 11, on the starboard quarter of *Terror*.

Arriving in area V–1, about 35 miles southwest of Okinawa, on 24 March, *Vigilance* and her sister mine-sweepers swept for moored mines until nightfall when they retired. She cut loose one moored mine on the 26th, three on the 27th, and one on the 28th. While per-forming these sweep operations, she served as MinRon 4 "destruction vessel," slated to destroy loose mines once they reached the surface. The ship sank several drifting floats and one moored mine with gunfire.

On the morning of the 28th, *Vigilance*'s lookouts spotted a Japanese "Kate" torpedo bomber and two "Val" dive-bombers attacking; and her gunners—along with those of the other ships in the unit—opened fire and blasted the "Kate" into pieces. The ship thus chalked up her first "sure assist" in downing the plane.

The landings commenced on 1 April. During the first three days of the invasion, *Vigilance* screened the un-loading transports off Hagushi beach. Then, after shifting to Kerama Retto for two days of logistics on 4 and 5 April, the minesweeper alternated between sweeping and screening operations for the ensuing week.

While *Vigilance* was patrolling five miles south of Kerama Retto on the afternoon of the 12th, a "flash red" alert was announced, and the ship's lookouts soon noted the presence of many enemy planes—all out of gun range. Suddenly, at 1456, the minesweeper noted black smoke pouring from *Whitehurst* (DE–634), a destroyer escort that had just been hit by a kamikaze while patrolling an adjacent sector. *Vigilance* altered course to close, accelerating to full speed as fire and rescue parties readied emergency fire-fighting and first aid equipment.

Meanwhile, *Whitehurst* circled, apparently out of control. Yet, when *Vigilance* caught up with the dam-aged ship and came alongside at 1530, the more serious fires on board the escort vessel had been controlled. *Vigilance*'s fire fighting and damage control parties helped to extinguish the remaining blaze and made emergency repairs.

However, the minecraft's prompt and efficient ren-dering of first aid was an even greater contribution. By 1535, 23 of the most seriously injured men from the escort's ship's company—and one dead man—had been transferred to *Vigilance* and taken to the mine-sweeper's mess hall for treatment. The ship's doctor, several officers, and enlisted men administered blood plasma and dressed wounds. The immediate injection of plasma and the efficient handling of the wounded saved 21 of the 23 casualties brought on board the minesweeper.

After placing Signalman 2d Class Thomas G. Barnes on board *Whitehurst* for temporary duty to handle the escort ship's communications—the destroyer escort's bridge force had been wiped out by the kamikaze—*Vigilance* proceeded to *Gosper* (APA–170) and trans-ferred the wounded to that attack transport. At 1854, *Vigilance* resumed her screening station off Kerama Retto.

Vigilance remained on patrol off those islands over the ensuing days—days which seemed comparatively quiet. However, on the morning of the 16th, alert look-outs sighted two planes—a "Val" and a "Frances"—off the ship's port quarter. Lt. (jg.) N. B. Norman, the officer of the deck, immediately ordered the gun watches on the 20-millimeter and 40-millimeter guns to com-mence firing, there not being time to call the ship to general quarters. *Vigilance*'s 20-millimeter guns com-menced firing on the "Val" when it was slightly abaft the beam, and the enemy plane then turned toward the ship before reversing course and heading for *Wilson* (DD–408). Eventually, the 20-millimeter fire from *Vigilance* scored; and the "Val" splashed some 300 yards ahead of the destroyer.

Meanwhile, the minesweeper's starboard 40-milli-meter mount took the "Frances" under fire. At a point 1,000 feet above and 100 yards from the port quarter of the nearby *Taluga* (AO–62), the "Frances" exe-cuted a wing-over and dived for the oiler. *Vigilance*'s Bofors continued firing until the plane was just above *Taluga*, at which point she ceased firing for fear of hitting the oiler. The "Frances" crashed *Taluga*'s bow, administering a glancing blow to the ship and blew some of the oiler's crew overboard. *Vigilance* fished three *Taluga* sailors from the water, who all agreed with the minesweeper's observers that the ship's gun-nery had proved accurate and effective in deflecting the suicide plane.

For the remainder of April and the first few days of May, *Vigilance* screened the landing operations. On two more occasions—on 18 April and on the 28th—*Vigilance* took passing Japanese planes under fire. In the first instance, she claimed to have shot down a "Jill"—one of four planes that closed the ship at night. Another of the four planes—believed to be a "Betty" bomber—strafed the ship but caused no dam-age. In the second case, the minesweeper shot down a snooping "Jake" floatplane at 0130 on the 28th.

The minecraft's patrol duties in May were high-lighted by two incidents. The first occurred on 4 May and the second on the 9th. In the first case, the ship was patrolling five miles south of Kerama Retto about sunset. Five miles to the north, five Japanese suicide planes headed for *Sangamon* (CVE–26). Combat air patrol (CAP) F4U Corsair fighters downed four, but the fifth crashed into the escort carrier at 1933. A burst of flame shot into the darkening skies; and soon the ship became a blazing inferno, ammunition and gasoline exploding at intervals and sending sheets of flame into the air to a height of what looked like hundreds of feet.

Screening ships and other vessels in the vicinity went to *Sangamon*'s assistance. After obtaining permission from her sector commander to do so, *Vigilance* departed her patrol area at 2035 and closed *Sangamon* to lend a hand. *Vigilance* located three swimming sailors blown overboard from the CVE and directed a nearby LCV(P) to pick them up and transfer them to a high-speed transport. By midnight, *Sangamon*'s fires were under control, and she was towed to an anchorage in Kerama Retto. At 0335 on the 5th, *Vigilance* formed up with *Forrest* (DMS–24), *Stern* (DE–187), and *Ringness* (APD–100) to conduct a combined search for survivors. At 1045, the search was abandoned, and *Vigilance* returned to her patrol station off Kerama Retto.

From 6 to 8 May, *Vigilance* underwent an availability at the fleet anchorage at Kerama Retto before returning to the screening line. The next day, while steaming on station Baker 10, four miles west of Kerama Retto, *Vigilance* manned her battle stations at 1845 when she received a "flash blue" air raid alert warning. Soon thereafter, the ship sighted a "Val" at 2,500 feet, three miles north. *Vigilance* opened fire with her 3-inch and 40-millimeter battery as the dive-bomber plunged toward the nearby *England* (DE–635).

England, on station Baker 11—three miles northeast of the minecraft, had attained fame throughout the fleet in the spring of 1944 by sinking six Japanese I-boats and earning a Presidential Unit Citation. Upon sighting the suicider, the destroyer escort started a hard right turn to present her beam to the attacker while her 3-inch antiaircraft battery pounded away. *Vigilance*, too, contributed to the flak above the twisting destroyer escort; gunfire from the ships blew off one wing of the suicider but failed to deflect the kamikaze from its one-way mission. The plane crashed into *England*'s starboard side, at the main deck below the bridge. A heavy explosion soon followed, and a burst of smoke and flame engulfed the destroyer escort's pilothouse and bridge.

Vigilance rang up full ahead and went to *England*'s assistance. While the minecraft was en route to the destroyer escort's side, another air battle ensued overhead. Two Corsairs shot down a "Val" which had possibly been attracted to the area by the burning *England*. As *Vigilance* attempted to overtake the stricken escort ship, her crew broke out fire and rescue equipment on the main deck and made the mess hall ready to receive wounded below. Still en route, sharp-eyed lookouts noted survivors in *England*'s wake, and the minecraft accordingly directed YMS–93 to pick up the swimmers. *Gherardi* (DMS–30) also closed the area to assist.

England, meanwhile, finally was brought under control and stopped about four miles east of where she had been kamikazed. At 1920, *Vigilance* pulled alongside the burning destroyer escort to find heavy fires blazing from the forward mess hall, up through the wardroom, forward 20-millimeter clipping room, radio room, pilothouse and flying bridge. A bomb, carried by the "Val" that had crashed the ship, had exploded in the mess hall. It wiped out the entire forward fire and rescue party, blew out the port side of the officers' quarters, opened the main deck, and tumbled a 3-inch gun over the side. A 3-inch, ready-service ammunition

box had fallen into the burning mess hall, and ammu nition was exploding.

Vigilance's fire and rescue party dragged on boar five fire hoses, two submersible pumps, one handy billy and a rescue breathing apparatus. Ruptured forwar water mains on board *England* had prevented th flooding of the forward magazines, so three hoses fror *Vigilance* and one found on *England*'s deck were traine down into the 3-inch ready box, stopping the detonatio of the ammunition. After 30 minutes of hard work, th forward 3-inch magazine was reported to be hal flooded, while the fires in the pilothouse, radio room and on the flying bridge were extinguished.

Because of the condition of *England*'s crew—man were shocked and dazed—the men from *Vigilance* ha to fight the fires largely themselves. Nine seriously injured *England* sailors, placed on stretchers, wer transferred to the minesweeper where they were given first aid and blood plasma. LSM–222 and PCE(R)– 853 lay alongside at 2015, sending two medical officer and three pharmacist's mates with additional medica supplies to handle the influx of casualties.

After two hours had elapsed—a time when the fre quent appearance of Japanese aircraft prohibited th use of lights and made the handling of lines, hoses, an damage control equipment difficult—*Vigilance* finally succeeded in extinguishing *England*'s fires and took th destroyer escort under tow. Underway for the northern entrance of Kerama Retto at 2135, the two ships ar rived at their destination two hours later. There, at th harbor entrance, *Gear* (ARS–34) took *England* unde tow and pulled her inside the anchorage. At that time the harbor was blanketed with smoke as enemy aircraf were again in the vicinity. *Vigilance* crept alongside *Gosper* at 0110 on 10 May and transferred *England*' casualties to the transport. *Gherardi* and YMS–93 soor arrived and transferred 25 more survivors to th transport.

Vigilance received a recommendation for a Navy Unit Commendation and her commanding officer, Lt. Jackson L. Morton, USNR, was later awarded a silver star fo his courage and level-headed action. *Vigilance* remained at anchor for the remainder of the day, replenishing medical supplies and damage control gear, before get ting underway on the 11th to sweep for mines in the vicinity of Tori Shima, in company with MinDiv 11 Upon completing the sweep at 1400 that afternoon *Vigilance* resumed her screening operations from 12 to 16 May.

The ship received fresh provisions on the 17th at anchor at Kerama Retto and returned to the screen ing line the next day. On 19 May, *Vigilance* got under way for the Marianas as part of Convoy OKA–4 and arrived at Saipan on the 24th. She shifted to Guam in company with *Gladiator* (AM–319) on the 25th and commenced two weeks of availability at the minecraft docks, Apra Harbor, Guam.

Upon the conclusion of the repairs, the minesweeper conducted ASW training exercises with *Trepang* (SS– 412) early on 12 June before departing Guam at 1755 to escort SS *Fairland* to Guam. Arriving at Tanapag Harbor the next day, she returned to Kerama Retto on 16 June in company with *Greene* (APD–36), *Opponent* (AM–269), and SS *Fairland* and SS *Cape Victory*.

Vigilance operated in the Ryukyus through the end of June and began July preparing for her next major operation, the sweeping of the East China Sea.

The minesweeper got underway on 4 July for area "Juneau," as part of Task Unit 39.11.4. Between 5 and 14 July, the ship accounted for four mines before under going logistics at Buckner Bay, Okinawa, from 16 to 17 July. A typhoon forced a general fleet movement to sea over the next four days, and *Vigilance* did not return until the 21st. Underway again for area "Juneau" on the 22d, the minesweeper and her sister ships spent the next week sweeping in the East China Sea. *Vigilance* contributed to the effort by locating and destroying three mines.

For the first five days in August, *Vigilance* remained at anchor at Buckner Bay. She got underway at 0558 on 6 August and escorted Convoy OKI–10 to San Pedro Bay, Leyte, Philippine Islands, arriving on 9 August. She moored alongside *Briareus* (AR–12) on the 10th for availability and, while her crew was enjoying movies on the forecastle that evening, she received the word that Japan was ready to surrender—news greeted with great rejoicing by all hands.

Vigilance remained alongside *Briareus* for 17 days before returning to Okinawa at the end of August. By that time, the war in the Pacific was over. She remained at Buckner Bay from 1 to 7 September and got underway at noon on the 8th, bound for Wakayama, Japan, to support the occupation of the erstwhile enemy's home islands. At 0430 on the 11th, *Vigilance* arrived at the southern entrance to Kii Suido and soon formed up in echelon formation to commence sweeping a channel—to a 120-foot depth—through Kii Suido to Wakayama. That evening she anchored at Wakayama Ko but resumed her labors early the following day and continued the routine for the next few days. She swept one mine on the 15th.

Worsening weather gave all signs of an approaching typhoon; and *Vigilance* was forced to anchor in various berths at Wakanoura Wan, off Honshu, between the 16th and 19th. As the storm reached its climax before dawn on the 18th, *LST–661* dragged her anchors and drifted down toward *Vigilance*'s berth. The minesweeper slipped her anchor and chain in an effort to avoid a collision; but the 90-knot wind pushed the LST inexorably toward the minecraft. Soon there came the crunch of steel on steel as the landing ship crashed into the minesweeper's starboard side, forward, bending in the bulwarks near the bow.

Eventually, *Vigilance* got underway and maneuvered inside the confused harbor before finally dropping anchor for the night to ride out the storm as it blew itself out. The dawn revealed three LST's aground and a YMS on her side on the rocks. After recovering her anchor and chain, *Vigilance* resumed minesweeping operations in the Japanese home waters. She swept off Honshu for the remainder of the month of September, anchoring upon occasion at Wakanoura Wan, and chalked up 16 more mines swept. Accompanying LCI's or PGM's sank by gunfire those mines which the sweeper cut loose. On the 24th, *Vigiliance* herself destroyed a mine with 20-millimeter and .30-caliber rifle fire.

After engineering repairs alongside *Patoka* (AG–125) in early October, *Vigilance* returned to the waters off Honshu to resume sweep operations, executing magnetic mine sweeps off Bishago Se and Iseno Umi. She returned to Tsu Ko to anchor on 12 October and there embarked passengers and loaded mail for transfer to Wakanoura Wan. After provisioning and fueling small craft to capacity, the minesweeper departed Tsu Ko at 1155 on 13 October and arrived at Wakanoura Wan early the following morning. Following another availability alongside *Patoka*, *Vigilance* tested her magnetic sweep gear before she returned to Bishago Se and Iseno Umi to resume sweep operations there.

Vigilance operated as pilot boat at the Yokkaichi anchorage, anchoring nightly in the Matoya Ko, rendezvousing with vessels off the harbor and leading them through the minefields to port. On 28 October, she shifted back to Wakanoura and remained there until noon of the following day for repairs to her radar. Reassigned duties as pilot ship soon thereafter, *Vigilance* returned to Iseno Umi and Matoya Ko on 31 October. During the operations off Nagoya, *Vigilance* had cleared the way for the evacuation of prisoners of war and the landing of American occupation forces. After performing similar operations in the Nagoya area through November, *Vigilance* departed Japanese waters on 17 December 1945, via Eniwetok and Pearl Harbor, bound for the United States. She operated locally out of San Francisco between January and November 1946 and alternated between San Diego and San Francisco into January of 1947. Decommissioned on 30 January 1947, the ship was placed in reserve on 16 April that same year. She remained inactive into the mid-1960's. During that period, she was reclassified as a fleet minesweeper, MSF-324, on 7 February 1955. Struck from the Navy list on 1 December 1966, the ship was transferred to the Government of the Philippines under a grant-in-aid on 19 August 1967. Renamed *Quezon*—in honor of the first President of the Philippine Commonwealth, Manuel Quezon—and classified as PS-70, the erstwhile minesweeper serves with the Philippine Navy into 1980.

Vigilance was awarded three battle stars for her World War II service.

Vigilant

I

(RC: t. 70; lbp. 40'; b. 17'8''; dph. 7'8''; a. 4 guns; cl. *Massachusetts*)

The first *Vigilant*—a schooner built in 1812 at Newport, R.I., by Benjamin Marble for the United States Revenue Cutter Service—was taken into the Navy during the War of 1812 and based at Newport, R.I., under the command of Capt. John Cahoone, USRCS.

Vigilant's first action came in the fall of 1813. The British privateer *Dart* had preyed upon Yankee shipping in Long Island Sound for some time, taking 20 to 30 vessels. She appeared off Newport on 4 October 1813 with two freshly caught prizes, and this braggadocio proved her undoing. Capt. Cahoone took 20 Navy volunteers on board to augment his regular crew and made sail to engage the brazen Britisher. *Vigilant* boldly sailed well within gun range of the more heavily armed sloop and loosed a broadside, which stunned the privateer. A boarding party from the revenue cutter quickly scrambled aboard the enemy vessel as she brushed alongside her quarry and quickly carried the Birton. *Vigilant* lost two men in the engagement, both of whom fell into the water and drowned while attempting to board.

After the cessation of hostilities with Great Britain in 1815, *Vigilant* resumed patrolling the New England coast. On 11 October 1817, *Vigilant* captured the brig *B*, of Bristol, in Vineyard Sound. Apparently the British vessel had used American shores to outfit for smuggling operations. The prize was, in the words of the *New York Post* for 23 October 1817, "libelled under the Act of the last Congress, to more effectively preserve the neutral relations of the United States."

In the spring of the following year, the revenue cutter continued her cruising off the eastern seaboard. On 17 May 1818, Capt. Cahoone learned that the Spanish brig *Belle Corunnes*—manned by a crew of Irishmen, Spaniards, and Britishers—lay in Block Island Sound. As his own ship was under repairs at the time, Cahoone embarked in a small gunboat with 10 volunteers. Proceeding from Newport, the revenue cutter captain and his men landed on the shores of Block Island Sound and found part of *Belle Corunnes*' cargo already landed. Placing a guard on the confiscated material—brandy and silks—Cahoone returned to Newport to hasten preparations of *Vigilant* for sea. Later that day, *Vigilant* embarked a detachment of artillerymen under Army Lt. Henry T. Evans and two artillery pieces. With the additional 18 men, the revenue cutter set sail.

Evans succinctly summed up what followed: "the desperadoes were over-awed by the superior force of the Revenue Cutter, and made little resistance; 25 of the crew were captured and the remainder, 11 in number, were captured soon thereafter." *Belle Corunnes* was eventually condemned and sold.

Vigilant maintained regular cruises in protection of American coastwise commerce out of Newport until 2 February 1830, when she was shifted to New Haven,

Conn. Returning later to Newport, she underwent an extensive overhaul in the fall of 1835 and, after a period of further service, was sold at Boston on 13 May 1842.

II

(Tug: dp. 300; l. 116′; b. 21′; dr. 9′ (mean); s. 12 k.; cpl. 46; a. 2 1-pdrs., 1 mg.)

The second *Vigilant*—originally named *George W. Pride*—was an iron-hulled, screw tug laid down in 1883 at Philadelphia, Pa., by William Cramp and Sons, and completed in 1888. She was acquired by the Navy from John D. Spreckels Brothers' Co., of San Francisco, at the outset of the Spanish-American War, and was commissioned on 6 April 1898.

Vigilant was stationed in the San Francisco region from 1898 to 1927, operating either at the Yerba Buena Naval Station or the Naval Training Station, San Francisco. Classified as YT-25 on 17 July 1920, *Vigilant*'s decommissioning date is uncertain. She was struck from the Navy list on 26 November 1927 and was sold to the Cary Davis Tug and Barge Co., of Seattle, Wash., on 25 April 1928.

III

(MB: t. 41; l. 72′0″; b. 14′0″; dr. 3′8″; cpl. 14; a. 1 1-pdr., 1 mg., 4 dc.)

The third *Vigilant* (SP-406) was a motorboat designed by Charles D. Mower; built in 1909 by Henry L. Blatz, of Philadelphia, Pa.; and originally named *Marguerite II*. Acquired by the Navy from E. B. Smith, of Philadelphia, *Vigilant* was commissioned on 19 May 1917 at the Philadelphia Navy Yard, Ens. John B. Yarnall, USNRF, in command.

The boat proceeded from Philadelphia to Essington, Pa., on 28 May for installation of armament, loaded ammunition at Fort Mifflin on 5 June and, two days later, reported to the 4th Naval District. Throughout the remainder of World War I, *Vigilant* patrolled the Delaware River and the coastal waters of the Middle Atlantic States, ranging from Atlantic City, N.J., to the mouth of he Chesapeake Bay. She remained alert to detect any U-boats which entered her patrol area as she carried messages, men, and mail to ships and stations within the 4th Naval District. Occasionally, she ventured out to sea to search for survivors of torpedoed merchantmen, as she did on 9 June 1918 when a U-boat had sunk SS *Del Rio*.

After the armistice ended hostilities, *Vigilant* proceeded to Philadelphia early in December for inactivation. She was decommissioned there on Christmas Eve 1918 and was returned to her owner.

IV

(CGC: dp. 220; l. 125′; b. 23′6″; dr. 9′; s. 11 k.; cpl. 38; a. 1 3″; cl. *Active*)

The fourth *Vigilant*—a 125-foot, steel-hulled, twin-screw, diesel-powered Coast Guard cutter—was completed in 1927 at Camden, N.J., by the American Brown Boveri Electric Corp. and was placed in service at Camden on 3 March 1927, Boatswain's Mate J. F. Morin, USCG, in charge.

After operating out of the Coast Guard base at Stapleton, N.J., into the spring of 1933, *Vigilant* shifted to Norfolk on 6 June, and, in 1935, to Ft. Pierce, Fla. The Navy took over Coast Guard vessels in the summer of 1941 for duty during the national emergency, but the Coast Guard cutter was still based at Ft. Pierce at the time of the Japanese attack against Pearl Harbor on 7 December 1941.

Fitted to service navigational aids, *Vigilant*—classified WPC-154—patrolled out of Ft. Pierce into early 1942. At 1350 on 19 February 1942, the cutter received a radio message reporting the torpedoing (later found

out to have been committed by *U-128*) of the tanker SS *Pan Massachusetts*. While the warship steamed to the area, SS *Elizabeth Massey* rescued the tanker's survivors and radioed that no assistance was necessary. Nonetheless, *Vigilant* remained in the area.

While off Melbourne, Fla., at 0555 on 22 February the cutter sighted a flare and altered her course to close. She soon found the burning tanker SS *Republic* which had been torpedoed an hour earlier by *U-504*.

At 0800, as *Vigilant* drew nearer, she discovered an overturned lifeboat alongside the blazing *Republic* with a man swimming nearby. She quickly maneuvered to within 50 feet of the man in the water. Suddenly, *Republic* blew up, enveloping the unfortunate man in flames and spraying oil on the rescuers. *Vigilant* remained perilously close to the raging flames and picked up two survivors, whom she later transferred to *Biddle* (DD-151) which had arrived on the scene. Eventually, *Vigilant* recovered six bodies and transferred them to *Biddle* before turning over the search to the destroyer.

Vigilant subsequently pursued a submarine contact on 9 May, believing it to be a U-boat thought to have been damaged earlier and seeking to escape by heading in a northerly direction from Miami. Joined by *Nike* (WPC-112), *Vigilant* conducted a fruitless search for the enemy submersible.

Vigilant's extant World War II diary entries end, for some reason, in 1942. It is known, however, that the vessel continued in service with the Coast Guard after World War II and was later stationed at Corpus Christi, Tex. The ship was reclassified a medium endurance cutter in the 1960's. She was decommissioned and sold in 1966.

Vigor

I

(AMc-110: dp. 195; l. 98′5″; b. 23′6″; dr. 10′6″ (max.); s. 10.0 k.; cpl. 17; a. 2 .50-cal. mg.; cl. *Accentor*)

The first *Vigor* (AMc-110)—a wooden-hulled, coastal minesweeper—was laid down on 6 August 1941 at Rockland, Maine, by the Snow Shipyard, Inc.; launched on 19 January 1942; sponsored by Mrs. Lawrence Carver; and placed in service at the Boston Navy Yard on 4 May 1942.

Following fitting out, *Vigor* departed Boston on 6 May and headed for the Virginia capes. Proceeding via Tompkinsville, N.Y., the coastal minesweeper arrived at Yorktown, Va., on 20 May for training at the Mine Warfare School. Upon completion of her exercises in the Tidewater area, *Vigor* operated off the eastern seaboard between Newport, R.I., and Norfolk, Va.—with her home yard at New York—for the remainder of the Atlantic war. Sailing from Norfolk, bound for Charleston, S.C., the warship arrived at the latter port on 8 August 1945.

Subsequently placed out of service at Charleston on 31 October 1945 and laid up in reserve in the Wando River, *Vigor* was declared surplus and made available for disposal by the Maritime Commission's War Shipping Administration. Struck from the Navy list on 16 November 1945, the erstwhile minecraft was sold on 13 November 1946.

II

(AM-473: dp. 775; l. 172′; b. 35′; dr. 10′; s. 14 k.; cpl. 70; a. 1 40mm., 2 .50-cal. mg.; cl. *Aggressive*)

The second *Vigor* (AM-473) was laid down on 16 June 1952 at Manitowoc, Wis., by the Burger Boat Co.; launched on 23 June 1953; sponsored by Mrs. Charles C. Kerwin; and commissioned at the Boston Naval Shipyard on 8 November 1954, Lt. Walter W. Schwartz in command.

USS *Vigor* (MSO–473) in the Gulf of Mexico, April 1960.

After brief duty at Boston, the minesweeper moved to Key West for shakedown training early in 1955. During the cruise, she was redesignated MSO–473 on 7 February. Minesweeper refresher training at Charleston, S.C., followed, and *Vigor* then began a tour of duty with the Naval Ordnance Laboratory at Port Everglades, Fla. Later that year, *Vigor* became a training ship, first for the Underwater Object Locator School at Key West and then for the Naval Mine Warfare School at Yorktown, Va. Early in 1956, she again headed south to participate in the annual Caribbean exercise, Operation "Springboard." During her cruise to the West Indies, *Vigor* made port calls at San Juan, Puerto Rico; and Fredricksted, St. Croix, in the Virgin Islands. Following her return to Charleston and operations out of that port, she got underway on 1 May for her first deployment to the Mediterranean Sea. During that cruise, she visited Harwich, England; Ostend, Belgium; and Lisbon, Portugal, as well as touching at the usual 6th Fleet ports of call along the Mediterranean coast. She concluded that cruise at Charleston on 6 October and resumed operations from that base.

Vigor continued that duty until the latter part of 1957, when she was reassigned to the Naval Mine Defense Laboratory at Panama City, Fla. From that new home port, the minesweeper operated with Mine Division 85 participating in various experimental projects conducted by the laboratory. For the next 14 years, she remained based at Panama City conducting operations for both the Mine Warfare Laboratory and with the Operational Test and Evaluation Force. During her assignment there, she also deployed to the Mediterranean five more times, operating with the 6th Fleet for six months at a time. Each time she returned to Panama City, she resumed normal duty which was broken periodically by overhauls at various locations.

On New Year's Day 1971, the ship's base was changed back to Charleston. She left Panama City on the 18th and arrived in Charleston on the 27th. After 15 months

of duty with the Mine Force, *Vigor* was decommissioned at Charleston on 4 April 1972. Simultaneously, her name was struck from the Navy list; and she was transferred to the government of Spain. As of the beginning of 1980, she remained an active unit of the Spanish Navy, serving under the name *Guadiana* (M 44).

Viking

I

(Yacht: dp. 218; l. 122'0'' (wl.); b. 21'0'' (wl.); dr. 8'6'' (mean); s. 11.75 k.; cpl. 43; a. 1 3-pdr., 3 6mm. mg.)

The first *Viking*—an iron-hulled, steam yacht built in 1883 at Chester, Pa., by John Roach—was acquired by the Navy on 22 April 1898 from Mr. Horace A. Hutchins for service in the Spanish-American War. Converted for naval service at New York, she was placed in commission there on 11 May 1898, Lt. Henry Minett in command.

Assigned to the North Atlantic Fleet as a dispatch ship, *Viking* remained at New York for the next two months. On 12 July, she departed New York bound for the blockading forces off the Cuban coast. After brief stops at Port Royal, S.C., and Key West, Fla., she joined the Fleet in Cuban waters on 28 July. After three weeks of duty carrying orders, messages, and passengers between ships on station on the blockade, *Viking* ended her brief war service without having participated in any combat. She headed back to Key West on 16 August, remained overnight, and then continued her voyage—via Port Royal—to Hampton Roads, Va. She remained in the Hampton Roads-Norfolk area until 8 September when she headed up Chesapeake Bay to Annapolis, Md. After a two-day visit, she returned to Norfolk on the 11th.

She was placed out of commission there on 22 September. *Viking* remained at Norfolk until 29 September 1899 at which time she was reactivated for a bit more than three weeks of service which ended on 23 October. On 9 December 1899, *Viking* was transferred to the War Department. No records telling of her Army service or of her ultimate disposition have been found.

The steel-hulled steam yacht *Viking*—built in 1909 at Wilmington, Del., by Pusey and Jones—was owned by George F. Baker, Jr., of New York City when inspected by the Navy for possible use as a section patrol vessel. Records concerning this ship are sparse. Although an order for her acquisition was issued by the Navy on 13 June 1917, and the ship received the classification SP–618, apparently she saw no active naval service. No deck logs or other documents which might substantiate any actual service have been found. She was returned to her owner sometime in late 1917—probably either in November or December.

II

(MB: t. 10; l. 42'0''; b. 10'0''; dr. 6'0''; s. 5.1 k.; a. none)

The second *Viking* (formerly named *Caesar*)—a wooden-hulled cabin motorboat built by the Navy in 1915 and then apparently sold into civilian ownership soon thereafter—was inspected by the Navy on 5 September 1918, assigned the classification SP–3314, and acquired from a Mrs. E. S. Wood on 24 September for use as a section patrol boat. While no deck logs for this vessel have been found, available records indicate that she operated in the 5th Naval District, probably in noncommissioned status. On 2 February 1919, the Secretary of the Navy authorized the Commandant of the 5th Naval District to dispose of the boat as "junk." She was struck from the Navy list on 19 February 1919 and sold the following day.

III

(Minesweeper No. 32: dp. 850; l. 180'; b. 35'6''; dr. 9'9½'' (mean); s. 14 k.; cpl. 78; a. none; cl. *Lapwing*)

The third *Viking* (ARS–1) was originally laid down as *Flamingo* (Minesweeper No. 32) on 18 October 1917 at Elizabethport, N.J., by the New Jersey Drydock and Transportation Co.; launched on 24 August 1918; sponsored by Miss Fanny Caroline Moritz, the daughter of Comdr. Albert Moritz, the inspector of minesweepers for the 3d Naval Distract; and commissioned at the New York Navy Yard on 12 February 1919, Lt. F. J. Mayer in command.

Flamingo fitted out at the New York Navy Yard and later shifted to Tompkinsville, Staten Island, N.Y., on 29 March. The minesweeper performed various towing jobs and carried stores locally in the 3d Naval District into the spring of 1919. On 10 April, she suffered damage in a collision with an unnamed Panama Railroad Co. tug, and underwent repairs at Port Richmond, Staten Island. Shifting to the New York Navy Yard soon thereafter, *Flamingo* began fitting out "for distant service."

Flamingo departed Tompkinsville on 18 May, bound for the Orkney Islands. Proceeding via Boston, the minesweeper arrived at Kirkwall, Scotland, on 5 June, to begin her tour of duty with the United States Minesweeping Detachment, North Sea. Along with American subchasers, chartered British trawlers, and fellow *Lapwing*-class sweepers, *Flamingo* would participate in the clearing of the North Sea Mine Barrage.

Laid by the United States Navy after America entered World War I, the barrier had served as a formidable obstacle for German U-boats based at North Sea ports. By 1919, however, the barrage hampered the resumption of peaceful commerce.

On 23 June, *Flamingo* transported officers and men from Kirkwall to Inverness, Scotland, and returned to her base in the evening carrying supplies for the detachment flagship, *Black Hawk* (Destroyer Tender No 9). The minesweeper then performed tugboat duty at Kirkwall between 25 June and 7 July. Four days later she sailed to assist in clearing group 11 of the mine barrage in the second phase of the fourth clearance operation conducted by the Minesweeping Detachment.

The first days were uneventful. On 15 July, *Flamingo* anchored for the night, as was usual practice, to the northward of the minefield. During the ensuing evening hours, strong winds and currents caused the ship to drag her anchor. She slowly worked southward from her original position. The next morning, when *Flamingo* weighed her anchor to get underway, she discovered that she had drifted into the minefield and had fouled one of the horned spheres in her anchor cable. The deadly device was trailing just beneath the fantail of the ship.

The mine exploded beneath *Flamingo*'s stern. The underwater blast badly damaged the rudder, disabled the capstan and generator, and dished in the ship's stern plating in several places. *Eider* (Minesweeper No 17) lent assistance and towed *Flamingo* to Invergordon, Scotland, for drydocking and repairs on 17 July.

Flamingo was ready to return to the base at Kirkwall by early in the next month. She transported a cargo of steel and lumber to *Black Hawk* on her return voyage, arriving at Kirkwall on 13 August. Two days later, the minesweeper towed her crippled sister ship *Pelican* (Minesweeper No. 27) to South Shields, England, for drydocking and repairs in the wake of her mining the previous month.

Later in August, *Flamingo* resumed her minesweeper duties with the detachment, working out of the Norwegian ports of Lervic, Stavanger, and Haugesund before returning to Kirkwall via Otters Wick, Orkneys, on 7 September. She subsequently participated in the final sweep of the mine barrage—the climactic sweep which detonated five mines, cut loose 47, and destroyed 50—into late September. Once the arduous and dangerous job was complete, *Flamingo* and her sister ships could head home to the United States for a well-earned rest. *Flamingo* departed Kirkwall on 1 October and—after a voyage which took the minecraft via Plymouth and Devonport, England; Brest, France; Lisbon, Portugal; the Azores; and Bermuda—eventually arrived at Tompkinsville on 20 November.

The pause at Tompkinsville was a brief one, however, for *Flamingo* was underway five days later—on 25 November—bound for the Portsmouth (N.H.) Navy Yard. She arrived on the 28th and soon commenced an overhaul. Assigned to the 1st Division, 2d Mine Squadron, Atlantic Fleet, on 1 July 1920, *Flamingo* received the classification AM–32 on 17 July, as the Navy adopted its modern system of alphanumeric hull numbers. The minesweeper operated with the 2d Mine Squadron into the autumn of 1920, until placed in reserve at the Portsmouth Navy Yard on 18 November.

Flamingo remained inactive for almost a year and one-half before an executive order of 25 March 1922 authorized the Navy to transfer the vessel to the Commerce Department, and she was accordingly decommissioned on 5 May 1922. Turned over to the Coast and Geodetic Survey for use as a survey vessel, at Portsmouth, on 23 January 1923, the erstwhile minecraft was renamed *Guide* on 1 March 1923.

Late in the year, after she had been converted and fitted out on the east coast, *Guide* departed New London bound for her new duty station, San Diego, Calif. On her voyage to the west coast, the ship made history by using—for the first time by a vessel of the Coast and Geodetic Survey—a sonic depth finder to measure and record the depth of the sea at points along her course. Before she reached San Diego—the date of her arrival has not been found, but she transited the

Panama Canal on 8 December—*Guide* had accumulated much data beneficial to the study of the movement of sound waves through water and measuring their velocity under varying conditions of salinity, density, and temperature.

Based at San Diego and surveying off the west coast of the United States, *Guide* performed her important duties for the Coast and Geodetic Survey for nearly two decades. Meanwhile, as war clouds gathered and tension mounted in Europe and the Far East in the late 1930's, the United States Navy expanded to meet the emergency—especially after the outbreak of hostilities following the German invasion of Poland in September 1939.

On 27 June 1941, *Guide* was transferred back from the Coast and Geodetic Survey to the Navy. Nearly one month later, on 25 July, work to convert the ship to a salvage vessel began at the San Diego Marine Construction Co. During the reconfiguration, on 5 August, the Navy renamed the ship *Viking* and classified her ARS–1. While the alterations were still in progress, Japanese aircraft attacked Pearl Harbor on 7 December 1941 plunging the United States into World War II. Placed "in service" on 3 January 1942, *Viking* was pronounced ready for duty on 12 February. Manned by a civilian crew and operated from San Diego by the Merritt, Chapman, and Scott salvage firm—a civilian company working under a contract let by the Bureau of Ships—*Viking* stood ready to perform salvage and rescue tasks in the 11th Naval District.

Between 3 and 6 July 1942, *Viking* assisted two local patrol craft, *YP–267* and *YP–269*, which had run aground off San Diego, towing them both back to port for repairs. From the ship's movement reports, *Viking* appears to have spent an uneventful autumn and winter at her home port. She shifted to San Francisco briefly in January 1943, en route to Guadalupe to perform emergency salvage operations under the aegis of the Commander, Western Sea Frontier. Returning to San Diego in February, the salvage vessel operated there into 1944.

On 27 October, *Viking* sailed for San Pedro for refit and returned to San Diego later in November. On the last day of 1944, *Viking* departed her home port in company with *Tenino* (ATF–115), bound for Clipperton Island. There, the two vessels joined *Seize* (ARS–26) to free the grounded *LST–563*. During the rescue operation, *Viking* suffered damage from heavy seas and put into San Diego for repairs soon thereafter.

The salvage vessel subsequently operated out of San Diego and San Pedro through the end of World War II in mid-August 1945. She performed tug and tow services with ships ranging in size from destroyers to LST's into the 1950's. In December of 1949, she aided the grounded steamer SS *Aristocratus* off the south point of Santa Rosa Island.

Eventually, *Viking*'s area of operations embraced Long Beach and Port Hueneme, Calif., as well as the San Diego locale. Relieved by *Gear* (ARS–34) as salvage vessel for the 11th Naval District, *Viking* was returned to Navy custody by the Merritt, Chapman, and Scott salvage firm. On 17 March 1953, she was authorized for disposal; and her name was struck from the Navy list on 19 April 1953.

She lay at the Naval Supply Depot, San Pedro, until sold on 22 July 1953 to Nathan Cohen and Son, Inc., of Los Angeles, Calif. The veteran of service in the United States Navy, as well as of the Coast and Geodetic Survey, was scrapped soon thereafter.

Vileehi

(Ketch: t. 54; l. 80'; b. 19'3''; dph. 11'3''; dr. 11'5''; s. 7 k.)

Vileehi—a wooden-hulled ketch with an auxiliary engine—was designed by Edson B. Schock and built in 1930 at San Diego, Calif., by the San Diego Marine

Construction Co. The vessel was acquired by the Navy from Hiram T. Horton of San Diego on 23 December 1941. Assigned to the 11th Naval District on 17 February 1942, *Vileehi* was given the designation IX–62 and placed in service on 26 February. She operated locally out of San Diego for the remainder of World War II and was placed out of service on 20 September 1945. Returned to her owner on 27 September, *Vileehi* was struck from the Navy list on 24 October 1945.

Villalobos

Ruy Lopez de Villalobos—a 16th century Spanish navigator and explorer—was given command of a force sent out by the Viceroy of Mexico to explore unknown islands in the southern seas of the Pacific. On 1 November 1542, Villalobos departed Mexico with five ships. In the course of his voyages, he discovered the Palaus, or the Western Caroline islands; and navigated the Philippine Archipelago, discovering them and naming them in honor of the reigning Spanish monarch, King Philip II. In 1546, the intrepid explorer died at Ambon, in what is now Indonesia.

I

(ScGbt: dp. 270; l. 156'2''; b. 23'0''; dr. 7'6'' (mean); s. 11.0 k.; cpl. 57; a. 4 3-pdrs., 2 1-pdrs.)

The first *Villalobos*—a steel-hulled, screw gunboat—was laid down in September 1895 at Hong Kong, British Crown Colony, by the Hong Kong and Whampoa Dock Co., for service with the Spanish Navy. Launched during the following year, she was completed in July 1896 and was based at Cavite, Philippine Islands, at the time of the Spanish-American War. Captured by the United States Army along with near-sisters *General Alava* and *Quiros*, *Villalobos* was acquired by the Navy on 21 February 1900 and commissioned at Cavite on 5 March 1900, Lt. Edward Simpson in command.

Departing Cavite on 13 March, *Villalobos* patrolled off the coast from Cape Santiago to Point Cueva, Buriad Island, maintaining a communication link with the marines guarding lighthouses at Santiago and Malabrigo and keeping a sharp lookout for traffic supplying the Philippine insurgents. Before the ship returned to to her home port on the 26th, she had destroyed seven bancas (small native boats) with a cargo valuing some $935.00 and also seized a brigantine, a schooner, and a banca which had all been engaged in smuggling.

After a brief period of rest at Cavite from 26 March to 1 April, *Villalobos* patrolled the coastline between Niac and Laguimanoc and cooperated with an Army detachment from Taal in seizing three bancas in the barrio of Hanahana and 11 at the barrio of San Luiz, towing them to Taal for not having licenses. During these operations, the gunboat also seized a sloop and a banca with two Americans on board and arrested them for cruising without proper identification and papers. Her third patrol from Cavite, commencing on 14 April, saw the ship transporting stores to the guards at Cape Santiago, Cape Malabrigo, and Cabra Island lighthouses before resuming routine communication duties with Army detachments at Batangas, Lucena, and Laguimanoc.

Her fourth patrol from Cavite found her returning to the vicinity of Laguimanoc, along the southwest coast of Luzon. She cooperated with *Indiana* (Battleship No. 1) and *Helena* (Gunboat No. 9) in supporting the 29th Army Division in securing Marinduque Island. The gunboat then carried dispatches from Marinduque to Batangas before returning with emergency rations for the troops. Furnishing supplies to the lighthouse keepers again occupied the ship before she returned to commerce-watching duties during which she seized three bancas for cruising without licenses. The ship also

The gunboat *Villalobos* in Chinese waters, about 1910. (NH 48493)

communicated with Army posts at Taal, Batangas, Laguimanoc, Buac, Santa Cruz, and visited Gazan.

She returned to Cavite on 10 May for a 10-day respite. Underway again on the 20th, she headed for the familiar region of the southwest coast of Luzon to resume her watch on local banca traffic and to serve as a communication link for Army posts with the "outside world." *Villalobos* seized three more bancas for operating without licenses and one for having insurgent papers on board, establishing a link between the last boat owner and forces then fighting the new American occupiers.

Army-cooperation duties included supporting the Army's landing detachments including the 30th Infantry at Bana Layley, and the 38th and 29th Infantry at Santa Cruz and Marlango. She then steamed back to Buac before supporting operations of the 30th Infantry at Unisan. During the land operations of the 28th Infantry, *Villalobos* blockaded Maricabau Strait and subsequently served on blockade duty off Nasugbu at the request of the American military governor there before carrying dispatches to Buac.

For the remainder of the year 1900 and into 1902, *Villalobos* conducted patrols in support of Army forces similar to those she had been carrying out since she was first commissioned. She continued to work off the northern and western coasts of Luzon and off Cebu. In between deployments, she was repaired at Cavite before returning to patrol duty in which she supported the Army occupation of Samar. On 20 November 1902, the gunboat was decommissioned at Cavite.

Recommissioned on 21 January 1903, *Villalobos* immediately commenced fitting out for service on the Yangtze River. She got underway for China on 7 February and stopped at Dasol Bay, Philippines, from 8 to 14 February to conduct a "hydrographic reconnaissance" of the bay in company with gunboat *Elcano*,

tender *Callao*, and collier *Pompey*. Underway again on the 14th, the squadron put into Hong Kong three days later and remained there until the 26th, when *Villalobos*, in company with *Pompey* and *Elcano*, sailed for Swatow, China. Leaving the collier at Swatow, *Villalobos* and *Elcano* proceeded to Pagoda Anchorage and thence moved on to Shanghai soon thereafter to inaugurate the United States Navy's Yangtze River Patrol. After a brief visit to this key Chinese seaport city, *Villalobos* pushed up the Yangtze on 27 March to Kiang-Yin to investigate conditions there and to check on the welfare of the American citizens living in the vicinity.

Thus the former Spanish gunboat commenced her service with the Yangtze Patrol—"showing the flag" on the mighty river of what the Chinese had called "the Middle Kingdom." China, once a power of stature perhaps unequalled, had become a collection of feuding states as strongmen leaders arose in various geographical areas to war on their neighbors. The Boxer Rebellion at the turn of the century—a scant three years before—had resulted in the "Boxer Protocol"—giving foreigners the right to station ships and men in the country to protect their nationals.

Villalobos steamed, in company with *Elcano*, to Chinkiang and thence via Nanking and Wuhu to Hankow where she arrived on 10 April. She spent the next five days awaiting a favorable rise in the river level to permit passage to I'Chang before she got underway on the 15th for Chenglin, Yochow, and Shasi. After arriving at I'Chang on 19 April, the ship headed back downriver and returned to Hankow on 5 May to investigate the possibility of making passage to Changsha for needed supplies. Proceeding thence to Yochow and Chin-Chi-wan, she met a party of American engineers mapping out a route for the Hankow to Canton Railway.

Cruising subsequently to Changsha, Siangtan, Chu-Chow, Yochow, and Hankow, *Villalobos* set out on 1 June for Kiukiang. She awaited three days to obtain a pilot for passage up the Kan River and Poyang Lake and, when one was finally obtained, got underway for Nanchang. However, upon discovering that the river level had fallen so rapidly, *Villalobos* proceeded no further but instead sent a whaleboat upstream for Nanchang to reconnoiter in accordance with orders from Admiral Robley D. Evans, Commander in Chief, Asiatic Fleet, who had wired the gunboat to investigate local conditions there.

On 6 June, the boat returned and reported that all was quiet at Nanchang, and *Villalobos* headed back downriver—briefly unaware that her visit had stirred up diplomatic waters. En route downriver, the gunboat's commander received a letter, via the American consul, from the local Tao-Tai (governor) who strongly protested *Villalobos'* visit—a protest which the consul seemed to sanction. When word reached Admiral Evans, the Commander in Chief responded that a French gunboat had earlier made the same trip and had followed the same procedures, and it had gone without a protest from the local Chinese authorities.

"Your visit with the *Villalobos* to Nanchang," wrote Evans to *Villalobos'* commander, "for the purpose of investigating the condition and providing for the protection of the lives and property of Americans is approved." The admiral continued: "It is my desire that, so far as practicable, similar visits be paid to all Americans having property or other lawful interests in China, that I may be kept fully informed regarding all things concerning their welfare." Referring to the Tao Tai's contention that the gunboats should stay away since the inhabitants of the district were "bad men," the Commander in Chief responded that this fact was all the more reason for more frequent visits.

Evans authorized *Villalobos'* commanding officer to inform any Chinese officials who might raise similar objections that the Fleet's gunboats "are always amply provided for dealing with 'bad men.'" The admiral admonished that if anything other than "proper respect" was shown to Americans in China, "severe and lasting punishment" would be meted out to those who dared to insult citizens of the United States. If the Chinese failed to provide "adequate and proper" protection, then gunboats flying the stars and stripes would do it for them. As if that were not enough, Evans wrote, "Our gunboats will continue to navigate Poyang Lake and other inland waters of China, wherever Americans may be, and where, by treaty with China, they are authorized to engage in business or reside for the purpose of spreading the Gospel."

When word of Evans' stand reached the American minister to China in Peking, Edward Conger, he sided with the Tao-Tai. Conger asked Evans by what authority he had sanctioned *Villalobos'* visit to Nanchang. The admiral responded that he had acted under no specific treaty—but rather, based his action on the broad principle of extending American protection to wherever this country's nationals resided for Gold, Glory, or Gospel. While communications between widely separated places often took weeks or even months and the matter passed to Washington and the State and Navy Departments, American gunboats continued to patrol Poyang Lake.

John Hay, the Secretary of State, wrote to Conger siding with Evans, whose position he considered "proper and correct." Furthermore, Evans at the time had had no knowledge of treaties that indirectly applied to American rights in China although they had been made with other nations. Article 52 of the British Treaty of 1858, made reference to "most-favored nation" treatment—unbeknownst to Evans—and applied directly to *Villalobos'* controversial visit. The admiral had thus established a precedent for the Asiatic Fleet that would be carried on until late in the 1930's.

Villalobos remained deployed on the Yangtze for the next 23 years, through various reorganizations and designations of what eventually became known as the Yangtze Patrol of the United States Asiatic Fleet. During World War I, the belligerent nations either withdrew their ships from Chinese waters or saw them interned. The vacuum thus created by the internment or redeployment of British, French, and German gunboats on the Yangtze left only the Americans available to "keep the peace." However, no major wars between factions and warlords occurred.

America's entry into the war soon resulted in internment for United States gunboats. While *Wilmington* (Gunboat No. 8) sailed for Manila within the allotted time to avoid forced internment, *Palos* (River Gunboat No. 1), *Monocacy* (River Gunboat No. 2), *Samar*, *Quiros*, and *Villalobos* all remained at Shanghai—maintained at 75 percent complement and occupying their time with usual and routine ship's maintenance work—until China entered the war on the side of the Allied and Associated Powers on 16 August 1917. At that time, *Villalobos* and her sister gunboats resumed their patrolling and continued it through the armistice and into the postwar years.

In March of 1921, the home port for the elderly former Spanish gunboats—*Villalobos*, *Quiros*, and *Elcano*—was changed officially from Manila to Shanghai. *Villalobos*—by now designated PG–42—patrolled the middle Yangtze in mid-1921, noting local conditions and continuing in her duty of standing ready to protect American lives and property should the need arise. The first flag officer commanding the Yangtze Patrol, Rear Admiral W. H. G. Bullard, felt that the venerable *Villalobos* and her near-sisters were "hopeless cases" in terms of upkeep, firepower, and living conditions; but they, nevertheless, remained on duty. However, by this point, there was not much for them to do, as the "war" between the warlords commanding Szechwan and Hupeh provinces had placed trigger-happy soldiers along both banks of the upper river, successfully halting river traffic. *Villalobos* reported on 22 July 1921 that "business is at a standstill" on both the middle and upper Yangtze River.

For the next five years, *Villalobos* continued her usual river activities, with occasional periods of upkeep at the Chinese-owned Kiangnan Dock and Engineering Works. In late August 1926, however, there were indications that there could be action in store for the gunboat at Hankow. Communist forces were on the march.

Underway on 27 August, the ship steamed upstream and passed Chinese warships at Kinkow, saw warlord soldiery along the banks, and spotted an occasional corpse floating with the tide—all of which indicated that further upstream there lay possibilities for trouble. After anchoring for the night, *Villalobos* got underway the next day only to soon run aground. While elsewhere in the Fleet such an incident would be grounds for a court-martial, in China the frequent capricious currents and changing river levels frequently resulted in such nautical mishaps. But with the river dropping one foot per day, if the ship were not soon refloated, she would be there until winter. Help soon happened by. A British Butterfield and Swire Line tug hove into sight towing a lighter. Closing the gunboat, the Briton came to the rescue, and *Villalobos'* crew transferred nearly everything portable—including ammunition and stores—to the tug's lighter. At the same juncture, *Pigeon* (AM–47)—a *Lapwing*-class minesweeper converted to a river gunboat—came by as well, headed downstream from Changsha while the river still allowed her to pass downriver safely. With her decreased draft, and the combined tugging efforts of *Pigeon* and the Butterfield and Swire boat, *Villalobos* shuddered free of the sandbar shortly thereafter and immediately began reloading of all stores and ammunition. When that task was completed, she resumed her passage.

After her delayed arrival, *Villalobos* remained at Changsha for the next four months until relieved by

Palos on 28 February. Proceeding downriver, *Villalobos* arrived at Hankow on 2 March, joining *Isabel* (PY–10)—flagship, Commander, Yangtzee Patrol, Rear Admiral H. H. Hough; *Truxtun* (DD–229); and *Pope* (DD–225). Unfortunately, the serene conditions prevailing in that area did not last long, for Chinese Nationalist forces swarmed into Nanking on 24 March and subjected American and British commercial installations to heavy attacks. On the 25th, Lt. Comdr. Earl A. MacIntyre ordered his crew to place more steel boiler-plate around vital control and gun positions on board *Villalobos* in expectation of action. Within two weeks, riots broke out in Hankow and looting commenced in the Japanese section of the city, prompting the Japanese to land forces to quell the disturbance. With the evacuation of Americans, *Villalobos* stood by, keeping watch on the scene with her guns cleared for action.

Ordered downriver to guard the American-owned Socony-Vacuum oil company's installation, *Villalobos* joined British gunboats HMS *Teal* and HMS *Scarab* in an uneventful watch. Relieved by *Palos* on 27 May, *Villalobos* departed Hankow and the middle-river area and sailed for Shanghai with the orders: "If fired upon, and source can be located, return and silence fire with suitable battery."

Meanwhile, while *Villalobos* and her ex-Spanish sisters were completing their tours on the Yangtze, six new gunboats were being built especially for Yangtze duty. The Secretary of the Navy's report for 1927 stated that *Villalobos* was in bad condition as regarding both hull and machinery and had little sale value. Thus, on 29 December 1927, President Calvin Coolidge authorized the destruction of *Villalobos* by gunfire; and the gunboat was placed out of commission on 29 May 1928. Struck from the Navy list on 4 October, the venerable gunboat was towed to sea and sunk in experimental destroyer gunnery exercises off the China coast on 9 October 1928.

II

(IX–145: dp. 4,398; l. 400′0″; b. 52′1″; dr. 29′5″; s. 10.0 k.; cpl. 133; a. 1 4″, 1 3″, 8 20mm.)

The second *Villalobos* (IX–145)—a tanker built as *William F. Herrin* at Newport News, Va., by the Newport News Shipbuilding and Drydock Co.—was launched on 4 February 1911. Initially sailing under the flag of the Associated Oil Co., the tanker was twice renamed prior to her Navy service—first as *Colorado* and then as *Typhoon*. On 19 October 1943, the Navy acquired the ship under a bareboat charter from the Maritime Commission's War Shipping Administration.

Although the Navy approved the name *Villalobos* for this venerable acquisition on 3 November 1943, subsequent records continued to refer to her as *Typhoon*. The war diary entries for Escort Division (CortDiv) 16; CortDiv 10; Commander, Central Pacific; and Task Group (TG) 51.6 all call the ship *Typhoon* through October 1944—11 months after the ship was ostensibly renamed. Documentary evidence for this ship's career is fragmentary at best, but as far as can be determined, she entered the war under her civilian name.

In any case, the ship sailed for the Pacific and soon supported Operation "Galvanic," the invasion of the Gilbert Islands. She fueled escort and screening ships in December 1943 while anchored in the lagoon of recently secured Tarawa Atoll. She subsequently embarked service troops and was assigned to TG 51.7, the Northern Garrison Group, for Operation "Flintlock," the conquest of the Marshall Islands. In company with SS *Titan* and escorted by *Sederstrom* (DE–31), *Typhoon* supported the occupation of Kwajalein and Majuro and completed her tanker and transport duties for the conquest of the Marshalls by 8 February 1944.

Meanwhile, American planning for the recapture of Guam and the capture of Saipan had proceeded apace.

Typhoon took part in these operations from 27 Jul to 9 August 1944. With TG 51.6, *Typhoon* continued to serve double duty as both tanker and transport. She commenced unloading at Apra Harbor, Guam, on August and completed the task on the 6th.

The ship then served in the western Pacific for the remainder of August and through September. As an element of TG 31.5, *Typhoon* departed Ulithi on 2 October, bound for Eniwetok. For the rest of 1944, as American forces pressed relentlessly onward toward the Japanese homeland, she labored as station tanker in the Ulithi-Eniwetok area.

About this time, the name *Villalobos* finally caught up with the tanker. She was classified as IX–145 and commissioned. Attached to Service Squadron 9, Service Force, Pacific Fleet, she continued providing the "black gold" necessary for the smooth wartime operations of the Fleet.

Departing Hollandia, New Guinea, on 15 April 1945 the tanker proceeded for Mios Woendi, Padaido Group Netherlands East Indies, and made port there on the 18th. *Villalobos* remained at Mios Woendi through the late spring and into the early summer, providing lubricants and other petroleum products for merchantmen cargo vessels, and Australian corvettes—ships whose fuel requirements were light.

During the ship's sojourn at Mios Woendi, she received the welcome news that Germany had unconditionally surrendered. A little over three months later, on 15 August, the venerable tanker got underway for the Philippines as the war in the Pacific finally came to an end. Stopping at Morotai on 18 August, en route, she arrived at Zamboanga on 19 August, dropping anchor in Basilan Strait.

Villalobos remained anchored at Mindanao through November as station tanker, providing fuel for small American cargo and merchant vessels. Directed to proceed to Palawan, the ship—with Army tug *YT–15* in tow—got underway on 7 November and made port at Puerto Princessa on 9 November. She then headed to San Pedro Bay, Leyte, and delivered her charge upon arrival.

Villalobos next reported to the Ship Repair Base, Manicani Island, off Samar. Soon after her arrival, a board of inspection and repairs convened, looked over the ship, and recommended that she be retained only until no longer needed. After lying off Manicani Island from 1 to 17 December, *Villalobos* steamed to Subic Bay and commenced preparations for going out of service.

Villalobos was decommissioned on 16 February 1946 and struck from the Navy list 10 days later. On 31 August 1948 in Manila, the Maritime Commission transferred the tanker to the Maritime Petroleum Society and Navigation Co., Genoa, Italy, for mercantile service.

The ship—as *Typhoon*—received three battle stars for her World War II service.

Vim

(PG–99: dp. 980; l. 205′0″; b. 33′0″; dr. 11′; s. 16 k.; cpl. 109; a. (Br.) 1 4″, 1 2-pdr., 6 20mm., 1 dcp (hh.); cl. *Action*)

When the United States entered World War II at the end of 1941, the Navy found itself sadly deficient in ocean escort-type vessels. A crash building program was instituted; but, to meet more immediate needs, the government contracted with shipbuilding firms in England and Canada to build Flower-class corvettes. *Vim* (PG–99) was one of those British-type escorts. She was launched on 1 April 1943 at the Collingwood Shipyard in England. Nine days later, however, she was transferred to the United Kingdom under the terms of the lend-lease agreement in return for another Flower-class corvette then under construction in Canada. The British renamed her *Statice* (K.281), and she served

524

the Royal Navy under the name through World War II. On 21 June 1946, she was returned to the United States Navy. Though carried on the Navy list as PG–99, the corvette never saw active service with the United States Navy. She was sold on 7 May 1947. To whom she was sold and to what purpose she was put is unknown.

Vincennes

A city in Knox County, Ind., on the Wabash River, 55 miles south of Terre Haute. Vincennes was founded in 1731 or 1732 by soldier-explorer Francois Marie Bissot, Sieur de Vincennes, and was the site of old Fort Vincennes, captured twice during the American Revolution—in December 1778 and February 1779—by the Virginian, George Rogers Clark.

I

(SlpW: t. 700; lbp. 127′; b. 33′9″; dr. 16′6″; cpl. 80; a. 18 guns)

The first Vincennes—one of 10 sloops-of-war whose construction was authorized by Congress on 3 March 1825—was laid down at New York in 1825; launched on 27 April 1826; and commissioned on 27 August 1826, Master Commandant William Bolton Finch in command.

During her 41 years of service in both peace and war, Vincennes compiled an outstanding record of unprecedented achievements in polar exploration, global cartography, and commercial expansion and protection. Her career paralleled that of the young, expanding, and confident American nation and began with her departure from New York on 3 September 1826.

Accompanied by Commodore Jacob Jones' frigate *Brandywine, Vincennes* rounded Cape Horn and cruised in the Pacific protecting American merchantmen and whalers until June 1829, when she received orders which sent her first to the Society Islands, then to the Sandwich (now Hawaiian) chain, and ultimately to Macao, China, which she reached early in 1830. From Macao, she sailed to the Philippines and put into Manila on 29 January. She got underway again on 5 February; sailed across the Indian Ocean; and arrived at Capetown, South Africa, 56 days later. After a brief stop at St. Helena, *Vincennes* returned to New York on 8 June 1830 to become the first American naval vessel to circumnavigate the globe.

Master Commandant Finch wrote of a voyage around the world that "none is more trying to a ship's qualities, hull, rigging and spars, and only such vessel as is most perfect in every respect, ought to undertake it." Finch also corrected earlier surveys of the Pacific Basin, discovering two islands west of the Society group and actually sailing over the charted location of a third.

Vincennes was decommissioned at New York on 10 June 1830; underwent extensive repairs at New York; and was then ordered to take up station in the West Indies to protect American commerce from pirates, Comdr. Edward R. Shubrick in command. She anchored at Pensacola, Fla., on 31 March 1831; visited Cuba and Jamaica in May; but—after yellow fever had broken out on board—returned to Pensacola in July. The vessel remained at Pensacola for nearly a year while the disease ran its course, finally put into the Portsmouth (N.H.) Navy Yard on 29 July 1832 and was decommissioned there on 19 August 1832 for extensive overhaul.

Placed back in commission on 1 June 1833, Comdr. Alexander S. Wadsworth in command, *Vincennes* de-

USS *Vincennes* in Disappointment Bay, Antarctica, during the Wilkes exploring expedition. (NH83178)

parted Portsmouth that autumn for her second Pacific cruise. She rounded Cape Horn early in 1834 with orders to visit the Fiji and Palau Islands, China, and Sumatra and search for shipwrecked and stranded American seamen. Following a more southerly route westward from South America than that taken previously by any American vessel, *Vincennes* became the first American warship to call at Guam. She arrived at Singapore on 24 January 1836, passed through the Straits of Malacca, and called at Quallah Battu on the west coast of Sumatra on 15 February. Continuing westward, *Vincennes* provisioned and watered at Capetown and St. Helena, and stood into Hampton Roads, Va., on 5 June 1836 to complete her second circumnavigation of the globe.

Decommissioned on 18 June 1836, *Vincennes* remained in ordinary at Norfolk, Va., for two years while receiving a thorough overhaul. By now, she had acquired a reputation for sturdiness and fine handling under sail and was selected as flagship for Lt. Charles Wilkes' United States South Sea Surveying and Exploring Expedition to the Antarctic and South Pacific. Accordingly, a new light deck was added to the ship at this time to provide better accommodations and improved weather protection for scientists and crew.

The expeditionary force sailed from Hampton Roads on 18 August 1838 and arrived at Madeira on 16 September. Lt. Wilkes and the civilian scientists on board *Vincennes* explored the interior and ports of the island before sailing on 25 September for Porto Praya, Cape Verde Islands, and Rio de Janeiro, Brazil, where the squadron arrived on 23 November. Repairs to the vessels occupied the remainder of the year, delaying departure for Antarctica until 6 January 1839.

Vincennes rounded Cape Horn easily and anchored in Orange Bay, located on the southeast coast of Hardy Peninsula 45 miles northwest of the cape, the scheduled jumping off place for the Antarctic exploration. Here, she established an observatory and remained to conduct surveys and local exploration while Lt. Wilkes and most of the rest of the squadron sailed south to the ice barrier. Following Lt. Wilkes' return on 30 March, *Vincennes* prepared for the voyage north, sailed for the coast of Chile on 17 April, and arrived at Valparaiso on 15 May. The expedition again followed its usual pattern of activity when in port. The ships were repaired and provisioned while the scientists and some of the officers made explorations inland. On 6 June, the squadron sailed for Callao, Peru, and arrived there on 30 June to complete repairs which could not be made at Valparaiso. On 13 July, *Vincennes* headed west for the Tuamotu Archipelago and, on 13 August, landed at Minerva Island in the Low Archipelago.

During August and September, the squadron made extensive surveys and explorations through the Tuamotu Islands and at Tahiti, Society Islands, contacting local natives and amassing a wealth of information on the anthropology, geology, history, botany, and zoology of these islands. *Vincennes* sailed westward on 29 September, bound for Samoa, reached Tutuila on 11 October, and anchored at Upolu on 26 November. Here, Lt. Wilkes took into custody a native murderer of an American seaman and also concluded an agreement with native chiefs on regulations governing affairs with American merchantmen and whalers. He also made the first thorough survey of the Samoan group, constructing charts still of great use today for checking land measurements.

The squadron left Apia, Samoa, on 10 November and headed for Australia to prepare for a second voyage to the Antarctic. After stopping at several small islands for botanical outings, the vessels stood off Sydney on 26 December. Continuing southward, all hands hastily prepared the vessel for an extended encounter with sub-zero temperatures and rough seas.

Vincennes sighted her first icebergs on 10 January 1840 and, by the evening of the 11th, a compact barrier of ice blocked further progress, forcing the vessel to heave to for the night. In the morning, she sailed west-ward, following the barrier as closely as possible. On the 16th, *Vincennes*' officers all agreed that what lay to the south could only be land; and, continuing west, *Vincennes* discovered Piner's Bay on 30 January. Wilkes reported that from this bay he ". . . saw the land gradually rising beyond the ice to the height of three thousand feet . . . It could be seen extending to the east and west of our position fully sixty miles . . . and now that all were convinced of its existence, I gave the land the name of the Antarctic Continent."

Vincennes continued westward, attempting to land, but was prevented from doing so by ice floes and raging seas. Finding her way blocked by an immense wall of ice on 17 February, *Vincennes* set sail for Sydney and arrived there on 11 March to replenish her stores. The coast along which the American vessel sailed is today called Wilkesland, a name given it on German maps as early as 1841.

Vincennes left Sydney on 19 March, bound for the Bay of Islands, New Zealand, and arrived there on the 30th to the relief of the other squadron vessels anxiously awaiting her overdue appearance. The vessel spent the next six months surveying the Fiji Islands and put into Honolulu, Oahu, in the Sandwich Islands, on 23 September. Once again, the officers and scientists on board *Vincennes* surveyed and explored the islands, making special observations of the volcanoes on Hilo. During their stay in the Sandwich group, the entire crew was lavishly entertained by Hawaiian King Kamehameha III.

Vincennes concluded her Hawaiian visit with a period of repairs and provisioning at Honolulu from 18 March to 5 April 1841. On the latter day, she sailed for the mouth of the Columbia River in the present state of Washington. Arriving at Cape Disappointment on 28 April, the squadron prepared to enter the river but found it impossible to cross the formidable bar without a skilled pilot. Since none was available, *Vincennes* set her course for the Strait of Juan de Fuca, where she arrived on 1 May. After anchoring at Port Discovery the next day, the expedition conducted surveys in the Vancouver Island area until 11 May, when *Vincennes* anchored off Fort Nisqually. Following additional experiments on land and expeditions into the interior, *Vincennes* returned to the strait on 20 June, anchoring at New Dungeness Roads. Thorough surveys of the creeks and inlets of the bay continued until 3 August, when the vessel weighed anchor and sailed for the mouth of the Columbia, arriving on 6 August.

Vincennes was dispatched to San Francisco, Calif., on 8 August with orders to survey the Sacramento River while awaiting the arrival of the remainder of the squadron. She dropped anchor in San Francisco Bay off Sausalito on 14 August and commenced her investigations. The remainder of the squadron presented itself on 19 October and aided *Vincennes* in completing the survey. The ships sailed for Oahu on 1 November, anchoring at Honolulu on the 17th. *Vincennes* again put to sea on the 27th and sighted Wake Island on 19 December. This important trio of islets now includes one named for Wilkes, and another for his chief scientist, naturalist Titian Ramsay Peale. Continuing westward, the survey-vessel anchored in Manila Bay on 11 January 1842.

Vincennes stood out of Manila on 21 January, bound for the Strait of Mindoro. She anchored off the island of Sulu on 2 February and, after concluding a treaty with the reigning sultan, sailed on to visit and survey the various islands of the Sulu Sea. The vessel put into Singapore Roads on 19 February to take on water and supplies for the long, westward trip home. She left Singapore on 26 February and touched at Capetown on 13 April and St. Helena on 1 May before arriving off Sandy Hook, N.J., on 10 June 1842, almost four years after the beginning of the expedition.

Vincennes was next assigned to the Home Squadron and placed under the command of Comdr. Franklin Buchanan, a distinguished officer destined to become the first Superintendant of the Naval Academy. She sailed to the West Indies and cruised off the Mexican coast protecting American interests until the summer of 1844. Though this duty proved relatively uneventful, *Vincennes* did rescue two grounded English brigs off the coast of Texas and received the thanks of the British government for this service. Buchanan was also ordered to prevent any attempted invasion by Mexico of the new Republic of Texas. Fortunately, this eventuality never materialized; and *Vincennes* returned to Hampton Roads on 15 August to enter dry dock.

On 4 June 1845, *Vincennes* sailed for the Far East under command of Capt. Hiram Paulding. She was accompanied by the ship-of-the-line *Columbus*, under the command of Capt. Thomas Wyman; and the two vessels formed a little squadron under the command of Commodore James Biddle, who carried a letter from Secretary of State John C. Calhoun to Caleb Cushing, American commissioner in China, authorizing Cushing to make the first official contact with the Japanese Government.

The squadron sailed for Macao by way of Rio de Janeiro and the Cape of Good Hope. Commodore Biddle arrived safely in Macao only to find that Cushing had already left for home and that his successor, Alexander H. Everett, was too ill to make the trip. Therefore, Biddle determined to conduct the negotiations himself. Accordingly, *Vincennes* and *Columbus* sailed for Japan on 7 July 1846 and anchored off Edo (Tokyo) on 19 July. The Japanese surrounded the vessels and allowed no one to land. Otherwise the visitors were treated with courtesy. However, Commodore Biddle's attempts to discuss the opening of feudal Japan to foreign trade were politely rebuffed, and the vessels weighed anchor on 29 July. *Columbus* returned to the United States by way of Cape Horn, but *Vincennes* remained on the China Station for another year before returning to New York on 1 April 1847. Here, she was decommissioned on the 9th, dry-docked, and laid up.

Vincennes remained in ordinary until 1849. Recommissioned on 12 November 1849, she sailed from New York exactly one month later, bound for Cape Horn and the west coast of South America. On 2 July 1850, while lying off Guayaquil, Ecuador, she harbored the Ecuadoran revolutionary General Elizalde for three days during one of that country's frequent civil disturbances. Sailing on to San Francisco, the vessel lost 36 members of her crew to the gold fever sweeping California at the time. Turning south, *Vincennes* cruised off South America until late 1851, closely monitoring the activities of revolutionaries ashore. She made a courtesy call to the Hawaiian Islands at the end of the year and proceeded thence to Puget Sound where she arrived on 2 February 1852. She anchored briefly there and returned via San Francisco and the Horn to New York where she arrived on 21 September and was decommissioned on the 24th.

Following repairs and a period in ordinary, *Vincennes* was recommissioned on 21 March 1853 and sailed into Norfolk on 13 May to join her second exploratory expedition, serving as flagship to Comdr. Cadwalader Ringgold's survey of the China Seas, the North Pacific, and the Bering Strait. Comdr. Ringgold was a veteran of the Wilkes expedition. The squadron stood out of Norfolk on 11 June 1843, rounded the Cape of Good Hope, and charted numerous islands and shoals in the Indian Ocean before arriving in China in March 1854. Here Commodore Matthew Calbraith Perry relieved Ringgold for medical reasons and gave command of the expedition to Lt. John Rodgers. *Vincennes* sailed on to survey the Bonin and Ladrone Islands and returned to Hong Kong in February 1855. The expedition sailed again in March and surveyed the islands between the Ryukyu chain and Japan, and then the Kurils. *Vincennes* left the squadron at Petropavlovsk, Russia, and entered the Bering Strait, sailing through to the northwest towards Wrangel Island. Ice barriers prevented the vessel from reaching this destination, but she came closer than any other previous ship. *Vincennes* returned to San Francisco in early October

and later sailed for the Horn and New York, where she arrived on 13 July 1856 to complete yet another circumnavigation of the globe.

Decommissioned four days later, the ship was laid up more than a year before being reactivated on 3 November 1857. Assigned to the African Squadron, *Vincennes* patrolled along the coast of the "Dark Continent," doing hot, difficult, and exhausting duty in the suppression of the slave trade. She returned home in the spring of 1860, was decommissioned on 3 April, and placed in ordinary at the Boston Navy Yard.

After the outbreak of the Civil War in April 1861, *Vincennes* was recommissioned on 29 June and assigned to duty in the Gulf Blockading Squadron. She arrived off Fort Pickens, Fla., on 3 September, and was ordered to assist in the occupation of Head of Passes, Mississippi River, and remain there on blockade duty. Though the Federal warships did successfuly deploy, on 12 October 1861 the Confederate metal-sheathed ram CSS *Manassas* and armed steamers *Ivy* and *James L. Day* drove the Union blockaders from Head of Passes, forcing *Richmond* and *Vincennes* aground. *Vincennes* was ordered abandoned and destroyed to prevent her capture, and a slow match was set to the vessel's magazine while her men took refuge on other ships. However, the magazine failed to explode; and, after the Confederate vessels withdrew early in the afternoon, *Vincennes* was refloated.

After the Confederate attack, the Union sloop-of-war continued on blockade duty off the Passes of the Mississippi, capturing the blockade-running British bark *Empress*, aground at North East Pass with a large cargo of coffee on 27 November. On 4 March 1862, she was ordered to proceed to Pensacola, Fla., to relieve *Mississippi* and spent the next six months shuttling between Pensacola and Mobile, Ala., performing routine patrol and reconnaissance duty. On 4 October, she was ordered to assume command of the blockade off Ship Island, Miss., and to guard the pass out of Mississippi Sound. While so deployed, boat crews from the vessel and *Clifton* captured the barge *H. McGuin* in Bay St. Louis, Miss., on 18 July 1863. *Vincennes* also reported the capture of two boats laden with food on 24 December.

Vincennes remained off Ship Island for the duration of the war and was laid up in ordinary at the Boston Navy Yard on 28 August 1865. The veteran world traveler was sold at public auction at Boston on 5 October 1867.

II

(CA–44: dp. 9,400; l. 588'0''; b. 61'10''; dr. 18'8''; s. 32.7 k.; cpl. 952; a. 9 8'', 8 5'', 8 .50-cal. mg., 2 3-pdrs, ac. 4; cl. *New Orleans*)

Vincennes (CA–44) was laid down on 2 January 1934 at Quincy, Mass., by the Bethlehem Shipbuilding Company's Fore River plant; launched on 21 May 1936; sponsored by Miss Harriet Virginia Kimmell, daughter of the mayor of Vincennes, Ind.; and commissioned on 24 February 1937, Capt. Burton H. Green in command.

The new heavy cruiser departed from Boston on 19 April 1937 for her shakedown cruise which took her to Stockholm, Sweden; Helsingfors (Helsinki), Finland; Le Havre, France; and Portsmouth, England.

Early in January 1938, *Vincennes* was assigned to Cruiser Division (CruDiv) 7, Scouting Force, and steamed through the Panama Canal to San Diego. In March, the ship participated in Fleet Problem XIX in the Hawaiian area before returning to San Pedro for operations off the west coast for the remainder of the year.

Following an overhaul at the Mare Island Navy Yard, Vallejo, Calif., which lasted through April 1939, the cruiser returned east; transited the Panama Canal on 6 June in company with *Quincy* (CA–39), *Tuscaloosa* (CA–37), and *San Francisco* (CA–38); and

527

anchored in Hampton Roads on the 13th. For the next two months, she operated out of Norfolk in the vicinity of the Chesapeake lightship and the southern drill grounds. On 1 September 1939—the day on which Hitler's legions marched into Poland and commenced hostilities in Europe—*Vincennes* lay at anchor off Tompkinsville, N.Y. She then began conducting Neutrality Patrols off the east coast, ranging into the Caribbean Sea and the Gulf of Yucatan, and continued these duties through the spring of 1940.

Late in May, as German troops were smashing Allied defenses in France, *Vincennes* steamed to the Azores and visited Ponta Delgada from 4 to 6 June 1940 before she proceeded on for French Morocco to load a shipment of gold for transport to the United States. While at anchor at Casablanca, the ship received word of Italy's declaration of war upon France—the "stab in the back" condemned by President Roosevelt soon thereafter. *Vincennes'* commanding officer, Capt. J. R. Beardall (later to become Naval Aide to the President), noted subsequently in his official report of the cruise that "it was apparent that the French bitterly resented this [the declaration of war] and despised Italy for her actions." After departing North African waters on 10 June, the cruiser returned to the United States to offload her precious metallic cargo and return to the drudgery of Neutrality Patrols.

Overhauling at Portsmouth Navy Yard, Norfolk, Va., into the first week of January 1941, *Vincennes* departed Hampton Roads on 7 January—in company with *Wichita* (CA–45), *New York* (BB–34), and *Texas* (BB–35)—bound for Guantanamo Bay, Cuba. Operating once again in the Caribbean, the heavy cruiser fired battle practice and gunnery exercises in company with *Wichita* through 18 January, when the two cruisers proceeded for Portland Bight, Jamaica, British West Indies. Conducting Neutrality Patrols from this port, *Vincennes* patrolled in company with other ships safeguarding neutral waters and America's recently acquired Caribbean bases.

Vincennes joined other Fleet units for landing exercises at Culebra, Puerto Rico, on 4 February 1941 and sent her 50-foot boats to assist in unloading and troop debarkation drills. She assisted *McCawley* (AP–10) and *Wharton* (AP–7) in landing men and material before taking station with Fire Support Group II. The cruiser then fired simulated gunfire support operations with her main and secondary batteries in exercises which foreshadowed her future combat role in the South Pacific.

For the remainder of February, the ship continued her landing support operations with Transport Divisions 2 and 7, anchoring on occasion at Mayaguez or Guayanilla, Puerto Rico. Conducting operations out of Puerto Rican waters, *Vincennes* called at Pernambuco, Brazil, on 17 March and got underway for Capetown, South Africa, on the 20th. Arriving to a warm welcome nine days later, the ship took on a large shipment of gold bullion to pay for arms purchased in the United States by the United Kingdom and then headed home on the 30th. En route to New York, she conducted exercises. After a brief post-voyage period of repairs, the heavy cruiser sailed for the Virginia capes, where she rendezvoused with *Ranger* (CV–4) and *Sampson* (DD–394); proceeded on to Bermuda; and dropped anchor in Grassy Bay on 30 April. She patrolled in the Caribbean and off the Atlantic coast of the United States through June. On occasion, she steamed in company with such ships as *Yorktown* (CV–5), *Augusta* (CA–31), *Ranger*, *Wichita*, or *Tuscaloosa*.

After continuing her duties with the Neutrality Patrol into the autumn as American naval forces in the North Atlantic found themselves engaged in a *de facto* war with Germany, *Vincennes* undertook another mission to South African waters. She left the east coast late in November with Convoy WS–12, American transports carrying British troops. On 7 December 1941, the cruiser fought its way through heavy seas.

Walls of water mercilessly pounded the ships of the convoy; and waves battered *Vincennes*, smashing a motor whaleboat to matchwood and ripping a Curtiss SOC Seagull floatplane from its "moorings" on the storm-lashed well-deck amidships. The plane was battered against the catapult silos and into the hangar doors before it was swept over the ship's side. By that evening, however, the ship learned that she was not only at war with the elements but with Japan as well. Japanese naval air forces had struck Pearl Harbor and plunged the United States into war.

After having safely convoyed her charges to Capetown, where she arrived on 9 December, *Vincennes* departed South African waters on the 16th, bound via Trinidad for Hampton Roads. Following her arrival at Norfolk on 4 January 1942, she shifted to New York four days later to be outfitted for war. Late in the month, she joined *Hornet* (CV–8) as the carrier conducted her shakedown training off the east coast of the United States.

Vincennes sailed from New York on 4 March, bound for the Pacific. She transited the Panama Canal on 11 March and proceeded via San Diego to San Francisco.

The heavy cruiser—now a part of Task Force (TF) 18, built around *Hornet*—departed San Francisco on 2 April. The carrier bore a strange deck cargo, 16 Army B–25 medium bombers slated to strike at Japan's heart. *Vincennes* rendezvoused with TF 16, built around *Enterprise* (CV–6) and, with the combined might of the two task forces, struck out westward across the Pacific, headed toward Japanese home waters.

On the morning of 18 April, when the American warships were still some 150 miles from the planned launch point, an unexpected hitch developed. Japanese trawlers sighted and reported the task force. Vice Admiral Halsey decided to fly off the bombers immediately. Accordingly, all 16 of the heavily loaded B–25's—laden with bombs and extra fuel—rose from *Hornet*'s spray-slicked flight deck and climbed unsteadily into the leaden gray skies. Although the daring raid inflicted only minimal materiel damage upon the Japanese homeland, it nevertheless packed a powerful morale-building "punch." When queried as to the base from whence the bombers had come, President Roosevelt said "from Shangri-La."

The combined *Enterprise* and *Hornet* task force retired eastward and made Pearl Harbor on 25 April. Departing again five days later, the ships, still screened by *Vincennes*, bent on speed toward the Coral Sea. However, they were too late to take part in the pivotal action which took place early in May in that beautiful body of water as planes from *Yorktown* (CV–5) and *Lexington* (CV–2) blunted the Japanese thrust toward strategic Port Moresby.

Vincennes' task force returned to Pearl Harbor on 26 May but got underway again on the 29th, bound for waters off Midway Island, which—according to American intelligence reports—a Japanese invasion force was approaching.

By 4 June, the heavy cruiser and her sister ship, *Astoria* (CA–34), were steaming north of Midway streamer of smoke before splashing into the sea.

At 1640, after American air attacks had crippled three of the four Japanese carriers, a group of torpedo planes—"Kates"—from Japanese carrier *Hiryu* approached from the north. TF 17's radar soon picked them up when 15 miles out, and *Yorktown* launched planes to intercept as her screen deployed to bring an optimum concentration of antiaircraft fire to bear upon the approaching enemy. Three minutes after the first plane was spotted, combat air patrol F4F Wildcats from the carrier splashed one "Kate." The Japanese torpedo plane spiraled from the sky trailing a long streamer of smoke before crashing into the sea.

Vincennes opened fire at 1644 with her 5-inch, 20-millimeter, and 1.1-inch antiaircraft batteries on the "Kates" approaching from the port side. Increasing her speed to 25 knots and slowly turning to starboard,

Vincennes kept her port guns trained on the enemy. While combing torpedo tracks, *Vincennes* bagged a "Kate" and sent it splashing into the sea 150 yards off her port bow.

The sharp, bitter action ended as quickly as it had begun. The Japanese had been driven off, but at a high cost for the Americans. *Yorktown*, mortally hit and listing to port, slowed to a halt, with smoke billowing from her wounded vitals. *Vincennes* altered course to follow *Astoria*'s movements around the carrier, screening the stricken warship from further air attacks. However, on 6 June, Japanese submarine *I-168* slipped through a screen of six destroyers and torpedoed *Yorktown* and destroyer *Hammann* (DD-412), sinking the latter. The carrier went down early on the 7th.

Returning to Pearl Harbor, *Vincennes* entered the navy yard for repairs and alterations which lasted until early July. She then conducted tactical exercises off the island of Hawaii with other ships of TF 11 before departing Hawaiian waters on 14 July to rendezvous with TF's 16, 18, and 62.

Screening for transport squadron "X-ray," slated to participate in the Guadalcanal landings, *Vincennes*, in company with *San Juan* (CL-54) and *Quincy*, joined TF 62 on 26 July. On the 27th, the cruiser conducted approach exercises for landing practice and simulated bombardment drills off Koro Island in the Fiji group. As flagship for Task Group (TG) 62.3, *Vincennes* remained on station in the covering force in the transport area before undertaking further approach and landing exercise support drills.

Following refueling and revictualing, the heavy cruiser formed up with the American armada making its way to the Solomons. *Vincennes*, screening transport division "Yoke," arrived off Guadalcanal on 7 August. At daybreak, beneath overcast skies, the ship catapulted her spotting planes and then unlimbered her main and secondary batteries to commence shore bombardment. While the thunder of the supporting ships' gunfire reverberated across the waters, marines disembarked from their landing craft and stormed ashore to meet initially light resistance on the island.

Shortly after 1320, Japanese planes launched a counterstrike. To sunward of the transports, *Vincennes* found herself in a favorable position to combat the attack and tracked the opposing planes—being among the first ships to open fire on the attackers. Forced to jettison their deadly loads prematurely, the Japanese retired without doing any damage; but not before *Vincennes* had bagged two of them. After sunset, *Vincennes*, *Quincy*, and *Astoria*—in company with *Helm* (DD-388) and *Jarvis* (DD-393)—retired to conduct screening patrols.

Returning to her covering duties at daylight, *Vincennes* arrived at transport area "X-ray," off Guadalcanal by daybreak. Two minutes before noon, Japanese bombers, intent on avenging their losses of the day before and disrupting the American landing, swooped down from Rabaul. Twenty-seven Mitsubishi G4M "Betty" bombers swept in, in a low-level torpedo attack, and ran a gauntlet of gunfire from the transports and their escorting cruisers and destroyers. Three thousand yards from the transports, *Vincennes*, as in the previous day's action, was again in favorable firing position and opened up with every gun in her battery, from 8-inch to 20-millimeter, that could bear on the attackers.

During the ensuing melee, the cruiser used her main-battery, 8-inch guns effectively, helping to down at least seven "Betties" which flew at an altitude of even 25 to 50 feet. The shell splashes from the main battery caused Japanese pilots to fly into walls of water or forced them to drastically alter their approaches. *Vincennes* dodged one torpedo which passed beneath her stern and evaded a bomb which fell off her port quarter. Unluckily, *Jarvis*, adjacent to the cruiser, took one torpedo hit which ultimately proved fatal to the ship.

Later, during the afternoon hours, aerial reconnaissance reported a Japanese surface force coming down from the base at Rabaul. These flights noted what was thought to be three Japanese cruisers, three destroyers, and two gunboats or seaplane tenders steaming south. While *Jarvis* limped away from Lunga Point, *Vincennes* and her sisters *Quincy* and *Astoria* steamed, as the northern escort force, to a position off Savo Island to screen the vulnerable transports which were still unloading off the invasion beaches. Capt. Frederick L. Riefkohl of *Vincennes* assumed that the enemy ships reportedly en route from Rabaul were going to launch and support another air attack early the following morning. He accordingly shaped night orders to be especially vigilant during the midwatch and fully expected an air attack at daybreak.

At about midnight on 8 August, Riefkohl retired to his sea cabin, adjacent to the pilothouse, after having been on the bridge continuously since 0445 that morning. Turning in at 0050 on 9 August, he left his ship in the hands of the executive officer, Comdr. W.E.A. Mullan.

Nearly an hour later, at about 0145, lookouts spotted flares and star shell to the southward, accompanied by the low rumble of gunfire. The sound of the general quarters alarm soon rang throughout the ship and stirred her to action. *Vincennes*' lookouts were seeing the elimination of the southern escort group, based around Australian heavy cruiser *Canberra* and *Chicago* (CA-29). Unbeknownst to the men manning the ships to the northward, a powerful enemy force was heading in their direction. Six cruisers and one destroyer under the command of Japanese Vice Admiral Gunichi Mikawa had turned north and were steaming directly towards *Vincennes* and her two sisters.

The first Japanese searchlight beams picked out *Vincennes*' splotchy camouflage shortly after 0155, and the American cruiser opened fire with her main battery turrets to shoot out the troublesome light. Within a minute, however, Japanese shells bracketed the ship; and *Vincennes* shuddered under the impact of the hail of steel screaming in from the ebony sky. Bridge, carpenter shop, "battle II," and radio antenna trunks all were hit in the first salvo.

Altering course to port, Riefkohl—who had leapt to the bridge at the alarm—rang down for increased speed; but, in the deafening din of battle, and with his ship and internal communications disrupted, it is doubtful that the order was received. Still moving at 19.5 knots, the heavy cruiser reeled under the impact of another group of direct hits.

Some of the shells in this group set afire the volatile planes in *Vincennes*' hangar space, and the resultant flames defied all attempts to put them out. A direct hit knocked the after antiaircraft director overboard. At 0200, *Vincennes* heeled to starboard in an attempt to evade the accurate enemy fire; but the probing Japanese gunners were not about to let the already sorely wounded ship escape. One or two "long lance" torpedoes then ripped into the ship's number 1 fireroom and put it out of action.

Losing steering control five minutes later, *Vincennes* was dead in the water within minutes. Rapidly hitting shells quickly reduced the ship's gunpower to a fraction of its original strength and before long snuffed it out entirely. Like a pummelled and reeling challenger in the boxing ring, *Vincennes* wallowed to a halt. Hit at least 57 times by 8- and 5-inch shells, the ship gradually assumed a more alarming list.

As if mercifully, at 0210, the Japanese ceased fire and retired, leaving Savo Island and the burning hulks of the three American cruisers of the northern force in their wakes. As *Vincennes*' list increased to port, Riefkohl circulated the command to abandon ship at 0230. Serviceable life jackets and rafts were broken out, and the crew began the sad task of abandoning ship. At 0240, the captain went down to the main deck and joined the last men to leave the sinking cruiser and jumped into the tepid waters of Savo Sound.

Riefkohl subsequently wrote a fitting epitaph: "The Magnificent *Vincennes*, which we were all so proud of, and which I had the honor to command since 23 April 1941, rolled over and then sank at about 0250, 9 August 1942, about 2½ miles east of Savo Island . . . Solomons Group, in some 500 fathoms of water."

Struck from the Navy list on 2 November 1942, *Vincennes* was awarded two battle stars for her participation in the Battle of Midway and the invasion of Guadalcanal.

III

(CL–64: dp. 10,000; l. 610'1''; b. 66'6''; dr. 20'0''; s. 33 k.; cpl. 992; a. 12 6'', 12 5'', 24 40mm., 21 20mm.; cl. *Cleveland*)

The third *Vincennes* (CL–64) was originally laid down as *Flint* (CL–64) on 7 March 1942 at Quincy, Mass., by the Bethlehem Shipbuilding Company's Fore River plant. While the ship was under construction, however, the Battle of Savo Island occurred in August 1942, during which engagement the heavy cruiser *Vincennes* (CA–44) had been sunk. In order to perpetuate the name, *Flint* was renamed *Vincennes* on 16 October 1942. Launched on 17 July 1943, *Vincennes* was sponsored by Mrs. Arthur A. Osborn, the former Miss Harriet V. Kimmell, who had sponsored the first cruiser of the name.

Commissioned on 21 January 1944, Capt. Arthur D. Brown in command, *Vincennes* fitted-out at her builders' yard into late February, undergoing her sea trials soon thereafter. From 25 February to the last day of March, *Vincennes* sailed to the British West Indies and back on her shakedown cruise. With brief stopovers in the Chesapeake Bay region, the new light cruiser "shook down" principally in the Gulf of Paria, near Trinidad.

After post-shakedown repairs and alterations, *Vincennes* became the flagship for Commander, Cruiser Division (CruDiv) 14, Rear Admiral Wilder D. Baker, who embarked in the light cruiser on 14 April with members of his staff. Other ships in the division included *Miami* (CL–89) and *Houston* (CL–81)—the latter perpetuating, like *Vincennes*, the name of a man-of-war lost earlier in action with Japanese surface units.

Departing Boston on 16 April, *Vincennes* subsequently transited the Panama Canal and ultimately reached Pearl Harbor, Territory of Hawaii, on 6 May. For the next week, the ship engaged in intensive training in the Hawaiian operating area. During one of the ship's in-port periods that interspersed the at-sea training evolutions, Admiral Chester W. Nimitz came on board *Vincennes* and presented her embarked flag officer with a Navy Cross—won for directing bombardment operations in the Aleutians.

With the shakedown and training phases of her career behind her, the sleek light cruiser put to sea on 24 May and left Pearl Harbor in her wake. After conducting exercises en route, *Vincennes* reached Majuro, in the Marshall Islands, six days later. A week later, she left Majuro as part of the mighty armada known as Task Force (TF) 58. At the helm of that powerful striking force, based around the fast carriers of the Fleet, was Vice Admiral Marc A. Mitscher.

Subsequently, *Vincennes* made her initial contact with the enemy. During the first strikes on the Bonins, Japanese aircraft in retaliatory raids went after the TF 58 flattops. *Vincennes*, in the screen, downed a "Betty"

The light cruiser *Vincennes* (CL–64), August, 1945, in the two-tone camouflage finish prevalent in the Pacific Fleet at that time. She is typical of the war-built *Cleveland*-class with the enlarged bridge of the later ships of this class. (80–G–38914)

bomber on 10 June. Her guns had drawn their first blood of the war. It would not be the last time.

In the days that ensued, *Vincennes* supported the carriers as they launched aircraft to smash Japanese positions on Saipan and Pagan Islands on 12 and 13 June. On the 16th, she was part of the group that conducted the first air strikes on Iwo Jima—an isle later to be remembered by many sailors and marines. During the key Battle of the Philippine Sea, *Vincennes'* gunners performed their tasks well, aiding materially in the barrage of gunfire that broke up several of the enemy's nevertheless persistent attacks.

On 23 June, Rear Admiral Baker shifted his flag to *Vincennes'* sistership *Miami*, releasing the erstwhile flagship to proceed to Eniwetok, in the Marshalls, for needed engineering repairs. Dropping anchor at Eniwetok on the 27th, *Vincennes* completed her repairs by the end of the month; she subsequently sailed to rejoin CruDiv 14, and Rear Admiral Baker broke his flag in the ship again on 7 July.

Departing Eniwetok on 14 July, *Vincennes* operated with TF 58 in the vicinity of Guam while the planes from the fast carriers conducted strikes on Japanese positions there from 18 to 21 July. She took part in further fast carrier task group strikes on Tinian, Rota, and Guam, through the 27th of the month. After continuing her support evolutions with the fast flattops, *Vincennes* headed for the Marianas, dropping her hook at Saipan on the last day of July.

Departing Saipan on 1 August, *Vincennes* resumed her operations with the carriers, making a high-speed run to the Bonins where planes from the carriers carried out air strikes on the 4th and 5th before retiring. The cruiser subsequently put into Eniwetok to replenish, anchoring there on the 11th, where Rear Admiral F. E. M. Whiting relieved Admiral Baker eight days later, breaking his flag at *Vincennes'* main on that day.

Assigned next to TF 34, *Vincennes* departed Eniwetok at the end of August and conducted tactical and gunnery exercises until joining TG 38.2 on 3 September. Early that month, the task group conducted strikes on Japanese positions in the Palau Islands on 6 September. The next day, 7 September, *Vincennes*, as part of Task Unit (TU) 38.2.5, under Rear Admiral Whiting, embarked on board, conducted the first shore bombardment on Japanese installations on Ngesebus, Peleliu, and Angaur Islands, the ship's captain subsequently recording that the coverage of the areas shelled was "excellent."

The operations against the Palaus, however, turned out to be only a curtain-raiser for the show to come— the recapture of the Philippines. *Vincennes* left the Palau group astern on 8 September for the southern Philippines. American carrier planes hit targets on the island of Mindanao on 9 and 10 September; the cruiser then screened the fast carriers as they conducted air strikes in the central Philippine Archipelago, hitting Negros, Leyte, Cebu, and the Bohol Islands from 12 to 14 September. *Vincennes* then proceeded to the operating areas off Luzon where carrier air strikes were launched against Japanese sites ashore on 21 and 22 September. The slate of air operations resumed again within a few days, *Vincennes* screening the flattops as their planes struck Leyte, Cebu, and Negros.

Vincennes left the operating areas soon thereafter, however, to replenish in the Carolines, reaching Ulithi on 1 October. Her stay in port was interrupted, however, by the presence of a typhoon in the vicinity. The light cruiser sortied for typhoon-evasion purposes on the 3d, returning to port two days later. Resuming and completing the replenishment chores at Ulithi, *Vincennes* subsequently weighed anchor on the 6th of October with TF 38.

Vincennes operated off Okinawa in the ensuing days, reaching the waters off that isle on 10 October. Planes from the carriers in the task groups conducted the first air strikes in that area while the ships in the screen stood poised for retaliation from shore. Many enemy planes closed the carriers and their escorting battleships, cruisers, destroyers, and destroyer escorts—most to no avail. Friendly fighters on combat air patrol (CAP) duties overhead proved invaluable, knocking down many enemy aircraft that ventured too close. Included in the bag were a "Betty" and a "Frances." The enemy knew no set time to attack—*Vincennes* observed a "Betty" being shot down within sight of the ship during the task force's fueling-at-sea evolutions the next day.

Vincennes and her sisters next shaped course for Formosa, as the fast carriers shifted their operating area to prepare the way for the upcoming onslaught against the Japanese-occupied Philippine Islands. En route to Formosa, Japanese planes frequently showed themselves, but maddeningly stayed out of range—persistent and pugnacious snoopers that always managed to slip away untouched.

On 12 October, the carriers began launching air strikes against Formosan sites; that afternoon, the task group gunners proved exceptional, downing a pair of "Betties" that ventured too close. *Vincennes* went to general quarters at 1855 on that day and remained at battle stations almost continuously for the next two days. At 1903, soon after the ship had manned her battle stations, *Vincennes* contributed to the flaming of two planes within 10 minutes time—one at 1903 and one at 1910. The cruiser maintained a steady rate of fire throughout the air attack that continued intermittently until 2045.

The strikes ceased at that point, but the respite provided the Americans proved only temporary—the determined Japanese came back again. Flares dropped from "snoopers" illuminated the entire task group, bathing the ships in an eerie light. Antiaircraft fire crisscrossed the night; one enemy plane tumbled in flames from the sky; *Vincennes* splashed another off her starboard quarter at 2340.

The operations in the vicinity of Formosa proved dangerous, to say the least. The persistent Japanese attacks had taken their toll: the light cruiser *Houston* and the heavy cruiser *Canberra* (CA–70) had taken torpedoes and were badly damaged, limping out of the battle zone. To protect their flight, "Cripple Division One" was formed. Put together on 16 October, the force served its purpose; *Vincennes* participated in the withdrawal, screening her crippled sistership and division mate, and *Canberra*.

Vincennes then operated in the vicinity of Visayas, in the Philippines, screening, as before, the fast carriers. Enemy snoopers closed the formation on several occasions; detected early on the 24th, a Japanese four-engined flying boat—an "Emily"—went down in flames to the guns of friendly fighters.

Meanwhile, the Battle for Leyte Gulf was shaping up. At 0325 on the 24th, *Vincennes* received reports of the presence of an enemy force. Four battleships, eight heavy cruisers, and 13 destroyers had been detected seven miles south of Buruncan Point, Mindanao Island. Enemy planes commenced a determined air attack; all ships in *Vincennes'* group maneuvered radically to avoid possible torpedoes.

At 0230 on the 25th, two enemy task groups were reported about 85 miles north of *Vincennes'* formation. At 0300, the light cruiser and her consorts headed north to engage; at 0733, an intercepted report from a search plane told of many enemy surface ships about 120 miles north and headed south at 20 knots. Aircraft from the fast carriers launched and took off on the hunt, conducting persistent strikes on the Japanese ships that resulted in heavy enemy losses.

Vincennes subsequently headed south toward the San Bernardino Strait in anticipation of making contact with the enemy ships, including stragglers, that were expected to transit the strait in retiring from the day's operations.

At 0026, *Vincennes'* radar plot disclosed a surface contact at a distance of 21,000 yards. *Vincennes*, *Miami*, and *Biloxi* (CL–80), escorted by Destroyer Division 103,

531

broke from the formation to attack. At 0054, gunflashes from *Vincennes* and her sisters' main battery split the night; both main and secondary batteries—6- and 5-inch guns—in company with the 5-inch guns of the destroyers, hurled salvoes at the enemy vessel. The vessel—tentatively identified as a cruiser—sank beneath the waves at 0149 as a result of the deluge of rapid shellfire.

Vincennes returned to former cruising grounds off Visayas on 28 October and off Luzon the following day. The ship experienced several determined air attacks on the 29th, but the CAP proved ready to accept the enemy's challenges, downing eight Japanese planes during the course of the raids.

Vincennes continued her vital screening duties on 5 and 6 November as carrier planes carried out strikes on Japanese positions and installations on Luzon. She then headed for the Carolines, reaching Ulithi on 9 November and dropping anchor. Replenishment completed, she stood out five days later to return to the combat zone in the Philippines.

By the time she returned, air strikes against Japanese positions on Luzon were well underway; enemy resistance—now taking on a fiercer aspect with more widespread use of the "kamikaze," proved heavy once more, several persistent air attacks occurring on the ships with which *Vincennes* was operating. *Hancock* (CV–19), *Intrepid* (CV–11), and *Cabot* (CVL–28) all took kamikazes. *Vincennes* blasted a second kamikaze heading for *Cabot*; others that managed to get by the CAP were taken under fire as well.

Subsequently, *Vincennes* returned to Ulithi for further replenishment and conducted exercises en route back to the battle zones. *Vincennes* then operated in support of carrier air strikes on Luzon on the 14th through 16th of December; during that time, *Vincennes'* senior aviator, Lt. Halbert K. Evans, led a rescue mission of cruiser-based floatplanes and performed such sterling service that he was later awarded the Air Medal.

Neptune's fury soon interrupted the unfolding pressure against the Japanese, however, when a typhoon swirled through the fleet on the 18th. The severe tropical storm generated gusts of wind up to 78 knots, whipping up mountainous seas. Fortunately for *Vincennes*, she was able to weather the storm without serious damage. After the storm had subsided, all available ships searched for the survivors of the three destroyers, *Spence* (DD–512), *Monaghan* (DD–354), and *Hull* (DD–350), which had tragically capsized in the typhoon.

After a Christmas respite at Ulithi from 24 to 30 December, *Vincennes* returned to the waters off Formosa, again screening the flattops. She subsequently entered the South China Sea in early January, encountering only two small enemy raids; night fighters ("friendlies") downed two enemy planes early on the morning of 10 January 1945.

Assigned areas east of Camranh Bay, Indochina, the task group to which *Vincennes* was attached conducted air strikes on shipping in that vicinity before proceeding west of Formosa for further strikes on that already-pounded isle, as well as the coast of China. Enemy air resistance, as before, proved heavy.

During subsequent attacks on Formosa, Japanese planes struck back. One pushed over into a steep dive shortly after noon on 21 January; as she screamed down at her target, *Vincennes* commenced firing at her. At 1209, the determined kamikaze plunged into *Ticonderoga* (CV–14). Fires soon broke out; the carrier began trailing a tell-tale plume of black smoke. She had been hit hard.

While ships rushed to *Ticonderoga*'s aid, the formation resumed a lookout for the determined Japanese. At 1246, *Vincennes* fired on enemy aircraft in the vicinity; three minutes later, the light cruiser teamed with *Miami* to blast a kamikaze from the sky and into the sea. The barrage of antiaircraft fire, however,

could not stop a second suicider which plunged into *Ticonderoga* at 1255.

After supporting strikes against Japanese positions on Okinawa, *Vincennes* returned to Ultihi for replenishment, reaching that place of rest on 26 January. Leaving the Carolines in her wake subsequently, the light cruiser departed Ulithi on 10 February, joining TG 58.1 that evening. During scheduled gunnery exercises, a radio control target drone crashed into the splinter shield of one of *Vincennes'* 40-millimeter mounts, bursting into flame. With utter disregard for their own safety, four sailors, Chief Boatswain's Mate Mack C. Miller, USN; Gunner's Mate 3d Class Carl C. Miller, USNR; Gunner's Mate 3d Class Buck E. Goebel, USNR; and Seaman 1st Class Paul G. Catarius, USNR, entered the mount and threw smoldering debris, as well as damaged and overheated ammunition over the side, thus preventing further damage. For their meritorious conduct, each man received commendation ribbons subsequently.

Repairing the superficial damage in the wake of the drone accident, *Vincennes* continued with TG 58.1 as it headed toward the Japanese home islands. Operating southeast of Honshu, the fast carriers conducted strikes on the Tokyo area and the southern Bonin Islands. The first carrier strikes conducted by the fast carrier planes hit Tokyo on the 16th; strikes that continued the following day, stepping up the pace of the war and carrying it to the Empire's veritable doorstep.

Over the days that ensued, carrier planes hit not only targets in Japan but on Chichi Jima, hitting Japanese airfields. More strikes against Tokyo itself took place on 25 February.

Four days later, the carriers launched their planes to hit Okinawa. On 1 March, *Vincennes*, *Miami*, *San Diego* (CL–53), and Destroyer Squadron 61, with Rear Admiral Whiting in *Vincennes* as unit commander, sailed for Okino Daito Shima and shelled Japanese installations there starting large fires ashore. For directing the successful bombardment mission, Rear Admiral Whiting was awarded the Bronze Star.

The following fortnight for *Vincennes* was spent primarily in operational training and replenishment away from the forward operating areas. Complete release from combat tensions was not enjoyed, however, for kamikazes struck Ulithi on 11 March, one crashing into the new carrier *Randolph* (CV–15) only three miles distant, and another crashing ashore.

Returning to the battle zone within a week's time, *Vincennes* steamed with TG 58.1 as it headed for Kyushu. After American carrier-based planes had hit Japanese installations on Kyushu, determined enemy attacks on the formation kept *Vincennes'* gunnery department busy on the 18th. A twin-engined bomber flew over the ship at 0506 on that day, at an altitude of 300 feet. The ship's gunfire scored hits on that enemy aircraft, as well as another one that crashed into the sea 3,000 yards astern, just 20 minutes later. At 0601, *Vincennes'* gunners scored again, splashing a Japanese plane close to *Wasp* (CV–18).

Firing at enemy aircraft continued at intervals throughout the balance of 18 and 19 March, with *Vincennes* contributing an outstanding performance; her antiaircraft fire control officer, 1st Lieutenant Henry M. Lamberton, USMCR, received a Bronze Star for his direction of that battery.

Vincennes operated east of Okinawa from 23 March through the 25th, while carriers in TG 58.1 sent off their planes to conduct air strikes against the Japanese on Okinawa. Two days later, the ship resumed operations east and southeast of the island earmarked for invasion and continued such operations through 5 April. On 31 March, two of *Vincennes'* floatplanes cooperated in rescuing a downed fighter pilot in spite of heavy enemy fire; Lt. Evans, commended earlier, received the Distingiushed Flying Cross, while Lt. (jg.) George A. Greenwood, USNR, and the two rear-seat men all received Air Medals.

On 1 April, the day of the initial assault on Okinawa, enemy air attacks came thick and fast. Ships of TG 58.1 smashed 12 enemy planes into the sea; *Vincennes* drew three assists in the action. At 1321, the ship experienced her narrowest escape in the war; an enemy aircraft, hit by the ship's gunfire, crashed only 50 feet astern.

Subsequently, *Vincennes* operated in various groups of Task Force 58 off Okinawa, supporting the fast carriers as they hit Okinawa and Kyushu. Frequent and persistent air attacks characterized the three weeks commencing on 7 April, while the invasion of Okinawa proceeded apace. CAP fighters shot down many of the attackers, but sometimes the attacks came in such force that ships in the formation would have to lay down barrages of antiaircraft fire to greet the enemy aircraft that had fought their way through the friendly fighters.

After another replenishment period at Ulithi, *Vincennes* rejoined the forces off Okinawa, remaining with TG 58.1. The light cruiser performed screening duties for the fast carriers as they hit Kyushu before being ordered to report for duty with the shore bombardment forces off Okinawa on 17 May. In company with sister-ship *Vicksburg* (CL–86), *Vincennes* complied and, for 27 of the next 30 days, shelled Japanese targets ashore, both day and night.

Vincennes' 6-inch guns fired 5,836 rounds; her 5-inch batteries contributed another 10,583 rounds to the shellings. Air spotters and shore fire control spotters recorded the effectiveness of the ship's fire in their subsequent reports: she destroyed a large "disappearing coastal gun" and concentrations of troops; direct hits were scored on mortar positions; destroyed nine gun emplacements; destroyed an ammunition dump with a direct hit; destroyed coastal batteries; and closed off the entrances to at least five caves. Her airmen proved a busy lot, Lt. Evans earning a gold star in lieu of his second DFC and Lt. (jg.) Greenwood earning a DFC; each man flew 10 spotting missions.

Vincennes fired her final salvoes on 16 June and then headed for the United States for a much-needed overhaul. Sailing via Pearl Harbor, *Vincennes* reached Mare Island Navy Yard on 8 July and remained there until the availability was completed in late August.

During that time, the war in the Pacific had drawn to a close with a battered but defiant Japan surrendering in mid-August. After her post-repair trials, *Vincennes* had shifted to San Diego on 29 August to commence her post-repair shakedown and refresher training in the waters off San Clemente Island.

Vincennes then participated in Operation "Magic Carpet" following her refresher training, sailing between Pearl Harbor and the west coast as a transport for returning sailors and marines. She continued her "Magic Carpet" assignment by sailing for the South Pacific that autumn, reaching Noumea, New Caledonia, to become the flagship for Rear Admiral Paul Hendren, Commander, South Pacific Area Force. On 25 October, the ship got underway to take Rear Admiral Hendren on an inspection tour of facilities at Guadalcanal; in the Russells; at Tulagi; at Espiritu Santo; and Efate, returning to Noumea on 5 November. During the course of that brief voyage, the ship passed near the spot where her namesake had gone down that furious night of combat on 8 and 9 August 1942 in the Battle of Savo Island.

Vincennes subsequently made two trips to New Zealand waters before returning home with 300 veterans embarked as passengers. Discharging them at San Francisco upon her arrival on 23 March 1946, the light cruiser sped to Mare Island where workmen soon commenced deactivating the ship.

Decommissioned on 10 September 1946, *Vincennes* never returned to active service with the Fleet. Struck from the Navy list on 1 April 1966, she was subsequently sunk as a target in missile experiments.

Vincennes earned six battle stars for her World War II service.

Vincent

(MB: t. 17; l. 49'0''; b. 10'7''; dr. 2'10''; s. 9.0 k.; cpl. 4; a. none)

Vincent—a wooden-hulled, single-screw, cabin motor-boat built in 1909 at Lynn, Mass., by Britt Brothers, boatbuilders—was acquired by the Navy on a free-lease basis from the Transfer Company of Norwich, Conn., for use as a section patrol craft and was assigned the identification number SP–3246.

Although listed in the 1918 *Ship's Data: U.S. Naval Vessels* as commissioned on 28 June 1917, there are no deck logs for the ship to give details of the ship's actual service. She was probably assigned to local patrol duties with the 3d Naval District and operated in that capacity at least through the end of World War I.

She was apparently decommissioned in the summer of 1919. The *Ship's Data* volume for 1919 lists the craft as being "returned to owner" on 28 June 1919. She was simultaneously struck from the Navy list.

Vindicator

(SwRam: t. 750; dr. 6'; s. 12 mph.; a. 1 100-pdr. P.r., 2 24-pdr. how., 1 12-pdr. r., 1 heavy 12-pdr.)

Vindicator—originally acquired by the Federal Government in 1863 at New Albany, Ind., for use by the Army during the Civil War—was transferred to the Navy in 1864; and commissioned on 24 May, Lt. Comdr. Thomas O. Selfridge in command.

Shortly after her transfer from the Army, *Vindicator* was reworked at Mound City, Ill., for use as a ram in the Mississippi Squadron. She was assigned Command to the 5th District of the squadron on 4 July and deployed off Natchez, Miss., later that month. While off Natchez, *Vindicator* and her squadron performed patrol and reconnaissance duties, and the mere presence and vigilance of the formidable Union gunboats there were credited with preventing a planned Confederate crossing of the river on 22 August.

Vindicator was transferred to the 6th District of the Mississippi River for duty in early November. During an expedition up the Yazoo River, *Vindicator* and the stern-wheeler *Prairie Bird* transported and covered Union cavalry forces in an attack on Confederate communications in western Mississippi on the 27th. The Federals destroyed the railroad bridge over the Big Black River and tore up tracks for a distance of 30 miles around. Major General Napoleon J. T. Dana praised the performance of the two gunboats, saying: "The assistance of the vessels of the Sixth Division Mississippi Squadron rendered the expedition a complete success."

Vindicator remained in the 6th District for the duration of the war and conducted a spirited, though unsuccessful, pursuit of the ram CSS *William H. Webb* off the mouth of the Red River in Mississippi on 23 and 24 April 1865. During the chase, Acting Master D. P. Slattery of *Vindicator* stoked his boilers to near bursting point, commenting that "Such was the spirit animating every officer, man, and boy that all seemed to vie with each other in the rapid and intelligent execution of each order."

Vindicator was withdrawn from service soon thereafter and laid up at Mound City, Ill., where she was partially dismantled in July. She was sold at public auction at Mound City to W. L. Hambleton on 29 November; redocumented *New Orleans* on 27 February 1866; and dropped from documentation in 1869.

The sidewheel river ram *Vindicator*.

Vinton

A county in southern Ohio—named in honor of Congressman Samuel Finlay Vinton. Born on 25 September 1792 in Hadley, Mass., Vinton graduated from Williams College in 1814 and was admitted to the Connecticut bar two years later. He moved to Ohio in 1816 and subsequently became a member of the U.S. House of Representatives from Ohio—serving from 1842 to 1851. Besides serving on committees dealing with public lands, roads, and canals, Vinton chaired the Ways and Means Committee during the Mexican War, from 1846 to 1848. President of the Cleveland and Toledo Railroad from 1853 to 1854, Vinton went to Washington, D.C., in 1862 to study the problems of the emancipated slaves who had sought refuge in the nation's capital. He died there on 11 May 1862.

(AKA–83: dp. 13,910; l. 459'2''; b. 63'0''; dr. 28'7''; s. 16.5 k.; cpl. 425; a. 1 5'', 8 40mm., 16 20mm.; cl. *Tolland*; T. C2–S–AJ3)

Vinton (AKA–83) was laid down under a Maritime Commission contract (MC hull 1393) on 20 June 1944 at Wilmington, N.C., by the North Carolina Shipbuilding Co.; launched on 25 August 1944; sponsored by Mrs. J. W. Kirkpatrick; acquired by the Navy under a loan-charter basis on 7 September 1944; converted to an attack cargo ship configuration at Baltimore, Md., by the Bethlehem Steel Company's Key Highway plant; and commissioned on 23 February 1945, Comdr. John D. Hoffman, USNR, in command.

Following shakedown training in Chesapeake Bay, *Vinton* sailed via the Panama Canal zone for the Central Pacific and arrived at Pearl Harbor on 16 April. She conducted training exercises in the Hawaiian operating area for a month and one-half before she weighed anchor on 30 May and got uderway for the Marianas. Two days out, the attack cargo ship was called upon to perform an errand of mercy when an ailing seaman from *Silversides* (SS–236) was transferred via *Gato* (SS–212) to *Vinton* for an emergency appendectomy. By the time the attack cargo ship arrived at Guam on 13 June, the submariner had recovered sufficiently to rejoin his ship.

Vinton remained at Guam until 25 June, when she headed for the Western Carolines. She arrived at Ulithi the next day, pushed on for the Ryukyus on 9 July, dropped anchor off Okinawa on the 13th and began unloading her cargo. Despite frequent kamikaze alerts and a typhoon evasion maneuver, her crew bent to the task of making inroads into the mountains of cargo in her holds. Returning to Ulithi on the 28th, *Vinton* departed the Western Carolines on the 30th and arrived at Pearl Harbor on 6 August. Slightly over a week later, the war was over. Japan—under the staggering weight of two atomic bombs and American armadas which ranged off her shores virtually unchallenged and unchecked—surrendered unconditionally by the 15th of August.

On 22 September, *Vinton* commenced her post-war operations supporting the fleet and its bases with cargo lifts to Tinian; Guam; Subic Bay, Philippine Islands; Manus, in the Admiralties; Batavia, Java; and Biak, New Guinea, before she returned to Manus en route home. Departing the Admiralties on 17 January 1946, the attack cargo ship arrived at San Francisco on 5 February.

Departing San Francisco Bay on 24 February, bound for the east coast, *Vinton* steamed via the Panama Canal and arrived at New York on 15 March. She was decommissioned on 16 March for return to the War Shipping Administration the following day. Struck from the Navy list on 5 June, she soon entered mercantile service as SS *Gulf Shipper* with the Gulf and South American Steamship Co. On 23 September 1964, the American President Lines, Inc., purchased the erstwhile attack cargo ship and renamed her *President Harding*. Subsequently, her ownership again changed hands on 29 September 1966, when she was purchased by the Pacific Far East Lines and renamed *America Bear*. In late 1969, the Columbia Steamship Company purchased the vessel for use in the Pacific freight trade and renamed her *Columbia Beaver*—in which livery she served until late 1972, and after which time her documentary trail runs cold.

Violet

A flowering herb known for its beautiful purple blossoms.

I

(ScTug: t. 166; l. 85'; b. 19'9''; dph. 11'9''; a. 1 12-pdr., 1 12-pdr. r.)

Violet—a wooden steam tug built as *Martha* in 1862 at Brooklyn, N.Y.—was purchased by the Navy at New York City on 30 December 1862 for use during the Civil War; and was commissioned at the New York Navy Yard on 29 January 1863.

Soon after her commissioning, *Violet* was dispatched to Newport News, Va., for duty as a tug with the North Atlantic Blockading Squadron. On 27 March, she received orders to proceed to the blockade off Cape Fear Inlet, near Wilmington, N.C., and finally arrived for duty in early April after a storm off Cape Hatteras, N.C., had forced her return to Hampton Roads in a sinking condition on 28 March.

While off Wilmington, the vessel performed double duty as both a tug and a blockader. On the night of 11 April, she chased and fired upon an unidentified steamer and, in the company of *Aries*, discovered the blockade-running British steamer *Ceres* aground and burning at the mouth of the Cape Fear River on 6 December. When *Ceres* floated free during the night, *Violet* seized her and extinguished the fire. *Violet*, herself, grounded on 20 December while attempting to refloat the Confederate blockade-running steamer *Antonica*. She lay aground for two nights and a day; and, at one time, salvagers feared she would become a total loss. However, after her guns had been heaved overboard, the vessel was refloated.

Early in 1864, *Violet* underwent repairs at the Norfolk Navy Yard, Va., and in April was assigned duty as a tug to the ironclad *Roanoke* off Newport News. Her orders were to maintain a vigilant nighttime and foul weather guard over the ironclad and be prepared to tow the warship to safety or run down any enemy vessels in the event of a Confederate attack. She performed this task until 20 July, when she was fitted with a torpedo device and reassigned to her old blockade station off the Cape Fear River. There, on the night of 7 August, she ran aground while proceeding to her inshore station, close to the shoal off Western Bar, N.C. Despite the efforts of both her crew and volunteers from other nearby vessels to float her off, the tides forced *Violet* harder aground. Finally, seeing that the situation was hopeless, *Violet*'s captain and crew fired her magazine to prevent capture, and the vessel blew up on the morning of the 8th.

(Tender: dp. 1,012; l. 170'0''; b. 32'0''; dr. 10'6''; s. 12 k.; a. 1 3'', 2 20mm., 2 dct.)

Violet—a steel-hulled, twin-screw navigational aid tender built in 1930 at Manitowoc, Wis.—was serving the Coast Guard at Baltimore, Md., by mid-1941 and came under naval control during World War II. Classified as WAGL-250 (a "miscellaneous tender"), she served under Navy orders for the duration of World War II.

Viper

Any one of the limbless reptiles of the family Viperidae. This family includes many dangerously venomous snakes inhabiting Europe, Asia, and Africa.

I

(Brig: t. 143; l. 73'; b. 23'8''; dph. 7'6''; cpl. 64; a. 12 guns)

The first *Viper*—originally the cutter *Ferret* designed by naval architect Josiah Fox and built at the Norfolk Navy Yard, Norfolk, Va., between 1806 and 1809 —was commissioned under her old name on 18 April 1809, Lt. Christopher Gadsden, Jr., in command.

Shortly after her commissioning, *Ferret* cruised along the coast of the Carolinas and Georgia to aid in the enforcement of the Embargo Act of 1807. She was renamed *Viper* during rerigging as a brig at the Washington Navy Yard in 1809 and 1810, and from Washington sailed to New Orleans, La., arriving there on 15 March 1811. *Viper* remained off the Gulf Coast enforcing the Embargo Act until the outbreak of the War of 1812. During the war, *Viper* proved woefully inadequate in deep water operations against the larger, more heavily gunned British warships and was captured by the 32-gun frigate HMS *Narcissus* off the coast of Belize, British Honduras, on 17 January 1813 and taken to New Providence in the Bahama Islands. Nothing is known of her subsequent career.

II

(Galley: l. 75'; b. 15'; dph. 4'; a. 1 24-pdr., 1 18-pdr. columbiad)

The second *Viper* was one of six large galleys hastily built and commissioned in the summer of 1814 at Vergennes, Vt., for use by Commodore Thomas Macdonough against the British on Lake Champlain.

Under the command of Lt. Francis Mitchell, *Viper* participated in the capture of the British squadron, under Commodore George Downie, off Plattsburg, N.Y., on 11 September 1814, where she helped drive the surviving enemy gunboats back towards Canada. This stunning American naval victory ended English attempts to invade and split the United States in two by way of the Lake Champlain-Hudson River corridor, immeasurably strengthening the American bargaining position during peace negotiations at Ghent. *Viper* remained with the squadron for the remainder of the war but, with the return of peace, was partialy dismantled and laid up at Whitehall, N.Y., until sold there at public sale in 1825.

Viper (Submarine No. 10)—was renamed *B–1* (*q.v.*) on 17 November 1911.

Vireo

A small, insectivorous, migratory bird common to the New World.

I

(Minesweeper No. 52: dp. 840; l. 187'10''; b. 35'5''; dr. 8'10''; cpl. 186; a. 2 3''; cl. *Lapwing*)

Vireo (Minesweeper No. 52) was laid down on 20 November 1918 by the Philadelphia Navy Yard; launched on 26 May 1919; sponsored by Mrs. E. S. Robert; and commissioned on 16 October 1919, Lt. Ernest R. Piercey in command.

Vireo was assigned to the Train, Atlantic Fleet, and operated along the east coast until she departed Norfolk on 8 January 1920 and headed for Cuban waters to join the Fleet for its annual winter maneuvers. Returning north three months later, she arrived back in Norfolk on 28 April. She was reclassified AM–52 on 17 July 1920.

In the following years, while some of her sisterships were decommissioned and laid up in reserve, *Vireo* continued in active service with the Fleet. From 1920 to 1932, she served off the east coast engaged in towing targets; transporting men, mail, and materiel; repairing buoys and beacons; and operating with the Atlantic and Scouting Fleets.

Viper (Submarine Torpedo Boat No. 10) heads up the East River toward the New York Navy Yard, with the piers and skyline of old Manhattan in the background. Canvas "dodgers" were rigged around the open bridges of these early submarines while on the surface to protect personnel from the water that came over the hull in anything but the flattest sea. (NR&L(O) 3992)

In July 1921, she towed several former German warships to sea off the Virginia capes, where they were sunk by aircraft in attempts to prove that capital ships were vulnerable to attack from the air. Between December 1930 and March 1931, *Vireo* served as plane guard for aircraft engaged in supporting the Nicaraguan-Puerto Rican aerial survey.

Late in 1931, *Vireo* received orders assigning her to the Pacific Fleet and duty with the Train, Base Force. Departing Norfolk on 2 January 1932, *Vireo* steamed—via Guantanamo Bay, Cuba, and the Panama Canal—to the west coast, arriving at San Pedro, Calif., on 6 March. Attached to the Pacific Fleet's Train, the minesweeper continued her Fleet support duties and ranged the Pacific from the California coast to Panama and the Hawaiian Islands.

With the emergence of an intransigent Japan and a tense Far Eastern situation, the focus of American Fleet operations shifted westward to Hawaii; and *Vireo* departed San Francisco on 10 November 1940, bound for Pearl Harbor. Soon after reaching Hawaiian waters, she commenced operations out of Pearl Harbor, towing target rafts, conducting minesweeping exercises, and performing towing service to some of the outlying islands of the Hawaiian group, including Palmyra and Johnston.

From 5 September to 7 October 1941, *Vireo* underwent a navy yard overhaul at the Mare Island Navy Yard before heading westward once again. On 7 December 1941, *Vireo* lay in a nest of her sisterships at the coal docks at Pearl Harbor, which included *Rail* (AM–26), *Bobolink* (AM–20), and *Turkey* (AM–13). Shortly before 0800 that morning, Japanese aircraft roared overhead. The marauders swept over the Fleet's base and devastated not only Peal Harbor, but outlying Army and Navy installations all over the island of Oahu.

In upkeep status, with her engines dismantled, *Vireo* nevertheless speedily entered the fight. While her gunners topside fought their mounts cooly and efficiently, the "black gang" below decks assembled the ship's engines and fired up the boilers to get underway. Her 3-inch guns expended some 22 rounds, and the men at her number 2 mount rejoiced when one of their shells exploded directly in the path of a Japanese bomber, causing the Nipponese plane to crash in a ball of fire.

When the Japanese attackers departed, they left behind them a swath of death and destruction. Beneath the oily pall of smoke settled the once-proud battleships of the Pacific Fleet, now battered and burnt. *Vireo* and some of her sister sweepers at Pearl Harbor received orders to assist the stricken *Califonia* (BB–44), sinking into the oil-stained ooze at berth F–3, off Ford Island.

While engaged in salvage operations alongside *California*, through January 1942, *Vireo* also served briefly as a tender to *Enterprise* (CV–6). The minesweeper carried ammunition to replenish "the Big E's" depleted stocks and prepare that ship for future forays against the Japanese empire.

After conducting minesweeping operations in the Pearl Harbor channel and other Hawaiian waters, *Vireo* underwent upkeep at Pearl Harbor between 10 and 13 February 1942. Following local operations near Honolulu and Pearl Harbor, she made brief runs to Johnston Island and the port of Hilo.

In April and May 1942, after another brief stretch around Pearl Harbor, *Vireo* conducted local patrols out of Hilo, sometimes in company with *Crossbill* (AMc–9) to conduct magnetic, acoustic, and mechanical minesweeping operations; and to patrol harbors with her echo-ranging and listening gear. From 23 to 24 April, *Vireo*, in company with *Crossbill* and *Sacramento* (PG–19), conducted a search for survivors of a downed Army plane off Pepeekeo Point, near Hilo, and found one body before she abandoned the task.

On 28 May 1942, under secret orders, *Vireo* and gasoline tanker *Kaloli* (AOG–13) departed Honolulu and headed for Midway Island. During the voyage, *Vireo* was reclassified as an ocean-going tug and redesignated AT–144 on 1 June 1942. While *Vireo* and her charge

Vireo (AT–144) at Pearl Harbor, August, 1942. (19–N–34748)

crept toward Midway at nine knots, two battle fleets steamed toward each other on a collision course. The American and Japanese Navies were squaring off for the decisive Battle of Midway.

Vireo and *Kaloli* hove to in Midway harbor on 3 June, amidst preparations there for defense of the island. Soon after the two American ships arrived, they received orders to proceed to a point 30 miles off Pearl and Hermes Reef, where they were to await further orders. Underway by 1910, *Vireo* and the gasoline tanker soon arrived at their assigned stations and lay to.

Air action the following day, 4 June 1942, was hot and heavy. Japanese carriers *Akagi*, *Kaga*, *Soryu*, and *Hiryu* were all crippled and sunk by American planes. However, American carrier *Yorktown* (CV–5) became the unfortunate victim of Japanese dive and torpedo bombers which heavily damaged the carrier, stopping her dead in the water, and forcing a severe list.

Lest the ship capsize before the crew could be removed, Capt. Elliot Buckmaster ordered *Yorktown* abandoned. When *Yorktown* stopped settling, Buckmaster concluded that the ship could possibly be saved. Accordingly, *Vireo* received a summons to take *Yorktown* in tow. The tug arrived on the scene by 1135 on 5 June and closed and maneuvered to pass *Yorktown* a towline, accomplishing this by 1308. *Vireo* and her unwieldy charge then labored painfully ahead, at a speed of under 3 knots, with a protective brood of destroyers standing by.

Vireo, hampered by a small rudder and inadequate engines for such a large tow, found itself confronted with the Herculean task of keeping the big carrier pointed into the wind and on course. The next day, *Hammann* (DD–412) secured alongside *Yorktown* to assist the salvage parties on the larger ship working to correct her trim and to repair her battle damage.

Around 1400 on the afternoon of 6 June, Japanese submarine *I–168* fired torpedoes at the nearly helpless targets. *Hammann*, mortally hit, broke in two and sank alongside the towering carrier, which also took two torpedoes. As the destroyer sank, her depth charges all went off at once, causing tremendous shock waves which convulsed swimmers in the water and violently wrenched the old tug. *Vireo* freed herself from the carrier by cutting the towing cable with an acetylene torch and then doubled back to commence rescue operations.

Up her sides clambered carriermen and destroyermen alike, while she maneuvered near the carrier's canting stern to take on board members of the salvage party who had chosen to abandon the carrier from there. She then proceeded to secure alongside the wounded flattop in the exact spot where *Hammann* had met her doom. *Yorktown* rolled heavily, her heavy steel hide pounding the lighter former minecraft's hull with a vengeance as the ships touched time and time again during the rescue operations. This mission completed, battered *Vireo* stood away from the sinking carrier, which sank shortly after dawn on the 7th.

Vireo's troubles, however, had only begun. Underwater explosions from *Hammann*'s depth charges had severely jostled the tug's rudder. As a result, it jammed as *Vireo* was entering the shipping channel at Midway harbor on 8 June, and she ran aground on a coral head, carrying away her echo-ranging gear and flooding her sound room. Repeated attempts to free herself only resulted in another grounding, so *Vireo* lay-to and called for a tow.

After arriving at Midway at the end of a towline from *YMT–12*, following another brush with a coral head which irreparably damaged the rudder, *Vireo* soon got underway for Pearl Harbor, this time behind *Seminole* (AT–65). Reaching Hawaiian waters on 17 June, she entered the navy yard at Pearl Harbor for emergency repairs which lasted from 18 to 30 June. Following this, she remained at the Pearl Harbor yard for a complete overhaul and drydocking.

Having concluded the refitting by 19 August, *Vireo* conducted post-repair trials before turning in all her mine gear on 25 August. Two days later, she got underway to escort SS *Gulf Queen* to the Fiji Islands, towing two barges. Upon her arrival at Suva on 11 September, the tug refueled, provisioned, and carried out minor repairs before heading for New Caledonia on 15 September. After arriving at Noumea five days later, on 20 September 1942, she commenced harbor operations under the control of Commander, Amphibious Forces, South Pacific (ComAmphibForSoPac). In accordance with verbal orders from ComAmphibForSo-

Pac, *Vireo*'s crew set about making camouflage nets and painting the ship green in preparation for her next assignment.

Arriving at Espiritu Santo on 8 October, she awaited further orders, spending four days at this port in the New Hebrides before setting out for the Guadalcanal area on 12 October, to take part in resupply operations for the marines at Henderson Field.

Since the initial landings on Guadalcanal on 7 August 1942, the campaign had been fought tooth and nail. Fierce land and sea battles had characterized the fighting since the early going. By this juncture, American aviation operations on Henderson Field had been so endangered by shellings, bad weather, and inadequate supplies, that the American situation was extreme.

With American aircraft using up gasoline at an alarming rate, that commodity ranked high on the list of priority supplies. Accordingly, a barge-towing operation was mounted in mid-October to ease the critical fuel situation on Guadalcanal.

The force to carry out this operation comprised *Alchiba* (AK–23), *Bellatrix* (AK–20), *Jamestown* (PG–55), *Meredith* (DD–434), *Nicholas* (DD–449), and *Vireo*, each pulling a barge carrying barrels of gasoline and quarter-ton bombs. Setting out from Espiritu Santo, the highly volatile convoy was spotted by Japanese aircraft on 15 October. All but *Vireo* and *Meredith* beat a hasty retreat.

Cautiously proceeding, the pair beat off a two-plane Japanese attack before they received word that Japanese surface ships were in the area. Only then did they reverse course. At noon, *Meredith* ordered old, slow, and vulnerable *Vireo* abandoned and took off her crew. *Meredith* then stood off to torpedo the tug at 1215 so that she would not fall into enemy hands intact. Suddenly, a whirlwind of destruction swept down from the sky and descended upon the destroyer. Like hawks, 27 planes from the Japanese carrier *Zuikaku* pounced on *Meredith* and deluged her with bombs, torpedoes, and bullets, sinking her in an instant.

Vireo and the two gasoline barges, however, drifted to leeward, untouched. One life raft, crammed with some of *Meredith*'s survivors, succeeded in overhauling the derelict tug and the men gratefully scrambled aboard. The barges and the tug were later found, intact. When a salvage party boarded *Vireo* on 21 October, the ship was dead in the water with no lights, no steam, and no power. After abortive attempts to light fires under the boilers, using wood, the tug had to be taken under tow by *Grayson* (DD–435). In company with *Grayson* and *Gwin* (DD–433), *Vireo* arrived safely at Espiritu Santo on 23 October.

With a new crew—the majority of her old complement lost in the ordeal with *Meredith*—she continued to operate in the Guadalcanal area with Task Force 62. She conducted resupply operations to Guadalcanal, towing barges loaded with precious gasoline and bombs and carrying out local escort for other, larger ships, engaged in the same vital duties.

On 3 December, in company with *Hilo* (AGP–2) and towing PT-boats, she departed Noumea and proceeded to Australia. Arriving at Cairns on 9 December, she spent the remainder of the year there, enjoying Christmas and New Year's Day in Australian waters before heading back to the combat area, arriving at Espiritu Santo on 9 January.

Operating out of the New Hebrides in early January, she assisted cruisers *Pensacola* (CA–24) and *Minneapolis* (CA–36) as they underwent repairs following damage received at Tassafaronga. Towing barges and firing target bursts for destroyers during gunnery practice off Guadalcanal, the tug continued her operations as before, between that island and Espiritu Santo and Noumea. It was dull and monotonous duty but necessary and vital, nonetheless.

In April 1943, as American forces advanced on the "island-hopping," "leap-frogging" campaigns against the Japanese in the South Pacific, Japanese Admiral Yamamoto initiated operation "I." Yamamoto aimed this stroke at Papua, in the hope of compensating for the loss of Guadalcanal, by destroying the American advance base there and thus slowing or stopping the Allied advance. The new Japanese thrust began on 7 April when large formations of Japanese planes swept down from Rabaul to attack American shipping in Lunga Roads between Guadalcanal and Tulagi.

Among these ships, there lay *Vireo*, engaged in her usual harbor activities. *Pathfinder* was engaged in taking soundings; also near were *Ortolan* (ASR–5) and *SC–521*. Shortly before the attack came, *Aaron Ward* (DD–483) passed by, escorting *LST–449*. Three Japanese dive bombers swooped down out of the sun and severely damaged the destroyer with their lethal loads. *Ortolan* and *Vireo* took the crippled *Aaron Ward* under tow, but the destroyer sank three miles short of Tulagi.

As the New Georgia campaign got underway and American forces advanced further up the chain of islands in the southwest Pacific, *Vireo* continued her operations out of Tulagi, Espiritu Santo, or Noumea. In the pre-dawn darkness of 13 July, the Battle of Kula Gulf was fought between Japanese and American surface forces, the latter augmented by New Zealand cruiser *Leander*. In the action which followed, *Honolulu* (CL–48), *St. Louis* (CL–49), and *Leander* were damaged. Later that day, *Vireo*, in company with *Rail* (AT–139) set out to assist in getting the cripples home and towed *Honolulu* to haven at government wharf, Tulagi, where temporary repairs to the cruiser's bow were made.

For the remainder of 1943 and on into 1944, *Vireo* followed the Fleet as it inched closer to Japan. In the rearward island areas, she continued her duties as a harbor tug and local escort vessel. On 15 May 1944, *Vireo* was reclassified as an ocean-going tug, old, and redesignated ATO–144.

In late July, American forces struck in northwestern New Guinea at Cape Sansapor. *Vireo* took part in these operations from 30 July to 2 August, engaged in the vital support activities necessary to support the successful landings.

After service in the South Pacific, the old tug moved northward with the invasion armada to liberate the Philippine Islands from the Japanese. On 18 October 1944, American troops stormed ashore on Leyte, keeping General MacArthur's promise to return to Philippine soil. *Vireo* operated in support of these landings into December. She departed Morotai on the 10th, bound for Biak. From there, she proceeded to Leyte, engaged in towing duties. Next—after touching at Hollandia, Manus, and Biak—she took part in the Okinawa operations in April and May 1945. Returning to Morotai, she engaged in towing operations again, this time to Tacloban on the island of Leyte, departing there on 25 May for Subic Bay. For the remainder of the war, she operated between the Philippine Islands and New Guinea, as American forces continued to sweep northward towards the Japanese home islands.

On 20 December 1945, after immediate postwar towing operations at Manila, Luzon, and Samar, she departed Philippine waters on 20 December 1945, in company with *Rail* (ATO–139) and *Whippoorwill* (ATO–169), and headed for the Marshalls. Following a brief stay at Eniwetok, *Vireo* got underway on 4 January 1946 and proceeded via Pearl Harbor to the west coast. She arrived at San Francisco, Calif., on 5 February and reported to the Commandant, 12th Naval District, for disposition.

As newer and more powerful fleet tugs supplanted the old converted minesweepers, the need for the old vessels decreased. Thus, on 18 April 1946, *Vireo* was decommissioned, declared surplus to Navy needs, and made available for disposal. Struck from the Navy list on 8 May 1946, *Vireo* was transferred from the Maritime Commission for disposal on 4 February 1947; but no records of her subsequent fate have survived.

Vireo received seven battle stars for her World War II service.

II

(MSC–205: dp. 412; l. 145'; b. 28'; dr. 12'; s. 12.8 k.; cpl. 40; a. 1 20mm., 2 .50-cal. mg., 1 81mm. M.; cl. *Redwing*)

Vireo (MSC–205) was laid down as AMS–205 on 14 September 1953 at the Bellingham Shipyards, Bellingham, Wash.; launched on 30 April 1954; sponsored by Mrs. Arvin E. Olsen; redesignated MSC–205 on 7 February 1955; and commissioned at the naval station at Tacoma, Wash., on 7 June 1955, Lt. (jg.) Leland E. Mench in command.

After completing tests and trials at Seattle, *Vireo* moved south at the beginning of July for shakedown training out of San Diego. The cruise occupied her until the second week in September at which time she began preparations for final acceptance trials to be conducted early in November. Upon passing those tests on the 4th, *Vireo* became an active unit of Mine Squadron (MinRon) 7. She operated from Long Beach, Calif., until 1 March 1956 when she stood out of that port, bound for the western Pacific. En route, she stopped at Pearl Harbor and, for the remainder of March and the entire month of April, the minesweeper conducted training operations in Hawaiian waters. She resumed her voyage westward on 9 May and arrived in Yokosuka, Japan, on the 31st.

Vireo served at Sasebo, Japan, as a unit of MinRon 3 for almost a decade and one-half. Her 14 years and 4 months in the Far East can be divided into two easily discernible periods. The first eight years, from June 1956 to July 1964, were devoted entirely to peacetime operations out of Sasebo. These included minesweeping exercises with other ships of the United States Navy and with units of the Japanese Maritime Self Defence Force as well as with navies of the Republic of Korea, Taiwan, and Thailand. She visited such diverse places as the Sea of Japan, the coast of Korea, the Philippine Islands, Okinawa, and the East and South China Seas. She punctuated her operations with port calls at Hong Kong, Okinawa, Keelung and Kaohsiung on Taiwan, Subic and Manila Bay in the Philippines, and at a host of Japanese ports including—among others—Beppu, Kobe, Kagoshima, Sasebo, and Yokosuka. The visits allowed her crew to rest after operations at sea, to replenish stores and supplies, and to refurbish the ship. During the crisis in 1958 over the Nationalist-held islands of Quemoy and Matsu, located just off the communist Chinese mainland, *Vireo* rushed from Japan to join American forces in the area and spent the months of September and October patrolling near the islands. In November, she resumed her routine peacetime minesweeping exercises, port calls, and occasional salvage or rescue operations. Activities such as these characterized her duty until mid-summer 1964.

The war in Vietnam dominated *Vireo*'s final six years in the Far East. In July 1964, just before the Tonkin Gulf incident gave impetus to an ever-widening American participation in combat in Vietnam, the minesweeper headed for Southeast Asian waters for a series of "special operations." Though she resumed her normal schedule early in August, the minesweeper began regular tours of duty on station off the South Vietnamese coast the following spring when an inshore patrol was established—under the code name Operation "Market Time"—to interdict the waterborne flow of arms to the Viet Cong insurgents. In carrying out her "Market Time" duties, *Vireo* patrolled stretches of the South Vietnamese coast relatively close inshore and stopped suspicious-looking craft—mostly junks but occasionally trawlers—to check their identity and to inspect cargoes and crews for illicit arms and communist infiltrators. During her first year on the patrol, she conducted five tours of duty—each of about two or three weeks duration—on junk surveillance assignments uncomplicated by any combat. Those periods were punctuated by port visits to her old haunts, normal mine exercises, and periods in port for upkeep and repair.

The year 1966, however, proved a different story altogether. After completing an overhaul at Sasebo, *Vireo* departed that port on 10 April to resume "Market Time" patrols off the coast of South Vietnam. Exactly one month later, while engaged in those operations, the minesweeper received her baptism of fire. At about 0430, USCGC *Point Grey* encountered a steel-hulled trawler trying to make a landfall near the mouth of the Cua Bo De River. The Coast Guard cutter received heavy .50-caliber gunfire when she tried to force the trawler to heave to for inspection but, while requesting assistance in the form of *Brister* (DER–327) and *Vireo*, succeeded in forcing the enemy ship aground. At a hasty conference on board *Brister*, it was decided to attempt to salvage the grounded gun runner. While USCGC *Point Grey* approached the trawler with a towline from *Vireo*, *Brister* launched her motor whaleboat to assist. The Coast Guard cutter received a withering machine gun fire from insurgents ashore as she neared the enemy. She answered that fire promptly, and *Vireo* joined in with 150 rounds of 20-millimeter. *Brister*, her battery masked by the cutter, could not bring her 3-inch guns to bear on the enemy. Ultimately, the Coast Guard cutter had to break contact and move off in order to get her wounded crewmen medical assistance. *Vireo* covered her retirement with 20-millimeter fire and provided a haven for *Brister*'s motor whaleboat while air strikes were called in to silence the enemy machine gun emplacements. Further air strikes eventually destroyed the trawler, and *Vireo* returned to "Market Time" duty. For participation in the action at Cua Bo De River, *Vireo* won the Navy Unit Commendation, and her commanding officer received the Bronze Star Medal.

Over the next four and one-half years, *Vireo* maintained her schedule of "Market Time" patrols alternated with unilateral and multilateral mining exercises and port visits at various places throughout the Orient. On 1 August 1970, *Vireo* learned that her home port had been changed from Sasebo to Long Beach, Calif., where she was scheduled to begin duty as a Naval Reserve training ship on 1 October. She departed Sasebo on 17 August and, after stops at Yokosuka and Pearl Harbor, arrived in Long Beach on 17 September. On 1 October, the minesweeper was placed out of commission. That same day, she departed Long Beach for her Naval Reserve duty station, Seattle, Wash. After four years and six months of operations along the northwest coast of the United States, *Vireo* began deactivation preparations on 1 April 1975. Three months later, on 1 July 1975, her name was struck from the Navy list. Though scheduled for disposal by sale at the time of her striking, as of May 1978, no such action appeared to have taken place.

Virginia

The first English colony in America and one of the original 13 states. Virginia ratified the constitution on 26 June 1788 to become the 10th state to enter the Union.

I

(Fr.: t. 681; l. 126'3½''; b. 34'4''; dph. 10'5½''; a. 24 12-pdrs., 6 4-pdrs., 6 swivel guns)

The first *Virginia*—one of 13 frigates authorized by the Continental Congress on 13 December 1775—was laid down in 1776 at Fells Point, Md., by George Wells; launched that August; and commissioned in the spring of 1777, Capt. James Nicholson in command.

The newly commissioned frigate's first orders directed her to attempt a run through the strong British naval blockade at the mouth of Chesapeake Bay and then, if successful, to head south to the West Indies and cruise in search of English merchantmen. However, her first sortie failed, as did four subsequent attempts to get to sea which she made in May, October, November, and December of 1777. These successive failures frustrated *Virginia*'s restive crew; and many deserted to join the numerous privateers scattered about the wharves of nearby Baltimore, Md.

By early January of 1778, the desertions had become so numerous that *Virginia* was unable to leave the docks. This situation prompted a series of ugly exchanges between Capt. Nicholson; his executive officer, Lt. Joshua Barney; and the governor of Maryland, Thomas Johnson. New recruits were finally procured through the auspices of the Maritime Committee of the Continental Congress, enabling *Virginia* to attempt another run past the blockade in mid-January. This latest dash went smoothly until HMS *Emerald* sighted *Virginia* near the Chesapeake capes. The British frigate pursued the Americans back towards Baltimore. *Virginia* tied up behind a water battery and chain stretched across the northwest branch of the Patapsco River, Md., between Whetstone Point and later Lazaretto Point, where she took on board 20 more seamen.

Later that month, when Capt. Nicholson again tried to run the blockade, he sent Lt. Barney ahead in the schooner *Dolphin* to reconnoiter the positions of the British warships. *Dolphin* sighted a large patrol vessel in Tangier Sound but outran her. Before rendezvousing with *Virginia*, the schooner recaptured a Baltimore sloop taken earlier. On the basis of Lt. Barney's report, Capt. Nicholson decided to abandon this latest attempt to get to sea and returned to Baltimore.

Virginia lay at anchor at Baltimore for two months repairing and reprovisioning. During this time, Barney was dispatched to York, Pa., to explain *Virginia*'s predicament to the Maritime Committee; and he returned in March with orders to make another attempt to get by the British as soon as possible. Awaiting Barney upon his arrival back in Baltimore were a letter of thanks from the Royal Navy for his kind treatment of *Dolphin*'s prisoners and a large English cheese.

Virginia left Baltimore late in March in obedience to the Maritime Committee's orders. Nicholson's plans called for *Virginia* to sail first to Annapolis, Md., to pick up a bay pilot promised by Governor Johnson. Completing this, the frigate and pilot vessel weighed anchor off Annapolis on 30 March and proceeded down the bay, plotting a night passage into the Atlantic. However, early on the morning of 31 March, *Virginia* grounded with a tremendous crash on the so-called Middle Ground between the capes, opposite the city of Hampton, Va. With a strong wind blowing astern, the surf pounded the frigate and forced her over. Her rudder snapped before she could be cleared and was soon lost. Once in the channel, *Virginia* was anchored and repairs begun.

At dawn, lookouts spotted *Emerald* and her fellow frigate HMS *Conqueror* approaching from seaward. Though *Virginia*'s guns remained undamaged, Capt. Nicholson ordered his barge broken out and went ashore with the ship's papers. Later that morning, the American frigate surrendered to Capt. Caldwell of *Emerald*. A Congressional court of inquiry into the fiasco cleared Capt. Nicholson of blame, and all the officers of the unlucky frigate saw action later during the Revolution.

Virginia, herself, was soon repaired and eventually purchased by the Royal Navy for use as the 32-gun frigate HMS *Virginia*. She was placed in service along the American coast and participated in the Penobscot operations of 1779 and the capture of Charleston, S.C., in 1780. At the end of the war she was condemned and sold.

II

(Sch.: t. 187; l. 50' on keel; b. 18'10''; dph. 8'6''; cpl. 70; a. 6 6-pdrs., 8 4-pdrs.)

The second *Virginia*—a schooner built in 1797 for the United States Revenue Cutter Service at Portsmouth, Va.—was transferred to the Navy for use in the unde-clared naval war against France in the early summer of 1798; and was commissioned on 25 June, Capt. Francis Bright in command.

In August 1798, *Virginia* received orders to join the frigate *Constitution* off the eastern seaboard of the United States for operations against suspected French warships and merchantmen. She remained on this station until December, when she was assigned identical duty in the West Indies between St. Christopher Island and Puerto Rico as part of the squadron commanded by Commodore Thomas Truxtun. While helping to defend American interests in the Caribbean, *Virginia*, assisted by *Richmond* and *Eagle*, captured the armed French schooner *Louis* and her cargo on 26 April 1799. Despite this success, in the following June, the fragile vessel was declared unfit for further naval service and was returned to the Revenue Cutter Service.

(SL: t. 2,633; lbp. 197'1½''; b. 53'; dph. 22'; cpl. 820; a. 74 guns; cl. *North Carolina*)

The next *Virginia* was one of nine, 74-gun warships authorized by Congress on 29 April 1816. She was laid down at the Boston Navy Yard, Mass., in May 1822; finished about 1825; and was kept on the stocks as naval policy and the expense involved discouraged launching or commissioning the "74s" except when the national interest clearly required it. *Virginia* remained on the stocks at Boston until she was broken up there starting in 1874.

III

(ScGbt.: dp. 581; l. 170'; b. 26'2''; dph. 14'8''; s. 9 k.; a. 6 24-pdr. how., 1 12-pdr. r.)

The third *Virginia* was originally the British merchantman *Pet* built at Dumbarton, Scotland, in 1861. *Pet* sailed as *Noe-Daquy* during the early months of the Civil War and, in December 1862, was acquired by a Havana merchant for use as a Confederate blockade runner. Renamed *Virginia*, the vessel was captured off Mugeres Island, Mexico, by *Wachusett* and *Sonoma* on 18 January 1863; was later purchased by the Navy from the New York prize court on 1 September; and was commissioned at the New York Navy Yard on 12 June.

Virginia was assigned duty with Rear Admiral David G. Farragut's West Gulf Blockading Squadron and, within a week of her commissioning, departed New York, bound for the Gulf of Mexico. En route, she touched briefly at Hampton Roads, Va., finally joining Farragut's squadron in July. However, further repairs and modifications were needed before the vessel could become a fully effective fighting unit; and the ship spent August and most of September at New Orleans undergoing overhaul.

Virginia finally returned to active duty in late September and was deployed along the coast of Texas for the duration of the war. There, she conducted numerous patrol and reconnaissance missions—which often took her up the rivers which empty into the gulf—and also compiled an impressive list of captures. Her first success was the seizure of the British blockade runner *Jenny* off the Texas coast with a cargo of cotton on 6 October. Between 2 and 14 November, *Monongahela*, *Owasco*, and *Virginia* convoyed and supported General Nathaniel Banks' successful landing at Brazos Santiago, Tex., near the mouth of the Rio Grande River. Here, *Virginia* also captured the British steamer *Matamoras* on the 4th and the English brig *Dashing Wave* on the 5th. This expedition began a Union offensive aimed both at wresting Texas from Confederate control and deterring French troops in Mexico from attempting to invade the state. On the 4th, Southern forces evacuated Brownsville, giving the Union a strong foothold at the Mexican border.

After the Rio Grande expedition, *Virginia* returned to blockade duty and found the waters off Texas a fertile breeding ground of smuggling activity. This was especially true of the area off San Luis Pass, Tex., and *Virginia* made most of her captures here. These included the British schooner *Mary Douglas* and her cargo of coffee, bananas, and linen which were seized on 15 February 1864, and the English schooner *Henry Colthirst* which she took on the 22d. On the 29th off Galveston, Tex., *Virginia* overhauled the Confederate schooner *Camilla* with a cargo of cotton. The sloop *Cassie Holt* was also captured at the same time, but she grounded off San Luis Pass and was burned. Once again off San Luis Pass, *Virginia* captured the sloop *Randall* on 8 March, the schooner *Sylphide* on the 10th, and the Mexican schooner *Juanita* on 11 April. However, *Juanita* grounded on the 13th and was recaptured with the loss of the prize crew. This incident was partially offset by the capture of the Mexican schooner *Alma* on the 19th and the seizure and destruction of the sloop *Rosina* on the 20th. *Virginia*'s last captures off San Luis Pass included the schooner *Experiment*, which she took on 3 May and subsequently destroyed and 94 stacked bales of cotton picked up ashore on the 7th and 8th.

Virginia returned to New Orleans in mid-May for badly needed repairs to her boilers. She remained at New Orleans until December, leaving on the 5th for the blockade off Galveston. Here, she captured the schooner *Belle* on 27 December and helped to destroy the side-wheel steamer *Acadia* in February 1865.

After the war ended in April 1865, *Virginia* sailed for Philadelphia on 17 July. The veteran blockader was sold at public auction at New York City to Perry Brothers on 30 November; was documented on 14 December; and was rerigged as a barge on 24 March 1885.

IV

(Battleship No. 13: dp. 14,980 (tl.); l. 441'3"; b. 76'2½"; dr. 23'9" (mean); s. 19.01 k. (tl.); cpl. 916; a. 4 12", 8 8", 12 6", 12 3", 24 1-pdrs., 4 .30-cal. Colt mg.; 4 21" tt.; cl. *Virginia*)

The fourth *Virginia* (Battleship No. 13) was laid down on 21 May 1902 at Newport News, Va., by the Newport News Shipbuilding and Dry Dock Co.; launched on 5 April 1904; sponsored by Miss Gay Montague, daughter of the Governor of Virginia; and commissioned on 7 May 1906, Capt. Seaton Schroeder in command.

After fitting out, *Virginia* conducted her "shaking down" cruise in Lynnhaven Bay, Va., off Newport, R.I., and off Long Island, N.Y., before she put into Bradford, R.I., for coal on 9 August. After running trials for the standardization of her screws off Rockland, Maine, the battleship maneuvered in Long Island Sound before anchoring off President Theodore Roosevelt's home, Oyster Bay, Long Island, from 2 to 4 September, for a Presidential review.

Virginia then continued her shakedown cruise before she coaled again at Bradford. Meanwhile, events were occurring in the Caribbean that would alter the new battleship's employment. On the island of Cuba, in August of 1906, a revolution had broken out against the government of President T. Estrada Palma. The disaffection, which had started in Piñar del Rio province, grew in the early autumn to the point where President Palma had no recourse but to appeal to the United States for intervention.

By mid-September, it had become apparent that the small Cuban constabulary (3,000 rural guards) was unable to protect foreign interests, and intervention would be necessary. Accordingly, *Virginia* departed Newport on 15 September 1906, bound for Cuba, and reached Havana on the 21st, ready to protect the city from attack if necessary. The battleship remained at Havana until 13 October, when she sailed for Sewall's Point, Va.

Virginia disembarked General Frederick Funston at Norfolk upon her arrival there and coaled before heading north to Tompkinsville to await further orders. She shifted soon thereafter to the New York Navy Yard where she was coaled and drydocked to have her hull bottom painted before undergoing repairs and alterations at the Norfolk Navy Yard from 3 November 1906 to 18 February 1907. After installation of fire control apparatus at the New York Navy Yard between 19 February and 23 March, the battleship sailed once more for Cuban waters, joining the fleet at Guantanamo Bay on 28 March.

Virginia fired target practices in Cuban waters before she sailed for Hampton Roads on 10 April to participate in the Jamestown Tricentennial Exposition festivities. She remained in Hampton Roads for a month, from 15 April to 15 May, before she underwent repairs at the Norfolk Navy Yard into early June. Subsequently reviewed in Hampton Roads by President Theodore Roosevelt between 7 and 13 June, *Virginia* shifted northward for target practices on the target grounds of Cape Cod Bay—evolutions that lasted from mid-June to mid-July. She later cruised with her division to Newport; the North River, New York City; and to Provincetown, Mass., before conducting day and night battle practice in Cape Cod Bay.

Returning southward early that autumn, *Virginia* underwent two months of repairs and alterations at the Norfolk Navy Yard, from 24 September to 24 November, before undergoing further repairs at the New York Navy Yard later in November. She subsequently shifted southward again, reaching Hampton Roads on 6 December.

Virginia spent the next 10 days preparing for a feat never before attempted—a round-the-world cruise by the battleships of the Atlantic Fleet. The voyage, regarded by President Roosevelt as a dramatic gesture to the Japanese—who had only recently emerged on the world stage as a power to be reckoned with—proved to be a signal success, with the ships performing so well as to confound the doomsayers who had predicted a fiasco.

The cruise began eight days before Christmas of 1907, and ended on Washington's Birthday, 22 February 1909. During the course of the voyage, the ships called at ports along both coasts of South America; on the west coast of the United States; at Hawaii; in the Philippines; Japan; China; and in Ceylon. *Virginia*'s division also visited Smyrna, Turkey, via Beirut, during the Mediterranean leg of the cruise. Both upon departure and upon arrival, the fleet was reviewed at Hampton Roads by President Roosevelt, whose "big stick" diplomacy and flair for the dramatic gesture had been practically personified by the cruise of the "Great White Fleet."

Following that momentous circumnavigation, *Virginia* underwent four months of voyage repairs and alterations at the Norfolk Navy Yard from 26 February to 26 June 1909. She spent the next year and three months operating off the eastern seaboard of the United States, ranging from the southern drill grounds, off the Virginia capes, to Newport, R.I. During that time, she conducted one brief cruise with members of the Naval Militia embarked and visited Rockport and Provincetown, Mass. For the better part of that time, she conducted battle practices with the fleet—evolutions only brokn by brief periods of yard work at Norfolk and Boston.

Virginia visited Brest, France, and Gravesend, England, from 15 November to 7 December and from 8 to 29 December 1909, respectively, before she—as part of the 4th Division, Atlantic Fleet—joined the Atlantic Fleet in Guantanamo Bay for drills and exercises. She subsequently operated in Cuban waters for two months, from 13 January to 13 March 1910, before she returned north for battle practices on the southern drill grounds.

541

Virginia departed Hampton Roads on 11 April, in company with *Georgia* (Battleship No. 15), and reached the Boston Navy Yard two days later. She underwent repairs there until 24 May before putting to sea for Provincetown. Over the next five days, *Virginia* operated with the collier *Vestal*, testing a "coaling-at-sea apparatus" off Provincetown and at Stellwagen's Bank, before she conducted torpedo practices. The battleship returned to the Boston Navy Yard on 18 June.

Virginia maintained her routine of operations off the eastern seaboard—occasionally ranging into Cuban waters for regularly scheduled fleet evolutions in tactics and gunnery—into 1913, a routine largely uninterrupted. In 1913, however, unrest in Mexico caused the frequent dispatch of American men-of-war to those waters. *Virginia* became one of those ships in mid-February, when she reached Tampico on the 15th of that month; she remained there until 2 March, when she shifted to Vera Cruz for coal. She returned to Tampico on 5 March and remained there for 10 days.

After another stint of operations off the eastern seaboard, ranging from the Virginia capes to Newport —a period of maneuvers and exercises varied by a visit to New York at the end of May 1913 for the dedication of the memorial to the battleship *Maine* (sunk in Havana Harbor in February 1898) and one to Boston in mid-June for Flag Day and Bunker Hill exercises— *Virginia* returned to Mexican waters in November. She reached Vera Cruz on 4 November and remained in port until the 30th, when she shifted to Tampico. She observed conditions in those ports and operated off the Mexican coast into January of 1914.

Returning to Cuban waters for exercises and maneuvers with the fleet, *Virginia* sailed for the Virginia capes in mid-March 1914. She maneuvered with the fleet off Cape Henry and in Lynnhaven Roads before she conducted gunnery drills at the wreck of *San Marcos* (ex-*Texas*) in Tangier Sound, Chesapeake Bay. *Virginia* subsequently held experimental gunnery firings on the southern drill grounds before she spent much of April drydocked at Boston.

The American occupation of Vera Cruz in April 1914 resulted in the sizeable deployment of American men-of-war to that port that lasted into the autumn. *Virginia* reached Vera Cruz on 1 May and operated with the fleet out of that port into early October, a period of time broken by target practice in Guantanamo Bay between 18 September and 3 October.

While war raged in Europe, *Virginia* continued her operations off the eastern seaboard of the United States, ranging from the southern drill grounds to the coast of New England and occasionally steaming to Cuban waters for winter maneuvers. She was placed in reserve on 20 March 1916, at the Boston Navy Yard, and was undergoing an extensive overhaul in the spring of 1917 when the United States declared war on Germany.

On the day America entered World War I, the United States government took steps to take over all interned German merchant vessels then in American ports. As part of that move, *Virginia* sent boarding parties to seize the German passenger and cargo vessels *Amerika*, *Cincinnati*, *Wittekind*, *Köln*, and *Ockenfels* on 6 April 1917.

Completing her overhaul at Boston on 27 August, *Virginia* sailed for Port Jefferson, N.Y., three days later, to join the 3d Division, Battleship Force, Atlantic Fleet. Over the ensuing 12 months, the battleship served as a gunnery training ship out of Port Jefferson and Norfolk; service interrupted briefly in early December 1917, when she became temporary flagship for Rear Admiral John A. Hoogewerff, Commander, Battleship Division 1. She subsequently became flagship for the 3d Division commander, Rear Admiral Thomas Snowden.

Overhauled at the Boston Navy Yard in the autumn of 1918, *Virginia* spent the remainder of hostilities engaged in convoy escort duties, taking convoys well over half-way across the Atlantic. She departed New York on 14 October 1918 on her first such mission, covering a convoy that had some 12,176 men embarked. After escorting those ships to longitude 22 degrees west, she put about and headed for home.

That proved to be her only such wartime mission, however, because the armistice was signed on 11 November 1918, the day before *Virginia* set out with a France-bound convoy, her second escort run into the mid-Atlantic. After leaving that convoy at longitude 34 degrees west, *Virginia* put about and headed for Hampton Roads.

The cessation of hostilities meant the return of the many troops that had been engaged in fighting the enemy overseas. Similar in mission to the "Magic Carpet" operation that followed the end of World War II, a massive troop-lift, bringing the "doughboys" back from "over there," commenced soon after World War I ended.

With additional messing and berthing facilities installed to permit her use as a troopship, *Virginia* departed Norfolk eight days before Christmas of 1918. Over the ensuing months, she conducted five round-trip voyages to Brest, France, and back. Reaching Boston on Independence Day 1919, ending her last troop lift, *Virginia* ended her transport service, having brought some 6,037 men back from France.

Virginia remained at the Boston Navy Yard, inactive, until decommissioned there on 13 August 1920. Struck from the Navy list and placed on the sale list on 12 July 1922, the battleship—reclassified prior to her inactivation to BB–13 on 17 July 1920—was subsequently taken off the sale list and transferred to the War Department on 6 August 1923 for use as a bombing target.

Virginia and her sistership *New Jersey* were taken to a point three miles off the Diamond Shoals lightship, off Cape Hatteras, N.C., and anchored there on 5 September 1923. The "attacks" made by Army Air Service Martin bombers began shortly before 0900. On the third attack, seven Martins, flying at 3,000 feet, each dropped two 1,100-pound bombs on *Virginia*—only one of them hit. That single bomb, however, "completely demolished the ship as such." An observer later wrote: "Both masts, the bridge, all three smokestacks, and the upperworks disappeared with the explosion and there remained, after the smoke cleared away, nothing but the bare hull, decks blown off, and covered with a mass of tangled debris from stem to stern consisting of stacks, ventilators, cage masts, and bridges."

Within one-half hour of the cataclysmic blast that wrecked the ship, her battered hulk sank beneath the waves. Her sistership ultimately joined her shortly thereafter. *Virginia*'s end, and *New Jersey*'s, provided far-sighted naval officers with a dramatic demonstration of air power and impressed upon them the "urgent need of developing naval aviation with the fleet." As such, the service performed by the old pre-dreadnought may have been her most valuable.

(SP–274: t. 91 (gross); l. 98'4''; b. 16'0''; dr. 5'6'' (aft); s. 13 k.; cpl. 14; a. 2 3-pdrs., 2 mg.)

Virginia—a yacht constructed in 1910 by the Elco Co. at Bayonne, N.J.—was purchased by the Navy on 5 May 1917 from Mr. Daniel W. Smith of New York City and delivered to the Government on 2 July. To avoid the confusion of having several ships of the same name, the Navy discarded her name and referred to her simply as *SP–274*, though references to her as *Virginia* (SP–274) in the *Navy Directory* for 1918 indicate that she probably retained her name informally. Commissioned on 10 August 1917, *SP–274* was assigned to the 9th Naval District section patrol; and, although the records are unclear, she probably operated out of Detroit, conducting patrols on Lake Michigan. She served until 12 August 1919, at which time her name was struck from the Navy list; and, by 18 March 1920, she had sunk at the Detroit Dock. Here again, the records are unclear with regard to whether she sank before or after being struck from the Navy list. In any event, her sunken hulk was sold to J. A. Nicholson of Morris Heights, N.J., on 1 April 1920.

(SP–746: t. 26; l. 61.6'; b. 10.4'; dr. 3'6'' (aft); s. 15 mph.; cpl. 6; a. 1 mg.)

Virginia—a motor boat built in 1906 at City Island, N.Y., and used by the Maine lobster warden—was acquired by the Navy on 13 July 1917 under free lease from the state of Maine. Though officially designated *SP–746* on the Navy list, *Virginia* retained her name informally while in naval service. The *Navy Directory* for 1918 lists her as *Virginia* (SP–746) and indicates that she was assigned to the 1st Naval District. The vessel, under the command of Boatswain A. D. Closson, USNRF, conducted patrols out of the section base located at Machias, Maine. She served the Navy until she was returned to her owner on 28 January 1919 when her name was struck from the Navy list.

(Sp–1965: t. 35 (gross); l. 61'; b. 15'8''; dr. 5' (aft); s. 8 mph.; cpl. 8)

Virginia—a two-masted, auxiliary schooner built in 1902 by F. W. McCullough at Norfolk, Va.—was ac-

quired by the Navy on Christmas Eve of 1917 under free lease from W. M. Holland of Norfolk. In Navy records, she does not appear as an active unit until July 1918—when she was listed in the *Navy Directory* as a unit of the 5th Naval District section patrol force —probably operating in and around Norfolk. Initially, she retained the name *Virginia* semi-officially and was so listed in several editions of the 1918 *Navy Directory*. However, after December 1918, she was carried on all Navy records as *SP–1965*, but frequently with a parenthetical *Virginia* added after the official designation. The schooner served the Navy until 3 January 1919 when her name was struck from the Navy list, and she was returned to her owner.

V

(CGN–38: dp. 9,473 (f.); l. 585'; b. 63'; dr. 30'6''; s. 30+ k.; cpl. 473; a. 2 mis. ln., 2 5'', Phalanx ASROC, Standard missile, Tartar, LAMPS, 6 15.5'' tt.; cl. *Virginia*)

The fifth *Virginia* (CGN–38) was laid down on 19 August 1972 by the Newport News Shipbuilding & Dry Dock Co. as a nuclear-powered, guided-missile frigate, DLGN–38; launched on 14 December 1974; sponsored by Miss Virginia S. Warner, daughter of the

The guided-missile cruiser *Virginia* (CGN–38).

Honorable John Warner, former Secretary of the Navy; reclassified a nuclear-powered, guided-missile cruiser and redesignated CGN–38 on 30 June 1975; and commissioned on 11 September 1976, Capt. George W. Davis, Jr., in command.

During the first six months of her commissioned service, *Virginia* ranged the eastern seaboard of the United States and cruised in the West Indies several times conducting a myriad of post-commissioning tests and shakedown training. On 25 April 1977, she entered the Norfolk Naval Shipyard for a five-month, post-shakedown availability. She completed her final sea trials on 28 September and began duty as an operational unit of the Atlantic Fleet. In November, she cruised along the New England and Canadian coasts, participating in antisubmarine warfare exercises. In December, she returned to the West Indies for missile firings on the Atlantic Fleet weapons range. She completed that mission on 13 December and reentered Norfolk three days later to begin holiday leave and upkeep in her home port. The beginning of 1978 found her still in Norfolk; but, by mid-month, she returned to sea in the Virginia capes operating area for a series of local operations. On 28 January, however, she departed Norfolk to return to the area along the Florida coast and in the West Indies for a series of special tests conducted under the auspices of the Office of the Chief of Naval Operations. The guided-missile cruiser returned to Norfolk on 23 March and resumed local operations.

That employment lasted until 23 August when she embarked upon a cruise to northern Europe to participate in Operation "Northern Wedding," a NATO exercise the purpose of which was to test the ability to reinforce NATO forces in western Europe. During that deployment, she visited Oslo in Norway, Rotterdam in the Netherlands, and Portsmouth in England. The warship departed the latter port on 3 October and reentered Norfolk on the 12th. On 16 November, she put to sea for training exercises in the Gulf of Mexico. During that voyage, she made a port visit at Mobile, Ala., and conducted naval gunfire support training at Vieques Island near Puerto Rico. She made another port visit to the island of St. Thomas on 6 and 7 December before heading home. *Virginia* reentered Norfolk on 11 December and began preparations for her first deployment to the Mediterranean which was scheduled to commence in early 1979.

Virginian

I

(Tug: t. 179 (reg.); l. 90'0''; b. 21'0''; dr. 7'9'' (mean); s. 8.0 k.; cpl. 15)

Virginian—a steamer built in 1904 at Camden, N.J., as *Blue Belle*—was acquired by the Navy at Philadelphia from the Southern Transportation Co., probably late in 1917. Apparently commissioned in January 1918, she served as a tug in the 5th Naval District—probably at Norfolk, Va.—through the end of World War I. On 12 May 1919, she was returned to her owner, and her name was struck from the Navy list.

II

(ScStr.: t. 7,914 (gross); l. 492'0''; b. 58'3''; dr. 31'9''; cpl. 106; tr. 4,771 (approx.); a. none)

The second *Virginian*, a transport, was originally built as the steel-hulled, twin-screw steamship *Maine*. Completed in 1903 at Sparrows Point, Md., by the Maryland Steel Co., *Maine* was operated by the Atlantic Transportation Co. until 1908. In that year, she was acquired by the American-Hawaiian Steamship Co. and renamed *Virginian*. Except for the brief period of service with the Navy in 1919, *Virginian* remained with that company, homeported in New York, into the 1940's.

Early in 1919, the Navy acquired the steamship for service with the Cruiser and Transport Force, United States Atlantic Fleet. She was commissioned at Hoboken, N.J., on 1 February 1919, Lt. Comdr. John S. Greene in command, and, soon thereafter, shifted to Fletcher's Dry Dock Co., Hoboken, for alterations and repairs. She remained at Fletcher's yard through the end of February.

On 11 March, *Virginian* got underway and anchored in New York harbor, abreast the Statue of Liberty. She then moved to pier 7, Bush Terminal, Brooklyn, N.Y., where she took on board cargo—billet steel, oats, and potatoes—and provisions for her crew. Repairs and alterations—necessary to convert the erstwhile merchant steamer to a troop ship—continued apace until she backed clear of her berth at 1713 on 21 March, with orders to proceed independently to France.

Virginian dropped anchor off Charpentier Point, near St. Nazaire, on 3 April, and shifted to that key seaport the following day. She unloaded her cargo there for the next two days before she began embarking Army troops for transport back to the United States. Her passengers included 74 officers and 4,097 men, from units that ranged from the 362d Infantry Machine Gun Co. to the 127th Convalescent Detachment. She got underway at 0740 on 8 April to return to the United States.

Arriving at the north side of Army dock number 7, Hoboken, on the morning of 20 April, *Virginian* discharged the troops before shifting to the Morse Dry Docks, Brooklyn, for repairs to her propellers. She shifted back to the Army dock at Hoboken on the 27th, only to get underway three days later to pick up returning doughboys for passage home.

Virginian reached St. Nazaire on the afternoon of 11 May, took on board 56 officers and 4,069 men, and departed that port on the 13th, bound for Hampton Roads. After a 12-day passage, the transport moored at the C&O docks at Newport News on the afternoon of 25 May and had all of the troops disembarked within an hour. After a brief period of upkeep and repairs at the Norfolk Navy Yard, Portsmouth, Va., *Virginian* again set sail for France.

The troop transport subsequently conducted two more round-trip voyages, bringing back men from "over there." She took the third group of troops back to Hampton Roads (the third voyage lasting from 1 to 25 June) and the fourth and final one to Hoboken (the voyage taking from 1 July to 3 August). After discharging the last troops, by 0945 on 4 August, *Virginian* began to prepare for demobilization. Over the next fortnight, yard workmen and ship's company bent to the task of taking down troop fittings, performing routine maintenance tasks, discharging ballasts, cleaning holds, and inventorying equipment. At 1600 on 19 August 1919, *Virginian* was decommissioned and formally turned over to the representative of the American-Hawaiian Steamship Co., Capt. John S. Greene (who had, incidentally, been the transport's first commanding officer). She subsequently resumed her mercantile service with the American-Hawaiian shipping firm, serving into the late 1940's. Her name ultimately disappeared from period shipping registers at the end of the decade.

Virgo

A zodiacal constellation located on the celestial equator due south of the handle of the Dipper. It is pictured as a woman holding a spike of grain and derives its name from the Latin word for virgin.

(AKA–20: dp. 13,910 (tl.); l. 459'3''; b. 63'0''; dr. 26'4'' (lim.); s. 16.5 k. (tl.); cpl. 473; a. 1 5'', 4 3''; cl. *Andromeda*; T. C2–S–B1)

Virgo (AKA–20) was laid down on 9 March 1943 at Kearny, N.J., by the Federal Shipbuilding & Drydock Co. under a Maritime Commission contract (MC hull

204); launched on 4 June 1943; sponsored by Miss Sharman Douglas; delivered to the Navy on 15 July 1943; and commissioned at the New York Navy Yard on 16 July 1943, Comdr. Clayton H. McLaughlin in command.

Virgo conducted her shakedown training in the Chesapeake Bay and off the Virginia capes in July and August and then departed Norfolk on 24 August, bound for the Pacific. She transited the Panama Canal on 31 August and arrived in San Diego, Calif., on 9 September. On the 15th, she continued her voyage west. The attack cargo ship entered Pearl Harbor on 21 September and began cargo operations—unloading some and taking on more. *Virgo* stood out of Pearl Harbor on 24 September and set a course for New Zealand. She arrived in Wellington on 6 October and began a series of landing craft exercises. The ship remained at Wellington until 1 November at which time she got underway for the New Hebrides Islands. She arrived in Havannah Harbor at the island of Efate to conduct training and make preparations for the forthcoming Gilberts and Marshalls invasions.

Virgo departed the New Hebrides on 13 November in company with a convoy bound for the Gilbert Islands. She arrived off Tarawa Atoll early on the morning of the 20th. While preparing to land marines on Betio Island, *Virgo* was straddled by four shells from a Japanese shore battery. However, air strikes and counter battery fire quickly silenced the offender, and *Virgo* resumed landing operations. She remained offshore while the marines carried out their bloody struggle—the bloodiest battle in American military history—to wrest control of the atoll from a well-fortified enemy. During that struggle and while the other islands of the atoll were cleared, *Virgo* remained in the vicinity of Tarawa. On 28 November, she cleared the Gilberts on her way to Hawaii. The attack cargo ship arrived in Pearl Harbor on 7 December. During the following six weeks, she practiced amphibious operations in the Hawaiian Islands in preparation for Operation "Flintlock," the assault and occupation of atolls in the Marshall Islands. On 22 January 1944, *Virgo* departed Oahu in company with Task Force (TF) 52, bound for the Marshalls. She arrived off Kwajalein Atoll early on the morning of 31 January and began launching boats and discharging troops. No untoward events occurred during her five-day stay at Kwajalein, and she departed the atoll on 4 February. The attack cargo ship arrived at Funafuti in the Ellice Islands on 8 February and remained there until the 19th when she got underway for Guadalcanal. The ship anchored in Port Purvis, Florida Island, on 24 February and began a series of amphibious training exercises in the southern Solomons.

That employment lasted until 27 March, on which day she got underway for Bougainville in the northern Solomons with elements of the Army's 25th Regimental Combat Team (RCT). She discharged those troops and their attending equipment at Bougainville on 28 March and departed that same day for New Guinea. *Virgo* entered Milne Bay, New Guinea, on 31 March and remained there until 4 April when she headed for Cape Sudest. The ship stopped at Cape Sudest from 5 to 14 April and then headed for the Beli Beli Islands. She reached that destination on the 15th and began loading elements of the Army's 24th RCT. Underway again on the 16th, *Virgo* set a course for Tanamerah Bay, New Guinea, where she arrived on 23 April. She unloaded the troops and their equipment and departed Tanamerah Bay on the 24th. She stopped at Cape Sudest on the 27th and arrived at Saidor on the 29th. There, she loaded men and equipment of the Army's 36th Infantry Division. On 1 May, the ship put to sea once again, bound for Aitape, New Guinea, where she arrived on the 3d and unloaded troops and equipment. Departing Aitape that same day, *Virgo* set a course via Cape Sudest for Guadalcanal where she arrived on 10 May. At Guadalcanal, the attack cargo ship loaded troops of the 1st Marine Provisional Brigade and began amphibious training exercises which lasted until 31 May.

On 4 June, she departed Guadalcanal with troops embarked for the invasion of the Mariana Islands. She stopped at Kwajalein from 9 to 11 June and then put to sea once again on the 12th. *Virgo*'s troops were not committed to the 15 June landings on Saipan. Instead, they made up a part of the floating reserve and were scheduled to land on Guam later in the month. However, Saipan proved to be a tougher nut to crack than expected; and, as a consequence, the Guam assault was delayed. After steaming around to the east of Saipan for several days—during which the 5th Fleet carriers destroyed the remnants of Japanese naval air power in the Battle of the Philippine Sea—she then put in at Eniwetok Atoll on 30 June to await reinforcements for the delayed invasion of Guam. The ship rode at anchor in Eniwetok until 17 July when she returned to sea and set a course back to the Marianas. On the 21st, she arrived off Guam, and her troops landed near Orote Peninsula. The attack cargo ship remained off Agate Bay until 27 July at which time she took leave of the Marianas on her way—via Eniwetok—to Espiritu Santo in the New Hebrides.

The ship arrived at Espiritu Santo on 6 August and, for the next month, conducted amphibious training there and at Guadalcanal. On 8 September, *Virgo* left Guadalcanal and shaped a course for the Palau Islands. She arrived off Peleliu Island early on the morning of 15 September, and her embarked troops stormed ashore at about 0830. She remained in the Palaus for almost a month supporting the troops in their difficult battle to subdue the Peleliu garrison. On 3 October, she departed the Palau Islands to return to Guadalcanal via the Russell Islands. She arrived at her destination on 12 October. The following day, the ship received orders to return to the United States and got underway almost immediately. After a non-stop voyage, *Virgo* arrived in San Francisco, Calif., on 29 October and, soon thereafter, began a two-month overhaul at the Hunters Point Navy Yard.

The attack cargo ship stood out of San Francisco on 4 January 1945 to return to the western Pacific. She stopped at Pearl Harbor from 10 to 28 January before continuing her voyage west. Along the way, *Virgo* also made a visit to Eniwetok before arriving in Ulithi on 13 February where she reported for duty with Service Squadron (ServRon) 10. Her tour of duty with ServRon 10 brought a change in mission for the ship. No longer did she serve as an assault cargo carrier engaged in amphibious operations. From that point forward, the attack cargo ship served as a straight cargo carrier. In that role, she supported the Iwo Jima operation in February by replenishing warships at sea. In April and May, *Virgo* performed similar services in support of the Okinawa campaign. In May, she began a return voyage to the United States, departing Okinawa on 15 May. En route, she made stops at Ulithi and at Pearl Harbor before arriving in San Francisco on 20 June. After a month in overhaul at Moore's Shipyard, *Virgo* headed back to the western Pacific on 3 August. However, she did not resume warlike activities because hostilities ceased on 15 August, four days before she arrived in the lagoon at Ulithi. The next day, she returned to sea with Task Group (TG) 30.8 to provision the ships of the 3d Fleet in Japanese waters. Finishing that mission early in September, *Virgo* arrived in Tokyo Bay on the 9th, a week after the formal surrender. She served as station store ship at Yokosuka for the occupation forces until 10 April 1946 at which time she headed back to the United States. The ship arrived in San Francisco on 14 May and began overhaul at the San Francisco Naval Shipyard.

She completed repairs in August and, on the 21st, began a series of voyages from the west coast to American bases in the Far East. She carried provisions and stores to bases in the Philippines, in the Marianas, in Japan, and in China. She also made side trips to Okinawa, the Admiralty Islands, and Korea. That routine lasted until the latter half of 1949. In October 1949, she began an overhaul at the Puget Sound Naval Shipyard which lasted until the beginning of 1950. Between 7 February and 31 March 1950, the attack cargo ship made a round-trip voyage from Oakland to Guam and back to San Diego. On 25 April, she departed San Diego for a voyage to the east coast of the United States. During that voyage, she transited the Panama Canal and visited both Bayonne, N.J., and Norfolk, Va. She returned to the west coast via the Panama Canal once more and arrived back in San Diego on 17 July.

While *Virgo* visited the east coast, conflict broke out in the Far East once again. On 25 June, troops of communist North Korea invaded the Republic of Korea (ROK) to the south. The United States, and later the United Nations, responded with support for South Korea against the aggressors. Thus, *Virgo* soon found herself supporting combat forces once more. On 19 August, she departed Port Chicago, Calif., with Navy passengers embarked and with a load of ammunition, bound ultimately for Korea. She stopped at Sasebo, Japan, from 6 to 15 September and then headed for Inchon, Korea. She arrived at Inchon on the 16th, the day following the amphibious landing carried out there. She remained in the Korean war zone, first at Inchon and later at Jinsen Ko, for about three weeks. During that time, the attack cargo ship provisioned minesweepers, a Canadian destroyer, an American destroyer and supplied ammunition to the troops ashore. She departed Korea on 7 October and returned to Japan where she visited Sasebo and Yokosuka before heading back to the United States on 1 November. After a stop at Pearl Harbor, the ship arrived in San Francisco on 19 November and began repairs at the Pacific Repair Co.

On 19 January 1951, *Virgo* departed San Francisco for her second tour of duty in the Korean combat zone. She arrived in Sasebo on 6 February to disembark passengers and unload ammunition. From Sasebo, the ship moved to Yokosuka at mid-month; and, from there, she headed for Korea. The attack cargo ship entered port at Pusan on 15 March but soon returned to sea to transfer ammunition to *Valley Forge* (CV–45) and to *Juneau* (CL–119). Following that, she returned to Sasebo for several days on the 19th. At the end of the month, she resumed ammunition resupply duty along the Korean coast, visiting Songjin, Wonsan, Suyong, and Pohang as well as replenishing ships at sea between port calls. She returned to Sasebo on 7 May and remained there until the 29th when she got underway to return to the United States. On 13 June, the attack cargo ship entered port at Long Beach Calif., and began overhaul at the Long Beach Naval Shipyard. She completed repairs in August and, after refresher training out of San Diego, loaded passengers and ammunition at Port Chicago in late September. On 5 October, she put to sea to return to the Far East. The ship arrived in Sasebo on 22 October, disembarked her passengers, and unloaded some ammunition before getting underway for the war zone once more. During that tour of duty, her mission consisted entirely of replenishments at sea in support of United Nations naval forces operating off the Korean coast. That assignment lasted until 12 August 1952 at which time she departed Yokosuka for home. She stopped at Pearl Harbor along the way and arrived in San Francisco on the 25th. *Virgo* then began an availability at the Triple "A" Machine Shop in San Francisco.

Virgo completed repairs in October and departed San Francisco on 1 November to resume duty in the Orient. She arrived in Sasebo on 19 November and remained there almost two months. On 3 January 1953, the ship stood out of Sasebo, bound for Korean waters. For the next five months, she resumed the familiar schedule

USS *Virgo* (AKA–20), 1959. (USN 1044326)

f replenishments at sea punctuated by ammunition deliveries at Korean ports and return trips to Sasebo or the purpose of restocking her own supplies. She completed her last mission early in June and, on the 8th, headed back to the United States. She reentered San Francisco on 28 June and entered the Mare Island Naval Shipyard for a three-month overhaul. While she underwent repairs, hostilities in Korea effectively ceased with the signing of an armistice on 19 July 1953. Thus, when she emerged from the shipyard late in September and prepared to resume voyages to the Far East, her missions lost their combat character.

Over the next five years, she continued to make voyages between the west coast and American bases in the Far East. Most frequently, she called at such ports as Sasebo and Yokosuka in Japan, Kaohsiung on the island of Taiwan, and Manila and Subic Bay in the Philippines. Less frequently, she stopped at the Japanese ports of Kure and Kobe, at Okinawa, Guam, and Hong Kong. At the end of that five years, on 3 April 1958, Virgo was decommissioned and berthed with the Columbia River Group, Pacific Reserve Fleet, located at Astoria, Oreg. On 1 July 1961, her name was struck from the Navy list; and she was transferred to the custody of the Maritime Administration. She was berthed with the National Defense Reserve Fleet located also at Astoria.

In September 1965, the Navy took custody of her once again, and her name was reinstated on the Navy list. On 1 November 1965, she was reclassified as an ammunition ship and redesignated AE–30. After almost a year of reactivation and rehabilitation work on the ship, Virgo (AE–30) was recommissioned at Seattle, Wash., on 19 August 1966, Capt. Harold R. MacMillan in command. She spent the remainder of 1966 engaged in shakedown training and independent ship's exercises along the west coast. In January of 1967, she loaded ammunition at Concord, Calif., in preparation for her first deployment to the western Pacific in support of the American effort in the Vietnamese civil war. She departed Concord on 12 January and arrived in Subic Bay on 6 February. There, she unloaded a part of her cargo before departing the Philippines on the 12th for replenishment missions in the Gulf of Tonkin. During the following six months, the ship made an equal number of replenishment voyages from Subic Bay to the warships operating in the Gulf of Tonkin to keep them supplied with ammunition. She punctuated those assignments with liberty calls at Subic Bay and at Hong Kong. Virgo headed back to the United States on 22 August. Almost a month later, on 21 September, she moored at the naval weapons station at Concord, Calif. She spent the remainder of the year engaged in normal operations out of her base at Concord.

During the first six weeks of 1968, Virgo loaded ammunition in preparation for and participation in the 1st Fleet exercise, Operation "Bead Stringer." In mid-February, she loaded ammunition for her second deployment to the western Pacific during the Vietnam conflict. On 26 February, she began her voyage west. The ship changed operational control to the 7th Fleet on 7 March and arrived in Subic Bay 12 days later. Once again, her assignment fell into a pattern of replenishment voyages to the ships operating in the Gulf of Tonkin. In six months' time, she made eight line wings from Subic Bay to the gulf bringing in new stocks of ammunition to refill the depleted magazines of American warships along the Vietnamese coast. She finished her last such mission early in October and returned to Subic Bay on the 10th. From there, she moved to Sasebo, Japan, for a four-day liberty call before getting underway for the United States on 23 October. The ammunition ship arrived back in Concord on 11 November, offloaded ammunition, and entered the Mare Island Naval Shipyard to begin post-deployment standdown. On 19 December, she moved to the Triple "A" shipyard to begin a six-week restricted availability.

Her repair period continued until the end of January 1969. On the 31st, she loaded ammunition at Concord in preparation for operations at sea with units of the 1st Fleet. Those missions—primarily to train new crew members—lasted until the beginning of April. After final loadout at Concord, she got underway for the Far East on 19 April. She arrived in Subic Bay on 14 May and, after two weeks of voyage repairs, began the familiar series of voyages between Subic Bay and Vietnamese waters to resupply 7th Fleet ships with ammunition. However, the increasing use of the fast combat support ship (AOE), which combined the features of both ammunition ship and oiler, relegated her to a reduced role.

During most of her eight line swings, Virgo either served as a backup for the AOE's or concentrated on replenishing the cruisers and destroyers operating close to the coast. The ammunition ship completed her eighth and final line period on 12 November and returned to Subic Bay on the 14th. On the 19th, Virgo got underway for Sasebo where she remained from the 23d to the 26th. On the latter day, she departed Sasebo and shaped a course for home. The ship arrived back in Concord on 13 December and began post-deployment leave and upkeep.

Standdown continued into January 1970. On 21 January, she began a restricted availability at the Bethlehem Steel shipyard located in San Francisco. Repairs complete on 16 February, Virgo moved back to Concord to load ammunition in preparation for operations at sea along the west coast. Refresher and type training occupied her time until 7 May at which time she departed San Francisco for the last western Pacific development of her Navy career. Virgo arrived in Subic Bay on 29 May and embarked upon the first of six line periods supplying ammunition to the warships off Vietnam. She completed her final line swing early in November and, after a stop at Sasebo, she got underway for home on 27 November. She arrived back at Concord on 12 December and began preparations for decommissioning. Virgo (AE–30) was decommissioned at Vallejo, Calif., on 18 February 1971, and her name was struck from the Navy list simultaneously. Subsequently transferred to the Maritime Administration for disposal, she was sold on 19 November 1973 to Taipei Hsieh, of Taiwan, for scrapping.

Virgo earned seven battle stars during World War II, nine battle stars for Korean War service, and 10 battle stars for service during the Vietnam conflict.

Vision

(MB: t. 13 (gross); l. 45'; b. 9'9''; dr. 2'9'' (mean); s. 18 k.; cpl. 8; a. 1 .30-cal. mg.)

Vision (SP–744)—a wooden-hulled, "express-cruiser," screw launch designed by Thomas V. Taylor and completed in 1916 at Watervliet, N.Y., by the Albany Boat Corp.—was acquired by the Navy on 3 July 1917 under free lease from L. E. Anderson; and was commissioned on the same day.

However, to avoid confusion with Vision (SP–1114), the Navy soon dropped the screw launch's name; and she served under her hull number, SP–744. Attached to the 2d Naval District, SP–744 operated out of Newport, R.I., on harbor and harbor entrance patrol duties. She also patrolled off the Naval War College and off Rose Island.

Following engine repairs from November 1917 to February 1918, SP–744 resumed patrols in the Newport area. On 23 June, the boat got underway southward for duty in the 8th Naval District. Proceeding via a succession of ports along the eastern seaboard from New London, Conn., to Charleston, S.C., Vision arrived at St. Augustine, Fla., on 15 October. She subsequently operated out of Miami, Fla., until she was decommissioned there on 22 January 1919 and returned to her owner.

I

(MB: t. 13 (gross) ; l. 67'6''; b. 12'6''; dr. 4' (mean) ; s. 12 k.; cpl. 9; a. 1 1-pdr.)

Vision (SP–1114)—a wooden-hulled motorboat completed in 1910 at Harrisburg, Tex., by William Nelson—was acquired by the Navy under a free lease from Haywood Nelms on 27 August 1917; and was commissioned the same day, Ens. Frank H. Nelms, USNRF, in command.

Assigned to the 3d section, 8th Naval District, *Vision* operated in the Gulf of Mexico off the Texas ports of Freeport, Sabine, Palacios, and Galveston. On occasion, she also conducted patrols off the entrance to the Brazos River and in Matagorda Bay.

Vision was towed by *SC–157* from Galveston to Harrisburg, was decommissioned on 19 December 1918, and was returned to her owner on the same day.

Visitor

(Tug: l. 63'6''; b. 15'0''; dr. 6'9''; s. 10.0 k.)

Visitor (SP–2266)—a tug built in 1883 at Baltimore, Md.—was acquired by the Navy on 17 April 1917 and was assigned to the 4th Naval District. *Visitor* served as a tug in the 4th Naval District—though probably not as a commissioned ship—for the remainder of World War I. In all likelihood, she operated at Philadelphia and on the Delaware River in an "in-service" status—although no documentation exists to corroborate that conjecture. In any event, she concluded her naval career in mid-December and was returned to her owner on the 17th. Her name was struck from the Navy list concurrently with her disposal.

Vital

Vital (AM–129)—an *Auk*-class minesweeper—was laid down on 1 January 1942 at Chickasaw, Ala., by the Gulf Shipbuilding Corp.; launched on 7 September 1942; sponsored by Miss E. Herrmann; and completed on 18 May 1943.

Turned over to the Royal Navy under provisions of the lend-lease agreement, *Vital* was renamed HMS *Strenuous* (J.338) and subsequently served in the British Navy for the duration of World War II. Returned to the United States Government after the war on 10 December 1946, the ship resumed her former classification, AM–129, but not her former name. She was carried on the Naval Vessel *Register* as *Strenuous* (AM–129), and in the 1 January 1947 edition of the *Naval Vessel Register* as merely AM–129. She was declared surplus on 23 April 1947 and sold by the State Department's Foreign Liquidation Commission to a foreign purchaser. She served in the merchant service until she was broken up for scrap in Germany in July 1956.

I

(MSO–474: dp. 775; l. 172'; b. 35'; dr. 10'; s. 14 k.; cpl. 70; a. 1 40mm., 2 .50-cal. mg.; cl. *Aggressive*)

Vital (MSO–474) was laid down as AM–474 on 3 October 1952 at Manitowoc, Wis., by the Burger Boat Co.; launched on 12 August 1953; sponsored by Mrs. Edwina Smith; redesignated MSO–474 on 7 February 1955; and commissioned on 9 June 1955 at the Boston Naval Shipyard, Lt. Bruce E. Prum in command.

Following shakedown and an availability at Charleston, S.C., *Vital* was deployed to the Mediterranean late in the spring of 1956. In addition to normal 6th Fleet operations and Mediterranean port visits, she participated in a special NATO minesweeping exercise conducted in the North Sea during September and October. The minesweeper returned to Charleston late

USS *Vital* (MSO–474), 1955. The white objects on her after decks are floats which support various types of mine sweeping gear. A large winch at the forward end of *Vital*'s fantail controls sweep wires; the conspicuous reel forward of this holds magnetic minesweeping cables (80–G–668767)

that fall and began operations along the southern Atlantic seaboard of the United States. In March 1957, she moved to the Gulf of Mexico for a three-month training period at the conclusion of which she returned to Charleston and resumed normal duty.

In July 1958, *Vital*'s home port was changed from Charleston to Panama City, Fla. From the latter port, she participated in experimental work with the Operational Test and Evaluation Force under the auspices of the Naval Mine Defense Laboratory. She remained based at that port for the next 12 and one-half years, departing periodically for deployments in foreign waters. The first break in her experimental work schedule came in August 1960 when she embarked upon a three-month cruise in the Caribbean. After returning to Panama City in November and resuming duty with the Mine Defense Laboratory, she remained so occupied until February of 1962, at which time the minesweeper headed across the Atlantic with the other units of Mine Division (MinDiv) 81 for a six-month tour of duty with the 6th Fleet in the Mediterranean. She arrived back in Panama City in August and resumed services to the Mine Defense Laboratory. Following 14 months of normal operations in the Gulf of Mexico, *Vital* headed south for a four-month assignment in the West Indies which she concluded at Panama City on 9 February 1964.

Upon the conclusion of that Caribbean deployment, *Vital* settled down to a routine of operations out of Panama City broken only by three Mediterranean deployments and an ascent of the Mississippi River in May of 1967 to participate in the Cotton Carnival at Memphis, Tenn. On 1 January 1971, *Vital* received word that her home port had changed back to Charleston. She arrived there on the 27th and, for the next 20 months, operated from that base as a unit of the Atlantic Fleet Mine Force. On 22 September 1972, *Vital* was decommissioned at Charleston. She was towed to Hampton Roads late in November and, on the 30th, placed in the Norfolk Group of the Atlantic Reserve Fleet. She remained there until struck from the Navy list in September 1977. At that time, she was scheduled to be sold; but no word of her final disposition was available as of May 1978.

Vitality

PG–100: dp. 980; l. 205'0''; b. 33'0''; dr. 11'; s. 16 k.; cpl. 109; a. (Br.) 1 4'', 1 2-pdr., 6 20mm., 1 dcp. (hh.))

During the first year and more after America entered the war against the Axis, the United States Navy suffered from an acute shortage of warships, particularly of antisubmarine warfare and escort types. To fill that need, an extensive ship construction and acquisition program was inaugurated. Part of that program consisted of placing orders with British and Canadian firms already tooled up to produce Flower-class corvettes. *Vitality* (PG–100) was such a ship. However, before she was launched on 15 April 1943 by the Midland Shipyard in Great Britain, she was traded to the Royal Navy under the terms of the lend-lease agreement for a similar ship being constructed in Canada. The British renamed her *Willowherb* (K.283), and she served in the Royal Navy for the duration of the war. On 11 June 1946, she was returned to the custody of the United States Navy. Though carried on the Navy list as PG–100 following the war, *Vitality* never actively served the United States Navy. She remained idle until sold on 7 May 1947. To whom she was sold and for what purpose is unknown, but one source indicates that she was not scrapped until 1961.

Vitesse

(MB: t. 18 (gross); l. 60'0''; b. 10'0''; dr. 3'0'' (mean); s. 22.0 k.; cpl. 7; a. 1 3-pdr., 1 Colt mg.)

Vitesse—a wooden-hulled motorboat built in 1917 at Greenport, Long Island, N.Y., by the Greenport Basin and Construction Co.—was acquired by the Navy in July 1917 from Charles Fry under a free lease. Assigned the designation SP–1192, *Vitesse* was commissioned at the Philadelphia Navy Yard on 18 July 1917, Machinist's Mate Second Class Charles Fry, USNRF, in temporary command. Eleven days later, on 29 July, Lt. (jg.) E. C. Sweeney, USNRF, assumed command.

Over the next few weeks, *Vitesse* remained in the Philadelphia area, fitting out. Her main battery, a single pedestal-mounted 3-pounder, was installed at the Essington Ship Building Co., Essington, Pa., on 3 August. Four days later, the boat received her secondary battery, a single Colt machine gun; and she took on ammunition at Fort Mifflin the following day. *Vitesse* ultimately departed Philadelphia on the afternoon of 9 August, carrying 1,000 hymn books for the chaplain at Cape May, N.J.—her assigned section base —as well as confidential publications for the commander of the harbor entrance patrol there.

Assigned to the 4th Naval District's harbor entrance patrol at the outset of her naval career, *Vitesse* performed her initial duty out of Sewall's Point and Cape May. She patrolled assigned sectors, usually off net defenses, speaking to and identifying passing naval and merchant vessels. In addition, she occasionally carried dispatches to other boats on patrol and stood by, ready to assist other nearby small craft in need of aid.

Vitesse escorted the yacht *Aloha* (SP–317), the flagship for Rear Admiral Cameron McR. Winslow, Inspector of Naval Districts, Atlantic Coast, when Admiral Winslow inspected the wreck of the steamer SS *Herbert Pratt* off Lewes, Del., on 4 and 5 June 1918. Later, on 30 September 1918, while operating temporarily out of the Corinthian Yacht Club, near Philadelphia, *Vitesse* embarked Rear Admiral James M. Helm, Commandant of the 4th Naval District, and Rear Admiral Hugo Osterhaus, USN (Ret.), from the Office of Naval Districts, as they toured Philadelphia harbor on an inspection trip.

After a final stint of patrol operations out of Lewes, Del., *Vitesse* departed that vicinity at 0605 on 24 November—13 days after the armistice and five days after the discontinuance of "military patrol" activities —and arrived at Fort Mifflin at 1600 to offload ammunition the same day. When that task was done, the motorboat proceeded on to pier 19, Philadelphia, arriving there at 1715 the same day. She remained there until decommissioned on 3 December 1918. Struck from the Navy list the following day, *Vitesse* was simultaneously returned to her owner.

Vittorio Emmanuele III

(Id. No. 3095: dp. 10,820; l. 380'; b. 53'9''; dr. 23'9''; dph. 29'3''; s. 10½ k.; cpl. 52; a. 1 5'', 1 3'')

Vittorio Emmanuele III (Id. No. 3095), a cargo steamer constructed in 1918 by the Seattle Construction & Drydock Co., was taken over by the Navy from the United States Shipping Board on 27 June 1918 and commissioned at Seattle, Wash., on 28 June 1918, Lt. Comdr. William A. Carleton, USNRF, in command.

Assigned to the Naval Overseas Transportation Service (NOTS), *Vittorio Emmanuele III* was refitted for naval service at Seattle. She departed that port on 5 July and set a course for Arica, Chile. She arrived at her destination on 30 July and loaded a cargo of nitrates. On 18 August, she stood out of Arica bound, via the Panama Canal, to Norfolk. The cargo ship entered Hampton Roads late in the month. At Norfolk, she loaded an Army cargo and, on 28 September, returned to sea, bound for New York and a rendezvous with a convoy bound for Europe. On 30 September, she departed New York with the convoy. The ship arrived in Brest, France, on 15 October and discharged her cargo. She then took on ballast and, on 3 November, set sail for home. After a coaling stop at Bermuda on 22 November, the cargo ship arrived back in Norfolk on the 28th. On 1 December, she got underway for Philadelphia, where she loaded another Army cargo. *Vittorio Emmanuele III* stood out of Philadelphia on 15 December and arrived in Quiberon, France, on 4 January 1919. After unloading her cargo at Quiberon, she moved to Brest where she loaded a return cargo. On 9 February, she headed back to the United States. The ship entered Philadelphia on 7 March, unloaded her cargo, and began preparations for decommissioning. *Vittorio Emmanuele III* was placed out of commission at Philadelphia on 4 April 1919, and she was returned to the United States Shipping Board. Her name was struck from the Navy list on 4 April also. Sold by the United States Shipping Board to G. E. Marsden sometime early in the 1920's, she operated in mercantile service—first as SS *Vittorio Emmanuele III* and after 1939 as SS *Vitorlock*—until early in 1947. At that time, her name disappeared from the merchant ship registers.

Vivace

(ScStr.: t. 66 (net); l. 118'0''; b. 12'0''; dph. 7'6''; dr. 4'3'' (aft); s. 22.0 k.; cpl. 12; a. 1 3-pdr., 1 1-pdr., 2 .30-cal. mg.)

Vixen—a composite-construction, screw-steam yacht designed by the noted naval architect, Charles L. Seabury—was built in 1904 at Morris Heights, N.Y., as a joint project of the firms of Charles L. Seabury Co. and the Gas Engine and Power Co. Later renamed *Vivace* and owned by the firms that built her, the yacht was inspected by the Navy for possible use as a section patrol craft and was assigned the classification SP–583.

"Enrolled and ordered delivered" on 18 June 1917, *Vivace* was commissioned on 20 September 1917 and was assigned to the 3d Naval District. No deck logs for this vessel are extant; but it is reasonable to surmise that she conducted local patrol operations in that district. One must assume that such operations were interspersed with the usual maintenance, upkeep, and training evolutions common to ships of her type. Listed as "out of commission" on 28 September 1918, *Vivace* was simultaneously struck from the Navy list. She was ultimately sold to Marvin Briggs, Inc., of Brooklyn, N.Y., on 16 April 1919, for junk.

Vixen

A female fox.

I

(Sch.: t. 170; l. 83'6''; b. 23'7½''; dph. 9'6''; cpl. 111; a. 12 18-pdr. car.)

The first *Vixen*—one of four vessels authorized by Congress on 28 February 1803—was built at Baltimore, Md., in the spring of 1803; and launched on 25 June, Lt. John Smith in command.

Designed especially for operations in the shoal waters off the coast of Tripoli, *Vixen* joined Commodore Edward Preble's squadron for duty in the Tripolitan War of 1801 to 1805 immediately upon her commissioning. She sailed from Baltimore on 3 August and deployed with the squadron off Gibraltar on 14 September. Commodore Preble dispatched *Vixen* and the frigate *Philadelphia* to Tripoli in October 1803 to establish the blockade there. However, *Vixen* soon departed in search of two Tripolitan warships and was not present when *Philadelphia* grounded and was captured on the 31st. Instead, she carried the dispatches announcing the loss of the frigate and the imprisonment of Capt. William Bainbridge, his officers, and crew back to Gibraltar in December.

Retribution for this latest, and by far most brazen outrage in a long series of depredations by the Tripoli pirates came swiftly and dramatically. Lt. Stephen Decatur, Jr., boarded and destroyed *Philadelphia* where she lay in Tripoli harbor on 16 February 1804, and Commodore Preble later followed this up with five heavy bombardments of the pirate state on 3, 7, 24, and 29 August, and on 3 September. *Vixen* participated in all these actions, and performed valuable tactical service by helping to coordinate the movements of the various American vessels. She was rerigged as a brig in September 1804, ostensibly to improve her sailing qualities, and was with the squadron, now under Commodore John Rodgers, in actions before Tunis in August 1805. The warship returned to the United States one year later in August 1806.

Vixen was placed in ordinary at the Washington Navy Yard immediately upon her return from the Mediterranean. She left the yard one year later and subsequently operated along the Atlantic coast under Lieutenants James Lawrence and Charles Ludlow. She continued this duty until the outbreak of the War of 1812, at which time she sailed along the southern coast under Master Commandant Christopher Gadsden, Jr., and, after his death on 28 August 1812, under Lt. George Washington Read. During one of her war cruises among the West Indies, *Vixen* was chased, intercepted, and captured by the 32-gun British frigate HMS *Southampton* on 22 November 1812. Both vessels were soon afterwards wrecked on Concepcion Island in the Bahamas, but the officers and crews all survived. Lt. Read, however, died of yellow fever in Jamaica before he could be exchanged.

II

(Brig: a. 14 guns)

The second *Vixen* was purchased by the Navy at Savannah, Ga., in 1813. She was captured at sea by the frigate HMS *Belvidera* on 25 December 1813 while sailing from Wilmington, N.C., to Newcastle, Del. without her armament or stores.

III

(SwGbt.: t. 240; l. 118'; b. 22'6''; dr. 7'; s. 7½ k.; cpl. 55; a. 1 8'' Sg., 2 32-pdr. car.)

The third *Vixen*—a wooden steamer orginally built for the Mexican Government by Brown & Bell of New York City—was purchased by the United States Navy in May of 1846 at the outset of the Mexican War.

Immediately after her purchase, *Vixen* was deployed off the Gulf Coast of Mexico with Commodore David Conner's blockade squadron. There, she performed numerous patrol and reconnaissance assignments and was helpful in securing the Mexican coast in preparation for combined Army-Navy movements inland. *Vixen* first saw action on 16 October 1846 when she participated in the unsuccessful attempt to take Alvarado, Mex., the most important Mexican port east of Vera Cruz. During the engagement, she towed the schooners *Bonita* and *Reefer* but, together with the rest of the American fleet, was unable to cross the bar off the port and soon broke off the attack.

After this initial failure, the squadron moved south in an attempt to cut off the Yucatan Peninsula from the rest of Mexico. Success hinged upon the capture of the coastal port of Frontera, at the mouth of the Tobasco River, followed by the surrender of the city of Tobasco, upstream. *Vixen* and the rest of the squadron maneuvered into position off Frontera on 23 October.

An early artist's rendition of USS *Vixen* after she was rerigged as a brig in 1804.

Commodore Matthew Calbraith Perry assumed command of the gunboat and, with the schooners *Bonita* and *Forward* in tow, dashed across the bar and captured the Mexican flotilla defending the port. *Vixen* and Perry ascended the Tobasco River on the 24th and 25th with other vessels of the squadron and finally secured Tobasco on the 26th after a three-shot bombardment of the city by *Vixen*.

Vixen returned to the blockade immediately after the successful conclusion of the Yucatan campaign and later participated in the capture of Laguna, Mex., on 20 September. She also assisted in the capture of Tampico, Mex., on 14 November and covered troop landings at Vera Cruz, the main military objective of the fleet, on 9 March 1847. After Mexican defenders rejected peace overtures, the American squadron attacked the city on the 23d; and, two days later, *Spitfire* and *Vixen* made a daring and visually spectacular close range assault upon defensive fortifications ashore. Vera Cruz finally surrendered unconditionally on the 28th. This stunning victory enabled General Winfield Scott to march on Mexico City by the shortest overland route and, as such, was the decisive action of the Mexican War.

Vixen conducted clean-up operations with the squadron for the duration of the war. After the ratification of the treaty of Guadalupe Hidalgo on 30 May 1848, she joined the Home Squadron and underwent repairs at the Washington Navy Yard in 1850. The gunboat was temporarily decommissioned at Pensacola, Fla., in 1853 after numerous fatal outbreaks of yellow fever swept her and underwent further repairs at the New York Navy Yard in 1854.

Vixen was sold in 1855.

IV

(SwGbt.: t. 300; a. 2 20-pdr. P.r.)

The fourth *Vixen* was acquired by the Navy from the Coast Survey on 26 August 1861 for use as a reconnaissance vessel during the Civil War; and was later commissioned on 31 July 1862.

Vixen left New York City bound for Port Royal, S.C., in October 1861 with orders to conduct survey work along the southern coast en route. Escorted by *Ottawa* and *Seneca*, she entered Port Royal Sound on 4 November to place buoys in the channel preparatory to Flag Officer Samuel F. Du Pont's planned attack there, and drew scattered fire from the Confederate naval squadron under Commodore Josiah Tattnall. The vessel conducted local surveys following the Union capture of the sound on the 7th, and reconnoitered St. Helena Sound, S.C., on the 24th. In early December, a second survey was taken of St. Helena and, on the 18th, *Pawnee*, *Seneca*, and *Vixen* took possession of North and South Edisto Rivers, S.C., and drove a Confederate force from Rockville, S.C. *Vixen* became disabled in January 1862 and was sent to the New York Navy Yard for repairs.

Vixen left the navy yard in August for Port Royal and duty with the South Atlantic Blockading Squadron. She arrived on the 12th and, on the 16th, received orders to report to the blockade at Ossabow Sound, Ga. The gunboat participated in the expedition against the Confederate works at Pocotaligo, S.C., on 21 to 23 October, and returned to the New York Navy Yard shortly thereafter. Here, she was decommissioned on 8 November to be repaired and returned to the Coast Survey.

The historical record detailing the remainder of *Vixen*'s career is incomplete. However, after her transfer to the Coast Survey, she conducted numerous explorations of the rivers and inlets along the coast of Florida in early 1863 and 1864. She also participated in several routine patrol and reconnaissance expeditions along the southeastern coast during this time.

Neosho (q.v.)—a single-turreted, wooden-hulled, river monitor built in 1862—was renamed *Vixen* on 15 June 1869. On 2 August 1869, she received her third and final name, *Osceola*.

V

(Yacht: dp. 806; l. 182'3"; b. 28'0"; dr. 12'8" (mean); s. 16.0 k.; cpl. 82; a. 4 6-pdrs., 4 1-pdrs.)

Josephine—a steel-hulled, schooner-rigged, steam yacht—was built in 1896 at Elizabethport, N.J., by Lewis Nixon and, at the time of her acquisition by the Navy on 9 April 1898, was owned by the Philadelphia financier Peter A. Brown Widener. Renamed *Vixen*, the erstwhile pleasure craft was armed and fitted out for naval service at the Philadelphia Navy Yard where she was commissioned on 11 April 1898, Lt. Alex Sharp in command.

Assigned to the North Atlantic Station, *Vixen* sailed for Cuban waters on 7 May and arrived off the coast of Cuba nine days later. For the duration of the "splendid little war," the graceful armed yacht performed a variety of duties, blockading and patroling, carrying mail and flags of truce, ferrying prisoners, establishing communications with Cuban insurgents ashore, and landing reconnaissance parties. Among her passengers embarked during that time was Colonel (later President) Theodore Roosevelt, of the famous "Rough Riders." Also aboard during that time period was Midshipman, later Admiral, Thomas C. Hart.

Between 13 and 17 June 1898, she took part in the bombardment of Santiago, Cuba, and, on 3 July 1898, took part in the Battle of Santiago.

On the latter occasion, the highlight of the ship's operations during the Spanish-American War, *Vixen* was patrolling off Santiago between 0935 and 0945 and was at a point some four miles to the westward of the distinctive landmark, the Morro Castle. At about 0940, a messenger reported to the captain, Lt. Sharp, that there had been an explosion inside the entrance to the harbor. Rushing on deck, Sharp almost immediately sighted the first Spanish vessel to sortie—the cruiser *Vizcaya*.

Sharp ordered full speed ahead and hard-a-port, a move taken in the nick of time because shells from his own ships—alerted to the sortie of Admiral Cervera's fleet—splashed in the water astern in the yacht's frothing wake. *Vizcaya* acknowledged the presence of the yacht in the vicinity when she sent a salvo toward her with her starboard bow guns. Fortunately for *Vixen*, the shells passed overhead, "all being aimed too high."

As *Vixen* gathered speed, she steered south by east, clearing the armored cruiser *Brooklyn*'s field of fire, about two points on *Vixen*'s port bow. The yacht then steered west by south, as Sharp wanted to steer a course parallel to that of the Spanish fleet that was then under fire from the other American ships. Unfortunately, the helmsman erred and steered southwest by

south—a mistake not discovered until *Vixen* had steered farther from the action.

Meanwhile, *Brooklyn* had engaged the leading ship of the Spanish fleet and was trading shell for shell in a spirited exchange of fire. Shells from *Cristobal Colon* passed over *Brooklyn*. One splashed "close ahead" and another splashed astern on the yacht's starboard beam. Several others passed directly overhead, a piece of bursting shell going through *Vixen*'s battle flag at her mainmast!

Vixen witnessed the battle as it unfolded, but, as her commanding officer observed, ". . . seeing that the Spanish vessels were out of range of our guns while we were well within range of theirs, we reserved our fire." In fact, *Vixen* did not fire upon the enemy ship until 1105, when she opened fire on the badly battered *Vizcaya*, which had gone aground, listing heavily to port. *Vixen*'s fire was short-lived for *Vizcaya*'s flag came down at 1107, and Lt. Sharp ordered cease fire. The yacht remained underway to participate in the chase of the last remaining heavy unit of the Spanish fleet, *Cristobal Colon*, until that Spanish warship struck early in the afternoon.

After the conclusion of hostilities with Spain later that summer, *Vixen* returned to the United States, reaching Staten Island, N.Y., on 22 September. She then shifted southward to Norfolk, arriving there on 19 October.

Subsequently placed in reserve there on 18 January 1899, *Vixen* was recommissioned on 17 March, sailing for Key West and the Caribbean on 21 May.

For the next seven years, *Vixen* operated in waters off Puerto Rico, conducting surveys, carrying mail, stores, and passengers for the fleet, interspersing those miscellaneous duties with annual voyages to Norfolk for overhauls. During that time, she also briefly served as tender for *Amphitrite* (Monitor No. 2), the station ship at Guantanamo Bay, and later herself held the assignment of station ship there. Her diligent service was often rewarded with commendations for the excellence of her surveying activities. She often carried out her duties in completely uncharted waters and under a variety of weather conditions.

Decommissioned at Pensacola, Fla., on 30 March 1906, *Vixen* remained there until 6 December 1907, when she was turned over on loan to the New Jersey State Naval Militia. Serving with that force until the American entry into World War I, *Vixen* was recommissioned on 2 April 1917. She patrolled off the eastern seaboard and, following the establishment of United States naval activities in the recently acquired Virgin Islands (purchased from Denmark), served as station ship at St. Thomas.

During her tour at that West Indian port, *Vixen* was classified as a converted yacht, PY–4, on 17 July 1920. Ultimately decommissioned on 15 November 1922, *Vixen* was struck from the Navy list on 9 January 1923. She was subsequently sold on 22 June 1923 to the Fair Oaks Steamship Corp., of New York.

VI

(PG–53: dp. 3,097; l. 333'2"; b. 46'7"; dr. 16'0"; s. 15 k.; cpl. 279; a. 4 3", 7 .50-cal. mg., 2 .30-cal. mg., 2 dct.)

Orion—a steel-hulled yacht built in 1929 at Kiel, Germany, by *Krupp Germania Werft*—was purchased from woolen manufacturer Julius Forstmann on 13 November 1940. Converted to a gunboat at Brooklyn, N.Y., by the Sullivan Drydock and Repair Co., the erstwhile pleasure craft was renamed *Vixen* and designated PG–53. Commissioned at her conversion yard on 25 February, with Comdr. Pal L. Meadows in command, *Vixen* got underway for the Caribbean on 5 March 1941.

During her shakedown cruise, the gunboat called at St. Thomas, Virgin Islands; San Juan, Puerto Rico;

Vixen (PG–53) at Philadelphia, 11 April 1944.

and Guantanamo Bay, Cuba, before heading north for Norfolk. She then cruised up the eastern seaboard to New London, Conn., and back to Norfolk again before she returned to New London on 23 May to assume duties as flagship for Commander, Submarines, Atlantic Fleet, Rear Admiral Richard S. Edwards.

The graceful gunboat served Admiral Edwards through the spring, summer, and fall months of the critical year, 1941. During this time, she participated in ceremonies off the Isle of Shoals, New Hampshire, on 22 June, honoring the deceased crew of *0–9*—a training submarine which had gone down during practice diving tests on 20 June and had failed to surface. From 30 July to 13 August, she took part in Fleet maneuvers off New River, N.C.; voyaged to Bermuda in October; and cruised to Argentia, Newfoundland; and Casco Bay, Maine, before returning to New London on 6 December—the day before Japan's attack on Pearl Harbor.

Vixen remained at New London until 20 December, when Commander, Submarines, Atlantic, hauled down his flag. That day, the gunboat got underway for Newport, R.I., where she went alongside the recently vacated flagship *Augusta* (CA–31) to pick up Admiral Ernest J. King's papers and belongings for transportation to the Washington Navy Yard. Earlier that day, King had flown from Quonset Point, R.I., to Washington to commence his tour of duty as Commander in Chief, United States Fleet. *Vixen* got underway on the day after Christmas and arrived at the nation's capital on the 28th. Two days later, on 30 December, Admiral King broke his four-starred flag at *Vixen*'s main. The gunboat served as his flagship, berthed at the Washington Navy Yard, until 17 June 1942 when she was relieved by *Dauntless* (PG–61).

While *Vixen* was undergoing the refit which followed, Admiral Royal E. Ingersoll, Commander in Chief, Atlantic Fleet, was laying plans for the yacht's future deployment. "I hope to get the *Vixen* in mid-July," he wrote an acquaintance on 10 June. "I will then be able to move to spots where there is more activity than here, and where I can see people, without their having to come to the 'mountain.' "

Vixen embarked Admiral Ingersoll at Newport on 21 July and got underway for Boston in company with *Charles F. Hughes* (DD–428). Over the subsequent months, the ship ranged up and down the eastern seaboard from Maine to the Caribbean isles. Calling at Portland, Maine; New London; Philadelphia; New York; Norfolk; Portsmouth, N.H.; Bermuda; the Dominican Republic; Trinidad; Curaçao—the ship's itinerary showed clearly that Ingersoll had mobility and was utilizing it to the fullest. From this base of operations, Ingersoll kept his finger on the pulse of German U-boat activity and the problems confronting the officers and ships under his command. Under his sagacious leadership, the Atlantic Fleet slowly, but surely, turned the tide against the dreaded Nazi submarines. His close contact with his commanders enabled Ingersoll to know local conditions and thus to deploy his forces where they could be most useful.

On 15 November 1944, Admiral Jonas H. Ingram relieved Ingersoll as Commander in Chief, Atlantic Fleet, and broke his flag in *Vixen*. Ingram, who had so successfully conducted United States-Brazilian relations during the period when he commanded American naval forces in the South Atlantic, would fly his flag in the gunboat through the end of hostilities, as the Atlantic Fleet continued to wear down the U-boat offensive. *Vixen* was decommissioned on 24 May 1946 and struck from the Navy list on 3 July 1946. Transferred to the War Shipping Administration, *Vixen* was sold on 21 January 1947.

On 16 June 1943, *PC–826*—formerly *Vixen*—was renamed *Venture* (q.v.) and redesignated PYc–51.

Voge

Richard George Voge—born on 4 May 1904 in Chicago, Ill.—completed the course at Harrison Technical High School in Chicago in 1921 and entered the Naval Academy later that year. He graduated on 4 June 1925 and received his ensign's commission.

His first assignment—three years in *Pittsburgh* (CA–4)—took him first to European waters for a year when his ship served as the flagship for the Commander, Naval Forces, Europe. During the last two years of that tour, he cruised the western Pacific while *Pittsburgh* carried the flag of the Commander in Chief,

Asiatic Fleet. That cruise afforded Voge his first hint of action in April and May of 1927 when Nationalist Chinese attempted to take Shanghai from the hands of the foreign forces which held the city. Voge served with the landing forces put ashore to deter the attack. Though the Chinese quickly captured the native sections of the city, they demurred at taking on the American and European forces protecting the International Settlement.

In early 1929, Voge returned to the United States from the Far East to attend the Submarine School at New London, Conn. After completing that course and qualifying for submarine duty, he spent the bulk of his remaining time at sea in submarines.

In January 1931, he went to the Far East to serve in *S–29* (SS–134) until June 1932 when he returned to the United States for war plans and intelligence training at the Great Lakes Naval Training Station. That assignment lasted from July 1932 to September 1933 when he became an instructor in marine engineering at the Naval Academy. In June 1935, Voge assumed command of *S–18* (SS–123) at Pearl Harbor. He remained in Hawaii—in command, first of *S–18* until May 1937, and then of *S–33*—until June 1937 when he departed in the latter submarine, bound for the east coast. *S–33* was decommissioned at Philadelphia in August 1937, and Voge was reassigned to the Naval Ordnance Plant at Baldwin on Long Island.

A four-month tour of duty as commissioning executive officer of *Rowan* (DD–405) from late September 1939 to late January 1940 followed the two years ashore at Baldwin. In mid-February 1940, Comdr. Voge returned to the Asiatic Fleet and assumed command of *Sealion* (SS–195), based at Cavite in the Philippines, and commanded that submarine until the opening day of American participation in World War II.

At the outbreak of hostilities on 8 December 1941 (West Longitude Time), Voge suffered the double ignominy of having his command caught in overhaul and, three days later, of losing her to enemy bombs while still at Cavite Navy Yard. Voge, however, quickly recovered from that blow, assumed command of *Sailfish* (SS–192) on 17 December, and led her on five successful war patrols during the first eight months of 1942. Until the Battles of Coral Sea and of Midway in May and June, respectively, only Pacific Fleet submarines like *Sailfish* were able to fight to impede the Japanese onslaught; and their war patrols provided the one bright spot for the Allied cause in the Pacific.

In August 1942, upon the completion of his fifth war patrol in *Sailfish*, Voge received orders to join the staff of Commander, Submarine Force, Pacific Fleet, as operations and combat intelligence officer. He retained that position, in which he was promoted to captain to date from 20 July 1943, until late in the war, when he was ordered to Washington, D.C., to serve in the Office of the Chief of Naval Operations.

On 1 November 1946, Capt. Voge was retired from the Navy and advanced to the rank of rear admiral. A little over two years later, Rear Admiral Voge died at the United Hospital at Port Chester, N.Y.

(DE–1047: dp. 2,400 (f.); l. 414'6''; b. 44'; dr. 24'6''; s. 27+ k.; cpl. 239; a. 2 5'', ASROC, 6 15.5'' tt.; cl. *Garcia*)

Voge (DE–1047) was laid down on 21 November 1963 at Bay City, Mich., by the Defoe Shipbuilding Co.; launched on 4 February 1965; sponsored by Mrs. Alice Voge Oetting, widow of Rear Admiral Voge; and commissioned at the Boston Naval Shipyard on 25 November 1966, Comdr. William F. Keller in command.

Voge remained at the Boston Naval Shipyard until 11 April 1967, completing her outfitting. On that day, she stood out of Boston, bound for her home port, Newport, R.I., whence she operated until mid-May. On 15 May, she departed Newport for her shakedown cruise, which lasted until 24 June and during which she operated out of Guantanamo Bay, Cuba. The ocean escort returned to Newport on 24 June and conducted local operations from there through the end of July. On 1 August, she reentered the Boston Naval Shipyard for her post-shakedown availability. That yard period occupied her for the remainder of 1967 and during the first two months of 1968.

In March 1968, she rejoined Escort Squadron (CortRon) 6 at Newport and began duty supporting the development and testing of sophisticated antisubmarine warfare tactics and related equipment. Her operations out of Newport continued through the end of 1968.

In February 1969, she began preparations for a brief cruise to northern Europe to participate in a NATO exercise. She departed Newport on 1 April and made her first port call—Lisbon, Portugal—later that month, after conducting hunter/killer ASW exercises with ships of the Spanish and Portugese navies. From Portugal, she moved to Spithead, England, for a Royal review of the NATO Fleet in celebration of the 20th anniversary of the treaty organization. In late May and early June, she made port visits to Cherbourg, France; Edinburgh, Scotland; and Bremen, Germany, conducting further hunter/killer exercises when at sea between ports.

From Bremen, *Voge* headed back to Newport and, en route home, encountered a submarine contact later confirmed as a Soviet "Yankee-type" submarine. *Voge* successfully applied hold-down tactics on the Russian submarine and later received the Meritorious Unit Commendation for her efforts. Upon completing the usual post-cruise leave and repair period, the ocean escort resumed her duties out of Newport, practicing and testing ASW tactics and testing newly developed ASW equipment. Such a routine occupied her until August 1970 when she entered the Boston Naval Shipyard for her first regular overhaul.

The warship completed her yard period late in January and spent February completing post-overhaul sea trials. After gunnery exercises in the Virginia capes operating area early in March, she got underway on the 12th for her refresher training cruise to the Guantanamo Bay operating area. The ocean escort returned to Newport on 10 May and, after a tender availability, resumed operations in the Narragansett Bay area. She continued that routine until the following spring when she crossed the Atlantic for bilateral United States-Spanish ASW exercises and another with ships of the Portugese Navy. *Voge* returned home through very heavy weather and reentered Newport on 24 April 1972.

The ocean escort immediately began preparations for her first deployment with the 6th Fleet in the Mediterranean Sea. On 13 June, the warship began her voyage to Rota, Spain, where she arrived on the 22d. During the ensuing six months, *Voge* joined other ships of the 6th Fleet in a series of unilateral and bilateral exercises and made port visits throughout the Mediterranean. Of special interest were her visit to the Turkish Naval War College on Heybeliada Island in the Sea of Marmara in early August and her participation in the multinational NATO Exercise "Deep Furrow" late in September. In early November, she was assigned special duty shadowing Soviet submarines reporting to and leaving the Mediterranean.

On one occasion, she followed a departing Soviet submarine some 300 miles into the Atlantic before breaking contact and returning to the Mediterranean. On 10 December, she completed turnover to her relief, *Du Pont* (DD–941), and set course for Newport where she arrived on the 18th.

After completing the usual month of post-deployment leave and repairs, *Voge* resumed normal east coast operations in January 1973. That routine occupied her through most of 1973 and included two major exercises in March, a brief tour as destroyer school ship in April, participation in bilateral exercises with ships of the French Navy in June, and a midshipman training cruise in July. She received orders changing her home port to Mayport, Fla., on 15 August; and, four days later, she got underway for the south. She arrived in Mayport on the 22d and began local operations which kept her busy until near the end of the year.

Late in December, the warship began preparations to return to the Mediterranean. On 4 January 1974, *Voge* stood out of Mayport on her way to join the 6th Fleet. She arrived in Rota on the 14th and relieved *Claude V. Ricketts* (DDG–5) before joining Task Group (TG) 60.1 near Golfe Juan, France, on the 19th. Again, the warship joined units of the 6th Fleet and of Allied navies in a series of unilateral and bilateral exercises as well as in at least one multilateral exercise. She again made port visits all along the Mediterranean littoral before she departed Rota on 24 June, for home.

After reentering Mayport on 3 July, the ship devoted July to post-deployment leave and upkeep; and a tender availability in Mayport, preparatory to regular overhaul, took care of August. On 4 September, she departed Mayport and, the following day, arrived in Charleston. She entered the Charleston Naval Shipyard late on the 6th and commenced a 10-month overhaul. While at Charleston, she was reclassified a frigate and redesignated FF–1047 on 1 July 1975.

A fortnight later, Voge's overhaul was completed, and the frigate returned to Mayport. Refresher training and naval gunfire support exercises engaged her until October, at which time she returned to Charleston for a three-month restricted availability to correct problems in her main propulsion plant. Late in December, the warship returned to Mayport.

Voge remained at her home port until mid-February 1976 when she put to sea to participate in exercises conducted in the Caribbean with units of the Netherlands and British navies. Upon her return to port, the frigate began preparations for her third deployment to the Mediterranean. After a brief visit to Charleston, S.C., she departed that port on 14 April and headed for Rota where she arrived on the 26th. During much of that deployment, port visits all along the Mediterranean punctuated a series of training exercises conducted with units of the 6th Fleet and from foreign navies. Late in the deployment, she also resumed surveillance duties on Soviet naval forces operating in the Mediterranean. On 28 August, while operating in the Ionian Sea near Greece, she collided with a Soviet E–2-class submarine and sustained serious structural damage that necessitated drydocking at Toulon, France. On 7 November, *Voge* successfully completed postdrydock sea trials and then headed for Rota for turnover. On the 20th, she stood out of Rota bound for Mayport. The frigate reentered her home port on 2 December.

Voge spent almost all of the ensuing seven months in port at Mayport, putting to sea only to test the main propulsion plant. On 11 July 1977, she headed back toward Rota in company with *Saratoga* (CV–60) and *Koelsch* (FF–1049) for duty with the 6th Fleet. However, she soon was ordered back to Mayport because of contaminated potable water tanks and reached home on the 13th. On the 27th, the frigate got underway and, after an independent transit of the Atlantic, finally arrived in Rota on 3 August. Again port visits and exercises—unilateral, bilateral, and multilateral—kept her busy during that tour of duty in the "middle sea." On 12 December, she changed operational control back to the 2d Fleet at Gibraltar and headed back toward Mayport. The frigate arrived home two days before Christmas and began post-deployment standdown.

Voge spent the first five months of 1978 engaged in training exercises out of Mayport. Early in June, she departed for the Bahamas where she provided services to submarines. The frigate then proceeded to Charleston to offload ammunition and continued on to Boston. On 12 July, *Voge* commenced a scheduled overhaul at Braswell Shipyard in South Boston which continued on into 1979.

Vogelgesang

Carl Theodore Vogelgesang—born on 11 January 1869 at North Branch, Calif.—was appointed a naval cadet (the name at that time applied to young men studying at the Naval Academy) on 6 September 1886. On 6 June 1890, he graduated from the Academy and began active duty on board *Alliance* as a passed naval cadet. At the completion of his requisite two years of sea duty before final graduation, he was commissioned an ensign on 14 July 1892 to date from 1 July 1892. Successive tours of duty on board *Adams* and *Mohican* occupied his time until 1895 when he was ordered to Washington, D.C., for duty in the Bureau of Navigation. Detached from that post on 29 August 1896, Ens. Vogelgesang reported to the gunboat *Bancroft* on 3 September. That ship remained his home through the Spanish-American War. Vogelgesang served in her during convoy escort missions and on blockade duty off Havana and near the Isle of Pines. Tours of duty in *Celtic* and at the New York Navy Yard in conjunction with the fitting out of *Kentucky* (Battleship No. 6) and *Wisconsin* (Battleship No. 9) followed. On 6 June 1904, he returned to the Bureau of Navigation for a two-year tour of duty as navigator on board *Louisiana* (Battleship No. 19), during which he attained the rank of lieutenant commander on 1 July 1905. A fifteen-month assignment from June 1906 to September 1907 was followed by his first command, *Mayflower*.

That tour of duty ended in March 1908 when he transferred to *Wisconsin* as navigator. In May 1909, Lt. Comdr. Vogelgesang reported for duty ashore once more, this time to study at the Naval War College at Newport, R.I. On 2 May 1911, near the end of his assignment at the war college, Vogelgesang was promoted to full commander. On 2 May 1912, he transferred to *Wyoming* (Battleship No. 32) to fit her out. When she was commissioned, he assumed duty as her executive officer. In late January 1914, Comdr. Vogelgesang was ordered to *Des Moines* (Cruiser No. 15) which he commanded until 23 October. On 21 November 1914, he reported for duty at the Naval War College and remained there until the beginning of 1917, when he became Chief of Staff to the Commander in Chief, Asiatic Fleet. Just after assuming the duties of that office, he received his promotion to captain, to date from 29 August 1916. In January 1918, Capt. Vogelgesang relinquished his position as Chief of Staff to the Commander in Chief Asiastic Fleet, and reported to Rio de Janeiro, Brazil, as senior officer of the American naval commission.

On 9 January 1919, Capt. Vogelgesang took charge of the fitting out of *Idaho* (Battleship No. 42) at Camden, N.J., and assumed command of her when that battleship was placed in commission on 24 March 1919. He commanded *Idaho* until June 1920 when he became the Chief of Staff to the Commander in Chief, Atlantic Fleet. A year later, Capt. Vogelgesang became Commandant, 3d Naval District, at New York. That tour of duty lasted until November 1922 when he received orders to organize and lead the United States Naval Mission to Brazil. For the next two years, he and his staff joined their Brazilian counterparts in reorganizing the Brazilian Navy. During his two years in Brazil, he helped to strengthen the warm and enduring friendship between that nation and the United States. Early in that assignment, he was promoted to rear admiral, to date from 16 October 1922. Rear Admiral Vogelgesang completed his mission in South America in January 1925 and returned to the United States on 7 February. On 3 April, he broke his flag in *New York* (BB–34) and became Commander, Battleship Division 2 of the Scouting Fleet. In June 1926, he was detached from command of Battleship Division 2 and took command of the Light Cruiser Division, Scouting Fleet. That tour of duty was abbreviated when Rear Admiral Vogelgesang entered the Naval Hospital, Washington, D.C., for treatment of a kidney ailment. He died there on 16 February 1927.

Vogelgesang (DE–284)—a *Rudderow*-class destroyer escort—was laid down by the Charleston Navy Yard sometime in 1943. However, before she was launched, her contract was cancelled on 10 June 1944.

I

(DD–862: dp. 2,425; l. 390′6″; b. 40′10″; dr. 18′6″; s. 34.6 k. (tl.); cpl. 345; a. 6 5″, 16 40mm., 5 21″ tt., 1 dcp. (hh.), 6 dcp., 2 dct.; cl. *Gearing*)

Vogelgesang (DD–862) was laid down on 3 August 1944 at Staten Island, N.Y., by the Bethlehem Steel Co.; launched on 15 January 1945; sponsored by Miss Senaide Vogelgesang; and commissioned on 28 April 1945 at the New York Navy Yard, Comdr. O. W. Spahr in command.

Vogelgesang conducted shakedown training out of Guantanamo Bay, Cuba, from mid-May to late June and returned to New York on the 24th for post-shakedown availability. In July, she moved to Newport, R.I., for gunnery exercises and, in August, began duty at Norfolk as a training platform for destroyer nucleus crews. In October, she interrupted her training schedule to take part in the Navy Day festivities at New York but resumed those duties in November. For the next two years, the destroyer operated out of Norfolk, along the east coast, and in the West Indies, conducting exercises both independently and in company with other units of the Atlantic Fleet. On 10 November 1947, she stood out of Norfolk on her first deployment to the Mediterranean Sea. She arrived at Gibraltar on 20 November and, after a little more than three months of exercises and port visits, departed the "middle sea" on 2 March 1948.

The warship arrived back in Norfolk on 11 March and resumed a normal schedule of 2d Fleet operations. She ranged up and down the east coast until 4 January 1949 at which time she headed back to the Mediterranean. *Vogelgesang* completed her second deployment to the 6th Fleet on 14 May, departed Gibraltar that day, reentered Norfolk on the 23d, and commenced a two-month upkeep period.

Over the next eight years, *Vogelgesang* alternated five deployments to the Mediterranean with tours of duty along the east coast and in the West Indies. In addition, she also visited northern European ports during the summer of 1956 while on a midshipman training cruise. Her five Mediterranean tours consisted of normal training operations with units of the 6th Fleet and with elements of Allied navies as well as port visits at various points throughout the Mediterranean. In 1957, there came a change in *Vogelgesang*'s routine of the previous eight years. She deployed to the Mediterranean once more in July; but, on this deployment, she added something new to her schedule. That new item was service in the Indian Ocean, for she added Aden and Massawa in Eritrea to her list of ports of call. In December, when she returned to the Mediterranean for another deployment with the 6th Fleet, she again transited the Suez Canal, repeated her former visits to middle eastern ports, and added Bahrein Island and Abadan, Iran, to her itinerary.

During the following nine years, *Vogelgesang* continue her schedule of alternating Mediterranean cruises and 2d Fleet operations. However, some special assignments highlighted her service. In 1961 and 1962, she provided support for the Project "Mercury" space shot.

On 1 March 1962, she entered the Boston Naval Shipyard to begin a fleet rehabilitation and modernization (FRAM) overhaul. For the next 10 months, she underwent extensive structural changes as well as equipment installation to improve greatly her antisubmarine warfare capabilities. She completed her FRAM conversion on 31 January 1963 and resumed normal operations out of Norfolk. In 1964, she participated in two binational exercises with Canadian ships,

CANUS SILEX in March and CANUS SLAMEX i September.

In October and November, she returned to Europea waters to participate in a large amphibious exercis Operation "Steel Pike I," carried out on the Atlanti coast of Spain. In January of 1965, the warship serve as part of the Project "Gemini" recovery force whic picked up an unmanned experimental Gemini spac capsule. In June, she deployed to the Mediterranea once again for a two-month tour of duty with the 6tl Fleet. *Vogelgesang* resumed 2d Fleet operations earl in September following another joint United States Canadian exercise in August on her way back fron Europe. On 3 December, she began her first regula overhaul since her FRAM conversion when she entere the Norfolk Naval Shipyard.

Vogelgesang completed overhaul and sea trials o 22 March 1966 and resumed normal duty with th Atlantic Fleet. That assignment lasted until 1 June a which time she and the other ships of Destroyer Squad ron (DesRon) 32 steamed out of Norfolk for a deploy ment to the western Pacific. Steaming by way of th Panama Canal, Pearl Harbor, and Guam, she and he colleagues reported for duty with the 7th Fleet a Subic Bay in the Philippines on 15 July. On the 19th she headed for the Gulf of Tonkin in the screen o *Constellation* (CVA–64). The task group arrived in th gulf on 28 July, and *Vogelgesang* provided antisub marine defense and plane guard services as the carrier' air group struck at targets in North Vietnam. On 1 August, the destroyer closed the shores of South Viet nam to provide gunfire support for troops operating ashore. On the night of 18 and 19 August, her 5-inc guns succeeded in breaking up a company-strength Vie Cong attack on a Popular Forces outpost near Dien Huong. Reports credited her main battery with killing 70 and wounding 40 of the attacking guerrillas. I addition to service in Vietnamese waters, the warship made visits to Hong Kong and Kaohsiung on Taiwan as well as periodic stops at Subic Bay for upkeep and replenishments. *Vogelgesang* concluded her only comba cruise during the Vietnam conflict on 10 November when she stood out of Subic Bay, bound—via the Indian Ocean, the Suez Canal, and the Mediterranean Sea— for Norfolk. She completed her round-the-world cruise at her home port on 17 December.

After post-deployment standdown, *Vogelgesang* re sumed her schedule alternating Mediterranean cruises with operations out of Norfolk. She spent the first 10 months of 1967 engaged in training operations along the east coast and in the West Indies. On 14 November 1967, the warship stood out of Norfolk for her first tour of duty with the 6th Fleet since 1965. On 24 November, she conducted turnover ceremonies at the Spanish island of Majorca and officially joined the 6th Fleet. For the next five months, the destroyer ranged the length and breadth of the Mediterranean, conduct ing training evolutions and making port visits. On 13 April 1968, she departed Malaga, Spain, to return to Norfolk.

After a 10-day transit, she reentered her home port on the 23d. She resumed normal 2d Fleet operations until 22 July at which time she departed Norfolk for a cruise to South American waters to participate in UNITAS IX, a series of multinational exercises with units of various Latin American navies. She concluded that assignment on 3 September when she reentered Norfolk.

Normal operations and a series of tender avail abilities in preparation for overhaul occupied her time from September of 1968 to June of 1969. On 2 June 1969, she departed Norfolk, en route to Boston. The warship entered the Boston Naval Shipyard and commenced regular overhaul on 5 June. She concluded sea trials successfully late in September and departed Boston on 3 October and arrived in Norfolk on the 5th. For the remainder of the year, the ship conducted post-repair exercises and refresher training in the Guantanamo Bay operating area. She returned to Norfolk on

14 December and remained in port for the rest of the year.

Normal operations out of Norfolk occupied her until 30 April 1970 at which time she embarked upon another Mediterranean tour of duty. She changed operational control to the 6th Fleet on 10 May and conducted turnover at Majorca between the 12th and the 17th. For the first four months of the deployment, *Vogelgesang* conducted normal 6th Fleet operations—port visits and training evolutions. However, early in September, she joined a special contingency force assembled in the eastern Mediterranean in response to Syrian intervention in the Jordanian civil war on the side of militant, antigovernment, Arab guerrillas. She cruised that portion of the sea from 5 September to 6 October. Finally, however, the American show of force succeeded in getting the Syrian forces to withdraw from Jordan, and *Vogelgesang* resumed normal operations with the 6th Fleet. On 8 November, she departed Palma de Majorca to return home.

The warship reentered Norfolk on 17 November and remained there through the end of the year. The destroyer resumed normal 2d Fleet operations early in 1971 and remained so occupied for the next 11 months. On 1 December 1971, she departed Norfolk for another tour of duty with the 6th Fleet in the Mediterranean. She arrived in port at Rota, Spain, on the 9th and conducted turnover ceremonies. For the following six months, *Vogelgesang* operated throughout the Mediterranean, engaged in the usual round of exercises and port visits. After turnover in Rota, the destroyer got underway on 23 June to return to Norfolk. On the 29th, she steamed into Hampton Roads and soon began a tender availability alongside *Sierra* (AD–18). She conducted operations out of Norfolk until 10 October at which time she began an extended repair period at the Norfolk Shipbuilding & Drydock Corp. The warship completed repairs on 26 January 1973 and finished sea trials by early February. She conducted normal operations for the remainder of the year, steaming as far south as the West Indies.

On 10 January 1974, *Vogelgesang* was transferred from DesRon 2 to DesRon 28 and reassigned to Naval Reserve training duty. On 1 March, her home port was changed from Norfolk to Newport, R.I. On 19 March, she headed out of Norfolk, bound for her new home port, where she arrived the following day. Since that time, *Vogelgesang* has operated at and out of Newport as a training platform for naval reservists, NROTC midshipmen, and OCS students. She alternated short periods at sea with weeks in port as a stationary training platform. Periodically, however, she has made extended training cruises down the east coast to the West Indies. As of the beginning of 1980, the destroyer continued to serve with the Naval Reserve training program, based at Newport, R.I.

Vogelgesang earned two battle stars for service during the Vietnam conflict.

Volador

One of several varieties of flying or sailing fishes named for a Spanish term meaning flying.

I

(Sch: t. 114; l. 110′0″; b. 23′5″; dr. 12′3″; dph. 11′6″; s. 7 k.)

The first *Volador*—a wooden-hulled schooner with an auxiliary engine—was designed by William Gardiner and built in 1926 at Wilmington, Calif., by William Muller. The vessel was acquired for the Navy by the Port Director, San Pedro, Calif., from W. L. Valentine, on 2 February 1942. Delivered to the Section Base, San Pedro, on that day, *Volador* was classified as a miscellaneous auxiliary, unclassified, IX–59, and was placed "in service" on 19 February 1942.

In July of that year, she was temporarily transferred Homeported at San Pedro, *Volador* operated locally under the aegis of the 11th Naval District into 1943. to the Coast Guard for operational training duties for Coast Guard district personnel.

On 17 August 1943, *Volador* was delivered to the War Shipping Administration which transferred the schooner to the War Department for operation by the Army. *Volador* (IX–59) was struck from the Navy list on 3 September 1943.

II

(SS–490: dp. 1,570 (surf.), 2,415 (subm.); l. 306′; b. 27′3″; dr. 15′5″; s. 20.25 k. (surf.), 8.75 k. (subm.); cpl. 85; a. 10 21″ tt., 1 5″; cl. *Balao*)

The second *Volador* (SS–490) was laid down on 15 June 1945 by the Portsmouth (N.H.) Naval Shipyard, but work on her construction was discontinued in January 1946. Her unfinished hulk remained on the ways until August 1947 when construction resumed. The submarine was launched on 21 May 1948; sponsored by Mrs. Dudley W. Morton; and commissioned on 1 October 1948, Comdr. H. A. Thompson in command.

Volador completed her builder's trials on 20 January 1949, left Portsmouth three days later, and stopped at Newport and New London before sailing for the Gulf of Mexico on 5 February. *Volador* arrived at New Orleans on 11 February and proceeded to the west coast, via Galveston and the Panama Canal, and arrived at San Diego on 11 March. The submarine conducted local operations along the California coast between San Diego and San Francisco until she departed San Diego on 13 October, bound for Hawaii. She arrived at Pearl Harbor on 7 November but returned to San Diego on the 18th and spent the remainder of 1949 as well as most of the following year on the west coast, conducting various training exercises. During that period, she also visited Portland, Vancouver, and Pearl Harbor. In June 1950, *Volador* embarked reserves at Treasure Island, Calif., and proceeded on a two-week reserve cruise to Hawaii. En route, the Korean War broke out; and the submarine spent two months training in Hawaiian waters before returning to San Diego for operations on the west coast that lasted into the summer of 1951.

The submarine departed San Diego on 21 July, bound, via Pearl Harbor, for Japan and arrived at Yokosuka on 15 August 1951. On 18 August, *Volador* got underway from Yokosuka for a period of special operations. Her orders directed the submarine to conduct an undetected reconnaissance patrol in the area of Hokkaido, Japan, for a four-week period, in order to keep Commander, Naval Forces Far East, informed of any Soviet or Chinese communist seaborne and airborne activity in that area. Throughout her patrol, the submarine identified and photographed numerous radar contacts and made rendezvous with *Ronquil* (SS–396) and *Tiru* (SS–416) to exchange patrol reports and other valuable information. On 15 September, *Volador* held ceremonies commemorating her 1,000th dive. After a 24-hour engineering run in Tsugaru Strait, she ended her patrol and arrived in Yokosuka on 22 September. From 11 to 15 November, *Volador* conducted ASW operations with *Hanson* (DD–832), *Mackenzie* (DD–836), and *Taussig* (DD–746) in the Atami area. From 16 November to 9 December, *Volador* participated in hunter/killer operations en route to Okinawa from Japan in company with Task Group (TG) 96.7. The submarine visited Buckner Bay, Okinawa, before heading home via Pearl Harbor.

Volador returned to San Diego in January 1952 and conducted local operations until early summer. She then spent three months in the Juan de Fuca Strait and the Puget Sound area before entering the Mare Island Naval Shipyard in October. During the five-month overhaul which followed, a new battery and an

Askania automatic depth control system were installed. Upon her return to San Diego, *Volador* provided services to ASW surface units, aircraft, and the Fleet Sonar School and participated in type training, Exercise "Pacphibex," and hunter/killer exercises. She departed San Diego on 7 August 1953 and arrived at Pearl Harbor on the 15th, received briefings by members of the Commander in Chief, Pacific Fleet, and the Commander, Submarines, Pacific staffs on 17 and 18 August and tested experimental sonar equipment at sea on 20 August.

On 22 August 1953, *Volador* began a period of special operations, departing Pearl Harbor for an Alaskan training cruise which kept her in northern waters until October 1953. Her patrol station was northeast of the St. Lawrence Bay; and, on 1 September, she made rendezvous with *Blackfin* (SS–322) off the southwest cape, St. Lawrence Island; the following day, she snorkeled to an area off Brook Bank, then proceeded to the Bering Strait area. *Volador* conducted a shipping reconnaissance patrol until the night of 27 September 1953 when she made rendezvous with and was relieved by submarine *Caiman* (SS–323). *Volador* arrived at Pearl Harbor on 7 October 1953. During her second patrol, she contacted a total of 63 ships and identified and photographed the majority of them.

Returning to San Diego, *Volador* rendered services and conducted type training there until May 1954, when she entered the Mare Island Naval Shipyard for overhaul. The yard work was completed in October 1954, and *Volador* returned to San Diego for local operations. Departing San Diego on 3 January 1955 for her second tour of duty in the Western Pacific (WestPac), *Volador* proceeded to Yokosuka, Japan, via Pearl Harbor. Upon arrival at Yokosuka on 26 January 1955, she conducted type training and furnished ASW services to a destroyer division and elements of the Japanese Maritime Self-Defense Force until 1 March 1955. Shen then completed two weeks of routine upkeep on 13 March, prior to departure for another period of special operations on the 14th.

Volador transited Tsugaru Strait and, on 19 March, commenced a submerged patrol on the lane between Vladivostok and La Perouse Strait which lasted until 8 April. She then commenced a transit of Tsugaru Strait and set a course back to Yokosuka where she moored on 11 April 1955. After the completion of this patrol, *Volador* was commended for excellent photography, correct identification of contacts, and accurate reporting of identifying characteristics regarding the 33 ships contacted.

Visiting Subic Bay, Hong Kong, and Pearl Harbor while en route, *Volador* returned to San Diego on 1 July. The submarine operated along the west coast for the next two years. In August 1957, *Volador* commenced another Far East deployment. She arrived at Pearl Harbor on 3 August and departed three days later for a 30-day patrol off Petropavlovsk, Kamchatka. Her mission was to gather intelligence information. Due to motor casualties nine days after arrival on station, she

departed the Petropavlovsk area on 25 August and arrived at Yokosuka five days later. During this patrol, *Volador* contacted 13 merchant ships and eight warships.

On 8 November 1957, the submarine arrived at Subic Bay for a scheduled upkeep and departed on 17 November for Yokosuka. *Volador* arrived at Yokosuka on 26 November; and, from 11 December through 4 January 1958, she conducted a special reconnaissance patrol in the Sea of Okhotsk. During this 17-day undetected special patrol, she completed her photographic mission in spite of severe ice and blizzard conditions. Returning to Japan, *Volador* departed Yokosuka on 9 January for Pearl Harbor. She arrived at Hawaii on 19 January and departed two days later for San Diego, arriving on 28 January 1958.

Volador remained at San Diego until 3 October, when she departed for Vancouver, Wash. Twenty guests of the Vancouver Navy League were embarked at Longview, Wash., for a ship's visit and disembarked upon arrival at Vancouver. *Volador* was welcomed by a gathering of about 500 citizens, plus the local high school band, and was presented a plaque in a simple ceremony on board. She departed Vancouver on 5 October and visited Seattle and Port Angeles, Wash., through the month of October. *Volador* visited Victoria, British Columbia, from 31 October through 3 November. HMCS *Antigonish* was the host ship, and wardroom officers were entertained on board and in the homes of the host's officers.

The submarine patrolled the areas of Esquimalt, Port Angeles, Tacoma, and Seattle until 22 November when she began her return trip to San Diego, arriving on 26 November. *Volador* operated in the San Diego-San Francisco area until 5 May 1959 when she entered the San Francisco Naval Shipyard at Hunters Point for overhaul.

Completing overhaul in October 1959, the submarine returned to San Diego for local operations until leaving for WestPac in late December. While thus deployed, *Volador* participated in many operations including amphibious Exercise "Blue Star" and SEATO Exercise "Sea Lion." Upon returning to San Diego, she participated in various local operations during the next 20 months.

Volador spent the early months of 1962 in local operations in the San Diego area until she conducted a reserve cruise from 4 to 11 April. Upon her return, she was placed 'in commission, in reserve" while undergoing FRAM Mk I conversion to a Guppy III configuration at the San Francisco Naval Shipyard. The submarine was saved from possible total destruction due to a spectacular pier fire at the shipyard on 9 and 10 November 1962 by the duty section led by the duty officer and the executive officer. In September 1962, *Volador* was returned to active service. The conversion was completed in February 1963. A 15-foot hull section was installed in addition to a large amount of new electronic, fire control, and sonar equipment, making *Volador* one of the most modern diesel-electric sub-

Volador (SS–490) as a *Guppy III* with an enlarged, streamlined sail. "Fins" on her deck are sonar transducer fairings.

marines in the Fleet. After trials in Puget Sound, Wash., she returned to San Diego in April 1963 to take part in local operations.

The submarine departed San Diego in September 1963 for another WestPac deployment. Near the conclusion of her tour, *Volador* conducted a special assignment which resulted in her receiving a commendation from the Commander, Submarine Force, United States Pacific Fleet, for "a mission of great value to the government of the United States." After returning to San Diego, she was assigned to local and Pacific coast operations.

In late 1964, *Volador* again distinguished herself by sending the ex-*Sea Devil* (SS-400) to the bottom after firing one homing torpedo in a weapons system evaluation test, making her the only submarine in the Navy to claim two peace-time "kills." Commander, Submarine Force, United States Pacific Fleet, awarded the "E" for overall performance "and for being adjudged the outstanding submarine in Submarine Squadron 5 in fleet intratype competition for fiscal year 1965.

Volador resumed operations on 3 January 1966 after a short period of holiday routine in San Diego alongside the submarine tender, *Nereus* (AS-17). The greater part of January was spent conducting weapons system accuracy trials at the Dabob Bay and Carr Inlet facilities in the Puget Sound area. *Volador* returned to San Diego on 3 February and conducted a week of refresher training commencing on 10 February. Following this, she began a three-week upkeep period during which she successfully underwent an administrative inspection and a nuclear weapons acceptance inspection. On 7 March 1966, *Volador* left port for a week of type training in the local operating areas during which time sound trials were conducted to investigate the problem of noisy propellers. She got underway on 4 April for a four-day restricted availability at the San Francisco Bay Naval Shipyard where new propellers were installed. The remainder of April and the period until 11 May were spent in the San Diego area conducting various tests and preparing for deployment to WestPac.

The submarine departed San Diego on 12 May and, after a four-day stopover in Pearl Harbor, reported to Commander, 7th Fleet, for operational control on 3 June and arrived at Yokosuka, Japan, on 6 June 1966.

Following an eight-day upkeep period for voyage repairs, *Volador* departed Yokosuka on 14 June to provide ASW services to ships and aircraft of the Japanese Maritime Self-Defense Force. Throughout the summer, she continued to conduct exercises and provide services which were made more meaningful by the mutual exchange of officers. The submarine operated in the areas of Yokosuka and Iwakuni, Japan, and Buckner Bay, Okinawa.

Volador was in upkeep status at Yokosuka from 15 to 23 September. She got underway for Hong Kong on 26 September, after shich she stopped at Kaohsiung and Midway Island and arrived at Pearl Harbor on 6 November. She departed two days later for San Diego. *Volador* arrived at her home port on 19 November and spent the remainder of 1966 in holiday leave and upkeep status. She was nominated for the Captain Edward F. Ney Memorial Award for the most outstanding general mess for 1966. On 1 July 1966, *Volador* was awarded the Squadron 5 award for fire control and weapons excellence.

Operations resumed on 15 January 1967 after a period of holiday routine alongside the Submarine Facility, Ballast Point, San Diego. The first half of 1967 was spent participating in various exercises, undergoing upkeep and repairs, and qualifying for a nuclear weapons technical proficiency inspection, a material inspection, and an operational readiness inspection.

Volador then departed San Diego on 24 July en route to Auckland, New Zealand. She made a two-day stop at Pago Pago, American Samoa, and arrived at Auckland on 15 August. The submarine participated in LONGEX 67, then departed for Subic Bay and arrived there on 10 September for five days of upkeep and voyage repairs. She participated in Exercise "Gillnet," visited Buckner Bay, Okinawa, and arrived at Yokosuka, Japan, on 26 September. The remainder of the year was spent conducting various operations out of Yokosuka.

On 1 January 1968, *Volador* was en route to Hong Kong for a port visit. She arrived back at Yokosuka, Japan, on the 24th to learn that her deployment was being indefinitely extended because of mobilization response to the capture of *Pueblo* (AGER-2) by the North Koreans. *Volador* departed for sea on 31 January and returned 31 days later. The submarine left Japan and made a two-day stopover at Pearl Harbor before arriving in San Diego on 29 March. The period until 26 June was spent in post-deployment upkeep and local operations. On 27 June, *Volador* departed for a regular shipyard overhaul in the San Francisco Naval Shipyard at Hunters Point at which time a Mk 48 fire control system was installed. Post-overhaul trials were conducted in the San Francisco operating area on 20 and 22 December, and the submarine finished the year at the San Francisco Naval Shipyard, Vallejo, Calif.

Throughout January and February 1969, *Volador* held sound and weapons trials in the Puget Sound area. The next two months were spent in upkeep and training before heading to the Pacific northwest for a quality assurance system test of the Mk 48 Astor torpedo. After the firings, while en route to home waters, a stop was made at Monterey, Calif., on 20 and 21 May to provide familiarization cruises for students of the Naval Postgraduate School, local members of the Navy League, and city leaders. The trip was an outstanding success and received wide dissemination through the local press media.

The submarine returned to San Diego and commenced an upkeep period and a final workup for deployment. *Volador* departed San Diego on 28 July 1969 for Yokosuka, Japan, via Pearl Harbor. During the Christmas holidays, *Volador* visited Bangkok, Thailand, enjoying the exotic sights and the Thai people and providing a week of services to the Royal Thai Navy. Leaving Bangkok on 26 December, the ship headed for Hong Kong and was en route as the year ended.

Volador left Hong Kong for two weeks of operations and liberty in Yokosuka, Japan, before returning to San Diego on 12 February 1970. The next month was a period of upkeep and rest for the crew. The following three months were filled with numerous exercises and drills to retrain the crew and to prepare for interfleet transfer to the east coast. *Volador* departed San Diego on 7 August for transit to the east coast via the Panama Canal. She arrived at her new home port of Charleston, S.C., and spent the remainder of 1970 there.

During the first few months of 1971, *Volador* conducted exercises and drills and underwent upkeep in preparation for deployment to the Mediterranean. On 19 April, she arrived at Rota, Spain, and commenced participation in Exercise "Dawn Patrol 71" with several NATO units on 23 April. Upon completion of this exercise on 12 May, *Volador* visited Piraeus, Greece; Augusta Bay, Sicily; Palma, Majorca; Villefranche, France; Gibraltar; Naples, Italy; and Malaga, Spain; and returned to Rota on 19 July for turnover. *Volador* departed for Charleston, S.C., on 21 July after spending three months in the Mediterranean Sea. On 1 August, she was diverted from her homeward transit to render assistance to the tanker M/T *Lacon*, a Liberian vessel which was on fire. *Volador* arrived at Charleston on 5 August and began a period of leave and upkeep until 20 September when she entered the Charleston Naval Shipyard, commencing a regular overhaul and battery renewal.

On 18 August 1972, *Volador* was transferred to Italy where she serves the Italian Navy as *Primo Longobordo* (S-501) into 1980.

Volador earned three campaign stars for service during the Vietnam War.

Volans

A Latin name for "flying fish," the constellation of stars joining Argo (Carina) in the southern sky.

(AKS–9: dp. 14,550 (lim.); l. 441'6"; b. 56'11"; dr. 28'4" (lim.); s. 12.5 k.; cpl. 214; a. 1 5", 1 3", 8 20mm.; cl. *Acubens*; T. EC2–S–C1)

Edward Preble was laid down under a Maritime Commission contract (MCE hull 772) on 19 October 1942 at South Portland, Maine, by the New England Shipbuilding Corp.; launched on 2 February 1943; sponsored by Miss Beverly Brown; renamed *Volans* and designated AKS–9 on 13 November 1943; and acquired by the Navy on 2 December 1943. Taken to the Tampa Bay Shipbuilding Co., Inc., *Volans* was converted for naval service at that yard, the work lasting into the following year. On 31 March 1944, *Volans* (AKS–9) was commissioned at Tampa, Comdr. Sherman R. Perie, USNR, in command.

Following her shakedown training in Chesapeake Bay and post-shakedown availability at the Norfolk Navy Yard, *Volans* loaded her initial cargo and got underway for the Canal Zone on 11 May 1944. After transiting the Panama Canal, the stores issue ship experienced a two-day layover at Balboa, on the Pacific side of the isthmian waterway, before she sailed on 28 May for the New Hebrides Islands.

Over the next year, *Volans* performed a vital service to the fleet as a stores issue ship. In the course of her important but unglamorous duties, she travelled from port to port, unescorted, proceeding independently from locales ranging from the Solomon Islands to the Carolines; and from the Palaus to the Admiralties. Ports of call included Guadalcanal; Tulagi; Emirau (Green Islands); Noumea, New Caledonia; the Russell Islands; Munda, New Georgia; Espiritu Santo, New Hebrides; Finschhafen and Hollandia, New Guinea; Manus; Ulithi; Kossol Roads; Peleliu; and the islands of Guam and Saipan. In addition, she also operated for a time out of Leyte in the Philippines.

Volans, in her unsung role, provided stores to the ships that took part in the initial carrier air strikes on Tokyo in January 1945 and to the ships that took part in landing operations at places such as Iwo Jima, Okinawa, and the Philippines. She serviced some 1,302 ships and facilities, filling 30,454 requisitions comprising an approximate 137,000 items. While at San Pedro Bay, Leyte, from 23 March to 5 April 1945, *Volans* experienced her busiest service. During that period, she issued supplies on a 24-hour basis, supporting the efforts to secure the Philippines and also to take Okinawa.

On 10 July 1945, *Volans* departed Ulithi for Seattle, Wash., and shipyard availability and arrived at her destination on 31 July. She was still under overhaul at the time of the Japanese surrender in mid-August and at the time of the formal surrender in Tokyo Bay in early September. On 25 September, *Volans* sailed for Okinawa and arrived there on 19 October.

Volans subsequently returned to Pearl Harbor in November and remained there until decommissioned on 17 June 1946. Towed to San Francisco for disposal, the former stores issue ship was delivered to the Maritime Commission at Suisun Bay, Calif., on 24 June 1947 and placed in the National Defense Reserve Fleet. Her name was struck from the Navy list on 17 July of the same year.

Volunteer

I

(SwGbt.: t. 209; dr. 5'; s. 6 mph.; a. 1 heavy 12-pdr. sb.)

The first *Volunteer*—originally a Confederate steamer captured off Natchez Island, Miss., by *Fort Hindman*

on 25 November 1863—was purchased by the Navy from the Springfield, Ill., prize court on 29 February 1864.

Volunteer was assigned to the Mississippi Squadron and performed valuable service as a patrol, dispatch, and tow steamer. Her one major engagement during the war occurred on 14 April 1864 when she helped to drive off a Confederate force which was attacking Fort Pillow, Tenn. After the end of the war in April 1865, *Volunteer* convoyed naval stores up and down the Mississippi River as Union naval forces in the West deactivated. That summer, she was decommissioned and laid up at Mound City, Ill., and was sold at public auction there to B. F. Goodwin on 29 November.

II

(Collier: dp. 16,100 (n.); l. 410'0"; b. 56'0"; dr. 30'6" (aft); s. 10.5 k.; cpl. 70)

The second *Volunteer* (Id. No. 3242) was launched on 18 May 1918 at Alameda, Calif., by the Bethlehem Shipbuilding Corp. for the United States Shipping Board. She was delivered to the Navy on 23 August 1918 and was placed in commission on that same day, Lt. Comdr. John G. Moreno, USNRF, in command.

Pressed into service as a collier, *Volunteer* set sail from San Francisco on 7 September, bound for the Far East. During that voyage, she made port calls at Shanghai and Hong Kong before arriving at Manila on 24 October. From there, she moved south to Iloilo on the island of Panay, located in the central Philippines. She reached that port on 6 November and, after a false start and a return for additional fuel, finally set course back to the United States on 8 December. *Volunteer* reached Oahu on New Year's Day 1919 and remained in Hawaii until the 9th when she got underway for the east coast. The collier arrived in New York City on 15 February 1919. Twelve days later, she was placed out of commission and was returned to the United States Shipping Board. Her name was struck from the Navy list on that same day, 27 February 1919. *Volunteer* remained in the possession of the United States Shipping Board until 1937 at which time she was sold to the Lykes Brothers-Ripley Steamship Co., of New Orleans, La. That company operated her under the name SS *Volunteer* until 1948 when her name disappeared from the mercantile lists.

Volunteer (SP–207)—a wooden-hulled motorboat built in 1906 at East Boothbay, Maine—was inspected during the summer of 1918 for duty with the section patrol. The 1918 *Naval Vessel Register*—which listed her as a "water boat"—indicates that she was commissioned in the Navy on 23 August 1918. However, that information is probably erroneous for two reasons: first, the 1919 edition of the *Naval Vessel Register* indicates that she was "not taken over," and she is not listed in the lists of district vessels found in the 1918 and 1919 issues of the *Navy Directory*. Second, there was another *Volunteer* (Id. No. 3242) which served in the Naval Overseas Transportation Service; and her commissioning date was, in fact, 23 August 1918. It seems likely that the compilers of the 1918 *Naval Vessel Register* confused the two ships and that *Volunteer* (SP–207) never saw service with the Navy.

Von Steuben

Friedrich Wilhelm Ludolf Gerhard Augustin von Steuben was born sometime in 1730 in Magdeburg in the Electorate of Brandenburg. The son of a lieutenant of engineers in the army of Frederick William I, King of Prussia and Elector of Brandenburg, he spent his early childhood in Russia where his father had entered the service of Czarina Anne at the command of Frederick William I. After the accession of Frederick

II to the Prussian throne, von Steuben returned to Germany with his father in 1740.

In 1747, at age 17, he became a cadet in a Prussian infantry regiment and, two years later, received his patent (commission) as an ensign. Von Steuben served with distinction during the Seven Years' War. His specific training and experience in general staff duties equipped him for his later role in the American Revolution.

His discharge from the army for obscure reasons in 1763 and subsequent financial difficulties caused him to seek service with the American Army in 1777. Stating that he wished no immediate compensation and would stake his fortunes upon the success of the Revolution, von Steuben reported to General Washington at Valley Forge in February 1778.

He was almost immediately successful in the training of the Continental Army in accordance with the exacting standards of the Prussian Army. Thereafter, the Continental Army proved itself, battalion for battalion, the equal in discipline of the best British regulars. He served with distinction with General Nathanael Greene in the Carolinas in 1780 and with General Lafayette at Yorktown in 1781.

Von Steuben became a citizen of the United States in 1783 and, following retirement from the army, resided in New York where he became one of the most popular figures in the city until his death in 1794.

I

(Id. No. 3017: dp. 23,500 (n.); l. 663′0″; b. 66′0″ (wl.); dr. 30′0″ (mean); dph. 39′3¼″; s. 23.0 k.; cpl. 975; a. 8 5″, 4 3″, 2 3″ AA., 4 1-pdrs., 8 mg.)

The first *Von Steuben* (Id. No. 3017)—a twin-screw, steam passenger ship constructed in 1901 by the *Aktiengesellschaft Vulcan* at Stettin, Germany—served the transatlantic passenger liner fleet of the North German Lloyd Lines as *Kronprinz Wilhelm* for 13 years carrying passengers between North America and the North Sea ports of Europe. When World War I broke out on 1 August 1914, the liner was in port at New York City. Two days later, she departed that port on orders from the German Admiralty and headed south to rendezvous with the cruiser SMS *Karlsruhe*. After a three-day voyage, she met the cruiser just to the north and west of the Bahama Islands. In just over two hours, *Karlsruhe* transferred two 8.8 cm. rapid fire guns, 290 rounds of 8.8 cm. ammunition, a machine gun, and 36 rifles as well as one officer, two non-commissioned officers, and 13 ratings. Just before the approach of HMS *Suffolk* abbreviated the rendezvous, *Kronprinz Wilhelm* was commissioned an auxiliary cruiser in the Imperial German Navy, *Kapitänleutnant* Thierfelder—formerly *Karlsruhe's* navigation officer—in command.

The proximity of the British cruiser forced the two German warships to cast off hastily and speed away in different directions. *Kronprinz Wilhelm* headed north for a time, then steered west and southwest, and she finally steadied up on a course generally east toward the Azores. She reached her destination on 17 August and rendezvoused with the German steamer SS *Walhalla* off St. Miguel Island. During the following four days, she coaled from *Walhalla* during the days; and the two ships steamed on a southerly course during the nights. After completing the coaling and provisioning operation, the newly commissioned commerce raider learned from German representatives at Las Palmas in the Canary Islands that no further coal would be available in the neighborhood of the Azores and the Canaries. Consequently, her commanding officer decided to head for the Brazilian coast where he hoped to find sources of coal more friendly to Germany or at least a greater choice of neutral ports in which to intern his ship if she should find herself unable to replenish her supplies from captured ships.

During the voyage to the Azores and thence to the South American coast, *Kronprinz Wilhelm* had to avoid contact with all shipping since she was not ready to embark upon her mission raiding Allied commerce. The guns had to be emplaced and a target for gunnery practice constructed. The crew—mostly reservists and civilians—received a crash course in their duties in a warship and in general naval discipline. A prize crew was selected and trained in the techniques of boarding prizes, inspecting cargo and ship's papers, and in using explosive charges to sink captured ships. Finally, all members of the crew were outfitted in some semblance of a naval uniform.

The crew worked at a feverish pace in order to be ready; and, by the time *Kronprinz Wilhelm* met *Karlsruhe's* tender SS *Asuncion* near Rocas Reef north of Cape San Roque on 3 September, preparations were nearly complete. And none too soon either for, at 2030 the following evening, the auxiliary cruiser encountered the British steamer SS *Indian Prince*. The merchantman stopped without the raider's firing a shot. Heavy seas, however, postponed the boarding until shortly after 0600 the following morning. The prize crew found a cargo composed largely of contraband; but, before sinking the ship, Thierfelder wanted to salvage as much of her supplies and fuel as he could—principally the latter. Continued heavy seas precluded the transfer until the afternoon of 8 September. *Indian Prince's* crew and passengers were brought over to *Kronprinz Wilhelm* at around 1400, and the two ships moved alongside each other immediately thereafter. Coaling started and continued throughout the night of 8 and 9 September. The following morning, the German prize crew detonated three explosive charges which sank *Indian Prince*. *Kronprinz Wilhelm* then headed south to rendezvous with several German supply ships.

Coal, more than any other factor, proved to be the key to the success of *Kronprinz Wilhelm's* cruise. The hope of finding that commodity had brought her to the coast of South America, and her success in locating sources of it kept her there. Initially, she replenished from German steamers sent out of South American ports specifically for that purpose. In fact, she spent the next month coaling from four such auxiliaries before she even contacted her next victim. That event occurred on 7 October, when she hailed the British steamer SS *La Correntina* well off the Brazilian coast in about the same latitude as Rio de Janeiro. The next day, the raider went alongside the captured ship to seize the prize's coal and cargo of frozen meat before sinking her. During the operation, she also improved her martial appearance—though not her actual military capability—when she took *La Correntina's* two ammunitionless 12 cm. guns and their splinter shields. Later, the raider mounted the additional guns aft and they were used for gun drills and to fire warning shots with modified, blank salute cartridges. She continued coaling and provisioning operations from *La Correntina* until 11 October when bad weather forced a postponement. On the 14th, she resumed the transfer of fuel but broke off again when she intercepted a wireless message indicating that her captive's sister ship SS *La Rosarina* had departed Montevideo two days earlier and would soon pass nearby. The prize crew placed the usual three explosive charges, and *La Correntina* sank that same day.

During the ensuing five months, *Kronprinz Wilhelm* cruised the waters off the coast of Brazil and Argentina. Her success in finding ships laden with coal and supplies combined with her luck and skill in evading British cruisers enabled the raider to capture 15 ships. Of that number, she sank 13 for sure; another she damaged severely by ramming, and it probably sank later. The remaining ship served as transportation into port for what had become an unbearable number of detainees on board after her 12th capture.

Late in March of 1915, the auxiliary cruiser headed north to rendezvous with another German supply ship at the equator. She arrived at the meeting point on the morning of the 28th and cruised in the neighborhood all day. That evening, she sighted a steamer in company with two warships—undoubtedly British—20 miles distant. Though *Kronprinz Wilhelm* did not know it at the time, she had just witnessed the capture of her supply ship, SS *Macedonia,* by two British cruisers. The raider steamed around in the general vicinity for several days, but the passage of each succeeding day further diminished her prospects of a successful rendezvous. Finally, a dwindling coal supply and an alarming increase in the sick list forced *Kronprinz Wilhelm* to make for the nearest neutral port. Early in the morning of 11 April, she stopped off Cape Henry, Va., and took on a pilot. At 1012 that morning, she dropped anchor off Newport News, Va., and ended her 72-day cruise during which she steamed 37,666 miles and destroyed just under 56,000 tons of Allied shipping.

Though interned, *Kronprinz Wilhelm* had not quite ended her wartime career. After she interned herself, *Kronprinz Wilhelm* was moved to Philadelphia. On 6 April 1917, the United States declared war upon the German Empire. That same day, the Collector of the Port of Philadelphia seized the former German raider in the name of the United States. On 22 May, President Wilson issued the executive order which empowered the Navy to take possession of the ship and to begin to repair her. On 9 June 1917, *Kronprinz Wilhelm* was renamed *Von Steuben* and commissioned in the United States Navy at Philadelphia, Lt. Charles H. Bullock in command.

Von Steuben began her Navy career as an auxiliary cruiser. Through the summer of 1917, her crew and workers at the Philadelphia Navy Yard prepared her to resume that role against her former masters. However, since the Allied and Associated Powers already maintained virtual control of the seas, their need for that type of ship was minimal. Accordingly, on 21 September, the Office of the Chief of Naval Operations telegraphed an order to the Commandant, Philadelphia Navy Yard, to assign her to transport duty upon completion of repairs to meet a more pressing need—the transportation of troops and supplies to Europe. The ship completed preparations by 29 Setember and put to sea that same day for her first voyage. During the next four weeks, she remained close to American shores, visiting Hampton Roads and New York in addition to Philadelphia.

On 31 October, she stood out of New York for her first transatlantic voyage under the American flag with 1,223 troops and passengers bound for Brest, France. At about 0605 on the morning of 9 November, *Von Steuben* received some damage when *Agamemnon,* another troop ship, collided with her during a zigzag. Both ships lost men overboard, and a few received injuries. In addition, two of her 5-inch guns and one of her 3-inch guns were damaged. Though her bow was opened to the sea, *Von Steuben* maintained 12 knots while the damage control party made repairs. The ship continued on with the convoy and arrived in Brest three days later. She disembarked passengers and unloaded cargo between 14 and 19 November; but she did not depart until the 28th.

On her way back to the United States, *Von Steuben* had to stop over at Halifax, Nova Scotia. At about 0914 on the morning of 6 December, she was about 40 miles from Halifax when lookouts spied a great flame and a high column of smoke in the direction of the port. Visual contact was followed rapidly by the concussion from the explosion of a French ammunition ship, *Mont Blanc,* in Halifax harbor. *Von Steuben* learned the facts when she entered the harbor at about 1430 that afternoon. A portion of the city had been devastated by the explosion and the fire which followed. She responded to the emergency by landing officers and men to patrol the city and assist in rescue efforts. The transport remained at Halifax until 10 December and then continued her voyage back to Philadelphia where she arrived on the 13th.

After debarking her passengers, *Von Steuben* got underway from Philadelphia again on 15 December. She coaled at Newport News on the 16th and remained there until the 20th when she returned to sea, bound for Guantanamo Bay, Cuba, where she disembarked marines. On 27 December, she got underway for the Canal Zone. The ship transited the canal on 29 December and entered the drydock at Balboa that afternoon. Over the next three weeks, she received repairs of the damage to her bow. On 20 January 1918, the ship floated out of the dock and then retransited the canal. After coaling at Colon, she departed the Canal Zone and headed back to the east coast. From 28 to 31 January, *Von Steuben* stopped at Newport News where she took on two new 5-inch guns and a 3-inch gun to replace those damaged in the collision with *Agamemnon.* On 1 February, she returned to Philadelphia to resume duty transporting troops to France.

On 10 February, *Von Steuben* stood down the Delaware River with another convoy. She reached her destination, Brest, without incident on the 24th, unloaded her troops and cargo, and set out on the return voyage five days later. At about 1620 on 5 March, a lookout spotted an object to port which resembled a submarine periscope. The alarm brought gun crews scurrying to their action stations, and they opened fire immediately. Before anyone realized that they were firing upon an innocuous piece of flotsam, a tragic accident occurred. The shell from one of her 5-inch guns exploded immediately upon leaving the barrel, and fragments struck three sailors. One died instantly, and the other two succumbed to their wounds later that night. *Von Steuben* coaled at Bermuda on 12 and 13 March and arrived at Norfolk on the 16th. After repairs and coaling, she moved on to Philadelphia to load troops and cargo for her third voyage to France.

Her next two voyages to France and back were uneventful, as was the New York-to-Brest leg of the following one. However, on the return voyage, she encountered a U-boat. At about 1230 on the afternoon of 18 June, one of her lookouts reported wreckage ahead. As she steamed closer, seven small boats under sail came into sight on the port bow about five miles away. *Von Steuben* began a zigzag approach to pick up what appeared to be boatloads of survivors from a sunken Allied ship. About 20 minutes later, her lookouts reported the wake of a torpedo approaching her bow from abaft the port beam. The gun crews manned their stations and began firing at the torpedo while the commanding officer ordered the wheel hard to starboard and all engines full astern in an effort to avoid the missile. Meanwhile, some of the gunners had shifted their attention to what they thought to be the periscope of *U–151,* the source of the torpedo bearing down upon *Von Steuben.* The ship's efforts to slow down and turn away from the torpedo were successful. It passed a few yards ahead of the ship, and *Von Steuben* delivered a desultory depth-charge barrage which subjected the submarine to a severe shaking.

The real losers in that brief, but sharp, exchange were the survivors of the British steamer *Dwinsk* adrift in those seven small boats. *U–151* had sunk their ship earlier and remained in the area to use them as decoys for other Allied ships such as *Von Steuben.* The possibility that they were simply decoys and that other submarines might be lurking about forced the ship to continue on without further investigation. That decision was further reinforced by the fact that the boats appeared empty. Credit for this must go to *Dwinsk*'s master who ordered his people to lie low in their craft so that other Allied ships would not be drawn into the waiting U-boat's trap. Fortunately, he and his men were saved eventually.

Von Steuben arrived in New York on 20 June and began preparations for another voyage to France. On the 29th, she embarked troops for passage to Europe; and the next day stood out of New York harbor and formed up with a convoy for the Atlantic crossing. At about noon on the third day out, a fire broke out in the forward cargo hold of *Henderson* (Transport No. 1). As the blaze grew in intensity, the transfer of the troops embarked became a necessary precaution; and *Von Steuben* approached the burning ship. Silhouetted by the flames, she would have made a perfect target for any U-boat in the vicinity, but she worked throughout the night and, by morning, had succeeded in embarking *Henderson*'s more than 2,000 troops. *Henderson* came about and made it safely back to the United States, while *Von Steuben* completed a somewhat cramped voyage at Brest on 9 July. Three days later, she headed back across the Atlantic with civilians and wounded soldiers returning to the United States after service in Europe. After a peaceful voyage, the transport reached New York on 21 July.

After a short repair period in late July and early August, the ship resumed duty transporting troops to Europe. Between late August and the armistice on 11 November, *Von Steuben* made three more round-trip voyages carrying troops to France and returning the sick and wounded to the United States. Though all three were peaceful passages by wartime standards, they were not uneventful. On the return voyage from the first of the three, she weathered a severe hurricane during which three of her complement were washed overboard and lost at sea, while several others received injuries. During the New York-to-Brest leg of the second, the influenza epidemic of 1918 struck the 2,700 troops she had embarked and resulted in 400 stretcher cases and 34 deaths.

Von Steuben returned to New York from her ninth wartime voyage on 8 November. On the 10th, she began repairs at the Morse Dry Dock & Repair Co., Brooklyn, N.Y. The next day, Germany signed the armistice which ended hostilities. The former commerce raider completed repairs on 2 March 1919 and put to sea to begin bringing troops home from France. She continued to serve the Navy until 13 October 1919 when she was decommissioned and turned over to the United States Shipping Board (USSB). Her name was struck from the Navy list on 14 October 1919; but, for almost five years, the ship continued to serve the United States under the auspices of the USSB, first as *Baron Von Steuben* and, after 1921, simply as *Von Steuben* again. Her name disappeared from mercantile records after 1923.

II

(SSBN–632: dp. 7,280 (f.) (surf.), 8,250 (subm.); l. 425'; b. 33'; dr. 32'; s. 20+ k.; cpl. 110; a. 16 Polaris mis., 4 21'' tt.; cl. *Lafayette*)

The second *Von Steuben* (SSBN–632) was laid down on 4 September 1962 at Newport News, Va., by the Newport News Shipbuilding & Dry Dock Co.; launched on 18 October 1963; sponsored by Mrs. Fred Korth; and commissioned on 30 September 1964, Comdr. John P. Wise (blue crew) and Comdr. Jeffrey C. Metzel (gold crew) in command.

During the fall of 1964, the fleet ballistic missile submarine completed two shakedown cruises—one for each crew—and a period of antisubmarine warfare (ASW) training between the two. On 22 December, the submarine's gold crew fired her first Polaris missile on the Atlantic missile range before returning to Newport News for Christmas. She changed crews again at the beginning of the new year, 1965, and returned to the missile range off Cape Canaveral (then called Cape Kennedy) where the blue crew fired its first missile. In February, after completing all initial training operations, she returned to Newport News.

In March, *Von Steuben* headed for her first duty assignment. The submarine joined Submarine Squadron (SubRon) 18 at Charleston, S.C., her new base of operations, and immediately began conducting classified deterrent patrols. Her primary mission was and is to deter aggression by providing a highly-mobile launch platform for her nuclear warhead-bearing Polaris missiles. Since her security and mission would be impaired should any potential enemy learn of her patrol routes and activities, that information is highly classified and cannot be recounted here. However, she has conducted more than 30 such patrols since her commissioning, at the rate of four or five per year.

At the end of her 11th patrol early in 1968, *Von Steuben* was reassigned to SubRon 16 and operated out of Rota, Spain, until the middle of 1969. During that assignment, she visited Groton, Conn., in the summer of 1968 for repairs at the Electric Boat Division of General Dynamics Corp., after which she resumed deterrent patrols out of Rota. In November 1970, she visited Groton once again, this time near the end of a 16-month overhaul during which she was modified to carry the newly developed Poseidon C–3 missile. She conducted post-conversion shakedown during the early months of 1971 and fired her first and second Poseidon missiles in February and March, respectively. She returned to Charleston and resumed deterrent patrols in May 1971. Since that time, she continued to make patrols out of Charleston and, recently, also from the submarine base at Holy Loch in Scotland.

Voyager

(MB: t. 35 (gross): l. 52'; b. 10'6''; dr. 4'; s. 9.5 k.; cpl. 9)

Voyager—a wooden-hulled motorboat built at Bay City, Mich., by the De Foe Boat and Motor Works—was acquired by the Navy from H. J. De Foe in July 1917 and given the designation SP–361. Although listed in the 1918 edition of *Ship's Data: U.S. Naval Vessels* as being delivered and commissioned on 25 July 1917, *Voyager*'s extant logs do not begin until 1 September 1917. Nevertheless, they indicate that the first men actually reported on board for duty as early as 13 July 1917—12 days before the delivery/commissioning date given in the *Ship's Data: U.S. Naval Vessels* for 1918.

Attached to the 9th, 10th, and 11th Naval District local patrol forces and based at Sault St. Marie for the duration of World War I, *Voyager* operated actively on the Great Lakes until winter ice stopped navigation. Her first recorded duty in September appears to have been standing off a navigable channel off Pipe Island, guarding the wreck of the U.S. Steel Corp. boat *Mitchell*, which was apparently blocking part of the channel.

Voyager operated out of Sault St. Marie into mid-November 1917 before she shifted to Detroit in company with the old gunboat *Isla de Luzon*. She was subsequently placed out of service between 18 and 21 November and was decommissioned "for the season" on the 23d. She remained inactive until 8 May 1918, when she was ordered to return to Sault St. Marie. Departing on that day, *Voyager* set out in company with *Isla de Luzon*, *Avis* (SP–382), *Mikawe* (SP–309), *Dicky* (SP–231), and *Raboco* (SP–310).

Rough weather during the first night of the voyage forced *Voyager* to drag anchor and run aground, but she was pulled off soon thereafter. Her motor broke down on 11 May, however, necessitating the SP boat's being towed back to her home port of Sault St. Marie. *Voyager* operated out of that Michigan port through the armistice of 11 November 1918 and was decommissioned on 13 May 1919. Simultaneously struck from the Navy list, *Voyager* was turned over to the Treasury Department for use by the United States Coast Guard at Chicago, Ill., on 15 September 1919.

Voyager operated out of Chicago until late in 1922, when she was shifted back to her former home port, Sault St. Marie. On 6 November 1923, the erstwhile patrol craft lost her name and became simply *AB–18*. Classified as a harbor patrol cutter, she served in that capacity into the late 1930's. After 1936, her name disappeared from Coast Guard ship registers.

Vreeland

Charles E. Vreeland—born on 10 March 1852 at Newark, N.J.—enlisted in the Navy as a naval apprentice early in 1866. After brief service in *Sabine*, he received a Presidential appointment as a midshipman at the Naval Academy on 27 July 1866. On 7 June 1870, he graduated from the academy as a passed midshipman and, at the end of July, reported on board the newly commissioned screw sloop *California*. On 28 September, he was detached from that ship and was ordered to proceed in *Severn* to duty in the screw sloop *Congress*, then cruising in the South Atlantic. He was later transferred to the screw sloop *Brooklyn* and, between 1871 and 1873, made a cruise in her to European waters. In July 1873, he was detached from *Brooklyn*. After successfully completing the required post-sea duty examination in October, he returned to sea in November in *Powhatan* and, less than a fortnight later, received his commission as an ensign.

Successive tours of duty in *Alert*, *Ashuelot*, and *Ticonderoga* followed; and, during that period, Vreeland received promotions to master and then to lieutenant. In November 1881, after a period ashore awaiting orders, he was posted to the Nautical Almanac Office, where charts and tables were prepared for use by naval officers in celestial navigation. In March 1884, Lt. Vreeland began a three-year tour at sea in *Hartford*, at the completion of which he went to the Bureau of Navigation for a two-year assignment. Upon leaving that duty in mid-April 1889, he took torpedo instruction at Newport, R.I. Then, a brief assignment with the Office of Naval Intelligence from July to September of 1889 preceded his reporting to the Coast Survey late in October. That employment lasted until the spring of 1893 when orders sent Vreeland to Europe as naval attache—first at Rome, then at Vienna, and finally in Berlin.

Lt. Vreeland returned home late in 1896, was posted to *Massachusetts* in mid-January 1897, and served in that battleship until transferred to *Helena* at the end of June. Vreeland was ordered to *Dolphin* as executive officer in April 1898, but he did not actually assume those duties until 24 August. Thus, he served in *Helena* through most of the brief Spanish-American War on blockade duty off Cuba until July. He was detached from *Dolphin* on 5 November 1898 and ordered to *Olympia;* however, those orders were changed in December, and he reported to *Concord* instead on the 30th. In March 1899, he became Lt. Comdr. Vreeland and, after completing assignments in *Concord*, *Monterey*, and *Baltimore*—all on the Asiatic station—he returned home on board the hospital ship *Solace* in March 1900. In April, he became a member of the Board of Inspection and Survey; and, during that assignment, he was promoted to full commander in mid-August 1901. In August 1902, he took charge of fitting out of the "New Navy" monitor *Arkansas* (later to be renamed *Ozark*) at Newport News, Va. When she was placed in commission on 28 October, he assumed command.

Two years later, Vreeland left his first command, *Arkansas*, and served ashore over the next two and one-half years, performing various special duties for the Navy Department. Initially, he was a member of and recorder for the board studying proposed changes to the New York Navy Yard. He was next assigned special duty in the Office of the Assistant Secretary of the Navy. While assigned to the Navy Department in Washington, Vreeland received his promotion to captain to date from 13 April 1906. Capt. Vreeland concluded that latest assignment in Washington on 17 April 1907 and, the following day, placed *Kansas* (Battleship No. 21) in commission at Camden, N.J. He commanded the new battleship for the next two years—a very auspicious time for it coincided with the cruise of the "Great White Fleet" around the world. Soon after the Fleet returned to Hampton Roads in February 1909, he relinquished command of *Kansas* and returned home to await orders. On 10 May, Capt. Vreeland took

over command of the Office of Naval Intelligence. That duty lasted until 8 December 1909 when, with his selection for promotion to rear admiral imminent, he broke his flag in *Virginia* (Battleship No. 13) as Commander, 4th Division, Atlantic Fleet. Nineteen days later, on the 27th, he became Rear Admiral Vreeland.

On 19 April 1911, he reported ashore for further duty in Washington. In his new assignment as Aide for Inspections, he approached the pinnacle of naval command. He became one of the four principal advisors of the Secretary of the Navy, George von L. Meyer, under the newly devised aide system for managing the Navy. During his tenure in that office, Rear Admiral Vreeland represented the Navy Department at the coronation of King George V of England and headed up the so-called "Vreeland Board" which reinvestigated the *Maine* disaster of 1898. The controversial report of that board—now considered erroneous—concluded that an external explosion sank the warship.

On 12 December, Rear Admiral Vreeland ended his tour of duty as Aide for Inspections and succeeded Rear Admiral Richard Wainwright as the Secretary's second Aide for Operations. While in that position—the forerunner to today's office of Chief of Naval Operations—Vreeland struggled to improve the defenses in the Philippines, agitated for increased naval construction, particularly of battle cruisers, and supported the development of American naval aviation. During his tenure as Aide for Operations, naval aviation found a permanent home at Pensacola, Fla. On 11 February 1913, Rear Admiral Vreeland relinquished his duties as Aide for Operations to Rear Admiral Bradley A. Fiske, the third and last man to hold the office under that title. Vreeland finished out his naval career as a member of both the General and Joint Boards. On 10 March 1914, he was transferred to the retired list. On 27 September 1916, after a retirement plagued by illness, Rear Admiral Vreeland died at Atlantic City, N.J.

(DE–1068: dp. 3,877 (f.); l. 438'; b. 47'; dr. 25'; s. 27+ k.; cpl. 245; a. 1 5", 4 15.5" tt., ASROC; cl. *Knox*)

Vreeland (DE–1068) was laid down on 20 March 1968 by the Avondale Shipyard at Westwego, La.; launched on 16 June 1969; sponsored by Mrs. Jamie L. Whitten, wife of the Congressman representing Mississippi's 2d Congressional District; and commissioned at Charleston, S.C., on 13 June 1970, Comdr. David R. Stefferud in command.

After fitting out at Charleston and shakedown training in the West Indies, *Vreeland* returned to Charleston to join Destroyer Squadron (DesRon) 4. She completed repairs in February 1971 and final contract trials in March and then began preparations for her first deployment to the Mediterranean area. The warship departed Charleston on 15 April and arrived in Rota, Spain, on the 25th. During the next six months, she steamed the length and breadth of the "middle sea" as a unit of the 6th Fleet. She visited numerous ports and participated in a host of exercises with American and Allied naval forces. She concluded that tour of duty at Gibraltar on 8 October when she changed operational control back to the 2d Fleet and headed home. The warship arrived in Charleston on the 16th and resumed 2d Fleet operations out of Charleston.

In the summer of 1972, the ship began preparations for another cruise in the Mediterranean Sea. That deployment, however, proved different than the previous one. Rather than deploying for six months and then returning home to Charleston, *Vreeland* received orders changing her home port to Athens, Greece. That assignment lasted for the next three years rather than the normal six months and included the relocation of *Vreeland* dependents to Athens—all as a part of the Navy's forward deployment program. During those three years, she performed the normal duties of a unit of the 6th Fleet, visiting ports, conducting exercises, and performing surveillance of Soviet ships operating in the Mediterranean.

On 1 July 1975, *Vreeland* was reclassified a frigate and redesignated FF–1068. Three days later, she departed Greece to begin her voyage back to the United States. The warship concluded that voyage and her three-year deployment at Philadelphia on 30 July. After post-deployment standdown, she moved south to Norfolk in September for repairs but returned to Philadelphia in October in time to participate in the Navy's 200th birthday celebration on the 13th. Duty as a surface warfare school ship and more repairs at Norfolk followed.

On 6 December, the frigate entered the Philadelphia Naval Shipyard where she spent the following year undergoing a major overhaul. Her refurbishing completed on 2 December 1976, the warship resumed duty as an active unit of the Fleet early in 1977. Refresher training and various qualification exercises out of her new home port, Mayport, Fla., occupied her during the first six months of 1977. On 25 July, she departed Mayport for a cruise to South America to participate in UNITAS XVIII, the annual series of exercises in which units of various South American navies join the United States Navy in practicing the skills of hemispheric defense. In November, she concluded her UNITAS cruise and reentered Mayport on the 25th. Leave and upkeep in port took up her time for the remainder of the year.

A part of January and February 1978 was devoted to a restricted availability for *Vreeland*. The frigate devoted the ensuing months to preparations for her forthcoming deployment to the Middle East. *Vreeland* departed from Mayport on 23 July in company with *Mullinix* (DD–944). Following fuel stops at Bermuda, the Azores, and Rota, Spain, the ships transited the Mediterranean and the Suez Canal and arrived at Port Sudan, Sudan, on 9 August. A turnover from *Glover* (AGFF–1) and *Barney* (DDG–6) was effected, and *Vreeland* joined the Middle East Force. The remainder of the year was spent in operations with that group. On 31 December, *Vreeland* and *Mullinix* retransited the Suez Canal on their return to the United States.

Vulcan

The Roman god of fire and metalworking who was known to the Greeks as Hephaestus. He was also a consort of Venus.

(ScStr: t. 1,909; l. 265'4''; b. 40'; dph. 15'6''; cpl. 197; a. 2 6-pdrs.)

Chatham—an iron-hulled, schooner-rigged screw steamship constructed at Philadelphia by the American Shipbuilding Co.—was completed in 1884 and acquired by the Navy on 2 May 1898 from the Merchants' and Miners' Transportation Co., of Baltimore, Md. Renamed *Vulcan*, the erstwhile merchantman underwent a metamorphosis to the Fleet's first repair ship. She was equipped with machine tools, forges, and foundries, and a large supply of widely varied stores. A large force of skilled mechanics rounded out her versatile crew. Commissioned on 31 May 1898 at the Boston Navy Yard, with Lt. Comdr. Ira Harris in command, *Vulcan* soon sailed for the Caribbean.

After proceeding via Newport News, Va., she arrived at Guantanamo Bay, Cuba, on 1 July in time to be present during the North Atlantic Fleet's bombardment that day of the Spanish forts at Aquadores. The ship served in Cuban waters for the duration of the brief war with Spain and performed yeoman service. On one occasion, while out on nightly patrol, her picket boat, commanded by Naval Cadet Louis G. Miller, drew some 200 shots from Spanish troops ashore. The Spaniards' fire—which the launch spiritedly returned—was ineffective; and all hands returned safely to the ship.

On 3 July, the American Fleet met and soundly trounced a Spanish squadron off Santiago, Cuba. Almost as soon as the smoke of that battle had cleared, the American Navy began making plans to salvage the Spanish vessels. *Vulcan* performed salvage work on the heavily damaged Spanish ships *Maria Theresa* and *Cristobal Colon*.

Vulcan remained in the Caribbean through the cessation of hostilities. Her services as the first ship of her type were exemplary and noteworthy. In the Bureau of Steam Engineering report for 1898, *Vulcan*'s performance was an "unqualified success and of great value in maintaining the efficiency of the fleet." In fact, *Vulcan*'s brief tour with the Fleet had proved to be so valuable to the Navy that the Chief of the Bureau of Steam Engineering recommended the acquisition of a second ship of her type to serve the ships of the Pacific Fleet.

By the end of August, reports from the repair ship further indicated that she had made repairs to 63 ships and supplied stores to 60. In addition, her "unusual facilities" and the 100 skilled mechanics on board enabled her to effect a wide variety of repairs—including hull work, gun mounts, dynamos, steam pipes, main piston rods for smaller ships, and "iron castings in considerable quantity." In the fall, with her tour thus completed, *Vulcan* sailed north on 30 October and proceeded to Norfolk, Va.

After shifting to the League Island Navy Yard, Philadelphia, Pa., in December 1898, *Vulcan* was decommissioned there on 12 January 1899 and sold on 3 July of the same year to her original owner. Renamed *Chatham*, the ship served the Merchants' and Miners' Transportation Co. until 1911 when her name disappeared from the shipping registers.

Vulcan—a steel-hulled, single-screw freighter built at Cleveland, Ohio, by the Globe Iron Works and completed in 1889—was inspected on 2 April 1918 at the 9th Naval District and designated Id. No. 2756. However, no records have been found showing that she was actually taken over for naval service.

II

(Collier No. 5: dp. 11,250; l. 403'; b. 53'; dr. 24'8'' (mean); dph. 29'6''; s. 12.82 k.; cpl. 82; a. none)

The second *Vulcan* (Collier No. 5) was laid down on 5 October 1908, at Sparrows Point, Md., by the Maryland Steel Co.; launched on 15 May 1909; and commissioned at the Norfolk Navy Yard on 2 October 1909.

For more than two years, *Vulcan* operated out of Norfolk, providing coal and stores for the ships of the Atlantic Fleet to support their operations off the east coast and in the West Indies. Placed out of service at the Portsmouth (N.H.) Navy Yard on 4 May 1912, the collier remained inactive until reactivated there and placed back in service on 25 February 1914.

Resuming her coaling operations with the Atlantic Fleet, *Vulcan* ranged from Portsmouth, N.H., to Guantanamo Bay, Cuba, and from Melville, R.I., to Vera Cruz, Mexico. In addition to carrying coal, she also transported stores and ordnance supplies for the Atlantic Fleet Cruiser Squadron.

During World War I, *Vulcan* served the Fleet Train, supplying coal for ships of the fleet. After hostilities ended, the collier was transferred to the Naval Overseas Transportation Service on 2 January 1919 and served that organization until she was returned to the Fleet Train on 23 June.

After routine operations through the remainder of that year and all of 1920, the collier sailed for European waters on 12 February 1921 to begin a tour of duty supporting American warships attempting to provide an element of stability there during the troubled postwar years. Arriving at Cherbourg, France, on 28 February, she discharged passengers and coaled

Chattanooga (PG–30) before sailing soon thereafter for Malta to deliver coal to *Pittsburgh* (CA–4) on 21 March.

Vulcan then sailed for the Adriatic and arrived at Pola, Italy, on 26 March. Sailing five days later, she reached Naples, Italy, on 3 April but soon got underway for Gibraltar to discharge cargo and passengers.

After returning to New York on 30 April, *Vulcan* was decommissioned at the Norfolk Navy Yard on 20 July. Following almost two years in reserve, the collier was struck from the Navy list on 26 April 1923. She was sold to N. Block and Co., of Norfolk, on 12 December 1923.

III

(AR–5: dp. 12,911; l. 530′; b. 73′4″; dr. 19′; s. 19.2 k.; cpl. 1,297; a. 4 5″, 4 .50-cal. mg.; cl. *Vulcan*)

Vulcan (AR–5) was laid down on 16 December 1939 at Camden, N.J., by the New York Shipbuilding Corp.; launched on 14 December 1940; sponsored by Mrs. James Forrestal, wife of the Under Secretary of the Navy; and commissioned at the Philadelphia Navy Yard on 14 June 1941, Comdr. Leon S. Fiske in command.

Following her shakedown cruise to San Juan, Puerto Rico, and Guantanamo Bay, *Vulcan* underwent post-shakedown repairs at the Philadelphia Navy Yard in mid-August. Assigned to the Atlantic Fleet Train on the 20th, the repair ship departed Philadelphia the following day and proceeded, via Casco Bay, Maine, to Argentia, Newfoundland.

By this time, the Atlantic Fleet was becoming more fully involved in the Battle of the Atlantic. In July 1941, at the request of the Icelandic government, the United States had occupied Iceland—the strategic island which, as the German geopolitician Karl Haushofer wrote, lay pointed "like a pistol . . . at the United States"—and had established bases at the barren ports of Reykjavik and Hvalfjordur. Marine wags soon nicknamed these places "Rinky Dink" and "Valley Forge," respectively.

Prompted by fears that the German battleship *Tirpitz* would break out into the Atlantic as her sister ship *Bismarck* had done in the spring of 1941, the Navy dispatched a task force to Iceland to deter such a move. Accordingly, the unit—designated Task Force (TF) 4 and based around *Wasp* (CV–7)—sailed from Argentia on 23 September. Besides the valuable carrier, the force included *Mississippi* (BB–41), *Wichita*

(CA–45), *Vulcan*, and a screen of four destroyers. A German U-boat, prowling to the southwest of Iceland, sighted the ships on the 26th but could not keep up with or identify the Americans. Having outpaced their adversary, TF 4 reached "Valley Forge" on 28 September.

While *Tirpitz* did not sortie, the U-boats continued their deadly forays against Allied shipping. By the fall of 1941, American destroyers were engaged in convoy operations half-way across the Atlantic, turning their charges over to British units at the MOMP (mid-ocean meeting point). On 4 September, *Greer* (DD–145) narrowly avoided being torpedoed after shadowing a German U-boat.

During the midwatch on 17 October 1941, *U–568* torpedoed *Kearny* (DD–432) while the latter was screening Convoy SC–48. With 11 bluejackets dead, *Kearny* limped into Reykjavik, a gaping hole and buckled plating disfiguring her starboard side below and aft of the bridge. *Vulcan* provided timely and effective assistance to the stricken warship. Since permanent repair facilities—such as a drydock—were nonexistent, *Kearny* pulled up alongside the repair vessel, and her port side was flooded to raise the torpedo hole above water level. Soon, *Vulcan*'s repair force had cut away the damaged plating and had fixed a patch. By Christmas 1941, *Kearny* could sail for the east coast and permanent repairs at Boston.

Operations in these inhospitable climes posed natural dangers as well—fog and storms frequently hampered operations and caused collisions. In November, *Niblack* (DD–424) was rammed by a Norwegian freighter. The destroyer had been scouring Iceland's coastal waters for a straying Icelandic merchant vessel when the accident occurred, costing *Niblack* an anchor and putting a hole in her side plating. *Vulcan* swiftly fixed the damage and patched the side, enabling the destroyer to resume her vital escort duties.

Vulcan remained in Iceland's chill and barren area into the spring of 1942. Meanwhile, on 7 December 1941, a Japanese task force had struck Pearl Harbor and severely crippled the battleships of the Pacific Fleet, plunging the United States into war on both oceans. *Vulcan*—bound for home in company with *Tarazed* (AF–13), *Livermore* (DD–429), and the familiar *Kearny*—departed "Valley Forge" on 26 April 1942 and arrived at Boston on 2 May. There, the repair ship underwent a drydocking before she returned northward to support the Fleet's operations in the North Atlantic. Based at Argentia from 16 June to 14 November, *Vulcan* shifted to Hvalfjordur and relieved

USS *Vulcan* (AR–5) shortly after World War II. (80–G–483373)

Melville (AD–2) there on 18 November. She remained at "Valley Forge" until she got underway on 6 April 1943, bound via Londonderry, Northern Ireland, for Hampton Roads.

After repairs at Norfolk from 8 to 22 June, *Vulcan* headed for the Mediterranean and arrived at Oran, Algeria, on the 27th. Shifting to Algiers in late June, *Vulcan* sent a fire and rescue party to the burning British ammunition ship *Arrow*. Three *Vulcan* sailors brought a boat alongside the flaming vessel and cut through her side plating to rescue British sailors trapped belowdecks. For their bravery and resourcefulness, the trio from the repair ship received decorations from the British government and Navy and Marine Corps medals from their own.

Vulcan remained based on the North African coast into the summer of 1944. In August and September, the repair ship supported the invasion of southern France and received her sole battle star for providing repair services to the ships and craft involved in the operation.

By late 1944, *Vulcan* was urgently required in the Pacific, and she accordingly departed the Mediterranean on 23 November 1944 in Convoy GUS–59. After voyage repairs at Norfolk which lasted into January 1945, the repair ship sailed for the South Pacific. Arriving at Guadalcanal on 9 February 1945, *Vucan* operated successively out of Tulagi, Noumea, and Ulithi for the remainder of the war. From Ulithi, *Vulcan* serviced the amphibious units which participated in the assault on the key island of Okinawa.

After hostilities with Japan ceased, *Vulcan* shifted to Okinawa and entered Buckner Bay in the wake of a destructive typhoon which had forced some ships aground and had severely damaged others. Repair work was well in hand by late September, when another typhoon threatened the anchorage. *Vulcan* led 17 merchantmen to sea in a typhoon evasion sortie—a mission successfully accomplished without loss or damage by 28 September.

Vulcan sailed for Japan immediately thereafter to support the occupation of the erstwhile enemy's home islands. Leading a group of service force ships and oilers through dangerous, still-mined waters, *Vulcan* arrived in Hiro Wan, near Kure, Japan, on 8 October. Here, the repair ship established an advance service unit to provide food, oil, and water to the ships of the occupation force based there. She also set up mail, medical, and recreational facilities ashore. In addition, she performed maintenance tasks on the diesel-powered vessels of the mine forces then clearing the waters around the Japanese home islands.

Vulcan also operated out of Kobe and Yokosuka into the new year. Departing Yokosuka on 9 March 1946, the repair ship sailed for the east coast of the United States, calling at Pearl Harbor and transiting the Panama Canal en route. She arrived at Brooklyn, N.Y., on 15 April 1946. *Vulcan* operated at Newport, R.I., until February 1954, when she shifted to Norfolk, Va.

The ship, supporting the Atlantic Fleet with repair services, was homeported at Norfolk into the mid-1970's. During this time, she conducted repairs, alterations, and overhauls on a wide variety of vessels. She called at ports from the Caribbean to Canada, providing repair services to the Fleet at such ports as Guantanamo Bay, San Juan, New York, and Boston, as well as Mayport, Fla., and Charleston, S.C.

When American intelligence pinpointed the presence of Russian missiles in Cuba in the fall of 1962, the United States and the Soviet Union stood "eyeball to eyeball" in the Caribbean. *Vulcan* sailed to San Juan, where she provided essential repair services to the ships operating on the "quarantine" line off Cuban shores to prevent the arrival of any further Russian military equipment. The ship also assumed an additional role as electronics and ordnance repair vessel as well. After supporting the Cuban blockade from 2 to 26 November, she returned to Norfolk to resume normal operations.

Only once in the 1960's and 1970's did *Vulcan* venture beyond her normal deployment bounds of the east coast and the Caribbean. In the fall of 1964, the repair ship sailed for Europe to participate in NATO exercises. Departing Norfolk on 8 September, bound for Scotland, she arrived at Greenock on 21 September.

After participating in NATO Exercise "Teamwork," *Vulcan* called at Antwerp, Belgium; Le Havre, France; and Rota, Spain, before participating in amphibious Exercise "Steel Pike I" off Huelva, Spain. She returned to Norfolk soon thereafter to again take up her regular duties.

Besides type and underway training exercises at sea, *Vulcan* made an occasional NROTC midshipman cruise and conducted individual ship exercises in between her regular long assignments as repair ship at Norfolk. Among the ships for which *Vulcan* provided availabilities was the intelligence ship *Liberty* (AGTR–5). Between 24 March and 21 April, *Liberty* lay alongside the repair ship before getting underway later that spring on the fateful overseas deployment in which she was attacked by Israeli planes and motor torpedo boats off El Arishon on the morning of 8 June 1967. In the 1970's, *Vulcan*'s itinerary included recreational and port visits to such places as Cartagena, Colombia; Ft. Lauderdale, Fla.; Halifax, Nova Scotia; and the more regular ports such as Charleston and Guantanamo Bay. During the ship's major overhaul in 1976, her long-time main battery—four 5-inch guns—was removed and replaced by four 20-millimeter guns.

Vulcan, as of April 1978, continued to serve at Norfolk as an Atlantic Fleet repair ship.

Vulcan received one battle star for her World War II service.

APPENDIX

TANK LANDING SHIPS (LST)

The British evacuation from Dunkirk in 1940 demonstrated to the Admiralty that the Allies needed relatively large, ocean-going ships capable of shore-to-shore delivery of tanks and other vehicles in amphibious assaults upon the continent of Europe. As an interim measure, three medium-sized tankers, built to pass over the restrictive bars of Lake Maracaibo, Venezuela, were selected for conversion because of their shallow draft. Bow doors and ramps were added to these ships which became the first tank landing ships (LST's). They later proved their worth during the invasion of Algeria in 1942, but their bluff bows made for inadequate speed and pointed up the need for an all-new design incorporating a sleeker hull.

At their first meeting at the Argentia Conference in August 1941, President Roosevelt and Prime Minister Churchill confirmed the Admiralty's views. In November 1941, a small delegation from the Admiralty arrived in the United States to pool ideas with the Navy's Bureau of Ships with regard to development of the required ship. During this meeting, it was decided that the Bureau of Ships would design these vessels.

Within a few days, John Niedermair of the Bureau of Ships sketched out an awkward-looking ship that proved to be the basic design for the more than 1,000 LST's which would be built during World War II. To meet the conflicting requirements of deep draft for ocean travel and shallow draft for beaching, the ship was designed with a large ballast system that could be filled for ocean passage and pumped out for beaching operations. The rough sketch was sent to Britain on 5 November 1941 and accepted immediately. The Admiralty then requested the United States to build 200 LST's for the Royal Navy under the terms of lend-lease.

The preliminary plans initially called for an LST 280 feet in length; but, in January 1942, the Bureau of Ships discarded these drawings in favor of specifications for a ship 290 feet long. Within a month, final working plans were developed which further stretched the overall length to 328 feet and called for a 50-foot beam

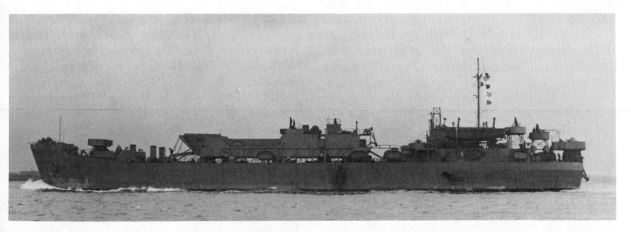

LST-229 with *LCT-583* secured on deck. LCT's were frequently carried to assault areas on the decks of LST's. On arrival off the beachhead, the LST was ballasted down to one side. The LCT, over 120 feet long and with an empty displacement of more than 150 tons, slid sideways into the water for loading. (NR&L(M) 37926)

569

and minimum draft of three feet 9½ inches. This scheme distributed the ship's weight over a greater area enabling her to ride higher in the water when in landing trim. The LST could carry a 2,100-ton load of tanks and vehicles. The larger dimensions also permitted the designers to increase the width of the bow door opening and ramp from 12 to 14 feet and thus accommodate most Allied vehicles. Provisions were made for the satisfactory ventilation of the tank space while the tank motors were running, and an elevator was provided to lower vehicles from the main deck to the tank deck for disembarking. By January 1942, the first scale model of the LST had been built and was undergoing tests at the David Taylor Model Basin in Washington, D.C.

In three separate acts dated 6 February 1942, 26 May 1943, and 17 December 1943, Congress provided the authority for the construction of LST's along with a host of other auxiliaries, destroyer escorts, and assorted landing craft. The enormous building program quickly gathered momentum. Such a high priority was assigned to the construction of LST's that the keel of an aircraft carrier, previously laid in the dock, was hastily removed to make place for several LST's to be built in her stead. The keel of the first LST was laid down on 10 June 1942 at Newport News, Va.; and the first standardized LST's were floated out of their building dock in October. Twenty-three were in commission by the end of 1942.

The LST building program was unique in several respects. As soon as the basic design had been developed, contracts were let and construction was commenced in quantity before the completion of a test vessel. Preliminary orders were rushed out verbally or by telegrams, telephone, and air mail letters. The ordering of certain materials actually preceded the completion of design work. While many heavy equipment items such as main propulsion machinery were furnished directly by the Navy, the balance of the procurement was handled centrally by the Material Coordinating Agency—an adjunct of the Bureau of Ships—so that the numerous builders in the program would not have to bid against one another. Through vigorous follow-up action on materials ordered, the agency made possible the completion of construction schedules in record time.

The need for LST's was urgent, and the program enjoyed a high priority throughout the war. Since most shipbuilding activities were located in coastal yards and were largely used for construction of large, deep-draft ships, new construction facilities were established along inland waterways. In some instances, heavy-industry plants such as steel fabrication yards were converted for LST construction. This posed the problem of getting the completed ships from the inland building yards to deep water. The chief obstacles were bridges. The Navy successfully undertook the modification of bridges and, through a "Ferry Command" of Navy crews, transported the newly constructed ships to coastal ports for fitting out. The success of these "cornfield" shipyards of the Middle West was a revelation to the long-established shipbuilders on the coasts. Their contribution to the LST building program was enormous. Of the 1,051 LST's built during World War II, 670 were constructed by five major inland builders.

By 1943, the construction time for an LST had been reduced to four months; and, by the end of the war, it had been cut to two months. Considerable effort was expended to hold the ship's design constant; but, by mid-1943, operating experience led to the incorporation of certain changes in the new ships. These modifications included: the replacing of the elevator by a ramp from the main deck to the tank deck, an increase in armament, and the addition of a distilling plant to make potable water. The main deck was strengthened to accommodate a fully-equipped landing craft, tank (LCT).

From their combat debut in the Solomons in June 1943 until the end of the hostilities in August 1945, the LST's performed a vital service in World War II. They participated in the invasions of Sicily, Italy, Normandy, and southern France in the European Theater and were an essential element in the island-hopping campaigns in the Pacific which culminated in the liberation of the Philippines and the capture of Iwo Jima and Okinawa.

The LST proved to be a remarkably versatile ship. A number of them were converted to become landing craft repair ships (ARL). In this design, the bow ramp and doors were removed, and the bow was sealed. Derricks, booms, and winches were added to haul damaged landing craft on board for repairs, and blacksmith, machine, and electrical workshops were provided on the main deck and tank deck.

Another successful conversion was the LST "Mother Ship." This version of the standard LST hull had two Quonset huts erected on the main deck to accommodate 40 officers. Bunks on the tank deck berthed an additional 196 men. A bake shop and 16 refrigeration boxes for fresh provisions augmented the facilities normally provided the crew. Four extra distilling units were added, and the ballast tanks were converted for storage of fresh water.

Thirty-eight LST's were converted to serve as small hospital ships. They supplemented the many standard LST's which removed casualties from the beach following the landing of their cargo of tanks and vehicles. For example, on D day, LST's brought 41,035 wounded men back across the English Channel from the Normandy beaches. Other LST's, provided with extra cranes and handling gear, were used exclusively for replenishing ammunition. They possessed a special advantage in this role, as their size permitted two or three LST's to go simultaneously alongside an anchored battleship or cruiser to accomplish replenishment more rapidly than standard ammunition ships. In the latter stages of World War II, some LST's were even fitted with flight decks from which small observation planes were sent up during amphibious operations.

Throughout the war, LST's demonstrated a remarkable capacity to absorb punishment and survive. Despite the sobriquet, "Large Slow Target," which was applied to them by irreverent crew members, the LST's suffered few losses in proportion to their number and the scope of their operations. Their brilliantly conceived structural arrangement provided unusual strength and buoyancy. Although the LST was considered a valuable target by the enemy, only 26 were lost due to enemy action, and a mere 13 were the victims of weather, reef, or accident.

A total of 1,152 LST's were contracted for in the great naval building program of World War II, but 101 were cancelled in the fall of 1942 because of shifting construction priorities. Of 1,051 actually constructed, 113 LST's were transferred to Great Britain under the terms of lend-lease, and four more were turned over

to the Greek Navy. Conversions to other ship types with different hull designations accounted for 116.

The end of World War II left the Navy with a huge inventory of amphibious ships. Hundreds of these were scrapped or sunk, and most of the remaining ships were put in "mothballs" to be preserved for the future. Consequently, construction of LST's in the immediate post-war years was modest. *LST–1153* and *LST–1154*, commissioned respectively in 1947 and 1949, were the only steam-driven LST's ever built by the Navy. They provided improved berthing arrangements and a greater cargo capacity than their predecessors.

The success of the amphibious assault at Inchon during the Korean War pointed up the utility of LST's once again. This was in contrast with the earlier opinion expressed by many military authorities that the advent of the atomic bomb had relegated amphibious landings to a thing of the past. As a consequence, 15 LST's of what were later to be known as the *Terrebonne Parish*-class were constructed in the early 1950's. These new LST's were 56 feet longer and were equipped with four, rather than two, diesel engines, which increased their speed to 15 knots. Three-inch 50-caliber twin mounts replaced the old twin 40-millimeter guns, and controllable pitch propellers improved the ship's backing power. On 1 July 1955, county or parish* names were assigned to LST's, which previously had borne only a letter-number hull designation.

In the late 1950's, seven additional LST's of the *De Soto County*-class were constructed. These were an improved version over earlier LST's, with a high degree of habitability for the crew and embarked troops. Considered the "ultimate" design attainable with the traditional LST bow door configuration, they were capable of 17.5 knots.

The commissioning of *Newport* (LST–1179) in 1969 marked the introduction of an entirely new concept in the design of LST's. She was the first of a new class of 20 LST's capable of steaming at a sustained speed of 20 knots. To obtain that speed, the traditional blunt bow doors of the LST were replaced by a pointed ship bow. Unloading is accomplished through the use of a 112-foot ramp operated over the

---

* Louisiana counties are called "parishes."

bow and supported by twin derrick arms. A stern gate to the tank deck permits unloading of amphibious tractors into the water or the unloading of other vehicles into a landing craft, utility (LCU) or onto a pier. Capable of operating with today's high speed amphibious squadrons consisting of LHA's, LPD's, and LSD's, the *Newport*-class LST can transport tanks, other heavy vehicles, and engineer equipment which cannot readily be landed by helicopters or landing craft. Thus, the utility of the LST seems to be assured far into the future.

LST–1

LST–1 was laid down on 20 July 1942 at Pittsburgh, Pa., by the Dravo Corp.; launched on 7 September 1942; sponsored by Mrs. Laurence T. Haugen; and commissioned on 14 December 1942, Lt. W. L. Chessman in command.

During World War I, *LST–1* was assigned to the European theater and participated in the following operations:

Sicilian occupation—July 1943
Salerno landings—September 1943
Anzio-Nettuno phase of operations on west coast of Italy—January to March 1944
Invasion of Normandy—June 1944

LST–1 was decommissioned on 21 May 1946 and was struck from the Navy list on 19 June 1946. On 5 December 1947, she was sold to the Ships Power and Equipment Co., of Barber, N.J., for scrapping.

LST–1 earned four battle stars for World War II service.

LST–2

LST–2 was laid down on 23 June 1942 at Pittsburgh, Pa., by the Dravo Corp.; launched on 19 September 1942; sponsored by Miss Nancy Jane Hughes; and commissioned on 9 February 1943.

During World War II, *LST–2* was assigned to the European theater and participated in the following operations:

North African occupation—early 1943
Sicilian occupation—July 1943
Salerno landings—September 1943
Invasion of Normandy—June 1944

LST–2 was decommissioned on 11 April 1946 and was struck from the Navy list on 5 June 1946. On 5 December 1947, she was sold to Bosey, Philippines.

LST–2 earned four battle stars for World War II service.

A Navy combat artist's view of Army DUKW's—amphibious trucks—on the tank deck of an LST, looking forward toward the open bow doors. Blowers, seen in the overhead, were of vital importance. Vehicles embarked in an LST's tank deck had to start their engines before the ship beached and opened its doors. If the space was not adequately ventilated, everyone on the tank deck could quickly be asphyxiated. (KN 21750)

LST-3

LST-3 was laid down on 29 June 1942 at Pittsburgh, Pa., by the Dravo Corp.; launched on 19 September 1942; sponsored by Mrs. A. C. Harlow; and commissioned on 8 February 1943.

During World War II, LST-3 was assigned to the European theater and participated in the following operations:

Sicilian occupation—July to August 1943
Invasion of southern France—August to September 1944

LST-3 was decommissioned sometime after World War II ended and was struck from the Navy list on 19 June 1946. On 10 September 1947, she was sold to the Boston Metals Co., of Baltimore, Md., for scrapping.

LST-3 earned two battle stars for World War II service.

LST-4

LST-4 was laid down on 4 July 1942 at Pittsburgh, Pa., by the Dravo Corp.; launched on 9 October 1942; sponsored by Mrs. J. Bartolo; and commissioned on 14 February 1943.

During World War II, LST-4 was assigned to the European theater and participated in the following operations:

Sicilian occupation—July 1943
Salerno landings—September 1943
West coast of Italy operations—Anzio-Nettuno advanced landings—January and February 1944; June 1944
Invasion of southern France—August and September 1944

LST-4 was decommissioned sometime after World War II ended and was struck from the Navy list on 19 June 1946. On 10 September 1947, she was sold to the Boston Metals Co., of Baltimore, Md., for scrapping.

LST-4 earned four battle stars for World War II service.

LST-5

LST-5 was laid down on 12 July 1942 at Pittsburgh, Pa., by the Dravo Corp.; launched on 3 October 1942; sponsored by Mrs. Wanetta Rose Barker; and commissioned on 22 February 1943.

During World War II, LST-5 was assigned to the European theater and participated in the following operations:

Sicilian occupation—July 1943
Salerno landings—September 1943
Invasion of Normandy—June 1944

LST-5 was decommissioned sometime after World War II ended and was struck from the Navy list on 1 August 1947. On 7 October 1947, she was sold to the Tung Hwa Trading Co., of Singapore, for scrapping.

LST-5 earned three battle stars for World War II service.

LST-6

LST-6 was laid down on 20 July 1942 at Wilmington, Del., by the Dravo Corp.; launched on 21 October 1942; sponsored by Mrs. H. E. Haven; and commissioned on 30 January 1943.

During World War II, LST-6 was assigned to the European theater and participated in the following operations:

Sicilian occupation—July 1943
Salerno landings—September 1943
Invasion of Normandy—June 1944

On 17 November 1944, she was mined and sunk in six fathoms of water while en route from Rouen, France, to Portland, England. She was struck from the Navy list on 22 December 1944.

LST-6 earned three battle stars for World War II service.

LST-7

LST-7 was laid down on 17 July 1942 at Pittsburgh, Pa., by the Dravo Corp.; launched on 31 October 1942; sponsored by Mrs. Anna Marvin; and commissioned on 2 March 1943.

During World War II, LST-7 was assigned to the European theater and participated in the following operations:

Sicilian occupation—July 1943
Salerno landings—September 1943
Invasion of Normandy—June 1944

LST-7 was decommissioned on 21 May 1946 and was struck from the Navy list on 19 June 1946. On 7 October 1947, she was sold to Mr. L. Lewis Green, Jr., of Charleston, S.C., for scrapping.

LST-7 earned three battle stars for World War II service.

LST-8

LST-8 was laid down on 26 July 1942 at Pittsburgh, Pa., by the Dravo Corp.; launched on 29 October 1942; sponsored by Mrs. Anne H. Johnston; and transferred to the United Kingdom on 22 March 1943.

LST-8 was returned from the United Kingdom on 1 June 1946 and was struck from the Navy list on 3 July 1946. On 5 December 1947, she was sold to Bosey, Philippines.

LST-9

LST-9 was laid down on 9 August 1942 at Pittsburgh, Pa., by the Dravo Corp.; launched on 14 November 1942; sponsored by Miss Katherine Moxin; and transferred to the United Kingdom on 19 March 1943.

LST-9 was returned to the United States Navy on 1 June 1946 and was struck from the Navy list on 3 July 1946. On 5 September 1948, she was sold to Bosey, Philippines.

LST-10

LST-10 was redesignated ARL-1 and named Achelous (q.v.) on 13 January 1943.

LST-11

LST-11 was laid down on 8 August 1942 at Pittsburgh, Pa., by the Dravo Corp.; launched on 18 November 1942; sponsored by Miss Virginia Fowler; and transferred to the United Kingdom on 22 March 1943.

LST-11 was returned to the United States Navy on 13 May 1946 and was struck from the Navy list on 5 June 1946. On 5 December 1947, she was sold to Bosey, Philippines.

LST-12

LST-12 was laid down on 16 August 1942 at Pittsburgh, Pa., by the Dravo Corp.; launched on 7 December 1942; sponsored by Mrs. Joseph Fay; and transferred to the United Kingdom on 25 March 1943.

LST-12 was returned to the United States Navy on 5 January 1946 and was struck from the Navy list on 20 March 1946. On 11 September 1947, she was sold to Washburn Wire Co., Philipsdale, R.I., for scrapping.

LST-13

LST-13 was laid down on 1 September 1942 at Pittsburgh, Pa., by the Dravo Corp.; launched on 5

January 1943; sponsored by Mrs. Jean A. Brackmann; and transferred to the United Kingdom on 3 April 1943.

LST–13 was returned to the United States Navy on 27 February 1946 and was struck from the Navy list on 5 June 1946. On 14 October 1947, she was sold to Luria Brothers and Co., Inc., of Philadelphia, Pa., for scrapping.

LST–14

LST–14 was redesignated AGP–5 and named *Varuna* (q.v.) on 25 January 1943.

LST–15

LST–15 was redesignated ARB–3 and named *Phaon* (q.v.) on 25 January 1943.

LST–16

LST–16 was laid down on 1 September 1942 at Wilmington, Del., by the Dravo Corp.; launched on 19 December 1942; sponsored by Mrs. Lois M. Alexander; and commissioned on 17 March 1943.

During World War II, LST–16 was assigned to the European theater and participated in the following operations:

North African occupation:
(a) Tunisian operations—July 1943
Sicilian occupation—September 1943
Salerno landings—September 1943
West coast of Italy operations:
(a) Anzio-Nettuno advanced landings—January and February 1944
Invasion of Normandy—June 1944

Following the war, LST–16 performed occupation duty in the Far East in September and November 1945. She was decommissioned on 8 March 1946 and was struck from the Navy list on 12 April 1946. On 5 December 1947, she was sold to Ships and Power Equipment Co., of Barber, N.J., for scrapping.

LST–16 earned five battle stars for World War II service.

LST–17

LST–17 was laid down on 21 September 1942 at Pittsburgh, Pa., by the Dravo Corp.; launched on 8 January 1943; sponsored by Mrs. Sarah H. Bankson; and commissioned on 19 April 1943, Lt. H. B. Gallagher, USCGR, in command.

During World War II, LST–17 was assigned to the European theater and participated in the following operation:

Invasion of Normandy—June 1944

Following the war, LST–17 performed occupation duty in the Far East intermittently from September through December 1945. She was decommissioned on 15 January 1946. On 15 November 1954, she was transferred to Commandant, 13th Naval District, for use as a mobile target, and was sunk on 15 August 1956 by torpedo fire.

LST–17 earned one battle star for World War II service.

LST–18

LST–18 was laid down on 1 October 1942 at Pittsburgh, Pa., by the Dravo Corp.; launched on 15 February 1943; sponsored by Miss Ruth Watt; and commissioned on 26 April 1943.

During World War II, LST–18 served in the Asiatic-Pacific theater and took part in the following operations:

Finschhafen occupation phase of the Eastern New Guinea operation—September 1943
Bismarck Archipelago operation:
(a) Cape Gloucester landings on New Britain —December 1943 and January 1944
(b) Admiralty Islands landings—March and April 1944
Hollandia operation—April and May 1944
Western New Guinea operations:
(a) Toem-Wakde-Sarmi area—May 1944
(b) Biak Island—June 1944
(c) Noemfoor Island—July 1944
(d) Cape Sansapor—July and August 1944
(e) Morotai landings—September 1944
Leyte landings—October and November 1944
Lingayen landings on Luzon—January 1945
Consolidation of the southern Philippines:
(a) Palawan Island landings—March 1945
(b) Visayan Islands landings—March and April 1945

Following the war, LST–18 performed occupation duty in the Far East until early November 1945. She returned to the United States and was decommissioned on 3 April 1946. She was struck from the Navy list on 17 April 1946 and was sold to the Suwannee Fruit & Steamship Co., of Jacksonville, Fla., on 31 October 1946 for conversion to merchant service.

LST–18 earned seven battle stars for World War II service.

LST–19

LST–19 was laid down on 22 October 1942 at Pittsburgh, Pa., by the Dravo Corp.; launched on 11 March 1943; sponsored by Mrs. Frances P. Gott; commissioned on 15 May 1943; and redesignated LSTH on 15 September 1945.

During World War II, LST–19 was assigned to the Asiatic-Pacific theater and participated in the following operations:

Gilbert Islands operation—November and December 1943
Marianas operation:
(a) Capture and occupation of Saipan—June and July 1944
Tinian capture and occupation—July 1944
Western Caroline Islands operations:
(a) Capture and occupation of southern Palau Islands—September and October 1944

Following the war, LST–19 performed occupation duty in the Far East in October and December 1945. She was decommissioned on 20 March 1946 and was struck from the Navy list on 1 May 1946. On 5 December 1947, she was sold to Ships and Power Equipment Co., of Barber, N.J., for scrapping.

LST–19 earned four battle stars for World War II service.

LST–20

LST–20 was laid down on 5 October 1942 at Pittsburgh, Pa., by the Dravo Corp.; launched on 15 February 1943; sponsored by Miss Anne B. Sylvester; and commissioned on 14 May 1943.

During World War II, LST–20 served in the Asiatic-Pacific theater and took part in the following operations:

Gilbert Islands operation—November and December 1943
Leyte landings—October 1944
Lingayen landings on Luzon—January 1945
Okinawa Gunto operation:
(a) Assault and occupation of Okinawa Gunto—April 1945

Following the war, LST–20 performed occupation duty in the Far East until early November 1945. She returned to the United States and was decommissioned on 3 April 1946. She was struck from the Navy list on 19 June 1946 and was transferred to the Maritime Administration on 8 October 1947 for disposal by scrapping.

LST–20 earned four battle stars for World War II service.

LST–21

LST–21 was laid down on 25 September 1942 at Wilmington, Del., by the Dravo Corp.; launched on 18 February 1943; sponsored by Mrs. Lillian M. Lloyd; and commissioned on 14 April 1943.

The tank landing ship was assigned to the European theater and participated in the Normandy invasion in June 1944.

Upon her return to the United States, the ship was decommissioned on 25 January 1946 and struck from the Navy list on 19 June 1946. She was sold to Louis Feldman, of Flushing, N.Y., on 12 March 1948 and was subsequently scrapped.

LST–21 earned one battle star for World War II service.

LST–22

LST–22 was laid down on 5 November 1942 at Pittsburgh, Pa., by the Dravo Corp.; launched on 29 March 1943; sponsored by Mrs. W. A. Barnes; and commissioned on 29 May 1943, Lt. L. N. Ditlefsen, USCG, in command.

During World War II, *LST–22* served in the Asiatic-Pacific theater and took part in the following operations:

Eastern New Guinea operation:
    (a) Saidor occupation—January and February 1944

Bismarck Archipelago operation:
    (a) Cape Gloucester, New Britain—December 1943, January and February 1944
    (b) Admiralty Islands landings—March and April 1944

Hollandia operation—April and May 1944

Western New Guinea operations:
    (a) Toem-Wakde-Sarmi area operation—May 1944
    (b) Biak Island operation—May and June 1944
    (c) Noemfoor Island operation—July 1944
    (d) Cape Sansapor operation—July and August 1944
    (e) Morotai landings—September 1944

Leyte landings—October and November 1944

Lingayen landings on Luzon—January 1945

LST–22 returned to the United States and was decommissioned on 1 April 1946. She was struck from the Navy list on 17 April 1946 and was sold to Ming-Sung Industrial Co., Ltd., of Shanghai, China, on 3 February 1947 to be converted for merchant service.

LST–22 earned six battle stars for World War II service.

LST–23

LST–23 was laid down on 27 October 1942 at Pittsburgh, Pa., by the Dravo Corp.; launched on 13 March 1942; sponsored by Mrs. Mary H. Miller; and commissioned on 22 May 1943.

During World War II, *LST–23* served in the Asiatic-Pacific theater and took part in the following operations:

Gilbert Islands operation—November and December 1943

Marshall Islands operation:
    (a) Occupation of Kwajalein and Majuro Atolls—February 1944

Marianas operation:
    (b) Capture and occupation of Saipan—June and July 1944

Tinian capture and occupation—July 1944

Western Caroline Islands operation:
    (a) Capture and occupation of southern Palau Islands—September and October 1944

Lingayen landings on Luzon—January 1945

On 15 September 1945, she was redesignated LSTH. Immediately after the war, *LSTH–23* performed occupation duty in the Far East until early December 1945. She returned to the United States and was decommissioned on 24 May 1946. She was struck from the Navy list on 3 July 1946 and was sold to the Kaiser Co., Inc., Seattle, Wash., on 6 April 1948 for scrapping.

LSTH–23 earned six battle stars for World War II service as *LST–23*.

LST–24

LST–24 was laid down on 19 November 1942 at Pittsburgh, Pa., by the Dravo Corp.; launched on 17 April 1943; sponsored by Mrs. Marguerite E. Davis; and commissioned on 14 June 1943.

During World War II, *LST–24* was assigned to the Asiatic-Pacific theater and participated in the following operations:

Marianas operation:
    (a) Capture and occupation of Guam—August 1944

Western New Guinea operation:
    (a) Morotai landings—September 1944

Leyte landings—October and November 1944

Okinawa Gunto operation:
    (a) Assault and occupation of Okinawa Gunto—March and June 1945

LST–24 was decommissioned on 26 February 1946 and was struck from the Navy list on 5 June 1946. On 23 December 1947, she was sold to the Humble Oil & Refining Co., of Houston, Tex., and was converted for merchant service.

LST–24 earned five battle stars for World War II service.

LST–25

LST–25 was laid down on 12 October 1942 at Wilmington, Del., by the Dravo Corp.; launched on 9 March 1943; sponsored by Miss Dolly Hemphill; and commissioned on 3 May 1943, Lt. J. B. Holmes, USCG, in command.

During World War II, *LST–25* served in the European and Asiatic-Pacific theaters and participated in the following operations:

Invasion of Normandy—June 1944

Okinawa Gunto operation:
    (a) Assault and occupation of Okinawa Gunto—May 1945

Navy Occupation Service, Asia—September and October 1945 and March 1946

China Service—October 1945 and March 1946

LST–25 was decommissioned on 2 August 1946 and was struck from the Navy list on 8 October 1946. On 31 March 1948, she was sold to the Kaiser Co., Inc., Seattle, Wash., for scrapping.

LST–25 earned two battle stars for World War II service.

LST–26

LST–26 was laid down on 16 November 1942 at Pittsburgh, Pa., by the Dravo Corp.; launched on 31 March 1943; sponsored by Mrs. Mathilda B. Coulter; and commissioned on 7 June 1943.

During World War II, *LST–26* served in the Asiatic-Pacific theater and took part in the following operations:

Bismarck Archipelago operation:
  (a) Cape Gloucester, New Britain—December 1943 and January 1944
Hollandia operation—April and May 1944
Western New Guinea operations:
  (a) Toem-Wakde-Sarmi area operation—May 1944
  (b) Biak Island operation—May and June 1944
  (c) Noemfoor Island operation—July 1944
  (d) Cape Sansapor operation—July and August 1944
  (e) Morotai landings—September 1944
Leyte landings—October and November 1944
Consolidation of the southern Philippines:
  (a) Mindanao Island landings—March 1945
She saw service in China from 3 to 10 October 1945.

Following the war, *LST–26* performed occupation duty in the Far East until early November 1945. She returned to the United States and was decommissioned on 1 April 1946. She was struck from the Navy list on 8 May 1946 and was sold to Arctic Circle Exploration, Seattle, Wash., on 17 June 1946 to be converted for merchant service.

LST–26 earned five battle star for World War II service.

LST–27

LST–27 was laid down on 10 December 1942 at Pittsburgh, Pa., by the Dravo Corp.; launched on 27 April 1943; sponsored by Mrs. R. R. Creed; and commissioned on 25 June 1943.

During World War II, *LST–27* was assigned to the European theater and participated in the following operations:
  Convoy UGS-36—April 1944
  Invasion of Normandy—June 1944

LST–27 was decommissioned on 9 November 1945 and was struck from the Navy list on 28 November 1945. On 15 December 1947, she was sold to the Rhode Island Navigation Co., of Newport, R.I., for scrapping.

LST–27 earned two battle stars for World War II service.

LST–28

LST–28 was laid down on 8 December 1942 at Pittsburgh, Pa., by the Dravo Corp.; launched on 19 April 1943; sponsored by Mrs. Michael Torick; and commissioned on 19 June 1943.

During World War II, *LST–28* was assigned to the European theater and participated in the following operations:
  Convoy UGS-36—April 1944
  Invasion of Normandy—June 1944

LST–28 was decommissioned on 16 August 1946 and was struck from the Navy list on 29 October 1946. On 19 May 1948, she was sold to George H. Nutman, of Brooklyn, N.Y., for scrapping.

LST–28 earned two battle stars for World War II service.

LST–29

LST–29 was laid down on 8 January 1943 at Pittsburgh, Pa., by the Dravo Corp.; launched on 17 May 1943; sponsored by Mrs. C. F. Lockton; and commissioned on 10 July 1943.

During World War II, *LST–29* was assigned to the Asiatic-Pacific theater and participated in the following operations:
  Gilbert Islands operation—November and December 1943
  Marshall Islands operation:

  (a) Occupation of Kwajalein and Majuro Atolls—January and February 1944
  (b) Occupation of Eniwetok Atoll—February and March 1944
Marianas operation:
  (a) Capture and occupation of Guam—July and August 1944
Okinawa Gunto operation:
  (a) Assault and occupation of Okinawa Gunto—May 1945

LST–29 was decommissioned on 11 March 1946 and was struck from the Navy list on 8 May 1946. On 17 June 1946, she was sold to the Foss Launch & Tug Co., of Seattle, Wash.

LST–29 earned four battle stars for World War II service.

LST–30

LST–30 was laid down on 12 January 1943 at Pittsburgh, Pa., by the Dravo Corp.; launched on 3 May 1943; sponsored by Mrs. C. B. Jansen; and commissioned on 3 July 1943.

During World War II, *LST–30* was assigned to the European theater and participated in the following operation:
  Invasion of Normandy—June 1944

LST–30 was decommissioned on 6 March 1946 and was struck from the Navy list on 8 May 1946. On 2 April 1947, she was sold to W. Horace Williams Co., of New Orleans, La., and was converted for merchant service.

LST–30 earned one battle star for World War II service.

LST–31

LST–31 was laid down on 2 February 1943 at Pittsburgh, Pa., by the Dravo Corp.; launched on 5 June 1943; sponsored by Mrs. Maurice Endres; and commissioned on 21 July 1943.

During World War II, *LST–31* served in the Asiatic-Pacific theater and took part in the following operations:
  Gilbert Islands operation—November and December 1943
  Marshall Islands operation:
  (a) Occupation of Kwajalein and Majuro Atolls—January and February 1944
  (b) Occupation of Eniwetok Atoll—February and March 1944
  Marianas operation:
  (a) Capture and occupation of Saipan—June through August 1944
  Tinian capture and occupation—July and August 1944
  Okinawa Gunto operation:
  (a) Assault and occupation of Okinawa Gunto—May 1945

Immediately following the war, *LST–31* performed occupation duty in the Far East until early January 1946. She returned to the United States and was decommissioned on 8 January 1946. On 1 July 1955, *LST–31* was named *Addison County* after a county in Vermont. Her name was struck from the Navy list on 11 August 1955, and she was sunk as a target.

Addison County earned five battle stars for World War II service as *LST–31*.

LST–32

LST–32 was laid down on 17 February 1943 at Pittsburgh, Pa., by the Dravo Corp.; launched on 22 May 1943; sponsored by Miss Dorothy M. Manko; and commissioned on 12 July 1943, Lt. Gardner P. Mulloy in command.

Overhead view of an early LST, June 1943. Note the forward upper-deck elevator, used to move vehicles to the tank deck for landing; the cargo hatch, just forward of the superstructure; and the relative lack of AA armament (one 40 mm and six 20mm guns).

During World War II, *LST–32* was assigned to the European theater and participated in the following operations:

Convoy UGS–36—April 1944
Invasion of southern France—August and September 1944

LST–32 was decommissioned in July 1946. She was recommissioned on 7 March 1951. On 1 July 1955, *LST–32* was assigned the name *Alameda County* after a county in California. She was reclassified *Alameda County* (AVB–1) on 28 August 1957, was decommissioned on 25 June 1962, and was struck from the Navy list that same month. On 20 November 1962, she was transferred to the Italian Navy.

Alameda County earned two battle stars for World War II service as *LST–32*.

LST–33

LST–33 was laid down on 23 February 1943 at Pittsburgh, Pa., by the Dravo Corp.; launched on 21 June 1943; sponsored by Mrs. Paul J. Walsh; commissioned on 4 August 1943; and transferred to the Greek Navy on 18 August 1943, with which she served through the remainder of World War II. She was sold to the government of Greece in January 1947 and served there as *Samos* (L–179). She was struck from the Navy list on 23 June 1947.

LST–34

LST–34 was laid down on 15 March 1943 at Pittsburgh, Pa., by the Dravo Corp.; launched on 15 June 1943; sponsored by Mrs. Verne C. Cobb; and commissioned on 26 July 1943.

During World War II, *LST–34* served in the Asiatic-Pacific theater and took part in the following operations:

Gilbert Islands operation—November and December 1943
Marshall Islands operation:
    (a) Occupation of Kwajalein and Majuro Atolls—January and February 1944
    (b) Occupation of Eniwetok Atoll—February and March 1944
Marianas operation:
    (a) Capture and occupation of Saipan—June 1944
Leyte landings—October and November 1944
Lingayen landings on Luzon—January 1945
Okinawa Gunto operation:
    (a) Assault and occupation of Okinawa Gunto—May 1945

Following the war, *LST–34* performed occupation duty in the Far East from March to November 1946. She returned to the United States and was decommissioned on 15 November 1946 and transferred to Military Government, Ryukyus. Her name was struck from the Navy list on 23 December 1947. She ran aground in the Far East in January 1949, and her hulk was abandoned.

LST–34 earned six battle stars for World War II service.

LST–35

LST–35 was laid down on 20 March 1943 at Pittsburgh, Pa., by the Dravo Corp.; launched on 30 June 1943; sponsored by Mrs. Samuel G. Cooper; and transferred to the government of Greece on 18 August 1943 with which she served through the remainder of World War II. She was sold to the government of Greece in January 1947 and served there as *Chios* (L–195). Her name was struck from the Navy list on 23 June 1947.

LST–36

LST–36 was laid down on 21 April 1943 at Pittsburgh, Pa., by the Dravo Corp.; launched on 10 July 1943; sponsored by Mrs. Franklin Keen; and transferred to the government of Greece on 23 August 1943 with which she served through the remainder of World War II. She was sold to the government of Greece in January 1947 and served there as *Lemnos* (L–158). Her name was struck from the Navy list on 23 June 1947.

LST–37

LST–37 was laid down on 1 April 1943 at Pittsburgh, Pa., by the Dravo Corp.; launched on 5 July 1943; sponsored by Mrs. Jack Domb; and transferred to the government of Greece on 18 August 1943. She ran aground off Bizerte, Tunisia, on 1 June 1944, and sank. Her name was struck from the Navy list on 12 August 1948.

LST–38

LST–38 was laid down on 14 April 1943 at Pittsburgh, Pa., by the Dravo Corp.; launched on 27 July 1943; sponsored by Miss Bertha Karpinski; and commissioned on 3 September 1943.

During World War II, *LST–38* was assigned to the Asiatic-Pacific theater and participated in the following operations:

Marshall Islands operation:
    (a) Occupation of Kwajalein and Majuro Atolls—January and February 1944
Bismarck Archipelago operation:
    (a) Admiralty Islands landings—March and April 1944
Hollandia operation—April 1944
Marianas operation:
    (a) Capture and occupation of Guam—July 1944

Following the war, *LST–38* was redesignated *LSTH–38* on 15 September 1945. She performed occupation duty in the Far East until mid-November 1945.

Upon her return to the United States, the ship was decommissioned on 26 March 1946 and struck from the Navy list on 1 May 1946. On 5 December 1947, she was sold to the Ships and Power Equipment Co., of Barber, N.J., and subsequently scrapped.

LSTH–38 earned four battle stars for World War II service as *LST–38*.

LST–39

LST–39 was laid down on 23 April 1943 by the Dravo Corp. at Pittsburgh, Pa.; launched on 29 July 1943; sponsored by Mrs. L. A. Mertz; and commissioned on 8 September 1943. She was assigned to the Pacific area during World War II but saw no combat action. She sank in the summer of 1944, and she was struck from the Navy list on 18 July 1944. She was later refloated, converted to a spare parts issue barge, and redesignated *YF–1079*. She served the Navy in that capacity until sometime between July 1945 and January 1946, by which time *YF–1079* disappeared from the Navy list.

LST–40

LST–40 was laid down on 3 June 1943 at Pittsburgh, Pa., by the Dravo Corp.; launched on 7 August 1943; sponsored by Miss Hilda Sambolt; and commissioned on 15 September 1943.

During World War II, *LST–40* was assigned to the Asiatic-Pacific theater and participated in the following operations:

Consolidation of the Solomon Islands:

(a) Consolidation of southern Solomons—June 1943

Marianas operation:
    (a) Capture and occupation of Saipan—June and August 1944

Tinian capture and occupation—July 1944

Okinawa Gunto operation:
    (a) Assault and occupation of Okinawa Gunto—May 1945

Following the war, LST–40 performed occupation duty in the Far East until mid-February 1946. She returned to the United States and was decommissioned on 18 February 1946. In February 1947, she was transferred to the United States Military Government, Korea, as a sale, and was struck from the Navy list on 5 March that same year.

LST–40 earned four battle stars for World War II service.

LST–41

LST–41 was laid down on 24 May 1943 at Pittsburgh, Pa., by the Dravo Corp.; launched on 17 August 1943; sponsored by Mrs. Mary Spisak; and commissioned on 24 September 1943, Lt. W. B. Dundon, USNR, in command.

During World War II, LST–41 was assigned to the Asiatic-Pacific theater and participated in the following operations:

Marshall Islands operation:
    (a) Occupation of Kwajalein and Majuro Atolls—January and February 1944

Hollandia operation—April 1944

Marianas operation:
    (a) Capture and occupation of Guam—July 1944

Western Caroline Islands operation:
    (a) Capture and occupation of southern Palau Islands—September and October 1944

Luzon operation:
    (a) Lingayen Gulf landing—January 1945

Following the war, LST–41 was redesignated LSTH–41 on 15 September 1945. She performed occupation duty in the Far East until late November 1945.

Upon her return to the United States, the ship was decommissioned on 25 April 1946 and struck from the Navy list on 19 June 1946. On 8 October 1947, she was sold to J. C. Berkwit & Co., of New York City, N.Y.

LSTH–41 earned five battle stars for World War II service as LST–41.

LST–42

LST–42 was laid down on 17 June 1943 at Pittsburgh, Pa., by the Dravo Corp.; launched on 17 August 1943; sponsored by Mrs. F. M. Leslie; and commissioned on 30 September 1943, Lt. Roy L. Guy in command.

During World War II, LST–42 was assigned to the Asiatic-Pacific theater and participated in the following operations:

Marshall Islands operation:
    (a) Occupation of Kwajalein and Majuro Atolls—January and February 1944
    (b) Occupation of Eniwetok Atoll—February and March 1944

Marianas operation:
    (a) Capture and occupation of Saipan—June and July 1944

Tinian capture and occupation—July 1944

Western Caroline Islands operation:
    (a) Capture and occupation of southern Palau Islands—September and October 1944

Iwo Jima operation:
    (a) Assault and occupation of Iwo Jima—February and March 1945

Following the war, LST–42 was redesignated LSTH–42 on 15 September 1945. She performed occupation duty in the Far East and service in China until early April 1946.

Upon her return to the United States, the ship was decommissioned on 26 July 1946 and struck from the Navy list on 25 September 1946. On 26 March 1948, she was sold to the Kaiser Co., Inc., of Seattle, Wash., and subsequently scrapped.

LSTH–42 earned five battle stars for World War II service as LST–42.

LST–43

LST–43 was laid down on 19 June 1943 at Philadelphia, Pa., by the Dravo Corp.; launched on 28 August 1943; sponsored by Mrs. C. A. Hill; and commissioned on 6 October 1943. She was assigned to the Asiatic-Pacific theater during World War II and participated in the occupation of Kwajalein and Majuro Atolls from 31 January to 8 February 1944. On 21 May 1944, she was lost through an accident. Her name was struck from the Navy list on 18 July 1944. She was raised but deemed beyond economical repair and was subsequently sunk by torpedoes in 1945.

LST–43 earned one battle star for World War II service.

LST–44

LST–44 was laid down on 7 July 1943 at Pittsburgh, Pa., by the Dravo Corp.; launched on 11 September 1943; sponsored by Mrs. F. E. Haeberle; and commissioned on 22 October 1943.

During World War II, LST–44 was assigned to the European theater and participated in the Normandy invasion from 6 to 25 June 1944. Following the war, she performed occupation duty in the Far East and service in China until mid-February 1946.

Upon her return to the United States, the ship was decommissioned on 20 February 1946. In 1947, she was transferred to the United States Army and was destroyed on 23 July 1947, cannibalized and scrapped. On 28 August 1947, her name was struck from the Navy list.

LST–44 earned one battle star for World War II service.

LST–45

LST–45 was laid down on 27 June 1943 at Pittsburgh, Pa., by the Dravo Corp.; launched on 31 August 1943; sponsored by Miss Lois C. Donnelly; and commissioned on 15 October 1943.

During World War II, LST–45 was assigned to the Asiatic-Pacific theater and took part in the following operations:

Marshall Islands operation:
    (a) Occupation of Kwajalein and Majuro Atolls—January and February 1944

Marianas operation:
    (a) Capture and occupation of Saipan—June through August 1944
    (b) Tinian capture and occupation—July and August 1944

Okinawa assault—March through June 1945

Following the war, LST–45 performed occupation duty in the Far East and saw service in China until late October 1945. Upon her return to the United States, the ship was decommissioned on 30 November 1948 and struck from the Navy list on 22 December that same year. On 25 February 1949, she was sold to the Foss Launch & Tug Co., of Seattle, Wash.

LST–45 earned four battle stars for World War II service.

LST–46

LST–46 was laid down on 20 July 1943 at Pittsburgh, Pa., by the Dravo Corp.; launched on 16 September

1943; sponsored by Mrs. J. J. Edson, Jr.; and commissioned on 3 November 1943.

During World War II, she was assigned to the European theater and participated in the Normandy invasion from 6 to 25 June 1944 and the invasion of southern France in August and September 1944. She was later transferred to the Asiatic-Pacific theater where she took part in the Okinawa assault in June 1945. Following the war, *LST-46* performed occupation duty in the Far East and service in China until mid-May 1946.

Upon her return to the United States, the ship was decommissioned on 6 June 1946 and struck from the Navy list on 19 June 1946. On 13 February 1948, she was sold to Bosey, Philippines, and resold to T. Y. Fong on the same date.

LST-46 earned three battle stars for World War II service.

LST-47

LST-47 was laid down on 30 July 1943 at Pittsburgh, Pa., by the Dravo Corp.; launched on 24 September 1943; sponsored by by Mrs. Clarence H. Vant; and commissioned on 8 November 1943.

The tank landing ship was initially assigned to the European theater and participated in the Normandy invasion in June 1944 and the invasion of southern France in August and September 1944. She was later transferred to the Asiatic-Pacific theater of operations where she took part in the Okinawa assault between 26 and 30 June 1945. Following the war, *LST-47* performed occupation duty in the Far East in the fall and winter of 1945 and early January 1946.

Upon her return to the United States, the ship was decommissioned on 11 January 1946 and transferred to the United States Army the same day. She was assigned to the Military Sea Transportation Service on 31 March 1952 and redesignated USNS *LST-47*. USNS *LST-47* was transferred to the Philippine Navy on 13 September 1976.

LST-47 earned three battle stars for World War II service.

LST-48

LST-48 was laid down on 8 August 1943 at Pittsburgh, Pa., by the Dravo Corp.; launched on 2 October 1942; sponsored by Mrs. A. E. Stacey; and commissioned on 16 November 1943.

The tank landing ship was initially assigned to the European theater and participated in the Normandy invasion between 6 and 25 June 1944 and the invasion of southern France between 15 August and 25 September 1944. She was later transferred to the Asiatic-Pacific theater of operations where she took part in the Okinawa assault between 30 May and 10 June 1945. Following the war, *LST-48* performed occupation duty in the Far East during the winter of 1945 and 1946.

Upon her return to the United States, the ship was decommissioned on 8 February 1946 and was struck from the Navy list on 5 December 1947. On 27 May 1948, she was sold to the Bethlehem Steel Co., of Bethlehem, Pa., and subsequently scrapped.

LST-48 earned three battle stars for World War II service.

LST-49

LST-49 was laid down on 17 August 1943 at Pittsburgh, Pa., by the Dravo Corp.; launched on 9 October 1943; sponsored by Mrs. Kathryn Saban; and commissioned on 20 November 1943.

The tank landing ship was initially assigned to the European theater and participated in the Normandy invasion between 6 and 25 June 1944 and the invasion of southern France between 15 August and 25 Sep-

tember 1944. She was later transferred to the Asiatic-Pacific theater of operations where she took part in the Okinawa assault between 8 and 30 June 1945. Following the war, *LST-49* performed occupation duty in the Far East and service in China until mid-March 1946.

Upon her return to the United States, the ship was decommissioned on 11 June 1946 and struck from the Navy list on 3 July 1946. She was sold to Bosey, Philippines, on 4 December 1947.

LST-49 earned three battle stars for World War II service.

LST-50

LST-50 was laid down on 29 August 1943 at Pittsburgh, Pa., by the Dravo Corp.; launched on 16 October 1943; sponsored by Mrs. Tito Tarquinio; and commissioned on 27 November 1943.

The tank landing ship was initially assigned to the European theater and participated in the Normandy invasion between 6 and 25 June 1944 and the invasion of southern France between 15 August and 25 September 1944. She was later transferred to the Asiatic-Pacific theater of operations where she took part in the Okinawa assault between 18 and 30 June 1945. Following the war, *LST-50* performed occupation duty in the Far East until early February 1946.

Upon her return to the United States, the ship was decommissioned on 6 February 1946 and was struck from the Navy list on 8 September 1952. On 14 November 1952, she was redesignated *ARB-13* and transferred to Norway as *Ellida* (A-534). She was returned to the United States on 1 July 1960 but was retransferred to Greece on 16 September 1960, and served with the Greek Navy as *Sakipia* (A-329).

LST-50 earned three battle stars for World War II service.

LST-51

LST-51 was laid down on 29 August 1943 at Pittsburgh, Pa., by the Dravo Corp.; launched on 22 October 1943; sponsored by Mrs. Charles A. Ward; and commissioned on 8 December 1943.

During World War II, *LST-51* was assigned to the European theater and participated in the following operations:

    Invasion of Normandy—June 1944
    Invasion of southern France—August and September 1944

She was then assigned to the Asiatic-Pacific theater and supported the occupation of Okinawa during May and June 1945.

Following the war, *LST-51* performed occupation duty in the Far East until March 1946. She returned to the United States and was decommissioned on 6 March 1946 and was struck from the Navy list on 31 October 1947. On 20 April 1948, she was sold to the Bethlehem Steel Co., of Bethlehem, Pa.

LST-51 earned three battle stars for World War II service.

LST-52

LST-52 was laid down on 16 September 1943 at Pittsburgh, Pa., by the Dravo Corp.; launched on 20 October 1943; sponsored by Mrs. Charles W. Crowley; and commissioned on 15 December 1943, Lt. (jg.) Robert H. Freeman, USNR, in command.

During World War II, *LST-52* was assigned to the European theater and participated in the Normandy invasion from 6 to 25 June. Immediately following the war, she was assigned to occupation duty in the Far East during the fall of 1945 and January 1946. She was decommissioned on 29 August 1946 and sunk as a target on 19 April 1948. Her name was struck from the Navy list on 30 April 1948.

LST–52 earned one battle star for World War II service.

LST–53

LST–53 was laid down on 24 September 1943 at Pittsburgh, Pa., by the Dravo Corp.; launched on 6 November 1943; sponsored by Mrs. Nicholas Spanard; and commissioned on 21 December 1943, Ens. Michael Stapleton in command.

During World War II, *LST–53* was assigned to the European theater and participated in the following operations:

    Invasion of Normandy—June 1944

    Invasion of southern France—August and September 1944

She was then assigned to the Asiatic-Pacific theater and supported the occupation of Okinawa during May and June 1945.

Immediately following the war, she was assigned to occupation duty in the Far East from September 1945 to January 1946. In September 1954, she was redesignated *APL–59*. She was transferred to the Republic of Korea in May 1955 and served that government as *Chang Su* (LST–811).

LST–53 earned three battle stars for World War II service.

LST–54

LST–54 was laid down on 3 October 1943 at Pittsburgh, Pa., by the Dravo Corp.; launched on 13 November 1943; sponsored by Miss Wanda Oleksiak; and commissioned on 24 December 1943.

During World War II, *LST–54* was assigned to the European theater and participated in the Normandy invasion from 6 to 25 June 1944. She was decommissioned on 5 November 1945 and was struck from the Navy list on 28 November 1945. On 22 March 1948, she was sold to the Townsend Transportation Co., of Bayonne, N.J., and subsequently scrapped.

LST–54 earned one battle star for World War II service.

LST–55

LST–55 was laid down on 10 October 1943 at Pittsburgh, Pa., by the Dravo Corp.; launched on 20 November 1943; sponsored by Mrs. Stephen Washensky; and commissioned on 6 January 1944.

During World War II, *LST–55* was assigned to the European theater and participated in the Normandy invasion from 6 to 25 June 1944. She was decommissioned on 11 December 1945 and was struck from the Navy list on 3 January 1946. On 26 March 1948, she was sold to the Ships & Power Equipment Corp., of Barber, N.J., and subsequently scrapped.

LST–55 earned one battle star for World War II service.

LST–56

LST–56 was laid down on 17 October 1943 at Pittsburgh, Pa., by the Dravo Corp.; launched on 27 November 1943; sponsored by Mrs. Robert G. Appleton; and commissioned on 10 January 1944, Lt. Raymond F. Willett in command.

During World War II, *LST–56* was assigned to the European theater and participated in the Normandy invasion from 6 to 25 June 1944. She was decommissioned on 23 May 1946 and was struck from the Navy list on 3 July 1946. On 5 December 1947, she was sold to the Ships & Power Equipment Corp., of Barber, N.J., and subsequently scrapped.

LST–56 earned one battle star for World War II service.

LST–57

LST–57 was laid down on 24 October 1943 at Pittsburgh, Pa., by the Dravo Corp.; launched on 4 December 1943; sponsored by Mrs. Edward Mays; and commissioned on 15 January 1944.

During World War II, *LST–57* served in the European theater and participated in the Normandy invasion from 6 to 25 June. Immediately following the war, she was assigned to occupation duty in the Far East during the fall of 1945. She was decommissioned on 24 January 1946 and placed in reserve. On 1 July 1955, *LST–57* was named *Armstrong County* after counties in Pennsylvania and Texas. Her name was struck from the Navy list on 11 August 1955, and she was sunk as a target in 1956.

Armstrong County earned one battle star for World War II service as *LST–57*.

LST–58

LST–58 was laid down on 31 October 1943 at Pittsburgh, Pa., by the Dravo Corp.; launched on 11 December 1943; sponsored by Mrs. L. H. Crawford; and commissioned on 22 January 1944.

During World War II, *LST–58* was assigned to the European theater and participated in the Normandy invasion from 6 to 25 June 1944. She was decommissioned on 7 November 1945 and was struck from the Navy list on 28 November 1945. On 30 November 1947, she was sold to the Northern Metals Co., of Philadelphia, Pa., and subsequently scrapped.

LST–58 earned one battle star for World War II service.

LST–59

LST–59 was laid down on 7 November 1943 at Pittsburgh, Pa., by the Dravo Corp.; launched on 18 December 1943; sponsored by Mrs. Richard A. Lewis; and commissioned on 31 January 1944, Lt. R. J. Mayer, USNR, in command.

During World War II, *LST–59* was assigned to the European theater and participated in the Normandy invasion from 6 to 25 June 1944. She was decommissioned on 21 January 1946 and was struck from the Navy list on 25 February 1946. On 18 September 1947, she was sold to the Southern Shipwrecking Co., of New Orleans, La., and subsequently scrapped.

LST–59 earned one battle star for service in World War II.

LST–60

LST–60 was laid down on 14 November 1943 at Pittsburgh, Pa., by the Dravo Corp.; launched on 24 December 1943; sponsored by Mrs. Daniel W. Mack; and commissioned on 7 February 1944, Lt. Carl E. Ellis in command.

During World War II, *LST–60* was assigned to the European theater and participated in the Normandy invasion from 6 to 25 June 1944. She was decommissioned on 27 June 1946 and was named *Atchison County* (LST–60) after counties in Kansas and Missouri on 1 July 1955. Her name was struck from the Navy list on 1 November 1958.

Atchison County earned one battle star for World War II service as *LST–60*.

LST–61

LST–61 was laid down on 24 June 1942 at Jeffersonville, Ind., by the Jeffersonville Boat & Machine Co.;

Maximum use had to be made of wartime shipping capability. Here, an LST has an LCT secured to her upper deck for transportation. In the LCT's well deck are nested an LCM and an LCVP; another LCVP is lashed to the deck just forward of the LCT's bow ramp. (80–G–43113)

launched on 8 November 1942; sponsored by Mrs. Corinne B. Redgrave; and commissioned on 5 February 1943, Lt. Norris G. Murphy, USNR, in command.

During World War II, *LST–61* was assigned to the European theater and participated in the Sicilian occupation in July 1943 and the Normandy invasion in June 1944. She was then assigned to the Asiatic-Pacific theater and took part in the following operation:

Western Caroline Islands operation:

    (a) Capture and occupation of southern Palau Islands—September and October 1944

LST–61 was decommissioned on 5 June 1946 and was struck from the Navy list on 19 June 1946. On 2 June 1947, she was sold to the Southern Trading Co., of Philadelphia, Pa., and converted for merchant service. She was subsequently scrapped in 1960.

LST–61 earned three battle stars for World War II service.

LST–62

LST–62 was laid down on 5 August 1942 at Jeffersonville, Ind., by the Jeffersonville Boat & Machine Co.; launched on 23 November 1942; sponsored by Mrs. Michael Zier; and commissioned in the Royal Navy on 3 March 1943. She was returned by the United Kingdom on 10 June 1946, and she was struck from the Navy list on 19 July 1946 On 12 May 1948, she was sold to the Northern Metals Co., Philadelphia, Pa., for scrapping.

LST–63

LST–63 was laid down on 6 August 1942 at Jeffersonville, Ind., by the Jeffersonville Boat & Machinery Co.; launched on 19 December 1942; sponsored by Mrs. W. H. Sweney; and commissioned in the Royal Navy on 15 March 1943. The tank landing ship never saw active service with the United States Navy. She was returned by the United Kingdom on 17 December 1945, and she was struck from the Navy list on 21 January 1946. On 27 May 1948, she was sold to the Northern Metals Co., of Philadelphia, Pa., and converted to merchant service.

LST-64

LST-64 was laid down on 13 August 1942 at Jeffersonville, Ind., by the Jeffersonville Boat & Machine Co.; launched on 8 January 1943; sponsored by Mrs. Frank H. Buening; and commissioned in the Royal Navy on 2 April 1943. The tank landing ship never saw active service with the United States Navy. She was returned by the United Kingdom, seriously damaged and beyond economical repair, in November 1945, and was struck from the Navy list on 5 December 1945. On 3 July 1946, she was sold to Rinaldo de Haag and subsequently scrapped.

LST-65

LST-65 was laid down on 14 August 1942 at Jeffersonville, Ind., by the Jeffersonville Boat & Machine Co.; launched on 7 December 1942; sponsored by Mrs. Elsie Middleton Love; and commissioned in the Royal Navy on 15 March 1943. The tank landing ship never saw active service with the United States Navy. She was returned by the United Kingdom on 5 January 1946, and her name was struck from the Navy list on 20 March 1946. On 4 May 1948, she was sold to the Northern Metals Co., of Philadelphia, Pa., and subsequently scrapped.

LST-66

LST-66 was laid down on 14 August 1942 at Jeffersonville, Ind., by the Jeffersonville Boat & Machine Co.; launched on 16 January 1943; sponsored by Mrs. A. C. Landwehr; and commissioned on 12 April 1943, Lt. Howard E. White, USCG, in command.

During World War II, LST-66 was assigned to the Asiatic-Pacific theater and participated in the following operations:
Bismarck Archipelago operation:
    (a) Cape Gloucester, New Britain—December 1943, January and February 1944
    (b) Admiralty Islands landing—February, March and April 1944
Eastern New Guinea operation:
    (a) Saidor occupation—January and February 1944
Hollandia operation—April and May 1944
Western New Guinea operations:
    (a) Toem-Wakde-Sarmi area operations—May 1944
    (b) Biak Island operation—June 1944
    (c) Noemfoor Island operation—July 1944
    (d) Cape Sansapor operation—July and August 1944
    (e) Morotai landings—September 1944
Leyte landings—October and November 1944
Lingayen landings on Luzon—January 1945
Consolidation of the southern Philippines:
    (a) Mindanao Island landings—March 1945
Borneo operations:
    (a) Balikpapan operation—July 1945
LST-66 was decommissioned on 26 March 1946 and struck from the Navy list on 1 May 1946. On 7 April 1948, she was sold to the Kaiser Co., Inc., of Seattle, Wash., for scrapping.
LST-66 earned eight battle stars for World War II service as well as the Navy Unit Commendation.

LST-67

LST-67 was laid down on 7 September 1942 at Jeffersonville, Ind., by the Jeffersonville Boat & Machine Co.; launched on 28 January 1943; sponsored by Mrs. William H. Lang; and commissioned on 20 April 1943.

During World War II, LST-67 was assigned to the Asiatic-Pacific theater and participated in the following operations:
Eastern New Guinea operation:
    (a) Finschhafen occupation—September 1943
    (b) Saidor occupation—January 1944
Bismarck Archipelago operation:
    (a) Cape Gloucester, New Britain—December 1943; January 1944
    (b) Admiralty Islands landing—March 1944
Hollandia operation—April and May 1944
Western New Guinea operations:
    (a) Toem-Wakde-Sarmi area operation—May 1944
    (b) Biak Island operation—May and June 1944
    (c) Noemfoor Island operation—July 1944
    (d) Cape Sansapor operation—July and August 1944
    (e) Morotai landings—September 1944
Leyte landings—October and November 1944
Borneo operations:
    (a) Tarakan Island operation—April and May 1945
    (b) Balikpapan operation—June and July 1945
Consolidation of the southern Philippines:
    (a) Visayan Islands landing—March 1945
LST-67 was decommissioned on 28 March 1946 and was struck from the Navy list on 8 May 1946. On 5 December 1947, she was sold to the Ships & Power Equipment Co., of Barber, N.J., for scrapping.
LST-67 earned seven battle stars for World War II service.

LST-68

LST-68 was laid down on 7 September 1942 at Jeffersonville, Ind., by the Jeffersonville Boat & Machine Co.; launched on 8 March 1943; sponsored by Mrs. Edna C. Crenshaw; and commissioned on 4 June 1943.

During World War II, LST-68 was assigned to the Asiatic-Pacific theater and participated in the following operations:
Bismarck Archipelago operation:
    (a) Cape Gloucester, New Britain—December 1943; January and February 1944
    (b) Admiralty Islands landings—March 1944
Eastern New Guinea operation:
    (a) Saidor occupation—January and February 1944
Hollandia operation—April 1944
Western New Guinea operations:
    (a) Biak Island operation—June 1944
    (b) Noemfoor Island operation—July 1944
    (c) Cape Sansapor operation—August 1944
    (d) Morotai landings—September 1944
Leyte landings—October and November 1944
Lingayen landings on Luzon—January 1945
Consolidation of the southern Philippines:
    (a) Visayan Islands landings—March 1945
LST-68 was decommissioned on 7 March 1946 and was struck from the Navy list on 5 June 1946. On 18 September 1947, she was sold to the Southern Ship-wrecking Co., of New Orleans, La., for scrapping.
LST-68 earned seven battle stars for World War II service.

LST-69

LST-69 was laid down on 7 September 1942 at Jeffersonville, Ind., by the Jeffersonville Boat & Machine Co.;

launched on 20 February 1943; sponsored by Mrs. S. F. Crum; and commissioned on 20 May 1943. She was assigned to the Asiatic-Pacific theater during World War II and participated in the Gilbert Islands operation in November and December 1943. She sank on 21 May 1944 as a result of fire and accidental explosion at Pearl Harbor, Hawaii. Her name was struck from the Navy list on 18 July 1944.

LST-69 earned one battle star for World War II service.

LST-70

LST-70 was laid down on 13 November 1942 at Jeffersonville, Ind., by the Jeffersonville Boat & Machine Co.; launched on 8 February 1943; sponsored by Mrs. George R. Bickel; and commissioned on 28 May 1943.

During World War II, *LST-70* was assigned to the Asiatic-Pacific theater and participated in the following operation:

Treasury-Bougainville operation:
    (a) Occupation and defense of Cape Torokina —November 1943
Bismarck Archipelago operation:
    (a) Green Islands landing—February 1944
Marianas operation:
    (a) Capture and occupation of Guam—July 1944
Iwo Jima operation:
    (a) Assault and occupation of Iwo Jima— February 1945
Okinawa Gunto operation:
    (a) Assault and occupation of Okinawa Gunto —April and May 1945

Following the war, *LST-70* performed occupation duty in the Far East in October and November 1945. She returned to the United States and was decommissioned on 1 April 1946. She was struck from the Navy list on 1 May 1946 and was sold to the Arctic Circle Exploration, Inc., of Seattle, Wash., on 1 July 1946, for scrapping.

LST-70 earned five battle stars for World War II service.

LST-71

LST-71 was laid down on 27 November 1942 at Jeffersonville, Ind., by the Jeffersonville Boat & Machine Co.; launched on 27 February 1943; sponsored by Mrs. Lew Murphy; and commissioned on 9 June 1943.

During World War II, *LST-71* was assigned to the Asiatic-Pacific theater and participated in the following operations:

Marianas operation:
    (a) Capture and occupation of Guam—July and August 1944
Treasury-Bougainville operation:
    (a) Treasury Island landing—November 1944
Okinawa Gunto operation:
    (a) Assault and occupation of Okinawa Gunto —April 1945

LST-71 was decommissioned on 25 March 1946 and was struck from the Navy list on 8 May 1946. On 23 January 1948, she was sold to the Atlantic & Pacific Packing Co., of Seattle, Wash., and subsequently converted for merchant service.

LST-71 earned three battle stars for World War II service.

LST-72

LST-72 was laid down on 20 December 1942 at Jeffersonville, Ind., by the Jeffersonville Boat & Machine Co.; launched on 17 March 1943; sponsored by Mrs. Audra Ehrhardt; and commissioned on 5 June 1943.

During World War II, *LST-72* was assigned to the European theater and participated in the Normandy invasion from 6 to 25 June 1944. Immediately following the war, she was assigned to occupation duty in the Far East from October 1945 to May 1946. She was decommissioned on 4 June 1946 and was struck from the Navy list on 19 June 1946. On 8 June 1948, she was transferred to the Philippine government.

LST-72 earned one battle star for World War II service.

LST-73

LST-73 was laid down on 10 December 1942 at Jeffersonville, Ind., by the Jeffersonville Boat & Machine Co.; launched on 29 March 1943; sponsored by Mrs. Bertha L. Johnston; and commissioned on 8 June 1943.

During World War II, *LST-73* was assigned to the European theater and participated in the Normandy invasion from 6 to 25 June 1944. Immediately following the war, she was assigned to occupation duty in the Far East during the fall of 1945. She was decommissioned on 13 July 1946 and was struck from the Navy list on 10 June 1947. On 31 March 1948, she was sold to the Kaiser Co., Inc., of Seattle, Wash., for scrapping.

LST-73 earned one battle star for World War II service.

LST-74

LST-74 was laid down on 1 January 1943 at Jeffersonville, Ind., by the Jeffersonville Boat & Machine Co.; launched on 31 March 1943; sponsored by Mrs. W. F. Satterlee; and commissioned on 15 June 1943.

During World War II, *LST-74* was assigned to the European theater and participated in the following operations:

Convoy UGS-36—April 1944
Invasion of southern France—August and September 1944

LST-74 was decommissioned on 21 December 1945 and was struck from the Navy list on 21 January 1946. On 22 September 1947, she was sold to the Southern Shipwrecking Co., of New Orleans, La., and subsequently scrapped.

LST-74 earned two battle stars for World War II service.

LST-75

LST-75 was laid down on 30 January 1943 at Jeffersonville, Ind., by the Jeffersonville Boat & Machine Co.; launched on 7 April 1943; sponsored by Mrs. Dorsey W. Brown; and commissioned on 21 June 1943.

During World War II, *LST-75* was assigned to the European theater and participated in the invasion of Nomandy in June 1944. Following the war, *LST-75* performed occupation duty in the Far East in November and December 1945 and service in China in July and August 1947. She returned to the United States and was decommissioned on 22 December 1947, and transferred to the Philippine government on 30 December 1947, serving that government as *Cotabato* (T-36). She was struck from the Navy list on 22 January 1948 and scrapped in 1964.

LST-75 earned one battle star for World War II service.

LST-76

LST-76 was laid down on 19 January 1943 at Jeffersonville, Ind., by the Jeffersonville Boat & Machine Co.; launched on 14 April 1943; sponsored by Mrs. Pauline Bower; and commissioned on 26 June 1943.

During World War II, *LST-76* was assigned to the European theater and participated in the following operations:

Convoy UGS–37—April 1944
   Invasion of southern France—August and September 1944
LST–76 was decommissioned on 24 December 1944 and transferred to the United Kingdom. She was returned to the United States Navy on 23 April 1946, and her name was struck from the Navy list on 19 June 1946. On 21 April 1948, she was sold to the Southern Trading Co., of Philadelphia, Pa., and subsequently converted for merchant service. However, she foundered off Cape Hatteras on 5 October 1951.

LST–76 earned two battle stars for World War II service.

LST–77

LST–77 was laid down on 20 February 1943 at Jeffersonville, Ind., by the Jeffersonville Boat & Machine Co.; launched on 21 April 1943; sponsored by Mrs. Anna Berry; and commissioned on 3 July 1943.

During World War II, *LST–77* was assigned to the European theater and participated in the following operations:
   Convoy UGS–37—April 1944
   Invasion of southern France—August and September 1944
LST–77 was decommissioned on 24 December 1944 and transferred to the United Kingdom. She was returned to the custody of the United States on 12 May 1946 and struck from the Navy list on 19 June 1946. On 7 November 1947, she was sold to Mr. James A. Hughes, of New York, N.Y., for scrapping.

LST–77 earned two battle stars for World War II service.

LST–78

LST–78 was laid down on 9 February 1943 at Jeffersonville, Ind., by the Jeffersonville Boat & Machine Co.; launched on 28 April 1943; sponsored by Mrs. Austin E. Overman; and commissioned on 8 July 1943.

During World War II, *LST–78* was assigned to the Asiatic-Pacific theater and participated in the following operations:
   Gilbert Islands operation—November and December 1943
   Marshall Islands operation:
      (a) Occupation of Kwajalein and Majuro Atolls—January and February 1944
   Marianas operation:
      (a) Capture and occupation of Guam—July 1944
   Occupation of Okinawa—May and June 1945
LST–78 was decommissioned on 8 March 1946 and struck from the Navy list on 8 May 1946. On 13 April 1948, she was sold to the Kaiser Co., Inc., of Seattle, Wash., for scrapping.

LST–78 earned four battle stars for World War II service.

LST–79

LST–79 was laid down on 28 February 1943 at Jeffersonville, Ind., by the Jeffersonville Boat & Machine Co.; launched on 8 May 1943; sponsored by Miss Virginia Lee Hughes; and commissioned on 7 July 1943. The tank landing ship never saw active service with the United States Navy. She was transferred to the United Kingdom on 17 July 1943 and was lost on 30 September 1943. On 11 October 1943, she was struck from the Navy list.

LST–80

LST–80 was laid down on 16 March 1943 at Jeffersonville, Ind., by the Jeffersonville Boat & Machine Co.;

launched on 18 May 1943; sponsored by Miss Jane G. Bonnie; and commissioned on 12 July 1943. The tank landing ship never saw active service with the United States Navy. She was transferred to the United Kingdom on 19 July 1943 and was lost in Royal Navy service in March 1945. On 11 July 1945, she was struck from the Navy list.

LST–81

LST–81 was laid down on 8 March 1943 at Jeffersonville, Ind., by the Jeffersonville Boat & Machine Co.; launched on 28 May 1943; sponsored by Miss Bettie Meador; and commissioned on 21 July 1943. She was decommissioned on 19 July 1943 and redesignated *ARL–5* on 20 July 1943. On 29 July 1943, she was transferred to the United Kingdom and served the Royal Navy as *LSE–1* until 21 May 1946 when she was returned to the United States. She was struck from the Navy list on 29 October 1946. On 20 August 1947, *LST–81* was sold to Argentina and served that government as *Ingeniero Iribas* (Q–21). She was sold by the Argentine Navy in 1967.

LST–82

LST–82 was laid down on 25 March 1943 at Jeffersonville, Ind., by the Jeffersonville Boat & Machine Co.; launched on 9 June 1943; sponsored by Mrs. G. D. Kellogg; redesignated *ARL–6* on 20 July 1943; and commissioned on 26 July 1943. On 2 August 1943, she was decommissioned and transferred to the United Kingdom as *LSE–2*. The tank landing ship never saw active service with the United States Navy. She was returned by the United Kingdom on 21 May 1946, and she was struck from the Navy list on 29 October 1946. On 20 August 1947, she was sold to Argentina as *Ingeniero Gadda* (Q–22) and served that government until she was decommissioned on 25 August 1960. She was sold by the Argentine Navy in 1967.

LST–83

LST–83 was redesignated ARL–4 and named *Adonis* (q.v.) on 26 August 1943.

LST–84

LST–84 was laid down on 13 April 1943 at Jeffersonville, Ind., by the Jeffersonville Boat & Machine Co.; launched on 26 June 1943; sponsored by Mrs. W. Raymond Brendel; and commissioned on 14 August 1943.

During World War II, *LST– 84* was assigned to the Asiatic-Pacific theater and participated in the following operations:
   Gilbert Islands operation:
      (a) Occupation of Kwajalein and Majuro Atolls—February 1944
   Marianas operation:
      (a) Capture and occupation of Saipan—June and July 1944
   Tinian capture and occupation—July 1944
   Assault and occupation of Iwo Jima—February and March 1945
Following the war, *LST–84* was redesignated *LSTH–84* on 15 September 1945. She performed occupation duty in the Far East until early March 1946.

Upon her return to the United States, the ship was decommissioned on 2 March 1946 and struck from the Navy list on 31 October 1947. On 20 April 1948, she was sold to the Bethlehem Steel Co., of Seattle, Wash., and subsequently scrapped.

LSTH–84 earned five battle stars for World War II service as *LST–84*.

LST–85 through LST–116

LST–85 through *LST–116* contracts were cancelled on 16 September 1942.

LST–117

LST–117 was laid down on 28 April 1943 at Jeffersonville, Ind., by the Jeffersonville Boat & Machine Co.; launched on 10 July 1943; sponsored by Mrs. Robert B. Sutherland; and commissioned on 27 August 1943.

During World War II, *LST–117* was assigned to the Asiatic-Pacific theater and participated in the following operations:

Marianas operation:
 (a) Capture and occupation of Guam—July 1944

Leyte landings—October 1944

Following the war, *LST–117* was redesignated *LSTH–117* on 15 September 1945. She performed occupation duty in the Far East until mid-February 1946.

Upon her return to the United States, the ship was decommissioned on 16 February 1946; redesignated *LST–117* on 6 March 1952; and transferred to MSTS for service as USNS *LST–117* (T-LST–117) on 31 March 1952. She was struck from the Navy list on 10 June 1973.

LST–117 earned two battle stars for World War II service.

LST–118

LST–118 was laid down on 21 April 1943 at Jeffersonville, Ind., by the Jeffersonville Boat & Machine Co.; launched on 21 July 1943; sponsored by Miss Dorothy Korrell; and commissioned on 6 September 1943, Lt. Clarence W. Lundberg in command.

During World War II, *LST–118* was assigned to the Asiatic-Pacific theater and participated in the following operations:

Hollandia operation—April 1944

Marianas operation:
 (a) Capture and occupation of Guam—July 1944

Leyte landings—October 1944

Following the war, *LST–118* was redesignated *LSTH–118* on 15 September 1945. She performed occupation duty in the Far East until early February 1946.

Upon her return to the United States, the ship was decommissioned on 8 February 1946 and struck from the Navy list on 29 September 1947. On 28 April 1948, she was sold to the Dulien Steel Products, Inc., of Seattle, Wash., and subsequently scrapped.

LSTH–118 earned three battle stars for World War II service as *LST–118*.

LST–119

LST–119 was laid down on 12 May 1943 at Jeffersonville, Ind., by the Jeffersonville Boat & Machine Co.; launched on 28 July 1943; sponsored by Mrs. Gilbert Coughlin; and commissioned on 1 September 1943, Lt. (jg.) R. D. Dewar, USNR, in command.

During World War II, *LST–119* was assigned to the Asiatic-Pacific theater and participated in the following operations:

Marshall Islands operation:
 (a) Occupation of Kwajalein and Majuro Atolls—January and February 1944

Marianas operation:
 (a) Capture and occupation of Saipan—June and July 1944

Upon her return to the United States, *LST–119* was decommissioned on 13 May 1946 and struck from the Navy list on 19 June 1946. On 17 May 1948, she was sold to Robert H. Beattie, Oil Transport Co., New Orleans, La., for conversion ʹto non-self-propelled operation.

LST–119 earned two battle stars for World War II service.

LST–120

LST–120 was laid down on 5 May 1943 at Jeffersonville, Ind., by the Jeffersonville Boat & Machine Co.; launched on 7 August 1943; sponsored by Miss Laura K. Richert; and commissioned on 22 September 1943.

During World War II, *LST–120* was assigned to the Asiatic-Pacific theater and participated in the following operations:

Marianas operation:
 (a) Capture and occupation of Saipan—June and July 1944
 (b) Tinian capture and occupation—July 1944

During the fall of 1945, *LST–120* performed postwar occupation duty in the Far East.

Upon her return to the United States, the ship was decommissioned on 7 January 1946. She was transferred to the United States Military Government for Korea as a sale in February 1947 and was struck from the Navy list on 5 March 1947.

LST–120 earned two battle stars for World War II service.

LST–121

LST–121 was laid down on 23 May 1943 at Jeffersonville, Ind., by the Jeffersonville Boat & Machine Co.; launched on 16 August 1943; sponsored by Mrs. H. A. Bayless; and commissioned on 29 September 1943, Lt. John P. Devaney, USNR, in command.

During World War II, *LST–121* was assigned to the Asiatic-Pacific theater and participated in the following operations:

Marshall Islands operation:
 (a) Occupation of Kwajalein and Majuro Atolls—January and February 1944

Marianas operation:
 (a) Capture and occupation of Saipan—June and July 1944
 (b) Tinian capture and occupation—July 1944

Western Caroline Islands operation:
 (a) Capture and occupation of southern Palau Islands—September and October 1944

Iwo Jima operation:
 (a) Assault and occupation of Iwo Jima—February 1945

Following the war, *LST–121* was redesignated *LSTH–121* on 15 September 1945. She performed occupation duty in the Far East until mid-November 1945.

Upon her return to the United States, the ship was decommissioned on 21 March 1946. On 14 April 1946, she was sold to the Sun Shipbuilding & Drydock Co., of Chester, Pa., for scrapping. She was struck from the Navy list on 1 May 1946.

LSTH–121 earned five battle stars for World War II service as *LST–121*.

LST–122

LST–122 was laid down on 4 June 1943 at Evansville, Ind., by the Missouri Valley Bridge & Iron Co.; launched on 9 August 1943; and commissioned on 3 September 1943, Lt. Samuel C. Pirie in command.

During World War II, *LST–122* was assigned to the Asiatic-Pacific theater and participated in the following operations:

Marshall Islands operation:
 (a) Occupation of Kwajalein and Majuro Atolls—January and February 1944

Hollandia operation—April 1944

Marianas operation:
  (a) Capture and occupation of Guam—July
      1944
Okinawa Gunto operation:
  (a) Assault and occupation of Okinawa Gunto
      —May 1945
Following the war, *LST–122* performed occupation
duty in the Far East and service in China until early
May 1946.
Upon her return to the United States, the ship was
decommissioned on 4 June 1946 and struck from the
Navy list on 3 July 1946. On 5 December 1947, she was
sold to Bosey, Philippines.
LST–122 earned four battle stars for World War II
service.

LST–123

LST–123 was laid down on 5 June 1943 at Evansville,
Ind., by the Missouri Valley Bridge & Iron Co.;
launched on 14 August 1943; sponsored by Mrs. C. B.
Enlow; and commissioned on 7 September 1943, Lt.
Francis P. Rossiter, USNR, in command.
During World War II, *LST–123* was assigned to the
Asiatic-Pacific theater and participated in the following
operations:
Marianas operation:
  (a) Capture and occupation of Guam—July
      1944
Leyte landings—October 1944
Lingayen landings in Luzon—January 1945
Following the war, *LST–123* was redesignated *LSTH–
123* on 15 September 1945. She performed occupation
duty in the Far East until mid-November 1945.
Upon her return to the United States, the ship was
decommissioned on 22 March 1946 and struck from the
Navy list on 1 May 1946. On 30 March 1948, she was
sold to the Sun Shipbuilding & Drydock Co., of Chester,
Pa., for scrapping.
LSTH–123 earned three battle stars for World War
II service as *LST–123*.

LST–124

LST–124 was laid down on 7 June 1943 at Evansville, Ind., by the Missouri Valley Bridge & Iron Co.;
launched on 18 August 1943; sponsored by Mrs. Hunt
Greathouse; and commissioned on 24 September 1943,
Ens. William A. Bartos in command.
During World War II, *LST–124* was assigned to the
Asiatic-Pacific theater and participated in the following
operations:
Marianas operation:
  (a) Capture and occupation of Saipan—June
      and July 1944
  (b) Tinian capture and occupation—June 1944
Okinawa Gunto operation:
  (a) Assault and occupation of Okinawa Gunto
      —May and June 1945
Upon her return to the United States, the ship was
decommissioned on 26 July 1946 and struck from the
Navy list on 28 August 1946. On 13 December 1947,
she was sold to the Kaiser Co., Inc., of Seattle, Wash.,
and subsequently scrapped.
LST–124 earned three battle stars for World War II
service.

LST–125

LST–125 was laid down on 8 June 1943 at Evans-
ville, Ind., by the Missouri Valley Bridge & Iron Co.;
launched on 23 August 1943; sponsored by Mrs. W. R.
Durham; and commissioned on 29 September 1943.
During World War II, *LST–125* was assigned to the
Asiatic-Pacific theater and participated in the following
operations:
Marianas operation:

  (a) Capture and occupation of Guam—July
      1944
Leyte landings—October 1944
Lingayen landings on Luzon—January 1945
Okinawa Gunto operation:
  (a) Assault and occupation of Okinawa Gunto
      —April 1945
Following the war, *LST–125* performed occupation
duty in the Far East and service in China until early
June 1946.
Upon her return to the United States, the ship was
decommissioned on 10 June 1946. She was sunk as a
target, by naval gunfire, on 14 August 1946, and
struck from the Navy list on 25 September 1946.
LST–125 earned four battle stars for World War II
service.

LST–126

LST–126 was laid down on 11 June 1943 at Evans-
ville, Ind., by the Missouri Valley Bridge & Iron Co.;
launched on 28 August 1943; sponsored by Mrs. Sam
B. Storm; and commissioned on 2 October 1943, Lt.
M. A. Cassell in command.
During World War II, *LST–126* was assigned to the
Asiatic-Pacific theater and participated in the following
operations:
Marshall Islands operation:
  (a) Occupation of Kwajalein and Majuro
      Atolls—January and February 1944
Marianas operation:
  (a) Capture and occupation of Saipan—June
      1944
Leyte landings—October 1944
Upon her return to the United States, the ship was
decommissioned on 17 June 1946 and struck from the
Navy list on 23 June 1947. On 14 June 1948, she was
sold to the Oil Transport Co., of New Orleans, La.,
for conversion to merchant service.
LST–126 earned three battle stars for World War II
service.

LST–127

LST–127 was laid down on 30 June 1943 at Evansville, Ind., by the Missouri Valley Bridge & Iron Co.;
launched on 31 August 1943; sponsored by Mrs. Paul
Johnson; and commissioned on 6 October 1943.
During World War II, *LST–127* was assigned to the
Asiatic-Pacific theater and participated in the following
operations:
Marshall Islands operation:
  (a) Occupation of Kwajalein and Majuro
      Atolls—January and February 1944
  (b) Occupation of Eniwetok Atoll—February
      1944
Marianas operation:
  (a) Capture and occupation of Saipan—June
      and July 1944
  (b) Tinian capture and occupation—July 1944
Western Caroline Islands operation:
  (a) Capture and occupation of southern Palau
      Islands—September and October 1944
Lingayen landings on Luzon—January 1945
Upon her return to the United States, the ship was
decommissioned on 11 March 1947 and struck from the
Navy list on 10 June 1947. On 11 June 1948, she was
sold to Walter W. Johnson Co. for scrapping.
LST–127 earned five battle stars for World War II
service.

LST–128

LST–128 was laid down on 20 June 1943 at Evansville, Ind., by the Missouri Valley Bridge & Iron Co.;
launched on 3 September 1943; sponsored by Mrs. Allen
H. Dame; and commissioned on 11 October 1943.

An Army Piper L–4 *Cub* artillery observation plane takes off from an LST at Anzio, 1944. *LST–386* had an improvised "flight deck" installed in 1943 and flew off four such planes during the landing on Sicily. Later LST modifications, like this one, could carry up to 10 planes and supported the Anzio landing and the invasion of southern France. During 1944, *LST–776* evaluated an experimental catapult for launching light planes, as well as Brodie gear. In this system, a cable was stretched between booms to one side of the ship, and planes were launched from a quick-release trolley. *LST–776* operated Marine OY–1's over Iwo Jima and Army L–4's at Okinawa. Helicopters began to operate from LST decks in 1949 as they continue to do today.

During World War II, *LST–128* was assigned to the Asiatic-Pacific theater and participated in the following operations:

    Marshall Islands operation:
        (a) Occupation of Kwajalein and Majuro Atolls—January and February 1944
    Marianas operation:
        (a) Capture and occupation of Saipan—June and July 1944
        (b) Tinian capture and occupation—July 1944
    Western Caroline Islands operation:
        (a) Capture and occupation of southern Palau Islands—September and October 1944

Following the war, *LST–128* performed occupation duty in the Far East until early March 1946.

Upon her return to the United States, the ship was decommissioned on 23 March 1946 and struck from the Navy list on 17 April 1946.

LST–128 earned four battle stars for World War II service.

LST–129

LST–129 was laid down on 1 July 1943 at Evansville, Ind., by the Missouri Valley Bridge & Iron Co.; launched on 8 September 1943; sponsored by Mrs. Henry Bohnsack; and commissioned on 23 October 1943, Lt. M. J. Prince, USNR, in command.

During World War II, *LST–129* was assigned to the Asiatic-Pacific theater and participated in the following operations:

Marianas operation:

(a) Capture and occupation of Saipan—June and July 1944

(b) Tinian capture and occupation—July 1944

Western Caroline Islands operation:

(a) Capture and occupation of southern Palau Islands—September and October 1944

LST–129 was redesignated *IX–198* on 5 December 1944 and was decommissioned on 20 January 1945. She was destroyed on 16 May 1946 and struck from the Navy list on 19 June 1946.

IX–198 earned three battle stars for World War II service as *LST–129*.

LST–130

LST–130 was laid down on 5 July 1943 at Evansville, Ind., by the Missouri Valley Bridge & Iron Co.; launched on 13 September 1943; sponsored by Ens. Marjorie M. Wilson, NC; and commissioned on 4 November 1943.

During World War II, *LST–130* was assigned to the Asiatic-Pacific theater and participated in the following operations:

Marianas operation:

(a) Capture and occupation of Saipan—June and August 1944

Okinawa Gunto operation:

(a) Assault and occupation of Okinawa Gunto —March and April 1945

Following the war, *LST–130* performed occupation duty in the Far East until early March 1946. Upon her return to the United States, she was decommissioned on 10 March 1946 and struck from the Navy list on 5 December 1947. On 27 May 1948, she was sold to the Bethlehem Steel Co., of Seattle, Wash., and subsequently scrapped.

LST–130 earned two battle stars for World War II service.

LST–131

LST–131 was laid down on 7 July 1943 at Evansville, Ind., by the Missouri Valley Bridge & Iron Co.; launched on 19 September 1943; sponsored by Mrs. Kenneth Still; and commissioned on 15 November 1943, Lt. John M. Tully, USNR, in command.

During World War II, *LST–131* was assigned to the Asiatic-Pacific theater and participated in the following operations:

Marianas operation:

(a) Capture and occupation of Saipan—June and July 1944

(b) Tinian capture and occupation—July 1944

Western Caroline Islands operation:

(a) Capture and occupation of southern Palau Islands—September and October 1944

Following the war, she performed occupation duty in the Far East until early January 1946. The ship was decommissioned on 20 May 1946 and struck from the Navy list on 10 June 1947. On 6 April 1948, she was sold to the Kaiser Co., Inc., of Seattle, Wash., and subsequently scrapped.

LST–131 earned three battle stars for World War II service.

LST–132

LST–132 was redesignated ARB–4 and named *Zeus* (q.v.) on 3 November 1943.

LST–133

LST–133 was laid down on 24 June 1943 at Seneca, Ill., by the Chicago Bridge & Iron Co.; launched on 2 November 1943; sponsored by Mrs. Bertha Hetelle; and commissioned on 29 November 1943, Lt. Floyd E. Richards in command.

During World War II, *LST–133* was assigned to the European and Asiatic-Pacific theaters and participated in the following operations:

Invasion of Normandy—June 1944

Okinawa Gunto operation:

(a) Assault and occupation of Okinawa Gunto —May and June 1945

After the war, she performed occupation duty in the Far East until late December 1945. She was used as a target in the Bikini atomic bomb tests in July 1946 and was decommissioned on 29 August that same year. On 11 May 1948, *LST–133* was sunk as a target and was stricken from the Navy list on 28 May 1948.

LST–133 earned two battle stars and the Navy Unit Commendation for World War II service.

LST–134

LST–134 was laid down on 14 June 1943 at Seneca, Ill., by the Chicago Bridge & Iron Co.; launched on 9 November 1943; sponsored by Miss Marguerite Markland; and commissioned on 7 December 1943.

During World War II, *LST–134* was initially assigned to the European theater and participated in the Normandy invasion between 6 and 25 June 1944, and the invasion of southern France in August and September 1944. She was later transferred to the Asiatic-Pacific theater of operations where she took part in the Okinawa assault in May and June 1945. Following the war, *LST–134* performed occupation duty in the Far East until early February 1946.

Upon her return to the United States, the ship was decommissioned on 17 February 1946 and struck from the Navy list on 31 October 1947. On 20 April 1948, she was sold to the Bethlehem Steel Co., of Seattle, Wash., and subsequently scrapped.

LST–134 earned three battle stars for World War II service.

LST–135

LST–135 was redesignated AGP–10 and named *Orestes* (q.v.) on 3 November 1943.

LST–136

LST–136 was redesignated ARL–8 and named *Egeria* (q.v.) on 3 November 1943.

LST–137

LST–137 was laid down on 23 October 1943 at Ambridge, Pa., by the American Bridge Co.; launched on 19 December 1943; sponsored by Mrs. J. A. Turek; and commissioned on 26 January 1944.

During World War II, *LST–137* was assigned to the European theater and took part in the invasion of Normandy from 6 to 25 June 1944. She was decommissioned on 20 November 1945 and struck from the Navy list on 5 December 1945. On 26 March 1948, she was sold to the Ships & Power Equipment Corp., of Barber, N.J., for scrapping.

LST–137 earned one battle star for World War II service.

LST–138

LST–138 was laid down on 27 October 1943 at Ambridge, Pa., by the American Bridge Co.; launched on 30 December 1943; and commissioned on 5 February 1944, Lt. John B. Wilson, USNR, in command.

During World War II, *LST–138* was assigned to the European theater and took part in the Normandy invasion between 6 and 25 June 1944.

Upon her return to the United States, the ship was decommissioned on 20 November 1945 and struck from the Navy list on 5 December 1945. On 16 June 1947, she was sold to Three Star Line, Inc., of Lake Charles, La., for conversion to merchant service.

LST–138 earned one battle star for World War II service.

LST–139

LST–139 was laid down on 3 November 1943 at Ambridge, Pa., by the American Bridge Co.; launched on 12 January 1944; and commissioned on 14 February 1944, Lt. Rex C. Gray, USNR, in command.

During World War II, *LST–139* was assigned to the European theater and took part in the invasion of Normandy between 6 and 25 June 1944.

Upon her return to the United States, she was decommissioned on 25 March 1946 and struck from the Navy list on 8 May 1946. On 22 April 1947, she was sold to the McWilliams Dredging Co., of New Orleans, La., for conversion to merchant service.

LST–139 earned one battle star for World War II service.

LST–140

LST–140 was laid down on 10 November 1943 at Ambridge, Pa., by the American Bridge Co.; launched on 8 January 1944; sponsored by Mrs. Hugh Robertson; and commissioned on 9 February 1944, Lt. Richard W. Mickelsen in command.

During World War II, *LST–140* was assigned to the European theater and participated in the UGS–36 Convoy operation in April 1944 and the invasion of southern France in August and September 1944.

Upon her return to the United States, she was decommissioned on 5 January 1946 and struck from the Navy list on 12 March 1946. On 18 September 1947, the ship was sold to the Southern Shipwrecking Co., of New Orleans, La., for scrapping.

LST–140 earned two battle stars for World War II service.

LST–141

LST–141 was laid down on 24 November 1943 at Ambridge, Pa., by the American Bridge Co.; launched on 16 January 1944; and commissioned on 16 February 1944.

During World War II, *LST–141* was assigned to the European theater and took part in the invasion of southern France in August and September 1944.

Upon her return to the United States, she was decommissioned on 18 December 1945 and struck from the Navy list on 7 February 1946. On 25 May 1948, the ship was sold to Hughes Bros. Inc., of New York, N.Y., for scrapping.

LST–141 earned one battle star for World War II service.

LST–142 through LST–156

LST–142 through *LST–156* contracts were cancelled on 16 September 1942.

LST–157

LST–157 was laid down on 25 June 1942 at Evansville, Ind., by the Missouri Valley Bridge & Iron Co.; launched on 31 October 1942; sponsored by Mrs. DeWitt C. Redgrave, Jr.; and commissioned on 10 February 1943.

During World War II, *LST–157* served in the European theater and participated in the following operations:

Sicilian occupation—July 1943
Salerno landings—September 1943
Invasion of Normandy—June 1944

Upon her return to the United States, the ship was decommissioned on 9 December 1944 and transferred to the United Kingdom. She was returned to the custody of the United States Navy on 11 April 1946 and struck from the Navy list on 5 June 1946. On 5 December 1947, she was sold to Bosey, Philippines.

LST–157 earned three battle stars for World War II service.

LST–158

LST–158 was laid down on 11 July 1942 at Evansville, Ind., by the Missouri Valley Bridge & Iron Co.; launched on 16 November 1942; sponsored by Mrs. H. S. Tullock; and commissioned on 10 February 1943.

During World War II, *LST–158* served in the European theater and participated in the following operations:

Sicilian occupation—July 1943
North African occupation:
    (a) Tunisian operations—May, June and July 1943

She was sunk off Licata, Sicily, on 11 July 1943 as a result of enemy aircraft action and was struck from the Navy list on 28 July 1943.

LST–158 earned two battle stars for World War II service.

LST–159

LST–159 was laid down on 19 July 1942 at Evansville, Ind., by the Missouri Valley Bridge & Iron Co.; launched on 21 November 1942; sponsored by Mrs. Adrian G. Wrucke; and commissioned on 13 February 1943. The tank landing ship never saw active service with the United States Navy. She was transferred to the United Kingdom on 3 March 1943 and returned to United States Navy custody on 23 April 1946. She was struck from the Navy list on 19 June 1946. On 27 April 1948, *LST–159* was sold to the Newport News Shipbuilding & Drydock Co., of Newport News, Va., for conversion to merchant service.

LST–160

LST–160 was laid down on 21 July 1942 at Evansville, Ind., by the Missouri Valley Bridge & Iron Co.; launched on 30 November 1942; sponsored by Mrs. Basil T. Kehoe; and commissioned on 18 February 1943. The tank landing ship never saw active service with the United States Navy. She was decommissioned on 4 March 1943 and transferred to the United Kingdom on 6 March 1943. The ship was returned to United States custody on 1 June 1946 and struck from the Navy list on 3 July 1946. On 5 December 1947, she was sold to Bosey, Philippines.

LST–161

LST–161 was laid down on 24 July 1942 at Evansville, Ind., by the Missouri Valley Bridge & Iron Co.; launched on 7 December 1942; sponsored by Mrs. Ashley Fancy; and commissioned on 28 February 1943. The tank landing ship never saw active service with the United States Navy. She was decommissioned on 14 March 1943 and transferred to the United Kingdom on 15 March 1943. The ship was returned to United States Navy custody on 5 January 1946 and struck from the Navy list on 20 March 1946. On 7 May 1948, she was sold to the Northern Metals Co., of Philadelphia, Pa., for scrapping.

LST–162

LST–162 was laid down on 24 July 1942 at Evansville, Ind., by the Missouri Valley Bridge & Iron Co.; launched on 3 February 1943; sponsored by Miss Marian Shapiro; and commissioned on 15 March 1943. The tank landing ship never saw active service with the United States Navy. She was decommissioned on 22 March 1943 and transferred to the United Kingdom. The ship was returned to United States Navy custody on 1 February 1946 and struck from the Navy list on 19 June 1946. She was sold to Luria Brothers and Co., Inc., of Philadelphia, Pa., on 9 October 1947 for scrapping.

LST–163

LST–163 was laid down on 10 August 1942 at Evansville, Ind., by the Missouri Valley Bridge & Iron Co.; launched on 4 February 1943; sponsored by Mrs. Monty H. Freeland; and commissioned on 24 March 1943. The tank landing ship never saw active service with the United States Navy. She was decommissioned on 29 March 1943 and transferred to the United Kingdom. The ship was returned to United States Navy custody on 29 November 1946 and was sold to Tung Hwa Trading Co., of Singapore, on 29 July 1947 and converted to merchant service. LST–163 was struck from the Navy list on 1 August 1947.

LST–164

LST–164 was laid down on 13 August 1942 at Evansville, Ind., by the Missouri Valley Bridge & Iron Co.; launched on 5 February 1943; sponsored by Mrs. Lloyd E. Miller; and commissioned on 30 March 1943. The tank landing ship never saw service with the United States Navy. The ship was decommissioned on 5 April 1943 and was transferred to the United Kingdom. She was returned to United States Navy custody on 29 November 1946 and struck from the Navy list on 1 August 1947. On 7 October 1947, she was sold to Tung Hwa Trading Co., of Singapore, and converted to merchant service.

LST–165

LST–165 was laid down on 7 September 1942 at Evansville, Ind., by the Missouri Valley Bridge & Iron Co.; launched on 2 February 1943; sponsored by Mrs. Frank Harrison; and commissioned on 3 April 1943. The tank landing ship never saw service with the United States Navy. The ship was decommissioned on 6 April 1943 and transferred to the United Kingdom. She was returned to United States Navy custody on 20 March 1946 and struck from the Navy list on 5 June 1946. LST–165 was sold to the Northern Metals Co., of Philadelphia, Pa., for scrapping.

LST–166

LST–166 was laid down on 7 September 1942 at Evansville, Ind., by the Missouri Valley Bridge & Iron Co.; launched on 1 February 1943; sponsored by Mrs. Vivian Massey; and commissioned on 22 April 1943, Lt. F. B. Bradley, USCG, in command.

During World War II, LST–166 was assigned to the Asiatic-Pacific theater and participated in the following operations:

Treasury-Bougainville operation:
  (a) Occupation and defense of Cape Torokina —December 1943
Marianas operation:
  (a) Capture and occupation of Saipan—June 1944
Okinawa Gunto operation:
  (a) Assault and occupation of Okinawa Gunto —April 1945

Following the war, LST–166 performed occupation duty in the Far East until the fall of 1945. She returned to the United States and was decommissioned on 3 May 1946. She was struck from the Navy list on 19 June 1946 and was sold to Dulien Steel Products, Inc., of Seattle, Wash., on 3 November 1947 for scrapping.

LST–166 earned three battle stars and the Navy Unit Commendation for World War II service.

LST–167

LST–167 was laid down on 19 September 1942 at Evansville, Ind., by the Missouri Valley Bridge & Iron Co.; launched on 25 February 1943; sponsored by Mrs. Harry J. Trainor; and commissioned on 27 April 1943, Lt. Edward C. Simons, USCG, in command.

During World War II, LST–167 was assigned to the Asiatic-Pacific theater and participated in the occupation of Vella Lavella in September 1943. She was severely damaged by a Japanese air attack at Vella Lavella, Solomon Islands, on 25 September 1943. Declared beyond economical repair, the ship was struck from the Navy list on 6 December 1943.

LST–167 earned one award of the Navy Unit Commendation and one battle star for World War II service.

LST–168

LST–168 was laid down on 26 September 1942 at Evansville, Ind., by the Missouri Valley Bridge & Iron Co.; launched on 25 February 1943; sponsored by Mrs. Merle Batey; and commissioned on 3 May 1943.

During World War II, LST–168 was assigned to the Asiatic-Pacific theater and participated in the following operations:

Eastern New Guinea operation:
  (a) Finschhafen occupation—September 1943
  (b) Saidor occupation—January 1944
Bismarck Archipelago operation:
  (a) Cape Gloucester, New Britain—December 1943, January and February 1944
  (b) Admiralty Islands landings—March 1944
Hollandia operation—April 1944
Western New Guinea operations:
  (a) Morotai landings—September 1944
Leyte landings—October and November 1944
Lingayen Gulf landings—January 1945
Mindanao Island landings—April 1945
Borneo operations:
  (a) Balikpapan operation—July 1945

Following the war, LST–168 performed occupation duty in the Far East in September and October 1945. She returned to the United States and was decommissioned on 14 March 1946. She was struck from the Navy list on 12 April 1946 and was sold to the Bethlehem Steel Co., of Bethlehem, Pa., on 9 April 1948 for scrapping.

LST–168 earned eight battle stars for World War II service.

LST–169

LST–169 was laid down on 1 October 1942 at Evansville, Ind., by the Missouri Valley Bridge & Iron Co.; launched on 26 February 1943; sponsored by Mrs. L. S. Oakes; and commissioned on 22 May 1943.

During World War II, LST–169 was assigned to the Asiatic-Pacific theater and participated in the following operations:

Gilbert Islands operation—November and December 1943
Marianas operation:
  (a) Capture and occupation of Saipan—June and July 1944
Leyte landing—October 1944

Following the war, *LST-169* performed occupation duty in the Far East until early December 1945. She returned to the United States and was decommissioned on 12 April 1946. She was struck from the Navy list on 19 June 1946 and was sold to Luria Steel & Trading Corp., of New York, N.Y., on 24 October 1947 for scrapping.

LST-169 earned three battle stars for World War II service.

LST-170

LST-170 was laid down on 9 October 1942 at Evansville, Ind., by the Missouri Valley Bridge & Iron Co.; launched on 27 February 1943; sponsored by Mrs. A. F. Sweet; and commissioned on 31 May 1943, Lt. T. N. Kelly, USCGR, in command.

During World War II, *LST-170* was assigned to the Asiatic-Pacific theater and participated in the following operations:

Bismarck Archipelago operation:

(a) Cape Gloucester, New Britain—December 1943

(b) Admiralty Islands landings—March 1944

Eastern New Guinea operation:

(a) Saidor occupation—January and February 1944

Hollandia operation—April and May 1944

Western New Guinea operations:

(a) Toem-Wakde-Sarmi area operation—May 1944

(b) Biak Island operation—May and June 1944

(c) Cape Sansapor operation—July and August 1944

(d) Morotai landing—September 1944

Leyte landings—October and November 1944

Luzon operations:

(a) Mindoro landings—December 1944

(b) Lingayen Gulf landing—January 1945

Consolidation of the southern Philippines:

(a) Mindanao Island landings—April 1945

Following the war, *LST-170* was decommissioned on 6 April 1946 and struck from the Navy list on 3 July 1946. On 5 November 1947, she was sold to the Biloxi Boatwrecking Co., of Biloxi, Miss., for scrapping.

LST-170 earned seven battle stars for World War II service.

LST-171

LST-171 was laid down on 20 October 1942 at Evansville, Ind., by the Missouri Valley Bridge & Iron Co.; launched on 28 February 1943; sponsored by Miss Martha J. Miller; and commissioned on 5 June 1943, Lt. Comdr. H. A. West in command.

During World War II, *LST-171* served in the Asiatic-Pacific theater and took part in the following operations:

Bismarck Archipelago operation:

(a) Cape Gloucester, New Britain—December 1943, January and February 1944

(b) Admiralty Islands landings—February and March 1944

Eastern New Guinea operation:

(a) Saidor occupation—January and February 1944

Western New Guinea operations:

(a) Biak Island operation—May and June 1944

(b) Cape Sansapor operation—July and August 1944

(c) Morotai landings—September 1944

Leyte landings—October and November 1944

Visayan Islands landings—March and April 1945

Borneo operations:

(a) Tarakan Island operation—April and May 1945

(b) Balikpapan operation—June and July 1945

Following the war, *LST-171* performed occupation duty in the Far East until late October 1945. She returned to the United States and was decommissioned on 21 May 1946. She was struck from the Navy list on 3 July 1946 and was sold to Boston Metals Co., of Baltimore, Md., on 26 September 1947 for scrapping.

LST-171 earned seven battle stars for World War II service.

LST-172

LST-172 was laid down on 24 December 1942 at Evansville, Ind., by the Missouri Valley Bridge & Iron Co.; launched on 12 May 1943; sponsored by Mrs. R. H. G. Mathews; and commissioned on 11 June 1943. She performed service in China until late May 1946. Upon her return to the United States, she was decommissioned on 8 June 1946 and struck from the Navy list on 9 June 1946. *LST-172* was sold to Bosey, Philippines, on 5 November 1947 and converted for merchant service.

LST-173

LST-173 was laid down on 24 December 1942 at Evansville, Ind., by the Missouri Valley Bridge & Iron Co.; launched on 24 April 1943; sponsored by Mrs. John McCone; and commissioned on 18 June 1943.

During World War II, *LST-173* served in the European theater and participated in the movement of Convoy UGS-36 in April 1944 and the invasion of southern France in August and September 1944. She was decommissioned and transferred to the United Kingdom on 24 December 1944 and was returned to United States Navy custody on 23 April 1946. On 19 June 1946, *LST-173* was struck from the Navy list. The ship was sold to Luria Brothers & Co., of Philadelphia, Pa., on 22 October 1947, for scrapping.

LST-173 earned two battle stars for World War II service.

LST-174

LST-174 was laid down on 1 January 1943 at Evansville, Ind., by the Missouri Valley Bridge & Iron Co.; launched on 21 April 1943; sponsored by Mrs. Elizabeth F. Maynard; and commissioned on 15 June 1943.

During World War II, *LST-174* was assigned to the European theater and participated in the movement of Convoy UGS-36 in April 1944 and the invasion of southern France in August 1944. She was decommissioned on 21 December 1945 and struck from the Navy list on 21 January 1946. On 30 January 1947, *LST-174* was sold to Ming-Sung Industrial Co., Ltd., of Shanghai, China, and converted for merchant service.

LST-174 earned two battle stars for World War II service.

LST-175

LST-175 was laid down on 6 January 1943 at Evansville, Ind., by the Missouri Valley Bridge & Iron Co.; launched on 18 April 1943; sponsored by Mrs. John Kuhn; and commissioned on 19 May 1943.

During World War II, *LST-175* served in the European theater and participated in the invasion of Normandy in June 1944. She was decommissioned on 1 March 1946 and struck from the Navy list on 8 May 1946. On 11 December 1947, she was sold to the Southern Shipwrecking Co., of New Orleans, La., for scrapping.

LST-175 earned one battle star for World War II service.

LST-176

LST-176 was laid down on 18 January 1943 at Evansville, Ind., by the Missouri Valley Bridge & Iron Co.; launched on 15 April 1943; sponsored by Mrs. L. J. Prues; and commissioned on 12 May 1943, Lt. J. S. Salt, USCGR, in command.

During World War II, LST-176 was assigned to the European theater and participated in the invasion of Normandy in June 1944. Following the war, LST-176 performed occupation duty in the Far East until early January 1946. She was decommissioned on 6 January 1946 and transferred to the Shipping Control Authority, Japan, and operated with a Japanese civilian crew. On 31 March 1952, she was redelivered to the United States Navy and served with the Military Sea Transportation Service as USNS T-LST-176 until she was stricken from the Navy list on 1 November 1973.

LST-176 earned one battle star for World War II service.

LST-177

LST-177 was laid down on 5 February 1943 at Evansville, Ind., by the Missouri Valley Bridge & Iron Co.; launched on 16 May 1943; sponsored by Mrs. James Gibson; and commissioned on 22 June 1943.

During World War II, LST-177 was assigned to the European theater and participated in the movement of UGS-36 in April 1944 and the invasion of southern France in August and September 1944. On 11 February 1946, the ship was decommissioned and was struck from the Navy list on 12 April 1946. On 13 March 1947, she was transferred to France as a sale. She served in the French Navy as Laita (L-9001) until she was decommissioned in January 1962 and converted to a port depot ship.

LST-177 earned two battle stars for World War II service.

LST-178

LST-178 was laid down on 6 February 1943 at Evansville, Ind., by the Missouri Valley Bridge & Iron Co.; launched on 23 May 1943; sponsored by Mrs. Charles Haglin; and commissioned on 21 June 1943.

During World War II, LST-178 was assigned to the European theater and participated in the movement of Convoy UGS-36 in April 1944 and the invasion of southern France in August and September 1944. LST-178 was decommissioned and transferred to the United Kingdom on 24 December 1944 and was returned to United States Navy custody on 12 December 1946. In November 1946, she was sold to the Egyptian Navy and was struck from the Navy list on 22 January 1947.

LST-178 earned two battle stars for World War II service.

LST-179

LST-179 was laid down on 7 February 1943 at Evansville, Ind., by the Missouri Valley Bridge & Iron Co.; launched on 30 May 1943; sponsored by Mrs. Milford M. Miller; and commissioned on 3 July 1943.

During World War II, LST-179 was assigned to the Asiatic-Pacific theater and participated in the Gilbert Islands operation during November and early December 1943. The ship was gutted by fire and sunk at Pearl Harbor, Hawaii, on 21 May 1944 and was struck from the Navy list on 18 July 1944. In November 1945, she was subsequently raised, stripped, and sunk by torpedo fire in an ordnance test.

LST-179 earned one battle star for World War II service.

LST-180

LST-180 was laid down in 8 February 1943 at Evansville, Ind., by the Missouri Valley Bridge & Iron Co.; launched on 3 June 1943; sponsored by Mrs. Samuel M. Galls; and commissioned on 29 June 1943.

On 10 July 1943, LST-180 was decommissioned and transferred to the United Kingdom. She was returned to United States Navy custody on 17 December 1945 and was struck from the Navy list on 21 January 1946. LST-180 was sold to the Ships & Power Equipment Co., of Barber, N.J., on 10 March 1948, and was converted for merchant service.

LST-181

LST-181 was laid down on 7 April 1943 at Jeffersonville, Ind., by the Jeffersonville Boat & Machine Co.; launched on 3 July 1943; sponsored by Mrs. T. J. Eifler; and commissioned on 21 August 1943.

During World War II, LST-181 was assigned to the Asiatic-Pacific theater and participated in the following operations:

Bismarck Archipelago operation:
    (a) Cape Gloucester, New Britain—February 1944
    (b) Admiralty Islands landings—March 1944
Hollandia operation—April and May 1944
Western New Guinea operation:
    (a) Toem-Wakde-Sarmi area operation—May 1944
    (b) Biak Island operation—June 1944
    (c) Noemfoor Island operation—July 1944

The American-built British LST-324 heads for the Anzio beachhead, January 1944. Barrage balloons were often flown from LST's to discourage strafing attacks by low-flying planes. Note the British surface-search radar above LST-324's wheelhouse.

(d) Cape Sansapor operation—July and August 1944

(e) Morotai landings—September 1944

Leyte landings—October and November 1944

Visayan Islands landings—March and April 1945

Borneo operations:

(a) Balikpapan operation—June and July 1945

LST–181 was decommissioned on 4 March 1946 and struck from the Navy list on 12 April 1946. On 9 December 1946, she was sold to the Construction Power Machinery Co., of Brooklyn, N.Y.

LST–181 earned seven battle stars for World War II service.

LST–182 through *LST–196*

LST–182 through *LST–196* contracts were cancelled on 16 September 1942.

LST–197

LST–197 was laid down on 15 June 1942 at Seneca, Ill., by the Chicago Bridge & Iron Co.; launched on 13 December 1942; sponsored by Mrs. Harriet Williamson; and commissioned on 5 February 1943, Lt. T. S. Medford, USNR, in command.

During World War II, *LST–197* was assigned to the European theater and participated in the following operations:

Sicilian occupation—July 1943

Salerno landings—September 1943

West coast of Italy operations:

(a) Anzio-Nettuno advanced landings—January through March 1944

Invasion of Normandy—June 1944

Following the war, *LST–197* performed occupation duty in the Far East until early November 1945. She returned to the United States and was decommissioned on 5 April 1946. She was struck from the Navy list on 5 June 1946 and sold to the Luria Steel & Trading Co., of New York, N.Y., on 31 October 1947 for scrapping.

LST–197 earned four battle stars and the Navy Unit Commendation for World War II service.

LST–198

LST–198 was laid down on 22 June 1942 at Seneca, Ill., by the Chicago Bridge & Iron Co.; launched on 17 January 1943; sponsored by Mrs. Martha Sherman; and commissioned on 15 February 1943.

On 27 February 1943, *LST–198* was decommissioned and transferred to the United Kingdom on 6 March 1943. The ship was returned to United States custody on 23 January 1946 and was struck from the Navy list on 20 March 1946. On 19 March 1948, she was sold to the Ships & Power Equipment Corp., of Barber, N.J., for scrapping.

LST–199

LST–199 was laid down on 27 June 1942 at Seneca, Ill., by the Chicago Bridge & Iron Co.; launched on 7 February 1943; sponsored by Mrs. Mary Bell; and commissioned on 1 March 1943. *LST–199* saw no service with the United States Navy. On 19 March 1943, she was decommissioned and transferred to the United Kingdom. On 27 March 1946, she was lost while on lease and was struck from the Navy list on 17 April 1946.

LST–200

LST–200 was laid down on 2 July 1942 at Seneca, Ill., by the Chicago Bridge & Iron Co.; launched on 20 February 1943; sponsored by Mrs. Mary Armstrong; and commissioned on 16 March 1943.

LST–200 saw no service with the United States Navy. On 25 March 1943, she was transferred to the United Kingdom and was returned to United States Navy custody on 27 February 1946. She was struck from the Navy list on 17 April 1946 and was sold to the Ships & Power Equipment Corp., of Barber, N.J., on 26 March 1948. She was later resold and converted for merchant service.

LST–201

LST–201 was laid down on 13 July 1942 at Seneca, Ill., by the Chicago Bridge & Iron Co.; launched on 2 March 1943; sponsored by Miss Loraine Johnson; and commissioned on 2 April 1943, Lt. Samuel D. LaRoue in command.

During World War II, *LST–201* was assigned to the Asiatic-Pacific theater and participated in the following operations:

Eastern New Guinea operations—November 1943 through April 1944

Hollandia operation—April 1944

Western New Guinea operations—May through August 1944

She was redesignated AGP–20 and named *Pontus* (*q.v.*) after a Greek god of the sea on 15 August 1944. She participated in the Leyte landing in November 1944 and, following the war, performed occupation duty in the Far East in November 1945. Decommissioned on 2 April 1946, *Pontus* was struck from the Navy list on 1 May 1946. She was transferred to the Maritime Commission on 26 November 1947 for disposal.

Pontus received one battle star for World War II service under her name and three more for World War II service as *LST–201*.

LST–202

LST–202 was laid down on 15 July 1942 at Seneca, Ill., by the Chicago Bridge & Iron Co.; launched on 16 March 1943; sponsored by Mrs. P. I. Birchard; and commissioned on 9 April 1943.

During World War II, *LST–202* was assigned to the Asiatic-Pacific theater and participated in the following operations:

Bismarck-Archipelago operations:

(a) Cape Gloucester, New Britain—December 1943, January and February 1944

(b) Admiralty Islands landings—February and March 1944

Eastern New Guinea operation:

(a) Saidor operations—January and February 1944

Hollandia operations—April and May 1944

Western New Guinea operations:

(a) Toem-Wakde-Sarmi operation—May 1944

(b) Noemfoor Island operation—July 1944

(c) Cape Sansapor operation—July and August 1944

(d) Morotai landings—September 1944

Leyte landings—October and November 1944

Following the war, *LST–202* performed occupation duty in the Far East until early November 1945. She returned to the United States and was decommissioned on 11 April 1946. She was struck from the Navy list on 28 August 1946 and was sold to the Bethlehem Steel Co., of Seattle, Wash., on 16 April 1948 for scrapping.

LST–202 earned five battle stars for World War II service.

LST–203

LST–203 was laid down on 2 July 1942 at Seneca, Ill., by the Chicago Bridge & Iron Co.; launched on

25 March 1943; sponsored by Miss Fay Horton; and commissioned on 22 April 1943. The ship ran aground on 1 October 1943 near Nanumea in the Ellice Islands and was declared a total loss. *LST-203* was struck from the Navy list on 6 March 1944.

LST-204

LST-204 was laid down on 24 July 1942 at Seneca, Ill., by the Chicago Bridge & Iron Co.; launched on 3 April 1943; sponsored by Mrs. Florence S. Jacobs; and commissioned on 27 April 1943.

During World War II, *LST-204* was assigned to the Asiatic-Pacific theater and participated in the following operations:

Eastern New Guinea operation:
    (a) Finschhafen occupation—September 1943
    (b) Saidor occupation—January and February 1944
Bismarck Archipelago operation:
    (a) Cape Gloucester, New Britain—December 1943, January, February and March 1944
Hollandia operation—April and May 1944
Western New Guinea operations:
    (a) Biak Island operation—June 1944
    (b) Noemfoor Island operation—July 1944
    (c) Cape Sansapor operation—July and August 1944
    (d) Morotai landings—September 1944
Leyte landings—October and November 1944
Lingayen Gulf landing—January 1945
Mindanao Island landings—March and April 1945

LST-204 was decommissioned on 23 February 1946 and was struck from the Navy list on 5 June 1946. On 8 October 1947, she was sold to the New Orleans Shipwrecking Corp., of Chicago, Ill., for scrapping.

LST-204 earned seven battle stars for World War II service.

LST-205

LST-205 was laid down on 5 August 1942 at Seneca, Ill., by the Chicago Bridge & Iron Co.; launched on 13 April 1943; sponsored by Mrs. Doris DeHaven; and commissioned on 15 May 1943.

During World War II, *LST-205* was assigned to the Asiatic-Pacific theater and participated in the following operations:

Gilbert Islands operation—November and December 1943
Biak Island operation—June 1944
Capture and occupation of Saipan—June and July 1944
Leyte landings—October and November 1944

Following the war, *LST-205* was redesignated *LSTH-205* on 15 September 1945. She performed occupation duty in the Far East until mid-December 1945.

Upon her return to the United States, the ship was decommissioned on 2 April 1946 and struck from the Navy list on 5 June 1946. On 4 June 1948, she was sold to Hughes Bros., Inc., of New York City, N.Y., for scrapping.

LSTH-205 earned four battle stars for World War II service as *LST-205*.

LST-206

LST-206 was laid down on 7 August 1942 at Seneca, Ill., by the Chicago Bridge & Iron Co.; launched on 21 April 1943; sponsored by Mrs. William Connor Laird; and commissioned on 7 June 1943.

During World War II, *LST-206* was assigned to the Asiatic-Pacific theater and participated in the following operations:

Bismarck Archipelago operation:
    (a) Cape Gloucester, New Britain—December 1943, January, February and March 1944
    (b) Admiralty Islands landings—March 1944
Hollandia operation—April and May 1944
Saidor occupation—January and February 1944
Western New Guinea operations:
    (a) Toem-Wakde-Sarmi area operation—May 1944
    (b) Biak Island operation—June 1944
    (c) Cape Sansapor operation—July and August 1944
    (d) Morotai landings—September 1944
Leyte landings—October and November 1944
Balikpapan operation—July 1945

LST-206 was decommissioned on 6 May 1946 and was struck from the Navy list on 5 June 1946. On 7 April 1948, she was sold to the Bethlehem Steel Co., of Seattle, Wash., for scrapping.

LST-206 earned six battle stars for World War II service.

LST-207

LST-207 was laid down on 7 September 1942 at Seneca, Ill., by the Chicago Bridge & Iron Co.; launched on 29 April 1943; sponsored by Mrs. Florence Horton Gillatt; and commissioned on 9 June 1943.

During World War II, *LST-207* was assigned to the Asiatic-Pacific theater and participated in the following operations:

Occupation and defense of Cape Torokina—November 1943
Green Islands landing—February 1944
Capture and occupation of Guam—July 1944
Leyte landing—October 1944
Assault and occupation of Okinawa Gunto—May 1945

Following the war, *LST-207* performed occupation duty in the Far East until mid-November 1945. She returned to the United States and was decommissioned on 20 March 1946. She was struck from the Navy list on 17 April 1946. On 19 December 1947, she was sold to the Ships & Power Equipment Corp., of Barber, N.J., for scrapping.

LST-207 earned five battle stars for World War II service.

LST-208

LST-208 was laid down on 7 September 1942 at Seneca, Ill., by the Chicago Bridge & Iron Co.; launched on 11 May 1943; sponsored by Mrs. Bernice Neurohr; and commissioned on 8 June 1943, Lt. Robert W. Emmons, USNR, in command.

During World War II, *LST-208* was assigned to the European theater and took part in the invasion of Normandy in June 1944. Following the war, *LST-208* performed occupation duty in the Far East until mid-May 1946. She returned to the United States and was decommissioned on 12 June 1946 and was struck from the Navy list on 3 July 1946. On 5 December 1947, she was sold to Bosey, Philippines.

LST-208 earned one battle star for World War II service.

LST-209

LST-209 was laid down on 7 September 1942 at Seneca, Ill., by the Chicago Bridge & Iron Co.; launched on 29 May 1943; sponsored by Mrs. C. A. Dalton; and commissioned on 10 June 1943.

During World War II, *LST-209* was assigned to the European theater and participated in the invasion of Normandy in June 1944. She returned to the United

States and was placed out of commission, in reserve, on 27 June 1946, and was transferred to the Military Sea Transportation Service for service as USNS *LST–209*. On 1 July 1955, she was named *Bamberg County* (LST–209) after a county in South Carolina. She was struck from the Navy list on 1 November 1958 and sold to Tolchester Lines, Inc., Arlington, Va., and resold to Dravo Corp., Pittsburgh, Pa., on 23 February 1961.

Bamberg County (LST–209) earned one battle star for World War II service as *LST–209*.

LST–210

LST–210 was laid down on 7 September 1942 at Seneca, Ill., by the Chicago Bridge & Iron Co.; launched on 1 June 1943; sponsored by Miss Ruth Hines; and commissioned on 6 July 1943.

During World War II, *LST–210* was assigned to the European theater and participated in the following operations:

> Convoy UGS–36—April 1944
> Alba and Pianosa landings—June 1944
> Invasion of southern France—August and September 1944

Following the war, *LST–210* was decommissioned on 8 December 1945 and struck from the Navy list on 3 January 1946. On 12 May 1948, the ship was sold to the Weeks Stevedoring Co., Inc., for non-self-propelled operation.

LST–210 earned three battle stars for World War II service.

LST–211

LST–211 was laid down on 7 September 1942 at Seneca, Ill., by the Chicago Bridge & Iron Co.; launched on 5 June 1943; sponsored by Mrs. Charles S. Pillsbury; and commissioned on 6 July 1943.

During World War II, *LST–211* was assigned to the European theater and participated in the following operations:

> Convoy UGS–37—April 1944
> Invasion of southern France—August and September 1944

Following the war, *LST–211* was decommissioned on 20 November 1945 and struck from the Navy list on 5 December that same year. On 26 March 1948, the ship was sold to the Ships & Power Equipment Corp., Barber, N.J., for scrapping.

LST–211 earned two battle stars for World War II service.

LST–212

LST–212 was laid down on 7 December 1942 at Seneca, Ill., by the Chicago Bridge & Iron Co.; launched on 12 June 1943; sponsored by Miss Catherine Trees; and commissioned on 6 July 1943.

During World War II, *LST–212* was assigned to the European theater and participated in the movement of Convoy UGS–37 in April 1944 and the invasion of Normandy in June 1944. She returned to the United States and was decommissioned on 15 November 1945 and was struck from the Navy list on 28 November 1945. On 24 July 1947, she was sold to Alfredo A. Lavalle, of New York, N.Y., and converted for merchant service.

LST–212 earned two battle stars for World War II service.

LST–213

LST–213 was laid down on 21 December 1942 at Seneca, Ill., by the Chicago Bridge & Iron Co.; launched on 16 June 1943; sponsored by Mrs. Marvin Sack; and commissioned on 7 July 1943.

During World War II, *LST–213* was assigned to the Asiatic-Pacific theater and participated in the following operations:

> Marianas operation:
> > (a) Capture and occupation of Saipan—June and July 1944
> > (b) Tinian capture and occupation—July 1944
> Leyte landings—October 1944

LST–213 was redesignated *LSTH–213* on 15 September 1945. The ship performed occupation duty in the Far East until late November 1945. She returned to the United States and was decommissioned on 11 March 1946 and was struck from the Navy list on 5 March 1947. On 26 June 1947, she was transferred as a sale to American Military Government, Korea.

LSTH–213 earned three battle stars for World War II service as *LST–213*.

LST–214

LST–214 was laid down on 29 December 1942 at Seneca, Ill., by the Chicago Bridge & Iron Co.; launched on 22 June 1943; sponsored by Mrs. Mabel Glenn; and commissioned on 7 July 1943. The tank landing ship never saw active service with the United States Navy. On 24 July 1943, she was transferred to the United Kingdom and was returned to United States Navy custody on 26 January 1946. She was struck from the Navy list on 12 April 1946. On 3 March 1947, she was sold to N. Block Co., of Norfolk, Va., for scrapping.

LST–215

LST–215 was laid down on 8 January 1943 at Seneca, Ill., by the Chicago Bridge & Iron Co.; launched on 26 June 1943; sponsored by Mrs. Frank T. Kegley; and commissioned on 12 July 1943. The tank landing ship never saw active service with the United States Navy. On 19 July 1943, she was transferred to the United Kingdom and was returned to United States Navy custody on 27 July 1946. She was struck from the Navy list on 29 October 1946 and was sold and converted for merchant service on 11 September 1947.

LST–216

LST–216 was laid down on 23 January 1943 at Seneca, Ill., by the Chicago Bridge & Iron Co.; launched on 4 July 1943; sponsored by Miss Ruth Curnick; and commissioned on 23 July 1943. The tank landing ship never saw active service with the United States Navy. On 4 August 1943, she was transferred to the United Kingdom and was sunk by an aircraft-launched torpedo off Cherbourg, France, on 7 July 1944. *LST–216* was struck from the Navy list on 13 November 1944.

LST–217

LST–217 was laid down on 2 February 1943 at Seneca, Ill., by the Chicago Bridge & Iron Co.; launched on 13 July 1943; sponsored by Mrs. C. H. Johnson; and commissioned on 30 July 1943. The tank landing ship never saw active service with the United States Navy. On 5 August 1943, she was transferred to the United Kingdom and was returned to United States Navy custody on 12 February 1946. She was struck from the Navy list on 5 June 1946. On 12 December 1947, she was sold to James A. Hughes, New York, N.Y., for scrapping.

LST–218

LST–218 was laid down on 11 February 1943 at Seneca, Ill., by the Chicago Bridge and Iron Co.; launched on 20 July 1943; sponsored by Mrs. Don

Leach; and was placed in reduced commission for ferrying to New Orleans on 5 August 1943. She was placed in full commission on 12 August that same year.

During World War II, *LST–218* was assigned to the Asiatic-Pacific theater and participated in the following operations:

Gilbert Islands operation—November and December 1943

Occupation of Kwajalein and Majuro Atolls—January and February 1944

Occupation of Eniwetok Atoll—February 1944

Capture and occupation of Saipan—June through August 1944

Capture and occupation of Tinian—July and August 1944

Following the war, *LST–218* performed occupation duty in the Far East until mid-January 1946. She was decommissioned on 19 January 1946 and transferred to the naval Shipping Control Authority for the Japanese Merchant Marine (SCAJAP). The ship was returned to United States Navy custody on 28 January 1950. On 15 November 1950, she was assigned to the Pacific Reserve Fleet at Bremerton where she was activated and transferred to the Republic of Korea Navy on 3 May 1955. She served that navy as *LST–809*.

LST–218 earned four battle stars for World War II service.

LST–219

LST–219 was laid down on 18 February 1943 at Seneca, Ill., by the Chicago Bridge & Iron Co.; launched on 27 July 1943; sponsored by Mrs. Anthony F. Nosek; and was commissioned on 19 August 1943.

During World War II, *LST–219* was assigned to the Asiatic-Pacific theater and participated in the capture and occupation of Guam in July 1944 and the Leyte landings in October 1944. Following the war, *LST–219* performed occupation duty in the Far East until mid-December 1946. She returned to the United States and was decommissioned on 29 November 1948 and struck from the Navy list on 22 December 1948. On 25 February 1949, she was sold to Foss Launch & Tug Co., of Tacoma, Wash.

LST–219 earned two battle stars for World War II service.

LST–220

LST–220 was laid down on 4 March 1943 at Seneca, Ill., by the Chicago Bridge & Iron Co.; launched on 3 August 1943; sponsored by Mrs. A. E. Ellerbee; and commissioned on 26 August 1943.

During World War II, *LST–220* was assigned to the Asiatic-Pacific theater and participated in the following operations:

Green Islands landing—February 1944

Hollandia operation—April 1944

Capture and occupation of Guam—July and August 1944

Leyte landings—October and November 1944

Following the war, *LST–220* returned to the United States and was decommissioned in March 1946 and destroyed and struck from the Navy list on 12 May 1948.

LST–220 earned four battle stars for World War II service.

LST–221

LST–221 was laid down on 9 March 1943 at Seneca, Ill., by the Chicago Bridge & Iron Co.; launched on 7 August 1943; sponsored by Mrs. Isabelle Chamness; and commissioned on 2 September 1943, Lt. Joseph H. Church, USNR, in command.

During World War II, *LST–221* was assigned to the Asiatic-Pacific theater and participated in the following operations:

Marshall Islands operations:

(a) Occupation of Kwajalein and Majuro Atolls—January and February 1944

(b) Occupation of Eniwetok Atoll—February and March 1944

Hollandia operation—April 1944

Capture and occupation of Guam—April 1944

Assault and occupation of Okinawa Gunto—April 1945

Following the war, *LST–221* performed occupation duty in the Far East until late January 1946. She returned to the United States and was decommissioned on 6 May 1946 and struck from the Navy list on 3 July 1946. On 4 March 1948, she was sold to Port Houston Iron Works, Inc., of Houston, Tex., for non-self-propelled merchant service.

LST–221 earned four battle stars for World War II service.

LST–222

LST–222 was laid down on 16 March 1943 at Seneca, Ill., by the Chicago Bridge & Iron Co.; launched on 17 August 1943; sponsored by Mrs. Ruth Clydedale; and commissioned on 10 September 1943.

During World War II, *LST–222* was assigned to the Asiatic-Pacific theater and participated in the following operations:

Occupation of Kwajalein and Majuro Atolls—January and February 1944

Capture and occupation of Saipan—June and July 1944

Tinian capture and occupation—July 1944

Capture and occupation of southern Palau Islands—September and October 1944

Following the war, *LST–222* was redesignated *LSTH–222* on 15 September 1945. She performed occupation duty in the Far East until early February 1946 and served with the Military Sea Transportation Service as *T–LST–222* from 31 March 1952 to 15 July 1972. On 15 July 1972, the tank landing ship was transferred to the Philippines as a loan, where, as of 1 January 1979, she remained active as *Mindoro Occidental* (LT–93).

LST–222 earned four battle stars for World War II service.

LST–223

LST–223 was laid down on 31 March 1943 at Seneca, Ill., by the Chicago Bridge & Iron Co.; launched on 24 August 1943; sponsored by Mrs. George S. Trees; and commissioned on 17 September 1943, Lt. Thomas S. Moulton, USNR, in command.

During World War II, *LST–223* was assigned to the Asiatic-Pacific theater and participated in the following operations:

Capture and occupation of Kwajalein and Majuro Atolls—January and February 1944

Capture and occupation of Saipan—June 1944

Leyte landings—October and November 1944

Following the war, *LST–223* performed occupation duty in the Far East until November 1945. On 15 September 1945, the ship was redesignated *LSTH–223*. She was transferred to the State Department for disposal on 13 March 1947.

LST–223 earned three battle stars for World War II service.

LST–224

LST–224 was laid down on 2 April 1943 at Seneca, Ill., by the Chicago Bridge & Iron Co.; launched on 31 August 1943; sponsored by Mrs. George P. Shoemaker; and commissioned on 23 September 1943.

During World War II, *LST-224* was assigned to the Asiatic-Pacific theater and participated in the following operations:

Marshall Islands operation:

    (a) Occupation of Kwajalein and Majuro Atolls—January and February 1944

    (b) Occupation of Eniwetok Atoll—February 1944

Capture and occupation of Saipan—June and July 1944

Tinian capture and occupation—July 1944

Capture and occupation of the southern Palau Islands—September and October 1944

Assault and occupation of Iwo Jima—February 1945

LST-224 was decommissioned on 22 March 1946, and struck from the Navy list on 17 April 1946. She was sold to the Bethlehem Steel Co., of Bethlehem, Pa., on 9 April 1948 for scrapping.

LST-224 earned five battle stars for World War II service.

LST-225

LST-225 was laid down on 14 April 1943 at Seneca, Ill., by the Chicago Bridge & Iron Co.; launched on 4 September 1943; sponsored by Miss Mary Oklesen; and commissioned on 2 October 1943.

During World War II, *LST-225* was assigned to the Asiatic-Pacific theater and participated in the following operations:

Capture and occupation of Saipan—June and July 1944

Tinian capture and occupation—July 1944

Capture and occupation of the southern Palau Islands—September and October 1944

Following the war, *LST-225* performed occupation duty in the Far East until mid-February 1946. She returned to the United States and was decommissioned on 30 July 1946 and struck from the Navy list on 28 August 1946. On 16 December 1947, she was sold to the Learner Co., of Oakland, Calif., for scrapping.

LST-225 earned two battle stars for World War II service.

LST-226

LST-226 was laid down on 16 April 1943 at Seneca, Ill., by the Chicago Bridge & Iron Co.; launched on 14 September 1943; sponsored by Mrs. Matthew Dekreon; and commissioned on 8 October 1943.

During World War II, *LST-226* was assigned to the Asiatic-Pacific theater and participated in the following operations:

Occupation of Kwajalein and Majuro Atolls—January and February 1944

Capture and occupation of southern Palau Islands—September and October 1944

Following the war, *LST-226* served in China from November 1945 through May 1946. She returned to the United States and was decommissioned on 8 June 1946 and struck from the Navy list on 19 June 1946. On 5 November 1947, she was sold to Bosey, Philippines, and converted for merchant service.

LST-226 earned two battle stars for World War II service.

LST-227

LST-227 was laid down on 10 May 1943 at Seneca, Ill., by the Chicago Bridge & Iron Co.; launched on 21 September 1943; sponsored by Mrs. C. B. Hellerson; and commissioned on 16 October 1943.

During World War II, *LST-227* was assigned to the Asiatic-Pacific theater and participated in the following operations:

Occupation of Kwajalein and Majuro Atolls—February 1944

Hollandia operation—April 1944

Capture and occupation of Guam—July 1944

Capture and occupation of southern Palau Islands—September and October 1944

Lingayen Gulf landing—January 1945

Assault and occupation of Okinawa Gunto—April and May 1945

Following the war, *LST-227* performed occupation duty in the Far East until mid-January 1946. She returned to the United States and was decommissioned on 22 January 1946. She served with the Shipping Control Authority, Japan, from 23 January 1946 to 6 June 1950. On 27 March 1955, she was transferred to Korea as a loan where she served as *Duk Bong* (LST-808) into the mid 1970's.

LST-227 earned six battle stars for World War II service.

LST-228

LST-228 was laid down on 20 May 1943 at Seneca, Ill., by the Chicago Bridge & Iron Co.; launched on 25 September 1943; sponsored by Mrs. Arthur B. Horton; and commissioned on 25 October 1943. The tank landing ship saw only brief active service with the United States Navy because, on 19 January 1944, she was grounded in the vicinity of Bahia Angra Island, Azores, and was declared beyond salvage and pronounced a total loss on 21 January 1944. *LST-228* was struck from the Navy list on 12 February 1944.

LST-229

LST-229 was laid down on 27 May 1943 at Seneca, Ill., by the Chicago Bridge & Iron Co.; launched on 5 October 1943; sponsored by Mrs. Kenneth E. Sandbach; and commissioned on 3 November 1943, Comdr. Harry R. Hayes in command.

During World War II, *LST-229* was assigned to the European theater and participated in the invasion of Normandy in June 1944. Following the war, *LST-229* performed occupation duty in the Far East and served in China until mid-December 1945. She returned to the United States and was decommissioned on 12 February 1946 and struck from the Navy list on 31 October 1947. On 7 April 1948, she was sold to the Consolidated Shipbuilding Corp., of Morris Heights, N.Y., for scrapping.

LST-229 earned one battle star for World War II service.

LST-230

LST-230 was laid down on 10 June 1943 at Seneca, Ill., by the Chicago Bridge & Iron Co.; launched on 12 October 1943; sponsored by Mrs. Lettie Reeks; and commissioned on 3 November 1943.

During World War II, *LST-230* was assigned to the European theater and participated in the invasion of Normandy in June 1944 and the invasion of southern France in August and September 1944. Following the war, *LST-230* performed occupation duty in the Far East in September 1945 and March 1946. She returned to the United States and was decommissioned on 4 March 1946 and was transferred to the Shipping Control Authority, Japan, on 31 March 1952, where she operated as T-*LST-230*. T-*LST-230* was transferred to the Philippine Navy on 13 September 1976.

LST-230 earned two battle stars for World War II service.

LST-231

LST-231 was redesignated ARL-7 and named *Atlas* (*q.v.*) on 3 November 1943.

LST–232 through LST–236

LST–232 through LST–236 contracts were cancelled on 16 September 1942.

LST–237

LST–237 was laid down on 9 February 1943 at Evansville, Ind., by the Missouri Valley Bridge & Iron Co., launched on 8 June 1943; sponsored by Mrs. Ralph Sollitt; and commissioned on 30 June 1943. The tank landing ship saw no active service with the United States Navy. On 12 July 1943, she was transferred to the United Kingdom and was returned to United States Navy custody on 11 February 1946. LST–237 was struck from the Navy list on 26 February 1946 and was sold to Bosey, Philippines, on 5 November 1947 and converted for merchant service.

LST–238

LST–238 was laid down on 5 March 1943 at Evansville, Ind., by the Missouri Valley Bridge & Iron Co.; launched on 13 June 1943; sponsored by Miss Ester Behme; and commissioned on 9 July 1943. The tank landing ship saw no active service with the United States Navy. On 16 June 1943, she was transferred to the United Kingdom and was returned to United States Navy custody on 13 February 1946. LST–238 was struck from the Navy list on 12 March 1946 and was sold to the Ships & Power Equipment Corp., of Barber, N.J., on 12 March 1948 for scrapping.

LST–239

LST–239 was laid down on 6 March 1943 at Evansville, Ind., by the Missouri Valley Bridge & Iron Co.; launched on 18 June 1943; sponsored by Mrs. Arthur L. Tomme; and commissioned on 13 July 1943. The tank landing ship saw no active service with the United States Navy. On 19 July 1943, she was transferred to the United Kingdom and was returned to United States Navy custody on 5 February 1946. LST–239 was struck from the Navy list on 5 June 1946; and, on 26 April 1948, she was sold to the Newport News Shipbuilding & Drydock Co., Newport News, Va., for conversion to non-self-propelled merchant operation.

LST–240

LST–240 was laid down on 7 March 1943 at Evansville, Ind., by the Missouri Valley Bridge & Iron Co.; launched on 25 June 1943; sponsored by Mrs. S. D. Bechtel; and commissioned on 27 July 1943, Lt. John K. Alges in command.

During World War II, LST–240 was assigned to the Asiatic-Pacific theater and participated in the following operations:

Marshall Islands operations:
  (a) Occupation of Kwajalein and Majuro Atolls—January and February 1944
  (b) Occupation of Eniwetok Atoll—February and March 1944
Capture and occupation of Saipan—June and July 1944

LST–240 was decommissioned on 3 May 1946 and struck from the Navy list on 23 June 1947. On 1 June 1948, she was sold to the Sun Shipbuilding & Drydock Co., of Chester, Pa., for scrapping.

LST–240 earned two battle stars for World War II service.

LST–241

LST–241 was laid down on 8 March 1943 at Evansville, Ind., by the Missouri Valley Bridge & Iron Co.; launched on 29 June 1943; sponsored by Mrs. Donald J. Siegel; and commissioned on 31 July 1943, Lt. James A. Shaw, USNR, in command.

During World War II, LST–241 was assigned to the Asiatic-Pacific theater and participated in the following operations:

Gilbert Islands operations—November and December 1943
Occupation of Kwajalein and Majuro Atolls—February 1944
Hollandia operation—April 1944
Capture and occupation of Guam—July 1944
Assault and occupation of Iwo Jima—February 1945
Assault and occupation of Okinawa Gunto—April 1945

Following the war, she performed occupation duty in the Far East until mid-October 1945. She returned to the United States and was decommissioned on 7 March 1946 and struck from the Navy list on 5 June 1946. On 29 September 1947, she was sold to the Southern Shipwrecking Co., of New Orleans, La., for scrapping.

LST–241 earned six battle stars for World War II service.

LST–242

LST–242 was laid down on 8 March 1943 at Evansville, Ind., by the Missouri Valley Bridge & Iron Co.; launched on 3 July 1943; sponsored by Mrs. Charles R. Duskey; and commissioned on 5 August 1943, Lt. (jg.) J. W. Winney, USNR, in command.

During World War II, LST–242 was assigned to the Asiatic-Pacific theater and participated in the following operations:

Gilbert Islands operation—November and December 1943
Marshall Islands operation:
  (a) Occupation of Kwajalein and Majuro Atolls—January and February 1944
  (b) Occupation of Eniwetok Atoll—February 1944
Capture and occupation of Saipan—June 1944
Leyte landings—October 1944

Following the war, LST–242 was redesignated LSTH–242 on 15 September 1945. She performed occupation duty in the Far East until early February 1946 when she returned to the United States. On 9 February 1946, she was decommissioned and transferred that same day to the Shipping Control Authority, Japan. She was struck from the Navy list on 31 October 1947.

LSTH–242 earned four battle stars for World War II service as LST–242.

LST–243

LST–243 was laid down on 26 April 1943 at Evansville, Ind., by the Missouri Valley Bridge & Iron Co.; launched on 9 July 1943; sponsored by Miss Marybeth Malsie; and commissioned on 9 August 1943, Lt. F. H. Blaske, USNR, in command.

During World War II, LST–243 was assigned to the Asiatic-Pacific theater and participated in the following operations:

Gilbert Islands operation—November and December 1943
Occupation of Kwajalein and Majuro Atolls—January and February 1944
Capture and occupation of Guam—July 1944
Capture and occupation of southern Palau Islands—September and October 1944
Lingayen Gulf landings—January 1945

Following the war, LST–243 was redesignated LSTH–243 on 15 September 1945. She performed occupation duty in the Far East until early January 1946 when she returned to the United States and was decommissioned on 9 January 1946. LSTH–243 was struck from

A Coast Guard artist conveys the feeling of LST operations under air attack in the South Pacific. Coast Guardsmen manned many wartime LST's as well as other types of patrol and landing ships and craft.

the Navy list on 17 July 1947. On 2 April 1948, she was sold to the Consolidated Shipbuilding Corp., of Morris Heights, N.Y., for scrapping.

LSTH–243 earned five battle stars for World War II service as *LST–243*.

LST–244

LST–244 was laid down on 1 May 1943 at Evansville, Ind., by the Missouri Valley Bridge & Iron Co.; launched on 14 July 1943; sponsored by Mrs. H. C. Price; and commissioned on 13 August 1943.

During World War II, *LST–244* was assigned to the Asiatic-Pacific theater and participated in the following operations:

    Gilbert Islands operation—November and December 1943

    Occupation of Kwajalein and Majuro Atolls—February 1944

    Capture and occupation of Guam—July and August 1944

    Assault and occupation of Okinawa Gunto—April 1945

LST–244 was decommissioned on 28 March 1946 and struck from the Navy list on 3 July 1946. On 11 June

1948, she was sold to the Sun Shipbuilding & Drydock Co., of Chester, Pa., for scrapping.

LST–244 earned four battle stars for World War II service.

LST–245

LST–245 was laid down on 7 May 1943 at Evansville, Ind., by the Missouri Valley Bridge & Iron Co.; launched on 17 July 1943; sponsored by Mrs. Conrad L. Walker; and commissioned on 22 August 1943, Lt. Matthew J. McCabe, USNR, in command.

During World War II, *LST–245* was assigned to the Asiatic-Pacific theater and participated in the following operations:

    Saidor occupation—January and February 1944

    Bismarck Archipelago operation:

        (a) Cape Gloucester, New Britain—February 1944

        (b) Admiralty Islands landings—March 1944

    Hollandia operation—April and May 1944

    Western New Guinea operations:

        (a) Toem-Wakde-Sarmi area operation—May 1944

        (b) Biak Island operation—June 1944

        (c) Noemfoor Island operation—July 1944

(d) Cape Sansapor operation—July and August 1944

(e) Morotai landings—September 1944

Leyte landings—October and November 1944

Lingayen Gulf landing—January 1945

Mindanao Island landings—April 1945

Balikpapan operation—June and July 1945

LST–245 was decommissioned on 1 April 1946 and struck from the Navy list on 8 May 1946. On 15 April 1948, she was transferred to the Maritime Administration for disposal.

LST–245 earned eight battle stars for World War II service.

LST–246

LST–246 was laid down on 12 May 1943 at Evansville, Ind., by the Missouri Valley Bridge & Iron Co.; launched on 22 July 1943; sponsored by Mrs. Joseph Shaw; and commissioned on 23 August 1943.

During World War II, *LST–246* was assigned to the Asiatic-Pacific theater and participated in the following operations:

Marshall Islands operation:

(a) Occupation of Kwajalein and Majuro Atolls—January and February 1944

(b) Occupation of Eniwetok Atoll—February 1944

Capture and occupation of Saipan—June and July 1944

Tinian capture and occupation—July 1944

Capture and occupation of southern Palau Islands —September and October 1944

Lingayen Gulf landing—January 1945

Assault and occupation of Okinawa Gunto—May 1945

Following the war, *LST–246* performed occupation duty in the Far East until early February 1946 when she returned to the United States and was decommissioned on 14 February 1946. On 26 June 1947, she was transferred to the United States Army and struck from the Navy list on 12 March 1948.

LST–246 earned six battle stars for World War II service.

LST–247

LST–247 was laid down on 17 May 1943 at Evansville, Ind., by the Missouri Valley Bridge & Iron Co.; launched on 30 July 1943; sponsored by Mrs. Wesley W. Allen; and commissioned on 26 August 1943, Lt. E. V. Converse, USNR, in command.

During World War II, *LST–247* was assigned to the Asiatic-Pacific theater and participated in the capture and occupation of Guam in July 1944. Following the war, *LST–247* was redesignated *LSTH–247* on 15 September 1945 and was decommissioned on 27 June 1946. She was struck from the Navy list on 15 August 1946. On 14 October 1947, the tank landing ship was sold to William E. Skinner for scrapping.

LSTH–247 earned one battle star for World War II service as *LST–247*.

LST–248 through LST–260

LST–248 through *LST–260* contracts were cancelled on 16 September 1942.

LST–261

LST–261 was laid down on 7 September 1942 at Ambridge, Pa., by the American Bridge Co.; launched on 23 January 1943; sponsored by Mrs. Harry F. Snyder; and commissioned on 22 May 1943.

During World War II, *LST–261* was assigned to the European theater and participated in the invasion of Normandy in June 1944. She was decommissioned on 22 February 1946 and struck from the Navy list on 28 March 1946. On 10 November 1947, she was sold to the Biloxi Boat Wrecking Co., of Biloxi, Miss., for scrapping.

LST–261 earned one battle star for World War II service.

LST–262

LST–262 was laid down on 7 September 1942 at Ambridge, Pa., by the American Bridge Co.; launched on 13 February 1943; sponsored by Mrs. Oscar Seidel; and commissioned on 15 June 1943.

During World War II, *LST–262* was assigned to the European theater and participated in the movement of Convoy UGS–36 in April 1944 and the invasion of Normandy in June 1944. She was decommissioned on 14 January 1946 and struck from the Navy list on 19 June 1946. On 9 December 1947, she was sold to N. Block & Co., of Norfolk, Va., for scrapping.

LST–262 earned two battle stars for World War II service.

LST–263

LST–263 was laid down on 7 September 1942 at Ambridge, Pa., by the American Bridge Co.; launched on 27 February 1943; sponsored by Mrs. Charles G. Baumgartner; and commissioned on 30 June 1943.

During World War II, *LST–263* was assigned to the European theater and participated in Convoy UGS–27 in April 1944 and the invasion of southern France in August and September 1944. She was decommissioned on 29 May 1946 and assigned to the Atlantic Reserve Fleet. On 1 July 1955, the ship was redesignated *Benton County* (LST–263) after nine counties of the United States. She was struck from the Navy list on 1 November 1958.

LST–263 earned two battle stars for World War II service.

LST–264

LST–264 was laid down on 21 September 1942 at Ambridge, Pa., by the American Bridge Co.; launched on 13 March 1943; sponsored by Mrs. James Dunn; and commissioned on 16 July 1943, Lt. R. W. Dale, Jr., USNR, in command.

During World War II, *LST–264* was assigned to the European theater and participated in the invasion of Normandy in June 1944. She was decommissioned on 11 January 1946 and struck from the Navy list on 19 June 1946. On 23 April 1948, she was sold to the Newport News Shipbuilding & Drydock Co., of Newport News, Va., for conversion to non-self-propelled mercantile operation.

LST–264 earned one battle star for World War II service.

LST–265

LST–265 was laid down on 31 October 1942 at Ambridge, Pa., by the American Bridge Co.; launched on 24 April 1943; sponsored by Miss Irene Louise Martin; and commissioned on 27 July 1943, Lt. George F. Sparks, USNR, in command.

During World War II, *LST–265* was assigned to the European theater and participated in the following operations:

Convoy UGS–36—April 1944

Elba and Pianosa landings—June 1944

Invasion of southern France—August and September 1944

LST–265 was decommissioned on 11 December 1945 and struck from the Navy list on 3 January 1946. On

20 February 1948, she was sold to Excello Corp., of New Haven, Conn., for conversion to merchant service.

LST–265 earned three battle stars for World War II service.

LST–266

LST–266 was laid down on 11 November 1942 at Ambridge, Pa., by the American Bridge Co.; launched on 16 May 1943; sponsored by Mrs. Joseph B. Barnwell; and commissioned on 4 August 1943.

During World War II, *LST–266* was assigned to the European theater and participated in Convoy UGS–26 in April 1944 and the invasion of Normandy in June 1944. She was decommissioned on 25 June 1947 and assigned to the Atlantic Reserve Fleet. On 1 July 1955, she was redesignated *Benzie County* (LST–266) after a county in Michigan. The ship was struck from the Navy list on 1 November 1958.

LST–266 earned two battle stars for World War II service.

LST–267

LST–267 was laid down on 21 November 1942 at Ambridge, Pa., by the American Bridge Co.; launched on 6 June 1943; sponsored by Mrs. D. L. See; and commissioned on 9 August 1943.

During World War II, *LST–267* was assigned to the Asiatic-Pacific theater and participated in the following operations:

> Capture and occupation of Saipan—June and July 1944
> Capture and occupation of Tinian—July 1944
> Capture and occupation of southern Palau Islands —September and October 1944
> Lingayen Gulf landing—January 1945
> Assault and occupation of Okinawa Gunto—March through June 1945

Following the war, *LST–267* performed occupation duty in the Far East and saw service in China until January 1946. She returned to the United States and was decommissioned on 25 June 1946 and struck from the Navy list on 31 July that same year. On 24 September 1947, the ship was sold to William E. Skinner for scrapping.

LST–267 earned five battle stars for World War II service.

LST–268

LST–268 was laid down on 26 November 1942 at Ambridge, Pa., by the American Bridge Co.; launched on 18 June 1943; sponsored by Mrs. W. Ward Powell; and commissioned on 19 August 1943.

During World War II, *LST–268* was assigned to the Asiatic-Pacific theater and participated in the following operations:

> Occupation of Kwajalein and Majuro Atolls— February 1944
> Tinian capture and occupation—July 1944
> Capture and occupation of southern Palau Islands —September and October 1944
> Lingayen Gulf landing—January 1945
> Assault and occupation of Okinawa Gunto—March through June 1945

Following the war, *LST–268* was redesignated *LSTH–268* on 15 September 1945, and she performed occupation duty in the Far East until early February 1946. She returned to the United States and was decommissioned on 16 February 1946 and struck from the Navy list on 31 October 1947. On 24 March 1948, she was sold to the Consolidated Shipbuilding Corp., of Morris Heights, N.Y., for scrapping.

LSTH–268 earned five battle stars for World War II service as *LST–268*.

LST–269

LST–269 was laid down on 28 December 1942 at Ambridge, Pa., by the American Bridge Co.; launched on 4 July 1943; sponsored by Mrs. J. J. Graham; and commissioned on 27 August 1943, Lt. F. C. Helm, USNR, in command.

During World War II, *LST–269* was assigned to the Asiatic-Pacific theater and participated in the following operations:

> Hollandia operation—April 1944
> Capture and occupation of Saipan—June and July 1944
> Leyte landings—October 1944
> Nasugbu at Manila Bay—January 1945

Following the war, *LST–269* performed occupation duty in the Far East until early February 1946. She returned to the United States and was decommissioned on 7 February 1946 and struck from the Navy list on 23 December 1947. On 28 May 1948, she was sold to the Bethlehem Steel Co., of Bethlehem, Pa., for scrapping.

LST–269 earned four battle stars for World War II service.

LST–270

LST–270 was laid down on 13 January 1943 at Ambridge, Pa., by the American Bridge Co.; launched on 18 July 1944; sponsored by Mrs. R. D. Seagraves; and commissioned on 8 September 1943, Lt. O. W. Barber in command.

During World War II, *LST–270* was assigned to the Asiatic-Pacific theater and participated in the following operations:

> Occupation of Kwajalein and Majuro Atolls— January and February 1944
> Hollandia operation—April 1944
> Capture and occupation of Guam—July 1944
> Leyte landings—October 1944

LST–270 was sold on 12 May 1950.

LST–270 earned four battle stars for World War II service.

LST–271

LST–271 was laid down on 21 January 1943 at Ambridge, Pa., by the American Bridge Co.; launched on 25 July 1943; sponsored by Mrs. J. F. DeGraaf; and commissioned on 1 September 1943.

During World War II, *LST–271* was assigned to the Asiatic-Pacific theater and participated in the following operations:

> Occupation of Kwajalein and Majuro Atolls— January and February 1944
> Capture and occupation of Saipan—June and July 1944
> Tinian capture and occupation—July 1944
> Capture and occupation of southern Palau Islands— September and October 1944
> Lingayen Gulf landing—January 1945

LST–271 returned to the United States and was decommissioned on 22 April 1946 and struck from the Navy list on 5 June 1946. On 15 April 1948, she was sold to the Basalt Rock Co., Inc., of Napa, Calif., for scrapping.

LST–271 earned five battle stars for World War II service.

LST–272

LST–272 was laid down on 9 February 1943 at Ambridge, Pa., by the American Bridge Co.; launched on 1 August 1943; sponsored by Mrs. J. P. D. Gerrese; and commissioned on 17 Seutember 1943, Lt. Heinrich Heine, USNR, in command.

During World War II, *LST–272* was assigned to the Asiatic-Pacific theater and participated in the following operations:

Occupation of Kwajalein and Majuro Atolls— January and February 1944

Occupation of Eniwetok Atoll—February and March 1944

Capture and occupation of Saipan—June and July 1944

Tinian capture and occupation—July 1944

Capture and occupation of southern Palau Islands —September and October 1944

Lingayen Gulf landing—January 1945

She returned to the United States and was decommissioned on 16 August 1946 and struck from the Navy list on 25 September 1946. On 5 April 1948, she was sold to the Bethlehem Steel Co., of Bethlehem, Pa., for scrapping.

LST–272 earned five battle stars for World War II service.

LST–273

LST–273 was laid down on 24 February 1943 at Ambridge, Pa., by the American Bridge Co.; launched on 8 August 1943; sponsored by Mrs. W. H. McComb; and commissioned on 24 September 1943.

During World War II, *LST–273* was assigned to the Asiatic-Pacific theater and participated in the following operations:

Marshall Islands operation:

(a) Occupation of Kwajalein and Majuro Atolls—January and February 1944

(b) Occupation of Eniwetok Atoll—February 1944

Capture and occupation of Saipan—June and July 1944

Tinian capture and occupation—July 1944

Capture and occupation of southern Palau Islands —September and October 1944

Lingayen Gulf landing—January 1945

Assault and occupation of Okinawa Gunto—April 1945

Following the war, *LST–273* performed occupation duty in the Far East until late October 1945. She returned to the United States and was decommissioned on 12 August 1946 and struck from the Navy list on 8 November 1946. On 3 November 1947, she was sold to the Hugo Neu Steel Products Corp., of New York, N.Y.

LST–273 earned six battle stars for World War II service.

LST–274

LST–274 was laid down on 11 March 1943 at Ambridge, Pa., by the American Bridge Co.; launched on 15 August 1943; sponsored by Mrs. R. F. Salmon; and commissioned on 28 September 1943, Lt. Russell E. Sard, Jr., USNR, in command.

During World War II, *LST–274* was assigned to the Asiatic-Pacific theater and participated in the occupation of Kwajalein and Majuro Atolls in January and February 1944 and the capture and occupation of Saipan in June and July 1944. She was decommissioned on 6 May 1946 and struck from the Navy list on 23 June 1947. On 29 June 1948, she was sold to the Alexander Shipyard, Inc., of New Orleans, La., and converted for merchant service.

LST–274 earned two battle stars for World War II service.

LST–275

LST–275 was laid down on 22 April 1943 at Ambridge, Pa., by the American Bridge Co.; launched on 22 August 1943; sponsored by Mrs. J. N. Walker; and commissioned on 5 October 1943.

During World War II, *LST–275* was assigned to the Asiatic-Pacific theater and participated in the capture and occupation of Saipan in June and August 1944 and the Tinian capture and occupation in July and August 1944. Following the war, *LST–275* performed occupation duty in the Far East until mid-February 1946. She returned to the United States and was decommissioned on 16 August 1946 and struck from the Navy list on 25 September 1946. On 5 April 1948, she was sold to the Bethlehem Steel Co., of Bethlehem, Pa., for scrapping.

LST–275 earned two battle stars for World War II service.

LST–276

LST–276 was laid down on 10 May 1943 at Ambridge, Pa., by the American Bridge Co.; launched on 29 August 1943; sponsored by Mrs. J. S. Ragland; and commissioned on 11 October 1943.

During World War II, *LST–276* was assigned to the Asiatic-Pacific theater and participated in the following operations:

Occupation of Kwajalein and Majuro Atolls—February 1944

Hollandia operation—April 1944

Capture and occupation of Guam—July 1944

Capture and occupation of southern Palau Islands—September and October 1944

Lingayen Gulf landing—January 1945

Following the war, *LST–276* was redesignated *LSTH–276* on 15 September 1945. She performed occupation duty in the Far East until mid-February 1946. The tank landing ship returned to the United States and was transferred to the Military Sea Transportation Service on 31 March 1952 for service as *LST–276* (T-*LST–276*) until she was struck from the Navy list on 10 June 1973 and sold.

LST–276 earned five battle stars for World War II service.

LST–277

LST–277 was laid down on 31 May 1943 at Ambridge, Pa., by the American Bridge Co.; launched on 5 September 1943; sponsored by Mrs. W. D. Guernsey; and commissioned on 24 October 1943.

During World War II, *LST–277* was assigned to the Asiatic-Pacific theater and participated in the following operations:

Occupation of Kwajalein and Majuro Atolls—February 1944

Capture and occupation of Saipan—June 1944

Leyte landings—October 1944

Nasugbu at Manila Bay operation—January 1945

Assault and occupation of Okinawa Gunto—March through June 1945

Following the war, *LST–277* performed occupation duty in the Far East until early February 1946 when she returned to the United States and was decommissioned on 12 February 1946. She served with the Shipping Control Authority, Japan, from 20 May 1949 until 31 March 1952. She was transferred on that date to the Military Sea Transportation Service where she served until struck from the Navy list on 1 February 1973. On 2 February 1973, she was sold to the Chilean Navy which she served as *Commandante Toro* (LST-97).

LST–277 earned five battle stars for World War II service.

LST–278

LST–278 was laid down on 16 June 1943 at Ambridge, Pa., by the American Bridge Co.; launched on 12 September 1943; sponsored by Mrs. R. F. Dickinson; and commissioned on 22 October 1943.

During World War II, *LST–278* was assigned to the Asiatic-Pacific theater and participated in the following operations:

Marianas operation:

    (a) Capture and occupation of Saipan—June and July 1944

    (b) Tinian capture and occupation—July 1944

Capture and occupation of southern Palau Islands—September and October 1944

LST–278 was decommissioned on 22 January 1945 and redesignated *Seaward* (IX–209) (*q.v.*) and recommissioned on 14 February 1945. She served as a barracks and post office at Ulithi until declared in excess of the Navy's needs and destroyed on 16 October 1946. She was struck from the Navy list on 22 May 1947.

LST–278 earned three battle stars for World War II service.

LST–279

LST–279 was laid down on 2 July 1943 at Ambridge, Pa., by the American Bridge Co.; launched on 19 September 1943; sponsored by Miss Marion Ruth Warsack; and commissioned on 25 October 1943, Lt. Charles A. Palm, USNR, in command.

During World War II, *LST–279* was assigned to the European theater and participated in the invasion of Normandy in June 1944. She returned to the United States and was decommissioned on 14 June 1955. On 1 July 1955, she was named *Berkeley County* (LST–279) after counties in South Carolina and West Virginia. The tank landing ship was transferred to Nationalist China on 30 June 1955 as *Chung Chie* (LST–218) and struck from the Navy list on 25 April 1960.

LST–279 earned one battle star for World War II service.

LST–280

LST–280 was laid down on 16 July 1943 at Ambridge, Pa., by the American Bridge Co.; launched on 26 September 1943; sponsored by Miss Lois Johnston; and commissioned on 2 November 1943.

During World War II, *LST–280* was assigned to the European theater and participated in the invasion of Normandy in June 1944. On 26 October 1944, she was transferred to the United Kingdom and returned to United States Navy custody on 11 April 1946. She was decommissioned on 13 April 1946 and struck from the Navy list on 5 June 1946. *LST–280* was sold to Bosey, Philippines, on 5 December 1947.

LST–280 earned one battle star for World War II service.

LST–281

LST–281 was laid down on 25 June 1943 at Ambridge, Pa., by the American Bridge Co.; launched on 30 September 1943; sponsored by Mrs. Mary Richards; and commissioned on 8 November 1943.

During World War II, *LST–281* was assigned to the European theater and participated in the invasion of Normandy in June 1944, and the invasion of southern France in August and September 1944. She was then assigned to the Asiatic-Pacific theater and participated in the assault and occupation of Okinawa Gunto in June 1945.

Following the war, *LST–281* performed occupation duty in the Far East until early February 1946. She returned to the United States and was decommissioned on 9 March 1946 and transferred to the Shipping Control Authority, Japan, on 20 May 1949. She served with the Military Sea Transportation Service as USNS

T–LST–281 from 31 March 1952 until struck from the Navy list on 19 May 1954 and sold.

LST–281 earned three battle stars for World War II service.

LST–282

LST–282 was laid down on 12 July 1943 at Ambridge, Pa., by the American Bridge Co.; launched on 3 October 1943; sponsored by Mrs. Carl B. Ihli; and commissioned on 12 November 1943.

During World War II, *LST–282* was assigned to the European theater and participated in the invasion of Normandy in June 1944 and the invasion of southern France in August 1944. On 15 August 1944, *LST–282* was sunk by a German radio-controlled bomb off southern France and struck from the Navy list on 16 September 1944.

LST–282 earned two battle stars for World War II service.

LST–283

LST–283 was laid down on 2 August 1943 at Ambridge, Pa., by the American Bridge Co.; launched on 10 October 1943; sponsored by Mrs. C. W. McNamee; and commissioned on 18 November 1943.

During World War II, *LST–283* was assigned to the European theater and participated in the invasion of Normandy in June 1944 and the invasion of southern France in August and September 1944. She performed occupation duty in the Far East between September and November 1945.

Upon her return to the United States, the ship was decommissioned on 13 June 1946 and struck from the Navy list on 22 January 1947. On 25 March 1947, she was sold to Northrup H. Castle, of Honolulu, Hawaii, for conversion to merchant service. She was purchased by Peru on 21 December 1951 for service in the Peruvian Navy as *Chimbote* (LST–34).

LST–283 earned two battle stars for World War II service.

LST–284

LST–284 was laid down on 9 August 1943 at Ambridge, Pa., by the American Bridge Co.; launched on 17 October 1943; sponsored by Mrs. R. R. Goll; and commissioned on 25 November 1943, Ensign W. H. Pennington in command.

During World War II, *LST–284* was assigned to the European theater and participated in the invasion of Normandy in June 1944 and the invasion of southern France in August and September 1944. She was then assigned to the Asiatic-Pacific theater and participated in the assault and occupation of Okinawa Gunto in May and June 1945. She performed occupation duty in the Far East until early November 1945.

Upon her return to the United States, the ship was decommissioned on 13 March 1946 and struck from the Navy list on 19 June 1946. On 11 December 1947, she was sold to the Southern Shipwrecking Co., of New Orleans, La., for scrapping.

LST–284 earned three battle stars for World War II service.

LST–285

LST–285 was laid down on 16 August 1943 at Ambridge, Pa., by the American Bridge Co.; launched on 24 October 1943; sponsored by Mrs. R. A. Shaw; and commissioned on 13 December 1943.

During World War II, *LST–285* was assigned to the European theater and participated in the invasion of

LST–788, –760, –724, and *LSM–264* land supplies through the debris of an assault beach on Iwo Jima, February 1945. The ships keep their propellers turning over to hold themselves in position. In the water are a DUKW and an LCPR; in the surf and on the beach are LVT's, DUKW's, trucks, bulldozers, and a crawler crane. Trucks at the right are towing 105mm howitzers inland from LST–724. A successful amphibious operation is the combined work of many men, using many types of ships, weapons, and vehicles.

Normandy in June 1944 and the invasion of southern France in August and September 1944.

Upon her return to the United States, the ship was decommissioned on 27 June 1947 and struck from the Navy list on 1 August 1947. On 26 March 1948, she was sold to the Kaiser Co., Inc., of Seattle, Wash., for scrapping.

LST–285 earned two battle stars for World War II service.

LST–286

LST–286 was laid down on 23 August 1943 at Ambridge, Pa., by the American Bridge Co.; launched on 27 October 1943; sponsored by Mrs. Lois Ethel Leseman; and commissioned on 11 December 1943.

During World War II, *LST–286* was assigned to the European theater and participated in the invasion of Normandy in June 1944 and the invasion of southern France in August and September 1944. She performed occupation duty in the Far East in September, November, and December 1945.

Upon her return to the United States, the ship was decommissioned on 26 March 1946 and struck from the Navy list on 8 May 1946. On 15 April 1948, she was sold to the Bethlehem Steel Co., of Bethlehem, Pa., for scrapping.

LST–286 earned two battle stars for World War II service.

LST–287

LST–287 was laid down on 30 August 1943 at Ambridge, Pa., by the American Bridge Co.; launched on 31 October 1943; sponsored by Mrs. Agnes Johnston; and commissioned on 15 December 1943, Lt. Frank P. Eldredge, USNR, in command.

During World War II, *LST–287* was assigned to the European theater and participated in the invasion of Normandy in June 1944. *LST–287* was transferred to the Military Sea Transportation Service on 29 May 1951 where she operated as USNS *LST–287*. USNS *LST–287* was later transferred to the Philippine Navy on 13 September 1976.

LST–287 earned one battle star for World War II service.

LST–288

LST–288 was laid down on 6 September 1943 at Ambridge, Pa., by the American Bridge Co.; launched on 7 November 1943; sponsored by Miss Virginia M. Plofchan; and commissioned on 20 December 1943.

During World War II, *LST-288* was assigned to the European theater and participated in the invasion of Normandy in June 1944 and the invasion of southern France in August and September 1944. She was then assigned to the Asiatic-Pacific theater and participated in the assault and occupation of Okinawa Gunto in May and June 1945. She performed occupation duty in the Far East in late 1945 and early 1946.

Upon her return to the United States, the ship was decommissioned on 6 March 1946. She served with the Shipping Control Authority, Japan, from 20 May 1949 to 14 June 1950. On 1 July 1955, the tank landing ship was redesignated *Berkshire County* (LST-288) after a county in Massachusetts. She was transferred to Korea, on loan, on 5 March 1956 where she served as *Ke Bong* (LST-810).

LST-288 earned three battle stars for World War II service.

LST-289

LST-289 was laid down on 14 September 1943 at Ambridge, Pa., by the American Bridge Co.; launched on 21 November 1943; sponsored by Mrs. Raymond Clapper; and commissioned on 31 December 1943, Lt. Harry A. Mettler, USNR, in command.

LST-289 was transferred to the United Kingdom on 9 December 1944 and returned to United States Navy custody on 12 October 1946. She was struck from the Navy list on 15 October 1946 and sold to the Netherlands as *Fendracht* on 30 January 1947 where she was converted for merchant service in 1956.

LST-290

LST-290 was laid down on 22 September 1943 at Ambridge, Pa., by the American Bridge Co.; launched on 5 December 1943; sponsored by Mrs. C. S. Garner; and commissioned on 10 January 1944.

During World War II, *LST-290* was assigned to the European theater and participated in the invasion of Normandy in June 1944.

Upon her return to the United States, the ship was decommissioned on 15 November 1945 and struck from the Navy list on 28 November 1945. On 23 December 1946, she was sold to Conlon and Tendler for conversion to merchant service.

LST-290 earned one battle star for World War II service.

LST-291

LST-291 was laid down on 25 September 1943 at Ambridge, Pa., by the American Bridge Co.; launched on 14 November 1943; sponsored by Mrs. John A. Parfitt; and commissioned on 22 December 1943, Ensign A. G. McNair in command.

During World War II, *LST-291* was assigned to the European theater and participated in the invasion of Normandy in June 1944. Upon her return to the United States, the ship was decommissioned on 18 June 1947 and struck from the Navy list on 19 May 1954. She was sunk as a target in July 1954.

LST-291 earned one battle star for World War II service.

LST-292

LST-292 was laid down on 30 September 1943 at Ambridge, Pa., by the American Bridge Co.; launched on 28 November 1943; sponsored by Mrs. Stuart Brown, Jr.; and commissioned on 5 January 1944.

During World War II, *LST-292* was assigned to the European theater and participated in the invasion of Normandy in June 1944. Upon her return to the United States, the ship was decommissioned on 25 January 1946 and struck from the Navy list on 12 April 1946. On 21 January 1948, she was sold to Hughes Bros., New York, N.Y., for scrapping.

LST-292 earned one battle star for World War II service.

LST-293

LST-293 was laid down on 5 October 1943 at Ambridge, Pa., by the American Bridge Co.; launched on 12 December 1943; sponsored by Mrs. R. E. Mason; and commissioned on 17 January 1944.

During World War II, *LST-293* was assigned to the European theater and participated in the invasion of Normandy in June 1944.

Upon her return to the United States, the ship was decommissioned on 3 December 1945 and struck from the Navy list on 19 December 1945. On 1 June 1949, she was sold to James Hughes, Inc., New York, N.Y., for scrapping.

LST-293 earned one battle star for World War II service.

LST-294

LST-294 was laid down on 12 October 1943 at Ambridge, Pa., by the American Bridge Co.; launched on 15 December 1943; sponsored by Mrs. J. S. Sohn; and commissioned on 20 January 1944, Ensign Edward J. Cantelope, USNR, in command.

During World War II, *LST-294* was assigned to the European theater and participated in the invasion of Normandy in June 1944.

Upon her return to the United States, the ship was decommissioned on 18 December 1945 and struck from the Navy list on 8 January 1946. On 13 October 1947, she was sold to Luria Bros. & Co., of Philadelphia, Pa.

LST-294 earned one battle star for World War II service.

LST-295

LST-295 was laid down on 19 October 1943 at Ambridge, Pa., by the American Bridge Co.; launched on 24 December 1943; sponsored by Miss Virginia Helen Valenta; and commissioned on 7 February 1944.

During World War II, *LST-295* was assigned to the European theater and participated in the invasion of Normandy in June 1944.

Upon returning to the United States, the ship was decommissioned on 28 December 1945 and struck from the Navy list on 12 April 1946. On 12 September 1947, she was sold to C. W. Edwards for conversion to merchant service.

LST-295 earned one battle star for World War II service.

LST-296 through LST-300

LST-296 through *LST-300* contracts were cancelled on 16 September 1942.

LST-301

LST-301 was laid down on 26 June 1942 at the Boston Navy Yard; launched on 15 September 1942; sponsored by Mrs. Margaret A. Caruso; and commissioned on 1 November 1942.

LST-301 performed no active service with the United States Navy. She was transferred to the United Kingdom on 6 November 1942 and returned to United States Navy custody on 20 March 1946. *LST-301* was transferred to the War Shipping Administration for disposition and struck from the Navy list in December 1947.

LST–302

LST–302 was laid down on 27 June 1942 at the Boston Navy Yard; launched on 15 September 1942; sponsored by Mrs. Elizabeth D. Walsh; and commissioned on 10 November 1942.

LST–302 was transferred to the United Kingdom on 14 November 1942 and returned to United States Navy custody on 5 January 1946. On 20 March 1946, she was struck from the Navy list and sold to Northern Metals Co., Philadelphia, Pa., on 11 December 1947 for scrapping.

LST–303

LST–303 was laid down on 3 July 1942 at the Boston Navy Yard; launched on 21 September 1942; sponsored by Mrs. Myrtle R. Doucette; and commissioned on 20 November 1942.

LST–303 was transferred to the United Kingdom on 21 November 1942 and returned to United States Navy custody on 1 June 1946. On 3 July 1946, she was struck from the Navy list and sold to Bosey, Philippines, on 5 December 1947.

LST–304

LST–304 was laid down on 3 July 1942 at the Boston Navy Yard; launched on 21 September 1942; sponsored by Mrs. Justine F. Dinn; and commissioned on 29 November 1942.

LST–304 was transferred to the United Kingdom on 30 November 1942 and returned to United States Navy custody on 29 November 1946. On 1 August 1947, she was struck from the Navy list and sold to Tung Hwa Trading Co., Singapore, on 7 October 1947 for conversion for merchant service.

LST–305

LST–305 was laid down on 24 July 1942 at the Boston Navy Yard; launched on 10 October 1942; sponsored by Miss Lillian R. Earley; and commissioned on 6 December 1942.

LST–305 was transferred to the United Kingdom on 7 December 1942. She was sunk by an Axis submarine off Anzio, Italy, on 20 February 1944 and struck from the Navy list on 16 May 1944.

LST–306

LST–306 was laid down on 24 July 1942 at the Boston Navy Yard; launched on 10 October 1942; sponsored by Mrs. Caroline De Simone; and commissioned on 11 December 1942, Lt. B. J. Bartram, USNR, in command.

During World War II, *LST–306* was assigned to the European theater and participated in the following operations:

  Sicilian occupation—July 1943
  Salerno landings—September 1943
  Invasion of Normandy—June 1944

Upon her return to the United States, the ship was decommissioned on 13 June 1946. She was redesignated *Bernalillo County* (LST–306) after a county in New Mexico on 1 July 1955 and struck from the Navy list on 1 February 1959. On 22 October 1959, she was sold to Ships, Inc., of Miami, Fla.

LST–306 earned three battle stars for World War II service.

LST–307

LST–307 was laid down on 15 September 1942 at the Boston Navy Yard; launched on 9 November 1942; sponsored by Miss Lauretta Watts; and commissioned on 23 December 1942, Lt. James B. Markham in command.

During World War II, *LST–307* was assigned to the European theater and participated in the following operations:

  Sicilian occupation—July 1943
  Salerno landings—September 1943
  Invasion of Normandy—June 1944

Following the war, *LST–307* performed occupation duty in the Far East until early March 1946. Upon her return to the United States, the ship was decommissioned on 13 June 1946 and struck from the Navy list on 31 July 1946. On 30 March 1948, she was sold to Kaiser Co., Inc., of Seattle, Wash., for scrapping.

LST–307 earned three battle stars for World War II service.

LST–308

LST–308 was laid down on 15 September 1942 at the Boston Navy Yard; launched on 9 November 1942; sponsored by Mrs. Elizabeth A. Haggerty; and commissioned on 2 January 1943.

During World War II, *LST–308* was assigned to the European theater and participated in the following operations:

  Sicilian occupation—July 1943
  Salerno landings—September 1943
  Invasion of Normandy—June 1944

Following the war, *LST–308* performed occupation duty in the Far East until late September 1946 and service in China in July and August 1946. Upon her return to the United States, she was decommissioned on 17 October 1946. On 5 December 1947, the ship was transferred to the State Department for disposition.

LST–308 earned three battle stars for World War II service.

LST–309

LST–309 was laid down on 22 September 1942 at the Boston Navy Yard; launched on 23 November 1942; sponsored by Miss Mildred M. Leydon; and commissioned on 11 January 1943, Lt. C. A. Lanborn, USNR, in command.

During World War II, *LST–309* was assigned to the European theater and participated in the following operations:

  Sicilian occupation—July 1943
  Salerno landings—September 1943
  Invasion of Normandy—June 1944

Following the war, *LST–309* performed occupation duty in the Far East until early November 1945.

Upon her return to the United States, the ship was decommissioned on 19 June 1946 and struck from the Navy list on 23 June 1947. On 1 June 1948, she was sold to the Humble Oil & Refining Co., Houston, Tex., and converted for merchant service.

LST–309 earned three battle stars for World War II service.

LST–310

LST–310 was laid down on 22 September 1942 at the Boston Navy Yard; launched on 23 November 1942; sponsored by Mrs. Inga M. Gustavson; and commissioned on 20 January 1943, Lt. W. P. Lawless, USNR, in command.

During World War II, *LST–310* was assigned to the European theater of war and participated in the Sicilian occupation in July 1943 and the invasion of Normandy in June 1944. Upon her return to the United States, she was decommissioned on 16 May 1945 and struck from the Navy list on 12 March 1946. On 28 January 1947, she was sold to the Boston Metals Co., of Baltimore, Md., for conversion to merchant service.

LST–310 earned two battle stars for World War II service.

LST–311

LST–311 was laid down on 7 September 1942 at the New York Navy Yard; launched on 30 December 1942; sponsored by Miss Marie L. Paternoster; and commissioned on 11 January 1943.

During World War II, *LST–311* was assigned to the European theater and participated in the following operations:

    Sicilian occupation—July 1943
    Salerno landings—September 1943
    Invasion of Normandy—June 1944

On 20 November 1944, *LST–311* was transferred to the United Kingdom and returned to United States Navy custody on 11 April 1946 and was decommissioned. She was struck from the Navy list on 5 June 1946 and sold to an unknown buyer on 5 December that same year. She was resold at a later date to T. Y. Fong.

LST–311 earned three battle stars for World War II service.

LST–312

LST–312 was laid down on 7 September 1942 at the New York Navy Yard; launched on 30 December 1942; sponsored by Mrs. Mary E. Storin; and commissioned on 9 January 1943, Lt. Charles L. Haslup, USNR, in command.

During World War II, *LST–312* was assigned to the European theater and participated in the following operations:

    Sicilian occupation—July 1943
    Salerno landings—September 1943
    Invasion of Normandy—June 1944

Upon her return to the United States, the ship was decommissioned on 12 July 1946 and struck from the Navy list on 15 August 1946. On 13 December 1947, she was sold to James A. Hughes, New York, N.Y., for scrapping.

LST–312 earned three battle stars for World War II service.

LST–313

LST–313 was laid down on 7 September 1942 at the New York Navy Yard; launched on 30 December 1942; sponsored by Mrs. Mary E. McCabe; and commissioned on 13 January 1943.

During World War II, *LST–313* was assigned to the European theater and participated in the Sicilian occupation in July 1943. The ship was sunk on 10 July 1943 off Gela, Sicily, by German aircraft. She was struck from the Navy list on 28 July 1943.

LST–313 earned one battle star for World War II service.

LST–314

LST–314 was laid down on 7 September 1942 at the New York Navy Yard; launched on 30 December 1942; sponsored by Mrs. Gertrude F. Holmes; and commissioned on 15 January 1943.

During World War II, *LST–314* was assigned to the European theater and participated in the following operations:

    Sicilian occupation—July 1943
    Salerno landings—September 1943
    Invasion of Normandy—June 1944

The tank landing ship was sunk by an enemy torpedo off Normandy on 9 June 1944. On 22 August 1944, she was struck from the Navy list.

LST–314 earned three battle stars for World War II service.

LST–315

LST–315 was laid down on 15 October 1942 at the New York Navy Yard; launched on 28 January 1943; sponsored by Miss Helen Clair Leuteritz; and commissioned on 3 February 1943.

During World War II, *LST–315* was assigned to the European theater and participated in the following operations:

    Sicilian occupation—July and August 1943
    Salerno landings—September 1943
    Invasion of Normandy—June 1944

The tank landing ship was transferred to the United Kingdom on 9 December 1944 and returned to United States Navy custody on 16 March 1946 and decommissioned. She was struck from the Navy list on 26 February 1946 and sold, on 5 December 1947, to Bosey, Philippines.

LST–315 earned three battle stars for World War II service.

LST–316

LST–316 was laid down on 15 October 1942 at the New York Navy Yard; launched on 28 January 1943; sponsored by Mrs. Pearl Magdalene Frick; and commissioned on 3 February 1943.

During World War II, *LST–316* was assigned to the European theater and participated in the following operations:

    Sicilian occupation—July 1943
    Salerno landings—September 1943
    Invasion of Normandy—June 1944

Upon her return to the United States, she was decommissioned on 24 May 1945 and struck from the Navy list on 12 March 1946. On 23 December 1946, she was sold to James Hughes, Inc., New York, N.Y., for conversion to marchant service.

LST–316 earned three battle stars for World War II service.

LST–317

LST–317 was laid down on 15 October 1942 at the New York Navy Yard; launched on 28 January 1943; sponsored by Mrs. Florence Whitehouse; and commissioned on 6 February 1943.

During World War II, *LST–317* was assigned to the European theater and participated in the following operations:

    Sicilian occupation—July 1943
    Salerno landings—September 1943
    Invasion of Normandy—June 1944

Upon her return to the United States, *LST–317* was decommissioned on 18 May 1945 and struck from the Navy list on 12 March 1946. On 22 January 1947, the tank landing ship was sold to A. G. Schoonmaker.

LST–317 earned three battle stars for World War II service.

LST–318

LST–318 was laid down on 15 October 1942 at the New York Navy Yard; launched on 28 January 1943; sponsored by Mrs. Emma V. Umstead; and commissioned on 8 February 1943.

During World War II, *LST–318* was assigned to the European theater and participated in the Sicilian occupation in July and August 1943. During this occupation duty, she was sunk, on 9 August 1943, by enemy aircraft off Coronia, Sicily. She was struck from the Navy list on 20 October 1943.

LST–318 earned one battle star for World War II service.

LST–319

LST–319 was laid down on 10 August 1942 at the Philadelphia Navy Yard; launched on 5 November 1942; and sponsored by Mrs. E. F. Stutzke.

On 15 December 1942, LST–319 was transferred to the United Kingdom and returned to United States Navy custody on 17 December 1945. She was struck from the Navy list on 21 January 1946 and sold to Ships & Power Equipment Corp., Barber, N.J., on 9 March 1948 and converted for merchant service.

LST–320

LST–320 was laid down on 10 August 1942 at the Philadelphia Navy Yard; launched on 5 November 1942; and sponsored by Miss Edith Elliott.

On 31 December 1942, LST–320 was transferred to the United Kingdom and returned to United States Navy custody on 23 April 1946. She was struck from the Navy list on 19 June 1946. On 4 October 1947, she was sold to the Southern Trading Co., Wilmington, Del., for scrapping.

LST–321

LST–321 was laid down on 10 August 1942 at the Philadelphia Navy Yard; launched on 5 November 1942; and sponsored by Miss Catherine Winkler.

On 31 December 1942, LST–321 was transferred to the United Kingdom and returned to United States Navy custody on 11 April 1946. The tank landing ship was struck from the Navy list on 10 June 1947 and sold to Bosey, Philippines, on 5 November 1947.

LST–322

LST–322 was laid down on 10 August 1942 at the Philadelphia Navy Yard; launched on 5 November 1942; and sponsored by Miss Nellie F. Ward.

On 9 January 1943, LST–322 was transferred to the United Kingdom and returned to United States Navy custody on 10 July 1946. On 29 October 1946, the tank landing ship was struck from the Navy list and sold to the government of Greece on 6 January 1947.

LST–323

LST–323 was laid down on 10 August 1942 at the Philadelphia Navy Yard; launched on 5 November 1942; and sponsored by Mrs. Raymond McDowell.

On 18 January 1943, LST–323 was transferred to the United Kingdom and returned to United States Navy custody and commissioned on 26 January 1946. She was decommissioned on 5 June 1946 and struck from the Navy list on 19 June 1946. On 9 October 1947, the tank landing ship was sold to Luria Bros. & Co., of Philadelphia, Pa., for scrapping.

LST–324

LST–324 was laid down on 10 August 1942 at the Philadelphia Navy Yard; launched on 5 November 1942; and sponsored by Mrs. James A. Boyle.

On 23 January 1943, LST–324 was transferred to the United Kingdom and returned to United States Navy custody on 1 June 1946. The tank landing ship was struck from the Navy list on 3 July 1946 and sold to Bosey, Philippines, on 13 February 1948.

LST–325

LST–325 was laid down on 10 August 1942 at the Philadelphia Navy Yard; launched on 27 October 1942; sponsored by Mrs. G. C. Wells; and commissioned on 1 February 1943, Lt. Ira Ehrensall, USNR, in command.

During World War II, LST–325 was assigned to the European theater and participated in the Sicilian occupation in July 1943 and the invasion of Normandy in June 1944. She was decommissioned on 2 July 1946 and struck from the Navy list on 1 September 1961. On 1 September 1964, LST–325 was transferred to Greece as grant aid where she remained active as Syros (L–144).

LST–325 earned two battle stars for World War II service.

LST–326

LST–326 was laid down on 12 November 1942 at the Philadelphia Navy Yard; launched on 11 February 1943; sponsored by Miss Mildred E. Kelly; and commissioned on 26 February 1943.

During World War II, LST–326 was assigned to the European theater and participated in the Sicilian occupation in July 1943, the Anzio-Nettuno advanced landings in January and February 1944, and the invasion of Normandy in June 1944.

On 9 December 1944, LST–326 was transferred to the United Kingdom and returned to United States Navy custody on 25 February 1946. She was decommissioned the following day and struck from the Navy list. She was sold to France on 5 April 1946.

LST–326 earned three battle stars for World War II service.

LST–327

LST–327 was laid down on 12 November 1942 at the Philadelphia Navy Yard; launched on 11 February 1943; sponsored by Miss Helen B. Higgins; and commissioned on 5 March 1943.

During World War II, LST–327 was assigned to the European theater and participated in the following operations:

Tunisian operations—July 1943
Sicilian occupation—July 1943
Salerno landings—September 1943
Anzio-Nettuno advanced landings — January through March 1944
Normandy invasion—June 1944

On 27 August 1944, LST–327 was severely damaged by an enemy mine in the English Channel. Upon her return to the United States, she was decommissioned on 19 November 1945 and struck from the Navy list on 5 December 1945. The tank landing ship was sold to the Sun Shipbuilding & Drydock Co., Chester, Pa., on 15 September 1948.

LST–327 earned five battle stars for World War II service.

LST–328

LST–328 was redesignated ARB-2 and named Oceanus (q.v.) on 25 January 1943.

LST–329

LST–329 was redesignated ARB-1 and named Aristaeus (q.v.) on 25 January 1943.

LST–330

LST–330 was redesignated AGP-4 and named Portunus (q.v.) on 25 January 1943.

LST–331

LST–331 was laid down on 12 November 1942 at the

Philadelphia Navy Yard; launched on 11 February 1943; sponsored by Miss Ruth Stout; and commissioned on 11 March 1943.

During World War II, *LST–331* was assigned to the European theater and participated in the following operations:

Tunisian operations—July 1943
Sicilian occupation—July 1943
Salerno landings—September 1943
Invasion of Normandy—June 1944

She was transferred to the United Kingdom on 20 November 1944 and returned to United States Navy custody and decommissioned on 16 March 1946. *LST–331* was struck from the Navy list on 26 February 1946 and sold to Bosey, Philippines, on 13 February 1948.

LST–331 earned four battle stars for World War II service.

LST–332

LST–332 was laid down on 29 October 1942 at the Philadelphia Navy Yard; launched on 24 December 1942; sponsored by Mrs. G. W. Henderson; and commissioned on 6 February 1943.

During World War II, *LST–332* was assigned to the European theater and participated in the following operations:

Sicilian occupation—July 1943
Salerno landings—September 1943
Invasion of Normandy—June 1944

LST–332 was decommissioned on 22 May 1945 and struck from the Navy list on 12 March 1946. On 17 October 1946, the tank landing ship was sold to the Suwannee Steamship Co., Charleston, S.C., for conversion to merchant service.

LST–332 earned three battle stars for World War II service.

LST–333

LST–333 was laid down on 17 July 1942 at the Norfolk Navy Yard; launched on 15 October 1942; sponsored by Mrs. Cornelius A. Kneeburg; and commissioned on 20 November 1942. She was torpedoed off Dellys, Algeria, on 22 June 1943 and struck from the Navy list on 6 July 1943.

LST–334

LST–334 was laid down on 17 July 1942 at the Norfolk Navy Yard; launched on 15 October 1942; sponsored by Mrs. W. M. Thompson; and commissioned on 29 November 1942, Lt. George Alyward, USNR, in command.

During World War II, *LST–334* was assigned to the Asiatic-Pacific theater and participated in the following operations:

Vella Lavella occupation—October 1943
Occupation and defense of Cape Torokina—November and December 1943
Capture and occupation of Guam—July and August 1944
Assault and occupation of Okinawa Gunto—April through June 1945

Following the war, *LST–334* performed occupation duty in the Far East until mid-October 1945. Upon her return to the United States, the ship was decommissioned on 24 April 1946 and struck from the Navy list on 5 June 1946. On 22 April 1948, she was sold to the Bethlehem Steel Co., Bethlehem, Pa., for scrapping.

LST–334 earned four battle stars and the Navy Unit Commendation for World War II service.

LST–335

LST–335 was laid down on 17 July 1942 at the Norfolk Navy Yard; launched on 15 October 1942; spon-

LST's took their share of the enemy's attention during World War II. *LST–599*'s crew fights flames off Okinawa on 3 April 1945 after a *kamikaze* exploded on deck. Although prophets of doom insisted that LST really meant Large, Slow Target, the type proved remarkably hardy. Of 1,117 LST's completed in Britain and the United States, 53 were lost to all causes during 1942–45. Twenty-six American LST's were lost to enemy action, and 13 more to the "perils of the sea."

sored by Mrs. B. V. McCandlish; and commissioned on 6 December 1942.

During World War II, *LST–335* was assigned to the European theater and participated in the following operations:

Sicilian occupation—July 1943
Salerno landings—September 1943
Invasion of Normandy—June 1944

Upon her return to the United States, the ship was decommissioned on 22 December 1945 and struck from the Navy list on 8 January 1946. She was sold to James A. Hughes, New York, N.Y., on 1 December 1947, for scrapping.

LST–335 earned three battle stars for World War II service.

LST–336

LST–336 was laid down on 17 July 1942 at the Norfolk Navy Yard; launched on 15 October 1942; sponsored by Mrs. Thomas B. Richey; and commissioned on 11 December 1942.

During World War II, *LST–336* was assigned to the European theater and participated in the following operations:

Sicilian occupation—July 1943
Salerno landings—September 1943
Invasion of Normandy—June 1944

She was decommissioned and transferred to the United Kingdom on 27 November 1944 and returned to United States Navy custody on 7 March 1946. *LST–336* was struck from the Navy list on 5 June 1946. On 22 October 1947, she was sold to Luria Bros. & Co., Inc., of Philadelphia, Pa.

LST–336 earned three battle stars for World War II service.

LST–337

LST–337 was laid down on 17 July 1942 at the Norfolk Navy Yard; launched on 8 November 1942; sponsored by Mrs. W. McL. Hague; and commissioned on 16 December 1942.

During World War II, *LST–337* was assigned to the European theater and participated in the following operations:

Sicilian occupation—July 1943
Salerno landings—September 1943
Invasion of Normandy—June 1944

LST–337 was transferred to the United Kingdom on 2 December 1944. She was returned to United States Navy custody and decommissioned on 16 March 1946. The tank landing ship was struck from the Navy list on 17 April 1946 and sold to Bosey, Philippines, on 5 December 1947.

LST–337 earned three battle stars for World War II service.

LST–338

LST–338 was laid down on 17 July 1942 at the Norfolk Navy Yard; launched on 8 November 1942; sponsored by Mrs. R. I. Coleman; and commissioned on 20 December 1942, Lt. D. A. Stratton, USNR, in command.

During World War II, *LST–338* was assigned to the European theater and participated in the following operations:

Sicilian occupation—July 1943
Salerno landings—September 1943
Invasion of Normany—June 1944

Upon returning to the United States, the tank landing ship was decommissioned on 6 May 1946 and struck from the Navy list on 23 June 1947. On 3 December 1947, she was sold to the Southern Trading Co., Philadelphia, Pa., for conversion to merchant service.

LST–338 earned three battle stars for World War II service.

LST–339

LST–339 was laid down on 17 July 1942 at the Norfolk Navy Yard; launched on 8 November 1942; sponsored by Mrs. F. B. Britt; and commissioned on 23 December 1942, Lt. John H. Fulweiler, USNR, in command.

During World War II, *LST–339* was assigned to the Asiatic-Pacific theater and participated in the following operations:

Consolidation of southern Solomons—June 1943
New Georgia Group operation:
(a) New Georgia-Rendova-Vangunu occupation—June and July 1943
(b) Vella Lavella occupation—August 1943
Occupation and defense of Cape Torokina—November 1943
Hollandia operation—April 1944
Western New Guinea operations:
(a) Biak Island operation—May and June 1944
(b) Noemfoor Island operation—June and July 1944
(c) Morotai landings—September 1944

Following the war, *LST–339* performed occupation duty in the Far East until mid-November 1945. Upon her return to the United States, the ship was decommissioned on 13 May 1946 and struck from the Navy list on 23 June 1947. On 16 October 1947, she was sold to the New Orleans Shipwrecking Corp., Chicago, Ill., for scrapping.

LST–339 earned four battle stars and the Navy Unit Commendation for World War II service.

LST–340

LST–340 was laid down on 17 July 1942 at the Norfolk Navy Yard; launched on 8 November 1942; sponsored by Mrs. A. W. Raab; and commissioned on 26 December 1942, Lt. William Villella in command.

During World War II, *LST–340* was assigned to the Asiatic-Pacific theater and participated in the following operations:

Consolidation of southern Solomons—June 1943
Capture and occupation of Saipan—June through August 1944
Tinian capture and occupation—July through August 1944

On 20 October 1944, she was redesignated IX–196 and named *Spark* (q.v.). The ship was decommissioned on 24 October 1944 and struck from the Navy list on 1 September 1945.

Spark earned three battle stars and the Navy Unit Commendation for service in World War II as *LST–340*.

LST–341

LST–341 was laid down on 21 August 1942 at the Norfolk Navy Yard; launched on 8 November 1942; sponsored by Miss Elizabeth R. Bisset; and commissioned on 28 December 1942.

During World War II, *LST–341* was assigned to the Asiatic-Pacific theater and participated in the following operations:

New Georgia Group operation:
(a) New Georgia-Rendova-Vangunu occupation—June and July 1943
(b) Vella Lavella occupation—August 1943
Occupation and defense of Cape Torokina—November 1943
Marianas operation:
(a) Capture and occupation of Saipan—June and July 1944
(b) Capture and occupation of Guam—July and August 1944
Leyte landings—October and November 1944

Following the war, *LST–341* performed occupation duty in the Far East in September and October 1945.

Upon her return to the United States, the ship was decommissioned on 14 March 1946 and struck from the Navy list on 12 April 1946. On 12 September 1946, she was sold to the Construction Power & Merchandising Co., of Brooklyn, N.Y., for conversion to merchant service.

LST–341 earned four battle stars and the Navy Unit Commendation for World War II service.

LST–342

LST–342 was laid down on 21 August 1942 at the Norfolk Navy Yard; launched on 8 November 1942; sponsored by Mrs. Philip H. Ryan; and commissioned on 31 December 1942.

During World War II, *LST–342* was assigned to the Asiatic-Pacific theater and participated in the New Georgia-Rendova-Vangunu occupation in July 1943. She was sunk by a Japanese torpedo off the Solomon Islands on 18 July 1943 and struck from the Navy list on 28 July 1943.

LST–342 earned one battle star and the Navy Unit Commendation for World War II service.

LST–343

LST–343 was laid down on 18 October 1942 at the Norfolk Navy Yard; launched on 15 December 1942; and commissioned on 9 January 1943, Lt. H. H. Rightmeyer in command.

During World War II, *LST–343* was assigned to the Asiatic-Pacific theater and participated in the following operations:

Consolidation of southern Solomons—June 1943
New Georgia-Rendova-Vangunu occupation—July 1943
Occupation and defense of Cape Torokina—December 1943
Capture and occupation of Guam—July and August 1944
Assault and occupation of Okinawa Gunto—April 1945

Following the war, *LST–343* performed occupation duty in the Far East until mid-January 1946. Upon her return to the United States, the ship was decommissioned on 27 January 1946. She was transferred to the United States Army Military Government in Korea on 21 February 1947 as a sale and struck from the Navy list on 5 March 1947.

LST–343 earned five battle stars and the Navy Unit Commendation for World War II service.

LST–344

LST–344 was laid down on 18 October 1942 at the Norfolk Navy Yard; launched on 15 December 1942; sponsored by Mrs. H. H. Ward; and commissioned on 14 January 1943, Lt. Maurice G. Jackson, USNR, in command.

During World War II, *LST–344* was assigned to the European theater and participated in the following operations:

Sicilian occupation—July 1943
Salerno landings—September 1943
Invasion of Normandy—June 1944

On 1 July 1955, she was named *Blanco County* (LST–344) after a county in south central Texas. The tank landing ship was decommissioned on 3 October 1969 and struck from the Navy list on 15 September 1974. She was sold for scrap.

LST–344 earned three battle stars for World War II service.

LST–345

LST–345 was laid down on 17 October 1942 at the Norfolk Navy Yard; launched on 15 December 1942;

sponsored by Mrs. John B. Brown; and commissioned on 21 January 1943.

During World War II, *LST–345* was assigned to the European theater and participated in the following operations:

Sicilian occupation—July 1943
Salerno landings—September 1943
Invasion of Normandy—June 1944

Following the war, *LST–345* was decommissioned on 5 December 1945 and struck from the Navy list on 3 January 1946. On 23 March 1948, she was sold to the Ships & Power Equipment Co., Barber, N.J., and scrapped.

LST–345 earned three battle stars for World War II service.

LST–346

LST–346 was laid down on 17 October 1942 at the Norfolk Navy Yard; launched on 15 December 1942; sponsored by Mrs. Felix X. Gygax, Jr.; and commissioned on 25 January 1943.

During World War II, *LST–346* was assigned to the European theater and participated in the following operations:

Sicilian occupation—July 1943
Salerno landings—September 1943
Invasion of Normany—June 1944

On 20 November 1944, she was transferred to the United Kingdom and returned to United States Navy custody on 2 May 1946. She was decommissioned on 4 May 1946 and struck from the Navy list on 19 June 1946. *LST–346* was sold to Bosey, Philippines, on 5 December 1947.

LST–346 earned three battle stars for World War II service.

LST–347

LST–347 was laid down on 10 November 1942 at the Norfolk Navy Yard; launched on 7 February 1943; sponsored by Mrs. J. M. Farrin; and commissioned on 7 February 1943.

During World War II, *LST–347* was assigned to the European theater and participated in the following operations:

Sicilian occupation—July 1943
Salerno landings—September 1943
Invasion of Normandy—June 1944

On 19 December 1944 she was transferred to the United Kingdom and returned to United States Navy custody in January 1948. On 23 January 1948, the ship was retransferred to France on lease and returned to United States Navy custody on 21 March 1949. *LST–347* was sold to France that same day. *LST–347* was struck from the Navy list on 28 April 1949.

LST–347 earned three battle stars for World War II service.

LST–348

LST–348 was laid down on 10 November 1942 at the Norfolk Navy Yard; launched on 7 February 1943; sponsored by Mrs. L. V. Honsinger; and commissioned on 9 February 1943.

During World War II, *LST–348* was assigned to the European theater and participated in the following operations:

Sicilian occupation—July 1943
Anzio-Nettuno advanced landings — January through March 1944

LST–348 was sunk by a submarine torpedo off Anzio, Italy, on 20 February 1944 and struck from the Navy list on 6 March 1944.

LST–348 earned two battle stars and the Navy Unit Commendation for World War II service.

LST-349

LST-349 was laid down on 10 November 1942 at the Norfolk Navy Yard; launched on 7 February 1943; sponsored by Mrs. C. O. Barclay; and commissioned on 11 February 1943.

During World War II, LST-349 was assigned to the European theater and participated in the Sicilian occupation in July 1943. She ran aground and sank off Ponza, Italy, on 26 February 1944 and was struck from the Navy list on 25 March 1944.

LST-349 earned one battle star for World War II service.

LST-350

LST-350 was laid down on 10 November 1942 at the Norfolk Navy Yard; launched on 7 February 1943; sponsored by Mrs. C. M. Terry; and commissioned on 13 February 1943.

During World War II, LST-350 was assigned to the European theater and participated in the following operations:

Sicilian occupation—July 1943
Salerno landings—September 1943
Invasion of Normandy—June 1944

LST-350 was redesignated Chandra (ARL-46) on 25 May 1945, but the redesignation was subsequently cancelled. The ship was decommissioned on 26 May 1945 and struck from the Navy list on 12 March 1946. On 2 December 1946, she was sold to the Suwannee Steam Ship Co., Charleston, S.C., and converted for merchant service.

LST-350 earned three battle stars for World War II service.

LST-351

LST-351 was laid down on 9 November 1942 at the Norfolk Navy Yard; launched on 7 February 1943; sponsored by Mrs. P. F. Wakeman; and commissioned on 24 February 1943.

During World War II, LST-351 was assigned to the European theater and participated in the following operations:

Sicilian occupation—July 1943
Salerno landings—September 1943
Anzio-Nettuno advanced landings — January through March 1944
Invasion of Normandy—June 1944

On 12 December 1944, she was transferred to the United Kingdom. The tank landing ship was struck from the Navy list on 15 October 1946 and returned to United States Navy custody on 10 December 1946. She was sold to the Netherlands sometime between 30 December 1946 and 17 June 1947.

LST-351 earned four battle stars for World War II service.

LST-352

LST-352 was laid down on 9 November 1942 at the Norfolk Navy Yard; launched on 7 February 1943; sponsored by Miss Virginia Henley; and commissioned on 26 February 1943.

During World War II, LST-352 was assigned to the European theater and participated in the following operations:

Sicilian occupation—July 1943
Salerno landings—September 1943
West Coast of Italy operations:
(a) Anzio-Nettuno advanced landings—January through March 1944
(b) Elba and Pianosa landings—June 1944
Invasion of southern France—August through September 1944

On 24 December 1944, she was transferred to the United Kingdom. The tank landing ship was returned to United States Navy custody on 2 August 1946 and struck from the Navy list on 29 October 1946. She was sold to Greece sometime between 21 November 1946 and 6 January 1947.

LST-352 earned four battle stars for World War II service.

LST-353

LST-353 was laid down on 15 July 1942 at the Charleston Navy Yard; launched on 12 October 1942; sponsored by Mrs. Estelle Lynette Cushman; and commissioned on 27 November 1942, Lt. L. E. Reynolds, Jr., USNR, in command.

During World War II, LST-353 was assigned to the Asiatic-Pacific theater and participated in the following operations:

Consolidation of southern Solomons—June 1943
New Georgia Group operation:
(a) New Georgia-Rendova-Vangunu occupation—July 1943
(b) Vella Lavella occupation—August 1943
Occupation and defense of Cape Torokina—November 1943

On 21 May 1944, she was sunk by internal explosion while moored at Pearl Harbor, Hawaii, and struck from the Navy list on 18 July 1944.

LST-353 earned three battle stars and the Navy Unit Commendation for World War II service.

LST-354

LST-354 was laid down on 15 July 1942 at the Charleston Navy Yard; launched on 13 October 1942; sponsored by Mrs. Jean Browne McCall; and commissioned on 27 November 1942, Lt. B. W. Robb, USNR, in command.

During World War II, LST-354 was assigned to the Asiatic-Pacific theater and participated in the following operations:

New Georgia Group operation:
(a) New Georgia-Rendova-Vangunu occupation—July 1943
(b) Vella Lavella occupation—August 1943
Occupation and defense of Cape Torokina—November 1943
Green Islands landing—February 1944
Capture and occupation of Saipan—June 1944
Assault and occupation of Iwo Jima—February 1945
Assault and occupation of Okinawa Gunto—April 1945

Following the war, LST-354 performed occupation duty in the Far East until mid-December 1945. She was decommissioned on 30 April 1946 and struck from the Navy list on 19 June 1946. On 16 December 1947, the tank landing ship was sold the the Southwest Steel Corp., of Pittsburgh, Pa., and subsequently scrapped.

LST-354 earned six battle stars and the Navy Unit Commendation for World War II service.

LST-355

LST-355 was laid down on 7 September 1942 at the Charleston Navy Yard; launched on 16 November 1942; sponsored by Mrs. Wendell E. Kraft; and commissioned on 22 December 1942, Lt. Norman L. Knipe, Jr., USNR, in command.

During World War II, LST-355 was assigned to the European theater and participated in the Salerno landings in September 1943 and the invasion of Normandy in June 1944.

Following the war, LST-355 performed occupation duty in the Far East until early March 1946. She was decommissioned on 6 March 1946 and struck from the Navy list on 31 October 1947. On 10 April 1948, the tank landing ship was sold to Consolidated Builders, Inc., Seattle, Wash.

LST–355 earned two battle stars for World War II service.

LST–356

LST–356 was laid down on 7 September 1942 at the Charleston Navy Yard; launched on 16 November 1942; sponsored by Mrs. Harold Rivington Parker; and commissioned on 22 December 1942, Lt. G. A. Jaguemot in command.

During World War II, *LST–356* was assigned to the European theater and participated in the following operations:

Sicilian occupation—July 1943
Salerno landings—September 1943
Invasion of Normany—June 1944

LST–356 returned to the United States and was decommissioned on 21 September 1945. On 1 July 1955, she was named *Bledsoe County* (LST–356) after a county in Tennessee. The tank landing ship was struck from the Navy list on 1 September 1960 and sold to the Mechanical Equipment Co., New Orleans, La., on 8 March 1961 and subsequently scrapped.

LST–356 earned three battle stars for World War II service.

LST–357

LST–357 was laid down on 24 October 1942 at the Charleston Navy Yard; launched on 14 December 1942; sponsored by Mrs. Richard Wilder Smith; and commissioned on 8 February 1943, Lt. J. C. Reynolds in command.

During World War II, *LST–357* was assigned to the European theater and participated in the Sicilian occupation in July 1943 and the invasion of Normandy in June 1944. Following the war, *LST–357* performed occupation duty in the Far East in October and November 1945. She returned to the United States and was decommissioned on 8 June 1946 and struck from the Navy list on 31 July 1946. On 1 April 1948, the tank landing ship was sold to the Bethlehem Steel Co., Bethlehem, Pa., and subsequently scrapped.

LST–357 earned two battle stars for World War II service.

LST–358

LST–358 was laid down on 24 October 1942 at the Charleston Navy Yard; launched on 15 December 1942; sponsored by Mrs. Robert Arthur Hinners; and commissioned on 8 February 1943.

During World War II, *LST–358* was assigned to the European theater and participated in the following operations:

Sicilian occupation—July 1943
Salerno landings—September 1943
Anzio-Nettuno advanced landings — January through March 1944
Invasion of southern France—August and September 1944

LST–358 was transferred to the United Kingdom on 24 December 1944. She was returned to United States Navy custody on 27 February 1946 and struck from the Navy list on 15 August 1946. On 3 October 1947, the tank landing ship was sold to the Southern Trading Co., Philadelphia, Pa., and subsequently scrapped.

LST–358 earned four battle stars for World War II service.

LST–359

LST–359 was laid down on 21 November 1942 at the Charleston Navy Yard; launched on 11 January 1943; sponsored by Mrs. Albert Miller Penn; and commissioned on 9 February 1943, Lt. James A. Ferreola in command.

During World War II, *LST–359* was assigned to the European theater and participated in the following operations:

Sicilian occupation—July and August 1943
Salerno landings—September 1943
Convoy KMS–31—November 1943
Anzio-Nettuno advanced landings — January through March 1944
Invasion of Normandy—June 1944

LST–359 was sunk on 20 December 1944 by a submarine torpedo in the eastern Atlantic. On 8 February 1945, she was struck from the Navy list.

LST–359 earned five battle stars and the Navy Unit Commendation for World War II service.

LST–360

LST–360 was laid down on 21 November 1942 at the Charleston Navy Yard; launched on 11 January 1943; sponsored by Mrs. Willard James Riddick; and commissioned on 9 February 1943.

During World War II, *LST–360* was assigned to the European theater and participated in the following operations:

Sicilian occupation—July and August 1943
Anzio-Nettuno advanced landings — January through March 1944
Invasion of Normandy—June 1944

The tank landing ship was transferred to the United Kingdom on 29 November 1944 and returned to United States Navy custody and decommissioned on 10 June 1946. She was struck from the Navy list on 15 August 1946 and sold on 8 October 1947.

LST–360 earned three battle stars for World War II service.

LST–361

LST–361 was laid down on 10 August 1942 at Quincy, Mass., by the Bethlehem Steel Co.; launched on 10 October 1942; sponsored by Mrs. Leverett Saltonstall; and delivered to and commissioned by representatives of the United Kingdom on 16 November 1942. She was returned to United States Navy custody on 7 March 1946 and struck from the Navy list on 5 June 1946. On 11 October 1947, the tank landing ship was sold to Luria Bros. & Co., Inc., of Philadelphia, Pa., for scrapping.

LST–362

LST–362 was laid down on 10 August 1942 at Quincy, Mass., by the Bethlehem Steel Co.; launched on 10 October 1942; sponsored by Mrs. Francis E. M. Whiting; and delivered to and commissioned by representatives of the United Kingdom on 23 November 1942. She was torpedoed and sunk by a German submarine on 2 March 1944. *LST–362* was struck from the Navy list on 28 April 1945.

LST–363

LST–363 was laid down on 2 September 1942 at Quincy, Mass., by the Bethlehem Steel Co.; launched on 26 October 1942; sponsored by Mrs. Kendall Preston; and delivered to and commissioned by representatives of the United Kingdom on 30 November 1942. The tank landing ship was returned to United States Navy custody on 26 January 1946 and struck from the Navy list on 12 April 1946. On 4 December 1947, she was sold to N. Block & Co., Norfolk, Va., for scrapping.

LST–364

LST–364 was laid down on 3 September 1942 at Quincy, Mass., by the Bethlehem Steel Co.; launched on 26 October 1942; sponsored by Mrs. Harold B. Buse; and delivered to and commissioned by representatives of the United Kingdom on 7 December 1942. She was sunk due to enemy action in February 1945 and struck from the Navy list on 11 July 1945.

LST–365

LST–365 was laid down on 14 October 1942 at Quincy, Mass., by the Bethlehem Steel Co.; launched on 11 November 1942; sponsored by Mrs. Miles Sherman; and delivered to and commissioned by representatives of the United Kingdom on 14 December 1942. She was struck from the Navy list on 15 October 1946 and returned to United States Navy custody on 10 December 1946. On 5 June 1947, the tank landing ship was sold to Fresh Frozen Foods, Ltd., Ayrshire, Scotland, for conversion for merchant service.

LST–366

LST–366 was laid down on 1 October 1942 at Quincy, Mass., by the Bethlehem Steel Co.; launched on 11 November 1942; sponsored by Mrs. Kenneth Blood; and delivered to and commissioned by representatives of the United Kingdom on 21 Dceember 1942. She was returned to United States Navy custody on 26 January 1946 and struck from the Navy list on 5 June 1946. The tank landing ship was sold to N. Block & Co., Norfolk, Va., for scrapping.

LST–367

LST–367 was laid down on 13 October 1942 at Quincy, Mass., by the Bethlehem Steel Co.; launched on 24 November 1942; sponsored by Mrs. Alfred W. Anthony, Jr.; and delivered to and commissioned by representatives of the United Kingdom on 29 December 1942. She was returned to United States Navy custody on 17 December 1945 and struck from the Navy list on 21 January 1946. On 18 March 1948, the tank landing ship was sold to the Great Atlantic Iron & Steel Corp. for scrapping.

LST–368

LST–368 was laid down on 13 October 1942 at Quincy, Mass., by the Bethlehem Steel Co.; launched on 24 November 1942; sponsored by Mrs. Joseph T. Hazen; and delivered to and commissioned by representatives of the United Kingdom on 4 January 1943. She was returned to United States Navy custody on 16 March 1943.

During World War II, LST–368 was assigned to the Asiatic-Pacific theater and participated in the occupation of Saidor in eastern New Guinea in February 1944. She returned to the United States and was decommissioned on 16 March 1946. The tank landing ship was struck from the Navy list on 17 April 1946 and was destroyed on 16 June 1948.

LST–368 earned one battle star for World War II service.

LST–369

LST–369 was laid down on 13 October 1942 at Quincy, Mass., by the Bethlehem Steel Co.; launched on 24 November 1942; sponsored by Mrs. Claude L. Turner; and commissioned on 8 January 1943.

During World War II, LST–369 was assigned to the European theater and participated in the following operations:

    Sicilian occupation—July 1943
    Salerno landings—September 1943
    Invasion of Normandy—June 1944

LST–369 was transferred to the United Kingdom on 29 November 1944 and returned to United States Navy custody on 29 November 1946. She was struck from the Navy list on 1 August 1947. On 7 October 1947, she was sold to the Tung Hwa Trading Co., Singapore.

LST–369 earned three battle stars for World War II service.

LST–370

LST–370 was laid down on 31 October 1942 at Quincy, Mass., by the Bethlehem Steel Co.; launched on 12 December 1942; sponsored by Mrs. Frederic F. Agens; and commissioned on 13 January 1943.

During World War II, LST–370 was assigned to the European theater and participated in the following operations:

    Sicilian occupation—July 1943
    Salerno landings—September 1943
    Invasion of Normandy—June 1944

LST–370 returned to the United States and was decommissioned on 7 January 1946. She was struck from the Navy list on 12 April 1946 and sold to Ming-Sung Industrial Co., Ltd., on 3 February 1947 and converted for merchant service.

LST–370 earned three battle stars for World War II service.

LST–371

LST–371 was laid down on 29 October 1942 at Quincy, Mass., by the Bethlehem Steel Co., launched on 12 December 1942; sponsored by Mrs. John E. Varney; and commissioned on 16 January 1943.

During World War II, LST–371 was assigned to the European theater and participated in the following operations:

    Sicilian occupation—July 1943
    Salerno landings—September 1943
    Invasion of Normandy—June 1944

On 17 November 1944, LST–371 was transferred to the United Kingdom. She was struck from the Navy list on 26 February 1946 and returned to United States Navy custody and decommissioned on 16 March 1946. The tank landing ship was sold to Bosey, Philippines, on 5 December 1947.

LST–371 earned three battle stars for World War II service.

LST–372

LST–372 was laid down on 14 November 1942 at Quincy, Mass., by the Bethlehem Steel Co.; launched on 19 January 1943; sponsored by Mrs. Paul W. Watson; and commissioned on 23 January 1943, Lt. Marvin F. Studebaker, USNR, in command.

During World War II, LST–372 was assigned to the European theater and participated in the following operations:

    Sicilian occupation—July 1943
    Salerno landings—September 1943
    Invasion of Normandy—June 1944

Following the war, LST–372 performed occupation duty in the Far East in October and November 1945 and saw service in China in December 1945 through March 1946. Upon her return to the United States, the ship was decommissioned on 9 July 1946 and struck from the Navy list on 15 August that same year. On 3 October 1947, she was sold to the Patapsco Scrap Corp., of Baltimore, Md., and subsequently scrapped.

LST–372 earned three battle stars for World War II service.

LST-373

LST-373 was laid down on 14 November 1942 at Quincy, Mass., by the Bethlehem Steel Co.; launched on 19 January 1943; sponsored by Mrs. Louis P. Davis; and commissioned on 27 January 1943.

During World War II, *LST-373* was assigned to the European theater and participated in the following operations:

Sicilian occupation—July 1943
Salerno landings—September 1943
Invasion of Normandy—June 1944

She was transferred to the United Kingdom on 9 December 1944. *LST-373* was returned to United States Navy custody and decommissioned on 16 March 1946. She was struck from the Navy list on 26 February 1946 and sold to Bosey, Philippines, on 5 November 1947.

LST-373 earned three battle stars for World War II service.

LST-374

LST-374 was laid down on 12 November 1942 at Quincy, Mass., by the Bethlehem Steel Co.; launched on 19 January 1943; sponsored by Mrs. Victor D. Herbster; and commissioned on 29 January 1943.

During World War II, *LST-374* was assigned to the European theater and participated in the Sicilian occupation in July and August 1943 and the invasion of Normandy in June 1944. She returned to the United States and was decommissioned on 29 May 1945 and struck from the Navy list on 12 March 1946. On 14 January 1947, the tank landing ship was sold to A. G. Schoonmaker.

LST-374 earned two battle stars for World War II service.

LST-375

LST-375 was laid down on 25 November 1942 at Quincy, Mass., by the Bethlehem Steel Co.; launched on 28 January 1943; sponsored by Mrs. Frederick C. Sachse; and commissioned on 2 February 1943.

During World War II, *LST-375* was assigned to the European theater and participated in the following operations:

Sicilian occupation—July 1943
Salerno landings—September 1943
Invasion of Normandy—June 1944

Following the war, *LST-375* performed occupation duty in the Far East in January and February 1946. She returned to the United States and was decommissioned on 18 July 1946 and struck from the Navy list on 10 June 1947. On 31 December 1948, the ship was sold to the Bethlehem Steel Co., Bethlehem, Pa., and subsequently scrapped.

LST-375 earned three battle stars for World War II service.

LST-376

LST-376 was laid down on 25 November 1942 at Quincy, Mass., by the Bethlehem Steel Co.; launched on 1 February 1943; sponsored by Mrs. Harold C. Pierce; and commissioned on 5 February 1943.

During World War II, *LST-376* was assigned to the European theater and participated in the following operations:

Sicilian occupation—July 1943
Salerno landings—September 1943
Invasion of Normandy—June 1944

LST-376 was torpedoed and sunk by a German surface craft in the English Channel on 9 June 1944 and struck from the Navy list on 28 June 1944.

LST-376 earned three battle stars for World War II service.

LST-377

LST-377 was laid down on 28 November 1942 at Quincy, Mass., by the Bethlehem Steel Co.; launched on 1 February 1943; sponsored by Mrs. Edward T. Dobbyn; and commissioned on 8 February 1943, Lt. A. C. Parks, USNR, in command.

During World War II, *LST-377* was assigned to the European theater and participated in the following operations:

Sicilian occupation—July 1943
Salerno landings—September 1943
Anzio-Nettuno advanced landings — January through March 1944
Invasion of Normandy—June 1944

Following the war, *LST-377* performed occupation duty in the Far East until early February 1946. The ship was decommissioned on 7 June 1946 and struck from the Navy list on 31 July 1946. On 1 April 1948, the tank landing ship was sold to the Bethlehem Steel Co., Bethlehem, Pa., and subsequently scrapped.

LST-377 earned four battle stars for World War II service.

LST-822 in the early 1950s. Except for the addition of a high bridge, she is essentially unmodified from her original appearance. The *LST-542*-class was built with a water-distilling plant and heavier armament than the earlier *LST-1*-class; this slightly decreased their payload.

LST-378

LST-378 was laid down on 12 December 1942 at Quincy, Mass., by the Bethlehem Steel Co.; launched on 6 February 1943; sponsored by Mrs. Herbert A. Hope; and commissioned on 10 February 1943.

During World War II, LST-378 was assigned to the European theater and participated in the following operations:

Sicilian occupation—July 1943
Salerno landings—September 1943
Anzio-Nettuno advanced landings — January through March 1944
Invasion of Normandy—June 1944

Following the war, LST-378 performed occupation duty in the Far East until mid-January 1946. She was decommissioned on 20 February 1946 and struck from the Navy list on 5 March 1947. On 1 June 1947, the tank landing ship was sold to the United States Military Government, Korea.

LST-378 earned four battle stars for World War II service.

LST-379

LST-379 was laid down on 12 December 1942 at Quincy, Mass., by the Bethlehem Steel Co.; launched on 6 February 1943; sponsored by Miss Elizabeth Virginia Collins; and commissioned on 12 February 1943, Lt. John T. Salistean in command.

During World War II, LST-379 was assigned to the European theater and participated in the following operations:

Sicilian occupation—July 1943
Salerno landings—September 1943
Anzio-Nettuno advanced landings — January through March 1944
Invasion of Normandy—June 1944

Following the war, LST-379 performed occupation duty in the Far East in September 1945. Upon her return to the United States, she was decommissioned on 28 February 1946 and struck from the Navy list on 20 March 1946. On 12 April 1948, the tank landing ship was sold to the Bethlehem Steel Co., Bethlehem, Pa., and subsequently scrapped.

LST-379 earned four battle stars for World War II service.

LST-380

LST-380 was laid down on 10 December 1942 at Quincy, Mass., by the Bethlehem Steel Co.; launched on 10 February 1943; sponsored by Mrs. D. J. Callahan; and commissioned on 15 February 1943.

During World War II, LST-380 was assigned to the European theater and participated in the following operations:

Sicilian occupation—July 1943
Salerno landings—September 1943
Invasion of Normandy—June 1944

LST-380 was transferred to the United Kingdom on 20 November 1944 and returned to United States Navy custody on 11 April 1946. On 7 June 1946, the tank landing ship was sold to the United States Military Government, Korea, and struck from the Navy list on 19 July 1946.

LST-380 earned three battle stars for World War II service.

LST-381

LST-381 was laid down on 10 December 1942 at Quincy, Mass., by the Bethlehem Steel Co.; launched on 10 February 1943; sponsored by Mrs. Everett Goodrich; and commissioned on 15 February 1943.

During World War II, LST-381 was assigned to the European theater of war and participated in the following operations:

Sicilian occupation—July 1943
Anzio-Nettuno advanced landings—January and February 1944
Invasion of Normandy—June 1944

LST-381 was transferred to the United Kingdom on 19 December 1944. She was decommissioned on 10 June 1946 and returned to United States Navy custody. The ship was struck from the Navy list on 19 July 1946. On 11 September 1947, she was sold and subsequently scrapped.

LST-381 earned three battle stars for World War II service.

LST-382

LST-382 was laid down on 10 December 1942 at Quincy, Mass., by the Bethlehem Steel Co.; launched on 3 February 1943; sponsored by Miss Emily F. Cass; and commissioned on 18 February 1943.

During World War II, LST-382 was assigned to the European theater and participated in the following operations:

Sicilian occupation—July 1943
Salerno landings—September 1943
Invasion of Normandy—June 1944

LST-381 was transferred to the United Kingdom on 29 November 1944. On 23 January 1948, she was transferred to France on lease and ultimately sold to France for further service on 21 March 1949. The tank landing ship was struck from the Navy list on 28 April 1949.

LST-382 earned three battle stars for World War II service.

LST-383

LST-383 was laid down on 16 June 1942 at the Newport News Shipbuilding & Drydock Co.; launched on 28 September 1942; sponsored by Mrs. Estelle Lynette Cushman; and commissioned on 27 October 1942.

During World War II, LST-383 was assigned to the European theater and participated in the following operations:

Sicilian occupation—July 1943
Salerno landings—September 1943
Anzio-Nettuno advanced landings — January through March 1944
Invasion of Normandy—June 1944

LST-383 was transferred to the United Kingdom on 20 November 1944. She was retransferred to the Netherlands East Indies Maritime Customs as a sale on 10 June 1946. On 3 July 1946, LST-383 was struck from the Navy list.

LST-383 earned four battle stars for World War II service.

LST-384

LST-384 was laid down on 16 June 1942 at the Newport News Shipbuilding & Drydock Co.; launched on 28 September 1942; sponsored by Miss Alice Palen; and commissioned on 2 November 1942.

During World War II, LST-384 was assigned to the European theater and participated in the following operations:

Sicilian occupation—July 1943
Salerno landings—September 1943
Anzio-Nettuno advanced landings—January and February 1944
Invasion of Normandy—June 1944

Following the war, LST-384 performed occupation duty in the Far East until mid-December 1945. Upon her return to the United States, she was decommissioned on 22 April 1946 and struck from the Navy list on 5 June 1946. On 8 April 1948, the tank landing ship was sold to Kaiser Co., Inc., Vancouver, Wash., and subsequently scrapped.

LST–384 earned four battle stars for World War II service.

LST–385

LST–385 was laid down on 19 June 1942 at the Newport News Shipbuilding & Drydock Co.; launched on 28 September 1942; sponsored by Miss Janet Lee Peebles; and commissioned on 6 November 1942.

During World War II, *LST–385* was assigned to the European theater and participated in the following operations:

> Sicilian occupation—July 1943
> Salerno landings—September 1943
> Convoy KMS–31—November 1943
> Anzio-Nettuno advanced landings—January and February 1944
> Invasion of Normandy—June 1944

She was transferred to the United Kingdom on 29 November 1944. The ship was struck from the Navy list on 26 February 1946. She was decommissioned on 16 March 1946 and returned to United States Navy custody. On 5 December 1947, *LST–385* was sold to Bosey, Philippines.

LST–385 earned five battle stars for World War II service.

LST–386

LST–386 was laid down on 9 June 1942 at the Newport News Shipbuilding & Drydock Co.; launched on 28 September 1942; sponsored by Miss Mary Randolph Scott; and commissioned on 10 November 1942.

During World War II, *LST–386* was assigned to the European theater and participated in the following operations:

> Tunisian operations—November 1942 through July 1943
> Sicilian occupation—July 1943
> Salerno landings—September 1943
> Anzio-Nettuno advanced landings—February and March 1944
> Invasion of Normandy—June 1944

LST–386 was transferred to the United Kingdom on 9 December 1944. She was struck from the Navy list on 15 October 1946. The ship was decommissioned and returned to United States Navy custody on 10 December 1946. On 5 June 1947, she was sold to Frozen Foods, Scotland, and converted for merchant service.

LST–386 earned five battle stars for World War II service.

LST–387

LST–387 was laid down on 20 June 1942 at the Newport News Shipbuilding & Drydock Co.; launched on 28 September 1942; sponsored by Miss Roberta Adele Fitzhugh; and commissioned on 17 November 1942.

LST–387 served in the European theater. On 22 June 1943, she was damaged by a German submarine torpedo, between Algiers and Bizerte, and subsequently repaired. The ship was decommissioned on 2 May 1946 and struck from the Navy list on 19 July 1946. On 22 December 1947, she was sold to the Northern Metals Co., Philadelphia, Pa., and scrapped.

LST–388

LST–388 was laid down on 20 June 1942 at the Newport News Shipbuilding & Drydock Co.; launched on 28 September 1942; sponsored by Miss Barbara Ann Besse; and commissioned on 20 November 1942.

During World War II, *LST–388* was assigned to the European theater and participated in the following operations:

> Tunisian operations—November 1942 through July 1943
> Sicilian occupation—July 1943
> Salerno landings—September 1943
> Invasion of Normandy—June 1944

After the war, she was decommissioned on 1 February 1947 and struck from the Navy list on 25 February 1947. On 7 April 1948, the ship was transferred to the Maritime Administration and later sold.

LST–388 earned four battle stars for World War II service.

LST–389

LST–389 was laid down on 20 June 1942 at the Newport News Shipbuilding & Drydock Co.; launched on 28 September 1942; sponsored by Miss Clara Elizabeth Ashe; and commissioned on 24 November 1942, Lt. George C. Carpenter, USNR, in command.

During World War II, *LST–389* was assigned to the European theater and participated in the following operations:

> Sicilian occupation—July 1943
> Salerno landings—September 1943
> Invasion of Normandy—June 1944

LST–389 was decommissioned on 12 March 1946. She was redesignated *Boone County* (LST–389) after eight counties in the United States on 1 July 1955 and struck from the Navy list on 1 June 1959. In May 1960, the ship was transferred to the government of Greece as grant aid where she served in the Royal Hellenic Navy as *Lesbos* (L–172).

LST–389 earned three battle stars for World War II service.

LST–390

LST–390 was laid down on 20 June 1942 at the Newport News Shipbuilding & Drydock Co.; launched on 15 October 1942; sponsored by Miss Robin Holzbach; and commissioned on 28 November 1942, Lt. W. J. C. Baker, USNR, in command.

During World War II, *LST–390* was assigned to the Asiatic-Pacific theater and participated in the following operations:

> Occupation and defense of Cape Torokina—November and December 1943
> Capture and occupation of Saipan—June 1944
> Capture and occupation of Iwo Jima—February 1945

Following the war, *LST–390* performed occupation duty in the Far East until early March 1946. Upon her return to the United States, she was decommissioned on 12 March 1946 and struck from the Navy list on 29 September 1947. On 3 April 1948, the tank landing ship was sold to Consolidated Builders, Inc., of Seattle, Wash., and subsequently scrapped.

LST–390 earned three battle stars and the Navy Unit Commendation for World War II service.

LST–391

LST–391 was laid down on 14 July 1942 at the Newport News Shipbuilding & Drydock Co.; launched on 28 October 1942; sponsored by Miss Katherine Wendell Blewett; and commissioned on 3 December 1942.

During World War II, *LST–391* was assigned to the European theater and participated in the following operations:

> Sicilian occupation—July 1943
> Salerno landings—September 1943
> Invasion of Normandy—June 1944

In May 1960, *LST–391* was transferred to Greece as grant aid where she served in the Royal Hellenic Navy as *Rodos* (L–157).

LST–391 earned three battle stars for World War II service.

LST-392

LST-392 was laid down on 14 July 1942 at the Newport News Shipbuilding & Drydock Co.; launched on 28 October 1942; sponsored by Miss Jane Lewis Irvine; and commissioned on 7 December 1942, Lt. Louis R. Lemaire, Jr., USNR, in command.

During World War II, LST-392 was assigned to the European theater and participated in the following operations:

Tunisian operations—May through July 1943
Sicilian occupation—July 1943
Salerno landings—September 1943
Invasion of Normandy—June 1944

Following the war, LST-392 was decommissioned on 12 April 1946 and struck from the Navy list on 19 June 1946. On 8 October 1947, the tank landing ship was sold to the H. H. Buncher Co., Pittsburgh, Pa., and subsequently scrapped.

LST-392 earned four battle stars for World War II service.

LST-393

LST-393 was laid down on 27 July 1942 at the Newport News Shipbuilding & Drydock Co.; launched on 11 November 1942; sponsored by Miss Lucy Jean Sorenson; and commissioned on 11 December 1942, Lt. John H. Halifax, USNR, in command.

During World War II, LST-393 was assigned to the European theater and participated in the following operations:

Sicilian occupation—July 1943
Salerno landings—September 1943
Invasion of Normandy—June 1944

Following the war, LST-393 returned to the United States and was decommissioned on 1 March 1946 and struck from the Navy list on 14 March 1947. On 28 March 1948, the tank landing ship was sold to the Sand Products Corp., Detroit, Mich., for conversion to merchant service.

LST-393 earned three battle stars for World War II service.

LST-394

LST-394 was laid down on 27 July 1942 at the Newport News Shipbuilding & Drydock Co.; launched on 11 November 1942; sponsored by Miss Dorothy Louise Comstock; and commissioned on 15 December 1942.

During World War II, LST-394 was assigned to the European theater and participated in the following operations:

Sicilian occupation—July 1943
Invasion of southern France—August through September 1944

The ship was transferred to the United Kingdom on 24 December 1944. She was decommissioned and returned to United States Navy custody on 12 May 1946. On 19 June 1946, the tank landing ship was struck from the Navy list and sold to N. Block & Co., Norfolk, Va., on 10 December 1947 and subsequently scrapped.

LST-394 earned two battle stars for World War II service.

LST-395

LST-395 was laid down on 28 September 1942 at the Newport News Shipbuilding & Drydock Co.; launched on 23 November 1942; sponsored by Miss Audrey Jane Terry; and commissioned on 19 Decemebr 1942, Lt. A. C. Forber, USNR, in command.

During World War II, LST-395 was assigned to the Asiatic-Pacific theater and participated in the following operations:

Consolidation of southern Solomons—June 1943

New Georgia Group operation:
(a) New Georgia-Rendova-Vangunu occupation—July 1943
(b) Vella Lavella occupation—August 1943
Occupation and defense of Cape Torokina—November 1943
Hollandia operation—April 1944
Western New Guinea operations:
(a) Biak Island operation—May 1944
(b) Cape Sansapor operation—July and August 1944
Balikpapan operation—June and July 1945
Mindanao Island landings—April 1945

Following the war, LST-395 performed occupation duty in the Far East until mid-October 1945. Upon her return to the United States, she was decommissioned on 19 April 1946 and struck from the Navy list on 1 May 1946. On 26 September 1947, the ship was sold to the Boston Metals Co., Baltimore, Md., and subsequently scrapped.

LST-395 earned six battle stars and the Navy Unit Commendation for World War II service.

LST-396

LST-396 was laid down on 28 September 1942 at the Newport News Shipbuilding & Drydock Co.; launched on 23 November 1942; sponsored by Miss Ann Hathaway Callis; and commissioned on 23 December 1942, Lt. E. W. White in command.

During World War II, LST-396 was assigned to the Asiatic-Pacific theater and participated in the following operations:

Consolidation of southern Solomons—June 1943
New Georgia Group operation:
(a) New Georgia-Rendova-Vangunu occupation—July 1943
(b) Vella Lavella occupation—August 1943

LST-396 was sunk by accidental fire and explosion off the Solomon Islands on 18 August 1943. She was struck from the Navy list on 3 September 1943.

LST-396 earned one battle star and the Navy Unit Commendation for World War II service.

LST-397

LST-397 was laid down on 28 September 1942 at the Newport News Shipbuilding & Drydock Co.; launched on 23 November 1942; sponsored by Miss Gretchen Lou White; and commissioned on 28 December 1942.

During World War II, LST-397 was assigned to the Asiatic-Pacific theater and participated in the following operations:

Consolidation of southern Solomons—June 1943
New Georgia Group operation:
(a) New Georgia-Rendova-Vangunu occupation—July 1943
(b) Vella Lavella occupation—August 1943
Occupation and defense of Cape Torokina—November and December 1943
Hollandia operation—April 1944
Western New Guinea operation:
(a) Biak Island operation—June 1944
(b) Noemfoor Island operation—July 1944
(c) Cape Sansapor operation—July and August 1944
(d) Morotai landings—September 1944
Leyte landings—November 1944
Lingayen Gulf landing—January 1945
Mindanao Island landings—March 1945

Following the war, LST-397 performed occupation duty in the Far East in October 1945. Upon her return to the United States, she was decommissioned on 26 April 1946 and struck from the Navy list on 5 June that same year. On 30 September 1947, LST-397 was sold to the Patapsco Scrap Corp., of Baltimore, Md., for scrapping.

LST-397 earned seven battle stars and the Navy Unit Commendation for World War II service.

LST-398

LST-398 was laid down on 28 September 1942 at the Newport News Shipbuilding & Drydock Co.; launched on 23 November 1942; sponsored by Miss Mary Sherwood Giese; and commissioned on 2 January 1943.

During World War II, *LST-398* was assigned to the Asiatic-Pacific theater and participated in the following operations:

Consolidation of southern Solomons—June 1943
New Georgia Group operations:
  (a) New Georgia-Rendova-Vangunu occupation—July 1943
  (b) Vella Lavella occupation—August 1943
Occupation and defense of Cape Torokina—November and December 1943
Capture and occupation of Guam—August 1944

Following the war, *LST-398* performed occupation duty in the Far East until mid-February 1946. Upon her return to the United States, she was decommissioned on 27 February 1946 and struck from the Navy list on 28 August 1947. On 28 March 1948, *LST-398* was sold to Consolidated Builders, Inc., Seattle, Wash.

LST-398 earned four battle stars and the Navy Unit Commendation for World War II service.

LST-399

LST-399 was laid down on 28 September 1942 at the Newport News Shipbuilding & Drydock Co.; launched on 23 November 1942; sponsored by Miss Valerie Macpherson; and commissioned on 4 January 1943.

During World War II, *LST-399* was assigned to the Asiatic-Pacific theater and participated in the following operations:

New Georgia Group operation:
  (a) New Georgia-Rendova-Vangunu occupation—July 1943
  (b) Vella Lavella occupation—August 1943
Treasury Island landing—October and November 1943
Capture and occupation of Guam—July 1944
Assault and occupation of Iwo Jima—February 1945
Assault and occupation of Okinawa Gunto—April 1945

Following the war, *LST-399* performed occupation duty in the Far East in the fall of 1945. Upon her return to the United States, she was decommissioned on 8 December 1945. The tank landing ship served with the Military Sealift Command as USNS *LST-399* (T-LST-399) from 31 March 1952 until struck from the Navy list on 1 November 1973 and subsequently scrapped.

LST-399 earned five battle stars and the Navy Unit Commendation for World War II service.

LST-400

LST-400 was laid down on 28 September 1942 at the Newport News Shipbuilding & Drydock Co.; launched on 23 November 1942; sponsored by Miss Judith Flaxington; and commissioned on 7 January 1943.

During World War II, *LST-400* was assigned to the European theater and participated in the Sicilian occupation in July 1943 and the invasion of Normandy in June 1944.

Following the war, *LST-400* was redesignated *Bradley County* (LST-400) on 1 July 1955 after counties in Arkansas and Tennessee. The tank landing ship was transferred to Taiwan as a grant in aid in September 1958 where she served as *Chung Suo* (LST-217). She was struck from the Navy list on 25 April 1960.

LST-400 earned two battle stars for World War II service.

LST-401

LST-401 was laid down on 17 August 1942 at Baltimore, Md., by the Bethlehem Fairfield Co.; launched on 16 October 1942; delivered to the United Kingdom on 30 November 1942 and commissioned in the Royal Navy that same day.

LST-401 never saw active service in the United States Navy. She served in the Royal Navy through the end of World War II and was returned to the custody of the United States Navy on 7 March 1946. On 5 June 1946, less than three months after her return, she was struck from the Navy list; and, on 11 October 1947, she was sold to Luria Brothers & Co., of Philadelphia, Pa.

LST-402

LST-402 was laid down on 21 August 1942 at Baltimore, Md., by the Bethlehem Fairfield Co.; launched on 9 October 1942; and transferred to the United Kingdom and commissioned on 9 December 1942. *LST-402* saw no active service in the United States Navy. The tank landing ship was decommissioned and returned to United States Navy custody on 24 September 1946 and struck from the Navy list on 10 June 1947. She was subsequently sold for scrap.

LST-403

LST-403 was laid down on 23 August 1942 at Baltimore, Md., by the Bethlehem Fairfield Co.; launched on 24 October 1942; and delivered to the United Kingdom and commissioned on 8 December 1942. *LST-403* saw no active service in the United States Navy. The tank landing ship was decommissioned and returned to United States Navy custody on 11 April 1946 and struck from the Navy list on 5 June 1946. On 5 December 1947, the ship was sold to Bosey, Philippines, for scrapping.

LST-404

LST-404 was laid down on 27 August 1942 at Baltimore, Md., by the Bethlehem Fairfield Co.; launched on 28 October 1942; and delivered to the United Kingdom and commissioned on 16 December 1942. *LST-404* saw no active service in the United States Navy. The tank landing ship was struck from the Navy list on 14 October 1944. She was decommissioned, returned to United States Navy custody on 21 October 1945, sold through the auspices of the State Department in November 1946, and subsequently scrapped.

LST-405

LST-405 was laid down on 30 August 1942 at Baltimore, Md., by the Bethlehem Fairfield Co.; launched on 31 October 1942; and delivered to the United Kingdom and commissioned on 28 December 1942. *LST-405* saw no active service in the United States Navy. The tank landing ship was sunk on 27 March while in Royal Navy service. *LST-405* was struck from the Navy list on 17 April 1946.

LST-406

LST-406 was laid down on 1 September 1942 at Baltimore, Md., by the Bethlehem Fairfield Co.; launched on 28 October 1942; and delivered to the United Kingdom and commissioned on 26 December 1942. *LST-406* saw no active service in the United States Navy. The tank landing ship was decommissioned and returned to United States Navy custody on 11 April 1946. She was struck from the Navy list on 10 June 1947. On 5 December 1947, *LST-406* was sold to Bosey, Philippines, for scrapping.

LST–407

LST–407 was laid down on 2 September 1942 at Baltimore, Md., by the Bethlehem Fairfield Co.; launched on 5 November 1942; and delivered to the United Kingdom and commissioned on 31 December 1942. LST–407 saw no active service in the United States Navy. The tank landing ship was damaged beyond repair on 24 April 1944 and beached off Baia, Italy. The hulk was accepted by the United States Navy on 6 May 1945. On 11 July 1945, LST–407 was struck from the Navy list. Sometime in July 1945, she was sold to a local Italian firm and scrapped.

LST–408

LST–408 was laid down on 9 September 1942 at Baltimore, Md., by the Bethlehem Fairfield Co.; launched on 31 October 1942; and delivered to the United Kingdom and commissioned on 23 December 1942. LST–408 saw no active service in the United States Navy. The tank landing ship was decommissioned and returned to United States Navy custody on 4 May 1946 and struck from the Navy list on 19 June 1946. On 5 December 1947, LST–408 was sold to Bosey, Philippines, and subsequently scrapped.

LST–409

LST–409 was laid down on 9 September 1942 at Baltimore, Md., by the Bethlehem Fairfield Co.; launched on 15 November 1942; and transferred to the United Kingdom and commissioned on 6 January 1943. LST–409 saw no active service in the United States Navy. The tank landing ship was decommissioned and returned to United States Navy custody on 2 July 1946 and struck from the Navy list on 29 October that same year. Sometime between 21 November 1946 and 6 January 1947, LST–409 was sold to Greece.

LST–410

LST–410 was laid down on 13 September 1942 at Baltimore, Md., by the Bethlehem Fairfield Co.; launched on 15 November 1942; and delivered to the United Kingdom and commissioned on 14 January 1943. LST–410 saw no active service in the United States Navy. The tank landing ship was struck from the Navy list on 26 February 1946. She was returned to United States Navy custody and decommissioned on 16 April 1947. On 13 February 1948, LST–410 was sold to Bosey, Philippines, and subsequently scrapped.

LST–411

LST–411 was laid down on 21 September 1942 at Baltimore, Md., by the Bethlehem Fairfield Co.; launched on 9 November 1942; and transferred to the United Kingdom and commissioned on 31 December 1942. LST–411 saw no active service in the United States Navy. The tank landing ship was lost in action on 1 January 1944 and struck from the Navy list on 13 November 1944.

LST–412

LST–412 was laid down on 24 September 1942 at Baltimore, Md., by the Bethlehem Fairfield Co.; launched on 16 November 1942; and transferred to the United Kingdom and commissioned on 26 January 1943. LST–412 saw no active service in the United States Navy. She was decommissioned and returned to United States Navy custody on 23 January 1946 and struck from the Navy list on 20 March 1946. On 16 December 1947, LST–412 was sold to the Northern Metals Co., Philadelphia, Pa., and subsequently scrapped.

LST–413

LST–413 was laid down on 10 October 1942 at Baltimore, Md., by the Bethlehem Fairfield Co.; launched on 10 November 1942; and transferred to the United Kingdom and commissioned on 5 January 1943. LST–413 saw no active service in the United States Navy. She was decommissioned and returned to United States Navy custody on 11 April 1946 and struck from the Navy list on 10 June 1947. On 5 December 1947, LST–413 was sold to Bosey, Philippines.

LST–414

LST–414 was laid down on 18 October 1942 at Baltimore, Md., by the Bethlehem Fairfield Co.; launched on 21 November 1942; and transferred to the United Kingdom and commissioned on 19 January 1943. LST–

LST–344 off Guam in the 1960s, with Army LCU–1517—descendant of the Navy's LCT of World War II—and vehicles on deck. Except for a tripod mast and additional 40mm guns, she is little changed from her original appearance.

414 saw no active service in the United States Navy. She was lost in action in August 1943 and struck from the Navy list on 24 November 1943.

LST–415

LST–415 was laid down on 29 October 1942 at Baltimore, Md., by the Bethlehem Fairfield Co.; launched on 21 November 1942; and transferred to the United Kingdom and commissioned on 19 January 1943. *LST–415* saw no active service in the United States Navy. She was torpedoed and beached off Thurrock, England, on 16 January 1945. The tank landing ship was returned to United States Navy custody and struck from the Navy list on 2 June 1945. The ship was sold to a local British firm in January 1948 and subsequently scrapped.

LST–416

LST–416 was laid down on 25 October 1942 at Baltimore, Md., by the Bethlehem Fairfield Co.; launched on 30 November 1942; and transferred to the United Kingdom and commissioned on 3 February 1943. *LST–416* saw no active service in the United States Navy. She was decommissioned and returned to United States Navy custody on 12 February 1946 and struck from the Navy list on 5 June that same year. On 23 April 1948, *LST–416* was sold to the Newport News Shipbuilding & Drydock Co., Newport News, Va., for conversion to merchant service.

LST–417

LST–417 was laid down on 29 October 1942 at Baltimore, Md., by the Bethlehem Fairfield Co.; launched on 24 November 1942; and transferred to the United Kingdom and commissioned on 29 January 1943. *LST–417* saw no active service in the United States Navy. She was decommissioned and returned to United States Navy custody on 31 May 1946 and struck from the Navy list on 3 July 1946. On 4 December 1947, *LST–417* was sold to James A. Hughes, New York, N.Y., and subsequently scrapped.

LST–418

LST–418 was laid down on 2 November 1942 at Baltimore, Md., by the Bethlehem Fairfield Co.; launched on 30 November 1942; and transferred to the United Kingdom and commissioned on 29 January 1943. *LST–418* saw no active service in the United States Navy. She was sunk on 20 April 1944 while in service with the Royal Navy. *LST–418* was struck from the Navy list on 16 May 1944.

LST–419

LST–419 was laid down on 1 November 1942 at Baltimore, Md., by the Bethlehem Fairfield Co.; launched on 30 November 1942; and transferred to the United Kingdom and commissioned on 8 February 1943. *LST–419* saw no active service in the United States Navy. She was decommissioned and returned to United States Navy custody on 4 May 1946 and struck from the Navy list on 8 July that same year. On 5 December 1947, *LST–419* was sold to Bosey, Philippines, and subsequently scrapped.

LST–420

LST–420 was laid down on 6 November 1942 at Baltimore, Md., by the Bethlehem Fairfield Co.; launched on 5 December 1942; and transferred to the United Kingdom and commissioned on 15 February 1943. *LST–420* saw no active service in the United States Navy. She was sunk on 28 November 1944 while in Royal Navy service. *LST–420* was struck from the Navy list on 2 June 1945.

LST–421

LST–421 was laid down on 11 November 1942 at Baltimore, Md., by the Bethlehem Fairfield Co.; on 5 December 1942; and transferred to the United Kingdom and commissioned on 26 January 1943. *LST–421* saw no active service in the United States Navy. She was decommissioned and returned to United States Navy custody on 29 November 1946 and struck from the Navy list on 1 August 1947. The tank landing ship was sold to the Tung Hwa Trading Co., Singapore, on 7 October 1947 and converted for merchant service.

LST–422

LST–422 was laid down on 12 November 1942 at Baltimore, Md., by the Bethlehem Fairfield Co.; launched on 10 December 1942; and transferred to the United Kingdom and commissioned on 4 February 1943. *LST–422* saw no active service in the United States Navy. The tank landing ship was lost in action while in Royal Navy service in January 1944. She was struck from the Navy list on 16 May 1944.

LST–423

LST–423 was laid down on 1 December 1942 at Baltimore, Md., by the Bethlehem Fairfield Co.; launched on 14 January 1943; and transferred to the United Kingdom and commissioned on 24 February 1943. *LST–423* saw no active service in the United States Navy. The tank landing ship was decommissioned and returned to United States Navy custody on 10 June 1946 and struck from the Navy list on 19 July that same year. On 29 December 1947, she was sold to the Northern Metals Co., Philadelphia, Pa., and subsequently scrapped.

LST–424

LST–424 was laid down on 17 November 1942 at Baltimore, Md., by the Bethlehem Fairfield Co.; launched on 12 December 1942; and transferred to the United Kingdom and commissioned on 1 February 1943. *LST–424* saw no active service in the United States Navy. The tank landing ship was decommissioned and returned to United States Navy custody on 7 January 1946 and struck from the Navy list on 21 May 1946. On 3 July 1946, she was sold to Rinaldo De Haag, Italy, and subsequently scrapped.

LST–425

LST–425 was laid down on 16 November 1942 at Baltimore, Md., by the Bethlehem Fairfield Co.; launched on 12 December 1942; and transferred to the United Kingdom and commissioned on 10 February 1943. *LST–425* saw no active service in the United States Navy. The tank landing ship was decommissioned and returned to United States Navy custody on 30 August 1946 and struck from the Navy list on 10 June 1947. She was sold on 8 October 1947.

LST–426

LST–426 was laid down on 16 November 1942 at Baltimore, Md., by the Bethlehem Fairfield Co.; launched on 11 December 1942; and transferred to the United

Kingdom and commissioned on 16 February 1943. *LST-426* saw no active service in the United States Navy. The tank landing ship was decommissioned and returned to United States Navy custody on 23 April 1946 and struck from the Navy list on 19 June that same year. On 2 December 1947, she was sold to N. Block & Co., Norfolk, Va., and subsequently scrapped.

LST-427

LST-427 was laid down on 22 November 1942 at Baltimore, Md., by the Bethlehem Fairfield Co.; launched on 19 December 1942; and transferred to the United Kingdom and commissioned on 16 February 1943. *LST-427* saw no active service in the United States Navy. The tank landing ship was decommissioned and returned to United States Navy custody on 11 April 1946 and struck from the Navy list on 10 June 1947. On 5 December 1947, she was sold to Bosey, Philippines, and subsequently scrapped.

LST-428

LST-428 was laid down on 22 November 1942 at Baltimore, Md., by the Bethlehem Fairfield Co.; launched on 22 December 1942; and transferred to the United Kingdom and commissioned on 9 February 1943. *LST-428* saw no active service in the United States Navy. The tank landing ship was decommissioned and returned to United States Navy custody on 10 June 1946 and struck from the Navy list on 19 July that same year. On 10 October 1947, she was sold to Luria Bros. and Co., Inc., Philadelphia, Pa., and subsequently scrapped.

LST-429

LST-429 was laid down on 16 November 1942 at Baltimore, Md., by the Bethlehem Fairfield Co.; launched on 11 January 1943; and transferred to the United Kingdom and commissioned on 20 February 1943. *LST-429* saw no active service in the United States Navy. The tank landing ship was sunk while in Royal Navy service in July 1943. On 24 November 1943, *LST-429* was struck from the Navy list.

LST-430

LST-430 was laid down on 25 November 1942 at Baltimore, Md., by the Bethlehem Fairfield Co.; launched on 31 December 1942; and transferred to the United Kingdom and commissioned on 19 February 1943. *LST-430* saw no active service in the United States Navy. The tank landing ship was decommissioned and returned to United States Navy custody on 26 January 1946 and struck from the Navy list on 8 May that same year. On 12 October 1947, she was sold to the Northern Metals Co., Philadelphia, Pa., and subsequently scrapped.

LST-431 through LST-445

Contracts for *LST-431* through *LST-445* were cancelled on 16 September 1942.

LST-446

LST-446 was laid down on 15 June 1942 at Vancouver, Wash., by Kaiser, Inc.; launched on 18 September 1942; and commissioned on 30 November 1942, Lt. H. A. Swartz, USNR, in command.

During World War II, *LST-446* was assigned to the Asiatic-Pacific theater and participated in the following operations:

Consolidation of southern Solomons — March through June 1943
New Georgia Group operation:
    (a) New Georgia-Rendova-Vangunu occupation—July and August 1943
    (b) Vella Lavella occupation—August 1943
Treasury-Bouganville operation:
    (a) Occupation and defense of Cape Torokina —November and December 1943
Green Islands landing—February 1944
Capture and occupation of Guam—July 1944
Assault and occupation of Okinawa Gunto—April 1945

Following the war, *LST-446* performed occupation duty in the Far East until mid-December 1945. Upon her return to the United States, the tank landing ship was decommissioned on 13 July 1946 and struck from the Navy list on 8 October that same year. On 10 February 1947, she was sold to the Suwannee Fruit & Steamship Co., of Jacksonville, Fla., for conversion to merchant service.

LST-446 earned six battle stars and the Navy Unit Commendation for service in World War II.

LST-447

LST-447 was laid down on 10 July 1942 at Vancouver, Wash., by Kaiser, Inc.; launched on 22 September 1942; and commissioned on 13 December 1942.

During World War II, *LST-447* was assigned to the Asiatic-Pacific theater and participated in the following operations:

Consolidation of southern Solomons—June 1943
Occupation and defense of Cape Torokina—November and December 1943
Green Islands landings—February 1944
Hollandia operation—April 1944
Capture and occupation of Guam—July and August 1944
Assault and occupation of Okinawa Gunto—April 1945.

The tank landing ship was sunk off Okinawa on 7 April 1945 following a kamikaze attack. She was struck from the Navy list on 2 June 1945.

LST-447 earned five battle stars and the Navy Unit Commendation for World War II service.

LST-448

LST-448 was laid down on 10 July 1942 at Vancouver, Wash., by Kaiser, Inc.; launched on 26 September 1942; and commissioned on 23 December 1942.

During World War II, *LST-448* was assigned to the Asiatic-Pacific theater and participated in the consolidation of the southern Solomons in June 1943 and the Vella Lavella occupation in October 1943. The tank landing ship was bombed and sunk on 5 October 1943 off the Solomon Islands. She was struck from the Navy list on 26 October 1943.

LST-448 earned two battle stars and the Navy Unit Commendation for World War II service.

LST-449

LST-449 was laid down on 10 July 1942 at Vancouver, Wash., by Kaiser, Inc.; launched on 30 September 1942; and commissioned on 31 December 1942.

During World War II, *LST-449* was assigned to the Asiatic-Pacific theater and participated in the following operations:

Consolidation of southern Solomons — April through June 1943
Occupation and defense of Cape Torokina—November and December 1943
Capture and occupation of Guam—July 1944

Assault and occupation of Iwo Jima—February 1945

Assault and occupation of Okinawa Gunto—April 1945

Following the war, *LST–449* performed occupation duty in the Far East until early November 1945. She returned to the United States and was decommissioned on 16 March 1946 and struck from the Navy list on 28 March that same year. On 27 January 1947, the tank landing ship was sold to a private purchaser for scrapping.

LST–449 earned five battle stars and the Navy Unit Commendation for World War II service.

LST–450

LST–450 was laid down on 10 July 1942 at Vancouver, Wash., by Kaiser, Inc.; launched on 4 October 1942; and commissioned on 6 January 1943.

During World War II, *LST–450* was assigned to the Asiatic-Pacific theater and participated in the following operations:

Capture and occupation of Saipan—June through July 1944

Tinian capture and occupation—July 1944

Assault and occupation of Okinawa Gunto—April 1945

Following the war, *LST–450* was redesignated *LSTH–450* on 15 September 1945. She performed occupation duty in the Far East until early December 1945. Upon her return to the United States, the tank landing ship was decommissioned on 8 April 1946 and struck from the Navy list on 17 April that same year. On 16 April 1948, the ship was sold to the Bethlehem Steel Co., of Bethlehem, Pa., and subsequently scrapped.

LSTH–450 earned three battle stars and the Navy Unit Commendation for World War II service as *LST–450*.

LST–451

LST–451 was laid down on 20 July 1942 at Vancouver, Wash., by Kaiser, Inc.; launched on 6 October 1942; and commissioned on 12 January 1943.

During World War II, *LST–451* was assigned to the Asiatic-Pacific theater and participated in the following operations:

Capture and occupation of Saipan—June and July 1944

Tinian capture and occupation—July 1944

Leyte landing—October 1944

Lingayen Gulf landing—January 1945

Assault and occupation of Okinawa Gunto—April 1945

Following the war, *LST–451* performed occupation duty in the Far East until mid-February 1946. She returned to the United States and was decommissioned on 22 July 1946 and struck from the Navy list on 25 September that same year. On 11 December 1947, the tank landing ship was sold to the Learner Co., Oakland, Calif., and subsequently scrapped.

LST–451 earned five battle stars and the Navy Unit Commendation for World War II service.

LST–452

LST–452 was laid down on 20 July 1942 at Vancouver, Wash., by Kaiser, Inc.; launched on 10 October 1942; and commissioned on 16 January 1943.

During World War II, *LST–452* was assigned to the Asiatic-Pacific theater and participated in the following operations:

Eastern New Guinea operation:
(a) Lae occupation—September 1943
(b) Finschhafen occupation—September 1943
(c) Saidor occupation—January 1944

Bismarck Archipelago operation:
(a) Cape Gloucester, New Britain—December 1943 through February 1944
(b) Admiralty Islands landings—March 1944

Hollandia operation—April through May 1944

Western New Guinea operations:
(a) Biak Islands operation—May and June 1944
(b) Cape Sansapor operation—July and August 1944
(c) Morotai landing—September 1944

Leyte landings—October 1944

Lingayen Gulf landing—January 1945

Balikpapan operation—June and July 1945

Following the war, *LST–452* saw service in China until mid-May 1946. She returned to the United States and was decommissioned on 12 June 1946 and struck from the Navy list on 3 July that same year. On 5 December 1947, the ship was sold to Bosey, Philippines.

LST–452 earned seven battle stars and the Navy Unit Commendation for World War II service.

LST–453

LST–453 was laid down on 28 July 1942 at Vancouver, Wash., by Kaiser, Inc., launched on 10 October 1942; sponsored by Mrs. Edward M. Argersinger; and commissioned on 21 January 1943, Lt. A. J. Hamre, USNR, in command.

During World War II, *LST–453* was assigned to the Asiatic-Pacific theater and participated in the following operations:

Eastern New Guinea operation:
(a) Supporting and consolidation operations— September through December 1943
(b) Finschhafen occupation—December 1943 through February 1944

Bismarck Archipelago operation:
(a) Arawe, New Britain—December 1943

LST–453 was redesignated ARL–40 and named *Remus* (q.v.) on 15 August 1944. On 15 July 1946, she was decommissioned and struck from the Navy list on 15 August that same year. She was sold to B. T. Jones on 16 December 1947 for scrapping.

LST–453 earned one battle star for World War II service.

LST–454

LST–454 was laid down on 10 July 1942 at Vancouver, Wash., by Kaiser, Inc.; launched on 14 October 1942; and commissioned on 26 January 1943, Lt. E. R. Swanton, USNR, in command.

During World War II, *LST–454* was assigned to the Asiatic-Pacific theater and participated in the following operations:

Eastern New Guinea operation:
(a) Lae occupation—September 1943
(b) Finschhafen occupation—September 1943
(c) Saidor occupation—January 1944

Admiralty Islands landings—February through March 1944

Hollandia operation—April 1944

Western New Guinea operations:
(a) Biak Island operation—May and June 1944
(b) Morotai landing—September 1944

Leyte landings—October and November 1944

Lingayen Gulf landings—January 1945

Visayan Island landings—March and April 1945

Balikpapan operation—June and July 1945

Following the war, *LST–454* returned to the United States and was decommissioned on 25 March 1946 and struck from the Navy list on 1 May that same year. On 3 October 1947, the ship was sold to the Patapsco Scrap Corp., of Baltimore, Md., and subsequently scrapped.

LST–454 earned eight battle stars for World War II service.

LST-455

LST-455 was laid down on 3 August 1942 at Vancouver, Wash., by Kaiser, Inc.; launched on 17 October 1942; and commissioned on 30 January 1943.

During World War II, LST-455 was assigned to the Asiatic-Pacific theater and participated in the Lae operation in September 1943. She was redesignated ARL-41 and named Achilles on 21 August 1944. Following her redesignation, Achilles took part in the Leyte landings in October and November 1944 and the Brunei Bay landing in June 1945.

After the war, Achilles returned to the United States and was decommissioned on 19 July 1946 and struck from the Navy list on 28 August that same year. On 8 December 1947, she was transferred to the Nationalist Government of the Republic of China.

LST-455 earned one battle star for World War II service. Achilles (ARL-41) earned two battle stars for World War II service.

LST-456

LST-456 was laid down on 10 July 1942 at Vancouver, Wash., by Kaiser, Inc.; launched on 20 October 1942; and commissioned on 3 February 1943, Lt. Asa L. Perdue, USNR, in command.

During World War II, LST-456 was assigned to the Asiatic-Pacific theater and participated in the following operations:
  Eastern New Guinea operation:
    (a) Lae occupation—September 1943
    (b) Saidor occupation—January and February 1944
  Bismarck Archipelago operation:
    (a) Cape Gloucester, New Britain—December 1943, February and March 1944
    (b) Admiralty Islands landings—March 1944
  Hollandia operation—April 1944
  Western New Guinea operations:
    (a) Toem-Wakde-Sarmi area operation—May 1944
    (b) Biak Island operation—May and June 1944
    (c) Cape Sansapor operation—July and August 1944
    (d) Morotai landing—September 1944
  Leyte landings—October 1944
  Lingayen Gulf landing—January 1945
  Mindanao Island landings—April 1945
  Balikpapan operation—June and July 1945

Following the war, LST-456 performed occupation duty in the Far East until early February 1946. She served with the Military Sea Transportation Service as USNS LST-456 from 31 March 1952 until she was struck from the Navy list on 15 June 1973. On 27 September 1973, the ship was sold to the Maritime Co. Ltd., Khorramshahr, Iran.

LST-456 earned eight battle stars for World War II service.

LST-457

LST-457 was laid down on 3 August 1942 at Vancouver, Wash., by Kaiser, Inc.; launched on 23 October 1942; and commissioned on 6 February 1943, Lt. John R. Riley, USNR, in command.

During World War II, LST-457 was assigned to the Asiatic-Pacific theater and participated in the following operations:
  Eastern New Guinea operation:
    (a) Lae occupation—September 1943
    (b) Saidor occupation—January and February 1944
  Bismarck Archipelago operations:
    (a) Cape Gloucester, New Britain—December 1943, January and February 1944
    (b) Admiralty Islands landings—March 1944
  Hollandia operation—April 1944
  Western New Guinea operation:
    (a) Toem-Wakde-Sarmi area operation—May 1944
    (b) Biak Island operation—May and June 1944
    (c) Noemfoor Island operation—July 1944
    (d) Morotai landings—September 1944
  Leyte landings—November 1944
  Visayan Island landings—March and April 1945
  Balikpapan operation—June and July 1945

Following the war, LST-457 performed occupation duty in the Far East until mid-October 1945. She returned to the United States and was decommissioned on 15 March 1946. The ship was struck from the Navy list on 29 September 1947. On 20 April 1948, she was sold to the Bethlehem Steel Co., of Bethlehem, Pa., and subsequently scrapped.

LST-457 earned seven battle stars for World War II service.

LST-458

LST-458 was laid down on 18 September 1942 at Vancouver, Wash., by Kaiser, Inc.; launched on 26 October 1942; and commissioned on 10 February 1943, Lt. F. W. Hinrichs, USNR, in command.

During World War II, LST-458 was assigned to the Asiatic-Pacific theater and participated in the following operations:
  Eastern New Guinea operation:
    (a) Lae occupation—September 1943
    (b) Saidor occupation—February 1944
  Bismarck Archipelago operation:
    (a) Cape Gloucester, New Britain—December 1943, January and February 1944
    (b) Admiralty Islands landings—March 1944
  Hollandia operation—April 1944
  Western New Guinea operations:
    (a) Toem-Wakde-Sarmi area operation—May 1944
    (b) Biak Island operation—June 1944
    (c) Noemfoor Island operation—July 1944
    (d) Cape Sansapor operation—August 1944
    (e) Morotai landings—September 1944
  Leyte landings—October and November 1944
  Mindanao Island landings—April 1945

Following the war, LST-458 performed occupation duty in the Far East until mid-October 1945. Upon her return to the United States, she was decommissioned on 15 April 1946 and struck from the Navy list on 3 July 1946. On 31 October 1947, the ship was sold to the Luria Steel & Trading Corp., of Philadelphia, Pa., and subsequently scrapped.

LST-458 earned six battle stars and the Navy Unit Commendation for World War II service.

LST-459

LST-459 was laid down on 22 September 1942 at Vancouver, Wash., by Kaiser, Inc.; launched on 29 October 1942; and commissioned on 13 February 1943.

During World War II, LST-459 was assigned to the Asiatic-Pacific theater and participated in the following operations:
  Bismarck Archipelago operation:
    (a) Cape Gloucester, New Britain—December 1943, January and February 1944
    (b) Admiralty Islands landings—March 1944
  Hollandia operation—April and May 1944
  Western New Guinea operations:
    (a) Biak Island operation—May and June 1944
    (b) Noemfoor Island operation—July 1944
    (c) Cape Sansapor operation—August 1944
    (d) Morotai landings—September 1944
  Leyte landings—November 1944

Lingayen Gulf landing—January 1945
Consolidation of the southern Philippines:
    (a) Mindanao Island landings—March 1945
    (b) Sulu Archipelago landings—April 1945
Following the war, *LST–459* performed occupation duty in the Far East until mid-November 1945. Upon her return to the United States, she was decommissioned on 12 April 1946 and struck from the Navy list on 19 June that same year. On 31 October 1947, the ship was sold to the New Orleans Shipwrecking Co., New Orleans, La., and subsequently scrapped.

LST–459 earned six battle stars for World War II service.

LST–460

LST–460 was laid down on 26 September 1942 at Vancouver, Wash., by Kaiser, Inc.; launched on 31 October 1942; and commissioned on 15 February 1943, Lt. Everett E. Weire in command.

During World War II, *LST–460* was assigned to the Asiatic-Pacific theater and participated in the following operations:
    Consolidation of southern Solomons—June 1943
    Vella-Lavella occupation—August 1943
    Treasury Island landing—November 1943
    Hollandia operation—April 1944
    Morotai landings—September 1944
    Leyte landings—November 1944
    Mindoro landing—December 1944

LST–460 was lost in action due to an enemy aircraft attack on 21 December 1944 off Mindoro, Philippines. She was struck from the Navy list on 19 January 1945.

LST–460 earned six battle stars and the Navy Unit Commendation for World War II service.

LST–461

LST–461 was laid down on 30 September 1942 at Vancouver, Wash., by Kaiser, Inc.; launched on 3 November 1942; sponsored by Mrs. Eugene E. Blazier; and commissioned on 18 February 1943, Lt. E. A. Bjork, USNR, in command.

During World War II, *LST–461* was assigned to the Asiatic-Pacific theater and participated in the following operations:
    Capture and occupation of Saipan—June and July 1944
    Tinian capture and occupation—July 1944
    Leyte landings—October 1944
    Manila Bay-Bicol operation:
        (a) Nasugbu—January 1945
    Lingayen Gulf landing—January 1945
    Assault and occupation of Okinawa Gunto—May 1945
Following the war, *LST–461* returned to the United States and was decommissioned on 2 September 1947 and struck from the Navy list on 16 September that same year. On 30 March 1948, the tank landing ship was sold to Consolidated Builders, Inc., of Seattle, Wash., and subsequently scrapped.

LST–461 earned five battle stars for World War II service.

LST–462

LST–462 was laid down on 4 October 1942 at Vancouver, Wash., by Kaiser, Inc.; launched on 6 November 1942; and commissioned on 21 February 1943, Lt. C. K. Ragan in command.

During World War II, *LST–462* was assigned to the Asiatic-Pacific theater and participated in the following operations:
    Hollandia operation—May 1944
    Western New Guinea operations:
        (a) Biak Island operation—May and June 1944

        (b) Noemfoor Island operation—July 1944
        (c) Cape Sansapor operation—July and August 1944
        (d) Morotai landings—September 1944
    Leyte landings—October 1944
    Lingayen Gulf landing—January 1945
    Balikpapan operation—July 1945
Following the war, *LST–462* returned to the United States and was decommissioned on 21 March 1946 and struck from the Navy list on 1 May that same year. On 15 December 1948, she was sold to Hughes Bros., Inc., New York, N.Y., and subsequently scrapped.

LST–462 earned four battle stars for World War II service.

LST–463

LST–463 was laid down on 6 October 1942 at Vancouver, Wash., by Kaiser, Inc., launched on 9 November 1942; and commissioned on 23 February 1943.

During World War II, *LST–463* was assigned to the Asiatic-Pacific theater and participated in the following operations:
    Cape Gloucester, New Britain—December 1943, January through March 1944
    Saidor occupation—January and February 1944
    Hollandia operation—April 1944
    Western New Guinea operations:
        (a) Biak Island operation—May and June 1944
        (b) Noemfoor Island operation—July 1944
        (c) Cape Sansapor operation—July and August 1944
        (d) Morotai landings—September 1944
    Leyte landings—October and November 1944
    Lingayen Gulf landing—January 1945
    Manila Bay-Bicol operation:
        (a) Nasugbu—January 1945
    Mindanao Island landings—April 1945
    Assault and occupation of Okinawa Gunto—June 1945
Following the war, *LST–463* returned to the United States and was decommissioned on 6 June 1946 and struck from the Navy list on 19 June that same year. On 3 November 1947, the tank landing ship was sold to Dulien Steel Products, Inc., of Seattle, Wash.

LST–463 earned nine battle stars for World War II service.

LST–464

LST–464 was laid down on 10 October 1942 at Vancouver, Wash., by Kaiser, Inc.; launched on 12 November 1942; and commissioned on 25 February 1943, Lt. Augustin K. Ridgway, USNR, in command.

During World War II, *LST–464* was assigned to the Asiatic-Pacific theater and participated in the following operations:
    Supporting and consolidations designated by Commander 7th Fleet—May through October 1944
    Leyte landings—October and November 1944
Following the war, *LST–464* was redesignated *LSTH–464* on 15 September and performed occupation duty in the Far East until late September 1945. The tank landing ship returned to the United States and was decommissioned on 16 April 1946 and struck from the Navy list on 19 June 1946. On 5 March 1948, she was sold to the Port Houston Iron Works, Inc., of Houston, Tex., for non-self-propelled operation.

LST–464 earned two battle stars and the Navy Unit Commendation for World War II service.

LST–465

LST–465 was laid down on 17 December 1942 at Vancouver, Wash., by Kaiser, Inc.; launched on 9 January

The landing craft repair ship *Satyr* (ARL–23), originally ordered as LST–852. Her bow doors are welded shut, and she has been equipped with booms and workshops for emergency repairs to amphibious craft in forward areas. Smaller craft can be lifted on board for repair or servicing.

1943; and commissioned on 27 February 1943, Lt. L. A. Smith, USNR, in command.

During World War II, *LST–465* was assigned to the Asiatic-Pacific theater and participated in the following operations:

Bismarck-Archipelago operation:
    (a) Cape Gloucester, New Britain—December 1943, January and February 1944
    (b) Admiralty Islands landings—March 1944
Saidor occupation—February 1944
Hollandia operation—April 1944
Western New Guinea operations:
    (a) Toem-Wakde-Sarmi area operation—May 1944
    (b) Morotai landings—September 1944
Leyte landings—October and November 1944
Lingayen Gulf landing—January 1945

Following the war, *LST–465* performed occupation duty in the Far East in October and November 1945. Upon her return to the United States, the tank landing ship was decommissioned on 8 March 1946 and struck from the Navy list on 12 April 1946. On 30 September 1947, she was sold to Patapsco Scrap Corp., Baltimore, Md., for scrapping.

LST–465 earned six batttle stars for World War II service.

LST–466

LST–466 was laid down on 14 October 1942 at Vancouver, Wash., by Kaiser, Inc.; launched on 18 November 1942; and commissioned on 1 March 1943.

During World War II, *LST–466* was assigned to the Asiatic-Pacific theater and participated in the following operations:

Eastern New Guinea operation:
    (a) Lae occupation—September 1943
    (b) Saidor occupation—January 1944
Bismarck Archipelago operation:
    (a) Cape Gloucester, New Britain—December 1943 and February 1944
    (b) Admiralty Islands landings—February and March 1944

Hollandia operation—April and May 1944
Western New Guinea operations:
    (a) Toem-Wakde-Sarmi area operation—May 1944
    (b) Biak Island operation—May and June 1944
    (c) Noemfoor Island operation—July 1944
    (d) Cape Sansapor operation—July and August 1944
Leyte landings—October 1944
Lingayen Gulf landing—January 1945
Borneo operation:
    (a) Tarakan Island operation—April and May 1945
    (b) Balikpapan operation—June and July 1945

Following the war, *LST–466* performed occupation duty in the Far East in October 1945 and saw service in China in November and December 1945. Upon her return to the United States, the tank landing ship was decommissioned on 8 March 1946 and struck from the Navy list on 12 April that same year. On 4 June 1948, she was sold to Hughes Bros., Inc., of New York, N.Y., and subsequently scrapped.

LST–466 earned seven battle stars for World War II service.

LST–467

LST–467 was laid down on 17 October 1942 at Vancouver, Wash., by Kaiser, Inc.; launched on 21 November 1942; and commissioned on 3 March 1943, Lt. Milton B. Taylor, USNR, in command.

During World War II, *LST–467* was assigned to the Asiatic-Pacific theater and participated in the following operations:

Lae occupation—September 1943
Cape Gloucester, New Britain—December 1943 and February 1944
Hollandia operation—April 1944
Western New Guinea operations:
    (a) Toem-Wakde-Sarmi area operation—May 1944

(b) Biak Island operation—June 1944
(c) Noemfoor Island operation—June and July 1944
(d) Cape Sansapor operation—August 1944
(e) Morotai landings—September 1944
Leyte landings—October and November 1944
Lingayen Gulf landing—January 1945
Consolidation of the southern Philippines:
(a) Palawan Island landings—March 1945
(b) Visayan Island landings—March 1945
Tarakan Island operation—April and May 1945
Following the war, *LST–467* returned to the United States and was decommissioned on 28 May 1946 and struck from the Navy list on 5 June 1946. On 22 November 1946, the tank landing ship was sold to the National Metal & Steel Corp., Terminal Island, Calif.

LST–467 earned seven battle stars and the Navy Unit Commendation for World War II service.

LST–468

LST–468 was laid down on 20 October 1942 at Vancouver, Wash., by Kaiser, Inc.; launched on 24 November 1942; and commissioned on 5 March 1943.

During World War II, *LST–468* was assigned to the Asiatic-Pacific theater and participated in the following operations:
Eastern New Guinea operation:
(a) Lae occupation—September 1943
(b) Saidor occupation—January and February 1944
Bismarck Archipelago operation:
(a) Cape Gloucester, New Britain—December 1943 and February 1944
(b) Admiralty Island landings—March 1944
Hollandia operation—April 1944
Western New Guinea operations:
(a) Biak Island operation—May and June 1944
(b) Noemfoor Island operation—July 1944
(c) Cape Sansapor operation—July and August 1944
(d) Morotai landings—September 1944
Leyte landings—October and November 1944
Lingayen Gulf landing—January 1945
Mindanao Island landings—April 1945
Following the war, *LST–468* returned to the United States and was decommissioned on 12 April 1946 and struck from the Navy list on 5 June that same year. On 30 September 1947, the tank landing ship was sold to the Patapsco Scrap Corp., Baltimore, Md., and subsequently scrapped.

LST–468 earned seven battle stars and the Navy Unit Commendation for World War II service.

LST–469

LST–469 was laid down on 23 October 1942 at Vancouver, Wash., by Kaiser, Inc.; launched on 27 November 1942; and commissioned on 8 March 1943.

During World War II, *LST–469* was assigned to the Asiatic-Pacific theater and participated in the following operations:
Hollandia operation—April 1944
Western New Guinea operations:
(a) Toem-Wakde-Sarmi area operation—May 1944
(b) Biak Island operation—May and June 1944
(c) Noemfoor Island operation—July 1944
(d) Cape Sansapor operation—July and August 1944
(e) Morotai landings—September 1944
Leyte landings—October 1944
Lingayen Gulf landing—January 1945
Following the war, *LST–469* performed occupation duty in the Far East until 24 October 1945 and saw

China service from 25 October to 2 November 1945. Upon her return to the United States, *LST–469* was decommissioned on 27 March 1946 and struck from the Navy list on 1 May that same year. On 13 December 1947, the tank landing ship was sold to Hughes Bros., Inc., New York, N.Y., for scrapping.

LST–469 earned four battle stars for World War II service.

LST–470

LST–470 was laid down on 26 October 1942 at Vancouver, Wash., by Kaiser, Inc.; launched on 30 November 1942; and commissioned on 9 March 1943, Lt. Richard McMahon, USNR, in command.

During World War II, *LST–470* was assigned to the Asiatic-Pacific theater and participated in the following operations:
Eastern New Guinea operation:
(a) Lae occupation—September 1943
(b) Saidor occupation—January 1944
Bismarck Archipelago operation:
(a) Cape Gloucester, New Britain—December 1943
(b) Admiralty Islands landing—March 1944
Hollandia operation—April 1944
Western New Guinea operations:
(a) Biak Island operation—May and June 1944
(b) Cape Sansapor operation—July and August 1944
(c) Morotai landings—September 1944
Leyte landings—October and November 1944
Lingayen Gulf landing—January 1945
Consolidation of the southern Philippines:
(a) Palawan Island landings—February and March 1945
(b) Mindanao Island landings—April 1945
Balikpapan operation—June and July 1945
Following the war, *LST–470* returned to the United States and was decommissioned on 4 March 1946 and struck from the Navy list on 5 June that same year. On 4 November 1947, the tank landing ship was sold to Dulien Steel Products, Inc., Seattle, Wash., and subsequently scrapped.

LST–470 earned eight battle stars and the Navy Unit Commendation for World War II service.

LST–471

LST–471 was laid down on 29 October 1942 at Vancouver, Wash., by Kaiser, Inc.; launched on 3 December 1942; and commissioned on 11 March 1943, Lt. Samuel C. Otto, USNR, in command.

During World War II, *LST–471* was assigned to the Asiatic-Pacific theater and participated in the following operations:
Lae occupation—September 1943
Leyte landing—October and November 1944
Lingayen Gulf landing—January 1945
Mindanao Island landings—March 1945
Balikpapan operation—June and July 1945
Following World War II, *LST–471* returned to the United States and was decommissioned on 26 February 1946 and struck from the Navy list on 12 April that same year. On 21 January 1948, the tank landing ship was sold to Hughes Bros., Inc., New York, N.Y., and subsequently scrapped.

LST–471 earned five battle stars for World War II service.

LST–472

LST–472 was laid down on 31 October 1942 at Vancouver, Wash., by Kaiser, Inc.; launched on 7 December 1942; sponsored by Mrs. Frank C. Huntoon; and commissioned on 13 March 1943.

During World War II, *LST–472* was assigned to the Asiatic-Pacific theater and participated in the following operations:

Consolidation of southern Solomons—June 1943

New Georgia-Rendova-Vangunu occupation—July 1943

Occupation and defense of Cape Torokina—November and December 1943

Green Islands landings—February 1944

Hollandia operation—April 1944

Western New Guinea operations:

(a) Toem-Wakde-Sarmi area operations—May 1944

(b) Biak Island operation—June 1944

(c) Noemfoor Island operation—July 1944

(d) Cape Sansapor operation—August 1944

(e) Morotai landings—September 1944

Mindoro landings—December 1944

LST–472 was sunk during action with the enemy off Mindoro Island, Philippines, on 21 December 1944 and struck from the Navy list on 19 January 1945.

LST–472 earned six battle stars and the Navy Unit Commendation for World War II service.

LST–473

LST–473 was laid down on 10 July 1942 at Vancouver, Wash., by Kaiser, Inc.; launched on 9 December 1942; and commissioned on 16 March 1943, Lt. R. W. Dillard in command.

During World War II, *LST–473* was assigned to the Asiatic-Pacific theater and participated in the following operations:

Lae occupation—September 1943

Leyte landings—October 1944

Lingayen Gulf landing—January 1945

Zambales-Subic Bay—January 1945

Mindanao Island landings—April 1945

Following the war, *LST–473* returned to the United States and was decommissioned on 18 March 1946 and struck from the Navy list on 17 April that same year. On 21 April 1948, the tank landing ship was sold to Hughes Bros., Inc., New York, N.Y., and subsequently scrapped.

LST–473 earned five battle stars for World War II service.

LST–474

LST–474 was laid down on 10 July 1942 at Vancouver, Wash., by Kaiser, Inc.; launched on 12 December 1942; and commissioned on 19 March 1943, Lt. R. W. Langworthy in command.

During World War II, *LST–474* was assigned to the Asiatic-Pacific theater and participated in the following operations:

Eastern New Guinea operation:

(a) Lae occupation—September 1943

(b) Saidor occupation—January 1944

Cape Gloucester, New Britain—December 1943

Hollandia operation—April 1944

Western New Guinea operations:

(a) Biak Island operation—May and June 1944

(b) Morotai landings—September 1944

Leyte landings—October and November 1944

Lingayen Gulf landing—January 1945

Mindanao Island landings—April 1945

Balikpapan operation—June and July 1945

Following the war, *LST–474* performed occupation duty in the Far East in September 1945. She returned to the United States and was decommissioned on 22 March 1946 and struck from the Navy list on 17 April that same year. On 17 December 1947, the ship was sold to the Ships and Power Equipment Corp., of Barber, N.J., and subsequently scrapped.

LST–474 earned eight battle stars for World War II service.

LST–475

LST–475 was laid down on 10 July 1942 at Vancouver, Wash., by Kaiser, Inc.; launched on 16 November 1942; and commissioned on 20 March 1943, Lt. Comdr. T. D. Blake, USNR, in command.

During World War II, *LST–475* was assigned to the Asiatic-Pacific theater and participated in the following operations:

Eastern New Guinea operation:

(a) Lae occupation—September 1943

(b) Saidor occupation—January 1944

Cape Gloucester, New Britain—December 1943 and January 1944

Hollandia operation—April 1944

Western New Guinea operations:

(a) Noemfoor Island operations—July 1944

(b) Cape Sansapor operation—July and August 1944

(c) Morotai landings—September 1944

Leyte landings—October and November 1944

Lingayen Gulf landing—January 1945

Following the war, *LST–475* performed occupation duty in the Far East until mid-October 1945. Upon her return to the United States, the ship was decommissioned on 24 April 1946 and struck from the Navy list on 5 June that same year. On 31 October 1946, she was sold to the Suwannee Fruit & Steamship Co., Jacksonville, Fla.

LST–475 earned six battle stars for World War II service.

LST–476

LST–476 was laid down on 5 August 1942 at Richmond, Calif., by Kaiser Co., Inc.; launched on 10 October 1942; and commissioned on 4 April 1943, Lt. W. J. Steffens, USNR, in command.

During World War II, *LST–476* was assigned to the Asiatic-Pacific theater and participated in the following operations:

Gilbert Islands operation—November and December 1943

Occupation of Kwajalein and Majuro Atolls—February 1944

Hollandia operation—April 1944

Capture and occupation of Guam—July and August 1944

Cape Sansapor operation—August 1944

Following the war, *LST–476* performed occupation duty in the Far East until early February 1946. Upon her return to the United States, *LST–476* was decommissioned on 12 February 1946 and struck from the Navy list on 31 October 1947. On 1 June 1948, the ship was sold to the Puget Sound Bridge & Dredging Co., of Seattle, Wash., and subsequently scrapped.

LST–476 earned five battle stars for World War II service.

LST–477

LST–477 was laid down on 12 August 1942 at Richmond, Calif., by Kaiser, Inc.; launched on 29 October 1942; and commissioned on 19 February 1942, Lt. Josiah K. Adams, USNR, in command.

During World War II, *LST–477* was assigned to the Asiatic-Pacific theater and participated in the following operations:

Gilbert Islands operation—November and December 1943

Occupation of Kwajalein and Majuro Atolls—February 1944

Capture and occupation of Guam—July 1944

Assault and occupation of Iwo Jima—February 1945

Following the war, *LST–477* was redesignated *LST(H)–477* on 15 September 1945. She performed occupation duty in the Far East until mid-February 1946. She returned to the United States and was struck from the Navy list on 28 August 1947. On 27 March 1948, the ship was sold to Consolidated Builders, Inc., of Seattle, Wash., and subsequently scrapped.

LST-477 earned four battle stars and the Navy Unit Commendation for World War II service.

LST–478

LST-478 was laid down on 17 August 1942 at Richmond, Calif., by Kaiser, Inc.; launched on 7 November 1942; and commissioned on 13 March 1943, Lt. H. F. Holmshaw in command.

During World War II, *LST-478* was assigned to the Asiatic-Pacific theater and participated in the following operations:

Gilbert Island operation—November and December 1943
Hollandia operation—April 1944
Capture and occupation of Guam—July 1944
Leyte landings—October 1944
Assault and occupation of Okinawa Gunto—April 1945

Following the war, *LST-478* performed occupation duty in the Far East until mid-March 1946. She returned to the United States and was decommissioned on 23 March 1946 and struck from the Navy list on 28 August 1947. On 25 March 1948, the ship was sold to Consolidated Builders, Inc., Seattle, Wash., for scrapping.

LST-478 earned five battle stars for World War II service.

LST–479

LST-479 was laid down on 25 August 1942 at Richmond, Calif., by Kaiser, Inc.; launched on 4 October 1942; and commissioned on 19 April 1943.

During World War II, *LST-479* was assigned to the Asiatic-Pacific theater and participated in the following operations:

Gilbert Islands operation—November and December 1943
Occupation of Kwajalein and Majuro Atolls—February 1944
Hollandia operation—April 1944
Capture and occupation of Guam—July 1944
Assault and occupation of Okinawa Gunto—March and April 1945

Following the war, *LST-479* returned to the United States and was decommissioned on 28 February 1946 and was struck from the Navy list on 28 March that same year. On 16 April 1948, the ship was sold to the Bethlehem Steel Co., Bethlehem, Pa., and subsequently scrapped.

LST-479 earned five battle stars for World War II service.

LST–480

LST-480 was laid down on 31 August 1942 at Richmond, Calif., by Kaiser, Inc.; launched on 29 October 1942; and commissioned on 3 May 1943.

During World War II, *LST-480* was assigned to the Asiatic-Pacific theater and participated in the Gilbert Islands operation in November and December 1943 and the occupation of Kwajalein and Majuro Atolls in February 1944. The ship was lost through an accident on 21 May 1944. She was struck from the Navy list on 18 July 1944.

LST-480 earned two battle stars for World War II service.

LST–481

LST-481 was laid down on 4 September 1942 at Richmond, Calif., by Kaiser, Inc.; launched on 2 December 1942; and commissioned on 15 May 1943.

During World War II, *LST-481* was assigned to the Asiatic-Pacific theater and participated in the following operations:

Gilbert Islands operation—November and December 1943
Occupation of Kwajalein and Majuro Atolls—January and February 1944
Hollandia operation—April 1944
Capture and occupation of Guam—July 1944
Assault and occupation of Iwo Jima—February 1945
Assault and occupation of Okinawa Gunto—April 1945

Following the war, *LST-481* performed occupation duty in the Far East until mid-November 1945. She returned to the United States and was decommissioned on 28 February 1946 and struck from the Navy list on 12 April 1946. On 16 April 1948, the ship was sold to the Bethlehem Steel Co., Bethlehem, Pa., and subsequently scrapped.

LST-481 earned six battle stars for World War II service.

LST–482

LST-482 was laid down on 14 September 1942 at Richmond, Calif., by Kaiser, Inc.; launched on 17 December 1942; and commissioned on 20 March 1943, Lt. R. L. Eddy, USNR, in command.

During World War II, *LST-482* was assigned to the Asiatic-Pacific theater and participated in the following operations:

Gilbert Islands operation—November and December 1943
Occupation of Kwajalein and Majuro Atolls—January and February 1944
Hollandia operation—April 1944
Capture and occupation of Guam—July 1944
Leyte landings—October 1944
Lingayen Gulf landing—January 1945

Following the war, *LST-482* was redesignated *LSTH-482* on 15 September 1945. She performed occupation duty in the Far East in November and December 1945. Upon her return to the United States, she was decommissioned on 23 February 1946 and redesignated *LST-482* on 6 March 1952. The tank landing ship was subsequently named *Branch County* (LST-482) on 1 July 1955 after a county in Michigan. Her name was struck from the Navy list on 11 August 1955. In early March 1956, the ship was sunk by naval gunfire and submarine-launched torpedoes in an exercise off San Diego, Calif.

LST-482 earned six battle stars for World War II service.

LST–483

LST-483 was laid down on 21 September 1942 at Richmond, Calif., by Kaiser, Inc.; launched on 30 December 1942; and commissioned on 3 May 1943.

During World War II, *LST-483* was assigned to the Asiatic-Pacific theater and participated in the following operations:

Capture and occupation of Saipan—June and July 1944
Tinian capture and occupation—July 1944
Leyte landings—October 1944
Assault and occupation of Okinawa Gunto—April 1945

Following the war, *LST-483* performed occupation duty in the Far East until early February 1946. Upon her return to the United States, she was decommissioned on 10 February 1946. The tank landing ship was redesignated *Brewster County* (LST–483) on 1 July 1955 after a county in Texas. Her name was struck from the Navy list on 11 August 1955, and she was later sunk as a target.

LST–483 earned four battle stars for World War II service.

LST–484

LST–484 was laid down on 28 September 1942 at Richmond, Calif., by Kaiser, Inc.; launched on 2 January 1943; and commissioned on 23 April 1943.

During World War II, *LST–484* was assigned to the Asiatic-Pacific theater and participated in the following operations:

> Gilbert Islands operation:
> > (a) Occupation of Kwajalein and Majuro Atolls—February 1944
> > (b) Occupation of Eniwetok Atoll—February and March 1944
> Capture and occupation of Saipan—June and July 1944
> Tinian capture and occupation—July 1944
> Assault and occupation of Okinawa Gunto—March through June 1945

Following the war, *LST–484* performed occupation duty in the Far East until mid-February 1946. Upon her return to the United States, she was decommissioned on 27 July 1946 and struck from the Navy list on 28 August that same year. On 13 December 1947, the ship was sold to Kaiser Co., Inc., Seattle, Wash., and subsequently scrapped.

LST–484 earned five battle stars for World War II service.

LST–485

LST–485 was laid down on 17 December 1942 at Richmond, Calif., by Kaiser, Inc.; launched on 9 January 1943; and commissioned on 19 May 1943.

During World War II, *LST–485* was assigned to the Asiatic-Pacific theater and participated in the following operations:

> Vella-Lavella occupation—September 1943
> Treasury Island landings—October through November 1943
> Capture and occupation of Saipan—June and August 1944
> Tinian capture and occupation—July and August 1944
> Assault and occupation of Okinawa Gunto—May through June 1945

Following the war, *LST–485* saw China service in January and February 1946 and performed occupation duty in the Far East until early March 1946. Upon her return to the United States, she was decommissioned on 30 July 1946 and struck from the Navy list on 28 August that same year. On 29 March 1948, the ship was sold to Kaiser Co., Inc., Seattle, Wash., and subsequently scrapped.

LST–485 earned five battle stars and the Navy Unit Commendation for World War II service.

LST–486

LST–486 was laid down on 31 December 1942 at Richmond, Calif., by Kaiser, Inc.; launched on 16 January 1943; and commissioned on 29 May 1943.

During World War II, *LST–486* was assigned to the Asiatic-Pacific theater and participated in the following operations:

> Capture and occupation of Saipan—June and July 1944
> Tinian capture and occupation—July 1944
> Leyte landings—October 1944
> Lingayen Gulf landing—January 1945

Following the war, *LST–486* was redesignated LSTH–486 on 15 September 1945. She performed occupation duty in the Far East until early January 1946. Upon her return to the United States, the ship was decommissioned on 13 January 1946. The tank landing ship was operated by the Shipping Control Authority, Japan, until destroyed on 23 July 1947. Her name was struck from the Navy list on 28 August 1947.

LST–486 earned four battle stars for World War II service.

LST–487

LST–487 was laid down on 2 January 1943 at Richmond, Calif., by Kaiser, Inc.; launched on 23 January 1943; and commissioned on 27 April 1943.

During World War II, *LST–487* was assigned to the Asiatic-Pacific theater and participated in the following operations:

> Capture and occupation of Saipan—June and July 1944
> Tinian capture and occupation—July 1944
> Capture and occupation of southern Palau Islands—September and October 1944
> Lingayen Gulf landing—January 1945
> Assault and occupation of Okinawa Gunto—May 1945

Following the war, *LST–487* performed occupation duty in the Far East until early November 1945. Upon her return to the United States, she was decommissioned on 15 March 1946 and struck from the Navy list on 1 May that same year. On 20 February 1948, the ship was sold to Brown & Root, of Houston, Tex., for merchant service.

LST–487 earned five battle stars for World War II service.

LST–488

LST–488 was laid down on 11 January 1943 at Richmond, Calif., by Kaiser, Inc.; launched on 5 March 1943; and commissioned on 24 May 1943.

During World War II, *LST–488* was assigned to the Asiatic-Pacific theater and participated in the following operations:

> Occupation and defense of Cape Torokina—November 1943
> Capture and occupation of Guam—July 1944
> Leyte landing—October 1944
> Lingayen Gulf landing—January 1945

Following the war, *LST–488* was redesignated LSTH–488 on 15 September 1945 and performed occupation duty in the Far East until early January 1946. Upon her return to the United States, she was decommissioned on 11 January 1946. She was redesignated LST–488 on 6 March 1952 and served with the Military Sea Transportation Service as USNS *LST–488* in the postwar period. The ship was transferred to the Republic of the Philippines as a lease on 15 July 1972.

LST–488 earned four battle stars and the Navy Unit Commendation for World War II service.

LST–489

LST–489 was redesignated ARL–2 and named *Amycus* (q.v.) on 13 January 1943.

LST–490

LST–490 was redesignated ARL–3 and named *Agenor* (q.v.) on 13 January 1943.

LST–491

LST–491 was laid down on 29 July 1943 at Evansville, Ind., by the Missouri Valley Bridge & Iron Co.;

launched on 23 September 1943; sponsored by Mrs. Barton Cook; and commissioned on 3 December 1943.

During World War II, *LST–491* was assigned to the European theater and participated in the invasion of Normandy in June 1944 and the invasion of southern France in August and September 1944. She was then assigned to the Asiatic-Pacific theater and took part in the assault and occupation of Okinawa Gunto in May and June 1945.

Following the war, *LST–491* performed occupation duty in the Far East until early January 1946. The tank landing ship returned to the United States and was decommissioned on 12 January 1946. She was loaned to the Japanese government on 31 March 1952 and operated under the Shipping Control Authority, Japan. The ship was later operated by MSTS (later MSC) Pacific. *LST–491* was struck from the Navy list in June 1975 and transferred to the Philippine Navy on 13 September 1976.

LST–491 earned three battle stars for World War II service.

LST–492

LST–492 was laid down on 3 August 1943 at Evansville, Ind., by the Missouri Valley Bridge & Iron Co.; launched on 30 September 1943; sponsored by Mrs. John A. Spruill; and commissioned on 8 December 1943.

During World War II, *LST–492* was assigned to the European theater and participated in the invasion of Normandy in June 1944 and the invasion of southern France in August and September 1945. She was then assigned to the Asiatic-Pacific theater and participated in the assault and occupation of Okinawa Gunto in May and June 1945.

Following the war, *LST–492* performed occupation duty in the Far East until early December 1945. Upon her return to the United States, she was decommissioned on 17 June 1946 and struck from the Navy list on 23 June 1947. On 24 February 1948, the tank landing ship was sold to Green's Bayou Transporters, Houston, Tex., for non-self-propelled operation.

LST–492 earned three battle stars for World War II service.

LST–493

LST–493 was laid down on 9 August 1943 at Evansville, Ind., by the Missouri Valley Bridge & Iron Co.; launched on 4 October 1943; sponsored by Mrs. Charles M. Hoagland; and commissioned on 13 December 1943.

During World War II, *LST–493* was assigned to the European theater and participated in the invasion of Normandy in June 1944. She grounded while attempting to enter Plymouth Harbor, England, on 12 April 1945 and was broken up and destroyed. The ship was struck from the Navy list on 19 May 1945.

LST–493 earned one battle star for World War II service.

LST–494

LST–494 was laid down on 10 August 1943 at Evansville, Ind., by the Missouri Valley Bridge & Iron Co.; launched on 11 October 1943; sponsored by Miss Marilyn Elise Stevens; and commissioned on 18 December 1943.

During World War II, *LST–494* was assigned to the European theater and participated in the invasion of Normandy in June 1944 and the invasion of southern France in August and September 1944. She was then assigned to the Asiatic-Pacific theater and took part in the assault and occupation of Okinawa Gunto in June

LST–983, with *LST–601* in the background, launches a Marine LVTP–5 for a waterborne landing. When carrying amphibious tractors, an LST could land her payload from offshore without beaching. Today's *Newport* (LST–1179)-class ships can debark amphibious vehicles from their stern gates.

1945. Following the war, *LST–494* performed occupation duty in the Far East until early March 1946 and saw China service from mid-March through late May 1946. Upon her return to the United States, she was decommissioned on 29 June 1946 and struck from the Navy list on 28 August that same year. On 12 August 1948, the ship was sold to Bosey, Philippines.

LST–494 earned three battle stars for World War II service.

LST–495

LST–495 was laid down on 14 August 1943 at Evansville, Ind., by the Missouri Valley Bridge & Iron Co.; launched on 16 October 1943; sponsored by Mrs. Arthur L. Nunn; and commissioned on 23 December 1943.

During World War II, *LST–495* was assigned to the European theater and participated in the invasion of Normandy in June 1944 and the invasion of southern France in August and September that same year. She was then assigned to the Asiatic-Pacific theater and took part in the assault and occupation of Okinawa Gunto in April and June 1945. Following the war, *LST–495* performed occupation duty in the Far East until late October 1945. Upon her return to the United States, she was decommissioned on 23 April 1946 and struck from the Navy list on 5 June 1946. On 8 April 1948, the ship was sold to Kaiser Co., Inc., of Seattle, Wash., and subsequently scrapped.

LST–495 earned three battle stars for World War II service.

LST–496

LST–496 was laid down on 24 August 1943 at Evansville, Ind., by the Missouri Valley Bridge & Iron Co.; launched on 22 October 1943; sponsored by Mrs. Fred McCutchan; and commissioned on 27 December 1943, Lt. Stanley H. Koch, USNR, in command.

During World War II, *LST–496* was assigned to the European theater and participated in the invasion of Normandy in June 1944. She was sunk by enemy mines off Omaha Beach, Normandy, on 11 June 1944. *LST–496* was struck from the Navy list on 22 August 1944.

LST–496 earned one battle star for World War II service.

LST–497

LST–497 was laid down on 26 August 1943 at Evansville, Ind., by the Missouri Valley Bridge & Iron Co.; launched on 27 October 1943; sponsored by Mrs. Paul H. Schmidt; and commissioned on 31 December 1943, Lt. C. V. Riley, USNR, in command.

During World War II, *LST–497* was assigned to the European theater and participated in the invasion of Normandy in June 1944. Following the war, she returned to the United States and was decommissioned on 18 December 1945 and struck from the Navy list on 8 January 1946. On 30 January 1948, the ship was sold to the Anglo-Canadian Pulp & Paper Mills, Quebec, Canada, for operation.

LST–497 earned one battle star for World War II service.

LST–498

LST–498 was laid down on 31 August 1943 at Evansville, Ind., by the Missouri Valley Bridge & Iron Co.; launched on 1 November 1943; sponsored by Mrs. Raymond M. Wall; and commissioned on 6 January 1944.

During World War II, *LST–498* was assigned to the European theater and participated in the invasion of Normandy in June 1944. She returned to the United States and was decommissioned on 8 November 1945 and struck from the Navy list on 28 November that same year. On 21 November 1947, the ship was sold to the Washburn Wire Co., of Philipsdale, R.I., and subsequently scrapped.

LST–498 earned one battle star for World War II service.

LST–499

LST–499 was laid down on 3 September 1943 at Evansville, Ind., by the Missouri Valley Bridge & Iron Co.; launched on 5 November 1943; sponsored by Mrs. Porter W. Kohlmeyer; and commissioned on 10 January 1944.

During World War II, *LST–499* was assigned to the European theater and participated in the invasion of Normandy in June 1944. She was sunk due to enemy action during the invasion on 8 June 1944, and her name was struck from the Navy list on 22 August 1944.

LST–499 earned one battle star for World War II service.

LST–500

LST–500 was laid down on 8 September 1943 at Evansville, Ind., by the Missouri Valley Bridge & Iron Co.; launched on 10 November 1943; sponsored by Mrs. Ben Moreell; and commissioned on 13 January 1944.

During World War II, *LST–500* was assigned to the European theater and participated in the invasion of Normandy in June 1944. She returned to the United States and was decommissioned on 18 July 1947. She was struck from the Navy list on 1 August 1947. On 20 April 1948, the ship was sold to the Southern Trading Co., of Wilmington, Del., for operation.

LST–500 earned one battle star for World War II service.

LST–501

LST–501 was laid down on 30 June 1943 at Jeffersonville, Ind., by the Jeffersonville Boat & Machine Co.; launched on 22 September 1943; sponsored by Miss Ellen B. Reed; and commissioned on 26 November 1943.

During World War II, *LST–501* was assigned to the European theater and participated in the invasion of Normandy in June 1944 and the invasion of southern France in August and September 1944. She was then assigned to the Asiatic-Pacific theater and took part in the assault and occupation of Okinawa Gunto in May and June 1945.

Following the war, *LST–501* performed occupation duty in the Far East until mid-October 1945. Upon her return to the United States, the ship was decommissioned on 20 August 1947 and struck from the Navy list on 29 September that same year. On 7 May 1948, she was sold to Consolidated Builders, Inc., Seattle, Wash., and subsequently scrapped.

LST–501 earned three battle stars for World War II service.

LST–502

LST–502 was laid down on 18 June 1943 at Jeffersonville, Ind., by the Jeffersonville Boat & Machine Co.; launched on 25 September 1943; sponsored by Mrs. Joseph Bronaugh; and commissioned on 8 December 1943.

During World War II, *LST–502* was assigned to the European theater and participated in the invasion of Normandy in June 1944 and the invasion of southern France in August and September 1944. She was then assigned to the Asiatic-Pacific theater and took part in the assault and occupation of Okinawa Gunto in May and June 1945.

Following the war, *LST–502* performed occupation duty in the Far East until early February 1946. Upon her return to the United States, the ship was decommissioned on 4 February 1946 and struck from the Navy list on 23 December 1947. On 20 May 1948, she was sold to Consolidated Builders, Inc., Seattle, Wash., and subsequently scrapped.

LST–502 earned three battle stars for World War II service.

LST–503

LST–503 was laid down on 29 July 1943 at Jeffersonville, Ind., by the Jeffersonville Boat & Machine Co.; launched on 8 October 1943; sponsored by Mrs. David E. Eppley; and commissioned on 8 December 1943, Lt. Sam H. Jones, USNR, in command.

During World War II, *LST–503* was assigned to the European theater and participated in the invasion of Normandy in June 1944. Following the war, *LST–503* returned to the United States and was decommissioned on 11 June 1946. She was transferred to the Republic of China on 4 April 1955 where she served as *Chung Kuang* (LST–216). The ship was struck from the Navy list on 25 April 1960.

LST–503 earned one battle star for World War II service.

LST–504

LST–504 was laid down on 21 July 1943 at Jeffersonville, Ind., by the Jeffersonville Boat & Machine Co.; launched on 19 October 1943; sponsored by Mrs. W. J. Griffin; and commissioned on 18 December 1943.

During World War II, *LST–504* was assigned to the European theater and participated in the invasion of Normandy in June 1944 and the invasion of southern France in August and September 1944. She was then assigned to the Asiatic-Pacific theater and took part in the assault and occupation of Okinawa Gunto in April and June 1945.

Following the war, *LST–504* performed occupation duty in the Far East until mid-January 1946. Upon her return to the United States, she was decommissioned on 22 January 1946. The ship was redesignated *Buchanan County* (LST–504) on 1 July 1955 after counties in Iowa, Missouri, and Virginia. She was struck from the Navy list on 11 August 1955 and sunk as a target in February 1956.

LST–504 earned three battle stars for World War II service.

LST–505

LST–505 was laid down on 6 August 1943 at Jeffersonville, Ind., by the Jeffersonville Boat & Machine Co.; launched on 27 October 1943; sponsored by Ensign Francis Nobis Berry, USNR; and commissioned on 27 December 1943, Lt. John A. Meadows in command.

During World War II, *LST–505* was assigned to the European theater and participated in the invasion of Normandy in June 1944 and the invasion of southern France in August and September 1944. She was then assigned to the Asiatic-Pacific theater and took part in the assault and occupation of Okinawa Gunto in May and June 1945. Following the war, *LST–505* performed occupation duty in the Far East until early February 1946 and saw service in China until mid-May that same year. Upon her return to the United States, she was decommissioned on 11 June 1946 and struck from the Navy list on 16 September 1947. On 13 February 1948, the ship was sold to Bosey, Philippines.

LST–505 earned three battle stars for World War II service.

LST–506

LST–506 was laid down on 19 August 1943 at Jeffersonville, Ind., by the Jeffersonville Boat & Machine Co.; launched on 4 November 1943; sponsored by Mrs. Frank Pigeon; and commissioned on 3 January 1944.

During World War II, *LST–506* was assigned to the European theater and participated in the invasion of Normandy in June 1944. Following the war, she returned to the United States and was decommissioned on 24 July 1947 and struck from the Navy list on 28 August that same year. On 4 December 1947, the ship was sold to the Southern Trading Co., Philadelphia, Pa., for operation.

LST–506 earned one battle star for World War II service.

LST–507

LST–507 was laid down on 8 September 1943 at Jeffersonville, Ind., by the Jeffersonville Boat & Machine Co.; launched on 16 November 1943; sponsored by Mrs. Raymond C. Fuller; and comissioned on 10 January 1944.

LST–507 was sunk by a German E-boat torpedo attack in the English Channel on 28 April 1944. She was struck from the Navy list on 9 June 1944.

LST–508

LST–508 was laid down on 18 September 1943 at Jeffersonville, Ind., by the Jeffersonville Boat & Machine Co.; launched on 10 Novembed 1943; sponsored by Mrs. Alexander Best; and commissioned on 14 January 1944, Lt. John G. Holmes, USNR, in command.

During World War II, *LST–508* was assigned to the European theater and participated in the invasion of Normandy in June 1944. Following the war, she returned to the United States and was decommissioned on 2 August 1946 and struck from the Navy list on 28 January 1947. On 25 March 1947, the ship was transferred to the State Department for disposal.

LST–508 earned one battle star for World War II service.

LST–509

LST–509 was laid down on 7 October 1943 at Jeffersonville, Ind., by the Jeffersonville Boat & Machine Co.; launched on 23 November 1943; sponsored by Lt. (jg.) Dorothy L. Nims, USCG(W); and commissioned on 20 January 1944, Lt. J. B. Malcom, USNR, in command.

During World War II, *LST–509* was assigned to the European theater and participated in the invasion of Normandy in June 1944. Following the war, *LST–509* returned to the United States and was redesignated *Bullock County* (LST–509) on 1 July 1955 after a county in Georgia. On 8 April 1970, the ship was decommissioned and leased to the Republic of Vietnam for service as *Qui Nhon* (HQ–504).

LST–509 earned one battle star for World War II service.

LST–510

LST–510 was laid down on 27 September 1943 at Jeffersonville, Ind., by the Jeffersonville Boat & Machine Co.; launched on 30 November 1943; sponsored by Mrs. C. P. Watson; and commissioned on 31 January 1944, Lt. G. P. Andrews in command.

During World War II, *LST–510* was assigned to the European theater and participated in the invasion of Normandy in June 1944. She returned to the United States and, on 1 July 1946, was decommissioned and assigned to the Pacific Reserve Fleet. On 1 July 1955, the ship was redesignated *Buncombe County* (LST–

510) after a county in North Carolina and was struck from the Navy list on 1 November 1958.

LST–510 received one battle star for World War II service.

LST–511

LST–511 was laid down on 22 July 1943 at Seneca, Ill., by the Chicago Bridge & Iron Co.; launched on 30 November 1943; sponsored by Mrs. James V. Gaynor; and commissioned on 3 January 1944, Lt. John Yacevich in command.

During World War II, *LST–511* was assigned to the European theater and participated in the invasion of Normandy in June 1944. Upon her return to the United States, she was decommissioned on 19 December 1945 and struck from the Navy list on 8 January 1946. On 17 February 1948, the ship was sold to the Anglo-Canadian Pulp & Paper Mills, Quebec, Canada, for operation.

LST–511 received one battle star for World War II service.

LST–512

LST–512 was laid down on 22 July 1943 at Seneca, Ill., by the Chicago Bridge & Iron Co.; launched on 10 December 1943; sponsored by Mrs. Gerry DeWane; and commissioned on 8 January 1944.

During World War II, *LST–512* was assigned to the European theater and participated in the invasion of Normandy in June 1944. She returned to the United States and, on 28 March 1947, was decommissioned and assigned to the Pacific Reserve Fleet. On 1 July 1955, the ship was redesignated *Burnett County* (LST–512) after a county in Wisconsin and was struck from the Navy list on 18 February 1957. On 11 October 1957, she was sold to the Peruvian Navy.

LST–512 received one battle star for World War II service.

LST–513

LST–513 was redesignated ARL–9 and named *Endymion* (q.v.) on 3 November 1943.

LST–514

LST–514 was redesignated ARB–5 and named *Midas* (q.v.) on 3 November 1943.

LST–515

LST–515 was laid down on 3 September 1943 at Seneca, Ill., by the Chicago Bridge & Iron Co.; launched on 31 December 1943; sponsored by Miss Rebekah Brown; and commissioned on 28 January 1944.

During World War II, *LST–515* was assigned to the European theater and participated in the invasion of Normandy in June 1944. Following the war, *LST–515* performed occupation duty in the Far East until mid-November 1952. She also saw postwar service with the Service Force, U.S. Atlantc Fleet.

Upon her return to the United States, she was redesignated *Caddo Parish* (LST–515) on 1 July 1955 after a parish (county) in Louisiana. The ship was decommissioned on 20 October 1955 and recommissioned on 2 August 1963. The tank landing ship performed service in Vietnam until transferred to the Republic of the Philippines as grant aid on 26 November 1969. She served the Philippine Navy as *Bataan* (LT–85).

LST–515 received one battle star for World War II service; and nine battle stars, one Navy Unit Commendation and one Meritorious Unit Commendation for Vietnam service.

LST–516

LST–516 was laid down on 6 September 1943 at Seneca, Ill., by the Chicago Bridge & Iron Co.; launched on 7 January 1944; sponsored by Mrs. R. R. Hansen; and commissioned on 31 January 1944, Lt. M. J. Miller in command.

During World War II, *LST–516* was assigned to the European theater and participated in the invasion of Normandy in June 1944. On 28 February 1947, she was decommissioned and, as a result of hostilities in Korea, recommissioned on 22 September 1950. She served in the Korean War and took part in the following campaigns:

    U.N. Summer-Fall Offensive—November 1951

    Second Korean Winter—January and February 1952

    Third Korean Winter—December 1952, January through April 1953

    Korea, Summer 1953—June through July 1953

Immediately following the Korean War, she continued to serve in the Korean area until 20 September 1953. Following her Korean service, she returned to the United States. She was named *Calaveras County* (LST–516) after a county in California on 1 July 1955. On 21 December 1955, the ship was decommissioned and struck from the Navy list on 1 October 1958.

LST–516 received one battle star for World War II service and four battle stars for Korean service.

LST–517

LST–517 was laid down on 10 September 1943 at Seneca, Ill., by the Chicago Bridge & Iron Co.; launched on 15 January 1944; sponsored by Miss Onita Watland Walker; and commissioned on 7 February 1944.

During World War II, *LST–517* was assigned to the European theater and participated in the invasion of Normandy in June 1944. Upon her return to the United States, she was decommissioned on 21 December 1945 and struck from the Navy list on 21 January 1946. On January 1947, the ship was transferred to the Maritime Administration for disposal.

LST–517 received one battle star for World War II service.

LST–518

LST–518 was redesignated ARB–6 and named *Nestor* (q.v.) on 3 November 1943.

LST–519

LST–519 was laid down on 17 September 1943 at Seneca, Ill., by the Chicago Bridge & Iron Co.; launched on 25 January 1944; sponsored by Miss Bonnie Faye Catherwood; and commissioned on 17 February 1944.

During World War II, *LST–519* was assigned to the European theater and participated in the movements of Convoy UGS–36 in April 1944 and the invasion of Normandy in June 1944. Following the war, she served with the Atlantic Fleet. Her primary mission was to dispose of condemned ammunition and radioactive waste material in deep water. *LST–519* returned to the United States and was named *Calhoun County* (LST–519) on 1 July 1955 after counties in 11 states of the United States. She was decommissioned on 8 November 1962 and struck from the Navy list that same day.

LST–519 received two battle stars for World War II service.

LST–520

LST–520 was laid down on 24 September 1943 at Seneca, Ill., by the Chicago Bridge & Iron Co.; launched on 31 January 1944; sponsored by Mrs. Jane G. Gongaware; and commissioned on 28 February 1944, Lt. E. J. Charette in command.

During World War II, *LST–520* was assigned to the European theater and participated in the invasion of Normandy in June 1944. She was then assigned to the Asiatic-Pacific theater and took part in the assault and occupation of Okinawa Gunto in May and June 1945.

Following the war, *LST–520* performed occupation duty in the Far East until early January 1946. Upon her return to the United States, she was decommissioned on 13 January 1946 and transferred to Shipping Control Authority, Japan, for operation from 13 January 1946 to 31 March 1952. The tank landing ship was transferred to the Republic of China for operation on 1 October 1958 and struck from the Navy list that same day.

LST–520 received two battle stars for World War II service.

LST–521

LST–521 was laid down on 4 October 1943 at Seneca, Ill., by the Chicago Bridge and Iron Co.; launched on 13 December 1943; sponsored by Mrs. Ruth Sexton; and commissioned on 9 February 1944, Lt. J. J. Kilthau in command.

During World War II, *LST–521* was assigned to the European theater and participated in the invasion of Normandy in June 1944. Upon her return to the United States, she was decommissioned on 21 October 1945. On 1 July 1955, the tank landing ship was redesignated *Cape May County* (LST–521) after a county in New Jersey. The ship was struck from the Navy list on 1 November 1959.

LST–521 earned one battle star for World War II service.

LST–522

LST–522 was laid down on 2 October 1943 at Seneca, Ill., by the Chicago Bridge & Iron Co.; launched on 11 February 1944; sponsored by Mrs. F. F. Loeb; and commissioned on 1 March 1944, Lt. Orton P. Jackson, USNR, in command.

During World War II, *LST–522* was assigned to the European theater and participated in the invasion of Normandy in June 1944. Following the war, *LST–522* performed occupation duty in the Far East and China service until mid-May 1946. Upon her return to the United States, she was decommissioned on 6 June 1946. On 18 October 1947, the ship was purchased by T. Y. Fong and struck from the Navy list on 22 January 1948.

LST–522 earned one battle star for World War II service.

LST–523

LST–523 was laid down on 15 October 1943 at Jeffersonville, Ind., by the Jeffersonville Boat & Machine Co.; launched on 6 December 1943; sponsored by Mrs. Cleona S. Rauth; and commissioned on 3 February 1944.

During World War II, *LST–523* was assigned to the European theater and participated in the invasion of Normandy in June 1944. On 19 June 1944, she was sunk by an enemy mine. The ship was struck from the Navy list on 22 August 1944.

LST–523 earned one battle star for World War II service.

LST–524

LST–524 was laid down on 4 October 1943 at Jeffersonville, Ind., by the Jeffersonville Boat & Machine Co.; launched on 13 December 1943; sponsored by Mrs. Mildred M. Anderson; and commissioned on 9 February 1944, Ens. E. B. Dodge in command.

During World War II, *LST–524* was assigned to the European theater and participated in the invasion of Normandy in June 1944. She was then assigned to the Asiatic-Pacific theater and took part in the assault and occupation of Okinawa Gunto in June 1945. Following the war, *LST–524* performed occupation duty in the Far East until early February 1946. She returned to the United States and was decommissioned on 4 February 1946 and struck from the Navy list on 31 October 1947. On 21 May 1948, the ship was sold to Consolidated Builders, Inc., Seattle, Wash., and subsequently scrapped.

LST–524 earned two battle stars for World War II service.

LST–525

LST–525 was laid down on 18 October 1943 at Jeffersonville, Ind., by the Jeffersonville Boat & Machine Co.; launched on 20 December 1943; sponsored by Mrs. Anna Mae Federspiel; and commissioned on 14 February 1944, Ens. James R. Stevens in command.

During World War II, *LST–525* was assigned to the European theater and participated in the following operations:

Convoy UGS–36—April 1944

Invasion of southern France—August and September 1944

Following the war, *LST–525* was decommissioned on 25 June 1946. She was recommissioned in October 1950 and performed services for the Amphibious Force, U.S. Atlantic Fleet, until decommissioned on 15 September 1954. On 1 July 1955, she was named *Caroline County* (LST–525) after counties in Maryland and Virginia. Again reactivated in mid-1965, *Caroline County* provided support and resupply for riverine forces in Vietnam in 1967 and 1968. She was struck from the Navy list on 15 September 1974.

LST–525 earned two battle stars for World War II service and four battle stars and the Meritorious Unit Commendation for Vietnam service.

LST–526

LST–526 was laid down on 30 October 1943 at Jeffersonville, Ind., by the Jeffersonville Boat & Machine Co.; launched on 27 December 1943; sponsored by Mrs. Edna Heath Kimball; and commissioned on 17 February 1944.

During World War II, *LST–526* was assigned to the European theater and participated in the movements of Convoy UGS–36 in April 1944 and the invasion of southern France in August and September 1944. She returned to the United States and was decommissioned on 21 December 1945 and struck from the Navy list on 21 January 1946. On 24 January 1947, the ship was sold to Chester D. Bentliff, Lake Charles, La., for operation.

LST–526 earned two battle stars for World War II service.

LST–527

LST–527 was laid down on 23 October 1943 at Jeffersonville, Ind., by the Jeffersonville Boat & Machine Co.; launched on 3 January 1944; sponsored by Mrs. Bliss A. Fox; and commissioned on 17 February 1944, Lt. W. R. Hammock in command.

During World War II, *LST–527* was assigned to the European theater and participated in the invasion of Normandy in June 1944. On 28 February 1945, she was decommissioned and, as a result of hostilities in Korea, recommissioned on 21 September 1950. She served in the Korean War and took part in the following campaigns:

LST's unload at Wonsan, Korea, in November 1950. The same ships and the same types of vehicles—note the assortment in the foreground—played much the same wartime roles that they had a few years earlier. The makeup of the LST force was cosmopolitan; 30 of 47 LST's engaged in the Inchon landing were manned by Japanese civilians operating under the Occupation authorities. LST's had a large share in the evacuation of the Tenth Corps from Hungnam in December 1950; this force also included South Korean ships. (80–G–707996)

Second Korean Winter—January and February 1952

Korea, Summer 1953—May and June 1953

Following her Korean service, she returned to the United States. She was named *Cassia County* (LST–527) after a county in Idaho on 1 July 1955. On 21 December 1956, the ship was decommissioned and struck from the Navy list on 1 October 1958. She was sunk as a target on 3 March 1959.

LST–527 earned one battle star for World War II service and two battle stars for Korean service.

LST–528

LST–528 was laid down on 13 November 1943 at Jeffersonville, Ind., by the Jeffersonville Boat & Machine Co.; launched on 11 January 1944; sponsored by Mrs. Madge Medlock Watt; and commissioned on 29 February 1944.

During World War II, *LST–528* was assigned to the European theater and participated in the invasion of Normandy in June 1944. She returned to the United States and was decommissioned in March 1954. The ship was named *Catahoula Parish* (LST–528) after a parish (county) in Louisiana on 1 July 1955. She was struck from the Navy list on 21 November 1960.

LST–528 earned one battle star for World War II service.

LST–529

LST–529 was laid down on 8 November 1943 at Jeffersonville, Ind., by the Jeffersonville Boat & Machine Co.; launched on 17 January 1944; sponsored by Mrs. Margaret S. Carey; and commissioned on 29 February 1944, Lt. G. L. Moore, USNR, in command.

During World War II, *LST–529* was assigned to the European theater and participated in the invasion of Normandy in June 1944. On 7 June 1946, she was decommissioned and, as a result of hostilities in Korea, recommissioned on 22 September 1950. She served in the Korean War and took part in the following campaigns:

U.N. Summer-Fall offensive—July and August 1951

Second Korean Winter—December 1951 through March 1952

Korea, Summer 1953—June and July 1953

Immediately following the Korean War, she continued to serve in the Korean area until July 1954. Following her Korean service, she returned to the United States. She was named *Cayuga County* (LST–529) after a county in New York on 1 July 1955. She was assigned as a logistic support ship for the Mariana and Bonin Islands in the late 1950's and remained there until transferred to the Republic of Vietnam on 17 December 1963.

LST–529 earned one battle star for World War II service and three battle stars for Korean service.

LST–530

LST–530 was laid down on 23 November 1943 at Jeffersonville, Ind., by the Jeffersonville Boat & Machine Co.; launched on 25 January 1944; sponsored by Mrs. Eloise K. Glass; and commissioned on 6 March 1944.

During World War II, *LST–530* was assigned to the European theater and participated in the invasion of Normandy in June 1944. She was then assigned to the Asiatic-Pacific theater and took part in the assault and occupation of Okinawa Cunto in June 1945.

Following the war, *LST–530* performed occupation duty in the Far East until mid-January 1946 when she returned to the United States and was decommissioned. The tank landing ship was transferred to the Military Sea Transportation Service on 31 March 1952 where it served as USNS *LST–530* until struck from the Navy list on 15 June 1973. On 17 September 1973, she was sold to S. S. Zee, Taipei, Taiwan, and subsequently scrapped.

LST–530 earned two battle stars for World War II service.

LST–531

LST–531 was laid down on 22 September 1943 at Evansville, Ind., by the Missouri Valley Bridge & Iron Co.; launched on 24 November 1943; sponsored by Mrs. Marion Yoder; and commissioned on 17 January 1944, Lt. William D. Bradley, USNR, in command.

During World War II, *LST–531* was sunk by a German E-boat torpedo attack in Lyme Bay, England, on 28 April 1944 while conducting a pre-invasion landing exercise.

LST–531 was struck from the Navy list on 9 June 1944.

LST–532

LST–532 was laid down on 24 September 1943 at Evansville, Ind., by the Missouri Valley Bridge & Iron Co.; launched on 28 November 1943; sponsored by Mrs. Fred M. Wyatt; and commissioned on 20 January 1944, Lt. Marinus Pilkington in command.

During World War II, *LST–532* was assigned to the European theater and participated in the invasion of Normandy in June 1944. Following the war, she operated with the Service Force, U.S. Atlantic Fleet. The ship was decommissioned on 8 June 1955 and renamed *Chase County* (LST–532) on 1 July 1955 after counties in Kansas and Nebraska. On 15 April 1967, she was transferred to the Military Sea Transportation Service and served as USNS *Chase County* until struck from the Navy list on 10 June 1973.

LST–532 earned one battle star for World War II service.

LST–533

LST–533 was laid down on 29 September 1943 at Evansville, Ind., by the Missouri Valley Bridge & Iron Co.; launched on 1 December 1943; sponsored by Mrs. H. D. Peoples; and commissioned on 27 January 1944, Lt. C. E. Hanks in command.

During World War II, *LST–533* was assigned to the European theater and participated in the invasion of Normandy in June 1944. Following the war, *LST–533* performed occupation duty in Europe until early February 1953. She was named *Cheboygan County* (LST–533) on 1 July 1955 after a county in Michigan. The ship was decommissioned on 1 December 1955 and recommissioned on 18 November 1961 and performed duties for the Service Force, U.S. Atlantic Fleet. The tank landing ship was again decommissioned in May 1969 and struck from the Navy list on 15 September 1974.

LST–533 earned one battle star for World War II service.

LST–534

LST–534 was laid down on 4 October 1943 at Evansville, Ind., by the Missouri Valley Bridge & Iron Co.; launched on 8 December 1943; sponsored by Mrs. C. S. Jones; and commissioned on 31 January 1944.

During World War II, *LST–534* was assigned to the European theater and participated in the invasion of Normandy in June 1944. On 22 June 1945, she was seriously damaged by a Japanese kamikaze attack. Following the war, *LST–534* performed occupation duty in the Far East until she was decommissioned on 2 November 1945. The ship was deemed beyond economical repair and towed to sea and sunk off Okinawa on 9 December 1945. She was struck from the Navy list on 3 January 1946.

LST–534 earned one battle star for World War II service.

LST–535

LST–535 was laid down on 19 October 1943 at Evansville, Ind., by the Missouri Valley Bridge & Iron Co.; launched on 21 December 1943; sponsored by Mrs. John L. Mullins; and commissioned on 4 February 1944, Lt. Martin L. Olson, USNR, in command.

During World War II, *LST–535* was assigned to the European theater and participated in the invasion of Normandy in June 1944. She was then assigned to the Asiatic-Pacific theater and took part in the assault and occupation of Okinawa Gunto in May and June 1945.

Following the war, *LST–535* performed occupation duty in the Far East until early January 1946 when she returned to the United States and was decommissioned on 14 January 1946. On 31 March 1952, the ship was transferred to the Military Sea Transportation Service where she served as USNS *LST–535* until transferred to the Republic of China and struck from the Navy list on 1' October 1958.

LST–535 earned two battle stars for World War II service.

LST–536

LST–536 was laid down on 19 October 1943 at Evansville, Ind., by the Missouri Valley Bridge & Iron Co.; launched on 27 December 1943; sponsored by Mrs. James M. Lavin; and commissioned on 9 February 1944.

During World War II, *LST–536* was assigned to the European theater and participated in the invasion of Normandy in June 1944. Following the war, *LST–536* performed occupation duty in the Far East until early January 1946. She returned to the United States and was decommissioned on 23 January 1946. On 21 February 1947, the ship was made available for disposal to the Republic of Korea and struck from the Navy list on 5 March 1947.

LST–536 earned one battle star for World War II service.

LST–537

LST–537 was laid down on 27 October 1943 at Evansville, Ind., by the Missouri Valley Bridge & Iron Co.; launched on 31 December 1943; sponsored by Mrs. Robert C. Dean; and commissioned on 9 February 1944.

During World War II, *LST–537* was assigned to the European theater and participated in the invasion of Normandy in June 1944. Following the war, *LST–537* performed occupation duty in the Far East and saw service in China until mid-January 1946. She returned to the United States, and was decommissioned on 29 May 1946 and transferred to the Republic of China. On 12 March 1948, the ship was struck from the Navy list.

LST–537 earned one battle star for World War II service.

LST–538

LST–538 was laid down on 29 October 1943 at Evansville, Ind., by the Missouri Valley Bridge & Iron Co.; launched on 5 January 1944; sponsored by Mrs. John W. Evans; and commissioned on 14 February 1944.

During World War II, *LST–538* was assigned to the European theater and participated in the movements of Convoy UGS–36 in April 1944 and the invasion of Normandy in June 1944. She returned to the United

States, and was struck from the Navy list on 26 February 1946 and decommissioned on 16 March that same year. On 5 December 1947, the ship was sold to Bosey, Philippines.

LST–538 earned two battle stars for World War II service.

LST–539

LST–539 was laid down on 9 November 1943 at Evansville, Ind., by the Missouri Valley Bridge & Iron Co.; launched on 10 January 1944; sponsored by Mrs. Peyton Koch; and commissioned on 17 February 1944.

During World War II, LST–539 was assigned to the European theater and participated in the movements of Convoy UGS–37 in April 1944 and the invasion of Normandy in June 1944. Following the war, LST–539 performed occupation duty in the Far East in October 1945 and saw service in China in December 1945. She returned to the United States and was decommissioned on 22 June 1946 and struck from the Navy list on 31 July that same year. On 22 April 1948, the ship was sold to the Bethlehem Steel Co., of Bethlehem, Pa., and subsequently scrapped.

LST–539 earned two battle stars for World War II service.

LST–540

LST–540 was laid down on 13 November 1943 at Evansville, Ind., by the Missouri Valley Bridge & Iron Co.; launched on 14 January 1944; sponsored by Ens. Elizabeth B. Mayer, USNR; and commissioned on 22 February 1944.

During World War II, LST–540 was assigned to the European theater and participated in the invasion of Normandy in June 1944. She was then assigned to the Asiatic-Pacific theater and took part in the assault and occupation of Okinawa Gunto in May and June 1945.

Following the war, LST–540 performed occupation duty in the Far East until early January 1946. She returned to the United States, and was decommissioned on 13 January 1946. The ship was transferred to Shipping Control Authority, Japan, where she was lost due to an operational accident on 20 August 1947. The tank landing ship was struck from the Navy list on 23 March 1949.

LST–540 earned two battle stars for World War II service.

LST–541

LST–541 was laid down on 22 November 1943 at Evansville, Ind., by the Missouri Valley Bridge & Iron Co.; launched on 25 January 1944; sponsored by Mrs. Earl B. Blackman; and commissioned on 28 February 1944.

During World War II, LST–541 was assigned to the European theater and participated in the invasion of Normandy in June 1944. Following the war, LST–541 returned to the United States and was decommissioned on 9 November 1945 and struck from the Navy list on 28 November that same year. On 22 March 1948, the ship was sold to the Townsend Transportation Co., of Bayonne, N.J., and subsequently scrapped.

LST–541 earned one battle star for World War II service.

LST–542

LST–542 was laid down on 29 November 1943 at Evansville, Ind., by the Missouri Valley Bridge & Iron Co.; launched on 28 January 1944; sponsored by Mrs. Robert C. Dean; and commissioned on 29 February 1944.

During World War II, LST–542 was assigned to the European theater and participated in the invasion of Normandy in June 1944. Following the war, LST–542 saw service as a part of the Amphibious Force, U.S. Atlantic Fleet. She was named Chelan County (LST–542) after a county in Washington on 1 July 1955. The ship was decommissioned in 1956 and struck from the Navy list on 1 November 1959.

LST–542 earned one battle star for World War II service.

LST–543

LST–543 was laid down on 6 December 1943 at Evansville, Ind., by the Missouri Valley Bridge and Iron Co.; launched on 1 February 1944; sponsored by Lt. (jg.) Helen C. Hanson, USNR; and commissioned on 6 March 1944, Lt. Robert F. Blake in command.

During World War II, LST–543 was assigned to the European theater and participated in the invasion of Normandy in June 1944. She was then assigned to the Asiatic-Pacific theater and took part in the assault and occupation of Okinawa Gunto in May and June 1945. Following the war, LST–543 performed occupation duty in the Far East and saw service in China until early May 1946. She returned to the United States and was decommissioned on 31 May 1946 and struck from the Navy list on 17 July 1947. On 5 December 1947, the ship was sold to Bosey, Philippines.

LST–543 earned two battle stars for World War II service.

LST–544

LST–544 was laid down on 8 December 1943 at Evansville, Ind., by the Missouri Valley Bridge & Iron Co.; launched on 4 February 1944; sponsored by Mrs. Maudie M. Marlow; and commissioned on 16 March 1944.

LST–544 saw no combat service with the United States Navy and was decommissioned on 9 August 1946 and struck from the Navy list on 25 September that same year. On 23 June 1948, the ship was sold to the Willamette Iron & Steel Co. for scrapping.

LST–545

LST–545 was laid down on 13 December 1943 at Evansville, Ind., by the Missouri Valley Bridge and Iron Co.; launched on 12 February 1944; sponsored by Mrs. Charles M. Wright; and commissioned on 23 March 1944.

Following World War II, LST–545 performed occupation duty in the Far East until early December 1945. She returned to the United States and was decommissioned on 29 August 1946. The tank landing ship was sunk as a target on 12 May 1948 and struck from the Navy list on 28 May that same year.

LST–546

LST–546 was laid down on 20 December 1943 at Evansville, Ind., by the Missouri Valley Bridge & Iron Co.; launched on 16 February 1944; sponsored by Mrs. W. J. Barbrick; and commissioned on 27 March 1944, Lt. William D. Silkworth in command.

Following World War II, LST–546 performed occupation duty in the Far East and saw service in China until early January 1946. She was transferred to the Military Sea Transportation Service on 31 March 1952 where she served as USNS LST–546. On 15 July 1972, the ship was decommissioned and transferred to the Republic of the Philippines as a lease.

LST–547

LST–547 was laid down on 24 December 1943 at Evansville, Ind., by the Missouri Valley Bridge & Iron

Co.; launched on 19 February 1944; sponsored by Mrs. Harold Jourdan; and commissioned on 30 March 1944.

Following World War II, LST–547 performed occupation duty in the Far East until mid-February 1946. She returned to the United States and was decommissioned on 28 February 1946 and struck from the Navy list on 31 October 1947. On 26 May 1948, the ship was sold to the Bethlehem Steel Co., of Bethlehem, Pa., and subsequently scrapped.

LST–548

LST–548 was laid down on 30 December 1943 at Evansville, Ind., by the Missouri Valley Bridge & Iron Co.; launched on 22 February 1944; sponsored by Mrs. Robert L. Koch; and commissioned on 3 April 1944.

During World War II, LST–548 was assigned to the European theater and participated in the invasion of Normandy in June 1944. She was then assigned to the Asiatic-Pacific theater and took part in the assault and occupation of Okinawa Gunto in June 1945. Following the war, LST–548 performed occupation duty in the Far East until early February 1946. She returned to the United States and was decommissioned on 15 February 1946. On 31 March 1952, LST–548 was transferred to the Military Sea Transportation Service where she served as USNS LST–548. The tank landing ship was struck from the Navy list on 1 January 1960.

LST–548 earned two battle stars for World War II service.

LST–549

LST–549 was laid down on 4 January 1944 at Evansville, Ind., by the Missouri Valley Bridge & Iron Co.; launched on 25 February 1944; sponsored by Mrs. E. A. Oberhuber; and commissioned on 5 April 1944.

During World War II, LST–549 was assigned to the Asiatic-Pacific theater and participated in the following operations:

    Morotai landings—September 1944
    Leyte landings—October and November 1944
    Lingayen Gulf landings—January 1945
    Mindanao Island landings—April 1945

Following the war, LST–549 performed occupation duty in the Far East and saw service in China until mid-February 1946. She returned to the United States and was decommissioned on 28 February 1946 and struck from the Navy list on 5 December 1947. On 23 May 1948, the ship was sold to Consolidated Builder's, Inc., of Morris Heights, N.Y., and subsequently scrapped.

LST–549 earned four battle stars for World War II service.

LST–550

LST–550 was laid down on 13 November 1944 at Evansville, Ind., by the Missouri Valley Bridge & Iron Co.; launched on 9 March 1944; sponsored by Mrs. Henry D. Hoover; and commissioned on 10 April 1944, Lt. V. A. Meehan, USNR, in command.

During World War II, LST–550 was assigned to the European theater and participated in the invasion of southern France in August and September 1944. She was then assigned to the Asiatic-Pacific theater and took part in the assault and occupation of Okinawa Gunto in June 1945.

Following the war, LST–550 performed occupation duty in the Far East until early January 1946. She returned to the United States and was decommissioned on 13 January 1946. On 31 March 1952, the ship was transferred to the Military Sea Transportation Service and served as USNS LST–550 until struck from the Navy list on 1 November 1973.

LST–550 earned two battle stars for World War II service.

LST–551

LST–551 was laid down on 15 January 1944 at Evansville, Ind., by the Missouri Valley Bridge & Iron Co.; launched on 11 March 1944; sponsored by Mrs. H. Edward Lannan; and commissioned on 14 April 1944.

During World War II, LST–551 was assigned to the European theater and participated in the invasion of southern France in August and September 1944. Following the war, LST–551 performed occupation service in Europe until early July 1945. The ship then performed post-World War II service with Commander, Amphibious Force, U.S. Atlantic Fleet until she was decommissioned on 10 June 1955.

On 1 July 1955, LST–551 was redesignated Chesterfield County (LST–551) after counties in South Carolina and Virginia. She was recommissioned on 21 December 1965 and operated off Vietnam in 1966 and 1967. Decommissioned once again, she was struck from the Navy list on 1 June 1970 and sold to Mitsui and Co., Japan, in February 1971 for scrapping.

LST–551 earned one battle star for World War II service and two for Vietnam service.

LST–552

LST–552 was laid down on 19 January 1944 at Evansville, Ind., by the Missouri Valley Bridge & Iron Co.; launched on 14 March 1944; sponsored by Mrs. Robert A. Burns; and commissioned on 19 April 1944, Lt. R. E. Sandvigen in command.

During World War II, LST–552 was assigned to the Asiatic-Pacific theater and participated in the following operations:

    Capture and occupation of southern Palau Islands
      —September and October 1944
    Leyte landings—October and November 1944
    Zambales-Subic Bay—January 1945
    Assault and occupation of Okinawa Gunto—April 1945

Following the war, LST–552 performed occupation duty in the Far East until mid-October 1945. Upon her return to the United States, the ship was decommissioned on 19 April 1946 and struck from the Navy list on 1 May that same year. On 3 November 1947, the tank landing ship was sold to Dulien Steel Products, Inc., of Seattle, Wash., and subsequently scrapped.

LST–552 earned four battle stars for World War II service.

LST–553

LST–553 was laid down on 24 January 1944 at Evansville, Ind., by the Missouri Valley Bridge and Iron Co.; launched on 16 March 1944; sponsored by Miss Agnes L. Maulding; and commissioned on 22 April 1944, Lt. John K. Alegeo in command.

During World War II, LST–553 was assigned to the Asiatic- Pacific theater and participated in the following operations:

    Capture and occupation of southern Palau Islands
      —September and October 1944
    Leyte landings—October and November 1944
    Lingayen Gulf landings—January 1945
    Zambales-Subic Bay—January 1945
    Assault and occupation of Okinawa Gunto—April
      through June 1945

Following the war, LST–553 conducted minesweeping operations in the waters surrounding the Japanese home islands as well as occupation duty in the Far East until early February 1947. She was decommissioned on 13 February 1947 and transferred to the U.S. Army at Yokohama, Japan. On 25 April 1947, the ship was struck from the Navy list.

LST–553 earned five battle stars for World War II service.

LST–554

LST–554 was laid down on 30 January 1944 at Evansville, Ind., by the Missouri Valley Bridge & Iron Co.; launched on 18 March 1944; sponsored by Mrs. T. R. Davis; and commissioned on 27 April 1944.

During World War II, *LST–554* was assigned to the Asiatic-Pacific theater and participated in the following operations:

> Capture and occupation of southern Palau Islands —September and October 1944
> Leyte landings—October and November 1944
> Lingayen Gulf landings—January 1945
> Assault and occupation of Okinawa Gunto—April 1945

LST–554 returned to the United States and was decommissioned on 20 July 1946 and struck from the Navy list on 25 September 1946. On 29 March 1948, the ship was sold to Kaiser, Inc., of Vancouver, Wash., and subsequently scrapped.

LST–554 earned four battle stars for World War II service.

LST–555

LST–555 was laid down on 5 February 1944 at Evansville, Ind., by the Missouri Valley Bridge & Iron Co.; launched on 22 March 1944; sponsored by Mrs. R. E. Sharp; and commissioned on 28 April 1944.

During World War II, *LST–555* was assigned to the Asiatic-Pacific theater and participated in the following operations:

> Capture and occupation of southern Palau Islands —September and October 1944
> Leyte landings—October and November 1944
> Zambales-Subic Bay—January 1945
> Assault and occupation of Okinawa Gunto—April through June 1945

The ship was badly damaged as a result of grounding off Wakayama, Japan, on 18 September 1945. Following the war, *LST–555* performed occupation duty in the Far East until early January 1946. She was decommissioned on 6 January 1946 and struck from the Navy list on 21 January that same year. Her hulk was destroyed by gunfire on 26 January 1946.

LST–555 earned four battle stars for World War II service.

LST–556

LST–556 was laid down on 4 February 1944 at Evansville, Ind., by the Missouri Valley Bridge & Iron Co.; launched on 7 April 1944; sponsored by Mrs. James C. Bradshaw; and commissioned on 1 May 1944.

During World War II, *LST–556* was assigned to the Asiatic-Pacific theater and participated in the following operations:

> Capture and occupation of southern Palau Islands —September and October 1944
> Leyte landing—October and November 1944
> Ormoc Bay landings—December 1944
> Mindoro landings—December 1944
> Zambales-Subic Bay—January 1945
> Assault and occupation of Okinawa Gunto—April and May 1945

Following the war, *LST–556* returned to the United States and was decommissioned on 14 March 1946 and struck from the Navy list on 12 April that same year. On 26 April 1948, the ship was sold to the Sun Shipbuilding & Drydock Co., of Chester, Pa., and subsequently scrapped.

LST–556 earned five battle stars for World War II service.

LST–557

LST–557 was laid down on 8 February 1944 at Evansville, Ind., by the Missouri Valley Bridge & Iron Co.; launched on 11 April 1944; sponsored by Mrs. Edward J. Baechle; and commissioned on 5 May 1944.

During World War II, *LST–557* was assigned to the Asiatic-Pacific theater and participated in the following operations:

> Capture and occupation of southern Palau Islands —September and October 1944
> Leyte landings—October and November 1944
> Lingayen Gulf landings—January 1945
> Assault and occupation of Okinawa Gunto—April 1945

Following the war, *LST–557* performed occupation duty in the Far East and saw service in China until late May 1946. The ship was decommissioned and transferred to the Republic of China as lend-lease on 29 May 1946. She was struck from the Navy list on 12 March 1948.

LST–557 earned four battle stars for World War II service.

LST–558

LST–558 was laid down on 11 February 1944 at Evansville, Ind., by the Missouri Valley Bridge & Iron Co.; launched on 14 April 1944; sponsored by Mrs. Henry Goodman; and commissioned on 8 May 1944, Lt. (jg.) H. A. Bisonet in command.

During World War II, *LST–558* was assigned to the Asiatic-Pacific theater and participated in the following operations:

> Capture and occupation of southern Palau Islands —September and October 1944
> Leyte landings—October and November 1944
> Lingayen Gulf landing—January 1945
> Zambales-Subic Bay—January 1945
> Assault and occupation of Okinawa Gunto—April 1945

Following the war, *LST–558* performed occupation duty in the Far East and saw service in China until early February 1946. The ship returned to the United States and was decommissioned on 13 February 1946 and struck from the Navy list on 16 September 1947. On 24 May 1948, the tank landing ship was sold to the Bethlehem Steel Co., of Bethlehem, Pa., for scrapping.

LST–558 earned four battle stars for World War II service.

LST–559

LST–559 was laid down on 14 February 1944 at Evansville, Ind., by the Missouri Valley Bridge & Iron Co.; launched on 18 April 1944; sponsored by Mrs. Carl J. Futter; and commissioned on 9 May 1944, Lt. Richard T. Smith, USNR, in command.

During World War II, *LST–559* was assigned to the Asiatic-Pacific theater and participated in the following operations:

> Capture and occupation of southern Palau Islands —September and October 1944
> Leyte landings—October and November 1944
> Lingayen Gulf landing—January 1945
> Assault and occupation of Okinawa Gunto—April 1945

Following the war, *LST–559* performed occupation duty in the Far East and service in China until mid-May 1946. Upon her return to the United States, she was decommissioned on 1 June 1946 and struck from the Navy list on 19 June that same year. On 5 December 1947, the tank landing ship was sold to Bosey, Philippines.

LST–559 earned four battle stars for World War II service.

LST–560

LST–560 was laid down on 22 February 1944 at Evansville, Ind., by the Missouri Valley Bridge & Iron Co.; launched on 21 April 1944; sponsored by Mrs. L. C. Holm; and commissioned on 2 May 1944.

During World War II, *LST–560* was assigned to the Asiatic-Pacific theater and participated in the following operations:

    Palawan Island landings—March 1945
    Visayan Island landings—March and April 1945
    Brunei Bay operation—June 1945

Following the war, *LST–560* performed occupation duty in the Far East until mid-October 1945. Upon her return to the United States, she was decommissioned on 17 May 1946 and struck from the Navy list on 19 June that same year. On 12 September 1946, the tank landing ship was sold to the Construction Power & Merchandising Co., of Brooklyn, N.Y.

LST–560 earned two battle stars for World War II service.

LST–561

LST–561 was laid down on 24 February 1944 at Evansville, Ind., by the Missouri Valley Bridge & Iron Co.; launched on 25 April 1944; sponsored by Miss Marie Meier; and commissioned on 15 May 1944.

During World War II, *LST–561* was assigned to the European theater and participated in the invasion of southern France in August and September 1944. She was decommissioned on 30 April 1946. Due to hostilities in Korea, the ship was recommissioned on 18 September 1950 and assigned to Commander, Amphibious Force, U.S. Pacific Fleet. She participated in the United Nations effort in Korea and performed services in the Far East, the Arctic, and off the west coast of CONUS. On 1 July 1955, she was redesignated *Chittenden County* (LST–561) after a county in Vermont. The tank landing ship was decommissioned again on 2 June 1958. Struck from the Navy list on 27 June 1948, *Chittenden County* was sunk as a target south of Oahu, Hawaii, on 21 October 1958.

LST–561 earned one battle star for World War II service and two for Korean service.

LST–562

LST–562 was laid down on 28 February 1944 at Evansville, Ind., by the Missouri Valley Bridge & Iron Co.; launched on 28 April 1944; sponsored by Mrs. D. A. Nordeen; and commissioned on 18 May 1944.

During World War II, *LST–562* was assigned to the Asiatic-Pacific theater and participated in the Morotai landings in September 1944 and the Tarakan Island operation in April and May 1945.

Following the war, *LST–562* performed occupation duty in the Far East until mid-December 1945. She was decommissioned on 21 May 1946 and struck from the Navy list on 3 July that same year. On 19 April 1948, the ship was sold to the Bethlehem Steel Co., of Bethlehem, Pa., and subsequently scrapped.

LST–562 earned two battle stars for World War II service.

LST–563

LST–563 was laid down on 4 March 1944 at Evansville, Ind., by the Missouri Valley Bridge & Iron Co.; launched on 1 May 1944; sponsored by Mrs. N. E. Senescall; and commissioned on 20 May 1944, Lt. J. B. Hockswender, USNR, in command.

During World War II, *LST–563* was grounded on Clipperton Island in the eastern Pacific, 670 miles southwest of Mexico, on 21 December 1944 and suffered extensive damage. After numerous unsuccessful at-

tempts to free her, *LST–563* was stripped and abandoned on 9 February 1945. She was struck from the Navy list on 23 February 1945.

LST–564

LST–564 was laid down on 5 March 1944 at Evansville, Ind., by the Missouri Valley Bridge & Iron Co.; launched on 4 May 1944; sponsored by Mrs. Frances Cassady; and commissioned on 25 May 1944.

During World War II, *LST–564* was assigned to the Asiatic-Pacific theater and participated in the Leyte landings in October 1944 and the assault and occupation of Okinawa Gunto from April until June 1945.

Following the war, *LST–564* performed occupation duty in the Far East until early November 1945. Upon her return to the United States, she was decommissioned on 8 March 1946 and struck from the Navy list on 1 May that same year. On 31 December 1948, the ship was sold to Brown & Root, Inc., of Houston, Tex., for operation.

LST–564 earned two battle stars for World War II service.

LST–565

LST–565 was laid down on 16 March 1944 at Evansville, Ind., by the Missouri Valley Bridge & Iron Co.; launched on 8 May 1944; sponsored by Mrs. Vergil P. Dyer; and commissioned on 25 May 1944.

During World War II, *LST–565* was assigned to the Asiatic-Pacific theater and participated in the following operations:

    Leyte landings—October 1944
    Mindoro landings—December 1944
    Zambales-Subic Bay—January 1945
    Assault and occupation of Okinawa Gunto—May 1945

Following the war, *LST–565* performed occupation duty in the Far East and saw service in China until mid-May 1946. Upon her return to the United States, she was decommissioned on 13 June 1946 and struck from the Navy list on 3 July that same year. The ship was disposed of on 21 June 1948.

LST–565 earned four battle stars for World War II service.

LST–566

LST–566 was laid down on 17 March 1944 at Evansville, Ind., by the Missouri Valley Bridge & Iron Co.; launched on 11 May 1944; sponsored by Mrs. George C. Martin; and commissioned on 29 May 1944.

Following World War II, *LST–566* performed occupation duty in the Far East and saw service in China until early March 1946. The ship was decommissioned on 11 March 1946 and transferred to the Military Sea Transportation Service on 31 March 1952 where she served as USNS *LST–566* until struck from the Navy list on 1 November 1973. USNS *LST–566* was transferred to the Philippine Navy on 13 September 1976.

LST–567

LST–567 was laid down on 20 March 1944 at Evansville, Ind., by the Missouri Valley Bridge & Iron Co; launched on 15 May 1944; sponsored by Miss Elizabeth Funkey; and commissioned on 1 June 1944.

During World War II, *LST–567* was assigned to the Asiatic-Pacific theater and participated in the following operations:

    Leyte landings—October and November 1944
    Lingayen Gulf landing—January 1945
    Assault and occupation of Okinawa Gunto—June 1945

In peace as well as in war, LST's have traditionally made themselves useful wherever heavy cargoes or equipment need hauling. Here a Seabee power shovel is landed from the Military Sea Transportation Service's *LST–325*.

Following the war, *LST–567* performed occupation duty in the Far East until late January 1946. She returned to the United States and was decommissioned on 28 January 1946 and struck from the Navy list on 31 October 1947. On 24 May 1948, the ship was sold to the Bethlehem Steel Co., of Bethlehem, Pa., and subsequently scrapped.

LST–567 earned three battle stars for World War II service.

LST–568

LST–568 was laid down on 21 March 1944 at Evansville, Ind., by the Missouri Valley Bridge & Iron Co.; launched on 18 May 1944; sponsored by Mrs. Arthur E. Owen; and commissioned on 3 June 1944.

During World War II, *LST–568* was assigned to the Asiatic-Pacific theater and participated in the following operations:

Leyte landing—October 1944
Lingayen Gulf landing—January 1945
Assault and occupation of Okinawa Gunto—April 1945

Following the war, *LST–568* performed occupation duty in the Far East until mid-October 1945. She was decommissioned on 4 March 1946 and struck from the Navy list on 20 March that same year.

LST–568 earned three battle stars for World War II service.

LST–569

LST–569 was laid down on 24 March 1944 at Evansville, Ind., by the Missouri Valley Bridge & Iron Co.; launched on 20 May 1944; sponsored by Mrs. George W. Lamb; and commissioned on 5 June 1944.

During World War II, *LST–569* was assigned to the Asiatic-Pacific theater and participated in the following operations:

Leyte landings—October and November 1944
Lingayen Gulf landings—January 1945
Zambales-Subic Bay—January 1945
Mindanao Island landings—April and May 1945

Following the war, *LST–569* performed occupation duty in the Far East and saw service in China untli mid-May 1946. The ship was decommissioned on 13 June 1946 and struck from the Navy list on 15 October that same year. On 5 December 1947, she was sold to Bosey, Philippines.

LST–569 earned four battle stars for World War II service.

LST–570

LST–570 was laid down on 14 April 1944 at Evansviille, Ind., by the Missouri Valley Bridge & Iron Co.; launched on 22 May 1944; sponsored by Mrs. L. J. Prues, Jr.; and commissioned on 9 June 1944, Lt. Frank A. Neun, USNR, in command.

During World War II, *LST–570* was assigned to the Asiatic-Pacific theater and participated in the Lingayen Gulf landing in January 1945 and the assault and occupation of Okinawa Gunto in April through June 1945. Following the war, *LST–570* performed occupation duty in the Far East and saw service in China until mid-November 1945. She returned to the United States and was decommissioned on 14 May 1946 and struck from the Navy list on 19 June that same year. On 31 December 1948, the ship was sold to the Patapsco Scrap Corp., Baltimore, Md.

LST–570 earned two battle stars for World War II service.

LST–571

LST–571 was laid down on 14 April 1944 at Evansville, Ind., by the Missouri Valley Bridge & Iron Co.; launched on 25 May 1944; sponsored by Mrs. Joseph H. Hayes; and commissioned on 14 June 1944, Lt. Walter A. Raleigh in command.

During World War II, *LST–571* was assigned to the Asiatic-Pacific theater and participated in the Lingayen Gulf landing in January 1945 and the assault and occupation of Okinawa Gunto from April to June 1945. Following the war, *LST–571* performed occupation duty in the Far East until early December 1945.

Upon her return to the United States, *LST–571* was decommissioned on 12 March 1946 and struck from the Navy list on 12 April that same year. On 17 August 1948, the ship was sold to the Port Houston Iron Works, Inc., of Houston, Tex., for non-self-propelled operation.

LST–571 earned two battle stars for World War II service.

LST–572

LST–572 was laid down on 15 April 1944 at Evansville, Ind., by the Missouri Valley Bridge & Iron Co.; launched on 29 May 1944; sponsored by Mrs. B. B. Dumville; and commissioned on 19 June 1944, Lt. James N. Kincanon in command.

During World War II, *LST–572* was assigned to the Asiatic-Pacific theater and participated in the assault and occupation of Okinawa Gunto in May and June 1945. Following the war, she performed occupation duty in the Far East until early March 1946.

LST–572 was decommissioned on 8 March 1946 and transferred to the Military Sea Transportation Service on 31 March 1952 where she operated as USNS *LST–572*. The ship was struck from the Navy list on 15 June 1973 and sold on 19 November that same year to Yi Ho Enterprise Corp.

LST–572 earned one battle star for World War II service.

LST–573

LST–573 was laid down on 15 April 1944 at Evansville, Ind., by the Missouri Valley Bridge & Iron Co.; launched on 31 May 1944; sponsored by Mrs. Ernest C. Stroebe; and commissioned on 21 June 1944.

During World War II, *LST–573* was assigned to the Asiatic-Pacific theater and participated in the following operations:

    Leyte landings—October and November 1944
    Mindoro landings—December 1944
    Consolidation of the southern Philippines:
        (a) Visayan Island landings—March and April 1945
        (b) Mindanao Island landings—March 1945

Following the war, *LST–573* performed occupation duty in the Far East until mid-January 1946. Upon her return to the United States, she was decommissioned on 24 January 1946 and struck from the Navy list on 31 October 1947. On 26 May 1948, the ship was sold to the Bethlehem Steel Co., of Bethlehem, Pa.

LST–573 earned three battle stars for World War II service.

LST–574

LST–574 was laid down on 16 April 1944 at Evansville, Ind., by the Missouri Valley Bridge & Iron Co.; launched on 5 June 1944; sponsored by Mrs. Earl Koester; and commissioned on 26 June 1944, Lt. (jg.) Francis Canny, USNR, in command.

During World War II, *LST–574* was assigned to the Asiatic-Pacific theater and participated in the following operations:

    Leyte landings—November 1944
    Lingayen Gulf landings—January 1945
    Mindanao Island landings—March 1945

Following the war, *LST–574* performed occupation duty in the Far East and saw service in China until mid-May 1946. She was decommissioned on 17 June 1946 and struck from the Navy list on 3 July that same year. On 5 November 1947, the ship was sold to Bosey, Philippines.

LST–574 earned three battle stars for World War II service.

LST–575

LST–575 was redesignated APB–41 and named *Wythe* (q.v.) on 31 March 1945.

LST–576

LST–576 was laid down on 3 May 1944 at Evansville, Ind., by the Missouri Valley Bridge & Iron Co.; launched on 12 June 1944; sponsored by Mrs. Joseph Perry; and commissioned on 8 July 1944.

During World War II, *LST–576* was assigned to the Asiatic-Pacific theater and participated in the Lingayen Gulf landing in January 1945 and the assault and occupation of Okinawa Gunto in April 1945. Following the war, *LST–576* performed occupation duty in the Far East until mid-December 1945. Upon her return to the United States, the ship was decommissioned on 14 May 1946 and struck from the Navy list on 9 June that same year. On 7 October 1947, she was sold to Leland Louis Green, Jr., of Charleston, S.C., for scrapping.

LST–576 earned two battle stars for World War II service.

LST–577

LST–577 was laid down on 3 May 1944 at Evansville, Ind., by the Missouri Valley Bridge & Iron Co.; launched on 16 June 1944; sponsored by Mrs. Christopher Roeder; and commissioned on 10 July 1944, Lt. Carl H. Stahl in command.

During World War II, *LST–577* was assigned to the Asiatic-Pacific theater and participated in the Leyte landings in November 1944 and the Lingayen Gulf landing in January 1945. She was sunk by a Japanese submarine-launched torpedo off the Philippines on 11 February 1945. The tank landing ship was struck from the Navy list on 30 March 1945.

LST–577 earned two battle stars for World War II service.

LST–578

LST–578 was laid down on 4 May 1944 at Evansville, Ind., by the Missouri Valley Bridge & Iron Co.; launched on 19 June 1944; sponsored by Mrs. A. B. Morris; and commissioned on 15 July 1944, Lt. D. C. Wooldridge in command.

During World War II, *LST-578* was assigned to the Asiatic-Pacific theater and participated in the following operations:

Leyte landings—November 1944
Lingayen Gulf landing—January 1945
Mindanao Island landings—March and April 1945

Following the war, *LST-578* performed occupation duty in the Far East until mid-March 1946. She was decommissioned on 22 March 1946 and transferred to the Military Sea Transportation Service on 31 March 1952 where she operated as USNS *LST-578*.

LST-578 earned three battle stars for World War II service.

LST-579

LST-579 was laid down on 4 May 1944 at Evansville, Ind., by the Missouri Valley Bridge & Iron Co.; launched on 22 June 1944; sponsored by Mrs. Mary Ellen Bonk; and commissioned on 21 July 1944, Lt. Hugh B. Severs, USNR, in command.

During World War II, *LST-579* was assigned to the Asiatic-Pacific theater and participated in the following operations:

Leyte landings—November 1944
Lingayen Gulf landing—January 1945
Mindanao Island landings—March and April 1945
Balikpapan operation—June and July 1945

Following the war, *LST-579* performed occupation duty in the Far East until mid-February 1946. She was decomissioned on 24 February 1946. On 31 March 1952, the ship was transferred to the Military Sea Transportation Service where she operated as USNS *LST-579*.

LST-579 earned four battle stars for World War II service.

LST-580

LST-580 was laid down on 17 May 1944 at Evansville, Ind., by the Missouri Valley Bridge & Iron Co.; launched on 26 June 1944; sponsored by Miss Mary Louise Rust; and commissioned on 25 July 1944, Lt. H. F. Guenzl in command.

During World War II, *LST-580* was assigned to the Asiatic-Pacific theater and participated in the Lingayen Gulf landings in January 1945 and the assault and occupation of Okinawa Gunto in April 1945. Following the war, *LST-580* performed occupation duty in the Far East until late January 1946. Upon her return to the United States, she was decommissioned on 29 January 1946 and struck from the Navy list on 31 October 1947. On 2 May 1948, the ship was sold to Consolidated Builders, Inc., Seattle, Wash., for scrapping.

LST-580 earned two battle stars for World War II service.

LST-581

LST-581 was laid down on 17 May 1944 at Evansville, Ind., by the Missouri Valley Bridge & Iron Co.; launched on 29 June 1944; sponsored by Mrs. Jack Rogers; and commissioned on 27 July 1944, Lt. O. F. Rapelyea in command.

During World War II, *LST-581* was assigned to the Asiatic-Pacific theater and participated in the assault and occupation of Okinawa Gunto in May and June 1945. Following the war, she performed occupation duty in the Far East until late January 1946. The ship was decommissioned on 28 January 1946 and transferred to the Military Sea Transportation Service on 31 March 1952 where she served as *LST-581* until struck from the Navy list on 1 June 1972. On 25 May 1973, *LST-581* was sold to Dongkuk Steel Co. of America, Inc., Los Angeles, Calif., for scrapping.

LST-581 earned one battle star for World War II service.

LST-582

LST-582 was laid down on 18 May 1944 at Evansville, Ind., by the Missouri Valley Bridge & Iron Co.; launched on 1 July 1944; sponsored by Miss Isabel Daniel; and commissioned on 31 July 1944.

During World War II, *LST-582* was assigned to the Asiatic-Pacific theater and participated in the assault and occupation of Okinawa Gunto in April 1945. Following the war, she performed occupation duty in the Far East until late January 1946. The ship returned to the United States and was decommissioned on 29 January 1946 and struck from the Navy list on 31 October 1947. On 24 May 1948, she was sold to Consolidated Builders, Inc., of Seattle, Wash., for scrapping.

LST-582 earned one battle star for World War II service.

LST-583

LST-583 was laid down on 18 May 1944 at Evansville, Ind., by the Missouri Valley Bridge & Iron Co.; launched on 5 July 1944; sponsored by Mrs. D. C. Hollis; and commissioned on 2 August 1944, Lt. Philip E. Acker, USNR, in command.

During World War II, *LST-583* was assigned to the Asiatic-Pacific theater and participated in the following operations:

Lingayen Gulf landing—January 1945
Zambales-Subic Bay—January 1945
Mindanao Island landings—March and April 1945

Following the war, *LST-583* performed occupation duty in the Far East until mid-December 1945. She was decommissioned in March 1946. The tank landing ship was named *Churchill County* (LST-583) on 1 July 1955 after a county in Nevada. The ship was recommissioned on 1 November 1960 and performed services for Commander, Amphibious Force, Atlantic Fleet, until she was again decommissioned in September 1968.

LST-583 earned three battle stars for World War II service.

LST-584

LST-584 was laid down on 8 May 1944 at Evansville, Ind., by the Missouri Valley Bridge & Iron Co.; launched on 8 July 1944; sponsored by Mrs. Paul Galbraith; and commissioned on 5 August 1944, Ens. D. B. Russell, USNR, in command.

During World War II, *LST-584* was assigned to the Asiatic-Pacific theater and participated in the Mindanao Island landings in March 1945 and the Tarakan Island operation in April and May 1945. Following the war, *LST-584* performed occupation duty in the Far East until mid-December 1945. She returned to the United States and was decommissioned on 12 April 1946 and struck from the Navy list on 3 July that same year. On 19 March 1948, the ship was sold to Green's Bayou Transporters, Houston, Tex., for non-self-propelled operation.

LST-584 earned two battle stars for World War II service.

LST-585

LST-585 was laid down on 31 May 1944 at Evansville, Ind., by the Missouri Valley Bridge & Iron Co.; launched on 12 July 1944; sponsored by Miss Barbara Harper; and commissioned on 8 August 1944, Lt. A. P. Morse, USNR, in command.

During World War II, *LST-585* was assigned to the Asiatic-Pacific theater and participated in the following operations:

Lingayen Gulf landing—January 1945
Mariveles-Corregidor—February 1945
Tarakan Island operation—April and May 1945

Following the war, *LST–585* performed occupation duty in the Far East and saw service in China until mid-July 1946. She returned to the United States and was decommissioned on 31 July 1946 and struck from the Navy list on 28 August that same year. On 5 October 1946, the ship was sold to the Netherlands East Indies.

LST–585 earned three battle stars for World War II service.

LST–586

LST–586 was laid down on 1 June 1944 at Evansville, Ind., by the Missouri Valley Bridge & Iron Co.; launched on 15 July 1944; sponsored by Mrs. J. R. Woods; and commissioned on 15 August 1944, Lt. Charles E. Ford, USNR, in command.

During World War II, *LST–586* was assigned to the Asiatic-Pacific theater and participated in the following operations:

Leyte landings—November 1944
Lingayen Gulf landing—January 1945
Mariveles-Corregidor—February 1945

Following the war, *LST–586* performed occupation duty in the Far East and saw service in China until early February 1946. She returned to the United States and was decommissioned on 17 February 1946 and struck from the Navy list on 29 September 1947. On 28 May 1948, the ship was sold to the Bethlehem Steel Co., of Bethlehem, Pa., and subsequently scrapped.

LST–586 earned three battle stars for World War II service.

LST–587

LST–587 was laid down on 2 June 1944 at Evansville, Ind., by the Missouri Valley Bridge & Iron Co.; launched on 19 July 1944; sponsored by Mrs. Charles F. Greever; and commissioned on 18 August 1944.

During World War II, *LST–587* was assigned to the Asiatic-Pacific theater and participated in the assault and occupation of Iwo Jima in February 1945 and the assault and occupation of Okinawa Gunto from April to June 1945. Following the war, *LST–587* performed occupation duty and saw service in China until early February 1946.

On 31 March 1952, the ship was transferred to the Military Sea Transportation Service where she served as USNS *LST–587* until struck on 1 June 1972. *LST–587* was sold to S. S. Zee, Taipei, Taiwan, on 17 September 1973 for scrapping.

LST–587 earned two battle stars for World War II service.

LST–588

LST–588 was laid down on 6 June 1944 at Evansville, Ind., by the Missouri Valley Bridge & Iron Co.; launched on 22 July 1944; sponsored by Mrs. A. J. Toulon; and commissioned on 19 August 1944.

During World War II, *LST–588* was assigned to the Asiatic-Pacific theater and participated in the assault and occupation of Iwo Jima in February 1945. Following the war, she performed occupation duty in the Far East and saw service in China until early May 1946. On 8 June 1946, the ship was decommissioned and struck from the Navy list on 3 July that same year. *LST–588* was sold to Bosey, Philippines, and delivered on 9 October 1948.

LST–588 earned one battle star for World War II service.

LST–589

LST–589 was laid down on 8 June 1944 at Evansville, Ind., by the Missouri Valley Bridge & Iron Co.; launched on 26 July 1944; sponsored by Mrs. Russel S. Gibson; and commissioned on 24 August 1944.

Following World War II, *LST–589* performed occupation duty in the Far East and saw service in China until mid-July 1946. She was decommissioned on 14 September 1946 and sold to Bosey, Philippines, on 17 December that same year. *LST–589* was struck from the Navy list on 23 April 1947.

LST–590

LST–590 was laid down on 19 June 1944 at Evansville, Ind., by the Missouri Valley Bridge & Iron Co.; launched on 29 July 1944; sponsored by Mrs. W. F. Broun; and commissioned on 26 August 1944, Ens. Boyd J. Arnett in command.

During World War II, *LST–590* was assigned to the Asiatic-Pacific theater and participated in the Tarakan Island operation from April to May 1945. Following the war, she performed occupation duty in the Far East until early February 1946. The ship was decommissioned on 2 February 1946. On 31 March 1952, *LST–590* was transferred to the Military Sea Transportation Service where she served as USNS *LST–590* until struck from the Navy list on 15 June 1973. The ship was sold to S. S. Zee, Taipei, Taiwan, on 17 September 1973 for scrapping.

LST–590 earned one battle star for World War II service.

LST–591

LST–591 was laid down on 21 June 1944 at Evansville, Ind., by the Missouri Valley Bridge & Iron Co.; launched on 2 August 1944; sponsored by Mrs. W. B. Parsons; and commissioned on 29 August 1944, Lt. Robert C. Allen in command.

During World War II, *LST–591* was assigned to the Asiatic-Pacific theater and participated in the Mindanao Island landings in March 1945. Following the war, she performed occupation duty in the Far East until early February 1946. The ship was decommissioned on 5 February 1946 and struck from the Navy list on 29 September 1947. On 24 May 1948, *LST–591* was sold to the Bethlehem Steel Co., of Bethlehem, Pa., for scrapping.

LST–591 earned one battle star for World War II service.

LST–592

LST–592 was laid down on 24 June 1944 at Evansville, Ind., by the Missouri Valley Bridge & Iron Co.; launched on 5 August 1944; sponsored by Mrs. John Dixon; and commissioned on 1 September 1944.

During World War II, *LST–592* was assigned to the Asiatic-Pacific theater and participated in the following operations:

Lingayen Gulf landing—January 1945
Mindanao Island landings—April through May 1945
Assault and occupation of Okinawa Gunto—June 1945

Following the war, *LST–592* performed occupation duty in the Far East until late November 1945. The ship returned to the United States and was decommissioned on 11 June 1946 and struck from the Navy list on 31 July that same year. On 23 October 1947, she was sold to the Boston Metals Corp., Baltimore, Md., for scrapping.

LST–592 earned three battle stars for World War II service.

LST–593

LST–593 was laid down on 28 June 1944 at Evansville, Ind., by the Missouri Valley Bridge & Iron Co.; launched on 9 August 1944; sponsored by Mrs. Olaf A.

Ragle; and commissioned on 5 September 1944, Lt. Fairfield P. Day, USNR, in command.

During World War II, *LST–593* was assigned to the Asiatic-Pacific theater and participated in the Mindanao Island landings from April to May 1945. Following the war, she performed occupation duty in the Far East until late October 1945. The ship returned to the United States and was decommissioned on 18 March 1946 and struck from the Navy list on 8 May that same year. On 28 May 1948, she was sold to the Alexander Shipyards, Inc., of New Orleans, La., for operation.

LST–593 earned one battle star for World War II service.

LST–594

LST–594 was laid down on 1 July 1944 at Evansville, Ind., by the Missouri Valley Bridge & Iron Co.; launched on 12 August 1944; sponsored by Mrs. Everett B. Wiley; and commissioned on 6 September 1944, Lt. Edgar Y. M. Henderson, USNR, in command.

Following World War II, *LST–594* performed occupation duty in the Far East and saw service in China until mid-February 1946. The ship was decommissioned on 21 February 1946 and was struck from the Navy list on 5 March 1947. On 4 June 1947, she was sold to the government of South Korea.

LST–595

LST–595 was laid down on 7 July 1944 at Evansville, Ind., by the Missouri Valley Bridge & Iron Co.; launched on 16 August 1944; sponsored by Mrs. Adlai Russell; and commissioned on 14 September 1944, Lt. A. C. Jackson, USNR, in command.

During World War II, *LST–595* was assigned to the Asiatic-Pacific theater and participated in the Palawan Island landings in March 1945 and the Visayan Island landings in March and April 1945. Following the war, she performed occupation duty in the Far East until January 1946. *LST–595* was decommissioned on 3 January 1946 and struck from the Navy list on 5 March 1947. On 31 May 1947, *LST–595* was sold to the government of South Korea.

LST–595 earned one battle star for World War II service.

LST–596

LST–596 was laid down on 11 July 1944 at Evansville, Ind., by the Missouri Valley Bridge & Iron Co.; launched on 21 August 1944; sponsored by Mrs. Palmer L. McMichael; and commissioned on 14 September 1944.

Following World War II, *LST–596* performed occupation duty in the Far East and saw service in China until mid-May 1946. She was decommissioned on 12 June 1946 and struck from the Navy list on 25 September that same year. The ship was sold to Bosey, Philippines, on 5 December 1947.

LST–597

LST–597 was laid down on 12 July 1944 at Evansville, Ind., by the Missouri Valley Bridge & Iron Co.; launched on 28 August 1944; sponsored by Mrs. Bernice C. Palmer; and commissioned on 19 September 1944.

During World War II, *LST–597* was assigned to the Asiatic-Pacific theater and participated in the following operations:

Palawan Island landings—March 1945
Visayan Island landings—March and April 1945
Assault and occupation of Okinawa Gunto—June 1945

Following the war, *LST–597* performed occupation duty in the Far East until early March 1946. Upon her return to the United States, the ship was decommissioned on 5 March 1946 and struck from the Navy list on 29 September 1947. On 31 May 1948, she was sold to the Bethlehem Steel Co., of Bethlehem, Pa., for scrapping.

LST–597 earned two battle stars for World War II service.

LST–598

LST–598 was laid down on 14 July 1944 at Evansville, Ind., by the Missouri Valley Bridge & Iron Co.; launched on 29 August 1944; sponsored by Mrs. Robert H. Vickery; and commissioned on 22 September 1944, Lt. Marion V. Reeder, USNR, in command.

During World War II, *LST–598* was assigned to the Asiatic-Pacific theater and participated in the assault and occupation of Okinawa Gunto in April and May 1945. Following the war, she performed occupation duty in the Far East and saw service in China until early June 1946. *LST–598* was decommissioned on 10 June 1946 and struck from the Navy list on 19 July that same year.

LST–598 earned one battle star for World War II service.

LST–599

LST–599 was laid down on 18 July 1944 at Evansville, Ind., by the Missouri Valley Bridge & Iron Co.; launched on 2 September 1944; sponsored by Mrs. J. M. Robinson; and commissioned on 27 September 1944, Lt. P. P. Roney in command.

During World War II, *LST–599* was assigned to the Asiatic-Pacific theater and participated in the assault and occupation of Okinawa Gunto in April 1945. Following the war, she performed occupation duty in the Far East and saw service in China until June 1946. The tank landing ship was decommissioned on 1 June 1946 and sold to Bosey, Philippines, on 5 December 1947. She was struck from the Navy list on 22 January 1948.

LST–599 earned one battle star for World War II service.

LST–600

LST–600 was laid down on 6 October 1943 at Seneca, Ill., by the Chicago Bridge & Iron Co.; launched on 28 February 1944; sponsored by Mrs. Helena Wilson Carpender; and commissioned on 20 March 1944.

Following World War II, *LST–600* performed occupation duty in the Far East until late February 1946. On 31 March 1952, she was transferred to the Military Sea Transportation Service where she operated as USNS *LST–600* until struck from the Navy list on 1 June 1969.

LST–601

LST–601 was laid down on 21 October 1943 at Seneca, Ill., by the Chicago Bridge & Iron Co.; launched on 4 March 1944; sponsored by Mrs. Celia Counter Finch; and commissioned on 25 March 1944, Lt. Ledbetter in command.

During World War II, *LST–601* was assigned to the European theater and participated in the invasion of southern France in August and September 1944. At the close of World War II, *LST–601* remained in active service under Commander, Amphibious Force, U.S. Atlantic Fleet. *LST–601* was redesignated *Clarke County* (LST–601) on 1 July 1955 after counties in Alabama, Georgia, Iowa, Mississippi, and Virginia. She was decommissioned on 23 November 1955. The ship was recommissioned on 28 July 1966. *Clarke County* performed service in the Vietnam theater during the period 1967 to 1970.

LST–601 received one battle star for World War II service, and six battle stars plus two awards of the Meritorious Unit Commendation for Vietnam service.

LST–602

LST–602 was laid down on 23 October 1943 at Seneca, Ill., by the Chicago Bridge & Iron Co.; launched on 9 March 1944; sponsored by Mrs. Adele R. Ziehm; and commissioned on 31 March 1944, Ens. John H. Mehus, USNR, in command.

During World War II, *LST–602* was assigned to the European theater and participated in the invasion of southern France in August and September 1944. In 1946, she was decommissioned and, as a result of hostilities in Korea, the ship was recalled to active service in 1950 and performed service in the Korean theater. On 1 July 1955, she was redesignated *Clearwater County* (LST-602) after counties in Idaho and Minnesota.

The tank landing ship was operated by the Air Force from September 1957 to September 1969 when she was transferred to the temporary custody of the Maritime Administration. She was struck from the Navy list on 1 May 1972 and sold to Mexico on 30 May 1972 where she served as *Manzanillo* (IA–02).

LST–602 earned one battle star for World War II service and two battle stars for Korean service.

LST–603

LST–603 was laid down on 5 November 1943 at Seneca, Ill., by the Chicago Bridge & Iron Co.; launched on 14 March 1944; sponsored by Mrs. Etla N. Hobart; and commissioned on 5 April 1944, Ens. William B. Sweet in command.

During World War II, *LST–603* was assigned to the European theater and participated in the invasion of southern France in August and September 1944. Following the war, she performed duties with the Amphibious Force, U.S. Atlantic Fleet, including one deployment to the Mediterranean in 1950. The ship was decommissioned on 12 May 1955. On 1 July that same year, she was redesignated *Coconino County* (LST-603) after a county in Arizona. She was recommissioned on 8 June 1966 and operated in the Vietnam theater commencing in 1966 until she was transferred to the Republic of Vietnam Navy on 4 April 1969 where she served as *Vung Tau* (HQ–503).

LST–603 received one battle star for World War II service, and six battle stars and two awards of the Meritorious Unit Commendation for Vietnam service.

LST–604

LST–604 was redesignated AGP–11 and named *Silenus* (q.v.) on 18 December 1943.

LST–605

LST–605 was laid down on 30 September 1943 at Seneca, Ill., by the Chicago Bridge & Iron Co.; launched on 29 March 1944; sponsored by Mrs. H. F. Stearns; and commissioned on 14 April 1944.

During World War II, *LST–605* was assigned to the Asiatic-Pacific theater and participated in the following operations:

> Leyte landing—October 1944
> Mindoro landing—December 1944
> Lingayen Gulf landing—January 1945

Assault and occupation of Okinawa Gunto—May and June 1945

Following the war, *LST–605* performed occupation duty in the Far East until mid-December 1945. She returned to the United States and was decommissioned on 24 May 1946 and struck from the Navy list on 3 July that same year. On 15 April 1948, the ship was sold to Kaiser Co., Inc., Vancouver, Wash., for scrapping.

LST–605 earned three battle stars and one award of the Navy Unit Commendation for World War II service.

LST–606

LST–606 was laid down on 27 November 1943 at Seneca, Ill., by the Chicago Bridge and Iron Co.; launched on 3 April 1944; sponsored by Mrs. George Milligan; and commissioned on 24 April 1944, Lt. William R. Brooks in command.

During World War II, *LST–606* was assigned to the Asiatic-Pacific theater and participated in the following operations:

> Capture and occupation of southern Palau Islands —September 1944
> Leyte landings—October and November 1944
> Lingayen Gulf landing—January 1945
> Assault and occupation of Okinawa Gunto—April through June 1945

Following the war, *LST–606* performed occupation duty in the Far East until mid-September 1945. Upon her return to the United States, she was decommissioned on 13 May 1946 and struck from the Navy list on 19 June that same year. On 19 April 1948, the ship was sold to the Bethlehem Steel Co., of Bethlehem, Pa., for scrapping.

LST–606 earned four battle stars for World War II service.

LST–607

LST–607 was laid down on 2 December 1943 at Seneca, Ill., by the Chicago Bridge & Iron Co.; launched on 7 April 1944; sponsored by Mrs. John Pirok; and commissioned on 24 April 1944.

During World War II, *LST–607* was assigned to the Asiatic-Pacific theater and participated in the capture and occupation of the southern Palau Islands from September to October 1944.

Following the war, *LST–607* performed occupation duty in the Far East until early January 1946. She was decommissioned on 11 January 1946 and transferred to the Military Sea Transportation Service on 31 March 1952 where she served as USNS *LST–607*. USNS *LST–607* was transferred to the Philippine Navy on 13 September 1976.

LST–607 earned one battle star for World War II service.

LST–608

LST–608 was laid down on 4 December 1943 at Seneca, Ill., by the Chicago Bridge & Iron Co.; launched on 11 April 1944; sponsored by Mrs. W. S. Martin; and commissioned on 15 April 1944.

During World War II, *LST–608* was assigned to the Asiatic-Pacific theater and participated in the following operations:

> Leyte landings—October and November 1944
> Lingayen Gulf landing—January 1945
> Assault and occupation of Okinawa Gunto—April 1945

Following the war, *LST–608* performed occupation duty in the Far East until early January 1946. She was decommissioned on 1 January 1946 and struck from the Navy list on 7 February 1947. On 31 May

LST–1110 follows the Coast Guard icebreaker *Bittersweet* (WAGL–389) through the ice off Point Barrow, Alaska, to supply one of the radar stations of the DEW (Distant Early Warning) Line, 1955. (80–G–709519)

1947, the ship was sold to the government of South Korea.

LST–608 earned three battle stars for World War II service.

LST–609

LST–609 was laid down on 10 December 1943 at Seneca, Ill., by the Chicago Bridge & Iron Co.; launched on 15 April 1944; sponsored by Mrs. Willard Maybauer; and commissioned on 15 May 1944.

During World War II, *LST–609* was assigned to the Asiatic-Pacific theater and participated in the following operations:

  Leyte landing—October 1944
  Mindoro landings—December 1944
  Zambales-Subic Bay—January 1945
  Assault and occupation of Okinawa Gunto—April 1945

Following the war, she was decommissioned on 4 January 1946 and struck from the Navy list on 21 January that same year. The ship was sold on 26 September 1947 to the Boston Metals Co., of Baltimore, Md., for scrapping.

LST–609 earned four battle stars for World War II service.

LST-610

LST-610 was laid down on 16 December 1943 at Seneca, Ill., by the Chicago Bridge & Iron Co.; launched on 19 April 1944; sponsored by Mrs. Patrick J. O'Herron; and commissioned on 15 May 1944.

During World War II, *LST-610* was assigned to the Asiatic-Pacific theater and participated in the following operations:

Capture and occupation of southern Palau Islands —September and October 1944

Leyte landing—October and November 1944

Lingayen Gulf landing—January 1945

Following the war, *LST-610* performed occupation duty in the Far East and saw service in China until mid-June 1946. She was decommissioned on 28 June 1946 and transferred to the military government of Okinawa on 18 September that same year. The ship was struck from the Navy list on 23 December 1947.

LST-610 earned three battle stars for World War II service.

LST-611

LST-611 was laid down on 17 December 1943 at Seneca, Ill., by the Chicago Bridge & Iron Co.; launched on 28 April 1944; sponsored by Mrs. Ray Hines; and commissioned on 15 May 1944, Lt. Roy E. Burton, Jr., USNR, in command.

During World War II, *LST-611* was assigned to the Asiatic-Pacific theater and participated in the following operations:

Leyte landing—October 1944

Mindoro landing—December 1944

The ship operated with the Amphibious Force, U.S. Pacific Fleet, following World War II and participated in the Inchon landings in September 1950 during the Korean War. On 1 July 1955, *LST-611* was redesignated *Crook County* (LST-611) after counties in Oregon and Wyoming. On 26 October 1956, the ship was placed in service, in reserve, in caretaker status.

LST-611 earned two battle stars for World War II service and three battle stars for Korean service.

LST-612

LST-612 was laid down on 18 December 1943 at Seneca, Ill., by the Chicago Bridge & Iron Co.; launched on 29 April 1944; sponsored by Mrs. Perry Arnold; and commissioned on 16 May 1944, Lt. John A. White in command.

During World War II, *LST-612* was assigned to the Asiatic-Pacific theater and participated in the following operations:

Leyte landing—October 1944

Mindoro landing—December 1944

Assault and occupation of Okinawa Gunto—April and June 1945

Following the war, *LST-612* performed occupation duty in the Far East and saw China service until early May 1946. She was decommissioned on 1 June 1946 and struck from the Navy list on 3 July that same year. On 5 December 1947, the ship was sold to Bosey, Philippines.

LST-612 earned three battle stars for World War II service.

LST-613

LST-613 was laid down on 21 January 1944 at Seneca, Ill., by the Chicago Bridge & Iron Co.; launched on 2 May 1944; sponsored by Mrs. W. D. Ford; and commissioned on 19 May 1944.

During World War II, *LST-613* was assigned to the Asiatic-Pacific theater and participated in the following operations:

Morotai landing—September 1944

Leyte landing—November 1944

Mindoro landing—December 1944

Lingayen Gulf landing—January 1945

Visayan Island landing—March 1945

Tarakan Island operation—April and May 1945

Following the war, *LST-613* performed occupation duty in the Far East until early January 1946. She was decommissioned on 6 January 1946 and transferred to the Military Sea Transportation Service on 31 March 1952 where she served as USNS *LST-613* until struck from the Navy list.

LST-613 earned five battle stars for World War II service.

LST-614

LST-614 was laid down on 28 January 1944 at Seneca, Ill., by the Chicago Bridge & Iron Co.; launched on 6 May 1944; sponsored by Mrs. Marjorie H. Elting; and commissioned on 22 May 1944, Lt. (jg.) P. S. Donovan, USNR, in command.

During World War II, *LST-614* was assigned to the Asiatic-Pacific theater and participated in the following operations:

Morotai landing—September 1944

Leyte landing—October 1944

Lingayen Gulf landing—January 1945

Mindanao Island landing—April 1945

Following the war, *LST-614* performed occupation duty in the Far East and saw service in China until mid-January 1946. She was decommissioned on 20 June 1946 and struck from the Navy list on 29 October that same year. On 13 February 1948, the ship was sold to Bosey, Philippines.

LST-614 earned four battle stars for World War II service.

LST-615

LST-615 was laid down on 4 February 1944 at Seneca, Ill., by the Chicago Bridge & Iron Co.; launched on 9 May 1944; sponsored by Mrs. Leo Marcoux; and commissioned on 26 May 1944.

During World War II, *LST-615* was assigned to the Asiatic-Pacific theater and participated in the Leyte landing in October 1944 and the assault and occupation of Okinawa Gunto in April 1945. Following the war, *LST-615* performed occupation duty in the Far East until mid-November 1945. She was decommissioned on 14 March 1946 and struck from the Navy list on 12 April that same year. On 7 April 1948, the ship was sold to Kaiser Co., Inc., Vancouver, Wash., and subsequently scrapped.

LST-615 earned two battle stars for World War II service.

LST-616

LST-616 was laid down on 12 February 1944 at Seneca, Ill., by the Chicago Bridge & Iron Co.; launched on 12 May 1944; sponsored by Mrs. Carrol McDaniel; and commissioned on 29 May 1944, Ens. Julian H. Rutherford, Jr., in command.

During World War II, *LST-616* was assigned to the Asiatic-Pacific theater and participated in the assault and occupation of Okinawa Gunto in March and April 1945. Following the war, the ship performed occupation duty in the Far East and saw service in China until early December 1945. She was decommissioned on 19 January 1946 and transferred to the Military Sea Transportation Service on 31 March 1952 where she served as USNS *LST-616*. *LST-616* was struck from the Navy list on 1 May 1961 and transferred to the government of Indonesia.

LST-616 earned one battle star for World War II service.

LST-617

LST-617 was laid down on 17 February 1944 at Seneca, Ill., by the Chicago Bridge & Iron Co.; launched on 15 May 1944; sponsored by Mrs. E. B. Payne; and commissioned on 1 June 1944, Lt. Howard J. Benward in command.

During World War II, LST-617 was assigned to the Asiatic-Pacific theater and participated in the following operations:

    Leyte landing—October 1944
    Mindoro landing—December 1944
    Lingayen Gulf landing—January 1945
    Assault and occupation of Okinawa Gunto—March
        through June 1945

Following the war, LST-617 performed occupation duty in the Far East until mid-December 1945. Upon her return to the United States, she was decommissioned on 24 May 1946 and struck from the Navy list on 3 July that same year. On 15 April 1948, the ship was sold to Kaiser Co., Inc., Vancouver, Wash., and subsequently scrapped.

LST-617 earned three battle stars for World War II service.

LST-618

LST-618 was laid down on 23 February 1944 at Seneca, Ill., by the Chicago Bridge & Iron Co.; launched on 19 May 1944; sponsored by Miss Anita Pierce; and commisioned on 3 June 1944.

During World War II, LST-618 was assigned to the Asiatic-Pacific theater and participated in the following operations:

    Leyte landing—October and November 1944
    Lingayen Gulf landing—January 1945
    Mindanao Island landings—April 1945

Following the war, LST-618 performed occupation duty in the Far East and saw China service until early July 1946. On 24 October 1946, she was transferred to United States Army custody and struck from the Navy list on 23 December 1947.

LST-618 earned three battle stars for World War II service.

LST-619

LST-619 was laid down on 8 March 1944 at Seneca, Ill., by the Chicago Bridge & Iron Co.; launched on 22 May 1944; sponsored by Mrs. Walter B. Colby; and commissioned on 5 June 1944.

During World War II, LST-619 was assigned to the Asiatic-Pacific theater and participated in the following operations:

    Leyte landings—October and November 1944
    Mindoro landings—December 1944
    Palawan Island landings—March 1945
    Visayan Island landings—March 1945

Following the war, LST-619 performed occupation duty in the Far East until mid-April 1946. Upon her return to the United States, she was decommissioned on 19 June 1946 and struck from the Navy list on 31 October 1947. On 27 May 1948, the ship was sold to Consolidated Builders, Inc., Seattle, Wash., for scrapping.

LST-619 earned three battle stars for World War II service.

LST-620

LST-620 was laid down on 11 March 1944 at Seneca, Ill., by the Chicago Bridge & Iron Co.; launched on 30 May 1944; sponsored by Mrs. V. A. Carpano; and commissioned on 17 June 1944.

During World War II, LST-620 was assigned to the Asiatic-Pacific theater and participated in the assault and occupation of Okinawa Gunto in May and June 1945. Following the war, she performed occupation duty in the Far East and saw service in China until early May 1946. The ship was decommissioned on 7 June 1946 and struck from the Navy list on 19 June that same year.

LST-620 earned one battle star for World War II service.

LST-621

LST-621 was laid down on 15 March 1944 at Seneca, Ill., by the Chicago Bridge & Iron Co.; launched on 2 June 1944; sponsored by Mrs. Josephine F. Madura; and commissioned on 21 June 1944, Lt. C. E. Watkins in command.

During World War II, LST-621 was assigned to the Asiatic-Pacific theater and participated in the assault and occupation of Okinawa Gunto in April and May 1945. Following the war, she performed occupation duty in the Far East until late December 1945. The ship was decommissioned on 10 June 1946 and struck from the Navy list on 31 July that same year. On 30 March 1948, she was sold to the Kaiser Co., Inc., Seattle, Wash., for scrapping.

LST-621 earned one battle star for World War II service.

LST-622

LST-622 was laid down on 15 March 1944 at Seneca, Ill., by the Chicago Bridge & Iron Co.; launched on 8 June 1944; sponsored by Mrs. Ray Menefee; and commissioned on 26 June 1944.

During World War II, LST-622 was assigned to the Asiatic-Pacific theater and participated in the Lingayen Gulf landing in January 1945 and the assault and occupation of Okinawa Gunto from March to June 1945. Following the war, LST-622 was decommissioned on 14 March 1946 and struck from the Navy list on 12 April that same year. On 13 April 1948, the ship was sold to Kaiser Co., Inc., Seattle, Wash., for scrapping.

LST-622 earned two battle stars for World War II service.

LST-623

LST-623 was laid down on 17 March 1944 at Seneca, Ill., by the Chicago Bridge & Iron Co.; launched on 12 June 1944; sponsored by Mrs. J. K. Esler; and commissioned on 29 June 1944.

During World War II, LST-623 was assigned to the Asiatic-Pacific theater and participated in the following operations:

    Leyte landings—October through November 1944
    Lingayen Gulf landing—January 1945
    Palawan Island landings—March 1945

Following the war, LST-623 performed occupation duty in the Far East and saw service in China until mid-February 1946. She was transferred to the Military Sea Transportation Service on 31 March 1952 where she operated as USNS LST-623.

LST-623 earned three battle stars for World War II service.

LST-624

LST-624 was laid down on 22 March 1944 at Seneca, Ill., by the Chicago Bridge & Iron Co.; launched on 16 June 1944; sponsored by Mrs. Agnes Reynolds; and commissioned on 3 July 1944, Lt. R. S. Salzer in command.

During World War II, LST-624 was assigned to the Asiatic-Pacific theater and participated in the following operations:

Lingayen Gulf landing—January 1945
Manila Bay-Bicol operations—January 1945
Assault and occupation of Okinawa Gunto—April 1945

Following the war, *LST–624* performed occupation duty in the Far East until early February 1946. She was decommissioned on 14 February 1946 and struck from the Navy list on 7 February 1947. On 1 June 1947, the ship was sold to the government of South Korea.

LST–624 earned three battle stars for World War II service.

LST–625

LST–625 was laid down on 30 March 1944 at Seneca, Ill., by the Chicago Bridge & Iron Co.; launched on 20 June 1944; sponsored by Miss Margaret Jones; and commissioned on 10 July 1944, Lt. George F. B. Capozzi, USNR, in command.

During World War II, *LST–625* was assigned to the Asiatic-Pacific theater and participated in the Lingayen Gulf landing in January 1945 and the assault and occupation of Okinawa Gunto in April 1945. Following the war, she performed occupation duty in the Far East until early February 1946. The ship was decommissioned on 11 February 1946 and transferred to the Military Sea Transportation Service on 31 March 1952 where she served as USNS *LST–625* until struck from the Navy list on 19 May 1954.

LST–625 earned two battle stars for World War II service.

LST–626

LST–626 was laid down on 31 March 1944 at Seneca, Ill., by the Chicago Bridge & Iron Co.; launched on 27 June 1944; sponsored by Miss Mary B. Ralston; and commissioned on 15 July 1944.

During World War II, *LST–626* was assigned to the Asiatic-Pacific theater and participated in the following operations:

Leyte landings—November 1944
Lingayen Gulf landing—January 1945
Mindanao Island landings—March 1945
Tarakan Island operation—April and May 1945
Brunei Bay operation—June and July 1945

Following the war, *LST–626* performed occupation duty in the Far East and saw service in China until early March 1946. She was decommissioned on 2 March 1946 and transferred to the Military Sea Transportation Service on 31 March 1952 where she served as USNS *LST–626* until struck from the Navy list on 1 June 1972. On 25 May 1973, the ship was sold to the Dongkuk Steel Co. of America, Inc., Los Angeles, Calif., for scrapping.

LST–626 earned four battle stars for World War II service.

LST–627

LST–627 was laid down on 8 April 1944 at Seneca, Ill., by the Chicago Bridge & Iron Co.; launched on 1 July 1944; sponsored by Mrs. C. H. Mattern; and commissioned on 20 July 1944, Lt. S. R. Parker, in command.

During World War II, *LST–627* was assigned to the Asiatic-Pacific theater and participated in the Lingayen Gulf landing in January 1945 and the assault and occupation of Okinawa Gunto in April 1945. Following the war, she performed occupation duty in the Far East and saw service in China until mid-May 1946. The ship was decommissioned on 6 June 1946 and sold to the government of the Netherlands East Indies on 15 June that same year. On 19 June 1946, *LST–627* was struck from the Navy list.

LST–627 earned two battle stars for World War II service.

LST–628

LST–628 was laid down on 10 April 1944 at Seneca, Ill., by the Chicago Bridge & Iron Co.; launched on 4 July 1944; sponsored by Mrs. P. G. Abernathy; and commissioned on 31 July 1944, Lt. Frank C. Siedenburg in command.

During World War II, *LST–628* was assigned to the Asiatic-Pacific theater and participated in the assault and occupation of Okinawa Gunto in May 1945. Following the war, she performed occupation duty in the Far East until early March 1946. The ship was decommissioned on 3 April 1946 and struck from the Navy list on 3 July that same year. She was sold to the Ships & Power Equipment Corp., of Barber, N.J., on 9 December 1947 for scrapping.

LST–628 earned one battle star for World War II service.

LST–629

LST–629 was laid down on 13 April 1944 at Seneca, Ill., by the Chicago Bridge & Iron Co.; launched on 8 July 1944; sponsored by Mrs. R. B. Douglass; and commissioned on 28 July 1944.

During World War II, *LST–629* was assigned to the Asiatic-Pacific theater and participated in the following operations:

Lingayen Gulf landing—January 1945
Mindanao Island landings—April 1945
Assault and occupation of Okinawa Gunto—June 1945

Following the war, *LST–629* saw service in China until late December 1945. The ship was decommissioned on 4 March 1946 and transferred to the Military Sea Transportation Service on 31 March 1952 where she served as USNS *LST–629*.

LST–629 earned three battle stars for World War II service.

LST–630

LST–630 was laid down on 14 April 1944 at Seneca, Ill., by the Chicago Bridge & Iron Co.; launched on 13 July 1944; sponsored by Mrs. Walter Dunnett; and commissioned on 4 August 1944.

During World War II, *LST–630* was assigned to the Asiatic-Pacific theater and participated in the following operations:

Mindoro landings—December 1944
Lingayen Gulf landing—January 1945
Mindanao Island landings—March through April 1945

Following the war, *LST–630* performed occupation duty in the Far East and saw service in China until mid-February 1946. She was decommissioned on 13 February 1946 and transferred to the Military Sea Transportation Service on 31 March 1952 where she served as USNS *LST–630* until struck from the Navy list on 15 June 1973. On 19 November 1973, she was sold to B. V. Dimex, Nijmegen, Netherlands, for scrapping.

LST–630 earned two battle stars for World War II service.

LST–631

LST–631 was laid down on 19 April 1944 at Seneca, Ill., by the Chicago Bridge & Iron Co.; launched on 18 July 1944; sponsored by Mrs. Theresa Colmone; and commissioned on 9 August 1944.

During World War II, *LST–631* was assigned to the Asiatic-Pacific theater and participated in the following operations:

Lingayen Gulf landing—January 1945
Zambales-Subic Bay—January 1945
Mindanao Island landings—March and April 1945

Following the war, *LST-631* performed occupation duty in the Far East until mid-December 1945. She was decommissioned on 24 May 1946 and struck from the Navy list on 3 July that same year. On 15 April 1948, the ship was sold to Kaiser Co., Inc., Seattle, Wash., and subsequently scrapped.

LST-631 earned three battle stars for World War II service.

LST-632

LST-632 was laid down on 26 April 1944 at Seneca, Ill., by the Chicago Bridge & Iron Co.; launched on 21 July 1944; sponsored by Mrs. William H. Hallenback; and commissioned on 12 August 1944, Ens. G. W. Chandler, USNR, in command.

During World War II, *LST-632* was assigned to the Asiatic-Pacific theater and participated in the following operations:

Lingayen Gulf landing—January 1945
Corregidor-Mariveles—February 1945
Mindanao Island landings—March through April 1945
Balikpapan operation—June and July 1945

Following the war, *LST-632* performed occupation duty in the Far East and saw service in China until mid-May 1946. She was decommissioned on 30 May 1946 and struck from the Navy list on 28 January 1947. The tank landing ship was destroyed as a target on 11 June 1948.

LST-632 earned four battle stars for World War II service.

LST-633

LST-633 was laid down on 3 May 1944 at Seneca, Ill., by the Chicago Bridge & Iron Co.; launched on 27 July 1944; sponsored by Miss Evelyn Martin; and commissioned on 17 August 1944.

During World War II, *LST-633* was assigned to the Asiatic-Pacific theater and participated in the assault and occupation of Okinawa Gunto from April to June 1945. Following the war, she performed occupation duty in the Far East until mid-February 1946. The ship was decommissioned on 15 February 1946 and struck from the Navy list on 29 September 1947. On 23 June 1948, she was sold to Consolidated Builders, Inc., Seattle, Wash., and subsequently scrapped.

LST-633 earned one battle star for World War II service.

LST-634

LST-634 was laid down on 13 May 1944 at Seneca, Ill., by the Chicago Bridge & Iron Co.; launched on 1 August 1944; sponsored by Mrs. R. F. Hendren; and commissioned on 22 August 1944, Lt. T. Little in command.

During World War II, *LST-634* was assigned to the Asiatic-Pacific theater and participated in the assault and occupation of Iwo Jima in February and March 1945. Following the war, she performed occupation duty in the Far East and saw service in China until early June 1946. The ship was decommissioned on 8 June 1946 and struck from the Navy list on 19 July that same year. On 23 June 1948, she was transferred to the Maritime Administration for disposal.

LST-634 earned one battle star for World War II service.

LST-635

LST-635 was laid down on 17 May 1944 at Seneca, Ill., by the Chicago Bridge & Iron Co.; launched on 7 August 1944; sponsored by Mrs. Isabelle Wurst; and commissioned on 26 August 1944, Lt. D. J. Lanphere in command.

Following World War II, *LST-635* performed occupation duty in the Far East and saw service in China until early June 1946. She was decommissioned on 7 June 1946 and transferred to the State Department for disposition on 19 July 1946.

LST-636

LST-636 was laid down on 22 May 1944 at Seneca, Ill., by the Chicago Bridge & Iron Co.; launched on 11 August 1944; sponsored by Mrs. Katherine R. Biehler; and commissioned on 31 August 1944, Lt. T. M. Hayes, Jr., USNR, in command.

During World War II, *LST-636* was assigned to the Asiatic-Pacific theater and participated in the Lingayen Gulf landing in January 1945 and the Mindanao Island landings in March and April 1945. She performed occupation duty in the Far East and saw service in China until early May 1946. The ship was decommissioned on 25 May 1946 and sold to Bosey, Philippines, on 5 December 1947. On 23 December 1947, she was struck from the Navy list.

LST-636 earned two battle stars for World War II service.

LST-637

LST-637 was laid down on 24 May 1944 at Seneca, Ill., by the Chicago Bridge & Iron Co.; launched on 18 August 1944; sponsored by Mrs. Elizabeth Ann Michaels; and commissioned on 5 September 1944, Lt. C. E. Helfrich, USNR, in command.

During World War II, *LST-637* was assigned to the Asiatic-Pacific theater and participated in the following operations:

Lingayen Gulf landing—January 1945
Visayan Island landings—March through May 1945
Tarakan Island operation—April and May 1945

Following the war, *LST-637* performed occupation duty in the Far East until late October 1945. She was decommissioned on 29 March 1946 and struck from the Navy list on 5 June that same year. On 18 December 1947, the ship was sold to the Ships & Power Equipment Corp., of Barber, N.J., and subsequently scrapped.

LST-637 earned three battle stars for World War II service.

LST-638

LST-638 was laid down on 25 May 1944 at Seneca, Ill., by the Chicago Bridge & Iron Co.; launched on 23 August 1944; sponsored by Mrs. Marjorie T. Twyman; and commissioned on 8 September 1944.

During World War II, *LST-638* was assigned to the Asiatic-Pacific theater and participated in the Palawan Island landings in March 1945 and the Visayan Island landings in April 1945. She performed occupation duty in the Far East and saw service in China until mid-May 1946. The ship was decommissioned on 8 June 1946 and struck from the Navy list on 12 March 1948. She was destroyed as a target on 15 June 1948.

LST-638 earned one battle star for World War II service.

LST-639

LST-639 was laid down on 26 May 1944 at Seneca, Ill., by the Chicago Bridge & Iron Co.; launched on 28 August 1944; sponsored by Mrs. Isabel C. Christofferson; and commissioned on 14 September 1944.

During World War II, *LST-639* was assigned to the Asiatic-Pacific theater and participated in the following operations:

Orleans Parish (LST–1069) at San Juan, Puerto Rico, early in 1957 as flagship and tender to Mine Squadron Four. Moored alongside are *Yazoo* (AN-92), *Robin* (MSC(O)–53), *Redpoll* (MSC(O)–57), *Ruff* (MSC(O)–54), with *Ostrich* (MSC(O)–29), *Reedbird* (MSC(O)–51), *Siskin* (MSC(O)–58), and *Egret* (MSC(O)–46) nested aft. In the foreground are six Canadian minesweepers which accompanied MinRon Four to the Caribbean for exercises. Berthed astern of *Orleans Parish* is the former LST–650, completed in 1945 as the landing-craft repair ship *Pandemus* (ARL–18) and also assigned to the mine force to maintain its diesel-powered ships.

Palawan Island landings—March 1945
Visayan Island landings—March 1945
Balikpapan operation—June and July 1945

Following the war, *LST–639* performed occupation duty in the Far East and saw service in China until mid-May 1946. She was decommissioned on 1 June 1946 and struck from the Navy list on 16 September 1947. On 5 December 1947, the ship was sold to Bosey, Philippines.

LST–639 earned two battle stars for World War II service.

LST-640

LST-640 was laid down on 27 May 1944 at Seneca, Ill., by the Chicago Bridge & Iron Co.; launched on 31 August 1944; sponsored by Mrs. Mary Frances Fox; and commissioned on 18 September 1944.

During World War II, LST-640 served in the Asiatic-Pacific theater and took part in the following operations:

Palawan Island landings—March 1945

Visayan Island landings—March and April 1945

Following the war, LST-640 performed service in China in March and April 1946. Upon her return to the United States, the ship was decommissioned on 30 April 1946 and struck from the Navy list on 19 July 1946.

LST-640 earned one battle star for World War II service.

LST-641

LST-641 was laid down on 1 June 1944 at Seneca, Ill., by the Chicago Bridge & Iron Co.; launched on 4 September 1944; and commissioned on 22 September 1944.

During World War II, LST-641 was assigned to the Asiatic-Pacific theater and participated in the assault and occupation of Iwo Jima in February 1945 and the assault and occupation of Okinawa Gunto from April through June 1945. She performed occupation duty in the Far East and saw service in China until mid-June 1946. The ship was decommissioned on 13 June 1946 and struck from the Navy list on 19 July that same year.

LST-641 earned two battle stars for World War II service.

LST-642

LST-642 was laid down on 5 June 1944 at Seneca, Ill., by the Chicago Bridge & Iron Co.; launched on 8 September 1944; sponsored by Mrs. Sylvia W. Nesbitt; and commissioned on 28 September 1944.

During World War II, LST-642 was assigned to the Asiatic-Pacific theater and participated in the assault and occupation of Iwo Jima in February and March 1945. She performed occupation duty in the Far East until mid-February 1947. The ship was decommissioned on 30 June 1947. LST-642 was abandoned at Barter Island, Alaska, on 10 February 1948 and struck from the Navy list on 19 February that same year.

LST-642 earned one battle star for World War II service.

LST-643

LST-643 was laid down on 10 June 1944 at Seneca, Ill., by the Chicago Bridge & Iron Co.; launched on 12 September 1944; sponsored by Lt. Cornelia W. Mattert, USNR; and commissioned on 2 October 1944.

During World War II, LST-643 was assigned to the Asiatic-Pacific theater and participated in the assault and occupation of Iwo Jima in February 1945 and the assault and occupation of Okinawa Gunto in April 1945. She performed occupation duty in the Far East until mid-January 1946. LST-643 was transferred to the Military Sea Transportation Service on 31 March 1952 where she operated as USNS LST-643 until struck from the Navy list on 15 June 1973. On 17 September 1973, the ship was sold to S. S. Zee, Taipei, Taiwan, for scrapping.

LST-643 earned two battle stars for World War II service.

LST-644

LST-644 was redesignated ARL-14 and named Minos (q.v.) on 14 August 1944.

LST-645

LST-645 was redesignated ARL-15 and named Minotaur (q.v.) on 14 August 1944.

LST-646

LST-646 was laid down on 30 June 1944 at Seneca, Ill., by the Chicago Bridge & Iron Co.; launched on 25 September 1944; sponsored by Mrs. Marie S. Pagoria; and commissioned on 13 October 1944.

During World War II, LST-646 was assigned to the Asiatic-Pacific theater and participated in the assault and occupation of Iwo Jima in February and March 1945. Following the war, LST-646 performed occupation duty in the Far East until early December 1945. She was decommissioned on 15 March 1946 and struck from the Navy list on 17 April that same year. On 11 May 1948, the ship was sold to J. Willis Smith & Bros. for scrapping.

LST-646 earned one battle star for World War II service.

LST-647

LST-647 was laid down on 5 July 1944 at Seneca, Ill., by the Chicago Bridge & Iron Co.; launched on 28 September 1944; sponsored by Mrs. Margaret H. Johnson; and commissioned on 19 October 1944.

During World War II, LST-647 was assigned to the Asiatic-Pacific theater and participated in the assault and occupation of Okinawa Gunto from March to June 1945. Following the war, she performed occupation duty in the Far East. The ship was decommissioned on 2 February 1946 and struck from the Navy list on 23 December 1947. On 25 May 1948, she was sold to the Bethlehem Steel Co., of Bethlehem, Pa., for scrapping.

LST-647 earned one battle star for World War II service.

LST-648

LST-648 was laid down on 7 July 1944 at Seneca, Ill., by the Chicago Bridge & Iron Co.; launched on 3 October 1944; sponsored by Mrs. Edith V. Vosburgh; and commissioned on 21 October 1944.

During World War II, LST-648 was assigned to the Asiatic-Pacific theater and participated in the assault and occupation of Iwo Jima in February 1945. Following the war, she performed occupation duty in the Far East until early February 1947. The ship was decommissioned on 14 February 1947 and struck from the Navy list on 25 February that same year and transferred to the United States Army.

LST-648 earned one battle star for World War II service.

LST-649

LST-649 was laid down on 19 July 1944 at Seneca, Ill., by the Chicago Bridge & Iron Co.; launched on 6 October 1944; sponsored by Miss Dorothy E. Otten; and commissioned on 26 October 1944.

During World War II, LST-649 was assigned to the Asiatic-Pacific theater and participated in the assault and occupation of Okinawa Gunto from March to June 1945. Following the war, she performed occupation duty in the Far East until early March 1946. On 31 March 1952, the ship was transferred to the Military Sea Transportation Service where she operated as USNS LST-649 until struck from the Navy list.

LST-649 earned one battle star for World War II service.

LST-650

LST-650 was redesignated ARL-18 and named Pandemus (q.v.) on 14 August 1944.

LST–651

LST–651 was laid down on 24 July 1944 at Seneca, Ill., by the Chicago Bridge & Iron Co.; launched on 16 October 1944; sponsored by Mrs. Mary Margaret Graham Aubry; and commissioned on 4 November 1944.

During World War II, LST–651 was assigned to the Asiatic-Pacific theater and participated in the assault and occupation of Okinawa Gunto in April 1945. Following the war, she performed occupation duty in the Far East until mid-January 1946. The ship was decommissioned on 23 January 1946 and struck from the Navy list on 5 December 1947. On 26 May 1948, LST–651 was sold to Consolidated Builders, Inc., Seattle, Wash., and subsequently scrapped.

LST–651 earned one battle star for World War II service.

LST–652

LST–652 was laid down on 24 July 1944 at Seneca, Ill., by the Chicago Bridge & Iron Co.; launched on 19 October 1944; sponsored by Mrs. Sadie M. Eveleigh; and commissioned on 1 January 1945, Lt. Richard N. Shaw, USNR, in command.

On 15 September 1945, she was redesignated LSTH–652. The ship performed occupation duty in the Far East until early March 1946. She was decommissioned on 5 March 1946. On 6 March 1952, the ship was redesignated LST–652 and transferred to the Military Sea Transportation Service on 31 March 1952 where she operated as USNS LST–652 until struck from the Navy list on 1 May 1961.

LST–653

LST–653 was laid down on 17 November 1943 at Ambridge, Pa., by the American Bridge Co.; launched on 23 January 1944; sponsored by Mrs. C. C. Smith; and commissioned on 1 April 1944, Lt. (jg.) H. C. Beasley, Jr., in command.

Following World War II, LST–653 performed occupation duty in the Far East until early February 1946. The ship was decommissioned on 3 February 1946 and struck from the Navy list on 5 March 1947. On 31 May 1947, LST–653 was sold to the government of South Korea.

LST–654

LST–654 was laid down on 9 December 1943 at Ambridge, Pa., by the American Bridge Co.; launched on 30 January 1944; sponsored by Miss Mary C. Nichols; and commissioned on 20 March 1944.

Following World War II, LST–654 performed occupation duty in the Far East and saw service in China until early June 1946. She was decommissioned on 12 June 1946 and transferred to the State Department for disposition and struck from the Navy list on 19 July 1946.

LST–655

LST–655 was laid down on 9 December 1943 at Ambridge, Pa., by the American Bridge Co.; launched on 6 February 1944; sponsored by Mrs. George T. Griffiths; and commissioned on 28 March 1944, Lt. Dudley D. Sumrall in command.

During World War II, LST–655 was assigned to the European theater and participated in the invasion of southern France in August and September 1944. She was then assigned to the Asiatic-Pacific theater and took part in the assault and occupation of Okinawa Gunto in June 1945. LST–655 performed occupation duty in the Far East and saw service in China until the spring of 1946. She was decommissioned on 31 May 1946 and transferred to the State Department for final disposition. LST–655 was struck from the Navy list on 3 July 1946.

LST–655 earned two battle stars for World War II service.

LST–656

LST–656 was laid down on 13 December 1943 at Ambridge, Pa., by the American Bridge Co.; launched on 18 February 1944; sponsored by Mrs. F. H. Dill; and commissioned on 7 April 1944.

During World War II, LST–656 was assigned to the European theater and participated in the invasion of southern France in August and September 1944. Following the war, she performed occupation duty in the Far East and saw service in China until late May 1946. The ship was decommissioned on 29 May 1946 and transferred to the State Department for disposition that same day. She was struck from the Navy list on 3 July 1946.

LST–656 earned one battle star for World War II service.

LST–657

LST–657 was laid down on 16 December 1943 at Ambridge, Pa., by the American Bridge Co.; launched on 25 February 1944; sponsored by Mrs. E. T. Owens; and commissioned on 10 April 1944, Lt. Eugene L. Berenbach, USNR, in command.

Following World War II, LST–657 performed occupation duty in the Far East and saw service in China until mid-February 1946. She was transferred to the Military Sea Transportation Service on 31 March 1952 where she served as USNS LST–657 until struck from the Navy list on 1 May 1961.

LST–658

LST–658 was laid down on 28 December 1943 at Ambridge, Pa., by the American Bridge Co.; launched on 13 March 1944; sponsored by Mrs. Joseph R. McDonald; and commissioned on 17 April 1944.

During World War II, LST–658 was assigned to the Asiatic-Pacific theater and participated in the following operations:

Capture and occupation of southern Palau Islands —September and October 1944
Leyte landings—October and November 1944
Lingayen Gulf landing—January 1945
Assault and occupation of Okinawa Gunto—April 1945

Following the war, LST–658 performed occupation duty in the Far East and saw service in China until late May 1946. She was decommissioned on 1 June 1946. The ship was transferred to the State Department for disposition and struck from the Navy list on 3 July 1946.

LST–658 earned four battle stars for World War II service.

LST–659

LST–659 was laid down on 31 December 1943 at Ambridge, Pa., by the American Bridge Co.; launched on 20 March 1944; sponsored by Mrs. A. N. Mellott; and commissioned on 20 April 1944.

During World War II, LST–659 was assigned to the European theater and participated in the invasion of southern France in August and September 1944. Following the war, she performed occupation duty in the Far East until early January 1946. The ship was decommissioned on 7 January 1946 and struck from the Navy list on 7 February 1947. On 25 May 1947, she was sold to the government of South Korea.

LST–659 earned one battle star for World War II service.

LST-660

LST-660 was laid down on 6 January 1944 at Ambridge, Pa., by the American Bridge Co.; launched on 24 March 1944; sponsored by Mrs. Robert Gibson; and commissioned on 26 April 1944.

During World War II, LST-660 was assigned to the Asiatic-Pacific theater and participated in the following operations:

Capture and occupation of southern Palau Islands —September and October 1944

Leyte landings—November 1944

Zambales-Subic Bay—January 1945

Assault and occupation of Okinawa Gunto—April 1945

Following the war, LST-660 performed occupation duty in the Far East until early January 1946. The ship was decommissioned on 26 April 1946 and struck from the Navy list on 5 June that same year. On 17 May 1948, she was sold to the Bethlehem Steel Co., of Bethlehem, Pa., and subsequently scrapped.

LST-660 earned four battle stars for World War II service.

LST-661

LST-661 was laid down on 9 January 1944 at Ambridge, Pa., by the American Bridge Co.; launched on 30 March 1944; sponsored by Mrs. J. H. Elder; and commissioned on 28 April 1944.

During World War II, LST-661 was assigned to the Asiatic-Pacific theater and participated in the capture and occupation of the southern Palau Islands in September and October 1944. Following the war, she performed occupation duty in the Far East until early April 1946. The ship returned to the United States and was decommissioned on 29 August 1946. On 25 July 1948, LST-661 was destroyed because of its unsalvageable condition and struck from the Navy list on 13 September that same year.

LST-661 earned one battle star for World War II service.

LST-662

LST-662 was laid down on 14 January 1944 at Ambridge, Pa., by the American Bridge Co.; launched on 5 April 1944; sponsored by Miss Louise Leahy; and commissioned on 2 May 1944.

During World War II, LST-662 was assigned to the Asiatic-Pacific theater and participated in the following operations:

Capture and occupation of southern Palau Islands —September and October 1944

Zambales-Subic Bay—January 1945

Assault and occupation of Okinawa Gunto—April 1945

Following the war, LST-662 was decommissioned on 19 December 1945 and struck from the Navy list on 8 January 1946. On 25 June 1946, the ship was sold to Arctic Circle Exploration, Inc., of Seattle, Wash.

LST-662 earned three battle stars for World War II service.

LST-663

LST-663 was laid down on 22 January 1944 at Ambridge, Pa., by the American Bridge Co.; launched on 8 April 1944; sponsored by Mrs. J. P. Delaney; and commissioned on 5 May 1944.

During World War II, LST-663 was assigned to the Asiatic-Pacific theater and participated in the following operations:

Capture and occupation of southern Palau Islands —September and October 1944

Leyte landings—October and November 1944

Assault and occupation of Okinawa Gunto—April through June 1945

Following the war, LST-663 returned to the United States and was decommissioned on 29 May 1946 and struck from the Navy list on 19 July that same year. On 11 December 1947, the ship was sold to the Southern Shipwrecking Co., of New Orleans, La., and subsequently scrapped.

LST-663 earned three battle stars for World War II service.

LST-664

LST-664 was laid down on 28 January 1944 at Ambridge, Pa., by the American Bridge Co.; launched on 13 April 1944; sponsored by Mrs. R. W. Caldwell, Jr.; and commissioned on 10 May 1944, Lt. John R. Burke in command.

During World War II, LST-664 was assigned to the European theater and participated in the invasion of southern France in August and September 1944. Following the war, she was transferred to the Military Sea Transportation Service on 19 April 1955 where she served as USNS LST-664 until struck from the Navy list on 15 June 1973. On 23 October 1973, the ship was sold to Majid Karoon, Khorramshahr, Iran, for scrapping.

LST-664 earned one battle star for World War II service.

LST-665

LST-665 was laid down on 5 February 1944 at Ambridge, Pa., by the American Bridge Co.; launched on 18 April 1944; sponsored by Mrs. L. L. Smith; and commissioned on 12 May 1944.

During World War II, LST-665 was assigned to the Euopean theater and participated in the invasion of southern France in August and September 1944. She was then assigned to the Asiatic-Pacific theater and took part in the capture and occupation of the southern Palau Islands in September and October 1944.

Following the war, LST-665 performed occupation duty in the Far East and saw service in China until mid-March 1946. She returned to the United States and was decommissioned on 11 June 1946 and struck from the Navy list on 3 July that same year. On 10 December 1947, the ship was sold to the Salco Iron & Metal Co. for scrapping.

LST-665 earned two battle stars for World War II service.

LST-666

LST-666 was laid down on 16 February 1944 at Ambridge, Pa., by the American Bridge Co.; launched on 24 April 1944; sponsored by Mrs. A. I. Hay; and commissioned on 16 May 1944.

During World War II, LST-666 was assigned to the Asiatic-Pacific theater and participated in the following operations:

Morotai landings—September 1944

Leyte landings—October and November 1944

Lingayen Gulf landing—January 1945

Zambales-Subic Bay—January 1945

Consolidation of the southern Philippines:

(a) Palawan Island landings—March 1945

(b) Visayan Island landings—March and April 1945

Balikpapan operation—June and July 1945

Following the war, LST-666 performed occupation duty in the Far East until early January 1946. She returned to the United States and was decommissioned on 20 June 1946 and struck from the Navy list on 31 July that same year. On 26 September 1947, the ship was sold to the Sun Shipbuilding & Dry Dock Co., of Chester, Pa.

LST-666 earned six battle stars for World War II service.

LST-667

LST-667 was laid down on 22 February 1944 at Ambridge, Pa., by the American Bridge Co.; launched on 27 April 1944; sponsored by Mrs. D. Hammerschmidt; and commissioned on 20 May 1944, Ens. W. S. Biernat in command.

During World War II, *LST-667* was assigned to the Asiatic-Pacific theater and participated in the following operations:

    Morotai landings—September 1944
    Leyte landings—November 1944
    Lingayen Gulf landings—January 1945
    Visayan Island landings—March and April 1945
    Tarakan Island operation—April and May 1945

Following the war, *LST-667* performed occupation duty in the Far East until mid-February 1946. She returned to the United States and was decommissioned on 5 June 1946 and struck from the Navy list on 3 July that same year. On 11 December 1947, the ship was sold to the Learner Co., of Oakland, Calif., for scrapping.

LST-667 earned five battle stars for World War II service.

LST-668

LST-668 was laid down on 6 March 1944 at Ambridge, Pa., by the American Bridge Co.; launched on 30 April 1944; sponsored by Mrs. Fred J. Kress; and commissioned on 23 May 1944, Lt. Milford E. Clark, USNR, in command.

During World War II, *LST-668* was assigned to the Asiatic-Pacific theater and participated in the following operations:

    Morotai landings—September 1944
    Leyte landings—October and November 1944
    Mindanao Island landings—April and May 1945
    Assault and occupation of Okinawa Gunto—June 1945

Following the war, *LST-668* returned to the United States and was decommissioned on 24 June 1946 and struck from the Navy list on 31 July that same year. On 26 May 1948, the ship was sold to the Bethlehem Steel Co., of Bethlehem, Pa., for scrapping.

LST-668 earned four battle stars for World War II service.

LST-669

LST-669 was laid down on 18 March 1944 at Ambridge, Pa., by the American Bridge Co.; launched on 3 May 1944; sponsored by Mrs. Faris Jones; and commissioned on 27 May 1944.

During World War II, *LST-669* was assigned to the Asiatic-Pacific theater and participated in the following operations:

    Leyte landings—October 1944
    Assault and occupation of Okinawa Gunto—April through June 1945

Following the war, *LST-669* performed occupation duty in the Far East until early March 1946. She returned to the United States and was decommissioned on 13 August 1946 and struck from the Navy list on 25 September that same year. On 10 May 1948, the ship was sold to the Bethlehem Steel Co., of Bethlehem, Pa., for scrapping.

LST-669 earned two battle stars for World War II service.

LST-670

LST-670 was laid down on 22 March 1944 at Ambridge, Pa., by the American Bridge Co.; launched on 6 May 1944; sponsored by Mrs. Gertrude Schumaker; and commissioned on 29 May 1944.

During World War II, *LST-670* was assigned to the Asiatic-Pacific theater and participated in the following operations:

    Leyte landing—October 1944
    Mindoro landings—December 1944
    Assault and occupation of Okinawa Gunto—March through June 1945

Following the war, *LST-670* returned to the United States and was decommissioned on 30 April 1946 and struck from the Navy list on 19 June that same year. The ship was sold on 10 February 1947.

LST-670 earned three battle stars for World War II service.

LST-671

LST-671 was laid down on 28 March 1944 at Ambridge, Pa., by the American Bridge Co.; launched on 11 May 1944; sponsored by Mrs. H. B. Taylor; and commissioned on 2 June 1944.

During World War II, *LST-671* was assigned to the Asiatic-Pacific theater and participated in the following operations:

    Leyte landings—October 1944
    Lingayen Gulf landing—January 1945
    Assault and occupation of Okinawa Gunto—April through June 1945

Following the war, *LST-671* performed occupation duty in the Far East until December 1945. She returned to the United States and was decommissioned on 25 June 1946 and struck from the Navy list on 15 August that same year. On 26 September 1947, the ship was sold to the Boston Metals Co., of Baltimore, Md., for scrapping.

LST-671 earned three battle stars for World War II service.

LST-672

LST-672 was laid down on 3 April 1944 at Ambridge, Pa., by the American Bridge Co.; launched on 14 May 1944; sponsored by Mrs. F. K. McDaniel; and commissioned on 5 June 1944.

During World War II, *LST-672* was assigned to the Asiatic-Pacific theater and participated in the following operations:

    Leyte landings—October 1944
    Assault and occupation of Okinawa Gunto—April through June 1945

Following the war, *LST-672* performed occupation duty in the Far East until April 1946. She returned to the United States and was decommissioned on 26 June 1946 and struck from the Navy list on 31 July that same year. On 2 January 1947, the ship was sold to the Suwannee Fruit & Steam Ship Corp., of Jacksonville, Fla.

LST-672 earned two battle stars for World War II service.

LST-673

LST-673 was laid down on 6 April 1944 at Ambridge, Pa., by the American Bridge Co.; launched on 22 May 1944; sponsored by Mrs. J. T. Ellis; and commissioned on 9 June 1944.

During World War II, *LST-673* was assigned to the Asiatic-Pacific theater and participated in the following operations:

    Leyte landings—October through November 1944
    Mindoro landings—December 1944

Lingayen Gulf landings—January 1945
Mindanao Island landings—April 1945
Balikpapan operation—June through July 1945

Following the war, *LST-673* performed occupation duty in the Far East until early March 1946. She returned to the United States and was decommissioned on 10 July 1946 and struck from the Navy list on 15 August that same year. On 27 October 1947, the ship was sold to the Moore Dry Dock Co. for scrapping.

LST-673 earned four battle stars for World War II service.

LST-674

LST-674 was laid down on 11 April 1944 at Ambridge, Pa., by the American Bridge Co.; launched on 26 May 1944; sponsored by Mrs. H. P. Anderson; and commissioned on 19 June 1944.

During World War II, *LST-674* was assigned to the Asiatic-Pacific theater and participated in the assault and occupation of Okinawa Gunto from 26 March through 30 June 1945. Following the war, she performed occupation duty in the Far East until late December 1945. Upon returning to the United States, the ship was decommissioned on 14 May 1946 and struck from the Navy list on 19 June that same year. On 26 May 1948, the tank landing ship was sold to the Bethlehem Steel Co., of Bethlehem, Pa., for scrapping.

LST-674 earned one battle star for World War II service.

LST-675

LST-675 was laid down on 16 April 1944 at Ambridge, Pa., by the American Bridge Co.; launched on 2 June 1944; sponsored by Mrs. H. B. Van Hook; and commissioned on 24 June 1944.

During World War II, *LST-675* was assigned to the Asiatic-Pacific theater and participated in the Lingayen Gulf landing in January 1945 and the assault and occupation of Okinawa Gunto in April 1945. She was grounded and suffered severe damage off Okinawa on 4 April 1945 and was ultimately determined to be unsalvageable. *LST-675* was decommissioned on 25 August 1945 and struck from the Navy list on 17 September that same year. In July 1957, her hulk was authorized by the Secretary of the Navy for donation to the government of the Ryukyus.

LST-675 earned two battle stars for World War II service.

LST-676

LST-676 was redesignated APB-42 and named *Yavapai (q.v.)* on 31 March 1945.

LST-677

LST-677 was redesignated APB-43 and named *Yolo (q.v.)* on 31 March 1945.

LST-678

LST-678 was redesignated APB-44 and named *Presque Isle (q.v.)* on 31 March 1945.

LST-679

LST-679 was laid down on 2 May 1944 at Ambridge, Pa., by the American Bridge Co.; launched on 20 June 1944; sponsored by Mrs. John Soboslay; and commissioned on 15 July 1944, Lt. N. A. Nelmes in command.

During World War II, *LST-679* was assigned to the Asiatic-Pacific theater and participated in the following operations:

Leyte landing—November 1944
Mindanao Island landings—April 1945

Following the war, *LST-679* performed occupation duty in the Far East until early April 1946. She returned to the United States and was decommissioned on 24 June 1946 and struck from the Navy list on 31 July that same year. On 25 May 1948, she was sold to the Bethlehem Steel Co., of Bethlehem, Pa., for scrapping.

LST-679 earned two battle stars for World War II service.

LST-680

LST-680 was laid down on 5 May 1944 at Ambridge, Pa., by the American Bridge Co.; launched on 26 June 1944; sponsored by Mrs. F. W. Leahy; and commissioned on 21 July 1944.

During World War II, *LST-680* was assigned to the Asiatic-Pacific theater and participated in the following operations:

Lingayen Gulf landing—January 1945
Zambales-Subic Bay—January 1945
Mindanao Island landings—April 1945

Following the war, *LST-680* performed occupation duty in the Far East until mid-April 1946. She returned to the United States and was decommissioned on 5 July 1946 and struck from the Navy list on 28 August that same year. On 14 May 1948, the ship was sold to the Bethlehem Steel Co., of Bethlehem, Pa., for scrapping.

LST-680 earned three battle stars for World War II service.

LST-681

LST-681 was laid down on 10 May 1944 at Ambridge, Pa., by the American Bridge Co.; launched on 1 July 1944; sponsored by Mrs. Pauline Taylor; and commissioned on 25 July 1944, Lt. (jg.) L. J. J. Spengler, USNR, in command.

During World War II, *LST-681* was assigned to the Asiatic-Pacific theater and participated in the following operations:

Lingayen Gulf landings—January 1945
Assault and occupation of Okinawa Gunto—April through June 1945

Following the war, *LST-681* performed occupation duty in the Far East until mid-March 1946. She returned to the United States and was decommissioned on 6 September 1946 and struck from the Navy list on 8 October that same year. On 9 October 1947, the ship was sold to William E. Skinner for scrapping.

LST-681 earned two battle stars for World War II service.

LST-682

LST-682 was laid down on 6 December 1944 at Jeffersonville, Ind., by the Jeffersonville Boat & Machine Co.; launched on 31 January 1944; sponsored by Mrs. Ethel M. Ward; and commissioned on 18 March 1944, Ens. R. B. Flynn in command.

During World War II, *LST-682* was assigned to the European theater and participated in the invasion of Normandy in June 1944. She was then assigned to the Asiatic-Pacific theater and took part in the assault and occupation of Okinawa Gunto in May and June 1945. Following the war, the ship performed occupation duty in the Far East until late February 1946. *LST-682* returned to the United States and was decommissioned on 30 July 1946 and struck from the Navy list on 25 September that same year. On 3 June 1948, she was sold to the Walter W. Johnson Co. for scrapping.

LST-682 earned two battle stars for World War II service.

Steuben County (LST–1138) in 1959. Her antiaircraft battery, 20-millimeter guns and director-controlled 40-millimeter twin mounts, is representative of the defensive armament of LST's at the end of World War II.

LST–683

LST–683 was laid down on 29 November 1943 at Jeffersonville, Ind., by the Jeffersonville Boat & Machine Co.; launched on 7 February 1944; sponsored by Mrs. Florence Robbins Bohr; and commissioned on 28 March 1944, Lt. Richard T. Paynter, USNR, in command.

Following World War II, *LST–683* performed occupation duty in the Far East and saw service in China until mid-February 1946. She returned to the United States and was decommissioned on 29 May 1946 and struck from the Navy list on 3 July that same year. The ship was sold to the Bethlehem Steel Co., of Bethlehem, Pa., on 26 May 1948 for scrapping.

LST–684

LST–684 was laid down on 13 December 1943 at Jeffersonville, Ind., by the Jeffersonville Boat & Machine Co.; launched on 12 February 1944; sponsored by Mrs. Florence M. Sussman; and commissioned on 3 April 1944, Lt. P. B. Welch, Jr., USNR, in command.

During World War II, *LST–684* was assigned to the Asiatic-Pacific theater and participated in the following operations:

    Capture and occupation of Guam—July and August 1944
    Assault and occupation of Iwo Jima—February 1945
    Assault and occupation of Okinawa Gunto—April through June 1945

Following the war, *LST–684* performed occupation duty in the Far East until mid-November 1945. She returned to the United States and was decommissioned on 25 November 1945 and destroyed on 22 March 1946. *LST–684* was struck from the Navy list on 5 June 1946.

LST–684 earned three battle stars for World War II service.

LST–685

LST–685 was laid down on 21 December 1943 at Jeffersonville, Ind., by the Jeffersonville Boat & Machine Co.; launched on 18 February 1944; sponsored by Miss Agnes J. Langley; and commissioned on 7 April 1944.

Following World War II, *LST–685* performed occupation duty in the Far East until mid-April 1946. She returned to the United States and was decommissioned on 22 July 1946. On 13 January 1947, the ship was placed in service and used for Naval Reserve training out of Tompkinsville, N.Y. She was inactivated on 2 June 1950 at Green Cove Springs, Fla. On 1 July 1955, she was redesignated *Curry County* (LST–685) after counties in New Mexico and Oregon. The tank landing ship was struck from the Navy list on 1 November 1958.

LST–686

LST–686 was laid down on 4 January 1944 at Jeffersonville, Ind., by the Jeffersonville Boat & Machine Co.; launched on 24 February 1944; sponsored by Mrs. Clara L. Vogt; and commissioned on 14 April 1944, Ens. H. A. May in command.

During World War II, *LST–686* was assigned to the Asiatic-Pacific theater and participated in the following operations:

    Leyte landings—October 1944
    Mindoro landings—December 1944
    Lingayen Gulf landing—January 1945
    Assault and occupation of Okinawa Gunto—March through May 1945

Following the war, *LST-686* performed occupation duty in the Far East and saw service in China until early April 1946. She returned to the United States and was decommissioned on 10 July 1946 and struck from the Navy list on 15 August that same year. On 17 September 1947, the ship was sold to Consolidated Builders, Inc., Seattle, Wash., for scrapping.

LST-686 earned three battle stars for World War II service.

LST-687

LST-687 was laid down on 28 December 1943 at Jeffersonville, Ind., by the Jeffersonville Boat & Machine Co.; launched on 28 February 1944; sponsored by Mrs. Emma D. Bott; and commissioned on 22 April 1944.

During World War II, *LST-687* was assigned to the Asiatic-Pacific theater and participated in the following operations:

Capture and occupation of southern Palau Islands —September and October 1944
Leyte landings—October and November 1944
Lingayen Gulf landing—January 1945
Assault and occupation of Okinawa Gunto—April through June 1945

Following the war, *LST-687* performed occupation duty in the Far East until early December 1945. She returned to the United States and was decommissioned on 24 May 1946 and struck from the Navy list on 3 July that same year. On 24 September 1947, the ship was sold to William E. Skinner for scrapping.

LST-687 earned four battle stars for World War II service.

LST-688

LST-688 was laid down on 17 January 1944 at Jeffersonville, Ind., by the Jeffersonville Boat & Machine Co.; launched on 5 March 1944; sponsored by Mrs. James R. Collier; and commissioned on 27 April 1944.

During World War II, *LST-688* was assigned to the Asiatic-Pacific theater and participated in the following operations:

Capture and occupation of southern Palau Islands —September and October 1944
Leyte landings—October and November 1944
Lingayen Gulf landing—January 1945
Assault and occupation of Okinawa Gunto—May and June 1945

Following the war, *LST-688* performed occupation duty in the Far East until early February 1956. She returned to the United States and was decommissioned on 5 August 1946 and struck from the Navy list on 25 September that same year. On 17 September 1947, the ship was sold to Consolidated Builders, Inc., Seattle, Wash., for scrapping.

LST-688 earned four battle stars for World War II service.

LST-689

LST-689 was laid down on 11 January 1944 at Jeffersonville, Ind., by the Jeffersonville Boat & Machine Co.; launched on 9 March 1944; sponsored by Mrs. Edith C. Smith; and commissioned on 2 May 1944, Lt. F. D. McKay, USNR, in command.

During World War II, *LST-689* was assigned to the Asiatic-Pacific theater and participated in the capture and occupation of the southern Palau Islands in September and October 1944. She returned to the United States and was decommissioned in March 1946. The tank landing ship performed no active post-World War II service. On 1 July 1955, the ship was redesignated *Daggett County* (LST-689) after a county in Utah. She was struck from the Navy list on 1 October 1959.

LST-689 earned one battle star for World War II service.

LST-690

LST-690 was laid down on 31 January 1944 at Jeffersonville, Ind., by the Jeffersonville Boat & Machine Co.; launched on 14 March 1944; sponsored by Mrs. Dorothy E. Bryant; and commissioned on 6 May 1944, Lt. Comdr. Ernest C. Reif, USNR, in command.

During World War II, *LST-690* was assigned to the European theater and participated in the invasion of southern France in August and September 1944. She was then assigned to the Asiatic-Pacific theater and took part in the assault and occupation of Okinawa Gunto in June 1945. Following the war, *LST-690* performed occupation duty in the Far East until late February 1946. She returned to the United States and was decommissioned on 23 July 1946 and struck from the Navy list on 28 August that same year. On 16 December 1947, the ship was sold to James A. Hughes, New York, N.Y., for scrapping.

LST-690 earned two battle stars for World War II service.

LST-691

LST-691 was laid down on 25 January 1944 at Jeffersonville, Ind., by the Jeffersonville Boat & Machine Co.; launched on 23 March 1944; sponsored by Mrs. Helen T. Briner; and commissioned on 12 May 1944.

During World War II, *LST-691* was assigned to the European theater and participated in the invasion of southern France in August 1944. Following the war, she performed occupation duty in the Far East until mid-December 1945. She returned to the United States and was decommissioned on 14 May 1946 and struck from the Navy list on 19 June that same year. On 4 November 1946, the ship was sold to Hughes Bros., Inc., of New York, N.Y.

LST-691 earned one battle star for World War II service.

LST-692

LST-692 was laid down on 7 February 1944 at Jeffersonville, Ind., by the Jeffersonville Boat & Machine Co.; launched on 31 March 1944; sponsored by Mrs. Alma D. Voelker; and commissioned on 10 May 1944, Lt. R. B. Carothers, USNR, in command.

During World War II, *LST-692* was assigned to the European theater and participated in the invasion of southern France in August and September 1944. Decommissioned in 1946, she was placed in the reserve fleet at Green Cove Springs, Fla., until reactivated in 1951. She performed active service during the Korean War and thereafter. *LST-692* was redesignated *Daviess County* (LST-692) on 1 July 1955 after counties in Indiana, Kentucky, and Missouri. The ship was struck from the Navy list on 1 June 1964 and transferred to the Military Sea Transportation Service where she operated as T-LST-692. *Daviess County* was transferred to the Philippine Navy on 13 September 1976.

LST-692 earned one battle star for World War II service and two battle stars for Korean service.

LST-693

LST-693 was laid down on 18 February 1944 at Jeffersonville, Ind., by the Jeffersonville Boat & Machine Co.; launched on 7 April 1944; sponsored by Miss Rose Mary Harrod; and commissioned on 15 May 1944, Lt. M. E. Hoag in command.

During World War II, *LST-693* was assigned to the Asiatic-Pacific theater and participated in the following operations:

Leyte landings—October and November 1944
Mindoro landings—December 1944
Zambales-Subic Bay—January 1945
Assault and occupation of Okinawa Gunto—April 1945

Following the war, LST–693 performed occupation duty in the Far East until mid-October 1945. She returned to the United States and was decommissioned on 1 May 1946 and struck from the Navy list on 3 July that same year. On 10 December 1947, the ship was sold to the Southern Shipwrecking Co., of New Orleans, La., for scrapping.

LST–693 earned four battle stars for World War II service.

LST–694

LST–694 was laid down on 14 February 1944 at Jeffersonville, Ind., by the Jeffersonville Boat & Machine Co.; launched on 16 April 1944; sponsored by Mrs. Ivy H. Wolf; and commissioned on 19 May 1944.

During World War II, LST–694 was assigned to the Asiatic-Pacific theater and participated in the following operations:

Morotai landings—September 1944
Leyte landings—October and November 1944
Lingayen Gulf landing—January 1945
Mindanao Island landings—April 1945
Balikpapan operation—June and July 1945

Following the war, LST–694 performed occupation duty in the Far East until mid-January 1946. The ship was decommissioned on 1 December 1947 and struck from the Navy list on 23 December that same year. She was transferred to the United States Army. On 1 March 1950, she was reacquired from the Army and transferred to the Military Sea Transportation Service, where she operated as USNS LST–694 until struck from the Navy list once again on 4 February 1958.

LST–694 earned five battle stars for World War II service.

LST–695

LST–695 was laid down on 28 February 1944 at Jeffersonville, Ind., by the Jeffersonville Boat & Machine Co.; launched on 24 April 1944; sponsored by Mrs. Ursula R. Vilsack; and commissioned on 22 May 1944.

During World War II, LST–695 was assigned to the Asiatic-Pacific theater and participated in the Morotai landings in September 1944 and the Leyte landings in October and November 1944. She was decommissioned on 6 November 1945 and struck from the Navy list on 28 November that same year. On 22 March 1946, the ship was sold to the George Pollack Co., of Stockton, Calif.

LST–695 earned two battle stars for World War II service.

LST–696

LST–696 was laid down on 25 February 1944 at Jeffersonville, Ind., by the Jeffersonville Boat & Machine Co.; launched on 27 April 1944; sponsored by Mrs. Samuel G. Shannon; and commissioned on 25 May 1944.

During World War II, LST–696 was assigned to the Asiatic-Pacific theater and participated in the following operations:

Morotai landings—September 1944
Leyte landings—November 1944
Lingayen Gulf landing—January 1945

Following the war, LST–696 performed occupation duty in the Far East until mid-April 1946. She returned to the United States and was decommissioned on 16 July 1946 and struck from the Navy list on 28 August that same year. On 19 May 1948, the ship was sold to the Bethlehem Steel Co., of Bethlehem, Pa., for scrapping.

LST–696 earned three battle stars for World War II service.

LST–697

LST–697 was laid down on 6 March 1944 at Jeffersonville, Ind., by the Jeffersonville Boat & Machine Co.; launched on 1 May 1944; sponsored by Mrs. Josephine B. Kieren; and commissioned on 30 May 1944, Ens. Lo Presti in command.

During World War II, LST–697 was assigned to the Asiatic-Pacific theater and participated in the following operations:

Morotai landings—September 1944
Leyte landings—November 1944
Lingayen Gulf landing—January 1945
Visayan Island landings—March and April 1945
Tarakan Island operation—April and May 1945

Following the war, LST–697 performed occupation duty in the Far East and saw service in China until mid-December 1945. She returned to the United States and was decommissioned on 12 July 1946 and struck from the Navy list on 28 August that same year. On 14 October 1947, the ship was sold to William E. Skinner for scrapping.

LST–697 earned five battle stars for World War II service.

LST–698

LST–698 was laid down on 14 March 1944 at Jeffersonville, Ind., by the Jeffersonville Boat & Machine Co.; launched on 5 May 1944; and commissioned on 3 June 1944.

During World War II, LST–698 was assigned to the Asiatic-Pacific theater and participated in the Leyte landings in October 1944 and the assault and occupation of Okinawa Gunto in April 1945. She was decommissioned on 26 November 1945 and struck from the Navy list on 5 December that same year. On 25 June 1946, the ship was sold to Arctic Circle Exploration, Inc., of Seattle, Wash.

LST–698 earned two battle stars for World War II service.

LST–699

LST–699 was laid down on 9 March 1944 at Jeffersonville, Ind., by the Jeffersonville Boat & Machine Co.; launched on 9 May 1944; and commissioned on 5 June 1944.

During World War II, LST–699 was assigned to the Asiatic-Pacific theater and participated in the following operations:

Leyte landings—November 1944
Lingayen Gulf landing—January 1945
Mindanao Island landings—April 1945

Following the war, LST–699 performed occupation duty in the Far East and saw service in China until mid-April 1946. She returned to the United States and was decommissioned on 24 June 1946 and struck from the Navy list on 31 July that same year. On 5 December 1947, the ship was sold to the Bethlehem Steel Co., of Bethlehem, Pa., for scrapping.

LST–699 earned three battle stars for World War II service.

LST–700

LST–700 was laid down on 22 March 1944 at Jeffersonville, Ind., by the Jeffersonville Boat & Machine Co.; launched on 13 May 1944; sponsored by Mrs. Leona M. Slack; and commissioned on 7 June 1944, Lt. C. W. Blodgett in command.

During World War II, LST–700 was assigned to the Asiatic-Pacific theater and participated in the Leyte landing in November 1944 and the Lingayen Gulf landing in January 1945. Following the war, LST–700 performed occupation duty in the Far East and saw service in China until mid-March 1946. She returned to the United States and was decommissioned on 27 July 1946 and struck from the Navy list on 28 August that same year. On 13 December 1947, the ship was sold to the Kaiser Co., of Vancouver, Wash., for scrapping.

LST-700 earned two battle stars for World War II service.

LST-701

LST-701 was laid down on 1 April 1944 at Jeffersonville, Ind., by the Jeffersonville Boat & Machine Co.; launched on 18 May 1944; sponsored by Mrs. Willie S. Etheridge; and commissioned on 13 June 1944.

During World War II, *LST-701* was assigned to the Asiatic-Pacific theater and participated in the following operations:

Lingayen Gulf landing—January 1945
Nasugbu—January 1945
Assault and occupation of Okinawa Gunto—April through June 1945

Following the war, *LST-701* returned to the United States and was decommissioned on 13 July 1946 and struck from the Navy list on 28 August that same year. On 27 October 1947, the ship was sold to the Moore Dry Dock Co., of Oakland, Calif., for scrapping.

LST-701 earned three battle stars for World War II service.

LST-702

LST-702 was laid down on 15 April 1944 at Jeffersonville, Ind., by the Jeffersonville Boat & Machine Co.; launched on 22 May 1944; sponsored by Mrs. Anne D. Wyatt; and commissioned on 19 June 1944.

During World War II, *LST-702* was assigned to the Asiatic-Pacific theater and participated in the assault and occupation of Okinawa Gunto in May and June 1945. Following the war, she performed occupation duty in the Far East and saw service in China until mid-April 1946. The ship returned to the United States and was decommissioned on 5 July 1946 and struck from the Navy list on 15 August that same year. On 23 October 1947, the tank landing ship was sold to Consolidated Builders, Inc., Seattle, Wash., for scrapping.

LST-702 earned one battle star for World War II service.

LST-703

LST-703 was laid down on 8 April 1944 at Jeffersonville, Ind., by the Jeffersonville Boat & Machine Co.; launched on 28 May 1944; sponsored by Mrs. Josephine S. Coe; and commissioned on 23 June 1944, Lt. W. C. Fisher in command.

During World War II, *LST-703* was assigned to the Asiatic-Pacific theater and participated in the following operations:

Leyte landings—October and November 1944
Zambales-Subic Bay—January 1945
Balikpapan operation—June and July 1945

Following the war, *LST-703* performed occupation duty in the Far East until late October 1945. She returned to the United States and was decommissioned on 10 June 1946 and struck from the Navy list on 31 July that same year. On 10 December 1947, the ship was sold to the Salco Iron & Metal Co. for scrapping.

LST-703 earned three battle stars for World War II service.

LST-704

LST-704 was laid down on 27 April 1944 at Jeffersonville, Ind., by the Jeffersonville Boat & Machine Co.; launched on 3 June 1944; sponsored by Mrs.

Dorothy B. Riefkin; and commissioned on 27 June 1944, Lt. W. H. Walshe, USNR, in command.

During World War II, *LST-704* was assigned to the Asiatic-Pacific theater and participated in the Leyte landings in October 1944 and the assault and occupation of Okinawa Gunto in April 1945. Following the war, *LST-704* performed occupation duty in the Far East until late December 1945. She returned to the United States and was decommissioned on 19 June 1946 and struck from the Navy list on 25 September that same year. On 26 May 1948, the ship was sold to the Basalt Rock Co., Inc., of Napa, Calif., for scrapping.

LST-704 earned two battle stars for World War II service.

LST-705

LST-705 was laid down on 21 April 1944 at Jeffersonville, Ind., by the Jeffersonville Boat & Machine Co.; launched on 7 June 1944; sponsored by Miss Rose Zeller; and commissioned on 4 July 1944.

During World War II, *LST-705* was assigned to the Asiatic-Pacific theater and participated in the following operations:

Leyte landings—November 1944
Lingayen Gulf landing—January 1945
Mindanao Island landings—March and April 1945

Following the war, *LST-705* performed occupation duty in the Far East until late February 1946. She returned to the United States and was decommissioned on 22 July 1946 and struck from the Navy list on 25 September that same year. On 8 December 1947, the ship was sold to the Learner Co., of Oakland, Calif., for scrapping.

LST-705 earned three battle stars for World War II service.

LST-706

LST-706 was laid down on 4 May 1944 at Jeffersonville, Ind., by the Jeffersonville Boat & Machine Co.; launched on 12 June 1944; sponsored by Miss Ethel C. Jones; and commissioned on 8 July 1944, Lt. Louis W. Schmidt, USNR, in command.

During World War II, *LST-706* was assigned to the Asiatic-Pacific theater and participated in the Leyte landings in November 1944 and the Lingayen Gulf landing in January 1945. Following the war, *LST-706* performed occupation duty in the Far East and saw service in China until mid-February 1946. She was decommissioned on 19 June 1946 and struck from the Navy list on 31 July that same year.

LST-706 earned two battle stars for World War II service.

LST-707

LST-707 was laid down on 1 May 1944 at Jeffersonville, Ind., by the Jeffersonville Boat & Machine Co.; launched on 16 June 1944; sponsored by Mrs. Lorine C. Deleuil; and commissioned on 13 July 1944.

During World War II, *LST-707* was assigned to the Asiatic-Pacific theater and participated in the following operations:

Leyte landings—November 1944
Lingayen Gulf landings—January 1945
Zambales-Subic Bay—January 1945
Mindanao Island landings—April 1945

Following the war, *LST-707* performed occupation duty in the Far East until late December 1945. She returned to the United States and was decommissioned on 28 May 1946 and struck from the Navy list on 3 July that same year. On 7 May 1948, the ship was sold to the Bethlehem Steel Co., of Bethlehem, Pa., and subsequently scrapped.

LST-707 earned four battle stars for World War II service.

LST-708

LST-708 was laid down on 9 May 1944 at Jeffersonville, Ind., by the Jeffersonville Boat & Machine Co.; launched on 20 June 1944; sponsored by Mrs. Charlotte R. Sherman; and commissioned on 17 July 1944.

During World War II, *LST-708* was assigned to the Asiatic-Pacific theater and participated in the assault and occupation of Okinawa Gunto from April through June 1945. Following the war, *LST-708* performed occupation duty in the Far East until early December 1945. She returned to the United States and was decommissioned on 28 May 1946 and struck from the Navy list on 3 July that same year. On 29 May 1948, the ship was sold to the Basalt Rock Co., of Napa, Calif., and subsequently scrapped.

LST-708 earned one battle star for World War II service.

LST-709

LST-709 was laid down on 18 May 1944 at Jeffersonville, Ind., by the Jeffersonville Boat & Machine Co.; launched on 24 June 1944; sponsored by Mrs. Sarah E. Lodewick; and commissioned on 21 July 1944, Lt. (jg.) George P. Cruickshank, USNR, in command.

During World War II, *LST-709* was assigned to the Asiatic-Pacific theater and participated in the following operations:

> Leyte landings—November 1944
> Palawan Island landings—January 1945
> Visayan Island landings—March and April 1945
> Assault and occupation of Okinawa Gunto—March 1945
> Brunei Bay operation—June 1945

Following the war, *LST-709* performed occupation duty in the Far East and saw service in China until mid-March 1946. She returned to the United States and was decommissioned on 3 July 1946 and struck from the Navy list on 15 August that same year. On 19 June 1948, the ship was sold to Consolidated Builders, Inc., of Seattle, Wash., and subsequently scrapped.

LST-709 earned four battle stars for World War II service.

LST-710

LST-710 was laid down at Jeffersonville, Ind., by the Jeffersonville Boat & Machine Co.; launched on 28 June 1944; sponsored by Mrs. Maude B. Shricker; and commissioned on 24 July 1944.

During World War II, *LST-710* was assigned to the Asiatic-Pacific theater and participated in the Lingayen Gulf landing in January 1945. She was redesignated APB-49 and named *Accomac* on 1 August 1945.

LST-710 earned one battle star for World War II service.

LST-711

LST-711 was laid down on 28 May 1944 at Jeffersonville, Ind., by the Jeffersonville Boat & Machine Co.; launched on 3 July 1944; sponsored by Mrs. Margaret C. Harris; and commissioned on 28 July 1944.

During World War II, *LST-711* was assigned to the Asiatic-Pacific theater and participated in the following operations:

> Lingayen Gulf landing—January 1945
> Mariveles-Corregidor—February 1945
> Tarakan Island operation—April and May 1945

Following the war, *LST-711* performed occupation duty in the Far East until mid-July 1946. She was decommissioned on 11 August 1946 and transferred to the United States Army. The ship was struck from the Navy list on 29 September 1947.

LST-711 earned three battle stars for World War II service.

LST-712

LST-712 was laid down on 22 May 1944 at Jeffersonville, Ind., by the Jeffersonville Boat & Machine Co.; launched on 7 July 1944; sponsored by Mrs. Elma Mae Goodhue; and commissioned on 2 August 1944.

During World War II, *LST-712* was assigned to the Asiatic-Pacific theater and participated in the following operations:

> Lingayen Gulf landing—January 1945
> Assault and occupation of Okinawa Gunto—April through June 1945

Following the war, *LST-712* performed occupation duty in the Far East until mid-December 1945. She returned to the United States and was decommissioned on 20 May 1946 and struck from the Navy list on 28 August that same year. On 27 May 1948, the ship was sold to the Basalt Rock Co., Napa, Calif., and subsequently scrapped.

LST-712 earned two battle stars for World War II service.

LST-713

LST-713 was laid down on 3 June 1944 at Jeffersonville, Ind., by the Jeffersonville Boat & Machine Co.; launched on 11 July 1944; sponsored by Mrs. Barbara A. Lawson; and commissioned on 7 August 1944.

During World War II, *LST-713* was assigned to the Asiatic-Pacific theater and participated in the following operations:

> Assault and occupation of Iwo Jima—February 1945
> Assault and occupation of Okinawa Gunto—April through June 1945

Following the war, *LST-713* performed occupation duty in the Far East until mid-February 1946. She returned to the United States and was decommissioned on 20 June 1946 and struck from the Navy list on 31 July that same year. On 21 May 1948, the ship was sold to the Bethlehem Steel Co., of Bethlehem, Pa., and subsequently scrapped.

LST-713 earned two battle stars for World War II service.

LST-714

LST-714 was laid down on 12 June 1944 at Jeffersonville, Ind., by the Jeffersonville Boat & Machine Co.; launched on 15 July 1944; sponsored by Mrs. Katherine C. Rowe; and commissioned on 11 August 1944, Lt. H. Van Voast, USNR, in command.

During World War II, *LST-714* was assigned to the Asiatic-Pacific theater and participated in the following operations:

> Leyte landings—November 1944
> Lingayen Gulf landing—January 1945
> Zambales-Subic Bay—January 1945
> Balikpapan operation—June and July 1945

Following the war, *LST-714* performed occupation duty in the Far East and saw service in China until early May 1946. She was decommissioned and transferred to the State Department on 10 May 1946 and struck from the Navy list on 19 June that same year.

LST-714 earned four battle stars for World War II service.

LST-715

LST-715 was laid down on 7 June 1944 at Jeffersonville, Ind., by the Jeffersonville Boat & Machine Co.; launched on 20 July 1944; sponsored by Mrs. Loudie S. Moffatt; and commissioned on 15 August 1944.

During World War II, *LST-715* was assigned to the Asiatic-Pacific theater and participated in the following operations:

Assault and occupation of Iwo Jima—February and March 1945

Assault and occupation of Okinawa Gunto—May and June 1945

Following the war, *LST–715* performed occupation duty in the Far East until mid-September 1945. She was decommissioned on 17 April 1946 and transferred to the United States Army on 28 June that same year. The ship was struck from the Navy list on 29 September 1946. Reacquired by the Navy on 25 July 1950, *LST–715* was redesignated *DeKalb County* (LST–715) after counties in six states of the United States on 1 July 1955. She was transferred to the Military Sea Transportation Service in December 1965 where she served as USNS *DeKalb County* until struck from the Navy list on 1 November 1973.

LST–715 earned two battle stars for World War II service.

LST–716

LST–716 was laid down on 16 June 1944 at Jeffersonville, Ind., by the Jeffersonville Boat & Machine Co.; launched on 25 July 1944; sponsored by Miss Nancy L. Duggins; and commissioned on 18 August 1944, Lt. Richard H. Perry in command.

During World War II, *LST–716* was assigned to the Asiatic-Pacific theater and participated in the following operations:

Assault and occupation of Iwo Jima—February 1945

Assault and occupation of Okinawa Gunto—May and June 1945

Following the war, *LST–716* performed occupation duty in the Far East and saw service in China until early June 1946. She was decommissioned on 12 June 1946. The ship was transferred to the Nationalist Government of the Republic of China under the terms of lend-lease on 7 February 1948. *LST–716* was struck from the Navy list on 12 March 1948.

LST–716 earned two battle stars for World War II service.

LST–717

LST–717 was laid down on 20 June 1944 at Jeffersonville, Ind., by the Jeffersonville Boat & Machine Co.; launched on 29 July 1944; sponsored by Miss Lou Anne Malsie; and commissioned on 23 August 1944, Lt. Karl F. Melde, USNR, in command.

During World War II, *LST–717* was assigned to the Asiatic-Pacific theater and participated in the following operations:

Palawan Island landings—January 1945

Mindanao Island landings—April 1945

Following the war, *LST–717* performed occupation duty in the Far East and saw service in China until early June 1946. She was decommissioned on 12 June 1946. On 17 February 1948, the ship was transferred to the Nationalist Government of the Republic of China under the terms of lend-lease. *LST–717* was struck from the Navy list on 12 March 1948.

LST–717 earned one battle star for World War II service.

LST–718

LST–718 was laid down on 28 June 1944 at Jeffersonville, Ind., by the Jeffersonville Boat & Machine Co.; launched on 3 August 1944; sponsored by Mrs. Helen N. DeGraw; and commissioned on 28 August 1944, Lt. R. A. Fisher, USNR, in command.

Following World War II, *LST–718* performed occupation duty in the Far East and saw service in China until early April 1946. She was decommissioned on 25 June 1946. On 18 June 1948, the ship was sold to Consolidated Builders, Inc., of Seattle, Wash., and subsequently scrapped. She was struck from the Navy list on 31 July 1948.

LST–719

LST–719 was laid down on 24 June 1944 at Jeffersonville, Ind., by the Jeffersonville Boat & Machine Co.; launched on 8 August 1944; sponsored by Mrs. Mary L. Mattingly; and commissioned on 31 August 1944, Lt. J. H. Ingram in command.

The advanced aviation base ship *Tallahatchie County* (AVB–2) was converted from LST–1154, one of two ships of the steam-powered *LST–1153*-class. Her after superstructure has been extended forward and her forecastle built up; electronic antennas and a heavy kingpost are mounted amidships. As an AVB, *Tallahatchie County* was designed to provide command and logistic facilities to a squadron of antisubmarine patrol planes operating from an improvised land base. Squadron equipment was carried in mobile vans, transported in *Tallahatchie County*'s tank deck, and landed over her bow ramp.

During World War II, *LST–719* was assigned to the Asiatic-Pacific theater and participated in the following operations:

    Palawan Island landings—March 1945
    Mindanao Island landings—April and May 1945

Following the war, *LST–719* performed occupation duty in the Far East and saw service in China until mid-February 1946. She returned to the United States and was decommissioned on 12 July 1946 and struck from the Navy list on 14 March 1947. On 4 November 1947, the ship was sold to the Moore Drydock Co., of Oakland, Calif., and subsequently scrapped.

LST–719 earned one battle star for World War II service.

LST–720

LST–720 was laid down on 7 July 1944 at Jeffersonville, Ind., by the Jeffersonville Boat & Machine Co.; launched on 12 August 1944; sponsored by Mrs. Ellen C. Harvey; and commissioned on 4 September 1944, Ens. J. D. Shepard in command.

During World War II, *LST–720* was assigned to the Asiatic-Pacific theater and participated in the following operations:

    Lingayen Gulf landing—January 1945
    Mindanao Island landing—March 1945

Following the war, *LST–720* performed occupation duty in the Far East and saw service in China until early April 1946. She returned to the United States and was decommissioned on 24 June 1946 and struck from the Navy list on 31 July that same year. On 23 October 1947, the ship was sold to Consolidated Builders, Inc., of Seattle, Wash., and subsequently scrapped.

LST–720 earned two battle stars for World War II service.

LST–721

LST–721 was laid down on 3 July 1944 at Jeffersonville, Ind., by the Jeffersonville Boat & Machine Co.; launched on 7 August 1944; sponsored by Mrs. Mary L. Hogan; and commissioned on 9 September 1944.

During World War II, *LST–721* was assigned to the Asiatic-Pacific theater and participated in the following operations:

    Visayan Island landings—March and April 1945
    Balikpapan operation—June and July 1945

Following the war, *LST–721* performed occupation duty in the Far East until mid-November 1945. She was decommissioned on 24 June 1946 and struck from the Navy list on 15 August that same year. The ship was reinstated on 21 November 1946. *LST–721* was restruck from the Navy list on 10 June 1947 and sold to Green's Bayou Transports, New Orleans, La., on 8 March 1948 for non-self-propelled operation.

LST–721 earned two battle stars for World War II service.

LST–722

LST–722 was laid down on 15 July 1944 at Jeffersonville, Ind., by the Jeffersonville Boat & Machine Co.; launched on 21 August 1944; sponsored by Miss Rosemary Furey; and commissioned on 13 September 1944.

During World War II, *LST–722* was assigned to the Asiatic-Pacific theater and participated in the following operations:

    Palawan Island landings—February and March 1945
    Mindanao Island landings—April 1945

Following the war, *LST–722* performed occupation duty in the Far East until April 1946. She was decommissioned on 13 July 1946. Recommissioned on 16 No-

vember 1951, the ship was assigned to the Amphibious Force, U.S. Atlantic Fleet, for duty. On 1 July 1955, *LST–722* was redesignated *Dodge County* (LST–722) after counties in Georgia, Minnesota, Nebraska, and Wisconsin. She was decommissioned again on 3 January 1956 and struck from the Navy list on 15 September 1974.

LST–722 earned one battle star for World War II service.

LST–723

LST–723 was laid down on 11 July 1944 at Jeffersonville, Ind., by the Jeffersonville Boat & Machine Co.; launched on 25 August 1944; sponsored by Mrs. Pearl L. White; and commissioned on 16 September 1944.

During World War II, *LST–723* was assigned to the Asiatic-Pacific theater and participated in the assault and occupation of Iwo Jima in February 1945 and the assault and occupation of Okinawa Gunto in April 1945. She was decommissioned on 20 July 1946 and struck from the Navy list on 10 June 1947. On 12 May 1948, the ship was sold to the Bethlehem Steel Co., of Bethlehem, Pa., and subsequently scrapped.

LST–723 earned two battle stars for World War II service.

LST–724

LST–724 was laid down on 20 July 1944 at Jeffersonville, Ind., by the Jeffersonville Boat & Machine Co.; launched on 29 August 1944; sponsored by Mrs. Frances M. Lively; and commissioned on 22 September 1944.

During World War II, *LST–724* was assigned to the Asiatic-Pacific theater and participated in the assault and occupation of Okinawa Gunto from April through June 1945. Following the war, she performed occupation duty in the Far East and saw service in China until late March 1946. *LST–724* returned to the United States and was decommissioned on 26 June 1946 and struck from the Navy list on 31 July that same year. On 23 September 1947, the ship was sold to William E. Skinner, New York, N.Y.

LST–724 earned one battle star for World War II service.

LST–725

LST–725 was laid down on 29 July 1944 at Jeffersonville, Ind., by the Jeffersonville Boat & Machine Co.; launched on 2 September 1944; sponsored by Mrs. Gladys D. Ogden; and commissioned on 25 September 1944.

During World War II, *LST–725* was assigned to the Asiatic-Pacific theater and participated in the assault and occupation of Iwo Jima in February 1945 and the assault and occupation of Okinawa Gunto from April through June 1945. She returned to the United States and was decommissioned on 1 May 1946 and struck from the Navy list on 3 July that same year. The ship was sold to the Southern Shipwrecking Co., of New Orleans, La., on 11 December 1947 for scrapping.

LST–725 earned two battle stars for World War II service.

LST–726

LST–726 was laid down on 26 July 1944 at Jeffersonville, Ind., by the Jeffersonville Boat & Machine Co.; launched on 6 September 1944; sponsored by Mrs. Ora M. Armstrong; and commissioned on 30 September 1944.

During World War II, *LST–726* was assigned to the Asiatic-Pacific theater and participated in the assault

and occupation of Iwo Jima in February 1945 and the assault and occupation of Okinawa Gunto in April 1945. Following the war, *LST–726* performed occupation duty in the Far East until late December 1945. She returned to the United States and was decommissioned on 25 June 1946 and struck from the Navy list on 31 July that same year. The ship was sold to the Bethlehem Steel Co., of Bethlehem, Pa., on 5 December 1947 for scrapping.

LST–726 earned two battle stars for World War II service.

LST–727

LST–727 was laid down on 8 August 1944 at Jeffersonville, Ind., by the Jeffersonville Boat & Machine Co.; launched on 10 September 1944; sponsored by Miss Sally Willis; and commissioned on 4 October 1944.

Following World War II, *LST–727* performed occupation duty in the Far East and saw service in China until mid-February 1946. She returned to the United States and was decommissioned on 26 July 1946 and struck from the Navy list on 28 August that same year. On 15 June 1948, the ship was sold to Steele Powers for operation.

LST–728

LST–728 was laid down on 3 August 1944 at Jeffersonville, Ind., by the Jeffersonville Boat & Machine Co.; launched on 14 September 1944; sponsored by Mrs. Helen E. Garrison; and commissioned on 10 October 1944.

During World War II, *LST–728* was assigned to the Asiatic-Pacific theater and participated in the assault and occupation of Okinawa Gunto from April through June 1945. Following the war, she performed occupation duty in the Far East and saw service in China until early March 1946. The ship was decommissioned on 18 June 1946 and struck from the Navy list on 31 July that same year. On 6 October 1947, *LST–728* was transferred to the Maritime Administration for disposal.

LST–728 earned one battle star for World War II service.

LST–729

LST–729 was laid down on 12 August 1944 at Jeffersonville, Ind., by the Jeffersonville Boat & Machine Co.; launched on 18 September 1944; sponsored by Mrs. Mary G. Rowell; and commissioned on 16 October 1944, Lt. (jg.) S. F. McCarthy in command.

Following World War II, *LST–729* performed occupation duty in the Far East and saw service in China until late September 1945. She returned to the United States and was decommissioned on 8 July 1946 and struck from the Navy list on 28 August that same year. On 27 October 1947, the ship was sold to the Moore Dry Dock Co., of Oakland, Calif., and subsequently scrapped.

LST–730

LST–730 was laid down on 13 December 1943 at Pittsburgh, Pa., by the Dravo Corp., Neville Island; launched on 29 January 1944; sponsored by Mrs. W. R. Nichols; and commissioned on 30 March 1944, Lt. Milo Hazard in command.

Following World War II, *LST–730* performed occupation duty in the Far East until early March 1946. She returned to the United States and was decommissioned on 8 June 1946 and struck from the Navy list on 31 July that same year. On 18 December 1947, the ship was sold to the Learner Co., of Oakland, Calif., and subsequently scrapped.

LST–731

LST–731 was laid down on 27 December 1943 at Pittsburgh, Pa., by the Dravo Corp., Neville Island; launched on 12 February 1944; sponsored by Mrs. A. J. Ackerman; and commissioned on 30 March 1944, Ens. K. S. McCann, Jr., in command.

During World War II, *LST–731* was assigned to the Asiatic-Pacific theater and participated in the following operations:

Capture and occupation of Guam—July and August 1944

Assault and occupation of Iwo Jima—February and March 1945

Following the war, *LST–731* was redesignated *LSTH–731* on 15 September 1945 and performed occupation duty in the Far East until mid-February 1946. She was decommissioned on 2 June 1950 and redesignated *LST–731* on 6 March 1952. The ship received the name *Douglas County* (LST–731) after counties in 12 states of the United States on 1 July 1955 and was struck from the Navy list on 1 November 1958.

LST–731 earned two battle stars for World War II service.

LST–732

LST–732 was laid down on 5 January 1944 at Pittsburgh, Pa., by the Dravo Corp., Neville Island; launched on 19 February 1944; sponsored by Miss Marian B. Ross; and commissioned on 10 April 1944.

Following World War II, *LST–732* performed occupation duty in the Far East and saw service in China until early June 1946. She was decommissioned on 7 June 1946 and transferred to the State Department for disposal. On 19 July 1946, the ship was struck from the Navy list.

LST–733

LST–733 was laid down on 16 January 1944 at Pittsburgh, Pa., by the Dravo Corp., Neville Island; launched on 26 February 1944; sponsored by Mrs. J. E. Shields; and commissioned on 15 April 1944, Lt. T. J. Tracy, USNR, in command.

During World War II, *LST–733* was assigned to the Asiatic-Pacific theater and participated in the following operations:

Leyte landings—October and November 1944

Mindoro landings—December 1944

Assault and occupation of Okinawa Gunto—April 1945

Following the war, *LST–733* performed occupation duty in the Far East until mid-April 1946. She returned to the United States and was decommissioned on 28 June 1946 and struck from the Navy list on 31 July that same year. On 17 September 1947, the ship was sold to Consolidated Builders, Inc., Seattle, Wash., and subsequently scrapped.

LST–733 earned three battle stars for World War II service.

LST–734

LST–734 was laid down on 25 January 1944 at Pittsburgh, Pa., by the Dravo Corp., Neville Island; launched on 4 March 1944; sponsored by Mrs. W. P. Spofford; and commissioned on 22 April 1944.

During World War II, *LST–734* was assigned to the Asiatic-Pacific theater and participated in the following operations:

Capture and occupation of southern Palau Islands —September and October 1944

Leyte landings—October and November 1944

Ormoc Bay landings—December 1944

Zambales-Subic Bay—January 1945

Assault and occupation of Okinawa Gunto—April through June 1945

Following the war, *LST–734* performed occupation duty in the Far East until late December 1945. She returned to the United States and was decommissioned on 7 May 1946 and struck from the Navy list on 5 June that same year. On 24 May 1948, the ship was sold to the Bethlehem Steel Co., of Bethlehem, Pa., and subsequently scrapped.

LST–734 earned four battle stars for World War II service.

LST–735

LST–735 was laid down on 30 January 1944 at Pittsburgh, Pa., by the Dravo Corp., Neville Island; launched on 11 March 1944; sponsored by Mrs. G. W. Fearnside; and commissioned on 26 April 1944, Lt. Theodore F. Aldous in command.

During World War II, *LST–735* was assigned to the Asiatic-Pacific theater and participated in the following operations:

Capture and occupation of Saipan—August 1944
Lingayen Gulf landing—January 1945
Zambales-Subic Bay—January 1945
Assault and occupation of Okinawa Gunto—March through June 1945

LST–735 was decommissioned in March 1946 and reactivated on 3 November 1950 when she performed service during the Korean War and after with Commander Mine Forces, Pacific.

LST–735 earned four battle stars for World War II service and three for Korean service.

LST–736

LST–736 was laid down on 2 February 1944 at Pittsburgh, Pa., by the Dravo Corp., Neville Island; launched on 18 March 1944; sponsored by Mrs. G. O. Griffin; and commissioned on 2 May 1944.

During World War II, *LST–736* was assigned to the Asiatic-Pacific theater and participated in the following operations:

Capture and occupation of southern Palau Islands —September and October 1944
Leyte landings—October and November 1944
Zambales-Subic Bay—January 1945
Assault and occupation of Okinawa Gunto—April through June 1945

Following the war, *LST–736* performed occupation duty in the Far East until early March 1946. She returned to the United States and was decommissioned on 20 June 1946 and struck from the Navy list on 31 July that same year. On 29 May 1948, the ship was sold to the Bethlehem Steel Co., of Bethlehem, Pa., and subsequently scrapped.

LST–736 earned four battle stars for World War II service.

LST–737

LST–737 was laid down on 13 February 1944 at Pittsburgh, Pa., by the Dravo Corp., Neville Island; launched on 25 March 1944; sponsored by Mrs. C. E. Walker; and commissioned on 6 May 1944, Lt. W. B. Kirk, USNR, in command.

During World War II, *LST–737* was assigned to the Asiatic-Pacific theater and participated in the following operations:

Capture and occupation of southern Palau Islands —September and October 1944
Leyte landings—October and November 1944
Ormoc Bay landings—December 1944
Lingayen Gulf landing—January 1945
Zambales-Subic Bay—January 1945
Assault and occupation of Okinawa Gunto—March through June 1945

Following the war, *LST–737* performed occupation duty in the Far East until early November 1946. She was decommissioned and transferred to the United States Army on 2 November 1946. The ship was struck from the Navy list on 29 September 1947.

LST–737 earned five battle stars for World War II service.

LST–738

LST–738 was laid down on 20 February 1944 at Pittsburgh, Pa., by the Dravo Corp., Neville Island; launched on 1 April 1944; sponsored by Mrs. John S. Mason; and commissioned on 9 May 1944, Lt. John T. Barnett, USNR, in command.

During World War II, *LST–738* was assigned to the Asiatic-Pacific theater and participated in the Leyte landings in October 1944 and the Mindoro landings in December that same year. On 15 December 1944, the ship was lost in action due to a Japanese aerial attack off Mindoro, Philippines. She was struck from the Navy list on 19 January 1945.

LST–738 earned two battle stars for World War II service.

LST–739

LST–739 was laid down on 27 February 1944 at Pittsburgh, Pa., by the Dravo Corp., Neville Island; launched on 8 April 1944; sponsored by Miss Jean Galbraith; and commissioned on 15 May 1944, Lt. Milton U. Sarezky, USNR, in command.

During World War II, *LST–739* was assigned to the Asiatic-Pacific theater and participated in the following operations:

Leyte landings—October 1944
Ormoc Bay landings—December 1944
Assault and occupation of Okinawa Gunto—April and May 1945

Following the war, *LST–739* performed occupation duty in the Far East until mid-December 1945. She returned to the United States and was decommissioned on 1 May 1946 and struck from the Navy list on 3 July that same year. On 1 March 1948, the ship was sold to the Tex-O-Kan Flour Mills Co., of Dallas, Tex., for operation.

LST–739 earned two battle stars for World War II service.

LST–740

LST–740 was laid down on 12 February 1944 at Pittsburgh, Pa., by the Dravo Corp., Neville Island; launched on 8 April 1944; sponsored by Miss A. Jean Blocker; and commissioned on 15 May 1944.

During World War II, *LST–740* was assigned to the Asiatic-Pacific theater and participated in the following operations:

Morotai landings—September 1944
Leyte landings—October and November 1944
Lingayen Gulf landing—January 1945
Mindanao Island landings—April 1945
Balikpapan operation—June and July 1945

Following the war, *LST–740* performed occupation duty in the Far East until late October 1945. She returned to the United States and was decommissioned on 8 March 1946 and struck from the Navy list on 12 April that same year. On 14 June 1948, the ship was sold to the Oil Transport Co., of New Orleans, La., for non-self-propelled operation.

LST–740 earned five battle stars for World War II service.

LST–741

LST–741 was laid down on 5 March 1944 at Pittsburgh, Pa., by the Dravo Corp., Neville Island; launched on 15 April 1944; sponsored by Mrs. Paul F. Meehan; and commissioned on 19 May 1944.

During World War II, *LST–741* was assigned to the Asiatic-Pacific theater and participated in the following operations:

    Morotai landings—September 1944
    Mindoro landings—December 1944
    Lingayen Gulf landing—January 1945
    Mindanao Island landing—April 1945

Following the war, *LST–741* was decommissioned on 9 August 1946 and struck from the Navy list on 25 September that same year. On 12 May 1948, the ship was sold to the Bethlehem Steel Co., of Bethlehem, Pa., and subsequently scrapped.

LST–741 earned three battle stars for World War II service.

LST–742

LST–742 was laid down on 12 March 1944 at Pittsburgh, Pa., by the Dravo Corp., Neville Island; launched on 22 April 1944; sponsored by Mrs. Harry Lester; and commissioned on 23 May 1944, Lt. Warren W. Holmes, USNR, in command.

During World War II, *LST–742* was assigned to the Asiatic-Pacific theater and participated in the following operations:

    Lingayen Gulf landing—January 1945
    Visayan Island landings—March and April 1945
    Tarakan Island operation—April and May 1945

Following the war, *LST–742* was decommissioned on 26 April 1946 and transferred to the United States Army on 28 June 1946. She was returned to the United States Navy and recommissioned on 1 September 1950. On 1 July 1955, she was redesignated *Dunn County* (LST–742) after counties in North Dakota and Wisconsin. The ship performed service during the Korean War followed by extensive service with Amphibious Force, U.S. Pacific Fleet, until decommissioned and struck from the Navy list on 1 February 1961. *Dunn County* (LST–742) was sold to Zidell Explorations, Inc., of Portland, Oreg., on 6 September 1961.

LST–742 earned three battle stars for World War II service and five battle stars for the Korean War.

LST–743

LST–743 was laid down on 20 February 1944 at Pittsburgh, Pa., by the Dravo Corp., Neville Island; launched on 19 April 1944; sponsored by Mrs. Jack M. Page; and commissioned on 23 May 1944.

During World War II, *LST–743* was assigned to the Asiatic-Pacific theater and participated in the Mindanao Island landings in March 1945 and the Tarakan Island landings in April and May 1945. Following the war, she performed occupation duty in the Far East until early January 1946. The ship was decommissioned on 23 April 1946 and struck from the Navy list on 19 June that same year. On 23 October 1947, *LST–743* was sold to the New Orleans Shipwrecking Co., of Chicago, Ill., for scrapping.

LST–743 earned two battle stars for World War II service.

LST–744

LST–744 was laid down on 1 March 1944 at Pittsburgh, Pa., by the Dravo Corp., Neville Island; launched on 29 April 1944; sponsored by Mrs. E. O. Stickel; and commissioned on 29 May 1944, Lt. Frank P. Bannen, USNR, in command.

During World War II, *LST–744* was assigned to the Asiatic-Pacific theater and participated in the following operations:

    Morotai landings—September 1944
    Leyte landings—October and November 1944
    Lingayen Gulf landing—January 1945
    Mindanao Island landings—April 1945

Following the war, *LST–744* performed occupation duty in the Far East and saw service in China until early March 1946. She returned to the United States and was decommissioned on 28 June 1946 and struck from the Navy list on 15 August that same year. On 4 March 1948, the ship was sold to the Port Houston Iron Works, Inc., of Houston, Tex., for non-self-propelled operation.

LST–744 earned four battle stars for World War II service.

LST–745

LST–745 was laid down on 19 March 1944 at Pittsburgh, Pa., by the Dravo Corp., Neville Island; launched on 29 April 1944; sponsored by Mrs. Paul Simon; and commissioned on 31 May 1944.

During World War II, *LST–745* was assigned to the Asiatic-Pacific theater and participated in the following operations:

    Leyte landings—October 1944
    Zambales-Subic Bay—January 1945
    Assault and occupation of Okinawa Gunto—May and June 1945

Following the war, *LST–745* performed occupation duty in the Far East until mid-February 1946. She returned to the United States and was decommissioned on 9 July 1946 and struck from the Navy list on 28 August that same year. On 26 September 1947, the ship was sold to the Boston Metals Co., of Baltimore, Md., for scrapping.

LST–745 earned three battle stars for World War II service.

LST–746

LST–746 was laid down on 26 March 1944 at Pittsburgh, Pa., by the Dravo Corp., Neville Island; launched on 6 May 1944; sponsored by Mrs. J. H. Jacobson; and commissioned on 3 June 1944.

During World War II, *LST–746* was assigned to the Asiatic-Pacific theater and participated in the following operations:

    Leyte landings—October and November 1944
    Mindoro landings—December 1944
    Lingayen Gulf landing—January 1945
    Zambales-Subic Bay—January 1945
    Mindanao Island landings—April 1945

Following the war, *LST–746* performed occupation duty in the Far East until mid-December 1945. She returned to the United States and was decommissioned on 1 May 1946 and struck from the Navy list on 3 July that same year. On 4 March 1948, the ship was sold to the Port Houston Iron Works, Inc., of Houston, Tex., for non-self-propelled operation.

LST–746 earned four battle stars for World War II service.

LST–747

LST–747 was laid down on 2 April 1944 at Pittsburgh, Pa., by the Dravo Corp., Neville Island; launched on 20 May 1944; sponsored by Mrs. Roy Uncapher; and commissioned on 15 June 1944.

During World War II, *LST–747* was assigned to the Asiatic-Pacific theater and participated in the Lingayen Gulf landing in January 1945 and the assault and occupation of Okinawa Gunto from April through June 1945. Following the war, she performed occupation duty in the Far East until mid-January 1946. The ship returned to the United States and was decommissioned on 20 June 1946 and struck from the Navy list on 31 July that same year. On 21 May 1948, the tank landing ship was sold to the Bethlehem Steel Co., of Bethlehem, Pa., for scrapping.

LST–747 earned two battle stars for World War II service.

Wexford County (LST–1168), about 1967. Her deck is marked as a helicopter landing area; ships of this class can land the heavy CH–46 *Sea Knight* and CH–53 *Sea Stallion*. She is armed with three 3-inch 50-caliber rapid-fire twin gun mounts, introduced after Korea to replace the earlier 40-millimeter weapons. The "shelves" along the sides of her hull are supports for pontoon causeway sections, often carried by LST's.

LST–748

LST–748 was laid down on 2 April 1944 at Pittsburgh, Pa., by the Dravo Corp., Neville Island; launched on 13 May 1944; sponsored by Mrs. C. McK. Lynch; and commissioned on 5 June 1944.

During World War II, *LST–748* was assigned to the Asiatic-Parific theater and participated in the Leyte landings in November 1944 and the Lingayen Gulf landing in January 1945. Following the war, *LST–748* performed occupation duty in the Far East and saw service in China until mid-March 1946. On 27 May 1948, she was transferred to the Maritime Administration for disposition.

LST–748 earned two battle stars for World War II service.

LST–749

LST–749 was laid down on 10 April 1944 at Pittsburgh, Pa., by the Dravo Corp., Neville Island; launched on 20 May 1944; sponsored by Mrs. George W. Scott; and commissioned on 23 June 1944, Lt. Ralph B. Flynn in command.

During World War II, *LST–749* was assigned to the Asiatic-Pacific theater and participated in the Leyte landings in October and November 1944. She was sunk by a Japanese aerial attack off the Philippines on 21 December 1944. The ship was struck from the Navy list on 19 January 1945.

LST–749 earned one battle star for World War II service.

LST–750

LST–750 was laid down on 7 April 1944 at Pittsburgh, Pa., by the Dravo Corp., Neville Island; launched on 30 May 1944; sponsored by Mrs. Clifford S. Heinz; and commissioned on 29 June 1944, Lt. Ralph W. Long, USNR, in command.

During World War II, *LST–750* was assigned to the Asiatic-Pacific theater and participated in the Leyte landings in October and November 1944. She was lost as a result of a Japanese aerial attack off Leyte, Philippines, on 28 December 1944. The ship was struck from the Navy list on 19 January 1945.

LST–750 earned one battle star for World War II service.

LST–751

LST–751 was laid down on 16 April 1944 at Pittsburgh, Pa., by the Dravo Corp., Neville Island; launched on 27 May 1944; sponsored by Mrs. John W. Oahler; and commissioned on 26 June 1944, Lt. Robert E. Garris, USNR, in command.

During World War II, *LST–751* was assigned to the Asiatic-Pacific theater and participated in the Leyte landings in November 1944 and the Lingayen Gulf landing in January 1945. Following the war, *LST–751* performed occupation duty in the Far East until mid-July 1946. She was decommissioned on 21 August 1946 and struck from the Navy list on 15 October that same year. On 13 November 1947, the ship was transferred to the Maritime Administration for disposal.

LST–751 earned two battle stars for World War II service.

LST–752

LST–752 was laid down on 23 April 1944 at Pittsburgh, Pa., by the Dravo Corp., Neville Island; launched on 3 June 1944; sponsored by Mrs. John K. Hill; and commissioned on 5 July 1944, Lt. Stephen A. McClean, USNR, in command.

During World War II, *LST-752* was assigned to the Asiatic-Pacific theater and participated in the Lingayen Gulf landing in January 1945 and the assault and occupation of Okinawa Gunto from April through June 1945. Following the war, she performed occupation duty in the Far East until mid-December 1945. The ship returned to the United States and was decommissioned on 7 June 1946 and struck from the Navy list on 19 July 1946. On 13 October 1947, the tank landing ship was sold to William E. Skinner, New York, N.Y., for scrapping.

LST-752 earned two battle stars for World War II service.

LST-753

LST-753 was laid down on 30 April 1944 at Pittsburgh, Pa., by the Dravo Corp., Neville Island; launched on 10 June 1944; sponsored by Mrs. C. F. Frye; and commissioned on 10 July 1944.

During World War II, *LST-753* was assigned to the Asiatic-Pacific theater and participated in the following operations:

Lingayen Gulf landing—January 1945
Mindanao Island landings—March and April 1945
Balikpapan operation—June and July 1945

Following the war, *LST-753* performed occupation duty in the Far East until early March 1946. She returned to the United States and was decommissioned on 25 June 1946 and struck from the Navy list on 31 July that same year. On 13 December 1947, the ship was sold to Kaiser Co., Vancouver, Wash., for scrapping.

LST-753 earned three battle stars for World War II service.

LST-754

LST-754 was laid down on 13 May 1944 at Ambridge, Pa., by the American Bridge Co.; launched on 6 July 1944; sponsored by Mrs. A. L. Provo; and commissioned on 29 July 1944.

During World War II, *LST-754* was assigned to the Asiatic-Pacific theater and participated in the Lingayen Gulf landings in January 1945, the Mariveles-Corregidor operation in February 1945, and the Mindanao Island landings in April 1945. Following the war, *LST-754* performed occupation duty in the Far East and saw service in China until late March 1946. She returned to the United States and was decommissioned on 20 June 1946 and struck from the Navy list on 31 July that same year. On 21 May 1948, the ship was sold to the Bethlehem Steel Co., of Bethlehem, Pa., for scrapping.

LST-754 earned three battle stars for World War II service.

LST-755

LST-755 was laid down on 20 May 1944 at Ambridge, Pa., by the American Bridge Co.; launched on 11 July 1944; sponsored by Mrs. L. W. Day; and commissioned on 3 August 1944, Lt. Hyman Harris, USNR, in command.

During World War II, *LST-755* was assigned to the Asiatic-Pacific theater and participated in the Lingayen Gulf landing in January 1945 and the Mindanao Island landings in April 1945. Following the war, she performed occupation duty in the Far East and saw service in China until late May 1946. On 29 May 1946, the ship was decommissioned and transferred to Nationalist China. She was struck from the Navy list on 12 March 1948.

LST-755 earned two battle stars for World War II service.

LST-756

LST-756 was laid down on 25 May 1944 at Ambridge, Pa., by the American Bridge Co.; launched on 15 July 1944; sponsored by Mrs. J. W. Small, Jr.; and commissioned on 8 August 1944, Lt. Frank L. Daum, USNR, in command.

During World War II, *LST-756* was assigned to the Asiatic-Pacific theater and participated in the assault and occupation of Iwo Jima in February 1945 and the assault and occupation of Okinawa Gunto in April through June 1945. She returned to the United States and was decommissioned on 5 April 1946 and struck from the Navy list on 17 April that same year. On 19 September 1946, the ship was sold to the Construction Power & Merchandising Co., of Brooklyn, N.Y.

LST-756 earned two battle stars for World War II service.

LST-757

LST-757 was laid down on 1 June 1944 at Ambridge, Pa., by the American Bridge Co.; launched on 21 July 1944; sponsored by Mrs. Beulah Schaefer; and commissioned on 15 August 1944, Lt. J. E. Clark, USNR, in command.

During World War II, *LST-757* was assigned to the Asiatic-Pacific theater and participated in the Lingayen Gulf landing in January 1945 and the Mindanao Island landings in April 1945. Following the war, she performed occupation duty in the Far East until late December 1945. The ship returned to the United States and was decommissioned on 28 May 1946 and struck from the Navy list on 3 July that same year. On 10 May 1948, she was sold to the Bethlehem Steel Co., of Bethlehem, Pa., for scrapping.

LST-757 earned two battle stars for World War II service.

LST-758

LST-758 was laid down on 5 June 1944 at Ambridge, Pa., by the American Bridge Co.; launched on 25 July 1944; sponsored by Mrs. F. D. Colburn; and commissioned on 19 August 1944.

During World War II, *LST-758* was assigned to the Asiatic-Pacific theater and participated in the assault and occupation of Iwo Jima in February 1945 and the assault and occupation of Okinawa Gunto in April through June 1945. Following the war, she performed occupation duty in the Far East until mid-September 1945. *LST-758* was decommissioned on 13 July 1946 and recommissioned on 3 November 1950 for service in the Korean War. She saw service in Korea until late July 1953. On 1 July 1955, the ship was redesignated *Duval County* (LST-758) after counties in Florida and Texas. Following the Korean War, she had extensive service with the Pacific and Atlantic Fleets through 1969. *LST-758* was decommissioned on 28 October 1969.

LST-758 earned two battle stars for World War II service and four battle stars for the Korean War.

LST-759

LST-759 was laid down on 11 June 1944 at Ambridge, Pa., by the American Bridge Co.; launched on 29 July 1944; sponsored by Mrs. N. B. Obbard; and commissioned on 25 August 1944, Lt. John A. Baybutt, USCGR, in command.

During World War II, *LST-759* was assigned to the Asiatic-Pacific theater and participated in the assault and occupation of Okinawa Gunto in April 1945. She was decommissioned in March 1946. On 1 July 1955, the ship was redesignated *Eddy County* (LST-759) (*q.v.*) after counties in New Mexico and North Dakota. The tank landing ship was berthed at the Columbia

River Group of the Pacific Reserve Fleet until struck from the Navy list on 1 October 1958.

LST-759 earned one battle star for World War II service.

LST-760

LST-760 was laid down on 15 June 1944 at Ambridge, Pa., by the American Bridge Co.; launched on 3 August 1944; sponsored by Mrs. Walton L. Carlson; and commissioned on 28 August 1944, Lt. R. T. A. McKenzie in command.

During World War II, *LST-760* was assigned to the Asiatic-Pacific theater and participated in the assault and occupation of Iwo Jima in February 1945 and the assault and occupation of Okinawa Gunto from April through June 1945. Following the war, she performed occupation duty in the Far East until early December 1945. The ship returned to the United States and was decommissioned on 24 May 1946 and struck from the Navy list on 3 July that same year. On 29 May 1948, she was sold to the Bethlehem Steel Co., of Bethlehem, Pa., for scrapping.

LST-760 earned two battle stars for World War II service.

LST-761

LST-761 was laid down on 18 June 1944 at Ambridge, Pa., by the American Bridge Co.; launched on 7 August 1944; sponsored by Mrs. H. A. Brainerd; and commissioned on 2 September 1944, Lt. H. A. Swagart, Jr., USCGR, in command.

During World War II, *LST-761* was assigned to the Asiatic-Pacific theater and participated in the assault and occupation of Iwo Jima in February and March 1945. She was decommissioned in March 1946 and assigned to the Columbia River Group of the Pacific Reserve Fleet. On 1 July 1955 the ship was named *Esmeraldo County* (LST-761) after an erroneous spelling of Esmeralda county in Nevada.

LST-761 earned one battle star for World War II service.

LST-762

LST-762 was laid down on 24 June 1944 at Amridge, Pa., by the American Bridge Co.; launched on 11 August 1944; sponsored by Mrs. Margaret M. Ewing; and commissioned on 5 September 1944, Lt. Franklin J. Ewers, USCGR, in command.

During World War II, *LST-762* was assigned to the Asiatic-Pacific theater and participated in the assault and occupation of Okinawa Gunto in April 1945. Following the war, she performed occupation duty in the Far East until mid-November 1945. The ship was decommissioned in 1946 and reactivated on 3 November 1950 for service in the Korean War. On 1 July 1955, she was redesignated *Floyd County* (LST-762) after counties in Georgia, Indiana, Iowa, Kentucky, Texas, and Virginia. Following the Korean War, she operated with the Pacific Fleet Amphibious Force, including extensive service off Vietnam from 1965 through 1968. *Floyd County* (LST-672) was again decommissioned on 3 September 1969 and struck from the Navy list.

LST-762 earned one battle star for World War II service, one for the Korean War, and three battle stars and an award of the Meritorious Unit Commendation for service in the Vietnam War.

LST-763

LST-763 was laid down on 29 June 1944 at Ambridge, Pa., by the American Bridge Co.; launched on 16 August 1944; sponsored by Mrs. A. J. Meade; and commis-

sioned on 8 September 1944, Lt. Alton W. Meekins, USCG, in command.

During World War II, *LST-763* was assigned to the Asiatic-Pacific theater and participated in the assault and occupation of Iwo Jima in February and March 1945 and the assault and occupation of Okinawa Gunto from April through June 1945. Following the war, she performed occupation duty in the Far East until mid-November 1945. The ship returned to the United States and was decommissioned on 29 April 1946 and struck from the Navy list on 15 August that same year. On 11 December 1947, *LST-763* was sold to the Southern Shipwrecking Co., of New Orleans, La., for scrapping.

LST-763 earned two battle stars for World War II service.

LST-764

LST-764 was laid down on 4 July 1944 at Ambridge, Pa., by the American Bridge Co.; launched on 21 August 1944; sponsored by Mrs. Guy Donoho; and commissioned on 13 September 1944, Lt. R. F. Nichols, USCGR, in command.

During World War II, *LST-764* was assigned to the Asiatic-Pacific theater and participated in the assault and occupation of Iwo Jima in February and March 1945. Following the war, she performed occupation duty in the Far East and saw service in China until mid-December 1945. The ship returned to the United States and was decommissioned on 30 April 1946 and struck from the Navy list on 3 July that same year. On 11 December 1947, the tank landing ship was sold to the Southern Shipwrecking Co., of New Orleans, La., for scrapping.

LST-764 earned one battle star for World War II service.

LST-765

LST-765 was laid down on 8 July 1944 at Ambridge, Pa., by the American Bridge Co.; launched on 26 August 1944; sponsored by Mrs. W. P. Douglas; and commissioned on 18 September 1944.

During World War II, *LST-765* was assigned to the Asiatic-Pacific theater and participated in the assault and occupation of Okinawa Gunto in May and June 1945. Following the war, *LST-765* performed occupation duty in the Far East until early December 1945. She returned to the United States and was decommissioned on 29 April 1946 and struck from the Navy list on 3 July that same year. On 16 December 1947, the ship was sold to B. T. Jones for scrapping.

LST-765 earned one battle star for World War II service.

LST-766

LST-766 was laid down on 13 July 1944 at Ambridge, Pa., by the American Bridge Co.; launched on 30 August 1944; sponsored by Mrs. C. E. Egeler; and commissioned on 25 September 1944.

Following World War II, *LST-766* performed occupation duty in the Far East and saw service in China until mid-October 1945. She was decommissioned on 19 March 1946 and struck from the Navy list on 5 June that same year. On 24 December 1946, the ship was sold to Pedro Bidegaray for operation.

LST-767

LST-767 was laid down on 19 July 1944 at Ambridge, Pa., by the American Bridge Co.; launched on 4 September 1944; sponsored by Mrs. Helen Stanhope; and commissioned on 30 September 1944, Lt. R. B. Seidman, USCGR, in command.

During World War II, *LST-767* was assigned to the Asiatic-Pacific theater and participated in the assault and occupation of Okinawa Gunto in April 1945. Following the war, she performed occupation duty in the Far East until early March 1946. The ship was decommissioned on 7 March 1946 and struck from the Navy list on 28 March that same year.

LST-767 earned one battle star for World War II service.

LST-768

LST-768 was laid down on 22 July 1944 at Ambridge, Pa., by the American Bridge Co.; launched on 8 September 1944; sponsored by Mrs. W. W. Slocum; and commissioned on 4 October 1944, Lt. B. R. Andrews, Jr., in command.

During World War II, *LST-768* was assigned to the Asiatic-Pacific theater and participated in the following operations:

    Assault and occupation of Iwo Jima—March 1945
    Assault and occupation of Okinawa Gunto—May and June 1945
    Fukuoka (Kyushu-Korea Area)—November and December 1945

Following the war, *LST-768* performed occupation duty in the Far East until mid-December 1945. She returned to the United States and was decommissioned on 15 April 1946 and struck from the Navy list on 5 June that same year. On 18 December 1947, the ship was sold to the Humble Oil & Refining Co., of Houston, Tex.

LST-768 earned three battle stars for World War II service.

LST-769

LST-769 was laid down on 28 July 1944 at Ambridge, Pa., by the American Bridge Co.; launched on 12 September 1944; sponsored by Mrs. Emma Farrah; and commissioned on 9 October 1944, Lt. Edwin B. Bertini in command.

During World War II, *LST-769* was assigned to the Asiatic-Pacific theater and participated in the assault and occupation of Okinawa Gunto from April through June 1945. Following the war, she performed occupation duty in the Far East until late November 1945. She returned to the United States and was decommissioned on 29 April 1946 and struck from the Navy list on 3 July that same year. On 11 December 1947, the ship was sold to the California Co. for operation.

LST-769 earned one battle star for World War II service.

LST-770

LST-770 was laid down on 1 August 1944 at Ambridge, Pa., by the American Bridge Co.; launched on 17 September 1944; sponsored by Mrs. B. A. McCormick; and commissioned on 13 October 1944, Lt. John H. Judge, USCGR, in command.

During World War II, *LST-770* was assigned to the Asiatic-Pacific theater and participated in the assault and occupation of Okinawa Gunto in March through June 1945. Following the war, she performed occupation duty in the Far East until late October 1945. The ship was decommissioned on 29 April 1946 and struck from the Navy list on 31 July that same year. On 6 February 1948, the tank landing ship was sold to Madison B. Wright for non-self-propelled operation.

LST-770 earned one battle star for World War II service.

LST-771

LST-771 was laid down on 5 August 1944 at Ambridge, Pa., by the American Bridge Co.; launched on 21 September 1944; sponsored by Mrs. Marion Morrow; and commissioned on 18 October 1944, Lt. T. L. Becton in command.

During World War II, *LST-771* was assigned to the Asiatic-Pacific theater and participated in the assault and occupation of Okinawa Gunto from March through June 1945. Following the war, she performed occupation duty in the Far East until mid-December 1945. She returned to the United States and was decommissioned on 14 May 1946 and struck from the Navy list on 5 June that same year. On 26 September 1947, the ship was sold to the Boston Metals Co., Baltimore, Md., for scrapping.

LST-771 earned one battle star for World War II service.

LST-772

LST-772 was laid down on 3 August 1944 at Seneca, Ill., by the Chicago Bridge & Iron Co.; launched on 24 October 1944; sponsored by Mrs. Elsie Jane Woodlief Arrington; and commissioned on 13 November 1944, Lt. George J. Nieman, USNR, in command.

During World War II, *LST-772* was assigned to the Asiatic-Pacific theater and participated in the assault and occupation of Okinawa Gunto from April through June 1945. Following the war, she performed occupation duty in the Far East until early December 1945. The ship was placed out of commission, in reserve, on 3 July 1946 and assigned to the Columbia River Group of the U.S. Pacific Reserve Fleet. Recommissioned on 3 November 1950, she saw extensive service during the Korean War. On 1 July 1955, she was redesignated *Ford County* (LST-772) after counties in Illinois and Kansas. *Ford County* was destroyed as a target ship on 19 March 1958 and struck from the Navy list that same day.

LST-772 earned one battle star for World War II service and six for Korean War service.

LST-773

LST-773 was redesignated AGP-16 and named *Antigone* (q.v.) on 14 August 1944.

LST-774

LST-774 was laid down on 5 August 1944 at Seneca, Ill., by the Chicago Bridge & Iron Co.; launched on 31 October 1944; sponsored by Mrs. Priscilla Winn Robertson; and commissioned on 20 November 1944, Lt. Joseph H. Gross, USNR, in command.

During World War II, *LST-774* was assigned to the Asiatic-Pacific theater and participated in the assault and occupation of Okinawa Gunto from April through June 1945. Following the war, she performed occupation duty in the Far East and saw service in China until mid-March 1946. *LST-774* returned to the United States and was decommissioned on 12 July 1946 and struck from the Navy list on 15 August that same year. On 17 September 1947, she was sold to Consolidated Builders, Inc., Morris Heights, N.Y., and subsequently scrapped.

LST-774 earned one battle star for World War II service.

LST-775

LST-775 was laid down on 22 April 1944 at Pittsburgh, Pa., by the Dravo Corp.; launched on 10 June 1944; sponsored by Mrs. William H. Evans; and commissioned on 15 July 1944, Lt. F. J. Rowe in command.

During World War II, *LST-775* was assigned to the Asiatic-Pacific theater and took part in the following operations:

Leyte landings—November 1944
Lingayen Gulf landing—January 1945
Zambales-Subic Bay—January 1945
Mindanao Island landings—April 1945

Following the war, *LST-775* performed occupation duty in the Far East until early March 1946. She was decommissioned on 15 July 1946.

LST-775 earned four battle stars for World War II service.

LST-776

LST-776 was laid down on 7 May 1944 at Pittsburgh, Pa., by the Dravo Corp.; launched on 17 June 1944; sponsored by Mrs. Douglas Pinquely; and commissioned on 20 July 1944, Lt. J. D. Copeland, USNR, in command.

During World War II, *LST-776* was assigned to the Asiatic-Pacific theater and participated in the assault and occupation of Iwo Jima in March 1945 and the assault and occupation of Okinawa Gunto in March and April 1945. Following the war, she performed occupation duty in the Far East until mid-October 1945. The ship returned to the United States and was decommissioned on 18 March 1946 and struck from the Navy list on 1 May that same year. On 17 January 1947, the tank landing ship was sold to *Compania Naviera y Commercial Perez Compano*, Buenos Aires, Argentina, for operation.

LST-776 earned two battle stars for World War II service.

LST-777

LST-777 was laid down on 4 May 1944 at Pittsburgh, Pa., by the Dravo Corp.; launched on 24 June 1944; sponsored by Mrs. George G. Kaszer; and commissioned on 25 July 1944.

During World War II, *LST-777* was assigned to the Asiatic-Pacific theater and participated in the following operations:

Zambales-Subic Bay—January 1945
Visayan Islands landings—April 1945

Following the war, *LST-777* performed occupation duty in the Far East until mid-April 1946. She returned to the United States and was decommissioned on 19 July 1946 and struck from the Navy list on 28 August that same year. On 7 May 1948, the ship was sold to the Bethlehem Steel Co., Bethlehem, Pa., and subsequently scrapped.

LST-777 earned two battle stars for World War II service.

LST-778

LST-778 was laid down on 14 May 1944 at Pittsburgh, Pa., by the Dravo Corp.; launched on 24 June 1944; sponsored by Mrs. D. M. Booth; and commissioned on 31 July 1944, Lt. Glendal T. Harper, USNR, in command.

During World War II, *LST-778* was assigned to the Asiatic-Pacific theater and participated in the following operations:

Lingayen Gulf landings—January 1945
Mindanao Island landings—April 1945

Following the war, *LST-778* performed occupation duty in the Far East until mid-October 1945. She returned to the United States and was decommissioned on 27 May 1946 and struck from the Navy list on 19 June 1946. On 23 October 1947, the ship was sold to the Boston Metals Corp., Baltimore, Md., for scrapping.

LST-778 earned two battle stars for World War II service.

LST-779

LST-779 was laid down on 21 May 1944 at Pittsburgh, Pa., by the Dravo Corp; launched on 1 July 1944; sponsored by Mrs. Andrew Vavrek; and commissioned on 3 August 1944, Lt. (jg.) Joseph A. Hopkins, USNR, in command.

During World War II, *LST-779* was assigned to the Asiatic-Pacific theater and participated in the following operations:

Assault and occupation of Iwo Jima—February 1945
Assault and occupation of Okinawa Gunto—April 1945

Following the war, *LST-779* performed occupation duty in the Far East and saw service in China until early April 1946. She was decommissioned on 18 May 1946 and struck from the Navy list on 19 July that same year. On 5 December 1947, the ship was sold to Bosey, Philippines.

LST-779 earned two battle stars for World War II service.

LST-780

LST-780 was laid down on 28 May 1944 at Pittsburgh, Pa., by the Dravo Corp.; launched on 10 July 1944; sponsored by Miss Anna May Ries; and commissioned on 7 August 1944, Lt. Theodore B. Clark in command.

During World War II, *LST-780* was assigned to the Asiatic-Pacific theater and participated in the assault and occupation of Okinawa Gunto in March and April 1945. Following the war, she performed occupation duty in the Far East until mid-September 1945. She returned to the United States and was decommissioned on 13 June 1946 and struck from the Navy list on 31 July that same year. On 27 October 1947, the ship was sold to the Moore Drydock Co., Oakland, Calif., for scrapping.

LST-780 earned one battle star for World War II service.

LST-781

LST-781 was laid down on 4 June 1944 at Pittsburgh, Pa., by the Dravo Corp.; launched on 15 July 1944; sponsored by Mrs. Stuart D. Brown; and commissioned on 18 August 1944.

During World War II, *LST-781* was assigned to the Asiatic-Pacific theater and participated in the assault and occupation of Okinawa Gunto in April 1945. She returned to the United States and was decommissioned on 27 June 1946 and struck from the Navy list on 15 August that same year. On 20 December 1947, the ship was sold to the Humble Oil & Refining Co., Houston, Tex., for operation.

LST-781 earned one battle star for World War II service.

LST-782

LST-782 was laid down on 11 June 1944 at Pittsburgh, Pa., by the Dravo Corp.; launched on 22 July 1944; sponsored by Mrs. Elizabeth R. Miser; and commissioned on 22 August 1944.

During World War II, *LST-782* was assigned to the Asiatic-Pacific theater and participated in the following operations:

Assault and occupation of Iwo Jima—February 1945
Assault and occupation of Okinawa Gunto—April 1945

Following the war, *LST-782* performed occupation duty in the Far East until mid-November 1945. She returned to the United States and was decommissioned on 14 May 1946 and struck from the Navy list on 5 June that same year. On 26 September 1947, the ship was sold to the Boston Metals Co., Baltimore, Md., for scrapping.

LST-782 earned two battle stars for World War II service.

LST-783

LST-783 was laid down on 14 May 1944 at Pittsburgh, Pa., by the Dravo Corp.; launched on 11 July 1944; sponsored by Mrs. John F. Hoffmeister; and commissioned on 14 August 1944, Lt. J. F. McAllister, USNR, in command.

During World War II, LST-783 was assigned to the Asiatic-Pacific theater and participated in the assault and occupation of Iwo Jima in March 1945. Following the war, she performed occupation duty in the Far East and saw service in China until mid-March 1946. LST-783 returned to the United States and was decommissioned on 22 August 1946 and struck from the Navy list on 16 June 1950. On 27 June 1950, the ship was sold to the Northern Metal Co., of Philadelpha, Pa., and subsequently scrapped.

LST-783 earned one battle star for World War II service.

LST-784

LST-784 was laid down on 18 June 1944 at Pittsburgh, Pa., by the Dravo Corp.; launched on 29 July 1944; sponsored by Mrs. Michael Ruzic; and commissioned on 1 September 1944, Lt. Daniel H. Miner, USCG, in command.

During World War II, LST-784 was assigned to the Asiatic-Pacific theater and participated in the assault and occupation of Iwo Jima in February and March 1945 and the assault and occupation of Okinawa Gunto in April through June 1945.

Following the war, LST-784 performed occupation duty in the Far East until mid-September 1945. She was decommissioned in March 1946 and assigned to the Columbia River Group of the Pacific Reserve Fleet. On 1 July 1955, the ship was redesignated *Garfield County*

(LST-784) (q.v.) after counties in Colorado, Montana, Nebraska, Oklahoma, Utah, and Washington.

LST-784 earned two battle stars for World War II service.

LST-785

LST-785 was laid down on 25 June 1944 at Pittsburgh, Pa., by the Dravo Corp.; launched on 5 August 1944; sponsored by Mrs. D. A. McFarlane; and commissioned on 4 September 1944, Lt. Myron E. Nichol, USCG, in command.

During World War II, LST-785 was assigned to the Asiatic-Pacific theater and participated in the assault and occupation of Iwo Jima in February 1945 and the assault and occupation of Okinawa Gunto from April through June 1945.

Following the war, LST-785 performed occupation duty in the Far East until early December 1945. She returned to the United States and was decommissioned on 3 May 1946 and struck from the Navy list on 5 June that same year. On 3 June 1948, the ship was sold to Walter W. Johnson Co. for scrapping.

LST-785 earned two battle stars for World War II service.

LST-786

LST-786 was laid down on 21 May 1944 at Pittsburgh, Pa., by the Dravo Corp.; launched on 22 July 1944; sponsored by Mrs. E. B. Keckler; and commissioned on 28 August 1944, Lt. Eli T. Ringler, USCG, in command.

During World War II, LST-786 was assigned to the Asiatic-Pacific theater and participated in the assault and occupation of Okinawa Gunto in May and June 1945. Following the war, she performed occupation duty in the Far East and saw service in China until mid-December 1945. LST-786 was decommissioned on 9 July 1946 and assigned to the Columbia River Group of the Pacific Reserve Fleet. On 1 July 1955, the ship

Windham County (LST-1170) ready for launching at Sturgeon Bay, Wisconsin. Note her shallow-draft hull form, with twin propellers and rudders.

was redesignated *Garrett County* (LST–786) (*q.v.*) after a county in Maryland. Recommissioned on 15 October 1966, *Garrett County* saw extensive service in the Vietnam War. She was transferred to the Republic of Vietnam Navy on 23 April 1971.

LST–786 earned one battle star for World War II service and the Presidential Unit Citation, the Navy Unit Commendation, and seven battle stars for the Vietnam War.

LST–787

LST–787 was laid down on 2 July 1944 at Pittsburgh, Pa., by the Dravo Corp.; launched on 12 August 1944; sponsored by Mrs. James Viziana; and commissioned on 13 September 1944, Lt. W. S. Lawrence in command.

During World War II, *LST–787* was assigned to the Asiatic-Pacific theater and participated in the following operations:

> Capture and occupation of Iwo Jima—February 1945
> Assault and occupation of Okinawa Gunto—April through June 1945

Following the war, *LST–787* performed occupation duty in the Far East until early November 1945. She returned to the United States and was decommissioned on 27 May 1946 and struck from the Navy list on 3 July that same year. On 7 May 1948, the ship was sold to the Bethlehem Steel Co., of Bethlehem, Pa., for scrapping.

LST–787 earned two battle stars for World War II service.

LST–788

LST–788 was laid down on 9 July 1944 at Pittsburgh, Pa., by the Dravo Corp.; launched on 19 August 1944; sponsored by Mrs. Gerard H. Nickerson; and commissioned on 18 September 1944, Lt. Walter R. Benson, USCGR, in command.

During World War II, *LST–788* was assigned to the Asiatic-Pacific theater and participated in the assault and occupation of Iwo Jima in February 1945 and the assault and occupation of Okinawa Gunto in April that same year. Following the war, she performed occupation duty in the Far East until late October 1945. The ship returned to the United States and was decommissioned on 16 April 1946 and struck from the Navy list on 5 June that same year. On 26 September 1947, *LST–788* was sold to the Boston Metals Co., of Baltimore, Md., for scrapping.

LST–788 earned two battle stars for World War II service.

LST–789

LST–789 was laid down on 1 June 1944 at Pittsburgh, Pa., by the Dravo Corp.; launched on 5 August 1944; sponsored by Mrs. Harry C. Story; and commissioned on 11 September 1944, Lt. H. M. Mulvey, USCGR, in command.

During World War II, *LST–789* was assigned to the Asiatic-Pacific theater and participated in the assault and occupation of Iwo Jima in February 1945 and the assault and occupation of Okinawa Gunto in April 1945. Following the war, *LST–789* performed occupation duty in the Far East until early November 1945. She returned to the United States and was decommissioned on 29 April 1946 and struck from the Navy list on 3 July that same year. The ship was sold to the California Co. on 11 December 1947 for operation.

LST–789 earned two battle stars for World War II service.

LST–790

LST–790 was laid down on 11 June 1944 at Pittsburgh, Pa., by the Dravo Corp.; launched on 19 August 1944; sponsored by Mrs. John Halifax; and commissioned on 22 September 1944.

During World War II, *LST–790* was assigned to the Asiatic-Pacific theater and participated in the assault and occupation of Iwo Jima in February 1945 and the assault and occupation of Okinawa Gunto in April 1945. Following the war, *LST–790* was redesignated *LST(H)–790* on 15 September 1945 and performed occupation duty in the Far East until mid-December 1945. She returned to the United States and was decommissioned on 27 May 1946 and struck from the Navy list on 3 July that same year. On 5 May 1948, the ship was sold to the Bethlehem Steel Co., of Bethlehem, Pa., for scrapping.

LST–790 earned two battle stars for World War II service.

LST–791

LST–791 was laid down on 16 July 1944 at Pittsburgh, Pa., by the Dravo Corp.; launched on 26 August 1944; sponsored by Mrs. John Fetsko; and commissioned on 27 September 1944.

During World War II, *LST–791* was assigned to the Asiatic-Pacific theater and participated in the assault and occupation of Okinawa Gunto from April through June 1945. Following the war, *LST–791* performed occupation duty in the Far East until mid-November 1945. She returned to the United States and was decommissioned on 28 May 1946 and struck from the Navy list on 3 July that same year. On 4 June 1948, the ship was sold to the Walter W. Johnson Co. for scrapping.

LST–791 earned one battle star for World War II service.

LST–792

LST–792 was laid down on 25 June 1944 at Pittsburgh, Pa., by the Dravo Corp.; launched on 2 September 1944; sponsored by Mrs. Ross Blaine; and commissioned on 2 October 1944.

During World War II, *LST–792* was assigned to the Asiatic-Pacific theater and participated in the assault and occupation of Iwo Jima in February 1945 and the assault and occupation of Okinawa Gunto from April through June 1945. Following the war, *LST–792* performed occupation duty in the Far East until late October 1945. She returned to the United States and was decommissioned on 29 April 1946 and struck from the Navy list on 19 July that same year. On 31 October 1946, the ship was sold to the Suwannee Fruit & S. S. Co., of Jacksonville, Fla.

LST–792 earned two battle stars for World War II service.

LST–793

LST–793 was laid down on 23 July 1944 at Pittsburgh, Pa., by the Dravo Corp.; launched on 2 September 1944; sponsored by Mrs. E. R. Gorman; and commissioned on 5 October 1944, Lt. George A. Miller, USCG, in command.

During World War II, *LST–793* was assigned to the Asiatic-Pacific theater and participated in the assault and occupation of Okinawa Gunto in March and April 1945. Following the war, *LST–793* performed occupation duty in the Far East until mid-September 1945. She returned to the United States and was decommissioned on 29 April 1946 and struck from the Navy list on 3 July that same year. On 16 December 1947, the ship was sold to Tex-O-Kan Flour Mills Co., of Dallas, Tex., for operation.

LST–793 earned one battle star for World War II service.

LST–794

LST–794 was laid down on 12 July 1944 at Pittsburgh, Pa., by the Dravo Corp.; launched on 16 September 1944; sponsored by Mrs. B. H. Gommel; and commissioned on 16 October 1944, Lt. W. C. Cain, USCGR, in command.

During World War II, *LST–794* was assigned to the Asiatic-Pacific theater and participated in the assault and occupation of Okinawa Gunto from April through June 1945. Following the war, *LST–794* performed occupation duty in the Far East and saw service in China until mid-December 1945. She was decommissioned on 9 July 1946 and assigned to the Columbia River Group of the Pacific Reserve Fleet. On 1 July 1955, the ship was redesignated *Gibson County* (LST–794) (*q.v.*) after counties in Indiana and Tennessee. She was sunk as a target for destruction by *Rasher* (SS–269) off the west coast of the United States on 22 May 1958. The tank landing ship was struck from the Navy list on 1 November 1958.

LST–794 earned one battle star for World War II service.

LST–795

LST–795 was laid down on 30 July 1944 at Pittsburgh, Pa., by the Dravo Corp.; launched on 9 September 1944; sponsored by Mrs. Heimo R. Iammi; and commissioned on 9 October 1944, Lt. Melvin H. Jackson, USCGR, in command.

During World War II, *LST–795* was assigned to the Asiatic-Pacific theater and participated in the assault and occupation of Iwo Jima in February 1945 and the assault and occupation of Okinawa Gunto from April through June 1945. Following the war, *LST–795* performed occupation duty in the Far East until mid-October 1945. She returned to the United States and was decommissioned on 29 April 1946 and struck from the Navy list on 19 July that same year. On 31 October 1946, the ship was sold to the Suwannee Fruit & S.S. Co., Jacksonville, Fla.

LST–795 earned two battle stars for World War II service.

LST–796

LST–796 was laid down on 6 August 1944 at Pittsburgh, Pa., by the Dravo Corp.; launched on 16 September 1944; sponsored by Mrs. J. A. Woodling; and commissioned on 20 October 1944.

During World War II, *LST–796* was assigned to the Asiatic-Pacific theater and participated in the assault and occupation of Okinawa Gunto from March through June 1945. Following the war, she performed occupation duty in the Far East and saw service in China until mid-December 1945. The ship returned to the United States and was decommissioned on 17 April 1946 and struck from the Navy list on 19 June that same year. On 22 September 1947, the tank landing ship was sold to the Southern Shipwrecking Co., of New Orleans, La., for scrapping.

LST–796 earned one battle star for World War II service.

LST–797

LST–797 was laid down on 21 August 1944 at Jeffersonville, Ind., by the Jeffersonville Boat & Machine Co.; launched on 22 September 1944; and commissioned on 20 October 1944.

During World War II, *LST–797* was assigned to the Asiatic-Pacific theater and participated in the assault and occupation of Okinawa Gunto in March and April 1945. Following the war, *LST–797* performed occupation duty in the Far East and saw service in China until early May 1946. She returned to the United States and was decommissioned on 28 June 1946 and struck from the Navy list on 31 July that same year. On 12 December 1947, the ship was sold to Consolidated Builders, Inc., of Morris Heights, N.Y., for scrapping.

LST–797 earned one battle star for World War II service.

LST–798

LST–798 was laid down on 17 August 1944 at Jeffersonville, Ind., by the Jeffersonville Boat & Machine Co.; launched on 26 September 1944; and commissioned on 26 October 1944, Lt. R. E. Hurt in command.

Following World War II, *LST–798* performed occupation duty in the Far East until mid-March 1946. She returned to the United States and was decommissioned on 16 July 1946 and struck from the Navy list on 15 August that same year. On 17 September 1947, the ship was sold to Consolidated Builders, Inc., of Morris Heights, N.Y., for scrapping.

LST–799

LST–799 was laid down on 25 August 1944 at Jeffersonville, Ind., by the Jeffersonville Boat & Machine Co.; launched on 3 October 1944; sponsored by Miss Mary R. Whalen; and commissioned on 28 October 1944, Lt. Daniel C. Millett, USNR, in command.

During World War II, *LST–799* was assigned to the Asiatic-Pacific theater and participated in the assault and occupation of Okinawa Gunto in April 1945. The ship was decommissioned and transferred to the United States Army on 6 May 1946. *LST–799* was returned to the United States Navy and recommissioned on 26 August 1950. She performed extensive service during the Korean War. On 1 July 1955, she was redesignated *Greer County* (LST–799) (*q.v.*) after a county in Oklahoma and assigned to the U.S. Pacific Fleet until she was struck from the Navy list on 1 November 1960 and sold for scrapping.

LST–799 earned one battle star for World War II service and the Navy Unit Commendation, the Korean Presidential Unit Citation, and nine battle stars for the Korean War.

LST–800

LST–800 was laid down on 29 August 1944 at Jeffersonville, Ind., by the Jeffersonville Boat & Machine Co.; launched on 10 October 1944; sponsored by Mrs. Roger C. Heimer; and commissioned on 2 November 1944, Lt. H. G. Chandler, Jr., in command.

Following World War II, *LST–800* performed occupation duty in the Far East until late October 1945. She returned to the United States and was decommissioned on 1 May 1946 and struck from the Navy list on 3 July that same year. On 22 December 1947, the ship was sold to the Humble Oil & Refining Co., of Houston, Tex., for operation.

LST–801

LST–801 was laid down on 6 September 1944 at Jeffersonville, Ind., by the Jeffersonville Boat and Machine Co.; launched on 14 October 1944; sponsored by Miss Jane E. Calhoun; and commissioned on 8 November 1944, Lt. Herbert G. Whitehead, USNR, in command.

During World War II, *LST-801* was assigned to the Asiatic-Pacific theater and participated in the assault and occupation of Okinawa Gunto from March through June 1945. Following the war, *LST-801* performed occupation duty in the Far East until early March 1946. She returned to the United States and was decommissioned on 18 July 1946 and struck from the Navy list on 18 August that same year. On 29 December 1947, the ship was sold to Pablo N. Ferrari & Co. for operation.

LST-801 earned one battle star for World War II service.

LST-802

LST-802 was laid down on 2 September 1944 at Jeffersonville, Ind., by the Jeffersonville Boat and Machine Co.; launched on 19 October 1944; sponsored by Mrs. Dolores Alberts; and commissioned on 13 November 1944, Lt. K. G. Adams, USNR, in command.

During World War II, *LST-802* was assigned to the Asiatic-Pacific theater and participated in the assault and occupation of Okinawa Gunto in May and June 1945. Following the war, *LST-802* performed occupation duty in the Far East until mid-April 1946. The ship was decommissioned on 21 July 1946 and transferred to the Shipping Control Authority, Japan, until returned to the Navy and recommissioned on 30 August 1950. She took part in the invasions of Inchon and Wonsan and the evacuation of Hungnam during the Korean War. Following conversion to a mine squadron flagship in 1954, she served with units of Mine Force, Pacific.

On 1 July 1955, *LST-802* was redesignated *Hamilton County* (LST-802) (*q.v.*) after counties in Florida, Illinois, Indiana, Iowa, Kansas, Nebraska, New York, Ohio, Tennessee and Texas. Loaned to Japan on 20 April 1960 under terms of the Military Assistance Program, *Hamilton County* was decommissioned on 30 June 1960 and struck from the Navy list on 1 July that same year.

LST-802 earned one battle star for World War II service and seven for the Korean War.

LST-803

LST-803 was laid down on 14 September 1944 at Jeffersonville, Ind., by the Jeffersonville Boat and Machine Co.; launched on 23 October 1944; sponsored by Mrs. Katie Bryant; and commissioned on 17 November 1944, Lt. Henry M. Parsons, USNR, in command.

During World War II, *LST-803* was assigned to the Asiatic-Pacific theater and participated in the assault and occupation of Okinawa Gunto from April through June 1945. *LST-803* performed occupation duty in the Far East until mid-May 1947. Following the war, *LST-803* saw service in the Marianas as a utility vessel until decommissioned on 26 March 1949. Recommissioned on 15 November 1950, she saw extensive service during the Korean War.

On 1 July 1955, *LST-803* was redesignated *Hampden County* (LST-803) (*q.v.*) after a county in Massachusetts. Following further service in the Pacific, she was once again decommissioned on 2 January 1958. *Hampden County* (LST-803) was struck from the Navy list on 17 April 1958 and sunk as a target on 26 September 1958.

LST-803 earned one battle star for World War II service and five for the Korean War.

LST-804

LST-804 was laid down on 10 September 1944 at Jeffersonville, Ind., by the Jeffersonville Boat and Machine Co.; launched on 27 October 1944; sponsored by Mrs. Carol B. Mann; and commissioned on 22 November 1944, Lt. R. Bull in command.

During World War II, *LST-804* was assigned to the Asiatic-Pacific theater and participated in the assault and occupation of Okinawa Gunto from April through June 1945. Following the war, *LST-804* performed occupation duty in the Far East and saw service in China until early May 1946. She was decommissioned on 24 May 1946 and transferred to the State Department for ultimate disposition. The ship was struck from the Navy list on 3 July 1946.

LST-804 earned one battle star for World War II service.

LST-805

LST-805 was laid down on 22 September 1944 at Jeffersonville, Ind., by the Jeffersonville Boat and Machine Co.; launched on 31 October 1944; and commissioned on 27 November 1944.

During World War II, *LST-805* was assigned to the Asiatic-Pacific theater and participated in the assault and occupation of Okinawa Gunto in June 1945. Following the war, *LST-805* performed occupation duty in the Far East until February 1946. She was decommissioned on 25 May 1946 and struck from the Navy list on 19 July that same year. On 5 November 1947, the ship was sold to Bosey, Philippines.

LST-805 earned one battle star for World War II service.

LST-806

LST-806 was laid down on 25 July 1944 at Evansville, Ind., by the Missouri Valley Bridge & Iron Co.; launched on 7 September 1944; sponsored by Mrs. Harold S. Miller; and commissioned on 28 September 1944.

During World War II, *LST-806* was assigned to the Asiatic-Pacific theater and participated in the Palawan Island landings in February and March 1945 and performed minesweeping operations in the Pacific from November 1945 through February 1946. She was decommissioned on 20 May 1946 and struck from the Navy list on 19 July that same year. On 20 November 1947, the ship was sold to Bosey, Philippines.

LST-806 earned two battle stars for World War II service.

LST-807

LST-807 was laid down on 29 July 1944 at Evansville, Ind., by the Missouri Valley Bridge & Iron Co.; launched on 11 September 1944; sponsored by Mrs. Barney C. King; and commissioned on 3 October 1944, Lt. J. D. Holder, USNR, in command.

During World War II, *LST-807* was assigned to the Asiatic-Pacific theater and participated in the assault and occupation of Iwo Jima in February 1945 and the assault and occupation of Okinawa Gunto in May and June 1945. Following the war, *LST-807* performed occupation duty in the Far East and saw service in China until mid-May 1946. She was decommissioned on 27 May 1946 and transferred to the State Department for disposition. The ship was struck from the Navy list on 3 July 1946.

LST-807 earned two battle stars for World War II service.

LST-808

LST-808 was laid down on 1 August 1944 at Evansville, Ind., by the Missouri Valley Bridge & Iron Co.; launched on 15 September 1944; sponsored by Mrs. W. I. Oliver; and commissioned on 29 September 1944.

During World War II, *LST-808* was assigned to the Asiatic-Pacific theater and participated in the assault and occupation of Iwo Jima in Feburary 1945 and the assault and occupation of Okinawa Gunto from April through June 1945. *LST–808* was torpedoed by a Japanese kamikaze off Ie Shima on 18 May 1945. Grounded on a reef following the torpedoing, she was destroyed on 11 November 1945 and struck from the Navy list.

LST–808 earned two battle stars for World War II service.

LST–809

LST–809 was laid down on 5 August 1944 at Evansville, Ind., by the Missouri Valley Bridge & Iron Co.; launched on 19 September 1944; sponsored by Mrs. H. G. Kipke; and commissioned on 10 October 1944.

During World War II, *LST–809* was assigned to the Asiatic-Pacific theater and participated in the assault and occupation of Iwo Jima in February 1945 and the assault and occupation of Okinawa Gunto from April through June 1945. Following the war, *LST–809* performed occupation duty in the Far East until early March 1946. She was decommissioned on 15 July 1946 and struck from the Navy list on 18 August that same year. On 19 May 1948, the ship was sold to the Bethleham Steel Co., of Bethlehem, Pa., for scrapping.

LST–809 earned two battle stars for World War II service.

LST–810

LST–810 was laid down on 8 August 1944 at Evansville, Ind., by the Missouri Valley Bridge & Iron Co.; launched on 21 September 1944; sponsored by Mrs. Leonard S. Shroyer; and commissioned on 13 October 1944.

During World War II, *LST–810* was assigned to the Asiatic-Pacific theater and participated in the assault and occupation of Okinawa Gunto from April through June 1945. Following the war, *LST–810* performed occupation duty in the Far East until early February 1946. She returned to the United States and was decommissioned on 18 July 1946 and struck from the Navy list on 28 August that same year. On 14 October 1947, the ship was sold to William E. Skinner, of New York City, N.Y., for scrapping.

LST–810 earned one battle star for World War II service.

LST–811

LST–811 was laid down on 12 August 1944 at Evansville, Ind., by the Missouri Valley Bridge & Iron Co.; launched on 23 September 1944; sponsored by Ens. Frances J. Russell, USNR(W); and commissioned on 18 October 1944, Lt. William J. Loeper, USNR, in command.

During World War II, *LST–811* was assigned to the Asiatic-Pacific theater and participated in the assault and occupation of Okinawa Gunto from March through June 1945. Following the war, *LST–811* performed occupation duty in the Far East until early March 1946. She returned to the United States and was decommissioned on 26 June 1946 and struck from the Navy list on 31 July that same year. On 4 November 1947, the ship was sold to Dulien Steel Products Inc., of Seattle, Wash., for scrapping.

LST–811 earned one battle star for World War II service.

LST–812

LST–812 was laid down on 14 August 1944 at Evansville, Ind., by the Missouri Valley Bridge & Iron Co.; launched on 27 September 1944; sponsored by Mrs. John J. Allan; and commissioned on 19 October 1944.

During World War II, *LST–812* was assigned to the Asiatic-Pacific theater and participated in the assault and occupation of Iwo Jima in February 1945 and the assault and occupation of Okinawa Gunto from April through June 1945. Following the war, *LST–812* performed occupation duty in the Far East until mid-December 1945. She returned to the United States and was decommissioned on 9 May 1946 and struck from the Navy list on 19 June that same year. On 25 May 1948, the ship was sold to the Bethlehem Steel Co., of Bethlehem, Pa., for scrapping.

LST–812 earned two battle stars for World War II service.

LST–813

LST–813 was laid down on 20 August 1944 at Evansville, Ind., by the Missouri Valley Bridge & Iron Co.; launched on 30 Sepember 1944; sponsored by Mrs. Pete Smith; and commissioned on 24 October 1944.

During World War II, *LST–813* was assigned to the Asiatic-Pacific theater and participated in the assault and occupation of Okinawa Gunto from March through May 1945. Following the war, *LST–813* performed occupation duty in the Far East until mid-April 1946. She returned to the United States and was decommissioned on 21 June 1946 and struck from the Navy list on 31 July that same year. On 12 June 1948, the ship was sold to the Walter W. Johnson Co. for scrapping.

LST–813 earned one battle star for World War II service.

LST–814

LST–814 was laid down on 25 August 1944 at Evansville, Ind., by the Missouri Valley Bridge & Iron Co.; launched on 4 October 1944; sponsored by Mrs. William B. Fletcher; and commissioned on 27 October 1944.

During World War II, *LST–814* was assigned to the Asiatic-Pacific theater and participated in the assault and occupation of Okinawa Gunto from March through May 1945. Following the end of the war, in September 1945, *LST–814* performed occupation duty in the Far East until mid-April 1946. During this period, she was severely damaged during a beaching operation off Sasebo, Japan, on 30 December 1945. The tank landing ship was decommissioned on 16 April 1946 and struck from the Navy list on 8 May that same year. *LST–814* was later sunk on 12 August 1946.

LST–814 earned one battle star for World War II service.

LST–815

LST–815 was laid down on 28 August 1944 at Evansville, Ind., by the Missouri Valley Bridge & Iron Co.; launched on 7 October 1944; sponsored by Miss Elizabeth Sweet; and commissioned on 30 October 1944.

During World War II, *LST–815* was assigned to the Asiatic-Pacific theater and participated in the assault and occupation of Okinawa Gunto from April through June 1945. Following the war, *LST–815* performed occupation duty in the Far East until early November 1945. She returned to the United States and was decommissioned on 6 September 1946. On 25 May 1948, the ship was sold to the Basalt Rock Co., Inc., for scrapping.

LST–815 earned one battle star for World War II service.

LST–816

LST–816 was laid down on 2 September 1944 at Evansville, Ind., by the Missouri Valley Bridge & Iron Co.; launched on 11 October 1944; sponsored by Mrs. Walter Smith; and commissioned on 2 November 1944, Lt. Charles Danziger, USNR, in command.

During World War II, *LST–816* was assigned to the Asiatic-Pacific theater and participated in the assault

and occupation of Iwo Jima in March and April 1945 and the assault and occupation of Okinawa Gunto in May and June 1945. Following the war, she performed occupation duty in the Far East until early April 1946. *LST–816* returned to the United States and was decommissioned on 29 June 1946 and struck from the Navy list on 31 July that same year. On 27 May 1948, the tank landing ship was sold to the Bethlehem Steel Co., Bethlehem, Pa., for scrapping.

LST–816 earned two battle stars for World War II service.

LST–817

LST–817 was laid down on 4 September 1944 at Evansville, Ind., by the Missouri Valley Bridge & Iron Co.; launched on 14 October 1944; sponsored by Mrs. Raymond Yelling; and commissioned on 7 November 1944, Lt. R. K. McInnes, USNR, in command.

During World War II, *LST–817* was assigned to the Asiatic-Pacific theater and participated in the assault and occupation of Okinawa Gunto from April through June 1945. Following the war, she performed occupation duty in the Far East until early November 1945. The tank landing ship returned to the United States and was decommissioned on 31 January 1947 and struck from the Navy list on 7 February that same year. On 25 May 1948, the ship was sold to the Basalt Rock Co., Inc., Napa, Calif., and subsequently scrapped.

LST–817 earned one battle star for World War II service.

LST–818

LST–818 was laid down on 8 September 1944 at Evansville, Ind., by the Missouri Valley Bridge & Iron Co.; launched on 18 October 1944; sponsored by Mrs. Roscoe B. Huffman; and commissioned on 9 November 1944, Lt. (jg.) Robert B. Bradley in command.

During World War II, *LST–818* was assigned to the Asiatic-Pacific theater and participated in the assault and occupation of Okinawa Gunto from March through June 1945. She returned to the United States and was decommisioned on 16 July 1946 and struck from the Navy list on 28 August that same year. On 17 September 1947, the ship was sold to Consolidated Builders, Inc., Seattle, Wash., and subsequently scrapped.

LST–818 earned one battle star for World War II service.

LST–819

LST–819 was laid down on 12 September 1944 at Evansville, Ind., by the Missouri Valley Bridge & Iron Co.; launched on 21 October 1944; sponsored by Mrs. Georgia E. Gilmore; and commissioned on 14 November 1944, Lt. George W. Ryerson, USNR, in command.

During World War II, *LST–819* was assigned to the Asiatic-Pacific theater and participated in the assault and occupation of Okinawa Gunto from April through June 1945. She returned to the United States and was decommissioned on 15 November 1946 and assigned to the Pacific Reserve Fleet.

Recommissioned on 8 September 1950, *LST–819* saw extensive service during the Korean War. The ship was decommissioned again on 24 June 1955. On 1 July 1955, *LST–819* was redesignated *Hampshire County* (LST–819) (*q.v.*) after counties in Massachusetts and West Virginia. Once more commissioned on 9 July 1966, *Hampshire County* supported the Navy's efforts off South Vietnam until decommissioned for the final time on 19 December 1970. The tank landing ship was struck from the Navy list in April 1975.

LST–819 received one battle star for World War II service and four for the Korean War. Additionally,

Hampshire County (LST–819) was awarded 10 battle stars, the Presidential Unit Citation, and the Navy Unit Commendation for the Vietnam War.

LST–820

LST–820 was laid down on 14 September 1944 at Evansville, Ind., by the Missouri Valley Bridge & Iron Co.; launched on 25 October 1944; sponsored by Mrs. Tom K. Smith; and commissioned on 16 November 1944, Lt. W. R. Evans in command.

During World War II, *LST–820* was assigned to the Asiatic-Pacific theater and participated in the assault and occupation of Okinawa Gunto in May and June 1945. Following the war, she performed occupation duty in the Far East until early October 1945. The tank landing ship returned to the United States and was decommissioned on 16 January 1946 and struck from the Navy list on 7 February that same year.

LST–820 earned one battle star for World War II service.

LST–821

LST–821 was laid down on 19 September 1944 at Evansville, Ind., by the Missouri Valley Bridge & Iron Co.; launched on 27 October 1944; sponsored by Mrs. Hugh Robertson, Sr.; and commissioned on 14 November 1944, Lt. C. J. Rudine, USNR, in command.

During World War II, *LST–821* was assigned to the Asiatic-Pacific theater and participated in the assault and occupation of Okinawa Gunto from April through June 1945. Following the war, she performed occupation duty in the Far East until early December 1945. *LST–821* returned to the United States and was decommissioned in March 1946 and assigned to the Pacific Reserve Fleet. On 1 July 1955, the ship was redesignated *Harnett County* (LST–821) (*q.v.*) after a county in North Carolina.

Recommissioned on 20 August 1966, *Harnett County* (LST–821) saw extensive service in the Vietnam War.

LST–821 earned one battle star for World War II service. Additionally, *Harnett County* (LST–821) earned nine battle stars, two awards of the Presidential Unit Citation, and three awards of the Navy Unit Commendation for the Vietnam War.

LST–822

LST–822 was laid down on 20 September 1944 at Evansville, Ind., by the Missouri Valley Bridge & Iron Co.; launched on 1 November 1944; sponsored by Mrs. Homer Seed; and commissioned on 23 November 1944, Lt. Robert N. McIntyre, USNR, in command.

During World War II, *LST–822* was assigned to the Asiatic-Pacific theater and participated in the assault and occupation of Okinawa Gunto in April and May 1945. Following the war, she performed occupation duty in the Far East until early March 1946. *LST–822* was decommissioned on 10 August 1946 and assigned to the Pacific Reserve Fleet. Recommissioned on 23 November 1950, she performed extensive service during the Korean War, including participation in the historic prisoner-of-war exchanges.

LST–822 was redesignated *Harris County* (LST–822) (*q.v.*) on 1 July 1955 after counties in Georgia and Texas. She was decommissioned for a second time in late 1955 and transferred to the Military Sea Transportation Service. *Harris County* was transferred to the Philippine Navy on 13 September 1976.

LST–822 earned one battle star for World War II service and four for Korean War service.

LST–823

LST–823 was laid down on 25 September 1944 at Evansville, Ind., by the Missouri Valley Bridge & Iron

Vernon County (LST–1161) lands vehicles over a pontoon causeway. These causeways came into standard use during World War II for landings on beaches where the gradient was too shallow to permit direct beaching. All LST's are fitted to carry causeway sections mounted on their sides and can tow additional sections if needed. When, as seen here, a long distance has to be covered, a number of LST's join their causeway sections together and take turns unloading.

Co.; launched on 4 November 1944; sponsored by Miss Olinda M. Brune; and commissioned on 28 November 1944, Lt. Robert T. Hanson, USNR, in command.

During World War II, *LST–823* was assigned to the Asiatic-Pacific theater and participated in the assault and occupation of Okinawa Gunto in June 1945. Following the war, she performed occupation duty in the Far East until early December 1945. The ship was decommissioned on 1 December 1945 and struck from the Navy list on 3 January 1946. In May 1947, the tank landing ship was sold to the Oklahoma-Philippines Co.

LST–823 earned one battle star for World War II service.

LST–824

LST–824 was laid down on 28 September 1944 at Evansville, Ind., by the Missouri Valley Bridge & Iron Co.; launched on 8 November 1944; sponsored by Mrs.

Harry W. Groot; and commissioned on 30 November 1944, Lt. Jesse D. Jones, USNR, in command.

During World War II, *LST–824* was assigned to the Asiatic-Pacific theater and participated in the assault and occupation of Okinawa Gunto from April through June 1945. Following the war, she performed occupation duty in the Far East until late September 1945. The ship was decommissioned on 15 May 1946 and assigned to the Pacific Reserve Fleet. The tank landing ship was redesignated *Henry County* (LST–824) (*q.v.*) on 1 July 1955 after counties in Alabama, Georgia, Illinois, Indiana, Iowa, Kentucky, Missouri, Ohio, Tennessee, and Virginia.

Recommissioned on 5 September 1959, *Henry County* performed extensive service with the Pacific Fleet and, commencing in 1965, participated in operations in the Vietnam theater. Later decommissioned again, *Henry County* was transferred to the Malaysian Navy where she served as *Sri Banggi* (A–1501).

LST–824 earned one battle star for World War II service and four for Vietnam service.

LST-825

LST–825 was laid down on 2 October 1944 at Evansville, Ind., by the Missouri Valley Bridge & Iron Co.; launched on 11 November 1944; sponsored by Mrs. John Spindler; and commissioned on 8 December 1944, Lt. Harry V. Hartsell in command.

During World War II, LST–825 was assigned to the Asiatic-Pacific theater and participated in the assault and occupation of Okinawa Gunto from April through June 1945. Following the war, she performed occupation duty in the Far East until early November 1945. The ship returned to the United States and was decommissioned on 22 May 1946 and assigned to the Pacific Reserve Fleet.

Recommissioned on 3 November 1950, she performed extensive service during the Korean War. On 1 July 1955, the tank landing ship was redesignated Hickman County (LST–825) (q.v.) after counties in Kentucky and Tennessee. She was decommissioned again on 20 May 1956. Recommissioned on 22 March 1963, Hickman County performed active service with the Atlantic Reserve Fleet until 1966 when she was transferred to the Service Force, Pacific Fleet, for service in Vietnam. In November 1969, Hickman County was sold to the Philippine government.

LST–825 earned one battle star for World War II service, two for the Korean War, and 10 for the Vietnam War.

LST-826

LST–826 was laid down on 6 October 1944 at Evansville, Ind., by the Missouri Valley Bridge & Iron Co.; launched on 14 November 1944; sponsored by Mrs. W. E. Haynie; and commissioned on 7 December 1944, Lt. John G. Mahler, USNR, in command.

During World War II, LST–826 was assigned to the Asiatic-Pacific theater and participated in the assault and occupation of Okinawa Gunto in May and June 1945. Following the war, she performed occupation duty in the Far East until early December 1945.

LST–826 earned one battle star for World War II service.

LST-827

LST–827 was laid down on 9 October 1944 at Evansville, Ind., by the Missouri Valley Bridge & Iron Co.; launched on 16 November 1944; sponsored by Mrs. Clark H. Woodward; and commissioned on 12 December 1944, Lt. R. L. Olander, USNR, in command.

During World War II, LST–827 was assigned to the Asiatic-Pacific theater and participated in the assault and occupation of Okinawa Gunto in May and June 1945. Following the war, the ship performed occupation duty in the Far East until mid-September 1945. She returned to the United States and was decommissioned on 7 June 1949 and assigned to the Pacific Reserve Fleet. Recommissioned on 3 November 1950, LST–827 saw extensive service during the Korean War. On 1 July 1955, she was redesignated Hillsborough County (LST–827) (q.v.) after counties in Florida and New Hampshire. Decommissioned again on 22 January 1958, Hillsborough County was struck from the Navy list on 28 March 1958. She was sunk as a target off the California coast on 14 August that same year.

LST–827 earned one battle star for World War II service and three for the Korean War.

LST-828

LST–828 was laid down on 13 October 1944 at Evansville, Ind., by the Missouri Valley Bridge & Iron Co.; launched on 22 November 1944; sponsored by Mrs. David M. Hammond; and commissioned on 13 December 1944, Lt. Richard P. Trenbeth, USNR, in command.

During World War II, LST–828 was assigned to the Asiatic-Pacific theater and participated in the assault and occupation of Okinawa Gunto from April through June 1945. Following the war, the ship performed occupation duty in the Far East until early January 1946. LST–828 was decommissioned on 22 April 1947. Usable equipment was removed, and the residual hulk was destroyed on 7 May 1947 in the Marianas. She was struck from the Navy list on 22 May 1947.

LST–828 earned one battle star for World War II service.

LST-829

LST–829 was laid down on 10 August 1944 at Ambridge, Pa., by the American Bridge Co.; launched on 26 September 1944; sponsored by Mrs. A. Tarasi; and commissioned on 23 October 1944, Lt. Harry A. Friedenberg, USCGR, in command.

During World War II, LST–829 was assigned to the Asiatic-Pacific theater and participated in the assault and occupation of Okinawa Gunto in March and April 1945. Following the war, she performed occupation duty in the Far East until early November 1945. LST–829 was transferred to the Maritime Administration for disposal on 19 March 1948.

LST–829 earned one battle star for World War II service.

LST-830

LST–830 was laid down on 15 August 1944 at Ambridge, Pa., by the American Bridge Co.; launched on 30 September 1944; sponsored by Mrs. J. C. Augsburger; and commissioned on 28 October 1944, Lt. Gordon Rowe, USCGR, in command.

During World War II, LST–830 was assigned to the Asiatic-Pacific theater and participated in the assault and occupation of Okinawa Gunto in April 1945. Following the war, she performed occupation duty in the Far East until mid-November 1945. The ship was decommissioned on 29 April 1946 and struck from the Navy list on 3 July that same year. On 8 July 1947, she was sold to Compania Naviera, Argentina, Buenos Aires, Argentina, for operation.

LST–830 earned one battle star for World War II service.

LST-831

LST–831 was laid down on 19 August 1944 at Ambridge, Pa., by the American Bridge Co.; launched on 6 October 1944; sponsored by Mrs. C. J. Connolly; and commissioned on 8 November 1944.

During World War II, LST–831 was assigned to the Asiatic-Pacific theater and participated in the assault and occupation of Okinawa Gunto from April through June 1945. Following the war, she performed occupation duty in the Far East until early November 1945. The tank landing ship was transferred to the Maritime Administration for final disposition on 19 December 1947.

LST–831 earned one battle star for World War II service.

LST-832

LST–832 was laid down on 25 August 1944 at Ambridge, Pa., by the American Bridge Co.; launched on 11 October 1944; sponsored by Mrs. J. Blessing; and commissioned on 4 November 1944, Lt. W. H. Young, USCGR, in command.

During World War II, LST–832 was assigned to the Asiatic-Pacific theater and participated in the assault and occupation of Okinawa Gunto from April through June 1945. Following the war, she performed occupation duty in the Far East until mid-December 1945. *LST–832* returned to the United States and was decommissioned on 30 April 1946 and struck from the Navy list on 3 July that same year. On 12 March 1948, the ship was sold to the Alexander Shipyards, Inc., New Orleans, La., for operation.

LST–832 earned one battle star for World War II service.

LST–833

LST–833 was laid down on 28 August 1944 at Ambridge, Pa., by the American Bridge Co.; launched on 16 October 1944; sponsored by Mrs. N. B. Ornitz; and commissioned on 10 November 1944.

During World War II, *LST–833* was assigned to the Asiatic-Pacific theater and participated in the assault and occupation of Okinawa Gunto from April through June 1945. Following the war, she performed occupation duty in the Far East and saw service in China until early January 1946. The ship returned to the United States and was decommissioned on 2 May 1946 and struck from the Navy list on 10 June 1947. On 13 May 1948, she was sold to the Alexander Shipyards, Inc., New Orleans, La., for operation.

LST–833 earned one battle star for World War II service.

LST–834

LST–834 was laid down on 2 September 1944 at Ambridge Pa., by the American Bridge Co.; launched on 20 October 1944; sponsored by Mrs. Harold Oberg; and commissioned on 10 November 1944, Lt. R. J. Bentley, USNR, in command.

During World War II, *LST–834* was assigned to the Asiatic-Pacific theater and participated in the assault and occupation of Okinawa Gunto in April 1945. Following the war, she performed occupation duty in the Far East and saw service in China until early June 1946. The ship returned to the United States and was decommissioned on 12 September 1946 and struck from the Navy list on 8 October that same year. On 13 December 1947, she was sold to Kaiser Co., Inc., Seattle, Wash., for scrapping.

LST–834 earned one battle star for World War II service.

LST–835

LST–835 was laid down on 6 September 1944 at Ambridge, Pa., by the American Bridge Co.; launched on 25 October 1944; sponsored by Mrs. I. Raphael; and commissioned on 20 November 1944, Lt. William H. McHenry in command.

During World War II, *LST–835* was assigned to the Asiatic-Pacific theater and participated in the assault and occupation of Okinawa Gunto in May and June 1945. Following the war, she performed occupation duty in the Far East until early November 1945. The ship was decommissioned in March 1946 and assigned to the Pacific Reserve Fleet. On 1 July 1955, she was redesignated *Hillsdale County* (LST–835) (q.v.) after a county in Michigan. The tank landing ship was struck from the Navy list in October 1959 and sold to Japan in April 1961 where she serves as *Shimokita* (LST–4002).

LST–835 earned one battle star for World War II service.

LST–836

LST–836 was laid down on 11 September 1944 at Ambridge, Pa., by the American Bridge Co.; launched on 29 October 1944; sponsored by Mrs. H. E. Hetu; and commissioned on 25 November 1944, Lt. Elmo J. Sullivan, USNR, in command.

During World War II, *LST–836* was assigned to the Asiatic-Pacific theater and participated in the assault and occupation of Okinawa Gunto in April 1945. Following the war, the ship performed occupation duty in the Far East until mid-December 1945. She was decommissioned on 25 July 1946 and assigned to the Pacific Reserve Fleet. Recommissioned on 3 November 1950, *LST–836* saw extensive service during the Korean War. On 1 July 1955, she was redesignated *Holmes County* (LST–836) (q.v.) after counties in Florida, Mississippi, and Ohio.

Commencing in 1965, *Holmes County* also saw service during the Vietnam War. Decommissioned again in early 1971, *Holmes County* was transferred to the government of Singapore on 1 July 1971 and renamed RS *Endurance*.

LST–836 earned one star for World War II service, three for the Korean War, and 12 battle stars and two awards of the Navy Unit Commendation for the Vietnam War.

LST–837

LST–837 was laid down on 15 September 1944 at Ambridge, Pa., by the American Bridge Co.; launched on 3 November 1944; sponsored by Mrs. H. G. Jetter; and commissioned on 29 November 1944, Lt. G. R. Keller, USNR, in command.

During World War II, *LST–837* was assigned to the Asiatic-Pacific theater and participated in the assault and occupation of Okinawa Gunto in April 1945. Following the war, she performed occupation duty in the Far East and saw service in China until mid-March 1946. The ship returned to the United States and was decommissioned on 28 June 1946 and struck from the Navy list on 15 August that same year. On 6 February 1948, she was sold to Madison B. Wright for non-self-propelled operation.

LST–837 earned one battle star for World War II service.

LST–838

LST–838 was laid down on 20 September 1944 at Ambridge, Pa., by the American Bridge Co.; launched on 8 November 1944; sponsored by Miss Margaret Foster; and commissioned on 4 December 1944, Lt. Allen T. Larkins, Jr., in command.

During World War II, *LST–838* was assigned to the Asiatic-Pacific theater and participated in the assault and occupation of Okinawa Gunto in April 1945. Following the war, the ship performed occupation duty in the Far East until early November 1945. She returned to the United States and was decommissioned on 7 August 1946 and assigned to the Pacific Reserve Fleet. On 1 July 1955, she was redesignated *Hunterdon County* (LST–838) (q.v.) after a county in New Jersey.

Recommissioned on 10 September 1966, *Hunterdon County* saw extensive service during the Vietnam War.

LST–838 earned one battle star for World War II service. Additionally, *Hunterdon County* earned seven battle stars, two awards of the Presidential Unit Citation, and four awards of the Navy Unit Commendation for the Vietnam War.

LST–839

LST–839 was laid down on 25 September 1944 at Ambridge, Pa., by the American Bridge Co.; launched on 12 November 1944; sponsored by Mrs. Arthur Lehner; and commissioned on 6 December 1944, Lt. Waldo F. McNeir in command.

During World War II, *LST–839* was assigned to the Asiatic-Pacific theater and participated in the assault

and occupation of Okinawa Gunto from April through June 1945. Following the war, the ship performed occupation duty in the Far East until mid-September 1945. She returned to the United States and was decommissioned in March 1946 and assigned to the Pacific Reserve Fleet. On 1 July 1955, she was redesignated *Iredell County* (LST–839) (*q.v.*) after a county in North Carolina.

Recommissioned on 18 June 1966, *Iredell County* saw extensive service during the Vietnam War. She was decommissioned again and transferred to the Indonesian Navy in July 1970 where she serves as *Teluk Bone*.

LST–839 earned one battle star for World War II service. Additionally, *Iredell County* earned 11 battle stars and single awards of the Presidential Unit Citation, the Navy Unit Commendation, and the Meritorious Unit Commendation for the Vietnam War.

LST–840

LST–840 was laid down on 28 September 1944 at Ambridge, Pa., by the American Bridge Co.; launched on 15 November 1944; sponsored by Mrs. C. W. Doerr; and commissioned on 11 December 1944, Lt. David McC. Bon, USNR, in command.

During World War II, *LST–840* was assigned to the Asiatic-Pacific theater and participated in the assault and occupation of Okinawa Gunto in April 1945. Following the war, the ship performed occupation duty in the Far East until mid-October 1945. She returned to the United States and was decommissioned on 1 June 1946 and assigned to the Pacific Reserve Fleet.

Recommissioned on 3 November 1950, *LST–840* performed extensive service during the Korean War. On 1 July 1955, she was redesignated *Iron County* (LST–840) (*q.v.*) after counties in Michigan, Missouri, Utah, and Wisconsin. Decommissioned again on 23 November 1957, *Iron County* was transferred to the Republic of China Navy on 1 July 1958, where she served as *Chung Fu* (LST–223). *Iron County* was struck from the Navy list on 6 February 1959.

LST–840 earned one battle star for World War II and four for the Korean War.

LST–841

LST–841 was laid down on 4 October 1944 at Ambridge, Pa., by the American Bridge Co.; launched on 20 November 1944; sponsored by Mrs. Rocco Palmer; and commissioned on 18 December 1944, Lt. Francis T. Carey, USNR, in command.

During World War II, *LST–841* was assigned to the Asiatic-Pacific theater and participated in the assault and occupation of Okinawa Gunto from April through June 1945. Following the war, the ship performed occupation duty in the Far East and saw service in China until mid-February 1946. She returned to the United States and was decommissioned on 25 June 1946 and struck from the Navy list on 23 June 1947. On 5 January 1948, the tank landing ship was sold to the California Co., New Orleans, La., for operation.

LST–841 earned one battle star for World War II service.

LST–842

LST–842 was laid down on 9 October 1944 at Ambridge, Pa., by the American Bridge Co.; launched on 24 November 1944; sponsored by Mrs. F. T. Hulet; and commissioned on 19 December 1944.

During World War II, *LST–842* was assigned to the Asiatic-Pacific theater and participated in the assault and occupation of Okinawa Gunto in June 1945. Following the war, the ship performed occupation duty in the Far East until mid-September 1945. She was

decommissioned on 30 December 1947 and transferred to the Philippine government. On 22 January 1948, the tank landing ship was struck from the Navy list.

LST–842 earned one battle star for World War II service.

LST–843

LST–843 was laid down on 13 October 1944 at Ambridge, Pa., by the American Bridge Co.; launched on 29 November 1944; sponsored by Mrs. R. S. Dyson; and commissioned on 23 December 1944, Lt. V. W. Tracy in command.

During World War II, *LST–843* was assigned to the Asiatic-Pacific theater and participated in the assault and occupation of Okinawa Gunto from April through June 1945. Following the war, the ship performed occupation duty in the Far East and saw service in China until early December 1947. She was decommissioned on 18 December 1947 and transferred to the Philippine government. On 22 January 1948, the tank landing ship was struck from the Navy list.

LST–843 earned one battle star for World War II service.

LST–844

LST–844 was laid down on 18 October 1944 at Ambridge, Pa., by the American Bridge Co.; launched on 3 December 1944; sponsored by Mrs. D. P. Cook; and commissioned on 30 December 1944, Lt. James F. Trawick in command.

During World War II, *LST–844* was assigned to the Asiatic-Pacific theater and participated in the assault and occupation of Okinawa Gunto in May and June 1945. Following the war, the ship performed occupation duty in the Far East until early November 1945. She returned to the United States and was decommissioned on 15 September 1947 and struck from the Navy list on 29 September that same year. On 28 June 1948, the tank landing ship was sold to the Humble Oil & Refining Co., Houston, Tex., for operation.

LST–844 earned one battle star for World War II service.

LST–845

LST–845 was laid down on 23 October 1944 at Ambridge, Pa., by the American Bridge Co.; launched on 7 December 1944; sponsored by Mrs. B. F. Fairless; and commissioned on 9 January 1945, Lt. Comdr. John Wildman, USNR, in command.

LST–845 participated in no combat operations during World War II but performed Asian occupation service following the war until the summer of 1946. Operating out of San Diego in the postwar years, she saw extensive service during the Korean War. On 1 July 1955, the ship was redesignated *Jefferson County* (LST–845) (*q.v.*) after counties in 25 states. Following further service with the Pacific Fleet, *Jefferson County* was decommissioned in early 1961. She was struck from the Navy list on 1 February 1961. On 22 August 1961, the tank landing ship was sold to Zidell Explorations, Inc., Portland, Oreg.

LST–845 earned six battle stars for the Korean War.

LST–846

LST–846 was laid down on 27 October 1944 at Ambridge, Pa., by the American Bridge Co.; launched on 12 December 1944; sponsored by Mrs. L. P. Quill; and commissioned on 9 January 1945.

Following World War II, *LST–846* performed occupation duty in the Far East and saw service in China until late April 1949. After postwar service, *LST–846* was decommissioned on 14 October 1949. Recommissioned on 3 November 1950, she performed service during the Korean War. On 1 July 1955, the ship was redesignated *Jennings County* (LST–846) (*q.v.*) after a county in Indiana.

Decommissioned again on 7 December 1955, *Jennings County* was once again commissioned on 11 June 1966 and conducted extensive operations during the Vietnam War. Decommissioned for a final time, she was struck from the Navy list on 25 September 1970.

LST–846 earned one battle star for the Korean War and two awards of the Presidential Unit Citation, four awards of the Navy Unit Commendation, and eight battle stars for the Vietnam War.

LST–847

LST–847 was laid down on 1 November 1944 at Ambridge, Pa., by the American Bridge Co.; launched on 17 December 1944; sponsored by Mrs. Eleanore Lott; and commissioned on 15 January 1945, Lt. G. A. Hoffman in command.

Following World War II, *LST–847* performed occupation duty and saw service in China until early March 1946. She returned to the United States and was decommissioned on 21 June 1946 and struck from the Navy list on 31 July that same year. On 13 May 1948, the ship was sold to the Alexander Shipyards, Inc., New Orleans, La., for operation.

LST–848

LST–848 was laid down on 6 November 1944 at Ambridge, Pa., by the American Bridge Co.; launched on 21 December 1944; sponsored by Mrs. F. D. Porter; and commissioned on 20 January 1945, Lt. R. P. Bentley, USNR, in command.

Following World War II, *LST–848* performed occupation duty in the Far East until early December 1945. She returned to the United States and was decommissioned on 10 August 1946 and assigned to the Pacific Reserve Fleet. On 1 July 1955, the ship was redesignated *Jerome County* (LST–848) (*q.v.*) after a county in Idaho.

Recommissioned on 7 December 1959, *Jerome County* operated with the Pacific Fleet in the early 1960's followed by extensive service in the Vietnam War. Decommissioned again on 1 April 1970, she was turned over, via lease, to the Republic of Vietnam Navy that same month.

LST–848 earned one award of the Presidential Unit Citation, one award of the Meritorious Unit Commendation, and five battle stars for the Vietnam War.

LST–849

LST–849 was laid down on 10 November 1944 at Ambridge, Pa., by the American Bridge Co.; launched on 30 December 1944; sponsored by Mrs. William B. Hetzel; and commissioned on 16 January 1945, Lt. Emil C. Hetzel in command.

During World War II, *LST–849* was assigned to the Asiatic-Pacific theater and participated in the assault and occupation of Okinawa Gunto in May and June 1945. Following the war, *LST–849* performed occupation duty in the Far East until mid-September 1945. She returned to the United States and was decommissioned on 13 June 1946 and assigned to the Pacific Reserve Fleet. On 1 July 1955, the ship was redesignated *Johnson County* (LST–849) (*q.v.*) after counties in 12 states. In January 1959, *Johnson County* was transferred to the Republic of Korea Navy where she served as *Wi Pong* (LST–812).

LST–849 earned one battle star for World War II service.

LST–850

LST–850 was laid down on 15 August 1944 at Seneca, Ill., by the Chicago Bridge & Iron Co.; launched on 3 November 1944; sponsored by Mrs. Mildred M. T. Honig; and commissioned on 27 November 1944, Lt. Perry B. Hazard in command.

During World War II, *LST–850* was assigned to the Asiatic-Pacific theater and participated in the assault and occupation of Okinawa Gunto from April through June 1945. Following the war, the ship performed occupation duty in the Far East until early October 1945. She returned to the United States and was decommissioned on 17 May 1946 and transferred to the Pacific Reserve Fleet. On 1 July 1955, she was redesignated *Juniata County* (LST–850) (*q.v.*) after a county in Pennsylvania. *Juniata County* was recommended for use as a target for destruction on 20 October 1958 and was struck from the Navy list on 1 November that same year.

LST–850 earned one battle star for World War II service.

LST–851

LST–851 was laid down on 10 August 1944 at Seneca, Ill., by the Chicago Bridge & Iron Co.; launched on 8 November 1944; sponsored by Mrs. Gertrude B. Van Trigt; and commissioned on 30 November 1944, Lt. Leo T. Tyburski in command.

During World War II, *LST–851* was assigned to the Asiatic-Pacific theater and participated in the assault and occupation of Okinawa Gunto in May 1945. Following the war, the ship performed occupation duty in the Far East until mid-October 1945. She returned to the United States and was decommissioned on 24 April 1946 and struck from the Navy list on 8 May that same year. On 30 September 1946, *LST–851* was sold to the Northwest Merchandising Service, Seattle, Wash.

LST–851 earned one battle star for World War II service.

LST–852

LST–852 was redesignated ARL–23 and named *Satyr* (*q.v.*) on 14 August 1944.

LST–853

LST–853 was laid down on 30 August 1944 at Seneca, Ill., by the Chicago Bridge & Iron Co.; launched on 17 November 1944; sponsored by Mrs. Ellen Scott De-Coursey; and commissioned on 11 December 1944, Lt. Charles B. Salsbury in command.

During World War II, *LST–853* was assigned to the Asiatic-Pacific theater and participated in the assault and occupation of Okinawa Gunto in May and June 1945. Following the war, the ship performed occupation duty in the Far East until early December 1945. She returned to the United States and was decommissioned on 24 July 1946 and assigned to the Pacific Reserve Fleet. On 1 July 1955, she was redesignated *Kane County* (LST–853) (*q.v.*) after counties in Illinois and Utah. *Kane County* was transferred to the Republic of Korea Navy on 22 December 1958 where she served as *Su Yong* (LST–813).

LST–853 earned one battle star for World War II service.

LST–854

LST–854 was laid down on 30 August 1944 at Seneca, Ill., by the Chicago Bridge & Iron Co.; launched on 20 November 1944; sponsored by Mrs. M. A. Menkol; and commissioned on 14 December 1944, Lt. E. J. Robeson in command.

Washtenaw County (LST-1166) tends river patrol craft in Vietnam. Her crew has christened the pontoon barge moored alongside the "LST 1166 Annex." Four other LST's were formally redesignated Patrol Craft Tenders (AGP) during the period between 1970 and 1972.

During World War II, *LST-854* was assigned to the Asiatic-Pacific theater and participated in the assault and occupation of Okinawa Gunto from April through June 1945. Following the war, the ship performed occupation duty in the Far East and saw service in China until early March 1949. She was decommissioned on 21 October 1949 and was recommissioned on 20 November 1950 and performed extensive service during the Korean War. On 1 July 1955, she was redesignated *Kemper County* (LST-854) (*q.v.*) after a county in Mississippi.

Continuing operations with the Pacific Fleet following the war, *Kemper County* participated in the support of the Republic of Vietnam commencing in 1965 until she was decommissioned once again on 28 May 1969.

LST-854 earned one battle star for World War II service, five for the Korean War, and one award of the Navy Unit Commendation and five battle stars for the Vietnam War.

LST–855

LST-855 was laid down on 6 September 1944 at Seneca, Ill., by the Chicago Bridge & Iron Co.; launched on 27 November 1944; sponsored by Mrs. Jeanne H. Hoerner; and commissioned on 21 December 1944, Lt. (jg.) Thomas P. Kierl in command.

Following World War II, *LST-855* performed occupation duty in the Far East and saw service in China until mid-June 1949. The ship was decommissioned on 15 February 1950. On 3 November 1950, *LST-855* was recommissioned and performed extensive service during the Korean War. On 1 July 1955, she was redesignated *Kent County* (LST-855) (*q.v.*) after counties in Delaware, Maryland, Michigan, Rhode Island, and Texas.

Following post-Korean operations with the Pacific Fleet, *Kent County* was again decommissioned on 22 January 1958 and destroyed as a target on 19 March that same year. She was struck from the Navy list on 19 March 1958.

LST-855 earned six battle stars for the Korean War.

LST–856

LST-856 was laid down on 16 September 1944 at Seneca, Ill., by the Chicago Bridge & Iron Co.; launched on 1 December 1944; sponsored by Mrs. Patricia Wiegand; and commissioned on 23 December 1944, Lt. Arthur E. Fisher in command.

During World War II, *LST-856* was assigned to the Asiatic-Pacific theater and participated in the assault and occupation of Okinawa Gunto in June 1945. Following the war, she performed occupation duty in the Far East and saw service in China until mid-February 1946. The tank landing ship returned to the

United States and was decommissioned on 29 May 1946 and struck from the Navy list on 3 July that same year. On 5 May 1948, she was sold to the Bethlehem Steel Co., Bethlehem, Pa., and subsequently scrapped.

LST-856 received one battle star for World War II service.

LST–857

LST-857 was laid down on 19 September 1944 at Seneca, Ill., by the Chicago Bridge & Iron Co.; launched on 6 December 1944; sponsored by Mrs. Beatrice S. Major; and commissioned on 29 December 1944, Lt. Roy C. Parlier in command.

During World War II, *LST-857* was assigned to the Asiatic-Pacific theater and participated in the assault and occupation of Okinawa Gunto in June 1945. Following the war, she performed occupation duty in the Far East until mid-December 1945. After postwar operations with the Pacific Fleet, *LST-857* performed extensive service during the Korean War. On 1 July 1955, the ship was redesignated *King County* (LST-857) (*q.v.*) after counties in Texas and Washington. In October 1957, she began conversion to an experimental guided missile test ship and was reclassified AG–157 on 17 May 1958. Decommissioned on 8 July 1960, *King County* was sold to Zidell Explorations, Inc., Portland, Oreg., on 25 April 1961.

LST-857 received one battle star for World War II service and seven battle stars for Korean service.

LST–858

LST-858 was redesignated ARL–26 and named *Stentor* (*q.v.*) on 14 August 1944.

LST–859

LST-859 was laid down on 26 September 1944 at Seneca, Ill., by the Chicago Bridge & Iron Co.; launched on 15 December 1944; sponsored by Mrs. Elsie M. Marcum; and commissioned on 6 January 1945, Lt. Daniel D. Kipnis in command.

During World War II, *LST-859* was assigned to the Asiatic-Pacific theater and participated in the assault and occupation of Okinawa Gunto in June 1945. After the war, she performed occupation duty in the Far East until early December 1945. Following postwar operations with the Pacific Fleet, *LST-859* saw extensive service during the Korean War. On 1 July 1955, the ship was redesignated *Lafayette County* (LST-859) (*q.v.*) after counties in Arkansas, Florida, Mississippi, Missouri, and Wisconsin: and a parish in Louisiana. Decommssioned on 15 August 1958, *Lafayette County* was transferred to the Republic of China Navy where she served as *Chung Cheng* (LST-224).

LST-859 received one battle star for World War II service and six battle stars for Korean service.

LST–860

LST-860 was laid down on 23 September 1944 at Seneca, Ill., by the Chicago Bridge & Iron Co.; launched on 19 December 1944; sponsored by Mrs. Marjorie C. Lindahl; and commissioned on 13 January 1945.

LST-860 conducted no combat operations during World War II. She was decommissioned on 1 June 1946 and struck from the Navy list on 3 July that same year. On 19 March 1948, the tank landing ship was sold to the Mechanical Equipment Export Co. for operation.

LST–861

LST-861 was laid down on 18 September 1944 at Jeffersonville, Ind., by the Jeffersonville Boat & Ma-

chine Co.; launched on 4 November 1944; sponsored by Miss Frances K. Gadjen; and commissioned on 30 November 1944.

During World War II, *LST-861* was assigned to the Asiatic-Pacific theater and participated in the assault and occupation of Okinawa Gunto in May and June 1945. Following the war, *LST-861* performed occupation duty in the Far East until mid-March 1946. She returned to the United States and was decommissioned on 10 March 1947 and struck from the Navy list on 4 April that same year. On 10 June 1948, the ship was sold to Kaiser Co., Inc., Seattle, Wash., and subsequently scrapped.

LST-861 received one battle star for World War II service.

LST–862

LST-862 was laid down on 26 September 1944 at Jeffersonville, Ind., by the Jeffersonville Boat & Machine Co.; launched on 9 November 1944; sponsored by Miss Angela Tolkacz; and commissioned on 4 December 1944, Lt. R. N. Moffett, USNR, in command.

During World War II, *LST-862* was assigned to the Asiatic-Pacific theater and participated in the assault and occupation of Okinawa Gunto from April through June 1945. Following the war, she performed occupation duty in the Far East and saw service in China until mid-April 1946. The tank landing ship was decommissioned in early 1946 and transferred to the Maritime Administration for disposal on 10 October 1947.

LST-862 received one battle star for World War II service.

LST–863

LST-863 was laid down on 11 October 1944 at Jeffersonville, Ind., by the Jeffersonville Boat & Machine Co.; launched on 14 November 1944; sponsored by Mrs. Eva L. Nolan; and commissioned on 9 December 1944.

During World War II, *LST-863* was assigned to the Asiatic-Pacific theater and participated in the assault and occupation of Okinawa Gunto from April through June. 1945. Following the war, she performed occupation duty in the Far East until mid-January 1946. The ship returned to the United States and was decommissioned on 19 June 1946 and struck from the Navy list on 31 July that same year. On 13 May 1948, she was sold to Hughes Bros., Inc., and subsequently scrapped.

LST-863 received one battle star for World War II service.

LST–864

LST-864 was laid down on 3 October 1944 at Jeffersonville, Ind., by the Jeffersonville Boat & Machine Co.; launched on 18 November 1944; sponsored by Mrs. Viola J. Wathen; and commissioned on 13 December 1944.

During World War II, *LST-864* was assigned to the Asiatic-Pacific theater and participated in the assault and occupation of Okinawa Gunto from April through June 1945. Following the war, she performed occupation duty in the Far East and saw service in China until mid-January 1947. She returned to the United States and was decommissioned on 1 May 1947 and struck from the Navy list on 22 May that same year. On 26 June 1948, the ship was sold to Consolidated Builders, Inc., Seattle, Wash., and subsequently scrapped.

LST-864 received one battle star for World War II service.

LST-865

LST-865 was laid down on 19 October 1944 at Jeffersonville, Ind., by the Jeffersonville Boat & Machine Co.; launched on 22 November 1944; sponsored by Mrs. Monetta S. Brendel; and commissioned on 16 December 1944.

Following the war, *LST-865* performed occupation duty in the Far East and saw service in China until mid-December 1947. She was decommissioned on 30 December 1947 and transferred to the Philippine Navy that same day where she served as *Albay* (LT-39). The ship was struck from the Navy list on 22 January 1948.

LST-866

LST-866 was laid down on 14 October 1944 at Jeffersonville, Ind., by the Jeffersonville Boat & Machine Co.; launched on 27 November 1944; sponsored by Mrs. Nellie Meehan; and commissioned on 21 December 1944.

During World War II, *LST-866* was assigned to the Asiatic-Pacific theater and participated in the assault and occupation of Okinawa Gunto in June 1945. Following the war, she performed occupation duty in the Far East and saw service in China until early April 1946. The ship returned to the United States and was decommissioned on 27 June 1946 and struck from the Navy list on 31 July that same year. On 25 September 1947, she was sold to Consolidated Builders, Inc., Seattle, Wash., and subsequently scrapped.

LST-866 received one battle star for World War II service.

LST-867

LST-867 was laid down on 23 October 1944 at Jeffersonville, Ind., by the Jeffersonville Boat & Machine Co.; launched on 1 December 1944; sponsored by Mrs. Kathryn V. Wise; and commissioned on 18 December 1944, Ens. V. Lopresti in command.

Following World War II, *LST-867* performed occupation duty in the Far East until early March 1946. She returned to the United States and was decommissioned on 2 July 1946 and struck from the Navy list on 31 July that same year. On 25 September 1947, the ship was sold to Consolidated Builders, Inc., Seattle, Wash., and subsequently scrapped.

LST-868

LST-868 was laid down on 31 October 1944 at Jeffersonville, Ind., by the Jeffersonville Boat & Machinery Co.; launched on 6 December 1944; sponsored by Mrs. Beatrice C. Hanley; and commissioned on 30 December 1944.

During World War II, *LST-868* was assigned to the Asiatic-Pacific theater and participated in the assault and occupation of Okinawa Gunto in June 1945. Following the war, she performed occupation duty in the Far East and saw service in China until mid-April 1946. *LST-868* returned to the United States and was decommissioned on 9 August 1946 and struck from the Navy list on 10 June 1947. On 19 December 1947, the ship was sold to the Northern Metals Co., Philadelphia, Pa., for scrapping.

LST-868 earned one battle star for World War II service.

LST-869

LST-869 was laid down on 27 October 1944 at Jeffersonville, Ind., by the Jeffersonville Boat & Machinery Co.; launched on 11 December 1944; sponsored by Mrs. Janie G. Ray; and commissioned on 6 January 1945, Lt. (jg.) E. J. Malloy in command.

Following World War II, *LST-869* performed occupation duty in the Far East and saw service in China until mid-April 1946. She returned to the United States and was decommissioned on 31 July 1946 and struck from the Navy list on 28 August that same year. On 26 December 1947, the ship was sold to Pablo N. Ferrari & Co. for operation.

LST-870

LST-870 was laid down on 4 October 1944 at Jeffersonville, Ind., by the Jeffersonville Boat & Machinery Co.; launched on 15 December 1944; sponsored by Mrs. Opal M. Burke; and commissioned on 10 January 1945.

Following World War II, *LST-870* performed occupation duty in the Far East until early February 1946. She returned to the United States and was decommissioned in June 1946 and struck from the Navy list on 28 August that same year. On 29 August 1947, the ship was sold to Consolidated Builders, Inc., Seattle, Wash., for scrapping.

LST-871

LST-871 was laid down on 9 November 1944 at Jeffersonville, Ind., by the Jeffersonville Boat & Machinery Co.; launched on 20 December 1944; and commissioned on 18 January 1945.

LST-871 was redesignated *LSTH-871* on 15 September 1945. Following World War II, *LSTH-871* performed occupation duty in the Far East until early May 1946. She returned to the United States and was decommissioned on 4 October 1946 and struck from the Navy list on 13 November that same year. On 30 June 1948, the ship was sold to the Humble Oil & Refining Co., Houston, Tex., for operation.

LST-872

LST-872 was laid down on 18 November 1944 at Jeffersonville, Ind., by the Jeffersonville Boat & Machinery Co.; launched on 28 December 1944; sponsored by Mrs. Carrie I. Morris; and commissioned on 22 January 1945.

LST-872 performed no combat service with the United States Navy and was decommissioned on 8 July 1946 and struck from the Navy list on 15 August that same year. On 27 October 1947, she was sold to the Northwest Merchandising Service for operation.

LST-873

LST-873 was laid down on 14 November 1944 at Jeffersonville, Ind., by the Jeffersonville Boat & Machinery Co.; launched on 3 January 1945; sponsored by Miss Florence A. Babb; and commissioned on 27 January 1945, Lt. Ned S. Holley in command.

Following World War II, *LST-873* performed occupation duty in the Far East until mid-February 1946. She returned to the United States and was decommissioned on 8 August 1946 and struck from the Navy list on 25 September that same year. On 20 May 1948, the ship was sold to Kaiser Co., Inc., Vancouver, Wash., for scrapping.

LST-874

LST-874 was laid down on 16 October 1944 at Evansville, Ind., by the Missouri Valley Bridge & Iron Co.; launched on 25 November 1944; sponsored by Mrs. Ernest B. Rainey; and commissioned on 18 December 1944.

During World War II, *LST–874* was assigned to the Asiatic-Pacific theater and participated in the assault and occupation of Okinawa Gunto from April through June 1945. Following the war, she performed occupation duty in the Far East until early January 1946. *LST–874* returned to the United States and was decommissioned on 29 May 1946 and struck from the Navy list on 3 July that same year. On 8 June 1948, the ship was sold to Donald P. Loker for operation.

LST–874 earned one battle star for World War II service.

LST–875

LST–875 was laid down on 18 October 1944 at Evansville, Ind., by the Missouri Valley Bridge & Iron Co.; launched on 29 November 1944; sponsored by Mrs. Karl R. Zimmermann; and commissioned on 22 December 1944, Lt. R. E. Euliss in command.

During World War II, *LST–875* was assigned to the Asiatic-Pacific theater and participated in the assault and occupation of Okinawa Gunto in May and June 1945. Following the war, she performed occupation duty in the Far East until mid-September 1945. She was decommissioned on 22 April 1946 and struck from the Navy list on 19 July that same year. On 2 July 1948, the ship was transferred to the Philippine Navy where she served as *Misamis Oriental* (LT–40).

LST–875 earned one battle star for World War II service.

LST–876

LST–876 was laid down on 21 October 1944 at Evansville, Ind., by the Missouri Valley Bridge & Iron Co.; launched on 2 December 1944; sponsored by Mrs. John S. Shochmake; and commissioned on 27 December 1944, Lt. John V. Quillan, Jr., USNR, in command.

During World War II, *LST–876* was assigned to the Asiatic-Pacific theater and participated in the assault and occupation of Okinawa Gunto in May and June 1945. Following the war, she performed occupation duty in the Far East and saw service in China until early April 1946. She returned to the United States and was decommissioned on 28 June 1946 and struck from the Navy list on 31 July that same year. On 4 November 1947, the ship was sold to W. A. Talbot for scrapping.

LST–876 earned one battle star for World War II service.

LST–877

LST–877 was laid down on 25 October 1944 at Evansville, Ind., by the Missouri Valley Bridge & Iron Co.; launched on 6 December 1944; sponsored by Mrs. E. L. Hardeman; and commissioned on 1 January 1945, Lt. George Lee Smith in command.

During World War II, *LST–877* was assigned to the Asiatic-Pacific theater and participated in the assault and occupation of Okinawa Gunto in June 1945. Following the war, she performed occupation duty in the Far East until early January 1946. Upon her return to the United States, she was decommissioned on 1 May 1946 and struck from the Navy list on 3 July that same year. On 15 January 1948, the ship was sold to the California Co. for operation.

LST–877 earned one battle star for World War II service.

LST–878

LST–878 was laid down on 30 October 1944 at Evansville, Ind., by the Missouri Valley Bridge & Iron Co.; launched on 9 December 1944; sponsored by Mrs. Richard L. Moorehead; and commissioned on 3 January 1945, Lt. Laurence Lattomus, USNR, in command.

Following the war, *LST–878* performed occupation duty in the Far East until late November 1945. Upon her return to the United States, she was decommissioned on 3 May 1946 and struck from the Navy list on 19 July that same year. On 5 November 1947, the tank landing ship was sold to Bosey, Philippines.

LST–879

LST–879 was laid down on 2 November 1944 at Evansville, Ind., by the Missouri Valley Bridge & Iron Co.; launched on 13 December 1944; launched by Mrs. Rella G. Heath; and commissioned on 5 January 1945.

During World War II, *LST–879* was assigned to the Asiatic-Pacific theater and participated in the assault and occupation of Okinawa Gunto from April through June 1945. Following the war, she performed occupation duty in the Far East until mid-November 1945. Upon her return to the United States, she was decommissioned on 26 June 1946 and struck from the Navy list on 25 September that same year. On 17 May 1948, the ship was sold to the Bethlehem Steel Co., Bethlehem, Pa., for scrapping.

LST–879 earned one battle star for World War II service.

LST–880

LST–880 was laid down on 6 November 1944 at Evansville, Ind., by the Missouri Valley Bridge & Iron Co.; launched on 16 December 1944; sponsored by Mrs. L. H. Quigley; and commissioned on 9 January 1945, Lt. (jg.) James T. Connolly in command.

Following World War II, *LST–880* performed occupation duty in the Far East until early December 1945. She was decommissioned on 1 October 1946 and assigned to the Atlantic Reserve Fleet at Green Cove Springs, Fla. Recommissioned on 20 August 1951, *LST–880* served with the Atlantic Fleet, including occupation duty in Europe, from June through November 1952. On 1 July 1955, the ship was redesignated *Lake County* (LST–880) (*q.v.*) after counties in 12 states. She was decommissioned on 25 November 1958. Declared unfit for further service, *Lake County* was used as a target ship for destruction.

LST–881

LST–881 was laid down on 10 November 1944 at Evansville, Ind., by the Missouri Valley Bridge & Iron Co.; launched on 20 December 1944; sponsored by Miss Pat Shobe; and commissioned on 15 January 1945.

Following World War II, *LST–881* performed occupation duty in the Far East until late September 1945. She returned to the United States and was decommissioned on 14 February 1947 and struck from the Navy list on 5 March that same year. On 24 November 1947, the ship was sold to E. G. Fontes & Co. for operation.

LST–882

LST–882 was laid down on 14 November 1944 at Evansville, Ind., by the Missouri Valley Bridge & Iron Co.; launched on 23 December 1944; sponsored by Mrs. John R. Brown; and commissioned on 18 January 1945.

Following World War II, *LST–882* performed occupation duty in the Far East until early March 1946. She returned to the United States and was decommissioned on 5 July 1946 and struck from the Navy list on 28 August that same year. On 4 November 1947, the ship was sold to the Moore Drydock Co., Oakland, Calif., for scrapping.

LST–883

LST–883 was laid down on 16 November 1944 at Evansville, Ind., by the Missouri Valley Bridge & Iron Co.; launched on 30 December 1944; sponsored by Mrs. L. D. McBride; and commissioned on 23 January 1945, Lt. Winfield H. Cook in command.

During World War II, *LST–883* was assigned to the Asiatic-Pacific theater and participated in the assault and occupation of Okinawa Gunto in June 1945. She was decommissioned on 20 April 1946 and transferred to the Army. Recommissioned on 1 July 1950, *LST–883* performed extensive service during the Korean War. On 1 July 1955, she was redesignated *La Moure County* (LST–883) (*q.v.*) after a county in North Dakota. Operating with the Pacific Fleet after the war, *La Moure County* was decommissioned again on 7 December 1959. Struck from the Navy list on 1 July 1960, the ship was sold to Zidell Explorations Corp., Portland, Oreg., on 30 November 1960.

LST–883 earned one battle star for World War II service and seven battle stars for the Korean War.

LST–884

LST–884 was laid down on 23 July 1944 at Pittsburgh, Pa., by the Dravo Corp.; launched on 30 September 1944; sponsored by Mrs. Michael Durkin; and commissioned on 10 October 1944.

During World War II, *LST–884* was assigned to the Asiatic-Pacific theater and participated in the assault and occupation of Iwo Jima in February 1945 and the assault and occupation of Okinawa Gunto in April 1945. She was decommissioned on 16 February 1946. Due to extensive damage resulting from a kamikaze attack on 1 April 1945, *LST–884*'s hulk was sunk on 6 May 1946. The ship was struck from the Navy list on 21 May 1946.

LST–884 earned two battle stars for World War II service.

LST–885

LST–885 was laid down on 13 August 1944 at Pittsburgh, Pa., by the Dravo Corp.; launched on 23 September 1944; sponsored by Mrs. Alvin H. Tutt; and commissioned on 26 October 1944.

During World War II, *LST–885* was assigned to the Asiatic-Pacific theater and participated in the assault and occupation of Okinawa Gunto in March and April 1945. Following the war, she performed occupation duty in the Far East until late November 1945. Upon her return to the United States, she was decommissioned on 29 April 1946 and struck from the Navy list on 3 July that same year. On 16 December 1947, the ship was sold to the Tex-O-Kan Flour Mills Co., Dallas, Tex., for operation.

LST–885 earned one battle star for World War II service.

LST–886

LST–886 was laid down on 20 August 1944 at Pittsburgh, Pa., by the Dravo Corp.; launched on 30 September 1944; sponsored by Mrs. C. S. Hamilton; and commissioned on 2 November 1944.

During World War II, *LST–886* was assigned to the Asiatic-Pacific theater and participated in the assault and occupation of Iwo Jima in March 1945 and the assault and occupation of Okinawa Gunto in April 1945. Following the war, she performed occupation duty in the Far East until mid-November 1945. Upon her return to the United States, she was decommissioned on 10 May 1946 and struck from the Navy list on 19 June that same year. On 20 May 1948, the ship was sold to Kaiser Co., Inc., Vancouver, Wash., for scrapping.

LST–886 earned two battle stars for World War II service.

LST–887

LST–887 was laid down on 27 August 1944 at Pittsburgh, Pa., by the Dravo Corp.; launched on 7 October 1944; sponsored by Mrs. F. J. Conroy; and commissioned on 7 November 1944, Lt. Loring O. Chandler, USCGR, in command.

During World War II, *LST–887* was assigned to the Asiatic-Pacific theater and participated in the assault and occupation of Okinawa Gunto from April through June 1945. Following the war, she performed occupation duty in the Far East until late October 1945. The ship was decommissioned on 23 July 1946 and assigned to the Pacific Reserve Fleet. Recommissioned on 3 November 1950, *LST–887* performed extensive service during the Korean War and with the Pacific Fleet thereafter. On 1 July 1955, she was redesignated *Lawrence County* (LST–887) (*q.v.*) after counties in 11 states of the United States. Decommissioned again on 22 March 1960, *Lawrence County* was struck from the Navy list on 1 November 1960 and sold to the Indonesian Navy where she served as *Tandjung Nusanixe* (LST–1).

LST–887 earned one battle star for World War II service and three for the Korean War.

LST–888

LST–888 was laid down on 11 August 1944 at Pittsburgh, Pa., by the Dravo Corp.; launched on 14 October 1944; sponsored by Mrs. Richard Connell; and commissioned on 13 November 1944, Lt. Walter V. Harlin in command.

During World War II, *LST–888* was assigned to the Asiatic-Pacific theater and participated in the assault and occupation of Okinawa Gunto from March through June 1945. Following the war, she performed occupation duty in the Far East until early April 1946. Upon her return to the United States, she was decommissioned on 2 September and assigned to the Atlantic Reserve Fleet at Green Cove Springs, Fla. On 1 July 1955, *LST–888* was redesignated *Lee County* (LST–888) (*q.v.*) after counties in 12 states of the United States. Struck from the Navy list on 21 September 1960, the ship was sold to Gulf Tampa Drydock, Inc., Tampa, Fla., on 18 April 1961 for scrapping.

LST–888 earned one battle star for World War II service.

LST–889

LST–889 was laid down on 3 September 1944 at Pittsburgh, Pa., by the Dravo Corp.; launched on 14 October 1944; sponsored by Mrs. Sylvester Hohl; and commissioned on 18 November 1944, Lt. Lon Hocker, Jr., USNR, in command.

During World War II, *LST–889* was assigned to the Asiatic-Pacific theater and participated in the assault and occupation of Okinawa Gunto from April through June 1945. Following the war, she performed occupation duty in the Far East until early December 1945. Upon her return to the United States, she was decommissioned on 28 May 1946 and struck from the Navy list on 19 July that same year. On 13 February 1948, the ship was sold to Bosey, Philippines.

LST–889 earned one battle star for World War II service.

LST–890

LST–890 was laid down on 10 September 1944 at Pittsburgh, Pa., by the Dravo Corp.; launched on 21 October 1944; sponsored by Mrs. Andrew Hetherington; and commissioned on 24 November 1944.

During World War II, *LST–890* was assigned to the Asiatic-Pacific theater and participated in the assault and occupation of Okinawa Gunto from April through

June 1945. Following the war, she performed occupation duty in the Far East until mid-October 1945. Upon her return to the United States, she was decommissioned on 24 May 1946 and struck from the Navy list on 3 July that same year. On 10 June 1948, the ship was sold to Kaiser Co., Inc., Vancouver, Wash., for scrapping.

LST–390 earned one battle star for World War II service.

LST–891

LST–891 was laid down on 21 August 1944 at Pittsburgh, Pa., by the Dravo Corp.; launched on 28 October 1944; sponsored by Miss Edyth Cole; and commissioned on 27 November 1944, Lt. James F. Brown in command.

During World War II, *LST–891* was assigned to the Asiatic-Pacific theater and participated in the assault and occupation of Okinawa Gunto in May 1945. Following the war, she performed occupation duty in the Far East until early December 1945. Upon her return to the United States, she was decommissioned on 2 July 1946 and struck from the Navy list on 31 July that same year. On 29 August 1947, the ship was sold to Consolidated Builders, Inc., Seattle, Wash., for scrapping.

LST–891 earned one battle star for World War II service.

LST–892

LST–892 was laid down on 17 September 1944 at Pittsburgh, Pa., by the Dravo Corp.; launched on 28 October 1944; sponsored by Mrs. P. D. Bowman; and commissioned on 30 November 1944, Lt. W. S. Miller in command.

During World War II, *LST–892* was assigned to the Asiatic-Pacific theater and participated in the assault and occupation of Okinawa Gunto from April through June 1945. Following the war, she performed occupation duty in the Far East until mid-February 1946. Upon her return to the United States, she was decommissioned on 5 July 1946 and struck from the Navy list on 28 August that same year. On 27 October 1947, the ship was sold to the Moore Dry Dock Co., Oakland, Calif., for scrapping.

LST–892 earned one battle star for World War II service.

LST–893

LST–893 was laid down on 24 September 1944 at Pittsburgh, Pa., by the Dravo Corp.; launched on 4 November 1944; sponsored by Mrs. John Schutt; and commissioned on 4 December 1944.

Following World War II, *LST–893* performed occupation duty in the Far East until early December 1945. Upon her return to the United States, she was decommissioned on 8 May 1946 and struck from the Navy list on 19 June that same year. On 29 May 1948, the ship was sold to the Bethlehem Steel Co., Bethlehem, Pa., for scrapping.

LST–894

LST–894 was laid down on 4 September 1944 at Pittsburgh, Pa., by the Dravo Corp.; launched on 11 November 1944; sponsored by Mrs. Robert C. Norris; and commissioned on 12 December 1944, Lt. F. N. Wood in command.

During World War II, *LST–894* was assigned to the Asiatic-Pacific theater and participated in the assault and occupation of Okinawa Gunto in April and May 1945. Following the war, she performed occupation duty in the Far East until late November 1945. The ship was decommissioned on 29 April 1946 and struck from the Navy list on 19 July that same year. On 5 December 1947, she was sold to Bosey, Philippines.

LST–894 earned one battle star for World War II service.

LST–895

LST–895 was laid down on 1 October 1944 at Pittsburgh, Pa., by the Dravo Corp.; launched on 11 November 1944; sponsored by Mrs. Frank Brooks; and commissioned on 16 December 1944.

During World War II, *LST–895* was assigned to the Asiatic-Pacific theater and participated in the assault and occupation of Okinawa Gunto from April through June 1945. Following the war, she performed occupation duty in the Far East until mid-September 1945. Upon her return to the United States, she was decommissioned on 17 August 1946 and struck from the Navy list on 12 March 1948. On 10 January 1952, the ship was sold to Babbidge & Holt Co., Inc., Portland, Oreg.

LST–895 earned one battle star for World War II service.

LST–896

LST–896 was laid down on 6 October 1944 at Pittsburgh, Pa., by the Dravo Corp.; launched on 18 November 1944; sponsored by Mrs. Russell D. Strouse; and commissioned on 20 December 1944, Lt. Vinton C. Vint in command.

York County (LST–1175). Like earlier LST's, these ships were often used to transport cargo; a cargo hatch at the after end of the upper deck is served by two heavy booms.

Following World War II, *LST–896* performed occupation duty in the Far East and saw service in China until early December 1945. She was decommissioned on 3 December 1945 and struck from the Navy list on 3 January 1946. Her typhoon-damaged hulk was destroyed on 8 March 1946.

LST–897

LST–897 was laid down on 19 September 1944 at Pittsburgh, Pa., by the Dravo Corp.; launched on 25 November 1944; sponsored by Mrs. Henry B. Taliaferro; and commissioned on 22 December 1944, Lt. Peter K. Peterson, USNR, in command.

During World War II, *LST–897* was assigned to the Asiatic-Pacific theater and participated in the assault and occupation of Okinawa Gunto in May and June 1945. Following the war, she performed occupation duty in the Far East and saw service in China until mid-March 1946. The ship returned to the United States and was decommissioned on 23 July 1946 and struck from the Navy list on 28 August that same year. On 15 June 1948, the tank landing ship was sold to Steel Powers for operation.

LST–897 earned one battle star for World War II service.

LST–898

LST–898 was laid down on 15 October 1944 at Pittsburgh, Pa., by the Dravo Corp.; launched on 25 November 1944; sponsored by Mrs. J. B. Mahwhinney; and commissioned on 29 December 1944, Lt. D. W. Kallock in command.

During World War II, *LST–898* was assigned to the Asiatic-Pacific theater and participated in the assault and occupation of Okinawa Gunto from April through June 1945. Following the war, she performed occupation duty in the Far East until mid-March 1946. The ship was decommissioned on 9 May 1946 and transferred to the Army. Recommissioned on 28 August 1950, *LST–898* performed extensive service during the Korean War and with the Pacific Fleet thereafter. On 1 July 1955, she was redesignated *Lincoln County* (LST–898) (*q.v.*) after counties in 24 states of the United States. Decommissioned again on 24 March 1961, *Lincoln County* was transferred to the Royal Thai Navy on 31 August 1962 where she served as *Cheng* (LST–2).

LST–898 earned one battle star for World War II service and six for the Korean War.

LST–899

LST–899 was laid down on 22 October 1944 at Pittsburgh, Pa., by the Dravo Corp.; launched on 2 December 1944; sponsored by Mrs. F. W. Trevorrow; and commissioned on 1 January 1945, Lt. A. H. Thornton in command.

Following World War II, *LST–899* performed occupation duty in the Far East and saw service in China until early April 1946. She returned to the United States and was decommissioned on 15 July 1946 and struck from the Navy list on 15 August that same year. On 5 December 1947, the ship was sold to the Bethlehem Steel Co., Bethlehem, Pa., for scrapping.

LST–900

LST–900 was laid down on 1 October 1944 at Pittsburgh, Pa., by the Dravo Corp.; launched on 9 December 1944; sponsored by Mrs. Felix R. Konkle; and commissioned on 6 January 1945, Lt. Neil A. McClaflin in command.

During World War II, *LST–900* was assigned to the Asiatic-Pacific theater and participated in the assault

and occupation of Okinawa Gunto in June 1945. Following the war, she performed occupation duty in the Far East until early November 1945. The ship was decommissioned on 15 May 1946 and assigned to the Pacific Reserve Fleet. On 1 July 1955, she was redesignated *Linn County* (LST–900) (*q.v.*) after counties in Iowa, Kansas, Missouri, and Oregon. The tank landing ship was transferred to the Republic of Korea on 2 December 1958 where she served as *Puk Han* (LST–815). *Linn County* was struck from the Navy list on 6 February 1959.

LST–900 earned one battle star for World War II service.

LST–901

LST–901 was laid down on 29 October 1944 at Pittsburgh, Pa., by the Dravo Corp.; launched on 9 December 1944; sponsored by Mrs. S. A. Evans; and commissioned on 11 January 1945, Lt. C. A. Henson in command.

Following World War II, *LST–901* performed occupation duty in the Far East until early September 1945. She was decommissioned on 9 August 1946 and assigned to the Pacific Reserve Fleet. Recommissioned on 30 November 1951, *LST–901* saw extensive service during the Korean War and the Vietnam War. On 1 July 1955, she was redesignated *Litchfield County* (LST–901) (*q.v.*) after a county in northwestern Connecticut. Decommissioned again on 6 December 1969, *Litchfield County* was sold to John S. Latsis, Inc., New York, N.Y., on 14 January 1977.

LST–901 earned two battle stars for the Korean War, and one award of the Navy Unit Commendation, one award of the Meritorious Unit Commendation, and six battle stars for Vietnam service.

LST–902

LST–902 was laid down on 5 November 1944 at Pittsburgh, Pa., by the Dravo Corp.; launched on 16 December 1944; sponsored by Mrs. Michael Grom; and commissioned on 15 January 1945, Lt. Everett J. Bondesen in command.

Following World War II, *LST–902* performed occupation duty in the Far East until early November 1945. She was decommissioned on 3 August 1946 and assigned to the Pacific Reserve Fleet. The ship was recommissioned on 18 January 1952 and saw service during the Korean War and with the Pacific Fleet thereafter. On 1 July 1955, she was redesignated *Luzerne County* (LST–902) (*q.v.*) after a county in eastern Pennsylvania. She was decommissioned on 30 November 1955 but was recommissioned once again on 29 March 1963 and operated extensively in Southeast Asia during the Vietnam War. Decommissioned for the final time, *Luzerne County* was struck from the Navy list on 12 August 1970.

LST–902 earned two battle stars for the Korean War and one award of the Meritorious Unit Commendation and 12 battle stars for Vietnam service.

LST–903

LST–903 was laid down on 15 October 1944 at Pittsburgh, Pa., by the Dravo Corp.; launched on 23 December 1944; sponsored by Mrs. E. W. Wilson; and commissioned on 20 January 1945, Lt. John B. Darrow in command.

Following World War II, *LST–903* performed occupation duty in the Far East until mid-October 1945. She was decommissioned on 10 September 1946 and assigned to the Pacific Reserve Fleet. On 1 July 1955, the ship was redesignated *Lyman County* (LST–903) (*q.v.*) after a county in South Dakota. *Lyman County* was designated a target ship on 20 October 1958 and struck from the Navy list on 1 November that same year. She was torpedoed and sunk by *Menhaden* (SS-377) on 28 March 1959 off the coast of Baja California.

LST-904

LST-904 was laid down on 12 November 1944 at Pittsburgh, Pa., by the Dravo Corp.; launched on 23 December 1944; sponsored by Miss Betty McCallen; and commissioned on 25 January 1945, Lt. James L. Randles, Jr., in command.

During World War II, *LST-904* was assigned to the Asiatic-Pacific theater and participated in the assault and occupation of Okinawa Gunto in June 1945. Following the war, she performed occupation duty in the Far East until early December 1945. The ship was decommissioned on 15 November 1946 and assigned to the Pacific Reserve Fleet. On 1 July 1955, she was redesignated *Lyon County* (LST-904) (*q.v.*) after counties in Iowa, Kansas, Kentucky, Minnesota, and Nevada. *Lyon County* was nominated as a target for destruction on 20 October 1958 and struck from the Navy list on 1 November that same year. She was sunk off the coast of Washington by *Capitaine* (SS-336) on 13 May 1959.

LST-904 earned one battle star for World War II service.

LST-905

LST-905 was laid down on 19 November 1944 at Pittsburgh, Pa., by the Dravo Corp.; launched on 30 December 1944; sponsored by Mrs. Paul Gulling; and commissioned on 20 January 1945.

During World War II, *LST-905* was assigned to the Asiatic-Pacific theater and participated in the assault and occupation of Okinawa Gunto in June 1945. Following the war, she performed occupation duty in the Far East until early December 1945. She was decommissioned on 11 September 1946 and assigned to the Pacific Reserve Fleet. On 1 July 1955, the ship was redesignated *Madera County* (LST-905) (*q.v.*) after a county in central California. Recommissioned on 30 March 1963, *Madera County* saw extensive service in the Vietnam War commencing in 1966. She was transferred to the Philippine Navy in November 1969 where she served as *Ilteos Norte* (LT-98).

LST-905 earned one battle star for World War II service, and one award of the Meritorious Unit Commendation and nine battle stars for Vietnam service.

LST-906

LST-906 was laid down on 24 January 1944 at Hingham, Mass., by the Bethlehem-Hingham Shipyard, Inc.; launched on 11 March 1944; sponsored by Mrs. Henry Levine; and commissioned on 27 April 1944.

During World War II, *LST-906* was assigned to the European theater and participated in the invasion of southern France in September 1944. She was decommissioned on 20 May 1945 after grounding off Leghorn, Italy, on 18 October 1944. The ship was struck from the Navy list on 22 June 1945 and sold for scrap.

LST-906 earned one battle star for World War II service.

LST-907

LST-907 was laid down on 31 January 1944 at Hingham, Mass., by the Bethlehem-Hingham Shipyard, Inc.; launched on 18 March 1944; sponsored by Miss Rosemary Leonard; and commissioned on 30 April 1944, Lt. Dale O. Morgan, USNR, in command.

During World War II, *LST-907* was assigned to the European theater and participated in the invasion of southern France in September 1944. She was decommissioned on 18 October 1946. On 25 November 1946, the ship was delivered to and commissioned in the Venezuelan Navy and struck from the Navy list that same date.

LST-907 earned one battle star for World War II service.

LST-908

LST-908 was laid down on 14 February 1944 at Hingham, Mass., by the Bethlehem-Hingham Shipyard, Inc.; launched on 28 March 1944; sponsored by Mrs. Charles E. Monorief; and commissioned on 8 May 1944.

During World War II, *LST-908* was assigned to the Asiatic-Pacific theater and participated in the following operations:

Leyte landings—October and November 1944
Mindoro landings—December 1944
Lingayen Gulf landings—January 1945
Zambales-Subic Bay—January 1945
Assault and occupation of Okinawa Gunto—April 1945

Immediately following World War II, *LST-908* performed occupation duty in the Far East until early April 1946. Upon her return to the United States, she was decommissieoned on 30 July 1946 and struck from the Navy list on 28 August that same year. On 3 October 1947, the ship was sold to Luria Bros. & Co., Philadelphia, Pa., for scrapping.

LST-908 earned four battle stars for World War II service.

LST-909

LST-909 was laid down on 19 February 1944 at Hingham, Mass., by the Bethlehem-Hingham Shipyard, Inc.; launched on 3 April 1944; and commissioned on 11 May 1944.

During World War II, *LST-909* was assigned to the Asiatic-Pacific theater and participated in the Lingayen Gulf landings in January 1945 and the assault and occupation of Okinawa Gunto in April 1945. Following the war, she performed occupation duty in the Far East until early February 1946. She returned to the United States and was decommissioned on 21 June 1946 and struck from the Navy list on 31 July that same year. On 19 May 1948, the ship was sold to Kaiser Co., Inc., Vancouver, Wash., for scrapping.

LST-909 earned two battle stars for World War II service.

LST-910

LST-910 was laid down on 23 February 1944 at Hingham, Mass., by the Bethlehem-Hingham Shipyard, Inc.; launched on 8 April 1944; sponsored by Mrs. Gerald Donovan; and commissioned on 24 May 1944, Lt. Harold V. Ruble in command.

During World War II, *LST-910* was assigned to the Asiatic-Pacific theater and participated in the following operations:

Battle of Surigao Strait—November 1944
Lingayen Gulf landing—January 1945
Zambales-Subic Bay—January 1945
Palawan Islands landings—February and March 1945
Mindanao Island landings—April and May 1945
Balikpapan operation—June and July 1945

Following the war, *LST-910* performed occupation duty in the Far East and saw service in China until early April 1946. She returned to the United States and was decommissioned on 27 June 1946 and struck from the Navy list on 31 July that same year. The ship was sold on 25 November 1948 to the Bethlehem Steel Co., Bethlehem, Pa., for scrapping.

LST-910 earned three battle stars for World War II service.

LST–911

LST–911 was laid down on 28 February 1944 at Hingham, Mass., by the Bethlehem-Hingham Shipyard, Inc.; launched on 12 April 1944; sponsored by Mrs. Christine Muir; and commissioned on 14 May 1944, Lt. M. T. Saffield in command.

During World War II, LST–911 was assigned to the Asiatic-Pacific theater and participated in the following operations:

Morotai landings—September 1944
Leyte landings—November 1944
Lingayen Gulf landings—January 1945
Mindanao Island landings—April 1945
Balikpapan operation—June and July 1945

Following the war, LST–911 performed occupation duty in the Far East until mid-April 1946. She returned to the United States and was decommissioned on 24 June 1946 and struck from the Navy list on 31 July that same year. On 25 September 1947, the ship was sold to the Puget Sound Bridge & Dredging Co., Seattle, Wash., for scrapping.

LST–912 earned four battle stars for World War II service.

LST–912

LST–912 was laid down on 5 February 1944 at Hingham, Mass., by the Bethlehem-Hingham Shipyard, Inc.; launched on 22 April 1944; sponsored by Mrs. Hazel B. Leppe; and commissioned on 21 May 1944, Lt. Lloyd R. White in command.

During World War II, LST–912 was assigned to the Asiatic-Pacific theater and participated in the following operations:

Morotai landings—September 1944
Leyte landings—November 1944
Lingayen Gulf landing—January 1945
Palawan Island landings—February and March 1945
Mindanao Island landings—April 1945

Following the war, LST–912 performed occupation duty in the Far East and saw service in China until mid-January 1949. On 1 July 1955, she was redesignated Mahnomen County (LST–912) (q.v.) after a county in northwestern Minnesota. The ship was decommissioned on 25 August 1955 and assigned to the Atlantic Reserve Fleet. Recommissioned on 27 March 1963, Mahnomen County performed extensive service in Southeast Asia, including Vietnam, before she grounded at Chulai, South Vietnam, on 30 December 1966 as a result of typhoon weather. Efforts to refloat her were unsuccessful, and she was struck from the Navy list on 31 January 1967. Mahnomen County was later demolished by the Navy Support Detachment at Chulai.

LST–912 earned four battle stars for World War II service and two battle stars for the Vietnam War.

LST–913

LST–913 was laid down on 15 March 1944 at Hingham, Mass., by the Bethlehem-Hingham Shipyard, Inc.; launched on 26 April 1944; and commissioned on 23 May 1944.

During World War II, LST–913 was assigned to the European theater and participated in the invasion of southern France in August and September 1944. She was then assigned to the Asiatic-Pacific theater and took part in the Leyte landings in November 1944 and the assault and occupation of Okinawa Gunto in June 1945.

Following the war, LST–913 performed occupation duty in the Far East until mid-December 1945. She returned to the United States and was decommissioned on 16 July 1946 and struck from the Navy list on 14 March 1947. On 18 June 1948, the ship was sold to the

Humble Oil and Refining Co., Houston, Tex., for operation.

LST–913 earned three battle stars for World War II service.

LST–914

LST–914 was laid down on 16 February 1944 at Hingham, Mass., by the Bethlehem-Hingham Shipyard, Inc.; launched on 18 April 1944; and commissioned on 18 May 1944, Lt. A. W. Meyer in command.

During World War II, LST–914 was assigned to the European theater and participated in the invasion of southern France in August and September 1944. She was then assigned to the Asiatic-Pacific theater and took part in the assault and occupation of Okinawa Gunto in May and June 1945. Following the war, the ship performed occupation duty in the Far East until mid-November 1945.

LST–914 was decommissioned on 26 June 1946 and loaned to the Army. Reverting to Navy control, LST–914 was recommissioned on 26 August 1950 and performed extensive service during the Korean War. Following the war, she conducted deployments to the western Pacific in 1954, 1956, and 1958. During this period, on 1 July 1955, the ship was redesignated Mahoning County (LST–914) (q.v.) after a county in Ohio. Decommissioned again on 5 September 1959, Mahoning County was sold to Zidell Explorations, Portland, Oreg., on 22 June 1960 for scrapping.

LST–914 earned two battle stars for World War II service and four battle stars and one award of the Navy Unit Commendation for the Korean War.

LST–915

LST–915 was laid down on 22 March 1944 at Hingham, Mass., by the Bethlehem-Hingham Shipyard, Inc.; launched on 3 May 1944; and commissioned on 27 May 1944.

Following World War II, LST–915 performed occupation duty in the Far East until early April 1946. She returned to the United States and was decommissioned on 25 June 1946 and struck from the Navy list on 31 July that same year. On 19 June 1948, the ship was sold to the Humble Oil and Refining Co., Houston, Tex., for operation.

LST–916

LST–916 was laid down on 22 March 1944 at Hingham, Mass., by the Bethlehem-Hingham Shipyard, Inc.; launched on 29 April 1944; and commissioned on 25 May 1944.

During World War II, LST–916 was assigned to the Asiatic-Pacific theater and participated in the following operations:

Leyte landings—October 1944
Lingayen Gulf landings—January 1945
Assault and occupation of Okinawa Gunto—April 1945

Following the war, LST–916 performed occupation duty in the Far East until mid-November 1945. She was decommissioned on 5 April 1946 and transferred to the Army on 28 June that same year. On 29 September 1947, she was struck from the Navy list; and, in 1949, LST–916 was lost in a typhoon at Okinawa.

LST–916 earned three battle stars for World War II service.

LST–917

LST–917 was laid down on 31 March 1944 at Hingham, Mass., by the Bethlehem-Hingham Shipyard, Inc.; launched on 6 May 1944; and commissioned on 28 May 1944.

During World War II, LST-917 was assigned to the Asiatic-Pacific theater and participated in the following operations:

Leyte landings—October 1944

Morotai landings—December 1944 and January 1945

Lingayen Gulf landing—January 1945

Mindanao Island landings—January 1945

Assault and occupation of Okinawa Gunto—March and April 1945

Following the war, LST-917 performed occupation duty in the Far East until mid-December 1945. She returned to the United States and was decommissioned on 24 May 1946 and struck from the Navy list on 3 July that same year. On 19 May 1948, the ship was sold to Kaiser Co., Inc., Vancouver, Wash., for scrapping.

LST-917 earned five battle stars for World War II service.

LST–918

LST-918 was laid down on 5 April 1944 at Hingham, Mass., by the Bethlehem-Hingham Shipyard, Inc.; launched on 7 May 1944; and commissioned on 29 May 1944, Lt. Paul Cherin, USNR, in command.

During World War II, LST-918 was assigned to the Asiatic-Pacific theater and participated in the Leyte landings in October 1944 and the assault and occupation of Okinawa Gunto from March through June 1945. Following the war, she performed occupation duty in the Far East until early January 1946. Upon her return to the United States, she was decommissioned on 12 June 1946 and struck from the Navy list on 31 July that same year. On 18 December 1947, the ship was sold to the Learner Co., Oakland, Calif., and subsequently scrapped.

LST-918 earned two battle stars for World War II service.

LST–919

LST-919 was laid down on 11 April 1944 at Hingham, Mass., by the Bethlehem-Hingham Shipyard, Inc.; launched on 17 May 1944; and commissioned on 31 May 1944.

During World War II, LST-919 was assigned to the Asiatic-Pacific theater and participated in the following operations:

Leyte landings—October and November 1944

Lingayen Gulf landing—January 1945

Mindanao Island landings—April 1945

Following the war, LST-919 performed occupation duty in the Far East and saw service in China until early April 1946. She returned to the United States and was decommissioned on 5 August 1946 and struck from the Navy list on 25 September that same year. On 10 January 1948, the ship was sold to Pablo N. Ferrari & Co. for operation.

LST-919 earned three battle stars for World War II service.

LST–920

LST-920 was laid down on 26 April 1944 at Hingham, Mass., by the Bethlehem-Hingham Shipyard, Inc.; launched on 29 May 1944; and commissioned on 17 June 1944.

During World War II, LST-920 was assigned to the Asiatic-Pacific theater and participated in the assault and occupation of Okinawa Gunto in June 1945. Following the war, she performed occupation duty and saw service in China until early March 1946. Upon her return to the United States, she was decommissioned on 8 July 1946 and struck from the Navy list

on 14 March 1947. On 17 June 1948, the ship was sold to the Standard Oil & Gas Co. for operation.

LST-920 earned one battle star for World War II service.

LST–921

LST-921 was laid down on 1 May 1944 at Hingham, Mass., by the Bethlehem-Hingham Shipyard, Inc.; launched on 2 June 1944; and commissioned on 23 June 1944.

LST-921 was torpedoed off the channel entrance to Bristol, England, on 14 August 1944. She was towed to port and stripped prior to decommissioning and disposal of the hulk. The ship was decommissioned on 29 September 1944 and struck from the Navy list on 14 October 1944.

LST–922

LST-922 was laid down on 26 April 1944 at Hingham, Mass., by the Bethlehem-Hingham Shipyard, Inc.; launched on 7 June 1944; and commissioned on 29 June 1944.

During World War II, LST-922 was assigned to the Asiatic-Pacific theater and participated in the following operations:

Lingayen Gulf landings—January 1945

Zambales-Subic Bay—January 1945

Palawan Islands landings—March 1945

Visayan Island landings—April 1945

Following the war, LST-922 performed occupation duty in the Far East and saw service in China until early March 1946. Upon her return to the United States, she was decommissioned on 8 July 1946 and struck from the Navy list on 28 August that same year. On 13 June 1948, the ship was sold to Walter W. Johnson Co. for scrapping.

LST-922 earned three battle stars for World War II service.

LST–923

LST-923 was laid down on 3 May 1944 at Hingham, Mass., by the Bethlehem-Hingham Shipyard, Inc.; launched on 11 June 1944; and commissioned on 6 July 1944, Lt. John T. Gordon in command.

During World War II, LST-923 was assigned to the Asiatic-Pacific theater and participated in the Lingayen Gulf landing in January 1945 and the assault and occupation of Okinawa Gunto in April through June 1945. Following the war, she performed occupation duty in the Far East until early April 1946. Upon her return to the United States, she was decommissioned on 10 July 1946 and struck from the Navy list on 15 August that same year. The ship was sold on 31 May 1948 to the Bethlehem Steel Co., Bethlehem, Pa., for scrapping.

LST-923 earned two battle stars for World War II service.

LST–924

LST-924 was laid down on 8 May 1944 at Hingham, Mass., by the Bethlehem-Hingham Shipyard, Inc.; launched on 17 June 1944; and commissioned on 10 July 1944.

During World War II, LST-924 was assigned to the Asiatic-Pacific theater and participated in the following operations:

Leyte landing—November 1944

Lingayen Gulf landings—January 1945

Visayan Island landings—March and April 1945

Tarakan Island operation—April and May 1945

Following the war, LST-924 performed occupation duty in the Far East and saw service in China until mid-May 1946. She was decommissioned on 13 June 1946 and struck from the Navy list on 3 July that same year. On 5 May 1947, the ship was sold to the Royal Navy of Thailand where it operated as *Angthong* (LST-1).

LST-924 earned four battle stars for World War II service.

LST-925

LST-925 was laid down on 10 May 1944 at Hingham, Mass., by the Bethlehem-Hingham Shipyard, Inc.; launched on 21 June 1944; and commissioned on 15 July 1944.

During World War II, *LST-925* was assigned to the Asiatic-Pacific theater and participated in the Lingayen Gulf landing in January 1945. She returned to the United States and was decommissioned on 26 November 1945 and struck from the Navy list on 5 December that same year. On 9 May 1948, the ship was sold to Consolidated Builders Inc., Seattle, Wash., for scrapping.

LST-925 earned one battle star for World War II service.

LST-926

LST-926 was laid down on 13 May 1944 at Hingham, Mass., by the Bethlehem-Hingham Shipyard, Inc.; launched on 24 June 1944; and commissioned on 20 July 1944, Lt. Floyd H. Gould in command.

During World War II, *LST-926* was assigned to the Asiatic-Pacific theater and participated in the Lingayen Gulf landing in January 1945 and the assault and occupation of Okinawa Gunto from April through June 1945. Following the war, she performed occupation duty in the Far East until late March 1946. The ship was decommissioned on 14 June 1946 and struck from the Navy list on 31 July that same year. On 13 June 1948, the tank landing ship was sold to the Walter W. Johnson Co. for scrapping.

LST-926 earned two battle stars for World War II service.

LST-927

LST-927 was laid down on 20 May 1944 at Hingham, Mass., by the Bethlehem-Hingham Shipyard, Inc.; launched on 28 June 1944; and commissioned on 4 July 1944.

During World War II, *LST-927* was assigned to the Asiatic-Pacific theater and participated in the Lingayen Gulf landing in January 1945 and the Mindanao Island landings in March and April 1945. She returned to the United States and was decommissioned on 20 July 1946 and struck from the Navy list on 8 October that same year. On 9 December 1947, the ship was sold to the Learner Co., Oakland, Calif., for scrapping.

LST-927 earned two battle stars for World War II service.

LST-928

LST-928 was laid down on 1 June 1944 at Hingham, Mass., by the Bethlehem-Hingham Shipyard, Inc.; launched on 5 July 1944; and commissioned on 30 July 1944, Lt. C. R. Stearns, USNR, in command.

During World War II, *LST-928* was assigned to the Asiatic-Pacific theater and participated in the assault and occupation of Iwo Jima in March 1945. She was decommissioned on 13 December 1946.

LST-928 earned one battle star for World War II service.

LST-929

LST-929 was laid down on 5 June 1944 at Hingham, Mass., by the Bethlehem-Hingham Shipyard, Inc.; launched on 8 July 1944; and commissioned on 2 August 1944.

During World War II, *LST-929* was assigned to the Asiatic-Pacific theater and participated in the assault and occupation of Iwo Jima in February 1945 and the assault and occupation of Okinawa Gunto from April through June 1945. On 15 September 1945, she was redesignated *LSTH-929*. Following the war, the ship performed occupation duty in the Far East and saw service in China until late May 1946. *LSTH-929* was decommissioned on 24 May 1946 and turned over to the Chinese Nationalist Navy. She was struck from the Navy list on 3 July 1946.

LST-929 earned two battle stars for World War II service.

LST-930

LST-930 was laid down on 9 June 1944 at Hingham, Mass., by the Bethlehem-Hingham Shipyard, Inc.; launched on 12 July 1944; sponsored by Mrs. C. M. Rocca; and commissioned on 6 August 1944, Lt. F. W. Grabowski in command.

During World War II, *LST-930* was assigned to the Asiatic-Pacific theater and participated in the assault and occupation of Iwo Jima in February 1945 and the assault and occupation of Okinawa Gunto from April through June 1945. On 15 September 1945, she was redesignated *LSTH-930* and performed occupation duty in the Far East until late October 1945. The ship returned to the United States and was decommissioned on 26 June 1946 and struck from the Navy list on 31 July that same year. On 8 June 1948, she was sold to the Humble Oil & Refining Co., Houston, Tex., for operation.

LST-930 earned two battle stars for World War II service.

LST-931

LST-931 was laid down on 13 June 1944 at Hingham, Mass., by the Bethlehem-Hingham Shipyard, Inc.; launched on 19 July 1944; and commissioned on 11 August 1944, Lt. E. L. Berenbach in command.

During World War II, *LST-931* was assigned to the Asiatic-Pacific theater and participated in the assault and occupation of Iwo Jima in February 1945 and the assault and occupation of Okinawa Gunto from April through June 1945. On 15 September 1945, she was redesignated *LSTH-931* and performed occupation duty in the Far East until late October 1945. The tank landing ship was decommissioned on 26 June 1946 and struck from the Navy list on 31 July that same year. On 12 June 1948, she was sold to the Walter W. Johnson Co. for scrapping.

LST-931 earned two battle stars for World War II service.

LST-932

LST-932 was laid down on 21 June 1944 at Hingham, Mass., by the Bethlehem-Hingham Shipyard, Inc.; launched on 22 July 1944; and commissioned on 15 August 1944, Lt. W. F. Jerome, USNR, in command.

During World War II, *LST-932* was assigned to the Asiatic-Pacific theater and participated in the Lingayen Gulf landing in January 1945 and the Mindanao Island landings in April and May 1945. Following the war, she performed occupation duty in the Far East and saw service in China until mid-February 1946. She returned to the United States and was decommissioned on 24 June 1946 and struck from the Navy list on 31 July

Graham County (LST–1176) at Vieques, Puerto Rico, in 1964. Note her bow door configuration, 3″/50 twin gun mounts, and radar-equipped gun directors.

that same year. On 29 March 1948, the ship was sold to the Standard Oil Co. for operation.

LST-932 earned three battle stars for World War II service.

LST-933

LST-933 was laid down on 23 June 1944 at Hingham, Mass., by the Bethlehem-Hingham Shipyard, Inc.; launched on 26 July 1944; sponsored by Miss Helen M. Long; and commissioned on 20 August 1944, Lt. (jg.) M. L. Stokes in command.

During World War II, *LST-933* was assigned to the Asiatic-Pacific theater and participated in the following operations:

Palawan Island landings—February and March 1945

Mindanao Island landings—April and May 1945

Assault and occupation of Okinawa Gunto—June 1945

Following the war, *LST-933* performed occupation duty in the Far East until mid-February 1946. She returned to the United States and was decommissioned on 2 July 1946 and struck from the Navy list on 15 August that same year. On 25 May 1948, the ship was sold to Hughes Bros., Inc., New York, N.Y., for scrapping.

LST-933 earned two battle stars for World War II service.

LST-934

LST-934 was laid down on 29 June 1944 at Hingham, Mass., by the Bethlehem-Hingham Shipyard, Inc.; launched on 29 July 1944; and commissioned on 25 August 1944.

During World War II, *LST-934* was assigned to the Asiatic-Pacific theater and participated in the following operations:

Palawan Island landings—March 1945

Visayan Islands landings—March and April 1945

Mindanao Island landings—April 1945

Assault and occupation of Okinawa Gunto—June 1945

Following the war, *LST-934* performed occupation duty in the Far East and saw service in China until early May 1946. She was decommissioned on 13 May 1946 and transferred to the State Department that same day. On 19 June 1946, the ship was struck from the Navy list.

LST-934 earned two battle stars for World War II service.

LST-935

LST-935 was laid down on 3 July 1944 at Hingham, Mass., by the Bethlehem-Hingham Shipyard, Inc.; launched on 5 August 1944; and commissioned on 29 August 1944, Lt. (jg.) Bruce B. Wells in command.

During World War II, *LST-935* was assigned to the Asiatic-Pacific theater and participated in the following operations:

Palawan Island landings—March 1945

Visayan Islands landings—March and April 1945

Mindanao Island landings—April 1945

Balikpapan operation—June and July 1945

Following the war, *LST-935* performed occupation duty in the Far East and saw service in China until mid-April 1946. She returned to the United States and was decommissioned on 2 July 1946 and struck from the Navy list on 15 August that same year. The ship was sold to Consolidated Builders, Inc., Seattle, Wash., on 29 August 1947 for scrapping.

LST-935 earned two battle stars for World War II service.

LST-936

LST-936 was laid down on 7 July 1944 at Hingham, Mass., by the Bethlehem-Hingham Shipyard, Inc.; launched on 9 August 1944; sponsored by Miss Dorothy M. Wadman; and commissioned on 1 September 1944.

During World War II, *LST-936* was assigned to the Asiatic-Pacific theater and participated in the Mindanao Island landings in March and April 1945. Upon her return to the United States, she was decommissioned on 17 May 1946 and struck from the Navy list on 5 June that same year. On 12 June 1948, the ship was sold to the Walter W. Johnson Co. for scrapping.

LST-936 earned one battle star for World War II service.

LST-937

LST-937 was laid down on 11 July 1944 at Hingham, Mass., by the Bethlehem-Hingham Shipyard, Inc.; launched on 12 August 1944; sponsored by Mrs. W. H. Hartt; and commissioned on 6 September 1944.

During World War II, *LST-937* was assigned to the Asiatic-Pacific theater and participated in the Mindanao Island landings in April 1945. Following the war, she performed occupation duty in the Far East and saw service in China until late May 1946. The ship was decommissioned on 24 May 1946 and transferred to the State Department on that date. She was struck from the Navy list on 3 July 1946.

LST-937 earned one battle star for World War II service.

LST-938

LST-938 was laid down an 14 July 1944 at Hingham, Mass., by the Bethlehem-Hingham Shipyard, Inc.; launched on 15 August 1944; and commissioned on 9 September 1944, Ens. W. H. Limes in command.

During World War II, *LST-938* was assigned to the Asiatic-Pacific theater and participated in the Mindanao Island landings in March and April 1945 and the Balikpapan operation in June and July 1945. Following the war, she performed occupation duty in the Far East and saw service in China until mid-May 1946. After serving as a Naval Reserve training ship, *LST-938* was decommissioned in December 1949 and assigned to the Atlantic Reserve Fleet. Recommissioned on 14 December 1951, she served as a Marine Corps training ship and was redesignated *Maricopa County* (LST-938) (*q.v.*) after a county in Arizona. She was decommissioned again on 29 February 1956. *Maricopa County* was struck from the Navy list on 1 June 1962 and transferred to the Vietnamese Navy on 12 July that same year where she served as *Da Nang* (HQ-501).

LST-938 earned two battle stars for World War II service.

LST-939

LST-939 was laid down on 21 July 1944 at Hingham, Mass., by the Bethlehem-Hingham Shipyard, Inc.; launched on 23 August 1944; sponsored by Mrs. William Lovett; and commissioned on 14 September 1944.

During World War II, *LST-939* was assigned to the Asiatic-Pacific theater and participated in the assault and occupation of Okinawa Gunto from April through June 1945. Following the war, she performed occupation duty in the Far East and saw service in China until mid-March 1946. Upon her return to the United States, she was decommissioned on 22 June 1946 and struck from the Navy list on 31 July that same year. On 12 June 1948, the ship was sold to the Walter W. Johnson Co. for scrapping.

LST-939 earned one battle star for World War II service.

LST-940

LST-940 was laid down on 25 July 1944 at Hingham, Mass., by the Bethlehem-Hingham Shipyard, Inc.; launched on 26 August 1944; and commissioned on 20 September 1944.

During World War II, LST-940 was assigned to the Asiatic-Pacific theater and participated in the assault and occupation of Iwo Jima in February 1945 and the assault and occupation of Okinawa Gunto in April 1945. Following the war, she performed occupation duty in the Far East and saw service in China until early April 1946. Upon her return to the United States, she was decommissioned on 13 July 1946 and struck from the Navy list on 28 August that same year. On 13 June 1948, the ship was sold to the Walter W. Johnson Co. for scrapping.

LST-940 earned two battle stars for World War II service.

LST-941

LST-941 was laid down on 28 July 1944 at Hingham, Mass., by the Bethlehem-Hingham Shipyard, Inc.; launched on 30 August 1944; sponsored by Mrs. Roland Gariepy; and commissioned on 22 September 1944.

During World War II, LST-941 was assigned to the Asiatic-Pacific theater and participated in the Palawan Island landings in March 1945 and the Visayan Islands landings in March and April 1945. Following the war, she performed occupation duty in the Far East until early October 1945. The ship returned to the United States and was decommissioned on 1 May 1946 and struck from the Navy list on 3 July that same year. On 28 March 1947, she was sold to Francis R. Stolz for operation.

LST-941 earned one battle star for World War II service.

LST-942

LST-942 was laid down on 1 August 1944 at Hingham, Mass., by the Bethlehem-Hingham Shipyard, Inc.; launched on 6 September 1944; and commissioned on 26 September 1944.

During World War II, LST-942 was assigned to the Asiatic-Pacific theater and participated in the Visayan Islands landings in April 1945. Following the war, she performed occupation duty in the Far East until mid-February 1946. LST-942 returned to the United States and was decommissioned on 26 June 1946 and struck from the Navy list on 31 July that same year. On 10 June 1948, the ship was sold to the Humble Oil & Refining Co., of Houston, Tex., for operation.

LST-942 earned one battle star for World War II service.

LST-943

LST-943 was laid down on 8 August 1944 at Hingham, Mass., by the Bethlehem-Hingham Shipyard, Inc.; launched on 9 September 1944; sponsored by Miss Margaret Clarke; and commissioned on 30 September 1944.

During World War II, LST-943 was assigned to the Asiatic-Pacific theater and participated in the assault and occupation of Iwo Jima in February 1945 and the assault and occupation of Okinawa Gunto in April 1945. Following the war, she performed occupation duty in the Far East until mid-April 1946. She returned to the United States and was decommissioned on 16 July 1946 and struck from the Navy list on 25 September that same year. On 4 November 1947, the ship was sold to the Moore Drydock Co., of Oakland, Calif., for scrapping.

LST-943 earned two battle stars for World War II service.

LST-944

LST-944 was laid down on 11 August 1944 at Hingham, Mass., by the Bethlehem-Hingham Shipyard, Inc.; launched on 13 September 1944; and commissioned on 4 October 1944.

During World War II, LST-944 was assigned to the Asiatic-Pacific theater and participated in the assault and occupation of Iwo Jima in February 1945 and the assault and occupation of Okinawa Gunto from April through June 1945. She returned to the United States and was decommissioned on 19 December 1945 and struck from the Navy list on 8 January 1946. On 26 September 1947, the ship was sold to the Boston Metals Co., of Baltimore, Md., for scrapping.

LST-944 earned two battle stars for World War II service.

LST-945

LST-945 was laid down on 11 August 1944 at Hingham, Mass., by the Bethlehem-Hingham Shipyard, Inc.; launched on 16 September 1944; and commissioned on 9 October 1944.

During World War II, LST-945 was assigned to the Asiatic-Pacific theater and participated in the assault and occupation of Okinawa Gunto from April through June 1945. Following the war, she saw service in China until early 1946. The ship returned to the United States and was decommissioned on 16 April 1946 and transferred to the Maritime Administration for disposition on 29 May that same year. She was struck from the Navy list on 19 July 1946.

LST-945 earned one battle star for World War II service.

LST-946

LST-946 was laid down on 15 August 1944 at Hingham, Mass., by the Bethlehem-Hingham Shipyard, Inc.; launched on 20 September 1944; sponsored by Miss Nancy Ruth Kerr; and commissioned on 12 October 1944, Ens. D. A. Schlarbaum in command.

During World War II, LST-946 was assigned to the Asiatic-Pacific theater and participated in the assault and occupation of Okinawa Gunto from March through May 1945. Following the war, she performed occupation duty in the Far East until mid-February 1946. She returned to the United States and was decommissioned on 25 June 1946 and struck from the Navy list on 31 July that same year. On 25 May 1948, the ship was sold to the California Co. for operation.

LST-946 earned one battle star for World War II service.

LST-947

LST-947 was laid down on 18 August 1944 at Hingham, Mass., by the Bethlehem-Hingham Shipyard, Inc.; launched on 23 September 1944; and commissioned on 15 October 1944, Lt. Rudolph Siemsson in command.

During World War II, LST-947 was assigned to the Asiatic-Pacific theater and participated in the assault and occupation of Okinawa Gunto in April 1945. Following the war, she performed occupation duty in the Far East until early July 1946. She was decommissioned on 16 August 1946 and struck from the Navy list on 15 October that same year. The ship was sold to Bosey, Philippines, on 5 December 1947.

LST-947 earned one battle star for World War II service.

LST-948

LST-948 was redesignated ARL-16 and named Myrmidon (q.v.) on 14 August 1944.

LST-949

LST-949 was laid down on 29 August 1944 at Hingham, Mass., by the Bethlehem-Hingham Shipyard, Inc.; launched on 30 September 1944; and commissioned on 23 October 1944, Lt. Thomas J. Twohig, USNR, in command.

During World War II, *LST-949* was assigned to the Asiatic-Pacific theater and participated in the assault and occupation of Okinawa Gunto from April through June 1945. On 15 September 1945, she was redesignated *LSTH-949* and performed occupation duty in the Far East until mid-April 1946. The ship returned to the United States and was decommissioned on 18 July 1946 and struck from the Navy list on 25 September that same year. On 30 June 1948, she was sold to the Humble Oil & Refining Co., of Houston, Tex., for operation.

LST-949 earned one battle star for World War II service.

LST-950

LST-950 was laid down on 1 September 1944 at Hingham, Mass., by the Bethlehem-Hingham Shipyard, Inc.; launched on 4 October 1944; sponsored by Mrs. C. C. Recca; and commissioned on 27 October 1944.

During World War II, *LST-950* was assigned to the Asiatic-Pacific theater and participated in the assault and occupation of Okinawa Gunto from April through June 1945. On 15 September 1945, she was redesignated *LSTH-950* and performed occupation duty in the Far East until early November 1945. She returned to the United States and was decommissioned on 23 September 1946 and struck from the Navy list on 10 June 1947. On 8 March 1948, the ship was sold to the Ships Power & Equipment Corp., of Barber, N.J., for scrapping.

LST-950 earned one battle star for World War II service.

LST-951

LST-951 was laid down on 8 September 1944 at Hingham, Mass., by the Bethlehem-Hingham Shipyard, Inc.; launched on 7 October 1944; sponsored by Mrs. O. P. Thomas, Jr.; and commissioned on 31 October 1944, Lt. L. J. Kelly in command.

During World War II, *LST-951* was assigned to the Asiatic-Pacific theater and participated in the assault and occupation of Okinawa Gunto from April through June 1945. On 15 September 1945, she was redesignated *LSTH-951* and performed occupation duty in the Far East until mid-January 1946. She was decommissioned on 8 August 1946 and struck from the Navy list on 25 September that same year. On 14 June 1948, the ship was sold to the Walter W. Johnson Co. for scrapping.

LST-951 earned one battle star for World War II service.

LST-952

LST-952 was laid down on 11 September 1944 at Hingham, Mass., by the Bethlehem-Hingham Shipyard, Inc.; launched on 11 October 1944; and commissioned on 3 November 1944.

During World War II, *LST-952* was assigned to the Asiatic-Pacific theater and participated in the assault and occupation of Okinawa Gunto from April through June 1945. On 15 September 1945, she was redesignated *LSTH-952* and performed occupation duty in the Far East and saw service in China until early May 1946. She returned to the United States and was decommissioned on 1 August 1946 and struck from the Navy list on 22 January 1947. On 10 October 1947, the ship was sold to Luria Bros. & Co., Inc., of Philadelphia, Pa., for scrapping.

LST-952 earned one battle star for World War II service.

LST-953

LST-953 was laid down on 15 September 1944 at Hingham, Mass., by the Bethlehem-Hingham Shipyard, Inc.; launched on 15 October 1944; and commissioned on 7 November 1944, Lt. T. W. Sexton in command.

During World War II, *LST-953* was assigned to the Asiatic-Pacific theater and participated in the assault and occupation of Okinawa Gunto in June 1945. On 1 July 1955, she was redesignated *Marinette County* (LST-953) (q.v.) after a county in northeastern Wisconsin. Earlier, she performed occupation duty in the Far East until early April 1946. Decommissioned on 12 November 1946 and assigned to the Atlantic Reserve Fleet, *Marinette County* was struck from the Navy list on 1 November 1958.

LST-953 earned one battle star for World War II service.

LST-954

LST-954 was redesignated ARL-17 and named *Numitor* (q.v.) on 14 August 1944.

LST-955

LST-955 was redesignated ARL-19 and named *Patroclus* (q.v.) on 14 August 1944.

LST-956

LST-956 was redesignated ARB-7 and named *Sarpedon* (q.v.) on 14 August 1944.

LST-957

LST-957 was laid down on 30 September 1944 at Hingham, Mass., by the Bethlehem-Hingham Shipyard, Inc.; launched on 30 October 1944; and commissioned on 20 November 1944, Lt. Samuel B. Wardwell, Jr., USNR, in command.

During World War II, *LST-957* was assigned to the Asiatic-Pacific theater and participated in the assault and occupation of Okinawa Gunto in April and May 1945. Following the war, she performed occupation duty in the Far East until early October 1945. The ship was decommissioned on 20 May 1946 and sold to Bosey, Philippines, on 5 December 1947. She was struck from the Navy list on 22 January 1948.

LST-957 earned one battle star for World War II service.

LST-958

LST-958 was laid down on 3 October 1944 at Hingham, Mass., by the Bethlehem-Hingham Shipyard, Inc.; launched on 31 October 1944; and commissioned on 25 November 1944.

During World War II, *LST-958* was assigned to the Asiatic-Pacific theater and participated in the assault and occupation of Okinawa Gunto in May and June 1945. Following the war, she performed occupation duty in the Far East until mid-October 1945. The ship was decommissioned on 14 March 1946 and struck from the Navy list on 28 March that same year. On 20 December 1946, the tank landing ship was sold.

LST-958 earned one battle star for World War II service.

LST-959

LST-959 was laid down on 6 October 1944 at Hingham, Mass., by the Bethlehem-Hingham Shipyard, Inc.; launched on 4 November 1944; and commissioned on 29 November 1944, Ens. J. H. Giesmann, Jr., in command.

During World War II, LST–959 was assigned to the Asiatic-Pacific theater and participated in the assault and occupation of Okinawa Gunto in June 1945. Following the war, she performed occupation duty in the Far East and saw service in China until mid-May 1946. She was decommissioned on 13 June 1946 and struck from the Navy list on 3 July that same year. On 10 June 1948, the ship was stripped and destroyed at Subic Bay, Philippines.

LST–959 earned one battle star for World War II service.

LST–960

LST–960 was laid down on 11 October 1944 at Hingham, Mass., by the Bethlehem-Hingham Shipyard, Inc.; launched on 8 November 1944; sponsored by Mrs. Helen Grande; and commissioned on 2 December 1944.

During World War II, LST–960 was assigned to the Asiatic-Pacific theater and participated in the assault and occupation of Okinawa Gunto in April and May 1945. Following the war, she performed occupation duty in the Far East and saw service in China until early April 1946. She returned to the United States and was decommissioned on 2 July 1946 and struck from the Navy list on 15 August that same year. On 4 April 1948, she was sold to Consolidated Builders, Inc., Seattle, Wash., for scrapping.

LST–960 earned one battle star for World War II service.

LST–961

LST–961 was laid down on 13 October 1944 at Hingham, Mass., by the Bethlehem-Hingham Shipyard, Inc.; launched on 11 November 1944; and commissioned on 6 December 1944.

During World War II, LST–961 was assigned to the Asiatic-Pacific theater and participated in the Palawan Island landings in March 1945 and the assault and occupation of Okinawa Gunto in May and June 1945. Following the war, she performed occupation duty in the Far East and saw service in China until mid-April 1946. She returned to the United States and was decommissioned on 23 July 1946 and struck from the Navy list on 28 August that same year. On 10 December 1947, the ship was sold to The Learner Co., Oakland, Calif., for scrapping.

LST–961 earned two battle stars for World War II service.

LST–962

LST–962 was redesignated ARL–22 and named Romulus (q.v.) on 14 August 1944.

LST–963

LST–963 was redesignated ARL–24 and named Sphinx (q.v.) on 14 August 1944.

LST–964

LST–964 was laid down on 24 October 1944 at Hingham, Mass., by the Bethlehem-Hingham Shipyard, Inc.; launched on 22 November 1944; sponsored by Mrs. Ailene Borland; and commissioned on 16 December 1944.

Following World War II, LST–964 performed occupation duty in the Far East and saw service in China until early April 1946. She was decommissioned on 27 June 1946 and struck from the Navy list on 15 August that same year. On 17 January 1947, the ship was sold to Compania Naviera y Commercial Perez Compano S.A. for operation.

LST–965

LST–965 was laid down on 27 October 1944 at Hingham, Mass., by the Bethlehem-Hingham Shipyard, Inc.; launched on 25 November 1944; and commissioned on 20 December 1944.

Following World War II, LST–965 performed occupation duty in the Far East until mid-October 1945. She returned to the United States and was decommissioned on 3 June 1946 and struck from the Navy list on 19 July that same year. On 23 October 1947, the ship was sold to the Boston Metals Corp., Baltimore, Md., for scrapping.

LST–966

LST–966 was redesignated AGP–15 and named Callisto (q.v.) on 14 August 1944.

LST–967

LST–967 was redesignated ARB–9 and named Ulysses (q.v.) on 14 August 1944.

LST–968

LST–968 was laid down on 7 November 1944 at Hingham, Mass., by the Bethlehem-Hingham Shipyard, Inc.; launched on 9 December 1944; sponsored by Mrs. John S. Eversole; and commissioned on 3 January 1945, Lt. (jg.) Rayburn M. Quinn in command.

Following World War II, LST–968 performed occupation duty in the Far East until early April 1946. She returned to the United States and was decommissioned on 2 July 1946 and struck from the Navy list on 15 August that same year. On 10 June 1948, the ship was sold to the Humble Oil and Refining Co., Houston, Tex., for operation.

LST–969

LST–969 was laid down on 10 November 1944 at Hingham, Mass., by the Bethlehem-Hingham Shipyard, Inc.; launched on 13 December 1944; and commissioned on 9 January 1945, Lt. (jg.) A. K. Price in command.

Following World War II, LST–969 performed logistic services between Hawaii and the west coast of the United States in 1945 and 1946 while assigned to the Pacific Fleet. She was decommissioned on 12 July 1946 and struck from the Navy list on 15 August that same year. On 25 April 1947, the ship was sold to Trailerships, Inc., for operation.

LST–970

LST–970 was laid down on 14 November 1944 at Hingham, Mass., by the Bethlehem-Hingham Shipyard, Inc.; launched on 16 December 1944; sponsored by Major Anne B. Cowan, WAC; and commissioned on 13 January 1945.

During World War II, LST–970 was assigned to the Asiatic-Pacific theater and participated in the assault and occupation of Okinawa Gunto in May and June 1945. Following the war, she performed occupation duty in the Far East and saw service in China until late February 1946. She returned to the United States and was decommissioned on 10 July 1946 and struck from the Navy list on 15 August that same year. On 25 April 1947, the ship was sold to Trailerships, Inc., for operation.

LST–970 earned one battle star for World War II service.

Grant County (LST–1174), with pontoon causeway sections stowed along her sides.

LST-971

LST-971 was redesignated ARL-13 and named *Menelaus* (*q.v.*) on 14 August 1944.

LST-972

LST-972 was laid down on 21 November 1944 at Hingham, Mass., by the Bethlehem-Hingham Shipyard, Inc.; launched on 22 December 1944; sponsored by Mrs. Margaret Avery; and commissioned on 22 January 1945.

Following World War II, LST-972 performed occupation duty in the Far East until early February 1946. She was decommissioned on 25 June 1946 and struck from the Navy list on 15 August that same year. On 29 May 1947, the ship was transferred to the Maritime Administration for disposal.

LST-973

LST-973 was laid down on 25 November 1944 at Hingham, Mass., by the Bethlehem-Hingham Shipyard, Inc.; launched on 27 December 1944; and commissioned on 27 January 1945.

Following World War II, LST-973 performed occupation duty in the Far East until early February 1946. She was decommissioned on 24 May 1946 and transferred to the Army. The ship was struck from the Navy list on 29 September 1947 but reinstated on 6 September 1950 for service during the Korean War. Decommissioned again on 7 November 1951, LST-973 was transferred to the French Navy that same date. She was struck from the Navy list for the second time on 20 November 1951.

LST-973 earned four battle stars and one award of the Navy Unit Commendation for Korean service.

LST-974

LST-974 was laid down on 28 November 1944 at Hingham, Mass., by the Bethlehem-Hingham Shipyard, Inc.; launched on 31 December 1944; and commissioned on 31 January 1945, Lt. A. C. Lane in command.

Following World War II, LST-974 performed occupation duty in the Far East and saw service in China until mid-May 1946. She was decommissioned and transferred to the State Department for disposal on 14 May 1946. The ship was struck from the Navy list on 19 June 1946.

LST-975

LST-975 was laid down on 1 December 1944 at Hingham, Mass., by the Bethlehem-Hingham Shipyard, Inc.; launched on 6 January 1945; sponsored by Miss Alice J. Varian; and commissioned on 3 February 1945, Lt. David S. Stanley in command.

Arriving in the Asiatic-Pacific theater at the end of the war, LST-975 conveyed troops and equipment between Philippine ports until she was decommissioned on 16 April 1946 at Subic Bay and turned over to the Army for Far East operations. She was recommissioned on 28 August 1950 and saw extensive service during the Korean War. The tank landing ship was named *Marion County* (LST-975) (*q.v.*) on 1 July 1955 after counties in 17 states. She alternated service with the Navy and MSTS until transferred under the Military Assistance Program to the Republic of Vietnam on 12 April 1962. *Marion County* operated with that country's navy as *Cam Ranh* (HQ-500). She was struck from the Navy list on 1 June 1963.

LST-975 earned six battle stars for Korean service.

LST-976

LST-976 was redesignated ARB-8 and named *Telamon* (*q.v.*) on 14 August 1944.

LST-977

LST-977 was redesignated AGP-14 and named *Alecto* (*q.v.*) on 14 August 1944.

LST-978

LST-978 was laid down on 15 December 1944 at Hingham, Mass., by the Bethlehem-Hingham Shipyard, Inc.; launched on 20 January 1945; sponsored by Mrs. Anna H. Phelan; and commissioned on 15 February 1945.

Following World War II, LST-978 performed occupation duty in the Far East until mid-December 1945. She returned to the United States and was decommissioned on 6 June 1946 and struck from the Navy list on 3 July that same year. On 10 December 1947, the ship was sold to the Salco Iron & Metal Co. for scrapping.

LST-979

LST-979 was laid down on 19 December 1944 at Hingham, Mass., by the Bethlehem-Hingham Shipyard, Inc.; launched on 23 January 1945; sponsored by Mrs. A. H. Balsley; and commissioned on 20 February 1945, Lt. Hunter A. Hogan, Jr., USNR, in command.

Following World War II, LST-979 performed occupation duty in the Far East and saw service in China until late March 1946. She returned to the United States and was decommissioned on 5 July 1946 and struck from the Navy list on 28 August that same year. On 4 November 1947, the ship was sold to the Moore Drydock Co., Oakland, Calif., for scrapping.

LST-980

LST-980 was laid down on 9 December 1943 at the Boston Naval Shipyard; launched on 27 January 1944; sponsored by Miss Imelda M. Munzing; and commissioned on 26 February 1944, Lt. W. F. Westfall in command.

During World War II, LST-980 was assigned to the European theater and participated in the invasion of Normandy in June 1944. Following the war, LST-980 saw extensive service with the Amphibious Fleet, Atlantic. Named *Meeker County* (LST-980) (*q.v.*) on 1 July 1955 after a county in Minnesota, she was decommissioned on 16 December 1955 and assigned to the Atlantic Reserve Fleet. Modernized and recommissioned on 23 September 1966, the tank landing ship operated in the Vietnam theater commencing in 1967 and ending in 1970.

LST-980 earned one battle star for World War II service and nine battle stars, the Meritorious Unit Commendation, and the Navy Unit Commendation for Vietnam service.

LST-981

LST-981 was laid down on 9 December 1943 at the Boston Navy Yard; launched on 27 January 1944; sponsored by Miss Helen Madden; and commissioned on 11 March 1944, Lt. Clyde A. Wilson in command.

During World War II, LST-981 was assigned to the European theater and participated in the invasion of Normandy in June 1944. Transferred to the Asiatic-Pacific theater, she engaged in the assault and occupation of Okinawa Gunto in May and June 1945. Following the war, she performed occupation duty in the

Far East until mid-May 1946. She returned to the United States and was decommissioned on 30 July 1946 and struck from the Navy list on 28 August that same year. On 12 December 1947, the ship was sold to the Salco Iron & Metal Co. for scrapping.

LST–981 earned two battle stars for World War II service.

LST–982

LST–982 was laid down on 22 December 1943 at the Boston Navy Yard; launched on 10 February 1944; sponsored by Mrs. Orrin R. Hewitt; and commissioned on 19 March 1944, Lt. (jg.) W. A. Breen, Jr., USNR, in command.

During World War II, *LST–982* was assigned to the European theater and participated in the invasion of Normandy in June 1944. Transferred to the Asiatic-Pacific theater, she engaged in the assault and occupation of Okinawa Gunto in May and June 1945. Following the war, she performed occupation duty in the Far East and saw service in China until mid-April 1946. The ship was decommissioned on 25 April 1946 and struck from the Navy list on 19 July 1946. On 5 December 1947, she was sold to Bosey, Philippines.

LST–982 earned two battle stars for World War II service.

LST–983

LST–983 was laid down on 22 December 1943 at the Boston Navy Yard; launched on 10 February 1944; sponsored by Mrs. Neal B. Farwell; and commissioned on 25 March 1944, Lt. Woodrow W. Weir, USNR, in command.

During World War II, *LST–983* was assigned to the European theater and participated in the invasion of Normandy in June 1944. Following the war, *LST–983* performed extensive service with the Amphibious Fleet, Atlantic. Renamed *Middlesex County* (LST–983) (*q.v.*) on 1 July 1955 after counties in Connecticut, Massachusetts, New Jersey, and Virginia, she was decommissioned on 10 January 1956 and assigned to the Atlantic Reserve Fleet. Recommissioned on 27 September 1961, *Middlesex County* operated in the Atlantic and Caribbean until decommissioning for the last time on 15 October 1969.

LST–983 earned one battle star for World War II service.

LST–984

LST–984 was laid down on 3 January 1944 at the Boston Navy Yard; launched on 25 February 1944; sponsored by Mrs. Charles J. Donahue; and commissioned on 1 April 1944, Ens. E. R. Baker in command.

Following World War II, *LST–984* performed occupation duty in the Far East until mid-March 1946. She was decommissioned on 25 June 1946 and struck from the Navy list on 31 July that same year. On 19 June 1948, the ship was sold to the Humble Oil & Refining Co., of Houston, Tex., for operation.

LST–985

LST–985 was laid down on 3 January 1944 at the Boston Navy Yard; launched on 25 February 1944; sponsored by Mrs. Charles E. Schofield; and commissioned on 7 April 1944.

Following World War II, *LST–985* performed occupation duty in the Far East and saw service in China until mid-March 1946. She returned to the United States and was decommissioned on 11 June 1946 and struck from the Navy list on 3 July that same year. On 13 October 1947, the ship was sold to William E. Skinner for scrapping.

LST–986

LST–986 was laid down on 15 January 1944 at the Boston Navy Yard; launched on 5 March 1944; and commissioned on 14 April 1944, Lt. Harold G. Waite, USNR, in command.

During World War II, *LST–986* was assigned to the Asiatic-Pacific theater and participated in the following operations:

Capture and occupation of Guam—July and August 1944

Lingayen Gulf landings—January 1945

Assault and occupation of Okinawa Gunto—April and May 1945

Following the war, *LST–986* performed occupation duty in the Far East until early March 1946. She returned to the United States and was decommissioned on 18 July 1946 and struck from the Navy list on 28 August that same year. On 4 November 1948, the ship was sold to the Moore Drydock Co., Oakland, Calif., for scrapping.

LST–986 earned three battle stars for World War II service.

LST–987

LST–987 was laid down on 2 February 1944 at the Boston Navy Yard; launched on 5 March 1944; and commissioned on 19 April 1944, Lt. William H. Pennington in command.

Following World War II, *LST–987* performed occupation duty in the Far East and saw service in China until mid-April 1946. She was decommissioned on 3 September 1946, but she continued training of Naval Reserves. *LST–987* entered the Atlantic Reserve Fleet at Green Cove Springs, Fla., in May 1950. On 1 July 1955, she was redesignated *Millard County* (LST–987) (*q.v.*) after a county in western Utah. The ship was struck from the Navy list on 1 June 1960 and sold to the Federal German Navy in August 1961.

LST–988

LST–988 was laid down on 10 February 1944 at the Boston Navy Yard; launched on 12 March 1944; sponsored by Mrs. Winfred K. Buckmaster; and commissioned on 25 April 1944, Lt. (jg.) Charles E. Craig in command.

During World War II, *LST–988* was assigned to the European theater and participated in the invasion of southern France in August and September 1944. Following the war, she performed occupation duty in the Far East until early April 1946. *LST–988* served as a Naval Reserve training ship until decommissioned on 13 June 1950 and assigned to the Atlantic Reserve Fleet. Recommissioned on 7 June 1951, *LST–988* operated as a unit of the Atlantic Fleet in the Atlantic, Caribbean, and the Mediterranean. On 1 July 1955, she was redesignated *Mineral County* (LST–988) (*q.v.*) after counties in Colorado, Montana, Nevada, and West Virginia. On 11 October 1957, *Mineral County* was decommissioned once again and stripped preparatory to her sinking as a target ship. She was struck from the Navy list on 27 September 1957.

LST–988 earned one battle star for World War II service.

LST–989

LST–989 was laid down on 10 February 1944 by the Boston Navy Yard; launched on 12 March 1944; sponsored by Mrs. Arthur L. Anderson; and commissioned on 28 April 1944, Ens. H. L. Campbell in command.

During World War II, *LST–989* was assigned to the European theater and participated in the invasion of southern France in August and September 1944. Following the war, *LST–989* performed occupation duty in the Far East and saw service in China until mid-April 1946. She was decommissioned on 7 October 1946 and struck from the Navy list on 13 November that same year. On 25 June 1948, the ship was sold to the Humble Oil & Refining Co., of Houston, Tex., for operation.

LST–989 earned one battle star for World War II service.

LST–990

LST–990 was laid down on 26 February 1944 at the Boston Navy Yard; launched on 27 March 1944; and commissioned on 1 May 1944, Lt. William C. Greenleaf, USNR, in command.

During World War II, *LST–990* was assigned to the Asiatic-Pacific theater and participated in the following operations:

    Capture and occupation of southern Palau Islands —September and October 1944

    Leyte landings—October and November 1944

    Zambales-Subic Bay—January 1945

    Assault and occupation of Okinawa Gunto—March through June 1945

Following the war, *LST–990* performed occupation duty in the Far East until early December 1945. She returned to the United States and was decommissioned on 10 July 1946 and struck from the Navy list on 25 September that same year. On 26 September 1947, the ship was sold to the Boston Metals Co., of Baltimore, Md., for scrapping.

LST–990 earned four battle stars for World War II service.

LST–991

LST–991 was laid down on 26 February 1944 at the Boston Navy Yard; launched on 27 March 1944; sponsored by Miss Dorothy Ann Govostes; and commissioned on 6 May 1944, Lt. Randall R. Shake, USNR, in command.

During World War II, *LST–991* was assigned to the Asiatic-Pacific theater and participated in the following operations:

    Capture and occupation of southern Palau Islands —September and October 1944

    Leyte landings—October and November 1944

    Lingayen Gulf landings—January 1945

    Zambales-Subic Bay—January 1945

    Assault and occupation of Okinawa Gunto—April through June 1945

Following the war, *LST–991* performed occupation duty in the Far East and saw service in China until early May 1946.

LST–991 earned five battle stars for World War II service.

LST–992

LST–992 was laid down on 5 March 1944 by the Boston Navy Yard; launched on 7 April 1944; sponsored by Mrs. Frances C. Landers; and commissioned on 10 May 1944, Lt. Stanley J. Kerr, USNR, in command.

During World War II, *LST–992* was assigned to the Asiatic-Pacific theater and participated in the assault and occupation of Okinawa Gunto in June 1945. Following the war, she performed occupation duty in the Far East and saw service in China until early April 1946. She returned to the United States and was decommissioned on 9 August 1946 and struck from the Navy list on 25 September that same year. On 13 June 1948, the ship was sold to the Walter W. Johnson Co. for scrapping.

LST–992 earned one battle star for World War II service.

LST–993

LST–993 was laid down on 7 March 1944 at the Boston Navy Yard; launched on 7 April 1944; sponsored by Mrs. Gladys L. Morey; and commissioned on 12 May 1944, Lt. A. W. Bates, USNR, in command.

During World War II, *LST–993* was assigned to the Asiatic-Pacific theater and participated in the following operations:

    Leyte landings—November 1944

    Lingayen Gulf landings—January 1945

    Tarakan Island operation—April and May 1945

Following the war, *LST–993* performed occupation duty in the Far East and saw service in China until early June 1946. She was decommissioned on 1 June 1946. On 7 February 1948, the ship was transferred to the Republic of China. She was struck from the Navy list on 12 March 1948.

LST–993 earned three battle stars for World War II service.

LST–994

LST–994 was laid down on 12 March 1944 by the Boston Navy Yard; launched on 17 April 1944; sponsored by Mrs. Lillian A. Finnerty; and commissioned on 17 May 1944, Lt. R. P. Gonder, USNR, in command.

During World War II, *LST–994* was assigned to the European theater and participated in the invasion of southern France in August and September 1944. Following the war, she performed occupation duty in the Far East and saw service in China until mid-April 1946. She returned to the United States and was decommissioned on 31 July 1946 and struck from the Navy list on 28 August that same year. On 23 December 1947, the ship was sold to Pablo N. Ferrari & Co. for operation.

LST–994 earned one battle star for World War II service.

LST–995

LST–995 was laid down on 12 March 1944 by the Boston Navy Yard; launched on 2 May 1944; and commissioned on 20 May 1944, Lt. (jg.) G. W. Chamberlin, USNR, in command.

During World War II, *LST–995* was assigned to the European theater and participated in the invasion of southern France in August and September 1944. Following the war, she performed occupation duty in the Far East until early April 1946. She returned to the United States and was decommissioned on 15 August 1946 and struck from the Navy list on 25 September that same year. On 4 November 1947, the ship was sold to the Northwest Merchandising Service for operation.

LST–995 earned one battle star for World War II service.

LST–996

LST–996 was laid down on 27 March 1944 at the Boston Navy Yard; launched on 2 May 1944; sponsored by Mrs. Ursula A. Hall; and commissioned on 23 May 1944, Ens. C. A. Leach, Jr., USNR, in command.

During World War II, *LST–996* was assigned to the European theater and participated in the invasion of southern France in August and September 1944. Transferred to the Asiatic-Pacific theater, she engaged in the assault and occupation of Okinawa Gunto in April through June 1945. She returned to the United States and was decommissioned on 22 April 1946 and struck from the Navy list on 8 May that same year. On 12 October 1947, the ship was sold to the Hugo Neu Steel Products Corp., New York, N.Y., for scrapping.

LST–996 earned two battle stars for World War II service.

LST–997

LST–997 was laid down on 27 March 1944 at the Boston Navy Yard; launched on 12 May 1944; sponsored by Mrs. Victoria V. Lynn; and commissioned on 27 May 1944, Lt. L. R. Dhuyvetter, USNR, in command.

During World War II, LST–997 was assigned to the European theater and participated in the invasion of southern France in August and September 1944. Following the war, she performed occupation duty in the Far East until mid-November 1945. She returned to the United States and was decommissioned on 7 March 1947 and struck from the Navy list on 4 April that same year. On 15 June 1948, the ship was sold to Consolidated Builders, Inc., Seattle, Wash., for scrapping.

LST–997 earned one battle star for World War II service.

LST–998

LST–998 was laid down on 8 April 1944 at the Boston Navy Yard; launched on 14 May 1944; sponsored by Miss Olga M. Lessa; and commissioned on 29 May 1944, Lt. R. W. Harter, USNR, in command.

Following World War II, LST–998 performed occupation duty in the Far East and saw service in China until late March 1946. She returned to the United States and was decommissioned on 26 June 1946 and struck from the Navy list on 31 July that same year. On 4 November 1948, the ship was sold to the Northwest Merchandising Service for operation.

LST–999

LST–999 was laid down on 8 April 1944 at the Boston Navy Yard; launched on 14 May 1944; sponsored by Miss Teresa C. McDevitt; and commissioned on 30 May 1944, Ens. V. L. Warner in command.

During World War II, LST–999 was assigned to the Asiatic-Pacific theater and participated in the following operations:

    Leyte landings—October 1944
    Mindanao Island landings—April 1945
    Assault and occupation of Okinawa Gunto—March through June 1945

LST–999 returned to the United States and was decommissioned on 29 July 1946 and struck from the Navy list on 25 September that same year. On 3 November 1947, the ship was sold to Dulien Steel Products, Inc., Seattle, Wash., for scrapping.

LST–999 earned three battle stars for World War II service.

LST–1000

LST–1000 was laid down on 18 April 1944 at the Boston Navy Yard; launched on 26 May 1944; and commissioned on 14 June 1944, Lt. Wesson S. Hertrais, USNR, in command.

During World War II, LST–1000 was assigned to the Asiatic-Pacific theater and participated in the assault and occupation of Okinawa Gunto in April 1945. Following the war, she performed occupation duty in the Far East and saw service in China until mid-April 1946. She returned to the United States and was decommissioned on 22 July 1946 and struck from the Navy list on 28 August that same year. On 13 June 1948, the ship was sold to Walter W. Johnson Co. for scrapping.

LST–1000 earned one battle star for World War II service.

LST–1001

LST–1001 was laid down on 18 April 1944 at the Boston Navy Yard; launched on 26 May 1944; sponsored by Mrs. Eva B. Rockett; and commissioned on 20 June 1944, Lt. Comdr. G. C. Masterson, USNR, in command.

During World War II, LST–1001 was assigned to the Asiatic-Pacific theater and participated in the assault and occupation of Okinawa Gunto in May and June 1945. Following the war, she performed occupation duty in the Far East until mid-September 1945. She returned to the United States and was decommissioned on 26 February 1946 and struck from the Navy list on 19 June that same year. On 23 October 1947, the ship was sold to the New Orleans Shipwrecking Corp., Chicago, Ill., for scrapping.

LST–1001 earned one battle star for World War II service.

LST–1002

LST–1002 was laid down on 3 May 1944 at the Boston Navy Yard; launched on 8 June 1944; sponsored by Mrs. Mary E. Nelson; and commissioned on 25 June 1944, Lt. S. Edelson, USNR, in command.

During World War II, LST–1002 was assigned to the Asiatic-Pacific theater and participated in the assault and occupation of Okinawa Gunto from April through June 1945. Following the war, she performed occupation duty in the Far East until mid-October 1945. The ship was decommissioned on 22 May 1946 and transferred to the State Department for disposition that same day. She was struck from the Navy list on 3 July 1946.

LST–1002 earned one battle star for World War II service.

LST–1003

LST–1003 was redesignated ARL–10 and named Coronis (q.v.) on 14 August 1944.

LST–1004

LST–1004 was laid down on 26 January 1944 at Quincy, Mass., by the Bethlehem Steel Co.; launched on 3 March 1944; and commissioned on 28 March 1944.

LST–1004 performed no combatant service during World War II. She was decommissioned on 27 June 1946 and struck from the Navy list on 7 February 1947. On 16 October 1947, the ship was sold to Consolidated Builders, Inc., Seattle, Wash., for scrapping.

LST–1005

LST–1005 was laid down on 2 February 1944 at Quincy, Mass., by the Bethlehem Steel Co.; launched on 11 March 1944; and commissioned on 6 April 1944.

Following World War II, LST–1005 performed occupation duty in the Far East until early 1946. She was decommissioned on 6 April 1946 after removal of all salvageable equipment following damage sustained in beaching operations. Her hulk was later destroyed. The ship was struck from the Navy list on 17 April 1946.

LST–1006

LST–1006 was laid down on 5 February 1944 at Quincy, Mass., by the Bethlehem Steel Co.; launched on 11 March 1944; and commissioned on 12 April 1944, Lt. Vardy D. Garvey in command.

During World War II, LST–1006 was assigned to the Asiatic-Pacific theater and participated in the following operations:

    Leyte landings—October 1944

Zambales-Subic Bay—January 1945

Assault and occupation of Okinawa Gunto—April through June 1945

Following the war, LST–1006 performed occupation duty in the Far East and saw service in China until late March 1946. She returned to the United States and was decommissioned on 26 July 1946 and struck from the Navy list on 28 August that same year. On 14 June 1948, the ship was sold to Steele Powers for operation.

LST–1006 earned three battle stars for World War II service.

LST–1007

LST–1007 was laid down on 8 February 1944 at Quincy, Mass., by the Bethlehem Steel Co.; launched on 20 March 1944; and commissioned on 15 April 1944.

During World War II, LST–1007 was assigned to the Asiatic-Pacific theater and participated in the Tarakan Island operation in April and May 1945. Following the war, she performed occupation duty in the Far East until late October 1945. She returned to the United States and was decommissioned on 2 March 1946 and struck from the Navy list on 12 April that same year. On 12 September 1946, the ship was sold to the Construction Power & Merchandising Co., of Brooklyn, N.Y.

LST–1007 earned one battle star for World War II service.

LST–1008

LST–1008 was laid down on 16 February 1944 at Quincy, Mass., by the Bethlehem Steel Co.; launched on 23 March 1944; and commissioned on 18 April 1944.

Following World War II, LST–1008 performed occupation duty in the Far East and saw service in China until early May 1946. She was decommissioned on 4 May 1946 and transferred to the State Department for disposition that same date. She was struck from the Navy list on 19 June 1946.

LST–1009

LST–1009 was laid down on 22 February 1944 at Quincy, Mass., by the Bethlehem Steel Co.; launched on 23 March 1944; and commissioned on 22 April 1944.

Following World War II, LST–1009 performed occupation duty in the Far East until mid-April 1946. She was decommissioned on 17 July 1946 and transferred to the United States Army. The ship was struck from the Navy list on 14 March 1947.

LST–1010

LST–1010 was laid down on 22 February 1944 at Quincy, Mass., by the Bethlehem Steel Co.; launched on 29 March 1944; and commissioned on 25 April 1944.

During World War II, LST–1010 was assigned to the European theater and participated in the invasion of southern France in August 1944. She was then assigned to the Asiatic-Pacific theater and took part in the assault and occupation of Okinawa Gunto in May and June 1945. Following the war, the ship performed occupation duty in the Far East until mid-January 1946. LST–1010 was transferred to the United States Army on 4 April 1947 and returned to United States Navy custody on 1 March 1950. She was later transferred to the Republic of Korea Navy on 22 March 1955 where she served as Un Pong (LST–807).

LST–1010 earned two battle stars for World War II service.

LST–1011

LST–1011 was laid down on 29 February 1944 at Quincy, Mass., by the Bethlehem Steel Co.; launched on 29 March 1944; and commissioned on 5 May 1944.

During World War II, LST–1011 was assigned to the European theater and participated in the invasion of southern France in August and September 1944. She was then assigned to the Asiatic-Pacific theater and took part in the assault and occupation of Okinawa Gunto in June 1945. Following the war, she performed occupation duty in the Far East until mid-February 1946. The ship returned to the United States and was decommissioned on 20 June 1946 and struck from the Navy list on 31 July that same year. On 12 June 1948, she was sold to the Walter W. Johnson Co. for scrapping.

LST–1011 earned two battle stars for World War II service.

LST–1012

LST–1012 was laid down on 4 March 1944 at Quincy, Mass., by the Bethlehem Steel Co.; launched on 8 April 1944; and commissioned on 30 April 1944, Lt. Comdr. M. J. Flowers, Jr., USNR, in command.

During World War II, LST–1012 was assigned to the European theater and participated in the invasion of southern France in August and September 1945. Following the war, she performed occupation duty in the Far East and saw service in China until early June 1946. The ship was decommissioned on 10 June 1946 and transferred to the State Department for disposal that same date. She was struck from the Navy list on 19 July 1946.

LST–1012 earned one battle star for World War II service.

LST–1013

LST–1013 was laid down on 13 March at Quincy, Mass., by the Bethlehem Steel Co.; launched on 16 April 1944; and commissioned on 2 May 1944, Lt. Charles K. Carroll, USNR, in command.

During World War II, LST–1013 was assigned to the Asiatic-Pacific theater and participated in the following operations:

Leyte landings—October 1944

Lingayen Gulf landings—January 1945

Assault and occupation of Okinawa Gunto—April through June 1945

Following the war, LST–1013 performed occupation duty in the Far East and saw service in China until early June 1946. She was decommissioned on 11 June 1946 and transferred to the State Department for disposition that same date. The ship was struck from the Navy list on 19 July 1946.

LST–1013 earned three battle stars for World War II service.

LST–1014

LST–1014 was laid down on 15 March 1944 at Quincy, Mass., by the Bethlehem Steel Co.; launched on 16 April 1944; and commissioned on 5 May 1944, Lt. William H. Weldon, USNR, in command.

During World War II, LST–1014 was assigned to the Asiatic-Pacific theater and participated in the following operations:

Capture and occupation of southern Palau Islands —September and October 1944

Leyte landings—November 1944

Assault and occupation of Okinawa Gunto—April through June 1945

Following the war, LST–1014 performed occupation duty in the Far East until late October 1945. She returned to the United States and was decommissioned

Marines, with *Ontos* antitank vehicles, coils of barbed wire, and cases of rations, on the deck of an LST off Vietnam. An LVTP is on the beach.

on 5 March 1946 and struck from the Navy list on 17 April that same year. On 12 September 1946, the ship was sold to the Construction Power & Merchandising Co., Brooklyn, N.Y.

LST–1014 earned three battle stars for World War II service.

LST–1015

LST–1015 was laid down on 22 March 1944 at Quincy, Mass., by the Bethlehem Steel Co.; launched on 20 April 1944; and commissioned on 8 May 1944.

During World War II, *LST–1015* was assigned to the Asiatic-Pacific theater and participated in the following operations:

Capture and occupation of southern Palau Islands —September through October 1944

Leyte landings—October and November 1944

Lingayen Gulf landings—January 1945

Assault and occupation of Okinawa Gunto—April 1945

Following the war, *LST–1015* performed occupation duty in the Far East and saw service in China until early May 1946. She was decommissioned on 6 May 1946 and transferred to the State Department for disposition that same date. The ship was struck from the Navy list on 19 June 1946.

LST–1015 earned four battle stars for World War II service.

LST–1016

LST–1016 was laid down on 25 March 1944 at Quincy, Mass., by the Bethlehem Steel Co.; launched on 25 April; and commissioned on 10 May 1944, Lt. John W. Chapman, USNR, in command.

During World War II, *LST–1016* was assigned to the Asiatic-Pacific theater and participated in the Mindanao Island landings in April 1945 and the Balikpapan operation in June and July 1945. Following the war, she performed occupation duty in the Far East until mid-February 1946. She returned to the United States and was decommissioned on 26 June 1946 and struck from the Navy list on 31 July that same year. On 9 December 1947, the ship was sold to the Learner Co., Oakland, Calif., for scrapping.

LST–1016 earned two battle stars for World War II service.

LST–1017

LST–1017 was laid down on 25 March 1944 at Quincy, Mass., by the Bethlehem Steel Co.; launched on 25 April 1944; and commissioned on 12 May 1944.

During World War II, *LST–1017* was assigned to the Asiatic-Pacific theater and participated in the following operations:

Morotai landings—September 1944

Leyte landings—November 1944

Lingayen Gulf landing—January 1945

Mindanao Island landings—April 1945

Brunei Bay operation—June and July 1945

Following the war, *LST–1017* performed occupation duty in the Far East and saw service in China until late June 1946. She was decommissioned on 29 June 1946 and transferred to the Republic of China on 14 December 1946. The ship was struck from the Navy list on 12 March 1948.

LST–1017 earned five battle stars for World War II service.

LST–1018

LST–1018 was laid down on 31 March 1944 at Quincy, Mass., by the Bethlehem Steel Co.; launched on 6 May 1944; and commissioned on 14 May 1944.

During World War II, *LST–1018* was assigned to the Asiatic-Pacific theater and participated in the following operations:

Morotai landings—September 1944

Leyte landings—November 1944

Lingayen Gulf landing—January 1945

Mindanao Island landings—April 1945

Balikpapan operation—June and July 1945

Following the war, *LST–1018* performed occupation duty in the Far East until mid-January 1946. She returned to the United States and was decommissioned on 16 August 1946 and struck from the Navy list on 23 June 1947. On 24 June 1948, the ship was sold to Consolidated Builders, Inc., Seattle, Wash., for scrapping.

LST–1018 earned five battle stars for World War II service.

LST–1019

LST–1019 was laid down on 31 March 1944 at Quincy, Mass., by the Bethlehem Steel Co.; launched on 6 May 1944; and commissioned on 17 May 1944, Lt. Comdr. Norman C. Ross, in command.

During World War II, *LST–1019* was assigned to the European theater and participated in the invasion of southern France in August and September 1944. Later transferred to the Asiatic-Pacific theater, she engaged in the assault and occupation of Okinawa Gunto in May and June 1945. Following the war, she performed occupation duty in the Far East until early April 1946. She returned to the United States and was decommissioned on 30 July 1946 and struck from the Navy list on 25 September that same year. On 28 June 1948, the ship was sold to the Humble Oil & Refining Co., Houston, Tex., for operation.

LST–1019 earned two battle stars for World War II service.

LST–1020

LST–1020 was laid down on 11 April 1944 at Quincy, Mass., by the Bethlehem Steel Co.; launched on 10 May 1944; and commissioned on 19 May 1944.

During World War II, *LST–1020* was assigned to the European theater and participated in the invasion of southern France in August and September 1944. Following the war, she performed occupation duty in the Far East and saw service in China until early April 1946. She returned to the United States and was decommissioned on 16 July 1946 and struck from the Navy list on 28 August that same year. On 13 June 1948, the ship was sold to the Walter W. Johnson Co. for scrapping.

LST–1020 earned one battle star for World War II service.

LST–1021

LST–1021 was laid down on 18 April 1944 at Quincy, Mass., by the Bethlehem Steel Co.; launched on 16 May 1944; and commissioned on 21 May 1944.

During World War II, *LST–1021* was assigned to the European theater and participated in the invasion of southern France in August and September 1944. She was transferred to the United Kingdom on 24 December 1944. The ship was returned to United States Navy custody and struck from the Navy list on 1 August 1947. On 7 October 1947, she was sold to Tung Hwa Trading Co., Singapore.

LST–1021 earned one battle star for World War II service.

LST–1022

LST–1022 was laid down on 18 April 1944 at Quincy, Mass., by the Bethlehem Steel Co.; launched on 16 May

1944; and commissioned on 24 May 1944, Lt. William D. Henderson in command.

During World War II, *LST-1022* was assigned to the Asiatic-Pacific theater and participated in the assault and occupation of Okinawa Gunto in June 1945. Following the war, she performed occupation duty in the Far East until early August 1946. She was decommissioned on 31 December 1947 and struck from the Navy list on 22 January 1948. On 28 June 1948, the ship was sold to R. G. Greive for scrapping.

LST-1022 earned one battle star for World War II service.

LST-1023

LST-1023 was laid down on 20 April 1944 at Quincy, Mass., by the Bethlehem Steel Co.; launched on 17 May 1944; and commissioned on 26 May 1944.

Following World War II, *LST-1023* performed occupation duty in the Far East until mid-April 1946. She returned to the United States and was decommissioned on 19 July 1946 and struck from the Navy list on 28 August that same year. On 18 June 1948, the ship was sold to the Humble Oil & Refining Co., Houston, Tex., for operation.

LST-1024

LST-1024 was laid down on 26 April 1944 at Quincy, Mass., by the Bethlehem Steel Co.; launched on 22 May 1944; and commissioned on 28 May 1944.

During World War II, *LST-1024* was assigned to the Asiatic-Pacific theater and participated in the Leyte landings in October 1944 and the assault and occupation of Okinawa Gunto in April and May 1945. Following the war, she performed occupation duty in the Far East until late December 1945. She returned to the United States and was decommissioned on 27 June 1946 and struck from the Navy list on 31 July that same year. On 12 March 1948, the ship was sold to Alexander Shipyards, Inc., for operation.

LST-1024 earned two battle stars for World War II service.

LST-1025

LST-1025 was laid down on 26 April 1944 at Quincy, Mass., by the Bethlehem Steel Co.; launched on 22 May 1944; and commissioned on 31 May 1944.

During World War II, *LST-1025* was assigned to the Asiatic-Pacific theater and participated in the following operations:

    Leyte landings—October and November 1944
    Zambales-Subic Bay—January 1945
    Visayan Islands landings—March 1945
    Tarakan Island operation—April and May 1945

Following the war, *LST-1025* performed occupation duty in the Far East until early January 1946. She returned to the United States and was decommissioned on 24 May 1946 and struck from the Navy list on 15 August that same year. On 11 June 1948, the ship was sold to the Walter W. Johnson Co. for scrapping.

LST-1025 earned four battle stars for World War II service.

LST-1026

LST-1026 was laid down on 8 May 1944 at Quincy, Mass., by the Bethlehem Steel Co.; launched on 2 June 1944; and commissioned on 7 June 1944, Lt. R. E. Parker, USNR, in command.

During World War II, *LST-1026* was assigned to the Asiatic-Pacific theater and participated in the Leyte landings in October and November 1944 and the Mindanao Island landings in March and April 1945. Following the war, she performed occupation duty in the Far East and saw service in China until mid-July 1946. She was decommissioned on 11 August 1946 and struck from the Navy list on 28 August that same year. On 5 December 1947, the ship was sold to Bosey, Philippines.

LST-1026 earned two battle stars for World War II service.

LST-1027

LST-1027 was laid down on 8 May 1944 at Quincy, *Mass.*, by the Bethlehem Steel Co.; launched on 2 June 1944; sponsored by Mrs. Harry A. Hassan; and commissioned on 7 June 1944.

During World War II, *LST-1027* was assigned to the Asiatic-Pacific theater and participated in the following operations:

    Leyte landings—November 1944
    Lingayen Gulf landings—January 1945
    Mindanao Island landings—March 1945

Following the war, *LST-1027* performed occupation duty in the Far East and saw service in China until early September 1946. She was decommissioned on 4 September 1946 and sold to Bosey, Philippines, on 20 January 1947. The ship was struck from the Navy list on 23 April 1947.

LST-1027 earned three battle stars for World War II service.

LST-1028

LST-1028 was laid down on 15 May 1944 at the Boston Navy Yard; launched on 18 June 1944; sponsored by Mrs. Susanna C. Curran; and commissioned on 7 July 1944, Lt. N. L. Knipe, Jr., USNR, in command.

During World War II, *LST-1028* was assigned to the Asiatic-Pacific theater and participated in the Lingayen Gulf landings in January 1945. She returned to the United States and was decommissioned on 19 November 1945 and struck from the Navy list on 5 December that same year. On 29 August 1947, the ship was sold to the Puget Sound Bridge & Dredging Co., Seattle, Wash., for scrapping.

LST-1028 earned one battle star for World War II service.

LST-1029

LST-1029 was laid down on 15 May 1944 at the Boston Navy Yard; launched on 18 June 1944; sponsored by Mrs. Stanley Madey; and commissioned on 13 July 1944, Lt. I. H. Vincent, USNR, in command.

During World War II, *LST-1029* was assigned to the Asiatic-Pacific theater and participated in the Lingayen Gulf landing in January 1945 and the assault and occupation of Okinawa Gunto from April through June 1945. Following the war, she performed occupation duty in the Far East until late October 1945. She returned to the United States and was decommissioned on 1 May 1946 and sold to the Suwannee Fruit & Steamship Co., Jacksonville, Fla., on 31 October 1946. The ship was struck from the Navy list on 10 June 1947.

LST-1029 earned two battle stars for World War II service.

LST-1030

LST-1030 was laid down on 27 May 1944 at the Boston Navy Yard; launched on 25 June 1944; sponsored by Miss Irene M. O'Brien; and commissioned on 19 July 1944, Lt. (jg.) S. W. Farnham, USNR, in command.

During World War II, *LST-1030* was assigned to the Asiatic-Pacific theater and participated in the Lingayen Gulf landing in January 1945 and the assault and occupation of Okinawa Gunto from April through June 1945. Following the war, she performed occupation duty in the Far East and saw service in China until late May 1946. The ship was decommissioned on 29 May 1946 and transferred to the Republic of China Navy on 17 February 1948 where she served as *Chung Chuan* (LST–221). She was struck from the Navy list on 12 March 1948.

LST–1030 earned two battle stars for World War II service.

LST–1031

LST–1031 was laid down on 27 May 1944 at the Boston Navy Yard; launched on 25 June 1944; sponsored by Mrs. Priscilla A. Daudelin; and commissioned on 25 July 1944, Lt. C. W. Price in command.

During World War II, *LST–1031* was assigned to the Asiatic-Pacific theater and participated in the assault and occupation of Okinawa Gunto in May and June 1945. She returned to the United States and was decommissioned on 18 December 1945 and struck from the Navy list on 8 January 1946. On 23 October 1947, the ship was sold to the Boston Metals Corp., of Baltimore, Md., for scrapping.

LST–1031 earned one battle star for World War II service.

LST–1032

LST–1032 was laid down on 9 June 1944 by the Boston Navy Yard; launched on 9 July 1944; sponsored by Mrs. Jennie M. Kneeland; and commissioned on 1 August 1944, Lt. J. M. Medina in command.

During World War II, *LST–1032* was assigned to the Asiatic-Pacific theater and participated in the assault and occupation of Iwo Jima in February 1945 and the assault and occupation of Okinawa Gunto from April through June 1945. Following the war, she performed occupation duty in the Far East until late October 1945. On 1 July 1955, she was redesignated *Monmouth County* (LST–1032) (*q.v.*) after a county in New Jersey. The ship was decommissioned on 14 November 1955 and assigned to the Atlantic Reserve Fleet. *Monmouth County* was recommissioned on 28 May 1963 and performed extensive service during the Vietnam War. Decommissioned again in 1970, *Monmouth County* was struck from the Navy list on 12 August 1970.

LST–1032 earned two battle stars for World War II service and one award of the Navy Unit Commendation, one award of the Meritorious Unit Commendation, and 11 battle stars for the Vietnam War.

LST–1033

LST–1033 was laid down on 9 June 1944 at the Boston Navy Yard; launched on 9 July 1944; sponsored by Miss Mary Theresa O'Donnell; and commissioned on 12 August 1944, Lt. J. W. Robinson, USNR, in command.

During World War II, *LST–1033* was assigned to the Asiatic-Pacific theater and participated in the assault and occupation of Iwo Jima in February 1945 and the assault and occupation of Okinawa Gunto from April through June 1945. Following the war, she performed occupation duty in the Far East and saw service in China until mid-July. She was redesignated *LSTH–1033* on 15 September 1945. The ship was decommissioned on 1 August 1946 and struck from the Navy list on 28 August that same year. On 5 December 1947, she was sold to Bosey, Philippines.

LST–1033 earned two battle stars for World War II service.

LST–1034

LST–1034 was laid down on 26 June 1944 at the Boston Navy Yard; launched on 4 August 1944; spon-

sored by Mrs. Edith A. Gannon; and commissioned on 26 August 1944, Lt. (jg.) Paul C. Greenwell, USNR, in command.

During World War II, *LST–1034* was assigned to the Asiatic-Pacific theater and participated in the Mindanao Island landings in April 1945. Following the war, she performed occupation duty in the Far East until early September 1946. The ship was decommissioned on 8 October 1946 and sold to the Netherlands East Indies on 28 October that same year. She was struck from the Navy list on 29 October 1946.

LST–1034 earned one battle star for World War II service.

LST–1035

LST–1035 was laid down on 26 June 1944 at the Boston Navy Yard; launched on 4 August 1944; sponsored by Mrs. Ella M. Kelleher; and commissioned on 1 September 1944, Lt. M. Perry in command.

During World War II, *LST–1035* was assigned to the Asiatic-Pacific theater and participated in the following operations:

   Palawan Island landings—March 1945
   Visayan Islands landings—March and April 1945
   Tarakan Island operation—April and May 1945

Following the war, *LST–1035* performed occupation duty in the Far East until mid-February 1946. She returned to the United States and was decommissioned on 6 June 1946 and struck from the Navy list on 3 July that same year. On 16 December 1947, the ship was sold to the Learner Co., Oakland, Calif., for scrapping.

LST–1035 earned two battle stars for World War II service.

LST–1036

LST–1036 was redesignated ARL–11 and named *Creon* (*q.v.*) on 14 August 1944.

LST–1037

LST–1037 was redesignated ARL–12 and named *Poseidon* (*q.v.*) on 14 August 1944.

LST–1038

LST–1038 was laid down on 29 October 1944 at Pittsburgh, Pa., by the Dravo Corp.; launched on 6 January 1945; sponsored by Mrs. Elwood Printz; and commissioned on 5 February 1945, Lt. Julius Wood in command.

During World War II, *LST–1038* was assigned to the Asiatic-Pacific theater and participated in the assault and occupation of Okinawa Gunto in May and June 1945. Following the war, she performed occupation duty in the Far East until early December 1945. She then operated as a training ship for naval reservists in the New York area. Decommissioned in 1949, *LST–1038* was assigned to the Atlantic Reserve Fleet berthed at Green Cove Springs, Fla. On 1 July 1955, she was redesignated *Monroe County* (LST–1038) (*q.v.*) after counties in 17 states. She was struck from the Navy list on 1 November 1958.

LST–1038 earned one battle star for World War II service.

LST–1039

LST–1039 was laid down on 26 November 1944 at Pittsburgh, Pa., by the Dravo Corp.; launched on 6 January 1945; sponsored by Mrs. Jack H. Johnston; and commissioned on 9 February 1945, Lt. G. E. Paris in command.

During World War II, *LST–1039* was assigned to the Asiatic-Pacific theater and participated in the assault and occupation of Okinawa Gunto in June 1945. Following the war, she performed occupation duty in the Far East until early April 1946. She returned to the United States and was decommissioned on 21 June 1946 and struck from the Navy list on 31 July that same year. On 2 September 1947, the ship was sold to the Columbia River Packers Association, Inc., for operation.

LST–1039 earned one battle star for World War II service.

LST–1040

LST–1040 was laid down on 3 December 1944 at Pittsburgh, Pa., by the Dravo Corp.; launched on 13 January 1945; sponsored by Mrs. Charles L. Hoffman; and commissioned on 13 February 1945, Lt. George E. Cooper, USNR, in command.

During World War II, *LST–1040* was assigned to the Asiatic-Pacific theater and participated in the assault and occupation of Okinawa Gunto in June 1945. Following the war, she performed occupation duty in the Far East and saw service in China until mid-July 1946. She was decommissioned on 23 September 1946 and sold to the Netherlands East Indies on 5 October that same year. On 23 April 1947, the ship was struck from the Navy list.

LST–1040 earned one battle star for World War II service.

LST–1041

LST–1041 was laid down on 12 November 1944 at Pittsburgh, Pa., by the Dravo Corp.; launched on 20 January 1945; sponsored by Mrs. D. W. Raegler; and commissioned on 19 February 1945.

Following World War II, *LST–1041* performed occupation duty in the Far East and saw service in China until mid-December 1945. She saw extensive service with the Atlantic Fleet for a decade. The ship was redesignated *Montgomery County* (LST-1041) (*q.v.*) on 1 July 1955 after counties in 18 states of the United States. She was decommissioned on 31 January 1956 and assigned to the Atlantic Reserve Fleet. The tank landing ship was struck from the Navy list on 1 June 1960 and sold to West Germany in August that same year.

LST–1042

LST–1042 was laid down on 10 December 1944 at Pittsburgh, Pa., by the Dravo Corp.; launched on 20 January 1945; sponsored by Mrs. A. M. Shields; and commissioned on 22 February 1945, Lt. Patrick Connolly, USNR, in command.

During World War II, *LST–1042* was assigned to the Asiatic-Pacific theater and participated in the assault and occupation of Okinawa Gunto in June 1945. Following the war, *LST–1042* performed occupation duty in the Far East and saw service in China until early May 1946. The ship was decommissioned on 9 May 1946 and struck from the Navy list on 19 June that same year.

LST–1042 earned one battle star for World War II service.

LST–1043

LST–1043 was laid down on 17 December 1944 at Pittsburgh, Pa., by the Dravo Corp.; launched on 27 January 1945; sponsored by Mrs. George W. Johnston; and commissioned on 24 February 1945, Lt. Clifford Off, Jr., USNR, in command.

Following World War II, *LST–1043* performed occupation duty in the Far East until late September 1945.

She returned to the United States and was decommissioned on 22 July 1946 and struck from the Navy list on 28 August that same year. On 10 December 1947, the ship was sold to the Learner Co., of Oakland, Calif., for scrapping.

LST–1044

LST–1044 was laid down on 25 November 1944 at Pittsburgh, Pa., by the Dravo Corp.; launched on 3 February 1945; sponsored by Mrs. J. D. Port; and commissioned on 2 March 1945, Lt. Frank P. Eldredge in command.

Following World War II, *LST–1044* performed occupation duty in the Far East and saw service in China until mid-April 1946. She returned to the United States and was decommissioned on 28 June 1946 and struck from the Navy list on 31 July that same year. On 8 January 1948, the ship was sold to Pablo N. Ferrari & Co. for operation.

LST–1045

LST–1045 was laid down on 22 December 1944 at Pittsburgh, Pa., by the Dravo Corp.; launched on 3 February 1945; sponsored by Mrs. William G. Rudge; and commissioned on 27 March 1945.

Following World War II, *LST–1045* performed occupation duty in the Far East until late February 1946. She returned to the United States and was decommissioned on 10 July 1946 and struck from the Navy list on 15 August 1946. On 9 December 1947, the ship was sold to James A. Hughes, New York, N.Y., for scrapping.

LST–1046

LST–1046 was laid down on 31 December 1944 at Pittsburgh, Pa., by the Dravo Corp.; launched on 10 February 1945; sponsored by Mrs. Florence M. Teepe; and commissioned on 28 March 1945, Lt. R. P. McGhie in command.

Following World War II, *LST–1046* performed occupation duty in the Far East and saw service in China until early April 1946. She returned to the United States and was decommissioned on 27 June 1946 and struck from the Navy list on 31 July that same year. The ship was sold to Consolidated Builders, Inc., Seattle, Wash., on 25 September 1947 for scrapping.

LST–1047

LST–1047 was laid down on 9 December 1944 at Pittsburgh, Pa., by the Dravo Corp.; launched on 17 February 1945; sponsored by Mrs. J. W. Deist; and commissioned on 28 March 1945, Lt Charles G. Wood in command.

Following World War II, *LST–1047* performed occupation duty in the Far East until mid-December 1945. The ship was decommissioned on 6 May 1946 and transferred to the Army on 25 June that same year. On 29 September 1947, she was struck from the Navy list.

LST–1048

LST–1048 was laid down on 7 January 1945 at Pittsburgh, Pa., by the Dravo Corp.; launched on 17 February 1945; sponsored by Mrs. L. P. Struble; and commissioned on 28 March 1945, Lt. Robert G. Stevenson in command.

Following World War II, *LST–1048* performed occupation duty in the Far East until mid-December 1945. She was decommissioned on 14 May 1946 and assigned to the United States Army. Following the outbreak of hostilities in Korea, she was recommissioned on 26 August 1950 and performed extensive service during that war. The ship was redesignated *Morgan County* (LST-1048) (*q.v.*) on 1 July 1955 for counties in 11 states of the United States. She was decommissioned again on 10 May 1956 and transferred to the Military Sea Transportation Service. Struck from the Navy list on 1 August 1959, she was sold to Ships, Inc., Miami, Fla., on 10 June 1960.

LST-1048 earned one battle star for the Korean War.

LST-1049

LST-1049 was laid down on 14 January 1945 at Pittsburgh, Pa., by the Dravo Corp.; launched on 24 February 1945; sponsored by Mrs. Walter Malec; and commissioned on 30 March 1945, Lt. Sheldon Potter, III, USNR, in command.

Following World War II, *LST-1049* performed occupation duty in the Far East until mid-April 1946. She was decommissioned on 18 July 1946 and struck from the Navy list on 19 February 1948. On 1 July 1949, the ship was sold to the Townsend Transportation Co., Bayonne, N.J.

LST-1050

LST-1050 was laid down on 23 December 1944 at Pittsburgh, Pa., by the Dravo Corp.; launched on 3 March 1945; sponsored by Mrs. Oscar Enigson, Jr.; and commissioned on 3 April 1945.

Following World War II, *LST-1050* performed occupation duty in the Far East and saw service in China until late January 1947. She was decommissioned and transferred to the Republic of China under the terms of lend-lease on 27 January 1947 where she served as *Chung Lien* (LST-209). The ship was struck from the Navy list on 12 March 1948.

LST-1051

LST-1051 was laid down on 21 January 1945 at Pittsburgh, Pa., by the Dravo Corp.; launched on 3 March 1945; sponsored by Mrs. Charles F. Posten; and commissioned on 7 April 1945.

Following World War II, *LST-1051* performed occupation duty in the Far East until early January 1946. She returned to the United States and was decommissioned on 7 May 1946 and struck from the Navy list on 5 June that same year. On 13 June 1948, the ship was sold to the Walter W. Johnson Co., for scrapping.

LST-1052

LST-1052 was laid down on 29 January 1945 at Pittsburgh, Pa., by the Dravo Corp.; launched on 6 March 1945; sponsored by Mrs. M. M. Lachowski; and commissioned on 15 April 1945.

Following World War II, *LST-1052* performed occupation duty in the Far East until early March 1946. She returned to the United States and was decommissioned on 11 July 1946 and struck from the Navy list on 15 August that same year. On 25 September 1947, the ship was sold to Consolidated Builders, Inc., Seattle, Wash., for scrapping.

LST-1053

LST-1053 was laid down on 6 January 1945 at Pittsburgh, Pa., by the Dravo Corp.; launched on 6 March 1945; sponsored by Mrs. William F. Thorpe; and commissioned on 23 April 1945.

Following World War II, *LST-1053* performed occupation duty in the Far East until early January 1946. She returned to the United States and was decommis-

sioned on 3 June 1946 and struck from the Navy list on 3 July that same year. On 8 June 1948, the ship was sold to the Humble Oil & Refining Co., Houston, Tex., for operation.

LST-1054

LST-1054 was laid down on 4 February 1945 at Pittsburgh, Pa., by the Dravo Corp.; launched on 17 March 1945; sponsored by Mrs. R. L. Stallings; and commissioned on 17 April 1945.

Following World War II, *LST-1054* performed occupation duty in the Far East until mid-April 1946. She returned to the United States and was decommissioned on 28 June 1946 and sruck from the Navy list on 31 July that same year. On 25 November 1947, the ship was sold to the Bethlehem Steel Co., Bethlehem, Pa., for scrapping.

LST-1055

LST-1055 was laid down on 10 February 1945 at Pittsburgh, Pa., by the Dravo Corp.; launched on 24 March 1945; sponsored by Mrs. R. T. Miles; and commissioned on 26 April 1945.

Following World War II, *LST-1055* performed occupation duty in the Far East until mid-February 1947. She was decommissioned on 13 February 1947 and transferred to the United States Army that same date. The ship was struck from the Navy list on 25 February 1947.

LST-1056

LST-1056 was laid down on 20 January 1945 at Pittsburgh, Pa., by the Dravo Corp.; launched on 24 March 1945; sponsored by Mrs. W. M. Harrison; and commissioned on 2 May 1945.

Following World War II, *LST-1056* performed occupation duty in the Far East and saw service in China until early July 1946. She was decommissioned on 12 July 1946 and sold to Bosey, Philippines, on 20 January 1947. The ship was struck from the Navy list on 10 June 1947.

LST-1057

LST-1057 was laid down on 17 February 1945 at Pittsburgh, Pa., by the Dravo Corp.; launched on 31 March 1945; sponsored by Mrs. E. W. McKinley; and commissioned on 7 May 1945.

Following World War II, *LST-1057* performed occupation duty in the Far East until early March 1946. The ship returned to the United States and was decommissioned on 5 August 1946 and struck from the Navy list on 25 September that same year. She was sold to Pablo N. Ferrari & Co. on 12 January 1948 for operation.

LST-1058

LST-1058 was laid down on 24 February 1945 at Pittsburgh, Pa., by the Dravo Corp.; launched on 7 April 1945; sponsored by Mrs. Harry Schoeffel; and commissioned on 16 May 1945.

LST-1058 performed no active service. She was decommissioned on 30 July 1946 and struck from the Navy list on 25 September that same year. On 13 June 1948, she was sold to the Walter W. Johnson Co. for scrapping.

LST-1059

LST-1059 was laid down on 3 March 1945 at Pittsburgh, Pa., by the Dravo Corp.; launched on 14 April

1945; sponsored by Mrs. Corinne G. Harris; and commissioned on 17 May 1945.

Following World War II, *LST-1059* performed occupation duty in the Far East and saw service in China until mid-July 1946. She was decommissioned on 14 September 1946 and sold to the Morrison Knudsen Co., Shanghai, China, on 14 January 1947. The ship was struck from the Navy list on 23 April 1947.

LST-1060

LST-1060 was laid down on 22 December 1944 at Hingham, Mass., by the Bethlehem-Hingham Shipyard, Inc.; launched on 29 January 1945; sponsored by Mrs. Alice M. Wiggin; and commissioned on 24 February 1945.

Following World War II, *LST-1060* performed occupation duty in the Far East and saw service in China until mid-July 1946. She was decommissioned on 7 September 1946 and struck from the Navy list on 23 April 1947. On 13 February 1948, the ship was sold to Bosey, Philippines.

LST-1061

LST-1061 was laid down on 26 December 1944 at Hingham, Mass., by the Bethlehem-Hingham Shipyard, Inc.; launched on 3 February 1945; sponsored by Mrs. Ada Smith; and commissioned on 1 March 1945, Lt. G. A. Johnson in command.

Following World War II, *LST-1061* performed occupation duty in the Far East until mid-September 1945. She returned to the United States and was decommissioned on 1 May 1946 and struck from the Navy list on 3 July that same year. On 1 March 1948, the ship was sold to the Texas Petroleum Co. for operation.

LST-1062

LST-1062 was laid down on 30 December 1944 at Hingham, Mass., by the Bethlehem-Hingham Shipyard, Inc.; launched on 6 February 1945; and commissioned on 5 March 1945, Lt. T. M. Robinson in command.

Following World War II, *LST-1062* performed occupation duty in the Far East until early April 1946. She returned to the United States and was decommissioned on 27 June 1946 and struck from the Navy list on 31 July that same year. On 25 November 1947, the ship was sold to the Bethlehem Pacific Coast Steel Corp. for scrapping.

LST-1063

LST-1063 was laid down on 3 January 1945 at Hingham, Mass., by the Bethlehem-Hingham Shipyard, Inc.; launched on 11 February 1945; and commissioned on 8 March 1945.

Following World War II, *LST-1063* performed occupation duty in the Far East until early April 1946. She was transferred to the Maritime Administration for disposal on 30 June 1948.

LST-1064

LST-1064 was laid down on 9 January 1945 at Hingham, Mass., by the Bethlehem-Hingham Shipyard, Inc.; launched on 14 February 1945; and commissioned on 12 March 1945, Lt. Leland H. Austin in command.

Following World War II, *LST-1064* performed occupation duty in the Far East until late December 1945. She was decommissioned on 21 August 1946 and redesignated *Nansemond County* (LST-1064) (q.v.) on 1 July 1955 after a county in southeastern Virginia. The ship was struck from the Navy list on 1 October 1959 and sold to Japan in April 1961 where she served

as *Shiretoko* (LST-4003). Reobtained from Japan in 1975, *Nansemond County* was transferred to the Philippines on 24 September 1976.

LST-1065

LST-1065 was laid down on 12 January 1945 at Hingham, Mass., by the Bethlehem-Hingham Shipyard, Inc.; launched on 17 February 1945; and commissioned on 16 March 1945.

Following World War II, *LST-1065* performed occupation duty in the Far East and saw service in China until early January 1946. She was decommissioned on 23 May 1946 and struck from the Navy list on 23 June 1947. On 17 January 1948, the ship was sold to *Compania Naviera y Commercial Perez Compano S.A.*, Buenos Aires, Argentina, for operation.

LST-1066

LST-1066 was laid down on 18 January 1945 at Hingham, Mass., by the Bethlehem-Hingham Shipyard, Inc.; launched on 21 February 1945; sponsored by Miss Cynthia L. Rowan; and commissioned on 20 March 1945, Lt. E. J. Gilman in command.

Following World War II, *LST-1066* performed occupation duty in the Far East until mid-December 1945. She was decommissioned in March 1946 and assigned to the Pacific Reserve Fleet. The ship was redesignated *New London County* (LST-1066) (q.v.) on 1 July 1955 after a county in southeastern Connecticut. She was recommissioned on 21 December 1965 and performed service in the Far East. Decommissioned again on 27 February 1967, *New London County* was transferred to the Military Sea Transportation Service. She was later sold to Chile where she serves as *Commandante Hemerdinger* (LST-88).

LST-1066 earned two battle stars for Vietnam service.

LST-1067

LST-1067 was laid down on 24 January 1945 at Hingham, Mass., by the Bethlehem-Hingham Shipyard, Inc.; launched on 27 February 1945; and commissioned on 24 March 1945, Lt. P. H. White in command.

Following World War II, *LST-1067* performed occupation duty in the Far East until early November 1945. She was decommissioned on 13 August 1946 and assigned to the Pacific Reserve Fleet. The ship was redesignated *Nye County* (LST-1067) (q.v.) on 1 July 1955 after a county in Nevada. She was recommissioned on 21 December 1965 and performed service in the Far East. Decommissioned again on 27 March 1967, *Nye County* was transferred to the Military Sea Transportation Service. She was later sold to Chile in August 1973 where she serves as *Commandante Araya* (LST-89).

LST-1067 earned two battle stars for Vietnam service.

LST-1068

LST-1068 was laid down on 31 January 1945 at Hingham, Mass., by the Bethlehem-Hingham Shipyard, Inc.; launched on 3 March 1945; sponsored by Mrs. Alice R. Wilbur; and commissioned on 27 March 1945, Lt. Clinton E. Voyles in command.

Following World War II, *LST-1068* performed occupation duty in the Far East until late November 1945. She was decommissioned on 9 August 1946 and assigned to the Pacific Reserve Fleet. Recommissioned on 8 September 1950, she performed extensive service during the Korean War. The ship was redesignated *Orange County* (LST-1068) (q.v.) on 1 July 1955 after counties in eight states of the United States. She was decommissioned again on 27 September 1957 and struck from the Navy list that same date. *Orange County* was subsequently sunk as a target vessel on 18 June 1958.

LST–1068 earned four battle stars for the Korean War.

LST–1069

LST–1069 was laid down on 7 February 1945 at Hingham, Mass., by the Bethlehem-Hingham Shipyard, Inc.; launched on 7 March 1945; sponsored by Mrs. James Whitfield; and commissioned on 31 March 1945, Lt. Lewis A. Rockwell in command.

Following World War II, *LST–1069* performed occupation duty in the Far East and saw service in China until late March 1946. She was decommissioned on 6 August 1946 and assigned to the Naval Reserve Program. Recommissioned on 11 January 1952, she was converted to a mine warfare flagship and logistic support vessel. The ship was redesignated *Orleans Parish* (LST-1069) (*q.v.*) on 1 July 1955 after a parish in Louisiana. Decommissioned again on 20 May 1966, *Orleans Parish* was transferred to the Military Sea Transportation Service where she operated in the Far East. *Orleans Parish* was transferred to the Philippines on 13 September 1976.

LST–1070

LST–1070 was redesignated AG–146 and named *Electron* (*q.v.*) on 27 January 1949.

LST–1071

LST–1071 was laid down on 13 February 1945 at Hingham, Mass., by the Bethlehem-Hingham Shipyard, Inc.; launched on 14 March 1945; and commissioned on 9 April 1945, Lt. W. C. Scott in command.

Following World War II, *LST–1071* performed occupation duty in the Far East until early December 1945. She was decommissioned on 10 June 1946 and assigned to the Pacific Reserve Fleet. Recommissioned on 3 January 1951, she operated for the next five years with the Amphibious Force, U.S. Atlantic Fleet. The ship was redesignated *Ouachita County* (LST-1071) (*q.v.*) on 1 July 1955 for a county in Arizona. She was decommissioned again on 15 February 1956 and berthed at Green Cove Springs, Fla., until she was struck from the Navy list on 1 November 1959.

LST–1072

LST–1072 was laid down on 16 February 1945 at Hingham, Mass., by the Bethlehem-Hingham Shipyard, Inc.; launched on 20 March 1945; sponsored by Mrs. Florence Mitchell; and commissioned on 12 April 1945.

Following World War II, *LST–1072* performed occupation duty in the Far East until early December 1945. She was transferred to the Military Sea Transportation Service on 2 April 1951 where she operated as USNS *LST—1072*. The ship was transferred to the Philippines on 13 September 1976.

LST–1073

LST–1073 was laid down on 20 February 1945 at Hingham, Mass., by the Bethlehem-Hingham Shipyard, Inc.; launched on 22 March 1945; and commissioned on 17 April 1945.

Following World War II, *LST–1073* performed occupation duty in the Far East until early November 1945. She was decommissioned on 5 August 1946 and assigned to the Pacific Reserve Fleet. The ship was recommissioned on 3 November 1950 and performed extensive service during the Korean War. On 1 July 1955, she was redesignated *Outagamie County* (LST–1073) (*q.v.*)

after a county in Wisconsin. She subsequently supported Navy operations in the Vietnam theater. *Outagamie County* was decommissioned again on 21 May 1971 and transferred to the Brazilian Navy where she saw service as *Garcia D'Avila* (G–28). The tank landing ship was struck from the Navy list on 1 December 1973.

LST–1073 earned five battle stars for the Korean War and eight battle stars for the Vietnam War.

LST–1074

LST–1074 was laid down on 24 February 1945 at Hingham, Mass., by the Bethlehem-Hingham Shipyard, Inc.; launched on 27 March 1945; and commissioned on 21 April 1945, Lt. John Gay in command.

LST–1074 performed occupation duty in the Far East until early December 1945. She was decommissioned on 4 September 1946 and assigned to the Pacific Reserve Fleet. The ship was redesignated *Overton County* (LST–1074) (*q.v.*) on 1 July 1955 after a county in Tennessee. The tank landing ship was struck from the Navy list on 1 November 1958.

LST–1075

LST–1075 was laid down on 5 March 1945 at Hingham, Mass., by the Bethlehem-Hingham Shipyard, Inc.; launched on 3 April 1945; and commissioned on 25 April 1945.

Following World War II, *LST–1075* performed occupation duty in the Far East and saw service in China until mid-December 1946. She was decommissioned and transferred to the Republic of China Navy on 18 December 1946. The ship was struck from the Navy list on 12 March 1948.

LST–1076

LST–1076 was laid down on 16 March 1945 at Hingham, Mass., by the Bethlehem-Hingham Shipyard, Inc.; launched on 14 April 1945; sponsored by Mrs. Lillian J. Ostler; and commissioned on 1 May 1945, Lt. Grover L. Rawlings, USNR, in command.

Following World War II, *LST–1076* performed occupation duty in the Far East until late September 1945. She was decommissioned on 13 June 1946 and assigned to the Pacific Reserve Fleet. The ship was redesignated *Page County* (LST-1076) (*q.v.*) after counties in Iowa and Virginia. Following modernization, she was recommissioned on 28 November 1960. *Page County* operated with the Pacific Fleet in the ensuing decade, including extensive service in Vietnam. She was decommissioned once again on 5 March 1971 and leased to the Greek Navy where she served as *Kriti* (L–171).

LST–1076 earned six battle stars for the Vietnam War.

LST–1077

LST–1077 was laid down on 21 March 1945 at Hingham, Mass., by the Bethlehem-Hingham Shipyard, Inc.; launched on 18 April 1945; and commissioned on 8 May 1945, Lt. I. W. Matthews in command.

Following World War II, *LST–1077* performed occupation duty in the Far East until late November 1945. She was decommissioned on 31 July 1946 and assigned to the Pacific Reserve Fleet. Recommissioned on 6 September 1950, *LST–1077* performed extensive service during the Korean War. She was decommissioned once again on 12 May 1955. The ship was redesignated *Park County* (LST-1077) (*q.v.*) after counties in Colorado, Montana, and Wyoming. She was later completely modernized and recommissioned on 9 April 1966 for service in the Vietnam War. *Park County* was decommissioned for the final time and transferred to the Mexican Navy in September 1971 where she served as *Rio Panuco* (IA–1).

LST–1077 earned five battle stars for the Korean War and one award of the Meritorious Unit Commendation, two awards of the Navy Unit Commendation, and 11 battle stars for the Vietnam War.

LST–1078

LST–1078 was redesignated AG–147 and named *Proton* (*q.v.*) on 27 January 1949.

LST–1079

LST–1079 was laid down on 30 March 1945 at Hingham, Mass., by the Bethlehem-Hingham Shipyard, Inc.; launched on 27 April 1945; and commissioned on 22 May 1945, Lt. William A. Putnam, Jr., USNR, in command.

LST–1079 was decommissioned in March 1946 and assigned to the Pacific Reserve Fleet. Recommissioned in October 1950, she operated with the Atlantic Fleet. On 1 July 1955, the ship was redesignated *Payette County* (LST–1079) (*q.v.*) after a county in Idaho. Decommissioned again on 1 November 1959 and struck from the Navy list that same date, she was sold to Zidell Explorations, Inc., Astoria, Oreg., on 18 May 1961.

LST–1080

LST–1080 was laid down on 5 April 1945 at Hingham, Mass., by the Bethlehem-Hingham Shipyard, Inc.; launched on 2 May 1945; and commissioned on 29 May 1945.

Following World War II, *LST–1080* performed occupation duty in the Far East until early December 1945. She was decommissioned on 29 August 1946 and assigned to the Pacific Reserve Fleet. The ship was recommissioned on 3 October 1950 and operated extensively during the Korean War. She was redesignated *Pender County* (LST–1080) (*q.v.*) on 1 July 1955 after a county in North Carolina. Decommissioned for the last time on 2 January 1958, *Pender County* was transferred to the Republic of Korea Navy in October 1958 where she served as *Hwa San* (LST–816). The tank landing ship was struck from the Navy list on 6 February 1959.

LST–1080 earned four battle stars for Korean War service.

LST–1081

LST–1081 was laid down on 13 November 1944 at Ambridge, Pa., by the American Bridge Co.; launched on 5 January 1945; sponsored by Mrs. J. L. Davidson, Jr.; and commissioned on 30 January 1945.

LST–1081 was decommissioned on 30 July 1946 and assigned to the Pacific Reserve Fleet. Recommissioned on 2 February 1951, she operated with the Amphibious Force, U.S. Atlantic Fleet. She was redesignated *Pima County* (LST–1081) (*q.v.*) on 1 July 1955 after a county in Arizona. The tank landing ship was decommissioned once again on 12 December 1956. Struck from the Navy list on 1 November 1958, she was sold in June 1960.

LST–1082

LST–1082 was laid down on 18 November 1944 at

Newport (LST–1179) in the Delaware River, August 1969.

Ambridge, Pa., by the American Bridge Co.; launched on 26 January 1945; sponsored by Mrs. Stephen Anzia; and commissioned on 7 February 1945, Lt. John B. Cameron, USNR, in command.

During World War II, *LST–1082* was assigned to the Asiatic-Pacific theater and participated in the assault and occupation of Okinawa Gunto in June 1945. Following the war, she performed occupation duty in the Far East until early December 1945. She was decommissioned on 5 August 1946 and assigned to the Pacific Reserve Fleet. Recommissioned on 6 September 1950, she performed extensive service during the Korean War. The ship was redesignated *Pitkin County* (LST–1082) (*q.v.*) on 1 July 1955 for a county in Colorado. She was decommissioned once again on 1 September 1955 and reassigned to the Pacific Reserve Fleet. Recommissioned on 9 July 1966, *Pitkin County* operated in the Vietnam theater for the next five years. She was decommissioned for the last time on 1 September 1971.

LST–1082 earned one battle star for World War II service, four battle stars for Korean War service, and two awards of the Navy Unit Commendation, one award of the Meritorious Unit Commendation, and 10 battle stars for Vietnam War service.

LST–1083

LST–1083 was laid down on 22 November 1944 at Ambridge, Pa., by the American Bridge Co.; launched on 14 January 1945; sponsored by Mrs. Orren Brown; and commissioned on 13 February 1945, Lt. Donald W. Homes in command.

During World War II, *LST–1083* was assigned to the Asiatic-Pacific theater and participated in the assault and occupation of Okinawa Gunto in June 1945. Following the war, she performed occupation duty in the Far East until early November 1945. She was decommissioned in August 1946 and assigned to the Pacific Reserve Fleet. Recommissioned on 8 September 1950, *LST–1083* performed extensive service during the Korean War. For the next decade, she operated with the Pacific Fleet. The ship was redesignated *Plumas County* (LST–1083) (*q.v.*) on 1 July 1955 after a county in California. She was decommissioned again on 22 August 1961. Following service with the Military Sea Transportation Service commencing in December 1965, *Plumas County* was struck from the Navy list on 1 June 1972.

LST–1083 earned one battle star for World War II service and three for the Korean War.

LST–1084

LST–1084 was laid down on 27 November 1944 at Ambridge, Pa., by the American Bridge Co.; launched on 19 January 1945; sponsored by Mrs. W. F. Shepherd; and commissioned on 19 February 1945, Lt. Lawrence E. Prehn in command.

Following World War II, *LST–1084* performed occupation duty in the Far East until September 1945. She was decommissioned on 13 August 1946 and assigned to the Pacific Reserve Fleet. Recommissioned on 3 November 1950, she performed extensive service during the Korean War. The ship was redesignated *Polk County* (LST–1084) (*q.v.*) on 1 July 1955 after 12 counties in the United States. For the next 14 years, the tank landing ship operated with the Pacific Fleet, including deployments to the Far East and the Vietnam theater. She was decommissioned for the final time on 3 October 1969 and was struck from the Navy list on 15 September 1974.

LST–1084 earned three battle stars for the Korean War and four battle stars for Vietnam War service.

LST–1085

LST–1085 was redesignated AG–148 and named *Colington* (*q.v.*) on 27 January 1949.

LST–1086

LST–1086 was laid down on 5 December 1944 at Ambridge, Pa., by the American Bridge Co.; launched on 28 January 1945; sponsored by Miss Julia L. Rowan; and commissioned on 24 February 1945, Lt. David J. Ward in command.

Following World War II, *LST–1086* performed occupation duty in the Far East and saw service in China until late March 1946. She was decommissioned on 7 August 1946 and assigned to the Atlantic Reserve Fleet. On 1 July 1955, the ship was redesignated *Potter County* (LST–1086) (*q.v.*) after counties in Pennsylvania, South Dakota, and Texas. The tank landing ship was transferred to Greece on 9 August 1960 where she served the Hellenic Navy as *Ikaria* (L–154).

LST–1087

LST–1087 was laid down on 11 December 1944 at Ambridge, Pa., by the American Bridge Co.; launched on 3 February 1945; sponsored by Mrs. Robert Maybin; and commissioned on 2 March 1945, Lt. H. C. Moses in command.

Following World War II, *LST–1087* performed occupation duty in the Far East and saw service in China until early April 1947. She was decommissioned on 11 August 1947 and struck from the Navy list on 29 September that same year. On 18 April 1948, the ship was transferred to the United States Army for operation.

LST–1088

LST–1088 was laid down on 16 December 1944 at Ambridge, Pa., by the American Bridge Co.; launched on 11 February 1945; sponsored by Mrs. A. J. Paddock; and commissioned on 27 March 1945, Lt. Sheldon Potter III in command.

Following World War II, *LST–1088* performed occupation duty in the Far East until early January 1946. She was decommissioned on 29 August 1946 and assigned to the Pacific Reserve Fleet. On 1 July 1955, the ship was redesignated *Pulaski County* (LST–1088) (*q.v.*) after seven counties in the United States. She was recommissioned on 21 May 1963 for service in the Atlantic Fleet. *Pulaski County* later served in Vietnam. In July 1967, the tank landing ship was transferred to the Military Sea Transportation Service for operation by a civilian crew.

LST–1088 earned two battle stars for Vietnam War service.

LST–1089

LST–1089 was laid down on 20 December 1944 at Ambridge, Pa., by the American Bridge Co.; launched on 17 February 1945; sponsored by Mrs. R. C. Robinson; and commissioned on 28 March 1945, Lt. Marvin A. Cohen in command.

Following World War II, *LST–1089* performed occupation duty in the Far East until early November 1945. She was decommissioned on 16 August 1946 and assigned to the Pacific Reserve Fleet. Recommissioned on 6 September 1950, *LST–1089* saw extensive service in Korea and later with the Pacific Fleet in the Far East and the eastern Pacific. On 1 July 1955, she was redesignated *Rice County* (LST–1089) (*q.v.*) after counties in Kansas and Minnesota. The ship was decommissioned again on 9 March 1960 and transferred to the West German Navy in October 1960 where she served as *Bochum* (N–120). *Rice County* was struck from the Navy list on 1 November 1960. She was later sold by the United States to the Turkish Navy in December 1972 where she served as *Sanlaktar* (A–580).

LST–1089 earned four battle stars for Korean War service.

LST–1090

LST–1090 was laid down on 28 December 1944 at Ambridge, Pa., by the American Bridge Co.; launched on 24 February 1945; sponsored by Mrs. R. B. Hunter; and commissioned on 2 April 1945, Lt. E. J. Doering, USNR, in command.

Following World War II, LST–1090 performed occupation duty in the Far East until early January 1946. She was decommissioned on 22 July 1946 and assigned to the Pacific Reserve Fleet. Recommissioned on 3 November 1950, LST–1090 performed extensive service during the Korean War and operated with the Pacific Fleet for the next decade. On 1 July 1955, the ship was redesignated Russell County (LST–1090) (q.v.) after counties in Alabama, Kansas, Kentucky, and Virginia. She was decommissioned for the last time on 5 April 1960 and struck from the Navy list on 1 November that same year.

LST–1090 earned three battle stars for Korean War service.

LST–1091

LST–1091 was laid down on 3 January 1945 at Ambridge, Pa., by the American Bridge Co.; launched on 3 March 1945; sponsored by Mrs. R. W. Robinson; and commissioned on 6 April 1945, Lt. Milton S. Johnston, USNR, in command.

Following World War II, LST–1091 performed occupation duty in the Far East until early January 1946. She was decommissioned on 5 July 1946 and assigned to the Pacific Reserve Fleet. On 1 July 1955, the ship was redesignated Sagadahoc County (LST–1091) (q.v.) after a county in Maine. The tank landing ship was transferred to the Republic of China Navy in October 1958 where she served as Chung Chih (LST–226). She was struck from the Navy list on 6 February 1959.

LST–1092

LST–1092 was redesignated ARVE–3 and named Aventinus (q.v.) on 8 December 1944.

LST–1093

LST–1093 was redesignated ARVA–5 and named Fabius (q.v.) on 8 December 1944.

LST–1094

LST–1094 was redesignated ARVE–4 and named Chloris (q.v.) on 8 December 1944.

LST–1095

LST–1095 was redesignated ARVA–6 and named Megara (q.v.) on 8 December 1944.

LST–1096

LST–1096 was laid down on 27 November 1944 at Jeffersonville, Ind., by the Jeffersonville Boat & Machine Co.; launched on 10 January 1945; sponsored by Mrs. Elizabeth L. Middleton; and commissioned on 2 February 1945, Lt. Lester W. Sperberg in command.

During World War II, LST–1096 was assigned to the Asiatic-Pacific theater and participated in the assault and occupation of Okinawa Gunto in May and June 1945. Following the war, she performed occupation duty in the Far East until mid-December 1945. She was decommissioned on 24 August 1946 and assigned to the Pacific Reserve Fleet. Recommissioned on 3 October 1950, LST–1096 saw extensive service during the Ko-

rean War. Following the Korean armistice in 1953, the tank landing craft continued to operate with the Pacific Fleet, alternating services along the west coast of the United States with deployments to the Far East. She was redesignated St. Clair County (LST–1096) (q.v.) on 1 July 1955 after counties in five states. During the period 1966 to 1969, St. Clair County performed logistic support duty off Vietnam. Decommissioned again on 26 September 1969, she was reassigned to the Pacific Reserve Fleet at Bremerton, Wash.

LST–1096 earned one battle star for World War II, three for Korea, and three battle stars and 1 award of the Navy Unit Commendation for Vietnam service.

LST–1097

LST–1097 was laid down on 22 November at Jeffersonville, Ind., by the Jeffersonville Boat & Machine Co.; launched on 16 January 1945; sponsored by Mrs. Susan A. Rash; and commissioned on 9 February 1945, Lt. Earl J. Lane in command.

During World War II, LST–1097 was assigned to the Asiatic-Pacific theater and participated in the assault and occupation of Okinawa Gunto in May and June 1945. Following the war, she performed occupation duty in the Far East until early November 1945. She was decommissioned on 19 December 1946 and assigned to the Pacific Reserve Fleet. On 27 January 1949, the ship was redesignated AG–149 and named League Island (q.v.). Recommissioned on 3 January 1951, the cargo stores ship performed service during the Korean War. Redesignated AKS–30, she continued service with the Pacific Fleet into 1956. Decommissioned again on 14 December 1956, League Island was struck from the Navy list on 1 April 1960 and sold for scrapping to the Hatch & Kirk Co., Seattle, Wash., on 24 April 1961.

LST–1097 earned one battle star for World War II service.

LST–1098

LST–1098 was redesignated ARST–1 and named Laysan Island (q.v.) on 8 December 1944.

LST–1099

LST–1099 was redesignated ARST–2 and named Okala (q.v.) on 8 December 1944.

LST–1100

LST–1100 was redesignated ARST–3 and named Palmyra (q.v.) on 8 December 1944.

LST–1101

LST–1101 was laid down on 22 November 1944 at Evansville, Ind., by the Missouri Valley Bridge & Iron Co.; launched on 3 January 1945; sponsored by Mrs. James J. Tolson; and commissioned on 26 January 1945, Lt. James M. Trotman, Jr., USNR, in command.

During World War II, LST–1101 was assigned to the Asiatic-Pacific theater and participated in the assault and occupation of Okinawa Gunto in June 1945. Following the war, she performed occupation duty in the Far East until early November 1945. The ship was decommissioned on 6 June 1946 and assigned to the Pacific Reserve Fleet. Recommissioned on 3 November 1950, LST–1101 performed extensive service during the Korean War. She was redesignated Saline County (LST–1101) (q.v.) after counties in five states of the United States. She continued to operate with the Pacific Fleet until she was again decommissioned on 9 March 1960. Struck from the Navy list on 1 November 1960, Saline

County was later transferred to the German Navy where she was converted to a minelayer and served as *Bottrop* (N121) until September 1971. In December 1972, she was sold to Turkey where she served in the Turkish Navy as *Bayraktar* (A–581).

LST–1101 earned one battle star for World War II service and five battle stars for Korean War service.

LST–1102

LST–1102 was laid down on 23 November 1944 at Evansville, Ind., by the Missouri Valley Bridge & Iron Co.; launched on 10 January 1945; sponsored by Mrs. Odette Snyder; and commissioned on 29 January 1945, Lt. L. J. Patterson, USNR, in command.

During World War II, *LST–1102* was assigned to the Asiatic-Pacific theater and participated in the assault and occupation of Okinawa Gunto in June 1945. Following the war, she performed occupation duty in the Far East and saw service in China until early October 1947. She was decommissioned on 21 November 1947 and assigned to the Pacific Reserve Fleet. The ship was redesignated AG–150 on 27 January 1949 and assigned the name *Chimon*, after an island off the coast of Connecticut, on 1 February 1949. Recommissioned on 27 December 1950, *Chimon* supported operations in the Korean War. Reclassified AKS–31 on 18 August 1951, she operated with the Pacific Fleet into 1957. Decommissioned again on 22 April 1958, *Chimon* was struck from the Navy list on 2 November 1959 and sold.

LST–1102 earned one battle star for World War II service.

LST–1103

LST–1103 was laid down on 28 November 1944 at Evansville, Ind., by the Missouri Valley Bridge & Iron Co.; launched on 13 January 1945; sponsored by Mrs. E. S. Paschall; and commissioned on 31 January 1945, Lt. Comdr. R. D. Foster, USNR, in command.

Following World War II, *LST–1103* performed occupation duty in the Far East until early March 1946. She was decommissioned on 18 June 1946 and struck from the Navy list on 23 June 1947. On 17 June 1948, the ship was sold to the Oil Transport Co., New Orleans, La., for non-self-propelled operation.

LST–1104

LST–1104 was laid down on 1 December 1944 at Evansville, Ind., by the Missouri Valley Bridge & Iron Co.; launched on 17 January 1945; sponsored by Mrs. Walter G. Koch; and commissioned on 8 February 1945, Lt. John F. Kelly, USNR, in command.

During World War II, *LST–1104* was assigned to the Asiatic-Pacific theater and participated in the assault and occupation of Okinawa Gunto in June 1945. Following the war, she performed occupation duty in the Far East and saw service in China until early April 1946. She was decommissioned on 8 July 1946. On 28 April 1947, the ship was sold to the Quarterman Corp. for operation. She struck from the Navy list on 22 May 1947.

LST–1104 earned one battle star for World War II service.

LST–1105

LST–1105 was laid down on 5 December 1944 at Evansville, Ind., by the Missouri Valley Bridge & Iron Co.; launched on 20 January 1945; sponsored by Mrs. William J. Peters; and commissioned on 13 February 1945, Lt. Lionel B. King, USNR, in command.

During World War II, *LST–1105* was assigned to the Asiatic-Pacific theater and participated in the assault and occupation of Okinawa Gunto in May and June

1945. Following the war, she performed occupation duty in the Far East until mid-February 1946. She was decommissioned on 29 May 1946 and struck from the Navy list on 19 June that same year. On 20 May 1948, the ship was sold to the California Co. for operation.

LST–1105 earned one battle star for World War II service.

LST–1106

LST–1106 was laid down on 9 December 1944 at Evansville, Ind., by the Missouri Valley Bridge & Iron Co.; launched on 24 January 1945; and commissioned on 16 February 1945, Lt. Jack Flinn, USNR, in command.

During World War II, *LST–1106* was assigned to the Asiatic-Pacific theater and participated in the assault and occupation of Okinawa Gunto in June 1945. Following the war, she performed occupation duty in the Far East until late September 1945. She was decommissioned on 2 August 1946 and struck from the Navy list on 8 October that same year. On 13 June 1948, the ship was sold to the Walter W. Johnson Co. for scrapping.

LST–1106 earned one battle star for World War II service.

LST–1107

LST–1107 was laid down on 13 December 1944 at Evansville, Ind., by the Missouri Valley Bridge & Iron Co.; launched on 29 January 1945; sponsored by Mrs. Frank Parks; and commissioned on 21 February 1945, Lt. G. P. Lynch in command.

Following World War II, *LST–1107* performed occupation duty in the Far East until mid-October 1945. She was decommissioned on 1 May 1946 and struck from the Navy list on 3 July that same year. On 28 February 1947, the ship was sold to Higgins, Inc., for operation.

LST–1108

LST–1108 was laid down on 16 December 1944 at Evansville, Ind., by the Missouri Valley Bridge & Iron Co.; launched on 1 February 1945; sponsored by Mrs. Edward H. Barnard; and commissioned on 27 February 1945, Lt. C. V. Lieb in command.

Following World War II, *LST–1108* performed occupation duty in the Far East until early December 1945. She was decommissioned on 15 August 1946 and struck from the Navy list on 25 September that same year. On 10 January 1948, the ship was sold to the Argentine Navy where she served as *Cabo San Vicente* (BDT–14).

LST–1109

LST–1109 was laid down on 21 December 1944 at Evansville, Ind., by the Missouri Valley Bridge & Iron Co.; launched on 6 February 1945; sponsored by Mrs. Paul H. Derrick; and commissioned on 28 February 1945, Lt. William A. McCaskill, USNR, in command.

Following World War II, *LST–1109* performed occupation duty in the Far East until early November 1945. She was decommissioned on 6 May 1946 and struck from the Navy list on 19 June that same year. On 13 June 1948, the ship was sold to the Walter W. Johnson Co. for scrapping.

LST–1110

LST–1110 was laid down on 28 December 1944 at Evansville, Ind., by the Missouri Valley Bridge & Iron Co.; launched on 9 February 1945; sponsored by Mrs. Sydney Kolb; and commissioned on 7 March 1945, Lt. Alton S. Lee, USNR, in command.

During World War II, *LST–1110* was assigned to the Asiatic-Pacific theater and participated in the assault and occupation of Okinawa Gunto in June 1945. Following the war, she performed occupation duty in the Far East and saw service in China until late January 1947. For the succeeding 10 years, *LST–1110* engaged in arctic resupply operations, operating out of ports on the California coast. On 1 July 1955, she was redesignated *San Bernardino County* (LST–1110) (*q.v.*) after a county in California. Decommissioned on 15 August 1958, *San Bernardino County* was transferred to the Republic of China Navy as *Chung Chiang* (LST–225). She was struck from the Navy list on 6 February 1959.

LST–1110 earned one battle star for World War II service.

LST–1111

LST–1111 was redesignated AKS–16 and named *Blackford* (*q.v.*) on 8 December 1944.

LST–1112

LST–1112 was redesignated AKS–17 and named *Dorchester* (*q.v.*) on 8 December 1944.

LST–1113

LST–1113 was redesignated AKS–18 and named *Kingman* (*q.v.*) on 8 December 1944.

LST–1114

LST–1114 was redesignated AKS–19 and named *Presque Isle* (*q.v.*) on 8 December 1944. Her name was later changed to *Vanderburgh* (*q.v.*) on 17 February 1945, and she was redesignated APB–45 on 7 March 1945.

LST–1115

LST–1115 was laid down on 29 September 1944 at Seneca, Ill., by the Chicago Bridge & Iron Co.; launched on 22 December 1944; sponsored by Mrs. Margaret Reed; and placed in reduced commission on 4 January 1945. She was subsequently decommissioned on 6 February 1945 and underwent conversion. *LST–1115* was later commissioned as *Pentheus* (ARL–20) (*q.v.*) on 7 June 1945.

LST–1116

LST–1116 was laid down on 2 October 1944 at Seneca, Ill., by the Chicago Bridge & Iron Co.; launched on 28 December 1944; sponsored by Mrs. Lucile H. Kelley; and commissioned on 9 January 1945. She was decommissioned on 15 February 1945, and underwent conversion and was recommissioned as *Proserpine* (ARL–21) (*q.v.*) on 31 May 1945.

LST–1117

LST–1117 was laid down on 10 October 1944 at Seneca, Ill., by the Chicago Bridge & Iron Co.; launched on 2 January 1945; sponsored by Mrs. Angeline C. Pattelli; and placed in reduced commission on 13 January 1945. *LST–1117* underwent conversion and was placed in full commission as *Tantalus* (ARL–27) (*q.v.*) on 5 June 1945.

LST–1118

LST–1118 was laid down on 17 October 1944 at Seneca, Ill., by the Chicago Bridge & Iron Co.; launched on 5 January 1945; sponsored by Mrs. F. E. Kittredge; and commissioned on 18 January 1945, Lt. Bernard M. Jacobsen, USNR, in command.

Decommissioned on 16 February 1945, *LST–1118* underwent conversion and was recommissioned as *Typhon* (ARL–28) (*q.v.*) on 18 June 1945.

LST–1119

LST–1119 was laid down on 19 October 1944 at Seneca, Ill., by the Chicago Bridge & Iron Co.; launched on 11 January 1945; sponsored by Mrs. M. D. Hembree; and placed in partial commission on 23 January 1945. *LST–1119* underwent conversion and was fully commissioned as *Diomedes* (ARB–11) (*q.v.*) on 23 June 1945.

LST–1120

LST–1120 was laid down on 20 October 1944 at Seneca, Ill., by the Chicago Bridge & Iron Co.; launched on 16 January 1945; sponsored by Mrs. Ruth Brown; and commissioned on 9 February 1945.

During World War II, *LST–1120* was assigned to the Asiatic-Pacific theater and participated in the assault and occupation of Okinawa Gunto in May and June 1945. Following the war, she performed occupation duty in the Far East and saw service in China until late January 1947. Decommissioned on 14 January 1948, the ship was struck from the Navy list on 19 February that same year. On 20 June 1948, she was sold to Consolidated Builders, Inc., Seattle, Wash., for scrapping.

LST–1120 earned one battle star for World War II service.

LST–1121

LST–1121 was laid down on 25 October 1944 at Seneca, Ill., by the Chicago Bridge & Iron Co.; launched on 19 January 1945; sponsored by Mrs. Willie Brown; and placed in partial commission on 31 January 1945, Lt. P. P. Wynn, USNR, in command.

LST–1121 underwent conversion to a battle damage repair ship and was commissioned as *Demeter* (ARB–10) (*q.v.*) on 3 July 1945.

LST–1122

LST–1122 was laid down on 30 October 1944 at Seneca, Ill., by the Chicago Bridge & Iron Co.; launched on 24 January 1945; sponsored by Mrs. Alice Schmidt; and commissioned on 14 February 1945, Lt. L. L. Hutchinson, USNR, in command.

Following World War II, *LST–1122* performed occupation duty in the Far East until late October 1945. Following occupation duty, *LST–1122* operated off the west coast of the United States until 1949. Decommissioned on 15 June 1949, she was assigned to the Pacific Reserve Fleet. Recommissioned on 3 November 1950, she performed extensive service during the Korean War.

On 1 July 1955, *LST–1122* was redesignated *San Joaquin County* (LST–1122) (*q.v.*) after a county in California. In the years that followed, the tank landing ship regularly deployed to the western and Central Pacific, operating in the Vietnam theater and the Trust Territories of the Pacific. *San Joaquin County* was decommissioned for a second time on 26 September 1969. She was struck from the Navy list on 1 May 1972 and subsequently scrapped.

LST–1122 earned five battle stars for the Korean War and one battle star for the Vietnam War.

LST–1123

LST–1123 was laid down on 1 November 1944 at Seneca, Ill., by the Chicago Bridge & Iron Co.; launched on 29 January 1945; sponsored by Miss Betty Lou Bailey; and commissioned on 19 February 1945, Lt. (jg.) John H. Cleaque III, USNR, in command.

After World War II, *LST-1123* performed occupation duty in the Far East until early November 1945. Following occupation duty, she operated off the west coast of the United States until the outbreak of the Korean War. She performed extensive service during the war, including the amphibious invasion at Inchon. She was redesignated *Sedgwick County* (LST-1123) (*q.v.*) after counties in Colorado and Kansas on 1 July 1955 and was decommissioned on 9 September that same year. Recommissioned on 4 June 1966, *Sedgwick County* participated in logistic support activities in the Vietnam theater.

Decommissioned again on 6 December 1969, *Sedgwick County* was assigned once again to the Pacific Reserve Fleet at Mare Island, Calif. She was struck from the Navy list on 15 March 1975 and transferred to the Malaysian Navy on 7 October 1976 where she served as *Rajah Jarom* (A-1502).

LST-1123 earned six battle stars for the Korean War and seven battle stars and one award of the Meritorious Unit Commendation for the Vietnam War.

LST-1124

LST-1124 was laid down on 6 November 1944 at Seneca, Ill., by the Chicago Bridge & Iron Co.; launched on 1 February 1945; sponsored by Miss Lillie Williams Kidd; and placed in partial commission on 3 March 1945.

LST-1124 underwent conversion to a landing craft repair ship and was commissioned as *Amphitrite* (ARL-29) (*q.v.*) on 28 June 1945.

LST-1125

LST-1125 was laid down on 15 November 1944 at Seneca, Ill., by the Chicago Bridge & Iron Co.; launched on 6 February 1945; sponsored by Mrs. June Elizabeth Reimer; and placed in reduced commission on 17 February 1945.

LST-1125 underwent conversion to a motor torpedo boat tender and was commissioned as *Brontes* (AGP-17) (*q.v.*) on 14 August 1945.

LST-1126

LST-1126 was laid down on 16 November 1944 at Seneca, Ill., by the Chicago Bridge & Iron Co.; launched on 9 February 1945; sponsored by Miss Gladys Minor Woodruff; and commissioned on 28 February 1945, Lt. F. C. Helm, USNR, in command.

Following World War II, *LST-1126* performed occupation duty in the Far East until early November 1945. For the next 25 years, she operated with the U.S. Pacific Fleet with numerous deployments to the western Pacific. She conducted extensive logistic support operations in the Vietnam theater during the period 1965 to 1970. She was redesignated *Snohomish County* (LST-1126) (*q.v.*) after a county in Washington on 1 July 1955. Decommissioned on 1 July 1970, *Snohomish County* was struck from the Navy list and sold to the Chin Ho Fa Steel & Iron Co., Ltd., Taiwan, in January 1971 for scrapping.

LST-1126 earned eight battle stars for Vietnam service.

LST-1127

LST-1127 was laid down on 23 November 1944 at Seneca, Ill., by the Chicago Bridge & Iron Co.; launched on 14 February 1945; sponsored by Mrs. Evelyn P. Adams; and commissioned on 26 February 1945, Lt. Adam W. Melohusky in command.

Decommissioned on 16 March 1945, *LST-1127* underwent conversion to a battle damage repair ship and was commissioned again as *Helios* (ARB-12) (*q.v.*) on 23 July 1945.

LST-1128

LST-1128 was laid down on 23 November 1944 at Seneca, Ill., by the Chicago Bridge & Iron Co.; launched on 19 February 1945; sponsored by Mrs. Marie Staat; and commissioned on 9 March 1945.

Following World War II, *LST-1128* performed occupation duty in the Far East and saw service in China until early February 1946. She was decommissioned on 29 July 1946 and assigned to the Pacific Reserve Fleet. On 1 July 1955, the ship was redesignated *Solano County* (LST-1128) (*q.v.*) after a county in California. She was struck from the Navy list on 1 November 1958 and transferred to the Indonesian Navy where she served as *Teluk Langsa* (LST-501).

LST-1129

LST-1129 was laid down on 29 November 1944 at Seneca, Ill., by the Chicago Bridge & Iron Co.; launched on 22 February 1945; sponsored by Mrs. Elizabeth P. Leatzow; and commissioned on 6 March 1945, Lt. J. K. Marshall in command.

Following World War II, *LST-1129* performed occupation duty in the Far East and saw service in China until mid-February 1946. She was decommissioned on 31 July 1946 and assigned to the Pacific Reserve Fleet. On 1 July 1955, the ship was redesignated *Somervell County* (LST-1129) (*q.v.*) after a county in Texas. She was struck from the Navy list on 1 November 1958.

LST-1130

LST-1130 was laid down on 5 December 1944 at Seneca, Ill., by the Chicago Bridge & Iron Co.; launched on 27 February 1945; sponsored by Miss Bessie F. Jipson; and commissioned on 20 March 1945, Lt. W. E. Johnson in command.

Following World War II, *LST-1130* performed occupation duty in the Far East and saw service in China until late November 1946. She was decommissioned and abandoned on 23 March 1948 following a grounding at Yap, Caroline Islands, which left the ship in a condition beyond economical repair. *LST-1130* was struck from the Navy list on 12 March 1948.

LST-1131

LST-1131 was laid down on 8 December 1944 at Seneca, Ill., by the Chicago Bridge & Iron Co.; launched on 2 March 1945; sponsored by Mrs. Patricia Ann Jacobsen; and commissioned on 15 March 1945, Lt. C. L. Haslup in command.

LST-1131 was decommissioned and underwent conversion to a landing craft repair ship, recommissioning as *Askari* (ARL-30) (*q.v.*) on 23 July 1945.

LST-1132

LST-1132 was laid down on 12 December 1944 at Seneca, Ill., by the Chicago Bridge & Iron Co.; launched on 7 March 1945; sponsored by Mrs. Hazel S. Witherspoon; and commissioned on 19 March 1945, Lt. P. P. Wynn in command.

Decommissioned on 31 March 1945, *LST-1132* underwent conversion to a landing craft repair ship, recommissioning as *Bellerophon* (ARL-31) (*q.v.*) on 21 July 1945.

LST-1133

LST–1133 was laid down on 16 December 1944 at Seneca, Ill., by the Chicago Bridge & Iron Co.; launched on 10 March 1945; sponsored by Mrs. Theodora S. Tillman; and placed in partial commission on 23 March 1945.

Decommissioned on 17 April 1945, *LST–1133* underwent conversion to a motor torpedo boat tender, recommissioning as *Chiron* (AGP–18) (*q.v.*) on 18 September 1945.

LST-1134

LST–1134 was laid down on 18 December 1944 at Seneca, Ill., by the Chicago Bridge & Iron Co.; launched on 16 March 1945; sponsored by Miss Ella J. Arne; and commissioned on 7 April 1945, Lt. C. R. Barheght, USNR, in command.

After World War II, *LST–1134* performed occupation duty in the Far East until early January 1946. Following occupation duty, she performed logistic duties in the western Pacific for the next four years and then participated in operations in support of the Korean War. After the war, she engaged in hauling cargo and passengers between the various Hawaiian Islands from 1951 to 1966.

On 1 July 1955, *LST–1134* was redesignated *Stark County* (LST–1134) (*q.v.*) after counties in Illinois, North Dakota, and Ohio. On 16 May 1966, *Stark County* was transferred to the Royal Thai Navy where she served as *Pangan* (LST–3). She was subsequently struck from the Navy list.

LST–1134 earned three battle stars for Korean War service.

LST-1135

LST–1135 was laid down on 26 December 1944 at Seneca, Ill., by the Chicago Bridge & Iron Co.; launched on 21 March 1945; sponsored by Mrs. Doris P. Syfert; and commissioned on 12 April 1945, Lt. L. A. Morgan in command.

Following World War II, *LST–1135* performed occupation duty in the Far East until late September 1946. She was decommissioned on 28 April 1948 and transferred to the Maritime Administration for disposal on 29 June 1948. *LST–1135* was struck from the Navy list on 12 August 1948.

LST-1136

LST–1136 was laid down on 27 December 1944 at Seneca, Ill., by the Chicago Bridge & Iron Co.; launched on 26 March 1945; sponsored by Mrs. Huberta J. Malsie; and commissioned on 6 April 1945, Lt. P. P. Wynn in command.

Decommissioned on 27 April 1945, *LST–1136* underwent conversion to a landing craft repair ship, recommissioning as *Bellona* (ARL–32) (*q.v.*) on 26 July 1945.

LST-1137

LST–1137 was laid down on 3 January 1945 at Seneca, Ill., by the Chicago Bridge & Iron Co.; launched on 30 March 1945; sponsored by Mrs. Dorothy L. Mahoney; and placed in reduced commission on 11 April 1945.

Decommissioned on 7 May 1945, *LST–1137* underwent conversion to a landing craft repair ship, recommissioning as *Chimaera* (ARL–33) (*q.v.*) on 7 August 1945.

LST-1138

LST–1138 was laid down on 6 January 1945 at Seneca, Ill., by the Chicago Bridge & Iron Co.; launched on 5 April 1945; sponsored by Mrs. Hattie R. Fox; and commissioned on 24 April 1945, Lt. D. C. Smith, USNR, in command.

Following World War II, *LST–1138* performed occupation duty in the Far East until early January 1946. After post-war operations with the Pacific Fleet, *LST–1138* saw extensive service during the Korean War.

San Bernardino (LST–1189) in January 1973. Her retracted bow ramp can be seen on deck. Heavy transport helicopters operate from the flight deck abaft her unusual odd-sized staggered stacks. The vehicle deck in the *Newport*-class, as in earlier LST's, extends nearly the length of the ship. Conventional vehicles land on the beach over the bow ramp, while amphibious types can debark offshore through a stern gate.

On 1 July 1955, she was redesignated *Steuben County* (LST–1138) (q.v.) after counties in Indiana and New York. She was struck from the Navy list on 1 February 1961 and sold to Zidell Explorations, Inc., Portland, Oreg., on 11 August 1961.

LST–1138 earned five battle stars for her Korean War service.

LST–1139

LST–1139 was laid down on 15 January 1945 at Seneca, Ill., by the Chicago Bridge & Iron Co.; launched on 9 April 1945; sponsored by Mrs. Helen G. Hines; and commissioned on 27 April 1945, Lt. John J. Flood, Jr., in command.

Following World War II, *LST–1139* performed occupation duty in the Far East until mid-December 1945. She was decommissioned on 20 July 1946 and struck from the Navy list on 15 August that same year. On 28 June 1948, the ship was sold to the Port Houston Iron Works, Inc., Houston, Tex., for non-self-propelled operation.

LST–1140

LST–1140 was laid down on 17 January 1945 at Seneca, Ill., by the Chicago Bridge & Iron Co.; launched on 13 April 1945; sponsored by Mrs. Eugenia L. Renkosik; and commissioned on 4 May 1945.

Following World War II, *LST–1140* performed occupation duty in the Far East until early November 1945. She was decommissioned on 3 June 1949 and struck from the Navy list on 15 August that same year. On 26 January 1950, the ship was sold to the Foss Launch & Tug Co., Seattle, Wash.

LST–1141

LST–1141 was laid down on 22 January 1945 at Seneca, Ill., by the Chicago Bridge & Iron Co.; launched on 18 April 1945; sponsored by Miss Gwendolyn K. Bartels; and commissioned on 9 May 1945, Lt. E. M. Biggs, USNR, in command.

Following World War II, *LST–1141* performed occupation duty in the Far East and saw service in China until mid-April 1949. She was decommissioned on 24 August 1949 and assigned to the Pacific Reserve Fleet. Recommissioned on 3 November 1950 due to the onset of the Korean War, *LST–1141* performed extensive service during that conflict. She was redesignated *Stone County* (LST–1141) (q.v.) after counties in Arkansas, Mississippi, and Missouri on 1 July 1955. The tank landing ship continued her operations with the Pacific Fleet, including service in Vietnam, through 1969. Decommissioned on 12 March 1970, *Stone County* was sold to the Royal Thai Navy on 15 August 1973 where she served as *Lanta* (LST–4). She was struck from the Navy list that same date.

LST–1141 earned four battle stars for Korean War service and five battle stars for Vietnam War service.

LST–1142

LST–1142 was laid down on 25 January 1945 at Seneca, Ill., by the Chicago Bridge & Iron Co.; launched on 23 April 1945; sponsored by Mrs. Emily S. Ekdahl; and commissioned on 12 May 1945.

Following World War II, *LST–1142* performed occupation duty in the Far East and saw service in China until early February 1946. She was decommissioned on 15 November 1946 and assigned to the Pacific Reserve Fleet. On 1 July 1955, the ship was redesignated *Strafford County* (LST–1142) (q.v.) after a county in New Hampshire. She was struck from the Navy list on 1 November 1958. In 1963, *Strafford County* was sold to the Foss Launch & Tug Co., Seattle, Wash., con-

verted to a barge, and operated under the name *Foss 202*.

LST–1143

LST–1143 was laid down on 31 January 1945 at Seneca, Ill., by the Chicago Bridge & Iron Co.; launched on 27 April 1945; sponsored by Mrs. Dorothea S. Freeman; and placed in reduced commission on 9 May 1945.

Decommissioned on 21 May 1945, *LST–1143* underwent conversion to a landing craft repair ship, commissioning as *Daedalus* (ARL–35) (q.v.) on 19 October 1945.

LST–1144

LST–1144 was laid down on 3 February 1945 at Seneca, Ill., by the Chicago Bridge & Iron Co.; launched on 2 May 1945; sponsored by Mrs. Evelyn B. Adams; and commissioned on 28 May 1945, Lt. T. R. Hopkins, USNR, in command.

Following the war, *LST–1144* was assigned to the Service Force, Atlantic Fleet, for which she operated on training and logistics missions into 1954. She was decommissioned on 11 February 1955 and assigned to the Atlantic Reserve Fleet. On 1 July 1955, the ship was redesignated *Sublette County* (LST–1144) (q.v.) after a county in Wyoming. She was struck from the Navy list on 1 June 1960. *Sublette County* was transferred to the Republic of China Navy in September 1961 where she served as *Chung Yeh* (LST–231).

LST–1145

LST–1145 was laid down on 5 February 1945 at Seneca, Ill., by the Chicago Bridge & Iron Co.; launched on 7 May 1945; sponsored by Mrs. Helen H. Davis; and placed in reduced commission on 18 May 1945.

Decommissioned on 11 June 1945, *LST–1145* underwent conversion to a landing craft repair ship, commissioning as *Gordius* (ARL–36) (q.v.) on 14 September 1945.

LST–1146

LST–1146 was laid down on 10 February 1945 at Seneca, Ill., by the Chicago Bridge & Iron Co.; launched on 11 May 1945; sponsored by Mrs. Margaret L. Hecht, Jr.; and commissioned on 30 May 1945, Lt. Warren A. Cushing, Jr., in command.

Following World War II, *LST–1146* performed occupation duty in the Far East until mid-November 1945. After occupation duty, *LST–1146* operated off the west coast of the United States for the next five years, principally occupied with resupply missions for Alaskan ports. During the Korean War, her resupply efforts were shifted to Korean ports. On 1 July 1955, she was redesignated *Summit County* (LST–1146) (q.v.) after counties in Colorado, Ohio, and Utah. From 1965 into 1969, *Summit County* saw extensive service in the Vietnam theater. She was transferred to the Maritime Administration in December 1969 and assigned to the Pacific Reserve Fleet at Suisun Bay, Calif. *Summit County* was sold to Ecuador on 1 November 1976.

LST–1146 earned one battle star for Korean War service and four battle stars for the Vietnam War.

LST–1147

LST–1147 was laid down on 12 February 1945 at Seneca, Ill., by the Chicago Bridge & Iron Co.; launched on 21 May 1945; sponsored by Mrs. Regina K. Hlubak; and placed in reduced commission.

LST–1147 underwent conversion to a landing craft repair ship and was commissioned as *Indra* (ARL–37) (*q.v.*) on 2 October 1945.

LST–1148

LST–1148 was laid down on 15 February 1945 at Seneca, Ill., by the Chicago Bridge & Iron Co.; launched on 23 May 1945; sponsored by Mrs. Helen M. Fay; and commissioned on 9 June 1945, Lt. Richard Goodhart, USCGR, in command.

Following World War II, *LST–1148* performed occupation duty in the Far East until mid-December 1945. She was decommissioned on 11 May 1946 and assigned to the Pacific Reserve Fleet. Recommissioned on 3 October 1950, *LST–1148* saw extensive service during the Korean War. She was redesignated *Sumner County* (LST–1148) (*q.v.*) after counties in Kansas and Tennessee on 1 July 1955. She continued to operate with the Pacific Fleet and supported operations in the Vietnam theater from 1965 to 1968. *Sumner County* was decommissioned once again on 9 October 1969 and assigned to the Atlantic Reserve Fleet at Orange, Tex.

LST–1148 earned one battle star for the Korean War, and one award of the Meritorious Unit Commendation and 10 battle stars for the Vietnam War.

LST–1149

LST–1149 was laid down on 23 February 1945 at Seneca, Ill., by the Chicago Bridge & Iron Co.; launched on 25 May 1945; and sponsored by Mrs. Eva B. Smith.

LST–1149 was placed in reduced commission and underwent conversion to a landing craft repair ship. She was commissioned as *Krishna* (ARL–38) (*q.v.*) on 3 December 1945.

LST–1150

LST–1150 was laid down on 1 March 1945 at Seneca, Ill., by the Chicago Bridge & Iron Co.; launched on 30 May 1945; sponsored by Mrs. Marie S. Budd; and commissioned on 20 June 1945, Lt. J. F. Carpenter, USCGR, in command.

Following World War II, *LST–1150* performed occupation duty in the Far East until early December 1945. She was decommissioned on 13 September 1946 and assigned to the Pacific Reserve Fleet. The ship was redesignated *Sutter County* (LST–1150) (*q.v.*) after a county in California on 1 July 1955. Recommissioned on 16 April 1966, she performed extensive service in the Vietnam theater from 1966 through 1970. Decommissioned for the final time on 1 December 1970, *Sutter County* remained with the Atlantic Reserve Fleet at Orange, Tex., until she was struck from the Navy list on 15 September 1974.

LST–1150 earned one award of the Navy Unit Commendation, one award of the Meritorious Unit Commendation, and eight battle stars for the Vietnam War as *Sutter County*.

LST–1151

LST–1151 was laid down on 3 March 1945 at Seneca, Ill., by the Chicago Bridge & Iron Co.; launched on 4 June 1945; sponsored by Mrs. Isabell H. Collins; and placed in reduced commission on 15 June 1945.

LST–1151 underwent conversion to a landing craft repair ship, commissioning as *Quirinus* (ARL–39) (*q.v.*) on 6 November 1945.

LST–1152

LST–1152 was laid down on 5 March 1945 at Seneca, Ill., by the Chicago Bridge & Iron Co.; launched on 8 June 1945; sponsored by Mrs. Alice H. Kline; and commissioned on 30 June 1945, Lt. Frank W. Hickson, Jr., USCGR, in command.

Following World War II, *LST–1152* performed occupation duty in the Far East until mid-December 1945. She was decommissioned on 1 July 1946 and assigned to the Pacific Reserve Fleet. On 1 July 1955, the ship was redesignated *Sweetwater County* (LST–1152) (*q.v.*) after a county in Wyoming. She was transferred to the Republic of China Navy on 21 October 1958 where she served as *Chung Ming* (LST–227). *Sweetwater County* was struck from the Navy list on 6 February 1959.

LST–1153

LST–1153 was laid down on 19 July 1945 at the Boston Navy Yard; launched on 24 April 1947; sponsored by Mrs. Lena Mickelson; and commissioned on 3 September 1947.

LST–1153 spent her entire career as a unit of the Amphibious Force, Atlantic Fleet, operating along the east coast of the United States interspersed with deployments to the Mediterranean. On 1 July 1955, she was redesignated *Talbot County* (LST–1153) (*q.v.*) after counties in Maryland and Georgia. She was decommissioned on 3 April 1970 and assigned to the Atlantic Reserve Fleet at Orange, Tex.

LST–1154

LST–1154 was laid down on 4 August 1945 at the Boston Navy Yard; launched on 19 July 1946; sponsored by Mrs. Wilder D. Baker; and commissioned on 24 May 1949, Comdr. Courtland T. Babcock in command.

From her commissioning until 1962, *LST–1154* alternated assignments for the Amphibious Force, Atlantic Fleet along the east coast of the United States with assignment to the 6th Fleet during periodic deployments to the Mediterranean. She was redesignated *Tallahatchie County* (LST–1154) (*q.v.*) after a county in Mississippi on 1 July 1955. She was converted to an advance aviation base ship and redesignated AVB–2 on 3 February 1962. For the remainder of her career, *Tallahatchie County* provided support to aviation units in the Mediterranean. She was decommissioned on 15 June 1970 and struck from the Navy list. *Tallahatchie County* was sold for scrap to *Contieri Navali Santa Maria*, Genoa, Italy, in July 1970.

LST–1155

The contract for *LST–1155* was cancelled on 7 January 1946.

LST–1156

LST–1156 was laid down on 2 January 1952 at Bath, Maine, by the Bath Iron Works; launched on 9 August 1952; sponsored by Miss Anne L. McCrea; and commissioned on 21 November 1952, Lt. Comdr. Henry L. Porter in command.

LST–1156 spent her entire career alternating assignments with the Amphibious Force, Atlantic Fleet, along the east coast of the United States and operations with the 6th Fleet while periodically deployed to the Mediterranean. She was redesignated *Terrebonne Parish* (LST–1156) (*q.v.*) after a parish in Louisiana on 1 July 1955. The ship was decommissioned on 29 October 1971 and transferred to the Spanish Navy where she served as *Velasco* (L–11).

LST–1157

LST–1157 was laid down on 3 March 1952 at Bath, Maine, by the Bath Iron Works; launched on 6 December 1953; sponsored by Mrs. John H. Spiller; and commissioned on 14 March 1954, Lt. Comdr. L. I. Reynolds in command.

Assigned to Amphibious Force, Pacific Fleet, *LST-1157* conducted numerous deployments to the western Pacific into 1964. She was redesignated *Terrell County* (LST-1157) (*q.v.*) after counties in Georgia and Texas on 1 July 1955. Commencing in 1964, *Terrell County* performed extensive service in the Vietnam theater. On 25 March 1971, the tank landing ship was decommissioned at the Puget Sound Naval Shipyard, Bremerton, Wash., and assigned to the Pacific Reserve Fleet.

LST-1157 earned one award of the Presidential Unit Citation, one award of the Navy Unit Commendation, three awards of the Meritorious Unit Commendation, and 12 battle stars for Vietnam service.

LST-1158

LST-1158 was laid down on 16 June 1952 at Bath, Maine, by the Bath Iron Works; launched on 11 April 1953; sponsored by Mrs. Joseph A. Callaghan; and commissioned on 20 June 1953, Lt. Comdr. Charles R. Patton in command.

Initially operating with the Amphibious Force, Atlantic Fleet, *LST-1158* transferred to the Pacific Amphibious Force in 1954. On 1 July 1955, she was redesignated *Tioga County* (LST-1158) (*q.v.*) after counties in New York and Pennsylvania. For the next decade, the tank landing ship alternated deployments to the western Pacific with operations off the west coast and the Hawaiian Islands. Commencing in 1965, *Tioga County* performed extensive logistic support duty in the Vietnam theater. On 25 November 1970, she was decommissioned and assigned to the Pacific Reserve Fleet at San Diego, Calif. She was assigned to the Military Sealift Command for service in 1972 and made available for final disposal in November 1973.

LST-1158 earned three battle stars for Vietnam service.

LST-1159

LST-1159 was laid down on 2 September 1952 at Bath, Maine, by the Bath Iron Works; launched on 2 July 1953; sponsored by Mrs. R. T. Cowdrey; and commissioned on 12 September 1953, Lt. Comdr. Stephen J. Nemeth in command.

Following shakedown, *LST-1159* was assigned to Amphibious Force, Pacific Fleet, in 1954. The tank landing ship alternated between operations off the west coast of the United States and deployments to the Far East during the ensuing decade. On 1 July 1955, she was redesignated *Tom Green County* (LST-1159) (*q.v.*) after a county in Texas. Commencing in 1965, *Tom Green County* performed extensive service in the Vietnam theater. This continued until the end of 1971, when the ship returned to the United States. Decommissioned on 5 January 1972, *Tom Green County* was transferred to the Spanish Navy where she served as *Conde del Vendito* (L-13).

LST-1159 earned four awards of the Navy Unit Commendation, two awards of the Meritorious Unit Commendation, and 12 engagement stars for service in Vietnam as *Tom Green County*.

LST-1160

LST-1160 was laid down on 18 December 1952 at Bath, Maine, by the Bath Iron Works; launched on 3 October 1953; sponsored by Mrs. Omar R. King; and commissioned on 19 December 1953, Lt. Comdr. J. W. Perkins in command.

Following commissioning and shakedown training, *LST-1160* was assigned to the Amphibious Force, Atlantic Fleet, for duty. She remained in this assign-

ment, alternating operations along the east coast of the United States with deployments to the Mediterranean and the Caribbean, throughout her active service. On 1 July 1955, the ship was redesignated *Traverse County* (LST-1160) (*q.v.*) after a county in Minnesota. She was decommissioned in 1970 and assigned to the Atlantic Reserve Fleet at Orange, Tex. On 7 June 1972, *Traverse County* was transferred to the Military Sealift Command (MSC).

LST-1161

LST-1161 was laid down on 14 April 1952 at Pascagoula, Miss., by the Ingalls Shipbuilding Corp.; launched on 25 November 1952; sponsored by Mrs. Hugh L. White; and commissioned on 18 May 1953, Lt. Comdr. D. E. Sutherlin in command.

Following shakedown training, *LST-1161* was assigned to the Amphibious Force, Atlantic Fleet, for duty. On 1 July 1955, she was redesignated *Vernon County* (LST-1161) (*q.v.*) after a parish in Louisiana and counties in Missouri and Wisconsin. On 6 June 1958, *Vernon County* was assigned to the Pacific Fleet. Later homeported in Yokosuka, the tank landing ship performed extensive service in the Vietnam theater. *Vernon County* was decommissioned on 14 June 1973 and transferred to Venezuela that same month where she served in the Venezuelan Navy as *Amazonas* (T-21).

LST-1161 earned one Presidential Unit Citation, three Navy Unit Commendations, three Meritorious Unit Commendations, and 14 battle stars for her Vietnam service as *Vernon County*.

LST-1162

LST-1162 was laid down on 21 July 1952 at Pascagoula, Miss., by the Ingalls Shipbuilding Corp.; launched on 23 January 1953; sponsored by Mrs. Wilbur G. Dees; and commissioned on 13 August 1953, Lt. Comdr. I. W. Matthews in command.

Following shakedown, *LST-1162* was assigned to the Amphibious Force, Atlantic Fleet, and, for the next 17 years, alternated operations along the east coast of the United States with deployments to the Mediterranean and the Caribbean. On 1 July 1955, the tank landing ship was redesignated *Wahkiakum County* (LST-1162) (*q.v.*) after a county in Washington. She was decommissioned on 16 October 1970 and transferred to the Military Sealift Command (MSC) on 10 April 1972.

LST-1163

LST-1163 was laid down on 4 August 1952 at Pascagoula, Miss., by the Ingalls Shipbuilding Corp.; launched on 17 March 1953; sponsored by Mrs. C. Richard Schaeffner; and commissioned on 17 September 1953, Lt. Comdr. Robert H. Steinkellner in command.

Following completion of shakedown training, *LST-1163* was assigned to the Amphibious Force, Atlantic Fleet, for duty. For the next 17 years, the ship alternated operations off the east coast of the United States with deployments to the Mediterranean and the Caribbean. On 1 July 1955, the tank landing ship was redesignated *Waldo County* (LST-1163) (*q.v.*) after a county in Maine. Decommissioned in October 1970, *Waldo County* was struck from the Navy list in November 1973.

LST-1164

LST-1164 was laid down on 22 September 1952 at Pascagoula, Miss., by the Ingalls Shipbuilding Corp.; launched on 15 May 1953; sponsored by Mrs. John A.

Furr; and commissioned on 26 October 1953, Lt. Comdr. Francis Kay in command.

Assigned to the Amphibious Force, Atlantic Fleet, *LST–1164* spent the next 18 years conducting a variety of operations off the east coast of the United States and in the Mediterranean and Caribbean. On 1 July 1955, the tank landing ship was redesignated *Walworth County* (LST–1164) (*q.v.*) after counties in South Dakota and Wisconsin. Decommissioned in April 1971, *Walworth County* was transferred to the Military Sealift Command (MSC) on 26 May 1972.

LST–1165

LST–1165 was laid down on 1 December 1952 at Pascagoula, Miss., by the Ingalls Shipbuilding Corp.; launched on 14 July 1953; sponsored by Mrs. Ralph K. James; and commissioned on 30 November 1953, Lt. Comdr. Robert R. Davis in command.

Assigned to the Amphibious Force, Atlantic Fleet, *LST–1165* was later transferred to the Pacific Fleet and homeported in Yokosuka, Japan. On 1 July 1955, the tank landing ship was redesignated *Washoe County* (LST–1165) (*q.v.*) after a county in Nevada. Commencing in 1965, *Washoe County* saw extensive service in the Vietnam theater providing combat and logistic support. Returning to the United States in 1970, she was decommissioned on 25 March 1971 and berthed at the Inactive Ship Facility, Bremerton, Wash. *Washoe County* was struck from the Navy list in November 1973.

LST–1165 earned one Presidential Unit Citation, one Navy Unit Commendation, one Meritorious Unit Commendation, and 11 battle stars for Vietnam service as *Washoe County*.

LST–1166

LST–1166 was laid down on 29 November 1951 at Sturgeon Bay, Wis., by the Christy Shipbuilding Corp.; launched on 22 November 1952; sponsored by Miss Dorothy Christenson; and commissioned on 29 October 1953, Lt. Comdr. Mack D. Ellis in command.

Assigned to the Amphibious Force, Atlantic Fleet, *LST–1166* conducted operations off the east coast of the United States with one deployment to the Mediterranean in 1956. Earlier, on 1 July 1955, she was redesignated *Washtenaw County* (LST–1166) (*q.v.*) after a county in Michigan. Transferred to the Pacific Fleet Amphibious Force in 1958, *Washtenaw County* was later homeported in Yokosuka, Japan, in 1960. Commencing in 1964, the tank landing ship performed extensive service in the Vietnam theater. Inactivated in August 1973, *Washtenaw County* was struck from the Navy list on 30 August 1973.

LST–1166 earned two Presidential Unit Citations, three Navy Unit Commendations, three Meritorious Unit Commendations, and 15 battle stars for Vietnam service as *Washtenaw County*.

LST–1167

LST–1167 was laid down on 11 January 1952 at Sturgeon Bay, Wis., by the Christy Shipbuilding Corp.; launched on 18 April 1953; sponsored by Mrs. Robert E. Wood; and commissioned on 10 March 1954, Lt. Comdr. Leamond F. Lacy in command.

Initially assigned to the Amphibious Force, Atlantic Fleet, *LST–1167* operated off the east coast of the United States and in the Caribbean and made one deployment to the Mediterranean prior to her transfer to the Pacific Fleet in 1958. On 1 July 1955, the tank landing ship was redesignated *Westchester County* (LST–1167) (*q.v.*) after a county in New York. In 1960, *Westchester County* was assigned the home port of Yokosuka, Japan, and spent the remaining years of

her active service in the Far East. Commencing in 1965, she performed extensive service in the Vietnam theater of operations. Decommissioned on 30 August 1973 at Yokosuka, *Westchester County* was assigned to the Inactive Ship Facility, Bremerton, Wash., in November of that year. On 27 August 1974, she was transferred to the Turkish Navy where she served as *Serdar* (L–402).

LST–1167 received three Navy Unit Commendations, two Meritorious Unit Commendations, and 15 engagement stars for Vietnam service as *Westchester County*.

LST–1168

LST–1168 was laid down on 27 February 1952 at Sturgeon Bay, Wis., by the Christy Shipbuilding Corp.; launched on 28 November 1953; sponsored by Mrs. Philip K. Wrigley; and commissioned on 15 June 1954, Lt. Comdr. V. W. Vanzant in command.

LST–1168 was initially assigned to the Amphibious Force, Atlantic Fleet, and, on 1 July 1955, was redesignated *Wexford County* (LST–1168) (*q.v.*) after a county in Michigan. In 1956, the tank landing ship was transferred to the Pacific Fleet. Commencing in 1965, *Wexford County* saw extensive service in support of operations in Vietnam. On 29 October 1971, she was decommissioned and transferred to the Spanish Navy where she served as *Martin Alvarez* (L–12). The ship was struck from the Navy list on 1 November 1976.

LST–1168 earned one Meritorious Unit Commendation and five battle stars for Vietnam service as *Wexford County*.

LST–1169

LST–1169 was laid down on 26 November 1952 at Sturgeon Bay, Wis., by the Christy Shipbuilding Corp.; launched on 22 August 1953; sponsored by Mrs. John L. Clarkson; and commissioned on 14 September 1954, Lt. Comdr. F. S. Handler in command.

Following shakedown training, *LST–1169* was assigned to the Amphibious Force, Atlantic Fleet. On 1 July 1955, she was redesignated *Whitfield County* (LST–1169) (*q.v.*) after a county in Georgia. *Whitfield County* was assigned to the Pacific Fleet in 1956 and was later homeported in Yokosuka, Japan. Commencing in 1965, the tank landing ship operated extensively in support of operations in the Vietnam theater. On 15 March 1973, *Whitfield County* was decommissioned; and, on 17 March 1977, she was transferred to the Greek Navy where she serves as *Kos* (L–116).

LST–1169 received one Presidential Unit Citation, three Navy Unit Commendations, three Meritorious Unit Commendations, and 15 battle stars for Vietnam service as *Whitfield County*.

LST–1170

LST–1170 was laid down on 21 April 1953 at Sturgeon Bay, Wis., by the Christy Shipbuilding Corp.; launched on 22 May 1954; sponsored by Mrs. Joseph R. McCarthy; and commissioned on 15 December 1954, Lt. Comdr. Max Wells in command.

Following shakedown training, *LST–1170* was assigned to the Amphibious Force, Atlantic Fleet. On 1 July 1955, the tank landing ship was redesignated *Windham County* (LST–1170) (*q.v.*) after counties in Connecticut and Vermont. She operated along the east coast of the United States and in the Caribbean and made one deployment to the Mediterranean before being transferred to the Amphibious Force, Pacific Fleet, in 1958. In 1960, the ship's home port was shifted from San Diego to Yokosuka, Japan, and she spent the remainder of her active service in the Far East. Commencing in 1965, *Windham County* performed extensive service in the Vietnam theater. On 1 June 1973,

Windham County was decommissioned and transferred to the Turkish Navy where it served as *Ertugrul* (L401).

LST–1170 earned one Presidential Unit Citation, three Navy Unit Commendations, three Meritorious Unit Commendations, and 14 battle stars for Vietnam service as *Windham County*.

DeSoto County (LST–1171)

DeSoto County (LST–1171) (*q.v.*) was named after counties in Florida, Louisiana, and Mississippi. She was laid down in September 1956 at Avondale, La., by the Avondale Marine Ways, Inc.; launched on 28 February 1957; sponsored by Mrs. C. Horton Smith; and commissioned on 10 June 1958, Lt. Comdr. Daniel A. York in command.

For almost the entire length of her active service, *DeSoto County* was assigned to the Amphibious Force, Atlantic Fleet. She interspersed operations off the east coast of the United States with frequent deployments to the Caribbean and the Mediterranean. The tank landing ship saw brief service in the Vietnam theater of operations in 1969. Decommissioned on 17 July 1972, *DeSoto County* was transferred to the Italian Navy where she served as *Nave Grado* (L9890).

DeSoto County earned one Meritorious Unit Commendation for service with the 6th Fleet in the Mediterranean and one battle star for Vietnam service.

LST–1172

The contract for *LST–1172* was cancelled in 1955.

Suffolk County (LST–1173)

Suffolk County (LST–1173) (*q.v.*) was named after counties in Massachusetts and New York. She was laid down on 17 July 1955 at the Boston Naval Shipyard; launched on 5 September 1956; sponsored by Mrs. Thomas P. O'Neill, Jr.; and commissioned on 15 August 1957, Lt. Comdr. James E. Brown in command.

Assigned to the Amphibious Force, Atlantic Fleet, following commissioning, *Suffolk County* spent her entire active service operating off the east coast of the United States interspersed with numerous deployments to the Caribbean and the Mediterranean. Decommissioned on 25 August 1972, *Suffolk County* was assigned to the Atlantic Reserve Fleet and berthed at Norfolk, Va.

Grant County (LST–1174)

Grant County (LST–1174) (*q.v.*) was named after counties in 15 states of the United States. She was laid down on 15 March 1956 at Avondale, La., by the Avondale Marine Ways, Inc.; launched on 12 October 1956; sponsored by Mrs. John Martin Higgins; and commissioned on 17 December 1957, Lt. Comdr. R. B. Nichols in command.

Assigned to the Amphibious Force, Atlantic Fleet, *Grant County* spent her entire active service operating off the east coast of the United States interspersed with deployments to the Caribbean and Mediterranean. Decommissioned on 15 January 1973, *Grant County* was transferred to the Brazilian Navy that same date where she served as *Duque de Caxias* (G–26).

York County (LST–1175)

York County (LST–1175) (*q.v.*) was named after counties in five states of the United States. She was laid down on 4 June 1956 at Newport News, Va., by the Newport News Shipbuilding & Drydock Co.; launched on 5 March 1957; sponsored by Mrs. William

C. France; and commissioned on 8 November 1957, Lt. Comdr. Warren M. Schafer, USNR, in command.

Upon commissioning, *York County* was assigned to the Amphibious Force, Atlantic Fleet. She spent her entire active service in operations conducted off the east coast interspersed with deployments to the Caribbean and the Mediterranean. Decommissioned on 17 July 1972, *York County* was transferred to the Italian Navy that same date where she served as *Nave Caorle* (L9891).

Graham County (LST–1176)

Graham County (LST–1176) (*q.v.*) was named after counties in Arizona, Kansas, and North Carolina. She was laid down on 4 February 1957 at Newport News, Va., by the Newport News Shipbuilding & Drydock Co.; launched on 9 September 1957; sponsored by Mrs. Ralph Otis Davis; and commissioned on 17 April 1958, Lt. Comdr. Gordon H. McCrea in command.

Assigned to the Amphibious Force, Atlantic Fleet, *Graham County* conducted operations off the east coast of the United States and in the Caribbean and Mediterranean for the next 14 years. Redesignated AGP–176 in 1972, her primary mission became the support of patrol gunboats, and her home port was changed to Naples, Italy. Decommissioned on 1 March 1977, *Graham County* was subsequently scrapped.

Lorain County (LST–1177)

Lorain County (LST–1177) (*q.v.*) was named after a county in Ohio. She was laid down on 9 August 1956 at Lorain, Ohio, by the American Shipbuilding Co.; launched on 22 June 1957; sponsored by Mrs. Albert D. Baumhart, Jr.; and commissioned on 3 October 1958, Lt. Comdr. Robert E. DuBois in command.

From the time of commissioning, *Lorain County* spent her entire period of active service with the Amphibious Force, Atlantic Fleet. For 14 years, she engaged in amphibious operations along the east coast of the United States supplemented with extended operations in the Caribbean and regular deployments as a unit of the 6th Fleet in the Mediterranean. Decommissioned on 1 September 1972, the tank landing ship was assigned to the National Defense Reserve Fleet at Norfolk, Va.

Wood County (LST–1178)

Wood County (LST–1178) (*q.v.*) was named after counties in Ohio, Texas, West Virginia, and Wisconsin. She was laid down on 1 October 1956 at Lorain, Ohio, by the American Shipbuilding Co.; launched on 14 December 1957; sponsored by Miss Margaret Ackerman; and commissioned on 5 August 1959, Lt. Comdr. Maxton M. Midgett in command.

Following commissioning, *Wood County* was assigned to the Amphibious Force, Atlantic Fleet. For 13 years, the tank landing ship alternated between operations on the east coast of the United States and deployments to the Caribbean and Mediterranean for participation in large scale amphibious training exercises. On 1 May 1972, *Wood County* was decommissioned and assigned to the National Defense Reserve Fleet at James River, Va.

Newport (LST–1179)

Newport (LST–1179) (*q.v.*) was laid down on 1 November 1966 at Philadelphia, Pa., by the Philadelphia Naval Shipyard; launched on 3 February 1968; sponsored by Mrs. Claiborne Pell; and commissioned on 7 June 1969, Comdr. Derwin T. Lamb in command.

Newport (LST–1179) tests her bow ramp. The upper sections of her bow hinge out to the sides to allow the landing ramp to be rigged out. This "over-the-bow" configuration enables ships of this class to combine the fine hull lines needed for higher speeds with the LST's traditional ability to land tanks and heavy vehicles directly onto a beach.

Assigned to the Amphibious Force, Atlantic Fleet, upon commissioning, *Newport* has alternated amphibious training operations along the east coast of the United States with extended deployments to the Caribbean and Mediterranean into 1980.

Manitowoc (LST–1180)

Manitowoc (LST–1180) (*q.v.*) was named after a city and county in eastern Wisconsin. She was laid down on 1 February 1967 at Philadelphia, Pa., by the Philadelphia Naval Shipyard; launched on 4 January 1969; sponsored by Mrs. Gaylord Nelson; and commissioned on 24 January 1970, Comdr. George T. Dyer, Jr., in command.

Following commissioning, *Manitowoc* was assigned to the Amphibious Force, Pacific Fleet. In the next three years, the tank landing ship conducted three deployments to the Far East in support of operations in the Vietnam theater. In January 1973, she shifted her home port to Little Creek, Va. Into 1978, *Manitowoc* alternated amphibious training operations along the east coast of the United States with deployments to the Caribbean and Mediterranean.

Manitowoc earned two battle stars for Vietnam service.

Sumter (LST–1181)

Sumter (LST–1181) (*q.v.*) was named after a city and county in South Carolina. She was laid down on 14 November 1967 at Philadelphia, Pa., by the Philadelphia Naval Shipyard; launched on 13 December 1969; sponsored by Mrs. Strom Thurmond; and commissioned on 20 June 1970, Comdr. James C. Hayes in command.

Following sea trials, *Sumter* was assigned to the Amphibious Force, Pacific Fleet, and homeported at Long Beach, Calif. The tank landing ship completed two deployments to the western Pacific in support of the United States effort in Vietnam and was transferred to the Atlantic Fleet in early 1973. Into 1978, *Sumter* was alternating operations along the east coast of the United States with deployments to the Caribbean and the Mediterranean.

Sumter earned two engagement stars for Vietnam service.

Fresno (LST–1182)

Fresno (LST–1182) was named for a city and county in California. She was laid down on 16 December 1967 at San Diego, Calif., by the National Steel & Shipbuilding Corp.; launched on 28 September 1968; sponsored by Mrs. Marilyn Hyde; and commissioned on 22 November 1969, Comdr. Stanislaus J. Sowinski in command.

Assigned to the Amphibious Force, Pacific Fleet, and homeported at San Diego, Calif., *Fresno* has alternated amphibious training operations along the west coast of the United States with regular, extended deployments to the western Pacific. She continues this regimen into 1980. *Fresno* saw extensive service during the latter stages of the Vietnam War.

Fresno earned two engagement stars for Vietnam service.

Peoria (LST–1183)

Peoria (LST–1183) (*q.v.*) was named after a city in Illinois. She was laid down on 22 February 1968 in San Diego, Calif., by the National Steel & Shipbuilding Corp.; launched on 23 November 1968; sponsored by Mrs. Robert H. Michel; and commissioned on 21 February 1970, Comdr. John T. Williams in command.

Assigned to the Amphibious Force, Pacific Fleet, upon commissioning, *Peoria* was homeported at San Diego, Calif. Into 1980, the tank landing ship has alternated amphibious training exercises along the west coast of the United States and off Hawaii with regular deployments to the western Pacific. *Peoria* provided logistic support for American forces in the Vietnam theater in 1971.

Peoria earned two battle stars for Vietnam service.

Frederick (LST–1184)

Frederick (LST–1184) was named after a city and county in Maryland. She was laid down on 13 April 1968 at San Diego, Calif., by the National Steel & Shipbuilding Corp.; launched on 8 March 1967; sponsored by Mrs. Kleber S. Masterson; and commissioned on 11 April 1970, Comdr. Robert A. Shaid in command.

Following shakedown, *Frederick* was assigned to the Amphibious Force, Pacific Fleet, and was homeported at San Diego. Since that time, *Frederick* has alternated amphibious training operations off the west coast of the United States with regular, extended deployments to the Far East.

Frederick earned one award of the Meritorious Unit Commendation and three battle stars for Vietnam service.

Schenectady (LST–1185)

Schenectady (LST–1185) (*q.v.*) was named after a county in New York. She was laid down on 2 August 1968 at San Diego, Calif., by the National Steel & Shipbuilding Corp.; launched on 24 May 1969; sponsored by Mrs. Charles E. Goodell; and commissioned on 13 June 1970, Comdr. David E. Sigsworth in command.

Assigned to the Amphibious Force, Pacific Fleet, *Schenectady* has alternated amphibious training operations along the west coast of the United States with regular, extended deployments to the Far East. She continues this routine into 1980.

Schenectady earned three battle stars for Vietnam service.

Cayuga (LST–1186)

Cayuga (LST–1186) was named after a county in New York. She was laid down on 28 September 1968 at San Diego, Calif., by the National Steel & Shipbuilding Corp.; launched on 12 July 1969; sponsored by Mrs. Luther C. Heinz; and commissioned on 8 August 1970, Comdr. William T. Hollenbach in command.

Following commissioning, *Cayuga* was assigned to the Amphibious Force, Pacific Fleet, with its home port at Long Beach, Calif. Into 1980, the tank landing ship has alternated amphibious training operations along the west coast of the United States with regular, extended deployments to the Far East.

Cayuga earned two battle stars for Vietnam service.

Tuscaloosa (LST–1187)

Tuscaloosa (LST–1187) (*q.v.*) was named after a county and city in Alabama. She was laid down on 23 November 1968 at San Diego, Calif., by the National Steel & Shipbuilding Corp.; launched on 6 September 1969; sponsored by Mrs. Thomas F. Connolly; and commissioned on 24 October 1970, Comdr. Harry W. Kinsley, Jr., in command.

Following commissioning, *Tuscaloosa* was assigned to the Amphibious Force, Atlantic Fleet, with its home port at San Diego, Calif. Into 1980, the tank landing ship has alternated amphibious training operations off the west coast of the United States with regular, extended deployments to the Far East.

Tuscaloosa earned one award of the Meritorious Unit Commendation and four battle stars for Vietnam service.

Saginaw (LST-1188)

Saginaw (LST-1188) (*q.v.*) was named after a county and city in central Michigan. She was laid down on 24 May 1969 at San Diego, Calif., by the National Steel & Shipbuilding Corp.; launched on 7 February 1970; sponsored by Mrs. James Harvey; and commissioned on 23 January 1971, Comdr. G. P. Brown in command.

Following her fitting out period, *Saginaw* was assigned to the Amphibious Force, Atlantic Fleet, with the home port of Little Creek, Va. Into 1980, the tank landing ship has alternated local amphibious training operations along the east coast of the United States and in the Caribbean with regular, sustained deployments to the Mediterranean.

San Bernardino (LST-1189)

San Bernardino (LST-1189) (*q.v.*) was named after a county and city in California. She was laid down on 12 July 1969 at San Diego, Calif., by the National Steel & Shipbuilding Corp.; launched on 28 March 1970; sponsored by Mrs. Walter H. Baumberger; and commissioned on 27 March 1971, Comdr. Francis L. Roach in command.

Following commissioning, *San Bernardino* was assigned to the Amphibious Force, Pacific Fleet, with the home port of San Diego, Calif. Into 1980, the tank landing ship has alternated amphibious training operations along the west coast of the United States with regular, sustained deployments to the western Pacific.

San Bernardino earned one battle star for Vietnam service.

Boulder (LST-1190)

Boulder (LST-1190) was named after a county and city in Colorado. She was laid down on 6 September 1969 at San Diego, Calif., by the National Steel & Shipbuilding Corp.; launched on 22 April 1970; sponsored by Mrs. Gordon L. Allott; and commissioned on 4 June 1971, Comdr. B. A. Troutman, Jr., in command.

Following commissioning at Long Beach, Calif., *Boulder* was assigned to the Amphibious Force, Atlantic Fleet, with the home port of Little Creek, Va. Into 1980, the tank landing ship alternated amphibious training operations along the east coast of the United States and in the Caribbean with regular, extended deployments to the Mediterranean.

Boulder received an award of the Meritorious Unit Commendation for removal and disposal of ordnance from the Suez Canal in 1974.

Racine (LST-1191)

Racine (LST-1191) (*q.v.*) was named after a county and city in Wisconsin. She was laid down on 13 December 1969 at San Diego, Calif., by the National Steel & Shipbuilding Corp.; launched on 15 August 1970; sponsored by Mrs. Edwin B. Hooper; and commissioned on 9 July 1971, Comdr. Daniel W. Anderson in command.

Following commissioning, *Racine* was assigned to the Amphibious Force, Pacific Fleet, with a home port of San Diego, Calif. In the years that followed, the tank landing ship alternated amphibious training operations along the west coast of the United States with regular, extended deployments to the western Pacific. *Racine* continued that cycle of operations into 1980.

Spartanburg County (LST-1192)

Spartanburg County (LST-1192) (*q.v.*) was named after a county in South Carolina. She was laid down on 7 February 1970 at San Diego, Calif., by the National Steel & Shipbuilding Corp.; launched on 7 November 1970; sponsored by Mrs. Neville Holcombe; and commissioned on 1 September 1971, Comdr. P. R. Royse in command.

Following commissioning, *Spartanburg County* transited the Panama Canal to her new home port, Little Creek, Va., where she was assigned to the Amphibious Force, Atlantic Fleet. Here, the tank landing ship commenced an operating cycle consisting of amphibious training exercises along the east coast of the United States and in the Caribbean interspersed with scheduled deployments to the Mediterranean. *Spartanburg County* maintained this cycle into 1980.

Fairfax County (LST-1193)

Fairfax County (LST-1193) was named for a county in Virginia. She was laid down on 28 March 1970 at San Diego, Calif., by the National Steel & Shipbuilding Corp.; launched on 19 December 1970; sponsored by Mrs. James W. O'Grady; and commissioned on 16 October 1971, Comdr. John F. Neese in command.

Following commissioning, *Fairfax County* transited the Panama Canal to her new home port, Little Creek, Va., where she was assigned to the Amphibious Force, Atlantic Fleet. Into 1980, the tank landing ship alternated amphibious training operations along the east coast of the United States and in the Caribbean with regular, extended deployments to the Mediterranean.

La Moure County (LST-1194)

The second *La Moure County* (LST-1194) was named after a county in North Dakota. She was laid down on 22 May 1970 at San Diego, Calif., by the National Steel & Shipbuilding Corp.; launched on 13 February 1971; sponsored by Mrs. Milton R. Young; and commissioned on 18 December 1971, Comdr. Robert B. Rogers in command.

Following commissioning, *La Moure County* transited the Panama Canal en route to her home port, Little Creek, Va., where she was assigned to the Amphibious Force, Atlantic Fleet. Since that time, into 1980, the tank landing ship has alternated amphibious training operations along the east coast of the United States and in the Caribbean with deployments to northern European waters and the Mediterranean.

Barbour County (LST-1195)

Barbour County (LST-1195) was named after counties in Alabama and West Virginia in the United States. She was laid down on 15 August 1970 at San Diego, Calif., by the National Steel & Shipbuilding Corp.; launched on 15 May 1971; sponsored by Mrs. J. Victor Smith; and commissioned on 12 February 1972, Comdr. John G. Schimming in command.

Following commissioning, *Barbour County* was assigned to the Amphibious Force, Pacific Fleet, with a home port of Long Beach, later changed to San Diego in August 1973. Into 1980, the tank landing ship alternated amphibious training operations off the west coast of the United States with regular, sustained deployments to the western Pacific.

Barbour County received the Meritorious Unit Commendation for Service in the Far East in 1975.

Harlan County (LST-1196)

Harlan County (LST-1196) was named after counties in Kentucky and Nebraska. She was laid down on 7 November 1970 at San Diego, Calif., by the National Steel & Shipbuilding Corp.; launched on 24 July 1971; sponsored by Mrs. Richard Capen; and commissioned on 8 April 1972, Comdr. Vernon C. Smith in command.

Following commissioning, *Harlan County* was assigned to the Amphibious Force, Atlantic Fleet, and transited the Panama Canal en route to her home port of Little Creek, Va. In the years that followed, the tank landing ship alternated amphibious training operations along the east coast of the United States and in the Caribbean with regular, sustained deployments to the Mediterranean. This cycle continued into 1980.

Barnstable County (LST–1197)

Barnstable County (LST–1197) was named after a county in Massachusetts. She was laid down on 19 December 1970 at San Diego, Calif., by the National Steel & Shipbuilding Corp.; launched on 2 October 1971; sponsored by Mrs. Frank P. Sanders; and commissioned on 27 May 1972, Comdr. Warren R. Ellsworth in command.

Following commissioning, *Barnstable County* was assigned to the Amphibious Force, Atlantic Fleet, and transited the Panama Canal en route to her new home port of Little Creek, Va. In the years that followed, the tank landing ship alternated between amphibious training operations along the east coast of the United States and in the Caribbean with regular, extended deployments to the Mediterranean and, in one instance in 1976, to northern Europe. She maintained this cycle into 1980.

Bristol County (LST–1198)

Bristol County (LST–1198) was named after counties in Massachusetts and Rhode Island. She was laid down on 13 February 1971 at San Diego, Calif., by the National Steel & Shipbuilding Corp.; launched on 4 December 1971; sponsored by Mrs. Robert Lee Townsend; and commissioned on 5 August 1972, Comdr. Donald L. Waggoner in command.

Following commissioning, *Bristol County* was assigned to the Amphibious Force, Pacific Fleet, with the home port of Long Beach. In the years that followed, the tank landing ship alternated amphibious training operations off the west coast of the United States with periodic, sustained deployments to the western Pacific. She maintained this cycle into 1980.

GUIDE TO THE SERIES

HISTORICAL SKETCHES:

"A" and "B" _____ VOLUME I
"C" through "F" _____ VOLUME II
"G" through "K" _____ VOLUME III
"L" and "M" _____ VOLUME IV
"N" through "Q" _____ VOLUME V
"R" and "S" _____ VOLUME VI
"T" through "V" _____ VOLUME VII
"W" through "Z" _____ VOLUME VIII

APPENDICES:

Aircraft _____ VOLUME V
Aircraft Carriers _____ VOLUME II
Aircraft Repair Ships _____ VOLUME IV
Aircraft Transports _____ VOLUME IV
Advance Aviation Base Ships _____ VOLUME IV
Amphibious Assault Ships _____ VOLUME IV
Amphibious Command Ships _____ VOLUME IV
Amphibious Transports Dock _____ VOLUME IV
Attack Cargo Ships _____ VOLUME IV
Attack Transports _____ VOLUME IV
Aviation Supply Ships _____ VOLUME IV
Battleships _____ VOLUME I
Cargo Ships and Aircraft Ferries _____ VOLUME IV
Civil War Naval Ordnance _____ VOLUME III
Classification of Naval Ships and Service Craft _____ VOLUME IV
Confederate Forces Afloat _____ VOLUME II
Cruisers _____ VOLUME I
Destroyers _____ VOLUME I
Destroyer Tenders _____ VOLUME IV
Dock Landing Ships _____ VOLUME IV
Eagle Class Patrol Craft _____ VOLUME VI
Escort Vessels _____ VOLUME I
High-Speed Transports _____ VOLUME IV
Historic Ship Exhibits _____ VOLUME III
Inshore Fire Support Ships _____ VOLUME IV
Lighter-than-Air Aircraft Tenders _____ VOLUME IV
Mechanized Artillery Transports _____ VOLUME IV
Minecraft _____ VOLUME V
Monitors _____ VOLUME III
Seaplane Tenders _____ VOLUME IV
Ships of the Line _____ VOLUME IV
Stone Fleet _____ VOLUME V

Submarine Chasers ------------------------------ VOLUME VI
Submarine Rescue Vessels ----------------------- VOLUME I
Submarine Tenders ------------------------------ VOLUME I
Submarines ------------------------------------- VOLUME I
Transport Submarines --------------------------- VOLUME IV
Torpedo Boats ---------------------------------- VOLUME I
Vehicle Landing Ships -------------------------- VOLUME IV

BIBLIOGRAPHY

Previous volumes of this series contain bibliographies of the widely varied historical literature of the United States Navy useful in fleshing out the condensed ship histories they contained. Rather than repeat these lists, this bibliography is restricted to more recently published books and earlier works which were used extensively in the research effort. It also lists the source materials which proved to be especially valuable in producing this new volume.

Readers who desire broader bibliographic assistance may refer to the Naval Historical Center's *United States Naval History: A Bibliography* which may be obtained through the Superintendent of Documents, Government Printing Office, Washington, D.C. 20402.

Unpublished Primary Sources

U.S. Coast Guard. *Records of the United States Coast Guard, 1789 to 1947.* Record Group 26, National Archives.

U.S. Navy. *Action Reports, 1941 to 1945 and 1950 to 1953.* Operational Archives Branch, Naval Historical Center, Washington, D.C.

———. *Area File, 1775 to 1910.* Record Group 45, National Archives. Miscellaneous naval documents arranged by date and geographical area.

———. *Cruising Reports 1898 to 1940.* Record Group 24, National Archives.

———. *Operation Plans, 1941 to 1945 and 1950 to 1953.* Operational Archives Branch, Naval Historical Center, Washington, D.C.

———. *Ships' Logs, 1801 to 1945.* Record Group 24, National Archives.

———. *Ships' Logs, 1945 to the present.* Washington National Records Center, Suitland, Maryland. Logs less than one year are held by the Office of the Chief of Naval Operations.

———. *Subject File 1775 to 1910.* Record Group 45, National Archives. Miscellaneous naval documents arranged by subject matter.

———. *War Diaries, 1941 to 1945 and 1950 to 1953.* Operational Archives Branch, Naval Historical Center, Washington, D.C.

———. *Records of the Board of Naval Commissioners, 1815 to 1842.* Record Group 45, National Archives.

———. *General Correspondence of the Bureau of Construction and Repair, 1850 to 1940.* Record Group 19, National Archives.

———. *Ships' Plans, 1794 to 1940.* Record Group 19, National Archives.

———. *Ship Source File, ca. 1920 to the present.* Ships' Histories Branch, Naval Historical Center, Washington, D.C.

———. *Letters of the Secretary of the Navy to Naval Officers, Men of War, 1798 to 1886.* Record Group 45, National Archives.

———. *Letters from Naval Officers, 1802 to 1886.* Record Group 45, National Archives.

———. *Records of the Immediate Office of the Secretary of the Navy, 1804 to 1946.* Record Group 80, National Archives.

Unpublished Secondary Sources

Clephane, L. P. *History of the Submarine Chasers in the World War.* Record Group 45, Subject File 1911 to 1927, ZOD, Box 802E, 168 pp., National Archives.

Stegmann, George H. *Statistical History of the Vessels of the U.S. Navy.* Ships' Histories Branch, Naval Historical Center, Washington, D.C.

Published Primary Sources

American States Papers: Naval Affairs. 4 vols. Washington: Gales and Seaton, 1834 to 1861. Contains early reports of the Secretaries of the Navy and other important documents.

U.S. Coast Guard. *Record of Movements, Vessels of the U.S. Coast Guard.* 2 vols. Washington: Government Printing Office, 1935. Covers the period from 1790 to 1933.

———. *Register of Commissioned and Warrant Officers.* Washington: Government Printing Office, published annually from 1917 to the present [title varies].

U.S. Congress. *Statutes at Large of the United States, Concurrent Resolutions, Recent Treaties, Conventions and Executive Proclamations* [title varies]. Boston and Washington: various publishers, 1845 to the present.

U.S. Navy. *Annual Report of the Secretary of the Navy.* Washington: various publishers, 1836 to the present. Reports prior to 1836 may be found in *American State Papers.*

———. *Navy and Marine Corps Awards Manual* (NAVPERS 15790). Revised ed. Washington: Government Printing Office, 1953.

———. *Navy Directory.* Washington: Government Printing Office, 1908 to 1942. Issued monthly 1908 to 1920; bimonthly and quarterly thereafter.

———. *Navy Register.* Washington: various publishers, 1800 to the present. Issued annually.

———. *Navy Yearbook.* Washington: Government Printing Office, 1903 to 1921.

———. *Ships' Data, U.S. Naval Vessels.* Washington: various publishers, 1911 to the present. Issued periodically.

———. *Movements of U.S. Vessels.* Washington: Government Printing Office, 1916. Covers 1866 to 1916.

Secondary Sources

Barbey, Daniel E. *MacArthur's Amphibious Navy.* Annapolis: United States Naval Institute, 1969.

Bauer, K. Jack. *Ships of the Navy, 1775 to 1969.* Troy, N.Y.: Rensselaer Polytechnic Institute, 1970.

Benham, Edith W., and Hall, Anne M. *Ships of the U.S. Navy and Their Sponsors, 1797 to 1913.* Norwood, Mass.: Plimpton Press, 1913.

———. *Ships of the U.S. Navy and Their Sponsors, 1913 to 1923.* Norwood, Mass.: Plimpton Press, 1925.

Breyer, Siegfried. *Battleships and Battle Cruisers, 1905-1970.* Garden City, N.Y.: Doubleday, 1973. 480 pp., illus., biblio.

Callahan, Edward W. *List of Officers of the Navy of the United States.* New York: L. R. Hammersley & Co., 1901.

Chapelle, Howard I. *The History of the American Sailing Navy: the Ships and Their Development.* New York: W. W. Norton, 1949.

Dulin, Robert O., Jr., & William H. Garzke, Jr. *Battleships; United States Battleships in World War II.* Annapolis: Naval Institute Press, 1976. 267 pp., illus., biblio.

Dyer, George C. *The Amphibians Came to Conquer.* Washington: United States Government Printing Office, 1972.

Elliott, Peter. *Allied Escort Ships of World War II: A Complete Survey.* Annapolis, Md.: Naval Institute Press, 1977. 575 pp., illus., appendices.

Emmons, George Fox. *The Navy of the United States from Commencement.* Washington: Gideon & Co., 1853.

Hooper, Edwin Bickford. *Mobility, Support, Endurance: A Story of Naval Operational Logistics in the Vietnam War.* Washington: Naval Nistory Division, 1972.

Jane, Fred T., *et. al.* (eds.). *Jane's Fighting Ships* [title varies]. London and New York: various publishers, 1897 to the present.

Lenton, H. T. *American Gunboats and Minesweepers* (World War II Fact Files series). New York: Arco Publishing Co., 1974. 64 pp., illus.

Liddell-Hart, Basil Henry. *History of the Second World War.* New York: G. P. Putnam's Sons, 1971.

Lytle, William M. *Merchant Steam Vessels of the United States 1807 to 1868.* Mystic, Conn.: The Steamship Historical Society of America, Pub. No. 6, 1952.

Naval Engineers Journal. Washington: American Society of Naval Engineers, 1889 to the present. Formerly the Society's *Journal.*

Neeser, Robert W. *Ship Names of the U.S. Navy.* New York: Moffat, Yard & Co., 1921.

————. *Statistical and Chronological History of the United States Navy.* 2 vols. New York: Macmillan Co., 1909.

Polmar, Norman. *Aircraft Carriers: A Graphic History of Carrier Aviation and Its Influence on World Events.* Garden City, N.Y.: Doubleday, 1969.

Preston, Anthony. *Battleships of World War I.* Harrisburg, Pa.: Stackpole Books, 1972.

Reilly, John C., Jr. *The American Destroyer, 1934–1945.* New York: Sterling, 1980.

Reilly, John C., Jr., & Robert L. Scheina. *American Predreadnought Battleships, 1886–1921; An Illustrated History.* Annapolis, Md.: Naval Institute Press, 1980.

Silverstone, Paul H. *U.S. Warships of World War I.* Garden City, N.Y.: Doubleday, 1970.

Watts, Anthony J. *Allied Submarines* (World War 2 Fact Files series), Arco, 1977. 64 pp., illus.

735

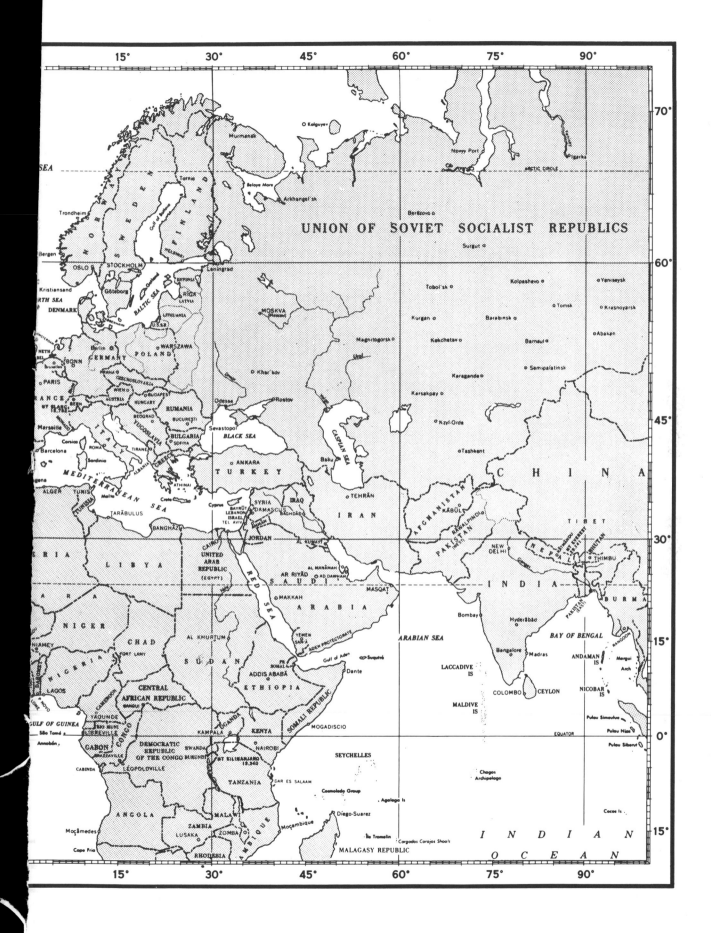